D1798296

COPINGER AND SKONE JAMES

on

COPYRIGHT

VOLUME ONE

COPINGER AND SKONE JAMES

on

COPYRIGHT

SIXTEENTH EDITION

BY

KEVIN GARNETT, M.A.
One of Her Majesty's Counsel

GILLIAN DAVIES, D.L., Ph.D.
Barrister

GWILYM HARBOTTLE, B.A. (Oxon)
Barrister

SWEET & MAXWELL

 THOMSON REUTERS

First edition by W.A. Copinger 1870
Second edition by W.A. Copinger 1881
Third edition by W.A. Copinger 1893
Fourth edition by J.M. Easton 1904
Fifth edition by J.M. Easton 1915
Sixth edition by F.E. Skone James 1927
Seventh edition by F.E. Skone James 1936
Eighth edition by F.E. Skone James 1948
Ninth edition by F.E. & E.P. Skone James 1958
Tenth edition by E.P. Skone James 1965
Eleventh edition by E.P. Skone James 1971
Second imprint by E.P. Skone James 1977
Twelfth edition by E.P. Skone James, John F. Mummery
    and J.E. Rayner James 1980
Thirteenth edition by E.P. Skone James, John F. Mummery,
    J.E. Rayner James and K.M. Garnett 1991
Fourteenth edition by K.M. Garnett, J.E. Rayner James
    and G. Davies 1999
Fifteenth edition by K.M. Garnett, G. Davies and G. Harbottle 2005
Sixteenth edition by K.M. Garnett, G. Davies and G. Harbottle 2011

Published in 2011 by Thomson Reuters (Legal) Limited
(Registered in England & Wales, Company No 1679046.
Registered Office and address for service:
100 Avenue Road, London NW3 3PF)
trading as Sweet & Maxwell
Typeset by Sweet & Maxwell's electronic publishing system.
Preliminary material typeset by LBJ Typesetting Ltd of Kingsclere
Printed and bound in Great Britain by CPI William Clowes Ltd, Beccles, NR34
7TL

For further information on our products and services, visit
www.sweetandmaxwell.co.uk

No natural forests were destroyed to make this product; only farmed
timber was used and re-planted

A CIP catalogue record for this book is available from the British Library

ISBN 978-0-414-04331-2

FOREWORD

The fact that the (unprecedented) third Supplement to the last edition of this work ran to 400 pages of text and 80 further pages of materials is some indication of the pace of development in the field of copyright today. And since then (October 2008) there have been another two years' worth of new legislation, case law and academic comment. How to deal with all this and the inevitable further developments in a work which, above all, we think should be a practitioners' book?

We take the view that a work of this kind should in the main be confined to an examination of what the law of the United Kingdom actually is. Where it is doubtful, we have of course tried to give a view but the fact remains that (regrettable though it may be to the paying client) there is no substitute for the hard beating out of difficult points before a sceptical tribunal. Even with this modest objective, the commentary on the current law alone (excluding the materials in Volume 2) runs to something over 2,000 pages and 1.5m words.

The point is perhaps brought home by the decisions of Mann J. and the Court of Appeal in *Lucasfilm*.[1] Until then, discussion of what constituted a "sculpture" was fairly limited, and not really advanced by an obviously correct decision that a model for a double-barrelled hypodermic syringe was not a sculpture.[2] But given a case in which the question became not merely crucial but also of real commercial significance, the issue was decided with the benefit of proper adversarial argument which came under the judicial hammer. The case makes the point that while we and other textbook and academic writers may take views on particular points, the law is only developed case by case, often unexpectedly. The fact that some arguments turn out to be right and some to be wrong highlights the problem for works of this kind: cases make the law, not textbook writers.

So what, then, of developments since the last edition of this work? The dominating feature is clearly that, like Sleeping Beauty, copyright law at a European level has awoken from a deep slumber. It is now undergoing an explosive development in the Court of Justice, sparked off mostly by issues arising out of the interpretation of the copyright Directives, in particular, the Information Society Directive. When the Preface to the last edition was written, the *British Horseracing Board* and *Fixtures Marketing* cases had just been decided but otherwise all seemed relatively peaceful. Since then, another 10 cases have been decided and, more to the point, there are currently twenty-four further copyright and related rights cases pending

[1] *Lucasfilm Ltd v Ainsworth* [2009] EWCA Civ 1328.
[2] *Metix v G H Maugham* [1997] F.S.R. 718

before the Court of Justice, of which over half concern the Information Society Directive. More references will clearly follow. In almost every sphere, United Kingdom copyright law is now overshadowed by one or more EU Directives, with the prospect of a reference to the Court of Justice to deal with points that are not *acte claire*.

Turning to the detail of what is new in this edition: in Chapter 3 the section on foreign works has been reordered with expanded coverage and this chapter, together with Chapters 6 and 18, has also required further extensive re-writing to deal with cases such as *Infopaq, Rafael Hoteles, Peek & Cloppenburg, Lucasfilm, Sawkins, Navitaire, Nova Productions, SAS Institute, QC Leisure, Baigent, Football Dataco* and *Newzbin* amongst others. Indeed, changes are to be found almost everywhere in the core of the book, contained in Chapters 3 to 8, to reflect the numerous developments in the case law here. Amongst others, these changes concern the problem areas of digitisation of works, transient copying, the extent of protection for software and databases, and the communication to the public right.

Chapter 9 deals with the extension of permitted acts in education and for libraries and archives, as well as the change of regime for playing sound recordings in clubs and broadcast sound recordings in public. In Chapter 10 we have explained the opening up of Crown copyright material to comply with the Directive on Public Sector Information by the introduction of the Open Government Licence. Chapter 13 (Design Right, etc.) includes coverage of a series of important cases including *Dyson v Qualtex, Procter & Gamble v Reckitt Benckiser* and *Grupo Promer* (General Court) and has an expanded section on unregistered community designs. Chapter 15 (Circumvention of Protection Measures, etc.) has coverage of *Nintendo v Playables, R v Gilham* and *R v Higgs*, and in Chapter 16 (Fraudulent Reception of Transmissions) we consider the references in *QC Leisure* and *Murphy*. In Chapter 19 the proposed amendments to the Public Lending Right Act to cover e-books are dealt with, and Chapter 20 (Artist's Resale Right) has been substantially revised to take account of experience in the administration of this new right and the question of whether it should be extended to deceased artists.

Chapter 21 has required substantial amendment to deal with the working-through of the Enforcement Directive, recent cases on the E-Commerce defences, the new Patents County Court rules and procedures, and the Digital Economy Act (the United Kingdom's attempt to grapple with the issues of file sharing and site blocking). Chapter 22 (Criminal Remedies, etc.) deals with the changes in penalties and the important procedural developments relating to customs seizure, and in Chapter 23 (International Treaties) as well as a full update there is coverage of the new Unesco Convention on Cultural Diversity and the latest draft of the Anti-Counterfeiting Trade Agreement (ACTA) dated mid-November 2010.

Chapter 24 (European Union Law) has required substantial rewriting to take account of the entry into force of the Lisbon Treaty on December 1,

2009 and the new EU Treaties on European Union (TEU) and on the Functioning of the European Union (TFEU). As mentioned above, there have been a substantial number of decisions of the Court of Justice on the interpretation of the copyright Directives and these are fully commented on. As a new feature we have reproduced in full all questions referred to the Court of Justice for a preliminary ruling under the various Directives. There are reports on all decisions to date arising from the Information Society Directive, including *Infopaq* and the decision in *Padawan* of October 21, 2010. As already indicated, no fewer than 13 cases are pending before the Court of Justice with questions arising under the Information Society Directive (and 11 further pending cases in related fields).

In Chapter 26 (Exploitation of Rights in Particular Industries) specialist contributing editors cover the major changes which are being made in the various industries to confront the problems and opportunities of the digital era, including digitisation of books, e-books, file sharing, screen scraping and the *SAS* case. In Chapter 28 (Control of the Exercise of Copyright, etc.) we deal with the new rules and new cases on jurisdiction and appeals in the Copyright Tribunal, and as regards competition, we cover *IMS Health* and the *Microsoft* interoperability and tying cases, with detailed sections on sports broadcasting and collecting societies. Chapters 27 (Collecting Societies) and 28 have been revised to take account of the new EU Treaties and EU case law and, finally, Chapter 29 (Tax) has been substantially rewritten.

After long thought we have dropped the Confidential Information and Passing Off chapters of the book. These chapters had a place when there were few other texts on these topics but this is no longer the case. Although the Confidential Information chapter had its origins in the common law copyright protection for unpublished works, the topics are today only distantly related.

Reviewers customarily bemoan the fact that purchasers have to pay for statutory and other materials (in the case of *Copinger*, these are to be found in Volume 2) which, one way or another, can today mostly be found in the internet. Time will of course tell, and the paying public will judge, whether the current publishing model is right, but we believe that the practitioner still appreciates being able to hold such material in the hand (if only just— Volume 2 of the last edition weighed well over $2\frac{1}{2}$lbs).

We have many people to thank. First, we have again been able to call upon a distinguished and experienced panel of contributing editors to deal not only with Design Right, database right and tax, but also with the industry specific topics in Chapter 26. We believe that the industry sections bring a valuable practical viewpoint to the more academic chapters dealing with pure law. We are grateful to Tom St Quintin (Hogarth Chambers) for updating Chapters 19 and 27.4 and Chris de Mauny (Hogarth Chambers) for updating Chapter 17. Then, there are many individuals who have helped us with basic research, checking and proofreading. Here we wish to acknowledge the contribution from Hogarth Chambers of Ben Longstaff. Further help has also come from Dr Gadi Oron (IFPI) for assistance with Chapter 23, Dr Maria Mercedes Frabboni (Queen Mary, University of London) and Martin Arthur Kuppers (Queen Mary, University of London) for their very valuable research assistance, Philippa Malas (of Lincoln's Inn) for work on Chapter 20 and Justin Goldspink (GSC Solicitors). Our clerks at Hogarth Chambers have been a great support, as too have been the members of Hogarth Chambers with their suggestions and help. Our publishers have worked harder than ever with us to bring out this edition under a tight time schedule. Modern printing techniques enable the late changes which authors always demand to be made but these impose additional burdens on publishers already grappling with the normal consequences of everything being delivered at the last possible moment. We are very grateful to them. Finally, we would like to thank our long-suffering spouses and close friends, who have put up with behaviour that probably only they can adequately describe.

As before, the present edition is also available online via Westlaw UK, and as part of the practice area specific Westlaw UK Intellectual Property service.

Comments from readers are always very welcome and we encourage readers to contact us at Hogarth Chambers, 5 New Square, Lincoln's Inn, London WC2A 3RJ or by email to copinger@hogarthchambers.com.

We have endeavoured to state the law as at September 30, 2010, unless indicated otherwise, but there have been many developments since then. Where possible we have taken them into account.

Kevin Garnett QC
Gillian Davies
Gwilym Harbottle

December 1, 2010

CONTENTS

Chapter One

Introduction—Classification and Scope of the Protection of Copyright,
Related Rights and Design Rights

Part I

Copyright

Chapter Two

Nature and History of Copyright

Chapter Three

Requirements for Copyright Protection

Chapter Four

Authorship of Copyright Works

Chapter Five

The Chain of Title

Chapter Six

Duration of Copyright

Chapter Seven

The Rights of a Copyright Owner: Primary Infringement

Chapter Eight

Secondary Infringement of Copyright

Chapter Nine

Permitted Acts

Chapter Ten

Crown Rights, Parliamentary Rights and the Rights of
International Organisation

Part II

Moral Rights

Chapter Eleven

Moral Rights

Part III

Rights in Performances

Chapter Twelve

Rights in Performances

Part IV

Design Right and the Protection of Works of Industrial Application

Chapter Thirteen

Design Right, Unregistered Community Design and the Protection of Works of Industrial Application

Part V

Miscellaneous Rights

Chapter Fourteen

Semiconductor Topographies

Chapter Fifteen

Circumvention of Protection Measures and Rights Management Information

Chapter Sixteen

Fraudulent Reception of Transmissions

Chapter Seventeen

Publication Right

Chapter Eighteen

Database Right

Chapter Nineteen

Public Lending Right

Chapter Twenty

Artist's Resale Right

Part VI

Remedies

Chapter Twenty One

Civil Remedies

Chapter Twenty Two

Criminal Remedies and Customs Seizure

Part VII

International Aspects

Chapter Twenty Three

International Treaties

Chapter Twenty Four

European Union Law

Chapter Twenty Nine

Taxation of Copyright

CONTENTS FOR VOLUME TWO

PART A

COPYRIGHT, DESIGNS AND PATENTS ACT 1988 AND RELATED MATERIALS

PART B

RELATED LEGISLATION AND MATERIALS

PART C

ORDERS IN COUNCIL

PART D

TABLES OF PARLIAMENTARY DEBATES

PART E

REPEALED STATUTES

PART F

COPYRIGHT CONVENTIONS AND AGREEMENTS

PART I

Related EU Instruments

PART J

Precedents and Court Forms

TABLE OF CASES

References are to paragraph numbers.

TABLE OF DECISIONS

TABLE OF STATUTES

TABLE OF STATUTORY INSTRUMENTS

References are to paragraph numbers.

TABLE OF TREATIES

References are to paragraph numbers.

TABLE OF CONVENTIONS

References are to paragraph numbers.

TABLE OF AGREEMENTS

References are to paragraph numbers.

TABLE OF EUROPEAN LEGISLATION

References are to paragraph numbers.

INTRODUCTION

CHAPTER ONE

INTRODUCTION—CLASSIFICATION AND SCOPE OF THE PROTECTION OF COPYRIGHT, RELATED RIGHTS AND DESIGN RIGHTS

"Copyright is the Cinderella of the law. Her rich older sisters, Franchises and Patents, long crowded her into the chimney-corner. Suddenly the fairy godmother, Invention, endowed her with mechanical and electrical devices as magical as the pumpkin coach and the mice footmen. Now she whirls through the mad mazes of a glamorous ball."[1]

Copyright is one of the three main branches of the law of intellectual property, along with patent law and trade mark law. Overshadowed for much of its history by the greater economic worth of patents and trade marks, at the beginning of the twenty-first century copyright has overtaken both in economic importance. The law of copyright, originally conceived to provide protection against unauthorised reproduction of books, faces unprecedented challenges from the accelerating pace of technological innovation and consequential new uses of works protected by copyright. Since copyright gives the owner the exclusive right to authorise or prohibit certain uses of his work by others, it is central to providing right owners with some element of control over the exploitation of their works in both traditional media and the new global networks of the information age.   **1–01**

Works protected by copyright and the rights related thereto discussed in this work represent a constantly increasing sector of the national economy[2] and of   **1–02**

---

[1] Z. Chafee, "Reflections on the Law of Copyright", XLV *Columbia Law Rev.* 503 and 719 (1945), 1.

[2] In 2007, the creative industries that are substantially dependent on copyright represented a major part of the UK economy, generating 7.3 per cent of Gross Value Added (GVA), which is comparable in size to the financial services industry. The sector grew by an average of 5 per cent per annum between 1997 and 2007. In 2007 exports of services by the creative industries amounted to 4.5 per cent of all goods and services exported. The creative sector also accounted for over 1.9 million jobs in 2006. Thus, the creative industries are important sources of wealth generation and employment. ("Staying ahead: the economic performance of the UK's creative industries", Report

world trade.[3] In the modern world, the law of copyright provides the legal framework not only for the protection of the traditional beneficiaries of copyright, the individual author, composer or artist, but also for the investment required for the creation of works by the major cultural industries, the publishing, film, broadcasting and recording industries, and the computer software industry. Copyright is important not only to the individuals and industries which depend upon it for their livelihood but it also impinges one way or another on the daily life of members of the public and business. Copyright protects a vast array of everyday items, including, for example on the private level, letters, photographs and home videos, and in business, all manner of advertisements, brochures, designs, documents, graphics, manuals and reports published or used by every firm in the country. No business can afford to be ignorant of the implications of copyright in its daily work. These implications are twofold: on the one hand, there is the copyright material created every day which is the subject of protection and of potential value and, on the other hand, there is the copyright protected material which is made use of in some way and in which rights must be cleared. For example, a newspaper proprietor publishes a daily paper in which copyright subsists; that paper, however, contains many articles, cartoons and photographs in which individual authors own the copyrights, all of which must be cleared and paid for before the newspaper can publish them. When an entrepreneur organises a concert, it is not enough to hire the performers and to ensure that their rights in the performance are respected; a licence to perform the musical works publicly must also be obtained. Likewise, the rights in works made available to the public by means of the internet must also be respected.

1. CLASSIFICATION OF THE RIGHTS DEALT WITH IN THIS WORK

A. COPYRIGHT GENERALLY

1–03   **The 1988 Act.** This work is about the law of copyright in the United Kingdom under the present copyright statute, the Copyright, Designs and Patents Act 1988 (the 1988 Act, as amended), and under the various international conventions and treaties on the subject to which the United Kingdom is party. Certain rights related to copyright also provided for under the 1988 Act, such as moral rights, rights in performances, design rights, rights in databases and rights in published editions are also covered. A number of other specific rights provided for by special legislation outside the 1988 Act and having a connection with copyright, such as the Public Lending Right (PLR) are also dealt with. A number of other specific rights provided for by special legislation outside the 1988 Act and having a connection with copyright, such as the Public Lending Right (PLR) and the new Artist's Resale Right (*Droit de Suite*) are also covered.

Copyright is the term used in English-speaking countries to describe the bundle of rights that are granted by statute, for limited periods of time and subject to certain permitted exceptions, in respect of original literary, dramatic, musical or artistic works, such as novels, plays, poems, musical compositions, paintings, sculptures, as well as of sound recordings, films, broadcasts and typographical arrangements of published editions. These are proprietary rights, giving the owner the right to do and to authorise other persons to do the acts restricted by the copy-

---

by the Work Foundation (Department for Culture, Media and Sport (DCMS)), June 2008; see also DCMS Creative Industries Economic Estimates, February 2010.
[3] International trade in goods protected by intellectual property was estimated to be about 5% of world trade in 2007 and constantly increasing (UNCTAD, World Investment Report 2007).

right law. Under the 1988 Act, these restricted acts include copying the work, issuing copies thereof to the public, renting or lending the work to the public, performing, showing or playing the work in public, communicating the work to the public and making an adaptation of the work or doing any of the acts restricted by copyright in relation to an adaptation. Communication to the public includes the broadcasting of the work and the making available to the public of the work by electronic transmission in such a way that members of the public may access it from a place and at a time individually chosen by them.

The 1988 Act deals separately with original literary, dramatic and musical works, databases, artistic works, sound recordings, films, broadcasts, published editions, and rights in performances and designs. A literary work has been given a definition in the Act that is broader than the normal concept of "a literary work". It is defined as meaning any work, other than a dramatic or musical work, which is written, spoken or sung, and including a table or compilation, a computer program, preparatory design material for a computer program, and a database. A dramatic work includes a work of dance or mime and a musical work means a work consisting of music, exclusive of any words or action intended to be sung, spoken or performed with the music. The term artistic work means a graphic work, photograph, sculpture or collage, irrespective of artistic quality, a work of architecture and a work of artistic craftsmanship.

For each category of work, the Act establishes the conditions under which copyright is to subsist, the duration of the protection and the acts restricted by the copyright.

(i) Distinction between authors' rights and related rights

Extent of protection. There are differences in the extent of protection afforded to these various categories of works, due partly to the international classification of the rights into so-called authors' rights in literary, dramatic, musical or artistic works, on the one hand, and so-called *related rights*, on the other hand. Authors' rights are protected in accordance with the Berne Convention for the Protection of Literary and Artistic Works 1886 (the Berne Convention) and the Universal Copyright Convention 1952 (the UCC) as well as the more recent WIPO Copyright Treaty 1996 (the WCT). The expression "related rights" in the narrow sense applies to the rights prescribed by the Rome Convention for the Protection of Performers, Producers of Phonograms and Broadcasting Organisations 1961 (the Rome Convention). Related rights in this narrow sense are sometimes also called "neighbouring rights", derived from the French expression *droits voisins du droit d'auteur*. Both expressions are used at the international level in a broader sense to describe not only the rights of beneficiaries of the Rome Convention but other newly introduced rights, such as, for example, certain rights afforded to publishers with respect to published editions and databases. In the United Kingdom, and other common law countries, the rights afforded to producers of sound recordings and broadcasters have always been described as "copyright", whereas in civil law countries these rights are generally described as related or neighbouring rights as opposed to authors' rights. The property rights that performers now enjoy in the United Kingdom are equivalent to copyright; in civil law countries, performers' rights are also considered to be related rights. The rights of two of the beneficiaries of the Rome Convention, performers and producers of phonograms, are also now protected under the WIPO Performances and Phonograms Treaty 1996 (the WPPT). **1–04**

International classification of rights. The international classification of the above rights is founded on the distinctions between the principles governing copyright protection in common law countries and those governing authors' **1–05**

rights (*droit d'auteur, derecho de autor, Urheberrecht*) in countries with a civil law tradition. Common law copyright has historically emphasised the protection of the "work" and has embraced new kinds of work, such as films, sound recordings, photographs and computer programs, as they have developed from advances in technology, admitting as the authors of such works both individuals and legal entities. Civil law authors' rights systems, by contrast, put emphasis on the individual author who is the creator of the work and, as a general rule, do not consider legal entities as eligible to be authors, since the author is considered to be the creator of the work in a personal sense, the work being deemed to emanate from the authors' personality.[4]

In the past, these distinctions had little impact on the domestic law of the United Kingdom. However, the wide-ranging harmonisation programme of the European Commission in the area of copyright and related rights law, which has now been in full swing for some years and is continuing, has had the effect of bridging the gaps between the common law and civil law systems in the Member States, and certain elements of the authors' rights approach to copyright have already found their way into UK law. One example of the introduction of such an element into UK law is the new right of the principal director of a film to be one of the authors of a film, along with the producer.[5] Another is the definition of originality introduced in relation to a literary work consisting of a database; this differs from the standard definition recognised by the law of the United Kingdom.[6] The Artist's Resale Right introduced in 2006, which gives living British artists the right to receive a royalty on the resale of their works, is another example of a civil law import.[7]

(ii) Copyright as intellectual property

1–06   **Copyright and industrial property distinguished.** Copyright as currently in force in the United Kingdom is defined in Ch.2, below. It belongs to the category of rights known as "Intellectual Property Rights", which concerns property rights granted for the results of creative activity, i.e. creations of the human intellect. Intellectual property rights comprise two main branches, copyright and industrial property. This work is concerned with copyright and rights related thereto; industrial property is concerned with the protection of inventions (patent law), industrial designs, trade marks, service marks and commercial names and designations as well as the law against unfair competition. International protection for industrial property is provided under the Paris Convention for the Protection of Industrial Property 1883, which affords protection to patents, utility models (petty patents), registered industrial designs, trademarks, service marks, trade names, indications of source or appellations of origin and the repression of unfair competition.[8]

B. Subject-Matter of this Work

1–07   This work is concerned with copyright in the broad sense of authors' and related

---

[4] This and other differences between the two approaches are discussed in paras 24–43 et seq., below.

[5] 1988 Act s.9(2)(ab); originally introduced by the Copyright and Related Rights Regulations 1996 (SI 1996/2967) December 1, 1996.

[6] 1988 Act s.3A.(2): "... [A] literary work consisting of a database is original if, and only if, by reason of the selection or arrangement of the contents of the database the database constitutes the author's own intellectual creation". This section was inserted by the Copyright and Rights in Databases Regulations 1997 (SI 1977/3032), with effect from January 1, 1998. On the subject of the standard of originality under UK law, see paras 2–01 and 3–125 et seq. below.

[7] The Artist's Resale Right Regulations 2006 (SI 2006/346); see Ch.20, below.

[8] Stockholm Act 1967.

rights as well as certain other rights connected thereto and covers the topics discussed below.

(i) Copyright

(a) *Authors' rights under the Berne Convention*

As seen in para.1–04, above, this covers original literary, dramatic, musical and artistic works protected in accordance with both the Berne and Universal Copyright Conventions and includes cinematographic works (films). The expression literary and artistic works is defined as follows by the Berne Convention[9]:

> "The expression 'literary and artistic works' shall include every production in the literary, scientific and artistic domain, whatever may be the mode or form of its expression, such as books, pamphlets and other writings; lectures, addresses, sermons and other works of the same nature; dramatic or dramatico-musical works; choreographic works and entertainments in dumb show; musical compositions with or without words; cinematographic works to which are assimilated works expressed by a process analogous to cinematography; works of drawing, painting, architecture, sculpture, engraving and lithography; photographic works to which are assimilated works expressed by a process analogous to photography; works of applied art; illustrations, maps, plans, sketches and three-dimensional works relative to geography, topography, architecture or science".

The expression "literary and artistic works" thus must be understood as including all such works capable of being protected. The definition lists a number of different kinds of works but the list is not exhaustive. The words "such as" make it clear that the list is purely illustrative and not limitative.[10] The United Kingdom as a member of the Berne Convention is obliged to afford protection to the works listed but is not prevented from providing copyright protection to other works. These works are protected in the United Kingdom for 70 years from the end of the calendar year in which the author dies, the period of protection having been increased from 50 years as a result of EC legislation adopted in 1993.[11] Rights in these works as provided by the 1988 Act are described in Chs 3, 7 and 8, below.

1–08

(b) *Rome Convention rights*

Copyright in the United Kingdom also provides protection to broadcasts and sound recordings; these rights include the protection guaranteed to producers of phonograms and broadcasters under the Rome Convention but are much more extensive than the minimum rights provided for therein. The period of protection of these works in the United Kingdom is 50 years from the end of the calendar year in which the work is made or first released[12] to the public. The rights in these works are also described in Chs 3, 7 and 8, below.

The other beneficiary of the Rome Convention, performers, do not benefit from copyright protection, as such, in the United Kingdom but enjoy non-property and

1–09

---

[9] Berne Convention art.2(1).

[10] *Guide to the Berne Convention* (World Intellectual Property Organisation, Geneva, 1978), para.2.6.

[11] Council Directive 93/98 [1993] OJ L290/9. The term of protection provided for by the Berne Convention is 50 years post mortem auctoris (pma).

[12] A recording is released when it is first published, played or shown in public, broadcast or included in a cable programme service.

property rights which also provide a higher level of protection than the Rome Convention. Rights in performances are discussed in Ch.12, below.[13]

As mentioned in para.1–04, above, performers and producers of phonograms also enjoy protection under the WPPT.

(c) *Other copyrights*

1–10   The 1988 Act also protects typographical arrangements of published editions as copyright works. Published editions are protected for a period of 25 years from the end of the calendar year in which they were first published. The rights in these works are described in Chs 3, 7, 8 and 17, below.

(ii) Authors' unwaivable right to rental remuneration

1–11   A right to equitable remuneration is guaranteed to any author who transfers his rental right concerning a sound recording or a film to the producer of the sound recording or film. Thus, even when the author has assigned or otherwise transferred his rental right to such a producer, he retains the right to equitable remuneration for the rental. This right to equitable remuneration may not be assigned at all except to a collecting society. This applies in the case of an author of a literary, dramatic, musical or artistic work, and the principal director of a film. The idea behind this provision is to protect authors who are perceived as being in a weak negotiating position vis á vis producers and therefore in need of a safeguard to prevent them giving up their rights. This right is described in para.7–101, below.

(iii) Moral rights of authors

1–12   Moral rights constitute certain specific rights that the author of an original literary, dramatic, musical or artistic work, and the director of a film, enjoys in his creation. Only the author personally can exercise these rights during his lifetime, since they are not assignable. Moreover, certain of these rights subsist in favour of the author, whether or not he is the owner of the copyright. These rights are distinct from the economic rights of authors and guarantee the personal connection between the author and his work. As a general rule, they continue to subsist until the copyright in the work has expired.

They include the following rights:
(a) Right to be identified as author or director of a work.
(b) Right to object to derogatory treatment of a work.
(c) Right to object to false attribution of authorship or directorship.
(d) Right to privacy of certain photographs and films.
These rights are described in Ch.11, below.

(iv) Rights in performances

1–13   Part II of the 1988 Act confers rights on performers and persons having recording rights.

(a) *Performers' economic rights in their performances*

1–14   These rights, described as performers' economic rights, are designed to protect

---

[13] See also paras 1–13 to 1–16, below.

performers against unauthorised recording or live broadcasting of their live performances and making a recording of such a broadcast. Performers are also guaranteed adequate control over and remuneration for the exploitation of recordings of their performances. Thus, their consent is required for copying a recording of a performance (reproduction right), issuing copies thereof to the public (distribution right) and for the rental or lending of such copies to the public (rental right). Consent is also required for making a recording of a performance available to the public by electronic transmission in such a way that members of the public may access the recording from a place and at a time individually chosen by them. This right is known as "the making available right". These four rights are property rights. Performers are also entitled to equitable remuneration from the owner of the copyright in the sound recording for the exploitation of a commercially published sound recording of their performance by means of public performance or communication to the public otherwise than by being made available as described in connection with the making available right, such as by inclusion in a broadcast or cable programme service and rental. This right to equitable remuneration may not be assigned, except to a collecting society for the purpose of enabling it to enforce the right on the performer's behalf. The rights expire 50 years from the end of the calendar year in which the performance takes place or is released to the public. These rights are described in Ch.12, below.

(b) *Exclusive recording rights*

These rights (also termed economic rights), introduced for the first time in the 1988 Act, benefit persons having an "exclusive recording contract" with a performer and who is thereby entitled to the exclusion of all other persons (including the performer) to make recordings of one or more of the performances of a performer with a view to their commercial exploitation, i.e. by sale, letting for hire, or showing or playing in public. "Recording" in relation to a performance, means a film or sound recording. In practice, this means a producer of a film or sound recording, who is party to and has the benefit of an exclusive recording contract to which the performance is subject, or to whom the benefit of such a contract has been assigned. The rights are infringed by anyone who, without the consent of the person having the recording rights or the performer, makes a recording of the whole or any substantial part of the performance or exploits a performance. The duration of these rights is the same as with respect to performers' rights in performances. These rights are also described in Ch.12, below. **1–15**

(c) *Performers' moral rights*

The WIPO Performers and Phonograms Convention (WPPT) 1996, to which the United Kingdom is a signatory, is the first international treaty to include provisions relating to moral rights for performers. The Treaty requires two moral rights to be afforded to performers, the right to claim to be identified as the performer of a performance (the right to be identified or the right of paternity) and the right to object to any distortion, mutilation or other modification of his performance that would be prejudicial to his reputation (the right to object to derogatory treatment, often referred to as the right of integrity).[14] The Performances (Moral Rights, etc.) Regulations 2006[15] has implemented these provisions in the United Kingdom in relation to any type of live performances and to sound recordings of any type of performance, regardless of whether that is made directly from **1–16**

---

[14] WPPT art.5.
[15] SI 2006/18.

the live performance or indirectly. These new rights are described also in Ch.11, below.

(v) Design right in original designs

1–17 Unregistered forms of protection for industrial designs include design right, unregistered European Community design and the protection of works of industrial application. A design is defined as "the design of any aspect of the shape or configuration (whether internal or external) of the whole or part of an article" (s.213(2) of the 1988 Act). It is concerned with what an article looks like or is intended to look like. It is not concerned with how an article performs its function, which is the concern of patent law. Industrial design covers a wide range of activity. An unregistered industrial design may be protected against acts of copying under the following bases: design right, introduced by the 1988 Act; unregistered European Community design under the Community Design Regulation 6/2002 and copyright. These rights are described in Ch.13, below.

(vi) Miscellaneous other specific rights

(a) *Protection of semiconductor topographies*

1–18 A design right in original semiconductor topographies (the etched patterns which make the electrical circuitry of integrated circuits) is provided by the Design Right (Semiconductor) Regulations 1989, as amended in 2006. A semiconductor product is a device performing an electronic function, utilising semiconducting properties of its constituent semiconductor layer(s). A semiconductor topography is a pattern which is either fixed or is intended to be fixed in a semiconductor layer or a layer of material provided over the semiconductor layer for the manufacture of a semiconductor device, and also includes an arrangement of such patterns in relation to each other. The requirement that a semiconductor topography must be original means that it must not be commonplace in the design field in question at the time of its creation. This right is dealt with in Ch.14, below.

(b) *Devices designed to circumvent copy protection*

1–19 Copies of copyright works of all kinds are now commonly made available to the public in an electronic form which is copy protected by so-called "protection measures", in order to prevent and discourage unauthorised reproduction (or piracy) of works. Copy protection measures are devices or technological measures which are applied to a copyright work and which prevent or restrict acts which are not authorised by the owner of the copyright. The 1988 Act thus provides legal protection for two categories of technical measures used by right holders to protect their works against unauthorised reproduction and other copyright infringements: measures to control access to works, for example, by encryption, and measures of copy control such as "copy management systems". Rights management information embedded in works in digital form is also protected. In these respects the relevant provisions of the EU Information Society Directive[16] have been transposed into UK law. The 1988 Act gives owners of copyright in

---

[16] Directive 2001/29 of the European Parliament and of the Council of May 22, 2001 on the Harmonisation of Certain Aspects of Copyright and Related Rights in the Information Society (OJ L167, June 22, 2001), transposed into UK law by the Copyright and Related Rights Regulations 2003 (SI 2003/2498).

computer programs the same rights against a person who makes or otherwise deals in devices or means specifically designed or adapted to circumvent copy protection systems as they have in respect of an infringement of copyright, including the right to delivery up and seizure of such articles. In relation to works other than computer programs, a new civil remedy has been introduced against any person who deliberately circumvents without authority effective technological measures used by right holders to protect their works. A new offence has also been created in relation to the dealing in devices and services which circumvent effective technological measures as well as a civil remedy in relation to that dealing. These civil and criminal remedies are available in respect of measures intended to protect rights in performances, publication rights and database rights, as well as copyright, and are available to the owner of the right as well as to the person issuing copies to the public. These rights are described in Ch.15, below.

(c) *Fraudulent reception of transmissions*

The 1988 Act has made it a criminal offence to fraudulently receive a programme included in a broadcasting service provided from a place in the United Kingdom with intent to avoid payment of any charge applicable to the reception of the programme. Similarly, it is an offence to make or otherwise deal in unauthorised decoders designed or adapted to enable an encrypted transmission, or any service of which it forms part, to be accessed in an intelligible form without payment of the fee charged by the person making the transmission (whether by the circumvention of any conditional access technology related to the transmission or service or by any other means). There are no civil remedies against the dishonest receiver of programmes or services. These provisions are described in Ch.16, below. **1–20**

(d) *25-year publication right*

This right, introduced by the Copyright and Related Rights Regulations 1996,[17] gives a person who, after the expiry of copyright protection, publishes[18] a previously unpublished work for the first time in the European Economic Area a property right equivalent to copyright for a limited period of 25 years. The right is granted without formality and supplements the rights publishers have in the typographical arrangement of their published editions. "Work" for the purpose of the right means a literary, dramatic, musical or artistic work, or a film. The right is described in Ch.17, below. **1–21**

(e) *The new sui generis Database right*

A database under the 1988 Act is a collection of independent works, data or other materials which are arranged in a systematic or methodical way, and which are individually accessible by electronic or other means. Such a database is now to be considered to be a literary work only if it is original in the sense that, by reason of the selection or arrangement of its contents, the database constitutes the author's own intellectual creation. There are, however, many databases which do not qualify as original literary works, because they are mere compilations of data. The creation of such databases may require considerable investment and labour and, therefore, deserve some degree of protection against unauthorised reproduction. For this reason, in response to EC legislation (the EC Council **1–22**

---

[17] SI 1996/2967.
[18] The publisher of the work must be, at the time of first publication, a national of an EEA state.

Directive on the legal protection of databases),[19] the Copyright and Rights in Databases Regulations 1997[20] incorporated into UK law the criterion of originality defined in the Directive for databases protected as literary works and introduced in addition a new sui generis property right in databases which do not meet that criterion (non-original databases), but in respect of which there has been a substantial investment in obtaining, verifying or presenting the contents of the database. It is an infringement of this right to extract or reutilise without consent all or a substantial part of the contents of the database. The right subsists for 15 years from the end of the calendar year in which the making of the database was completed. These rights are described in Ch.18, below.

(f) Public lending right

1–23 The Public Lending Right Act 1979 set up a scheme to provide remuneration to be paid out of public funds to authors of books lent out to the public by local library authorities in the United Kingdom. This is not a copyright but an assignable property right for the benefit of authors of books only; no other category of author may benefit from it. Authors must be nationals or residents of a country within the European Economic Area. The right subsists from the date of the book's first publication until 50 years from the end of the year of the author's death.[21] The scheme is described in Ch.19, below.

(g) Artist's Resale Right

1–24 A new intellectual property right, the artist's resale right, previously unknown to the law of the United Kingdom, has been created by The Artist's Resale Right Regulations 2006, which entered into force on February 14, 2006.[22] The new right was introduced in implementation of the European Directive on the resale right for the benefit of the author of an original work of art.[23] Artist's resale right consists in the entitlement of artists to receive a royalty on the resale of their works, provided that an art market professional is involved in that sale and the sale price is above a specified minimum threshold. The minimum threshold established by the Regulations is the equivalent of EUR 1,000, and the royalty set is 4 per cent of the sale price. For the time being, the royalty is payable on the sale of works by living artists only. The right lasts for as long as the copyright in the work subsists, which is normally for 70 years after the death of the artist. The right is inalienable. The right is described in a Ch.20, below.

C. INTELLECTUAL PROPERTY RIGHTS NOT DEALT WITH IN THIS WORK

(i) Registered designs

1–25 Design right in original designs, referred to in para.1–17, above, is to be distinguished from the protection conferred on registered designs under the Registered Designs Act 1949, as amended by the Registered Design Regulations 2001, which were introduced in implementation of the EC Directive on the Legal Protection of Designs 1998 and the Community Design Regulation 6/2002. A detailed discussion of the law of registered designs under both UK and EC law is outside the scope of this work but Ch.13 contains an outline of the relevant law.

---

[19] Directive 96/9 of March 11, 1996.
[20] SI 1997/3032.
[21] Public Lending Right Act 1979 ss.1(7), 4(2) and 6.
[22] SI 2006/346.
[23] Directive 2001/84/EC of the European Parliament and of the Council, dated September 27, 2001.

(ii) Patents for inventions

Under the Patents Act 1977,[24] the patent system provides monopoly protection **1–26** for a period of 20 years from the date of filing an application for a patent for an invention which is susceptible of industrial application, new and involves an inventive step. Patents are granted only after search and examination procedures designed to ensure that inventions meet those requirements of patentability. The patent law of the United Kingdom is in line with the European Patent Convention (EPC) 1973, as revised in 2000, which established a common system of law for the grant of patents in the Contracting States.[25] The United Kingdom became party to the EPC on October 7, 1977. Thus, applicants for patents in the United Kingdom may apply for a national patent at the United Kingdom Patent Office and/or for a European patent at the European Patent Office (EPO), designating whichever of the currently 37 Member States of the EPC in which protection is sought, including the United Kingdom, if desired. If a European patent is granted, it confers on its proprietor (with effect from the date of the mention of its grant in the European Patent Bulletin) in each Contracting State in respect of which it is granted the same rights as would be conferred by a national patent. At the international level, patents are protected under the Paris Convention for the Protection of Industrial Property 1883, to which the United Kingdom is also party.

There are a number of exclusions from patentability under the law of the United Kingdom and the EPC. The following may not be regarded as inventions: discoveries, scientific theories and mathematical methods; aesthetic creations; schemes, rules and methods for performing mental acts, playing games or doing business and programs for computers, as such; as well as, finally, presentations of information.[26] Computer programs are, as seen above, considered as literary works in terms of copyright protection; this means that the expression of the computer program is protected but not its underlying idea. In 2004, the European Union reached political agreement on a common position on a proposal for an EU Directive on the patentability of computer implemented inventions, stipulating that for a computer-implemented invention to be patentable it must meet the other requirements of patentability, namely, industrial applicability, novelty and inventive step. However, in July 2005, the European Parliament rejected the Council common position and the legislative procedure was closed. The proposed Directive would have confirmed the present position under the EPC. Meanwhile, the EPO continues its existing practice.[27]

---

[24] On patent law in the UK, see S. Thorley, et al., *Terrell on the Law of Patents* 16th edn (London: Sweet and Maxwell, 2006).

[25] On the law and practice relating to the EPC, see *Case Law of the Boards of Appeal of the European Patent Office*, 6th edn (Munich: EPO 2010); *European National Patent Decisions Report* (Munich: EPO DG3, 2005); N. Fox, *A Guide to the EPC 2000* 4th edn (London: CIPA, 2010); G. Paterson, *The European Patent System* 2nd edn (London: Sweet and Maxwell, 2001); Singer and Stauder, *The European Patent Convention: A Commentary* 3rd edn (London: Sweet and Maxwell/Carl Heymanns Verlag KG, 2003). As of August 31, 2010, the EPO had the following 37 Contracting States: Albania, Austria, Belgium, Bulgaria, Croatia, Cyprus, Czech Republic, Denmark, Estonia, Finland, France, Germany, Greece, Hungary, Iceland, Ireland, Italy, Latvia, Liechtenstein, Lithuania, Luxembourg, Macedonia, Malta, Monaco, Netherlands, Norway, Poland, Portugal, Romania, San Marino, Slovakia, Slovenia, Spain, Sweden, Switzerland, Turkey and the United Kingdom. Serbia acceded to the EPC on July 15, 2010 and consequently the EPC will enter into force for Serbia on October 1, 2010. States which at present recognise European patents on request (known as "extension States") are: Bosnia and Herzegovina, Montenegro and Serbia.

[26] EPC art.52(2).

[27] See Opinion of the Enlarged Board of Appeal of the EPO in case G3/08 of May 12, 2010, which confirmed the approach of the EPO regarding the patentability of computer programs under the EPC.

(iii) Registered trade marks

1–27   The third main branch of intellectual property law concerns trade marks.[28] A
registered trade mark is an item of personal property and acts as a distinctive sign
to protect the value of reputation and goodwill in trade and to distinguish the
goods and services of one trading enterprise from those of another. A trade mark
can be a very valuable item of intellectual property because it can come to be associated in the minds of the public with the reputation of a company and the quality of the goods and services it provides. Trade marks also protect the consumer.
Trade mark law has been harmonised within the European Community[29] and this
EC legislation was implemented by the Trade Marks Act 1994. The Act defines a
trade mark as being "any sign capable of being represented graphically which is
capable of distinguishing goods or services of one undertaking from those of another" and gives examples, such as words (including personal names), designs,
letters, numerals, or the shape of goods or their packaging. There is a registration
system for trade and service marks, following examination of the distinctiveness
of the mark and search and examination of prior registrations for the same goods
and services and those of the same description. The Act also provides for the
registration of collective marks, which are marks distinguishing the goods or services of members of the association which is the proprietor of the mark from
those of other undertakings. The duration of registration is 10 years from the date
of filing.

A European Community Trade Mark Office has been established at Alicante in
Spain and began to accept applications for registration on January 1, 1996, following the entry into force of the Council regulation on the Community Trade
Mark in 1994.[30] Only marks which can have effect throughout the Community as
a whole will be accepted, since the Community trade mark has a unitary character
having equal effect throughout the Community.

(iv) Malicious falsehood

1–28   Malicious falsehood, also referred to as injurious falsehood, is a tort which is
available to provide protection against forms of unfair trading, such as false statements which are damaging to a trader's reputation or business.[31] The basis of the
action is an untrue statement maliciously published about a plaintiff's business
which is calculated to cause pecuniary damage. Under the Defamation Act 1952,
proof of special damage is not necessary if the statement was calculated to cause
pecuniary damage to the plaintiff and was published in writing or some other permanent form, or was made in respect of any office, profession, calling, trade or
business held or carried on by him at the time of publication.

(v) Rights of confidence

1–29   The law of breach of confidence is based on equity and has been developed by
case law; the 1988 Act provides that any rule of equity relating to breaches of
trust or confidence is not affected thereby.[32] According to this judge-made doctrine, a person who has received information in confidence must not use it or pub-

---

[28] See D. Kitchin et al., (eds), *Kerly's Law of Trade Marks and Trade Names* 14th edn (London:
Sweet and Maxwell, 2005).
[29] Council Directive of December 21, 1988 to approximate the laws of Member States relating to
trade marks [1989] OJ L40/1.
[30] [1994] OJ L11.
[31] See *Copinger* 13th edn, paras 21–50 et seq.
[32] CDPA 1988 s.171(1)(e).

lish it in breach of the obligation of confidence. The right to restrain the publication of a work on the ground of breach of confidence is in some ways broader than copyright, because it may protect ideas and information which copyright does not protect, thus raising questions relating to the public interest and freedom of expression.[33]

(vi) Authors' and copyright owners' goodwill

The tort of passing off may be committed in relation to copyright works without infringing copyright but by causing damage to the interests of the author or owner of the copyright. For example, questions commonly arise in relation to copyright works as to the protection of titles of works, the names of the authors and fictional characters, and the general goodwill and reputation attaching both to the copyright work and its author.[34]   **1–30**

(vii) Plant Varieties Act 1997

The protection of plant varieties is now governed by the Plant Varieties Act 1997, which replaced the Plant Varieties and Seeds Act 1964. The 1964 Act had created a special scheme of protection outside the patent system and provided a monopoly right to breeders or discoverers of plant varieties The new Act brings the law of the United Kingdom on this subject into line with the revised 1991 version of the Convention for the Protection of New Varieties of Plants 1961 (UPOV), and with the EC Regulation on Community Plant Variety Rights 1994.[35] It should be noted that a grant of EU rights gives protection throughout the European Union and that EU rights and UK rights cannot operate simultaneously.[36]   **1–31**

Plant breeders' rights may be granted for varieties of all plant genera and species. "Variety" means a plant grouping within a single botanical tax on of the lowest-known rank having certain defined characteristics, i.e. that it can be: (i) defined by the expression of the characteristics resulting from a given genotype or combination of genotypes, (ii) distinguished from any other plant grouping by the expression of at least one of those characteristics, and (iii) considered as a unit with regard to its suitability for being propagated unchanged. To qualify for protection, a variety must be distinct, uniform, stable and new. Plant breeders' rights in the United Kingdom are granted to applicants after official testing by the Controller of the Plant Variety Rights Office.

The United Kingdom is party to the Convention for the Protection of New Varieties of Plants 1961 (UPOV), as revised in 1991. The Patents and Plant Variety Rights (Compulsory Licensing) Regulations 2002, which came into force on

---

[33] See *Copinger* 15th edn, Ch.20, and R. G. Toulson and C. Phipps, *Confidentiality* (London: Sweet and Maxwell, 2006) and K. Brearley and S. Bloch, *Employment Covenants and Confidential Information* 3rd edn (Bloomsbury Professional, 2009).

[34] See *Copinger* 15th edn Ch.21, C. Wadlow, The *Law of Passing Off* 3rd edn (London: Sweet and Maxwell, 2004), D. Young, *Passing Off* 3rd edn (1994) and D. Kitchin et al., (eds) *Kerly's Law of Trade Marks and Trade Names* 14th edn (London: Sweet and Maxwell, 2005).

[35] Council Regulation EC 2100/94 of July 27, 1994 on Community Plant Variety Rights (OJ L227, September 1, 1994) which came into operation in the UK on April 27, 1995. See also the UK Patents and Plant Variety Rights (Compulsory Licensing) Regulations 2002.

[36] The UK, however, allows UK plant breeders' rights to be suspended whilst EU plant variety rights are exercised, which allows UK rights to be re-invoked if EU Plant Variety rights are terminated. These arrangements only apply where an EU plant variety right follows the grant of a UK right and not vice versa. The UK and EU systems of plant breeders' rights are administered by the UK Plant Varieties Office and the EU Plant Variety Office, respectively. See also the *Plant Breeders' Rights Handbook* and *Guide to the Plant Varieties Act 1997*, available from the UK Plants Variety Office and Seeds Division website: *http://www.defra.gov.uk/planth/pvs/default.htm*

March 1, 2002, established a new regulatory framework for compulsory licences and cross-licences between holders of patents and plant breeders' rights. The Regulations implemented in the United Kingdom the provisions of European Directive 98/44/EC on the legal protection of biotechnological inventions[37]; the Directive provides for compulsory licensing of plant breeders' rights and patent rights in circumstances where the existence of one right hinders the acquisition or exploitation of the other right.

(viii) Protection of the Olympic and Paralympic Symbols

1–32   The Olympic Symbol, etc. (Protection) Act 1995,[38] as amended by the London Olympic Games and Paralympic Games Act 2006, which entered into force on March 30, 2006, establish the Olympics and Paralympics association rights. The 1995 Act conferred exclusive rights in relation to the use of the Olympic symbol, the Olympic motto and certain words associated with the Olympic Games, such as Olympic, Olympiad and Olympian and created a right known as "the Olympics association right" which is infringed by unauthorised usage of any of the protected words or symbols. The 1995 Act provided for certain permitted acts in relation to the right as well as for civil remedies and criminal sanctions in relation to infringement of the right. The 2006 Act has created the same rights in relation to the Paralympic symbol and motto and certain protected words such as Paralympiad, Paralympian and Paralympic. The Act also makes provision in connection with the Olympic Games and Paralympic Games that are to take place in London in the year 2012. It also expanded the scope of protection to prevent an unauthorised person from doing anything likely to create in the public mind an association between the 2012 London Olympics and that person, or the goods and services provided by that person.

The Olympic symbol is also protected under the terms of an international agreement, the Treaty on the Protection of the Olympic Symbol, adopted at Nairobi on September 26, 1981. The Treaty prescribes that States party thereto are obliged to refuse or to invalidate the registration as a mark and to prohibit by appropriate measures the use, as a mark or other sign, for commercial purposes, of any sign consisting of or containing the Olympic symbol, except with the authorisation of the International Olympic Committee. The United Kingdom is not a party to the Treaty; nor did it sign the Treaty at the time it was open for signature.[39]

2. SCOPE OF SUCH RIGHTS GENERALLY

A. INTER-RELATIONSHIP OF RIGHTS

1–33   **Copyright as bundle of rights.** Copyright gives the copyright owner a bundle of property rights. Thus, the owner has the right to do or to authorise other persons to do the various acts restricted by the copyright law, including, for example, inter alia to reproduce, rent out and broadcast the work and to communicate it to the public. The right to control each of these acts is generally exercisable separately. However, these rights may overlap with other rights such as moral

---

[37] art.12.

[38] The Olympic Symbol, etc. (Protection) Act 1995 (c.32), brought into force by SI 1995/2472, September 20, 1995.

[39] The Treaty was open for signature at Nairobi until December 31, 1982, and at Geneva until June 30, 1983. As of October 15, 2010, the Treaty had 48 Member States (for up-to-date status see the WIPO website at *http://www.wipo.int* [Accessed November 15, 2010]).

rights, so that in a given situation there may be infringement of the right of reproduction as well as of the moral right to be identified as the author. Rarely, the exercise of rights is mutually exclusive, as in the case of the protection given to those original designs which are not protected by copyright but which are protected by means of the separate registered design right described above.

Similarly, where more than one right owner has rights in a work, these rights subsist and may be exercised independently. For example, in relation to a sound recording, separate rights subsist with respect to: (a) the music and lyrics embodied in it; (b) the fixation of the performances recorded on it; and (c) the sound recording itself. Someone who wishes to exploit the sound recording must, therefore, acquire or clear all these separate rights. Any unauthorised exploitation will be actionable by any individual right owner.

Copyright is essentially not a positive but a negative right. Thus, for example, no provision of the Copyright Act confers on the owner of copyright in a literary work the right to publish it. The Act gives the owner of the copyright the right to *prevent* others from doing that which the Act recognises the owner alone has the right to do.[40]

B. EXCLUSIVITY AND EXCEPTIONS

Checks and balances on exclusive rights. Copyright is not a monopoly, since it **1–34** does not prevent competition from similar works which have been created independently. However, the rights afforded by copyright and related rights are exclusive property rights, which, if exercised oppressively to prevent access to works, or to make such access too expensive, could be contrary to the public interest. The need for a balance between the rights owners, on the one hand, and the interest of the public in access to protected works, on the other hand, has given rise to various statutory limitations on and exceptions to copyright and related rights. The most important limitation is the restriction of the term of protection of copyright and other rights. Other limitations, often referred to as exceptions, restrict the exclusive rights of owners of the rights with regard to certain uses of their works. The main such exceptions in the United Kingdom are certain permitted acts, for example, for research and private study and for the purposes of criticism and review. There are also statutory exemptions in favour of education and libraries. Finally, the licensing of works by rights owners and their respective collecting societies is subject to the control of the Copyright Tribunal to prevent potential abuse of exclusive rights.[41]

C. MODERN PERCEPTION OF RATIONALE FOR PROTECTION

Purpose of copyright and related rights. Works protected by copyright are **1–35** generally the expression of creative authorship. Copyright provides the framework required to induce authors and other right owners to create and to reward them for their work, i.e. one purpose of copyright is to encourage and reward human endeavour. It acts as an incentive also to publishers and others to invest in the dissemination and exploitation of works for the ultimate benefit of the public. A second rationale for copyright is that stimulating creativity benefits the public. The rationale for copyright is equally valid for related rights. Thus, these rights are regarded as worthy of protection in the public interest. It follows, that, where there is a conflict between the interests of right owners in receiving adequate

---

[40] *Ashdown v Telegraph Group Ltd* [2001] EWCA Civ 1142; [2002] Ch. 149; [2002] R.P.C. 5.
[41] The powers of the Copyright Tribunal are described in paras 28–81 et seq., below.

reward and those of the public in access to works, there is a need to balance the conflicting interests.[42]

1–36   **Balancing private and public interests.** The question of balance is an increasingly delicate matter. Copyright law has been adapted continually to technological advances, as new works and new uses of works have resulted from technical progress. Technical advances accelerated throughout the twentieth century and are continuing to do so. The most recent developments, combining digital and telecommunications technologies, make it possible to distribute copyright works instantaneously throughout the world and to reproduce them at will. This makes the role of Government in balancing the need to define and guarantee the core rights of copyright owners, on the one hand, with the interest of the general public in obtaining access to works, on the other hand, correspondingly difficult. The plethora of legislation adopted by the European Community and the United Kingdom on the subject in the past 20 years bears witness to the constant need to adapt copyright to new circumstances resulting from technical advances and to the difficulty of this process. One controversial area where it is particularly difficult to establish a proper balance is that of private use, including private copying by means of file sharing, since works are now disseminated in digital form so widely and recording techniques make high-quality copying of copyright works so easy.[43]

D. TERRITORIALITY AND ENFORCEMENT OF RIGHTS

1–37   **Territorial nature of rights.** As a rule, copyright and related rights are granted with respect to a particular territory only and give protection to nationals of that territory alone; protection and the possibility of enforcing rights stops at the national borders except in so far as protection is extended outside the territory by bilateral or multinational treaties with other countries. The protection of works of foreign origin within the territory will also depend on such treaties.[44]

1–38   **Enforcement.** The law of the United Kingdom as regards enforcement of rights is described in Chs 21 and 22, below. The extent to which the rights of UK nationals may be enforced abroad depends on a network of international treaties and regional and bilateral agreements, mentioned at paras 1–40 et seq., below and described in more detail in Ch.23, below. However, in recent years, the trade implications associated with the marketing of copyright goods have multiplied, mainly because the problems associated with the enforcement of intellectual property rights generally have escalated. In 2008, the Organisation for Economic Co-operation and Development (OECD) estimated that the value of international trade in counterfeit and pirated products could have accounted for USD 200 billion in 2005. At the time, this amount was larger than the national GDPs of about 150 economies.[45] In 2009, updated estimates published by the OECD suggest that counterfeit and pirated goods in international trade grew steadily over the period 2000–2007 and could amount to USD 250 billion in 2007. The share of counterfeit and pirated goods in world trade is also estimated to have increased from 1.85 per cent in 2000 to 1.95 per cent in 2007. While numerically small this increase is significant, given that world trade more than doubled over that period. These figures do not include domestically produced and consumed products or

---

[42] The rationale for copyright is discussed in more detail in para.2–05, below.

[43] See Ch.21, below, on the subject of file sharing.

[44] Regarding the protection of UK works abroad, see Ch.25, below; as regards the protection of foreign works in the UK, see Chs 3 (6) and 23, below.

[45] *The Economic Impact of Counterfeiting and Piracy* (OECD, 2008).

the significant volume of non-tangible pirated digital products which are distributed via the internet.[46] As the OECD pointed out in its 2008 report, if these items were added, the total magnitude of counterfeiting and piracy worldwide could well be several hundred billion dollars more.

International measures. The increasing share of counterfeit and pirated goods in world trade in the 1980s and early 1990s led to intellectual property rights becoming an important issue in the trade negotiations of the GATT Uruguay Round, which resulted in the adoption of the Agreement on Trade-Related Aspects of Intellectual Property (TRIPs) in 1994.[47] The TRIPs Agreement set minimum standards of protection for intellectual property rights generally, including copyright and related rights, and provided for improved international enforcement measures to fight against international piracy of copyright protected material. The past 20 years has also seen a great deal of activity on the international copyright front which resulted in the adoption in December 1996 of the WIPO Copyright Treaty (WCT) and the WIPO Performances and Phonograms Treaty (WPPT),[48] the aim of which is to give right owners a better level of international protection in the digital age against piracy of all kinds. The Treaties are frequently referred to as the WIPO Internet Treaties. The resulting international obligations imposed on the United Kingdom and the vastly increased trade in copyright goods mean that these rights are no longer a matter for the domestic law of the United Kingdom alone. Moreover, as mentioned at paras 1–41 et seq., below, the United Kingdom's membership of the European Union and the creation of the single market have made it necessary for the copyright law to be adapted to the laws of its European partners.   **1–39**

E. International Standards for the Protection of Copyright and Related Rights

(i) International treaties

Principal influential treaties. Towards the end of the nineteenth century, the expansion of international trade resulting from the industrial revolution fostered a recognition of the need for reciprocal protection of works between countries, and this led in the first place to the adoption of the Berne Convention in 1886.[49] The Berne Convention is based on the principle of national treatment, according to which each Member State affords the protection of its national law to nationals of the other Member States. This principle did not basically interfere with the territorial nature of copyright law. The other major international conventions in this field, including the Universal Copyright Convention 1952 (UCC) (which provides a lower level of protection than the Berne Convention for authors and therefore a refuge for countries unwilling to accept the obligations of Berne), and the Rome Convention for the Protection of Performers, Producers of Phonograms and Broadcasting Organisations 1961 (the Rome Convention) are also based on national treatment. The history and scope of these Conventions, as well as the Convention for the Protection of Producers of Phonograms against the Unautho-   **1–40**

---

[46] *Magnitude of Counterfeiting and Piracy of Tangible Products: An Update, November 2009* (OECD, 2009).

[47] The Agreement on Trade-Related Aspects of Intellectual Property Rights (the TRIPs Agreement) is Annex 1C to the Agreement establishing the World Trade Organisation adopted at Marrakesh on April 15, 1994. See D. Gervais, *The TRIPs Agreement* 3rd edn (London: Sweet and Maxwell, 2008).

[48] The WCT and the WPPT came into force respectively on March 6, 2002 and May 20, 2002.

[49] As regards The Berne Convention, see paras 23–04 et seq., below.

rised Duplication of their Phonograms 1971 (the Phonograms Convention), the Convention relating to the Distribution of Programme-carrying Signals Transmitted by Satellite 1974 (the Satellite Convention) and the TRIPs Agreement (mentioned above) are described in Ch.24, below. All these treaties set minimum standards of protection for the categories of rights owner which they aim to protect, and these standards must be implemented by any state which adheres to the treaty in question. Should a Contracting State fail to meet its obligations under these treaties, generally there is no remedy; only the TRIPs Agreement carries sanctions with it.

The more recently adopted WCT and WPPT are also analysed at paras 23–66 et seq. and paras 23–119 et seq., below.

(ii) European Union

1–41   **Impact of EU law.** The accession of the United Kingdom to the present European Union in 1973 and the establishment of the single market has also had a considerable impact on trade in copyright goods and on the law of copyright. The application of the principle of the free flow of goods within the single market, according to which once such goods have been put on the market in one country with the consent of the rights owner they may be freely exported to another, meant that problems arose in connection with the differences in copyright protection in the various Member States. In the mid-1980s the Commission of the then European Communities recognised the need for some measure of harmonisation of the laws of copyright and related rights, and embarked on a programme of approximation of laws which is continuing. This programme, including the legislation already adopted in the form of Directives and future legislation currently under consideration, as well as its likely impact on UK copyright law, is described in Ch.24, below. The impact of EU law generally, and in particular competition law, on the exercise of rights under the 1988 Act is also explained in Ch.24, below.

(iii) Regional and bilateral treaties

1–42   **Regional treaties.** Until the UCC was adopted in 1952, the United States of America and many Latin American countries remained outside the international copyright community. Instead, a series of Pan-American conventions were adopted between 1889 and 1946 to provide a degree of reciprocal protection for copyright as between the Contracting Parties. These are described at paras 23–178 et seq., below.

There are also a number of Conventions concerned with the protection of copyright and related rights adopted under the auspices of the Council of Europe between 1958 and 2003, which are dealt with at paras 23–181 et seq., below.

1–43   **Bilateral treaties.** In the nineteenth century, as a rule, national copyright laws denied any protection to works of foreign authors, and what protection did exist resulted from bilateral treaties. The importance of these treaties has been superseded by the international conventions mentioned above. However, the European Union and the United States of America both make a point of including requirements for the respect of copyright and related rights in bilateral trade agreements which they enter into with third countries.

3. GENERAL SCHEME OF PROTECTION

Scheme of Protection

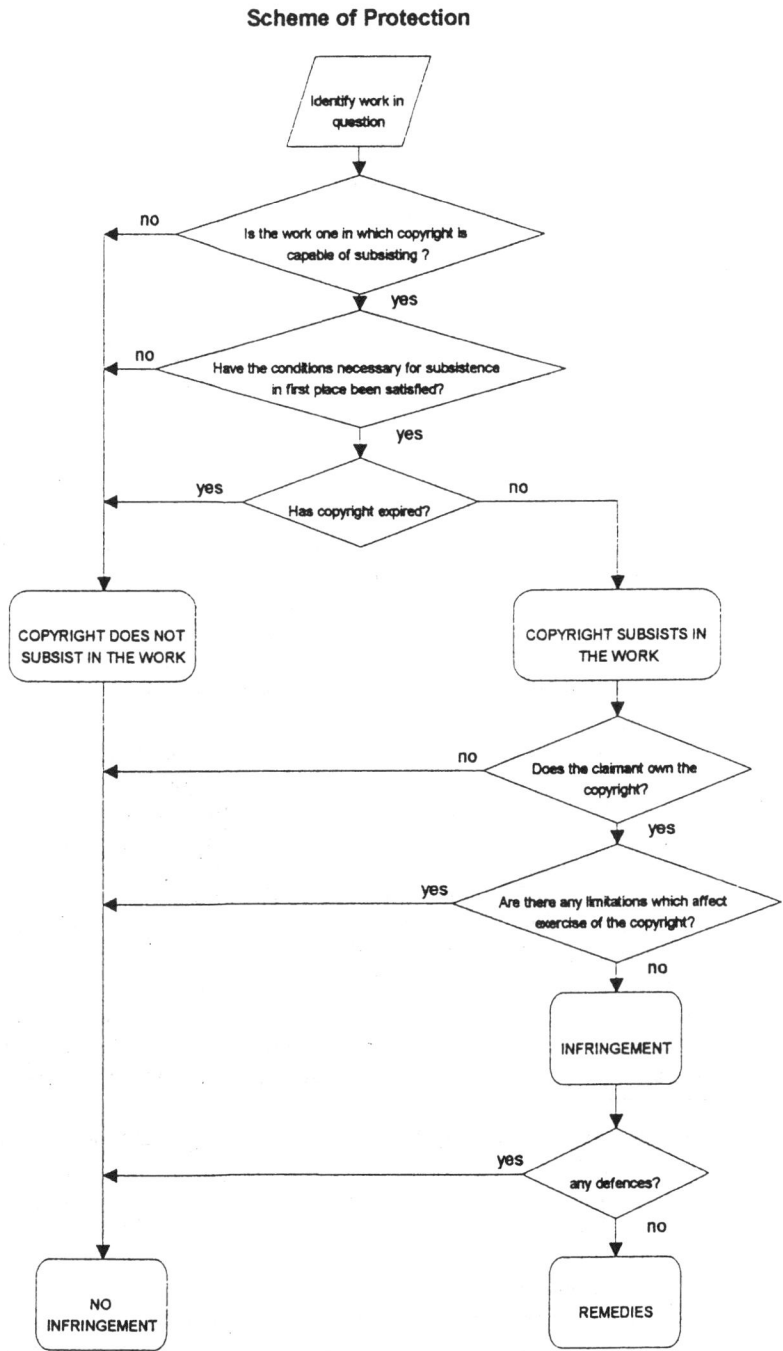

Approaching a copyright problem. The reader who is faced with a copyright **1–44** problem, or a problem concerning any of the related and other rights described above, will no doubt hope to find the answers to any queries regarding the law in this work. The following guide aims to assist the reader to analyse his problem in such a way that he can identify the relevant chapter and find the information he needs. The steps are described in terms of copyright but they are equally applicable to problems arising out of the other rights discussed in this work.

First, the reader should identify the work in question. Might it be a literary, dramatic, musical or artistic work, or a film, a sound recording, a broadcast or other subject-matter of protection? The subject-matter of copyright protection is discussed at paras 3–02 et seq., below.

Then the following questions should be asked:

1. Is the work in fact one in which copyright is capable of subsisting, i.e. does it fit within the definitions of the works protected by the 1988 Act? (cf. paras 3–02 et seq., below).

2. Does copyright subsist in the work now (i.e. at the time the question is posed)? The answer to this depends on the answers to the next two questions:

    (a) Were the conditions necessary for its subsistence in the first place satisfied? Was the work reduced to writing or fixed in some other material form? (cf. paras 3–107 et seq., below). Were the originality requirements satisfied? (cf. paras 3–125 et seq., below). Did the work qualify for protection either by reason of the nationality of its author or, if published, the place of publication? (cf. paras 3–154 et seq., below). As regards the nationality of the author, is the author a British national, a national of the European Economic Area (EEA) or of a country to which protection has been extended under one or other of the international conventions to which the United Kingdom is party? (cf. paras 3–192 et seq. and Ch.23 below). Are there any other qualifying conditions for subsistence of copyright? (cf. paras 3–154 et seq., below).

    (b) Has the copyright expired? In the case of a work in which the duration is connected with the life of the author, the question is whether the author is still alive and, if not, whether he has been dead for more than 70 years or not. In the case of a broadcast, performance or sound recording, the question is when was the work first made or released to the public? For other works, e.g. typographical arrangements of published editions, the crucial question is when was the work first published? (cf. Ch.6, below).

3. Who is the author of the work (cf. Ch.4, below)? Who owns the copyright (cf. Ch.5, below)? These questions may be straightforward to answer but are not necessarily so. These rights are transferable and each constituent part of the bundle of rights which make up copyright may be assigned separately.

    To find out who owns the relevant right at any particular time, it is necessary to pose the following questions:

    (a) Who was the first owner of the copyright in question (cf. Ch.5.1)? To determine this it is usually necessary to know who the author of the work was (cf. Ch.4, below).

    (b) Has ownership of the particular right in which the reader is interested since been transmitted to another person? Assignments of copyright only take effect if they are in writing, signed by or on behalf of the assignor. Questions relating to the chain of ownership are discussed in Ch.5, below.

4. What rights does the copyright prima facie include, i.e. what are the acts restricted by the copyright? The 1988 Act establishes a specific list of restricted acts for each category of work (cf. Chs 7 and 8, below). What

are the moral rights of the copyright owner? (cf. Ch.11, below). How long do all these rights last? (cf. Chs 6 and 11, below).

5. In the particular circumstances, are there any reasons why such exclusive rights are not available for dealing with in a non-litigious context or are there any defences to an infringement claim in a litigious context? This question concerns the limitations imposed by statute on the exercise of copyright. Apart from limitations on the duration of protection, the 1988 Act also limits the scope of copyright protection by providing for exceptions by means of certain permitted acts (cf. Ch.9, below). In relation to infringement of copyright, a number of statutory defences are available. These questions are discussed in Ch.21, below.

6. Are the rights, although exercisable, subject to any form of control? Collective licensing of rights through collecting societies representing one or more categories of right owners is common practice. Such societies provide a convenient mechanism for licensing and administering those rights which it would be difficult for right owners to exercise individually, such as, broadcasting and public performance rights. These societies normally represent the vast majority of those representing a particular category of right owner and the danger exists that they could abuse what amounts to a monopolistic position. The Copyright Tribunal exists to control the licensing practices of these societies; any party to a negotiation may in certain circumstances refer a dispute to the Tribunal for resolution. The law relating to collecting societies is discussed in Ch.27, below, and that concerning control of the exercise of copyrights and related rights in Ch.28, below.

7. In the case of infringement, what remedies are available? The enforcement of rights by action in civil and criminal proceedings and other enforcement measures are dealt with in Chs 21 and 22, below.

PART I

COPYRIGHT

CHAPTER TWO

NATURE AND HISTORY OF COPYRIGHT

Contents   *Para.*

1. NATURE OF COPYRIGHT

Copyright defined. Copyright under the Copyright, Designs and Patents Act **2–01**
1988 ("the 1988 Act") is a property right which subsists in a number of different
kinds of works, such as original literary, dramatic, musical or artistic works,
sound recordings, films or broadcasts and the typographical arrangement of
published editions.[1] A "copyright work" means any such work in which copyright subsists.[2] Literary, dramatic, musical and artistic works must comply with
the criterion of originality in order to be protected. In UK law, "original" means
that the work must originate from its author and must not be copied from another
work.[3] It does not mean that the work must be the expression of original or inventive thought; the originality required relates to the expression of the thought.[4] The
standard of originality is low and depends on the author having expended sufficient independent skill, labour and judgement to justify copyright protection for
the result.[5]

Copyright springs into life immediately on creation of the work. Thus, the
work is protected as soon as it is recorded, in writing or otherwise, on paper,
canvas, tape, disc, film or other recording medium from which it is capable of being reproduced.[6] Unlike the case of other intellectual property rights, such as
patents and trade marks, there are no formalities required for copyright to subsist
and no system of registration of rights.[7] Thus, it is not necessary to apply to any
authority in order to enjoy copyright protection: "The law of copyright rests on a
very clear principle: that anyone who by his or her own skill and labour creates
an original work of whatever character shall, for a limited period, enjoy an

---

[1] CDPA 1988 s.1(1). A new publication right was introduced by the Copyright and Related Rights
Regulations 1996 (SI 1996/2967) s.16; this gives a person who, after the expiry of copyright
protection, publishes for the first time a previously unpublished work a property right equivalent
to copyright for a period of 25 years (see Ch.17, below). See M. Wyburn, "Giving credit where it
is due: the da Vinci Code Litigation" [2007] Ent. L.R. 18(3), 96 and 18(4), 131.

[2] CDPA 1988 s.1(2).

[3] *University of London Press Ltd v University Tutorial Press Ltd* [1916] 2 Ch. 601 at 608. As
regards the criterion of originality in other jurisdictions, see paras 25–43 et seq., below.

[4] See para.2–06, below.

[5] *Kelly v Morris* (1865–66) L.R. 1 Eq. 697; *Karo Step* [1977] R.P.C. 255 at 273. As to originality
generally, see paras 3–125 et seq., below. Note that a higher criterion of originality is required in
the case of databases: "A literary work consisting of a database is original if, and only if, by reason of the selection or arrangement of the contents of the database the database constitutes the
authors' own intellectual creation", (CDPA 1988 s.3A(2)).

[6] CDPA 1988 s.3(2) in relation to literary, dramatic and musical works.

[7] This was not always the case. Registration (originally with the Stationers' Company) was required
to acquire copyright under the first copyright law, the Statute of Anne 1709 (cf. para.2–16,
below). After the copyright law was revised in 1842 (cf. para.2–19, below), the requirement for
registration was maintained not as a pre-condition for statutory copyright but as a condition precedent to taking an enforcement action. The copyright arose automatically on publication (Copyright Act 1842 ss.13, 24).The requirement of registration was abolished by the 1911 Act to
comply with the UK's international obligations under the Berlin Act of the Berne Convention.

exclusive right to copy that work. No one else may for a season reap what the copyright owner has sown".[8]

Copyright gives the owner of the copyright in a work of any description the exclusive right to do certain acts in relation to the copyright work. This includes the right to copy the work itself and also to use the work in other ways protected under the law. These protected uses are issuing copies of the work to the public, renting or lending copies of the work to the public, performing, showing or playing the work in public, communicating the work to the public and making an adaptation of the work, or doing any of the above in relation to an adaptation. Communication to the public includes the broadcasting of the work and the making available to the public of the work by electronic transmission in such a way that members of the public may access it from a place and at a time individually chosen by them. These acts are known as the acts restricted by copyright[9] and are also often referred to as the copyright owner's economic rights. A person who does any of the acts restricted by copyright without the licence (i.e. agreement) of the copyright owner infringes the copyright in the work, unless the acts are otherwise excused,[10] and is liable to have legal action taken against him. Both civil remedies and criminal penalties are available for the enforcement of copyright.[11] In addition to these economic rights, so-called "moral rights" subsist in favour of the author, director or commissioner of certain descriptions of copyright work, irrespective of whether he is the owner of the copyright. These rights include the right to be identified as the author of a literary, dramatic, musical or artistic work or as director of a film, the right to object to derogatory treatment of certain copyright works and the right to object to having a work falsely attributed to oneself as author, as well as the right to privacy of certain photographs and films.[12]

2–02   The meaning of the expression "copyright" has changed over the years with the development of copyright law to extend protection to new subject-matter and to extend the classes of acts which constitute infringement. Before the 1911 Act, the expression "copyright" was confined to the right of multiplying copies and did not include the performing right in dramatic or musical works.[13] At that time, copyright subsisted at common law in respect of unpublished works (except for drawings, paintings and photographs) and by statute for published works (including unpublished drawings, paintings and photographs)[14] and it is uncertain whether the expression "copyright" was used before that date only in relation to the right to restrain publication of published works, or so as to include also the right of an author to restrain publication of his unpublished works.[15]

After the 1911 Act, the expression "copyright" in the United Kingdom came to be used to mean all the rights conferred by the 1911 Act upon authors, composers and artists in respect of their literary, dramatic, musical and artistic works.[16] Copyright, however, although now expressed as the exclusive right to do certain

---

[8] See *Designers Guild Ltd v Russell Williams (Textiles) Ltd* [2000] 1 W.L.R. 2416; [2001] F.S.R. 11, HL at para.2, per Lord Bingham of Cornhill.

[9] CDPA 1988 s.16.

[10] Because the acts constitute "permitted acts", see Ch.9, below.

[11] CDPA 1988 Ch.VI ss.96, et seq.

[12] CDPA 1988 s.2 and Ch.IV ss.77, et seq. (and see Ch.11, below). See also G. Davies and K. Garnett Q.C., *Moral Rights* (London: Sweet and Maxwell, 2010).

[13] See *Pollock CB, Chappell v Purday*, 153 E.R. 491; [1845] 14 M. & W. 303.

[14] Fine Arts Copyright Act 1862 (25 & 26 Vict. c.68).

[15] *Re Dickens* [1935] Ch. 267.

[16] See Copyright Act 1911 s.1(2).

acts,[17] essentially gives the right owner the right to restrict others from doing those acts or to authorise them to do them, and, when copyright is referred to as "an exclusive right", the emphasis is on the word "exclusive". Thus, the 1988 Act, whilst not defining "copyright" otherwise than as a property right,[18] which is transmissible as personal or moveable property,[19] provides that the owner of the copyright in a work has the exclusive right to do the acts restricted by the copyright in a work of that description specified in the 1988 Act.[20] Copyright is infringed by a person who, without the licence of the copyright owner, does, or authorises another to do, any of the restricted acts[21] set out in various sections of the 1988 Act.[22]

Thus, the essence of copyright is the owner's right to take action to prevent others from engaging in specified kinds of activity without the owner's permission. Under the 1988 Act, that right is limited to activities taking place in the United Kingdom.[23] Although usually classified as a moveable,[24] copyright shares some of the characteristics of immoveables in the sense that the rights are territorially limited, and from this it follows that copyright is situate in the country whose law governs its existence. Given that the relevant provisions of the 1988 Act extend to England and Wales, Scotland and Northern Ireland[25] this means that what is often referred to as "United Kingdom copyright" is situate or located in the United Kingdom.[26] Copyright is thus territorial in extent and, as a matter of UK law, there is no such thing as global or world-wide copyright.[27]

Ownership of copyright. According to the 1988 Act, the author, in relation to a work, means the person who creates it.[28] In relation to a literary, dramatic, musical or artistic work, the author will be the individual who wrote the book or play, composed the music or painted or created the artistic work. In the case of literary, dramatic, musical or artistic work which is computer-generated,[29] the author is taken to be the person by whom the arrangements necessary for making the work are undertaken. In relation to other copyright works, the author and person who creates the work is taken to be the producer in the case of sound recordings; the producer and the principal director in the case of films; the person making the broadcast in the case of broadcasts, or, in the case of a broadcast which relays another broadcast by reception and immediate re-transmission, the person making that other broadcast,[30] and, in the case of typographical arrangements of published editions, the publisher.[31] The author of a work is the first owner of copyright in it, except where a literary, dramatic, musical, artistic work or film is made by an employee in the course of his employment, in which case, subject to any agree-

2–03

---

[17] CDPA 1988 s.16(1).
[18] s.1(1).
[19] s.90(1). See also Ch.5, below.
[20] ss.2(1) and 16(1). See also Chs 7 and 8, below.
[21] s.16(2).
[22] ss.17–21.
[23] s.16(1).
[24] s.90(1).
[25] s.207.
[26] See *Peer International Corp v Termidor Music Publishers Ltd* [2002] EWHC 2675, Ch. D., paras 22, 23, citing Dicey, Morris and Collins, *The Conflict of Laws* 14th edn, para.22–051 and *Novello & Co Ltd v Hinrichsen Edition Ltd* [1951] Ch. 1026; (1951) 68 R.P.C. 243.
[27] *Peer International Corp v Termidor Music Publishers Ltd* [2002] EWHC 2675, Ch. The decision on these aspects was not affected by the decision on appeal in *Peer* [2003] EWCA Civ. 1156.
[28] CDPA 1988 s.9(1). See also Ch.4, below.
[29] s.9((3).
[30] s.9(2)(b).
[31] s.9(2)(d).

ment to the contrary, his employer is the first owner of any copyright in the work.[32] Copyright is generally alienable and may be transferred or assigned, in whole or in part, and the owner of copyright may license one or more specific uses of his work.[33]

2–04   **Limitations on copyright.** Copyright protection is limited in duration as well as in other respects, certain exceptions being permitted to the exclusive rights it affords. The term of protection for an original literary, dramatic, musical or artistic work and for films generally expires at the end of the period of 70 years from the end of the calendar year of the death of the author or authors, and in the case of works of unknown authorship, from making or making the work available to the public.[34] As regards computer-generated works, sound recordings and broadcasts (i.e. works where the author is generally a corporate body rather than an individual), copyright subsists for a period of 50 years from making or making available to the public.[35] The duration of copyright in typographical arrangements of published editions subsists for 25 years from the end of the calendar year in which the work was first published.[36] Other limitations on copyright protection include numerous exceptions in favour of the general public, such as, for example, fair dealing for the purpose of research and private study, criticism, review and reporting current events and certain acts done for the purpose of instruction in educational establishments and done in libraries,[37] and many others.

Since copyright law does not create a monopoly, it has been argued that the basic protection which the law of copyright affords, namely that of preventing unlawful reproduction, should extend without limit of time. Prior to the 1911 Act, unpublished literary (and other) works had a perpetual right at common law. But such right ended on publication, after which an author had to base his claim for protection upon his statutory right, if any.[38] However, common law copyright was abolished by the 1911 Act, which provided that no person should be entitled to copyright or any similar right otherwise than under and in accordance with the provisions of that Act, or of any other statutory enactment for the time being in force.[39] The 1956 Act[40] and the 1988 Act[41] contain similar provisions. Nevertheless, an unlimited statutory term for unpublished literary (and other) works was created by the 1911 Act,[42] and continued by the 1956 Act,[43] but not by the 1988 Act, except in the case of works of unknown authorship.[44] However, a new property right equivalent to copyright has recently been introduced for persons who, after the expiry of copyright protection, publish for the first time a previously unpublished work.[45] The 1988 Act[46] also ended the perpetual copyrights granted to

---

[32] s.11.

[33] See paras 5–66 et seq. and 5–198 et seq., below. Note, however, that certain moral rights and rights to equitable remuneration are not alienable. The new artist's resale right is also inalienable.

[34] CDPA 1988 ss.12(1) and 13B. See also Ch.6, below.

[35] ss.12(7), 13A and 14.

[36] SI 1996/2967 s.16(6) and CDPA 1988 s.15.

[37] CDPA 1988 Ch.III ss.28, et seq. See also Ch.9, below.

[38] *Donaldson v Beckett*, 1 E.R. 837; [1774] 4 Burr. 2408; as to other works, see *Albert (Prince) v Strange*, 41 E.R. 1171; (1849) 1 Mac. & G. 25. See also para.2–17, below.

[39] Copyright Act 1911 s.31.

[40] Copyright Act 1956 s.46(5).

[41] CDPA 1988 s.171(2).

[42] Copyright Act 1911 s.17(1).

[43] Copyright Act 1956 s.2(3), 3(4).

[44] CDPA 1988 ss.9(4), (5), 12 and Sch.1 para.12. See paras 6–48 et seq., below.

[45] The Copyright and Related Rights Regulations 1996 s.16.

[46] CDPA 1988 Sch.1 para.13.

universities and colleges by the Copyright Act 1775,[47] which had been preserved by the 1911 Act,[48] as well as by the 1956 Act.[49]

Justifications for copyright. The underlying principles on which the modern international system of copyright and authors' rights is founded are generally considered to be fourfold: natural law, just reward for labour, stimulus to creativity and social requirements.[50] According to natural law, the author has an exclusive natural right of property in the results of his labour and should have control over the publication of his work as well as the right to object to any unauthorised modification or other attack on the integrity of his work. The principle of just reward for labour supposes that authors deserve to be remunerated when their work is exploited. Moreover, copyright provides the economic basis for the investment required to create some works, such as films, sound recordings and works of architecture and to publish others. These investments will not be made unless there is a reasonable expectation of obtaining a return on them. Just reward for labour in turn provides a stimulus to creativity; copyright presupposes that the guarantee of protection and the possibility of controlling and being paid for the exploitation of works encourages authors to create. As Anthony Trollope said: "Take away from English authors their copyrights, and you would very soon take away from England her authors".[51]

2–05

Finally, it is considered a social requirement in the public interest that authors and other rights owners should be encouraged to publish their works so as to permit the widest possible dissemination of works to the public at large. These four fundamental principles are cumulative and interdependent and are applied in the justification of copyright in all countries, although different countries give varying emphasis to each of them. To generalise, it is true to say that in the development of modern copyright laws, the economic and social arguments are given more weight in the Anglo-American laws of common-law tradition, whereas, in Continental law countries with civil law systems, the natural law argument and the protection of the author are given first place.

In the United Kingdom, the justifications for copyright legislation have centred historically on the economic and social arguments. While the need to protect the natural rights of authors and to encourage creativity by protecting the products of their intellects has always been recognised, as well as the need to ensure an adequate reward for authors and creators for their efforts, the copyright system aims to encourage the dissemination of ideas and knowledge to the general public. There is also a concern to balance the interest of authors in protection of their works, on the one hand, with the interest of the public in access to works on the other. Thus, the copyright law in the United Kingdom has created rights and regularly adapted the law to provide authors and other owners of rights with protection with respect to new developments in technology, but at the same time conditions and limitations have been imposed on these rights. The protection of

---

[47] 15 Geo. 3, c.53 and see paras 6–84 et seq., below.

[48] Copyright Act 1911 s.33.

[49] Copyright Act 1956 s.46(1). In this regard, it is, perhaps, surprising that the CDPA 1988 created a new perpetual non-copyright right. Such right is a right for the Hospital for Sick Children, Great Ormond Street, to receive royalties in respect of certain acts of exploitation of the play *Peter Pan* by Sir James Matthew Barrie, notwithstanding that the copyright in such work expired on December 31, 1987. CDPA 1988 ss.149 and 301 and Sch.6 and see para.6–52, below.

[50] S M Stewart, *International Copyright and Neighbouring Rights* 2nd edn (London: Butterworths, 1989), paras 1.01 et seq.; G. Davies, *Copyright and the Public Interest* 2nd edn (London: Sweet & Maxwell, 2002), pp.9 et seq.

[51] A. Trollope, *Autobiography* (London: William Blackwood and Sons, 1883), Ch.6.

copyright, along with other intellectual property rights,[52] is considered as a form of property worthy of special protection because it is seen as benefiting society as a whole and stimulating further creative activity and competition in the public interest.[53]

2–06 **No copyright in ideas.** Copyright is a property right,[54] but copyright law is concerned, in essence, with the negative right of preventing the copying of material.[55] It is not concerned with the reproduction of ideas, but with the reproduction of the form in which ideas are expressed.[56] "Ideas, it has always been admitted,… are free as air."[57] Copyright is not a monopoly, unlike patents and registered designs, which are.[58] Thus, if it can be shown that two precisely similar works were in fact produced wholly independently of one another, there can be no infringement of copyright by one of the other.[59] The position is that, if the idea embodied in the plaintiff's work is sufficiently general, the mere taking of that idea will not infringe. If, however, the idea is worked out in some detail in the plaintiff's work and the defendant reproduces the expression of that idea, then there may be an infringement.[60] In such a case, it is not the idea which has been copied but its detailed expression.[61] This fundamental and internationally recognised principle of copyright law has in recent times been given express recognition in the TRIPs Agreement and in the WIPO Copyright Treaty (WCT), both of which provide that "Copyright protection extends to expressions and not to ideas, procedures, methods of operation or mathematical concepts as such".[62] This principle may be illustrated by the House of Lords case, *Designers Guild*, where Lord Hoffmann in his judgment discussed the question of what is really meant by the notion that there is no copyright in ideas, and what is the basis of the so-called

---

[52] See Introduction, para.1–06, above.

[53] "The exclusive rights which are granted by national copyright, patent, trademark and design laws are granted because it is in the public interest to grant them": *Copyright and Designs Law*, Report of the Committee to consider the Law on Copyright and Designs, Chairman: The Honourable Mr Justice Whitford (the Whitford Report), March 1977, HMSO, Cmnd.6732, para.84. "The Government's broad aims in this revision of copyright law are to ensure continued protection for those who create copyright works while at the same time recognising that the public has a substantial interest in the availability of their works": *Intellectual Property and Innovation*, DTI White Paper, April 1986, HMSO, Cmnd.9712, para.4.

[54] CDPA 1988 ss.1(1), 90(1) and 96(2); cf. Copyright Act 1956 s.36(1) and Copyright Act 1842 s.25.

[55] *George Hensher Ltd v Restawhile Upholstery (Lancs.) Ltd* [1976] A.C. 64; [1974] F.S.R. 173 at 98; *Fraser v Thames Television Ltd* [1984] Q.B. 44 at 60; *Performing Right Society Ltd v Rangers FC Supporters Club* [1975] R.P.C. 626 at 633; *British Leyland Motor Corp v Armstrong Patents Co Ltd* [1986] A.C. 577; [1986] R.P.C. 279 at 302.

[56] See *Jefferys (C) v Boosey (T)*, 10 E.R. 681; (1855) 4 H.L.C. 815; *Donoghue v Allied Newspapers Ltd* [1938] Ch. 106 at 109 and 110; *Gleeson v H. R. Denne Ltd* [1975] R.P.C. 471; *Gomme (E.) Ltd v Relaxateze Upholstery Ltd* [1976] R.P.C. 377; *Catnic Components Ltd v Hill & Smith Ltd* [1981] F.S.R. 60; *LB (Plastics) Ltd v Swish Products Ltd* [1979] R.P.C. 551, HL; *LA Randall Pty Ltd v Millman Services Pty Ltd* (1977–1978) 17 A.L.R. 140; *Kleeneze Ltd v DRG (UK) Ltd* [1984] F.S.R. 399; *George Ward (Moxley) Ltd v Richard Sankey Ltd* [1988] F.S.R. 66; *Green v Broadcasting Corp of New Zealand* [1989] R.P.C. 700; *Designers Guild Ltd v Russell Williams (Textiles) Ltd* [2000] 1 W.L.R. 2416; [2001] F.S.R. 11, HL, para.24. And see CDPA 1988 s.3(2).

[57] A. Birrell, *The Law and History of Copyright in Books* (London: Cassell and Co., 1899), p.167.

[58] See *British Leyland Motor Corp v Armstrong Patents Co Ltd* [1986] A.C. 577; *LB (Plastics) Ltd v Swish Products Ltd* [1979] R.P.C. 551, HL, at 570. Although, cf. *Tate v Fulbrook* [1908] 1 K.B. 821 at 832, 833 and *Green v Broadcasting Corp of New Zealand* [1989] 2 All E.R. 1056 at 1058.

[59] *Corelli v Gray* (1913) 29 T.L.R. 570; *Rees v Melville* [1911–1916] Mac. C.C. 96 at 168; *Hollinrake v Truswell* [1894] 3 Ch. 420; *Libraco Ltd v Shaw Walker Ltd* (1913) 30 T.L.R. 22; *Wesman v McNamara* [1923–1928] Mac. C.C. 121; *Francis Day & Hunter Ltd v Bron* [1963] Ch. 587; and see paras 7–13 et seq., below.

[60] See *IBCOS Computers Ltd v Barclays Mercantile Highland Finance Ltd* [1994] F.S.R. 275.

[61] See also para.7–13, below.

[62] TRIPs Agreement art.9(2); WCT art. 2.

ideas/expression dichotomy.[63] He first pointed out that all copyright works have as their *basis* an idea, in that all works are the expression of the author's ideas, represented by his decision to use certain modes of expression rather than others. The point usually made is a different one, or rather two different ones, since the distinction which the cases make between ideas and the expression of ideas in fact has two quite separate elements:

(1) A work may express certain "ideas" but those ideas are not protected by the copyright which subsists in the work because they have no connection with the particular subject-matter of the work, whether it be literary, dramatic, musical or artistic, etc. Thus, a literary work which describes a system or invention does not entitle the copyright owner to protection for the invention.[64] In such cases, the expression of the idea in the literary work may well attract copyright protection but the operation of the system itself, or the working of the inventive process, will not reproduce the literary expression which is the subject-matter of copyright.

(2) A work may contain the expression of an "idea" but that expression, as contained in the work, may not be protected because it is not original or so commonplace as not to form a substantial part of the work. The example given was the case of *Kenrick & Co v Lawrence & Co*,[65] where the subject-matter was an artistic work representing a human hand in the act of voting. This category should, it is suggested, in fact be understood as applying to a number of separate types of cases, namely those, (a) where because the idea was so well known to the author from the work of others that its expression required no sufficient skill and labour (an unusual type of case in practice), or (b) where the idea has been expressed in such a trivial manner as not to satisfy the originality test and thus to merit protection, or (c) where, and this is the most usual type of case, the expression of the idea merits copyright protection but the defendant has not appropriated the skill and labour of the author in giving form to that expression. This was the situation in *Kenrick v Lawrence*. If the defendant there had made greater borrowing of the plaintiff's skill in representing a voter's hand, there would have been an infringement. Applied to the facts of *Designers Guild*, one of the features of the claimant's work consisting of a design for fabric was the combination of evenly spaced stripes over which flowers were scattered. If that was all that had been copied, the mere idea of combining stripes and flowers in a design would not have represented sufficient skill and labour to merit protection from copying. "Particularly in relation to cases of artistic copyright, the more abstract and simple the copied idea, the less likely it is to constitute a substantial part. Originality tends to lie in detail with which the basic idea is presented."

So also, in *Designers Guild Ltd*, Lord Hoffmann emphasised that while an artistic technique, such as a type of brushstroke, could not be protected by copyright, the results of a particular technique, in terms of the visual effects produced using them, could be.[66]

A more recent case in this area is the *Da Vinci Code* case.[67] The claimants asserted that the novel *The Da Vinci Code* was a non-textual infringement of the

---

[63] *Designers Guild Ltd v Russell Williams (Textiles) Ltd* [2000] 1 W.L.R. 2416; [2001] F.S.R. 11, HL, per Lord Hoffmann, at para.24.

[64] See, e.g. *Kleeneze Ltd v DRG (UK) Ltd* [1984] F.S.R. 399

[65] *Kenrick & Co v Lawrence & Co* (1890) 25 Q.B.D. 99.

[66] *Designers Guild Ltd v Russell Williams (Textiles) Ltd* [2000] 1 W.L.R. 2416.

[67] *Baigent and Leigh v The Random House Group Ltd* [2007] EWCA Civ 247; [2007] F.S.R. 24. See also *SAS Institute Inc v World Programming Ltd* [2010] EWHC 1829 (Ch).

copyright in their book *The Holy Blood and the Holy Grail (HBHG)*, which was presented as a book of non-fiction. They alleged that their book contained a "central theme" of 15 interconnected points and that this theme had been infringed. The trial judge held that there was no infringement, finding that there was actually no central theme to *HBHG* and that the alleged theme of the claimants was a construct for the litigation.

An appeal against the decision was dismissed.[68] The appeal court agreed with the trial judge's finding that what the defendant had taken from *HBHG* amounted to generalised propositions, at too high a level of abstraction to qualify for copyright protection; what was taken was not the product of the application of skill and labour by the authors of *HBHG* in the creation of their literary work. It lay on the wrong side of the line between ideas and their expression. The court also endorsed the judge's finding that the central theme was not a theme of *HBHG* at all, but rather was no more than a selection of features of *HBHG* collated for forensic purposes.

2–07   **Development of law of copyright.** Copyright law was first introduced in the United Kingdom in response to the need to protect the new printing trade against the unauthorised copying of books (piracy). Ever since, it has developed to keep pace with the introduction of new technologies. As copyright law developed in the eighteenth and nineteenth centuries it was mainly concerned with the field of literature and the arts but, following the advances in technology of the twentieth century, the protection given by copyright law has been considerably expanded over the years, both with respect to the subject-matter of protection and also to the classes of acts which constitute infringement. Thus, today, not only is protection given to literary, dramatic, musical and artistic works (with, for instance, computer programs and databases being protected as literary works[69]), but also to sound recordings, films, broadcasts, and the typographical arrangements of published editions.[70] Infringement of copyright was originally limited to copying but the acts restricted by copyright now cover the issue of copies to the public, the rental or lending of works to the public, the performance, showing or playing the work in public, communicating the work to the public and making an adaptation of the work or doing any of the above in relation to an adaptation.

2. HISTORY OF COPYRIGHT

2–08   **Antiquity.** It is helpful to an understanding of the modern law of copyright to study its history—to see how it has developed from its origins to the present day.

Copyright is a comparatively modern concept, born in the late fifteenth century, following the invention of printing, which for the first time made it possible to produce multiple copies of books quickly and comparatively cheaply. The classical world did not recognise copyright as such; there is no mention of any such concept in Justinian although there is plenty of evidence that Greek and Roman authors were greatly concerned to be identified as the author of their works and that their authorship should be recognised.[71] The word plagiarism, the practice of copying the work of another and passing it off as the copier's own, derives from

---

[68] *Baigent v Random House Group Ltd* [2007] EWCA Civ 247.

[69] CDPA 1988 s.3. A literary work now, expressly, includes preparatory design material for a computer program. See paras 3–11 et seq., below.

[70] See paras 3–02 et seq., below.

[71] A. Birrell, *The Law and History of Copyright in Books* (London: Cassell and Co., 1899), pp.41 et seq.; S.M. Stewart, *International Copyright and Neighbouring Rights* 2nd edn (London: Butterworths, 1989), p.13; G.H. Putnam, *The Question of Copyright* 2nd edn (New York: The Knickerbocker Press, 1896).

the Latin *plagiarius*, an abductor or kidnapper, and has been condemned as an immoral and contemptible practice from the earliest historical times, but in those days there was no law against it. In today's terms, classical authors were concerned that their moral rights be respected, but they enjoyed no economic rights. The earliest copyright case of which there is any record is an Irish sixth-century case involving St Columba, who, while on a visit to the monastery of his former teacher, Abbot Finnian, copied the latter's psalter; Finnian demanded the return of the copy and getting no satisfaction referred the dispute to the King, who ruled in his favour: "to every cow her calf and consequently to every book its copy".[72]

Before the invention of printing, there was little practical need for legal protection of authors against the copying of their works. To start with, the bulk of the population was illiterate and had no use for books. Moreover, the copying of manuscripts was a painstaking and time-consuming occupation mainly done by monks and limited to the copying of religious works for religious orders and the royal courts of Europe. The possibility of printing multiple copies of books cheaply resulted in a new market for books for a public which had not previously had access to the manuscripts which, in the past, had been available only to the most privileged members of society.

Early control of printing. Throughout its history, as already noted, copyright law has been closely linked to developments in technology. It was only after the introduction of printing that any serious question as to the copyright in literary works could be expected to arise. An early statute of Richard III in 1483[73] encouraged the printing of books, and permitted their importation, but this statute was repealed 50 years later on protectionist grounds, it being alleged, in the preamble of the repealing statute in 1533,[74] that such a "marvellous number of printed books" were imported into the realm to the prejudice of the "King's natural subjects", who "have given themselves so diligently to learn and exercise the said craft of printing, that at this day there be within this realm a great number cunning and expert in the said science or craft of printing as able to exercise the said craft in all points as any stranger in any other realm or country". A similar plea was urged on behalf of the bookbinders, who, "having no other faculty wherewith to get their living, be destitute of work and likely to be undone, except some reformation herein be had".[75]

As the number of printers increased in England, the King assumed a prerogative of granting printing privileges, and the earliest copyright protection took the form of printers' licences granted by the Sovereign to regulate the book trade and to protect printers against piracy.[76] These privileges became a source of considerable profit to the Crown[77] and in time were used as an instrument of censorship by the authorities.

Original charter of the Stationers' Company. In 1556, the original charter of the Stationers' Company was granted by the Catholic Queen Mary and her

2–09

2–10

---

[72] R.R. Bowker, *Copyright, its history and its law* (Houghton Mifflin, 1912), p.3; and see G. Putnam, *Books and their makers during the Middle Ages, 1476–1600* (New York, 1962).

[73] 1 Ric. 3, c.9.

[74] 25 Hen. 8, c.15.

[75] This statute is the prototype of the American "manufacturing clause", which provided that foreign works were protected only if printed in the USA. This clause was repealed only by the US Copyright Act 1976.

[76] An Act of Henry VIII (*Cum privilegio regali ad imprimendum solum*) set up the system of privileges for the printing of books in England in 1529.

[77] For a discussion of the prerogative and its residual status in the UK, see *Monotti* in [1992] 9 E.I.P.R. 305.

consort, Philip II of Spain.[78] It was the declared object of the Crown at that time to prevent the propagation of the reformed religion, and it seems to have been thought that this could be brought about most effectively by imposing the severest restrictions on the publishing trade and the press to prevent the publishing of seditious and heretical books and pamphlets. Until 1640, the Crown, using the Star Chamber as its instrument, rigorously enforced several decrees and ordinances of that Chamber regulating the manner of printing, the number of presses permitted to operate throughout the Kingdom, and prohibiting all printing against the force and meaning of any of the statutes or laws of the realm. This restrictive jurisdiction was enforced by the use of summary powers of search, confiscation and imprisonment, free of any obstruction from Parliament.

2–11   **Decrees of the Star Chamber.** In the same year 1556, by a decree of the Star Chamber, it was forbidden, amongst other things, to print contrary to any ordinance, prohibition, or commandment in any of the statutes or laws of the realm, or any injunction, letters patent, or ordinances set forth, or to be set forth, by the Queen's grant, commission or authority. By a later decree, this time in the reign of Mary's Protestant sister, Elizabeth I, dated June 23, 1585, every book was required to be licensed, and all persons were prohibited from printing: "any book, work, or copy against the form or meaning of any restraint contained in any statute or laws of this realm, or in any injunction made by Her Majesty, or her Privy Council; or against the true intent and meaning of any letters patent, commissions, or prohibitions under the great seal, or contrary to any allowed ordinance set down for the good government of the Stationers' Company".

In 1623, a proclamation was issued to enforce this decree; reciting that it had been evaded, amongst other ways "by printing beyond the sea such allowed books, works, or writings, as have been imprinted within the realm, by such to whom the sole printing thereof by letters patent or lawful ordinance or authority doth appertain".

In 1637, the Star Chamber codified its law on book licensing and printing and again decreed that "no person is to print or import (if printed abroad) any book or copy which the Company of Stationers, or any person, hath or shall, by any letters patent, order or entrance in their register book, or otherwise, have the right, privilege, authority, or allowance, solely to print".[79]

2–12   **First Licensing Act.** In 1640, however, the Star Chamber was abolished; with the Cromwellian revolution, the King's authority was set at naught; all the regulations of the press, and restraints previously imposed upon unlicensed printers by proclamations, decrees of the Star Chamber and charter powers given to the Stationers' Company were deemed, and certainly were, illegal. The scandalous nature of some libellous publications induced Parliament to pass an ordinance in 1643 which prohibited printing, unless the book was first lawfully licensed and entered in the register of the Stationers' Company. The ordinance prohibited printing of any such licensed book without the consent of the owner, or importing it (if printed abroad), upon pain of forfeiting the same to the owner or owners of the copies of the said books, and "such further punishment as shall be thought fit". The provision necessarily presupposed the property to exist; it would have been of no effect if there had been no admitted owner. An owner could not at that time have existed otherwise than by common law. In 1647, 1649 and 1652 fur-

---

[78] Confirmed by Elizabeth I in 1559.
[79] 4 Burr. 2312.

ther ordinances were passed in similar terms.[80] Finally, in 1662 the Licensing Act was passed[81] which likewise prohibited the printing of any book unless first licensed and entered in the register of the Stationers' Company. It ordered that no person should presume to print "any heretical, seditious, schismatical, or offensive books or pamphlets, wherein any doctrine or opinion shall be asserted or maintained which is contrary to the Christian faith, or the doctrine or discipline of the Church of England, or which shall, or may, tend to be to the scandal of religion or the church, or the government or governors of the church, state, or commonwealth, or of any corporation or particular person or persons whatever". It further prohibited the publication of unlicensed books, prescribed regulations as to printing and empowered the King's messengers, and the master and wardens of the Stationers' Company, to seize books suspected of containing matters hostile to the Church or Government. It was necessary to print at the beginning of every licensed book the certificate of the licenser to the effect that the books contained nothing "contrary to the Christian faith, or the doctrine or discipline of the Church of England, or against the state and government of this realm, or contrary to good life or good manners, or otherwise, as the nature and subject of the work shall require". To prevent fraudulent changes in a book after it had been licensed, a copy was required to be deposited with the licenser when application was made for a licence.

The Act further prohibited any person from printing or importing, without the consent of the owner, any book which any person had the sole right to print by virtue of letters patent, or "by force or virtue of any entry or entries thereof duly made or to be made, in the register book of the said Company of Stationers, or in the register book of either of the universities". The penalty for piracy was forfeiture of the books and six shillings and eight pence for each copy, half to go to the King, and half to the owner. The sole property of the owner is here acknowledged in express terms as a common law right; and so the legislature which passed that Act must have recognised the concept that the productions of the brain could be the subject-matter of property. To support an action on this statute, ownership of the book had to be proved or the plaintiff could not have recovered, because the action was to be brought by the owner who was to have a half share of the penalty. The various provisions of this Act in effect prevented piracy, without actions at law or Bills in equity. Cases of disputed property did, however, arise. Some of them were between different patentees of the Crown; in some the point was whether the property belonged "to the author, from his invention and labour, or the King, from the subject-matter".

End of the Licensing Acts. The Licensing Act 1662 was continued by several **2–13** Acts of Parliament, but expired in May 1679. The system had fallen into disrepute because the power of members of the Stationers' Company to claim copyright in perpetuity had led to high prices and a lack of availability of books. Powerful arguments were also being heard in favour of freedom of the press. The control of the book trade exercised by the Stationers' Company was broken with the result that piracy flourished. Soon thereafter, a case is reported in Lilly's Entries of Hilary Term,[82] in which action was brought for printing 4,000 copies of the Pilgrim's Progress, of which the plaintiff was the true proprietor, as a result of which he had lost the profit and benefit of his copy.

---

[80] It has been questioned whether these clauses were applicable to anybody other than members of the Stationers' Company—i.e. whether they were more than by-laws for the regulation of the members inter se, but it is doubtful whether any such restricted interpretation can be put upon their scope.

[81] 13 & 14 Car. 2, c.33.

[82] 31 Car. 2, B.R. *Ponder v Brady, Lilly's Entries*, 67; see Carter, 89; 4 Burr. 2317; Skinner 234; 1 Mod. 257.

2–14   Ordinances of the Stationers' Company. In 1681, all legislative protection having ceased, the Stationers' Company adopted an ordinance, or byelaw of its own, which recited that several members of the company had "great part of their estates in copies", that by ancient usage of the company, when any book or copy was duly entered in their register to any member, such person had always been reputed and taken to be the proprietor of such book or copy, and ought to have the sole printing thereof. The ordinance further recited that this privilege and interest had of late been often violated and abused; and it then provided a penalty against such violation by any member or members of the company, where the copy had been duly entered in their register. This ordinance was an attempt by the members of the Stationers' Company, who on finding their property in copies of books ("their estates in copies, which belonged to them by the common law") no longer under the protection of the Licensing Act, to provide for the failure of legislation and to regulate the printing trade themselves, although the ordinance was, of course, only applicable to their own members. The ordinance, however, shows what the common law right was then deemed to be. The situation was much the same as if an association of persons were to agree that any one of their number should pay a penalty for violating the acknowledged rights of property of any other person in the association, provided such rights were duly entered in their common records. It would not be an attempt to create the right, but it would justly be regarded as acknowledgment of the existence of such a right.[83]

In another byelaw, passed in 1694, it was stated that copies were constantly bargained and sold amongst the members of the company as their property, and bequeathed to their children and others for legacies and to their widows for maintenance; and it was provided that, if any member should, without the consent of the member by whom the entry was made, print or sell the same, he should pay a fine of 12 pence for every copy.

2–15   New legislation sought. Parliament was regularly petitioned, therefore, for a new Licensing Act. The booksellers argued that failure to continue exclusive rights of printing had resulted in disincentives to writers. Without some form of protection to encourage authors, the public interest would be harmed by the decreased flow of works.[84]

To the submissions of the members of the Stationers' Company were added in 1690 the plea of the philosopher, John Locke, who, although opposed to licensing as leading to unreasonable monopolies injurious to learning, demanded a copyright for authors which he justified by the time and effort expended in the writing of the work which should be rewarded like any other work.[85]

In one of the petitions presented to the House of Commons in support of applications to Parliament in 1709 for a Bill to protect copyright, the last clause or paragraph was as follows:

"The liberty now set on foot of breaking through this ancient and reasonable usage is no way to be effectually restrained but by an Act of Parliament. For by common law, a bookseller, can recover no more costs than he can prove damage, but it is impossible for him to prove the tenth, nay, perhaps, the hundredth part of the damage he suffers; because a thousand counterfeit

---

[83] G.T. Curtis, *A Treatise on the Law of Copyright* (Boston: C.C. Little and J. Brown, 1847), p.38.

[84] L. Patterson, *Copyright in Historical Perspective* (Nashville: Vanderbilt University Press, 1968), p.142.

[85] J. Locke, *Two Treatises of Government* (1690), P. Laslett, (ed.) (Cambridge University Press, 1988), para.27. And see J. Locke, "Memorandum to Edward Clark", cited in M. Rose, *Authors and Owners, the Invention of Copyright* (Harvard University Press, 1994), pp.32, 33. Ahead of his time, Locke also advocated limiting the term of protection to a period of from 50 to 70 years after the death of the author.

copies may be dispersed into as many hands over the kingdom, and he not be able to prove the sale of them. Besides, the defendant is always a pauper, and so the plaintiff must lose his costs of suit. (No man of substance has been known to offend in this particular, nor will any ever appear in it.) Therefore, the only remedy by the common law is to confine a beggar to the rules of the King's Bench or Fleet, and there he will continue the evil practice with impunity. We therefore pray that confiscation of counterfeit copies be one of the penalties to be inflicted on offenders".[86]

The Statute of Anne 1709. In response to these applications, in 1709, the first Copyright Act was passed and came into force on April 10, 1710.[87] The Statute of Anne was the first copyright law, as such, in the world and it is the foundation on which the modern concept of copyright was built.[88] Two of the principles established by the Statute of Anne were revolutionary at the time: recognition of the author as the fountainhead of protection and adoption of the principle of a limited term of protection for published works.[89] It was not the first English statute to deal with copyright but the first to be adopted by Parliament as opposed to royal decree and the first to be unconnected with censorship. According to its Preamble, the Act responded to several objectives: the encouragement of learning, the prevention of the practice of piracy for the future, and the "encouragement of learned men to compose and write useful books". The Act gave authors of books already printed the sole right and liberty of printing them for a term of 21 years from the date of entry into force of the Act, and of books not then printed the sole right of printing for 14 years, with a proviso that, after the expiration of the said term of 14 years, the sole right of printing or disposing of copies should return to the authors thereof, if they were then living, for another term of 14 years. Thus the statutory copyright was not to be limited to the members of the Guild and it was not to exist in perpetuity.

The title to the copy of a book had to be registered before publication with the Stationers' Company, and nine copies had to be delivered to certain libraries. Penalties for infringement were severe: infringing books were subject to forfeiture and a fine of a penny for every sheet copied. This resulted in a steep fine when many copies of a substantial book were pirated. The fine was divided equally between the Crown and the complainant. It is of interest to note that the Act also expressly provided that the importation and sale of books in Greek and other foreign languages printed "beyond the seas" should remain unaffected by its provisions. The idea that foreign authors also merited protection was not yet ripe.

The question of literary property. In 1731, 21 years after the Statute of Anne came into force, the stationers' monopoly on printing books already in print when the Statute had come into force expired. Printers in Scotland and in the provinces issued new editions of old books and the London booksellers sought means to prevent this in a series of cases brought before both the English and

2–16

2–17

---

[86] 4 Burr. 2318.

[87] 8 Anne, c.19.

[88] "The unfortunately conceived and unhappily expressed statute of Queen Anne, which, however, has the honour of being the first copyright statute at law to be found in the *Corpus Juris* of any State, either of ancient or modern times", per A. Birrell, *The Law and History of Copyright in Books* (London: Cassell and Co.,1899), p.68; cf. also G. Davies, *Copyright and the Public Interest* 2nd edn (London: Sweet & Maxwell, 2002), pp.11 et seq.

[89] Lord Hailsham of St. Marylebone in *Halsbury's Laws of England* 4th edn (London: Butterworths, 1974), Vol.9.

Scottish courts.[90] The booksellers argued that, at common law, and regardless of the expiry of the statutory period of protection, authors had a perpetual right to authorise printing, rights which had been assigned to them.[91] It was not disputed that the manuscript of a work was the property of the author and that prior to publication his right to it could continue indefinitely. The question was posed only with regard to published works and the argument raged over whether copyright was an inalienable form of property arising from the act of creation or a limited right of control or monopoly bestowed by Statute. The issue was first decided in favour of the perpetual right by a majority of the Court of King's Bench in the case of *Millar v Taylor* in 1769.[92] The Court held that there was a common law right of an author to his copy stemming from the act of creation and that that right was not taken away by the Statute of Anne. The decision was finally overturned, however, by the House of Lords in *Donaldson v Beckett*[93] in 1774, a case which decided that copyright was the deliberate creation of the Statute of Anne and thereafter treated as statutory property. Thus, the effect of the Statute of Anne was to extinguish the common law copyright in published works, while leaving the common law copyright in unpublished works unaffected. Such rights were abolished by the 1911 Act.[94]

The universities and colleges, alarmed at the consequence of this decision, applied for and, in 1775, obtained an Act of Parliament[95] establishing in perpetuity their right to all the copies given or bequeathed to them or which might thereafter be given to or acquired by them. Such rights were abolished by the 1988 Act.

2–18   **Copyright Acts 1709/1833.** The Statute of Anne remained in force, virtually unchanged, until superseded by the Copyright Act of 1842, although it was amended from time to time to add to the list of protected works. The 1709 Act protected only literary works, "books and other writings" but gradually engravings, prints, lithographs and works of sculpture were added.[96] In 1777, musical and dramatic compositions were held to be books within the meaning of the Statute of Anne.[97] However, the duration of copyright was somewhat varied by s.4 of the Copyright Act 1814,[98] which replaced the two contingent 14-year periods of protection by a single term of 28 years, calculated from the day of first publication, or the natural life of the author, if he was still living at the expiration of that period. In 1833, the Dramatic Copyright Act[99] provided for a public performance right in dramatic works.

---

[90] *Millar v Taylor*, 98 E.R. 201; 4 Burr. 2301; *Donaldson v Beckett*, 1 E.R. 837; 4 Burr. 2407; *Hinton v Donaldson* (1773) Mor 8307. For accounts of English cases in the mid-eighteenth century see A. Birrell, *The Law and History of Copyright in Books* (London: Cassell and Co., 1899), pp.99 et seq.; D. Saunders, "Purposes or Principle? Early Copyright and the Court of Chancery", [1993] 12 E.I.P.R. 452. The Scottish cases are described in H.L. MacQueen, "Copyright, Competition and Industrial Design", 2nd edn *Hume Papers on Public Policy: Vol.3, No.2* (Edinburgh University Press, 1995). See also R.S. Tompson, "Scottish Judges and the Birth of British Copyright", *The Juridical Review*, Pt 1 (1992) 1.

[91] B. Kaplan, *An Unhurried View of Copyright* (Columbia University Press, 1967), p.12. See also M. Rose, "Author as Proprietor: Donaldson v Beckett and the Genealogy of Modern Authorship", in *Of Authors and Origins, Essays on Copyright Law*, B. Sherman and A. Strowel (eds) (Oxford: Clarendon Press, 1994).

[92] *Millar v Taylor*, 4 Burr. 2301.

[93] (1774) 4 Burr. 2407.

[94] See para.2–30, below.

[95] 15 Geo. 3, c.53: and see Copyright Act 1801 (41 Geo. 3, c.107).

[96] See paras 2–19 to 2–24, below.

[97] *Bach v Longman*, 98 E.R. 1274; (1777) 2 Cowp. 623 and see para.2–22, below.

[98] 54 Geo. 3, c.156.

[99] Dramatic Literary Property Act 1833 (3 & 4 Will. c.15).

Copyright Act 1842.[100] The 1709 and 1814 Acts were repealed by the Copyright   **2–19**
Act 1842. From 1837 to 1842, in spite of the opposition of Lord Macaulay, the
celebrated historian and politician, Mr Serjeant Talfourd had used his best endeavours and expended all his eloquence to accomplish its passing. In contending
for an extension of the period during which protection was afforded to literary
works to 60 years after the death of the author, he argued:

> "There is something peculiarly unjust in bounding the term of an author's
> property by his natural life, if he should survive so short a period as 28
> years. It denies to age and experience the probable reward it permits to
> youth—to youth, sufficiently full of hope and joys to slight its promises. It
> gives a bounty to haste, and informs the laborious student, who would wear
> away his strength to complete some work which the world will not willingly
> let die, that the more of his life he devotes to its perfection, the more limited
> shall be his interests in its fruits. It stops the progress of remuneration at the
> moment it is most needed; and when the benignity of nature would extract
> from her last calamity a means of support and comfort to the survivors—at
> the moment when his name is invested with the solemn interest of the
> grave—when his eccentricities or frailties excite a smile or a shrug no lon-
> ger—when the last seal is set upon his earthly course, and his works assume
> their place among the classics of his country—your law declares that his
> works shall become your property, and you requite him by seizing the patri-
> mony of his children".[101]

Macaulay opposed extending the period of protection beyond the life of the
author at all, being convinced that to do so would "inflict grievous injury on the
public, without conferring any compensating advantage on men of letters". He
emphasised that "no natural right of property" could survive the original
proprietor. "The system of copyright has great advantages, and great disadvantages ... The advantages ... are obvious. It is desirable that we should have a supply of good books; we cannot have such a supply unless men of letters are liberally remunerated: and the least objectionable way of remunerating them is by a
monopoly. Yet monopoly is an evil. For the sake of the good we must submit to
the evil; but the evil should not last a day longer than is necessary for the purpose
of securing the good."[102]

The 1842 Act as adopted represented a compromise, extending the period of
literary copyright to the life of the author and seven years after his death, or a
term of 42 years from publication, whichever should be the longer, or, if
published after the author's death, 42 years from publication. Literary copyright
covered material such as books and pamphlets, sheet music, maps, charts and
plans. The performing right extended for the same period. The 1842 Act
contained provisions for registration at Stationers' Hall. This was not compulsory,
but had to be done before any action could be brought against infringers. In spite
of its defects, both in substance and in draftsmanship, the 1842 Act remained the
governing statute as to literary copyright until it was repealed by the 1911 Act.[103]

Engraving copyright. In the realm of artistic copyright, engravings were the first   **2–20**
to receive legislative protection. In 1734, the Engraving Copyright Act[104] was
passed, conferring copyright upon these for a term of 14 years.

No provision was made in this Act for the protection of any work of which the

---

[100] 5 & 6 Vict. c.45.
[101] *Hansard*, Vol.56, cols 1841, 342/3.
[102] *Hansard*, Vol.56, cols 1841, 344.
[103] 1 & 2 Geo. 5, c.46.
[104] 8 Geo. 2, c.13.

engraver was not also the designer; and this has been accounted for by the fact that Hogarth, by whose influence the Act was introduced,[105] was invariably the designer as well as the engraver of his celebrated works.

The Engraving Copyright Act of 1766[106] was passed to remedy this oversight, and extended protection to any person making an engraving from the original work of another, provided that they bore the copyright owner's name and the publication date. It also prolonged the period of protection to 28 years from the date of first publication. A further Act, the Prints Copyright Act of 1777,[107] improved the remedies for piracy; the Prints Copyright Act of 1836[108] extended the provisions of the Engravings Acts to Ireland, and the International Copyright Act of 1852[109] to prints taken by lithography or other mechanical process.

2–21 **Sculpture copyright.** Works of sculpture were the next to be protected, by the Sculpture Copyright Act 1814,[110] the term of protection being 14 years from first publication, with a further reversionary term of 14 years to the author, if then living and provided he had not meanwhile divested himself of the copyright.

2–22 **Musical and dramatic copyright.** Musical and dramatic compositions were held to be "books" within the meaning of the Copyright Acts relating to literary works[111]; but the performing right was not statutorily protected until the year 1833, when the Dramatic Copyright Act, commonly known as Bulwer Lytton's Act,[112] conferred an exclusive right of public performance for 28 years, with a reversionary period to the author for the residue of his life, provided the work was printed and published; if the work was not printed or published, the term of protection was uncertain.

Bulwer Lytton's Act only referred to dramatic pieces, but s.20 of the Literary Copyright Act 1842[113] dealt with the performing rights in both musical and dramatic pieces, and extended protection to the performing rights in both classes of works for a similar period to that provided for the duration of copyright in books, namely, a period of 42 years from first public representation or performance, or the life of the author and seven years after, whichever should be the longer: and 42 years from first public representation or performance for posthumous pieces.

Certain abuses arose with respect to the performing rights in musical works. In particular, a man named Wall gained considerable notoriety by purchasing performing rights and enforcing payment of "penalties" (royalties)—which were fixed at 40s. a performance by Bulwer Lytton's Act—from innocent infringers. This led to the passing of the Copyright (Musical Compositions) Acts of 1882 and 1888,[114] which required that notice of reservation of rights of public performance of any musical composition should be printed on every published copy thereof and left the question of payment of costs and amount of penalties to the discretion of the court.

---

[105] Hogarth's series of engravings "A Harlot's Progress", published in 1732, had been very popular and widely pirated.

[106] 6 Geo. 3, c.38.

[107] 17 Geo. 3, c.57.

[108] 6 & 7 Will. 4, c.59.

[109] 15 & 16 Vict. c.12, s.14.

[110] 54 Geo. 3, c.56.

[111] *Bach v Longman*, 98 E.R. 1274; (1777) 2 Cowp. 623, *Storace v Longman* (1809) 2 Camp. 26, note; and see para.2–18, above.

[112] 3 & 4 Will. 4, c.15.

[113] 5 & 6 Vict. c.45. Lectures were protected by the Lectures Copyright Act 1835 (5 & 6 Will. 4, c.65).

[114] 45 & 46 Vict. c.40; 51 and 52 Vict. c.17.

Owing to the injury caused to proprietors of the copyright in musical composi- **2–23**
tions by the practice of selling pirated copies of songs and music through street
hawkers, and the difficulty of finding any substantial person to proceed against
for infringement, the Musical (Summary Proceedings) Act 1902, and the Musical
Copyright Act 1906,[115] were passed providing summary methods of procedure
against infringers of musical copyright. Both these last-mentioned Acts remained
unrepealed by the 1911 Act, but were repealed by the 1956 Act.

Painting, drawing and photographic copyright. Paintings, drawings and **2–24**
photographs were protected, for the first time, by the Fine Arts Copyright Act
1862.[116] This Act sought to protect paintings, drawings and photographs for the
term of the life of the author and seven years after his death, but to obtain the full
benefit of the Act, registration at Stationers' Hall was necessary. However, the
wording of the Act was such as to produce the somewhat remarkable result that,
unless the work was commissioned, so as to vest the copyright initially in the
person commissioning the work, the copyright was lost altogether upon the first
sale of the work unless, on that occasion, there was some written instrument
signed by the artist dealing with the copyright, either by way of express assignment to the purchaser, or by way of express retention by the artist.[117] This requirement probably also applied to works of foreign origin, the copyright in which
was secured in the United Kingdom by Convention or Order in Council, though it
seems unlikely that foreign artists would have been aware of this peculiar provision of English law on a first sale to a dealer in their own country.

Royal Commission of 1875. Having regard to the number of Acts in force deal- **2–25**
ing with different branches of the law of copyright, a consolidating statute was
urgently required. In 1875, a Royal Commission was appointed to inquire into
the working of the Copyright Acts, and the Commissioners presented their Report
in 1878.[118] In this Report they stated[119]:

> "The first observation which a study of the existing law suggests is that its
> form, as distinguished from its substance, seems to us bad. The law is wholly
> destitute of any sort of arrangement, incomplete, often obscure, and, even
> when it is intelligible upon long study, it is in many parts so ill-expressed
> that no one who does not give such study to it can expect to understand it.
> The common law principles, which lie at the root of the law, have never
> been settled. The well-known cases of *Millar v Taylor*, *Donaldson v Beck-*
> *ett*, and *Jefferys v Boosey* ended in a difference of opinion amongst many of
> the most eminent judges who have ever sat upon the Bench. The 14 Acts of
> Parliament which deal with the subject were passed at different times be-
> tween 1735 and 1875.[120] They are drawn in different styles, and some are
> drawn so as to be hardly intelligible. Obscurity of style, however, is only
> one of the defects of these Acts. Their arrangement is often worse than their
> style. Of this the Copyright Act of 1842 is a conspicuous instance".

The Commission recommended that the law should be codified and clarified
and entertained "no doubt that the interest of authors and the public alike requires
that some specific protection should be afforded by legislation to owners of
copyright". It is also of interest to note that the Commission made a strong recommendation to the Government of the day to enter into a bilateral copyright

---

[115] 2 Edw. 7, c.mus; 6 Edw. 7, c.36.
[116] 25 & 26 Vict. c.68.
[117] *Copinger* 4th edn, pp.366, 367.
[118] Report of the Commissioners, C.2036, HMSO (1878).
[119] Report of the Commissioners, C.2036, HMSO (1878), paras 7, 8, 9.
[120] Several more were added between 1875 and 1910.

agreement with the United States of America in order to provide for reciprocal protection for British and US authors.[121]

2–26   **The Berne Convention.** Despite the recommendations of the Commission, no consolidating statute was passed and it was the involvement of this country in the preparatory work on the Berne Convention which finally gave the necessary impetus for reform. In 1886, the United Kingdom was represented at the Conference of Powers held at Berne, which resulted in the framing of the Berne Convention for the Protection of Literary and Artistic Works (the Berne Convention),[122] which the United Kingdom ratified with effect from December 5, 1887. Prior to the Conference, the International Copyright Act, 1886,[123] was passed, making the necessary alterations and additions to the International Copyright Act 1844[124] to enable the United Kingdom to give the required protection to foreign authors. The main changes to the existing copyright law were, first, that registration and deposit in the United Kingdom of foreign works were no longer required; second, an exclusive right to produce or import translations was granted in respect of foreign works, extending for the full term of the copyright in the original work. A further effect of the 1886 Act was to apply British copyright law to works originating in British possessions. This meant that a work produced in one of the possessions received protection not only in the United Kingdom but in all of the rest of them.[125]

However, the Berne Convention did not give rise to a comprehensive reform of the UK law at that stage. It was not until after the revision conference in Berlin held in 1908, where a number of modifications were introduced to the Berne Convention, including the principle that protection under the Convention should be free from compliance with any formalities and a period of protection of the life of the author and 50 years thereafter, that it was recognised that the law had to be revised if the United Kingdom was to join with the other Powers and be in a position to give foreigners the protection required by the revised Act of the Convention.

2–27   **1909 Copyright Committee.** In 1909, therefore, a Committee was appointed to consider and make recommendations for changes to the copyright law required by the Berlin Act. The Committee examined the Berlin Act article by article to see which, if any, amendments were required to the law of this country. After hearing evidence, it reported to Parliament,[126] generally approving the provisions of the Berlin Act, and recommending the passing of a consolidating and amending Act, saying: "It would be a great advantage if the British law were placed on a plain and uniform basis, and that basis were one which is common so far as practicable to the nations which join in the Convention".[127]

2–28   **Copyright Act 1911.** The Copyright Act 1911, which was aimed at giving effect

---

[121] There was at the time no protection for British authors in the USA and British works were being widely pirated; see Report of the Commissioners, C.2036, HMSO (1878), paras 233–252.

[122] cf. paras 23–04 et seq., below. See also I. Davis, "A Century of Copyright: the United Kingdom and the Berne Convention", (1986), *Copyright*, p.177.

[123] 49 & 50 Vict. c.33.

[124] 7 & 8 Vict. c.12. This empowered the Crown to issue orders in Council extending copyright protection in the UK to cover works first published in foreign countries. Orders could specify shorter terms of copyright for foreign works than for British ones, and registration and deposit were required to secure protection for foreign works.

[125] On November 28, 1886, an Order in Council was issued under the 1886 Act extending the protection of the Berne Convention to all British dominions.

[126] Report of the Committee on the Law of Copyright, Cmd.4976 (1909).

[127] Report of the Committee on the Law of Copyright, Cmd.4976 (1909), p.7.

to these recommendations, received the Royal Assent on December 16, 1911.[128] This Act repealed all previous statutes on the subject of literary and artistic copyright, with the exception of the Musical (Summary Proceedings) Copyright Act of 1902 and the Musical Copyright Act of 1906,[129] and one section of the Fine Arts Copyright Act of 1862.[130] The 1911 Act came into force on July 1, 1912.[131]

The 1911 Act brought about several major reforms in order to comply with the Berlin Act of the Berne Convention on all points where it conflicted with the previous law of the United Kingdom. The requirement for registration, a leftover from the days of the Stationers' Company, was abolished altogether in conformity with one of the main principles of the Berne Convention, namely that protection under the Convention should not be subject to any formalities; the Act extended the term of protection to the international standard of life plus 50 years and gave authors of literary, dramatic, or musical works, the sole right to make any record, perforated roll, cinematograph film, or other contrivance by means of which the work could be mechanically performed or delivered.[132] Works of architecture were protected as artistic works and choreographic works as dramatic works. For the first time, the Act also provided that copyright should subsist in records, perforated rolls, and other contrivances by means of which sounds may be mechanically reproduced (sound recordings), in like manner as if such contrivances were musical works. The term of copyright for such contrivances was 50 years from making.[133]

The adoption of the term of protection of 50 years *post mortem auctoris* (pma) to conform with the Berlin Act and international practice was subject to an important proviso. At any time after the expiration of 25 years from the death of the author of a published work, a compulsory licence permitted reproduction subject to payment by the publisher to the author's heirs of a 10 per cent royalty.[134] There was a similar provision under which, at any time after the death of the author of a literary, dramatic or musical work which had been published or performed in public, application could be made to the Judicial Committee of the Privy Council to require the owner of the copyright to grant a licence allowing reproduction or performance of the work in public, if he had refused consent.[135]

2–29 Films were not specifically protected but that gap was remedied by the courts in 1912, when it was held that each frame of a film was a photograph, i.e. an artistic work.[136] In addition to the new rights given to authors to make cinematographic films and sound recordings of their works, certain doubtful areas of the law were clarified, the author being given a dramatisation right, a translation right and a public performance right in musical works. In 1934, the courts held that the copyright in sound recordings, of which the maker or producer was the author, also included a performance right separate from that in the works recorded.[137]

2–30 **Abolition of common law copyright.** The 1911 Act also abolished common law

---

[128] 1 & 2 Geo. 5, c.46. For a survey of the law of copyright immediately prior to the Copyright Act 1911, see *Copinger* 12th edn, pp.1105–1333.
[129] See paras 2–22 and 2–23, above.
[130] See para.2–24, above.
[131] Copyright Act 1911 s.37(2)(a).
[132] s.1(2)(d).
[133] s.19.
[134] s.3.
[135] s.4.
[136] *Barker v Hutton* (1912) 28 T.L.R. 496.
[137] *Gramophone Co Ltd v Stephen Cawardine & Co.* [1934] Ch. 450.

copyright in unpublished works.[138] Except in the cases of paintings, drawings and photographs,[139] unpublished works received no statutory protection prior to the commencement of the 1911 Act,[140] but were protected, if at all, under the common law.[141] This was a perpetual right for unpublished works which ceased on publication, after which an author had to base his claim for protection upon his statutory right, if any. The nature of this common law protection was fully discussed in *Re Dickens*,[142] in which one of the questions at issue was whether the common law right in an unpublished manuscript passed under a bequest, taking effect before the passing of the 1911 Act, of "all my private papers". The Court of Appeal held that the right was an incorporeal right existing independently of the property in the manuscript and one which did not pass to a legatee or donee on a bequest or gift of the manuscript itself.

2–31   **Committee of 1951.** The influence of the Berne Convention continued to make itself felt. The Convention was further revised at Rome in 1928 and at Brussels in 1948.[143] Following the Brussels Conference, in 1951, a further Committee was appointed "to consider and report whether any, and, if so, what changes are desirable in the law relating to copyright in literary, dramatic, musical and artistic works with particular regard to technical developments and to the revised international convention for the protection of literary and artistic works signed at Brussels in June 1948 and to consider and report on related matters". The Committee also took into consideration the preparatory work on the Universal Copyright Convention (UCC) which was subsequently signed at Geneva in 1952 under the auspices of UNESCO.[144] This Committee, after hearing evidence, reported to Parliament[145] recommending that Her Majesty's Government should accede to the Convention as revised at Brussels in 1948, and proposing a number of changes in the law.

2–32   **Copyright Act 1956.** A Bill to give effect to these recommendations received the Royal Assent on November 5, 1956.[146] This Act repealed the 1911 Act (except ss.15, 34 and 37[147]), the Musical (Summary Proceedings) Copyright Act of 1902 and the Musical Copyright Act of 1906 as well as the outstanding section of the Fine Arts Copyright Act of 1862. It came into force on June 1, 1957,[148] and was amended by the Design Copyright Act 1968.

The 1956 Act duly repealed the compulsory licence provisions of ss.3 and 4 of the 1911 Act, which were no longer permitted under the Brussels Act of the Berne Convention and made other limited changes to the law to enable the United Kingdom to ratify it. For example, it introduced a specific right to object to false

---

[138] See para.2–17, above.

[139] *Tuck & Sons v Priester* [1887] 19 Q.B.D. 48; Fine Arts Copyright Act 1862 (25 & 26 Vict. c.68), s.1.

[140] Copyright Act 1911 s.37(2)(a).

[141] *Donaldson v Beckett.* 1 E.R. 837; (1774) 4 Burr. 2408; *Millar v Taylor*, 98 E.R. 201; (1769) 4 Burr. 2303; *Jefferys v Boosey*, 10 E.R. 681; [1855] 4 H.L.C. 815; *Beckford v Hood* (1798) 7 T.R. 620; *Mayall v Higbey*, 158 E.R. 837; (1862) 1 H. & C. 148; *Macmillan & Co v Dent* [1907] 1 Ch. 107; *Mansell v Valley Printing Co.* [1908] 2 Ch. 441; *Bowden Bros. v Amalgamated Pictorials Ltd* [1911] 1 Ch. 386; *Albert (Prince) v Strange*, 41 E.R. 1171; (1849) 1 M. & G. 25.

[142] *Re Dickens* [1935] Ch. 267.

[143] cf. in general paras 23–04 et seq. and specifically para.23–08, below.

[144] As a result this Convention is variously referred to as the Universal, Geneva or UNESCO Convention.

[145] Report of the Committee on the Law of Copyright, Cmd.8662 (1952).

[146] 4 & 5 Eliz. 2 c.74.

[147] ss.34 and 37(2) were repealed by the Statute Law (Repeals) Act 1986 (c.12); s.15 concerned the delivery of copies to the British Museum and other libraries.

[148] SI 1957/863, see *Copinger* 12th edn, para.1735.

attribution of authorship.[149] In addition, it introduced reforms to deal with technical advances affecting copyright since the passage of the 1911 Act. For the first time, specific protection for 50 years from publication for films (cinematographic works), for sound and television broadcasts and for published editions of works was introduced. The performance right in sound recordings recognised by the *Cawardine* case in 1934 was confirmed. The Act also established the Performing Right Tribunal to which disputes over the terms of broadcasting and public performance licences for the use of musical works and sound recordings by broadcasters and others could be referred.

No protection for performers. Performers were not protected under the 1956 Act.   **2–33**

Protection under the criminal law against misappropriation of their performances was first introduced in 1925. A series of statutes—the Performers' Protection Acts 1958–1972—subsequently extended the protection available to them, establishing summary offences against making recordings or films of performances, performing them in public and broadcasting performances without the written consent of the performer.

Committee of 1973. The pace of technical development, allied to the continuing   **2–34**
evolution of the Berne Convention, which was revised in Stockholm in 1967 and again in Paris in 1971, prompted the setting up of a new departmental Committee in 1973 to consider and report whether any, and if so what, changes were desirable in the law relating to copyright as provided in particular by the 1956 Act and the Design Copyright Act 1968, including the desirability of retaining the system of protection of industrial designs by the Registered Designs Act 1949. There was specific exclusion from the terms of reference of "any consideration of the merits of lending to the public as one of the acts restricted by copyright in a work". The Public Lending Right Act 1979 in fact established a non-copyright scheme to provide authors with remuneration paid out of public funds in respect of the lending of books in an entirely separate legislative process.[150]

The Committee, after receiving written and oral evidence, reported to Parliament.[151] The report proposed simplification of the general structure of the Copyright Act 1956 and a whole series of reforms aimed at rationalising and updating the law. Apart from recommending the repeal of registered design monopoly protection as then provided by the Registered Designs Act 1949, other major recommendations were made to take account of the problems raised by new technical developments since the 1951 Committee had reported. Attention was drawn to the impact of this new technology on the methods by which works could be reproduced, on the techniques for recording sounds and sequences of visual images and on computer technology. The report also contained recommendations in relation to the United Kingdom's obligations under various international conventions having regard, in particular, to the revision of the Berne Convention at Stockholm in 1967 and at Paris in 1971, and of the Universal Copyright Convention at Paris in 1971 as well to the Rome Convention for the Protection of Performers, Producers of Phonograms and Broadcasting Organisations (the Rome Convention), which had been adopted in 1961.[152]

The report was acclaimed as a highly valuable contribution to the copyright debate but legislation did not follow for over a decade. During this period, the Government legislated on an ad hoc basis to amend the Copyright Act 1956 to

---

[149] 1956 Act s.43 (cf. CDPA 1988 s.84).
[150] See Ch.19, below and Vol.2 B3.i.
[151] Report of the Committee to consider the Law on Copyright and Designs, Cmnd.6732 (1977).
[152] See Ch.23, below.

deal with such urgent matters as improved remedies against piracy, which had become a real scourge as a result of new technology facilitating reproduction techniques, and the protection of computer software and cable programmes; these measures were contained in particular in the Copyright Act 1956 (Amendment) Act 1982, the Copyright (Amendment) Act 1983, the Cable and Broadcasting Act 1984 and the Copyright (Computer Software) Amendment Act 1985. The Government also produced a series of consultative documents on copyright law reform.[153] These culminated only in 1986 with a White Paper outlining the Government's legislative intentions.[154]

2–35   **Semiconductor products.** By the Semiconductor Products (Protection of Topography) Regulations 1987[155] a topography right, similar to copyright, was given to the designs of semiconductor products. These regulations were made on August 20, 1987, and came into force on November 7, 1987.

2–36   **Copyright, Designs and Patents Act 1988.** In October 1987, a Bill was introduced into the House of Lords which, as its title suggests, was not limited to copyright. In fact, it contained seven parts, only one of which was concerned with copyright and new statutory moral rights, the others being concerned with such matters as new statutory performers' rights, a new design right and amendments to the Registered Designs Act 1949. Other provisions were concerned with patents and Patent Agents and Trade Mark Agents. The Bill received the Royal Assent on November 15, 1988.[156]

The 1988 Act, inter alia, repealed the whole of the 1956 Act, the Copyright (Computer Software) Amendment Act 1985, and the Performers' Protection Acts 1958, 1963 and 1972, but did not repeal s.15 of the 1911 Act (concerning the delivery of copies of newly published books to the British Museum and other libraries) which was left unrepealed by the 1956 Act and the Statute Law (Repeals) Act 1986.[157]

The 1988 Act incorporated the previous ad hoc amendments to the 1956 Act which had dealt with remedies against piracy and protection with respect to computer software and cable programmes. It also introduced specific protection with respect to satellite broadcasting and cable programmes for their operators and for right owners, granted the right to control rental to the authors of films and phonograms (under UK law at the time in both cases the producers) and computer programs, created moral rights for authors and film directors to enable the United Kingdom to ratify the Paris Act of the Berne Convention, replaced the Performing Right Tribunal with a Copyright Tribunal with extended powers over collecting societies and provided civil rights of action for performers and producers of phonograms against unauthorised exploitation of performances. More controversially, it created a new perpetual non-copyright right in favour of the Hospital for Sick Children, Great Ormond Street.[158]

2–37   Another controversial issue, which the 1988 Act failed to legislate upon, was so-called private copying, i.e. the non-commercial copying of sound recordings and audiovisual works for personal and domestic use. By the 1980s, private copying had become a major unauthorised use of copyright works, a use which still

---

[153] Reform of the Law relating to Copyright, Designs and Performers' Protection, Cmnd.8302, HMSO, July 1981. Intellectual Property Rights and Innovation, Cmnd.9117, December 1993. The Recording and Rental of Audio and Video Copyright Material, Cmnd.9445, February 1985.
[154] Intellectual Property and Innovation, Cmnd.9712, HMSO, 1986.
[155] SI 1987/1497: see *Copinger* 13th edn, para.A–565 and Ch.14, below.
[156] c.48: see Vol.2 A1.
[157] c.12.
[158] CDPA 1988 s.301 and Sch.6. See fn.49, above.

escapes the control of the copyright owners. In 1977[159] the Whitford Committee had recommended that a "levy" on recording equipment, similar to that operated in the Federal Republic of Germany at the time, should be implemented. The Government in its Green Paper published in 1981,[160] then invited public debate on the issue, but said that it was not convinced of the need for a levy.

Following this consultation, the Government published a White Paper in 1986[161] in which it stated that it had decided to introduce a "levy" on blank audio tapes. This decision, which was announced in the Queen's speech[162] setting out the Government's programme in June 1987, was subsequently overturned and the subject was dropped from the Bill introduced later that year and, in spite of major discussions of the issue in both Houses of Parliament, remained excluded from the 1988 Act.[163] The issue has remained controversial and, to date, the Government has maintained its opposition to the introduction of any royalty or levy system to provide remuneration to right owners for private copying.[164]

Semiconductor products. There have also been new regulations concerned with the design of semiconductor products[165] which revoked the earlier regulations.[166] Further amendments have been made by the Design Right (Semiconductor Topographies) (Amendment) Regulations 1991 (SI 1991/2237), the Design Right (Semiconductor Topographies) (Amendment) Regulations 1992 (SI 1992/400) and the Design Right (Semiconductor Topographies) (Amendment) Regulations 1993 (SI 1993/2497).[167]   **2–38**

Developments. In the 22 years since the 1988 Act entered into force, it has been amended continuously, mainly to implement EC Directives on the subject of copyright and related rights resulting from the European Commission's programme for the harmonisation of such laws within the European Union. This programme, the resulting Directives and their implementation in the United Kingdom, is described in detail in Ch.24 of this work. Suffice it to say here that the amendments required to the 1988 Act have concerned the provisions regarding the legal protection of computer programs, the protection of performers, producers of sound recordings and films and broadcasting organisations, rental and lending rights, rights concerning satellite broadcasting and cable retransmission, rights in databases and, most importantly of all, the period of protection, which has been extended to 70 years pma with respect to literary, artistic and musical works, including films and computer programs.[168]   **2–39**

More recently, the United Kingdom has transposed into the 1988 Act the EC

---

[159] *Copyright and Designs Law,* Report of the Committee to consider the Law on Copyright and Designs; Chairman, the Hon. Mr Justice Whitford, Cmnd.6732 (1977).

[160] *Reform of the Law Relating to Copyright, Designs and Performer's Protection: A Consultative Document,* Cmnd.8302 (1981) Ch.3, para.23.

[161] *Intellectual Property and Innovation, presented to Parliament by the Secretary of State for Trade and Industry by Command of Her Majesty,* Cmnd.9712 (1986).

[162] Queen's Speech: June 25, 1987. The Copyright Bill, without provisions for royalties for private copying was introduced in October 1987.

[163] cf. para.24–159, below.

[164] In this respect, it should be noted that the EC Directive 2001/29 (the Information Society Directive) provides in art.5(2)(b) that private copying is permitted "on condition that the rightholders receive fair compensation which takes account of the application or non-application of technological measures". See para.24–115, below.

[165] SI 1989/1100 (see Vol.2 B9) as amended by the Design Right (Semiconductor Topographies) (Amendment) Regulations 2006, SI 2006/1833, which came into force on August 1, 2006.

[166] SI 1987/1497: see para.2–35, above and Ch.14, below.

[167] See Ch.14, below

[168] See paras 24–43 et seq., below. SI 1992/3233 on Copyright—The Copyright (Computer Programs) Regulations 1992 (came into force January 1, 1993) implementing Council Directive 91/250 of May 14, 1991 on the legal protection of computer programs; SI 1995/3297, the Duration of Copyright and Rights in Performances Regulations (came into force January 1, 1996)

Directive on the harmonisation of certain aspects of copyright and related rights in the information society.[169] The Directive harmonises rights in certain key areas, primarily to meet the challenge of the internet and e-commerce, and digital technology in general. It also deals with exceptions to these rights and legal protection for the technological aspects of rights management systems. The Copyright and Related Rights Regulations 2003 therefore amended the 1988 Act in the following respects: the definition of broadcasting has been updated to take account of new electronic transmission techniques and the internet; a new restricted act of communication to the public of a work has been defined; performers have been accorded a making available right; the permitted acts in relation to copyright works and rights in performances, the so-called exceptions to copyright have been amended to conform with the Directive; protection for right owners against the circumvention of technical protection measures applied to copyright works and against the removal or alteration of electronic rights management information is introduced. Further substantial amendments to the 1988 Act were made by the Broadcasting Act 1990,[170] including the creation of two new forms of compulsory licence concerned with the inclusion of sound recordings (but not the music on the sound recordings) in broadcasts and cable programmes, and the provision of information about broadcast programmes.[171] The Broadcasting Act 1990 has itself been amended by the Broadcasting Act 1996, which in turn further amended the 1988 Act. In addition, the 1988 Act has been amended by The Copyright, etc. and Trade Marks (Offences and Enforcement) Act 2002, The Copyright (Visually Impaired Persons) Act 2002 and The Legal Deposit Libraries Act 2003.

Since the 15th Edition of this work was published in 2005, the 1988 Act has been further amended by regulation in order to transpose further EC Directives into the law of the United Kingdom. The regulations include: the Performances (Moral Rights, etc.) Regulations 2006,[172] which entered into force on February 1, 2006; the Artist's Resale Right Regulations 2006,[173] which entered into force on February 14, 2006; and the Intellectual Property (Enforcement, etc.) Regulations 2006,[174] which entered into force on April 29, 2006.

2–40   **The influence of EU harmonisation on UK copyright law.** The 1988 Act in the form in which it was first adopted may be seen as the last copyright legislation to be passed in the United Kingdom free of the influence of the harmonisation programme of the European Union. Historically, since preparatory work began in the 1870s on the international standards later incorporated in the Berne Convention, the law of copyright in the United Kingdom developed independently, while taking account of international norms and obligations under the various copy-

---

implementing Council Directive 93/98 of October 29, 1993 harmonising the term of protection of copyright and certain related rights. SI 1996/2967, Copyright and Related Rights Regulations (came into force December 1, 1996) implementing the Directive on rental right and lending right and on certain rights related to copyright in the field of intellectual property of November 19, 1992 (92/100 [1992] OJ L346/61) and the Directive on the co-ordination of certain rules concerning copyright and rights related to copyright applicable to satellite broadcasting and cable retransmission of September 27, 1993 (93/83 [1993] OJ L248/15); SI 1997/3032, the Copyright and Rights in Databases Regulations 1997 (came into force January 1, 1998) implementing Directive of the Parliament and Council 96/9 [1996] OJ L77/20.

[169] Directive 2001/29 (OJ L167/10, 22.6.2001), transposed into UK law by the Copyright and Related Rights Regulations 2003, SI 2003/2498, which came into force on October 31, 2003.

[170] c.42. The provisions of this Act came into force on various dates: see the Broadcasting Act 1990 (Commencement No.1 and Transitional Provisions) Order 1990 (SI 1990/2347 (c.61)); see also Vol.2 A2.ii.

[171] Broadcasting Act 1990 ss.175 and 176.

[172] SI 2006/18.

[173] SI 2006/346.

[174] SI 2006/1028.

right and related rights conventions to which this country has adhered in the meantime. Moreover, since the United Kingdom was traditionally influential in the intergovernmental negotiations leading to the adoption of the multinational conventions, and many other countries throughout the English-speaking world and the Commonwealth had copyright laws based on that of the United Kingdom, the conventions as adopted took account of the British tradition of copyright and were broadly compatible with it. Moreover, the Berne and UCC Conventions, and in particular, the Rome and Phonograms Conventions and the TRIPs Agreement,[175] did not impose doctrinal approaches to the protection of authors and other beneficiaries of copyright, but left it to national legislators to implement the standards required as they saw fit. Thus, for example, over 100 years' membership of the Berne Convention, while, as has been seen, having considerable influence on the development of the United Kingdom's copyright law, did not fundamentally alter the approach of the copyright law. The Convention evolved in such a way as to provide a bridge between the approaches of the common law and civil law systems in many respects. The influence of the harmonisation programme of the European Commission, however, on the United Kingdom's copyright law is altogether more far-reaching, introducing elements of the civil law authors' rights approach.[176] This process will continue, since the harmonisation programme of the Commission is not yet complete and areas of copyright law not so far affected will be dealt with. As mentioned above and described in detail in Ch.24, below, the EC Directive on copyright and related rights in the information society adopted in April 2001[177] has been implemented in the United Kingdom. The Directive deals with issues relevant to the use of copyright material in the information society, the internet and e-commerce, in particular, the rights of reproduction and communication to the public (electronic transmission, including digital broadcasting and "on demand" services). It also limits the type and scope of permitted exceptions to these rights and provides legal protection for technological measures used to safeguard rights and identify and manage copyright materials (such as copy protection systems and digital watermarks and encryption systems). One of its main aims was to bring the laws of the EU Member States into conformity with the new international Treaties adopted in December 1996, the WIPO Copyright Treaty (WCT) and the WIPO Performances and Phonograms Treaty (WPPT). The Directive required Member States to transpose its provisions into their national laws before December 22, 2002; the United Kingdom failed to meet this deadline but the Directive was transposed into the law of the United Kingdom by the Copyright and Related Rights Regulations 2003.[178]

As regards the impact of the EU Directives in the area of copyright, it should be noted that as recently pointed out by Mr Justice Arnold in *SAS Institute Inc v World Programming Limited*, domestic legislation, and in particular legislation specifically enacted or amended to implement a European directive, must be construed by the UK courts so far as is possible in conformity with, and to achieve the result intended by, the directive.[179] Moreover, a European Directive falls to be interpreted according to the principles of interpretation of EU legislation developed by the Court of Justice of the European Union (CJEU). The basic rule

---

[175] cf. Introduction, paras 1–04, 1–08 and 1–09, above, and Ch. 23, below.

[176] cf. Introduction, para.1–05, above, and paras 24–43 et seq., below, and e.g. paras 24–62 and 24–86.

[177] See para.2–39 and fn.169, above.

[178] Copyright and Related Rights Regulations (SI 2003/2498), cf para.2–39, fn.169, above.

[179] *SAS Institute Inc. v World Programming Limited* [2010] EWHC 1829 (Ch), para.163. Cf. *Marleasing SA v La Comercial Internacional de Alimentación SA* (C–106/89) [1990] ECR I–4135 at para.8.

of such interpretation is the following: "According to settled case law, in interpreting a provision of Community law it is necessary to consider not only its wording, but also the context in which it occurs and the objectives pursued by the rules of which it is part".[180] In the light of these now established principles, on matters concerning copyright the UK courts must interpret the 1988 Act in conformity with EU legislation and decisions of the CJEU and the relevant international treaties.

The EC harmonisation programme will continue. In October 2005, the Commission adopted a recommendation on management of online rights in musical works.[181] The recommendation puts forward measures for improving the EU-wide licensing of copyright for online services. It may be that the recommendation will be followed in due course by a Directive if insufficient progress is made.[182] Furthermore, in a recent review of the EC legal framework in the field of copyright and related rights the Commission announced that it is working towards the objective of codifying the *acquis communautaire*, i.e. the existing body of EC law in this field.[183] The first stage in codifying the *acquis communautaire* was reached in December 2006, when the Rental and Related Rights Directive 92/100/EEC and the Term Directive 93/98/EEC were both repealed and replaced by new codified texts, which take account of amendments made to the two Directives by subsequent EC legislation, such as, for example, the Information Society Directive 2001/29/EC. These new Directives are codifying measures only.[184] In the meantime, a new codified version of the Computer Software Directive was adopted in April 2009.[185]

Over the past five years, the European Commission has continued to be active on the copyright front and has published a number of studies and reports on the future of copyright in Europe. Two major studies have been published on the *aquis communautaire* in this field. The first, published in November 2006, examined the *aquis communautaire* with a view to its consolidation and to filling in gaps and inconsistencies in the current legislation.[186] The second, published in February 2007, examined the implementation and effect of the Information Society Directive 2001/29/EC in Member States' laws in the light of the development of the digital market.[187] Both these reports make recommendations for amendments to the *acquis communautaire*.[188] In July 2008, these reports were followed by a new Green Paper on "Copyright in the Knowledge Economy" described as the basis for consultation on the long-term future of copyright policy in Europe.[189]

More recently, the Commission has published a series of documents concerned with the future of the European digital single market. In October 2009, it published an internal reflection document on the future challenges facing creative

---

[180] *SAS Institute Inc.* [2010] EWHC 1829, para.165.

[181] Commission Recommendation of May 18, 2005, on collective cross-border management of copyright and related rights for legitimate online music services (2005/737/EC).

[182] Commission Press Release, IP/05/1261, October 12, 2005. For recent developments, see paras 27–22 and 27–24, below.

[183] cf. Ch.24, below, paras 24–164 et seq.

[184] New Directives 2006/115/EC and 2006/116/EC dated December 27, 2006, see paras 24–59 and 24–84, below.

[185] COM(2008)23 final, June 17, 2008, see paras 24–51 et seq., below.

[186] B. Hugenholtz et al., "The Recasting of Copyright and Related Rights for the Knowledge Economy", Institute for Information Law, University of Amsterdam, November 2006.

[187] L. Guibault and G. Westkamp et al., "Study on the Implementation and Effect in Member States' Laws of Directive 2001/29/EC", Institute for Information Law, University of Amsterdam, in co-operation with the Queen Mary Intellectual Property Research Centre, University of London, February 2007.

[188] The Commission subsequently published a staff working document reporting on the application of the Information Society Directive (SEC(2007) 1556, November 30, 2007.

[189] Directive 2009/24/EC of April 23, 2009, on the legal protection of computer programs (codified version).

content in the digital single market in which possible European Union targeted legislative action and the possibility of establishing a European Copyright Law by means of an EU Regulation was discussed.[190] It was stated that the Commission intended to take a proactive role in order to ensure a culturally diverse and rich online content for consumers, while creating adequate possibilities for remuneration and improved conditions in the digital environment for rightholders. In the course of 2010 to date, this reflection document has been followed by three further reports: (1) a Green Paper entitled "Unlocking the potential of cultural and creative industries";[191] (2) "A New Strategy for the Single Market" by former Commissioner Mario Monti;[192] and (3) a new Commission Communication "A Digital Agenda for Europe".[193] The Green Paper announced the Commission's intention inter alia to create a true single market for online content and services, with a balanced regulatory framework governing the management of intellectual property rights, measures to facilitate cross-border online content services, the fostering of multi-territorial licences, and adequate protection and remuneration for right holders.[194] The Monti report proposes a number of initiatives for creating a digital single market and estimates that the European Union could gain 4 per cent of GDP by stimulating its fast development by 2020. In this context, among the Monti report's key recommendations are proposals for an EU copyright code, including an EU framework for copyright clearance and management as well as proposals for a legal framework for EU-wide online broadcasting.[195] The document "A Digital Agenda for Europe" announces that the Commission will take action inter alia to simplify copyright clearance, management and cross-border licensing by enhancing the governance, transparency and pan-European licensing for (online) rights management by proposing a framework Directive on collective rights management in 2010; further it will propose a Directive on orphan works also in 2010.[196] The remaining months of 2010, therefore, are likely to bring forward several new proposals for EU legislation leading to further harmonisation. The impact on UK copyright law and practice of a possible movement towards an EU Copyright Code imposed by EU Regulation cannot be overestimated.

UK developments. Meanwhile much attention has been paid over the same period to the intellectual property regime in the United Kingdom. A series of major reports and consultation papers affecting copyright and related rights have been published since the 15th Edition of this work was published in 2005. The conclusions of these reports will influence future UK legislation and the position of the United Kingdom in future discussions on the new harmonisation measures within the European Union. These reports are the following: (1) The Gowers Review of Intellectual Property (the Gowers Review), published in December 2006; (2) The Review of the Copyright Tribunal, published by the UK Intellectual Property Office in May 2007; (3) The Report of the House of Commons Culture, Media and Sport Committee, entitled "New Media and the Creative Industries" (HC 509–1,

2–41

---

[190] *Creative Content in a European Digital Single Market: Challenges for the Future*, A Reflection Document of DG INFSO and DG Markt, October 22, 2009.

[191] Green Paper *Unlocking the potential of cultural and creative industries*, COM(2010) 183 of April 27, 2010.

[192] *A New Strategy for the Single Market-At the Service of Europe's Economy and Society*, Report to the President of the European Commission by Mario Monti, May 9, 2010.

[193] *A Digital Agenda for Europe*, Communication from the Commission to the European Parliament, the Council, the European Economic and Social Committee and the Committee of the Regions, COM(2010) 245, May 19, 245.

[194] COM(2010) 183, p.8.

[195] Monti Report, fn.192, above, pp.44 et seq

[196] COM(2010) 245, pp.8 et seq.

Fifth Report of Session 2006–07); (4) "Taking forward the Gowers Review of Intellectual Property: Proposed Changes to Copyright Exceptions", UKIPO, January 2008 and December 2009; (5) © the Future—Developing a copyright agenda for the 21st Century, UKIPO, December 2008; (6) "Digital Britain—Final Report",[197] UKIPO, June 2009; (7) "© the way ahead—A Strategy for Copyright in the Digital Age", Department for Business Innovation and Skills, UKIPO, October 2009.

The Gowers Review was set up by the Government to establish whether the intellectual property system in the United Kingdom was "fit for purpose in an era of globalization, digitization and increasing economic specialization". It concluded that the system was not in need of a radical overhaul but suggested that there was room for reform in a number of areas, including some concerning copyright. The specific suggestions and proposals are referred to in this work in the context of their subject-matter. Not all the recommendations are within the purview of the UK Government, being subject to EU legislation, but the recommendations are timely in view of the European Commission's own review of the *acquis communautaire* and its digital single market programme. Meanwhile, following on from the Gowers Review, in the course of 2008 and 2009, the UK Government launched separate consultations on recommendations made in the review for changes to the law with regard to certain copyright exemptions relating to music licensing, on the one hand, and exceptions and limitations, on the other.[198]

The Review of the Copyright Tribunal examines the subject of copyright and the role of the collecting societies. The Review's recommendations are discussed in Ch.27, below, and make some far-reaching proposals for organisational reform of the Copyright Tribunal and its procedures.

The House of Commons report considered the impact on the creative industries of recent and future developments in digital convergence and media technology and the effect on these industries of piracy and counterfeiting as well as unauthorised dissemination of creative content. It considered also the question where the balance should lie between the rights of creators and the expectations of consumers. The report concluded by addressing a series of recommendations to Government, some of which would require amendments to the law of copyright and related rights.

The BIS/UKIPO Copyright Strategy document published in October 2009 considered how copyright can tackle the challenges of the digital age and proposed action to improve access to orphan works, enable extended collective licensing, encourage the development of model contracts and clauses, and tackle illegal P2P file-sharing and declared its willingness to consider European action on the subject of private, non-commercial use of copyright material.

The first legislative action to address the digital market in the United Kingdom is the Digital Economy Act 2010[199] which deals inter alia with online infringement of copyright and file sharing. It imposes obligations on internet service providers aimed at the reduction of online infringement. A full explanation of this important new legislation is given in Ch.21, below.

For the time being the new UK Government has announced that it is conducting a review of copyright policy.

However, it is abundantly clear that further legislative initiatives may be

---

[197] Cm 7650 June 2010.

[198] UKIPO consultation on the future of copyright in the digital age (January 8–April 8, 2008); UKIPO consultation "Music Licensing Review" on copyright exemptions for public performance of music (July 1–October 31, 2008).

[199] 2010 Ch.24 of April 8, 2010.

foreseen, following all the above EU and UK consultations, reports and proposals, to adapt the present law of copyright in the United Kingdom and at the level of the European Union to the challenges of the European digital single market.

The future. The challenges to copyright presented by the digital and online 2–42 environment of the so-called information society, with the possibility of works protected by copyright being recorded, stored and made available on demand in digital form all over the world through electronic communications networks such as the internet, and with the threat of unlimited, perfect-quality copies being made of them, have long ceased to be matters for the United Kingdom alone. Indeed, even a harmonised legislative response from the European Union will not suffice to protect rights owners adequately. Only a global approach will provide the protection required; the WCT and WPPT need to attract a membership at least as wide as that of the Berne Convention in a very short time-span if the present lack of protection and spiralling digital piracy of copyright-protected material is to be brought under control.

Until recently, it was generally supposed that technology would provide the capability for rights owners to use digital tools, such as encryption, copy protection devices and embedded rights management information, to control and monitor online exploitation of their works, and specific measures to protect these systems against circumvention devices designed or marketed for infringement purposes are envisaged and given legal protection by the WCT and WPPT and the EC Information Society Directive, as well as by the 1988 Act. To date, however, these technical tools of protection (technical protection measures (TPMs)) have not been effectively harnessed to provide the required protection for works protected by copyright and related rights. In fact it is now becoming clear that TPMs are not the answer to digital online piracy. There are two main reasons for this: the first is "tech literacy", that is, consumers familiar with the technology are easily able to circumvent TPMs, and to illegally download and disseminate protected works, and the second is the fact that non-technical consumers dislike TPMs and resist marketing solutions which use them as they make access to works more difficult for them. Thus, as a general rule, right owners cannot rely only on TPMs to control access to works. They are effective in certain markets, such as subscription and streaming services, but they are perhaps best regarded as being of limited applicability and perhaps best deployed only when the specific market conditions allow. Right owners are concentrating, therefore, instead, on diversifying their markets by offering consumers new ways to buy and access works. One way forward much in the limelight at present is for right owners to cooperate with Internet Service Providers (ISPs) to deter illegal file sharing on ISP networks.

Technical advance has long been the motor for the development of the law of 2–43 copyright. The legislator must ensure that the basic principles of copyright protection are applied to and enforced in the new digital environment, if rights owners are to be persuaded to continue to provide content for online services. It is also in the interest of service providers and the general public that there should be certainty about the extent of the rights available, so as to facilitate contractual arrangements and rights management so that the potential of the information society and the digital market can be realised for the benefit of rightholders and consumers.

2009 marked the 300th Anniversary of the adoption of the Statute of Anne 1709, which was not only the first copyright law to be adopted in England but also the first copyright statute in the world. "In changing the conceptual nature of copyright, it became the most important single event in copyright history".[200] The Statute of Anne is the universal foundation on which the modern concept of copyright law was built. It was the product of a new communications technology, the printing press, just as the modern law of copyright has to adapt to the new technologies driving cultural production and the new means of reproduction and dissemination of copyright works in the present day. The Act embodied principles which continue to inform the copyright debate today: its stated purpose was to encourage learning and it recognised the individual author as the fountainhead of protection. It aimed to prevent the practice of piracy, which continues to afflict copyright owners and the cultural industries and to concern the international community, and to encourage "learned men to compose and write useful books".[201] In the public interest, the Statute limited the term of protection. In adapting the copyright law to the needs of the 21st Century, the challenge is to respect the fundamentals of the law and to meet the needs of both creators and the public interest alike.[202]

---

[200] Lord Hailsham of St Marylebone *Halsbury's Laws of England*, 4th edn (London: Butterworths, 1974) Vol. 9. See also L. Bently, U. Suthersanen, and P. Torremans (eds), *Global Copyright: Three Hundred Years Since the Statute of Anne, from 1709 to Cyberspace*, (Edward Elgar, 2010).

[201] Statute of Anne 1709 s.1.

[202] On the future of copyright, see: E. Derclaye (ed), *Research Handbook on the Future of EU Copyright* (Edward Elgar, 2009); B. Fitzgerald, "Copyright 2010: The Future of Copyright", E.I.P.R. 2008, 30(2), 43; C. Geiger, "The future of copyright in Europe: striking a fair balance between protection and access to information", I.P.Q. 2010, 1.

CHAPTER THREE

REQUIREMENTS FOR COPYRIGHT PROTECTION

1. INTRODUCTION

3–01   **Introduction.** This chapter deals with the question of whether copyright subsists in a particular subject matter. Today, this matter is governed by the Copyright, Designs and Patents Act 1988.[1] The first stage of the inquiry is to identify whether the particular subject matter is capable of being a copyright work under the 1988 Act; the second stage is to consider whether the requirements laid down in the Act for subsistence of copyright in such subject matter are met. The first stage is dealt with in Section 2, "Subject Matter of Protection", and the second stage is dealt with in Sections 3, 4, and 5, "Fixation", "Originality" and "Qualifying Conditions". Section 6 deals with "Foreign Works", and Section 7 with the circumstances in which protection may be denied to works.

2. SUBJECT MATTER OF PROTECTION

A. Introduction: Copyright Works

3–02   **Introduction: copyright works.** The approach of the 1988 Act is to provide that copyright can subsist, subject to the conditions for subsistence being met,[2] only in specified categories of what in the Act are referred to as "works". In every case, therefore, the question whether copyright subsists in a particular subject matter first involves the question whether the subject matter falls within one of the specified categories of works. The works in which copyright can subsist under the 1988 Act are described in s.1(1) of the 1988 Act as follows:

(a) original literary, dramatic, musical or artistic works,

(b) sound recordings, films or broadcasts, and

(c) the typographical arrangement of published editions.

    Works of these descriptions in which copyright subsists are referred to in the 1988 Act as copyright works.[3] Each of these categories of works is discussed in turn in this Section.

3–03   **Categorisation of works.** The history of statutory copyright protection[4] is a history of steady enlargement of the extent of protection by the addition of new categories of protected subject matter, as technology has advanced or a need has been perceived to protect the fruits of human endeavour. Statutory protection was first accorded to books (1709) (which included musical and dramatic compositions), then to engravings (1734), sculptures (1814), prints and lithographs (1852), paintings, drawings and photographs (1862), mechanical contrivances for the reproduction of sound (1911), films (in their own right), broadcasts and typographical arrangements of published works (1956), cable programmes (1985)[5] and computer programs (1985). The introduction of specific legislation to deal with a particular category of work has often been preceded by attempts to fit the work into an existing category, sometimes successfully and other times not. Although the origins of this categorisation lie in the piecemeal development of the extension of protection to new subject matter, the need to retain such categorisation has been driven, first, by the need for definition, so as to be able to determine what falls within and what falls outside protection, and, secondly, by the need to make different provisions for different kinds of works.

---

[1] See s.1. As to works made before the commencement of the 1988 Act, see para.3–07, below.

[2] CDPA 1988 ss.1(1) and 153.

[3] CDPA 1988 s.1(2). Note that in the civil law copyright systems, subject matters such as sound recordings, broadcasts and some films are not regarded as "works", this being an expression reserved for the creation of human authors.

[4] As to common law copyright in unpublished works, see Ch.2.

[5] Now protected under the heading of broadcasts, see para.3–84, below.

It is a legacy of this piecemeal development that the description given to the categories into which a particular subject matter is subsumed may often be misleading. Thus, the terms literary and artistic works in the context of the Berne Convention must be given a much wider meaning than those terms have traditionally been given in the United Kingdom legislation, including, as they do under the Berne Convention, musical works, dramatic works and films. In the United Kingdom, the example can be given of the protection of computer programs and tables of figures as literary works. An earlier example was the protection of sound recordings as musical compositions under the 1911 Act.

Are the categories always mutually exclusive? In some cases, the 1988 Act **3–04** makes it clear that certain categories of copyright work are mutually exclusive or what the boundaries of certain categories are. Thus it is expressly stated that a literary work cannot be a dramatic or musical work; a musical does not include any words or action intended to be sung, spoken or performed with the music; a photograph cannot also be part of a film[6]; and a soundtrack associated with a film is part of the film.[7] Occasionally, a subject matter may appear to fall into several categories at the same time but on closer examination it turns out to be a composite creation in which there is embodied more than one copyright work. So, for example, in relation to a song, there is separate protection for the words and for the music.[8] Other works may embody a number of underlying works, for example a film, where in addition to the copyright in the film itself[9] there will be independent protection for the score, the screenplay and other works such as any novel on which the film is based.

Apart from cases where the Act specifically provides for mutual exclusion and apart from "composite" creations, it now seems clear that a single subject matter of creation can, depending on the circumstances, fall at the same time into two or more categories of copyright work. Unless the categories are expressly stated by the Act to be mutually exclusive, the only question is whether the subject matter in fact falls within the descriptions in question. Thus in *Norowzian v Arks Ltd (No.2)*,[10] the Court of Appeal held that the categories in subss.1(1)(a) ("original literary, dramatic, musical or artistic works") and 1(1)(b) ("sound recordings, films or broadcasts") were not mutually exclusive. It followed that since the proper definition of a dramatic work is a work of action, with or without words or music, which is capable of being performed before an audience,[11] and a film could in appropriate circumstances fit this description, a film can be protected both as a "film" and as a dramatic work, assuming the work satisfies the definitions of each kind of work. The reasons why the court took the view that these categories were not mutually exclusive were simply that (a) there was no express requirement of mutual exclusivity in the 1988 Act[12] and (b) the absence of any requirement of originality in subs.1(b) was sufficient ground for no exclusion to be implied.[13] This is consistent with the earlier view expressed by Jacob J. in

---

[6] CDPA ss.3(1), 3(2) and 4(2), respectively.

[7] CDPA s.5B(2).

[8] *Redwood Music Ltd v B. Feldman & Co Ltd* [1981] R.P.C. 337; *Electronic Techniques (Anglia) Ltd v Critchley Components Ltd* [1997] F.S.R. 401, 413. Contrast the position in France, where words which accompany music are treated as part of a single musical work (with the consequence, in the past, of benefiting from the longer term of protection accorded to musical works).

[9] As to which, see para.3–79, below.

[10] *Norowzian v Arks Ltd (No.2)* [2000] F.S.R. 363.

[11] See para.3–32, below.

[12] The fact that the 1956 Act s.48(1) expressly provided that a dramatic work did not include a cinematograph work whereas the 1988 Act was silent on the point was also said to support the conclusion, although Nourse L.J. thought that it would be unsafe to base any construction of the provisions of the 1988 Act on those of the 1956 Act.

[13] Buxton L.J. also considered that the United Kingdom's obligations under the Berne Convention required that any work of cinematography within the meaning of the Berne Convention was

Anacon Corp Ltd v Environmental Research Technology Ltd[14] that the visual part of a circuit diagram might be both a literary work and an artistic work (the literary work consisting of the table or compilation of information to be read from the diagram, namely the components, and how the components were interconnected).[15] It seems, however, that this view was regarded as wrong in *Electronic Techniques (Anglia) Ltd v Critchley Components Ltd*,[16] where Laddie J., although accepting[17] that a circuit diagram could be a literary and an artistic work provided information could be read from it, and thus holding that the particular circuit diagram in that case was a literary work to the extent that it listed six components, said[18]: "... although different copyrights can protect simultaneously a particular product and an author can produce more than one copyright work during the course of a single episode of creative effort, ... it is quite another thing to say that a single piece of work by an author gives rise to two or more copyrights in respect of the same creative effort. The categories of copyright work are, to some extent, arbitrarily defined.... In the case of a borderline work, I think there are compelling arguments that the author must be confined to one or other of the possible categories. The proper category is that which most nearly suits the characteristics of the work in issue." Laddie J. took the view that the circuit diagram in *Anacon* was correctly regarded as a literary work to the extent that it consisted of a list or compilation of components whose identity could be read from the diagram but that the information as to how one component was connected to another, which could be deduced from the lines representing the connecting wiring, was not part of any literary work since it was purely visual information. As was pointed out in *Sandman v Panasonic U.K. Ltd*,[19] however, it is not clear that this is a correct reading of *Anacon* or why, if it is legitimate to look at written symbols for components to ascertain their nature, the lines which interconnect the symbols on a circuit diagram are not merely symbols for interconnections which can be "read" in order to understand their starting points and ending points and how they cross over each other or connect together. The conflict which exists between *Anacon* and *Electronic Techniques* was examined by Pumfrey J. in *Sandman*,[20] where he reached the conclusion that two such copyrights might subsist side by side. He gave as examples an e.e. cummings poem about a cat, written in the shape of a two-dimensional cat, and a Chinese calligraphic work.

Part of the confusion arises because of the way in which the question is often expressed, for example, by asking whether a work (in the singular) can be both a literary work and an artistic work. The better approach in such a case is to ask whether a single form of expression can, for example, be both a literary work and an artistic work. It is suggested that, to the extent that the subject matter comes within the definition of a literary work in that it conveys information or ideas in a form which can be written, spoken or sung,[21] it is a literary work and, to the extent that it comes within the meaning of an artistic work in that it conveys

---

included within a "dramatic work", as that expression was to be understood in the 1988 Act. See para.3–32, below.

[14] *Anacon Corp Ltd v Environmental Research Technology Ltd* [1994] F.S.R. 659, although acknowledging that he had not heard proper argument on the point.

[15] See also *Comprop Ltd v Moran* [2002] E.C.D.R. CN 4; [2002] J.L.R. 222 (Royal Ct of Jersey) where it was noted that a map might be both an artistic work and a literary work, the literary work consisting in the written information which could be read from the map.

[16] *Electronic Techniques (Anglia) Ltd v Critchley Components Ltd* [1997] F.S.R. 401.

[17] *Electronic Techniques (Anglia) Ltd v Critchley Components Ltd* [1997] F.S.R. 401 at 412.

[18] *Electronic Techniques (Anglia) Ltd v Critchley Components Ltd* [1997] F.S.R. 401 at 413.

[19] *Sandman v Panasonic U.K. Ltd* [1998] F.S.R. 651.

[20] Although again without full argument.

[21] See para.3–11, below.

purely visual information or ideas,[22] it is an artistic work. It is suggested that there is no objection in principle to a single form of expression being protected as both kinds of work: it is both a literary work and an artistic work.

At first sight, difficulties might be thought to arise as a result of the same subject matter being classified as two different kinds of work.[23] Thus, for example, the rights associated with a copyright work vary according to the description of the work,[24] as do the acts in relation to a copyright work which are permitted (and thus which do not amount to an infringement of copyright).[25] Again, the categorisation of works also has importance beyond copyright protection, as the same descriptions of works are used in relation to moral rights protection[26] and rights in performances.[27] However, the question in each case is whether the subject matter is a literary work, or an artistic work, etc. and to the extent that it is one or more of these, then the statutory consequences will follow.

What categories are not exclusive? It follows from the above that the categories of literary and artistic works are not mutually exclusive and also that a single form of expression can be both a dramatic work and a film. Since, like a film, some broadcasts can be described as works of action, with or without words or music, which are capable of being performed before an audience, it seems that the same subject matter can be both a dramatic work and a broadcast. Apart from cases in which the 1988 Act expressly delimits categories of works, most, if not all other categories are mutually exclusive simply because of the way in which they are defined. **3–05**

What amounts to a "work"? For many purposes, it is important to identify precisely the "work" in question, for example because infringement is defined to take place when an unlicensed act takes place in relation to the "work as a whole or any substantial part of it".[28] This question is partly tied up with such questions as what amounts to a *literary*, etc. work,[29] and partly with what amounts to an *original* work.[30] A "work" is a thing which satisfies the statutory description of a literary, dramatic, etc., work. At the end of the particular process of creation, one must look at what has been created and assess whether it is a literary, etc. work and then whether it is an original work. The creation of a work may of course extend over a period of time, and be the subject to revisions. At each interval in the process of creation there is likely to have been created a new copyright work, even though as yet incomplete in the mind of the author.[31] Assuming this is so, it is, however, generally not appropriate to say of the final product of creation that it is composed of a number of separate works, each corresponding to a stage in the creative process. It is a single work,[32] albeit that there are also a number of ante- **3–06**

---

[22] See paras 3–51 et seq., below.

[23] As recognised in *Electronic Techniques (Anglia) Ltd v Critchley Components Ltd* [1997] F.S.R. 401.

[24] See Ch.7, below.

[25] See Ch.9, below.

[26] See CDPA 1988 s.77(1).

[27] CDPA 1988 s.180(2).

[28] See s.16(3)(a) of the 1988 Act and paras 7–25 et seq., below.

[29] As to which see, e.g. paras 3–11 et seq., below.

[30] As to which see paras 3–125 et seq., especially para.3–135, below.

[31] *Brighton v Jones* [2004] EWHC 1157 (Ch); [2005] F.S.R. 16 (first scenes of a dramatic work); *Taylor v Rive Droite Music Ltd* [2004] EWHC 1605 (Ch), para.247 (on appeal, but not on this point: [2005] EWCA Civ 1300; [2006] E.M.L.R. 4); *IPC Media Ltd v Highbury-Leisure Publishing Ltd (No.2)* [2004] EWHC 2985 (Ch); [2005] F.S.R. 20, para.5.

[32] In *Ladbroke (Football) Ltd v William Hill (Football) Ltd* [1964] 1 W.L.R. 273, the House of Lords refused to regard a work of compilation as made up of its constituent elements for the purposes of an infringement claim.

cedent works.[33] Circumstances may exist which justify regarding a constituent part of a larger entity as in itself a copyright work, but this will only be where the part in question could fairly be regarded as so separable from the material with which it is collocated as itself to constitute a copyright work.[34] Subject to this unusual type of case, it is clear that a claimant cannot choose to divide up the subject matter of a "work" into small parts, or into "a legal millefeuilles" of successive works,[35] claiming that each part is "a work" thereby, for example, making it easier for him to establish that a substantial part of it has been copied by cherry picking particular features.[36]

3–07   **Old works: transitional provisions**. What is the position of a work made before the commencement of the 1988 Act (August 1, 1989)? To be a protected work, it must fall within the description of protected subject matter under the 1988 Act itself. Since, however, the Act provides that copyright in a pre-1988 Act work only subsists after commencement if copyright subsisted in it immediately before commencement,[37] it follows that in theory one must ask whether the work also fell within one of the descriptions of protected subject matter under the previous Copyright Act, namely the Copyright Act 1956.[38] Save in relation to works for which there are special transition provisions,[39] there is, however, no need to go through this step because the 1988 Act has been framed in such a way as to include all previous descriptions of protected subject matter. If a work falls within one of the descriptions of protected work under the 1988 Act, one can therefore safely assume that it fell within one of the descriptions of protected work under the pre-existing law.[40]

---

[33] In *CCH Canadian Ltd v Law Society of Upper Canada* [2002] 4 F.C. 213 (Canada Fed CA) (reversed on appeal, but not on this point, at [2004] S.C.C. 13), the question as to what is a "work" was answered by the Federal Court of Appeal of Canada as follows: "… one must decide whether the material in question is capable of existing outside of the context in which it is published, communicated, displayed, performed or otherwise disseminated. If a production is distinctive and reasonably able to stand alone, then it may be deemed a work in itself rather than a part of another work. However, if a production is dependent upon surrounding materials such that it is rendered meaningless or its utility largely disappears when taken apart from the context in which it is disseminated, then that component will instead be merely a part of a work" (Linden J.A., Sharlow J.A. agreeing). Rothstein J.A. suggested that a work was something which was complete or perhaps substantially complete. It is suggested that neither of these tests is correct. A work is something which conforms to the statutory description of the particular kind of work.

[34] *Coffey v Warner/Chappell Music Ltd* [2005] EWHC 449 (Ch); [2005] F.S.R. 34, para.12, citing *Coogi Australia Pty Ltd v Hysport International Pty Ltd* (1998) 157 A.L.R. 247 (Fed Ct of Aus).

[35] per Laddie J. in *IPC Media Ltd v Highbury-Leisure Publishing Ltd* [2004] EWHC 2985 (Ch); [2005] F.S.R. 20 at para.23.

[36] See *Ladbroke (Football) Ltd v William Hill (Football) Ltd* [1964] 1 W.L.R. 273, where the House of Lords refused to regard a work of compilation as made up of its constituent elements for the purposes of an infringement claim. See also *IPC Media Ltd v Highbury-Leisure Publishing Ltd* [2004] EWHC 2985 (Ch); [2005] F.S.R. 20 at para.23 and *Coffey v Warner/Chappell Music Ltd* [2005] EWHC 449 (Ch) at paras 8 to 10.

[37] CDPA 1988 Sch.1 para.5(1).

[38] The approach under the 1956 Act was different to that under the 1988 Act. The 1956 Act provided a self-contained code as to protected works, making certain adjustments to that code in relation to works made before the 1956 Act came into force. See Sch.7 of that Act.

[39] As, for example, in the case of films, which became protected for the first time as such by the 1956 Act. See para.3–81, below.

[40] Note that although CDPA 1988 Sch.1 para.35 provides that every work in which copyright subsisted under the 1956 Act immediately before commencement is to be deemed to satisfy the requirements of Pt I of the Act "as to qualification for copyright protection", this only refers to the qualification provisions referred to in s.9(3), not the question of whether the work falls within one of the descriptions of protected works.

B. LITERARY WORKS

(i) History of protection

Oldest category of protected works. As already pointed out,[41] the category of literary works is the oldest category of protected works. Historically, it was not a category which was capable of exhaustive definition. Even in the early days of statutory protection for this category, when the protected subject matter was described as "books", it was necessary to add a definition which extended the category beyond what would ordinarily have been understood by that expression.[42]   **3–08**

Literary works under the 1911 and 1956 Acts. Neither statute attempted a complete definition of the term "literary work". The 1911 Act merely stated that a literary work included maps, charts and plans as well as table and compilations.[43] The inclusion of maps, charts and plans followed the previous categorisation of these works as literary works[44] and compilations were expressly included to ensure that such works, which had previously been protected as "books", remained protected.[45] The 1956 Act repeated this, as to tables and compilations, consigning maps, charts and plans to the more logical category of artistic works, as part of the definition of a drawing.[46]   **3–09**

The Berne Convention. By the time the composite definition of literary and artistic works came to be formulated in the Berne Convention, a lengthy list of examples had to be included, in order to demonstrate the width of these two expressions. The definition of "literary and artistic works" in art.2(1) thus includes "every production in the literary, scientific and artistic domain, whatever may be the mode or form of its expression, such as books, pamphlets and other writings; lectures, addresses, sermons and other works of the same nature".   **3–10**

(ii) Literary works in general

Statutory definition: literary work. By s.3(1) of the 1988 Act, a literary work is defined to mean any work, other than a dramatic or musical work, which is written, spoken or sung. The definition continues by stating that a literary work includes a table or compilation (other than a database), a computer program, preparatory design material for a computer program, and, separately, a database. These specific examples of literary works are discussed below. Writing is further defined[47] as including any form of notation or code,[48] whether by hand or otherwise and regardless of the method by which, or the medium in or on which   **3–11**

---

[41] See para.3–03, above.
[42] The Literary Copyright Act 1842 (5 & 6 Vict. c.45), s.2 defined books as every volume, part, or division of a volume, pamphlet, letterpress sheets, music sheets, maps, charts and plans.
[43] Copyright Act 1911 s.35(1).
[44] See para.3–08, above.
[45] Parliamentary Debates, Fifth Series, House of Lords (1911) Vol.X, HMSO, at 211, Lord Gorell.
[46] Copyright Act 1956 s.48(1): " 'literary work' includes any written table or compilation". But see *Comprop Ltd v Moran* [2002] E.C.D.R. CN 4; [2002] J.L.R. 222 (Royal Ct of Jersey), as to logic of the 1911 Act in classifying a map as a literary work.
[47] CDPA 1988 s.178, and the term "written" is to be construed accordingly.
[48] Notation was included in the definition under the 1956 Act s.48(1). The reference to code was new in the 1988 Act. A dictionary definition (OED) of notation is any set of symbols or characters used to represent numbers, quantities, etc. Presumably, also, a set of symbols or characters, such as the alphabet, used to represent words is equally a form of notation. If so, it is not clear what the addition of the word "code" in the 1988 Act adds.

it is recorded.[49] The reference to a work which is written, spoken or sung clearly limits the nature of the protected subject matter to expressions by means of words[50] or by things which convey information by written means.[51] Quite apart for the need for fixations,[52] the reference to the need for a literary work to be written, i.e. recorded, emphasises that the work relied on must be recorded in one of the specified ways.[53]

3–12   **Exclusion of musical and dramatic works.** The express exclusion of dramatic and musical works from the definition of literary work was new in the 1988 Act.[54] The way the exclusion is formulated means that if the work is properly a dramatic or musical work then it cannot be a literary work. This is unlikely to give rise to much difficulty in practice, nor, today, does much turn on whether a work is a literary, dramatic or musical work.[55]

3–13   **Protected subject matter.** As has been seen, under both the 1911 and 1956 Acts the protected subject matter was a "literary work", and what was protected was an "original literary work". This expression "original literary work" could be broken down into its constituent words, each of which added a shade of meaning to the composite whole. In particular, the word "original" has a particular significance in a copyright context,[56] so that in the past the analysis sometimes proceeded by asking whether the subject matter was a "literary work" and then whether it was an "original literary work". Even the expression "literary work" could be broken down by asking whether the subject matter came within the adjectival description of being "literary" and then whether it constituted a "work",[57] although this was more unusual. In fact, in some of the cases it is not easy to deduce whether the issue being addressed was whether the work was a literary work or an original literary work.[58] Although a warning was given against treating the expression "original literary work" other than as a composite expres-

---

[49] This part of the definition also enlarged the processes by which the notation can be written. The definition in the 1956 Act referred to "whether by hand or by printing, typewriting or any similar process". This made the distinction clear between something which was in handwriting, and something which was typed or printed, both of which processes may involve the use of the hand. The current definition is less elegant, in that the reference to "by hand" must presumably be read as "in handwriting"; the last part, however, clearly is intended to cover writing by means of a word processor or other electronic process, where the writing may be stored in computer memory or other electronic carrier.

[50] Sounds which are sung, but which do not consist of words in any human language, would, it is suggested, be a musical work, and therefore would be excluded from being a literary work.

[51] As in *Sandman v Panasonic U.K. Ltd* [1998] F.S.R. 651 and *Anacon Corp Ltd v Environmental Research Technology Ltd* [1994] F.S.R. 659, discussed in para.3–04.

[52] See para.3–107.

[53] *Navitaire Inc v easyJet Airline Co Ltd (No.1)* [2004] EWHC 1725 (Ch); [2005] E.C.D.R. 17, para.83, where "complex commands" for a computer program were held not to constitute literary works.

[54] Whilst it had been recognised that in the case of songs under the 1956 Act the words and music were the subject of separate copyrights as literary and musical works, respectively, and to that extent the categories were mutually exclusive (see *Redwood Music Ltd v B. Feldman & Co Ltd* [1981] R.P.C. 337), this was not necessarily so between dramatic and literary works.

[55] The distinction, which had been of some importance under the 1911 Act, was already less important under the 1956 Act. Under the 1988 Act, the distinction has little importance, save possibly in the realm of infringement and as regards the restricted act of making an adaptation of a work, the definition of which is different in the case of each category of work (see CDPA 1988 s.21(3)(a) and (b)).

[56] See paras 3–125 et seq., below.

[57] As in *Exxon Corporation v Exxon Insurance Consultants International Ltd* [1982] Ch. 119; [1982] R.P.C. 69, at 143, per Stephenson L.J.: "I am not sure whether this can be said to be a 'work' at all; I am clearly of the opinion that it cannot be said to be a literary work"; and at 132, where Graham J. observed that the word "Jabberwock" could not be a "literary *work*" (his emphasis). See also *Apple Computer v Computer Edge* [1984] F.S.R. 481 at 495 (Fed Ct of Aus).

[58] Of course, if it was held that the work was entitled to copyright protection as an *original* literary

sion,[59] the need to do so was (and still is) sometimes unavoidable.[60] The 1988 Act might be thought to have legitimised a compartmentalised analysis, since a literary work is now defined "as *meaning* any *work*, other than a dramatic or musical work, which is written, spoken or sung ...", thereby emphasising the need for there to be "a work" in the first place, the words "written, spoken or sung" going to the issue of whether or not the work is a literary or some other kind of work. Despite this change in the way in which literary work is defined, it remains a composite expression and the pre-1988 Act cases will remain relevant[61]; nevertheless it will sometimes be legitimate to ask whether or not the subject matter is a "work".[62]

Written, spoken or sung. It has been said that since the definition of literary work in the 1988 Act (i.e. anything written spoken or sung which is not a dramatic or musical work) was new it is "essential to eschew any attempt at further definition".[63] However, some analysis of the definition is called for. The words are not concerned with the question of fixation of the work[64]; their purpose is to define what is a *literary* work. The common theme underlying the words "written, spoken or sung" is that of the expression of ideas or information by means of words, or at least writing which conveys information.[65] The reference to the possibility of the work being sung does not mean that the music of a song can be a literary work,[66] merely that singing is one possible means of expression using words. In the case of a spoken or sung work, the form of communication will necessarily involve the use of language. Whilst the voice need not be a human voice,[67] a communication by sign language would not appear to be capable of being a literary work (even if the requirement of fixation were satisfied by the communication being recorded on film), unless and until the work is written, spoken or sung. In the case of a written communication, the extended definition of writing so as to include any form of notation or code makes it clear that the writing need not be in the form of ordinary human language, provided it conveys

3–14

---

work, it must have been a necessary part of the decision, or a matter of concession, that the work was a literary work.

[59] *Exxon Corporation v Exxon Insurance Consultants International Ltd* [1982] Ch. 119; [1982] R.P.C. 69, per Stephenson L.J. at 139 ("... it is the expression as a whole in the context of the Act which has to be construed.") and per Oliver L.J. at 144 ("... for my part I do not think that the right way to apply a composite expression is, or at any rate is necessarily, to ascertain whether a particular subject matter falls within the meaning of each of the constituent parts, and then to say that the whole expression is merely the sum total of the constituent parts. In my judgment it is not necessary, in construing a statutory expression, to take leave of one's commonsense ....").

[60] For example, under s.84 the right to complain of false attribution arises in relation to a literary work, not an original literary work. See *Noah v Shuba* [1991] F.S.R. 14, where the same kind of issue arose under s.43 of the 1956 Act.

[61] Not least because of s.172(2) of the 1988 Act, which provides that a provision of Pt I of the Act which corresponds to a provision of the previous law is not to be construed as departing from previous law merely because of a change of expression. Nevertheless, care should be taken when considering cases decided before the 1911 Act because what was at issue there was not whether the work was a literary work but whether it was a "book" within the meaning given to that expression (see para.3–08, above and *Exxon Corporation v Exxon Insurance Consultants International Ltd* [1982] Ch. 119, per Graham J., at 130).

[62] See, e.g. *R. Griggs Group Ltd v Evans* [2003] EWHC 2914 (Ch), para.17, [2004] F.S.R. 31 (upheld on appeal: [2005] EWCA Civ 11; [2005] F.S.R. 31) where it was said that copyright could not exist in the expression "Dr Martens" because it was not a "work" In *Navitaire Inc v easyJet Airline Co Ltd* [2004] EWHC 1725 (Ch); [2006] R.P.C. 3 at para.80, Pumfrey J. held that it was clear that single words in isolation were not literary works. See further fn.61.

[63] *Navitaire Inc v easyJet Airline Co Ltd* [2004] EWHC 1725 (Ch); [2006] R.P.C. 3, at para.79.

[64] This is the concern of CDPA 1988, s.3(2); see paras 3–107 et seq., below.

[65] As in *Sandman v Panasonic U.K. Ltd* [1998] F.S.R. 651 and *Anacon Corp Ltd v Environmental Research Technology Ltd* [1994] F.S.R. 659, discussed in para.3–04.

[66] This is made clear by s.3(1), which defines a musical work as a work consisting of music, exclusive, inter alia, of any words intended to be sung with it.

[67] A person who speaks with the assistance of a computer-generated voice is expressing his thoughts in speech.

something and is capable of being understood, and indeed, the communication need not be in a form which is directly readable or intelligible to a human being.[68] The "writing" may even take the form of a diagram, provided information can be read from it.[69] In general, however, in every case the question is what is the work which lies behind, and is the subject of the communication. What matters is the message, not the medium. A message, expressed in writing, speech or song, will be capable of being a literary work. That is not, however, to confuse the expression of the message with its contents. It is with the expression and the form of that expression that copyright is concerned, not the content. This has particular consequences in relation to the issue of originality,[70] but in the present context it is this which distinguishes ideas and works, the latter being the subject matter of protection, not the former.[71]

Two points arise from this. First, a work conceived in the mind of a person, even though he uses words in his mind to formulate his thoughts, is not a literary work. It remains, at this stage, in the realm of ideas which have not been given any expression. The definition requires the work to be written, spoken or sung; it does not refer to a work which is *intended* to be written, spoken or sung.[72] Secondly, once a work is written, spoken or sung, it does not matter, for the purposes of its being a literary work, whether it was thought out as to its form and content before it was written, spoken or sung.[73] Thus, a person who gives an oral description from memory of an event is using speech to communicate information, and what is spoken by him will be a literary work, as this term is defined for the purposes of the 1988 Act, just as much as it would be if the person, being mute, communicated his recollection in writing.[74] Whether the spoken recollection is a copyright work will depend inter alia on whether it remains merely a spoken recollection, or becomes fixed, by being recorded in some way.[75] Similarly, a person who delivers a carefully thought out (but not previously written down) speech is delivering a literary work, as is a judge who delivers an *ex tempore* judgment.[76]

3–15   **"Literary" work.** The term "literary" work has never implied any requirement that the work must have any literary style or merit.[77] Rather, the word "literary" refers to the nature of the work, that is, one in which the expression is conveyed

---

[68] Examples of other forms of notation or code are Braille, Morse code, shorthand, and computer-readable code; a work "written" in any of these will be a literary work.

[69] *Anacon Corp Ltd v Environmental Research Technology Ltd* [1994] F.S.R. 659; *Sandman v Panasonic U.K. Ltd* [1998] F.S.R. 651. See, further, para.3–17, below.

[70] See paras 3–107 et seq., below.

[71] See, for a helpful discussion as to the distinction between the concept of a work and its expression in a detailed and concrete form, *Plix Products Ltd v Frank M. Winstone (Merchants)* [1984] 3 I.P.R. 390 at 418, per Pritchard J.: [1986] F.S.R. 63; affirmed [1985] 1 N.Z.L.R. 376, CA; [1986] F.S.R. 608. See also para.3–18, below.

[72] This is irrespective of the lack of fixation of such work; but contrast the position of a musical work, discussed as para.3–48, below.

[73] The issue of originality is a separate matter, and is discussed below.

[74] In *Gould Estate v Stoddart Publishing* [1996] Can. Abr. 3000, it was held that copyright did not subsist in an oral statement, because it was not a literary creation. The decision appears to have been based on the lack of permanence of such expression, but this is to confuse the requirement of fixation with the nature of the work itself.

[75] See further paras 3–114 et seq., below.

[76] It had been suggested that a literary work under the 1956 Act was required to be expressed in some form of notation (see *Copinger* 12th edn, pp.53, 85); the introduction of the words spoken or sung into the definition of a literary work in the 1988 Act makes it clear that there is no such requirement (following the recommendation of the 1977 Copyright Committee, Cmnd.6732, para.609 (viii)). See *Hansard*, HL Vol.490, cols 828–829 and Vol.493, cols 1058–1059. For a discussion of the problems in connection with copyright in spoken words, see Phillips in [1989] E.I.P.R. 231.

[77] See, e.g. *University of London Tutorial Press Ltd v University Tutorial Press Ltd* [1916] 2 Ch. 601 at 608, approved in *Ladbroke (Football) Ltd v William Hill (Football) Ltd* [1964] 1 W.L.R.

by means of words or writing.[78] This point is now given statutory force by the fact that the word "literary" does not appear in the statutory definition of literary work in the 1988 Act at all: the only requirement is that it be a "work" which is "written, spoken or sung". Quite apart for the need for fixation,[79] the reference to the possibility of a literary work being written, i.e. recorded, emphasises that in these cases the work relied on must be recorded in one of the specified ways.[80]

As already noted, in decisions under previous Acts little emphasis was placed on the individual words "literary" and "work" as opposed to the composite expression "literary work". Nevertheless, these cases provide a clear idea of what amounts to a literary work. For many years, the classic definition of a literary work has been something which is intended to afford another pleasure in the form of literary enjoyment or which is intended to convey information or instruction through the medium of writing, speech or song.[81] Although this definition will serve most purposes, and helps in borderline cases, it is clearly not exhaustive in that a work written for purely personal reasons, and without any intention of it being communicated to anyone, and thus not intended to afford another person literary pleasure, instruction or information, is nevertheless clearly capable of being a literary work.[82] A computer program is also not intended to convey instruction or information to another *person* but probably always was,[83] and is now expressly, a literary work. Also expressly protected are other works which might not ordinarily be thought of as "literary works" such as tables and compilations. For this reason, the usefulness of the above definition has been doubted, as being "from a different world",[84] it at the same time being accepted that while to concentrate on the word "literary" can mislead, it must not be ignored.[85] There is no bright line test and it has been said that to attempt definitions ad hoc (such as, does it convey information or emotion?) is unhelpful: in the end, the question is merely whether a written artefact is to be accorded the status of a copyright work having regard to the kind of skill and labour expended, the nature of copyright

---

273, per Lord Pearce at 291; *Winterbottom v Wintle* (1947) 50 W.A.L.R. 58 (no literary merit required for a list).

[78] See *University of London Tutorial Press Ltd* [1916] 2 Ch. 601, per Peterson J., at 608: "The word 'literary' seems to be used in a sense somewhat similar to the use of the word 'literature' in political or electioneering literature and refers to written or printed matter" and *Ladbroke (Football) Ltd v William Hill (Football) Ltd* [1964] 1 W.L.R. 273, per Lord Pearce at 291: "[The words] are used to describe work which is expressed in print or writing ...". Today, of course, these statements should be understood as extending to spoken or sung matter, the emphasis being on the fact that the communication is by means of words.

[79] See paras 3–114 et seq.

[80] *Navitaire Inc v easyJet Airline Co Ltd (No.1)* [2004] EWHC 1725 (Ch), para.83, where "complex commands" for a computer program were held not to constitute literary works: only by analysing the source code could it be seen that a computer operating it would recognise the commands and perform the desired function, this being a feature of computer programs written in "procedural languages". The fact that the complex commands were not recorded was purely a result of the way the claimant's program had been written. The same result could have been achieved by recording the command names and their syntax expressly and using a program known as a parser generator to construct a parser that recognised such commands accompanied by arguments according to such a syntax. The commands and their syntax would then be recognisable as such in the source code of the parser generator. In that case, the copyright owner would be able to point to a written work describing exactly how the alleged infringer's program parsed the code and the consequences would be "very different".

[81] *Exxon Corporation v Exxon Insurance Consultants International Ltd* [1982] Ch. 119; [1982] R.P.C. 69, in which the Court of Appeal approved the definition of a literary work given by Davey L.J. in *Hollinrake v Truswell* [1894] 3 Ch. 420 at 427–428 as being something which "is intended to afford either information and instruction or pleasure in the form of literary enjoyment".

[82] As noted in *International Business Machines Corporation v Spirales Computers Inc* (1984) 12 D.L.R. (4th) 351 (Fed Ct of Can). As to the definition in *Exxon* not being exhaustive, see also *Apple Computer v Computer Edge* [1984] F.S.R. 481 at 495 (Fed Ct of Aus).

[83] See para.3–28, below.

[84] *Navitaire Inc v easyJet Airline Co Ltd* [2004] EWHC 1725 (Ch); [2006] R.P.C. 3, at para.79.

[85] *Navitaire Inc v easyJet Airline Co Ltd* [2004] EWHC 1725 (Ch), at para.80.

protection and its underlying policy.[86] It is not sufficient to say that the purpose of the Act is to protect original skill and labour and it is not of much weight either that other forms of protection may be available.[87]

In most cases, however, whether or not a work satisfies this requirement will not present any particular problem and, as will be seen, there is a vast array of different types of works which without argument have been afforded protection as literary works. What are more instructive are those cases, few in number, in which protection has been denied on this ground. So, for example, protection was denied to the single invented word "Exxon" on the grounds that by itself it conveyed no information, provided no instruction, gave no pleasure and was simply an "artificial combination of four letters of the alphabet which serves a purpose only when used in conjunction with other English words …".[88] Protection was similarly denied to the expression "Dr Martens"[89] and to individual invented words consisting of user commands for a computer booking system.[90] To similar effect is the observation that the word "Jabberwock" is not a literary work, only becoming part of a literary work and having meaning when it is embodied in Lewis Carroll's poem.[91] The European Court of Justice has also observed that words as such do not constitute elements covered by copyright protection, although this was in the context of a discussion of originality rather than subject matter.[92] In South Africa, protection has been similarly denied to the invented single word "LePacer" on the grounds that it was meaningless.[93] Protection as a literary work was also denied to the layout of the body of the diary, i.e. the way in which the days and dates were set out with spaces for notes, etc.[94] Before the 1911 Act, protection was denied to a cardboard device in the shape of a sleeve for the human arm intended for use in dressmaking[95] since by itself it

---

[86] *Navitaire Inc v easyJet Airline Co Ltd* [2004] EWHC 1725 (Ch), at para.80.

[87] *Navitaire Inc v easyJet Airline Co Ltd* [2004] EWHC 1725 (Ch), at para.80, noting that in *Exxon Corporation v Exxon Insurance Consultants International Ltd* [1982] Ch. 119, plenty of skill and labour had gone into the creation of the name "Exxon".

[88] *Exxon Corporation v Exxon Insurance Consultants International Ltd* [1982] Ch. 119, per Oliver L.J. at 144. And see Graham J., at first instance, at 130: "… though invented and therefore original, [it] has no meaning and suggests nothing in itself. To give it substance and meaning, it must be accompanied by other words or used in a particular context or juxtaposition." Since the word could be written, spoken or sung, presumably today the case might be decided on the grounds that it was not a "work", as to which, see Stephenson L.J. at 143G.

[89] *R. Griggs Group Ltd v Evans* [2003] EWHC 2914 (Ch), para.17, (upheld on appeal: [2005] EWCA Civ 11): "Dr Martens" not a "work".

[90] *Navitaire Inc v easyJet Airline Co Ltd* [2004] EWHC 1725 (Ch), at para.80: "… clear that single words in isolation are not to be considered as literary works."

[91] *Exxon Corporation v Exxon Insurance Consultants International Ltd* [1982] Ch. 119, per Graham J. at 132.

[92] *Infopaq International A/S v Danske Dagblades Forening* (C–5/08) [2009] E.C.R. I–6569: words "… considered in isolation are not as such an intellectual creation of the author who employs them. It is only through the choice, sequence and combination of those words that the author may express his creativity in an original manner and achieve a result which is an intellectual creation."

[93] *Kinnor (Pty) Ltd v Finkel T/A Harfin Agencies* (June 1, 1990, WLD 9059/90, Sup Ct of S.A.), leaving open the question whether the expression "Le Pacer" (two words) should be regarded differently as meaning, in the context of watches, a watch that paces other watches. *Sed quaere*, since by itself the expression means virtually nothing, and conveys no literary pleasure, instruction or information or, per *Navitaire*, should not be accorded the status of a copyright work having regard to the kind of skill and labour expended, the nature of copyright protection and its underlying policy. See also *Procter & Gamble Pharmaceuticals v Novopharm* [1996] Can. Abr. 299, in which it was held that it was arguable that copyright could subsist in the invented name "ASACOL". Again, *sed quaere*.

[94] *G. A. Cramp & Sons Ltd v Frank Smythson Ltd* [1944] A.C. 329. This decision appears to have been reached independently of any question of originality.

[95] The device was curved so as to represent a human arm above and below the elbow and had printed on it the words "top curve line; under curve line; under arm curves; measure round the thick part of the arm; measure round the thick part of the elbow; measure round the knuckles of the hand;" together with curved lines relating to the words "under arm curves" and scales of

conveyed no information or instruction[96]; simple instructions pasted on the outside of a moneybox as to what to do with it[97]; an article described as a child's trick, consisting of an envelope with some simple words printed on the outside and, inside, a card board device and a verse by Longfellow.[98]

From some of the older decisions it might be thought that provided the words in question convey at least some information or instruction, even if they are unlikely to give any pleasure, then they will amount to a literary work. This is not the correct position, however, in that protection has been denied to expressions which, although they clearly have some meaning by themselves, have been considered too trivial.[99] Thus it was held that instructions on the use of a product, namely: "Follow clinic procedure for aftercare. If proper procedures are followed, no risk of viral infections can occur" did not, on their own, afford *sufficient* information, instruction or literary enjoyment to qualify for protection.[100] It might be thought that the instructions did convey some information or instruction, and the issue of sufficiency could perhaps have been decided the question of originality, not literary work. On the other hand, the instructions were of such a banal nature that probably no one would pay any attention to them or thus receive information or instruction from them. The same comment can be made about the observation that the expression "Avoid the predicament of being without your glasses" was too trivial to merit protection.[101]

In accordance with these general principles, and despite this small number of cases denying protection as literary works, virtually every product of writing, speech or song is likely to be a literary work and a vast array of works have been protected as such, whether the product of substantial creative endeavour such as

---

inches and half-inches relating to the words "measure round the thick part of the arm," and "measure round the thick part of the elbow". The device also had certain holes in it and was intended for actual use in cutting out sleeves, and was not merely a set of instructions as to how to do so.

[96] *Hollinrake v Truswell* [1894] 3 Ch. 420. Lord Herschell and Lindley L.J. decided the case on the basis that the words and figures were not merely directions for the use of the device but were a part of the device itself, without which it could not be used, and except in connection with which they had no use. It was not therefore a "volume, part or division of a volume, pamphlet, sheet of letterpress, sheet of music, map, chart, or plan separately published" within the meaning of the 1842 Act, not being separately published nor being a publication complete in itself, but only a direction on a device, to be understood and used with it. And see also *Davis v Comitti* 52 L.T. (N.S.) 539 (printed portions for use on face of barometer, such as "high winds", etc.; meaningless unless used with barometer). There is no objection in principle, however, to instructions for use of a device being the subject of copyright: see *Meccano Ltd v Anthony Horden & Sons Ltd* [1918] S.R. (N.S.W.) 606. Davey L.J. decided *Hollinrake v Truswell* on what would now be regarded as the conventional ground that the sleeve chart gave no information or instruction and was not calculated to afford literary enjoyment or pleasure. As noted in *Meccano Ltd v Anthony Horden & Sons Ltd*, the claimant was in effect seeking to copyright a tool. The instructions, apart from the tool, were meaningless.

[97] *Warren v Foster Bros. Clothing Co* (1906) 51 Sol. Jo. 145, on the basis, following *Hollinrake v Truswell* [1894] 3 Ch. 420, that the words only had use in relation to the box and therefore formed part of the box, and were thus not to be separately published. It was expressly left undecided whether the words had any literary merit on the grounds that the result would be the same either way.

[98] *Cable v Marks* (1882) 52 L.J. 107. The device cast a shadow resembling da Vinci's " *Ecce Homo*". The words were: "Entered at Stationers' Hall. Key enclosed. The Christograph: The Christian's Puzzle. Suitable for all sects and denominations—Every family should have it. Price, with Key, sixpence."

[99] These decisions therefore appear to give emphasis to the word "work" rather than the word "literary", although arguably this is something that might be better left to the issue of originality.

[100] *Noah v Shuba* [1991] F.S.R. 14 at 32, 33. This part of the decision was, however, obiter.

[101] *Kirk v J & R. Fleming Ltd* [1928–1935] Mac.C.C. 44. This comment was made as part of a wider decision on whether a number of commonplace sentences (of which the one quoted in the text formed part) strung together for the purposes of an advertisement constituted an original literary work. The basis of the decision as a whole appears to have been lack of originality, rather than the inherent inability of such phrases to amount to a literary work. See para.3–131, below, and note *Victoria v Pacific Technologies (Australia) Pty Ltd (No.2)* [2009] F.C.A. 737; [2009] 81 I.P.R. 525 (Fed. Ct. of Aus.), where protection was denied to the words "Help-Help-Driver-in-Danger-Call-Police-Ph.000" for lack of originality.

novels, newspaper articles or examination papers or more mundane things such as ordinary letters, written advertisements, rules for games and formulae. In this area of protected subject matter, the issue is usually whether the work is original or not, so that cases in which the point has been argued have been relatively rare.[102] Leaving aside cases about compilations and tables,[103] the following types of works have been protected: ordinary business letters[104]; examination papers[105]; a manual of instructions for a toy, being complete in itself[106]; a form for use in correspondence courses[107]; material included in a diary consisting of the months, dates and days, with a three-month calendar[108]; a formula using symbols and numbers[109]; and a programme and a race card for greyhound racing.[110] A host of other mundane works have been protected without any argument on the point, for example, trade circulars,[111] consignment notes,[112] the rules of a game,[113] and rules of a trade association.[114]

3–16   **Names and titles as literary works.** In the same vein is the reluctance of English courts to confer copyright protection on titles of newspapers, magazines, books and the like. In relation to books in particular, the title normally forms part of a copyright work consisting of the book as a whole and the issue here may be whether the copying of the title amounts to the taking of a substantial part of the whole work.[115] General statements can nevertheless be found in non-copyright cases to the effect that there is no property in a name or title standing alone unless it is the subject of goodwill or a registered trade mark.[116] In *Chilton v Progress Printing and Publishing Co*,[117] what amounted to a claim to copyright in individual names for horses was refused.[118] Much the same approach has been applied in

---

[102] The full variety of cases in which the subject matter has accepted without argument as a literary work can be seen from the cases on originality: see paras 3–131 et seq., below.

[103] As to which, see para.3–21, below.

[104] *British Oxygen Co Ltd v Liquid Air Ltd* [1925] Ch. 383, applied in *Tett Bros. Ltd v Drake & Gorham Ltd* [1928–1935] Mac.C.C. 492; *Musical Fidelity Ltd v Vickers* [2002] EWHC 1000 (Ch) (although coming as a matter of surprise to two members of the Court of Appeal: *Musical Fidelity Ltd v Vickers* [2002] EWCA Civ 1989, paras 28, 33; [2003] F.S.R. 50); *Cembrit Blunn Ltd v Apex Roofing Services LLP* [2007] EWHC 111 (Ch), paras 240, 241. See also "Copyright in Letters" printed as an addendum in [1905–1910] Mac.C.C. at para.241.

[105] *University of London Press Ltd v University Tutorial Press Ltd* [1916] 2 Ch. 601.

[106] *Meccano Ltd v Anthony Horden & Sons Ltd* [1918] S.R. (N.S.W.) 606, distinguishing *Hollinrake v Truswell* [1894] 3 Ch. 420.

[107] *Southern v Bailes* [1894] 38 S.J. 681, although it is not clear precisely what the copyright work was.

[108] *Waylite Diaries CC v First National Bank Ltd* [1993] (2) S.A. 128, (High Ct of S.A.).

[109] *Bookmakers' Afternoon Greyhound Services Ltd v Wilf Gilbert (Staffordshire) Ltd* [1994] F.S.R. 723 (formula describing how to do a calculation, and which could be set out at length using ordinary language). Copyright did not subsist, however, in the dividend forecasts which were produced by using the formula.

[110] *Bookmakers' Afternoon Greyhound Services Ltd v Wilf Gilbert (Staffordshire) Ltd* [1994] F.S.R. 723. Such a programme is probably more accurately classified as a compilation.

[111] *Coral Index Ltd v Regent Index Ltd* [1970] F.S.R. 13

[112] *Van Oppen & Co Ltd v Leonard Van Oppen* (1903) R.P.C. 617.

[113] *Caley (A. J.) & Son Ltd v Garnett (G.) & Sons Ltd* [1936–1945] Mac.C.C. 99.

[114] *Co-operative Union Ltd v Kilmore, etc. Ltd* [1912] 47 I.L.T. 7.

[115] Which will almost invariably not be the case. See, e.g. *Francis Day and Hunter Ltd v Twentieth Century Fox Corp Ltd* [1940] A.C. 112; *Ladbroke (Football) Ltd v William Hill (Football) Ltd* [1964] 1 W.L.R. 273.

[116] See, e.g. *Tavener Rutledge Ltd v Trexapalm Ltd* [1975] F.S.R. 479, at 483 (no copyright or other property in the invented name "Kojak" by itself); *Miss World (Jersey) Ltd v James Street Productions Ltd* [1981] F.S.R. (C.A.) 309 at 311 (no property or copyright in a title such as "Miss World"); *Kean v McGivan* [1982] F.S.R. 119 (no property in the name "Social Democratic Party"); *Mirage Studios v Counter-Feat Clothing Co Ltd* [1991] F.S.R. 145, at 154 ("... there is a rule in copyright that you can have no copyright in a name ...").

[117] *Chilton v Progress Printing and Publishing Co* [1895] 2 Ch. 29.

[118] The claimant published in its newspapers the names of horses which were tipped to win races in

relation to titles for books, newspapers, etc.,[119] sometimes coupled with the expression of a fear of conferring a monopoly on part of the English language.[120] On this basis, copyright protection has been denied to titles, such as *Splendid Misery* for a book,[121] *The Lawyer's Diary 1986* for a diary,[122] *The Licensed Victuallers' Mirror* for a newspaper,[123] *The Man Who Broke the Bank at Monte Carlo*[124] and *Nellie the Elephant*[125] as titles for songs, *Opportunity Knocks* for a television game-show,[126] and "*Dr Martens*" for the name of boots.[127] The courts have, however, been careful not to rule out the possibility of such protection in appropriate circumstances,[128] although in practice no case has ever gone this far. The only concrete example which has been given judicially is the now archaic practice of the title-page of a book consisting of an extended passage of text.[129] In *Lamb v Evans*,[130] protection was granted to an elaborate series of headings arranged alphabetically in a trade directory and provided in four languages but this

---

the forthcoming week; each day the defendant published the names of horses which were tipped to win that day by various tipsters, including the claimant's tip. The basis of the decision was that the announcement of the name of a horse was not a protectable subject matter, being only an expression of the tipster's opinion. There is, however, nothing in principle to prevent the expression of someone's opinion being a literary work and today the case would probably be decided on the basis that while the claimant's newspaper as a whole was entitled to copyright, the taking of a single word from it could not amount to an infringement. For further comment on the case, see *Independent Television Publications Ltd v Time Out Ltd* [1994] F.S.R. 64.

[119] *Dick v Yates* (1881) 18 Ch. D. 76 (James L.J.: "... there cannot in general be any copyright in the title or name of a book."); *Licensed Victuallers' Newspaper Co v Bingham* (1888) 38 Ch. D. 139 (Bowen L.J.: "... there is no copyright in the title of a newspaper"); *Francis Day and Hunter Ltd v Twentieth Century Fox Corp Ltd* [1940] A.C. 112 at 123 ("... a title is not by itself a proper subject matter of copyright. As a rule a title does not involve literary composition, and is not sufficiently substantial to justify a claim to protection"). These cases overruled the earlier cases of *Weldon v Dicks* (1878) 10 Ch. D. 247 and *Mack v Petter* (1872) L.R. 14 Eq. 431, where such protection was conferred but which can be explained as passing off cases, as the law is now understood. See *Dick v Yates* and *Francis Day and Hunter Ltd v Twentieth Century Fox Corp Ltd*, cited earlier in this footnote.

[120] See, *e.g. Rose v Information Services Ltd* [1978] F.S.R. 254 at 255.

[121] *Dick v Yates* (1881) L.R. 18 Ch. D. 76. It may well have been, however, that protection was denied on the grounds of lack of originality rather than because the title was not capable of protection: see the judgments of Jessel M.R. and Lush L.J.

[122] *Rose v Information Services Ltd* [1978] F.S.R. 254. Again, however, the ground of the decision may have been lack of originality.

[123] *Licensed Victuallers' Newspaper Co v Bingham* (1888) L.R. 38 Ch. D. 139.

[124] *Francis Day and Hunter Ltd v Twentieth Century Fox Corp Ltd* [1940] A.C. 112, where the House of Lords, at 123, apparently considered that although there might have been a certain amount of originality in choosing the title it was not a literary work.

[125] *Animated Music Ltd's Trade Mark* [2004] E.C.D.R. 27 (Trade Mark Registry).

[126] *Green v Broadcasting Corp of New Zealand* [1989] R.P.C. 469, at 475.

[127] *R. Griggs Group Ltd v Evans* [2003] EWHC 2914 (Ch), para.17 (obiter); [2004] F.S.R. 31.

[128] See, e.g. *Francis Day and Hunter Ltd v Twentieth Century Fox Corp Ltd* [1940] A.C. 112, above, at 123, noting that the general rule "does not mean that in particular cases a title may not be on so extensive a scale, and so important in character, as to be the proper subject of protection against being copied", citing *Dick v Yates* (1881) L.R. 18 Ch. D. 76); *Ladbroke (Football) Ld v William Hill (Football) Ltd* [1964] 1 W.L.R. 273 (per Lord Hodson at 286, saying that *Dick v Yates* and *Francis Day and Hunter* "do not support the proposition that, as a matter of law, copyright cannot subsist in titles. No doubt they will not as a rule be protected, since alone they would not be regarded as a sufficiently substantial part of the book or other copyright document to justify the preventing of copying by others." See also Graham J. at first instance in *Exxon Corp v Exxon Insurance Ltd* [1982] Ch. 119 at 131: "Nothing I have said above is intended to suggest that I consider that a word which is used as a title can, as a matter of law, never in any circumstances be the subject of copyright, and I would disagree with dicta in previous cases to the contrary effect. Such a word would, however, I think, have to have qualities or characteristics in itself, if such a thing is possible, which would justify its recognition as an original literary work rather than merely as an invented word. It may well turn out not to be possible in practice, but, as at present advised, I consider that the mere fact that a single word is invented and that research or labour was involved in its invention does not in itself, in my judgment, necessarily enable it to qualify as an original literary work ...".

[129] See *Dick v Yates* (1881) L.R. 18 Ch. D. 76, approved on this point in *Francis Day and Hunter Ltd v Twentieth Century Fox Corp Ltd* [1940] A.C. 112 at 123.

[130] *Lamb v Evans* [1893] 1 Ch. 218.

seems to have been a compilation case rather than a pure "title" case.[131] It has been held arguable that a headline on a website consisting of the words "Bid to Save Centre after Council Funding Cock-up", which had been put together for the purpose of imparting information, was protected by copyright,[132] but this was based on a concession that a headline could be a literary work.

3–17   **Literary work: code and other forms of notation.** It is not necessary that the work should convey any information to the ordinary reader. A work which is written in code is "in writing"[133] and is thus protectable even though it may mean nothing to the person who does not have the key. In the "code cases"[134] protection was conferred on lists of short words which had been carefully selected in order that, when transmitted in Morse code, mistakes were less likely to occur with them than with other words. Users of the codes attributed their own meanings to the words, and thus used the lists simply as a source of appropriate code words. By itself, each word had no particular meaning[135] and the cases are therefore properly regarded as compilation cases rather than authorities for the proposition that a work written in code is protectable.[136] Nevertheless, they are relevant because the argument that nothing could qualify as a literary work which did not involve an appreciation of the meaning of words was rejected.[137] In the same way, a work written in a foreign language that few people would understand is nonetheless a literary work, as is a work of which the only embodiment or record is a digital one stored in computer memory, such that it cannot be appreciated without the aid of suitable equipment. It has also been suggested that a list of electrical components identified on a wiring diagram using only their technical symbols is a literary work,[138] and on this basis it seems that even a line on such a diagram may be protected as part of a literary work if it would be understood as an instruction to connect component A to component B.[139]

3–18   **Copyright in ideas.** It is often stated that there is no copyright in ideas (the

---

[131] Bowen L.J., however said that the headings were "the result of literary labour, both as regards *the composition of the headings themselves* and their collocation or concatenation in the book" (emphasis added) and in *Ladbroke (Football) Ltd v William Hill (Football) Ltd* [1964] 1 W.L.R. 273, Lord Hodson cited *Lamb v Evans* [1893] 1 Ch. 218 as good authority for the protection of headings in a proper case. For a more modern case in which *Lamb v Evans* was applied, see *Desktop Marketing Systems Ltd v Telstra Corp Ltd* [2002] FCAFC 112 (Fed Ct of Aus), 55 I.P.R. (2002) 1, although since doubted in *IceTV Pty Ltd v Nine Network Australia Pty Ltd* [2009] HCA 14 (High Ct of Aus).

[132] *The Shetland Times v Wills* [1997] F.S.R. 604.

[133] CDPA 1988 s.178.

[134] i.e. *Anderson (D. P.) & Co Ltd v The Lieber Code Co* [1917] 2 K.B. 469; *Ager v P. & O. Steam Navigation Co* (1884) 26 Ch. D. 637; *Ager v Collingridge* (1886) 2 T.L.R. 291.

[135] In *Anderson (D.P.) & Co Ltd v The Lieber Code Co* [1917] 2 K.B. 469, the words were made up and had no inherent meaning; in the *Ager* cases (*Ager v P. & O. Steam Navigation Co* (1884) 26 Ch. D. 637 and *Ager v Collingridge* (1886) 2 T.L.R. 291), the words had been selected from various languages.

[136] See, e.g. Graham J. in *Exxon Corporation v Exxon Insurance Consultants International Ltd* [1982] Ch. 119, at 129; [1982] R.PC. 69, noting that it was the whole collection of many thousand words that was protected. Similarly, in *Pitman v Hine* (1884) 1 T.L.R. 39, a large collection of examples of shorthand words was protected, although the issue there was not subsistence but copying.

[137] This formed part of the *ratio* in *Anderson (D.P.) & Co Ltd v The Lieber Code Co* [1917] 2 K.B. 469. In *Ager v P. & O. Steam Navigation Co* (1884) 26 Ch. D. 637 copyright in the lists was not in issue and, in *Ager v Collingridge, Anderson* (1886) 2 T.L.R. 291, was merely applied.

[138] *Anacon Corp Ltd v Environmental Research Technology Ltd* [1994] F.S.R. 659; *Electronic Techniques (Anglia) Ltd v Critchley Components Ltd* [1997] F.S.R. 401.

[139] See the analysis of *Anacon Corp Ltd v Environmental Research Technology Ltd* [1994] F.S.R. 659, and *Electronic Techniques (Anglia) Ltd v Critchley Components Ltd* [1997] F.S.R. 401, in *Sandman v Panasonic U.K. Ltd* [1998] F.S.R. 651.

"ideas/expression dichotomy")[140] but without further explanation it is a dangerous proposition: no work will be denied copyright protection simply because it
can be categorised as one which "only" expresses ideas. In a general sense, of
course, all copyright works have as their basis an idea, in that all works are the
expression of the author's ideas, represented by his decision to use certain modes
of expression rather than others.[141] As discussed above, however, it is not the
concern of copyright to protect ideas unless and until the ideas have found expression in the form of a work of a category recognised as deserving of protection.[142]
The expression of ideas in writing, speech or song will almost always produce a
literary work save in the rare cases discussed in the preceding paragraphs. The
protection given by copyright to the expression of those ideas then becomes a
matter of the scope of the exclusive rights which are conferred on the copyright
owner in the work, in particular, what amounts to infringement by way of the taking of a substantial part of the work. It follows that once the ideas have been
expressed in the form of a literary work, it is the form of expression which is the
subject of protection, not the ideas, which themselves may be freely extracted
from the work and absorbed and used by others to produce their own works so
long as the form of expression of the copyright work is not also taken.[143] There
are a number of further aspects to this. First, although a work may express certain
ideas, it may be that those ideas are not protected by the copyright which subsists
in the work because they have no connection with the particular subject matter.
Thus a literary work which describes a system or invention does not entitle the
copyright owner to protect the invention since the operation of the system or the
working of the invention does not reproduce the literary expression which is the
subject of copyright.[144] Again, the particular expression of ideas may not be
protected because the expression is not original or the ideas are so commonplace
that the expression which has been copied does not form a substantial part of the
work.[145] As to this, the idea may have been so well known to the author from the
work of others that its expression required no sufficient skill and labour (an
unusual type of case in practice), or the idea may have been expressed in such a

---

[140] Innumerable cases could be cited, e.g. *IPC Media Ltd v Highbury-Leisure Publishing Ltd* [2004]
EWHC 2985 (Ch); [2005] F.S.R. 20, per Laddie J., para.14: "The law of copyright has never
gone as far as to protect general themes, styles or ideas. ... Such general concepts are not put out
of bounds to others by the law of copyright", although he went on to explain more precisely what
is meant by such a statement.

[141] *Designers Guild Ltd v Russell Williams (Textiles) Ltd* [2000] 1 W.L.R. 2416, per Lord Hoffmann
at 2422.

[142] See, e.g. *Donoghue v Allied Newspapers Ltd* [1938] Ch. 106, per Farwell J., at 109: "This at any
rate is clear beyond all question, that there is no copyright in an idea, or in ideas. A person may
have a brilliant idea for a story, ... and which appears to him to be original; but if he communicates that idea to an author ..., the production which is the result of the communication of
the idea to the author ... is the copyright of the person who has clothed the idea in form ..., and
the owner of the idea has no rights in that product."

[143] See, again, for example, *Donoghue v Allied Newspapers Ltd* [1938] Ch. 106, per Farwell J. at
110: "... that in which copyright exists is the particular form of language by which information
which is to be conveyed is conveyed ... It is not until [the idea] is ... reduced into writing or into
some tangible form that there is any copyright, and the copyright exists in the particular form of
language in which ... the information or the idea is conveyed to those who are intended to read it
...". In this respect, however, it is to be noted that the form of expression of a literary work does
not mean only the actual language in which that work is written; it may include the selection, and
arrangement in a particular order, of incidents, whether factual or fictional. See, for an example
of the extent of protection given to a traditional literary work, *Ravenscroft v Herbert and New
English Library* [1980] R.P.C. 193. For a more recent statement of the general propostion, see
also *London General Holdings Ltd v USP Plc* [2005] EWCA Civ 931; [2006] F.S.R. 6, paras 29
and 44.

[144] *Designers Guild Ltd v Russell Williams (Textiles) Ltd* [2000] 1 W.L.R. 2416, citing the example
of *Kleeneze Ltd v D.R.G. (U.K.) Ltd* [1984] F.S.R. 399. For a further discussion on this point, see
para.7–12, below.

[145] *Designers Guild Ltd v Russell Williams (Textiles) Ltd* [2000] 1 W.L.R. 2416, citing as an example
Kenrick v Lawrence & Co (1890) 25 Q.B.D. 99.

trivial fashion that the expression does not form a substantial part of the work as a whole. The most usual type of case is where the expression of the idea may merit protection but the defendant has not appropriated the author's skill and labour in giving form to that expression.[146] As already stated, these issues in the end all relate to questions of infringement, not subsistence of copyright, and are considered in Ch.7.

3–19 **Copyright in news.** The same kind of considerations apply to literary works whose principal purpose is to communicate news, and indeed it is often stated that there is no copyright in news.[147] Again, however, taken by itself this is not a correct statement of UK law: the fact that the content of a literary work is news does not prevent that work from being capable of protection by copyright. What is protected is the form of expression of that content.[148] In general terms, the information itself, once stripped of its particular form of expression and robbed of any work of compilation with other material, may be freely used, as with any other literary work. Again, however, this issue relates to the question of infringement, not subsistence of copyright.[149] Newspapers themselves are more properly regarded as compilations of literary and (usually) artistic works. News can also sometimes be protected as confidential information before publication.[150]

3–20 **Copyright in information.** Much the same can be said about statements that there can be no copyright in "mere" information. Merely because the work consists in essence of pure information, even if the work is the only source of that information, does not mean that copyright does not subsist in it.[151] See the following paragraphs, however, as to information in the form of tables, compilations or databases.

(iii) Tables, compilations and databases

3–21 **Tables, compilations and databases.** Whether called a table, compilation or database, such works have long been protected as copyright works, but copyright protection has never been conferred on systems as such, or on methods of indexing or retrieval of such material.[152] Until January 1, 1998, s.3(1) of the Act defined

---

[146] This was the situation in *Kenrick v Lawrence & Co* (1890) 25 Q.B.D. 99. If the defendant there had made greater borrowing of the artist's skill in representing the voter's hand, there would presumably have been an infringement. See paras 7–66 et seq., below, for further discussion of this point generally.

[147] For example, art.2(8) of the Berne Convention provides that the protection of the Convention is not to apply to "news of the day or to miscellaneous facts having the character of mere items of press information."

[148] *Walter v Steinkopff* [1892] 3 Ch. 489, per North J.; *Wilson v Lukepy* [1875] 1 V.L.R. 127; and see *Football League Ltd v Littlewoods Pools Ltd* [1959] Ch. 637, per Upjohn J., at 651 ("... there can be no copyright in information or in an opinion per se. Copyright can only be claimed in the composition or language which is chosen to express the information or opinion").

[149] See para.7–44, below.

[150] Such news was protected before the 1911 Act either on this basis or under common law copyright in the wire service cases, e.g. *Exchange Telegraph Co Ltd v Central News Ltd* [1897] 2 Ch. 48; *Exchange Telegraph Co Ltd v Gregory & Co* [1896] 1 Q.B. 147; *Press Association Ltd v Northern and Midland Reporting Agency* [1905–10] Mac. C.C. 306.

[151] *Football League Ltd v Littlewoods Pools Ltd* [1959] Ch. 637. The plaintiff had created the fixture lists for all the professional football leagues, and so a person who wished to reproduce a substantial part of the fixture lists would inevitably infringe, absent any defence such as fair dealing or, today, public interest or anti-competitive practices. See also *Fraser v Evans* [1969] 1 Q.B. 349 at 362, per Lord Denning, M.R.: Information is not the subject of copyright, but only "the literary form in which the information is dressed".

[152] See *Libraco Ltd v Shaw Walker Ltd* (1913) 30 T.L.R. 22 (a card index system with cards of different colours and headings for filing particulars of employees, and carrying only simple words

a literary work as including a table or compilation[153] and made no express reference to databases, which would normally have come within the description of either a table or a compilation. With effect from this date, however, the Act was amended to exclude a database from the description "table or compilation",[154] and a database is now a separate category of literary work. Thus, as the Act now stands, a literary work is defined to include (a) a database and (b) a table or compilation other than a database.[155] Tables or compilations may often be databases, and vice versa, and the reason why it is necessary to make a distinction between tables and compilations which are databases and those which are not is to be found in the Database Directive.[156] This Directive, as well as creating a new sui generis right in databases,[157] also provided that copyright should subsist in databases if, but only if, by reason of the selection or arrangement of its contents, the database constituted the author's own intellectual creation.[158] This test is higher than the normal originality requirement for such works under United Kingdom copyright law[159] and so it became necessary to introduce a two-tier system of copyright protection: protection for databases (which, as defined, will include many tables and compilations) which satisfy the new and higher test of originality, and protection for tables and compilations which are not also databases as defined. Tables and compilations which are also databases but which, although satisfying the traditional, low UK test of originality, do not satisfy the new higher test of originality therefore no longer qualify for copyright protection.[160] They may of course qualify for database right protection.

Databases: statutory definition.[161] Since it is now of fundamental importance to know whether a table or compilation is also a database, it is logical to consider what amounts to a database within the meaning of the Act before considering what amounts to a table or compilation.[162] The term "database" has to be construed in accordance with the Database Directive and its recitals, and the intention of the Directive is to give the term a wide scope, unencumbered by considerations of a formal, technical or material nature.[163] Thus, for example, according to art.1(1), the Directive concerns the legal protection of databases "in any form". A database is defined to mean a collection of independent works, data or other materials arranged in a systematic or methodical way and individually accessible by electronic or other means.[164] Recital 17 of the Directive provides that a database should be understood to include (a) literary, artistic, musical or other collections of works, (b) collections of other material such as texts, sounds, images, numbers, facts and data, and (c) collections of independent works, data

3–22

---

such as "name" and "address": "useless and conveyed no meaning"). See also *Cartwright v Wharton* [1912] O.L.R. 357 (system of indexing).

[153] s.48(1) of the 1956 Act referred to "any" rather than "a" table or compilation, but it was not considered that this altered the previous law: *Football League Ltd v Littlewoods Pools Ltd* [1959] Ch. 637 at 650, per Upjohn J. Tables and compilations had been included in the category of literary works under the 1911 Act: s.35(1); see para.3–09, above.

[154] By the Copyright and Rights in Databases Regulations 1997 (SI 1997/3032).

[155] CDPA 1988 ss.3(1)(d) and (a) respectively.

[156] Council Directive 96/9 of March 14, 1996 on the legal protection of databases.

[157] See generally as to database rights, Ch.18.

[158] Database Directive 96/9 art.3(1).

[159] As to which, see paras 3–129 and 3–146.

[160] As to the transitional position, see para.3–147.

[161] The reader is also referred to the discussion in Ch.18.

[162] In theory, there may be databases which are not tables or compilations, but it is hard to imagine an example.

[163] *Fixtures Marketing Ltd v Organismos prognostikon agonon podosfairou AE(OPAP)* (C–444/02) [2005] 1 C.M.L.R. 16, para.20.

[164] Database Directive 96/9 art.1(2), implemented by CDPA 1988 s.3A(1), introduced by the Copyright and Rights in Databases Regulations 1997 (SI 1997/3032) with effect from January 1, 1998.

or other materials, the common requirement being that such collections should be systematically or methodically arranged and individually accessible. For these purposes it is irrelevant whether the collection is made up of materials created by the author of the database himself or by someone else, or of materials falling within both those categories, and a database does not have to be its maker's own intellectual creation to be classified as such.[165] Classification as a database is dependent on the existence of a collection of "independent" materials, that is to say, materials which are separable from one another without their informative, literary, artistic, musical or other value being affected.[166] For this reason, recital 17 makes it clear that a recording of an audiovisual, cinematographic, literary or musical work as such does not fall within the scope of the Directive.[167] What thus makes something a database is the collection and systematic arrangement of works, data or other materials (referred to in the Directive as "contents"),[168] and the object of the Directive is to ensure harmonised protection for works which are created in this way, whilst preserving any rights which may exist in the individual components which make up the database.[169] While recital 21 of the Directive makes it clear that it is not necessary for the systematic or methodical arrangement to be physically apparent, the recital implies that the collection should be contained in a fixed base of some sort, and include either technical means such as electronic, electromagnetic or electro-optical processes (see recital 13), or other means, such as an index, a table of contents, or a particular plan or method of classification, to allow the retrieval of any independent material contained within it.[170] The Act implements this by providing that the contents should be individually accessible "by electronic or other means".[171] This condition makes it possible to distinguish a database within the meaning of the Directive, characterised by a means of retrieving each of its constituent materials, from a collection of materials providing information without any means of processing the individual materials which make it up.[172] What is not clear is what is meant by "other means" and, in particular, whether a collection of data which is accessible by purely physical means, for example by reference to the index to a book, or even by simple visual examination of a book's contents, satisfies the definition. In this respect, recital 14 at least makes it clear that Directive extends to non-electronic databases, so that purely hard-copy databases therefore seem to be covered. The reference to a collection of independent works, data or other materials embraces the items which may be the subject of a compilation, and the reference to collection and arrangement in a systematic or methodical way covers the acts of selection, compilation and arrangement of those things. Certain types of works are (somewhat unnecessarily) specifically excluded from protection as a database, namely computer programs used in the making or operation of cinematographic,

---

[165] *Fixtures Marketing Ltd v Organismos prognostikon agonon podosfairou AE(OPAP)* (C–444/02) [2005] 1 C.M.L.R. 16, paras 25, 26, the criterion of originality being relevant only to the assessment whether a database qualifies for the copyright protection.

[166] *Fixtures Marketing Ltd v Organismos prognostikon agonon podosfairou AE(OPAP)* (C–444/02) [2005] 1 C.M.L.R. 16, para.29.

[167] *Fixtures Marketing Ltd v Organismos prognostikon agonon podosfairou AE(OPAP)* (C–444/02) [2005] 1 C.M.L.R. 16, para.29.

[168] *Football Dataco Ltd v Brittens Pools Ltd* [2010] EWHC 841 (Ch); [2010] R.P.C. 17, para.51.

[169] *Football Dataco Ltd v Brittens Pools Ltd* [2010] EWHC 841 (Ch), paras 51, 67, noting at para.69 that the individual contents may or may not be entitled to copyright, depending on the facts.

[170] *Fixtures Marketing Ltd v Organismos prognostikon agonon podosfairou AE(OPAP)* (C–444/02) [2005] 1 C.M.L.R. 16, para.30.

[171] CDPA 1988 s.3A(1)(b).

[172] *Fixtures Marketing Ltd v Organismos prognostikon agonon podosfairou AE(OPAP)* (C–444/02) [2005] 1 C.M.L.R. 16, para.31.

literary or musical works as such.[173] It is also stated that "as a rule, the compilation of several recordings of musical performances on a CD[174] does not come within the scope of the Directive, both because, as a compilation, it does not meet the conditions for copyright protection and because it does not represent a substantial enough investment to be eligible under the *sui generis* right".[175] In summary, the term database in the Directive refers to any collection of works, data or other materials, separable from one another without the value of their contents being affected, and including a method or system of some sort for the retrieval of each of its constituent materials.[176] Programs or scripts creating a database are not properly part of the database, even though they define its "arrangement" and "structure".[177] Again, material which may be entered into database programs in order to change the structure of the database by adding or subtracting fields or adding or removing datasets, or metadata defining the fields and datasets or the tables, rows or columns, are not to be regarded as databases, these being protected, (if at all) as computer programs.[178]

Examples of databases. Many of the earlier cases provide examples of what would now be regarded as databases,[179] but a modern example of the application to the definition is the *Football Dataco Ltd* case.[180] This concerned a series of football fixture lists, where the date and the time of and the identity of the two teams playing in both home and away matches were covered by the concept of independent materials within the meaning of art.1(2) of the Directive in that they had autonomous informative value. The data concerning the date, the time and the identity of the teams for a particular match had an independent value in that they provided interested third parties with relevant information. Further, the arrangement, in the form of a fixture list, of the dates, times and names of the teams in those various football matches met the conditions as to systematic or methodical arrangement and individual accessibility of the constituent materials of that collection. The fact that lots had to be drawn to decide the pairing of the teams was irrelevant.[181] 3–23

Table or compilation. A dictionary definition of a table is an arrangement of numbers, words or items of any kind, in a definite and compact form, so as to exhibit some set of facts, or relations, in a distinct and comprehensive way.[182] A dictionary definition of the verb "to compile" is to construct a written or printed 3–24

---

[173] Recital 23.

[174] Nevertheless, it seems that electronic databases may include devices such as CD-ROMs, CD-Is, and presumably DVDs, pursuant to recital 22 of the Directive.

[175] Directive, recital 19. It follows that such compilations may be databases, as defined, but will not generally receive protection. In *Football Dataco Ltd v Brittens Pools Ltd* [2010] EWHC 841 (Ch), para.84, it was noted that the recital is not specific as to precisely why such a compilation would not be protected by copyright, but that it must be referring to the requirement that the selection be the author's own intellectual creation. See, further, para.3–148.

[176] *Fixtures Marketing Ltd v Organismos prognostikon agonon podosfairou AE(OPAP)* (C–444/02) [2005] 1 C.M.L.R. 16, para.32, and the ECJ's formal ruling on this point.

[177] *Navitaire Inc v easyJet Airline Co Ltd* [2004] EWHC 1725 (Ch); [2006] R.P.C. 3, per Pumfrey J., obiter at para.274.

[178] *Navitaire Inc v easyJet Airline Co Ltd* [2004] EWHC 1725 (Ch), per Pumfrey J., obiter at para.274, noting also that such metadata also probably do not fall within the definition of "database" because they are not a collection of data.

[179] See para.3–22.

[180] *Football Dataco Ltd v Brittens Pools Ltd* [2010] EWHC 841 (Ch); [2010] R.P.C. 17.

[181] *Football Dataco Ltd v Brittens Pools Ltd* [2010] EWHC 841 (Ch). See also *Fixtures Marketing Ltd v Organismos prognostikon agonon podosfairou AE(OPAP)* (C–444/02) [2005] 1 C.M.L.R. 16, paras 33–35.

[182] *Oxford English Dictionary*. So a table of measurements for machine parts was a "table": *Purefoy Engineering Co v Sykes Boxall & Co* (1955) 72 R.P.C. 89, at 102. In *Statuscard Australia Pty Ltd v Rotondo* [2008] Q.S.C. 181 at para.98, it was held that a framework for displaying data on a

work out of materials collected from various sources.[183] Whilst the two terms clearly overlap, and the term compilation is often used in this work to cover both, the essential characteristic of a table lies in what determines the arrangement between the items contained in the table, that of a compilation lies in the gathering together of the items. A collection of literary works in an anthology is a clear example of a compilation but any collection of separate items which can be written, spoken or sung will qualify too. As a matter of terminology, a database will almost inevitably also be a table or compilation.[184] But a table or compilation requires that there has been some tabulation or compiling, respectively. The mere coming together of items will not be enough. Thus, a collection of commands for the operation of a computer program was refused protection as a compilation since there was no *compilation* of commands, only an "accretion" by virtue of their individual formulation. The collection of command names and syntax was never designed as such and the only influence that one command or set of commands had on the others was that it was necessary that they should all have different names.[185] The items which are arranged together in a table or assembled in a compilation may, individually, be entitled to copyright; such individual copyright remains independent of the separate copyright in the table or compilation.[186]

3–25   **Tables and compilations other than databases**. As already noted, any database will almost inevitably be a table or compilation but it may be wondered whether there can be a table or compilation which is not also a database. The reference to a database being a collection of independent works, data or other materials[187] would seem to cover all forms of tables or compilations[188] and so the only points of departure can be tables or compilations in which the materials are either (a) not arranged in a systematic or methodical way or (b) not individually accessible by electronic or other means. Most tables or compilations are arranged according to some system or method, if only an alphabetical or chronological one. Although it is not clear, it would seem that it is (b) which is critical. Non-electronic databases are included in the definition of databases,[189] and the problem of knowing what is meant by "other means" has already been referred to. Although a collection of poems or a newspaper in ordinary hard copy form is a compilation, and although technically each item is individually accessible by looking in an index or opening the pages, it must be questioned whether it was the intention of the Directive to bring such works within its scope.[190] At present this remains an open question.

3–26   **Collections of literary and artistic works**. A database can clearly consist of literary, artistic and other works,[191] even though it is included in the category of a literary work. As for a compilation, is it is suggested that the items which are

---

computer screen comprising coloured boxes with column headings was not a table or compilation because it had no content; it was probably a drawing (see further para.3–131 of this work).
[183] *Oxford English Dictionary*.
[184] As to tables or compilations that are not databases, see para.3–25.
[185] *Navitaire Inc v easyJet Airline Co Ltd* [2004] EWHC 1725 (Ch); [2006] R.P.C. 3, although the main reason was that the commands amounted to a computer language (see para.3–30, below).
[186] See, e.g. *Purefoy Engineering Co Ltd v Sykes Boxall & Co Ltd* [1955] 72 R.P.C. 89; *Longman Group Ltd v Carrington Technical Institute Board of Governors* [1991] 2 N.Z.L.R. 574; (1990) 20 I.P.R. 264 (High Ct of NZ). In the same way, the making of the table or compilation will require the licence of the owner of the copyright in the individual items, unless less than a substantial part of those works are taken.
[187] CDPA 1988 s.3A(1).
[188] See para.3–24, above. The word "independent" appears to refer merely to the materials having a significance or existence apart from each other, a feature of any table or compilation.
[189] Database Directive 96/9, recital 14.
[190] See the discussion at paras 18–05 et seq., below.
[191] Database Directive 96/9, recital 17.

compiled together again need not themselves be literary material, and that a compilation may consist of a mixture of literary and artistic material, or even exclusively of artistic material.[192] Newspapers and magazines are obvious examples of such works, as are atlases, books of street maps, catalogues, art gallery and exhibition guides,[193] and a story told in a series of pictures.[194] Indeed, if it were otherwise, where skill and labour has been expended in choosing and arranging artistic works as part of a larger composite work, the result would not be protected. Such works were protected as books under the pre-1911 Copyright Acts,[195] so that protection was given to works consisting entirely of illustrations with no, or virtually no, text, such as trade catalogues,[196] as well as trade catalogues consisting of text and illustrations,[197] and also map books[198] and other works containing both text and illustrations.[199] In relation to these works, even where the work contained text, copyright was held to be infringed where artistic material only had been taken,[200] showing that protection must have extended to the selection of the artistic material as part of the book. Protection for such works, now as compilations, continued after the passing of the 1911 Act.[201]

The only doubt about the point arises under the present wording of the 1988 Act, which defines a literary work as meaning a work which is *written*,[202] spoken or sung, and "accordingly" as including compilations (other than databases). Arguably, a work which partly or wholly consists of artistic material is not, or to the extent that it consists of artistic material is not, "written". If, however, such works were no longer compilations under the 1988 Act, this would represent a change in the law and it seems unlikely that Parliament intended to remove protection for this category of work. It is suggested that the express inclusion of

---

[192] *The Football Association Premier League Ltd v Panini UK Ltd* [2003] EWCA Civ. 995; [2004] 1 W.L.R. 1147; [2004] F.S.R. 1, per the "provisional view" of Mummery L.J. (obiter, and acknowledging that the point had not been argued). It is suggested that Mummery L.J.'s provisional view is correct and it accords with art.2(5) of the Berne Convention, which requires protection to be given to collections of literary or artistic works, which, by reason of the selection and arrangement of their contents, constitute intellectual creations.

[193] All cited as examples by Mummery L.J. in *The Football Association Premier League Ltd v Panini UK Ltd* [2004] 1 W.L.R. 1147. But see *Woodtree Pty Ltd v Zheng* [2007] F.C.A. 1922 at para.32, where it was held to be even arguable that a layout for a box label comprising a photograph and several short lines of explanatory text and numbers was a compilation.

[194] Each picture will constitute a separate artistic work. However, the structure and plot of the story, the creation of which may itself be presumed to have involved time, skill and labour, are found only in the arrangement of the pictures, one with another, and there seems no reason why this effort should not give rise to a separate copyright as a compilation.

[195] Although "books" had an extended definition: see para.3–08, above.

[196] *Grace v Newman* (1875) L.R. 19 Eq. 623; *Maple & Co v Junior Army and Navy Stores* (1882) 21 Ch. D. 369, overruling *Cobbett v Woodward* (1872) L.R. 14 Eq. 407; *Davis v Benjamin* [1906] 2 Ch. 491).

[197] *Bogue v Houlston* 5 De G. & Sm. 267; *Hotten v Arthur* (1863) 1 H. & M. 603; *W. Marshall & Co Ltd v A.H. Bull Ltd* (1901) 85 L.T. 77.

[198] *Cary v Longman & Rees* [1801] 1 East. 358; 102 E.R. 139; *Cary v Kearsley* [1802] 4 Esp. 168; 170 E.R. 679; *Cary v Faden* (1799) 5 Ves. Jun. 23; 31 E.R. 453, although it is not clear to what extent these contained artistic works in the form of maps as opposed to itineraries, information about distances, etc.

[199] e.g. *Comyns v Hyde* (1895) 72 L.T. 250.

[200] *Bogue v Houlston*, 5 De G. & Sm. 267; *W. Marshall & Co Ltd v A.H. Bull Ltd* (1901) 85 L.T. 77; *Comyns v Hyde* (1895) 72 L.T. 250.

[201] See *Masson, Seeley & Co Ltd v Embosotype Manufacturing Co* (1924) 41 R.P.C. 160 (catalogue of type consisting of drawings plus text; the argument that a catalogue was not protected as a literary work because the law had been changed by the omission of "book" as a protected subject matter was rejected, applying the meaning given to "literary work" in *University of London Press v University TutorialPress* [1916] 2 Ch. 601). *Purefoy Engineering Co Ltd v Sykes Boxall & Co Ltd* [1955] 72 R.P.C. 89 (trade catalogue comprising literary and artistic elements). The same result was achieved under the equivalent provisions of the Australian statute: *Kalamazoo (Aust.) Pty Ltd v Compact Business Systems Pty Ltd* [1990] 1 Qd. R. 231; (1985) 5 I.P.R. 213 (Sup Ct of Queensland): accounting forms consisting of words, lines and boxes held to be a compilation.

[202] For this purpose, something which is written includes something in notation or code, by hand or otherwise: CDPA 1988 ss.178, 3(1).

"compilation" in the definition, a word which has a well-established meaning in a copyright context, carries much greater force than the argument that the word "accordingly" restricts compilations to works which are wholly written.[203]

3–27   **Example of tables and compilations.** Historically, the issue in cases involving compilations, etc. has seldom been whether the essential characteristic of a compilation is satisfied, but rather whether the work is original[204] or has been infringed.[205] Provided the subject matter can reasonably be called a table, compilation or database, it will almost always fall within the statutory description.[206] Ultimately, however, the test remains the same as the general test for a literary work, namely whether the subject matter provides information, instruction or pleasure in the form of literary enjoyment[207] or whether, perhaps, it satisfies a more general test, namely that it is a written artefact which is to be accorded the status of a copyright work having regard to the kind of skill and labour expended, the nature of copyright protection and its underlying policy.[208] Thus on the one hand copyright has been denied to a list of names which conveys no useful information,[209] and a card index system with cards of different colours and headings for filing particulars of employees, and carrying only simple words such as "name" and "address"[210]; but on the other hand copyright was conferred on tables comprising grids of five-letter sequences for a monthly newspaper competition since they provided information to a competitor, telling him whether he had won or lost.[211] Arguments that there can be no copyright in "mere" information or lists have been rejected.[212] Examples of the variety of cases where compilations have been protected, often without argument, are: schedules of broadcasting programmes,[213] school textbooks consisting of compilations of different mate-

---

[203] And see CDPA 1988 s.172(2). But see *Monotti* [1993] E.I.P.R. 156, arguing that a collection made up wholly of artistic material cannot now be a compilation while collections of literary and artistic material may be, the position being unclear.

[204] As to which, in the case of compilations, see paras 3–146 et seq., below.

[205] As to which see Ch.7, below.

[206] In *Ladbroke (Football) Ltd v William Hill (Football) Ltd* [1964] 1 W.L.R. 273, at 278, Lord Reid pointed out that cases in which copyright has been denied to a compilation are comparatively few.

[207] *Express Newspapers v Liverpool Daily Post and Echo* [1985] 1 W.L.R. 1089; [1985] F.S.R. 306; *Real Estate Institute of N.S.W. v Wood* (1923) 23 S.R. (N.S.W.) 349 (copyright in a compilation if it supplies "intelligible information"). In *Kalamazoo (Aust.) Pty Ltd v Compact Business Systems Pty Ltd*, [1990] 1 Qd. R. 231, (1985) 5 I.P.R. 213 (Sup Ct of Queensland), however, this test was rejected when conferring copyright on accounting forms consisting of words, lines and boxes which conveyed no information or instruction by themselves, it being said that the relevant test was whether there was intellectual input in the forms, it being the case on the facts that they were designed and presented in a way which would produce meaningful results for the user. This, however, would seem to go to the issue of originality.

[208] *Navitaire Inc v easyJet Airline Co Ltd* [2004] EWHC 1725 (Ch); [2006] R.P.C. 3, at para.80. See para.3–24.

[209] *Weatherby & Sons v International Horse Agency and Exchange Ltd* [1910] 2 Ch. 297 at 304.

[210] See *Libraco Ltd v Shaw Walker Ltd* (1913) 30 T.L.R. 22 (index was "useless and conveyed no meaning"). See also *Cartwright v Wharton* [1912] O.L.R. 357 (system of indexing).

[211] *Express Newspapers v Liverpool Daily Post and Echo* [1985] 1 W.L.R. 1089, distinguishing *Exxon Corporation v Exxon Insurance Consultants International Ltd* [1982] Ch. 119; [1982] R.P.C. 69.

[212] *British Broadcasting Co v Wireless League Gazette Publishing Co* [1926] Ch. 433 (applying *University of London Press v University Tutorial Press* [1916] 2 Ch. 601), followed in *Independent Television Publications Ltd v Time Out Ltd* [1984] F.S.R. 64.

[213] *British Broadcasting Co v Wireless League Gazette Publishing Co* [1926] Ch. 433; *Independent Television Publications Ltd v Time Out Ltd* [1984] F.S.R. 64; *RTÉ v Magill TV Guide* [1990] F.S.R. 561 (High Ct of Ireland). There may be copyright in a written schedule of programmes, but not in a compilation of the programmes as they are broadcast during the day in accordance with the schedule: *FWS Joint Sports Claimants v Copyright Board* (1992) 22 I.P.R. 429; (1991) 81 D.L.R. 412 (Fed CA of Canada). For a full discussion of some of the television listings cases in the United Kingdom, Australia, New Zealand and Europe, see Watts and Durie in [1992] 4 Ent. L. R. 133.

rials,[214] a book of scientific questions and answers,[215] directories of all kinds,[216] trade brochures,[217] a report on various collieries, with plans and an appendix,[218] lists of registered bills of sale and deeds of arrangement extracted from publicly available sources,[219] a list of foxhunts and associated information,[220] a list of Stock Exchange prices,[221] biographical notes of prominent golfers published in a golf annual,[222] a list of brood mares with their sires and a list of stallions with daughters at stud,[223] a list of weights and acceptances for horse racing,[224] a list of recently published books,[225] a list of characteristics of racehorses,[226] a list of customers,[227] a price list,[228] a manual of classified information for the use of motor car insurers,[229] a business manual,[230] an alphabetical list of railway stations,[231] chronological fixture lists of football clubs,[232] football pool coupons,[233] columns of birth and death announcements in a newspaper,[234] contract forms,[235] forms of writs,[236] a series of book-keeping forms,[237] sheets of election results,[238] tables comprising grids of five-letter sequences for a monthly newspaper competition,[239] a list of three letter mnemonics,[240] and an electronic circuit diagram.[241] Arrays of numerous single-character columns and rows on computer screens, which were

---

[214] *Educational Co of Ireland Ltd v Fallon Bros Ltd* [1919] 1 I.R. 62; *Ghafur v Jwala* [1921] A.I.R. All. 95; *Leanie v Pillans* [1843] 5 Dunl. (Ct of Sess.) 416.

[215] *Jarrold v Houlston* (1857) 3 K. & J. 708.

[216] *Kelly v Morris* (1866) L.R. 1 Eq. 697; *Morris v Ashbee* (1868) L.R. 7 Eq. 34; *Morris v Wright* (1870) 5 Ch. 279; *Matthewson v Stockdale* (1806) 12 Ves. 270; *Fax Directories (Pty) Ltd v S.A. Fax Listings C.C.* (1990) 2 S.A.L.R. 164 (Sup Ct of S.A.).

[217] *Maple & Co v Junior Army and Navy Stores* (1882) 21 Ch. D. 369.

[218] *Kenrick v Danube Collieries, etc. Co Ltd* (1891) 39 W.R. 473.

[219] *Trade Auxiliary Co v Middlesbrough, etc. Association* (1889) 40 Ch. D. 425; *Cate v Devon, etc. Newspaper Co* (1889) 40 Ch. D. 500; *T.M. Hall & Co v Whittington & Co* [1892] 18 V.L.R. 525.

[220] *Cox v Land and Water Journal Co* (1869) L.R. 9 Eq. 324.

[221] *Exchange Telegraph Co Ltd v Gregory & Co* [1896] 1 Q.B. 147.

[222] *Nisbet (J.) & Co Ltd v The Golf Agency* (1907) 23 T.L.R. 370.

[223] *Weatherby & Sons v International Horse Agency and Exchange Ltd* [1910] 2 Ch. 297.

[224] *Winterbottom v Wintle* (1947) 50 W.A.L.R. 58.

[225] *J. Whitaker & Sons Ltd v Publishers' Circular Ltd* [1946–47] Mac. C.C. 10.

[226] *Portway Press Ltd v Hague* [1957] R.P.C. 426, and see *Caboverbury Park Race Course Co Ltd v Hopkins* (1932) 49 W.N. (N.S.W.) 27; *Demerara Turf Club v Phang* (1963) 6 W.I.R. 177 and *Ascot Jockey Club Ltd v Simons* (1968) 64 W.W.R. 411.

[227] *Flocast Australia Pty Ltd v Purcell* 39 I.P.R. 177.

[228] *Payen Components South Africa Ltd v Bovis Gaskets C.C.* (1996) 33 I.P.R. 406 (South Africa).

[229] *Underwriters Survey Bureau Ltd v Amer. Home Fire Ass. Co* (1939) 4 D.L.R. 89.

[230] *Flocast Australia Pty Ltd v Purcell* 39 I.P.R. 177.

[231] *Blacklock (H.) & Co Ltd v Arthur Pearson (C.) Ltd* [1915] 2 Ch. 376; *Leslie v Young (J.) & Sons Ltd* [1894] A.C. 335.

[232] *Football League Ltd v Littlewoods Pools Ltd* [1959] Ch. 637.

[233] *Ladbroke (Football) Ltd v William Hill (Football) Ltd* [1964] 1 W.L.R. 273.

[234] *John Fairfax & Sons Pty Ltd v Australian Consolidated Press Ltd* [1960] S.R. (N.S.W.) 413.

[235] *Capital Finance Co v Bowmaker (Commercial) Ltd* [1964] R.P.C. 463; *Capital Finance Co v Lombank Ltd* [1964] R.P.C. 467; *Real Estate Institute of N.S.W. v Wood* (1923) 23 S.R. (N.S.W.) 349

[236] *Alexander (W.) v Mackenzie (R.)* (1846) 9 Sess. Cas.D. 748.

[237] *Kalamazoo (Aus.) Pty Ltd v Compact Business Systems Pty Ltd* [1990] 1 Qd. R. 231 (Sup Ct of Queensland).

[238] *Press Association Ltd v Northern and Midland Reporting Agency* [1905–1910] Mac. C.C. 306.

[239] *Express Newspapers v Liverpool Daily Post and Echo* [1985] 1 W.L.R. 1089; [1985] F.S.R. 306. Each of the 750 tables was a separate work.

[240] *Microsense Systems Ltd v Control Systems Technology Ltd* noted at [1992] I.P.D. 15006 (the three-letter mnemonics comprised the language code for communication with a pelican crossing controller).

[241] *Anacon Corporation Ltd v Environmental Research Technology Ltd* [1994] F.S.R. 659 (the diagram showed a large amount of writing and symbols and was a list of components together with information as to how they were connected).

only capable of displaying printable characters, some of which could be seen in the underlying computer code, were properly to be viewed as tables.[242]

(iv) Computer programs and preparatory design material for a computer program

3–28   **History of protection of computer programs.** Computer programs were not expressly referred to in the UK copyright legislation until 1985,[243] nor in any major copyright convention until 1996.[244] However, by the time of the 1977 Copyright Committee,[245] there was already a widely held view, not only in the United Kingdom, but also internationally, that computer programs should be considered as falling within the category of literary works. The Committee recommended that computer programs should be treated as literary works under UK copyright law.[246] This approach was followed in several interlocutory decisions in the first half of the 1980s.[247] The Copyright (Computer Software) Amendment Act 1985 removed any residual doubt about the protection of software under United Kingdom copyright law by confirming that the 1956 Act applied to computer programs, including programs made before the 1985 Act,[248] as it applied in relation to a literary work, regardless of any other copyright protection which also subsisted. The 1985 Act did not attempt to define a computer program. The 1988 Act dealt with computer programs slightly differently, but to the same effect, by introducing a computer program as a specific type of literary work in the definition of literary work in s.3(1).

The need to harmonise the treatment of computer programs under the national laws of the Member States led to the adoption of the Directive on the legal protection of computer programs ("the Software Directive"),[249] which required Member States to protect computer programs as literary works within the meaning of the Berne Convention, and expressly provided that protection should extend to the expression in a form of program but not to "ideas and principles" which underlie any element of it (including its interfaces),[250] and that to be protected a program must be original in the sense that it was the author's own intellectual creation.[251] The Software Directive was implemented in the United Kingdom with effect from January 1, 1993 by the Copyright (Computer Programs) Regulations 1992.[252] Specific aspects of the implementation of the Directive in the United Kingdom are discussed elsewhere,[253] but it should be noted that although some provisions of the Directive were implemented more or less verbatim, other provisions of the

---

[242] *Navitaire Inc v easyJet Airline Co Ltd* [2004] EWHC 1725 (Ch); [2006] R.P.C. 3 at para.96. However, they were not protected because they were "ideas which underlie ... interfaces" in the sense used in art.1(2) of the Software Directive, providing the static framework for the display of the dynamic data which it was the task of the software to produce.

[243] Copyright (Computer Software) Amendment Act 1985 (c.41).

[244] WIPO Copyright Treaty, adopted December 1996.

[245] Cmnd.6732, Ch.9.

[246] 1977 Copyright Committee, para.520(i).

[247] Reported decisions in which the issue arose include *Gates v Swift* [1982] R.P.C. 339, *Sega Enterprises v Richards* [1983] F.S.R. 73 and *Thrustcode Ltd v W.W. Computing Ltd* [1983] F.S.R. 502.

[248] *Milltronics Ltd v Hycontrol Ltd* [1990] F.S.R. 273.

[249] Council Directive 91/250, adopted on May 14, 1991, [1991] OJ L122/42. For a discussion of the background to the Directive, see paras 24–47 et seq., below. The Directive has since been replaced by a consolidated version: Council Directive 2009/24/EC. There has been some re-ordering of the recitals and articles but for present purposes the substance remains the same: *SAS Institute Inc v World Programming Ltd* [2010] EWHC 1829 (Ch), para.155.

[250] art.1(2).

[251] art.1(3).

[252] SI 1992/333.

[253] See, as to originality and permitted acts, paras 3–132 and 9–149 et seq. respectively.

Directive were apparently considered not to differ from existing United Kingdom law, with the result that in these areas no change was made to the language of the Act.[254] Nevertheless, it is particularly important to refer to the Directive when applying the 1988 Act to computer programs, to ensure that the proposed application is consistent with the terms of the Directive, and in fact a court today will usually refer only to the Directive, on the basis that if the Act means what it should, the Directive has been properly implemented, and if not, the Directive has not been properly implemented.[255]

So far as concerns the wider international stage, with the adoption of the 1996 WIPO Copyright Treaty ("WCT") and the TRIPs Agreement, computer programs are to be protected as literary works within the meaning of art.2 of the Berne Convention. The protection applies to computer programs, whatever may be the mode or form of their expression (art.4 WCT). Although art.10 of TRIPs adopts a slightly different wording ("computer programs whether in source or object code"), according to two agreed statements attached to the Treaty the scope of protection for computer programs under art.4 of the Treaty "is consistent with Article 2 of the Berne Convention". Thus, it is to be understood that computer programs are to be treated as "works" within the meaning of literary and artistic works as defined in art.2 of the Berne Convention. Although art.1(2) of the Software Directive is differently worded from TRIPs and the WCT, and in particular refers to "ideas and principles" rather than "ideas, procedures, methods of operation and mathematical concepts", the distinction it draws is essentially the same. If and in so far as there is any difference, however, art.9(2) of TRIPs and art.2 of the WIPO Copyright Treaty make it clear that art.1(2) of the Software Directive must be broadly interpreted.[256]

Overall, not only should those parts of the 1988 Act relating to copyright in computer programs be interpreted in accordance with the Software Directive,[257] but United Kingdom courts are also obliged, both as a matter of domestic and as a matter of EU law, to interpret both European and domestic legislation in conformity with the wording and purposes of the relevant international agreements to which the European Union is a party, namely TRIPs and the WCT,[258] both of which are intended to be confirmatory of the position under art.2 of the Berne Convention.[259] As a result, UK courts must interpret the 1988 Act so as to protect "expressions" and not "ideas, procedures, methods of operation and mathematical concepts as such."[260] Although UK law has formally changed in this respect,[261] it is not considered that the substantive law has changed: this is how the courts had previously interpreted the 1988 Act and earlier copyright Acts.

What is a computer program? The 1988 Act does not attempt any definition of   **3–29**
a computer program.[262] The Directive provides only a partial definition, by includ-

---

[254] As to criticism of the way on which the Directive was implemented, see *Nova Productions Ltd v Mazooma Games Ltd* [2007] EWCA Civ 219; [2007] R.P.C. 25, at para.28.

[255] *Navitaire Inc v easyJet Airline Co Ltd* [2004] EWHC 1725 (Ch); [2005] E.C.D.R. 17, at para.88.

[256] *SAS Institute Inc v World Programming Ltd* [2010] EWHC 1829 (Ch), para.208.

[257] *Nova Productions Ltd v Mazooma Games Ltd* [2007] EWCA Civ 219, para.27.

[258] *Nova Productions Ltd v Mazooma Games Ltd* [2007] EWCA Civ 219, para.38; *SAS Institute Inc v World Programming Ltd* [2010] EWHC 1829 (Ch), paras 168, 200.

[259] *SAS Institute Inc v World Programming Ltd* [2010] EWHC 1829 (Ch), para.204.

[260] *SAS Institute Inc v World Programming Ltd* [2010] EWHC 1829 (Ch), para.205.

[261] *SAS Institute Inc v World Programming Ltd* [2010] EWHC 1829 (Ch), para.205.

[262] The position was the same under the Copyright (Computer Software) Amendment Act 1985, cf. the definition introduced into the Australian Copyright Act 1968 by amendment in 1984: a set of statements or instructions to be used directly or indirectly in a computer in order to bring about a certain result.

ing preparatory design material within the term.[263] However, the Directive does give some further guidance by providing that protection under the Directive shall apply to a computer program in any form,[264] and expressed in any form,[265] and it thus includes a version of a computer program in source code[266] as well as in other forms. In general terms, however, the protectable subject matter of a computer program is the language or code written by programmer and the design and the structure of the program.[267] The Directive provides that protection does not extend to ideas and principles which underlie any element of a computer program, including those which underlie its interfaces.[268] The background to this exclusion of ideas and principles is elaborated in the recitals to the Directive. Recital 10 outlines the desirability of standardisation and interoperability; recital 11 confirms that only the expression of a computer program is protected and that ideas and principles which underlie any element of a program, including those which underlie its interfaces, are not protected by copyright. Thus to the extent that logic, algorithms and programming languages comprise ideas and principles, those ideas and principles are not protected. In accordance with the legislation and case-law of the Member States and the international copyright conventions, the expression of those ideas and principles is to be protected by copyright.

3–30   **Nature of protected subject matter.** The question of what is the subject matter of copyright in a computer program usually arises in relation to what is the scope of protection of a computer program, and thus what amounts to an infringement, rather than whether the program itself is a protected work, a question which in isolation does not often give rise to difficulties.[269] Nevertheless because the question is complex, and the discussion often runs the questions of protected subject matter, originality and infringement together, it may be helpful to say something about it here. In simple cases, where for example some or all of the source code can be seen to have been literally copied, the nature of the protected subject matter is not in doubt. Problems which have arisen are mainly concerned with allegations of non-literal copying, and whether the subject matter of a copyright in such works extends to (i) programming languages, (ii) interfaces or (iii) the functionality of a computer program.

> (1) The "well-known" dichotomy between an idea and its individual expression is intended to apply and does to copyright in computer software just as with other literary works,[270] so that there is no protection for ideas which are not the result of the skill and labour of the programmer and which do not find expression in the program.[271]
>
> This applies not just to the ideas which underlie a particular element, or

---

[263] 2009/24/EC art.1(1); and see para.3–31, below.

[264] Recital 7, including a program which is incorporated into hardware.

[265] art.1(2).

[266] *Ibcos Computers Ltd v Barclays Mercantile Highland Finance Ltd* [1994] F.S.R. 275 at 296, disapproving the statement in *Total Information Processing Systems Ltd v Daman Ltd* [1992] F.S.R. 171 at 181 to the contrary. In *Saphena Computing Ltd v Allied Collection Agencies* [1995] F.S.R. 616, it was assumed that separate copyrights attach to the source code and object code of a computer program. Whether this is so will depend on whether each is original.

[267] *Cyprotex Discovery Ltd v The University of Sheffield* [2003] EWHC 760 (TCC); [2004] R.P.C. 4, para.78 (upheld on appeal, although this point was not in issue: [2004] EWCA Civ 380; [2004] R.P.C. 43).

[268] 2009/24/EC art.1(2).

[269] So, in none of the cases cited later in the text was there any apparent difficulty in identifying the computer program relied on, invariably taking the form of the source code and/or preparatory design material.

[270] *Nova Productions Limited v Mazooma Games Limited* [2007] EWCA Civ 219; [2007] R.P.C. 25, para.31; *SAS Institute Inc v World Programming Ltd* [2010] EWHC 1829 (Ch), para.210.

[271] *Nova Productions Ltd v Mazooma Games Ltd* [2007] EWCA Civ 219, para.44, approving the

building block, of a program,[272] since where an "idea" is sufficiently general then, even if an original work embodies it, the mere taking of that idea will not infringe. But if the "idea" is detailed, then there may be infringement. It is a question of degree.[273]

(2) It is necessary to distinguish between "expressions" on the one hand and "ideas, procedures, methods of operation and mathematical concepts as such" on the other. What is protected by copyright in a computer program is the form of expression of the program itself. Other things which are conveyed by or described in the program, of which "ideas, procedures, methods of operation and mathematical concepts" is a non-exhaustive list, are not protected.[274] The distinction is one between different kinds of skill, judgement and labour. Skill, judgement and labour in devising ideas, procedures, methods of operation and mathematical concepts is not protected by the copyright in a computer program. What is protected by copyright in a computer program is with the skill, judgement and labour in devising the form of expression of the program as a literary work.[275]

(3) *Programming languages.* As the law stands, while the expression of a program in a particular language is entitled to copyright, computer languages themselves are not included in protection afforded to computer programs, and this principle extends to ad hoc languages such as defined user command interfaces.[276] For this purpose it is irrelevant how the language of the interface is defined, whether this done formally or only by the code that recognises it.[277] The intention of the Directive is to keep the language free for use, but not the particular ideas expressed in it in any particular case.[278] The statement in recital 11 "*to the extent* that ... programming languages comprise ideas and principles, those ideas and principles are not protected under this Directive" should not be construed as if it were an operative provision in an English statute. It is there to guide courts as to the purpose of art.1(2). When read in its proper context in recital 11, the words "to the extent that" are to be understood as meaning "in as much as".[279]

(4) *Functionality.* Whether the scope of the copyright in a computer program includes its functionality, so that copyright in source code is infringed by another program whose source code is completely different but which reproduces the former's functionality, clearly comes under the heading of infringement.[280] The argument sometimes put is that the manner in which a machine behaves under the control of a program represents part of the skill and labour that went into the program. To copy an operating machine in this manner avoids the need to conduct any systems analysis or the pro-

---

statement of Kitchin J., at first instance: *Nova Productions Limited v Mazooma Games Limited* [2006] EWHC 24 (Ch), para.24

[272] *Nova Productions Limited v Mazooma Games Limited* [2007] EWCA Civ 219, per Jacob L.J. at paras 32.

[273] *Nova Productions Limited v Mazooma Games Limited* [2007] EWCA Civ 219, per Jacob L.J. at para.33, citing his own judgment in *Ibcos Computers v Barclays Mercantile* [1994] F.S.R. 275 at p.291.

[274] *SAS Institute Inc v World Programming Ltd* [2010] EWHC 1829 (Ch), para.206, observing that thereby a line is drawn between copyright protection and the public domain, citing Reinbothe and von Lewinski, The WIPO Treaties 1996: Commentary and Legal Analysis (London: Butterworths, 2002), pp.46–47.

[275] *SAS Institute Inc v World Programming Ltd* [2010] EWHC 1829 (Ch), para.207.

[276] *Navitaire Inc v easyJet Airline Co Ltd* [2004] EWHC 1725 (Ch) at para.88.

[277] *Navitaire Inc v easyJet Airline Co Ltd* [2004] EWHC 1725 (Ch), at para.88.

[278] *Navitaire Inc v easyJet Airline Co Ltd* [2004] EWHC 1725 (Ch), at para.88.

[279] *SAS Institute Inc v World Programming Ltd* [2010] EWHC 1829 (Ch), para.217.

[280] See para.7–57.

duction of functional specifications. Although the copyist has not avoided the need to write software to achieve the desired result, he has avoided the need to identify the result by any of the normal methods of analysis that either precede or accompany the writing of a substantial piece of business software.[281] However, as the law at present stands, although copyright protection is not limited to the text of the source code of the program, but also extends to protecting the design of the program, that is, its "structure, sequence and organisation",[282] there is a distinction between protecting the design of the program and protecting its functionality: it is perfectly possible to create a computer program which replicates the functionality of an existing program, yet whose design is quite different.[283] It is not, without more, an infringement of the copyright in a computer program to create another computer program which has the same functionality.[284] The key issue is "the nature of the skill and labour"[285]; copyright in a computer program (including any preparatory design material) protects the skill, judgement and labour in devising the form of expression of the program (including any preparatory design material), that is to say, its design and source code. The skill, judgement and labour that goes into understanding and elucidating a computer program in order to write another program with same functionality is the wrong kind of skill, judgement and labour to be protected by copyright in the resulting computer program (including any preparatory design material).[286] The functions of a computer program cannot in this respect be compared to the plot of a novel or play. A plot is protected because it is part of the work's expression and the correct analogy with a computer program is with the program's design. The functions of a computer program have no counterpart in the case of a novel or play because such works have no function in this sense.[287] The fact that copyright may in some cases protect works which are wholly utilitarian is irrelevant: what is protected in such works is the skill and labour in devising the form of expression of the work.[288] In this respect the courts should be astute not to extend the protection of the Directive into a region where only the functional effects of a program are in issue, and a line should be

---

[281] As argued in *Navitaire Inc v easyJet Airline Co Ltd* [2004] EWHC 1725 (Ch). See paras 114, 115.

[282] *SAS Institute Inc v World Programming Ltd* [2010] EWHC 1829 (Ch), para.232, noting that if there were any doubt about this, then the conferring of protection on "preparatory design material" confirms it.

[283] *SAS Institute Inc v World Programming Ltd* [2010] EWHC 1829 (Ch), para.232.

[284] *Nova Productions Limited v Mazooma Games Limited* [2006] EWCA Civ 1044; *SAS Institute Inc v World Programming Ltd* [2010] EWHC 1829 (Ch), para.232; *Navitaire Inc v easyJet Airline Co Ltd* [2004] EWHC 1725 (Ch), at para.86; *Ibcos Computers Ltd v Barclays Mercantile Highland Finance Ltd* [1994] F.S.R. 275.

[285] *Navitaire Inc v easyJet Airline* [2004] EWHC 1725 (Ch) at para.129; *SAS Institute Inc v World Programming Ltd* [2010] EWHC 1829 (Ch), para.233. Earlier discussion, to the effect that where the expression of an idea is inseparable from its function, it forms part of the idea and is not entitled to copyright protection, must now be considered as wrong. The concept, which had a brief flowering in *Total Information Processing Systems Ltd v Daman Ltd* [1992] F.S.R. 171 at 181, was disapproved by Jacob J. in *Ibcos Computers Ltd v Barclays Mercantile Highland Finance Ltd* [1994] F.S.R. 275 at 290–292, and was derived from a line of United States authorities such as *Lotus Development Corp v Paperback Software International* (1990) 740 F. Supp. 37 (Massachusetts Dist Ct); (1990) 18 I.P.R. 1 at 25 and *Computer Associates International Inc v Altai Inc* (1992) 23 I.P.R. 385 (US CA) (and see also *Autodesk Inc v Dyason* [1992] R.P.C. 575 at 583 (High Ct of Aus)).

[286] *SAS Institute Inc v World Programming Ltd* [2010] EWHC 1829 (Ch), para.233.

[287] *SAS Institute Inc v World Programming Ltd* [2010] EWHC 1829 (Ch), para.234, following *Navitaire Inc v easyJet Airline Co Ltd* [2004] EWHC 1725 (Ch).

[288] *SAS Institute Inc v World Programming Ltd* [2010] EWHC 1829 (Ch), para.235, discussing the example of *Anderson v Lieber Code Co* [1917] 2 KB 469 (copyright in a telegraphic code of invented five letter words).

drawn between the embodiment of a function as expressed in the actual software and the "superset" of that software, i.e., its functionality,[289] and thus between the concepts of idea v expression.[290]

(5) *Interfaces*. The Directive is concerned only with the protection of computer programs as literary works, and therefore has no impact on literary, artistic or other works that may associated with them.[291] Thus for example, depending on the underlying technology, screen displays may properly be characterised as tables or as artistic works.[292] Beyond this, however, the copyright in a computer program does not protect "interfaces", which are described in the Software Directive as the parts of the program which provide for the "logical and, where appropriate, physical interconnection and interaction ... required to permit all elements of software and hardware to work with other software and hardware and with users in all the ways they are intended to function."[293] Not only is this supported by the legislative history of the Directive,[294] but also art.6, which provides for a limited right to obtain information about interfaces by the process of "decompilation",[295] proceeds on the basis that users are free to copy interfaces.[296] On the basis that it is the policy of the Software Directive to exclude both computer languages and the underlying ideas of the interfaces from protection, then it should not be possible to circumvent these exclusions by seeking to identify some overall function or functions that it is the sole purpose of the interface to invoke, and relying on those instead.[297] As a matter of policy also, to permit the "business logic" of a program to attract protection through the literary copyright afforded to the program itself would be an unjustifiable extension of copyright protection into a field where it is probably not appropriate.[298]

(6) Because, however, none of the points relating to language, functionality or interfaces is considered to be *acte clair*, they have been referred to European Court of Justice (Case C–406/10).[299]

The copyright in a computer program should be clearly distinguished from the copyright in any separate subject matter which may be stored in memory or streamed and which is enabled to be displayed, printed, heard or seen in some

---

[289] *Navitaire Inc v easyJet Airline Co Ltd* [2004] EWHC 1725 (Ch), at para.94.

[290] *Navitaire Inc v easyJet Airline Co Ltd* [2004] EWHC 1725 (Ch), at para.94, acknowledging that some might think this was to draw the line too far on the side of expression, such hesitancy, however, being described in *SAS Institute Inc v World Programming Ltd* [2010] EWHC 1829 (Ch), para.218 as being "perfectly consistent with the distinction between expressions and ideas, procedures, methods of operation and mathematical formulae."

[291] *Navitaire Inc v easyJet Airline Co Ltd* [2004] EWHC 1725 (Ch), 3 at paras 93, 94. The potential for tension between protection of programs and closely associated data and data structures is acknowledged in the Database Directive, which specifically provides that copyright protection should not apply to computer programs used in the making or operation of databases accessible by electronic means: art.1(3).

[292] *Navitaire Inc v easyJet Airline Co Ltd* [2004] EWHC 1725 (Ch), at para.96 (where text-based screen displays were held to be tables and graphic-based displays artistic works).

[293] Recital 10.

[294] As to which, see *SAS Institute Inc v World Programming Ltd* [2010] EWHC 1829 (Ch).

[295] art.6, implemented by CDPA 1988 s.50B, entitles third parties to obtain information about interfaces by decompiling the object code of a program where the necessary information is not available from either (i) published sources such as manuals, (ii) common standards or (iii) observation, study or testing of the program. See para.9–151.

[296] *SAS Institute Inc v World Programming Ltd* [2010] EWHC 1829 (Ch), para.226.

[297] *Navitaire Inc v easyJet Airline Co Ltd* [2004] EWHC 1725 (Ch), at para.130.

[298] *Navitaire Inc v easyJet Airline Co Ltd* [2004] EWHC 1725 (Ch), at para.130.

[299] *SAS Institute Inc v World Programming Ltd* [2010] EWHC 1829 (Ch), para.238, taking the view that the Court of Appeal in *Nova Productions Ltd v Mazooma Games Ltd* [2006] EWCA Civ 1044 did not decide that the question was *acte clair* either. For this and other pending references, see paras 24–55 et seq.

form by means of the running of the program. Whether any infringement takes place in this event will depend on a detailed analysis in each case of what is stored in memory and what is produced by the running of the program.[300]

3–31   **Preparatory design material for a computer program.** The Software Directive specifically provides that the term computer program should include preparatory design material for computer programs.[301] This is slightly amplified in the recitals to the Directive, which explain that preparatory design work is included provided that the nature of the preparatory work is such that a computer program can result from it at a later stage.[302] This requirement was implemented in the United Kingdom by the addition of a new category of literary work, referred to as preparatory design material for a computer program.[303] It is questionable whether the Software Directive has been correctly implemented in this respect, since it appears to contemplate a single copyright in a computer program, not two, one in the preparatory work and the other in the program itself.[304]

At a practical level, given the relatively low originality threshold applied in UK copyright law, it is does not seem that any additional protection is given by the express inclusion of preparatory design materials as a separate category of protectable literary works. Written notations produced in preparation for writing a computer program would have been entitled to protection in any event as a literary work. More important, perhaps, is the fact that the protection of preparatory design material for a computer program does not mean that ideas by way of preparatory design work are protected: what is protected under this heading is such a work as a literary work, namely the expression of the designs which are to go into the ultimate programme, not the ideas themselves.[305] There are no transitional provisions in relation to preparatory design materials, giving rise to the question of what protection is available for such materials produced before 1993 and not otherwise entitled to protection.[306]

C. DRAMATIC WORKS

(i) History of protection

3–32   **History of protection.** In order to understand the nature of the protection currently given to dramatic works, it is particularly important to understand the his-

---

[300] Modern examples of such an analysis can be found in such cases as *Navitaire Inc v easyJet Airline Co Ltd* [2004] EWHC 1725 (Ch); *Nova Productions Ltd v Mazooma Games Limited* [2006] EWHC 24 (Ch); on appeal [2006] EWCA Civ 1044; *SAS Institute Inc v World Programming Ltd* [2010] EWHC 1829 (Ch).

[301] Directive 2009/24/EC art.1(1).

[302] Recital 7.

[303] CDPA 1988 s.3(1)(c).

[304] *Nova Productions Ltd v Mazooma Games Ltd* [2007] EWCA Civ 219; [2007] R.P.C. 25 at para.28, per Jacob L.J. observing that there may be cases where it would make a difference, for example where there are different authors for the program and its preparatory design material, thus making it unclear when "the copyright" expires, or where there are different dealings in the 'two' copyrights. However, it is suggested that this is to construe the Directive too strictly, given that separate copyrights may subsist in successive versions of the computer program itself (i.e. considered as something separate from the preparatory design material), there seems no objection in classifying preparatory design material separately. Note, however, the definition of adaptation, which applies to a computer program, but makes no reference to preparatory materials for a computer program: s.21(3)(ab).

[305] *Nova Productions Limited v Mazooma Games Limited* [2007] EWCA Civ 219, para.50, making the point that the Software Directive needed to make such a provision because not all member states protected such works (para.51).

[306] The Computer Programs Directive expressly provides that its provisions shall apply to programs (which term in the Directive includes preparatory design material) created before January 1, 1993: art.9(1).

tory of their protection. Dramatic works were protected under the early copyright statutes as literary works, but the performing right in such works was not given statutory protection until the Dramatic Copyright Act 1833.[307] The protection was extended to musical works by the Literary Copyright Act 1842.[308] To constitute a dramatic work, it had to be more than just "dramatic", in particular it had to be a work of action. A work which was intended to be sung by a singer in character costume but without action could not therefore be a dramatic work.[309] Under these Acts, a dramatic work also had to be capable of being printed and published to obtain copyright protection,[310] so that no dramatic copyright subsisted in scenic effects, the make-up of the actors or any unscripted "stage-business"[311] or other unscripted pantomime or dumb show[312] or dance.[313] As will be seen, the need for the existence of some work capable of being printed and published disappeared under the 1911 Act, and therefore such old cases are of limited help in establishing what constitutes a dramatic work under the modern law.

The 1911 Act. By the time of the 1911 Act, protection under the Berne Convention extended to dramatic and dramatico-musical works, choreographic works and entertainments in dumb show, the acting form (or "*mise en scène*") of which was fixed in writing or otherwise.[314] These terms were reflected in the definition of a dramatic work in the 1911 Act, which was defined to include any piece for recitation, choreographic work or entertainment in dumb show, the scenic arrangement or acting form of which was fixed in writing or otherwise.[315] The definition was clearly not exclusive, since it did not refer to the most common type of dramatic work, namely a play consisting of words and action intended to be performed in front of an audience. The Act clearly now for the first time extended protected to works without words, such as works of dance and mime; it is unclear to what extent scenic arrangements or effects were protected.[316]   **3–33**

Films as dramatic works. A further change under the 1911 Act was that a dramatic work was also defined to include any cinematograph production where the arrangement or acting form or the combination of incidents represented gave   **3–34**

---

[307] 3 & 4 Will. 4, c.15, under which the performing right was given to authors of any tragedy, comedy, play, opera, farce or other dramatic piece of entertainment.

[308] 5 & 6 Vict., c.45, which also now defined the protected subject matter, namely "dramatic piece", to mean and include every tragedy, comedy, play, opera, farce or other scenic, musical, or dramatic entertainment (s.2).

[309] *Fuller v Blackpool Winter Gardens* [1895] 2 Q.B. 429 (CA); *Tate v Fullbrook* [1908] 1 K.B. 821 at 832, per Farwell L.J. The work would be a literary work, as to any words, and a musical work as to the music.

[310] *Tate v Fullbrook* [1908] 1 K.B. 821;

[311] *Tate v Fullbrook* [1908] 1 K.B. 821, although contrary to the dictum of Brett J. in *Chatterton v Cave* (1876) as reported in 33 L.T. 255: situations and scenic effects "are more peculiarly the subject of copyright than words themselves."

[312] *Karno v Pathé Frères Ltd* (1908) 99 L.T. 114, applying *Tate v Fullbrook* [1908] 1 K.B. 821. An appeal was dismissed on other grounds: (1909) 100 L.T. 260. In *Lee v Simpson* (1847) 3 C.B. 871, the written introduction to an otherwise unscripted pantomime was protected, but it is not clear that the protection extended to the pantomime itself.

[313] *Bishop v Viviana & Co* [1905–1910] Mac. C.C. 211, again applying *Tate v Fullbrook* [1908] 1 K.B. 821.

[314] Berne Convention art.2.

[315] Copyright Act 1911, s.35(1).

[316] In *Tate v Thomas* [1921] 1 Ch. 503, it seems to have been held that no copyright could subsist in mere scenic effects since they could not be printed or published, relying on *Tate v Fullbrook* [1908] 1 K.B. 821. But this represented the pre-1911 position, which did not apply under the wording of the 1911 Act. It may be that the real ground of the decision in *Tate v Thomas* was that the relevant elements in the drama were not sufficiently certain or fixed. See the judgment at 511. The *mise en scène* was held to be the subject of copyright in *Perkin v Ray* [1911–16] Mac.C.C. 288, where there was clearly a reasonably well-defined script, consisting of a number of sketches loosely hung together, with scripted jokes.

the work an original character.[317] While the individual frames of a film could therefore be protected as photographs,[318] a film which satisfied these additional requirements of originality could therefore also be protected as a dramatic work[319] and be "performed" by being shown to an audience.[320] A film of a sporting event was held not to be a dramatic work because it did not involve any acting form or arrangement, and was therefore not a "cinematograph *production*", and even if it was a "production" it had no original character.[321] Even an edited film of a sporting event was held not to be a dramatic work, since the editing did not give rise to the drama, which was inherent in the event itself,[322] although a suitably edited version of a naturally occurring event might be.[323]

3–35   **The 1956 Act.** To an extent, the 1956 Act maintained this approach, defining dramatic work as including a choreographic work or entertainment in dumb show if reduced to writing in the form in which the work or entertainment was to be presented.[324] The Act no longer contained any reference to scenic arrangements and was assumed to have limited the scope of the definition and to confine protection to something which had dramatic action without regard to any elements of background or production.[325] In addition, a dramatic work was now expressly defined to exclude a cinematograph film (as distinct from a scenario or script for a cinematograph film),[326] and a new form of copyright protection was conferred on cinematograph films of all kinds, whether having a degree of original character or not.[327] A film could not therefore also be a dramatic work.

3–36   **The Berne Convention.** Dramatic and dramatic-musical works, and choreographic works and entertainments in dumb show are all protectable under the general rubric of "literary and artistic works", as are cinematograph works and works expressed by an analogous process.[328] Article 14bis of the Convention also provides that cinematograph works are to be protected as original works, and that the owner of the copyright in them is to enjoy the same rights as the owners of other original works.

---

[317] Copyright Act 1911 s.35(1). This "new" category of dramatic work and the wording followed from the 1908 Berlin Revision to the Berne Convention, by which it was provided that cinematograph productions should be protected as literary or artistic works, if, by the arrangement of the acting form or the combination of the incidents represented, the author had given the work a personal and original character (art.14(2)). As has been pointed out (S. Ricketson and J.C. Ginsburg, *International Copyright and Neighbouring Rights, The Berne Convention and Beyond* 2nd edn (Oxford: Oxford University Press, 2006), para.8–32), the necessity for such a provision was questionable since such works should already have been protected as dramatic or dramatico-musical works, albeit expressed in what was then a novel form, and the requirement of personal and original character was implicit for such works.

[318] As an artistic work: Copyright Act 1911 s.35(1). See *Pathé Frères v Bancroft* [1928–35] Mac.C.C. 403.

[319] *Nordisk Films Co Ltd v Onda* [1917–1923] Mac.C.C. 337.

[320] *Copinger* 5th edn, p.80.

[321] *Canadian Admiral Corp Ltd v Rediffusion Inc* (1954) 20 C.P.R. 75 (Excheq Ct of Can), citing *Copinger* 8th edn, p.221.

[322] *Australian Olympic Committee v Big Fights Inc* (1999) 46 I.P.R. 53 (Fed Ct of Aus).

[323] *Australian Olympic Committee v Big Fights Inc* (1999) 46 I.P.R. 53 (Fed Ct of Aus).

[324] Copyright Act 1956, s.48(1).

[325] *Copinger* 9th edn, p.61.

[326] *Copinger* 9th edn, p.61.

[327] Copyright Act 1956 s.13. The 1952 Gregory Committee Report (Cmnd.8662) had noted that the requirement of original character in s.35(1) of the 1911 Act was probably to deprive films such as newsreels of any protection, and took the view that the Berne Convention did not require that films should have an original character. See para.100. Pre-1956 Act films which had qualified under the 1911 Act as dramatic works continued to be treated as dramatic works under the 1956 Act (1956 Act Sch.7 para.15) and did not qualify as cinematograph films (ibid. Sch.7 para.14).

[328] Berne Convention art.2(1).

(ii) Under the 1988 Act

Meaning of "dramatic work". The 1988 Act continues the general approach of **3–37** the earlier Acts in that, unlike the cases of literary and musical works, it does not attempt a comprehensive definition of a dramatic work, merely stating that it includes a work of dance or mime.[329] Although it is expressly provided that a literary work cannot be a dramatic work,[330] there is no express exclusion, unlike in the case of the 1956 Act, of the possibility of a film being a dramatic work. Whether or not this was deliberate,[331] the effect has been to reintroduce the possibility of a film being a dramatic work.[332] As to what comes within the general description of "dramatic work", the expression is at large and should therefore be given its natural and ordinary meaning, which is that it is a work of action, with or without words or music, which is capable of being performed before an audience.[333] This definition brings out the point that a distinguishing characteristic of a dramatic work is that it must be capable of being performed, but also that not all works which are capable of being performed are dramatic works. It is possible, in one sense, to perform a literary work (for example, by reciting a poem), or a musical work (for example, by singing a song), or even an artistic work (for example, by the once popular entertainment of recreating well-known paintings or statues by *tableaux vivants*, using actors, in suitable attitudes but silent and motionless), but these possibilities do not make such works dramatic works: they are not works of action. A work consisting of words intended to be spoken or sung, whether in costume or not, would not therefore be a dramatic work unless the performance of the words is to be accompanied by action.[334] Similarly, the assembly of a scene to be viewed or to be the subject of a photograph, even if incorporating human actors, does not constitute a dramatic work, as it lacks the necessary element of action.[335] For the same reason, backdrops and scenic arrangements produced as the setting in which a play is to be performed do not themselves constitute, nor are part of, a dramatic work.[336] No matter how "dramatic" the work, however, it must be one which is capable of performance if it is to be protected as a dramatic work. So where a film had been made of a man dancing but had then been edited (or "jump-cut") in such a way that the dancer's movements as portrayed in the film could not have been performed by a human actor, the actions which had been recorded in the edited film were not themselves a dramatic work because they were not capable of performance.[337] Similarly, the "visual experience generated by" coin-operated computer games based on the theme of pool was not capable of amounting to a dramatic work. The game was

---

[329] CDPA 1988 s.3(1).

[330] s.3(1). See *Nova Productions Limited v Mazooma Games Limited* [2006] EWHC 24 (Ch); [2006] R.P.C. 14, para.118.

[331] There was no recommendation in the 1977 Whitford Committee Report (Cmnd.6732) that this be done, and no reference to the point in the subsequent White Paper or Parliamentary debates.

[332] See para.3–39, below.

[333] *Norowzian v Arks Ltd (No.2)* [2000] F.S.R. 363, CA per Nourse L.J., said by him to be substantially a distillation of existing dictionary and textbook definitions; *Nova Productions Limited v Mazooma Games Limited* [2006] EWHC 24 (Ch); [2006] R.P.C. 14, para.115. See also the cases decided under the earlier Acts, referred to above.

[334] Contrast works of dance and mime, which clearly predicate action in their performance.

[335] *Creation Records v News Group Newspapers* [1997] E.M.L.R. 444 (the arrangement of a scene including members of a group and other props to be photographed for the cover of their album). The same applies to *tableaux vivants*.

[336] Although they may, of course, be protected as artistic works, either in themselves (e.g. the painted backdrop) or as based on prior drawings (e.g. the stage layout). As noted above, the position has altered with successive Copyright Acts.

[337] *Norowzian v Arks Ltd (No.2)* [2000] F.S.R. 363 at 367. Although the Court of Appeal held that the film was not a recording of a dramatic work, it ruled that the film itself was a dramatic work. See para.3–39, below. The observation in *Aristocrat Leisure Industries Pty Ltd v Pacific Gaming Pty Ltd* 50 I.P.R. (2001) 29 (Fed Ct of Aus), that a *script* for an animated cartoon could be a

not intended to be or capable of being performed in front of an audience. Although the game had a set of rules, the sequence of images presented on screen depended very much on the way the game was played. Thus, there was insufficient unity in the game for it to be capable of performance.[338]

3-38   **Dramatic v musical works.** Whilst a dramatic work cannot, by definition,[339] also be a literary work, the same is not the case as between a dramatic and a musical work. If a dramatic work includes music, the musical elements are capable of copyright protection as a musical work,[340] but it would seem that the work as a whole is still capable of protection as a dramatic work.[341] The importance of the distinction between a dramatic work or musical work, and a literary work, already much less important under the 1956 Act than it had been under the law prior to 1911, ceases to be of any importance under the 1988 Act.

3-39   **A film as a dramatic work.** As has been seen, the status of a film as a possible dramatic work has altered with successive Copyright Acts. The removal of the exclusion which existed under the 1956 Act which prevented a dramatic work also being a film[342] means that a film can once more be a dramatic work, provided that it is a work of action.[343] The requirement that a dramatic work be capable of performance can be satisfied in the case of a film, since its visual and acoustic presentation to an audience will amount to performance.[344] As to what distinguishes films which are works of action from other films, it does not seem that there is any requirement that in order to be a dramatic work the film should record the actions of a human being.[345] If this is right, films in which the action is portrayed by animals or by cartoon characters may therefore be dramatic works, provided there is action, as also, it would seem, may a film which consists entirely of a record of naturally occurring events, such as a volcano erupting, particularly where the film has been edited to increase the dramatic impact.[346] Again, there seems no reason why a film of a sporting event should not be a dramatic work, particularly where it has been edited to increase its impact. In contrast, a documentary film or a filmed interview will generally not be a work of action. If the film records action which is taking place in front of the lens, it will be a

---

dramatic work does not generally represent the position under UK law since, usually, the action cannot be performed by a human actor. See the main text, below.

[338] *Nova Productions Limited v Mazooma Games Limited* [2006] EWHC 24 (Ch), para.116. In any event, the particulars of similarity relied on in support of the claim for infringement were analogous to those relied on in the *Green v Broadcasting Corp of New Zealand* [1989] R.P.C. 700 (see para.3–43): they were not capable of performance; they did not have sufficient certainty, being drawn at a very high level of generality; they were simply aspects of the game (para.117).The conclusion that the games were not protected as dramatic works was not challenged on appeal: [2007] EWCA Civ 219; [2007] R.P.C. 25 at para.3.

[339] CDPA 1988 s.3(1); see paras 3–04 and 3–12, above.

[340] Which will exclude any words or action intended to be sung, spoken or performed with it: s.3(2).

[341] In the terminology of the Berne Convention, the work is a dramatico-musical work (art.2(1)).

[342] CDPA 1988 s.48(1); see above.

[343] *Norowzian v Arks Ltd (No.2)* [2000] F.S.R. 363. Buxton L.J. also considered that the United Kingdom's obligations under the Berne Convention required that any work of cinematography within the meaning of the Berne Convention was included within a "dramatic work", as that expression was to be understood in the 1988 Act. As noted elsewhere (para.3–04), the Court of Appeal held that there was no objection to a film being protected both as a film under CDPA 1988 s.5B and as dramatic work under s.3. To be protected as a dramatic work, it must of course be an *original* dramatic work. Further, per Buxton L.J., the United Kingdom's obligations under the Berne Convention required that any work of cinematography within the meaning of the Berne Convention was included within a "dramatic work", as that expression was to be understood in the 1988 Act.

[344] *Norowzian v Arks Ltd (No.2)* [2000] F.S.R. 363 This was also the position under the 1911 Act: see above.

[345] In *Norowzian v Arks Ltd (No.2)* [2000] F.S.R. 363, the sequence of actions recorded on the edited film could not have been performed in the same way by a human being.

[346] See, further, para.3–34, above.

dramatic work; whether or not it will be an *original* dramatic work will depend, it seems, on whether the filmmaker adds anything of dramatic significance to the action which is taking place, for example, by choice of camera angle, lighting or editing.[347] The possibility of a film being a dramatic work is of general significance because the film copyright will only be infringed by the copying of the actual record of sounds and visual images, that is, tape-to-tape copying and the like.[348] If copyright also subsists in the film as a dramatic work, this copyright may be infringed by the re-creation of a substantial part of the dramatic work without any copying of the actual record of the images and sounds.

Many films of action are also recordings of a dramatic work. This dramatic work may already have been recorded, for example in a screenplay, or may have been recorded for the first time when the film was shot. Nevertheless, the fact that almost all films in their final version are the product of editing means that the film itself will often be a dramatic work distinct from the earlier or underlying dramatic works. This will be so particularly in the case of films containing sequences made using special effects or editing which could not be performed by live actors.[349]

Pre-1988 Act films as dramatic works. The protection which previously existed for films which had qualified as dramatic works under the 1911 Act[350] continues: they are still protected as dramatic works under the 1988 Act.[351] This is clearly significant for the protection of old (pre-1956 Act) films. The position of films made under the 1956 Act, i.e. between June 1, 1957 and August 1, 1989, is more difficult. Even though a film made in this period could not have enjoyed any protection as a dramatic work, is the effect of the 1988 Act to confer copyright for the first time on such films if they qualify as dramatic works? The Act contains no transitional provisions which expressly deal with the point, only the general provision that copyright does not subsist in a work which was made before August 1, 1989 unless copyright subsisted in it immediately before that date.[352] In one sense, copyright may have subsisted in such a film before commencement *qua* cinematograph film under s.13 of the 1956 Act, even if not as a dramatic work under s.2. It is suggested, however, that the transitional provision should be read as meaning that copyright does not subsist in a dramatic work which was made before August 1, 1989 unless copyright subsisted in it as a dramatic work immediately before that date, so that films made in this period cannot also be dramatic works. Otherwise, the effect of the Act, apparently unintended, will have been to create a whole new raft of copyright works when arrangements and agreements may have been entered into on the basis that no such copyright existed.

3–40

A broadcast as a dramatic work. On the same basis that a film can be a dramatic work, a broadcast which is a work of action can also, it seems, be a dramatic work.[353]

3–41

No requirement as to form. There is no particular requirement as to the form

3–42

---

[347] As to originality in dramatic works, see paras 3–125 et seq., below.

[348] *Norowzian v Arks Ltd (No.1)* [1998] F.S.R. 394.

[349] For further discussion on the issues raised, see Stamatoudi, "'Joy'; for the Claimant: Can a film be protected as a dramatic work?" [2000] I.P.Q. 117; Arnold, "Joy: A Reply" [2001] I.P.Q. 10.

[350] See para.3–33, above. After repeal of the 1911 Act, protection for such films continued under the 1956 Act: Sch.7 para.15.

[351] Sch.1, para.7(2). The protection extends to films made before June 1, 1957: ibid.

[352] Sch.1, para.5(1).

[353] See the observation of Somers J. in *Green v Broadcasting Corp of New Zealand* [1989] R.P.C. 469 (High Ct of NZ), at 477, that the actual broadcast programme of each game show might have been a dramatic work, even though the court held that there was no dramatic copyright in any scripts.

which a work has to take in order to be a dramatic work. In many cases it is obvious whether a work is a dramatic work, in the sense discussed above. A play is a prime example of a dramatic work and a screenplay is another.[354] Further, as with a literary work, what has to be considered for present purposes is the message, not the medium. Leaving aside the separate requirement of fixation of the work before copyright can subsist in it,[355] there is nothing in the modern law which requires a play to be written down before it can constitute a dramatic work. An author may, therefore, conceive the entirety of a play in his head, and get the actors to perform it by oral instruction and direction. Such a work is nonetheless a dramatic work for the purposes of the 1988 Act. Similarly, a piece of mime which the originator has developed in his mind and perfected by practice is a dramatic work, notwithstanding that he has never written down any part of it.

3–43   **Elements or features of a dramatic work.** The elements or features which make a work a dramatic work are many and varied, and in the case of an obvious example of a dramatic work, such as a play or a screenplay, will be readily identifiable as the dialogue and the acting directions, usually found in the stage directions. However, in order for a work to constitute a dramatic work there must be sufficient certainty of its subject matter.[356] In the case of a play or a screenplay, this presents little problem, since what knits the separate incidents together so that they can be performed as an entity is the structure of the work, or the plot, which comprises the setting, the characters, and their inter-relationship and development. In the case of subject matter which does not fall into any of the obvious types of dramatic work, however, this requires not only that there should be identifiable with sufficient certainty elements or features in such subject matter which are of a dramatic nature in the sense discussed above, but also that those features or elements should be sufficiently linked or connected so as to be capable of performance.[357] This ultimately turns on the facts of the particular case, but in applying this test it has been held that a computer game was not a dramatic work[358] and that a sports game did not constitute a choreographic work (and therefore was not a dramatic work), even though parts of the game were intended to follow a pre-determined plan.[359] There seems no reason in principle, however, why other features commonly found in dramatic presentations, such as sound and light effects, should not be capable of being part of a dramatic work, provided they are sufficiently certain and capable of being linked together with other elements of the action.

---

[354] See the discussion in *Hansard*, HL Vol.490, col.830.

[355] See further paras 3–117 et seq., below.

[356] *Green v Broadcasting Corporation of New Zealand* [1989] R.P.C. 700 (where this was a further reason why the format in that case failed to qualify as a dramatic work); *Nova Productions Limited v Mazooma Games Limited* [2006] EWHC 24 (Ch); [2006] R.P.C. 14, para.113; *Tate v Thomas* [1921] 1 Ch. 503. See also *Tate v Fullbrook* [1908] 1 K.B. 821 (a case under the pre-1911 law in which it was held that "gags" inserted into the piece by the performer and which were changed from time to time by the performer, could not be the subject of protection as a dramatic work). As to literary characters, see Klement, "Copyright Protection of Unauthorised Sequels under the Copyright, Designs and Patents Act 1988" [2007] 1 Ent. L.R. 13 and McCutcheon, "Property in Literary Characters: Protection under Australian Copyright Law" [2007] 4 E.I.P.R. 140.

[357] This latter requirement was identified by the Privy Council in *Green v Broadcasting Corporation of New Zealand* [1989] R.P.C. 700; in that case the features claimed as constituting the format of a television show, being unrelated to each other except as accessories to be used in the presentation of some other dramatic or musical performance, lacked the essential characteristic of sufficient unity to be capable of performance. See also *Nova Productions Limited v Mazooma Games Limited* [2006] EWHC 24 (Ch), para.113.

[358] *Nova Productions Limited v Mazooma Games Limited* [2006] EWHC 24 (Ch), para.116. The conclusion that the games were not protected as dramatic works was not challenged on appeal: [2007] EWCA Civ 219; [2007] R.P.C. 25, at para.3.

[359] *FWS Joint Sports Claimants v Copyright Board* (1991) 22 I.P.R. 429 (Fed CA of Canada), citing *Tate v Fulbrook* [1908] 1 K.B. 821 and *Green v Broadcasting Corporation of New Zealand* [1989] R.P.C. 700.

Television show formats. It is sometimes said that there can be no copyright in **3–44** television show formats, particularly game show formats. This conclusion is often said to follow from the decision in *Green v Broadcasting Corporation of New Zealand*,[360] where effectively a claim to the copyright in the format for the game show *Opportunity Knocks* failed. However, the claim there suffered from a number of fundamental defects. No scripts were available at trial,[361] and all that could be inferred was that such scripts as there had been did no more than express a general idea or concept for a talent quest. The characteristic features of the show which were repeated in each performance and in respect of which a claim was made for the dramatic format consisted merely of the title, the use of the catch phrases "For [name of the competitor], opportunity knocks", "This is your show folks, and I do mean you" and "Make up your mind time", the use of a "cla-pometer" to measure audience reaction to competitors' performances and the use of sponsors to introduce competitors. The other material (the acts of the perform-ers in the talent show, the questions and answers in the quiz show, etc.) changed with each broadcast and there was therefore no sufficient certainty as to their subject matter. As to the fixed elements, they were unrelated to each other except as accessories to be used in the presentation of some other dramatic or musical performance and therefore lacked sufficient unity to be capable of performance.[362] There is no reason in principle, however, why a format should not be protectable as a dramatic work if it contains a sufficient record of how the show is to be presented.[363] Today, such formats, in addition to recording the central idea of the show or game, will often contain scripted spoken elements, directions for what the participants should do at particular stages, and details for the staging, lighting and sound effects. A useful test to determine whether there is a protectable dramatic work is to ask whether, using the written script or other record as a basis, it is possibly to present a coherent and meaningful show which is capable of being performed.[364] Whether another game show infringes will depend on whether or not a substantial part has been taken.[365]

Nature of copyright in a dramatic work. As with a literary work,[366] the idea for **3–45** a dramatic work is not itself protected by copyright. What is protected is the form in which that idea is expressed. Whilst, as discussed above, a work will only be a dramatic work if it is a work of action capable of being performed before an audi-ence, the *performance* of any actors must be distinguished from the *work*. The work may enjoy protection as a dramatic work; the performance of any actors may give rise to quite separate rights under Pt II of the Act.[367] A copyright dramatic work confers on the owner the exclusive rights to do various acts in re-

---

[360] *Green v Broadcasting Corporation of New Zealand* [1989] R.P.C. 700.

[361] Although there was evidence that there had once been some scripts, no reconstructions were produced.

[362] Similarly, it has been held that news and current affairs programmes comprising video clips, interviews and discussion, lacked the choreography required to constitute them dramatic works: *Television N.Z. v Newsmonitor Services* [1994] 2 N.Z.L.R. 91 (High Ct of NZ). Under the New Zealand Act s.2, a dramatic work is defined to include a chorographic work if reduced to writing in the form in which it is to be presented; a film cannot be a dramatic work. Of course, the script for a television broadcast for a news or current affairs programme could itself constitute a literary work: ibid.

[363] Despite lobbying, the Government has resisted efforts to make specific provision for the protec-tion of game show formats. Although consultation has taken place (see, e.g. the 1994 and 1996 DTI Consultation Papers), nothing has come of this.

[364] *Hutton v Canadian Broadcasting Corporation* (1989) 29 C.P.R. (3rd) 398 (High Ct of Canada) in which it was held that there was sufficient dramatic incident and seminal storyline in the concept of a television series to qualify it as a dramatic work.

[365] As to which, see para.7–63, below.

[366] See para.3–18, above.

[367] See Ch.12.

lation to the work as a whole or a substantial part of it; a qualifying performance confers on the owner of the performers' right various rights in relation to the performance. The unauthorised copying of a performance of a dramatic work may thus separately infringe the rights of the owners of the copyright and the performers' right. Again, a person may give a performance which is an ad-lib performance. This may either be as part of a work, as where the author has left the performer to improvise without direction from the author, or it may constitute the entire performance. In the former case, the improvisation may be part of the dramatic structure of the work, but what the actor actually does while improvising cannot, it is suggested, be part of the original dramatic work.[368]

D. MUSICAL WORKS

(i) History of protection

3–46   **Early protection.** Musical scores were protected under the early Copyright Acts only as literary works, and thus only from unauthorised reproduction in printed or sheet music form. When a performing right was first introduced under the Dramatic Copyright Act 1833,[369] it applied only to dramatic, not musical works. This was remedied by the Literary Copyright Act 1842.[370] Such statutes contained no definition of a musical work.[371] Musical works were protected as a separate category of works under the 1911 Act and under the 1956 Act, but again neither Act contained a definition of a musical work.

3–47   **Berne Convention.** Musical works are protected under the Berne Convention as musical compositions, with or without words.[372]

(ii) Under the 1988 Act

3–48   **Statutory definition: musical work.** The 1988 Act "defines" a musical work as a work consisting of music, exclusive of any words or action intended to be sung, spoken or performed with the music.[373] A dictionary definition of music is "sounds in melodic or harmonic combination, whether produced by voice or instruments",[374] but this definition is too restrictive for present purposes, as sounds which are neither in melodic nor harmonic combination may equally be recognised to be music. While an essential ingredient of a musical work is obviously that it be capable of being sensed by the human ear, mere sounds are not necessarily music.

---

[368] Although it may become part of a new dramatic work if recorded. In the case of a truly improvised and unrecorded performance, whilst this will not be a performance of a dramatic work, it is suggested that this will still be a dramatic performance for the purposes of Pt II of the 1988 Act, given the subtle difference between the wording of s.180(2)(a) and (c), which seems designed to cover this very possibility. Note that a performance of a variety act or similar presentation (which would often contain much unscripted material) is specifically such a performance: s.180(2)(d).

[369] 3 & 4 Will. 4, c.15.

[370] 5 & 6 Vict., c.45.

[371] In a number of cases, the question arose whether a particular work was a dramatic piece as well as a musical work: *Russell v Smith* (1848) 12 Q.B. 217; *Clark v Bishop* (1872) 25 L.T. 908; *Roberts v Bignell* (1887) 3 T.L.R. 552; *Fuller v The Blackpool Winter Gardens, etc. Co Ltd* [1895] 2 Q.B. 429.

[372] Berne Convention art.2(1).

[373] CDPA 1988 s.3(1); as already noted there was no definition of musical work in the Copyright Act 1911 or in the Copyright Act 1956. See also the comment of Jacob L.J. in *Hyperion Records Ltd v Sawkins* [2005] EWCA Civ 565, at para.73: "The definition of 'music' is not a definition at all — its obvious purpose is just to separate out lyrics or choreographical directions or the like. They go into a different 'box' for copyright purposes, for instance lyrics into 'literary works' and choreographical works into 'dramatic works.'"

[374] *Oxford English Dictionary*. The now repealed Musical (Summary Proceedings) Copyright Act 1902 (2 Edw. 7, c.15) s.3, defined a musical work as any combination of melody and harmony.

"In the absence of a special statutory definition of music, ordinary usage assists: as indicated in the dictionaries, the essence of music is combining sounds for listening to. Music is not the same as mere noise. The sound of music is intended to produce effects of some kind on the listener's emotions and intellect. The sounds may be produced by an organised performance on instruments played from a musical score, though that is not essential for the existence of the music or of copyright in it. Music must be distinguished from the fact and form of its fixation as a record of a musical composition. The score is the traditional and convenient form of fixation of the music and conforms to the requirement that a copyright work must be recorded in some material form. But the fixation in the written score or on a record is not in itself the music in which copyright subsists. There is no reason why, for example, a recording of a person's spontaneous singing, whistling or humming or of improvisations of sounds by a group of people with or without musical instruments should not be regarded as 'music' for copyright purposes."[375]

The emphasis on the fact that music is not the same as mere noise but is intended to produce effects of some kind on the listener's emotions and intellect, is also consistent with the history of protection of musical works and types of works held to be protected under the earlier Acts,[376] something which, it is suggested, is relevant to an understanding of this category of work.[377] The relevant intention is that of the author-composer, and it is irrelevant whether he is successful in the attempt to affect the listener's emotions or intellect.[378] In music copyright the sounds are more important than the notes, as is shown by the fact that it is possible to infringe a musical work without taking the actual notes.[379] In principle, there is no reason for regarding the actual notes of music as the only matter covered by musical copyright, any more than, in the case of a dramatic work, only the words to be spoken by the actors are covered by dramatic copyright.[380] Accordingly, it is wrong in principle to single out the notes as uniquely significant for copyright purposes and to proceed to deny copyright to the other elements that make some contribution to the sound of the music when performed, such as performing indications, tempo and performance practice indicators, if they are the product of a person's effort, skill and time, bearing in mind the relatively modest level of the threshold for a work to qualify for protection.[381] As with other forms of work, it is not legitimate to define a work by cherry-picking parts of a piece of music so as to increase the changes of establishing copying of a substantial part.[382]

To the extent that notation or words are written down and are intended to represent sounds which qualify as music in the above sense, it seems that they are excluded from the definition of literary work, even though they can in one sense

---

[375] *Sawkins v Hyperion Records Ltd* [2005] EWCA Civ 565; [2005] 1 W.L.R. 3281; [2005] R.P.C 32, para.53, per Mummery L.J., with whom Mance L.J. and Jacob L.J. appear to have agreed (see paras 71 and 72).

[376] See para.3–46.

[377] See the comparable discussion on the nature of "sculptures" in *Lucasfilm Ltd v Ainsworth* [2009] EWCA Civ 1328; [2010] F.S.R. 10, discussed at para.3–60.

[378] Compare *Lucasfilm Ltd v Ainsworth* [2009] EWCA Civ 1328 at para.71.

[379] *Sawkins v Hyperion Records Ltd* [2005] EWCA Civ 565, para.54, citing *Austin v Columbia Gramophone Co* [1917–1923] Mac.C.C. 398).

[380] *Sawkins v Hyperion Records Ltd* [2005] EWCA Civ 565, para.55.

[381] *Sawkins v Hyperion Records Ltd* [2005] EWCA Civ 565, para.56.

[382] *Coffey v Warner/Chappell Music Ltd* [2005] EWHC 449 (Ch); [2005] F.S.R. 34, paras 10, 11, where the claimant sought to identify a musical work as "comprising the combination of vocal expression, pitch contour and syncopation of and around the words *"does it really matter"*, i.e. the combination of these three features. The work should have been identified by reference to the surrounding melody, ie the notes, their duration and rhythm.

be read.[383] While words which are sung with music do not form part of the musical work, the human voice can constitute a part of the overall orchestration of a musical work, as with a musical instrument in a band or an orchestra.[384] A passage of silence set within musical sounds and intended to be appreciated as part of those sounds is clearly part of the musical work as a whole. It is doubtful that a passage of silence by itself is capable of being a musical work, even if claimed by the author or critics to be such.

3–49   **No requirement as to form.** There is no requirement in the statutory definition of a musical work that the music must be expressed in writing or other notation. However, as with a literary and a dramatic work, for music to be the subject matter of copyright it must satisfy the requirement as to fixation.[385] A composer who composes a piece of music entirely in his head, therefore, will be creating a musical work for the purposes of the 1988 Act.[386] Equally, where a musician plays music which has not previously been composed, what is produced is a musical work. In any such case, however, no copyright will be capable of subsisting in such work until it is fixed, and for the purposes of the 1988 Act the date the musical work is made will be the date it is first fixed, not when it was first conceived or performed.[387]

3–50   **Musical work also a dramatic work.** The definition of a musical work makes it clear that it does not include words intended to be sung or spoken with the music or action intended to be performed with the music.[388] No doubt, first, the intention being referred to is the intention of the author of the music and, secondly, the material time for establishing the intention is the time the author creates the music. Any such words, if they constitute a literary work,[389] are treated as a separate work, entitled to a separate copyright, and the mutually exclusive nature of the two types of works is strictly maintained. However, as already pointed out,[390] a dramatic work may include music: the music will be entitled to a separate copyright, notwithstanding that the music also forms an integral part of the dramatic work, as in the case of a work of dance written to music, or an opera. This question is of little importance, since the owner of copyright in a dramatic work has the same rights as those enjoyed by the owner of copyright in a musical work.

E. ARTISTIC WORKS

(i) History of protection

3–51   **Early protection.** Artistic works have successively become the subject of protection under the Copyright Acts as new processes have developed. Engravings, prints and lithographs were the earliest group of such works to be given protection, under the Engraving Copyright Acts of 1734 and 17668 Geo. 2, c.13; 7 Geo.

---

[383] See CDPA 1988, s.3(1). And see the statement by Jacob J. in *Anacon Corp v Environmental Research Technology* [1994] F.S.R. 659 at 663, where, having suggested that a diagram could be a literary work provided it was all written down and contained information which could be read by somebody, as opposed to being appreciated simply with the eye, he said: "Similarly musical notation is written down but needs expressly to be taken out of the definition of 'literary work'".

[384] *Hayes v Phonogram Ltd* [2002] EWHC 2062 (Ch).; [2003] E.C.D.R. 11, para.50.

[385] By being recorded in writing or otherwise: CDPA 1988 s.3(2); see para.3–119, below.

[386] Contrast the position with a literary work, discussed at para.3–14, above.

[387] s.3(2).

[388] CDPA 1988 s.3(1). This provision was introduced to avoid any doubt about the distinction between the music itself, on the one hand, and words to be sung or performed with music on the other: *Hansard*, Vol.490, col.837.

[389] See para.3–15, above.

[390] See para.3–38, above.

3, c.38. and the Prints Copyright Act 1777.[391] Sculptures followed, under the Sculpture Copyright Act 1814,54 Geo. 3, c.56. and paintings, drawings and photographs were first protected under the Fine Arts Copyright Act 1862.[392] Works of artistic craftsmanship and works of architecture first became separately entitled to copyright protection under the 1911 Act.

Berne Convention. With the exception of works of architecture, all such works were included in the original definition of literary and artistic works in the Berne Convention.[393]

3–52

(ii) Artistic works in general

Statutory definition: artistic work. By s.4(1) of the 1988 Act, an artistic work means:

3–53

(a) a graphic work, photograph, sculpture or collage, irrespective of artistic quality;

(b) a work of architecture being a building or a model for a building; or

(c) a work of artistic craftsmanship.

Artistic quality. Works described under sub-para.(a) are artistic works, regardless of whether they have any "artistic quality".[394] The definition of an artistic work under the 1911 Act did not contain such words,[395] but it was generally considered that the word "artistic" was merely used as a generic term to include the different processes of creating works set out in the definition section and that, provided that a work was produced by one of such processes, and that its creation involved some skill or labour on the part of the artist, it was protected.[396] The use of the word "artistic" was thought to equate to the use of the word literary in connection with literary works, which, as already pointed out,[397] was held to refer only to the nature of the material being written or printed and not to its literary quality. This contrasts with the position in the case of artistic works falling within sub-paras (b) and (c), where such words do not occur.[398] While this remains generally true, the position today is more complicated, particular as regards works that also depict something functional. Thus it is it can seen that copyright protection in artistic works is defined as above by reference to various categories of work with no apparent distinction between their aesthetic merits and appeal and their functionality. So, as will be seen, a graphic work such as a diagram or plan which is designed to have only practical utility is still protected as an artistic work. The key to copyright protection is that the work created by the author falls within one or other of the descriptions contained in the 1988 Act: i.e. that it is

3–54

---

[391] 17 Geo. 3, c.57.

[392] 25 & 26 Vict., c.12.

[393] Berne Convention art.2(1). Works of architecture were first included in the Berlin Act (1908). Art.2(1) of the Convention now includes within the description of "artistic works" every production in the artistic domain, whatever may be the mode or form of its expression, such as works of drawing, painting, architecture, sculpture, engraving and lithography, photographic works and works "expressed" by a process analogous to photography, works of applied art, illustrations, maps, plans, sketches and three-dimensional works "relative" to geography, topography, architecture or science.

[394] This was also the position under the Copyright Act 1956 s.3(1)(a). These words were deliberately retained in the 1988 Act, so as to avoid any doubt that artistry was not a requirement for protection as an artistic work: *Hansard*, HL Vol.490, cols 839, 840.

[395] Copyright Act 1911 s.35(1).

[396] Thus, merely commercial designs were protected under the Copyright Act 1911: *Waters v Huygen (M.A) & Co* [1923–1928] Mac. C.C. 17; *Purefoy Engineering Co Ltd v Sykes, Boxall & Co Ltd* (1955) 72 R.P.C. 89.

[397] See para.3–15, above.

[398] As to these works, see paras 3–62 and 3–65, below.

such a work. It does not depend upon a further analysis or identification of its design features.[399] The fact that a work has design features which also entitle it to registration as a design in those respects therefore says little about how to define the limits of copyright protection. Nevertheless, there are limits, and not all works which fall within the literal description of the categories in the Act will be protected. This is most clearly the case for the category of sculpture, this description connoting that the work must also have been created by an artist's hand with the intention that it be a work of art and thus that it contains some element of artistic expression, however unsuccessful.[400] Whether the same is true of the other categories of artistic work will be discussed in turn.

3–55   **Nature of copyright in artistic works.** The essential nature of an artistic work is that it is a thing to be *looked* at in some manner or other. What matters is that which is *visually* significant.[401] It follows from this and ordinary copyright principles that the ideas conveyed by an artistic work, however original, are not protected by copyright, only the expression of those ideas in the form of an artistic work,[402] although of course every element in the expression of an artistic work will usually be the expression of an idea on the part of the artist, representing his choice to paint one thing rather than another, or to use one colour or brush technique rather than another, and so on, and it is the expression of these ideas which is protected.[403] In the case of simple artistic works, the protection given by copyright is therefore relatively weak, as shown by *Kenrick & Co v Lawrence & Co*.[404] There, the claimant had the idea of producing cards on which were printed a hand holding a pencil in the act of making a cross within a square, to be used at elections by illiterate voters. The defendants then published similar cards with a hand holding a pencil, but the hand in the defendants' cards was in a slightly different position, though the idea was clearly taken from the claimant's cards. It was held that the defendants had not infringed the claimant's copyright. There was no copyright in the idea; the defendants' work did not substantially reproduce the form of the claimant's, and the claimant was not entitled to prevent anyone from producing such a simple design as a hand in a square in any form.[405]

3–56   **Simple artistic works.** Provided that the subject matter can be fairly said to fall

---

[399] *Lucasfilm Ltd v Ainsworth* [2009] EWCA Civ 1328; [2010] F.S.R. 10, para.43.

[400] *Lucasfilm Ltd v Ainsworth* [2009] EWCA Civ 1328.

[401] *Anacon Corp v Environmental Research Technology* [1994] F.S.R. 659, applying *Interlego AG v Tyco Industries Ltd* [1988] R.P.C. 343 at 373, per Lord Oliver, himself drawing on the phrase "visually significant" used by Whitford J. in *Rose Plastics GmbH v William Beckett & Co (Plastics) Ltd* [1989] F.S.R. 113.

[402] See, e.g. *Entec (Pollution Control) v Abacus Mouldings* [1992] F.S.R. 332, per Nicholls L.J. at 348; *Donoghue v Allied Newspapers Ltd* [1938] Ch. 106, per Farwell J., at p.109: "This at any rate is clear beyond all question, that there is no copyright in an idea, or in ideas. A person may have a brilliant idea ... for a picture ..., and which appears to him to be original; but if he communicates that idea to ... an artist ..., the production which is the result of the communication of the idea to ... artist ... is the copyright of the person who has clothed the idea in form, ... and the owner of the idea has not rights in that product." And again, at 110: "... that in which copyright exists is the particular form of language by which information which is to be conveyed is conveyed. If the idea, however original, is nothing more than an idea, and is not put into ... any form of expression such as a picture, then there is no such thing as copyright at all. It is not until it is ... reduced into ... some tangible form that there is any copyright, and the copyright exists in ... the particular form of the picture by which ... the information or the idea is conveyed to those who are intended to look at it."

[403] *Designers Guild Ltd v Russell Williams (Textiles) Ltd* [2000] 1 W.L.R. 2416, at 2423.

[404] *Kenrick & Co v Lawrence & Co* (1890) 25 Q.B.D. 99.

[405] But there was copyright in the claimant's drawing and if the drawing had been more closely reproduced, copyright would no doubt have been infringed. See also *George Ward (Moxley) Ltd v Richard Sankey Ltd* [1988] F.S.R. 66, where Whitford J. adopted a similar approach to the copying of an idea for the design of flower pots; *Entec (Pollution Control) Ltd v Abacus Mouldings* [1992] F.S.R. 332 at 348 (Nicholls L.J.) (drawings for a septic tank comprising simple pencil sketches of commonplace shapes with dimensions on them: what were crucial were the dimensions written on the drawings and it was these that had been copied) and *Mirage Studios v*

within one of the categories of protected subject matter (drawing, diagram, etc.), it will in principle be protectable, even though it is elementary or commonplace,[406] the issue in the case of simple works being one rather of originality.[407] All that it is necessary is that there be some visual significance in the product of the artist's work. It may be that certain very simple creations are not protectable at all[408] but the boundary here is not very clear.[409] It has been suggested that the notion of an "artistic *work*" carries with the word "work" the notion of the exercise of some degree of skill and labour[410] but it is suggested this is an issue best left to the question of originality.

(iii) Graphic works

Statutory definition: graphic work. The term graphic work was new in the 1988 Act, and is defined to include any painting, drawing, diagram, map, chart or plan, engraving, etching, lithograph, woodcut or similar work The definition of "graphic work" in subs.4(2) is inclusive, i.e. it is not restricted to the specific exemplars given.[411]

    (a) *Painting.* A painting is not further defined, but is a word in ordinary usage in the English language, and should be given its ordinary meaning.[412] One meaning given in the dictionary[413] is a representation of objects or figures by means of colours laid on a surface. This is clearly too restrictive, in referring to a representation of objects or figures, to act as a comprehensive definition for the purposes of the 1988 Act, since it would exclude much abstract art, where the use of colour alone may be the essential element of the painting. Nevertheless, applying this definition, it has been held that the term did not embrace facial make-up.[414] It is unclear to what extent a work made by painting, irrespective of artistic quality, must at least be intended to be a work of art to be enjoyed as a visual thing, and thus in which there must be some element of artistic expression, however unsuccessful.[415] For example, do the painted walls of domestic house constitute a painting? Of course it may be argued that even if it does, it does

3–57

Counter-Feat Clothing Co Ltd [1991] F.S.R. 145 at 154 (where Browne-Wilkinson V.-C. observed that the concept of a humanoid turtle of an aggressive nature receiving protection was a "difficult concept").

[406] *British Northrop Ltd v TexteamBlackburn Ltd* [1974] R.P.C. 344.

[407] As to which, see para.3–130, below.

[408] *British Northrop Ltd v Texteam Blackburn Ltd* [1974] R.P.C. 344, at 68 (a line drawn with a ruler stated to be not "a very promising subject for copyright"; *Karo Step Trade Mark* [1977] R.P.C. 255 (straight line or circle not protectable); *Rose v Information Services Ltd* [1987] F.S.R. 254 (single vertical line doubted to be a work of originality).

[409] See, e.g. *Waylite Diaries CC v First National Bank Ltd* [1993] (2) S.A. 128, (High Ct of S.A.), where the straight lines dividing up the pages of an ordinary diary were held to be artistic works.

[410] *Karo Step Trade Mark* [1977] R.P.C. 255. See the similar discussion in relation to literary works at para.3–15.

[411] *Nova Productions Limited v Mazooma Games Limited* [2006] EWHC 24 (Ch); [2006] R.P.C. 14, para.100.

[412] *Merchandising Corporation of America Inc v Harpbond Ltd* [1983] F.S.R. 32.

[413] *Oxford English Dictionary.*

[414] *Merchandising Corporation of America Inc v Harpbond Ltd* [1983] F.S.R. 32 (facial make-up of pop singer Adam Ant), decided in part on the basis that facial make-up was not painting on a surface. However, there is no requirement as to fixation in relation to artistic works (see para.3–121, below) and even then there would seem to be no good reason in principle why the face or any part of the body should not be considered a surface, so that facial or body make-up should constitute an artistic work (consider the example of a clown's particular facial make-up, which is his personal "trade mark").

[415] Compare *Lucasfilm Ltd v Ainsworth* [2009] EWCA Civ 1328; [2010] F.S.R. 10, where it was held that works of sculpture must have this quality. It is not entirely clear what Jacob L.J. meant when he said (para.43): "A graphic work … can comprise a painting which (however bad it may be in artistic terms) is unlikely to be anything but decorative."

have the relevant degree of originality, but this is not the point. Given the nature and history of protection of such works,[416] it is suggested that a work which is made by painting does have to satisfy the further test referred to above.

(b) *Drawing, diagram.* It is reasonably clear from the nature of the works in this category which have been held to be protected that a work which has been made by drawing or some other form of delineation does not have to be a work of art to be enjoyed as a visual thing, and thus in which there must be some element of artistic expression.[417] Thus a diagram can include such things as a circuit diagram[418] and a flow chart.[419] In Australia it has been held that when considering whether something is a "drawing", the crucial question is whether it is "designed to convey 'semiotic' meaning (i.e. to be read as a text) or rather a visual look and feel (i.e. to be understood as a design)".[420] Thus where design drawings for T-shirts comprised words and slogans in stylised text and a picture of a bull, it was considered that consumers would purchase the T-shirts because the selection and arrangement of the various elements (text, colour, font, shape, and so on), which had been carefully made to form an aesthetically pleasing visual "look and feel" in the same way that any picture or drawing did. Accordingly, the designs qualified for protection as "drawings".[421] A layout for a box label comprising a photograph and several short lines of explanatory text and numbers has been held not to be a drawing,[422] while a framework for displaying data on a computer screen comprising coloured boxes with column headings has been held probably to be a drawing.[423] The meaning of drawings or diagrams has been stretched to include works which, although containing some visually significant elements, are in reality little more than written instructions for creating an article that has visual appeal,[424] but it is suggested that to the extent that a work includes material that can be read rather than appreciated visually, it

---

[416] See para.3–51.

[417] Again, compare *Lucasfilm Ltd v Ainsworth* [2009] EWCA Civ 1328.

[418] But, where the diagram showed a large amount of writing and symbols and was a list of components together with information as to how they were connected, it was held also capable of protection as a compilation (which gave wider protection against unlicensed copying): *Anacon Corporation Ltd v Environmental Research Technology Ltd* [1994] F.S.R. 659; see para.3–17, above. As to whether the same work can be both a literary work and artistic work, see para.3–04, above.

[419] A flow chart produced as preparatory design material for a computer program will now be capable of protection as a literary work; see para.3–31, above.

[420] *Elwood Clothing Pty Ltd v Cotton On Clothing Pty Ltd* [2008] F.C.A. 447 at para.15. Upheld on appeal [2008] FCAFC 197; [2009] 80 I.P.R. 566.

[421] *Elwood Clothing Pty Ltd v Cotton On Clothing Pty Ltd* [2008] F.C.A. 447 at paras 16, 17. Upheld on appeal [2008] FCAFC 197; [2009] 80 I.P.R. 566.

[422] *Woodtree Pty Ltd v Zheng* [2007] F.C.A. 1922 (Fed. Ct. of Aus.), paras 25–29; in s.10(1) of the Australian Copyright Act 1968 the term "drawing" is defined as including "a diagram, map, chart or plan".

[423] *Statuscard Australia Pty Ltd v Rotondo* [2008] Q.S.C. 181 at para.111, although as such it was insufficiently original to attract protection, being too simple and too much determined by its function.

[424] *Lerose Ltd v Hawick Jersey International Ltd* [1973] F.S.R. 15 (point patterns for knitting machines containing, in addition to a visual representation of the pattern, instructions in the form of hieroglyphics, figures in the margins and words appearing underneath to enable a machine operator to set a knitting machine so that what emerges from it has the pattern reproduced upon it); *Vermaat v Boncrest Ltd* [2001] F.S.R. 43 (drawings for patchwork bedspread covers and cushions consisting of drawings in the form of grids of numbered squares and a border, on each of which was placed a code-number corresponding to the numbers of differently coloured swatches of material, which were also fixed to the drawing).

can only be a literary work.[425] If it were otherwise, purely written instructions describing how to make an artistic work could be protected as an artistic work, and infringed by the making of the artistic work, which is clearly not the correct position.[426] All these types of work are static. Accordingly, a series of still images which provides the illusion of movement, whether created by drawing for a cartoon film or by a computer, is not protected as an artistic work distinct from the individual images.[427] A drawing does not cease to exist because the original lines have been cut around to produce a paper pattern without lines,[428] and it appears that it does not even require production by means of a pen or pencil or similar means, but that it denotes that the work is a product of an author who represents his ideas by use of line or delineation. Thus it has been held that labels made by cutting out various parts and sticking them on the appropriate background were capable of constituting a drawing.[429]

(c) *Map, chart or plan.* Such works may be of real or imaginary things.[430] A map may be protected as both an artistic work and as a literary work, and, as to the latter it seems, either as a compilation of written and artistic material[431] or, to the extent that it contains information that can be read, purely as a literary work.[432]

(d) *Engravings, etchings, lithographs and woodcuts.* These are all works intended to produce a representation by a similar or analogous process. In the case of an engraving, the representation is made by incisions on a surface, traditionally being wood, metal or stone, but this could include rubber or plastic.[433] In the case of an etching, the process involves the eating away of the surface, usually by the use of an acid. It is not clear what is added by reference to a lithograph and a woodcut, since these are usually understood to be no more than examples of these processes carried out on particular surfaces, namely stone and wood, respectively. It has been held that there is no requirement that an engraving must be something that could be regarded as the work of an artist,[434] and presumably the same could be said of etchings, lithographs, and woodcuts. Although the various other decisions cited below do not themselves throw doubt on this, the point was not discussed there and today the point must be doubtful given the Court of Appeal decision in *Lucasfilm Ltd v Ainsworth* relating to what constitutes a sculpture.[435] Those decisions in which works of a purely utilitarian nature have been held to be engravings would appear now to be contrary to the underlying purpose for protecting such works. Thus dies and moulds for making products have been held to be protect-

---

[425] See *Interlego AG v Tyco Industries Inc* [1989] A.C. 217 at 265C; [1988] R.P.C. 343. The law has developed differently in New Zealand: see *ABB Ltd v New Zealand Insulators Ltd* [2006] NZHC 1072 at para.176.

[426] See paras 7–12 and 7–37, below.

[427] *Nova Productions Ltd v Mazooma Games Ltd* [2007] EWCA Civ 219 at para.16.

[428] *Radley Gowns Ltd v Spyrou* [1975] F.S.R. 455 at 466. In any event, the original drawing with lines does not cease to exist as a copyright work following its destruction (see para.3–111) and the paper pattern without lines will reproduce the outline of the copyright work.

[429] *Ornstin Ltd v Quality Plastics* (Aldous J.) noted only at [1990] I.P.D. 13027. As to such a work being a collage, see para.3–61.

[430] As to protection of maps and plans of imaginary things, see *Braithwaite Burn & Co v Trustees of the Port of Madras* (1956) 2 Mad. L.J. 486.

[431] See para.3–26.

[432] *Comprop Ltd v Moran* [2002] J.L.R. 222 (Royal Ct of Jersey).

[433] *James Arnold and Co Ltd v Miafern Ltd* [1980] R.P.C. 397 (rubber stereos used for printing onto transfer paper).

[434] *Hi-Tech Autoparts Ltd v Towergate Two Ltd (No.1)* [2002] F.S.R. 15; cf. *Metix (U.K.) Ltd v G.H. Maughan (Plastics) Ltd* [1997] F.S.R. 718, as to which see para.3–60, below.

[435] *Lucasfilm Ltd v Ainsworth* [2009] EWCA Civ 1328.

able as engravings,[436] although it is difficult to see what aspect of the process of engraving is employed in making such moulds or dies. The better view would seem to be that engraving requires some process of cutting, incision, marking or otherwise working a surface, and that a mould or die made in the ordinary way would not be an engraving.[437] An engraving is typically made on a flat surface but need not be.[438] What constitutes an engraving is not limited to the appearance of that which is left by cutting away the surface but includes the internal shape and texture of cuts below the surface and any other part that affects the final appearance of the print made from it.[439] Nevertheless, not all cutting away of material from a plate constitutes engraving, so that, for example, cutting a rod into sections would not qualify.[440] Not only is the plate whose surface has been cut into with an engraving tool an "engraving", but so also is the object produced by using this plate, since "engraving" can and usually does mean an image produced from an engraved plate.[441] The position was clearer on this point under the 1956 Act, which defined an engraving to include not only any etching, lithograph or woodcut, but also any "print or similar work". Under the 1988 Act, the relevant protected works are "any engraving, etching, lithograph, woodcut or similar work", without any further definition of "engraving" and without any reference to a "print". It would be surprising, however, if the 1988 Act had the effect of abolishing copyright in works in which copyright subsisted immediately before commencement,[442] and presumably the position in relation to prints under the 1988 Act remains as it was before.[443]

3–58   **Examples of graphic works.** As with other composite categories of work, examples of works which have been held to fall within the category merely go to illustrate the wide variety of types of work which have gained protection. Further, many of the cases are now mainly of historical significance only, given the

---

[436] *Wham-O Manufacturing Co v Lincoln Industries Ltd* [1985] R.P.C. 127 (High Ct of NZ) (moulds for making frisbees); *Mayceys Confectionery Ltd v Beckmann* (High Ct of NZ), noted at [1995] E.I.P.R. D- 101 (rubber moulds taken from plaster of Paris model for confectionery "crocodiles"—the report at 30 I.P.R. 331 is concerned with *quantum* only; subsistence was not in issue on the appeal, reported at 33 I.P.R. 543

[437] See *Gabrin v Universal Music Operations Ltd* [2003] EWHC 1335 (Ch), para.30, [2004] E.C.D.R. 4; *Greenfield Products Pty Ltd v Rover-Scott Bonnar Ltd* (1990) 95 A.L.R. 275 (Fed Ct of Aus) (discussed by Ricketson in [1990] E.I.P.R. 421); *Talk of the Town Pty Ltd v Hagstrom* (1990) 19 I.P.R. 649 at 655 (Fed Ct of Aus)), not following *Wham-O Manufacturing Co v Lincoln Industries Ltd* [1985] R.P.C. 127 (High Ct of NZ).

[438] *Talk of the Town Pty Ltd v Hagstrom* (1990) 19 I.P.R. 649 (Fed Ct of Aus), correcting the statement on this point in *Greenfield Products Pty Ltd v Rover-Scott Bonnar Ltd* (1990) 95 A.L.R. 275 (Fed Ct of Aus).

[439] *Hi-Tech Autoparts Ltd v Towergate Two Ltd (No.1)* [2002] F.S.R. 15, para.39 (steel plate which had been worked with a boring tool to produce grooved circles with circular and conical edges, to be used as a stamp to produce rubber, anti-slip mats, held to be an engraving). The court also rejected the argument that what is protected in the category of "any engraving, etching, lithograph, woodcut or similar work" are works which are concerned with the final appearance of the two-dimensional print taken from the work as a plate, such that the protectable skill and labour is only that which has any impact on the appearance of the print.

[440] *Hi-Tech Autoparts Ltd v Towergate Two Ltd (No.1)* [2002] F.S.R. 15.

[441] *Hi-Tech Autoparts Ltd v Towergate Two Ltd (No.1)* [2002] F.S.R. 15, paras 36 and 39; *Hi-Tech Autoparts Ltd v Towergate Two Ltd (No.2)* [2002] F.S.R. 16, para.16, following James *Arnold & Co Ltd v Miafern Ltd* [1980] R.P.C. 397 at 403, and *Wham-O Manufacturing Co v Lincoln Industries Ltd* [1985] R.P.C. 127.

[442] Copyright does not automatically subsist under the 1988 Act in works in which copyright subsisted under the 1956 Act; para.35 of Sch.1 to the 1988 Act relates only to the requirements as to qualification for protection, not categories of protected works.

[443] The point appears to have been glossed over in *Hi-Tech Autoparts Ltd v Towergate Two Ltd* [2002] F.S.R. 15; [2002] F.S.R. 16. Nevertheless, the requirement that in order for copyright to subsist the engraving should be original obviously presents problems in the case of such derivative prints. See para.3–137, below.

effect of the restriction placed on the copyright in designs for the shape or configuration of articles by s.51 of the Act, and protection of such designs now falls mainly within the scope of design right.[444]

In the case of graphic works, examples demonstrate that simplicity is not enough to prevent copyright subsisting in a graphic work as an artistic work, and drawings for screws, studs, bolts, metal bars, rivets and washers (all carefully drawn to scale) have been held protectable.[445] Drawings for standard parts for vehicles such as engines and gearboxes[446] and exhausts,[447] and engineering drawings generally,[448] have been held capable of protection as artistic works. Protection has been conferred on the artistic part of a simple trade mark,[449] designs for packaging,[450] mastheads and newspaper logos,[451] and to a signature and Union emblem.[452]

Point patterns for knitted fabrics,[453] and drawings for clerical shirts[454] have been protected as artistic works. In cases concerned with dress designs, infringement used often to be alleged in the design sketch, cutting patterns and prototype garment.[455] Such a sketch is undoubtedly a work in which copyright is capable of subsisting.[456] Where cutting patterns have been made by first drawing an outline

---

[444] See para.9–160 and Ch.13, below.

[445] *British Northrop Ltd v Texteam Blackburn Ltd* [1974] R.P.C. 344, and see para.3–56, above, as to simplicity in general. But even if simple, such drawings must be original, see further paras 3–131 et seq., below.

[446] *Nichols Advanced Vehicle Systems Inc v Rees* [1979] R.P.C. 127.

[447] *L.B. (Plastics) Ltd v Swish Products Ltd* [1979] F.S.R. 145; *Kwik Lok Corporation v W.B.W. Engineers Ltd* [1975] F.S.R. 237; *British Leyland Motor Corp v T.I. Silencers Ltd* [1981] F.S.R. 213; *British Leyland Motor Corp v Armstrong Patents Co Ltd* [1972] F.S.R. 481.

[448] See cases cited in the previous footnote.

[449] *Karo Step Trade Mark* [1977] R.P.C. 255 (a circle contained with four quarter-arcs of circles); *AUVI Pte Ltd v Seah Siew Tee* (1991) 24 I.P.R. 41; [1995] F.S.R. 288 (High Ct of Singapore) (logo consisting of four letters in a stylised form); *R. Griggs Group Ltd v Evans* [2003] EWHC 2914 (Ch), para.18, [2004] F.S.R. 31 (logo for boots, being word or phrase drawn in stylised way) (on appeal but not on this point: [2005] EWCA Civ 11; [2005] F.S.R. 31; [2005] E.C.D.R. 30). Compare *Kinnor (Pty) Ltd v Finkel T/A Harfin Agencies*, W.L.D. 9059/90, Stranex Judgments on Copyright 352, and noted at [1990] 5 Ent. L.R. E-84, (Sup. Ct of S.A.), where it was held that a representation of a logo for "LePacer", with the loop of the "P" being elongated for the full length of the word, was not an original artistic work, being simply a different way of writing what was still the letter "P". See also *Australian Chinese Newspapers Pty Ltd v Melbourne Chinese Press Pty Ltd* [2003] F.C.A. 878 (on appeal *Melbourne Chinese Press Pty Ltd v Australian Chinese Newspapers Pty Ltd* (2004) 63 I.P.R. 38), in which it was conceded that a logo consisting of three characters in a particular calligraphic style used for a newspaper masthead was a copyright work.

[450] *Charles Walker & Co Ltd v The British Picker Co Ltd* [1961] R.P.C. 57; *Taverner Rutledge Ltd v Specters, Ltd* [1959] R.P.C. 83; *Frank & Hirsch (Pty) Ltd v A. Roopanand Brothers (Pty) Ltd* (1994) 29 I.P.R. 465 (CA of S.A.) (artwork for audio cassette wrappers). *Henkel KgaA v Holdfast New Zealand Ltd* [2006] NZSC 102; (2006) 70 IPR 624; [2007] 1 N.Z.L.R. 336 at paras 36, 47 (design drawing for packaging comprising a combination of "common form" elements of a glue bottle affixed to a card of a dominant blue primary colour with pictures of two uses and a list of applications; but note that in England the claim would have probably fallen foul of s.51 of the 1988 Act).

[451] *IPC Magazines Ltd v MGN Ltd* [1998] F.S.R. 431 (the logo "Woman" used as the masthead of a magazine). In *News Group Newspapers Ltd v Mirror Group Newspapers (1986) Ltd* [1989] F.S.R. 126, it was assumed that the masthead of *The Sun* was capable of being protected as an artistic work, subject to its originality. In *Emap National Publications Ltd v Security Publications Ltd* [1997] F.S.R. 891 it was conceded that copyright subsisted in the claimant's oval lozenge logo for its publication *Popular Classics*.

[452] *Daily Telegraph*, March 1, 1977 (use of facsimile of Mr Clive Jenkins' signature and his Union's emblem).

[453] As to diagrams: *Lerose Ltd v Hawick Jersey International Ltd* [1973] F.S.R. 15. But see para.3–57, above.

[454] *Gleeson v H.R. Denne Ltd* [1975] R.P.C. 471.

[455] *Radley Gowns Ltd v Costas Spyrou* [1975] F.S.R. 455 is just one example.

[456] See, e.g. *J. Bernstein Ltd v Sidney Murray Ltd* [1981] R.P.C. 303, 328.

of the pattern, copyright is capable of subsisting in them as graphic works,[457] and in theory copyright is capable of subsisting in a prototype garment as a work of artistic craftsmanship.[458]

Typeface designs are clearly protectable under the 1988 Act.[459] They were also considered capable of protection under the 1956 Act as artistic works, at least as to designs of individual letters, although doubt was expressed as to whether designs for fonts (i.e. complete sets of lettering) qualified as artistic works.[460] Designs for individual letters were protected under the 1911 Act as artistic works,[461] as also were fonts.[462]

Graphical user interface computer screens, which had been drawn by selecting from a palette of available objects things such as command buttons, toggle buttons, checkboxes, scrolling lists and so on and moving them around on a form until a satisfactory layout had been achieved, have been held to be artistic works. It did not matter that they were recorded only in the complex code which displayed them.[463] The icons which appeared on the screens were also protected as artistic works, "albeit minor".[464] Also considered as artistic works have been bitmap (digital image) files created using computer tools such as the mouse and on-screen tools such as notional brushes and pencils and the screen colour palette (the files creating a visual effect which was very similar to a painting or drawing) and composite frames generated by the computer program using the bitmap files.[465]

(iv) Photographs

3–59   **Statutory definition: photograph.** A photograph is defined to mean a recording of light or other radiation on any medium on which an image is produced or from which an image may by any means be produced, and which is not part of a film.[466] Save for the last clause, this definition is new and is so worded to ensure that such things as holograms are capable of protection as artistic works by being

---

[457] See *Radley Gowns Ltd v Costas Spyrou* [1975] F.S.R. 455; *Merlet v Mothercare Plc* [1984] F.S.R. 358. The point was conceded in *House of Spring Gardens Ltd v Point Blank Ltd* [1983] F.S.R. 213 (High Ct of Ireland).

[458] See paras 3–65 et seq., below.

[459] The 1988 Act proceeds on the assumption that designs for typefaces qualify for protection as artistic works: see, e.g. ss.54 and 55 and *Hansard*, HL Vol.490, col.844; HL Vol.493, col.1068. S.78 defines "typeface" as including an ornamental motif used in printing, and see paras 9–163 et seq., below. Designs for typefaces are excluded from the effect of s.51 (see s.51(1) and para.9–160, below). See generally on the protection of software fonts, *Watts & Blakemore* Protection of software fonts in UK law [1995] E.I.P.R. 133. The 1977 Whitford Committee Report recommended (Cmnd.6732, para.538) that the UK should ratify the Vienna Agreement on the Protection of Typefaces, signed by the UK on June 12, 1973 (Cmnd.5754, set out in Vol.2 F9), but to date the UK has not done so.

[460] See the Whitford Committee Report, paras 524 and 529.

[461] *Millar & Lang Ltd v Polak* [1908] 1 Ch. 433 (designs of distinctive individual letters for Christmas cards; *Roland Corporation v Lorenzo & Sons (Pty) Ltd* (1991) 22 I.P.R. 245 (Fed Ct of Aus) (logo devices consisting of depictions of single letters).

[462] *Stephenson, Blake & Co v Grant, Legros & Co Ltd* (1916) 33 R.P.C. 406, following *Maple & Co v Junior Army and Navy Stores* (1882) 21 Ch. D. 369 and *Davis v Benjamin* [1906] 2 Ch. 491.

[463] *Navitaire Inc v easyJet Airline Co Ltd* [2004] EWHC 1725 (Ch); [2006] R.P.C. 3, para.97. It seems that the contrary was not seriously argued (see para.74).

[464] *Navitaire Inc v easyJet Airline Co Ltd* [2004] EWHC 1725 (Ch) at para.99.

[465] *Nova Productions Limited v Mazooma Games Limited* [2006] EWHC 24 (Ch); [2006] R.P.C. 14. The case concerned coin operated computer games based on the theme of pool. The computer program built up composite images by combining individual bitmap images, for example of the table, the cue and the balls (para.104). All this was common ground on appeal: [2007] EWCA Civ 219 at para.12.

[466] CDPA 1988 s.4(2). Compare the definition in the Copyright Act 1956, s.48(1): any product of photography or any process akin to photography, other than a part of a cinematograph film. For an interesting review of the early history of protection of copyright in photographs, see Deazley, "Photography, copyright, and the South Kensington experiment" [2010] I.P.Q. 293–311.

photographs.[467] The definition also covers a photograph recorded digitally, since what is recorded is still light or other radiation, and the reference to the medium is unrestricted. The reference to light or other radiation ensures that a photograph taken by x-ray or infra-red or other process is nonetheless a photograph for the purposes of the Act. The last clause of the definition, which in this respect follows the definition in the 1956 Act, excludes a single frame of a film from being capable of protection as a photograph. A single frame of a film is, however, protectable as part of a film.[468]

(v) Sculptures

Definition: sculpture. Sculpture is defined in the 1988 Act to include a cast or model made for purposes of sculpture,[469] but the 1988 Act does not otherwise define what is a sculpture. The ordinary dictionary meaning of the art of sculpture is the art of forming representations of objects or abstract designs in the round or in relief by chiselling stone, carving wood, modelling clay, casting metal or similar processes.[470] While, as will be seen, this is not a sufficient definition for the purposes of the Act, it may be taken as a starting point so that, for example, an arrangement of a scene for the purpose of a photograph being taken for the cover of a record album was held not to constitute a sculpture, as no element in the composition had been carved, modelled or made in any of the other ways in which a sculpture was made.[471] Beyond this, however, the difficulty in identifying what constitutes a "sculpture" is partly that the word can be used to describe not only a physical object but also the process by which the object is created, e.g. moulding or carving material into a desired shape or, in the case of a metal cast sculpture, by creating the necessary cast or mould. Objects which are essentially utilitarian in nature can be created, often by mass-production, from an intermediate mould or cast which can thus be said to have been sculptured. Following the Court of Appeal decision in *Lucasfilm Ltd v Ainsworth*[472] it is now clear, however, that such works are in general not sculptures within the meaning of the Act since the word must not be interpreted divorced from its legislative history.[473] When so interpreted, broadly speaking sculpture has to be a work at least intended to be a work of art in which there must be some element of artistic expression, however unsuccessful.[474] There is no precise, comprehensive or exclusive definition of

3–60

---

[467] See *Hansard*, HL Vol.495, col.1065.

[468] CDPA s.17(4) and para.7–81, below. See generally, *Football Association Premier League Ltd v QC Leisure* [2008] EWHC 1411, (Ch); [2008] F.S.R. 32; [2008] 3 C.M.L.R. 12, at paras 224–7.

[469] CDPA 1988 s.4(2), repeating the definition in s.48(1) of the Copyright Act 1956.

[470] *Oxford English Dictionary*, applied in *Breville v Thorn EMI* [1995] F.S.R. 77. But see later in the text as to the status of this decision.

[471] *Creation Records v News Group Newspapers* [1997] E.M.L.R. 444. See also *Jarman & Platt Ltd v I. Barget Ltd* [1977] F.S.R. 260, CA: the headnote only records that at trial it had been held that settings or arrangements of furniture were not capable of attracting copyright but it is not clear under what category of artistic work protection was claimed.

[472] *Lucasfilm Ltd v Ainsworth* [2009] EWCA Civ 1328; [2010] F.S.R. 10.

[473] *Lucasfilm Ltd v Ainsworth* [2009] EWCA Civ 1328, para.21, citing in particular the Act of 1798 (38 Geo III. C.71), Sculpture Copyright Act of 1814, Copyright Acts 1911, 1956 and CDPA 1988. Ultimately, the issue has to be determined by reference to the copyright provisions of the 1988 Act themselves. In this, the fact that a model or cast which qualifies as a sculpture may have design features which also entitle it to registration as a design in those respects does not help to define the limits of copyright protection since these are different issues. While a work of sculpture in the traditional fine art sense would undoubtedly have the qualities of eye appeal necessary to make its shape registrable as a design, the converse does not follow: *Lucasfilm Ltd v Ainsworth* [2009] EWCA Civ 1328, para.44.

[474] *Lucasfilm Ltd v Ainsworth* [2009] EWCA Civ 1328, paras 66, 70, approving the decision of Mann J. at first instance, *Lucasfilm Ltd v Ainsworth* [2008] EWHC 1878 (Ch).

"sculpture" sufficient to determine the issue in any given case[475] and a multi-factorial approach must therefore be adopted, using a number of guidance factors which should act as signposts, rather than points of principle or hard and fast rules.[476] These are as follows[477]:

    (i) Some regard has to be had to the normal use of the word.

    (ii) Nevertheless, the concept can be applicable to things going beyond what one would normally expect to be art in the sense of the sort of things that one would expect to find in art galleries.

    (iii) It is inappropriate to stray too far from what would normally be regarded as sculpture.

    (iv) No judgment is to be made about artistic worth.

    (v) Not every three dimensional representation of a concept can be regarded as a sculpture. Otherwise every three dimensional construction or fabrication would be a sculpture, and that cannot be right.

    (vi) It is of the essence of a sculpture that it should have, as part of its purpose, a visual appeal in the sense that it might be enjoyed for that purpose alone, whether or not it might have another purpose as well. The purpose is that of the creator. Sculpture thus connotes a three-dimensional work made by an artist's hand.[478] An artist (in the realm of the visual arts) creates something because it has visual appeal which he wishes to be enjoyed as such. He may fail, but that does not matter (no judgments are to be made about artistic merit). It is the underlying purpose that is important.

    (vii) The fact that the object has some other use does not necessarily disqualify it from being a sculpture, but it still has to have the intrinsic quality of being intended to be enjoyed as a visual thing. The issue does not turn on the purpose for which the object is actually used but on the purposive nature of the object, i.e. its intrinsic quality of being intended to be enjoyed as a visual thing. The purpose of the object is not determinative but simply one of the relevant guides to whether it qualifies as a sculpture.[479]

    (viii) The process of fabrication is relevant but not determinative. A purely functional item, not intended to be at all decorative should not be treated as a sculpture simply because it is (for example) carved out of wood or stone.

Point (vii) highlights a grey area in which, even on the approach outlined in points (i)–(vi), there may be difficulties in drawing the line between sculpture and an object which, though well designed, does not qualify as such. Nevertheless, a line has to be drawn somewhere and some form of differentiation made, since otherwise almost any moulded version of a functional object will be included in the definition.[480]

In accordance with these principles, it can now be said that the following were

---

[475] The attempt to devise such a definition being "not possible or wise": *Lucasfilm Ltd v Ainsworth* [2009] EWCA Civ 1328, para.77.

[476] *Lucasfilm Ltd v Ainsworth* [2009] EWCA Civ 1328, para.77, approving the reasoning of Mann J. at first instance, *Lucasfilm Ltd v Ainsworth* [2008] EWHC 1878 (Ch), para.118.

[477] *Lucasfilm Ltd v Ainsworth* [2009] EWCA Civ 1328, para.71, approving the approach of Mann J. at first instance, *Lucasfilm Ltd v Ainsworth* [2008] EWHC 1878 (Ch).

[478] Approving in particular the decision of Laddie J. in *Metix v G H Maugham* [1997] FSR 718.

[479] *Lucasfilm Ltd v Ainsworth* [2009] EWCA Civ 1328, para.75.

[480] *Lucasfilm Ltd v Ainsworth* [2009] EWCA Civ 1328, para.75. See also the observations of Mann J. at first instance (*Lucasfilm Ltd v Ainsworth* [2008] EWHC 1878 (Ch), at para.118(viii)). "A pile of bricks, temporarily on display at the Tate Modern for two weeks, is plainly capable of being a sculpture. The identical pile of bricks dumped at the end of my driveway for two weeks preparatory to a building project is equally plainly not. One asks why there is that difference, and the answer lies, in my view, in having regard to its purpose. One is created by the hand of an artist, for artistic purposes, and the other is created by a builder, for building purposes. I appreciate

correctly held to have been sculptures: metal models of soldiers, being artistic depictions of mounted yeoman and cast from a model which had been made with recognisable artistic skill[481]; a plastic model of a wolf-cub's head produced from a papier-mâché mould in order to be used as a totem by the Boy Scouts Association, even though made with the intention of being reproduced in large quantities[482]; three-dimensional depictions of animals made out of wire, even though some of these were also functional in that they incorporated a candle holder, but nevertheless being decorative and made with a degree of skill in the medium employed and which were designed to have aesthetic appeal to potential purchasers.[483] Further, it can now be said that the following were correctly held *not* to have been sculptures: moulds used for making cartridges for "flow mixers", these having the appearance of a double-barrelled hypodermic syringe through which different chemicals were passed using a plunging mechanism and then mixed to create a chemical reaction[484]; a model of a dental impression tray[485]; a helmet and armour created for a character in a *Star Wars* film,[486] and toys based

---

that this example might be criticised for building in assumptions relating to what it seeks to demonstrate, and then extracting, or justifying, a test from that, but in the heavily subjective realms of definition in the artistic field one has to start somewhere."

[481] *Britain v Hanks* (1902) 86 LT 765, decided under the Sculpture Copyright Act 1814. The contention that the models were mere toys of no artistic merit was rejected by the trial judge; "... the model soldier in *Britain* might be played with, but it still, apparently, had strong purely visual appeal which might be enjoyed as such." See *Lucasfilm Ltd v Ainsworth* [2008] EWHC 1878 (Ch), at para.118(vii).

[482] *Pytram v Models (Leicester)* [1930] 1 Ch 639 (obiter) but the Court of Appeal in *Lucasfilm Ltd v Ainsworth* [2009] EWCA Civ 1328, at para.60 saw no reason to doubt its correctness: the object in question was an artistic creation of an animal's head which was in a real sense a sculpture within the meaning of the 1911 Act.

[483] *Wildash v Klein* (2004) 61 IPR 324 (Sup. Ct. N. Terr., Aus), clearly thought to have been correct by the English Court of Appeal in *Lucasfilm Ltd v Ainsworth* [2009] EWCA Civ 1328, and see *Lucasfilm Ltd v Ainsworth* [2008] EWHC 1878 (Ch), at para.118(vii): "... the Critters in *Wildash* had other functions, but they still had strong purely visual appeal."

[484] *Metix v G H Maugham* [1997] F.S.R. 718 (design considered obviously intended to have a purely industrial application and no reason why the word "sculpture" should be extended far beyond the meaning which that word has to ordinary members of the public; nothing to suggest that the manufacturers of the moulds considered themselves, or were considered by anybody else, to be artists when they designed the moulds or that they were concerned in any way with the shape or appearance of what they were making, save for the purpose of achieving a precise functional effect; nothing to suggest that any consideration of appeal to anything other than functional criteria was in mind or achieved). The decision was implicitly clearly approved by the Court of Appeal in *Lucasfilm Ltd v Ainsworth* [2009] EWCA Civ 1328, e.g. at para.68. The doubts about *Metix (UK) Ltd v G.H. Maughan* expressed in *Hi-Tech Autoparts Ltd v Towergate Two Ltd (No.1)* [2002] F.S.R. 15, para.47, must now be taken as incorrect. It should be noted that *Metix* turned on a pleading point, there being no direct pleading of a work of sculpture, only a plea that certain moulds were sculptures. It was held that if this plea was sufficient, it meant that any mould would be a sculpture, which was clearly not the case.

[485] *J & S Davis (Holdings) v Wright Health Group* [1988] R.P.C. 403 (the submission that the mould was a sculpture was in fact rejected largely on the grounds of its ephemeral nature but the substance of the decision was clearly approved by the Court of Appeal in *Lucasfilm Ltd v Ainsworth* [2009] EWCA Civ 1328, at para.67: "The only remarkable thing about the case is that anyone could have thought the work in question could remotely be considered a 'sculpture'".

[486] *Lucasfilm Ltd v Ainsworth* [2008] EWHC 1878 (Ch), at paras 121, 122: "The purpose of the helmet was that it was to be worn as an item of costume in a film, to identify a character, but in addition to portray something about that character—its allegiance, force, menace, purpose and, to some extent, probably its anonymity. It was a mixture of costume and prop. But its primary function is utilitarian. While it was intended to express something, that was for utilitarian purposes. While it has an interest as an object, and while it was intended to express an idea, it was not conceived, or created, with the intention that it should do so other than as part of character portrayal in the film." Accordingly, it did not have the necessary quality of artistic creation. Approved by the Court of Appeal, *Lucasfilm Ltd v Ainsworth* [2009] EWCA Civ 1328 at para.80: "Although invented, the helmet and armour are still recognisable as such and have a function within the confines of the film as the equipment of the stormtrooper. They are, to that extent, no different from and serve the same purpose as any real helmet or armour used in a film. The judge made this point by referring to the primary function of the helmet and armour as being utilitarian and lacking in artistic purpose. This is simply a shorthand for the application of the various considerations set out in his [judgment]."

on the *Star Wars* characters.[487] On the other hand, the following would not today be held to be sculptures[488]: a preparatory wooden model for what became the Frisbee[489] and plastic shapes produced in order to create moulds for the heated plates in a sandwich toaster.[490]

It has been held that objects which are not intended to have any permanent existence do not fall within the definition of sculpture[491] but this factor seems to be irrelevant.[492]

(vi) Collages

3–61   **Collages**. A collage is now specifically included as an artistic work.[493] No definition of a collage is provided or was apparently considered to be necessary,[494] and a dictionary definition of collage is "an abstract form of art in which photographs, pieces of paper, newspaper cuttings, string, etc. are placed in juxtaposition and glued to the pictorial surface".[495] Consistent with this, it has been held that a collage involves the use of glue or adhesive in the process of making a work.[496] While a collage may be a protected work "irrespective of its artistic quality,"[497] it must be a work of visual art[498] in the same sense, it is suggested, as in the case of a sculpture[499] so that a purely functional product would not be protected.[500]

---

[487] *Lucasfilm Ltd v Ainsworth* [2008] EWHC 1878 (Ch), at para.123. They were intended primarily for the purposes of play. They were not made for the purposes of their visual appearances as such but to look like the costumes worn in the film. It was highly unlikely that they would be displayed and admired as such.

[488] As to the cases next cited in the text, see *Lucasfilm Ltd v Ainsworth* [2008] EWHC 1878 (Ch), at para.118(vii): "I would respectfully disagree with the conclusions reached by the judges in those cases that things were sculptures. Those decisions, in my view, would not accord with the ordinary view of what a sculpture is, and if one asks why then I think that the answer is that … there is no intention that the object itself should have visual appeal for its own sake, and every intention that it be purely functional."

[489] *Wham-O v Lincoln Industries* [1985] R.P.C. 127. See *Lucasfilm Ltd v Ainsworth* [2009] EWCA Civ 1328, at para.65: "The model was not intended to be a depiction of any animate object … nor was it made as the model for an abstract work of art", and at para.66: "A total or almost total emphasis on the manner of creation, as in … Wham-O produces a result which offends common sense and in our view is wrong."

[490] *Breville Europe v Thorn EMI* [1995] F.S.R. 77. As to this, see *Lucasfilm Ltd v Ainsworth* [2009] EWCA Civ 1328, at para.66: "No ordinary citizen–indeed no ordinary lawyer – would regard a sandwich toaster or any part of it as a work of sculpture–even if it did produce 'scalloped' sandwiches", and at para.66: "A total or almost total emphasis on the manner of creation, as in *Breville* … produces a result which offends common sense and in our view is wrong." The judge's further observation in *Breville* that "for example, carved wooden patterns intended for the purpose of casting mechanical parts in metal or plastic might well be susceptible of protection" must also be considered to have been wrong.

[491] *Davis (J & S) (Holdings) Ltd v Wright Health Group Ltd* [1988] R.P.C. 403 (dental impression trays).

[492] See *Metix (UK) Ltd v G.H. Maughan* [1997] F.S.R. 718, making the point that a sculpture in ice is nonetheless a sculpture, although see *Merchandising Corporation of America Inc v Harpbond Ltd* [1983] F.S.R. 32 (no copyright in short-lived fixation of painting) and the comment on this case in para.3–57, above.

[493] There was some doubt as to whether a collage fell within the definition of an artistic work under the 1956 Act. If not, then it seems there is no protection created before August 1, 1989. See CDPA 1988 Sch.1 para.5(1).

[494] *Hansard*, HL Vol.495, col.1067.

[495] *Oxford English Dictionary*. And see *Creation Records v News Group Newspapers* [1997] E.M.L.R. 444

[496] *Creation Records v News Group Newspapers* [1997] E.M.L.R. 444, holding that the arrangement of a scene for the purpose of a photograph being taken for the cover of an album could not constitute a collage. It was also suggested that the intrinsically ephemeral nature of the assemblage prevented it being a collage, *sed quaere*.

[497] CDPA 1988 s.4(1)(a).

[498] *Creation Records v News Group Newspapers* [1997] E.M.L.R. 444.

[499] See para.3–60, above.

[500] Such as, for example, the labels made by cutting out various parts and sticking them on the ap-

(vii) Works of architecture

History of protection of works of architecture. Works of architecture, as **3–62** distinct from the plans, drawings and sketches of such works, were first made the subject of copyright protection under the 1911 Act.[501] This followed the revision of the Berne Convention in 1908, as a result of which the definition of literary and artistic works was extended to require protection to be granted to illustrations, maps, plans, sketches and three-dimensional works "relative", inter alia, to architecture.[502] Under the 1911 Act, an artistic work was therefore defined to include "architectural works of art",[503] this expression being in turn defined to mean any building or structure having an artistic character or design, in respect of such design, or any model for such building or structure, but the protection given by the Act was confined to the artistic character and design, and did not extend to processes or methods of construction.[504] Copyright could therefore now subsist in a building, as distinct from a copyright in the plans on which the building was based.[505] Under the 1956 Act, an artistic work was defined to include works or architecture, being either buildings or models for buildings,[506] a building being defined to include any structure.[507] Express reference to artistic character or design, and to the nature of protection, was now omitted but it is thought that this did not produce any substantial alteration in the law. While drawings were protected "irrespective of artistic quality",[508] the omission of these words in respect of architectural works maintained, in effect, the requirement under the 1911 Act that such works, in order to be architectural works, must have some artistic character.

Statutory definition: work of architecture. A work of architecture is defined by **3–63** the 1988 Act as being a building or a model for a building,[509] and a building is defined as including any fixed structure, or a part of a building or fixed structure.[510] The reference to a part of a building or structure was introduced to remove any doubt that an extension to a building is included.[511] Although the word "building" is found in a number of other Acts, probably little help as to what constitutes a building is to be obtained from them: the definition was deliberately wide, and was intended to include structures designed by engineers, rather than architects, such as a bridge.[512] It is suggested that a building or structure must be of such a character as is usually erected upon, or constructed under the ground and that in each case it involves something of substance, with an element of permanence. If a building or structure has these characteristics, then it will be entitled to protection, not only as a whole, but in individual architectural features, including internal features of design.[513] On this basis a chimney-piece might, it is thought, be entitled to copyright and it has been held that a garden, consisting of a layout

---

propriate background, which were protected as drawings in *Ornstin Ltd v Quality Plastics* (Aldous J.), noted at [1990] I.P.D. 13027.

[501] Copyright Act 1911 s.35(1).
[502] Berlin Act art.2(1).
[503] Copyright Act 1911 s.35(1)—although the remedies for the infringement of those works were considerably curtailed: s.9.
[504] Copyright Act 1911 s.35(1).
[505] *Meikle v Maufe* [1941] 3 All E.R. 144.
[506] Copyright Act 1956 s.3(1)(b).
[507] s.48(1).
[508] s.3(1)(a).
[509] CDPA 1988 s.4(1)(b), in identical terms to the definition in s.3(1)(b) of the Copyright Act 1956.
[510] CDPA 1988 s.4(2).
[511] *Hansard*, HL Vol.493, col.1069.
[512] *Hansard*, HL Vol.493, col.1071.
[513] *Meikle v Maufe* [1941] 3 All E.R. 144.

including steps, walls, ponds and other structures in stone, was capable of protection as "a structure".[514]

In view of what has been said, it is questionable whether the introduction in the 1988 Act of the qualification "fixed" to the term "structure" is helpful.[515] Presumably fixed means fixed to the ground, and is intended to denote a degree of permanence,[516] but the term may itself introduce argument as to the degree and duration of fixation which is envisaged and could result in some arbitrary distinctions between works capable of protection as architectural works and others which are not. For example, a construction such as a summer house, which rested by its own weight on the ground but was not otherwise fixed to the ground, would, unless it was a "building", seem by this requirement to be excluded from being a work of architecture, although it would be capable of being a work of architecture if fixed to the ground in any way (even if such fixing was intended to be only temporary).

A model will be protected as a work of architecture if it is a model "for" a building. It is suggested that this is deliberately different from a model "of" a building. The word "for" implies a purposive connection between the making of the model and the intended building. In this respect a model is, like architects' plans and drawings, a preparatory work in the process of producing the design for the building or structure. This would exclude from a work of architecture a model made as a model (whether of an existing or imaginary building) which was not made for the purpose of showing the architectural form of the intended building or structure. Such a model would be capable of protection, if at all, as a work of artistic craftsmanship.[517]

3–64   **Artistic character or design of architectural work.** The necessity under the 1911 and 1956 Acts that a work of architecture should have an artistic character or design has already been noted and it is suggested that the position is the same under the 1988 Act.[518] It is suggested that such artistic character need not involve any aesthetic judgment,[519] but may reside in the process of design of the building or structure. In the case of the vast majority of structures in respect of which the issue might arise as to whether they were works of architecture, this is, in practice, likely not to be a problem. It is, however, possible to conceive of a structure which would require to be designed but which might not be considered to qualify as a work of architecture.[520]

(viii) Works of artistic craftsmanship

3–65   **Early protection for works of artistic craftsmanship.** Protection was first given

---

[514] *Vincent v Universal Housing Co Ltd* [1928–35] Mac. C.C. 275.

[515] The word "fixed" was intended to distinguish protected structures from those which were not intended to be protected, such as moveable engineering structures (e.g. a ship): *Hansard*, HL Vol.493, col.1071.

[516] It is suggested that, for example, a building constructed as part of a garden display at the Chelsea Flower Show would satisfy this requirement, even though it was intended to be demolished at the end of the show (and consider the example of the Crystal Palace, erected in Hyde Park for the duration of the Great Exhibition).

[517] See para.3–65, below.

[518] As with the 1956 Act, the 1988 Act, although stating that an artistic work includes a graphic work, photograph, sculpture or collage, "irrespective of artistic quality" (s.4(1)(a)), makes no such qualification in the case of a work of architecture.

[519] In *Blake v Warren* [1928–1935] Mac.C.C. 268 (an official referee's decision), it was held that the requirement of "artistic character or design" in the 1911 Act required something apart from the "common stock of ideas", rather something that "strikes the eye as uncommon". But it is suggested that this is to apply a test which is virtually one of novelty, which was not the correct position.

[520] For example, an underground concrete water sump, or the foundations for a building, comprising the concrete raft and the piles to be driven into the ground.

to such works by the 1911 Act.[521] Previously, protection in this area was given only to works of "the fine arts"[522] and the intention of the 1911 Act was to extend protection to works produced under the influence of the Arts and Crafts movement, with its emphasis on the applied or decorative arts.[523] Although the term was not defined in the 1911 Act, the intention was thus to give protection to works of genuine artistry such as pottery, embroidery, and other forms of craftsmanship which might not otherwise be protected as artistic works.[524] The 1956 Act continued this protection and, similarly, provided no definition of this category of artistic work.[525]

Berne Convention. Work of artistic craftsmanship is not a term which is derived from the Berne Convention.[526] **3–66**

Works of artistic craftsmanship under the 1988 Act. As with the previous Acts, the 1988 Act does not attempt to define this description of artistic work. Indeed, it was considered that no satisfactory definition of what is a work of artistic craftsmanship could be given in the statute.[527] In addition to this, matters are not helped by the fact that the leading case, in the House of Lords,[528] was handicapped by what was probably a mistaken concession,[529] and that even then the House of Lords did not speak with one voice.[530] The starting point[531] for considering whether a work is a work of artistic craftsmanship is that the phrase imports two separate requirements combined in the same work: artistic quality and craftsmanship. Had the intention merely been to protect works of craftsmanship, irrespective of artistic quality, the word artistic would have been omitted from the phrase. This is emphasised by the absence, in relation to this description of artistic work, of the words "irrespective of artistic quality", which accompany the description of artistic works included in s.4(1)(a) of the 1988 Act.[532] Although shades of meaning can be extracted from both the words "artistic" and "craftsmanship",[533] the phrase "work of artistic craftsmanship" is in the end a **3–67**

---

[521] Copyright Act 1911 ss.1 and 35(1).

[522] i.e. to paintings, drawings and photographs under the Fine Arts Copyright Act 1862; and see the preamble to the Act.

[523] *George Hensher Ltd v Restawile Upholstery (Lancs) Ltd* [1976] A.C. 64, per Lord Simon at 90; [1974] F.S.R. 173.

[524] The latter point was confirmed, in the case of the 1956 Act at least, by the fact that an artistic work was defined to include works of artistic craftsmanship "not falling within either of the preceding paragraphs", i.e. paras 3(1)(a) and (b), setting out the other categories of artistic works. The omission, in the 1988 Act, of these extra words is not considered to have effected any change in the law.

[525] Copyright Act 1956 s.3(1)(c).

[526] Berne Convention art.2(1) merely refers to works of "applied art" as being included in the definition of literary and artistic works.

[527] See *Hansard*, HL Vol.490, col.847. The High Court of Australia has concluded that it would be unwise to seek to define the term: *Swarbrick v Burge: Burge v Swarbrick* [2007] HCA 17.

[528] *George Hensher Ltd v Restawile Upholstery (Lancs) Ltd* [1976] A.C. 64.

[529] The defendants had conceded at trial, probably wrongly in the view of each of the members of the House of Lords, that a prototype for piece of "knock-up" furniture was a work of craftsmanship. The only issue was thus whether it was a work of " *artistic* craftsmanship".

[530] As was pointed out by Lord Kilbrandon in *George Hensher Ltd v Restawile Upholstery (Lancs) Ltd* [1976] A.C. 64 at 98, the House of Lords rejected definitions of "artistic" framed by the trial judge, the Court of Appeal, counsel for the claimants and two by counsel for the defendants; further, each member of the House of Lords hearing the appeal provided a definition of his own.

[531] For a helpful review of the cases, see *Coogi Australia Pty Ltd v Hysport International Pty Ltd* (1998) 157 A.L.R. 247 (Fed Ct of Aus).

[532] Although in *George Hensher Ltd v Restawile Upholstery (Lancs) Ltd* [1976] A.C. 64 at 95, Lord Simon observed that it was no doubt because the Act is concerned with works of artistic craftsmanship, and not with artistic works of craftsmanship, that it was unnecessary to repeat these words, which refer to artistic merit.

[533] See paras 3–68 and 3–69, below.

composite phrase that should be construed as a whole.[534] For a work to be regarded as one of artistic craftsmanship, it should be possible to say that the creator was both a craftsman and an artist.[535] It has been suggested that determining whether a work is a work of artistic craftsmanship does not turn on assessing the beauty or aesthetic appeal of work or on assessing any harmony between its visual appeal and its utility, but on assessing the extent to which the particular work's artistic expression, in its form, is unconstrained by functional considerations. Accordingly, the more constrained the designer is by functional considerations, the less likely the work is to be a work of artistic craftsmanship. It is a matter of degree.[536]

3–68 **Craftsmanship**. Obviously, unless the work is one of craftsmanship it cannot qualify for protection at all.[537] Did the work's creation reflect an exercise of craftsmanship, a concept in part requiring "a manifestation of pride in sound workmanship" and a "rejection of the shoddy, meretricious, the facile"?[538] A craftsman can be regarded as someone who makes a thing in a skilful way, as well as taking a justified pride in his workmanship,[539] so that a work of craftsmanship will involve the exercise of skill on the part of the creator in using the materials of which the article is made and the devices by which those materials are turned into an article.[540] It has been said that such a work presupposes special training, skill and knowledge for its production.[541] Such skills are not confined to handicraft skills but may involve skills in the use of machines,[542] even a computer-controlled machine, provided the resulting work is a manifestation of the creator's skill with the machine, knowledge of materials and pride in workmanship.[543] The issue in each case will be one of fact, on which lay and expert evidence will be admissible.[544]

3–69 **Artistic**. Clearly, not all works of craftsmanship are works of artistic craftsmanship.[545] What is required is that the work should have some real artistic or aesthetic quality,[546] but it does have to be a work of art,[547] or a "work of fine

---

[534] *George Hensher Ltd v Restawile Upholstery (Lancs) Ltd* [1976] A.C. 64, per Lord Simon at 91; *Lucasfilm Ltd v Ainsworth* [2008] EWHC 1878 (Ch); [2008] E.C.D.R. 17 at para.130(i). The judge's decision on the issue of "artistic craftsmanship" was not contested in the Court of Appeal: *Lucasfilm Ltd v Ainsworth* [2009] EWCA Civ 1328.

[535] *Bonz Croup (Pty) Ltd v Cooke* [1994] 3 N.Z.L.R. 216, followed in *Vermaat v Boncrest Ltd* [2001] F.S.R. 43 and found to be "helpful" in *Lucasfilm Ltd v Ainsworth* [2008] EWHC 1878 (Ch); [2008] E.C.D.R. 17 at para.131.

[536] *Swarbrick v Burge: Burge v Swarbrick* [2007] HCA 17 (High Ct of Aus), paras 83, 84.

[537] *George Hensher Ltd v Restawile Upholstery (Lancs) Ltd* [1976] A.C. 64 at 80; [1974] F.S.R. 173.

[538] *George Hensher Ltd v Restawile Upholstery (Lancs) Ltd* [1976] A.C. 64 at 91, per Lord Simon; *Merlet v Mothercare Plc* [1986] R.P.C. 115; *Bonz Group (Pty) Ltd v Cooke* [1994] 3 N.Z.L.R. 216; *Guild v Eskandar Ltd* [2001] F.S.R. 645. It has been said that a work of craftsmanship suggests a durable, useful, handmade object (*Hensher*, per Lord Reid, at 77), but clearly this is not a definition, and does not apply in all cases: see the further discussion in the text.

[539] *Bonz Group (Pty) Ltd v Cooke* [1994] 3 N.Z.L.R. 216, found to be "helpful" in *Lucasfilm Ltd v Ainsworth* [2008] EWHC 1878 (Ch); [2008] E.C.D.R. 17 at para.131; *Vermaat v Boncrest Ltd* [2001] F.S.R. 43.

[540] *Bonz Group (Pty) Ltd v Cooke* [1994] 3 N.Z.L.R. 216; *Vermaat v Boncrest Ltd* [2001] F.S.R. 43.

[541] *George Hensher Ltd v Restawile Upholstery (Lancs) Ltd* [1976] A.C. 64 at 91 per Lord Simon, following *Cuisenaire v Reed* [1963] V.L.R. 719 and *Cuisenaire v South West Imports Ltd* [1968] 1 Ex.C.R. 493 514. But it is suggested in particular that special training is not necessarily required.

[542] *George Hensher Ltd v Restawile Upholstery (Lancs) Ltd* [1976] A.C. 64 at 90, 91, per Lord Simon.

[543] *Coogi Australia Pty Ltd v Hysport International Pty Ltd* (1998) 157 A.L.R. 247 (Fed Ct of Aus).

[544] See the discussion as to evidence in relation to "artistic", para.3–69, below.

[545] See the discussion of different kinds of craftsmanship by Lord Simon in *George Hensher Ltd v Restawile Upholstery (Lancs) Ltd* [1976] A.C. 64 at 91; [1974] F.S.R. 173.

[546] *George Hensher Ltd v Restawile Upholstery (Lancs) Ltd* [1976] A.C. 64 at 85H, 8E, 96G; *Cui-*

art".[548] It should therefore be possible to regard the creator as an artist as well as a craftsman[549] and an artist has been described as someone with creative ability who produces something which has aesthetic appeal.[550] The requirement of artistic quality clearly requires a judgment by the court as to whether the work is artistic or not, but this does not mean that it is for the court to make its own value judgment as to whether the work has this quality. The issue is one of fact to be determined in the light of the evidence[551] on an objective basis.[552] The evidence may be of various types. First, evidence of the intentions of the maker, in particular whether or not he had the conscious purpose of creating a work of art, is admissible, relevant and important, although not a paramount or determining consideration.[553] It should also be treated with caution and tested against the contemporary documents.[554] If the maker did have this intention, then provided he has not manifestly failed, it will be a work of art in the required sense.[555] Second, evidence from ordinary members of the public that they do or would value the work for its appearance or get pleasure or satisfaction from it, whether on an emotional or intellectual level, is relevant.[556] Third, expert evidence, although not a necessity,[557] will be admissible from those who have special capabilities or qualifications for forming an opinion, and whose evidence will command respect,[558] in particular those who are acknowledged artist-craftsmen or who teach in the field.[559] If the maker already has other works to his name which are acknowledged to be artistic, this will be relevant.[560] The fact that it is also a utilitarian article does not mean that it cannot have artistic or aesthetic qualities[561] nor is the presence of non-functional features the test of aesthetic quality.[562] The level of aesthetic appeal to be applied is, however, higher than

---

senaire v Reed [1963] V.L.R. 719 at 730; *Merlet v Mothercare plc* [1986] R.P.C. 115 at 124 (does the work have artistic appeal in itself?); *Bonz Group (Pty) Ltd v Cooke* [1994] 3 N.Z.L.R. 216 at 224.

[547] *Lucasfilm Ltd v Ainsworth* [2008] EWHC 1878 (Ch); [2008] E.C.D.R. 17, per Mann J. at para.130(i), rejecting Walton J.'s analysis in *Merlet v Mothercare plc* [1986] R.P.C. 115 at 125 of the majority view of the House of Lords in *George Hensher Ltd v Restawile Upholstery (Lancs) Ltd* [1976] A.C. 64, although adopted in *Guild v Eskandar Ltd* [2001] F.S.R. 645.

[548] The purpose of the provision was originally to extend to works of applied art the protection formerly given to works of fine art: *Coogi Australia Pty Ltd v Hysport International Pty Ltd* (1998) 157 A.L.R. 247 (Fed Ct of Aus)

[549] *Bonz Group (Pty) Ltd v Cooke* [1994] 3 N.Z.L.R. 216; adopted in *Vermaat v Boncrest Ltd* [2001] F.S.R. 43. This aspect of the *Bonz Group* decision was described as "helpful" in *Lucasfilm Ltd v Ainsworth* [2008] EWHC 1878 (Ch), at para.131.

[550] *Bonz Group (Pty) Ltd v Cooke* [1994] 3 N.Z.L.R. 216; adopted in *Vermaat v Boncrest Ltd* [2001] F.S.R. 43 and found to be "helpful" in *Lucasfilm Ltd v Ainsworth* [2008] EWHC 1878 (Ch), at para.131.

[551] *George Hensher Ltd v Restawile Upholstery (Lancs) Ltd* [1976] A.C. 64, at 78C, 87B, 94G, 96H; *Merlet v Mothercare Plc* [1986] R.P.C. 115, Walton J. adopting the approach which he considered favoured by the majority of the House of Lords in *Hensher*.

[552] *George Hensher Ltd v Restawile Upholstery (Lancs) Ltd* [1976] A.C. 64 at 81F/G.

[553] *George Hensher Ltd v Restawile Upholstery (Lancs) Ltd* [1976] A.C. 64 at paras 78F, 81G, 95B; *Merlet v Mothercare Plc* [1986] R.P.C. 115 at para 126; *Lucasfilm Ltd v Ainsworth* [2008] EWHC 1878 (Ch); [2008] E.C.D.R. 17, at para.130(i).

[554] *Swarbrick v Burge: Burge v Swarbrick* [2007] HCA 17 (High Ct of Aus), paras 65, 69.

[555] *George Hensher Ltd v Restawile Upholstery (Lancs) Ltd* [1976] A.C. 64 at 81; *Merlet v Mothercare Plc* [1986] R.P.C. 115 at 126; *Bonz Group (Pty) Ltd v Cooke* [1994] 3 N.Z.L.R. 216.

[556] *George Hensher Ltd v Restawile Upholstery (Lancs) Ltd* [1976] A.C. 64 at 78, 87. But note the warning against mere "eye-appeal" being sufficient, below.

[557] *Lucasfilm Ltd v Ainsworth* [2008] EWHC 1878 (Ch); [2008] E.C.D.R. 17, at para.130(iv).

[558] *George Hensher Ltd v Restawile Upholstery (Lancs) Ltd* [1976] A.C. 64 at 82, 87.

[559] *George Hensher Ltd v Restawile Upholstery (Lancs) Ltd* [1976] A.C. 64 at 94.

[560] *George Hensher Ltd v Restawile Upholstery (Lancs) Ltd* [1976] A.C. 64.

[561] *George Hensher Ltd v Restawile Upholstery (Lancs) Ltd* [1976] A.C. 64, at 79, 86; *Coogi Australia Pty Ltd v Hysport International Pty Ltd* (1998) 157 A.L.R. 247 (Fed Ct of Aus).

[562] *Coogi Australia Pty Ltd v Hysport International Pty Ltd* (1998) 157 A.L.R. 247 (Fed Ct of Aus), and see the observation of Lord Simon in *George Hensher Ltd v Restawile Upholstery (Lancs)*

mere visual appeal.[563] The question is therefore not concluded by evidence that the appearance of the work is such that some members of the public are motivated to acquire the article "on especial account" thereof[564]; it must have some aesthetic quality, and the fact that a segment of the public can be found who have been motivated to buy the work simply because of its visual appeal is not enough.[565] Whether a work is one of artistic craftsmanship must be decided by looking at the work in isolation, not when placed in juxtaposition with something else, where the ensemble may be "artistic".[566]

3–70   **Other points**. A work intended to be reproduced in articles of mass-production can as a matter of principle be a work of artistic craftsmanship, although this fact may cast doubt on whether it is truly one of artistic craftsmanship.[567] In the case, for example, of a mass-produced run of fabric which repeats a design, if any part is to be a work of artistic craftsmanship, copyright first subsists when the first fixation of the work is made. Copyright does not subsist in every length of fabric bearing the design.[568] It is not essential for such a work to be the product of the efforts of a single artist-craftsman. It is enough that two or more people have combined to design and make the ultimate product if it satisfies the two criteria of craftsmanship and aesthetic quality,[569] provided, it is suggested, that the authors are joint authors of the work.[570]

3–71   **Examples: copyright conferred**. There are relatively few cases in which copyright has been conferred on works under this heading.[571] Works in respect of which protection has been conferred include: hand-knitted woollen sweaters,[572] fabric with a highly textured surface comprising a complex multi-coloured design

---

[563] *Ltd* [1976] A.C. 64 at 93B that in the context of the arts and crafts movement, the antithesis between function and beauty is a false one.

[563] *George Hensher Ltd v Restawile Upholstery (Lancs) Ltd* [1976] A.C. 64, at 79C, 81E, 84F, 86, 93E, 95F.

[564] *Coogi Australia Pty Ltd v Hysport International Pty Ltd* (1998) 157 A.L.R. 247 (Fed Ct of Aus).

[565] *Coogi Australia Pty Ltd v Hysport International Pty Ltd* (1998) 157 A.L.R. 247 (Fed Ct of Aus).

[566] *Merlet v Mothercare Plc* [1986] R.P.C. 115 at 124 (rain-cape for mother and baby not to be viewed as worn by mother and child). In *Guild v Eskandar Ltd* [2001] F.S.R. 645 at 700, Rimer J. questioned whether it was not at least permissible to view a garment as arranged on a mannequin.

[567] In *George Hensher Ltd v Restawile Upholstery (Lancs) Ltd* [1976] A.C. 64; [1974] F.S.R. 173, Lord Reid at [1976] A.C. 77 said that he found it difficult to conceive a work of artistic craftsmanship as being an object which was only intended as a step in a commercial operation and which had no value in itself, although he made it clear that this was not intended to be an authoritative statement. In *Guild v Eskandar Ltd* [2001] F.S.R. 645, sample garments made as prototypes for mass production were held to be neither artistic nor works of craftsmanship.

[568] *Coogi Australia Pty Ltd v Hysport International Pty Ltd* (1998) 157 A.L.R. 247 (Fed Ct of Aus).

[569] *Bonz Group (Pty) Ltd v Cooke* [1994] 3 N.Z.L.R. 216; *Vermaat v Boncrest Ltd* [2001] F.S.R. 43, such an approach considered to be "sensible" in *Lucasfilm Ltd v Ainsworth* [2008] EWHC 1878 (Ch); [2008] E.C.D.R. 17, at para.131, provided there was a sufficient nexus between the two people.

[570] A single copyright work cannot have more than one author unless the authors are joint authors: para.4–04, below. For a work to qualify as a work of joint authorship, the contribution of each must not be distinct from that of the other: see paras 4–34 and 4–37, below. If, therefore, one author is responsible for the elements of artistry and the other for the elements of craftsmanship, and their contributions are distinct, then it seems that there cannot be a work of artistic craftsmanship. And see *Burke etc. Ltd v Spicers Dress Designs* [1936] Ch. 400: any copyright which might have subsisted in the prototype garment did not vest in the firm which executed the design because the firm's servants, who made the garment from a third party's design, did not originate any artistic element which might subsist. See also *Lucasfilm Ltd v Ainsworth* [2008] EWHC 1878 (Ch); [2008] E.C.D.R. 17, at para.131, suggesting (but not deciding) that there must be sufficient "nexus" between artist and craftsman.

[571] In several cases, the issue has been held arguable at the interim stage, e.g. *Radley Gowns Ltd v Costas Spyrou* [1975] F.S.R. 455 at 466 (prototype garments); *Shelley Films Ltd v Rex Features Ltd* [1994] E.M.L.R. 134 (a film set).

[572] *Bonz Group (Pty) Ltd v Cooke* [1994] 3 N.Z.L.R. 216; compare the cases referred to below where protection has been denied to prototype garments.

with 3D elements, produced using a computer-controlled knitting machine to realise the creative idea,[573] a range of pottery[574] and items of dinnerware.[575]

Examples: copyright denied. There have been many failed attempts made to bring works within this category. They include a prototype sofa for a range of "knock-up" furniture,[576] a set of rods, specifically designed for teaching mathematics,[577] a prototype of a cape for a mother and child,[578] a frock,[579] sample garments made as prototypes for mass production,[580] "moving sand pictures",[581] a lounge suite,[582] sample patchwork bedspreads and cushion covers,[583] a corkscrew,[584] a full scale "plug" or form for moulds for a racing yacht,[585] and helmets and armour created for the *Star Wars* films.[586]

3–72

F. SOUND RECORDINGS

(i) History of protection

Pre-1912. Reproduction of sounds first became a copyright issue in 1886, the year of the Berne Convention. However, the issue was not whether protection should be granted to such reproductions, which by their very nature fell outside the scope of the Convention,[587] but whether the rights of authors of musical compositions should extend to prevent the unauthorised mechanical reproduction of their compositions. The issue was resolved against the mechanical reproduction

3–73

---

[573] *Coogi Australia Pty Ltd v Hysport International Pty Ltd* (1998) 157 A.L.R. 247 (Fed Ct of Aus). The operator was skilled in textile computer-aided machine operation and had used his knowledge of the material properties of textiles.

[574] *L. & J.E. Walter Enterprises (Pty) Ltd v Kearns* (High Ct of Zimbabwe) noted at [1990] 4 Ent. L. R. E-61.

[575] *Commissioner of Taxation v Murray* (1990) 92 A.L.R. 671 (Fed Ct of Aus).

[576] *George Hensher Ltd v Restawile Upholstery (Lancs) Ltd* [1976] A.C. 64; [1974] F.S.R. 173, where the evidence was wholly inadequate to establish that the furniture in question merited the epithet "artistic".

[577] *Cuisenaire v Reed* [1963] V.R. 719; *Cuisenaire v South West Imports Ltd* [1968] 1 Ex.C.R. 493; 37 Fox's C.P.C. 81 (no craftsmanship in the making of the rods as no skill was involved in cutting or colouring them; nor were they artistic).

[578] *Merlet v Mothercare Plc* [1984] F.S.R. 358, not a work of art, but a basic commodity.

[579] *Burke etc. Ltd v Spicers Dress Designs* [1936] Ch. 400: although the claim in fact failed on the question of title.

[580] *Guild v Eskandar Ltd* [2001] F.S.R. 645 (simple machine-made garments for which there was no evidence of any special elements of craftsmanship going into their manufacture and no sufficient evidence that their designer intended to create works of art or regarded herself as an artist. Even if all that was necessary to qualify as a work of art was that the work satisfied the aesthetic emotions of a substantial section of the public, there was no adequate evidence of this either); *Muscat v Le* (2004) 204 A.L.R. 335.

[581] *Komesaroff v Mickle* [1988] R.P.C. 204 (Sup Ct of Victoria).

[582] *Dress Designs (Pty) Ltd v G. Y. Lounge Suite Mfgs (Pty) Ltd* (1991) 2 S.A.L.R. 455 (Sup Ct of S.A., Witwatersrand Local Division)—a utilitarian product only.

[583] *Vermaat v Boncrest Ltd* [2001] F.S.R. 43: although the making of the articles by the seamstress might have been a work of craftsmanship, it was not sufficiently artistic.

[584] *Sheldon and Hammond Pty Ltd v Metrokane Inc* (2004) 61 I.P.R. 1.

[585] *Swarbrick v Burge: Burge v Swarbrick* [2007] HCA 17 (High Ct of Aus), para.73 (because matters of visual and aesthetic appeal had been subordinated to achievement of the purely functional aspects required for a successfully marketed "sports boat" and thus for the commercial objective).

[586] *Lucasfilm Ltd v Ainsworth* [2008] EWHC 1878 (Ch) at para.134 (they were works of craftsmanship but insufficiently "artistic" to qualify for protection: their purpose was not to appeal to the aesthetic at all or to do anything more than what was necessary to give the correct impression in the film of the character inside).

[587] The aim of the Convention was to protect the rights of authors in their literary and artistic creations; devices for the reproduction of music involved technical or industrial rather than artistic creativity.

of musical airs being regarded as an infringement of copyright.[588] At that time, the only mechanical means generally known for reproducing music were musical boxes and "Barbary" organs, and musical composers did not feel that they were abandoning rights of any great value by agreeing to this derogation of their rights.[589] It was not long, however, before instruments were being invented which were capable of reproducing not one or two tunes, but any number of tunes and even the words of songs, by means of perforated rolls, discs and cylinders. The popularity of such devices was soon established, to the concern of composers, who sought to test whether the manufacture and sale of these contrivances was an infringement of their copyright. The result, in the United Kingdom, was that such actions failed.[590]

3–74   **The 1911 Act.** At the conference in Berlin in 1908, the Berne Convention was revised to require protection to be given to composers against reproductions of their works by mechanical means.[591] By this time, a considerable industry for the manufacture of such mechanical contrivances had developed in the United Kingdom. The manufacturers lobbied the Parliamentary Committee, formed in 1909 to report to Parliament on what changes to British law were required to implement the Berlin Act for the introduction of a form of compulsory licence, but the majority of the Committee recommended allowing musical composers full control over the reproduction of their works by mechanical means.[592] The Copyright Bill was originally drafted to this effect. However, further lobbying by the manufacturers achieved the introduction of what became s.19 of the 1911 Act, the short effect of which was to compel a musical composer, if he had granted a licence to one person to reproduce his work mechanically, to grant to any other person a licence to reproduce the same work in like manner upon payment of a certain royalty.

It was s.19 of the 1911 Act which also gave to the manufacturers of such mechanical contrivances the protection they had sought against unauthorised copying of their devices, by according protection to records, perforated rolls and other contrivances by means of which sounds might be mechanically reproduced. The 1911 Act did not, however, create a new category of copyright work for this purpose, but provided that such mechanical contrivances were to be protected in the same manner as if they were musical works.[593] This effectively gave the maker of the contrivance the same exclusive rights as were enjoyed by the author of a musical composition.[594] The protection was extended to such contrivances as already existed at July 1, 1912, when the 1911 Act took effect.[595]

3–75   **The 1956 Act.** The link between mechanical contrivances and musical compositions became increasingly anomalous, with the development of technology and the manufacture and sale of recordings of other than musical works. Following the recommendation of the 1952 Copyright Committee, the 1956 Act introduced

---

[588] By the declaration contained in art.3 of the Final Protocol.

[589] This provision had been requested by the Swiss delegates, to protect what was a Swiss national industry.

[590] See *Boosey v Whight* [1899] 1 Ch. 836, affirmed on appeal: [1900] 1 Ch. 122; *Newmark v The National Phonograph Co Ltd* (1907) 23 T.L.R. 439; *Monckton v The Gramophone Co Ltd* (1912) 106 L.T. 84. The composers had better success in Italy and Belgium, and partial success in France (the provision was interpreted as not permitting reproduction of the words of a song).

[591] Berlin Act art.13.

[592] Cd.4976 (1909).

[593] Copyright Act 1911 s.19(1).

[594] Including the performing right, although this was not fully appreciated until the decision in *Gramophone Co Ltd v Stephen Cawardine & Co* [1934] Ch. 450.

[595] Copyright Act 1911 s.19(8).

a separate regime of protection for sound recordings in their own right.[596] A sound recording was defined as the aggregate of the sounds embodied in and capable of being reproduced by means of a record of any description.

Under the 1911 Act, the soundtrack of a film enjoyed its own protection as a mechanical contrivance under s.19. Under the 1956 Act, a film soundtrack was excluded from the definition of a sound recording[597] and was treated as part of the film.[598]

Conventions and EU Directives. Protection for sound recordings first became the subject of international convention under the Rome Convention.[599] This defines a phonogram as any exclusively aural fixation of sounds of a performance or of other sounds.[600] The Convention requires signatories to grant national treatment to producers of sound recordings who are nationals of a contracting state or where the sound was recorded in a contracting state or published in a contracting state. The United Kingdom's adherence to the Convention did not require amendment to be made to the 1956 Act. At the European level, the scope of protection for sound recordings is the subject of various Directives. This is dealt with in Ch.6.   **3–76**

(ii) Under the 1988 Act

Statutory definition: sound recording. Sound recordings are protected as a separate description of works under s.1(1)(b) of the 1988 Act.[601] A sound recording is defined as a recording either of sounds from which the sounds may be reproduced, or of the whole or any part of a literary, dramatic or musical work, from which sounds reproducing the work or part of the work may be produced.[602] The first limb of the definition is intended to cover a recording where there is no underlying work, such as a recording of people talking, or of other sounds such as the sounds of wildlife, whereas the second limb is intended to cover the recording of the performance of works which may themselves be the subject of separate copyrights. There is clearly a large degree of overlap between these two limbs of the definition.[603] In the case of a recording of a performance of a work, the protection granted to the sound recording is separate from any rights in the performance itself and to any recording rights which may exist in relation to the performance.[604]   **3–77**

The definition makes it clear that the nature of the carrier, that is the physical medium on which the sound recording is stored, is irrelevant, as is also the

---

[596] Copyright Act 1956 s.12(1) and (2).

[597] Copyright Act 1956 s.12(9).

[598] Copyright Act 1956 s.13(10).

[599] The International Convention for the Protection of Performers, Producers of Phonograms and Broadcasting Organisations signed at Rome on October 26, 1961. See, generally, Ch.24.

[600] art.3(b); for the text of the Convention, see Vol.2 F5.

[601] Following the position adopted under the 1956 Act s.12(1) and (2). This had not been the position under the 1911 Act; see para.3–74, above.

[602] CDPA 1988 s.5A; re-enacting the previous definition which was contained in s.5(1). The renumbering is a consequence of the introduction by the Duration of Copyright and Rights in Performances Regulations 1995 (SI 1995/3297) of the new provisions as to films, now contained in s.5B.

[603] This was accepted during the debate of this provision: see *Hansard*, HL Vol.490, col.855. Since the definition in the 1956 Act was equally apt to cover both sorts of recordings, it is not clear why it was thought necessary to change the definition from the shorter and simpler one contained in the 1956 Act s.12(9), which was: the aggregate of the sounds embodied in and capable of being reproduced by means of a record of any description.

[604] i.e. rights granted under Pt II of the 1988 Act; as to which see Ch.12.

method by which the sounds are reproduced or produced.[605] As a matter of definition, therefore, a film soundtrack (that is the sound recording accompanying a film and synchronised onto the film) is a sound recording for the purposes of the 1988 Act.[606]

3–78   **Soundtracks of films.** The 1988 Act, as originally enacted, introduced a change in the treatment of soundtracks of films by including them in the definition of sound recordings. Under the 1956 Act, soundtracks were expressly excluded from the definition of sound recordings,[607] and the definition of a cinematograph film under that Act included sounds embodied in any soundtrack associated with the film.[608] The position from August 1, 1989, therefore, was that the soundtrack of a film, including a soundtrack existing at that date,[609] was entitled to copyright protection as a sound recording.[610]

However, since January 1, 1996, the position has reverted to what it was under the 1956 Act, in that although the definition of a sound recording remains unaltered, a soundtrack accompanying a film, including a soundtrack in existence at that date,[611] is, since such date, to be treated as part of the film for the purposes of Pt I of the 1988 Act.[612]

G. FILMS

(i) History of protection

3–79   **The position pre-1912.** At the time of their early development, at the end of the nineteenth century, films were not protected in their own right, but only as a series of photographs.[613] Photographs were required to be protected under the Berne Convention,[614] although not then included in the principal category of literary and artistic works.[615] Cinematograph productions were first required to be protected under Berne as a result of revision of the Convention at the Berlin Conference in 1908.[616] Protection was to be granted to cinematograph productions as literary or artistic works if, by the arrangement of the acting form or the combination of the incidents represented, the author gave the work a personal and original character.

3–80   **The position under the 1911 Act.** Under the 1911 Act, there was still no copyright in a film as such. As had been the position before, a film was regarded as a

---

[605] CDPA 1988 s.5A.

[606] This was not the position under the 1956 Act s.12(9), which expressly excluded a soundtrack associated with a cinematograph film. But see, as to the position now, para.3–78, below.

[607] Copyright Act 1956 s.12(9).

[608] Copyright Act 1956 s.13(9).

[609] CDPA 1988 Sch.1 para.8(1); subject to the provisions of para.8(2).

[610] This reverted to the position under the 1911 Act, under which the soundtrack of a film was separately protected as a contrivance by means of which sounds might be mechanically reproduced.

[611] reg.26(1) of the Duration of Copyright and Rights in Performances Regulations 1995 (SI 1995/3297).

[612] CDPA 1988 s.5B(2); introduced by the Duration of Copyright and Rights in Performances Regulations 1995 (SI 1995/3297). For an example, see *Football Association Premier League Ltd v QC Leisure* [2008] EWHC 1411 (Ch); [2008] F.S.R. 32, para.198.

[613] Under the Fine Arts Copyright Act 1862 (25 & 26 Vict., c.68). There was no protection for the acting performance as a dramatic work under the Dramatic Copyright Act 1833 (3 & 4 Will. 4, c.15), because of the requirement that such a work had to be capable of being printed and published: *Tate v Fullbrook* [1908] 1 K.B. 821.

[614] Berne Convention art.3.

[615] Berne Convention art.2.

[616] Berlin Act art.14(2).

series of photographs, each photograph being capable of protection as an artistic work.[617] Protection was maintained by the 1911 Act in respect of any films so protected immediately before July 1, 1912.[618] In addition, under the 1911 Act the production was protected as a dramatic work where the arrangement or acting form, or the combination of incidents represented, gave the work an original character.[619] The soundtrack was protected as a contrivance by means of which sounds might be mechanically reproduced.[620] There was also a separate literary or dramatic copyright in any scenario or script.[621]

The position under the 1956 Act. Following the recommendation of the 1952 Copyright Committee, the 1956 Act introduced a separate regime for the protection of cinematograph films in their own right.[622] A cinematograph film was defined as any sequence of visual images recorded on material of any description (whether translucent or not) so as to be capable, by the use of that material, either of being shown as a moving picture, or of being recorded on other material (whether translucent or not) by the use of which it can be so shown.[623] This definition made it clear that the work which was the subject of protection was the content of the film, that is, the sequence of visual images, regardless of the medium on which it was recorded. The definition expressly made a film soundtrack part of the film.[624] **3–81**

(ii) Under the 1988 Act

Statutory definition: film. Under the 1988 Act, a film is defined as a recording on any medium from which a moving image may by any means be produced.[625] This definition retains the essential element of a moving image,[626] found in the definition of a cinematograph film contained in the 1956 Act,[627] but is otherwise in a much simplified form which removes any doubt that may have existed as to whether the definition under the 1956 Act covered video recordings.[628] The scope of protection for films is the subject of various EU Directives, and is dealt with in Ch.6. **3–82**

Soundtracks of films. Film soundtracks, protected under the 1956 Act as part of **3–83**

---

[617] *Pathé Pictures Ltd v Bancroft* [1928–1935] Mac. C.C. 403; *Barker, etc. Ltd v Hulton (E.) & Co Ltd* (1912) 28 T.L.R. 496; *Nordisk Films Co Ltd v Onda* [1917–1923] Mac. C.C. 337.

[618] Copyright Act 1911 s.24(1).

[619] Copyright Act 1911 s.35(1), reflecting art.14(2) of the Berlin Act.

[620] Copyright Act 1911 s.19(1).

[621] *Milligan v The Broadway Cinema Productions Ltd* (1923) S.L.T. 35.

[622] Copyright Act 1956 s.13.

[623] s.13(10).

[624] s.13(9).

[625] CDPA 1988 s.5B(1); re-enacting the previous definition which was contained in s.5(1). The re-numbering is a consequence of the introduction by the Duration of Copyright and Rights in Performances Regulations 1995 (SI 1995/3297) of new provisions as to authorship of films and duration of the term of copyright in films.

[626] A single frame of a film cannot therefore itself constitute a film, nor is it protectable as a photograph (see para.3–59, above), although it is protectable as part of a film: see CDPA 1988 s.17(4) and para.7–81, below and *Football Association Premier League Ltd v QC Leisure* [2008] EWHC 1411 (Ch); [2008] F.S.R. 32 at paras 224–7. As to the position under the 1956 Act, see *Spelling Goldberg Productions Inc v B.P.C. Publishing* [1981] R.P.C. 283.

[627] See para.3–81, above.

[628] Following the recommendation of the 1977 Copyright Committee, Cmnd.6732, paras 889 and 916, that this should be made clear, notwithstanding their view that video recordings were within the definition in the 1956 Act. Note that a film, if it is a work of action, may be protected both as a "film" within the meaning of the Act and as a dramatic work: *Norowzian v Arks Ltd (No.2)* [2000] F.S.R. 363. See para.3–39, above, for a discussion of this case.

the film,[629] became entitled to copyright separately as sound recordings under the 1988 Act as originally enacted,[630] but since January 1, 1996 are to be treated, once again, as part of the film.[631]

H. BROADCASTS

(i) History of protection

(a) *Introduction*

3–84   Today, there are gathered together under the one heading of "broadcasts" what had previously been two separate protected subject matters, namely broadcasts consisting of wireless transmissions (which were called simply broadcasts) and broadcasts by cable (which were called cable programmes). With effect from October 31, 2003, there is a single protected subject matter only, namely broadcasts. This history of protection deals with each in turn.

(b) *History of protection of wireless broadcasts*

3–85   **No protection of broadcasts under 1911 Act.** The 1911 Act gave no protection to broadcasts as such.[632]

3–86   **Position under the** 1956 Act. As a result of strong representations made to it, the 1952 Copyright Committee recommended that a broadcasting authority should have the right to prevent the copying of its programmes and should also have a performing right in television programmes, but not in sound programmes.[633] These recommendations were partly taken up in s.14 of the 1956 Act,[634] which conferred a variety of exclusive rights by way of copyright in respect of television and sound broadcasts made by the British Broadcasting Corporation or by the Independent Broadcasting Authority[635] from a place in the United Kingdom. This right was conferred, however, only in respect of television and sound broadcasts made after June 1, 1957.[636]

3–87   **Broadcasts under the 1988 Act as originally enacted.** This protection continued under the 1988 Act, although the distinction between television and sound broadcasts was abandoned in favour of a single composite definition. A

---

[629] See para.3–75, above.

[630] CDPA 1988 s.5(1).

[631] Following the introduction of s.5B(2) by the Duration of Copyright and Rights in Performances Regulations 1995 (SI 1995/3297).

[632] In so far as a programme which was broadcast included a literary, dramatic or musical work in which copyright subsisted, the act of broadcasting did not infringe that copyright but the public performance of the material which has broadcast, or its reproduction on a record or other device, would have constituted an infringement of that copyright, if unlicensed. In so far as the material which was broadcast did not enjoy copyright protection itself, a performance by a person who received the broadcast in a public place did not involve an infringement of copyright, nor was it an infringement of copyright to record the performance on a record or other device. This applied, in particular, to broadcasts of outside events, such as sporting events, processions, and historic occasions.

[633] Cmnd.8662, paras 117, 186 and 192.

[634] The Act went further than the recommendations and conferred a performing right protecion on sound recordings.

[635] Formerly the Independent Television Authority: Sound Broadcasting Act 1972 (c.31) s.1, repealed and replaced by Independent Broadcasting Authority Act 1973 (c.19) ss.1, 38 and 39.

[636] Copyright Act 1956 Sch.7 para.17.

broadcast was defined as a transmission by wireless telegraphy[637] of visual images, sounds or other information which was either capable of being lawfully received by members of the public, or was transmitted for presentation to members of the public.[638]

(c) *Cable transmissions*

No protection until January 1, 1985. Cable programme services, or diffusion services as they were originally known, were not the subject of copyright protection in the United Kingdom either under the 1911 Act, or under the 1956 Act as originally enacted. This led to the 1977 Copyright Committee recommending that cable companies should enjoy a copyright in originated transmissions, just as broadcasters did under the 1956 Act.[639] This recommendation was implemented by the introduction into the 1956 Act of s.14A by the Cable and Broadcasting Act 1984.[640] The new right did not apply to cable programmes included in a cable programme service before January 1, 1985.[641]   **3–88**

The 1988 Act, as enacted. This regime was altered by the 1988 Act. The protected subject matter was now called a cable programme and comprised what was transmitted by cable.[642] However, not all transmissions by cable were protectable as cable programmes, only those items included in a "cable programme service".[643] A cable programme service was defined as a service consisting wholly or mainly in sending visual images, sounds or other information by means of a telecommunications system[644] other than one which was a transmission by wireless telegraphy.[645] In order to give rise to a cable programme in which copyright could subsist, the cable service had to be aimed at an audience of more than one, in that it had to be a service for sending information for reception either at two or more places (whether for simultaneous reception or at different times in response to requests by different users) or for presentation to members of the public.[646] An internet website, which allowed information to be sent to members of the public who accessed the website, was considered arguably to satisfy this definition and to be a cable programme service.[647]   **3–89**

A number of services were excluded from the definition of cable programme

---

[637] Defined as the sending of electro-magnetic energy over paths not provided by a material substance constructed or arranged for that purpose: CDPA 1988 s.178. This definition was amended with effect from December 1, 1996 to exclude transmissions of microwave technology between terrestrial fixed points (reg.8 of the Copyright and Related Rights Regulations 1996 (SI 1996/2967)). This amendment had little effect on what was a broadcast, given the further requirement that a broadcast had to be intended for reception by the public.

[638] CDPA 1988 s.6(1).

[639] Cmnd.6732, para.468(x).

[640] c.46.

[641] The commencement date of s.22 of the Cable and Broadcasting Act 1984; see Copyright Act 1956 s.14A(11).

[642] CDPA 1988 s.1(1)(b).

[643] CDPA 1988 s.7(1), as enacted; this had also been the position under s.14A of the 1956 Act.

[644] CDPA 1988 s.7(1). A telecommunications system was defined by s.178 to be a means for conveying visual images, sounds or other information by electronic means.

[645] CDPA 1988 s.7(1) and see s.178 for the definition of wireless telegraphy. This exclusion ensured that the subject matter of a transmission could not qualify for copyright protection both as a broadcast and as a cable programme.

[646] CDPA 1988 s.7(1). This aspect of the definition would, it is suggested, have excluded an email service from qualifying as a cable programme service, notwithstanding that the electronic signals were conveyed by cable. It would in any event have been excluded by the provisions of s.7(2)(a), as to which see later in the text. See, in this respect, *Hansard*, HL Vol.495, col.616.

[647] See *The Shetland Times v Wills* [1997] E.M.L.R. 277, approved, obiter, in *Sony Music Entertainment (UK) Ltd v Easyinternetcafe Ltd* [2003] EWHC 62; [2003] F.S.R. 48 (Ch), at para.47. The website contained articles and photographs taken from a local newspaper.

service by s.7(2) of the 1988 Act.[648] The first exception was aimed at interactive services. Thus there was excepted a service or part of a service which had as an essential feature not only the transmission of visual images, sounds or other information to the recipient but also the reception from the recipient of information (other than signals sent for the operation or control of the service).[649] The words in brackets ensured that the service was not excepted merely because the recipient could exercise a choice as to what was transmitted to him, for example, by selecting, in the case of a video on-demand cable service, the particular film or programme which he wished to see. The effect of this exception, together with those words, was to ensure that those parts of an interactive service in which sound, images or other information were conveyed to the user were within the definition of a cable programme service, so that those elements transmitted were capable of being protected as cable programmes, whilst those elements that were genuinely interactive (the placing of an order or the inputting of data) were not part of a cable programme service, and therefore were not capable of being protected by copyright as a cable programme.[650] The remaining exceptions dealt with services which were not truly aimed at the public. They included: a service run for the purposes of a business, or by an individual for domestic purposes, and which was entirely within the control of such business or individual, and was not connected to any other telecommunications system[651]; a service operating in or connecting premises in single occupation (except where the services formed part of the amenities provided for residents or inmates of premises run as a business) and not connected to any other telecommunications system[652]; and a service run for persons providing broadcasting or cable programme services or programmes for such services.[653]

(d) *International Conventions*

3–90   **The protection of broadcasts under international conventions.** The first international convention to deal with broadcasts was the European Agreement on the Protection of Television Broadcasts.[654] This Convention applied to the visual and sound elements of television broadcasts, but not to sound-only broadcasts.

---

[648] CDPA 1988 s.7(1) excluded any service which was excepted, or to the extent that it was excepted, by s.7(2) of the 1988 Act. The reference to the extent to which a service was excepted meant that merely because some elements of the service fell within an exception, the remainder of the service was not excluded from being a cable programme service. Thus, an item transmitted as part of the service which was not excepted was a cable programme, whilst an item transmitted as part of the service which was excepted has not.

[649] CDPA 1988 s.7(2)(a).

[650] See *Hansard*, HL Vol.138, cols 113, 114 and Vol.501, cols 204–206.

[651] CDPA 1988 s.7(2)(b) and (c). The latter was intended to ensure that a system which was entirely domestic, i.e. comprising equipment in the private home which was not linked to any outside cable system, was not a cable programme service: *Hansard*, HL Vol.490, col.867. The exception excluded therefore, an internal telephone system in domestic or business premises, but not if it was linked to British Telecom's network or to some other network.

[652] CDPA 1988 s.7(2)(d). This exception excluded a computer network in an office, provided it was not connected to an external network, but the words in brackets ensured that cable systems in hotels, hostels, residential homes, etc. were not excepted, so that items transmitted on such services (for example, announcements of interest to the residents concerning activities, weather, local news, etc.) were capable of being cable programmes in which copyright might subsist.

[653] CDPA 1988 s.7(2)(e). Programmes made for broadcast are often transmitted by cable to the place from which they are to be broadcast; similarly, broadcasts may be transmitted by cable to a cable operator, for inclusion in that cable operator's service; this exception ensured that when such transmissions were made by others as part of a service provided for the programme maker and broadcaster, respectively, such a service was not itself treated as a cable programme service.

[654] Concluded at Strasbourg on June 22, 1960 and which was ratified by the UK on October 30, 1963 and entered into force on May 18, 1964. For the text of this Convention see Vol.2 F3.

The Rome Convention[655] provided protection for all forms of broadcasting, defined as the transmission by wireless means for public reception of sounds, or of images and sounds.[656] These Conventions did not require any amendment to be made to the 1956 Act, but resulted in protection being applied to foreign broadcasts by Orders in Council made under the 1956 Act.

(e) *European Directives*

The Rental and Related Rights Directive,[657] the Satellite and Cable Directive[658] and subsequently the Information Society Directive,[659] required Member States to grant broadcasting organisations various rights in relation to their broadcasts,[660] and thus recognised broadcasts as being entitled to protection (as a "related right"). Cable broadcasters were to some extent regarded as broadcasters for these purposes.[661] No amendment needed to be made to the definitions of the protected subject matter in order to implement these Directives but, as will be seen, substantial amendments to their definitions became necessary as part of the implementation of the Information Society Directive.   **3–91**

(f) *The 1988 Act, as amended*

Introduction. Under the 1988 Act as enacted, as under the 1956 Act, the definitions used in relation to the protected subject matters of a broadcast and a cable programme were also used to determine what amounted to an infringement of copyright (i.e. to define the acts restricted by copyright) by way of the unlicensed broadcasting or cable transmission of a work.[662] Thus, for example, a "broadcast" was defined for the purposes of the protected subject matter, and the same definition was used when it came to the restricted act of "broadcasting" a work. The same applied to the protected subject matter of "cable programme" and the restricted act of including a work in a "cable programme service". The Information Society Directive[663] required the United Kingdom to alter the nature of these restricted acts, particularly in relation to transmission of a work by means of an on-demand service, and this in turn caused the United Kingdom to alter the definitions of the protected subject matter. The result has been that the link which had previously existed between the protected subject matter and the acts restricted by copyright has been broken. These amendments were made by the Copyright and Related Rights Regulations 2003.[664]   **3–92**

Broadcast: basic definition. With effect from October 31, 2003, a broadcast means an electronic transmission of visual images, sounds or other information which (a) is transmitted for simultaneous reception by members of the public and is capable of being lawfully received by them, or (b) is transmitted at a time determined solely by the person making the transmission for presentation to   **3–93**

---

[655] The International Conventions for the Protection of Performers, Producers of Phonograms and Broadcasting Organisations, signed at Rome on October 26, 1961, and which was also ratified by the UK on October 30, 1963 and entered into force on May 18, 1964. See Ch.23. For the text, see Vol.2 F5.

[656] Rome Convention art.3(f).

[657] Directive 92/100. This Directive and its amendments have now been codified as Directive 2006/115/EC: [2006] OJ L376/28. The new Directive took effect on January 16, 2007: art.15.

[658] Directive 93/83.

[659] Directive 2001/29.

[660] See arts 2, 3 of the Rental and Related Rights Directive and arts 7–10 of Directive 2006/115/EC.

[661] See arts 7(2) and (3) of Directive 2006/115/EC.

[662] i.e. in CDPA 1988 s.20.

[663] Directive 2001/29.

[664] SI 2003/2498, coming into force on October 31, 2003.

members of the public, and which is not an excepted internet transmission.[665] The subject matter of protection under s.1(1)(b) of the 1988 Act is therefore the transmission, not the works which happen to be included in the transmission. The essential element of this definition, namely that copyright is capable of subsisting in visual images, sounds and information which are broadcast, remains as before. The definition is intended to be technologically neutral, that is, it should embrace both wireless transmissions and cable transmissions of a broadcast character.[666] The definition therefore no longer contains any reference to wireless telegraphy and requires simply that the transmission be an electronic one.[667] Thus it covers both wireless transmissions and transmissions by cable and the like, or those which are partly one and partly the other.

3–94   **Broadcast to "the public".** It is implicit in the concept of a broadcast as a means of communication that the communication should be intended for wide simultaneous dissemination, that is, to more than one person at the same time. This is made clear by the fact that in order for a transmission to be a broadcast for these purposes, it must either be transmitted for simultaneous reception by members of the public or be transmitted for presentation to members of the public. While the expression "the public" has a wide meaning,[668] the relevant sector is cut down by other parts of the definition, considered in the following paragraphs.

3–95   **Transmission of visual images, sounds or other information.** These were the expressions used in the 1988 Act in the case of both a broadcast and a cable programme. "Other information" was probably intended to cover data transmissions of the kind sent in the vertical blanking interval.[669]

3–96   **Broadcast: the first limb.** The expressions "transmitted for simultaneous reception by members of the public" and "capable of being lawfully received by them" are grounded in the original definition of broadcast in the 1988 Act.[670] It clearly covers the traditional form of broadcast, where there is no possibility of the recipient being able to influence the time or content of the transmission. Capability of reception implies merely that the electronic signals can be captured and reproduced by members of the public by means of appropriate equipment.[671]

3–97   **Capable of lawful reception.** The requirement that the broadcast should be capable of being lawfully received introduces an important qualification. In the present context, it has two aspects: first, it prevents those transmissions which are not intended for public consumption from falling within the definition of a broadcast, particularly those transmissions by wireless telegraphy which are not intended for public reception; and secondly, encrypted broadcasts. As to the first aspect, in the United Kingdom it remains illegal to use wireless telegraphy appa-

[665] CDPA 1988 s.6(1), as amended. References to broadcasting are to be construed accordingly: ibid. As to excepted internet transmissions, see para.3–101, below.

[666] See the Government Conclusions on the Patent Office's Consultation Paper of August 7, 2002, para.3.6.

[667] Electronic is defined as meaning actuated by electric, magnetic, electro-magnetic, electro-chemical or electro-mechanical energy: CDPA 1988 s.178.

[668] See, e.g. the expression "to the public", considered in Ch.7.

[669] A business sprang up in the 1980s whereby BBC Worldwide sold data carrying capacity in the BBC's broadcasts to companies and other organisations that needed to transmit data to recipients located across the country.

[670] CDPA 1988 s.6(1)(a): "a 'broadcast' means a transmission by wireless telegraphy ... which is capable of being received by members of the public".

[671] Reception, in this context, also includes reception of the broadcast relayed by means of a telecommunications system, such as a cable network (CDPA 1988 s.6(5)). Telecommunications system means a system for conveying visual images, sounds or other information by electronic means (s.178).

ratus, which includes a radio receiver, without a licence under the Wireless Telegraphy Act 1949, unless the use of the apparatus is exempted by regulation.[672] Apparatus used only for the reception of messages sent by authorised broadcasting stations or by licensed amateur stations is exempt, and therefore the use by a member of the public of equipment which is lawfully available for purchase for the purpose of receiving such signals is lawful without a licence. However, the use of such equipment for the reception of other radio transmissions without a licence remains unlawful. This will include transmissions by the police and emergency authorities, irrespective of whether such transmissions are unencrypted or not. There are therefore many transmissions which are capable of being received by members of the public on equipment which can be lawfully purchased in this country, but which are nevertheless excluded from being broadcasts for the purposes of the 1988 Act, because reception of such broadcasts by a member of the public is illegal in the United Kingdom. It is also illegal intentionally to intercept a communication in the course of its transmission by means of a public telecommunication system.[673] Communications by and to mobile telephones cannot therefore fall within the definition of a broadcast, as they may not be lawfully received except by the member of the public for whom they are intended.[674] A licence is, however, required for the lawful use of a television receiver, but since such licence is available to any member of the public, on payment of the required fee, any broadcast which can be received on such a television set is capable of being lawfully received by members of the public, for the purposes of this definition.

Lawful reception of encrypted broadcast. Section 9(2) of the 1988 Act contains special provisions defining what amounts to lawful reception in the case of encrypted broadcasts. The Act does not define an encrypted broadcast but in general it is a broadcast transmitted in an encoded form such as not to be receivable in an intelligible form without the reception being passed through appropriate decoding equipment. Encryption enables the broadcaster to control access to its broadcast, by controlling the supply of the appropriate decoding equipment, and thus to obtain payment by subscription or on the basis of use. Without further provision, the mere reception of an encrypted broadcast would not amount to unlawful reception. In the case of such a transmission, therefore, the Act provides that test of capability of reception by the public is satisfied only if the decoding equipment necessary to unscramble the signals has been made available to members of the public by or with the authority of the person making the transmission or the person providing the contents of the transmission.[675] If, therefore, decoding equipment which enables the broadcast to be viewed or heard has been available to the public, for example by the issue of smart cards to subscribers, the broadcast becomes one which is lawfully capable of reception and therefore a protectable subject matter, whether or not any particular individual who receives the signal has lawful possession of a smart card.[676] Making the necessary decoding equipment available only to specific individuals (or companies) would not, it

3–98

---

[672] See the Wireless Telegraphy Act 1949, s.1(1); see also ibid s.5(1)(b)(i) under which it is an offence to use any wireless telegraphy apparatus with intent to obtain information as to the content of any message (whether sent by means of wireless telegraphy or not) of which neither the person using the apparatus nor the person on whose behalf he is acting is an intended recipient.

[673] Regulation of Investigatory Powers Act 2000 s.1.

[674] A different conclusion was reached by the High Court of Australia on the wording of the Australian Copyright Act 1968, in the light of its legislative history. *Telstra Corporations Ltd v Australia Performing Rights Associations Ltd* [1997] I.P.R. 294. See also the discussion in *Hansard*, HL Vol.490, cols. 860–866.

[675] CDPA 1988 s.6(2).

[676] There are various offences relating to the unauthorised use and supply of decoding equipment (see CDPA 1988 ss.297, 297A, etc. and Ch.15) but these do not affect the question of whether the broadcast itself is protected by copyright.

is suggested, be making it available to members of the public, and therefore would not satisfy this limb of the definition of a broadcast.[677]

3–99   **Broadcast, the second limb: transmitted for presentation to the public.** This limb is also grounded in the original definition of broadcast in the 1988 Act.[678] It is designed to bring within the definition transmissions which are intended by the transmitter to be played or shown to the public rather than simply being received by them.[679] It is clearly meant to include transmissions of a different kind from those covered by the first limb and does not refer to the ordinary kind of broadcasts which are transmitted for simultaneous reception by members of the public and which may also happen to be shown or played to members of the public by the recipient, for example in a pub.[680] Rather it is intended to cover those transmissions which are not transmitted for general reception by the public but by particular individuals or companies for presentation to the public. The definition does not specify how the broadcast might be presented to the public. One obvious example is the broadcast by encrypted satellite transmission of a sporting event to specific locations where the public is invited to attend for the purpose of viewing the broadcast. In such a case, the necessary decoding equipment will have been supplied to the locations, but will not have been made available to the public generally. Such a transmission is clearly a broadcast, in that it satisfies the second limb of the definition (but not the first). Similarly, an encrypted transmission of music to specific locations such as shops, pubs, restaurants, arcades, etc. for presentation to the public as background music at such locations, where the necessary decoding equipment is made available only to those locations,[681] will qualify as a broadcast under the second limb of the definition (but not, it is suggested, under the first).

3–100   **On-demand services.** The requirements that the transmission either be for simultaneous reception by the public or for reception at a time determined solely by the person making the transmission means that an on-demand or on-request transmission is not a broadcast for this purpose, except in the unlikely event of a request triggering a general transmission.[682] This marks a major change from the protection previously given to on-request or on-demand cable transmissions, which were protected under s.7 as enacted[683] and which are thus no longer protected.[684] It also represents one of the key distinctions now made between broadcasting as a protected subject matter and the new restricted act of com-

---

[677] But, if the transmission was intended for presentation to the public via these individuals or companies by means of the decoding equipment, then the second limb of the definition would be satisfied; see para.3–99, below.

[678] CDPA 1988 s.6(1)(b): "a 'broadcast' means a transmission by wireless telegraphy ... which is ... transmitted for presentation to members of the public."

[679] See the Government's conclusions on the Patent Office's Consultation Paper of August 7, 2002, para.3.9.

[680] Such transmissions are not "transmitted... *for* presentation to members of the public." If it had been the intention simply to refer to this kind of broadcast, there would be no need for the second limb at all.

[681] A service known as narrowcasting, in contrast to broadcasting.

[682] Although the Government seems to have taken a different view (see the Government's conclusions on the Patent Office's Consultation Paper of August 7, 2002, para.3.9, explaining the reason for introducing the words "at a time determined solely by the person making the transmission"), the requirement under the second limb that the transmission be for presentation to members of the public would in any event rule out virtually all on-demand transmissions.

[683] Under which a cable programme service was defined, amongst other things, as a service for reception at two or more places at different times in response to requests by different users.

[684] The reason given for this is that such services, which will inevitably rely on the transmission of recordings, will usually already contain protectable subject matter such as films and sound recordings, if not also other underlying works. It was therefore considered that there was no need to protect a cable programme as a species of copyright work, as apposed to its contents, unless it was in the nature of a broadcast: See the Government Conclusions on the Patent Office's Con-

munication of a work to the public. As will be seen, internet transmissions are in general excluded from broadcasts, leaving only internet transmissions of a broadcast character. "Near on-demand" services, by which programmes are repeatedly transmitted at frequent intervals, clearly fall within the definition of a broadcast.[685]

Excepted internet transmissions. "Internet transmissions" are generally   **3–101**
excepted from the definition of broadcast by s.9(1A). The only kind of "internet transmission" which qualifies as a broadcast is: (a) a transmission taking place simultaneously on the internet and by other means, or (b) a concurrent transmission of a live event, or (c) a transmission of recorded moving images or sounds forming part of a programme service offered by the person responsible for making the transmission, being a service in which programmes are transmitted at scheduled times determined by that person.[686] The Act contains no definition of "internet transmission" or "the internet". The general intention is said to have been to include within the protected subject matter internet transmissions or webcasts which are in the nature of a conventional broadcast and not, for example, the transmission of ordinary web pages.[687] The obvious type of internet transmission included under (a) is a webcast where a simultaneous conventional broadcast of the material is taking place by radio or television, but it is not confined to cases where the simultaneous transmission is a broadcast as defined, the only requirement being that it should be a transmission other than on the internet. A single simultaneous transmission to a private person, and not generally to or for reception by the public, would appear to be sufficient. It does not have to be a broadcast. As to the second case, (b), there is no definition of "live event", but it no doubt refers to any event happening in real time, such as a sports event, an unfolding news item or a simple piece spoken live to the camera, and thus excludes any transmission of an event which has been pre-recorded (except to the extent that the recording forms part of a "live event"). It will include webcasts of live events where there is no simultaneous conventional broadcast. The third category, (c), will include a webcast of any pre-recorded material provided it is transmitted as part of a service and in accordance with a pre-determined schedule. It does not appear that the schedule must be one that has been published (although usually it will be), only that such a schedule has been fixed by the person responsible for the transmission and that the transmission is in accordance with that schedule. The essential point is that the transmission must not be part of an on-demand service, that is, as to both as to its timing and content, it is not transmitted in direct response to a request from the recipient.

Immediate re-transmissions. The Act, as now amended, also provides that the   **3–102**
relaying of a broadcast by its reception and immediate re-transmission is to be regarded as a separate act of broadcasting from the making of the broadcast which is so re-transmitted.[688] The effect of this is that the re-transmission is itself a pro-

sulation Paper of August 7, 2002, para.3.6. While this may true, it does not necessarily follow that the "broadcaster" will be the owner of such rights.

[685] See the Government Conclusions on the Patent Office's Consultation Paper of August 7, 2002, para.3.11.

[686] CDPA 1988 s.6(1A).

[687] See the Government's conclusions on the Patent Office's Consultation Paper of August 7, 2002, para.3.11. The transmission of emails is already effectively excluded by the lack of any transmission to the public: ibid, para.3.11.

[688] CDPA 1988 s.6(5A).

tectable broadcast. This was previously the position in relation to wireless broadcasts[689] but was not the position in relation to cable programmes.[690]

3–103 **Transitional provisions.** The amended provisions of the Act apply to works made before October 31, 2003[691] and so a broadcast which satisfies the above provisions of s.9 as amended but which did not fall within the unamended provisions will have been protectable as from October 31, 2003. The main category of newly protected works would appear to be immediate cable retransmissions of broadcasts, in which copyright now subsists.[692] Nevertheless, no act done before this date is to be regarded as an infringement of any such new broadcasting right.[693] Further, nothing in the amending regulations is to affect any agreement made before December 22, 2002 and no act done after October 31, 2003 in pursuance of an agreement made before December 22, 2002, is to be regarded as an infringement of any new broadcasting right.[694] As to works which qualified as broadcasts or cable programmes but which no longer do so, there are no saving provisions and it appears that they are no longer entitled to copyright. This is not likely to affect any old-style (wireless) broadcasts, but only cable programmes which were not of a broadcast nature.

I. Typographical Arrangements of Published Editions

3–104 **Background to protection for typographical arrangements.** The origin of this right can be traced to two developments in the publishing industry, one of them artistic and the other technological. The first was the great improvement in typographical design which was associated with the arts and crafts movement in the last two decades of the nineteenth century and the first two of the twentieth. A new font could be registered as a design but the typographic layout of a particular book, which may have taken considerable skill and effort, was not as such protected. The second was the development since the First World War of the technique of photo-lithography, which enabled printing plates to be made by photographic means. The skill and labour which had gone into the typographical design of fine editions of classical works (themselves out of copyright) could be appropriated by other publishers who used photo-lithography to make facsimile copies.[695] The 1952 Copyright Committee therefore recommended protection for typographical arrangements[696] and this was brought about by s.15(1) of the 1956 Act, which gave copyright protection to typographical arrangements of published editions of one or more literary, dramatic or musical works.

Although the United Kingdom has therefore given copyright protection to typographical arrangements of published editions since 1957, such protection is not required under the terms of the Berne Convention or any European Directive, and has not generally existed in other countries,[697] including many other European Member States. Similar considerations to those which led to the introduction of this protection in the United Kingdom resulted, however, in the creation

---

[689] Copyright was only denied to broadcasts which *infringed* the copyright in another broadcast or cable programme: s.6(6).

[690] Copyright was denied to a cable programme if it was included in a cable programme service by reception and immediate re-transmission of a broadcast: s.7(6)(a).

[691] Copyright and Related Rights Regulations 2003 r.31(1).

[692] See para.3–102, above.

[693] Copyright and Related Rights Regulations 2003 reg.31(2).

[694] Copyright and Related Rights Regulations 2003 regs 32(1), (2).

[695] *Newspaper Licensing Agency Ltd v Marks & Spencer Plc* [2001] UKHL 38; [2003] 1 A.C. 551; [2002] R.P.C. 4.

[696] Cmnd.8662, paras 308 and 310.

[697] A similar type of provision was tabled by WIPO for inclusion in its model Copyright Act, but was abandoned in 1987; see *Hecker* [1995] E.I.P.R. 75.

throughout the Community of a publication right,[698] to protect those who first publish a previously unpublished work at a time when copyright in the work has expired. Whilst the term of protection under this right and under the typographical arrangement right is the same,[699] the two provisions are, however, different in their application. In some ways the publication right is of wider application, in that it covers first publication of previously unpublished artistic works and films,[700] but in others it is of narrower application, in that it applies only to first publication of works in which copyright has expired.[701]

Statutory definition: typographical arrangement of a published edition. 3–105
Typographical arrangements of published editions are protected under s.1(1)(c) of the 1988 Act. For the purposes of that provision, "published edition" means a published edition of the whole or any part of one or more literary, dramatic or musical works.[702] The reference to the edition having been published must be construed in accordance with the definition of publication in the Act.[703] It is to be noted that there is no requirement that the work itself should still be, or indeed should ever have been, the subject of copyright,[704] although it must qualify under the Act as a literary, dramatic or musical work.[705] The definition deliberately excludes typographical arrangements of artistic works from protection. Typographical arrangement implies the layout of words or symbols on the printed page, to which the publisher has made a contribution. Where artistic works are included in a book, the publisher merely reproduces the work. In such a case, the protection of the copy of the artistic work rests solely on the copyright in the original work.[706]

Published edition. In this context, the term "published edition" is the language 3–106
of the publishing trade.[707] In the context of works comprising a number of literary works, such as newspapers, the "edition" referred to in the expression "published edition" is therefore the product, generally between covers, which the publisher offers to the public.[708] The words "one or more" in the definition of a published

---

[698] Pursuant to art.4 of Council Directive 2006/116/EC, harmonising the term of protection of copyright and certain related rights; see, generally, Ch.24. This aspect of the Directive was originally implemented by reg.16 of The Copyright and Related Rights Regulations (SI 1996/2967), with effect from December 1, 1996.

[699] i.e. 25 years from the end of the year of publication; see Chs 6 and 17, respectively.

[700] Typographical arrangements of published editions do not include artistic works (see para.3–105, below), or films.

[701] Neither subsistence of copyright, nor its expiry, in the work is a requirement for protection for the typographical arrangement of a published edition; see para.3–105, below. Also, each new typographical arrangement of a published edition is entitled to its own protection, whereas the publication right applies only on the first publication of the previously unpublished work.

[702] CDPA 1988 s.8(1), in the same terms as s.15(1) of the 1956 Act.

[703] CDPA 1988 s 175(1). See paras 3–174 et seq., below.

[704] Compare the new publication right, granted in respect of the first publication of a previously unpublished work after copyright in the work has expired; see generally Ch.17.

[705] See *Machinery Market Ltd v Sheen Publishing Ltd* [1983] F.S.R. 431.

[706] See *Hansard*, HL Vol.490, cols 870, 871. In *X Ltd v Nowacki* [2003] EWHC (Ch) 1928 at para.52, the layout of wording designed to be stamped on the underside of tableware, the words being set in various different fonts, was held to be an artistic work, and thus a separate copyright work from any copyright that might subsist in typographical arrangement of the words under CDPA 1988 s.1(1)(c).

[707] *Newspaper Licensing Agency Ltd v Marks & Spencer Plc* [2001] UKHL 38; [2003] 1 A.C. 551.

[708] *Newspaper Licensing Agency Ltd v Marks & Spencer Plc* [2001] UKHL 38, approving *Nationwide News Pty Ltd v Copyright Agency Ltd* (1995) 128 A.L.R. 285 (Fed Ct of Aus) and disapproving *Machinery Market Ltd v Sheen Publishing Ltd* [1983] F.S.R. 431, which had proceeded on the unchallenged but incorrect assumption that copyright subsisted in the typographical arrangement of a single advertisement appearing in a newspaper, i.e. in the arrangement of a single literary work rather than the whole newspaper.

edition[709] show that one may have a single published edition of more than one literary work and that there is therefore no necessary congruence between the concept of an edition and the underlying works.[710] "Published edition" does not therefore refer to the published edition of each literary work appearing in the newspaper[711] but to the published edition of the whole newspaper.[712] While there may be borderline cases in which two or more distinct products are offered simultaneously at a single price, such as a newspaper with typographically distinct supplements or "inserts", it is unlikely that the point will matter in practice, because it is unlikely to affect the question of infringement (see para.7–85, below). Similarly, in the case of a work such as an anthology of poems, the published edition copyright will subsist in the typographical arrangement of the entire collection contained between the two covers, and not of a number of copyrights consisting of the typographical arrangement of each poem.[713]

3. FIXATION

A. FIXATION IN GENERAL

3–107   **Introduction.** It is a long-established principle of copyright law that copyright does not subsist in a work unless and until the work takes some material form. This principle is known as the requirement of fixation. The reasons for this principle are practical. Since copyright is a form of monopoly in relation to the subject matter which is protected, there must be certainty as to what that subject matter is.[714] This is necessary both so as to be able to prove the existence of the work and to establish what the work consists of, so that it can be judged whether the work has been copied or otherwise infringed. Fixation also provides a limit to the monopoly, ensuring that the protection accorded to the work does not extend beyond the expression of the work to the ideas or information contained or represented in it. This is necessary in holding a balance between the author's interests and society's interests. Further, fixation provides a defined moment when the work takes existence, essential for the purpose of applying the rules as to the status of its author.

3–108   **Fixation under the Berne and Rome Conventions.** The principle of fixation is of general application, and is referred to both in the Berne Convention[715] and in the Rome Convention.[716] Of the subject matter protected under the Rome Conven-

---

[709] "'published edition' ... means a published edition of the whole or any part of one or more literary, dramatic or musical works".

[710] *Newspaper Licensing Agency Ltd v Marks & Spencer Plc* [2001] UKHL 38; [2003] 1 A.C. 551.

[711] With the consequence that the newspaper as a whole does not consist of many published editions.

[712] *Newspaper Licensing Agency Ltd v Marks & Spencer Plc* [2001] UKHL 38.

[713] *Newspaper Licensing Agency Ltd v Marks & Spencer Plc* [2001] UKHL 38.

[714] See *Tate v Fullbrook* [1908] 1 K.B. 821; *Tate v Thomas* [1921] 1 Ch. 503; and *Green v Broadcasting Corporation of New Zealand* [1989] R.P.C. 700, PC, discussed at para.3–43, above, in relation to dramatic works. See also *IPC Media Limited v Highbury-Leisure Publishing Limited* [2004] EWHC 2985 (Ch); [2005] F.S.R. 20 at paras 7 and 8, and *Baigent v The Random House Group Limited* [2006] EWHC 719 (Ch); [2006] E.M.L.R. 16 at para.156, citing the need for certainty as a reason for the absence of copyright protection for ideas at a high level of abstraction: "if what is asserted to be infringed is so general that it cannot be certain that would lead to a conclusion that it is [at] such a level of abstraction that no protection should be afforded to it". This statement was not the subject of comment in the Court of Appeal: [2007] EWCA Civ 247; [2007] R.P.C. 25; [2007] E.M.L.R. 14; [2007] E.C.D.R. 6.

[715] Berne Convention art.2(2), which provides that it is for Union Countries to prescribe any requirements of fixation.

[716] In various articles relating to the protection of performances and phonograms. However, the

tion, fixation is a requirement in the definition of a phonogram.[717] It has no application to a broadcast, which is essentially of an ephemeral nature.

Distinction between fixation and requirement as to form of a work. Whilst the principle of fixation requires that the work be reduced to a material form (for example in the case of a literary work, that it be recorded, in writing or otherwise), this is a separate matter from any requirement as to the form a particular work should take (in the case of a literary work, that it be written, spoken or sung). The requirement as to a particular form is an integral part of the description of the work; unless it is in that form, it does not constitute a work of that description. The requirement as to reduction to a material form is part of the conditions which the designated work must satisfy in order to qualify for copyright protection. Where there is a requirement as to a particular form, and this is met, the requirement as to fixation may also be met, but this is not necessarily so,[718] and this coincidence, when it does occur, should not obscure the distinction between the two. The distinction has not always been clear under earlier Copyright Acts,[719] which tended to describe any requirement as to fixation as being a requirement as to the particular form of the work, but this distinction is clearly made in the 1988 Act.

3–109

Material not in a permanent form. The courts have often experienced a difficulty in according a work copyright protection where the first embodiment of the work is considered to have or to have had a transient or ephemeral existence.[720] This is to confuse the requirement that the work should take a material form before copyright subsists with a requirement that such form should be permanent, or have a degree of permanence. It also confuses the physical material on or in which the work is first reduced to a material form with the copyright work, which continues to exist whatever happens to the first embodiment of the work. There is no reason in principle why a work which was always intended to have a fleeting existence should not be protected by copyright, if it otherwise satisfies the conditions for copyright to subsist in it.

3–110

Separate existence of work and material on which fixed. It follows from what has been said that the work, once fixed, continues to have a separate, disembodied, existence from the material form in which it is fixed. The record of the work may, indeed, be entitled to its own copyright as a separate work.[721] This is so even in those cases where the statute has prescribed a particular form as part of the description of the work itself. Destruction of the material form in which the work was fixed does not destroy the work itself, nor the copyright which came into existence upon its being fixed.[722] This is equally so in the case where the expression of the work which qualifies it as a work takes the material form in which the work is fixed, as is the case in many artistic works, for example a painting or a sculpture.

3–111

---

principle has most application in relation to works protected under Berne, that is, in the United Kingdom, to literary, dramatic, musical, artistic and cinematograph works.

[717] It is referred to in relation to a performance, but is not a requirement for protection of a performance.

[718] See, e.g. *Hadley v Kemp* [1999] E.M.L.R. 589 (words and music of songs in existence before being recorded for the first time).

[719] For a good example, see the discussion in para.3–118, below in relation to dramatic works.

[720] This was particularly the case where an intermediate work made in the course of an industrial process was sought to be protected as a work of sculpture; see the discussion at para.3–60, above. See also *Merchandising Corporation of America Inc v Harpbond* [1983] F.S.R. 32, where the court apparently took the view that no copyright could subsist in a face painting because it was too ephemeral.

[721] e.g. a dramatic work first recorded on film.

[722] If this were not so, copyright in a painting could not be infringed if the painting had been destroyed, since infringement is defined by reference to the exclusive right of the copyright owner to "copy the work": see CDPA 1988 s.16(1)(a).

3–112 **Immaterial by whom fixed.** Since fixation addresses the issue of the definition of the work, and proof as to its existence and content, there is no reason of principle why the person who creates the work and the person who fixes the work should be the same. The functions of creation and fixation are distinct, as in the case of a person who first records the spoken words of another. Copyright protects the skill and labour of the author, and once he has created and expressed his work, it is immaterial how his work comes to be fixed.

3–113 **Fixation under the** 1988 Act. As will be seen, prior to the 1988 Act, the requirement of fixation tended to be expressed as an aspect of the definition of a particular work. The 1988 Act gives clear expression to the requirement of fixation as a separate requirement and in doing so reflects the principles as to fixation discussed above.

B. LITERARY, DRAMATIC AND MUSICAL WORKS

3–114 Fixation is now an express requirement for copyright to subsist in a literary, dramatic or musical work, the Act providing that copyright does not subsist in a literary, dramatic or musical work until it is recorded, in writing or otherwise.[723] The form of fixation required by the Act for these works is thus expressed in wide terms. The width is in the "or otherwise", which makes it clear that the nature of the medium on which the record is made is irrelevant.[724] The Act also makes it clear that the work may be recorded for the purposes of fixation by someone other than the author, and that it is immaterial whether this takes place with the author's consent or not.[725]

3–115 **Fixation of a literary work.** In the case of a literary work, the definition of the work as being a work which is written, spoken or sung[726] makes it clear that the definition of the work does not now contain its own requirement as to fixation, since writing is only one form which such a work can take, and speaking and singing, whilst forms of expression, are not a reduction of the work to a recorded form. This definition means that an original *ex tempore* speech, lecture or judgment is capable of being protected as a literary work once delivered, provided that some record of it, whether in shorthand or by some technical recording means, was made when it was delivered. Similarly, the lyrics of a song, even though not previously written down, are capable of being protected as a literary work once they are sung, provided that the singing is recorded, as will often be the case when such performance is given as part of a recording session in a studio.

Since it is immaterial by whom the literary work is in fact recorded,[727] if an author dictates a work to another who makes a record of it by whatever means, he will acquire copyright in his material as a literary work at the moment it is recorded. This is on the basis that the person dictating the material is in fact the author of it; it is immaterial that the other is not an employee.[728] Similarly, in the case of an original *ex tempore* speech, lecture or judgment which is recorded by another by some means, the person delivering the same is entitled to copyright in the speech, lecture or judgment, whilst the person recording the same will be entitled to a separate (but necessarily dependent) copyright, i.e. as a as a literary work if the record is in written form (e.g. a form of shorthand) or as a sound re-

---

[723] CDPA 1988 s.3(2).

[724] The definition of writing is discussed at para.3–11, above.

[725] CDPA 1988 s.3(3), following the recommendation of the 1977 Copyright Committee, Cmnd.6732, para.609(viii).

[726] Discussed at para.3–14, above.

[727] CDPA 1988 s.3(3).

[728] See *Donoghue v Allied Newspapers Ltd* [1938] Ch. 106, and para.4–10, below.

cording if by some technical means which can reproduce the spoken words. Again, the pop musician who performs a song comprising lyrics composed in his head creates a literary work when he sings such lyrics in a recording studio and they are recorded, and it is immaterial that the sound recording is made by the recording studio or the record company. In such cases, there will be separate copyrights, often in separate ownership, in the literary work and the recording.

Fixation of literary works under earlier Acts. The 1956 Act did not contain any such clear requirement as to fixation but contained provisions relating to the time when a literary, dramatic or musical work was "made",[729] and it would seem that a work had to be "made" before copyright could subsist in it.[730] In this context, references to the time at which a work was made were to be taken as references to the time at which it was first reduced to writing or some other material form.[731] It was unclear whether, for example, the recording on tape of a literary work amounted to reduction of the work to some material form; the view expressed in earlier editions of *Copinger* was that some form of notation was required.[732] Under equivalent provisions of the Irish Act it has been decided that reduction of the work onto tape is not sufficient on the grounds that "the symbol which comprises the notation must be capable without more of being understood"[733] but this seems doubtful. There is no requirement that the literary content of the material form be directly accessible by a human being. The 1911 Act contained no equivalent provision and the position under that Act is uncertain. Under the earlier Acts, statutory copyright did not subsist in mere spoken words.[734]

Fixation of a dramatic work. Under the 1988 Act, any form of recording of a dramatic work is sufficient to satisfy the requirement of fixation.[735]

Fixation of dramatic works under earlier Acts. Under the 1911 Act, a dramatic work was expressly defined as something which was fixed in writing or otherwise.[736] Although expressed as a requirement of the form of a dramatic work, this requirement was really no more than a fixation requirement, since it acknowledged that a dramatic work could exist independently of the particular form in which it was fixed. Under the 1956 Act,[737] however, a dramatic work was required to be reduced to writing. This requirement therefore operated much more restrictively than a mere requirement as to fixation, and effectively restricted the description of the work to one particular form in which a dramatic work could take material form. The result was that a work which was considered to be a dramatic work in which copyright subsisted under the 1911 Act, such as a sketch which was not written down, but was recorded on film at the moment of performance, was not a dramatic work under the 1956 Act. The 1988 Act has restored the position, in this respect, to what it was under the 1911 Act.

3–116

3–117

3–118

---

[729] See Copyright Act 1956 ss.2(1) (qualification), 4(2), 4(4) (ownership).

[730] See, e.g. the 1977 Whitford Committee Report, Cmnd.6732, at para.590: "Speeches and lectures delivered extempore do not acquire copyright unless and until fixed."

[731] Copyright Act 1956 s.49(4). Writing was defined to include any form of notation, whether by hand or by printing, typewriting or any similar process: s.48(1).

[732] *Copinger* 12th edn, pp.53, 85. But see Somers J. in *Green v Broadcasting and Corporation of New Zealand* [1989] R.P.C. 469 (High Ct of NZ.), at 477: "There is much force in the submission that writing is but one method of giving a work the degree of certainty necessary to justify the monopoly conferred by the Act and that the same security can be obtained by fixing it in other tangible forms."

[733] *Gormley v EMI Records Ltd* [2000] E.C.D.R. 31 (Sup Ct of Ireland).

[734] For a review of the position, see Brennan and Christie, "Spoken Words and Copyright Subsistence in Anglo-American Law" [2000] I.P.Q. 309.

[735] See s.3(2) and para.3–114, above.

[736] Copyright Act 1911 s.35(1).

[737] Copyright Act 1956 s.48(1).

3–119 **Fixation of a musical work.** In contrast to a literary work, which must be expressed in writing, speech or singing before it can exist as a literary work, a musical work may exist as such in the mind of its composer as well as when it has been merely played or sung.[738] However, such work cannot be the subject of copyright under the 1988 Act until it is fixed, in any of the same ways that literary and dramatic works may also be fixed, that is, by it being recorded, in writing or otherwise.[739] The approach in the 1988 Act to fixation is of particular importance in relation to much modern music, which is played straight onto a recording device without having first been written down. So, as with the lyrics,[740] the pop musician who performs a song comprising music composed in his head creates a copyright musical work when he plays such music in a recording studio and it is recorded, and it is immaterial that the sound recording is made by the recording studio or the record company. In such cases, there will be separate copyrights, often in separate ownership, in the musical work and in the recording.

It follows from the combination of s.3(1) and (2) of the 1988 Act that if A improvises a tune in B's presence, then A has created a musical work. However, at that point the tune is not protected by copyright, as it is neither written down nor otherwise recorded. If B carries the tune away in his head and subsequently records it, then by such act by B the tune may become protected by copyright. However, B is not the author of the tune, as he is not the person who created it.[741] Although it is B's act in recording the tune which caused the tune to be the subject of copyright, upon such recording taking place it would seem clear that A is the owner of any copyright thereby subsisting in the tune and could therefore sue B for infringing his copyright.[742]

3–120 **Fixation of musical works under earlier Acts.** The position is the same as in relation to literary works, considered above.

3–121 **Fixation of artistic works.** Artistic works are not made subject to a specific requirement of fixation under the 1988 Act, but the nature of each of the types of work which fall within the definition of artistic work is such that the work will have taken a material form.[743] The position was the same under the earlier Acts.[744]

C. SOUND RECORDINGS, FILMS, BROADCASTS AND TYPOGRAPHICAL ARRANGEMENTS

3–122 **Sound recordings and films.** The 1988 Act contains no express requirement of fixation in relation to these works; their nature is such that it is unnecessary to specify separately any fixation requirement, since such works can only exist in

---

[738] *Hadley v Kemp* [1999] E.M.L.R. 589 (music of songs in existence before being recorded for the first time).

[739] CDPA 1988 s.3(2).

[740] See para.3–115, above.

[741] See CDPA 1988 s.9(1), and Ch.4.

[742] Subject to the evidential difficulty that A would face in proving that he, and not B, was in fact the author of the tune.

[743] The conception of a work of art, such as a painting or a sculpture, does not itself constitute the making of an artistic work for the purposes of the 1988 Act. It is the execution of the concept by painting the scene or sculpting the form which produces the artistic work. Drawings or sketches produced in preparation for the execution of such a work may, of course, be entitled to copyright as artistic works in their own right. See also *ABB Ltd v New Zealand Insulators Ltd* [2006] NZHC 1072 at para.158: the mere specification of a colour to be used in manufacturing a label is not protected in the absence of any drawing, graphic design or other object that could be said to be the original example of the labelling concept.

[744] CDPA 1988 s.49(4) did not apply to artistic works.

some material form.[745] Thus the Act defines each work by reference to a "record-ing"[746] which must, of course, therefore exist in a material form. The definitions provide, following the principle of fixation discussed above, that the medium on which the recording exists in each case is irrelevant.[747] Again, therefore, this makes it clear that the work has an existence independent of the medium. The po-sition was the same under the 1956 Act. No copyright subsists in a film as such made before the commencement of the 1956 Act; and under the 1911 Act, copy-right subsisted in sound recordings as if they were musical works.[748]

Fixation of broadcasts. The 1988 Act requires no fixation for broadcasts. The   **3–123**
position was the same under the 1956 Act.

Fixation of typographical arrangements of published editions. Fixation is not   **3–124**
specifically referred to as a requirement for subsistence of copyright in a typographical arrangement of a published edition, but the nature of a typographi-cal arrangement satisfies the principle of fixation. The position was the same under the 1956 Act.

4. ORIGINALITY

A. LITERARY, DRAMATIC, MUSICAL AND ARTISTIC WORKS

(i) Introduction

Statutory provision. Under s.1(1)(a) of the 1988 Act it is a requirement for the   **3–125**
subsistence of copyright in a literary, dramatic, musical and artistic work that the work should be original. This was the position under the equivalent provisions of the 1956[749] and 1911 Acts.[750] As with these earlier Acts, there was no definition of "original" in the 1988 Act as originally enacted, and this remains the position as regards a definition of general application; a definition of originality was introduced by amendment[751] specifically in relation to a database, when a database was itself introduced as a new sub-category of a literary work.[752] Decisions on the question of originality under the 1911 and 1956 Acts therefore remain valid under the 1988 Act.[753]

History of requirement of originality. Under the piecemeal legislation which   **3–126**
existed before the 1911 Act, there was no general statutory requirement of originality for copyright works. On the one hand, neither the Literary Copyright Act 1842, 5 & 6 Vict., c.45; this gave copyright protection to books, which were defined to include not only books in the ordinary sense, but other printed material such as pamphlets and letterpress sheets, and also music sheets, maps, charts and plans. nor the Engravings Copyright Act 1766, 7 Geo. 3, c.38. used the expres-sion "original" while, on the other hand, the Sculpture Copyright Act 1814, 54

---

[745] Cinematograph works are classed as literary and artistic works under the Berne Convention, and art.2(2) therefore applies to them. Sound recordings are specifically described in terms of fixation in the Rome Convention: art.3(b).

[746] CDPA 1988 ss.5A(1), 5B(2).

[747] CDPA 1988 ss.5A(1), 5B(2).

[748] Copyright Act 1911 s.19(1).

[749] Copyright Act 1956 ss.2(1) and (2), and 3(2) and (3).

[750] Copyright Act 1911 s.1(1).

[751] CDPA 1988 s.3A(2); introduced by the Copyright and Rights in Databases Regulations 1997 (SI 1997/3032) with effect from January 1, 1998.

[752] See para.3–146, below.

[753] And see CDPA 1988 s.171(3).

Geo. 3, c.56. and the Fine Arts Copyright Act 1862, 25 & 26 Vict., c.68. referred respectively to "original sculptures" and "every original painting, drawing and photograph". So far as the 1842 Act was concerned, only a low level of creativity on the part of the author was required. This was demonstrated by the House of Lords decision in *Walter v Lane*,[754] where it was held that a reporter was entitled to copyright in his verbatim report of a public speech. Since the statute did not contain any express requirement as to originality,[755] it might have been thought that the introduction of an express statutory requirement of originality by the 1911 Act brought about a change in the law. Decisions under the 1911 Act, however, established that the test of originality remained a low one, and the better view was therefore that there had been no change in the law.[756] The matter was resolved in *Express Newspapers Plc v News (UK) Ltd*,[757] where the court held that *Walter v Lane* remained good law.

3–127   **The Berne Convention and TRIPs.** Originality is not expressed to be a requirement for protection under the Berne Convention or TRIPs. The concept behind the Berne Convention is, however, to accord protection to authors in respect of their intellectual creations.[758] This implies that the product so created is the result of the individual's own intellectual efforts, and, therefore, in this sense is original to him. The degree of originality required for the protection of works the subject of Berne varies widely amongst the countries adhering to Berne, as also does the approach to different types of works.[759] The United Kingdom has, from before 1911, adopted a low threshold of originality as qualifying a work for protection.[760]

---

[754] *Walter v Lane* [1900] A.C. 539.

[755] Lord Halsbury L.C. specifically referred as a basis for his decision in *Walter v Lane* [1900] A.C. 539 to the absence of "original" in the statute (ibid. at 594) but Lord Davey considered that the fact no originality or literary skill was required for the report had less to do with this than the principle that a person should not avail himself of another's skill, labour and expense, by copying his work (ibid. at 552).

[756] See earlier editions of *Copinger*; cf. *Roberton v Lewis* [1976] R.P.C. 169 (decided in 1960), where Cross J. suggested that in view of the introduction of the word "original" into the 1911 and 1956 Acts, it was at least arguable that *Walter v Lane* [1900] A.C. 539 was no longer good law. The point was left open in *Sifam Electrical Instrument Co Ltd v Sangamo Weston Ltd* [1973] R.P.C. 899, at 910. In *L.B. (Plastics) Ltd v Swish Products Ltd* [1979] F.S.R. 145, Whitford J., noting the point, nevertheless observed that the cases since the 1911 Act had established that no originality of thought was required for subsistence of copyright.

[757] *Express Newspapers Plc v News (UK) Ltd* [1990] F.S.R 359 (Browne-Wilkinson V.-C.), following the decision of the High Court of Australia in *Sands McDougall Proprietary Ltd v Robinson* (1917) 23 C.L.R. 49. In *Sawkins v Hyperion Records Ltd* [2005] EWCA Civ 565; [2005] 1 W.L.R. 3281; [2005] R.P.C. 32, Mummery L.J. stated (at para.33) that *Walter v Lane* remained good law, citing the *Express Newspapers* case. Jacob L.J., while noting (at para.79) that the Court of Appeal had not been presented with a full frontal attack on *Walter v Lane*, accepted that it was "highly probable" that *Walter v Lane* was still good law and went on to express the view that the reasoning in the *Sands McDougall* case adopted in the *Express Newspapers* case was "right". Mance L.J. (at para.71) agreed with both judgments. See, however, Gravells, "Authorship and Originality: the Persistent Influence of *Walter v Lane*" [2007] I.P.Q. 267, arguing that reliance in the present day on *Walter v Lane* is "at best inappropriate and at worst misconceived".

[758] See, for example, Berne Convention art.2(5), in relation to compilations. See S. Ricketson and J.C. Ginsburg, *International Copyright and Neighbouring Rights, The Berne Convention and Beyond* 2nd edn (Oxford: Oxford University Press, 2006), para.8–05.

[759] In *CCH Canadian Ltd v Law Society of Upper Canada* [2004] S.C.C. 13, the differences were summarised by the Supreme Court of Canada, as follows: "There are competing views on the meaning of 'original' in copyright law. Some courts have found that a work that originates from an author and is more than a mere copy of a work is sufficient to ground copyright. See, for example, *University of London Press Ltd v University Tutorial Press Ltd*, [1916] 2 Ch. 601; *U & R Tax Services Ltd v H & R Block Canada Inc* (1995), 62 C.P.R. (3d) 257 (F.C.T.D.). This approach is consistent with the "sweat of the brow" or "industriousness" standard of originality, which is premised on a natural rights or Lockean theory of "just desserts", namely that an author deserves to have his or her efforts in producing a work rewarded. Other courts have required that a work must be creative to be "original" and thus protected by copyright. See, for example, *Feist Publications Inc v Rural Telephone Service Co*, 499 U.S. 340 (1991); *Tele-Direct (Publications) Inc v American Business Information Inc*, [1998] 2 F.C. 22, CA. This approach is also consistent

EC Directives. As part of the harmonisation of national copyright laws, two of the Directives adopted by the EC contain what amounts to a definition in similar terms of originality for the purposes of their respective subject matter. The first was the Directive on the legal protection of computer programs[761] ("the Software Directive") and the second was the Directive on the legal protection of databases ("the Database Directive").[762] The Software Directive requires that a computer program shall be protected if it is original in the sense that it is the author's own intellectual creation,[763] and specifies that no other criteria, in particular as to the qualitative or aesthetic merits of the program, shall be applied in determining whether or not a computer program is an original work.[764] No change was made to the 1988 Act when the Directive was implemented, presumably on the basis that the law under the 1988 Act was considered to be already in line with the requirements of the Directive.[765] The Database Directive adopted a similar approach to the Software Directive, and provided that copyright protection should be accorded to databases which, by reason of the selection or arrangement of their contents, constitute the author's own intellectual creation,[766] and that no other criteria should be applied to determine their eligibility for copyright protection.[767] When, however, the Database Directive was implemented,[768] a definition of originality was introduced into the 1988 Act in relation to a database to reflect the terms of the Directive.[769] The reference in both Directives to the work being the author's own intellectual creation reflects the use of this phrase in the Berne Convention.[770] It should be noted that the Term Directive[771] provided that photographs "which are original in the sense that they are the author's own intellectual creation" should be protected.[772] Since, however, Member States were permitted to provide for the protection of other photographs,[773] the United Kingdom was not required to make any change on implementation, even assuming that this test was different from that applied by the 1988 Act in relation to

---

with a natural rights theory of property law; however it is less absolute in that only those works that are the product of creativity will be rewarded with copyright protection. It has been suggested that the "creativity" approach to originality helps ensure that copyright protection only extends to the expression of ideas as opposed to the underlying ideas or facts. See *Feist, supra,* at p. 353."

[760] Described a "a more relaxed view" by S. Ricketson and J.C. Ginsburg, *International Copyright and Neighbouring Rights, The Berne Convention and Beyond* 2nd edn (Oxford: Oxford University Press, 2006), para.8–05, as being contrary to the spirit, if not the letter, of the Convention. But note the comment by McGechan J. in *Glogau v Land Transport Safety Authority of New Zealand* [1999] 1 N.Z.L.R. 257 (CA of NZ) that where the degree of originality is low it is unlikely that anything other than almost exact copying will be an infringement; conversely in the case of works involving a high degree of originality. As to the correlation between the degree or originality and the substantial part test for infringement, see paras 7–28 and 7–30, below.) In consequence, applying a low threshold test of originality causes no real harm.

[761] Council Directive 91/250, adopted on May 14, 1991; [1991] OJ L122/42.

[762] Directive 96/9 of the European Parliament and Council, of March 11, 1996; [1996] OJ L77/20.

[763] See art.1(3) of Directive 91/250 and *Infopaq International A/S v Danske Dagblades Forening,* Case C–5/08 [2009] ECR I–6569.

[764] Software Directive 91/250 art.1(3).

[765] Whether the United Kingdom was correct not to make any amendment in relation to computer programs is considered below in para.3–132.

[766] See art.3(1) of Directive 96/9, and *Infopaq International A/S v Danske Dagblades Forening* (C–5/08) [2009] E.C.R. I–6569.

[767] Directive 96/9; recital 16 adds that no aesthetic or qualitative criteria shall be applied in determining eligibility for protection.

[768] By the Copyright and Rights in Databases Regulations 1997 (SI 1997/3032). As to the new database right introduced by these Regulations, see Ch.18.

[769] As part of the new s.3A. See para.3–148, below.

[770] See, e.g. art.2(5).

[771] The Term Directive and its amendments have now been codified in Directive 2006/116/EC [2006] O.J. L372/12.

[772] art.6 of Directive 2006/116/EC.

[773] art.6 of Directive 2006/116/EC.

photographs.[774] These Directives have in a sense been overtaken by Information Society Directive,[775] which provides a broad protection right for authors' works.[776] This Directive is also based on the principle[777] that the protection of subject-matters as authors' works presupposes that they are intellectual creations,[778] and that copyright as protected under the Directive applies only in relation to a subject-matter which is original in the sense that it is its author's own intellectual creation.[779] At present, the effect of these Directives has not been to alter the general law of the United Kingdom as regards originality as it is applied in practice (the originality required for a copyright database is clearly an exception[780]) and it seems likely that this will remain the position. The Directives do not lay down any very clear test of originality and although the test or originality under UK law is low in comparison to that of some Member States, it is generally based on the principle that a work should be the author's own intellectual creation.

(ii) Principles of originality

3–129 **Expression, not content.** Copyright protection is given to literary, dramatic, musical and artistic works and not to ideas,[781] and therefore it is original skill or labour in execution of the work, and not originality of thought, which is required.[782] Original, in this connection, does not mean that the work must be the expression of original or inventive thought; the originality required relates to the expression of thought.[783] The general policy of copyright is to prevent the unauthorised copying of certain material forms of expression resulting from intellectual exertions of the human mind and, subject to various exceptions, it can be used to prevent copying of a substantial part of the relevant form of expression, but it does not prevent use of the information, thoughts or emotions expressed in the copyright work. This explains why the threshold requirement of an "original" work has been interpreted as not imposing objective standards of novelty, usefulness, inventiveness, aesthetic merit, quality or value.[784] A work may thus be "complete rubbish and utterly worthless, but copyright protection may be available for it, just as it is for the great masterpieces of imaginative literature, art and music."[785] The position in this respect under the Copyright Acts may be contrasted with the standard required for registered designs under the Registered Designs

---

[774] See para.3–144, below. But note the aside in *Infopaq International A/S v Danske Dagblades Forening*, Case C–5/08 [2009] ECR I–6569, para.35, that photographs are protected by copyright *only* if they are original in the sense that they are their author's own intellectual creation.

[775] Directive 2001/29 on the harmonisation of certain aspects of copyright and related rights in the information society.

[776] See para.7–10, and *Infopaq International A/S v Danske Dagblades Forening*, (C–5/08) [2009] E.C.R. I–6569.

[777] See recitals 4, 9 to 11, and 20, and the preamble.

[778] Based on the overall objectives of the Directive and international law, particularly the general scheme to be found in arts 2(5) and (8) of the Berne Convention.

[779] *Infopaq International A/S v Danske Dagblades Forening* (C–5/08) [2009] E.C.R. I–6569, noting that the same is true for computer programs, databases and photographs.

[780] See para.3–146 et seq.

[781] See para.3–18, above, and the discussion in *Plix Products Ltd v Frank M. Winstone (Merchants)* [1986] F.S.R. 63 at 92.

[782] *L.B. (Plastics) Ltd v Swish Products Ltd* [1979] F.S.R. 145. The sentence in the text was cited with approval in *Martin v Polyplas Manufacturers Ltd* [1969] N.Z.L.R. 1046 at 1050.

[783] *University of London Press Ltd v University Tutorial Press Ltd* [1916] 2 Ch. 601 at 608, per Petersen J., cited with approval in: *Macmillan & Co Ltd v Cooper (K. & J.)* (1923) 40 T.L.R. 186 at 190; *British Broadcasting Co v Wireless League Gazette Publishing Co* [1926] Ch. 433 at 440; *Ladbroke (Football) Ltd v William Hill (Football) Ltd* [1964] 1 W.L.R. 273 at 277; and see *Ascot Jockey Club Ltd v Simons* (1968) 64 W.W.R. 411.

[784] *Sawkins v Hyperion Records Ltd* [2005] EWCA Civ 565; [2005] 1 W.L.R. 3281; [2005] R.P.C. 32, at para.31.

[785] *Sawkins v Hyperion Records Ltd* [2005] EWCA Civ 565, at para.31.

Act 1949, which is generally one of novelty, so that, if a design in fact resembles an existing design, it may not be registered, even though the designer of the second design arrived at this design entirely independently of the first design.

Nature of skill or labour required.[786] A work need only be "original" in the **3–130** limited sense that the author originated it by his efforts rather than slavishly copying it from the work produced by the efforts of another person.[787] Here, there are two interconnecting strands involved.[788] First, the work must originate from the author, in the sense that it must not be slavishly copied from another work, for, as discussed below, in such a case the copyist does not ordinarily obtain copyright in his copy.[789] As will be seen, however, the work may nevertheless be original even though the author has drawn on knowledge common to himself and others,[790] or has used already existing material.[791] Second, whether or not the author has drawn on other material, what is required is the expenditure of more than negligible or trivial effort or relevant skill in the creation of the work.[792] As to this, while it is clear that the standard of originality required by the Copyright Acts is a low one,[793] it is otherwise almost impossible to state in any precise terms the amount of knowledge, labour, judgment, skill or taste which the author of a work must bestow on its creation in order for the work to acquire copyright.[794] There is no guiding principle as to the *quantum* of labour, skill or judgment required.[795] It is a question of fact and degree and thus has to be determined on the facts of the particular case.[796] United Kingdom law has traditionally regarded mere labour in the creation of a work as sufficient to make it original, whether or not there is also skill involved.[797] As to what is meant by skill or judgment in this context, the following is a helpful statement by the Supreme Court of Canada:

> "By skill, I mean the use of one's knowledge, developed aptitude or practised ability in producing the work. By judgment, I mean the use of one's capacity for discernment or ability to form an opinion or evaluation by

---

[786] Sometimes the cases refer to labour, skill or *judgment* being required. In this work, judgment will for the most part be treated as being an aspect of the skill required for creation of a work.

[787] *Sawkins v Hyperion Records Ltd* [2005] EWCA Civ 565; [2005] 1 W.L.R. 3281; [2005] R.P.C. 32 at para.31.

[788] See *Ultra Marketing (UK) Ltd v Universal Components Ltd* [2004] EWHC 468 (Ch) at para.51, where the question of originality was correctly broken down into these two stages.

[789] See para.3–133, below.

[790] *University of London Press Ltd v University Tutorial Press Ltd* [1916] 2 Ch. 601 at 608, per Petersen J.; *Macmillan & Co Ltd v Cooper (K. & J.)* (1923) 40 T.L.R. 186 at 188, in which Lord Atkinson cited with approval *Emerson v Davies*, Storey's U.S. Rep. 768 (1845); *Ladbroke (Football) Ltd v William Hill (Football) Ltd* [1964] 1 W.L.R. 273, at, e.g. 291 (Lord Pearce). And see *Dutt (S.K.) v Law Book Co* [1954] A.L.J. 125; *Gouindan v Gopalakrishna Kone* (1955) Mad.W.N. 369.

[791] See further paras 3–134 et seq., below.

[792] *Ladbroke (Football) Ltd v William Hill (Football) Ltd* [1964] 1 W.L.R. 273 at 287; *Autospin (Oil Seals) v Beehive Spinning* [1995] R.P.C. 683, at 694 (drawings of oil seals). In *Hyperion Records Ltd v Sawkins* [2005] EWCA Civ 565, Mummery L.J. stated (at para.31) that a work need only be "original" in the limited sense that the author originated it by his efforts rather than "slavishly" copying it from the work produced by the efforts of another person; while Jacob L.J. stated (at para.85) the question in terms of whether the claimant's work went beyond mere "servile copying". Mance L.J. (at para.71) agreed with both judgments.

[793] See some of the examples cited later in the text.

[794] See, per Lord Atkinson in *Macmillan & Co Ltd v Cooper (K. & J.)* (1923) 40 T.L.R. 186, PC; the decision of the Privy Council was approved by the House of Lords in *G.A. Cramp & Sons Ltd v Frank Smythson Ltd* [1944] A.C. 329 at 335, and *Ladbroke (Football) Ltd v William Hill (Football) Ltd* [1964] 1 W.L.R. 273 at 179, 282.

[795] As was pointed out by Maugham J. in *Cambridge University Press v University Tutorial Press Ltd* (1928) 45 R.P.C. 335.

[796] *Macmillan & Co Ltd v Cooper (K. & J.)* (1923) 40 T.L.R. 186, per Lord Atkinson; *G.A. Cramp & Sons Ltd v Frank Smythson Ltd* [1944] A.C. 329, at p.335; *Biotrading & Financing v Biohit* [1996] F.S.R. 393 at 395; [1998] F.S.R. 109, CA at 116.

[797] See, e.g. the compilation cases at para.3–146, below.

comparing different possible options in producing the work. This exercise of skill and judgment will necessarily involve intellectual effort. The exercise of skill and judgment required to produce the work must not be so trivial that it could be characterized as a purely mechanical exercise. For example, any skill and judgment that might be involved in simply changing the font of a work to produce 'another' work would be too trivial to merit copyright protection as an 'original' work."

And in conclusion:

"While creative works will by definition be 'original' and covered by copyright, creativity is not required to make a work 'original'."[798]

Simplicity, as such, is not enough to prevent copyright subsisting unless extreme, such as in a straight line,[799] or a circle[800] and indeed there are relatively few cases in which copyright has been denied on the grounds of lack of originality.[801] Copyright has been denied to a work written when drunk,[802] but in principle there is no reason why a work created under the influence of alcohol or drugs should not be regarded as original if it has some meaning or significance[803] and is not simply gibberish. Also, as already noted,[804] it is sometimes difficult to know whether cases have been decided on the basis that the work is not a *literary*, etc. work or that it is not an *original* work, and the reader is referred to the earlier discussion on this point and the cases referred to there. It has sometimes been said that as a rough practical test "what is worth copying is worth protecting",[805] but this should be applied with caution since otherwise the most trivial of works will be protected if copying has taken place,[806] and it can become a misleading rhetorical device.[807]

(iii) Non-derivative works

3–131   Where an author creates a work without reference to any existing subject matter, it will be rare that it will lack originality merely by reason of its simplicity or banality. The European Court of Justice has, for example, observed that words as such do not constitute elements covered by copyright protection, since words "... considered in isolation are not as such an intellectual creation of the author who

---

[798] *CCH Canadian Ltd v Law Society of Upper Canada* [2004] SCC 13 (Sup Ct of Can). Note, however, that the court decided that, under the Canadian statute, originality required more than mere labour, and thus a higher test of originality than that laid down in *University of London Press Ltd v University Tutorial Press Ltd* [1916] 2 Ch. 601, (and lower than the test laid down by the US court in *Feist Publications Inc v Rural Telephone Service Co* 199 U.S. 340 (1991)). In this, Canadian law is thus different from UK law.

[799] *British Northrop Ltd v Texteam Blackburn Ltd* [1974] R.P.C. 344.

[800] *Karo Step Trade Mark* [1977] R.P.C. 255; *Gleeson v H.R. Denne Ltd* [1975] R.P.C. 471, at 482 (suggesting that there could be no copyright in simple figures such as squares, circles or crosses); *Duriron Inc v Hugh Jennings Ltd* [1984] F.S.R. 1 (no originality in rough and inaccurate representation of pipe of varying size, not drawn to scale); but see *Solar Thomson Engineering Co Ltd v Barton* [1977] R.P.C. 537 (copyright probably subsisted in drawing of three concentric circles, drawn to precise measurements).

[801] See para.3–131, below.

[802] *Fournet v Pearson Ltd* (1897) 14 T.L.R. 82.

[803] What of Coleridge's *Kubla Khan*?

[804] See para.3–13, above.

[805] *University of London Press Ltd v University Tutorial Press Ltd* [1916] 2 Ch. 601 at 610, per Peterson J.; *Ladbroke (Football) Ltd v William Hill (Football) Ltd* [1964] 1 W.L.R. 273, (per Lord Reid at 279: "I think that there is much wisdom in the reference by Petersen J. to the "rough practical test that what is worth copying is prima facie worth protecting—in *University of London Press Ltd* ...").

[806] *Ibcos Computers Ltd v Barclays Mercantile Highland Finance Ltd* [1994] F.S.R. 275; *Network Ten Pty Ltd v TCN Channel None Pty. Ltd* [2004] HCA 14; (2004) 59 I.P.R. 1. See also para.7–31, below.

[807] *Baigent v The Random House Group Ltd* [2007] EWCA Civ 247; [2007] F.S.R. 24 at para.97, per Lloyd L.J., Rix L.J. and Mummery L.J. agreeing.

employs them. It is only through the choice, sequence and combination of those words that the author may express his creativity in an original manner and achieve a result which is an intellectual creation."[808] Copyright has been denied previously to simple phrases,[809] titles for books and magazines,[810] and the general arrangement and layout of a diary (i.e. the ways in which the days and dates were set out, with spaces for notes).[811] In relation to artistic works, simple divisions of a diary page, although regarded as artistic works, have been denied copyright on this ground.[812] While it has been doubted that copyright could subsist in simple drawings such as squares, circles or crosses,[813] and copyright has been denied to a rough and inaccurate representation of a pipe,[814] and to sketches of designs for a flag,[815] copyright has been held to subsist in a series of circles drawn in a regular array,[816] logos,[817] and held "probably" to subsist in a precise drawing of three concentric circles.[818] Originality may lie in the mere selection of the elements to use in a work, as where the creator is presented with a choice between two different versions or even where a variant has been created by a mistake.[819] Originality can also subsist in the mere selection of colours to be used in an artistic work.[820] Where the author has created a work by following some method, design or formula, it is irrelevant that by the same process another person could produce, or

---

[808] *Infopaq International A/S v Danske Dagblades Forening*, Case C–5/08 [2009] ECR I–6569, para.45.

[809] *Kirk v J. & R. Fleming Ltd* [1928–1935] Mac.C.C. 44; *R. Griggs Group Ltd v Evans* [2004] F.S.R. 31 (on appeal, but not on this point: [2005] EWCA Civ 11; [2005] F.S.R. 31; [2005] E.C.D.R 30) ("Dr Martens"); *Victoria v Pacific Technologies (Australia) Pty Ltd (No 2)* [2009] F.C.A. 737; [2009] 81 I.P.R. 525 (Fed. Ct. of Aus.) (the words "Help-Help-Driver-in-Danger-Call-Police-Ph.000" not original); but compare *Sunlec International Pty Ltd v Electropar Ltd* [2009] 79 I.P.R. 411 (High Ct. of N. Z.) (slogan: "Field Friendly—The best choice for fieldwork" even if the language taken was from the common stock of the English language, slogan used language in a succinct and relatively memorable way: held original).

[810] See para.3–16, above.

[811] *Frank Smythson Ltd v G.A.Cramp & Sons Ltd* [1943] Ch. 133, CA. These aspects of the diary were regarded as a literary work, and was probably a table or compilation. For the decision on the further compilation aspects of the case in the House of Lords, see para.3–147, below. See also *Statuscard Australia Pty Ltd v Rotondo* [2008] Q.S.C. 181. In s.10(1) of the Australian Copyright Act 1968 the term "drawing" is defined as including "a diagram, map, chart or plan". Applying that definition it was held that a framework for displaying data on a computer screen comprising coloured boxes with column headings was probably a drawing, but as such was insufficiently original to attract protection (para.109), being too simple and too much determined by its function (para.111).

[812] *Waylite Diaries CC v First National Bank Ltd* [1993] (2) S.A. 128 (High Ct of S.A.) following the Court of Appeal decision in *Frank Smythson Ltd v G.A.Cramp & Sons Ltd* [1943] Ch. 133 (the diary, devised for bank managers, consisted of (a) lines dividing up pages and (b) months, dates and days, and a three-month calendar); cf. *Artifakts Design Group Ltd v N.P. Rigg Ltd* [1993] 1 N.Z.L.R. 196 (copyright subsisted in original artwork for the covers and other parts of corporate diaries).

[813] *Gleeson v H.R. Denne Ltd* [1975] R.P.C. 471 at 482.

[814] *Duriron Inc v Hugh Jennings Ltd* [1984] F.S.R. 1.

[815] *Commercial Signs v General Motors Products of Canada Ltd* (1937) 2 D.L.R. 310. The design consisted of four stars and were merely enlargements of an original drawing with colouring and lettering added.

[816] *Hi-Tech Autoparts Ltd v Towergate Two Ltd* [2002] F.S.R. 15 at para.17.

[817] See para.3–58, above, and also *R. Griggs Group Ltd v Evans* [2004] F.S.R. 31 (on appeal, but not on this point: [2005] EWCA Civ 11; [2005] F.S.R. 31) (skill and labour used to draw word or phrase in a stylised way).

[818] *Solar Thomson Engineering Co Ltd v Barton* [1977] R.P.C. 537.

[819] *Guild v Eskandar Ltd* [2003] F.S.R. 3. In that case, the feature had been introduced by an error in the manufacture of a prototype. The decision proceeded on the basis that the "adoption of the mistake may not contribute much by way of labour but it can certainly be the product of skill" (see para.48). Where the feature is merely one of a number of features which go to make up the whole work, such that a judgment is made between different possible versions, the decision seems unobjectionable. Caution needs to taken not to extend the principle too far. See, e.g. *A. Fulton Co Ltd v Grant Barnett & Co Ltd* [2001] R.P.C. 257 at para.42. If a machine makes a substantial change to a work, there may in reality be no human author of what results. As to computer-generated works, see para.3–149.

[820] *Coogi Australia Pty Ltd v Hysport International Pty Ltd* (1998) 157 A.L.R. 247 (Fed Ct of Aus).

has already produced, an identical work, provided the author has worked out the result for himself. Thus works such as mathematical tables have been protected, even though identical tables have previously been published.[821] Although the idea or information embodied in the tables may not be novel, the result of the author's labour of compilation is a set of tables upon which the author has done original work. Again, for example, a collection of precedents constructed by following the general directions of a statute will be entitled to copyright, although any two persons with a knowledge of the subject would be bound to arrive at a similar result.[822] The same point can be made in relation to works of reference, such as directories or maps, where it is irrelevant that two persons can in theory independently arrive at the same result.[823]

3–132   **Computer programs.** Computer programs are protected as literary works and as such are subject to the ordinary requirement of originality of the 1988 Act. No amendment was made to the Act on the implementation of the Software Directive, despite the requirement in the Directive that a computer program "shall be protected if it is original in the sense that it is the author's own intellectual creation" and that "no other criteria shall be applied to determine its eligibility for protection."[824] From this it can only be concluded that it was thought that such a requirement was fully consistent with the meaning of "original" in the 1988 Act, as it has come to be interpreted by the courts in relation to works generally.[825] Since the requirement of originality has been viewed as meaning no more than that the work must be the product of the author's own skill and labour,[826] it would seem that this conclusion is correct, but in any event the Act must be construed in accordance with the Directive.[827] To date, no point has been taken in any reported case that a computer program lacks originality. The nature of the protected subject matter of a computer program has already been discussed[828] and it is important to make a distinction between different kinds of skill, judgement and labour. What is protected by copyright in a computer program is the skill, judgement and labour in devising the form of expression of the program as a literary work,[829] and it is to this aspect of the work that the inquiry as to originality must be directed.[830] Other things which may be conveyed by or described in the program, including ideas, procedures, methods of operation and mathematical concepts, are not protected and are thus not relevant to the inquiry.[831]

---

[821] *Bailey v Taylor* (1830) 1 Russ. & My. 73 (tables of values of leases and annuities; subsistence of copyright was not, however, in issue).

[822] *Alexander (W.) v Mackenzie (R.)* (1846) 9 Sc.Sess.Cass. (2nd Ser.) 748 at 755 (held, although the work was not one of genius, or novel, it required care and exertion of mind).

[823] As to such works, see paras 3–146 et seq., below.

[824] Software Directive 91/250 art.1(3). Note also that the eighth recital of the Software Directive provides that in respect of the criteria to be applied in determining whether or not a computer program is an original work, no tests as to the qualitative or aesthetic merits of the program are to be applied.

[825] The European Commission has noted the fact that the United Kingdom has not expressly implemented this part of the Directive and has observed that it remains to be seen whether this will lead to an over-extensive protection of computer programs in the United Kingdom (see the Commission's report of April 10, 2000 (COM/2000/0199 final) on the implementation and effects of the Software Directive).

[826] See para.3–130, above.

[827] *Navitaire Inc v easyJet Airline Co Ltd* [2004] EWHC 1725 (Ch) at para.88; [2005] E.C.D.R. 17; *SAS Institute Inc v World Programming Ltd* [2010] EWHC 1829 (Ch), para.205.

[828] See para.3–28 et seq.

[829] *SAS Institute Inc v World Programming Ltd* [2010] EWHC 1829 (Ch), para.207.

[830] So, in *Vitof Ltd v Altoft* [2006] EWHC 1678 (Ch), para.143, it was accepted that computer code, 10 per cent of which was either different from or a modified version of part of a previous version, was original since it had not been slavishly copied.

[831] *SAS Institute Inc v World Programming Ltd* [2010] EWHC 1829 (Ch), para.206, observing that

(iv) Derivative works

Mere copy. Whether a work counts as original where skill, labour and judgment   **3–133**
has been expended merely in the process of copying, is a matter of degree. What
has to be considered is the extent to which the "copyist" is a mere copyist—
merely performing an easy mechanical function. The more that this is so the less
is his contribution likely to be taken as "original". In the end the question is one
of degree—how much skill, labour and judgment in the making of the copy is
that of the creator of the copy? Both individual creative input and sweat of brow
may be involved and will be factors in the overall evaluation.[832] "Reproductions
requiring great talent and technical skill may qualify as protectable works of
authorship, even if they are copies of pre-existing works. This would be the case
for photographic and other high quality replicas of works of art."[833] A work need
only be "original" in the limited sense that the author originated it by his efforts
rather than slavishly copying it from the work produced by the efforts of another
person.[834] This modern statement of the law must be taken as having superseded
previous statements to the effect that skill, labour and judgment merely in the
process of copying cannot confer originality, and that a mere copyist cannot have
protection for his copy[835] and all the older cases must be read with this statement
in mind. Nevertheless it no doubt remains generally true that particularly where
the copy is in the same medium as the original, there must be more than an exact
reproduction or facsimile enlargement or reduction if the copy is to secure copyright;[836] there must usually be some element of material alteration or embellishment which suffices to make the totality of the new work an original work.[837] In
this, the quality of the alteration is likely to be more important than the quantity.
In the case of a literary work, what is significant is the form of literary expression[838] and, in the case of an artistic work, the visual impact of the alteration or
embellishment on the work as a whole is more important than its technical
significance.[839] It is originality in relation to visually significant matters that is
important here.[840] Mere change of scale will therefore not normally be regarded

---

thereby a line is drawn between copyright protection and the public domain, citing Reinbothe and
von Lewinski, *The WIPO Treaties 1996: Commentary and Legal Analysis* (London: Butterworths, 2002), pp.46–47

[832] *Sawkins v Hyperion Records Ltd* [2005] EWCA Civ 565; [2005] 1 W.L.R. 3281; [2005] R.P.C.
32 at para.83, per Jacob L.J. (with which Mance L.J. agreed).

[833] Prof. Jane Ginsberg, The Concept of Authorship in Comparative Copyright Law, *http://
ssrn.com.abstract__id=368481*), cited with approval by Jacob L.J. in *Sawkins v Hyperion Records Ltd* [2005] EWCA Civ 565 at para.83.

[834] *Sawkins v Hyperion Records Ltd* [2005] EWCA Civ 565, per Mummery L.J., at para.31, Mance
L.J. agreeing.

[835] Principally per Lord Oliver (obiter) in *Interlego A.G. v Tyco Industries Inc* [1989] A.C. 217 at
262H–263A, approving, at 261; [1988] R.P.C. 343; *British Northrop Ltd v Texteam Blackburn
Ltd* [1974] R.P.C. 344. See also per Lord James in *Walter v Lane* [1900] A.C. 539 at 554; *Leslie v
Young (J.) & Sons* [1894] A.C. 335; *Barfield v Nicholson* (1824) 2 Sim.St. 1. The Court of Appeal in the design right case of *Dyson Limited v Qualtex (UK) Limited* [2006] EWCA Civ 166;
[2006] R.P.C. 31, felt better able to understand the *Interlego* decision having seen the drawings.
"As soon as you see the two drawings you see they are of the same thing, not surprisingly for
they are both for the same article, a Lego brick with 4×2 studs on the top. The differences, such
as they are, are nearly all in what is written on the drawing. There is one very minor visual difference in that the 1968 brick had a small portion on the top of the inside which was to allow flow of
plastic–the so-called 'flow rib'. You have to look hard to find it". See Jacob L.J. at para.86.

[836] *The Reject Shop v Manners* [1995] F.S.R. 870 (facsimile enlargement).

[837] *Interlego A.G. v Tyco Industries Inc* [1989] A.C. 217 at 262H–263A.

[838] *Gormley v EMI Records Ltd* [2000] E.C.D.R. 31 (Sup Ct of Ireland) (child's endeavours to repeat
a Bible story resulted in some change of language but did not create an original literary work: the
story was told in the same way).

[839] *Ornstin Ltd v Quality Plastics* noted at [1990] I.P.D. 13027 (Aldous J.)

[840] *Ultra Marketing (UK) Ltd v Universal Components Ltd* [2004] EWHC 468 (Ch) at para.10.

as visually significant.[841] If the original, in the case of an artistic work, is used merely as a model to give the idea of the new work, then the new work may well be entitled to protection, but if the result is simply a slavish copy, it will not usually be protected. Thus, protection has been denied to precise copies of existing drawings for children's building bricks,[842] tracings made from sections cut from a three-dimensional casting,[843] and an engraving copied from an existing engraving.[844] Photographs, which in one sense will always be a copy of what is before the camera lens, and which may more specifically be a copy of an existing artistic work, create their own problems as regards originality, and the principles discussed above are not easily applied to them; they are discussed separately below.[845]

3–134   **Other use of existing subject-matter.** As has been seen, where the author has produced his result without reference to any pre-existing subject-matter, it is immaterial that the result is not novel, or that anyone else could have produced the same result, or that the idea or scheme from which the result has been produced is open to the public. But where the author has made use of existing subject-matter, greater difficulty arises, and it has to be determined whether he has expended sufficient independent skill and labour to justify copyright protection for his result.[846] In determining whether the work is original and entitled to copyright, the work must be looked at as a whole and if, notwithstanding that the author has used existing subject-matter, he has expended a degree of independent skill, labour and judgment, even if it is only in the process or copying, he will be entitled to copyright protection for his work as a whole.[847] It is wrong to attempt to isolate parts which are not original and argue that copyright subsists only in the remainder.[848]

3–135   **Works in the course of creation.** Many works are not created in their final form at one sitting. The status of a work in the course of creation will depend on the degree of skill and labour applied at any particular stage.[849] As soon as sufficient skill and labour have been devoted to it to make it an original work, copyright will subsist in it even though the work may be incomplete and the author intends to do further work on it. Thus even the first section of the first chapter of a literary

---

[841] *Drayton Controls (Engineering) Ltd v Honeywell Control Systems Ltd* [1992] F.S.R. 245, per Knox J. at 260.

[842] *Interlego A.G. v Tyco Industries Inc* [1989] A.C. 217 at 263 D/E.

[843] *J. & S. Davis (Holding) Ltd v Wright Heath Group Ltd* [1988] R.P.C. 403 at 412.

[844] *Re Martin (T.J.)* (1884) 10 V.L.R. 196.

[845] See para.3–144, below.

[846] *Cala Homes (South) v Alfred McAlpine Homes East Ltd* [1995] F.S.R. 818; *Martin v Polyplas Manufacturers Ltd* [1969] N.Z.L.R. 1046.

[847] *Sawkins v Hyperion Records Ltd* [2005] EWCA Civ 565; *Ladbroke (Football) Ltd v William Hill (Football) Ltd* [1964] 1 W.L.R. 273; *Redwood Music Ltd v Chappell & Co Ltd* [1982] R.P.C. 109. Examples of cases where this test has been satisfied include: *Sawkins v Hyperion Records Ltd* [2005] EWCA Civ 565 (new edition early music, with corrections, etc.); *Macmillan Publishers Ltd v Thomas Reed Publications Ltd* [1993] F.S.R. 455 (sufficient work and skill in producing nautical charts from admiralty charts); *Cala Homes (South) v Alfred McAlpine Homes East Ltd* [1995] F.S.R. 818 (architect expended sufficient effort and skill in producing a new design with a combination of features from preceding designs); *Kilvington Bros Ltd v Goldberg* (1957) 8 D.L.R. (2d) 768 (artistic designs for tombstones original even though containing many features of existing designs: the creator's designs came from his own mind): and *Henkel KgaA v Holdfast New Zealand Ltd* [2006] NZSC 102; (2006) 70 IPR 624; [2007] 1 N.Z.L.R. 336 at para.47 (design drawing showing a combination of "common form" elements of a glue bottle affixed to a card of a dominant blue primary colour with pictures of two uses and a list of applications).

[848] *Ladbroke (Football) Ltd v William Hill (Football) Ltd* [1964] 1 W.L.R. 273; *Nouveau Fabrics Ltd v Voyage Decoration Ltd* [2004] EWHC 895 (Ch). Nevertheless, an analysis of what parts of a work were truly original and what parts were derived from existing material may become relevant when it comes to deciding the issue of substantial part for infringement purposes. See para.7–30 at (j), below.

[849] See also para.3–06, above.

work may qualify as a copyright work. As sections are added to the work, new copyright works will come into existence provided, in each case, the additions are the product of sufficient skill and labour. The final work should, however, be regarded as a single copyright work, although technically there will remain in the background a family of underlying works.[850]

Successive versions. A similar point arises where a work goes through succes-   **3–136**
sive revisions in the course of its creation and development. Successive revisions to a complete work, as in the case of revisions to an author's manuscript, may of course result in separate copyright works if the revisions are the product of new skill and labour.[851] The important issue is usually the originality of later versions, although copyright will continue to subsist in the earlier versions, whatever use is made of the material contained in it.[852] The issue as to the originality of later versions, or whether the claimant has identified the correct work to rely on, used frequently to arise in relation to revisions of engineering drawings.[853] One question is whether it is only the revision, rather than the whole of the revised drawing, which is entitled to the newly created copyright. In *L.B. (Plastics) Ltd v Swish Products Ltd*,[854] it was held that where there has been a previous drawing or a model from which a new drawing is prepared, or some sketches have been made which are in part redrawn, the new drawing will be entitled to copyright as a whole where there has been sufficient relevant skill and labour in producing it. Whether it is so entitled to copyright will usually depend on whether there has been the addition of some element of material alteration or embellishment which suffices to make the totality of the work an original work.[855] This is a matter of fact and degree; even an alteration or addition which is quantitatively small may, if material, suffice to create an original work.[856] However, there is no single test for deciding whether or not a drawing is original by reference to how much skill or labour has been expended on its creation; a distinction must be made between what is visually significant, where skill and labour expended are highly important, and work which is not visually significant, where skill and labour involved is not relevant.[857] Even if such a revised or updated drawing is entitled to copyright, there may be problems in establishing infringement of such a work in that the courts, in considering whether a substantial part has been taken, will disregard the parts which have been taken without alteration from the pre-existing works in which the claimant does not own copyright.[858] Generally, however, a defendant can expect to receive short shrift from the court where he attempts to take points about successive versions of work, for example arguing that the earliest works

---

[850] See *Sweeney v Macmillan Publishers Ltd* [2002] R.P.C. 35 at para.33. See also *A v B* [2001] E.M.L.R. 1006, where it was pointed out that the first entry, and each successive entry in a diary, will be entitled to copyright protection on its own, as well as the diary as a whole, provided each entry was the product of sufficient skill and labour.

[851] *Sweeney v Macmillan Publishers Ltd* [2002] R.P.C. 35 at para.34; *IPC Media Ltd v Highbury-Leisure Publishing Ltd* [2004] EWHC 2985 (Ch); [2005] F.S.R. 20 at para.5.

[852] *L.A. Gear Inc v Hi-Tec Sports Plc* [1992] F.S.R. 121, CA, followed in *Biotrading & Financing v Biohit* [1998] F.S.R. 109, CA. See also *Ray v Classic FM* [1998] F.S.R. 622; *Macmillan Publishers Ltd v Thomas Reed Publications Ltd* [1992] F.S.R. 455; *Ultra Marketing (UK) Ltd v Universal Components Ltd* [2004] EWHC 468 (Ch) at para.19.

[853] The problem may still arise in relation to design right, which has supplanted copyright in such cases. See Ch.13, below.

[854] *L.B. (Plastics) Ltd v Swish Products Ltd* [1979] F.S.R. 145.

[855] *Interlego A.G. v Tyco Industries Inc* [1989] A.C. 217 at 263C; [1988] R.P.C. 343, per Lord Oliver.

[856] See para.3–133, above.

[857] *Drayton Controls (Engineering) Ltd v Honeywell Control Systems Ltd* [1992] F.S.R. 245, per Knox J. at 259, applying *Interlego A.G. v Tyco Industries Inc* [1989] A.C. 217. See also *Biotrading & Financing v Biohit* [1996] F.S.R. 393; [1998] F.S.R. 109, CA.

[858] See *Warwick Film Productions Ltd v Eisinger* [1969] Ch. 508; and see para.7–30 at (j), below.

have not been disclosed by the claimant and that the later ones must be unoriginal, being copies of the earlier drawings with only insignificant alterations.[859] The reality, as has been pointed out, is that either the later drawings will as a whole be original or, if not, they are evidence of what earlier, and original, drawings looked like. Occasionally, however, the point becomes important, for example because the earlier works are no longer entitled to copyright or because the claimant does not own the copyright in the whole chain of works.[860]

3–137   **Change of medium or form.** It is often said that changing the expression of a work from one medium or form to another will entitle the new work to copyright. As a generalisation, this is true but it is no more than another way of saying that skill and labour expended on the creation of a work confers originality. The work of a reporter in faithfully reporting a speech delivered orally is an example of the expenditure of skill and labour in connection with a change of medium which has been held to entitle a work to protection.[861] An example of a change of form is the work of a translator, which has long been entitled to protection.[862]

In relation to artistic works, a change of medium will often entitle a reproduction of an existing artistic work to independent protection. Thus it has been said that a two-dimensional drawing of a three-dimensional object would qualify as an original work.[863] A further example is an engraving, which is often a copy, but the engraver's work will usually be original in the sense that he has employed skill and judgment in its production,[864] even where the engraving is a close copy of an existing work such as a painting or drawing. An engraver of the classical kind uses means which are very different from those of the painter or draughtsman whose work he copies, producing his effect by the management of light and shade (the "*chiaroscuro*"), using different lines and dots,[865] which usually requires a high degree of skill and labour.[866] Even in the case of an engraving of a mundane kind,[867] there will usually be skill and labour involved,[868] but copyright has been denied to an engraving which was merely a copy of another engraving.[869] As

---

[859] *L.A. Gear Inc v Hi-Tec Sports Plc* [1992] F.S.R. 121, CA at 136, (followed in *Biotrading & Financing v Biohit* [1998] F.S.R. 109, CA), where the point that each successive drawing was entitled to copyright was described as "so obvious that it needs no authority to support it", even though each drawing might have contained only a minor variation or been just a copy. See per Nourse L.J. at 136.

[860] *Biotrading & Financing v Biohit* [1996] F.S.R. 393 at 395; *Ultra Marketing (UK) Ltd v Universal Components Ltd* [2004] EWHC 468 (Ch) (where the claimant did not own the copyright in the later drawings).

[861] See *Walter v Lane* [1900] A.C. 539. As to the status of this decision, see para.3–133.

[862] *Byrne v Statist Co* [1914] 1 K.B. 622; *Wyatt v Barnard* (1814) 3 V. & B. 77 (translation of patent specification). Translations are required to be protected under art.2(3) of the Berne Convention. For a general discussion of the position of the translator, see *Vaver* in [1994] E.I.P.R. 159.

[863] *L.B. (Plastics) Ltd v Swish Products Ltd* [1979] F.S.R. 145, per Whitford J.; this seems to have been accepted as correct in *Interlego A.G. v Tyco Industries Inc* [1989] A.C. 217; [1988] R.P.C. 343.

[864] Engravings were the first works in the field of artistic copyright to receive statutory protection, by the Engraving Copyright Act 1734. See para.2–20, above. Despite the wording of the earlier Acts, which referred to something that was invented and designed, it was never necessary that an engraving be of a totally new subject to qualify for protection, so that engravings of things taken from nature, or of buildings, were always protected: *Blackwell v Harper* (1740) 2 Atk. 92.

[865] *Newton v Cowie* (1827) 4 Bing. 234 at 246.

[866] *Martin v Polyplas Manufacturers Ltd* [1969] N.Z.L.R. 1046 (copyright in three-dimensional engravings of two-dimensional designs for coins, requiring "great delicacy and intense application").

[867] As to what constitutes an engraving, see para.3–57, above.

[868] As in *Hi-Tech Autoparts Ltd v Towergate Two Ltd* [2002] F.S.R. 15, where an engraver had copied a plan drawing of a series of circles in a regular array to produce a three-dimensional plate having grooved circles with conical and vertical sides. The skill and labour resided in designing the grooves and in combining the grooved circles with the final layout of the circles. See para.32.

[869] *Re Martin* (1884) 10 V.L.R. 196. This decision must be open to doubt in the light of *Sawkins v*

noted earlier,[870] it seems that the meaning of "engraving" is wide enough to include prints and other forms of work made from an engraved plate or stamp, these forms of work therefore being capable of attracting copyright as engravings in their own right. In a number of cases in which this point has been made, consideration does not, however, appear to have been given to the question of originality in relation to the print.[871] In most cases, particularly where the prints are made by some kind of industrial process, it seems doubtful that any print could be an original work. The question will usually turn on what skill and labour, rather than mechanical acumen, is involved in realising that which is visually different between the plate and the print.

New version of existing work. In the case of a new edition of an existing work, **3–138** the issue will be whether any original work has been done by the editor.[872] Such work may consist of additions to, or alterations of, the text which, if they are not merely trivial, but are material so as to make the totality of the work original, will be protected in the same way as any original literary work, whether they form a substantial part of the complete work or not.[873] Alternatively, such work may consist of a new arrangement of the existing subject matter. It follows, therefore, that where a work not out of copyright is edited, there may be two copyrights, that in the original text and that in the new edition. Exploitation of the new edition will require the consent of the owners of the copyright in both works. In the same way, there will often be originality in a new or revised version of an existing dramatic work,[874] provided more than just a few words are added.[875] Where a claimant reconstructed an ancient text from a large number of incomplete fragments (the Dead Sea Scrolls) by using his knowledge of linguistics and religious law to interpolate missing sections, the result was an original work, even though the intention was to recreate, as nearly as possible, the ancient text.[876]

New arrangement or adaptation of music. Any substantially new arrangement **3–139**

Hyperion Records Ltd [2005] EWCA Civ 565; [2005] 1 W.L.R. 3281; [2005] R.P.C. 32: see para.3–133.

[870] See para.3–57.

[871] See, e.g. *Hi-Tech Autoparts Ltd v Towergate Two Ltd (No.1)* [2002] F.S.R. 15; *Hi-Tech Autoparts Ltd v Towergate Two Ltd (No.2)* [2002] F.S.R. 16; *James Arnold & Co Ltd v Miafern Ltd* [1980] R.P.C. 397; and *Wham-O Manufacturing Co v Lincoln Industries Ltd* [1985] R.P.C. 127.

[872] The distinction drawn in the cases on this topic before 1911 is not now relevant. Under the Literary Copyright Act 1842, no action could be brought in respect of infringement of copyright in a book unless the book was duly registered at Stationers' Hall. Consequently, if a new edition was registered, and the date of publication entered as the date of its publication of the new edition, the question was whether the new edition, regarded as a whole, was a new book or not. If it was, the registration was correct, and an action for infringement of the book could be brought; if it was not, and the new edition was merely the old book with slight variations, then the registration was invalid. See *Thomas v Turner* (1886) 33 Ch. D. 292; *Black (A. & C.) Ltd v Murray (A.) & Son* (1870) 9 Sc. Sess. Cas. (3rd Ser.) 341; *Hedderwick v Griffin* (1841) 3 Dunl. (Ct of Sess.) 383.

[873] *Interlego A.G. v Tyco Industries Inc* [1990] A.C. 217, PC, per Lord Oliver at 263C, and see *Black v Murray* (1870) 9 Ct. Sess. (3rd series) (new edition of works of Walter Scott, with notes); *Jogesh Chandra Chaudhuri v Mohim Chandra Rai* [1914] C.W.N. 1078. The position is much the same as in relation to an author's successive revisions to his manuscript. See para.3–136, above.

[874] *Hatton v Keane* (1859) 7 C.B. 268 (new version of one of Shakespeare's plays, with certain alterations in the text, original music, scenic effects, and other accessories); *Tree v Bowkett* (1896) 74 L.T. 77 (play altered by addition of two scenes, and so altered as to make it the plaintiff's; *Christoffer v Poseidon Film Distributors Ltd* [2000] E.C.D.R. 487 (Homer's *Odyssey* subjected to considerable reworking).

[875] *Tree v Bowkett* (1896) 74 L.T. 77; *Ashmore v Douglas-Home* [1987] F.S.R. 553 (no sufficient additions).

[876] *Eisenman v Qimron* [2001] E.C.D.R. 73 (Sup Ct of Israel). On this decision, see Burton Ong "Originality from copying: fitting recreative works into the copyright universe" [2010] I.P.Q. 165. It follows, perhaps curiously, that if the reconstruction ultimately produces a work which is identical to the original work, the reconstruction will be a new copyright work. See also para.3–139, below as to musical works.

or adaptation of an existing piece of music is entitled to copyright.[877] What matters in relation to a musical work is its sound as appreciated by the human ear[878] and thus, in the present context, what is important is the contribution made to the sound by the arranger or adapter. If A makes a piano score of the music of B's opera,[879] or if he writes an arrangement of an existing melody,[880] A has, in each case, produced an original musical work. The work does not have to be inventive, in the sense of creating music which did not exist before.[881] Painstaking work in restoring a score to what the composer probably intended, and correcting errors and filling in omissions may therefore qualify as original work, provided the resulting sound is different from existing versions of the musical work which the restorer worked on.[882] So a new transcription of a long out-of-copyright work was held to be entitled to copyright where the author had selected which manuscript to use, transcribed the manuscripts into modern notation, making them playable or more easily playable, corrected errors, inserted material from other sources, included the "figured bass" (notation which provides guidance to the player of the bass-line above the continuous bass), and inserted "advisory" or courtesy indications, such as tempo and ornamentation.[883] This had not been mere servile copying but had had the practical value of making the work playable. His re-creative work had been such as to create something really new using his own original (not merely copied) work.[884] There is therefore no reason why technical skill alone should not in appropriate circumstances be sufficient and, for example, in relation to an arrangement, no great skill or labour is required for the purpose of conferring copyright.[885] The work of transcribing a piece of music into notation will usually be enough to make the new work original; even though the transcriber may not have created new sounds, the work will usually be original on the basis of *Walter v Lane*.[886]

3–140   **Abridgments, précis and abstracts.** These are all examples of the same process,

---

[877] *Redwood Music Ltd v Chappell & Co Ltd* [1982] R.P.C. 109.

[878] See para.3–48, above.

[879] *Wood v Boosey* (1867) L.R. 3 Q.B. 223, affirming (1866) L.R. 2 Q.B. 340, where it was held, under the pre-1911 Act law, that the test was whether the arrangement was a new and substantive work in itself. In *Redwood Music Ltd v Chappell & Co Ltd* [1982] R.P.C. 109 at 116, it was held that this test was consistent with the originality requirement of the 1911 Act. It is suggested, however, that although an arrangement which is a new and substantive work in itself will clearly be original, this is not the determining test. See also *Boosey v Fairlie* (1877) 7 Ch. D. 301.

[880] *Austin v Columbia Gramophone Co Ltd* [1917–1923] Mac. C.C. 398; *Lover v Davidson* (1856) 1 C.B. (N.S.) 182; *Leader v Purday* (1848) 7 C.B. 4.

[881] *Sawkins v Hyperion Records Ltd* [2004] EWHC 1530 (Ch) at para.65 [2005] EWCA Civ 565; [2005] 1 W.L.R. 3281; [2005] R.P.C. 32. See paras 32 to 36, 71 and 77 to 86.

[882] *Sawkins v Hyperion Records Ltd* [2004] EWHC 1530 (Ch) at paras 32 to 36, 71 and 77. See also para.3–138, above and the case of *Eisenman v Gimron* [2001] E.C.D.R. 73 (Sup Ct of Israel) referred to there. For a full discussion of the decision in *Sawkins*, see Rahmatian, "The concepts of 'musical work' and 'originality' in UK copyright law— *Sawkins v Hyperion* as a test case" [2009] 40 IIC 560 and Burton Ong "Originality from copying: fitting recreative works into the copyright universe" [2010] I.P.Q. 165.

[883] *Sawkins v Hyperion Records Ltd* [2005] EWCA Civ 565, per Mummery L.J., paras 42 and 43, the Court of Appeal upholding the first instance decision: [2004] EWHC 1530 (Ch).

[884] *Sawkins v Hyperion Records Ltd* [2005] EWCA Civ 565, per Jacob L.J, who upheld the first instance decision on the basis that even in relation to the piece in respect of which the author had made the fewest interventions, he had started by choosing which original manuscript(s) to use (in fact using mainly two out of four, using one to correct ambiguities in the other), and had then checked every note and supplied 27 "corrections" (i.e. his personal evaluation as to what note the original composer (Lalande) really intended), supplied many suggestions for the figured bass, and put the whole into modern notation. He had thus re-created Lalande's work using a considerable amount of personal judgment (para.86). Mance L.J. agreed with both judgments (para.71).

[885] *Redwood Music Ltd v Chappell & Co Ltd* [1982] R.P.C. 109; *Godfrey v Lees* [1995] E.M.L.R. 307.

[886] *Walter v Lane* [1900] A.C. 539. This had been doubted by Cross J. in *Roberton v Lewis* [1976] R.P.C. 169, but the observation seems to have been based partly on an arguably wrong view of *Walter v Lane*. In *Hyperion Records Ltd v Sawkins* [2005] EWCA Civ 565 at para.84, on the basis that *Walter v Lane* was probably still good law, Jacob L.J. stated that a transcription of a

by which a larger work is reduced to a shorter summary.[887] Copyright will subsist in such works if they required skill and labour in their creation. However, the reduction of the size of a work merely by copying some of its parts and omitting others without the application of any skill or labour in the selection of what to retain and what to reject generally confers no copyright.[888]

Headnotes and case summaries. The digest of a law report in the form of a headnote or a case summary is a species of abridgment. Whether viewed as a separate brief report or as an independent deduction from the report, in principle there is clearly sufficient exertion of skill and labour to render a headnote or case summary the subject of copyright. It is something for which much skill and thought is often required, so as to express in clear and concise language the principle of law to be deduced from the decision, or the facts and circumstances which bring the case within some principle or rule of law or of practice:[889]

3–141

> "The authors must select specific elements of the decision and can arrange them in numerous different ways. Making these decisions requires the exercise of skill and judgment. The authors must use their knowledge about the law and developed ability to determine legal *ratios* to produce the headnotes. They must also use their capacity for discernment to decide which parts of the judgment warrant inclusion in the headnotes. This process is more than just a mechanical exercise."[890]

Indexes. An index will often be a work of separate creation from the main work. As such, the decision as to what to include will usually require the exercise of skill and judgment. The creator must choose the headings and then both decide what to include under those headings and how to describe the items included by a short summary.[891] Even, therefore, if the index is properly to be regarded as a database it will be entitled to copyright as such.[892]

3–142

Works infringing other works. Copyright can, as a matter of principle, subsist in an infringing work.[893] Whether it does so or not will depend on whether the pirated work has involved the expenditure by its author of time, skill and labour, and it is suggested that this is so whether the entire work consists of pirated material, or merely part of it, provided that its originator has expended time, skill and labour on the material pirated. A particular example of such a pirated work is an

3–143

---

musical work would be original, citing the example of the 14-year-old Mozart's transcription of Allegri's unpublished *Miserere* after he had heard it at a performance in the Vatican.

[887] Note that the 1988 Act, in the defence provided under s.60 in relation to the copying of abstracts of articles on scientific or technical subjects, recognises that an abstract of an article can be entitled to its own copyright. It used to be important to know what constituted a true abridgment since a true abridgment, being a new and useful work, was often not regarded as an infringement. See *Gyles v Wilcox* (1740) 2 Atk. 141; *Ganga'vishnu Shrikisanda's v Moreshuar Ba'Puj Hegishte* [1889] I.L.R. 13 Bom. 358; *Macmillan & Co Ltd v Cooper (K. & J.)* (1923) 40 T.L.R. 186, citing earlier editions of this work. The same is not true today. See para.7–31 at (e), below.

[888] As in *Macmillan & Co Ltd v Cooper (K. & J.)* (1923) 40 T.L.R. 186. See also the discussion of this case in relation to compilations at paras 3–146 et seq., below.

[889] *Sweet v Benning* (1855) 16 C.B. 459 at 491; *Ragunthan v All India Reporter Ltd* [1971] 4 A.I.R. Bom. 48.

[890] *CCH Canadian Ltd v Law Society of Upper Canada* [2004] SCC 13 (Sup Ct of Can). For this purpose, the headnote was taken to include the summary of the case, catchlines, statement of the case, case title and case information. Case summaries were similarly regarded as original, since a "summary of judicial reasons is not simply a copy of the original reasons. Even if the summary often contains the same language as the judicial reasons, the act of choosing which portions to extract and how to arrange them in the summary requires an exercise of skill and judgment".

[891] *CCH Canadian Ltd v Law Society of Upper Canada* [2004] SCC 13 (Sup Ct of Can) (index of legal cases); *Blacklock (H.) & Co Ltd v Arthur Pearson (C.) Ltd* [1915] 2 Ch. 376 at 384 (index to a new edition of a railway timetable).

[892] See para.8–148.

[893] See the discussion at para.3–307, below.

unauthorised translation of a copyright work, where the translator may have expended considerable time, skill and labour in producing the translation, entitling the translation to its own copyright.[894] Such works may give rise to particular problems when it is alleged that this copyright has itself been infringed; the result may depend on whether what has been copied was the subject of edited or unedited copying.[895]

(v) Photographs; films as dramatic works

3–144 Photographs present their own problems in relation to originality.[896] The essence of a photograph is that it should capture something for the purpose of its being reproduced for subsequent viewing. In one sense a photograph is always, therefore, a copy of something. Photography is a process which is a mixture between a mechanical process and a creative process; the balance between these two elements may vary enormously in any given case, yet the product is in each case a photograph. In the United Kingdom, copyright law has never distinguished between a photograph which is the result of a purely mechanical process, that is the operation of the shutter caused by the button being depressed, and that which is the result of the expenditure of much time and skill by the photographer in obtaining the right conditions for the photograph that he wishes to achieve.[897] Although art.6 of the Term Directive[898] required Member States to protect photographs which are original "in the sense that they are the author's own intellectual creation", Member States were permitted to protect "other" photographs. The United Kingdom did not amend the 1988 Act in this respect when implementing the Directive, or introduce a lesser category of photographs, and so the law as to what amounts to an original photograph was not altered.[899]

The copyright status of photographs was for some time in some doubt following the obiter remarks of Lord Oliver in *Interlego AG v Tyco Industries Inc*,[900] where he said:

> "Take the simplest case of artistic copyright, a painting or a photograph. It takes great skill, judgment and labour to produce a good copy by painting or to produce an enlarged photograph from a positive print, but no one would reasonably contend that the copy painting or enlargement was an 'original' artistic work in which the copier is entitled to claim copyright. Skill, labour or judgment merely in the process of copying cannot confer originality."

---

[894] It will of course remain dependent on the copyright in the work infringed in the sense that the exploitation of the translation will require the licence of the owner of the copyright in the original; see para.3–307, below.

[895] See, for example, *Warwick Film Productions Ltd v Eisinger* [1969] Ch. 508; *ZYX Music GmbH v King* [1995] 3 All E.R. 1 (on appeal, but not on this point: [1997] 2 All E.R. 129, CA).

[896] Particularly in the context of infringement, when it has to be determined what aspects of a photograph are protected by the copyright which subsists in it. As to what is protected by the copyright in a photograph, see *Bauman v Fussell* [1978] R.P.C. 485 (decided in 1953) and para.7–71, below. For a full discussion of the topic, see Michalos, *The Law of Photography and Digital Images* (London: Sweet & Maxwell, 2004). and Deazley "Photography, copyright, and the South Kensington experiment" [2010] I.P.Q. 293–311.

[897] For a discussion as to the differing approaches of other Union Countries, to the protection of photographs, see S. Ricketson and J.C. Ginsburg, *International Copyright and Neighbouring Rights, The Berne Convention and Beyond* 2nd edn. (Oxford: Oxford University Press, 2006), para.8–57.

[898] Council Directive 93/98 harmonising the term of protection of copyright and related rights. See now art.6 of Directive 2006/116/EC, the codified version of the Term Directive and its amendments.

[899] But note the aside in *Infopaq International A/S v Danske Dagblades Forening* (C–5/08) [2009] E.C.R. I–6569, para.35, that photographs are protected by copyright *only* if they are original in the sense that they are their author's own intellectual creation. The Court does not appear to have had in mind the possibility of lower protection at the national level.

[900] *Interlego AG v Tyco Industries Inc* [1989] A.C. 217.

However, this statement must now be considered, as a generality, to be wrong, being inconsistent with *Walter v Lane*.[901] It has also been decided by a court in the United States that, as a matter of English law and based on Lord Oliver's statement, particular photographs of paintings were not original since there was no element of "material alteration or embellishment" from the original work[902]; the photographs were effectively no different from photocopies.[903] However, this decision must, for the same reason, now also be taken to have been wrong.[904]

In terms of what is original for the purpose of determining whether copyright subsists in a photograph, the requirement of originality is again low. So, photographs of various antiques were held to be original where they were taken with a view to exhibit particular qualities of the objects, including their colours, features (for example, glaze in pottery) and other details.[905] It was assumed for these purposes that some degree of skill was involved in the lighting, angling and judgment of the positions and the selection of the objects.[906] In fact, it seems that the test of originality may be satisfied by little more than the opportunistic pointing of the camera and the pressing of the shutter button[907] and there seems no reason of principle why there should be any distinction between the photograph which is the result of such a process and a photograph which is intended to reproduce a work of art, such as a painting or another photograph.[908] Provided that the author can demonstrate that he expended some small degree of time, skill and labour in producing the photograph (which may be demonstrated by the exercise of judgment as to such matters as the angle from which to take the photograph, the lighting, the correct film speed, what filter to use, etc.), the photograph ought to be entitled to copyright protection, irrespective of its subject matter.[909]

Film or broadcast as a dramatic work. It has already been seen that a film or broadcast, if it is a work of action, will also be a dramatic work.[910] From the point of originality, such works are similar in some respects to photographs. Taking a

3–145

---

[901] See *Hyperion Records Ltd v Sawkins* [2005] EWCA Civ 565; [2005] 1 W.L.R. 3281; [2005] R.P.C. 32, per Jacob L.J. (with whom Mance L.J. agreed) at para.83. See further, para.3–133, above. It should be pointed out that Lord Oliver was not concerned in *Interlego* with photographs or this particular issue, and no argument appears to have been addressed to the Privy Council on the point. In any event, his obiter remarks about photographs were directed at the making of an enlargement from a positive, not the taking of a photograph itself.

[902] *The Bridgeman Art Library Ltd v Corel Corp*, 25 F. Supp. 2d 421 (S.D.N.Y.) 1998 and 36 F. Supp. 2d 191, applying the words of Lord Oliver in *Interlego AG v Tyco Industries Inc* [1989] A.C. 217 at 262H–263A.

[903] i.e. applying *The Reject Shop Plc v Manners* [1995] F.S.R. 870, on this point. *Graves' Case* (1869) L.R. 4 Q.B. 715, was distinguished on the grounds of its antiquity and the "subsequent development" of the law of originality, presumably a reference to *Interlego*.

[904] It is also suggested that the analogy of a photocopier made in the *Bridgeman* decision is a poor one, given the disparity of the skill and labour involved. See further on the *Bridgeman* case: Garnett, "Copyright in Photographs" [2000] E.I.P.R. 229; Deazley, "Photographing Paintings in the Public Domain: A Response to Garnett" [2001] E.I.P.R. 179; Stokes, "*Graves' case* revisited in the USA—The Bridgeman Art Library v. The Corel Corporation" [2000] Ent. L.R. 104; Stokes, letter, [2001] E.I.P.R. 354; Michalos, *The Law of Photography and Digital Images* (London: Sweet & Maxwell, 2004).

[905] *Antiquesportfolio.com v Rodney Fitch & Co Ltd* [2001] F.S.R. 23.

[906] *Antiquesportfolio.com v Rodney Fitch & Co Ltd* [2001] F.S.R. 345.

[907] *Antiquesportfolio.com v Rodney Fitch & Co Ltd* [2001] F.S.R. 345, approving a paragraph in the previous edition of this work containing this statement.

[908] See *Graves' Case* (1869) 4 L.R.Q.B. 715, in which copyright was held to subsist under the Fine Arts Copyright Act 1862 in photographs of engravings, themselves made from paintings. See also *Hansard*, HL Vol.493, col.1073. "The question whether one photograph is a copy of another of the same subject matter will have to be decided by the usual test—is it original? Has it involved skill and effort on the part of the photographer?".

[909] Compare *The Reject Shop v Manners* [1995] F.S.R. 870, where copyright was held not to subsist in an enlarged photocopy.

[910] See para.3–39, above, and *Norowzian v Arks Ltd (No.2)* [2000] F.S.R. 363.

film as an example, where the action in the film has been produced or enhanced by the process of editing, no particular problem arises. Where, however, the action takes place in front of the lens, presumably the resulting film will usually only be original if the filmmaker has added something of dramatic significance, for example by way of camera angle, lighting or editing.

(vi) Compilations, tables and databases

3–146   **Compilations, tables and databases.** The labour and skill employed in gathering, selecting or arranging existing subject-matter traditionally resulted in copyright protection being given to the resulting work. Such protection was originally conferred either by way of a table or a compilation[911] but with effect from January 1, 1998 there are now two categories of work to be considered, namely (a) databases and (b) tables and compilations which are not databases, and for works made on or after March 27, 1996 the test of originality differs in relation to each category.[912] In particular, although the Database Regulations[913] apply to databases created before as well as after January 1, 1998,[914] where a database was created before March 27, 1996[915] and copyright subsisted in it immediately before January 1, 1998, copyright will continue to subsist in the database for the remainder of its copyright term.[916] It follows that the "old" originality test is to be applied in relation to all compilations and tables made before March 27, 1996 and to tables and compilations made after this date if they are not also databases. The "new" originality test must be applied to all compilations and tables made after this date which are also databases (as well as any other work which is a database). The "old" test will be discussed first.

3–147   **The "old" originality requirement.** The relevant skill and labour may be directed to the compiling of the contents, their selection from a larger number of items, or to their arrangement.[917] Originality in this context will depend upon the degree of skill, labour and judgment involved in preparing the compilation.[918] In particular, since the nature of a compilation or table is that it supplies intelligible information,[919] it is skill and labour directed to this object which is relevant. As to selection, there are only a few cases in which the labour of selection was regarded as so negligible that copyright protection was refused. For example, copyright was denied to the selection of various common tables for insertion into a pocket diary,[920] a local railway timetable relating to a particular town compiled from a

---

[911] CDPA 1988 s.3(1)(a); Copyright Act 1911 s.35; Copyright Act 1956 s.48(1).

[912] This is the effect of the amendments introduced by the Copyright and Rights in Databases Regulations 1997 (SI 1997/3032), implementing the Database Directive 96/9. See para.3–21, above, for a discussion of these categories.

[913] See the previous footnote.

[914] reg.27. Member States were required to implement the Database Directive by this date: art.16(1).

[915] The date of the Directive was March 11, 1996.

[916] reg.29(1).

[917] Although art.2(5) of the Berne Convention stipulates that protection is to be conferred on collections of literary or artistic works such as encyclopaedias and anthologies which, by reason of the selection and arrangement of their contents, constitute intellectual creations, it does not follow that only such compilations are to be protected, since the Convention imposes minimum standards only.

[918] *Interlego A.G. v Tyco Industries Inc* [1989] A.C. 217 at 262; [1988] R.P.C. 343, referring to *Macmillan & Co Ltd v Cooper* 40 T.L.R. 186; *G.A. Cramp & Son Ltd v Frank Smythson Ltd* [1944] A.C. 329; and the speeches of Lord Reid and Lord Hodson in *Ladbroke (Football) Ltd v William Hill (Football) Ltd* [1964] 1 W.L.R. 273 at 277, 285, 287.

[919] *Real Estate Institute of N.S.W. v Wood* (1923) 23 S.R. (N.S.W.) 349. See para.3–24, above.

[920] *G.A. Cramp & Sons Ltd v Frank Smythson Ltd* [1944] A.C. 329 (the claimants claimed originality in a choice of seven tables for the diary: (a) a calendar for the year, (b) a selection of "days

larger timetable,[921] a selection of passages from North's translation of Plutarch's life made simply by omitting certain passages,[922] a list of greyhounds written down in the order in which they were drawn from a hat[923] and to the linking together of three computer programs.[924] By contrast, protection has been given under this head to a wide variety of works and originality has seldom been in issue, the argument usually being about infringement. Thus, compilations of works of literature, such as selections of poems or prose compositions have been protected as original works,[925] as have selections of incidents from real life[926] and selections of quotations from an interview.[927] Equally, trade directories,[928] telephone directories,[929] maps,[930] trade catalogues,[931] lists of horses,[932] race cards,[933] soccer fixture lists,[934] listings of programmes to be broadcast,[935] bridge

---

and dates" for the year, (c) postal rates, (d) equivalents of metric and imperial weights and measures, (e) lighting-up times, (f) an empire and foreign timetable (i.e. the equivalent time to noon at Greenwich), and (g) a percentage table. The compiler was dead and no evidence was called as to the process of selection).

[921] *Leslie v J. Young & Sons* [1894] A.C. 335, HL (although the timetable was "convenient and useful for the inhabitants of that town, ... it does not require either such labour or such ingenuity in its preparation as to render it fit subject-matter for copyright". See the comment of Lord Macmillan on the case in *G.A. Cramp & Sons Ltd v Frank Smythson Ltd* [1944] A.C. 329 at 337. A compilation of circular journeys from the town was, however, held to be original).

[922] *Macmillan & Co Ltd v K. & J. Cooper* (1924) 40 T.L.R. 186 (North's translation contained about 40,000 words, of which about 20,000 words were selected. On the other hand, various notes to the selected text were protected, though of a commonplace nature and at least in part themselves selected from older sources).

[923] *Greyhound Racing Association Ltd v Shallis* [1923–1928] Mac. C.C. 370.

[924] *Total Information Processing Systems Ltd v Daman Ltd* [1992] F.S.R. Note, however, that in *Ibcos Computers Ltd v Barclays Mercantile Highland Finance Ltd* [1994] F.S.R. 275 at 290, Jacob J. considered that the general proposition that copyright cannot subsist in a compilation of computer programs was wrong.

[925] *Macmillan & Co v Suresh Chunder Deb* (1890) 17 Indian L.R. (Calcutta) 951 (PC) (Palgrave's *Golden Treasury*).

[926] See *Harman Pictures N.V. v Osborne* [1967] 1 W.L.R. 723 (choice of incidents from the Charge of the Light Brigade); *Poznanski v London Film Production Ltd* [1936–1945] Mac. C.C. 107 (book about Catherine the Great); *MacGregor v Powell* [1936–1945] Mac. C.C. 233 (compilation about the evacuation of St Kilda in 1930, although the headnote appears to go further than the report); and *Ravenscroft v Herbert & Anor* [1980] R.P.C. 193. In none of these cases, however, was originality of the work in issue.

[927] *Express Newspapers plc v News (UK) Ltd* [1990] F.S.R. 359 at 360 (sufficient skill and judgment in selection of quotations from an interview lasting over eight and a half hours).

[928] e.g. *Kelly v Morris* (1886) L.R. 1 Eq. 697; *Morris v Ashbee* (1868) L.R. 7 Eq 34. For further examples of directory cases, see other footnotes to this paragraph and para.7–47, below.

[929] *Desktop Marketing Systems Ltd v Telstra Corp Ltd* 55 I.P.R. (2002) 1.

[930] *Macmillan Publishers Ltd v Thomas Reed Publications Ltd* [1992] F.S.R. 455 (sufficient work in selection of information such as depth soundings, geographical features, buoys, etc. in producing nautical charts).

[931] *Hotten v Arthur* (1863) 1 H. & M. 603 (list of rare books, manuscripts, etc. relating to an estate, with anecdotes, comments and descriptions); *Grace v Newman* (1875) L.R. 19 Eq. 623 (compilation of sketches of tombstones); *Maple & Co v Junior Army and Navy Stores* (1882) 21 Ch. D. 369 (overruling *Cobbett v Woodward* (1872) L.R. 14 Eq. 407, to the contrary); *Harpers Ltd v Barry, Henry & Co Ltd* (1892) 20 Sess. Cas. (4th Ser.) 133; *Collis v Cater Ltd* (1898) 78 L.T. 613, *Lamb v Evans* [1893] 1 Ch. 218 (list of advertisements). Illustrations in trade catalogues may be individually protected as artistic works, although text and illustrations together may be protected as a compilation; see para.3–26, above.

[932] *Weatherby & Sons v International Horse Agency and Exchange Ltd* [1910] 2 Ch. 297.

[933] *Bookmakers' Afternoon Greyhound Services Ltd v Wilfred Gilbert (Staffordshire) Ltd* [1994] F.S.R. 723, following *Demerara Turf Club v Phang* [1963] W.I.R. 177 (Sup Ct of British Guyana); *Ascot Jockey Club Ltd v Simons* [1968] 64 W.W.R. 411 (Sup Ct of Can); *British Columbia Jockey Club v Standen (Winibar Publications)* [1984] 4 W.W.R. 537 (Sup Ct of Brit. Columbia), distinguishing *Greyhound Racing Association v Shallis* [1923–1928] Mac. C.C. 370, noted earlier in this paragraph, where the list was compiled merely by drawing the names from a hat.

[934] *Ladbroke (Football) Ltd v William Hill (Football) Ltd* [1964] 1 W.L.R. 273.

[935] *British Broadcasting Co v Wireless League Gazette Publishing Co* [1926] 1 Ch. 433; 42 T.L.R. 370; *Independent Television Productions Ltd v Time Out Ltd* [1984] F.S.R. 64.

tallies[936] and other mundane material[937] can be the subject-matter of copyright as original compilations. It is, of course, always open to question whether the component parts of a catalogue are original or merely taken from a common source, but a catalogue is generally a compilation upon which the compiler will have exercised skill and judgment in its creation. As to the gathering of information into a table or compilation, it has never been the position under English law that compilations compiled merely using "sweat of the brow" and not involving skill and judgment in the selection of their constituent parts were not protected as original works.[938] This can be seen, for example, from *Collis v Cater*[939] where it was held that copyright subsisted in a "dry" list of ordinary medicines sold by a chemist, arranged in alphabetical order, which had required labour, or expense and trouble, but no literary skill, in its compilation. The same is true of the directory cases,[940] where originality may lie in the humdrum though painstaking accumulation of information. Another example is *Football League Ltd v Littlewood Pools Ltd*,[941] where copyright was held to subsist in a chronological list of football matches taken from a larger list, painstaking hard work and attention to accuracy being all that was required in its creation.[942]

It is sometimes argued that a distinction should be made between the skill and labour required for the compiling of information and the skill and labour required for the presentation of it, only the latter being relevant for the purposes of the originality requirement and copyright protection. Thus, with regard to the creation of a Football League fixture list, which required skill to arrange the dates on which the teams should play each other, it was argued that the working out of the dates had been done for the purposes of the League's activities and not for the compilation of its fixture list.[943] Again, in the case of the creation of football pool coupons, it was argued that while skill and labour might have been involved in working out which bets to offer, there was no sufficient skill and labour in writing out the bets.[944] The argument is usually founded on a statement of Lord Evershed's in *Purefoy Engineering Company Ltd v Sykes, Boxall & Co Ltd*.[945] There, the claimants made standard parts to be used by customers in the manufacture of jigs, and the defendants copied these jigs, as they were entitled to do. The claimants also made a catalogue of their parts, and it was argued that the defendants had copied the catalogue indirectly, by copying the claimants' parts. In the course of rejecting the argument, Lord Evershed said:

"... the contents of the catalogue described the parts made and offered by

---

[936] *Stevenson (A.) v Crook (H.F.)* [1938] Ex. (Can.) 299 (tables of combinations of the players worked out so as to avoid repetition of partners, much skill and labour being involved in their creation; originality *was* in issue).

[937] e.g. *Skybase Nominees Pty Ltd v Fortuity Ltd* (1996) 36 I.P.R. 529 (Fed Ct of Aus) (compilation of weight loss programmes, requiring great skill and judgment, and expense); *Olympic Amusements Pty Ltd v Milwell Pty Ltd* (1998) 162 A.L.R. 199 (scales of prizes to be awarded by gaming machines to standard poker hands, whose working out was a complex and highly skilled affair).

[938] In this the law of the UK differs from that of the US, as laid down in such decisions as *Feist Publications Inc v Rival Telephone Service Co* 499 U.S. Ct. 340 (1991).

[939] *Collis v Cater* (1898) 78 L.T. 613, approved in *Purefoy Engineering Co Ltd v Sykes Boxall & Co Ltd* (1955) 72 R.P.C. 89, CA at 99 and *Ladbroke (Football) Ltd v William Hill (Football) Ltd* [1964] 1 W.L.R. 273.

[940] See the cases cited earlier in this paragraph. For a very full and modern discussion of the principles in such cases, see *Desktop Marketing Systems Ltd v Telstra Corp Ltd* 55 I.P.R. (2002) 1 (Fed Ct of Aus).

[941] *Football League Ltd v Littlewood Pools Ltd* [1959] Ch. 637.

[942] *Football League Ltd v Littlewood Pools Ltd* [1959] Ch. 637 at 656.

[943] *Football League Ltd v Littlewoods Pools Ltd* [1959] Ch. 637 at 653 et seq.

[944] *Ladbroke (Football) Ltd v William Hill (Football) Ltd* [1964] 1 W.L.R. 273 at 278.

[945] *Purefoy Engineering Company Ltd v Sykes, Boxall & Co Ltd* (1955) 72 R.P.C. 89. The issue in the case was not, however, subsistence of copyright but whether the defendants had copied. See paras 7–34 and 7–37, below.

the plaintiffs. And the considerable skill and labour devoted by the plaintiffs in making their selection was devoted to the selection of the range of goods in which the plaintiffs were to trade and not for the purpose of bringing into existence the literary work, namely, the catalogue. No doubt skill and labour were employed for the latter purpose, but skill and labour of a different order. The selected range of goods existed or was capable of existing for trading purposes independently altogether of the plaintiffs' catalogue or of any catalogue."

Although such a defence is theoretically possible,[946] arguments of this kind have invariably failed, the reasons given being that the purpose of accumulating the information has in fact been to reduce it to a written or otherwise protectable form[947] and that a line cannot be drawn between the effort involved in developing ideas and that minimal effort required in setting those ideas down on paper.[948]

The "new" originality requirement for databases. As already noted, as far as copyright protection is concerned, databases are now excluded from the category of a table or compilation, and are to be treated as a separate type of literary work[949]; for practical purposes this change will be relevant for all databases created after March 27, 1996.[950] A database is the only work to be singled out in the 1988 Act to have its own definition of originality. Echoing the wording of art.3(1) of the Database Directive, s.3A(2) of the 1988 Act now provides that a database is original if, and only if, by reason of the selection or arrangement of the contents of the database, the database constitutes the author's own intellectual creation.[951] This new condition for subsistence of copyright in a database "raised the bar" so far as concerns the previously accepted notion of originality for the subsistence of copyright in the United Kingdom.[952] Although the recital 15 of the Directive states that this criteria should be "defined to" the fact that the selection or the arrangement of the contents of the database is the author's own intellectual creation, this seems to be an error in translation and a better rendering would be "confined to" or "limited to".[953]

What constitutes a database for present purposes has already been

3–148

---

[946] *Ladbroke (Football) Ltd v William Hill (Football) Ltd* [1964] 1 W.L.R. 273, per Lord Hodson at 287: "It may well be that there are cases in which expenditure of time and money has been laid out which cannot properly be taken into account as skill and labour involved in bringing into existence the literary work, be it catalogue or other compilation."

[947] *Football League Ltd v Littlewoods Pools Ltd* [1959] Ch. 637 at 655, followed in *Ladbroke (Football) Ltd v William Hill (Football) Ltd* [1964] 1 W.L.R. 273.

[948] *Ladbroke (Football) Ltd v William Hill (Football) Ltd* [1964] 1 W.L.R. 273, per Lord Hodson at 287. A further example is *Autocaps (Aust.) Pty Ltd v Pro-Kit Pty Ltd* (1999) 46 I.P.R. 339 (Fed Ct of Aus), where the compilation consisted of a list of replacement radiator and fuel tank caps, with an indication of which vehicles they were suitable for. It was held that preparatory work in determining which cap suited a particular vehicle was relevant for the purposes of originality. A similar case is *TS & B Retail Systems Pty Ltd v 3Fold Resources Pty Ltd (No 3)* [2007] FCA 151.

[949] See paras 3–21 et seq., above.

[950] In theory it may also affect databases created on or before this date but which were not then in copyright. See reg.29(1) of the Database Regulations.

[951] The use of the words "if, and only if" reflect the additional requirement in art.3(1) of the Database Directive 96/9 that "no other criteria shall be applied to determine their eligibility for that protection": *Football Dataco Ltd v Brittens Pools Ltd* [2010] EWHC 841 (Ch); [2010] R.P.C. 17, para.63. The wording of the Directive is also found in art.5 of the 1996 WIPO Copyright Treaty, dealing with compilations of data or other material.

[952] *Football Dataco Ltd v Brittens Pools Ltd* 2010 EWHC 841 (Ch), para.53.

[953] *Football Dataco Ltd v Brittens Pools Ltd* 2010 EWHC 841 (Ch), para.68, contrasting the French words " *se limiter au*" and the German word " *beschränkt*", and that it was plainly the intention of the Database Directive not to leave in place a patchwork of national laws protecting (by reference to a variety of different standards) the turning of independent works, data or other materials into a database.

considered.[954] It is relevant to keep in mind that the kind of work which is the subject matter of protection is different from that protected by the sui generis database right[955]: the purpose of copyright harmonised by the Directive is to provide encouragement for creative endeavour, and differs in this respect from the sui generis right, which is designed to encourage investment in particular types of data gathering. As regards the kind of work of selection or arrangement of the contents of the database which is relevant to the issue of originality, it is not confined to selection or arrangement performed after the data is finally created, and it thus includes selection decisions which are taken in the course of creating data, in particular as to the actual contents of the database, such work necessarily involving the choice of adopting one alternative and rejecting others. It is then necessary to focus on the skill and labour which was actually concerned with this type of selection and arrangement, and to exclude that which was not. The statement in recital 12[956] that "as a rule" the compilation of several recordings of musical performances on a CD does not fall within the scope of the Directive makes it clear that not everything which originates with the author will satisfy the Directive's originality test, the implication being that such a selection does not involve enough of the author's individual creativity. How much creativity is required is not made clear in the Directive, and will no doubt vary from case to case, but the requirement imposes a significant qualitative factor on the test, requiring some subjective contribution by the author. A collection made by "sweat of the brow" will therefore not satisfy the requirement, nor will computer-generated databases. Although the court will not apply a qualitative or subjective assessment (in the sense of judging whether the work is good or bad) in applying the test to the finished work,[957] the author must have exercised judgment, taste or discretion (good, bad or indifferent) in selecting or arranging the contents of the database. Thus mere rote application of particular rules to the selection will not be enough, e.g. all poems written by someone between 1900 and 1910, whereas, it seems, a selection by someone of their 1,000 favourite poems would be. Finally, although there is no requirement to demonstrate aesthetic or qualitative criteria, there must be a quantitative baseline of originality before protection is acquired.[958] So, in the example given, the quantity of 1,000 poems would clearly satisfy this test. In general in this respect, the hurdle is not very high.[959]

Overall the task for the court is therefore to: (i) identify the data which has been collected and arranged in the database; (ii) analyse the work which went into the creation of the database by collecting and arranging the data so identified, isolating the work which is properly regarded as selection and arrangement; (iii) ask whether the work of selection and arrangement was the author's own intellectual creation and in particular whether it involved the author's judgment,

---

[954] See para.3–21 et seq.

[955] As to which see Ch.18. This and the following passage in the text are based on the judgment in *Football Dataco Ltd v Brittens Pools Ltd* [2010] EWHC 841 (Ch), paras 83–91.

[956] "Whereas, as a rule, the compilation of several recordings of musical performances on a CD does not come within the scope of this Directive, both because, as a compilation it does not meet the conditions for copyright protection and because it does not represent a substantial enough investment to be eligible under the sui generis right."

[957] See recital 16.

[958] See *British Horseracing Board Ltd v William Hill Organisation Ltd* [2001] R.P.C. 31.

[959] *Football Dataco Ltd v Brittens Pools Ltd* [2010] EWHC 841 (Ch), para.89, the court finding helpful the decision of the German *Oberlandesgericht* in *Pharma Intranet Information AG v IMS Health GmbH & Co. OHG* [2005] E.C.C. 12, where a distinction was made between the purely deterministic and that which allows sufficient room for individual creative work, and where the view was taken that not very much "room for manoeuvre" is required to enable the creation of a copyright work (subject to the CD example of recital 19, where the room for manoeuvre in choosing recordings to put on a CD may be very large indeed, but something more than a "small coin" was required for originality).

taste or discretion; (iv) finally ask whether such work is quantitatively sufficient to attract copyright protection.

Applying these principles, a database of football fixtures for the English professional football leagues was found to satisfy the database originality test where: (i) the collected data included at least (a) the *dates* on which matches in general were to be played, (b) the *matches* which were to be played and (c) the *dates* of specific matches; (ii) the work of selection of that data isolated from all the other work done by the claimants consisted of the exercise of choice over the dates on which the fixtures were to be played and the identity of the teams to play in each match on those dates[960]—although the overall list of matches in any league was ultimately a "given", there was undoubted selection in the choice of dates and the decisions as to which match was to be played on which date; (iii) there were numerous stages in the process of allocation of matches to dates, and in the selection of the dates themselves, where judgment and discretion in the relevant sense had to be exercised[961]; and (iv) the quantum of relevant work involved in producing the lists for any of the leagues was considerable and was made more complex by the fact that no two fixtures could be freely interchanged without affecting others.[962]

(vii) Computer generated works

The 1988 Act contemplates that there may be literary, dramatic, musical or artistic works that are generated by computer in circumstances that there is no human author of the work in the ordinary sense. Where this is the case, the author is to be taken as the person by whom the arrangements necessary for the creation of the work are undertaken,[963] and this can clearly be a company as well as a human being. It is not clear how the requirement of originality is to be applied in these circumstances, in particular the requirement that the work be the product of at least some skill and labour. The difficulty will often be overcome by a readiness to find a human author, even in a process which is highly computer assisted,[964] but in principle there will always remain a class of works in respect of which this is not possible. It is suggested that the relevant skill and labour is that of the person by whom the arrangements necessary for the creation of the work were undertaken.   **3–149**

B. SOUND RECORDINGS AND FILMS

Sound recordings and films: copies of previous sound recordings or films.   **3–150**
Originality, as such, is not a requirement for the subsistence of copyright in sound recordings or films,[965] and the 1988 Act only provides that copyright does not subsist in a sound recording or film which is, or to the extent that it is, a copy

---

[960] Even if this work was not correctly characterised as "selection", then it was held to be "arrangement", proceeding from the starting materials of (i) the clubs in the league and (ii) the dates of the rounds of matches, to produce an arrangement which brought them together.

[961] In this respect the "author's intellectual creation" did not require the reader of a database to be able to identify the author.

[962] *Football Dataco Ltd v Brittens Pools Ltd* [2010] EWHC 841 (Ch), paras 93–98. Compare *Pennwell Publishing (UK) Ltd v Ornstein* [2007] EWHC 1570 (QB) at para.107(f), where the Judge stated (obiter) that he was far from persuaded that the exercise of assembling a list of the details of 1,650 contacts which was maintained on an Outlook system and in an Excel spreadsheet met the standard of originality required for database copyright protection.

[963] CDPA 1988 s.9(3).

[964] See, e.g. *Express Newspapers plc v Liverpool Daily Post & Echo Plc* [1985] F.S.R. 306.

[965] An amendment to the original Bill seeking to introduce the requirement of originality as regards sound recordings, films, broadcasts and cable programmes and typographical arrangements of published editions was opposed, on the basis that lack of originality in content for such works

taken from a previous sound recording or film.[966] This applies whether such copy was authorised or not. Under the 1956 Act there was no requirement of originality and no equivalent provision.

C. Broadcasts

3–151   **Broadcasts.** There is no originality requirement as such in relation to broadcasts. The 1988 Act merely provides that copyright does not subsist in a broadcast which infringes, or to the extent that it infringes, the copyright in another broadcast.[967] The 1988 Act therefore adopts a different approach in relation to broadcasts than it does in relation to sound recordings and films.[968] Although a broadcast which is an authorised repeat of an earlier broadcast is thus entitled to its own copyright,[969] it is provided that such copyright expires at the same time as that in the original broadcast.[970] It would seem that where the broadcast repeats an earlier broadcast but contains new material, the entirety of the subsequent broadcast will be protected as such for its own full term of copyright.[971]

3–152   **Cable programmes.** With effect from October 31, 2003, cable programmes are no longer protected as a separate subject matter,[972] and the rights in relation to such works have since that date been subsumed within the enlarged category of a "broadcast". The amendments to the 1988 Act which have brought this about apply to works, and thus cable programmes, which were made before October 31, 2003,[973] and so the above provisions relating to "broadcasts" must be applied to those works which were formerly regarded as cable programmes and which are now protected as broadcasts.

D. Typographical Arrangements

3–153   **Copies of previous typographical arrangements.** Under s.8(2) of the 1988 Act, copyright does not subsist in the typographical arrangement of a published edition if, or to the extent that, it reproduces the typographical arrangement of a previous edition.[974] Reproduction is not now a defined term under the 1988 Act,[975] and, strictly, the reference should have been to copying, not reproducing, since copying is defined, in relation to typographical arrangements, as the making of a facsimile copy of the arrangement.[976] In the context, this is clearly what was intended, and no doubt "reproduces" in s.8(2) will be so construed.

---

was irrelevant, and all that was required was to exclude copyright to the extent that the work was taken from an existing work: *Hansard*, HL Vol.493, cols 1057.

[966] CDPA 1988 ss.5A(2), 5B(4). See *Hansard*, HL Vol.493, cols 1073, 1074 as to how these provisions came to be worded as they are. An argument that copyright does not subsist in a work to the extent that it is a copy of films from which it was taken is a question which should come under the heading of reproduction of a substantial part, rather than subsistence: *Football Association Premier League Ltd v QC Leisure* [2008] EWHC 1411 (Ch), para.183; [2008] F.S.R. 32.

[967] CDPA 1988 s.6(6).

[968] The reason for the different wording is explained in *Hansard*, HL SCE, col.50.

[969] The rationale of this provision is that a repeat broadcast is not made from a recording of the first broadcast. It will be made from a recording made at the same time as or even before the first broadcast. For copyright protection to be adequate, therefore, each repeat must be given its own copyright, albeit for an abbreviated time. See *Hansard*, HL Vol.490, col.1163.

[970] CDPA 1988 s.14(5) and (6).

[971] This would appear to follow from general principles, and s.14(5) of the 1988 Act does not use the phrase "or to the extent that it is a repeat".

[972] See paras 3–88 et seq., above.

[973] The Copyright and Related Rights Regulations 2003 (SI 2003/2498), reg.31(1).

[974] CDPA 1988 s.8(2); re-enacting Copyright Act 1956 s.15(1), proviso.

[975] As it was under the 1956 Act (s.48(1)).

[976] CDPA 1988 s.17(5); facsimile is defined as including a copy which is reduced or enlarged in scale (s.178).

5. QUALIFYING CONDITIONS

A. INTRODUCTION

Qualification for copyright protection. The 1988 Act, after enumerating the **3–154** descriptions of works in which copyright may subsist,[977] provides, in relation to all such works, that copyright does not subsist in such works unless the requirements set out in c.IX of the Act with respect to qualification for copyright protection are met.[978] Chapter IX contains a common set of provisions for the subsistence of copyright in published and unpublished works of all descriptions,[979] with special provision being made in the case of broadcasts.[980] These provisions apply to works coming into existence on or after August 1, 1989. Works which already existed at that date, and which are referred to in this section of this work as existing works,[981] are subject to a different regime and, as a general rule, copyright under the 1988 Act subsists in such a work only if copyright subsisted in it immediately before August 1, 1989, that is, under the 1956 Act.[982] It is therefore necessary to deal separately with works coming into existence on or after August 1, 1989[983] and those in existence at that date.[984]

B. WORKS COMING INTO EXISTENCE ON OR AFTER AUGUST 1, 1989

(i) Introduction

Two bases of qualification. For all descriptions of works coming into existence **3–155** on or after August 1, 1989,[985] the 1988 Act provides two bases on which copyright protection may be obtained. The first basis is by reference to the status of the author, irrespective of whether the work has been published or not.[986] The requirements, broadly, relate to the nationality, citizenship or residence of the author. The second basis, which applies to works which have been published, is by reference to the country in which the work was first published being met.[987] The requirements, broadly, are that the country should be one to which the provisions of the 1988 Act extend,[988] or have been applied in recognition of that country's protection of works of UK origin. In the case of broadcasts, the 1988 Act maintains this dual basis of qualification, but replaces the concept of publication (which, as it involves the issue of copies of the work to the public, has no application to such works) with that of the making of a broadcast, and the second

---

[977] CDPA 1988 s.1(1); see paras 3–02 et seq., above.

[978] CDPA 1988 ss.1(3) and 153(1). The scheme of the 1956 Act was different, in that qualifying conditions were set out in the sections dealing with each category of works: Copyright Act 1956 ss.2(1) and (2), 3(2) and (3), 12(1) and (2), 13(1) and (2), 14(1) and 15(1).

[979] CDPA 1988 ss.154 and 155; see para.3–155, below.

[980] CDPA 1988 s.156; see para.3–184, below.

[981] CDPA 1988 Sch.1 para.1(3). This term, however, can have different meanings in different statutory contexts; see para.6–12, below.

[982] Sch.1 para.5. This general rule is subject to the important exception that an existing work may first gain protection under the 1988 Act by virtue of first publication in a relevant country or by the inclusion, for the first time, of the country of its author's nationality in an Order made under s.159 of the Act: Sch.1 para.5(2)(a) and (b); see further para.3–192, below.

[983] Section B, paras 3–155 et seq., below.

[984] Section C, paras 3–185 et seq., above.

[985] Except in respect of works the copyright in which belongs to the Crown to which special provisions apply: see Ch.10.

[986] CDPA 1988 s.154; and see paras 3–160 et seq., below.

[987] s.155; and see paras 3–174 et seq., below.

[988] See para.3–159, below.

basis for qualification for such works is by reason of the requirements being met as to the country from which the broadcast is made (i.e. transmitted).[989]

3–156   **Origin of two bases.** The two bases reflect the fact that in the early days of the development of copyright protection there were two parallel systems of protection: that accorded under statute, and that accorded under the common law. So far as early statutory protection was concerned, this was aimed exclusively at works which were published,[990] and, before the advent of international conventions to protect copyright works of other countries, it was natural that only those works which were published in the United Kingdom should be protected. Unpublished works continued to be protected by common law copyright,[991] where what mattered was whether the individual was subject to the common law, which was so in the case of an individual who was a subject of the Crown or who lived in England under the protection of the common law. This distinction between published and unpublished works also found expression in the Berne Convention, which required protection to be extended to works of authors who were nationals of a country of the Union, if unpublished or if first published in a country of the Union.[992] This was the position adopted in the United Kingdom under the 1911 Act, which abolished common law copyright and provided that copyright should subsist under that Act in the case of published works only if first published in the United Kingdom or a country to which the Act extended, and in the case of unpublished works only if the author was at the date of the making of the work a British subject or resident within a country to which the Act extended.[993]

3–157   **Time at which qualification requirements must be met.** The qualification requirements themselves all relate to a situation at a specific time (generally when the work was made or first published, as the case may be), from which it would follow that, if those requirements are met at the required time, later events (for example, the author ceasing to be a qualifying person or the country of first publication ceasing to be one to which the 1988 Act extends) are irrelevant to the continued subsistence of copyright. That this is the case in relation to works made on or after August 1, 1989, is made clear, in that the 1988 Act specifically provides that it is sufficient for copyright to subsist in a work if the qualification requirements of c.IX[994] are once satisfied in respect of that work, and that copyright does not cease to subsist in that work by reason of any subsequent event.[995]

3–158   **Alternative nature of the two bases: published works.** Under the 1988 Act, the two bases are entirely independent of each other. In the case of unpublished works, the only possible basis for qualification remains by reference to the status of the author. In the case of published works, the two bases are now true alternatives, in that all that is necessary for copyright to subsist in a published work is that the requirements relating to one basis should be satisfied. Although, for the

---

[989] ss.153(1)(c) and 156; and see para.3–184, below.

[990] This continued to be so until the 1911 Act, with the exception of the Fine Arts Copyright Act 1862 (25 & 26 Vict., c.68), which applied to paintings, drawings and photographs, whether published or unpublished, whose author was a British subject or resident in the British Dominions.

[991] Such protection was lost on publication: *Donaldson v Beckett* (1774) 4 Burr. 2408; *Beckford v Hood* (1798) 7 T.R. 620; *Jefferys (C.) v Boosey (T.)* (1855) 4 H.L.C. 815.

[992] Berne Convention art.4(1).

[993] Copyright Act 1911 s.1(1).

[994] The reference to the requirements of CDPA 1988 c.IX means that this principle does not apply in the case of works made before August 1, 1989, which are not governed by c.IX, but by the rules in force under the 1956 Act (see ibid. Sch.1 para.5).

[995] CDPA 1988 s.153(3). This was not so under the 1956 Act, since a work entitled to copyright by reason of the nationality of its author would subsequently have lost protection by first publication in a country to which the 1956 Act was not extended or applied; see *Copex Establishment v Flegon*, The Times, August 18, 1967, and *Bodley Head v Flegon* [1972] R.P.C. 587.

reasons discussed above, publication has been historically the more important basis, as regards most types of work coming into existence after August 1, 1989, the application of the provisions of the 1988 Act to an increasing number of countries[996] and the loosening of the link required between an individual and such a country means that it is much more probable that inquiry as to the status of the author will prove the easier basis on which to establish subsistence of copyright under the 1988 Act. This is therefore the basis which is discussed first below.

Extension and application of the provisions of the 1988 Act. Before setting out the different bases on which copyright protection may be obtained under the 1988 Act, it is necessary to explain briefly the difference between the extension and the application of the provisions of the Act to other countries.[997] Extension is used to describe the situation where the provisions of the Act apply in a country because they are the law of that country. Under the 1911 Act and, to a lesser extent, under the 1956 Act, the provisions of those Acts were extended to a number of colonies and dependent territories,[998] but Pt I of the 1988 Act extends only to England and Wales, Scotland and Northern Ireland.[999] Application is used to describe the situation where the provisions of the Act are made applicable to a country to which they do not extend, so that works which are first published in that country or are made by authors who, in the case of individuals, are citizens or subjects of, or are domiciled or resident in, such country, or, in the case of companies, are incorporated under the laws of that country, will be treated in the same way as works first published in the United Kingdom or made by a qualifying person.[1000]   **3–159**

(ii) By reference to the status of the author

Two bases on which status of author may qualify work for protection. There are two different routes by which the status of the author may qualify the work for protection under the 1988 Act. Both depend on the nature of the link which the author has with a particular country. The first is by reason of the author being a qualifying person, where the link is with the United Kingdom[1001]; the second is by reason of the link the author has with a country to which the provisions of the 1988 Act have been applied by Order in Council made under section 159 of the Act.[1002] In each case the link required may be broadly summarised as nationality of, or domicile or residence in, that country, or, in the case of a legal person, incorporation under the laws of that country.   **3–160**

Qualifying person. A work[1003] qualifies for copyright protection if its author was   **3–161**

---

[996] See para.3–159, below.

[997] These matters are discussed more fully in Section 6, Foreign Works, paras 3–192 et seq., below.

[998] See paras 3–270 et seq., below.

[999] CDPA 1988 s.157(1). Although there is power to extend Pt I to the Channel Islands, the Isle of Man or any colony (s.157(2)) by Order in Council, no such Order has been made; for the current position in the Channel Islands, the Isle of Man and Hong Kong, see further paras 3–272 to 3–278, below.

[1000] By an Order in Council made under CDPA 1988 s.159. As to Orders made under this section, and the countries to which Pt I has been applied, see paras 3–202 et seq., below.

[1001] CDPA 1988 s.154(1); the subsection refers to a country to which Pt I extends, but this effectively means England and Wales, Scotland and Northern Ireland.

[1002] CDPA 1988 s.154(2); see para.3–159, above.

[1003] These provisions apply to all descriptions of works; broadcasts could not qualify for protection under the 1956 Act by reason of their author being a qualified person; see further para.3–86, above.

at the material time a qualifying person.[1004] In the case of an individual, this means a person who enjoys what may be described for brevity as an extended form of British nationality, or who is domiciled or resident in the United Kingdom or in a country to which the relevant provisions of the Act extend.[1005] In the case of a body corporate, this means a body incorporated under the laws of the United Kingdom or of another country to which the relevant provisions of the Act extend.[1006]

3–162   **British nationality.** The extended form of British nationality comprises the terms British citizen, British overseas territories citizen, British national (Overseas), British overseas citizen, British subject and British protected person as these are defined in the British Nationality Act 1981.[1007]

3–163   **British citizen.** This status is principally acquired through birth in the United Kingdom to a parent who is a British citizen or who is settled, that is ordinarily resident, in the United Kingdom; other methods of acquisition include by descent, that is birth outside the United Kingdom to a person who is a British citizen, by adoption, by naturalisation or, in appropriate circumstances, by registration.[1008]

3–164   **British overseas territories citizen.** This status is conferred on citizens of a number of specified countries.[1009]

3–165   **British National (Overseas).** This means a person who is so defined under the Hong Kong (British Nationality) Order 1986.[1010]

3–166   **British Overseas citizenship.** This is a residual category for citizens of the United Kingdom and Colonies who do not acquire, under the 1981 Act, British citizenship or British Dependent Territories citizenship.[1011]

[1004] The term used in the 1956 Act was "qualified person" (see Copyright Act 1956 ss.2(1), 3(2), 12(1) and 13(1)), but the concept remains the same (see Copyright Act 1956 s.1(5)).

[1005] CDPA 1988 s.154(1). This effectively means England and Wales, Scotland and Northern Ireland, see para.3–184, below.

[1006] CDPA 1988 s.154(1). This effectively means England and Wales, Scotland and Northern Ireland, see para.3–160, above. The 1956 Act adopted the same test for corporate bodies being qualified persons, but the 1911 Act had referred to such bodies "having an established place of business". This remains the test in relation to certain existing works: see para.3–159, above.

[1007] 1981 (c.61) (as amended); the Act came into force on January 1, 1983 and repeals the definitions of British subject and Commonwealth citizen formerly contained in the Interpretation Act 1978 (c.30) Sch.1.

[1008] British Nationality Act 1981 ss.1–14 and see the British Nationality (Hong Kong) Act 1990 (c.34), the British Nationality (Hong Kong) Act 1997 and the Hong Kong (War Wives & Widows) Act 1996 (c.41).

[1009] British Overseas Territories Act 2002, (c.8) s.1(1); British Nationality Act 1981 ss.16–25 (ss.19–21 repealed by the Nationality, Immigration and Asylums Act 2002 ss.15, 161, Sch.2 para.1(d) and Sch.9). The countries are those specified in Sch.6, namely: Anguilla, Bermuda, British Antarctic Territory, British Indian Ocean Territory, Cayman Islands, Falkland Islands (as amended by the British Nationality Act (Amendment of Schedule 6) Order 2001/3497, with effect from December 4, 2001, by removal of "and Dependencies"), Gibraltar, Hong Kong (since removed with effect from July 1, 1997, by the Hong Kong (British Nationality) Order 1986 (SI 1986/948) as amended by the Hong Kong (British Nationality) (Amendment) Order 1993 (SI 1993/1795)), Montserrat, Pitcairn, Henderson, Ducie and Oeno Islands, St Christopher and Nevis (since removed by the Saint Christopher & Nevis Modification of Enactments Order 1983 (SI 1983/882)), St Helena Ascension and Tristan da Cunha (words substituted for "and Dependencies" by British Nationality Act 1981 (Amendment of Schedule 6) Order 2009/2744, with effect November 14, 2009), South Georgia and the South Sandwich Islands (inserted by British Nationality Act 1981 (Amendment of Schedule 6) Order 2001 (SI 2001/3497) art.2(b)), Sovereign Base Areas of Akrotiri and Dhekelia, Turks and Caicos Islands and Virgin Islands.

[1010] SI 1986/948 as amended by the Hong Kong (British Nationality) (Amendment) Order 1993 (SI 1993/1795) and the British Overseas Territories Act 2002.

British subject. A British subject under the 1981 Act[1012] is a person who im-   **3–167**
mediately before that Act came into force was a British subject without citizenship or was a British subject by virtue of being a former citizen of Eire, under the
British Nationality Act 1948,[1013] or was a British subject by registration under the
British Nationality Act 1965.[1014]

British protected person. This means a person declared to be such by an Order   **3–168**
in Council made in relation to any territory which was a former protectorate,
protected state or United Kingdom trust territory within the meaning of those
terms under the British Nationality Act 1948[1015] and who is *not* a citizen of certain
specified territories mentioned in Sch.3 to the British Nationality Act 1981.[1016]

Domicile. No attempt is made, in the 1988 Act, to define domicile, the meaning   **3–169**
of which is therefore left to the general law to determine.[1017] Domicile may be
obtained either by birth, operation of law,[1018] or by choice. Domicile of origin
prevails in the absence of a domicile of choice, that is, if a domicile of choice has
never been acquired or, if once acquired, has been abandoned. Further, a domicile of choice is acquired when a person fixes voluntarily his sole or chief residence in a particular place with an intention of continuing to reside there for an
unlimited time.[1019] A domicile of choice may be abandoned when, after departure
from a country, a person no longer has an intention to return there.[1020]

Residence. As with the concept of domicile, the 1988 Act does not attempt to   **3–170**
define residence, and the meaning of residence in the 1988 Act is therefore left to

---

[1011] British Nationality Act 1981 ss.26–29 (s.28 repealed by the Nationality, Immigration and
Asylums Act 2002 Sch.2 para.1(2), with effect November 7, 2002); as to the status of citizenship
of the United Kingdom and Colonies, see the British Nationality Act 1948 (11 & 12 Geo. 6, c.56)
now almost entirely repealed by the British Nationality Act 1981.
[1012] British Nationality Act 1981 ss.30–35.
[1013] British Nationality Act 1948 ss.2, 13 and 16, now repealed by the British Nationality Act 1981.
[1014] 1965 (c.34), repealed by the British Nationality Act 1981.
[1015] British Nationality Act 1948 ss.30 and 32, now repealed (save as to s.32(3)) by the British
Nationality Act 1981.
[1016] British Nationality Act 1981 s.38; the territories mentioned are: Antigua and Barbuda, Australia,
The Bahamas, Bangladesh, Barbados, Belize, Botswana, Brunei (inserted by the British Nationality (Brunei) Order 1983 (SI 1983/1699), Cameroon (inserted by the British Nationality (Cameroon and Mozambique) Order 1998 (SI 1998/3161), art.2), Canada, Republic of Cyprus, Do-
minica, Fiji, The Gambia, Ghana, Grenada, Guyana, India, Jamaica, Kenya, Kiribati, Lesotho,
Malawi, Malaysia, Maldives (inserted by the Brunei & Maldives Act 1985 s.1, Sch., para.8),
Malta, Mauritius, Mozambique (inserted by the British Nationality (Cameroon and Mozambique)
Order 1998 (SI 1998/3161), art.2), Namibia (inserted by the Namibia (British Nationality) Order
1990 (SI 1990/1502), Nauru, New Zealand, Nigeria, Pakistan (inserted by the Pakistan (British
Nationality) Order 1989 (SI 1989/1331), Papua New Guinea, Rwanda, (inserted by the British
Nationality (Rwanda) Order 2010/246, with effect from March 10, 2010), Saint Lucia, Saint Vin-
cent and the Grenadines, Saint Christopher & Nevis (inserted by the Saint Christopher & Nevis
Modification of Enactments Order 1983 (SI 1983/882), Seychelles, Sierra Leone, Singapore, Solomon Islands, South Africa (inserted by the British Nationality (South Africa) Order 1994 (SI
1994/1634), Sri Lanka, Swaziland, Tanzania, Tonga, Trinidad and Tobago, Tuvalu, Uganda,
Vanuatu, Western Samoa, Zambia, Zimbabwe. Under the British Nationality Act 1981 s.37,
citizens of these territories are Commonwealth citizens and will not, as from the commencement
of that Act, by the fact of their citizenship of that country be British subjects (as they were under
s.1(3) of the British Nationality Act 1948).
[1017] Other statutory definitions for particular purposes (see for example, Civil Jurisdiction and Judgments Act 1982 (c.27), ss.41–46, defining domicile for the purposes of that Act) may not therefore
be of much assistance. For a fuller discussion of domicile, see Dicey & Morris, *Conflict of Laws*
14th edn (London: Sweet & Maxwell, 2008), Ch.6, ss.1 and 2.
[1018] See Domicile and Matrimonial Proceedings Act 1973 (c.45).
[1019] *In the Estate of Fuld, decd. (No.3)* [1968] P. 675; *Plummer v I.R.C.* [1988] 1 W.L.R. 292.
[1020] See *Buswell v I.R.C.* [1974] 1 W.L.R. 1631; *Re Flynn* [1968] 1 W.L.R. 103; and *I.R.C. v Bullock*
[1976] 1 W.L.R. 1178.

the general law.[1021] Where there is nothing to show that the term residence is used in a more extensive sense, it denotes the place where an individual eats, drinks and sleeps, or where his family or his servants eat, drink and sleep.[1022] It seems clear that it implies something more permanent than a visit, but the degree of permanence is hard to define.[1023] It is suggested that it will be sufficient to show that the author, at the time the work was made, was living at a place within the country in question as his home.[1024]

3–171   **Foreign works.** An author who is a citizen or subject of, or domiciled or resident in, or, in the case of a corporate body, is incorporated under the law of a foreign country to which Pt I of the 1988 Act has been applied by an Order under s.159, is not by such fact brought within the definition of a qualifying person (although he may be a qualifying person if he otherwise satisfies the requirements of that definition). The works of such authors qualify independently for copyright protection by virtue of the author being, at the material time, a citizen or subject of, or domiciled or resident in or, in the case of a corporate body, incorporated under the law of such country.[1025]

3–172   **Material time.** The material time for the purposes of satisfying the test as to the author of a literary, dramatic, musical or artistic work being a qualifying person is, in the case of an unpublished work, when the work was made, or if the making of the work extended over a period, a substantial part of that period,[1026] and, in the case of a published work, when the work was first published, or, if the author had died before first publication, immediately before his death.[1027] A literary, dramatic or musical work is made when it is recorded in writing or otherwise;[1028] there is no equivalent definition as to when an artistic work is made.[1029] In the case of an artistic work which is completed, there would seem to be no difficulty in treating it as being made, for these purposes, when the making of the work is completed.[1030] However, there seems no reason why a work which the artist leaves unfinished (for whatever reason) should be denied copyright protection,[1031] and such a work should be treated as made for these purposes when the artist abandons

---

[1021] For a fuller discussion of residence, see Dicey & Morris, *Conflict of Laws* 14th edn (London: Sweet & Maxwell, 2008), Ch.6, s.3.

[1022] *R. v The Overseers of Norwood* (1866) L.R. 2 Q.B. 457; *Sinclair v Sinclair* [1968] P. 189; *R. v Barnet L.B.C. Ex p. Shah* [1983] 2 A.C. 309, HL.

[1023] See *MacRae v MacRae* [1949] P. 397 and *Stransky v Stransky* [1954] P. 428.

[1024] For cases on residence decided under the Income Taxes Acts, see: *Lloyd (T.) v S.I.R.* (1883) 11 Sess. Cas. (4th Ser.) 687; *Levene v C.I.R.* [1928] A.C. 217; *C.I.R. v Lysaght* [1928] A.C. 234; and *Reed v Clark* [1986] Ch. 1; and see *Cicutti v Suffolk* [1981] 1 W.L.R. 558 (a case under the Education Act) and *R. v Sec. State Ex p. Margueritte* [1983] 1 Q.B. 180 (a case under the British Nationality Act).

[1025] Under CDPA 1988 s.154(2); whether a person is a citizen or subject of, or domiciled in, a foreign country will depend on the application of that country's law, these being matters of a person's status under that law; it is suggested that residence is a factual concept, and will be judged by what the term means in English law, as to which see para.3–170, above. As to foreign works generally, see paras 3–192 et seq.

[1026] CDPA 1988 s.154(4)(a). As to who is the author of such works, see ibid., s.9(1) and paras 4–09 et seq., below.

[1027] s.154(4)(b).

[1028] s.3(2), re-enacting s.49(4) of the 1956 Act; writing includes any form of notation or code, whether by hand or otherwise: CDPA 1988 s.178. Making is not therefore the same as the first creation of the work, e.g. music may be composed, and even performed, before it is "made" for the purposes of the 1988 Act; see paras 3–49 and 3–119, above.

[1029] Nor was there under the 1956 Act. In *Mak Hau-Shing v Oriental Press Group Ltd* [1996] 1 H.K.L.R. 245 it was held that copyright subsisted in a photograph as soon as the shutter had opened and closed.

[1030] Compare the general provision in relation to works in existence at August 1, 1989 that when the making extended over a period the work shall be taken to have been made when its making was completed: CDPA 1988 Sch.1 para.1(3).

[1031] See paras 3–06 and 3–135, above.

finishing the work or when he dies. The material time for the purposes of satisfying the test as to the author of sound recordings, films and broadcasts being a qualifying person is also when they were made.[1032] In the case of films and sound recordings, as with artistic works, there is no definition of when such works are made,[1033] nor is there any specific provision, such as in the case of literary, dramatic, musical and artistic works,[1034] to deal with the situation (which is likely to be the case for most films) where the making extends over a period of time. It is suggested, again, that such works should be treated as made for these purposes when their making is complete.[1035] In the case of a wireless broadcast, the definition as to the place where it is made, contained in s.6(4) of the 1988 Act, also effectively defines the moment when it is made, which is when the programme-carrying signals are introduced into an uninterrupted chain of communication.[1036] In relation to cable broadcasts, the broadcast is no doubt made when the signals are introduced into the cable network leading to the recipient. In relation to typographical arrangements of a published edition, the work is made when the edition was first published.[1037]

Works of joint authorship. Where the work is a work of joint authorship,[1038] the work qualifies for copyright protection if at the material time any of the authors satisfies the above requirements, but only those authors who satisfy such requirements are taken into account when determining ownership and duration of the copyright so subsisting.[1039]   **3–173**

(iii) By reference to the place of first publication

(a) *Publication in general*

Publication: generally. As stated above, a literary, dramatic, musical or artistic work, typographical arrangement of a published edition, a sound recording or a film qualifies for copyright protection if it is first published in the United Kingdom, or in another country to which the relevant provisions of the 1988 Act have been applied.[1040] Publication, in relation to all works in which copyright may subsist under the 1988 Act, means the issue of copies of the work to the public.[1041] It follows that a work cannot be orally published.[1042] The reference to copies in the plural is deliberate, and there can be no publication of a work of   **3–174**

[1032] CDPA 1988 s.154(5)(a) and (b). As to who is the author of such works, see ibid., s.9(2) and paras 4–48 et seq. and 4–54 et seq., below.
[1033] cf. Copyright Act 1956 s.12(8), which provided that a sound recording was made when the first record embodying the recording was produced.
[1034] See earlier in this paragraph.
[1035] Compare the general provision in relation to works in existence at August 1, 1989 that when the making extended over a period the work shall be taken to have been made when its making was completed: CDPA 1988 Sch.1 para.1(3).
[1036] Which, in the case of a satellite broadcast, includes the uplink. As to who is the author of such works, see CDPA 1988 s.9(2) and paras 4–62 et seq., below.
[1037] CDPA 1988 s.154(5)(d). As to who is the author of such works, see ibid., s.9(2) and paras 4–67 et seq., below.
[1038] As to which see para.4–32 et seq., below.
[1039] CDPA 1988 s.154(3); and also for the purpose of determining whether the work is anonymous or pseudonymous under s.57.
[1040] CDPA 1988 s.155(1) and (2). See para.3–159, above and para.3–207, below.
[1041] CDPA 1988 s.175(1).
[1042] Thus delivery of a lecture from notes does not constitute publication of the notes: see para.3–180, below. Public performance of a dramatic work had been held to be publication of the work, prior to the 1911 Act changing the law in this respect: see para.3–180, below.

which there exists only a single example.[1043] Indeed, the issue of copies must be such that it is intended to satisfy the reasonable requirements of the public and not be merely colourable, or else it does not constitute publication.[1044] It is suggested that this remains the position, notwithstanding the amendment[1045] of the expression "issue of copies", in the context of the restricted act of issue of copies to the public, but expressed to apply to references to the expression in Pt I, to include reference to the issue of the original.[1046] The term "copy'" must be construed in accordance with the provisions contained in s.17 of the 1988 Act defining copying and copies.[1047] For the issue of copies to constitute publication, it must have been done by or with the licence of the copyright owner.[1048]

3–175   **First publication: simultaneous publication.** Publication for these purposes means first publication of the work. The 1988 Act provides that publication in one country shall not be regarded as other than the first publication by reason of simultaneous publication elsewhere, and for this purpose publication elsewhere within the previous 30 days shall be treated as simultaneous.[1049] What is frequently in copyright law described as simultaneous publication therefore means any two or more publications which take place within a period of 30 days. Under the 1911 Act, the relevant provision provided a period of 14 days only.[1050] This period continued to apply under the 1956 Act,[1051] in the case of a publication taking place before June 1, 1957, and, by virtue of the transitional provisions in the 1988 Act,[1052] this period still remains applicable in relation to existing works published before such date.[1053]

3–176   **Copies of the work.** Publication involves the issue of copies of the work to the public. "Copies" must be construed in accordance with s.17 of the 1988 Act.[1054] Section 17 provides specific rules as to what are to be treated as copies in the case of various different categories of works. Whilst these rules are expressed in the context of the acts restricted by copyright, they are clearly equally applicable to the question of what are copies for the purposes of publication under s.175 of the Act. The question remains, however, as to how exact the copies of the work issued to the public must be in order to constitute publication of that work. In this respect, the general provision that the doing of a restricted act in relation to a work is to be taken to include the doing of that act in relation to a substantial part of the work,[1055] has no application. If the "substantial part" test does not apply, do the copies have to be copies of the entirety of the work in order for their issue to constitute publication of the work? It is suggested that minor variations between the copies and the original will not prevent issue of the copies being publication of the original and that the test should be whether the whole work has in substance

---

[1043] Save, now, in the case of a work of architecture: CDPA 1988 s.175(3); see para.3–180, below. A writer of a private letter does not publish the letter by sending it to his correspondent, although by sending it to a newspaper for publication he would be licensing its publication by the newspaper. Compare the amendment of the restricted act of issuing copies of the work to the public (CDPA 1988 s.18(1)).

[1044] CDPA 1988 s.175(5), re-enacting s.49(2)(b) of the 1956 Act; see further, para.3–178, below.

[1045] By the Copyright and Related Rights Regulations 1996 (SI 1996/2967) with effect from December 1, 1996.

[1046] CDPA 1988 s.18(4).

[1047] s.17(1); see further para.3–181, below.

[1048] ss.175(6) and 178.

[1049] CDPA 1988 s.155(3). As did the Copyright Act 1956 s.49(2)(d).

[1050] Copyright Act 1911 s.35(3).

[1051] Copyright Act 1956 Sch.7 para.33(1).

[1052] CDPA 1988 Sch.1 para.5(1) and para.35.

[1053] See further as to existing works, paras 3–185 et seq., below.

[1054] CDPA 1988 s.17(1).

[1055] CDPA 1988 s.16(3).

been made available to the public. If what has been made available is something different in material respects from the original work, then the latter work has not been made available to the public and so has not been published. At most, what has been published is the work in the form of the copies.[1056]

When copies of a work are issued to the public. In order for a work to be 3–177 published, not only must the copies of the work be made, but they must be issued to the public.[1057] Issue for the purposes of sale is not essential,[1058] although, if copies are issued for such a purpose, that would amount to publication.[1059] A presentation of copies on the part of the author to individuals, or to a limited class,[1060] or even the sending of advance copies to the press for review, would not, it is thought, be publication, but gratuitous circulation generally would seem to be so.[1061] Thus, in *Prince Albert v Strange*,[1062] Queen Victoria and Prince Albert had given to their close friends lithographic copies of drawings and etchings which they had made for their own amusement, but this was held not to amount to publication of the works. In *Infabrics Ltd v Jaytex Shirt Co Ltd*,[1063] the Court of Appeal thought that an offer or exposure for sale would not be publication but that any consequent sale which resulted in the issue of reproductions of the work to the public would constitute publication. However, it is suggested that if such offer or exposure for sale is sufficient to show that there was an intention to satisfy the demands of the public, should such demand arise, then that will be treated as publication.[1064]

Colourable publication. For the issue of copies of the work to the public to con- 3–178 stitute publication it must be intended to satisfy the reasonable requirements of the public and not be merely colourable.[1065] The question as to what is a merely colourable publication arose in *Francis, Day & Hunter v Feldman & Co*,[1066] in which the claimants claimed to be the owners of the copyright in a song. On May 5, 1913 they sent one copy to the British Museum and filed one copy at their London office. They also sent four copies to the agent for receiving copies for the university libraries. They exposed six copies for sale on the counter in the retail department of their business premises in London. They did not advertise the song, and there was no immediate demand for it, but subsequently it became a great success and was the subject of large sales. It was held that the publication in England, on May 5, 1913, was not "colourable only", and that it was sufficient to

---

[1056] See, e.g. *Sweeney v Macmillan Publishers Ltd* [2002] R.P.C. 35 at para.42, confirming that for this purpose publication means publication of the whole work, not just a substantial part of it. If what is published is the latest in a series of revisions to a work, then what is published is the text set out in that latest, published version and not the text of the previous versions, which will remain unpublished.

[1057] See, as to sufficiency of evidence of publication, *Warner Bros Inc v The Roadrunner Ltd* [1988] F.S.R. 292.

[1058] See *British Northrop Ltd v Texteam Blackburn Ltd* [1974] R.P.C. 344.

[1059] *White v Geroch* (1819) 2 B. & Ald. 298; *Blanchett v Ingram* (1887) 3 T.L.R. 687.

[1060] For example, the issue of copies of the Oscar statuette to Acadamy Award winners was held not to be publication: *Oscar Trade Mark* [1980] F.S.R. 429.

[1061] *Novello v Sudlow* (1852) 12 C.B. 177; subject to the requirement that the issue of copies must be intended to satisfy the reasonable requirements of the public and not be merely colourable, as to which see para.3–178, below.

[1062] *Prince Albert v Strange* (1849) 1 M. & G. 25.

[1063] *Infabrics Ltd v Jaytex Shirt Co Ltd* [1980] Ch. 282, per Buckley L.J. at 292 (expressing the same view as to a sale by private treaty); reversed on appeal as to the meaning of publication for the purposes of infringement: [1982] A.C. 1; [1981] F.S.R. 261 HL.

[1064] See *British Northrop Ltd v Texteam Blackburn Ltd* [1974] R.P.C. 344 and see *Francis Day & Hunter v Feldman & Co* [1914] 2 Ch. 728 discussed at para.3–178, below.

[1065] CDPA 1988 s.175(5), re-enacting Copyright Act 1956 s.49(2)(b) and Copyright Act 1911 s.35(3).

[1066] *Francis, Day & Hunter v Feldman & Co* [1914] 2 Ch. 728.

show that there was an intention to satisfy the demands of the public if such demand should arise.[1067]

On the other hand, where the nature of the publication deliberately disregards the requirements of the public, it will not amount to publication.[1068]

3–179   Place of publication. In cases where the place of first publication is material, it would appear that it is the place where copies are first put on offer to the public.[1069] In the Canadian case of *Grossman v Canada Cycle Co*[1070] the posting in Canada of copies of a newspaper to subscribers in the United Kingdom was held not to amount to publication in the United Kingdom. However, since the persons receiving the newspapers in the United Kingdom were subscribers, and had therefore requested to be supplied with the newspapers, it is difficult to see why this would not constitute publication in the United Kingdom, subject to the quantity of copies being sufficient in accordance with the cases discussed above, particularly if the subscriptions had been obtained by reason of advertisement in the United Kingdom of the availability of the newspaper by subscription.

(b) *Literary, dramatic, musical and artistic works and typographical arrangements of published editions*

3–180   Publication: literary, dramatic, musical and artistic works and typographical arrangements of published editions. In addition to the general definition of publication,[1071] the 1988 Act provides that in the case of a literary, dramatic, musical or artistic work, publication includes making such a work available to the public by means of an electronic retrieval system.[1072] In relation to literary, dramatic, musical and artistic works, a copy means a reproduction of the work in any material form, including one stored electronically.[1073] The issue of records embodying such a work is therefore also publication under the 1988 Act.[1074]

The performance or communication to the public[1075] of a literary, dramatic or

---

[1067] In *Copex Establishment v Flegon, The Times*, August 18, 1967, 169 copies of the claimant's book in the Russian language had been placed on sale at more than 50 booksellers in the United Kingdom. On the first occasion of sale the demand did not exceed the supply, but, since the publicity given to the case, there had been extra demand which had exceeded the supply and it was intended to satisfy that demand. It is suggested that this satisfied the test of publication (the issue was not determined as undertakings were given).

[1068] See the example of the samizdat publication in *Bodley Head v Flegon* [1972] R.P.C. 587, which, being clandestine, was considered deliberately to disregard the requirements of the Russian public, because such requirements could neither be lawfully voiced by potential readers nor satisfied by the author.

[1069] *British Northrop Ltd v Texteam Blackburn Ltd* [1974] R.P.C. 344. As to publication in parts, see *Low v Ward* (1868) L.R. 6 Eq. 415. The Court of Appeal in *Infabrics Ltd v Jaytex Shirt Co Ltd* [1980] Ch. 282, per Buckley L.J. at 292, expressed the view that offer for sale would not be publication.

[1070] *Grossman v Canada Cycle Co* [1901–1904] Mac. C.C. 36.

[1071] CDPA 1988 s.175(1); see para.3–174, above.

[1072] s.175(1)(b).

[1073] s.17(1), (2).

[1074] This was excluded from being publication under the 1956 Act s.49(2)(a).

[1075] "Communication to the public" has a special meaning, namely communication to the public by electronic transmission, and it includes (a) the broadcasting of the work and (b) the making available to the public of the work by electronic transmission in such a way that members of the public may access it from a place and at a time individually chosen by them (i.e. by way of an on-demand service). See CDPA 1988 s.20(2) and para.7–112, below, for a full discussion. In order to achieve consistency with s.175(1)(b), however (see the earlier text of this paragraph), there is excepted from this exclusion any such communication for the purposes of an electronic retrieval system (s.175(4)(a)(ii)).

musical work does not constitute publication.[1076] Where lectures, addresses, speeches and sermons have been recorded in writing or some other form, and are thus capable of being protected as literary works,[1077] they do not become published by being delivered in public, since such delivery falls within the definition of performance of such works,[1078] and is therefore excluded from constituting publication.[1079] However, such works may be published by the issue of reports, or even of copies of notes, with the licence of the author. A lecturer would probably be held to license publication if he delivered his lectures knowing reporters were present, subject to any express or implied obligation on the part of those hearing the lecture to the contrary.[1080]

An artistic work is not published by being exhibited.[1081] Although, in relation to three-dimensional artistic works, a copy includes a copy in two dimensions,[1082] a work of architecture in the form of a building or a model for a building, a sculpture or a work of artistic craftsmanship is not published by the issue to the public of copies of a graphic work representing, or photographs of, such work.[1083] Having regard to these provisions, therefore, a three-dimensional artistic work, or a work of artistic craftsmanship, can only be published by the issue of three-dimensional copies of such a work; for example, in the case of a work of sculpture, by copies cast from the original work. A work of architecture in the form of a building, or an artistic work incorporated into a building, is treated as published when constructed.[1084] The issue to the public of copies of a film including an artistic work,[1085] and the communication to the public of the work,[1086] do not constitute publication of the artistic work.[1087]

In relation to typographical arrangements of published editions, copy is defined as meaning a facsimile copy of the arrangement.[1088] Facsimile is not itself defined,

---

[1076] CDPA 1988 s.175(4)(a); this follows the position under the 1956, and 1911, Acts. The 1911 Act effected a change in this respect, in that public performance of a dramatic work had previously been held to constitute publication: *Boucicault v Delafield* (1863) 1 H. & M. 597; *Boucicault v Chatterton* (1877) 5 Ch. D. 267; *Caird v Sime* (1887) 12 App.Cas. 326; *Walter v Lane* [1900] A.C. 539; *Falcon v The Famous Players Film Co Ltd* [1926] 2 K.B. 474 CA.

[1077] *University of London Press Ltd v University Tutorial Press Ltd* [1916] 2 Ch. 601; and see para.3–115, above.

[1078] CDPA 1988 s.19(2); re-enacting the previous position in relation to such works, under the Copyright Act 1956 ss.49(2)(a) and 48(1), and, before that, the Copyright Act 1911 s.1(3).

[1079] CDPA 1988 s.175(4)(a)(i).

[1080] See *Nicols v Pitman* (1884) 26 Ch. D. 374; *Caird v Sime* (1887) 12 App. Cas. 326 and, now, CDPA 1988 s.58. In an American case, *Keene (L.) v Kimball (M.)* (1860) 16 Gray (82 Mass.) 545, Hoar J. said: "The student who attends a medical lecture may have a perfect right to remember as much as he can, and afterwards to use the information thus acquired in his own medical practice, or to communicate it to students or classes of his own, without involving the right to commit the lecture to writing, for the purpose of subsequent publication in print or by oral delivery."

[1081] CDPA 1988 s.175(4)(b)(i). This was also the case under the 1956 Act: see s.49(2)(a). It was held, prior to 1911, that exhibition of a painting in a public gallery, the rules of which forbade the public to copy, was not a publication of the work: *Turner v Robinson* (1860) 10 Ir.Ch. 121 at 510.

[1082] CDPA 1988 s.17(3); as under the 1956 Act s.48(1).

[1083] CDPA 1988 s.175(4)(b)(ii). As to the meaning of graphic work, see s.4(2) and para.3–57, above.

[1084] CDPA 1988 s.175(3). This was not so under the 1956 Act: s.49(2)(a). It was doubted whether such a work could ever be published under the 1956 Act, save possibly by the issue to the public of paintings or drawings of the work: see *Copinger* 12th edn, pp.265, 266.

[1085] CDPA 1988 s.175(4)(b)(iii); "inclusion" is not defined, but this is not intended to cover the situation where the film is properly a reproduction of the work, for example a cartoon film which reproduces each of the artistic works comprising the drawings for the film; such drawings are published by the issue of copies of the film in which they are reproduced: *Warner Bros Inc v The Roadrunner Ltd* [1988] F.S.R. 292.

[1086] Otherwise than for the purpose of an electronic retrieval system: CDPA 1988 s.175(4)(b)(iv). As to the meaning of "communication to the public" in this context, see paras 7–120 et seq., below.

[1087] CDPA 1988 s.175(4)(b)(iv).

[1088] s.17(5).

other than as including a copy which is reduced or enlarged in scale,[1089] but its ordinary meaning is an exact reproduction. From this it necessarily follows that the copies must be identical (save for any enlargement or reduction) to the original typographical arrangement, but, again, if the copies only relate to part of the typographical arrangement and not the whole, their issue will not constitute publication of the typographical arrangement as a whole.[1090]

3–181   **What is a reproduction?** Although, therefore, the 1988 Act refers, for the purposes of publication of a literary, dramatic, musical or artistic work, to the issue of copies,[1091] because of the terms of s.17 of that Act which define copying and copies in relation to such works by reference to reproduction,[1092] it remains necessary to consider, for the purposes of publication of such works, what is a reproduction. Since it was considered necessary to provide specifically that the issue of copies of graphic works representing, and of photographs of, works of architecture, sculptures and works of artistic craftsmanship should not constitute publication,[1093] it appears to have been considered by the legislature that such graphic works and photographs would have been copies, and therefore reproductions, for the purposes of publication. Thus, the issue to the public of authorised graphic works or photographs of a painting, which, it would follow, are reproductions for these purposes, would constitute publication of such painting. Similarly, by excluding publication by the issue to the public of copies of a film in which the artistic work is included,[1094] it appears to have been considered that such inclusion would have constituted reproduction for the purposes of publication.[1095] This approach to "reproduction" for the purposes of publication is in accordance with the decision under the 1956 Act in *Merchant Adventurers Ltd v M. Grew & Co Ltd*,[1096] that drawings for light-fittings were published by the sale to the public of the three-dimensional fittings made from the drawings on the basis that "reproduction" in s.49(2)(c) of the 1956 Act should not be given a more restricted meaning than "reproduction" in s.48(1) of that Act where it was defined as including three-dimensional reproductions of two-dimensional artistic works. Nevertheless, questions may arise in relation to other works. For instance, if A were to translate his manuscript work and publish the translation before the original, would that be a publication of the original? It is suggested that it would not, and that the proper view of the matter is that where what is published so differs from the original that it is capable of existing as a separate copyright work, it is this separate copyright work which is published, not the original. This reasoning would apply to a dramatisation of an unpublished novel as well as to a translation. Thus, it is suggested that the publication of a pianoforte arrangement of an opera, or that of a few of the orchestral parts, would not be a publication of the opera

---

[1089] s.178.

[1090] See s.16(3)(a) and para.3–176, above; it is suggested that such issue would constitute publication of the copied part.

[1091] CDPA 1988 s.175(1)(a); cf. Copyright Act 1956 s.49(2)(c). See para.3–174, above.

[1092] s.17(2).

[1093] s.175(4)(b)(ii); re-enacting, as regards works of architecture and sculptures, the former provisions of the 1911 Act (s.1(3)) and of the 1956 Act (s.49(2)(a)).

[1094] CDPA 1988 s.175(4)(b)(iii).

[1095] This would remain so, however, in the case of a cartoon film, which in the true sense is a copy of the drawings produced for the film; such drawings would be published by the issue of copies of the film to the public: see *Warner Bros Inc v The Roadrunner Ltd* [1988] F.S.R. 292.

[1096] *Merchant Adventurers Ltd v M. Grew & Co Ltd* [1972] Ch. 242; [1971] F.S.R. 233; and see *Sifam Electrical Instruments Co Ltd v Sangamo Weston Ltd* [1971] F.S.R. 337 and *British Northrop Ltd v Texteam Blackburn Ltd* [1973] F.S.R. 241.

itself.[1097] These views are confirmed by the fact that the making of an adaptation of a work is treated as distinct from reproduction.[1098]

(c) *Sound recordings and films*

Publication: sound recordings. Copy is not further defined in the 1988 Act in relation to sound recordings. Nor does the 1988 Act provide a specific definition of publication in relation to sound recordings.[1099] Although the issue of records reproducing the whole sound recording clearly remains the issue of copies of the recording, and therefore publication of the sound recording under the 1988 Act, it is less clear whether, under the 1988 Act, the issue of records which reproduce part only of a sound recording is a publication of the whole sound recording, as it was under the 1956 Act.[1100] Playing a sound recording in public does not constitute publication, nor does its communication it to the public.[1101]   **3–182**

Publication: films. Similarly, the 1988 Act contains no definition of publication specifically in relation to films other than the general definition of issue of copies to the public. The definition given in the 1956 Act as the sale, letting on hire, or offer for sale or hire, of copies of the film to the public,[1102] is not repeated in the 1988 Act. This definition was wider than the ordinary definition of publication (issue of copies to the public), but still gave rise to the question whether letting on hire of copies merely to exhibitors, rather than to the general public, constituted publication. The absence in the 1988 Act of any specific definition of publication in relation to films would appear to resurrect all the problems previously thought to exist under the 1911 Act,[1103] as to what constitutes publication of a film, since, in particular, the first issue of copies is usually the letting of copies on hire to exhibitors. In relation to a film, a copy includes a photograph of the whole or a substantial part of any image forming part of such work.[1104] Showing a film in public does not constitute publication, nor does its communication to the public.[1105]   **3–183**

(iv) By reference to the place of transmission

Broadcasts. As stated above, whilst the general qualifying conditions otherwise   **3–184**

[1097] *Boosey v Fairlie* (1877) 7 Ch. D. 301.
[1098] CDPA 1988 ss.17(1) and 21(1).
[1099] The definition given in the 1956 Act s.12(9), as the issue to the public of records embodying the recording or any part of it, is not repeated in the 1988 Act.
[1100] By virtue of the words "or any part thereof" included in the definition in s.12(9) of the 1956 Act; cf. CDPA 1988 s.172, is the omission of these words in the 1988 Act "merely a change of expression"? Contrast the position in relation to literary, dramatic, musical and artistic works and typographical arrangements, discussed at para.3–176, above. It is suggested that the better view is that this change of wording is deliberate, and intended to bring sound recordings into line with the position applying to other works in this respect.
[1101] CDPA 1988 s.175(4)(c). For the meaning of communication to the public in this context, see para.7–121.
[1102] Copyright Act 1956 s.13(10).
[1103] Prior to the 1956 Act enlarging the definition of publication in relation to films, films had been regarded as unpublished works, because of the definition of publication in the 1911 Act (s.1(3)) as issue of copies to the public.
[1104] CDPA 1988 s.17(4); it was open to question under the 1956 Act whether a single frame could be a copy of a film for the purposes of publication (see *Spelling Goldberg Productions Inc v B.P.C. Publishing* [1981] R.P.C. 283); if the present definition applies equally for the purposes of subsistence as for infringement, then this question would seem to be answered, but such a result would be so anomalous that it is suggested that such a construction of copies for the purposes of subsistence by publication cannot be correct (cf. the position in relation to sound recordings discussed at para.3–182, above).
[1105] CDPA 1988 s.175(4)(c). For the meaning of communication to the public in this context, see para.7–121.

applicable to all works by reference to the author are applicable to broadcasts,[1106] the nature of a broadcast means that the alternative basis of qualification by reference to the place of first publication requires modification, to refer to the place of transmission.[1107] Thus, copyright subsists in a broadcast if it is made from a place which is either in the United Kingdom,[1108] or in a country to which the relevant provisions of the 1988 Act have been applied.[1109] The place where a wireless broadcast is made is defined as the place where the programme-carrying signals are introduced into an uninterrupted chain of communication, which in the case of a satellite broadcast includes the uplink.[1110] The place where a cable broadcast is made is not defined, but is no doubt the place where the signals are introduced into the cable network that leads to the recipient.

C. EXISTING WORKS

3–185   **Qualification by reference to country of first publication.** Under the 1911 Act, the subsistence of copyright in a published work depended solely on the place of first publication, and consequently copyright could often be lost or gained by publication. This was so, in particular, in relation to works emanating from the United States of America, since, by Order in Council, copyright was extended to the unpublished works of subjects or residents of the United States, but not to works first published there.[1111] The position was different under the 1956 Act, and subsistence of copyright in published works depended, not only upon the place of first publication but also, whatever that place, on whether the author was a qualified person when the work was first published or, if he died before publication, on whether he was a qualified person immediately before his death.[1112]

3–186   **Importance of determining when a work is published: existing works.** The new provisions of the 1956 Act, referred to in para.3–185, above, did not apply to works which were first published before the commencement of the 1956 Act.[1113] Consequently, it remained, under the 1956 Act, of substantial importance to determine whether or not a work was published. Even in the case of an existing work published after the commencement of the 1956 Act, the date for determining whether or not the author was a qualified person was different, so that if the work was not first published in the United Kingdom or in another country to which the relevant provisions of the 1988 Act extended, it was necessary to ascertain different information about the author to that which was relevant while the work remained unpublished. Moreover, the term of copyright in certain cases ran from first publication.[1114] While the term of copyright in relation to photographs taken after the commencement of the 1988 Act now does not run from first publication,[1115] and the position is now different in relation to works first published in the United States of America, following that country becoming

---

[1106] CDPA 1988 s.155; see para.3–115, above.
[1107] s.156.
[1108] s.156(1).
[1109] s.156(2); as to the countries to which the relevant provision have been applied, see paras 3–202 et seq., below.
[1110] s.6(4), replacing with effect from December 1, 1996 the provision as originally enacted, which was to similar effect but applied only to satellite broadcasts.
[1111] S.R. & O. 1915 No.130.
[1112] Copyright Act 1956 ss.2(2), 3(3).
[1113] i.e. June 1, 1957: Copyright Act 1956 Sch.7 para.1.
[1114] e.g. published photographs and sound recordings.
[1115] See para.6–09, below.

a signatory to the Berne Convention,[1116] whether a work was published, and if so when and where, are questions which remain important under the 1988 Act in many cases in respect of works in existence before the commencement of that Act, particularly in relation to the term of copyright in such works.[1117]

Existing works. An existing work, for the purposes of the 1988 Act, is a work the making of which was both begun and completed before August 1, 1989.[1118] Unlike the definition of material time for the purposes of satisfying the test as to the requirements for subsistence of copyright by reference to a work's author,[1119] in the case of a work the making of which extended over a period of time, it is the time of completion of the making of the work alone which governs whether the new provisions of the 1988 Act as to subsistence apply to the work. Nevertheless, where the making of the work was begun before, but completed after, August 1, 1988, it may still be necessary to consider the position during the making of the work prior to such date in order to determine whether copyright subsists in the work by reference to the requirements as to authorship being satisfied.[1120]

3–187

Subsistence of copyright in existing works. The 1988 Act provides that copyright subsists in an existing work after August 1, 1989 only if it subsisted immediately before such date, or if it is published after such date in accordance with the requirements as to first publication contained in s.154 of that Act.[1121] The new provisions as to subsistence of copyright introduced by the 1988 Act are, therefore, not to apply to events which occurred before August 1, 1989.[1122] For example, if copyright did not subsist under the 1956 Act in a musical work, but records reproducing that work had been released in the United Kingdom prior to August 1, 1989,[1123] such release does not operate to confer copyright on the work after commencement. Similarly, copyright will not subsist by virtue of publication under the 1988 Act in a work of architecture in the form of a building which was constructed prior to commencement.[1124] On the other hand, if copyright did subsist in an existing work under the 1956 Act, then copyright continues to subsist under the 1988 Act, irrespective of whether the requirements for subsistence set out in the 1988 Act are in fact satisfied in relation to such work.[1125] This approach to existing works in effect preserves the importance of the previous law under the 1956 Act in relation to such works. Thus, in relation to photographs taken, and sound recordings made, before June 1, 1957, the requirement as to qualification by reference to the author where it is a corporate body being incorporated under the laws of a country, continues to mean, under the 1988 Act, in relation to such works, a reference to such body having its established place of business in such country.[1126]

3–188

Existing works: special provisions. The general approach of the 1988 Act to

3–189

[1116] See para.3–269, below.
[1117] CDPA 1988 Sch.1 para.5(1) and para.12, and see Ch.6, below.
[1118] CDPA 1988 Sch.1 para.2.
[1119] See para.3–154, above.
[1120] See para.3–154, above.
[1121] CDPA 1988 Sch.1 para.5(1) and (2)(a); but see, as to foreign works, para.3–190, below.
[1122] Save in respect of works which are not existing works, because although their making began before commencement it was completed after such date: see para.3–187, above.
[1123] An act which did not constitute publication of the musical work under the Copyright Act 1956 (s.49(2)(a)), but which does under the 1988 Act; see para.3–180, above.
[1124] CDPA 1988 s.175(3); and see para.3–180, above.
[1125] CDPA 1988 Sch.1 para.35.
[1126] This being the definition of qualified persons which were corporate bodies under the 1911 Act, as preserved under the Copyright Act 1956 Sch.7 para.39(4).

existing works, discussed above,[1127] is supplemented by specific transitional provisions to ensure that copyright is not conferred on certain existing works which did not enjoy copyright protection under the Copyright Act 1956.

Thus, copyright does not subsist under the 1988 Act in an artistic work made before June 1, 1957, which at the time it was made constituted a design capable of registration under the Registered Designs Act 1949 and was used, or intended to be used, as a model or pattern to be multiplied by industrial process.[1128]

The same approach of maintaining the existing law is taken in relation to certain existing films, film soundtracks and broadcasts. Thus no copyright subsists under the 1988 Act in films as such made before June 1, 1957, but provision is made for preserving the dramatic and artistic copyright in such films corresponding to the rights so subsisting by virtue of the 1911 Act.[1129] Film soundtracks made before August 1, 1989 are now treated as sound recordings, not, as previously, as part of the film. However, for certain purposes, including subsistence of copyright, they continue to be treated as if they were part of the film.[1130] Wireless broadcasts made before June 1, 1957 and broadcasts by cable before January 1, 1985 are not entitled to copyright protection.[1131]

3–190   **Foreign existing works.** The only exception to the principle that events occurring before August 1, 1989 cannot entitle existing works to copyright protection if they did not enjoy such protection under the 1956 Act,[1132] is in relation to existing foreign works, which may qualify for copyright protection after commencement by virtue of an Order made under s.159 of the 1988 Act applying Pt I of that Act to a country to which those provisions do not extend.[1133]

The point is of most significance in relation to existing American works made before June 1, 1957, in particular old American films, and which did not qualify for copyright protection under the 1956 Act until the adherence of the United States of America to the Berne Convention led to the inclusion of that country in Sch.1 of the Order applying the 1956 Act to such works.[1134] The wording of that Order made it clear that such previously unprotected works could qualify for copyright protection under the 1956 Act either by virtue of a publication which took place in the United States of America before June 1, 1957, or by reason of the author being a citizen, resident or subject of such country.[1135] This alteration in protection afforded to foreign existing works has greatly diminished the importance previously attributed to the question of whether it was possible to publish old American films, a question upon which the copyright protection in the United Kingdom of such films in turn depended.[1136]

The position under the 1988 Act is the same, originally by virtue of the provi-

---

[1127] See para.3–188, above.

[1128] CDPA 1988 Sch.1 para.6; this maintains the position as it was under the Copyright Act 1956 Sch.7 para.8 and Sch.8 para.2.

[1129] CDPA 1988 Sch.1 para.7; this maintains the position as it was under the Copyright Act 1956 Sch.7 paras 14, 15 and 16.

[1130] CDPA 1988 Sch.1 para.8.

[1131] CDPA 1988 Sch.1 para.9, as amended; this maintains the position as it was under the Copyright Act 1956 Sch.7 para.17 and s.14A (added, with effect from January 1, 1985, by the Cable and Broadcasting Act 1984 ss.22–24 (now repealed)).

[1132] i.e. the principle underlying CDPA 1988 Sch.1 para.5(1) discussed at para.3–188, above.

[1133] CDPA 1988 Sch.1 para.5(2); and see paras 3–192 et seq., below.

[1134] The Copyright (International Conventions) Order 1979 (SI 1979/1715) as amended with effect from March 8, 1989 by the Copyright (International Conventions) (Amendment) Order 1989 (SI 1989/1570).

[1135] Copyright (International Conventions) Order 1979 (SI 1979/1715), Sch. para.6.

[1136] See *Copinger* 12th edn, p.797.

sions of an Order made under s.159 of the Act.[1137] Such Order contained its own "transitional" provisions intended to deal with the situation where, prior to such work becoming protected in the United Kingdom, a person committed himself to investment with a view to exploitation of the work in a way which was, after the work became protected, an infringement of copyright.[1138]

Unprotected work qualifying for protection. Although the Orders in Council made under the Copyright Acts to comply with the Berne Convention and Universal Copyright Convention must make the event more unusual than in the past,[1139] circumstances may still occur in which an unpublished work was unprotected in the United Kingdom, but subsequently became protected by reason of its publication here.[1140] For instance, apart from international arrangements, a foreign artist does not, by exhibiting his painting in the United Kingdom, become entitled to copyright here. Until he has issued copies to the public, any person is at liberty (unless acting in breach of confidence or contract) to copy the original work and to sell those copies in the United Kingdom. This, being done without the licence of the artist, does not constitute publication of the work,[1141] and therefore, if the artist himself subsequently issues reproductions to the public in the United Kingdom (or another country to which the 1988 Act is applied or to which its provisions are extended), he thereby gains copyright in the United Kingdom in his original. What then is the position of the first copyist? Clearly, he cannot be sued for piracy merely because he has in his possession copies of the work, for those copies were lawfully made and the subsequent acquisition of copyright by the author cannot, prima facie, have a retrospective effect so as to render an act unlawful which was perfectly lawful at the time it was committed.[1142] It is equally clear that the copyist cannot make or print any further copies (even from the copies he has already made). However, it is not so clear whether he can dispose of copies which he has on hand at the date when the artist acquired his copyright. Under the 1956 Act, it was suggested that the test remained whether copies were lawfully made when made, and, if so, their subsequent sale could not give rise to an infringement.[1143] The case was considered to be analogous to that of a person who has assigned his copyright, or granted a licence to publish for a term which has expired. It was held, under the old law, that an assignor could dispose of copies manufactured before the date of his assignment, and that a licensee could do the same with regard to copies manufactured before his licence ran out.[1144] The position would appear to be different under the 1988 Act, in that the putting into circulation of copies not previously put into circulation now con-

3–191

[1137] The Copyright (Application to Other Countries) (No.2) Order 1989 (SI 1989/1293), paras 2(1) and (2). See now the Copyright and Performances (Application to Other Countries) Order 2008 (SI 2008/677), below at **C1**.

[1138] See para.7(1) and (2) of the 1979 Order and now art.7 of the Copyright and Performances (Application to Other Countries) Order 2008 (SI 2008/677), below at **C1**.

[1139] But, as to the particular problem caused in relation to existing works by the retrospective effect given under the Order in Council to the United States of America becoming a signatory to the Berne Convention, see para.3–269, below.

[1140] See *Copex Establishment v Flegon*, The Times, August 18, 1967, where the authoress was Mrs Svetlana Alliluyeva, Stalin's daughter; and see *Bodley Head v Flegon* [1972] R.P.C. 587.

[1141] CDPA 1988 ss.175(6) and 178.

[1142] This is the approach taken under the various Orders in Council in relation to acts which were lawful when done, where previously unprotected works become protected in the United Kingdom; see para.3–190, above.

[1143] See Copyright Act 1956 s.5(3).

[1144] *Taylor v Pillow* (1869) L.R. 7 Eq. 418 (a case of assignment); *Howitt v Hall* (1862) 6 L.T. 348 (a case of licence); cf. the dicta to the contrary with regard to gramophone records under the Copyright Act 1911 s.2(2): *Monckton v Pathé Frères Ltd* [1914] 1 K.B. 395.

stitutes an infringement, if done without the copyright owner's licence, irrespective of whether the copies were infringing copies when made.[1145]

6. PROTECTION OF FOREIGN WORKS

A. Introduction and Scheme of this Section

3–192   **Relevance of foreign connection provisions**. If a work does not (or cannot be shown to) presently qualify for copyright protection by reason of the basic qualification provisions,[1146] it is very likely still to qualify by reason of a connection with a foreign country. Just as with the basic qualification provisions, there are three types of relevant connection: by reference to the author, by reference to the place of first publication and (in the case of a broadcast) by reference to the country from which the broadcast was made.

3–193   **The present law**. In order to find out whether a work qualifies in this way at the present time, it is necessary to consider the current Order in Council dealing with the matter, presently the Copyright and Performances (Application to Other Countries) Order 2008 (which came into force on April 6, 2008) ("the 2008 Order").[1147] With some exceptions and limitations, if the country in question is listed in the Schedule to the Order, and the Act is stated to apply to works in the relevant category which are connected with that country in a relevant manner, the work qualifies for protection. This is so even if the work is an "existing work", that is to say it was made before the commencement of the 1988 Act on August 21, 1989.[1148]

3–194   **Relevance of previous law**. The previous law may however be relevant for a number of reasons. First, the 2008 Order and its predecessors provide a defence to infringement proceedings for persons who have incurred expenditure in relation to acts which became infringements by reason of a work qualifying under the Order in question. In order to see whether such a defence applies it is necessary to look at the terms of the actual Order which caused the work to qualify, because the terms of these defences have changed over the years.

Secondly, it may be necessary to know whether copyright subsisted in a work at a particular date in the past, not only when considering infringement but also when considering the effect of agreements, assignments or licences. As might be expected, the 2008 Order and its predecessors are not retrospective in the sense that they do not confer copyright as from the creation of the work but only from the date they came into force. It follows such Orders provide no assistance in finding out whether a work qualified for copyright protection by reason of a connection with a foreign country at a date before they came into force. For that it is necessary to consider the earlier law.

Thirdly, para.5(1) of Sch.1 to the 1988 Act provides that copyright subsists in an existing (pre-commencement) work after commencement if copyright subsisted in it immediately before commencement. It follows that if for some reason qualification cannot be achieved by applying the 1988 Act it may nevertheless be achieved by applying the provisions of the 1956 Act.

3–195   **Nature of the previous law**. Protection for foreign-connected works has gener-

---

[1145] CDPA 1988 s.18.

[1146] As to which see paras 3–154 to 3–191, above.

[1147] SI 2008/677. This Order has been amended by SI 2009/2745, which came into force on November 12, 2009 and contains provisions limited to Bermuda. See Vol.2 C4.

[1148] The present law is dealt with in paras 3–200 et seq., below.

ally been based on reciprocity between the United Kingdom and other countries. In general, therefore, there is no protection for works with a foreign connection in respect of a period during which there was no reciprocal protection for works connected to the United Kingdom. In some cases the reciprocal protection may exist but only in partial form and it is therefore necessary to examine the terms of the Order to ascertain the scope of the protection it provides.

Coverage of the earlier law in this section. The earlier law is dealt with in   **3–196**
chronological order, starting with the position prior to the commencement of the 1911 Act[1149] and going on to deal with the position while that Act was in force, followed by the position while the 1956 Act was in force. Special sections are devoted to the law of the United States.[1150] The coverage is not intended to be comprehensive. Comprehensive accounts of the law at particular dates are contained in earlier editions of this work.[1151]

Extension of the Act to British colonies and dependencies. The qualification   **3–197**
provisions referred to above need to be seen in the context of the provisions of the 1911, 1956 and 1988 Acts which permitted their provisions to be extended to British colonies, dependencies and similar territories. These provisions (which are of diminishing importance) are dealt with separately, starting with the law under the 1988 Act and then dealing with the previous law in chronological order.[1152]

Other foreign connected works. Special provision is made by the 1988 Act in   **3–198**
respect of works made by officers and employees of certain international organisations and in relation to unpublished literary, dramatic, musical or artistic works of unknown authorship where there is evidence that the author (or, in the case of a joint work, any of the authors) was a qualifying individual by connection with a country outside the United Kingdom. These provisions are dealt with in separate paragraphs.[1153]

States which denounce conventions, alter their territory or disappear.   **3–199**
Complex issues arise when a state denounces an international convention, alters its territorial extent or ceases to exist (whether as a result of being taken over by another country or by being broken up). No attempt is made to deal with the international aspects of these issues in this section. The position under the Berne Convention is covered at length in the leading text on the subject.[1154] In respect of other conventions, recourse must be had to general principles of international law.[1155]

Section 153(3) of the 1988 Act provides that if the qualification requirements of the 1988 Act are once satisfied in respect of a work, copyright does not cease to subsist by reason of any subsequent event. This provision is in the most general terms and would appear to overcome even the disappearance of the country in question. However, there was no similar provision in the 1911 or 1956 Acts.

[1149] paras 3–224 et seq., below.
[1150] paras 3–233, 3–239, 3–244 and 3–269 below.
[1151] For the dates of such editions, see the endpapers of this one.
[1152] paras 3–270 et seq., below.
[1153] paras 3–301 and 3–303, below.
[1154] Ricketson and Ginsberg *International Copyright and Neighbouring Rights* (2006) paras 17.35 et seq.
[1155] See 61 *Halsbury's Laws* 5th edn *International Relations Law* and the standard texts.

Denunciations of the Berne Convention have been rare.[1156] In the United Kingdom they have generally been dealt with by the making of an Order revoking the relevant Order in Council so far as applicable to that country or deleting the name of the country. There is no consistent policy as to how this is done. In two cases[1157] no express provision was made for acquired rights. In the remaining cases,[1158] express provision was made to preserve existing rights.

The position of a country which incorporates territory of another country ought not (it is thought) to create many difficulties. The question whether a person is a national of such a country will no doubt be determined by the local law while the question whether the work was first published within the territory of the country will (so far as it matters) depend on the scope of the territory at the relevant time.

The position of a country which has disappeared is not so clear. One example is Germany, which was replaced by two separate countries after the Second World War. The reference to "Germany" remained in the 1933 Order[1159] until 1957 when that Order was revoked and replaced by the 1957 Order,[1160] which referred only to the Federal Republic and Land Berlin. The revocation of the 1933 Order did not affect rights which had been acquired under it by reason of a connection with "Germany".[1161] However, it would seem that works made in the Federal Republic between the end of the war and the commencement of the 1957 Order or in the Democratic Republic between the end of the war and its accession to the Berne Convention were not protected during that period. The position was further complicated by the fact that it is not clear whether the Democratic Republic was a member of the Berne Union before 1970.[1162]

B. WORKS AND OTHER SUBJECT MATTER CONNECTED WITH FOREIGN COUNTRIES OTHER THAN COLONIES, DEPENDENT TERRITORIES AND SIMILAR COUNTRIES

(i) Provisions of the 1988 Act

3–200   **Existing (pre-commencement) works.** The general approach is to apply the provisions of the 1988 Act to existing works as they apply to works coming into existence after commencement, subject to any provision to the contrary contained in Sch.1 to the Act.[1163]

3–201   **The basic method of qualification under the 1988 Act.**[1164] A work may qualify for protection either by reference to its author or by reference to the place where it was first published.[1165] Copyright subsists in a work if the author was a "qualifying person" at the material time. If the work is unpublished, the material time is when the work was made. If the work is published, the material time is when the

---

[1156] Ricketson and Ginsberg *International Copyright and Neighbouring Rights* (2006) paras 17.34 et seq.

[1157] Liberia (see S.R.&O. 1929 No.657) and Upper Volta (SI 1971/1850).

[1158] Montenegro (see S.R.&O. 1899 No.594), Hayti (as it was then spelt) (SI 1943/383), Indonesia (SI 1960/200) and Syria (SI 1962/397).

[1159] S.R.&O. 1933 No.253.

[1160] SI 1957/1523.

[1161] This is the effect of art.5 of the Order, which applied the Interpretation Act 1889 to the Order as if it were a statute and s.38(2)(c) of the 1889 Act which preserved existing rights when a statute repealed a statutory instrument.

[1162] Ricketson and Ginsburg *International Copyright and Neighbouring Rights* (2006) para.17.68. The Federal Republic and East Berlin were added to SI 1972/673 in 1973: see SI 1973/772.

[1163] CDPA 1988 Sch.1 para.3.

[1164] See generally paras 3–154 to 3–191, above.

[1165] For the meaning of the term "publication", see paras 3–174 et seq., above.

work was published or, if the author had died before that time, immediately before his death.[1166] An individual is a qualifying person if he is a British citizen, a British Dependent Territories Citizen, a British National (Overseas), a British Overseas Citizen, a British subject or a British protected person; or domiciled or resident in the United Kingdom or another country to which the relevant provisions of Pt 1 of the Act extend.[1167] A work also qualifies for publication if it was first published in the United Kingdom or another country to which the relevant sections of Pt I of the Act extend.[1168] A broadcast qualifies for protection if it was made from a place in the United Kingdom or another country to which the relevant sections of Pt I of the Act extend.[1169]

Power to apply Pt 1 of the 1988 Act to other countries. By s.159 of the 1988 Act, Her Majesty is authorised, by Order in Council, to make provision for applying any of the provisions of Pt I of the Act dealing with copyright, in the case of a country[1170] to which such Part does not extend, so as to secure that those provisions:　　　　　　　　　　　　　　　　　　　　　　　　　　　　　　　　　3–202

  (a) apply in relation to persons who are citizens or subjects of that country or are domiciled or resident there, as they apply to persons who are British citizens or are domiciled or resident in the United Kingdom, or
  (b) apply in relation to bodies incorporated under the law of that country as they apply in relation to bodies incorporated under the law of a part of the United Kingdom, or
  (c) apply in relation to works first published in that country as they apply in relation to works first published in the United Kingdom, or
  (d) apply in relation to broadcasts made from that country as they apply in relation to broadcasts made from the United Kingdom.

Any such Order can be made subject to exceptions and modifications, and may apply either generally or in relation to specified classes of works or classes of cases. A statutory instrument containing an Order in Council under s.159 is subject to annulment in pursuance of a resolution of either House of Parliament.

Countries in relation to which such an Order may be made. An Order may be made in relation to any country to which the copyright Part of the 1988 Act does not extend. The present position is that the copyright Part of the 1988 Act extends to England and Wales, Scotland and Northern Ireland.[1171] There is power to extend it by Order to any of the Channel Islands, the Isle of Man and any colony.[1172] Although such Orders have been made in relation to Bermuda[1173] and Gibraltar,[1174] they have since been revoked.[1175] It follows that such an Order may be made in relation to any country other than England and Wales, Scotland and Northern Ireland.　　　　　　　　　　　　　　　　　　　　　　　　　　　　　　　3–203

Limitation on power to apply the 1988 Act. The operation of s.159 is based on the principle of reciprocity between the United Kingdom and other countries. In　3–204

[1166] CDPA 1988 ss.155(1) and 3(4).
[1167] These terms are considered elsewhere: paras 3–164 et seq., above. Separate provision is made for bodies corporate in subs.154(1)(c).
[1168] CDPA 1988 s.155. For "extension" of the Act, see paras 3–270 et seq., below.
[1169] CDPA 1988 s. 156. For "extension" of the Act, see paras 3–270 et seq., below.
[1170] "Country" includes any territory: CDPA 1988 s.178.
[1171] CDPA 1988 s.157(1).
[1172] CDPA 1988 s.157(2). This power is discussed in more detail elsewhere.
[1173] The Copyright (Bermuda) Order 2003 (SI 2003/1517).
[1174] The Copyright (Gibraltar) Order 2005 (SI 2005/853).
[1175] By the Copyright (Bermuda) Revocation Order 2009 (SI 2009/2749), and the Copyright (Gibraltar) Revocation Order 2006 (SI 2006/1039).

general, therefore, there is to be no protection for works with a connection to a particular foreign country if or to the extent that there is no protection in that country for works connected with the United Kingdom. Accordingly, the power to make such Orders is limited in that an Order is not to be made in relation to a country,[1176] other than a "Convention country" or another Member State of the European Community, unless Her Majesty is satisfied that provision has been or will be made under the law of that country in respect of the class of works to which the Order relates, giving adequate protection to the owners of copyright under Part I of the 1988 Act. A "Convention country" is a country which is a party to a Convention relating to copyright to which the United Kingdom is also a party.[1177]

3–205 **Effect of such an Order.** If and to the extent that an Order has been made in relation to works connected to a particular country, they are put on the same footing as works connected with the United Kingdom.[1178] As will be seen from the next paragraph, the inclusion of a country in such an Order is not irreversible. However, as is the case in relation to works which qualify for protection by reason of a connection with the United Kingdom, once a work qualifies for protection, that protection cannot be lost.[1179]

3–206 **Power to curtail protection.** The counterpart to s.159 of the 1988 Act is s.160. This section gives power to deprive citizens or subjects of countries not giving adequate protection to "British works", of copyright under the 1988 Act. This power arises if the laws of a country[1180] fail to give adequate protection to "British works", or to one or more classes of such works. A "British work" is a work of which the author was a qualifying person at the material time within the meaning of s.154 of the 1988 Act.[1181] It seems to follow that the absence of protection for works first published in the United Kingdom is not a basis for curtailing protection in this way. In the given circumstances, an Order in Council can be made providing, either generally or in respect of specified classes of cases, that works first published after a date specified in the Order do not qualify for copyright protection by virtue of such publication if at the time of their first publication the authors are citizens or subjects of the country designated by the Order and not domiciled or resident in the United Kingdom or another country to which the relevant provisions of Pt I of the 1988 Act extend,[1182] or are bodies incorporated under the laws of the designated country. Such an Order may be made in respect of literary, dramatic, musical and artistic works, sound recordings and films. No such Order has yet been made. A statutory instrument containing an Order in Council under s.160 of the 1988 Act is subject to annulment in pursuance of a resolution of either House of Parliament.

(ii) Orders in Council under the 1988 Act

3–207 **General.** Successive Orders in Council have been made under the 1988 Act. Each has been amended (in some cases more than once) and each has revoked its predecessor. These revocations will not have affected rights which had already

---

[1176] See para.3–202, above.
[1177] CDPA 1988 s.159(3) and (4).
[1178] CDPA 1988 ss.154(2) and (3), 155(2) and 156(2). As to existing works, see Sch.1 para.5, in particular para.5(2)(b) and para.35.
[1179] CDPA 1988 s.153(3).
[1180] See para.3–202, above.
[1181] See paras 3–161 et seq., above.
[1182] See, as to countries ceasing to be colonies, CDPA 1988 s.158(2)(a).

accrued under the revoked orders.[1183] The Orders' basic structure falls into two types but is not thought that there is any substantive difference between the two approaches.

(a) The present Order and the 2005–2007 Orders

General. The present Order is the Copyright and Performances (Application to Other Countries) Order 2008 (which came into force on April 6, 2008).[1184] It was preceded by Orders structured in the same way which were made in 2005 (which came into force on May 1, 2005),[1185] 2006 (which came into force on April 6, 2006)[1186] and 2007 (which came into force on April 6, 2007).[1187] Since they are structured in the same way, these Orders are considered together.

3–208

Comparison with previous Orders made under the 1988 Act. The previous Orders under the 1988 Act are dealt with below.[1188] The Orders made since 2005 differ from them in a number of respects. First, in contrast with the previous Orders, the 2005 and subsequent Orders have simply applied all relevant provisions of Pt I of the 1988 Act in relation to specified countries "so that" those provisions apply in relation to individuals or companies connected to, works first published in and (as the case may be) broadcasts made from such countries as they apply to individuals or companies connected to, works first published in or (as the case may be) broadcasts made from the United Kingdom. This structure reverts to that adopted in the Orders made under the 1956 Act.[1189] It is not thought that there is any substantive difference between the two approaches. Secondly, the 2005 and subsequent Orders also deal with performances (which had hitherto been dealt with separately).[1190] Thirdly, the 2005 and subsequent Orders do not include provision that nothing in them is to be taken to derogate from para.35 of Sch.1 to the 1988 Act, which provides that every work in which copyright subsisted under the 1956 Act immediately before commencement of the 1988 Act was deemed to qualify for protection under the 1988 Act. Paragraph 35 is however referred to in the Explanatory Note to each Order, which also reminds the reader that the effect of s.153(3) of the 1988 Act is that the Order does not affect works in which copyright already subsists. Evidently it is no longer thought necessary to make express reference to para.35 in the text of the Order. Fourth, the saving provisions in art.7 of the pre-2005 Orders are not repeated in the same form. This is discussed below. In the discussion which follows, the term "relevant connection" is used to mean a connection between a particular work and a particular country of the type referred to in one of ss.153 to 156 of the 1988 Act.

3–209

Literary, dramatic, musical and artistic works, films and the typographical arrangements of published editions. Article 2(1) of each of the 2005 to 2008 Orders provides that all the provisions of Pt I of the 1988 Act, insofar as they relate to literary, dramatic, musical and artistic works, films and the typographical arrangement of published editions, apply in relation to the countries listed in the second column of the table set out in the Schedule to the Order so that those provisions apply:

3–210

[1183] This follows from CDPA 1988 s.153(3) and, more generally, from Interpretation Act 1978 ss.16(1)(c) and 23(1).
[1184] SI 2008/677. This Order has been amended by SI 2009/2745, which came into force on November 12, 2009 and contains provisions limited to Bermuda.
[1185] SI 2005/852.
[1186] SI 2006/316.
[1187] SI 2007/273.
[1188] paras 3–216 et seq., below.
[1189] See e.g. the Copyright (International Conventions) Order 1979 (SI 1979/1715).
[1190] See *Copinger* 15th edn, para.12–25.

(a) in relation to persons who are citizens or subjects of, or are domiciled or resident in, those countries as they apply to persons who are British citizens or are domiciled or resident in the United Kingdom,

(b) in relation to bodies incorporated under the laws of those countries as they apply in relation to bodies incorporated under the law of a part of the United Kingdom, and

(c) in relation to works first published in those countries as they apply in relation to works first published in the United Kingdom.[1191]

Article 2(2) of each of the 2005 to 2008 Orders provides that where a literary, dramatic, musical or artistic work was first published before June 1, 1957 (the date of commencement of the 1956 Act) it shall not qualify for copyright protection by reason of s.154 of the 1988 Act (qualification by author).[1192]

Each of the countries listed in the second column of the table in the Schedule to each Order qualifies for inclusion on one or more of the following bases: it is a party to the Berne Convention, the Universal Copyright Convention or the Agreement establishing the World Trade Organisation (including TRIPs); it is a Member State of the European Community or the European Free Trade Agreement; or it is otherwise considered to give adequate protection under its law.[1193]

3–211　**Sound recordings.** Article 3(1) of each of the 2005 to 2008 Orders provides that with certain exceptions all the provisions of Pt I of the 1988 Act, insofar as they relate to sound recordings, apply in relation to the countries listed in the third column of the table set out in the Schedule to the Order so that those provisions apply:

(a) in relation to persons who are citizens or subjects of, or are domiciled or resident in, those countries as they apply to persons who are British citizens or are domiciled or resident in the United Kingdom,

(b) in relation to bodies incorporated under the laws of those countries as they apply in relation to bodies incorporated under the law of a part of the United Kingdom, and

(c) in relation to works first published in those countries as they apply in relation to works first published in the United Kingdom.

Article 3(2) in effect lays out three separate regimes. The first applies to countries whose entry in the third column of the table includes an asterisk, that is countries which are parties to the Rome Convention[1194] or are Member States of the European Community or the European Free Trade Agreement or otherwise give adequate protection under their laws.[1195] All the provisions of Pt I of the 1988 Act so far as applicable to sound recordings apply in relation to these countries.

The second regime applies to countries listed in the third column of the table and marked with a hash (#). This regime applies to countries which are parties to the WIPO Performances and Phonograms Treaty[1196] but not to the Rome Convention. At the time the Orders were made, the United Kingdom had not ratified the WIPO Performances and Phonograms Treaty, but had agreed to do so

---

[1191] S.155(3) of the Act provides that for these purposes publication in one country is not to be regarded as other than first publication by reason of simultaneous publication elsewhere and for this purpose publication elsewhere within the 30 previous days is to be treated as simultaneous.

[1192] This reproduces art.2(2)(a)(i) of the 1989 to 1999 Orders. Otherwise, however, the complex limitations in art.2(2) and (3) of those Orders no longer apply.

[1193] See the Explanatory Note to each Order. See generally Chs 23 and 24 below.

[1194] See paras 23–88 et seq., below.

[1195] See the Explanatory Note to each Order.

[1196] See paras 23–119 et seq., below.

together with the European Community and with the other Member States.[1197] Protection was therefore accorded to Contracting Parties in anticipation of ratification on the basis that upon ratification those countries would provide protection under their laws.[1198] All the provisions of Pt I so far as applicable to sound recordings apply to these countries except ss.18A (infringement by rental and lending to the public) insofar as it applies to lending, 19 (infringement by playing in public), 20 (infringement by communication to the public) so far as it concerns broadcasting, 26 (secondary infringement by provision of apparatus for infringing performance, etc.), 107(2A) (criminal liability for communicating to the public) so far as it concerns broadcasting and 107(3) (criminal liability for playing in public).

The third regime applies to all other countries listed in the third column of the table. All the provisions of Pt I so far as applicable to sound recordings apply to these countries except ss.18A (insofar as it applies to lending), 19, 20, 26, 107(2A) and 107(3).

Broadcasts. For the purposes of the 2005 to 2008 Orders a distinction is drawn between wireless and non-wireless broadcasts. Article 4 deals with wireless broadcasts and art.5 deals with other broadcasts.   **3–212**

Wireless broadcasts. Article 4(1) provides that with certain exceptions and subject to certain provisos, all the provisions of Pt I of the 1988 Act, insofar as they relate to wireless broadcasts, apply in relation to the countries listed in the fourth column of the table set out in the Schedule to the Order so that those provisions apply: **3–213**

   (a) in relation to persons who are citizens or subjects of, or are domiciled or resident in, those countries as they apply to persons who are British citizens or are domiciled or resident in the United Kingdom,

   (b) in relation to bodies incorporated under the laws of those countries as they apply in relation to bodies incorporated under the law of a part of the United Kingdom, and

   (c) in relation to broadcasts made from those countries as they apply in relation to broadcasts made from the United Kingdom.

The effect of arts 4(1) and 4(2) is that where a country's entry in the fourth column of the table does not include an asterisk, the protection granted to broadcasts connected with it is not limited in extent (see below, however, for duration). These countries are parties to the Rome Convention,[1199] Member States of the European Community or the European Free Trade Agreement or otherwise give adequate protection under their laws.[1200]

Where, however, a country's entry includes an asterisk, the following provisions of Pt I do not apply: ss.18A (infringement by rental and lending to the public), 19 (infringement by showing or playing in public), but only insofar as it relates to broadcasts other than television broadcasts, 20 (infringement by communication to the public), except in relation to broadcasting by wireless telegraphy, 26 (secondary infringement by provision of apparatus for infringing performance, etc.) but only insofar as it relates to broadcasts other than television broadcasts and 107(2A) (criminal liability for communicating to the public)

[1197] In accordance with Council Decision 2000/278/EC [2001] OJ L89/6 (see Vol.2 I1). The United Kingdom ratified this Treaty on December 14, 2009 with effect from March 14, 2010.

[1198] See the Explanatory Note to each Order.

[1199] See paras 23–88 et seq., below.

[1200] See the Explanatory Note to each Order.

except in relation to broadcasting by wireless telegraphy. The asterisked countries are parties to the TRIPs agreement[1201] but not to the Rome Convention.[1202]

The effect of art.4(3) and 4(4) is that the provisions of Pt I of the 1988 Act do not apply in relation to wireless broadcasts made before the date which is specified against each country's entry in the fourth column of the table set out in the Schedule. Paragraph 9(b) of Sch.1 to the 1988 Act provides that no copyright subsists in a broadcast made before the commencement of the Copyright Act 1956 on June 1, 1957. Accordingly, that is the earliest date which may be so specified. The other date which is frequently specified is January 1, 1996, the date on which the TRIPs agreement took effect.[1203]

Article 4(5) provides that for the purposes of s.14(5) of the 1988 Act (which concerns the term of copyright in repeat broadcasts) any wireless broadcast which does not qualify for copyright protection shall be disregarded.

3–214   **Non-wireless broadcasts.** Article 5 of the 2005 to 2008 Orders provides that all the provisions of Pt I of the 1988 Act, insofar as they relate to non-wireless broadcasts, apply in relation to the countries indicated in the fifth column of the table set out in the Schedule so that those provisions apply:

    (a) in relation to persons who are citizens or subjects of, or are domiciled or resident in, those countries as they apply to persons who are British citizens or are domiciled or resident in the United Kingdom,

    (b) in relation to bodies incorporated under the laws of those countries as they apply in relation to bodies incorporated under the law of a part of the United Kingdom, and

    (c) in relation to broadcasts made from those countries as they apply in relation to broadcasts made from the United Kingdom.

The countries in the fifth column are Member States of the European Community or the European Free Trade Agreement or otherwise considered to give adequate protection under their laws. The effect of para.9(b) of Sch.1 to the 1988 Act is that protection does not extend to broadcasts made by cable before January 1, 1985.[1204]

3–215   **Saving provision.** Article 7 of the 2005 to 2008 Orders begins with the concept of an "excluded act", which is defined as an act in respect of which two requirements are satisfied at a time when the act neither infringed nor was restricted by copyright or moral rights. The requirements are first, that a person (called in the Orders "A") must have incurred expenditure or liability in connection with the act; and secondly, that that person must either have begun in good faith to do that act or to have made in good faith effective and serious preparations to do the act.

Article 7(2) provides that where a person (called in the Orders "B") acquires (relevantly) copyright or moral rights pursuant to the Order in question, A has the right to continue to do the excluded act or to do the excluded act (as the case may be) even though the excluded act infringes or is restricted by such rights.

Article 7(3) provides that where B or his exclusive licensee pays reasonable compensation to A, art.7(2) no longer applies and accordingly the act becomes an infringement.

Article 7(4) provides that where B offers to pay compensation to A but they cannot agree on the amount, either may refer the matter to arbitration.

It will be noted that the 2005 to 2008 Orders use the words "pursuant to this

---

[1201] See paras 23–136 et seq., below.
[1202] See the Explanatory Note to each Order.
[1203] See paras 23–88, et seq., below.
[1204] See the Explanatory Note to the Orders.

Order". It appears to follow that where a person in the position of B acquired copyright pursuant to an earlier Order the relevant saving provision is that contained in the earlier Order.

Despite the change in terminology, and apart from the introduction of a reference to moral rights, there only appears to be one substantive difference between the new and old saving provisions. In particular, no attempt has been made to resolve any of the difficulties with the old saving provision.[1205] The one substantive difference is the requirement that the doing of the act or (as the case may be) the making of the preparations for the act should have been in good faith. Presumably this is intended to cover the possibility that a person might have incurred the expenditure or liability and commenced the act or preparations for it with notice that a particular country had become a party to a relevant convention but that the Government had not yet made provision for this by the making of an Order listing that country. It is not clear what degree of notice will be considered sufficient to deprive a person of good faith.

(b) *Orders made between 1989 and 2004*

General. Earlier Orders under the 1988 Act were made in 1989 (which came into force on August 1, 1989),[1206] 1993 (which came into force on May 4, 1993)[1207] and 1999 (which came into force on July 22, 1999).[1208] In general, each of these Orders applied relevant parts of ss.153 to 156 of the 1988 Act to individuals or companies connected to, works first published in and broadcasts made from specified countries as they applied to individuals or companies connected to, works first published in or broadcasts made from the United Kingdom. The Orders then went on to provide that where copyright subsisted in a work as a result, the whole of Pt I of the 1988 Act applied in relation to that work. The Orders then set out certain modifications and exceptions based on the absence of reciprocal protection in relation to certain types of work. Each of the Orders then provided that nothing in them was to be taken to derogate from para.35 of Sch.1 to the 1988 Act, which provides that every work in which copyright subsisted under the 1956 Act immediately before commencement of the 1988 Act is deemed to qualify for protection under the 1988 Act.[1209] Finally, each Order contained a saving provision.[1210]

3–216

Literary, dramatic, musical and artistic works, films and the typographical arrangements of published editions: general. Article 2(1) of each Order provided that in relation to these works, ss.153 to 155 of the 1988 Act[1211] applied:

(a) in relation to citizens of subjects of a country specified in Sch.1 to the Order or were domiciled there as they applied to British citizens or persons domiciled in the United Kingdom;

3–217

[1205] For the old saving provisions, see para.3–223, below.

[1206] The Copyright (Application to Other Countries (No. 2) Order 1989 (SI 1989/1293). This replaced SI 1989/988 which never came into force. It was amended twice. The first amendment was by SI 1989/2415, which came into force on January 29, 1990. The second amendment was by SI 1990/2153, which came into force on November 29, 1990.

[1207] The Copyright (Application to Other Countries) Order 1993 (SI 1993/942), which took account of the reunification of Germany. This Order too was amended twice, by SI 1994/263 which came into force on March 11, 1994, and by SI 1995/2987, parts of which came into force on December 15, 1995 and other parts of which came into force on January 1, 1996.

[1208] The Copyright (Application to Other Countries) Order 1999, SI 1999/1751. This was amended once, by SI 2003/774.

[1209] art.6.

[1210] art.7. This is considered below (para.3–223).

[1211] That is, the sections dealing with qualification in general, qualification by reference to author and qualification by reference to country of first publication respectively.

(b) in relation to bodies incorporated under the law of such a country as they applied in relation to bodies incorporated under the law of a part of the United Kingdom; and

(c) in relation to works first published in such a country as they applied in relation to works first published in the United Kingdom.[1212]

The countries listed in Sch.1 to the 1989 and 1993 Orders were at the time the Order in question was made parties to the Berne Convention or the Universal Copyright Convention or both or were otherwise considered to give adequate protection under their law.[1213] In 1995 the 1993 Order was amended so that the list included countries which were at the time the Order was amended parties to the Berne Convention or the Universal Copyright Convention or the Agreement Establishing the World Trade Organisation (including TRIPS)[1214] or some or all of these or were otherwise considered to give adequate protection under their law. In the 1999 Order the list was further amended so that it included countries which at that time were parties to any of these three treaties or were Member States of the European Community or were otherwise considered to give adequate protection under their law. Article 2(3) of each Order provided that with one minor exception,[1215] where copyright subsisted in relation to a work by virtue of art.2(1), the whole of the copyright Part of the 1988 Act applied to that work.

3–218   **Literary, dramatic, musical and artistic works, films and the typographical arrangements of published editions: exceptions and modifications**. Each Order contained a number of important exceptions and modifications. First, each Order provided that a literary, dramatic, musical or artistic work would not qualify under art.2(1) by reference to its author if it was first published before June 1, 1957.[1216] Second, such a work would not qualify under art.2(1) if it was first published before August 1, 1989[1217] and at the "material time" the author was not a "relevant person". For these purposes, the expression "material time" had the same meaning as in the 1988 Act, that is (relevantly) the date of first publication or (if the author had died before that) immediately before his death.[1218] A "relevant person" was a Commonwealth citizen, a British protected person, a citizen or subject of any country specified in Sch.1 to the Order, or a person resident or domiciled in the United Kingdom, another country to which the relevant provisions of the copyright Part of the 1988 Act extended or a country specified in Sch.1 to the Order. Third, works connected with countries which at the time of the Order were parties to the Universal Copyright Convention alone only had protection if published after the date on which the Convention was considered to have entered into force in those countries. This was achieved by providing that no work would qualify under art.2(1) if it was first published before a date or the earliest date specified in Sch.1 to the Order in respect of the only country or countries relevant to the work for the purposes of qualification under art.2(1). The specified date was the date on which the Convention was considered to have entered into force in the relevant country. Fourth, there was a similar date restriction in relation to works connected with Taiwan. Fifth, where a work qualified under art.2(1), the whole of Pt 1 of the 1988 Act applied to it except that the

---

[1212] s.155(3) of the Act provides that for these purposes publication in one country is not to be regarded as other than first publication by reason of simultaneous publication elsewhere and for this purpose publication elsewhere within the 30 previous days is to be treated as simultaneous.

[1213] See the preamble to Sch.1 to each Order. For the Berne Convention, see paras 23–04 et seq., below. For the Universal Copyright Convention, see paras 23–79 et seq., below.

[1214] See paras 23–136 et seq., below.

[1215] See the next paragraph.

[1216] The date of commencement of the 1956 Act.

[1217] The date of commencement of the 1988 Act.

[1218] CDPA 1988 s.154(4)(b). See para.3–172, above.

permitted acts in relation to artistic works consisting of the design of a typeface were limited.[1219] Sixth, each of the 1989 and 1993 Orders also contained specific exceptions in relation to Indonesia, Singapore and Taiwan.[1220] The 1999 Order contained a specific exception in relation to Taiwan,[1221] but this was deleted in 2003.[1222] Finally, the whole of each Order was subject to a general saving provision, which is considered below.[1223]

Sound recordings. Article 3 of each Order provided that art.2 applied to sound   **3–219** recordings as it applies to films but with modifications. In each case, the main modification was to provide that the owners of copyright in sound recordings[1224] which qualified only by reason of their connection with certain countries did not gain the full range of rights comprised in the copyright and in particular did not gain the right of public performance. This was achieved by providing that specified sections of the 1988 Act applied only if at least one of the countries relevant to the work for the purposes of art.2(1) was specified in Sch.2 to the Order. The sections were 19 (infringement by performance, showing or playing in public), 20 (infringement by broadcasting or inclusion in a cable programme service[1225]), 26 (provision of apparatus for infringing performances) and 107(3) (criminal provisions in relation to performance, showing or playing in public). The countries listed in Sch.2 were at the time the Order was made parties to the Rome Convention for the Protection of Performers, Producers of Phonograms and Broadcasting Organisations. The 1989 and 1993 Orders also contained specific provisions relating to Indonesia which were revoked in 1994.[1226]

Broadcasts. Article 4(1) of each Order provided that in relation to broadcasts,   **3–220** ss.153, 154 and 156 of the 1988 Act[1227] applied:

(a) in relation to citizens or subjects of a country specified in Sch.3 to the Order or persons domiciled there as they applied to British citizens or persons domiciled in the United Kingdom;

(b) in relation to bodies incorporated under the law of such a country as they applied in relation to bodies incorporated under the law of a part of the United Kingdom; and

(c) in relation to broadcasts made from such a country as they applied in relation to broadcasts made from the United Kingdom.

Schedule 3 to the 1989 Order contained a list of countries which were either parties to the Rome Convention for the Protection of Performers, Producers of Phonograms and Broadcasting Organisations[1228] or the European Agreement on the Protection of Television Broadcasts[1229] or both or were otherwise considered

---

[1219] art.2(3). For these permitted acts, see paras 9–163 et seq., below.

[1220] Sch.4.

[1221] Sch.5(2).

[1222] By the Copyright (Application to Other Countries)(Amendment) Order 2003 (SI 2003/774), which came into force on April 22, 2003.

[1223] para.3–223, below.

[1224] The 1989 Order excluded film soundtracks accompanying a film from this exception. The two later Orders did not. Since January 1, 1996 a soundtrack accompanying a film has been treated as part of the film: see CDPA 1988 s.5B, inserted by SI 1995/3297. It is not clear why the removal of this exclusion was effected as early as 1993.

[1225] Note that with effect from October 31, 2003, s.20 was amended (by SI 2003/2498) to cover communication to the public.

[1226] See art.3(b). This provision was revoked by SI 1994/203, which came into force on March 11, 1994.

[1227] That is, the sections dealing with qualification in general, qualification by reference to author and qualification by reference to place of first transmission respectively.

[1228] See para.23–88, below.

[1229] See Vol.2 F3.

to give adequate protection under their law.[1230] In 1995 this was amended so that it included countries which at that time were parties to either of these treaties or to the Agreement Establishing the World Trade Organisation (including TRIPS) or were otherwise considered to give adequate protection under their law.[1231] In the 1999 Order the list was further amended so that it included countries which at that time were parties to any of these three treaties or were Member States of the European Community or were otherwise considered to give adequate protection under their law.

3–221   **Broadcasts: exceptions and modifications**. First, Sch.3 to the 1989 and 1993 Orders identified some countries as "television only" and provided that if qualification was by reference to such a country, copyright subsisted in the broadcast only if it was a television broadcast.[1232] No such exception appeared in the 1999 Order. Second, all three orders provided that copyright did not subsist in a broadcast by virtue of art.4(1) if the broadcast was made before the "relevant date",[1233] that is the date or (as the case might be) the earliest of the dates specified in Sch.3 in respect of the country or countries relevant for the purposes of art.4(1).[1234] In the case of treaty members, the dates were those on which the countries in question acceded to the relevant convention. Third, the Orders provided that where copyright subsisted in a broadcast by virtue of art.4(1), the whole of the copyright Part of the 1988 Act applied in relation to the broadcast except that for the purposes of the duration of copyright in repeats,[1235] a broadcast was to be disregarded if it was made before the "relevant date"[1236] and a cable programme was to be disregarded if it was included in a cable programme service before the later of the relevant date and January 1, 1985.[1237] Fourth, with effect from January 1, 1996, the Orders provided that in relation to broadcasts qualifying for protection by reason of their connection to certain countries,[1238] subs.16(1)(b) of the 1988 Act did not apply at all and subss.16(1)(d) and 16(1)(c) only applied in part. The effect of this was that where qualification was by reference to such a country, the copyright owner had no right to prevent the issue of copies of the broadcast to the public, the inclusion of the work in a cable programme service or (in the case of broadcasts other than television broadcasts) the performance, showing or playing the work in public.[1239] The countries in question appeared to be countries which were parties to the Agreement Establishing the World Trade Organisation (including TRIPS) but not to the Rome Convention for the Protection of Performers, Producers of Phonograms and Broadcasting Organisations or the European Agreement on the Protection of Television Broadcasts. Finally, as was the case with other copyright works, specific provision was made for certain individual countries in Sch.5 to the Order.

3–222   **Cable programmes.** The 1989 and 1993 Orders provided that in respect of Singapore they applied in relation to cable programmes as they applied in relation to

---

[1230] Preamble to Sch.3.
[1231] See the Copyright (Application to Other Countries) (Amendment) Order 1995 (SI 1995/2987) art.3(b)(i), which came into force on January 1, 2006.
[1232] art.4(2).
[1233] See art.4(3) of the 1989 and 1993 Orders and art.4(2) of the 1999 Order.
[1234] Where different dates were specified for television and non-television broadcasts, this was the date appropriate to the type of broadcast in question.
[1235] CDPA 1988 s.14(2) until January 1, 1996 when s.14(2) was replaced by a new s.14(5): Duration of Copyright and Rights in Performances Regulations 1995 (SI 1995/3297).
[1236] See earlier in this paragraph for the meaning of this expression.
[1237] See art.4(4) of the 1989 and 1993 Orders and art.4(3) of the 1999 Order.
[1238] Marked in Sch.3 by an asterisk.
[1239] See Sch.4(3) to the 1993 Order as amended by SI 1995/2987 and Sch.5(3) to the 1999 Order.

broadcasts, but with limitations.[1240] In the 1999 Order this provision was extended to many other countries, being Member States of the European Community or countries considered to give adequate protection under their law.[1241] For these purposes, the "relevant date" was January 1, 1985.[1242]

Saving provision. Article 7 of each Order was a saving provision designed to protect people who had incurred financial commitments in relation to acts which at the time were not restricted but became restricted as a result of the Order. It was expressed to apply in relation to works made before August 1, 1989 (the date of commencement of the copyright Part of the 1988 Act) in which copyright under the 1956 Act did not subsist and to works made on or after August 1, 1989 in which copyright did not subsist. If copyright subsequently subsisted in such a work by virtue of the Order, and a person had incurred expenditure or liability in connection with, for the purpose of or with a view to the doing of an act which at the time was not an act restricted by the copyright in the work, the act was not a restricted act unless the owner of the copyright or his exclusive licensee (if any) paid such compensation as, failing agreement, might be determined by arbitration. The effect appeared to be that unless and until compensation was paid the act was not an infringement but once compensation had been paid it might become one. On a literal interpretation this would have meant that having paid compensation the copyright owner might then sue the person who committed the act for damages and injunctive relief. In theory such acts might attract criminal liability, but this would conflict with the general principle that criminal liability must not be imposed retrospectively. The provision gave rise to a number of other potential difficulties, not least as to the assessment of any compensation and the costs of any arbitration proceedings. In fact, however, art.7 does not appear to have come before the courts.

3–223

(iii) Position before the 1911 Act

The International Copyright Act 1838. The first statute to deal with the question of copyright protection in the United Kingdom (and the Dominions of the Crown) for works originating abroad was the International Copyright Act 1838.[1243] The preamble to the Act recited that it was "desirable to afford Protection within Her Majesty's Dominions to the Authors of Books first published in Foreign Countries, and their Assigns, in cases where Protection shall be afforded in such Foreign Countries to the Authors of Books first published in Her Majesty's Dominions, and their Assigns". Section 1 of the Act permitted her Majesty by Order in Council to direct that the authors of specified books published in specified foreign countries should have the sole liberty of printing such books in the United Kingdom and the Dominions of the Crown for such term as the Order might direct. There were further provisions including in relation to the term of such copyright. However, no Orders in Council were ever made under the 1838 Act. It seems that the reasons for this included the fact that

3–224

[1240] art.4(6), art.5.
[1241] art.4(5), Sch.4.
[1242] Sch.5 para.1.
[1243] An Act for securing to Authors, in certain Cases, the Benefit of International Copyright, 1&2 Vict. c.59.

the term of UK copyright was shorter than the equivalent term in other countries[1244] and that the 1838 Act was limited to books.[1245]

3–225   **The International Copyright Act 1844: general.** The 1838 Act was repealed and replaced by the International Copyright Act 1844.[1246] The 1844 Act recited that the powers in the 1838 Act were "insufficient to enable Her Majesty to confer upon Authors of Books first published in Foreign Countries Copyright of the like Duration, and with the like Remedies for the Infringement thereof, which are conferred and provided" by that Act "with respect to Authors of Books first published in the British Dominions"; and that the 1838 Act did not apply to dramatic pieces, musical compositions, prints or sculptures. The provisions of the 1844 Act were modelled on those of the 1838 Act, but extended to books, prints, articles of sculpture and other works of art.[1247]

3–226   **The International Copyright Act 1844: specific provisions.** Section 2 of the 1844 Act empowered Her Majesty by Order in Council to direct that as respects classes of books, prints, articles of sculpture and other works of art specified in the Order which were first published in a foreign country specified in the Order after a date so specified, copyright should subsist for such period as might be specified in the Order, not exceeding the period conferred on such works which were first published in the United Kingdom.[1248] The effect of such an Order was to be to confer the same rights in respect of the work as subsisted in respect of a work first published in the United Kingdom, subject to any limitation as to term which the Order might contain.[1249] The Act went on to make analogous provision in respect of dramatic pieces and musical compositions first publicly represented or performed in countries to which such an Order related, the effect of an Order in relation to such works being to confer the same protection throughout the British dominions as was granted to dramatic pieces and musical compositions which were first represented or performed in the British dominions.[1250] The Act provided that no Order in Council should have any effect unless it was stated that reciprocal protection had been secured.[1251] Such Orders were to be revocable but without prejudice to rights acquired before the revocation.[1252] In addition the Act provided that no rights should be acquired in respect of works first published outside Her Majesty's dominions otherwise than under the Act.[1253] By this time the term of UK copyright had been extended[1254] and the Act proved more successful than its predecessor, resulting in the signature of treaties with Prussia (1846) and a number of other German states.[1255] These treaties were implemented by Orders in Council under the 1844 Act.[1256]

3–227   **Developments between 1851 and 1886.** In 1851 a Convention was concluded with France which provided that authors of works of literature (including transla-

---

[1244] See Deazley, R. (2008) "Commentary on International Copyright Act 1838", in *Primary Sources on Copyright (1450–1900)*, L. Bently & M. Kretschmer (eds) *http://www.copyrighthistory.org/* [Accessed September 20, 2010].

[1245] *Copinger* 3rd edn, p.567.

[1246] An Act to amend the law relating to International Copyright, 7&8 Vict. c. 12.

[1247] s.2.

[1248] s.2.

[1249] ss.3 and 4.

[1250] s.5.

[1251] s.14.

[1252] s.17.

[1253] s.19.

[1254] By the Copyright Act 1842. See para.2–22, above.

[1255] For a list of the Conventions entered into prior to the Berne Convention, see the Order in Council of November 28, 1887, which is reproduced in *Copinger* 4th edn, App.B, pp.c-cii.

[1256] For an example, see *Copinger* 1st edn App.(B.) p.c.

tions) and art published in England should have the same protection in France as French authors had there and vice versa.[1257] Because the Convention extended beyond the terms of the 1844 Act (not least because it included translations) it needed to be ratified by an Act of Parliament and this was done by the passage of a new International Copyright Act in 1852.[1258] The 1952 Act extended the provisions of the 1844 Act to translations and made other amendments to its terms. Meanwhile, additional treaties were entered into with other German states and with Belgium, Spain, Sardinia, Italy and Germany itself. Again these treaties were implemented by Order in Council.[1259] Further amendments were made to the 1852 Act by the International Copyright Act 1875.[1260]

The International Copyright Act 1886. Following the agreement of a draft of   **3–228** the Berne Convention in 1885, the International Copyright Act 1886[1261] was passed with a view to enabling Her Majesty to accede to the Berne Convention.[1262] The 1886 Act amended and clarified the 1844, 1852 and 1875 Acts and provided that it should be construed together with them (together "the International Copyright Acts").[1263] The result was a framework for the making of Orders in Council giving effect to the Berne Convention.

Provisions of the 1886 Act. The basic principle of the Berne Convention was   **3–229** that authors of any one of the countries of the Berne Copyright Union should enjoy the same rights in the other countries of the Union in respect of their works whether published or unpublished which were enjoyed by the authors of those other countries.[1264] The 1886 Act referred to the grant by Orders in Council of reciprocal protection to works first "produced" in countries to which such Orders related. The term "produced" was defined to mean as the case required "published or made, or performed or represented".[1265] The Berne Convention provided that the rights granted by it could not exceed the term of protection granted in the work's country of origin.[1266] Accordingly, the 1886 Act provided that the International Copyright Acts and any Order made under them should not confer any greater right or longer term of copyright in a work than that enjoyed in the foreign country in which the work was first produced.[1267] The Berne Convention provided for a right to make or authorise the making of translations which was to last for 10 years from the end of the year in which the original was published in one of the countries of the Union.[1268] The 1886 Act provided for such a right but that it should cease if an authorised translation had not been produced within 10 years of the end of the year in which the book was first produced.[1269]

Application of the 1886 Act to existing works. The Berne Convention applied   **3–230** to existing works provided they had not yet fallen into the public domain in their

---

[1257] *Copinger* 1st edn, p.227.
[1258] The International Copyright Act 1852, 15 & 16 Vict. c.12.
[1259] See *Copinger* 3rd edn, p.578.
[1260] 38 Vict. c.12.
[1261] 49 & 50 Vict. c. 33.
[1262] See the preamble.
[1263] s.1(3).
[1264] art. 2. For a fuller account, see paras 23–04 et seq., below.
[1265] s.11. In the case of a painting, what mattered was where the work was published rather than where it was made: *Hanfstaengl v American Tobacco Co* [1895] 1 Q.B. 347.
[1266] art.2. The country of origin was defined as the country in which the work was first published or if such publication took place simultaneously in several countries of the Union, that one of them in which the shortest term of protection was granted by law. The country of origin of unpublished works was the country to which the author belonged.
[1267] s.2(3).
[1268] art.5.
[1269] s.5.

country of origin.[1270] However, in the absence of any special conventions on the topic, the manner in which this principle was to be applied was for domestic legislation.[1271] Accordingly, s.6 of the 1886 Act provided that where an Order in Council was made under the International Copyright Acts, the author or publisher of a work which was produced before the Order came into operation should have the same rights and remedies as if the Acts and the Order had applied to the work at the date it was produced. The Act went on to provide that where any person had lawfully produced any work in the United Kingdom before the date of publication of the Order, nothing in the section should diminish or prejudice any rights or interests arising from or in connection with such production which were subsisting and valuable at that date. In summary, the International Copyright Acts were retrospective in the sense that they were deemed to have applied to a work at the date of its production. However, they did not confer any rights in respect of activities which predated the publication of the Order. In addition, the author or owner would not be able to prevent acts committed after the publication of the Order if to do so would prejudice subsisting and valuable "rights" or "interests". Such "rights" might include new copyrights created by bestowing additional labour on an existing foreign work which was unprotected at the time the labour was carried out. Such "interests" might include the interests of a publisher who had invested capital in the production of a work and depended for the return of that capital on the sale of copies of stock and perhaps a new edition.[1272]

3–231   **The 1887 Order in Council.** On November 28, 1887, an Order in Council was issued pursuant to the International Copyright Acts. With effect from December 6, 1887, the Order revoked the previous Orders made under those Acts and gave effect to the Berne Convention.[1273] It granted protection in Her Majesty's dominions to "literary or artistic works"[1274] first "produced"[1275] in Belgium, France, Germany, Haiti, Italy, Spain, Switzerland and Tunis.[1276] It expressly limited the term of such protection to that enjoyed in the country in which the work was first produced. In accordance with the Acts, it provided that a work first produced simultaneously in two or more countries of the Union was deemed to have been first produced in the country in which the term of copyright in the work was shortest.[1277]

3–232   **Further Orders in Council prior to the 1911 Act.** A further Order in Council published on March 7, 1898 applied the Paris Act of the Berne Convention to Germany, Belgium, Spain, France, Italy, Luxembourg, Monaco, Switzerland and Tunis.[1278] An Order in Council published on April 30, 1894 gave effect to a separate treaty with Austria-Hungary with effect from May 11, 1894.[1279]

3–233   **United States works prior to the 1911 Act.** There was no copyright treaty between Great Britain and the United States during this period, and it was not until

---

[1270] art.14. See now art.18(1) of the Paris Act and *Experience Hendrix LLC v Purple Haze Records Ltd* [2007] EWCA Civ 501, [2007] F.S.R. 31, at para.30.

[1271] This was the combined effect of art.14 of the Convention and para.4 of the final protocol. See now art.18(3) of the Paris Act.

[1272] For more detail and an account of the authorities, see *Copinger* 5th edn, pp.292–298.

[1273] *Copinger* 4th edn, App.B, p.c-cii.

[1274] Defined in s.11 of the 1886 Act as "every book, print, lithograph, article of sculpture, dramatic piece, musical composition, painting, drawing, photograph, and other work of literature and art" to which the copyright legislation then in force extended (see also art.4 of the Berne Convention).

[1275] See para.3–229 for the meaning of this expression.

[1276] art.2.

[1277] arts 3 and 5.

[1278] *Copinger* 4th edn, App.B, p.cvi.

[1279] *Copinger* 4th edn, App.B, p.cx.

1891, after the passage of the "Chace Act", that British authors could obtain any effective protection for their works in that country. The Chace Act was repealed by the Copyright Act 1909, under which British authors could obtain some protection for their works, by virtue of a proclamation by the President of the United States to the effect that British law granted to citizens of the United States the benefit of copyright on substantially the same basis as its own citizens.[1280] American citizens were in fact able to obtain copyright in their works by first publishing them in England, or simultaneously[1281] in England or a Convention country and America; and they could, no doubt, sue in England in respect of any publication in breach of trust or confidence.

(iv) Position under the 1911 Act

Existing works. The International Copyright Acts were repealed by the 1911 Act.[1282] However, with certain modifications, the 1911 Act provided that any person entitled to copyright immediately before commencement (July 1, 1912) obtained copyright under the 1911 Act for the term for which it would have subsisted if the 1911 Act had been in force at the date when the work was made and the work had been entitled to copyright under that Act.[1283] In relation to published foreign works, the position depended on whether there had been a relevant Order in Council.[1284] In relation to unpublished works, the position is more complex. It seems that existing unpublished literary, dramatic and musical works, together with sculptures created on or after July 1, 1862, were protected irrespective of the existence of a relevant Order in Council but that existing foreign unpublished paintings, drawings and photographs were only protected if there was a relevant Order in Council.[1285]   **3–234**

The basic method of qualification under the 1911 Act. There were two regimes, depending on whether the work was or was not published. In short, if a literary, dramatic, musical or artistic work was a published work, it qualified for protection if it was first published[1286] within a part of the Dominions of the Crown to which the 1911 Act extended.[1287] If such a work was unpublished, it qualified for protection if the author was at the date of its making a British subject or resident within such parts of the Dominions of the Crown.[1288] As a result of these rules, copyright could often be lost or gained by publication.   **3–235**

Qualification provisions of the 1911 Act relating to foreign works. Consistently with the provisions referred to in the previous paragraph,[1289] s.29(1) of the 1911 Act provided that His Majesty might, by Order in Council, direct that the Act (except such parts if any as might be specified) should apply: **3–236**

(a) to works first published in a foreign country to which the Order related, in like manner as if they were first published within the parts of His Majesty's dominions to which the Act extended;

[1280] See *Copinger* 13th edn, para.18–23.

[1281] As to the meaning of this expression, see para.3–175, above.

[1282] s.36 and Sch.2.

[1283] s.24(1). Specific provision was made for the reversion of copyright to the author in the event that the term under the 1911 Act exceeded that previously available (s.24(1)(b)—see paras 5–152 et seq., below) and for the protection of persons who had acquired "subsisting and valuable" rights or interests before July 26, 1910 (s.24(1)(b)).

[1284] See paras 3–231 and 3–232, above.

[1285] See paras 17–26 et seq., below for a detailed account.

[1286] For the meaning of published, see paras 3–174 et seq., above.

[1287] For the complex provisions about extending the Act outside the United Kingdom see paras 3–285 et seq., below.

[1288] s.1(1).

[1289] And in contrast to the 1886 Act and Orders in Council made under that Act.

(b) to literary, dramatic, musical and artistic works, or any class of such works, the authors of which were at the time of the making of the work subjects or citizens of a foreign country to which the Order related, in like manner as if the authors were British subjects;

(c) in respect of residence in a foreign country to which the Order related, in like manner as if such residence were residence in the parts of His Majesty's Dominions to which the Act extended.

Upon the making of such an Order, subject to the provisions of Pt II of the Act ("International Copyright") and of the Order, the Act should apply accordingly. Section 29 of the 1911 Act provided that before making such an Order: "His Majesty shall be satisfied that that foreign country has made, or has undertaken to make, such provisions, if any, as it appears to His Majesty expedient to require for the protection of works entitled to copyright under this Act".

3–237   **The 1912 Order in Council.** A general Order in Council was made on June 24, 1912[1290] for the purpose of applying the 1911 Act, in accordance with s.29, to works originating in countries of the Berne Copyright Union. The Order revoked the Orders in Council made under the International Copyright Acts as from the date of its commencement so far as regarded the parts of His Majesty's dominions to which it applied.[1291] However, it provided that neither such revocation nor anything else in the Order should prejudicially affect any right acquired or accrued before its commencement by virtue of any of the revoked Orders.[1292] The Order stated that it extended to all the then countries of the Berne Copyright Union[1293] and then followed the wording of s.29(1) in applying the provisions of the 1911 Act (including those as to existing works) to works first published in such countries, works the authors of whom were subjects or citizens of such countries at the time they were made and in respect of residence in like manner as if residence had been residence in the parts of the Dominions of the Crown to which the 1911 Act extended.[1294]

3–238   **The 1912 Order: restrictions and limitations.** The Order went on to provide that the term of copyright conferred by it was not to exceed that conferred by the law of the country of origin of the work.[1295] The term "country of origin" was to have the same meaning as in art.4 of the Berne Convention.[1296] Various other restrictions and limitations were imposed in respect of those countries which had made reservations to the Berne Convention.[1297] In respect of existing translations, it was provided that rights extinguished by virtue of s.5 of the International Copyright Act 1886, that is by virtue of non-publication in the English language within 10 years, should not be revived by the Order.[1298] Finally, the Order provided that the copyright in musical works to which the Order applied which had been published before the commencement of the 1911 Act should include mechanical rights where no contrivances had been made or sold in Dominions of the Crown

---

[1290] S.R. & O. 1912 No.913. This is reproduced (without its Schedules) in *Copinger* 5th edn, pp.652–657.

[1291] art.(6). The date of commencement of the Order in the United Kingdom was July 1, 1912 and the date of commencement in any part of the dominions to which the Order applied was the day on which the 1911 Act came into operation in such part: art.(8).

[1292] art.(6).

[1293] That is, Belgium, Denmark and the Faroe Islands, France, Germany and the German Protectorates, Haiti, Italy, Japan, Liberia, Luxemburg, Monaco, Norway, Portugal, Spain, Sweden, Switzerland and Tunis: art.(1).

[1294] art.(2).

[1295] art.(2), proviso para.(iii).

[1296] art.(4).

[1297] art.(2), proviso paras (i), (iii).

[1298] art.2, proviso para.(iv).

before the commencement of the Order.[1299] Subsequent Orders were made between 1913 and 1933, as necessity arose, by reason of countries joining the Berne Copyright Union or altering their reservations to the Berne Convention.[1300]

1914–1918 wartime legislation: the United States. By an Order in Council dated February 3, 1915,[1301] made under s.29 of the 1911 Act, the protection of that Act was extended to unpublished works whose authors were citizens of or resident in the United States at the time they were made.[1302] But works first published in America had no protection in this country. By an Order in Council dated February 9, 1920,[1303] the 1911 Act was applied to works first published in the United States between August 1, 1914 and the termination of the war, which had not been republished in the British Empire (except the self-governing dominions[1304]) prior to February 2, 1920, provided the work was published in such area not later than six months after the termination of the war. It would appear that, if an authorised publication was made in the area in question after the 14 days allowed by the 1911 Act, but before February 2, 1920, advantage could not be taken of this Order. The 1915 and 1920 Orders were revoked by the first Order in Council to be made under the 1956 Act.[1305] **3–239**

1914–1918 wartime legislation: works of enemy origin. Prior to the commencement of the 1914–1918 War, Germany, as a member of the Berne Convention, and Austria-Hungary by a special copyright treaty, had been given, by Orders in Council, rights in this country in respect of works published in those countries, or whose authors were subjects of, or residents in those countries.[1306] Where works were made or published before the outbreak of the war, the copyright in this country, if the property of an enemy, became liable, under the Trading with the Enemy Acts 1914 to 1918, to be vested in the Public Trustee as the Custodian of Enemy Property.[1307] With regard to works made or published in an enemy country after the outbreak of the war, it was doubted whether any copyright in this country was acquired, though the Orders in Council creating such copyright do not appear to have been revoked. To remove these doubts it was provided, by the Trading with the Enemy (Copyright) Act 1916,[1308] that the copyright created by these Orders in Council in enemy works should subsist and should be vested in the Custodian of Enemy Property. A large number of enemy copyrights were vested in the Custodian in the course of the war, and licences were granted in respect of the publication of such works in this country. **3–240**

Revesting after the 1914–1918 war. The Treaties of Peace provided for the revesting of such copyrights, but subject to severe disabilities. The terms upon which the revesting took place are set out, as regards Germany and Austria, in an **3–241**

[1299] art.3.
[1300] For a list, see Sch.4 to the 1933 Order in Council, reproduced in *Copinger* 7th edn at p.436–437. Some of these Orders were reproduced in previous editions of Copinger. See the 5th edn, pp.657–662 and the 6th edn, pp.429–442.
[1301] S.R. & O. 1915/130. See *Copinger* 8th edn, p.468.
[1302] *Oscar Trade Mark* [1979] R.P.C. 173 on appeal to the Court from the Registrar [1980] F.S.R. 429.
[1303] S.R. & O. 1920/257.
[1304] In *Warner Brothers Inc v The Roadrunner Ltd* [1988] F.S.R. 292, it was held that, under the 1942 Order, this area did include the self-governing dominions: but see Copyright Act 1911 ss.25 and 29, and para.3–244, below.
[1305] See para.3–253 below.
[1306] See above, paras 3–231 and 3–232.
[1307] 4 & 5 Geo. 5, c.87, s.4(1); 8 & 9 Geo. 5, c.31, s.8.
[1308] 6 & 7 Geo. 5, c.32.

Order in Council of November 9, 1920,[1309] made under the powers conferred by the Trading with the Enemy Act 1914, and the Treaty of Peace Orders 1919 and 1920, and, as regards Hungary, in an Order in similar terms dated August 16, 1921. These Orders reserved power to the Board of Trade to grant licences, but the provisions of these Orders were revoked in 1930,[1310] so that, subject to any licences which may have been granted, it appears that the owner of the work was again beneficially entitled to it. In order, however, to follow the title to such works, it may still be necessary to consider the effect of this legislation upon German, Austrian and Hungarian works made or published before the termination of the war, that is, in the case of Germany, before January 10, 1920,[1311] in the case of Austria, July 16, 1920, and in the case of Hungary, August 31, 1921,[1312] since such works, if vested in the Custodian at any time, became revested, subject to the disabilities and restrictions created by the Peace Treaties and set out in the Orders in Council above referred to.

3–242   **The 1933 Order.** By an Order[1313] dated March 16, 1933, all previous Orders made under the 1911 Act were revoked. The Order was expressed to relate to the then 33 other members of the Berne Copyright Union,[1314] and followed the essential terms of the 1912 Order. Under this Order, as under previous Orders, the term of protection was limited to that conferred by the law of the country of origin of the work. Following the 1933 Order a series of other Orders were made under the 1911 Act.[1315]

3–243   **Saving provision.** The 1933 Order contained a saving provision[1316] which applied where any person had before the date of the Order taken any action whereby he had incurred any expenditure or liability in connection with the reproduction or performance of any work in a manner which at the time was lawful or for the purpose of or with a view to the performance of a work at a time when such reproduction or performance would, but for the making of the Order, have been lawful. In such circumstances, nothing in the Order was to diminish or prejudice any rights or interest arising from, or in connection with such action which were subsisting and valuable at that date unless the person who by virtue of the Order became entitled to restrain such reproduction or performance agreed to pay such compensation as failing agreement might be determined by arbitration.

3–244   **1939–1945 wartime legislation: the United States.** By an Order in Council dated August 6, 1942, as amended by an Order in Council dated October 9, 1950,[1317] the 1911 Act was applied to works first published in the United States between September 3, 1939, and December 29, 1950, which had not been

---

[1309] S.R. & O. 1920/2119.

[1310] Order in Council May 17, 1930 (S.R. & O. 1930/341).

[1311] By Order in Council of February 9, 1920, made under the Termination of the Present War (Definition) Act 1918 (8 & 9 Geo. 5, c.59).

[1312] By Order in Council August 10, 1921, made under that Act.

[1313] S.R. & O. 1933 No.253; *Copinger* 8th edn, p.459.

[1314] That is, Austria, Belgium, Brazil, Bulgaria, Czecho-Slovakia, Free City of Dantzig, Denmark with the Faroe Islands, Estonia, Finland, France with Algeria and Colonies, Germany, Greece, Hayti, Hungary, Italy, Japan with Korea, Formosa, Japanese Saghalien and Kwantung Leased Territory, Leichtenstein, Luxembourg, Monaco, Morocco (French Zone), Netherlands with the Netherlands East Indies, Norway, Poland, Portugal with Colonies, Roumania, Siam, Spain with Colonies, Surinam and Curacao, Sweden, Switzerland, Syria and Lebanon, Tunis and Yugo-Slavia.

[1315] They are listed in Sch.5 to the Copyright (International Conventions) Order 1957 (SI 1957/1523), which repealed them: see art.3, which preserved rights acquired under them.

[1316] art.3.

[1317] S.R. & O. 1942 No.1579; SI 1950/1641 The four Orders were repealed by the 1957 Order.

published in the British Empire (except the self-governing dominions[1318]) within 14 days of the publication in the United States. In order to take advantage of this Order publication must have been made not later than December 28, 1950.[1319] The 1942 Order came into operation on the date of its publication in the *London Gazette*, March 10, 1944. While persons taking action before the commencement of the 1942 Order, on the assumption that no copyright existed, were given certain protection for accrued rights and interests, it remains obscure whether, if an authorised publication was in fact made, the owner thereof had a title by relation back.

1939–1945 wartime legislation: works of enemy origin. By s.5 of the Patents, **3–245** Designs, Copyright and Trade Marks (Emergency) Act 1939,[1320] provision was made for the preservation of enemy copyrights and the continuing in force of Orders in Council made under the Copyright Act in relation to enemy countries. The result was that the war did not affect the creation or continuance of British copyrights in works originating in enemy countries. The 1939 Act[1321] also continued in force licences granted by enemies to persons resident in the United Kingdom, subject to control. The Act[1322] also gave power to the comptroller to grant licences in respect of enemy copyrights, and to vary existing licences.[1323] In consequence of these provisions, few copyrights were vested in the Custodian under the ordinary trading with the enemy legislation, matters being dealt with by leaving the copyrights vested in enemies and granting licences as required. Certain German copyrights might, however, have been affected by virtue of the Enemy Property Act 1953,[1324] in consequence of the exercise by, or on behalf of, the Crown of the rights thereby conferred.

(v) Position under the 1956 Act

(a) *Provisions of the 1956 Act*

Existing works. The provisions of the 1956 Act were treated as having always **3–246** applied to works in existence at its commencement, subject to the modifications contained in Sch.7 to the Act.[1325] Those modifications included a provision that existing works made before July 1, 1912,[1326] could not qualify for protection under the 1956 Act unless they were protected under the 1911 Act immediately before the commencement of the 1956 Act.[1327]

The basic method of qualification under the 1956 Act. As was the case under **3–247**

[1318] In *Warner Brothers Inc v The Roadrunner Ltd* [1988] F.S.R. 292, it was held that, under the 1942 Order, this area did include the self-governing dominions: but see Copyright Act 1911 ss.25 and 29.

[1319] See *Plantation Wood (Lancing) Ltd's Applications for a Trade Mark* [1958] R.P.C. 400.

[1320] (2 & 3 Geo. 6, c.107). The 1939 Act was amended by the CDPA 1988 (s.303(1) and (2) and Schs 7 and 8) to take account of design right: and see Copyright Act 1956 Sch.7 para.44(b), CDPA 1988 Sch.1 para.4(2).

[1321] Patents, Designs, Copyright and Trade Marks (Emergency) Act 1939 s.1.

[1322] ss.1 and 2.

[1323] The nature and effect of these powers was discussed in *Novello & Co Ltd v Eulenburg (E.) Ltd* [1950] 1 All E.R. 44 and *Novello & Co Ltd v Hinrichsen Edition Ltd* [1951] Ch. 595, 1026.

[1324] (1 & 2 Eliz. 2, c.52), most of which was repealed by the Statute Law (Repeals) Act 1976 (c.16).

[1325] Sch.7 para.45(1).

[1326] The date of commencement of the 1911 Act.

[1327] Sch.7 para.35.

the 1911 Act, there were two regimes, depending on whether the work was or was not published.[1328]

Copyright subsisted in unpublished works whose author was a "qualified person" at the time the work was made.[1329] An individual was a qualified person if he was a British subject, a British protected person, a citizen of the Republic of Ireland or domiciled or resident in the United Kingdom or another country to which a relevant provision of the Act extended.[1330]

As was the case under the 1911 Act, copyright subsisted in published works if first publication took place in the United Kingdom or another country to which the relevant section of the Act extended. However, by contrast with the 1911 Act, copyright also subsisted in a published work if the author was a qualified person at the time the work was first published or (in the case of works not published during the author's lifetime) was a qualified person immediately before his death.[1331] This additional ground of qualification, which gave effect to the Universal Copyright Convention,[1332] which the United Kingdom ratified with effect from September 27, 1957, meant that copyright would not necessarily be lost by first publication in the wrong country.

These provisions applied to existing (pre-commencement) works but without the provision that published works might qualify by reference to the status of their author.[1333] Thus the qualification conditions of the 1911 Act continued to apply to such works.

3–248   **Preservation of Orders in Council made under the 1911 Act.** In order to prevent Orders in Council made under the 1911 Act lapsing immediately upon the commencement of the 1956 Act and its repeal of the 1911 Act, it was provided[1334] that such Orders, and all the provisions of the 1911 Act required for the purposes of any proceedings arising out of the operation of such continuance, were to continue in force until the occurrence of whichever of the following events first occurred, that was to say:

    (a) the revocation of the Order under the 1911 Act;

    (b) the coming into operation of an Order under the 1956 Act in the case of the foreign country in question; and

    (c) the expiration of the period of two years from the repeal of the 1911 Act.

3–249   **Power to apply the 1956 Act to other countries.** By s.32 of the 1956 Act, Her Majesty was authorised, by Order in Council, to make provision for applying any of the provisions of that Act, in the case of a country to which those provisions did not extend, so as to secure that those provisions:

    (a) applied in relation to literary, dramatic, musical or artistic works, sound recordings, cinematograph films or editions first published in that country as they applied to such works first published in the United Kingdom;

    (b) applied in relation to persons who, at a material time, were citizens or subjects of that country as they applied in relation to British subjects;

    (c) applied in relation to persons who, at a material time, were domiciled or resident in that country as they applied in relation to persons domiciled or resident in the United Kingdom;

[1328] For the meaning of the term "publication", see paras 3–174 et seq., above.
[1329] ss.2(1) and 3(2).
[1330] s.1(5)(a). Separate provision was made for bodies corporate in subs.1(5)(b).
[1331] ss.2(2) and 3(3).
[1332] See para.23–79 et seq.
[1333] Sch.7 para.1.
[1334] By Copyright Act 1956 Sch.7 para.40, which was repealed by Statute Law (Repeals) Act 1986 (c.12).

(d) applied in relation to bodies incorporated under the laws of that country as they applied in relation to bodies incorporated under the laws of any part of the United Kingdom;

(e) applied in relation to television broadcasts and sound broadcasts made from places in that country by one or more organisations constituted in or under the laws of that country as they applied in relation to television broadcasts and sound broadcasts made by the British Broadcasting Corporation or the Independent Broadcasting Authority[1335]; and

(f) applied in relation to cable programmes sent from places in that country as they applied in relation to cable programmes sent from places in the United Kingdom.[1336]

Any such Order in Council could have been made subject to exceptions and modifications, and could have applied either generally or in relation to specified classes of works or classes of cases.

Limitation on power to apply the 1956 Act. The power to make such Orders was, however, limited, in that an Order was not to be made applying any of the provisions of the 1956 Act in the case of a country, other than a country which was a party to a Convention relating to copyright to which the United Kingdom was also a party, "unless Her Majesty is satisfied that, in respect of the class of works or other subject-matter to which those provisions relate, provision has been or will be made under the laws of that country whereby adequate protection will be given to owners of copyright under this Act". This limitation was in slightly different language from that contained in the similar provisions in the 1911 Act.[1337]   3–250

Self-governing dominions. Whilst s.29 of the 1911 Act enabled Orders in Council to be made in respect of works originating in "a foreign country", s.32 of the 1956 Act applied to works originating in any country. This is because the 1911 Act extended, or was capable of being extended, throughout the British Empire, including the self-governing dominions, whereas the 1956 Act was only capable of being extended to the Isle of Man, the Channel Islands and any colony.[1338] Consequently, protection of works originating in a self-governing dominion or member of the Commonwealth had to be provided by Order in Council in the same way as in the case of a foreign country.   3–251

Power to curtail protection. The 1956 Act gave[1339] power to deprive citizens or subjects of countries not giving adequate protection to British works, of copyright under that Act, but this power does not appear to have been used.   3–252

(b) *Orders in Council under s.32 of the 1956 Act*

The 1957 Order. By an Order in Council made under s.32 of the 1956 Act, and coming into operation on September 27, 1957,[1340] the provisions of the 1956 Act relating to literary, dramatic, musical and artistic works, sound recordings, cinematographic films and published editions of literary, dramatic or musical   3–253

[1335] See Independent Broadcasting Authority Act 1973 (c.19), ss.1, 38 and 39; repealed by Broadcasting Act 1981 (c.68), s.65(4) and Sch.9, but 1973 Act amendment preserved by 1981 Act para.7, Sch.8.

[1336] Sub-para.(f) was added by the Cable and Broadcasting Act 1984 (c.46).

[1337] As to which, see para.3–236, above.

[1338] Copyright Act 1956 s.31 and see para.3–292, below.

[1339] Copyright Act 1956 s.35.

[1340] SI 1957/1523. *Copinger* 12th edn, p.2105. The date is the date on which the Universal Copyright Convention took effect so far as Great Britain is concerned.

works[1341] were applied in the case of the countries specified in Sch.1 to that Order, being countries which had adhered to the Berne or Universal Copyright Conventions as follows.[1342] First, they were applied in relation to such works, recordings, films or editions first published in such countries as they applied in relation to such works, recordings, films or editions first published in the United Kingdom. Second, they were applied in relation to the citizens or subjects of such countries, and to persons domiciled or resident in such countries, as they applied to British subjects or persons domiciled or resident in the United Kingdom. Third, they were applied in relation to bodies incorporated under the laws of such countries as they applied in relation to bodies incorporated under the law of any part of the United Kingdom. The general effect of the Order, therefore, was that all such works were to be treated as if they had been first published in the United Kingdom, or had been made by British subjects, persons domiciled or resident in the United Kingdom, or UK companies, as the case may have been. The Order revoked the Orders in Council made under the 1911 Act.[1343]

3–254   **Operation of the 1957 Order.** The Order applied to works irrespective of whether or not they existed at the date of its commencement. It contained a number of exceptions and limitations which were applicable to all the works to which it applied and some additional limitations and exceptions which applied only to works which existed at the date of its commencement. Finally, it contained saving provisions both in relation to persons who had incurred expenditure or liability in relation to non-infringing activities which became infringing by reason of the Order and in relation to works (if any) which ceased to be protected by reason of the revocation of the Orders made under the 1911 Act.

3–255   **The 1957 Order. Restrictions and limitations: all works.** There were two respects in which the copyright differed from that in a work qualifying under the basic method. The first concerned the term of such copyright and was general, and the second was of a limited character in respect of the copyright in sound recordings.

3–256   **The 1957 Order. Term of copyright.** By analogy with earlier Orders, the Order provided that the term of copyright in a work protected under its provisions was not to exceed that granted by the country of origin of the work without formality, other than that specified in the Universal Copyright Convention, to a British work of the same class.[1344] "British work" meant a work made by a British subject resident in the United Kingdom, or by a company incorporated under the laws of the United Kingdom, and which, if published, was first published in the United Kingdom.[1345] There was an exception to this in the case of works first published in the United States during the periods of the two world wars which already enjoyed copyright in the United Kingdom by virtue of the Wartime Orders mentioned above.[1346]

This provision was cancelled by an Order[1347] which came into operation on August 11, 1958, so that the normal term under the 1956 Act was applicable to all such works. But this amending Order was not to revive copyrights, so that it may still be necessary to consider the provisions of the original Order if, under

---

[1341] The provisions applied were Pts I and II with the exception of s.14, which concerned television and sound broadcasts.

[1342] art.1(a)–(c).

[1343] art.3 and Sch.5.

[1344] art.1, Proviso, para.(ii).

[1345] art.4(1).

[1346] Proviso, para.(vi). For the Orders, see paras 3–239 and 3–244, above.

[1347] The Copyright (International Conventions) (Amendment) Order 1958 (SI 1958/1254).

such provisions, the term would have expired between September 27, 1957, and August 11, 1958. This will involve knowledge of the relevant foreign law, and of the meaning of "country of origin" in the Order.

The 1957 Order. Meaning of "country of origin". Owing to the requirements of the various Conventions and the complications ensuing as a result of the simultaneous publication of works in a number of countries, the expression "country of origin" received a complicated definition in the 1957 Order[1348] which may be shortly summarised as follows:

    3–257

In the case of a work which was published in a country belonging to either of the Conventions it meant, if first published in such a country and not simultaneously published elsewhere, that country.

In the case of simultaneous publication, which meant, in the case of publications occurring before the commencement of that Order, publications within 14 days of one another, and, in any other case, within a period of 30 days of one another, there were four classes of case. If a work was simultaneously published in a Berne country and a non-Berne country, the country of origin was the Berne country. If the work was simultaneously published in a Universal Copyright Convention country and a country which was not a member of either Convention, the country of origin was the Universal Copyright Convention country. If a work was simultaneously published in several Berne countries, the country of origin was the country giving the shortest term of protection. If a work was simultaneously published in a number of Universal Copyright Convention countries and not in a Berne country, the country of origin was the country giving the shortest term of protection.

In the case of a work which was unpublished or first published in a country which did not belong to either Convention, the country of origin was the country whose laws gave the longest term of protection to such a work of the following, namely, the country of which the author was a subject or citizen, the country in which the author was domiciled, the country in which the author was resident or, where the author or maker was a body corporate, the country in which such body was incorporated.

The 1957 Order. Sound recordings. The provision about sound recordings was that, in relation to various specified countries,[1349] the acts restricted by the copyright in a sound recording conferred by the 1956 Act as applied by the Order were not to include causing the recording to be heard in public or broadcasting the recording.

    3–258

The 1957 Order. Restrictions and limitations: existing works. The provisions of the 1957 Order applied to works existing at its commencement, subject to the exceptions already noted and to certain further qualifications:

    3–259

(a) In the first place, copyright was not to subsist by virtue of the 1957 Order in any work by reason only of its publication before the commencement of the Order in a country which was a party to the Universal Copyright Convention, but which was not a country of the Berne Copyright Union.[1350] There was an exception to this in the case of works first published in the United States during the periods of the two world wars

---

[1348] art.4(2).
[1349] That is, those listed in Sch.1 other than those listed in art.1, Proviso, para.(ii).
[1350] Proviso, para.(i).

which already enjoyed copyright in the United Kingdom by virtue of the Wartime Orders mentioned above.[1351]

(b) Second, specific provision was made in relation to the statutory recording licence in respect of musical works and their associated words. Under the 1911 and 1956 Acts, one of the preconditions for the exercise of that licence was that records should have been made in or imported into the United Kingdom with the licence of the copyright owner. That precondition did not apply if the work in question had been first published before the commencement of the 1911 Act. The reason for this was that mechanical rights were first conferred by the 1911 Act.[1352] The effect of para.1 of Sch.4 to the Order was that in respect of the countries listed this precondition was disapplied from a specified date, which is stated to be the date when the mechanical right was first conferred in relation to works connected with that country.[1353] In respect of many countries, the date was the date of commencement of the 1911 Act but in respect of many others the date was later.

(c) Third, provision was made in relation to mechanical rights in respect of musical works in which copyright subsisted immediately before the commencement of the Order by virtue of an Order made under the 1911 Act. The effect of para.2 of Sch.4 to the Order was that if such a work had been published before a specified date, the mechanical right did not apply if before that date a record had been lawfully made or placed on sale in the United Kingdom. The date was stated to be the date when the mechanical right was first conferred in relation to works connected with that country.

(d) Fourth, provision was made in relation to mechanical rights in respect of musical works in which copyright did not subsist immediately before the commencement of the Order by virtue of an Order made under the 1911 Act. The effect of para.3 of Sch.4 to the Order was that if such a work had been published before the commencement of the Order, the mechanical right did not apply if a record had been lawfully made or placed on sale in the United Kingdom before the commencement of the Order.

(e) Fifth, provision was made in relation to sound recordings to which the 1911 Act applied immediately before the commencement of the Order. The 1956 Act provided that no copyright subsisted under that Act in a sound recording made before commencement of the 1911 Act unless a "corresponding" copyright subsisted at that date.[1354] Such a "corresponding" copyright subsisted if the making of the sound recording would not have infringed the copyright in another recording if the 1911 Act had been in force at the time the sound recording was made.[1355] The effect of para.4 of Sch. 4 to the Order was to apply these provisions to sound recordings originating in the countries to which the Order applied as from the date which was stated to be the date when the mechanical right was first conferred in relation to works connected with that country rather than the date of commencement of the 1911 Act. The paragraph went on to provide that in the case of any other sound recording the date in question was the date of commencement of the Order.

(f) Finally, there was a general provision that, in Sch.7 to the 1956 Act, refer-

---

[1351] Proviso, para.(vi). For the Orders, see paras 3–239 and 3–244, above.

[1352] See generally *Copinger* 12th edn, para.838.

[1353] In fact, the date appears to be the date on which the provisions of the 1911 Act applied to the territory of the state so identified.

[1354] Sch.7 para.13.

[1355] Copyright Act 1911 s.19(8).

ences to the commencement of that Act, or to the repeal of any provision of the 1911 Act, were to be treated, in relation to any work or other subject-matter in which copyright subsisted by virtue of the Order, as references to the commencement of the Order.

The 1957 Order: translations. The Order provided[1356] that nothing in the 1956 Act, as applied by the Order, was to be construed as reviving any right to make, or restrain the making of, or any right in respect of, translations, if such right had ceased before the commencement of that Order. This referred, in particular, to certain provisions of the Copyright (Rome Convention) Order 1933 made under the 1911 Act restricting the translation rights in works originating in certain countries because these countries also restricted translation rights.[1357]

3–260

The 1957 Order: saving provisions. The Order contained saving provisions both in relation to persons who had incurred expenditure or liability in relation to non-infringing activities which became infringing by reason of the Order and in relation to works (if any) which ceased to be protected by reason of the revocation of the Orders made under the 1911 Act. The first such provision[1358] was in the same terms as that contained in the 1933 Order, as to which see above.[1359] The second such provision[1360] provided that where copyright subsisted by virtue of any of the Orders made under the 1911 Act which were revoked by the 1957 Order, and copyright did not subsist in the work by art.1 of the Order, copyright should continue to subsist in the work as if the Order under the 1911 Act had not been revoked. It was not clear whether this provision simply preserved the copyright for the two-year period mentioned in para.40 of Sch.7[1361] or amounted to a positive Order under s.32 of the 1956 Act, continuing the copyright in such works for its full term.

3–261

Subsequent Orders under the 1956 Act: general. The 1957 Order was amended on a number of occasions and subsequent Orders (themselves often amended) were made in 1964, 1972 and 1979.[1362] Each of the 1964, 1972 and 1979 Orders revoked its predecessor.[1363] It is assumed that these revocations did not revive copyrights,[1364] but this is by no means entirely clear. By a separate Order made in 1961 the provisions of the 1956 Act were applied to foreign television broadcasts for the first time.[1365] Its provisions (as amended) were subsumed within the 1972 and 1979 Orders. Between 1979 and the commencement of the 1988 Act, specific orders were made in relation to Taiwan, Singapore and Indonesia.[1366] The 1979

3–262

[1356] art.1 proviso (v).

[1357] S.R. & O. 1933 No.253, art.2, proviso (ii); see also proviso (vi).

[1358] In art. 2.

[1359] para.3–243.

[1360] In art.3.

[1361] See para.3–248 above.

[1362] By the Copyright (International Conventions) Orders 1964, 1972 and 1970, SI 1964/690, 1972/673 and 1979/1715. They are reproduced in *Copinger* 12th edn, paras 2117 to 2152.

[1363] See art.19(2) of the 1964 Order, art.11 of the 1972 Order and art.11 of the 1979 Order.

[1364] See art.11, 1964 Order and art.2(2) 1972 Order and Interpretation Act 1889, s.38 (52 & 53 Vict., c.63) and Interpretation Act 1978 (c.30) ss.16, 21, 23.

[1365] See the Copyright (Foreign Television Broadcasts) Order 1961 (SI 1961/993), amended by SI 1962/165. Both these Orders were repealed by the 1964 Order which catered more fully for broadcasts (see below).

[1366] See, respectively The Copyright (Taiwan) Order 1985 (SI 1985/1777), the Copyright (Singapore) Order 1987 (SI 1987/940) and the Copyright (Sound Recordings) Indonesia Order 1988 (SI 1988/797).

Order and all subsequent Orders made under the 1956 Act were revoked and replaced after the commencement of the 1988 Act.[1367]

3–263   **Provisions of the 1964, 1972 and 1979 Orders.** Like the 1957 Order, each of the 1964, 1972 and 1979 Orders applied the provisions of the 1956 Act relating to literary, dramatic, musical and artistic works, sound recordings, cinematographic films and published editions of literary, dramatic or musical works in the case of specified countries as they applied in relation to works, persons and bodies corporate connected to the United Kingdom.[1368]

3–264   **The 1964, 1972 and 1979 Orders: broadcasts.** The 1964, 1972 and 1979 Orders also provided[1369] that the provisions of s.14 of the 1956 Act, so far as they related to sound broadcasts, were to apply in relation to sound broadcasts made from places in a number of named countries by any organisation constituted under the laws of such countries as they applied to broadcasts made from places in the United Kingdom by the British Broadcasting Corporation ("the BBC"). The Orders also provided[1370] that the provisions of s.14 of the 1956 Act, so far as they related to television broadcasts, were to apply in relation to television broadcasts made from places in another series of countries by any organisation constituted under the laws of such countries as they applied to television broadcasts made by the BBC or the Independent Broadcasting Authority. The Orders provided in effect that copyright should not subsist in a broadcast made before the date on which the provisions of the 1956 Act were applied to it.[1371]

3–265   **Operation of the 1964, 1972 and 1979 Orders.** Like the 1957 Order, each of the 1964, 1972 and 1979 Orders applied both to works created before and after its commencement, included a variety of restrictions and limitations on its operation and included saving provisions.

3–266   **The 1964, 1972 and 1979 Orders. Restrictions and limitations: all works.** The limitation on the term of copyright to that of the country of origin of the work, which was contained in the 1957 Order but removed from it in 1958, was not revived. However, as before,[1372] each of the Orders provided that in relation to various specified countries,[1373] the acts restricted by the copyright in a sound recording conferred by the 1956 Act as applied by the Order were not to include causing the recording to be heard in public or broadcasting the recording.[1374]

3–267   **The 1964, 1972 and 1979 Orders. Restrictions and limitations: existing works.**

      (a) The prohibition on works or other subject matter qualifying for protection by reason only of publication before September 27, 1957 in a country which was a party to the Universal Copyright Convention but which was not a country of the Berne Copyright Union[1375] was continued.[1376] However, in the subsequent Orders a date later than September 27, 1957

[1367] By the Copyright (Application to Other Countries) (No. 2) Order 1989 (SI 1989/1293).

[1368] art.1 of the 1964 Order and art.3 of the 1972 and 1979 Orders.

[1369] 1964 Order art.8 and Sch.5. 1972 Order art.8 and Sch.4. 1979 Order art.8 and Sch.4.

[1370] 1964 Order art.9 and Sch.6. 1972 Order art.9 and Sch. 1979 Order art.9 and Sch.5.

[1371] See arts 8 and 9.

[1372] See para.3–258, above.

[1373] That is, those listed in Sch.1 other than those listed in Sch.3.

[1374] art.3 of the 1964 Order and art.5 of the 1972 and 1979 Orders.

[1375] para.3–259, above.

[1376] art.2(2) of the 1964 Order and art.4(2)(b) of the 1972 and 1979 Orders.

was specified for some such countries.[1377] In such cases the date specified was the date on which the provisions of the 1956 Act were first applied by previous Orders other than the 1957 Order to the country in question. Once more, there was an exception to this in the case of works first published in the United States during the periods of the two world wars which already enjoyed copyright in the United Kingdom by virtue of the Wartime Orders mentioned above.[1378] Other countries were specifically excepted as well.[1379]

(b) The restrictions and limitations relating to mechanical rights and sound recordings contained in the 1957 Order[1380] were not repeated in the 1964, 1972 or 1979 Orders.

(c) The general provision that, in Sch.7 to the 1956 Act, references to the commencement of that Act, or to the repeal of any provision of the 1911 Act were to be treated, in relation to any work or other subject-matter in which copyright subsisted by virtue of the Order, as references to the commencement of the 1957 Order, was repeated,[1381] but in relation to some countries which were parties to the Universal Copyright Convention but not countries of the Berne Copyright Union the relevant date was a later date.[1382] Again, in such cases the date specified was the date on which the provisions of the 1956 Act were first applied by previous Orders other than the 1957 Order to the country in question.

The 1964, 1972 and 1979 Orders: saving provisions and translations. The saving provision contained in the 1957 Order relating to persons who had incurred expenditure or liability in relation to non-infringing activities was continued as was the provision in relation to translations.[1383]   **3–268**

(c) *United States works under the 1956 Act*

Copyright under the 1956 Act was originally conferred in respect of works of US origin by reason of that country's adherence to the Universal Copyright Convention, but the provisions of the Orders conferring this right were not retrospective in relation to published works except in so far as such works had already acquired copyright under wartime Orders made under the 1911 Act.[1384] However, this position changed after the United States acceded to the Paris Act of the Berne Convention with effect from March 1, 1989. The 1979 Order was amended, as from March 8, 1989, in such a way as to remove US works from the limit on protection in such Order of works first published in the United States before September 27, 1957,[1385] other than in accordance with the wartime Orders. As this amendment granted copyright to works not previously entitled thereto, the amending Order contained a general provision preserving existing rights of persons who, before the commencement of such Order, had incurred expenditure or liability in connection with the reproduction or performance of any work or other subject-matter. This amendment would appear to make reliance on the   **3–269**

[1377] See Sch.2 to the Orders.
[1378] Proviso, para.(vi). For the Orders, see paras 3–239 and 3–244.
[1379] art.4 of the 1964 Order; art. 4(3) of the 1972 and 1979 Orders.
[1380] para.3–259, above.
[1381] art.2(1) of the 1964 Order and art.4(1) of the 1972 and 1979 Orders.
[1382] art.2((3) of the 1964 Order and art.4(2)(a) of the 1972 and 1979 Orders.
[1383] See paras 3–261 and 3–260, above.
[1384] See paras 3–239 and 3–244, above.
[1385] The Copyright (International Conventions) Order 1979 (SI 1979/1715), as amended by the Copyright (International Conventions) (Amendment) Order 1989 (SI 1989/157).

wartime Orders of less importance. Of course many existing works would have obtained United Kingdom protection, under the 1956 Act, by having been simultaneously published in the United Kingdom or a Berne Convention country, without the necessity of reliance upon such Orders in Council.

C. EXTENSION OF UNITED KINGDOM COPYRIGHT LEGISLATION TO COLONIES, DEPENDENCIES ETC.

(i) Introduction

3–270   **"Extension".** The "extension" of a particular copyright statute to another country or territory is a distinct concept from the "application" of provisions of the Act to works first published in or made by citizens or subjects of another country. A statute can only be extended to another country or territory over which the UK government has the power to legislate or which has agreed that the statute should apply. The fact that a UK copyright statute has been extended to a particular country or territory does not necessarily mean that it applies in identical terms in that country or territory: the power to extend may include a power to modify the statute's application in the country or territory concerned and that power may have been exercised. Moreover, the effect of the extension of a provision of the various copyright statutes appears to have differed over time.

3–271   **Historical overview.** The Literary Copyright Act 1842 expressly extended copyright to every part of the British dominions. However, other nineteenth-century acts did not have this effect. At the Colonial Conference of 1910, resolutions were passed generally recognising the desirability of obtaining a uniform code of copyright laws which should apply throughout the King's dominions but insisting at the same time, that, at any rate, self-governing colonies ought not to be bound by any Imperial Copyright Act, or be made party to any convention or treaty entered into by the home government, without the assent of those colonies, and that all colonies ought to have the right to make local modifications in the law.[1386] Accordingly, the 1911 Act was extended in general terms throughout the King's dominions, but the self-governing dominions were given rights to decide whether or not it should operate within their territories. In fact, they all adopted the 1911 Act and, in consequence, the 1911 Act operated throughout the British Commonwealth. The 1956 Act, by contrast, was framed so that it could only extend to the United Kingdom, the Isle of Man, the Channel Islands, colonies and protected territories. The 1988 Act can only extend to the United Kingdom (including United Kingdom territorial waters and British ships, aircraft and hovercraft), the Channel Islands, the Isle of Man and colonies and at the present time the copyright part of it is not in fact extended beyond the United Kingdom at all.

(ii) Position under 1988 Act

3–272   **Extension of the 1988 Act to other countries.** Power is given, by s.157 of the 1988 Act,[1387] to extend the copyright provisions of the 1988 Act and Orders in Council made thereunder, by Order in Council to any of the Channel Islands, the Isle of Man or any colony.[1388] This power does not extend to self-governing dominions or the Republic of Ireland. The extending Orders in Council can

---

[1386] Report of Colonial Conference 1910 (Cd.5272).
[1387] See also CDPA 1988 s.304(3), (4) and (5).
[1388] CDPA 1988 s.157(2) and (3): and see s.304(6).

extend such provisions and Orders in Council subject to exceptions and modifications.[1389]

Power of such other countries to modify the 1988 Act. The legislature of any country to which the copyright provisions of the 1988 Act have been extended may, under s.157 of the 1988 Act, modify or add to such provisions in their operation as part of the law of that country. But such modifications or additions are limited to adapting such provisions to the circumstances of the country concerned as regards procedure and remedies or as regards works qualifying for copyright protection by virtue of a connection with that country.[1390]   **3–273**

Effect where the 1988 Act is so extended. As is explained below,[1391] where the 1956 Act and Orders in Council thereunder had been extended, common conditions for obtaining copyright protection existed throughout the area to which that Act and Orders in Council were so extended, with the advantages resulting therefrom.   **3–274**

However, the situation does not appear to have been continued in its entirety by the 1988 Act. Thus, by s.157(1) of the 1988 Act, that Act is to extend to England and Wales, Scotland and Northern Ireland,[1392] and the countries to which the 1988 Act can be extended by Order in Council are more limited than under the 1956 Act in that they do not include protected territories.[1393] Further, copyright under the 1988 Act does not, as under the 1956 Act, appear to cover the right to do and restrain the doing of certain acts in countries to which the Act has been extended, as well as in the United Kingdom. Thus, by s.2 of the 1988 Act, the copyright owner is given the exclusive right to do the restricted acts specified in Ch.II of Pt 1 of that Act, and the various sections in Ch.II, which also cover infringement, appear to be limited to the doing of acts in the United Kingdom.[1394] Again, s.90(2) of the 1988 Act does not, like s.36(2)(b) of the 1956 Act, contain a provision for partial assignments as to one or more countries. Finally, the 1988 Act contains no provision similar to s.31(4) of the 1956 Act[1395] under which proceedings could be brought in the United Kingdom in respect of an act done in a country to which the 1988 Act had been extended.

On the other hand, certain of the conditions for qualifying for copyright protection under the 1988 Act are similar to those under the 1956 Act[1396] in that, for instance, by s.154(1) of the 1988 Act, individuals domiciled or resident in a country to which the copyright provisions of the 1988 Act have been extended and bodies incorporated under the law of such a country are included. Also included, by s.155(1) of the 1988 Act, are works first published in such a country as are, by s.156(1) of that Act, broadcasts made from a place in such a country.

The result of this would appear to be that, although the relevant provisions of the 1988 Act can be extended to another country, as could the provisions of the 1956 Act, and although, as under the 1956 Act, a person resident in a country to which the 1988 Act has been extended, for instance, may get copyright under the

---

[1389] CDPA 1988 s.157(2) and (3).

[1390] CDPA 1988 s.157(4).

[1391] See para.3–294.

[1392] See CDPA 1988, s.161 and para.38, Sch.1 as to the territorial waters of the UK and the UK sector of the continental shelf. See also s.162 and para.39, Sch.1 as to British ships, aircraft and hovercraft.

[1393] See para.3–292, below.

[1394] See CDPA 1988 ss.16–27, in particular ss.16, 18, 22, 24 and s27, and compare Copyright Act 1956 ss.1(1) and (2), 5 and 16.

[1395] See para.3–296, below.

[1396] See, for instance, Copyright Act 1956 ss.1(5), 2(1) and (2), 3(2) and (3), 12(1) and (2), 13(1) and (2) and 15(1).

1988 Act, nonetheless whereas under the 1956 Act, an act done in a country to which the 1956 Act had been extended could be an infringement of copyright under the 1956 Act as well as of copyright under the 1956 Act as extended to that country, it will not now be an infringement of copyright under the 1988 Act to do an act in a country to which the 1988 Act has been extended. This will, if at all, only be an infringement of that country's law, that is the 1988 Act as extended to that country.

3–275   **Countries ceasing to be colonies.** Section 158 of the 1988 Act contains certain provisions applicable where the country to which the copyright provisions of that Act have been extended ceases to be a colony of the United Kingdom.[1397] If that happens, such a country is, as from the date on which it ceases to be a colony, not to be treated as a country to which such copyright provisions extend for the purposes of s.160(2)(a)[1398] and of ss.163 and 165.[1399] Nonetheless it is to continue to be treated as a country to which such copyright provisions extend for the purposes of qualification for copyright protection[1400] until an Order in Council is made in respect of that country under s.159 of the 1988 Act,[1401] or an Order in Council is made declaring that it shall cease to be so treated by reason of the fact that such copyright provisions as part of the law of that country have been repealed or amended.[1402] A statutory instrument containing such a declaratory Order in Council is subject to annulment in pursuance of a resolution of either House of Parliament.[1403]

3–276   **Dependent Territories: general.** The 1956 Act was extended to the Isle of Man and a number of other countries,[1404] but not, except to a limited extent, to the Channel Islands, where the 1911 Act remained in force.[1405] The 1988 Act, para.36, Sch.1, contains provisions dealing with what are defined as dependent territories, that is any of the Channel Islands, the Isle of Man or any colony.[1406]

3–277   **Channel Islands.** Paragraph 36(1) of Sch.1 to the 1988 Act provides that the 1911 Act is to remain in force as part of the law of any dependent territory in which it was in force immediately before the commencement of the copyright provisions of the 1988 Act, such as the Channel Islands, until such provisions come into force in that territory by virtue of an Order under s.157 of the 1988 Act (extension),[1407] or in the case of the Channel Islands, the 1911 Act is repealed by Order under para.36(3). Certain provisions of the 1956 Act were, in fact, extended to the Channel Islands, (as well as to the Isle of Man and certain other countries), by Order in Council,[1408] and para.36(2) of Sch.1 to the 1988 Act provides that an Order in Council in force immediately before such commencement which extends to any dependent territory any provisions of the 1956 Act shall remain in force as part of the law of that territory until the copyright provisions of the 1988 Act come into force in that territory by virtue of an Order under s.157 of the 1988 Act (extension), and while it remains in force such an Order may be varied under the

---

[1397] CDPA 1988 s.158(1) and (2).

[1398] See para.3–206, above.

[1399] See Ch.10.

[1400] CDPA 1988 ss.154–156.

[1401] See para.3–202, above.

[1402] CDPA 1988 s.158(3). As to countries in which the 1911 Act or the 1956 Act is in force ceasing to be a colony, see CDPA 1988 Sch.1 para.36(5).

[1403] CDPA 1988 s.158(4).

[1404] See para.3–278, above.

[1405] See para.3–277, below.

[1406] CDPA 1988 Sch.1 para.36(6).

[1407] See para.3–272, above, and see CDPA 1988 s.157(5).

[1408] The Copyright Act 1956 (Transitional Extension) Order 1959 (SI 1959/103).

provisions of the 1956 Act under which it was made. It would appear, therefore, that, until an Order is made under the 1988 Act, the position in the Channel Islands remains the same. At the moment no such Orders have been made.[1409]

As to the future, presumably the Order in Council extending certain provisions of the 1956 Act to the Channel Islands[1410] will go if, and when, an Order is made in respect of the Channel Islands under s.157 of the 1988 Act. So far as the 1911 Act is concerned, this will remain in force in the Channel Islands until an Order is made under s.157 or the Act is repealed by an Order under para.36(3). Paragraph 36(3) provides that, if it appears to Her Majesty that provision with respect to copyright has been made in the law of any of the Channel Islands otherwise than by extending the copyright provisions of the 1988 Act, Her Majesty may by Order in Council repeal the 1911 Act as it has effect as part of the law of that territory. However, if such an Order is made, it will be made, apparently, in a situation where the copyright provisions of the 1988 Act have not been extended to the Channel Islands. If that be so, it is unclear what is to happen to the Order extending certain provisions of the 1956 Act to the Channel Islands,[1411] since, although para.36(3) also refers to revoking an Order extending the 1956 Act, this appears, when taken with para.36(2)(b), only to relate to the Isle of Man.

Finally, para.36(4) provides that a dependent territory in which the 1911 or 1956 Act remains in force is to be treated, in the law of the countries to which the copyright provisions of the 1988 Act extend, as a country to which such provisions extend. Further, that those countries are to be treated in the law of such a territory as countries to which the 1911 Act or, as the case may be, the 1956 Act extends. The Channel Islands are dependent territories but, again, this is not entirely clear since certain provisions of the 1956 Act have been extended to the Channel Islands.[1412]

Isle of Man. Paragraph 36(2) of Sch.1 to the 1988 Act provides that an Order in Council in force immediately before the commencement of the copyright provisions of the 1988 Act which extends to any dependent territory, such as the Isle of Man, any of the provisions of the 1956 Act, is to remain in force as part of the law of that territory until such provisions come into force in that territory by virtue of an Order under s.157 of the 1988 Act (extension), or in the case of the Isle of Man, the Order is revoked by Order under para.36(3), and while it remains in force such an Order may be varied under the provisions of the 1956 Act under which it was made.   **3–278**

As at the commencement of the 1988 Act, the 1956 Act had been extended to the Isle of Man.[1413] The copyright provisions of the 1988 Act were never so extended. Instead, with effect from July 1, 1992, an Order was made under s.159 of the Act applying ss.153 to 156 of the Act to works, broadcasts and cable programmes connected with the Isle of Man as they apply to works connected with the United Kingdom.[1414] At the same time, the Order extending the 1956 Act to the Isle of Man was revoked pursuant to para.36(3).[1415] The 1992 Order was revoked with effect from May 1, 2005 by art.8(a) of the Copyright and Perfor-

---

[1409] Note, however, that CDPA 1988 ss.297 to 299 (fraudulent reception and unauthorised decoders) have been extended to Guernsey (by SI 1989/1997—Vol.2 A4.viii) and that the protection afforded by CDPA 1988 ss.297 and 298 has been extended to transmissions provided from Guernsey (by SI 1989/2003). See Vol.2 A4.ix.

[1410] The Copyright Act 1956 (Transitional Extension) Order 1959 (SI 1959/103).

[1411] The Copyright Act 1956 (Transitional Extension) Order 1959 (SI 1959/103).

[1412] The Copyright Act 1956 (Transitional Extension) Order 1959 (SI 1959/103).

[1413] See para.3–293, below.

[1414] The Copyright (Application to the Isle of Man) Order 1992 (SI 1992/1313).

[1415] By the Copyright (Isle of Man) (Revocation) Order 1992 (SI 1992/1306).

mances (Application to Other Countries) Order 2005.[1416] That Order and its replacement[1417] having been revoked, the position in respect of works and broadcasts connected with the Isle of Man is now governed by the terms of the Copyright and Performances (Application to Other Countries) Order 2008.[1418]

3–279   **Hong Kong.** Certain provisions of the 1956 Act, not including s.32 of that Act, were extended to Hong Kong by Orders in Council.[1419] Further, para.36(2) of Sch.1 to the 1988 Act, which provides that such Orders in Council are to remain in force until an Order is made under s.157 of the 1988 Act, also provides that, while they remain in force, they may be varied under the provisions of the 1956 Act under which they were made. Such a variation was made by a further Order in Council with effect from April 12, 1990.[1420] The effect of this further Order in Council was to extend to Hong Kong s.32 of the 1956 Act suitably amended. Section 32 of the 1956 Act enabled Her Majesty, by Order in Council, to apply the provisions of the 1956 Act to countries to which they did not extend,[1421] and the amended s.32 extended to Hong Kong enabled the Governor of Hong Kong by Order to apply provisions of the 1956 Act to such countries. By reason of para.36(1)(a) and (2)(a) of Sch.1 to the 1988 Act, the position remained the same until Hong Kong ceased to be a colony immediately before July 1, 1997.[1422]

3–280   **Other dependent territories.** By reason of para.36(1)(a) and (2)(a) of Sch.1 to the 1988 Act, the position will remain the same as it was before commencement of the 1988 Act until an Order is made under s.157 of the 1988 Act. Paragraph 36(4) deals with the relationship between a dependent territory and other countries whilst the 1911 or 1956 Act remains in force in such territory. The only other Orders which have been made under s.157 concerned Bermuda and Gibraltar. Various provisions of Pt 1 of the 1988 Act, subject to modifications, were extended to Bermuda with effect from such date as the Governor of Bermuda might appoint by proclamation published in the Gazette of Bermuda.[1423] That Order was revoked with effect from November 12, 2009.[1424] Provision has been made in the past for the extension with modifications of provisions of Pt I of the 1988 Act to Gibraltar,[1425] but such provision too has been revoked.[1426] Works, broadcasts and performances connected with Bermuda and Gibraltar are now governed by the Copyright and Performances (Application to Other Countries) Order 2008 as amended.[1427]

3–281   **Non-dependent territories.** By virtue of para.39(2) of Sch.7 to the 1956 Act, certain countries were to be treated as countries to which the 1956 Act extended. Paragraph 37 of Sch.1 to the 1988 Act contains provisions dealing with such of those countries which were not immediately before the commencement of the copyright provisions of the 1988 Act dependent territories. "Dependent territory"

[1416] SI 2005/852.

[1417] The Copyright and Performances (Application to Other Countries) Order 2006 (SI 2006/316).

[1418] SI 2008/677. See, generally, paras 3–207 et seq., above.

[1419] The Copyright (Hong Kong) Order 1972 (SI 1972/1724) and the Copyright (Hong Kong) (Amendment) Order 1979 (SI 1979/910).

[1420] The Copyright (Hong Kong) (Amendment) Order 1990 (SI 1990/588).

[1421] See paras 3–249 et seq., above.

[1422] See 13 *Halsbury's Laws* 5th edn, para.727.

[1423] See the Copyright (Bermuda) Order 2003 (SI 2003/1517).

[1424] By the Copyright (Bermuda) Revocation Order 2009 (SI 2009/2749).

[1425] See most recently the Copyright (Gibraltar) Order 2005 (SI 2005/853).

[1426] By the Copyright (Gibraltar) Revocation Order 2006 (SI 2006/1039).

[1427] SI 2008/677. See in particular as to Bermuda the Copyright and Performances (Application to Other Countries) (Amendment) Order (SI 2009/2745).

means any of the Channel Islands, the Isle of Man or any colony,[1428] and para.37(1) provides that Her Majesty may by Order in Council conclusively declare for the purposes of para.37 whether a country[1429] was a country to which the 1956 Act extended or was treated as such a country. Such an Order was made in 1990 ("the 1990 Order")[1430] and the list of countries to which the 1956 Act extended or which were treated as such is as follows: Botswana, Dominica, Gambia, Grenada, Guyana, Jamaica, Kiribati, Lesotho, St Christopher-Nevis, St Lucia, Seychelles, Solomon Islands, Swaziland, Tuvalu and Uganda.[1431]

Paragraph 37(2) provides that a country to which para.37 applies is to be treated as a country to which the copyright provisions of the 1988 Act extend for the purposes of ss.154 to 156 of the 1988 Act (qualification for copyright protection) until an Order in Council is made in respect of that country under s.159 of the 1988 Act (application),[1432] or an Order in Council is made declaring that it shall cease to be so treated by reason of the fact that the provisions of the 1956 Act or, as the case may be, the 1911 Act, which extended there as part of the law of that country have been repealed or amended. A statutory instrument containing an Order in Council under para.37 is subject to annulment in pursuance of a resolution of either House of Parliament.[1433] The 1990 Order declares that Botswana, Seychelles, Solomon Islands and Uganda shall cease to be treated as countries to which Pt I of the 1988 Act extends for the purposes of s.154 to 156 of the 1988 Act by reason of such repeal or amendment. With the exception of Kiribati and Tuvalu, the remaining countries to which the 1956 Act extended or was treated as having extended by reason of the 1990 Order are the subject of an Order in Council under the 1988 Act.[1434]

(iii) Position before the 1911 Act

Law prior to 1911 Act. The Literary Copyright Act 1842 expressly extended copyright to every part of the British dominions,[1435] but none of the Acts relating to artistic or dramatic copyright contained any similar provision. The Fine Arts Copyright Act 1862 did refer to the British dominions, giving copyright in all works made in the British dominions or elsewhere,[1436] but it was held that there was nothing in that Act to extend the copyright throughout the British dominions, the provisions of ss.8 and 10 providing for the recovery of the penalties in England, Scotland and Ireland, and forbidding the importation into the United Kingdom of copies made in any part of the British dominions indicating a contrary intention.[1437]

3–282

Whilst, therefore, a British author publishing a literary work in the United Kingdom obtained, under the Literary Copyright Act 1842, an imperial copyright extending throughout the British dominions, and was thus enabled to prevent piracies in any colony, a British artist, first publishing in the United Kingdom, obtained no imperial copyright, but, if he desired to prevent infringements in a colony, needed to acquire local copyright according to the laws of the particular colony.

[1428] CDPA 1988 Sch.1 para.36(6).
[1429] "Country" includes any territory: CDPA 1988 s.178.
[1430] See the Copyright (Status of Former Dependent Territories) Order 1990 (SI 1990/1512).
[1431] See Sch.1 to the Order.
[1432] See para.3–202, above.
[1433] CDPA 1988 Sch.1 para.37(3).
[1434] See now the Copyright and Performances (Application to Other Countries) Order 2008 as amended.
[1435] (5 & 6 Vict., c.45) s.29.
[1436] (25 & 26 Vict., c.68) s.1.
[1437] *Graves (Henry) & Co Ltd v Gorrie* [1903] A.C. 496.

3–283   **Rights of colonial authors in United Kingdom.** Conversely, it was held that the Literary Copyright Act 1842 did not confer copyright in the United Kingdom on works first published in the colonies.[1438] This grievance was removed by the International Copyright Act 1886, which, by section 8, provided that the Copyright Acts should, subject to the provisions of the Act of 1886, apply to a literary or artistic work first produced in a *British possession* in like manner as they applied to a work first produced in the United Kingdom: provided (a) that the enactments respecting the registry of the copyright in such work should not apply if the law of such possession provided for the registration of such copyright; and (b) that where such work was a book, the delivery to any persons or body of persons of a copy of any such work should not be required. If, therefore, in the particular colony there was no provision for registration, then the registration needed to be effected in this country.

The result was that any work produced in the colonies became entitled to the same copyright as it would have obtained if it had been first produced in the United Kingdom, but that, although literary works published in the United Kingdom obtained copyright throughout the dominions, this was not the case with regard to artistic works.

3–284   **Foreign reprints.** By s.17 of the Literary Copyright Act 1842, all persons, other than the proprietor of the copyright or persons authorised by him, were forbidden to import into any part of the British dominions, for sale or hire, any printed book first composed or written or printed and published within the United Kingdom, in which there should be copyright, and reprinted in any country or place out of the British dominions, under penalty of £10, and double the value of the books.[1439] Complaints arose, especially from Canada, with regard to this prohibition. It was contended that, in the sparsely populated colonies, where the circulating library system did not prevail, the price of English books was practically prohibitive, whilst English publishers were afraid to issue special cheap colonial editions, because they would not be able to prevent their re-importation into Great Britain. With a view to remedying these grievances, the Act commonly known as the Foreign Reprints Act was passed in 1847,[1440] enabling the Crown, by Order in Council, to suspend the prohibition against importation into the colonies of English copyright works, subject to their making suitable provisions for the protection of British authors. Under this Act, numerous Orders in Council were issued by virtue of which cheap foreign reprints of copyright works were permitted to be imported into various colonies.

(iv) Position under the 1911 Act

3–285   **Provisions of the 1911 Act.** The provisions of the 1911 Act relating to the British possessions were contained in ss.25 to 28. The countries subject to the Crown were divided into three classes: (a) dominions of the Crown, other than self-governing colonies; (b) self-governing colonies, meaning thereby the Dominion of Canada, the Commonwealth of Australia, the Dominion of New Zealand, the Union of South Africa, and Newfoundland[1441]; and (c) protectorates and Cyprus.

3–286   **Non self-governing colonies and protectorates.** The provisions of the 1911 Act relating to the colonies, other than the self-governing dominions, and to the

---

[1438] *Routledge v Low* (1868) L.R. 3 H.L. 100.
[1439] And see the Customs Consolidation Act 1876 (39 & 40 Vict., c.36), ss.151 and 152; and *Black v Imperial Book Co Ltd* (1903) 5 Ontario L.R. 184; (1905) 21 T.L.R. 540.
[1440] Its official title is the Colonial Copyright Act 1847 (10 & 11 Vict., c.95).
[1441] Copyright Act 1911 s.35(1).

protectorates and Cyprus, were comparatively simple. Section 25(1) enacted that that Act, "except such of the provisions thereof as are expressly restricted to the United Kingdom,[1442] shall extend throughout His Majesty's dominions", subject to a saving in respect of a self-governing dominion. Section 28 enabled His Majesty by Order in Council to extend the 1911 Act to any territories under his protection, and to Cyprus, "and, on the making of any such Order, this Act shall, subject to the provisions of the Order, have effect as if the territories to which it applies or Cyprus were part of His Majesty's dominions to which this Act extends." The legislature of any British possession to which the 1911 Act extended had, however, power to modify, or add to, any of the provisions of that Act in its application to the possession.[1443]

Thus, for the purposes of copyright, the colonies, other than the self-governing colonies, were treated as parts of the United Kingdom, and British copyright extended to all such colonies, and, vice versa, colonial copyright extended to the United Kingdom, except those modifications and additions to the British Act which the legislature of any colony should make, those only applying locally. Similarly, the following protectorates, to which by an Order in Council[1444] dated June 24, 1912, the British Act was extended, were equally considered for copyright purposes to be part of the United Kingdom, namely, Cyprus, the Bechuanaland Protectorate, East Africa Protectorate, Gambia Protectorate, Gilbert and Ellice Islands Protectorate, Northern Nigeria Protectorate, Northern Territories of the Gold Coast, Nyasaland Protectorate, Northern Rhodesia, Southern Rhodesia, Sierra Leone Protectorate, Somaliland Protectorate, Southern Nigeria Protectorate, Solomon Islands Protectorate, Swaziland and Uganda Protectorate. Further, the British Act was extended to Palestine by an Order in Council of March 21, 1924, to Tanganyika by an Order in Council of April 16, 1924, to the Federated Malay States by Order in Council[1445] of February 12, 1931, and to British Cameroons by Order in Council of March 16, 1933. Most of such colonies and protectorates passed local laws regarding the seizure by the customs of infringing copies and introducing penal provisions similar to those contained in s.11 of the 1911 Act, such laws being authorised by s.27 of that Act.

The 1911 Act came into force in the above-mentioned possessions (including the Channel Islands other than Jersey) on July 1, 1912, except that it came into force in the Isle of Man on July 5, 1912, in India on October 30, 1912, in Papua on February 1, 1913, and in Jersey on March 8, 1913. The 1911 Act came into force in the above-mentioned protectorates at the dates referred to in the respective Orders.

Self-governing dominions. The self-governing dominions all became dominions to which the 1911 Act extended.[1446] Section 25(1) of the 1911 Act provided that that Act should not extend to the self-governing dominions unless declared by the legislature of any dominion so to apply, either without modifications, or with modifications relating exclusively to procedure and remedies, or necessary for its application to the dominion. Newfoundland adopted the 1911 Act without modifications. The Commonwealth of Australia and the Union of South Africa made certain modifications.

Canada and New Zealand did not adopt this procedure, but passed independent Acts on similar lines to the 1911 Act. By s.25(2) of the 1911 Act it was provided

3–287

[1442] i.e. Copyright Act 1911 ss.11 and 12, relating to summary remedies.
[1443] Copyright Act 1911 s.27: and see *Rediffusion (Hong Kong) Ltd v Att-Gen of Hong Kong* [1970] A.C. 1136, and *Butterworth and Co (Publishers) Ltd v Ng Sui Nam* [1987] R.P.C. 485.
[1444] S.R. & O. 1912 No. 912.
[1445] S.R. & O. 1931 No.105.
[1446] As regards the Republic of Ireland, see para.3–288, below.

that, if the Secretary of State certified, by notice published in the *London Gazette*, that any self-governing dominion had passed legislation under which works, the authors whereof were, at the date of the making of the works, British subjects resident elsewhere than in the dominion or (not being British subjects) were resident in the parts of His Majesty's dominions to which that Act extended, enjoyed within the dominion rights substantially identical with those conferred by that Act, then, whilst such legislation continued in force, the dominion should, for the purposes of the rights conferred by that Act, be treated as if it were a dominion to which that Act extended.

The Canadian Act of 1921 complied with the provisions of this section in its terms, and the New Zealand Act of 1913 also complied with them when coupled with an Order of the Executive Council made thereunder of March 27, 1914. The Secretary of State in fact certified, in respect of both dominions, under s.25(2), in 1923 as to Canada and in 1914 as to New Zealand.[1447]

3–288   The Republic of Ireland. By an Order in Council dated October 27, 1930, made in pursuance of the Irish Free State (Consequential Provisions) Act 1922,[1448] the Irish Free State was deemed to be a self-governing dominion for the purposes of the 1911 Act, and, by a further Order in Council dated October 27, 1930, made in pursuance of s.26(3) of the 1911 Act, the 1911 Act was declared to apply to works first published in the Irish Free State and to works of which the authors were, at the time of making the work, resident in the Irish Free State, provided that there was to be no right to prevent the translation into English of literary or dramatic works in Irish if an authorised translation was not made within 10 years from publication. This Order in Council was preserved by the provisions of para.40(4) of Sch.7 to the 1956 Act,[1449] but was repealed by the Copyright (International Conventions) Order 1957[1450] which applied the 1956 Act to the Republic of Ireland as a Berne Convention country.

The 1911 Act was repealed in the Irish Free State by an Irish Free State Act[1451] passed in 1927 but, since this was thought to create doubts as to subsisting copyrights,[1452] a further Act was passed in 1929[1453] declaring that, so far as was necessary for the subsistence in the Irish Free State of copyrights, the 1911 Act and every Order made thereunder should be deemed to continue to have full force and effect in the Irish Free State. A new Copyright Act was passed on April 8, 1963, to replace the existing law.[1454] For the present position, see Ch.25.

3–289   International arrangements with dominions. With regard to any international arrangements which were made by the United Kingdom, it was provided that any Order in Council made under s.29 of the 1911 Act[1455] was to apply to all His Majesty's dominions, except the self-governing dominions and any other possession specified in the Order.[1456] Accordingly, the various Orders in Council which were made under that section applied the Order to all the dominions, colonies and possessions of the Crown, with the exception of the self-governing dominions,

---

[1447] See *Mansell v Star Printing, etc. Ltd* [1937] A.C. 872 and *Walt Disney Productions v (H.) John Edwards Publishing Co Pty Ltd* (1954) 71 W.N. (N.S.W.) 150.

[1448] 13 Geo. 5, c.2.

[1449] Repealed by Statute Law (Repeals) Act 1986 (c.12), but see s.2 thereof.

[1450] *Copinger* 12th edn, p.2105: see Copyright (International Conventions) Order 1979 (SI 1979/1715), as amended.

[1451] Industrial and Commercial Property (Protection) Act 1927, No.16 of 1927. See *Copinger* 9th edn, App.E.

[1452] *Performing Right Society Ltd v Bray U.D.C.* [1930] A.C. 377.

[1453] Copyright (Preservation) Act 1929, S.R. & O. No.25 of 1929. See *Copinger* 9th edn, App.E.

[1454] Copyright Act (S.R. & O. No.10 of 1963).

[1455] See para.3–236, above.

[1456] Copyright Act 1911 s.30(1) and (3).

and also to Cyprus and the protectorates to which the Copyright Act was by Order in Council extended.[1457] With regard to the self-governing dominions the 1911 Act authorised the Governor in Council of any such dominion to which that Act extended to make, as respects that dominion, the like Orders as the Crown in Council was, under ss.29 and 30 of that Act, authorised to make with regard to dominions other than self-governing dominions, and the provisions of those sections were, with the necessary modifications, to apply accordingly.[1458] Orders in Council were, under this power, or a similar power in their own Acts, made by Australia, New Zealand, Newfoundland and the Union of South Africa, while the same effect was produced by the terms of the Canadian Act itself.

Repeal by dominions of pre-1911 legislation. It is to be noted that s.26(1) of the 1911 Act gave to the legislature of any self-governing dominion power to repeal any enactment relating to copyright, including the 1911 Act. All the dominions repealed the legislation prior to the 1911 Act which applied to them.   **3–290**

(v) Position under the 1956 Act

Repeal of the 1911 Act in the United Kingdom. Paragraph 41 of Sch.7 to the 1956 Act provided that, in so far as the 1911 Act, or any Order in Council made thereunder, formed part of the law of any country other than the United Kingdom at a time after that Act had been wholly or partly repealed in the law of the United Kingdom, it should, so long as it formed part of the law of that country, be construed and have effect as if that Act had not been so repealed.[1459] The repeal of the 1911 Act in the United Kingdom, therefore, did not affect its operation, either in colonial territories, or in the self-governing dominions.   **3–291**

Extension of the 1956 Act to other countries. Power was given, by s.31 of the 1956 Act, to extend that Act and Orders in Council made under that Act, by Order in Council, to the Isle of Man, any of the Channel Islands, any colony,[1460] any country outside HM dominions in which for the time being Her Majesty had jurisdiction, and any country consisting partly of one or more colonies and partly of one or more such countries as are last mentioned. Such Orders in Council could have extended the 1956 Act subject to exceptions and modifications. By extending provisions of the Act, such provisions became the law of the country to which they had been extended. No Order in Council was made extending the main provisions of the 1956 Act to the Channel Islands, and so the 1911 Act remained in force there.[1461]   **3–292**

Extension Orders under the 1956 Act.   **3–293**
(i) Orders in Council under the 1956 Act were extended to various countries, either by the Orders in Council themselves,[1462] or by other Orders in Council.[1463] The 1956 Act and various Orders in Council thereunder were extended, by Orders in Council, to the following countries: the Isle of

---

[1457] See para.3–286, above.

[1458] Copyright Act 1911 s.30(2).

[1459] See, as to repeal of the 1911 Act as part of the law of any country in the Commonwealth, the Copyright Act 1956 (Transitional Extension) Order 1959 (SI 1959/103).

[1460] See *Rediffusion (Hong Kong) Ltd v Att-Gen of Hong Kong* [1970] A.C. 1136.

[1461] Copyright Act 1911 ss.25(1) and 37(2)(c). The date the Act of 1911 came into operation in the Channel Islands was July 1, 1912, except for Jersey when the date was March 8, 1913. S.37(2) was repealed by Statute Law (Repeals) Act 1986 (c.12).

[1462] See, for instance, the Copyright (International Conventions) Order 1979 (SI 1979/1715) as amended and the Copyright (Singapore) Order 1987 (SI 1987/940).

[1463] See, for instance, the Copyright (Singapore) (Amendment) Order 1987 (SI 1987/1030), the Copyright (Taiwan) (Extension to Territories) Order 1987 (SI 1987/1826), the Copyright (Taiwan

Man as from May 31, 1959,[1464] Sarawak as from January 1, 1960,[1465] Gibraltar as from June 1, 1960,[1466] Fiji as from February 1, 1961,[1467] Uganda as from January 1, 1962,[1468] Zanzibar as from January 1, 1962,[1469] Bermuda as from August 6, 1962,[1470] North Borneo as from August 6, 1962,[1471] the Bahamas as from October 11, 1962,[1472] the Virgin Islands as from October 11, 1962,[1473] the Falkland Islands as from June 10, 1963,[1474] St Helena and dependencies as from June 10, 1963,[1475] Seychelles as from June 10, 1963,[1476] Kenya as from July 4, 1963,[1477] Mauritius as from May 21, 1964,[1478] Montserrat as from November 5, 1965,[1479] St Lucia as from November 5, 1965,[1480] Bechuanaland as from December 4, 1965,[1481] Cayman Islands as from December 4, 1965,[1482] Grenada as from January 1, 1966,[1483] British Guiana as from February 5, 1966,[1484] British Honduras as from June 16, 1966,[1485] Saint Vincent as from July 5, 1967,[1486] Hong Kong as from December 12, 1972,[1487] and the British Indian Ocean Territory as from May 14, 1984.[1488] Each Order contained exceptions and modifications which varied according to local circumstances.

(ii) The Copyright (Computer Software) Amendment Act 1985[1489] was to be construed as one with the 1956 Act[1490] so that the provisions thereof could be extended to other countries like the provisions of the 1956 Act. The

---

Order) (Isle of Man Extension) Order 1987 (SI 1987/1833) and the Copyright (Singapore) (Amendment) Order 1988 (SI 1988/1297).

[1464] The Copyright (Isle of Man) Order 1959 (SI 1959/861), the Copyright (Isle of Man) Order 1970 (SI 1970/1437) and the Copyright (Isle of Man) Order 1971 (SI 1971/1848): these three Orders were revoked and repealed by the Copyright (Isle of Man) Order 1986 (SI 1986/1299). See also the Copyright Act 1956 (Transitional Extension) Order 1959 (SI 1959/103).

[1465] The Copyright (Sarawak) Order 1959 (SI 1959/2215).

[1466] The Copyright (Gibraltar) Order 1960 (SI 1960/847), as amended by the Copyright (Gibraltar) (Amendment) Order 1985 (SI 1985/1986).

[1467] The Copyright (Fiji) Order 1961 (SI 1961/60).

[1468] The Copyright (Uganda) Order 1961 (SI 1961/2462).

[1469] The Copyright (Zanzibar) Order 1961 (SI 1961/2463), as amended by the Copyright (Zanzibar) (Amendment) Order 1962 (SI 1962/629).

[1470] The Copyright (Bermuda) Order 1962 (SI 1962/1642), as amended by the Copyright (Bermuda) (Amendment) Order 1985 (SI 1985/1985). The Copyright (Bermuda) Order 1962 was revoked by the Copyright (Bermuda) Order 2003 (SI 2003/1517). See now SI 2008/677.

[1471] The Copyright (North Borneo) Order 1962 (SI 1962/1643).

[1472] The Copyright (Bahamas) Order 1962 (SI 1962/2184).

[1473] The Copyright (Virgin Islands) Order 1962 (SI 1962/2185), as amended by the Copyright (Virgin Islands) (Amendment) Order 1985 (SI 1985/1988).

[1474] The Copyright (Falkland Islands) Order 1963 (SI 1963/1037).

[1475] The Copyright (St Helena) Order 1963 (SI 1963/1038).

[1476] The Copyright (Seychelles) Order 1963 (SI 1963/1039).

[1477] The Copyright (Kenya) Order 1963 (SI 1963/1147).

[1478] The Copyright (Mauritius) Order 1964 (SI 1964/689).

[1479] The Copyright (Montserrat) Order 1965 (SI 1965/1858), as amended by the Copyright (Montserrat) (Amendment) Order 1985 (SI 1985/1987).

[1480] The Copyright (St Lucia) Order 1965 (SI 1965/1859).

[1481] The Copyright (Bechuanaland) Order 1965 (SI 1965/2009).

[1482] The Copyright (Cayman Islands) Order 1965 (SI 1965/2010).

[1483] The Copyright (Grenada) Order 1965 (SI 1965/2158).

[1484] The Copyright (British Guiana) Order 1966 (SI 1966/79).

[1485] The Copyright (British Honduras) Order 1966 (SI 1966/685).

[1486] The Copyright (St Vincent) Order 1967 (SI 1967/974).

[1487] The Copyright (Hong Kong) Order 1972 (SI 1972/1724), as amended by the Copyright (Hong Kong) (Amendment) Order 1979 (SI 1979/910) and the Copyright (Hong Kong) (Amendment) Order 1990 (SI 1990/588).

[1488] The Copyright (British Indian Ocean Territory) Order 1984 (SI 1984/541).

[1489] c.41.

[1490] Copyright (Computer Software) Amendment Act 1985 s.4(2).

provisions of the 1985 Act were accordingly extended to the Isle of Man[1491] and to a number of other countries.[1492]

Effect where the 1956 Act was so extended. Copyright was defined, in s.1(1) of the 1956 Act, as the exclusive right to do and authorise others to do certain acts in the United Kingdom or in any other country to which the provisions of that Act extended, and, to the extent that the 1956 Act and Orders in Council thereunder had been so extended, common conditions for obtaining copyright protection existed throughout the area to which that Act and Orders in Council were so extended. Thus, the definition of "qualified person", in s.1(5) of the 1956 Act, included a person domiciled or resident in the United Kingdom or in another country to which any provision of that Act extended, and a body incorporated under the laws of any such country. Further, "first publication", in ss.2(2) and 3(3) of that Act, included first publication in the United Kingdom or in another country to which the section extended. Similar provisions occurred in ss.12(2), 13(2) and 15(1) of the 1956 Act and also as to infringement, in ss.1(2), 5 and 16. Further, by s.36(2)(b) of the 1956 Act, an assignment of copyright could be limited so as to apply to any one or more, but not all, of the countries in relation to which the owner of the copyright had by virtue of that Act the exclusive right to do certain acts.

3–294

The advantages of having such common conditions for obtaining and enforcing copyright throughout that area were, however, diminished by reason of some countries in that area becoming independent and in some cases enacting their own copyright legislation.[1493] A further consequence of independence was that many such countries became countries to which the provisions of the 1956 Act were applied,[1494] rather than extended.

Power of such other countries to modify the 1956 Act. While the legislature of any country to which any provisions of the 1956 Act had been extended, as aforesaid, could have modified or added to those provisions in their operation as part of the law of that country, no such modifications or additions, except in so far as they related to procedure and remedies, were to be made so as to apply to any work or other subject-matter unless the qualification of authorship or publication arose with reference to that other country.[1495] In fact numerous modifications of a minor character were embodied in the Orders in Council.

3–295

Proceedings in the United Kingdom. It was further provided[1496] that, for the purposes of any proceedings under the 1956 Act in the United Kingdom, where the proceedings related to an act done in a country to which any provisions of that Act extended subject to exceptions, modifications or additions, the procedure and remedies were to be in accordance with that Act in its operation as part of the law of the United Kingdom; but, if the act did not constitute an infringement of copyright in its operation as part of the law of the country where the act was done, it was not to be treated as constituting an infringement of copyright under that Act in its operation as part of the law of the United Kingdom. Presumably the usual conditions would have applied in respect of service out of the jurisdiction but, subject to this, it appears that a defendant could have been sued in the United Kingdom in respect an infringement in a colony, provided that the act

3–296

[1491] The Copyright (Isle of Man) Order 1986 (SI 1986/1299).
[1492] The Copyright (Computer Software) (Extension to Territories) Order 1987 (SI 1987/2200).
[1493] See para.3–300.
[1494] See the Copyright (International Conventions) Order 1979 (SI 1979/1715), as amended.
[1495] Copyright Act 1956 s.31(3); and see *Rediffusion (Hong Kong) Ltd v Att-Gen of Hong Kong* [1970] A.C. 1136.
[1496] Copyright Act 1956 s.31(4).

of infringement would have been an infringement by the law of the colony if the proceedings had been brought there, but the procedure and remedies would have been those of the United Kingdom.

3–297 **Position as to colonial territories and self-governing dominions distinguished.** So far as the colonial territories were concerned, the making of the necessary Orders in Council created a similar situation to that existing under the 1911 Act. But, so far as concerned the self-governing dominions, these were outside the operation of the 1956 Act, and works originating in their territory were only protected in the United Kingdom in the same manner as works originating in foreign countries were protected, that is to say, by Order in Council under s.32 of the 1956 Act, applying the provisions of the 1956 Act to works originating in such countries.[1497]

3–298 **Position in period before Orders in Council made.** To provide for the interim period after the commencement of the 1956 Act, and before Orders were made extending or applying that Act to colonial and self-governing territories, provision was made in paragraph 39 of Schedule 7 to that Act. The effect of this paragraph appeared to be that, until any such Order was made, for the purposes of construing any reference in any provision of that Act to countries to which that provision extended, such provision was treated as extending to the territory in question whether it was a self-governing territory or not. The Copyright (International Conventions) Order 1957, which came into operation on September 27, 1957,[1498] applied the 1956 Act in respect of works originating in the self-governing dominions, that position being continued by the Copyright (International Conventions) Order 1964,[1499] then by the Copyright (International Conventions) Order 1972,[1500] and then by the Copyright (International Conventions) Order 1979.[1501] Works originating in other Commonwealth territories would have remained protected by virtue of para.39 until the making of Orders in Council extending the 1956 Act to them.

3–299 **The Republic of Ireland.** The Republic of Ireland was treated as a self-governing dominion to which the 1911 Act did not extend, and copyright protection was afforded to works originating in that country by an Order in Council made under s.26(3) of the 1911 Act. After the commencement of the 1956 Act, therefore, para.40(4) of Sch.7 to that Act[1502] applied in relation to the Irish Republic, and it was accordingly treated as a foreign country in respect of which an Order in Council under s.29 of the 1911 Act had been made. But the Republic of Ireland was one of the countries in respect of which protection was given by virtue of the Copyright (International Conventions) Order 1957,[1503] then by the Copyright (International Conventions) Order 1964,[1504] then by the Copyright (International Conventions) Order 1972,[1505] and then by the Copyright (International Conventions) Order 1979.[1506] The 1956 Act itself, in defining "qualified person", included an individual who was a citizen of the Republic of Ireland, but not a body corporate incorporated under the laws of the Republic, and the Republic of

---

[1497] See paras 3–253 et seq.
[1498] SI 1957/1523.
[1499] SI 1964/690.
[1500] SI 1972/673.
[1501] SI 1979/1715.
[1502] Repealed by Statute Law (Repeals) Act 1986 (c.12), but see s.2 thereof.
[1503] SI 1957/1523.
[1504] SI 1964/690.
[1505] SI 1972/673.
[1506] SI 1979/1715.

Ireland was not a country to which that Act extended for the purpose of the provisions regarding first publication.

International arrangements with dominions. As the 1956 Act could not have been extended to the self-governing dominions, international protection there depended upon the 1911 Act, and Orders in Council made under that Act, so long as that Act was in force there. In so far as the self-governing dominions passed new Copyright Acts of their own, the nature of international protection there falls to be determined according to the provisions of those Acts.[1507]   3–300

D. INTERNATIONAL ORGANISATIONS

Position under the 1956 Act. Section 33 of the 1956 Act provided for the conferring of copyright by Order in Council upon original literary, dramatic, musical or artistic works made by or under the direction or control of an international organisation, whether or not such organisation had the legal capacity of a body corporate.[1508] The section also applied where such a work was first published by or under the direction or control of such an organisation. The section also dealt with duration and ownership of such copyright.   3–301

Position under the 1988 Act. Section 168 of the 1988 Act[1509] contains provisions for conferring copyright on original literary, dramatic, musical and artistic works made by officers or employees of, or published by an international organisation and which do not qualify for copyright protection under ss.154 or 155 of the 1988 Act.[1510] In such circumstances the organisation is to be the first owner of such copyright.[1511] Such copyright subsists until the end of the period of 50 years from the end of the calendar year in which the work was made or such longer period as may be specified by Order in Council for the purpose of complying with the international obligations of the United Kingdom.[1512] Any work in which copyright subsisted by virtue of s.33 of the 1956 Act immediately before commencement of the copyright provisions of the 1988 Act is to be deemed to satisfy the requirements of s.168(1) of the 1988 Act, but otherwise s.168 does not apply to works made or, as the case may be, published before such commencement. Copyright in any such work which is unpublished continues to subsist until the date on which it would have expired in accordance with the 1956 Act, or the end of the period of 50 years from the end of the calendar year in which the copyright provisions of the 1988 Act come into force, whichever is the earlier.[1513]   3–302

An international organisation means an organisation the members of which include one or more states,[1514] and the international organisations to which s.168 of the 1988 Act applies are those to which Her Majesty has by Order in Council declared that it is expedient that such section should apply.[1515] Such an organisation is to be deemed to have, and to have had at all material times, the legal capacities of a body corporate for the purpose of holding, dealing with and enforcing copyright and in connection with all legal proceedings relating to

---

[1507] See also the Copyright (Status of Former Dependent Territories) Order 1990 (SI 1990/1512).

[1508] This did not apply to works made or published before the commencement of the 1956 Act (Sch.7, para.27). See Copyright (International Organisations) Order 1957 (SI 1957/1524), *Copinger* 12th edn, p.2116.

[1509] The corresponding provision of the Copyright Act 1956 was s.33.

[1510] See CDPA 1988 s.153(2) and (3).

[1511] s.168(1), and see s.11(3).

[1512] s.168(3), and see s.12(5).

[1513] Sch.1 para.44.

[1514] s.178.

[1515] s.168(2). See Vol.2 C1 and CDPA 1988 s.302 as to the giving of financial assistance to international organisations.

copyright.[1516] A statutory instrument containing an Order in Council under s.168 of the 1988 Act is subject to annulment in pursuance of a resolution of either House of Parliament.[1517] By the Copyright (International Organisations) Order 1989,[1518] s.168 was applied to the United Nations, the Specialised Agencies of the United Nations and the Organisation of American States;

The 1988 Act also contains provisions relating to moral rights in works in which copyright originally vested in an international organisation.[1519]

E. ANONYMOUS UNPUBLISHED WORKS: FOLKLORE

3–303   **The 1988 Act.** Section 169 of the 1988 Act contains provisions (which were new in the 1988 Act) conferring copyright, in certain circumstances, on unpublished literary, dramatic, musical or artistic works of unknown authorship[1520] where there is evidence that the author (or, in the case of a joint work, any of the authors) was a qualifying individual by connection with a country outside the United Kingdom. A qualifying individual is a person who at the material time (within the meaning of s.154 of the 1988 Act)[1521] was a person whose works qualified under that section for copyright protection.[1522] Section 169(2) of the 1988 Act further provides that if under the law of that country a body is appointed to protect and enforce copyright in such works, Her Majesty may by Order in Council designate that body for the purposes of that section. No such Order has yet been made. Such a designated body is to be recognised in the United Kingdom as having authority to do in place of the copyright owner anything, other than assign copyright, which it is empowered to do under the law of that country, in particular bringing proceedings in its own name.[1523] Section 169 of the 1988 Act does not apply if there has been an assignment of copyright in the work by the author of which notice has been given to the designated body, and nothing in that section is to affect the validity of an assignment of copyright made, or licence granted, by the author or a person lawfully claiming under him.[1524] A statutory instrument containing an Order in Council under s.169 of the 1988 Act is subject to annulment in pursuance of a resolution of either House of Parliament.[1525]

7. WORKS DENIED PROTECTION

3–304   **Copyright is a creature of statute.** The 1988 Act accords copyright to the works described in s.1(1) which meet the requirements for subsistence of copyright set out in s.153 and c.IX of the Act, discussed above. Nowhere in the 1988 Act[1526] is the existence of that right qualified by considerations such as public policy, which do not, therefore, affect the question of the subsistence of copyright in a work. Thus, copyright will subsist in a work which otherwise satisfies the requirements of the Act, even though the work may be considered by some to be libellous, im-

---

[1516] s.168(4). See, as to presumptions, CDPA 1988 ss.104(2)(b) and (3) and 107(6). See, as to exceptions from infringement, s.57(2)(b).
[1517] s.168(5).
[1518] SI 1989/989.
[1519] ss.79(7)(b) and 82(1)(c) and (2): "sufficient disclaimer" s.178.
[1520] As to "unknown authorship", see CDPA 1988, s.9(4) and (5). "Folklore" is not referred to in s.169, only in the side note thereto.
[1521] See paras 3–161 et seq., above.
[1522] CDPA 1988, s.169(5).
[1523] s.169(3).
[1524] s.169(6).
[1525] s.169(4).
[1526] The position has been the same in successive copyright enactments.

moral, obscene, scandalous, irreligious, to involve deception of the public or where its exploitation would otherwise be contrary to public policy.[1527]

Although copyright will subsist in such works, the court retains a jurisdiction to refuse to enforce some or all of the rights of a copyright owner, on the grounds of public interest or otherwise.[1528] It had previously been held that the courts had only a limited, residual jurisdiction to decline to allow its process to be used in cases relating to the nature of the work, and that otherwise the permitted act provisions of the Act[1529] provided a complete code striking the balance between the interests of the public and the copyright owner.[1530] This residual jurisdiction was said to apply in cases where the work was: (i) immoral, scandalous or contrary to family life; (ii) injurious to public life, public health and safety or the administration of justice; or (iii) liable to incite or encourage others to act in a way referred to in (ii).[1531] While the court has refused to enforce copyright claims in a variety of such cases, it is now established that the limits of the defence of public interest in particular are not circumscribed or confined to these categories and the circumstances in which public interest can override rights of copyright are not capable of precise categorisation or definition.[1532] Indeed, a further category of public interest has now been identified, namely, cases where the rights of the copyright owner must give way to the right to freedom of expression under art.10 of the European Convention on Human Rights.[1533] While these are all matters which in principle go to a defence to a copyright claim rather than issues of subsistence of copyright, they are for convenience dealt with here.

Historically, this jurisdiction has been founded on the rule that it is against public policy to enforce the exclusive rights of copyright where the exploitation of such rights would itself be against the public interest.[1534] Before the fusion of the courts of equity and law, the decisions took the form of a refusal by a court of equity to grant an injunction, leaving the copyright owner to pursue such remedy as he might have at law,[1535] although sometimes all forms of relief were denied.[1536] Today, no doubt, the nature of the exercise of the jurisdiction will vary according to the circumstances. Sometimes it will be sufficient to deny a claimant an injunction, leaving him to such remedy as he may have in damages; sometimes public

---

[1527] Note, however, that in *Glyn v Weston Feature Film Co Ltd* [1916] 1 Ch. 261 at 269, Younger J. stated said that copyright could not subsist in a work of a grossly immoral tendency, but it is suggested that the better view is that copyright subsists but will not necessarily be enforced.

[1528] *Ashdown v Telegraph Group Ltd* [2001] EWCA (Civ) 1142; [2002] Ch. 149; [2002] R.P.C. 5, which establishes that a defence of public interest is generally available to copyright claims. See further in the text. The jurisdiction to deny relief is preserved by CDPA 1988 s.171(3): "Nothing in this Part affects any rule of law preventing or restricting the enforcement of copyright, on grounds of public interest or otherwise". The equivalent provision under the 1956 Act (s.46(4)) was rather more limited, referring only to any rule of equity relating to breaches of trust or confidence. For an illuminating discussion of the law in England and Wales, Australia and the United States, see Sims: "The Denial of Copyright on Public Policy Grounds" [2008] E.I.P.R. 189.

[1529] See Ch.9.

[1530] *Hyde Park Residence Ltd v Yelland* [2001] Ch. 143; [2000] R.P.C. 604, Mance L.J. dissenting. The jurisdiction was said to relate to the nature of the work itself and not the particular use intended to be made of it, since copyright is assignable: see per Aldous L.J., at para.66.

[1531] See *Hyde Park Residence Ltd v Yelland* [2001] Ch. 143, per Aldous L.J. at para.66. It had already been established that the defence was not confined to cases in which the claimant had been guilty of some inquity or wrongdoing. See *Lion Laboratories Laboratories v Evans* [1985] Q.B. 526 at 537, 538, 550. In previous editions of this work, the jurisdiction was described as consisting of cases where the court had considered the work to be libellous, immoral, obscene, scandalous or irreligious, or to involve deception of the public.

[1532] *Ashdown v Telegraph Group Ltd* [2001] EWCA (Civ) 1142.

[1533] *Ashdown v Telegraph Group Ltd* [2001] EWCA (Civ) 1142.

[1534] See, e.g. *Stockdale v Onwhyn* (1826) 5 B. & C. 173.

[1535] See, e.g. *Walcot v Walker* (1802) 7 Ves. 1; *Lawrence v Smith* (1822) Jac. 471.

[1536] See, e.g. *Stockdale v Onwhyn* (1826) 5 B. & C. 173; *Glyn v Weston Feature Film Co Ltd* [1916] 1 Ch. 261.

policy will require that any pecuniary remedy be denied as well. Further, there is no reason in principle why, in relation to the same work, relief should not be refused in some circumstances but granted in others. So, for example, if a claimant is seeking to restrain dissemination of a grossly immoral or pornographic work in order to preserve the market for himself, an injunction might no doubt be refused, but if the work was always intended to be kept private or the claimant has come to regret having made it in the first place, there seems no good reason in principle why an injunction should not be granted,[1537] and indeed it would be in the public interest to do so. Again, while an injunction to restrain dissemination of a confidential document may be refused where there is an overriding right to freedom of expression, which requires that the contents of the document be made public, once the contents have received sufficient publicity and the public interest requirement has been satisfied, there is no reason in principle to deny relief in respect of others who seek to make a profit out of further exploitaion of the work.

3–305 **Works immoral, scandalous or contrary to family life.** There have been various cases where the courts have refused to grant relief on these grounds. For example, works have been denied protection on the grounds of gross immorality or indecency,[1538] or their libellous[1539] or irreligious[1540] content. In one curious case, relief was granted in respect of leaflet purporting to be the imaginary will of Adolf Hitler.[1541] Such readiness on the part of the judges in the past to apply their own views in deciding what works should be refused protection gave rise to criticism.[1542] In the present day, in which the public perception of such matters is different, the courts can be expected to reflect this difference and to take an attitude which is far less protective of the public. Attitudes to what amounts to unacceptable irreligious material have changed,[1543] and at least in relation to sexual conduct protection is only likely to be refused to a work considered as having a grossly immoral tendency by present-day standards.[1544]

3–306 **Works injurious to public life, public heath and safety, or the administration of justice.** Examples of cases in this category are those where the work involves

---

[1537] *Southey v Sherwood* (1817) 2 Mer. 435, 438.

[1538] *Stockdale v Onwhyn* (1826) 5 B. & C. 173 (a book of memoirs of Harriette Wilson, a courtesan); *Glyn v Weston Feature Film Co Ltd* [1916] 1 Ch. 261 (work of "grossly immoral tendency"); *Goeie Hoop Vitgewers (Ecendoms) B.P.K. v Central News Agency* (1953) (2) S.A. 843 (morbid presentation of sordid details of practice and acts of prostitution, likely to corrupt the young and inexperienced). But cf. *Pastickniak v Dojacek* [1923–28] Mac.C.C. 423 (book's contents merely "coarse and nasty", rather than suggesting lust, sexual passion or gross indecency).

[1539] *Walcot v Walker* (1802) 7 Ves. 1 (criminally libellous publication); *Southey v Sherwood* (1817) 2 Mer. 435; *Stocksdale v Onwhyn* (1826) 5 B. & C. 173 (where the book also contained passages that were slanderous); *Hime v Dale* (1809) 2 Camp. 27n (no protection if work contained so gross a libel as to affect public morals).

[1540] *Lawrence v Smith* (1822) Jac. 471; *Murray v Benbow* (1822) Jac. 474n. (injunction refused in respect of Lord Byron's poem "Cain").

[1541] *A. Bloom & Sons Ltd v Black* [1936–1945] Mac.C.C. 274 (the leaflet was described as coarse and nasty, and deprived of merit of any sort).

[1542] Story J., in referring to Lord Eldon's decisions in cases cited on this point, said (2 Story's Eq. Jur. at 938): "If a court of equity, under colour of its general authority, is to enter upon all the moral, theological, metaphysical, and political inquiries, and if it is to decide dogmatically upon the character and bearing of such discussions, and the rights of authors growing out of them, it is obvious that absolute power is conferred over the subject of literary property, which may sap the very foundations on which it rests, and retard, if not entirely suppress, the means of arriving at physical as well as at metaphysical truth".

[1543] See *R. v Lemon* [1979] A.C. 617, involving an alleged blasphemous libel concerning the Christian religion published in the magazine *Gay News*.

[1544] This was the view adopted by Browne-Wilkinson V.-C. in *Stephens v Avery* [1988] Ch. 449 (a confidential information case), noting the difficulty caused by the fact that there no longer exists an accepted code of sexual morals. In *Mak Hau-Shing v Oriental Press Group Ltd* [1996] 1 H.K.L.R. 245, the court said that it would refuse to enforce copyright in photographs if they were indecent, obscene or otherwise of a grossly immoral tendency, or perhaps where, if they were merely mildly pornographic, the subject of the photographs had been subjected to coercion.

a deception of the public. Thus, a claim failed where the copyright work was falsely held out to be a translation from the German of an author who had a high reputation for works of that kind, and the object had been to deceive purchasers and to give the work a value which it would not otherwise have had.[1545] The same principle was applied where the claimant published an illustrated catalogue of trucks, trolleys and barrows made by him which contained pages headed "Inventor, patentee, and sole maker" and "Slingsby's Patents", despite the claimant having no English patent for the various articles represented.[1546] The catalogue also contained pictures of buildings on which the claimant's name was written in large letters, although the claimant did not occupy the whole of them. The defendant had copied the claimant's catalogue, but the claimant was refused an injunction on the grounds that the catalogue was calculated to deceive the public (as to the claimant having patents and as to its building), and that the claimant was attempting to obtain trade regardless of the manner in which it was obtained. No doubt relief would be refused in respect of a work intended to be used to further some illegal purpose, such as unlawful betting[1547] or an unlawful restraint of trade,[1548] or for a work written in breach of confidence.[1549]

Works infringing other works. Today it is clear that copyright can subsist in a work which itself infringes copyright in an earlier work,[1550] and the issue is whether the court will enforce such copyright. As to this, a work which itself is an infringement of an earlier work, but which otherwise satisfies the requirements for copyright to subsist in the work,[1551] will normally be entitled to protection, subject to the right of the owner of the earlier copyright work to receive a share of any sum recovered.[1552] The position might possibly be different if some moral obloquy was involved in the creation of the later work.[1553]   **3–307**

Copyright and freedom of expression. Where the right to freedom of expression under art.10 of the European Convention on Human Rights comes into potential conflict with the rights of a copyright owner, the permitted act provi-   **3–308**

[1545] *Wright v Tallis* (1845) 1 C.B. 893.

[1546] *Slingsby v Bradford Patent Truck, etc. Co* [1905] W.N. 122; [1906] W.N. 51, approved in *Att.-Gen. v Guardian Newspapers Ltd (No.2)* [1990] 1 A.C. 109, at 294 per Lord Jauncey; [1989] 2 F.S.R. 181. In *Hayward Bros v Lely & Co* (1887) 56 L.T. 418, the claimant's catalogue included one item which was described as patented, which indeed it had been, but the patent expired a short time after publication. An injunction was refused as to those parts where a mistatement was made.

[1547] This seems to have been accepted in *Barnard v White & Co* [1923–1928] Mac.C.C. 218, although there the particular activity involved, namely credit betting on football matches, was not unlawful and so relief was granted.

[1548] Again, this seems to have been accepted in *British Oxygen Co Ltd v Liquid Air Ltd* [1925] Ch. 383, although there it was held that the copyright work being relied on, a business letter, had been written as a legitimate act in furtherance of trade.

[1549] See *Att-Gen v Guardian Newspapers Ltd (No.2)* [1990] 1 A.C. 109, HL at 262, 275–276, 294, although Lord Griffiths, at 276, considered that the copyright would in those circumstances have belonged to the person to whom the confidence was owed (in that case, the Crown), so that presumably there would have been no objection to the Crown relying on copyright to prevent dissemination of the work. Lord Jauncey, at 294, considered that no one could have been prevented from copying the work.

[1550] *Redwood Music Ltd v Chappell & Co Ltd* [1982] R.P.C. 109 at 120 (Goff J.), applying *Wood v Boosey* (1866) L.R. 2 Q.B. 340; (1867) L.R. 3 Q.B. 223 at 229 (arrangement of a score of an opera held to be subject of copyright, notwithstanding that its publication without the authority of the composer of the original opera would be an infringement). See also *Vitof Ltd v Altoft* [2006] EWHC 1678 (Ch) at para.147.

[1551] As to whether such a work qualifies as original, see para.3–141, above. In some of the older cases, relief was refused on the ground that the work was infringing: see e.g. *Cary v Faden* (1799) 5 Ves. 23. *Sailendra Nath De v Chayanika Chire Mandir* (1950) 55 Cal.W.N. 713; *Gouindan. v Gopalakrishna Kone* [1955] Mad.W.N. 369.

[1552] *ZYX Music GmbH v King* [1995] F.S.R. 566; [1995] 3 All E.R. 1 at 9h to 11b, per Lightman J.

[1553] *ZYX Music GmbH v King* [1995] 3 All E.R. 1 at 10g. See also *Cary v Faden* (1799) 5 Ves. 23.

sions of the 1988 Act, in particular the fair dealing provisions, will usually provide a defence. There may, however, be exceptional and rare cases where this is not the case, even construing the 1988 Act as generously as possible to accommodate the right. In such circumstances, and where the art.10 right is paramount in the public interest, a court would be bound to deny the copyright owner any relief the effect of which would be to prevent that freedom of expression.[1554] Usually, this will involve the denial of an injunction, although not a claim to damages or an account of profits.[1555] The topic is considered in more detail elsewhere.[1556]

[1554] *Ashdown v Telegraph Group Ltd* [2001] EWCA (Civ) 1142; [2002] Ch. 149; [2002] R.P.C. 5.
[1555] *Ashdown v Telegraph Group Ltd* [2001] EWCA (Civ) 1142. An earlier case where this occurred was *Lion Laboratories v Evans* [1985] Q.B. 526, where an injunction restraining publication of confidential memoranda which cast doubt on the accuracy of the breathalysers, and thus the safety of convictions, was refused on the grounds of public interest. A fair dealing defence was not, however, argued and today it seems likely that such a defence would succeed, obviating the need for reliance on a separate public interest defence.
[1556] See para.22–82, below.

AUTHORSHIP OF COPYRIGHT WORKS

1. INTRODUCTION

This chapter is concerned with who is to be regarded as the "author" of the various categories of copyright works. Establishing the identity of the author of a copyright work is important for a number of reasons: **4–01**

(a) Whether a work qualifies for protection at all may depend on the status of the author.[1]

(b) It is usually necessary to know who the author of the work was in order to determine who was the first owner of the copyright.[2]

(c) For many works, the term of copyright is calculated by reference to the date of death of the author.[3]

(d) In the case of many copyright works, the author has important moral rights and a right to remuneration from rental of certain copies of his works.[4]

It is particularly important to keep in mind the distinction between the author of a work and the owner of the copyright in it. Thus, for example, the author of a work created by an employee is the employee but the first owner of the copyright in the work will generally be the employer.[5] Again, confusion can arise unless it is remembered that the term of copyright is not dependent on the identity of the owner of the copyright but in general only on the identity of the author. So too,

---

[1] See Ch.3, above.

[2] See Ch.5, below. But note that the author will not necessarily be the first owner of the copyright.

[3] See Ch.6, below.

[4] As to moral rights, see Ch.11, below. As to the unwaivable right to remuneration, see paras 5–107 and 7–101, below.

[5] As to works of employees, see paras 5–11 et seq., below.

although copyright may be transferred by assignment or operation of law, the moral rights of the author and his right to remuneration from rental of copies cannot be transferred in this way. They remain with the author until his death.[6] Likewise, the artist's resale right is not assignable and may not be waived.[7]

4–02 **Authorship a matter of status.** Authorship is a question of status and fact, not agreement. An agreement between parties as to who the author is, or should be, cannot therefore confer the status of authorship on someone who was not in law the author.[8]

4–03 **Conflict with civil law systems of copyright.** For many years there has existed a conflict between common law and civil law systems of copyright law in the approach to the status of an author and indeed what works qualify for copyright protection.[9] Although this conflict has not in the past been of great practical significance to practitioners in the United Kingdom, it has become increasingly important, particularly with the steps which have been taken to harmonise the copyright laws of the Member States of the European Union.[10] The conflict has its origins in the different approach to the rationale of copyright protection. In the civil law, or *droit d'auteur*, systems, a work must be a work of personal, intellectual creation to be worthy of "author's right" protection. The works protected by author's right are therefore original literary, dramatic, musical and artistic works.[11] As such, they are regarded as part of the personality of the author. An author has both economic rights, enabling him to benefit from the exploitation of his work but also, and no less significant, moral rights, enabling him to decide whether his work should be published at all and, if it is published, to control the form of publication, to prevent his work from being distorted or mutilated ("the right of integrity"), and the right to be identified as its creator ("the paternity right"). In relation to his economic rights, the civil law systems recognise that authors may have a weak bargaining position and so tend to place obstacles in the way of out-and-out alienation of the author's right. These may take the form of restrictions or presumptions against alienation[12] or the conferring on an author of the right to receive remuneration from the exploitation of his work, a right which cannot be alienated. A further economic right of authors, which was formerly alien to the common law system, is the artist's resale right, known as the "*droit de suite*", which gives authors of certain works a right to a continuing interest on successive sales of their work. One consequence of the attitude that author's right

---

[6] CDPA 1988 ss.93B, 94. As to the transfer of moral rights on death, see CDPA 1988 s.95. As to moral rights generally, see Ch.11, below. As to the transfer of the unwaivable right to remuneration on death, see s.93B(2) and, generally, para.7–101, below.

[7] The Artist's Resale Right Regulations 2006 (SI 2006/346) regs 7(1) and 8(1). As to the transfer of the resale right on death, see reg.9. As to the artist's resale right generally, see Ch.20, below.

[8] An agreement between two people as to who is to be regarded as the author may nevertheless create an estoppel as between them, as was argued in *Beggars Banquet Records Ltd v Carlton Television Ltd* [1993] E.M.L.R. 349.

[9] Inevitably, the distinction between common law and civil law systems is not cut and dried. At the extremes are, on the one hand, the laws of France (the ideological leaders), Italy, Spain, Portugal and the countries of Latin America and, on the other, those of the United Kingdom, together with countries which have been part of the British Commonwealth, and the United States. Countries such as Germany, Austria, Switzerland, the Nordic countries and Japan, while owing their ideology to other civil law systems, have developed certain aspects of it in different ways. See Stewart, *International Copyright and Neighbouring Rights*, 2nd edn, paras 1.13 et seq, and also Burkitt,. "Copyright Culture—The History and Cultural Specificity of the Western Model of Copyright" [2001] I.P.Q. 146.

[10] For a survey of the position, see para.24–05 et seq., below.

[11] Films form a hybrid category. See para.4–47, below.

[12] The German and Austrian laws do not allow assignment of the author's right. French law provides that the author's right in the work of an employee belongs to him unless expressly assigned to the employer. As to the contrasting position under UK law, see paras 5–11 et seq., below.

is a personal right which springs from an individual's creativity is that copyright works cannot be created by a corporation, so that record producers, film producers and broadcasters are not entitled to any author's right in the sound recordings, films or broadcasts that they produce. To the extent that such things are protected, they are generally protected by way of related (or neighbouring[13]) rights.[14]

The common law system, on the other hand, has taken a more commercial and pragmatic view towards copyright, the rationale being to reward those who spend time, skill and effort in creating intangible property of the kind which can be exploited by being reproduced, performed, broadcast, etc. This is done by conferring copyright on their works and thus the exclusive right to control their exploitation. Further, in the purest form of the system, market forces are given a free hand in relation to matters of ownership and transferability of the copyright. Although, therefore, the actual intellectual creator of literary, dramatic, musical and artistic works is accorded the status of author, he may well have no "economic" rights. An example would be where the work was created by him in the course of his employment. Until the 1988 Act, he had few moral rights either[15] and it was only with the passing of that Act that the United Kingdom belatedly introduced a code of such rights, albeit subject to many limitations.[16] Again, the artist's resale right was only introduced into the law of the United Kingdom to bring it into conformity with an EU Directive on the subject.[17] Further, "works" such as sound recordings, films and broadcasts are protected as copyright works, the right generally being conferred in the first instance on those who have assumed the financial risk of their creation. The framers of the 1988 Act had no ideological difficulty in describing such persons as "authors".[18]

The conflicts between the two systems have clearly emerged in the framing of the EC Directives dealing with the term of copyright[19] and the rental right.[20] Thus, the United Kingdom has been obliged to accede to directors of films the status of author[21] and to authors an unwaivable right to remuneration in respect of the rental of certain copies of their works.[22] Other tensions are emerging, for example in relation to the question of the originality required as a condition for subsistence of copyright in a work. Whereas common law systems tend to confer copyright protection on any work on which substantial skill or labour has been expended,[23] civil law systems often impose a higher test.[24] This divergence has,

---

[13] "Related" is the UC terminology.

[14] Together with the rights of performers. A film is a hybrid category, sometimes being protected by author's right, being regarded as the product of the intellectual creation of the director, screenplay writer, film crew, leading actors, composer of the music, etc. sometimes by way of a related or neighbouring right, and sometimes both. See Stewart, *International Copyright and Neighbouring Rights*, 2nd edn.

[15] As to the limited range of these which existed before the 1988 Act, see Ch.11, below.

[16] See generally, Ch.11, below.

[17] Directive 2001/84/EC on the Resale Right for the Benefit of the Author of an Original Work of Art, of October 13, 2001.

[18] CDPA 1988, s.9(1). In reality, however, the expression is used as a shorthand and not in the ordinary meaning of that word. The 1956 Act used the expression "maker" in relation to such works. See paras 4–43 *et seq.*, below.

[19] Directive 93/98.

[20] Directive 92/100.

[21] See para.4–48, below.

[22] See paras 5–114 and 7–101, below.

[23] Although note the rejection in the United States of a "sweat-of-the-brow" test for copyright in compilations: *Feist Publications Inc. v Rival Telephone Service Co.* 499 U.S. Ct 340.

[24] The case of photographs is a particular example. See Stewart, *International Copyright and Neighbouring Rights* (2nd ed.).

for example, seen the creation of a two-tier Community scheme of protection for databases.[25]

4–04 **More than one author.** Where more than one person has been involved in the process of creation, a number of different regimes may apply:

(a) What they produce may consist of a number of distinct parts or works, as for example with an encyclopaedia, of which each part has a separate author.[26]

(b) Successive persons may have worked separately to produce successive versions of a work, each building on the efforts of his predecessor: each version is a separate work and each version has a separate author.[27]

(c) The efforts of the various persons in producing a work may have been collaborative and not distinct, in which case authorship of the work will be joint.[28]

(d) The contributions of some of the individuals may be of such a slight nature that they are not in law "authors" at all.[29]

4–05 **Transitional provisions.** The law relating to authorship of copyright works has changed from time to time. Save in relation to moral rights, the 1988 Act is framed so as to avoid any retrospective change in the identity of the author of a work caused by an alteration of the law. This is achieved by a transitional provision in the 1988 Act[30] to the effect that the law which was in force when a work was made must be applied to determine who was the author of the work. The effect is shown by the following table.

Date when work made	Act to be applied
On or after August 1, 1989	The 1988 Act
On or after June 1, 1957 but before August 1, 1989	The 1956 Act
On or after July 1, 1912, but before June 1, 1957	The 1911 Act
Before July 1, 1912	The Acts then in force.[31]

For this purpose, where the making of a work extended over a period, the work is to be taken as having been made when its making was completed.[32] The position is different in relation to moral rights, where the identity of the author of a work made before August 1, 1989 must be determined in accordance with the provisions of the 1988 Act alone.[33]

4–06 **Works of unknown authorship.** The identity of an author is to be regarded as unknown if it is not possible for a person to ascertain his identity by reasonable enquiry; but if his identity is once known it is not subsequently be regarded as unknown.[34] Such works are often referred to as "orphan works". Problems can arise, for example, in a situation where someone else wishes to use the work, and

---

[25] See para.3–21 and Ch.18, below.

[26] But note that there will usually also be a separate copyright work consisting of the encyclopaedia as a whole, considered as a compilation, with its own author or authors. See para.4–37, below.

[27] See para.4–35 et seq., below, and, for example, *Robin Ray v Classic FM Plc* [1998] F.S.R. 622, 638; *Brighton v Jones* [2004] EWHC 1157 (Ch); [2005] F.S.R. 16.

[28] As to works of joint authorship, see paras 4–32 et seq., below.

[29] See para.4–35, below.

[30] CDPA 1988 Sch.1, para.10.

[31] See para.4–31, below.

[32] CDPA 1988 Sch.1 para.1(3).

[33] Sch.1 para.10.

[34] CDPA 1988 s.9(5).

in relation to the calculation of the term of copyright, if it is not possible to establish who the author was. Special provision is made for such cases.[35]

Presumptions. Various statutory presumptions can be relied on, in legal proceedings, to discharge the burden of proving who was the author of a work. These are considered elsewhere.[36]   **4–07**

2. LITERARY, DRAMATIC, MUSICAL AND ARTISTIC WORKS

The 1988 Act defines "author" generally as meaning the person who creates the   **4–08** work.[37] In the case of literary, dramatic, musical and artistic works, no further definition of this expression is given.[38] With limited exceptions,[39] the 1956, 1911 and earlier Acts contained no definition of "author" at all but in the light of the interpretation given to the expression "author" under these earlier Acts, there has not been any change in the law in terms of who is to be regarded as the author of a work of these types.[40] The question of authorship of these categories of work can therefore be considered without reference to the date when the work was created.

Meaning of "author". In the present context, it will not normally be hard to   **4–09** determine who is the person who created the work and therefore who was the author of it. As is discussed elsewhere,[41] copyright is concerned with the protection of the original expression in some material form of ideas, information, etc. and not the ideas, information, etc. themselves.[42] In general terms, therefore, the author of a work is the person who originates the protectable elements of the work, whether the language used, dramatic incident, musical content or design, as the case may be. Although this will usually be the person who puts down the work on the page, etc. it need not necessarily be so, as can be appreciated from the earlier example of a shorthand secretary, or an amanuensis, who clearly is not the author of the work in question.[43] The author is therefore not necessarily the person responsible for the actual fixation of the work (although he usually will be) but rather the person who is responsible for creating, selecting or gathering together the detailed concepts, data or emotions which are found in the work.[44]

With very limited exceptions,[45] the "author" of these categories of work must be   **4–10**

---

[35] See, for example, CDPA 1988 ss.12(4) (duration of copyright) and 57 (acts permitted on assumption as to expiry of copyright or death of author of anonymous or pseudonymous works). See paras 6–46 and 9–170, below, respectively.

[36] See para.22–260, below.

[37] CDPA 1988 s.9(1). The Artist's Resale Right Regulations 2006 (SI 2006/346) also defines the author, in relation to a work, as the person who creates it (reg.2).

[38] Save in relation to computer-generated works. As to these, see para.4–13, below.

[39] Relating to photographs and mechanical contrivances. See paras 4–29 and 4–33, below, respectively.

[40] "The word 'author' has never been defined, although it has always been taken to be the person who created the work." See the Whitford Committee Report (Cmnd.6732), para.539. Note also CDPA 1988 s.172, which provides for the general continuity of the law.

[41] See para.7–13, below.

[42] As to the meaning of "original" in this context, see paras 3–129 et seq., above.

[43] See para.4–16, below.

[44] *Cala Homes (South) Ltd v Alfred McAlpine Homes East Ltd* [1995] F.S.R. 818; *Ray v Classic FM* [1998] F.S.R. 622 (emphasising the need for direct responsibility for what is recorded). See the further discussion on this point later in this chapter.

[45] Relating to computer-generated works and old photographs. See paras 4–13 and 4–27, below.

a natural person.[46] The fact that one person is acting as employee of another cannot affect the question of authorship,[47] nor can the fact that one person is an agent for another unless, perhaps, he acts in accordance with his principal's precise instructions, so as to be, in effect, an extension of his principal's hand in recording his principal's work. In the same way, a designer who is head of a design team is not the author of drawings made by other members of the team.[48]

4–11   **Author of non-language content.** Although true for most cases, statements that whoever originates the language of a literary or dramatic work is the author need to be regarded with caution where the real essence, or protectable element, of the copyright work consists of or includes elements such as plot or structure. A typical example of such a case is where one person suggests details of a plot for a dramatic work and another clothes the plot with words and stage directions. This is considered in more detail below,[49] but in principle a person who suggests the plot of a dramatic work may be one of its authors provided his suggestions are sufficiently substantial, well defined and original. This will be a matter of degree. In the same way, the person responsible for originating the structure of a computer program may be one of the authors of the computer program.[50] A case where someone contributes detailed incidents of plot, characterisation, etc. but not the actual language, to a "pure" literary work, such as a novel, is less likely to arise in practice. Nevertheless, there is no reason in principle why a person who makes such a contribution should not be an author of the work, provided again that what he contributes is sufficiently defined, detailed and original.[51] In all such cases, it is necessary to identify the products of the skill and labour which made the work "original", and thus protected, and then ask who was responsible for them.

4–12   **Derivative works.** In many cases a work is derived from an existing work. Common examples are a translation of a work, the dramatisation of a novel, a photograph of a painting and an arrangement of a musical work, but a derivative version can take many forms, even a simple revision of the earlier work. Whether in such cases a new copyright work is created will depend on whether sufficient skill and labour was expended upon it[52] but, assuming that it was, the person who was responsible for that skill and labour will be the author of the new work. So where A's work is independently translated by B, B is the author of the translation.[53] A of course remains the author of his original work but he is not the co-author or joint author with B of the translation.[54] The same is true where B simply revises A's work, for example, by correcting and improving it. The final position will depend on the amount and value of the corrections and improvements. If the independent skill and labour expended by B is such as to

---

[46] See, e.g. CDPA 1988 s.12(1) and *Fax Directories (Pty) Ltd v SA Fax Listings CC* [1990] 2 S.A.L.R. 164 (Local Division of Sup. Ct of SA).

[47] *Shepherd v Conquest* 139 E.R. 1140; (1856) 17 C.B. 427, where the employer merely suggested the subject matter and had no share in the design or execution of the work which, so far as any originality belonged to it, flowed from the mind of the person employed. Employment may, however, affect the separate question of ownership: see paras 5–11 et seq., below.

[48] *Nichols Advanced Vehicle Systems Inc v Rees* [1979] R.P.C. 127, 139.

[49] See para.4–22, below.

[50] See para.4–21, below.

[51] See, e.g. *Ibcos Computers Ltd v Barclays Mercantile Highland Finance Ltd* [1994] F.S.R. 275, 302.

[52] See para.3–134, above.

[53] *Byrne v Statist Co* [1914] 1 K.B. 622.

[54] As to joint authorship, see paras 4–32 et seq., below.

create a new copyright work, then he will be author of it.[55] If not, there will be no new copyright work and A will remain the author of the original work. B will have been the author of the alterations but their nature will not have been such as to attract any protection under the law of copyright. If B's contribution was substantial in the above sense and it was the result of collaboration with A and the contributions of each were not distinct, then they will have been joint authors.[56]

Where a new copyright work is created by B from A's work, the rights of the owner of the copyright in A's work will depend upon how much of A's work remains in B's work. If B's work contains a substantial reproduction of A's work, then A's licence will be required to exploit it, as well as B's, for otherwise such exploitation will amount to an infringement of A's copyright. If B's work does not contain a substantial reproduction of A's work, then A's licence is not required.[57]

Some of the earlier cases on the point are confusing:

In *Springfield v Thame*[58] the claimant journalist (A) had sent an account of an incident he had witnessed to a newspaper. For the purposes of publication, a sub-editor (B) of the newspaper compiled an account of the facts in abbreviated form, reducing A's piece from 83 lines to 18 lines in length and such that it became in substance a different statement of the facts. The piece was copied and published by the defendant (C) in another newspaper with only slight further alterations. A's action against C failed on the ground that B was the "author" of the published version, not A. While this was clearly correct on the facts, it is suggested that this approach confuses the issue of authorship and infringement. A could not in any event have been the author of the published piece since he was not responsible for the alterations, although he was of course the author of the original account. An alternative and, it is suggested, better way of looking at the point would have been to say that the piece published by C did not infringe the copyright in A's original account.[59]

In *Samuelson v Producers Distributing Co Ltd*,[60] an actor (B) made alterations to the script for a dramatic sketch which had been written by A, the altered version then being performed on the stage with considerable success. B's work amounted to a reconstruction of the original with alterations and omissions. Although the script was different, various phrases or passages from the old script remained the same, together with the characters and staging. It was held that A was the "author" of the altered sketch. It is, however, important to see what the issue in the case was. The defendant had produced a film which had been misrepresented in advertisements to be a film of the sketch as performed. Although the question of authorship was in issue on the pleadings, it being alleged that A was the owner of the copyright in the final version (B's), the cause of action by the date of trial was passing off, it being conceded that the film did not infringe the copyright in the sketch. At issue was whether A was entitled to be recognised as the author of the sketch and thus whether he

---

[55] As in *Tree v Bowkett* (1896) 74 L.T. 77, where the claimant had made additions and alterations to an existing dramatic work, principally one entirely new scene and one altered scene. Clearly the work which he had done was substantial.

[56] As to joint authorship, see paras 4–32 et seq., below.

[57] The examples assume that A and B are the owners of the copyright in their respective works.

[58] (1903) 89 L.T. 242

[59] (1903) 89 L.T. 242, 243: what C had published was news, not the claimant's expression of it (see para.7–44, below).

[60] (1932) 48 R.P.C. 580.

had a cause of action in passing off.[61] It is suggested that the decision is not helpful on the issue of authorship of a copyright work. In fact, A had been credited as the "author" of the sketch as performed on the stage and B made no claim to own the copyright in his version. It is suggested that had infringement of copyright been in issue, the true analysis is that A was the author of the work consisting of the original script and B was the author of the work consisting of the resulting sketch.

4–13 **Computer-generated works.** Few people would have any difficulty with the concept that someone who uses word-processing software to write a document is the author of that document. The software is a tool for writing, it does not supply the necessary ingredient of "originality", i.e. the skill and labour required for the composition of the document. Software can, however, assist in the creative process to a much greater degree. Many types of software, for example, enable complex images and structures to be designed with the assistance of graphical libraries and rules. Software can perform extremely complex calculations to generate data for scientific and other uses, and from this generate complex outputs, including music, still or moving images, and other computer programs. The question then arises as to whether a work created with the aid of such software has a human author, and if so, who it is. In many cases, of course, the software will merely be a tool used by an individual to create a work.[62] When framing the 1988 Act, however, it was recognised that there may be circumstances when it may be impossible to identify a human author of such a work, the only immediate human involvement perhaps being the activation of a machine. Against this eventuality, the 1988 Act provides for a special category or works, namely those which are "computer-generated", being those works generated by a computer in circumstances such that there is no human author.[63] In relation to such works, the author is to be taken to be the person by whom the arrangements necessary for the creation of the work are undertaken.[64] This definition uses the same terminology as is used in relation to the definition of "producer" in the context of determining the author of a sound recording and a film.[65] So, where arcade video games generated composite frames, each of which was a computer-generated work, then the arrangements necessary for the creation of the works were considered to have been undertaken by the person who had devised the appearance of the various elements of the game and the rules and logic by which each frame was generated and who had written the relevant computer program. The player of the game was not, however, an author of any of the artistic works created in the successive frame images. His input was not artistic in nature and he had contributed no skill or labour of an artistic kind. Nor had he undertaken any of the arrangements necessary for the creation of the frame images. All he had done was to play the game.[66]

The differences between such works and works of which there is a human author are significant. Not only is the question of authorship and thus ownership affected but also there is a problem in understanding how a computer-generated

---

[61] As to this claim, see Ch.21, below.

[62] As in *Express Newspapers Plc v Liverpool Daily Post & Echo Plc* [1985] 1 W.L.R. 1089; [1985] F.S.R. 306, a case decided under the 1956 Act, where it was held that the computer and computer programs used to produce a work were simply tools of the person controlling them, just as with a conventional pen.

[63] CDPA 1988, s.178.

[64] s.9(3).

[65] See paras 4–42 and 4–49, below.

[66] See *Nova Productions Ltd v Mazooma Games Ltd* [2006] EWHC 24 (Ch), para.106 (affirmed on appeal [2007] EWCA Civ 219; [2007] E.C.D.R. 6).

work could satisfy the requirement of originality under the Act.[67] In addition, the term of protection for such works is only 50 years from the end of the calendar year in which the work was made.[68]

Pre-1988 Act computer-generated works. It is not clear whether there were in fact any such works, but since the 1956 Act contained no such provision it would appear that in cases where there was no human author, there was no copyright in the work under that Act. There can thus be no copyright in the work under the 1988 Act.[69]   **4–14**

A. LITERARY WORKS

Cases of difficulty sometimes arise where one person is responsible for the fixing of the work in some material form for the first time[70] but another may have contributed some or all of the content. At one extreme is the case of a someone who merely records in writing another's spoken words. At the other is the case of a writer who uses the idea for a story which has been given to him.[71] Inevitably there are intermediate cases. The various situations are considered in turn.[72]   **4–15**

Mere amanuensis. It is clear that a person who merely takes down, word for word, the text of a work originated and dictated by another is not the author of the work which is thus recorded.[73] Such a person, sometimes referred to as a "mere amanuensis",[74] has not played any part in originating the expression of the ideas or information contained in the work. In the same way, where A extemporises and B reduces the results to some permanent form, either simultaneously or, relying on his memory, later, A is the author of the work which is thus created.[75]   **4–16**

Reporters and others as authors. Another category of cases is where a person (B), although in one sense merely reproducing the words of another (A), exercises substantial skill and labour in reducing it into some material form. As has been pointed out[76] in such cases, there may be two copyright works in existence. First, that of which A is the author, he being the originator of the words spoken by him. If he is speaking from a prepared text, copyright may already subsist; if he is speaking extempore, copyright will only come into existence when the first record of the words is made by B. The second copyright work is B's record, of which B is the author, having exercised substantial skill and labour in reducing it into that form. So, a reporter who exercises sufficient skill and labour in reporting the words spoken by another is to be regarded as the author of his work.[77] So too, where a medium wrote down what she claimed had been told her by a spirit, do-   **4–17**

---

[67] See paras 3–129 et seq., above.

[68] CDPA 1988 s.12(3). See para.6–49, below.

[69] See CDPA 1988 Sch.1 para.5(1).

[70] No copyright will subsist in a literary, dramatic or musical work until it is recorded, in writing or otherwise. CDPA 1988 s.3(2). As to fixation, see para.3–113, above. As to artistic works, see para.3–121, above.

[71] The person who had the idea may be able to prevent its use by the person to whom he communicated it on the grounds of breach of confidence.

[72] The question can also be approached from the perspective of joint authorship. See paras 4–35 et seq., below.

[73] *Donoghue v Allied Newspapers Ltd* [1938] Ch. 106, 109.

[74] See, e.g. *Donoghue v Allied Newspapers Ltd* [1938] Ch. 106, 109.

[75] It may well be that the record of the work created by B will be a separate copyright work, of which B is the author. See the next paragraph.

[76] See paras 3–115 and 3–126 et seq., above.

[77] *Walter v Lane* [1900] A.C. 539; *Express Newspapers Plc v News (U.K.) Plc* [1990] 1 W.L.R. 1320; [1991] F.S.R. 36 both considered correct in *Sawkins v Hyperion Records Ltd* [2005] EWCA Civ 565 (see para.3–133, above); *Cala Homes (South) Ltd v Alfred McAlpine Homes East Ltd*

ing so at great speed and reproducing in archaic English what she said was communicated to her in an unknown tongue, she was clearly the author of the resulting work.[78] The difference between this type of case and the work of a mere amanuensis is that the amanuensis has exercised no relevant skill and labour in rendering the spoken word into a more permanent form. The work is not original.

4–18 **Biographies, reminiscences and "ghosted" works.** Accounts of the lives of famous personalities are often written on the basis of information supplied by them to a writer. In many cases ghost writers are employed to write such stories in the name of, or "with", the personality in question, who may not have the literary ability or time to do so himself. The normal principle applies in relation to such accounts, whether "ghosted" or not, namely that the author is the person who originated the literary expression. If, as often happens, the subject of the account provides details of incidents from his own life as the basis of articles or stories in which these incidents are written up by another, but does not take any part in producing the particular form of language in which the information is conveyed and which is the subject-matter of copyright, he is not the author of the written work.[79] But the position may be different if the writer uses the words actually spoken by the personality to a significant extent.[80]

4–19 **Originator of plot of a novel.** The copyright in a novel can be infringed if its plot is taken and turned into a dramatised version without any language copying.[81] It is only where the plot is worked out in some detail that this is likely to be so[82] but it follows that the person who originated these details, and who may not have been the same person as the person who clothed it in words, is one of its authors. Where the two have collaborated they are likely to be joint authors[83] but if one person has recorded details of the plot and another has independently worked them up into a novel there will be two copyright works, each with its own author.[84] A dramatisation of the novel which takes sufficient incidents of plot will require the consent of the owner of the copyright in the first work.

4–20 **"Author" of collective or composite work.** In the case of collective or composite works, such as encyclopaedias, there will be distinct copyrights, namely, the copyright in the entire work and the copyright in the various separate contributions. The person who gathers together and arranges the entire work will be the author of the whole work, considered as a compilation.[85] The fact that he is assisted in this by others will not make him any the less the author if it is he who

---

[1995] F.S.R. 818. See, however, N.P. Gravells, "Authorship and Originality: The Persistent Influence of Walter v Lane", 26. I.P.Q. 3, 267.

[78] *Cummins v Bond* [1927] 1 Ch. 167. The result would have been the same if the source of the communication had been a real person. Eve J. rejected the suggestion that the spirit, who had been "domiciled on the other side of the inevitable river" for some 1,900 years was the true author, this being a matter for solution by others "more competent" to decide than he.

[79] *Evans v E. Hulton & Co Ltd* [1923–28] Mac.C.C. 51 (a freelance detective); *Donoghue v Allied Newspapers Ltd* [1938] Ch. 106 (a famous jockey); *Housden v Marshall* [1959] 1 W.L.R. 1 (another jockey); *Chaplin v Leslie Frewin (Publishers) Ltd* [1966] Ch. 71 (Charlie Chaplin's son).

[80] This possibility was left open in *Thrustcode Ltd v WW Computing Ltd* [1983] F.S.R. 502, 507. If both are responsible for the final form of the language, then they may be joint authors. See paras 4–32 et seq., below. Where what is recounted are the actual words spoken in conversation by others, no doubt these will not be original to the writer, but in practice it is unlikely that such account would be verbatim.

[81] i.e. by making an "adaptation" of it. See CDPA 1988 s.21, *Kelly v Cinema Houses Ltd* [1928–1935] Mac.C.C. 362, 367 and para.7–140, below.

[82] The point is more clearly illustrated in the cases relating to dramatic works since plot detail is a well established element of a dramatic work. See para.7–63, below.

[83] As to joint authors, see paras 4–32 et seq., below.

[84] See also para.4–35, below.

[85] In *Waterlow Publishers Ltd v Rose* [1995] F.S.R. 207, the Court of Appeal considered that the provisions of s.20 of the 1956 Act, which provided for certain presumptions as to authorship in

compiled and arranged the information.[86] As to the separate contributions, the authors of these will be the persons who wrote them. Thus where a person has written the entries in a work such as a directory using information supplied by others he will be the author of those entries, unless he has done nothing more than simply copy such information verbatim.[87]

Author of computer program. No changes to the basic rules of authorship were required to implement the authorship requirements of the Computer Software Directive.[88] Computer programs are often written by more than one person and it is common for questions to arise as to whether they are works of joint authorship or whether the program, or package of programs, are distinct works.[89] Often, contributions are at different levels, one person being mainly responsible for the overall structure of the program, another for the detailed coding.   **4–21**

Computer programs are written in programming languages, some of which contain a high level of inbuilt intelligence which is carried through into the final program by use of terms from the language. The use of such complex programming languages may in an extreme position raise the issue as to whether the resulting program has a human author or is a computer-generated work.[90]

B. DRAMATIC WORKS

The author of a dramatic work will be the person who has originated the protectable elements of the work. It is sometimes said that a person who suggests the plot of a dramatic work is not an author, but the statement needs to treated with care.[91] Thus, it is established that the copyright in a dramatic work may be infringed by the copying of its plot, even where the language itself is not taken.[92] It follows that the person who originates the protectable elements of plot is an author. Clearly, however, someone who has a mere idea for a play, however   **4–22**

---

civil proceedings (see now CDPA 1988 s.104), contemplated that there might be cases in which there was no identifiable author of a compilation, in which case the presumptions would apply. However, it is hard to understand why this should be so. It may be difficult as a matter of fact to identify the author of a compilation (although no more so than with many other works) and the presumptions may help to prove authorship, but these are different matters.

[86] *Scott v Stanford* (1866–67) L.R. 3 Eq. 718, cited with approval in *Elanco Products Ltd v Mandops (Agricultural Specialists) Ltd* [1980] R.P.C. 213.

[87] *James Nisbet & Co Ltd v The Golf Agency* (1907) 23 T.L.R. 370. In *Black (A and C) Ltd v Claude Stacey Ltd* [1929] 1 Ch. 177 it was held that even if the written information provided by third parties for such entries was used verbatim, the author of each contribution was the compiler of the directory who had asked for the information and not the third party. It is doubted whether this can be correct. The subject matter was *Who's Who* and the ruling was based on the proposition that where material is given to a compiler for publication by him, the provider cannot be the author. With respect this confuses the issues of authorship and the right to use material. The decision purportedly followed that in *James Nisbet & Co Ltd v The Golf Agency*, above, which concerned a similar publication. There, however, the compilers of the entries had sent out written questionnaires from which the entries were compiled. They did not simply copy what was sent to them. It is clear, therefore, that the compilers were responsible for the language used. Had they simply copied the material, the position might have been different (see 371). In relation to a copyright database, as defined in the 1988 Act, it will be necessary to identify the person who has created the original, and then protectable, subject matter, in respect of which such works now receive protection. See para.3–148, above.

[88] Directive 91/250 of December 16, 1986. Article 2.1 provided that: "The author of a computer program shall be the natural person or group of natural persons who has created the program ...". See now Directive 2009/24/EC, art.2.1.

[89] As to joint authorship, see paras 4–32 et seq., below.

[90] As to which, see para.4–13, above.

[91] It is suggested that the reasoning in *Hatton v Kean* (1859) 7 C.B. (N.S.) 268, where the claimant provided the defendant with the elements of music for a dramatic work, that it was the defendant who was the author of the whole work and that the claimant was not an author, would not be followed today, the distinction not being drawn there between the issues of authorship and ownership.

[92] See para.7–63, below.

good, is not an author if it is not he who has clothed it with the form in which the idea is realised.[93] So, for example, it was not enough to make a person an author where he had suggested an idea and some dramatic incidents for a dramatic sketch,[94] or even a few catch lines, together with some scenic effects and "stage business".[95] Again, where one person (A) suggested to another that he, B, write a dramatic version of an existing book and A then made critical suggestions which led to whole scenes being rewritten, helped with the stage craft but contributed nothing to the eventual dialogue apart from an occasional line and idea, A was not an author.[96] Even more clearly, where a theatre proprietor sent a writer to see and adapt an existing play, the proprietor was not the author of the result, having had no part in the design or execution of that which gave it its originality.[97] Where the dramatic work takes the form of a film,[98] the author will be the person or persons who were directly responsible for originating the action which is portrayed by the film: this will usually include the director and the editor of the film. The author of the screenplay, and of any other underlying works such as a novel, will not, it is suggested, be "authors" of the dramatic work which is the film. They are authors of their separate dramatic or literary works. The film itself, if it is a work of action,[99] will be a new dramatic work, although based on the underlying works, and the authors of this new dramatic work will be those who realised the transformation of the underlying works onto film, often adding further dramatic material of their own in the process.[100]

C. MUSICAL WORKS

4–23   Disputes as to authorship of musical works are relatively common, particularly in the field of popular music where a good deal of informality often accompanies their creation. Disputes where one person claims to have been involved in making a contribution to the final form of a piece of music usually arise in the context of a work of joint authorship, which is dealt with separately,[101] but problems can arise where one person claims to have arranged an existing musical work. If the arrangement is sufficiently original to qualify as a new copyright work,[102] then the "arranger" will be the author of it.[103]

D. ARTISTIC WORKS

4–24   **"Author" of artistic works.** In the case of artistic works the author will be the

---

[93] *Donoghue v Allied Newspapers Ltd* [1938] Ch. 106.

[94] *Tate v Fullbrook* [1908] 1 K.B. 821. To the same effect is *Bagge v Miller* [1917–23] Mac.C.C. 178, where only the idea for a one-act dramatic sketch was provided, all the work of its execution being another's.

[95] *Tate v Thomas* [1921] 1 Ch. 503.

[96] *Wiseman v Weidenfeld & Nicolson Ltd* [1985] F.S.R. 525.

[97] *Shepherd v Conquest* (1856) 17 C.B. 427.

[98] As to a film being a dramatic work, see para.3–39, above. Note that the author of the dramatic work which takes the form of a film may be different from the author of the separate copyright work which is the film. As to the author of the copyright work which is a film, see para.4–56 et. seq., below.

[99] See para.3–39, above.

[100] Although the film may be based on underlying works, it will almost inevtiably be original, not least because of the skill and labour involved in the change of medium and in realising a screenplay.

[101] See paras 4–32 et seq., below.

[102] As to which, see paras 3–125 et seq., above.

[103] As in *Hyperion Records Ltd v Sawkins* [2005] EWCA Civ 565; [2005] 1 W.L.R. 3281; [2005] R.P.C. 32. See para.3–139.

person who is most nearly the effective cause of the final representation.[104] Others may have had the idea for the work but what is relevant is what is done in creating the material form in which the idea is expressed.[105] To be an author, a person must have played a substantial role in putting the artistic work on the material in question.[106] In the ordinary case it will be the person whose hand fixes the picture upon the paper, canvas, etc. who is the author. So for example, where a person conceived of the idea of a card to help illiterate voters, consisting of a picture of a hand holding a pencil in the act of completing a cross but, being unable to draw, employed another, under his direction, to execute the idea, the latter was the author of the work.[107] By contrast, in theory, no doubt a person might have such close control over the application of pencil or paint to paper by another that he might be the sole author but it seems unlikely to arise often in practice. An example might be the case where an artist directs his apprentice precisely where and how to apply paint to a partially completed work. A more likely outcome in most cases will be joint authorship, as where a person who, although he did not actually put pen to paper, made such an input into the work, by way, for example, of providing preliminary sketches, stipulating the form of the final design and shepherding the design as it evolved, that he could be said to have provided part of the skill and effort involved in creating the detailed design which was found on the paper.[108] The fact that a person may have used computer software as a tool to assist him in creating the drawing will not make him any the less the author of it.[109]

Derivative artistic works. Artistic works are often based on pre-existing works. **4–25** Historically important examples are engravings and lithographs made for the purpose of the mass reproduction of illustrations in books and periodicals. With modern printing techniques, the process of reproducing illustrations for publication tends to be largely mechanical but problems can still arise today, for example in relation to an existing artistic work which is photographically reproduced. In such cases, the main question is usually whether a new copyright work has been created, that is, whether the new work is original.[110] Hand-produced engravings and lithographs will usually be so.[111] If a new copyright work is in fact created, the author will be the person who made it, notwithstanding that the work may be derived from an earlier work.

Works of architecture. It will be recalled that for the purpose of the Copyright **4–26**

---

[104] *Nottage v Jackson* (1883) 11 Q.B.D. 627, where Brett M.R. also observed at 631: "Persons who draw Acts of Parliament will sometimes use phrases that nobody else uses …. Whoever, in ordinary life, talks of 'the *author*' of a painting?". The expression, however, now has a clear meaning in copyright law, and Brett M.R. went on: "Yet one can easily make out what is meant by the author of a painting or a drawing. The author of a painting is the man who paints it; and the author of a drawing is the man who draws it".

[105] *Plix Products Ltd v Frank M Winstone (Merchants)* [1986] F.S.R. 63, 81 (High Ct of NZ).

[106] *Kenrick & Co v Lawrence & Co* (1890) 25 Q.B.D. 99. Note, however, that unlike literary, dramatic and musical works, there is no express requirement that as a condition of subsistence an artistic work must be reduced to some material form, but presumably until it is fixed in some form it cannot be said to exist. See CDPA 1988 s.3(2) and para.3–113, above.

[107] *Kenrick & Co v Lawrence & Co* (1890) 25 Q.B.D. 99. The possibility of the two being joint authors was left open, although this seems unlikely to have been the correct position on the facts. See para.4–35, below. In *Nottage v Jackson* (1883) 11 Q.B.D. 627, to the same effect, the illustration was given of one person saying to another: "Go and draw that lady with a dog at her feet, and in one hand holding a flower". The former would not be one of the authors of the resulting drawing.

[108] *Cala Homes (South) Ltd v Alfred McAlpine Homes East Ltd* [1995] F.S.R. 818. As to joint authorship, see paras 4–32 et seq., below.

[109] *Husqvarna Forest & Garden Ltd v Bridon New Zealand Ltd* (1997) 38 I.P.R. 513 (High Ct of NZ). As to the general problem of computer-assisted works, see para.4–13, above.

[110] As to this question, see paras 3–125 et seq., above.

[111] See para.3–137, above.

Acts, a work of architecture consists of either a building or structure, or a model for a building or structure.[112] It does not include any architectural drawing.[113] As also explained elsewhere,[114] copyright will only subsist in a work of architecture if it has some artistic character.[115] The author will be the person who was the effective cause[116] of the shape and design of the building.[117] In most cases this will be the same person as the author of any plans, certainly where the building is constructed following such plans. In cases where a builder constructs the building without reference to any plans, the builder will be the author of any work of architecture which results.

4–27 **Photographs.** Photographs form a special category of work in that not only is the general concept of authorship sometimes difficult to apply but also under the 1911 and 1956 Acts the meaning of author was modified by express provision. As already noted,[118] the law which was in force when a work was made must be applied to determine who was the author of the work. The position under the 1988 Act is examined first.

4–28 **Photographs: the 1988 Act.** The provisions of the 1988 Act determine who is the author of a photograph made on or after August 1, 1989. In contrast to the 1911 and 1956 Acts, the 1988 Act contains no special provisions as to authorship of photographs. The general principle therefore applies, namely, that the author of a photograph is the person who creates it.[119] This represents a return to the position which existed before the passing of the 1911 Act, which simply used the expression "author" in this context.[120] In most cases there will be no difficulty in identifying the author of a photograph: it will be the "photographer". In some cases, however, the subject matter of the photograph may have been carefully arranged or composed by one person and the shutter operated by another. In such a case it will be the former who is the author, he being the effective cause of the final result,[121] and in general terms the author of a photograph will be the person

---

[112] CDPA 1988 s.4(1)(b); Copyright Act 1956 s.3(1)(b); Copyright Act 1911 s.35(1). See para.3–63, above.

[113] An architectural drawing is of course capable of protection, but as a drawing or plan and not as a work of architecture. See para.3–62, above.

[114] See para.3–64, above.

[115] Further, under the 1911 Act, copyright only subsisted *to the extent* of any artistic character or design. See s.35(1) and para.7–76, below.

[116] See para.3–64, above.

[117] *Meikle v Maufe* [1941] 3 All E.R. 144, where the argument that the builder was the author was rejected. Earlier editions of *Copinger* note the unreported case of *Jackson v Jones* (1934), where Farwell J. is reported to have held that the author was the builder and not the architect, but the factual basis of the decision is unknown.

[118] See para.4–05, above.

[119] CDPA 1988 s.9(1).

[120] Fine Arts Copyright Act 1862 s.1. The change effected by the 1988 Act followed the recommendation of the Whitford Committee that the author of a photograph should be defined as the person responsible for its composition (see Cmnd.6732, para.587). For a detailed discussion of this topic, see Garnett and Abbott, "Who is the 'Author' of a Photograph?" [1998] 6 E.I.P.R. 204.

[121] *Nottage v Jackson* (1883) 11 Q.B.D. 627, 632, 637, applied in *Wooderson v Raphael Tuck & Sons* (1887) 4 T.L.R. 57. In *Melville v Mirror of Life Co* [1895] 2 Ch. 531, the claimant's son undertook most of the arrangement and execution of a portrait photograph. The claimant, who ran a photographic business, for the most part stood by and looked on. It was held that the claimant was the author since everything had been done under his direction and by his agent. If the basis of the decision was that the son was merely carrying out his father's directions as to the posing of the subject, etc. then the decision is unexceptional (see, for example, *Nottage v Jackson*, at 632). If, however, as seems to have been the case on the facts, the steps taken by the son were not so directed then it is suggested that the true position was that the son was an author. (Since the father had held up his hand at the critical moment to indicate the direction in which the subject was to look they may in fact have been joint authors, assuming this to have added significantly to the final effect.) The fact that one person may have been acting on behalf of another in such circumstances may affect the question of ownership, but this is a different issue.

who expended relevant skill and labour in its production.[122] What amounts to sufficient skill and labour to make a person an author of a photograph will be a question of degree in each case. Merely showing the photographer where photographs should be taken from is unlikely to be enough.[123] No doubt if the person who operated the shutter also made a contribution to the final result by, for example, choosing particular camera settings, he too would be an author.[124] The important, and sometimes difficult, step is to determine what it is that makes the photograph original,[125] but once this is done, the author can then be identified as the person responsible for those elements in the work.[126]

Photographs: the 1911 and 1956 Acts. Specific definitions of "author" were contained in the 1911 and 1956 Acts in the case of photographs such that any problem in identifying the "author" of a photograph was largely avoided,[127] although certainty was achieved at the price of potential capriciousness. The position is as follows: **4–29**

   (a) In relation to photographs taken on or after July 1, 1912, but before June 1, 1957, the 1911 Act applies. This Act defined the author as the person who owned the original negative from which the photograph was directly or indirectly derived at the time when such negative was made.[128]

   (b) In relation to photographs taken on or after June 1, 1957 but before August 1, 1989, the 1956 Act applies. This Act defined the author as being the person who, at the time when the photograph was taken, was the owner of the material on which it was taken.[129]

There is in practice no difference in the two definitions. It will be noted that the author of a photograph as defined for these purposes may have been someone quite different from the person who would have been the author had the 1988 Act applied.[130] Indeed the "author" may have had little relation to the actual photographer and may have been a company.[131]

---

[122] *Ellis v Marshall (H) & Son* (1895) 64 L.J.Q.B. 757; *Creation Records Ltd v News Group Newspapers Ltd* [1997] E.M.L.R. 444, 450.

[123] *Stackemann v Paton* [1906] 1 Ch. 774, 779. In this case, however, authorship of one of the photographs was denied to the person who had arranged members of a school cricket team into poses as if they were playing a match. It is suggested that this must have been a borderline case and might be decided differently today.

[124] In the course of the passage of the Copyright Bill through Parliament, an amendment which would have had the effect of making the "photographer" the author in all circumstances was resisted, it being pointed out on behalf of the Government that: "In certain cases someone other than the person who operates the camera will make a substantial creative contribution to the final image—perhaps in the darkroom, perhaps in composing the picture through the viewfinder without actually pressing the button—and it would not be right to deny him a copyright in it on the grounds that he was not the actual photographer." (*Hansard*, HL Vol.490, col.883.)

[125] See para.3–144, above.

[126] See *Baumann v Fussell* [1978] R.P.C. 485, 487.

[127] See *Nottage v Jackson* (1883) 11 Q.B.D. 627, where Brett M.R. observed: "I should like to know whether the person who drew this Act of Parliament [the Fine Arts Copyright Act 1862, 25 & 26 Vict. c.68] was clear in his mind as to who can be the *author* of a photograph".

[128] s.21.

[129] s.48(1).

[130] For example the case of a press photographer using film stock belonging to a newspaper proprietor. And see *Australian Olympic Committee v Big Fights Inc* (1999) 46 I.P.R. 53 (Fed. Ct of Aus.), for a case where the question of ownership of original film stock had to be investigated many years after the event (the 1956 Olympic Games in Melbourne).

[131] The use of the word "person" clearly included such a possibility. See, for example, the wording of s.21 of the 1911 Act. This possibility did not raise any difficulty when determining the term of copyright in photographs since this was to be reckoned without reference to the date of death of any author. It has, however, caused a problem with the implementation of the Term Directive. See the next paragraph.

4–30 **Pre-1988 Act photographs and the Term Directive.** Under the Regulations[132] which extended the term of UK copyright, photographs were in general granted an extended term of copyright for the life of the author and 70 years thereafter. The Regulations contain transitional provisions whose effect is to extend and in certain cases revive the copyright in some works in existence at the commencement date of the Regulations, in particular for present purposes, some photographs made while the 1911 and 1956 Acts were in force.[133] As has been seen, under the 1911 and 1956 Acts, the author, as defined by those Acts, may not have been a natural person yet the Regulations defined the new term of copyright in such works by reference to the date of the author's death. By a subsequent clarifying regulation,[134] the author of such works is to be taken to be, for the purpose of the Regulations relating to the extended or revived term only, the author as determined in accordance with the 1988 Act, namely, the person who created it.[135] This will in all cases be a natural person, identified in accordance with the principles stated above. The identity of the author for all other purposes is not affected.

E. PRE-1911 ACT WORKS

4–31 There will still be many copyright works in existence which were made before the coming into force of the Copyright Act 1911 on July 1, 1912. This is not simply because of the longevity of some authors. Even before the extension of the term of copyright to life and 70 years,[136] a copyright work written by a 20-year-old in 1910, who died in 1960, would have remained in copyright until 2010.[137] Furthermore, at the passing of the 1988 Act there were many unpublished, pre-1911 Act copyright works which still had a potentially indefinite term of copyright, or whose period had only started to run in recent years.[138]

There is no difficulty in principle in stating who was the author of an unpublished work protected at common law: it will have been the creator of it. As to works protected by statute, the various statutes generally either simply referred to the "author" of the various works or, as noted below, dealt only with who was the first owner of the copyright. The relevant Acts and works dealt with are as follows[139]:

    (a) "Books" (defined to mean every volume, part or division of a volume, pamphlet, sheet of letter-press, sheet of music, map, chart or plan separately published) and dramatic works (i.e. every tragedy, comedy, play, opera, farce, or other scenic, musical or dramatic entertainment): Literary Copyright Act 1842.[140]

    (b) Lectures: Lectures Copyright Act 1835.[141]

    (c) Tragedies, comedies, plays, operas, farces or any other dramatic piece of

---

[132] The Duration of Copyright and Rights in Performances Regulations 1995 (SI 1995/3297), Vol.2 A3.ii. These implemented the Directive 93/98, harmonising the term of copyright.

[133] For a full discussion of the effect of these Regulations, see Ch.6, below.

[134] Copyright and Related Rights Regulations 1996 (SI 1996/2967) reg.19.

[135] See para.4–28, above.

[136] See Ch.6, below.

[137] And will now remain in copyright until 2030.

[138] See paras 6–44 et seq., below. The works which had an indefinite term of copyright were, broadly, literary, dramatic and musical works and engravings which had not been published in the author's lifetime. Although the term of copyright in all such works has now started to run, it will be many years before such terms expire.

[139] See Vol.2 E5, for these Acts and paras 6–23 et seq., below, for a discussion of the term of copyright in these works.

[140] 5 & 6 Vict. c.45. See Vol.2 E5.vii. Musical scores and books of words were protected under this Act.

[141] 5 & 6 Will. 4 c.65. See Vol.2 E5.vi.

entertainment: Dramatic Copyright Act 1833.3 & 4 Will. 4 c.15. See Vol.2 E5.v. As noted in the text of point (a), above, musical scores and books of words were protected under the Literary Copyright Act 1842. The performing rights in dramatic works only were protected by the 1833 Act, but ss.20 and 21 of the 1842 Act extended the protection to both musical and dramatic compositions.

(d) Engravings, etchings and workings in mezzotinto or chiaroscuro, prints taken by lithograph, or any other mechanical process for multiplying prints: Engravings Copyright Acts 1734, 1766; International Copyright Act 1852.8 Geo. 2 c.13 ("... every person who shall invent and design, engrave, etch, or work ... or from his own works shall cause to be designed and engraved, etched, or worked ... [any print] shall have the sole right and liberty of printing and reprinting the same ..."), 7 Geo. 3 c.38 and 15 & 16 Vict. c.12, respectively. See Vol.2 E5.i and E5.ii. The 1734 Act did not make provision for protection of any work of which the engraver was not also the designer. This was remedied by the 1766 Act, which extended protection, subject to conditions, to the work of any person making an engraving from the original work of another. Section 14 of the 1852 Act brought prints taken by lithograph, etc. within the scope of the earlier Acts relating to engravings.

(e) Sculptures: Sculpture Copyright Act 1814.[142]

(f) Paintings, drawings and photographs: Fine Arts Copyright Act 1862 25 & 26 Vict. c.68. See Vol.2 E5.ix.

3. JOINT AUTHORSHIP: LITERARY, DRAMATIC, MUSICAL AND ARTISTIC WORKS

Introduction. As has been noted,[143] circumstances may arise where there are joint authors of a work. Since the passing of the 1911 Act, the concept of joint authorship has been defined by statute. Before that date it was not defined. Despite slight differences in wording between the 1911, 1956 and 1988 Acts,[144] there has not been any change in the law in relation to this issue[145] and indeed the Acts reflect the position as it existed before the passing of the 1911 Act.[146] Nevertheless, it is technically still necessary to bear in mind that the question of joint authorship must be approached in accordance with the law in force when the work was made.[147]   **4–32**

Importance of distinction between joint authors and co-authors.[148] Whether a work is one of joint authorship or whether there are co-authors is not merely an academic question but has important consequences. For example, the term of copyright in work will depend on the question, as will issues of ownership and infringement.   **4–33**

Definition. A work of joint authorship is defined by the 1988 Act to mean "a   **4–34**

---

[142] 54 Geo. 3 c.56 ("... every person who shall make or cause to be made any new and original sculpture ... shall have the sole right and property ..."). See Vol.2 E5.iv.

[143] See para.4–04, above.

[144] See fn.150, below.

[145] The point was conceded, with apparent judicial approval, in *Cala Homes (South) Ltd v Alfred McAlpine Homes East Ltd* [1995] F.S.R. 818.

[146] See *Copinger's Law of Copyright*, 4th edn, p.109.

[147] See para 4–05, above.

[148] The expression "co-authors" is used here to describe, e.g. the case where two or more authors make distinct contributions to a work. See para.4–04, above, and, e.g. the second limb of the definition of "collective work" in CDPA 1988 s.178.

work produced by the collaboration of two or more authors in which the contribution of each author is not distinct from that of the other author or authors".[149] It is not necessary that all should contribute to the same extent.[150] As to these requirements[151]:

    (a) To be a work of joint authorship, all the collaborators must answer the description of an "author", as that concept is properly to be understood.[152]

    (b) Since collaboration is required, a work is not a work of joint authorship unless it is made in furtherance of some common design.[153]

    (c) If the contributions are distinct or separate, it is not a work of joint authorship.[154]

There is no additional requirement that there must be a joint intention to create a joint work, in the sense that each author must intend the other to be a joint author.[155] The above three issues are considered in turn below. Whether a work is a work of joint authorship is a question of fact not agreement.[156]

4–35   **All collaborators must be "authors".** All must therefore make some contribution to the literary, dramatic, musical or artistic form in which copyright subsists.[157] The question is whether the collaborator takes a part in producing the matter which is the subject of copyright,[158] i.e. whether he has contributed the right kind of skill and labour and in sufficient amount.[159] It may helpful to break this requirement down into four elements: (1) the collaborator must make a con-

---

[149] CDPA 1988 s.10(1). The definition in the 1956 Act s.11(3) was the same except that the word "separate" was used, rather than "distinct". (Note that one of the O.E.D. definitions of "distinct" is "separate" and also CDPA 1988 s.172, which provides that a provision corresponding to a provision of the previous law should not be construed as departing from previous law merely because of a change of expression.) The 1911 Act also used the word "distinct", defining a work of joint authorship as "a work produced by the collaboration of two or more authors in which the contribution of one author is not distinct from the contribution of the other author or authors" (s.16(3)). The expression "collective work" as used in the Copyright Act 1911 s.35(1), and CDPA 1988 ss.79(6), 81(4), 116(4)(a) and 178 has a different meaning. See para.5–118, below.

[150] *Levy v Rutley* (1871) L.R. 6 C.P.

[151] See *Ray v Classic FM* [1998] F.S.R. 622l, 636 for an equivalent formulation of these three principles.

[152] See para.4–35, below.

[153] *Levy v Rutley* (1871) L.R. 6 C.P. 523; *Heptulla v Orient Longman Ltd* [1989] F.S.R. 598 (Delhi High Ct); *Glogau v Land Transport Safety Authority of New Zealand* [1997] 3 N.Z.L.R. 353 (High Ct of NZ). See, further, para.4–36, below.

[154] See para.4–37, below.

[155] *Beckingham v Hodgens* [2003] EWCA Civ 143; [2004] E.C.D.R. 6, not following *Neudorf v Nettwerk Productions* [1999] R.P.C. 935 (Sup. Ct of British Columbia). As to the statement in *Levy v Rutley* (1871) L.R. 6 C.P., that for a work to be one of joint authorship there should be a "joint labouring in furtherance of a common design", the "common design" referred to there is not an intention that the work should be one of joint authorship but is a reference to the need for a joint process in the creation of the work.

[156] See para.4–38, below and, for example, *Samuelson v Producers Distributing Co Ltd* [1932] 1 Ch. 201; (1932) 48 R.P.C. 580, 586 and *Wiseman v George Weidenfeld & Nicolson Ltd* [1985] F.S.R. 525.

[157] *Wiseman v George Weidenfeld & Nicolson Ltd* [1985] F.S.R. 525.

[158] *Evans v E Hulton & Co Ltd* [1923–1928] Mac.C.C. 51, 56; *Ray v Classic FM* [1998] F.S.R. 622, 636.

[159] *Fylde Microsystems Ltd v Key Radio Systems Ltd* [1998] F.S.R. 449; *Godfrey v Lees* [1995] E.M.L.R. 307 (a joint author must make a significant and original contribution to the creation of the work). For an analysis of the role of the soloist as regards works of joint authorship, see Arnold "Reflections on 'The Triumph of Music': copyrights and performers' rights in music" [2010] I.P.Q. 153–164, concluding that (1) it will often be the case that a recorded piece of music created through performance is sufficiently original over any antecedent musical work to attract copyright and (2) that piece of music will often be a work of joint authorship between some or all of the musicians. Also cited Bently, "Authorship of Popular Music in UK Copyright Law" (2009) 12(2) Information, Communication & Society 179 and Rahmatian, "The Concepts of 'Musical Work' and 'Originality' in UK Copyright Law—Sawkins v Hyperion as a Test Case" (2009) 40 I.I.C. 560.

tribution of some sort[160]; (2) it must have been significant[161]; (3) it must have been original; and (4) it must have been a contribution to the creation of the work.[162] The last element may often be crucial, in the sense that a contribution which does not find itself expressed in the final work will not be relevant.[163] In general as to this requirement, the skill and labour need not be contributed in an amount equal to that of the other co-author or co-authors,[164] and need not be of the same kind, so that, for example, someone whose principal role is to arrange the songs written by his collaborators can be a joint author.[165] It will be a matter of fact and degree whether his contribution was large enough to make him a joint author.[166] It follows that if one person is merely the medium for transmitting to paper, canvas, etc. the original work of another, the former is not an author and the work is not a work of joint authorship. Looking at the other side of the coin, a person who merely suggests the idea, without contributing anything to the literary, dramatic or other form in which copyright subsists, is not a joint author. A situation can clearly arise, however, where two people make a contribution to the work's final expression, one being the person actually responsible for committing the work to paper, the other providing an input into what is recorded.[167] But the fact that two persons may have divided up the labour of creating a work will not make them joint authors if only one person is responsible for the skill and labour involved in final expression of their efforts.[168] For the same reason, a person who revises and makes minor additions to an existing work cannot be a joint author.[169]

Examples of cases where this principle has been established include those where one person (A) had recounted the events of his life to another (B), who had agreed to write A's biography, B making notes from which drafts were prepared which A and B then went over together, making amendments, A correcting the final draft line by line[170]; where three people all took part in the design of new models of chairs and settees, one being primarily responsible for the conception but all three taking part in the realisation of that conception in consultation with each other[171]; where two people who were intimately associated and contemplating marriage had collaborated on a book on poliomyelitis, having both worked in a hospital treating an epidemic, one supplying much information to the other and it being impossible to tell who had written which lines[172]; where members of a

---

[160] So the fact that an author needed to obtain the approval of a government department for the contents and form of a work, and that the department laid down certain requirements, did not make the department a joint author of the work: *Glogau v Land Transport Safety Authority of New Zealand* [1999] 1 N.Z.L.R. 257 (Ct of App. of NZ).

[161] Emphasised in *Brighton v Jones* [2004] EWHC 1157 (Ch); [2005] F.S.R. 16, para.34(1).

[162] *Hadley v Kemp* [1999] E.M.L.R. 589.

[163] As to this fourth element, and for emphasis on the fact that the author must contribute to the expression which the law protects, as opposed simply to "ideas", see also *Brighton v Jones* [2004] EWHC 1157 (Ch); *Neudorf v Nettwerk Productions Ltd* [2000] R.P.C. 935 (Sup. Ct of British Columbia).

[164] *Levy v Rutley* (1871) L.R. 6 C.P. 523; *Godfrey v Lees* [1995] E.M.L.R. 307.

[165] *Godfrey v Lees* [1995] E.M.L.R. 307.

[166] *Stuart v Barrett* [1994] E.M.L.R. 448; *Fylde Microsystems Ltd v Key Radio Systems Ltd* [1998] F.S.R. 449.

[167] *Cala Homes (South) Ltd v Alfred McAlpine Homes East Ltd* [1995] F.S.R. 818; *Brighton v Jones* [2004] EWHC 1157 (Ch).

[168] *Fylde Microsystems Ltd v Key Radio Systems Ltd* [1998] F.S.R. 449; *Ray v Classic FM* [1998] F.S.R. 622. The principle needs to be applied with caution in the case of works of compilation, where the relevant skill and labour will often include the gathering or selection of material. See para.4–20, above.

[169] He would also of course not be a joint author if there were no collaboration and their contributions were distinct.

[170] *Heptulla v Orient Longman Ltd* [1989] F.S.R. 598 (Delhi High Ct).

[171] *George Hensher Ltd v Restawhile Upholstery (Lancs.) Ltd* [1976] A.C. 64; [1974] F.S.R. 173.

[172] *Taylor v Prior* (1956) *The Author*, LXVII, No.3 at 60.

pop group sat down and composed pieces of music together[173]; where one person contributed the orchestral arrangements to songs otherwise written by members of a pop group[174]; where one person collaborated with a second to amend the lyrics of a rap song written by the latter to give them an authentic rap feel, resulting in an adaptation which was held to be both significant and original in the copyright sense[175]; where one architect engaged another to help him produce house designs and gave precise instructions as to the features to be incorporated into each house, often with the aid of sketches, checked each drawing produced and marked on it or otherwise made clear the alterations which he required.[176]

Examples of cases in which the claim of joint authorship has not been made out include those where one person had suggested the title of a dramatic sketch, together with various incidents and a few catch lines and odd words, but others had actually written the material[177]; where one person recounted his life's adventures to another, the latter being solely responsible for the form of words[178]; where one person (A) suggested to another (B) that he, B, write a dramatic version of an existing book and A made critical suggestions which led to whole scenes being rewritten, helped with the stage craft but contributed nothing to the eventual dialogue apart from an occasional line and idea[179]; where the claimant had written software for the defendant's mobile telephones and the defendant claimed joint authorship on the basis that he had made an extensive and technically sophisticated contribution in that he had provided (a) the specification for the software (but without saying how the specification was to be achieved), (b) the technical information to enable the software to communicate with the hardware, (c) various parameters for the software, (d) help in developing the software by testing and reporting faults and bugs, and (e) suggestions as to what was the cause of some of the faults (but without providing the software solution to them)[180]; where the defendant had made a number of suggestions as to what a cataloguing system for classical music broadcasts should contain but where the claimant had been responsible for all the final content[181]; where the claimants were members of a pop group to whom the defendant, another member, brought virtually finished songs, and the claimants then applied their skills as performers to the playing of the songs (as a result of which they were recorded for the first time) but did not make any significant contribution to the words or music of them[182]; where a director of a play suggested changes to a play but the playwright was responsible for turning the suggestions into the words and action which ap-

[173] *Stuart v Barrett* [1994] E.M.L.R. 448. By contrast, mere "tinkering" by a member with a song written before he joined did not make him a joint author: *Fisher v Brooker* [2009] UKHL 41; [2009] 1 W.L.R. 1764; [2009] F.S.R. 25.
[174] *Godfrey v Lees* [1995] E.M.L.R. 307.
[175] *Brown v Mcasso Music Production Ltd* (PCC) Patents County Court [2005] F.S.R. 40.
[176] *Cala Homes (South) Ltd v Alfred McAlpine Homes East Ltd* [1995] F.S.R. 818, described as an exceptional case in *Ray v Classic FM* [1998] F.S.R. 622, and one in which the actual draftsmen were essentially only "scribes" of the architect.
[177] *Tate v Thomas* [1921] 1 Ch. 503. The former's contributions to the subject matter of the copyright work were described as "insignificant and negligible". To similar effect are *Tate v Fullbrook* [1908] 1 K.B. 821, where the contributions consisted of the general ideas on which the sketch was based, and *Bagge v Miller* [1917–23] Mac.C.C. 178, where only the bare idea for a one-act dramatic sketch was provided, all the work of execution of the idea being another's. But see, as to plot, para.4–22, above.
[178] *Evans v E Hulton & Co Ltd* [1923–1928] Mac.C.C. 51. cf. *Heptulla v Orient Longman Ltd* [1989] F.S.R. 598 (Delhi High Ct).
[179] *Wiseman v Weidenfeld & Nicolson Ltd* [1985] F.S.R. 525.
[180] *Fylde Microsystems Ltd v Key Radio Systems Ltd* [1998] F.S.R. 449. For a similar case where a claim to joint authorship of computer programs failed, see *Cyprotex Discovery Ltd v The University of Sheffield* [2003] EWHC 760 (TCC); [2004] R.P.C. 4 at para.84 (upheld on appeal, although this point was not in issue: [2004] EWCA Civ 380; [2004] R.P.C. 44).
[181] *Ray v Classic FM* [1998] F.S.R. 622.
[182] *Hadley v Kemp* [1999] E.M.L.R. 589.

peared in the script.[183] In *Kenrick v Laurence*,[184] where one person had conceived the idea for a drawing but it had been executed by another, it was suggested[185] that they might be joint authors. Unless, however, the former had made an actual contribution to final artistic form, which clearly was not the case on the facts, it is suggested that this would have been wrong.

Collaboration required. There must be collaboration for authorship to be joint. **4–36** The work of the authors must be in prosecution of a joint design or joint labouring in furtherance of a common design.[186] So where an author was commissioned to write a play by a theatre proprietor who subsequently made alterations to the author's work, without reference to him, the resulting work was not one of joint authorship.[187] Again, if an existing musical work composed by A is independently arranged by B, the resulting work is not a work of joint authorship. The proper analysis is that is that A is the author of the original work and B is the author of the arrangement.[188]

Contributions distinct. The fact that the contribution can be identified in the **4–37** final work does not mean it is distinct; the issue is whether it forms an integral part of the work, without which the work would be different in character.[189] If the contributions of each author are distinct, then what is produced will not be a work of joint authorship but works of separate authorship, even if they were acting pursuant to a common design. Each person will be the author of the part which he has contributed, each being a separate work.[190] An example would be an encyclopaedia, where there will usually be a large number of copyright works consisting of the individual entries, each having its separate author. In the case of such works it will be unusual if there is not also a further copyright work, being the encyclopaedia considered as a whole, with its own author or authors who have brought the works together.

Agreement as to joint authorship. There is some authority for the proposition **4–38** that where there has been some collaboration, a person can be a joint author if this is something which has been agreed, even though he was not one of the authors of the work in the legal sense.[191] It is suggested that this cannot be right.

---

[183] *Brighton v Jones* [2004] EWHC 1157.

[184] (1890) 25 Q.B.D. 99 (see para.4–24, above).

[185] (1890) 25 Q.B.D. 99, 106.

[186] *Levy v Rutley* (1871) L.R. 6 C.P. 523; *Heptulla v Longman Orient Ltd* [1989] F.S.R. 598 (Delhi High Ct); *Glogau v Land Transport Safety Authority of New Zealand* [1997] 3 N.Z.L.R. 353C (High Ct of NZ); *Neudorf v Nettwerk Productions Ltd* [2000] R.P.C. 935 (Sup. Ct of British Columbia).

[187] *Levy v Rutley* (1871) L.R. 6 C.P. 523. To the same effect is *Samuelson v Producers Distributing Co Ltd* (1932) 48 R.P.C. 580, where an actor made alterations to a dramatic sketch he had been sent. As to the actual decision in this case, see para.4–12, above.

[188] See *Brighton v Jones* [2004] EWHC 1157; [2005] F.S.R. 16 and para.4–12, above, for a general discussion of derivative works, where it is pointed out that the consent of the owner of the copyright in the original work will of course be required for the exploitation of the arranged version.

[189] So, a violin part which had been written specially by the claimant for a song was not distinct from the other contributions to the music. Although it was possible to identify the violin part separately in terms of musical notation, the part was dependent on what was already there. It would have sounded odd and have lost meaning played on its own. The final musical expression, which is what audiences would hear, was a joint one. See *Beckingham v Hodgens* [2003] EWCA Civ 143; [2004] E.C.D.R. 6 at para.46.

[190] In *Levy v Rutley* (1871) L.R. 6 C.P. 523, it was said, obiter, that if two persons, in prosecution of a pre-concerted joint design, had written different portions of a play such that each portion was the sole production of one or the other, they might be "co-authors". See also *Fisher v Brooker* [2009] UKHL 41; [2009] 1 W.L.R. 1764; [2009] E.C.D.R. 17.

[191] See, e.g. *Prior v Lansdowne Press Pty Ltd* [1977] R.P.C., discussed at fn.193, below.

Authorship is a question of status and fact, not agreement[192] and each person must answer the description of author. In the same way, if one person is solely responsible for the creation of a work, the fact that he made the work pursuant to a common design with another for its creation cannot make that other person one of the authors of the work.

4–39   **Rights of joint authors inter se and against third parties.** So far as concerns copyright, the question of the rights of co-authors as between themselves or as against third parties arises in the context of ownership of copyright rather than authorship, and is therefore considered in Ch.5. The regulation of moral rights as between co-authors is considered in Ch.11.

4. SOUND RECORDINGS, FILMS, BROADCASTS AND TYPOGRAPHICAL ARRANGEMENTS

4–40   **Introduction.** It has already been noted that the use in the 1988 Act of the term "author" in relation to these classes of works is not generally a happy one, and has been the subject of criticism. Save now in relation to films, however, the expression is not in fact used otherwise than as shorthand in the process of identifying the first owner of the copyright. As to this, the first owner is broadly identified with whoever was responsible for the financial risk behind the creation of the work, although the position in relation to films has now changed. Consistently with this approach, "authors" of these categories of works are not generally granted moral rights in respect of these works. There are two exceptions to this: the director of a copyright film, since the passing of the 1988 Act; and the performer in the case of broadcast performances and sound recordings, since the entry into force on February 1, 2006, of The Performances (Moral Rights, etc.) Regulations 2006.[193]

A. SOUND RECORDINGS

4–41   Sound recordings have been protected as such since the passing of the 1956 Act. Under the 1911 Act they were in effect protected as musical works, although with the passing of the 1956 Act these existing works became protectable as sound recordings rather than as musical works.[194] The copyright in all pre-1911 Act sound recordings will by now have expired.[195]

4–42   **The 1988 Act.** The question of authorship of sound recordings made after August 1, 1989 is governed by the authorship provisions of the 1988 Act.[196] As to this, the general principle under the 1988 Act, namely that the author of a work means

---

[192] See *Levy v Rutley* (1871) L.R. 6 C.P. 523, 531. The point was accepted on all sides in *Wiseman v George Weidenfeld & Nicolson Ltd* [1985] F.S.R. 525, 529. The confusion often arises because of the close connection in many cases between the concepts of authorship and ownership. Thus where two or more persons each provide some input to the final form of a work, it will often be agreed between them, expressly or impliedly, that they will own the copyright jointly. As to whether such agreement will in fact make them joint owners, either at law or in equity, in *Prior v Lansdowne Press Pty Ltd* [1977] R.P.C. 511 (Sup. Ct of Victoria) one person had made no contribution to the text of a book but had helped to compile the material, and was a party with the two actual contributors to the publishing agreement in which they were all collectively described as "the Author" and was named in the book as published as one of its authors. He was held to be a joint author. At issue was the share of the damages which one of the other writers was entitled to. It is suggested that the decision that he was joint author was wrong, although it may well have been correct to treat him as a joint owner.

[193] See Ch.11, below.

[194] Copyright Act 1956 Sch.7 para.11.

[195] Sch.7 para.11.

[196] See para.4–05, above. The one exception relates to sound recordings made after August 1, 1989

the person who created it, is modified such that this person is to be taken to be the producer, defined as the person by whom the arrangements necessary for the making of the recording are undertaken.[197] This latter expression is also to be found in the provisions of the 1988 and 1956 Acts dealing with films, so that the authorities in that context[198] are relevant here. In the normal commercial context of producing a sound recording, this person will usually be the person who has, for example, engaged or hired the equipment, studio, record producer, engineer, session musicians and any other personnel. In many cases this will be a record company but clearly many permutations are possible. The word "undertaken" implies that it is the person directly responsible for such arrangements, particularly in the financial sense, who is the author.[199] One who merely commissions or finances the making of the recording, not being directly responsible for making the various payments, is unlikely to be the author.[200] The wording of the 1988 Act is clearly directed at the usual situation of the making of a commercial sound recording. The wording is less apt to cover the case where, for example, a recording is informally made by a person who simply turns on a tape recorder when others are performing. In such a case presumably it will the person who is responsible for bringing the tape recorder and making any necessary adjustments to it who will be the "author".

In each case the issue will be one of fact. For example, in one case a person (A), requiring some recordings to be made for a particular purpose, engaged a musician (B) to make them. B was to set up a studio and musicians at his own expense in return for a fee that would enable him to make a profit. B (1) commissioned and paid for the musical arrangements that were made, (2) booked, arranged for and paid all the musicians and engineers and (3) discharged all the incidental expenses. A was nevertheless held to be the author.[201] The person who "made" the recording clearly will not necessarily be the person by whom the arrangements necessary for the making of the recording were undertaken.[202]

The 1956 Act. There is no-one who can properly be described as the "author" of a sound recording made before August 1, 1989.[203] The 1956 Act used the expression "maker" rather than "author". It is, however, convenient to consider the provisions here.   **4–43**

but whose making was commissioned before that date. The provisions of the 1956 Act apply to such recordings. As to these, see para.4–43, below.

[197] CDPA 1988 ss.9(2)(aa), 178. The expression "producer" was introduced into the 1988 Act with effect from December 1, 1996 by the Copyright and Related Rights Regulations 1996 (SI 1996/2967) and derives from art.2.1 of the Rental and Related Rights Directive (92/100). Previously s.9(2)(a) of the 1988 Act simply defined the author of a sound recording as being the person by whom the arrangements necessary for the making of the recording were undertaken. The effect of the amendment is to introduce an extra layer of definition but not to change the substantive law.

[198] See para.4–49, below.

[199] *Re FG (Films) Ltd* [1953] 1 W.L.R. 483.

[200] *Beggars Banquet Records Ltd v Carlton Television Ltd* [1993] E.M.L.R. 349.

[201] *A&M Records Ltd v Video Collection International Ltd* [1995] E.M.L.R. 25. The facts of the case must have been very close to the borderline. The real issue was the ownership of the copyright in the sound recording and it was held in the alternative that A was entitled in equity to the copyright on the basis of an implied term of B's engagement by A (as to which see para.5–177, below). Had the case been decided under the 1956 Act it would have been possible to achieve the same result by applying the commissioning provisions of the Act (s.12(4)). See para.5–43, below.

[202] *A&M Records Ltd v Video Collection International Ltd* [1995] E.M.L.R. 25. In *Beggars Banquet Records Ltd v Carlton Television Ltd* [1993] E.M.L.R. 349 (a case concerning films rather than sound recordings) it was said that the words of the section must be construed in the light of the words of CDPA 1988 s.9(1), which provides that the expression author "means the person who creates" the work. If by this it was intended to mean that it is relevant to consider who was responsible for the intellectual creation of the results of the recording it is suggested that this is wrong. CDPA 1988 s.9(2) redefines "author" without reference to any direct responsibility for the creative process and the suggestion is contrary to the authorities cited here and in relation to films on the wording of s.9(2).

[203] Or whose making was commissioned before that date. See CDPA 1988 Sch.1 para.11(2).

The 1956 Act provided that the maker of a sound recording was the person who owned the first record embodying the sound recording at the time when the recording was made.[204] This person is clearly not necessarily the same as the person who made the arrangements necessary for the making of the recording,[205] so that the positions under the 1956 and 1988 Acts are different. Thus, in many cases where a recording studio was hired and recording tape supplied by the studio as part of its hire services, the studio will have been the maker although not responsible for any other costs or creative input.[206] Nice questions as to the title of the tape may thus affect the question of who was the maker.[207]

4–44   **1911 Act sound recordings.** As noted above, these became protectable under the 1956 Act as sound recordings rather than musical works, and this treatment is continued by the 1988 Act. Nevertheless, the 1911 Act must now be referred to in order to determine who the authors of such works were.[208] Unlike the 1956 Act, the 1911 Act actually spoke in terms of an "author" of such works, since they were equated with musical works.[209] The author was, however, deemed to be the person who was the owner of the original "plate"[210] from which the recording was derived, at the time when it was made.[211] The definition was therefore to the same effect as the equivalent provision in the 1956 Act.

4–45   **Pre-1911 Act sound recordings.** As noted above, the copyright in such works will by now have expired.

4–46   **Film soundtracks.** The question of the authorship of film soundtracks is considered under its own heading, below.

B. Films

4–47   **Introduction.** The treatment of films, and their "authorship", has been the subject of much change over the years.[212] In effect, three different regimes have existed:

Regime 1. That which has applied since July 1, 1994, the effective date of

---

[204] Copyright Act 1956 s.12(8).

[205] In *Springsteen v Flute International Ltd* [2001] E.M.L.R. 654, tape recordings of an artist's performance were made by a partnership as part of its preparations for the promotion of the artist. On the assumption that one of the partners had bought the tapes, it was held that he had done so on behalf of the partnership and that they had become the property of the partnership. It was irrelevant whether or not he had been reimbursed.

[206] Note, however, that the potentially capricious effect of the Act was lessened by s.12(4), thereby a person who commissioned the making of a sound recording became the owner of the copyright (see para.5–43, below).

[207] Precisely this kind of problem arose in *Springsteen v Flute International Ltd* [2001] E.M.L.R. 654. The dispute concerned the ownership of sound recordings made over 25 years previously. One party had made the arrangements for the recordings to be made at a recording studio and had duly paid the studio (although not in circumstances amounting to a commissioning). Although it was probable that the recording studio had provided the blank tapes which were used, it was held, in the absence of any evidence to the contrary, that the arrangement was that the blank tapes would become the property of the other party immediately before they were used for recording purposes.

[208] See para.4–05, above.

[209] See the Copyright Act 1911 s.19(1).

[210] "Plate" was defined inter alia to mean any appliance by which records, perforated rolls or other contrivances for the acoustic representation of any work were intended to be made. See Copyright Act 1911 s.35(1).

[211] Copyright Act 1911 s.19(1).

[212] Note that in relation to a work made after the commencement of the 1988 Act, a film which is a work of action may also be protected as a dramatic work. See para.3–39, above. The author of the dramatic work which takes the form of a film may be different from the author of the separate copyright work which is the film. As to the author of a dramatic work, see para.4–22, above.

the amendments made to the 1988 Act to implement the Rental and Re-lated Rights Directive.[213]

Regime 2. That which applied between June 1, 1957, the date of the com-ing into force of the 1956 Act, and July 1, 1994. In this period, the 1956 Act and 1988 Act, as unamended, were successively in force, but their ef-fect was the same.

Regime 3. That which applied before June 1, 1957, relating to films made before the coming into force of the 1956 Act, when films were not protected as such and only the constituent elements, namely the dramatic work embodied in the film, the photographs forming the frames and the sound track were capable of individual protection.

Under the 1956 Act and the 1988 Act as originally enacted, the United Kingdom did not treat films as works having a true author, in the sense of having an individual who was responsible for the intellectual creation of the subject mat-ter of the film, and in general terms conferred copyright on the person most closely responsible for the financial risk involved in making of the film.[214] Other systems, particularly civil law systems, have regarded films differently and have treated them as true authors' works, having "authors" properly so-called, for example, the screenplay writer, director, lighting cameraman, leading actors and composers of musical works for the film.[215] This difference in approach first came to a head with the Rental and Related Rights Directive,[216] which required, for the purpose of conferring the rental right,[217] that the principal director of a cinematographic or audiovisual work be considered as its author or one of its authors.[218] In fact before implementing the Rental Directive, the United Kingdom implemented the Directive harmonising the term of copyright,[219] which contained a similar requirement,[220] although when implementing the Term Directive, the United Kingdom merely enacted a provision whereby the term of copyright in a film was to be calculated by reference to the date of death of various specified individuals, including the principal director, and did not alter the law as to authorship.[221] However, the Term Directive required the United Kingdom to make the principal an author for all purposes by July 1, 1997 and although the Rental and Related Rights Directive only required the principal director be made

---

[213] Directive 92/100.

[214] See para.4–49, below.

[215] See Stewart, *International Copyright and Neighbouring Rights*, 2nd edn, p.129. The Berne Convention had applied to cinematograph works since 1908, but from the outset adherence to the Convention left Member States free to determine authorship of films. See art.14bis(2)(a) and S. Ricketson and J.C. Ginsburg, *International Copyright and Neighbouring Rights, The Berne Convention and Beyond*, 2nd edn (Oxford University Press, 2006), paras 7–07 et seq.

[216] Directive 92/100.

[217] As to this right, see para.7–93, below.

[218] art.2.2. Fears had been expressed by the United Kingdom, amongst other Member States, that the requirement in the Directive that the principal director of a film be recognised as one of its authors would cause difficulties with regard to a film's exploitation. As part of a compromise when reaching a common position on the Directive, the Commission therefore agreed to produce a report on the question, this being finally produced on December 9, 2002 (IP/02/1824). The report concluded that the fears had been unfounded and that any potential difficulties had been or could be overcome by contractual arrangements between films producers and directors. See the report at *http://www.europa.eu.int/comm/internal_market/en/intprop/news/index.htm*.

[219] Directive 93/98.

[220] Directive 93/98 art.2.1. The Community was faced with conflicting systems of law in relation to the treatment of films and particularly how the term of copyright was calculated. The fact that the principal director had already been accorded a rental right was one of the factors which influenced the decision to calculate the term of copyright in films by reference, inter alia, to the date of death of the principal director. See, e g Dworkin, "Authorship of Films and the European Commission Proposals for Harmonising the Term of Copyright" [1993] E.I.P.R. 151.

[221] CDPA 1988 s.13B, as amended by the Duration of Copyright and Rights in Performances Regula-tions 1995 (SI 1995/3297).

an author for the limited purpose of the rental right, the law relating to authorship was duly changed when implementing the Rental Directive.

Regime 1

4–48   **Films made on or after July 1, 1994.**[222] In relation to such films, but only as from December 1, 1996,[223] the definition of author in the 1988 Act as being the person who created the work[224] is further defined such that the author or authors are to be taken to be the producer and the principal director of the film.[225] Unless the producer and the principal director were the same person, a film is to be treated as a work of the joint authorship of these two persons.[226]

4–49   **Producer.** The producer is defined as the person by whom the arrangements necessary for the making of the film were undertaken.[227] This expression has already been considered in the context of sound recordings.[228] This definition was also used in the 1956 Act in the context of films, the expression "maker" in that Act being the equivalent of "producer",[229] so that decisions under that Act are still relevant in this context. The producer, as so defined, will normally be the producer as that expression is also understood in the film industry, rather than, for example, the camera operator.[230] He will be the person responsible for the arrangements, particularly in the financial sense.[231] For example, where a shell company acted purely as nominee and agent for another company, which was in reality providing the finance and control, the shell company was not the maker.[232] In contrast, where a company (A), whose promoters had had the idea for a film and were the joint directors, paid for the purchase of the film stock and the fares for the crew and participants, A was the maker of the film, notwithstanding that the finance was in fact provided by a television company for whom the film was being made. Everything which was done in the making of the film was done on A's behalf. An individual who had been engaged as cameraman and who may have played some part in the direction of the film, and another company associated with him which was to have been responsible for the cutting and editing, were not co-makers and had no interest in the copyright.[233] So, again, where a company had initiated a project for a film, organised the activity necessary for it to be made and paid for it, that person was the maker and not the local company whose help had necessarily been invoked to help shoot the film in mainland

---

[222] Where the making of the film extended over a period, it is to be taken to have been made when its making was completed. See reg.25(2).

[223] The Copyright and Related Rights Regulations 1996 (SI 1996/2967) reg.36(1). The starting date of July 1, 1994 derives from art.13.4 of the Rental and Related Rights Directive. See para.4–51, below, as to transitional provisions.

[224] s.9(1).

[225] s.9(2)(ab).

[226] s.10(1A). As to joint authorship of films generally, see para.4–59, below.

[227] CDPA 1988 s.178, as amended.

[228] See para.4–42, above. As with sound recordings, the expression "producer", although new to UK law (cf. in the context of the Rome and Berne Conventions), simply forms an extra layer of definition.

[229] See para.4–52, below.

[230] *Adventure Film Productions Ltd v Tulley* [1993] E.M.L.R. 376.

[231] *Re FG (Films) Ltd* [1953] 1 W.L.R. 383.

[232] *Re FG (Films) Ltd* [1953] 1 W.L.R. 483, a case decided under the Cinematograph Films Act 1938, where the relevant expression, as in the 1956 Act, was in fact "maker" rather than "producer". See para.4–52, below.

[233] *Adventure Film Productions SA v Tulley* [1993] E.M.L.R. 376, decided under the 1956 Act. See para.4–59, below, as joint authorship in such circumstances.

China.[234] Where a television documentary was made about a group of schoolboys on an expedition, the idea for the film was that of a youth worker who had arranged and organised funding for the expedition, including the travel and accommodation costs of the freelance camera operator and sound recordist. A television company supplied a "script" consisting of the kinds of things to be filmed, paid the remuneration of the camera operator and sound recordist and supplied film equipment. The camera operator and sound recordist decided on what scenes and sequences would be filmed but took into account suggestions from the youth worker and others. In financial terms the youth worker's contribution was much greater than that of the television company. The youth worker and television companies jointly were held by the trial judge to be "the person by whom the arrangements necessary for the making of the film were undertaken".[235]

The principal director. This expression, which is derived from art.2.1 of the Rental Directive, is not further defined.[236]   **4–50**

Transitional. Although the new provisions only took effect as from December 1, 1996, they apply to films made after July 1, 1994,[237] a provision which has some difficult consequences. These, however, relate mainly to the question of ownership of the copyright and so are considered in the next chapter.   **4–51**

Regime 2

In this period, two different statutes apply, although they are to the same effect: **4–52**

(a) **Films made before July 1, 1994: the 1988 Act.** In relation to films made after August 1, 1989 but before July 1, 1994, the original provisions of the 1988 Act apply. These provided that the person who created a film, and who was thus the author of it, was to be taken to be the person by whom the arrangements necessary for the making of the film were undertaken.[238] The meaning of this expression has already been considered.

(b) **The 1956 Act.** The provisions of the 1956 Act, which apply to all films made between June 1, 1957 and August 1, 1989,[239] were to the same effect, namely, that the maker of a cinematograph film was the person by whom the arrangements necessary for the making of the film were undertaken.[240]

Regime 3

Pre-1956 Act films. There is no copyright in cinematograph films as such made before June 1, 1957.[241]   **4–53**

[234] *Century Communications Ltd v Mayfair Entertainment U.K. Ltd* [1993] E.M.L.R. 335.
[235] *Seven Network Operations v TCN Channel Nine Pty Ltd* [2005] FCAFC 144; (2005) 66 IPR 101. On appeal, Lindgren J. agreed with this conclusion (para.15); Finkelstein J. expressed the view that it was "probably incorrect" but had not been challenged on appeal (para.89). Edmonds J. took the view that the film had been made as a joint venture; accordingly, the film company and the youth worker were "multiple owners": the film company took rights to broadcast the film while the youth worker took all other rights (para.117).
[236] A new presumption is available in proceedings to help prove who was the principal director. See CDPA 1988 ss.105(5) and (6) and para.21–269, below.
[237] See the Copyright and Related Rights Regulations 1996 reg.36(1).
[238] CDPA 1988 s.9(2)(a).
[239] See para.4–05, above.
[240] s.13(10). It will be recalled that the expression "maker" rather than "author" was used in the 1956 Act.
[241] CDPA 1988 Sch.1 para.7(1).

C. FILM SOUNDTRACKS

4–54   **Introduction.** The position of film soundtracks has been complicated by the changes which have been made from time to time in the way they are treated. The dilemma is as follows. Should a soundtrack be treated as part of the film copyright, or should it be treated as a separate copyright work, that is, a sound recording, even when part of the film? It is the varying answers to this question that have produced the complications.[242]

4–55   **Film soundtracks made on or after August 1, 1989: the 1988 Act as amended.** With effect from January 1, 1996, but in relation to all soundtracks,[243] the 1988 Act now provides that the soundtrack accompanying a film is to be treated as part of the film.[244] This is not, however, to affect any copyright subsisting in a film soundtrack as a sound recording.[245] Copyright therefore subsists independently in a sound recording which forms the soundtrack of a film and, in the usual way, its author will be the producer, that is, the person by whom the arrangements necessary for its making were undertaken.[246] The film copyright will, however, also include the soundtrack. The film, taken as a whole and therefore including the soundtrack, will have its own author or authors. These will be the producer and, in relation to films made on or after July 1, 1994, the principal director.[247]

The position can be illustrated as follows. If the recording of sounds was made separately, and not as part of the record of moving images, the recording will be a sound recording in the normal way and have its own author. It will remain as a separate copyright work with its own author even when the sound recording is united with the record of moving images, although the separate copyright work consisting of the film will now include the recording which forms the soundtrack. As to this, the author of the film must be determined, amongst other matters,[248] by asking who undertook the arrangements necessary for the making of the film as a whole, which will include the uniting of the sound recording with the film. Depending on whether the sound recording was made especially for the film or whether it was a pre-existing recording or recordings, this will involve asking who undertook the necessary arrangements for the making of a new sound recording or the selection of the existing sound recording, respectively, and then in each case who then undertook the arrangements necessary to have the recording united with the record of moving images. Where, alternatively, the soundtrack was made in the course of a live shoot, there will still be two copyright works created, the film, with its soundtrack, and the sound recording which is embodied in the soundtrack of the film. Each will have its own author or authors, determined according to the above rules, although in this case they will often be one and the same person or persons.

4–56   **Film soundtracks made on or after August 1, 1989 but before January 1, 1996: the transitional position under the 1988 Act as amended.** As has been

---

[242] See para.3–78, above, for a fuller discussion of the position of soundtracks.

[243] Note that in relation to questions of authorship and ownership, the 1988 Act is only of relevance to works made on or after August 1, 1989. See para.4–05, above. See below as to the treatment of film soundtracks made before this date.

[244] CDPA 1988 s.5B(2), inserted by Duration of Copyright and Rights in Performances Regulations 1995 (SI 1995/3297). The effective date is provided for by reg.26(1). This treatment of soundtracks only applies for the purposes of Pt I of the Act, i.e. the provisions dealing with copyright and moral rights.

[245] s.5B(5).

[246] See para.4–42, above.

[247] See paras 4–47 et seq., above.

[248] The role of the principal director must not be overlooked in relation to films made on or after July 1, 1994.

seen, the amended provisions of the 1988 Act apply as from January 1, 1996 to those earlier soundtracks. What is the position of these works?[249] Under the original provisions of the 1988 Act, copyright subsisted in a film soundtrack as a sound recording in its own right and the film copyright did not include the soundtrack.[250] In the usual way, the author of the soundtrack was the person by whom the arrangements necessary for the making of the soundtrack were undertaken.[251] The film, which was not to be regarded as including the soundtrack for these purposes, would have had its own author or authors, determined in accordance with the normal rules. The effect of the amendments to the 1988 Act as they apply to these existing works was therefore to enlarge retrospectively the scope of the film copyright and thus possibly to alter or enlarge retrospectively the class of persons who were the authors of such films. The possible effect of this on the ownership of the film copyright and its consequences are considered when dealing with the question of first ownership of the copyright.[252]

Film soundtracks made on or after June 1, 1957 but before August 1, 1989: **4–57** **the 1956 Act.** Under the 1956 Act the sounds embodied in any soundtrack associated with a cinematograph film were to be taken to be included in the film.[253] Copyright therefore subsisted in such a soundtrack as part of the copyright in the cinematograph film and not as a separate sound recording. The maker of the film was therefore the person who undertook the necessary arrangements for the making not only of the record of visual images but also the soundtrack. Again, however, a sound recording made separately from the film would have had its own, separate copyright, with its own "maker". The 1988 Act now provides that film soundtracks to which the 1956 Act applied are to be treated as sound recordings and not as part of the film.[254] This might have created difficulties with regard to the ownership of the copyright in such sound recordings but the 1988 Act provides that the "author" of such a film is to be treated as having been the "author" of the sound recording.[255] Thus, it seems, whoever was the maker of the cinematograph film[256] will be treated as having been the "author" of the soundtrack which is now to be regarded as a sound recording.

Film soundtracks: the 1911 Act. Copyright does not subsist in a film as such **4–58** made before June 1, 1957[257] so that film soundtracks made before this date are protected as sound recordings and their author will be determined accordingly.[258]

D. JOINT AUTHORSHIP OF SOUND RECORDINGS AND FILMS

The 1988 Act. In general, sound recordings and films to which the 1988 Act ap- **4–59** plies may be works of joint authorship.[259] If the overall agreement between two persons is that one of them is to be the producer of a film, the fact that the other

---

[249] It should be remembered that this discussion is not concerned with soundtracks made before August 1, 1989, since the authorship provisions of the 1988 Act only apply to works made on or after that date. See para.4–05, above.

[250] CDPA 1988 s.5.

[251] See para.4–42, above.

[252] See paras 5–52 et seq., below.

[253] Copyright Act 1956 ss.12(9), 13(9).

[254] CDPA 1988 Sch.1 para.8(1). This provision has not been altered by the changes introduced to the treatment of film soundtracks by Duration of Copyright and Rights in Performances Regulations 1995.

[255] CDPA 1988 Sch.1 para.8(2). The use of the expression "author" in relation to such 1956 Act works appears to be inappropriate.

[256] i.e. the person who undertook the arrangements necessary for its making.

[257] CDPA 1988 Sch.1 para.7(1).

[258] See para.4–44, above.

[259] A difficulty may be thought to arise because a work of joint authorship is defined as meaning "a

makes the arrangements for a particular location will not make the two of them joint authors in this sense.[260] As already seen,[261] a film made on or after July 1, 1994, will always be a work of joint authorship unless the producer and principal director are one and the same person.

4–60   **The 1956 Act: films.** It was implicit that the express provisions of the 1956 Act relating to joint authorship related only to literary, dramatic, musical and artistic works since it was only in relation to such works that the expression "author" could be applied.[262] Since a 1956 Act film did not have any "authors", it could not have been a work of joint authorship, but there seems no reason why there should not have been joint "makers" of a film.[263]

4–61   **1956 Act and 1911 Act sound recordings.** Again, there seems no reason why there should not have been joint makers or authors, respectively, of sound recordings made under these Acts, where the original recording or plate, respectively, was jointly owned.[264]

E. BROADCASTS

4–62   **The 1988 Act.** It has already been seen[265] that with effect from October 31, 2003, the definition of "broadcast" has been altered in the course of implementation of the Information Society Directive, and the expression now also includes within its scope what used to be cable programmes.

As with sound recording and films, the concept of an "author" of a broadcast is an uneasy one but the expression is used only as a means to identify the first owner of the copyright. Thus, in relation to broadcasts made on or after August 1, 1989, the 1988 Act provides that the person who creates the work, and who is thus the author of it, is to be taken to be the person making the broadcast or, in the case of a broadcast which relays another broadcast by reception and immediate retransmission, the person making that other broadcast.[266] The 1988 Act further provides that references to the person making the broadcast are to the person transmitting the programme if he has responsibility to any extent for its contents, and to any person providing the programme who makes with the person transmitting it the arrangements necessary for its transmission.[267] In this context, the reference to a "programme" is to any item included in a broadcast. This definition applies to broadcasts, as now defined, whether made before or after October 31, 2003, the effective date of the Regulations which amended the defintion of the "broadcast".[268] Since the new definition includes within in it everything that was a broadcast under the 1988 Act as enacted, this does not give rise to any difficulties.

---

work produced by the collaboration of two or more authors in which the contribution of each author is not distinct from that of the other author or authors" (s.10(1)), and the author of a sound recording or film may not actually "produce" the work at all. It is suggested there is nothing in this. See, e.g. s.10(1A) of the 1988 Act. The possibility of joint authorship was accepted without argument in *Beggars Banquet Records Ltd v Carlton Television Ltd* [1993] E.M.L.R. 349.

[260] *Adventure Film Productions Ltd v Tulley* [1993] E.M.L.R. 376.

[261] See para.4–48, above.

[262] See the wording of s.11(3) of the 1956 Act.

[263] As suggested in *Adventure Film Productions Ltd v Tulley* [1993] E.M.L.R. 376. The Whitford Committee noted that there were no provisions in the 1956 Act dealing with "joint makers" of films and sound recordings, in contrast to the provisions relating to joint authors, and recommended the making of equivalent provision (see Cmnd.6732, para.584).

[264] See the previous last footnote to para.4–60, above.

[265] See para.3–93, above.

[266] CDPA 1988 s.9(2)(b).

[267] s.6(3).

[268] The Copyright and Related Rights Regulations 2003 (SI 2003/2498) para.31(1).

Cable programmes. In relation to cable programmes which are "broadcasts"   **4–63**
within the new definition of this expression, the author is the person set out above.
As to those cable programmes which came into existence between August 1,
1989 and October 31, 2003 which are still entitled to copyright,[269] the author was
previously defined to be the person providing the cable programme service in
which the programme was included.[270] This definition has, however, been repealed along with s.7 of the Act, and in relation to these cable programmes,
which are now to be regarded as broadcasts, the new, general definition of author
of a broadcast apparently applies. It is not clear whether there will have been any
cable programmes in respect of which the person providing the cable programme
service in which the programme was included will have been someone different
from the person "making" the transmission, as that expression is defined. If so, it
seems that as at October 31, 2003 there will have been a retrospective change of
authorship of the work and potentially, therefore, of ownership.

Joint authors. Where more than one person is to be taken as making the   **4–64**
broadcast in accordance with the above definition, then the broadcast is to be
treated as a work of joint authorship.[271]

The 1956 Act. The 1956 Act did not use the expression "author" in relation to   **4–65**
what were broadcasts as defined under that Act, identifying only the person who
was entitled to first ownership, namely the BBC or the IBA, as the case may have
been.[272] In relation to what were described as cable programmes, there was no
copyright in cable programmes included in a cable programme service before
January 1, 1985.[273] As to cable programmes which came into existence after this
date, the 1956 Act, as amended, did not make provision for any person to be the
author of a cable programme, simply stating that the person providing the cable
programme service in which a cable programme was included should be entitled
to the copyright in such a work.[274]

Pre-1956 Act broadcasts. There is no copyright in broadcasts made before June   **4–66**
1, 1957.[275]

F. TYPOGRAPHICAL ARRANGEMENTS

The 1988 Act. In relation to a typographical arrangement of a published edition   **4–67**
made after August 1, 1989, the person who created the work, and who is thus the
author of it, is to be taken to be the publisher of it.[276]

The 1956 Act. The 1956 Act, which applies to typographical arrangements made   **4–68**
before August 1, 1989,[277] did not provide for an author of such works. The Act
simply stated that the publisher was to be entitled to the copyright subsisting in a
published edition under that Act.[278]

Pre-1956 published editions. It appears that the 1956 Act applied to pre-1956   **4–69**
Act published editions, since that Act contained no relevant transitional

---

[269] See para.3–93, above.
[270] CDPA 1988 s.9(2)(c).
[271] CDPA 1988 s.10(2).
[272] Copyright Act 1956 s.14(2).
[273] s.14A(11), as inserted by the Cable and Broadcasting Act 1984; CDPA 1988 Sch.1 para.9(b).
[274] Copyright Act 1956 s.14A(3), as inserted by the Cable and Broadcasting Act 1984.
[275] CDPA 1988 Sch.1 para 9(a).
[276] CDPA 1988 s.9(2)(d). As to the meaning of "publisher", see s.175(1).
[277] See para.4–05, above.
[278] Copyright Act 1956 s.15(2).

provisions. However, the 25-year term in respect of such works[279] will have expired.

---

[279] Copyright Act 1956 s.15(2).

Chapter Five

THE CHAIN OF TITLE

1. THE FIRST OWNER OF COPYRIGHT

A. Introduction

Introduction. In many circumstances it will be important to know who is the   **5–01**
owner of the copyright in a work. This involves asking, first, who was the first
owner of the legal title to the copyright and, secondly, whether that title has since
devolved on some other person. The question of first ownership is considered in

this section, the issue of devolution of title in the next. It must also be borne in mind that although the legal title may be vested in one person, some other person may be entitled to the copyright in equity. This will often have significant consequences and is considered in the later section on equitable title.

5–02 **Distinction between ownership of copyright and physical material.** It is important to bear in mind that, subject to limited exceptions,[1] the identity of the first owner of the copyright in a work may be quite different from the person who is owner of the physical material or other medium on or in which the copyright work is first recorded or fixed. The question arises more usually in the context of transfer of title, where the principle is the same, namely that the transfer of the medium on which the work was first fixed does by itself operate to transfer the copyright.[2] Often, of course, the author will own the paper, ink, canvas, paint, etc., by means of which the work is fixed but even where he does not, this does not affect the question of first ownership.

5–03 **Transitional provisions.** The rules relating to first ownership of copyright have altered from time to time. As with authorship, the provisions of the 1988 Act have been framed so as to avoid any retrospective alteration in the identity of the first owner of the copyright. This is achieved by a transitional provision to the effect that the law which was in force when the work was made must be applied to determine who was the first owner of the copyright.[3] The effect is shown by the following table:

Date when work made	Act to be applied
On or after August 1, 1989	The 1988 Act
On or after June 1, 1957 but before August 1, 1989	The 1956 Act
On or after July 1, 1912, but before June 1, 1957	The 1911 Act
Before July 1, 1912	The Acts then in force[4]

For this purpose, where the making of a work extended over a period, the work is to be taken as having been made when its making was completed.[5]

5–04 **Presumptions.** Various presumptions can be applied, in civil proceedings, to determine who the owner of the copyright was at certain times.[6] These are considered elsewhere.[7]

5–05 **Crown and Parliamentary copyright, copyright of certain international organisations.** A quite separate regime applies to these works, which is considered elsewhere.[8]

B. LITERARY, DRAMATIC, MUSICAL AND ARTISTIC WORKS

(i) Author as first owner

5–06 **The general rule.** The general rule under all the Copyright Acts in relation to

---

[1] i.e. first ownership of pre-1988 Act photographs and sound recordings. See paras 4–29, above (with 5–06) and 5–42, below, respectively.
[2] See para.5–68, below.
[3] CDPA 1988 Sch.1 para.10.
[4] See para.5–40, below.
[5] CDPA 1988 Sch.1 para.1(3).
[6] CDPA 1988 ss.104–106.
[7] See paras 21–260 et seq., below.
[8] See Ch.10, below.

these works has always been that the author is the first owner of the copyright.[9] The question of who the author of these works is has already been considered.[10] The remainder of this chapter is concerned with exceptions to this general rule.

Joint authors. As an extension of this principle, where the authors are joint authors,[11] then the general rule is that these authors will be the first owners of the copyright, holding as joint owners.[12]
    5–07

(ii) Works of employees

Introduction. In contrast to the position under many civil law or *droit d'auteur* systems,[13] it has for many years been the position under UK law, as an exception to the general rule stated above, that an employer is prima facie entitled to the copyright in the work made by his employee.[14]
    5–08

The 1988, 1956 and 1911 Acts. The full statement of the rule under all these Acts is that where a literary, dramatic, musical or artistic work is or was made by an employee in the course of his employment under a contract of service or apprenticeship, his employer is the first owner of any copyright in the work, subject to any agreement to the contrary.[15] The rule is subject to qualification in relation to pre-1988 Act works of employees of proprietors of newspapers and the like, and certain other contributions to newspapers.[16] Save in relation to such works, however, the rule is the same in relation to all works made on or after July 1, 1912. The position in relation to works before that date is considered separately.[17]
    5–09

Equitable ownership and licence. It must always be borne in mind that, even if the legal title to the copyright does not vest in the employer as first owner under these rules, it will often be a term of the contract of the author's engagement that the "employer" should own the copyright or at least have some rights to use the work. A number of possibilities then arise:
    5–10

    (a) If the contract amounts to a valid assignment of future copyright,[18] the copyright will vest in the "employer" as soon as it comes into existence.

    (b) If the contract does not amount to such an assignment but it is nevertheless a term of the contract, express or implied, that the "employer" should own the copyright, then although the legal title will remain with the

---

[9] CDPA 1988 s.11(1); Copyright Act 1956 s.4(1); Copyright Act 1911 s.5(1); as to the earlier Acts, see para.5–40, below.

[10] See Ch.4, above.

[11] As to joint authorship, see para.4–32, above.

[12] CDPA 1988 ss.11(1) and 10(3); Copyright Act 1956 s.4(1) and Sch.3 para.6. The 1911 Act contained no such express provisions but it is suggested the position is clear. As to the incidents of co-ownership, see para.5–72, below.

[13] See para.4–03, above.

[14] This position reflects the views of the Whitford Committee in its report (Cmnd. 6732) that "... as a matter of principle, if a person is employed to do a job of work and paid for his services according to the nature of those services, the product of his labour should, subject to any agreement to the contrary, belong to his employer ...". See para.571 of the report and also para.5–26, below. The Committee rejected submissions that the general rule should always be that the author/employee should be the first owner of the copyright in his work. The Committee's recommendation (para.574) that, if a work was exploited by the employer in a way not in the contemplation of the parties at the time of its making, the employee should have a statutory right to an award, was not accepted. Compare the position under the Patents Act 1977 s.40, as amended. For the choice of law issues which may arise, see Torremans, "Authorship, Ownership of Rights and Works Created by Employees: Which Law Applies" [2005] 6 E.I.P.R. 220.

[15] CDPA 1988 ss.11(2) and 178; Copyright Act 1956 ss.4(4) and (5); Copyright Act 1911 s.5(1)(b).

[16] See paras 5–29 and 5–30, below.

[17] See paras 5–31 et seq., below.

[18] As to which, see paras 5–108 et seq., below.

author, the "employer" will own the copyright in equity provided he is
entitled to enforce the contract.[19]

(c) Alternatively, it may appear from the terms of the author's engagement
that even though the "employer" was not to be the owner of the copyright,
the "employer" was to be entitled to use the results of the author's work to
some extent. The result of this will be that the "employer" will have a
licence to use the work, the terms of which, including whether it is sole
and exclusive, will depend on the terms of the engagement.[20]

5–11   **Employees' works: the issues.** The rule stated above raises the following questions:

(a) Was the author employed under a contract of service?

(b) Was the work made in the course of the author's employment?

(c) Was there a relevant agreement to the contrary?

In practice, it can sometimes be difficult to be sure of the answers to these
questions and this can cause a dilemma where, for example, a prospective
employer-claimant is contemplating seeking urgent interim relief. There are four
possible courses of action: first, to take the risk that the contract is one of service,
etc, and sue in the employer's name alone; secondly, to obtain an assignment
from the author (together with accrued causes of action) before issuing proceedings in the name of the employer; thirdly, to join the author as co-claimant;
fourthly, where there is a dispute between them or the author is not willing to co-
operate, to join the author as a defendant.[21] The first course of action clearly
contains the greatest risk.

5–12   **Was the author employed under a "contract of service"?**[22] There are many
cases outside the copyright field on this issue,[23] and the concepts of an employee
and a contract of service are well understood and have the same meanings in the
1988 Act as they do elsewhere.[24] The distinction is between a "contract of service" and a "contract for services".[25] The two expressions indicate, for example,
the distinction between a person engaged to do some specific work under a
considerable measure of control, extending not only to the work which he does
but also to the way in which he does it, on the one hand, and that of a person
engaged more in the capacity of an independent contractor, for example professionally, on the other.[26] A contract of service will exist if three conditions are
satisfied: (a) the servant agrees that, in consideration of a wage or other remuneration, he will provide his own work and skill in the performance of some work
for his master; (b) he agrees, expressly or impliedly, that in the performance of

---

[19] See paras 5–174 et seq., below.

[20] As to licences, see paras 5–198 et seq., below

[21] This option assumes that if he is not the legal owner of the copyright then, at worst, the
"employer" is either the equitable owner or an exclusive licensee within the meaning of the 1988
Act (as to which, see para.5–207, below). If he is none of these things, the action for infringement
of copyright will fail. The need to join the author as defendant arises from the requirement that
the legal owner or the exclusive licensor, as the case may be, must be joined as a party, although
note that an interim injunction may nevertheless be obtained in these cases without having joined
the author. See the separate treatment of these two situations at paras 5–190 and 5–210, below.

[22] The recommendation of the Whitford Committee (Cmnd. 6732, para.575), that the only question
should be whether the work was made in the course of employment, was not accepted. The Committee's comment (para.568) was that the expression "contract of service", if intelligible at all, is
only intelligible to lawyers.

[23] Often in the field of income tax and previously in the field of the Workman's Compensation Acts.

[24] *Ultraframe (UK) Ltd v Fielding* [2003] EWCA Civ 1805, para.19; [2004] R.P.C. 24 (a design
right case).

[25] *Beloff v Pressdram Ltd* [1973] R.P.C. 765 at 769.

[26] *Stevenson Jordan & Harrison Ltd v Macdonald & Evans* [1952] 1 T.L.R. 101, per Evershed
M.R.

that work he will be subject to the other's control in a sufficient degree to make that other master; and (c) the other provisions of the contract are consistent with its being a contract of service.[27] There is an "irreducible minimum of mutual obligations necessary to create a contract of service", in the sense of an obligation to provide work and a corresponding obligation to undertake it.[28] As to these, the degree of control is important, but is no longer regarded as the determining factor.[29] There must, however, be some degree of control, not necessarily in the sense of direction and control exercised by actual supervision, or the possibility of such supervision, but in the sense of ultimate authority over the worker in the performance of his work so that he is subject to the employer's orders and directions.[30] One feature of the difference is that under a contract of service, a person is usually employed as part of the business, and the work is done as an integral part of the business, whereas under a contract for services, the work, although done for the business, is not integrated into it, but is only an accessory to it.[31] But these represent the extreme positions and a more useful test is whether the person who performed the work did so as a person in business on his own account. In answering this question, no strict rules can be laid down as to the relative weight which should be attached to the various considerations which apply. As already stated, the degree of control is important but is no longer regarded as the determining factor. Other factors which may be important are whether the person provides his own equipment, hires his own helpers, what degree of financial risk he takes, what degree of responsibility for investment and management he has, and whether and how far he has an opportunity of profiting from sound management in the performance of his task.[32] A contract of employment may be casual rather than regular[33] but a series of more or less back-to-back individual contracts of engagement, at the end of each of which there was no mutual obligation to offer/accept work, could still lead to a finding that they amounted to a single period of continuous employment.[34] Evaluation of the position is not a mechanical exercise of checking off the various factors but of evaluating the whole picture painted from the accumulation of detail.[35] The terms of the contract as a whole need to be looked at, giving attention particularly to the substantive obligations and rights of each party, so as to determine whether they are more

---

[27] *Ready Mixed Concrete (South East) Ltd v Minister of Pensions and National Insurance* [1968] 2 Q.B. 497, taken to be "the safest starting point" in *Montgomery v Johnson Underwood Ltd* [2001] I.C.R. 819 and applied in *Ultraframe (UK) Ltd v Fielding* [2003] EWCA Civ 1805, para.21; [2004] R.P.C. 24.

[28] *Carmichael v National Power Plc* [1999] 1 W.L.R. 2042; *Montgomery v Johnson Underwood Ltd.* [2001] I.C.R. 819.

[29] See *Market Investigations* [1969] 2 Q.B. 173, at p.185. The degree of control can be particularly important in the case of professional persons, who are often employed under contracts of service. See *Morren v Swinton and Pendlebury BC* [1965] 1 W.L.R. 576; *Whittaker v Minister of Pensions and National Insurance* [1967] 1 Q.B. 156. A mix of mutuality and control was applied in *Weight Watchers (UK) Ltd v Revenue and Customs Commissioners* [2010] UKFTT 54 (TC); [2010] S.T.I. 1620. Compare *Littlewood (t/a JL Window & Door Services) v Revenue and Customs Commissioners* [2009] S.T.C. (SCD) 243 (insufficient degree of control). The control element was also applied in *Autoclenz Ltd v Belcher* [2009] EWCA Civ 1046; [2010] I.R.L.R. 70.

[30] *Humberstone v Northern Timber Mills* (1949) 79 C.L.R. 389, 404, applied in *Montgomery v Johnson Underwood Ltd* [2001] I.C.R. 819.

[31] *Humberstone v Northern Timber Mills* (1949) 79 C.L.R. 389, per Denning L.J. The test of "is the person doing business on his own account?" from *Market Investigations* was referred to in *Smith v Reliance Water Controls Ltd* [2003] EWCA Civ 1153; [2004] E.C.C. 38.

[32] *Market Investigations Ltd v Minister of Social Security* [1969] 2 Q.B. 173 at 184, 185. Approved in *Lee Ting Sang v Chung Chi-Keung* [1990] 2 A.C. 374 at 382, PC.

[33] *Hall v Lorimer* [1994] 1 W.L.R. 209, CA.

[34] *Cornwall CC v Prater* [2006] EWCA Civ 102.

[35] *Hall v Lorimer* [1994] 1 W.L.R. 209 at 216, CA.

strongly indicative of one form of relationship rather than the other.[36] The test of whether the person is in business on his own account may not be so helpful in the case of a person carrying on a profession or vocation, when it may be more important to bear in mind the traditional contrast between a servant and an independent contractor, the extent to which he is dependent upon or independent of a particular paymaster for the financial exploitation of his talents being of significance.[37] Whether a person is engaged under a contract of service or not is a question of law depending upon the facts[38]: the question is always what was the true legal relationship between the parties.[39] Although parties cannot alter the nature of their relationship by putting a new label on it, where the situation is in doubt or ambiguous, so that it can be brought under one relationship or the other, it is open to the parties, by agreement, to stipulate what the legal situation between them should be.[40]

A number of examples in the copyright and related fields show that each case turns on its own facts[41]:

Cases where a contract of service established

5–13
(a) A "dress editress" of a periodical, engaged to recommend artists, visit shops, supervise fashion artists, write dress articles and correspondence, her duties being of a general nature.[42]

(b) A chief dancer of a ballet company, engaged as choreographer as well as a dancer, required to give his exclusive services to the company, attend all performances as required and superintend all necessary rehearsals, in return for a monthly salary.[43]

(c) A part-time interviewer for a market research company, required to follow the company's detailed instructions on interviewing and as to who to interview (although beyond the company's actual control when in the field), but free as to when to do the work within a given period and to work for other organisations.[44]

(d) A full-time political and lobby correspondent of a national newspaper, paid an annual salary, who is an active member of the editorial staff with an office in the newspaper building, and discusses the content of her articles with, but is not dictated to by, the editor.[45]

---

[36] *Barnett v Brabyn* [1996] S.T.C. 716.

[37] *Hall v Lorimer* [1994] 1 W.L.R. 209 at 218, CA, where it was pointed out that a self-employed author working at home may have none of the usual trappings of a business.

[38] *O'Kelly v Trusthouse Forte plc* [1984] Q.B. 90 distinguished in *Cornwall CC v Prater* [2006] EWCA Civ 102. Where the entire contract is contained in a written agreement, the matter is purely one of law. See, e.g. *McMeechan v Secretary of State for Employment* [1995] I.C.R. 444, EAT. Otherwise it will be necessary to determine, as a question of fact, what the contract was. An appellate court should only interfere with the trial court's finding of fact if there was no evidence to support the finding. See *Lee Ting Sang v Chung Chi-Keung* [1990] 2 A.C. 374, PC.

[39] *Protectacoat Firthglow Ltd v Szilagyi* [2009] EWCA Civ 98; [2009] I.C.R. 835 (holding that the judge had been entitled to find that certain partnership and service agreements were shams). The focus should be on discovering the actual legal obligations between the parties based on all the evidence: *Autoclenz Ltd v Belcher* [2009] EWCA Civ 1046.

[40] *Massey v Crown Life Insurance Co* [1978] 1 W.L.R. 676.

[41] Quite apart from the fact that each case turns on its own facts, care must be taken in relying on the earlier cases, decided when the degree of control exercised was considered a decisive factor.

[42] *Re Beeton & Co* [1913] 2 Ch. 279. She was therefore a "servant" within the meaning of the Companies (Consolidation) Act 1908 s.209.

[43] *Massine v De Basil* [1936–45] Mac.C.C. 223.

[44] *Market Investigations Ltd v Minister of Social Security* [1969] 2 Q.B. 173.

[45] *Beloff v Pressdram Ltd* [1973] F.S.R. 33.

(e) A designer of cars employed as chief engineer and designer for a fixed term and at an annual salary.[46]

(f) A professional, salaried dancer engaged full-time during specified hours by Sadlers Wells, the company having first call on his services but, subject to that, he being permitted to obtain outside work.[47]

(g) Three entertainers engaged at a holiday camp for a summer season, each through an agent, and each responsible for own tax and national health contributions. and where the employer did not dictate content of performances.[48]

No contract of service

(a) A person engaged by a fashion magazine at a monthly salary to supply   **5–14** fashion drawings and not to do any other work until such work was completed, working at her home or her studio and doing odd jobs for others; not a "servant" within the meaning of the Companies (Consolidation) Act 1908 s.209. Nor was a writer engaged to provide weekly articles for the magazine, but not on an exclusive basis and not being required to attend its offices.[49]

(b) University examiners employed to prepare examination papers and mark the answers, for which they received a lump sum, they being free to do so at their own convenience, subject to a deadline, it being left to their own skill and judgment to decide what questions to be asked having regard to the syllabus and standard of examination, and not being part of the staff of the university and having regular employment in other educational establishments.[50]

(c) Two newspaper reporters, one employed to attend certain sporting meetings and provide reports for which he was paid a rate per diem, the other employed to write a number of weekly sporting articles for which he was paid an annual salary. Neither worked at the newspaper's offices, nor were they bound to render their exclusive services to the newspaper, nor were they under the newspaper's general control.[51]

(d) A music hall artiste engaged to appear with another artiste as a comedy duo at a specified theatre for one week, subject to a large number of regulations designed for the proper working of the theatre, but his performance depending entirely on his skill, personality and artistry, with which the management had no right to interfere, the amount and degree of control being the significant factor.[52]

(e) A person engaged as a screenplay writer for a sequel to a successful film, with various milestones for its preparation being specified, the production company having the right to require revisions but not to tell him how to go about his work or what he was to do, the writer being paid a fee payable by instalments and a share of the net profit.[53]

(f) A member of what was in effect a co-operative of musicians forming an orchestra. Although technically engaged by a company, each member was

---

[46] *Nichols Advanced Vehicle Systems Inc v Rees* [1979] R.P.C. 127.
[47] *Fall v Hitchen* [1973] 1 W.L.R. 286.
[48] *Warner Holidays v Secretary of State for Social Services* [1983] I.C.R. 440 (QBD) ("employed earners").
[49] *Re Beeton & Co* [1913] 2 Ch. 279. Cf. example (a) ("dress editress"), above.
[50] *University of London Press Ltd v University Tutorial Press Ltd* [1916] 2 Ch. 601.
[51] In *Re Ashley & Smith Ltd* [1917–23] Mac.C.C. 54.
[52] *Gould v Minister of National Insurance* [1951] 1 K.B. 731.
[53] *Hexagon Pty Ltd v Australian Broadcasting Commission* [1976] R.P.C. 628.

a shareholder and if asked: "Who is your employer?" would have replied: "We don't have a boss, we run ourselves through a company, and we hire 11 administrators to do it."[54]

(g) Freelance musicians engaged by an orchestra company on a session-by-session basis, being free to accept or refuse engagements as they wished.[55]

(h) A well-known expert in classical music, engaged at an hourly rate to advise on the composition and compilation of a radio station's repertoire, the contract making provision for him to pursue other business interests and to work when and where he wanted, without supervision or control.[56]

(i) A performer under an agreement with a management company pursuant to which the latter agreed "to render its services ... to use its best endeavours in the promotion and furtherance of the career and interest of the performer" in return for a percentage of the performer's income while the performer agreed to render to the management company his exclusive services for a term.[57]

5–15   **Company directors.** The position of a company director sometimes causes difficulty because a director will not necessarily be employed under a contract of service, even where he is an executive director.[58] The fact that a managing director, as part of his management activities, from time to time acts as if he were a servant or employee does not make him an employee for this purpose.[59] If he is so employed, the ordinary rule applies. If he is not, the legal title to the copyright will not vest in the company but the fiduciary duties which he owes as a director and officer will usually mean that he holds on trust for the company any copyright in work he does qua director.[60]

5–16   **Owner-directors of companies.**[61] Where a person owns the entire share capital of a company or a controlling interest and is also a director or shadow-director, it can be even more difficult to know whether he has a contract of employment with the company.[62] The first question may be whether there is a genuine contract between the director and the company at all, as to which, facts such as how and for what reasons the alleged contract came into existence and what each party did in relation to the contract are likely to be important. The next question will usually be whether any such contract, assuming it is not a sham, was a contract of employment, as to which the above types of considerations will be relevant. This issue is not determined by the fact that he owns a controlling shareholding, and it will be relevant to ask whether there are directors other than, or additional to, the

---

[54] *Winfield v London Philharmonic Orchestra Ltd* [1979] I.C.R. 726.

[55] *Addison v London Philharmonic Orchestra Ltd* [1981] I.C.R. 261.

[56] *Ray v Classic FM plc* [1998] F.S.R. 622. The contract also expressly stated that the relationship was one of an independent contractor providing services and not that of employer and employee.

[57] *Experience Hendrix LLC v Purple Haze Records Ltd* [2007] EWCA Civ 501; [2007] F.S.R. 31 at paras 68–69. The agreement was a management agreement, and had nothing to do with vesting copyright in the management company.

[58] *Parson v Albert J. Parson & Sons Ltd* [1979] F.S.R. 254. In *Gardex Ltd Sorata Ltd* [1986] R.P.C. 623, it was held that the work was done in the course of a managing director's employment, but it is not clear that there was any evidence of a contract of employment.

[59] *Antocks Lairn Ltd v I. Bloohn Ltd* [1972] R.P.C 219 at 221; *Wilden Pump & Engineering Co v Fusfield* (1985) 8 I.P.R. 250.

[60] *Antocks Lairn Ltd v I. Bloohn Ltd* [1972] R.P.C. 219. See para.5–180, below.

[61] Generally as to the status of shareholders and directors, see *Secretary of State for Business, Enterprise and Regulatory Reform v Neufeld* [2009] EWCA Civ 280.

[62] On this question generally, see *Ultraframe (UK) Ltd v Fielding* [2003] EWCA Civ 1805; [2004] R.P.C. 24. For examples of a sole director/shareholder's employment status as regards an agreement with a third party, see *First Word Software Ltd v Revenue and Customs Commissioners* [2008] S.T.C. (SCD) 389; *Dragonfly Consulting Ltd v Revenue & Customs Commissioners* [2008] S.T.C. (SCD) 430.

shareholder and whether the constitution of the company gives him rights such that in reality he is answerable only to himself and incapable of being dismissed. If he is a director, it may be relevant to ask whether he is entitled under the articles to vote on matters on which he is personally interested, such as his contract of employment. Again the conduct of the parties under the contract may well be relevant.[63] As a practical matter, it may be useful to ask questions such as: Was the individual, as shareholder and director, under an obligation to be at work a certain number of hours a week, or to do things such as create copyright works in return for wages?[64]

Partners. A partner of a firm is not "employed" by his partners or the partnership and so the partner will be the first owner of the legal title to a work created by him.[65] On the other hand, the copyright in a work created by an employee of the firm in the course of his employment under a contract of service will vest in the partners.[66]   **5–17**

Course of employment. In order for the copyright to vest in an employer, it is not sufficient merely that the work is made by an author who is employed under a contract of service. It must also be made in the course of that employment. This involves asking, first, whether the work which was done was the kind of work which the employee was engaged to do and, if it was, whether the work was in fact done in the course of that employment at all. The questions often merge into one another.   **5–18**

Scope of employment. This involves a consideration of the terms of the contract of service. Where there is no express contract of employment or no definitive statement of the employee's duties, it will be relevant to consider whether the work was done during normal office hours and using materials provided at the employer's expense and for his benefit and at his request, but these are not conclusive factors[67] since an employee will often do things for his employer which he is not expressly contracted to do.[68] Each case must, of course, depend on its own facts. The question to ask is, was the author employed to do the kind of work in question? Under the contract, could he have been ordered to do the work and would it have been a breach of contract for the employee then not to do it?[69] A contract of employment often evolves in the course of time so that it may be unsafe to have regard only to the terms contained in an initial written contract of employment.[70]   **5–19**

Work done outside course of employment. The fact that work is done outside normal working hours does not necessarily mean that the work is not done in the course of employment. Indeed for many employees today there is no clear   **5–20**

---

[63] Ibid., para.20.

[64] Ibid., para.25.

[65] As to the equitable title, see para.5–181, below.

[66] As to the rights of the partners amongst themselves, see, again, para.5–181, below.

[67] *Intercase UK Ltd v Time Computers Ltd* [2003] EWHC (Ch) 2988; [2004] E.C.D.R. 8.

[68] *Stevenson Jordan and Harrison Ltd v MacDonald & Evans* [1952] 1 T.L.R. 101 at 111.

[69] *Stevenson Jordan and Harrison Ltd v McDonald & Evans* [1952] 1 T.L.R. 101 at 113. In *Sun Newspapers Ltd v Whippie* (1928) 28 S.R. (N.S.W.) 473, an illustration made by an employee was beyond the scope of his employment and he could have refused to do it. Nevertheless the employer was held to have acquired the legal title. This was on the basis that the "respective rights of the parties in the original drawing were intended to be the same as their rights in the drawings made under the contract", so that the drawing was "considered to have been made in the course of his employment". It is suggested that this conclusion was wrong, although no doubt the employer was entitled to the copyright in equity.

[70] *LIFFE Administration and Management v Pinkava* [2007] EWCA Civ 217; [2007] R.P.C. 30 at paras 56, 58.

demarcation of the hours of work. It is suggested that if the work is within the scope of employment[71] and was done for the benefit of the employer, it will have been done in the course of employment.

5–21 **Work done outside course of employment: "Moonlighting".** Where the work falls within the scope of employment but is not done in the course of employment, for example, being done outside office hours and not for the employer's benefit, and the results of which might later be used in competition, the employee may be in breach of his fiduciary duty by not disclosing the work to his employer. Although an employee may make use of his leisure for his profit, he may not secretly set himself up to do in his spare time something which would inflict harm on his employer's business.[72] The consequence of this may either be that the copyright is held on constructive trust for the employer, or the employee will not be allowed to set up a claim that the work was not done in the course of his employment.[73]

5–22 **Work done in breach of contract of employment.** It does not follow from the fact that an employee has acted in breach of his contract of employment that he is also in breach of a fiduciary duty. Contractual duties of good faith and loyalty, or trust and confidence, are not automatically to be equated with fiduciary obligations. In all cases it is necessary to examine the particular duties of the employee and see whether in the circumstances he must act solely in the interests of his employer. In the case of the creation of copyright works, the question may be whether the employee had a duty to use his skill and expertise for his employer's benefit alone and thus create such works for his employer.[74] So, where an employee, working undercover for a film maker, had secretly filmed events inside his employer's film parlour, there had been no breach which brought this principle into operation. There was no breach of confidence involved and he was therefore free to describe what he had seen, whether in writing or otherwise. He could thus not be a trustee of such a description and for the same reason he could not be a trustee of a photograph or film he had made, whether covert or not.[75]

5–23 **Course of employment: examples.** Examples help to illustrate the point:

(a) A person permanently employed on the editorial staff of a newspaper and who was specially requested by the proprietors to translate and summarise a speech, which he did in his own time, independently of his ordinary duties and for a separately negotiated fee, was not acting in the course of his employment. What he had done was not in pursuance of any duty owed to his employer.[76]

(b) A management consultant, who prepared and wrote lectures for delivery to universities and societies dealing with the business in which he was

[71] See the previous paragraph.
[72] *Hivac Ltd v Park Royal Scientific Instruments Ltd* [1946] 1 Ch. 169 at 178, cited in *Ultra Marketing (UK) Ltd v Universal Components Ltd* [2002] EWHC 2285 (Ch), where an employee was not held to be in breach of any duty by creating a copyright work outside his employment. The employee was known to have personal interests and the work he created would never have been part of an actual or intended business of the company.
[73] See *Missing Link Software v Magee* [1989] F.S.R. 361; *Service Corp plc v Channel Four Television Corp* [1999] E.M.L.R. 83. As to an equitable title, see paras 5–179 et seq., below.
[74] *Nottingham University v Fishel* [2001] R.P.C. 367. It was accepted that an employer might be entitled in equity to the copyright in a work created by an employee otherwise than in the course of his employment if it had been created in breach of his fiduciary duty to his employer, for example in breach of his contractual duty to use his expertise for his employer alone or where the work contained confidential information belonging to his employer.
[75] *Service Corp International PLC v Channel Four Television Corp* [1999] E.M.L.R. 83.
[76] *Byrne v Statist Co* [1914] 1 K.B. 622. Having paid for the work, the newspaper proprietor was no doubt entitled to the copyright in equity. See para.5–177, below.

employed, did not do so in the course of his employment.[77] This was so notwithstanding that (1) the giving of lectures was helpful to the company in that it served as an advertisement and, on that account, he was paid the expenses he incurred and (2) that it was, in a sense, part of the services rendered by him for the benefit of the company. It was not part of his regular duties and he could not have been ordered to give the lectures. On the other hand, a report which he had written for a client about its business when on assignment to the client was written in the course of his employment even though it was written largely after hours. The difference was that this was written as part of his work as a servant of the company but the lectures were written as an accessory to the contract and not as part of it. The decision was made having regard to the general consideration that someone engaged to deliver a series of lectures would, in the absence of clear terms to the contrary, be entitled to the copyright in them.[78]

(c) A consultant epidemiologist who wrote, at home, in the evenings and at weekends but not at the instigation of his employers, a guide on hygiene in relation to skin-piercing activities, did not do so in the course of his employment.[79] This was so notwithstanding that he had not undertaken the writing of the book in any private capacity and its preparation was part of his official duties which fell within the terms of his conditions of service and was his employer's publication.

Unincorporated association. The legal title in the copyright in a work created **5–24** by a member of an unincorporated association will usually belong to that member but its ownership will be subject to the rules of the association.[80]

Apprenticeship. An apprentice is someone who is engaged to another for the **5–25** purpose of learning his trade or calling, the nature of the contract being that the master teaches and the other serves the master with the intention of learning.[81] The purpose of apprenticeship is to learn a craft, trade or a profession such that when the apprenticeship is completed the apprentice becomes qualified in that trade or profession.[82]

Agreement to the contrary. The 1988 Act provides, as did the 1956 and 1911 **5–26** Acts, that these employment provisions are subject to any agreement to the contrary.[83] The agreement must have been made before the work came into existence.[84] Such a term may be express, whether in writing[85] or oral, or implied, for example, as a result of a long-standing practice adopted by an employer

---

[77] *Stevenson, Jordan & Harrison Ltd v Macdonald & Evans* [1952] 1 T.L.R. 101.

[78] *Stevenson, Jordan & Harrison Ltd v Macdonald & Evans* [1952] 1 T.L.R. 101 at 107, citing the example of Professor Maitland's law lectures to students at Cambridge. Further examples given were lectures or lessons given orally to students by a doctor on the staff of a hospital or a teacher on the staff at a school who, for his own convenience, puts the lectures into writing, this being useful as an accessory to his contracted work but not part of it. See p.111 of the report.

[79] *Noah v Shuba* [1991] F.S.R. 14, following *Stevenson, Jordan & Harrison Ltd v Macdonald & Evans* [1952] 1 T.L.R. 101. Note that because the presumption of ownership contained in s.20(2) of the 1956 Act applied, the burden of proof to show that the claimant had made the work in the course of employment was on the defendant.

[80] In *Massie & Renwick Ltd v Underwriters' Survey Bureau Ltd* [1940] S.C.R. 218 (Can.), it was held that in the particular circumstances, the copyrights belonged to the members as tenants in common.

[81] *Clapham v St Pancras* (1860) 6 Jur. N.S. 700; *Horan v Hayhoe* [1904] 1 K.B. 288 (in which the element of instruction is again emphasised).

[82] *Wiltshire Police Authority v Wynn* [1981] Q.B. 95.

[83] CDPA 1988 s.11(2); Copyright Act 1956 s.4(5); Copyright Act 1911 s.5(1).

[84] *Noah v Shuba* [1991] F.S.R. 14. A contract made afterwards may, of course, amount to an assignment or an agreement to assign.

[85] As in *Christopher Bede Studios Ltd v United Portraits Ltd* [1958] N.Z.L.R. 250.

whereby the employee retains the copyright.[86] The agreement must be one such that (a) notwithstanding the existence of a contract of employment, the title to works created during its course should not vest in the employer, and (b) it is legally effective.[87] Generally, it will no doubt be hard for an employee to establish such an implied term. The normal inference from employment and payment will be that copyright should belong to the employer.[88]

5–27   **Employees as joint authors.** The position as to first ownership where one of the authors is acting in the course of his employment under a contract of service and the other is not, or is employed by a different employer, is unclear. Arguably the provisions of the Copyright Acts making the employer the first owner of the copyright[89] do not apply since the references in the 1988 and 1956 Acts to the author of a work are to be taken to be references to all authors in the case of a work of joint authorship.[90] Whatever the position as to the legal title in such circumstances, however, the employer will almost inevitably be entitled in equity to his employee's interest in the work.

(iii) Works made for publication in a newspaper, magazine or similar periodical

5–28   For many years, special provision was made regarding the ownership of copyright in works made by employees for publication in newspapers, etc. The 1988 Act makes no such provision for this category of work, so that the general rule under the Act relating to works of employees[91] applies. In relation to such works made before August 1, 1989, however, the rules under the earlier Acts are still relevant. The regime under these Acts was a half-way house between that applying to employees in general and that relating to non-employees. Under the provisions, newspaper and other proprietors acquired a limited or restricted copyright, extending only to press publication. The absence of such a provision in the 1988 Act effected a substantial change in the law in this area. As will be seen, the 1988 Act also brought about a major change in the existing rights to these works made under the 1911 Act.[92]

5–29   **The 1956 Act.** The provisions of this Act must be applied in relation to all such works made between June 1, 1957, and August 1, 1989.[93] The Act provided that where a literary, dramatic or artistic work was made by the author in the course of the author's employment by the proprietor of a newspaper, magazine or similar periodical under a contract of service or apprenticeship, and was so made for the purpose of publication in a newspaper, magazine or similar periodical, then

---

[86] *Noah v Shuba* [1991] F.S.R. 14.

[87] *Ray v Classic FM plc* [1998] F.S.R. 622. Presumably for this purpose a "legally effective" agreement means an agreement which has the force of a contract.

[88] *Lawrence & Bullen Ltd v Aflalo* [1904] A.C. 17, applying *Sweet v Benning* (1855) 16 C.B. 459, followed in *Lamb v Evans* [1893] 1 Ch.D. 218, all cases decided under the Copyright Act 1842 s.18, as to which, see para.5–31, below. See also the remarks of the Whitford Committee in its report, quoted in the footnote to para.5–08, above.

[89] See para.5–08, above.

[90] CDPA 1988 s.10(3); Copyright Act 1956 Sch.3 para.6. The 1911 Act did not contain any such express provision.

[91] See para.5–08, above.

[92] See para.5–30, below. It was submitted to the Whitford Committee that this type of provision in fact reflects a fair balance between the interests of employer and employee in all cases. The Committee's conclusion in relation to all works of employees, however, was that certainty and practicability were important and that it was generally undesirable to separate ownership of the various rights comprised in the copyright, this being best left to agreement between the parties in individual cases (Cmnd. 6732, para.574).

[93] See para.5–03, above.

the proprietor should be entitled to the copyright in the work in so far as the copyright related to publication of the work in any newspaper, magazine or similar periodical, or to reproduction of the work for the purpose of its being so published; but in all *other* respects the author should be entitled to any copyright subsisting in the work by virtue of that Act.[94]

What is meant by "in the course of employment" under a "contract of service or apprenticeship" has already been discussed.[95] It should be noted that this provision did not apply to musical works. In the equivalent provision of the Australian Copyright Act, it was held that a "newspaper" was a publication containing a narrative of recent events and occurrences, published regularly at short intervals from time to time.[96] Supplementary advertising material and "fliers" inserted in newspapers can also be part of a newspaper, if they are of the kind of material apt to be found as an integral part of it.[97] The newspaper proprietor's copyright does not include the right to make photocopies of the journalist's work for use in a press clippings service, since this does not constitute publication or reproduction for the purposes of publication in a newspaper.[98] It is suggested that for the same reason the right of storage and exploitation of a journalist's work in an online data retrieval service is not within the proprietor's copyright.

While the operation of the subsection might have been excluded by agreement, it could not have been extended by an agreement. Thus the proprietor could not, merely by agreement, acquire the legal title to more than the newspaper right in the work under this section unless the agreement amounted to a valid assignment of the balance of the copyright[99] or, where, for example, the agreement was only oral, an equitable title to it.[100] If the work was not made by an employee under a contract of service, but by a paid independent contributor, there is an argument that the equitable right to the entire copyright ought not to have vested in the proprietor unless there was something more than mere engagement and payment from which a contract to that effect could be inferred. Otherwise such a contributor would have been in a worse position than one who was employed under a contract of service, for the latter was deemed to have the general rights of publication reserved to him. In the end, however, the question will depend on what were the terms of the contract, express or implied.

The 1911 Act. The provisions of this Act must be applied in relation to all such works made on or after July 1, 1912, but before June 1, 1957.[101] This Act contained a similar provision to that found in the 1956 Act, namely, that where a work made in the course of employment by an employee under a contract of service or apprenticeship was an article or other contribution to a newspaper, magazine or similar periodical, there was to be deemed to be reserved to the author a right to restrain the publication of the work otherwise than as part of a newspaper, magazine or similar periodical.[102] The effect of this provision was to give the copyright to the employer while apparently giving the employee a bare statutory

5–30

---

[94] s.4(2). The subsection had effect subject to any agreement excluding its operation and to Pt VI of the Act, which includes provisions relating to devolution of title: s.4(5), (6).

[95] See paras 5–11 et seq., above.

[96] *De Garis v Nevill Jeffress Pidler Pty Ltd* (1990) 18 I.P.R. 292 (Fed. Ct of Aus.), applying *D.C.T. v Rotary Offset Press Pty Ltd* (1971) 45 A.L.J.R. 518 (High Ct of Aus.).

[97] *John Fairfax & Sons Ltd v D.C.T.* (1988) 15 N.S.W.L.R 620C (Sup. Ct of N.S.W.) followed in *De Garis v Nevill Jeffress Pidler Pty Ltd*, above.

[98] *De Garis v Nevill Jeffress Pidler Pty Ltd*, above.

[99] As to which, see paras 5–83 et seq., below.

[100] As to the acquisition of an equitable title, see paras 5–177 et seq., below.

[101] See para.5–03, above.

[102] s.5(1)(b).

right to restrain publication by his employer[103] and others.[104] The employer was entitled to restrain infringements by others, relying on his copyright.[105] The effect of this provision has not been continued by the 1988 Act.[106] It therefore appears that today the author has no rights and the employer is to be regarded as having been the first owner of the entire copyright in such works. If correct, this represents a substantial change brought about by the 1988 Act.

5–31   **Pre-1911 Act works.** The Literary Copyright Act 1842 contained an ill-drafted section[107] under which the copyright in an "encyclopaedia, review, magazine, periodical work, or work published in a series of books or parts, or any book whatsoever" vested in the proprietor in certain circumstances. The proprietor had to prove that (a) he employed the writer to compose the articles; (b) the articles were composed on terms that the copyright should belong to the proprietor; and (c) the articles were paid for by him.[108] It is thought that this section applied only to works of the character of encyclopaedias, magazines and periodicals.[109] It was held that such a term could be implied and need not be express. Whether a term could be implied depended in the usual way upon the inferences of fact to be drawn from the nature of the contract and all the circumstances.[110] The general rule was that it was unreasonable to suppose that a person paid for the right to publish another's contributions in an encyclopaedia leaving it open to the other to publish his contributions the next day in a separate form.[111] The section also provided that the author was to be at liberty, after the lapse of 28 years from the date of publication, to publish his articles in a separate form. The 1988 Act continues this right, by providing that where a work made before July 1, 1912 consists of an essay, article or portion forming part of and first published in a review, magazine or other periodical or work of a like nature, the copyright is subject to any right of publishing the essay, article or portion in a separate form to which the author was entitled at the commencement of the 1911 Act, or would, if that Act had not been passed, have become entitled under s.18 of the 1842 Act.[112]

(iv) Commissioned artistic works

Commissioned works generally

5–32   None of the Copyright Acts has ever contained a general provision relating to the

---

[103] *Nicol v Barranger* [1917–1923] Mac.C.C. 219; *Sun Newspapers Ltd v Whippie* (1928) 28 S.R. (N.S.W.) 473.

[104] *Nicol v Barranger* [1917–1923] Mac.C.C. 219. This point was left open in *Sun Newspapers Ltd v Whippie* (1928) 28 S.R. (N.S.W.) 473, but seems clear.

[105] *Nicol v Barranger* [1917–1923] Mac.C.C. 219 at 228.

[106] The 1911 Act was repealed by the 1956 Act and although the effect of this provision was continued by the 1956 Act (see Sch.7 para.3 and Sch.8 para.1), the 1956 Act was itself repealed by the 1988 Act without equivalent provision being made.

[107] s.18.

[108] Actual payment was necessary: *Richardson v Gilbert* (1851) 1 Sim. (N.S.) 336; *Brown v Cooke* [1874] 16 L.J. Ch. 140; *Collingridge v Emmott* [1887] 57 L.T. 864.

[109] See, e.g. *Copinger* (4th edn), p.110 and wording of the complementary right conferred on the author, as now preserved by the 1988 Act (see below, in the body of the text). cf. *Ward, Lock & Co Ltd v Long* [1906] 2 Ch. 550, deciding that the section extended to books generally.

[110] *Lawrence, etc., Ltd v Aflalo* [1904] A.C. 17, following *Sweet v Benning* (1855) 16 C.B. 459. To the same effect is *Lamb v Evans* [1893] 1 Ch. 218; *Chantrey, etc., Co v Dey (T.H.)* (1912) 28 T.L.R. 499. No such term was made out or sufficiently pleaded in either *Bishop of Hereford v Griffin* (1848) 16 Sim. 190 or *Walter v Howe* (1881) 17 Ch.D. 708.

[111] *Lawrence, etc., Ltd v Aflalo* [1904] A.C. 17.

[112] CDPA 1988 Sch.1 para.18. Similar transitional provisions were contained in the Copyright Act 1911 Sch.1 and the Copyright Act 1956 Sch.7 para.37.

commissioning of all categories of works. Subject therefore to the special provisions made in the pre-1988 Acts which are discussed below, the general rule is that the first legal owner of the copyright in a work whose making was commissioned will be the author, i.e. the person who creates it.[113] Even where this general rule applies, it should nevertheless be borne in mind that in many cases where a work is made pursuant to a contract of commission, it will be a term of the contract, express or implied, that the commissioner will be entitled to the copyright. Provided that the commissioner is entitled to enforce the contract, he will thus be the equitable owner of the copyright.[114] Alternatively, if the agreement on its true construction amounts to an assignment of future copyright and complies with the relevant formalities, then the copyright will vest in the commissioner on the coming into existence of the copyright.[115] At its lowest, the commissioner is likely to have some sort of licence to use the work.[116]

Although containing no general rule, the earlier Copyright Acts contained important provisions relating to the commissioning of particular categories of works, and these still continue to apply in relation to works made before August 1, 1989.[117] Those relating to artistic works are considered here. Commissioned sound recordings are considered when dealing with sound recordings.[118] While the 1988 Act did not continue the regime relating to the first ownership of copyright in certain commissioned works,[119] the Act does contain other sections which relate to commissioning. Thus, the Act creates a moral right entitling a person to a right of privacy in respect of photographs which were commissioned for private and domestic purposes.[120] The ownership of design right may also be affected where the design was commissioned.[121] Decisions under the earlier Acts as to what amounts to commissioning may therefore also be applicable in construing these provisions.

Commissioned artistic works under the 1956 Act. The provisions of the 1956   **5–33** Act apply to determine questions of first ownership of copyright in works made between June 1, 1957 and August 1, 1989.[122] The 1956 Act provided that, where a person commissioned the taking of a photograph, or the painting or drawing of a portrait, or the making of an engraving, and paid or agreed to pay for it in money or money's worth, and the work was made in pursuance of that commission, the person who so commissioned the work should be entitled to any copyright subsisting under that Act.[123]This provision was expressed to be subject to provisions of the Act relating to the works of employees of newspaper proprietors

---

[113] See para.5–06, above.
[114] As to equitable title, see para.5–178, below.
[115] See CDPA 1988 s.91, the Copyright Act 1956 s.37 and para.5–108, below.
[116] See the similar discussion in relation to works made for an "employer", para.5–10, above.
[117] CDPA 1988 Sch.1 para.11(2).
[118] See para.5–43, below.
[119] The majority recommendation of the Whitford Committee, which was not accepted, was that, subject to any agreement to the contrary, the author should retain the copyright in all cases, subject to the commissioner having an exclusive licence to use the work for the purposes contemplated by the parties, and also the right to restrain other exploitation to which he could reasonably have objected (Cmnd. 6732, para.577).
[120] CDPA 1988 s.85(1).
[121] See paras 13–90 and 13–111, below.
[122] See para.5–03, above. The commissioning provisions of the 1956 Act also apply to works made after August 1, 1989 but which were commissioned before that date (CDPA 1988 Sch.1 para.11(2)). Where a work was made after June 1, 1957, but pursuant to a contract made before that date, the provisions of the 1911 Act apply (Copyright Act 1956 Sch.7 para.3), as to which, see para.5–35, below.
[123] s.4(3).

and the like.[124] It was also subject to any agreement excluding the operation of the section[125] and to Pt VI of the Act, which included provisions relating to devolution of title.[126]

5–34   **The 1956 Act.** Various points arise under these provisions:

(a) *"Engraving", "photograph" and "portrait"*.[127] "Engraving" was defined as including any etching, lithograph, woodcut, print, or similar work, not being a photograph, and "photograph" was defined as any product of photography or any process akin to photography, other than part of a cinematograph film.[128] There was no definition of a "portrait" in the Act.[129] Whether a picture is a portrait or not will no doubt depend upon what is the main purpose of the picture.[130] If it is to represent the likeness of a person, it is nonetheless a portrait because of the presence of subordinate accessories in the picture. It is fairly clear that a portrait may include the likeness of more than one individual, but that, on the other hand, the mere fact that real persons happen to be delineated in a picture does not necessarily make that picture a portrait.[131] So, a picture of the Duke of Schomberg sitting, clad in armour, upon horseback, a battle scene forming the background of the picture, was a portrait.[132] Again, a picture painted by a spiritualist medium of a dead person whom he had not seen, was a "portrait". This was because it was intended to represent the deceased person as that person was when living, and that it was nonetheless a portrait because the "model" that the artist used was entirely subjective.[133] On the other hand, a picture, although said to be "of" a real person but not based on any life study or representation of him and therefore not bearing any likeness, would not be a portrait.[134]

(b) *When did the copyright vest?* The copyright will have vested as soon as the work came into existence.[135] It follows that the commissioner became

---

[124] See para.5–29, above. The application of this saving is unclear but presumably the intention was to make it clear that where, for example, a newspaper proprietor requested an employee to take a particular photograph, the split ownership provisions of s.4(2), considered above, should apply.

[125] See s.4(5). The parties might therefore agree, expressly or impliedly, that the copyright should remain with the author, as was found to be the case in *Gabrin v Universal Music Operations Ltd* [2003] EWHC 1335 (Ch), para.25.

[126] s.4(6). The effect of this saving was presumably to make it clear that the parties to the commissioning might effectively transfer the title to some third party or that the commissioner himself might do so.

[127] Vaisey J. pointed out in *Leah v Two Worlds Publishing Co Ltd* [1951] Ch. 393, without drawing any conclusions, that whereas engravings and photographs involve particular methods of production, the word "portrait" can cover all methods of pictorial representation. In its report (Cmnd. 6732), the Whitford Committee noted that, portraits aside, no one had been able to suggest any valid ground for treating photographs and engravings differently from other commissioned works. See para.561 of the report.

[128] 1956 Act s.48(1). Cinematograph film was itself defined as any sequence of visual images recorded on material of any description (whether translucent or not) so as to be capable, by the use of that material (a) of being shown as a moving picture or (b) being recorded on other material (whether translucent or not) by the use of which it can be shown: s.13(10).

[129] The dictionary definition of the word is "a figure drawn, painted or carved upon a surface to represent some object, now, almost always, a likeness of a person, especially of the face, made from life …" (Shorter O.E.D.). Clearly, however, a portrait does not necessarily have to be made from "life". See *Leah v Two Worlds Publishing Co Ltd* [1951] Ch. 393, discussed below.

[130] See *Apple Corps Ltd v Cooper* [1993] F.S.R. 286 at 293.

[131] *Duke of Leeds v Earl Amherst* (1845) 14 L.J. Ch. 73. The issue arose on the construction of a will.

[132] *Duke of Leeds v Earl Amherst* (1845) 14 L.J. Ch. 73.

[133] *Leah v Two Worlds Publishing Co Ltd* [1951] Ch. 393 (decided under the 1911 Act, as to which, see below).

[134] *Duke of Leeds v Earl Amherst*, above, at 81.

[135] *Apple Corps Ltd v Cooper* [1993] F.S.R. 286.

the owner of the copyright whether or not the work was accepted[136] or even completed.[137]

(c) *What amounts to a commissioning?* In general, the word "commission" means "order".[138] This means more than "request" or "encourage".[139] There must therefore come into existence a contract with mutual obligations, namely an obligation to create the work and an obligation to pay.[140] While well-known personalities will often agree to their photograph being taken, even in a studio, without any commission by them being made, this is less likely to happen in the case of people in the ordinary walk of life, since in the latter case the photographer is unlikely to take the risk of no prints being ordered.[141] Of course, if there was either payment or an agreement to pay, it will normally be easy to conclude that a work was commissioned but it does not necessarily follow that this was so. The commissioning must obviously have taken place before the work is made.[142]

(d) *Work subcontracted.* If a person ordered a work to be made by another, who then subcontracted the necessary labour, the person ordering the work would in the normal case have been entitled to the copyright in the work. This is on the basis that the person ordering the work commissioned all necessary articles to be made even though unaware of the need for them.[143] This principle assumes, however, that the subcontracted work was itself subject to the commissioning provisions of the Act.[144] The position would be different if, for example, the subcontractor had reserved the copyright.[145]

(e) *Was there an agreement to pay?*[146] While a commissioning does not necessarily imply an obligation to pay, it will often do so. Indeed, the usual meaning of "commission" involves both the ordering of work to be done and the coming under an obligation to pay for that work, irrespective of whether any product of that work is purchased.[147] Everything, however, will depend on the circumstances as to whether any agreement was made at all and, if so, whether it included a provision for payment. In the case of a portrait photograph, for example, the question will be whether, if the sitter declines to buy any copies of the photograph, the photographer is entitled to a fee or the cost of the work and labour done in the making of the copyright work.[148] In the ordinary case where a professional photographer, painter or engraver is commissioned, the court will readily imply

---

[136] *Apple Corps Ltd v Cooper* [1993] F.S.R. 286.
[137] *Art Direction Ltd v U.S.P. Needham (N.Z.) Ltd* [1977] 2 N.Z.L.R. 12, decided under the similar provision of the New Zealand Act.
[138] *Plix Products Ltd v Frank M. Winstone (Merchants)* [1986] F.S.R. 63.
[139] *Plix Products Ltd v Frank M. Winstone (Merchants)* [1986] F.S.R. 63.
[140] *Ultraframe (UK) Ltd v Fielding* [2003] EWCA Civ 1805, para.30; [2004] R.P.C. 24. As to the obligation to pay, see further in the text.
[141] *Sasha Ltd v Stoenesco* (1929) 45 T.L.R. 350.
[142] *Plix Products Ltd v Frank M. Winstone (Merchants)* [1986] F.S.R. 63; *Apple Corps Ltd v Cooper* [1993] F.S.R. 286.
[143] *James Arnold and Co Ltd v Miafern Ltd* [1980] R.P.C. 397.
[144] See the reservation in *Apple Corps Ltd v Cooper* [1993] F.S.R. 286 at 297.
[145] See 1956 Act s.4(5).
[146] Note that the 1988 Act, when dealing with commissions in relation to the moral right of privacy in relation to photographs and films, refers only to commissioning, without the further requirement of an agreement to pay (s.85(1)). The provision dealing with the design right, however, refers to a "commission for money or money's worth" (s.263(1)).
[147] *Plix Products Ltd v Frank M. Winstone (Merchants)* [1986] F.S.R. 63.
[148] *Sasha Ltd v Stoenesco* (1929) 45 T.L.R. 350; *Hartnett v Pinkett* (1953) 103 L.J. 204 (Cty Ct).

that the commissioner is to pay for the work.[149] But a professional photographer will often be willing to attend occasions such as a wedding or the taking of a school photograph without any agreement for payment but simply in the expectation that people will order prints from him. In such a case, he will have retained the copyright. As already noted, in the case of well-known personalities, a photographer may also be willing to take photographs without any commission or assurance of payment.[150] An agreement to pay, of course, requires a consensus so that where the commissioner had an intention to pay, perhaps only if requested, but this was not known to the maker of the work, this will not suffice. Neither will expectation of payment by the maker if the commissioner had not agreed to pay.[151]

(f) *What the payment must have been for.* The payment or agreement to pay must have been for the making of the copyright work, not the physical embodiment of the work itself. The payment is the *quid pro quo* for the copyright.[152] In the context of a photograph, for example, the fact that prints or even the negative was paid for will not therefore be sufficient, although clearly the cost of the work of taking the photograph may in fact be built into the price of making copies.[153] So, too, the fact that the creator of the work is commissioned and paid for his time and expenses, and payment is also made for a licence to use the works, will not be sufficient if the payment was not also for the making of the works.[154] Again, in the context of an engraving, payment for a run of the finished product with a built-in or separate charge for the costs of tooling will not necessarily be payment for the making of the work.[155] Such cases will turn on the nice question of precisely what the payment was to be for.

(g) *Money or money's worth.* Under the earlier Acts, the issue was whether "valuable" or "good" consideration had been given. These cases are considered below but it is suggested that they are not of great assistance when considering the provisions of the 1956 Act. "Money's worth" refers to the case where the price or consideration for the making of the work was something other than money, for example services to be rendered or property other than money.[156] Whether the giving of access to private premises or a famous personality will amount to payment in money's worth will depend on the precise circumstances, although usually it will not. In any event it is likely to be rare that such access will have been provided by way of payment for the making of the photographs.[157]

(h) *When must the agreement to make the work and to pay, or payment, have been made?* Since the vesting of the copyright in the commissioner takes place, if at all, when the work is first made, all the elements referred to in the section must be present at this moment. It follows that the commissioning and thus also either the payment or the agreement to pay must

---

[149] *Boucas v Cooke* [1903] 2 K.B. 227, analysed in *Apple Corps Ltd v Cooper* [1993] F.S.R. 286 citing the example of a sitter approaching the photographer without any prior invitation.
[150] *Sasha Ltd v Stoenesco* (1929) 45 T.L.R. 350.
[151] *Apple Corps Ltd v Cooper* [1993] F.S.R. 286.
[152] *Apple Corps Ltd v Cooper* [1993] F.S.R. 286.
[153] *Sasha Ltd v Stoenesco* (1929) 45 T.L.R. 350.
[154] *Gabrin v Universal Music Operations Ltd* [2003] EWHC 1335 (Ch), para.24; [2004] E.C.D.R. 4.
[155] *Plix Products Ltd v Frank M. Winstone (Merchants)* [1986] F.S.R. 63.
[156] See *Secretan v Hart* [1969] 1 W.L.R. 1599.
[157] The cases under the earlier Acts in which such questions arose are considered below.

have been made before this time.[158] Payment made after the event without obligation will not, therefore, of itself have operated to vest the copyright in the commissioner.[159] In such circumstances, the copyright will only have been transferred to the commissioner if it was part of a separate transaction by which the legal title was validly assigned.[160] Alternatively in such a case, the commissioner may thereby have acquired an equitable title if the payment was part of an agreement which included, expressly or impliedly, the acquisition of the copyright.[161]

Commissioned artistic works under the 1911 Act. The provisions of the 1911 Act apply to determine questions of first ownership of copyright in works made between July 1, 1912, and June 1, 1957.[162] The 1911 Act provided[163] that where, in the case of an engraving,[164] photograph[165] or portrait,[166] the plate[167] or other original was ordered by some other person than the author, and was made for valuable consideration in pursuance of that order, then, in the absence of any agreement to the contrary, the person by whom such plate or other original was ordered was the first owner of the copyright. The 1911 and 1956 Acts, although expressed in different words seem generally to have been to the same effect, although it is possible that "money or money's worth" in the 1956 Act had a narrower meaning than "valuable consideration", which is considered below. The above discussion as to what amounted to a "commissioning" under the 1956 Act is relevant in considering what amounted to an "ordering" under the 1911 Act.[168]   **5–35**

Valuable consideration. This expression was also used in the 1862 Act, considered below, which in addition used the expression "good" consideration. Valuable consideration usually consists of some right, interest, profit or benefit accruing to one party, or some forbearance, detriment, loss or responsibility given, suffered or undertaken by the other.[169] It clearly includes money or money's worth, but excludes a consideration which is illusory or merely nominal. Some of the cases on this point are not easy to reconcile: **5–36**

(a) Where a claimant was in the business of taking and selling photographs of well-known sporting celebrities and requested and was allowed to take a photograph of one such person, on terms that the photographer be allowed

---

[158] *Apple Corps Ltd v Cooper* [1993] F.S.R. 286; *Ultraframe (UK) Ltd v Fielding* [2003] EWCA Civ 1805, para.30; [2004] R.P.C. 24. See also *Gabrin v Universal Music Operations Ltd* [2003] EWHC 1335 (Ch), para.24; [2004] E.C.D.R. 4, where no agreement to acquire and pay for any of the photographs was made before they were taken. The agreement to acquire the copyright in particular photographs was made after the event, and for a further consideration.

[159] *Leah v Two Worlds Publishing Co Ltd* [1951] Ch. 393, where the agreement to pay for a portrait was only made after it had been seen.

[160] As to assignments of copyright, see paras 5–83 et seq., below.

[161] As to equitable titles, see para.5–177, below.

[162] See para.5–03, above. The 1911 Act also applied to works made after June 1, 1957 but which were commissioned by a contract made before that date (see the footnotes to para.5–33, above).

[163] s.5(1)(a).

[164] Defined to include etchings, lithographs, wood-cuts, prints and other similar works, not being photographs: s.35(1). This is identical to the 1956 Act definition.

[165] Defined to include a photo-lithograph and any work produced by any process analogous to photography: s.35(1). This is similar to the 1956 definition, except that the 1956 Act excluded any photograph forming part of a cinematograph film. Under the 1911 Act, films were not protected as such but the individual frames were protected as photographs.

[166] As to the meaning of this, see the earlier discussion of the 1956 Act provisions.

[167] Defined to include any stereotype or other plate, stone, block, mould, matrix, transfer, or negative used or intended to be used for printing or reproducing copies of any work: s.35(1).

[168] See, for example, *Boucas v Cooke* [1903] 2 K.B. 227 and *Sasha Ltd v Stoenesco* (1929) 45 T.L.R. 350, referred to above in the discussion of the 1956 Act provisions.

[169] *Fleming v New Zealand Bank* [1900] A.C. 577.

to print and sell copies, the celebrity was held thereby to have given good and valuable consideration.[170]

(b) Where a celebrity agreed to a request by a photographer to sit for her photograph, without any charge being made by the photographer, this did not amount to good or valuable consideration.[171]

(c) Where a firm of photographers took photographs of school premises and pupils with the permission of the proprietors, it being clearly understood that no one was compelled to buy any prints, the photographers reasonably speculating that they would in fact make sales to pupils and others, it was held that the proprietors had given "good", although apparently not "valuable", consideration by permitting the photographers to have access to private premises and showing them around.[172]

5–37   **The 1911 Act: "Other original".** The meaning of this expression is unclear. It seems that it was not just the copyright in the engraving, photograph or portrait which the commissioner acquired. Thus, a sketch produced with the intention of its being reproduced in a newspaper was held to be within the section on the basis that it was the "original" of the newspaper illustration.[173] A sketch which, had it been accepted, was intended by its maker for use as the original of an engraving would not be an "original" if it was never in fact accepted or so used.[174]

5–38   **Pre-1911 Act commissioned artistic works.** There was a similar provision in the Fine Arts Copyright Act 1862[175] to the effect that, where a painting, drawing or the negative of any photograph was "made or executed for or on behalf of any person for a good or a valuable consideration", the copyright belonged to "the person for or on whose behalf the same shall be so made or executed".[176] Under this Act it was necessary, if the commissioned author wished to retain the copyright, for him to do so in writing. The differences between the 1911 Act and the 1862 Act were that: (1) under the 1911 Act writing was not required if the artist desired to retain his copyright—the proviso only said "in the absence of any

---

[170] *Melville v Mirror of Life Co* [1895] 2 Ch. 531. The claim that the copyright had vested in the celebrity failed, however, on the wording of the 1862 Act in that the photograph had not been made or executed "for or on his behalf". See below.

[171] *Ellis v Marshall (H.) & Son* (1895) 64 L.J.Q.B. 757. Again, the claim also failed because the photographs were not taken "for or on her behalf". *Melville v Mirror of Life Co* [1895] 2 Ch. 531, was decided 15 days earlier and not cited.

[172] *Stackemann v Paton* [1906] 1 Ch. 774. *Melville v Mirror of Life Co* [1895] 2 Ch. 531 was apparently not cited. *Ellis v Marshall (H.) & Son* (1895) 64 L.J.Q.B. 757 was distinguished on the basis that the judge there had found that the only consideration given by the celebrity was that he had taken the trouble to walk up to the photographer's room and sit in his chair, and this was neither good nor valuable. It is suggested that even if the decision that the proprietors of the school had given good consideration was correct, the case was wrongly decided since the photographs had not been made "for or on behalf of" the proprietors (see, again, the wording of the 1862 Act, below). Farwell J. seems to have been influenced by the conclusion that the proprietors would not conceivably have allowed a photographer to publish photographs of the inside of a girls' school (including that of the French governess in her bedroom), a factor which, it is suggested, was irrelevant on this point.

[173] *Nicol v Barranger* [1917–23] Mac.C.C. 219. Although it is not clear from the report, it seems that an engraving was made from the sketch so that it could be reproduced in the newspaper, and thus that the sketch was the "original" of the engraving (see the specific reference to "engravings" in the quotation of s.5(1)(a) at p.226). In *Con Planck Ltd v Kolynos Inc* [1925] 2 K.B. 804, a sketch which was intended to be reproduced by lithographic process for advertisement purposes was held itself to be a "lithograph". Sed quaere.

[174] *Toronto Carton Co v Manchester McGregor Ltd* [1935] 2 D.L.R. 94, decided under the similar provisions of the Canadian Act. It seems, although this was not decided, that the sketches were also not made for valuable consideration in pursuance of any order, having been made in the hope only that they would be accepted and paid for.

[175] 25 & 26 Vict., c.68.

[176] As to this provision, see above and *Petty v Taylor* [1897] 1 Ch. 465; *Boucas v Cooke* [1903] 2 K.B. 227.

agreement to the contrary"; (2) the 1862 Act referred to a work "made" for an-other, whereas the 1911 Act spoke of a plate or original "ordered" by some other person; (3) as already noted, the 1862 Act used the expression "a good or a valu-able consideration," whereas the 1911 Act only had the words "valuable consideration"; (4) the 1862 Act referred to any painting or drawing, not just a portrait.

Limits as to commissioning. It has already been pointed out that the provisions **5–39** of the Copyright Acts relating to commissioned works are limited in scope. Gen-erally, it was only commissioned engravings and photographs that vested in the commissioner, together with commissioned portraits, by whatever means produced. This was capable of producing unexpected severances of copyright in the case of commercial art. Consider, for example, the case of an advertiser who placed an order for an advertisement. He would have been the owner of the final engraving or photograph comprising the advertisement, having commissioned it. But the advertisement probably started life as a sketch or drawing, unaffected by this subsection,[177] so that there will have been an outstanding copyright in the sketch or drawing which will not have vested in the advertiser as a result of the commission and which might have caused trouble if the advertiser wished to repeat the main design in a new advertisement.[178]

(v) Pre-1911 Act works

Pre-1911 Act works. The position of pre-1911 Act works has already been **5–40** discussed in the context of authorship.[179] As to unpublished works which were protected at common law, the author will have been the first owner. As to works protected by statute, the general position was that the author was the first owner, the exceptions being:

(a) *Books, etc.,*[180] protected under the Literary Copyright Act 1842.[181] Where the work was published posthumously, the copyright belonged to the owner of the manuscript.[182]

(b) *Encyclopaedias, reviews, magazines, periodical works, works published in a series of books or parts, or any book*, protected under the Literary Copyright Act 1842.[183] This exception is considered in the section dealing with works made for publication in a newspaper, etc.[184]

(c) *Lectures*, protected under the Lectures Copyright Act 1835.[185] The first owner was the author or the person to whom he had sold or otherwise conveyed "the copy thereof".[186]

(d) *Engravings, etchings, lithographs, etc.*, protected under the Engravings

---

[177] Although see the discussion of the expression "other original" in the 1911 Act, above.
[178] See, for example, the comments in *Plix Products Ltd v Frank M. Winstone (Merchants)* [1986] F.S.R. 63. It is doubtful whether many such problems remain today. In any event, it should be remembered that the equitable title to the copyright in the sketch or drawing may nevertheless have vested in the advertiser, or at least he is likely to have acquired some form of licence. See para.5–177, below.
[179] See para.4–31, above.
[180] See para.4–31, above, for what was included within this description.
[181] 5 & 6 Vict., c.45.
[182] Copyright Act 1842 s.3. See para.5–134, below, as to the effect of a bequest of a manuscript.
[183] 5 & 6 Vict., c.45.
[184] See para.5–31, above.
[185] 5 & 6 Will. 4, c.65.
[186] See Lectures Copyright Act 1835 s.1.

Copyright Acts 1734, 1766 and the International Copyright Act 1852.[187] The first owner was the person who either engraved, etc., any work or who caused it to be engraved, etc.[188] Thus a person who had arranged for lithographs to be made to help follow the course of the Franco-Prussian war and who provided the engraver with rough sketches and other materials was the first owner of the copyright in the engraving, even though he could not draw himself.[189]

(e) *Paintings, drawings and photographs* protected under the Fine Arts Copyright Act 1862.[190] The exception made for commissioned works has already been considered in the context of commissioned works generally.[191]

(f) *Sculptures*, protected under the Sculpture Copyright Act 1814.[192] The first owner was the person who made or caused the work to be made.[193]

C. Sound Recordings and Films

(i) Sound recordings

5–41   **The 1988 Act.** With one exception,[194] the question of first ownership of copyright in sound recordings made after August 1, 1989 is governed by the provisions of the 1988 Act. As with other works, these provide that the first owner is the author.[195] As has already been discussed, this person is to be taken to be the producer, that is, the person by whom the arrangements necessary for the making of the recording are undertaken.[196] The meaning of this expression has already been considered.[197] There are no provisions dealing with the case where the arrangements are made by an employee in the course of his employment since where this happens clearly it will be the employer who is the "producer".

5–42   **The 1956 Act.** This Act applies in the case of sound recordings made on or after June 1, 1957 but before August 1, 1989, or whose making was commissioned before the latter date.[198] The 1956 Act provided that, save in relation to commissioned sound recordings, the first owner of the copyright was the "maker". As already seen, the maker of a sound recording was defined to be the person who owned the first record embodying the sound recording at the time when the recording was made.[199]

5–43   **1956 Act commissioned sound recordings.** In a case where a person commissioned the making of a sound recording and paid or agreed to pay for it in money or money's worth, and the record was made in pursuance of that commission,

---

[187] 8 Geo. 2, c.13, 7 Geo. 3, c.38 and 15 & 16 Vict., c.12, respectively.

[188] See s.1 of the 1734 and 1766 Acts.

[189] *Stannard v Harrison* (1871) 19 W.R. 811.

[190] 25 & 26 Vic., c.68.

[191] See para.5–38, above.

[192] 54 Geo. 3, c.56.

[193] See Sculpture Copyright Act 1814 s.1.

[194] See the next paragraph.

[195] CDPA 1988 s.11(1).

[196] CDPA 1988 s.9(2)(aa). The expression "producer" was introduced into the 1988 Act by the Copyright and Related Rights Regulations 1996 and derives from the Rental and Related Rights Directive, 2006/115/EC. The effect of the amendment was to introduce an extra layer of definition but not to change the law. See the footnote to para.4–42, above.

[197] See para.4–42, above.

[198] See CDPA 1988 Sch.1 para.11(2).

[199] Copyright Act 1956 s.12(8). See para.4–43, above. The Whitford Committee did not recommend any change in this area, noting that the industry seemed content with the position as it was, no doubt in the light of the commissioning provisions, considered below (Cmnd. 6732, para.581).

that person and not the maker was the first owner of the copyright, in the absence of any agreement to the contrary.[200] The question of commissioning has already been discussed in relation to artistic works.[201] The same principles apply. As already noted, this provision tempered the potentially capricious effect of the "maker" provisions, above.

The 1911 Act. As already noted,[202] these works became protectable under the 1956 Act as sound recordings rather than musical works and this treatment is continued by the 1988 Act. Nevertheless, the 1911 Act must now be referred to in order to determine who the first owner of the copyright in these works was.[203] As has been seen, the author and thus the first owner was deemed to be the person who was the owner of the original "plate"[204] from which the recording was derived, at the time when it was made.[205] There were no provisions in the 1911 Act relating to commissioned sound recordings.   **5–44**

Pre-1911 Act sound recordings. The copyright in such works will by now have expired.[206]   **5–45**

Film soundtracks. The topic of film soundtracks is considered under its own heading, below.   **5–46**

(ii) Films

Introduction. As already seen,[207] three different regimes in effect operate in relation to films: first, those made on or after July 1, 1994; secondly those made before July 1, 1994 but on or after June 1, 1957; thirdly, those made before this date.   **5–47**

(a) *Regime 1*

Films made on or after July 1, 1994. The consequence of the authorship provisions of the 1988 Act, as amended,[208] is that as from December 1, 1996,[209] the first owners of the copyright in such films will be the producer and the principal director, or where employed, etc., his or their employers.[210] The expressions   **5–48**

---

[200] Copyright Act 1956 s.12(4). For an example of a decision as to who, on the facts, owned the record, see *Silly Wizard Ltd v Shaughnessy* [1984] F.S.R. 163 (Ct of Sess.).

[201] See paras 5–32 et seq., above.

[202] See paras 4–41 and 4–44, above.

[203] See para.5–03, above.

[204] Plate was defined, inter alia, to mean any appliance by which records, perforated rolls or other contrivances for the acoustic representation of any work were intended to be made. See the Copyright Act 1911 s.35(1).

[205] Copyright Act 1911 s.19(1).

[206] See the Copyright Act 1956 Sch.7 para.11.

[207] See para.4–47, above.

[208] See para.4–48, above.

[209] Copyright and Related Rights Regulations 1996 (SI 1996/2967) reg.36(1). The starting date of July 1, 1994 derives from art.13(4) of the Rental Directive (92/100). See the next paragraph in the text as to transitional provisions.

[210] CDPA 1988 ss.9(2)(ab) and 11(2). In IP/02/1824, see para.4–47, fn.219, on the question of authorship of cinematograph or audiovisual works, the Commission has stated its view that the effect of s.11(2) "seem[s] to exclude the principal director from having rights in the work". The Commission therefore stated its intention to examine how far this was consistent with the provisions of the Rental Directive (92/100) which stipulate that the principal director is to be regarded as one of the authors of a film. S.11(2) is of course expressly made subject to any agreement to the contrary, and there is also nothing in the Directive which prohibits an employer or film producer acquiring the principal director's interest in the film copyright. Indeed, the main thrust of the Report is that the existence of contractual arrangements between film producers and directors

"producer" and "principal director" have already been considered.[211] Unless the producer and the principal director are the same person, these first owners will be joint owners.[212]

5–49 **Transitional.** Although these provisions only apply as from December 1, 1996, they apply in relation to films made on or after July 1, 1994.[213] This creates a potential difficulty in that between July 1, 1994 and December 1, 1996 there will have been films brought into existence whose copyright first belonged to whoever undertook the arrangements necessary for their making. Such a person may well have entered into arrangements relating to the copyright, whether the granting of licences or the assignment of the copyright. What is the effect of the fact that, as from December 1, 1996, the principal director is also to be regarded as one of the authors of these films and that therefore he, or his employer and also the employer of the producer, if any, are to be regarded as first owners of the copyright? The Regulations contain a limited saving provision, providing that it is not an infringement of the principal director's interest to do anything after December 1, 1996 in pursuance of arrangements for the exploitation of the film made before November 19, 1992.[214] The effect seems to be that as from November 19, 1992, parties are to be taken to have known that the law would be changed and thus that arrangements made after this date without the principal director's consent will not bind him so far as anything done after December 1, 1996 is concerned.

(b) *Regime 2*

5–50 Two statutes applied successively during this period but their effect is the same:
  (a) **Films made before July 1, 1994: the 1988 Act.** In relation to films made on or after August 1, 1989 but before July 1, 1994, the effect of the 1988 Act is that the first owner of the copyright is the person by whom the arrangements necessary for the making of the film were undertaken.[215]
  (b) **The 1956 Act.** The provisions of the 1956 Act, which apply to all films made between June 1, 1957 and August 1, 1989,[216] were to the same effect. Thus the Act provided that the first owner of the copyright was the maker, namely the person by whom the arrangements necessary for the making of the film were undertaken.[217]

(c) *Regime 3*

5–51 **Pre-1956 Act films.** There is no copyright in cinematograph films as such made before June 1, 1957.[218]

(iii) Film soundtracks

5–52 **Film soundtracks made on or after August 1, 1989: the 1988 Act as amended.**

---

has avoided any potential obstacles to the normal exploitation of films. The Rental Directive and its amendments have now been codified as Directive 2006/115/EC.

[211] See para.4–48, above.

[212] CDPA 1988 s.10(1A). As to joint authorship of films generally, see para.4–59, above.

[213] Copyright and Related Rights Regulations (SI 1996/2967) reg.36(1).

[214] The date of the Rental and Related Rights Directive 92/100 which led to the introduction of these provisions. The Rental Directive and its amendments have now been codified as Directive 2006/115/EC.

[215] CDPA 1988 ss.11(1) and 9(2)(a), as enacted. See para.4–52, above.

[216] See paras 4–07 and 5–03, above.

[217] Copyright Act 1956 s.13(10). It will be recalled that the expression "maker" rather than "author" was used in the 1956 Act.

[218] CDPA 1988 Sch.1 para.7(1).

The complicated provisions relating to "authorship" of film soundtracks have already been considered.[219] It will be recalled that a soundtrack accompanying a film is now to be treated as part of the film but this is not to affect any copyright subsisting in the film soundtrack as a sound recording.[220] The present position is therefore that the first owner of the copyright in a sound recording which forms the soundtrack of a film will be the author of the sound recording, namely, the person by whom the arrangements necessary for its making were undertaken (the "producer").[221] In relation to films made on or after July 1, 1994, the first owner or owners of the copyright in the film, of which the soundtrack is now to be treated as forming part, will be, as from December 1, 1996, the producer and principal director or their employers. In relation to films made after August 1, 1989 but before July 1, 1994, the first owner will have been the producer alone. The meaning of these expressions in the context of film soundtracks has already been discussed.[222]

Film soundtracks made on or after August 1, 1989 but before January 1, 1996: the transitional position under the 1988 Act as amended. The new provisions in the 1988 Act whereby a soundtrack which accompanies a film is to be taken to be part of the film were introduced with effect from January 1, 1996 but are to apply to soundtracks made before that date.[223] As has been seen, under the original provisions of the 1988 Act, copyright subsisted in a film soundtrack as a sound recording in its own right and the film copyright did not include the soundtrack.[224] Who owns that part of the film copyright which includes the soundtrack? What is the position about acts done in relation to the sound recording before January 1, 1996? Transitional provisions provide that whoever was the owner of the copyright in the film immediately before January 1, 1996 is to have from that date what are termed "corresponding rights" as copyright owner in the existing soundtrack which is now to be treated as part of the film.[225] The "corresponding rights" are presumably the rights which correspond to those which the owner of the copyright has in a film, with accompanying soundtrack, made after January 1, 1996. These rights are without prejudice to the rights of the owner of the sound recording copyright which exists in the soundtrack.[226] Generally acts done and arrangements made in relation to the sound recording before this date are saved. Thus the Regulations provide that anything done under or in relation to the copyright in the sound recording continues to have effect, so far as concerns the soundtrack, in relation to the film as in relation to the sound recording.[227] A licence to exploit the sound recording as a film soundtrack would therefore remain good. Again, anything done after January 1, 1996 in pursuance of arrangements for the exploitation of the sound recording made before that date will not infringe the copyright in the film.[228]

5–53

Film soundtracks: the 1956 Act. The position of these works has already been

5–54

---

[219] See paras 4–54 et seq., above.

[220] CDPA 1988 s.5B(2), (5). It will be recalled that in relation to questions of authorship and first ownership, it is only in relation to works made after August 1, 1989 that the 1988 Act applies.

[221] CDPA 1988 s.9(2)(aa). See para.4–42, above.

[222] See paras 4–55 et seq., above.

[223] Duration of Copyright and Rights in Performances Regulations 1995 reg.26(1).

[224] CDPA 1988 s.5. This discussion of the ownership provisions of the 1988 Act of course only relates to works made after August 1, 1989.

[225] Duration of Copyright and Rights in Performances Regulations 1995 reg.26(2). This provision obviously includes the particular case under consideration, that is, first ownership.

[226] reg.26(2) and see also CDPA 1988 s.5B(5).

[227] reg.26(3).

[228] reg.26(4).

considered.[229] The 1988 Act provides that film soundtracks to which the 1956 Act applied[230] are now to be treated as sound recordings and not as part of the film and further provides that the first owner of the copyright in such a film is to be treated as having been the first owner of the copyright in the sound recording.[231] Thus, it seems, whoever was the maker of the cinematograph film[232] will be treated as having been the first owner of the soundtrack which is now to be regarded as a sound recording rather than a film.

5–55   **Film soundtracks: the 1911 Act.** Copyright does not subsist in a film as such made before June 1, 1957[233] so that film soundtracks made before this date are protected as sound recordings and the first owner of copyright will be determined accordingly.[234]

(iv) Joint first ownership of copyright in sound recordings and films

5–56   **The 1988 Act.** Sound recordings and films to which the 1988 Act applies may be the works of joint authorship and thus joint first ownership.[235] As already seen,[236] a film made after July 1, 1994, will always be a work of joint first ownership unless the producer and principal director are one and the same person.

5–57   **The 1956 Act: films.** As already noted,[237] there seems no reason why there should not have been joint makers and thus joint first owners of the copyright in these works.

5–58   **The 1956 and 1911 Acts: sound recordings.** Since an original "plate" or recording could in principle have been jointly owned, there seems no reason why such works could not have had joint first owners.[238]

D. BROADCASTS

5–59   **The 1988 Act.** It has already been seen[239] that with effect from October 31, 2003, the definition of "broadcast" was altered as part of the amendments to implement the Information Society Directive, and the expression now also includes within its scope cable broadcasts and internet transmissions transmissions which are in the nature of broadcasts. In relation to broadcasts made after August 1, 1989, the 1988 Act provides that the first owner of the copyright is the author and thus the person making the broadcast or, in the case of a broadcast which relays another broadcast by reception and immediate re-transmission, the person making that other broadcast.[240] The question of who is the person making the broadcast has already been considered.[241]

5–60   **Cable programmes.** In relation to cable programmes which constitute "broadcasts" within the new definition of this expression, the first owner of the copy-

---

[229] See para.4–57, above.
[230] i.e. those made between June 1, 1957 and August 1, 1989.
[231] CDPA 1988 Sch.1 para.8(2).
[232] As to which, see para.4–52, above.
[233] CDPA 1988 Sch.1 para.7(1).
[234] See para.4–53, above.
[235] See para.4–59, above.
[236] See para.4–49, above.
[237] See para.4–60, above.
[238] As to the ordinary rule relating to first ownership of such works, see para.4–35, above.
[239] para.3–93, above.
[240] CDPA 1988 s.9(2)(b).
[241] See para.4–62, above.

right is the person determined in accordance with the above rule. This now applies to all cable broadcasts coming into existence after August 1, 1989. As to those cable programmes which came into existence between August 1, 1989 and October 31, 2003 which are now entitled to copyright as broadcast,[242] the author and thus first owner of the copyright was previously defined as the person who created the cable programme, being the person providing the cable programme service in which the programme was included.[243] This definition has, however, now been repealed along with s.7 of the Act, and in relation to these cable programmes, which are now to be regarded as broadcasts, the new, general definition of author and thus first owner apparently applies. As pointed out when dealing with the authorship provisions,[244] it is not clear whether there will have been any cable programmes in respect of which the person providing the cable programme service in which the programme was included will have been someone different from the person "making" the transmission, as that expression is defined. If so, it seems that as at October 31, 2003 there will have been a retrospective change of authorship of the work and potentially, therefore, of ownership.

Joint authors. Where more than one person is to be taken as making the broadcast in accordance with the above definition, then the broadcast is to be treated as a work of joint authorship and thus joint first ownership.[245]   **5–61**

The 1956 Act. Under the 1956 Act the BBC or the IBA, as the case may have been, were the persons entitled to the copyright in broadcasts made by them.[246] In relation to what were described as cable programmes, there is no copyright in cable programmes included in a cable programme service before January 1, 1985.[247] As to cable programmes made after this date, the 1956 Act, as amended, stated that the person providing the cable programme service in which a cable programme was included should be entitled to the copyright in such a work.[248]   **5–62**

Pre-1956 Act broadcasts. There is no copyright in broadcasts made before June 1, 1957.[249]   **5–63**

E. TYPOGRAPHICAL ARRANGEMENTS

The 1988 Act. In relation to a typographical arrangement of a published edition made after August 1, 1989, the first owner of copyright is the author, that is, the publisher of it.[250]   **5–64**

The 1956 Act. Under the 1956 Act, the publisher was to be entitled to the copyright subsisting in a published edition.[251]   **5–65**

---

[242] See para.3–93, above.
[243] CDPA 1988 s.9(2)(c).
[244] See para.4–63, above.
[245] CDPA 1988 s.10(2).
[246] Copyright Act 1956 s.14(2). See para.4–65, above.
[247] s.14A(11), as inserted by the Cable and Broadcasting Act 1984; CDPA 1988 Sch.1 para.9(b).
[248] Copyright Act 1956 s.14A(3), as inserted by the Cable and Broadcasting Act 1984.
[249] CDPA 1988 Sch.1 para.9(a).
[250] CDPA 1988 s.9(2)(d). As to the meaning of "publisher", see s.175(1).
[251] Copyright Act 1956 s.15(2).

2. TRANSMISSION OF TITLE

A. INTRODUCTION

5–66   Today, copyright is a statutory property right,[252] being a thing in action,[253] which is transmissible by assignment or by operation of law as personal or moveable property.[254] This section is concerned with transfers of the legal title. Transfers of the equitable title are dealt with later.

5–67   **The root of title.** Copyright has two features which combine to create difficulties when it comes to establishing title. The first is the potential longevity of many works, the period of copyright for literary, dramatic, musical and artistic works and films now being the lifetime of the author plus 70 years. Many works made in the nineteenth century are therefore still in copyright. The second is the absence of any system of registration of title,[255] or the existence of any rule whereby a good title can be deduced from a transfer made at least a certain number of years ago,[256] or a concept equivalent to a possessory title to land.[257] The result is that, if required, the title to a work has to be proved by establishing a chain of title from the first owner through to the present claimant.[258] If the work is an old one, or is one which has passed through the hands of several owners this may present difficulties in obtaining the necessary evidence and is also likely to be expensive. Apart from insurance, however, there is no short cut if a purchaser requires title to be fully deduced. In the context of litigation, suggestions that the burden of proof be altered such that the defendant should be required to prove that the claimant does *not* own the copyright have been rejected.[259] A claimant has two means of mitigating the problem as the law stands today, neither of them usually being very effective in practice. The first is to serve a notice to admit the various facts which establish the claimant's title,[260] thereby throwing the risk of having to pay the costs of proving title on the defendant, whatever the result of the action. The second, where the appropriate material is available, is to seek to rely on one or more of the various statutory presumptions.[261] Occasionally, too, a claimant may be able to invoke the maxim *omnia paesumunter rite esse acta.* So, for example, where a party has "acquired" the copyright by purchase and there has been a long course of dealing by him on the basis that he owns the copyright, without objection from anyone who might have a rival claim, a court may be able to infer that everything was done to carry out the intention of the parties, and that therefore title was transferred by a valid assignment.[262]

5–68   **Distinction between transfer of title to copyright and to physical material.** It

---

[252] CDPA 1988 s.1(1).

[253] *Orwin v Att Gen* [1998] F.S.R. 415 at 421.

[254] CDPA 1988 s.90.

[255] Compare patents, registered trade marks and registered designs.

[256] Compare, in the case of unregistered land, the Law of Property Act 1925 s.23.

[257] There can be no "possession" of copyright: *Chaplin v Leslie Frewin (Publishers) Ltd* [1966] Ch. 71.

[258] It may of course be the case that an old agreement can no longer be found or is known to have been lost. In such circumstances, it is permissible to adduce secondary evidence of it and its contents, and the court will attach such weight to that evidence as is appropriate in all the circumstances. The old "best evidence" rule no longer applies: *Springsteen v Masquerade Music Ltd* [2001] E.M.L.R. 654, CA.

[259] See, e.g. the Gregory Committee Report in 1952 (Cmnd. 8662, para.286) and the Whitford Committee Report in 1977 (Cmnd. 6732, para.729). In general, the Gregory Committee concluded that the burden which a copyright owner may have to labour under is something he has to expect in return for the great benefits conferred by a copyright system that requires no registration or fee.

[260] i.e. under CPR r.32.18.

[261] As to these, see paras 21–17 et seq., below.

[262] *Dennison v Ashdown* (1897) 13 T.L.R. 226, following *Dennison v Boosey* (Unreported) to the

is important to recognise that ownership of copyright in a work is distinct from the ownership of the physical material in which the copyright work may happen to be embodied. Just as the owner of the physical material on or in which a copyright work is first recorded is not necessarily the first owner of the copyright,[263] so the transfer of title to the original physical material does not by itself to operate to transfer the title to the copyright[264] any more than an assignment of copyright operates by itself transfer title to the physical material on which the work may be embodied. Copyright is not a chattel and so cannot be passed by delivery.[265] Thus, to take an obvious example, the purchaser of a book or DVD becomes the owner of the physical article but he does not thereby become the owner of any part of the copyright in the works reproduced in it. The copyright in the literary work remains with the copyright owner, who enjoys and is entitled to enforce all the exclusive rights of copying, publication, adaptation, sale, rental and so on conferred on him by copyright law. The purchaser does not acquire by his purchase any right, either by way of assignment or licence, to exercise any of those exclusive rights. In the case of the purchase of the physical material on which the copyright work was first fixed, for example an author's manuscript or an original painting, it may not be so obvious that the mere fact of purchase includes neither the right to make copies of it nor the right to prevent the author or artist or anyone else from making copies.[266] It is, nevertheless, the fact that such a purchaser can only obtain the right to make copies of the work he has purchased by taking an assignment of copyright or entering into some form of licence. It has been said that there are occasions when the retention of the copyright by the vendor of an article, such as a picture, involves an "unnatural dissociation of two kinds of property" and, consequently, the court will lean towards construing a document given at the time of the sale as an assignment of copyright.[267] It is, however, suggested that today, with perhaps a greater appreciation of the commercial value of copyright and the ease of duplication, there are few if any works of which it can be said that the separation of the copyright and its physical embodiment involves any unnatural dissociation. In the end, and in the absence of any express terms, the issue will be what terms, if any, are to be implied from the circumstances of the sale.[268]

In the same way, the sale of an article by means of which a work can be easily reproduced (for example, a copy of it in digital form or of artwork in the form of negatives) does not by itself convey the copyright in the work.[269] The contract of sale may of course expressly or impliedly include a term whereby the copyright is also agreed to be sold.[270] More frequently, a contract of sale of such an article will, by necessary implication, include a licence to use the article for some limited purposes and thus to do what would otherwise be an infringement. This subject is

---

same effect. The copyright work had been purchased at an auction of a music publishers' plates and copyrights.
[263] See para.5–02, above.
[264] *Nicol v Barranger* [1917–1923] Mac.C.C. 219.
[265] *Performing Right Society Ltd v London Theatre of Varieties Ltd* [1924] A.C. 1 at 26.
[266] Unless the purchaser can frame an action in, for example, contract, confidence or trust.
[267] *London Printing, etc., Alliance Ltd v Cox* [1891] 3 Ch. 291 at 304. In fact, there was no dispute that the contract included the sale of the copyright as one of its terms, the only issue being whether the copyright was intended to pass at once or later.
[268] See *Wilson v Weiss Art Pty Ltd* (1995) 31 I.P.R. 423 at 432 (Fed. Ct of Aus.).
[269] *Cooper v Stephens* [1895] 1 Ch. 567 (where the sale of printing blocks included a licence for the purchaser, but no one else, to use them), followed in *Marshall (W.) & Co Ltd v Bull (A.H.) Ltd* (1901) 85 L.T. 77, CA.
[270] Even so, the copyright will only be transferred if the formalities for an assignment of the legal title are satisfied, and this will depend on the form and substance of the contract. As to formalities, see para.5–85, below.

dealt with elsewhere.[271] There are also circumstances in which the courts will hold that the vendor of an article may not derogate from his grant by asserting his copyright against a purchaser in order to prevent him from repairing the article. This is also considered elsewhere.[272]

5–69   **Letters, manuscripts, etc.** For the same reasons, while the property in a letter will usually pass to the recipient,[273] the copyright will remain with the writer. Ownership of copyright apart, and depending on the circumstances, the recipient may at one extreme have a licence to publish it[274] or, at the other, be liable in an action for breach of confidence for disclosing its contents. The position in relation to manuscripts submitted to a publisher is considered elsewhere.[275]

5–70   **Bequest of original materials.** The one exception to this general rule applies in the case of a bequest of the original material on which a work is recorded or embodied. This exception is considered in detail below.[276]

5–71   **Transfer of title by one joint owner.** Where the legal title of one joint owner is assigned to a third party, the third party will become the joint legal owner of the copyright together with the other joint owners.

5–72   **Transfer of copyright by "foreign" transaction.** Whether, and to what extent, UK copyright is assignable is a matter of the law of the United Kingdom.[277] Where the proper law of the instrument is foreign law, the instrument must therefore comply with the formal requirements of the 1988 Act[278] if it is to transfer UK copyright but at the same time if, as an agreement, it is invalid under that law (for example because some formality has not been observed) it will not be effective to transfer the UK copyright.[279] An act purporting to expropriate UK copyright which is not recognised by English law will be of no effect.[280]

5–73   **Transfer of foreign copyrights.** An assignment may, on its true construction, show an intention to pass foreign copyrights, or rights equivalent to UK copyright, as well as the copyright conferred by the Copyright, Designs and Patents Act 1988. It should be borne in mind that the rules relating to the transfer of such foreign rights will be governed by the law of the particular foreign system and not that of the United Kingdom.

5–74   **Summary of law affecting transfers of title.** Before considering what amounts to an effective transfer of the legal title, it is convenient to summarise the legal effect of the various kinds of possible transaction.

5–75   *Transmission of legal title.* In the case of an effective and immediate transmission of the legal title, whether of the whole or part of the copyright[281]:
     (a) If the transferee was a bona fide purchaser for value without notice he will

---

[271] See para.5–217, below.

[272] See para.5–235, below.

[273] *Pope v Curl* (1741) 2 Atk. 341; *Oliver v Oliver* (1861) 11 C.B. (N.S.) 139.

[274] As with a letter written to a newspaper for publication. See para.5–224, below.

[275] See paras 26–55 et seq., below.

[276] See para.5–131, below.

[277] *Peer International Corp v Termidor Music Publishers Ltd* [2002] EWHC 2675 (Ch); [2004] R.P.C. 22, para.24, citing Dicey & Morris, *The Conflict of* Laws, 13th edn (London: Sweet & Maxwell), r.118(1)(b) and *Campbell Connolly & Co Ltd v Noble* [1963] 1 W.L.R. 252 at 255.

[278] CDPA 1988 s.90(3). See para.5–85, below.

[279] *Peer International Corp v Termidor Music Publishers Ltd* [2002] EWHC 2675 (Ch); [2004] RPC 22, para.25; [2003] EWCA Civ 1156; [2004] Ch. 212, CA, para.7.

[280] *Peer International Corp v Termidor Music Publishers Ltd* [2003] EWCA Civ 1156.

[281] See, as to partial assignments, paras 5–97 et seq., below.

take free of any prior equitable interests, including those of any equitable assignee. He will also take free of any earlier licences granted by the copyright owner.[282] In all other cases, he will take subject to such equities or licences. His title will be secure against anyone to whom his assignor subsequently purports to assign the copyright or to grant any licence, whether or not the latter had notice of the previous transfer.

(b) The transferee can sue for infringement in his own name without adding any other party.[283]

Creation of equitable title. An event which does not pass the legal title immediately may nevertheless result in the creation of an equitable title in the transferee. This commonly arises in the following situations[284]:   **5–76**

(a) A purported but defective assignment of the legal title will usually be construed as an agreement to assign and thus operates as an equitable assignment of the copyright, provided it is specifically enforceable, in particular, provided that it is supported by consideration.

(b) Whether or not it satisfies the technical requirements for an assignment of the legal title, the transaction may on its true construction amount to an agreement to assign rather than a purported immediate assignment. If the agreement is specifically enforceable, the assignee will again be entitled to the copyright in equity. Where such an agreement amounts to an agreement to assign the copyright in an existing work at some future time,[285] the assignee's equitable title will arise when that time comes.

The position of someone who acquires an equitable title only can be summarised as follows:[286]

(a) He can rely on his equitable title to bring proceedings for infringement but usually he can only succeed at trial if he has by then perfected his legal title by taking an assignment from the legal owner or, in the absence of such an assignment, if he has joined the legal owner of the copyright, either as claimant or defendant.

(b) His title is not binding on a bona fide purchaser of the legal title without notice of the equitable title. He is therefore liable to be sued and otherwise have his rights defeated by such legal owner.

(c) Except as against such a purchaser of the legal title, however, he will have a defence of consent to any action for infringement brought by the legal owner.

These various situations are discussed in more detail in the following sections of this work.

Licence only. Alternatively, the effect of the transaction, while not amounting to an assignment either in law or equity, may amount to a licence. This may be: **5–77**

(a) An exclusive licence, which, depending on its form, may give the licensee a right to bring an action for infringement against third parties[287]; or

(b) A non-exclusive licence which complies with the requirements of s.101A

---

[282] See CDPA 1988 s.90(4) and para.5–78, below.
[283] But see para.5–95, below, as to accrued causes of action, and paras 5–207 et seq., below, as to exclusive licensees.
[284] See paras 5–175 et seq., below, for a full discussion of this topic.
[285] As to the special case of an assignment of the copyright in a "future work", see para.5–108, below.
[286] Again, see paras 5–190 et seq., below, for a full discussion of this topic.
[287] See paras 5–207 et seq., below.

of the 1988 Act,[288] which will confer on the licensee a right to bring an action for infringement against third parties but which will otherwise merely provide a defence to an action for infringement brought by the copyright owner; or

(c) Some lesser licence, which will merely provide a defence to an action for infringement brought by the copyright owner.[289]

5–78   **The effect of a valid transfer of the legal title.** The position in outline has already been discussed, but an owner generally has an unfettered right to transfer his copyright and the transferee will take free of any obligations or burdens to which he was subject. This general rule is subject to three limitations.

(a) First, where there are outstanding equitable interests[290] then, except in the case of a bona fide purchaser for value without actual or constructive notice, the transferee will take subject to such equities. Thus if the owner held the legal title on trust for another or, for example, had granted an option to another to acquire the copyright, the transferee is liable to be divested of the copyright at the suit of the owner of the equitable right.

(b) Secondly, and again except in the case of a bona fide purchaser for value without actual or constructive notice, a transferee will be bound by any licence granted by the copyright owner.[291]

(c) Thirdly, a transferee may possibly be bound by contractual obligations of his predecessor under the doctrine of "benefit and burden". This is considered in more detail in para.5–80 ("Assignor's rights to royalties, etc.")

Equities and licences created by a predecessor of the transferor will similarly bind the transferee unless, at some stage in the chain, the legal title has been acquired by a purchaser for value without notice.[292] These rules are obviously a trap for an assignee, who takes the risk of not investigating his assignor's title.

5–79   **Agreement not to assign.** If the copyright owner has contracted not to assign the copyright, it is suggested that an assignment in breach of that agreement will nevertheless be effective to transfer the legal title. The same is true where he has agreed not to assign the copyright without first obtaining consent. The opposite conclusion has, however, been reached in New Zealand, on the grounds that an agreement, express or implied, not to assign rights in personam, or not to assign them without consent, should generally be specifically enforced as between the immediate parties, unless there is some strong reason why that course should not be adopted.[293] However, the reasoning does not appear to give full weight to the fact that copyright is a property right. The fact that a copyright owner has agreed to pay royalties or share profits with another will not by itself be sufficient to give rise to an implied term not to transfer the copyright.[294]

5–80   **Assignor's rights to royalties, etc.** In general, where an owner assigns copyright in return for a promise to pay royalties, he cannot sue a third party to whom the copyright has been assigned for those royalties unless a novation of the original

---

[288] As to which, see paras 5–213, below.

[289] See para.5–198, below.

[290] As to such interests, see paras 5–174 et seq., below

[291] CDPA 1988 s.90(4).

[292] As to this rule in relation to licences, see CDPA 1988 s.90(4).

[293] *New Zealand Payroll Software Systems Ltd v Advanced Management Systems Ltd* [2003] 3 N.Z.L.R. 1, applying *Linden Gardens Trust Ltd v Lenesta Sludge Disposals Ltd* [1994] 1 A.C. 85.

[294] *Sims v Marryat* (1851) 17 Q.B. 281.

contract has taken place: no privity of contract exists between them.[295] The assignor retains his contractual rights against his assignee but obviously these may be worthless in the event of the assignee's insolvency.[296] In *Barker v Stickney*,[297] various grounds were advanced for making the subsequent purchaser liable for royalties but were all rejected:

(a) An unpaid vendor's lien. *Held*: the assignor/vendor had accepted the assignee/purchaser's covenant to pay royalties in satisfaction of his claim for the price and was therefore not an unpaid vendor.

(b) A charge on the copyright. *Held*: a charge could only arise if it had been clearly and expressly created, and this was not the case.[298]

(c) A burden which ran with the copyright, on the general principle stated in *De Mattos v Gibson*.[299] *Held*: since it was settled law[300] that a purchaser of a chattel is not bound by mere notice of stipulations entered into by his vendor, and there was nothing to distinguish a chose in action such as copyright from chattels or land, a person acquiring copyright was not bound by notice of his predecessor's promise.

As to the burden of the obligation to pay royalties running with the copyright, it has since been confirmed that the *De Mattos v Gibson* principle would not, even at its fullest extent, assist because it only enables negative restrictions to be enforced, not positive obligations.[301] An alternative argument which possibly still remains open is the principle of "benefit and burden".[302] In order to succeed here, however, it seems that it will be necessary to show that on the transfer from the original assignee the copyright had been transferred subject to the transferee discharging the obligation to pay royalties.[303] A simple transfer of the copyright, or of the benefit of the contract, which did not make it clear that the original assignee did not intend to remain liable for payment of royalties, would, it seems not be enough.[304] This rule is mitigated somewhat for assignments made after May 11, 2000 by the Contracts (Rights of Third Parties) Act, 1999. This permits some types of third party to enforce a term of a contract either if the contract expressly provides that he may[305] or if the term purports to confer a benefit on him.[306] However, the original assignor is not normally able to ensure that subsequent assignments will be in terms that confer rights on him under the Act. For this and other reasons, therefore, it is always in the interests of an author who depends upon the continued payment of royalties or performance of other

---

[295] *Bagot Pneumatic Tyre Co v Clipper Pneumatic Tyre Co* [1902] 1 Ch. 146 and see *Beswick v Beswick* [1968] A.C. 58. See Adams, "The Passing of the Burden of Royalty Payments" [2007] I.P.Q. 403.

[296] As in *Re Grant-Richards Ex p. Deeping* [1907] 2 K.B. 33. The limited protection given by the Bankruptcy Act 1914 given to an author in the case of a publisher's insolvency is discussed at para.5–82, below.

[297] [1919] 1 K.B. 121. But see Adams, " *Barker v Stickney* revisited" [1998] I.P.Q. 113, arguing that *Barker v Stickney* was wrongly decided.

[298] But see Adams, *Barker v Stickney* revisited" [1998] I.P.Q. 113, suggesting that today a court may be more ready to imply a charge.

[299] (1859) 4 De G. & J. 276.

[300] Applying *Taddy & Co v Sterious & Co* [1904] 1 Ch. 354; *McCruther v Pitcher* [1904] 2 Ch. 306; and *Dunlop Tyre Co Ltd v Selfridge & Co Ltd* [1915] A.C. 847.

[301] See *Swiss Bank Corp v Lloyds Bank Ltd* [1979] Ch. 584.

[302] See *Tito v Waddell (No.2)* [1977] Ch. 106.

[303] See *Tito v Waddell (No.2)* [1977] Ch. 106 at 302 and *Law Debenture Corp. v Ural Caspian Oil Corp. Ltd* [1993] 1 W.L.R. 138 at 147.

[304] But see *John v James* [1991] F.S.R. 397 where it seems to have been taken for granted that an assignee who acquires the benefit of an original publisher's rights will take subject to any burden of exploitation, including the ordinary burden of accounting to the writer for his contractual entitlement to royalties.

[305] Contracts (Rights of Third Parties) Act, 1999 s.1(1)(a).

[306] s.1(1)(b). This subsection does not apply if "on a proper construction of the contract it appears that the parties did not intend the term to be enforceable by the third party"— s.1(2).

contractual obligations, to enter into a licence for the exploitation of his work rather than an assignment.

5–81 **The fiduciary duties of a publisher-assignee.** A publisher who takes an assignment of copyright in return for an agreement to pay royalties may be subject to fiduciary duties in addition to his contractual duties. The existence and scope of any such duty will be subject to the express terms of the agreement,[307] but, where the agreement is silent, the nature of the duty will have to be worked out from the other terms and surrounding circumstances. Generally, it seems that a publisher will have a fiduciary duty to account for monies received and to exploit the copyright only in a way which the publisher honestly considers to be for the joint benefit of the parties.[308] Other duties may be implicit from the relationship, for example, one not to make any profit for himself which is not brought into account when computing the writer's royalties, such that the publisher will be in breach by setting up overseas subsidiaries to deduct greater sums than are justified by the work involved. Factors which may be relevant here include whether[309]:

(a) the agreement is to endure for the full term of copyright;

(b) the works in question comprise all works written by the author during the term of the agreement;

(c) the entire copyright is assigned to the publisher;

(d) the publisher has complete control over the method of exploitation;

(e) the exploitation is for the benefit of the publisher alone or for their joint benefit, such that the agreement is in the nature of a joint venture, the author having to place trust and confidence in the publisher over the manner in which the publisher discharges its exploitation functions;

(f) it is implicit that the publisher is to account for a fixed share of royalties from only one pool, including sales from home and overseas markets, such that it is implicit that there would not be some other pool, for example sums earned by wholly owned overseas subsidiaries, in which the author is not to share.

5–82 **Bankruptcy Act 1914.** This Act gave some protection to authors by preventing a publisher's trustee in bankruptcy from selling or authorising the sale of copies of his work or dealing with his interests in the copyright except on terms which ensured that the author would receive such royalties as would have been payable by the publisher.[310] The provision has been repealed,[311] but continues to have effect in relation to any transaction entered into before the commencement of the Insolvency Act 1986.[312]

---

[307] *Kelly v Cooper* [1993] A.C. 205 at 215, PC.

[308] *John v James* [1991] F.S.R. 397.

[309] These were the factors considered relevant in *John v James* [1991] F.S.R. 397 in imposing such a duty on the publisher.

[310] Bankruptcy Act 1914 s.60. The section did not apply where the publisher was a company (*Re Health Promotion Ltd* [1932] 1 Ch. 65). As to whether the provision was applicable where the publisher had a mere licence, see *Henham v Alston Rivers Ltd* [1911–1916] Mac.C.C. 330 and *Copinger*, 12th edn, para.1162.

[311] Insolvency Act 1985, as replaced by the Insolvency Act 1986.

[312] Insolvency Act 1986 Sch.11 para.15.

B. TRANSFER OF LEGAL TITLE BY ASSIGNMENT

(i) General

Introduction. As already noted, copyright is today transmissible by assignment as personal or moveable property.[313]   **5–83**

Transitional. It may be necessary in the case of old works to consider the effect of transactions entered into before the passing of the 1988 Act. With the exceptions which will be noted, the law on assignments under the 1988 Act is to the same effect as that under the previous Acts. The 1988 Act provides that any document made before August 1, 1989, which affected the ownership of the copyright in a work made before that date (an "existing work"), or which transferred an interest or right in respect of the copyright in such a work, is to have the corresponding operation in relation to copyright in the work under the 1988 Act.[314] The effect of this is that if an assignment was effective to transfer the copyright or an interest in the copyright conferred under the earlier Acts, then it is effective to transfer the copyright or the corresponding interest conferred by the 1988 Act. The Act also provides that expressions used in pre-August 1, 1989 documents are to be construed in accordance with their effect immediately before this date.[315]   **5–84**

There should also be borne in mind the general provisions contained in the 1988 Act for securing the continuity of the law so far as the new copyright provisions (i.e. the provisions of the 1988 Act relating to copyright[316]) re-enact, with or without modification, earlier provisions. The following general principles are laid down[317]:

   (a) A reference in an instrument or other document to copyright, or to a work or other subject matter in which copyright subsists, which apart from the 1988 Act would be construed as referring to copyright under the 1956 Act, is to be construed, so far as may be required for continuing its effect, as being, or as the case may require, including, a reference to copyright under the 1988 Act or to works in which copyright subsists under that Act.[318]

   (b) A reference (express or implied) in an instrument or other document to a provision repealed by the 1988 Act is to be construed, so far as may be required for continuing its effect, as a reference to the corresponding provision of that Act.[319]

(ii) Requirements for a valid assignment

Requirements for valid assignment of the legal title: the 1988 Act. An assign-   **5–85**

---

[313] CDPA 1988 s.90.

[314] CDPA 1988 Sch.1 para.25(1). The effect of this provision, no more but no less, is to preserve the legal effect of a pre-commencement assignment or agreement to assign. It does not attempt to legislate as to the effect of such a document and only preserves such effect as the document originally had. See *Novello & Co Ltd v Keith Prowse Music Publishing Co Ltd* [2004] EWHC 766 (Ch), para.9; [2004] R.P.C. 48. The decision of Patten J. was upheld on appeal: [2004] EWCA Civ 1776; [2005] R.P.C. 23. The 1956 Act (Sch.7 para.28(1)) contained a provision to similar effect. As to the 1911 Act, see s.24(1) and paras 5–152 et seq., below.

[315] CDPA 1988 Sch.1 para.25(2). See the previous footnote as to this provision's effect, which is the same as para.25(1). Sch.7 para.28(2) of the 1956 Act was to similar effect, adding that this was so "notwithstanding that a different meaning is assigned to them for the purpose of this Act."

[316] CDPA 1988 Sch.1 para.1(1).

[317] These general principles have effect subject to any specific transitional provision or saving and to any express amendment made by the 1988 Act. See Sch.1 para.4(6).

[318] CDPA 1988 Sch.1 para.4(2).

[319] Sch.1 para.4(5).

ment of the legal title to copyright is not effective unless it is in writing signed by or on behalf of the assignor.[320] "Writing" includes any form of notation or code, whether by hand or otherwise and regardless of the method by which, or medium in, or on which, it is recorded.[321] No notice to anyone is required to perfect the transfer.[322] Minors[323] can own and dispose of copyrights in the same way as adults, but subject to the usual rules as to infants' contracts.[324] In the case of a body corporate, the requirement that the assignment should be signed by or on behalf of any person is satisfied by the affixing of its seal.[325] An assignment may also of course be executed by a company by it being signed by someone on the company's behalf. If the assignment is signed on behalf of the assignor, the person so signing must obviously have the authority of the assignor in order to transfer the copyright.[326] A receiver appointed by the court over partnership assets, which include copyrights, will usually have authority to sign an assignment of any copyright "on behalf of" the partners.[327] A receiver appointed out of court under a debenture will invariably have sufficient authority by virtue of the terms of the debenture to enable him to dispose of the company's property and execute documents on its behalf.

5–86   **Assignments under the 1956 and 1911 Acts.** The provisions under these Acts relating to the formal requirements for an assignment of existing copyright were to the same effect as those of the 1988 Act.[328]

5–87   **What words will effect an assignment?** An assignment of copyright does not have to be in any special form, other than in writing, signed by or on behalf of the assignor.[329] Thus any written, signed instrument may constitute an assignment of copyright even though the word "copyright" is not used in the document if, on its true construction, it was intended that the copyright should thereby pass.[330] Thus, for example, the copyright would be carried by general expressions such as "all right and title in the business" or "the assets" of the business if the copyright formed part of the assets of that business and it is apparent from the surrounding circumstances that this is what was intended.[331] In the same way, it is not necessary that the words "grant" or "assign" be used if an intention to assign the copy-

---

[320] CDPA 1988 s.90(3). See Vol.2 J1.i, for a precedent of an assignment of copyright.

[321] s.178.

[322] *Performing Right Society Ltd v London Theatre of Varieties Ltd* [1924] A.C. 1. As to assignment of accrued causes of action, see para.5–95, below.

[323] See the Family Law Reform Act 1969 (c.46).

[324] *Chaplin v Leslie Frewin (Publishers) Ltd* [1966] Ch. 71.

[325] CDPA 1988 s.176(1). This provision was new in the 1988 Act. Where the company does not have a common seal, a document signed by a director and the secretary, or by two directors, and expressed to be executed by the company, has the same effect as if executed under the company's common seal. See the Companies Act 1985 s.36A(4).

[326] *Beloff v Pressdram Ltd* [1973] F.S.R. 33; *Heptulla v Orient Longman Ltd* [1989] F.S.R. 598 at 610.

[327] *Murray v King* [1986] F.S.R. 116 (Fed. Ct of Aus.). The reasoning (pp.129, 137) was that although the receiver was not the agent of the partners and was not in "possession" (sic—see the footnote to para.5–67, above) of the copyright, the partners must nevertheless have been taken to have anticipated the possibility of a receiver being empowered by the court to sell the assets in a receivership (p.129), since otherwise they might not obtain that to which they were entitled (p.137). The sale could therefore be said to be on the partners' behalf.

[328] Copyright Act 1956 s.36; Copyright Act 1911 s.5(2). As to pre-1911 Act assignments, see paras 5–96 et seq., below.

[329] See para.5–85, above.

[330] *Cray Valley Ltd v Deltech Europe Ltd* [2003] EWHC (Ch) 728, para.69; *Murray v King* [1986] F.S.R. 116 (Fed. Ct of Aus.); *Greenfield Products Ltd v Rover-Scott Bonnar Ltd* [1990] A.I.P.C. 90–667. As already noted (see para.5–72, above), whether, and to what extent, UK copyright is assignable is a matter of UK law. Where the agreement is governed by foreign law, it must be construed in accordance with that law.

[331] *Cray Valley Ltd v Deltech Europe Ltd* [2003] EWHC (Ch) 728, para.69; *Murray v King* [1986]

right can be gathered from the context.[332] Many transactions are informal in nature and it is often difficult to determine whether the intention of the party in signing a document was to transfer the copyright or simply grant or confirm the grant of a licence. This topic is dealt with elsewhere,[333] but in general the whole background may need to be looked at to discover the parties' true intention. Where the signed document forms part of a transaction in which a copyright work was made for a purchaser, and where it is clear that it was contemplated by both that the purchaser was to have exclusive use of the work, it may be easy to conclude that copyright was intended to pass with the physical subject matter. On this basis, the wording on mere invoices[334] or receipts[335] has been held to amount to an assignment.

Assignment of "copyright": extent of assignment. As an item of property, copyright can in principle, and in the absence of express restriction on its assignability, be disposed of in any lawful way that the owner wants.[336] Copyright is made up of a bundle of various rights. The extent to which a partial assignment of these rights is permissible is considered below but in general an assignment of "copyright" will operate, in the absence of contrary intention, to convey to the assignee all the rights which go to make up the copyright.[337] An assignor should therefore always take care that the assignment is drawn in such a way as not to carry rights in excess of those intended to be assigned.   **5–88**

Future rights. In general, an assignment expressed to include future rights cannot operate to transfer the legal title to such rights and will at best operate as an agreement to assign, i.e. an equitable assignment.[338] A statutory exception exists in relation to "future copyright." The topic is considered in more detail later in this chapter.[339]   **5–89**

Subject matter of grant. If there is ambiguity in the subject matter of the grant, extrinsic evidence may be adduced to identify it.[340]   **5–90**

Extent of assignment: new technologies. It is not always clear whether an assignment includes rights which are exercisable by means of technologies which   **5–91**

F.S.R. 116 (Fed. Ct of Aus.); *Greenfield Products Ltd v Rover-Scott Bonnar Ltd* [1990] A.I.P.C. 90–667.

[332] See *Lacy v Toole* (1867) 15 L.T. 512 (an agreement to "let A have" a certain work in discharge of a debt owing to A, sufficient to pass the copyright in the work to A); *British Actors Film Co Ltd v Glover* [1918] 1 K.B. 299 (agreement by the copyright owner to let, and by the defendant to hire, the "right of performing" a comic opera for a term construed as an assignment (or at least an equitable assignment)).

[333] See para.5–206, below.

[334] As in *London Printing, etc., Alliance Ltd v Cox* [1891] 3 Ch. 291 (the words on an invoice, "For pastel picture and entire copyright, 'On the Threshold', £52 10s." sufficient to pass the copyright, the circumstances of the case showing that the title to the copyright was intended to pass at the same time as the picture itself); *Ornamin (UK) Ltd v Bacsa Ltd* [1964] R.P.C. 293 (invoice expressed to be for "two designs for children's plates").

[335] As in: *Savory (E.W.) Ltd v The World of Golf Ltd* [1914] 2 Ch. 566, where the words on a receipt, "Received of Messrs. E.W.S., Ltd, the sum of £2 6s. 6d. for five original card designs, inclusive of all copyrights. Subjects: Four Golfing subjects; one Teddy Bear painting" were held to be a sufficient assignment of the copyright; *Glogau v Land Transport Safety Authority of New Zealand* [1997] 3 N.Z.L.R. 353 (High Ct of N.Z.): "This receipt is to be regarded as full and final payment for unencumbered ownership of the intellectual property and copyright …"; *Comprop Ltd v Moran* [2002] J.L.R. 222 (Royal Ct. of Jersey), where the vendor wrote: "I hereby acknowledge receipt of the sum of £25,614.00 … for the purchase of all copyrights …".

[336] *Crosstown Music Company 1, LLC v Rive Droite Music Ltd* [2010] EWCA Civ 1222, at para.37.

[337] See, for example, CDPA 1988 ss.1(1) and 2(1).

[338] See paras 5–108 and 5–177 et seq., below.

[339] See paras 5–108 et seq., below.

[340] *Savory (E.W.) Ltd v The World of Golf Ltd* [1914] 2 Ch. 566; *The Photocrom Co Ltd v H. & W. Nelson Ltd* [1923–1928] Mac.C.C. 293; *Comcorp (Pty) Ltd v Quipmor CC* (1997) 2 S.A. 599.

were not known at the date of the assignment. This is a question which more frequently arises in the context of commercial licences, and is considered there.[341]

5–92   **Assignor may not reproduce the work.** An author who has assigned the copyright in his work may, like any other person, be restrained by the assignee from reproducing or authorising others to reproduce the work.[342] There is no reservation of such a right in the assignment unless it can be shown that, in the circumstances of the case, it is necessary to imply it to give business efficacy to the transaction.[343]

5–93   **Separate assignments of derivative works.** Where an author has created a second work by using material derived from an earlier work, what is the effect of separate assignments of each work? The point may arise where an author has created several drafts or sketches before the final version of the work. Where the first assignment in time is of the earlier work, the second assignment cannot operate to vest in the assignee any rights which the assignor no longer owns and thus cannot vest in the assignee rights of copyright in the earlier work. He will only have exclusive rights in relation to material which is found only in the later work. Thus, if in exploiting the later work he reproduces a substantial part of the earlier work, he will infringe. His rights as against the first assignee and third parties extend only to the right to complain of exploitation of a substantial part of the new material contained in his work. He cannot of course complain about exploitation of the earlier work itself. If the later work is so far removed from the earlier that although references from the one can be found in the other, the later work does not in fact reproduce any substantial part of it, then they are two independent copyright works and can be exploited independently.

Where the first assignment in time is of the later work, then its effect will depend on its construction but prima facie an assignee of the copyright in the later work can maintain an action for infringement against a person using the first work to the extent it can be said to "reproduce" the later work.[344] This is on the basis that the assignment of the second work must generally be taken to include an assignment of the copyright in the preceding works to the extent that they are found in the final work. Otherwise the assignment would be valueless if confined only to what was new in the final work. The assignment could of course be expressly framed to have this effect.

A similar problem can arise if there is a single assignment of copyright which does not expressly state what is the subject matter of the assignment. Does the assignment extend to all works or only the latest in time? The answer depends on the intention of the parties as gathered from the words used in the assignment when construed against the factual background.[345] Relevant factors may include whether the parties are likely to have contemplated that the assignor should be free to exploit the earlier work and the consequences of the titles to the distinct copyright works becoming separated.

5–94   **Assignment not bona fide: a sham.** The court will always look behind the legal form to the reality of the transaction. The court will regard an assignment as bogus if, though in proper legal form, it was intended to take effect otherwise

---

[341] See paras 5–206 et seq., below.

[342] CDPA 1988 s.64 provides a limited exception in the case of artistic works. See para.9–193, below.

[343] *Performing Right Society Ltd v Harlequin Record Shops Ltd* [1979] F.S.R. 233 at 241.

[344] *Metzler & Co (1920) Ltd v Curwen (J.) & Sons Ltd* [1928–1935] Mac.C.C. 127. Technically, of course, material taken from the earlier work will not reproduce the later work, there being no causal connection.

[345] *Comprop Ltd v Moran* [2002] J.L.R. 222 (Royal Ct. of Jersey), para.104.

than as an assignment in substance and reality.[346] The court will, however, give effect to an assignment which is intended to be in all respects an out and out assignment, even though it was contemplated at the time of the assignment that the assignee would thereby be assisted or enabled to bring proceedings for infringement of the copyright against a third party.[347]

Assignment of accrued causes of action. Where litigation is contemplated and an assignment of copyright is taken to enable an action to be brought or the claimant's legal title perfected, care should also be taken to assign accrued causes of action in respect of past infringements. Otherwise a claimant may be met by a defence that he is not entitled to relief in respect of these acts. The legal title to such accrued causes of action may be passed by an absolute assignment in writing under the assignor's hand coupled with the giving of express notice in writing of the assignment to the infringer.[348] If suitably drafted,[349] therefore, and once notice has been given, the same instrument can be effective in law to transfer not only the copyright but also the rights of action accrued to and vested in the assignor in respect of past infringements of that copyright. Where there is no express mention in the assignment of accrued causes of action, it will be a matter of construction to determine whether the parties in fact intended to transfer such rights. Until notice is given to the infringer,[350] the assignment of the accrued causes of action will only operate in equity[351] so that, as a matter of caution, notice of such assignment should be given to the prospective defendant before the issue of proceedings.[352]

5–95

Pre-1911 Act assignments. The copyright in unpublished works protected at common law could seemingly be transferred orally.[353] An assignment of the copyright in a published literary work either had to be in writing[354] or, if the title had been registered at Stationers' Hall, could be effected by making an entry of the assignment in the register.[355] As regards published musical and dramatic works, the musical scores and books of words were protected as literary works,[356] but an assignment of the copyright did not convey the performing right unless an

5–96

---

[346] *Landeker & Brown v Woolff (L.)* (1907) 52 S.J. 45 (assignment of copyright executed subject to an undertaking that assignee would not reproduce the work without the assignor's consent, the purpose being to enable the assignee to bring an action without joining the assignor, who was a foreigner); *Dennison v Ashdown* (1897) 13 T.L.R. 226; *Beloff v Pressdram Ltd* [1973] F.S.R. 33.

[347] *Beloff v Pressdram Ltd* [1973] F.S.R. 33; *Husqvarna Forest & Garden Ltd v Bridon New Zealand Ltd* (1997) 38 I.P.R. 513 (High Ct of N.Z.) (assignment to local distributor with (apparently) a right to call for a reassignment).

[348] i.e. under the Law Property Act 1925 s.136. Such an assignment will rarely savour of maintenance or champerty since an assignment of a cause of action simultaneously with a property right to which it is ancillary, or of a cause of action in respect of which the assignee has a genuine commercial interest in taking and enforcing for his own benefit, is valid. See *Trendtex Trading Corp v Crédit Suisse* [1982] A.C. 679 at 703 (per Lord Roskill). What is objectionable is trafficking in litigation: *Camdex International Ltd v Bank of Zambia* [1998] Q.B. 22.

[349] As, e.g. in *Beloff v Pressdram* [1973] F.S.R. 33; *Infabrics Ltd v Jaytex Shirt Co Ltd* [1978] F.S.R. 451 at 461. For a precedent, see Vol.2 J1.i.

[350] An assignment of copyright does not of course require the giving of notice.

[351] No consideration is required: *Holt v Heatherfield Trust Ltd* [1942] 2 K.B. 1 at 4.

[352] The assignee may nevertheless commence an action relying on his equitable title: *Weddell v J.A. Pearce & Major* [1988] Ch. 26 at 41. If by no other means, it seems that the legal title will usually be perfected in the course of the action by the assignment being referred to or disclosed: *Weddell v J.A. Pearce & Major*, above. See also *The Aiolos* [1983] 2 Lloyd's Rep.25 at 34, but cf. *Compania Colombiana de Seguros v Pacific Steam Navigation Co* [1965] 1 Q.B. 101.

[353] See *Copinger* 4th edn, p.142.

[354] *Leyland v Stewart* (1876) 4 Ch.D. 419. It was generally considered that such an assignment did not have to be attested. See *Cumberland v Copeland* (1862) 1 Hurl. & C. 194; but see 8 Jur.(N.S.), Part II, p.148.

[355] Literary Copyright Act 1842 s.13.

[356] i.e. under the Literary Copyright Act 1842 ss.20 and 21.

entry to that effect was made in the register at Stationers' Hall.[357] The assignment of the copyright in an engraving probably had to be in writing, attested by two witnesses,[358] and in a work of sculpture, by deed, attested by two witnesses.[359] In the case of a painting, drawing or photograph, it had to be in writing, signed by the proprietor of the copyright or his agent.[360]

(iii) Partial assignments

(a) *Extent of permissible assignments*

5–97   **Partial assignments.** A copyright owner will often wish to divide up the copyright, parcelling out different rights to different persons and, in general, it is permissible to do this. Thus, the 1988 Act makes it clear that there can be separate and independent owners of the copyright in respect of the doing of different acts, or different classes of acts, and at different times. Where different persons are in consequence of partial assignments entitled to different aspects of copyright in a work, the "copyright owner" for the purposes of, for example, infringement, is the person who is entitled to the aspect of the copyright relevant for the purpose of the Act.[361] The Act thus creates separate rights which can be dealt with separately.[362] The divisions which a copyright owner may desire to make will be into different modes of exploitation, different periods of time and different territories. These are considered in turn, below.

5–98   **Extent of permissible assignments: the 1988 Act.** The 1988 Act provides that an assignment may be partial, that is, limited so as to apply to:
   (a) one or more, but not all, of the things the copyright owner has the exclusive right to do;
   (b) part, but not the whole, of the period for which the copyright is to subsist.[363]

As already noted, such a partial assignment will vest in the assignee a proprietary interest in the copyright and enable him to sue in his own name for infringement of that right by third parties. As already mentioned, copyright can in principle, and in the absence of express restriction on its assignability, be disposed of in any lawful way that the owner wants.[364] The permissible extent of an assignment is determined by the above provisions of the 1988 Act, and in this neither the common law rules relating to personal property nor the provisions of s.136 of the Law of Property Act 1925 are relevant.[365]

5–98A   **"Floating Reverter".** A valid assignment may be made of copyright for a period that is not fixed, certain or known at the date of assignment, but depends on future events, for example by way of a contractual provision for reversion of copyright to the assignor in the event of default by the assignee in its

---

[357] Literary Copyright Act 1842 s.22.

[358] See the reasoning in *Jefferys v Boosey* (1854) 4 H.L.C. 815 at 994, 995.

[359] Sculpture Copyright Act 1814 (54 Geo. 3, c.56) s.4.

[360] Fine Arts Copyright Act 1862 (25 & 26 Vict. c.68) s.3.

[361] CDPA 1988 s.173(1).

[362] *J. Albert & Sons Pty Ltd & Others v Fletcher Construction Co Ltd* [1976] R.P.C. 615 (Sup. Ct of N.Z.).

[363] CDPA 1988 s.90(2).

[364] *Crosstown Music Company 1, LLC v Rive Droite Music Ltd* [2010] EWCA Civ 1222, at para.37.

[365] *Crosstown Music Company 1, LLC v Rive Droite Music Ltd* [2010] EWCA Civ 1222, at paras 35, 92.

obligations.[366] Such a provision, if construed as such, operates as an assignment and not as an agreement to assign.

Particular means of exploitation. As already stated, the 1988 Act provides that an assignment of copyright may be "limited so as to apply to one or more, but not all, of the things the copyright owner has the exclusive right to do." Section 16 of the Act sets out the various "acts" which he has the exclusive right to do, for example, the right to copy the work, perform it in public, broadcast it, etc. The word "things", rather than "acts", was used in s.90(2)(a) with the intention of making it clear that an assignment of copyright may be limited to narrower classes of exploitation than these principal categories of "acts".[367] So, as well as divisions into such rights as the reproduction, public performing or broadcasting right,[368] further subdivisions are possible, for example the right to reproduce a work on records (often referred to as the "mechanical right"), broadcast it by satellite, and so on. By way of further example, there seems no reason why an assignment cannot be made of the right to perform a work "professionally".[369]   **5–99**

It seems clear that it was the intention to be able to sub-divide copyright not just into different modes of exploitation, as above, but also into exploitation for different purposes in relation to particular modes, for example, the right to reproduce and publish the work in book form,[370] or in hardback or paperback form. In previous editions of this work,[371] doubt was expressed as to whether this was possible, taking the case of the example of a grant of "serial rights", and arguing that since the infringing act of reproduction took place, if at all, when printing took place, it could not be determined at that stage whether the pages would be bound up for a single publication or for publication in parts over a period, so that it would be impossible to know at that stage whether an infringement had occurred or who was the proper claimant. It is suggested, however, that establishing the purpose for which the work was printed would be a matter for evidence. Such an approach is adopted elsewhere in the 1988 Act.[372] Certainly under the earlier Acts, which appear to have been to the same effect, the validity of such a division was accepted without argument.[373]

Particular means of exploitation: the 1956 Act. The 1956 Act was to the same effect. Thus, the structure of the 1956 Act was that various acts, such as the reproduction of a work, its performance in public, broadcasting, etc., were "restricted" by the copyright, the copyright owner having the exclusive right to do these acts.[374] The Act then provided that an assignment might be limited to one or more, but not all, of the classes of acts which the owner of the copyright had the exclusive right to do, including any one or more classes of acts not separately designated as being restricted by the copyright, but falling within any of the classes of acts so designated.[375]   **5–100**

Particular means of exploitation: the 1911 Act. The effect of the 1911 Act was   **5–101**

---

[366] *Crosstown Music Company 1, LLC v Rive Droite Music Ltd* [2010] EWCA Civ 1222.

[367] See *Hansard*, HL Vol.493, col.1342; HL Vol.495, cols 667 and 668.

[368] As to the primary rights of a copyright owner, see Ch.7, below.

[369] *British Actors Film Co Ltd v Glover* [1918] 1 K.B. 299, decided under the 1911 Act but which seems to have been to the same effect. See para.5–101, below.

[370] See *Hansard*, HL, Vol.493, col.1342; HL Vol.495, cols 667 and 668.

[371] See, e.g. *Copinger*, 13th edn, para.5–19.

[372] So that, for example, whether the decompilation of a computer program amounts to an infringement apparently depends on the purpose for which the decompilation is carried out. See CDPA 1988 s.50B, especially subs.(3)(d).

[373] See para.5–101, below.

[374] See the Copyright Act 1956 s.1(1).

[375] Copyright Act 1956 s.36(2)(a). Note, for example, that s.4(2) of the Act expressly provided for such a split of the copyright. Again, the assignee of such a limited right was then to be taken to be

the same. The Act provided that the right of copyright, being the sole right to do various acts, for example, to reproduce a work or perform it in public,[376] might be assigned either wholly or partially.[377] The right so given to part with the copyright limited as to the means of exploitation was clearly recognised.[378]

5–102   **Time.** It is clear that copyright may be assigned for a period less than the whole term of copyright.[379] This may be for a fixed term starting immediately or in the future, or for a period that is not fixed, certain or known at the data of the assignment.[380] At the end of the period, the legal title "reverts" to the assignor.[381] The position was the same under the earlier Acts.[382] A common problem which arises under such a grant is the right of the assignee, after the end of the term, to continue to deal with articles made by him during the term. This is dealt with elsewhere.[383]

5–103   **Different territories: the 1988 Act.** It is a common feature of international copyright for a copyright owner to want to divide up the right between different territorial areas, whether by assignment or grant of exclusive licences. This may be because the copyright owner does not have the means to exploit the work abroad himself, and so must find another to take this burden on, or for other commercial reasons.[384] Two points need to be borne in mind in this connection. First, the assignment of the rights conferred under foreign systems of law will be governed by those systems. As to this, the present treatment is concerned only with the question of whether it is possible to effect a subdivision of the limited territorial copyright conferred by the 1988 Act. Secondly, the partition of an intellectual property right between different territories in an attempt to create separate markets may fall foul of rules relating to the free movement of goods and anti-competitive practices. The latter topic is dealt with elsewhere.[385]

The 1988 Act confers on the copyright owner the exclusive right to do various acts "in the United Kingdom".[386] It is suggested that the copyright conferred by the 1988 Act cannot be sub-divided into rights for the different countries which make up the United Kingdom or even smaller areas. This is because, firstly, the Act, while making express provision for partial assignments in terms of different acts and different times, makes no provision as to different areas. Secondly, although the copyright can be divided up into one or more of the "things" which the copyright owner has the exclusive right to do, the things which the copyright owner has the exclusive right to do are set out in s.16, and these confer the exclusive right to do various acts "in the United Kingdom", and not "or in part

---

the owner of the copyright in respect of its application to the particular limited class of act: s.49(5).

[376] Copyright Act 1911 s.1(2).

[377] s.5(2); and where an assignee became entitled to any right comprised in the copyright, he was to be treated, as respects the right so assigned, as the owner of the copyright: s.5(3).

[378] *British Actors Film Co Ltd v Glover* [1918] 1 K.B. 299 (right to perform a work "professionally"); *Jonathan Cape Ltd v Consolidated Press Ltd* [1954] 1 W.L.R. 1313 (right to publish in "volume form"); *Canadian Performing Right Society v Famous Players Canadian Corp. Ltd* (1927) 60 O.L.R. 280 and 614 (assignment of performing right).

[379] CDPA 1988 s.90(2).

[380] *Crosstown Music Company 1, LLC v Rive Droite Music Ltd* [2010] EWCA Civ 1222.

[381] *Crosstown Music Company 1, LLC v Rive Droite Music Ltd* [2010] EWCA Civ 1222, at para.102.

[382] See the Copyright Act 1956 s.36(2)(c), the Copyright Act 1911 s.5(2) and, as to the earlier acts, *Copinger*, 4th edn, p.147 and, e.g. *Horrit v Hall* (1862) 6 L.T. 348.

[383] See para.26–66, below.

[384] For example, it is common for music publishers and recording companies to operate through a system of assignments or exclusive licences of the copyright in favour of different companies in different territories.

[385] See Ch.29, below.

[386] See CDPA 1988 s.16(1). The UK consists of England, Wales, Scotland and Northern Ireland: Interpretation Act 1978 Sch.1.

thereof". Thirdly, if UK copyright could be so divided it would apparently mean, for example, that the owner of the copyright "in Scotland" would have the right to prevent the making of copies of a work in England, relying on the provision in s.16 that the owner of the copyright has the exclusive right to copy the work "in the United Kingdom". This result could only be prevented by adding words to the statute so as to limit the rights of the copyright owner to the territory of his grant.[387] Again, it is difficult to see how the owner of the copyright "in Scotland" could prevent the "importation" into Scotland of copies unlawfully made in England, since the Act only makes it an infringement to import infringing copies "into the United Kingdom". *A fortiori*, it is suggested that the division of the copyright into smaller areas, for example counties, is not possible. The effect of a purported assignment of the copyright in "England" would, it is suggested, not be to vest any proprietary interest in the "assignee". At best he would only obtain contractual rights against the "assignor".

Different territories: the 1956 Act. At a first reading, the effect of the provisions of the 1956 Act might appear to have been to produce a different result. It is suggested, however, that this was not the case. Thus the Act expressly provided that an assignment of copyright might be limited to one or more of the countries in relation to which the owner had the exclusive right.[388] The different wording arises because under the 1956 Act (and the 1911 Act), unlike the 1988 Act, the Act as a whole, including the infringement provisions, might be extended to other countries.[389] An assignment might therefore be limited to one of these other countries but could not, it is suggested, and for the same reasons as apply to the 1988 Act, have been limited to a territory smaller than the United Kingdom.   **5–104**

Different territories: the 1911 Act. It is suggested that the position was the same under the 1911 Act, which permitted an assignment "either wholly or partially, and either generally or subject to limitations to the United Kingdom or any self-governing Dominion or other part of His Majesty's Dominions to which this Act extends".[390] There is, however, some authority to suggest that local divisions of the copyright were possible. For example, it was said that since the Act recognised the right to part with the copyright subject to restrictions as to time, place or otherwise, so as to make the grantee of the limited right which he acquired the actual owner of that limited part of the copyright, an assignee of the right to perform a work "in the provinces" was therefore the owner of the copyright to that extent.[391] But the point was not argued,[392] and it is suggested that the better view is that an assignment could not have been made in respect of an area smaller than the United Kingdom (or one of the Dominions).[393]   **5–105**

Pre-1911 Act assignments. It is not clear whether, under the law prior to 1911, copyright was divisible as to territory. It is thought that statutory copyright was not.[394]   **5–106**

---

[387] It is suggested that s.173(1) is insufficient to do this.

[388] Copyright Act 1956 s.36(2)(b).

[389] See the Copyright Act 1956 ss.31 and 1(2). As to the extension of the Copyright Acts to other countries generally, see paras 3–271 et seq., above.

[390] Copyright Act 1911 s.5(2).

[391] *British Actors Film Co Ltd v Glover* [1918] 1 K.B. 299.

[392] The argument was whether, because of its other provisions, the grant took effect as a licence only. It was not argued that an assignment limited to a particular area was not possible at all. See p.305.

[393] See, for example, *Copinger*, 8th edn, p.109.

[394] See *Copinger*, 4th edn, p.146 and *Jefferys (C.) v Boosey (T.)* (1855) 4 H.L.C. 815 at 993 (copyright conferred on every part of British Dominions not divisible; assignment limited to UK or smaller regions therefore void); *Taylor v Neville* (1878) L.J. Q.B. 254 (no legal right to present a

(b) *Presumption of transfer of rental right*

5–107   **Presumption of transfer of rental in case of film production agreement.** The EC Directive on Rental, Lending and Related Rights[395] required Member States to confer on authors and performers an unwaivable right to remuneration from the rental of fixations of their works and performances on sound recordings and films where they had parted with such rental right. Although Member States were at the same time required to provide for a presumed transfer of a performer's rental right on the conclusion of a film production agreement, it was left to the discretion of Member States whether to make a similar provision in the case of authors. After consultation, the United Kingdom chose to exercise this option by introducing provisions which mirror those which apply to performers.[396]

Section 93A thus provides that where an agreement concerning film production is concluded between an author and a film producer,[397] the author is to be presumed, unless the agreement provides to the contrary, to have transferred to the film producer any rental right[398] in relation to the film arising by virtue of the inclusion of a copy of the author's work in the film.[399] For this purpose, "author" means an author, or prospective author, of a literary, dramatic, musical or artistic work.[400] The section therefore does not apply to an agreement between a film producer and the principal director of the film, even though the principal director is now to be taken as one of the authors of a film.[401] Nor does it apply, for example, to an agreement between the film producer and the "author" of any sound recording used in the film.

The presumption does not apply to any rental right in relation to the film arising by virtue of the inclusion in the film of a screenplay, dialogue or music specifically created for and used in the film.[402] This will exclude the operation of the section in the case of many of the works in relation to which a film production agreement is usually concluded. Often of course, such an agreement will be concluded in relation to a work, such as a novel or a piece of music, which already exists and was not written specifically for the film. In the case of such works, and works created specifically for and used in the film other than the screenplay, dialogue or music, the question is then whether the agreement "concerns" film production. This expression is vague[403] but clearly is intended to refer to an agreement between an author and film producer relating to the use of the author's work in a particular film.

The section therefore appears to provide an exception to the general rule relating to assignments, namely that an assignment of copyright must be in writing and signed by or on behalf of the copyright owner. Thus, it seems that any agreement, whether written or oral, and if written, whether or not signed, will be sufficient to bring the section into play and effect a transfer of the rental right by virtue of the presumption of an effective transfer. Some doubt is thrown on this

---

work "in London" can be assigned); cf. *Holt v Woods* (1896) 17 N.S.W.R. 36 (distinction drawn between right to reproduce a work—not divisible—and right to present performance of a work—divisible; right to perform a work in Australia therefore assignable).

[395] Directive 2006/115/EC: [2006] OJ L376/28.

[396] See CDPA 1988 s.191F and para.12–49, below.

[397] A film "producer" means the person by whom the arrangements necessary for the making of the film are undertaken. CDPA 1988 s.178.

[398] "Rental right" means the exclusive right of a copyright owner to authorise or prohibit the rental of copies of the work. See CDPA 1988 s.178, and para.7–93 et seq., below.

[399] CDPA 1988 s.93A(1).

[400] s.93A(2).

[401] See s.9(2)(ab) and para.4–48, above. As an author, however, he will potentially be able to bargain for a share in any profits made from rental of the film.

[402] s.93A(3).

[403] The wording is taken from art.3(4) of Directive 2006/115/EC.

conclusion, however, by the wording of subs.(4), which provides that where s.93A applies, the absence of signature by or on behalf of the author does not exclude the operation of the s.91(1). This latter section provides that an agreement by which "future copyright" is purported to be assigned will be effective to vest the legal title in the assignee if the agreement is signed by or on behalf of the prospective owner.[404] In relation to a work which is not yet in existence, s.93A(4) therefore makes it clear that the presumption of a transfer will apply even in the absence of a signed agreement. It might be thought to follow from this specific provision and the omission of any corresponding provision in relation to existing works that the absence of signature from an agreement relating to existing works was fatal to the operation of s.93A. There seems no logical justification for such a conclusion: indeed it seems likely that these provisions of the Directive were intended to apply to oral agreements as well as written ones in all cases.[405] If an *effective* transfer is to be presumed then, the presumption must be that the transfer was made by means sufficient to vest the legal title in the film producer, i.e. by an assignment in writing signed by or behalf of the copyright owner. Probably the wording of s.93A(4) was inserted out of unnecessary caution.

Although the section refers to a "presumption" (the word used in the Directive), the presumption is rebuttable if the agreement provides to the contrary. The use of the concept of a presumption was imported from the Directive, but the section appears to be similar in effect, if not in wording, to the employment provision in s.11(2) of the 1988 Act, which provides that where a work is made by an employee in the course of his employment, his employer is the first owner of the copyright subject to any agreement to the contrary. The new section does not say whether the agreement to the contrary must be express or can be implied but it is suggested that an implied agreement to the contrary will be enough.[406] In practice of course, such agreements will usually contain express provision dealing with the rights granted to the film producer.

The Act further provides that the reference in the section to an agreement concluded between an author and a producer includes any agreement having effect between those persons, whether made by them directly or through intermediaries.[407] It is not clear what the purpose or result of these words is, since if the agreement has "effect" between the parties, whether concluded directly or through "intermediaries" (i.e. presumably, agents), it will amount in law to an agreement "concluded" between them. The Directive requires, in the similar provision relating to performers,[408] that the presumption is to apply where the agreement is concluded "individually or collectively" between the parties, the latter

---

[404] For a full discussion of the section, see para.5–108 et seq., below.

[405] See, e.g. Reinbothe & von Lewinski, *The* EC Directive on Rental and Lending Rights and on Piracy (London: Sweet & Maxwell, 1993), p.57.

[406] Compare, for example, the operation of s.11(2), where an implied agreement to the contrary is sufficient to oust the employer/employee provisions of the section (see *Noah v Shuba* [1991] F.S.R. 14) and of the Copyright Act 1842, where an implied agreement was held sufficient for the purposes of s.18: see *Lawrence, etc., Ltd v Aflalo* [1904] A.C. 17, following *Sweet v Benning* (1855) 16 C.B. 459. To the same effect is *Lamb v Evans* [1893] 1 Ch. 218 and *Chantrey, etc., Co v Dey (T.H.)* (1912) 28 T.L.R. 499. See generally, para.5–31, above. Note that Art.3(4) of Directive 2006/115/EC speaks in terms of "contractual *clauses* to the contrary", but it is not thought this terminology was intended to exclude the operation of any implied term. See, e.g. Reinbothe & von Lewinski, *The* EC Directive on Rental and Lending Rights and on Piracy (Sweet & Maxwell, 1993), p.58.

[407] CDPA 1988 s.93(A)(5).

[408] Directive (92/100), Art.2.5. And see also CDPA 1988 s.191F.

presumably referring to the possibility of some kind of collective bargaining,[409] and this may be the reason for the wording in the Act.[410]

Section 93A applies to an agreement whenever made[411] although in relation to an agreement concluded before December 1, 1996 there is no exclusion of the presumption in relation to screenplay, dialogue or music specifically created for the film under s.93A(3).[412]

(iv) Assignments of "future" copyright and future rights

(a) *"Future" copyright works*

5–108   Where parties enter into arrangements concerning a work to be made in the future, it is often highly convenient if the vesting of the legal title can be dealt with at the time, rather than having to deal with this by a separate assignment once the work has been created. This may, for example, happen where a work is being commissioned or where an author is regularly creating copyright works and he has entered into an agreement for their exploitation or control by a publisher or a collecting society. Statute apart, however, the general law is that a work must be in existence before its ownership can be assigned at law.[413] An assignment of an expectancy, if made for consideration, will only be treated as a contract to assign. If, on creation of the subject matter, the legal ownership duly vests in the assignor, the beneficial interest and thus equitable ownership will be all that vests in the assignee.[414] Under the general law, therefore, an assignment of the copyright in all works then or thereafter belonging to the assignor would amount to a valid assignment of the legal title in respect of all copyrights vested in the assignor at the date of the assignment and an agreement to assign future and after-acquired copyrights. As seen below, however, this general rule was expressly altered by the 1956 Act, enabling parties to enter into an agreement which will effect the vesting of the legal title in the assignee as soon as a future work is created.

5–109   **Transitional.** The 1988 Act applies to all relevant agreements made after June 1, 1957 but not to any assignment or agreement made before that date.[415] The normal rule therefore applies to these earlier assignments: the legal title cannot have been passed in this way.

5–110   **Transfer of future copyright: the 1988 Act.** Subsection 91(1) of the 1988 Act provides that:

> "Where by an agreement made in relation to future copyright, and signed by or on behalf of the prospective owner of the copyright, the prospective owner purports to assign the future copyright (wholly or partially) to another person, then if, on the copyright coming into existence, the assignee or an-

---

[409] See, e.g. Reinbothe & von Lewinski, *The EC Directive on Rental and Lending Rights and on Piracy* (Sweet & Maxwell, 1993), p.58.

[410] cf. the more usual form in, e.g. s.90, that an assignment be signed "by or on behalf of" the assignor.

[411] See the Copyright and Related Rights Regulations 1996 (SI 1996/2967), reg.32(1). It appears that reg.27(1), which provides that, except as otherwise expressly provided, nothing in the Regulations is to affect an agreement made before November 19, 1992, is overridden by reg.32(1).

[412] Copyright and Related Rights Regulations 1996 (SI 1996/2967), reg.32(1).

[413] *Sweet v Shaw* (1839) 8 L.J. Ch. 216; *Colburn v Duncombe* (1838) 9 Sim. 151.

[414] *Performing Right Society Ltd v London Theatre of Varieties Ltd* [1924] A.C. 1; *Wah Sang Industrial Co v Tackmay Industrial Co Ltd* [1980] F.S.R. 303 at 309.

[415] CDPA 1988 Sch.1 para.26(1). The provisions of s.37 of the 1956 Act were substantially to the same effect, and altered the existing law, hence the transitional date.

other person claiming under him would be entitled as against all other persons to require the copyright to be vested in him, the copyright shall vest in the assignee or his successor in title by virtue of this subsection."[416]

A number of points arise under this provision:

(a) "Future copyright" is defined as copyright which will or may come into existence in respect of any future work or class of works or on the occurrence of a future event.[417] "Prospective owner" is to be construed accordingly and includes a person who is prospectively entitled to copyright by virtue of such an agreement as is mentioned in the provision.[418]

(b) Assignments of future copyright can only be made by written agreement. Purported assignments which fall outside this description will at best operate as equitable assignments.[419]

(c) Unlike an assignment of existing copyright, which does not require consideration or an "agreement", it seems that a specifically enforceable agreement is necessary under the section. This follows not only from the use of the word "agreement", in contrast to "writing" in the case of an assignment of existing copyright,[420] but also from the fact that the title will only vest if the assignee is entitled, as against all other persons, and thus including the assignor, to require the title to be vested in him by the assignor.[421] An assignment of future copyright must therefore not only be in writing but also be supported by sufficient consideration. An assignment by way of deed only will not suffice.

(d) It might be thought to follow that if, when the work comes into existence, the assignee has lost the right to specific performance of the agreement, for example, because he has failed to honour relevant obligations of the agreement on his side, no automatic vesting under s.91(1) will take place. However, in *Peer International Corp v Editora Musical de Cuba*,[422] it was held that an assignment of future copyright was good to transfer the equitable title despite the fact that the contract had by virtue of a foreign decree been abrogated before the copyright came into existence.[423]

(e) The expression "entitled as against all other persons" apparently refers to the rules of priority which would have applied apart from the Act if the assignee had been claiming specific performance of the agreement to assign the copyright to him. So, for example, where the prospective owner purports to assign the future copyright to two persons by separate assignments, the first in time will become the owner unless he has so acted to cause his equity to be postponed.

---

[416] See Vol.2 J1.ii for a precedent of an assignment of future copyright.
[417] CDPA 1988 s.91(2). As to the reference to the occurrence of a future event, a work may be in existence but not yet entitled to copyright because none of the qualifying conditions for subsistence has yet been satisfied.
[418] s.91(2).
[419] See para.5–175, below.
[420] See CDPA 1988 s.90(3).
[421] The drafting of the section seems clearly to have started from the position which existed before the passing of the 1956 Act, under which an assignee of future copyright could at most acquire an equitable title. The section also appears to be somewhat tautologous in that if the section operates at all, the title will automatically vest and so there will be no one against whom the assignee can assert the right to require vesting of the copyright. Presumably the words "apart from the operation of this section" should be read into subs. (1) after the words "would be entitled".
[422] [2002] EWHC 2675 (Ch); [2004] R.P.C. 22 (not affected on this point by the decision on appeal [2003] EWCA Civ 1156; [2004] Ch. 212, CA).
[423] This decision was reached relying on *Re Lind, Industrials Finance Syndicate Ltd v Lind* [1915] 2 Ch. 345 (not following *Collyer v Isaacs* (1881) 19 Ch.D. 342), for the general principle that such an assignment creates an equitable charge arising immediately upon the property coming into existence, and thus is an independent and higher right than the contractual right to an assignment.

(f) The section is not limited to cases where the prospective owner is the author of the work. Thus, an employer may make an effective assignment of the copyright in a work to be made by his employee.[424]

(g) It also follows from the definition of "prospective owner" that an effective assignment may be made not only by the prospective first owner, but also by the prospective assignee of the future copyright from him, and so on.

(h) Since the legal title vests in the assignee the moment the work is created, the subsequent avoidance of the agreement, for example on the grounds that the assignor was an infant, will not operate to revest the title in the assignor.[425]

5–111   **Assignments made under the 1956 Act.** As already noted, assignments of future copyright made under the 1956 Act are now governed by the 1988 Act. In fact, the 1956 Act, although worded slightly differently, was, apart from one provision, to the same effect.[426] The only difference is that the 1956 Act expressly dealt with the case where the person who would have been entitled to the copyright died before the copyright came into existence, the Act providing that the copyright was then to devolve as if it had subsisted immediately before his death and he had then been the owner of the copyright.[427] The effect of this provision has been preserved.[428]

5–112   **Pre-1956 Act assignments.** As already noted, the provisions of the 1988 Act relating to assignments of future copyright do not apply to agreements made before June 1, 1957. As to these, the provisions of the earlier Acts relating to assignments[429] had no application to a document purporting to assign the copyright in a future copyright work, since there was no owner in existence who could execute an assignment.[430] The legal title therefore vested in the author or other first owner when the work came into existence, although a purported assignment might be enforced as an equitable assignment.[431]

(b) *Assignments of future rights*

5–113   Although a copyright work may exist at the date of the assignment, new or extended rights may subsequently be brought into existence by statute in relation to that work. Recent examples are the rental right,[432] the extended rights in re-

---

[424] As to works of employees, see paras 5–08 et seq., above.

[425] *Chaplin v Leslie Frewin (Publishers) Ltd* [1966] Ch. 71. The assignor may of course be able to establish grounds, for example, undue influence, for an order that the copyright be revested in him.

[426] Copyright Act 1956 s.37.

[427] s.37(2).

[428] Thus, although this provision has been repealed, its repeal does not affect its operation in relation to an agreement made before commencement of the 1988 Act on August 1, 1989. See CDPA 1988 Sch.1 para.26(2).

[429] For example, the Copyright Act 1911 s.5(2), (3).

[430] *Performing Right Society Ltd v London Theatre of Varieties Ltd* [1924] A.C. 1. The position was the same before the 1911 Act. See *Colburn v Duncombe* (1838) 9 Sim. 151; *Sweet v Shaw* (1839) 3 Jur. 217. The decision in *Ward, Lock & Co Ltd v Long* [1906] 2 Ch. 550, might suggest the contrary, Kekewich J. holding that, in the context of a publishing agreement, "an agreement to assign in matters of this kind is quite as good as a direct assignment in words, is enforceable in equity, and as between businessmen is complete", with the consequence that an equitable title prevailed over that of a later assignee of the legal title. It is suggested that as a matter of principle the decision was wrong.

[431] As to equitable ownership generally, see para.5–174, below.

[432] i.e. the right of a copyright owner to authorise or prohibit the rental of copies of the work. See para.7–93, below.

spect of the extended and revived term of copyright,[433] the extended rights in sound recordings,[434] and the communication to the public right.[435] The effect of a pre-existing grant on these rights will depend in the first instance on any transitional provisions. For example, in the case of rights to the extended and revived terms of copyright which came into being as a result of the increase in the term of copyright from life and 50 years to life and 70 years, and to the extended rights in sound recordings, express provision is made.[436] As to the example of the rental right as a new right, it is clear that the right subsists in relation to works made before the coming into force of the amending Regulations.[437] The same is true in relation to the communication to the public right.[438] Since there are no other relevant transitional provisions, it therefore appears to follow that a pre-amendment assignment of the "copyright" will carry with it the rental right and the communication to the public right in the absence of any contrary intention in the assignment: it is part of the "copyright" in the work. This can be more clearly seen in relation, for example, to the exclusive right to issue copies of the work to the public,[439] a right which was first introduced in its present form by the 1988 Act.[440] Again, this right clearly exists in relation to works which were made before the commencement of the 1988 Act.[441] The effect of the transitional provisions in the Act is that any assignment of the "copyright" made before commencement will, subject to any term in the assignment to the contrary effect, carry the copyright as conferred by the 1988 Act,[442] and thus the complete bundle of rights included within the copyright, including the exclusive right to issue copies of a work to the public. The general effect of the 1956 Act seems to have been the same, for example in relation to the exclusive right to broadcast a work which the Act introduced.[443] An example to the opposite effect was the mechanical right introduced by s.19 of the 1911 Act. Under the previous law, the owner of the copyright in a musical work did not enjoy the exclusive right to make copies of it in the form of sound recordings, or "mechanical contrivances".[444] This position was changed by the 1911 Act[445] but at the same time it was provided that an assignment of the copyright in a musical work made before commencement should not carry the new mechanical right, which was instead to belong to the author or his personal representatives.[446]

Although, therefore, as a matter of general law a present assignment of future rights cannot operate to transfer the legal title to such rights and will only operate as an agreement to assign,[447] this rule may be altered by transitional provisions. Certainly, the use of such expressions in an assignment as "the whole of the prop-

---

[433] See para.6–13 et seq., below.

[434] See para.6–57 et seq., below.

[435] See para.7–112 et seq., below.

[436] See paras 5–137 et seq. and 5–146 et seq., below, respectively, where it is explained that the position is the same in relation to the increased term of copyright introduced by the Copyright Act 1911.

[437] See the Copyright and Related Rights Regulations 1996 (SI 1996/2967) reg.26(1), and para.7–100, below.

[438] Copyright and Related Rights Regulations 2003 (SI 2003/2498) reg.31(1).

[439] See CDPA 1988 s.18, paras 7–87 et seq., below.

[440] Under the 1956 Act, an exclusive right of first publication existed, which was rather different in its effect. See the footnotes to para.7–87, below.

[441] CDPA 1988 Sch.1 para.3.

[442] Sch.1 para.25(1).

[443] See the Copyright Act 1956 s.2(5)(d) and Sch.7 para.28(1).

[444] *Boosey v Whight* [1900] 1 Ch. 122.

[445] Copyright Act 1911 s.1(2)(d).

[446] s.19(7)(c).

[447] See, e.g. para.5–108, above.

erty, copyright and interest, present or future, vested or contingent" will often be wide enough to show an intention to assign such future rights.[448]

(v) Limitations on the right to assign

(a) *Right to equitable remuneration where rental right transferred*

5–114   Substantial amendments were made to the 1988 Act to implement the EC Directive on rental and lending rights,[449] one effect of which was to confer on an owner of copyright a comprehensive right to control the rental and lending of copies of the copyright work. At the same time, there was created in favour of an author of a literary, dramatic, musical or artistic work, and the principal director of a film, a right to receive equitable remuneration for such rental where the rental right concerning a sound recording or film had been transferred to the producer of the sound recording or film.[450] This right ("the equitable remuneration right") is not strictly a right of copyright and is considered further elsewhere,[451] but it should be noted here that the Act places restrictions on the ability of the author to assign such right, hence the use of the expression "the unwaivable right to remuneration."[452]

Thus, s.93B of the Act provides that the equitable remuneration right may not be assigned by the author except to a collecting society for the purpose of enabling the society to enforce the right on his behalf.[453] Although the right cannot be assigned by the author, it is however transmissible by testamentary disposition or by operation of law as personal or moveable property.[454] Any person into whose hands the right passes on such a transmission may himself assign or transmit it.[455] No formalities are prescribed,[456] but presumably such an assignment can be effected in law by a transfer complying with s.136 of the Law of Property Act 1925, and in equity by a more informal assignment.[457]

(b) *Reversionary rights under the 1911 Act*

5–115   The 1911 Act contained a limitation on the power of an author to part with his interest in his copyright for longer than 25 years after his death, making any attempt to do so by him ineffective. The object of this limitation was to protect authors and their heirs from the consequences of the imprudent disposition of the fruits of their special talent and, originality,[458] but for the reasons which are discussed below, the benefits conferred by this limitation were largely illusory.

---

[448] See *Redwood Music Ltd v B. Feldman & Co Ltd* [1978] R.P.C. 429 at 444; [1979] R.P.C. 385, CA at 394.

[449] Council Directive 2006/115/EC [2006] OJ L376/28 as implemented by the Copyright and Related Rights Regulations 1996 (SI 1996/2967).

[450] A similar right was created in favour of performers. See CDPA 1988 s.191G and para.12–49, below.

[451] See para.7–101, below.

[452] See art.4 of Directive 92/100. See now art.5 of Directive 2006/115/EC.

[453] CDPA 1988 s.93B(2). For this purpose, a collecting society means a society or other organisation which has as its main object, or one of its main objects, the exercise of the equitable remuneration right on behalf of more than one author. See s.93B(7).

[454] s.93B(2).

[455] s.93B(2).

[456] cf. the formalities prescribed for an assignment of copyright by s.90(3).

[457] See *Snell's Equity*, 31st edn (London: Sweet & Maxwell), paras 3–12 et seq.

[458] *Redwood Music Ltd v B. Feldman & Co Ltd & Others* [1979] R.P.C. 385 at 402; *Chappell & Co Ltd v Redwood Music Ltd* [1981] R.P.C. 337.

Following a recommendation of the Gregory Committee in 1952,[459] the provision was repealed by the 1956 Act but its effect was continued in respect of assignments entered into before the Act's commencement. This state of affairs has been continued by the 1988 Act, with some further amendments and clarification. This limitation, therefore, still has important implications for agreements entered into before June 1, 1957 and can be something of a trap.

As the limitation now stands,[460] its effect is that where the author of literary, dramatic, musical or artistic work was the first owner of the copyright in it, no assignment of the copyright or grant of any interest in it by him (otherwise than by will) made after the passing of the 1911 Act[461] and before June 1, 1957 is to be operative to vest in the assignee or grantee any rights with respect to the copyright in the work beyond the expiration of 25 years from the death of the author.[462] This means that, unless some further assignment has been made since June 1, 1957 (see below), any such assignment or grant will only have operated until the end of this 25-year period.

"Grant of any interest". It is unclear what these words mean in this context.   **5–116**
Their use derives from the original provisions of the 1911 Act which provided, first, that the owner of the copyright in a work might assign the right, either wholly or partially, and might grant "any interest in the right by licence", but that no such assignment or grant should be valid unless it was in writing and signed by the owner or his agent.[463] The words of the reverter proviso then went on to apply in the case of any "assignment" or "grant of any interest" in the copyright by the author/first owner. It was clear that a mere consent, even oral or implied from conduct, although always a defence to a claim for infringement,[464] did not amount to the grant of an interest in the copyright such that, for example, the person with the benefit of the consent could sue a third-party infringer.[465] It seems, therefore, that a distinction was being drawn between such consents and some other, more formal licences in writing by which a proprietary interest in the copyright was granted coupled with a licence to exercise it.[466] What might have amounted to such a grant has always been unclear,[467] but it is suggested the section was intended to apply to a grant which, although it could have been the subject of an assignment, was in fact by way of exclusive licence.[468]

---

[459] Cmnd. 8662. In fact the reasons for the repeal were other than the illusory nature of the benefit. See further, below, para.5–124, below.

[460] As now set out in CDPA 1988 Sch.1 para.27, which governs the position today: *Novello & Co Ltd v Keith Prowse Music Publishing Co Ltd* [2004] EWHC (Ch) 766, para.7; [2004] R.P.C. 48. And see paras 22 to 24 of the judgment of Lloyd J. in the Court of Appeal: *Novello & Co Ltd v Keith Prowse Music Publishing Co Ltd* [2004] EWCA Civ 1776; [2005] R.P.C. 23. The provision was originally contained in the proviso to s.5(2) of the 1911 Act and its effect was continued by the 1956 Act Sch.8 para.6 and Sch.7 para.28.

[461] i.e. on December 16, 1911.

[462] CDPA 1988 Sch.1 para.27(1). Given the fact that para.25 of Sch.1 preserves the effect of pre-1988 Act assignments (see para.581, above), para.27 may have been unnecessary, but it follows the pattern of the 1956 Act and may in any event have been necessary to preserve the statutory vesting of the reversionary interest in the author's personal representatives (see para.5–117, below): *Novello & Co Ltd v Keith Prowse Music Publishing Co Ltd* [2004] EWWCA Civ 1776, para.11.

[463] Copyright Act 1911 s.5(2).

[464] See the 1911 Act s.2(1) and para.5–198, below.

[465] See para.5–198, below.

[466] See *British Actors Film Co Ltd v Glover* [1918] 1 K.B. 299 at 307, 308.

[467] In cases where the question might have arisen, the agreement was construed as an assignment and not a licence, and so did not have to be answered. See *British Actors Film Co Ltd v Glover* [1918] 1 K.B. 299; *Jonathan Cape Ltd v Consolidated Press Ltd* [1954] 1 W.L.R. 1313. But see *Kinekor Film (Pty) Ltd v Movie Time* [1976] (1) S.A. 649.

[468] See *Copinger*, 8th edn, p.115. Note that today an exclusive licence in writing from the copyright

5–117   **Further points.** The following further points should be noted:

(a) A first assignment of copyright or grant of an interest in respect of pre-1956 Act works made by the author on or after June 1, 1957 are unaffected by the limitation. The assignee or grantee takes freely under the terms of the instrument. The position of an author who on or after June 1, 1957 deals with the reversionary interest in a work which was the subject of pre-June 1, 1957 assignment or grant by him is considered below.[469]

(b) As the law stood under the 1911 Act, an author could not assign the legal title to the copyright in a "future" work of his, such an assignment at best operating as an agreement to assign, creating an equitable interest in the assignee.[470] To the extent that an author purportedly assigned or granted an interest in the last 25 years of the term of copyright in a future work of his, including a work made on or after June 1, 1957, it will have been inoperative to do so.[471]

(c) As a general rule, the reversionary interest in the copyright expectant on the determination of the 25-year period will, on the death of the author, devolve on his legal personal representatives as part of his estate.[472] If, however, the author has executed a further assignment on or after June 1, 1957 which includes the reversionary interest, this will now take full effect. This is made clear by express statutory provision in the case of assignments made on or after August 1, 1989,[473] and has been established also to be the position in the case of an assignment made between June 1, 1957 and August 1, 1989.[474] An author who had purported to assign away the copyright in his work for the full term before June 1, 1957 may therefore at any time since then freely dispose of his reversionary interest.

(d) The devolution of the reversionary interest on the "legal personal representatives" probably refers only to those obtaining an English grant but in any event certainly does not extend to heirs, next-of-kin, devisees, legatees or creditors in respect of whom no grant or order of any court, English or foreign, has been made as to title to or as to the vesting of the deceased's personal property.[475] Accordingly, where there were no "legal personal representatives" in this sense the reversionary rights vested in

---

owner confers procedural but not proprietary rights on the licensee. See paras 5–207 et seq., below. See further, as to the 1911 Act and exclusive licences, para.5–212, below.

[469] As to assignments made before the passing of the 1911 Act, see further, para.5–120, below.

[470] Such an agreement, or any purported assignment, could not in any event have been effective at that time to transfer the legal title to the promisee. See para.5–108, above.

[471] This was made clear by the wording of the proviso to s.5(2) of the 1911 Act, which provided that any agreement entered into by the author as to the disposition of the reversionary interest was to be null and void. See *Novello & Co Ltd v Keith Prowse Music Publishing Co Ltd* [2004] EWHC 766 (Ch), para.21; [2004] R.P.C. 48.

[472] CDPA 1988 Sch.1 para.27(2), thus effecting a statutory revesting of the reversionary period without the need for any re-assignment. See *Novello & Co Ltd v Keith Prowse Music Publishing Co Ltd* [2004] EWHC 766 (Ch), para.10.

[473] CDPA 1988 Sch.1 para.27(2) .

[474] *Novello & Co Ltd v Keith Prowse Music Publishing Co Ltd* [2004] EWHC 766 (Ch). The decision of Patten J. was upheld on appeal: see [2004] EWCA Civ 1776; [2005] R.P.C. 23. The Whitford Committee thought that whether an author could assign the reversion after the commencement of the 1956 Act was not free from doubt and recommended that, to the extent it was not already clear, it ought to be provided that an author might be able to do so at any time. See Cmnd. 6732, paras 620 and 622. The draftsman of the 1988 Act presumably also thought that the position was unsettled but took the view that any doubt should be resolved by the courts rather than risk altering established rights by statute. This is probably why the 1988 Act only makes express provision for the position after the commencement of that Act. See *Novello & Co Ltd v Keith Prowse Music Publishing Co Ltd* [2004] EWHC 766 (Ch), para.13 and para.24 of the judgment of Lloyd J on appeal ([2004] EWCA Civ 1776).

[475] *Peer International Corporation v Termidor Music Publishers Ltd* [2006] EWHC 2883 (Ch); [2007] E.C.D.R. 1, para.72. As to the doubt, see fn.472.

the Public Trustee (para.71).[476] The term probably also includes executors named in the will of a person who has died domiciled abroad even if they have not proved the will in England and Wales.[477]

(e) Nothing in these provisions affects three kinds of assignment relating to reversionary interests, namely[478]:

(i) An assignment of the reversionary interest by a person to whom it has been assigned. A person to whom the reversion had been assigned by the personal representatives (see next paragraph) might therefore have himself assigned it at any time, as may a person to whom the author, after June 1, 1957 has assigned the reversion (see previous paragraph).

(ii) An assignment of the reversionary interest after the death of the author by his personal representatives or any person becoming entitled to it. Any such assignment by the personal representatives is therefore valid, even made while the 1911 Act was in force.[479] There is therefore no requirement that the personal representatives must wait until the reversion falls in. The purpose of the Act was only to prevent a disposal by the author.[480]

(iii) Any assignment of the copyright after the reversionary interest has fallen in.

(f) Nothing in the provision is to be construed as applying to the assignment of the copyright in a collective work, or to a licence to publish a work or part of a work as part of a collective work.[481]

(g) The limitation applied to partial assignments of copyright just as it did to assignments of the whole copyright in a work.[482]

(h) The reverter provision applies not only to an assignment of the copyright, but also to the "grant of any interest in [the copyright]", such as, for example, the grant of an exclusive licence extending into the period starting 25 years after the death of the author.[483]

(i) The reverter only applies in cases where the author was the first owner of the copyright. The author may not have been the first owner where the work was made by him in the course of his employment or where the work was a commissioned engraving, photograph or portrait.[484] The first owner of the copyright in such cases was at liberty to assign it for the full term.

---

[476] *Peer International Corporation v Termidor Music Publishers Ltd* [2006] EWHC 2883 (Ch), where the authors had died intestate and there had been no English grant.

[477] *Redwood Music Ltd v B. Feldman & Co Ltd* [1979] R.P.C. 1. In *Peer International Corporation v Termidor Music Publishers Ltd* [2006] EWHC 2883 (Ch), Lindsay J. stated that the reasoning in Redwood was "not above doubt" (para.68), particularly insofar as the judge (Robert Goff J.) had relied by analogy on the provisions of section 19 of the Revenue Act 1889 (para.70). Lindsay J.'s preferred, alternative construction of the term "legal personal representatives" are stated in the text (at fn.470). Clearly, the decision in *Redwood v Feldman* is inconsistent with Lindsay J.'s preferred construction but presumably is reconcilable because the claimants in Redwood claimed through named executors as opposed to heirs, etc. (It is however noteworthy that Lindsay J. took the view that there might well have been a US grant: para.(67).)

[478] CDPA 1988 Sch.1 para.27(3). These provisions were not contained in the 1911 or 1956 Acts but their inclusion in the 1988 Act did not, it is thought, change the existing position. They were inserted for clarification. See the Whitford Committee Report, Cmnd. 6732, paras 620 and 622.

[479] *Chappell & Co Ltd v Redwood Music Ltd* [1981] R.P.C. 337 at 347.

[480] As to the consequence of this in practice, see para.5–123, below.

[481] CDPA 1988 Sch.1 para.27(4). See, further, para.5–118, below.

[482] *Redwood Music Ltd v Francis Day & Hunter Ltd* [1978] R.P.C. 429 at 449.

[483] See, for example, the reference in subpara.(4) to a licence to publish a work as part of a collective work. See para.5–116, above, as to the meaning of "grant of any interest".

[484] Copyright Act 1911 s.5(1)(a) and (b). See paras 5–09 and 5–35, above, respectively.

5–118   **Reverter does not apply to collective works.** The reverter does not apply "to the assignment of the copyright in a collective work or a licence to publish a work or part of a work as part of a collective work".[485] A collective work means: (a) an encyclopaedia, dictionary, year book, or similar work; (b) a newspaper, review, magazine, or similar periodical; and (c) any work written in distinct parts by different authors, or in which works or parts of works of different authors are incorporated.[486] In a collective work, there may be several distinct copyrights, namely, the copyright in the complete work, considered as a whole, in addition to the various copyrights in the distinct contributions to the work. Thus, an anthology enjoys a copyright of its own, as a compilation arising out of the original literary effort and judgment involved in the selection and arrangement of the subject-matter of the compilation. The copyright in the compilation is additional to, and independent of, and different from whatever copyright or copyrights may subsist in the component parts of the compilation. On the other hand, in the case, for example, of a song, there is no copyright in it as an entity: the words and the music each attract separate copyrights. A disposition of the copyright in a compilation, as distinct from the disposition of the copyright in the separate parts, is excepted from the application of the reverter provision.[487] An "assignment" of the copyright in a compilation, if a collective work, could therefore have been made for the full period of copyright, as could a licence to publish a contribution as part of the collective work. But assignments of the copyright in the contributions themselves could not have been made for the full period. The expression "the copyright in a collective work" refers only to that "compilation copyright" which exists, if at all, in addition to and apart from any separate copyright which may exist in the constituent parts of the collective work: it does not refer to the copyright in the separate constituent parts. Thus, in the case of a song, assignments of the distinct copyrights in the words and music written by different persons will not have been effective beyond the expiration of 25 years after the death of the respective authors. There is no independent copyright attributable to a song as a compilation and, therefore, nothing to fall within the exception to the proviso. What purports, however, to be an assignment of copyright in a work for use only as part of a collective work may amount to no more than a licence for that purpose and fall within the second half of the exception.[488]

5–119   **Works of joint authorship.** Although the reverter provision does not apply to collective works it does apply to works of joint authorship.[489] The 1911 Act provided that:

> "references in this Act to the period after the expiration of any specified number of years from the death of the author shall be construed as references to the period after the expiration of the like number of years from the death of the author who dies first or after the death of the author who dies last, whichever period may be the shorter."[490]

The effect of this would appear to be that, where the reversion takes place, it takes place in respect of the shares of both joint authors at the same time. The date of reversion is ascertained by substituting, for the period after the expiration of 25 years from the death of the author referred to in the reverter provision, ei-

---

[485] CDPA 1988 Sch.1 para.27(4).

[486] CDPA 1988 Sch.1 para.27(5). The wording repeats that of the 1911 Act s.5(2), proviso, hence the particular language.

[487] *Chappell & Co Ltd v Redwood Music Ltd* [1981] R.P.C. 337; *Redwood Music Ltd v B. Feldman & Co Ltd* [1979] R.P.C. 385; *Redwood Music Ltd v Chappell & Co Ltd* [1982] R.P.C. 109.

[488] *Chappell & Co Ltd v Redwood Music Ltd* [1981] R.P.C. 337; *Redwood Music Ltd v B. Feldman & Co Ltd* [1979] R.P.C. 385; *Redwood Music Ltd v Chappell & Co Ltd* [1982] R.P.C. 109.

[489] *Redwood Music Ltd v B. Feldman & Co Ltd* [1979] R.P.C. 1; [1979] R.P.C. 385 at 406.

[490] Copyright Act 1911 s.16(1).

ther the period after the expiration of 25 years from the death of the author who dies first, or the period after the death of the author who dies last, whichever period is the shorter. The operation of the provision in the case of published joint works is illustrated in the following two examples in which A and B are joint authors of the relevant work:

(a) A dies first. B dies five years later. The period of copyright remaining after B's death was 45 years (now 65 years), whereas the period remaining after the expiration of 25 years from the death of A will be only 25 (now 45) years and will therefore be the shorter period. Reversion will therefore take place 25 years after the death of A.

(b) A dies first. B does not die until 30 years later. In this case, the shorter remaining period of copyright is the period of 20 years (now 40) after the death of B. Reversion will therefore take place on the death of B.

It follows from these examples that it is impossible to know at the time of A's death when the reversion will occur, or, indeed, if it will occur at all. This can only be known on the death of B, the author who dies last.

The 1988 Act provides that any document made before August 1, 1989 which had any operation affecting the ownership of the copyright in an existing work or creating, transferring or terminating any interest, right or licence in respect of the copyright in an existing work, has the corresponding operation in relation to copyright in the work under the 1988 Act.[491] The position was the same under the 1956 Act.[492] Thus an assignment of a share in the copyright in a work of joint authorship to which the reverter provision applied, operates, in relation to the copyright subsisting under the 1988 Act, as it would have done in relation to the copyright subsisting under the 1911 Act.[493] The position under the 1956 Act was the same. It would also appear that, where an assignment was made in respect of a work of joint authorship before 1956, and the copyright was still subsisting at the commencement of the 1956 Act, then the work enjoyed the extended term, ascertained by reference to the author who died last.

Reverter applies to pre-1911 Act works, but not to pre-1911 Act assignments.   **5–120**
The references in the reverter provision contained in the 1911 Act to "the copyright" referred to the copyright as conferred by the 1911 Act and not the rights which existed previously.[494] An assignment or grant made before the commencement of the 1911 Act which dealt with the copyright in an existing work was therefore unaffected by the reverter provision.[495] This is clearly so in the case of assignments made before the passing of the Act but even in the case of assignments made between the passing and commencement of the Act, the express reference in the reverter provision to an assignment made "after the passing" of the Act did not affect assignments made in this period of the pre-1911 Act rights. It concerned only assignments of the future copyright in works which might come into existence after the commencement of the Act.[496] On the other hand, the provision applies to assignments made by an author after commencement in respect of pre-commencement works, since the subject matter of the assignment will

---

[491] CDPA 1988 Sch.1 para.25(1). See also *Novello & Co Ltd v Keith Prowse Music Publishing Co Ltd* [2004] EWHC 766 (Ch); [2004] R.P.C. 48. The decision of Patten J. was upheld on appeal: see [2004] EWCA Civ 1776; [2005] R.P.C. 23.

[492] Copyright Act 1956 Sch.7 para.25(1).

[493] *Redwood Music Ltd v B. Feldman & Co Ltd* [1979] R.P.C. 1; [1979] R.P.C. 385 at 406.

[494] *Coleridge-Taylor v Novello & Co Ltd* [1938] Ch. 850.

[495] Such assignments were, however, governed by the provisions of s 24 of the 1911 Act. See paras 5–152 et seq., below.

[496] *Coleridge-Taylor v Novello & Co Ltd* [1938] Ch. 850. Such an assignment could pass the equitable title but not the legal one.

necessarily have been the new copyright which was conferred by the 1911 Act on such works.[497]

5–121   **Doubt as to photographs.** It is uncertain whether the reverter provision applies to photographs, the copyright in which was for a period of 50 years from the date of the making of the negative, and which first vested in the owner of the negative, who was "deemed" to be the author of the work.[498] It would seem that the draftsman of the reverter provision overlooked the fact that in the case of these works, the period of copyright protection bore no relation to the life of the author, and that the author might have been a company. Although, therefore, the words of the reverter provision are prima facie wide enough to cover photographs, it is suggested that it does not in fact apply to such works.[499] One reason for excluding photographs from the provision is that, as noted, a corporation could have been the "author" of such works and, in such a case, the reverter provision could have no possible application. Again, one reason for fixing the period of 25 years from the death of an author as the limit of the assignability of copyright was because, at that date, a work ceased to have exclusive copyright, and any person—including, of course, the assignee of the copyright, who then ceased to have the benefit of his assignment—could have reproduced the work for sale upon a royalty basis.[500] It is, however, doubtful whether a photograph could have been exploited upon this basis.[501] The assignee of the copyright in a photograph whose author died shortly after the making of the negative or plate would therefore be in a worse position as compared to an assignee of, say, literary copyright. Again, the provision refers to the interest of the author after the termination of the period of his assignment as "the reversionary interest in the copyright expectant on the termination of that period". If works for which the existence of any reversionary period was problematical (for the author of a photograph might live for 25 years after the making of the photograph) were intended to be included, it might have been expected that there would have been added, after the words "reversionary interest", the words "if any".

5–122   **Arrangements and adaptations.** After the copyright in the work had been assigned by the author-first owner, original arrangements or adaptations of the work may have been made by or with the licence of the assignee and given rise to fresh and independent copyrights in the arrangements or adaptations. These copyrights will vest in the person who made the arrangements or adaptations, or his employer, assignee, etc. At the end of the 25-year period they do not revert to the author of the original work from which the arrangements or adaptations were made because he was not the first owner of the copyright in them. All that reverts to him is the copyright in the underlying work of which he was the author and first owner. This is the case even with arrangements and adaptations which were made without the licence of the author-first owner after the reversion has taken place.[502]

5–123   **Illusory nature of the benefits conferred by the reverter.** The reverter provision was inserted in the 1911 Act in the interest of an author's family, to prevent,

---

[497] *Chappell & Co Ltd v Redwood Music Ltd* [1982] R.P.C. 109.

[498] Copyright Act 1911 ss.19 and 21.

[499] A similar doubt previously existed in relation to "mechanical contrivances", which were protected under the 1911 Act as musical works (see s.19 of the 1911 Act). Such 1911 Act works are now protected as sound recordings and are thus clearly outside the scope of the reverter provision, which applies only to literary, dramatic, musical and artistic works.

[500] 1911 Act s.3, proviso. See *Copinger*, 12th edn, paras 296 et seq.

[501] See *Copinger*, 12th edn, para.303.

[502] *Redwood Music Ltd v Chappell & Co Ltd* [1982] R.P.C. 109.

if possible, a successful author from making improvident contracts for the fruits of his talent and originality to the detriment of his dependants.[503] The reversionary interest became an asset of the author's estate and assignable immediately upon his death by his personal representatives or by a beneficiary after assent.[504] It might therefore have been sold by his personal representatives for the payment of his debts and, even if not required for that purpose, it was frequently the duty of the executors to realise the interest for the purpose of winding up the author's estate.[505] Even where the author made a specific bequest of his reversionary interest in his copyright, the specific legatee would probably be ready to sell that interest at once, rather than wait for a chance of income 25 years later. The amount which a purchaser would be prepared to give for a reversionary interest in a copyright falling into possession 25 years later was not likely to have been very large, particularly bearing in mind that he would in any event be entitled to publish the work upon payment of a royalty and also that, if he did purchase, he could for the same reason not acquire an exclusive right.[506] It was also the fact that in the case of works originating in the United States of America, the descendants of a deceased author often executed assignments in favour of publishers with the primary purpose of transferring to the publishers the renewal rights in the works arising under American law at the expiration of 28 years from the date of first publication. Such agreements may, on their true construction according to the proper law of the agreements, have been effective to transfer to the publishers the reversionary copyright arising under English law.[507]

Recommendation of 1952 Copyright Committee. The Gregory Committee recommended that this provision should not be continued on the ground that since it was recommending the omission of the right to publish works on compulsory royalty terms at the end of the 25-year period,[508] the reverter provision should also go, taking the view that it had been inserted so as to give the compulsory royalty to the personal representatives of the author.[509] These recommendations were carried into effect by the 1956 Act, together with transitional provisions which, together with clarifications and further amendment, are contained in the 1988 Act, as discussed above.   **5–124**

C. Transmission by Testamentary Disposition and Operation of Law

As has been seen, the 1988 Act provides that copyright is transmissible by testamentary disposition or by operation of law, as personal or moveable property.[510] On such a transmission, copyright may be divided up in the same way as it can be by a partial assignment.[511] Note that title to UK copyright, being property situate in the United Kingdom, cannot be taken away by foreign   **5–125**

---

[503] *Redwood Music Ltd v B. Feldman & Co Ltd* [1979] R.P.C. 385 at 402; *Chappell & Co Ltd v Redwood Music Ltd* [1981] R.P.C. 337 at 344.

[504] *Chappell & Co Ltd v Redwood Music Ltd* [1981] R.P.C. 337 at 344.

[505] For instance, the rule well known to equity lawyers as the rule in *Howe v Lord Dartmouth* (1802) 7 Ves. 137 would apply. cf. *Pickering v Evans* [1921] 2 Ch. 309.

[506] Copyright Act 1911 s.3.

[507] Although there is no necessary implication that they do so when they are executed in the context of American renewal rights. See *Redwood Music Ltd v B. Feldman & Co Ltd* [1979] R.P.C. 385 at 403; *Chappell & Co Ltd v Redwood Music Ltd* [1981] R.P.C. 337 at 350.

[508] 1911 Act s.3. See para.5–160, below.

[509] Cmnd.8662, para.23.It is unclear from the Parliamentary debates at the time that this was in fact the case. See also para.5–115, above, as to the objective of the reverter provision.

[510] CDPA 1988 s.90(1). S.36(1) of the 1956 Act made the same provision. There was no express provision to this effect in the 1911 Act but it is thought it was to the same effect.

[511] CDPA 1988 s.90(2). As to such assignments, see paras 5–97 et seq., above.

governmental decree or act. This is simply an application of the wider rule that English law will not enforce foreign laws which purport to have extra-territorial effect.[512]

(i) Death

5–126   On the death of an owner, his copyrights will devolve on his personal representative.[513] Subject to payment of debts and administration expenses, the copyrights will be held by the personal representative for the benefit of the person to whom the owner has bequeathed them or, if he died intestate, his next-of-kin.

5–127   **In whom vested on death.** Where a person dies testate and domiciled in England or Wales, having appointed an executor who survives him, his copyrights will vest on his death in his executor.[514] A subsequent grant of probate does not operate to vest the copyrights in him: they are already vested. The grant is merely the proof which an English court requires to establish his appointment.[515] On the other hand, where a person domiciled in England or Wales dies intestate, or dies testate but without having appointed an executor entitled to probate, or an executor who survives him,[516] his copyrights will vest by operation of law in the Public Trustee on death.[517] It is only on the grant of letters of administration that the copyrights will vest in the administrator,[518] whose title does not in general relate back to the date of death.[519]

The distinction between the two situations is crucial. Since an executor's title dates from the moment of death, he may start an infringement action without obtaining a grant. If his title is put in issue, he will merely have to obtain a grant by the date of the trial to prove it.[520] For the same reason, an executor has sufficient title to assign the copyright before obtaining a grant. On the other hand, if an infringement action is started by a prospective administrator before obtaining a grant, he will have had no title at the date of the issue of the writ and the action is likely to be irremediably bad.[521] The subsequent obtaining of the grant will not

---

[512] See *Peer International Corp v Termidor Music Publishers Ltd* [2003] EWCA Civ 1156; [2004] Ch. 212; [2004] R.P.C. 23, applying *Bank voor Handel en Scheepvaart NV v Slatford* [1953] 1 Q.B. 248 and holding *Lorentzen v Lydden & Co Ltd* [1942] 2 K.B. 202 to have been wrongly decided. In *Peer*, a decree of the communist government of Cuba made in 1960 had the purported effect of divesting owners of their copyright, but was held to be of no effect in relation to UK copyright.

[513] Williams, Mortimer and Sunnucks on *Executors, Administrators and Probate*, 19th edn (London: Sweet & Maxwell), pp.606 et seq.

[514] Williams, Mortimer and Sunnucks on *Executors, Administrators and Probate*, 19th edn, p.606.

[515] Williams, Mortimer and Sunnucks on *Executors, Administrators and Probate*, 19th edn, p.503.

[516] No grant of probate will be issued in these circumstances, only a grant of letters of administration with the will annexed. See *In the Goods of Pryse (Deceased)* [1904] P. 301.

[517] Administration of Estates Act 1925 s.9, as amended by s.14 of the Law of Property (Miscellaneous Provisions) Act 1994.

[518] Administration of Estates Act 1925 s.9.

[519] Williams, Mortimer and Sunnucks on *Executors, Administrators and Probate*, 19th edn, p.504.

[520] In some circumstances a party may be able to obtain a stay of the action pending a grant.

[521] *Redwood Music Ltd v B. Feldman & Co Ltd* [1979] R.P.C. 1. As to the sufficiency of title at the date of the writ generally, see para.21–38, below. For the exceptional cases in which title of an administrator is regarded as "relating back" to a time before the grant, see Williams, Mortimer and Sunnucks on *Executors, Administrators and Probate*, 19th edn, p.505. In *Peer International Corporation v Termidor Music Publishers Ltd* [2006] EWHC 2883 (Ch); [2007] E.C.D.R. 1, Lindsay J. appeared to reject an argument that although there was no grant of letters of administration, a claimant which had obtained assignments from all those entitled on intestacy could sue for declaratory relief on the basis that it had a better title than anyone else in equity (para.80). The claimant's application to be appointed administrator of the copyrights or for an accountant to be so appointed also failed on the facts (paras 85 and 86).

save it. In the same way he has no title to assign.[522] Where urgent action needs to be taken and there is no executor, the appropriate course is to obtain a limited or special grant (*ad colligenda bona*) or obtain the appointment of a receiver by the court. Whether title is claimed by an executor or administrator, the primary way of proving the grant is the production of the grant itself. In its absence, secondary evidence is admissible, but may be of little weight.[523]

Death of person with foreign domicile. The position as to the immediate vesting of the copyrights of a person dying domiciled abroad is not very clear and is complicated by the fact that, unlike the position under English and other common law systems, civil law systems generally provide for the immediate and automatic transmission of property to the heirs or universal legatee.[524] The position seems to depend on whether the question is one of administration or succession. On the one hand, questions regarding the succession of moveables (which for this purpose would include copyright[525]) are governed by the law of the deceased's domicile. On the other, under English law, questions regarding the administration of an estate are treated as governed by the law of the country from which the personal representative derives his authority. A grant issued by a foreign court has no operation in England or Wales, so to establish title here a personal representative will need to obtain an English grant and thus the administration will be governed by English law. It is suggested that under English law, the immediate vesting of a deceased person's property is a matter of administration not succession.

    5–128

As to the authorities, where a foreigner dies testate, appointing an executor who survives him, and the law of his domicile on this issue is the same as the law of England, it seems that his copyrights vest in the executor.[526] An action may therefore be started by him, or by persons claiming through him, before obtaining a grant. Where a foreigner dies intestate or without appointing an executor who survives him, it appears that his English copyrights vest in the Public Trustee until a grant is obtained.[527] No action may therefore be brought before such a grant is obtained.

Literary executors. It is common practice for an author to appoint separate

    5–129

---

[522] Although if he subsequently obtains a grant, the title may be perfected by virtue of the doctrine of "feeding the estoppel".

[523] *Gabrin v Universal Music Operations Ltd* [2003] EWHC (Ch) 1335; [2004] E.C.D.R. 4 (although wrongly holding that the old "best evidence" rule applies—see para.5–67, above, and *Springsteen v Masquerade Music Ltd* [2001] E.M.L.R. 654, CA).

[524] See Cheshire and North, *Private International Law* 13th edn (Butterworths, 1999), p.975.

[525] Although the 1988 Act states that copyright is transmissable as personal or moveable property (s.90(1)), copyright shares some of the characteristics of immoveables in the sense that the rights of copyright are territorially limited, so that copyright is regarded as situate in the country whose law governs its existence. UK copyright is therefore situate in the UK. See *Peer International Corp v Termidor Music Publishers Ltd* [2002] EWHC (Ch) 2675; [2004] R.P.C. 22 and para.2–02, above.

[526] *Redwood Music Ltd v B. Feldman & Co Ltd* [1979] R.P.C. 1. But note that the decision appears to have proceeded on the basis that the issue of the vesting was governed by the law of domicile (the State of Michigan). cf. *Mackay v Mackay* [1912] 2 S.L.T. 445. Also, note that in *Peer International Corporation v Termidor Music Publishers Ltd* [2006] EWHC 2883 (Ch), the correctness of the statement in *Redwood Music Ltd v B. Feldman & Co Ltd* that "English copyright which forms part of the estate of a testator who dies domiciled abroad can vest in the executors appointed in his will, without any Grant of Probate or Letters of Administration in this country", on which the passage in the text is based, was questioned. It was common ground that this statement was obiter (para.64). Lindsay J. stated that the reasoning in Redwood was "not above doubt" (para.68), particularly insofar as the judge (Robert Goff J.) had relied by analogy on the provisions of s.19 of the Revenue Act 1889 (para.70). In the event, however, Lindsay J. was able to distinguish Redwood on the basis that the deceased in *Peer* had all died intestate (para.71).

[527] *Novello & Co Ltd v Hinrichsen Edition Ltd* [1951] Ch. 1026; (1951) 68 R.P.C. 243 (executor dying before testator); *Redwood Music v B Feldman & Co Ltd* [1981] R.P.C. 337; *Novello & Co Ltd v Eulenburg (E.) Ltd* [1950] 1 All E.R. 44 at 46, CA. The decisions were, however, obiter, and see fn.521 as to the doubt about the position.

executors of his literary estate, often having particular experience in the field.[528] Where no relevant trusts are declared by the will, the executors' primary obligation will be to sell the property in order to wind up the estate,[529] but there is nevertheless a discretion to postpone sale for its better administration.[530] This power may be particularly valuable where the immediate sale of the literary estate would not realise its full potential.[531] A properly drawn will appointing literary executors will vest in the literary executors not only the author's copyrights but also his manuscripts and the benefit of his publishing contracts and provide for express powers to postpone sale and manage the exploitation of the copyrights.

5–130   **Title from personal representative.** Title may be derived from a personal representative by assignment or assent. Where the personal representative sells the copyright, title should be passed by way of assignment. Where copyright has been bequeathed, title should be made by assent. An assent, although usually in writing, may be oral or even implied from conduct,[532] and operates to vest the property in the beneficiary by operation of law. Where a personal representative has died with copyright still vested in him, the title will devolve on his personal representative. If he has no executor, a special grant will be needed.[533]

(ii) Bequest of an unpublished work

5–131   The 1988 Act supplies a rule of construction affecting the title to copyright works where the physical object originally embodying the work passes under a specific or general bequest in a will. It therefore operates as a limited exception to the general principle that a transfer of the ownership of a physical object embodying a copyright work does not operate to transfer the copyright. Earlier Acts contained rules of more limited application and in order to preserve the effect of these rules the provisions of the 1988 Act therefore vary, depending on the date of death.

5–132   **Death on or after August 1, 1989.** This rule applies where a person is entitled under a specific or general bequest to an original document or other thing recording or embodying a literary, dramatic, musical or artistic work which was unpublished before the testator's death. In such a case, unless a contrary indication appears from the will or codicil, the bequest is to be construed as including the copyright in the work in so far as the testator was the owner of the copyright immediately before his death.[534] A similar rule applies in the case of an unpublished sound recording or film where a person is entitled under a bequest to the original thing containing the recording or film.[535] The rule applies whether or not the testator is the author and thus it applies, for example, where an assignee of the copyright owns original manuscripts. The rule applies whether the bequest is specific or general and whether the person is entitled under the bequest beneficially or otherwise, for example, as trustee on trust.

---

[528] The literary estate will of course be available, with the testator's other property, for the payment of debts and expenses in the course of administration: Administration of Estates Act 1925 s.32(1).

[529] And where life interests are involved, the rule in *Howe v Lord Dartmouth* (1802) 7 Ves. 137 will need to be considered.

[530] Administration of Estates Act 1925 s.39(1)(iii) and, in the case of an intestate s.33(1). As to the effect of this power on the power to trade or carry on a business, see Williams, Mortimer and Sunnucks on *Executors, Administrators and Probate*, 19th edn, p.767.

[531] It will often be the case that the market for the literary estate will in practice be limited to the author's publisher.

[532] Williams, Mortimer and Sunnucks on *Executors, Administrators and Probate*, 19th edn, p.1154; *Redwood Music Ltd v B. Feldman & Co Ltd* [1979] R.P.C. 1.

[533] See generally, Williams, Mortimer and Sunnucks on *Executors, Administrators and Probate*, 19th edn, pp.363 et seq.

[534] CDPA 1988 s.93.

[535] s.93.

Death before August 1, 1989 but after June 1, 1957. The rule is more limited, **5–133** applying only to a bequest of an original document embodying a work, and thus only to literary, dramatic, musical and artistic works.[536] This reflects the more limited provision which was contained in the 1956 Act.[537]

Death before June 1, 1957. The above provisions do not apply where a testator **5–134** died before the commencement of the 1956 Act.[538] In such an event, the rule is even more limited, applying only to the author of an unpublished or unperformed literary, dramatic or musical work. Here, the ownership after his death of a manuscript of his is prima facie proof of the copyright being with the owner of the manuscript where such ownership was acquired under a testamentary disposition made by the author.[539] This provision reflects the position under the 1911 Act[540] and perhaps that which existed before then.[541] It had no application to bequests by anyone other than the author, in particular, assigns from him, or to artistic works.

(iii) Bankruptcy

On an owner's bankruptcy, the copyright in a work is held initially by the Official **5–135** Receiver as receiver and manager,[542] and, on the appointment of the trustee in bankruptcy of the copyright owner passes, to him by operation of law without any assignment in writing.[543] The copyright in any work acquired by or, devolving on the bankrupt after the commencement of his bankruptcy and before his discharge does not automatically vest in the trustee, but may be the subject of a claim by him.[544] Although the benefit of an unexecuted contract for personal services by the bankrupt will not vest in a trustee,[545] the trustee is entitled to sums of money such as publishing royalties or distributions from collecting societies due in respect of works completed before the bankruptcy and not depending on performance of further obligations on the author's part.[546] In the absence of any claim to post-bankruptcy works themselves, the trustee is not entitled to sums arising from such works.[547]

(iv) Execution

There is no process whereby copyright can be directly taken in execution by a **5–136** judgment creditor of the copyright owner[548] even, it seems, by the appointment of a receiver by way of equitable execution.[549] Of course, royalties due to the judgment debtor may be subject to process of execution, such as attachment in garnishee proceedings.

---

[536] CDPA 1988 Sch.1 para.30(1)(b).
[537] Copyright Act 1956 s.38 and Sch.7 para.29(1).
[538] CDPA 1988 Sch.1 para.30(1)(a).
[539] Sch.1 para.30(2).
[540] Copyright Act 1911 s.17(2).
[541] See *Wilis v Curtois* (1838) 1 Beav. 189. Note, also, the provisions of s.3 of the Copyright Act 1842, under which the copyright in every "book" published after the author's death was to belong to the proprietor of the manuscript.
[542] Insolvency Act 1986 s.287.
[543] CDPA 1988 s.90(1) and the Insolvency Act 1986 ss.283 and 306.
[544] Insolvency Act 1986 s.307.
[545] *Bailey v Thurston & Co Ltd* [1903] 1 K.B. 137 at 145–146.
[546] *Performing Right Society Ltd v Rowland* [1997] 3 All E.R. 336.
[547] *Performing Right Society Ltd v Rowland* [1997] 3 All E.R. 336.
[548] See *Re Baldwin* (1858) 2 De G. & J. 230. But compare *Planet Earth Productions Inc v Rowlands* (1990) 69 D.L.R. (4th) 715 (Ontario S.C.), although there the wording of the relevant statute included choses in action.
[549] *Edwards & Co v Picard* (1909) 78 L.J. K.B. 1108 (a patent case).

3. RIGHTS IN EXTENDED AND REVIVED TERMS OF COPYRIGHT

A. The Extended and Revived Terms under the Term Directive

(i) Introduction

5–137   As discussed elsewhere,[550] compliance with the Council Directive 93/98 harmonising the term of copyright required the United Kingdom to extend the term of copyright for many works[551] to the life of the author and 70 years after his death.[552] This was achieved by the Duration of Copyright and Rights in Performances Regulations 1995, which came into force on January 1, 1996. In the case of works which were the subject of existing UK copyright protection on this date, this meant extending the term for a further 20 years. In addition, where the UK term of copyright had already expired by December 31, 1995 but the work was, on July 1, 1995, still protected in another EEA state under legislation relating to copyright or related rights, the UK copyright in such works was revived for the remainder of the 70-year post mortem term.[553] It followed that the Regulations needed to deal with two separate issues, namely, ownership of the copyright during the extended term and ownership of the revived term of copyright.

The Directive did not stipulate who such owners should be. In each case, there were three alternative candidates: first, the original author; secondly, first owner of the copyright, who otherwise stood to be deprived of the windfall of the extended or revived term; thirdly, the owner of the copyright immediately before the expiry of the old term. As will be seen, in respect of the extended term, the Regulations confer the extended copyright on the person who is or was the owner of the copyright at the end of the old term. In respect of the revived term, the general effect of the Regulations is to confer the right either on the person who was the owner of the copyright immediately before it expired or, if that person had died or ceased to exist before January 1, 1996, the original author or his personal representatives. In this respect, the Regulations appear to operate in a rather arbitrary manner.

(ii) Ownership of the extended and revived terms

5–138   **Ownership of the extended term generally.** In the case of works which were the subject of UK copyright on December 31, 1995, the person who was the owner of the copyright at that date became, as from January 1, 1996, the owner of the full, extended term.[554] Thus whoever was the owner of the copyright on December 31, 1995, whether he was the original, first owner or someone deriving title from him, became the owner of the new, longer term. The exception to this rule is where the copyright owner on December 31, 1995 was owner for a term less than the full, old term of life and 50 years, for example under an assignment for a more limited period. In this case, whoever was entitled to the reversionary

---

[550] See Ch.6, below.

[551] i.e. literary, dramatic, musical and artistic works, and films.

[552] More precisely, to a term being the author's life and a period ending 70 years from the end of the calendar year in which the author died. See CDPA 1988 s.12(1) as amended by the Duration of Copyright and Rights in Performances Regulations 1995 (SI 1995/3297). Previously, the term of copyright for such works was a period ending 50 years from the end of the calendar year in which the author died.

[553] For a full discussion of the effect of the Regulations, see Ch.6, below.

[554] Duration of Copyright and Rights in Performances Regulations 1995 (SI 1995/3297) reg.18(1).

interest expectant on the termination of the lesser term became entitled to the extended term.[555]

Ownership of the revived term. In the first instance, the Regulations provide   **5–139**
that the person who was the owner of the copyright in the work immediately before the copyright expired became, as from January 1, 1996, the owner of any revived copyright.[556] Effectively, therefore, the last owner of the expired copyright became the owner of copyright for the rump of the post mortem period, even if he only acquired the copyright a short time before the expiry of the old term. Where, however, this person had died before January 1, 1996, or being a legal person, such as a company, had ceased to exist before this date, the revived term was to belong to the author of the work or his personal representatives,[557] except in the case of a film, when the right was to belong to the principal director of the film or his personal representatives.[558] Where the right vested in personal representatives in this way, it was to be held by them for the benefit of the person who would have been entitled to the right had it been vested in the deceased person immediately before his death and devolved as part of his estate.[559] This provision has two notable effects. First, whether or not the revived copyright vested in the author depended entirely on whether the former copyright owner died or ceased to exist before January 1, 1996, an event which had no bearing on who had the greater moral claim to the benefit of the revived term. The second is that where the former owner had died, then, except in the case of films, it was the author or his estate, which benefited.[560] This was so even where the author never owned the copyright, for example where the work was made by him in the course of his employment under a contract of service. The position was similar in relation to films where the former copyright owner had died or ceased to exist: the revived right belonged to the principal director, a person who previously would have had no interest in the copyright.

(iii) Transitional provisions

(a) *Pre-commencement assignments and licences*

Pre-commencement assignments. Since the owner of the extended term became   **5–140**
the owner "as from" January 1, 1996 ("commencement"), he could assign or deal with the extended term of copyright, together with his interest in what was the remainder of the old term, from that date. What, however, is the effect of attempted dealings in the extended term before that date? In general, the legal title to property which is not yet in existence cannot be passed, and a purported assignment will at best take effect as an agreement to assign,[561] so that all that can be achieved by such an assignment, if it was given for consideration, is the passing of the equitable title to the extended or revived term. The position is to some extent dealt with by the Regulations, which provide that:

"Where, by an agreement made before commencement in relation to

---

[555] reg.18(2).
[556] Duration of Copyright and Rights in Performances Regulations 1995 (SI 1995/3297) reg.19(1)(b).
[557] As to the vesting in an author's personal representatives, see the similar wording of the proviso to the 1911 Act s.5(2) proviso, now re-embodied in CDPA 1988 Sch.1 para.27(2). As to the effect of this proviso, see paras 5–117 et seq., above.
[558] Duration of Copyright and Rights in Performances Regulations 1995 (SI 1995/3297) reg.19(2)(a).
[559] reg.19(3).
[560] It is only in the case of films that the author might still be alive.
[561] See para.5–108, above.

extended or revived copyright,[562] and signed by or on behalf of the prospective owner of the copyright, the prospective owner purports to assign the extended or revived copyright (wholly or partially) to another person, then if, on commencement the assignee or another person claiming under him would be entitled as against all other persons to require the copyright to be vested in him, the copyright shall vest in the assignee or his successor in title by virtue of this paragraph".[563]

It follows that where this paragraph applies, the legal title to the extended or revived term will have vested in the assignee on January 1, 1996. It should be noted that an agreement for which there was no consideration will not carry such rights since the assignee would not be entitled to a decree of specific performance vesting the copyright in him.[564] The wording of the Regulation is similar to that used elsewhere in the Act in relation to the assignment of future rights and, perhaps partly as a result, is not as clear as it might be.[565] First, it is not clear what is added by the qualifying condition that the agreement should be one "in relation to" extended or revived copyright. If the prospective owner purports to assign such copyright, then presumably the agreement will have been one "in relation to" such copyright; if not, the provision is of no operation anyway. In any event, the main issue is likely to be whether the prospective owner purported to deal with the revived or extended copyright. This will be a matter of construing the agreement in the light of the surrounding circumstances. Many assignments include as a matter of standard form words such as "all extensions and renewals of copyright" in defining the subject matter of the grant and such words may help in reaching the conclusion that the extended or revived term was intended to be included. Even in such a case, however, there may still be an issue as to whether there was an intention to assign "the" extended or revived term of UK copyright when neither party had it in contemplation as opposed, for example, to any extensions under existing foreign systems of law. Many assignments, of course, simply define the subject matter of the grant as "the copyright". It is suggested that the normal meaning to be placed on such words is that all possible rights were intended to be assigned so that such an assignment will carry the extended or revived term.

The second issue arises on the further requirement that the assignee or his successor should have been entitled on January 1, 1996 to have "the copyright" vested in him. It is here that the repetition of the wording used in s.91(1) and elsewhere in the 1988 Act gives rise to difficulties. The common case which will arise in practice is no doubt the one of a pre-commencement assignment of copyright, the issue being whether it will carry the extended or revived right. In such a case, "the copyright", as it existed before commencement, will already be vested in the assignee. It therefore seems inappropriate to speak in terms of the assignee still being entitled on commencement to require "the copyright" to be vested in him. This comment applies even in the case of a pre-commencement assignment expressly limited to the extended or revived term. Clearly, a purposive construction must be given to the provision and it therefore seems that the words "the copyright" should be understood as referring to the extended or revived copyright.

---

[562] "Extended copyright" is defined as any copyright which subsists by virtue of the provisions of the 1988 Act as amended by the Regulations ("the new provisions") after the date on which it would have expired under the 1988 Act as unamended ("the 1988 provisions"). Similarly, "revived copyright" is defined to mean any copyright which subsists by virtue of the new provisions after having expired under the 1988 provisions or any earlier enactment relating to copyright. See Duration of Copyright and Rights in Performances Regulations 1995 (SI 1995/3297) reg.17.

[563] reg.20(1).

[564] cf. the similar situation in respect of assignments of future copyright. See para.5–110, above.

[565] cf. CDPA 1988 ss.91 (future copyright—see para.5–110, above), 191C (future performer's property rights—see para.12–44, below) and s.223 (future design right—see para.13–120, below).

Licences by prospective owners. Provision is made as to who is bound by   **5–141**
licences granted by prospective owners of the extended or revived terms. Thus it
is provided that a licence granted by a prospective owner of extended or revived
copyright is binding on every successor in title to his interest, or prospective
interest, in the right, except a purchaser in good faith for valuable consideration
and without actual or constructive notice of the licence or a person deriving title
from such a purchaser.[566] For this purpose, a prospective owner also includes a
person who is prospectively entitled to any extended or revived copyright by
virtue of such an agreement.[567] Thus, licences granted in respect of the extended
or revived term by a person to whom the extended or revived term was
prospectively assigned will bind his successors. Again, the wording of the relevant regulation has been imported from s.91(3) of the 1988 Act without, perhaps,
sufficient thought being given to its new context. Clearly, the reference to the
prospective owner includes all pre-commencement owners of the copyright since
they were, unknowingly, prospective owners of the new rights. Again, presumably the reference to the licence granted by such an owner must be a reference to
a licence granted by him in respect of the extended or revived term. Usually, no
doubt, a licence agreement will have made no express reference to the extended
or revived term. Separate provision is made as to the effect of existing licences in
relation to the extended term, considered below, and the interrelationship of the
two provisions is not clear. No provision is made in relation to the revived term.[568]

The effect of existing licences and agreements: the extended term. Before   **5–142**
January 1, 1996 many copyright owners will have granted a licence or entered
into an agreement affecting the right to exploit a work. What is the effect of this
in relation to the extended term? Two different but interrelated regulations have
to be considered in such cases.

(a) First, it is provided that where any copyright licence or any term or condition of an agreement relating to the exploitation of a copyright work
subsisted immediately before January 1, 1996 in relation to a work in
which copyright then subsisted, and was not to expire before the old period of copyright, then it is to have effect during the period of any extended
period of copyright, subject to any agreement to the contrary.[569] So where,
for example, a licence was granted for the whole of the old term of copyright, it will continue for the extended term unless the agreement provided
otherwise. In the same way, any terms or conditions of the licence, for
example as to payment, will continue for the extended term. The position
is the same where the licence, or the terms or conditions of the agreement,
were imposed by the Copyright Tribunal.[570] One odd effect of these provisions is that if a pre-commencement licence was granted for some future
term expiring at the end of the old term of copyright, but which had not
yet started to run at commencement, the licence will not continue to have
effect into the extended period.

(b) Secondly, as has already been seen, a licence granted by a prospective
owner of the extended term in respect of the interest will generally bind
his successors in title. If, therefore, the licence granted continues to have
effect during the extended period, successors to the original licensor will
be bound.

---

[566] Duration of Copyright and Rights in Performances Regulations 1995 (SI 1995/3297) reg.20(2).
[567] reg.20(3).
[568] But note that a licence of right is available in respect of the revived term. See para.5–145, below.
[569] Duration of Copyright and Rights in Performances Regulations 1995 (SI 1995/3297) reg.21(1).
No doubt the agreement may be express or implied. cf. para.5–156, above.
[570] reg.21(2).

(b) *Effect of things done in relation to revived copyright before commencement*

5–143 Where the copyright in a work had expired, acts may well have been done in relation to the work on the basis that it was, and would remain, in the public domain and therefore no licence to do the acts was required from anybody. Article 10(3) of the Term Directive provides that any revival of the term is to be without prejudice to any acts of exploitation performed before implementation of the Directive and that Member States are required to adopt measures to protect acquired rights of third parties. The detail of such measures, however, was left to the discretion of Member States, provided that they did not have the overall effect of preventing the application of the new terms of protection laid down by the Directive.[571] To achieve this, the Regulations therefore had to deal with a number of situations.

(a) First, it is provided that no act done before commencement[572] is to be regarded as an infringement of any revived copyright in a work.[573] It follows that no copying of the work before this date will have been an infringement and such copies will not be infringing copies for the purposes of any act of sale, etc, whether pre- or post-commencement.[574] Prima facie, however, the issue of such copies to the public after commencement would be an infringement, but the extent to which this will be so is limited, as discussed below.

(b) Secondly, it is not an infringement to do anything after commencement in pursuance of arrangements made before January 1, 1995 at a time when copyright did not subsist in the work.[575] Provided therefore that relevant "arrangements" were made before this date, it will not be an infringement to do anything "in pursuance" of those arrangements. For this purpose, "arrangements" means arrangements for the exploitation of the work.[576] So, for example, if steps were taken to stage a performance of a public domain work, such as the hiring of a venue, the engagement of the performers and the building of sets, it will not be an infringement of copyright to perform the work pursuant to those arrangements after commencement. It is not clear whether this would still be the case if the public demand for the work led to an extended run of several years and in different venues, although if the arrangements which were made contemplated such a possibility, it is suggested it would. As to what will suffice as "arrangements", they are not limited to arrangements by way of contract but do not extend to all kinds of acts done, or steps of any kind taken: the acts must be of some degree of solidity or certainty, such that it can be said that acts done later are done "in pursuance of" the arrangements.[577] So, where a defendant had done a great deal of work on a new edition of a book which was then out of copyright, and had had various encouraging discussions with publishers but had not yet concluded a contract with them, neither the discussions nor the work on the new edition amounted to "arrangements" within the meaning of the regulations.[578] Where, however, all or a great deal of the preparatory work had been done before January 1, 1995 on the basis of an understanding or negotiations between the author and publisher relating to its publication, this would probably suffice.

---

[571] *Butterfly Music Srl v Carosello Edizioni Musicali E Discografichi Srl* [2000] E.C.D.R. 1 (E.C.J.).
[572] i.e. January 1, 1996.
[573] Duration of Copyright and Rights in Performances Regulations 1995 (SI 1995/3297) reg.23(1).
[574] As to infringement by dealing in infringing copies, see Ch.8.
[575] reg.23(2)(a).
[576] reg.23(5).
[577] *Sweeney v Macmillan Publishers Ltd* [2002] R.P.C. 35, at para.57.
[578] ibid.

(c) Thirdly, it will not be an infringement to issue to the public copies of the work made before July 1, 1995[579] at a time when copyright did not subsist in the work.[580] So, in the case of the example given above in relation to the printing of copies of the work, provided those copies were made before July 1, 1995, the issue of those copies to the public will not be an infringement. As already pointed out, such copies will not be infringing copies.

It may well have happened that while a work was in the public domain, other works were made which incorporated the public domain work. The exploitation of the new work could thus be prevented by the revival of copyright if no provision were made dealing with this. The Regulations therefore provide that in two circumstances it is not an infringement of the revived copyright in a work (the "old work") to do anything after commencement in relation to a literary, dramatic, musical or artistic work or a film made before commencement, or made in pursuance of arrangements made[581] before commencement (a "new work"), which contains a copy of the old work or is an adaptation of the old work:

(a) The first circumstance is where the new work was made before July 1, 1995[582] at a time when copyright did not subsist in the old work.[583] So, where a book was written before July 1, 1995 incorporating material from an old work in which copyright has since revived, it will not be an infringement to print and distribute copies of that book or do anything else "in relation to" it, for example, make a film based upon it. The Regulation will apply where, for example, the work is incorporated into a play or film although not where it is incorporated into a sound recording. The Regulation contemplates that there must be a new "work" brought into existence in which there will be found a copy or adaptation of the public domain work.

(b) The second circumstance is where the new work was made in pursuance of arrangements made before July 1, 1995 at a time when copyright did not subsist in the old work.[584] Thus even if the new work was not itself made before July 1, 1995, provided it was made in pursuance of arrangements made before this date, nothing done in relation to the new work will be an infringement.

(c) *The revived term: further provisions*

Revived copyright: owner not known. It can often be difficult to establish the identity of a copyright owner, particularly in relation to an old work. This problem is accentuated in cases of revived copyright since (a) the work may have been out of copyright for some time so that there will have been no authorised publisher or other person exploiting the work in the market in recent years who can be found and (b) where the revived copyright became the property of the author or his personal representatives rather than the last owner of the copyright,[585] it may be very difficult to establish who became the new copyright owner. To alleviate this problem, the Regulations provide that it is not an infringement of the revived

5–144

---

[579] This is the date by which Member States were required to implement the Directive. See art.13(1).
[580] reg.23(1)(b).
[581] See the text earlier in the paragraph as to the meaning of "arrangements made".
[582] As already noted, this is the date by which Member States were required to implement the Directive.
[583] reg.23(3)(a).
[584] reg.23(3)(b).
[585] See the Duration of Copyright and Rights in Performances Regulations 1995 (SI 1995/3297), reg.19(2) and para.5–139, above.

copyright in a work to do, after 1995, anything which is a restricted act in relation to the work if the act is done at a time when, or is done in pursuance of arrangements made[586] at a time when, the name and address of the person entitled to authorise the act cannot by reasonable inquiry be ascertained.[587]

5–145   **Use of revived copyright work as of right.** The rights of the revived copyright owner are substantially cut down by the availability of a compulsory licence to anyone who gives notice of his intention to exploit the work. In order to avail himself of such a licence, a person merely has to give reasonable notice of his intention to the copyright owner, stating when he intends to begin such acts. The licence will be subject to the payment of such reasonable royalty or other remuneration as may be agreed or determined in default of agreement by the Copyright Tribunal but the licence will come into effect whether or not the parties have come to any agreement as to royalties or other remuneration and whether or not this has been determined by the Tribunal. It appears that the requirement of "reasonable" notice is of little significance, not least because the copyright owner can do nothing to stop the intended acts once notice in proper form is given, and that thus very short notice is sufficient.[588] These provisions are considered in more detail elsewhere.[589]

B. Rights in the Extended Term of Copyright in Sound Recordings under the Information Society Directive

(i) Introduction

5–146   As discussed elsewhere,[590] one of the possible effects of the implementation of the Information Society Directive,[591] with its amendment of art.3(2) the Term Directive[592] was to extend the term of copyright in sound recordings. Because of this, the implementing regulations[593] contained transitional and other provisions which are similar to those in the regulations relating to the more general extension of the term of copyright dealt with in the previous section ("the Term Regulations").[594] For this purpose, the Regulations define the expression "extended copyright" to mean any copyright in a sound recording which subsists by virtue of the amended Act after the date on which it would have expired before amendment.[595]

(ii) Ownership of the extended copyright

5–147   The Regulations provide that the person who was the owner of the copyright in a sound recording immediately before October 31, 2003 became, as from that date, the owner of any extended copyright in that sound recording.[596] This provision therefore differs from that in the Term Regulations relating to the general extension of copyright, so far as concerns a person who was, on October 31, 2003, the

---

[586] See para.5–143, above, as to the meaning of "arrangements made".
[587] reg.23(4).
[588] *Sweeney v Macmillan Publishers Ltd* [2002] R.P.C. 35, at para.63.
[589] See paras 28–41 et seq., below.
[590] See para.6–57, below.
[591] 2001/29.
[592] 93/100, amended by art.11(2) of the Information Society Directive 2001/29, and since replaced by 2006/116/EC.
[593] Copyright and Related Rights Regulations 2003 (SI 2003/2498).
[594] There is no *revival* of any copyright under the regulations considered in the present section.
[595] reg.30(1C).
[596] Copyright and Related Rights Regulations 2003 (SI 2003/2498) reg.36.

owner of the copyright for *less* than the old term.[597] In this, the Regulations seem rather arbitrary.

(iii) Transitional provisions

(a) *Pre-commencement assignments, licences and agreements*

Pre-commencement assignments. The Regulations contain a provision dealing with the effect of an agreement made before October 31, 2003 whereby the prospective owner of the extended copyright in a sound recording purported to assign the extended copyright. If, on commencement, the assignee or person claiming under him would have been entitled to require the copyright to be vested in him, the copyright vested in him automatically.[598] The provision is similar to that contained in the Term Regulations, and the same comments apply.[599]   **5–148**

Licences by prospective owners. As with the Term Regulations, a licence granted by a prospective owner of the extended copyright in a sound recording is binding on successors in title, except a purchaser for value without actual or constructive notice of the licence.[600]   **5–149**

The effect of existing licences and agreements. Any copyright licence or any term or condition of an agreement relating to the exploitation of a sound recording which subsisted immediately before October 31, 2003 and which would not have expired before the end of the term of copyright under the unamended provisions of the Act, is to continue to have effect during the period of any extended copyright, subject to any agreement to the contrary.[601] The same applies to any licence, term or condition imposed by order of the Copyright Tribunal.[602] The Term Regulations contain identical provisions.[603]   **5–150**

(b) *Effect of things done in relation to extended copyright before commencement*

The Regulations make a number of savings similar to those found in the Term Regulations: (1) no act done before October 31, 2003 is to be regarded as an infringement of any extended copyright[604]; (2) nothing in the Regulations is to affect any agreement made before December 22, 2002[605]; (3) no act done after October 31, 2003, in pursuance of an agreement made before December 22, 2002, is to be regarded as an infringement of any extended copyright.[606] The comments made in relation to the equivalent provisions of the Term Regulations apply equally to these provisions, except that it should be noted that the expression   **5–151**

---

[597] See para.5–138, above.
[598] Copyright and Related Rights Regulations 2003 (SI 2003/2498) reg.37(1)
[599] See para.5–140, above.
[600] Copyright and Related Rights Regulations 2003 (SI 2003/2498) reg.37(2). "Prospective owner" is defined in reg.30(1). See the comment on the similar provisions of the Term Regulations in para.5–141, above.
[601] Copyright and Related Rights Regulations 2003 (SI 2003/2498) reg.38(1).
[602] reg.38(2).
[603] See para.5–142, above.
[604] Copyright and Related Rights Regulations 2003 (SI 2003/2498) reg.31(2).
[605] reg.32(1).
[606] reg.32(2).

used now is "in pursuance of any agreement" rather than "in pursuance of any arrangements",[607] clearly a more strict test.[608]

C. Rights in the Extended Term under the 1911 Act

5–152 **Introduction.** The term of copyright conferred by the 1911 Act in respect of published works was longer than that subsisting under the pre-existing law,[609] and this longer term was conferred on existing works which were still in copyright at the commencement date of the 1911 Act.[610] Subject to the important transitional provisions considered below, whoever was the owner of the relevant right immediately before commencement became entitled to the corresponding copyright conferred by the 1911 Act, including, therefore, the copyright during the period of any extended term. This meant that where the author had assigned or granted an interest in the old right for the whole of the old term, a windfall might have been produced for the assignee or grantee. In such a case, it was therefore provided that the assignment or grant continued until the old period of copyright would have run out, at which date the unexpired term of copyright revested in the author or his personal representatives, subject to two alternative rights of the original assignee or grantee to continue to exploit the work. The 1956 Act sought to maintain the rights of the various interested parties and the 1988 Act continues this regime. To understand the position today it is necessary, first, to examine the nature of the provisions in the 1911 Act and then to see how these have been carried through by the 1956 and 1988 Acts.

5–153 **The substituted rights under the 1911 Act.** As to the provisions of the 1911 Act, first, it is important to examine how the Act operated generally in the case of pre-1911 Act rights. Before the passing of the 1911 Act, a right of copyright existed at common law to restrain the publication of and other dealings with certain categories of unpublished works. Copyright also subsisted by force of statute in published works of various descriptions (and certain unpublished works), giving the owner the right to restrain reproduction, etc., of such works. Further, in relation to works which could be performed, namely musical and dramatic works, there similarly existed two distinct public performance rights, namely a right at common law to restrain the public performance of works which had not previously been performed in public, and a statutory right to restrain performance of works which had been publicly performed. Under the 1911 Act, these rights were coalesced into one, "substituted", right of copyright. Thus the owner of the pre-1911 Act copyright, whether statutory or common law, became entitled to the substituted right of copyright conferred by the 1911 Act, and common law copyright was abolished.[611] As to the performing right, a person who before the 1911 Act was the owner, whether at common law or under statute, of the performing right, but not the copyright, in a musical or dramatic work became the owner of a substituted right of copyright, being the sole right to perform the work in public, to the exclusion of all other rights comprised in the copyright. Similarly, a person who owned the copyright, but not the performing right, in a musical or dramatic work, became the owner of a substituted right of copyright,

---

[607] reg.23(2)(a) of the Term Regulations, dealing with revived copyright.

[608] See the discussion at para.5–143, above.

[609] So, for example, whereas the term for published works under the Literary Copyright Act 1842 was the life of the author and seven years, or 42 years from publication, whichever was the longer, the term of copyright for such works under the 1911 Act was the lifetime of the author and 50 years after his death. The period of copyright in many unpublished works under the pre-1911 Act law was perpetual.

[610] Copyright Act 1911 s.24(1).

[611] Copyright Act 1911 s.24(3).

being the copyright to the exclusion of the sole right to perform the work or any substantial part of it in public.[612] Again, the common law performing right was abolished.

Ownership of the 1911 Act term. In general terms, the 1911 Act provided that whoever was entitled to a pre-1911 Act right which was still subsisting at commencement[613] became the owner of the substituted right, or to the same interest in such substituted right, for the term for which it would have subsisted had the 1911 Act been in force when the work was made. In general terms, this meant that the owner of the old right as at commencement became the owner of the new, substituted right of copyright for the whole of the new term of copyright.   **5–154**

The revesting proviso. As already indicated, the one qualification to this applied where an author, being the first owner of the old right, had assigned or granted an interest for the whole of the old term. In such a case, the 1911 Act provided[614] that where the author of a pre-1911 Act right which was subsisting at commencement[615] had assigned the right or granted any interest in it for the whole term of the right, then at the date when, but for the passing of the Act, the right would have expired, the substituted right conferred by the Act should, in the absence of express agreement, pass to the author of the work.[616] Any interest in the work created before commencement, and still then subsisting, determined.[617] The general intention was therefore to preserve the extended term for the benefit of authors or their estates.   **5–155**

Express agreement. The words "in the absence of express agreement" meant "in the absence of an agreement expressly referring to the substituted right identified as such".[618] The agreement must therefore have been one made in clear contemplation of these provisions of the Act. It follows that an agreement made before the passing of the 1911 Act referring in general terms to copyright, however wide, for example, "present or future, vested or contingent", would not fall within this description.[619] However, a further assignment, after commencement, of the "copyright" would prima facie have carried the full, extended term.   **5–156**

Relation to 1911 Act reverter provision. As has been seen,[620] the 1911 Act contained a provision whereby authors were unable to dispose of their interest in their works for the last 25 years of the term of copyright. Any attempt to do so resulted in the copyright reverting to their personal representatives at the beginning of this period. However, the references in this reverter provision to "the copyright" referred to the copyright as conferred by the 1911 Act and not the rights which existed previously.[621] An assignment or grant made before the commencement of the 1911 Act which dealt with the copyright in an existing work was therefore unaffected by the reverter provision.   **5–157**

Partial assignment or grant for less than old term. The above provision only applied to the case of an assignment or grant of an interest covering the whole   **5–158**

---

[612] s.24, Sch.1.
[613] July 1, 1912.
[614] Copyright Act 1911 s.24(1), proviso.
[615] July 1, 1912.
[616] For this purpose, the expression "author" included the legal personal representatives of a deceased author. See s.24(2).
[617] s.24(1), proviso.
[618] *Chappell & Co Ltd v Redwood Music Ltd* [1981] R.P.C. 337.
[619] *Chappell & Co Ltd v Redwood Music Ltd* [1981] R.P.C. 337.
[620] See para.5–115, above.
[621] *Coleridge-Taylor v Novello & Co Ltd* [1938] Ch. 850.

term of copyright. If, therefore, the author had parted with his copyright for a period less than the whole of the original term, he had a reversionary interest which would automatically confer upon him the substituted right, which would become exercisable by him upon the falling in of his reversion. It is unclear whether the proviso applied in the situation where the author had assigned or granted a right to one person for a portion of the old term, and then to another for the residue of that term. It is suggested that, in accordance with the policy underlying the section, it did apply.[622] The proviso must also have applied where the assignment or grant was made at some time after the work was created, so that it will not strictly have been for the "whole term of the right", but for the whole of the remaining term of the right. Otherwise the proviso would have been of almost no application.

5–159   **Assignment by a person other than the author.** It is important to note that the proviso only applied to a case where the assignment or grant was made by "the author" of the work. Where the copyright vested in the first instance in any person other than the author,[623] then a suitably worded pre-1911 Act assignment or grant by such person would have been effective to pass to the assignee or grantee the benefit of the extended term conferred by the 1911 Act.

5–160   **Rights of assignee or grantee notwithstanding revesting.** Although the benefit of any extended term of copyright conferred by the 1911 Act prima facie vested in the original author of the work, and not in his assignee or grantee, it was considered unfair to deprive the assignee or grantee of the right to reap any advantage from the market which he might have created. The 1911 Act therefore provided that the person who, immediately before the date when the copyright would have expired under the repealed statutes, was the owner of any right or interest in the copyright was entitled to two, alternative options, as follows:

> *First option.* He was entitled to call for an assignment of the right or the grant of a similar interest in it for the remainder of the extended term of the right. This right had to be exercised by notice and was to be for such consideration as, failing agreement, was determined by arbitration.[624] The notice referred to had to be given not more than one year, and not less than six months, before the date on which the right would have so expired, and to be sent by registered post to the "author"[625] or, if the author could not with reasonable diligence be found, advertised in the London Gazette and in two London newspapers.[626] It is suggested that the true construction of this option was that a person who had obtained an assignment of the old term of copyright was entitled to an assignment of the right, but not to the grant of an interest, and, similarly, that a person who had obtained a grant of an interest for the whole of the old term was entitled to a "similar" grant for the residue of the new term, but not to an assignment of the right.

> *Second option.* Alternatively, he was entitled, without taking any such assignment or grant, to continue to reproduce or perform the work on a non-

---

[622] But note that the transitional provisions of the 1956 Act, which summarise the application of the revesting proviso, refer to the grant of "an" interest in the right, rather than "any" interest. See the Copyright Act 1956 Sch.7, para.38(a).

[623] As, for example, in the case of articles written for collective works, where in certain circumstances the copyright first vested in the proprietor. See the Literary Copyright Act 1842 s.18 and para.5–31 and 5–40, above.

[624] The giving of this notice presumably bound the person giving it to purchase the right or interest.

[625] As noted, this expression included his personal representatives: see Copyright Act 1911 s.24(2).

[626] It is not clear how the assignment or grant, as the case may have been, was to be obtained if the author or his personal representatives could not be found. The person giving the notice, however, would presumably obtain at least an equitable title.

exclusive basis,[627] subject to the payment of royalties to the author, if demanded, but otherwise in the same manner as before.[628] No notice had to be given by the assignee or grantee and the demand for such royalties had to be made by the author within three years after the date on which the right would have expired, otherwise any right was forfeited. The royalties were to be of such amount as, failing agreement, was determined by arbitration.

The second option and collective works. Where the assignee or grantee took   5–161
the second option, the rights of the author were further qualified in the case of collective works.[629] As to pre-1911 Act collective works, it often happened that the copyright in an article contributed to a collective work vested, ab initio, in the proprietor of the work.[630] In that case there would have been no assignment by "the author", and the proviso had no application.[631] The extended term of copyright would belong to the proprietor of the collective work.[632] If, however, the copyright did not originally vest in the proprietor of the collective work, but was the property of the author, then, in accordance with the revesting proviso, the benefit of the extended term would belong to the author or his personal representatives, notwithstanding any subsequent assignment or grant for the whole term. In this situation, the Act provided that where the assignee or grantee for the whole term was also the proprietor of the collective work, he was to be entitled, during the extended term of copyright, to continue to reproduce the work without any payment to the author.[633] He could, however, only reproduce "in like manner as theretofore", so that under this option he could not reproduce an article contributed to the collective work, except as part of that collective work.

Provisions of the 1956 Act. When the 1956 Act was passed, two classes of cases   5–162
had to be considered, namely (a) cases in which the pre-1911 Act copyright term would by then have expired but the extended term under the 1911 Act had not yet done so and, (b) cases in which the pre-1911 Act term would not yet have expired (and where the term conferred by the 1911 Act had not done so either).

The 1956 Act: where the pre-1911 Act term would have already expired. In   5–163
this situation, the substituted right would already have revested in the author in accordance with the proviso, either unencumbered or subject to the rights of the former assignee or grantee under one or other of the two options. These rights will usually have either been exercised or been forfeited, although there may have been a number of cases where the old term would have expired only shortly before commencement of the 1956 Act[634] so that they remained exercisable. The transitional provisions of the 1956 Act provided that, if before commencement any event had occurred or notice had been given which, in accordance with the terms of the revesting proviso, had any operation affecting the ownership of the right conferred by the 1911 Act in relation to the work, or creating, transferring or terminating an interest, right or licence in respect of that right, that event or notice was to have the corresponding operation in relation to the copyright in the

---

[627] *Loew's Inc v Littler* [1958] Ch. 650.
[628] *Loew's Inc v Littler* [1958] Ch. 650.
[629] For the definition of "collective work", see s.35 of the 1911 Act and para.5–118, above.
[630] i.e. under s.18 of the Literary Copyright Act 1842. See paras 5–31 and 5–40, above, and *Lawrence, etc., Ltd v Aflalo* [1904] A.C. 17.
[631] See para.5–155, above.
[632] Subject to the concurrent right of the author, if the collective work was of a periodical nature, and not otherwise, to publish his article in "separate form" when 28 years had elapsed since the original publication. See the note to Sch.1 to the 1911 Act and para.5–31, above.
[633] Copyright Act 1911 s.24 proviso (a)(ii).
[634] On June 1, 1957.

work under the 1956 Act. It followed, therefore, that where the copyright under the 1911 Act had revested in the author or his personal representative under the proviso, the copyright conferred by the 1956 Act vested in him also, and the operation of any notice given under the first option was also preserved. It was further provided that any right which, at a time after the commencement of the 1956 Act, would, by virtue of the revesting proviso, have been exercisable in relation to the work or to the right conferred by the 1911 Act, if the 1956 Act had not been passed, should be exercisable in relation to the work, or to the copyright therein under the 1956 Act, as the case might be.[635] This preserved the right conferred upon the assignee under the second option, and the right to exercise the first option, if still available.

5–164 **The 1956 Act: where the pre-1911 Act term would not yet have expired.** In this situation, the assignee or grantee would, immediately before commencement, still have been entitled to his interest for the remainder of the old term. As to this, the 1956 Act provided that if the substituted right conferred by the 1911 Act would have reverted to the author or his personal representatives at the end of the pre-1911 Act term in accordance with the revesting proviso, and this date fell after the commencement of the 1956 Act, then on that date:

(a) the copyright in the work conferred by the 1956 Act was to revert to the author or his personal representatives as the case might be; and

(b) any interest of any other person in that copyright which subsisted on that date, by virtue of any document made before the commencement of the 1911 Act, was thereupon to determine.[636]

Nevertheless, as already seen, any right which after the commencement of the 1956 Act would have been exercisable if the 1956 Act had not been passed, was to be exercisable in relation to the copyright conferred by the 1956 Act. This preserved the right of the assignee or grantee under the two options. The effect of the 1956 Act was therefore to continue the regime of the 1911 Act.

5–165 **Provisions of the 1988 Act.** The 1988 Act continues the effect of these provisions. Thus:

(a) If, before the commencement of the 1988 Act (August 1, 1989), any event occurred or notice was given which, by virtue of the above transitional provisions of the 1956 Act, had any operation in relation to copyright in the work under that Act, the event or notice has the corresponding operation in relation to copyright conferred by the 1988 Act.[637] This preserved the revesting of copyright which had already taken place and the corresponding rights of assignees and grantees under the two options.

(b) Any right which, immediately before commencement of the 1988 Act, would by virtue of these provisions of the 1956 Act have been exercisable in relation to the work or copyright in it, is exercisable in relation to the work or copyright in it under the 1988 Act.[638] This preserves the rights of assignees and grantees in the future to exercise the two options.

(c) Finally, if in accordance with the above provisions of the 1956 Act, copyright would, on a date after the commencement of the 1956 Act, have reverted to the author or his personal representatives and that date falls after August 1, 1989, the copyright in the work is to revert to the author or his personal representatives, as the case may be, and any interest of any

---

[635] Copyright Act 1956 Sch.7 para.38(3).
[636] Copyright Act 1956 Sch7 para.38(4).
[637] CDPA 1988 Sch.1 para.28(2).
[638] Sch.1 para.28(3).

other person in the copyright which subsists on that date, by virtue of any document made before the commencement of the 1911 Act, is to thereupon determine.[639] This provides for the revesting of copyright in accordance with the proviso where the old term would have come to an end after the commencement of the 1988 Act.

4. JOINT AUTHORS AND JOINT OWNERS

The topic of joint authorship and ownership is dealt with in detail as it arises in connection with various issues such as authorship, ownership, etc. A summary of the important points only is given here.

5–166

Joint authorship.[640] A work of joint authorship is one produced by the collaboration of two or more authors in which the contribution of each author is not distinct from that of the other or others.[641] This requires that (a) each contributor must answer the description of an "author", (b) there must have been collaboration between them and (c) their contributions must not have been distinct. A film will now always be a work of joint authorship of the producer and principal director, unless they are one and the same person.[642]

5–167

Subsistence of copyright in works of joint authorship. Where the subsistence of copyright depends on the author satisfying one of the qualifying conditions of the 1988 Act, then if any one of the authors satisfies those requirements the work will qualify for copyright protection.[643] Where a work qualifies for protection by this route, however, only those authors who satisfy the requirements are to be taken into account in deciding who is the first owner of copyright, determining the duration of copyright and whether the defence under s.57 of the Act (anonymous or pseudonymous works) applies.[644]

5–168

Joint authors as first owners of copyright. Where a work is one of joint authorship, the general rule is that the authors will be joint first owners of the copyright.[645] As such, they will usually hold the copyright as tenants in common rather than as joint tenants, this being the natural inference in the context of the creation of a copyright work. The matter, however, is one of agreement and the circumstances may show a contrary intention.[646] For example, there may be a strong inference that the property of husband and wife was intended to be held as joint tenants.[647] Where the first owners hold the copyright as tenants in common,

5–169

---

[639] Sch.1 para.28(4).
[640] See paras 4–32 et seq., above, for a detailed treatment of joint authorship.
[641] CDPA 1988 s.10(1).
[642] s.10(1A).
[643] CDPA 1988 s.154(3). See Ch.3, above, for a detailed treatment of this topic.
[644] s.154(3).
[645] See para.5–07, above. The exception is where the authors were employed under contracts of service. As to this situation, see para.5–08, above.
[646] The statement in *Lauri v Renad* [1892] 3 Ch. 402 at 413, per Kekewich J., to the effect that this is always so is, it is suggested, wrong and is based on an incorrect reading of *Powell v Head* (1879) L.R. 9 Ch. 518. In this latter case, the owners in question were each assignees of a share of the copyright from the first owner and so were clearly tenants in common. It is also suggested that a similar statement in previous editions of this work, upon which the dicta in *Prior v Lansdowne Press Pty Ltd* [1977] R.P.C. 511, *Dixon Projects Pty Ltd v Masterton Homes Pty Ltd* (1996) 36 I.P.R. 136 and *Acorn Computers Ltd v MCS Microcomputer Systems Pty Ltd* (1984) 4 I.P.R. 214 were built, and the statement in *Ray v Classic FM plc* [1998] F.S.R. 622 that joint authors hold copyright as tenants in common, were also wrong.
[647] *Mail Newspapers plc v Express Newspapers plc* [1987] F.S.R. 90 (copyright in wedding photographs).

the shares will usually be equal,[648] but there is no rule as to this[649] and the circumstances may indicate otherwise, for example where the authors have agreed otherwise or[650] are parties to a publishing agreement which provides for an unequal split in royalties.[651]

5–170   **Transmission of title.** One joint owner may assign his interest in the copyright.[652] On the death of one joint tenant, his interest in the copyright will pass to his co-owners by survivorship.[653] On the death of one tenant in common, his interest passes to his personal representatives as part of his estate.[654]

5–171   **Term of copyright.** The present position under the 1988 Act is that the copyright in a literary, dramatic, musical or artistic work of joint authorship expires 70 years after the death of the last of the authors to die.[655]

5–172   **Licence by one joint owner only.** One of several joint owners cannot grant a licence which is binding on his co-owners.[656] Nor can he grant a statutory exclusive licence to a third party, since he is not "the" copyright owner.[657]

5–173   **Rights of co-owners inter se.** One co-owner can sue his co-owners for infringement of copyright for doing any of the acts restricted by the copyright which have been committed without his licence. This is because the reference in s.16(2) to acts done without the "licence" of the copyright owner is to be taken as a reference to all the copyright owners.[658] One co-owner therefore has no right to exercise the rights of a copyright owner alone, not even if he accounts to his co-owners for a share of any profits: the rights of his co-owners are not limited to an account.[659] One co-owner can also sue third parties for infringement and obtain an injunction and damages without joining his co-owners.[660] Probably, one tenant in common can only recover damages for the injury done to his share.[661]

---

[648] As in *Redwood Music Ltd v B. Feldman & Co Ltd* [1979] R.P.C. 1 at 4.

[649] *Bamgboye v Reed* [2002] EWHC 2922 (QB), para.40; [2004] E.M.L.R. 5. And see, e.g., *Fisher v Brooker* [2006] EWHC 3239 (Ch); [2007] F.S.R. 12 at paras 96 and 98, where a 40 per cent share was awarded (para.98). This finding was not challenged on appeal: [2009] UKHL 41.

[650] *Hayes v Phonogram Ltd* [2002] EWHC 2062 (Ch); [2003] E.C.D.R. 11, para.5.

[651] As in *Prior v Lansdowne Press Pty Ltd* [1977] R.P.C. 511 (Sup. Ct of Victoria). Again, it is suggested that the statement in *Ray v Classic FM plc* [1998] F.S.R. 622 that joint authors hold the copyright as tenants in common in equal shares is wrong.

[652] See para.5–71, above. The effect of an assignment by one joint tenant will be to sever the joint tenancy.

[653] See *Mail Newspapers plc v Express Newspapers plc* [1987] F.S.R. 90.

[654] As to transmission on death generally, see para.5–125, above.

[655] CDPA 1988 s.12(8). This only summarises the present position. The reader is referred to Ch.6, below, for the detailed discussion on the term of copyright.

[656] CDPA 1988 s.173(2). The earlier Copyright Acts did not make express provision for this but the position was the same. See *Copinger*, 12th edn, para.372 and *Powell v Head* (1879) 12 Ch. D. 686.

[657] See CDPA 1988 s.173(2). As to statutory exclusive licences, see paras 5–208 et seq., below. It is suggested that the statement in *Mail Newspapers plc v Express Newspapers plc* [1987] F.S.R. 90 that this follows from the fact that one co-owner cannot prevent his co-owners from doing of any of the acts restricted by the copyright is incorrect. He *can* do so (see the following paragraph).

[658] CDPA 1988 ss.16(2) and 173(2); *Ray v Classic FM plc* [1998] F.S.R. 622. The position was the same under the earlier Acts, although not so explicit. See *Cescinsky v George Routledge & Sons Ltd* [1916] 2 K.B. 325.

[659] *Ray v Classic FM plc* [1998] F.S.R. 622, above.

[660] *Lauri v Renad* [1892] 3 Ch. 402; *Prior v Lansdowne Press Pty Ltd* [1977] R.P.C. 511; *Acorn Computers Ltd v MCS Microcomputer Systems Ltd* (1985) A.L.R. 389; *Waterlow Publishers Ltd v Rose* [1995] F.S.R. 207; *Cala Homes (South) Ltd v Alfred McAlpine Homes East Ltd* [1995] F.S.R. 818 at 836; *Dixon Projects Pty Ltd v Masterton Homes Pty Ltd* (1996) 36 I.P.R. 136.

[661] *Prior v Lansdowne Press Pty Ltd* [1977] R.P.C. 511.

5. EQUITABLE OWNERSHIP

It happens frequently that the legal and beneficial titles to a copyright work become separated. This Section is concerned with the circumstances in which this occurs, how the equitable title can be transferred and what the incidents of equitable ownership are.

5–174

A. CREATION OF AN EQUITABLE TITLE

There are no set rules which determine the circumstances in which an equitable title arises. By definition, it occurs on an event which results in the legal and beneficial titles becoming separated. Although an express declaration of trust is the clearest example of the creation of an equitable interest,[662] the usual commercial cases arise either on the creation of the work or on a later, ineffective, attempt to transfer the legal title. Writing is not necessary to create an equitable interest, whether created by trust or otherwise, although it is necessary for the purpose of assigning such interest.[663]

5–175

(i) Equitable title arising on creation of a work

The identity of the first legal owner of the copyright in a work is determined by the application of the relevant statutory provisions, which have already been considered. In many cases, however, the circumstances in which the work is made mean that the beneficial owner is in fact some person other than the legal owner, either because this is what the parties agreed[664] or as a consequence of some fiduciary or trust relationship that exists between them.

5–176

Equitable title by virtue of contract. There is no limit to the variety of contractual situations in which parties may agree that the copyright in a work yet to be created will belong to someone other than the first legal owner. Contracts pursuant to which the making of a work is commissioned are a common example, and are considered separately, below. If the contract contains a valid assignment of the future legal title in the work to be created, then the legal title will vest in the assignee when the work is made.[665] Often, however, the agreement is silent or ineffectual to transfer the future legal title, but if the intention of the parties, express or implied, is that a party other than the first legal owner should be entitled to the copyright, then that party will acquire an equitable title in the copyright when the work is made, provided that he is entitled to enforce his claim in equity to have the title vested in him by the legal owner.[666] This will often be the case where the author was paid to create the work.[667] The consequence of such an ar-

5–177

---

[662] For an example of such a declaration in a commercial context, see *The Photocrom Co Ltd v H. & W. Nelson Ltd* [1923–1928] Mac.C.C. 293.

[663] See para.5–189, below.

[664] The identity of first legal owner is determined by statute. It cannot be altered by agreement, save in relation to employees' works and "future" works (as to which see paras 5–26 and 5–108, above, respectively).

[665] As to such an assignment of the future copyright, see para.5–108, above.

[666] Note that it seems that the equitable title may remain good even if the assignee has lost the right to enforce the contract before the legal title is perfected. See *Peer International Corp v Editora Musical de Cuba* [2002] EWHC (Ch) 2675; [2004] R.P.C. 22, where the contract in question had been abrogated by virtue of a foreign decree. Presumably, however, the equitable title would be lost if the assignee had lost the right to specific performance of the agreement because of his own conduct. The decision on these aspects was not affected by the decision on appeal: [2003] EWCA Civ 1156; [2004] Ch. 212; [2004] R.P.C. 23; [2003] E.M.L.R. 34.

[667] *Massine v de Basil* [1936–1945] Mac.C.C. 223; *John Richardson Computers Ltd v Flanders* [1993] F.S.R 497.

rangement will be that the copyright is held on trust by the legal owner,[668] and the legal owner must transfer the legal title if called upon to do so.[669] Thus the agreement may contain an express provision that the copyright in the work should belong to the other party[670] amounting to an agreement to sell it,[671] or merely an implied term to this effect.[672] In this context, a purported assignment of future copyright which is for some reason ineffectual to transfer the legal title when the work is made[673] will be construed as an agreement to assign the copyright[674] and, if supported by consideration, will therefore be sufficient to vest an equitable title in the assignee as soon as the work comes into existence. Alternatively, the agreement may be to assign the copyright when called upon to do so, in which case the equitable title will arise when a request to assign is made.[675] It follows that an agreement for which there is no sufficient consideration will be ineffective to create an equitable title, as will a contract in respect of which the right to specific performance has been lost.[676] On the other hand, an oral agreement supported by sufficient consideration can clearly be effective to do so, whether or not the consideration has been executed.[677]

5-178   **Commissioned works.** It has already been seen that, except in certain pre-1988 Act cases,[678] a person who commissions a work to be made by another does not thereby become the first legal owner of the copyright. His interest in the copyright, if any, will depend on the terms of the contract. Where the terms expressly deal with the copyright, little difficulty usually arises.[679] Where, on the other hand, the matter is one of implication it can be very hard to determine what the true position is. There are many circumstances where a work is prepared by A for B which do not result in B acquiring any interest in the copyright: the result of the transaction may simply be that B becomes entitled to the property in the physical material created and to a licence to use it for the particular purpose envisaged by the parties, but does not become equitable owner of the copyright.[680] In accordance with general principles, a term to the effect that the commissioner is to be entitled to the copyright will only be implied where it is necessary to give business efficacy to the contract and the implied term satisfies the officious bystander test. Almost inevitably, however, some term will have to be implied, even if only that the commissioner is licensed to use the work, for the general principle is that:

---

[668] *Nichols Advanced Vehicle Systems Inc v Rees* [1979] R.P.C. 127 at 139; *John Richardson Computers Ltd v Flanders* [1993] F.S.R 497 at 516.

[669] *R. Griggs Group Ltd v Evans* [2003] EWHC 2914 (Ch), para.33; [2004] F.S.R. 31; upheld on appeal [2005] EWCA Civ 11; [2005] F.S.R. 31. Note the suggestion in that case (para.56) that if the commissioned author had been mistaken as to scope of the project and had undercharged as a result, he might be able to resist a demand that he assign the copyright without being paid an increased fee.

[670] As in *University of London Press Ltd v University Tutorial Press Ltd* [1916] 2 Ch. 601. But such an agreement may of course, on its true construction, and if the formalities are complied with, amount to a valid assignment.

[671] *Simms v Marryat* (1851) 17 Q.B. 281.

[672] Most commonly, this arises in the context of commissioned works, which are considered below, together with the topic of when such a term can be implied.

[673] As to which see para.5–110, above.

[674] *Performing Right Society v London Theatre of Varieties Ltd* [1924] A.C. 1; *Wah Sang Industrial Co v Takmay Industrial Co Ltd* [1980] F.S.R. 303.

[675] *Hexagon Pty Ltd v Australian Broadcasting Commission* [1976] R.P.C. 628.

[676] *Levy v Rutley* (1871) L.R. 6 C. p.523.

[677] *Western Front Ltd v Vestron Inc* [1987] F.S.R. 66; *Wah Sang Industrial Co v Takmay Industrial Co Ltd* [1980] F.S.R. 303.

[678] See paras 5–33 et seq. and 5–43, above.

[679] As in *Ward, Lock & Co Ltd v Long* [1906] 2 Ch. 550; *Hazlitt v Templeman* (1866) 13 L.T. 593 (agreements to assign the copyright in a book yet to be written, a very common example).

[680] See, e.g. *Nicol v Barranger* [1917–23] Mac.C.C. 219; *Cooper v Stephens* [1895] 1 Ch. 567. See para.5–221, below, as to the further examples of such licences.

"the engagement for reward of a person to produce material of a nature which is capable of being the subject of copyright implies a permission, or consent, or licence in the person giving the engagement to use the material in the manner and for the purpose in which and for which it was contemplated between the parties that it would be used at the time of the engagement".[681]

The question will be whether the term to be implied is one for a non-exclusive licence, an exclusive licence or an assignment of the copyright, in whole or part: on the facts, was the agreement one whereby the author sold his copyright[682] or merely one whereby he granted some form of licence? In accordance with modern, general principles, the term implied should go no further than is necessary to fill the lacuna in the express terms of the contract, so that if the implication of a licence of some kind will meet this need, no agreement to assign should be implied.[683] It might be thought that the difficulty with the rigid application of this principle is that in almost every case in which it would be otherwise appropriate to imply an agreement to assign (as to which, see the next paragraph), business efficacy could be given to the agreement by implying the grant of an exclusive licence, since in such a case the grantee would be entitled to exploit the work to the exclusion of all others, including the grantor.[684] This is not so, however, since it is only in the case of a statutory exclusive licence that the licensee obtains rights which, for present purposes, are sufficiently close to those of an assignee of the copyright, in particular, a right to sue in his own name for infringements by third parties. In many cases, the agreement in question will not satisfy the requirements for the grant of a statutory exclusive licence, which must be in writing and signed by or on behalf of the owner of an existing copyright work.[685] In any event, the remedies of an exclusive licensee are not necessarily as good as those of a copyright owner.[686] If, therefore, the commissioner may need to enforce the copyright against third parties and have exclusive control over the work, this will point to it being implicit that he should own the copyright.[687]

Circumstances in which an agreement to assign the copyright are likely to be implied include those where the work is made specifically for the commissioner's business and at his expense and neither party can have contemplated that the maker of the work would have any genuine use for it himself.[688] It will be necessary to consider in particular the price paid. Where the agreement provides for

---

[681] *Beck v Montana Constructions Pty Ltd* [1964–1965] N.S.W.R. 229 approved in *Blair v Osborne & Tomkins* [1971] 2 Q.B. 78, CA.

[682] See, e.g. *Ironside v H.M. Attorney-General* [1988] R.P.C. 197 and *Ray v Classic FM plc* [1998] F.S.R. 622 at 640, which contains a review of the relevant principles.

[683] *Ray v Classic FM plc* [1998] F.S.R. 622, at 642, applying *Liverpool City Council v Irwin* [1977] A.C. 239. In *R. Griggs Group Ltd v Evans* [2005] EWCA Civ 11; [2005] F.S.R. 31 at para.14, the summary of the law on this topic in *Ray v Classic FM* was described by the Court of Appeal as "masterful".

[684] And see *Ray v Classic FM plc* [1998] F.S.R. 622 at 644, suggesting that today an assignment is rarely likely to be implied, an exclusive licence usually being sufficient. So in *Wrenn v Landamore* [2007] EWHC 1833 (Ch), where the defendant had been engaged by the claimant to write software for use in interfaces between car radios and third party audio equipment, it was held to be sufficient to imply an exclusive licence. Such a licence would be sufficient to enable the claimant to market interfaces embodying the software. Admittedly, there were other circumstances also indicating an exclusive licence only: see further in the text.

[685] CDPA 1988 s.92(1). See para.5–208, below, for a detailed discussion of the formalities required for the grant of an exclusive licence. Note also the suggestion referred to in para.5–205 that it is possible that there can be such a thing as an implied equitable statutory exclusive licence which would entitle the licensee to call for a statutory exclusive licence in the same way as an informal assignee is entitled to call for a legal assignment.

[686] *R. Griggs Group Ltd v Evans* [2003] EWHC (Ch) 2914, para.58, upheld on appeal: [2005] EWCA Civ 11; [2005] F.S.R. 31.

[687] *R. Griggs Group Ltd v Evans* [2003] EWHC 2914 (Ch), upheld on appeal: [2005] EWCA Civ 11. See also *Durand v Molino* [2000] E.C.D.R. 320.

[688] As in *A&M Records Ltd v Video Collection International Ltd* [1995] E.M.L.R. 25; *Harold Drabble Ltd v The Hycolite Manufacturing Co* (1928) 44 T.L.R. 264 (although note the sugges-

the payment of a royalty, this may indicate an exclusive licence rather than an assignment, since otherwise the maker might have no effective rights in the event of non-payment of royalties, whereas a licence can be terminated on an accepted repudiation.[689] It is sometimes argued that the maker needs to retain the copyright to be able to secure further payment in the event of unforeseen use being made of the work. Of course, if he has already been paid the proper rate for the use of the work for all purposes throughout the world the argument is disposed of,[690] but in any event a right to further payment for unforeseen or undisclosed further use may be implied in some cases. In other cases, the maker may indeed retain the copyright and so be able to prevent such further use: it depends on the circumstances.[691] The impact of an assignment on the maker and whether it could sensibly have been intended that he should retain the copyright obviously needs to be considered.[692] The fact that the maker may have made use of underlying works supplied and owned by the commissioner, such as preliminary drafts or sketches, so that the commissioned work could not be used by the maker without infringing the copyright in these underlying works, will also support such an implication.[693] Again, where the maker works as part of a team with employees of the commissioner, this may justify the implication.[694] On the other hand, where it is contemplated that the work may be sold by the maker to others[695] or where it incorporates elements that the maker made previously or is likely to use again in his business, such as standard routines employed by a software writer, together with additions that are specific to the commissioner's business, an intention that the commissioner should own the entire copyright is unlikely to be implied.[696] Obviously the fact that the maker disowns any claim to any beneficial interest

---

tion in *Ray v Classic FM plc* [1998] F.S.R. 622, that the decision may only have been that a licence was implied); *Warner v Gestetner Ltd* (unreported but cited in *Saphena Computing Ltd v Allied Collection Agencies Ltd* [1995] F.S.R. 616 at 634), and also cited as an example in *Ray v Classic FM plc* [1998] F.S.R. 622, at 642; *Pasterfield v Denham* [1999] F.S.R. 168 (advertising leaflets commissioned by a local authority to promote a local tourist attraction); *Durland v Molino* [2000] E.C.D.R. 320 (commissioned painting of restaurateur and others participating in restaurant business, reproductions of it and the original to be used in the business); *R. Griggs Group Ltd v Evans* [2003] EWHC (Ch) 2914, upheld on appeal: [2005] EWCA Civ 11 (defendant commissioned to produce a logo for shoes); *Lucasfilm Ltd v Ainsworth* [2009] EWCA Civ 1328; [2010] F.S.R. 10.

[689] *Wrenn v Landamore* [2007] EWHC 1833 (Ch), para.37.

[690] *R. Griggs Group Ltd v Evans* [2005] EWCA Civ 11, even though the defendant had been told (and believed) that only limited use would be made of the work.

[691] *R. Griggs Group Ltd v Evans* [2005] EWCA Civ 11.

[692] *Ray v Classic FM plc* [1998] F.S.R. 622, at 642.

[693] Again, cited as an example in *Ray v Classic FM plc*, above, at 642. However, it by no means follows that whenever the commissioner has some right in respect of a contribution of a different nature to the overall project, he will obtain exclusive rights to everything produced within that project. It all depends on the circumstances: *Clearsprings Management Ltd v BusinessLinx Ltd* [2005] EWHC 1487 (Ch); [2006] F.S.R. 3, at para.37.

[694] *Ray v Classic FM plc* [1998] F.S.R. 622, citing as examples *Nichols Advanced Vehicle Systems Inc v Rees* [1979] R.P.C. 127 at 139, and *Sofia Bogrich v Shape Machines*, unreported November 4, 1994. However, where the maker's contribution to the work of such a team is distinct and it is clear that the parties would have intended the maker to be free to use it or would have been indifferent to such use, an assignment is both unnecessary and unworkable: *Clearsprings Management Ltd v BusinessLinx Ltd* [2005] EWHC 1487 (Ch); [2006] F.S.R. 3 at para.36. The case concerned computer software. Both parties contemplated that the maker would re-use the code created for the project in question. The court implied a non-exclusive licence together with a restriction on the maker using information about the commissioner's operating procedures for purposes other than those of the commissioner.

[695] *Saphena Computing Ltd v Allied Collection Agencies Ltd* [1995] F.S.R. 616.

[696] But in *Wrenn v Landamore* [2007] EWHC 1833 (Ch), the defendant had been engaged by the claimant to write software for use in interfaces between car radios and third party audio equipment. A licence was implied which extended to the source code both so as to enable source code to be compiled into object code in the manufacture of interfaces but also to enable the software to be developed by others, as the defendant appeared to have envisaged might happen (para.38). The source code included a so-called "emulation layer", which had been written by the defendant prior to his involvement with the claimant. It was contended on behalf of the defendant

will make it easier in practice for the commissioner to establish his equitable title.[697] Care may need to be taken with some of the older cases, decided when the modern principles relating to the implication of terms into a contract had not yet been worked out or in which they were not rigorously applied, for example with such statements as:

> "... where a man employs another to write an article, or to do anything else for him, unless there is something in the surrounding circumstances, or in the course of dealing between the parties, to require a different construction, it is to be understood that the writing or other thing is produced on terms that the copyright shall belong to the employer".[698]

Employee not under a contract of service. The legal title to most works made by an author in the course of his employment under a contract of service will belong to his employer.[699] Where this is not the case, the work may nevertheless have been made in circumstances that a term is to be implied that the copyright should belong to whoever has engaged or employed the author.[700]   **5–179**

Company directors and other fiduciaries. Where the work is created by some-one who stands in a fiduciary relationship with another, such that he cannot be heard to say that he created the work for his own benefit, he will usually hold the copyright in trust for that other person. So, for example, a director or de facto director of a company who is not employed under a contract of service[701] may nevertheless hold the copyright in works he makes for the company on trust and will have to assign the copyright to the company when called upon to do so.[702] This will usually be so because the director will have created the work for the company's business, using the company's property and in the company's time.[703] There is, however, no rule that works created by a director for his company are   **5–180**

---

that the licence should exclude the source code or alternatively that it should exclude the emulation layer. This argument was rejected but the grounds for rejecting the alternative argument are not easy to understand (para.42). The point did not arise on appeal: [2008] EWCA Civ 496.

[697] As in *Merchant Adventurers Ltd v M. Grew & Co Ltd* [1973] R.P.C. 1.

[698] *Sweet v Benning* (1855) 16 C.B. 459, per Maule J. Note also that the suggestion in *Ray v Classic FM plc* [1998] F.S.R. 622, at 643, that cases decided before the passing of the 1956 Act are generally likely to be of little guidance since before then an exclusive licensee had no right to sue in his own name (see para.5–211 to 5–212, below). As seen above, however, it will often not be possible to create a statutory exclusive licence by implication.

[699] CDPA 1988 s.11(2). See paras 5–213 et seq., below.

[700] As in *Massine v De Basil* [1936–45] Mac.C.C. 223; *Sweet v Shaw* (1839) 8 L.J. Ch. 216 (law reports prepared for future publication). See also the reasoning in *Sweet v Benning* (1855) 16 C.B. 459, quoted in para.5–178, above.

[701] As, e.g., in *Parsons v Albert J. Parsons & Sons Ltd* [1979] F.S.R. 254; *Wilden Pump & Engineering Co v Fusfield* (1985) 8 I.P.R. 250 and *Ultraframe (UK) Ltd v Fielding* [2003] EWCA Civ 1805; [2004] R.P.C. 24. Where a work is made by a director in the course of his employment under a contract of service, the copyright will, of course, subject to any agreement to the contrary, belong to the company. See paras 5–15 et seq., above, and *Gardex Ltd v Sorata Ltd* [1986] R.P.C. 623; *Erica Vale Australia Pty Ltd v Thompson & Morgan (Ipswich) Ltd* (1994) 29 I.P.R. 589 at 632.

[702] *Antocks Lairn Ltd v I. Bloohn Ltd* [1971] F.S.R. 490; *Kambrook Distributing Pty Ltd v Delaney* (1984) 4 I.P.R. 79 at 89; *A-One Accessory Imports Ltd v Off Road Imports Pty Ltd* (1994) 34 I.P.R. 306 (Fed. Ct of Aus.), suggesting that work done by two persons intended to be for the benefit of a company which they later acquired and became directors of was held in trust for the company. See also *Vitof Ltd v Altoft* [2006] EWHC 1678 (Ch) at paras 144 to 147, citing with approval all but the last sentence of this paragraph, together with *Charly Acquisitions Ltd v Immediate Records Inc* (Pumfrey J., February 7, 2002) at paras 78 to 79 and the trade mark case of *Ball v The Eden Project Ltd* [2002] F.S.R. 43, and also holding (at paras 148 to 149), following the *A-One* case, that the copyright in source code created in contemplation of the incorporation of a company and for its benefit was held on trust for the company.

[703] See the analysis in *Ultraframe (UK) Ltd v Fielding* [2003] EWCA Civ 1805; [2004] R.P.C. 24.

always held on trust: it will depend on what, if anything, has been agreed.[704] In particular, it is always open to the shareholders of a company to agree that a director should retain property he has created or to relieve him of any liability for any breach of duty, provided that to do so is not ultra vires the company or a fraud on its creditors.[705] In the case of a sole shareholder-director, however, it will often be difficult to show that the company has agreed to this.[706] Again, where a work is made by an employee outside office hours, but in breach of his fiduciary duty to his employer, the employer may be entitled to the copyright in equity.[707] It is an open question whether an employer is entitled in equity to the copyright in a former servant's work containing information which he remained under a duty of confidence to keep secret.[708]

5–181   **Partners.** Where a work is made by one partner in the ordinary course of the partnership business and for the purposes of the partnership, the copyright in the work will become partnership property, in the sense that as between the partners it is to be regarded as an asset of the partnership.[709] In the absence of a written assignment, however, the legal title will remain with the partner who was the author and will not devolve upon the partners. The other partners' right is to have the copyright applied for the benefit of the partnership.[710] The same will apply to copyright brought into the partnership as capital.[711] Where such rights are partnership assets, the assignment by that partner of his rights to a third party will not be void: it may affect the process of accounting between the co-partners but the co-partners will have no right to require the third party to reassign the rights.[712]

(ii) Equitable title arising subsequent to creation of work

5–182   There are many circumstances in which the legal and equitable titles become separated on an event subsequent to the creation of a copyright work. Most frequently this happens in a transaction which amounts to an agreement to assign the copyright.

5–183   **Agreement to assign.** Where an agreement made for consideration contains an obligation to assign the copyright in an existing work, an equitable title will be

---

[704] *Wilden Pump & Engineering Co v Fusfield* (1985) 8 I.P.R. 250 (director of one-man company receiving royalties for designs from company: inconsistent with holding copyright in trust).

[705] *Ultraframe (UK) Ltd v Fielding* [2003] EWCA Civ 1805, at para.39; [2004] R.P.C. 24. It will, however, be ultra vires the company to distribute assets to a shareholder otherwise than by distribution of a profit lawfully made or by lawful reduction or return of capital, and allowing a shareholder-director to retain rights of copyright will normally involve either one or other of these steps: *Ultraframe*, at para.39.

[706] *Ultraframe (UK) Ltd v Fielding* [2003] EWCA Civ 1805.

[707] *Missing Link Software v Magee* [1989] F.S.R. 361; *Service Corp International plc v Channel Four Television Corp*, [1999] E.M.L.R. 83.

[708] See *Attorney-General v Guardian Newspapers Ltd (No.2)* [1990] 1 A.C. 109 at 263A; [1989] 2 F.S.R. 181, HL; *Att Gen v Blake* [1998] Ch. 439; [1997] Ch. 84. In *Att Gen v Blake*, at first instance, Sir Richard Scott V.C. indicated that although he would have felt constrained by *Lister & Co v Stubbs* (1890) 45 Ch. D. 1 and *Halifax Building Society v Thomas* [1996] Ch. 217 to hold that the employer (in that case the Crown) was not so entitled, his view was that in the light of Privy Council decision in *Att Gen for Hong Kong v Reid* [1994] 1 A.C. 324, disapproving *Lister*, the law should be otherwise. For the decision in the House of Lords, see [2001] 1 A.C. 268.

[709] *Meikle v Mauffe* [1941] 3 All E.R. 144; *Roban Jig & Tool Co Ltd v Taylor* [1979] F.S.R. 130; *Murray v King* [1986] F.S.R. 116 (Fed. Ct of Aus.); *Ibcos Computers Ltd v Barclays Mercantile Highland Finance Ltd* [1994] F.S.R. 275; cf. *Coffey's Registered Designs* [1982] F.S.R. 227, where the partnership business was not concerned with producing designs.

[710] *O'Brien v Komersaroff* (1982) 56 A.L.J.R. 681.

[711] *Ibcos Computers Ltd v Barclays Mercantile Highland Finance Ltd* [1994] F.S.R. 275.

[712] *Bourne v Davis* [2006] EWHC 1567 (Ch) at paras 25 and 29 (a performers' property rights case).

created.[713] The agreement may be oral or implied. A vesting order may be made to transfer the legal title.[714] Where the obligation arises at some future time, the assignee will acquire an equitable title when that time comes,[715] assuming the agreement then to be specifically enforceable.[716] The obligation to assign may arise at some fixed, future time or be a matter of the assignee's choice.[717] Until that time arrives, the assignee has a sufficient equitable interest in the copyright to entitle him to protection, for example, to prevent disposal of the copyright by the assignor.[718] Except as against a purchaser of the legal title for value without notice, the assignee will be entitled to the copyright against anyone to whom the legal owner has assigned the copyright in breach of his contract with the assignee.

Imperfect legal assignment. The requirements for a valid, immediate assignment of the legal title to a copyright work have already been considered,[719] as has the special case of an assignment of a future copyright work.[720] An invalid assignment of the legal title to an existing work will be treated as an agreement to assign, and thus an equitable assignment, if supported by sufficient consideration.[721]   **5–184**

Assignment of after-acquired works. It is a common feature of music publishing and other similar agreements that a party agrees to assign not only works which he owns at the date of the assignment but also works which he subsequently acquires from other parties. Such an agreement will rarely operate as a legal assignment of the title to the works when they are acquired[722] and at best the assignee will therefore usually only acquire an equitable title.[723] Such agreements should therefore always contain a covenant for further assurances.   **5–185**

(iii) Other equitable interests: options, pre-emptions and equitable mortgages

Option to acquire. Although an agreement whereby a party is granted an option to acquire the copyright in a work will not create any equitable title to the copyright before exercise of the option, it will create a sufficient equitable interest to entitle the grantee to an injunction to restrain exploitation of the work by a third-party assignee from the grantor, unless the third party is a purchaser for value without notice.[724] Such options are a common feature of publishing agreements in the literary and music fields, and in the film industry.   **5–186**

Right of pre-emption or first refusal. It is common in many fields for the copy-   **5–187**

---

[713] See *The Photocrom Co Ltd v H. & W. Nelson Ltd* [1923–1928] Mac.C.C. 293. S.90(3) is only concerned with transfers of the legal title: *Lakeview Computers plc v Steadman*, unreported November 26, 1999, CA.

[714] *Lakeview Computers plc v Steadman*, No. PTA + A 1999/7282/1, November 26, 1999, CA.

[715] *Hexagon Pty Ltd v Australian Broadcasting Commission* [1976] R.P.C. 628.

[716] But see *Peer International Corp v Editora Musical de Cuba* [2002] EWHC (Ch) 2675; [2004] R.P.C. 22 and the comment in the footnotes to para.5–177, above, on this case.

[717] As in *Hexagon Pty Ltd v Australian Broadcasting Commission* [1976] R.P.C. 628; *Colburn v Duncombe* 9 Sim. 151 (agreement to deliver a "regular assignment" when called upon to do so). As to an assignment of the copyright in a "future work", see para.5–108, above.

[718] *Macdonald (E.) Ltd v Eyles* [1921] 1 Ch. 631.

[719] See para.5–85, above.

[720] See para.5–108, above.

[721] *Wah Sang Industrial Co v Takmay Industrial Co Ltd* [1980] F.S.R. 303 (Ct of Appeal of Hong Kong).

[722] The provisions of CDPA 1988 s.91, relating to assignments of future copyright, will only catch such works if they are works of "future copyright" and the assignor is a "prospective owner" within the meaning of the section (see para.5–110, above).

[723] *Performing Right Society Ltd v London Theatre of Varieties Ltd* [1924] A.C. 1 at 13.

[724] *Macdonald (E.) Ltd v Eyles* [1921] 1 Ch. 631.

right owner to grant another the right of pre-emption or first refusal to a work. Such a grant, if given for consideration, will give the grantee an equitable interest which can be enforced against not only the grantor but also all others except a purchaser for value without notice.

5–188 **Equitable mortgage.** The creation of, and rights incidental to, an equitable mortgage are considered elsewhere.[725]

B. Transfer of Equitable Interest

5–189 Although no formalities are required for the creation of an equitable interest, the assignment of an equitable title to copyright is governed by the Law of Property Act 1925, which provides that a disposition of an equitable interest subsisting at the time of the disposition must be in writing, signed by the person disposing of the same, or by his agent lawfully authorised in writing or by will.[726] The combined effect of the 1988 Act and the Law of Property Act 1925 is therefore that any assignment of copyright, whether it be of the legal or equitable interest, must be in writing.[727] As with the legal title, the disposal of the physical property in which the copyright work may happen to be embodied, such as a manuscript or painting, does not carry with it the equitable title.[728]

C. Incidents of Equitable Ownership

5–190 **Right to bring proceedings.** An equitable owner is entitled to institute proceedings for infringement of copyright and to obtain an interim injunction, thereby protecting his interest.[729] Normally, however, an equitable owner by himself cannot obtain judgment at trial,[730] even a final injunction, because of the risk to the defendant that he will be exposed to a second claim by a legal owner, in particular a bona fide purchaser for value without notice claiming under the legal owner.[731] Before judgment, therefore, the equitable owner must either perfect his title by taking an assignment from the legal owner or, alternatively, join the legal owner, either as claimant or defendant.[732] Until he does so, the proceedings are li-

---

[725] See para.5–196, below.

[726] Law of Property Act 1925 s.53(1)(c); *Lakeview Computers plc v Steadman*, No. PTA + A 1999/ 7282/1, November 26, 1999, CA; *Comprop Ltd v Moran* [2002] J.L.R. 222 (Royal Ct of Jersey) at para.97.

[727] *Roban Jig & Tool Co Ltd v Taylor* [1979] F.S.R. 130 at 143; see *Performing Right Society Ltd v London Theatre of Varieties Ltd* [1924] A.C. 1 at 18; *Wah Sang Industrial Co v Takmay Industrial Co Ltd* [1980] F.S.R. 303 at 309 (Ct of Appeal of Hong Kong).

[728] *Nicol v Barranger* [1917–1923] Mac.C.C. 219. See also para.5–68, above.

[729] *Mawman v Tegg* (1826) 2 Russ. 385; *Sweet v Shaw* (1839) 8 L.J. Ch. 216; *Sweet v Cater* 11 Sim. 572; *Hodges v Welsh* (1840) 2 Ir. Eq. R. 266; *Performing Right Society Ltd v London Theatre of Varieties Ltd* [1924] A.C. 1 at 14, 35; *Merchant Adventurers Ltd v Grew & Co* [1972] Ch. 242 at 252; *Roban Jig & Tool Co Ltd v Taylor* [1979] F.S.R. 130 at 135; *Wah Sang Industrial Co v Takmay Industrial Co Ltd* [1980] F.S.R. 303; *Orwin v Att Gen* [1998] F.S.R. 415.

[730] See *University of London Press v University Tutorial Press* [1916] 2 Ch. 601; *Orwin v Att Gen*, above.

[731] *Performing Right Society Ltd v London Theatre of Varieties Ltd* [1924] A.C. 1 at 14; *Weddell v J.A. Pearce & Major* [1988] Ch. 26; *Batjac Productions Inc v Simitar Entertainment (UK) Ltd* [1996] F.S.R. 139, at 150.

[732] *Orwin v Att Gen* [1998] F.S.R. 415 at 423; *Batjac Productions Inc v Simitar Entertainment (UK) Ltd* [1996] F.S.R. 139, at 152; *Three Rivers District Council v Bank of England* [1996] Q.B. 292 at 309. Note that an equitable assignor can only bring proceedings by himself if, with the agreement of the assignee, he sues as trustee for the assignee, and in that event his representative capacity should be revealed in accordance with CPR r.16.2(3). If he sues, attempting to recover for himself, the assignee must be joined. See *Three Rivers District Council v Bank of England* at 308B.

able to be stayed.[733] This is, however, a rule of practice not law, although it will be departed from only very sparingly. Thus, there may be special cases where the equitable owner can sue alone, for example because of the impossibility of getting an assignment from the legal owner and the great inconvenience of joining him, his conduct,[734] or other exceptional circumstances.[735] An important factor will be the evaluation of the risk to the defendant of a further claim by the legal owner. A helpful parallel may be drawn with the power of the court to grant leave to an exclusive licensee to proceed without joining the copyright owner.[736]

Rights as against legal owner. By definition, except as against a purchaser of the legal title for value without notice, the equitable owner has a right to an assignment of the legal title, which may be enforced by a decree for specific performance or an order vesting the copyright in him.[737] Even before such assignment, it seems that he is entitled to the remedies available under the 1988 Act as against the bare legal owner.[738] **5–191**

Rights as between equitable owners. The normal equitable rule applies, namely that the title of the first equitable owner in time will prevail, except that the first owner may lose his prior claim through his own misconduct.[739] Except in such circumstances, therefore, the first owner in time will be entitled to an assignment of the legal title from the legal owner in priority to the second owner, and to an injunction against the second owner.[740] **5–192**

Defence to an action for infringement. An equitable owner will have a defence to a claim for infringement, except one brought by a bona fide purchaser of the legal title for value without notice. **5–193**

6. MORTGAGES AND CHARGES

The express giving of security over a specific copyright work or works has historically not been a common feature of copyright law but is becoming more so. An exception has been the film and related industries where the sums required to fund the making of a film are such that the financiers will usually require some form of security (usually a mortgage) over the film and underlying works (such as the screenplay) to protect their investment. Apart from this, it is of course an everyday feature of commercial life for companies to provide fixed and floating charges over their assets by way of a debenture to secure bank or other loans. Caught up in such charges will be any copyright works belonging to the company. **5–194**

Mortgages. As with any mortgage, the characteristic of a mortgage of copyright is the transfer of the copyright to another as a security for the payment of a debt **5–195**

---

[733] *Weddell v J.A. Pearce & Major* [1988] Ch. 26.

[734] *Performing Right Society Ltd v London Theatre of Varieties Ltd* [1924] A.C. 1 at 18.

[735] As in *William Brandt's Sons & Co v Dunlop Rubber Co* [1905] A.C. 454 at 462, where the defendant disclaimed a wish to have the legal owner joined.

[736] See CDPA 1988 s.102(1) and para.5–210, below.

[737] See, e.g. the Trustee Act 1925 s.51; *R. Griggs Group Ltd v Evans No.1* [2003] EWHC (Ch) 2914, para.34; [2004] F.S.R. 31 (on appeal [2005] EWCA Civ 11; [2005] F.S.R. 31); *R. Griggs Group Ltd v Evans No.2* [2004] EWHC (Ch) 1088, para.51; [2005] Ch. 153; [2004] F.S.R. 48.

[738] *Vitof Ltd v Altoft* [2006] EWHC 1678 (Ch) at para.174. See also *Cableship Ltd v Williams*, noted at [1991] I.P.D. 14205 and *John Richardson Computers Ltd v Flanders* [1993] F.S.R. 497. It is not clear whether the remedies were granted in the latter case as a matter of equity. In *Ibcos Computers Ltd v Barclays Mercantile Highland Finance Ltd* [1994] F.S.R. 275, no such point was taken.

[739] See *Snell's Equity*, 31st edn, paras 4–43 et seq.

[740] *Sims v Marryat* (1851) 17 Q.B. 281 at 292.

or the discharge of some other obligation for which it is given.[741] A legal mortgage of copyright is formally effected by an assignment of the copyright by the mortgagor coupled with a covenant by the mortgagee to reassign on repayment of the debt or discharge of the obligation.[742] A legal mortgage must therefore be in writing, signed by or on behalf of the mortgagor-copyright owner.[743] Where it is contemplated that the mortgagor will need to exploit the work during the term of the mortgage, the mortgage will need to include a grant back of a licence, usually an exclusive licence, to allow for this. Where finance is being provided for the making of a work, a legal mortgage can be created relying on the provisions of s.91 of the 1988 Act.[744] An attempt to create a mortgage otherwise than by these means will at best create an equitable mortgage, the rights of the equitable mortgagee then being at risk as against a person who bona fide acquires the legal title by way of purchase for value (whether on a sale or, for example, another mortgage) without notice of the equitable mortgagee's interests. It should be noted that a purported assignment by way of mortgage may not, on its proper construction, be effective to pass the legal title to the copyright, so that the mortgage created thereby will be merely equitable.[745]

A legal mortgagee, having the legal title vested in him, can sue in his own name for infringements of copyright, although in his conduct of the action he must bear in mind that he holds the copyright as a mere security for his debt. The mortgagor, who retains an interest in the copyright by way of the equity of redemption, also has a sufficient title to start proceedings to restrain infringements of copyright and thus protect his interest,[746] but must join the mortgagee or redeem the mortgage before trial.[747] Where the mortgage includes the grant back of an exclusive licence to the mortgagor, the mortgagor will have additional title to sue.[748]

5–196   **Equitable mortgages.** An equitable mortgage may arise on an ineffectual attempt to create a legal mortgage, for example, where the mortgage has not been signed by, or on behalf of the mortgagor, or is merely oral. An equitable owner of copyright may mortgage his interest; such a mortgage must also be in writing signed by, or on his behalf.[749]

5–197   **Charges.** An equitable charge over copyright is created when the owner agrees to give another rights over the copyright as security for a loan or other obligation.[750] This is formally effected by the owner agreeing that the copyright should stand charged with the repayment of the loan or discharge of the obliga-

---

[741] *Santley v Wilde* [1899] 2 Ch. 474.

[742] See *Snell's Equity*, 31st edn, para.35–16.

[743] See CDPA 1988 s.90(3) and para.5–85, above. For a precedent of a legal mortgage, see Vol.2 J1.vii.

[744] This section enables the legal assignment of "future copyright". See para.5–110, above.

[745] See *Chitty on Contracts*, 30th edn, para.19–004, for a discussion of the circumstances in which a purported assignment of a chose in action may not be an effective legal assignment. Section 90(1) of the 1988 Act does not expressly provide that an assignment must be "absolute" or "not by way of charge only" (cf. s.136 of the Law of Property Act 1925), but it would seem that a purported assignment of copyright which is conditional (for example, expressed to be only until the debt is repaid, or only to take effect on default) will not be an "assignment" within s.90(1). See, e.g. *Hearst Corp v Stark* 639 F. Supp.970 (N.D. Cal. 1986) and *Pantone, Inc v A.I. Friedman Inc* 294 F. Supp.545 (1968). However, a mortgage in ordinary form with a proviso for reassignment upon repayment of the mortgage is an absolute assignment for the purposes of Law of Property Act 1925 s.136. See *Tancred v Delagoa Bay and East Africa Rly Co* (1889) 23 Q.B.D. 239; *Hughes v Pump House Hotel Co* [1902] 2 K.B. 190.

[746] *Hardacre v Armstrong* [1905–1910] Mac.C.C. 1.

[747] See para.5–190, above.

[748] As to an exclusive licensee's right to bring proceedings, see para.5–209, below.

[749] i.e. so as to satisfy the Law of Property Act 1925 s.53(1)(c). See para.5–189, above.

[750] *London County and Westminster Bank Ltd v Tompkins* [1918] 1 K.B. 515.

tion, but the same result is achieved where the owner agrees to pay a debt out of the copyright or its proceeds of sale.[751] In the case of many company debentures, the charge will be a floating one,[752] enabling the company to deal freely with copyright works created or acquired in the course of the business until the charge crystallises. Neither the legal nor equitable title is transferred to the chargee and in principle the chargee merely has the right to have the copyright realised by judicial process to obtain repayment of the loan.[753] A well-drafted charge will, however, provide remedies such as the power to appoint a receiver to enable the chargee to realise his security without recourse to proceedings.

7. LICENCES AND RELATED ISSUES

A. INTRODUCTION

The 1988 Act confers on the copyright owner the exclusive right to do the various acts restricted by the copyright.[754] An infringement of copyright occurs if one of those acts is done without his licence.[755] A licence therefore passes no interest but merely makes lawful that which would otherwise be unlawful[756]; it is a permission which carries with it immunity from proceedings.[757] A mere licence from the copyright owner confers no proprietary interest on the licensee enabling him, for example, to bring proceedings in his own name,[758] unless coupled with the grant of some other interest, for example, the right to take property away.[759] Statute apart, even an exclusive licence, which is merely the leave to do a thing coupled with a promise not to do, or give anyone else permission to do, that thing, gives the licensee no right to sue in his own name for infringement nor any other proprietary interest.[760] In copyright law, this general rule is altered by statute in the case of exclusive licences which comply with prescribed formalities.[761] The 1998 Act confers on such a licensee a procedural status which enables him to

5–198

---

[751] See *Swiss Bank Corp v Lloyds Bank Ltd* [1979] Ch. 548 at 569.

[752] The usual form of debenture often does not include copyrights in the property secured by way of fixed charge or mortgage; more normally this is included in a floating charge of the undertaking and all other assets of the company, both present and future.

[753] See *Snell's Equity*, 31st edn, para.34–03.

[754] CDPA 1988 s.16(1).

[755] s.16(2).

[756] *Canon Kabushiki Kaisha v Green Cartridge Co (Hong Kong) Ltd* [1997] A.C. 728 at 735; [1997] F.S.R. 817 (P.C.), citing *Thomas v Sorrell* (1674) Vaughan 330, 351. See also *Muskett v Hill* (1840) 5 Bing. N.C. 694; *Nicol v Barranger* [1917–23] Mac.C.C. 219 at 243; *Frisby v BBC* [1967] Ch. 932 at 948.

[757] *British Actors Film Co Ltd v Glover* [1918] 1 K.B. 299.

[758] *Neilson v Horniman* (1909) 26 T.L.R. 188 (sole licence), following *London Printing and Publishing Alliance (Ltd) v Cox* [1891] 3 Ch. 291 and *Heap v Hartley* (1889) 42 Ch. D. 461. The suggestions in *Young v Odeon Music House Pty Ltd* (1976) 10 A.L.R. 153 at 161, and *Sega Enterprises Ltd v Galaxy Electronics Pty Ltd* (1997) 39 I.P.R. 577, based on a passage in *Halsbury's Laws of England*, 4th edn, Vol.9, para.880, that a non-exclusive licensee may sue for infringement if the copyright owner is joined as co-claimant, are submitted to be wrong, and based on a mistaken reading of *Neilson v Horniman*.

[759] *Heap v Hartley* (1889) 42 Ch.D. 461 at 470 (a patent case).

[760] *Heap v Hartley* (1889) 42 Ch.D. 461; *C.B.S. United Kingdom Ltd v Charmdale Record Distributors Ltd* [1980] F.S.R. 289 at 295. It is suggested that the statement in *Wilson v Weiss Art Pty Ltd* (1995) 31 I.P.R. 423 (Fed. Ct of Aus.) at 433 that: "The grant of an irrevocable and exclusive licence for consideration must create, in equity, in favour of the licensee, an interest in the copyright, no different from that created in favour of an assignee by an equitable assignment, except for the right, in an appropriate case, to call for a legal assignment" is incorrect as a matter of English law.

[761] See CDPA 1988 s.101, and paras 5–208 and 22–20, below. CDPA 1988 s.101A also confers procedural remedies on certain non-exclusive licensees. See paras 5–213 and 22–30, below.

bring proceedings but otherwise the rule is unchanged: an exclusive licensee has no proprietary interest in the copyright.[762]

5–199 **Formalities.** Except in relation to the particular procedural status conferred by statute on certain licensees,[763] there is no requirement that a licence be in writing or comply with other formalities. A licence can therefore be oral, or be implied into a contract, whether on the grounds of business efficacy or trade practice and custom. It may be gratuitous and inferred from conduct only.

5–200 **Licence granted by one joint owner.** A licence granted by one of several joint owners will not bind the others, and a person acting on the strength of it will be liable to the others in an infringement action.[764]

5–201 **Position of licensee.** A licence granted by a copyright owner is binding on every successor in title to his interest in the copyright, except a purchaser in good faith for valuable consideration and without notice (actual or constructive) of the licence, or a person deriving title from such a purchaser.[765] References to doing anything with or without the licence of the copyright owner are to be construed accordingly.[766] The licensee of copyright, to the extent of the licence, can therefore do acts restricted by the copyright as against the owner and anyone claiming under the owner, except a purchaser for value without notice. Where the licence permits the licensee to authorise others to do acts restricted by the copyright or to grant sub-licences to others, then those other persons will be in a similar position in relation to acts done within the scope of their authorisation or sub-licence.[767]

5–202 **Transitional.** The 1988 Act provides that any document made, or event occurring, before August 1, 1989 which had any operation creating, transferring or terminating any licence in respect of the copyright in any work made before that date will have the corresponding operation in relation to the work under the 1988 Act.[768] Generally, licences granted before this date have the same effect in relation to copyright conferred under the 1988 Act as do licences granted after this date. A number of exceptions are considered separately, below.

5–203 **Compulsory licences.** There are a number of cases in which a licence, or a right

---

[762] *C.B.S. United Kingdom Ltd v Charmdale Record Distributors Ltd* [1980] F.S.R. 289.

[763] See paras 5–209 and 5–215, below.

[764] CDPA 1988 s.173(2).

[765] CDPA 1988 s.90(4). This statutory rule was first introduced by the 1956 Act (s.36(4)). Before then it had been established that an assignee for value without notice took free of any licence (see *London Printing, etc, Alliance Ltd v Cox* [1891] 3 Ch. 291 at first instance—the decision was reversed on other grounds on appeal) and although it was assumed that a purchaser *with* notice took subject to the licence (see, e.g. *Copinger*, 8th edn, p.114), it is not clear what the basis for this was since a mere licence did not create an equitable interest. The point was left open at first instance in the *London Printing* case. It is suggested that the need for the statutory rule indicates that a mere licence would not otherwise bind a subsequent assignee.

[766] CDPA 1988 s.90(4). A licence granted by the prospective owner of copyright, including the prospective owner of any extended or revived copyright, is similarly binding upon every successor in title to his interest (or prospective interest) in the right: CDPA 1988 s.91(3), the Duration of Copyright and Rights in Performances Regulations 1995 (SI 1995/3297) reg.20(2), and the Copyright and Related Rights Regulations 2003 (SI 2003/2498) reg.37(2).

[767] The 1956 Act contained express provision to this effect (s.49(7)) which is not repeated in the 1988 Act, but presumably the law has not changed.

[768] CDPA 1988 Sch.1 para.25(1). The effect of this provision is to preserve the legal effect of a pre-commencement licence. It does not attempt to legislate as to the effect of such a document and only preserves such effect as the document originally had. See *Novello & Co Ltd v Keith Prowse Music Publishing Co Ltd* [2004] EWHC 766 (Ch), para.9; [2004] R.P.C. 48. The decision of Patten J. was upheld on appeal: see [2004] EWCA Civ 1776; [2005] R.P.C. 23.

to call for one, is conferred by statute, rather than arising by agreement. These are considered elsewhere.[769]

B. ASSIGNMENT OR LICENCE?

A frequent problem in this area is to determine whether a particular agreement amounts to an assignment of copyright, in whole or part, or merely a licence, in particular, an exclusive licence.

5–204

Importance of the distinction. Given that an exclusive licensee may, if the agreement complies with the statutory formalities,[770] have sufficient title to sue infringers, it might be thought that it is of little importance today whether the instrument amounts to an assignment or exclusive licence.[771] In many respects, however, the distinction is vital and has important consequences. The differences arise from the proprietary nature of an assignee's title as opposed to that of a licensee. They can be summarised as follows:

5–205

(a) The rights of a licensee, whether exclusive or non-exclusive, are not proprietary: they derive only from his contract, if any, together with such extra protection as the 1988 Act gives him. Thus his licence will not bind a purchaser from the copyright owner acting in good faith for valuable consideration and without notice of the licence. In contrast, an assignee's title, being a proprietary one, is good against all subsequent dealings, including of course a purported, subsequent purchaser from his assignor.

(b) An exclusive licensee's right to assign the benefit of his licence or grant sub-licences will be subject to the terms of his licence. Even if he is entitled to assign the benefit of the licence, the right to exercise the licence will remain subject to whatever terms were originally imposed. In contrast, an assignee has a proprietary title which he can assign,[772] and his assignee will take the copyright free of any contractual restrictions or other encumbrances which may exist, save only any subsisting licences or other equities, these binding all except a bona fide purchaser without notice. Thus, for example, a failure to pay royalties due under the original agreement may, in the case of a licence, enable a licence to be revoked but, in the case of an assignment, cannot lead to recovery of the copyright which has been assigned. This distinction is highly significant, for example in relation to the different consequences on the death or insolvency of an assignee and a licensee.[773]

(c) As a matter of the general law, a licensee has no title to sue. The right to sue given to certain licensees is a statutory right only and in the case of exclusive licensees is subject to the procedural limitation that without leave he cannot proceed with the action unless he joins his licensor. An assignee, whether of whole or part of the copyright, can sue in his own name.[774]

(d) In his dealings with the copyright work, an exclusive licensee must act within the scope of the licence. Otherwise he will infringe. So, for

[769] See Ch.28, below.
[770] See para.5–209, below.
[771] See, e.g. *Chaplin v Leslie Frewin (Publishers) Ltd* [1966] Ch. 71 at 93. Sometimes, of course, it clearly does not matter, as in *Ironside v HM Att Gen* [1988] R.P.C. 197, where the defence of either (equitable) assignment or licence was sufficient to defeat the claim.
[772] He may, of course, be in breach of contract, for example of a term granting option or pre-emption rights, by doing so.
[773] See para.5–80, above, as to the obligations which may bind a successor in title.
[774] Except where he has granted an exclusive licence of concurrent rights, when without leave he may not proceed with the action unless he joins the exclusive licensee. See CDPA 1988 s.102(1).

example, he may not alter the work if the licence does not permit this. On the other hand, an assignee of the copyright and his successors may deal with the work as they please, for example by altering or adapting it, subject only to any moral rights which the author has[775] and, in the assignee's case, to any contractual restrictions which bind him.

(e) A statutory exclusive licensee cannot himself grant an exclusive sub-licence which will enable the sub-licensee to sue in his own name.[776]

For these reasons, therefore, it is always in the interests of an author who depends upon the continued payment of royalties or performance of other contractual obligations to enter into an exclusive licence for the exploitation of his work rather than an assignment.

5–206   **Principles of construction.** In each case it is of course a matter of construction of the instrument in question whether the parties intended that there should be transferred a proprietary interest in the copyright or merely that the grantee should be given a permission to exploit the work, coupled perhaps with contractual restraints on the grantor as to his own exploitation. The distinction is often a fine one.[777] The position is made complicated by the fact that rights of the copyright owner are defined in terms of the "exclusive right" to do the various acts restricted by the copyright.[778] A grant of "exclusive" or "sole and exclusive" rights is therefore ambiguous,[779] being equally consistent with an assignment or a licence.Where such an expression is used, as it often is, the other terms of the agreement must be considered to determine whether the grant was intended to operate by way of assignment[780] or licence.[781]

The following limited principles can be extracted from the cases:

(a) An assignment need not use the word "assign" or "grant", provided the intention to assign otherwise appears from the context.[782] Obviously, however, the use of words such as "assign" or "licence" helps to indicate

---

[775] As to such rights, see Ch.11, below.

[776] The position is the same in relation to non-exclusive licensees who have a right to sue by virtue of CDPA 1988 s.101A. See para.5–214, below.

[777] See the comments in *Western Front Ltd v Vestron Inc* [1987] F.S.R. 66 at 75–76.

[778] CDPA 1988 s.16(1). The wording of the 1956 Act was the same (s.1(1)). The 1911 Act defined copyright as the "sole" right to do various acts.

[779] *Re "Clinical Obstetrics"* [1905–1910] Mac.C.C. 176; *Booth v Richards* [1905–1910] Mac.C.C. 284. See however *JHP Ltd v BBC Worldwide Ltd* [2008] EWHC 757 (Ch); [2008] F.S.R. 29 at para.13: an exclusive licence "most consistent" with "grant" of the "sole and exclusive right" to publish in book form.

[780] Cases where such a grant has been construed as an assignment include: *Messager v British Broadcasting Corp* [1929] A.C. 151 (the grant of the sole and exclusive right of representing and performing a play—other provisions insufficient to cut down this "plain grant"); *Jonathan Cape Ltd v Consolidated Press Ltd* [1954] 1 W.L.R. 1313 (a grant of the exclusive right to print and publish a work in volume form); *Loew's Incorporated v Littler* [1958] Ch. 650 (sale and purchase of sole rights of production of a work in the English language); *Chaplin v Leslie Frewin (Publishers) Ltd* [1966] Ch. 71 (agreement that publishers should have the exclusive right of producing, publishing and selling a work in volume form); *JHP Ltd v BBC Worldwide Ltd* [2008] EWHC 757 (Ch) (sole and exclusive right to publish in book form).

[781] Cases where such a grant has been construed as an exclusive licence include: *Stevens v Benning* (1855) 1 K. & J. 168, affirmed at 6 D.M. & G. 223 (grant construed as sole licence to print and publish); *In re Jude's Musical Compositions* [1907] 1 Ch. 651 (grant of sole and exclusive right to print and publish in volume form); *"Clinical Obstetrics* [1905–1910] Mac.C.C. 176 (an agreement giving another the whole (sic) and exclusive right to print and publish a work); *Sampson Low, Marston & Co, Ltd v Duckworth & Co* [1923–1928] Mac.C.C. 205 (an agreement ceding and assigning to another the exclusive right to publish a work, including the right to arrange any translation or reprint in whatever manner thought fit); *C.I.R. v Longmans Green & Co Ltd* [1928–1935] Mac.C.C. 345 (the grant of the exclusive right of translation and publication); *Frisby v British Broadcasting Corp* [1967] Ch. 932 (exclusive right to televise a play).

[782] *Stevens v Benning* (1855) 1 K. & J. 168 at 6 D.M. & G. 223; *Chaplin v Leslie Frewin (Publishers) Ltd* [1966] Ch. 71 at 94. And see also *British Actors Film Co Ltd v Glover* [1918] 1 K.B. 299 (agreement by A to let, and by B to hire, the right of performing a work: partial assign-

the parties' intentions one way or the other,[783] but even then they are not conclusive.[784] Generally, parties may not disguise the reality of the transaction by applying inappropriate labels to it.[785]

(b) The commercial significance to either party of the grant operating either as a licence or an assignment will be a relevant factor.[786]

(c) If the word "copyright" is used elsewhere in the agreement but not in the words of grant, this may point to a licence on the principle that since the parties had the concept of copyright in mind they would have used the word in the grant if copyright was intended to pass.[787]

(d) Sometimes, the fact that the agreement has continuing obligations, for example to pay royalties as opposed to a one-off lump sum, has influenced a decision that the agreement was a licence[788] but again this is not conclusive.[789] Probably little weight would be given to this fact today since many agreements which are clearly assignments do provide for payments of royalties rather than a lump sum.

(e) Agreements for profit sharing generally indicate a licence.[790]

(f) The fact that the circumstances show that the grantor relied on the personal skill and discretion of the grantee points to a licence.[791] Nevertheless, agreements of this kind often contain an unambiguous assignment.

(g) The fact that the agreement provides for the "reversion" of the right in certain events indicates an assignment,[792] but the absence of such a clause is not fatal to an assignment, since, if necessary, it can be implied.[793]

(h) Assistance can sometimes be obtained if the agreement provides for who is to sue in case of an infringement. Since, however, the parties often do not understand the principles involved, this can be of limited help.

---

ment); *Bairstow v Terry* [1924] 2 Ch. 316 (agreement for A to have entire rights in play inalienably: assignment of performing right).

[783] *Neilson v Horniman* (1909) 25 T.L.R. 684 (grant of "sole licence" not an assignment). In both *"Clinical Obstetrics"* [1905–1910] Mac.C.C. 176 and *Sampson Low, Marston & Co, Ltd v Duckworth & Co* [1923–1928] Mac.C.C. 205, the absence of any reference to "assigns" of the grantee was held to point to a licence.

[784] *Messager v British Broadcasting Corp* [1929] A.C. 151 (parties to assignment described as "licensors" and "licensees").

[785] *Street v Mountford* [1985] A.C. 809; *A.G. Securities v Vaughan* [1900] 1 A.C. 417. cf. *Massey v Crown Life Insurance Co* [1978] 1 W.L.R. 676, CA.

[786] *Wilson v Weiss Art Pty Ltd* (1995) 31 I.P.R. 423 (Fed. Ct of Aus.)

[787] As in *"Clinical Obstetrics"* [1905–1910] Mac.C.C. 176; *Sampson Low, Marston & Co, Ltd v Duckworth & Co* [1923–1928] Mac.C.C. 205.

[788] *Re Jude's Musical Compositions* [1906] 2 Ch. 595, affirmed on slightly different grounds at [1907] 1 Ch. 651; *Sampson Low, Marston & Co, Ltd v Duckworth & Co* [1923–1928] Mac.C.C. 205. See also *R. Griggs Group Ltd v Evans* [2003] EWHC (Ch) 2914, para.58; [2004] F.S.R. 31 (upheld on appeal: [2005] EWCA Civ 11; [2005] F.S.R. 31), noting that an exclusive licence is more appropriate where the consideration is payment of royalties rather than a lump sum. See also *JHP Ltd v BBC Worldwide Ltd* [2008] EWHC 757 (Ch); [2008] F.S.R. 29, at para.13.

[789] As in, e.g. *Messager v British Broadcasting Corp Ltd* [1929] A.C. 151 (although not one of the grounds relied on by the court).

[790] *Stevens v Benning* (1855) 1 K. & J. 168, affirmed at 6 D.M. & G. 223; *Reade v Bentley* (1858) 3 K. & J. 271; *Hole v Bradbury* (1879) 12 Ch.D. 886; *Sampson Low, Marston & Co Ltd v Duckworth*, above.

[791] *Re "Clinical Obstetrics"* [1905–1910] Mac.C.C. 176; *Sampson Low, Marston & Co, Ltd v Duckworth & Co* [1923–1928] Mac.C.C. 205.

[792] *Messager v British Broadcasting Corp. Ltd* [1929] A.C. 151, at 155; *Loew's Incorporated v Littler* [1958] Ch. 650 at 663. However, reference to "reversion" of the rights is not conclusive: *JHP Ltd v BBC Worldwide Ltd* [2008] EWHC 757 (Ch); [2008] F.S.R. 29 at para.14(d). Such a "floating reverter" is perfectly valid: *Crosstown Music Company 1, LLC v Rive Droite Music Ltd* [2010] EWCCA Civ 1222.

[793] *Chaplin v Leslie Frewin (Publishers) Ltd* [1966] Ch. 71. Note also that a provision for a reverter may not be necessary at all, since copyright can be assigned for part only of the term of copyright. See CDPA 1988 s.90(2)(b) and para.5–102, above.

C. EXCLUSIVE LICENCES

(i) Introduction

5–207   A sole licence is often understood to be one where the licence is coupled with a contractual promise that the licensor will not grant a licence to any other party, the licensor himself remaining free to exercise the licensed rights. In contrast, a sole and exclusive licence, or, more shortly, an exclusive licence, is one where there is included a promise that the licensor will not himself exercise any of the rights the subject of the licence. As has been seen,[794] as a matter of general law an exclusive licence, whether oral or written, confers no proprietary interest in the copyright, merely the usual incidents of a licence but coupled with contractual remedies against the licensor in the event of any breach of exclusivity provisions. So for example, statute apart, an exclusive licensee has no right to bring an action in his own name and no remedy against a third party to whom the licensor may have subsequently granted a licence or assigned the copyright. Exclusive licences are, however, of great commercial convenience and since the passing of the 1956 Act such licensees have enjoyed a statutory procedural status entitling them to bring actions against infringers in their own name.[795]

(ii) Statutory exclusive licences

5–208   **Statutory exclusive licence: the 1988 Act.** For the purposes of the 1988 Act, an "exclusive licence" is a licence in writing, signed by or on behalf of the copyright owner, authorising the licensee to the exclusion of all other persons, including the person granting the licence, to exercise a right which would otherwise be exercisable exclusively by the copyright owner.[796] Since an exclusive licensee has the same rights and remedies as if the licence had been an assignment,[797] it follows that the rights granted by such a licence must be such as to be capable of forming the subject matter of a valid assignment of copyright and, likewise, that whatever is capable of forming the subject matter of a valid assignment of copyright is capable of being the subject of an exclusive licence.[798] The extent to which copyright is divisible by way of assignment is dealt with elsewhere[799] but it should be noted that an assignment of copyright cannot be made in respect of, for example, "England" or some smaller area, such as London. It follows that a statutory exclusive licence cannot be granted covering such a limited area either and that will take effect in contract only. Two matters also follow from the requirement that the licence be signed "by or on behalf of the copyright owner"— first, that a statutory exclusive licensee cannot himself grant a statutory exclusive licence by way of sub-licence. If such a grant is permitted by the terms of the head licence, it will of course create a valid contractual sub-licence, giving the sub-licensee protection in an infringement action brought by the copyright owner and contractual rights against his own licensor. Secondly, it seems that a statutory exclusive licence cannot be granted in respect of a future copyright work[800]: at the date of the grant there is no "copyright owner" by whom or on whose

---

[794] See para.5–198, above.
[795] The position of an exclusive licensee before the passing of the 1956 Act was uncertain. See para.5–212, below.
[796] CDPA 1988 s.92(1).
[797] s.101(1).
[798] *Sega Enterprises Pty Ltd v Galaxy Electronics Pty Ltd* (1998) 39 I.P.R. 577.
[799] See para.5–97, above.
[800] See CDPA 1988 s.92 and cf. the wording of s.91.

behalf the licence can be granted.[801] A statutory exclusive licence may be granted in respect of any act which the copyright owner has the exclusive right to do and is not limited to those acts which fall within s.16 of the Act. A statutory exclusive licence may therefore be granted in respect of the importation of infringing copies,[802] but not the right to sell licensed copies of a work since the right to sell such copies is not an exclusive right of the copyright owner.[803] No doubt, however, such an agreement could often be construed as a grant of the exclusive right to issue copies of the work to the public,[804] which would amount to a statutory exclusive licence. Where the licensor reserves to himself rights which are also the subject of the grant to the licensee, the licence obviously is not exclusive. Where some rights are reserved, it will depend on the construction of the licence whether there is any overlap with the rights granted.[805] It is possible that there can be such a thing as an implied equitable statutory exclusive licence which would entitle the licensee to call for a statutory exclusive licence in the same way as an informal assignee is entitled to call for a legal assignment.[806] In order to establish an equitable statutory exclusive licence it would presumably have to be shown that the parties had agreed and that the licence should have the characteristics of a statutory exclusive licence, in particular that the licence should be committed to writing signed by the licensor and that the licensee should be entitled to bring infringement proceedings.

Rights of statutory exclusive licensee. A statutory exclusive licensee has, except against the copyright owner, the same rights and remedies in respect of matters occurring after the grant of the licence as if the licence had been an assignment.[807] Such rights and remedies are concurrent with the rights and remedies of the copyright owner, and references to the copyright owner are to be construed accordingly.[808] These provisions are purely procedural, entitling the exclusive licensee to enforce the proprietary rights of the copyright owner. The exclusive licensee is not himself the owner of the copyright, is not treated as such owner (otherwise than for procedural purposes) and is not entitled to the copyright.[809] It is, however, a "right over property" and is thus a "non-cash asset" for the purposes of s.320 of the Companies Act 1985.[810]

5–209

Generally, the right of a statutory exclusive licensee to sue for infringement of copyright is exercisable only against third-party infringers but not assignees or

---

[801] cf. the similar problem which arose before the 1956 Act in respect of assignments of future copyright. See *Performing Right Society Ltd v London Theatre of Varieties Ltd* [1924] A.C. 1 and para.5–112, above.

[802] *Biotrading & Financing OY v Biohit Ltd* [1998] F.S.R. 109.

[803] See the wording of CDPA 1988 s.92(1) and also *Avel Pty Ltd v Multicoin Amusements Pty Ltd* (1990) 18 I.P.R. 443 (High Ct of Aus.). cf. *Broderbund Software Inc v Computermate (Australia) Pty Ltd* (1991) 22 I.P.R. 215. In *PM Sulcs & Associates Pty Ltd v Detroit Diesel-Allison Australia Pty Ltd* (1997) 39 I.P.R. 328 (Fed. Ct of Aus.), the point whether an exclusive licence to use and license the use of a computer program was capable of amounting to an exclusive licence to reproduce the work was held not sufficiently clear for summary determination.

[804] See CDPA 1988 s.18.

[805] See, e.g. *Sega Enterprises Pty Ltd v Galaxy Electronics Pty Ltd* (1998) 39 I.P.R. 577, where the grant of the exclusive right to exhibit films in games arcades, coupled with a reservation to enable the licensor to supply its own arcades, was held capable of being a grant of a valid exclusive licence to exhibit in arcades other than those of the licensor. See also *Young v Odeon Music House Pty Ltd* (1976) 10 A.L.R. 153.

[806] *Wrenn v Landamore* [2008] EWCA Civ 496 at para.46, per Mummery L.J., without deciding the point.

[807] CDPA 1988 s.101(1).

[808] s 101(2).

[809] *C.B.S. United Kingdom Ltd v Charmdale Record Distributors Ltd* [1980] F.S.R. 289.

[810] *Ultraframe (UK) Ltd v Fielding (No.2)* [2005] EWHC 1638 (Ch); [2006] F.S.R. 17 (a design right case). Indeed, an exclusive licensee is often spoken of as having an "interest" in the copyright. See e.g. *Chaplin v Leslie Frewin (Publishers) Ltd* [1966] Ch. 71 at 94.

licensees claiming under the copyright owner. As to licensees from the copyright owner, this follows from s.101(3) of the 1988 Act, which provides that, in any action brought by the exclusive licensee, a defendant may avail himself of any defence which would have been available to him if the action had been brought by the copyright owner. It also follows that if the owner of the copyright has granted or subsequently grants a licence conflicting with the exclusive licence, the other licensee will be protected in proceedings for infringement of copyright brought by the exclusive licensee, since he could have relied upon his licence in an action brought by the owner of the copyright. The same applies to a licensee "by estoppel" from the copyright owner.[811] In such a case, the only remedy of the exclusive licensee is in damages against the owner of the copyright,[812] and possibly an injunction to restrain him from granting further licences.

As against a licensor who acts in conflict with the exclusive licence, the licensee's remedies are restricted to claims for breach of contract. As against the licensor's assigns, the licensee would, statute apart, have no remedy. This is because even though the assignee might take subject to the licence,[813] he would not assume the burden of the contractual obligations of the licensor nor, since he is the copyright owner, would he be liable in an action for infringement of copyright.[814] To deal with this situation, it is provided that a licensee under an exclusive licence has the same rights as against a successor in title who is bound by the licence[815] as he has against the person granting the licence.[816] The effect of this seems to be that the contractual obligations of the licensor are imposed by statute on his successors, except a bona fide purchaser for value without notice and his successors. This provision was new in the 1988 Act and does not apply in relation to an exclusive licence granted before August 1, 1989.[817]

5–210 **Necessity to join owner of copyright as party.** Where an action for infringement of copyright brought by the copyright owner or an exclusive licensee relates to an infringement in respect of which they have concurrent rights of action, the copyright owner or, as the case may be, the exclusive licensee, may not, without the leave of the court, proceed with the action unless the other is either joined as a claimant or added as a defendant.[818] In many cases the copyright owner will be unwilling to join in the action as co-claimant or take any active part in the action. In such a case, if he is joined as a defendant, he will not be liable for any costs in the action unless he takes part in the proceedings.[819] These provisions requiring joinder of the copyright owner do not affect the granting of interim relief on an application by a copyright owner or exclusive licensee alone.[820] An exclusive licensee may therefore start an action and obtain interim relief without joining the copyright owner (and vice versa). Thereafter, he may proceed in the absence of the owner of the copyright only with the leave of the court and will usually be required to join the owner, for otherwise the defendant

---

[811] *JHP Ltd v BBC Worldwide Ltd* [2008] EWHC 757 (Ch); [2008] F.S.R. 29.
[812] *See Simms v Marryat* (1851) 17 Q.B. 281 (grant of exclusive right impliedly including a warranty of sufficient title).
[813] See CDPA 1988 s.90(4) and para.5–201, above.
[814] See s.101(1) and also s.16(2).
[815] i.e. anyone other than a bona fide purchaser for value without notice and his successors. See CDPA 1988 s.90(4) and para.5–201, above.
[816] s.92(2).
[817] Sch.1 para.29.
[818] CDPA 1988 s.102(1).
[819] s.101(2).
[820] s.102(3).

will be at risk from a subsequent claim by the owner.[821] Leave to proceed without the copyright owner may be particularly appropriate where he is dead and no grant has been taken to his estate or he cannot be found or is otherwise unavailable.[822]

Special provisions as to damages and account of profits. The fact that both the   **5–211** copyright owner and the exclusive licensee have a concurrent right of action means that special provision has to be made for the assessment of damages or an account of profits in such cases. These provisions apply whether or not the copyright owner and the exclusive licensee are both parties to the action. They are as follows[823]:

(a) *Damages.* In such cases, the court, in assessing damages, must take into account the terms of the licence and any pecuniary remedy already awarded or available to either the copyright owner or the exclusive licensee in respect of the infringement.

(b) *Account of profits.* No account of profits shall be directed if an award of damages has been made, or an account of profits has been directed, in favour of the other of them in respect of the infringement. If an account of profits is directed, the court must apportion the profits between the copyright owner and the exclusive licensee as the court considers just, subject to any agreement between them.

(c) *Delivery up and right of seizure.* Special provision is also made for applying for delivery up orders and for the exercise of the right of seizure of infringing copies. The copyright owner is under an obligation to notify any exclusive licensee having concurrent rights before applying for a delivery up order or exercising the right of seizure of infringing copies. The court may on the application of the licensee make such order for delivery up or, as the case may be, prohibiting or permitting the exercise by the copyright owner of the right of seizure, as it thinks fit having regard to the terms of the licence.[824]

Transitional. The 1988 Act provides that in relation to any document or event   **5–212** occurring before August 1, 1989 which had any operation in creating any interest, right or licence in respect of a work which was then in existence, it is to have the corresponding operation in relation to copyright in the work under the 1988 Act.[825] The effect of licences entered into before this date therefore needs to be considered.

(a) *The 1956 Act.* The provisions of the 1956 Act were to substantially the same effect as those now contained in the 1988 Act.[826] The procedural status conferred on exclusive licensees by the 1988 Act is therefore also conferred on licensees under a statutory exclusive licence granted between June 1, 1957 and August 1, 1989.

---

[821] cf. the requirement that an equitable owner must join the legal owner before judgment. See para.5–190, above.

[822] See *Bodley Head Ltd v Flegon* [1972] 1 W.L.R. 680; [1972] F.S.R. 21, where, by consent, leave was given to proceed without joining the copyright owner, the dissident author Solzhenitsyn.

[823] CDPA 1988 s.102(4).

[824] s.102(5).

[825] CDPA 1988 Sch.1 para.25(1). The effect of this provision is to preserve the legal effect of a pre-commencement licence. It does not attempt to legislate as the effect of such a document and only preserves such effect as the document originally had. See *Novello & Co Ltd v Keith Prowse Music Publishing Co Ltd* [2004] EWHC (Ch) 766, para.9; [2004] R.P.C. 48 (upheld on appeal: [2004] EWCA Civ 1776; [2005] R.P.C. 23).

[826] Copyright Act 1956 s.19. The exception is that the 1956 Act did not contain a provision which corresponds to s.92(2) of the 1988 Act, which gives an exclusive licensee rights against a successor in title to his licensor who is bound by the licence. See para.5–209, above. Sch.1 para.9, of the 1988 Act expressly provides that s.92(2) does not apply to a licence granted before August 1, 1989.

(b) *The* 1911 Act. There were no provisions relating to exclusive licences contained in the 1911 Act which correspond to those contained in the 1988 Act. Prima facie, therefore, an exclusive licensee under a grant made between July 1, 1912 and June 1, 1957 enjoys no special status today. The 1911 Act, however, provided that a copyright owner might "grant any interest in the right by licence".[827] It was never resolved what this provision meant and in particular whether it was sufficient to confer on a licensee, particularly an exclusive licensee, a legal interest in the copyright such as would, for example, enable him to sue in his own name.[828] An argument against such a construction is that whereas the Act expressly provided that the assignee under a partial assignment was to be treated as the owner of such part, no such provision was made in relation to a grantee by way of licence.[829] In *British Actors Film Co Ltd v Glover*,[830] the view was expressed, obiter, that the expression referred to the case of grant of an interest coupled with a licence to exercise it, as distinct from an assignment or partial assignment on the one hand or a simple consent on the other. It is not clear, however, what the former might have been, other than an assignment. If the true effect of the 1911 Act was indeed to confer a proprietary interest on an exclusive licensee, then the licence is to have a "corresponding operation" under the 1988 Act. It seems doubtful, however, that this can be the procedural status which is now conferred by the 1988 Act on exclusive licensees, since this status does not correspond to the operation of a pre-1956 Act exclusive licence, whatever this might have been.

(c) *Pre*-1911 Act. Before the passing of the 1911 Act, an exclusive licensee had no proprietary interest in the copyright enabling him to sue in his own name.[831]

D. LICENCES GRANTED UNDER SECTION 101A

5–213   **Introduction.** When the Information Society Directive[832] was implemented by the Copyright and Related Rights Regulations 2003,[833] a new s.101A was inserted giving certain non-exclusive licensees the right to bring proceedings for infringement of copyright. The original thinking behind this provision was to enable service providers and others to act against those using their networks to transmit infringing material in circumstances where they are neither the owners nor exclusive licensees of rights in the content they transmit, but the owner of copy-

---

[827] Copyright Act 1911 s.5(2). No such grant was valid unless it was in writing signed by the owner of the relevant right: ibid.

[828] It was because of this uncertainty that the Gregory Committee recommended in 1952 that the status of an exclusive licensee be made clear, as was done by the 1956 Act. See Cmnd.8662, para.276. See also para.5–116, above.

[829] See Copyright Act 1911 s.5(3). It was suggested in previous editions of this work that the legislature inserted the provision to cover the case of a grant which was, in substance, a partial assignment but, in form, was expressed as a licence, and that the real effect of this provision was to make it easier to construe such a document as a partial assignment. This would not affect the law relating to documents which were licences only in the narrower sense, either because they were not exclusive or because they purported to deal with rights which were not susceptible of separate assignment.

[830] [1918] 1 K.B. 299. The point was left open in *Jonathan Cape Ltd v Consolidated Press Ltd* [1954] 1 W.L.R. 1313.

[831] *Heape v Hartley* (1889) 42 Ch.D. 461; *The London Printing and Publishing Alliance Ltd v Cox* [1891] 3 Ch. 291; *Neilson v Horniman* (1909) 26 T.L.R. 188.

[832] Directive 2001/29.

[833] SI 2003/2498.

right in the content wishes them to be able to act.[834] In fact, the provision is of general scope and not restricted to service providers or licences to transmit works in networks.

Applicable licences. A non-exclusive licensee may now bring proceedings, provided the licence (i) is in writing and is signed by or on behalf of the copyright owner; and (ii) expressly grants the non-exclusive licensee a right of action under the section.[835] The first limb uses the same wording as is found in s.92(1), defining exclusive licensee, and means that to be effective the licence must be signed by or on behalf of the copyright owner, and not for example by an exclusive licensee. The second limb is likely to reduce greatly the application of the section, since it appears that there must be an express reference to the section in the licence for it to be effective. It is unlikely to become a matter of standard drafting to include such a reference, because in most commercial cases, the copyright owner will not wish to give the licensee a right to sue independently of him.   **5–214**

The right to bring proceedings. The section limits the circumstances in which such a licensee can bring proceedings. He may only bring an action if the infringing act "was directly connected to a prior licensed act of the licensee".[836] This rather curiously worded provision presumably means that the infringing act must be one which would fall within the scope of the licence, and must have been committed at a time when the licence was in force. It is not clear, however, whether it means something more. In particular, is it necessary that the licensee has previously done an act which falls within the scope of his licence? In other words, in order to trigger the right to sue, must the licensee be already acting pursuant to the licence? It is also not clear what is the intended effect of the words "*directly connected* to the prior licensed act" and, in particular, whether anything more is intended than that the infringing act must fall within the scope of the licence, or, if anything more is intended, precisely what. In the case of a defendant using a service provider's network to transmit infringing material, it is unlikely that the defendant's act of infringement will have any kind of connection with the licensed actions of the service provider other than use of its network. Generally, this seems a confusingly worded provision if the intention was to simply to enable: **5–215**

> "service providers [and others] to be able to act against infringements connected to their activities in circumstances where they are neither the owner nor exclusive licensee of rights in content they transmit, but the owner of copyright in the content wishes them to be able to act".[837]

Procedural provisions. The other provisions are more straightforward and follow the example of s.92 and the rights of exclusive licensees. Thus, the non-exclusive licensee is to have the same rights and remedies available to him as the copyright owner would have had if he had brought the action,[838] and the licensee's   **5–216**

---

[834] See Government's Conclusions on the Patent Office's Consultation Paper of August 7, 2002 and the Transposition Notice accompanying the Regulations.

[835] CDPA 1988 s.101A(1)(b). For these purposes, a non-exclusive licensee is defined to mean the holder of a licence authorising him to exercise a right which remains exercisable by the copyright owner: s.101A(6). A s.101A licence may therefore be granted by a partial owner of copyright in respect of his partial interest, or some lesser interest; the s.101A right will come to an end when the copyright owner's interest terminates (which would be the usual position in any event).

[836] CDPA 1988 s.101A(1)(a).

[837] See the Government's Conclusions on the Patent Office's Consultation Paper of August 7, 2002, para.8.6.

[838] CDPA 1988 s.101A(2).

rights are to be concurrent with those of the copyright owner.[839] Further, in any action brought by the licensee, a defendant may avail himself of any defence which would have been available to him if the action had been brought by the copyright owner.[840] Finally, the procedural provisions of ss.102(1) to (4) are to apply to the non-exclusive licensee as they apply to an exclusive licensee.[841]

E. IMPLIED AND INFORMAL LICENCES

5–217   **Implied licences.** Implied licences frequently cause difficulties. Since it will be the defendant who will have raised the issue of licence as a defence, no doubt the onus will be upon him to establish its existence and extent.[842] Where the licence is alleged to arise in a contractual context, a term will only be implied if it is necessary to give business efficacy to the contract and it satisfies the "officious bystander" test, and not simply because it is reasonable.[843] The test is an objective one.[844] Where a work is made by an independent contractor to be used by another for certain purposes, in circumstances such that the copyright is retained by the contractor,[845] some licence to use the work must be implied in favour of the latter if the contract is otherwise silent on the point. In such cases the principle to be applied is that "the engagement for reward of a person to produce material of a nature which is capable of being the subject of copyright implies a permission, or consent, or licence in the person giving the engagement to use the material in the manner and for the purpose in which and for which it was contemplated between the parties that it would be used at the time of the engagement".[846] The implied licence extends no further than the minimum which is necessary to give business efficacy to the contract.[847] In a case where the licence is gratuitous and informal,[848] however, the position is different. Thus, where the work is supplied knowing that it will be used for a particular purpose, the licence may be limited to that purpose,[849] but where the purpose is left vague, the extent of the licence is unlikely to be confined to the immediate purposes which the parties had in mind.[850] No

---

[839] s.101A(3). References in the relevant provisions of Pt I of the Act to the copyright owner are to be construed accordingly: ibid.

[840] s.101A(4).

[841] s.101A(5).

[842] *Noah v Shuba* [1991] F.S.R. 14; *De Garis v Neville Jeffries Pidler Pty Ltd* (1990) I.P.R. 292 at 302 (Fed. Ct of Aus.). Technically, however, it will be for the claimant to establish his cause of action by proving that the acts in question were done without licence. See *Computermate Products (Aust) Pty Ltd v Ozi-Soft Pty Ltd* (1988) 83 A.L.R. 492; *Avel Pty Ltd v Multicoin Amusements Pty Ltd* (1990) 97 A.L.R. 19 (High Ct of Aus.); *Devefi Pty Ltd v Mateffy Pearl Nagy Pty Ltd* [1993] R.P.C. 493 (Fed. Ct of Aus). Usually, however, this evidential burden is discharged by the claimant's formal evidence that consent was not given.

[843] *Liverpool City Council v Irwin* [1977] A.C. 239; *Shell UK Ltd v Lostock Garage Ltd* [1976] 1 W.L.R. 1187 at 1197, 1200; *Sport International Bossum B.V. v Hi-Tec Sports Ltd* [1988] R.P.C. 329. *Ray v Classic FM plc* [1998] F.S.R. 622; *R. Griggs Group Ltd v Evans No.1* [2005] EWCA Civ 11; [2005] F.S.R. 31.

[844] *Redwood Music Ltd v Chappell & Co Ltd* [1982] R.P.C. 109 at 128.

[845] For example, because the contract expressly so provides or where it is not a term of the contract (express or implied) that the copyright should belong to the other.

[846] *Beck v Montana Constructions Pty Ltd* [1964–65] N.S.W.R. 229, approved by the Court of Appeal in *Blair v Osborne & Tomkins* [1971] 2 Q.B. 78. See also, e.g. *Ironside v HM Att Gen* [1988] R.P.C. 197.

[847] *Stovin-Bradford v Volpoint Ltd* [1971] Ch. 1007; *R. & A. Bailey & Co Ltd v Boccaccio Pty Ltd* (1988) 77 A.L.R. 177; *De Garis v Neville Jeffries Pidler Pty Ltd* (1990) I.P.R. 292 (Fed. Ct of Aus.); *Ray v Classic FM plc* [1998] F.S.R. 622.

[848] As in *Barrett v Universal-Island Records Ltd* [2006] EWHC 1009 (Ch); [2006] E.M.L.R. 21, where since the claimants did not know that they were entitled to any copyright, there could be no intention to create legal relations and accordingly any implied licence could not be contractual (para.362).

[849] See *Trumpet Software Pty Ltd v Ozemail Pty Ltd* (1996) 34 I.P.R. 481 at 500.

[850] *Brighton v Jones* [2004] EWHC (Ch) 1157, para.76; [2005] F.S.R. 16. In *Barrett v Universal-*

doubt the test is objective: for what purposes would a reasonable person in the shoes of the licensee consider he could use the work?

Licences implied from trade practice or custom. It is clearly possible that a **5–218** trade custom or practice may exist whereby works are accepted on all sides as being liable to be copied, etc. The usual difficulty will be to show that the usage or custom is invariable, certain and general,[851] as opposed to mere common practice.[852]

Licences implied from conduct. A licence can also arise as a result of conduct, **5–219** without the existence of any contractual relation. So, for example, the payment and acceptance of royalties or other sums in respect of the exploitation of the copyright can evidence the recipient's consent to the acts of the payer[853] and such a licensee can rely on the acceptance of royalties as a clear indication that the licensor confirms the continuation in force of the licence.[854] In such a case, the test is an objective one, namely whether, viewing the facts objectively, the words and conduct of the alleged licensor, as made known to the alleged licensee, indicated that the licensor consented to what the licensee was doing.[855]

Effect of estoppel and acquiescence. Where a copyright owner stands back and **5–220** allows another to assume that no objection will be taken to the exploitation of the work, the effect may be that the copyright owner will become estopped from asserting that there was no consent or that any consent has been revoked. The ordinary principles of estoppel or acquiescence will operate.[856] In *Fisher v Brooker*, the claimant had contributed to a composition but left the band soon afterwards, making no claim to the copyright. His co-writer (the defendant) and his publishing company continued to exploit the composition for almost 40 years. The claimant claimed that such exploitation was pursuant to an implied licence,

---

Island Records Ltd [2006] EWHC 1009 (Ch); [2006] E.M.L.R. 21, where the claimants had participated in the recording of songs for inclusion in an album for distribution to the public, at a time when the means of mechanical reproduction of music were limited to vinyl records and cassettes, it was held (obiter) that any implied licence would have extended not only to the making of such records and cassettes but also to the making of CDs and DVDs, which the judge described as "a more technologically advanced means of reproducing the same work in essentially the same form" (para.360). The judge went on to hold that it would not have been necessary to imply an *exclusive* licence: if the claimants had wanted to license others to perform any songs in which they had copyright or to perform them themselves, they should have been free to do so.

[851] See *Chitty on Contracts*, 30th edn, para.13–018. In *Express Newspapers Plc v News (UK) Ltd* [1990] F.S.R. 359, the suggestion that there was a trade custom between newspaper publishers that one newspaper was free to reproduce news stories appearing in another, particularly the quoted words of an interviewee, was held sufficiently arguable to go to trial.

[852] *De Garis v Neville Jeffries Pidler Pty Ltd* (1990) I.P.R. 292 (Fed. Ct of Aus.). Such a licence will not be implied from the fact that copying habitually takes place: *Walter v Steinkopff* [1892] 3 Ch. 489; *USP Strategies v London General Holdings Ltd* [2002] EWHC (Ch) 2557. See also *Banier v News Group Newspapers Ltd* [1997] F.S.R. 812 (where it was said to be common practice, after one newspaper has published a photograph, for other newspapers to publish without waiting to obtain a formal licence; held: the practice, if it existed, amounted to the taking of a commercial risk and was unlawful). As to any custom in the Press, see para.5–224, below.

[853] *Redwood Music Ltd v Francis Day & Hunter Ltd* [1978] R.P.C. 429; *Redwood Music Ltd v Chappell & Co Ltd* [1982] R.P.C. 109.

[854] *Leofelis SA v Lonsdale Sports Ltd* [2007] EWHC 451 (Ch) at para.56, holding that there is no principled distinction between the circumstances of landlord and a tenant and those of the licensor of a trade mark and his licensee. The point was referred to on appeal but without any final decision: [2008] E.T.M.R. 63 at para 88–91.

[855] *Redwood Music Ltd v Chappell & Co Ltd* [1982] R.P.C. 109.

[856] See, e.g. *Godfrey v Lees* [1995] E.M.L.R. 307; *Ibcos Computers Ltd v Mercantile Highlands Finance Ltd* [1994] F.S.R. 275; *Baillieu v Australian Electoral Commission* (1996) 33 I.P.R. 494 (Fed. Ct of Aus.). The argument failed on the facts in *Banier v News Group Newspapers Ltd* [1997] F.S.R. 812; *KMA Corp Pty Ltd v G & F Productions Pty Ltd* (1997) 38 I.P.R. 243; *Beckingham v Hodgens* [2003] EWCA Civ 143; [2003] E.C.D.R. 6 and *Brighton v Jones* [2004] EWHC 1157 (Ch); [2005] F.S.R. 16.

which he purported to revoke. At first instance,[857] it was held that the claimant's contribution entitled him to a 40 per cent share and declarations as to joint authorship and joint ownership were granted, together with a declaration that the implied licence had been revoked and an order for an inquiry as to damages in respect of infringement during the period after the revocation. The claim for restitution of past licence fees was dismissed on the ground that there was an implied licence. Defences of laches, acquiescence and estoppel were rejected. The judgment was for the most part upheld in the House Lords[858] since the mere passage of time could not, itself, undermine a claim and, for it to do so, laches would need to be established. However, laches can only bar equitable relief, and a declaration as to the existence of a long-term property right, recognised as such by statute, is not equitable relief. The defendants had not demonstrated any acts during the course of the delay which had resulted in a "balance of justice" justifying the refusal of the relief to which the claimant would otherwise be entitled. They could not show any prejudice resulting from the delay, and, even if they could, the benefit they had obtained from the delay would outweigh any such prejudice.

5–221   **Examples of implied licences.** As already noted, where a copyright work is made by A at the request of B but in circumstances that the copyright does not belong either in law or in equity to B, some licence must usually be implied if use is to be made of the work for the purposes contemplated by both parties. There are many examples of such implied licences and each case turns on its own facts and is subject to whatever other contractual terms may have been agreed. For example, the production of an advertisement by an advertising agency for a client was held to include a licence to use the advertisement for as long as the client wished,[859] and the commission of designs of coins to include a licence from the designer to use the designs for the coinage and proof sets.[860] Depending on the circumstances, the supply of source code by a software house to a customer may imply a licence to use it to fix errors in the object code.[861] A common situation which gives rise to the implication of a licence is the sale of an article by means of which a work can be easily reproduced.[862] Again, the extent of any implied term will turn on the minimum terms that are required to give the contract business efficacy and to satisfy the "officious bystander" test, and not on some lesser test of what is reasonable.[863] Neither will the court imply a licence to reproduce a work for commercial purposes from the sale of an article simply because there is no express restriction on the use of a copyright work which is embodied in it.[864] The following examples in this field can be noted: the retail sale of a pattern book containing knitting patterns generally includes a licence to make garments for personal use but not in commercial quantities[865]; of a directory, to obtain information from it but not the right to copy it for the purpose of producing a rival directory[866]; of a book of legal precedents, the right to reproduce the precedents in the ordinary course of practice but not in a competing work; of a book of code

---

[857] [2006] EWHC 3239 (Ch); [2007] F.S.R. 12.
[858] *Fisher v Brooker* [2009] UKHL 41; [2009] 1 W.L.R. 1764; [2009] F.S.R. 25.
[859] *Drabble (Harold) Ltd v The Hycolite Manufacturing Co* (1928) 44 T.L.R. 264.
[860] *Ironside v HM Att Gen* [1988] R.P.C. 197.
[861] *Saphena Computing Ltd v Allied Collection Agencies Ltd* [1995] F.S.R. 616 at 637 (the statutory right of a lawful user of a computer program under CDPA 1988 s.50C to copy it for the purpose of correcting errors only applies to errors in *that* program).
[862] Whether in these circumstances the seller in fact has the right to grant any licence is of course a separate issue.
[863] *Creative Technology Ltd v Aztech Systems Pte Ltd* [1997] F.S.R. 491 (CA of Singapore); *Ray v Classic FM plc* [1998] F.S.R. 622.
[864] *Roberts v Candiware Ltd* [1980] F.S.R. 352.
[865] *Roberts v Candiware Ltd* [1980] F.S.R. 352
[866] *Waterlow Directories Ltd v Reed Information Services Ltd* [1992] F.S.R. 409.

words, the right to reproduce the code in sending messages but not the right to publish a competing work[867]; of printing blocks, the right of the purchaser, but not others, to use them.[868] A further situation which has given rise to a body of case law is the case of architects' drawings and is considered separately, below.[869]

Betts v Willmott: as already indicated, the courts, when implying a term, have generally drawn the line at what is necessary to give a contract business efficacy. Commonwealth courts, in particular, have refused to import the so-called "*Betts v Willmott*" principle from patent law, which is to the following effect:

> "When a man has purchased an article he expects to have control of it, and there must be some clear and explicit agreement to the contrary to justify the vendor in saying that he has not given the purchaser his licence to sell the article, or to use it wherever he pleases as against himself".[870]

In rejecting this approach, the courts have pointed to the old form of a grant of letters patent, which gave the patentee the exclusive right to "make, use exercise and vend" the invention, which required the implication of some such term into the contract of sale of a patented article if the sale was not to be futile. In contrast, the law of copyright does not prevent the ordinary use of a copy of a copyright work and therefore no similar implication is required.[871] So, the sale of an article in one jurisdiction without any territorial restriction on resale does not imply or carry the right to import it into another jurisdiction and to do so may therefore infringe the importation right.[872] The principle established by the European Court of Justice that the putting of a trade marked product onto the market outside the EEA does not constitute consent on the part of the trade mark proprietor to the product thereafter being marketed within the EEA applies equally to causes of action in copyright (and designs).[873] Again, the ordinary retail sale of test or diagnostic software as part of a larger software package does not include a licence to run the software for the purpose of understanding its functionality so as to make a competing product.[874] For an attempt to rely on *Betts v Wilmott* as a defence to a claim in relation to the sale of "illicit devices", see para.16–23 of this work.

Computer programs. Computer programs are unlike most other copyright works in that in the course of their ordinary use they are almost inevitably copied. Clearly some licence to use the program for ordinary purposes is implied into the normal contract of sale and purchase if no express provision is otherwise made.[875] In fact, amendments made to the 1988 Act to implement the Software Directive[876] provide that certain acts in relation to computer programs are permitted and therefore not infringing, so that the question of licence does not arise. These

5–222

[867] *Ager v Peninsular & Oriental Steam Navigation Co* (1884) 26 Ch.D. 637.
[868] *Cooper v Stephens* [1895] 1 Ch. 567; *Marshall (W.) & Co Ltd v Bull (A.H.) Ltd* (1901) 85 L.T. 77.
[869] See paras 5–232 et seq., below.
[870] See *Betts v Willmott* (1871) L.C. 6 Ch. App. 239 at 245 and also *National Phonograph Co of Australia Ltd v Menck* [1911] A.C. 336.
[871] *Time-Life International (Nederlands) B.V. v Interstate Parcel Express Co Pty Ltd* [1978] F.S.R. 251 at 270 (High Ct of Aus.); *Creative Technology Ltd v Aztech Systems Pte Ltd* [1997] F.S.R. 491 (Ct of App. of Singapore).
[872] *Time-Life International (Nederlands) B.V. v Interstate Parcel Express Co Pty Ltd* [1978] F.S.R. 251; *R. & A. Bailey & Co Ltd v Boccaccio Pty Ltd* (1988) 77 A.L.R. 177.
[873] *KK Sony Entertainment v Pacific Game Technology (Holding) Ltd* [2006] EWHC 2509 (Ch).
[874] *Creative Technology Ltd v Aztech Systems Pte Ltd* [1997] F.S.R. 491.
[875] As to the effect of "shrink-wrap" and "click-wrap" licences, see *Beta Computers (Europe) Ltd v Adobe Systems (Europe) Ltd* [1996] F.S.R. 367 (Ct of Sess.), and para.27–372, below.
[876] Council Directive 91/250.

provisions are considered in detail elsewhere[877] but in summary the following acts are not infringements:

(a) The making of back-up copies by a lawful user, any contractual term to the contrary being void[878];

(b) The decompilation of a program by a lawful user to obtain necessary information for the creation of an independent program, any contractual term to the contrary being void[879];

(c) The observation, study or testing of the functioning of the program by a lawful user in order to determine the ideas and principles which underlie any element of the program, if the user does so while performing any of the acts of loading, displaying, running, transmitting or storing the program which he is entitled to do, any contractual term to the contrary being void[880];

(c) To copy the program in the course of lawful use or to correct errors, subject to any contractual term to the contrary.[881]

5–223 **Databases.** In the same way, amendments to the 1988 Act to implement the Database Directive[882] have introduced a class of permitted act in relation to the use of databases that might otherwise have been covered by licence. Thus, the Act provides that it is not an infringement of copyright in a database for anyone who has a right to use it to do anything which is necessary for the purposes of access to and use of its contents, any contractual term to the contrary being void.[883]

5–224 **Letters and the Press.** The nature of the agreement to be implied when an author submits an article or other manuscript for publication is considered elsewhere.[884] Since, when a letter is written to a newspaper with a view to publication, the copyright remains with the writer, a licence to publish is clearly implied.[885] As to other letters, whether the recipient of a letter has a licence to reproduce and publish it will obviously depend upon the circumstances, but prima facie such publication will be an infringement.[886] Before the 1911 Act, letters might be published to vindicate the character of the receiver[887] but it is thought that no such defence could now be relied upon in an action for infringement of copyright[888]: a defendant would have to establish that his conduct amounted to fair dealing or was within one of the other classes of permitted acts,[889] or was in the public interest.[890] Commonly photographic agencies will submit prints or transparencies to newspapers on the understanding that the paper is at liberty to use them, when a recognised fee will be paid. The legal effect of this arrangement will usually be that the agency makes an offer to permit the newspaper to use the photograph in

---

[877] See paras 9–149 et seq., below.

[878] CDPA 1988 ss.50A and 296A.

[879] ss.50B and 296A.

[880] ss.50BA and 296A.

[881] ss.50C.

[882] Council Directive 96/9.

[883] CDPA 1988 ss.50D and 296B. See para.9–156.

[884] See paras 26–55 et seq., below.

[885] The extent to which alterations may be made is considered, see para.5–228, below.

[886] See, e.g. *British Oxygen Co Ltd v Liquid Air Ltd* [1925] Ch. 383; *Tett Bros Ltd v Drake & Goreham Ltd* [1928–1935] Mac.C.C. 492 (commercial correspondence).

[887] *Perceval (Lord and Lady) v Phipps* (1813) 2 V. & B. 19; *Lytton (Earl of) v Devy* (1884) 52 L.T. 121; *Labouchere v Hess* (1898) 77 L.T. 559; *Folsom v Marsh* (1841) 2 Story (Amer.) 100; *Howard v Gunn* (1863) 32 Beav. 462. cf. *Palin v Gathercole* (1844) 1 Col.C.C. 565.

[888] See *British Oxygen Co Ltd v Liquid Air Ltd* [1925] Ch. 383.

[889] See Ch.9, below.

[890] See para.22–93, below.

return for a fee, which offer is accepted by publication.[891] Like all offers made without consideration, however, it may be revoked by notice, and thereafter the newspaper has no right to publish photographs which have already been submitted.[892] There may be a custom in the Press that one newspaper may copy from another the quoted words of a third party,[893] but otherwise a licence will not be implied from the fact that copying, for example by one newspaper of another, is habitually carried on.[894]

F. Construction and Terms of Licences

Difficulties usually arise where the licence is either wholly implied, in which case all the terms have to be worked out, or only partly express, leaving other terms to be implied. The important questions to decide are usually: what persons are entitled to the benefit of the licence; the extent of the permitted use; and the licence's duration.   **5–225**

Persons entitled to benefit. The original licensee may be the only person entitled to the benefit of the licence[895] or it may extend beyond him, for example, to his workmen or professional advisers.[896] A licence may even be so expressed as to extend to the world at large.[897] In all cases, the licence will need to be construed carefully.[898]   **5–226**

Licence personal or otherwise not assignable. The benefit of a licence may be assignable or the circumstances of the grant of the licence and its terms may justify the conclusion that it was intended to be personal to the licensee and not capable of vicarious performance. Thus a licence will not be assignable where it was granted to the licensee because of his personal skill or reputation,[899] as is often the case with publishing contracts and other agreements where the licensee is entrusted with the exploitation of a work made by the licensor.[900] The fact that the licensee is a partnership[901] or even a limited company[902] or that the agreement   **5–227**

---

[891] *Bowden Bros v Amalgamated Pictorials Ltd* [1911] 1 Ch. 386.

[892] *Bowden Bros v Amalgamated Pictorials Ltd* [1911] 1 Ch. 396.

[893] *Express Newspapers plc v News (UK) Ltd* [1990] F.S.R. 359, where, on an application for summary judgment, the point was treated as being arguable.

[894] *Walter v Steinkopff* [1892] 3 Ch. 489; *Banier v News Group Newspapers Ltd* [1997] F.S.R. 812.

[895] As in *Cooper v Stephens* [1895] 1 Ch. 567.

[896] *Blair v Osborne & Tomkins* [1971] 2 Q.B. 78.

[897] *Mellor v Australian Broadcasting Commission* [1940] A.C. 491; *Computermate Products (Aust) Pty Ltd v Ozi-Soft Pty Ltd* (1988) 83 A.L.R. 492; cf. *Plix Products Ltd v Frank M. Winstone (Merchants)* [1986] F.S.R. 63. Note that a general licence has been granted in respect of the reproduction of the designs for the Euro coins. See [2002] O.J. C318, November 13, 2002, p.3.

[898] As in *Booth v Edward Lloyd Ltd* (1909) 26 T.L.R. 549, where a licence to A to print and publish was held to permit A to print and supply books to B, with B's name as printer and publisher, for sale to the public by B, the reason given being that if a licensor wished to restrict his licensee to printing and publishing *in his own name*, he should expressly do so. Sed quaere: and surely B was the "publisher".

[899] *Stevens v Benning* (1855) 1 K. & J. 168; *Reade v Bentley* 3 K. & J. 271 (licences to publishers); *Messager v British Broadcasting Corp. Ltd* [1927] 2 K.B. 543, reversed on other grounds [1929] A.C. 151 (licence by composer to theatrical agent); *Dorling v Honnor Marine Ltd* [1964] Ch. 560 at 568 (licence to build sailing dinghies).

[900] In *Hales v T. Fisher Unwin Ltd* [1923–1928] Mac.C.C. 31, the licence was held to be personal even though the author admitted that he was so poor he would agreed to anyone publishing his work if promised a royalty.

[901] *Hole v Bradbury* (1879) 12 Ch.D. 886; *Sampson Low, Marston & Co, Ltd v Duckworth* [1923–1928] Mac.C.C. 205, where the licence was construed to extend to the partnership as it might be constituted from time to time but not to a limited company formed to take over the business.

[902] *Griffith v Tower Publishing Co Ltd* [1897] 1 Ch. 21; *Hales v T. Fisher Unwin Ltd* [1923–1928] Mac.C.C. 31.

is made with a publisher "and his assigns"[903] does not mean that the identity of the licensee was irrelevant and that the licence may therefore be assigned. Where a licence is on its terms not assignable, or is assignable only on certain conditions, for example only with the licensor's consent, a purported assignment which does not comply with the licence terms will not, as against third parties, vest any rights in the assignee.[904]

5–228   **Alterations.** Whether a party who is not the copyright owner and who has only a licence to reproduce a work is entitled to make alterations to it will in part depend upon the terms of the licence and will now also turn on an author's right not to have his work subjected to derogatory treatment, a topic which is considered elsewhere.[905] As to the terms of the licence, the licence may expressly or impliedly require that use of the work be in an unaltered form or that no substantial alteration be made, and a court will readily imply a term into any contract limiting the right to make alterations[906] particularly, it is thought, in cases where matters of judgment or opinion are involved.[907] In cases of a more commercial character, it is suggested that a limitation on the right to make at least insubstantial alterations and additions will be less easily implied. In the absence of any prohibition or limitation, however, the licensee may make alterations, even substantial ones.[908] The position of a licensee should be contrasted with that of an assignee, who is generally free to alter a work as he sees fit, subject only to any moral rights of the author and the law of passing off and defamation.

Thus the alteration of even one line in a play may be beyond the scope of a production company's licence,[909] but insubstantial changes to an architect's plans may be permitted.[910] A limited consent to alter an article submitted for publication may be implied, for example to reduce it in length to fit the available space,[911] particularly perhaps where it has been prepared hurriedly to meet a deadline. A court will readily imply a term that no substantial alteration may be made to a signed article without the author's consent.[912] In the case of a letter to a newspaper written for publication, the newspaper not only has the implied right to publish it but also, by customary implication, the right to alter it, so long as the alterations are not of a nature to affect the credit or literary reputation of the writer. Today, the letters page of a newspaper usually sets out terms on which letters are accepted for publication.

5–229   **New technologies.** Questions frequently arise both in the context of licences and assignments as to whether a grant made before the advent of a particular technology extends to exploitation by use of that technology. Thus, should the grant be limited to what was known to the parties at the time or should it extend to the new technology if the words of the grant are in fact wide enough to cover it? The

---

[903] See *Booth v Richards* [1905–1910] Mac.C.C. 284.

[904] *Hospital for Sick Children v Walt Disney Productions Inc* [1968] Ch. 52; [1967] F.S.R. 152; *Devefi Pty Ltd v Mateffy Pearl Nagi Pty Ltd* [1993] R.P.C. 493 (Fed. Ct of Aus.); *Beck v Montana Constructions Pty Ltd* [1964–1965] N.S.W.R. 229; and, generally, *Linden Gardens Trust Ltd v Lenesta Sludge Disposals Ltd* [1994] 1 A.C. 85; *Hendry v Chartsearch Ltd* [1998] C.L.C. 1382.

[905] See Ch.11, below.

[906] *Frisby v British Broadcasting Corp* [1967] Ch. 932; *Messager v British Broadcasting Corp Ltd* [1927] 2 K.B. 543.

[907] See *Joseph v National Magazine Co Ltd* [1959] Ch. 14; *Gilbert v Workman* [1905–1910] Mac.C.C. 235 (where the point was conceded).

[908] *Frisby v British Broadcasting Corp* [1967] Ch. 932; *Cox v Cox* (1853) 11 Hare 118.

[909] *Frisby v British Broadcasting Corp* [1967] Ch. 932. But the line was considered by the author to be the key line of the play.

[910] See the cases discussed below in relation to architects' plans.

[911] As was conceded in *Joseph v National Magazine Co Ltd* [1959] Ch. 14.

[912] *Joseph v National Magazine Co Ltd* [1959] Ch. 14, approved in *Frisby v British Broadcasting Corp* [1967] Ch. 932.

answer to this question is a matter of construction. Modern agreements often grant the right to exploit works using such expressions as "by all means whether known or unknown" and here the intention is clearly to cover future technologies. The difficult cases are where no such expression is used.

If the grant is wide enough in its terms to include the new technology, then it is capable of including the new rights even if such rights were unknown or the parties did not have such a possibility in mind.[913] So, a grant of the "exclusive right of production" of a play in 1880 included the right to make a film of it, even though films were then unknown.[914] Again, a grant (or reservation) of "moving picture rights" made in 1919 was capable of carrying the right to make a sound film[915] since talkies were a species of moving pictures with essentially the same form and area of exploitation.[916] But this conclusion will yield to the parties' intention as drawn from the actual agreement, as where the new rights were unknown and the parties contemplated a single exercise of the principal right,[917] the agreement containing a warranty that the author owned all "cinematograph rights", but the grant being only of "moving picture" rights, the former clearly meaning something more than the latter, and it being impossible to make a "moving picture" of the voice.[918] Where the right granted is exclusive or amounts to an assignment and the new right cannot be exploited separately from the old (as with the right to make a talking picture, which cannot be exploited without the moving picture rights), it may be helpful to ask whether it is likely that the parties really intended to divide the right to exploit the new right between them.[919] Obviously all other terms of the agreement need to be considered.[920] If the agreement provides for the payment of royalties on sales, and the royalty provisions are not workable in the case of sales in the new medium, this may indicate that the parties did agree to exploitation by this means. Where a licence to exploit a work has to be implied, it will extend no further than to acts which were in the contemplation of the parties at the time and what was necessary to give business efficacy to the agreement.[921] An implied licence will therefore seldom, if ever, extend to technologies which were unknown at the date of the agreement.

Effect of non-compliance with licence terms. A licence will usually contain terms, express or implied, relating to its exercise, for example that agreed fees be paid or that no alterations be made. The question then often arises as to the position of a licensee who does not observe such terms. If he simply does something for which he does not have permission, he will be acting beyond the terms of the licence and thus infringing. Thus a person may have a licence to print and sell

5–230

---

[913] *Hospital for Sick Children v Walt Disney Productions Inc* [1968] Ch. 52; [1967] F.S.R. 152. It is suggested that the views to this effect expressed by the Court of Appeal at 65, 73 and 78, although obiter, and differing from those of the trial judge ([1966] 1 W.L.R. 1055), were correct.

[914] *Serra v Famous-Lasky Film Service Ltd* (1922) 127 L.T. 109.

[915] *Serra v Famous-Lasky Film Service Ltd* (1922) 127 L.T. 109.

[916] *L.C. Page & Co v Fox Film Corp* (1936) 83 Fed. Rep. (2d.) 196. See also *J.C. Williamson Ltd v Metro-Goldwyn-Mayer Theatres Ltd* (1937) 56 C.L.R. 567 (High Ct. of Aus.)—grant in 1924 excluding all motion picture film rights, although future use of talkies by this time contemplated. Both decisions were followed in *Hospital for Sick Children v Walt Disney Productions Inc* [1968] Ch. 52. "Talkies" first became a technological possibility in about 1923 and a commercial reality in about 1927.

[917] e.g. the making of a single film, as in *Hospital for Sick Children v Walt Disney Productions Inc* [1968] Ch. 52.

[918] *Pathé Pictures Ltd v Bancroft* [1928–1935] Mac.C.C. 403.

[919] *J.C. Williamson Ltd v Metro-Goldwyn-Mayer Theatres Ltd* (1937) 56 C.L.R. 567.

[920] For a discussion of some of the cases on the point in the United States, as they apply to the acquisition of internet rights, see Radcliffe, "New Media Convergence: Acquiring Rights to Existing Works for the Internet under U.S. Law" [2001] E.I.P.R. 172.

[921] *Ray v Classic FM plc* [1998] F.S.R. 622 at 643. See, however, *Barrett v Universal-Island Records Ltd* [2006] EWHC 1009 (Ch), para.5–217, above.

copies of a work but not to authorise its public performance,[922] to use another's work but not to claim it as his own,[923] nor to make alterations,[924] with the result that if he does these latter things he infringes. Alternatively, a term may amount to a condition precedent to the exercise of the licence so that failure to comply with the term will again mean that what is done is an infringement. Thus it may be a condition precedent for the right to use a song in a film that the composer be credited, or at least that someone else should not be credited.[925] On the other hand, if the licence is given in return for a promise by the licensee, the licensor's only remedy may be in damages. This will often be the position where the promise in question is to make a one-off payment by the licensee.[926] Whether or not such a term is a condition precedent, or a term whose breach will allow the licensor to revoke the licence, will depend upon the proper construction of the licence agreement.[927] Where the licence contains continuing obligations on the part of the licensee, for example to pay royalties, it is suggested that non-payment or other default amounting to a repudiation of the contract will usually entitle the licensor to accept the repudiation and thus bring the licence to an end on the basis that, as a matter of construction, the licence was granted only so long as the licensee adhered to the terms of the agreement.[928]

5–231   **Revocation and termination.** In the absence of special circumstances, a licence can be granted on any terms as to determination which the licensor wishes to agree with the licensee.[929] Thus, a provision entitling the licensor to determine the licence in the event of the licensee's insolvency, even bearing in mind that it may only take effect after the bankruptcy or liquidation of the licensee, is in principle unobjectionable.[930] A licence, if coupled with a contract not to revoke it (for example, a contractual licence for a fixed term) is irrevocable[931] except in accordance with its express terms or on the occasion of a relevant breach by the licensee (see below). If a contractual licence does not expressly or impliedly provide for its duration, it is revocable on reasonable notice, as is a gratuitous licence.[932] A licence which is personal and thus unassignable by the licensee[933] will terminate on the licensee's insolvency[934] or death.[935] To be effective, a notice must purport to revoke the licence or otherwise make it clear that the licensor considers the licence to be at an end and not, for example, simply propose terms for its continuance.[936] A letter from a licensor which is in fact a repudiation of a licence agreement does not constitute a notice to terminate the licence pursuant

---

[922] *Williams v Feldman* [1911–1916] Mac.C.C. 98.

[923] *Blair v Osborne & Tomkins* [1971] 2 Q.B. 78.

[924] *Frisby v British Broadcasting Corp* [1967] Ch. 932.

[925] *Miller v Cecil Film Ltd* [1937] 2 All E.R. 464.

[926] *Ng v Clyde Securities Ltd* [1976] N.S.W.L.R. 443.

[927] *Ng v Clyde Securities Ltd* [1976] N.S.W.L.R. 443.

[928] See, e.g. *Jay v Benning* (1855) 1 K. & J. 168 at 174; *"Clinical Obstetrics"* [1905–1910] Mac.C.C. 176.

[929] *Perpetual Trustee Co Ltd v BNY Corporate Trustee Services Ltd* [2009] EWCA Civ 1160; [2010] Ch. 347 at para.81.

[930] *Perpetual Trustee Co Ltd v BNY Corporate Trustee Services Ltd* [2009] EWCA Civ 1160; [2010] Ch. 347 at para.81.

[931] *Hurst v Picture Theatres Ltd* [1915] 1 K.B. 1; *British Actors Film Co Ltd v Glover* [1918] 1 K.B. 299; *Williams v Feldman* [1911–1916] Mac.C.C. 98; *Winter Garden Theatre (London) Ltd v Millennium Productions Ltd* [1948] A.C. 173; *Hounslow London BC v Twickenham Garden Developments Ltd* [1971] Ch. 233.

[932] *Edwards v Cotton* (1903) 19 T.L.R. 34; *Hart v Hayman, etc, Ltd* [1911–1916] Mac.C.C. 301. See further, below.

[933] See para.5–227, above.

[934] *Lucas v Moncrieff* (1905) 21 T.L.R. 683.

[935] *Messager v British Broadcasting Corp Ltd* [1927] 2 K.B. 543, reversed on other grounds: [1929] A.C. 151.

[936] *Redwood Music Ltd v Chappell & Co Ltd* [1982] R.P.C. 109.

to an express or implied term unless it is otherwise clear that the licence is being revoked.[937] Thus, if the licensor purports to revoke a revocable licence, but gives no notice or insufficient notice of revocation, the licensee cannot ignore the revocation and treat the licence as subsisting.[938] On the other hand, the licensee cannot be treated as a wrongdoer for continuing to do what the licence permitted him to do until the expiry of the period which would have constituted reasonable notice.[939] Although a gratuitous licence may in general be revoked at any time, where the licensor has led the licensee to believe that it would not be revoked and the licensee has acted on that basis, the licensor may find himself estopped from revoking it, or from asserting his equitable and legal rights after any revocation.[940] Where there is a dispute as to title, the person revoking the licence should be in a position to produce proof of his title to the copyright before he can effectively revoke the licence.[941]

G. ARCHITECTS' PLANS AND WORKS OF ARCHITECTURE

Many of the problems connected with licences are illustrated by cases concerning architects' plans.[942] Although the property in the physical plans prepared by an architect for a client usually belongs to the client,[943] the architect will usually remain the owner of the copyright in them.[944] The architect may also of course own the copyright in models for the building, or the building itself, as works of architecture. Unless the client has acquired the copyright in such works, he may not copy any of them unless he has some licence to do so. If nothing is said, it is usually clear that some licence to use the plans must be implied but, first, what is the extent of the use covered by the licence? For example, is it limited to an application for planning permission alone, or does it extend to obtaining planning permission and thereafter for use in constructing and repairing the building in accordance with the plans, perhaps as modified?[945] Secondly, who is entitled to the benefit of the licence? Is it the original client, or the original client and for instance anyone to whom he sells the site with the benefit of the planning permission, and in either case is the licence dependent upon the architect having been paid his fee?

5–232

Examples. A claimant had prepared plans for a client for the purpose of obtain-

5–233

---

[937] *Decro-Wall S.A. v Marketing Ltd* [1971] 1 W.L.R. 361 at 382 (letter purporting to accept repudiation, itself amounting to a repudiation, not sufficient notice under agreement terminable on 12 months' notice).

[938] *Dorling v Honnor Marine Ltd* [1964] Ch. 560; *Godfrey v Lees* [1995] E.M.L.R. 307. The distinction between this situation and a *Decro-Wall* type of case can be a fine one.

[939] *Dorling v Honnor Marine Ltd* [1964] Ch. 560 at 567; *Martin-Baker Aircraft Co Ltd v Canadian Flight Equipment Ltd* [1955] 2 Q.B. 556; (1955) 72 R.P.C. 236.

[940] As in *Godfrey v Lees* [1995] E.M.L.R. 307 and *Brooker v Fisher* [2009] UKHL 41. Such an estoppel may, depending on the facts, be terminable on reasonable notice: see *Barrett v Universal-Island Records Ltd* [2006] EWHC 1009 (Ch), para.363. But the incurring of expenditure by the licensee will not automatically make the licence irrevocable: *Hart v Hayman, Christy and Lilly Ltd* [1911–1916] Mac.C.C. 301. The revocation of a licence will not affect contracts or arrangements entered into prior to the revocation: *Barrett v Universal-Island Records Ltd* [2006] EWHC 1009 (Ch); [2006] E.M.L.R. 21, para.366, following *Brighton v Jones* [2004] EWHC 1157 (Ch); [2005] F.S.R. 16.

[941] *Redwood Music Ltd v Chappell & Co Ltd* [1982] R.P.C. 109.

[942] Today, use of an architect's plans will usually be governed by standard terms of the architect's engagement, such as the RIBA conditions. See para.5–234, below.

[943] *Gibbon v Pease* [1905] 1 K.B. 810; *Inala Industries Pty Ltd v Associated Enterprises Pty Ltd* [1960] Q.S.R. 562. The property in all notes, sketches and other material used by the architect in preparation of the plans will usually remain with the architect: *Leicestershire County Council v Faraday & Partners Ltd* [1941] 2 K.B. 205; *Chantrey Martin v Martin* [1953] 2 Q.B. 286.

[944] The standard term of the RIBA conditions so provides.

[945] It should be remembered that the reconstruction of a building will not infringe the copyright in any plans at all. See CDPA 1988 s.65 and para.9–195, below.

ing full planning permission to build two houses on a site and had been paid the full-scale fee under the RIBA conditions for that work. The site was sold after planning permission had been obtained and the plans were then used by another firm in erecting houses on the site. It was held that in the circumstances the claimant had impliedly licensed the use of the plans for all purposes connected with the erection of that building on that site in substantial accordance with them, whether by the client or by the purchasers of the plot, and by their surveyors or workmen, and such that they might make copies of the plans for that purpose.[946] This conclusion was reached on a consideration of the then RIBA conditions under which the architect was paid for his work in stages and which envisaged that the architect's engagement might not run its full course, so that it would be wrong in principle for the architect to be able to hold the client to ransom such that the client would almost inevitably have to retain him, particularly where the scale fees fully compensated the architect for the work actually done.[947] The principle applied was that:

> "the payment for sketch plans includes a permission or consent to use those sketch plans for the purpose for which they were brought into existence, namely, for the purpose of building a building in substantial accordance with them and for the purpose of preparing any necessary drawings as part of the task of building the building".[948]

But where an architect charged a nominal amount purely for the purposes of preparing plans for a planning application, the amount being much less than the appropriate scale fee, no licence was implied further than one enabling the plans to be used for that purpose.[949] The reason why a nominal fee will be charged in many such cases is that if the planning application is refused the money spent by the client will be thrown away, whereas if it is granted the architect may expect to be engaged under the building contract and earn substantial fees,[950] or at least to be further compensated.[951] Every case will, however, depend upon its own facts,[952] and it may be that a licence would be implied even if the architect had not been paid full-scale fees for the work done up to a particular stage, but had been asked to remain as architect for the project and had refused or demanded unreasonable terms for doing so.[953]

Where the architect has retained the copyright, there will often be sound reasons for this. For example, he may thereby be able to prevent the plans being used for purposes other than the specific building contemplated.[954] But where a licence can be implied for all purposes connected with the erection of buildings in accordance with plans, the licence will usually extend to making changes to them which are not substantial or to adding detail to them, for example for the

---

[946] *Blair v Osborne & Tomkins* [1971] 2 Q.B. 78.

[947] See the analysis in *Stovin-Bradford v Volpoint Ltd* [1971] Ch. 1007.

[948] *Blair v Osborne & Tomkins* [1971] 2 Q.B. 78, the Court of Appeal citing with approval this passage from *Beck v Montana Constructions Pty Ltd* [1964–1965] N.S.W.R. 229.

[949] *Stovin-Bradford v Volpoint* [1971] Ch. 1007. See also *Parramatta Design & Developments Pty Ltd v Concrete Pty Ltd* [2005] FCAFC 138: where an architect had gratuitously provided plans to a joint venture in order to keep the venture going, obtain planning permission and see the development constructed by the joint venture partners, it was held that the implied licence did not extend to a purchaser of the site.

[950] *Stovin-Bradford v Volpoint* [1971] Ch. 1007, per Salmon L.J. at 1019.

[951] *Stovin-Bradford v Volpoint* [1971] Ch. 1007, per Megaw L.J. at 1022.

[952] *Stovin-Bradford v Volpoint* [1971] Ch. 1007.

[953] *Stovin-Bradford v Volpoint* [1971] Ch. 1007, per Megaw L.J. at 1022, and per Salmon L.J. at 1019, citing the example of an architect of wide renown; and see also *Beck v Montana Constructions Pty Ltd* [1964–1965] N.S.W.R. 229.

[954] *Blair v Osborne & Tomkins* [1971] 2 Q.B. 78, per Widgery L.J. at 86.

purpose of obtaining building regulation approval.[955] The licence will usually extend to successors in title to the property,[956] or the assignees from the original client,[957] and will extend to reproducing the plans in a leaflet intended to be shown to prospective purchasers of the building.[958] It will usually enable the owner and his successors in title and contractors to repair or renovate the building, particularly where this has become necessary because of the architect's own fault.[959] It will not, however, extend to permit someone to remove the architect's name from the plans and put them forward as his own, although in such cases the damage resulting may be small.[960]

Whether the architect can stop the use of his plans where he is unpaid will depend upon whether payment was a condition precedent, or whether non-payment can be treated as a repudiatory act allowing the architect to terminate any licence. It has been said that one of the purposes of the architect retaining copyright is to enable him to prevent the use of his work by others who have paid him no fee,[961] but in the usual type of case, particularly where payment is not expected to be made at the outset, it is thought that the correct analysis will be that the licence is given in return for a promise to pay, recoverable by action.[962] Where the original client has become insolvent, and the site has passed into another's hands, this remedy may of course be worthless.[963] Where, however, the architect's consent has been given gratuitously, he may later withdraw it.[964]

Current RIBA conditions. The terms on which a client may use an architect's   **5–234**
plans may of course be regulated by the express terms of his appointment. The current edition of the RIBA standard conditions of appointment makes more detailed provision than the conditions considered in the earlier cases. They provide that the client may reproduce the plans for purposes related to the project on the site or part of the site to which they relate. Those purposes expressly include the operation, maintenance, repair, reinstatement, alteration, extension, promotion, leasing and sale of the building. This licence is subject to numerous qualifications, including the following. First, the design may not be used for any extension of the project or any other project unless a licence fee is specified in the agreement. Second, if the use occurs between the last provision by the architect of services and practical completion, the client must (a) if the architect has not completed detailed proposals under Work Stage D obtain the architect's consent (not to be unreasonably withheld) and/or (b) pay a reasonable licence fee if none is specified in the agreement. Third, the architect can suspend the licence on seven days' notice if the client is in default of payment of any fees or other amounts due. Use of the licence "may be resumed" on receipt of the outstanding

---

[955] *Blair v Osborne & Tomkins* [1971] 2 Q.B. 78; see also *Barnett v Cape Town Foreshaw Board* [1978] F.S.R. 176 (Cape Div. Ct) but cf. *Netupsky v Dominion Bridge Co Ltd* (1969) 68 W.W.R. 529. The point was left open in *Hunter v Fitzroy Robinson and Partners* [1978] F.S.R. 167. Regard should also be had to an architect's right to object to derogatory treatment of his work. See Ch.11, below.

[956] *Blair v Osborne & Tomkins* [1971] 2 Q.B. 78.

[957] *Hunter v Fitzroy Robinson and Partners* [1978] F.S.R. 167.

[958] *Robert Allan & Partners v Scottish Ideal Homes*, 1972 S.L.T. (Sh Ct) 32. The use of drawings or photographs of buildings in such circumstances may now also be permissible by virtue of s.63 of the 1988 Act. See para.9–191, below.

[959] *ADI Ltd v Destein* (1983) 141 D.L.R. (3d) 370.

[960] *Blair v Osborne & Tomkins* [1971] 2 Q.B. 78, where the claimant was awarded £2. Note that there is also an architect's moral right to be identified as the author of his work. See Ch.11, below.

[961] *Blair v Osborne & Tomkins* [1971] 2 Q.B. 78, per Widgery L.J. at 86.

[962] *Ng v Clyde Securities Ltd* [1976] N.S.W.L.R. 443.

[963] As in *Ng v Clyde Securities Ltd,* [1976] N.S.W.L.R. 443.

[964] *Katz v Cytrynbaum* (1984) 2 D.L.R. (4th) 52, following *Hart v Hayman, Christy & Lilly Ltd* [1911–1916] Mac.C.C. 301.

amounts. Generally, the benefit of the agreement, and therefore any licence, is stated not to be assignable without the consent in writing of the architect. This is obviously a powerful weapon in the hands of the architect and a trap for any successor to the client.[965]

H. THE RIGHT TO REPAIR

5–235   **Implied licence: the right to repair.** Before the decision of the House of Lords in *British Leyland Motor Corp Ltd v Armstrong Patents Co Ltd*,[966] there were a number of decisions to the effect that a purchaser of an article was entitled, by virtue of an implied licence from the vendor, to reproduce a copyright work if this was done in the course of repair of the article. Such decisions were reached by analogy with patent cases where the old form of the letters patent[967] forced the court to imply some licence to enable the purchaser of a patented article to use it and thus repair it. The licence in such cases extended no further than enabling the purchaser to prolong the life of the article by repair but not to entitle him to make a new article under the cover of repair.[968] The cases decided in relation to copyright established that such a licence extended to enable the purchaser to make spare parts himself and to have such parts made for him,[969] and probably to have two or more made at the same time against the future breakdown of the article.[970] The licence did not, however, extend to the world at large so as to enable a manufacturer to make spare parts in anticipation of future orders,[971] nor to enable the manufacturer to copy any plans to which he might have had access, as opposed to working backwards from the part which he was going to replace.[972]

5–236   **Non-derogation from grant: the right to repair.** The use by the courts of an implied licence theory was artificial and gave rise to obvious difficulties, for example, where there was no privity of contract between the manufacturer of the original article and its owner or the spare part manufacturer. The principle was largely abandoned by the House of Lords in the *British Leyland* case, where the question arose whether an independent manufacturer of replacement car exhaust systems could be stopped by the owner of the copyright in the manufacturing drawings for such systems. Two alternative bases were propounded for denying such a remedy. First, that the purchaser of an article such as a car has an inherent right to repair it, so that the common law will not allow a copyright owner to assert a monopoly right to detract from the rights of ownership, thus affecting the

---

[965] As in *Dorrans v The Shand Partnership* [2004] E.C.D.R. 21, which concerned an earlier version of the RIBA Conditions. The benefit of the agreement was stated not to be assignable without the architect's consent. The architect produced plans for a potential developer of a site in support of a planning application. Planning permission was granted but the purchase fell through. It was held that given the prohibition on assignment there was no basis for construing the expression "the Client" as extending to future proprietors of the property, nor was there room for an implied term to that effect.

[966] [1986] A.C. 577.

[967] "To make, use, exercise and vend" the invention.

[968] *Dunlop Pneumatic Tyre Co v Neal* [1899] 1 Ch. 807; (1899) 16 R.P.C. 247; *Sirdar Rubber Co Ltd v Wallington Weston & Co* (1907) 24 R.P.C. 539. The concept of an implied licence to repair in the case of patented articles has now been abandoned. The question in all cases is whether the defendant has "made" the patented article. See *United Wire Ltd v Screen Repair Services (Scotland) Ltd* [2001] R.P.C. 439, HL.

[969] *Solar Thomson Engineering Co Ltd v Barton* [1977] R.P.C. 537; *Gardner & Sons Ltd v Paul Sykes Organisation Ltd* [1981] F.S.R. 281, and *Weir Pumps Ltd v C.M.L. Pumps Ltd* [1984] F.S.R. 33.

[970] *British Leyland Motor Corp Ltd v Armstrong Patents Co Ltd* [1984] F.S.R. 591; *Hoover plc v George Hulme Ltd* [1982] F.S.R. 565.

[971] *British Leyland Motor Corp Ltd v Armstrong Patents Co Ltd* [1984] F.S.R. 591; *Hoover plc v George Hulme Ltd* [1982] F.S.R. 565.

[972] i.e. by reverse engineering. See *Weir Pumps Ltd v C.M.L. Pumps Ltd* [1984] F.S.R. 33.

value and use of the article sold.[973] Secondly, by an extension of the principle of non-derogation from grant, it was held that a grantor would not be allowed to derogate from his grant by using intellectual property retained so as to render property granted by him unfit or materially unfit for the purpose for which the grant was made.[974]

The full extent of this doctrine as applied to the field of copyright was never fully worked out[975] and now that the transitional provisions relating to the introduction of design right[976] and the corresponding restriction on the ability to rely on copyright in relation to designs for spare parts[977] have worked themselves out,[978] the principle is likely to be of little importance. This is because s.51 essentially abolished industrial copyright as it had previously been recognised under the 1956 Act, so that there is no further need for a spare part exception in relation to industrial designs since there is no right from which the exception is needed.[979] In addition, there is no room for a spare part exception in relation to design right,[980] because the question of spare parts was specifically considered by Parliament when introducing design right and no such right was provided for. Nor is there any room for it in relation to computer programs or database right, since these have both been the subject of complete statutory codes following implementation of the respective Community Directives.[981] In relation to other forms of copyright work, the Information Society Directive[982] permits Member States to make an exception to the reproduction and distribution rights in connection with the repair of equipment,[983] and while the United Kingdom did not introduce any provision taking advantage of this on implementation, it is arguable that any residual right to repair under UK law would come within this.[984] What follows is therefore a summary of the law on this topic as it stood before its development was arrested.

It was recognised by the House of Lords in *British Leyland Motor Corp Ltd*[985] that it was a novel application of the principle of non-derogation from grant to prevent a party exercising a statutory right and indeed subsequently the Privy Council has suggested that the true basis of the decision was one of public policy, namely to prevent a manufacturer from controlling the after-market in spare parts.[986] Thus any suggestion that it should be extended will be treated with

---

[973] per Lord Bridge at 625.

[974] per Lord Templeman at 641, relying on *Browne v Flower* [1911] 1 Ch. 219.

[975] There is nothing in the 1988 Act which apparently affects the general application of the *British Leyland* principle (see, e.g. CDPA 1988 s.172(3)), but see the further discussion in the text.

[976] See Ch.13, below. The defence was not taken away with the passing of the 1988 Act: *Flogates Ltd v Refco Ltd* [1996] F.S.R. 935.

[977] i.e. CDPA 1988 s.51. See paras 13–301 et seq., below.

[978] CDPA 1988 Sch.1 para.19. See para.13–340 et seq., below.

[979] *Mars UK Ltd v Teknowledge Ltd* [2000] F.S.R. 138.

[980] See Ch.13, below.

[981] Namely, the Software Directive (91/250) and the Database Directive (96/9). Namely, the Software Directive (91/250) and the Database Directive (96/9).

[982] Directive 2001/29.

[983] art.5(3)(l). Generally, however, the Directive is without prejudice to provisions concerning design rights (see art.9). See Ch.9, below, for a discussion on the effect of the Directive on the exceptions to rights permitted to Member States.

[984] Any such exception would, however, have to comply with the three-step test in art.5, i.e. it should only apply in certain special cases which do not conflict with a normal exploitation of the work or other subject-matter and do not unreasonably prejudice the legitimate interests of the right-holder. As to this, see para.23–32, below.

[985] [1986] A.C. 577 at 627.

[986] *Canon Kabushiki Kaisha v Green Cartridge Co (Hong Kong) Ltd* [1997] A.C. 728; [1997] F.S.R. 817.

caution.[987] Certainly, the principle does not go so far as to enable the owner of the article to do whatever is necessary to keep it in running order,[988] and neither is it sufficient to ask mechanistically whether the "spare part" can properly be regarded as a separate entity or as an accessory of a larger entity.[989] The true basis of the principle combines two features. First, does the manufacture of the part constitute repair of a kind which the ordinary man who bought the article would assume he could do without infringing any rights of the manufacturer? Secondly, would the exercise of the property right unquestionably operate against the interests of consumers? Evaluation of the second feature may require asking whether the purchaser of the original article would normally evaluate the cost of purchasing the replacement parts during the lifetime of the article when making his decision to purchase.[990] Various other principles can be stated:

(a) In a case where a question of patent protection simultaneously arose,[991] the principles applicable in such cases still applied and the principle of non-derogation from grant did not and perhaps should not have been invoked.[992]

(b) None of the "repair" cases decided under the implied licence principle were disapproved on their facts and the result in each case was presumably not wrong.

(c) The principle enabled the owner of an article to have a replacement part made either by himself or by another, as before, but also enabled a supplier to manufacture such stock in advance of anticipated orders.[993]

(d) The principle appears to go further than that applied in relation to patent cases in that the copyright owner was not entitled to complain of the manufacture of an entirely new part as opposed to simply the repair of an existing one.[994]

(e) The distinction between the two principles is further emphasised by the fact that the right to repair and thus reproduce copyright works could not apparently be withheld even by express terms of the contract of purchase.[995]

(f) A subcontractor who designed a part for a manufacturer, knowing the

---

[987] *Canon Kabushiki Kaisha v Green Cartridge Co (Hong Kong) Ltd* [1997] A.C. 728; *Mars UK Ltd v Teknowledge Ltd* [2000] F.S.R. 138.

[988] *Canon Kabushiki Kaisha v Green Cartridge Co (Hong Kong) Ltd* [1997] A.C. 728.

[989] *Canon Kabushiki Kaisha v Green Cartridge Co (Hong Kong) Ltd* [1997] A.C. 728 citing *Dennion Manufacturing Co v Alfred Holt and Co Ltd* (1987) 10 I.P.R. 612 (plastic tags for attaching price labels to garments by means of a gun not "spare parts" for gun).

[990] Compare the position in *British Leyland* where the decision as to what make of car to buy was probably not influenced by the cost of occasional replacement of the exhaust, with that in the *Canon Kabushiki* case, where the cost of replacement printer cartridges was substantial in relation to the cost of the whole printer and was likely to have been an important part of the choice between rival makes. The principle suggests that the argument of the claimant in *Flogates Ltd v Refco Ltd* [1996] F.S.R. 935 that the defence did not apply to parts which were regularly worn out and whose replacement cost was a major factor for a prospective buyer was probably correct.

[991] As it did in the *Solar Thomson Engineering Co Ltd v Barton* [1977] R.P.C. 537.

[992] *British Leyland Motor Corp Ltd v Armstrong Patents Co Ltd* [1986] A.C. 577, per Lord Bridge at 625; [1986] F.S.R. 221. Lord Templeman, who gave the other leading speech, did not expressly deal with the point. See also *Dellareed Ltd v Delkim Developments* [1988] F.S.R. 329. Note, however, that principle in patent cases no longer rests on the concept of an implied licence: *United Wire Ltd v Screen Repair Services (Scotland) Ltd* [2001] F.S.R. 24, HL.

[993] *British Leyland Motor Corp Ltd v Armstrong Patents Co Ltd* [1986] A.C. 577 at 625.

[994] As in the *British Leyland* case itself. This also appears to have been the position established under the implied licence cases. See *Gardner & Sons Ltd v Paul Sykes Organisation Ltd* [1981] F.S.R. 281 and *Weir Pumps Ltd v C.M.L. Pumps Ltd* [1984] F.S.R. 33.

[995] *British Leyland Motor Corp Ltd v Armstrong Patents Co Ltd* [1986] A.C. 577 at 643.

purpose for which it was to be used, could not assert his copyright against the purchaser.[996]

(g) The right did not permit a defendant to take copies of the claimant's drawings directly[997] or, presumably, to make articles from such copies.

(h) Where the purchaser would not normally have been able or have expected to repair the article, the principle did not apply.[998]

(i) The right did not permit a purchaser to repair goods which were not of merchantable quality. His remedy was to return the goods or claim damages.[999]

(j) The copying of a work to help produce a compatible and competing product did not fall within the principle.[1000]

I. Transitional Provisions

General principles. As has already been noted, any document made or event occurring before the commencement of the 1988 Act (i.e. August 1, 1989) which had any operation affecting the ownership of the copyright in an existing work or creating, transferring or terminating an interest, right or licence in respect of the copyright in an existing work, has the corresponding operation in relation to copyright in the work under the 1988 Act.[1001] In addition, expressions used in such documents are to be construed in accordance with their effect immediately before commencement.[1002] The general effect of these provisions is therefore that one should first consider the operation of a pre-commencement licence when it was created. It is then to have the corresponding operation under the 1988 Act. Although these provisions of the 1988 Act apply in general to all existing works (i.e. works made before commencement of the 1988 Act), including works in existence at the commencement of the 1911 Act or the 1956 Act, there are modifications in special cases in the application of certain provisions of the 1988 Act to existing works. These are now summarised.   **5–237**

Exclusive licences. The effect of an exclusive licence granted before the 1956 Act came into force has already been considered,[1003] as has the fact that s.92(2) of the 1988 Act, dealing with the rights of an exclusive licensee against successors in title to the licensor, does not apply in relation to a licence granted before August 1, 1989.[1004]   **5–238**

1911 Act reversionary rights. It has already been seen that assignments under the 1911 Act were in certain cases subject to a proviso limiting the ability of an author to assign the last 25 years of the term of copyright. This limitation also applied to those licences which amounted to a grant of an interest in the   **5–239**

---

[996] *British Leyland Motor Corp Ltd v Armstrong Patents Co Ltd* [1986] A.C. 577 at 643.
[997] *Warman International Ltd v Envirotech Australia Pty Ltd* (1986) 67 A.L.R. 253 (Fed. Ct of Aus.).
[998] *Saphena Computing Ltd v Allied Collection Agencies Ltd* [1995] F.S.R. 616.
[999] *Fylde Microsystems Ltd v Key Radio Systems Ltd* [1998] F.S.R. 449.
[1000] *Creative Technology Ltd v Aztech Systems Pte Ltd* [1997] F.S.R. 491 (Ct of App. of Singapore).
[1001] CDPA 1988 Sch.1 para.25(1).
[1002] Sch.1 para.25(2).
[1003] See para.5–237, above.
[1004] See paras 5–209 and 5–237, above.

copyright.[1005] The effect of this limitation has already been considered when dealing with assignments.[1006]

5–240   **1911 Act s.24.** It has been seen that since the term of copyright under the 1911 Act was, in general, longer than that subsisting under the pre-existing statute law, the 1911 Act contained provisions under which assignments or licences subsisting at the commencement of that Act should determine when the old period of copyright ran out, and the 1911 Act copyright thereafter revested in the author or his personal representatives. The continuing effect of these provisions has been dealt with in the section dealing with assignments.

[1005] See the proviso to s.5(2) of the Copyright Act 1911, as now re-enacted in CDPA 1988 Sch.1 para.27. As to the meaning of the "grant of any interest", see paras 5–116 and 5–237, above.
[1006] See para.5–116, above.

CHAPTER SIX

DURATION OF COPYRIGHT

1. INTRODUCTION

Introduction. The need to establish the duration of copyright in a particular   **6–01**
work may arise in a variety of contexts. Thus, it may be important to establish
that copyright in a particular work has already expired before undertaking an act
of exploitation of that work which would otherwise need to be licensed. In an infringement action, it will be necessary to establish not only that the requirements
for copyright to subsist in the work have been met, but that copyright continued
or continues to subsist throughout the period of alleged infringement. It may also
be important to establish for how long in the future the work may be expected to
enjoy protection, a matter as much of concern to those on both sides of transactions involving the copyright in the work as to those who are waiting for the
copyright to expire, so that they may freely exploit the work once it falls into the
public domain.

In the case of a recently created work in which copyright is established to
subsist, the question of the duration of copyright in such work is a relatively
straightforward matter. It involves identifying the appropriate description of the

work for the purposes of the 1988 Act,[1] ascertaining (in the case of some works) the identity of its author[2] and, if dead, the year of his death, or, in the case of other works, the date of the creation or first exploitation of the work, and identifying the rule applying to the particular work amongst the rules as to duration contained in ss.12 to 15A of the 1988 Act.

However, in relation to all but the most recently created works, the question of the duration of copyright subsisting in the work is a much more complex matter, since the identification of the applicable period of protection will involve considering the rules as to duration not only under the current statutory regime, but under each preceding statutory regime, back to that which was in force when the work was created. This is not because successive Copyright Acts have maintained in force the earlier statutory regime as to duration for existing works,[3] since each Act has proceeded on the general principle that its own rules as to duration apply as much to new works as to existing works. However, the history of the term of copyright protection in the United Kingdom is one of progressive extensions to the term, and as each successive statutory regime as to duration has replaced its predecessor, it has usually retained, through transitional provisions, certain aspects of the previous regime, which continue to apply to works created under that previous regime. Since, until the amendments made to the 1988 Act in 1996,[4] each regime has replaced its predecessor, it was, before this latest amendment of the 1988 Act, necessary only to consider the transitional provisions in the 1988 Act in order to determine whether the current rules are modified in their application to a particular existing work, whatever the date of creation of that work.

However, the very question of the subsistence of copyright under the current regime, in a work created before that regime was introduced, requires consideration as to whether that work remained protected immediately prior to the commencement of the subsequent regime, and this in turn requires consideration of the duration of protection applied to that work under the preceding regime. If the work was created before that preceding regime came into force, then the same consideration has to be given to the duration of protection applied to the work under the earlier preceding regime. For this purpose, it has always been necessary to consider not only the principal rules of that earlier regime, but also its transitional provisions.

It is this retrospective aspect which makes the question of the duration of the copyright in a work under the current provisions of the 1988 Act a matter of considerable complexity, which is increased as the date of the creation of the work falls within each earlier period in the following table:

Date when work made	*Provisions to be considered*
On or after January 1, 1996	(i) the 1988 Act as amended[5]

---

[1] See CDPA 1988 s.1(1), and Ch.3, above.

[2] As to who is the author of a work, see Ch.4, above.

[3] As is the case, for example, regarding the question of who is the author of a work; see para.4–10, above.

[4] As explained in para.6–16, below, the transitional provisions of the Regulations, which amended the CDPA 1988, did not follow this practice, and require the position to be considered also under the CDPA 1988 as it was before amendment by the Regulations.

[5] By the Duration of Copyright and Rights in Performance Regulations 1995 (SI 1995/3297), see para.6–13, below.

Date when work made	Provisions to be considered
On or after August 1, 1989 but before January 1, 1996	(i) as above; and (ii) the 1988 Act as originally enacted and the transitional provisions contained in regs 12 to 16 of the Duration Regulations[6]
On or after June 1, 1956 but before August 1, 1989	(i) and (ii) as above; and (iii) the transitional provisions contained in para.12 of Sch.1 to the Act; and (iv) the 1956 Act and the transitional provisions contained in paras 2, 11 and 14 of Sch.7 to the Act
On or after July 1, 1912 but before June 1, 1956	(i), (ii), (iii) and (iv) as above; and (v) the 1911 Act
Before July 1, 1912	(i), (ii), (iii), (iv) and (v) as above; and (vi) the Acts then in force

The scheme of this chapter is to describe the history of the term of protection that has applied in the United Kingdom, first, against the background of international developments, and then making certain points of general application to existing works under each of the regimes that has applied since before 1911, before setting out the specific rules as to the duration of copyright in the different descriptions of works protected by copyright under the 1988 Act, dealing in each case with the current rules and then any particular rules applicable to existing works of that description under the transitional provisions of the 1988 Act.

2. THE HISTORY OF THE DEVELOPMENT OF THE TERM OF COPYRIGHT PROTECTION

What is a fair term for copyright? The history of the development of the term **6–02** of copyright protection in the United Kingdom is one of progressive extension of the term of protection,[7] and might be thought to reflect a development towards a consensus as to what is considered to be the fair term for such protection. The debate as to what should be the proper period of protection, which was first raised in the United Kingdom when literary works were first accorded copyright under statute, by the Statute of Anne 1709,[8] has continued over the succeeding years without any general consensus emerging. In the early days of the debate, the argument was between those who contended, in the interest of literature, for a very short period; and others who contended, in the same interest, for perpetuity.

---

[6] The transitional provisions of the Duration Regulations amending the CDPA 1988 do not follow this practice, and require the position to be considered also under the CDPA 1988 as it was before amendment by the Duration Regulations, see also para.6–14, below.

[7] As has been the case with most other countries adhering to Berne; a notable exception was the reduction in the term accorded to Berne works by Spain in November 1987; see the footnotes to para.6–10, below.

[8] 8 Anne c.19; see para.2–16, above, and see generally as to the history of the development of copyright, Ch.2 above, and A. Robinson "The Life and Terms of UK Copyright in Original Works" [1997] 2 Ent. L.R. 60.

The Gregory Committee was faced with these conflicting views.[9] The debate has been rekindled on each occasion that copyright protection has been extended to a new description of work, or when attempts are made to revise the term of protection at international level through the revision of the various international conventions. The 1977 Copyright Committee considered submissions that the term should be extended to a period of life of the author plus 70 years thereafter, but concluded that the case for extension had not been made out, and that the then current period should remain.[10] The debate was revived in the context of the extension of the term of protection required in the United Kingdom, and throughout the territory of the European Union by Council Directive 93/98,[11] in relation to works of EEA origin,[12] and were recently with the Commission's proposals for reform of the term of protection for sound recordings and performers' rights.[13]

Those who argue in favour of a restricted period for copyright speak of it as a monopoly[14]; whilst upholders of copyright in perpetuity speak of the author's right to prevent others multiplying copies of his work as a right of property. The issue of what is a fair term of copyright cannot be decided by such attempts to categorise copyright, but by a consideration of opposing public interests which are to be balanced. On the one hand, there is the public interest in ensuring access to creative works,[15] which argues for limiting the term of protection. On the other hand, there is the public interest in encouraging creative effort and its dissemination, which argues for extending the term of protection so as both to provide adequate rewards for the author and his publisher for their creative and business endeavour, and to protect the author's right to maintain the integrity of his work.[16]

Thus, whilst it is generally accepted, today, that the liberal arts cannot be expected to flourish in a country possessing inadequate copyright laws, at the same time clearly some limit must be set on copyright protection. The longer the period of protection, the greater the practical difficulty of tracing title to a kind of

---

[9] Perpetuity at one extreme, a fixed period of 15 years from publication at the other. The Gregory Committee itself was of the view that all periods of copyright are arbitrary, there being no ideal period: Report of the Committee on the Law of Copyright, 1952, Cmnd.8662, para.16.

[10] Report of the Committee to consider the Law on Copyright and Designs, Cmnd.6732, para.637; and see, generally, paras 625–636.

[11] [1993] OJ L290/9, and see paras 6–10 to 6–12, below. As to the interrelationship between the European Union and the European Economic Area, see para.24–01, below. Directive 93/98/EEC has been repealed and replaced by Directive 2006/116/EC, without prejudice to the obligations of the Member States relating to the time-limits for transposition into national law of the Directives, and their application. Directive 2006/116/EC is a consolidating measure, taking into account amendments to the Term Directive made by the Information Society Directive (Directive 2002/29/EC), and has not made any substantive changes to the law. However, it should be noted that the numbering of the recitals and articles of the two directives differ somewhat. References in this work are to the new codified directive unless otherwise indicated.

[12] See, for example, S. Ricketson "The Copyright Term" (1992) 6 I.I.C. 755; S. von Lewinski in (1992) 6 I.I.C. 785; G. Dworkin "Authorship of Films and the European Commission Proposals for Harmonising the Term of Copyright" [1993] 5 E.I.P.R. 151; P. Parrinder "The Dead Hand of European Copyright" [1993] 11 E.I.P.R. 391; L. Kurlantzick "Harmonisation of Copyright Protection" [1994] 11 E.I.P.R. 463; G. Davies *Copyright and the Public Interest* 2nd edn (London: Sweet & Maxwell, 2002); Mr Justice Laddie "Copyright: Over-strength, Over-regulated, Over-rated?" [1996] 5 E.I.P.R. 253; J. Antill and P. Coles "Copyright Duration: The European Community Adopts 'Three Score Years and Ten'" [1996] 7 E.I.P.R. 379.

[13] See paras 6–61 and 24–90.

[14] As to how far this is correct, see para.1–33, above.

[15] Embodied in art.27(1) of the Declaration Human of Rights, which provides: "Everyone has the right freely to participate in the cultural life of the community, to enjoy the arts and to share in scientific advancement and its benefits". See also para.1–35, above.

[16] Protection of the author's economic and moral rights is also embodied in the Declaration of Human Rights, art.27(2) of which provides: "Everyone has the right to the protection of the moral and material interests resulting from any scientific, literary or artistic production of which he is the author". See also para.1–35, above.

property of which there can be no physical possession.[17] Also, at least as regards published works, it is unreasonable to give to the remote successors of the author, long after his death, a monopoly in what has in fact been made public by exploitation. That is particularly so in relation to works which by their nature involve an element of industrial enterprise, as distinct from individual literary, musical or artistic creativity, and the tendency has been to accord such works a shorter, usually fixed, period of protection.

The adoption of a term of 50 years pma. At the Conference of the Powers held   **6–03**
at Berlin in 1908 for the purpose of considering what modifications ought to be made to the Berne Convention,[18] it was decided that the minimum period of protection accorded to an author of a literary or artistic work[19] should be 50 years *post mortem auctoris*,[20] that is, during his life and for a period of 50 years after his death.[21] This was accordingly the term adopted by the United Kingdom in the Copyright Act 1911 for all literary, dramatic, musical and artistic works, with certain minor exceptions.[22] This position had the very considerable advantage over the position under the law in the United Kingdom before 1911, in that the date of publication no longer had any bearing on the period of copyright protection, save in certain excepted cases. Under the law prior to 1911, which gave an alternative period of copyright for literary works, either for the life of the author and seven years after his death or a gross period of 42 years from the date of publication, whichever should be the longer,[23] the works of the same author were liable to fall into the public domain at different times. The change introduced by the 1911 Act has been followed in subsequent Copyright Acts, so that since 1911 all the literary, dramatic, musical and artistic works of the same author will, save in certain excepted cases,[24] fall into the public domain at the same time. Furthermore, since such date the term has depended on proof of the date of death,[25] which is generally much easier to secure than proof of date of first publication.

Brussels Act. The Brussels Act, resulting from a further conference to revise the   **6–04**
Berne Convention held at Brussels in 1948, maintained the standard period of 50 years from the death of the author.[26] However, the definition of literary and artistic works was revised expressly to include cinematographic and photographic works,[27] and in respect of these works the term of protection was to be that given by the law of the country in which protection was claimed, but was not to exceed the term fixed in the country of origin of the work.[28] The Brussels Act provided (with the object of removing any uncertainty which might otherwise arise through

---

[17] See para.5–67, above.

[18] The Convention of the International Union for the Protection of Literary and Artistic Works signed at Berne on September 9, 1886; see Ch.23.

[19] Such expression in the Convention encompasses every production in the literary, scientific and artistic domain, including dramatic and musical works: art.2.

[20] Often abbreviated to "pma".

[21] This was therefore the period provided for in the Berlin Act (1908).

[22] Copyright Act 1911 s.3; photographs and sound contrivances were entitled to a straight term of 50 years from their making ((ss.21 and 19 respectively) and literary, dramatic and musical works first published after the death of the author were entitled to a term of 50 years from publication (s.17)).

[23] Under the Copyright Act 1842 (5 & 6 Vict. c.45); see para.2–18, above.

[24] i.e. certain photographs and those literary, dramatic and musical works first published posthumously, see fn.19, above.

[25] Save in the case of works of unknown authorship, as to which see para.6–48, below.

[26] Brussels Act art.7(1); and see Ch.23, below.

[27] Brussels Act art.2(1). Certain types of cinematographic works had been protected since the Berlin Act 1908 (art.14.(2)). Certain types of photographic works had been protected under the Berne Convention since its inception, but photographic works in general were only included in art.2(1) in the Brussels Act 1948.

[28] Brussels Act art.7(3).

difficulty in determining the precise date of death or other event) that the term of protection should always be deemed to begin on January 1 of the year following the event.[29] The necessary changes to give effect to this rule of calculation were introduced in the 1956 Act. This rule has been maintained in subsequent revision of the Berne Convention,[30] and has remained the rule in the United Kingdom under the 1988 Act.[31]

6–05   **Universal Copyright Convention.** The Universal Copyright Convention of 1952, provided, as does the Paris revision of 1971 of this Convention, that the Convention States should give to works of Convention nationals, or works first published in Convention States, protection for the period given to their own nationals, but in any event a minimum of 25 years.[32] As this minimum was less than that required by the Brussels Act (1948) (and by subsequent revisions of the Berne Convention), the United Kingdom, in formulating the term of protection under the 1956 and 1988 Acts in relation to such works, had regard to the Berne Convention as so revised.

6–06   **Revision to Berne Convention: Stockholm and Paris Acts.** The Berne Convention was further revised at conferences held at Stockholm in 1967 and Paris in 1971. The resulting Acts made no revision to the standard period of 50 years from the death of the author.[33] However, the Stockholm Act introduced a minimum term of protection in relation to films, which has been retained in the Paris Act, as an alternative to the standard period, of 50 years after the work was made available to the public.[34] As regards photographic works, the Stockholm Act introduced a minimum term of 25 years from the making of such work, which was retained in the Paris Act.[35] However, the World Copyright Treaty (WCT) 1996 provides that, in respect of photographic works, the Contracting Parties shall not apply the provisions of art.7(4) of the Berne Convention,[36] which provides:

> "It shall be a matter for legislation in the countries of the Union to determine the term of protection of photographic works and that of works of applied art in so far as they are protected as artistic works; however, this term shall last at least until the end of a period of twenty-five years from the making of such a work."

The result is that parties to the WCT are obliged to protect photographs as artistic works for the life of the author and fifty years after his death in accordance with art.7(1) of the Paris Act of the Berne Convention.

6–07   **The Rome Convention.** Whilst films and photographs have been assimilated to literary and artistic works, so far as the provisions of the Berne Convention are concerned, sound recordings and other works which have become protected as new technology has developed in the course of the century following the ratification of the Berne Convention, such as broadcasts, have been the subject of other

---

[29] Brussels Act art.7(6).
[30] See now art.7(5) (Paris Act 1971).
[31] This rule of calculation was adopted as mandatory under the Term Directive art.8; see para.6–10, below.
[32] See Ch.23, below.
[33] art.7(1) in each Act.
[34] art.7(2) in each Act.
[35] art.7(4) in each Act.
[36] WCT art.9.

international conventions, principally the Rome Convention.[37] This Convention is based on the principle of according national treatment to the works originating in other Contracting States; however, as regards the term of protection of its beneficiaries, performers, producers of phonograms and broadcasting organisations, it stipulates a minimum period of 20 years computed from the end of the year in which:

(a) the fixation was made—for phonograms and for performances incorporated therein;

(b) the performance took place—for performances not incorporated in phonograms;

(c) the broadcast took place—for broadcasts.

Certain other international conventions relating to such works do stipulate for a minimum period, but that minimum has tended to be low, reflecting the lowest period adopted amongst the contracting states.[38]

The TRIPs Agreement and the WPPT. Under the Agreement on Trade-Related   **6–08**
Aspects of Intellectual Property 1994 (the TRIPs Agreement),[39] the term of protection accorded to performers and producers of phonograms shall last at least until the end of a period of 50 years computed from the end of the calendar year in which the fixation was made or the performance took place. Broadcasts benefit from a minimum term of 20 years from the end of the calendar year in which the broadcast took place.[40] The WIPO Performances and Phonograms Treaty 1996 (WPPT),[41] provides also for a minimum of 50 years for performers and producers of phonograms. For performances, the term is computed, as under the TRIPs Agreement, from the end of the year in which the performance was fixed in a phonogram; for producers, the period is calculated from the end of the year in which the phonogram was published, or failing such publication within 50 years from fixation of the phonogram, 50 years from the end of the year in which the fixation was made.[42]

The 1988 Act as originally enacted. The 1988 Act, as originally enacted,   **6–09**
provided two basic periods for protection for works in which copyright subsists under the Act, reflecting the distinction, referred to above,[43] as to whether the creation of the work involved an element of industrial or technical enterprise, as distinct from individual literary, musical or artistic creativity. Thus, the 1988 Act originally provided for all[44] literary, dramatic, musical and artistic works a period of protection lasting until the end of the period of 50 years from the end of the

---

[37] The International Convention for the Protection of Performers, Producers of Phonograms and Broadcasting Organisations agreed at Rome, October 26, 1961; for the text see Vol.2 F5.

[38] For example, the European Agreement on the Protection of Television Broadcasts agreed at Strasbourg, June 22, 1960, stipulated a minimum period of protection of 10 years in respect of television broadcasts: art.2(1); for the text of the Agreement see Vol.2 F3. This minimum was increased to 20 years by a Protocol agreed at Strasbourg on January 22, 1965; for the text, see Vol.2 F3.i. The Convention for the Protection of Producers of Phonograms against Unauthorised Duplication of their Phonograms, agreed at Geneva October 29, 1971, stipulates for a minimum period of protection in respect of sound recordings of 20 years: art.4; for the text see Vol.2 F8.

[39] See Ch.23, paras 23–136 et seq., below.

[40] TRIPs Agreeament art.14(5).

[41] See Ch.23, paras 23–136 et seq., below.

[42] WPPT art.17.

[43] See para.6–02, above; also reflecting the United Kingdom's international obligations under the different conventions discussed at paras 6–03 to 6–07, above.

[44] Following the recommendation of the 1977 Copyright Committee, Cmnd.6732, para.656, that such period should be the maximum period of protection for all such works.

calendar year in which the author died,[45] and for sound recordings, films, broadcasts and cable programmes a period of protection lasting until the end of the period of 50 years from the making of such work.[46] Solely in relation to typographical arrangements of published editions, the 1988 Act provided a period of 25 years from the end of the year in which the edition was first published.[47]

6–10   **European harmonisation of the term of protection.** Decisions of the European Court of Justice had highlighted the need for harmonisation in the national copyright laws of the Member States, if differences between such laws were not to continue to impede the establishment of an internal market.[48] This was particularly so as regards the differences which existed in the term of protection accorded under such laws.[49] This led to the adoption by the Council of the European Communities, on October 29, 1993, of Directive 93/98 harmonising the term of protection of copyright and certain related rights (the Term Directive).[50]

The objective of the Term Directive was to harmonise in the laws of the Member States:

(1) the period of copyright protection for authors to a period of 70 years after the death of the author;

(2) the period of related rights protection to a period of 50 years;

(3) the manner of calculation of the period of protection; and

(4) the protection afforded to the works of non-Community nationals.

The works required to be given the benefit of the extended term under (1) are those which are treated as literary or artistic works under the Berne Convention,[51] which are those works defined under the 1988 Act as literary, dramatic, musical and artistic works and films. The benefit of the extension is to be given to existing works which were protected in any Member State on January 1, 1995.[52]

The choice of a period of protection of 70 years after the author's death has been criticised as extending a term which many already considered to be too long.[53] The rationale expressed in the Duration Directive for this choice is that the minimum term of protection under Berne of life of the author and 50 years after his death was intended to provide protection for the author and the first two generations of his descendants, and that the average lifespan in the Community had grown longer to the point where this term was no longer sufficient to cover two generations.[54] However, the reality of the matter is that the Commission, in formulating the proposal, had to take account of the fact that certain Member States had exercised their right under Berne to accord a longer period of

---

[45] Subject to exceptions in the case of computer-generated works (see para.6–49, below) and works of unknown authorship (see para.6–48, below).

[46] This remains the position in relation to sound recordings (see para.6–58, below) and broadcasts (see para.6–79, below) but is no longer so in respect of films (see paras 6–70 et seq., below).

[47] This remains unchanged; see para.6–83, below.

[48] See generally paras 24–39, et seq., below.

[49] See *EMI Electrola GmbH v Patricia Im- und Export Verwaltungsgesellschaft GmbH* (Case 341/87) [1989] E.C.R. 79; and paras 24–40 et seq., below. And as to harmonisation generally in the European Union, see paras 24–43 et seq., below.

[50] [1993] OJ L290/9. As already noted, Directive 93/98/EEC has been repealed and replaced by Directive 2006/116/EC. See also the discussion of the Directive at para.24–19, below.

[51] Term Directive art.1(1) and see Berne, art.2, set out at paras 1–08 et seq., above.

[52] Term Directive art.10(2) and art.13(1) of Directive 93/98/EC; as also is the term provided for in (2).

[53] See, in particular, P. Parrinder "The Dead Hand of European Copyright" [1993] 11 E.I.P.R. 391; Mr Justice Laddie "Copyright: Over-strength, Over-regulated, Over-rated?" [1996] 5 E.I.P.R. 253.

[54] Even assuming the validity of the premise, the logic of the extension is open to challenge: see the articles by P. Parrinder and Mr Justice Laddie, cited in the previous footnote.

protection.[55] Thus, the period of protection of such works after the death of the author varied from 70 years in Germany,[56] to 60 years in Spain,[57] in respect of all such works, to 70 years in France in respect of musical works, with or without words.[58] Faced with this disparity, there was little choice but to harmonise the term of protection upwards, otherwise transitional provisions which would have been required to protect vested rights would have effectively postponed, to a large extent and for far too long,[59] the progress to the smooth operation of the internal market which was the principal objective of the harmonisation.[60]

The term of related rights protection to be accorded under the Duration Directive is also to apply to works protected in any Member State on January 1, 1995.[61] Not surprisingly, given the low minimum terms required under international conventions in relation to works not falling within Berne, there was a much wider variation in the laws of the Member States in the term of protection accorded to such works. Thus, in relation to sound recordings, the period of protection varied from 20 years to 50 years,[62] calculated variously from creation (fixation) or release (publication).[63] There was an equally large disparity in the term of protection accorded to broadcasts.[64] Applying the same imperative, the Directive required harmonisation of the term upwards, to 50 years, in respect of sound recordings, broadcasts and films[65] (as distinct from the protection to be accorded to films as cinematographic or audiovisual works[66]).

For the same reason of ensuring that the harmonising effect of the Directive's provisions would not be unduly delayed, it was necessary to ensure that the extended term would apply equally throughout the Community to existing works, even if such works had fallen into the public domain in one or more Member States.[67] This led to the adoption by the Council of the European Communities, on October 29, 1993, of Directive 93/98 harmonising the term of protection of copyright and certain related rights, which has since been repealed and replaced by a codifying Directive 2000/116/EC.[68] These Directives are collectively referred to hereafter as "the Term Directive".

The Information Society Directive. Although not principally concerned with   **6–11**

---

[55] art.7(6) (Paris Act 1971).

[56] A period which had been adopted in 1965.

[57] The term of protection in Spain had been reduced in November 1987 from 80 years pma (the period which had operated since 1879) to 60 years pma, but with transitional provisions continuing to protect vested rights.

[58] The Directive seeks to explain such longer terms as introduced to offset the effect of the world wars on the exploitation of authors' works (Duration Directive 93/98, recital 6). This had certainly been given as the reason for Germany extending the term of protection from 50 years pma to 70 years pma in 1965. Other countries had introduced specific extensions for wartime works: Belgium, 10 years; Italy, 12 years (repealed by the law of February 6, 1996, implementing the Duration Directive); France, six and eight years respectively in relation to each World War and 30 years in respect of works whose author was killed in action.

[59] Term Directive, recital 10.

[60] Term Directive, recitals 3 and 12.

[61] Term Directive art.10(2) and art.13(1) of Directive 93/98/EEC.

[62] In 1993: 20 years (Luxembourg); 25 years (Germany); 30 years (Italy); 40 years (Spain); 50 years (Austria, Denmark, France, Greece, Ireland, the Netherlands, Portugal, United Kingdom).

[63] Fixation: Denmark, France, Greece, the Netherlands, Luxembourg, Portugal; publication: Ireland, Spain, United Kingdom. Germany applied both criteria, and Italy applied a criterion of deposit.

[64] Through 25 years (Germany, Norway, Finland, Iceland); 40 years (Spain); 50 years (Denmark, France, United Kingdom); to unlimited (Italy).

[65] Term Directive art.3(2), (3) and (4) respectively.

[66] art.2(1); see further paras 6–69 and 6–64, below.

[67] Directive 93/98/EEC, recital 25.

[68] [2006] OJ L372.

further harmonisation of the term of copyright, this Directive[69] made a small adjustment to the period of protection of sound recordings, in order to comply with the 1996 WIPO Performances and Phonograms Treaty (see para.6–10, below). This is considered in more detail later in this chapter.

6–12   **Further international harmonisation of the term of protection.** The harmonisation brought about as between the laws of the Member States of the European Union by the Term Directive in relation to the term of protection of copyright and related rights has to some extent been mirrored by further progress at harmonisation at the international wider level. Thus, as regards sound recordings and broadcasts, the TRIPS agreement[70] provided for a minimum term of 50 years and 20 years for such works respectively.[71] The WIPO Performances and Phonograms Treaty[72] has completed this harmonisation by providing for a term of protection of 50 years in respect of sound recordings.[73] As regards such works, therefore, the position within the European Union is likely to be reflected on the international level, as countries adopt legislation to give effect to this WIPO Treaty.

That is not the position, however, as regards the term of protection in respect of those authors' works which are the subject of the Berne Convention. Whilst recent Community legislation has brought about harmonisation of the term of protection as between the laws of the Member States of the European Union upwards to the level of life plus 70 years, the standard period of protection for those works outside the European Union remains the life of the author and the period of 50 years after his death.[74] This is the standard adopted in the TRIPS agreement[75] and subsequently in the WIPO Copyright Treaty.[76] It is unlikely at present that the international community will progress to extending the period of protection for works falling within Berne to life plus 70 years.

That there would be this disparity between the term of protection accorded such works within the European Union and outside was recognised by the Duration Directive, which is deliberately framed to require Member States to accord the extended term of protection only to works of Community origin.[77] In the case of such works not of Community origin, Member States are required to apply comparison of terms, rather than national treatment.[78] This requirement is subject to any international obligation the Member States may otherwise have to accord a longer period of protection to such works.[79]

---

[69] Directive 2001/29 of the European Parliament and of the Council on the harmonisation of certain aspects of copyright and related rights in the information society (May 22, 2001).

[70] The Agreement on Trade-related Aspects of Intellectual Property Rights concluded at Geneva on December 15, 1993: art.9.

[71] arts 14(2), (3) and (5).

[72] Concluded at the WIPO Diplomatic Conference in Geneva, December 20, 1996.

[73] art.17(2).

[74] See para.6–05, above. The United States is a notable exception, where, following the increase in the term applied by Member States in Europe and the application of "comparison of terms" (see further in the text and para.6–19, below), the standard term was also increased to life and 70 years pma.

[75] The Agreement on Trade-related Aspects of Intellectual Property Rights concluded at Geneva on December 15, 1993: art.9.

[76] Concluded at the WIPO Diplomatic Conference in Geneva, December 20, 1996: art.1(4). An earlier suggestion that the term should be similarly increased under the Berne Convention was not carried through; see para.24–84, below.

[77] Term Directive, recital 21 and art.7.

[78] Term Directive art.7(1); see further paras 6–18 to 6–20, below.

[79] Term Directive art.7(2) and (3).

3. THE PRESENT POSITION UNDER THE 1988 ACT AS AMENDED

Implementation of the Duration Term Directive in the United Kingdom.   6–13
Member States were given until July 1, 1995 to introduce the provisions necessary to implement the Term Directive.[80] The United Kingdom did so by the Duration of Copyright and Rights in Performances Regulations 1995 (the Duration
Regulations),[81] with effect from January 1, 1996.[82] The 1988 Act did not require
amendment to provide for a term of 50 years for related rights, or as to the manner of calculation of the period of protection, as its original provisions were already in accordance with the requirements of the Directive in these respects.[83]
Some amendment was required to deal with the protection afforded to the works
of non-Community nationals,[84] and extensive amendment and new provisions
were required to deal with the extension of the period of protection to 70 years
and its application to existing works.[85] Before dealing with the present position in
the United Kingdom with respect to the different descriptions of works protected
by copyright under the 1988 Act as so amended, some comments of general applicability to all such works, except typographical arrangements, are necessary in
order to understand the full implications of the amended provisions, particularly
for works made before January 1, 1996.

The transitional provisions of the Duration Regulations. In addition to the   6–14
amendments required to ss.12 to 15 of the 1988 Act in order to give effect to the
Term Directive in respect of works coming into existence after January 1, 1996,
transitional provisions were also required, to ensure, in accordance with the
policy mentioned above which lies behind the Directive,[86] that the benefit of the
extended term is applied in the United Kingdom to any work of EEA origin
protected under the law of any one EEA state on July 1, 1995. The Duration
Regulations achieve this by providing that the 1988 Act as amended[87] is to apply
not only to works coming into existence after commencement[88] but also to three
categories of existing works. An existing work, for the purposes of the Regulations, is one made before January 1, 1996,[89] irrespective of when, before that
date, it was made. The three categories of existing works to which the new provisions are to be applied are:

---

[80] art.13(1) of Directive 93/98/EEC.

[81] SI 1995/3297. The relevant sections of the 1988 Act, both before amendment and as amended,
are set out at Vol.2 A1. The text of those provisions of the Regulations not incorporated into the
Act is set out at Vol.2 A3.ii. For the discussion in Parliament of the Regulations, see *Hansard*,
H.C. Vol.268, cols 1254–1272, December 18, 1995.

[82] The United Kingdom was therefore late in implementing the Directive, in theory exposing the
United Kingdom to an action by private parties for damages: see, as to the effect of Directives,
Cases C–6 and C–9/90, *Francovich v Italy* and *Boniface v Italy* [1991] E.C.R. 5357. The delay
was explained by the Government as due to the complexity of the drafting and consultative
exercise which was required: *Hansard*, H.C. Vol.268, col. 1254, December 18, 1995. Implementation throughout the Union was piecemeal (see the table of implementation at para.24–140,
below), with other countries being late (out of the 15 countries, only Belgium, Denmark, Germany and Ireland implemented the Directive before July 1, 1995).

[83] That is in respect of the matters set out in (2) and (3) in para.6–10, above; see paras 6–04 and
6–09, above.

[84] See paras 6–17 to 6–20, below.

[85] See, as to literary, dramatic, musical and artistic works, paras 6–53 et seq., below, as to sound
recordings, paras 6–57 et seq., below and as to films paras 6–69 et seq., below. The particular
problems as to ownership of the extended (and revived) term of copyright created by the Regulations and the protection of acquired rights are dealt with at paras 5–137 et seq., above.

[86] See paras 6–10 to 6–12, above.

[87] The provisions of the Act as so amended are referred to as "the new provisions": reg.12(2).

[88] reg.16(a); the Regulations came into force on January 1, 1996: reg.1(2).

[89] reg.14(1)(a). The term "existing work" is therefore used to describe both works existing before
January 1, 1996 and also works existing before August 1, 1989 (see CDPA 1988 Sch.1 para.1(3)),
depending on the context. In this part of the work, it is used with the former meaning.

   (i) existing works first qualifying for protection after January 1, 1996[90];

  (ii) existing works in which copyright subsisted immediately before that date[91]; and

 (iii) existing works in which copyright expired before December 31, 1995 but which were protected on July 1, 1995 in another EEA state.[92]

6–15   **Existing works first brought into protection by the Regulations.** Given the extent of copyright protection accorded by the 1988 Act (and its predecessors) prior to January 1, 1996, there is no obvious example which can be given of an existing work which had not enjoyed copyright protection at any time before that date, but which is brought within protection by the new provisions. No doubt this class of existing work was included out of caution, and emphasises the objective that, whatever the position which governed before January 1, 1996, the new provisions are to govern the position thereafter.

6–16   **Existing copyright works.** Existing copyright works are defined as those existing works in which copyright subsisted immediately before January 1, 1996.[93] In the case of the principal category of authors' works, previously benefiting from a term of 50 years pma, this will include all the works of authors who died on or after January 1, 1945. The application of the new provisions to this class of existing works is, however, subject to the important qualification that if copyright would have subsisted in the work under the provisions of the 1988 Act before amendment for a longer period, then that is the period which continues to apply to the work.[94] Whilst this qualification will not apply to the majority of existing copyright works, it has particular application to existing copyright works which had not, prior to January 1, 1996, been published or otherwise commercially exploited, and were enjoying a period of protection under the 1988 Act, as unamended, which was not limited in time.[95] This qualification nevertheless has the unfortunate consequence, already described, that it is in all cases necessary to consider the position of an existing copyright work under the two distinct regimes, before the current period of its term of protection can be determined with certainty.[96]

    The further period of protection which, subject to this qualification, will apply to existing works (20 years in the case of existing literary, dramatic, musical and artistic works and a potentially longer period in the case of films) is referred to in the Regulations as "extended copyright",[97] and is subject to special rules as to its ownership[98] and savings in respect of existing licences, agreements, etc.[99]

6–17   **Existing works in the public domain in the United Kingdom but protected in another EEA state on July 1, 1995.** Before the amendment of the 1988 Act by the Duration Regulations, the determination of the term of protection of a work in the United Kingdom was entirely a matter of applying the relevant rules of the law of the United Kingdom, and this was so whether the country of origin of that

---

[90] reg.16(b); see para.6–15, below.

[91] reg.16(c); see para.6–16, below.

[92] reg.16(d); see paras 6–17 et seq., below.

[93] reg.14(1)(b). Time is a continuum, and this therefore includes works in which copyright would otherwise have expired at midnight on December 31, 1995; see *Hansard*, H.C. Vol.268, col.1265, December 18, 1995.

[94] reg.16(c) and reg.15(1).

[95] See further, paras 6–53 to 6–56, below.

[96] See the beginning of the Chapter: para.6–01, above.

[97] reg.17.

[98] regs 18 and 20; discussed at para.5–137, above.

[99] reg.21; discussed at para.5–142, above.

work was the United Kingdom or a foreign country. This was because the United Kingdom had not, as a general rule, exercised the right under Berne to apply comparison of terms to the works of other Berne Convention countries, but simply applied, through the inclusion of such countries in the relevant Order in Council under s.159, national treatment to such works.

Under the 1988 Act as amended, and in relation to works made before January 1, 1996, it is now necessary to consider the position as to the term under the regime applicable in the United Kingdom, and then, if that leads to the conclusion that copyright in the United Kingdom had expired before December 31, 1995 (that is had expired on December 31, 1994 or before), it remains necessary to consider the position of that work under the laws of the other EEA states.[100] If the work continued to benefit from copyright protection in any one of those countries, then it must be given a revived term of protection in the United Kingdom, so that copyright expires in that work throughout the whole of the EEA at the same time. For this purpose it does not matter that the work has never enjoyed copyright protection in the United Kingdom.[101] As regards rights holder who are not Community nationals, the Directive applies where the work at issue was, on July 1, 1995, protected as such in at least one Member State and where the holder of such rights benefited, at that date, from the protection provided for by those national provisions.[102]

As indicated above, a degree of harmonisation as to the manner of calculation of the term in respect of authors' works had been achieved amongst Berne Convention countries.[103] For those EEA states that had, like the United Kingdom, adopted that method of calculation,[104] the reference to copyright subsisting in another EEA state on July 1, 1995 effectively refers to works which remained in protection on January 1, 1995.

Since, however, as indicated above,[105] a number of EEA states had already accorded a term of protection for certain categories of authors' works of 70 years pma, the effect of this provision was to bring back into copyright in the United Kingdom a large number of such works of authors who died on or after January 1, 1925 and before January 1, 1945. The period of copyright which such works enjoy is that part of the period of 20 years which remains, depending on how recently before January 1, 1945 the author died. The further period of protection which applies to such works is referred to in the Regulations as "revived copyright".[106]

In the case of an author who died on January 1, 1925, and benefited from a period of protection for his works of 70 years pma in Germany, for example, that work would have fallen into the public domain in the United Kingdom as from January 1, 1976. Such a work should, under the Term Directive,[107] have enjoyed a revived period of copyright in the United Kingdom until December 31, 1995.

---

[100] An EEA state is a state which is a contracting party to the Agreement on the European Economic Area signed at Oporto on May 2, 1992, as adjusted by the Protocol signed at Brussels on March 17, 1993: CDPA 1988 s.172A.

[101] *Sony Music Entertainment (Germany) GmbH v Falcon Neue Medien Vertrieb GmbH* (C–240/07) [2009] E.C.R. I–263; [2009] E.C.D.R. 12, the Court of Justice ruling that the term of protection laid down by Directive is applicable, pursuant to art.10(2), where the subject matter at issue has at no time been protected in the Member State in which the protection is sought.

[102] *Sony Music Entertainment (Germany) GmbH v Falcon Neue Medien Vertrieb GmbH* (C–240/07) [2009] E.C.R. I–263; [2009] E.C.D.R. 12.

[103] See para.6–04, above.

[104] A few had not, calculating the term from the date of death or other event, for example Belgium (and also Iceland and Liechtenstein).

[105] See para.6–10, above. Austria, also, amongst EEA states, had applied a period of 70 years pma since 1936.

[106] reg.17.

[107] Term Directive art.10(2) and art.13(1) of Directive 93/98/EEC.

However, because of the late implementation of the Directive in the United Kingdom, the effect of the provisions is effectively to deny such work any period of revived copyright.[108] So far as the United Kingdom is concerned, therefore, the shortest period of revived copyright will have been from January 1, 1996 to December 31, 1996, applicable in the case of an author who died on or after January 1, 1926 and before January 1, 1927, and whose work benefited from a period of 70 years pma in, for example, Germany. At the other end of the scale is the case of the author who died on or after January 1, 1944 and before January 1, 1945 and whose work benefited from a period of protection of 70 years pma in Germany. In his case, the work will benefit from revived copyright under reg.16(d) for a period of 19 years lasting from January 1, 1996 until December 31, 2014.

Revived copyright is subject to special rules as to its ownership,[109] savings in respect of moral rights,[110] and for acts done when the work was in the public domain,[111] and is subject to a form of statutory licence.[112]

6–18   **The *Phil Collins* Case.** The discussion above of reg.16(d) has concentrated on the application of the new provisions in the United Kingdom to a work which was still in copyright in another EEA state in 1995, but which had fallen into the public domain in the United Kingdom before that date. The examples given to demonstrate the application of this provision were of works which benefited from the longer period of protection granted in another EEA state, for example Germany, which that state granted under its own laws. Unlike the United Kingdom, such countries have traditionally applied comparison of terms to the works of other nationals or of which the country of origin was another Berne Convention country, as they were entitled to do. Thus, whilst the work of a German author who died in 1944 was entitled to a term of copyright in Germany expiring on December 31, 2014, a comparable work of an English author was entitled, under the comparison of terms approach, to a term of protection in Germany expiring on December 31, 1974.

However, for an EEA state to apply comparison of terms to such effect is a breach of its obligations under European law, in that it amounts to discrimination on the basis of nationality. The Court of Justice, in its decision in the joined cases of *Phil Collins v Imtrat HandelsGmbH* and *Verwaltung-gesellschaft mbH v EMI Electrola GmbH*[113] held that such discrimination was not permissible as being contrary to what is now art.6 of the Treaty.[114] It is, therefore, not only the works of the nationals of such countries, or even the works of which such a country is the country of origin, which benefit from the revival in the United Kingdom of copyright, pursuant to art.10(2) of the Term Directive, but all works of which the authors are nationals of an EEA state or of which such a state is the country of origin,[115] or where the work at issue was, on July 1, 1995, protected as such in at

[108] reg.16(d) applies to such a work, but such revived copyright is effectively nullified by reg.23(1), which provides that nothing done before January 1, 1996 shall infringe revived copyright in a work.
[109] regs 19 and 20; discussed at para.11–88, below.
[110] reg.22; discussed at para.5–143, above.
[111] reg.23; discussed at para.5–145, above.
[112] regs 24 and 25; discussed at para.5–148, above.
[113] Cases 92 and 326/92, [1993] 3 C.M.L.R. 773.
[114] For the text of art.6, see Vol.2 G. The prohibition against discrimination by a Member State applies equally in cases where the author has died before the EEC Treaty comes into force in the Member State concerned: *Land Hessen v G Ricordi & Co Bühnen- und Musikverlag GmbH* (C–360/00) [2003] F.S.R. 11.
[115] For a discussion of the effect of this decision in the context of the Term Directive, see the article by Dworkin and Sterling in [1994] E.I.P.R. 187.

least one Member State and where the holder of such rights benefited, at that date, from the protection provided for by those national provisions.[116]

Country of origin: authors' works. The concept of the country of origin of a   **6–19** work has existed under Berne as a means of determining which foreign works a Convention country is obliged to treat under its own laws as enjoying protection.[117] However, this concept had not previously required definition in UK Copyright Acts, as the policy of the 1988 Act and its predecessors had been to apply the same term of protection to a work which qualifies by reason of its being first published in, or its author being domiciled or resident in, a country to which the relevant provisions of the 1988 Act had been applied,[118] as to a work of that type which qualified by reason of its being first published in, or its author being a British subject or being domiciled or resident in the United Kingdom.[119] This is no longer the position, and the 1988 Act now contains a comparison of terms provision, in that in respect of works of non-EEA origin, the normal rule of life plus 70 years is not to apply unless that is the term which applies in the country of origin. The term of protection for such a work in the United Kingdom is limited to the term which that work enjoys in the country of origin. This change was required in order to implement the Term Directive.[120]

The country of origin of a work for the purposes of the application of the provisions relating to duration of copyright[121] is determined by the provisions contained in s.15A of the 1988 Act,[122] which follow closely the provisions in Berne. Thus, the country of origin of a work first published in a Berne Convention country[123] is that country[124]; if the work is first published simultaneously[125] in two or more countries only one of which is a Berne Convention country, then that country is the country of origin of the work.[126]

Country of origin: EEA states. Since the only purpose in introducing the   **6–20** concept of the country of origin into the 1988 Act is to be able to distinguish between works whose country of origin is an EEA state[127] and those whose country of origin is not, further rules are contained in s.15A defining the country of origin in the case of EEA states. If the work is published simultaneously in two or more countries, of which two or more are Berne Convention countries, then if any one

---

[116] *Sony Music Entertainment (Germany) GmbH v Falcon Neue Medien Vertrieb GmbH* (C–240/07) [2009] E.C.R. I–263; [2009] E.C.D.R. 12, ruling on the issue whether national provisions governing the protection of rightholders who are not Community nationals constitute national provisions within the meaning of art.10(2) of Directive 2006/116.

[117] See Brussels Act art.4(3), and now Paris Act 1971 art.5(4).

[118] i.e. by an Order in Council under CDPA 1988 s.159. A definition of country of origin was contained in the Copyright (International Conventions) Order 1957 (SI 1957/1523), para.4(2). See *Copinger* 12th edn, para.1392.

[119] Whilst the United Kingdom could consistent with its international obligations have applied comparison of terms to such works, it traditionally favoured applying national treatment. As to application of the provisions of the 1988 Act to foreign works generally, see paras 3–192 et seq., above.

[120] See para.6–10, above.

[121] Stated to be generally for the purposes of Pt I of the CDPA 1988, but the concept has no relevance other than in relation to term.

[122] Introduced by the Duration Regulations.

[123] That is a country which is a party to any Act of the International Convention for the Protection of Literary and Artistic Works signed at Berne on September 9, 1886: CDPA 1988 s.15A(6)(a).

[124] CDPA 1988 s.15(2); Berne art.5(4)(a).

[125] That is, published within 30 days of first publication: CDPA 1988 s.15A(6)(b).

[126] CDPA 1988 s.15A(3); Berne (Paris Act 1971) art.5(4)(b).

[127] An EEA state is a state which is a contracting party to the Agreement on the European Economic Area signed at Oporto on May 2, 1992, as adjusted by the Protocol signed at Brussels on March 17, 1993: CDPA 1988 s.172A.

of those countries is an EEA state, that country is the country of origin,[128] but if not, then that Berne Convention country which grants the shorter or shortest period of copyright protection is the country of origin.[129] Where the work is unpublished, or is first published in a country which is not a Berne Convention country, then the general rule is that the country of origin of the work is that country of which the author is a national.[130] The general rule is subject to exceptions in the case of films, where the country of origin is that country in which the maker of the film has his headquarters, is domiciled or resident,[131] and works of architecture or artistic works incorporated into a work of architecture, where the country of origin is that country in which the work of architecture is situated.[132] In both cases the exception applies only if that country is a Berne Convention country.

6–21   Country of origin: other works. The 1988 Act does not refer to the country of origin other than in respect of works defined in the Berne Convention (which include films).[133] In respect of sound recordings and broadcasts, the Act refers to the author of such works being a national of an EEA state.[134] The construction of references in the 1988 Act to an EEA state is subject to special transitional provisions, which are designed to ensure that the benefit of the new provisions is applied to works whenever any EEA state regards that work as published in an EEA state,[135] or as originating in an EEA state,[136] or regards its author as a national of an EEA state.[137]

4. THE EFFECT OF TRANSITIONAL PROVISIONS ON THE TERM OF EXISTING WORKS

6–22   Introduction. Before dealing with the current rules as to the duration of copyright in the different descriptions of work in which copyright subsists under the 1988 Act, it is necessary, for the reasons described above,[138] to provide an outline of the development of the term of protection in the United Kingdom through the various Acts leading up to the 1988 Act, and to describe how each Act has dealt, through transitional provisions, with works existing at the date of its commencement. Since, in the case of works made under earlier regimes, it is necessary to consider each successive regime, it is convenient to start with the position before 1912 and end with the position under the transitional provisions of the 1988 Act.

A. THE LAW BEFORE THE 1911 ACT

6–23   Unpublished works. The 1911 Act abolished common law copyright[139] with effect from July 1, 1912. Unpublished works were previously protected at common

---

[128] CDPA 1988 s.15A(4)(a). Presumably, in the case where two or more are EEA states, then "those countries" are the "country of origin".

[129] CDPA 1988 s.15A(4)(b), following, by analogy, Berne Convention art.5(4)(a).

[130] CDPA 1988 s.15A(5)(c).

[131] CDPA 1988 s.15A(5)(a).

[132] CDPA 1988 s.15A(5)(b).

[133] See CDPA 1988 ss.12(6) and 13B(7).

[134] See CDPA 1988 ss.13A(4) and 14(3).

[135] In the case of a work first published before July 1, 1995: reg.36(1)(a).

[136] In the case of a film made before July 1, 1995 and whose maker was regarded by such state as domiciled or resident in that state: reg.36(1)(b).

[137] In the case of the author of a work made before July 1, 1995: reg.36(1)(c).

[138] See para.6–01, above.

[139] Copyright Act 1911 s.31.

law, and, therefore, any work[140] unpublished on July 1, 1912 was protected under the 1911 Act.

Literary copyright. The governing statute was the Literary Copyright Act   **6–24**
1842,[141] which provided in relation to "books" (that is every volume, part, or division of a volume, pamphlet, letterpress sheet, music sheet, map, chart and plan[142]) a period of protection of the longer of seven years after the death of the author or 42 years from publication.[143] The protection accorded to such works included the literary rights in musical and dramatic works. Any such work published on or after July 1, 1870, or any work the author of which died on or after July 1, 1905, was, therefore protected under the 1911 Act,[144] notwithstanding that there had been no registration of the copyright.[145]

Lectures. Limited protection was granted to published lectures under the Lectur-   **6–25**
ers Copyright Act 1835.[146] The period of protection was 28 years from publication.[147] Speeches and lectures delivered in public and without restrictions lost all right to protection, unless certain onerous formalities were complied with.[148] But a report of a speech might be entitled to copyright.[149]

Musical and dramatic works. Musical scores and books of words were   **6–26**
protected as literary works under the Literary Copyright Act 1842.[150] The statutes relating to the performing rights were the Dramatic Copyright Act 1833,[151] which originally only applied to dramatic works, and ss.20 and 21 of the Literary Copyright Act 1842, which applied to both musical and dramatic compositions. The effect of these provisions was to protect the performing rights in a musical or dramatic work which had been published as a book for the longer of seven years after the death of the author or 42 years from the date of the first public representation or performance of the work. If the work had not been published as a book, but was in manuscript form only, the term of the performing rights was doubtful.[152] In the case of musical, but not dramatic works, it was essential to the preservation of performing rights that a notice of reservation of those rights should be printed on the title page of every publication of work published after 1882.[153] No musical work, therefore, published after 1882, but before July 1, 1912, which omitted to print such notice of reservation obtained any performing rights under the 1911 Act.

Engravings, prints and lithographs. As regards engravings and prints, the main   **6–27**
statutes in force before the 1911 Act were the Engraving Copyright Acts of 1734

---

[140] But see para.6–29, below as to paintings, drawings and photographs.
[141] 5 & 6 Vict. c.45.
[142] Literary Copyright Act 1842 s.2.
[143] Literary Copyright Act 1842 s.3; as to the terms and conditions applying to such copyright, see *Copinger* 12th edn, paras 1107 and 1108.
[144] See para.6–31, below.
[145] *Savory (E.W.) Ltd v The World of Golf Ltd* [1914] 2 Ch.566.
[146] 5 & 6 Will. 4, c.65.
[147] Lecturers Copyright Act 1835 s.4.
[148] See *Copinger* 12th edn, para.1112.
[149] *Walter v Lane* [1900] A.C. 539; and see para.3–137, above.
[150] See para.6–24, above.
[151] 3 & 4 Will. 4, c.15.
[152] The Dramatic Copyright Act 1833 did not prescribe any term in such a case, and it is not clear that this was altered by the Literary Copyright Act 1842.
[153] For the terms and conditions applying to such copyright, see *Copinger* 12th edn, paras 1114 and 1115.

and 1766[154] and the Prints Copyright Act 1777.[155] Prints taken by lithograph, or any other mechanical process for multiplying prints, were brought under the earlier Acts relating to engravings by the International Copyright Act 1852.[156] The term of protection was 28 years from the date of publication, provided the name of the author and the date of first publication was engraved on the plate and printed on each copy.[157] In order, therefore, to be entitled to protection under the 1911 Act, engravings must have been published since June 30, 1884, and have had the name of the author and date of first publication printed on every copy.

6–28   **Sculptures.** Works of sculpture were protected under the Sculpture Copyright Act 1814.[158] The term of protection was 14 years from first publication, and a further 14 years if the first proprietor was then living and had not divested himself of the copyright. The name of the sculptor and date of first publication had to be put on the work.[159] The following works of sculpture made before July 1, 1912, therefore, received no protection under the 1911 Act: (a) all works published before July 1, 1884; (b) all works published between June 30, 1884 and July 1 1898, unless the author was then living; and (c) all works published before July 1, 1912, which did not bear the name of the sculptor and the date of first publication.

6–29   **Paintings, drawings and photographs.** By the Fine Arts Copyright Act 1862,[160] a painting, drawing or photograph made in the British Dominions or elsewhere was entitled to a term of protection (if its author was a British subject or resident in the British Dominions) for the period of the life of the author and seven years after his death. The statutory term of protection commenced from the date of the making of the work, whether the same was published or not; although, if the work was unpublished, a common law copyright existed in parallel to the statutory copyright, which probably expired at the same time as the statutory protection. Further, except in the case of works executed on commission, copyright was liable to be destroyed if the author did not, upon the first sale of his work, reserve the copyright to himself in writing.[161] It consequently follows that no painting, drawing or photograph made before July 1, 1912 was entitled to protection under the 1911 Act if the author had died before July 1, 1905, or if he had failed to reserve the copyright in the work on its first sale (in the case of a work not executed on commission). Non-registration under the 1862 Act did not disentitle the work to copyright (although it prevented an infringement action being brought in respect of the period prior to registration).[162]

6–30   **Non-protected works.** Works of architecture (except architects' plans, which were protected as artistic works), choreographic works, pantomimes and musical and other records were not entitled to any copyright under the law before July 1, 1912, and with the exception of mechanical contrivances for reproducing sounds,[163] none of these works, if made or published before July 1, 1912, was entitled to protection under the 1911 Act.

---

[154] 8 Geo. 2, c.13; 7 Geo. 3, c.38.
[155] 17 Geo. 3, c.57.
[156] 15 & 16 Vict. c.12; s.14.
[157] As to terms and conditions applying to such copyright, see *Copinger* 12th edn, para.1120.
[158] 54 Geo. 3, c.56.
[159] As to terms and conditions applying to such copyright, see *Copinger* 12th edn, para.1121.
[160] 25 & 26 Vict. c.68.
[161] As to the terms and conditions applying to such copyright, see *Copinger* 12th edn, para.1123.
[162] See *Copinger* 12th edn, para.1122.
[163] Such works were protected under the 1911 Act by virtue of s.19(8).

B. THE 1911 ACT

General position under the 1911 Act: existing works. The approach of the   6–31
1911 Act to works in existence at its commencement[164] was to provide that any
person entitled to copyright under the previous law at that date thereupon obtained
copyright, as defined by the Act of 1911, subject to certain modifications in respect of rights forming part of the copyright under the 1911 Act which had not
previously existed. In relation to works in existence before July 1, 1912, it
therefore remains necessary to consider the law as it stood before that date in order to determine whether there was a subsisting copyright at that date. This differs from the approach in both the 1956 and 1988 Acts, under which all questions
of subsistence and term in relation to existing works depend upon the provisions,
respectively, of those Acts.

General rule as to term. The term adopted under the 1911 Act for all literary,   6–32
musical, dramatic and artistic works, with certain exceptions, was the period of
the life of the author and 50 years after his death.[165] The period was calculated
from the date of death. The exceptions were photographs and certain works first
published posthumously, and contrivances for the reproduction of sounds.

Photographs. Photographs, which included films (which were treated as a series   6–33
of photographs), were granted a fixed period of protection of 50 years from the
date of the making of the original negative.[166]

Posthumous works. Literary, dramatic and musical works and engravings, in   6–34
which copyright subsisted at the date of the death of the author, and which
remained unpublished at that date, were entitled under the 1911 Act to an
unlimited period of copyright until first publication of the work, when they
became entitled to a further period of 50 years from that date. Publication, in this
context, included, in the case of a dramatic or musical work, being performed in
public, and, in the case of a lecture, being delivered in public.[167]

Mechanical instruments. Records, perforated rolls and other contrivances by   6–35
means of which sounds might be mechanically reproduced, were protected in the
same manner as if they were musical works, but were granted a period of protection of 50 years from the making of the original plate from which the contrivance
was derived.[168]

Films. As stated above, films were protected under the 1911 Act as a series of   6–36
photographs.[169] Films were also capable of protection as dramatic works,[170] and a
film in which copyright subsisted as a dramatic work was entitled to the standard
period of protection for such works, namely the life of its author and the period of
50 years after his death.

C. THE 1956 ACT

General position under the 1956 Act: existing works. The approach adopted   6–37

---

[164] July 1, 1912.
[165] Copyright Act 1911 s.3.
[166] Copyright Act 1911 s.21.
[167] Copyright Act 1911 s.17(1).
[168] Copyright Act 1911 s.19(1).
[169] See para.6–33, above.
[170] The definition of dramatic work under the 1911 Act included any cinematograph production
where the arrangement or acting form or the combination of incidents represented gave the work
an original character: s.35(1). See para.3–34, above.

by the 1956 Act to works in existence at its commencement[171] was to treat its provisions as having always applied to such works, subject to any modifications contained in Sch.7 to the Act.[172]

6–38 **General rule as to term.** The 1956 Act made no change in the standard period of protection for literary, musical, dramatic and artistic works, which remained the period of the life of the author and 50 years after his death. However, under the 1956 Act, this period was calculated from the end of the year in which the death or other relevant event occurred.[173] The general rule was subject to exceptions in the case of certain works first published posthumously, and photographs.

Literary, dramatic and musical works,[174] and engravings[175] which remained unpublished at the author's death were entitled to protection for an unlimited period until first published, when they became entitled to a further fixed period of 50 years from the end of the year in which publication took place.

Photographs were entitled to protection for a fixed period of 50 years from the end of the year in which they were first published.[176]

Sound recordings were granted protection of unlimited duration while they remained unpublished, and on publication became entitled to protection for a further period of 50 years from the end of the year in which publication occurred.

Films became subject to their own regime, and, in general,[177] were granted protection of unlimited duration while they remained unpublished, and on publication became entitled to protection for a further period of 50 years calculated from the end of the year in which publication occurred.

Broadcasts, which were first given protection under the 1956 Act, were granted a fixed period of 50 years after the end of the year in which they were first broadcast.

6–39 **Transitional provisions.** In the case of works existing at June 1, 1957 the general rules as to term therefore applied to such works, with modification in the case of existing photographs and in the case of joint works. Exceptions were also made in the case of existing sound recordings and films.

6–40 **Existing photographs.** The term of copyright in a photograph taken before June 1, 1957 was the period of 50 years from the end of the year in which it was taken, and not from the end of the year in which the photograph was published.[178]

6–41 **Existing works of joint authorship.** There was no copyright under the 1956 Act[179] in a work of joint authorship in which the copyright expired before June 1, 1957 under the provisions of the 1911 Act as to joint works,[180] which provided for such works a term which was the longer of (a) the period of 50 years from the death of the author who died first or (b) the life of the author who died last.

6–42 **Existing sound recordings.** In respect of sound recordings existing before June

---

[171] June 1, 1957.
[172] Copyright Act 1956 Sch.7 para.45(1).
[173] Copyright Act 1956 ss.2(3) and 3(4).
[174] Copyright Act 1956 proviso to s.2(3).
[175] Copyright Act 1956 proviso (a) to s.3(4).
[176] Copyright Act 1956 s.3(4), proviso (b).
[177] Depending on whether they were registrable or not.
[178] Copyright Act 1956 Sch.7 para.2.
[179] Copyright Act 1956 Sch.7 para.10.
[180] Copyright Act 1911 s.16(1).

1, 1957, the term of protection was fixed at 50 years from the end of the year in which they were made.[181]

Existing films. Films made before June 1, 1957 were excluded from copyright as films, but retained their protection as a series of photographs and as dramatic works, as under the 1911 Act.[182]   **6–43**

D. THE 1988 ACT

General position under the 1988 Act: existing works. The general approach of the 1988 Act to works existing at August 1, 1989[183] was to apply its provisions to such works as they apply in relation to works coming into existence after that date, subject to any express provision to the contrary contained in the transitional provisions of Sch.1 to the Act.[184] The general principles underlying the schedule were stated to be that existing copyright should not be lost; that existing works not in copyright should not suddenly acquire it; that existing copyright owners should not suddenly find themselves with a right substantially less valuable than already enjoyed; and that others exploiting or dealing with existing works should not find themselves unable to continue.[185] Although this statement of principles would not have prevented the extension of the rights of owners of copyright in existing works in which copyright subsisted immediately before August 1, 1989, the approach taken in the 1988 Act as regards duration is to preserve the position which existed under the previous applicable legislation by specific provisions contained in para.12 of Sch.1 to the Act.   **6–44**

General rule as to term. The 1988 Act retained as the standard period of protection for Berne works, other than films, the period of the life of the author and a further period of 50 years after the end of the year of his death.[186] This term of protection was for the first time applied to photographs, which had hitherto enjoyed a fixed period of protection, not dependent on the life of their author.   **6–45**

The period of protection accorded to sound recordings, films, broadcasts and cable programmes[187] remained the same as it had been under the 1956 Act,[188] save that the possibility for sound recordings and films to enjoy protection for an unlimited time while they remained unpublished, was removed.

Transitional provisions. The application of the general rules as to duration contained in ss.12 to 15 of the Act is therefore modified in relation to existing works by the specific provisions contained in para.12 of Sch.1 to the Act, affecting posthumous works, photographs, works of unknown authorship, sound recordings and films. These exceptions are dealt with more fully in the following sections of this chapter, in respect of each of the works concerned.[189]   **6–46**

---

[181] Copyright Act 1965 Sch.7 para.11.

[182] Copyright Act 1965 Sch.7 paras 15 and 16.

[183] The date of commencement of the 1988 Act.

[184] CDPA 1988 Sch.1 para.3.

[185] *Hansard*, H.L. Vol.492, col. 582.

[186] CDPA 1988 s.12.

[187] CDPA 1988 ss.13 and 14. As to cable programmes, see below.

[188] As amended, in the case of cable programmes, which became protected by the amendments introduced by the Cable and Broadcasting Act 1984.

[189] Note that the Gowers Review of Intellectual Property of December 2006, recommended inter alia that policy makers should adopt the principle that the term and scope of protection for IP rights should not be altered retrospectively in the future: Recommendation 4.

5. LITERARY, DRAMATIC, MUSICAL AND ARTISTIC WORKS

A. WORKS MADE ON OR AFTER JANUARY 1, 1996

6–47 **General position.** By s.12(2) of the 1988 Act,[190] the normal period of protection for literary, dramatic, musical and artistic works coming into existence after commencement of the Duration Regulations[191] lasts until the end of the period of 70 years from the end of the calendar year in which the author died. In the case of a work of joint authorship, this means the death of the last of the authors to die.[192] This remains the period whether or not at the author's death such works have been published or otherwise publicly exploited.[193] This general rule is subject to special provisions applying to works of unknown authorship[194]; computer-generated works[195]; and works the copyright in which belongs to the Crown,[196] to the Houses of Parliament,[197] or to certain international organisations.[198] These provisions apply to all photographs, irrespective of whether they involve the author's own intellectual creation.[199]

6–48 **Works of unknown authorship: "orphan works".** The right of an author to preserve his anonymity in relation to his work, without thereby forfeiting copyright protection for the work, is recognised under the Berne Convention.[200] This creates a practical difficulty in applying the normal rule as to term, being fixed as it is by reference to the date of death of the author. The 1988 Act provides a distinct regime for determining the term of protection of anonymous and pseudonymous works, at the same time providing that acts which would otherwise infringe the copyright in such works are in certain circumstances permitted.[201] Such works coming into existence after commencement of the Duration Regulations[202] enjoy a period of copyright protection lasting for 70 years from the end of

---

[190] As amended by the Duration Regulations (SI 1995/3297) which came into force January 1, 1996: reg.1(2).

[191] For the purposes of the Regulations, "commencement" means January 1, 1996: reg.12(1). The new provisions as to term apply to such works by virtue of reg.16(a).

[192] CDPA 1988 s.12(8), and see generally paras 4–32 et seq., above. Note that the European Commission has published a proposal for a Directive to amend the present Term Directive 2000/116/EC to provide, inter alia, for a uniform means of calculating the term of protection applying to a musical composition with words, which contains the contributions of several authors, within the EU. Such a composition would be treated as if it were a work of joint authorship, whether or not this composition with words would qualify otherwise as a work of joint authorship. For details of the proposal, see para.25–90, below.

[193] This was the position under the CDPA 1988 before amendment. Under the 1956 Act, the period was different depending on whether on not publication or other public exploitation had taken place before the author's death; see para.6–38, above, and para.6–53, below.

[194] CDPA 1988 s.12(3); and see para.6–48, below.

[195] CDPA 1988 s.12(7) and see para.6–49, below.

[196] CDPA 1988 s.12(9) and see para.10–01, below.

[197] CDPA 1988 s.12(9) and see para.10–64, below.

[198] CDPA 1988 s.12(9) and see para.3–282, above.

[199] As was the case under the 1988 Act before amendment. The United Kingdom has never made a distinction as regards the term of protection between photographs involving the author's intellectual creation and others, such as news photographs. Such a distinction was permissible under the Berne Convention (Paris Act 1971 art.7(4)) and remained permissible under the Term Directive art.6. See, for a discussion of the history of protection of photographs under the Berne Convention, S. Ricketson and J.C. Ginsburg, *International Copyright and Neighbouring Rights, The Berne Convention and Beyond* 2nd edn (Oxford: Oxford University Press, 2006), para.8.48 et seq.

[200] See now art.7(3) and also art.15 (Paris Act 1971).

[201] See CDPA 1988 s.57, and para.9–170, below.

[202] January 1, 1996; see regs 12(1), 1(2).

the year in which the work was made,[203] unless within that period the work has been made available to the public, in which case the period lasts for 70 years from the end of the year in which it was first made available to the public.[204]

A work is of unknown authorship if it is not possible for a person to ascertain the identity of the author by reasonable inquiry.[205] Once the identity of an author is known, it shall not subsequently be treated as unknown.[206] If the identity of the author becomes known before the end of the 70-year period from the end of the year in which the work was made, or in which it was first made available to the public, as the case may be, then the term of protection for such work becomes subject to the normal rule, that is 70 years from the end of the year in which the author died.[207] In the case of a work of joint authorship, it is only to be treated as a work of unknown authorship if all the authors are unknown; if the identity of any one or more authors is known, then the term is determined by applying the normal rule under s.12(2) of the 1988 Act to that author or authors.[208]

The phrase "first made available to the public" clearly covers publication, that is the issue of copies to the public,[209] but is wider in that it also includes public performance of a literary, dramatic or musical work, public exhibition of an artistic work or of a film in which it is included, and the communication to the public of any such work, provided in each case that no account is taken of any unauthorised act.[210] The definition of the term "first made available to the public" is specific to s.12.[211] The provision is silent as to whether it is sufficient that a substantial part of the work should have been made available to the public through such means, rather than the work in its entirety, in order for the extended term to apply. In the context of infringement, that is the doing without the necessary licence of an act which is restricted by the copyright,[212] it is sufficient for the act to be done in relation to a substantial part of the work, rather than as to its

---

[203] CDPA 1988 s.12(3)(a); prior to the amendment of s.12, the equivalent provision in s.12(2) referred not to the making of the work, but to when it was first made available to the public, thus effectively giving such a work which was never made available to the public a perpetual copyright. This provision, together with s.57(1), before it was amended by the Duration Regulations (which permitted acts in respect of anonymous and pseudonymous works on the assumption as to the expiry of copyright), was in accordance with art.7(4) of Berne (Paris Act 1971). The change was required in order to bring the position into line with art.1(4) of the Term Directive. See further as to existing anonymous and pseudonymous works, para.6–53, below.

[204] CDPA 1988 s.12(3)(b).

[205] Note that the Gowers Review of Intellectual Property, HM Treasury, November 2006, proposed that the European Commission should amend Directive 2001/29/EC (the Information Society Directive) to introduce an exception to copyright to permit the use of a genuine "orphan work", provided that the user has performed a reasonable search and, where possible, gives attribution. Gowers also recommended that UKIPO should issue clear guidance on the parameters of a "reasonable search" for orphan works, in consultation with rights holders, collecting societies, rights owners and archives, when an orphan works exception comes into being.

[206] CDPA 1988 s.9(5).

[207] CDPA 1988 s.12(4). This provision does not repeat the express provision in s.12(2) as originally enacted that this shall not apply if the identity of the author becomes known after the end of that period, but this is clearly implicit from the wording of s.12(2); it was not expressed in the equivalent provision in the 1956 Act (see Copyright Act 1956 Sch.2 para.2) but was considered implicit., and see *Hansard*, H.L. Vol.493, cols 1083, 1084.

[208] CDPA 1988 s.9(4) and s.12(8)(a)(ii) and (b).

[209] As to what is publication of such works, see paras 3–132 et seq., above. That availability to the public was intended to include, but be wider than, publication was confirmed in the debate on this provision: *Hansard*, H.L. Vol.490, col.1158; H.C. SCE, cols 116–120.

[210] CDPA 1988 s.12(5). "Communication to the public" has a defined meaning for these purposes, namely the communication to the public of the work by electronic transmission, which includes (a) the broadcasting of the work and (b) the making available to the public of the work by electronic transmission in such a way that members of the public may access it from a place and at a time individually chosen by them (i.e. by way of an on-demand service). See s.20(2). For a full discussion of the term, see paras 7–112 et seq., below. For the meaning of unauthorised, see CDPA 1988 s.178.

[211] CDPA 1988 s.12(5).

[212] i.e. under CDPA 1988 s.16; and see paras 7–25 et seq., below.

entirety.[213] The acts referred to as constituting making the work available to the public are all acts which are in themselves restricted by the copyright in such works, and it might be argued therefore that the opening words of s.16(3)[214] apply to such acts in the context of s.12. However, it is thought that the better view is that the provision contained in s.16(3) is specific to the context of infringement, where it is understandable that it should be enough to do the restricted act in relation to a substantial part of the work. The context of s.12 is more similar to the context of publication for the purposes of subsistence of copyright, rather than for the purposes of infringement. As was the position under the 1956 Act in relation to publication,[215] there is no reason of policy why the statutory "substantial part" test should apply in the context of determining whether the work is entitled to the extended period of protection. Nevertheless, if, as it is suggested is correct, the substantial part test does not apply, there clearly must be some degree to which the work as performed, or broadcast, etc., is not in every respect required to be identical to the whole work, or else a performance would rarely constitute making the work available. It is suggested that the test is whether in substance the whole work has been made available to the public. If the work performed or broadcast, etc. is different in material respects from the whole work, then the latter work has not been made available by this means to the public. At most, a different, lesser work, has been made available to the public.[216]

6–49   **Computer-generated works.** Computer-generated literary, dramatic, musical and artistic works, that is works generated by a computer in circumstances such that there is no human author of the work,[217] are subject to a special rule, reflecting the fact that they do not have a human author,[218] and are entitled only to a fixed period of 50 years from the end of the year in which the work was made.[219]

6–50   **Works of non-EEA origin.** Where the country of origin of the work is not an EEA state[220] and the author of the work is not a national of an EEA state,[221] the new provisions require the application of the principle of comparison of terms, in that the term of protection for such work is that to which it is entitled in the country of origin of the work, provided that such term does not exceed the standard period for such works or the period applicable to works of unknown authorship under s. 12, as may be appropriate.[222]

B. Works made before January 1, 1996

6–51   **General position.** The new provisions of the 1988 Act apply to literary, musical,

---

[213] CDPA 1988 s.16(3)(a).

[214] "References in this Part to the doing of an act restricted by the copyright in a work ...".

[215] See the Copyright Act 1956 s.49(1) proviso and s.49(2), the effect of which was to exclude the application of the substantial part test in the context of publication.

[216] Since in such a case the alteration to the work has been authorised (or else the question does not arise), it may therefore be that this other work is the work which enjoys the extended period of protection, while the work as a whole does not, although this presents difficult conceptual problems.

[217] CDPA 1988 s.178.

[218] That is, as the work's creator in the sense meant by s.9(1) of the 1988 Act. Such a work may nevertheless be treated as having a human author by reason of s.9(3) of the 1988 Act, where such person undertakes the arrangements necessary for the creation of the work; see generally as to authorship of computer-generated works, para.4–13, above.

[219] CDPA 1988 s.12(7), to the same effect as s.12(3) as originally enacted.

[220] As to which see para.6–19, above.

[221] As to which see para.6–20, above.

[222] CDPA 1988 s.12(6);

dramatic and artistic works made before January 1, 1996[223] and which first qualify for copyright protection after that date[224] or in which copyright subsisted immediately before that date,[225] irrespective of whether the work was made before August 1, 1989. These existing works (other than computer-generated works[226]) therefore benefit from the extended term of protection lasting until the end of the period of 70 years from the end of the calendar year in which the author died. In the case of existing copyright works, the application of the new provisions is subject to the important qualification that if the period of protection for a work under the 1988 Act before its amendment by the Duration Regulations would have been longer, then that period continues to apply to the work.[227] Thus, in respect of such works, it remains necessary to consider the rules for the duration of the term of protection both under the Act as amended and as originally enacted, in order to determine which provides the longer term.

General position under the 1988 Act (before amendment). The general approach of the 1988 Act to works existing at August 1, 1989[228] was to apply its provisions to such works as they apply in relation to works coming into existence after that date, subject to any express provision to the contrary.[229]   **6–52**

It was the general policy of the 1988 Act to abolish the possibility for perpetual copyright, previously enjoyed by certain works. Where the 1988 Act achieved this, it substituted a fixed term of 50 years commencing on January 1, 1990.

In accordance with this policy,[230] the 1988 Act abolished the perpetual copyrights which were enjoyed by universities and colleges, originally under the Copyright Act 1775,[231] in respect of certain works, providing that such rights shall continue to subsist until December 31, 2039 and will then expire.[232] Given the nature of these works, this remains the position under the 1988 Act as amended.

The 1988 Act also abolished,[233] with exceptions, the perpetual copyright previously possible for unpublished literary, dramatic, musical works and engravings and photographs,[234] and transitional provisions, found in para.12 of Sch.1 to the 1988 Act, apply this rule to works existing at August 1, 1989. However, the new provisions now apply to such works, and in relation to existing works of unknown authorship,[235] posthumously published existing works[236] and photographs,[237] it is necessary to consider the effect of these transitional provisions in the light of the amendment of the 1988 Act.

---

[223] The commencement date for the Duration Regulations (SI 1995/3297); see para.6–14, above.

[224] Duration Regulations, reg.16 (b); see generally para.6–15, above.

[225] Defined as existing copyright works: reg.16(c); this means works in which copyright subsisted from January 1, 1995 to December 31, 1995, and includes those works in which, apart from the effect of the Duration Regulations, copyright would have expired at midnight on December 31, 1995; see para.6–16, above.

[226] Which remain entitled to a fixed term of 50 years from the end of the year in which they were made; see para.6–24, above.

[227] reg.16(c) and reg.15(1); see para.6–16, above.

[228] The date of commencement of the 1988 Act.

[229] CDPA 1988 Sch.1 para.3. See, generally, paras 6–44 to 6–46, above.

[230] And following the recommendation of the 1977 Copyright Committee, Cmnd.6732, para.656(iii).

[231] 15 Geo. 3, c.53; and see further paras 6–84 et seq., below.

[232] CDPA 1988 Sch.1 para.13.

[233] Following the recommendation of the 1977 Copyright Committee, Cmnd.6732, para.656.

[234] Copyright Act 1956 ss.2(3) and 3(4) (works posthumously published) and Sch.2 para.2 (works of unknown authorship).

[235] See para.6–53, below.

[236] See paras 6–54 and 6–55, below.

[237] See para.6–56, below.

On the other hand, the 1988 Act introduced a new exception[238] in relation to the play *Peter Pan* by Sir James Barrie, the copyright in which expired on December 31, 1987, by giving to the trustees of The Hospital for Sick Children, Great Ormond Street, London a perpetual right to receive a royalty in respect of the public performance and certain other forms of exploitation[239] of such work, so long as the Hospital continues to have a separate identity and have purposes which include the care of sick children.[240] Whilst these provisions remain unaffected by the amendments made to the 1988 Act by the Duration Regulations, the play itself is a work which benefits from a revived copyright under the new provisions, which will expire on December 31, 2007. During the period of revived copyright, therefore, the trustees will benefit from the more extensive rights available to the copyright owner under s.16 of the 1988 Act,[241] rather than the limited right granted under Sch.6.

6–53   **Existing literary, dramatic, musical and artistic works (except photographs) of unknown authorship.** The amended provisions relating to literary, dramatic, musical and artistic works of unknown authorship apply to existing anonymous and pseudonymous works.[242] However, the new provisions are different, in setting the initial period of copyright protection by reference to a period calculated from the end of the year in which the work was made.[243] The previous provisions referred to a period calculated from the end of the year in which the work was first made available to the public by being published or otherwise publicly exploited,[244] thus providing an unlimited period of protection for such works until they became publicly exploited.

However, under the transitional provisions of the 1988 Act,[245] such literary, dramatic, musical and artistic works (except photographs) of unknown authorship made before August 1, 1989, and which had been published[246] before August 1, 1989 continued to enjoy the period of protection that they would have enjoyed under the 1956 Act, that is for a period of 50 years from the end of the year in which the work was first published.[247] In the case of such works, therefore, the term will be calculated under the new provisions, as the longer period of 70 years from the end of the year in which they were first published.

The potentially unlimited period of protection for such works made before August 1, 1989 and not published before that date was taken away by the transitional provisions of the 1988 Act.[248] In its place, such works were given a fixed period of 50 years from January 1, 1990, unless made available to the public within that period, when the term would continue for a period of 50 years from the end of the year in which that occurred. In the case of such works made before January 1, 1970, therefore, the initial term will be 50 years from January

---

[238] CDPA 1988 s.301 and Sch.6.

[239] i.e. commercial publication or communication to the public: CDPA 1988 Sch.6 para.2(1).

[240] CDPA 1988 Sch.6 para.7(2).

[241] But subject to the general limitations applicable to all revived copyrights; see para.6–17, above.

[242] See para.6–48, above, but see para.6–56, below, as to photographs.

[243] CDPA 1988 s.12(3)(a) (as amended); this change was required in order to implement art.1(3) of the Term Directive 93/98.

[244] CDPA 1988 s.12(2) (as originally enacted); as to what constitutes being made available to the public, see para.6–48, above.

[245] CDPA 1988 Sch.1 para.12(3); as to existing photographs of unknown authorship, see para.6–56, below.

[246] That is the previous narrower criterion, not the new wider criterion of being made available to the public.

[247] Copyright Act 1956 Sch.2 para.2.

[248] CDPA 1988 Sch.2 para.12(3)(b), as amended by the Copyright and Related Rights Regulations 2003 (SI 2003/2498) to correct the errors made on the original implementation of the Term Directive.

1, 1990, this being longer than 70 years from the end of the year in which they were made. In the case of such works made on or after January 1, 1970, the new provisions will provide the longer initial term of 70 years from the end of the year in which they were made. In each case, the initial term will be extended if the work is made available to the public within the initial term, but in the case of a work governed by the old provisions, for a further period of 50 years, and in the case of a work governed by the new provisions, for a further period of 70 years.

In the case of works of unknown authorship made on or after August 1, 1989 and before January 1, 1996, the possibility of an unlimited initial term of copyright remains.[249] In respect of such works, therefore, it will be necessary to wait and see whether the new or the old provisions will provide the longer term. This will depend on whether the work is made available to the public within the period of 70 years from the end of the year in which it was made; if it is, then the new provisions will provide the longer term, (because the second period will be a further 70, not 50 years), but if it is not, then the old provisions will inevitably provide the longer term.

Posthumously published existing literary, dramatic and musical works. In   **6–54**
the case of works of a known author made after August 1, 1989, the date of publication of such works is not relevant to the term of their protection and neither, therefore, is any distinction made between such works published during the life of their author and those published posthumously. However, a distinction was made under the 1956 Act, and literary, dramatic and musical works which at the author's death had not been published, performed in public, offered for sale to the public on records, broadcast or included in a cable programme, continued to enjoy copyright protection until the end of the period of 50 years from the end of the calendar year in which they were first published or otherwise publicly exploited in any of those ways.[250] This distinction is maintained by the transitional provisions of the 1988 Act in relation to works made before August 1, 1989. Where such works had been publicly exploited in this manner before August 1, 1989, and the 50-year period had begun to run, the 1988 Act maintained that period as the term of protection for such works.[251] The new provisions accord such works the standard period of 70 years pma. The term for such works will therefore now depend on whether they were first publicly exploited within 20 years of the author's death, in which case the new provisions will provide the longer term, but if not, then the old provisions will provide the longer term.

Where such works had not been publicly exploited before August 1, 1989, the 1988 Act substituted a fixed term of protection for such works, of 50 years from January 1, 1990.[252] In respect of such works, therefore, the term will depend on whether the author died on or after January 1, 1969. If he did, then the new provisions will provide the longer term of 70 years pma, but if he died before that date, then the old provisions will apply, as providing the longer term.

The discussion above would appear to apply equally to such works made before June 1, 1957 as made after that date, as the 1956 Act contained no relevant transitional provisions.[253]

Posthumously published existing engravings. The provisions relating to   **6–55**

---

[249] This is difficult to understand, in the light of the removal of the possibility of unlimited protection for such works made before August 1, 1989.
[250] Copyright Act 1956, proviso to s.2(3); this included doing such acts in relation to an adaptation of the work: ibid., s.2(4).
[251] CDPA 1988 Sch.1 para.12(2)(a).
[252] CDPA 1988 Sch.1 para.12(4)(a).
[253] These provisions were substantially to the same effect as s.17(1) of the Copyright Act 1911, save

posthumously published works in the 1956 Act did not apply in general to artistic works, but similar provisions applied to engravings.[254] Engravings which at the author's death had not been published continued to enjoy copyright protection until the end of the period of 50 years from the end of the calendar year in which they were first published.[255] These provisions were maintained in relation to engravings made before August 1, 1989 by the transitional provisions of the 1988 Act. In the case of such engravings which had been published before August 1, 1989, and in respect of which the 50-year period had begun to run, the 1988 Act maintained that period as the term of protection for such works.[256] The new provisions accord such works the standard period of 70 years pma. The term for such works will therefore now depend on whether they were first publicly exploited within 20 years of the author's death, in which case the new provisions will provide the longer term, but if not, then the old provisions will provide the longer term.

Where such engravings had not been published before August 1, 1989, the 1988 Act substituted a fixed term of protection for such works, of 50 years from January 1, 1990.[257] In respect of such engravings, therefore, the term will depend on whether the author died on or after January 1, 1970. If he did, then the new provisions will provide the longer term of 70 years pma, but if he died before that date, then the old provisions will apply, as providing the longer term.

The discussion above would appear to apply equally to such engravings made before June 1, 1957 as made after that date, as the 1956 Act again contained no relevant transitional provisions.[258]

6–56   **Existing photographs.** As indicated above,[259] photographs taken on or after August 1, 1989 became assimilated to other artistic works, enjoying a term of protection calculated from the death of the author.[260] Under the 1988 Act as originally enacted, this was a period of 50 years from the end of the calendar year in which the author dies.[261] Under the new provisions, that term is increased to a period of 70 years from the end of the calendar year in which the author dies.[262]

Under the 1956 Act, photographs had enjoyed indefinite protection while they remained unpublished, and once published enjoyed a period of protection of 50 years from the end of the year in which publication occurred,[263] and, accordingly, the question of whether the identity of the author was known or not did not arise. The transitional provisions of the 1988 Act maintain this distinction in relation to photographs made before August 1, 1989, and whether the identity of their author is known or not does not affect their term.[264]

In the case of photographs taken on or after June 1, 1957 (whether or not of unknown authorship) and which had been published before August 1, 1989, and in respect of which the 50-year period had therefore begun to run, the 1988 Act

---

that the issue of records of a work may not have constituted publication of the work under that Act.

[254] See para.6–38, above.

[255] Copyright Act 1956 s.3(4), proviso, sub-para.(a).

[256] CDPA 1988 Sch.1 para.12(2)(b).

[257] CDPA 1988 Sch.1 para.12(4)(b).

[258] See also paras 6–39 et seq., above.

[259] See para.6–45, above.

[260] Following the recommendation of the 1977 Copyright Committee, Cmnd.6732, para.656. The general provisions as to works of unknown authorship contained in s.12(2) (as unamended) therefore became applicable to photographs.

[261] CDPA 1988 s.12(1) (before amendment).

[262] See para.6–47, above. The new provisions as to works of unknown authorship contained in s.12(3) apply to photographs.

[263] Copyright Act 1956 s.3(4), proviso, sub-para.(b).

[264] CDPA 1988 Sch.1 para.12(3).

retained that period as the term of protection for such works.[265] The new provisions accord such photographs the standard period of 70 years pma, and apply the general provisions as to works of unknown authorship. Which provision will provide for the longer term will depend on the respective dates of publication and of the author's death. For example, in the case of a photograph taken in 1960, and whose author dies in 1961, and which is published in 1980, the old provisions provide a term which expires on December 31, 2030 (end of 50 years after the end of the calendar year in which publication took place), and the new provisions provide a term which expires on December 31, 2031 (end of 70 years from the end of the year in which the author died, assuming his identity is known). The new provisions will therefore apply to such photographs.

In the case of photographs taken on or after June 1, 1957 but which remained unpublished at August 1, 1989, the 1988 Act removed the indefinite protection and substituted a fixed period of 50 years from January 1, 1990.[266] The new provisions accord such photographs the standard term of 70 years after the end of the year in which the author dies. As regards such photographs, therefore, unless the author died before January 1, 1969, the new provisions will provide the longer term.

As regards photographs taken before June 1, 1957, these were accorded a fixed term of protection of 50 years from the end of the year in which they were taken.[267] This term was retained in respect of such photographs under the 1988 Act and applied whether the photograph had been published or not.[268] The new provisions of the 1988 Act accord such photographs the standard period of 70 years pma. As regards such photographs, therefore, whether the new provisions or the old provisions as to term will apply to them, will depend on the respective dates of when the photograph was taken and of the author's death. For example, a photograph taken in 1955 and whose author died in 1995 would have a term of protection expiring on December 31, 2005 under the old provisions, and on December 31, 2065 under the new provisions, which would therefore apply to such a photograph to accord it a considerable period of extended copyright.[269]

As has been explained above, when the 1988 Act introduced the change, in respect of photographs, from a fixed term of protection to a term of 50 years pma, the new term did not apply to photographs which had been taken before August 1, 1989. The amendment of the 1988 Act, as indicated above, is not so restricted, with the effect that the new term of 70 years pma will become applicable to many photographs which had already fallen into the public domain in the United Kingdom. For example, in the case of a photograph taken in 1918 by an author who died in 1990, such photograph would have had a term of protection under the 1956 Act expiring on December 31, 1968. The photograph would have remained in the public domain in the United Kingdom after August 1, 1989, notwithstanding that its author was still alive. However, on January 1, 1996, such a photograph became entitled to revived copyright in the United Kingdom, (as-

---

[265] CDPA 1988 para.12(2)(c); the purpose of the transitional provisions being to maintain the shorter period of protection in force when the photograph was taken.

[266] CDPA 1988 Sch.1 para.12(4)(c).

[267] Copyright Act 1956 Sch.7 para.2. This in substance maintained the period of protection accorded to such photographs under the Copyright Act 1911 s.21 (50 years from the making of the original negative from which the photograph was directly or indirectly derived); see para.6–40, above.

[268] CDPA 1988 Sch.1 para.12(2)(c).

[269] As to which see para.6–16, above.

suming that it remained in copyright in at least one EEA state[270] on July 1, 1995)[271] expiring on December 31, 2060.[272]

6. SOUND RECORDINGS

6–57 **Introduction.** The position of sound recordings has been complicated by a number of factors. First, as enacted, the 1988 Act dealt with films and sound recordings together, but separate treatment was then required in order to implement the Term Directive. Second, the Information Society Directive[273] made minor changes to the treatment of phonograms in the Term Directive in order to give effect to the 1996 WIPO Phonograms and Performances Treaty. This is turn required minor changes to be made to the 1988 Act, and at the same time provisions had to be made to deal with the possibile extension of copyright in sound recordings which resulted.[274]

A. SOUND RECORDINGS MADE ON OR AFTER JANUARY 1, 1996

6–58 **General position.** In relation to a sound recording made after commencement of the Duration Regulations,[275] copyright expires at the end of the period of 50 years from the end of the calendar year in which it was made,[276] or, if published before the end of that period, 50 years from the end of the calendar year in which it was published,[277] or that if during that period the recording is not published but is made available to the public by being played in public or communicated to the public,[278] 50 years from the end of the calendar year in which it was first so made available.[279] In determining whether a sound recording has been published, played in public or communicated to the public, no account is to be taken of any unauthorised act.[280]

6–59 **History of amendments.** Before amendment of the 1988 Act to implement the Information Society Directive,[281] copyright in a sound recording was to expire at the end of the period of 50 years from the end of the calendar year in which it was made,[282] or, if released before the end of that period, 50 years from the end of the calendar year in which it was released. These provisions reproduced the previous provisions in the 1988 Act as originally enacted,[283] save that they only applied to sound recordings (films being treated similarly to other works covered by the Berne Convention and being given their own separate rules as to duration[284]) and were made subject to the new provisions relating to works which are not of EEA

---

[270] See para.6–20, above.
[271] By reg.16(d) of the Duration Regulations (SI 1995/3297).
[272] As to the limitations of revived copyright, see para.6–17, above.
[273] Directive 2001/29 of the European Parliament and of the Council of May 22, 2001 on the harmonisation of certain aspects of copyright and related rights in the information society.
[274] See paras 6–59 et seq., below.
[275] January 1, 1996; reg.12(1).
[276] CDPA 1988 s.13A(2)(a).
[277] CDPA 1988 s.13A(2)(b). As to the meaning of published, see CDPA 1988 s.175.
[278] As to the meaning of this expression, see paras 7–112 et seq., below.
[279] CDPA 1988 s.13A(2)(c).
[280] CDPA 1988 s.13A(3).
[281] By the Copyright and Related Rights Regulations 2003 (SI 2003/2498) reg.29, with effect from October 31, 2003.
[282] CDPA 1988 s.13A(2)(a).
[283] CDPA 1988 s.13(1) (as originally enacted).
[284] s.13B and see para.6–70, below.

origin.[285] The concept of a "release" of a sound recording had been introduced by the 1988 Act in relation to sound recordings (and films), to define the acts of public exploitation upon which the sound recording (and film) became entitled to the further term of copyright. Following the amendment of the 1988 Act by the Duration Regulations, this concept remained, with some modification, applicable to sound recordings but not to films, which were given their own rules as to duration.[286] The amendment made on implementation of the Information Society Directive replaces the concept of release with the acts of publication, playing in public and communication to the public. Because this gives rise to the possibility of the term being extended, provision is made as to ownership of the extended term[287] and as to existing licences and agreements.[288] Similarly, because these amendments also give rise to the possibility of the term being otherwise shortened, it is expressly provided that copyright in an existing sound recording is to continue to subsist until the date it would have expired under the Duration Regulations 1995[289] if that date is later than the date on which copyright would expire under the Act as now amended.[290]

The possibility of the further term of protection being accorded to sound recordings from the date of their public exploitation had existed under the 1956 Act, but was triggered by publication, reflecting the similar position in relation to literary, dramatic, musical and artistic works. However, publication of a sound recording occurred only when records embodying the sound recording were issued to the public, and did not occur when the sound recording was played or shown in public, or was broadcast or included in a cable programme service.[291] Before amendment to implement the Information Society Directive, that was still the position as regards publication.[292] The concept of release introduced by the 1988 Act included, but was wider than, publication and under the provision before its amendment, a sound recording or film was released not only when it was first published, but also when it was broadcast or included in a cable programme service or, in the case of a film or film soundtrack, when the film was first shown in public,[293] provided that in each case no account was to be taken of any unauthorised act.[294] The substituted provision which defined, with effect from January 1, 1996, what constituted release of a sound recording repeated the previous provision, but in addition included the act of playing the sound recording in public, an act which had not previously caused the sound recording to be released. As already seen, the Act as it now stands contemplates the further period of protection arising once a sound recording is either published, played in public or communicated to the public.[295]

Limit imposed on term. The second difference introduced by the 1988 Act was that, whilst under the 1956 Act copyright in unpublished sound recordings (and films) continued without limit in time until they were first published, and then   **6–60**

---

[285] CDPA 1988 s.13A(4) and (5) and see para.6–62, below.
[286] See paras 6–70 et seq., above.
[287] By the Copyright and Related Rights Regulations 2003 (SI 2003/2498) regs 36, 37. See para.5–147, above.
[288] reg.38. See paras 5–148 et seq., above.
[289] i.e. under reg.15.
[290] Copyright and Related Rights Regulations 2003 (SI 2003/2498) reg.39.
[291] Copyright Act 1956 s.12(9); the same position applied in relation to films: s.13(10).
[292] CDPA 1988 s.175(4)(c).
[293] CDPA 1988 s.13(2).
[294] CDPA 1988 s.13(2); for the full meaning of unauthorised, see s.178.
[295] The concept of a sound recording being included in a cable programme service has now been assimilated into the single act of communication to the public. See paras 7–112 et seq., below, as to the meaning of this.

expired at the end of 50 years from first publication,[296] the 1988 Act set a limit on the term for unreleased sound recordings of 50 years from the end of the calendar year in which they were made.[297] This remains the position. It is only if a sound recording is published, played in public or communicated to the public within such period that it will then enjoy copyright protection for a further period of 50 years from the end of the calendar year in which such act occurs.[298] The maximum possible period of copyright protection for a new sound recording or film is therefore 101 years.[299]

6–61   **Proposals for reform.** The fact that many famous sound recordings were falling into the public domain led to calls from the recording industry and performers to prolong the period of protection afforded to them to 70 years or more. In May 2007, support for an increase in the term of protection to at least 70 years came from the House of Commons Culture, Media and Sport Committee in its report entitled "New Media and the Creative Industries".[300] However, the Gowers Review of Intellectual Property of December 2006 recommended against requesting the European Union to consider such an extension (Recommendation 3) and the Department of Culture, Media and Sport announced on July 27, 2007, that it would not support extending the term of protection of either producers of sound recordings or performers. Meanwhile, however, on July 16, 2008, the European Commission published a proposal for a Directive amending the present term Directive 2000/116/EC to extend the term of copyright protection for producers of sound recordings from 50 to 95 years. The extension will apply to phonograms whose initial term of protection of 50 years has not expired at the date of adoption of the proposed Directive. For details of the proposals, which provide also for the same increase in the term of protection for performers with respect to their performances fixed in phonograms, see paras 12–38 and 24–90, below. Meanwhile, in January 2009, the European Economic and Social Committee (ECOSOC) adopted an opinion on the proposal, recommending inter alia an extension of protection for fixations of performances from 50 to 85 years.[301] Subsequently, in April 2009, the European Parliament approved a text which sets the term at 70 years.[302] The matter is still pending before the Council of the European Union.[303]

6–62   **Works of non-EEA origin.** Where the author of a sound recording[304] is not a

---

[296] Copyright Act 1956 ss.12(1) and (3), and 13(1) and (3) (although a limit of 50 years after registration was set in respect of films required to be registered under certain enactments: s.13(3)(a), as amended by the Films Act 1985 (c.21) s.7(2)).

[297] See now, CDPA 1988 s.13A(2)(a). This changed followed the recommendation of the 1977 Copyright Committee, Cmnd.6732 para.656(ii).

[298] CDPA 1988 ss.13A(2)(b), (c).

[299] CDPA 1988 ss.13A(2)(b), (c). Taking the extreme example of a sound recording made on January 1 in one year and not, for example, published until some time in the 51st year after that; for example: made January 1, 1996, published December 31, 2046, copyright expires December 31, 2096.

[300] Fifth Report of Session 2006–2007, HC 509–1, dated May 1, 2007, Recommendation 28.

[301] Opinion of the European Economic and Social Committee on the "Proposal for a European Parliament and Council Directive amending Directive 2006/116/EC of the European Parliament and of the Council on the term of protection of copyright and related rights, September 4, 2008 (COM (2008) 464 final—2008/0157 (COD) OJ 2009/C 182/07).

[302] European Parliament legislative resolution of April 23, 2009, on the proposal for a directive of the European Parliament and of the Council amending Directive 2006/116/EC of the European Parliament and of the Council on the term of protection of copyright and related rights (P6 TA(2009)0282). See also Commission press release IP/09/627 of April 23, 2009.

[303] See, further, para.24–90. For a critical response to the proposal, see the statement of the Max Planck Institute for Intellectual Property, Competition and Tax Law [2008] I.I.C. 586.

[304] As to who is the author of a sound recording, see para.4–41, above.

national of an EEA state,[305] the Act as amended requires the application of the principle of comparison of terms, in that the term of protection for such a work is that to which it is entitled in the country of which the author is a national, provided that such term does not exceed the standard period for such works under s.13A.[306] This rule is subject to exception, to the extent that it would place the United Kingdom in breach of an international obligation assumed before October 29, 1993,[307] in which case the standard rule applies.[308] In the present context, this is effectively a reference to the United Kingdom's obligations under the Rome Convention,[309] under which the United Kingdom is obliged to accord national treatment to the sound recordings produced by nationals of, or first published in, other Contracting States.[310] In relation to such sound recordings, therefore, the United Kingdom will continue to accord them the standard term under s.13A(2), through the inclusion of such Contracting States in Orders in Council made under s.159 of the Act.[311]

Film soundtracks. Under the 1956 Act, a film soundtrack was treated as part of the film and not as a sound recording.[312] This was reversed by the 1988 Act as originally enacted.[313] The effect of the Duration Regulations was to restore the position to that which existed under the 1956 Act, and a soundtrack accompanying a film is to be treated as part of the film for the purposes of Pt I of the Act.[314] The amended provisions applying to films therefore apply to film soundtracks.[315]   **6–63**

B. SOUND RECORDINGS MADE BEFORE JANUARY 1, 1996

General position. The provisions of the 1988 Act following amendment by the Duration Regulations applied to sound recordings made before January 1, 1996[316] and which first qualified for copyright protection after that date[317] or in which copyright subsisted immediately before that date,[318] irrespective of whether the sound recording was made before August 1, 1989. The amended provisions introduced no change in the duration of the standard term of protection for sound recordings, but amended the concept of release to include playing the record in public.[319] This amendment in the Act to the concept of release was not stated to be applicable only prospectively, and the deliberate general retrospective ap-   **6–64**

---

[305] As to which see paras 6–20 and 6–21, above.

[306] CDPA 1988 s.13A(4).

[307] That is the date the original Term Directive 93/98/EC was adopted.

[308] CDPA 1988 s.13A(5).

[309] International Convention for the Protection of Performers, Producers of Phonograms and Broadcasting Organisations, signed at Rome, October 26, 1961, ratified by the United Kingdom on October 30, 1963.

[310] art.5.

[311] See further para.3–202, above.

[312] See para.3–78, above. The 1956 Act reversed the previous position, under which film soundtracks were treated as recordings: 1911 Act s.19(1).

[313] CDPA 1988 s.5(1); and see para.3–78, above.

[314] CDPA 1988 s.5B(2); as to the problems to which this gives rise, see P. Kamina, "The Protection of Film Soundtracks under British Copyright after the Copyright Regulations 1995 and 1996" [1998] Ent. L.R. 153.

[315] See further para.6–72, below.

[316] The commencement date for the Duration Regulations reg.1(2).

[317] Duration Regulations reg.16(b); see generally para.6–15, above.

[318] Duration Regulations reg.16(c); this means works in which copyright subsisted from January 1, 1995 to December 31, 1995, and includes those works in which, apart from the effect of the Duration Regulations, copyright would have expired at midnight on December 31, 1995; see para.6–16, above.

[319] CDPA 1988 s.13A(3), now repealed (see below); and see para.6–59, above.

plication of the new provisions[320] would suggest that the amended concept applied to events taking place before January 1, 1966. This was subject to the overriding principle that such application was not to result in a shorter term of protection being applicable to an existing sound recording in which copyright subsisted immediately before January 1, 1996.[321] The same applies following the further amendment to replace the concept of release with the acts of publication, playing in public and communication to the public.[322] Thus, in respect of such works, it remains necessary to consider the rules for the duration of the term of protection both under the Act as amended and as originally enacted, in order to determine which provides the longer term.

6–65   **Sound recordings made on or after August 1, 1989 and before January 1, 1996.** A sound recording made between such dates and which has been played in public or communicated to the public before January 1, 1996, but has not otherwise been published, broadcast or included in a cable programme service, will therefore now be treated as released on the date on which such act took place, with the consequence that the 50-year term will run from the end of the calendar year in which the act took place.[323] However, the retrospective effect of the amended provisions cannot result in a shorter term of protection than would otherwise have applied under the 1988 Act before its amendment.[324]

6–66   **Sound recordings made on or after June 1, 1957 and before August 1, 1989.** These sound recordings are existing works for the purposes of the 1988 Act.[325] The general approach of the 1988 Act in treating existing works in the same way as new works[326] is modified by the transitional provisions of the Act,[327] which preserve in relation to such works the former distinction based on publication,[328] so that under the 1988 Act as originally enacted the wider concept of release did not therefore apply to such works.

6–67   **Existing published sound recordings.** Thus, the term of copyright for a sound recording made on or after June 1, 1957 and before August 1, 1989 and which was published[329] before August 1, 1989 continues until the date on which it would have expired under the 1956 Act;[330] that is until the end of 50 years from the end of the calendar year in which it was so published.[331] Whether the term of protection for such a sound recording is shorter under the new provisions, therefore, will depend on whether any acts are done in relation to the sound recording which amount to its playing in public or communication to the public before the sound recording was published. If so, then the old provisions may provide the longer term, depending on the respective dates of making of the sound recording and its eventual publication. If, as will often be the case, broadcasting and playing of the sound recording in public take place at the same time as records of the sound recording are issued to the public, then there will be no distinction between the term under the new and old provisions. Nevertheless, there will be cases where

---

[320] reg.16(c).

[321] reg.16(c) and reg.15(1).

[322] Copyright and Related Rights Regulations 2003 reg.39. The possibility of the term being extended has also been noted, in para.6–59, above.

[323] CDPA 1988 s.13A(2)(b), (c).

[324] See para.6–64, above.

[325] CDPA 1988 Sch.1, para.1(3).

[326] CDPA 1988 Sch.1 para.3.

[327] Sch.1 para.12(2)(d) and para.12(5)(a).

[328] Copyright Act 1956 s.12(9).

[329] That is, in accordance with the definition in Copyright Act 1956 s.12(9).

[330] CDPA 1988 Sch.1 para.12(2)(d).

[331] See Copyright Act 1956 s.12(3).

the distinction is material. For example, in the case of a recording made in 1940 of a public performance which was then broadcast in 1940, but which was not published by the issue of records of the recording until 1988, the new provisions provide a term expiring on December 31, 1990, whilst the old provisions provide a term expiring on December 31, 2038, which is therefore the applicable term.

Existing unpublished sound recordings. Sound recordings made on or after **6–68** June 1, 1957 and before August 1, 1989, and which remained unpublished at that date,[332] were given a further period of protection of 50 years from January 1, 1990, regardless, therefore, of how long ago they were made.[333] At the end of that period the term of copyright expires, unless publication takes place during that period, when protection continues for a further period of 50 years after the calendar year in which publication took place.[334] Whether the term of protection for such a sound recording will be that under the new provisions or the old provisions will depend on whether the recording has been published, and, if so, the respective dates of the making of the recording and its being first published. Thus, in the case of a recording made in 1960 of a public performance but which has not to date been published or released, the copyright in that recording will expire under the old provisions on December 31, 2039, unless by then it has been published, in which case the copyright will expire 50 years after the end of the year in which it is published, and will expire under the new provisions on December 31, 2010, unless by then it has been played in public or communicated to the public, in which case copyright will expire 50 years after the end of the year it which such an act takes place. Unless such recording is published,[335] therefore, before December 31, 2010, the old provisions will be applicable providing the longer term. In the case of a recording which was made in 1960 of a public performance and which was broadcast later in 1960, but was not published by the issue of records of the recording until 1995, the new provisions provide a term expiring on December 31, 2010, whilst the old provisions provide a term expiring December 31, 2045, which is therefore the applicable term.

Sound recordings made before June 1, 1957. The 1988 Act as originally **6–69** enacted maintained, by its transitional provisions,[336] the term of protection accorded to such sound recordings under the 1956 Act,[337] which was the fixed period of 50 years from the end of the year in which the recording was made.[338] Thus, under the old provisions of the 1988 Act copyright in all sound recordings made before January 1, 1945 will have expired on December 31, 1994, at the latest, the period of protection not being affected or extended by any subsequent publication of the sound recording. The amended provisions will not apply to such a sound recording, since copyright did not subsist in it immediately before January 1, 1996.[339] This assumes that the sound recording was not still in copyright on July 1, 1995 in another EEA state.[340] On the other hand, the amended provisions will apply to a sound recording made on or after January 1, 1945 and

---

[332] The criterion remains that of publication, not release; see para.6–72, above.

[333] CDPA 1988 Sch.1 para.12(5)(a).

[334] CDPA 1988 Sch.1 para.12(5)(a).

[335] By the issue of copies to the public, not by any other act which constitutes release.

[336] CDPA 1988 Sch.1 para.12(2)(d).

[337] Copyright Act 1956 Sch.7 para.11. By ibid., para.13 the term of protection was maintained for works before July 1, 1912, provided they had enjoyed copyright under the 1911 Act, by virtue of s.19(8) of that Act. However, copyright in all such recordings expired under the 1956 Act by July 1, 1962, at the latest.

[338] This was the period that had been accorded such works under the Copyright Act 1911 s.19(1), save that it ran from the date of making of the recording.

[339] SI 1995/3297, reg.14(1)(b) and reg.16(c).

[340] Whilst no other EEA state has accorded sound recordings a greater term than 50 years, it is pos-

before June 1, 1957.[341] The term of protection for such a recording will inevitably be either the same or longer under the amended provisions, and this is so whether the recording has been published or not. In the case of such recordings which have been published, the difference between the term under the amended provisions and the old will be the greater the longer the interval between the making of the recording and its first being published. Thus, in the case of a sound recording made in 1945 and first published in 1995, copyright expires under the old provisions on December 31, 1995, but on December 31, 2045 under the amended provisions, which is therefore the applicable term. In the case of a sound recording made in 1957 (before June 1, 1957), and first published in 1995, copyright expired on December 31, 2007 under the old provisions and on December 31, 2045 under the amended provisions, which is therefore the applicable term. In the case of a sound recording made in 1957 (before June 1, 1957) and published in 1958, copyright expired on December 31, 2007 under the old provisions, and on December 31, 2008 under the amended provisions, which is still therefore the applicable term.

7. FILMS

A. FILMS MADE ON OR AFTER JANUARY 1, 1996

6–70 **General position.** The amended provisions introduced by the Duration Regulations brought about a major change in the period of protection accorded to films. Previously, films were treated in the United Kingdom as original works in accordance with art.14*bis*(1) of the Berne Convention, which provides that a cinematographic work shall be protected as an original work and that the owner of copyright in a cinematographic work shall enjoy the same rights as the author of an original work. The Berne Convention provides also that ownership of copyright in a cinematographic work shall be a matter for legislation in the country where protection is claimed.[342] The United Kingdom recognised the film producer as the author of the film and protected films for 50 years from the end of the year in which it was made,[343] thus affording films a regime of protection similar to that of phonograms. At the international level, however, films remain protected under the Berne Convention as cinematographic works, whereas phonograms are subject to the related rights regime of the Rome Convention. Under the amended provisions of the 1988 Act, films are now treated similarly to other authors' works so far as the term of protection is concerned.

In relation to a film made after January 1, 1996, therefore, the term of protection is to last until the end of 70 years from the end of the calendar year in which the last of a number of designated persons dies. The persons designated for this purpose are: the principal director, the author of the screenplay, the author of the dialogue and the composer of music specially created for and used in the film.[344] If there is no-one falling within this list of designated persons, then the film is to

---

sible that differences in the criterion as to when such period commences might result in such a sound recording being still protected on July 1, 1995 in an EEA state, in which case the new provisions would apply to it by virtue of reg.16(d).

[341] And possibly in the case of one made on or after January 1, 1944 and before January 1, 1945; see the previous footnote.

[342] art.14*bis*(2)(a).

[343] But see para.6–74, below.

[344] CDPA 1988 s.12(2) (as amended).

be entitled to a fixed period of protection of 50 years from the end of the year in which it was made.[345]

This list of designated persons follows the list set out in the Term Directive,[346] which also provides that the designation of such persons is irrespective of whether they are co-authors of the film. The earlier Rental Directive[347] had already provided that Member States should harmonise their laws as to authorship of films to provide that the principal director should be designated as the author or one of the authors of a film,[348] and this requirement was repeated in the Term Directive.[349] Section 9 of the 1988 Act was amended by the Regulations implementing the Rental Directive to provide that the authors of a film are to be taken to be the producer and the principal director.[350]

The scheme of the Term Directive would appear to provide for two distinct sets of rights in films, one in films as cinematographic or audiovisual works, to be treated as authors' works, the other in films as the recording of the work, to be treated as a work protected by related rights. Thus, the Directive provided a term of 70 years after the end of the year in which the last of the designated list of persons dies[351] and, separately, a fixed term of 50 years after fixation in respect of the first fixation of the film,[352] which was to belong to the producer of the film.[353] Before the amendment of the 1988 Act, the United Kingdom granted the rights in the film, protected as a recording, to the producer of the film, as its sole author.[354] In amending the authorship provisions to include the principal director as a co-author, and changing the term of protection to the period of 70 years pma, the United Kingdom has implemented the provisions of the Term Directive, but in doing so it has amalgamated what would appear to be considered by the Term Directive as two different sets of rights in two different works into one set of rights in a single work.[355]

Films of unknown "authorship". Before the amendment of the 1988 Act, films **6–71** were granted a fixed period of protection not dependent on the life of an author, and the provisions as to works of unknown authorship were not applied to films. As a consequence of the change in the period of protection of films now being dependent on the lives of various individuals, new provisions had to be introduced by the Duration Regulations dealing with films where the identity of the designated individuals is unknown. As noted above,[356] of these persons, only the principal director is treated as an author of the film, so the provisions contained in s.13B (3) to (6) of the 1988 Act are different from, but closely reflect, the similar provisions applying to literary, dramatic, musical and artistic works of unknown

---

[345] CDPA 1988 s.13B(9). An example of such a film might be a home movie; this will depend on the meaning given to "the principal director".

[346] art.2(2).

[347] Council Directive 92/100 on rental right and lending right and on certain rights related to copyright, November 19, 1992, [1992] OJ L346/61; see para.25–59, below.

[348] Rental Directive art.2(2).

[349] Term Directive art.2(1).

[350] CDPA 1988 s.9(2)(ab), as amended with effect from December 1, 1996, by the Copyright and Related Rights Regulations 1996 (SI 1996/2967).

[351] art.2(2), referred to above.

[352] Defined as a cinematographic or audiovisual work or moving images, whether or not accompanied by sound: art.3(3).

[353] art.3(3).

[354] CDPA 1988 s.9(2)(a) (as unamended).

[355] Whether this properly implements the Duration Directive is questionable; see P. Kamina "Authorship of Films and Implementation of the Term Directive: The Dramatic Tale of Two Copyrights" [1994] 8 E.I.P.R. 319, and "British Film Copyright and the Incorrect Implementation of the EC Copyright Directives" [1998] Ent. L.R. 109; see also G. Dworkin, "Authorship of Films and the European Commission Proposals for Harmonising the Term of Copyright" [1993] 5 E.I.P.R. 151.

[356] See para.6–70, above.

authorship.[357] The identity of any of the individuals is only to be treated as unknown if it is not possible to ascertain the identity of that person by reasonable enquiry.[358] If the identity of any such person is once known, it shall not subsequently be treated as unknown.[359]

These provisions only apply where the identity of none of the designated persons is known.[360] If the identity of any one of the designated persons is known, then the period of 70 years is to run from the death of that person.[361] If the identity of none of the designated persons is known, then the period of protection is a fixed period of 70 years from the end of the year in which the film was made,[362] unless within that period the film has been made available to the public, in which case the period lasts for 70 years from the end of the year in which it was first made available to the public.[363] As with literary, dramatic, musical and artistic works of unknown authorship, if the identity of any of the designated persons becomes known during the period of protection (but not afterwards), then the period of protection will be the period of 70 years from the end of the year in which that person, or the last of those persons, died.[364]

For the purposes of these provisions, a film is made available to the public not only when it is published by the issue of copies of the film to the public, but also when it is shown in public or communicated to the public.[365]

6–72 **Film soundtracks.** As indicated above,[366] a film soundtrack is treated under the amended provisions of the 1988 Act as part of the film, thus reversing the position under the 1988 Act as originally enacted, and restoring the position to that which existed under the 1956 Act, which itself had reversed the position existing under the 1911 Act. The primary purpose of treating a soundtrack as part of the film is to harmonise the regimes applicable to the audio and visual elements of a film.[367]

6–73 **Films of non-EEA origin.** Where the country of origin of a film[368] is not an EEA state,[369] the amended provisions require the application of the principle of comparison of terms, in that the term of protection for such a film is that to which it is entitled in its country of origin, provided that such term does not exceed the period which would apply under the rules discussed in para.6–70, above.

B. FILMS MADE BEFORE JANUARY 1, 1996

6–74 **General position.** The amended provisions of the 1988 Act apply to films made

---

[357] See para.6–48, above.

[358] CDPA 1988 s.13B(10); to the same effect as s.9(5), which does not apply since the provisions do not refer to the identity of the author being unknown.

[359] CDPA 1988 s.13B(10)

[360] CDPA 1988 s.13B(3). This is not, of course, the same as there being no such persons, as to which see para.6–70, above.

[361] CDPA 1988 s.13B(3).

[362] CDPA 1988 s.13B(4)(a).

[363] CDPA 1988 s.13B(4)(b).

[364] CDPA 1988 s.13B(5).

[365] CDPA 1988 s.13B(6). For the meaning of communicated to the public, see paras 7–112 et seq., below, for the meaning of unauthorised see s.178. This parallels the definition of "making available to the public" in relation to literary, dramatic, musical and artistic works in s.12(5); see para.6–48, above.

[366] See para.6–60, above.

[367] As to the problems which the assimilation of the soundtrack to the film creates, see P. Kamina, "The Protection of Film Soundtracks under British Copyright after the Copyright Regulations 1995 and 1996" [1998] Ent. L.R. 153.

[368] As to which see paras 6–19 and 6–20, above.

[369] As to which see para.6–20, above.

before January 1, 1996[370] and which first qualify for copyright protection after that date,[371] or in which copyright subsisted immediately before that date.[372] This remains subject to the overriding principle that such application is not to result in a shorter term of protection being applicable to an existing sound recording in which copyright subsisted immediately before January 1, 1996.[373] Thus, in respect of such works, it remains necessary to consider the rules for the duration of the term of protection both under the Act as amended and as originally enacted, in order to determine which provides the longer term.

Films made on or after August 1, 1989 and before January 1, 1996. A film made on or after August 1, 1989 and before January 1, 1996 was entitled to a period of protection of 50 years from the end of the year in which it was made,[374] or if released during that period, to a further period of 50 years from the end of the year in which it was released.[375] The amended provisions apply to such a film, and, assuming that there is at least one person falling within the list of designated persons for that film, the amended provisions will usually provide the longer term. However, in the case of a film made in 1995, in respect of which there is no designated person,[376] and which is not released until 2045, the period of protection under the amended provisions will expire on December 31, 2045, and under the original provisions on December 31, 2095, which is therefore the applicable term. Similarly, in the case of a film made in 1995, in respect of which the last of the designated persons died in 2010, and which is not released until 2045, the period of protection under the amended provisions will expire on December 31, 2080, and under the original provisions on December 31, 2095, which is therefore the applicable term.

6–75

Films made on or after June 1, 1957 and before August 1, 1989. A film made on or after June 1, 1957 and before August 1, 1989, if registrable,[377] was entitled to a period of protection of 50 years from the end of the year in which it was registered.[378] If the film was not registrable, it was entitled to a period of protection of unlimited duration while it remained unpublished, and thereafter for a further 50 years from the end of the year in which it was published.[379] Under the transitional provisions of the 1988 Act, such a film, if registrable, or if not registrable but which had been published before August 1, 1989, remains entitled to the period of protection which it enjoyed under the 1956 Act.[380] Publication in the case of a film means by the issue of copies of the film to the public.[381] In the case of a film which was not registrable, and which had not been published before August 1, 1989, such a film remains entitled to a further fixed period of protection expiring on December 31, 2039, unless before that date it is published, in

6–76

---

[370] The commencement date for the Duration Regulations; reg.1(2).

[371] Duration Regulations reg.16(b); see generally para.6–15, above.

[372] Duration Regulations reg.16(c); this means works in which copyright subsisted from January 1, 1995 to December 31, 1995, and includes those films in which, apart from the effect of the Duration Regulations, copyright would have expired at midnight on December 31, 1995; see para.6–16, above.

[373] reg.16(c) and reg.15(1).

[374] CDPA 1988 s.13(1)(a) (as unamended).

[375] CDPA 1988 s.13(1)(b) (as unamended). As to what constitutes release of a film for these purposes, see para.6–57, above.

[376] See para.6–70, above.

[377] Under Pt III of the Cinematograph Films Act 1938 (1 & 2 Geo. 6, c.17) or Pt II of the Films Act 1960 (8 & 9 Eliz. 2, c.57): Copyright Act 1956 s.31(1).

[378] Copyright Act 1956 s.13(3)(a); as amended by the Films Act 1960 and the Films Act 1985 (c.21) s.7(2) (which repealed the Films Act 1960).

[379] Copyright Act 1956 s.13(3)(b).

[380] CDPA 1988 Sch.1 para.12(2)(e).

[381] As to what constitutes publication of a film, see para.3–132, above.

which case it will enjoy a further period of protection of 50 years from the end of the year in which it is published.[382]

6–77 **Films made before June 1, 1957.** Films made before June 1, 1957 were not entitled to protection as films, but as a series of photographs and as dramatic works.[383] The period of protection to which such a film is entitled under the old provisions of the 1988 Act is therefore that applicable to photographs[384] and to dramatic works[385] made before that date. The amended provisions are expressly made to apply to films made before June 1, 1957, in so far as they are protected as photographs or dramatic works.[386] Each set of provisions will therefore have to be applied to the facts relating to such a film, which will include ascertaining who is to be treated as the author of such works,[387] before its term can be ascertained.

6–78 **Film soundtracks.** The amended provisions relating to the treatment of film soundtracks apply to film soundtracks existing at January 1, 1996 as to film soundtracks made on or after that date, but with transitional rules relating to ownership and to acts done before January 1, 1996.[388]

8. BROADCASTS

6–79 **General position.** Under the 1988 Act as amended, copyright in a broadcast expires at the end of the period of 50 years from the end of the calendar year in which the broadcast was made.[389] As has been seen,[390] the definition of broadcast has been altered as part of the implementation of the Information Society Directive, with the result that cable programmes are no longer protected as such: cable broadcasts are now protected simply as broadcasts, whenever they were made. The ordinary term of copyright in broadcast therefore applies to those cable broadcasts which are now protected simply as broadcasts.

6–80 **Broadcasts existing before January 1, 1996.** The current provision of the 1988 Act as to the standard term of protection of broadcasts in effect re-enacts without alteration the provision as it was before the 1988 Act was amended by the Duration Regulations.[391] No distinction therefore requires to be made in considering the term of protection of broadcasts between those existing before January 1, 1996 and those coming into existence after that date. The same provision applies to broadcasts made before commencement of the 1998 Act.[392] Wireless broadcasts were first accorded protection in the United Kingdom under the 1956 Act,[393] which did not apply to wireless broadcasts made before June 1, 1957. The transitional provisions of the 1988 Act applied only to existing wireless broadcasts in which copyright subsisted before August 1, 1989,[394] and expressly

---

[382] CDPA 1988 Sch.1 para.12(5)(b).

[383] See para.6–43, above.

[384] See para.6–56, above.

[385] See para.6–52, above.

[386] Duration Regulations reg.13.

[387] As to which see above at paras 4–29 et seq., (photographs) and paras 4–22 et seq., (dramatic works).

[388] Duration Regulations reg.26(1) and see para.5–53, above.

[389] CDPA 1988 s.14(2).

[390] See para.3–92, above.

[391] CDPA 1988 s.14(1).

[392] CDPA 1988 Sch.1 para.12(6).

[393] Copyright Act 1956 s.14.

[394] CDPA 1988 Sch.1 para.12(6).

maintain this position as to wireless broadcasts made before June 1, 1957.[395] No distinction therefore requires to be made in considering the term of protection of wireless broadcasts between those existing before August 1, 1989 and those coming into existence after that date. The position in relation to those cable programmes which are now protected as broadcasts appears to the same, in that they are simply to be regarded as "broadcasts". It should be noted, however, that cable programmes were first accorded protection in the United Kingdom only under the 1956 Act[396] as amended by the Cable and Broadcasting Act 1984,[397] which did not apply to cable programmes included in a cable programme service before January 1, 1985.[398] The transitional provisions of the 1988 Act applied only to existing cable programmes in which copyright subsisted before August 1, 1989,[399] and expressly maintain this position as to broadcasts made by cable before January 1, 1985.[400]

Repeat broadcasts. Copyright in a repeat broadcast expires at the same time as the copyright in the original broadcast.[401] A repeat broadcast is one which is a repeat of a broadcast previously made,[402] but disregarding any wireless broadcast, whether sound or television, made before June 1, 1957, and broadcasts by cable made before January 1, 1985.[403] This means, in effect, that no addition to the term of copyright can be acquired by virtue of a repetition of a broadcast. However, if a repetition involves any substantial alteration of the material, then presumably the broadcast will be a new broadcast, and, at least as regards the additional material, will be entitled to a new copyright having its own term of 50 years from broadcast.[404] The rationale of this provision is that a repeat broadcast is not made from a recording of the first broadcast. It will be made from a recording made at the same time as, or even before the first broadcast. For copyright protection to be adequate, therefore, each repeat must be given its own copyright, albeit for an abbreviated time.[405] **6–81**

Works of non-EEA origin. Where the author of a broadcast[406] is not a national of an EEA state,[407] the new provisions require the application of the principle of comparison of terms, in that the term of protection for such a work is that to which it is entitled in the country of which the author is a national, provided that such term does not exceed the standard period for such works under s.14.[408] This rule is subject to exception, to the extent that it would place the United Kingdom **6–82**

---

[395] CDPA 1988 Sch.1 para.9, as amended by the Copyright and Related Rights Regulations 2003 (SI 2003/2498) Sch.1 para.16; preserving, in respect of broadcasts, the effect of Sch.7 para.18 of the 1956 Act.

[396] Copyright Act 1956 s.14A.

[397] c.46

[398] The commencement date of s.22 of the Cable and Broadcasting Act 1984; see Copyright Act 1956 s.14A(11).

[399] CDPA 1988 Sch.1 para.12(6).

[400] CDPA 1988 Sch.1 para.9, as amended by the Copyright and Related Rights Regulations (SI 2003/2498) Sch.1 para.16 .

[401] CDPA 1988 s.14(5) (as amended), re-enacting in similar terms ibid., s.14(2) (as originally enacted), to the same effect as the Copyright Act 1956 s.14(3) and 14A(4).

[402] CDPA 1988 s.14(6) (as amended), re-enacting in similar terms ibid., s.14(3) (as originally enacted), to the same effect as Copyright Act 1956 ss.14(3) and 14A (4).

[403] CDPA 1988 Sch.1 para.9.

[404] See further paras 3–151 and 3–152, above.

[405] See *Hansard*, H.L. Vol.490, col.1163.

[406] As to who is the author of such a work, see para.5–57, above.

[407] As to which see para.6–20, above.

[408] CDPA 1988 s.14(3).

in breach of an international obligation assumed before October 29, 1993,[409] in which case the standard rule applies.[410] In the present context, this is effectively a reference to the United Kingdom's obligations under the Rome Convention,[411] under which the United Kingdom is obliged to accord national treatment to the broadcasts either made by a broadcasting organisation whose headquarters is situated in another Contracting State, or transmitted from another Contracting State.[412] In relation to such broadcasts, therefore, the United Kingdom will continue to accord them the standard term under s.14(2), through the inclusion of such Contracting States in Orders in Council made under s.159 of the Act.[413]

9. TYPOGRAPHICAL ARRANGEMENTS OF PUBLISHED EDITIONS

6–83   **Typographical arrangements.** Copyright in the typographical arrangement of a published edition expires at the end of the period of 25 years from the end of the calendar year in which the edition was first published.[414] The same provision applies to typographical arrangements of an edition published before commencement.[415] Protection for typographical arrangements of published editions was first provided by the 1956 Act[416] and although it appeared that the protection was accorded to such works whether they first came into existence before or after June 1, 1957,[417] given the limited period of protection granted to such works, protection for any such works first published before June 1, 1957 had already expired before August 1, 1989.[418]

The protection accorded to typographical arrangements of published editions now exists alongside the new publication right, introduced by the Rental Regulations.[419]

10. RIGHTS OF CERTAIN UNIVERSITIES AND COLLEGES

6–84   **Perpetual copyrights.** The Copyright Act 1775[420] had conferred on certain universities and colleges perpetual copyrights in books which were given or bequeathed to them for the advancement of learning and other purposes of education. The 1775 Act and the rights which it had created survived a succession of subsequent Copyright Acts,[421] until the Act was repealed by the Copyright Act 1911, which provided that no person was to be entitled to copyright or any similar right otherwise than in accordance with the provisions of the 1911

---

[409] That is the date the Duration Directive 93/98 was adopted.

[410] CDPA 1988 s.14(4).

[411] International Convention for the Protection of Performers, Producers of Phonograms and Broadcasting Organisations, signed at Rome, October 26, 1961, ratified by the United Kingdom on October 30, 1963.

[412] Rome Convention art.6.

[413] See further para.3–202, above.

[414] CDPA 1988 s.15. Such works are not literary or artistic works within the meaning of art.2 of the Berne Convention, and this provision remained unamended by the Duration Regulations (SI 1995/3297); it is in the same terms as s.15(2) of the 1956 Act.

[415] CDPA 1988 Sch.1 para.12(6); and see para.4–68, above.

[416] See para.3–104, above.

[417] See *Copinger* 12th edn, para.181.

[418] No doubt this is why the transitional provisions of the 1988 Act do not make any reference to such works, although Sch.1 para.12(6) would ensure that s.15 applied to such works in any event.

[419] The Copyright and Related Rights Regulations 1996 (SI 1996/2967) reg.16, implementing the Duration Directive 93/98 art.4; see generally as to the publication right, Ch.17.

[420] 15 Geo. 3, c.53.

[421] See, as to the intervening history, para.6–87, below.

Act or another statutory enactment for the time being in force.[422] Nevertheless, the 1911 Act preserved those copyrights which the universities and colleges had already acquired under the 1775 Act.[423] With the repeal of the 1775 Act, no further copyrights could be acquired by those institutions after July 1, 1912. Section 33 of the 1911 Act, along with virtually the whole of the Act, was repealed by the 1956 Act, which similarly provided that no copyright or right in the nature of copyright should subsist otherwise than by virtue of the 1956 Act or some other enactment in that behalf.[424] Nevertheless, again, the existing rights of these universities and colleges were preserved by the 1956 Act.[425]

Abolition of the perpetual copyrights. The 1977 Copyright Committee   **6–85** considered that these surviving perpetual copyrights enjoyed by the universities and colleges were anomalous, served little purpose and, although probably harmless, should be abolished.[426] This recommendation was implemented by the 1988 Act. The 1988 Act repealed the 1956 Act and, like its two predecessors, provided in s.171(2) that, subject to certain saved rights listed in s.171(1), no copyright right or right in the nature of copyright shall subsist otherwise than by virtue of Pt I of the 1988 Act or some other enactment in that behalf. Section 171(1) did not include those existing rights of the universities and colleges amongst the list of saved rights. Nonetheless, these rights were preserved by the transitional provisions in the 1988 Act for a further limited period of 50 years from the end of the year in which the 1988 Act came into force.[427] Thus the rights conferred on universities and colleges by the Copyright Act 1775 continue to subsist until December 31, 2039. During this final period, the rights are subject to other provisions in Pt I of the Act, namely: c.III (acts permitted in relation to copyright works;[428]) c.VI (remedies for infringement), c.VII (provisions with respect to copyright licensing) and c.VIII (the Copyright Tribunal).[429]

Origin of the rights. In 1534, Henry VIII granted letters patent to the University   **6–86** of Cambridge empowering the Chancellor, Masters and Scholars of that University to appoint University printers although, apparently, no printing actually took place until 50 years later. Similar letters patent were granted to the University of Oxford by Charles I in 1632, although Oxford University had, it seems, begun printing in 1585. The granting by the Crown to the Universities of Oxford and Cambridge of patents to print Bibles and Prayer Books is dealt with elsewhere.[430] Immediately after, and in consequence of, the decision in *Donaldson v Beckett*,[431] the universities secured the passing of the Copyright Act 1775[432] enabling the two universities in England (Oxford and Cambridge), the four universities in Scotland (St Andrews, Glasgow, Edinburgh and Aberdeen), and the several colleges of Eton, Westminster, and Winchester, to hold in perpetuity

---

[422] Copyright Act 1911 s.31.
[423] Copyright Act 1911 s.33. The remedies and penalties for infringement of those rights were those granted under the 1911 Act.
[424] Copyright Act 1956 s.46 (5).
[425] Copyright Act 1956 s.46(1); proceedings for infringement now had to be brought under the 1956 Act.
[426] Report of the Committee to consider the Law on Copyright and Designs; Cmnd.6732, paras 648, 649.
[427] CDPA 1988 Sch.1 para.13(1).
[428] But in relation to the acts permitted by CDPA 1988 s.57, it is provided that the assumption in s.57(1)(b)(i) as to expiry of copyright is not to apply in relation to such rights: ibid., Sch.1 para.15(2)(b).
[429] CDPA 1988 Sch.1 para.13(2).
[430] See para.10–04, below.
[431] (1774) 4 Burr. 2408; and see para.2–16, above.
[432] 15 Geo. 3, c.53.

the copyright in books given or bequeathed to them for the advancement of useful learning and other purposes of education.

The right was to exist in all such books as had been before 1775, or should thereafter be, given or bequeathed by the authors of the same, or their representatives, to or in trust for those universities, or any colleges, or any of them, for the beneficial purpose of education within them or any of them.

The privilege in favour of the universities and colleges was to extend only to their own books, so long as they were printed at the college press and for their sole benefit. A power was given to the universities and colleges by the Act, to sell or dispose of the copyright given or bequeathed to them, but if they should delegate, grant, lease, or sell the copyright of any book, or allow any person to print it, their privilege was to cease to exist. The copyright of any work presented to the universities was required to be registered at Stationers' Hall within two months after any such gift came to the knowledge of the officers of the university or college. Special penalties were imposed for any infringement of copyright.

6–87   **Subsequent history of the rights.** By the Copyright Act 1801,[433] a similar right to copyright was given to Trinity College, Dublin. The Literary Copyright Act 1842 Act[434] repealed the 1801 Act, but not the 1775 Act. Nevertheless, by s.27 of the 1842 Act, the rights of the universities (including Trinity College, Dublin) and of the colleges were saved from the operation of that Act. As indicated above,[435] the 1775 Act was repealed by the 1911 Act, which also repealed the 1842 Act. The effect of this repeal was therefore that in so far as any rights of Trinity College, Dublin, were saved by the 1842 Act, they appear to have been lost altogether upon the 1911 Act coming into force.

11. ABANDONMENT OF COPYRIGHT

6–88   It has been said that an author may by his conduct, or by his express desire, abandon his copyright, and give to the public a right to publish his work before the time when his copyright would expire.[436] There is no direct authority on the point,[437] and it is difficult to say what amount of evidence the courts would require as to the fact of a dedication of a copyright to the public. Clearly mere non-exploitation by the copyright proprietor of his rights will not give grounds for such a plea of abandonment.[438] The argument that British Leyland had abandoned its copyright in its drawings of exhaust pipes was advanced in *British Leyland Motor Corp v Armstrong Patents Co Ltd*, but was rejected by Foster J. who considered that it was extremely difficult to divest oneself of a legal right.[439] A similar argument that the claimant's predecessor in title had released its copy-

---

[433] 41 Geo. 3, c.107.

[434] 5 & 6 Vict. c.45.

[435] See para.6–82, above.

[436] In *Millar v Taylor* (1769) 4 Burr. 2303 at 2346; *Platt v Button* (1813) 19 Ves.447; *Rundell v Murray* (1821) Jac. 311 at 316. As to the separate issue of whether an author can ever abandon his manuscript, see *Moorhouse v Angus & Robertson (No.1) Pty* [1981] 1 N.S.W.L.R. 700 and para.26–56, below.

[437] See *Mellor v Australian Broadcasting Commission* [1940] A.C. 491; *Romesh Chowdhry v Kh. Ali Mohamad Nowsheri* [1965] A.I.R. Jammu and Kashmir 101.

[438] See *Weldon v Dicks* (1878) 10 Ch. D. 247, in which the argument that the proprietor of the copyright in a book had lost his copyright by non-publication for a period of 12 years, during which the book had been allowed to remain out of print, was rejected.

[439] *British Leyland Motor Corp v Armstrong Patents Co Ltd* [1982] F.S.R. 481 at 492; although it would appear that *Millar v Taylor* (1769) 4 Burr. 2303 at 2346; *Platt v Button* (1813) 19 Ves.447; *Rundell v Murray* (1821) Jac. 311 were not cited to the judge. See also CDPA 1988 s.153(3) which, in the context of qualification for copyright protection, provides that, once the qualification requirements are satisfied, copyright does not cease to subsist by reason of any subsequent event.

right to the public domain, or had licensed the world to make copies, was rejected by the High Court of New Zealand in *Plix Products Ltd v Frank M. Winstone (Merchants).*[440]

In *Catnic Components Ltd v Hill & Smith Ltd*,[441] Whitford J. expressed the view that a patentee, by applying for a patent must be deemed, upon publication, to have abandoned his copyright in drawings the equivalent of the patent drawings. The basis for this view was that a patentee in applying for a patent necessarily makes an election accepting that, in return for a potential monopoly, the material disclosed by him in the specification must, upon publication, be deemed to be open to be used by the public, subject only to such monopoly rights as he may acquire on his application for the patent and during the period for which his monopoly remains in force, whatever be the reason for the determination of the monopoly rights. This view was, however, obiter to the actual decision in the case, and the Court of Appeal, whilst upholding the learned judge's finding of non-infringement, declined to comment on the question of abandonment.[442] The view expressed by Whitford J. has not subsequently been endorsed in the courts of England and Wales.[443] However, Aldous J., in *Merrell Dow Pharmaceuticals Inc. and Another v N.H. Norton & Co. Ltd*,[444] pointed out that Whitford J.'s statement of the law was made without the benefit of considering *Werner Motors Ltd. v A.W. Gamage Ltd.*[445] In the latter case, the Court of Appeal had held that there was no basis for putting an applicant to an election between a patent for an article and registration of a design for the shape of a similar article. Aldous J. also referred to the fact that since 1982, a considerable body of judicial opinion, albeit in other jurisdictions, had pointed out the difficulty of accepting Whitford J.'s statement as the law.[446]

---

[440] [1986] F.S.R. 63 at 87–88; affirmed on appeal (but this point not being the subject of the appeal): [1986] F.S.R. 608. See also para.5–226, above, and the cases cited there.

[441] [1978] F.S.R. 405. The 1977 Copyright Committee, Cmnd.6732, para.915, recommended that any copyright in drawings reproduced in a patent specification should cease when the patent ceases to be in force.

[442] [1979] F.S.R. 619, CA.

[443] The point was treated as arguable by Slade J. in *General Electric Co v Turbine Blading Ltd.* [1980] F.S.R. 510, on an application in a copyright action for discovery of patent drawings, and Falconer J. distinguished *Catnic (Catnic Components Ltd v Hill and Smith* [1978] F.S.R. 405) on its facts, without deciding its correctness on this point in *Gardex Ltd v Serata Ltd* [1986] R.P.C. 623. See also Whitford J. in *Rose Plastics GmbH v William Beckett & Co (Plastics) Ltd* [1989] F.S.R. 113 at 123–4.

[444] [1994] R.P.C. 1.

[445] (1904) 21 R.P.C. 621.

[446] *House of Spring Gardens Ltd v Point Blank Ltd.* [1983] F.S.R. 213 at 269 (High Court of Ireland, affirmed on appeal: [1985] F.S.R. 327); *Ogden Industries Pty Ltd v Kis (Australia) Ltd* [1983] F.S.R. 619 (Supreme Court of New South Wales); *Wham-O Manufacturing Co v Lincoln Industries ltd* [1982] R.P.C. 281 at 297 (High Court of New Zealand); and, in particular, *Interlego AG v Tyco Industries Inc* [1989] A.C. 217; [1987] F.S.R. 409, where the point was fully discussed at 455 (Court of Appeal of Hong Kong).

CHAPTER SEVEN

THE RIGHTS OF A COPYRIGHT OWNER: PRIMARY INFRINGEMENT

1. INTRODUCTION

Copyright is a statutory property right, the rights of property granted being the **7–01** exclusive right to do various "restricted acts" in relation to the copyright work. Being a property right, the rights of a copyright owner can be sold or licensed, in contrast to purely personal rights such as moral rights.[1] In a commercial context, therefore, it is common to ask what are the *rights* of a copyright owner which are available or need to be obtained. As to enforcement of those rights, the remedy for invasion of a copyright owner's exclusive rights by a third party is, by statutory definition, an action for infringement. In the context of litigation, therefore, it is common to ask what are the acts that amount to an *infringement*. These two viewpoints merely represent a different side of the same coin. Infringement only occurs if one of the exclusive rights of the copyright owner has been invaded.

Primary and secondary infringement. This chapter is concerned with the **7–02** exclusive rights which are conferred on a copyright owner and what amounts to an infringement of those rights. In addition, however, the 1988 Act provides additional remedies to copyright owners in respect of various dealings in relation to copyright works and infringing copies. The common and necessary ingredients of these remedies are that (a) they only arise when some other infringing act has already occurred or is assumed to have occurred ("the primary infringement") and (b) the liability of a defendant is dependent on establishing some degree of "guilty" knowledge on his part. The acts in respect of which these remedies are available are also classified as infringements and although they are not strictly

---

[1] See Ch.11.

invasions of any of the exclusive property rights which are expressly conferred on the copyright owner, yet in some sense these remedies do constitute additional rights of the copyright owner.[2] It is common to classify these infringements as "secondary" infringements,[3] being secondary to the primary act of infringement which takes place. Secondary infringements are discussed in the next chapter.

7–03   **European Directives.** A number of Directives have prescribed a patchwork of rights in the copyright and related rights fields. Most recently, the Information Society Directive[4] has prescribed a coherent scheme for a number of basic rights for various rights owners, namely (1) an exclusive right of reproduction, (2) an exclusive right of communication to the public and (3) an exclusive right of distribution of copies. There were already in existence a number of Directives prescribing a piecemeal scheme of protection for rights owners, namely, and in historical order, the Software Directive,[5] the Rental and Related Rights Directive,[6] the Satellite and Cable Directive[7] and the Database Directive.[8] The effect of these Directives will be considered in relation to the various rights of copyright owners under UK law as they arise.

7–04   **The rights: basic definitions.** The rights of the copyright owner are defined to be the exclusive right to do the following acts in the United Kingdom[9]:

(a) copy the work ("the reproduction right"[10]);

(b) issue copies of the work to the public ("the distribution right");

(c) rent or lend the work to the public ("the rental and lending rights");

(d) perform, show or play the work in public ("the public performance right"[11]);

(e) communicate the work the work to the public ("the communication to the public right");

(f) make an adaptation of the work, or to do any of the above acts in relation to an adaptation of the work ("the adaptation right").

These various rights are described as the acts "restricted by the copyright" in a work.[12] They are the subject of more detailed statutory definition as discussed later in this chapter.

7–05   **Infringement: the basic definitions.** Copyright is infringed by a person who, without the licence of the copyright owner, does, or authorises another to do, any of the acts restricted by the copyright.[13] Not only is copyright therefore infringed by anyone who does one of the restricted acts without licence, but also by anyone

---

[2] They can, for example, be the subject of a licence: *Biotrading & Financing OY v Biohit Ltd* [1998] F.S.R. 109.

[3] See, e.g. the heading to CDPA 1988 ss.22 et seq.

[4] Directive 2001/29.

[5] Or Computer Program Directive 91/250/EC, since replaced by Council Directive 2009/24/EC.

[6] Directive 92/100, since replaced by Directive 2006/115/EC.

[7] Directive 93/83.

[8] Directive 96/9.

[9] CDPA 1988 ss.2(1), 16(1).

[10] This and the following descriptions of the various rights are used as a convenient shorthand but are not, apart from the rental right, part of any statutory definition.

[11] Caution should be taken when speaking of the public performance right since in some circumstances, for example in relation to the administration of rights by the Performing Rights Society Ltd, the expression performing right includes other rights, e.g. the right to broadcast.

[12] CDPA 1988 s.16(1).

[13] CDPA 1988 s.16(2).

who without licence *authorises* the doing of any such act.[14] An infringing act of authorisation is a separate tort from the infringing act so authorised.[15] In addition, copyright is infringed:

(a) by the doing of any of these acts not only in relation to the whole of a work but also in relation to any substantial part of it[16];

(b) by the doing of any of these acts indirectly as well as directly, it being immaterial whether any intervening acts themselves infringe copyright.[17]

The doing of any of these acts by any person other than the copyright owner or one who has his permission is therefore an infringement unless the act falls within one of the statutory permitted acts[18] or is otherwise excusable.[19] Each wrongful exercise of an exclusive right constitutes a separate tort. Apart from these acts, however, other dealings with a work do not constitute a primary infringement. It is thus not an infringement of copyright to read a hard copy of a book, even if an infringing copy,[20] or to resell a legitimate copy which was purchased in a bookshop.[21]

Licence; permitted acts. It is a necessary ingredient of the tort that the act in question was done without the licence of the copyright owner. This topic is considered in detail elsewhere.[22] There is also a large class of so-called permitted acts which, although falling within the description of one or more of the restricted acts, may be done without infringing copyright. These acts are considered in Ch.9.   **7–06**

Innocence or ignorance not a defence. It is a characteristic of all these rights of the copyright owner that the right is infringed whether or not the defendant appreciated that what he was doing infringed copyright or whether he intended to infringe.[23] Copyright is a proprietary right and is infringed by invasion of the right, except to the extent that the statute provides otherwise. Innocence is therefore not a defence to a claim for primary infringement of copyright.[24] A limited defence to a claim in damages (but not to any other relief) is available where the defendant proves that at the time of the infringement he did not know, and had no reason to believe, that copyright subsisted in the work in question.[25] The defence is of very limited application.[26]   **7–07**

Infringement actionable without damage. Copyright is a right of property and is actionable without having to show damage, this not being one of the ingredients of the tort.[27]   **7–08**

---

[14] In addition, of course, the ordinary rules as to liability for inciting or procuring the commission of a tort apply. See paras 21–42 et seq., below.

[15] *Ash v Hutchinson & Co (Publishers) Ltd* [1936] Ch. 489.

[16] CDPA 1988 s.16(3)(a). As to the meaning of substantial part, see paras 7–25 et seq., below.

[17] CDPA 1988 s.16(3)(b). See para.7–15, below.

[18] See para.7–06, below.

[19] e.g. because it is in the public interest. See para.21–93, below.

[20] Reading a copy of a book stored in digital form raises other issues, because reproduction of the work inevitably takes place in the process. See para.7–19, below.

[21] But note that to put into circulation a licensed copy of a work which had not previously been put into circulation is an infringement. See CDPA 1988 s.18 and paras 7–87 et seq., below.

[22] See paras 5–195, et seq.

[23] *Baigent v The Random House Group Ltd* [2007] EWCA Civ 247; [2007] F.S.R. 24 at para.97, per Lloyd L.J., Rix L.J. and Mummery L.J. agreeing.

[24] See, e.g. *Mansell v Valley Printing Company* [1908] 2 Ch. 441; *Lee Simpson* 136 E.R. 349; (1847) 3 C.B. 871. See, further, para.7–24, below.

[25] CDPA 1988 s.97(1).

[26] See paras 21–75 et seq., below.

[27] See the definition of infringement in CDPA 1988 s.16(2) and *Weatherby & Sons v International*

2. THE REPRODUCTION RIGHT

A. INTRODUCTION

7–09   The exclusive right to prevent copying or reproduction of a work is the most fundamental, and historically the oldest, right of a copyright owner.

7–10   **European Directives.** A number of Directives have dealt with various aspects of the reproduction right. Most recently, and most importantly, the Information Society Directive[28] has defined the scope of the acts covered by the reproduction right which Member States are obliged to confer in relation to authors' works[29] and related rights subject matter,[30] the intention being to ensure legal certainty within the internal market.[31] Thus the Directive provides for an exclusive right to authorise or prohibit the direct or indirect, temporary or permanent reproduction of such subject matter by any means and in any form, in whole or in part.[32] The main object of the protection is to introduce a "high level" of protection, in particular for authors to enable them to receive an appropriate reward for the use of their works in order to be able to pursue their creative and artistic work[33] and the acts covered and protection given by this Directive must be construed broadly.[34] Before that, a number of other Directives had made piecemeal provision relating to the reproduction of various types of subject matter. Thus, the Software Directive[35] provided for an exclusive right of the permanent or temporary reproduction of computer programs, by any means and in any form, in part or in whole, including situations where the loading, displaying, running, transmission or storage of the program necessitated such reproduction.[36] Next, the Rental and Related Rights Directive[37] provided, in relation to phonogram producers for their phonograms, film producers for their films and broadcasting organisations for their broadcasts, for an exclusive right to authorise or prohibit direct or indirect reproduction.[38] Finally, the Database Directive[39] provides, in relation to copyright databases, for an exclusive right to carry out or authorise the temporary or permanent reproduction of the database by any means and in any form, in whole or in part.[40] In relation to all of these requirements, it would seem that UK law as contained in the 1988 Act was already compliant with them, such that no amendment to the reproduction right was required when other provisions of these Directives were

---

Horse Agency & Exchange Ltd [1910] 2 Ch. 297, at 305, applied in *Hawkes & Son (London) Ltd v Paramount Film Service Ltd* [1934] Ch. 593.

[28] Directive 2001/29.

[29] i.e. the rights in Berne copyright works, namely, literary, dramatic, musical, artistic works, and works of cinematography considered as authors' works.

[30] i.e. rights conferred on producers of sound recordings and films, and broadcasters. The rights of performers are considered separately, in Ch.12, below.

[31] See recital 21 of Directive 2001/29.

[32] art.2.

[33] *Infopaq International A/S v Danske Dagblades Forening* (C–5/08) [2009] ECR I–6569, paras 41, 43, although it is not made clear what constitutes a "high level" of protection.

[34] *Infopaq International A/S v Danske Dagblades Forening* (C–5/08) [2009] ECR I–6569, referring to recital 21.

[35] Directive 91/250/EC, now replaced by 2009/24/EC.

[36] art.4.

[37] Directive 92/100, now replaced by Directive 2006/115/EC.

[38] art.7. This article has now been deleted and replaced by arts 2(b), (c), (d) and (e) of the Information Society Directive (2001/29), above, to equivalent effect.

[39] Directive 96/9.

[40] art.5.

implemented. In any event, however, s.17 of the 1988 Act must be construed in conformity with, in particular, the Information Society Directive.[41]

Common considerations. In one form or another, the reproduction right exists   **7–11**
today in relation to every category of copyright work.[42] Each such category is considered in turn in this chapter[43] but some points are common to all categories, namely:

(1) The right is the exclusive right of *copying*.[44] For the right to be infringed, two elements have to be established, (a) a sufficient degree of objective similarity between the copyright work and the alleged infringement and (b) that this was the result of the copyright work having been copied, i.e. that there is a causal connection between the two.

(2) As with all rights of a copyright owner, the exclusive right relates not only to the entire work but also any substantial part of it.

(3) Again, as with all other such rights, the exclusive right is the right to copy the work either directly or indirectly.

(4) In relation to all categories of work, the exclusive right extends to the making of copies which are transient or incidental to some other use of the work.[45]

These issues are considered separately in this introductory section.

Sufficient similarity. As already stated, there must be a sufficient objective   **7–12**
similarity between the copyright work and alleged copy. This has two aspects:

(a) First, the allegedly infringing work must in some real sense represent the claimant's.[46] Thus a literary work consisting of instructions will not be infringed by the making of an article in accordance with those instructions[47] and an artistic work such as a circuit diagram will not be infringed by describing it or its contents in words, no matter how detailed.[48] Another example, from the law as it stood before 1911, is that piano rolls and cylinders for music boxes did not amount to "copies" of sheet music.[49] The question in these cases is not whether the defendant has used the claimant's work, but whether he has reproduced it, a question that should be answered from a common sense point of view.[50]

(b) Secondly, even if the defendant's work does represent the claimant's in

---

[41] *Football Association Premier League Ltd v QC Leisure* [2008] EWHC 1411, para.219; [2008] F.S.R. 32.

[42] CDPA 1988 s.17(1).

[43] The basic right is the subject of different statutory rules of interpretation in relation to each category, these rules being part definition and part elucidation.

[44] The right is necessarily limited to the exclusive right to do an act whereby a copy comes into existence which did not exist before. The right does not include an exclusive right to alter a version of a work without producing a new copy. See *Thèberge v Gallerie d'Art du Petit Champlain Inc* 210 DLR (4th) 385 (Sup Ct of Can) and para.7–66, below.

[45] CDPA 1988 s.17(6). But note the permitted act in relation to the making of transient and incidental copies provided for by s.28A. See para.9–61, below and see, further in para.7–19, below.

[46] *Purefoy Engineering Co Ltd v Sykes Boxall & Co. Ltd* (1955) 72 R.P.C. 89 at 99.

[47] *Interlego A.G. v Tyco Industries Inc* [1989] A.C. 217 at 265. See the discussion in relation to literary works at para.7–37, below, for further examples.

[48] *Anacon Corp Ltd v Environmental Research Technology Ltd* [1994] F.S.R. 659. This is not to say that something made by following a written or verbal description of an artistic work may not infringe the copyright in the artistic work. See below.

[49] *Boosey v Whight* [1900] 1 Ch. 122. Sheet music was protected as a "book" under the Literary Copyright Act 1842. The law is now different.

[50] *Designers Guild Ltd v Russell Williams (Textiles) Ltd* [2001] 1 W.L.R. 2416; [2008] F.S.R. 11. See also paras 2–06 and 7–13, for a discussion of the ideas/expression dichotomy and *Autospin (Oil Seals) Ltd v Beehive Spinning* [1995] R.P.C. 683, which contains a provocative discussion of the problem.

this sense, there will be no infringement if there is no *sufficient* objective similarity between it and the copyright work.[51] Even if a copyright work has been used as a reference or is the inspiration for what the defendant has done, this by itself is not enough if there is no such similarity. For example, a defendant may have derived his work from the claimant's but may have done so in such a way, either deliberately or through incompetence, that what he produces does not amount to a copy in law.[52] The issue here is whether a substantial part of the copyright work has been copied,[53] an issue which is perhaps the most common and often the most difficult question arising in everyday copyright law. This is considered further, below.

7–13   **Ideas versus expression.** In dealing with the question of copying, there should be borne in mind the well-established principle that there is no copyright in mere ideas, concepts, schemes, systems or methods.[54] Rather, the object of copyright is to prevent the copying of the particular form of expression in which these things are conveyed. If the expression is not copied, copyright is not infringed.[55] Thus, to be liable, the defendant must have made a substantial use of the form of expression; he is not liable if he has taken from the work the essential idea, however original, and expressed the idea in his own form, or used the idea for his own purposes. Protection of this kind can only be obtained, if at all, under patent law or the law relating to confidential information. This principle finds expression in many of the cases, to the effect, for example, that it is no infringement of the copyright in a literary or dramatic work to take its basic idea or general plot[56] or of an artistic work to take the general idea.[57] It is, however, impossible to define the boundary between mere taking of general concepts and ideas on the one hand and copying in the copyright sense on the other, and wherever the line is drawn it will often seem arbitrary.[58] Further, it should be noted that UK courts are also obliged, both as a matter of domestic and as a matter of EU law, to interpret both European and domestic legislation in conformity with the wording and purposes of the relevant international agreements to which the European Union is a party,

---

[51] *Francis Day & Hunter Ltd v Bron* [1963] Ch. 587 at 614.

[52] *Billhöffer Maschinenfabrik GmbH v Dixon & Co Ltd* [1990] F.S.R. 105.

[53] This applies both to the case where a part of the work has been taken and to the case where the whole work has been copied, but in an altered form.

[54] There are many statements in the cases to this effect. For modern examples, see *L.B. (Plastics) Ltd v Swish Products Ltd* [1979] F.S.R. 145, HL; *Johnstone Safety Ltd v Peter Cook (Int.) Plc* [1990] F.S.R. 161, CA; *Harman Pictures N.V. v Osborne* [1967] 1 W.L.R. 723 at 728; *IPC Media Ltd v Highbury-Leisure Publishing Ltd* [2004] EWHC 2985 (Ch); [2005] F.S.R. 20 at para.14; *Hyperion Records Ltd v Sawkins* [2005] EWCA Civ 565; [2005] 1 W.L.R. 3281; [2005] R.P.C. 32, per Mummery L.J. (with whom Mance L.J. agreed) at para.29: "copyright can be used to prevent copying of a substantial part of the relevant form of expression, but it does not prevent use of the information, thoughts or emotions expressed in the copyright work." For older examples, see *Hollinrake v Truswell* [1894] 3 Ch. 420; *McCrum v Eisner* (1917) 87 L.J. Ch. 99.

[55] *Hollinrake v Truswell* [1894] 3 Ch. 420 at 424, 427.

[56] *Wilmer v Hutchinson & Co Ltd* [1936–1945] Mac. C.C. 13. There are many similar examples in the field of dramatic works. See paras 7–63 et seq., below.

[57] *Kenrick & Co v Lawrence & Co* (1890) 25 Q.B.D. 99 (drawing of hand filling in voting slip, made to help illiterate voters, not infringed by use of the same concept); *Gleeson v H.R. Denne Ltd* [1975] F.S.R. 250 (idea for design of ecclesiastical collar). See further, para.7–69, below.

[58] *IPC Media Ltd v Highbury-Leisure Publishing Ltd* [2004] EWHC 2985 (Ch); [2005] F.S.R. 20, per Laddie J. at para.14, citing Judge Learned Hand in *Nichols v Universal Pictures Co* 45 F 2nd 119 (2nd Cir. 1930): "Upon any work, and especially upon a play, a great number of patterns of increasing generality will fit equally well, as more and more of the incident is left out. The last may perhaps be no more than the most general statement of what the play is about, and at times may consist of only its title; but there is a point in this series of abstractions where they are no longer protected, since otherwise the playwright could prevent the use of his 'ideas', to which, apart from their expression, his property is never extended." (p.121).

namely TRIPs and the WCT,[59] both of which are intended to be confirmatory of the position under art.2 of the Berne Convention.[60] As a result, so far as relates to computer programs, UK courts must interpret the 1988 Act so as to protect "expressions" and not "ideas, procedures, methods of operation and mathematical concepts as such."[61] Although UK law has formally changed in this respect,[62] it is not considered that the substantive law has changed: this is how the courts had previously interpreted the 1988 Act and earlier copyright Acts.

As with all such general statements of principle, however, it must be treated with caution and not taken too far. It is not a correct statement of English law that because a copyright work contains the expression of an idea it may be copied; nor that if there is only one way of expressing an idea, then that way cannot be the subject of copyright[63]; nor that where the expression of an idea is inseparable from its function, it forms part of the idea and is not entitled to copyright protection.[64] The distinction drawn in the case law between ideas and the expression of ideas in fact supports two distinct propositions.[65] The first is that a copyright work may express certain ideas which are not protected because they have no connection with the literary, dramatic, musical or artistic nature of the work. Thus a literary or artistic work which describes a system or invention does not entitle the author to claim protection for his system or invention as such and however striking or original the idea may be, others are (in the absence of patent protection) free to express it in works of their own.[66] The other proposition is that certain ideas expressed by a copyright work are not protected because, although they are ideas of a literary, dramatic or artistic nature, they are not original, or they are so commonplace as not to form a substantial part of the work.[67] The correct position is therefore that although copyright cannot prevent the copying of a general idea, where the idea has been worked out in detail in the form of writing, drawings, etc. it will be an infringement if the labour which went into the expression of the idea is appropriated. In such a case, it is not the idea which has been copied but its detailed expression.[68] Thus the law of copyright is concerned not with originality of ideas but with the original expression of thought (in the case of a literary work, for example, the expression in writing).[69] The originality which is required, and thus the protection conferred, relates to the expression of thought.[70] In each case, it will be a matter of degree whether the line which divides

---

[59] *Nova Productions Ltd v Mazooma Games Ltd* [2007] EWCA Civ 219, para.38; [2007] R.P.C. 25; *SAS Institute Inc v World Programming Ltd* [2010] EWHC 1829 (Ch), paras 168, 200.

[60] *SAS Institute Inc v World Programming Ltd* [2010] EWHC 1829 (Ch), para.204.

[61] *SAS Institute Inc v World Programming Ltd* [2010] EWHC 1829 (Ch), para.205.

[62] *SAS Institute Inc v World Programming Ltd* [2010] EWHC 1829 (Ch), para.205.

[63] See the criticisms of *Total Information Processing Systems Ltd v Daman Ltd* [1992] F.S.R. 171 and *John Richardson Computers Ltd v Flanders* [1993] F.S.R. 497 in *Ibcos Computers Ltd v Barclays Finance Ltd* [1994] F.S.R. 275.

[64] Such statements were sometimes made in relation to computer programs, drawing on US authorities. See, e.g. *Autodesk Inc v Dyason* [1992] R.P.C. 575 at 583 (High Ct of Aus), citing *Lotus Development Corp v Paperback Software International* 740 F.Supp. 37 at 25 (U. Dis Ct).

[65] *Designers Guild Ltd v Russell Williams (Textiles) Ltd* [2000] 1 W.L.R. 2416; [2001] E.C.D.R. 10; [2001] F.S.R. 11.

[66] As in *Kleeneze Ltd v. D.R.G. (U.K.) Ltd* [1984] F.S.R. 399.

[67] As in *Kenrick & Co v. Lawrence & Co* (1890) 25 Q.B.D. 99.

[68] *L.B. (Plastics) Ltd v Swish Products Ltd* [1979] F.S.R. 145, HL; *William Hill (Football) Ltd v Ladbroke (Football) Ltd* [1980] R.P.C. 539 at 546; *Leco Instruments (U.K.) Ltd v Land Pyrometers Ltd* [1982] R.P.C. 140 (an idea put into permanent form may be the subject of copyright).

[69] *Ibcos Computers Ltd v Barclays Finance Ltd* [1994] F.S.R. 275.

[70] *University of London Press Ltd v University Tutorial Press Ltd* [1916] 2 Ch. 601 at 608, cited with approval in *Ladbroke (Football) Ltd v William Hill (Football) Ltd* [1964] 1 W.L.R. 273 at 277.

the copying of an idea from copying of its expression has been overstepped.[71] For the same reason, care should be taken when it is said that there is no copyright in news. The original expression of a news story is certainly capable of being the subject matter of copyright and of being infringed by the appropriation of that expression.[72]

7–14   **Causal connection.** As has been pointed out,[73] where the claimant's and the defendant's works are similar, there are four possible explanations: the defendant's work was copied from the claimant's; the claimant's from the defendant's; both from a common source; or mere chance or coincidence.[74] It is only in the first case that an infringement of the claimant's work can have occurred. Although the concept of copying is expressed differently in relation to the different categories of work, the underlying principle is that there can be no infringement unless use has been made, directly or indirectly, of the copyright work.[75] Copyright is not a monopoly right and no infringement occurs by an act of independent creation.[76] This is often expressed as saying there must be a causal connection between the copyright work and an infringing work.[77] This is one of the ways in which copyright differs from true monopoly rights such as patents and registered designs. In the case of the latter rights, a person can infringe even though he has arrived at his result by independent creation.

7–15   **Indirect copying.** Although there must be a causal connection between the claimant's and the defendant's work for there to be any infringement, this connection need not be direct. The 1988 Act makes clear what has always been the position, namely, that copyright may be infringed indirectly by copying something which is itself a copy of the claimant's work.[78] Indeed, in most cases of alleged infringement the copying is done indirectly, the plagiarist never having seen the original manuscript, drawing, etc. only the published work or other thing derived from the original work. The position is the same whether or not the intervening work is of a nature capable of enjoying copyright or is itself an in-

---

[71] *Ibcos Computers Ltd v Barclays Finance Ltd* [1994] F.S.R. 275. So, in *Bowater Windows Ltd v Aspen Windows Ltd* [1999] F.S.R. 780, a particular technique for selling double glazing had been given expression in the form of documents used by salesmen used in the course of their "pitch". Only the form in which the technique had been expressed in the documents could be protected, not the technique itself. In that case the sales technique was common in the industry and the defendant had not copied the detailed expression of the technique from the claimant's documents. There was therefore no infringement even though the claimant's documents had been the inspiration for the defendant's. (Although there had been some copying of expression from the claimant's documents, there had been no sufficient skill and labour expended on these parts to make the amount copied a substantial part.)

[72] The matter is considered further at para.7–44, below.

[73] *Corelli v Gray* (1913) 29 T.L.R. 570.

[74] The possibility of coincidence should never be ruled out, for: "We constantly in life meet with coincidences which suggest a common origin, but which, when investigated and examined, are found to be nothing but coincidences. Experience shews that it is not merely probable, but certain, that improbable events will happen." See *Lucas v Cooke* (1879) 13 Ch. D. 872 at 879. Of course, the more commonplace the subject matter, the less improbable is the explanation of coincidence.

[75] *L.B. (Plastics) Ltd v Swish Products Ltd* [1979] F.S.R. 145, HL.

[76] *L.B. (Plastics) Ltd v Swish Products Ltd* [1979] F.S.R. 145, HL; *Francis Day & Hunter Ltd v Bron* [1963] Ch. 587 at 617; *Corelli v Gray* (1913) 29 T.L.R. 570; *Wesman v McMara* [1923–1928] Mac.C.C. 121.

[77] *Francis Day & Hunter Ltd v Bron* [1963] Ch. 587, at 614.

[78] CDPA 1988 s.16(3)(b). It has always been the law that it is irrelevant by what intermediate sources the defendant copied. See, e.g. *British Leyland Motor Corp. Ltd v Armstrong Patents Co Ltd* [1986] A.C. 577; [1986] F.S.R. 221, HL; *King Features Syndicate Inc v O. & M. Kleeman Ltd* [1940] Ch. 523 at 806, CA (the point was no longer in issue by the time the case reached the House of Lords). As to examples of pre-1911 Act cases, see *Ex p. Beal* [1868] L.R. 3 Q.B. 387; *Cate v Devon, etc. Newspaper Co* [1889] 40 Ch. D. 500; *Hanfstaengl v H.R. Baines & Co. Ltd* [1895] A.C. 20, HL.

fringement of copyright[79] and even if there is no intervening work as such at all. Thus an artistic work is capable of being infringed where the link between it and the copy is a written[80] or verbal[81] description, if the description is nevertheless sufficient to enable a copy of the artistic work to be made. The latter point underlines the risk that, even if an independent designer is employed in an attempt to avoid infringement, it may be necessary to give him so much information that the work he produces is still a copy.[82] A defendant may even infringe by giving a designer very loose instructions and then prompting him to produce, for example by trial and error, a result which eventually resembles the copyright work.[83] Where it is alleged that the original copyright work has been copied via some intervening work, care must be taken when comparing the alleged infringing work with the intervening work, since the vital comparison is between the alleged infringement and the original work.[84]

Even though copying may take place indirectly, it is still necessary to prove an unbroken chain between the claimant's and the defendant's work. It must therefore be shown that the intermediate copy is itself either a direct or indirect copy of the copyright work.[85] Often this turns out not to be the case, particularly where the claimant's work is derived from another work or article and the defendant has copied that other work or article.[86] This situation frequently arose where the claimant's work, for example a drawing, turned out not to be at the head of the chain but to have been made to record an existing article, the latter being what the defendant had actually copied.[87] The "intermediate" stage must in some real and intelligible sense be a copy or description of the work in which copyright subsists. Thus where a defendant compiled a catalogue from the range of machinery parts sold by the claimant, thereby bringing into being a catalogue substantially similar to the claimant's, the copyright in the claimant's catalogue was not infringed. This was because the machinery parts offered by the claimant did not in any proper sense amount to a reproduction of the descriptions of those parts in the catalogue.[88]

Access. The need for a causal connection obviously implies the need to show that the alleged infringer had access, either directly or indirectly, to the copyright work.[89] The issue of proof of copying is considered below, but if there is suf-

7–16

---

[79] *Hanfstaengl v H.R. Baines & Co. Ltd* [1895] A.C. 20, HL (copies of claimant's paintings made via *tableaux vivants*, not themselves capable of amounting to an infringement).

[80] *Plix Products Ltd v Frank M. Winstone (Merchants) Ltd* [1986] F.S.R. 63 at 608 (CA of NZ).

[81] *Ultra Marketing (UK) Ltd v Universal Components Ltd* [2004] EWHC 468 (Ch), para.15, applying *Plix Products Ltd v Frank M. Winstone (Merchants) Ltd* [1986] F.S.R. 63, and *Solar Thomson Engineering Co Ltd v Barton* [1977] R.P.C. 537. See also *Gleeson v H. R. Denne Ltd* [1975] F.S.R. 250 (no infringement, on the facts).

[82] *Solar Thomson Engineering Co Ltd v Barton* [1977] R.P.C. 537.

[83] *House of Spring Gardens Ltd v Point Blank Ltd* [1983] F.S.R. 213 (High Ct of Ireland); *LED Builders Pty. Ltd v Eagle Homes Ltd* (1996) 35 I.P.R. 215 (Fed Ct of Aus).

[84] As in *Johnstone Safety Ltd v Peter Cook (International) Plc* [1990] F.S.R. 161.

[85] *Johnstone Safety Ltd v Peter Cook (International) Plc* [1990] F.S.R. 161; *Billhöffer Maschinenfabrik GmbH v Dixon & Co Ltd* [1990] F.S.R. 105 at 108.

[86] Examples are *Toole v Young* [1873] 9 Q.B. 523; *Schlesinger v Bedford* (1890) 63 L.T. 762 (in both cases, the defendant's independent dramatisation of a novel had not been copied from claimant's dramatisation); *Lucas v Cooke* (1879) 13 Ch. D. 872 (copyright in engraving of painting not infringed by subsequent copy taken from painting); *The Duriron Co Incorp v H. Jennings & Co. Ltd* [1984] F.S.R. 1 (claimant's articles not made from drawings relied on).

[87] *Autospin (Oil Seals) Ltd v Beehive Spinning* [1995] R.P.C. 683. These types of cases are less likely to arise today. See para.7–65.

[88] *Purefoy Engineering Co Ltd v Sykes Boxall & Co Ltd* (1955) 72 R.P.C. 89. The skill and labour of the claimant which had been copied was that which had gone into selecting the parts and not into compiling the catalogue.

[89] *L.B. (Plastics) Ltd v Swish Products Ltd* [1979] F.S.R. 145, HL.

ficient similarity between the works, this will raise a prima facie case of access and thus causation.[90]

7–17   **Proof of copying.**[91] It is for the claimant to prove copying, this being a question of fact,[92] the standard being the ordinary civil standard.[93] In most cases copying can only be deduced by inference from all the surrounding circumstances because normally there will be no evidence from anyone "being present and looking over the [defendant's] shoulder" at the time he designed or made his work.[94] The case will therefore normally start with establishing substantial similarity combined with the possibility of access.[95] Where there is substantial similarity, this is prima facie evidence of copying[96] and also of access.[97] Once a prima facie case is established in this way, it is often said that a shift in the evidential burden takes place which the party charged may refute by evidence of independent creation[98] or by giving some alternative explanation for the similarities.[99] The task of the judge is then to decide, on the evidence as a whole, whether or not there has been copying.[100] This can be summarised by saying that proof of sufficient similarity, coupled with proof of the possibility of access, raises a prima facie case or inference of copying for the defendant to answer.[101] This "shifting" of the burden of proof is, however, merely one of plain, rational thought,[102] and in reality the burden of proof always remains with the party alleging copying, since proof of sufficient similarity merely places on the defendant an obligation to give an explanation of that similarity, which the court then considers together with all the other facts.[103]

Naturally, even if an inference of copying can be drawn, it may be rebutted by the defendant's evidence that he did not copy.[104] The fact that the defendant denies copying is some evidence to rebut the inference but is obviously not

---

[90] *Francis Day & Hunter Ltd v Bron* [1963] Ch. 587 at 612.

[91] See also para.7–67, below, for a discussion of this issue in relation to artistic works.

[92] *Ibcos Computers Ltd v Barclays Finance Ltd* [1994] F.S.R. 275 at 296.

[93] *Biotrading & Financing OY v Biohit Ltd* [1998] F.S.R. 109 at 121.

[94] *Sifam Electrical Instrument Co. Ltd v Sangamo Weston Ltd* [1971] F.S.R. 337.

[95] In *L.B. (Plastics) Ltd v Swish Products Ltd* [1979] F.S.R. 145, Lord Wilberforce speaks of "proof" of access but it is suggested that this goes too far. Proof of the possibility of access is surely enough.

[96] *King Features Syndicate v O. & M. Kleeman Ltd* [1941] A.C. 417 at 436.

[97] *Francis Day & Hunter Ltd v Bron* [1963] Ch. 587 at 612. Of course, if it is very unlikely that a defendant could have had access to the claimant's work, this will weaken the inferential case.

[98] *L.B. (Plastics) Ltd v Swish Products Ltd* [1979] F.S.R. 145; *King Features Syndicate Inc v O. & M. Kleeman* [1941] A.C. 417. If the defendant calls no evidence, a court is therefore entitled to find copying proved: *Mathieson v Universal Stock Exchange* [1901–1904] Mac.C.C. 80; *Cadieux v Beauchimin* [1901–1904] Mac.C.C. 4 (Sup Ct of Can).

[99] *Billhöffer Maschinenfabrik GmbH v Dixon & Co Ltd* [1990] F.S.R. 105 at 107.

[100] *L.B. (Plastics) Ltd v Swish Products Ltd* [1979] F.S.R. 145, HL.

[101] *Francis Day & Hunter Ltd v Bron* [1963] Ch. 587, at 612, 614; *Designers Guild Ltd v Russell Williams (Textiles) Ltd* [2001] 1 W.L.R. 2416, per Lord Millett at para.39; [2001] F.S.R. 11. See also *Baigent v The Random House Group Ltd* [2007] EWCA Civ 247; [2007] F.S.R. 24 at paras 4, 122.

[102] *Ibcos Computers Ltd v Barclays Finance Ltd* [1994] F.S.R. 275 at 297; cited with approval in *Creative Technology Ltd v Aztech Systems Pte. Ltd* [1997] F.S.R. 491 at 501 (CA of Singapore). See also *EPI Environmental Technologies Inc v Symphony Plastic Technologies plc* [2006] EWCA Civ 3; [2006] 1 W.L.R. 495 (note), per Jacob L.J. at para.8: "[The] reasoning is not so much a rule of law as one of rational weighing of evidence. It is simply this: if the degree of similarity between the work alleged to have been copied and the alleged piratical work is unlikely to have come about by coincidence, it is for the defendant to prove that it was."

[103] *EPI Environmental Technologies Inc v Symphony Plastic Technologies Plc* [2006] EWCA Civ 3, per Buxton L.J., at para.65, citing *Francis Day & Hunter v Bron* [1963] 1 Ch 587, Willmer L.J., at p 612, who had characterised as "quite untenable" a suggested wider rule, which would have the effect of placing a burden of proof on the alleged copier.

[104] *De Manduit v Gaumont, etc. Corp. Ltd* [1936–1945] Mac.C.C. 292.

conclusive[105]: it has to be weighed against all the other evidence. A bare denial of copying without any explanation of the similarities is, however, unlikely to be convincing.[106] On the other hand, where there is a respectable defence of, for example, common source, functional necessity or hackneyed theme, the absence of other tell-tale similarities may mean that the defendant's evidence can easily be accepted.[107] Thus where two works are claimed to have been based on earlier materials, similarities in incident and situations, although affording prima facie evidence of copying, may not be sufficient to override a denial of copying coupled with an explanation of similarities by reference to the sources.[108] While for the purposes of the "substantial part" test it is the similarities between the works which matter, not the differences,[109] in the context of copying, the unimportant parts of two works may contain unexplained similarities which are probative of copying.[110] But it is important not to be misled, since: "In copyright cases, chipping away and ignoring all the bits which are undoubtedly not copied may result in the creation of an illusion of copying in what is left."[111] Again, although an alleged infringing article and a copyright drawing may appear similar when viewed from one angle, when viewed from another they may appear so dissimilar that any inference of copying is dispelled.[112] Evidence of unlikely similarities will usually have to be of the most cogent kind before it can be preferred to the sworn evidence of a respectable and responsible person which the court would otherwise accept.[113] On the other hand, the similarities may be so great that his evidence could never be believed.[114] The fact that a witness who denies copying is disbelieved will not necessarily prove copying[115] since it constitutes no positive evidence,[116] but it can clearly be brought into the balance.[117] The fact that the defendant has copied other works before may be probative[118] and, in limited circumstances, similar fact evidence may be relied upon to rebut the suggestion of coincidence.[119] The type of evidence which will help prove copying obviously varies with each case, but unexplained similarities in style, content and so on usually play a part.[120] Indeed it is often in the repetition of mistakes, redundancies, idiosyncrasies and the like that a plagiarist is caught out, for "… it is the resemblances in *inessentials*, the small, redundant, even mistaken elements of the copyright work, which carry the greatest weight. This is because they are least likely to have been the result of independent design"[121] and may "shed a flood of

---

[105] *Francis Day & Hunter Ltd v Bron* [1963] Ch. 587, at 614.

[106] *Harman Pictures N.V. v Osborne* [1967] 1 W.L.R. 723.

[107] As in *Deeks v Wells* [1928–1935] Mac.C.C. 353; *Thomas Forman & Sons Ltd v Balding & Mansell* [1928–1935] Mac.C.C. 501.

[108] See, e.g. *Poznanski v London Film Production Ltd* [1937–1945] Mac.C.C. 107.

[109] *Entec (Pollution Control) Ltd v Abacus Mouldings* [1992] F.S.R. 332. See para.7–30, below at (g).

[110] *Billhöfer Maschinenfabrik GmbH v Dixon & Co Ltd* [1990] F.S.R. 105; *Ibcos Computers Ltd v Barclays Mercantile Highland Finance Ltd* [1994] F.S.R. 275.

[111] *IPC Media Ltd v Highbury-Leisure Publishing Ltd* [2004] EWHC 2985 (Ch); [2005] F.S.R. 20 at para.11.

[112] *Gomme Ltd v Relaxateze Upholstery Ltd* [1976] R.P.C. 377.

[113] *Deeks v Wells* [1928–1935] Mac.C.C. 353, CA.

[114] *Robl v Palace Theatre (Ltd)* (1911) 28 T.L.R. 69.

[115] *L.B. (Plastics) Ltd v Swish Products Ltd* [1979] F.S.R. 145, HL.

[116] *Johnstone Safety Ltd v Peter Cook (International) Plc* [1990] F.S.R. 161 at 175; *Billhöffer Maschinenfabrik GmbH v Dixon & Co Ltd* [1990] F.S.R. 105.

[117] *Designers Guild Ltd v Russell Williams (Textiles) Ltd*, [2000] 1 W.L.R. 2416, at p.2419, recording the approach of the trial judge; [2001] F.S.R. 11.

[118] See para.22–276, below.

[119] See para.22–276, below.

[120] There are many examples of such cases and it is not helpful to cite individual examples.

[121] *Billhöfer Maschinenfabrik GmbH v T.H. Dixon & Co Ltd* [1990] F.S.R. 105 at 123; cited in *Ibcos*

light on the real source of the more substantial similarities."[122] Obviously, where a number of passages in a work are proved to have been copied (e.g. because of mistakes), other passages which are the same in both works may be assumed also to have been copied.[123]

7-18   **The role of expert witnesses.** Expert witnesses are often called in infringement actions.[124] Their usual function will be to examine the similarities and differences which are said to exist between the two works, where necessary explaining the technicalities involved, and help the court reach a conclusion on whether and to what extent the similarities are or are not probative of copying.[125] This may involve setting the similarities against what is usual or commonly done in the field and an examination of other sources which were available to the defendant.[126] In cases of technical complexity, such as computer software infringement, they may be essential in order to explain the presence and significance of what seem to be similarities between the two works.[127] In music copyright cases, expert evidence is almost invariably called to educate the court in the nuances of melody, rhythm, orchestration and even lyrics,[128] and to identify and explain common or unusual musical figures.[129] This is so even though similarities between two musical works are often apparent to the most uneducated in music. Such witnesses can also play a role in identifying what is important or essential about a work and therefore help the court decide whether a substantial part of the claimant's work has been reproduced, where this issue arises.[130] Although an expert's opinion as to whether or not copying has taken place is admissible,[131] it is important to appreciate the limitations of the expert's role, which is not to evaluate the factual

---

Computers Ltd v Barclays Finance Ltd [1994] F.S.R. 275 at 297 and *Creative Technology Ltd v Aztech Systems Pte. Ltd* [1997] F.S.R. 491 at 501 (CA of Singapore).

[122] *L.B. (Plastics) Ltd v Swish Products Ltd* [1979] F.S.R. 145, per Lord Hailsham.

[123] *Mawman v Tegg* (1826) 2 Russ. 385; *Ibcos Computers Ltd v Barclays Finance Ltd* [1994] F.S.R. 275 at 303. Proof of copying of an insubstantial part may therefore support the proof of copying of a substantial part.

[124] As to the ordinary duties of an expert witness, see *"The Ikarian Reefer"* [1993] F.S.R. 562; *Cala Homes (South) Ltd v Alfred McAlpine Homes East Ltd* [1995] F.S.R. 818; *Autospin (Oil Seals) Ltd v Beehive Spinning* [1995] R.P.C. 683.

[125] *Virgin Atlantic Airways Ltd v Premium Aircraft Interiors Group* [2009] EWHC 26 (Pat); [2009] E.C.D.R. 11 at para.37 (first instance).

[126] *Baumann v Fussell* [1978] R.P.C. 485. An example is *Nicolv Barranger* [1917–1923] Mac.C.C. 219. See also *IPC Media Ltd v Highbury-Leisure Publishing Ltd* [2004] EWHC 2985 (Ch); [2005] F.S.R. 20 at paras 40 and 43.

[127] As in *Ibcos Computers Ltd v Barclays Finance Ltd* [1994] F.S.R. 275.

[128] For the importance of expert evidence in cases involving allegations of copying rap lyrics, see *Confetti Records v Warner Music UK Ltd* [2003] EWHC 1274; [2003] E.C.D.R. 31 and *Brown v Mcasso Music Production Ltd* [2005] EWCC 1 (Cpwt); [2005] F.S.R. 40 at para.10.5.

[129] In *Barrett v Universal-Island Records Ltd* [2006] EWHC 1009 (Ch); [2006] E.M.L.R. 21, (exceptionally) no expert evidence was called. One issue was as to whether the addition of an "instrumental bridge" to an existing work was sufficient to give rise to a new copyright work. The Judge was asked to listen to both works and then reach a view without the assistance of expert evidence. The Judge held that in principle this was "not the way to proceed" (para.355) and stated that in the absence of expert evidence he was unable to reach any conclusion about whether the bridge was an original composition, a question of interpretation or performance or part of an overall arrangement of the song as a whole (para.356).

[130] See *Ibcos Computers Ltd v Barclays Finance Ltd* [1994] F.S.R. 275, at 301, where the importance was emphasised of an expert separating the two issues: (1) are there any indicia of copying? (2) if so, has a substantial part been taken?

[131] Civil Evidence Act 1972 s.3 allows the giving of expert evidence on *any* issue in the proceedings: *Designers Guild Ltd v Russell Williams (Textiles) Ltd* [1998] F.S.R. 803, at 811; *IPC Media Ltd v Highbury Leisure Publishing Ltd* [2004] EWHC 1967 (Ch), para.15.

evidence[132] or to decide the issues of copying or substantial part, these being for the court and the court alone.[133]

Works recorded in digital form. The growth of digital storage and transfer of **7–19** works via the internet has a number of copyright implications. Whereas, traditionally, most works can be enjoyed simply and freely by, for example, reading the book in which the work has been printed, or watching or listening to the work being performed,[134] works which are recorded in digital form usually cannot be sensibly enjoyed without being copied again for the particular purpose, for example into transient computer memory (and often again onto a screen). The restricted act of copying is therefore usually implicated in uses of works recorded in digital form. Thus, although the traditional enjoyment of works has not required any form of licence, enjoyment of works in digital form will often do so. Usually, of course, such use is impliedly licensed on the sale of a physical carrier of the digital copy, but where the material is supplied online, it raises the possibility of other charging models. Even in the case where use is licensed on the sale of a physical carrier, such licence may be limited in extent.[135]

Transient and incidental copying; copying by electronic means. Article 2 of **7–20** the Information Society Directive provides that the reproduction right includes the exclusive right of temporary reproduction by any means and in any form.[136] It was not necessary to alter UK law to give effect to this.[137] Thus and unless it constitutes a permitted act,[138] any fleeting but unlicensed copying of a work will therefore infringe, whether, for example, taking the form of the fleeting presence of a work in computer memory,[139] the presentation of text or an image on a computer or television screen[140] or writing on a blackboard.[141] As will be seen, in relation to literary, dramatic, musical and artistic works, copying also expressly

---

[132] *Virgin Atlantic Airways Ltd v Premium Aircraft Interiors Group* [2009] EWHC 26 (Pat); [2009] E.C.D.R. 11 at para.37 (first instance).

[133] *IPC Media Ltd v Highbury-Leisure Publishing Ltd* [2004] EWHC 2985 (Ch); [2005] F.S.R. 20 at paras 40 to 42; *Baumann v Fussell* [1978] R.P.C. 485; *Deeks v Wells* [1928–1935] Mac.C.C. 353, CA .

[134] Public performance, etc. of most works is of course a restricted act, for which the performer is responsible.

[135] For example, an article may be sold in one territory on terms that it is for use in that territory only, in which case any use in another territory which involves reproduction of a copyright work will be unlicensed. See *Kabushi Kaisha Sony Computer Entertainment Inc v Owen* [2002] E.W.H.C. 45 (Ch); [2002] E.C.D.R. 27.

[136] Note that an attempt to include in the 1996 WIPO Copyright Treaty and WIPO Performances and Phonograms Treaty provisions to the effect that temporary and transient copying were restricted acts was abandoned in the face of opposition, although in an "Agreed Statement on the Reproduction Right" it was confirmed that: "The reproduction right ... and the exceptions permitted thereunder, fully apply in the digital environment, in particular to use of works in digital form. It is understood that the storage of a protected work in digital form in an electronic medium constitutes a reproduction ...". In other words, notwithstanding a clear statement that digitisation is an infringing act, the position with respect to temporary and transient storage was left open so far as the international treaty position is concerned. For a detailed discussion of these Treaties, see paras 23–66 and 23–119, below.

[137] Thus CDPA 1988 s.17(6) already provided that the exclusive reproduction right extends to the making of copies which are transient or incidental to some other use of the work.

[138] Particularly, in this context, an act permitted by s.28A. See para.9–61, below.

[139] *Kabushiki Kaisha Sony Computer Entertainment Inc. Ball* [2004] EWHC 1738 (Ch), para.13; [2005] F.S.R. 9.

[140] *Football Association Premier League Ltd v QC Leisure* [2008] EWHC 1411 (Ch); [2008] F.S.R. 32 at paras 231–233 (broadcast comprising graphics, devices and logos together with various films); *UEFA v Briscomb* [2006] EWHC 1628 (Ch), although Kitchin J. doubted in the former case whether those who framed the CDPA ever contemplated this. However, the position was the same under the 1956 Act, even though it did not contain such an express provision. See *Bookmakers' Afternoon Greyhound Services Ltd v Wilf Gilbert (Staffordshire) Ltd* [1994] F.S.R. 723 at 738.

[141] An older example was the representation of a painting or sculpture by human figures, i.e. as a *tableau vivant*. See para.7–66, below.

includes the storing of the work in any medium by electronic means.[142] The combination of the two provisions makes it clear that the fleeting copying of such works in computer memory is one of the exclusive rights of the copyright owner. In each case, however, it will be necessary to examine precisely what has been copied. A difficult issue arises where for example only very small fragments of a work are displayed on a screen or have been successively copied in RAM or other temporary memory as part of the incidental processing of the whole of the work for some other use. An example might be the copying which takes place in the memory of a decoder while decoding an encrypted broadcast film, various fragments of the film being stored sequentially and then successively destroyed such that at any one time the decoder holds copies only a very small number of frames in one part of its memory.[143] Other examples are a DVD player which in the course of displaying a film on a screen reads data from the DVD and copies small fragments to a temporary memory which are held there only fleetingly before being replaced by further fragments[144] and the buffering which takes place in temporary memory when a broadcast is streamed over the internet. Assuming for present purposes that none of these fragments by themselves constitutes a substantial part of the whole work,[145] no "copy" is made of the relevant work as a whole and so no copying of the work takes place for the purposes of the Act.[146] In particular, it is not appropriate to consider the fragments on a cumulative or rolling basis in cases such as those above, where the fragmentary copies relied upon are successively destroyed as an inherent part of the process.[147] The restricted act of making a transient copy of the work (or of a substantial part of it) requires that the copy or substantial part must be embodied in the transient copy, not a series of different transient copies which are stored one after the other in the transient memory.[148] Nevertheless, there is an outstanding referral to the European Court of Justice on the issue of transient copying.[149]

7–21   **Who commits the act of copying?** In the era of electronic communications and the use of other new technologies, it may often be crucial to know who commits the actual act of copying which is the exclusive right of the copyright owner. The question may arise in the comparatively simple case of a fax transmission: who is

---

[142] CDPA 1988 s.17(2). It was clear since at least 1985, and probably before, that under UK copyright law, storage in computer memory had been a restricted act. The Copyright (Computer Software) Amendment Act 1985 s.2, provided that "[r]eferences in the Copyright Act 1956 ... to the reproduction of any work in a material form, shall include reference to storage of that work in computer."

[143] The facts in *Football Association Premier League Ltd v QC Leisure* [2008] EWHC 1411 (Ch), para.217.

[144] The facts in *Australian Video Retailers Association Ltd v Warner Home Video Pty Ltd* (2002) 53 I.P.R. 242 (Fed Ct. of Aus).

[145] As was found to be the case in *Football Association Premier League Ltd v QC Leisure* [2008] EWHC 1411 (Ch), para.224.

[146] *Football Association Premier League Ltd v QC Leisure* [2008] EWHC 1411 (Ch), para.227, also approving the reasoning in *Australian Video Retailers Association Ltd v Warner Home Video Pty Ltd* (2002) 53 I.P.R. 242 (Fed Ct. of Aus) that: "It is clear that neither the whole nor any substantial part of a cinematograph film or motion picture is ever embodied in the RAM of a DVD player or personal computer at any given time. The mere fact that, over a period of time, being the time taken to play the motion picture or cinematograph film, tiny parts of it are sequentially stored in the RAM of the DVD player or personal computer does not mean that the motion picture or cinematograph film is embodied in such a device."

[147] *Football Association Premier League Ltd v QC Leisure* [2008] EWHC 1411 (Ch), para.227, also rejecting the argument that the "little and often" doctrine might apply (see para.7–32).

[148] *Football Association Premier League Ltd v QC Leisure* [2008] EWHC 1411 (Ch), paras 227, 228. See, however, further in the text as to the referral of this (and other) questions to the European Court of Justice.

[149] See *Football Association Premier League Ltd v QC Leisure* [2008] EWHC 1411 (Ch), where, amongst other issues, the following question was referred: Does the reproduction right in art.2 extend to the creation of transient images on a television screen? For other questions referred, relating to the issue of "little and often", see para.7–29.

the "person who ... *does*" the restricted act of copying the work.[150] A more complex case is where digital information is sent via an electronic network such as the internet, often broken down into small packets, when it will usually may be stored transiently in computers provided by intermediate service providers, before being stored more permanently, although still in electronic form, by the eventual recipient. Although such intermediaries will often be able to rely on the protection conferred on them following the implementation into UK law of both the E-Commerce Directive[151] and the Information Society Directive,[152] the threshold question may still arise in such cases as to who does the act of copying. The problem may be acute, not only because in the course of such a transfer copying may take place in several jurisdictions, but also because the service providers will generally have no means of knowing whether the copies which are being made in their computers are licensed or not, and will often be unable to control what is passed through or received by their computers. The primary act of infringement by copying is a tort of strict liability, so that the consequences are clearly of fundamental importance.[153] These questions require the application of copyright law in a new context but this does not mean that the ordinary principles should not be applied. The question always remains the same: who "does" the act of copying? Who is the human person who is the most proximate cause of the act being done?[154] Thus, in the simple example of a photocopier provided by a library, a member of the public who uses the photocopier to make a copy is clearly the person who copies the work, not the librarian nor the owner of the library nor the supplier of the photocopying equipment. In the technically more complex case of the sending of a fax, where the sender causes a copy to be made automatically by the recipient's remote fax machine, it is suggested that the sender is the person who is responsible for copying the work which is sent, not the person in control of the receiving fax machine.[155] In the case of network transmissions, the problem is in essential respects no different.[156] Although the service provider makes available the facilities for making the copy, it is suggested its employees, servants or agents do not themselves copy the work if this is done as a result of an automatic process which is activated by the receipt of a transmission. So, where copyright works were attached to emails and sent to a person's email address where they "arrived" in the inbox on the person's home computer, it was held that the act of sending the emails caused a reproduction of the copyright works on the defendant's email server.[157] Other potential grounds of liability need to be considered in all these cases, of course, in particular whether the defendant has authorised the copying of the work,[158] or is liable as a joint infringer, or for hav-

---

[150] See CDPA 1988 ss.16(2), (1).

[151] See para.21–100, below.

[152] See para.9–19, below.

[153] It was for this reason, of course, that the liability of service providers was modified by the E-Commerce (2000/31) and Information Society (2001/29) Directives.

[154] So, in *Football Dataco Ltd v Sportradar GmbH* [2010] EWHC 2911 (Ch), where material on the defendants' website could be accessed and reproduced by members of the public clicking on the relevant window, it was conceded that it was not the defendants who so reproduced the material but the members of the public.

[155] See the observations of Peter Smith J. in *Sony Music Entertainment (UK) Ltd v Easyinternetcafe Ltd* [2003] EWHC 62 (Ch); [2003] F.S.R. 48, at para.33, although he appears to have taken the view that the owner of the machine would not be liable because he would be "an involuntary copier". It is suggested, however, that he is not a copier at all.

[156] *Sony Music Entertainment (UK) Ltd v Easyinternetcafe Ltd* [2003] EWHC 62 (Ch).

[157] *Woolworths Ltd v Olson* [2004] NSWSC 849; (2004) 63 I.P.R. 258.

[158] See generally *C.B.S. Songs Ltd v Amstrad Plc* [1988] A.C. 1013; [1988] R.P.C. 567, HL and *Amstrad Consumer Electronics Plc v British Phonographic Industry Ltd* [1986] F.S.R. 159, CA, and see paras 7–130 et seq., below, for a detailed discussion of authorisation.

ing procured or incited the copying.[159] The Act also creates a liability in the case of a person who transmits a work by means of a telecommunication system, knowing or having reason to believe that infringing copies will be made by means of the reception of the transmission[160] but it would seem that this provision is unnecessary since the person will be strictly liable for the act of reproduction. In the case of a service provider which has enabled the onward transmission of the work through its networks, consideration will also need to be given as to whether it has communicated the work to the public.[161] In relation to these potential grounds of liability, it will be necessary to examine the facts of each case, particularly the relationship between the service provider and the third parties involved, and whether the service provider assumes responsibility to any extent for policing what is stored, for example by way of monitoring the content or reserving the right to intervene. It is suggested, however, that a purely passive service provider would not be liable for the act of copying. There remains the possibility of obtaining an injunction against the service provided under s.97A of the Act.[162]

7–22   **Where does the act of copying take place?** The problem is obviously acute in the case of internet and other electronic transmissions. If a defendant in jurisdiction A using electronic means causes a work which is stored in jurisdiction B to be transmitted and stored in computer memory situated in jurisdiction C, where does the act of copying take place? No doubt it will be necessary to examine the technical processes involved to see where the work was copied as a matter of actual physical fact but otherwise it is suggested that the approach should not be over-technical.[163] In the example, the physical act of copying took place in jurisdiction C (perhaps also in B) and C is where it should be regarded as having taken place so far as any act of infringement by the defendant is concerned, even though the defendant caused the copying to take place at a distance.

7–23   **File sharing.** Where infringing copies of a work are made via the process of file sharing or P2P copying, multiple acts of infringement may take place, and each must be analysed separately.[164] Thus it may involve such primary acts of infringement as (1) permanent copying of a work in electronic form (2) transient copying (3) communication of the work to the public[165] and (4) authorisation of copying, for example by either by the sender or by the internet service provider. In the present context, a person who seeks out a work via a file-sharing network and causes it to be downloaded onto his computer obviously thereby commits the act of reproducing it.

7–24   **Ignorance no excuse; subconscious copying.** As already pointed out, since copyright is a proprietary right, ignorance is no defence to an infringement claim.[166] If, therefore, the defendant's work has been copied from the claimant's, either directly or indirectly, the fact that the defendant was unaware that the work

---

[159] See para.22–35, below.
[160] CDPA 1988 s.24(2). See para.8–15.
[161] i.e. within the meaning of CDPA 1988 s.20. The issue used to be whether the provider was operating a cable programme service (see para.7–84, below), as held arguably to be the case in *Shetland Times Ltd v Wills* [1997] F.S.R. 604 (approved, obiter, in *Sony Music Entertainment (UK) Ltd v Easyinternetcafe Ltd* [2003] EWHC 62 (Ch) at para.47.
[162] See para.21–121, and also para.21–288 as to the provisions of the Digital Economy Act 2010.
[163] See, e.g. the pragmatic approach adopted in *KK Sony Entertainment v Pacific Game Technology (Holding) Ltd* [2006] EWHC 2509 (Ch).
[164] For a general discussion of the problems involved, and the attempt by the United Kingdom to deal with them via the Digital Economy Act 2010, see para.21–288.
[165] As to which see para.7–112 et seq.
[166] See para.7–146, above.

he was copying in this way existed, or was the claimant's or was the subject of copyright, or whether he thought he had a licence, provides no defence to a claim for primary infringement although, in very limited circumstances, it may affect the remedy.[167] Nor would a blind person, or someone who was illiterate or who simply chose not to look at the thing he is copying, have a defence.[168] It also follows that a defendant's intentions, whether it was to copy or infringe copyright or not, are irrelevant. It is sometimes alleged that there has been "subconscious copying" that is, subconscious use of the claimant's work rather than conscious use by deliberate copying. Such a possibility often arises in musical copyright cases, where a songwriter may have been exposed to many melodies and other musical devices over the years which he may subconsciously call upon when writing a work. Since the issue of copying does not depend on any question of "knowledge" but, in this respect, only causation, it is suggested that if the reason for the substantial similarity between two works is that the maker of the defendant's work unconsciously or subconsciously drew on the claimant's work as his source, then copying will have occurred. The possibility has in fact been accepted in a number of cases without argument.[169] In the one case where the matter has been argued, the result was inconclusive,[170] although it was emphasised that the fact that the maker of the defendant's work did not believe there was any causal connection between the two works is irrelevant.[171] The problem will in most cases be one of proof. With a work of any complexity, it is unlikely that a person who remembered enough of it to be able to recreate it would be unaware of what he was doing. With a more simple work such as a popular song, if the evidence that no conscious copying took place is accepted then it may be difficult to prove that the reason for the similarity is a causal link between the two works rather than an independent creation, particularly in a field where almost every musical device can be found to have been used somewhere else before. A particularly difficult situation may arise where the defendant is accused of copying an earlier work of his own which he no longer has the right to reproduce, since it may be very hard for him to put out of his mind completely the earlier work.[172]

---

[167] See CDPA 1988 s.97(1) and para.21–87, below.

[168] *Sony Music Entertainment (UK) Ltd v Easyinternetcafe Ltd* [2003] EWHC 62 (Ch); [2003] F.S.R. 48, at para.36 (obiter).

[169] *Sinanide v La Maison Kosmeo* (1927) 44 T.L.R. 371 (reversed on other grounds on appeal); *Gleeson v Denne (H.R.) Ltd* [1975] R.P.C. 471; *Johnstone Safety Ltd v Peter Cook (International) Ltd* [1990] F.S.R. 161; *John Richardson Computers Ltd v Flanders* [1993] F.S.R. 497; *EMI Music Publishing Ltd v Papathanassiou* [1993] E.M.L.R 306; *Jules Rimet Cup Ltd v The Football Association Ltd* [2007] EWHC 2376 (Ch); [2008] F.S.R. 10 at para.31. In *G. Ricordi & Co v Clayton & Waller Ltd* [1928–1935] Mac.C.C. 154, the possibility of subconscious copying was accepted but not established on the facts. In *Rees v Melville* [1911–1916] Mac.C.C. 168, it was established that the defendant might unconsciously (or indeed consciously) have retained some recollection of the claimant's play but as no substantial part was reproduced, there was no infringement. Subconscious misuse of information has been held sufficient to found a breach of confidence claim: *Seager v Copydex Ltd* [1967] 1 W.L.R. 923 at 921; [1967] F.S.R. 211.

[170] *Francis Day & Hunter Ltd v Bron* [1963] Ch. 587. Diplock L.J. felt unable to deal with the matter without evidence of the mental processes involved. Upjohn L.J. declined to express a view. *G. Ricordi & Co (London) Ltd v Clayton & Waller Ltd* [1928–1935] Mac.C.C. 154, ibid. was apparently cited as the only English authority on the point (see at 612), although a number of US authorities were relied on. In *Andritz Sprout-Bauer Australia Pty Ltd v Rowland Engineering Sales Pty Ltd* (1993) 28 I.P.R. 29 (Fed Ct of Aus), the concept was clearly accepted.

[171] *Francis Day & Hunter Ltd v Bron* [1963] Ch. 587, per Diplock L.J. at 625. Willmer L.J. expressed the opinion (at 614) that whether or not the defendant was consciously aware of a causal connection was irrelevant.

[172] *Industrial Furnaces Ltd v Reeves* [1970] R.P.C. 605 at 623 (conscious copying found in the facts); *Galago Publishers (Pty) Ltd v Erasmus* [1989] 1 S.A. 276 at 293. Note that in the case of artistic works there is a limited defence under CDPA 1988 s.64 for an artist who does not repeat or imitate the main design of his earlier work. See para.9–193, below.

B. SUBSTANTIAL PART

7–25   Introduction. The law has never allowed a defendant to escape liability on the grounds that he has not copied the claimant's work exactly; less than complete copying has always been an infringement. In this, the underlying rationale of the law of copyright is to protect and adequately reward the interests of authors and copyright owners and to prevent others from unfairly appropriating the benefit of the effort, skill and labour which went into a work's creation.[173] On the other hand, it has never been the law that copying of any part of a work, no matter how small, is unlawful; copyright should not be allowed to become an instrument of oppression and extortion.[174] Some use of a copyright work is clearly permissible, for the Act does not prohibit use of "any" part, even if that part was the product of skill and labour,[175] only of a "substantial part".[176] It is in arriving at the dividing line that the difficulty arises. Although the issue arises in relation to all the exclusive rights of the copyright owner, not merely the reproduction right, it most often arises and is mostly easily discussed in the present context.

Where the copying is not exact copying of the whole work, the use which has been made of the claimant's work can usually be characterised as either (a) the exact use of part of the work only (as where extracts from a literary work have been taken verbatim) or (b) some reworking of the whole of it (as where the whole of a literary work has been paraphrased, dramatised or translated into another language; an entire artistic work imitated in some way; or a complete musical work altered) or (c) a combination of these. As to these:

(a) The issue in the first category is simply whether the part which has been taken is a substantial part, applying the tests set out below.

(b) Where the whole work has been imitated, modified or otherwise altered without exact copying of any part, the issue has historically sometimes been treated as being whether the use amounts to the copying of the whole of the claimant's work[177] and sometimes whether the copying is of a substantial part.[178] These cases were also sometimes characterised as ones of "colourable imitation" or "colourable alteration" of the claimant's

---

[173] *Designers Guild Ltd v Russell Williams (Textiles) Ltd* [2001] 1 W.L.R. 2416, at 2432 (Lord Scott) and per Lord Bingham at 2418; [2001] F.S.R. 11: "The law of copyright rests on a very clear principle: that anyone who by his or her own skill and labour creates an original work of whatever character shall, for a limited period, enjoy an exclusive right to copy that work. No one else may for a season reap what the copyright owner has sown". See also, e.g. *Hanfstaengl v Empire Palace* [1894] 3 Ch. 109 at 128, CA; *Hawkes & Son (London) Ltd v Paramount Film Service Ltd* [1934] Ch. 593 at 602.

[174] *Hanfstaengl v Empire Palace* [1894] 3 Ch. 109 at 128, CA; *Hawkes & Son (London) Ltd v Paramount Film Service Ltd* [1934] Ch. 593 at 602, and also *Chappell & Co v D.C. Thompson & Co* [1928–1935] Mac.C.C. 467. Admittedly, in *Hanfstaengl* one of the examples of oppression and extortion of which Lindley L.J. was thinking was the possibility of preventing fair reviews of plays, etc. a matter which then fell to be decided under the heading of copying, but which would now be dealt with under the heading of fair dealing (see paras 9–23 et seq., below). This does not apply to the other examples he cites, or the decisions in *Hawkes* and *Chappell*, decided under the 1911 Act.

[175] *Electronic Techniques (Anglia) Ltd v Critchley Components Ltd* [1997] F.S.R. 401 at 409. In *Designers Guild Ltd v Russell Williams (Textiles) Ltd* [2001] 1 W.L.R. 2416, at 2418, Lord Bingham described the substantial part test as amounting to the realistic recognition that no real injury is done to the copyright owner if no more than an insignificant part of the copyright work is copied.

[176] CDPA 1988 s.16(3)(a). As to the reference in art.2 of the Information Society Directive 2001/29, art.2, to reproduction in whole or "in part", see para.7–27.

[177] As in *Sillitoe v McGraw-Hill Book Co (U.K.) Ltd* [1983] F.S.R. 545 at 550. And see the analysis in *Spectravest Inc v Aperknit Ltd* [1988] F.S.R. 161 at 170.

[178] As in *King Features Syndicate Inc v O. & M. Kleeman* [1941] A.C. 417, HL, at 424; *Bauman v Fussell* [1978] R.P.C. 485, CA.

work.[179] The use of the expression was continued in the 1911 Act, which defined an infringing copy as including any copy or colourable imitation of a work[180] (in addition to defining "copyright" as the sole right to produce or reproduce the work or any substantial part of it[181]) but was no longer included as part of the definition of infringement in the 1956 or 1988 Acts.[182] Although the expression is sometimes still used,[183] it is suggested that since the ordinary meaning of colourable is that the change is designed to disguise the fact that use has been made of the claimant's work,[184] it does not add to the discussion of what amounts to impermissible copying. The defendant's state of mind, in particular whether the changes were made deliberately in an attempt to throw off the suspicion of copying, is irrelevant.[185] The only relevant question is whether there has been a copying of a substantial part of the claimant's work. In order to answer this question, it is necessary to identify, first, what elements or features of the copyright work have been taken and then, secondly, to ask whether those elements or features amount to a substantial part of the copyright work, applying the tests set out below.[186] The approach is therefore no different in principle to that applied in relation to the first category of cases, although it is more difficult to apply because of the requirement to identify, as a first step, the elements or features which have been taken. It may be tempting, particularly in cases of artistic or musical works where it is often difficult to describe in words what has been taken, to ask whether the offending work looks or sounds like the copyright work or, conversely, to reach a conclusion that since it does *not* look or sound like the copyright work, no substantial part has been taken. This approach is incorrect, however, and may lead to the wrong conclusion.[187]

(c) In the third class of case, it is again necessary to identify what part or parts of the copyright work have been copied and then ask whether they amount to a substantial part of the whole work.

Although, therefore, types of copying can be differently categorised, the test remains the same.

Substantial part and permitted uses. The question of what amounts to a substantial part is not answered simply by balancing the interests of the author or   **7–26**

---

[179] Thus in early editions of this work, for example, infringements were classified as: (1) reprinting the whole verbatim; (2) reprinting a part verbatim; (3) imitating the whole or part or by reproducing the whole or part with colourable alterations; (4) reproduction under an abridged form and; (5) translation. See *Copinger* 4th edn (1904), pp.155(a) and 170(b).

[180] s.35(1).

[181] s.1(2).

[182] Although the expression is still used in the separate context of what constitutes publication of a work for the purposes of satisfying the qualification provisions of the Act. Thus CDPA 1988 s.175 states that references to publication "do not include publication which is merely colourable and not intended to satisfy the reasonable requirements of the public".

[183] See, e.g. *Designers Guild Ltd v Russell Williams (Textiles) Ltd* [2001] 1 W.L.R. 2416, per Lord Millett, at 2425: "The reproduction may be exact or it may introduce deliberate variations involving altered copying or colourable imitation as it is sometimes called"; *Sillitoe v McGraw-Hill Book Co (U.K.) Ltd* [1983] F.S.R. 545 at 550, where passages of the claimant's work had been rendered into *oratio obliqua*: "... 'reproduction' for copyright purposes, embraces a colourable imitation", and also *Norowzian v Arks Ltd* [1998] F.S.R. 394 (a colourable imitation to "all intents and purposes is a copy of the original work, albeit that there might be certain relatively minor changes to it").

[184] See, e.g. *Catnic Components Ltd v Hill & Smith Ltd* [1981] F.S.R. 60 and *Rodi and Weinenberger A.G. v Henry Showell Ltd* [1968] F.S.R. 100, both patent cases, and also *Emerson v Davies* (1845) 3 Story (Amer.) 768 at 793.

[185] As to " *animus furandi*", see para.7 31, sub para.(d)

[186] *Designers Guild Ltd v Russell Williams (Textiles) Ltd* [2001] 1 W.L.R. 2416.

[187] As happened in the Court of Appeal in *Designers Guild Ltd v Russell Williams (Textiles) Ltd*, reported at [2000] F.S.R. 121. See the decision in the House of Lords [2000] 1 W.L.R. 2416.

copyright owner against the general public interest in being able to reproduce parts of a work for certain purposes, since this latter interest can to a large extent be assumed to be safeguarded by the various permitted acts to which today the rights of the copyright owner are subject. Indeed, these two issues have been kept separate since the passing of the 1911 Act. Thus copyright is only infringed if a substantial part of the claimant's work has been taken. If this issue is decided against a defendant, the question may then arise as to whether his actions fall with any of the permitted acts. The extent of such acts is today the subject of a defined code.[188]

7–27   **The Information Society Directive.**[189] This Directive now governs the restricted act of reproduction of a copyright work. Article 2 of the Directive defines the reproduction right by reference to reproduction "in whole or in part" but does not define this concept further. As now established by the European Court of Justice,[190] the expression has to be construed having regard to the wording and context of the Directive, and in the light of the overall objectives of both the Directive and international law. In this, the Information Society Directive is based on the principle that copyright protection applies only in relation to subject-matter which is original in the sense that it is its author's own intellectual creation.[191] The various individual parts of a work will therefore enjoy protection under the Directive provided that they contain elements which are the expression of the intellectual creation of the author of the work. As a corollary, there will only be reproduction of a substantial part of a work where what has been reproduced represents the expression of the intellectual creation of the author of that work.[192] The scope of the protection conferred by the Directive should be broadly interpreted and so it is possible that a relatively small part of a work may contain within it the expression of the intellectual creation of the author and thus be a protectable part of a work.[193] It is for the national court in each case to make this determination.

The expression reproduction of "a part" in the Directive therefore does not mean any part, however small, and is clearly to be equated with expression "substantial part" in the 1988 Act.[194] As will be seen, the substantial part test as developed by the UK courts is in line with the test propounded by the Court of Justice and thus although reference must now be made to the Directive in

---

[188] See CDPA 1988 ss.28, para 8–76 and Ch.9, below.

[189] 2001/29/EC.

[190] *Infopaq International A/S v Danske Dagblades Forening* (C–5/08 [2009] ECR I–6569, upon which this and the following passage in the text are based.

[191] As to which, the directive follows the general scheme of the Berne Convention, in particular arts 2(5) and (8), which is that the protection of subject-matters as artistic or literary works presupposes that they are intellectual creations. The same is true for computer programs, databases and photographs, which are protected by copyright only if they are original in the sense that they are their author's own intellectual creation.

[192] *SAS Institute Inc v World Programming Ltd* [2010] EWHC 1829 (Ch) at para.244, applying *Infopaq International A/S v Danske Dagblades Forening* Case C–5/08 [2009] E.C.R. I–6569; [2009] E.C.D.R. 16 at paras 31–48.

[193] In *Infopaq International A/S v Danske Dagblades Forening* (C–5/08) [2009] ECR I–6569, itself, which was concerned with whether 11 consecutive words taken from a newspaper article constituted a part of the whole work for these purposes, the ECJ indicated that it was possible that such isolated sentences, or even certain parts of sentences in the text in question, might convey to the reader the originality of the newspaper article and thus an expression of the author's own intellectual creation.

[194] When implementing the Directive, the United Kingdom correctly assumed that the Directive did not require Member States to provide an exclusive right of reproduction literally in relation to any part, but only to any "creative" part, which it considered essentially to correspond with the UK substantial part test. See the Government Conclusions on the Patent Office's Consultation Paper of August 7, 2002.

determining this question, it does not appear that UK law has changed in this respect.

Substantial part: the test.[195] The Court of Appeal has warned against trying to define the term "substantial part", on the grounds that the quest is only "a path to a dictionary and to the dubious substitution or addition of other words which do not help to answer the crucial question of fact",[196] but some elucidation is necessary if only to better understand the expression and in this the decided cases help in identifying the relevant necessary and sufficient conditions for substantiality.[197] The essential test is whether the defendant's work has been produced by the substantial use of those features of the claimant's work which, by reason of the knowledge, skill and labour employed in their production, constitute it an original copyright work. The test has been put in a number of similar ways. Has the infringer incorporated a substantial part of the independent skill, labour, etc. contributed by the original author in creating the copyright work?[198] Has there been a substantial appropriation of the independent labours of the author?[199] Has there been an appropriation of a part of the work on which a substantial part of the author's skill and labour was expended?[200] Has there been an over-borrowing of the skill, labour and judgment which went into the making of the claimant's work?[201] Has the defendant made a substantial use of those features of the claimant's work in which copyright subsists?[202] It is therefore often important to ask what are the features of the claimant's work which made it an original work and thus which gave rise to its protection under the law of copyright in the first place. For example, with a literary work it may be the skill or effort in expressing thoughts or information in words, or the collecting together and presentation of other material; with a dramatic work, the working out of details of character and plot; with a musical work, the composition of a melody or its orchestration; with an artistic work, the arrangement and representation of subject matter; and so on. If substantial use has been made of these features, then a substantial part will have been taken.

7–28

Old law. As already noted, although it has always been the law that a defendant could not escape infringement by using less than the whole of the claimant's work, it was only with the passing of the 1911 Act that the "substantial part" test was expressly included as part of the statutory definition of infringement.[203] Although this was intended to give effect to previous decisions, which are therefore sometimes still good authority,[204] caution must be used in referring to pre-1911 Act cases since the issue of what might properly be taken of a claimant's work was often bound up with questions which would now fall within the description of "fair dealing" or permitted acts, again a topic which was not then part of any

7–29

---

[195] The equivalent of this paragraph of the 15th edition was described in *R. v Gilham* [2009] EWCA Crim 2293; [2010] Crim L.R. 407, as a helpful summary of the law.

[196] *Baigent v The Random House Group Ltd* [2007] EWCA Civ 247; [2007] F.S.R. 24, per Mummery L.J. at para.144, Rix L.J. agreeing.

[197] *Baigent v The Random House Group Ltd* [2007] EWCA Civ 247, per Mummery L.J. at para.145.

[198] *Designers Guild Ltd v Russell Williams (Textiles) Ltd* [2001] 1 W.L.R. 2416, per Lord Scott at 2431.

[199] *Ladbroke (Football) Ltd v William Hill (Football) Ltd* [1964] 1 W.L.R. 273 at 288.

[200] *Cantor Fitzgerald v Tradition (U.K.) Ltd* [2000] R.P.C. 95.

[201] *Ibcos Computers Ltd v Barclays Finance Ltd* [1994] F.S.R. 275. Although in *Cantor Fitzgerald v Tradition (U.K.) Ltd* [2000] R.P.C. 95, it was thought not helpful to rephrase the test by asking whether there has been an "overborrowing", since this does not add any further useful criteria.

[202] *Krisarts S.A. v Briarfine Ltd* [1977] F.S.R. 557, at 562.

[203] Copyright Act 1911 s.1(2). Under the Literary Copyright Act of 1842, which granted the exclusive right to print or otherwise multiply copies of "books", a book was defined to include every "volume, part or division of a volume". See s.2.

[204] *Chappell & Co v D.C. Thompson & Co* [1928–1935] Mac.C.C. 467.

statutory code. Thus the question often asked, before the 1911 Act, was whether any "unfair use" had been made of the claimant's work.[205]

7–30   **Substantial part: a question of mixed fact and law.** The issue of substantial part is a mixture of law and fact in the sense that it requires the court to apply a legal standard to the facts as found.[206] It is a matter of degree in each case[207] and has to be considered having regard to all the circumstances. In the end it is often a matter of impression,[208] in the sense that it generally involves taking into account a number of factors of varying degrees of importance and deciding whether they are sufficient to bring the whole within the legal description of "substantial part", as to which it may be difficult to give precise reasons for arriving at a conclusion one way or the other.[209] There are always borderline cases over which reasonable minds may differ.[210] For these reasons, and since the question involves the application of a "not altogether precise" legal standard to a combination of features of varying importance, an appeal will not lie against the decision unless the judge misdirected himself[211] or there was no evidence to support it.[212] It can be a matter which is suitable for determination on an application for summary judgment if this is the only live issue and no further relevant evidence will be available at trial.[213]

Although it is perhaps the most common and difficult of all questions which arise in copyright cases, limited assistance is obtained from the authorities. This is because after the application of the general principles discussed below, the matter, as already noted, often becomes one of impression. A court will therefore frequently move from a citation of one or more of the general principles and an enunciation of the relevant factors to a conclusion on the particular facts of the

[205] See, e.g. *Weatherby & Sons v International Horse Agency and Exchange Ltd* [1910] 2 Ch. 297.
[206] *Designers Guild Ltd v Russell Williams (Textiles) Ltd* [2001] 1 W.L.R. 2416, per Lord Hoffmann at 2423, although in *King Features Syndicate Inc v O. & M. Kleeman* [1941] A.C. 417, HL, per Viscount Maugham at 424, it was described as a question of fact. In the past, it has been described as a jury question (*Beere v Ellis* (1889) 5 T.L.R. 330, applying *Planche v Braham* 4 Bing. N.C. 19), although no doubt the jury had to be directed as to the law.
[207] *Ladbroke (Football) Ltd v William Hill (Football) Ltd* [1964] 1 W.L.R. 273 at 283; *Leco Instruments (U.K.) Ltd v Land Pyrometers Ltd* [1982] R.P.C. 140.
[208] *Merchandising Corporation of America v Harpbond* [1983] F.S.R. 32. *Handi-Craft Company v B Free World Ltd* [2007] EWHC 10 (Pat); [2007] E.C.D.R. 21 at para.171 (on appeal but not on this point [2008] EWCA Civ 868).
[209] *Designers Guild Ltd v Russell Williams (Textiles) Ltd* [2001] 1 W.L.R. 2416, at 2420, 2426.
[210] *Designers Guild Ltd v Russell Williams (Textiles) Ltd* [2001] 1 W.L.R. 2416.
[211] *Designers Guild Ltd v Russell Williams (Textiles) Ltd* [2001] 1 W.L.R. 2416 at 2418, 2423, applying *Pro Sieben Media A.G. v Carlton U.K. Television Ltd* [1999] 1 W.L.R. 605, 612–613; [2000] E.C.D.R. 110, and *Norowzian v Arks Ltd (No. 2)* [2000] F.S.R. 363, 370. See also *Bauman v Fussell* [1978] R.P.C. 485 at 487, 490, where the actual decision may have been surprising on its facts but the Court of Appeal, having come to the conclusion that the trial judge had correctly approached the issue as one of fact, was not prepared to interfere with his finding. Note also that where the decision on substantial part is based partly on assistance given by expert witnesses, the trial judge may be in a better position than the Court of Appeal to assess the importance of various elements of the claimant's work, even if the credibility of witnesses is not in issue. This may be an additional reason for the Court of Appeal not to interfere with the trial judge's decision: see *Designers Guild Ltd v Russell Williams (Textiles) Ltd* [2001] 1 W.L.R. 2416, at para.28, *per* Lord Hoffmann.
[212] *Bauman v Fussell* [1978] R.P.C. 485, at 489.
[213] Sometimes the application is by the alleged infringer who seeks a declaration of non-infringement, arguing that even if all other matters, such as copying, were established, the material which is alleged to have been taken still does not amount to a substantial part. Sometimes the judge hearing such an application will be in as good a position as the trial judge to reach a decision on the point, assuming that the copyright owner is not able to persuade the court that, for example, disclosure may throw light on the extent of copying, as in *Leco Instruments (U.K.) Ltd v Land Pyrometers Ltd* [1982] R.P.C. 140 (*sed quaere*), sometimes not, as in *Allen v Bloomsbury Publishing plc* [2010] EWHC (Ch). Generally, see para.21–259, below.

case without further analysis. Generally, therefore, it is not useful to refer to particular decisions as to the quantity taken.[214]

As to the general principles, the application of the substantial part test varies with the type of work, whether literary, dramatic, musical, artistic and so on. These categories will be considered separately, but some general propositions can be stated:[215]

(a) As already stated, the overriding question is whether, in creating the defendant's work, substantial use has been made of the skill and labour which went into the creation of the claimant's work and thus those features which made it an original work.

(b) The quality or importance[216] of what has been taken is much more important than the quantity.[217] The issue thus depends therefore not just on the physical amount taken but on its substantial significance[218] or importance to the copyright work,[219] so that the quality, or importance, of the part is frequently more significant than the proportion which the borrowed part bears to the whole. In this context, expressions such as "quality" or "importance" need to be properly understood. A literary work may convey a very important idea but, as already discussed, the law of copyright is concerned with the protection of the expression of such ideas, not the idea itself. In the same way, a drawing may contain important information, but it is the draftsman's work which the law protects, not the information as such.[220] Quality and importance must therefore be understood in terms of the features of the work which made it an original work in the first place. It follows that the quality relevant for the purposes of substantiality in the case of a literary work refers to the originality of that which has been copied. In the case of an artistic work, it is the originality of the artistic expression of that which has been copied.[221] And so on.

(c) Depending on the circumstances, the question may depend on whether what has been taken is novel or striking, or is merely a commonplace arrangement of words or well-known material.[222] In this respect it may be a helpful shortcut to ask whether the part taken could itself be the subject of copyright,[223] although this should not be used as a substitute for the proper and full test of substantial part.[224] In any event it is in reality merely a restatement of the basic question, which is whether use has been made of those features of the claimant's work which, by reason of the skill and la-

---

[214] See, e.g. *Bramwell v Halcomb* (1836) 3 My. & Cr. 737 at 738: "It is useless to refer to any particular cases as to quantity."

[215] Cited in part in *SAS Institute Inc v World Programming Ltd* [2010] EWHC 1829 (Ch), at para.169.

[216] *Catnic Components Ltd v Hill & Smith Ltd* [1981] F.S.R. 60.

[217] There are statements in many authorities to this effect. See, *e.g. Ladbroke (Football) Ltd v William Hill (Football) Ltd* [1964] 1 W.L.R. 273 at 276; *Designers Guild Ltd v Russell Williams (Textiles) Ltd* [2001] 1 W.L.R. 2416, at 2422, 2425, 2431. See also *Bramwell v Halcomb* (1836) 3 My. & Cr. 737 (all the "vital part of another's book, though it might be but a small proportion of the book in quantity").

[218] *Ladbroke (Football) Ltd v William Hill (Football) Ltd* [1964] 1 W.L.R. 273, at 283.

[219] *Designers Guild Ltd v Russell Williams (Textiles) Ltd* [2001] 1 W.L.R. 2416, per Lord Millett, at 2426.

[220] The difficult subject of what is protected by an artistic work is considered more fully later in this chapter.

[221] *Designers Guild Ltd v Russell Williams (Textiles) Ltd* [2001] 1 W.L.R. 2416, and see the comment on this aspect of the case in *Newspaper Licensing Agency Ltd v Marks & Spencer Plc* [2001] UKHL 38; [2003] 1 A.C. 551; [2002] R.P.C. 4.

[222] *Ladbroke (Football) Ltd v William Hill (Football) Ltd* [1964] 1 W.L.R. 273, at 276.

[223] So, in *A v B* [2001] E.M.L.R. 1006, copies of two pages from a personal daily diary were held to amount to a substantial part of the whole diary since the first entry in the diary, and each successive entry, would have been entitled to copyright protection on their own.

[224] *Ladbroke (Football) Ltd v William Hill (Football) Ltd* [1964] 1 W.L.R. 273 at 277.

bour employed in their production, constitute it an original copyright work.

(d) As a corollary of the last point, the more simple or lacking in substantial originality the copyright work, the greater the degree of taking will be needed before the substantial part test is satisfied. In the case of works of little originality, almost exact copying will normally be required to amount to infringement.[225]

(e) The more abstract and simple a copied idea, the less likely it is to constitute a substantial part. Originality, in the sense of the contribution of the author's skill and labour, tends to lie in the detail with which the basic idea is presented.[226]

(f) In general it is wrong to dissect the claimant's work, taking each part which has been copied and asking whether each part could be the subject of copyright if it had stood alone: "... it is wrong to take the parts of the original copyright work that have been copied in the alleged infringing work, to isolate them from the whole original copyright work and then to conclude that 'a substantial part' of the original copyright work has not been copied because there was no copyright in the copied parts on their own."[227] It is the work as a whole which must be considered,[228] particularly where the originality of the work lies in the creation of the work as a whole. If there is no originality in the creation of the work as a whole, for example where the work is simply a collection of subsidiary works assembled without any sufficient skill or labour, the proper analysis is that there is not one work but rather a number of works. In such a case it would be proper to take each subsidiary work by itself.[229] But this is not a question of substantial part but of identifying the real copyright work or works in issue. A claimant cannot divide up "the work" into small sections, so as to improve his case by arguing that a substantial part of a small section has been taken.[230]

(g) It is wrong to concentrate on the dissimilarities between the works: what is important is a comparison between the copyright work considered as a whole and those elements which have been taken from it.[231] The extent to which the defendant's work is different from the claimant's is irrelevant

---

[225] *Glogau v Land Transport Safety Authority of New Zealand* [1999] 1 N.Z.L.R. 257 (CA of NZ).

[226] *Designers Guild Ltd v Russell Williams (Textiles) Ltd* [2001] 1 W.L.R. 2416, at 2423, per Lord Hoffmann: "Copyright law protects foxes better than hedgehogs", explained by Arden LJ in L. *Woolley Jewellers Ltd v A & A Jewellery Ltd* [2002] EWCA Civ 1119; [2003] F.S.R. 15 at paras 9, 10 as follows: "... it appears that it is a reference to a fragment of Greek poetry of the seventh century BC, with which the late Sir Isaiah Berlin begins his famous essay on Tolstoy: 'There is a line among the fragments of a Greek poet Archilochus which says "The fox knows many things, but the hedgehog knows one big thing".' (The Hedgehog and the Fox: An Essay on Tolstoy's View of History by Isaiah Berlin. (1953, as revised in 1978) (Phoenix) (1999) p.3)." Arden LJ added that, as Sir Isaiah Berlin had pointed out. "... scholars have differed about the correct interpretation of these 'dark' words. They may, on the one hand, mean no more than that the fox, for all his cunning, is defeated by the hedgehog's one defence. But the fragment may also be taken figuratively as contrasting those with a single central vision and organising principle as against those who pursue many ends, often unrelated or contradictory. It was, I think, in the figurative sense that Lord Hoffmann was using his metaphor."

[227] See *Baigent v The Random House Group Ltd* [2007] EWCA Civ 247; [2007] F.S.R. 24, per Mummery L.J. at paras 131, 132, with whom Rix L.J. agreed.

[228] *Designers Guild Ltd v Russell Williams (Textiles) Ltd* [2001] 1 W.L.R. 2416, at 2421.

[229] As in *Leslie v Young & Sons* [1894] A.C. 335.

[230] *Coffey v Warner/Chappell Music Ltd* [2005] EWHC 449 (Ch); [2005] F.S.R. 34; [2006] E.M.L.R. 2, at paras 8 to 10, applying *Coogi Australia Pty Ltd v Hysport International Pty Ltd* (1998) 157 A.L.R. 247 (Fed Ct of Aus).

[231] *Designers Guild Ltd v Russell Williams (Textiles) Ltd* [2001] 1 W.L.R. 2416, at 2418, 2422. See also *Entec (Pollution Control) Ltd v Abacus Mouldings* [1992] F.S.R. 332; *Biotrading & Financing OY v Biohit Ltd* [1998] F.S.R. 109 at 121.

and, in the context of artistic works for example, it is wrong to ask whether the defendant's work looks, or does not look like, like the claimant's.[232]

(h) At this stage it is also wrong merely to compare the similarities between the works where not all the similarities are due to copying. What matters is the significance of what has been copied.

(i) If copying is established or admitted, it is wrong to jump to the conclusion that a substantial part was taken,[233] for copying can clearly occur which falls short of the taking of a substantial part. Nevertheless, where a finding of copying has been made as a result of the inference drawn from the similarities between the two works, it is likely to follow that a substantial part has been taken, although the question still needs to be considered independently.[234] While a finding of copying based in inference may not conclude the issue of copying, in many cases it is almost bound to do so.[235] An exception to this general approach will be where copying has been established because of the presence of a small and non-substantial number of unexplained similarities, the only explanation for which is copying.[236] The court may of course go on to make a finding, based on this small number of points in common, that copying on a larger scale has taken place,[237] but unless it does so, the court will not be justified in a holding that there has been copying of a substantial part.

(j) If what has been taken from the claimant's work is material which was not original to the maker of the work, because for example it was copied from another work, then it should be disregarded in deciding this issue.[238] If, however, part of the originality of the claimant's work consisted of the choosing and collecting together of unoriginal material, and the defendant has made unfair use of *this* labour and skill, then the test will be satisfied. This can often be seen in compilation cases,[239] but other types of works will also often contain elements taken from earlier works but combined in a new way. In such cases, "old" material which has been copied should not be disregarded: all of what was copied should be taken into account, keeping in mind what it was that made the claimant's work original.[240] On the other hand, "that which would not attract copyright except by reason of its collocation will, when robbed of that collocation, not be a substantial part of the copyright".[241] It is, therefore, often important to isolate what is the real worth of a work from the copyright point of view, in particular

---

[232] *Designers Guild Ltd v Russell Williams (Textiles) Ltd* [2001] 1 W.L.R. 2416; *Baumann v Fussell* [1978] R.P.C. 485; *Spectravest Inc v Aperknit Ltd* [1988] F.S.R. 161 at 170; *Monsoon Ltd v India Imports of Rhode Island Ltd* [1993] F.S.R. 486. An examination of the differences may of course highlight the similarities: *Biotrading & Financing OY v Biohit Ltd* [1998] F.S.R. 109.

[233] *Ibcos Computers Ltd v Barclays Finance Ltd* [1994] F.S.R. 275 at 301.

[234] *Designers Guild Ltd v Russell Williams (Textiles) Ltd* [2001] 1 W.L.R. 2416, at 2418, per Lord Bingham, at 2426, per Lord Millett.

[235] *Designers Guild Ltd v Russell Williams (Textiles) Ltd* [2001] 1 W.L.R. 2416: cf. the view of Lord Scott, that such a finding would be determinative of the issue of substantiality as well as copying. The other Law Lords do not appear to have agreed, and it is suggested that it is wrong as a matter of principle. In *Nova Productions Ltd v Mazooma Games Ltd* [2007] EWCA Civ 219; [2007] R.P.C. 25, it was considered that Lord Scott's observation was confined to the facts of the case and did not lay down any general principle: para.26.

[236] As sometimes happens in the case of directories, where deliberate mistakes, or "sleepers", are placed in the copyright work in order to detect infringers, or in the case of computer programs, which often contain redundant sections of code.

[237] As in *Comprop Ltd v Moran* [2002] J.L.R. 222 (Royal Ct of Jersey).

[238] *Warwick Film Productions Ltd v Eisinger* [1969] Ch. 508.

[239] See para.7–47, below.

[240] *Biotrading & Financing OY v Biohit Ltd* [1998] F.S.R. 109 at 122 (designs for parts of pipettes including shapes taken from earlier drawings but combined with new shapes).

[241] *Ladbroke (Football) Ltd v William Hill (Football) Ltd* [1964] 1 W.L.R. 273 at 293.

what parts of the work constitute the original contribution of the author and thus represent the skill or labour of his creation.

(k) Although statements to precisely the opposite effect can be found,[242] the relevant question is not whether the part which has been taken forms a substantial part of the defendant's work but whether a substantial part of the claimant's work has been taken. Indeed, whether the part taken forms either a small or a substantial part of the defendant's work is irrelevant.[243] The overall appearance of the defendant's work may therefore be very different from the copyright work while nevertheless infringing.[244] Of course, if the defendant's work is of any substance and a large proportion of it has been copied from the claimant's, it may easily follow that an unlawful appropriation of the claimant's labours had been made.

(l) In the case of some works, such as works of reference, it may be that a greater amount of copying is permissible than with other works, such as novels. This is on the basis that one of the purposes of the author was to add to the stock of human knowledge, so that there may be attributed to him an intention that the material in his work, if it is not to become sterile, may be used by the reader with the consequence that the law will allow wider use of such a work.[245] The right of copyright does not extend to clothing information, facts, ideas, theories and themes with exclusive property rights, so as to enable a claimant to monopolise historical research or knowledge and prevent the legitimate use of historical and biographical material, theories propounded, general arguments deployed, or general hypotheses suggested (whether they are sound or not) or general themes written about.[246] It is suggested, however, that the principle, if it exists, is of limited application, perhaps to historical works only,[247] and is certainly not applicable to all reference works.[248] There seems no good reason why the normal rule should not be that the copyright owner is presumed to have intended that such use should be made of his work as the law generally allows in the case of copyright works and no more. Any wider right to use could only be the subject of one of the permitted acts or some implied licence, a limited concept.

7–31   Other considerations. A number of other considerations were sometimes put forward in the past as helping to decide whether a substantial part has been taken but today need to be treated with caution:

(a) Are the two works in competition? Has the value of the claimant's work been diminished? Is the market for the claimant's work likely or unlikely to be affected? Tests of these kind were sometimes applied[249] but it is suggested that today they need to be used with caution. Obviously, if it can be

---

[242] e.g. *Neale v Harmer* (1897) 13 T.L.R. 209.

[243] *Designers Guild Ltd v Russell Williams (Textiles) Ltd* [2001] 1 W.L.R. 2416, per Lord Millett at 2425. The same point is made in *Cantor Fitzgerald v Tradition (U.K.) Ltd* [2000] R.P.C. 95, at 133. See also *Nova Productions Limited v Mazooma Games Limited* [2006] EWHC 24 (Ch); [2006] R.P.C. 14 at para.122; on appeal [2007] EWCA Civ 219; [2007] R.P.C. 25.

[244] *Nova Productions Limited v Mazooma Games Limited* [2006] EWHC 24 (Ch), [2006] R.P.C. 14, [2006] E.M.L.R. 14 at para.122 (on appeal [2007] EWCA Civ 219; [2007] R.P.C. 25).

[245] *Ravenscroft v Herbert* [1980] R.P.C. 193 at 205.

[246] *Baigent v The Random House Group Limited* [2006] EWHC 719 (Ch); [2006] E.M.L.R. 16 at para.176.

[247] This was the subject matter in *Ravenscroft*.

[248] *Comprop Ltd v Moran* [2002] J.L.R. 222 (Royal Ct of Jersey).

[249] See the statement of Story J. quoted in *Folsom v Marsh* (1841) 2 Story 100 at 116, cited with approval in *Scott v Stanford* (1867) L.R. 3 Eq. 718, that: "… we must, in deciding questions of this sort, look to … [inter alia] … the degree in which the use may prejudice the sale, or diminish the profits, or supersede the objects, of the original work". In *Weatherby & Sons v International*

seen that the market for lawful reproductions of the claimant's work has been adversely affected, this may be because a substantial part has been taken, particularly if the reason for this is that the public regards the defendant's work as an adequate substitute for the claimant's.[250] Care needs to be taken, however, since this decline may simply be the result of lawful (i.e. non-infringing) competition. Conversely, it is possible to imagine many cases where the businesses of the claimant and the defendant do not compete, but unfair advantage of the claimant's skill and labour may yet have been taken.[251] In such a case it is difficult to see why the absence of competition should help answer the question in favour of the defendant. Where, however, the two works are clearly in the same market and compete, and the claimant's work would be expected to suffer if a substantial part had been taken, the absence of any injury may be a helpful indication.

(b) A rough practical test which is sometimes applied is: "what is worth copying is worth protecting".[252] An indication of the value of what was taken may, of course, be the fact that the defendant has chosen to take it rather than rely on his own efforts.[253] Clearly, however, the test needs to be applied with caution since otherwise the copying of any part of a work would amount to an infringement: at best it should serve as a guide only[254] and at worst it is a misleading rhetorical device.[255] The practice of "sampling" musical works and sound recordings, discussed later, and the use of "Ringtones", may be appropriate cases for the application of this test. The test can also have no real application where the whole point of the defendant's work was to refer to works such as the claimant's, for example, in a work of criticism or reference.

(c) On the same principle, it has been said that the basis of copyright law is the Seventh Commandment: "Thou shalt not steal",[256] but this is not particularly helpful since it does not identify what it is permissible to take.

Horse Agency and Exchange Ltd [1910] 2 Ch. 297, Parker J. stated that the nature of the two works and the likelihood or unlikelihood of competition was not only relevant but might be the determining factor in a case. But see fn.252 as to this case. Another example is *Cambridge University Press v University Tutorial Press Ltd* (1928) 75 R.P.C. 335, where this factor was described as useful, although not determinative. Older cases on the point include *Dodsley v Kinnersely* (1737) 1 Amb. 402; *Gyles v Wilcox* (1740) 2 Atk. 141; *Hawkesworth v Newbery* (1776) Lofft. 755; *Bell v Whitehead* (1839) 8 L.J. Ch. 141; cf. e.g. *Dickens v Lee* (1844) 8 Jur. 183, suggesting that the claimant is the best person to judge whether his work is harmed. And note also *Nova Productions Limited v Mazooma Games Limited* [2007] EWCA Civ 21 at para.26, where Jacob L.J. observed in passing: "... the games, being different from one another, are not competitive in the sense that one would do as a substitute for the other."

[250] As, e.g. with an abridgment or other edited version.

[251] Thus in *Weatherby & Sons v International Horse Agency and Exchange Ltd* [1910] 2 Ch. 297, Parker J. went on to say (see fn.250) that unfair use of the claimant's work might be made even where there is no likelihood of competition, since copyright is a right of property. For an example, see *Kipling v Genatosan Ltd* [1917–1923] Mac.C.C. 203, where four lines from Kipling's "If" were used in an advertisement for the defendant's medicinal preparation. Held: an infringement.

[252] *University of London Press Ltd v University Tutorial Press Ltd* [1916] 2 Ch. 601 at 610, cited with approval in *Ladbroke (Football) Ltd v William Hill (Football) Ltd* [1964] 1 W.L.R. 273 at 288.

[253] *Campbell v Scott* (1842) 11 Sim. 31, per Shadwell V.-C. at 39: "I do not think that it is necessary for me to consider whether the selections in this case are the very cream and essence of all that [the claimant] ever wrote; but it is pretty plain that they would not have been inserted in the Defendant's work, unless the party who selected them thought that they were very attractive in themselves".

[254] *Ibcos Computers Ltd v Barclays Mercantile Highland Finance Ltd* [1994] F.S.R. 275; *Cantor Fitzgerald v Tradition (U.K.) Ltd* [2000] R.P.C. 95, at 133; *Network Ten Pty Ltd v TCN Channel None Pty Ltd* [2004] HCA 14, 59 I P R 1 (2004).

[255] *Baigent v The Random House Group Ltd* [2007] EWCA Civ 247; [2007] F.S.R. 24 at para.97, per Lloyd L.J., Rix L.J. and Mummery L.J. agreeing.

[256] e.g. *MacMillan & Co. Ltd v Cooper* (1923) 40 T.L.T. 186, PC, at p.187.

As a statement it can neither enhance the rights of an owner nor extend the ambit of infringement.[257] It also does not emphasise the real basis of copyright law, which is that one man must not be permitted to appropriate the result of another's labour.[258]

(d) Has there been an *animus furandi*[259] on the part of the defendant, in the sense of an intention on his part to take for the purpose of saving himself labour?[260] Historically, this test was sometimes applied,[261] but today the defendant's intentions are to be regarded as irrelevant,[262] as is whether use of the claimant's work is openly acknowledged or not.[263] The concept is a red herring in modern copyright law, and should no longer be invoked.[264]

(e) Has the defendant expended a sufficient amount of skill and labour on his work such that it qualifies as an original work itself? Is the defendant's work itself a useful work, not being just a copy of the claimant's? This test was often applied in the older cases[265] but today is no longer good law.[266]

7–32   **"Little and often".** A problem arises where a defendant regularly takes a small amount of material from the claimant's works, for example, a few statistics each week from figures published by the claimant. Assuming that the taking of the material from just one issue is not enough of itself to amount to an infringement, does the defendant infringe by his cumulative actions? The same problem arises where a defendant takes a large number of small segments from a digital work. There are two types of situation to be considered, first, where the takings are made from different copyright works, secondly, where the takings are all made from the same copyright work:

(1) In *Trade Auxiliary Co v Middlesborough, etc. Association,*[267] the claimant published a nationwide weekly list of all bills of sale and deeds of arrangement which had been registered, running to about 400 items. The

---

[257] *C.B.S. Songs Ltd v Amstrad Plc* [1988] A.C. 1013; [1988] R.P.C. 567, per Lord Templeman at 1057.

[258] *L.B. (Plastics) Ltd v Swish Products Ltd* [1979] F.S.R. 145, HL. And see *Autospin (Oil Seals) Ltd v Beehive Spinning* [1995] R.P.C. 683, per Laddie J. at 700 suggesting that it is because the claimant has so often blatantly stolen the results of the claimant's labours in many cases that the courts have applied this principle with "almost evangelical fervour". Compare the more correct aphorism: "No one else may for a season reap what the copyright owner has sown": *Designers Guild Ltd v Russell Williams (Textiles) Ltd* [2001] 1 W.L.R. 2416, per Lord Bingham at 2418.

[259] i.e. an intention of stealing.

[260] *Jarrold v Houlston* (1857) 3 K. & J. 708. The distinction made is usually between those cases where a defendant has taken the claimant's work and promulgated it as his own, and works of criticism, abridgement, etc. where there is no disguise of the source.

[261] See, e.g. *Carey v Kearsley* (1802) 4 Esp. 168; *Mawman v Tegg* (1826) 2 Russ. 385; *Lewis v Fullarton* (1839) 2 Beav. 6; *Reade v Lacy* (1861) 1 J. & H. 524. However, the principle was also applied in the relatively modern case of *Ravenscroft v Herbert* [1980] R.P.C. 193, at 203, 207.

[262] See para.7–07, above.

[263] This only becomes relevant in the context of fair dealing. See paras 9–23 et seq., below.

[264] *Baigent v The Random House Group Ltd* [2007] EWCA Civ 247; [2007] F.S.R. 24 at para.97, per Lloyd L.J., Rix L.J. and Mummery L.J. agreeing.

[265] A sample of such cases includes: *Gyles v Wilcox* (1740) 2 Atk. 141; *Carey v Kearsley* (1802) 4 Esp. 168; *Wilkins v Aikin* (1810) 17 Ves. 422; *Mawman v Tegg* (1826) 2 Russ. 385; *Bramwell v Halcomb* (1836) 3 My. & Cr. 737; *Dickens v Lee* (1844) 8 Jur. 183; *Spiers v Brown* (1858) 6 W.R. 352; *Hotten v Arthur* (1863) 1 H. & M. 603. *Glyn v Weston Feature Film Co* [1916] 1 Ch. 261 is a later example.

[266] *Schweppes Ltd v Wellingtons Ltd* [1984] F.S.R. 210, followed in *Williamson Music Ltd v Pearson Partnership* [1987] F.S.R. 97. The headnote in *Joy Music Ltd v Sunday Pictorial Newspapers (1920) Ltd* [1960] 2 Q.B. 60 is incorrect: *Williamson Music*. In *Henkel KgaA v Holdfast New Zealand Ltd* [2006] NZSC 102; (2006) 70 IPR 624; [2007] 1 N.Z.L.R. 336 at para.49, the Supreme Court of New Zealand stated that if the defendant's work was of sufficient originality to amount to a copyright work, there would have been no infringement. This approach does not accord with English law.

[267] *Auxiliary Co v Middlesborough, etc. Association* (1889) 40 Ch. D. 425.

defendant took details which were of local interest to readers of its publication, amounting to about four per week, and was held to have infringed.[268] In *Cate v Devon and Exeter Constitutional Newspaper Co*,[269] brought by the same claimants, the defendant similarly took a small number of entries for its local readership[270] and was held to have infringed on the ground that all that was material for the purpose of the defendant's newspaper had been taken and copied exactly and systematically, week by week, as of right. It is suggested, however, that in so far as each work is a separate copyright work, each must be looked at separately to see whether a substantial part of *that* work has been taken. It is not legitimate to combine separate works and ask whether a substantial part of the combination has been appropriated. If, of course, the claimant's work can be regarded as one serial work published in instalments, the position may be different,[271] but it is suggested that this is likely to be an artificial solution.[272] It is also not easy to see why, as a matter of principle, if a defendant acts lawfully by taking an extract from one publication, his actions should become unlawful if repeated in relation to successive publications, however aggravating his conduct might be to the claimant.[273] These two cases have since been explained as having been decided at a time when the relevant statute contained no reference to substantial part, and the only issue was whether the infringement was sufficiently minimal as not to warrant the grant of an injunction: they did not decide that a "substantial part", as that expression is now understood, had been taken.[274] Whether or not this is correct, it is suggested that the cases would not be decided in the same way today. So, where there had been regular copying of small extracts (each not a substantial part in itself) from successive editions of newspapers, and thus separate copyright works, it was held that this did not cumulatively amount to the taking of a substantial part.[275]

(2) In *Football League Ltd v Littlewoods Pools Ltd*,[276] the claimant had produced a chronological list of the 2,000 or so weekly Football League championship fixtures to be played in the season. Each fortnight, the defendant copied the list of the fixtures being played by the 90 or so clubs for that fortnight for the purpose of preparing its pools coupons. There was, therefore, only one copyright work which was alleged to have been infringed, the case being that small amounts had been repeatedly taken. The defendant was held to have infringed, relying on *Cate*, and the decision has since been regarded as correctly decided on the basis that the statutory requirement of substantial part was satisfied by the repeated, systematic copying from the same work, such that the entire list was in the end copied.[277] On the facts, however, it is suggested that each fortnightly list was clearly an infringement of the whole chronological list and it was

---

[268] The then relevant Act, the 1842 Act, contained no express "substantial part" test. The defendant argued that the use was *de minimis*.

[269] *Auxiliary Co v Middlesborough, etc. Association* (1889) 40 Ch. D. 500.

[270] In one case, a single entry only. See p.507 of the report.

[271] See the suggestion to this effect made in *Electronic Techniques (Anglia) Ltd v Critchley Components Ltd* [1997] F.S.R. 401.

[272] For example, if the various lists made for the claimant in the two cases had been made by different authors, although each employed by the claimant, they would clearly be different works.

[273] See *Electronic Techniques (Anglia) Ltd v Critchley Components Ltd* [1997] F.S.R. 401 for a discussion of some of the illogical results which follow from the decision in *Cate*.

[274] *Newspaper Licensing Agency Ltd v Marks & Spencer Plc* [2001] UKHL 38; [2003] 1 A.C. 551; [2002] R.P.C. 4.

[275] *Newspaper Licensing Agency Ltd v Marks & Spencer Plc* [2001] UKHL 38.

[276] *Football League Ltd v Littlewoods Pools Ltd* [1959] Ch. 637.

[277] *Newspaper Licensing Agency Ltd v Marks & Spencer Plc* [2001] UKHL 38.

unnecessary to call in aid the cumulative effect of the defendant's actions. In contrast, if, for example, a local newspaper had each week published the details of the one match being played by its local club, the publication of that one fixture in the first week would surely not infringe, and the newspaper's actions could surely not become infringing in the future by some process of accumulation.[278] Otherwise, presumably it would follow that an infringement would occur once the cumulative amount taken went past the threshold of a substantial part. Presumably, it would then also follow that at this point all previous copying would retrospectively become an infringement, and that what was previously not an infringing copy would now become an infringing copy. This type of conclusion shows the difficulty with the point. The position might well be different if, at the beginning of the season, the newspaper had published a complete list of all matches to be played by the club that season. The problem can also arise today with the transient copying of small fragments of a work in temporary computer memory. Such fragments should generally not be considered on a cumulative or rolling basis, particularly where they are successively destroyed as an inherent part of the process: the substantial part must be embodied in the transient copy, not in a series of different transient copies which are stored one after the other.[279] In *Infopaq International A/S v Danske Dagblades Forening*,[280] the European Court of Justice was concerned with a data capture process that allowed for the reproduction of multiple extracts from protected works, a process which reproduced an extract of 11 words each time a search word appeared in the relevant work. The court ruled that the reproduction of 11 words might of itself amount to a substantial part of the work in question[281] but also observed that the process increased the likelihood that the defendant would make reproductions in part within the meaning of the Directive "… because the cumulative effect of those extracts may lead to the *reconstitution of lengthy fragments* which are liable to reflect the originality of the work in question …" (emphasis added). It thus seems that the court did not consider that the cumulative taking of short, non-infringing fragments without their reconstitution into longer, infringing fragments would be an infringement. In any event, however, there is an outstanding referral to the European Court of Justice which should throw further light on this issue.[282]

7–33   **Parodies and burlesques.** The fact that a defendant's work may be a parody or

---

[278] See, again, *Electronic Techniques (Anglia) Ltd v Critchley Components Ltd* [1997] F.S.R. 401, for a discussion of the illogicalities involved. Laddie J. there suggested that a defendant's conduct might be viewed as one continuous act, a proposition which is again suggested to be artificial. As Laddie J. himself points out at 409, a small amount of copying is permissible, even though the labour of the claimant is thereby appropriated.

[279] *Football Association Premier League Ltd v QC Leisure* [2008] EWHC 1411 (Ch); [2008] F.S.R. 32, [2008] 3 C.M.L.R. 12 at para.227. Although Kitchin J. stated that he was not reaching a conclusion as to the above doubts about the doctrine as expressed in *Electronic Techniques (Anglia) Ltd v Critchley Components Ltd* [1997] F.S.R. 401, it is suggested that the case is a clear example of the second category of "little and often". Kitchin J. in any event referred the issue to the European Court of Justice—see subsequently in the text.

[280] *Infopaq International A/S v Danske Dagblades Forening* (C–5/08) [2009] ECR I–6569.

[281] See para.7–27.

[282] *Football Association Premier League Ltd v QC Leisure* [2008] EWHC 1411 (Ch). The question referred relates to a case where sequential fragments of a film, musical work or sound recording (such as frames of digital video and audio) are created (i) within the memory of a decoder or (ii) in the case of a film on a television screen, and the whole work is reproduced if the sequential fragments are considered together but only a limited number of fragments exist at any point in time. The questions referred are: (a) is the question of whether those works have been reproduced in whole or in part to be determined by the rules of national copyright law relating to what constitutes an infringing reproduction of a copyright work, or is it a matter of interpretation of art.2 of the Information Society Directive? (b) If the latter, should the national court consider all of the

burlesque of the claimant's is not a relevant consideration when considering the issue of substantial part.[283] The test remains the same, whether in the context of literary,[284] dramatic,[285] musical[286] or artistic works.[287] The point is discussed further in relation to these classes of works.

C. LITERARY, DRAMATIC, MUSICAL AND ARTISTIC WORKS

In relation to literary, dramatic, musical and artistic works, the exclusive right of copying is defined to mean the right of reproducing the work in any material form.[288] For this purpose, reproducing a work in material form includes storing it in any medium by electronic means[289] and making transient copies or ones which are incidental to some other use.[290] Although in other contexts the word "reproduce" is sometimes used in the neutral sense of producing something similar, whether by copying or not,[291] it is clear that in the present context that the word "reproduce" essentially means "copy".[292] However, even though the two words are now often used interchangeably in this context, historically the expression "copy" encompassed a narrower class of act than simply "reproduce in any material form". For example, under the law before the 1911 Act, a musical work was not copied by the making of a mechanical device which could reproduce the musical work in terms of sound.[293] The later Acts made clear that in the case of literary, dramatic or musical works, references to reproducing a work were to include their reproduction in the form of a record or film.[294] Although the 1988

7–34

---

fragments of each work as a whole, or only the limited number of fragments which exist at any point in time? If the latter, what test should the national court apply to the question of whether the works have been reproduced in part within the meaning of that article?

[283] *Schweppes Ltd v Wellingtons Ltd* [1984] F.S.R. 210; *Williamson Music Ltd v Pearson Partnership* [1987] F.S.R. 97. Whether there can be a "fair dealing" defence in the case of parodies is considered elsewhere. See para.9–46, below. The government has decided not to alter the 1988 Act in response to Information Society Directive (2000/31/EC), which allows exceptions to be made in respect of such uses (see art.5.3(k)). See the responses to the government's consultation paper on the Gowers Review of December 2006 at *http://www.ipo.gov.uk/pro-policy/consult/consult-live/consult-gowers2.htm* [Accessed March 23, 2010].

[284] *Williamson Music Ltd v Pearson Partnership* [1987] F.S.R. 97.

[285] *Glyn v Weston Feature Film Co* [1916] 1 Ch. 261; *Carlton v Mortimer* [1917–1923] Mac.C.C. 194.

[286] *Francis Day & Hunter Ltd v Feldman & Co* [1914] 2 Ch. 728; *Williamson Music Ltd v Pearson Partnership* [1987] F.S.R. 97.

[287] *Twentieth Century Fox Film Corp. Ltd v Anglo Amalgamated Film Distributors Ltd*, *The Times*, January 22, 1965; *Schweppes Ltd v Wellingtons Ltd* [1984] F.S.R. 210; *A.G.L. Sydney Ltd v Shortland County Council* [1990] A.I.P.C. 90–661 (Fed Ct of Aus) (parody of advertisement by advertisement).

[288] CDPA 1988 s.17(2).

[289] CDPA 1988 s.17(2)

[290] CDPA 1988 s.17(6). See para.7–20 as to transient copying.

[291] In *Purefoy Engineering Co. Ltd v Sykes, Boxall & Co. Ltd* (1954) 72 R.P.C. 89, Evershed M.R. at 99, gave the example of the effects of a naturally occurring event, such as a storm, being "reproduced" by a later storm.

[292] *British Leyland Motor Corp. Ltd v Armstrong Patents Co. Ltd* [1986] A.C. 577 per Lord Griffiths at 646; [1986] F.S.R. 221; *Ladbroke (Football) Ltd v William Hill (Football) Ltd* [1964] 1 W.L.R. 273 at 276; *Purefoy Engineering Co. Ltd v Sykes, Boxall & Co. Ltd* (1954) 72 R.P.C. 89; *Norowzian v Arks Ltd* [1998] F.S.R. 394 (the words "reproducing the work in any material form" is a "commonsense explanation of what copying in relation to a literary work must mean. What is protected is the work itself").

[293] See *Boosey v Whight* [1900] 1 Ch. 122, decided under the 1842 Copyright Act, where it was held that perforated rolls for mechanical organs were not "copies" of the claimant's sheet music. However, under the 1842 Act, the claimants were the owners not of a musical work as that expression would now be understood but of the copyright in sheet music, and thus the exclusive right of multiplying copies of those sheets, i.e. essentially as a book. The law was changed by the 1911 Act. See s.1(2)(b) of that Act.

[294] Copyright Act 1956 s.48(1). The Copyright Act 1911 s.1(2)(d) was to the same effect.

Act does not contain such express provision, there can be no doubt that the law has not changed on this point.[295]

7–35   **Reproduction versus adaptation.** In relation to literary, dramatic and musical works, there exists a separate category of restricted act, namely the making of an adaptation, this being expressly defined, but including for example in relation to a literary work, a translation or a dramatisation of it.[296] The whole topic is discussed in more detail under the heading of "Adaptation"[297] but it is suggested, although the point is not clear, that in some cases at least, a version of a work may amount to both a reproduction of it and an adaptation of it.

(i) Literary works

(a) *Introduction*

7–36   The general principles have already been considered. As has been pointed out, copying of a literary work may take place not only when the work is reproduced in the same medium, for example in writing or in print, but also when reproduction occurs in some other material form. So, for example, a song lyric is copied when it is reproduced on a sound carrier such as a compact disc and a written work is copied when it is stored in digital form on the hard disk of a computer. As with all categories of works, the making of transient or incidental copies amounts to copying just as much as the making of permanent copies.[298]

7–37   **Defendant's work must represent claimant's.** It has already been pointed out that in general terms a work is not reproduced unless what has been produced represents the work in some real sense. A description in a novel of a scene from nature is thus not infringed by a drawing made to depict that scene. So, in the context of a literary work, the copyright in a book which described a method of teaching mathematics was not infringed by making a series of coloured rods which demonstrated that method,[299] the copyright in written instructions for the making of a garment was not infringed by making the garment,[300] and the copyright in the words and numerals in knitting guides was not infringed by making garments to those instructions.[301] Again the copyright in a book of recipes would not be infringed by making a dish according to one of the recipes.[302]

The problem can also arise in relation to literary works that consist of tables or compilations. Such works are obviously infringed by their unlicensed and substantial reproduction in the form of another written table or compilation, but do other forms of copying amount to a reproduction in a material form? In particular, is a list of components or articles reproduced for these purposes by assembling those components, either loosely or in the form of a composite article? The question was discussed, although not answered, in *Anacon Corp. Ltd v*

---

[295] *Norowzian v Arks Ltd* [1998] F.S.R. 394. And see also CDPA 1988 s.172(2): no departure from previous law merely as a result of a change of expression.

[296] CDPA 1988 s.21.

[297] See para.7–137, below.

[298] CDPA 1988 s.17(6). See, however, s.28A and para.9–19, below, as to the permitted act of making transient or incidental copies.

[299] *Cuisenaire v Reed* [1963] V.R. 719; *Cuisenaire v South West Imports Ltd* [1968] 1 Ex.C.R. 493.

[300] *Lambretta Clothing Co Ltd v Teddy Smith (UK) Ltd* [2003] EWHC 1204 (Ch), at para.78; [2003] R.P.C. 41 (first instance only).

[301] *Brigid Foley Ltd v Ellott* [1982] R.P.C. 433.

[302] *J & S Davis (Holdings) Ltd v Wright Health Group Ltd* [1988] R.P.C. 403 at 414; *Edge Pty Ltd v Apple Computer Inc* (1986) 65 A.L.R. 33 at 61.

Environmental Research Technology Ltd,[303] where Jacob J. held that copyright subsisted in a circuit diagram both as an artistic work[304] and a literary work, the literary work consisting of the written information which the diagram contained, even though it was largely in the form of code (i.e. symbols for electrical components and how they interconnected). It was held that the literary copyright was infringed by the making of a "net list", that is, a list of all the components, and what other components they were connected to and where, since the net list reproduced the information found in the literary work. Whether the literary copyright was also infringed by the making of a circuit from the circuit diagram was left undecided, but with the indication that while the mere presence of the components on a circuit board would not make it an infringement, if the components were marked then it might do so, on the grounds that one could then read the information from the circuit board. In *Sandman v Panasonic U.K. Ltd*,[305] Pumfrey J. expressed the view that a circuit would be a reproduction of a circuit diagram considered as a literary work because it would contain all the literary content of the copyright work, even though it would require analysis for it to be extracted. It is not clear whether Pumfrey J. was referring to a case in which the components were marked, and indeed he added that the question might turn on the facts. If the question turns on whether the components are marked or not, it is suggested that this is an artificial distinction, for there seems no good reason to distinguish between cases where the components carry a written description, or one where the components are, for example, colour-coded in accordance with industry conventions or the manufacturer's system, or one where they are unmarked and require destructive analysis to determine what they are. It also is artificial, because if interconnects are part of the literary information which makes up the literary work[306] such interconnects will not be "marked" but could be "read" by a visual inspection of their layout.

(b) *Substantial part: general considerations*

General considerations. The general question of what amounts to a substantial   **7–38**
part has already been considered. There will only be reproduction of a substantial part of a literary work where what has been reproduced represents the expression of the intellectual creation of the author of that literary work.[307] No clear principle can be laid down on how or where to draw the line between the legitimate use of the ideas expressed in a literary work and the unlawful copying of their expression. Thus, it is not necessary for the actual language of the copyright work to be copied or even for similar words to be used, tracking the language of the copyright work like a translation. It is sufficient to establish that there has been substantial copying of the original collection, selection, arrangement, and structure of literary material, even of material that is not in itself the subject of copyright. It is not, however, sufficient for the alleged infringing work simply to replicate or use items of information, facts, ideas, theories, arguments, themes and so on derived from the original copyright work.[308]

Wholly new versus derivative works. Two separate types of cases can be identi-   **7–39**

---

[303] *Anacon Corp. Ltd v Environmental Research Technology Ltd* [1994] F.S.R. 659.
[304] Which had not been infringed: see para.7–66, below.
[305] *Sandman v Panasonic U.K. Ltd* [1998] F.S.R. 651.
[306] See para.3–17, above.
[307] *SAS Institute Inc v World Programming Ltd* [2010] EWHC 1829 (Ch) at para 244, applying *Infopaq International A/S v Danske Dagblades Forening* Case C–5/08 [2009] E.C.R. I–6569; [2009] E.C.D.R. 16 at paras 31–48.
[308] *Baigent v The Random House Group Limited* [2007] EWCA Civ 247; [2007] F.S.R. 24.

fied in relation to literary works, first, where the claimant's work is essentially a new work, such as a novel, poem, etc., where no part of it was derived from other sources, and, secondly, where the claimant's work is to some extent derivative, having been created by drawing on earlier works or other source material. Where the claimant's work is wholly original in the first sense, the question of substantial part is uncomplicated by the presence in the claimant's work of unoriginal material. In the case of a derivative work on the other hand, a number of complicating factors may arise. The first is that an explanation of independent creation rather than copying as the reason for similarities in the works may be more credible. The second is that a work of this kind may be protected on two levels, (a) the actual language used to convey the information, etc. and (b) the work of compilation in selecting and presenting the materials. Copyright in such a work may be infringed if there has been substantial copying of the protectable work of compilation[309] although little language copying.[310] Thirdly, and related to this, where the claimant's work contains extracts from other works, it may be necessary to examine closely what it is that the defendant has taken and what it was that made the claimant's work original, i.e. what was the nature of the relevant labour or skill which the claimant contributed. If what has been taken was not original to the claimant's work, because for example it was itself taken from another work, there will be no infringement unless the originality of the claimant's work consisted of the choosing and bringing together of such material and it is this labour and skill which has been appropriated.

7–40   **Non-literal or non-textual copying.** It is not essential for the purposes of infringement that the very words used in the claimant's work have been taken. As the cases about précis, etc. discussed below, clearly show, so-called non-textual copying[311] may amount to an infringement just as much as literal copying. The principle is not confined to précis and the like, however, but extends to any case in which there has been a substantial taking of the original skill and labour of the author in expressing his ideas, thoughts, etc. Thus the copyright in a historical work was infringed where there was a substantial taking of the information which the author had assembled,[312] and a novel may be infringed where a substantial amount of the incident, plot and characterisation has been copied in another novel.[313] Many of the cases on the point relate to dramatic works, or the dramatisation of literary works,[314] but the general point of principle is the same. So in the "Da Vinci Code" case,[315] it was alleged that the "central theme" of a work of "historical conjecture" had been taken, consisting of a series of "points" arranged

---

[309] See para.7–46 (databases).

[310] The copyright protection afforded to compilations is considered in the next section.

[311] Although see the criticism of the use of such "loose non-statutory terminology", as being misleading, in *Baigent v The Random House Group Limited* [2007] EWCA Civ 247; [2007] F.S.R. 24, by Mummery L.J. at paras 140–142, giving the example of the reproduction of an original anthology of out of copyright poetry in which the text would be copied but the infringement would lie in the selection and arrangement of the poems.

[312] *Ravenscroft v Herbert* [1980] R.P.C. 193.

[313] *Designers Guild Ltd v Russell Williams (Textiles) Ltd* [2001] 1 W.L.R. 2416, per Lord Hoffmann at 2422; *Cantor Fitzgerald v Tradition (U.K.) Ltd* [2000] R.P.C. 95; *Brighton v Jones* [2004] EWHC 1157 (Ch); [2005] F.S.R. 16; *Christoffer v Poseidon Film Distributors Ltd* [2000] E.C.D.R. 487, citing *Ravenscroft v Herbert* [1980] R.P.C. 193, and *Harman Pictures NV v Osborne* [1967] 1 W.L.R. 723, although on the facts *Christoffer* appears to have been a case of the copying of a dramatic work by the making of a film and other preparatory acts; *Autospin (Oil Seals) Ltd v Beehive Spinning* [1995] R.P.C. 683 at 697, although citing the example of a novel being turned into a play, a clear case of infringement by making an adaptation. See para.7–124, below. For a discussion of the authorities on the copying of literary features of fictional characters, see McGee and Scanlan, "Copyright in Character, Intellectual Property Rights and the Internet" Parts I [2005] 8 Ent. L.R. 209 and II [2006] 1 Ent. L.R. 15.

[314] See paras 7–63 and 7–140, below.

[315] *Baigent v The Random House Group Limited* [2007] EWCA Civ 247.

in chronological order. As always, it was important to analyse the nature of the work alleged to have been infringed. It was accepted that copyright existed in the claimants' work by reason of the skill and labour expended in the original composition and production of it and the original manner or form of expression of the results of research, such original expression including not only the language in which the work was composed but also the original selection, arrangement and compilation of the raw research material. The copyright did not, however, extend to clothing information, facts, ideas, theories and themes with exclusive property rights, so as to enable a claimant to monopolise historical research or knowledge and prevent the legitimate use of historical and biographical material, theories propounded, general arguments deployed, or general hypotheses suggested (whether they are sound or not) or general themes written about. What had been taken by the defendant amounted to generalised propositions, at too high a level of abstraction to qualify for copyright protection, because it was not the product of the application of skill and labour by the claimants in the creation of their literary work. It lay on the wrong side of the line between ideas and their expression.[316] The individual elements of the claimants' work which appeared in the defendant's work were not of a sufficiently developed character to amount to a substantial part. They were too generalised, consisting of an assortment of items of historical fact and information, virtual history, events, incidents, theories, arguments and propositions. There were no detailed similarities of language or "architectural" similarities in the detailed treatment or development of the collection or arrangement of incidents, situations, characters and narrative, such as was normally found in cases of infringement of literary or dramatic copyright. The common aspects were differently expressed, collected, selected, arranged and narrated. The use of items of information, fact and so on derived from assembled research material was not, in itself, "a substantial part" of the claimants' work simply because it had taken time, skill and effort to carry out the necessary research.[317]

Wholly "new" literary work: verbatim extracts. Quantity is not the appropriate test: the question depends on the qualitative importance of the part that has been copied, assessed in relation to the copyright work as a whole.[318] Thus the taking of four lines out of 32 from a serious poem[319] or 11 words from a newspaper article[320] may be infringements, yet four lines consisting of some 20 quite simple words having no sort of literary merit taken from the refrain of a popular song may not be.[321]   **7–41**

Abstracts, précis and other abridgments. A version of another work, whether it involves the verbatim reproduction of the actual language of part of another work or is merely a paraphrase of it will, if it in any real sense acts as a substitute for the original, almost inevitably involve the reproduction of a substantial part of it. So, in a modern case,[322] the copyrights in two novels and a play were infringed by study notes produced for schools which reproduced either verbatim or in *ora-*   **7–42**

---

[316] *Baigent v The Random House Group Limited* [2007] EWCA Civ 247, per Lloyd L.J., Rix L.J. and Mummery L.J. agreeing, in this respect upholding the judge's findings: [2006] EWHC 719 (Ch); [2006] E.M.L.R. 16.

[317] *Baigent v The Random House Group Limited* [2007] EWCA Civ 247 paras 154–156.

[318] *Designers Guild Ltd. v. Russell Williams (Textiles) Ltd* [2001] 1 W.L.R. 2416; [2001] FSR 11, at para.61, Lord Scott of Foscote.

[319] As in *Kipling v Genatosan Ltd* [1917–1923] Mac.C.C. 203: the four lines forming the "essential part of the crescendo" of Kipling's "If".

[320] *Infopaq International A/S v Danske Dagblades Forening* (C–5/08) [2009] ECR I–6569.

[321] As in *Chappell & Co v D.C. Thompson & Co* [1928–1935] Mac.C.C. 467. The decision was clearly influenced by the fact that the words were being used by the defendant as part of a serial story and therefore caused no damage to the claimant's work as part of a popular song.

[322] *Sillitoe v McGraw-Hill Book Co. (U.K.) Ltd* [1983] F.S.R. 545.

tio obliqua between five and 10 per cent of the works. It was under this heading that the question in many of the early cases arose as to whether copying a part of the claimant's work was an infringement[323] but the reasoning in most of these cases would not be good law today, turning as they often did on whether the claimant's work had been prejudiced or whether the defendant's work itself had involved independent judgment or was useful.[324]

More difficult are the cases where a work has been summarised, not with the purpose of being a substitute, but to provide an outline of the contents. No rule can be laid down but it is suggested that if the author of the précis has not simply taken the shortcut of repeating various passages from the claimant's work, and thus used another's labours, but instead by his own efforts and in his own words distilled the essence of the ideas being expressed into a short piece, infringement is unlikely.[325] In contrast, where a work is summarised in detail so as give a complete picture of the claimant's work, infringement is likely.[326] A helpful example is *Valcarenghi v The Gramophone Co. Ltd*,[327] where the plots of various operas had been summarised in the defendant's publication, along with other historical details about the works. The defendant was held not to have infringed where the plots had been summarised, some in very bare outline only, others in more detail, but in neither case having the effect of transposing them into short stories.

7–43   **Parodies, etc.** The general principle here has already been discussed. The fact that the defendant's intention may have been to parody the claimant's work is no defence if what has been taken is a substantial part of it, the test being unaffected the defendant's motives. Of course, with most parodies of literary works it will be the style rather than the actual words which has been copied. Unless there has been substantial copying of language, there will usually be no infringement.[328]

7–44   **Newspaper reports.** Although it is often said that there is no copyright in news, just as there is no copyright in ideas or information, copyright can clearly subsist in the form in which news is expressed[329] and will be infringed if the expression

---

[323] Some of the old cases include: *Gyles v Wilcox* (1740) 2 Atk. 141 (work colourably shortened only); *Bell v Walker* (1784) 1 Brick 450 and *Story v Holcombe* (1847) 4 McLean 306 (facts, and terms in which they were related, the same); *Butterworth v Robinson* (1801) 5 Ves. 709 (law reports repeated verbatim, leaving out only the headnotes); *D'Almaine v Boosey* (1835) 1 Y. & C. Ex. 288 (whole chapters taken); *Sweet v Benning* (1855) 15 C.B. 459 (headnotes from law reports repeated verbatim); *Saunders v Smith* (1883) 3 My. & Cr. 711 (law reports).

[324] See para.7–31, above for a discussion of some of the factors which are suggested not to be relevant today.

[325] Rightly or wrongly, much is likely to depend on the perceived purpose of the defendant's work, in particular whether it was to take advantage of the claimant's work for his own benefit. Note also the permitted act contained in CDPA 1988 s.60 which allows the copying of the claimant's own abstract of a scientific or technical article, where there is one. See para.9–163, below.

[326] See, e.g. *Sillitoe v McGraw-Hill Book Co (U.K.) Ltd* [1983] F.S.R. 545, where the copyright in a play was held to be infringed by detailed, scene-by-scene summaries, described by the judge as "more than a synopsis of the play". Admittedly the infringement amounted to an adaptation of the play (i.e. conversion into a non-dramatic work) rather than a reproduction, but it is suggested the same result would have followed if the claimant's work been a literary rather than a dramatic work.

[327] [1928–1935] Mac.C.C. 301. Again, strictly, the case was concerned with infringement by the making of an adaptation (i.e. turning a dramatic work into a non-dramatic one) rather than by reproduction.

[328] Which was the position in *Williamson Music Ltd v Pearson Partnership* [1987] F.S.R. 97 where the words of Oscar Hammerstein II's lyrics for "There is Nothin' Like a Dame" were parodied, but not copied, in an advertisement for a bus service. (The music for the advertisement was, however, sufficiently like Richard Rogers' to attract an interim injunction.)

[329] *Walter v Steinkopff* [1892] 3 Ch. 489. See para.3–19, above.

of that story has been reproduced.[330] The difficult balance here is between protecting a journalist's literary effort as against the wider public interest in dissemination of news to the public at large.[331] It has been pointed out that if the law is too restrictive in this area, a newspaper which obtained a scoop from an exclusive and confidential source would have a monopoly in the story.[332] So where a news story about a drowning man was reduced from a piece of some 83 lines to one of 18, becoming in effect a restatement of the facts, there was no infringement.[333] On the other side of the line, where one newspaper had taken from another verbatim quotations attributed to an interviewee running to some 154 words, infringement was established.[334] Even the taking of 11 words may be enough, if they contain within them the expression of the intellectual creation of the author.[335] As always, it is important to analyse the true nature of the claimant's work. Thus, if the originality lies in the selection, collecting together and presentation of information, so that the work has elements of a "compilation copyright"[336] then an infringement is likely if the defendant, in covering the same story, has simply saved the effort of doing this work himself. So, a wire news service was held to have infringed the copyright in three cocoa crop reports on the basis that the most important and interesting parts of the reports had been taken, including a number of direct quotations and statistical information.[337]

(c) Compilations, tables, databases and other works of reference

Compilations generally. Disputes frequently arise over whether a work containing information or material obtained from elsewhere has been copied or, if this is admitted or proved, as to what use can properly be made of such a work. Copying is often suspected because works such as compilations relating to the same subject matter will of necessity often have similarities. It should be borne in mind in this area that although a claimant's work may contain much material that is not original, the value of the work may lie in the searching out and selection of such material. The general principle, discussed in more detail below, is that even where two such works will inevitably contain similarities, the maker of the second must do for himself what was done in the making of the first.[338] A defendant is not entitled to make unfair use of the labour or skill which was expended on the production of the claimant's work. It is in this area that copying can often be detected by the repetition of mistakes, redundant features and even innocuous material deliberately included to trap pirates ("seeds" or "sleepers").

7–45

---

[330] The cases in this area are mostly concerned with the question of whether copyright subsists in a news story, rather than whether a substantial reproduction has occurred.

[331] CPDA 1988 s.30(2) provides that fair dealing with a work for the purpose of reporting current events is not an infringement if accompanied by a sufficient acknowledgment. See generally para.9–44, below. But as between trade rivals, the dealing may not be fair and it may be inappropriate to provide any acknowledgment.

[332] *Express Newspapers Plc v News (U.K.) Ltd* [1990] 1 W.L.R. 1320 at 1325; [1991] F.S.R. 36. Sir Nicolas Browne-Wilkinson V.-C. suggested that the escape from a finding of infringement might lie in the fair dealing provisions (see above) or the implication of an implied licence. Both these solutions have difficulties in practice and it is suggested the first question must always be whether a substantial part of the journalist's work has been reproduced.

[333] *Springfield v Thame* (1903) 89 L.T. 242. In fact, the case was decided on the rather confusing ground that the author of the original piece was not the author of the rewritten version (as to which, see para.4–12, above), but the point was also made that what the defendant had published was news, not the claimant's expression of it.

[334] *Express Newspapers Plc v News (U.K.) Ltd* [1990] 1 W.L.R. 1320. Although there is no discussion of the point, it is implicit in the judgment that a substantial part had been taken. And see also *Walter v Steinkopff* [1892] 3 Ch. 489, where substantial passages were taken from the claimant's newspaper.

[335] *Infopaq International A/S v Danske Dagblades Forening* (C–5/08) [2009] ECR I–6569

[336] See para.7–47, below.

[337] *PCR Ltd v Dow Jones Telerate Ltd* [1998] F.S.R. 170.

[338] *Kelly v Morris* (1866) L.R. 1 Eq. 697. See para.7–47, below.

7–46   **Databases.** Many literary works include, to a greater or lesser extent, material which has been gathered from other sources. Such works may range from "pure" literary works, for example, a work of a historical nature, through anthologies, to a bare list of data, amounting to a table, compilation or database.[339] In considering this topic today, it must be borne in mind that following the implementation of the Database Directive[340] databases are treated differently from other literary works of this kind. The topic is considered in detail elsewhere[341] but in outline:

(a) Although tables and compilations are not defined by the 1988 Act, they generally comprise works in which information or ideas have been gathered from other sources and presented in a single work. From a copyright point of view, their value lies in the labour of compiling, selecting and presenting the material. Historically, such works were treated as original and thus protected even though their creation might have involved no intellectual effort but only mere labour.[342] As will be seen in the next paragraph, databases are now excluded from the class of literary works consisting of a "table or compilation".

(b) Historically, a "database" would have fallen within the description of a table or compilation, but databases, as defined by the Act, are now excluded from this category and treated as a separately defined category of literary work.[343] A database for this purpose is defined to be a collection of independent works, data or other materials which (a) are arranged in a systematic or methodical way and (b) are individually accessible by electronic or other means.[344] As to this:

  (i) A "database", so defined, made after March 27, 1996[345] will be protected as a literary work if and only if it satisfies a modified originality test, namely, that by reason of the selection and arrangement of its contents it constituted the author's own intellectual creation.[346] "Sweat-of-the-brow" works which fall within the definition of database but which are not original in this sense are therefore now excluded from copyright protection.

  (ii) A database within this definition but which is now excluded from copyright protection because it fails the modified originality test may yet be protected under the separate, sui generis database extraction right if there was substantial investment in obtaining, verifying or presenting the contents of the database.[347]

  (iii) A database which was made on or before March 27, 1996[348] and was in copyright on January 1, 1998[349] (i.e. which satisfied the old originality test) will continue to enjoy copyright protection for its full term under s.12 of the 1988 Act.[350] Obviously these works will become of increasingly less importance.

---

[339] See CDPA 1988 s.3(1). A historical work which includes information which has been collected from other sources can of course be regarded, *pro tanto*, as a compilation.

[340] Council Directive 96/9, implemented by the Copyright and Rights in Databases Regulations 1997 (SI 1997/3032).

[341] See Ch.18, below.

[342] So called "sweat-of-the-brow" works. See para.3–147, above.

[343] CDPA 1988 s.3(1).

[344] Precisely what is included within this definition is discussed elsewhere. See paras 3–22, above and 18–05, below.

[345] Copyright and Rights in Databases Regulations 1997 reg.29(1)(a).

[346] CDPA 1988 s.3A(2). As to the requirement of originality, see paras 3–146 et seq.

[347] See the Copyright and Rights in Databases Regulations 1997 reg.13(1) and Ch.18.

[348] Copyright and Rights in Databases Regulations 1997 reg.29(1)(a).

[349] i.e. the commencement date of the Database Regulations.

[350] Copyright and Rights in Databases Regulations 1997 regs 29(1), (2).

Questions of copyright infringement therefore vary, depending of the precise categorisation of the work, as follows:

(a) Pre-March 28, 1996 copyright databases, and tables and compilations (not being databases) whenever made.

(b) Post-27 March 1996 copyright databases.

(c) Databases entitled to the sui generis database right.[351]

There are also other respects in which these works are treated differently. Thus the exclusive right of making an adaptation of a work has a different meaning in relation to a database than for other literary works[352] and databases are also treated differently in relation to some of the permitted acts.[353]

Substantial part: pre-March 28, 1996 copyright databases, and tables and compilations (not being databases) whenever made. Many of the database cases in this category will now be only of historical significance, for example the "directory" cases referred to below, but they nevertheless exemplify the general principles involved and remain valid as regards tables and compilations. So, as regards this category of works, a defendant may not unfairly take advantage of the labour which has been expended by another in making the compilation, etc.: "No man is entitled to avail himself of the previous labour of another for the purpose of conveying to the public the same information."[354] The defendant must himself therefore carry out the work which is necessary to produce the work,[355] or at least do so by some other means than taking the shortcut of using the claimant's work.[356] Even to copy the claimant's work but then to go to the source to check that the information is correct will be an infringement.[357] It is irrelevant that the plan, arrangement or layout of the claimant's work may not have been copied if the labour of compilation or selection has been appropriated.[358] The fact that the information in the claimant's work is not available from any other source, as for example in case of television programme schedules or football fixture lists, does not excuse copying.[359]

7–47

This is not to say that no part of the claimant's labour may be used: a single piece of information may be taken since this will not represent a substantial part of the claimant's work.[360] Again, many other legitimate uses may of course be made of such works, particularly if they were intended to be used as reference works. Thus, a person may use a claimant's work to find sources which he might not otherwise have thought of,[361] and he is then entitled to quote from those sources provided that the end result is not simply to reproduce the claimant's

---

[351] See Ch.18.

[352] See CDPA 1988 s.21(3)(ac).

[353] See CDPA 1988 ss.29(1A) and 50D and Ch.9.

[354] *Scott v Sandford* (1867) L.R. 3 Eq. 723.

[355] *Kelly v Morris* (1866) L.R. 1 Eq. 697 ("he must count the milestones for himself"); *Cox v Land and Water Journal Co* (1869) L.R. 9 Eq. 324 ("... it is information they must get at their own expense, as a result of their own labour, and they are not to be entitled to the results of the labours undergone by others").

[356] *Independent Television Publications Ltd v Time Out Ltd* [1984] F.S.R. 64 at 69.

[357] *Kelly v Morris* (1866) L.R. 1 Eq. 697; *Morris v Ashbee* (1868) L.R. 7 Eq. 34; *Moffat and Paige Ltd v Gill* (1902) 86 L.T. 465, CA; *Waterlow Publishers Ltd v Rose* [1995] F.S.R. 207.

[358] *Kelly v Morris* (1866) L.R. 1 Eq. 697; *Morris v Ashbee* (1868) L.R. 7 Eq. 34; *Moffat and Paige Ltd v Gill* (1902) 86 L.T. 465, CA; *Waterlow Publishers Ltd v Rose* [1995] F.S.R. 207.

[359] *Independent Television Publications Ltd v Time Out Ltd* [1984] F.S.R. 64 at 69; *Football League Ltd v Littlewoods Pools Ltd* [1959] 1 Ch. 637.

[360] The statement in *Kelly v Morris* (1866) L.R. 1 Eq. 697 at 702 that a defendant may not take a single word from a map or single line from a directory without infringing goes too far. It is suggested that the doubt about this statement expressed in *Waterlow Directories Ltd v Reed Information Services Ltd* [1992] F.S.R. 409 is clearly correct.

[361] *Jarrold v Houlston* (1857) 3 K. & J. 708.

work of compilation or selection.[362] Again, the claimant's work may be consulted and used to check the accuracy of what the defendant has himself done,[363] or to check whether there is anything which he has forgotten.[364] There will of course be no infringement if no copying or other restricted act takes place. A person can therefore use a work such as directory to contact the listed names as many times as he wishes.[365] If, however, in the course of doing so or afterwards he writes down or makes some other record of a substantial amount of the information obtained from the claimant's work, then he is likely to have infringed. On the other hand, if having contacted the names and obtained information from them, he publishes that information without reproducing the compilation of names and contact details, he will not infringe. Although no case directly decides the point,[366] it is suggested that infringement may occur even where the copying occurs by the recording of the names and addresses on separate pieces of paper, for example on envelopes to be sent out as part of a mail-shot. It is suggested that the real issue here will often not be whether a substantial part of the claimant's work has been reproduced but whether such use was licensed. In particular, the important point may be whether the use was for a competing purpose, for example to compile a rival directory, or whether it was for a legitimate purpose such as to canvass non-competing business from those identified in the directory. In the former case, whether the names and addresses were copied out onto one or separate pieces of paper cannot alter the fact that the defendant has appropriated the labour and skill of the claimant's work of compilation. In the latter case, it may be strongly argu-able that the defendant is using the directory for the very purpose for which it was made available by the claimant, so that such use is licensed. An important distinction can also be made between different kinds of compilations. A work such as a trade directory is intended to be used in a different manner from a work such as an anthology of poetry. The limits of any such implied licence are, however, reasonably clear: in no case will use of the claimant's work be autho-rised for the production of a second work of a competing nature.[367]

A difficult point is whether any distinction is to be drawn between the labour involved in gathering or compiling the information and that involved in present-ing it. Compilation cases have been said to be based essentially upon a claimant being able to establish the requisite degree of skill and labour in making the compilation, as distinct from that of ascertaining that information,[368] and, again, that "... it is the product of the labour, skill, and capital of one man which must not be appropriated by another, not the elements, the raw material ... upon which the labour and skill and capital of the first have been expended".[369] Clearly no copyright protection could be claimed for a work consisting simply of a figure for the height of a mountain, no matter how much skill, effort and labour had gone

---

[362] *Morris v Wright* (1870) L.R. 5 Ch. App. 279; *Pike v Nicholas* (1870) L.R. 5 Ch. App. 251.

[363] *Kelly v Morris* (1866) L.R. 1 Eq. 697; *Scott v Stanford* (1867) L.R. 3 Eq. 718.

[364] *Jarrold v Houlston* (1857) 3 K. & J. 708.

[365] Pre-March 28, 1996 directories will of course seldom be of practical use today, and later works of this kind will usually be databases. Nevertheless, the passages in the text which follow will use the present tense.

[366] The point was left open in *Waterlow Directories Ltd v Reed Information Services Ltd* [1992] F.S.R. 409.

[367] *Waterlow Directories Ltd v Reed Information Services Ltd* [1992] F.S.R. 409.

[368] *Elanco Products Ltd v Mandops (Agricultural Specialists) Ltd* [1980] R.P.C. 213; *PCR Ltd v Dow Jones Telerate Ltd* [1998] F.S.R 170. But see the reservations expressed by Whitford J. in *Independent Television Publications Ltd v Time Out Ltd* [1984] F.S.R. 64, at 69.

[369] *Macmillan & Co Ltd v Cooper* (1924) 40 T.L.R. 186 at 188, cited with approval in *Interlego A.G. v Tyco Industries Inc* [1989] A.C. 217 at 260, although the words were spoken in the context of the requirement of originality generally, and particularly, in *Interlego*, in the context of whether a mere copy is capable of being an original work.

into the survey and calculations required.[370] With compilations, however, it is clearly not simply the skill and labour of the author of the work in presenting the information in a digestible or useful way which is protected. The whole merit of many works of this kind is that someone has spent substantial time and effort in collecting together or choosing the raw material which is the basis of the compilation, and it is this skill and effort which the law protects.[371] The skill and effort is not literary in any conventional sense, but as a matter of convenience it is protected as a literary work.[372]

Examples. These principles may be illustrated by reference to some of the cases: **7–48**

(a) *Directories: the older cases.*[373] Three leading nineteenth-century cases illustrate many of the points. In *Kelly v Morris*[374] the claimant published a street directory for London, including the names and addresses of residents. The defendant infringed where a large number of entries had been copied from the claimant's directory and canvassers were then sent to the addresses to see if the information was correct. This information was then copied into the defendant's rival directory, even where it had not been possible to verify the information. The same result followed in *Morris v Ashbee*,[375] where the claimant's work consisted of a London trade directory giving the names and occupations of merchants, traders and businessmen, arranged in a classified list in alphabetical order. The defendant cut out entries from this directory and then sent representatives to call on each person to verify the information and obtain permission to use it. This information was then printed in his own directory. In contrast, in *Morris v Wright*,[376] although the defendant had similarly cut out the entries from the claimant's directory and sent out representatives, he had not yet published his directory and at the date of the interim hearing there was no evidence that he had actually copied any entry, this issue being left to trial. There was therefore no infringement established.[377]

(b) *Directories: later cases.* The claimant compiled a directory of names and addresses of lawyers. The defendant copied 1,600 out of 12,620 entries onto a word processor and, using these, sent out canvassing letters for the purpose of preparing its own directory. Held: an infringement.[378] The same result followed where a defendant used the claimant's directory to send out 50,000 forms to solicitors containing proposed entries for the recipients to approve and correct.[379] Thus in these directory cases it was

---

[370] See, e.g. *Bookmakers' Afternoon Greyhound Services Ltd v Wilf Gilbert (Staffordshire) Ltd* [1994] F.S.R. 723, at 735 (no copyright in individual dividend forecast).

[371] *Autospin (Oil Seals) Ltd v Beehive Spinning* [1995] R.P.C. 683 at 698.

[372] *Autospin (Oil Seals) Ltd v Beehive Spinning* [1995] R.P.C. 683.

[373] As already noted, this and the next group of cases are today likely to be only of historical significance.

[374] *Kelly v Morris* (1866) L.R. 1 Eq. 697.

[375] *Morris v Ashbee* (1868) L.R. 7 Eq. 34.

[376] *Morris v Wright* (1870) L.R. 5 Ch. 279.

[377] The defendant had altered his *modus operandi* in the light of the decision in *Morris v Ashbee* (1868) L.R. 7 Eq. 34. See the analysis of these three cases in *Waterlow Directories Ltd v Reed Information Services Ltd* [1992] F.S.R. 409. Other older cases include *Mathewson v Stockdale* (1806) 2 Russ. 385; *Kelly v Hooper* (1840) 4 Jur. 21; *Cornish v Upton* (1861) 4 L.T. 862.

[378] *Waterlow Directories Ltd v Reed Information Services Ltd* [1992] F.S.R. 409. It was the copying of the claimant's list onto a word processor which was held to amount to an infringement. As noted above, the question as to whether the printing of the names and addresses onto separate envelopes was also an infringement was left open.

[379] *Waterlow Publishers Ltd v Rose* [1995] F.S.R. 207. See also *Fax Directories (Pty) Ltd v S.A. Fax Listings* [1990] 2 S.A.L.R. 164; (1992) S.A. 64 (D) (Sup. Ct of S.A.).

the effort and skill expended in finding out who lives where, etc. which merited protection.[380]

(c) *Catalogues*.[381] The claimant published a number of works on fruiting plants. The defendant compiled his own catalogue of plants, in the course of which he put specimens of fruit trees in front of him and compared their appearance with the descriptions in various publications, including the claimants'. Where the description tallied exactly, he copied the claimant's description, otherwise making the necessary alterations. Where he could not obtain a specimen, he copied the description from the claimant's work. Held: an infringement.[382]

(d) *Statistical information*. The claimant compiled statistical information as part of a crop forecasting service, the information consisting of details of the growing crop, weather and soil information, and so on. The information was presented as part of a report to subscribers. The defendant infringed by passing on to commodity traders the "essential" part of the information extracted from the reports.[383]

(e) *Technical data*. The claimant published information about a chemical on labels on the outside of containers, the information having been compiled from a number of public domain sources. The defendant infringed by producing a label which contained much of the same information and which had been obtained from the claimant's label. The result would have been different if the defendant had itself looked at all the available information, including that on the claimant's label, and then made its own choice about what to include and how to express it, even though the result might have been very similar to the claimant's. What it was not entitled to do was to take advantage of the skill and judgment of the claimant and save itself the trouble and cost of assembling the information.[384]

(f) *Dictionaries, encyclopaedias, etc.*[385] The claimant produced an educational scientific book in the form of questions and answers. The concept was not new and the material itself not original. The defendant infringed where he had used portions of the book mixed in with his own labour.[386]

(g) *Anthologies, etc.*

(1) The defendant infringed where he copied the selection of poems in Palgrave's *Golden Treasury*, the selection requiring "extensive reading, careful study and comparison, and the exercise of taste and judgment."[387] Again, where the claimant had prepared an annotated, potted version of *As You Like It* for use in schools, the defendant infringed by copying the substance of the work. It was said that, in relation to a series of quotations, to take the reference given by the claimant and to go and see if it is correctly copied and, if so, to use it with other added material:

"... is to leave out the whole merit; the felicity of the quota-

---

[380] *Autospin (Oil Seals) Ltd v Beehive Spinning* [1995] R.P.C. 683, at 698.

[381] Post-March 27, 1996 works in this and the next two categories of works (statistical information, technical data) may or may not be databases, depending on what basis they were compiled.

[382] *Hogg v Scott* (1873) L.R. 18 Eq. 444.

[383] *PCR Ltd v Dow Jones Telerate Ltd* [1998] F.S.R. 170. See also *Scott v Stanford* (1867) L.R. 3 Eq. 718 (statistics of coal imports).

[384] *Elanco Products Ltd v Mandops (Agrochemical Specialists) Ltd* [1979] F.S.R. 46.

[385] Post-March 27, works in this and the next categories of works, even if databases, will often be copyright works, although this will depend on what basis they were compiled.

[386] *Jarrold v Houlston* (1857) 3 K. & J. 708. See also *Mawman v Tegg* (1826) 2 Russ. 385; cf. *Jarrold v Heywood* (1870) 18 W.R. 279 (on the facts, no copying).

[387] *MacMillan & Co v Suresh Chunder Deb* (1890) 17 I.L.R. 951 (Calcutta), approved in *MacMillan & Co Ltd v Cooper* (1923) 40 T.L.R. 186, PC.

tion; its adaptability to a particular end; its illustration of a particular characteristic. All these things enter into the choice of one quotation as apart from another. This is a process which may involve gifts both of knowledge and intelligence. The aptness of quotation does not depend on the particular page or number of lines in which it is found … it does not entitle you to annexe the skill and judgement and taste which has dictated the selection."[388]

(2) But where the claimant's work consisted of the life of Alexander, compiled by taking selected passages amounting to about one-half of the standard translation of Plutarch's work and knitting them together with a word or two of connecting material to make a connected narrative, the defendant did not infringe by reproducing those passages, there being no sufficient skill or taste in what had been done by the author of the claimant's work in this respect.[389]

(3) A more difficult case arose where a study of Hazlitt's essays had been published consisting of 13 of the 127 published essays, chosen to represent his work, together with a lengthy introduction and notes, the whole work being prescribed for an examination course. Of the 127 essays, 30 to 40 were well known and likely to be the starting point for any edition, and of which four or five were so well known as to be inevitably included in such a collection. Other collections had also been published, for example one of 23 essays containing 12 of the claimant's 13. The defendant published a selection of 20 essays, including the 13 chosen by the claimant (albeit in a different order), and which were marked with an asterisk to indicate that they were prescribed. In a decision which was described as being close to the line,[390] it was held that there was no infringement, relevant factors being that the claimant's introduction and notes (which were part of the prescribed materials) had not been taken; part of the merit of the claimant's work lay in its arrangement, which had not been copied; the inclusion of the 13 essays was not motivated to gain an advantage from the choice made in the claimant's work but to cater for the needs of students; the claimant's work was much more elaborate and knowledgeable and its sales unlikely to be affected by the defendant's.[391]

(h) *Historical works.* Although there is no monopoly in historical facts, protection will be given to a work which is the result of skill and effort in researching and presenting the material.[392] Thus where the claimant's work consisted of a historical account of the charge of the Light Brigade, compiled from the various sources, it appeared that the defendant's film script had made extensive use of that work, thus saving the labour of the

---

[388] *Moffat and Paige Ltd v Gill* (1902) 86 L.T. 465, CA. See also *Blackie & Sons Ltd v The Lothian Book Publishing Co, etc. Ltd* (1921) 29 C.L.R. 396 (annotated version of *King Henry V*).

[389] *MacMillan & Co Ltd v Cooper* (1923) 40 T.L.T. 186, PC. However, the defendant infringed by copying the notes which accompanied the text. See also *Longman v Winchester* (1809) 16 Ves. 269 at 271.

[390] *Cambridge University Press v University Tutorial Press Ltd* (1928) 75 R.P.C. 335. The case was clouded by the fact that the defendant had published an earlier edition which clearly infringed, and was obviously also partly motivated by the wish to publish a work which contained the prescribed essays.

[391] Some of these factors would today be considered as irrelevant.

[392] Although note that slightly greater leeway may be given to the borrowing of material from historical works than from other kinds. See para.7–30, above, at (l) and *Ravenscroft v Herbert* [1980] R.P.C. 193.

research and presentation, even though much other material was added: injunction granted.[393] Again, where a claimant had written a semi-historical, semi-mystical account of the spear which pierced the side of Christ, the defendant's novel infringed where about 4 per cent of the claimant's work had been copied in order to give the defendant's book historical authenticity, there being both language and non-language copying.[394] In contrast, where the defendant had used the claimant's work to find sources for his book on the origin of the English nation, and had then gone to those sources and quoted from them and not the claimant's work, he did not infringe, even though in the result the works were quite similar.[395] Again, where all that had been taken from a semi-fictional historical work consisted of generalised propositions, there was no infringement since these were at too high a level of abstraction to qualify for copyright protection, and was not the product of the application of skill and labour expended in the creation of the literary work. It lay on the wrong side of the line between ideas and their expression.[396]

(i) *Maps, etc.* As well as being artistic works, maps may also be regarded as compilations.[397] The general topic of maps is, however, considered in relation to artistic works.

(j) *Fixture lists.* The claimant produced a list of League football matches for the entire season. The defendant produced a fortnightly pools coupon having taken the matches for that fortnight from the claimant's list. Held: an infringement.[398]

(k) *Programme schedules.* Where the claimant produced a schedule of forthcoming television programmes, the defendant's listings magazine compiled using information from the claimant's schedules infringed.[399]

(l) *Betting coupons, etc.* A defendant infringed where it had copied the layout and betting system worked out by the claimant for its pools coupons.[400]

(m) *Computer programs.* While each computer program may be entitled to protection in its own right,[401] a suite of computer programs may be protected quite independently as a compilation if sufficient labour and skill has been expended in assembling them.[402]

---

[393] *Harman Pictures N.V. v Osborne* [1967] 1 W.L.R. 723. The decision was an interim one only but a strong case of copying was made out in the absence of any explanation from the defendant.

[394] *Ravenscroft v Herbert* [1980] R.P.C. 193.

[395] *Pike v Nicholas* (1869) L.R. 5 Ch. App. 251. It seems that a feature which led to both works being similar was that both were written as entries to a competition and it was likely that the prize committee would favour an entry written with a particular slant.

[396] *Baigent v The Random House Group Limited* [2007] EWCA Civ 247; [2007] F.S.R. 24, per Lloyd L.J., and Mummery L.J. agreeing, in this respect upholding the judge's findings: [2006] EWHC 719 (Ch); [2006] E.M.L.R. 16. See the more detailed discussion in para.7–40.

[397] *Anacon Corp. Ltd v Environmental Research Technology Ltd* [1994] F.S.R. 659; *Comprop Ltd v Moran* [2002] J.L.R. 222 (Royal Ct of Jersey).

[398] *Football League Ltd v Littlewood Pools Ltd* [1959] Ch. 637. The case was decided by reference to the "little and often" principle (see para.7–29, above), but it is suggested that the material taken each fortnight was a substantial part of the season's list. For examples of race card cases, see *Bookmakers' Afternoon Greyhound Services Ltd v Wilf Gilbert (Staffordshire) Ltd* [1994] F.S.R. 723; *Demerara Turf Club v Phang* [1963] W.I.R. 177 (Sup Ct of Brit Guyana); *Ascot Club Ltd v Simoms* [1968] 64 W.W.R. 411 (Sup Ct of Canada); *British Columbia Jockey Club v Standen* [1984] 4 W.W.R. 537 (Sup Ct of Brit Columbia).

[399] *Independent Television Publications Ltd v Time Out Ltd* [1984] F.S.R. 64. But as to programme listings now, see the Broadcasting Act 1990 s.176 and Sch.17 and paras 29–09, below et seq.

[400] *Ladbroke (Football) Ltd v William Hill (Football) Ltd* [1964] 1 W.L.R. 273.

[401] See para.7–54, below.

[402] *Ibcos Computers Ltd v Barclays Mercantile Highland Finance Ltd* [1994] F.S.R. 275, disapproving *Total Information Processing Systems Ltd v Daman Ltd* [1992] F.S.R. 171.

Rearrangement or scrambling of pre-March 28, 1996 databases, and of tables and compilations not being databases, whenever made. Sometimes a defendant takes a list of data prepared by another and presents it in a different order. It is suggested that whether or not this amounts to an infringement will depend upon where the originality of the claimant's work lay. If at least part of the originality lay in compiling or assembling the information, then the defendant will infringe by using the results of that labour even in a rearranged form.[403] If, on the other hand, this was not the case, for example because the information was readily available or was gathered without any labour or skill in selection, but the originality lay in the manner of its presentation, which the defendant has not copied, there will be no infringement.

7–49

Post-27 March 1996 copyright databases. With these works, the crucial question will often be whether the work is entitled to copyright protection at all. Once this is established, since the threshold originality requirement is different for these works,[404] the substantial part test will also be different. Thus, whether a substantial part has been taken must be assessed by reference to the author's work of intellectual creation in selecting or arranging the contents of the database.[405] Many of the older cases discussed in the previous paragraphs will still be relevant although caution must be taken in implying them blindly. For example, a post-27 March 1996 copyright database may have been made using not only work of intellectual creation in selecting or arranging its contents but also "sweat of the brow" labour in assembling data in accordance with that selection or arrangement. It is only where there has been a taking of a substantial part of the expression of the former kind of work that there will have been an infringement.

7–50

Rearrangement or scrambling of post-March 27, 1996 copyright databases.[406] Again, what is protected here is author's work of intellectual creation in selecting or arranging the contents of the database. Where therefore the contents have been re-arranged or scrambled, the question of substantial part will need to be assessed in the light of the author's work of selection rather than his work of arrangement.

7–51

"Little and often." Compilations are particularly susceptible to having small amounts regularly taken from them for a defendant's specialist needs. This general problem had already been discussed.[407]

7–52

(d) *Computer programs*

Introduction. Perhaps more than with other works, questions of infringement of computer programs require an analysis of the protected subject matter. This has been dealt with in Ch.3, where it is noted that the discussion often runs the issues

7–53

---

[403] See, e.g. *Independent Television Publications Ltd v Time Out Ltd* [1984] F.S.R. 64; *British Columbia Jockey Club v Standen* (1986) 22 D.L.R. (4th) 467. In *Demerara Turf Club v Phang* (1963) W.I.R. 177, it was held that the publication in the defendant's coupon of a list of names of horses in a race, taken from the claimant's programme and coupon, but in a scrambled form, was an infringement. The point was left open in *Football League Ltd v Littlewoods Pools Ltd* [1959] Ch. 637. See also *Robertson v The Thomson Corporation* (2004) 243 D.L.R. (4th) 257 (C.A. Ontario): the reproduction of the contents of a newspaper in an online database was not an infringement of the compilation copyright.

[404] See para.3–148, above.

[405] See para.3–148, above. Note that in *Football Dataco Ltd v Brittens Pools Ltd* [2010] EWHC 841 (Ch); [2010] R.P.C. 17, the question of whether the database there was an original copyright database was decided as a preliminary issue, so that the question of any infringement did not arise for decision.

[406] See para.7–49 for an introduction to this topic.

[407] See para.7–30, above.

of protected subject matter and infringement together, and the reader is referred to that treatment.[408] In general, copying may take the form of: (a) the exact or literal reproduction of all or part of the program (textual copying), (b) reproduction of the program in a re-written form, perhaps in a different language, (c) reproduction on a higher level, such as the reproduction of the structure of the program, (d) or copying of the computer language, or the interfaces or function of the program. In the usual way, the 1988 Act defines the restricted acts in respect of all works including computer programs by reference to "the work as a whole or any substantial part of it" and while the Software Directive defines the restricted acts by reference to reproduction "in any form, in part or in whole", the Directive's meaning must be limited to reproduction of a substantial part.[409] It should also be noted that where an arrangement or altered version of the program is made, or a version of the program is made in which it is converted into or out of a computer language or code, or into a different computer language or code, this will amount to an adaptation of the program as well, perhaps, as a reproduction of it.[410] It should also be borne in mind that such things as data files and suites of programs may contain other kinds of copyright works as well as, or rather than, a computer program.[411]

7–54   **Textual copying.** One of the features of a computer program that sets it apart from other literary works is that for most practical purposes it cannot be perceived, accessed or used without being copied into computer memory, albeit invisibly to the user.[412] Since it is made clear that reproduction of a computer program includes transient or incidental copying,[413] as well as the storing of the program in any medium by electronic means, the restricted act of copying is likely to be committed in every form of use. Not only will the storage of a program inevitably involve its reproduction in computer memory,[414] but even the ordinary acts of transient copying between different parts of a computer system incidental to the running of the programme will normally do so. This is recognised in the Computer Software Directive,[415] art.4(a) of which provides that, subject to exceptions, the exclusive rights of the owner of copyright in a computer program "shall include the right to do or to authorize … the permanent or temporary reproduction of a computer program by any means and in any form, in part or in whole. In so far as loading, displaying, running, transmission or storage of the computer program necessitate such reproduction, such acts shall be subject to authorization by the rightholder." The result is that for all practical purposes any unlicensed use of a computer program is liable to be an infringement if not subject to one of the permitted acts.[416] This protection for computer programs is a very valuable weapon in the hands of copyright owners, given the ease of copy-

---

[408] See para.3–30.

[409] Since otherwise it would require the copying of insubstantial parts to be an infringement, which would be absurd. See *Nova Productions Ltd v Mazooma Games Ltd* [2007] EWCA Civ 219; [2007] R.P.C. 25 at para.29. See also the decision in *Infopaq International A/S v Danske Dagblades Forening* (C–5/08) [2009] ECR I–6569.

[410] See CDPA 1988 ss.21(3)(ab), (4). See para.7–143.

[411] See, e.g. *Ibcos Computers Ltd v Barclays Mercantile Highland Finance Ltd* [1994] F.S.R. 275.

[412] For a description of the copying which occurs during the development, maintenance and running of a computer program, see *Cantor Gaming Ltd v Gameaccount Global Ltd* [2007] EWHC 1914 (Ch); [2008] F.S.R. 4 at paras 35–45.

[413] CDPA 1988 s.17(6).

[414] *Ocular Sciences Ltd v Aspect Vision Care Ltd* [1997] R.P.C. 289 at 418.

[415] Directive 91/250 of May 14, 1991.

[416] As to such acts, it should be borne in mind that there are a number of permitted acts which are specific to computer programs, namely the making of back-up copies; decompilation to make a compatible program; observing, studying and testing the functioning of a program; and acts necessary for the lawful use of a program, including error correction: see CDPA 1988 ss.50A–50C and paras 9–132 et seq., below. Note, however, that the permitted act provisions of s.28A, which

ing of such works. The need for users to have a licence to use the program provides a strong foundation for controlling use, to be compared, for example, with the rights of owners of copyright in other works, who, presented with a defendant who is using a suspected pirate copy of a work, may need to be sure that the knowledge requirements applicable to acts of secondary infringement are satisfied before effective action can be taken.[417]

The general principles in relation to infringement of computer programs are no different from those relating to other types of literary works.[418] In the usual way, in the case of purely textual copying, what must be compared is the claimant's program with the alleged infringing work, almost inevitably another program.[419] It is not necessary to examine every part of the defendant's program to establish reproduction of a substantial part. A comparison of samples will be sufficient if they are representative.[420]

With computer programs in particular, it is the presence of similar redundancies, mistakes and idiosyncrasies in coding, as opposed to standard routines, which reveal the hand of the copyist.[421] Computer code typically evolves, both during initial development and subsequently through testing and upgrading. As a result, it is common to find that there is residual and redundant code left within the program. Just as some directory and list publishers introduce "sleepers" or "seed" entries into their works,[422] some programmers also deliberately include "smoking guns" into their code, with no function other than to assist in proving copying. In addition, true and permanent deletion of computer code is difficult. "Deleted" files are often merely re-indexed rather than being deleted, and can be readily retrieved. More sophisticated tools exist for endeavouring to retrieve files which have been deliberately overwritten. Copies of programs and data are also routinely made and stored as part of computer or network backups, and may provide useful snapshot proof of the development process, despite deliberate attempts to destroy the evidence. Careful analysis of code can also reveal evidence of copying at the level of comments and notes in the human-generated program code.[423] It follows that, although copying may be easier in the digital world, proof of copying may also be easier.

Textual copying: substantial part. In the common case of flagrant piracy of a computer program, there will usually be exact reproduction of the whole program by simple duplication, and proving identity is a purely mechanical task. Where there has been literal copying of part only of the program, however, the issue is whether that part constitutes a substantial part, the question here being in principle no different than in other copyright cases. The function of the law of copyright is to protect the relevant skill and labour of the author, so that infringement occurs if there has been an appropriation of a part of the work on which a substantial

7–55

---

relate to the making of transient or incidental copies, do not apply to computer programs (or databases).

[417] In particular, possession in the course of business, knowing or having reason to believe the article is an infringing copy. See Ch.8, below.

[418] See para.7–36.

[419] *Thrustcode Ltd v W.W. Computing Ltd* [1983] F.S.R. 502; *Apple Computers Inc. v Mackintosh Computers Ltd* (1990) 71 D.L.R. 95.

[420] *Ibcos Computers Ltd v Barclays Mercantile Highland Finance Ltd* [1994] F.S.R. 275; *Accounting Systems 2000 (Developments) Pty Ltd v C.C.H. Australia Ltd* (1993) 114 A.L.R. 355 (Fed Ct of Aus).

[421] As in *Ibcos Computers Ltd v Barclays Mercantile Highland Finance Ltd* [1994] F.S.R. 275; *Creative Technology Ltd v Aztech Systems Pte. Ltd* [1997] F.S.R. 491 (Ct of App of Singapore); *Cantor Fitzgerald v Tradition (U.K.) Ltd* [2000] R.P.C. 95

[422] See paras 7–45 and 7–17, above.

[423] As happened in *Ibcos Computers Ltd v Barclays Mercantile Highland Finance Ltd* [1994] F.S.R. 275.

part of the author's skill and labour was expended.[424] The copying of a small amount of code is unlikely to amount to an infringement[425] particularly if, for example, the writing of that part involved no great skill or labour, as in the case of commonplace routines. In the context of computer software, it is also dangerous to import tests sometimes used in relation to other types of works, such as, how important or essential is the part taken when compared to the whole of the claimant's work?[426] This is because in relation to a computer program, the slightest semantic error may cause the program not to run or cause it to produce the wrong result. In this sense, the smallest part of a program, and one containing no relevant originality, may be vitally important.[427] The fact that two devices produce the same output in response to a command or produce the same result or "look" the same does not necessarily mean that there is any similarity between the actual code of the two computer programs: at a lower level each may be structured and written entirely differently.[428] The question of possible infringement by non-textual copying in such cases is dealt with in the following paragraphs.

7–56   **Non-textual copying: ideas only.** Article 1.2 and recitals 13 and 15 of the Software Directive make it clear that the "idea/expression" dichotomy applies to copyright in computer software.[429] For these purposes, ideas are not protected if they have nothing to do with the nature of the work, i.e. a computer program having all the necessary coding in order to function.[430] Accordingly, the exclusion of "ideas" is not limited only to exclusion of ideas which "underlie an element of the program"[431] but extends to exclusion of mere ideas as to what the program should do.[432] It is therefore necessary to distinguish between "expressions" on the one hand, the form of which is protected, and other things which are conveyed by or described in the program, of which "ideas, procedures, methods of operation and mathematical concepts" as such, is a non-exhaustive list, which are not protected.[433] Skill, judgement and labour in devising ideas, procedures, methods of operation and mathematical concepts is therefore not protected but rather the

---

[424] *Cantor Fitzgerald v Tradition (U.K.) Ltd* [2000] R.P.C. 95; *Ibcos Computers Ltd v Barclays Mercantile Highland Finance Ltd* [1994] F.S.R. 275, although there Jacob J. propounded the test as being whether there has been an "overborrowing" of the author's skill and labour, a test which was doubted by Pumfrey J. in *Cantor Fitzgerald v Tradition (U.K.) Ltd*, since it did not add any further useful criteria.

[425] See *Creative Technology Ltd v Aztech Systems Pte. Ltd* [1997] F.S.R. 491 (two sections of code consisting of 7 and 12 lines respectively and forming about 4% of the total program were not enough to amount to a substantial part).

[426] See para.7–35, above at (b).

[427] *Cantor Fitzgerald v Tradition (U.K.) Ltd* [2000] R.P.C. 95. In *Autodesk Inc v Dyason* [1992] R.P.C. 575, the High Court of Australia held that the copying of a 127-bit "look-up table", a series of numbers stored within a program and being part of a "lock-and-key" security device, amounted to an infringement, even though the numbers had been randomly generated and thus had required no programming skill to create them and were unlikely to have qualified for copyright protection had they stood alone. The decision does not form part of English law: *Cantor Fitzgerald v Tradition (U.K.) Ltd* [2000] R.P.C. 95. For further criticism of the decision, see *Lahore* [1992] E.I.P.R. 428, *Prescott* [1992] E.I.P.R. 191 and the doubts expressed in *Autodesk Inc v Dyason (No.2)* [1993] R.P.C. 259.

[428] *John Richardson Computers Ltd v Flanders* [1993] F.S.R. 497; *Autodesk Inc v Dyason* [1992] R.P.C. 575 (High Ct of Aus); *News Datacom Ltd v Satellite Decoding Systems* [1995] F.S.R. 201; *Admar Computers Pty Ltd v Ezt Systems Pty Ltd* (1997) 38 I.P.R. 659.

[429] *Nova Productions Ltd v Mazooma Games Ltd* [2007] EWCA Civ 219; [2007] R.P.C. 25 at para.31, on appeal from [2006] EWHC 24 (Ch); [2006] R.P.C. 14.

[430] *Nova Productions Ltd v Mazooma Games Ltd* [2007] EWCA Civ 219 at para.35, applying *Designers Guild Ltd v Russell Williams (Textiles) Ltd* [2000] 1 W.L.R. 2416.

[431] As to which, see recital 13 of the Software Directive: *Nova Productions Ltd v Mazooma Games Ltd* [2007] EWCA Civ 219 at para.36.

[432] *Nova Productions Ltd v Mazooma Games Ltd* [2007] EWCA Civ 219 at para.35.

[433] *SAS Institute Inc v World Programming Ltd* [2010] EWHC 1829 (Ch), para.206, observing that thereby a line is drawn between copyright protection and the public domain, citing Reinbothe and

skill, judgement and labour in devising the form of expression of the program as a literary work.[434] These concepts are reinforced by the fact that the Directive is to be construed in accordance with TRIPS,[435] art.9.2 of which provides that "copyright protection shall extend to expressions and not to ideas", laying down a positive rule as to the point beyond which copyright protection may not go.[436] Thus where an idea, function or concept is sufficiently worked out and expressed in computer code, being the result of independent skill and labour, that expression is protected and the copying of a substantial part of that expression is a restricted act.[437]

Non-textual copying: structure. Where the expression of the structure of a   **7–57** computer program represents a substantial part of the skill and labour of the programmer of the copyright work, infringement may occur by it being reproduced, including the overall structure at a high level of abstraction.[438] Nevertheless, while protection is not limited to the text of the source code, but extends to protecting the design of the program, that is, its "structure, sequence and organisation",[439] there is a distinction between protecting the design of the program and protecting its functionality: it is perfectly possible to create a computer program which replicates the functionality of an existing program, yet whose design is quite different.[440] Here, it is dangerous, and indeed wrong, to draw an analogy between computer programs and dramatic or other types of works, where infringement can clearly occur even where language copying has not taken place.[441] Computer programs are different from other kinds of literary works and present peculiar problems for copyright law.[442] First, two completely different computer programs can produce a result which is identical not only at some level of abstraction, but at any level of abstraction. This is so even if the author of one has had no access at all to the other but only to its results. Second, it is wrong to say that a computer program has a "plot": rather it amounts to a set of instructions. There is no theme, there are no events and there is no narrative flow. It is merely a series of pre-defined operations intended to achieve a desired result in response to the requests of the customer.[443] Rather, in each case, it will be a matter of degree, applying the usual tests, whether a substantial part has been taken. In the end, this will be a matter for the court's value judgment, helped, especially in this

---

von Lewinski, *The WIPO Treaties 1996: Commentary and Legal Analysis* (Butterworths, 2002), pp.46–47

[434] *SAS Institute Inc v World Programming Ltd* [2010] EWHC 1829 (Ch), para.207.

[435] *Nova Productions Ltd v Mazooma Games Ltd* [2007] EWCA Civ 219 at para.38, applying *Schieving-Nijstad v Groeneveld* (C–89/99) [2001] E.C.R. I–5851; [2002] F.S.R. 22, although noting that the Software Directive predates TRIPs, a point not considered relevant in *SAS Institute Inc v World Programming Ltd* [2010] EWHC 1829 (Ch), paras 168, 200.

[436] *Nova Productions Ltd v Mazooma Games Ltd* [2007] EWCA Civ 219 at para.38.

[437] See *Ibcos Computers Ltd v Barclays Mercantile Highland Finance Ltd* [1994] F.S.R. 275 and para.7–13, above.

[438] *Ibcos Computers Ltd v Barclays Mercantile Highland Finance Ltd* [1994] F.S.R. 275; *John Richardson Computers Ltd v Flanders* [1993] F.S.R. 497; *Cantor Fitzgerald v Tradition (U.K.) Ltd* [2000] R.P.C. 95 (no substantial copying of these elements on the facts). Indeed this was common ground in *Navitaire Inc v easyJet Airline Company* [2004] EWHC 1725 (Ch); [2006] R.P.C. 3.

[439] *SAS Institute Inc v World Programming Ltd* [2010] EWHC 1829 (Ch), para.232, noting that if there were any doubt about this, then the conferring of protection on "preparatory design material" confirms it.

[440] *SAS Institute Inc v World Programming Ltd* [2010] EWHC 1829 (Ch), para.232.

[441] As to which, see para.7–63, above.

[442] *Navitaire Inc v easyJet Airline Company* [2004] EWHC 1725 (Ch), paras 112, 125; *SAS Institute Inc v World Programming Ltd* [2010] EWHC 1829 (Ch), para.198.

[443] *Navitaire Inc v easyJet Airline Company* [2004] EWHC 1725 (Ch), para.125. Pumfrey J. went on to consider an analogy: If a chef develops a recipe for a pudding, that will be a literary work. If a competitor, after much culinary labour, but without using the original recipe, succeeds in emulating the result and records his recipe, the resulting record will not be an infringement of the origi-

field, by expert evidence. In this respect it is wrong to incorporate jurisprudence from the United States,[444] particularly insofar as this involves carrying out an "abstraction and filtration" process whereby there is first systematically excluded from consideration various elements of the claimant's program, as follows: (1) elements which result from the expression of an idea where there is only one way to express that idea, (2) elements which result from the description of the same facts which can only be described in a particular way, and lastly (3) elements taken from the public domain, and then, when this process is complete, what is left of the claimant's program is compared with the defendant's work. The law of the United States differs from the United Kingdom in this area.[445]

7-58   **Non-textual copying: function, language and interfaces.** These principles as to "ideas" apply to all aspects of non-textual copying. Programs are often designed to emulate the functions of or closely resemble the manner or appearance in operation of another "target" program, without the designer ever having had access to the source code of the target or without the designer in the process producing source code that has any textual identity with the target.[446] As the law as present stands, such similarities do not amount to copying of a substantial part of the target program: "merely making a program which will emulate another but which in no way involves copying the program code or any of the program's graphics is legitimate".[447] The "business function" embodied in a program does not form part of the relevant skill and labour of the kind protected by copyright.[448] If the policy of the Software Directive was to exclude both computer languages and the underlying ideas of the interfaces from protection, then it should not be possible to circumvent those exclusions by seeking to identify some overall function which it was the sole purpose of the interface to invoke and relying on that instead.[449]

7-59   **Interfaces.** There is no protection for "interfaces", being the parts of the program which provide for the "logical and, where appropriate, physical interconnection and interaction ... required to permit all elements of software and hardware to work with other software and hardware and with users in all the ways they are intended to function."[450] Indeed, the Software Directive proceeds on the basis that users will be free to copy interfaces.[451]

7-60   **Computer languages.** Computer languages as such are not included in protec-

---

nal recipe even though the end result, the plot and purpose of both (the pudding) is the same (para.127).

[444] As was done in *John Richardson Computers Ltd v Flanders* [1993] F.S.R. 497, applying the principles adopted in *Computer Associates Ltd v Altai Inc* 23 U.S.P.Q. 2d. 1241 (2nd. Cir. 1992).

[445] See *Ibcos Computers Ltd v Barclays Mercantile Highland Finance Ltd* [1994] F.S.R. 275.

[446] As in *Navitaire Inc v easyJet Airline Company* [2004] EWHC 1725 (Ch); [2006] R.P.C. 3, para.129, where the defendant had commissioned a system which was substantially indistinguishable from the claimant's system in respect of its user interface, that is, the appearance which the running software presented to the user. Thus, the defendant's system acted on identical or very similar inputs to those of the claimant's system and produced very similar results. The defendant and its software developer never had access to the source code of the claimant's system and accordingly the source codes were quite different. The claimant nevertheless contended that this taking of its "business logic" was analogous to the taking of the plot of a novel or play, as to which see para.7–40.

[447] *Nova Productions Ltd v Mazooma Games Ltd* [2007] EWCA Civ 219; [2007] R.P.C. 25 at para.52, on appeal from *Nova Productions Limited v Mazooma Games Limited* [2006] EWHC 24 (Ch): see paras 134, 248 and 253, and applying *Navitaire Inc v easyJet Airline Company* [2004] EWHC 1725 (Ch); [2005] E.C.D.R. 17.

[448] *Navitaire Inc v easyJet Airline Company* [2004] EWHC 1725 (Ch).

[449] *Navitaire Inc v easyJet Airline Company* [2004] EWHC 1725 (Ch).

[450] Software Directive, recital 10.

[451] *SAS Institute Inc v World Programming Ltd* [2010] EWHC 1829 (Ch), para.226, citing art.6, implemented by CDPA 1988 s.50B, which entitles third parties to obtain information about interfaces by decompiling the object code of a program where the necessary information is not

tion afforded to computer programs, and this principle extends to ad hoc languages such as defined user command interfaces.[452] The intention of the Directive is to keep the language free for use, while giving protection to the particular ideas expressed in it in any particular case.[453]

Preparatory design material. Although copyright in computer programs **7–61** extends to copyright in preparatory design work for computer programs, this does not mean that copyright extends to such material even to the extent that it consists of ideas as to what the program should do. Thus if the defendant's program does what is set out in the preparatory design material, this does not mean that it infringes. The Directive expressly extends protection to preparatory design material but it does not provide that protection extends to ideas contained in such material. The reason such express provision was made is not that it was intended that protection should extend beyond the literary expression of such material to the ideas contained in it but because not all Member States necessarily provided such protection.[454]

Reference to the European Court of Justice. Because none of the various points **7–62** relating to language, functionality or interfaces are not considered to be *acte clair*, they have been referred to European Court of Justice (Case 406/10).[455]

(ii) Dramatic works

In the case of dramatic works which are written or otherwise recorded in words, **7–63** if the language itself has been copied, no special considerations apply. However, a basic distinction between literary works and dramatic works is that the choice of dramatic incident and the arrangement of situation and plot may constitute, to a much greater extent, the real value of a dramatic work. This section of the chapter is primarily concerned with whether infringement of a dramatic work can occur where only situations and plot, but not language, have been reproduced. This commonly happens, for example, where a play is based on another play, or a film upon a play. Infringement by turning a dramatic work into a non-dramatic work, and vice versa, is considered under the heading of infringement by making an adaptation, but here too the question can arise as to whether copying of incident and plot, without language copying, can amount to an infringement. It should be remembered that dramatic works include not only plays and screenplays but also works of dance and mime.[456]

A dramatic work may be infringed by a second dramatisation which reproduces dramatic incidents without using or imitating language.[457] It is thus not necessary that the words in the dialogue should be the same, for the situations and incidents,

---

available from either (i) published sources such as manuals, (ii) common standards or (iii) observation, study or testing of the program. See 9–151.

[452] *Navitaire Inc v easyJet Airline Co Ltd* [2004] EWHC 1725 (Ch); [2005] E.C.D.R. 17 at para.88. See para.3–30(5).

[453] *Navitaire Inc v easyJet Airline Co Ltd* [2004] EWHC 1725 (Ch), at para.88.

[454] *Nova Productions Ltd v Mazooma Games Ltd* [2007] EWCA Civ 219; [2007] R.P.C. 25 at para.51.

[455] *SAS Institute Inc v World Programming Ltd* [2010] EWHC 1829 (Ch), para.238, taking the view that the Court of Appeal in *Nova Productions Limited v Mazooma Games Limited* [2006] EWCA Civ 1044 did not decide that the question was *acte clair* either. Note also the pending reference in *Bezpečnostní softwarová asociace (Security software association) v Ministerstvo kultury ČR (Ministry of Culture of the Czech Republic)* (C–393/09): "Should Article 1(2) of 91/250/EEC be interpreted as meaning that the phrase 'the expression in any form of a computer program' also includes the graphic user interface of the computer program or part thereof?" For these and other pending references, see para.24–55.

[456] CDPA 1988 s.3(1).

[457] *Designers Guild Ltd v Russell Williams (Textiles) Ltd* [2000] 1 W.L.R. 2416; *Cantor Fitzgerald v*

and the way in which the ideas are worked out and presented, may form a part of the real value of the whole work. Regard should be had to the dramatic value and importance of what has been taken, even though the part may in fact be small and the actual language not copied. On the other hand, the fundamental idea of two plays may be the same, but if worked out separately and on independent lines they may be so different as to bear no real resemblance to one another.[458]

Care should be taken in reaching the conclusion that copying has taken place simply because of the presence in both works of stock incidents, whether found in other dramatic works or drawn from historical or fictional sources.[459] If there are incidents in common between the two works which can be found in other sources or which are well-used dramatic ideas, it may be that no copying took has taken place or, even if there was copying, there may be no infringement if there was no originality in the part copied or the defendant's piece has been worked out in a different way.[460] More of the reported cases fail on these grounds[461] than have succeeded. In this area, help as to what amounts to protectable elements of plot and situation can be also obtained from cases concerned with infringement by adaptation, whether the dramatisation of a non-dramatic work or vice versa.[462] Of course in every case copying must be proved. Thus even if there are sufficient similarities between the two works to establish an inference of copying, this inference can be rebutted by the defendant's evidence that no copying took place.[463]

(iii) Musical works

7–64   As with literary and dramatic works, the copying of a musical work can take place not only by its reproduction in the form of sheet music but also by its reproduction in the form of recordings of the music, whether on conventional sound carriers such as records, tapes, CDs and films, but also in data files stored in computer memory. If a musical work has been arranged or transcribed, this

---

Tradition (U.K.) Ltd [2000] R.P.C. 95, at 133; *Christoffer v Poseidon Film Distributors Ltd* [2000] E.C.D.R. 487 (copying of a dramatic work by the making of a film and other preparatory acts); *Brighton v Jones* [2004] EWHC 1157 (Ch); [2005] F.S.R. 16 (incorporation of scenes from preparatory script into final script). Cases decided before the passing of the 1911 Act must be read with caution because there was some doubt whether the copyright in a dramatic work could be infringed unless actual words and phrases were used or colourably imitated. If scenes or points of drama were taken (*Chatterton v Cave* (1878) 3 App. Cas. 483) or, in the case of a musical drama, words of some of the songs (*Planché v Braham* (1838) 4 Bing. N.C. 17), but not the embodiment of the plot in words to any substantial extent, there was no infringement (*Schlotz v Amasis Ltd & Fenn* [1905–1910] Mac.C.C. 216; but see *Nethersole v Bell* [1901–1904] Mac.C.C. 64). See *Sutton Vane v Famous Players Film Co Ltd* [1928–1935] Mac.C.C. 6 and *Kelly v Cinema Houses Ltd* [1928–1935] Mac.C.C. 362 for a review of the position.

[458] *Rees v Melville* [1911–1916] Mac.C.C. 96 and 168. See also *Sutton Vane v Famous Players Film Co. Ltd* [1928–1935] Mac.C.C. 6; *Bolton v British International Pictures Ltd* [1936–1945] Mac.C.C. 20; *Poznanski v London Film Production Ltd* [1936–1945] Mac.C.C. 107; *Ashmore v Douglas-Home* [1987] F.S.R. 553; *Harman Pictures N.V. v Osborne* [1967] 1 W.L.R. 723; *Telstra Corp Ltd v Royal & Sun Alliance Insurance Ltd* I.P.R. 57 (2003) 453.

[459] *Harman Pictures N.V. v Osborne* [1967] 1 W.L.R. 723 at 728.

[460] In the unusual case of *Norowzian v Arks Ltd (No.2)* [2000] F.S.R. 363, the technique used in the claimant's work had been copied, but the actual dramatic story told by the defendant's work was quite different.

[461] Examples of such cases are: *Rees v Melville* [1911–1916] Mac.C.C. 96 and 168; *Robl v Palace Theatre* (1911) 28 T.L.R. 69; *Bagge v Millar* [1917–1923] Mac.C.C. 179; *Dagnall v British and Dominion Film Corporation Ltd* [1928–1935] Mac.C.C. 391; *Wilmer v Hutchinson & Co Ltd* [1936–1945] Mac.C.C. 13; *Bolton v British International Pictures Ltd* [1936–1945] Mac.C.C. 20; *Poznanski v London Film Production Ltd* [1936–1945] Mac.C.C. 107; *De Manduit v Gaumont, etc. Corp. Ltd* [1936–1945] Mac.C.C. 292; *Ashmore v Douglas-Home* [1987] F.S.R. 553.

[462] See, e.g. *Corelli v Gray* (1913) 29 T.L.R. 570; *Harman Pictures N.V. v Osborne* [1967] 1 W.L.R. 723, and paras 7–140 and 7–141, below.

[463] As in *Sutton Vane v Famous Players Film Co Ltd* [1928–35] Mac.C.C. 6; *De Manduit v Gaumont, etc. Corp Ltd* [1936–1945] Mac.C.C. 292.

may also constitute infringement by making an adaptation of it,[464] a topic which is considered separately. In dealing with questions of infringement of musical works by copying, it should be remembered that words or action intended to be sung, spoken or performed with the music are not included within the definition of a musical work: they are protected as literary or dramatic works.[465]

As to whether a substantial part of a musical work has been copied, the question remains whether the alleged infringement has made use of a substantial part of the skill, labour and taste of the original composer.[466] It is common practice in music copyright cases to call expert evidence to identify and explain the significance of similarities and differences between the works.[467] Although the court is often helped by such evidence, the issue of substantial part does not depend solely on a note for note comparison but must be determined by the ear as well as by the eye,[468] for the most uneducated in music can recognise that an altered work of music is, in effect, the same as or is derived from the original work.[469] In undertaking the comparison, the works as a whole should be considered, and it is wrong to isolate certain features and concentrate on those.[470] It is clear that a relatively short part of a work can amount to a substantial part,[471] particularly if what has been taken is the vital or essential part of the work,[472] as opposed to being musical commonplace.[473] A relevant question may be whether the amount taken is so small that it is impossible to recognise the original work,[474] or whether it can still be recognised, but where the part taken has been added to other material it is important not to fall into the trap of asking whether the defendant's work sounds like the claimant's: the correct comparison is between the part taken by the defendant and the claimant's work, not between the defendant's work and the claimant's work.[475] Where the claimant's work contains material that was not original to him, then in the usual way these parts should be left out of the comparison exercise and attention centred on those parts which were original.[476]

Particularly in the field of popular music, the vital or essential part of the work may be a short refrain or hook line. The problem here becomes even more acute where a work has been "sampled", i.e. where a short piece of the work is taken and often repeated many times in the making of a new recording. The same point arises in relation to "ringtones". The piece taken is often the most distinctive part of the original work and thus immediately recognisable, which is of course the reason why it was taken. In cases of this kind, it will be relevant to ask whether

---

[464] i.e. under CDPA 1988 s.21(3)(b).

[465] CDPA 1988 s.3(1).

[466] *Francis Day & Hunter Ltd v Bron* [1963] Ch. 587.

[467] As to the role of expert evidence generally, see paras 7–18, above and 22–278, below.

[468] *D'Almaine v Boosey* (1835) 1 Y. & C. Ex. 288; *Austin v Columbia Gramophone Co Ltd* [1917–1923] Mac.C.C. 398; *Francis Day & Hunter Ltd v Bron* [1963] Ch. 587. Other cases on the point include *Boosey v Fairlie* (1877) 7 Ch. D. 301; on appeal (1879) 4 App. Cas. 711; see also *Leader v Purday* (1848) 7 C.B.4; *Wood v Boosey* (1867) L.R. 2 Q.B. 340, L.R. 3 Q.B. 223.

[469] *D'Almaine v Boosey* (1835) 1 Y. & C. Ex. 288; *Francis Day & Hunter Ltd v Bron* [1963] Ch. 587.

[470] *Betsen v CBS United Kingdom Ltd* [1994] E.M.L.R. 467 (drum and bass line only of popular song alleged to be similar); *Coffey v Warner/Chappell Music Ltd* [2005] EWHC 449 (Ch); [2005] F.S.R. 34.

[471] *Austin v Columbia Gramophone Co Ltd* [1917–1923] Mac.C.C. 398; *G. Ricordi & Co., etc. Ltd v Clayton and Waller Ltd* [1928–1935] Mac.C.C. 154 (eight bars sufficient, although not in fact copied); *Hawkes & Son (London) Ltd v Paramount Film Service Ltd* [1934] Ch. 593 (28 bars of "Colonel Bogey" copied, amounting to just under a minute's worth of composition lasting about four minutes); *Francis Day & Hunter Ltd v Bron* [1963] Ch. 587.

[472] *Francis Day & Hunter Ltd v Bron* [1963] Ch. 587.

[473] *EMI Music Publishing Ltd v Papathanasiou* [1993] E.M.L.R. 306.

[474] *Hawkes & Son (London) Ltd v Paramount Film Service Ltd* [1934] Ch. 593.

[475] *Designers Guild Ltd v Russell Williams (Textiles) Ltd* [2001] 1 W.L.R. 2416.

[476] *Sawkins v Hyperion Records Ltd* [2004] EWHC 1530 (Ch); [2005] R.P.C. 4, upheld on appeal: *Hyperion Records Ltd v Sawkins* [2005] EWCA Civ 565; [2005] 1 W.L.R. 3281.

the piece which was copied was the result of any particular inventiveness on the part of the original author or was, for example, merely a hackneyed phrase.[477] The rule of thumb that "what is worth copying is worth protecting" may be appropriate in this context but must be applied with caution.[478]

Even where the material in common is sufficient to amount to a substantial part, it of course still has to be established that the reason for this is copying.[479] It is in the field of music copyright cases in particular that the difficult issue of subconscious copying can often arise.[480]

(iv) Artistic works

7–65   **Designs for articles.** The whole topic of the copying of artistic works cannot today be discussed without an appreciation of the fundamental changes to the law in this area made by the 1988 Act. Before the 1988 Act, the gradual appreciation that copyright was capable of subsisting in artistic works such as engineering drawings and other designs for utilitarian objects, and might be infringed by indirectly copying the three-dimensional objects which had been made from those drawings, resulted in a good deal of controversy, culminating judicially in the House of Lords' decision in *British Leyland*.[481] In response, s.51 of the 1988 Act effected a fundamental change in the approach to works of this kind by cutting down the ambit of the copyright in relation to such works while at the same time providing a more limited form of protection by way of design right.[482] The matter is considered in detail elsewhere[483] but can be summarised as follows:

(a) Certain works are now classified as design documents, namely those which contain any record of a "design", whether in the form of a drawing, a written description, a photograph, data stored in a computer or otherwise. For this purpose a "design" means the design of any aspect of the shape or configuration (whether internal or external) of the whole or part of an article, other than surface decoration. A drawing for a machine part is therefore a design document, since it contains a record of the shape and configuration of the whole of an article.

(b) With certain exceptions, the Act then provides that in relation to a design document as so defined, it is not an infringement of any copyright in it to make an article to the design or to copy an article made to the design.[484] It is therefore not an infringement of the copyright in a drawing for a machine part to make a machine part from it. Nor is it an infringement of the copyright in the drawing to make a machine part by copying another machine part which was itself made from the drawing.

---

[477] See, e.g. *EMI Music Publishing Ltd v Papathanasiou* [1993] E.M.L.R. 306, not a sampling case but where the only thing in common was a four-note sequence, described as "musical commonplace".

[478] As to this rule of thumb, see para.7–31, at (b). The problem also arises in relation to the copying of sound recordings (see para.7–79, below).

[479] See, e.g. *G. Ricordi & Co, etc. Ltd v Clayton and Waller Ltd* [1928–1935] Mac.C.C. 154 (substantial similarity but defendant's evidence of no copying accepted).

[480] As to subconscious copying, see para.7–24, above.

[481] *British Leyland Motor Corp v Armstrong Patents Co Ltd* [1986] A.C. 577. Note that the Court of Appeal, [1986] A.C. 577; [1986] F.S.R. 221, rejected the argument that the prevention of three-dimensional reproduction of functional designs by way of copyright protection was unlawful under art.30 of the Treaty of Rome: see *Entec (Pollution Control) Ltd v Abacus Mouldings* [1992] F.S.R. 332.

[482] The 1988 Act contained transitional provisions such that works made before the commencement of the Act (August 1, 1989) were unaffected by these provisions for a period of 10 years from that date, although in the last five years of this period, licences of right were available.

[483] See Ch.13, below.

[484] CDPA 1988 s.51.

(c) The exceptions referred to above concern design documents or models recording or embodying a design for an artistic work or a typeface. These are still infringed by making an article to that design or by copying an article made to that design. Thus the copyright in a design document consisting of preliminary sketches for a sculpture is infringed by the unlicensed making of a sculpture to that design, since the design document records a design for an artistic work. A design for a machine part does not fall within this exception because a machine part is not an artistic work.

(d) It is also not an infringement of the copyright to issue to the public, or include in a film or broadcast, anything the making of which was, by virtue of the above provisions, not an infringement of that copyright.

These provisions must therefore be borne in mind when approaching any question of infringement concerning an artistic work which consists of a representation of an article, or which is itself a three-dimensional work. The provisions apply not merely to functional or utilitarian objects such as machine parts but also, for example, to designs for items of clothing in so far as the design relates to aspects of shape or configuration. It also follows that many of the earlier cases relating to infringement of artistic works, and which are referred to below, will be of no direct application today and are useful only in so far as they exemplify general principles.

Reproduction: general principles. The copying of an artistic work can take place by its reproduction in any material form,[485] even for example in a form by which it cannot be directly seen, such as data stored in computer memory.[486] The 1988 Act also specifically provides that a two-dimensional artistic work may be infringed by the making of a copy in three dimensions and a three-dimensional work infringed by making a copy in two dimensions.[487] An artistic work consisting of a two-dimensional representation of a three-dimensional object is therefore infringed by copying it in the form of the three-dimensional object, whether directly (i.e. from the artistic work itself) or indirectly (e.g. by copying an object itself made from the artistic work).[488] The copyright in a drawing of a human figure may thus be infringed by copying it in the form of a sculpture, and the copyright in a sculpture infringed by taking a photograph of it.[489] The change of medium or dimension may make it more difficult to see that the three-dimensional work is a copy, but this is only a question of degree.[490] It makes no difference, it is suggested, that after it was made the copy became bound up with other items

7–66

---

485 CDPA 1988 s.17(2).

486 CDPA 1988 s.17(2). And see *Autospin (Oil Seals) Ltd v Beehive Spinning* [1995] R.P.C. 683 at 698. See also *Australian Chinese Newspapers Pty Ltd v Melbourne Chinese Press Pty Ltd* [2003] F.C.A. 878 (upheld on appeal *Melbourne Chinese Press Pty Ltd v Australian Chinese Newspapers Pty Ltd* (2004) 63 I.P.R. 38): copyright in a logo consisting of three characters in a particular calligraphic style was infringed by making a similar version using a computer typesetting program.

487 CDPA 1988 s.17(3). There was some doubt about this prior to the 1911 Act (see *Hanfstaengl v Empire Palace* [1894] 2 Ch. 1, where it was held on the facts of that case that *tableaux vivants* were not infringements of copyright in pictures, although the House of Lords considered that as a matter of law this was possible: see [1895] A.C. 20), but any doubt about this was laid to rest by the 1911 Act: see *Bradbury, Agnew & Co v Day* (1916) 32 T.L.R. 349 and *King Features Syndicate v O. & M. Kleeman Ltd* [1940] 1 Ch. 531 (at first instance) and [1941] A.C. 417, followed in *Walt Disney Productions v H. John Edwards Publishing Co Pty Ltd* (1954) 71 W.N. (N.S.W.) 150. Although see *Autospin (Oil Seals) Ltd v Beehive Spinning* [1995] R.P.C. 683, suggesting that there was never any doubt.

488 *British Leyland Motor Corp v Armstrong Patents Co Ltd* [1986] A.C. 577; [1986] R.P.C. 279, HL; *Canon Kabushiki Kaisha v Green Cartridge Co. (Hong Kong) Ltd* [1997] A.C. 728; [1997] F.S.R. 817.

489 Although note the defence provided by CDPA 1988 s.62.

490 *King Features Syndicate v O. & M. Kleeman Ltd* [1940] Ch. 523 (at first instance). But note *Burke, etc. Ltd v Spicers Dress Designs* [1936] Ch. 400 (dress held not to amount to a reproduc-

such that it no longer resembles the copyright work or a substantial part of it. Before alteration it was a copy and if it can be disassembled it can be seen to be a copy again.[491] It has already been pointed out[492] that copying can take place where the link between the artistic work and the copy is only a written or verbal description, and that a work may also be infringed by the designer being given very loose instructions and then corralled into producing something which eventually resembles the copyright work. There is no copying, however, where no new copy of the work is brought into existence. So where a defendant transferred an image from a poster onto canvas by physically lifting the ink from the poster, leaving a blank piece of paper behind, there was no copying.[493]

The 1956 Act contained a special defence such that the copyright in a two-dimensional artistic work was not infringed by a three-dimensional copy if the copy did not appear to a non-expert to be a reproduction of the two-dimensional work.[494] This provision was not repeated in the 1988 Act but its abolition has not widened the scope of what constitutes a reproduction of an artistic work.[495]

In order to see whether an artistic work has been reproduced, it is permissible to examine a greatly magnified form of the alleged infringing article.[496] However, the copy must in some real sense represent the artistic work, so that the copyright in an artistic work such as a map or diagram which contains information in a visual as opposed to a literary form is not infringed by reproducing the data in a literary form, such as a table.[497] Nor is the copyright in such an artistic work infringed by producing something which has a wholly different visual appearance, even though the information conveyed may be the same.[498] Again, there is no artistic copyright in such matters as dimensions or other written material re-

---

tion of perspective drawing), a case decided very much on its own facts, and not followed in *Gleeson v H.R. Denne Ltd* [1975] R.P.C. 471; *Radley Gowns Ltd v Coftas Spyrou* [1975] F.S.R. 455; *J. Bernstein Ltd v Sidney Murray Ltd* [1981] R.P.C. 303.

[491] See *Muscat v Le* (2004) 204 A.L.R. 335, disapproving *Merlet v Mothercare Plc* [1984] F.S.R. 358, where Walton J. had held that a cape was not a reproduction of a cutting pattern because in its sewn-up form it did not resemble the pattern.

[492] See para.7–15, above.

[493] *Thèberge v Gallerie d'Art du Petit Champlain Inc* 210 D.L.R. (4th) 385 (Sup Ct of Can). See also *Benchmark Building Supplies Ltd v Mitre 10 (New Zealand) Ltd* (2004) 58 I.P.R. (stickers superimposed on claimant's posters) and *Frost v Olive Series Publishing Co* (1908) 22 TLR 649 (mounted pictures from pamphlets sold as cards).

[494] Copyright Act 1956 s.9(8), which provided that: "The making of an object of any description which is in three dimensions shall not be taken to infringe the copyright in an artistic work in two dimensions, if the object would not appear, to persons who are not experts in relation to objects of that description, to be a reproduction of the artistic work." There were few cases in practice where the defence succeeded, although see, e.g. the remarks in *S.W.Hart Ltd v Edwards Hot Water Systems* [1986] F.S.R. 575 (High Ct of Aus). The section came under repeated criticism for the difficulties in its interpretation.

[495] *Anacon Corp. Ltd v Environmental Research Technology Ltd* [1994] F.S.R. 659, rejecting the argument that s.9(8) of the Copyright Act 1956 recognised that there might be certain kinds of artistic works which only an expert could recognise as infringements, so that certain things are now infringements which were not before. However, it must also be arguable that any case which would have come within the old s.9(8) defence should still not be an infringement, since if the alleged infringing article cannot be seen by anyone other than an expert to "reproduce" the copyright work, why should a court find it to be so?

[496] *Guildford Kapwood Ltd v Embassy Fabrics Ltd* [1983] F.S.R. 567, where the court compared a greatly magnified version of the defendant's garment with the claimant's lapping diagram, used in a particular knitting process.

[497] *Anacon Corp. Ltd v Environmental Research Technology Ltd* [1994] F.S.R. 659. But in such a case it is important to bear in mind that copyright may subsist in the data as a separate literary work (namely a table or compilation) and, if so, the copyright in this work may be infringed by reproduction of the data. See paras 3–17 et seq. and 7–37 above at (i). See also *Sandman v Panasonic U.K. Ltd* [1998] F.S.R. 651.

[498] Copyright in an artistic work consisting of a circuit diagram will thus not be infringed by copying it in the form of another circuit diagram with a wholly different visual appearance, or by copying it in the form of a circuit board which has a wholly different visual appearance. See the cases cited in the previous footnote. Note, however, that in *Mackie Designs Incorporated v Behringer Specialised Studio Equipment (U.K.) Ltd* [1999] R.P.C. 717, a circuit diagram was held to be

corded on an artistic work, so that if these are all that the defendant has copied, the artistic copyright will not be infringed: a reproduction must in some way be a copy or representation of the original.[499] Written instructions and other material may of course be referred to, to see whether there is any causal link between the three-dimensional work and the drawing.[500] Associated drawings may be looked at together to see if there has been an infringement,[501] but where it is alleged that the copyright in two separate drawings has been infringed by one composite work, each drawing must be considered separately.[502] Where a claimant's works consist of a large number of similar drawings, as in the case of characters created for a cartoon series, a defendant may well not have copied any one particular drawing but rather an amalgam of the distinguishing features of a character. In such cases, a defendant will not escape by arguing that the claimant cannot identify the particular work copied.[503] There is a problem where the "artistic work" is recorded in the form of a data file: is the record of dimensions, etc., an artistic or a literary work (being a table, etc.), and if the latter, is copyright infringed by reproducing the data in a form recognisable to the human eye as an artistic work? The approach to such problems should be a common sense one, namely: has the work been reproduced?[504]

If an artistic work consists of the representation of some internal part of an object which is not directly visible, it is permissible to dissect the object, for example to make a cross section. If from the sectioned article, the artistic work can be seen to have been copied, this is sufficient for the purposes of infringement.[505] The same applies where the drawing is itself a sectional drawing of a three-dimensional object,[506] although the application of both these principles has been greatly reduced by s.51 of the 1988 Act, considered above.

Proof of copying. Whether or not copying has taken place is established using   **7–67**
the usual forensic means already discussed.[507] In a case where the court is asked to infer copying by reason of the similarities between the works, the first step should be to identify those features of the defendant's work which it is alleged have been copied from the copyright work. The court should then undertake a visual comparison of the two works, noting the similarities and the differences. The

---

design document within the meaning of s.51 and therefore the copyright in such a diagram would in any event not be infringed by making an article to that design. See Ch.13 and para.13–317, below. As to the possibility of infringement of the literary work which may be recorded in a circuit diagram, see para.7–37, abaove.

[499] *Catnic Components Ltd v Hill & Smith Ltd* [1981 F.S.R. 60, approved in *Interlego Industries A.G. v Tyco Industries Inc* [1989] A.C. 217; [1988] R.P.C. 343. See also *The Duriron Company Inc v Hugh Jennings & Co Ltd* [1984] F.S.R. 1; *Brigid Foley Ltd v Ellott* [1982] R.P.C. 433 (written knitting guides not infringed by manufacture of garments); *Davis (J & S) (Holdings) Ltd v Wright Health Group Ltd* [1988] R.P.C. 403 at 414. See, generally, on this point, para.7–37, above.

[500] *British Leyland Motor Corporation v Armstrong Patents* [1984] F.S.R. 591, CA; *Interlego A.G. v Tyco Industries Inc* [1987] F.S.R. 409 (CA, Hong Kong) and [1989] A.C. 217, 265; [1988] R.P.C. 343, PC. This point often arose in connection with s.9(8) of the 1956 Act, referred to above.

[501] *Rose Plastics GmbH v William Beckett & Co. (Plastics) Ltd* [1989] F.S.R. 113, relying on *Solar Thomson Engineering Co v Barton* [1971] F.S.R. 233; [1977] R.P.C. 537 at 559. See also *Merchant Adventurers Ltd v M. Grew & Co Ltd* [1972] Ch. 242; [1971] F.S.R. 233.

[502] *Biotrading & Financing OY v Biohit Ltd* [1998] F.S.R. 109; *UPL Group Ltd v Dux Engineers Ltd* [1989] 3 N.Z.L.R. 135 at 143.

[503] *King Features Syndicate Inc v O. & M. Kleeman Ltd* [1941] A.C. 417, applied in *BBC Worldwide Ltd v Pally Screen Printing Ltd* [1998] F.S.R. 665.

[504] See *Autospin (Oil Seals) Ltd v Beehive Spinning* [1995] R.P.C. 683. Arguably, the data file can be regarded as an artistic work because it is simply the record of the shape, etc of the work, just as are the lines drawn on a page.

[505] *Solar Thomson Engineering Co Ltd v Barton* [1977] R.P.C. 537.

[506] There are many examples in the cases. See, e.g. *Johnstone Safety Ltd v Peter Cook (International) Plc* [1990] F.S.R. 161.

[507] See para.7–17, above.

purpose of this examination is to judge whether the particular similarities relied on are sufficiently close, numerous or extensive to be more likely to be the result of copying than coincidence, not to see whether the overall appearance of the two designs is similar. Similarities which are commonplace, unoriginal, the result of common subject matter or external constraints, such as dimensions to which both works are subject,[508] or consist of general ideas can usually be disregarded at this stage because they are not probative of copying. This is not a hard and fast rule, however, because an overall impression of sufficient similarity, leading to an inference of copying, can arise from a combination of elements which by themselves are not original.[509] If the claimant demonstrates sufficient similarity, not in the works as a whole but in the features which he alleges have been copied, and establishes that the defendant had prior access to the copyright work, it will then be for the defendant to satisfy the judge that, despite the similarities, they did not result from copying. Although this inquiry is directed to the similarities rather than the differences, the differences may nevertheless be important because they may indicate an independent source and so rebut any inference of copying. But differences in the overall appearance of the two works due to the presence of features of the defendant's work about which no complaint is made are not material.[510]

7–68   **Inexact reproduction: imitation and substantial part.** Once it has been established that the defendant's work represents the claimant's in the sense discussed above and that the similarities between the works are the result of copying, then, except in the case of exact copying, the question will be whether the defendant's work is a copy of a substantial part of the claimant's. The general principles relating to inexact reproduction have already been discussed. Since it is the object of copyright in cases of this kind to ensure that the skill and effort of the creator are rewarded,[511] it has to be determined whether the maker of the defendant's work used a substantial part of those features of the claimant's work upon the creation of which skill and labour was employed. Have the essential features and substance of the copyright work been adopted?[512] As to this, in accordance with general principles, the elements or features which have been copied must first be identified and then compared with the copyright work as whole.[513] A claimant is not entitled to select only parts of his work, claiming copyright in those, so as to establish infringement by reproduction of just those parts.[514] By the same token, a defendant is not entitled to dissect the copyright work, taking each part which has been copied and asking whether each part could be the subject of copyright if it had stood alone. The inquiry should be directed to what has

---

[508] *Nicol v Barranger* [1917–1923] Mac.C.C. 219, CA.

[509] *Nouveau Fabrics Ltd v Voyage Decoration Ltd* [2004] EWHC 895 (Ch), pointing out that otherwise an inference of copying could never be made where the originality of the copyright work lay in its combination of existing elements or features.

[510] This paragraph is based on the speech of Lord Millett in *Designers Guild Ltd v Russell Williams (Textiles) Ltd*, [2000] 1 W.L.R. 2416 at 2425.

[511] *British Leyland Motor Corp Ltd v Armstrong Patents Co Ltd* [1983] F.S.R. 50 (at first instance).

[512] *Hanfstaengl v Baines & Co* [1895] A.C. 20 at 31; *Merchant Adventurers Ltd v M. Grew & Co Ltd* [1971] F.S.R. 233; *Drayton Controls (Engineering) Ltd v Honeywell Control Systems Ltd* [1992] F.S.R. 245.

[513] *Designers Guild Ltd v Russell Williams (Textiles) Ltd* [2001] 1 W.L.R. 2416. In *Spectravest Inc v Aperknit Ltd* [1988] F.S.R. 161, Millett J., as he then was, suggested, citing *Baumann v Fussell* [1978] R.P.C. 485, that it may be a useful approach to start by identifying that part of the copyright work which is *alleged* to have been reproduced and deciding first whether that part constitutes a substantial part of the copyright work, applying the usual qualitative test, and then deciding whether that part *is* a copy. In the light of what was said in *Designers Guild Ltd v Russell Williams (Textiles) Ltd*, however, to which Lord Millett was a party, this is not the right approach.

[514] *Merchandising Corporation of America Inc v Harpbond Ltd* [1983] F.S.R. 32.

been reproduced rather than what has not.[515] Because of this, it is wrong to decide the question by asking whether the defendant's work looks like the claimant's.[516] An action for infringement of copyright is not concerned with the appearance of the defendant's work but with its derivation. The basis of the complaint is not that the defendant's work resembles the copyright work but that the defendant has copied all or a substantial part of it. Thus the overall appearance of the defendant's work may be very different from the copyright work, but it does not follow that the defendant's work does not infringe the plaintiff's copyright.[517] A visual comparison of the two designs is therefore not only unnecessary, but likely to mislead.[518] It used to be said[519] that the question of substantial part could generally be answered merely by a comparison of the two works, and that a useful test of a copy was something which came so near to the original as to give every person seeing it the idea created by the original[520] or, alternatively, that which comes so near to the original as to suggest that original to the mind of every person seeing it.[521] This must now be regarded as wrong,[522] certainly to the extent that it suggests that if the defendant's work does *not* give the idea of or suggest the copyright work, the substantial part test is not satisfied. Obviously, if the defendant's work does give the idea of or suggest the copyright work, this may be because there has been substantial copying, but even this may not be the case for the reasons given below. This kind of approach is more appropriate in relation to the threshold question of whether there has been copying.[523]

In deciding the question of substantial part, it may be helpful to bear in mind that the essential nature of an artistic work is that it is a thing to be looked at, and what is important is what is visually significant.[524] In this context "visually significant" means visually significant to the person to whom the work would normally be addressed.[525] In the case of an artistic work, whether the part reproduced is substantial may therefore depend upon how important that part is to the recognition and appreciation of the work.[526] So, where a logo was alleged to have been copied the correct approach was held to be to compare the original logo with the allegedly infringing logo at the same sort of distance from the eye at which a purchaser or user of an object to which the logo was affixed or printed would be

---

[515] *Designers Guild Ltd v Russell Williams (Textiles) Ltd* [2001] 1 W.L.R. 2416; *Baumann v Fussell* [1978] R.P.C. 485.

[516] *Designers Guild Ltd v Russell Williams (Textiles) Ltd* [2001] 1 W.L.R. 2416; *Baumann v Fussell* [1978] R.P.C. 485.

[517] *Designers Guild Ltd v Russell Williams (Textiles) Ltd* [2001] 1 W.L.R. 2416, per Lord Millett, at 2425.

[518] *Designers Guild Ltd v Russell Williams (Textiles) Ltd* [2001] 1 W.L.R. 2416, at 2426.

[519] See, e.g. *Copinger*, 14th edn, para.7–82.

[520] *West v Francis* (1822) 5 B. & Ald. 737 at 743; cited with approval in the House of Lords in *King Features Syndicate v O. & M. Kleeman Ltd* [1941] A.C. 417, although note that this form of definition is not complete, as it does not take into account the necessity of proving actual copying: see *Merchant Adventurers Ltd v M. Grew & Co Ltd* [1971] F.S.R. 233 at 237.

[521] *Hanfstaengl v W.H. Smith & Sons* [1905] 1 Ch. 519 at 524; see *Catnic Components Ltd v Hill & Smith Ltd* [1975] F.S.R. 529, [1979] F.S.R. 619, CA; *Lerose Ltd v Hawick Jersey International Ltd* [1973] F.S.R. 15; *Antocks Lairn Ltd v I. Bloohn Ltd* [1971] F.S.R. 490; and see *Twentieth Century Fox Film Corp v Anglo Amalgamated Film Distributors Ltd* (1965) 109 S.J. 107.

[522] See *Designers Guild Ltd v Russell Williams (Textiles) Ltd* [2000] 1 W.L.R. 2416 and the general discussion of the "substantial part" issue, para.7–30, above.

[523] See para.7–67, above.

[524] *Rose Plastics GmbH v William Beckett & Co (Plastics) Ltd* [1988] R.P.C. 343; [1989] F.S.R. 113, adopted in *Interlego Industries A.G. v Tyco Industries Inc* [1989] A.C. 217 and applied in *Johnstone Safety Ltd v Peter Cook (International) Plc* [1990] F.S.R. 161.

[525] *Billhöfer Machinenfabrik GmbH v T. H. Dixon & Co. Ltd* [1990] F.S.R.105: in the case of an engineering drawing, "visually significant" means visually significant to an engineer and not an ordinary member of the public.

[526] *Catnic Components Ltd v Hill & Smith Ltd* [1982] R.P.C. 183 at 223, approved in *Interlego Industries A.G. v Tyco Industries Inc* [1989] A.C. 217 and applied in *Johnstone Safety Ltd v Peter Cook (International) Plc* [1990] F.S.R. 161.

likely to see it.[527] Where the purpose of the artistic work is to convey information, the importance of the part reproduced may thus fall to be judged by how far it contributes to the conveying of that information.[528] Nevertheless, it must be born in mind that what is protected is the skill and labour devoted to making the artistic work, not the skill and labour devoted to developing the idea or invention communicated.[529] The limit of protection in the case of an artistic work is its visual characteristics, not the technical ideas that it embodies.[530]

7–69   Since the question of substantiality has to be judged by asking whether there has been a substantial taking of those features of the copyright work upon the creation of which skill and labour was employed, it follows that if the defendant has merely reproduced a part of the copyright work on which no skill and labour was expended, so that it had no originality, there will be no infringement.[531] Thus if the copyright work is based partly upon an earlier work, and all that has been appropriated is the work of the earlier artist, there will have been no substantial copying of the copyright work.[532] Again, there is no copyright in an idea or functional concept as such, so that if this is all that the defendant has copied, and he has not appropriated the claimant's labour in expressing that idea in the form of an artistic work, there will be no infringement.[533] Generally speaking, the more abstract and simple the copied idea, the less likely it is to constitute a substantial part of the copyright work. Originality, in the sense of the contribution of the author's skill and labour, tends to lie in the detail with which the basic idea is presented.[534] Copyright protection is no broader where the work embodies a novel or inventive idea than where it represents a commonplace object.[535] But where an idea or concept has been expressed in some artistic work using sufficient skill and labour to make it a copyright work, then the copyright will be infringed by copying that expression.[536] Artistic techniques and skills, for example types of brushwork, cannot generally be the subject of copyright, so if this is all that has been copied, this will not amount to the taking of a substantial part. The principle cannot be taken too far, however, because the use of techniques will result in visual effects forming part of the artistic work and if these effects have been reproduced, this will be relevant to the overall issue of substantial part.[537] Again, in the case of a drawing of a utilitarian article, it is not correct to attempt to separate the skills of the creator of the copyright work into

---

[527] *Handi-Craft Company v B Free World Ltd* [2007] EWHC 10 (Pat); [2007] E.C.D.R. 21 at para.172 (on appeal but not on this point: [2008] EWCA Civ 868).

[528] *Entec (Pollution Control) Ltd v Abacus Mouldings* [1992] F.S.R. 332 (at first instance: in the case of a manufacturing drawing, reproduction of a substantial part means reproduction of the dimensions and spatial arrangements which are important for the purpose of manufacturing the article).

[529] *Catnic Components Ltd v Hill & Smith Ltd* [1981] F.S.R. 60, approved in *Interlego Industries A.G. v Tyco Industries Inc* [1989] A.C. 217.

[530] *Ultra Marketing (UK) Ltd v Universal Components Ltd* [2004] EWHC 468 (Ch), para.51.

[531] *Merchandising Corporation of America Inc v Harpbond Ltd* [1983] F.S.R. 32.

[532] See, e.g. para.7–30, above at (j).

[533] *L.B. (Plastics) Ltd v Swish Products Ltd* [1979] F.S.R. 145; *Johnstone Safety Ltd v Co v Peter Cook (International) Plc* [1990] F.S.R. 161; *Mono Pumps (N.Z.) v Amalgamated Pumps* [1992] 1 N.Z.L.R. 728.

[534] *Designers Guild Ltd v Russell Williams (Textiles) Ltd* [2001] 1 W.L.R. 2416, at 2423: "Copyright law protects foxes better than hedgehogs." See fn.227 to para.7–30, above at (e).

[535] *Catnic Components Ltd v Hill & Smith Ltd* [1979] F.S.R. 619, CA.

[536] *Catnic Components Ltd v Hill & Smith Ltd* [1979] F.S.R. 619, CA; *Leco Instruments (U.K.) Ltd v Land Pyrometers Ltd* [1982] R.P.C. 140, CA. For examples of cases where the idea has been copied but not the expression, see *Kenrick & Co v Lawrence & Co* (1890) 25 Q.B.D. 99 (idea of illustration of human hand in the act of voting, as an aid to illiterate voters); *Gleeson v H.R. Denne Ltd* [1975] R.P.C. 471 (concept for design of clerical collars); *Kleeneze Ltd v D.R.G. (U.K.) Ltd* [1984] F.S.R. 399 (concept for draught excluder); *George Ward (Moxley) Ltd v Richard Sankey Ltd* [1988] F.S.R. 66 (idea of sleeve for "nested" flower pots). For a general discussion of the problem of idea *versus* expression, see para.7–13, above.

[537] *Designers Guild Ltd v Russell Williams (Textiles) Ltd* [2001] 1 W.L.R. 2416. There, the creator

those which were purely "artistic" and those which were directed to giving the article its operational efficiency, perhaps at the direction of an engineer, and thus argue that if no use has been made of the former skills there will have been no infringement.[538] The fact that the claimant's work may have been the inspiration for the defendant's will not of itself make the defendant's work an infringement,[539] although if the "feeling and character" of the claimant's work has been taken this will be a relevant, but not conclusive, consideration.[540] Again as has been seen, the test of infringement is not affected by the fact that the defendant's work may be a parody of the claimant's.[541]

Once it is established that there has been a substantial use of the claimant's work, it does not matter that the defendant has used a different medium, or that the infringing work has been derived indirectly from the claimant's. It is equally an infringement of copyright whether the size of the copy has been increased or reduced,[542] or the dimensions altered.[543] A copy of another's work will not escape infringement merely by the omission or substitution by the defendant of features in the claimant's work,[544] or by combining part of the claimant's work with his own or another's in producing the final result.[545] Minor or trivial differences will not prevent one work from being a reproduction of another.[546]

Simple artistic works. Where the work is simple, or one representing ordinary objects, the first issue is usually whether the work is sufficiently original to make it a copyright work.[547] Once this had been established, the fact that the work may be described as simple does not help a defendant if he has in fact copied, that is, taken advantage of the skill and labour of the claimant in making the work.[548] On the other hand, where the work is indeed simple, a defendant may more easily be able to show that while he may have copied the concept, he did not take advantage of the claimant's labour in expressing it, i.e. did not copy what was visually significant, but rather did this by his own efforts.[549] A simple article may look like another but the question is whether the author used his own skill to create the

7–70

---

of the claimant's work had used a technique that had produced a distinctive impression of looseness and boldness combined with lightness and fragility, and this effect had been copied: see p.2421.

[538] *British Leyland Motor Corp Ltd v Armstrong Patents Co Ltd* [1986] A.C. 577 at 621; [1986] F.S.R. 221, HL, although cases of this kind will now usually only be relevant in the case of design right. It has been said that where the claimant's design has been indirectly copied but only to the extent of features that are purely functional, there is no infringement: see *George Ward (Moxley) Ltd v Richard Sankey Ltd* [1988] F.S.R. 66, per Whitford J., citing the dissenting judgment of Lord Griffiths in *British Leyland*. It is suggested that this is clearly wrong.

[539] *Baumann v Fussell* [1978] R.P.C. 485.

[540] *Baumann v Fussell* [1978] R.P.C. 485; *Brooks v Religious Tract Society* (1897) 45 W.R. 476; *Antiquesportfolio.com v Rodney Fitch & Co Ltd* [2001] F.S.R. 345 at 355 (photographs).

[541] *Twentieth Century Fox Film Corporation v Anglo Amalgamated Film Distributors Ltd* (1965) 109 S.J. 107.

[542] *Johnstone Safety Ltd v Peter Cook (Int.) Plc* [1990] F.S.R. 161 at 174; *Auvi Trade Mark* [1995] F.S.R. 288 at 296; *Antiquesportfolio.com v Rodney Fitch & Co Ltd* [2001] F.S.R. 345.

[543] *Wham-O Manufacturing Co v Lincoln Industries Ltd* [1985] R.P.C. 127 (CA of NZ); *Johnstone Safety Ltd v Peter Cook (Int.) Plc* [1990] F.S.R. 161; *Alan Nuttall v Equipashop Ltd*, noted at [1992] I.P.D. 15097 (what is substantial cannot be defined by inches or measurement).

[544] *Brooks v Religious Tract Society* (1897) 45 W.R. 476.

[545] *London Stereoscopic, etc. Co Ltd (The) v Kelly* (1888) 5 T.L.R. 169; *Weldons Ltd v United Press Ltd* [1905–1910] Mac.C.C. 293.

[546] *British Northrop Ltd v Texteam Blackburn Ltd* [1973] F.S.R. 241; *S.W. Hart & Co Pty Ltd v Edwards Hot Water Systems* [1986] F.S.R. 575; *Interlego A.G. v Tyco Industries Inc* [1987] F.S.R. 409.

[547] As to which, see para.3–131, above.

[548] *Cala Homes (South) Ltd v Alfred McAlpine Homes East Ltd* [1995] F.S.R. 818. So, in *Handi-Craft Company v B Free World Ltd* [2007] EWHC 10 (Pat); [2007] E.C.D.R. 21 (on appeal but not on this point: [2008] EWCA Civ 868), the copyright in a relatively simple logo was held to be infringed: para.172.

[549] *Entec (Pollution Control) Ltd v Abacus Mouldings* [1992] F.S.R. 332.

design or was in substance merely copying.[550] Thus, generally, the more simple and commonplace the drawing, the more clearly must the alleged infringement adhere to it if liability is to be established,[551] and in the case of works of little originality, almost exact copying will normally be required to establish infringement.[552] It follows that in the case of simple drawings, the labour of creation may have been so slight that there will be no infringement unless there is an almost exact reproduction of the drawing.[553]

7–71   **Reproduction of photographs.** Photographs are commonly reproduced photographically or by some other facsimile process, but they may also be reproduced by a drawing, painting or even by another photograph for which the subject matter was specially posed or selected.[554] These cases sometimes cause difficulties, and it is important to understand what it is that the copyright in a photograph protects, namely the author's work of origination.[555] Thus where a photographer takes a photograph of some public event or naturally occurring scene, a defendant who uses the photograph to obtain an accurate impression of the relative positions of the individuals or objects in the scene, but otherwise recreates the scene in his own style, will usually not infringe. This is because the relative positions of the individuals or objects are not the work of the photographer.[556] This may even be the case where the scene is not commonplace and the photograph may have been the inspiration for the defendant's work.[557] But where the defendant has in addition recreated the feeling and artistic character of the claimant's work this may be sufficient to amount to an infringement if a substantial portion of the claimant's skill and labour has thereby been taken.[558] So also where the photographer has arranged the subject-matter of the photograph to create a particular design[559] or has composed his photograph to include a particular selection of features which the defendant has copied.[560] In each case it is a matter of degree.[561] The copying, however, must be of the photograph. Thus where a defendant took a photograph of a scene which had been arranged by the claimant,

---

[550] *Dyson Limited v Qualtex (UK) Limited* [2006] EWCA Civ 166; [2006] R.P.C. 31, para.90, citing the example of *British Northrop Ltd v Texteam Blackburn Ltd* [1974] R.P.C. 57, where the point related to drawings for simple things such as a washer.

[551] *Constructions Pty Ltd v Foskett Pty Ltd* (1991) 20 I.P.R. 666 (Fed Ct of Aus.); *Dixon Investments Pty Ltd v Hall* (1990) 18 I.P.R. 481 (Fed Ct of Aus.).

[552] *Glogau v Land Transport Safety Authority of New Zealand* [1999] 1 N.Z.L.R. 257 (CA of NZ).

[553] *Politechnika Ipari Szovetkezet v Dallas Print Transfers Ltd* [1982] F.S.R. 529.

[554] *Antiquesportfolio.com v Rodney Fitch & Co Ltd* [2001] F.S.R. 345, at 355, approving this passage, although only obiter.

[555] As to the issue of the originality of a photograph, see para.3–144, as to the author of a photograph, see paras 4–27 et seq., above. For a full discussion of the various issues, see Michalos, *The Law of Photography and Digital Images* (London: Sweet & Maxwell, 2004). Note, however, the pending reference *Eva-Maria Paine v Standard Verlags GmbH, Axel Springer AG, Süddeutsche Zeitung GmbH, Spiegel-Verlag Rudolf Augstein GmbH & Co KG and Verlag M. DuMont Schauberg Expedition der Kölnischen Zeitung GmbH & Co KG* (C–145/10): "Are Article 1(1) of Directive 2001/29 in conjunction with Article 5(5) thereof and Article 12 of the Berne Convention for the Protection of Literary and Artistic Works ... particularly in the light of Article 1 of the First Additional Protocol to the European Convention for the Protection of Human Rights and Fundamental Freedoms (ECHR) ... and Article 17 of the Charter of Fundamental Rights of the European Union, to be interpreted as meaning that photographic works and/or photographs, particularly portrait photos, are afforded 'weaker' copyright protection or no copyright protection at all against adaptations because, in view of their 'realistic image', the degree of formative freedom is too minor?"

[556] *Baumann v Fussell* [1978] R.P.C. 485.

[557] *Baumann v Fussell* [1978] R.P.C. 485

[558] *Brooks v Religious Tract Society* (1897) 45 W.R. 476; *Baumann v Fussell* [1978] R.P.C. 485.

[559] *Baumann v Fussell* [1978] R.P.C. 485.

[560] *Krisarts S.A. v Briarfine Ltd* [1977] F.S.R. 557.

[561] The equivalent passage in the 14th edn, down to this point, was approved in *Antiquesportfolio.com v Rodney Fitch & Co Ltd* [2001] F.S.R. 345, at 355, with a particular emphasis on the points that it is the "author's work of origination which is protected", and that there may be infringement

he did not infringe the copyright in the claimant's photograph of the same scene because there was no causal link between the two photographs.[562]

Reproduction of scenes from painting, etc. The same kind of problem may arise where the claimant's work is a painting or drawing of a scene. Even if the scene is a well-known one, the artist may well have made an original contribution to his picture by his choice of viewpoint, the balance of features in the foreground, middle ground and background, and the other details. A defendant who makes a substantial use of these features will infringe.[563]   **7–72**

Maps and diagrams. The normal rules apply to what might be called the purely artistic features of a map.[564] In the case of maps, however, copyright will subsist not only in the outlines of the various features but also in the selection, arrangement and presentation of the various parts, such as towns, lakes, rivers, etc. If the defendant has copied the claimant's selection, amounting to a substantial part, he will have infringed.[565] It should also be borne in mind that such works are usually not only artistic works, but in some respects are also compilations of information, and in this respect are to be treated as literary works.[566] The artistic copyright may therefore be infringed by reproduction in the form of a substantially similar map and the literary work may be infringed by the reproduction in some other form, for example a table of the information which the map contains. In either case, to escape infringement a defendant must himself carry out the survey, gather the information and do whatever else is necessary to compile the work, and not simply appropriate the claimant's labour.[567]   **7–73**

Architects plans and works of architecture. Copyright may subsist in both architects' plans and in works of architecture themselves (i.e. buildings or models for buildings[568]). Although architects may therefore be concerned with infringements of a number of different rights, disputes in this area most usually concern infringements of plans by the making of other plans and the construction of buildings from such plans.   **7–74**

Infringement of plans. Copyright in an architect's plan is infringed if a substantial part of the skill and labour used in creating the work has been taken.[569] The copying of the same methods of construction, if they do not find expression in the claimant's artistic work and the defendant's plan or building, will not constitute an infringement. Naturally it will be more difficult to establish copying of a design for an ordinary building since the similarities may be explained by the fact that each architect has drawn on common experience or sources.[570] However, this only goes to the matter of proof: if a claimant's original design for an ordinary building has been copied, the fact that the design is simple does not afford a   **7–75**

---

where the defendant has "recreated the feeling and artistic character of the [claimant's] work". The case contains a number of examples of copying of photographic works.

[562] *Creation Records Ltd v News Group Newspapers Ltd* [1997] E.M.L.R. 444. There was also no copyright in the scene itself.

[563] *Krisarts S.A. v Briarfine Ltd* [1977] F.S.R. 557.

[564] Some of the older cases include *Carnon v Bowles* 2 Bro.C.C. 80; *Cary v Longman* (1801) 1 East. 357; *Cary v Faden* 5 Ves. 24.

[565] *Geographia Ltd v Penguin Books Ltd* [1985] F.S.R. 208; see also *General Drafting Co Inc v Andrews* 37 F. 2d 54.

[566] *Anacon Corp Ltd v Environmental Research Technology Ltd* [1994] F.S.R. 659.

[567] *Longman v Winchester* (1809) 16 Ves. 269 (two maps, if both accurate, may be much the same, but the labour and expense of a survey must be undertaken by each); *Kelly v Morris* (1866) L.R. 1 Eq. 697, is to the same effect.

[568] CDPA 1988 s.4(1)(a).

[569] *Cala Homes (South) Ltd v Alfred McAlpine East Ltd* [1995] F.S.R. 818.

[570] See, e.g. *Beck v Montana Constructions Pty Ltd* [1964–1965] N.S.W.R. 229 at 232.

defence.[571] In the usual way, the alleged infringement, even if derived from the claimant's work, must bear a sufficient resemblance to the part copied.[572]

An architect's plans may be copied in the form of a building which reproduces the plans. Thus a drawing of an elevation for a building can be infringed by a building which reproduces the elevation, this being a reproduction of the claimant's work in a "material form".[573] The more difficult case is where floor plans are copied. Here it may be thought more difficult to say that the plans have been infringed if the only way to see the resemblance would be either to demolish the building to floor level or to recreate the floor plan by measurement of the building. Nevertheless it seems reasonably clear that if it can be proved by such means, or by reference to the plans which it is proved the defendant used to construct the building, that the layout is substantially similar, then the copyright in the claimant's plans will have been infringed by the construction of the building, since the plans will have been reproduced in a "material form".[574]

7–76   **Infringement of building or model for building.** It should be borne in mind that, unlike other artistic works, copyright does not subsist in a building or model for a building "irrespective of artistic quality".[575] It is suggested that infringement is therefore confined to copying that in which copyright subsists, namely the features of the building having artistic quality.[576] It should also be borne in mind that the copyright in a building is not infringed by making a graphic work,[577] photograph or film of it, or broadcasting a visual image of it.[578] Infringement is therefore largely confined to making a three-dimensional copy, whether in the form of another building or a model. The same applies to a model for a building if it is situated in a public place or in premises open to the public.[579]

7–77   **Other permitted acts.** It should also be noted that the copyright in a building, or in any drawings or plans in accordance with which the building was lawfully constructed, is not infringed by anything done for the purposes of reconstructing that building.[580]

D.   SOUND RECORDINGS

7–78   There is no extended definition in the 1988 Act of "to copy" in relation to sound recordings. It is therefore an infringement of the copyright in a sound recording

---

[571] *Cala Homes (South) Ltd v Alfred McAlpine East Ltd* [1995] F.S.R. 818 (see the Annexes to the report for an analysis and illustrations of the designs held to infringe).

[572] *Collier Constructions Pty Ltd v Foskett Pty Ltd* (1991) 20 I.P.R. 666 (Fed Ct of Aus)—copyright in floor plans for a house, which included the room divisions, windows, entrances and various fittings, not infringed by the reproduction of the outline only in an advertisement comparing overall sizes). See also *Dixon Investments Pty Ltd v Hall* (1990) 18 I.P.R. 481 (Fed Ct of Aus) and the cases cited there; *Eagle Homes Pty Ltd v Austec Homes Pty Ltd* (1997) 39 I.P.R. 565. For the particular difficulties posed by plans for so-called "project homes", see *Tamawood Ltd v Henley Arch Pty Ltd* [2004] FCAFC 78; 61 I.P.R. 378.

[573] *Chabot v Davies* (1936) 155 L.T. 525; [1936] 3 All E.R. 221.

[574] This was accepted without argument in *Cala Homes (South) Ltd v Alfred McAlpine East Ltd* [1995] F.S.R. 818. Note also that it is permissible to examine a cross section of what the defendant has made to establish infringement. See para.7–66, above. See also *Lend Lease Homes Pty Ltd v Warrigal Homes Pty Ltd* [1970] 3 N.S.W.R. 265, where the difficult case of *Burke, etc. Ltd v Spicers Dress Designs* [1936] Ch. 400 was distinguished.

[575] See CDPA 1988 s.4(1)(a).

[576] See *Meikle v Maufe* [1941] 3 All E.R. 144, although note that under the 1911 Act copyright was conferred on a building or structure having an artistic character or design *in respect of such character or design*. See s.35(1).

[577] This expression includes a painting, drawing or plan. For the full definition, see CDPA 1988 s.4(2).

[578] See CDPA 1988 s.62, and para.9–188, below for a fuller discussion of these permitted acts.

[579] CDPA 1988 s.62, and para.9–188, below for a fuller discussion of these permitted acts.

[580] CDPA 1988 s.65. See para.9–195.

to copy it[581] or a substantial part of it,[582] either directly or indirectly[583] and whether transiently or incidentally to some other use.[584] Although the Act does not expressly state that copying takes place by storing the sound recording in a medium by electronic means,[585] it clearly does so.

What is protected by the copyright in a sound recording is the particular recording of sounds on the sound carrier.[586] The copyright in a sound recording is therefore infringed by making a copy of those sounds, directly or indirectly, from that recording but not by making a new recording of identical or similar sounds independently, for example by recording a new performance by musicians of the same music.[587] Nor is it an infringement of the copyright in a sound recording to make a transcription in some form of notation of the sounds which have been recorded, for example in the form of sheet music. In any of these cases, of course, any copyright in the work which is recorded on the recording may be infringed by such means.

Substantial part. The issue of what amounts to a substantial part of a sound re-   **7–79**
cording frequently arises because of the practice of "sampling", that is, the process of taking a small part of a recording and repeating it, together with other material, to form a new recording. The problem is a difficult one because a very small and musically unexceptional part of a recording of a popular piece of music may yet be instantly recognisable. Indeed, this is usually the very reason why the part has been taken and, by the repeated use of the extract, the defendant draws on the popularity of the claimant's work to attract the public for his own benefit. The rule of thumb that "what is worth copying is worth protecting" should be applied with caution.[588]

Film soundtracks. The treatment of film soundtracks has changed over the years.   **7–80**
The topic is discussed in detail elsewhere,[589] but for present purposes the soundtrack accompanying a film is today to be treated as part of the film.[590] Where, therefore, a film soundtrack has been copied, this is to be regarded as the copying of a film rather than of a sound recording.[591]

E. FILMS

It is an infringement of the copyright in a film to make a copy of it,[592] or a   **7–81**
substantial part of it,[593] whether directly or indirectly[594] and whether transiently

---

[581] CDPA 1988 ss.16(1)(a), 17(1).

[582] s.16(3)(a).

[583] s.16(3)(b).

[584] s.17(6), although note the permitted act provisions of s.28A in relation to transient or incidental use.

[585] cf. s.17(2), which only applies in the case of copying of literary, dramatic, musical and artistic works.

[586] "Sound recording" means: (a) a recording of sounds, from which the sounds may be reproduced, or (b) a recording of the whole or any part of a literary, dramatic or musical work, from which sounds reproducing the work or part may be produced. See CDPA 1988 s.5A(1).

[587] *Norowzian v Arks Ltd* [1998] F.S.R. 394; *CBS Records Australia Ltd v Telmak Teleproducts (Aust.) Pty Ltd* (1988) 79 A.L.R. 604; *Polygram Records Inc v Raben Footwear Pty Ltd* (1996) 35 I.P.R. 426 (Fed Ct of Aus).

[588] See para.7–31, at (b), and compare the position in relation to musical works, para.7–53, above. See also *Tackaberry* in [1990] Ent. L.R. 87 (for a review of the Canadian authorities) and *Bently and Sherman* in [1992] Ent. L.R. 158.

[589] See para.3–78.

[590] CDPA 1988 s.5B(2).

[591] CDPA 1988 s.5B(3)(c).

[592] CDPA 1988 ss.16(1)(a), 17(1).

[593] CDPA 1988 s.16(3)(a).

or incidental to some other use.[595] As with a sound recording, it is not expressly stated that copying of a film includes storing it by electronic means, but again it clearly does so.[596] Again, the copyright in a film is infringed if the recorded moving images are directly or indirectly copied but not if the same or similar images are created independently, for example by reshooting the subject matter of the film.[597] Again, however, underlying works such as the screenplay may be infringed by such means. What amounts to a substantial part is a question of fact and degree and depends upon both quality and quantity of what has been taken, and the fact that the copied part is very short is not decisive.[598] Thus clips lasting only a few seconds taken from films of football matches lasting 90 minutes were held to be substantial parts of the films: they reproduced incidents of particular interest to the viewers, such as goals, near misses, demonstrations of particular skill and the like, and sufficient footage was shown to enable the viewers to appreciate the incidents.[599] The position was not quite the same under the 1956 Act, which did not contain a "substantial part" test in the case of a film, so that the copying of a single frame constituted an infringement.[600] This position has, however, been preserved, in that under the 1988 Act copying in relation to a film includes making a photograph of the whole or any substantial part of any image forming part of the film.[601] This provision is, however, limited in effect, in the sense that the definition of a photograph excludes any image which is part of a film,[602] a film being defined as something from which a moving image may be produced.[603] So, whereas a photograph of a single frame of a film will amount to a copy of the film, a copy consisting of a number of photographs of frames will not do so if a moving image, however short, can be produced from that copy.[604] Otherwise the substantial part test in relation to a film would have no application, since even a very short and insignificant clip would come within the "photograph" provision, which is clearly intended to relate to "stills" from a film. Again, however, underlying works such as the screenplay may be infringed by such means.

It has been seen that in relation to films made after July 1, 1994 the author of a film is to be taken, as from December 1, 1996 to be the principal director of the

---

[594] CDPA 1988 s.16(3)(b).

[595] CDPA 1988 s.17(6), although note the permitted act provisions of s.28A in relation to transient or incidental use.

[596] This was not disputed in *Football Association Premier League Ltd v QC Leisure* [2008] EWHC 1411 (Ch).

[597] *Norowzian v Arks Ltd* [1998] F.S.R. 394; *Zeccola v Universal City Studios Inc.* (1982) 46 A.L.R. 189 and *Telmak Teleproducts Australia Pty Ltd v Bond International Pty Ltd* (1985) 5 I.P.R. 203 (although see the subsequent decision in the case reported at (1987) 9 I.P.R. 440, where the question was left open).

[598] *Football Association Premier League Ltd v QC Leisure* [2008] EWHC 1411 (Ch); [2008] F.S.R. 32 at para.209.

[599] *Football Association Premier League Ltd v QC Leisure* [2008] EWHC 1411 (Ch) at para.209.

[600] *Spelling Goldberg Productions Inc v B.P.C. Publishing Ltd* [1981] R.P.C. 283

[601] CDPA 1988 s.17(4). This gives statutory effect to the judicial interpretation of the 1956 Act (see *Spelling Goldberg Productions Inc v B.P.C. Publishing Ltd* [1981] R.P.C. 283): *Football Association Premier League Ltd v QC Leisure* [2008] EWHC 1411 (Ch); [2008] F.S.R. 32 at para.224.

[602] CDPA 1988 s.4(2).

[603] CDPA 1988 s.5B(1).

[604] *Football Association Premier League Ltd v QC Leisure* [2008] EWHC 1411 (Ch) at para.224. See, however, *R. v Gilham* [2009] EWCA Crim 2293 at 23; [2010] E.C.D.R. 5, where the court of appeal seems to have cast doubt on whether this is consistent with what was said by Jacob L.J. in *R. v Higgs* [2008] EWCA Crim 1324; [2008] F.S.R. 34 or Laddie J. in *Sony v Ball* [2004] EWHC 1738 (Ch); [2005] F.S.R. 9; [2004] E.C.D.R. 33. It is not clear, however, whether the Court of Appeal was criticising this statement of Kitchin J., and in any event it is suggested that Jacob L.J. had overlooked the kind of careful analysis which formed the basis of Kitchin J.'s decision.

film, as well as the producer.[605] This is clearly likely to have an effect on the ownership of the copyright in such films and thus on the question of infringement. Transitional provisions therefore provide that where arrangements were made before November 19, 1992[606] for the exploitation of any such film, the rights which the principal director now has are not infringed by anything done after December 1, 1996 in pursuance of such arrangements.[607]

Film soundtracks. As already noted, for present purposes the soundtrack accompanying a film is today to be treated as part of the film.[608] Where, therefore, a film soundtrack has been copied, this is to be regarded as the copying of a film rather than of a sound recording.[609]
    7–82

F. Broadcasts

No further definition of "copying" in relation to a broadcast is given in the 1988 Act other than that, as with films, it includes making a photograph of the whole or any substantial part of any image forming part of the broadcast.[610] The usual substantial part test applies.[611] It should be noted, however, that the making in domestic premises for private and domestic use of a photograph of the whole or any part of an image forming part of a broadcast, or a copy of such a photograph, does not infringe any copyright in the broadcast.[612] In the usual way, it will also be an infringement to copy the whole or any substantial part of the broadcast,[613] whether directly or indirectly[614] or transiently or incidentally to some other use[615] or store it by electronic means.
    7–83

Cable programmes. It has already been noted that, with effect from October 31, 2003, there is no longer a separate category of copyright work consisting of a cable programme, only a "broadcast".[616] Since that date, any work in which copyright may have subsisted as a cable programme can now only be protected as a broadcast, provided of course that it satisfies the qualifying conditions for a broadcast under the amended provisions of the 1988 Act.[617]
    7–84

G. Typographical Arrangements

The Act provides that in relation to the typographical arrangement of a published edition, copying means making a facsimile copy of the arrangement.[618] "Facsimile copy" is defined to include a copy which is reduced or enlarged in scale.[619] The ubiquitous practice of the unlicensed scanning, photocopying and faxing of
    7–85

---

[605] See CDPA 1988 s.9(2)(ab) and para.4–48, above.

[606] The effective date of the Rental and Related Rights Directive.

[607] The Copyright and Related Rights Regulations 1996 (SI 1996/2967) reg.36(2).

[608] CDPA 1988 s.5B(2).

[609] CDPA 1988 s.5B(3)(C)

[610] CDPA 1988 s.17(4). See para.7–81 as to the effect of this provision.

[611] CDPA 1988 s.16(3)(a). See also *TCN Channel Nine Pty Ltd v Network Ten Pty Ltd* [2005] FCAFC 53, (2005) 65 I.P.R. 571 (no special rules apply in the case of broadcasts).

[612] s.71. See para.9–216.

[613] s.16(3)(a).

[614] s.16(3)(b).

[615] s.17(6).

[616] See paras 3–84 et seq.

[617] See paras 3–92 et seq. and Interpretation Act 1978 s.16.

[618] CDPA 1988 s.17(5). In *Machinery Market Ltd v Sheen Publishing Ltd* [1983] F.S.R. 431, decided under the 1956 Act, the defendants were held liable although it was their printers who had made the reproductions. It is not clear whether the printers were treated simply as the defendants' agents, although no doubt the defendants were liable for having authorised the infringement.

[619] CDPA 1988 s.178.

published works are everyday examples of such infringements. Where the text of a published work is electronically scanned and the image then converted into a text file by character recognition software, the act of scanning will amount to copying of the typographical arrangement but the subsequent conversion or storage of the text will not do so. This is because the software will generate the typographical arrangement afresh.

7–86   **Substantial part.** As seen elsewhere,[620] the protected work in the case of typographical arrangement copyright is the whole of the product which a publisher offers to the public whether, in the case of a book, that which is between the covers or, in the case of a newspaper, the whole newspaper. The issue of substantial part must be judged by applying the normal rule that substantiality is about quality rather than quantity. As to the relevant quality, this again must be considered by reference to the reason why copyright protection is conferred on the work, which is to protect and reward the investment of skill and labour in the presentation and layout of the edition.[621]

The question is therefore whether there has there been a copying of sufficient of the relevant skill and labour expended on the creation of the edition's typographical arrangement. This depends not upon the proportion which the part taken bears to the whole but on whether the copy can be said to have appropriated the presentation and layout of the edition. In the case of traditional book publishing,[622] the skill and labour involved is the skill in designing the pages and the labour and capital in setting up the type and keeping it standing. In the case of a newspaper, the skill and labour devoted to the typographical arrangement is principally expressed in the overall design. It is not the choice of a particular typeface, the precise number or widths of the columns, the breadth of margins or the relationship of headlines and strap lines to the other text, the number of articles on a page or the distribution of photographs and advertisements, but the combination of all of these into pages which give the newspaper as a whole its distinctive appearance. In some cases, that appearance will depend upon the relationship between the pages; for example, having headlines rather than small advertisements on the front page. Usually, however, it will depend upon the appearance of any given page. It is therefore unlikely that the skill and labour which has gone into the typographical arrangement of a newspaper will be sufficiently expressed in anything less than a full page since the particular fonts, columns, margins and so forth are "the typographical vocabulary in which the arrangement is expressed".[623] So, where a defendant had made reprographic copies of individual articles from newspapers, this did not amount to the copying of a substantial part of the typographical arrangement of the whole newspaper. The defendant had not "reproduced anything that could be regarded as either resembling the newspaper concerned or having newspaper-like qualities".[624]

---

[620] See para.3–106, above.

[621] *Newspaper Licensing Agency Ltd v Marks & Spencer* [2001] UKHL 38; [2003] 1 A.C. 551; [2002] R.P.C. 4, approving *Nationwide News Pty Ltd v Copyright Agency Ltd* (1994) 30 I.P.R. 159; (1995) 34 I.P.R. 53 (Fed Ct of Aus).

[622] This was the field of activity in mind when this form of protection was originally created by the 1956 Act; the purpose of the copyright was originally to protect the publisher against competition from pirate photo-lithographic copies of the edition.

[623] *Newspaper Licensing Agency Ltd v Marks & Spencer* [2001] UKHL 38, per Lord Hoffmann at para.23; [2003] 1 A.C. 551.

[624] *Newspaper Licensing Agency Ltd v Marks & Spencer* [2001] Ch. 257, CA, per Mance L.J. and approved by the House of Lords [2001] UKHL 38.

3. THE ISSUE OF COPIES TO THE PUBLIC: THE DISTRIBUTION RIGHT

The distribution right. One of the acts restricted by the copyright in all works is   **7–87**
the issue of copies of the work to the public, often called the "distribution right".[625]
Broadly, this means the act of first release onto the market of any particular copy
of the work, including "the original". Infringement by issue of copies to the public was a new concept introduced by s.18 of the 1988 Act and represented a
substantial departure from the previous law, under which "publication" of a literary, dramatic, musical or artistic work was an infringement.[626] Decisions under
the earlier law are of little assistance in interpreting s.18.

The Berne and Rome Conventions. There has been little consistency amongst   **7–88**
the countries which are parties to these Conventions in their approach to a right
to control the distribution of works and related rights subject matter, and thus the
Conventions do not lay down any general exclusive right in this area.[627]

EC Directives. The distribution right has been the subject of a number of EC   **7–89**
Directives, two of which have necessitated amendments to s.18,[628] namely the
Computer Software Directive, which dealt with computer programs,[629] and the
Rental and Related Rights Directive, which dealt with related rights subject
matter.[630] Most recently, art.4 of the Information Society Directive[631] has required
Member States to provide for a general distribution right[632] but no change to the
1988 Act was required to be made by way of implementation of this aspect of the
Directive.[633]

Issue to the public: meaning.[634] As s.18 now stands, the expression "the issue to   **7–90**
the public of copies of a work" means:

    (a) The act of putting into circulation in the EEA[635] copies not previously put
        into circulation in the EEA by or with the consent of the copyright owner;
        or

---

[625] See, e.g. the references in the Information Society Directive, referred to subsequently in the text.

[626] The expression "publishing" in this context did not mean the issuing of works to the public, but rather making public what had previously not been made public in the United Kingdom: *Infabrics Ltd v Jaytex Ltd* [1982] A.C. 1; [1981] F.S.R. 261. A defendant could therefore only be liable under this head if copies of the work had never before been issued to the public in the United Kingdom. For confirmation of the change in the law, see *The British Phonographic Industry Ltd v Mechanical-Copyright Protection Society Ltd (No. 2)* [1993] E.M.L.R. 86 at 98, n.9.

[627] See Ricketson and Ginsburg, *The International Copyright and Neighbouring Rights* 2nd edn (OUP), para.11.45.

[628] As to the transitional provisions relating to these amendments, see *Copinger* 14th edn, para.7–110.

[629] art.4 of the Directive required Member States to provided the rightholder with an exclusive right in relation to any form of distribution to the public of the original program or copies. It was implemented by the Copyright (Computer Programs) Regulations 1992 (SI 1992/3233).

[630] art.9 of the Directive required Member States to provide an exclusive distribution right in respect of sound recordings, films (the producer's right) and broadcasts. It was implemented by the Copyright and Related Rights Regulations 1996 (SI 1996/2967). The Rental and Related Rights Directive and its amendments have now been codified as Directive 2006/115/EC: [2006] OJ L376/28. Art.9 of the original Directive is now art.9 of Directive 2006/115.

[631] Directive 2001/29.

[632] Member States are required to provide for authors, in respect of the original of their works or of copies of them, with the exclusive right to authorise or prohibit any form of distribution to the public by sale or otherwise: art.4 (the distribution right in relation to related rights subject matter is dealt with in similar terms by art.9 of the Rental and Related Rights Directive, 92/100).

[633] As to whether the Directive was correctly implemented in this respect, see para.7–91, concerning the loan, hiring and importation of copies.

[634] See generally on the distribution right, Philips and Bently, "Copyright Issues: The Mysteries of Section 18" [1999] E.I.P.R. 133.

[635] The "EEA" means the European Economic Area: CDPA 1988 s.172A(1).

(b) The act of putting into circulation outside the EEA copies not previously put into circulation in the EEA or elsewhere.[636]

For this purpose, "issue to the public of copies of a work" does not include:

(c) any subsequent distribution, sale, hiring or loan of copies previously put into circulation[637]; or

(d) any subsequent importation of such copies into the United Kingdom or another EEA state,

except insofar as para.(a) above applies to putting into circulation in the EEA copies previously put into circulation outside the EEA.[638]

Further, the expression "the issue of copies" is to be understood as including the issue of the "original" work.[639] Thus the putting into circulation of an original painting for the first time is a restricted act. The section originally made further provision for the case of rental of copies of certain works, but rental is now exclusively the subject of the separate rental right under s.18A, considered later in this chapter.[640]

Generally, s.18 must be interpreted in accordance with the Information Society Directive, which provides that: (a) the right includes the exclusive right to control "distribution of the work incorporated in a tangible article"; (b) the first sale in the Community of the original of a work or copies thereof by the rightholder or with his consent exhausts the right to control resale of that object in the Community but the right is not to be exhausted by a sale outside the Community; and (c) the distribution right is without prejudice to the provisions relating to the rental and lending rights contained in the Rental and Lending Rights Directive.[641]

In accordance with the Information Society Directive, the Act therefore makes the act of putting particular copies of a work into circulation in the United Kingdom for the first time a restricted act, even where the work has already been published in the sense that other copies of the work have previously been put into circulation in the United Kingdom. So, for example, the putting into circulation of a further 10 copies of a work which has already been published is a restricted act. It is also clear that it does not matter for this purpose whether the further copies are licensed or unlicensed.[642] A trader who therefore acquires a number of copies of a work which were made with the licence of the copyright owner but who does not have the owner's express or implied licence to put them into circulation will infringe if he does so.[643]

7-91   On the wording of the section, it might appear that copyright could be infringed by the act of putting copies into circulation outside the United Kingdom, not only anywhere in the EEA but even anywhere in the world outside the EEA. This cannot be correct. Not only is the whole basis of copyright, both as generally understood under UK law and internationally, territorial[644] but the words of s.18 are subject to the general words of s.16, namely that "[the] owner of the copyright in a work has, in accordance with the following provisions of this Chapter,

---

[636] CDPA 1988 s.18(2). For this purpose, the issue of the film sound track which accompanies a film constitutes the issuing of a film, not the issuing of a sound recording: CDPA 1988 s.5B(3)(c).

[637] But see CDPA 1988 s.18A: infringement by rental or lending.

[638] CDPA 1988 s.18(3).

[639] CDPA 1988 s.18(4). See also art.4 of the Information Society Directive.

[640] See para.7–93.

[641] Recital 28. As to the Rental and Lending Rights Directive (2006/115/EC), see para.7–93.

[642] *Nelson v Rye* [1996] F.S.R. 313 at 339.

[643] Assuming that those copies had not previously been put into circulation. Normally, of course, he will have an implied if not express licence to do so. See *Nelson v Rye* [1996] F.S.R. 313, at 339.

[644] i.e. the right which each state confers by way of copyright is essentially domestic, and is concerned with the rights of the owner within that state.

the exclusive right to do the following acts *in the United Kingdom* … (b) to issue copies of the work to the public."[645] As originally enacted, s.18(2) provided that "References in this Part to the issue to the public of copies of a work are to the act of putting into circulation copies not previously put into circulation, in the United Kingdom or elsewhere, and not to (a) any subsequent distribution, sale, hiring or loan of those copies, or (b) any subsequent importation of those copies into the United Kingdom …". The change introduced to give effect to the Computer Software Directive[646] did not materially affect the sense of the section.[647] It was only the changes made as part of the implementation of the Rental and Related Rights Directive[648] which introduced the present wording. There is nothing in the Directive itself or the purposes which underlie it which suggests that a revolutionary broadening of the territoriality of the scope of infringement was intended. Section 18 must also be construed consistently with the provisions of the Information Society Directive, under which the right is only to be exhausted by the first sale or other transfer of ownership in the Community but not by first sale outside the Community.[649] It is suggested that the present wording has come about because when implementing the Rental and Related Rights Directive the draughtsman concentrated on giving effect to the Community principle of exhaustion of rights, while seeking to deny any question of international exhaustion, that is, to make it clear that while the act of putting a copy of a work into circulation in the EEA should exhaust that right within the EEA, the act of putting that copy into circulation anywhere outside the EEA should not do so. In doing so, the draughtsman focused on dealing with the past history of the copy (i.e. whether it had been put into circulation and, if so, where) and overlooked that, in doing so, the clarity of the geographic limitation of the basic exclusive right had been lost. It is therefore suggested that the effect of the section is as follows:

(a) If the copy of the work has never before been put into circulation anywhere in the world, the act of putting it into circulation in the United Kingdom for the first time is a restricted act.

(b) If the copy has previously been put into circulation within the EEA by or with the consent of the copyright owner, then the act of putting it into circulation in the United Kingdom is not a restricted act. In Community terms, the distribution right is exhausted by the consensual first act of distribution.

(c) If the copy has previously been put into circulation in a country outside the EEA, but not within the EEA, then the act of putting it into circulation in the United Kingdom is a restricted act.

---

[645] As to the territorial scope of UK copyright see *Peer International Corp v Termidor Music Publishers* [2002] EWHC 2675 (Ch); [2004] R.P.C. 22. And see *ABKCO Music v Music Collection International Ltd* [1995] R.P.C. 657 on the difference in the territorial scope of CDPA 1988 s.16 (limited to the United Kingdom) and the tort of authorisation (not so limited).

[646] By the Copyright (Computer Programs) Regulations 1992 (SI 1992/3233).

[647] The 1992 Regulations introduced, after the words "References in this Part to the issue to the public of copies of a work are", in CDPA 1988 s.18(2), the words "except where the work is a computer program" and a further subsection relating to computer programs: "(3) References in this Part to the issue to the public of copies of a work where the work is a computer program are to the act of putting into circulation copies of that program not previously put into circulation in the United Kingdom or any other member State, by or with the consent of the copyright owner, and not to (a) any subsequent distribution, sale, hiring or loan of those copies, or (b) any subsequent importation of those copies into the United Kingdom; except that the restricted act of issuing copies to the public includes any rental of copies to the public."

[648] By the Copyright and Related Rights Regulations 1996 (SI 1996/2967). The Rental and Related Rights Directive and its amendments have now been codified as Directive 2006/115/EC.

[649] Recital 28. See also *KK Sony Entertainment v Pacific Game Technology (Holding) Ltd* [2006] EWHC 2509 (Ch), para.17, accepting that the jurisprudence of the ECJ in relation to Community exhaustion of rights applies equally to actions in copyright, and that in particular putting a product onto the market outside the EEA does not constitute consent on the part of the rightsowner to the product thereafter being marketed within the EEA.

(d) Whether the act of putting the copy into circulation in a country other than the United Kingdom is an infringement of copyright is a matter for the law of that state, not that of the United Kingdom.

As to what acts amount to issuing to the public, or putting a copy into circulation, the latter expression is not further defined but suggests a release of a copy onto the market such that it may be passed on to other members of the public. It is not clear whether for this purpose the plural includes the singular, so that the release of a single copy is a restricted act, but as a matter of principle there seems no good reason why it should not do so.[650] It might be thought that some help as to what acts might be included within the expression is to be derived from the references in subs.(3)(a) and (b) to "subsequent" acts of importation, distribution, sale, hire and loan, the inference being that any such act can amount to putting a copy into circulation (provided that it is not "subsequent" to an earlier issue to the public). In the case of acts of sale and distribution, it is easy to see that such acts might well usually have the effect of releasing copies onto the market. However, the Information Society Directive defines the right by reference to "any form of distribution to the public by sale or otherwise"[651] and the European Court of Justice has made it clear that in the case of distribution otherwise than by sale, the right is not engaged unless ownership in the article passes (it presumably being implicit that in the case of distribution by sale ownership also passes).[652] Although therefore the act of the first loan or hire may have the effect of releasing a copy into circulation, this will not be *free* circulation, and does not amount to issue to the public. The acts of the rental and lending of copies of a work to the public are restricted acts under s.18A[653] and the Court of Justice has made it clear that the rental right is not exhausted by the sale or other acts of release into circulation of a copy of the work,[654] nor by other acts of rental.[655] The exclusion by the Act of "any subsequent ... loan or hiring ... of copies previously put into circulation" from the restricted act of issue to the public therefore appears to be unnecessary and misleading. Finally, as to importation, it is difficult to see how the mere act of importation could amount to putting copies into circulation, particularly if, for example, the copies were not then released to the public.[656] It is clear that the act of offering or exposing copies for sale is not capable of amount-

---

[650] This is clearly so in the case of the rental and lending right, and some support is given by the fact that the issue of the "original" is now a restricted act. The point was left open in *Microsoft Corp v Electro-wide Ltd* [1997] F.S.R. 580.

[651] art.4.1

[652] *Peek & Cloppenburg KG v Cassina SpA* (C–456/06) [2008] E.C.R. I–2731 (ECJ). The case concerned the question whether the exhibition of articles of furniture in a shop window or a shop showroom, where the public was able to try them out, amounted to a distribution to the public by sale *or otherwise*, within the meaning of the Information Society Directive. The referring court asked whether it could be assumed that there was a distribution to the public otherwise than by sale where third parties were able to make use of the works without there being any transfer of *de facto* power to dispose of those items, or where works were shown publicly without the public being able to make use of them. The ECJ reinterpreted this question as being whether the concept of distribution to the public otherwise than through the sale must be interpreted as meaning that it includes, first, granting to the public the right to use reproductions of a work protected by copyright without the grant of use entailing a transfer of *ownership* and, secondly, exhibiting those reproductions to the public without actually granting a right to use them. The answer to this question was then stated to be that the concept of distribution to the public, otherwise than through sale, applies only where there is a transfer of the ownership of that object. As a result, "neither granting to the public the right to use reproductions of a work protected by copyright nor exhibiting to the public those reproductions without actually granting a right to use them can constitute such a form of distribution."

[653] As to this, see further below.

[654] *Metronome Musik GmbH v Music Point Hokamp GmbH* [1999] F.S.R. 576, ECJ.

[655] *Foreningen AF Danske Videogramdistributorer v Laserdisken* [1999] E.M.L.R. 681, ECJ.

[656] While the inclusion of this act in CDPA 1988 s.18(3)(b) suggests that there are circumstances where importation could amount to an issue to the public, the better view is that this is also the result of muddled drafting. The intention as expressed in Parliament seems clearly to have been

ing to putting copies into circulation.[657] It is an open question whether the sale to the public of an article subject to a retention of title clause constitutes an issue to the public.[658]

It is less clear what constitutes the restricted act of putting copies into circulation where there is a chain of distribution. Thus in the common type of case, the chain of distribution will start with the manufacturer or importer of the goods, which are then sent to a wholesaler, who in turn distributes them to retailers, who then sells them to the public. Who, in this chain, puts the goods into circulation? The Act must be construed in accordance with the Information Society Directive, which makes it clear that the right is exhausted by first sale in the Community[659] and so the question must be answered in accordance with ordinary exhaustion of rights principles.[660] The producer or importer at the head of the chain is the principal cause of the goods being put into eventual circulation, and it is therefore suggested that it is this person who is liable for the primary act of infringement of issuing copies of the work to the public, even though it is not he who deals directly with the public. Although it is the Directive which governs here, the Act in fact provides some support in view of the express provision that any *subsequent* distribution, sale, hiring or loan of copies previously put into circulation does not amount to an infringement, indicating that it is only the person at the head of the distribution chain who is liable under this section. The only other person who might sensibly be described as putting the copies into circulation would be the retailer at the end of the distribution chain, being the person who has direct contact with the public. As will be seen,[661] however, in relation to the acts of importation, sale and distribution of *infringing* copies, the persons responsible for such acts are generally liable only if they have knowledge, actual or constructive, that they are dealing with infringing copies. A construction which made the person at the end of the distribution chain liable for the primary act of infringement of issuing copies to the public would thus render the requirement of guilty knowledge nugatory in the case of dealings with infringing copies.[662]

Importation cases. In importation cases, it is also not always clear who is the person who "issues" the relevant copy, or even when or where this takes place, in particular in the case of a seller physically situated abroad but selling via a website directed to persons in the United Kingdom. Is it the seller situated abroad or the purchaser situated in the United Kingdom? It would seem that the act takes place when, and in the place where, the copy is delivered to a member of the   **7–92**

---

that mere importation could not amount to infringement. See *Hansard*, cols 214, 215 (November 2, 1988) (Lord Young).

[657] *Peek & Cloppenburg KG v Cassina SpA* (C–456/06) [2008] E.C.R. I–2731 (ECJ). But see CDPA 1988 s.24(1)(d), under which such acts in relation to infringing copies can amount to a secondary infringement.

[658] On a strict view of *Peek & Cloppenburg KG v Cassina SpA* (C–456/06) [2008] E.C.R. I–2731 (ECJ), it does not, because property does not pass. However, the Court of Justice was not concerned with a retention of title case.

[659] Recital 28.

[660] See para.24–20 et seq, below.

[661] See Ch.8, below.

[662] Note that in *The Football Association Premier League Ltd v Panini UK Ltd* [2003] EWCA Civ. 995; [2004] 1 W.L.R. 1147; [2004] F.S.R. 1, Mummery L.J. assumed that where a defendant had imported copies and then distributed them to distributors, it was the distributors who issued the copies to the public, not the defendant (presumably there were no further distributors in the chain so that the distributors sold direct to the public). On this basis the defendant might have been liable for importing, selling, distributing, etc., infringing copies, with knowledge, or for authorising the issue of copies to the public by the distributors, but not for the act of issue to the public itself. The point, however, had not been argued and it is suggested that the conclusion was incorrect. The obiter view of Paterson J., in *Video Ezy International (NZ) Ltd v Roadshow Entertainment (NZ) Ltd* [2002] N.Z.L.R. 855, at 862, was to the same effect. See, again also, Philips and Bently, "Copyright Issues: The Mysteries of Section 18" [1999] E.I.P.R. 133.

public.[663] Beyond this, the authorities to date are not entirely satisfactory. In *KK Sony Entertainment v Pacific Game Technology (Holding) Ltd*[664] the court was concerned with the sale of an article by a Hong Kong company via a website to a UK consumer who had paid by credit card. It is unclear where the property in the goods passed, although the defendant had asserted that this was in Hong Kong.[665] This sale was alleged inter alia to amount to an issue of the article to the public in the United Kingdom. Applying the trade mark cases in this field,[666] it was held on the facts that the website conveyed to a reasonable consumer an *offer for sale* within the United Kingdom (or the EEA).[667] This is not controversial, but then, without more, it was held that the infringing acts alleged, including that of issue to the public, had been perpetrated not in Hong Kong but in the EEA, the judge stating: "…it would make no sense if intellectual property rights in the EEA could be avoided merely by setting up a website outside the EEA crafted to sell within it. Were the acts of which complaint is made to have been committed physically within the EEA they would unarguably have been infringing acts. I cannot see how the electronic intermediary of a website which focussed at least in part on the EEA would make them any less so." In *Independiente Ltd v Music Trading On-Line (HK) Ltd*[668] CDs were ordered online by consumers in the United Kingdom from the defendant based in Hong Kong who despatched them directly to the consumers using the Hong Kong and UK postal services. As in the *KK Sony* case the defendant's website was clearly intended to have effect in the United Kingdom to attract consumers. This time it was common ground that property passed before the CDs were delivered to the Hong Kong postal services. It was also common ground that a copy is "issued to the public" when it is "delivered" to a member of the public.[669] The defendant contended that delivery took place when the CDs were delivered to the Hong Kong postal authorities and accordingly that the person responsible for putting them into circulation in the United Kingdom was the consumer. It was held, however, that although the normal rule is that where the seller is authorised or required to send the goods to the buyer, delivery to the carrier is presumed to be delivery of the goods to the buyer,[670] in the case of sales of goods to a buyer who "deals as consumer" this rule is disapplied[671] so that the goods remain at the seller's risk during transit. Accordingly, it was the defendant who had delivered the CDs to the consumer when the CD in question was delivered by the postal authorities to the consumer in the United Kingdom, and so was liable for having issued them to the public.[672]

Neither case is entirely satisfactory. The *KK Sony* case was decided on a summary judgment application in the absence of the defendants and the *Independiente* case sits uneasily with the House of Lords decision in *Sabaf SpA v MFI*

---

[663] *Independiente Ltd v Music Trading On-Line (HK) Ltd* [2007] EWHC 533 (Ch); [2007] F.S.R. 21 at para.42.

[664] [2006] EWHC 2509 (Ch), decided on an application for summary judgment but in the absence of the defendants.

[665] After recording this assertion and then various other allegations, the judge stated that "these" submissions were rejected or were to be discounted in the face of practical realities (see para.25). However, it is not clear precisely which submissions were being rejected or discounted or, if the assertion as to passing of property was rejected, why it was.

[666] e.g. *Euromarket Designs Inc v Peters* [2001] F.S.R. 20.

[667] para.23.

[668] [2007] EWHC 533 (Ch); [2007] F.S.R. 21.

[669] See para.42.

[670] Sale of Goods Act 1979 s. 32(1).

[671] Sale of Goods Act 1979 s.32(4).

[672] The Judge's conclusion would have been the same even if the site had not been intended to have effect in the United Kingdom to attract consumers: para.51.

Furniture Centres Ltd,[673] albeit cited in the judgment, in which the question of who was responsible for an importation was determined without regard to the technicalities of the contract of sale (although the contractual position was referred to). It is suggested that in such cases what is required is the application of a broad common sense view rather than an application of the technicalities of the law of sale of goods, a law which was developed for the purpose of regulating the legal position between buyer and seller rather than that between right holder and alleged infringer. In both cases a seller of goods had set up the arrangements to deliver the goods to a purchaser, being a member of the public situated in the United Kingdom. An issue to the public of the goods in the United Kingdom had clearly taken place and the only person who realistically could be said to have done so was the seller.

4. THE RENTAL AND LENDING RIGHTS

Background. Historically, the right to control the rental or lending of legitimate   **7–93** copies was not one of the rights within the bundle of rights conferred on copyright owners.[674] The 1988 Act as enacted contained a limited exclusive right to control the rental of copies of certain works which was directed at the limited rental market which then existed. Thus in relation to sound recordings, films and computer programs, the exclusive right of issuing copies to the public under s.18 included the exclusive right of rental of copies of such works to the public.[675] No such right was given in relation to the literary, dramatic, musical or artistic works which might be included in such media or which were otherwise the subject of rental, for example in the form of books. However, under the Public Lending Right Act 1979 as implemented by the Public Lending Right Scheme 1982, a separate right had been conferred on a limited class of authors under which they were entitled to payment out of a central fund in respect of books lent to the public by local library authorities. The public library lending of computer programs, sound recordings and films did not fall within the Public Lending Right Scheme but was treated as rental under s.18, even though no payment might be made.[676] Implementation of the Rental and Related Rights Directive required the United Kingdom to grant an exclusive right of rental and lending in relation to a much wider class of works than those referred to above.[677] Although Member States were prima facie required to provide an exclusive right of lending in respect of such works, they were permitted to derogate from this right in respect of "public lending", provided that authors obtained remuneration for this. The United Kingdom chose to exercise this right of derogation, and such remuneration is now provided under an amended Public Lending Right Scheme.[678] The necessary

---

[673] [2004] UKHL 45; [2005] R.P.C. 10 (see para.8–14).

[674] Although they had the right to control such dealings in infringing copies. See the Copyright Act 1956 s.5(3)(a).

[675] CDPA 1988 s.18(2). For this purpose "rental" included any arrangement under which a copy of a work was made available (a) for payment (in money or money's worth), or (b) in the course of a business, as part of services or amenities for which payment was made, in either case on terms that it would or might be returned. See s.178 as enacted. Whether the first act of rental of copies of these and other types of work might constitute issue to the public was unclear. S.18 was amended, with effect from January 1, 1993, to introduce a new subs.(3) dealing solely with computer programs, but under which the rental of copies to the public remained a restricted act. See the Copyright (Computer Programs) Regulations 1992 (SI 1992/3233).

[676] See CDPA 1988 Sch.7 para.8, as enacted.

[677] For a detailed discussion of the background to the Rental Directive, see Reinbothe and von Lewinski, *The EC Directive on Rental and Lending Rights and on Piracy* (1993). The Rental and Related Rights Directive and its amendments have now been codified as Directive 2006/115/EC.

[678] See Ch.19, below.

amendments to the 1988 Act were made with effect from December 1, 1996.[679] The scheme of the 1988 Act, as amended, is that both rental and lending of copies of a work to the public are restricted acts, that is, they are two of the exclusive rights of the copyright owner, but if the lending of a book by a public library is within the Public Lending Right Scheme, or is by a prescribed library or archive, it amounts to a permitted act and is therefore not an infringement.[680] Provision is also made for the Secretary of State to provide for the lending to the public of defined categories of works to be treated as licensed, subject only to payment of a reasonable royalty.[681] As already pointed out, the first rental or lending of a work is not an act restricted by the distribution right.

7–94   **The Berne and Rome Conventions.** There has been little consistency amongst countries which are parties to these Conventions in their approach to a right to control the rental or lending of works and related rights subject matter, and thus the Conventions do not lay down any general exclusive right in this area.[682]

7–95   **Applicable works.** The rental and lending right only applies to certain categories of works, namely: (a) literary, dramatic and musical works; (b) artistic works other than (i) works of architecture in the form of a building or a model for a building, and (ii) works of applied art; and (c) films and sound recordings.[683] As to the works excluded from these categories, the Rental and Related Rights Directive provides that the rights should not extend to "buildings",[684] the intention being to exclude the possibility of an architect or copyright owner being able to control the leasing of property.[685] In fact, the 1988 Act goes further than the Directive in that models for buildings are also excluded, an exclusion that appears to be in breach on the Directive. The exception in the case of works of "applied art" is also provided for by the Directive,[686] the expression not being defined further either by the Directive or the 1988 Act. It is an expression that is also found in the Berne Convention,[687] and refers broadly to articles to which an artistic work has been applied, usually by an industrial process. The distinction is between works of applied art and works of pure art. The intention is again to prevent the owner of the copyright in designs for such articles as cars or items of crockery from controlling their rental.[688]

7–96   **Rental right.** The rental of copies of any of the above categories of works, or the original,[689] to the public is a restricted act. The Directive defines "rental" as the making available for use, for a limited period of time and for direct or indirect economic or commercial advantage[690] and is therefore aimed at the ordinary commercial rental of a work. The Act defines rental in slightly wider terms, namely as the making a copy of the work available for use, *on terms that it will*

---

[679] By the Copyright and Related Rights Regulations 1996 (SI 1996/2967).
[680] CDPA 1988 s.40A. See para.9–108, below.
[681] CDPA 1988 s.66. See paras 9–178 and 28–45, below.
[682] For a discussion, see Ricketson and Ginsburg, *The International Copyright and Neighbouring Rights* 2nd edn (OUP), para.11.38.
[683] For this purpose, the rental or lending of the film sound track which accompanies a film constitutes the rental or lending of a film, not the issuing of a sound recording: CDPA 1988 s.5B(3)(c).
[684] Directive 92/100 art.2.3. See now Directive 2006/115 art.3(2).
[685] See Reinbothe and von Lewinski, *The EC Directive on Rental and Lending Rights and on Piracy* (1993), p.53.
[686] Directive 92/100 art.2.3. See now Directive 2006/115, art.3(2).
[687] See art.2(1), and especially art.2(7). See Ricketson and Ginsburg, *The International Copyright and Neighbouring Rights* 2nd edn (OUP), para.8.59.
[688] Reinbothe and von Lewinski, *The EC Directive on Rental and Lending Rights and on Piracy* (1993), p.53.
[689] CDPA 1988 s.18A(6).
[690] art.2.1(1).

or may be returned, for direct or indirect economic or commercial advantage.[691] The reference to the possibility that the work "may" be returned is unclear, but can hardly include an arrangement whereby a copy of a work is sold to a purchaser but on terms that it can be brought back and some part of the money refunded or another work taken in exchange. As is so often the case, the wording of the Directive should be referred to directly. The more limited provisions of the 1988 Act as originally enacted made it clear that rental included the making available of a work in the course of a business, as part of services or amenities for which payment was made.[692] This was clearly aimed at including the making available of copies of videos to hotel guests. The existing provisions are not so explicit but it is suggested that the words "indirect economic or commercial advantage" would catch such rental.[693] The European Court of Justice has made it clear that rental right is not exhausted by the sale or other acts of release into circulation of a copy of the work,[694] nor by other acts of rental.[695]

The lending right. The lending of copies of any of the above categories of works, or the original,[696] to the public is also a restricted act. The Directive defines lending as the making available for use, for a limited period of time and not for direct or indirect economic or commercial advantage, when it is made through establishments which are accessible to the public.[697] Again, the Act defines the term slightly differently, and incorrectly, as making a copy of the work available for use, *on terms that it will or may be returned*, otherwise than for direct or indirect economic or commercial advantage, through an establishment which is accessible to the public. The word "establishment" is not defined either in the Act or the Directive. The expression clearly includes, but is not limited to, public libraries. Although the restricted act is confined to lending to the public, the Directive and the Act nevertheless expressly provides that lending between establishments accessible to the public, for example from one library to another, is not a restricted act.[698] As to what constitutes direct or indirect economic or commercial advantage, the Directive and the Act make it clear that the mere making of a payment which does not go beyond what is necessary to cover the operating costs of the establishment is not to amount to such an advantage.[699]

7–97

Common considerations. In the case of both the rental and the lending right, the rights only apply where copies are made available "to the public". This expression clearly requires that the public at large has access to the work, for example by means of a high-street rental outlet, library or mail order scheme. It apparently excludes the rental or loan of the work or a copy by one private individual or concern to another. Both rights only concern the making available "for use". In most cases, of course, the copy will have been made available in order to be read, listened to or otherwise enjoyed. It would seem that in relation to an artistic

7–98

---

[691] CDPA 1988 s.(2)(a).
[692] CDPA 1988 s.178, as enacted.
[693] The expression "for direct or indirect commercial advantage" is taken directly from Directive 2006/15. See art.1(2).
[694] *Metronome Musik GmbH v Music Point Hokamp GmbH* [1999] F.S.R. 576, ECJ.
[695] *Foreningen AF Danske Videogramdistributorer v Laserdisken* [1999] E.M.L.R. 681, ECJ.
[696] CDPA 1988 s.18A(6).
[697] art.2.1(b).
[698] Recital 10 of Directive 2006/115; CDPA 1988 s.18A(4).
[699] Recital 11 of Directive 2006/115; CDPA 1988 s.18A(5).

work, "use" would include the lending of it to a member of the public so that it can be viewed or enjoyed in private.[700]

7–99   **Excluded acts.** Three classes of acts are excluded from both the rental and lending rights:

(a) The making available of the original work or copies for the purpose of public performance, playing or showing in public, or communication to the public.[701] Thus, for example, the rental of a film to a cinema for public showing is not a restricted act.[702]

(b) The making available of the work or copies for the purpose of exhibition in public.[703]

(c) The making available of the work or copies for on-the-spot reference use.[704] Thus an organisation which allows users to have access to a work but not to take it away does not rent or lend the work for this purpose.

7–100   **Transitional.** Section 18A, by which the rental and lending right was conferred, came into force on December 1, 1996[705] and is subject to transitional provisions, most of which will by now have worked themselves out.[706] Two provisions only need to be mentioned here. First, the amended provisions apply to works made both before and after this date.[707] The second depends on an understanding of the distinction made in the transitional provisions between "new" and other rights. A new right is a right which arose by virtue of the implementing Regulations to authorise or prohibit an act in relation to a copyright work, but excluding a right which corresponded to a right which existed immediately before commencement of the Regulations. Thus the exclusive rights of rental in relation to literary works (other than computer programs), dramatic and musical works and the limited class of artistic works were all new rights, unlike the exclusive right of rental in relation to computer programs, films and sound recordings.[708] In relation to the lending right, all such rights were new rights.[709] In a case where before December 1, 1996 the owner or prospective owner of the copyright in a literary, dramatic, musical or artistic work authorised another to make a copy of that work, the new rental and lending rights in relation to that copy are to belong not to the copyright owner but to the person so authorised, subject to any agreement to the contrary.[710]

7–101   **Unwaivable right to remuneration.** It is a feature of the rental right,[711] but not

---

[700] The making available of the work or copy for the purpose of exhibition in public is expressly excluded. See para.7–99, below.

[701] Recital 10 of Directive 2006/115; CDPA 1988 s.18A(3)(a).

[702] Of course, the showing in public of the film would itself require the consent of the owners of the copyright in the film and of the underlying rights. See CDPA 1988 s.19 and paras 7–137 et seq., below.

[703] Recital 10 of Directive 2006/115; CDPA 1988 s.18A(3)(b).

[704] Recital 10 of Directive 2006/115; CDPA 1988 s.18A(3)(c).

[705] Copyright and Related Rights Regulations 1996 (SI 1996/2967) regs 1(2), 4.

[706] For these provsions, see *Copinger*, 14th edn, para.7–117.

[707] Copyright and Related Rights Regulations 1996 (SI 1996/2967) reg.26(1).

[708] Although the definition of "rental" under the 1988 Act as enacted (see fn.676 above) was slightly different from the current definition, it is suggested that the rights in relation to these works now conferred by s.18A do "correspond" to the rights conferred under CDPA 1988 s.18, as enacted.

[709] The new lending right does not correspond to the rights of certain authors under the Public Lending Right Scheme, since those rights do not include any right to authorise or prohibit the lending of their works. Again, it is suggested that the rights of copyright owners in respect of the public library lending of computer programs, sound recordings and films, which was treated as rental under CDPA 1988 s.18 and which did not fall within the Public Lending Right Scheme (see para.7–93, above), do not correspond to the new lending right.

[710] Copyright and Related Rights Regulations 1996 (SI 1996/2967) reg.31.

[711] i.e. the exclusive right to rent or authorise the rental of the work. CDPA 1988 s.178.

the lending right, that with effect from December 1, 1996[712] authors of certain works are entitled to limited "unwaivable" rights to remuneration in respect of rental of their work. The authors in question are the authors of literary, dramatic, musical and artistic works, and the principal directors of films. Where such an author transfers the rental right, so far as it concerns use of the work in a sound recording or film, to the producer of the sound recording or film, he retains the right to "equitable remuneration" for any rental of his work.[713] Thus, for example, an author who assigns the right to use his screenplay in a film to the film producer, where such assignment includes the right to rent copies of the film to the public, retains a right to remuneration from such rental. This right cannot be excluded or restricted by contract.[714] The limitations on the ability to assign this right are considered elsewhere[715] as are the provisions of the Act for determining the amount of such remuneration.[716] The right of the author to remuneration appears to be a sui generis right and is not strictly a right of copyright, since his rights are limited to his claim for remuneration and he cannot, for example, prevent the further rental of copies if he is not paid. His only right is a claim for remuneration against the owner of the rental right for the time being, that is, the person to whom the rental right was transferred or his successor in title.[717]

Transitional. The right to equitable remuneration arose with effect from December 1, 1996.[718] Where a right to equitable remuneration would otherwise have arisen on the transfer by an author of his rental right under s.93B, no such right shall in fact arise in respect of any rental after that date of a sound recording or film made in pursuance of an agreement entered into before July 1, 1994.[719] The only exception is where, before January 1, 1997, the author or any successor in title of his notified the person by whom the remuneration would be payable that he intended to exercise such right.[720]   **7–102**

5. PERFORMANCE, SHOWING OR PLAYING OF A WORK IN PUBLIC: THE PUBLIC PERFORMANCE RIGHT

Literary, dramatic and musical works. It is an act restricted by the copyright in a literary, dramatic or musical work to perform the work in public.[721] For this purpose, "performance" is defined to include delivery in the case of lectures, addresses, speeches and sermons[722] and, in general, includes any mode of visual or acoustic presentation, including presentation by means of a sound recording, film or broadcast of the work.[723] These latter expressions are all further defined.[724] Thus, in addition to the obvious ways in which such works may be performed, a literary or musical work embodied in a sound recording may be performed by its being played by means of the sound recording. In relation to a dramatic work, if   **7–103**

---

[712] For transitional provisions, see the Regulations and *Copinger* 14th edn, para.7–119.
[713] CDPA 1988 s.93B(1).
[714] CDPA 1988 s.93B(5).
[715] See para.5–114, above.
[716] See para.28–125, below. In the absence of agreement, it will be determined by the Copyright Tribunal. See CDPA 1988 s.93C.
[717] CDPA 1988 s.93B(3).
[718] Copyright and Related Rights Regulations 1996 (SI 1996/2967) regs.1(1) and (4).
[719] reg.33.
[720] reg.33.
[721] CDPA 1988 s.19(1).
[722] CDPA 1988 s.19(2)(a).
[723] CDPA 1988 s.19(2)(b).
[724] "Sound recording": CDPA 1988 s.5A(1); "film": s.5B(1); "broadcast": s.6(1).

the incidents of the plot are visually presented to a substantial degree, this will amount to an infringement, even though the same language is not used.[725] There is no equivalent right in respect of showing an artistic work in public.[726] In the usual way, it is not only an infringement to do such acts in relation to the work as a whole but also in relation to any substantial part of it.[727] Again, it is a separate infringement to authorise such acts.[728]

7–104   **Sound recordings, films and broadcasts.** In relation to a sound recording, film or broadcast, the playing or showing of the work in public is a restricted act.[729] Thus, for example, the playing of a sound recording in public by means of a record player or sound system would amount to a public performance not only of the literary or musical works embodied in it, but also of the sound recording itself. Again, these rights are infringed by doing such acts in relation to a substantial part of the work and by authorising such acts.[730]

7–105   **International conventions.** In general terms, this provision implements art.11 of the Berne Convention,[731] which is directed to public performance rights which, in so far as they involve an act of communication, do so at the place where that communication originates.[732] This article has not been made the subject of any harmonising measure at the European level and so to this extent the right remains a matter of national law.[733]

7–106   **Communication to the public versus performance.** It is clear that the expressions "performance", "playing" and "showing" used in the above senses include the doing of such acts by means of a radio or television set.[734] Thus, for example, the playing of a radio or television in public will amount to a public performance of works of the above descriptions embodied in the broadcast, and of the broadcast itself.[735] However, the act of broadcasting is not itself a public performance of the works included in the broadcast but amounts to the separate restricted act of communication of the works to the public.[736] The essential difference is that the acts of performance, playing and showing in public all connote that the public is present where these acts takes place, whereas broadcasting to the public, etc. connotes a communication from one place to another place where the public is present.

7–107   **The person liable for the infringement.** In the case of a public performance

---

[725] See para.7–63, above.

[726] As noted in *Football Association Premier League Ltd v QC Leisure* [2008] EWHC 1411 (Ch); [2008] F.S.R 32, para.265.

[727] CDPA 1988 s.16(3)(a).

[728] CDPA 1988 s.16(2).

[729] CDPA 1988 s.19(3). For this purpose, the playing of the film sound track which accompanies a film constitutes the showing of a film, not the playing of a sound recording: CDPA 1988 s.5B(3)(a), (b).

[730] As in *Football Association Premier League Ltd v QC Leisure* [2008] EWHC 1411 (Ch); [2008] F.S.R. 32, where the showing on television of action replays lasting a few seconds each represented a substantial part of the film of a football match: see paras 208–209 of the judgment and para.7–81 of this work.

[731] "Authors of dramatic, dramatico-musical and musical works shall enjoy the exclusive right of authorizing: (i) the public performance of their works, including such public performance by any means or process; (ii) any communication to the public of the performance of their works."

[732] *Football Association Premier League Ltd v QC Leisure* [2008] EWHC 1411 (Ch); [2008] F.S.R. 32, para.259, although apparently mis-reading art.11*bis*(1)(iii).

[733] *Football Association Premier League Ltd v QC Leisure* [2008] EWHC 1411 (Ch); [2008] F.S.R. 32, para.259.

[734] i.e. apparatus for receiving visual images or sounds conveyed by electronic means. See, e.g. CDPA 1988 s.19(2)(b) and the wording of s.19(4). See s.178 for the definition of "electronic."

[735] See the various cases referred below in relation to the expression "in public".

[736] See paras 7–112 et seq., below and CDPA 1988 s.20.

through the human agency of actors, singers, etc. there will usually be no difficulty in determining who is the performer. Again, where recorded music is played in a club it will be the operator of the equipment who is primarily liable for the performance of the lyrics and music, and the playing of the sound recording. Where the works are played by the use of such means as radios, televisions or sound system, the person liable for the primary act of infringement will be the person who actually operates the apparatus by means of which the sounds or images are produced.[737] Other persons may of course be liable for having authorised such acts of primary infringement,[738] and persons who provide the premises or apparatus for such performances may be liable for acts of secondary infringements.[739] The Act makes it clear that in the case of a performance, playing or showing of a work in public by means of an apparatus for receiving visual images or sounds conveyed by electronic means, neither the person by whom the visual images or sounds are sent (e.g. a broadcaster) nor, in the case where the work is performed by individuals, the performers themselves, are to be regarded as responsible for the infringement.[740]

"In public." The expression "in public", was also used in this context in the 1956 and 1911 Acts,[741] and has been the subject of numerous decisions. Whether a particular performance takes place in public or not is in one sense a question of law, in that the true meaning of the words "in public" is a matter of law, but in every case it is obviously a question of fact whether the facts of the case do or do not fall within that meaning.[742] The chief guide in answering the question should be common sense.[743]   **7–108**

The distinction to be made is between performances which are public and those which are domestic or quasi-domestic in character, that is, those in which the members of the audience are present in their capacity as members of the particular home circle.[744] A useful test is whether the persons coming together to form the audience are bound together by a domestic or private tie, or by an aspect of their public life.[745] In drawing this distinction, it is also the character of the audience which is crucial[746] and in particular it is the relationship of the audience to the owner of copyright which is important rather than its relationship to the

---

[737] See, e.g. *Performing Right Society Ltd v Hammond's Bradford Brewery Co Ltd* [1934] Ch. 121, followed in *Canadian Performing Right Society Ltd v Ford Hotel* [1935] 2 D.L.R. 391 and *Performing Right Society Ltd v Gillette* [1943] 1 All E.R. 413. See also *Messager v British Broadcasting Co Ltd* [1929] A.C. 151.

[738] See paras 7–146 et seq., below.

[739] i.e. under CDPA 1988 ss.25 and 26. These secondary acts of infringement are considered in Ch.8.

[740] CDPA 1988 s.19(4). There was some doubt whether under the 1911 Act broadcasting itself constituted a public performance of the works embodied in it. See *Messager v British Broadcasting Co Ltd* [1927] 2 K.B. 543; *Performing Right Society Ltd v Hammond's Bradford Brewery Co Ltd* [1934] Ch. 121. cf. *Mellor v Australian Broadcasting Commission* [1940] A.C. 491. See also *Canadian Admiral Corporation Ltd v Rediffusion Inc* (1954) Ex. C.R. 382; *Chappell & Co. Ltd v Associated Radio Co of Australia Ltd* [1925] V.L.R. 350; *Remick (J.H.) & Co v American Auto-Accessories Co* [1923–1928] Mac.C.C. 173. Under the 1956 Act, broadcasting or including a work in a cable programme was expressly excluded from the definition of performance (s.48(5)) and was a separate act of infringement.

[741] Copyright Act 1956 ss.2(5)(c), 12(5)(b), 13(5)(b), 14(4)(c); Copyright Act 1911 s.1(2). Under the law before 1911, the performance, to be an infringement of copyright, had to be presented at a place of dramatic entertainment. But it was held that this condition was fulfilled if the performance was at any place in public (*Russell v Smith* (1848) 12 Q.B. 217). The 1911 Act gave effect to the decisions under the earlier law. See, for example *Glenville v Selig Polyscope Co* (1911) 27 T.L.R 554.

[742] *Jennings v Stephens* [1936] Ch. 469; *Harms (Inc) Ltd v Martins Club Ltd* [1927] 1 Ch. 526.

[743] *Ernest Turner, etc. Ltd v Performing Right Society Ltd* [1943] Ch. 167.

[744] *Duck v Bates* (1884) 13 Q.B.D. 843; *Jennings v Stephens* [1936] Ch. 469.

[745] *Australian Performing Right Association Ltd v Commonwealth Bank of Australia* (1992) 25 I.P.R. 157 at 171.

[746] *Jennings v Stephens* [1936] Ch. 469.

performer.[747] If it can be said that the audience is one which the owner of the copyright might fairly consider as part of his public then this indicates that the performance was "in public",[748] particularly where the members of the audience are enjoying the work under conditions where they would normally pay for the privilege in one form or another.[749] It has been said that the key to the construction of these words is that what is intended to be protected is the value of the author's invention.[750] Consistent with this, it has also been said that it is the duty of the court to protect the rights of persons such as authors and composers, according to a fair construction of the Act, such that it is important to ask whether the public's demand for their works may be affected by such performances.[751]

Always bearing in mind that it is the character of the audience and its relationship to the copyright owner which is crucially important, various other tests have been discussed in the cases. Thus, clearly, if the public at large is freely admitted, the performance will almost certainly be in public, but the performance may also be in public if only a limited portion of the public is allowed to attend, for example the members of a club and their guests.[752] On the other hand, the mere fact that guests are present at what would otherwise be a private performance will not make it public.[753] The number of persons present is a relevant consideration, but nevertheless a performance may be in public even though the audience is very small.[754] Whether the performance is given with a view to monetary profit may be relevant,[755] but it is of very limited importance whether the actual performers are paid. Thus performers often give their services to the public for free, whereas they are often paid when the occasion is undoubtedly private.[756] The fact that no charge is made for admission is of itself also of little importance.[757] The kind of place at which the performance occurs may be an indication of the type of performance, but clearly a private performance may be given in what is normally a public room, and a public performance may be given in a private house.[758] As already noted, it is important to consider whether the performance is likely to injure the owner of the copyright in the sense that some of the audience might be willing to pay to see or hear such a performance,[759] and whether the demand for the author's work might otherwise be diminished.[760] Thus if the person responsible for the performance would be likely to pay for a licence rather than have such performance stopped, then clearly the copyright owner will suffer by an unlicensed performance,[761] although obviously it is not in every such case that the performance will be in public.

7–109   While bearing in mind that each case must be considered separately on its own facts, the following are examples of cases in which performances have been regarded as having taken place in public: the putting on of a drama by an amateur

---

[747] *Jennings v Stephens* [1936] Ch. 469; *Ernest Turner, etc. Ltd v Performing Right Society Ltd* [1943] Ch. 167; *Performing Right Society Ltd v Rangers F.C. Supporters Club* [1975] R.P.C. 626.
[748] *Jennings v Stephens* [1936] Ch. 469.
[749] *Performing Right Society Ltd v Rangers F.C. Supporters Club* [1975] R.P.C. 626.
[750] *Duck v Bates* (1884) 13 Q.B.D. 843.
[751] *Jennings v Stephens* [1936] Ch. 469.
[752] *Harms (Inc.) Ltd v Martans Club Ltd* [1927] 1 Ch. 526.
[753] *Jennings v Stephens* [1936] Ch. 469.
[754] *Jennings v Stephens* [1936] Ch. 469
[755] *Harms (Inc.) Ltd v Martans Club Ltd* [1927] 1 Ch. 526.
[756] *Jennings v Stephens* [1936] Ch. 469.
[757] *Harms (Inc.) Ltd v Martans Club Ltd* [1927] 1 Ch. 526.
[758] *Jennings v Stephens* [1936] Ch. 469.
[759] *Harms (Inc.) Ltd v Martans Club Ltd* [1927] 1 Ch. 526.
[760] *Jennings v Stephens* [1936] Ch. 469.
[761] *Performing Right Society Ltd v Harlequin Record Shops Ltd* [1979] 1 W.L.R. 851.

company for a charitable object, the public being admitted upon payment of money or by the issue of tickets generally[762]; the performance of music by a dance band at a proprietary dinner and dance club at which members and their guests were present, the membership being selective and by election but being drawn by invitation to the public[763]; a dramatic performance given at a village Women's Institute, even though the performers were all members of a neighbouring Institute, no one was present except members and no charge was made (all the adult female members of the village were, however, in practice eligible to join the Institute)[764]; the playing of gramophone records and the radio over loudspeakers to workers at a factory during working hours[765]; the playing of video cassettes in the presence of 11 employees, the general public being unable to see or hear, the purpose being to instruct the employees[766]; the performance of orchestral music in the lounge of a hotel, the audience consisting of residents of the hotel and members of the public who had dined there[767]; the playing of television in the open areas of a public house[768]; the playing of a radio in a public house's private room, but which the public was freely able to use as a saloon bar[769]; the playing of a radio in a private room of a public house, but which could be heard in the adjoining public bar[770]; the playing of a radio in a private room adjoining a restaurant, but which could be heard in the restaurant, the principle being that the performance took place wherever it could be heard[771]; the performance of music to an audience consisting of members of a social club and their guests[772]; the playing of records in record shops to which the public was encouraged to enter without payment or invitation, the purpose and effect being to increase the sale of records, the evidence being that most record shop proprietors would pay for the necessary licence rather than be prevented from playing such records.[773] No doubt the performance of works to inmates of prisons is "in public".

On the other hand, the putting on of a play by children or adults at home would obviously not be in public, being domestic and private.[774] The same would apply to a play put on for friends in a house hired for the occasion.[775] A performance given by an amateur dramatic club to nurses, attendants and others connected

---

[762] Given as an example in *Duck v Bates* (1884) 13 Q.B.D. 843.

[763] *Performing Right Society Ltd v Hammond's Bradford Brewery Co Ltd* [1934] Ch. 121.

[764] *Jennings v Stephens* [1936] Ch. 469.

[765] *Ernest Turner, etc. Ltd v Performing Right Society Ltd* [1943] Ch. 167. This case is reported jointly with *Performing Right Society Ltd v Gillette Industries Ltd*, where the facts were very similar.

[766] *Australian Performing Right Association Ltd v Commonwealth Bank of Australia* (1992) 25 I.P.R. 157.

[767] *Performing Right Society Ltd v Hawthornes Hotel (Bournemouth) Ltd* [1933] Ch. 855.

[768] *Football Association Premier League Ltd v QC Leisure* [2008] EWHC 1411 (Ch); [2008] F.S.R. 32, para.266.

[769] *Performing Right Society Ltd v George* (unreported, but referred to in *Performing Right Society Ltd v Camelo* [1936] 3 All E.R. 557).

[770] *Performing Right Society Ltd v George*, obiter, but relied on in *Performing Right Society Ltd v Camelo* [1936] 3 All E.R. 557; and see *Australian Performing Right Association Ltd v Canterbury-Bankstown League Club Ltd* [1964–65] N.S.W.R. 138.

[771] *Performing Right Society Ltd v Camelo* [1936] 3 All E.R. 557.

[772] *Performing Right Society Ltd v Rangers F.C. Supporters Club* [1975] R.P.C. 626.

[773] *Performing Right Society Ltd v Harlequin Record Shops Ltd* [1979] 1 W.L.R. 851. See also *Canadian Admiral Corporation Ltd v Rediffusion Inc* [1954] Ex. C.R. 382; *Australasian Performing Right Association Ltd v Tolbush Pty Ltd* (1986) 62 A.L.R. 521; and see *South African, etc Ltd v Trust Butchers (Pty)* [1978] 1 S.A.L.R. 1052.

[774] Given as an example in *Duck v Bates* (1884) 13 Q.B.D. 843.

[775] *Duck v Bates* (1884) 13 Q.B.D. 843.

with a hospital, to which admission was free, the expenses being borne by the governors of the hospital, was held not to be in public.[776]

7–110   Hotel bedrooms, etc. An unresolved question is whether, for example, where music or a television programme is relayed to hotel bedrooms, in which the music or programme is then listened to or watched by the occupants, this amounts to a public performance. Whether the operation of such a system amounts to the communication of works to the public by the hotelier is a separate matter, and does not provide any real assistance.[777] It has been decided in the Exchequer Court of Canada[778] that the performance of material by way of television in private homes, the material having been received by subscribers to a cable service, did not amount to public performance on the grounds that the character of the audience was purely domestic, and even a large number of "private" performances could not be in public. It might therefore be argued that the character of the audience in separate hotel bedrooms is similar, each hotel bedroom being the occupant's "home" for the night, and each performance being "private".[779] In a decision of the Supreme Court of New South Wales,[780] however, the issue arose whether the watching of television sets by the occupants of motel rooms, to which films were relayed by means of a video cassette recorder and cables, amounted to public performance. The plaintiff's case was argued primarily on the basis that the presentation of a film in a single room, even to only one person, amounted to public performance. It was held that such presentation was in fact in public since the character of the audience was as guests of the motel and not as individuals in a private or domestic situation. In that capacity the guests were paying for the accommodation and the benefits which went with it.

7–111   Permitted acts. There are important exceptions relating to the public performance of sound recordings and broadcasts, which are considered elsewhere.[781]

6. THE COMMUNICATION TO THE PUBLIC RIGHT

(i) Introduction and background

7–112   The communication to the public right. With effect from October 31, 2003,

---

[776] *Duck v Bates* (1884) 13 Q.B.D. 843, described there by Brett M.R. as a borderline and extreme case; see also the comments on this decision in *Jennings v Stephens* [1936] Ch. 469 and *Harms (Inc.) Ltd v Martans Club Ltd* [1927] 1 Ch. 526. Note also the odd case of *Brown v Mcasso Music Production Ltd* [2005] EWCC 1 (Cpwt); [2005] F.S.R. 40, where a "showreel" including an infringing copy of a musical work had been archived to a sub-site within the defendant's website, described by the Judge as "a sort of electronic waste basket—or at any rate a locked cupboard", with a view to disposing of it because it was no longer considered to be useful, current publicity. However, it could be accessed by members of the public, if only by someone with considerable competence with computers. The Judge held (para.50, obiter) that the availability of the material was not a performance of the work in public. Presumably it was not a performance either, but the point appears to have arisen because of the way the claimant put his case.

[777] See CDPA 1988 s.20, and paras 7–112 et seq. So, in *Sociedad General de Autores y Editores de España (SGAE) v Rafael Hoteles SL* (C–306/05) [2007] Bus. L.R. 521; [2007] E.C.D.R. 2, the Court of Justice observed that for the purposes of the "communication to the public right" the private or public nature of the place where the communication takes place is immaterial, and that the right would be meaningless if it did not also cover communications carried out in private places. See paras 50, 51.

[778] *Canadian Admiral Corporation Ltd v Rediffusion Inc* [1954] Ex.C.R. 382.

[779] See, e.g. *Mellor v Australian Broadcasting Commission* [1940] A.C. 491 at 500; but cf. *Messager v British Broadcasting Co. Ltd* [1927] 2 K.B. 543.

[780] *Rank Film Production Ltd v Dodds* [1983] 2 N.S.W.L.R. 553; see also *Hotel Mornington AB v Föreningen Svenska Tonsättares Internationella Musikbyrö (STIM)* [1982] E.C.C. 171 (Sup Ct of Sweden); *Teosto v A Taxi Driver* [2004] E.C.D.R. 3 (Sup. Ct. of Finland) (provision of music by taxi driver to his customers).

[781] i.e. under CDPA 1988 ss.67, 72. See Ch.9, below.

and as part of the implementation of the Information Society Directive s.20 of the 1988 Act was amended to introduce a new exclusive right, the communication to the public right, in place of the two separate exclusive rights which previously existed, namely, the broadcasting right and the cable programme right. As will be seen, the new right broadly assimilated these two separate rights, but was also extended to what may loosely be called the on-demand availability right, particularly as it relates to communications via the internet.[782]

The old broadcasting and the cable programme rights. The exclusive right of broadcasting a work to the public via a wireless service was first provided for by the Copyright Act 1956, and the exclusive right of transmitting a work to the public via a cable service was first provided for following amendment to the 1956 Act by the Cable and Broadcasting Act 1984.[783] These rights were separate and distinct from the exclusive right of performing a work in public. At the same time, broadcasts and cable programmes were themselves protected as "works". This scheme was broadly continued under the 1988 Act as originally enacted, which provided that broadcasting a work and including a work in a cable programme service were both restricted acts. "Cable programme service" was given a convoluted definition but broadly meant a service consisting of sending visual images, sounds or other information by means of a telecommunications system.   **7–113**

The Berne Convention and the 1996 WIPO Copyright Treaty. The 1971 Paris Act of the Berne Convention provides an incomplete regime in this field. Thus, art.11*bis* of the Convention provides that in relation to Berne literary and dramatic works there is to be an exclusive right of authorising the broadcasting of these authors' works, or their communication to the public by any other means of wireless diffusion, and of authorising the communication of these works to the public by wire. Article 11 of the Convention provides that in relation to Berne dramatic, dramatico-musical and musical works, there is to be an exclusive right of authorising the communication to the public of the *performance* of these author's works, by any means or process. Article 8 of the 1996 WIPO Copyright Treaty[784] was intended to provide a more comprehensive regime, with the result that in relation to literary and artistic works there is to be an exclusive right of authorising any communication to the public, by wire or wireless means, including the right of making the works available to the public in such a way that members of the public may access them from a place and at a time individually chosen by them (the "on-demand availability right"), this being intended to cover internet and similar transmissions.   **7–114**

The Rome Convention and 1996 WIPO Performances and Phonograms Treaty. Under the Rome Convention, phonogram producers are provided only with the possibility of a limited right to equitable remuneration in the case of the broadcasting or communication to the public of their commercially published phonograms,[785] but not with a general broadcasting or communication to the public right. The 1996 WIPO Performances and Phonograms Treaty goes further than this by providing that phonogram producers shall have a right to equitable remuneration in respect of the broadcasting or communication to the public of   **7–115**

---

[782] The extent to which such transmissions fell with the cable programme right was never entirely clear. See para.7–120, below.

[783] See ss.2(5)(d), (e), 3(5)(c), (d), 12(5)(c), 13(5)(c), (d), 14(4)(d) of the 1956 Act as amended. The cable right was originally described as the right to include a work in a diffusion service and subsequently as the right to include a work in a cable programme service.

[784] As to the WIPO Copyright Treaty, see para.23–66, below.

[785] Rome Convention art.12.

their commercially published recordings,[786] and an exclusive right in relation to the making available of their recordings via an on-demand service.[787] No general exclusive right of communication to the public is provided for. Under the Rome Convention, broadcasters are to be provided with an exclusive right in relation to the rebroadcasting of their works and a limited communication to the public right in the case of television broadcasts.[788]

7–116   **The Rental and Related Rights Directive.** In this area, the scope of the Rental and Related Rights Directive was limited. It merely prescribed a right for phonogram producers to share in equitable remuneration for the broadcasting of their commercially published sound recordings.[789]

7–117   **The Directive on Satellite Broadcasting and Cable Retransmission.** This Directive was of more general scope in that authors were to have an exclusive right in relation to the broadcasts of their works by satellite.[790]

7–118   **The Information Society Directive.** One of the objectives of the Information Society Directive was to give effect to the 1996 WIPO Treaties. Article 3(1) of the Directive therefore provides that in relation to authors' rights works, Member States are to provide an exclusive right to authorise or prohibit any communication to the public of the work, by wire or wireless means (i.e. broadcasting generally),[791] as well as an "on-demand right", that is, the right to make a work available to the public by wire or wireless means in such a way that members of the public may access it from a place and at a time individually chosen by them.[792] In relation to related rights subject matter, as has been seen, an equitable right of remuneration for producers of phonograms in respect of the broadcasting or communication to the public of their commercially published phonograms had already been provided for by the Rental and Related Rights Directive. The Information Society Directive did not make any further provision concerning a broadcasting right related to this and other related rights subject matter, but required that an exclusive on-demand right be provided for in respect of such subject matter.[793]

7–119   **Overview.** Acts which fall within the description of communication to the public under s.20 are different in nature from the restricted acts of performing, or showing or playing, a work in public under s.19. The restricted act of communication to the public in art.3 of the Information Society Directive and s.20 is concerned with cases where a work is communicated to a public which is not present at the place where the communication originates,[794] whereas the restricted act of public performance, etc., is concerned with performances which take place in the presence of a public audience. As such, the communication to the public right is addressed to the subject matter of art.11*bis*(1) of the Berne Convention[795] but not to

---

[786] WIPO Copyright Treaty art.15.

[787] WIPO Copyright Treaty art.14.

[788] WIPO Copyright Treaty art.13.

[789] The Rental and Related Rights Directive and its amendments have now been codified as Directive 2006/115/EC.

[790] Directive on Satellite Broadcasting and Cable Retransmission art.2.

[791] Information Society Directive art.3(1)

[792] Information Society Directive art.3(1)

[793] Information Society Directive art.3(2).

[794] See recitals 22 and 23 of the Information Society Directive 2001/29 and art.3, which refers to communication by wire or wireless means. The point is made clear by CDPA 1988 s.20, which refers to communication by electronic transmission.

[795] Authors of literary and artistic works shall enjoy the exclusive right of authorizing: (i) the

the subject matter of art.11(1),[796] which is directed to public performance rights which, in so far as they involve an act of communication, do so at the place where that communication originates.[797] Thus, as has been seen, in the case where a work is performed in public by means of a broadcast,[798] the communication is to be regarded as originating in the loudspeaker of the television or radio set where the public is present, and not at the place of transmission of the broadcast.

(ii) The communication to the public right: introduction

Implementation of the Information Society Directive. Although the restricted act of inclusion of a work in a cable programme service in the 1988 Act probably extended to "on request" services,[799] the definition of a cable programme service was extremely convoluted and was not considered by the Government to be a particularly "clear or transparent" way of ensuring that the requirements of the Information Society Directive were fulfilled.[800] A new right was therefore introduced which includes within in it both the exclusive right to broadcast a work, whether by wireless means or by cable, and the on-demand right prescribed by the Directive. In doing so, the link which had previously existed between, on the one hand, the protected subject matters of a "broadcast" and a "cable programme" and, on the other, the restricted acts of broadcasting a work or including a work in a cable programme service, was abandoned. On the one hand, there now exists the single protected subject matter of a "broadcast", which includes within it wireless broadcasts and cable transmissions in the nature of broadcasts, but not internet transmissions of a non-broadcast kind, in particular, not on-demand transmissions. On the other, there is now an exclusive right of communicating a work to the public by electronic means, which includes wireless and cable broadcasts and, in addition, on-demand transmissions by electronic means, whether wireless or by wire, or partly one and partly the other.

The right defined. It is an act restricted by the copyright in all categories of work, apart from a published edition of a typographical arrangement, to communicate the work to the public.[801] Communication to the public is for this purpose defined to mean the communication to the public by electronic transmission, and to include:

(a) The broadcasting of the work;
(b) The making available to the public of the work by electronic transmission in such a way that members of the public may access it from a place and at a time individually chosen by them.[802]

It is important to appreciate that although two particular instances of com-

7–120

7–121

---

broadcasting of their works or the communication thereof to the public by any other means of wireless diffusion of signs, sounds or images; (ii) any communication to the public by wire or by rebroadcasting of the broadcast of the work, when this communication is made by an organization other than the original one; (iii) the public communication by loudspeaker or any other analogous instrument transmitting, by signs, sounds or images, the broadcast of the work.

[796] "Authors of dramatic, dramatico-musical and musical works shall enjoy the exclusive right of authorizing: (i) the public performance of their works, including such public performance by any means or process; (ii) any communication to the public of the performance of their works."

[797] *Football Association Premier League Ltd v QC Leisure* [2008] EWHC 1411 (Ch); [2008] F.S.R. 32, para.259, although apparently misreading arts 11(1) and 11*bis*(1). As to the art.11(1) right, see para.7–105.

[798] See paras 7–103 and 7–106, above.

[799] *Shetland Times Ltd v Wills* [1997] F.S.R. 604 (Ct of Sess).

[800] See the Government Conclusions on the Patent Office's Consultation Paper of August 7, 2002, para.3.1.

[801] CDPA 1988 s.20(1), as amended by the Copyright and Related Rights Regulations 2003 (SI 2003/2498), with effect from October 31, 2003.

[802] CDPA 1988 s.20(2).

munication to the public by electronic means are specified, *any* act which falls within the description of a communication to the public by electronic means is an act restricted by the copyright in a work. The discussion which follows will deal first with the two particular instances and then the more general definition of the restricted act.

7–122   **Works subject to the right.** The communication to the public right is a right which subsists in relation to literary, dramatic, musical and artistic works, and sound recordings, films and broadcasts.[803] It therefore does not subsist in relation to typographical arrangements of published editions, which was also the position in relation to the pre-amendment rights.[804]

7–123   **Transitional provisions.** The Regulations implementing the Information Society Directive contain a number of transitional provisions, the only one of likely remaining relevance being that the amendments apply to works whenever made.[805]

(iii) Broadcasting

7–124   **Broadcasting the work.** The definition of "broadcast" has already been considered in relation to the protected subject matter of a broadcast.[806] The earlier discussion is not repeated here, except to say that a broadcast means an electronic transmission of visual images, sounds or other information which is transmitted for simultaneous reception by members of the public and is capable of being lawfully received by them, or is transmitted at a time determined solely by the person making the transmission for presentation to members of the public.[807] It therefore includes both wireless transmissions and transmissions by wire, i.e. cable transmissions, and to some extent has assimilated the previous restricted acts of: (a) broadcasting (which was limited to a transmission by wireless telegraphy) and (b) inclusion in a cable programme service. Excepted from this definition of broadcasting, however, is any internet transmission unless it is: (a) a transmission taking place simultaneously on the internet and by other means, or (b) a concurrent transmission of a live event, or (c) a transmission of recorded images or sounds forming part of a programme service offered by the person responsible for making the transmission, being a service in which programmes are broadcast at scheduled times by that person.[808] Such internet transmissions are similar in nature to "ordinary" broadcasts and for this reason are included within the scope of a broadcast. To the extent that internet transmissions are excluded from the definition of broadcast, they may still fall within the making available right, considered further below.[809]

7–125   **Who is the person who broadcasts?** The person who is liable for the restricted act of communicating a work to the public, in the case where the communication takes place by way of a broadcast, is obviously the person who "broadcasts" the work. It is not so obvious, however, who this person actually is. Is it, for example,

---

[803] CDPA 1988 s.20(1). For this purpose, the communicating of the film sound track which accompanies a film constitutes the communication of a film, not the communication of a sound recording: CDPA 1988 s.5B(3)(b).

[804] Such a right was not within the scope of Directive 2001/29.

[805] The Copyright and Related Rights Regulations 2003 reg.31(1).

[806] See paras 3–93 et seq., above.

[807] CDPA 1988 s.6(1).

[808] CDPA 1988 s.6(1A).

[809] The distinction may be important for performers, although not for owners of copyright in commercially published sound recordings, because if the transmission is a broadcast but not an ondemand transmission, there will only be a right to equitable remuneration.

the person who operates the transmission equipment, or the person who has responsibility for feeding the programme-carrying signals into the transmission process, or the person who is responsible for the programme content, or some other person? The Information Society Directive says nothing about who is to be regarded as communicating a work to the public. Before amendment of the Act, the position was reasonably clear.[810] Thus, s.6(3) of the Act provided that references to the person: (a) making the broadcast (which then meant a wireless broadcast but not a cable broadcast), (b) broadcasting a work, or (c) including a work in a broadcast, were to the person transmitting the "programme" (which meant any item included in the broadcast) if that person had responsibility to any extent for its contents.[811] In addition to that person, where any other person provided the programme (which meant any item included in the broadcast) and made the arrangements necessary for its transmission with the person transmitting it, that other person was also be taken to have broadcast the work.[812] It seemed clear that this definition of "broadcasting a work" applied to the restricted act of broadcasting the work under s.20.[813] Section 6(3) therefore provided an extended definition of who was the broadcaster in the case of wireless broadcasts. The position following amendment is no longer as clear as it was, both in relation to wireless broadcasts and cable broadcasts. Thus, although s.6(3) still provides that references to a person "making a broadcast or a transmission which is a broadcast" (which now includes both wireless and cable transmissions of the defined kind) are to the persons referred to above,[814] it does not now say anything about who is to be regarded as "broadcasting" the work. The principal purpose of the definition in s.6(3) of the person who "makes" a broadcast appears to be identify the author of, and thus first owner of the copyright in, a broadcast.[815] In contrast, and on a literal reading, the restricted act of broadcasting is not concerned with who "makes" the broadcast but who broadcasts the work. It is nevertheless the case that for the purposes of broadcasting by satellite, which is a sub-class of the restricted act of broadcasting, the broadcaster is clearly to be regarded as the person who "makes" the broadcast[816] and it is suggested that it is reasonably clear that the person who makes the broadcast is the broadcaster.[817]

Where does the act of broadcasting take place? There was a prolonged debate over whether a broadcast should be regarded as occurring at the place where the signals are transmitted (the "emission theory") or at the place where they are received, or both. As far as the European Community and satellite broadcasts are concerned, this debate was resolved in favour of the emission theory by EC Direc-

7–126

---

[810] Under the 1956 Act, where there were no precisely equivalent definitions, the broadcaster was held to include anyone participating in the broadcast, for example, the programme contractors and even, it seems, the performers. *Independent Television Companies Association Ltd v Performing Right Society Ltd*, *The Times*, February 23, 1982; *The Association of Independent Radio Contractors Ltd v Phonographic Performance Ltd* (1980) (unreported). "Broadcasting" was limited to transmissions by wireless telegraphy.

[811] CDPA 1988 s.6(3).

[812] CDPA 1988 s.6(3).

[813] See the words "in this Part" in CDPA 1988 s.6(3).

[814] i.e. to the person transmitting the "programme" if that person had responsibility to any extent for its contents and also to any other person who provides the programme and who makes the arrangements necessary for its transmission with the person transmitting it.

[815] See, e.g. the wording of CDPA 1988 s.9(2)(b).

[816] See CDPA 1988 s.6A.

[817] See also *Murphy v Media Protection Services Ltd* [2007] EWHC 3091 (Admin); [2008] 1 W.L.R. 1869; [2008] F.S.R. 15 at para.39, where it was said (obiter) with regard to the provisions of CDPA 1988 s.297 that the persons who had editorial responsibility for the composition of schedules of television programmes so far as the transmitted broadcast was concerned were the broadcasters.

tive 93/83 on Satellite Broadcasting and Cable Retransmission.[818] Effect was given to the Directive by amendments made to the 1988 Act by the Copyright and Related Rights Regulations 1996, as now refined following implementation of the Information Society Directive. Thus any infringement of copyright by communication of a satellite broadcast to the public takes place in the country from which the broadcast is made and the reception of broadcasts in other Member States cannot be prevented by copyright owners or licensees in those other countries, where the copyright might be owned by or licensed to someone different.[819] In fact, the 1988 Act goes further than the Directive and expressly applies the emission theory to wireless broadcasts of all kinds, not just satellite broadcasts.[820] The position in relation to broadcasts by cable is not expressly provided for and is less clear:

7–127   (i) *Wireless broadcasts.* First, in the case of a wireless broadcast, the 1988 Act now provides that the place from where the broadcast is made is the place where, under the control and responsibility of the person making the broadcast, the programme signals are introduced into an uninterrupted chain of communication ending with the receiver.[821] In the case of a satellite transmission, this chain is to include the chain leading to the satellite and down towards the earth.[822] These provisions make it clear that in the case of wireless transmissions, what matters for the purposes of infringement is the place from which the signals are first introduced into the chain of communication and not the place where a signal is receivable or its footprint falls. The fact that the signal may not be receivable in the United Kingdom therefore does not affect a broadcaster's potential liability under the 1988 Act if the chain of communication of the signals starts in the United Kingdom. By the same token, the fact that a broadcast can be received in the United Kingdom does not mean that the restricted act of broadcasting is taking place in the United Kingdom: it will not do so if the broadcast was made from another country in accordance with the above rules.

There are two situations in which a satellite broadcast which is made from outside the EEA in accordance with the above definition is in fact treated as being made from within the EEA.[823] In the context of UK copyright law, this becomes important when the place from which the broadcast is made is treated as being within the United Kingdom when otherwise it would not be so. Both situations arise where the law of the country from which the broadcast is actually made fails to provide a minimum level of protection for authors and performers, and in particular fails to provide:

(a) Exclusive rights in relation to broadcasting equivalent to the exclusive

---

[818] See Directive 93/83 art.1.2(a), (b).

[819] *Football Association Premier League Ltd v QC Leisure* [2008] EWHC 1411 (Ch); [2008] F.S.R. 32 at para.290, adding that the purpose of the Directive was to simplify the life of the broadcaster by subjecting it to the laws of only one Member State in relation to its acts of communication to the public by satellite: para.295. Thus the Directive does not prevent parties from dividing up rights as such (see recital 16, subject to the competition rules in art.81 (ex art.85)) but, if they do, they must accept that licensees in the country of reception cannot complain about a communication by satellite to the public in that country of works for which they hold the relevant rights.

[820] As noted in *Football Dataco Ltd v Sportradar GmbH* [2010] EWHC 2911 (Ch) at paras 66, 67.

[821] CDPA 1988 s.6(4), as amended with effect from December 1, 1996 by the Copyright and Related Rights Regulations 1996 (SI 1996/2967). As already noted, the Directive only required this definition in the case of broadcasts by satellite, but the amendment applied to all types of wireless broadcast, presumably on the basis that the emission theory correctly represented the law in the case of terrestrial wireless broadcasts as well. S.6(4), as enacted, provided that the place from which a broadcast was made was, in the case of a satellite transmission, the place from which the signals carrying the broadcast were transmitted to the satellite.

[822] CDPA 1988 s.6(4), as amended with effect from December 1, 1996 by the Copyright and Related Rights Regulations 1996 (SI 1996/2967).

[823] These two cases are prescribed by the Satellite and Cable Directive. See recital 20 and art.1(2)(d).

rights of broadcasting conferred on authors of literary, dramatic, musical and artistic works, films and broadcasts by s.20 of the 1988 Act[824];

(b) A right in relation to live broadcasting equivalent to that conferred on a performer in relation to the live broadcasts of his performances under s.182(1)(b) of the 1988 Act[825]; and

(c) A right for authors of sound recordings and performers to share in a single equitable remuneration in respect of the broadcasting of such sound recordings.[826]

The first situation is where the broadcast is made from such a country but the place from which the programme-carrying signals are transmitted to the satellite ("the uplink station") is located in an EEA State. In this situation, the latter place is treated as being the place from which the broadcast is made and the person operating the uplink station is treated as being the person making the broadcast. Where this place is within the United Kingdom, therefore, the unlicensed broadcast is liable to be an infringement under the 1988 Act for which the person operating the uplink is liable. The second situation is where the uplink station is not located in an EEA State but a person who is established within an EEA State has commissioned the making of the broadcast. In this situation, he will be treated as making the broadcast and the place in which he has his principal establishment in the EEA shall be treated as the place from which the broadcast was made. Again, therefore, an infringement under the 1988 Act may occur where this place is within the United Kingdom.

(ii) Broadcasts by cable. As to broadcasts by cable (i.e. by wire), neither the Act nor any Directive makes any provision as to where the broadcast takes place.[827] Where the broadcast is initiated in one country and received in another (for example between the Republic of Ireland and Northern Ireland), where does the broadcast take place? Since the United Kingdom has applied the emission theory to wireless broadcasts of all kinds, it is suggested that the theory is also to be applied to broadcasting by cable, so that broadcasting by this means occurs at the place where the signals originate. All such transmissions are now "broadcasts" and it is suggested that no distinction should be drawn between different types of transmission.

7–128

Re-broadcasts. Where a broadcast is relayed by its reception and immediate re-transmission, this is to be regarded as a separate act of broadcasting from the making of the original broadcast.[828] It was always the case that rebroadcasting a work fell within the restricted act of broadcasting. An important exception exists, however, in the case of cable re-transmission of wireless broadcasts by cable.[829]

7–129

An issue often arises where broadcast signals are received by, for example, a hotelier, and then relayed to guests either in the public spaces within the hotel or to private places, such as hotel bedrooms. Two questions can arise, namely, do the actions of the hotelier amount to a re-broadcast and, if so, is this a communication to the public? The second question is dealt with below under the heading of "Communication to the public" but, as to the first, this depends on a

---

[824] i.e. the section presently under consideration.

[825] See Ch.12, below.

[826] Again, in fact the United Kingdom confers no such right on authors of sound recordings, although the owner of the copyright in a sound recording has the exclusive right to control its exploitation. Performers have such a right by virtue of CDPA 1988 s.182D.

[827] CDPA 1988 s.6(4), which states where a broadcast takes place from, applies only to wireless broadcasts.

[828] CDPA 1988 s.6(5A). This provision was introduced to establish that such a broadcast also qualifies for copyright protection.

[829] i.e. under CDPA 1988 s.73. See para.9–205, below.

technical evaluation of what takes place after the broadcast signal is received by the hotelier. So where signals were received by main aerial of a hotel and then distributed by wire to each of the television sets in the various rooms of the hotel guests, this was clearly a re-broadcast.[830] In contrast, where a publican simply received a broadcast signal by satellite, which was then decoded and displayed on a television screen in the bar, he had not effected any retransmission by wire or otherwise.[831] Communication to the public is concerned with the transmission of the work to members of the public who are not present at the place where the communication originates as opposed to public performance, which so far as it concerns an act of communication at all, concerns communication at the place where the communication originates.[832]

7-130   **Communication to the public.** In the case of ordinary broadcasts which are intended for reception by members of the public, this is not usually an issue[833]: a communication to the public takes place even though the signals may have been intended largely for reception in people's private homes.[834] Problems arise, however, where the broadcast (often a rebroadcast) takes place on a much smaller scale, as for example, with the relay of a signal by hotelier to hotel guests, either in the public areas of the hotel or, more problematically, in hotel bedrooms. The European Court of Justice[835] has ruled that in determining this issue "communication to the public" must be interpreted broadly, such an interpretation being es-

---

[830] *Sociedad General de Autores y Editores de España (SGAE) v Rafael Hoteles SL* (C–306/05) [2007] Bus. L.R. 521; [2007] E.C.D.R. 2, where this point was not in dispute: see the analysis in *Football Association Premier League Ltd v QC Leisure* [2008] EWHC 1411 (Ch); [2008] F.S.R. 32, at para.260.

[831] *Football Association Premier League Ltd v QC Leisure* [2008] EWHC 1411 (Ch), per Kitchin J., expressing a provisional view, and referring the following question to the Court of Justice: (a) Is a copyright work communicated to the public by wire or wireless means within the meaning of art.3 of Directive 2001/29/EC where a satellite broadcast is received at a commercial premises (for example a bar) and communicated or shown at those premises via a single television screen and speakers to members of the public present in those premises? (b) Is the answer to (a) affected if: (i) the members of the public present constitute a new public not contemplated by the broadcaster (in this case because a domestic decoder card for use in one Member State is used for a commercial audience in another Member State)? (ii) the members of the public are not a paying audience according to national law? (iii) the television broadcast signal is received by an aerial or satellite dish on the roof of or adjacent to the premises where the television is situated? (c) If the answer to any part of (b) is yes, what factors should be taken into account in determining whether there is a communication of the work which has originated from a place where members of the audience are not present? See also the related reference in *Union of European Football Associations v Euroview Sport Ltd* [2010] EWHC 1066 (Ch) and further pending references noted at para.24–125 et seq., below. For the background, see [2010] EWHC 1066 (Ch) at paras 17 to 32.

[832] *Football Association Premier League Ltd v QC Leisure* [2008] EWHC 1411 (Ch), at para.259.

[833] See, e.g. *Lagardère Active Broadcast v Société pour la perception de la rémunération équitable (SPRE)* (C–28/04) [2005] 3 C.M.L.R. 48, a case concerned with the Satellite and Cable Directive (93/83/EEC), where the satellite in question operated on frequency bands which were reserved for closed, point-to-point communication, and the signals were not intended for reception by the public within the meaning of art.1(2)(a).

[834] Compare the quite different issue of what amounts to a performance "in public". See para.7–108.

[835] *Sociedad General de Autores y Editores de España (SGAE) v Rafael Hoteles SL* (C–306/05) [2007] Bus. L.R. 521, [2007] E.C.D.R. 2. See also *Organismos Sillogikis Diakhirisis Dimiourgon Theatrikon kai Optikoakoustikon Ergon v Divani Acropolis Hotel and Tourism AE* (C–136/09). Note also the pending references *SCF-Consorio Fonografici v Marco del Corse* (C–135/10): "Does the broadcasting, free of charge, of phonograms within private dental practices engaged in professional economic activity, for the benefit of patients of those practices and enjoyed by them without any active choice on their part, constitute 'communication to the public' or 'making available to the public' for the purposes of the application of Article 3(2) (b) of Directive 2001/ 29/EC?"; *Phonographic Performance (Ireland) Ltd v Ireland* (C–162/10): "Is a hotel operator which provides in guest bedrooms televisions and/or radios to which it distributes a broadcast signal a "user" making a "communication to the public" of a phonogram which may be played in a broadcast for the purposes of Article 8(2) of Codified Directive 2006/115/EC?"; *Circul Globus Bucureşti (Circ & Variete Globus Bucureşti) v Uniunea Compozitorilor şi Muzicologilor din România* (C–283/10): "Is Article 3(1) of 2001/29/EC 1 to be interpreted to the effect that 'communication to the public' means: (a) exclusively communication to the public where the public is not present at the place where the communication originates, or (b) also any other communica-

sential to achieve the principal objective of the Information Society Directive, which is to establish a high level of protection of, inter alios, authors, allowing them to obtain an appropriate reward for the use of their works, in particular on the occasion of communication to the public.[836] A general approach is required, having regard to whether the communication is also receivable in public parts of the hotel and taking into account particularly the facts that: (a) usually, hotel customers quickly succeed each other; (b) as a general rule, a fairly large number of persons are involved, so that they may be considered to be a public; (c) the cumulative effects of making the works available to such potential television viewers means that this type of communication could become very significant. It is therefore of little relevance that the only recipients are the occupants of rooms and that, taken separately, they are of limited economic interest for the hotel. It is also relevant that the communication is made by an broadcaster other than the original one, and to a public which is different from the public to which the original broadcast was addressed.[837] Further, the action by a hotel by which it gives access to a broadcast work to its customers must be considered an additional service performed with the aim of conferring some benefit on the customer. While, therefore, the mere provision of physical facilities such as television sets does not constitute, as such, a communication within the meaning of the Directive,[838] the nature of hotel rooms does not preclude the communication of a work by means of television sets from constituting communication to the public. In this it does not matter that there may be customers who have not switched in their television sets.

(iv) Making the work available on demand

The on-demand right. The second category of communication to the public right (the so-called on-demand right) is the act of making available a work to the public by electronic transmission in such a way that members of the public may access it from a place and at a time individually chosen by them.[839] The wording of this provision follows closely that of arts 3.2 and 3.3 of the Information Society Directive, which are themselves based on art.8 of the 1996 WIPO Copyright Treaty and arts 10 and 14 of the 1996 WIPO Performances and Phonograms Treaty. The Directive states expressly that the transmission may be by wire or wireless means, so that the right encompasses both wireless transmissions and transmissions by cable, but this is implicit in s.20 from the fact that the communication must be by electronic transmission. The essential difference between this right and the "broadcasting" right is of course that in the case of the broadcasting right the work is transmitted at a time determined by the broadcaster with a view to its simultaneous reception by the public at large, whereas in relation to the on-demand right the transmission is to a single recipient, who initiates the transmission and chooses when and where to receive it.

7–131

---

tion of a work which is carried out directly in a place open to the public using any means of public performance or direct presentation of the work?"; and *Bezpečnostní softwarová asociace (Security software association) v Ministerstvo kultury ČR (Ministry of Culture of the Czech Republic)* (C–393/09): "Should Article 1(2) of 91/250/EEC be interpreted as meaning that the phrase 'the expression in any form of a computer program' also includes the graphic user interface of the computer program or part thereof? If so, does television broadcasting, whereby the public is enabled to have sensory perception of the graphic user interface of a computer program or part thereof, albeit without the possibility of actively exercising control over that program, constitute making a work or part thereof available to the public?" See, further, para.24–125 et seq., below.

[836] See recitals 9 and 10.
[837] Although this will almost always be the case with a re-broadcast.
[838] See recital 27 of the Directive.
[839] CDPA 1988 s.20(2)(b).

7-132   **What constitutes the act of making a work available and who is liable?** Neither the Act nor the Directive says anything further about this. The important point to emphasise is that it is the act of making a work available to the public *by electronic transmission*, and *in such a way that the public can access it*, which matters. Thus, where A makes a work available to B, an internet service provider, so that B can make it available to the public in this way, it is suggested that it is the act of B in making it available by electronic transmission such that the public can access it which is the restricted act. Although A has made the work available, he has not made the work available to the public by electronic transmission, etc., although of course he may be liable for having authorised that act or as a joint tortfeasor. In each case, it will be necessary to examine the facts to see who has committed the restricted act.[840]

7-133   **File sharing.** Making a work available to the public will often be one of the acts of infringement committed during the course of unlawful file-sharing. So, connecting a computer to the internet where the computer is running peer-to-peer software, and where music files containing copies of copyright works are placed in a shared directory, amounts to communication to the public of those works by the person in control of the computer ("the uploader").[841] A more difficult question is whether the operator of a website which members of the public make use of to engage in unlawful file-sharing commits the act of communication work to the public, when those works are only transmitted between the file-sharers and not by the operator of the service. In each case the facts must be closely examined to analyse what has taken place. So, a defendant was held to have communicated works to the public where it had provided a service which enable its customers to identify films available from other customers (file-sharers) using its cataloguing and indexing system and then to download those films using a facility which it provided. The service was not merely passive in providing a link to a film of interest which was available from a third party but amounted to an intervention in a material way to make the claimants' films easily available to a new audience, that is to say, the defendant's customers. Its customers would have considered that the defendant was making available to them the films in the defendant's index.[842]

7-134   **When does the act of making available occur?** Unlike the restricted act of broadcasting, there appears to be no requirement that any transmission actually takes place before the restricted act takes place: the restricted act is the making available of the work so that members of the public "may" access it. For example, therefore, it is suggested that as soon as a work becomes available on an internet service provider's servers, the restricted act is committed, and will continue to be committed until the work is no longer available.[843]

7-135   **Where does the act of making available take place?** This will often be a vital

---

[840] It is important to note, however, that a person who makes a work available within the meaning of s.20 may have a defence available to him, particularly of "hosting", "caching" or "mere conduit" under the E-Commerce Regulations (see paras 21–100 et seq., below).

[841] *Polydor Ltd v Brown* [2005] EWHC 3191 (Ch), para.7. For a general discussion of the problem, and the UK's approach to it via the Digital Economy Act 2010, see para.21–288, below.

[842] *Twentieth Century Fox Film Corporation v Newzbin Ltd* [2010] EWHC 608 (Ch); [2010] F.S.R. 21, para.125.

[843] See *Polydor Ltd v Brown* [2005] EWHC 3191 (Ch), where it was apparently not considered necessary that there should have been an actual transmission. This approach is also consistent with *Sociedad General de Autores y Editores de Espana v Rafael Hoteles SA* (C–306/05) [2007] Bus. L.R. 521, [2007] E.C.D.R. 2, concerning the provision by cable re-broadcast of television programmes to hotel bedrooms, where the Court of Justice held that for there to be a communication to the public it was sufficient that the work was made available in such a way that the public might access it: para.43. In the same way, an infringement can continuously take place by the exposure of an infringing copy for sale under CDPA 1988 s.24(1).

point where the transmission in question has occurred across national boundaries. In principle it resurrects the arguments which existed as to the place where a broadcast should be regarded as occurring. The 1988 Act is not particularly clear in that it provides only that exclusive right is infringed if a person does the restricted act *in the United Kingdom* of making a work available to the public in such a way that members of the public may access if from a place and at a time chosen by them.[844] Art.3.2 of the Information Society Directive, which must be referred to as the primary source, is more general but still unclear in this respect, providing that Member States shall provide for the exclusive right to authorise or prohibit the making available to the public of a work in such a way that the public may access it from a place and at a time individually chosen by them. As the UK case law stands, however, the act of making available to the public by online transmission is committed and committed only where the transmission takes place[845] and thus (presumably) where the servers, etc., are situated from which the communication carrying the work originates. While, therefore, the placing of data on a server in one state can make the data available to the public in another state, this does not mean that the party who has made the data available has committed the act of making available by transmission in the state of reception.[846] It follows that the kind of considerations which apply in the case of the distribution right do not apply,[847] namely that where a work is sold to a person with the intention that he receives it in the United Kingdom, it is irrelevant that the person selling the work is situated outside the United Kingdom, whether within the EEA or elsewhere.

It is also not clear from the Directive whether infringement is committed by the mere passive act of making it available such that the public *may* access it, or only when an act of communication of the work via such an on-demand service takes place, but the latter seems to be the correct position.[848] In this respect it is to be noted that the Directive (and the 1988 Act) classifies the on-demand right as a sub-category of the more general right of *communication* to the public.[849]

The whole topic seems likely to become the subject of a reference to the European Court of Justice in due course.[850]

(v) Other forms of communication to the public by electronic means

The acts of broadcasting a work and making it available on-demand are merely   **7–136**

---

[844] CDPA 1988 ss.16(1), (2), 20(1), (2). The Government declined to make express provision in relation to this question, taking the view that it was neither necessary nor appropriate given that the Information Society Directive was silent on the point. See the Government Conclusions on the Patent Office's Consultation Paper of August 7, 2002, para.3.5.

[845] *Football Dataco Ltd v Sportradar GmbH* [2010] EWHC 2911 (Ch) at para 74 dealing with the similar right in relation to the sui generis database right (see para.18–28, below), and thus applying, in effect, the "emission theory" to such transmissions, and rejecting arguments that: (1) such theory only applies in the case of satellite broadcasts; (2) the emission theory would make the right to prevent online transmission worthless, the court taking the view that the right would still prevent transmission or re-transmission in a state to which the Directive applies and any further use of the database within the state of reception if the transmission originated from outside the EU would infringe other exclusive rights; and (3) that to apply the theory would be tantamount to applying a rule of exhaustion as soon as a digital work was published, the court noting that there is no question of subsequent infringing acts ceasing to be actionable.

[846] *Football Dataco Ltd v Sportradar GmbH* [2010] EWHC 2911 (Ch) at para.74.

[847] See para.7–92, above.

[848] *Football Dataco Ltd v Sportradar GmbH* [2010] EWHC 2911 (Ch) at para.74 ("... the act of making available to the public by online *transmission* is committed and committed only where the *transmission* takes place" (emphasis added).

[849] See arts 3(1) and (2) and recital 23.

[850] In *Football Dataco Ltd v Sportradar GmbH* [2010] EWHC 2911 (Ch) at para.96, the judge acknowledged that the place where the act of making available by online transmission occurs was a question of importance and was not acte claire, but declined to make a reference on the grounds that a reference would be determinative of the case before him.

two specified kinds of the more general restricted act of communication of a work to the public by electronic means. As to what acts might fall outside two specified kinds but within the more general restricted act, it is easier to say what acts do not fall within the general restricted act at all. For example, the reference to a communication to the public means that point-to-point electronic communications initiated by the sender, such as emails, will not fall within the scope of the restricted act.

7. THE ADAPTATION RIGHT

7–137   One of the acts restricted by the copyright in any literary, dramatic or musical work is the right to make an adaptation of the work.[851] Further consideration is given below as to the meaning of "adaptation" in this context, but there is an unclear dividing line between what amounts to a reproduction of a work and what amounts to an adaptation of a work. Thus, for example, although the making of a translation of a literary or dramatic work is expressly included within the definition of making an adaptation, it can clearly be argued that a translation is also a reproduction of the original work, assuming that a substantial use was thereby made of the skill and labour of its author.[852] Other acts expressly brought within the definition of making an adaptation, considered below, provide even clearer examples. The concept of an exclusive right to make an adaptation of a work was first introduced by the 1956 Act, partly to bring under one head a number of separate exclusive rights provided for under the 1911 Act,[853] and partly to make it clear that certain other acts were also within the exclusive rights of the copyright owner.[854] The concept has been continued by the 1988 Act and in subsequent amendments made to it. The Act provides that no inference is to be drawn from the provisions relating to the making of an adaptation as to what does or does not amount to copying of a work,[855] and since there is no reason in principle why the same act cannot fall within two separate classes of restricted act, it is suggested that in some cases the same act may infringe both the reproduction right and the adaptation right.

In general, an adaptation is made when it is recorded, in writing or otherwise.[856] If the restricted act extended no further than the *making* of an adaptation, the right would be of limited value but the Act provides that not only is the making of an adaptation a restricted act but it is also a restricted act to reproduce an adaptation in any material form, issue copies of it to the public, perform it in public or communicate it to the public.[857] For this purpose it is immaterial whether the adaptation itself was recorded in the above sense when any such further act was done.[858] This provision makes it clear, for example, that copyright in a musical work may be infringed by performing an adaptation of it on stage, even though the adaptation itself is never recorded.

In the usual way, it is a restricted act not only to do any of the above acts in re-

---

[851] CDPA 1988 ss.16(1)(e), 21(1).

[852] But note that there is some authority, referred to below, that a translation of a literary work is not a "copy" of it.

[853] i.e. the "translation" and "dramatisation" rights (see ss.1(2)(a), (b) and (c) of the Copyright Act 1911).

[854] i.e. the "strip-cartoon" right and the right to make an arrangement or transcription of a musical work (see ss.2(6)(a)(iv) and (b) of the Copyright Act 1956).

[855] CDPA 1988 s.21(5).

[856] CDPA 1988 s.21(1). For this purpose, writing includes any form of notation or code, whether by hand or otherwise and regardless of the method by which, or medium in or on which, it is recorded. CDPA 1988 s.178.

[857] CDPA 1988 s.21(2).

[858] CDPA 1988 s.21(2).

lation to the work as a whole but also in relation to any substantial part of it. Further, copyright is infringed not only by anyone who does one of these restricted acts without the licence of the copyright owner, but also by anyone who authorises the doing of such an act without licence.

Literary and dramatic works

The expression "adaptation" is defined by reference to particular categories of work. Thus, in relation to a literary or dramatic work, other than a computer program or a database, the 1988 Act defines "adaptation" to mean: **7–138**

(a) a translation of the work;
(b) a version of a dramatic work in which it is converted into a non-dramatic work or, as the case may be, a version of a non-dramatic work in which it is converted into a dramatic work;
(c) a version of the work in which the story or action is conveyed wholly or mainly by means of pictures in a form suitable for reproduction in a book, or in a newspaper, magazine or similar periodical.[859]

Translation.[860] Although "translation" commonly means the turning of a work from one human language into another, it is suggested that the word is wide enough to include the conversion of a work into code or Braille.[861] It should be noted that two separate rights may exist where there has been a translation, namely the right of the owner of the copyright in the original work to restrain reproduction, etc. of the original or any translated form, and the right of the owner of the copyright in the translation to restrain reproduction of his translation. Anyone wishing to reproduce a particular translation should therefore obtain a licence from the owner of the copyright in both the original and the translation.[862] The position will be the same even where the translation was unauthorised since, although an infringement, it will be entitled to copyright.[863]   **7–139**

Dramatisation of non-dramatic works. Infringements of this kind may occur when a novel is turned into a play or a screenplay for a film.[864] In such cases there may of course be sufficient copying of language for the defendant's dramatic work to be a reproduction of the plaintiff's work. However, even where there is   **7–140**

---

[859] CDPA 1988 s.21(3)(a).
[860] Pre-Copyright Act 1911 cases on this point need to be approached with caution since there was some doubt, prior to the 1911 Act, whether copyright in a work could be infringed by making a translation of it: *Burnett v Chetwood* (1817) 2 Mer. 441; cf. *Cate v Devon, etc. Newspaper Co* (1889) 40 Ch. D. But see *Copinger* 4th edn, pp.187 et seq., arguing strongly for the opposite view. The 1911 Act made it clear that the exclusive rights to produce, reproduce, perform and publish a work included the exclusive right to do these acts in relation to any translation of the work (see s.1(2)(a)). As noted above, the Copyright Act 1956 introduced the concept of the restricted act of making an adaptation of a work, which was defined to include the making of a translation (see ss.2(5), (6)(a)(iii)).
[861] If not, then such acts must presumably be regarded as amounting to a reproduction of a work, since otherwise they would not be restricted acts at all, a curious result. But see *Apple Computer, Inc v Mackintosh Computers Ltd* (1988) 44 D.L.R. (4th) 74.
[862] *Murray v Bogue* (1853) 1 Drew. 353 at 368.
[863] *Redwood Music Ltd v Chappell & Co Ltd* [1982] R.P.C. 109; *ZYX Music v King* [1995] 3 All E.R. 1 (at first instance); and see para.3–307, above.
[864] Again, care must be taken with the earlier cases on this point. Before the passing of the Copyright Act 1911, it did not constitute an infringement to convert a novel or other non-dramatic work into a dramatic work, provided there was no substantial language copying (see *Read v Conquest* (1861) 9 C.B. (N.S.) 755; *Tinsley v Lacey* (1863) 32 L.J. Ch. 535; *Warne & Co v Seebohm* (1888) 39 Ch. D. 73. Under the Copyright Act 1911 it was expressly provided that the exclusive rights to produce, reproduce, perform and publish a work included the right to convert a non-dramatic work into a dramatic work, and vice versa (see ss.1(2)(b), (c)). The law was thus changed: see *Corelli v Gray* (1913) 30 T.L.R. 116. The Copyright Act 1956 introduced the concept of the restricted act of making an adaptation of a work, which was defined to include similar rights

no language copying but, for example, the defendant has to a substantial extent taken the incidents and plot from the plaintiff's novel and turned them into a dramatic work, this will amount to an infringement by the making of an adaptation.[865] The issues which arise here are similar to those which arise in relation to the reproduction of one dramatic work by another.[866] Thus the question is whether the situations or plot have been copied from the novel and then represented in dramatic form.[867] This is not to say that mere ideas or a character can be protected in this way, certainly if the character or ideas are not novel,[868] but if the combination of events which has been taken is not merely trivial, but amounts to a substantial part, there will be an infringement.[869] Examples from the cases include infringements by dramatising a novel in the form of a play, a sketch,[870] a script for a film or a film itself,[871] or a short story in the form of a ballet.[872] In the case of a historical work, which the claimant has compiled from various sources, it will in the usual way be necessary to examine whether the incidents in common between the two works which the defendant has dramatised have been taken by him from the claimant's work or from those other sources.[873]

7–141   **Conversion of dramatic into non-dramatic work.**[874] As in the case of non-dramatic works, a dramatic work may be infringed simply by its language being reproduced to a substantial extent. Even where there has not been such copying, however, the copyright in a dramatic work may be infringed if it is converted into a non-dramatic form. Thus where the events and conversations in a play were described in detail, scene by scene, constituting more than just a synopsis, this was held to be an adaptation.[875] It made no difference that the descriptions formed part of a larger work and were interspersed with commentaries and other writings. On the other hand, short synopses of operas are unlikely to be infringements of the operatic works if the operas are described shortly and in very bare outline.[876] The position would presumably be different if numerous incidents were reproduced.

7–142   **Strip cartoon.** As has been seen, in relation to a literary or dramatic work, "adaptation" includes a version of the work in which the story or action is conveyed wholly or mainly by means of pictures in a form suitable for reproduction in a

---

(ss.2(6)(i), (ii)). However, to turn a novel into a film would have been to reproduce the novel, not to have made an adaptation of it (see s.48(1)—definitions of "dramatic work" and "reproduction").

[865] *Corelli v Gray* (1913) 30 T.L.R. 116. Again, arguably it will also amount to copying of the work, where part of the merit of the literary work was its plot, characterisation, etc.

[866] See para.7–63, above.

[867] *Kelly v Cinema Houses Ltd* [1928–1935] Mac.C.C. 362.

[868] *Kelly v Cinema Houses Ltd* [1928–1935] Mac.C.C. 362; *Dagnall v British and Dominion Film Corporation Ltd* [1928–1935] Mac.C.C. 391 (a case of infringement of a dramatic work by reproduction); *Harman Pictures N.V. v Osborne* [1967] 1 W.L.R. 723.

[869] *Kelly v Cinema Houses Ltd* [1928–1935] Mac.C.C. 362; *Fernald v Jay Lewis Productions Ltd* [1975] F.S.R. 499; cf. *MacGregor v Powell* [1936–1945] Mac.C.C. 233; *De Mandnit v Gaumont British Picture Corporation Ltd* [1936–1945] Mac.C.C. 292.

[870] *Corelli v Gray* (1913) 30 T.L.R. 116.

[871] *Fernald v Jay Lewis Productions Ltd* [1975] F.S.R. 499 (infringement by taking a single episode from a semi-fictional story, itself consisting of 12 episodes, and dealt with in only four out of 126 pages of the book); *Zeccola v Universal City Studios Inc* (1982) 46 A.L.R. 189.

[872] *Holland v Vivian Van Damm Productions Ltd* [1936–1945] Mac.C.C. 69.

[873] *Harman Pictures N.V. v Osborne* [1967] 1 W.L.R. 723.

[874] See the footnotes to para.7–140, above, dealing with the earlier law.

[875] *Sillitoe v McGraw-Hill Book Co (U.K.) Ltd* [1983] F.S.R. 545.

[876] *Valcarenghi v The Gramophone Co Ltd* [1928–1935] Mac.C.C. 301, where it was found that the defendants had not infringed, not having transposed the work into a novel or short story.

book, or in a newspaper, magazine or similar periodical.[877] A pictorial representation of the plot of a book or a play will therefore constitute infringement even though no words are used in the representation.

Computer programs. In the early days of the debate about software protection, **7–143** there was concern whether infringement could be avoided by arguments about the distinctions between the levels of code involved in the translation from what was written by the human author (source code) to the lowest level of code, on which the computer operated (machine code), or by arguing that there was no infringement if a program was re-written in a different computer language. The Copyright (Computer Software) Amendment Act 1985 addressed these issues by specifically providing that a version of a program in which it was converted into or out of a computer language or code, or into a different computer language or code, was an adaptation of the program.[878] This approach was substantially repeated in the 1988 Act, by means of a special definition of "translation", and thus adaptation, so far as computer programs were concerned.[879] As part of the implementation of the Computer Software Directive,[880] the wording was modified to mirror more closely the wording of art.4(b) of the Directive. Thus the 1988 Act now provides that in relation to a computer program, "adaptation" means an arrangement or altered version of it, or a translation of it, a translation for these purposes including a version of the program in which it is converted into or out of a computer language or code or into a different computer language or code.[881] Perhaps because of the pervasiveness of copying in the digital environment, relatively little attention has been given to this restricted act. The cases are usually treated as ones of mere reproduction. The section clearly covers cases where, as with the translation of a traditional literary work from one human language to another, a program written in one programming language is rewritten in another, with similarities of structure and nomenclature, where these are consistent with the programming environment.

Database. In relation to a copyright database, adaptation means an arrangement **7–144** or altered version of the database, or a translation of it.[882] The expression "translation" is not further defined in relation to database and so has the ordinary meaning used in relation to literary and dramatic works other than computer programs.

Musical works. In relation to musical works, the 1988 Act defines adaptation to **7–145** mean an arrangement or transcription of the work.[883]

8. AUTHORISATION

As already noted, copyright is infringed not only where an act restricted by the **7–146** copyright in a work is done without consent, but also where a person authorises

---

[877] This right was expressly included for the first time in the Copyright Act 1956. Before then there was doubt whether such an act amounted to an infringement.

[878] Copyright (Computer Software) Amendment Act 1985 s.1(2).

[879] s.21(4), as enacted, provided that: "In relation to a computer program a 'translation' includes a version of the program in which it is converted into or out of a computer language or code or into a different computer language or code, otherwise than incidentally in the course of running the program".

[880] 91/250, as implemented by the Copyright (Computer Programs) Regulations 1992 (SI 1992/3233).

[881] CDPA 1988 ss.21(3)(ab), (4). Provision is now made by CDPA 1988 s.50C for the incidental running of a program.

[882] CDPA 1988 s.21(3)(ac). The subsection was introduced by the Copyright and Rights in Databases Regulations 1997 (SI 1997/3032). See paras 7–45 et seq., above as to infringement of copyright databases.

[883] CDPA 1988 s.21(3)(b).

the doing of such an act.[884] The meaning of "authorised" in this context is discussed below, but where a person is liable for having authorised an infringement he will also often be liable as a joint tortfeasor or for having procured the infringing act.[885] Also, of course, he may be vicariously liable for the acts of his servants or agents done with his authority.[886] "Authorisation" is a separate act of infringement from the act which is itself authorised.[887] It does not apply to indirect acts of infringement.[888]

7–147   **Jurisdiction.** Although no infringement is committed by the doing of any of the restricted acts unless the act takes place in the United Kingdom,[889] infringement by authorisation of any of those acts occurs even if the act of authorisation takes place outside the jurisdiction.[890]

7–148   **Meaning of "authorise".** Authorisation means the grant or purported grant, which may be express or implied, of the right to do the act complained of, whether the intention is that the grantee should do the act on his own account, or only on account of the grantor.[891] An expression which has often been used as equivalent to the word "authorise" is "sanction, approve and countenance",[892] but this must be treated with caution, particularly in so far as the word "countenance" is equivalent to the word "condone".[893] Thus, in general, an authorisation "can only come from someone having or purporting to have authority, and an act is not authorised by someone who merely enables or possibly assists or even encourages another to do that act, but does not purport to have any authority which he can grant to justify the doing of the act".[894] Some of the older cases need to be read with caution in the light of this modern statement of the law.

Clearly a person will have authorised an act if he formally grants the right to

---

[884] CDPA 1988 s.16(2). The position was the same under the 1956 and 1911 Acts: Copyright Act 1956 s.1(1); Copyright Act 1911 s.1(2).

[885] As to which, see *CBS Songs Ltd v Amstrad Plc* [1988] A.C. 1013 at 1057; [1988] R.P.C. 567, HL; *Amstrad Consumer Electronics Plc v British Phonographic Industry Ltd* [1986] F.S.R. 159, CA and paras 21–42 et seq., below.

[886] *Performing Right Society Ltd v Mitchell and Booker, etc. Ltd* [1924] 1 K.B. 762; *Canadian Performing Right Society v Canadian National Exhibition Association* [1934] 4 D.L.R. 154. It was questioned whether the word "authorise" added anything to the law when first introduced in the 1911 Act (see, e.g. *Performing Right Society v Ciryl Theatrical Syndicate Ltd* [1924] 1 K.B. 1), but it had been held before then that a person was only liable for infringements committed by his servants or agents (see, e.g. *Karno v Paté Frères Ltd* (1909) 100 L.T. 260) and the effect of the Copyright Act 1911 was clearly to overrule this (*Falcon v Famous Players Film Co* [1926] 2 K.B. 474). See also *Fiel v Lemaire* (1939) 4 D.L.R. (Can.) 561

[887] *Ash v Hutchinson and Co. (Publishers) Ltd* [1936] Ch. 489; *ABKCO Music v Music Collection International Ltd* [1995] R.P.C. 657.

[888] Although the Report of Whitford Committee, Cmnd. 6732, recommended at para.749(iii) that it should.

[889] CDPA 1988 s.16(1).

[890] *ABKCO Music v Music Collection International Ltd* [1995] R.P.C. 657; *Football Dataco Ltd v Sportradar GmbH* [2010] EWHC 2911 (Ch) at para.30.

[891] *CBS Songs Ltd v Amstrad Plc* [1988] A.C. 1013; [1988] R.P.C. 567, HL citing, with apparent approval, Atkin L.J.'s statement in *Falcon v Famous Players Film Co.* [1926] 2 K.B. 474 at 499.

[892] *Falcon v Famous Players Film Co.* [1926] 2 K.B. 474, per Bankes L.J., following *Monckton v Pathé Frères Pathephone Ltd* [1914] 1 K.B. 395 and *Evans v E. Hulton & Co. Ltd* (1924) 131 L.T. 534. The phrase is meant to be read conjunctively: *Pensher Security Door Co Ltd v Sunderland City Council* [2000] R.P.C. 249, CA.

[893] *Amstrad Consumer Electronics Plc v British Phonographic Industry Ltd* [1986] F.S.R. 159, CA, per Lawton L.J. at 207, approved in *CBS Songs Ltd v Amstrad Plc* [1988] A.C. 1013 at 1055. It has been said that in this context "countenance" must be understood in its strongest dictionary meaning, namely, "give approval to, sanction, favour, encourage": *CCH Canadian Ltd v Law Society of Upper Canada* [2004] S.C.C. 13 (Sup. Ct. of Canada); [2004] F.S.R. 44, citing *The New Shorter Oxford English Dictionary* (1993), Vol.1, p.526.

[894] Per Whitford J. in *CBS Inc v Ames Records & Tapes Ltd* [1982] Ch. 91 at 106; [1981] R.P.C. 407, approved in *Amstrad Consumer Electronics Plc v British Phonographic Industry Ltd* [1986] F.S.R. 159 at 211, CA and in *CBS Songs Ltd v Amstrad Plc* [1988] A.C. 1013 at 1055; [1988] R.P.C. 567, HL.

do the act in contemplation that it will in fact be done,[895] or simply gives permission for it to be done.[896] Likewise, a person who asks another to do an act, the former having the power to give or refuse permission to do that act, will usually be taken to have authorised it,[897] and a person who commissions another to produce an article will usually impliedly grant him the right to make it and thus authorise him to do so.[898] Cases where a person simply puts the means of doing the infringing act into another's hands are more difficult.[899] A person does not necessarily authorise an act to be done merely because he intentionally puts into another's hands the means by which the infringing act can be done if those means can also be used for a perfectly legitimate purpose,[900] even where it is known that they will in fact inevitably be used for an infringing purpose.[901] This will be so particularly if the supplier has no control over how the means will be used,[902] since it is the essence of a grant or purported grant that the grantor has some degree of actual or apparent right to control the relevant actions of the grantee.[903] It follows that merely passing on something which will inevitably be used for infringement does not amount to authorising, and a lender or seller of an article does not authorise infringing use.[904] Something more is required, and in this a crucial factor will often be whether the defendant had any control over the use of the product once sold.[905] Where the defendant does retain control over the means in question, the facts may warrant a finding of implicit authorisation.[906] Generally whether a grant or purported grant to do the relevant act can be implied will depend on all the relevant circumstances including, in particular, the nature of the relationship between the alleged authoriser and the primary infringer, whether the equipment or other material supplied constitutes the means used to infringe, whether it is inevitable it will be used to infringe, the degree of control which the supplier retains and whether he has taken any steps to prevent infringement.[907] The older cases state that: (a) authorisation may be inferred from acts which fall

---

[895] *Evans v E. Hulton & Co Ltd* (1924) 131 L.T. 534.

[896] As in *ABKCO Music v Music Collection International Ltd* [1995] R.P.C. 657.

[897] *Standen Engineering Ltd v A. Spalding & Sons Ltd* [1984] F.S.R. 554, held in *Pensher Security Door Co Ltd v Sunderland City Council* [2000] R.P.C. 249, CA, not to have been impliedly overruled by *CBS Songs Ltd v Amstrad Plc* [1988] A.C. 1013.

[898] *Pensher Security Door Co Ltd v Sunderland City Council* [2000] R.P.C. 249.

[899] Whether or not the supply of equipment amounts to authorisation, such acts may well amount to secondary infringement. This is considered elsewhere; see paras 8–19 et seq., below.

[900] See the cases cited in the examples given below at para.7–149, below.

[901] *Amstrad Consumer Electronics Plc v British Phonographic Industry Ltd* [1986] F.S.R. 159 at 211, CA, and *CBS Songs Ltd v Amstrad Plc* [1988] A.C. 1013, HL, disapproving *RCA Corporation v John Fairfax & Sons Ltd* [1982] R.P.C. 91 (Sup Ct of New South Wales) on this point.

[902] *Vigneux v Canadian Performing Right Society Ltd* [1945] A.C. 108, cited with approval by Lawton and Glidewell LL.J. in the Court of Appeal in *Amstrad Consumer Electronics Plc v British Phonographic Industry Ltd* [1986] F.S.R. 159, whose judgments were themselves approved by the House of Lords in *CBS Songs Ltd v Amstrad Plc* [1988] A.C. 1013, HL.

[903] Per Slade L.J. in *Amstrad Consumer Electronics Plc v British Phonographic Industry Ltd* [1986] F.S.R. 159, whose judgment was approved by the House of Lords, in *CBS Songs Ltd v Amstrad Plc* [1988] A.C. 1013, HL. See also *RCA Corporation v John Fairfax & Sons Ltd* [1982] R.P.C. 91.

[904] *Philips Domestic Appliances and Personal Car BV v Salton Europe* [2004] EWHC 2092 (Ch) at para.44, applying the words of Lord Templeman in *CBC Songs Ltd v Amstrad Consumer Electronics PLC* [1988] A.C. 1013.

[905] *Philips Domestic Appliances and Personal Car BV v Salton Europe* [2004] EWHC 2092 (Ch) at para.44.

[906] *Moorhouse v University of New South Wales* [1976] R.P.C. 15, and *Amstrad Consumer Electronics Plc v British Phonographic Industry Ltd* [1986] F.S.R. 159 at 211.

[907] *Twentieth Century Fox Film Corporation v Newzbin Ltd* [2010] EWHC 608 (Ch); [2010] F.S.R. 21, para.90, emphasising that these are matters to be taken into account and may or may not be determinative, depending upon all the other circumstances. This summary was described as "helpful" in *Football Dataco Ltd v Sportradar GmbH* [2010] EWHC 2911 (Ch) at para.29.

short of being positive and direct; (b) even indifference may be sufficient[908]; and (c) whether what the defendant has done amounts to an authorisation will often be a matter of impression,[909] particularly in the case of advertisements which appear to encourage a particular activity.[910] In each case, it is no doubt a question of fact as to the true inference to be drawn from the conduct of the defendant,[911] but today it is likely to be a rare case that a sufficient inference can be drawn from such actions (or inaction). The mere failure to prevent infringement taking place when it could have been stopped will not amount to authorisation.[912] Ignorance of the fact that what will be done will be an infringement does not affect the question of liability.[913]

7–149   **Examples of "authorisation".** Many of the older reported cases are concerned with authorisation of the public performance of works. Where this question arises in the context of a performance in a place of public entertainment, the question of liability under s.25 of the Act will usually also arise.[914] As to authorisation, where a person engages performers for a public occasion, but in his absence and without his knowledge and without him suspecting, they perform works in infringement of copyright, he is clearly not liable for authorising, even though he has the power to direct them what to perform and to dismiss them if they refuse.[915] The older cases suggest that the position may be different if that person does not care whether the performance is an infringement or not and is present when it is given,[916] and also that where a person engages performers, and then approves a list of proposed titles which they submit, this will amount to authorisation.[917] These examples, must however, be regarded with caution in the light of the modern approach in *CBS Songs v Amstrad*, above. The facts of each case need to be looked at to see whether, for example, the performers looked to the person engaging them to give them the necessary permission to perform the material; or whether this was regarded as the performers' responsibility; or whether, for example, this was a matter to which no thought was given by either party. It is suggested that it is only in the first of these cases that there can have been authorisation. Simply approving a list of works to be performed can hardly amount to authorisation, since it does not reveal enough about what the assumptions were. It has been said that a broadcaster who knows that his broadcast will

---

[908] *Performing Right Society v Ciryl Theatrical Syndicate Ltd* [1924] 1 K.B. 1.

[909] *RCA Corporation v John Fairfax & Sons Ltd* [1982] R.P.C. 91.

[910] *WEA International Inc v Hanimex Corporation Ltd* (1987) 77 A.L.R. 456.

[911] *WEA International Inc v Hanimex Corporation Ltd* (1987) 77 A.L.R. 456

[912] *Durand v Molino* [2000] E.C.D.R. 320 (occupier of premises who at the public unveiling of a painting did not act to prevent a photographer taking a photograph of it did not thereby authorise its reproduction).

[913] *Performing Right Society Ltd v Bray U.D.C.* [1930] A.C. 377, PC. Although note *Brintons Ltd v Feltex Furnishings of New Zealand Ltd* [1991] 2 N.Z.L.R. 677 (High Ct of NZ) where it was held that a person who merely authorised another to make an article could not be liable for infringement unless he knew that the article was a copy of another work. The decision was apparently being based on the proposition that "there can only be copying if the infringer knows he is copying." This is not a correct statement of the law under CDPA 1988.

[914] See para.8–17, below.

[915] *Performing Right Society v Ciryl Theatrical Syndicate Ltd* [1924] 1 K.B. 1.

[916] *Monaghan v Taylor* (1885) 2 T.L.R. 685, a case decided before the Copyright Act 1911, where the issue was whether the defendant had caused or permitted a place to be used for public entertainment. See also *Bolton v London Exhibitions Ltd* (1898) 14 T.L.R. 550; *Green v Irish Independent Co Ltd* [1899] 1 I.R. 386; *Colburn v Simms* (1843) 2 Ha. 543 at 547.

[917] *Performing Right Society Ltd v Bray U.D.C.* [1930] A.C. 377, PC. See also *Australasian Performing Right Association Ltd v Canterbury-Bankstown Leagues Club Ltd* [1964–1965] N.S.W.R. 138; and *Australasian Performing Right Association Ltd v Koolman* [1969] N.Z.L.R. 273.

be performed in public at hotels and other public places authorises such public performance, but this cannot be correct.[918]

As already indicated, cases in which the defendant provides the means by which the infringement is committed sometimes cause difficulties. Again, in this context the question will sometimes also arise as to whether an act of secondary infringement under ss.24 or 26 has been committed.[919] Where a person places an order for the manufacture of an article upon another, the former having the power to prevent such manufacture, and supplies an example of the article to be copied, this will usually amount to authorisation.[920] Again, where a person sold the rights in a manuscript with a view to its publication, such publication being bound to infringe, this amounted to authorisation.[921] Where defendants hired out to a cinema proprietor a film whose exhibition was bound to be an infringement, they were held to have authorised that act.[922] It has been held that the seller of a record authorises its use,[923] which may on the particular facts be true, but whether he authorises its infringing use is a different question, since it may be used for non-infringing purposes, for example, performance in private.[924] The mere sale of a record would not today be held to be an authorisation of the public performance of the musical work embodied in it. Thus where a record library lent out records and simultaneously offered blank tapes for sale at a discount, it was held that no authorisation of home taping had occurred.[925] Usually a seller of a computer program will authorise its use,[926] and since any use of a program will inevitably involve its reproduction,[927] it is likely that where such use is unlicensed, or is not subject to one of the permitted acts,[928] and is thus an infringement, the seller will also infringe by authorising such use.

In *Amstrad*,[929] where the defendant sold hi-fi systems which included the facility for the high-speed duplication of cassette tapes, this was held not to amount to authorisation even though the almost inevitable consequence would be that purchasers would use such equipment to make infringing copies. Again, in *Vigneux*,[930] the supply of a coin-operated juke box on hire for a fixed rent to a restaurant, and of the records for use in it, did not, on the facts, amount to authorisation of public performance, the supplier having no control over the use of the

---

[918] Per Viscount Maugham in *Mellor v Australian Broadcasting Commission* [1940] A.C. 491. The point was not argued. A broadcaster has no control over whether or not an appropriate public performance licence is obtained.

[919] See paras 8–15 and 8–19, below.

[920] *Standen Engineering Ltd v A. Spalding & Sons Ltd* [1984] F.S.R. 554.

[921] *Evans v E. Hulton & Co. Ltd* (1924) 131 L.T. 534.

[922] *Falcon v Famous Players Film Co.* [1926] 2 K.B. 474; *Fenning Film Service Ltd v Wolverhampton, etc. Cinemas Ltd* [1914] 3 K.B. 1171; compare, prior to the Copyright Act 1911, *Glenville v Selig Polyscope Co* (1911) 27 T.L.R. 554; see also *Karno v Pathé Frères Ltd* (1909) 100 L.T. 260.

[923] *Monckton v Pathé Frères Pathephone Ltd* [1914] 1 K.B. 395.

[924] The proposition from *Monckton* cited in the text was apparently approved by the House of Lords in *CBS Songs Ltd v Amstrad Plc* [1988] A.C. 1013; [1988] R.P.C. 567, on the basis that in the *Monckton* case "a performance of the musical work by the use of the record was bound to be an infringing use and the record was sold for that purpose." But only a *public* performance of a musical work is bound to be an infringement. Playing the record in private will not be.

[925] *CBS Inc v Ames Records & Tapes Ltd* [1982] Ch. 91; [1981] R.P.C. 407. See also *A. & M. Records Inc v Audio Magnetics Incorporated (U.K.) Ltd* [1979] F.S.R. 1; *Paterson Zochonis Ltd v Merfarken Packaging Ltd* [1983] F.S.R. 273.

[926] *Ibcos Computers Ltd v Barclays Mercantile Highland Finance Ltd* [1994] F.S.R. 275.

[927] See para.7–19, above.

[928] See Ch.9, below.

[929] *CBS Songs Ltd v Amstrad Plc* [1988] A.C. 1013.

[930] *Vigneux v Canadian Performing Right Society Ltd* [1945] A.C. 108. The case was decided under the special provisions of the Canadian Act and the decision on "authorisation" was strictly obiter, but affirmed by the Supreme Court of Canada in *Muzak Corp v Composers, Authors and Publishers Association of Canada* [1953] S S.C.R. 182. See also *Georges de Tervagne v Town of Beloeil*, (1993) 50 C.P.R. (3d) 419, and the next footnote.

machine or as to whether it was available to customers. But a case on similar facts was distinguished in the later Australian decision of *Winstone*, where it was held that the fact that the defendant supplied the records for use in the juke box gave the defendant sufficient control over its use to amount to authorisation.[931] Again, in *Moorhouse*,[932] another Australian case, where a university provided copying machines close to its library, retaining control over them and over the books which were copied using the machines, and having reasonable grounds to suspect that infringements might occur if no adequate precautions to prevent this happening were taken, this was held to amount to authorisation. *Moorhouse* has not been followed by the Supreme Court of Canada in *CCH Canadian*[933] in a similar factual situation, the important points being that not all works in the library were copyright works, some users would have had a defence of fair dealing, and the library had posted a notice above the photocopiers disclaiming responsibility for infringing copies. How an English court would decide cases on these facts today is uncertain[934] but each case has to be looked at on its own facts. If a defendant supplies music equipment to another on the basis the user must obtain whatever licences are necessary to play the music in public,[935] this could hardly justify a finding of authorisation.[936] If, however, the basis on which the equipment was supplied by the defendant was that music could be played without fear of any infringement, since all necessary permissions had been obtained, the position would be different. As already noted, the 1988 Act widened the categories of secondary infringements to include the provision of apparatus, with knowledge, for the purpose of an infringing performance.[937] In the case of a photocopier made available by a library or photocopy shop, it is suggested that the decision in *CCH Canadian* is a better guide than that in *Moorhouse*. In contrast, the sale and supply of the decoder cards to enable customers to view encrypted broadcasts will almost inevitably amount to authorisation. Such a decoder card has one purpose only, which is to permit the customer to have access to what he would otherwise be denied and in this sense it is an authorisation in physical form. In absence of a statement or some other indication to the contrary, the supply of

---

[931] *Winstone v Wurlitzer, etc.* [1946] V.L.R. 338. However, in *Vigneux*, the defendant also supplied the records for use in the juke box and to this extent the case seems hard to distinguish on the facts, although this was not a matter which was commented on by the court. See also the comments of Whitford J. in *CBS Inc v Ames Records & Tapes Ltd* [1982] Ch.91. *Vigneux* was also distinguished in *Winstone* on the ground that in *Winstone* the juke box was provided on a profit-sharing arrangement rather than a fixed fee, so that the arrangement was a joint venture for which the defendant was liable.

[932] *Moorhouse v University of New South Wales* [1976] R.P.C. 151 (High Ct of Aus). There are extensive provisions in the CDPA 1988 regulating the extent of copying permitted by libraries. See paras 9–115 et seq., below.

[933] *CCH Canadian Ltd v Law Society of Upper Canada* [2004] SCC 13 (Sup Ct); [2004] F.S.R. 44, stating that *Moorhouse* was not consistent with the previous British and Canadian approaches to the question. The court also applied the principle, extracted from Canadian authorities, that courts should presume that a person who authorises an activity does so only so far as it is in accordance with the law, although this presumption may be rebutted if it is shown that a certain relationship or degree of control existed between the alleged authoriser and the persons who committed the copyright infringement. It is suggested that this is not a principle of English law.

[934] Dicta from *Vigneux* were cited in the Court of Appeal and the House of Lords in the *Amstrad* decisions, but the decision on the facts was not commented upon. *Winstone* was cited to the House of Lords in *CBS Songs Ltd v Amstrad* [1988] A.C. 1013 but not commented upon. *Moorhouse* appears to have been regarded in *Amstrad Consumer Electronics Plc v British Phonographic Industry Ltd* [1986] F.S.R. 159 as correct on its own facts, which justified a finding of implicit authorisation: at 211.

[935] For example from Performing Right Society Ltd or Phonographic Performance Ltd (as to which see paras 27–65 and 27–66, below, respectively).

[936] See, e.g. *Keays v Dempster* [1994] F.S.R. 554 (author merely choosing photographs for his book, leaving it to the publisher to clear any rights).

[937] See paras 8–19 et seq., below.

decoder cards to customers will almost always therefore constitute authorisation to use the decoder cards for the purpose for which they were supplied.[938]

File sharing. Authorisation will often be an act of infringement which takes place in the case of unlawful file sharing.[939] However, the facts need to be examined in detail to analyse what has taken place, particularly where it is alleged that the operator of website has authorised infringement by members of the public who have used the website to engage in unlawful file-sharing. So, for example, such an operator was found to have infringed where its customers were able to access a system which provided a searching and indexing facility and a guide to the materials posted by third parties (file-sharers) on Usenet, such that they could search and browse not only by reference to the names of particular works but also, for example, by reference to genre. This facility extended beyond indexing and categorisation and saved members the task of manually locating and identifying items of interest, and further identified the individual user who had posted the content to Usenet, together with details of particular works available to be shared. Upon the press of a button, the facility also created a file which was delivered to the member's computer where it might be stored and which, when run by the member, caused a copy to be made on the member's computer of works made available by another file-sharer. Once, therefore, a work was entered onto the defendant's index, use of the facility was bound to result in that work being copied. In the context of the other features of defendant's operation, the facility provided the means for infringement, was created by the defendant and was entirely within the defendant's control. Also significant was the fact that a very large proportion of the content of the indexed works was commercial and so very likely to be protected by copyright. This had not led the defendant to install some kind of filtering system which, on the evidence, it could easily have done. On the contrary, it had actively engaged editors to make reports on various copyright works, had rewarded them for so doing and had instructed and guided them to include URLs in their reports. The contractual restrictions which had been placed upon editors and members in relation to infringing activity were held to be window dressing, being inconsistent with the structure and operation of the defendant's system and the advice given to editors both generally and specifically. Moreover, the defendant had taken no steps to remove editors who, to the defendant's knowledge, had posted reports on infringing materials. So far as the defendant's members were concerned they had been given ready access to all the films and programmes in the various categories of copyright works, with detailed information about them and the facility to download them. A reasonable member would therefore deduce from the defendant's activities that it purported to possess the authority to grant any required permission to copy any film that a member might choose from the listed categories of works and that the defendant had sanctioned, approved and countenanced the copying of the claimants' works.[940]

Other matters. Obviously, unless the act authorised is itself an infringement, no

7–150

7–151

---

[938] *Football Association Premier League Ltd v QC Leisure* [2008] EWHC 1411 (Ch); [2008] F.S.R. 32 (sale of cards to publicans to enable customers to watch television programmes in pubs), Kitchin J. observing that decoder cards were quite different to the twin-tape recorders the subject of the *Amstrad* decision which might or might not have been used to perform the allegedly infringing activities and that there was nothing inherent in the sale which suggested that Amstrad had the authority to allow those activities to be carried out.

[939] For a general discussion of the problem, the UK's approach to it via the Digital Economy Act 2010, see para.21–288, below.

[940] *Twentieth Century Fox Film Corporation v Newzbin Ltd* [2010] EWHC 608 (Ch); [2010] F.S.R. 21. For derisions on the facts in other jurisdictions, see *Cooper v Universal Music Australia Pty Ltd* [2006] FCAFC 187 and *Roadshow Films Pty Ltd v iiNet Ltd (No3)* [2010] FCA 24.

act of authorisation can amount to an infringement either.[941] It is unclear whether, in order for the tort of authorisation to be complete, the act authorised must itself have been committed. There is authority that this is the correct position,[942] and if it were otherwise an instruction to do an act which was revoked before the act was carried out would be an infringement, although in suitable circumstances a case for a *quia timet* injunction could no doubt be made out.[943] So, where a defendant had the copyright owner's consent to distribute a film, and had consequently authorised its showing in public by third-party exhibitors, he was not liable for authorisation where the copyright owner later revoked his consent before the showings had taken place.[944] Nevertheless, the point must be in doubt following the decision in *MCA Records Inc v Charly Records Ltd*[945] There, a licence had been granted by a defendant more than six years before the writ had been issued, but some infringing acts committed under the licence had taken place within the six-year period. The issue was whether the acts of authorisation had also taken place within this period. By analogy with cases concerning the grant of an unlawful subtenancy, it was held that the authorisation was a one-off event which had taken place on the grant of the licence and was not renewed from time to time as each act of infringement was committed. Further, and probably obiter, it was held that authorisation "is complete when the authorisation is effected; it is not a tort which is completed only once an infringing act is carried out in pursuance of the authorisation". However, none of the above cases to the contrary effect are referred to in the judgment, and it is not clear whether they were cited to the court.[946] Of course, such a ruling has attractions as a matter of practice, not least because otherwise a licensor might be liable over the full term of the licence, which might last as long as the term of copyright in the work or works in question. Against this, the copyright owner will usually have no means of knowing of the act of authorisation until, at the earliest, an act of infringement under the licence is committed. Again, from the copyright owner's point of view, a licensor is often of greater financial worth than a licensee when it comes to pursuing any claim for damages or profits.

It has been said that it is necessary to plead some specific authorisation of an actual breach of copyright affecting a particular claimant, and that it is not sufficient to plead authorisation at large.[947] However, it is suggested that there is no reason in principle why a sufficiently clear act of authorisation should not amount to an infringement even though not addressed to a specific person.

---

[941] *ABKCO Music & Records Inc v Music Collection International Ltd* [1995] R.P.C. 657 at 660; *Nelson v Rye* [1996] F.S.R. 313; *Composers, Authors and Publishers Association of Canada Ltd v CTV Television Network Ltd* [1968] S.C.R. 676, at 680.

[942] *Performing Right Society Ltd v Mitchell and Booker, etc. Ltd* [1924] 1 K.B. 762 at 773; *Moorhouse v University of New South Wales* [1975] R.P.C. 454 at 467; *RCA Corporation v John Fairfax & Son Ltd* [1982] R.P.C. 91; *Copyright Agency Ltd v Haines* [1982] F.S.R. 331; *WEA International Inc v Hanimex Corp. Ltd* (1987) 77 A.L.R. 456.

[943] *RCA Corporation v John Fairfax & Sons Ltd* [1982] R.P.C. 91 (*quia timet* injunction refused); *WEA International Inc v Hanimex Corp. Ltd* (1987) 77 A.L.R. 456.

[944] *Century Communications Ltd v Mayfair Entertainment U.K. Ltd* [1993] E.M.L.R. 335.

[945] [2000] E.M.L.R. 743. *Fenning Film Service Ltd v Wolverhampton, etc. Cinemas Ltd* [1914] 3 K.B. 1171 may be authority to the same effect (see, e.g. *Performing Right Society Ltd v Mitchell and Booker, etc. Ltd* [1924] 1 K.B. 762).

[946] See further, Dickens, "When Is an Authorisation an Authorisation?" [2000] E.I.P.R. 339.

[947] *A. & M. Records Inc v Audio Magnetics Incorporated (U.K.) Ltd* [1979] F.S.R. 1.

SECONDARY INFRINGEMENT OF COPYRIGHT

1. INTRODUCTION

The 1988 Act provides for a class of secondary infringements, the principal   **8–01**
characteristic of which is that it is a necessary ingredient of the tort that the defendant must have a degree of "guilty knowledge" before he can be liable. The acts are termed secondary because they generally depend upon a primary act of infringement having first taken place, for example the making of an infringing copy.[1] The 1988 Act does not provide that a person who authorises a secondary act of infringement is liable, although a person may nevertheless be liable for such an act under the common law, for example as a joint tortfeasor.[2]

The 1988 Act provides for three broad classes of secondary infringement. The first consists of various dealings with infringing copies, the second of providing the means for making infringing copies and the third of permitting or enabling infringing performances to take place. The three classes will be considered in turn.

2. DEALINGS IN INFRINGING COPIES

A. INTRODUCTION

The main acts of secondary infringement concern dealings with infringing copies.   **8–02**
Thus the copyright in a work is infringed by any person who, without the licence of the copyright owner:
   (a) possesses in the course of a business,
   (b) sells or lets for hire, or offers or exposes for sale or hire,
   (c) in the course of a business exhibits in public or distributes, or
   (d) distributes otherwise than in the course of a business to such an extent as to affect prejudicially the owner of the copyright,
an article which is, and which he knows or has reason to believe is, an infringing

---

[1] This is an oversimplification in the case, e.g. of importation. See para.8–05, below.
[2] As to authorisation, see para.7–146, above, and as to joint tortfeasors see para.21–42, below. Note that the 1977 Copyright ("Whitford") Committee, Cmmd.6732, para.749(iii), recommended that persons authorising indirect infringements should be liable.

copy of the work.[3] The copyright in a work is also infringed by any person who, without the licence of the copyright owner, imports into the United Kingdom, otherwise than for his private and domestic use,[4] an article which is, and which he knows or has reason to believe is, an infringing copy of the work.[5] These provisions are principally directed, not to manufacturers, but to third parties who deal in infringing articles supplied to them,[6] and enable a copyright owner to limit the further dissemination of such copies. The need for a claimant to prove the element of "guilty knowledge" reflects the fact that traders and others may handle infringing copies without necessarily suspecting or having the means of knowing that they are infringing. As already noted, there may be circumstances in which someone who sells or distributes infringing copies is also liable for the primary act of infringement of issuing copies to the public,[7] in respect of which "guilty knowledge" is not an element. The point is discussed in relation to the treatment of issue to the public.[8] To an extent, these secondary rights granted to copyright owners can be regarded as an aspect of the distribution right although, of course, they only relate to infringing copies and not legitimate copies.

B. INFRINGING COPY

8–03   An article is an infringing copy if its making constituted an infringement of the copyright in the work in question.[9] An article is also an infringing copy if:

(a) it has been or is proposed to be imported into the United Kingdom, and

(b) its making in the United Kingdom would have constituted an infringement of the copyright in the work in question, or a breach of an exclusive licence agreement relating to that work.[10]

There are also a number of provisions in the 1988 Act whereby copies of works whose making did not constitute an infringement of copyright, because statutory exemptions applied, are nevertheless to be treated as infringing copies in certain subsequent events.[11] These provisions are dealt with elsewhere.[12] A device such as a silicon wafer or other temporary computer memory in which a work is only fleetingly copied is nonetheless an article for this purpose.[13] Where in any proceedings it is proved that an article is a copy of a work, and that copyright subsists or has at any time subsisted in the work, then for the purposes of deciding whether the article is an infringing copy it is to be presumed until the contrary is proved that the article was made at a time when copyright subsisted in the work.[14] An article becomes an infringing article because of the manner in which it is made and so whether it is an infringing article must be determined by refer-

---

[3] CDPA 1988 s.23.

[4] In the context of CDPA 1988 s.85 the taking of a photograph for "private and domestic purposes" has been said to envisaged ordinary home life or "something close to it": *Mahmood v Galloway* [2006] EWHC 1286 (QB); [2006] E.M.L.R. 26, para.18.

[5] s.22.

[6] *Paterson Zochonis Ltd v Merfarken Packaging Ltd* [1983] F.S.R. 273.

[7] i.e. under CDPA 1988 s.18.

[8] See para.7–91, above.

[9] CDPA 1988 s.27(2). Although for the purposes of infringement the 1988 Act only applies in relation to acts done after August 1, 1989, the article dealt in may of course have been made before this date. For the purposes of determining whether an article is an infringing copy, the 1956 Act is to be applied in relation to an article made after June 1, 1957 and before August 1, 1989, and the 1911 Act is to be applied to an article made before June 1, 1957 (see CDPA 1988 Sch.1 para.14(3)). In relation to articles made on or after August 1, 1989, the 1988 Act is to be applied.

[10] s.27(3). As to the definition of an exclusive licence, see s.92(1) and para.5–208, above.

[11] s.27(6).

[12] See Ch.9, below.

[13] *Kabushiki Kaisha Sony Computer Entertainment Inc (also trading as Sony Computer Entertainment Inc.) v Ball* [2004] EWHC 1738 (Ch); [2004] E.C.D.R. 33; [2005] F.S.R. 9.

[14] CDPA 1988 s.27(4).

ence to that moment. It is irrelevant whether it remains in that state.[15] Thus a silicon chip and other forms of computer memory are capable of being an "article" and for present purposes it does not matter that a copy of a work is to be found in the chip only transiently: for this short period of time it is capable of being an infringing article.[16] An article such as a door does not cease to be an "article" simply because it becomes integrated into a building.[17]

The making was an infringement. Little more needs to be said about this   **8–04** ingredient. The making of the copy will have been an infringement if the reproduction right was thereby infringed.[18]

Imported copies. An article will also be an infringing copy if its making in the   **8–05** United Kingdom would have constituted an infringement of copyright or a breach of an exclusive licence agreement relating to that work. This definition therefore proceeds on a hypothetical basis as to the place and circumstances in which the article was made. The assumption which has to be made is that the copy was made in the United Kingdom by the person who actually made it.[19] The section therefore covers the cases where:

(a) The article was made abroad by a third party who has no interest in the copyright and no licence of any kind.

(b) The article was made abroad by a person who owned the copyright in that territory (but not in the United Kingdom) or who had a licence in that territory (but not for the United Kingdom).

(c) The article was made abroad by a person who owned the copyright in the United Kingdom but who had granted an exclusive licence for the United Kingdom.[20] In this case, the making of the copy by the copyright owner in the United Kingdom would not have constituted an infringement of copyright but would have constituted a breach of the exclusive licence. It is therefore an infringing copy.[21]

Thus the owner of the UK copyright, or the UK exclusive licensee, can object to the importation of and subsequent dealings in copies made abroad without his licence, subject to EC law principles.[22] This is so even though the articles made abroad were legitimately purchased there on the open market (so-called "grey copies"), since the sale of articles in the ordinary course of business in one territory without restriction on resale does not carry with it any implied licence to import and sell those articles in another territory.[23] The purchaser obtains the same rights as the purchaser of any other chattel, and the rights which flow from acquisition and ownership do not involve any such implied licence.[24] United Kingdom copyright law has never recognised the principle of "international

---

[15] *Kabushiki Kaisha Sony Computer Entertainment Inc v Ball* [2004] EWHC 1738 (Ch); [2004] E.C.D.R. 33; [2005] F.S.R. 9, para.15.

[16] *Kabushiki Kaisha Sony Computer Entertainment Inc v Ball* [2004] EWHC 1738 (Ch), para.15.

[17] *Pensher Security Door Co. Ltd v Sunderland City Council* [2000] R.P.C. 249, CA.

[18] As to the reproduction right, see CDPA 1988 s.17 and paras 7–09 et seq., above.

[19] See *C.B.S. Ltd v Charmdale Record Distributors Ltd* [1981] Ch. 91; [1980] F.S.R. 289; *Polydor Ltd v Harlequin Record Shops Ltd* [1980] F.S.R. 194 and 362, CA. These cases were decided under the slightly different provisions of ss.5(2) and (3) of the 1956 Act.

[20] As to the meaning of exclusive licence, see CDPA 1988 s.92 and paras 5–208 et seq., above.

[21] The position under the 1956 Act was different. See *C.B.S. Ltd v Charmdale Record Distributors Ltd* [1981] Ch. 91 and *Polydor Ltd v Harlequin Record Shops Ltd* [1980] F.S.R. 194 and 362, CA.

[22] See para.8–06, below.

[23] See para.5–221.

[24] *Time-Life International (Nederlands) N.V. v Interstate Parcel Express Co. Pty Ltd* [1978] F.S.R. 251; *Polydor Ltd v Harlequin Record Shops* [1980] F.S.R. 362; *Penguin Books Ltd v India Book Distributors* [1985] F.S.R. 120; *R. & A. Bailey & Co. Ltd v Boccaccio Pty Ltd* (1988) 77 A.L.R.

exhaustion", and is now bound by European Directives not to do so in relation to sales outside the European Community.[25]

8–06 **The European Communities Act 1972.** The 1988 Act expressly provides that nothing in the provisions of the 1988 Act shall be construed as applying to an article which may be lawfully imported into the United Kingdom by virtue of any enforceable Community right within the meaning of s.2(1) of the European Communities Act 1972.[26] Thus if an article is in free circulation within the European Economic Area it will not be an infringing copy for any purpose.[27] This point is reinforced by a number of provisions in European Directives in this field, dealing with the question of exhaustion of rights. Thus, most recently, art.4(2) of the Information Society Directive[28] stipulates that the distribution right is not exhausted within the Community in respect of the original or copies of the work, except where the first sale or other transfer of ownership in the Community of that object is made by the rightholder or with his consent. This does not apply in relation to first sale outside the Community.[29] Similar provision had been made in earlier Directives dealing with computer programs,[30] related rights subject matter[31] and copyright databases.[32] The bare fact that an article has been sold in a Community territory, and the owner did not prevent it, will not be enough to raise a defence in the absence of any evidence that the copyright owner knew that the sale was taking place and could have prevented it, and by inference must be taken to have authorised it.[33] In *Independiente Ltd v Music Trading On-Line (HK) Ltd* [2007] EWHC 533 (Ch); [2007] F.S.R. 21, the Judge appeared on one reading of para.[21] of his judgment to assimilate the test for whether an article has been placed on the market in the EEA with the consent of the copyright owner with that applicable in the field of trade marks. This is plainly right: see *Mastercigars Direct Ltd v Hunters & Frankau Ltd* [2007] EWCA Civ 176; [2007] R.P.C. 24; [2007] E.T.M.R. 44 (now the leading trade mark case on this point in this jurisdiction) at para.14. In the latter case, the Court of Appeal accepted certain propositions (paras 16, 17) which can be adapted to the copyright field as follows:

(1) For there to be consent such consent must relate to each individual item of the product in respect of which exhaustion of rights is pleaded.

(2) Consent to the marketing of goods within the EEA may be implied where it is to be inferred from facts and circumstances which unequivocally demonstrate that the copyright owner has renounced his right to oppose placing of the goods on the market within the EEA.

(3) Implied consent cannot be inferred from:

(a) the fact that the copyright owner has not communicated his opposi-

---

177; *Computermate Products (Aus) Pty Ltd v Ozi-Soft Pty Ltd* (1988) 83 A.L.R. 492. As to implied licences generally, see para.5–217 et seq., above.

[25] See para.8–06, below.

[26] CDPA 1988 s.27(5).

[27] *KK Sony Entertainment v Pacific Game Technology (Holding) Ltd* [2006] EWHC 2509 (Ch), (exhaustion principles apply to copyright works). As to the effects of Community law generally, see Ch.24, below.

[28] Directive 2001/29/EC.

[29] Recital 28. Indeed, it is not open to Member States to provide that the distribution right in respect of the original or copies of a work is exhausted where the first sale or other transfer of ownership is made by the holder of that right or with his consent outside the Community: *Laserdisken ApS v Kulturministeriet* (C–479/04) [2007] 1 C.M.L.R. 6; [2006] E.C.D.R. 30.

[30] Computer Programs Directive 91/250 art.5(c).

[31] Rental and Related Rights Directive 92/100 art.9(2). The Rental and Related Rights Directive and its amendments have now been codified as Directive 2006/115/EC: [2006] OJ L376/28.

[32] Database Directive 96/9 art.5(c).

[33] *EMI Records Ltd v The CD Specialists Ltd* [1992] F.S.R. 70. Again, see more generally, Ch.25.

tion to marketing within the EEA to all subsequent purchasers of goods placed on the market outside the EEA; or
(b) the fact that the goods carry no warning of a prohibition on their being placed on the market within the EEA; or
(c) the fact that the copyright owner has transferred the ownership of the goods without imposing a contractual reservation and that, according to the law governing the contract, the rights transferred include, in the absence of such a reservation, an unlimited right of resale or at least a right to market the goods within the EEA.
(4) The onus lies on the defendant to prove consent express or implied.

C. TERRITORIAL EXTENT

Unlike the case of primary acts of infringement,[34] and the equivalent provisions of the 1956 Act,[35] the acts of secondary infringement, apart from importation, are not restricted in express terms in the 1988 Act to acts done in the United Kingdom. It is suggested, however, that it is clear that they are. This Part of the Act is extended in the first place only to England and Wales, Scotland and Northern Ireland,[36] and the general principle of statutory construction is that unless the contrary is expressly enacted, English legislation does not extend to acts of foreigners committed outside the jurisdiction.[37] Thus if an article whose making in the United Kingdom constituted an infringement of copyright, and which was thus an infringing copy, subsequently came into the hands of someone in a foreign jurisdiction, it would be surprising if the legislature intended that person should become liable under the 1988 Act for selling the article in the foreign jurisdiction even where he had the necessary knowledge.

8–07

In these circumstances, the provision that an "infringing copy" may include one which is "proposed" to be imported into the United Kingdom requires explanation, since it apparently expressly contemplates a situation in which a dealing with an article which has not yet been imported into the United Kingdom may be an infringement. First, although to "import" is not defined in the Act, it probably means to bring an article from abroad into port, such that the carriage is ended or its continuity is in some way broken.[38] Secondly, an act done on a British ship, aircraft or hovercraft will be treated as being done in the United Kingdom[39] and, in addition, the territorial waters of the United Kingdom are to be treated as part of the United Kingdom.[40] It follows that acts can be done in what is the United Kingdom for the purposes of the Act, for example on board a British ship, in relation to articles which are "proposed to be imported into the United Kingdom". If this is correct, then it would be an infringement of copyright to possess, with knowledge, a piratical article on board a British ship if it was proposed to import it into the United Kingdom, but it would not be an infringement to possess such an article on board a British ship if the article was neither made in the United Kingdom nor had ever been imported into the United Kingdom and it was not proposed to import it.

---

[34] See CDPA 1988 s.16(1).
[35] Copyright Act 1956 ss.5(2), (3), 16(2), (3). See also *Def Lepp Music v Stuart-Brown* [1986] R.P.C. 273, confirming that the provisions of the 1956 Act were expressly confined to acts done in the UK or other countries to which the Act was extended. The same principle underlies the decision in *Pearce v Ove Arup Partnership Ltd* [2000] Ch. 403.
[36] CDPA 1988 s.157(1).
[37] See *Ex parte Blain* (1879) 12 Ch. D. 522; *Clark v Oceanic Contractors Inc.* [1983] 2 A.C. 130; *ABKCO Music v Music Collection International Ltd* [1995] R.P.C. 657.
[38] See para.8–14, below, in relation to infringement by importation.
[39] CDPA 1988 s.162.
[40] s.161.

D. Knowledge

8–08 **Necessity to prove knowledge.** As has been seen, in relation to secondary infringements, it is necessary to prove that the defendant knew or had reason to believe he was dealing with an article which was an infringing copy of the work. Two states of mind are therefore sufficient for this purpose: actual knowledge or constructive knowledge. The 1988 Act effected a change of the law in this area: under the 1911 and 1956 Acts a defendant was liable only if he knew the making of the copy was an infringement,[41] although some of the cases decided under these provisions came close to making a defendant liable who had only constructive knowledge.[42] The clear intention behind these provisions of the 1988 Act was to relax the requirement of guilty knowledge in favour of a claimant.[43] Cases decided under the 1956 and 1911 Acts[44] are therefore generally not useful authorities for the purpose of construing the constructive knowledge limb of the 1988 Act.[45]

8–09 **Actual knowledge.**[46] The question is one of fact and will usually turn on the evidence of the defendant's actions and what he knew and did. The burden of proof is on the claimant and has been described as a heavy one.[47] Strictly, turning a blind eye, or "Nelsonian" knowledge, is a case of actual knowledge since the defendant merely averts his gaze from what he knows to be there. A person who deliberately refrains from inquiry and shuts his eyes to that which is obvious to him (and which he therefore knows) cannot therefore be heard to say that he lacks the requisite knowledge.[48] The provisions, however, contemplate specific knowledge about the circumstances in which a specific article was made and it may be that a defendant's general knowledge that an article may be an infringing copy will not be sufficient to fix him with knowledge, for example, where he is in possession of a large number of articles, some of which he knows may infringe and some of which may not.[49] Under the 1956 Act, a defendant was taken to have had actual knowledge if he knew all the relevant facts but was under a mistake of law or ignorant as their effect.[50] This is still good law[51] although the point is now likely to be academic in the light of the alternative constructive knowledge limb.

8–10 **Constructive knowledge.** The words "has reason to believe" should be construed in accordance with their ordinary meaning. In particular:

---

[41] Copyright Act 1956 ss.5(2), (3), 16(2), (3). For the cases decided on this point, see the next footnote and *Van Dusen v Kritz* [1936] 2 K.B. 176; *R.C.A. Corporation v Custom Cleared Sales Pty Ltd* [1978] F.S.R. 576; applied in *Politechnika v Dallas Print Transfers Ltd* [1982] F.S.R. 529; *Hoover Plc v George Hulme Ltd* [1982] F.S.R. 565 and *Hooi v Brophy* (1984) 52 A.L.R. 710. See also *International Business Machines Corp. v Computer Imports Ltd* [1989] 2 N.Z.L.R. 395.

[42] See, e.g. *Albert v Hoffnung & Co. Ltd* [1921] 22 S.R. (N.S.W.) 75, followed in *Infabrics Ltd v Jaytex Shirt Co. Ltd* [1978] F.S.R. 451 (at first instance). See also *Gramophone Co. Ltd v Music Machine (Pty) Ltd* [1973] 3 S.A.L.R. 188.

[43] See, e.g. the White Paper: Intellectual Property and Innovation, Cmnd.9712, para.12.12.

[44] Such as *Van Dusen v Kritz* [1936] 2 K.B. 176; *Hoover Plc v George Hulme (Stockport) Ltd* [1982] F.S.R. 565.

[45] *LA Gear Inc. v Hi-Tec Sports Plc* [1992] F.S.R. 121.

[46] Cases decided under the 1956 and 1911 Acts are potentially relevant on the issue of actual knowledge, but borderline cases will no doubt usually be decided now under the constructive knowledge limb.

[47] *Infabrics Ltd v Jaytex Shirt Co. Ltd* [1978] F.S.R. 451 (at first instance); *Sillitoe v McGraw-Hill Book Co.* [1983] F.S.R. 545.

[48] *Columbia Picture Industries v Robinson* [1987] Ch. 38; [1986] F.S.R. 367.

[49] *Columbia Picture Industries v Robinson* [1987] Ch. 38. The point is of limited importance now, given the alternative constructive knowledge test.

[50] *Sillitoe v McGraw-Hill Book Co.* [1983] F.S.R. 545 (decided under the 1956 Act). See also *International Business Machines Corp. v Computer Imports Ltd* [1989] 2 N.Z.L.R. 395 at 418.

[51] *ZYX Music GmbH v King* [1997] 2 All E.R. 129, CA, applying *Sillitoe v McGraw-Hill Book Co.* [1983] F.S.R. 545.

(a) "Reason to believe" involves a concept of knowledge of facts from which a reasonable man would arrive at the relevant belief. The test is thus an objective one;

(b) Facts from which a reasonable man might *suspect* the relevant conclusion are not enough;

(c) The section connotes the allowance of a period of time to enable the reasonable man to evaluate the facts to convert them into a reasonable belief.[52]

The reasonable man will be taken to be a reasonable man in the position of the defendant and with his knowledge and experience.[53] If a defendant has knowledge of relevant facts giving grounds for belief that is all that is necessary: it is no defence that the defendant did not in fact believe the copies to be infringing[54] or for a defendant to say that although he knew the facts he nevertheless believed that as a matter of law no infringement would be committed, even if this was on the basis of legal advice.[55] Mere suspicion, however, is not enough.[56] Where a person is not aware that he is dealing in infringing goods, he must therefore be given notice of the facts, commonly by letter, before a prima facie case can be made that further dealings by him will amount to infringement. Sufficient information must be given to suggest to the recipient that an infringement will be committed if he continues to deal in the articles in question. The information must not be of such a general nature that the recipient can form no proper view as to what is being alleged.[57] Thus usually it will be necessary to identify the copyright work in question, and if a copy is not supplied then at least facilities should be offered for its inspection. It is not, however, necessary for a person to have seen a copy of the relevant copyright work before he can be said to have reason to believe that an article is an infringing copy. Each case will turn on its own facts. For example, where a claim of infringement is made against a person who knows that his article is similar to and has probably been copied from the claimant's corresponding article, and a reasonable man would know that the claimant's article was made from drawings in which copyright subsisted, he will have "reason to believe" for this purpose.[58] As to the period of notice, as already noted, a period of time must be allowed to enable the reasonable man to evaluate the facts to convert them into a reasonable belief,[59] or for what may be grounds for suspicion to harden into grounds for belief,[60] whether or not the defendant actually believes it. A person is not fixed with knowledge at the instant he receives notice of a claim. A period of 14 days is often taken as sufficient[61] but in each

---

[52] *LA Gear Inc. v Hi-Tec Sports Plc* [1992] F.S.R. 121, CA; *Linpac Mouldings Ltd v Eagleton Direct Export Ltd* [1994] F.S.R. 545, CA.

[53] *ZYX Music GmbH v King* [1995] F.S.R. 566 at 578 (knowledge of reasonable record distributor in defendant's position); *Raben Footwear Pty Ltd v Polygram Records Inc.* (1997) 37 I.P.R. 417 (regard to be had "to the knowledge, capacity and circumstances of the particular defendant").

[54] *Nouveau Fabrics Ltd v Voyage Decoration Ltd* [2004] EWHC 895, Ch. D.

[55] *ZYX Music GmbH v King* [1997] 2 All E.R. 129, CA, applying *Sillitoe v McGraw-Hill Book Co.* [1983] F.S.R. 545 (decided under the 1956 Act). See also *International Business Machines Corp. v Computer Imports Ltd* [1989] 2 N.Z.L.R. 395 at 418. In *Handi-Craft Company v B Free World Ltd* [2007] EWHC 10 (Pat); [2007] E.C.D.R. 21, on appeal but not on this point [2008] EWCA Civ 868, while acknowledging that ignorance of the law was not an excuse, the court observed that it was all the more important when it is intended to make laymen defendants in infringement actions that proper advance notice is given, para.172.

[56] *ZYX Music GmbH v King* [1995] 3 All E.R. 1.

[57] *Hoover Plc v George Hulme Stockport Ltd* [1982] F.S.R. 565.

[58] *Pensher Security Door Co. Ltd v Sunderland City Council* [2000] R.P.C. 249, CA.

[59] *L.A. Gear Inc. v Hi-Tec Sports Plc* [1992] F.S.R. 121, CA. For the earlier cases, which were to the same effect, see, e.g. *Van Dusen v Kritz* [1936] 2 K.B. 176; *R.C.A. Corporation v Custom Cleared Sales Pty Ltd* [1978] F.S.R. 576.

[60] *Nouveau Fabrics Ltd v Voyage Decoration Ltd* [2004] EWHC 895, Ch. D.

[61] See, e.g. *Infabrics Ltd v Jaytex Ltd* (at first instance) [1978] F.S.R. 451.

case it will be a question of fact.[62] A defendant is not bound to accept the claimant's assertions, although he cannot simply ignore them.[63] A defendant who does so, and who therefore is a person who has reason to *suspect*, is capable of becoming a person with reason to *believe* if he carries out no sensible inquiries, and does absolutely nothing in the face of continued assertions of the copyright by the owner.[64] What he must do is evaluate the assertions, a process which will, in many cases, require him to make reasonable inquiries, and the result of those inquiries will be taken into account in assessing whether he has reason to believe.[65] Sometimes a relatively long time may be needed for the defendant to make proper inquiries and obtain what information he can.[66]Where a defendant's knowledge consists only of assertions of infringement, or of disputed facts, whether made in correspondence or pleadings, this is not enough.[67] Thus where there is a dispute between A and B about whether certain articles infringe, and C deals in those articles knowing of the dispute but does not know and does not have the means of knowing what is the correct position, he does not have sufficient knowledge for this purpose should A's version of events subsequently turn out to be correct[68]: he does not have knowledge of the relevant facts. Probably the knowledge of an agent would be imputed to his principal.[69] It has been said, in a different context, that where a trader goes into the market and finds what appears to be a novel product, it is not incumbent upon him, in the absence of some special circumstance, to enquire of the person offering the product whether there are any copyright complications involved in dealing with the product. He is entitled to assume that the vendor is in a position toon to sell what he offers to sell.[70] The burden of satisfying the court that a defendant has sufficient knowledge lies on the claimant.[71]

E. PARTICULAR ACTS

8–11   **Possession.** Copyright in a work is infringed by any person who, without the licence of the copyright owner, and with the necessary knowledge, possesses an infringing copy in the course of a business.[72] "Business" is defined as including a trade or profession.[73] The business in question must be that of the possessor, and

---

[62] See, e.g. *Sillitoe v McGraw-Hill Book Co.* [1983] F.S.R. 545. Where the defendant had to make inquiries of manufacturers abroad, nine days was held insufficient in *Rexnold Inc. v Ancon Ltd* [1983] F.S.R. 662, but 21 days sufficient in *Monsoon Ltd v India Imports of Rhode Island Ltd* [1993] F.S.R. 21.

[63] *Nouveau Fabrics Ltd v Voyage Decoration Ltd* [2004] EWHC 895, Ch. D.

[64] *Nouveau Fabrics Ltd v Voyage Decoration Ltd* [2004] EWHC 895, Ch. D., although it is not clear, on this basis, when reason to suspect will become reason to believe.

[65] *Nouveau Fabrics Ltd v Voyage Decoration Ltd* [2004] EWHC 895, Ch. D.

[66] In *Nouveau Fabrics Ltd v Voyage Decoration Ltd* [2004] EWHC 895, Ch. D., six months elapsed between the letter before action and the defendant having reason to believe.

[67] The paragraph down to this point in the 14th edition was approved as an accurate statement of the law in *Vermaat v Boncrest Ltd (No.2)* [2002] F.S.R. 21.

[68] *Hutchinson Personal Communications Ltd v Hook Advertising Ltd* [1995] F.S.R. 365; *Metix (UK) Ltd v G.H. Maughan (Plastics) Ltd* [1997] F.S.R. 718.

[69] *R.C.A. Corporation v Custom Cleared Sales Pty Ltd* [1978] F.S.R. 576.

[70] *Quaker Oats Co. Ltd v Alltrades Distributors Ltd* [1981] F.S.R. 9. The context was a consideration of factors relevant to the grant of interlocutory relief. As to the effect of a copyright notice on imported goods, see *Clarke, Irwin & Co. v C. Cole & Co.* (1960) 22 D.L.R. (2d) 183; and also *Godfrey, etc., Ltd v Coles Book Stores Ltd* [1974] 40 D.L.R. (3d) 346 and *Simon & Schuster Inc. v Coles Book StoresLtd* [1976] 61 D.L.R. (3d) 590.

[71] *Springsteen v Flute International Ltd* [1999] F.S.R. 180.

[72] This provision was new in the 1988 Act. The Whitford Committee had recommended only that possession in the course of trade of imported copies should be an infringement: Cmnd.6732, para.749(ii).

[73] CDPA 1988 s.178.

not that of some other person who sold it to him[74] for otherwise every member of the public who knowingly bought an infringing copy from a business would be liable for possession, which is clearly not the Act's intention. Although the business in question is not limited to that of doing business in articles of that kind,[75] possession of such articles must be part of the ordinary course of the business, so that possession which is only incidental to a business will not amount to possession in the course of that business.[76] Otherwise a party's solicitor might become liable if he came into possession of an infringing article while acting for him, which would be absurd.[77] In the case of a local authority, some of its activities can be properly described as business activities and some not. In each case it will depend on the nature of the activity. For example, a local authority carrying out its duty to provide street lighting is not engaged in a business activity but the ownership, management, regulation, control and letting of flats pursuant to a local authority's powers under the Housing Acts is a business activity.[78] "Possession" in this context is not confined to cases where a party is in possession of an article with a view to its dissemination to some other party. Possession with a view to retention is also an infringement.[79]

Sale, etc. It is an infringement to offer or expose for sale or hire an infringing copy, whether in the course of a business or not. The exhibition of an infringing article in public is also an infringement but only if done in the course of a business. It is not an infringement under these provisions to invite offers for sale, for example by sending out a price list.[80] Nor does a person infringe copyright who merely attempts to effect a sale but who does not in the course of doing so commit one of the specific acts of infringement, such as the offer or exposure of the copy for sale.[81] Where articles were concealed from view at a trade exhibition and were produced only to those who asked to see them, but were not for sale even though a brochure and price list referring to them were openly available, they were held to be neither offered for sale nor exposed for sale and, arguably, not even exhibited in public.[82] Whether a sale has taken place will be judged on the normal objective basis, and the fact that one party had no subjective intention to enter into a contract or legal relationship, for example on a trap purchase, is irrelevant.[83] Where a defendant has delivered copies of a work on a "sale or return basis" he is not liable for any subsequent sale because he cannot demand the return of the copies.[84]

8–12

Distribution. To be an infringement, the distribution must either be in the course of a business or to such an extent as to affect prejudicially the owner of the copyright. It is not, however, easy to imagine a case in which distribution is nei-

8–13

---

[74] See *Reid v Kennett* (1986) Crim.L.R. 456, decided under the Copyright Act 1956 s.21(4A).
[75] *LA Gear Inc. v Hi-Tec Sports Plc* [1992] F.S.R. 121, CA.
[76] *Pensher Security Door Co. Ltd v Sunderland City Council* [2000] R.P.C. 249, CA.
[77] *Pensher Security Door Co. Ltd v Sunderland City Council* [2000] R.P.C. 249, CA. This view is supported by a statement made by the Government when resisting an amendment to s.24. It was said that a person who was merely looking after an article for a friend would have "custody or control" of it, but that the friend would have "possession" of it. *Hansard*, HL, Vol.490, col.1216. (Note, however, that the words "in the course of a business" were subsequently added to the definition of the infringing act of possession.)
[78] *Pensher Security Door Co. Ltd v Sunderland City Council* [2000] R.P.C. 249, CA (possession of infringing doors an integral part of the council's business activity of managing and letting flats).
[79] *Pensher Security Door Co. Ltd v Sunderland City Council* [2000] R.P.C. 249, CA.
[80] *Norgren Co. v Technomarking*, The Times, March 3, 1983.
[81] *Wolff v Wood*, The Times, October 31, 1903; *Britain v Kennedy* (1903) 19 T.L.R. 122.
[82] *LA Gear Inc. v Hi-Tec Sports Plc* [1992] F.S.R. 121, CA.
[83] *Phillips v Holmes* [1988] R.P.C. 613.
[84] *Schofield & Sims Ltd v Gibson (R.) & Sons Ltd* [1928–1935] Mac.C.C. 64; but cf. *E.W. Savory Ltd v The World of Golf Ltd* [1910–1916] Mac.C.C. 149.

ther in the course of a trade or business nor prejudicial to the owner of the copyright, except perhaps where only a few copies are distributed to persons who would never have bought the work anyway.

8–14   **Importation.** No definition of what amounts to importation is contained in the Act. Generally, an article is imported when it is brought from abroad into port or, in the case of carriage by aircraft, landed.[85] It is thought that the carriage must be ended or its continuity in some way broken,[86] so that an article is not imported if the vessel in which it is carried merely enters a port of call on its way to its final destination.[87] Nor is an article imported if the vessel carrying it merely enters the territorial waters of the United Kingdom[88]; the goods must be physically received and become subject to the English Court's jurisdiction.[89] But an article will be imported even though it is landed only with the purpose of transporting it across the territory to another state.[90] The position may be different if the goods are landed involuntarily, for example, as a result of a hijack or bad weather[91] and where goods are brought into the United Kingdom under the Community "inward processing" procedure they will not have been imported (within the meaning of s.10(4)(c) of the Trade Marks Act 1994) because they will not have been released for circulation or become "Community goods".[92] As to who is the importer, once the fact of importation has been established, it should not normally be necessary to resort to the technicalities of the contract of sale.[93]

The onus is on the importer to show, if he can, that the article was only imported for private or domestic use. Note that provision is also made for the owner of the copyright to restrict unlawful importation by giving notice to the Commissioners of Customs and Excise. The matter is dealt with elsewhere.[94]

3. PROVIDING THE MEANS OF MAKING INFRINGING COPIES

8–15   The Act contains provisions making persons liable who knowingly possess or provide the means for making infringing copies. Whether or not such acts may also amount to the separate tort of authorising an infringement is dealt with elsewhere.[95] Thus the copyright in a work is infringed by a person who, without the licence of the copyright owner:

(a) makes,

(b) imports into the United Kingdom,

---

[85] See, e.g. *Wilson v Chambers & Co. Pty Ltd* (1926) 38 C.L.R. 138. For a definition of when an article is imported for Customs and Excise purposes, see the Customs and Excise Management Act 1979 s.5.

[86] *Wilson v Chambers & Co. Pty Ltd* (1926) 38 C.L.R. 138.

[87] *Canada Sugar Refining Co. v R.* [1898] A.C. 735.

[88] *R. v Bull* (1974) 48 A.L.J.R. 232.

[89] *LA Gear Inc. v Hi-Tec Sports Plc* [1992] F.S.R. 121, CA.

[90] *Mattel Inc. v Tonka Corp.* [1992] F.S.R. 28 (High Ct of Hong Kong); *Gramophone Company of India Ltd v Pandey* [1985] F.S.R. 136.

[91] *Mattel Inc. v Tonka Corp.* [1992] F.S.R. 28 (High Ct of Hong Kong).

[92] *Eli Lilly & Company v 8PM Chemists Ltd* [2008] EWCA Civ 24; [2008] F.S.R.12, following *Class International BV v Colgate-Palmolive Co* (C–405/03) [2005] E.C.R. I–8735.

[93] *Sabaf SpA v MFI Furniture Centres Ltd* [2004] UKHL 45; [2005] R.P.C. 10 (a patent case), where the Italian manufacturer of infringing goods had sold them to an English company and arranged their transport to England on behalf of the English company, which reimbursed the cost of doing so. Property passed in Italy. As a matter of the law of international carriage of goods by road, the contract of carriage was presumed to have been made on behalf of the consignee and owner of the goods. On this basis, the manufacturer was not the importer but also the manufacturer was not the importer because no matter who had contracted with the carrier, the English company was the importer, para.41. The manufacturer might have been liable for the importation as a joint tortfeasor but no such contention was made, para.40.

[94] See paras 22–69 et seq., below.

[95] See para.7–146, above.

(c) possesses in the course of a business, or

(d) sells or lets for hire, or offers or exposes for sale or hire,

an article specifically designed or adapted for making copies of that work, know-ing or having reason to believe that it is to be used to make infringing copies.[96] Again, a "business" is defined as including a trade or profession.[97] The reference to an article "specifically designed or adapted for making copies of that work" makes it clear that dealing in an article which is generally designed for making copies, such as a photocopier or tape-recorder, will not fall within this provision. Rather, the provision is directed to dealings in articles such as photographic negatives, moulds, master recordings and the like which may be used to make copies of specific works.[98] The article does not itself have to be an infringing copy.

The copyright in a work is also infringed by a person who, without the licence of the copyright owner, transmits the work by means of a telecommunications system (otherwise than by communication to the public), knowing or having rea-son to believe that infringing copies of the work will be made by means of the reception of the transmission in the United Kingdom or elsewhere.[99] "Telecom-munications system" is defined as meaning a system for conveying visual im-ages, sounds or other information by electronic means.[100] This provision will make it an infringement, for example, to fax a work knowing that infringing cop-ies will then be made at the receiving end. In such a case, the person transmitting the work will often also have infringed by copying the work before, or in the course of, transmission. Where the transmission is by way of communication to the public, an act of primary infringement will of course also occur.[101] The provi-sion that an infringement will occur under the present section if the sender knows or has reason to believe that infringing copies will then be made "elsewhere" than in the United Kingdom appears to be designed to prevent works being electronically exported for copying overseas. The provision appears to be of limited application, however, since the definition of "infringing copy" is gener-ally limited to copies either made in the United Kingdom or which have been or are intended to be imported into the United Kingdom.

4. PERMITTING OR ENABLING PUBLIC PERFORMANCE

Introduction. As has been seen, the exclusive rights of performance, playing and showing of various works in public are primary rights, restricted by the copyright in such works. In addition to the general liability of persons who authorise such infringements, the 1988 Act also makes provision for secondary acts of infringe-ment in cases where the defendant gave permission for premises to be used for performances or supplied the means by which such works were seen or heard in public. The wording of the 1988 Act makes it clear that a person can only be li-able under these provisions where there is already some other person liable for the primary infringement.   **8–16**

---

[96] CDPA 1988 s.24(1).

[97] s.178.

[98] An amendment during the passage of the Bill to alter the wording of the section to "an article designed for making copies of that class of works" was successfully resisted. See also *Hansard*, HL, Vol.490, col.1217, and the report of the debates of the House of Commons Standing Com-mittee E in 1988, col.166.

[99] CDPA 1988 s.24(2). But see para.7–21, above, suggesting that the sender may also be liable for the primary act of infringement by reproduction.

[100] s.178, where "electronic" is also defined.

[101] See para.7–112, above.

8–17 **Permitting use of premises.** The Act provides that where the copyright in a literary, dramatic or musical work is infringed by a performance at a place of public entertainment, any person who gave permission for that place to be used for the performance is also liable for the infringement, unless when he gave permission he believed on reasonable grounds that the performance would not infringe copyright.[102] For this purpose, "place of public entertainment" includes premises which are occupied mainly for other purposes but are from time to time made available for hire for the purposes of public entertainment.[103] The effect of the Act appears to be to make the defendant liable for the actual act of infringement by performance, presumably jointly with whoever is liable for that infringement.

8–18 **Permission.** One of the crucial questions will often be whether permission was given for the use of the premises for the performance. The question whether the defendant committed the separate tort of authorising the performance will often arise at the same time.[104] As to permission, the giving of permission for use of the premises generally is not sufficient since the permission must be for the premises to be used for the performance complained of. Under the equivalent provisions of the 1911 Act it was said that a person does not permit what he cannot control, and does not permit the use of a place for the performance of a work if he does not know that the work is going to be performed.[105] Thus where a person permits premises to be used knowing which works will be performed, this will be sufficient to establish "permission", but not if the music to be performed is left to the performers and the defendant has no knowledge of what in fact will be performed.[106] Permission may be inferred from acts which fall short of being direct and positive, and may be inferred from indifference, but permission will not be inferred from a mere general authority to use a theatre for the performance of musical or dramatic works.[107] In an Australian case, it was held that the owners of a hall who, under the terms of their contract of letting, could not prevent the performance of which complaint is made, did not "permit" the performance.[108]

8–19 **Provision of apparatus, etc.** The 1988 Act makes further provision for secondary infringement where the copyright in a work is infringed by the public performance of a work or by the playing or showing of it in public. Thus various categories of person may also be liable where such infringement has occurred by means of apparatus for playing sound recordings, showing films or receiving visual images or sounds conveyed by electronic means.[109] Again, the wording of the 1988 Act makes it clear that a person can only be liable under these provisions where there is already some other person liable for the primary infringement.

First, a person who supplies the apparatus, or any substantial part of it, is liable for the infringement if, when he supplied the apparatus or part:

   (a) he knew or had reason to believe that the apparatus was likely to be so used as to infringe copyright, or

---

[102] CDPA 1988 s.25(1).

[103] ibid., s.25(2).

[104] As to which, see para.7–146, above.

[105] *Performing Right Society Ltd v Ciryl Theatrical Syndicate Ltd* [1924] 1 K.B. 1.

[106] *Monaghan v Taylor* (1885) 2 T.L.R. 685, cited in *Performing Right Society Ltd v Ciryl Theatrical Syndicate Ltd* [1924] 1 K.B. 1. See also *ACUM (Society of Authors and Composers) v R.K. Orel Events Ltd* (Civil Case 7779/03, Haifa Magistrates Court) [2004] Ent. L.R. N-67, which is to the same effect.

[107] *Performing Right Society Ltd v Ciryl Theatrical Syndicate Ltd* [1924] 1 K.B. 1.

[108] *Australian Performing Right Association Ltd v Adelaide Corporation* (1928) 40 C.L.R. 481; see also *Canadian Performing Right Society v Canadian National Exhibition Association* (1934) 4 D.L.R. 154; but cf. *Australian Performing Right Association v Turner (J) & Son* (1927) 27 S.R. (N.S.W.) 344.

[109] CDPA 1988 s.26(1).

(b) in the case of apparatus whose normal use involves a public performance, playing or showing, he did not believe on reasonable grounds that it would not be so used as to infringe copyright.[110]

Presumably, an infringement in the first case would occur where, for example, a person supplied a television for use in public, such as in a public house, knowing that no sufficient licence had been obtained. The second kind of case might arise where, for example, a juke box was supplied for use in public, or specialised equipment for use in a discotheque. Although the burden of proof as to the requisite degree of knowledge appears still to rest with the claimant, the intention in this latter kind of case appears to make that burden easier to discharge. In the ordinary type of case it will no doubt be sufficient to prove that the supply of apparatus has continued after a warning letter has been received.

Secondly, an occupier of premises who gives permission for the apparatus to be **8–20** brought onto the premises is also liable for the infringement if, when he gave permission, he knew or had reason to believe that the apparatus was likely to be so used as to infringe copyright.[111] Again, this kind of case might arise where the occupier of a public house or discotheque allows equipment to be brought onto the premises knowing that no sufficient licence has been obtained.

Thirdly, a person who supplies a copy of the sound recording or film used to infringe copyright is also liable for the infringement if when, he supplied it, he knew or had reason to believe that what he supplied, or a copy made directly or indirectly from it, was likely to be so used as to infringe copyright.[112] Persons who knowingly supply records for use in jukeboxes are therefore likely to be caught by this provision.

---

[110] s.26(2).
[111] CDPA 1988 s.26(3).
[112] CDPA 1988, s.26(4).

CHAPTER NINE

PERMITTED ACTS

Contents

Contents　　　　　　　　　　　　　　　　　　　　　　　　　*Para.*

Contents   *Para.*

1. GENERAL INTRODUCTION

Chapter III Pt I, of the 1988 Act, containing some 67 sections, permits certain **9–01** acts which would otherwise amount to copyright infringement. Since the 1988 Act was originally enacted, various sections have been added and a large number of amendments made in order to comply with European legislation. These "permitted acts"[1] are in general designed to balance the interests of copyright owners with the public interest, and some of the provisions show up important conflicts between the two.[2] More generally, the permitted acts should be viewed alongside the requirement of substantial taking[3] and the restrictive way in which some of the exclusive rights of the copyright owner are drawn, in particular the exclusive right to perform a work, which only applies to performances in public. The possible existence of an implied licence needs also to be borne in mind.[4]

The Berne Convention, and the "three-step test". The Berne Convention[5] al- **9–02** lows for exceptions to be made to the rights in works protected under the Convention in certain specified cases.[6] The permitted act provisions take advantage of these provisions, which are dealt with as they arise in the course of this chapter. As well as allowing for such specific exceptions, however, the Berne Convention also contains in art.9(2) a general dispensation in the following terms: "It shall be a matter for legislation in the countries of the Union to permit the reproduction of [literary and artistic[7]] works in certain special cases, provided such reproduction does not conflict with the normal exploitation of the work and does not unreasonably prejudice the legitimate interests of the author". The three requirements, namely that such permission may be granted (a) in certain special cases, where the reproduction (b) does not conflict with the normal exploitation of the work and (c) does not unreasonably prejudice the legitimate interests of the author, are known as the Berne "three-step" test. The meaning and significance of the three-step test is considered elsewhere.[8] Although the three-step test has never been

---

[1] The various permitted acts are sometimes referred to as defences, but strictly speaking this is not the case, cf. CDPA 1988 s.97.

[2] Moreover, it is important to recognise that the permitted acts serve a number of disparate functions and take effect in a variety of ways. For example, a number of the provisions only take effect in the absence of a licensing agreement (see, e.g. CDPA 1988 ss.35, 36, 60, 74 and corresponding text, below).

[3] CDPA 1988 s.16(3)(a). See further, paras 7–25, et seq., above.

[4] See further, paras 5–217 et seq., above.

[5] See Ch.23, below.

[6] See Berne Convention arts 2*bis* (1), (2), 10 and 10*bis*.

[7] The concept of a literary or artistic work is wider under Berne than under UK legislation. See Ch.23, below.

[8] See paras 23–33 and 23–142, below.

incorporated into UK copyright legislation it has in principle been taken into account when framing a number of the permitted act provisions.[9]

9–03   **The Rome Convention.** The Rome Convention 1961,[10] which for present purposes is concerned with the rights in relation to phonograms and broadcasts,[11] permits contracting states to provide for exceptions to such rights in cases of (a) private use, (b) use of short excerpts in connection with the reporting of current events, (c) the ephemeral fixation by a broadcasting organisation by means of its own facilities and for its own broadcasts and (d) use solely for the purposes of teaching or scientific research.[12] In addition to this, however, contracting states are also permitted to provide for the same kinds of limitations to these rights as they provide in connection with the protection of literary and artistic works.[13] As with the Berne Convention, the 1988 Act contains provisions taking advantage of these permitted exceptions, which are considered in this chapter as they arise.

9–04   **The TRIPS Agreement.** The TRIPS Agreement 1994 requires Members to confine limitations or exceptions to the protection granted to Berne Convention works to cases complying with the three-step test[14] and, in the case of subject matter protected under the Rome Convention, to those provided for by the Rome Convention.[15]

9–05   **The WIPO Copyright Treaty and the WIPO Performances and Phonograms Treaty 1996.** The WCT provides for limitations and exceptions to the rights granted provided that they comply with the three-step test.[16] The WPPT permits the same kinds of limitations or exceptions with regard to the protection of performers and producers of phonograms as they provide for, in their national legislation, in connection with the protection of copyright in literary and artistic works, provided also that they are in conformity with the three-step test.[17]

9–06   **European Directives.** Various European Directives have made piecemeal provision affecting exceptions which Member States either must or may make to the various rights which are the subject matter of such Directives. First, arts 5 and 6 of the Software Directive[18] required certain limited exceptions to be made to the rights relating to computer programs; no others were permitted. These exceptions either fell within existing permitted act provisions of the 1988 Act or were implemented by amendment.[19] Second, art.5 of the Rental and Related Rights Directive[20] permits certain derogations from the public lending right, which the United Kingdom took advantage of by the introduction of ss.36A and 40A into the 1988 Act.[21] Article 10 of the same Directive permits specified exceptions to be made to the rights prescribed in relation to phonograms, films and broadcasts, but also permits Member States to make limitations of the same kind as are

---

[9] For examples of cases which are generally considered to fall within this permitted exception, see S. Ricketson and J.C. Ginsburg, *International Copyright and Neighbouring Rights, The Berne Convention and Beyond* 2nd edn (Oxford University Press, 2006), paras 13.31 et seq.
[10] See Ch.23, below.
[11] As to the Rome Convention and performers, see Ch.12, below.
[12] Rome Convention art.15(1).
[13] Rome Convention art.15(2).
[14] TRIPS art.13. See, however, with respect to the law of the European Community, para.24–115, below.
[15] TRIPS art.14(6).
[16] WCT art.10.
[17] WPPT art.16.
[18] Directive 2009/2/EC (amended consolidated text).
[19] See paras 9–149 et seq., below.
[20] Directive 2006/116/EC (amended consolidated text).
[21] See paras 9–197 and 28–45, below, respectively.

provided in the case of literary and artistic works. No amendments were made to the 1988 Act arising out these matters. Thirdly, the Database Directive[22] required Member States to make what was in effect an exception to rights of copyright in databases[23] and allowed Member States to provide for certain other limitations or exceptions to these rights, including exceptions of a kind that were traditionally allowed under national copyright laws.[24] Section 50D was introduced into the 1988 Act to give effect to the former requirement[25] but no other amendments were made. Fourth and finally, but most significantly, the Information Society Directive[26] attempted a degree of harmonisation across the whole field of permitted exceptions. This Directive is considered in more detail below. It should also be borne in mind that the E-Commerce Directive[27] provides for horizontal, or across the board, defences whose aim is to limit the liability of intermediary internet service providers to actions of all kinds (and not just for copyright infringement) arising out of the transmission and storage of information in their electronic networks. Subject to various safeguards, liability in respect of any damages and for any other pecuniary remedy or for any criminal sanction is therefore to be excluded for the activities of "mere conduit", "caching" and "hosting" of information. These exclusions, which are in the nature of defences rather than permitted acts, have been implemented into UK law[28] and are discussed in more detail in Ch.21.

The Information Society Directive. This Directive[29] merits discussion in greater detail here. It had two objectives in the area of permitted acts. The first, which overlaps with that of the E-Commerce Directive, relates to the harmonisation provision in art.2 of the Information Society Directive which requires Member States to provide rightholders with the exclusive right to prevent or authorise the temporary reproduction of the subject-matter of their rights.[30] This exclusive right extends to temporary or transient reproductions in computer memory. It was considered that some provision had to be made, however, such that this right would not unduly interfere with the proper functioning of electronic networks or lawful use of works in electronic form. This has been achieved by a mandatory requirement in the Directive that liability for transient acts of reproduction in the course of the transmission of material through networks or lawful use is to be exempted from the reproduction right.[31] This objective, which was controversial,[32] is limited in scope in its implementation. It is considered in more detail later in this chapter.[33] The second objective was more general, and more ambitious. It was to achieve harmonisation amongst Member States across the entire range of permitted exceptions or limitations. A justification for the Directive in its final form can be found in recital 31, where it is stated that the existing exceptions and limitations provided by Member States needed to be "reassessed

9–07

---

[22] Directive 96/9.

[23] art.6(1).

[24] arts 6(2), (3)

[25] See para.9–156, below.

[26] Directive 2001/29/EC

[27] Directive 2000/31/EC.

[28] By the Electronic Commerce (EC Directive) Regulations 2002 (SI 2002/2013).

[29] Directive 2001/29/EC.

[30] As to this right, see para.7–20, above.

[31] Although there is an overlap here with the E-Commerce Directive, the provisions are complementary and operate in parallel. See recital 16 of the Information Society Directive 2001/29/EC.

[32] There were those who argued that the exclusive right in respect of such transient reproduction in networks should not have been made part of the reproduction right in the first place. See, e.g. A Dietz, "The Protection of Intellectual Property in the Information Age—The Draft EU Copyright Directive of November 1997" [1998] I.P.Q. 335.

[33] See paras 9–19 et seq., below.

in the light of the new electronic environment." Such differences, it was said, had "direct negative effects on the functioning of the internal market" which might well have "become more pronounced in view of the further development of trans-border exploitation of works and cross-border activities". In order to ensure the proper functioning of the internal market, such exceptions and limitations therefore needed to "be defined more harmoniously", although the degree of the harmonisation needed to be "based on the impact on the smooth functioning of the internal market".[34] In its first incarnations, the draft Directive provided for a small and closed class of exceptions.[35] As perhaps could have been predicted, the objective ran into opposition, with Member States arguing for retention of their own particular exceptions. In its final form, recital 32 proclaims that the final list of exceptions takes due account of the different legal traditions in Member States, while at the same time aiming to ensure a functioning internal market. In reality, what has been achieved is a poor form of harmonisation, with no less than 19 separate permitted exceptions or limitations, many of which are of a general nature or have further subdivisions, coupled with a save-all provision which allows Member States to retain their existing exceptions in the case of analogue uses of minor importance, but not digital, uses. The Directive fails to achieve harmonisation because, save only the case of the exception mandated by art.5(1) for the making of transient and incidental copies, referred to above, all the permitted exceptions are optional, that is, Member States are free to choose whether or not to take advantage of them. This part of the Directive is a harmonisation measure only in the sense that the class of permitted acts is closed, so that Member States are not able to provide exceptions outside these cases.[36] Particular, although perhaps predictable, areas of failure were in relation to private copying and reprographic copying, it being one of the principal original aims of the Directive to harmonise the laws of Member States in this area. In the end, no effective consensus could be achieved on these issues, and the matter has been left such that Member States may, but are not required to, permit private copying and reprographic copying. If they do so, however, it is only to be on terms that right holders receive fair compensation.[37]

The various exceptions or limitations allowed by the Directive are dealt with in this chapter as they arise in the context of the various permitted acts. Some general comments can be made about them here, however. The first is that the permitted exceptions are concerned only with the exclusive rights which are the subject matter of the Directive, namely the reproduction right, the distribution

---

[34] Harmonisation to this degree has never been attempted by the signatories to the Berne Convention (see generally, S. Ricketson and J.C. Ginsburg, *International Copyright and Neighbouring Rights, The Berne Convention and Beyond* 2nd edn (Oxford: Oxford University Press, 2006), or the Rome Convention, and it must be also doubted whether the workings of the Internal Market were in the past affected in any substantial way by the patchwork of exceptions which existed within the Community. Of course, the effects in the future in a digital environment are more uncertain.

[35] See, e.g. the 1997 Proposal, COM (97) 628 final.

[36] See also recital 32, which states that the Directive provides for an exhaustive enumeration of exceptions and limitations to the reproduction right and the right of communication to the public. Thus, the UK may not introduce any new exception. However, this did not deter the Gowers Review of Intellectual Property (HM Treasury Report, December 2006) from making a number of recommendations for additional exceptions, see para.9–13, below.

[37] For some of the extensive literature on the Information Society Directive and these exceptions, see T. Heide, "The Approach to Innovation under the Proposed Copyright Directive: Time for Mandatory Exceptions?" [2000] I.P.Q. 215; M. Wing & E. Kirk, "European/US Copyright Law Reform: Is a Balance Being Achieved?" [2000] I.P.Q. 138; T.C. Vinje, "Should We Begin Digging Copyright's Grave?" [2000] E.I.P.R. 551; B. Hugenholtz, "Why the Copyright Directive is Unimportant, and Possibly Invalid" [2000] E.I.P.R. 499.

right and the communication to the public right,[38] these being the rights prescribed by arts 2, 3 and 4. The Directive is thus not directly concerned with exceptions which Member States may make to rights of public performance.[39] As already noted, earlier Directives have dealt with permissible or mandatory exceptions to the particular rights the subject of those Directives and for the most part the Information Society Directive leaves those Directives untouched.[40] Further, the Directive does not permit exceptions to all three rights indiscriminately. Thus, the first category of exceptions, in art.5(2), are permitted only in relation to the reproduction and distribution rights,[41] while the second category, in art.5(3), are permitted in relation to all three rights.[42] An exception permitted only under art.5(2) cannot therefore be applied in relation to the communication to the public right. Finally, art.5(5) of the Directive restates the requirement of the three-step test in art.9(2) of the Berne Convention, by stating that the exceptions and limitations permitted by the Directive shall only be applied in certain special cases which do not conflict with a normal exploitation of the work or other subject-matter and do not unreasonably prejudice the legitimate interests of the right holder.[43] When taking advantage of particular permitted exceptions Member States therefore must frame their legislation to comply with the three-step test.

Amendments to the 1988 Act. While many of the existing permitted act provisions of the 1988 Act fell within these permitted exceptions, many did not. In the latter case, the Act has been amended as discussed in detail later in this Chapter by reference to individual permitted acts. In cases where the Directive permits, but does not require, Member States to make exceptions and where there was no existing equivalent permitted act in the 1988 Act, the United Kingdom has taken a minimalist approach and only introduced new provisions required by the Directive.[44] As with previous legislation in this field, the 1988 Act does not contain any express reference to the three-step test, which the Directive requires to be applied. Rather, the legislation has been framed with this requirement in mind.[45] However, the fact that the three-step test is now part of European law means that it will be possible to challenge the implementation of the Directive by way of infraction proceedings in the European Court of Justice. A number of tidying up amendments have also been made to reflect the change to s.20, whereby the restricted acts of broadcasting a work and including a work in a cable programme service have been replaced by the composite restricted act of communicating a work to the public. **9–08**

Transitional provisions. Regulations to amend the 1988 Act and implement the **9–09**

---

[38] The exclusive right to communicate authors' works to the public (art.3(1)) and the exclusive right to make related rights subject matter available to the public (art. 3(2)) are in this chapter referred to together as the "communication to the public right", the compendious title given to these rights by the 1988 Act.

[39] See recitals 23 and 24 of the Information Society Directive 2001/29/EC.

[40] As will be seen, however, the Information Society Directive also amends provisions of the Rental and Related Rights Directive dealing with permitted exceptions or limitations, and this has affected the exceptions permitted in respect of the public performance of sound recordings. See paras 9–181 and 9–200, et seq., below.

[41] An exception to the distribution right is only permissible where a corresponding exception has been made to the reproduction right, and then only to the extent justified by the purpose of the permitted act of reproduction. See art.5(4).

[42] Although see the preceding note for the limitation on the distribution right.

[43] See para.9–02, above.

[44] See, e.g. the Patent Office's Consultation Paper of August 7, 2002 and the Analysis of Responses and Government Conclusions, and the Transposition Note to the Implementing Regulations (SI 2003/2498). No doubt this attitude was also influenced by the lack of Parliamentary time and Government's ability to make amendments to the 1988 Act by Statutory Instrument using its powers under the European Communities Act 1972 s.2.

[45] See the Analysis of Responses and Government Conclusions to the Patent Office's Consultation Paper of August 7, 2002, para.5.2 and the Transposition Note.

Information Society Directive came into force on October 31, 2003.[46] As a matter of the general law, whether or not an act committed before this date constituted an infringement or fell within the permitted act provisions must be determined in accordance with the law then in force.[47] In addition, however, the Regulations provide that the provisions of the 1988 Act as they stood *before* amendment shall continue to apply to anything done *after* commencement in completion of an act begun before commencement which was permitted by those unamended provisions.[48] A more general saving provides that nothing in the Regulations is to affect any agreement made before December 22, 2002[49] and no act done after October 31, 2003, in pursuance of an agreement made before December 22, 2002, shall be regarded as an infringement of any new or extended right arising by virtue of the Regulations.[50]

9–10   **Permitted exceptions and copy protection devices.** A further problem which the Information Society Directive had to deal with was the conflict between the provisions of the Directive requiring or allowing exceptions to rights of copyright owners and related right holders and the provisions of the Directive which aim to prevent the circumvention of copy-protection devices. For details of these latter provisions, which implement the 1996 WIPO Copyright and Performances and Phonograms Treaties, see Ch.15. In brief, Member States are required to provide legal protection against the circumvention of copy protection devices, and against the manufacture of and commercial dealings in products or services which achieve this. Where a work is available in electronic form, so that any access to it will inevitably involve copying, it follows that there may be a conflict between the general public policy of permitting uses of the work which do not unreasonably prejudice the right holder and the right holder's ability to control any use of the work via copy protection devices. The Directive in the end offered no clear solution to this highly contentious issue and passed the problem on to Member States. Thus, the Directive requires that in relation to certain of the permitted exceptions, and in the absence of voluntary measures taken by right holders, Member States are to take "appropriate measures" to ensure that right holders make available to the beneficiary of the exception the means of benefiting from it.[51] These provisions are not, however, to apply to works or other subject-matter made available to the public on agreed contractual terms by way of an on-demand service.[52] The reasoning is that where material is available under licence by way of an on-demand service, the contractual provisions of the licence should prevail over any general right, although it is questionable whether this does not run against the whole spirit and purpose of permitted use in cases where this is founded on public interest considerations.

9–11   **Implementation by the 1988 Act.** The United Kingdom's answer to the

---

[46] The Copyright and Related Rights Regulations 2003 (SI 2003/2498).
[47] Interpretation Act 1978 s.16.
[48] SI 2003/2498 reg.33.
[49] As to this date, see Information Society Directive art.10.
[50] SI 2003/2498 reg.32.
[51] Information Society Directive art.6(4) and recital 51. Such measures are to be made available only to the extent necessary to enable a benefit to be obtained from that exception and only where that beneficiary has legal access to the protected work or subject-matter concerned. Art.6(4) also provides that when art.6 "is applied in the context of" the Rental and Lending Directive (2006/116/EC (amended and consolidated text) and the Database Directive (96/9/EC), "this paragraph" is to apply *mutatis mutandis*. The apparent purpose of this is that in the case of the exceptions which those Directives provide for, a similar regime as to voluntary or appropriate measures is to apply, although presumably only where there is an equivalent exception.
[52] i.e. where the subject-matter is made available in such a way that members of the public may access it from a place and at a time individually chosen by them. See the penultimate paragraph of art.6(4) and also recital 53 of the Information Society Directive.

problems posed by art.6 of the Directive is contained in s.296ZE of the Act, which is considered in more detail in Ch.15. In short, where the presence of a copy protection device prevents a person from carrying out one of a limited list of permitted acts[53] then a complaint can be made to the Secretary of State. If the Secretary of State establishes that there is no subsisting voluntary measure or agreement enabling such use, he may give directions so as to ensure that the means of carrying out the permitted act, to the extent necessary so as to benefit from the permitted act, are made available to the complainant.[54] These provisions do not apply to computer programs, which are subject to the different regime of permitted exceptions imposed by the Software Directive.[55] It is worth noting here that, amongst others, these provisions do not apply to the permitted acts of making temporary copies, under s.28A, or fair dealing for the purposes of criticism, review or news reporting. The Act leaves unanswered the question which the Directive itself failed to address, namely how are any means enabling the relevant permitted act to be limited to that purpose, as opposed to enabling access to or use of the work for all purposes?[56]

The Impact of the Human Rights Act on the Permitted Acts. The Human Rights Act 1998 came into force on October 1, 2000 and with it the European Convention on Human Rights, including the right under art.10 to freedom of expression, became part of the domestic law of the United Kingdom. The right to freedom of expression may impinge on the 1988 Act in a number of ways: (1) it may affect the circumstances in which copyright will be enforced[57]; (2) it may affect the application of the permitted act sections of the Act; and (3) in circumstances where the permitted act sections of the Act do not apply, it may provide an additional defence, essentially on the grounds of public interest.[58] In the area of the permitted act sections of the 1988 Act, the impact of the art.10 right of freedom of expression is most likely to be felt in relation to the fair dealing provisions of the Act. It is therefore considered under that heading, below.[59]   **9–12**

The Gowers Review and subsequent UK Government consultations. The Gowers Review of Intellectual Property (HM Treasury Report, December 2006), made a series of recommendations as to exceptions. Some of these require modifying the Information Society Directive 2001/29/EC as they are not currently permitted under the Directive. The recommendations proposed amending the exceptions in the 1988 Act by: **9–13**

1. Creating a new exception for transferring ("format shifting") e.g. music from a CD to the hard drive of a computer.
2. Allowing educational establishments to copy broadcasts and extracts for distance learners.
3. Extending the current "fair dealing" exception for research and private study to apply to sound recordings, broadcasts and film.
4. Permitting libraries and archives to make more than one copy and to

---

[53] Sch.5A to the 1988 Act sets out the list of the permitted acts to which these provisions apply, the intention being to conform with the list set out in art.4 of the Information Society Directive.

[54] CDPA 1988 ss.296ZE(2), (3).

[55] Directive 2009/24/EC (amended and consolidated text), arts 5 and 6.

[56] The right holder is to make available means "to the extent necessary to benefit from that exception or limitation". See art.6(4) of the Directive.

[57] See para.3–304, above.

[58] See paras 21–93 et seq., below. The decision in *Hyde Park Residence Ltd v Yelland* [1999] R.P.C. 655, that the provisions of the 1988 Act spell out a complete code of exceptions to copyright, and that there is therefore no room for any more general defence that the acts of the defendant were in the public interest, must now be regarded as wrong: *Ashdown v Telegraph Group Ltd* [2001] EWCA Civ 1142; [2002] Ch. 149; [2002] R.P.C. 5.

[59] See para.9–26, below.

format shift as long as this is only for preservation purposes. The Government is also considering the viability of extending this to include museums and galleries.

5. Creating a new exception for parody, caricature and pastiche.[60]

In January 2008, the IPO launched the first stage of a two-part consultation with a document entitled: "Taking forward the Gowers Review of Intellectual Property: Proposed changes to copyright exceptions".[61] The paper did not address the recommendations which had an impact on EC law but stated that they were being pursued with the EC Commission. The paper put forward a number of options and a series of meetings were later held with stakeholders to discuss them. Subsequently, in December 2009, the IPO issued a further paper "Taking Forward the Gowers Review of Intellectual Property: Second Stage Consultation on Copyright Exceptions".[62] This second stage of the consultation includes an analysis of the responses received during the first stage of the consultation, an outline of the Government's proposals and draft legislation. The legislative proposals focus on the three recommendations now being taken forward concerning educational provisions; preservation by libraries and archives; and fair dealing for research and private study purposes. Details of these proposals are given below in the relevant sections of this Chapter.[63]

The Gowers Review also considered the problem of orphan works and proposed that the IPO should issue clear guidance on the parameters of a "reasonable search" for orphan works, in consultation with rights holders, collecting societies, rights owners and archives (Recommendation 14a).[64] In the meantime, the subject of orphan works has been addressed by the UK Digital Economy Act 2010.[65]

9–14 **Copyright exemptions for public performance of recorded music.** In July 2009, the UK Government launched a new consultation in respect of certain copyright exemptions which apply to the playing of recorded music in public by charities and not-for-profit organisations. It published its response to the consultation in November 2009 and announced its intention to repeal the exemptions. The Government's proposal is discussed in s.16, below.

9–15 **EC Green Paper.** In 2008, the European Commission published a Green Paper "Copyright in the Knowledge Economy"[66] to launch a debate on the long-term future of copyright policy. It considered the exceptions outlined in the Information Society Directive and their impact on the dissemination of research, science and educational materials. The Green Paper focused in particular on the exceptions to copyright which are most relevant in this context, namely: the exceptions for the benefit of libraries and archives and for teaching and research purposes.; It also considers the exception for the benefit of people with a disability and looks

---

[60] Summary of the Gowers Review Recommendations as to exceptions in © *The Way Ahead – A Strategy for Copyright in the Digital Age* (IPO/BIS), October 2009, p.32.
[61] Available on the IPO website, *http://www.ipo.gov.uk* [Accessed October 22, 2010]. The consultation period ended on April 8, 2008. Subsequently, the IPO published a brief summary of responses to the consultation paper.
[62] *http://www.ipo.gov.uk/consult-gowers2.pdf* [Accessed October 22, 2010]
[63] See sections 4B, 6 and 7, below.
[64] As regards the EU position on orphan works, see para.9–173, below.
[65] C.24 of April 8, 2010, which entered into force on June 8, 2010. For details and the orphan works provisions see Ch.21, below.
[66] COM(2008) 466/3, July 16, 2008.

at a possible exception for user created content. The UK Government issued a response to the Green Paper in December 2008.[67]

2. INTRODUCTORY PROVISIONS

The permitted acts are grouped together into 14 categories: introductory (which **9–16** includes the making of temporary copies),[68] general (which includes the fair dealing exceptions of research and private study and criticism, review and news reporting as well as incidental inclusion of copyright material),[69] visual impairment,[70] education,[71] libraries and archives,[72] public administration,[73] computer programs,[74] databases,[75] designs,[76] typefaces,[77] works in electronic form,[78] miscellaneous provisions relating to literary, dramatic, musical and artistic works,[79] miscellaneous provisions relating to the lending of works and playing of sound recordings,[80] miscellaneous provisions relating to films and sound recordings (including the playing of sound recordings for purposes of clubs, societies, etc.)[81] and miscellaneous provisions relating to broadcasts (including incidental recording for purposes of broadcasts and recording for purposes of time-shifting).[82] This chapter considers each category in turn, with the exception of the provisions relating to designs and the provisions establishing compulsory licences, which are only dealt with in outline.[83] Defences under European law and the E-Commerce Directive, and the public interest defence are dealt with elsewhere.[84] Finally, the Broadcasting Act 1990 imposes a statutory duty on broadcasters to supply information about their programmes and confers a statutory licence on publishers enabling such information to be reproduced and published.[85] Although the 1988 Act was not amended to give effect to this, the 1990 Act provides that the 1988 Act is to have effect as if the relevant provisions of the 1990 Act were included in Ch.III of the 1988 Act. These provisions are nevertheless considered under the topic of compulsory licences.[86]

The Act provides that the permitted acts are to be construed independently of each other, so that just because an act does not fall within one provision does not mean that it is not covered by another.[87] In addition, the Act expressly provides that the provisions are to apply to works of every description, except where a more limited class of works is specified.[88] Again, if, by virtue of the permitted acts, an act may be done in relation to a literary, dramatic or musical work and

---

[67] Available on the IPO website: *http://www.ipo.gov.uk* [Accessed October 22, 2010].
[68] CDPA 1988 ss. 28 and 28A, paras 9–19 et seq., below.
[69] ss.29, 30 and 31, paras 9–23 et seq., below.
[70] ss.31A–31F, paras 9–68, et seq., below.
[71] ss.32–36A, paras 9–96 et seq., below.
[72] ss.37–44A, paras 9–110 et seq., below.
[73] ss.45–50, paras 9–140 et seq., below.
[74] ss.50A–50C, paras 9–149 et seq., below.
[75] s.50D, paras 9–156 et seq., below.
[76] s.50D, paras 9–158 et seq., below.
[77] ss.54–55, paras 9–163 et seq., below.
[78] s.56, para.9–168, below.
[79] ss.57–65, paras 9–170 et seq., below.
[80] s.66, paras 9–197 et seq., below.
[81] ss.66A–67, paras 9–198 et seq., below.
[82] ss.68–75, paras 9–206 et seq., below.
[83] They are considered in detail in Chs 13 and 28, respectively.
[84] See Chs 24 and 21, respectively.
[85] Broadcasting Act 1990 s.176 and Sch.17.
[86] See Ch.28, below.
[87] CDPA 1988 s.28(4).
[88] s.28(2).

the work is itself an adaptation of another work there will be no indirect infringement of that other work.[89]

The fact that an act may be done without infringing copyright does not, however, mean that such an act will not be a breach of some other right or obligation, such as an express contractual term, restricting the doing of any of the specified acts.[90] Thus if a work is supplied to a library under an agreement whereby no part of it is to be copied, but such a copy is made regardless, the library will be in breach of contract, even though there may be no infringement of copyright.[91]

Since the provisions only apply once infringement has been established, procedurally the onus will be on the defendant to prove that one of the exceptions applies.[92] As derogations from the owner's property rights, the courts have occasionally adopted the approach of construing these provisions strictly against the defendant.[93] The matter is one of ordinary statutory construction, however,[94] and the permitted act provisions are to be regarded as an integral part of the Copyright Act, rather than a mere defence.[95] Indeed it is clear that the provisions are to be construed liberally in favour of the defendant, particularly where freedom of expression considerations exist[96]

9–17   **Private use.** Although not formally recognised in the structure of the Act, there are a very small number of permitted acts which relate to the use of a copyright work for private and domestic purposes. For example, there are provisions which permit the copying of a broadcast for the purpose of "time-shifting" and which allow photographs to be taken of part of a television broadcast.[97] Other permitted acts, whilst not specifically confined to the private sphere, are clearly relevant to the copying or use of a work in this context. Under this heading also fall exceptions relating to private study and to the playing of sound recordings for the purposes of a club or society.[98] It should also be remembered that certain acts are not an infringement at all if either done in private (performance of a work, s.19) or done for private and domestic purposes (importation of an infringing copy, s.22). Taken together, these provisions are undoubtedly important, but it would be a mistake to view them as marking a clearly defined boundary between acceptable private use and activities which pose a substantial threat to the copyright

---

[89] s.76.

[90] s.28(1).

[91] This seems entirely obvious, but research conducted during the passage of the Bill showed that there was considerable confusion over this issue: Hansard HL, Vol.501, cols 227–228. S.28(1) has a more limited effect in relation to computer programs, databases and broadcasts.

[92] *Sillitoe v Mcgraw Hill Book Co* [1983] F.S.R. 545 at 558.

[93] See *Beloff v Pressdram Ltd* [1973] F.S.R. 33; *Distillers Co (Biochemicals) Ltd v The Times Newspapers Ltd* [1975] Q.B. 613. Also see *The Longman Group Ltd v Carrington Technical Institute Board of Governors* [1991] 2 N.Z.L.R. 574 (High Court of NZ).

[94] *CCH Canadian Ltd v Law Society of Upper Canada* [2002] 4 F.C. 213, Can. Fed. CA (for the next note for decision of the Supreme Court).

[95] See, e.g. *CCH Canadian Ltd v Law Society of Upper Canada* [2004] SCC 13 (Can. Sup. Ct): "The fair dealing exception .   .   . is a user's right. In order to maintain the proper balance between the rights of a copyright owner and users' interests, it must not be interpreted restrictively.   .   . 'User rights are not just loopholes. Both owner rights and user rights should therefore be given the fair and balanced reading that befits remedial legislation.'," citing D. Vaver, *Copyright Law* (Toronto: Irwin Law, 2000) p.171.

[96] See para.9–26, below.

[97] CDPA 1988 ss.70 and 71, respectively. In relation to rights in performances, an exception (former s.182(2)) allowing a recording of a performance to be made where it was for the private and domestic use of the person making the recording was repealed by the Copyright and Related Rights Regulations 1996 (SI 1966/2967), with effect from December 1, 1966. The permitted acts in relation to rights in performances are listed in Sch.2 to the 1988 Act and are described in Ch.12, s.6, below.

[98] ss. 29, 67 and 72(1B)(a) and related exemptions. Note that on November 12, 2009, the Government announced its intention to repeal the latter provisions.

owner's interests.[99] While it has been the ambition for some time to bring in European legislation to harmonise provisions relating to private copying, little progress has been made.[100] In particular, the Information Society Directive failed to achieve harmonisation in this respect, merely permitting, but not requiring, Member States to provide for a private copying exception on condition that the right holder receive fair compensation.[101] The United Kingdom did not take advantage of this permitted exception when implementing the Directive.

Criminal offences. The structure of the Act might suggest that the permitted acts can only be relied upon in civil actions, but they apply equally in the context of criminal offences,[102] since if the act was permitted it cannot have been an infringement or an offence.[103]   9–18

3. GENERAL PROVISIONS

THE MAKING OF TEMPORARY COPIES

Introduction: The Information Society Directive. The Directive requires that an exemption be made from the reproduction right in the case of certain transient or incidental reproductions. The requirement applies to all forms of subject-matter with which the Directive is concerned, but not to computer programs or databases.[104] As has already been seen,[105] the exemption was legislated for since it was felt that otherwise the temporary reproduction right required by art.2 would unduly interfere with the proper functioning of electronic networks and lawful use.[106] Article 5(1) accordingly provides that temporary acts of reproduction, which are transient or incidental and an integral and essential part of a technological process and whose sole purpose is to enable (a) a transmission in a network between third parties by an intermediary, or (b) a lawful use of a work or other subject-matter to be made, and which have no independent economic significance, shall be exempted from the reproduction right provided for in art.2.[107] It is   9–19

---

[99] In this context it should be noted that Government declined to introduce a levy on blank tapes as a solution to the ubiquitous problem of "home taping" of copyright works, both in the 1988 Act as enacted and when implementing the Information Society Directive (see 2001/29 art.5(2)(b)). Subject to a fairly narrow set of exceptions, private copying therefore remains an infringing act. For a comparative analysis of the problems in this area see G. Davies and M. Hung, *Music and Video Private Copying* (London: Sweet and Maxwell, 1993).

[100] See the *Follow-Up to the Green Paper on Copyright and Related Rights in the Information Society*, Com (96) 586 final, pp.9–12.

[101] See Information Society Directive, 2001/29 art.5(2)(b).

[102] CDPA 1988 s.107 and see Ch.23, below.

[103] s.107(1)(e), (2)(b), (3)(b). Also see *Thames & Hudson Limited v Design and Artists Copyright Society Limited* [1995] F.S.R. 153.

[104] See Information Society Directive (2001/29) art.1(2). Works of these types are subject to the provisions of arts 5 and 6 of the Software Directive and art.5 of the Database Directive respectively, which provide their own code of exceptions. Art.5(1) of the Software Directive in particular provides that temporary acts of reproduction of a computer program shall not require authorisation by the right holder where they are necessary for the use of the computer program by the lawful acquirer in accordance with its intended purpose. The exceptions permitted in the case of computer programs are dealt with by ss.50A–50D of the 1988 Act respectively.

[105] See para.7–20, above.

[106] There were those who argued that the exclusive right in respect of such transient reproduction in networks should not have been made part of the reproduction right in the first place. See, e.g. A. Dietz, "The Protection of Intellectual Property in the Information Age—The Draft EU Copyright Directive of November 1997" [1998] I.P.Q. 335.

[107] Member States are, obviously perhaps, not permitted to make an exception to the distribution right in relation to copies so made, in contrast to the position in relation to copies made by acts of reproduction permitted under arts 5(2) and (3): see art.5(4).

the only mandatory "exception"[108] in the Directive and required the United Kingdom to amend the 1988 Act by the introduction of an entirely new s.28A, since under s.17(6) of the Act copying is defined to include the making of copies which are transient or incidental to some other use of the work. As will be seen, the wording of art.5(1) was implemented virtually verbatim. The Government declined to refine the wording further to take into account the three-step test which art.5(5) imposes as a further requirement on this and all other exceptions,[109] it being the Government's understanding that the Commission of the European Union took the view that the test had already been taken into account when framing art.5(1), so that it would be inappropriate to add the test.[110] Recital 33 of the Directive amplifies art.5 by stating that to the extent that any use meets the above conditions, the exception "should include acts which enable browsing as well as acts of caching to take place, including those which enable transmission systems to function efficiently, provided that the intermediary does not modify the information and does not interfere with the lawful use of technology, widely recognised and used by industry, to obtain data on the use of the information". The Government also declined to implement any part of this wording on the grounds that, in line with what was understood to be the Commission's view, it was "inappropriate".[111]

9–20　　**The 1988 Act as amended.** Section 28A of the 1988 Act implements art.5(1) virtually verbatim. Thus, the section provides that copyright in a literary work (other than a computer program or a database), or in a dramatic, musical or artistic work, the typographical arrangement of a published edition,[112] a sound recording or a film, is not infringed by the making of a temporary copy which is transient or incidental, which is an integral and essential part of a technological process and the sole purpose of which is to enable:

  (a) a transmission of the work in a network between third parties by an intermediary; or

  (b) a lawful use of the work;

and which has no independent economic significance.

　　It will be noted, first, that in line with the Directive, the permitted act of making temporary copies does not extend to computer programs or copyright databases. More generally, the permitted act is directed to two quite different situations, namely copying which enables the transmission of a work in a network and copying which enables some lawful use of a work. In each case, however, there are common requirements:

  (1) The permitted act only extends to the restricted act of copying. If, for example, as part of the same process, the work is communicated to the

---

[108] The terminology of art.5(1) is ambivalent, in that it speaks of temporary acts of reproduction as being "exempted" from the right, whereas arts 5(2) and (3) speak of the acts referred to there as being allowable "exceptions or limitations" to the relevant rights. Nevertheless, art.5 is generally headed "Exceptions and Limitations" and recital 33 speaks of art.5(1) as being an "exception". Presumably Member States are free to implement art.5(1) either by defining the reproduction right in terms that exclude the exclusive right to do or authorise these temporary acts or by providing a separate exception, which is what the United Kingdom has done.

[109] As to this test, see para.9–02, above. In the context of the Information Society Directive, (2001/29/EC) see also J. Griffiths, "The 'three-step test' in European Copyright Law—problems and solutions", [2009] I.P.Q. 428.

[110] See the Government Conclusions to the Patent Office's Consultation Paper of August 7, 2002, para.4.2. This is despite that fact that the art.5(1) exception for temporary copies is made expressly subject to the three-step test in art.5(5).

[111] See the previous note.

[112] The copyright conferred on typographical arrangements of published editions by the United Kingdom (see paras 7–85 et seq., above) was not within the ambit of the Directive. Unless CDPA 1988 s.28A extended to such works, however, the operation of the exception in the case of literary works in facsimile form (e.g. pdf format) would be seriously affected.

public via the internet, there is no defence under this provision to the act of communication.

(2) The permitted act only extends to the making of a temporary copy of the work. "Temporary" is not defined in the Act or in the Directive but necessarily implies that the copy will be deleted, destroyed or will otherwise disappear within some limited, although not necessarily short, time. An essential nature of a temporary copy is that it lacks permanence, usually, in the present context, by virtue of the nature of the physical copy in question. A copy made in RAM, which ceases to exist when a computer is turned off or when that part of memory is required for some other purpose, or a copy displayed on a computer screen, are both no doubt temporary copies in this sense. Recital 33 of the Directive, set out above, indicates that temporary copies made to enable browsing or caching are capable of falling within the exception. Copies made in RAM or on a computer screen to enable browsing will no doubt therefore normally fall within the exception. Presumably a cached copy may itself amount to a temporary copy and thus be permitted, although such copies may often be stored for substantial periods of time.[113]

(3) The copy must not only be temporary but also be transient or incidental. Transience reinforces the requirement that the copy be temporary, but also adds the notion that the lifetime of the copy is short or fleeting. "Incidental" connotes that the making of the copy is incidental to some other purpose, or is the means to some other end. A copy of a work displayed on a computer screen will normally be transient (although not if it remains displayed for a substantial length of time) but not incidental: the display of the copy is likely to be the very reason why the process has been initiated. A copy made in RAM in order that some process can be carried out on it, in particular, in order that it may be transmitted in a network, may or may not be transient but will be usually only incidental to that larger purpose. Again, a cached copy will often be more than transient but perhaps can be regarded as being incidental in that it merely enables easier access to the work in the near future. In all of this, it must of course be remembered that the exception does not apply to computer programs or databases.

(4) The copying must take place as an integral and essential part of a technological process. "Technological process" is not defined but is a very general term. A temporary copy made in writing on a piece of paper which is then thrown away might be temporary and transient, but it would not usually be part of a technological process. The requirement that it be integral implies that the copying is part of a process whereby the copying is integrated with other steps in the process. The requirement that the copying is an essential part of the process implies that without the copying the process will fail to achieve its designed objective.

(5) The making of the copy must have no independent economic significance. The important word to emphasise here is "independent", which presumably means independent of the network transmission or the lawful user. Some acts of temporary copying may well have economic significance. For example, some users may be willing to pay to be able to see the temporary display of a work on a screen. If, however, the display is to enable the lawful use of the work, it would seem that the display does not have an economic significance independent of the lawful use. As has been

---

[113] The maker of cached copies will in any event normally have a defence under r.18 of the Electronic Commerce (EC Directive) Regulations 2002 (SI 2002/2013). See para.21–108, below.

seen, recital 33 of the Directive contemplates that the exception should include acts which enable browsing to take place.[114]

9–21   **Transmissions in networks.** Where the above conditions are satisfied, copying will be permitted when it is to enable the transmission of the work in a network between third parties by an intermediary. None of these expressions is defined.[115] This limb of the exception is obviously aimed primarily at copying which takes place by intermediaries such as service providers. Copying of a work other than the one to be transmitted is not permitted, nor is any alteration of the work by the intermediary.[116] It would also appear that the copying must be to enable transmission of the work *by* the intermediary. Copying of a work to enable transmission of the work *to* an intermediary for onward transmission to a further recipient is therefore not permitted. Nor does the section permit unlicensed copying by the further recipient. The fact that an infringement of copyright has been committed by the sender, or will be committed by the recipient of the transmission, does not affect the intermediary's exemption from liability, even if he knows or has reason to believe that an infringement is taking place. In such circumstances, however, it may be possible to obtain an injunction against the service provider under s.191JA of the Act.[117] The E-Commerce Regulations,[118] which implement the E-Commerce Directive,[119] provide an overlapping defence in this area.

9–22   **Lawful use.** Again, where the conditions set out in s.28A are satisfied, temporary copying to enable "lawful use" will be permitted. Although the Act does not define lawful use, recital 33 of the Directive states that a use "should be considered lawful where it is authorised by the right holder or not restricted by law". No doubt the latter type of use includes any case where another of the permitted act provisions applies or where some other defence can be relied on. As to "lawful use" generally, if the making of a temporary copy is to enable a use which is licensed, the making of that copy will often itself fall within the scope of the licence, so that the permitted act provisions of s.28A will not need to be relied on. Again, if the enabled use is lawful by virtue of a permitted act, for example the making of a copy of a work for the purpose of private study under s.29(1C), then the making of such a temporary copy would in any event usually be permit-

---

[114] In *Football Association Premier League Ltd v QC Leisure* [2008] EWHC 1411 (Ch); [2008] 3 C.M.L.R. 12, the Court has referred to the CJEU two questions on the interpretation of the Information Society Directive (2001/29/EC) with regard to the expression "independent economic significance" in art.5(1) of the Directive (implemented in the UK by s.28A CDPA 1988), as follows: Q5(a) Are transient copies of a work created within a satellite television decoder box or on a television screen linked to the decoder box, and whose sole purpose is to enable a use of the work not otherwise restricted by law, to be regarded as having "independent economic significance" within the meaning of art.5(1) of Directive 2001/29/EC by reason of the fact that such copies provide the only basis upon which the rights holder can extract remuneration for the use of his rights? (b) Is the answer to Question 5(a) affected by (i) whether the transient copies have any inherent value; or (ii) whether the transient copies comprise a small part of a collection of works and/or other subject-matter which otherwise may be used without infringement of copyright; or (iii) whether the exclusive licensee of the rights holder in another Member State has already received remuneration for use of the work in that Member State? The case is pending under case C–403/08 [2008] OJ C301/19 joined with C–429/08 [2008] OJ C301/26 (*Karen Murphy v Media Protection Services Ltd* [2008] EWHC 1666 (Admin); [2008] F.S.R. 33). See also *Union of European Football Associations (UEFA) v Euroview Sport Ltd* [2010] EWHC 1066 (Ch), where Arnold J., has referred similar questions to the court and invited it to consider whether the reference should proceed with the *Premier League* case given the similar legal and factual issues (pending case C–228/10) and see C. Stothers, "Copyright and the EC Treaty: music, films and football", [2009] E.I.P.R. 272.

[115] Recital 33 of the Information Society Directive 2001/29 qualifies "transmission" with the word "efficient".

[116] Recital 33.

[117] See para.21–119, below.

[118] The Electronic Commerce (EC Directive) Regulations 2002 (SI 2002/2013).

[119] Directive 2001/31/EC.

ted under s.29(1C), since it would be likely to fall within the ambit of dealing with the work for the permitted purpose of private study.[120] The same appears to be true in relation to other permitted acts. Nevertheless, the effect of s.23A is to make the position clearer.

In relation to acts which are not expressly licensed there is often doubt about the full extent of the licence. In these cases, the effect of this permitted act provision is to make it clear that acts which "enable" lawful use will not be infringements of copyright, and so to avoid technical arguments about the scope of the licence. The key question will be whether the use is lawful.

4. THE FAIR DEALING PROVISIONS

A. OVERVIEW

Introduced in 1911, the fair dealing provisions provide three important limitations to owners' rights, namely, fair dealing for the purposes of non-commercial research or private study, fair dealing for the purposes of criticism or review and fair dealing for the purpose of news reporting. Before the 1911 Act there were no statutory exceptions to copyright infringement in the United Kingdom, unlike in many civil law countries, which have long provided such provisions.[121] Nevertheless, the question of what amounted to "fair dealing" frequently arose under the law prior to 1911 in determining whether the use which had been made of the plaintiff's work was sufficient to constitute infringement.[122] As such, this question was often not distinguished from the issue of whether a substantial part of the plaintiff's work had been taken.[123] Since the 1911 Act, the two issues have been quite distinct. It is only when the court has determined that a substantial part has been taken that any question of fair dealing arises.

As noted above, under the 1988 Act fair dealing is permitted for the purposes of private study or non-commercial research, criticism or review or the reporting of current events. Other types of dealing are not permitted no matter how "fair" they may be.[124] This restricted approach can be contrasted with the fair use provisions under US law,[125] which only provides guidelines as to what amounts to fair

9–23

---

[120] See paras 9–35 et seq., below.
[121] English and French versions of some of these early provisions can be found in A. Birrell, *Seven Lectures on the Law and History of Copyright in Books* (London: Cassell & Co, 1899) pp.182–185.
[122] e.g. *Wilkins v Aikin* (1810) 17 Vesey 422; *Scott v Stanford* (1867) L. R. 3 Eq. 718; *Bradbury v Hotten* (1872) L.R. 8 Ex. 1; *Smith v Chato* (1874) 31 L.T. 77. Prior to the 1911 Act, however, no cases had arisen on the question of whether there was a right to copy a work for the purposes of private study.
[123] In particular see *Bradbury v Hotten* (1872) L.R. 8 Ex. 1, but cf. *Bell v Whitehead* (1839) 8 L.J., N.S. (Equity) 141. For a review of the history of fair dealing in the UK, see A. Sims, "Strangling their creation: the court's treatment of fair dealing in copyright law since 1911", [2010] I.P.Q. 192. See also R. Burrell: "Reining in Copyright Law. Is Fair Use the Answer?" [2001] I.P.Q. 361.
[124] "It is fair dealing directed to and consequently limited to and to be judged in relation to the approved purposes. It is dealing which is fair for the approved purposes and not dealing which might be fair for some other purpose or fair in general", per Ungoed-Thomas J. in *Beloff v Pressdram* [1973] F.S.R. 33; "The provisions are not to be regarded as mere examples of a general wide discretion vested in the courts to refuse to enforce copyright where they believe such refusal to be fair and reasonable", per Laddie J. in *Pro Sieben Media AG v Carlton UK Television Ltd* [1998] F.S.R. 43 at 49 (reversed by the Court of Appeal, [1999] 1 W.L.R. 605; [1999] F.S.R. 610, but not with any disapproval of this statement) . For further discussion, see J. Griffiths "Preserving Judicial Freedom of Movement—Interpreting Fair Dealing in Copyright Law" [2000] I.P.Q. 164.
[125] Copyright Act 1976, 17 U.S.C., s.107. M. de Zwart, "A historical analysis of the birth of fair dealing and fair use: lessons for the digital age" [2007] I.P.Q. 1, 60.

use[126] and which are available in relation to all types of work. The Whitford Committee had recommended that a similar approach be adopted in the United Kingdom,[127] but this was rejected by the Government, together with a proposal to rename the defence "fair use" or "fair practice".[128] The argument against a codified system such as that in the United Kingdom is that a more flexible approach allows the courts to develop the law on a case-by-case basis as new problems emerge.[129]

9–24   **The Berne Convention.**[130] Article 10(1) of the Convention provides that it is permissible to make "quotations" from a work which has already been lawfully made available to the public, provided that the making is compatible with fair practice, and their extent does not exceed that justified by the purpose, including quotations from newspaper articles and periodicals in the form of press summaries. Where such use is made, however, "mention" must be made of the source, and of the name of the author if it appears on the work.[131] "Lawfully made available to the public" is a broader concept than that of a "published work" and would include, for example, a public performance or electronic dissemination. Furthermore, there is no requirement under the article that the work be made available to the public with the author's consent, only that this has been lawfully done. Thus "lawfully made available to the public" might include a situation where a work is made available by virtue of a compulsory licence. Presumably, however, it would not include a situation where a work has only been distributed to a narrow category of persons.[132] As to use for the purposes of reporting current events, a number of provisions of the Convention are in theory relevant. First, art.2(8) excludes protection for "news of the day or to miscellaneous facts having the character of mere items of press information".[133] Secondly, art.10*bis*(1) provides for a limited class of exception, permitting "the reproduction by the press, the broadcasting or the communication to the public by wire of articles published in newspapers or periodicals on current economic, political or religious topics, and of broadcast works of the same character", provided a due acknowledgment is made. However, this is of little application in the present context since it does not apply if the right has been expressly reserved. Thirdly, art.10*bis*(2) states that it is for individual countries "to determine the conditions under which, for the purpose of reporting current events by means of photography, cinematography, broadcasting or communications to the public by wire, literary or artistic works seen or heard in the course of the event may, to the extent justified by the informatory purpose, be reproduced and made and available to the public". This article is in effect dealing with incidental inclusion of works (see

---

[126] *Sony Corporation of America v Universal City Studios* (1984) 464 U.S. 417. This approach has been criticised for ignoring the principle of statutory construction noscitur a sociis (i.e. that the meaning of a doubtful word may be ascertained by reference to the meaning of words associated with it). See P. Goldstein, *Copyright* (Boston: Little, Brown & Co, 1989) para.10.2.1.

[127] Report of the Committee to Consider the Law on Copyright and Designs, Cmnd. 6732, paras 672–677.

[128] *Hansard*, HL Vol.491, cols 85–89. Although it was accepted that "dealing" is somewhat deceptive, in that it implies some form of transaction, it was retained on the grounds that the phrase is understood by lawyers and others in the field.

[129] See Ll. L. Weinreb, "Fair's Fair: A Comment on the Fair Use Doctrine," (1990) 103 Harv. L. Rev. 1137.

[130] For a full discussion of exceptions permitted under the Berne Convention, see paras 23–28 et seq., below.

[131] Berne Convention art.10(3).

[132] As in *Hubbard v Vosper* [1972] 2 Q.B. 84, CA. See S. Ricketson and J.C. Ginsburg, *International Copyright and Neighbouring Rights, The Berne Convention and Beyond* 2nd edn (Oxford: Oxford University Press, 2006), paras 13–39 to 13–43.

[133] As to the doubtful nature of the exception, see S. Ricketson and J.C. Ginsburg, *International Copyright and Neighbouring Rights, The Berne Convention and Beyond* 2nd edn (Oxford: Oxford University Press, 2006), paras 8–104 to 8–106.

para.9–61, below), and is not of general application in relation to reporting of current events.

The Information Society Directive. A number of provisions of the Directive ap- **9–25** ply in the area of fair dealing, and required several changes to be made to the 1988 Act. First, whereas the 1988 Act originally provided that fair dealing with a work for the purposes of "research" was permitted, art.5(3)(a) of the Directive in effect stipulates that such acts must be of a non-commercial nature. The Act has therefore been amended to restrict this permitted act to research for a "non-commercial" purpose. Secondly, art.5(2)(b) effectively requires the private study provision to be restricted to private study of a non-commercial nature, and the Act has been amended to make this clear. Thirdly, whereas the Act originally provided that fair dealing with a work for the purposes of criticism or review was permitted where the work was either published or unpublished, art.5(3)(d) of the Directive stipulates that such use shall be permitted only where the use relates to a work or other subject-matter which has already been lawfully made available to the public.[134] The Act has been amended accordingly. Fourth, although in some cases of fair dealing the Act required a "sufficient acknowledgment" of the work and its author to be made, no such acknowledgment was required in the case of fair dealing for the purposes of research or private study. The Directive has changed this. These amendments all took effect from October 31, 2003.[135]

The Human Rights Act.[136] Consideration is given to the Human Rights Act **9–26** 1998 elsewhere[137] but it has a potentially significant impact in the context of the fair dealing provisions, where the art.10 right to freedom of expression will often overlap with the permitted acts of criticism, review and reporting of current events. In cases where it is necessary to reproduce a substantial part of a work for these purposes, the fair dealing provisions will usually permit this and thus the freedom of expression requirements of the Act will be satisfied. The requirement of fairness, particularly in the context of a dealing for the purposes of reporting current events, will normally be flexible enough to enable a court to reflect properly the public interest in freedom of expression and, in particular, the freedom of the press.[138] There may, nevertheless, be rare cases where the right of freedom of expression will come into irreconcilable conflict with the protection

---

[134] This provision has clearly been taken from art.10(1) of the Berne Convention. See para.9–24, above.

[135] The Copyright and Related Rights Regulations 2003 (SI 2003/2498) para.1.

[136] What follows in this paragraph is based on *Ashdown v Telegraph Group Ltd* [2001] EWCA Civ 1142; [2002] Ch. 149; [2002] R.P.C. 5. But see *HRH Prince of Wales v Associated Newspapers Ltd* [2006] EWHC 522 (Ch); [2006] E.C.D.R. 20. The case related to an application by the Prince of Wales (W) for summary judgment against a newspaper publishing company (N) for reproducing without consent private journals obtained illegally via a breach of confidence. It was held that when balancing W's right to privacy under the Human Rights Act 1998 Sch. Pt I art.8, against N's right to freedom of expression under art.10 of the 1998 Act, it was impossible to say that N's disclosures from a particular journal's contents were necessary in a democratic society for the protection of the rights and freedoms of others, and that W's entitlement to confidentiality in respect of that journal should be overridden. The extracts quoted from the journal formed a substantial part, both qualitatively and quantitatively, of the whole, and there was no real prospect that the defence of fair dealing under s.30(2) of the 1988 Act would succeed. An appeal against the decision was dismissed ([2006] EWCA Civ 1776). The Court of Appeal held that N's publication of the information did not in the circumstances constitute fair dealing for the purposes of reporting current events; nor did N have any defence of fair dealing for the purposes of criticism or review.

[137] See paras 3–304, above and 21–93 et seq., below.

[138] This approach requires that decisions made before the Human Rights Act came into force as to what amounts to "fair" dealing should not be regarded as inflexible, although they are still important. The question which needs to be asked is: are the facts of the case such that the importance of freedom of expression outweighs the conventional considerations established by the earlier authorities as to what is "fair"? See *Ashdown*.

afforded by the 1988 Act, notwithstanding the express exceptions to be found in the Act, even when these expressions are construed liberally in favour of the user[139] and a flexible approach is adopted in relation to what is "fair" use. Examples might be where the reporting in question cannot realistically be said to be of "current events",[140] where the reporting of current events in the public interest can only effectively be done by the use of a photograph[141] or where there is a sufficient public interest in the criticism or review of a work which has not previously been made available to the public.[142] In these circumstances, a court would be bound, in so far as it is able, to apply the Act in a manner that accommodates the right of freedom of expression. The possible methods of doing so would be to refuse the discretionary relief of an injunction, leaving the claimant to his remedy in damages (which will usually be the appropriate course), or by invoking the public interest defence.[143]

9–27   **Approach to construction.** Some consideration has already been given as to how the permitted act provisions should be construed.[144] In general, the fair dealing provisions involve issues on which a trial judge comes to a judgmental conclusion after taking into account a number of factors. As such, his decision should not be disturbed by the Court of Appeal unless it proceeded from some error of principle or is clearly unsustainable.[145] As to the various expressions, "criticism or review" and "reporting current events", these are expressions which should be interpreted liberally and their precise boundaries cannot be plotted: the nearer any use comes to the boundaries, unplotted as they are, the less likely is the use to be "fair".[146] All the fair dealing provisions use the words "for the purpose of". As to whether this expression imports an objective or subjective test, it is important to construe the composite phrases "for the purpose of non-commercial research" and "for the purpose of private study", etc. rather than each single word. When this is done, the precise mental element on the part of the user ceases to be of great importance. The words "in the context of" or "as part of an exercise in" could be substituted for "for the purpose of" without any significant change of meaning. The task of the court is to consider the use made of the work and then ascertain what the perceived purpose of that use was. The user's subjective intention might well be relevant to the issue of whether the dealing was "fair", but it is wrong for a court to put itself in the user's shoes to decide what the purpose was.[147]

9–28   **Preparatory dealings.** In cases where there has been dissemination of a work for the purposes of criticism, review or reporting of current events, there will usually

---

[139] See para.9–27, below.

[140] A case suggested in *Ashdown*.

[141] Such use falls outside the permitted act provisions. See para.9–54, below.

[142] Again, such use falls outside the permitted act provisions. See para.9–37, below. The facts of *Hubbard v Vosper* [1972] 2 Q.B. 84, CA might be such a case.

[143] See para.21–93, below.

[144] See para.9–16, above.

[145] *Pro Sieben Media AG v Carlton UK Television Ltd* [1999] 1 W.L.R. 605; [1999] F.S.R. 610, approved by the House of Lords in *Designers Guild Ltd v Russell Williams (Textiles) Ltd* [2001] F.S.R. 113.

[146] *Pro Sieben Media AG v Carlton UK Television Ltd* [1999] 1 W.L.R. 605. The same is no doubt true of the expressions "non-commercial research" and "private study".

[147] *Pro Sieben Media AG v Carlton UK Television Ltd* [1999] 1 W.L.R. 605. It was said there that to do so would, for example, encourage journalists to give implausible evidence as to their intentions if encouraged to think that a sincerely held belief as to the actual purpose would be sufficient. See *Pro Sieben*, above, at 620 and *Hyde Park Residence Ltd v Yelland* [2001] Ch. 143; [2000] R.P.C. 604. If, however, the purpose is to discover whether the use fell within the ambit of the statute, there seems no good reason why both the user's actual intentions and also the impact of the use on the intended recipient should not be of help. If implausible evidence is given on behalf of the defendant, then it is unlikely to be believed.

be other, preparatory acts of copying, especially where dissemination takes place via one of the established forms of media. In such a case, the preparatory acts will also have been carried out "for the purpose" of the relevant act.[148] In those cases where a sufficient acknowledgment is required, this raises a difficult issue as to whether the acknowledgment must be made in respect of these preparatory acts as well as the acts of dissemination.[149]

B. Non-Commercial Research and Private Study

(i) Introduction

The general aim of these provisions is to give students and non-commercial researchers greater access to copyright works. By granting a limited right to copy articles and small sections of other works, these groups are repeatedly able to consult sources to which they may not have ready access, provided that the copying remains within the bounds of what is fair (see para.9–58, below). As was the case under the 1956 Act, the exceptions apply only to literary, dramatic, musical and artistic works, thus "it is possible to make copies of parts of plays for the purposes of studying drama, but no equivalent loophole exists in relation to film footage".[150] There are also provisions covering the typographical arrangement of a published edition.[151] These exceptions fail to reflect the increasing importance of non-textual media for both study and research and means, for example, that a researcher is not permitted to copy part of a sound recording under this section, even though there would be no infringement of the underlying musical work in doing so.[152] In this connection, it should be noted that the Gowers Review of Intellectual Property (HM Treasury, December 2006) recommended that the fair dealing exceptions permitting private copying for the purposes of research for a non-commercial purpose should be extended to cover all forms of content, including for the first time sound recordings, films and broadcasts. The recommendation relates to the copying, not the distribution of media (Recommendation 9). In December 2009, the IPO announced in a second stage consultation on copyright exceptions that the Government now proposes to extend s.29 to include sound recordings, films and broadcasts. In its view this would eliminate many of the rights clearance problems and enable individuals to make their own "fair dealing" copies. However, mindful of the fact that it may be appealing to copy such works purely for "entertainment" purposes, the Government intends to restrict the permitted acts relating to these additional works to those who are members of an educational establishment, and for the purposes of private study or research

9–29

---

[148] *Pro Sieben Media AG v Carlton UK Television Ltd* [1999] 1 W.L.R. 605; [1999] F.S.R. 610. There, the defendant had made a copy of the whole of the claimant's television programme before deciding to use a short extract. Although there was little evidence about the circumstances in which this was done, the Court of Appeal accepted that it was copied simply in order for it to be available to the editor to consider whether to use an extract from it. Since the ultimate use of the extract was for the purpose of criticism or review, the making of the complete copy was for the same ultimate purpose. See also *Time Warner Entertainment Ltd v Channel 4 Television Corporation Plc* [1994] E.M.L.R. 1; *Television New Zealand v Newsmonitor Services Ltd* (1993) 27 I.P.R. 441 (High Ct of New Zealand) at 467.

[149] See, further, para.9–33, below.

[150] *Pro Sieben Media AG v Carlton UK Television Ltd* [1998] F.S.R. 43 at 48, but note the limited educational exception that exists in relation to films: CDPA 1988 s.32(2) and see para.9–100, below.

[151] 1988 Act s.29(2).

[152] Note that the combined effect of ss.19(1) and 2(1) of the 1911 Act was to permit such acts.

being undertaken at that establishment. In its view, this should minimise the potential risks of unauthorised use and give some assurance to right holders.[153]

(ii) Non-commercial research

9–30   **Introduction: the Information Society Directive.** The Directive permits Member States to make an exception to the reproduction right, to the communication to the public right, and to the distribution right, in the case of use "for the sole purpose of scientific research, as long as the source, including the author's name, is indicated, unless this turns out to be impossible, and to the extent justified by the non-commercial purpose to be achieved".[154] Recital 42 also provides that when applying the exception or limitation for non-commercial scientific research purposes, the non-commercial nature of the activity in question should be determined "by that activity as such" and the organisational structure and the means of funding of the establishment concerned are not to be the decisive factors in this respect. A number of preliminary points can be made about this. First, although the Directive refers to "scientific" research, it is reasonably clear that this includes the humanities.[155] Secondly, the source of the work will usually have to be indicated. Thirdly, in the rather convoluted language of the Directive, it is clear that the purpose of the research must be non-commercial and the extent of any exception is to be limited to the extent justified by that non-commercial purpose.

9–31   **The 1988 Act, as amended.** The Act required amendment to comply with the non-commercial nature of the permitted exception and the requirement of recognition of the source. Thus, the Act now provides that fair dealing with a literary,[156] dramatic, musical or artistic work for the purposes of research for a non-commercial purpose does not infringe any copyright in the work, provided it is accompanied by a sufficient acknowledgment,[157] unless this is impossible, for reasons of practicability or otherwise.[158] Previously, fair dealing was permitted in the case of any form of research, other than in the case of a database.[159] As it happens, the Whitford Committee had recommended that commercial research

---

[153] "Taking forward the Gowers Review of Intellectual Property: Second Stage Consultation on Copyright exceptions", para.187, and see proposed amendments to s.29 in the draft Regulations attached to this document at p.47: "The Copyright (Permitted Acts) (Amendment) Regulations 2010", ss.1 to 4. The complete document is available on the IPO website, *http://www.ipo.gov.uk* [Accessed October 22, 2010]. The consultation period ended on March 31, 2010.

[154] Information Society Directive, 2001/29 arts 5(3)(a), (4). An exception is permitted to the distribution right only to the extent justified by the purpose of the authorised act of reproduction: art.5(4).

[155] Note that although art.6 of the Database Directive 96/9 also refers to scientific research, recital 36 of that Directive makes it clear that this term covers "both the natural sciences and the human sciences."

[156] Note, however, that special rules apply to computer programs with the result that they are effectively taken out of this provision. See para.9–39, below.

[157] CDPA 1988 s.29(1), as amended.

[158] CDPA 1988 s.29(1B). See Joint Guidelines on Copyright and Academic Research: Guidelines for researchers and publishers in the Humanities and Social Sciences, British Academy and Publishers Association, April 2008.

[159] As enacted, no distinction was made by the 1988 Act as to databases either. However, implementation of the Database Directive (96/9) required the permitted act of fair dealing with a database for the purpose of research to be restricted to non-commercial research, and also that such fair dealing be accompanied by a sufficient acknowledgment. See s.29(5), as introduced by the Copyright and Rights in Databases Regulations (SI 1997/3032). With the changes made to implement the Information Society Directive 2001/29, however, it was no longer necessary to distinguish between databases and other literary works, and s.29(5) has therefore been deleted.

should be excluded from the scope of fair dealing[160] but this did not survive lobbying from British industry.[161] In the case of the typographical arrangement of a published edition, fair dealing for the purposes of research or private study does not infringe any copyright in the arrangement, and no acknowledgment is required at all.[162]

"Research for a non-commercial purpose." The expressions "research" and "non-commercial purpose" no doubt have to be construed consistently with the Directive,[163] but in the end they are ordinary English words.[164] In the equivalent Australian provision, "research" has been held to have its ordinary dictionary meaning, namely, the "diligent and systematic inquiry or investigation into a subject in order to discover facts or principles".[165] Quite what the limits are of non-commercial research is not clear. Although, as already noted, recital 42 provides that the *non-commercial* nature of the activity in question should be determined "by that activity as such" and that the organisational structure and the means of funding of the establishment concerned (where there is one, presumably) are not the *decisive* factors in this respect, this does not provide a great deal of extra clarity. Presumably any research which, at the time it is conducted, is contemplated or intended should be ultimately used for a purpose which has some commercial value will not be within the permitted act. "Commercial" in general means engaged in commerce, which suggests an activity by way of trade, but the expression no doubt encompasses any activity conducted with a view to making a profit. What is relevant is the purpose of the research, not the larger purpose of the researcher. Thus, in the case of research carried out by an employee of a not-for-profit organisation but with a view to raising funds for the organisation, it seems that the research would be for a commercial purpose. The purpose may no doubt be internal, that is, research to be used to produce something which has a commercial value (a product, or the supply of professional services, for example), or external, where the research is published as part of a larger commercial enterprise (the publication of a book with a view to profit, for example).

9–32

Sufficient acknowledgment. If it is not to be an infringement, the dealing must be accompanied by a sufficient acknowledgment, except "where this would be

9–33

---

[160] That this was the committee's view is evident from paras 676–677. Also see Hansard, HL Vol.491, col.93.

[161] See *Hansard*, HL Vol.493, cols 1153–1157. Reliance was placed on the transaction cost argument, that is to say, that any revenue raised from licensing agreements would be swallowed up by the costs of administering such agreements (see *Hansard*, HL Vol.491, cols 92–94). It is instructive to contrast the position in the United States, where the ready availability of licences has meant that the reproduction of single copies of articles for commercial research purposes does not amount to fair use (*American Geophysical Union v Texaco Inc.* 60 F.3d 913 (2d Cir. 1994)).

[162] CDPA 1988 s.29(2). Typographical arrangements are treated differently from other works under s.29 because they are not subject to the Information Society Directive. Although there has been an amendment to s.29(2), the effect is to preserve the position in relation to such works as it was before an amendment was made to s.29(1).

[163] The Government did not amend the section to restrict any dealing, in the words of the Directive, to "scientific" research, taking the view that the breadth of the term was such that it did not appear to add anything. See the Government Conclusions on the Patent Office's Consultation Paper of August 7, 2002, para.5.4.

[164] *HM Stationery Office v Green Amps Ltd* [2007] EWHC 2755 (Ch). Held that s.29 required both that what would otherwise be the act of infringement was for the purposes of research and that such research should be for a non-commercial purpose. The defendant downloaded maps for a "mapping tool" which at the time of litigation still had R & D status. As the end use of the downloaded maps was to make a commercial toolkit, the judge found that the research was for a commercial purpose. See also E. Derclaye, *Case Comment* [2008] E.I.P.R. 30(4), 162.

[165] *De Garis v Neville Jeffress Pidler Pty Ltd* (1990) 18 I.P.R. 292 (Fed. Ct of Australia) at 298–299. Also see *Television New Zealand v Newsmonitor Services Ltd* (1993) 27 I.P.R. 441 (High Ct of New Zealand) at 463.

impossible for reasons of practicality or otherwise". This requirement was introduced as a result of art.5(3)(a) of the Directive, which permits such use, "as long as the source, including the author's name, is indicated" unless "this turns out to be impossible". As will be seen, the basic requirement of sufficient acknowledgment was already part of UK law as applied to other cases of fair dealing, and is defined to mean an acknowledgment identifying the work in question by its title or other description and identifying the author unless (a) in the case of a published work, it is published anonymously[166]; or (b) in the case of an unpublished work, it is not possible to ascertain the identity of the author by reasonable inquiry.[167] In the case of s.29(1), the requirement therefore has two layers of dispensation. First, the general requirement of sufficient acknowledgment is dispensed with where the work is published anonymously or, in the case of an unpublished work, where the author cannot reasonably be ascertained. Secondly, even where, for example, the work was published under the author's name, acknowledgment is also dispensed with where it would be impossible for reasons of practicality or otherwise to name him.[168] Such cases are likely to be rare, but may arise where the version of the work used for the dealing no longer bears the author's name. No doubt the words "for reasons of practicality or otherwise" were added in the Act because the wording of the Directive ("unless this turns out to be impossible"), taken literally, impose a test that could hardly ever be satisfied, and this was not the intention of the Directive. Dispensation in cases where acknowledgment would be "impossible for reasons of practicality" suggests a situation where it is not practical, using all reasonable endeavours, to establish the name of the author or title of the work in the time available before the dealing in question. Cases where it is "otherwise" impossible suggest a situation where no amount of inquiry would have revealed this information. It should be noted that although the Act does not require the work or author to be named where the work has been published anonymously, even where these details are in fact known, this is not consistent with the Directive, which requires identification in such circumstances. It might have been better simply to adopt the words of the Directive in the form "...as long as the source, including the author's name, is indicated, unless this turns out to be impossible for reasons of practicality or otherwise".

In other cases where acknowledgment is required by the Act, namely criticism, review and the reporting of current events, the "dealing" in question usually involves some form of public dissemination of the work, in which event the acknowledgment has some purpose and value for the author. In the case of research, however, the dealing may be wholly private.[169] Is the researcher required to place the name of the author of the work and the title on every copy he makes? It may be that the Directive, which refers to the source being "indicated", does not require this and only contemplates the source being named when some communication of the work to a another person actually takes place, but a literal reading of the Act requires an acknowledgment in the case of every dealing. In some cases of research of a private nature the dealing can no doubt be brought within the private study exception, which does not require acknowledg-

---

[166] For example, see *PCR Ltd v Dow Jones Telerate Ltd* [1998] F.S.R. 170, in particular, at 184.
[167] CDPA 1988 s.178.
[168] In *Fraser-Woodward v BBC* [2005] EWHC 472; [2005] F.S.R. 36, it was held that sufficient acknowledgment of the author did not require express identification. All that was required was that there was an identification and it was a question of fact whether there was or not.
[169] See para.9–23, above, on the choice of the word "dealing." The making of a single copy in the course of research is clearly a dealing. If it were otherwise the act of copying could not be brought within the section at all.

ment[170] but this will not always be the position. It seems that in this latter type of case an acknowledgment is required to avoid infringement.

Form of acknowledgment. The acknowledgment of the work may take the form   **9–34** of identification of its title or some other description of it. Identification of the author is required unless, in the case of a published work, it is published anonymously, or in the case of an unpublished work, it is not possible for a person to ascertain the identity of the author by reasonable enquiry.[171] Identification need not be by reference to the author's proper name, particularly if this would be unlikely to have any particular significance or would be meaningless to the bulk of the intended audience.[172] Use of a pseudonym by which an author is known to the public will therefore be sufficient. There is authority that the acknowledgment must recognise the position or claims of the author and that it is not sufficient that the title of the work and the identity of the author are immediately revealed in the text[173] but this seems doubtful. The Directive, for its part, merely requires that the source, including the author's name, be "indicated". It is important to emphasise that the acknowledgment must identify the author of the work, not the copyright owner.[174] If the part of the work which is used itself reproduces a substantial part of an underlying work then the underlying work must also be acknowledged. This may prove to be a trap for the unwary.[175]

(iii) Private study.

The Directive. Articles 5(2)(b) and (4) of the Information Society Directive   **9–35** permit Member States to provide an exception to the reproduction right and to the distribution right in the case of reproductions on any medium made by a natural person for private use and for ends that are neither directly nor indirectly commercial, on condition that the right holder receive fair compensation. Although the existing provisions of the 1988 Act permitted fair dealing with a literary, dramatic, musical or artistic work for the purposes of private study,[176] it was clearly felt that this might not exclude private study for a commercial end. Logistically, the Directive also required that dealings for the purposes of commercial research be dealt with differently from dealings for the purposes of private study. The Act has therefore been amended to place the private study exception in a new subsection[177] and to define private study so as to exclude any study which is directly or indirectly for a commercial purpose.[178] No acknowledgment is required in the case of this permitted act. Again, in the case of the typographical arrangement of a published edition, fair dealing for the purposes of private

---

[170] See paras 9–35 et seq., below.

[171] CDPA 1988 s.178.

[172] *Pro Sieben Media AG v Carlton UK Television Ltd* [1999] 1 W.L.R. 605; [1999] F.S.R. 610; *Newspaper Licensing Agency Ltd v Marks and Spencer Plc* [1999] R.P.C. 536 CA. See further as to the form of acknowledgment, para.9–57, below.

[173] *Sillitoe v McGraw-Hill Book Co* [1983] F.S.R. 545 at 565. In that case the defendant published study notes of various works to help students prepare for examination. It was quite clear what the title of work was and who was its author, but it was said that there was nothing by way of "acknowledgment"; the work was treated, so far as appearances went, as if it were a non-copyright work.

[174] *Express Newspapers Plc v News (UK) Ltd* [1990] F.S.R. 359 at 367.

[175] This does not apply where the work in question is an adaptation. In this instance only the adaptation itself need be acknowledged; the underlying work from which the adaptation is made need not be: CDPA 1988 s.76 and see para.9–16, above.

[176] CDPA 1988 s.29(1). As with fair dealing for the purposes of research, an amendment was made to exclude databases but this is no longer relevant See the notes to para.9–31, above.

[177] s.29(1C).

[178] s.178. This amendment was said to be "for the avoidance of doubt". See the Transposition Note on implementation.

study does not infringe copyright in such an arrangement.[179] It will be noted that no amendment has been made to restrict this permitted act to dealings by way of copying and distribution of copies so made, no doubt on the premise that private study will not involve other classes of acts restricted by the copyright. More significantly, no amendment has been made to provide right holders with any compensation for this form of copying. The Government's view was apparently that private copying of this kind does not prejudice right holders in any substantial way, so that "fair" compensation would either be zero or of such little amount that it would be swallowed up by the transaction costs involved in establishing and running any scheme.[180]

9–36   The Gowers Review of Intellectual Property (HM Treasury, December 2006) recommended (Recommendation 8) that a limited private copying exception should be introduced in the United Kingdom by 2008 to permit format shifting (i.e. transferring a work from, e.g. a CD to an MP3 player or from a video tape to DVD) for works published after the date that the law comes into effect. It proposed that there should be no accompanying compensation, although it is questionable whether this would be in conformity with art.5(2)(b) of the Information Society Directive 2001/29/EC. In January 2008, the IPO launched a consultation document: "Taking forward the Gowers Review of Intellectual Property: Proposed changes to copyright exceptions", in which it made the following proposal:

1. Format shifting only (from, e.g. CD to MP3 player)
2. By an individual solely for his own benefit (not family and friends)
3. No retention of copies if no longer in possession of the original (to avoid, e.g. resale of originals once copies had been made)
4. To apply only to legitimately acquired works.

This proposal proved controversial and in December 2009 the Government announced in its second-stage consultation on taking forward the Gowers Review that it did not currently consider it appropriate to introduce a narrow UK-only format shifting exception. Instead, it proposed to encourage the European Union to look at options that benefit consumers, including the possibility of a broad exception to copyright for non-commercial use.[181] In addition it will continue to pursue other measures in the United Kingdom which facilitate easier access to works, including those incorporated within the Digital Economy Act 2010.[182]

9–37   **Private study and non-commercial purpose.** In Australia, "study" has been held to have its ordinary meaning, namely: (1) The application of the mind to the acquisition of knowledge, as by reading, investigation or reflection; (2) The cultivation of a particular branch of learning, science or art (as in the study of law); (3) A particular course of effort to acquire knowledge (as in the pursuance

---

[179] s.29(2). See the notes to para.9–20, above.
[180] See the Government Conclusions on the Patent Office's Consultation Paper of August 7, 2002, para.5.6 and Transposition Note. The Government also relied on recital 35 of the Directive, which provides that "When determining the form, detailed arrangements and possible level of such fair compensation, account should be taken of the particular circumstances of each case. When evaluating these circumstances, a valuable criterion would be the possible harm to the rightholders resulting from the act in question. In cases where rightholders have already received payment in some other form, for instance as part of a licence fee, no specific or separate payment may be due. ...In certain situations where the prejudice to the rightholder would be minimal, no obligation for payment may arise." See, again, the Government Conclusions on the Consultation Paper and the Transposition Note.
[181] "Taking Forward the Gowers Review of Intellectual Property: Second Stage Consultation of Copyright Exceptions", IPO, December 11, 2009, paras 133 et seq., at para 171.
[182] "Taking Forward the Gowers Review of Intellectual Property: Second Stage Consultation of Copyright Exceptions", IPO, December 11, 2009, paras 133 et seq., at para.172. See also on the Digital Economy Act 2010, Ch.21, below.

of medical studies); (4) A thorough examination and analysis of a particular subject.[183] There is clearly some overlap with the expression "research", considered above. The meaning of commercial in this context has also already been considered in the context of research. The mere fact that a work is reproduced for the purposes of private study will not, in itself, mean that the use amounts to a fair dealing. Thus, for example, it was no defence under the previous provisions of the Act to reproduce a work in the form of study notes to be used by examination students[184] and the position would be the same today.

(iv) Common considerations

Copying by a person other than the student or researcher. The Act makes extensive provision as to the circumstances in which copies may be made for the purposes of private study or non-commercial research by others. In the case of libraries the Act provides that copying by a librarian or his agent is not permitted if it goes beyond what is permissible under the provisions which specifically relate to copying by such persons.[185] In addition, the Act provides that in any other case, copying by a person other than the researcher or student himself is not fair dealing if the person doing the copying knows or has reason to believe that it will result in copies of substantially the same material being provided to more than one person at substantially the same time and for substantially the same purpose.[186] The Act, therefore, provides only a limited exception in the case of any copying done by a person other than the person actually engaged in the non-commercial research or private study. Thus it appears clear that there is no defence under this section if a teacher makes multiple copies of a work for use by classroom students. On the other hand, it seems that a student or researcher may ask another to make a copy of a work provided that the section is otherwise satisfied.

9–38

Computer programs. Two special provisions apply in the case of computer programs. The Software Directive[187] allows only a limited category of exceptions to the rights prescribed in relation to such works. Two exceptions are relevant in the present context of fair dealing. First, art.5(3) of the Directive stipulates that there is to be an exception to allow a person having a right to use a copy of a program to observe, study or test the functioning of the program in order to determine the ideas and principles which underlie any element of the program, if this is done while performing any of the acts of loading, displaying, running, transmitting or storing the program which he is entitled to do. At the time of implementation of the Software Directive by the United Kingdom, this requirement was clearly considered to be catered for by the provisions of s.29 as they then stood, which permitted fair dealing for the purposes of commercial as well as non-commercial research or private study. With the amendment of the Act to restrict this permitted act to non-commercial research or private study, this was no longer the case. New ss.29(4A) and 50BA have therefore been added to deal with this. Thus, s.50BA provides, in the words of the Directive, that it is not an infringement of copyright for a lawful user of a copy of a computer program to

9–39

[183] *De Garis v Neville Jeffress Pidler Pty Ltd* (1990) 18 I.P.R. 292 (Fed. Ct of Australia) at 298–299. Also see *Television New Zealand v Newsmonitor Services Ltd* (1993) 27 I.P.R. 441 (High Ct of New Zealand) at 463.
[184] *Sillitoe v McGraw Hill Book Co* [1983] F.S.R. 545.
[185] CDPA 1988 s 29(3)(a). This relates to s.38 (copying by librarians: articles in periodicals) and s.39 (copying by librarians: parts of published works). See paras 9–116 and 9–117, below.
[186] s.29(3)(b).
[187] Council Directive 91/250/EEC.

observe, study or test the functioning of the program in order to determine the ideas and principles which underlie any element of the program if he does so while performing any of the acts of loading, displaying, running, transmitting or storing the program which he is entitled to do. A line between acts permitted under s.50BA and those permitted under the fair dealing provisions is drawn by s.29(4A), which provides that it is not fair dealing to observe, study or test the functioning of a computer program in order to determine the ideas and principles which underlie any element of the program, these being acts which are permitted if they fall within s.50BA.

The second relevant exception prescribed by the Software Directive is to permit decompilation of a computer program so as to obtain information necessary to achieve interoperability between that program and another program. This topic is discussed elsewhere[188] but effect was given to this provision of the Directive by s.50B—introduced by the Copyright (Computer Programs) Regulations 1992.[189] A line was again drawn between the two categories of permitted acts, by s.29(4), which provides that it is not fair dealing to convert a program expressed in a low-level language into a version expressed in a higher-level language or in the course of so doing to copy it, these being acts permitted if done in accordance with s.50B.

C. CRITICISM OR REVIEW

9–40   **Introduction.** Criticism or review of a work has always been permitted and since the 1911 Act has been the subject of statutory provision.[190]

9–41   **The Information Society Directive.** Articles 5(3)(d) and (4) of the Directive permit Member States to provide an exception to the reproduction, distribution and communication to the public rights in the case of quotations for purposes such as criticism or review, provided (a) that they relate to a work or other subject-matter which has already been lawfully made available to the public, and (b) that, unless this turns out to be impossible, the source, including the author's name, is indicated, and (c) that their use is in accordance with fair practice, and to the extent required by the specific purpose.[191] Except in one respect, the existing provision in s.30(1) of the 1988 Act allowing fair dealing for the purposes of criticism or review was consistent with the Directive. The expression "quotations" is clearly borrowed from the art.10 of the Berne Convention[192] and no doubt includes use of a substantial part of a work in some form other than an unaltered textual quotation, and also use of an artistic work. The one respect in which the 1988 Act clearly did not comply with the Directive was that the Act permitted fair dealing with an unpublished work as well as a published work.[193] The Act has therefore had to be amended in this respect.

9–42   **The 1988 Act.** As the Act now stands, fair dealing with a work for the purpose of criticism or review, of that or another work or of a performance of a work, does not infringe any copyright in the work provided that it is accompanied by a suf-

---

[188] See para.9–151, below.

[189] SI 1992/3233.

[190] Sometimes, it could no doubt be argued that review or criticism of a work is impliedly authorised by the copyright owner putting the work before the public. Without s.30, however, there is a danger that only favourable or insipid reviews would be permitted. cf. *Chatterton v Cave* (1878) 3 App.Cas. 483 at 492.

[191] An exception to the distribution right is permitted only to the extent justified by the purpose of the authorised act of reproduction: art.5(4).

[192] See para.9–24, above.

[193] The fact that the work was unpublished might, however, have affected the question of whether the dealing was fair. See paras 9–58 et seq., below.

ficient acknowledgment and provided that the work has previously been made available to the public.[194]

For the purposes of criticism or review. The proper approach to the construction of these expressions has already been considered.[195] In Australia, the words "criticism" and "review" have both been given their dictionary definitions. Thus "criticism" has been defined as: (1) The act or art of analysing and judging the quality of a literary or artistic work, etc. (as in literary criticism). (2) The act of passing judgment as to the merits of something. (3) A critical comment, article or essay.[196] "Review" has been defined as: "a critical article or report, as in a periodical, on some literary work, commonly some work of recent appearance; a critique".[197] "Criticism" can thus be seen as describing the "critical application of the mental faculties", whilst "review" describes the results of such a process.[198] Criticism may be strongly expressed and unbalanced, the issue then usually being whether the use is fair dealing.[199]

9–43

Criticism or review "of a work". It is not necessary for the parts of the work selected for the criticism or review to be representative of the work as a whole. Criticism of a single aspect of a work is therefore capable of constituting fair dealing.[200] The requirement that the criticism or review be of "a work" or a performance of "a work" is construed liberally. The criticism or review need not be confined to the literary style or merit of the work but may extend to the thoughts underlying it, for example the doctrine or philosophy[201] or ideas and events[202] expounded in the work or, for example, to criticism of works constituting the fruits, and thus the practice, of "cheque-book" journalism,[203] and even to criticism of a decision to withdraw a work from circulation.[204] Nevertheless, what is required is that the copying should take place as part of and for the purposes of criticising or reviewing the work in question. If it is done for some other purpose it will not suffice.[205] The fact that there is another purpose, such as education, as

9–44

---

[194] CDPA 1988 s.30(1). Note that this provision applies to all categories of work (see s.28(2)).

[195] See para.9–23, above.

[196] *De Garis v Neville Jeffress Pidler Pty Ltd* (1990) 18 I.P.R. 292 at 299.

[197] *De Garis v Neville Jeffress Pidler Pty Ltd* (1990) 18 I.P.R. 292.

[198] *De Garis v Neville Jeffress Pidler Pty Ltd* (1990) 18 I.P.R. 292.

[199] *Pro Sieben Media AG v Carlton UK Television Ltd* [1999] 1 W.L.R. 605, [1999] F.S.R. 610, CA. An author's remedy for unbalanced criticism which still amounts to fair dealing will lie, if anywhere, in the law of defamation: *Pro Sieben*.

[200] *Time Warner Entertainment Ltd v Channel 4 Television Corporation Plc* [1994] E.M.L.R. 1.

[201] *Hubbard v Vosper* [1972] 2 Q.B. 84. In *Fraser-Woodward Ltd v BBC* [2005] EWHC 472 the criticism and/or review was of two things, of the photographs themselves and the philosophy behind them. It was held that the ideas or philosophy underlying a certain style of journalism could be subject to criticism which fell within s.30 of the CDPA 1988 and the use of the photographs was held to amount to fair dealing under s.30(1) of the CDPA 1988.

[202] *Distillers Co (Biochemicals) Ltd v The Times Newspapers Ltd* [1975] Q.B. 613.

[203] *Pro Sieben Media AG v Carlton UK Television Ltd* [1999] 1 W.L.R. 605, [1999] F.S.R. 610. The works criticised were the claimant's television programme and newspapers in general.

[204] *Time Warner Entertainment Ltd v Channel 4 Television Corporation Plc* [1994] E.M.L.R. 1. Although the film was arguably only reviewed in order to facilitate criticism of the plaintiff's decision to withdraw the work from circulation, there was still a review of the film, and the review of the film and the criticism of the decision not to allow the film to be shown in the United Kingdom were inseparable.

[205] *Ashdown v Telegraph Group Ltd* [2001] EWCA Civ 1142; [2002] Ch.149; [2002] R.P.C. 5 (no criticism or review of the copyright work, only of the actions of certain individuals); *Banier v News Group Newspapers Ltd* [1997] F.S.R. 812 (no defence of fair dealing for the purposes of criticism or review when a newspaper copied a rival's photograph since the defendant's purpose had been to report a news story).

well as the purpose of criticism or review, will not, in itself, prevent the defence of fair dealing applying, although this may affect the question of fairness.[206]

9–45   **Work reproduced need not be the work criticised.** The exception is available whether the work reproduced is the work criticised or not.[207] Thus in criticising one work it is permissible to quote from other comparable works for the purpose of exemplifying the criticism. Again, in criticising a work in a foreign language, it is permissible to quote from an English translation even though there is no criticism of the translation as such. Nevertheless, under the 1956 Act the criticism or review had to be of a "work" and since a performance is not a "work" it followed that the defence probably could not have been relied upon when, for example, quoting passages of a play in reviewing a performance of it. Under the 1988 Act the defence is available in such circumstances.[208] There is no requirement that the work performed be a copyright work so that, for example, it would seem that the section would apply in the case of a review of an extempore performance of which no record is made.

9–46   **Caricature, parody or pastiche.**[209] Unlike some other countries, there has never been a specific statutory exception for these kinds of treatment in the United Kingdom. Although art.5(3)(k) of the Information Society Directive permits Member States to provide an exception in the case of caricature, parody or pastiche, the United Kingdom has not taken advantage of this, except in so far as the existing UK law of criticism or review already permits such acts. As parody depends upon recognition of the work being parodied, the substantial part requirement will sometimes be satisfied.[210] Where this is the case the parody will infringe unless the dealing falls within one of the statutory exceptions, the most likely being fair dealing for the purpose of criticism or review. This issue has yet to be addressed directly by the courts in the United Kingdom,[211] but in the United States it is clear that a parody may fall within the fair use doctrine as a form of criticism.[212] However, even if parody were to be accepted as a form of criticism two difficulties would remain. First, there is the requirement of sufficient

---

[206] *Sillitoe v Mcgraw Hill Book Co* [1983] F.S.R. 545, and see paras 9–58 et seq., below.

[207] CDPA 1988 s.30(1); the position under the 1956 Act was the same: Copyright Act 1956 s.6(2).

[208] s.30(1). Fair dealing with a performance for the purpose of criticism or review, of that or another performance, will also not infringe any separate rights in the performance, s.189 and Sch.2 para.2.

[209] For an exploration of the different meanings attached to these and other terms see Gredley and Maniatis, "Parody: A Fatal Attraction? Part 1: The Nature of Parody and its Treatment in Copyright" [1997] 7 E.I.P.R. 339.

[210] See paras 7–33 and 7–43, above, as the substantial part test in relation to infringement by parody. There is unlikely to be taking of a substantial part where there is a mere "conjuring up" of the work. See Gredley and Maniatis, "Parody: A Fatal Attraction? Part 1: The Nature of Parody and its Treatment in Copyright" [1997] 7 E.I.P.R. 339. In general, a substantial part of the work is much more likely to be taken when parodying an artistic work or a musical work than when parodying a literary work.

[211] In *Williamson Music v The Pearson Partnership Ltd* [1987] F.S.R. 97, the point seems to have been accepted as a possibility.

[212] In particular, see the judgment of the Supreme Court in *Campbell v Acuff-Rose Music, Inc.* (1994) 127 L. Ed 2d 500. Also see Nimmer, *Nimmer on Copyright* (New York: Matthew Bender, 1981) pp.13–212 to 13–230. More generally, see *The Parody Defence to Copyright Infringement: Productive Fair Use After Betamax* (1984) 97 Harv. L. Rev. 1395. For a more critical view of parodies see Dube J. in *MCA Canada Ltd-MCA Canada Ltee et al. v Gillberry & Hawke Advertising Agency Ltd* (1976) 28 C.P.R. (2d) 52. If parody were to be accepted as a form of criticism then in one respect UK law would prove to be more flexible than its American counterpart. In some US cases a distinction has been drawn between cases where a work itself is parodied and cases of satire, where part of a work is used to provide a critique of individuals or institutions or society in general: *Metro-Goldwyn-Mayer, Inc. v Showcase Atlanta Coop. Productions Inc.* (1979) 479 F. Supp. 351; *MCA Inc. v Wilson* (1981) 677 F.2d 180; *Campbell v Acuff-Rose Music, Inc.* (1994) 127 L. Ed 2d 500 (per Justice Kennedy, concurring). The broad definition of criticism which has been adopted in the United Kingdom which allows the reviewer to look "behind" a

acknowledgment (see para.9–48, below). Whilst such acknowledgment is by no means impossible,[213] it runs counter to ordinary publishing practice and imposes a rather artificial obligation on the parodist, as one of the benchmarks against which a parody can be judged is its success in making a connection with the work being parodied without any form of express reference. Moreover, the author of the work being parodied may well prefer not to be identified. The second obstacle is the possibility that the parody may amount to a derogatory treatment of the work,[214] as to which there is no fair dealing defence. The possibility of a derogatory treatment claim exists despite the fact that although a parody may be prejudicial to an author's reputation in a broad sense, it will not usually be presented as the creation of the author and is, therefore, much closer to an adverse review than to a case where a work is altered in order to meet some commercial objective.

The Gowers Review of Intellectual Property (HM Treasury, December 2006), noting that the Information Society Directive 2001/29/EC specifically allows for an exception for "caricature, parody or pastiche", recommended that such an exception to copyright be created by the year 2008 (Recommendation 12). The rationale for the proposal was that an exception to cover parody in the United Kingdom would reduce transaction costs across Europe and create value. In January 2008, the IPO launched a consultation document: "Taking forward the Gowers Review of Intellectual Property: Proposed changes to copyright exceptions", in which it asked about the potential impact and benefits of a new exception on this subject.[215] In December 2009, in its second stage consultation on copyright exceptions, the Government announced that it did not believe that there was sufficient justification to introduce a new exception for parody in the United Kingdom at present. Most respondents had expressed no interest in the exception and of those who commented on it opinions were quite polarised. It concluded that there is scope for further debate within the EU context about the potential for a non-commercial use exception which if implemented could cover some parody.[216]

Work must have been made available to the public. It has been seen that the   **9–47**
art.5(3)(d) of the Information Society Directive limits the permitted exception to criticism or review relating to subject-matter which has already been lawfully made available to the public, and the 1988 Act has had to be amended to comply with this requirement. The Government seems to have taken the view, correctly it is suggested, that the Directive prohibits substantial use of a work which has not been made available to the public for criticism or review of *that* work or another work (whether publicly available or not), but not use of a work which is publicly available for the purposes of criticism or review of another work which is not publicly available.

---

work (see para.9–44, above), would seem to make it more likely that some cases of satire would also fall within the fair dealing defence.

[213] Both the author and the publisher were acknowledged in *Campbell v Acuff-Rose Music, Inc.* (1994) 127 L. Ed 2d 500.

[214] See CDPA 1988 ss.80, 89 and see paras 11–46 et seq., below, and Gredley and Maniatis, "Parody: A Fatal Attraction? Part 1: The Nature of Parody and its Treatment in Copyright" [1997] 7 E.I.P.R. 339. The author would have to establish that there was an addition to, deletion from or alteration to or adaptation of the work or some part of the work and that the parody distorted or mutilated the work or was otherwise prejudicial to his reputation.

[215] Consultation document, IPO, January 2008, p.8. Available on the IPO website, *http://www.ipo.gov.uk* [Accessed October 22, 2010]. The consultation period ended on April 8, 2008. Subsequently, the IPO published a brief summary of responses to the consultation paper. See also P. Groves, "Pistache?—A Consultation Paper" [2008] Ent. L.R. 19(5), 89.

[216] "Taking Forward the Gowers Review of Intellectual Property: Second Stage Consultation of Copyright Exceptions", IPO, December 11, 2009, paras 292 et seq., at para.324. The Government also stated that it did not accept that an exemption for parody is necessary for the CDPA to be compliant with art.10 of the ECHR.

The Act therefore now states that fair dealing with a work for the purposes of criticism or review is only permissible where the work has been made available to the public. For this purpose, a work is to be regarded as having been made available to the public if it has been made available by any means, including (a) the issue of copies to the public; (b) making the work available by means of an electronic retrieval system; (c) the rental or lending of copies of the work to the public; (d) the performance, exhibition, playing or showing of the work in public; (e) the communication to the public of the work.[217] The possibility of the right to freedom of expression under the Human Rights Act 1998 overriding the 1988 Act in the case of works not made available to the public has already been noted.[218]

9–48   Sufficient acknowledgment. As enacted, the 1988 Act required that any dealing with a work for the purpose of criticism or review had to be accompanied by a "sufficient acknowledgment".[219] No amendment was made to this provision on implementation of the Information Society Directive, which requires that in the case of criticism or review of a work the source, including the author's name, be indicated, unless this turns out to be impossible.[220] The meaning of "sufficient acknowledgment" and the extent to which this differs from the terms of the Directive have already been considered.[221]

D. REPORTING CURRENT EVENTS

9–49   Introduction. It has always been accepted that fair use of a work should be allowed for the purposes of news reporting and since the 1911 Act this has had statutory recognition.[222] The defence is intended to protect the role of the media in informing the public about matters of current concern to the public.[223] In many cases, of course, a news reporting exception is unnecessary since current events can be reported without infringing copyright, as the law of copyright does not confer a monopoly over a particular set of facts.[224] This would be to ignore, however, the authority which can be given to a news story by a quotation from an original document and thus the public interest in learning of the very words

---

[217] CDPA 1988 s.30(1A), which also provides that in determining whether a work has been made available to the public no account is to be taken of any unauthorised act .

[218] See para.9–26, above.

[219] CDPA 1988 s.30(1). This requirement was first introduced in the 1956 Act in order to bring the position in the United Kingdom in line with art.10 of the Berne Convention: Report of the Copyright Committee, 1952 (Cm. 8662), para.42. Art.10 of the Berne Convention is itself intended to ensure protection for the author's paternity right: Ricketson, *The Berne Convention for the Protection of Literary and Artistic Works 1886–1986* (London: Kluwer, 1987) p.500. No acknowledgment or attribution of authorship was required under s.2(1)(i) of the 1911 Act: *Johnstone v Bernard Jones Publications Ltd* [1938] Ch. 599 at 606.

[220] Information Society Directive, 2001/29 art.5(3)(d).

[221] See para.9–33, above.

[222] Copyright Act 1911 s.2(1)(i), where the permitted act was "newspaper summary".

[223] *Ashdown v Telegraph Group Ltd* [2001] EWCA Civ 1142; [2002] Ch.149; [2002] R.P.C. 5. It was also observed there that a system of law whereby the media should have to pay compensation for the right to use a work might discourage the participation by the press in matters of public concern, applying the reasoning of *Bladet Tromso v Norway* [1999] 29 E.H.R.R. 125 and *Tolstoy Miloslavsky v United Kingdom* [1995] 20 E.H.R.R. 442. However, there has never been any question of applying a compulsory licence in this area. The important issue is the ability of the media to use material without the threat of an injunction.

[224] *Ashdown v Telegraph Group Ltd* [2001] EWCA Civ 1142. It was also observed there that a system of law whereby the media should have to pay compensation for the right to use a work might discourage the participation by the press in matters of public concern, applying the reasoning of *Bladet Tromso v Norway* [1999] 29 E.H.R.R. 125 and *Tolstoy Miloslavsky v United Kingdom* [1995] 20 E.H.R.R. 442. However, there has never been any question of applying a compulsory licence in this area. The important issue is the ability of the media to use material without the threat of an injunction.

used.[225] Moreover, such quotations place readers in a better position to make their own judgment, rather than relying upon that of the journalist.[226]

The Berne Convention. The various provisions of the Berne Convention have already been noted.[227]   **9–50**

The Information Society Directive. Articles 5(3)(c) and (4) of the Information Society Directive permit Member States to provide an exception to the reproduction, distribution and communication to the public rights in the case of use of works or other subject-matter in connection with the reporting of current events, to the extent justified by the informatory purpose and as long the source, including the author's name, is indicated, unless this turns out to be impossible.[228] The Act needed only a slight amendment to the sufficient acknowledgement requirement in order for it to comply with the Directive.   **9–51**

The 1988 Act. The Act provides that fair dealing with a work (other than a photograph) for the purpose of reporting current events does not infringe any copyright in the work provided that it is accompanied by a sufficient acknowledgment,[229] except where the reporting of current events is by means of a sound recording, film or broadcast, when no such acknowledgment is required where this would be impossible for reasons of practicality or otherwise.[230]   **9–52**

For the purpose of reporting current events. The general approach to the construction of this provision has already been considered[231]: it is clear that the expression will be construed liberally. Substituting other expressions for "current events", such as "current affairs" or "news" does not provide much assistance.[232] Current events are not confined to specific and very recent happenings,[233] particularly where the ramifications of the event continue to be a matter of public debate and concern.[234] The exception is not confined to the reporting of current events in a general news programme and includes, for example, the reporting of sports events in a sports news bulletin.[235] The work itself need not be "current", provided that it is used properly to report current events.[236] The events reported must, however, be current and not just a newsworthy matter of history, so that a newspaper was not able to rely on this section in using the death of the Duchess   **9–53**

---

[225] *Ashdown v Telegraph Group Ltd* [2001] EWCA Civ 1142.

[226] For a general discussion of the problems in this area see Johnston, "Copyright and Freedom of the Media: A Modest Proposal" [1996] 1 E.I.P.R. 6.

[227] See para.9–24, above.

[228] An exception to the distribution right is permitted only to the extent justified by the purpose of the authorised act of reproduction: art.5(4). Art.5(3)(c) also provides for a more restricted exception in the case of reproduction by the press, communication to the public or making available of published articles on current economic, political or religious topics or of broadcast works or other subject-matter of the same character, in cases where such use is not expressly reserved, and as long as the source, including the author's name, is indicated.

[229] CDPA 1988 s.30(2).

[230] s.30(3).

[231] See para.9–27, above.

[232] *Pro Sieben Media AG v Carlton UK Television Ltd* [1999] 1 W.L.R. 605; [1999] F.S.R. 610, CA.

[233] *Pro Sieben Media AG v Carlton UK Television Ltd* [1999] 1 W.L.R. 605.

[234] *Ashdown v Telegraph Group Ltd* [2001] EWCA Civ 1142; [2002] Ch.149; [2002] R.P.C. 5 (where the "event" consisted of a meeting which had taken place two years previously; while the issues identified by the defendant in its articles might not themselves have been "events", the existence of those issues could help to demonstrate the continuing public interest in the meeting). In *Hyde Park Residence Ltd v Yelland* [2001] Ch. 143; [1999] R.P.C. 655, the Court of Appeal considered that it was arguable that the events surrounding the death of Diana Princess of Wales were still current a year later, at a time when the investigation into the death was still continuing.

[235] *British Broadcasting Corp v British Satellite Broadcasting* [1992] Ch. 141 and see the Broadcasting Act 1996 s.137 (see para.9–56, below).

[236] *Associated Newspapers Group Plc v News Group Newspapers Ltd* [1986] R.P.C. 515.

of Windsor as an excuse to reprint correspondence.[237] The fact that a work has recently been published will not, of itself, mean that it is fair to reproduce it for the purposes of commenting on that fact[238] but sometimes the media coverage of an event may itself be a current event which it is fair to report[239] although this will often be a "bootstraps" argument of little merit.[240] In deciding whether the work is being used for this purpose, a useful test may be whether it is reasonably necessary to refer to the work in order to deal adequately with the events in question.[241] The work must be used for "reporting current events" and not for editorial or other purposes.[242] It would seem that the "reporting" must consist of reporting to the public at large in some general sense and not the reporting to a closed circle for some commercial purpose.[243]

9–54   **Photographs.** As has been seen, photographs are excluded from the ambit of the permitted act. The reason for this is that it was said that use of photographs in the context of news reporting could never be fair, such that the matter needed to be put beyond doubt.[244] It is suggested, however, that while many of the situations which would cause concern, such as the use by newspapers of a rival's photograph, would in any event probably not be fair (see para.9–58, below), it would have been preferable to leave the matter open to allow for the exceptional case.[245]

9–55   **The Human Rights Act.** It has already been noted[246] that the limitation in the fair dealing provision to the reporting of *current events*, and the exclusion of photographs from the ambit of s.30(2), may be the occasion, in a rare case, for the art.10 right to freedom of expression overriding the provisions of the 1988 Act.

9–56   **Avoidance of certain terms relating to news reporting.** As has been seen,[247] in general the permitted acts only relate to the question of copyright infringement and do not affect any other right or obligation. It is therefore possible to exclude the operation of the permitted acts contractually. However, in order to ensure that

---

[237] *Associated Newspapers Group Plc v News Group Newspapers Ltd* [1986] R.P.C. 515.

[238] *Associated Newspapers Group Plc v News Group Newspapers Ltd* [1986] R.P.C. 515.

[239] *Newspaper Licensing Agency Ltd v Marks and Spencer Plc* [2001] Ch. 257; [2001] R.P.C. 76, CA, Peter Gibson L.J. disagreeing); *Pro Sieben Media AG v Carlton UK Television Ltd* [1999] 1 W.L.R. 605, [1999] F.S.R. 610 (volume and intensity of media interest sufficient to bring the media coverage itself within the ambit of the current events which were being reported); *Hyde Park Residence Ltd v Yelland* [2001] Ch.143, [1999] R.P.C. 655 (media coverage generated by statements made by Mr Al Fayed concerning the relationship between his son and Diana Princess of Wales); *PCR Ltd v Dow Jones Telerate Ltd* [1998] F.S.R. 170 (defendant's articles reported the fact that the plaintiff's commodity report had been published and that it had affected the market; held, the defendant's articles were written for the purpose of reporting current events).

[240] *Ashdown v Telegraph Group Ltd* [2001] EWCA Civ 1142.

[241] *Associated Newspapers Group Plc v News Group Newspapers Ltd* [1986] R.P.C. 515 at 519.

[242] *Hyde Park Residence Ltd v Yelland* [2001] Ch. 143.

[243] *Newspaper Licensing Agency Ltd v Marks and Spencer Plc* [2001] Ch. 257 CA, per Peter Gibson L.J.: Chadwick L.J. disagreed. Mance L.J. declined to express a concluded view, but indicated that it was difficult to extend the exception to the reporting of current events for private commercial purposes, and that although in some instances private reporting might be in the public interest (for example reporting to the Cabinet or other official bodies), an extension of the exception to all reporting for any purpose was "debatable".

[244] See next note.

[245] This was in fact the Government's original intention. In the event, resistance from the photographic community and the National Union of Journalists proved such that the Government thought better of it: *Hansard*, HL Vol.501, cols 236–237. Note that a photograph which is part of a film is not to be regarded as a photograph under the 1988 Act: CDPA 1988 s.4(2). cf. *Barker Motion Photography Ltd v Hulton and Co Ltd* (1912) 28 T.L.R. 496. Also see *Banier v News Group Newspapers Ltd* [1997] F.S.R. 812: no defence of fair dealing for the purposes of criticism or review when a newspaper copied a rival's photograph since the defendant's purpose had been to report a news story.

[246] See para .9–26, above.

[247] See para.9–16, above.

extracts of sports programmes remain available for news reporting purposes, a more restricted rule applies to broadcasts. The Broadcasting Act 1996 thus provides that a provision in an agreement is void in so far as it purports to prohibit or restrict the communication to the public of any visual images taken from a broadcast, where the communication is covered by fair dealing for the purpose of reporting current events.[248]

Sufficient acknowledgment. As originally enacted, the 1988 Act required suf-   **9–57** ficient acknowledgment except where the news reporting was by means of a sound recording, film or broadcast. This exception reflected the practical difficulties which it was thought broadcasters and others might experience in identifying the work in question in the time available to them.[249] The Information Society Directive, however, requires acknowledgment in all circumstances in the context of reporting current events, unless this "turns out to be impossible",[250] and so the Act needed amendment. The result is something of a mess. The basic requirement of sufficient acknowledgment has been left unchanged but in the case of the reporting of current events by means of a sound recording, film or broadcast the Act now states that no acknowledgment is required where this would be impossible for reasons of practicality or otherwise. The meaning of "sufficient acknowledgment" and the other implications of these requirements have already been considered.[251] In the case of the reporting of current events, the "author" of the work used may well be a company,[252] and in such a case the acknowledgment can properly take the form of the name by which the company is known to the intended readership or audience, rather than the full company name,[253] or even a simple logo.[254]

E. THE CONCEPT OF FAIRNESS

Introduction. The expression "fair dealing" was also used in the 1956 and 1911   **9–58** Acts. In addition to the above categories of dealing, the issue of fair dealing now has also to be considered in the context of educational use.[255] Although rather different policy considerations are involved with the various different fair dealing provisions, namely non-commercial research, private study, criticism, review, the reporting of current events and educational use, similar criteria of "fairness" are employed in considering whether the use in question amounts to "fair" dealing.[256] Unlike the position in the United States of America, there are no statu-

---

[248] Broadcasting Act 1996 s.137 as amended by SI 2003/2498. This provision should be read alongside the provisions of that Act relating to listed events: ss.97–105.

[249] *Hansard*, HL Vol.491, cols 115–116.

[250] Information Society Directive, 2001/29 art.5(3)(c).

[251] See para.9–33, above.

[252] As in the case of sound recordings, films, broadcasts and typographical arrangements of published editions.

[253] *Newspaper Licensing Agency Ltd v Marks and Spencer Plc* [2001] Ch.257 CA; [1999] R.P.C. 536 CA (newspaper publisher was sufficiently identified by the name of the newspaper which it published and with which it was identified in the public mind, rather than its actual name).

[254] *Pro Sieben Media AG v Carlton UK Television Ltd* [1999] 1 W.L.R. 605; [1999] F.S.R. 610 (the claimant sufficiently identified by its logo, consisting of a stylised figure 7, particularly in the light of the facts that it was the means by which it was accustomed to identify itself and the use of the full, correct name (Pro Sieben Media AG) would have been unlikely to have any particular significance to the bulk of the audience).

[255] Under CDPA 1988 s.32(2A) copyright in specified works is not infringed by copying in the course of instruction or of preparation for instruction, provided, amongst other things, the copying is fair dealing with the work. See para.9–100, below.

[256] See *British Broadcasting Corp v British Satellite Broadcasting* [1992] Ch.141, in particular, at 148.

tory criteria of "fairness" under UK copyright law,[257] although the test that has been judicially developed incorporates a number of similar considerations. As already noted,[258] in cases where the dealing brings into play the art.10 right to freedom of expression, pre-Human Rights Act cases as to what amounts to fair dealing should not be applied inflexibly. Considerations of public interest are paramount and it should be asked whether the facts of the case are such that the importance of freedom of expression outweighs the conventional considerations established by the earlier authorities.[259]

9–59   **An objective test.** Fairness should be judged by the objective standard of whether a fair-minded and honest person would have dealt with the copyright work in the manner in which the defendant did, for the relevant purposes.[260] Ultimately the decision must be a matter of impression.[261]

9–60   **Relevant considerations.** Relevant factors to be taken into account in judging whether the dealing was fair have been identified in various cases. None is determinative and the weight to be attached to them will vary from case to case. In particular, the various factors will carry different weight according to the type of dealing. Cases of fair dealing for purposes of criticism, review and the reporting of current events usually raise more difficult problems than cases of non-commercial research and private study. The three most important factors have been identified to be[262]:

(1) The degree to which the alleged infringing use competes with exploitation of the copyright work by the owner. This is likely to be a most important factor. Clearly, if a criticism or review of a work competes with it in the sense that the criticism or review will act as an acceptable substitute to the public, this will be highly relevant. The test should be understood as referring not just to competition with the actual form of media in which the claimant exploits his work but any form of activity which potentially affects the value of the copyright work.[263] The mere existence of commercial rivalry is not conclusive, however. So, even where the claimant and de-

---

[257] cf. United States Copyright Act 1976, 17 U.S.C., s.107.

[258] See para.9–26, above.

[259] *Ashdown v Telegraph Group Ltd* [2001] EWCA Civ 1142; [2002] Ch.149; [2002] R.P.C. 5. See also *Fraser-Woodward Ltd v BBC* [2005] EWHC 472; [2005] F.S.R. 36 where Mann J. set out the basic principles on which fair dealing are to be assessed. First, regard should be had to the motives of the user; second, fair dealing is a matter of impression; third, the amount of the work used is relevant and excessive use could render the use unfair; fourth, the court can have regard to the purpose of the use made, i.e. is it a genuine piece of criticism or review, or something else? In addition, as regards substantiality, particular care should be taken with photographs; lastly, the "three-step" test of the Berne Convention should be respected. Cf. T. Theobald, "Copyright Infringement or is it Just Fair Dealing"[2005] Ent. L.R. 16(6), 153–156.

[260] *Hyde Park Residence Ltd v Yelland* [2001] Ch. 143; [1999] R.P.C. 655, applied in *Newspaper Licensing Agency Ltd v Marks and Spencer Plc* [2001] Ch. 257; [2001] R.P.C. 76, CA.

[261] *Hubbard v Vosper* [1972] 2 Q.B. 84 at 92–95. Also see *Johnstone v Bernard Jones Publication* [1938] Ch. 599.

[262] *Ashdown v Telegraph Group Ltd* [2001] EWCA Civ 1142; [2002] Ch.149; [2002] R.P.C. 5. These correspond to the three factors identified by Lord Denning MR in *Hubbard v Vosper* [1972] 2 Q.B. 84, in the more limited context of fair dealing for the purposes of criticism or review, namely, (1) the number and the extent of the quotations and the extracts; (2) the use made of the quotations and the extracts: if they have been used for a rival purpose then that may well be unfair; (3) the proportion of the work consisting of quotations and extracts as compared with the proportion of the work consisting of comment and analysis. cf. United States Copyright Act 1976, U.S.C. 17, s.107 which lists four factors to be taken into consideration when deciding whether a use is fair: (1) The purpose and character of the use, including whether such use is of a commercial nature or is for non-profit educational purposes; (2) The nature of the copyrighted work; (3) The amount and substantiality of the portion used in relation to the copyrighted work as a whole; and (4) The effect of the use upon the potential market for or value of the copyrighted work.

[263] Thus contrast *Pro Sieben Media AG v Carlton UK Television Ltd* [1999] 1 W.L.R. 605; [1999]

fendant were both involved in the broadcasting of sports programmes, their trade rivalry did not prevent the defendant's use of short extracts from some of the claimant's programmes being fair.[264] The mere fact that, in the case of criticism, review or reporting of current events, the use is for a commercial purpose[265] clearly does not prevent the dealing from being fair.[266]

(2) Whether the work has been published or not. If the work is unpublished, no dealing is likely to be fair.[267] Since the amendment made to the 1988 Act to remove "unpublished" works altogether from the ambit of fair dealing for the purposes of criticism or review,[268] this factor is only of relevance in cases of non-commercial research, private study, the reporting of current events and educational use. It seems that this principle may not be as relevant in the case of government documents.[269] Furthermore, even if a work has not been published to the world at large, it may have been circulated to a sufficiently wide circle so that it is fair to publish sections of it by way of reporting current events.[270]

(3) The extent of the use and the importance of what has been taken. In many cases this will be a highly important factor,[271] particularly if the defendant has taken the most interesting and valuable part from the claimant's work.[272] In most cases there will a grey area between the threshold of substantial part (below which no infringement occurs in any event) and a use which is so substantial as to be unfair. Here, a useful test may be whether it was necessary to use as much as the defendant did for the relevant purpose.[273] This reasoning should not be used, however, to attempt to pare off "unnecessary" parts from defendant's work to make a case of unfair use: there will be no precise boundary line between what is fair and unfair. Occasionally, it may be fair to reproduce the whole of a work,

---

F.S.R. 610 (defendant's television programme criticising chequebook journalism did not in any real sense represent unfair competition with the claimant's exploitation of its rights) with *Ashdown v Telegraph Group Ltd* [2001] EWCA Civ 1142; [2002] Ch.149 (the defendant's publication destroyed a part of the value of the claimant's memoirs which it had been his intention to sell).

[264] *British Broadcasting Corp v British Satellite Broadcasting* [1992] Ch.141.

[265] In the case of research or private study, of course, the fact that the dealing is for a commercial purpose will take it outside the permitted act provisions.

[266] Although note that in *Newspaper Licensing Agency Ltd v Marks and Spencer Plc* [2001] Ch. 257; [2001] R.P.C. 76 Chadwick L.J. considered that a dealing by a person for his own commercial advantage, and to the actual or potential commercial disadvantage of the copyright owner, would not be fair dealing unless there was some overriding element of public advantage which justified the subordination of the rights of the copyright owner. Peter Gibson L.J. considered that the dealing in that case (an internal news clippings service) would have been fair, since the commercial motives and intentions of the defendant could not be impugned and it was not in competition with the claimant, for example, by selling the material to others.

[267] *Ashdown v Telegraph Group Ltd* [2001] EWCA Civ 1142. In *British Oxygen Company Ltd v Liquid Air Ltd* [1925] Ch. 383 at 393, it was said that any dealing which resulted in publication of a previously unpublished document could not be fair, but this clearly goes too far. It is a highly relevant factor only: *Beloff v Pressdram* [1973] F.S.R. 33.

[268] See para.9–42, above. Strictly, it is where a work has not been "made available to the public" that the permitted act no longer applies.

[269] *Commonwealth of Australia v John Fairfax and Sons Ltd* [1981] 55 A.L.J.R. 45 at 50.

[270] *Hubbard v Vosper* [1972] 2 Q.B. 84 (although that case was concerned with criticism or review).

[271] See also as to this factor, *Pro Sieben Media AG v Carlton UK Television Ltd* [1999] 1 W.L.R. 605; [1999] F.S.R. 610, CA. It was said in *Independent Television Publications v Time Out* [1984] F.S.R. 64 at 75, that once it is established that a substantial part of a work has been taken then no defence of fair dealing will be likely to succeed, but this is clearly wrong as a matter of principle.

[272] See also the emphasis given by Mance L.J. to the intrinsic worth or merit of the work in question in *Hyde Park Residence Ltd v Yelland* [2001] Ch.143; [1999] R.P.C. 655 at 392.

[273] *PCR Ltd v Dow Jones Telerate Ltd* [1998] F.S.R. 170; *Associated Newspapers Group Plc v News Group Newspapers Ltd* [1986] R.P.C. 515.

particularly if it is very short[274] and it may well be fair to copy the whole of a longer work if this is preparatory to making a decision as to which parts to use for a relevant dealing.[275]

Other relevant factors may be:

(4) The motives of the alleged infringer: for example, was the use merely dressed up in the guise of criticism or review?[276]

(5) The purpose of the use: was the use necessary at all to make the point in question?[277]

(6) The fact that the copy of a previously unpublished work was obtained by the defendant by theft or other misappropriation.[278] Where the work has previously been published, the method used to obtain the copy appears to be of little relevance.[279]

F. General Provisions: Incidental Inclusion of Copyright Material

9–61   **Introduction.** Section 31 of the Act provides that the copyright in a work is not infringed by its incidental inclusion in an artistic work, sound recording, film or broadcast.[280] Where, by virtue of these provisions, the making of a copy was not an infringement of copyright in a work, then the issue to the public of such copies, or the playing, showing or communication to the public, of anything whose making was not an infringement of copyright, will not infringe the copyright in the work either.[281]

There would seem to be three justifications for such a provision. First, in relation to photographers, sound recording and film makers and broadcasters, it is justifiable on the grounds that it will often be very difficult to obtain permission from the owners of all the works reproduced in the photograph, sound recording, film or broadcast. Consider the live broadcast of a sporting event. Without such a provision a broadcaster might infringe copyright by broadcasting a sound recording which is being played over the public address system or by including shots of an advertising hoarding.[282] A second justification is that the incidental use of a work will in any event not detract from the market for the original and in certain

---

[274] See Megaw L.J. in *Hubbard v Vosper* [1972] 2 Q.B. 84 at 98 who gives the melancholy example of a parishioner who, wishing to complain about an epitaph on a tombstone, sets it out in full in a letter to the parish magazine.

[275] *Pro Sieben Media AG v Carlton UK Television Ltd* [1999] 1 W.L.R. 605; *Time Warner Entertainment Ltd v Channel 4 Television Corporation Plc* [1994] E.M.L.R. 1. Also see *Television New Zealand v Newsmonitor Services Ltd* (1993) 27 I.P.R. 441 (High Ct of New Zealand) at 467: "In my view it is a fair dealing with a television broadcast to tape the whole program for the purpose of extracting material from it if that extraction does not go beyond the bounds of fair dealing and if the tape is not used for any other purpose and is then destroyed".

[276] *Pro Sieben Media AG v Carlton UK Television Ltd* [1999] 1 W.L.R. 605.

[277] *Hyde Park Residence Ltd v Yelland* [2001] Ch. 143; [1999] R.P.C. 655 (use of stills from video footage of Diana Princess of Wales not necessary to make the point).

[278] *Hyde Park Residence Ltd v Yelland* [2001] Ch. 143, per Mance L.J. at 393; *Ashdown v Telegraph Group Ltd* [2001] EWCA Civ 1142; *Beloff v Pressdram* [1973] F.S.R. 33. *Fraser-Woodward Ltd v BBC* [2005] EWHC 472.

[279] *Time Warner Entertainment Ltd v Channel 4 Television Corp Plc* [1994] E.M.L.R. 1.

[280] The 1956 Act (which only applied to artistic works) was more restrictive in that it provided that there was no infringement of copyright if the work's inclusion "is only by way of background or is otherwise only incidental to the principal matters represented". Copyright Act 1956 s.9(5).

[281] CDPA 1988 s.31(2).

[282] See *Hansard*, HL Vol.491, col.123. Normally, of course, the intention of the advertiser will have been to have the hoarding included in the broadcast. See, for example, *Football Association Premier League v QC Leisure* [2008] EWHC 1411 (Ch); [2008] F.S.R. 32, where, in the context of the filming and broadcasting of a sporting event, it was held that the inclusion of the sound recording and musical work embodied in the Premier League Anthem, which had been played over the public address system at the stadium during the player line up and picked up by microphones, was entirely incidental (paras 198 et seq. of the judgment).

circumstances may even enhance it. This point has been accepted in a number of US cases, with the result that incidental inclusion has been held to fall within the fair use defence, there being no specific provisions in the US Act dealing with this matter.[283] The third justification for such a provision is that it allows, e.g. film makers and broadcasters a degree of artistic freedom by allowing them to set the activities of their characters in a wide variety of settings. Thus no special permission is needed to film against the background of a play being performed in a theatre.[284] Indeed without some form of exception an artist, photographer, film maker or broadcaster could not even include images of a building in his work without infringing the architect's copyright.[285] Overall, these provisions have a great deal of importance for photographers, advertisers, sound recording and film makers as well as broadcasters.

Berne Convention. The permitted act of incidental inclusion partly corresponds to art.10*bis*(2) of the Berne Convention. This article states that it is for individual countries "to determine the conditions under which, for the purpose of reporting current events by means of photography, cinematography, broadcasting or communications to the public by wire, literary or artistic works seen or heard in the course of the event may, to the extent justified by the informatory purpose, be reproduced and made available to the public". Section 31 is clearly wider than this, and presumably is justified under the general exception for special cases permitted by art.9(2).[286]   **9–62**

The Information Society Directive. The Directive permits Member States to provide an exception to the reproduction, distribution and communication to the public rights in the case of the incidental inclusion of a work or other subject-matter in other material.[287] This was consistent with the existing provisions of the 1988 Act and no amendment was therefore required, other than that brought about by the changed definition of broadcasting and the new right of communication to the public.   **9–63**

Incidental. Special provision is made for what constitutes incidental inclusion in the case of a musical work[288] but, apart from this, the word "incidental" is an ordinary descriptive English word and was deliberately left undefined in the Act.[289] It has been said that it is impossible to provide a definition that will be satisfactory for all purposes: what is incidental will depend on all the circumstances of the case.[290] Resort should not therefore be had to dictionaries, *Hansard*, the 1956 Act or substitute words or expressions.[291] "Incidental" in this context does not mean unintentional,[292] and indeed is not confined to unintentional or non-deliberate inclusion. Nor is a valid distinction to be made between use of a copy-   **9–64**

---

[283] See further, *Mura v Columbia Broadcasting Systems Inc.* (1965) 245 F. Supp. 587; *Italian Book Corp v American Broadcasting Cos* (1978) 458 F. Supp. 65.

[284] See also Sch.2 para.3(1): no infringement of rights in the performance.

[285] But also see s.62.

[286] See para.9–02, above.

[287] Information Society Directive 2001/29 arts 5(3)(i), (4). The exception to the distribution right is permitted only to the extent justified by the purpose of the authorised act of reproduction: art.5(4).

[288] CPDA s.31(3), see para.9–67, below.

[289] *The Football Association Premier League Ltd v Panini UK Ltd* [2003] EWCA Civ. 995; [2004] 1 W.L.R. 1147; [2004] F.S.R. 1.

[290] *The Football Association Premier League Ltd v Panini UK Ltd* [2003] EWCA Civ. 995.

[291] *The Football Association Premier League Ltd v Panini UK Ltd* [2003] EWCA Civ. 995. The decision in *IPC Magazines Ltd v MGN Ltd* [1998] F.S.R. 431, that the word "incidental" bears its ordinary dictionary meaning of casual, inessential, subordinate, or merely background, per the Oxford Dictionary, must presumably be regarded as over-elaborate, although not wrong as such.

[292] *The Football Association Premier League Ltd v Panini UK Ltd* [2003] EWCA Civ. 995. This is clear from CDPA 1988 s.31(3), as to which, see para.9–67, below.

right work which is "incidental" and that which is "integral" to the work in which it is included, and there is no necessary dichotomy between the two in this context. But that does not mean that its inclusion either is, or is not, incidental. The only question is whether the inclusion of the copyright work in the relevant artistic work, sound recording, film or broadcast was or was not incidental, and that turns on the question: why, having regard to the circumstances in which the relevant work was made, was the copyright work included?[293] Depending on the circumstances, consideration can be given not only to the aesthetic reasons for including it but also to the commercial ones. This is particularly so where the work was made primarily for commercial reasons.[294] For this purpose it will be irrelevant to consider the subjective intentions of the person creating the work in which the copyright work is included.[295]

9–65   **The relevant acts.** In relation to incidental inclusion it may be particularly important to focus on the relevant acts which are alleged to be an infringement. In a case in which articles or things have been made and then issued to the public or disseminated in some other way, such acts being the alleged infringing acts, it is important (a) to examine the circumstances when these things or articles were made, and (b) whether or not the articles or things are artistic works, sound recordings, films or broadcasts. As to (a), it is only the circumstances which existed at the time when the things were made which are relevant to the question of incidental inclusion, and not those which existed at the time of some antecedent act, for example when a preparatory copy of the copyright work was first made. As to (b), it is only where the copyright work is incidentally included in one of these categories of work that the exception in s.31 applies. Thus it should be noted, for example, that where artistic works are published as part of a newspaper, magazine, etc. the whole publication may be a compilation and thus a literary work.[296] The individual images as they appear in the compilation are artistic works in their own right but this does not prevent the entirety being a compilation. To the extent that the publication is a compilation it would seem that the section cannot apply so as to permit acts done in relation to the compilation.[297]

---

[293] *The Football Association Premier League Ltd v Panini UK Ltd* [2003] EWCA Civ. 995. *Fraser-Woodward Ltd v BBC* [2005] EWHC 472; [2005] F.S.R. 36.

[294] *The Football Association Premier League Ltd v Panini UK Ltd* [2003] EWCA Civ. 995. Note also the suggestion in *IPC Magazines Ltd v MGN Ltd* [1998] F.S.R. 431, that it may be helpful to assess the impact of the defendant's work without the presence of the claimant's. There, the defendant had reproduced the front cover of the claimant's magazine (a copyright work) for the purposes of a comparative advertisement for its own magazine in a television programme. It was held that the inclusion was not incidental: the impact of the advertisement would have been lost entirely if the front cover of the claimant's magazine had not been used. Its inclusion was an essential and important feature of the advertisement.

[295] *The Football Association Premier League Ltd v Panini UK Ltd* [2003] EWCA Civ. 995, per Chadwick L.J. at para.27 and Mummery L.J. at para.39, where it was considered irrelevant to consider what might have been in the mind of the employee making the work or of those to whom it was distributed. In *IPC Magazines Ltd v MGN Ltd* [1998] F.S.R. 431 it was also held that whether or not the inclusion was "incidental" was an objective question, in the sense that it was not relevant to call evidence of the intentions of the defendant or of the perceptions of those who may have seen the use made. A different view was taken at first instance in *Panini* [2002] EWHC 2779 (Ch), namely that the question might be partly subjective and partly objective, on the grounds that for the purposes of CPDA 1988 s.31(3) (see para.9–65, below) it is a relevant consideration that the work was deliberately included, a subjective matter, and that it would be odd if the test differed between the two subsections. This approach must presumably be regarded as having been overruled by the Court of Appeal although it is difficult to see why, if the intentions of the person making the subsidiary work are known, this should not be a relevant consideration.

[296] See para.3–26, above.

[297] *The Football Association Premier League Ltd v Panini UK Ltd* [2003] EWCA Civ. 995; [2004] 1 W.L.R. 1147; [2004] F.S.R. 1, although the point was expressly left open by the Court of Appeal,

The decision in *Panini*. In *The Football Association Premier League Ltd v Pa-*   **9–66**
nini UK Ltd,[298] photographs of soccer players wearing their club strip were
reproduced in the form of stickers to be inserted into a collector's album, and in
the form of further images printed in the album itself. The photographs
reproduced the club or Premier League emblems or logos, which were copyright
artistic works. The stickers and albums had been made abroad and the acts of infringement alleged were (it seems) the importation of copies of copyright works,
and the offer for sale, sale and distribution of those copies to distributors, all with
the knowledge that they were infringing copies, and the authorisation of the issue
to the public by the distributors of the stickers and albums. The question identified by the Court of Appeal was whether the emblems and badges printed on the
players' strip had been incidentally included in the stickers and in the album
when those stickers and albums were made. This question was therefore to be
answered by examining the circumstances which existed at that time and not at
the time when the original photographs were made, or by asking what were the
subjective intentions, motives, views or states of mind of the photographer or the
employee producing the stickers or album, or the distributors or collectors. On
the facts, the answer to the question why the logos and emblems were included in
the stickers and the album was self evident. The objective, when creating the image of the player as it appeared on the sticker and the album was to produce
something that was attractive to the collector. As part of that objective it was
important that the players appeared in what was recognisably their authentic club
strip and for this purpose the club logos and emblems needed to be apparent. The
inclusion of these copyright works was essential to the object for which the image of the players was produced on the stickers and albums.[299]

In *Panini* there was no claim brought against the original photographer alleging that the taking of his photographs had been an infringement.[300] If there had
been such a claim, then for the purposes of any defence under s.31(1) it would
clearly have been relevant to examine the circumstances as they existed at the
time when the photographs were made. It is possible (although highly unlikely in
a case such as *Panini*) that the making of the photographs would not have been
an infringement (because their inclusion then was incidental) but their reproduction on stickers would have been (because they were not incidentally included at
that stage), or vice versa. For example, the photographer might have chosen his
subject-matter for reasons having nothing to do with the included copyright material, and may even have been oblivious to it, but the eventual user might have
chosen the image precisely because the included material suited his commercial
purposes.

The test in *Panini* was applied in *Fraser-Woodward Ltd v BBC*,[301] in a case
where damages were sought for infringement of F's copyrights in 14 photographs.
The photographs were of a celebrity couple and their family and had been

---

not having been argued. The reason given for not advancing the argument was that it would be
startling if a defence which was available in relation to the making and distribution of individual
artistic works ceased when the artistic work was combined with other works. This reasoning was
doubted by Mummery L.J. (who alone in the Court of Appeal dealt with the point), with good
reason it is suggested. Any oddity in the result is due to the fact that the Act has prescribed a
limited class of works to which the exception applies. Assuming that a collection of artistic
works and written material can correctly be described as a compilation (which, again, it is suggested is the case), there seems no room for argument on the point.

[298] [2003] EWCA Civ. 995.

[299] As already noted, the collection of artistic works with other written material in the album was
arguably a compilation and thus a literary work. If this was correct, then whatever the position
may have been in relation to the stickers, acts relating to the making and distribution of the
albums as a whole could not have been within CDPA 1988 s.31. Since, however, the images
were clearly not incidentally included in the albums in any event, and the point had not been
argued, the question was left open by the Court of Appeal.

[300] See para.31 of the judgment.

[301] *Fraser-Woodward Ltd v BBC* [2005] EWHC 472 (Ch); [2005] F.S.R. 36.

originally published in various tabloid newspapers by licence. The question of incidental inclusion arose in relation to one of the photographs which had appeared on screen for some four seconds within a newspaper headline. The court found that the headline appeared as an example of a sensational headline and in that context the small photo was incidental. It was there because it happened to be there in the original headline. While it might have been there to lend interest to the original headline, its appearance in the programme shot was in everyday terms, incidental.[302]

9–67 **Musical works, etc.** A musical work, words spoken or sung with music, or so much of a sound recording or broadcast as includes a musical work or such words, is not to be regarded as incidentally included if it is deliberately included.[303] Here, it becomes relevant to know the subjective intentions of the maker of the artistic work, sound recording, film or broadcast in which the work is included.[304] It would seem that the burden of proof lies on the person alleging infringement. This provision would prevent it from being argued that, for example, the intentional inclusion of background music (of whatever kind) in a film or television programme to add colour is not an infringement of copyright, but would generally allow the filming of an event at which music happens to be played if it was not the film-maker's intention that it should include music.[305] It may be relevant to ask: was the decision to start filming dictated to any extent by whether or not music was playing? This special provision was the result of lobbying by the music industry: other groups did not appear to see any grounds for concern, perhaps because they did not consider that non-musical works were likely to be used in the same way or to the same extent.[306] The extension of this exclusion to prevent the reproduction of a sound recording or broadcast in so far as either includes part of a musical work means that even if permission is obtained from the owner of the musical work for this use it would still not be possible to make a film with recorded music deliberately playing in the background without obtaining the permission of the owner of the copyright in the sound recording.[307] The decision in *Football Association Premier League v Q.C. Leisure*[308] provides an example of incidental use of a musical work and sound recording. In the context of the filming and broadcasting of a sporting event, the Premier League Anthem, a musical work embodied in a sound recording, was played over the public address system at the stadium during the player line-up and picked up by microphones. However, there had been no intention specifically to include the sound of the Anthem in the broadcast and those responsible for the broadcast were quite unconcerned as to whether the Anthem was playing at all, let alone

[302] *Fraser-Woodward Ltd v BBC* [2005] EWHC 472 (Ch), para.86.

[303] CDPA 1988 s.31(3). It seems that the phrase "words spoken or sung with music" must have been intended to refer to words which are being spoken or sung to music at the time of their inclusion, rather than referring to "a literary work consisting of words intended to be spoken or sung with music", which is used in a later section of the Act (s.77(3)). However, this seems unnecessarily restrictive and would catch, for example, Tony Hancock's rendition of the words of a Government health campaign to the tune of *Lied Der Deutschen* (*The Blood Donor*, BBC Video, 1994).

[304] *The Football Association Premier League Ltd v Panini UK Ltd, at first instance*, [2002] EWHC 2779, Ch. D; [2003] F.S.R. 38

[305] cf. *Hawkes and Son (London) Ltd v Paramount Film Service Ltd* [1934] Ch. 593 (newsreel of opening of the Royal Hospital School which included a snatch from "Colonel Bogey" played by a boys' band). Also see *Hansard*, HL Vol.491, cols 123, 124 and the Report of the Debates of the House of Commons Standing Committee E in 1988, cols 218–220.

[306] See *Hansard*, HL Vol.491, col.124.

[307] It is not clear why the nature of any underlying works should have a bearing on the way in which the sound recording or broadcast can be treated. It may be that this extension was intended to prevent a defendant from relying on the argument that it was the sound recording or broadcast that was deliberately included and not the underlying musical work.

[308] *Football Association Premier League Ltd v QC Leisure* [2008] EWHC 1411 (Ch); [2008] F.S.R. 32.

whether it could be heard by viewers. The court formed the conclusion that neither the broadcasters nor the viewers of the broadcasts attached any importance to whether the Anthem could be heard. The objective was to show the players line up and convey the sense of excitement and anticipation in the stadium but the inclusion of the anthem was not essential for this purpose. Thus, it held that the inclusion of the Anthem was entirely incidental.[309]

5. VISUAL IMPAIRMENT

A. THE CORE PROVISIONS

Introduction. Before the general implementation of the Information Society Directive, the 1988 Act had been prospectively amended by the Copyright (Visually Impaired Persons) Act 2002 to introduce a new series of permitted acts to enable versions of works to be made which are more accessible by visually impaired persons. Research had indicated that, with the exception of a few commercial publishers of large-print and audio books, most publishers did not find it economic to publish works adapted to suit the needs of visually impaired people. While rightholders did not on the whole insist on a royalty for the making of such versions, the process of obtaining consents on a case-by-case basis was often a long-drawn-out and thus expensive process. The fact that the making of these versions was not an activity which was of any real commercial significance for the majority of rightholders, and thus did not damage their economic interests, contributed to the shaping of the 2002 Act, which restricts the permitted acts to those of a non-commercial nature. Indeed, where publishers do make such versions available, the permitted act provisions do not apply. These permitted acts are thus designed to be compliant with the Berne three-step test.[310] The Act came into force on October 31, 2003,[311] immediately after the Regulations implementing the Directive.[312] The Act must be read in a way that is compatible with the requirements of the E-Commerce Regulations.[313]

9–68

The Information Society Directive. Recital 43 to the Information Society Directive provides that it is "important for the Member States to adopt all necessary measures to facilitate access to works by persons suffering from a disability which constitutes an obstacle to the use of the works themselves, and to pay particular attention to accessible formats". The Directive therefore permits Member States to provide an exception to the reproduction right, the communication to the public right and the distribution right, in the case of uses for the benefit of people with a disability, which are directly related to the disability and of a non-commercial nature, to the extent required by the specific disability. The exception

9–69

---

[309] *Football Association Premier League* para.202.

[310] See paras 9–02, above and 23–33, below.

[311] The Copyright (Visually Impaired Persons) Act 2002 (Commencement) Order 2003 (SI 2003/2499). For the background, see the Patent Office Consultation Paper (Copyright and Visually Impaired People, available at *http://www.ukipo.org/benefit.pdf* and *http://www.ukipo.org/response-benefit.pdf* [Accessed November 16, 2010]). For a critique of the Act, see K. Garnett, "The Copyright (Visually Impaired Persons) Act 2002" [2003] E.I.P.R. 25(11), 522–527. See also D. Bradshaw, "Making Books and Other Copyright Works Accessible, without Infringement, to the Visually Impaired: A Review of the Practical Operation of the Applicable, and Recently-Enacted, UK Legislation" I.P.Q. 2005, 4, 335–360.

[312] The Copyright (Visually Impaired Persons) Act 2002 (Commencement) Order 2003 (SI 2003/2499) para.2.

[313] The Electronic Commerce (EC Directive) (Extension) Regulations 2003 (SI 2003/115).

to the distribution right is permitted only to the extent justified by the purpose of the authorised act of reproduction.[314]

9–70   **Subsequent international developments.** Since the passage of the 2002 Act, the United Nations Convention on the Rights of Persons with Disabilities has entered into force and has been ratified by the United Kingdom and the members of European Union.[315] Article 9 of the Convention requires States Parties to take appropriate measures to ensure that persons with disabilities have equal access to information and communications which are open to the public. Article 21 requires States Parties to take all appropriate measures to ensure that persons with disabilities can exercise the right to freedom of expression and opinion including the freedom to seek, receive and impart information and ideas on an equal basis with others and through all forms of communication of their choice. This includes an express obligation to urge private entities that provide services to the general public to provide information and services in accessible and usable formats for persons with disabilities.[316] Article 30 requires States Parties to take all appropriate measures to ensure that persons with disabilities enjoy access to cultural materials, television programmes, films, theatre and other cultural activities in accessible formats and (in accordance with international law) to ensure that laws protecting intellectual property rights do not constitute an unreasonable or discriminatory barrier to access by persons with disabilities to cultural materials. In 2010, WIPO's Standing Committee on Copyright and Related Rights discussed various proposals (including one from the European Union) for a treaty for improved access to works protected by copyright by persons with a print disability.

9–71   **Subsequent European developments.** The Commission's proposal for a Directive on the principle of equal treatment (2008) makes reference to equal treatment for persons with disabilities in relation to access to and supply of goods and services.[317] In its Communication on Copyright in the Knowledge Economy (2009)[318] the Commission noted the following. First, only 5 per cent of books published in Europe each year were converted into accessible formats and a lack of harmonisation of the disability exception to copyright was hampering the cross-border transfer of accessible material. Secondly, concerns had been expressed about the effect in this field of technological protection measures.[319] Thirdly, while persons with disabilities advocated a standard mandatory EU-wide copyright exception, publishers preferred to proceed on the basis of voluntary schemes. The Commission concluded that publishers should continue to be encouraged to increase access.[320] It also stated that it would organise a stakeholder forum to consider the range of issues and possible policy responses by reference to the standards set in the UN Convention.[321] Issues to be considered included how to encourage the unencumbered export between Member States of converted works while ensuring that right holders were adequately remunerated; the mutual recognition and free movement of accessible material; and the accessibility of

---

[314] See Information Society Directive, 2001/29, arts 5(3)(b) and (4).

[315] The Convention entered into force on May 3, 2008. It was signed by the United Kingdom on June 8, 2009 and ratified by the United Kingdom on August 7, 2009.

[316] art.21(c).

[317] COM (2008) 426 final art. 3.

[318] COM (2009) 532 final.

[319] Note however that a recent study found little hard evidence of this: Akester *Technological accommodation of conflicts between freedom of expression and DRM: the first empirical assessment* (2009) p.100. See *http://www.law.cam.ac.uk* [Accessed October 8, 2010].

[320] In this context the Commission mentioned TPMs and contractual terms which did not recognise the exception as particular problems to be overcome.

[321] See previous paragraph.

online content. Thereafter, the Commission stated, it would assess whether further initiatives were required.

The core provisions. Sections 31A to 31F of the 1988 Act contain three core **9–72** provisions: (1) a provision enabling a "visually impaired person" to make an "accessible copy" of a work; (2) a provision enabling certain approved bodies to make accessible copies of a work for visually impaired persons; and (3) a provision enabling such approved bodies to hold "intermediate" copies of works, being copies necessarily created during the making of accessible copies. It can therefore be seen that there are two fundamental concepts: (a) a "visually impaired person" and (b) an "accessible" copy.

Visually impaired person. A visually impaired person is defined in s.31F(9) as a **9–73** person: (1) who is blind; (2) who has an impairment of visual function which cannot be improved, by the use of corrective lenses, to a level that would normally be acceptable for reading without a special level or kind of light; (3) who is unable, through physical disability, to hold or manipulate a book; or (4) who is unable, through physical disability, to focus or move his eyes to the extent that would normally be acceptable for reading. The definition of a visually impaired person is therefore not restricted to persons whose visual functions are impaired. It extends, for example, to persons who cannot hold a book because of severe rheumatoid arthritis.

Accessible. The provisions are concerned with copies of works which are "accessible" **9–74** to a visually impaired person. A copy of a copyright work is to be taken to be accessible to a visually impaired person only if it is as accessible to him as it would be if he were not visually impaired.[322]

Accessible copy. An accessible copy, in relation to a copyright work, is defined **9–75** as meaning a version which provides improved access to the work for a visually impaired person.[323] From the use of the word "version" it follows that an accessible copy includes not only a version made by "copying" the work within the meaning of s.17(2) of the Act but also one by making an adaptation of the work within the meaning of s.21. Copying of a work could include the making of an enlarged photocopy or the making of a copy of a literary, dramatic or musical work in the form of a sound recording or film, such as a talking book, video cassette or DVD. The making of an adaptation of a work would include the making of a version of a work in braille.[324] For this purpose, an accessible copy also includes one which has facilities for navigating around the work, such as an index or search facility, but does not include one which has: (a) changes that are not necessary to overcome problems caused by visual impairment; or (b) changes which infringe the right not to have the work subjected to derogatory treatment.[325]

Lawful possession and lawful use. Many of the new provisions are dependent **9–76** on there being "lawful possession" or "lawful use" of a copy of a copyright work from which the accessible copy is made. Situations where this may occur include not only those where a retail copy has been bought by the user but also where a lawful copy has been lent to him, whether by another member of the public or a library.

Other permitted acts. It should be remembered, of course, that there are other **9–77**

---

[322] CDPA 1988 s.31F(2).
[323] CDPA 1988 s.31F(3).
[324] i.e. a translation. See s.21(3)(a)(i).
[325] s.31F(4). As to changes which might infringe the right not to have the work subjected to derogatory treatment, see Ch.11, below.

provisions of the 1988 Act which permit dealings with copyright works (for example fair dealing for the purposes of private study) which may be applicable in the case of visually impaired persons. These are not affected.

B. MAKING FOR PERSONAL USE OF VISUALLY IMPAIRED PERSON

9–78   **The main provisions.** Section 31A permits the making of an accessible copy of a copyright work for the personal use of a visually impaired person. The section recognises that in some cases the visually impaired person may easily be able to make the copy himself (as in the case of an enlarged photocopy) while in other cases he may not (the making of a copy in braille, for example). The section only applies where a visually impaired person already has lawful possession or lawful use of a copy (referred to as a "master copy") of the whole or part of a literary, dramatic, musical or artistic work, or a published edition, but it is not accessible to him because of his visual impairment.[326] The exception is not restricted to published works. In these circumstances, it is not an infringement of copyright in the work, or in the typographical arrangement of the published edition, for an accessible copy of the master copy to be made for the visually impaired person's personal use.[327] It follows that the copy does not have to be made by the visually impaired person, provided he had lawful possession or use of the master copy in the first place, the copy is made for him for his personal use, and the copy is made from the master copy. A making of a copy in such circumstances by a friend or a copy shop would therefore not be an infringement. Where in such a case the person making the copy charges for it, the sum charged must not exceed the cost of making and supplying the copy.[328] Presumably the effect of this is to make the charging of an excessive sum unlawful and, if an excessive sum is paid, the excess will be recoverable. The requirements also make it clear that the section will not enable multiple copies to be made, either by a visually impaired person or for visually impaired persons generally.[329] As to the phrase "for his personal use", this can be distinguished from the phrase "for his private and domestic use" which is an expression used elsewhere in the Act.[330] Use for the visually impaired person's business or profession is therefore permitted provided the use is personal to him, and it seems that the section will also enable an employer to make an accessible copy for an employee who is a visually impaired person, assuming that the visually impaired person has possession of the master copy in the course of his employment and the accessible copy is for his personal use in the course of his employment.

9–79   **Restrictions on the permitted act.** There are certain restrictions to this exception. First, it does not apply where the master copy is of a musical work, or part of a musical work, and the making of an accessible copy would involve recording a performance of the work or part of it.[331] Thus accessible copies of musical works may not be made from sound recordings, and the rights in the

---

[326] CDPA 1988 s.31A(1).
[327] s.31A(1).
[328] s.31A(5).
[329] This is emphasised both by the section heading ("Making a single accessible copy for personal use"), although this wording is not found in the section itself, and the exchanges in the Parliamentary debates, in which, as elsewhere, this exception has been referred to as the "one-for-one" exception.
[330] See, for example, s.22.
[331] CDPA 1988 s.31A(2)(a).

sound recordings themselves and those of performers are thus preserved.[332]
Second, the exception does not apply where the master copy is of a database, or
part of a database, and the making of an accessible copy would infringe copyright
in the database.[333] The reason for this is that the Database Directive[334] permits
only limited derogations from any copyright which may subsist in a database[335]
and none of these derogations are directly applicable to the case of visually
impaired persons. In any event, any database may well be one in which the separate and parallel sui generis database right subsists, whether or not copyright also
subsists in it,[336] so that the making of an accessible copy may well infringe
database right. Given the potentially wide meaning of a database, these are
important limitations on the operation of these provisions.[337] Thirdly, the exception does not apply in relation to the making of an accessible copy for a particular
visually impaired person if, or to the extent that, copies of the copyright work are
commercially available, by or with the authority of the copyright owner, in a
form that is accessible to that person.[338] This too is an important restriction on the
permitted act. The reasoning for it is that if accessible copies of the work are
commercially available then the ability to make further accessible copies by way
of a permitted act would interfere with the normal exploitation of the work and
thus contravene the Berne three-step test. There is no requirement, however, that
the commercially available copies should be available at a price which is either
reasonable or one which the visually impaired person can afford.

Sufficient acknowledgment. The Act contains an ill-drafted provision dealing   **9–80**
with information that must accompany an accessible copy. Thus, where an accessible copy is made under s.31A, the copy must be accompanied by (a) a statement that the copy has been made under the section and (b) a sufficient
acknowledgment.[339] "Sufficient acknowledgment" has its usual meaning under
the Act, namely an acknowledgment identifying the work in question by its title
or other description, and identifying the author.[340] Presumably one of the objects
of this provision is to ensure, so far as reasonably possible, that such copies will
not be misused in the hands of third parties (as to which, see below). Such provision is not required by the Information Society Directive and it seems onerous
and rather unrealistic in the case of one-off copies made by or for individual visually impaired persons. The effect of non-compliance is also obscure, since the
section merely states that the accessible copy "must" be accompanied by the relevant statements. It would seem that at best all that is created is a statutory duty, a
breach of which will be actionable at the suit of the copyright owner. By way of
contrast, the effect of the fair dealing provisions of ss.29(1), 30(1) and (2) of the
Act, which also require there to be a sufficient acknowledgment, is that unless
there is such an acknowledgment the exceptions do not apply, so that the dealing
will be an infringement, no matter how "fair".

---

[332] Since an accessible copy is defined as a version which provides improved access to the work for a
visually impaired person, this restriction seems hardly necessary.

[333] s.31A(2)(b). As to what constitutes a database, see s.3A(1), and para.3–22, above.

[334] Database Directive 96/9.

[335] See art.6.

[336] See para.3–22, above.

[337] The point was noted by the Commission in its Green Paper *Copyright in the Knowledge Economy*
COM (2008) 466/3 p.4 and acknowledged by the UK Government in its response. However, the
point was not mentioned in the Commission's subsequent Communication *Copyright in the
Knowledge Economy* COM (2009) 532 final.

[338] s.31A(3).

[339] CDPA 1988 s.31A(4).

[340] CDPA 1988 s.178. See also para.9–33, above. The requirement is dispensed with in the case of
anonymously published works and unpublished works where it is not possible to ascertain the
identity of the author by reasonable inquiry: s.178.

C. USE OF ACCESSIBLE COPY

9–81   Introduction. A complicated and poorly drafted regime applies following the making of an accessible copy, the general effect of which is to restrict the use which may be made of such copies.[341] The basic position is of course that where an accessible copy is made by or for a visually impaired person under s.31A(1) it will not be an infringing copy, so that the holding of the copy, or the passing of the copy from the visually impaired person to another person, whether or not also a visually impaired person, would not be an infringement.[342] The Act alters this prima facie position in a number of ways.

9–82   Holding of an accessible copy. The Act deals first with the position of a person who "holds" an accessible copy made under s.31A(1). Section 31A(6) provides that if a person holds an accessible copy made under s.31A(1) when he is not entitled to have it made under that subsection, the copy is to be treated as an infringing copy. The use of the expression "when he is not entitled to have it made" is not very apt. Presumably what is meant is "when he would not be entitled to have such a copy made for him".[343] Obviously, if the provisions of s.31A(1) were not complied with when the copy was made it will always have been an infringing copy and the section is not directed to this. Rather, the section is directed to two situations: first, where the person in question is the visually impaired person who made or for whom the accessible copy was originally made; secondly, where the accessible copy comes into the hands of some other person. The general effect in either case is that if and so long as such a person is a visually impaired person who would have been able to make or have made another such copy for him for his personal use under s.31A(1), a non-infringing accessible copy will remain a non-infringing copy. Otherwise it will become an infringing copy. The wording makes it reasonably clear that this person must at all times also have lawful possession or lawful use of a "master copy".[344] This seems harsh. For example, where a visually impaired person borrows a book at his local library to make an enlarged copy to read at home, the copy will become an infringing copy once he gives the book back. Admittedly, his possession will not amount to an infringement nor will the copy be liable to be delivered up unless the possession happens to be in the course of a business.[345] It would appear that a copy can pass in and out of the status of being an infringing copy, depending on the position of the holder. It also follows that where an accessible copy is transferred from one visually impaired person to another, it will become an infringing copy in the transferee's hands unless (a) the copy also provides that person with improved access to the work, i.e. he suffers from a similar kind of impairment; (b) he also has lawful possession or use of a master copy of the work; and (c) the copy is for his personal use. In addition, it should be noted that under the provisions considered below, the copy may in fact already have become an infringing copy by virtue of the particular type of transfer.

---

[341] As will be seen, the intended effect of the provisions is reasonably clear and was also partly explained by the Parliamentary Under Secretary of State for Trade and Industry in Parliament: "A visually impaired person may keep an accessible copy that they were entitled to have made, or are entitled to have transferred to them, only if they still have what is referred to in the Bill as a 'master copy' of the copyright material. It is not legal under the exception for a visually impaired person to make an accessible copy and pass it on to another visually impaired person who does not have a master copy. Nor is it possible for a visually impaired person to keep an accessible copy when they have handed on the master copy to someone else". (Standing Committee D, May 1, 2002, Col.16.)

[342] Assuming that such acts did not amount to an issue of copies to the public within the meaning of CDPA 1988 s.18.

[343] Compare the rather happier wording of the CDPA 1988 s.31B(9), dealt with below.

[344] As to the meaning of "master copy", see para.9–78, above.

[345] See ss.24(1)(c) and 99(1)(a).

Unless further provision were made, it would also follow from this that where a master copy had been supplied to a person for the purpose of making an accessible copy for a visually impaired person under s.31A(1), the accessible copy, when made, would be an infringing copy in the maker's hands. It is therefore provided that subs.(6) does not apply where the person holding the accessible copy is a person who has lawful possession of the master copy and intends to transfer the accessible copy to a visually impaired person who "is entitled to have the accessible copy made under subsection (1)".[346] The same comment as is made above can be made about the inapt wording of this provision.

Commercial dealings. The Act contains relatively straightforward provisions aimed at making commercial dealings with an accessible copy an infringement. Thus, if an accessible copy which, apart from s.31A(1), would be an infringing copy is subsequently dealt with: (a) it is to be treated as an infringing copy for the purposes of that dealing; and (b) if that dealing infringes copyright, it is to be treated as an infringing copy for all subsequent purposes.[347] For this purpose, "dealt with" means sold or let for hire or offered or exposed for sale or hire or communicated to the public.[348] This provision follows the form of similar provisions relating to other permitted acts.[349] A person who sells an accessible copy, knowing or believing it to be an infringing copy (which it will be by virtue of s.31A(9)—and ignorance of the law will not be a defence) will thus infringe, even if the sale is to a visually impaired person who would be entitled under s.31A(1) to have such a copy made for him. As will be seen, there is an uneasy overlap between this provision and the next set of provisions, dealing with other transfers of accessible copies.

9–83

Other transfers of accessible copies. Section 31A(7) deals with cases where a person who holds an accessible copy made under s.31A(1) "may" transfer it to some other person. Thus, it is provided that a person who holds an accessible copy made under subs.(1) "may" transfer it to two categories of transferee. First, under subs.(7)(a), to a visually impaired person "entitled to have the accessible copy made under subsection (1)", that is, presumably, to a person who would be entitled to have such a copy made for him. Secondly, under subs.(7)(b), to a person who has lawful possession of "the" master copy and intends to transfer the accessible copy to the first category of person. Taken by themselves, these provisions would appear to be of limited scope. Presumably the expression "may transfer" simply means that a person who carries out such an act does so without infringing copyright. The cases in which a person may hold an accessible copy without it becoming an infringing copy have already been considered. If the copy is not an infringing copy in the hands of the transferor then of course the transfer will not be an infringing act except in the perhaps rare case of the transfer amounting to the issue, rental or lending of "copies" to the public under ss.18 or 18A. The fact that the copy may become an infringing copy in the hands of the transferee under s.31A(6) will not affect this either way. If, on the other hand, the copy is an infringing copy in the hands of the transferor, the act of transfer would only be an infringement if the transfer amounted to a sale, letting for hire or distribution, with the requisite degree of knowledge, under s.23(d). Subsection (7) cannot, however, be read without reference to subs.(8), which provides for circumstances in which a transfer of an accessible copy "is" an infringement of copyright. It provides that the transfer by a person of an accessible copy made

9–84

---

[346] See s.31A(6) and (7).
[347] CDPA 1988 s.31A(9).
[348] s.31A(10).
[349] s.31A(10).

under subs.(1) to another person is an infringement of copyright by the transferor unless he has reasonable grounds for believing that the transferee is a person falling within subs.(7)(a) or (b) (as to which, see above). The subsection therefore appears to provide for a new category of infringement, namely the transfer of an accessible copy in the defined circumstances, whether or not the act of "transfer" also happens to be one of the existing acts of primary or secondary infringement. The reference to "another person" is clearly to a person who does not fall within subss.(7)(a) or (b). On such an infringing transfer, the accessible copy will necessarily become an infringing copy by virtue of the "holding" provisions of s.31A(6).

D. THE MAKING OF MULTIPLE COPIES

9–85   **Introduction.** Section 31B enables the making of multiples copies for visually impaired persons. The general safeguard is that such copies can only be made by an approved body. For this purpose an approved body means an educational establishment or a body that is not conducted for profit.[350] As will be seen, there are circumstances in which the Secretary of State may deny the application of the section to certain approved bodies. Section 31B applies where an approved body has lawful possession of a copy (referred to, again, as a "master copy") of the whole or part of (a) a commercially published literary, dramatic, musical or artistic work; or (b) a commercially published edition. Section 31B therefore differs from s.31A in that it only applies where the work in question has been "commercially published".[351] In these circumstances, it is not an infringement of copyright in the work, or in the typographical arrangement of the published edition, for the body to make, or supply, accessible copies for the personal use of visually impaired persons to whom the master copy is not accessible because of their impairment. For this purpose, "supply" includes lending[352] and "lending" means making it available for use, otherwise than for direct or indirect economic or commercial advantage, on terms that it will or may be returned.[353] A loan is not to be treated as being for direct or indirect economic or commercial advantage if a charge is made for the loan which does not exceed the cost of making and supplying the copy.[354] If the approved body charges for supplying a copy made under this section, the sum charged must not exceed the cost of making and supplying the copy.[355]

9–86   **Restrictions.** There are a number of restrictions which apply. First, there are restrictions which are similar to those applying under s.31A. Thus s.31B(1) does not apply if the master copy is of a musical work, or part of a musical work, and the making of an accessible copy would involve recording a performance of the work or part of it.[356] Again, it does not apply if the master copy is of a database, or part of a database, and the making of an accessible copy would infringe copyright in the database.[357] Further, it does not apply in relation to the making of an accessible copy if, or to the extent that, copies of the copyright work are commercially available, by or with the authority of the copyright owner, in a form

---

[350] CDPA 1988 s.31B(12). "Educational establishment" has its usual definition under s.174.
[351] As to this expression, see s.175 and para.11–11, below.
[352] s.31B(13).
[353] s.31F(6).
[354] s.31F(6), (7). The definition of lending in s.18A does not apply: s.31F(8).
[355] s.31B(6).
[356] CDPA 1988 s.31B(2)(a).
[357] s.31B(2)(b).

that is accessible to the same or substantially the same degree.[358] Finally, it does not apply in relation to the supply of an accessible copy to a particular visually impaired person if, or to the extent that, copies of the copyright work are commercially available, by or with the authority of the copyright owner, in a form that is accessible to that person.[359] Secondly, there are similar requirements as to information and acknowledgment. An accessible copy made under s.31B must be accompanied by (a) a statement that it is made under the section and (b) a sufficient acknowledgment.[360] Thirdly, where the approved body is an educational establishment, it "must" ensure that the copies will be used only for its educational purposes. Presumably the only remedy for non-compliance is for breach of statutory duty. Fourthly, if the master copy is in copy protected electronic form, any accessible copy made of it under the section must, so far as it is reasonably practicable to do so, incorporate the same, or equally effective, copy protection, unless the copyright owner agrees otherwise.[361] Again, presumably the remedy for non-compliance is for a breach of statutory duty.

Subsequent dealings. As with s.31A, there are a number of provisions which affect subsequent dealings. If an accessible copy which would be, but for the subsection, an infringing copy is subsequently dealt with, (a) it is to be treated as an infringing copy for the purposes of that dealing; and (b) if that dealing infringes copyright, it is to be treated as an infringing copy for all subsequent purposes.[362] For this purpose, "dealt with" again means sold or let for hire or offered or exposed for sale or hire or communicated to the public.[363] Further, if an approved body continues to hold an accessible copy made under the subsection when it would no longer be entitled to make or supply such a copy under that subsection, the copy is to be treated as an infringing copy. Unlike s.31A, there are no other comparable provisions whereby accessible copies made under s.31B become infringing copies in the hands of other persons, or whereby certain transfers become infringements.

9–87

Approved bodies and the Secretary of State's powers. Although the Act speaks in terms of "approved bodies", such bodies are not approved in any real sense of the word and the Act therefore contains provisions enabling the Secretary of State to take steps if there is evidence of abuse. Thus, the Secretary of State may make an order under s.31E if it appears to him that the making of multiple copies by an approved body under s.31B has led to infringement of copyright on a scale which, in the Secretary of State's opinion, would not have occurred if s.31B had not been in force.[364] Such an order may prohibit one or more named approved bodies, or one or more specified categories of approved body, from acting under s.31B[365] and may disapply the provisions of s.31B in respect of the making of copies of a description so specified.[366] Such an order is exercisable by statutory instrument subject to annulment in pursuance of a resolution of either House of Parliament.[367] Where the Secretary of State is proposing to make an order he must first consult (a) such bodies representing copyright owners as he thinks fit;

9–88

---

[358] s.31B(3).
[359] s.31B(4).
[360] s.31B(5).
[361] s.31B(8). As to copy protection devices, see Ch.15, below.
[362] CDPA 1988 s.31B(10).
[363] s.31B(11).
[364] CDPA 1988 s.31E.
[365] s.31E(2).
[366] s.31E(3).
[367] s.31F(11).

and (b) such bodies representing visually impaired persons as he thinks fit.[368] If the Secretary of State proposes to make an order which includes a prohibition he must, before making it, consult (a) if the proposed order is to apply to one or more named approved bodies, that body or those bodies; (b) if it is to apply to one or more specified categories of approved body, such bodies representing approved bodies of that category or those categories as he thinks fit.[369]

9–89 **Record keeping and notices.** An approved body must keep records of accessible copies made under s.31B and of the persons to whom they are supplied and allow the copyright owner or a person acting for him, on giving reasonable notice, to inspect the records at any reasonable time.[370] Further, within a reasonable time of making the accessible copy the approved body must (a) notify each relevant representative body; or (b) if there is no such body, notify the copyright owner.[371] For this purpose a relevant representative body is a body which (a) represents particular copyright owners, or owners of copyright in the type of copyright work concerned; and (b) has given notice to the Secretary of State of the copyright owners, or the classes of copyright owner, represented by it.[372] The Secretary of State has power by regulations to prescribe (a) the form in which or (b) the procedure in accordance with which any such notices must be given.[373] Such power is exercisable by statutory instrument subject to annulment in pursuance of a resolution of either House of Parliament.[374] The requirement to notify the copyright owner under the above provision does not apply if it is not reasonably possible for the approved body to ascertain the name and address of the copyright owner.[375] There are no prescribed sanctions for breaches of any of these provisions and presumably they are actionable as breaches of statutory duty.

E. INTERMEDIATE COPIES

9–90 **Introduction.** Where multiple copies are made by an approved body under s.31B it may often be necessary to make relatively expensive intermediate copies as part of the manufacturing process. The policy of the Act is not to waste that expenditure if possible. Section 31C(1) therefore provides that an approved body which is entitled to make accessible copies under s.31B "may hold" an intermediate copy of the master copy which is necessarily created during the production of the accessible copies. It seems clear from subs.(2) that the effect of the words "may hold" is that the intermediate copy is not to be treated as an infringing copy in the hands of the body while the conditions of the subsection continue to be satisfied. An intermediate copy is not itself defined but is clearly a copy which was made, directly or indirectly, from the master copy and from which, directly or indirectly, multiple copies are subsequently made, the making of which was a necessary and integral part of the manufacturing process. There is no reason why there may not be more than one intermediate copy in the manufacturing chain.

The subsection goes on to provide that the approved body "may hold" an intermediate copy only (a) if and so long as the approved body continues to be entitled to make accessible copies of that master copy; and (b) for the purposes of the production of further accessible copies. If the intermediate copy is held in breach

---

[368] s.31E(4).
[369] s.31E(5).
[370] CDPA 1988 s.31C(6).
[371] s.31C(7).
[372] s.31C(8).
[373] s.31F(10).
[374] s.31F(11).
[375] s.31C(9).

of these provisions it is to be treated as an infringing copy.[376] It follows that if the approved body no longer has lawful possession of the master copy, or if the copies of the work in a form that is accessible to the same or substantially the same degree become commercially available, the intermediate copy will immediately become an infringing copy. A body holding such a copy in the course of a business and with the requisite degree of knowledge will thus become liable for infringement by possession. Although the Act states that the approved body may only hold the intermediate copy for the purposes of the production of further accessible copies, it is reasonably clear that once a manufacturing run has been completed the body may continue to hold the intermediate copy pending any decision to make further copies provided, of course, that meanwhile it does not use it for some other purpose.

Making intermediate copies available. The Act goes on to make provision enabling an approved body to make an intermediate copy available to other approved bodies for the same purpose. Thus s.31C(3) provides that an approved body "may lend or transfer" the intermediate copy to another approved body which is entitled to make accessible copies of the work or published edition under s.31B. Lending for this purpose has the same extended definition as it does for the purposes of s.31B.[377] The mere lending or transfer of such a copy would not ordinarily be an infringement unless it fell within the provisions of either s.18 or 18A but, as with ss.31B(7) and (8), it seems that s.31C(3), taken with s.31(4), creates a new act of infringement. Thus, s.31C(4) provides that the loan or transfer by an approved body of an intermediate copy to another person is an infringement of copyright by the lender or transferor unless he has reasonable grounds for believing that the borrower or transferee: (a) is another approved body which is entitled to make accessible copies of the work or published edition under s.31B; and (b) will use the intermediate copy only for the purposes of the production of further accessible copies. As with s.31B, the effect of these provisions is presumably that the loan or transfer to a person who does not fall within this description is an infringement unless the lender or transferor reasonably believes that he does so. The borrower or transferee will of course only be entitled to make further accessible copies if he has lawful possession of a master copy (whether from the lender or transferor, or another copy). As to whether he "will use the intermediate copy" only for this purpose, presumably it will be a question of fact whether this is his intention. If the approved body charges for lending or transferring the intermediate copy, the sum charged must not exceed the cost of the loan or transfer.[378]

9–91

   Although the wording is not entirely happy, an approved body which holds an intermediate copy following such a loan or transfer presumably "may" continue to hold it under subs.(1) provided it remains entitled to make accessible copies and holds it for the purposes of doing so. It too may lend or transfer it to another approved body.[379]

Record keeping and notices. As with s.31B, there are requirements on approved bodies to keep records and give certain notices in relation to intermediate copies. Thus an approved body must (a) keep records of any intermediate copy lent or transferred under this section and of the persons to whom it is lent or transferred; and (b) allow the copyright owner or a person acting for him, on giving reason-

9–92

---

[376] CDPA 1988 s.31C(2).
[377] As to which, see above and CDPA 1988 ss.31F(6), (7) and (8).
[378] s.31C(5).
[379] s.31C(3).

able notice, to inspect the records at any reasonable time.[380] Again, within a reasonable time of lending or transferring an intermediate copy under this section, the approved body must (a) notify each relevant representative body; or (b) if there is no such body, notify the copyright owner.[381]

F. LICENSING SCHEMES

9-93 **Introduction.** Just as the policy of the Act is not to permit the making of accessible copies where copies of the work in question are commercially available, it is also the policy of the Act not to permit such activities where a relevant licensing scheme is in force. Section 31D therefore provides that the ability of an approved body to make multiple copies under s.31B does not apply to the making of an accessible copy in a particular form if three conditions are satisfied: (a) a licensing scheme operated by a licensing body is in force under which licences may be granted by the licensing body permitting the making and supply of copies of the copyright work in that form; (b) the scheme is not unreasonably restrictive; and (c) the scheme and any modification made to it have been notified to the Secretary of State by the licensing body. Section 31D(2) provides that a scheme is unreasonably restrictive if it includes a term or condition which: (a) purports to prevent or limit the steps that may be taken under s.31B or 31C; or (b) has that effect.[382] Nevertheless, subs.(2) does not apply if (a) the copyright work is no longer published by or with the authority of the copyright owner; and (b) there are reasonable grounds for preventing or restricting the making of accessible copies of the work.[383] Finally, if s.31B or 31C is displaced by a licensing scheme, the scheme can be referred to the Copyright Tribunal.[384] As with notices under s.31C, the Secretary of State has power by regulations to prescribe (a) the form in which or (b) the procedure in accordance with which any notice required under s.31D(1) must be given.[385]

9-94 **The Secretary of State's powers.** As with the provisions relating to the making of multiple copies by approved bodies, the Secretary of State has powers to make orders in the case of licensing schemes. Thus he may make an order if it appears to him that the making of copies under a licence granted under a licensing scheme that has been notified under s.31D has led to infringement of copyright on a scale which, in the Secretary of State's opinion, would not have occurred if the licence had not been granted.[386] Such an order may prohibit one or more named approved bodies, or one or more specified categories of approved body, from acting under a licence of a description specified in the order and the order may disapply the provisions of a licence, or a licensing scheme, of a description specified in the order in respect of the making of copies of a description so specified.[387] As with the powers in relation to s.31B, the power is exercisable by statutory instrument subject to annulment in pursuance of a resolution of either House of Parliament[388] and the Secretary of State must consult specified bodies before any such order is

---

[380] CDPA 1988 s.31C(6).
[381] s.31C(7).
[382] CDPA 1988 s.31D(2).
[383] s.31D(3).
[384] s.31D(4). As to the reference of a scheme to the Copyright Tribunal, see paras 28–84 et seq., below.
[385] s.31F(10).
[386] CDPA 1988 s.31E(1).
[387] s.31E(2) and (3).
[388] s.31F(11).

made.[389] Where an approved body is prohibited by an order from acting under a licence, it may not apply to the Copyright Tribunal under s.121(1) in respect of a refusal or failure by a licensing body to grant such a licence.[390]

Schemes. Schemes have been published by the Copyright Licensing Agency Ltd   **9–95**
("CLA") and the Music Publishers Association Ltd ("MPA"). The present version of the CLA's scheme[391] permits the making and distribution to visually impaired persons of accessible copies of original published editions of books journals, magazines and other periodicals within the CLA's repertoire. The MPA's scheme[392] covers the making of copies in print or "electronic graphic form" of compositions within its repertoire.

6. EDUCATION

Introduction. One of the clearest examples of a strong public interest in limiting   **9–96**
copyright protection is in the field of education. However, just because education is a worthy cause does not mean that some form of blanket exception to copyright should be allowed. It must be remembered that it is works made for educational purposes that will often be copied in educational establishments. A wide exemption would therefore undermine the market for such works, so that a publisher would be unlikely to invest in their production. In the event, the exceptions relating to education are in many respects quite limited, even when viewed alongside the available licensing agreements and other sections of the 1988 Act, such as the exceptions relating to libraries and fair dealing for the purposes of non-commercial research or private study. The exceptions are an expansion of the even more modest provision made in the 1956 Act and before that the 1911 Act.[393]

The Berne Convention. Article 10(2) of the Convention states that it is a matter   **9–97**
for individual countries to permit the use of works for illustration in publications, broadcasts, sound recordings or films for teaching, provided this is compatible with fair practice. The acts permitted by the 1988 Act in this area appear to fall within this.

The Information Society Directive. Recital 14 to the Directive states that the   **9–98**
Directive should seek to promote learning and culture by protecting works and other subject-matter while permitting exceptions or limitations in the public interest for the purpose of education and teaching. Articles 5(2)(c) and (4) go on to permit Member States to make an exception to the reproduction and distribution rights in respect of specific acts of reproduction made by educational establishments, which are not for direct or indirect economic or commercial advantage.[394] Articles 5(3)(a) and (4) also permit an exception to be made to the reproduction right, to the communication to the public right, and the distribution right, for the sole purpose, amongst other things, of illustration for teaching, as long as the source, including the author's name, is indicated, unless this turns out to be impossible, to the extent justified by the non-commercial purpose to be

---

[389] ss.31E(4) and (5).
[390] s.31E(6).
[391] Published on May 28, 2010. See *http://www.cla.co.uk* [Accessed October 1, 2010]. It is understood that this scheme has been notified to the Secretary of State (email exchange with Shantilal Shah, Licensing Administrator of the CLA, October 2010).
[392] Dated October 31, 2003. See *http://www.mpaonline.org.uk* [Accessed October 1, 2010].
[393] See s.6(6) of the 1956 Act and s.2(1)(iv) of the 1911 Act.
[394] The exception to the distribution right is permitted only to the extent justified by the purpose of the authorised act of reproduction: Information Society Directive, 2001/29 art.5(4).

achieved.[395] Recital 42 to the Directive indicates that when applying the exception or limitation for non-commercial educational purposes the non-commercial nature of the activity in question is to be determined by that activity as such. The organisational structure and the means of funding of the establishment concerned are not the decisive factors in this respect. Overall, these requirements necessitated a number of changes to the permitted acts under the 1988 Act dealing with education, in particular to provide for sufficient acknowledgment and to restrict the permitted acts to non-commercial purposes.

9–99   **Educational establishment.** With the exception of s.32, which deals with instruction and examination in a broad sense (see paras 9–100 to 9–102, below), the education exceptions in ss.33 to 36A are confined to educational establishments. "Educational establishment" is defined by the Act as including any school, which is itself defined by reference to the various Education Acts.[396] Apart from any school, the term includes any other educational establishment specified by the Secretary of State under his powers under s.174(1)(b) of the 1988 Act.[397] In addition, these provisions have been extended to apply to teachers employed by a local authority to give instruction to pupils unable to attend an educational establishment.[398] While it was the Government's view that copying for educational purposes or instruction in educational establishments under these exceptions would very largely be for a non-commercial activity, it could not be confident that this would invariably be so, for example in relation to some educational activity in some further education establishments.[399] Amendments were therefore made to various provisions to limit the permitted acts to a non-commercial activity. These are considered in turn, below.

A. DOING THINGS FOR THE PURPOSES OF INSTRUCTION OR EXAMINATION

9–100   **Instruction.** Section 32(1) of the Act provides that the copyright in a literary, dramatic, musical or artistic work is not infringed by its being copied in the course of instruction or of preparation for instruction, provided the copying (a) is done by a person giving or receiving instruction, (b) is not done by means of a reprographic process and (c) is accompanied by a sufficient acknowledgment, and provided the instruction is for a non-commercial purpose.[400] No acknowledgment is required where this would be impossible for reasons of practicality or

---

[395] Again, the exception to the distribution right is permitted only to the extent justified by the purpose of the authorised act of reproduction.

[396] CDPA 1988 s.174(3). The Acts in question are the Education Act 1996 (c.56), the Education (Scotland) Act 1962 (c.47) (see also the Education (Scotland) Act 1980 (c.44)) and the Education and Libraries (Northern Ireland) Order 1986 (SI 1986/594 (NI 3)).

[397] See the Copyright (Educational Establishments) Order 2005 (SI 2005/223), at Vol.2 A4.xiii, which defines "educational establishment" very broadly to include universities, other providers of higher education as defined in certain statutes, providers of further education as provided in certain statutes and theological colleges. In the context of its consultation on the scope of ss.35 and 37 of the 1988 Act, the Government has rejected a suggestion that the definition of educational establishment be extended to museums, galleries, libraries and archives: see the UK IPO document Taking Forward the Gowers Review of Intellectual Property: Second Stage Consultation on Copyright Exceptions, December 2009 para.70. See *http://www.ukipo.org* [Accessed October 3, 2010].

[398] See the Copyright (Application of Provisions relating to Educational Establishments to Teachers) (No.2) Order 1989 (SI 1989/1067) at Vol.2 A4.iv made under s.174(2) of the CDPA 1988.

[399] See the Government Conclusions on the Patent Office's Consultation Paper of August 7, 2002, para.5.8.

[400] CDPA 1988 s.32(1). As to the limited exception provided for reprographic copying, see CDPA 1988 s.36, para.9–107, below.

otherwise.[401] The requirements of sufficient acknowledgment and non-commercial purpose were introduced in 2003.[402] "Reprographic process" is defined by the Act as meaning a process (a) for making facsimile copies, or (b) involving the use of an appliance for making multiple copies, and includes, in relation to a work held in electronic form, any copying by electronic means, but does not include the making of a film or sound recording.[403] Thus, for example, it seems that a teacher may copy onto a blackboard a substantial part of a literary work, and pupils may copy it down. The teacher may not, however, photocopy the same material for use by students in the absence of a licensing agreement. Similarly, a teacher would not be entitled to photocopy material onto an acetate for use on an overhead projector, even though the same material could be copied onto an acetate by hand. The meaning of sufficient acknowledgment has already been considered.[404] It should be noted that the acknowledgment does not have to be in writing, which may be important in the context of classroom teaching. As to the copying being "for a non-commercial purpose", this expression has also been considered in the context of fair dealing.[405] Strictly, what is relevant here is the purpose of the instruction, not the purpose of the copying or the purpose of the educational establishment, although no doubt these matters will be of some relevance in assessing the purpose of the instruction. The relevant purpose appears to be that of either the giver or the receiver of the instruction. In the case of the latter, instruction received by way of general school or university education is presumably not received for a commercial purpose but instruction received in the course of professional or other vocational training with a view to a qualification would appear to be received for a commercial purpose. As to the giver of the instruction, the requirement of non-commercial purpose would no doubt be satisfied in the case of most educational establishments but not in the case of commercial organisations offering courses to fee-paying students.

In relation to a sound recording, film or broadcast, copyright is not infringed by its being copied by making a film or film sound-track in the course of instruction, or of preparation for instruction, in the making of films or sound-tracks, provided the copying (a) is done by a person giving or receiving instruction and (b) is accompanied by a sufficient acknowledgment, and provided the instruction is for a non-commercial purpose.[406]

Section 32(2A) provides that in relation to a literary, dramatic, musical or artistic work which has been made available to the public, copyright is not infringed by its being copied in the course of instruction or of preparation for instruction, provided the copying (a) is fair dealing with the work, (b) is done by a person giving or receiving instruction, (c) is not done by means of a reprographic process, and (d) is accompanied by a sufficient acknowledgment.[407] There is clearly a large overlap between s.32(2A) and s.32(1). Section 32(2A) was introduced to take advantage of art.5(3)(d) of the Information Society Directive, apparently on the basis that the article is not limited to criticism or review, these

---

[401] s.32(3A).
[402] By SI 2003/2498.
[403] s.178, where "facsimile copy" and "electronic" are also defined.
[404] See para.9–33, above.
[405] See para.9–32, above.
[406] CDPA 1988 s.32(2). Again, no acknowledgment is required where this would be impossible for reasons of practicality or otherwise: s.32(3A).
[407] s.32(2A). No acknowledgment is required where this would be impossible for reasons of practicality or otherwise: s.32(3A) The meaning of "made available to the public" has the same meaning here as under the fair dealing provisions of s.30(1A): s.32(2B). As to permitted acts of reprographic copying in the case of educational uses, see s.36 and para.9–107, below.

being only examples of the permitted use.[408] The important difference between s.32(2A) and s.32(1) is that copying in the course of instruction for a commercial purpose is permitted provided, of course, that the work has been made available to the public and it amounts to fair dealing. What amounts to fair dealing has already been considered.[409] In deciding whether a dealing is fair, the fact that the instruction is for a commercial purpose will be a factor to be considered, but will not be conclusive. Also relevant will be the amount of copying and the reason for the copying.

9–101   **Examinations.** The 1988 Act also provides that copyright is not infringed by anything done for the purposes of an examination by way of setting the questions, communicating the questions to the candidates or answering the questions, provided that the questions are accompanied by a sufficient acknowledgment.[410] The requirement of sufficient acknowledgment is new and clearly raises an obstacle where the point of the question is to test the candidate's knowledge of the name of the work or its author. The provision does not extend to the making of a reprographic copy of a musical work for use by an examination candidate in performing the work.[411] "Reprographic copy" refers to copying by a reprographic process.[412] Thus it will not be permissible to photocopy sheet music for candidates taking a musical test instead of buying or hiring the sheet music.[413]

9–102   **Subsequent dealings with copies.** If by virtue of the above provisions the making of a copy of a work was not an infringement of copyright, but such a copy is subsequently dealt with, that is (a) sold, let for hire, offered or exposed for sale or hire, or (b) communicated to the public (unless that communication is itself, by virtue of s.32(3), not an infringement of copyright), then it is to be treated as an infringing copy for the purpose of that dealing.[414] Once such an infringement has occurred, the copy will be treated as an infringing copy for all subsequent purposes, and not just for the purpose of that dealing.[415] Thus, for example, possession in the course of business, with the requisite degree of knowledge, subsequent to such a dealing, will also amount to an infringement.[416] The purpose of these provisions is to prevent the commercial exploitation of copies made for educational purposes. As to the knowledge required to make such a dealing an infringement, in accordance with the usual principles it will be sufficient if the defendant has knowledge of the relevant facts. His ignorance of these particular provisions, being matters of law, will be irrelevant.[417] Thus, if the person dealing with a copy of a work knows or has reason to believe that it is a copy made for educational purposes, that dealing will almost inevitably amount to a secondary infringement under s.23 of the Act.

---

[408] This provision was introduced "to maintain existing flexibility in this area". See the Patent Office Consultation Paper of August 7, 2002 and the Transposition Note on implementation of the Directive by SI 2003/2498.

[409] See para.9–58, above.

[410] CDPA 1988 s.32(3). No acknowledgment is required where this would be impossible for reasons of practicality or otherwise: s.32(3A).

[411] s.32(4).

[412] s.178 and see para.9–100, above.

[413] This provision reflects the vulnerability of this publishing sector. See further, Gurnsey, *Copyright Theft* (Aldershot: Aslib Gower, 1995).

[414] CDPA 1988 s.32(5), s.27(6). Communication to the public was introduced as a further form of dealing on implementation of the Information Society Directive because of the possible commercial nature of such acts. See the Government Conclusions on the Patent Office's Consultation Paper of August 7, 2002, para.5.11.

[415] s.32(5).

[416] s.23(a).

[417] See Ch.8, above.

B. Anthologies for Educational Use

The Act contains a very limited exception which allows for the inclusion of a **9–103** "short passage" from a published literary or dramatic work in a collection which is intended for use in educational establishments.[418] In order to fall within this exception four conditions must be satisfied. First, the collection must be described as being for use in educational establishments both in its title and in any advertisements issued by or on behalf of the publisher. Secondly, it must consist "mainly of material in which no copyright subsists". Thirdly, the work from which the passage is taken must itself not be intended for use in an educational establishment. Finally, the inclusion must be accompanied by a sufficient acknowledgment.[419] Moreover, even if the above conditions are satisfied, no more than two excerpts from copyright works by the same author may be published in collections by the same publisher over any period of five years.[420] In relation to any given passage this reference to excerpts from works by the same author (a) includes excerpts from works created by him in collaboration with another and (b) if the passage in question is from a collaborative work, "works by the same author" is to be taken to include excerpts from works by any of the authors.[421] Thus, within a five-year period, it seems that a publisher who had already taken an excerpt from a work by A and an excerpt from a work by B, could not take an excerpt from a work created by A and B, even though he could take another excerpt from a work created by A or B individually. The utility of this exception is further diminished by the lack of certainty involved in the concept of a "short passage". Logically this must refer to something greater than a "substantial part", but otherwise the concept is undefined. The courts may therefore be forced into a general consideration of the "fairness" of the use in question.[422] The requirement that the collection should "mainly consist of material in which no copyright subsists" (itself rather vague) is also extremely restrictive. It would not be possible, for example, for a publisher to rely on this section if he wished to include a short extract of a work in a collection consisting mainly of material in which he owned the copyright. A publisher might, however, be able to rely on fair dealing for the purposes of criticism or review in such circumstances.[423]

C. Performing, Playing or Showing a Work in the Course of Activities of Educational Establishments

The performance of a literary, dramatic or musical work before an audience **9–104** consisting of teachers and pupils at an educational establishment and other persons directly connected with the activities of the establishment (a) by a teacher or pupil in the course of the activities of the establishment, or (b) at the establishment by any person for the purposes of instruction, is not to be regarded as a pub-

---

[418] CDPA 1988 s.33(1). References in the section to the use of a work "in an educational establishment" are to any use for the purposes of such an establishment: s.33(4). The purpose of this subsection was to make sure that the exception applies to institutions such as the Open University, where use of the work would take place mostly in the home of the student rather than on the premises of the institution itself: *Hansard*, HL Vol.493, col.1166.

[419] See para.9–33, above.

[420] s.33(2).

[421] s.33(3).

[422] See paras 9–58 et seq., above.

[423] See paras 9–40 et seq., above.

lic performance for the purposes of infringement of copyright.[424] Similarly, the playing or showing of a sound recording, film or broadcast before such an audience at an educational establishment for the purposes of instruction is not a playing or showing of the work in public for the purposes of infringement of copyright.[425] Reference has already been made to the definition of an "educational establishment."[426] "Teacher" and "pupil" are defined to mean any person who gives and any person who receives instruction respectively.[427] As to the persons who may be "directly connected with the activities" of such an establishment, the Act provides that a person is not for this purpose directly connected with the activities of the educational establishment simply because he or she is the parent of a pupil at the establishment.[428] This exclusion of parents was felt to be necessary in order to comply with the Berne Convention, which does not allow for the granting of exceptions in relation to a public performance.[429] Thus a school play to which all parents or the parents of participants are invited will constitute a public performance and may infringe copyright accordingly.[430] If, however, parents were present because they had some special role in relation to the particular performance, for example, by assisting backstage, they would seem to fall within the exception. In any event, the unforeseen presence of one or two parents would probably not, in itself, render the performance a public one.[431] Other persons "directly connected with the activities" of the establishment might include caretakers and similar employees.[432]

D. Recording of Broadcasts

9–105 Modern teaching methods make extensive use of visual media, particularly video, as this helps keep student attention by introducing an element of variety and on occasion allows information to be presented more efficiently. In recognition of this, the Act allows a recording of a broadcast,[433] or a copy of such a recording, to be made by or on behalf of an educational establishment,[434] provided that this is to be used for the educational purposes of that establishment, and provided that it is accompanied by a sufficient acknowledgment of the broadcast and that the educational purposes are non-commercial.[435] If these conditions are satisfied, such recording will not infringe copyright in the broadcast, or in any work

---

[424] CDPA 1988 s.34(1). The Information Society Directive is not concerned with the public performance right and so its provisions do not have to be taken into account in relation to s.34.

[425] s.34(2).

[426] See para.9–99, above.

[427] s.174(5).

[428] s.34(3).

[429] See *Hansard*, HL Vol.493, col.1167. This is presumably why, in the case of this "permitted" act, the 1988 Act does not speak in terms of it not being an infringement but redefines it so as not to amount to the restricted act of public performance.

[430] But see *Duck v Bates* (1884) 13 Q.B.D. 843. cf. *Jennings v Stephens* [1936] 1 Ch. 469. As to what constitutes a performance in public more generally, see paras 7–103 et seq., above.

[431] See *Hansard*, HL Vol.493, col.1167.

[432] *Hansard*, HL Vol.493, col.1168. Although this example was given in Parliament it would be possible to argue that whilst caretakers and the like are connected with the running of the school they are not directly connected with its "activities".

[433] The Government has rejected a suggestion that this exception should be extended to "on demand" services but retains an open mind on the issue: see the UK IPO document Taking Forward the Gowers Review of Intellectual Property: Second Stage Consultation on Copyright Exceptions, December 2009 para.90. See *http://www.ukipo.org* [Accessed November 16, 2010].

[434] The Government has rejected a suggestion that for the purposes of ss.35 and 36 of the 1988 Act the definition of educational establishment be extended to museums, galleries, libraries and archives: see the UK IPO document Taking Forward the Gowers Review of Intellectual Property: Second Stage Consultation on Copyright Exceptions, December 2009 para.70. See *http://www.ukipo.org* [Accessed November 16, 2010].

[435] CDPA 1988 s.35(1). Such a recording can then be shown to students in accordance with s.34 (see para.9–104, above).

included in it.[436] The requirements of sufficient acknowledgment and non-commercial purpose are new. Copyright is also not infringed where a recording of a broadcast or a copy of such a recording, whose making was by virtue of the above provisions not an infringement of copyright, is communicated to the public by a person situated within the premises of an educational establishment provided that the communication cannot be received by any person situated outside the premises of that establishment.[437] These provisions do not apply, however, if or to the extent that the Secretary of State has certified a licensing scheme for these purposes under s.143 of the Act.[438] Even if a scheme has been certified, however, the matter can still be referred to the Copyright Tribunal, should an educational establishment feel that the proposed terms are unreasonable. The Act thus provides an incentive to owners to offer licences on reasonable terms. In this instance the Act benefits educational establishments not by conferring a limited privilege upon them, but rather by strengthening their bargaining position as against copyright owners. The section also contains provisions of the kind already discussed making it an infringement to deal in copies made under the protection of this section.[439]

Proposed extension of the exception. The Gowers Review[440] recommended that   **9–106**
s.35 should be amended so as to extend to the communication of broadcasts to distance learning students who were not located within the educational establishment.[441] In order to ensure that access to such material should not be generally available to the public, it proposed that such students would need to access the material securely via a virtual learning environment (VLE).[442] In December 2009, the Government indicated its intention to extend the exception so that it applied to the communication of broadcasts from the premises of educational establishments to teachers and pupils,[443] situated outside the premises who were authorised by the educational establishment to receive them.[444] Educational establishments would be required to take all reasonable steps to ensure that only authorised persons accessed the material.[445] No further use would be permitted.[446]

E. REPROGRAPHIC COPYING

Section 36 of the 1988 Act provides an exception to allow to a limited extent the   **9–107**

---

[436] s.35(1).
[437] s.35(1A). This provision was introduced because otherwise the deletion of s.7 would have meant that cable transmission within an educational establishment of recordings of broadcasts made under the s.35 exception would require authorisation, whereas it had previously been exempt by virtue of s.7(2)(d). See the Analysis of Responses and Government Conclusions on the Patent Office's Consultation Paper of August 7, 2002, para.5.9.
[438] s.35(2) and see, as to licensing schemes so far certified, para.28–63, below.
[439] s.35(3) and see para.9–102, above. Under this section, however, "dealt with" means sold or let for hire, offered or exposed for sale or hire, or communicated from within the premises of an educational establishment to any person situated outside those premises.
[440] Gowers Review of Intellectual Property HM Treasury, December 2006.
[441] Recommendation 2; see also para.4.18.
[442] A VLA is a software system designed to facilitate the task of teachers in the management of educational courses for their students.
[443] It was considered that these expressions were broad enough to include support staff and persons assisting pupils: see paras 125 and 126.
[444] Taking Forward the Gowers Review of Intellectual Property: Second Stage Consultation on Copyright Exceptions (UKIPO; see http://www.ukipo.org [Accessed November 16, 2010]) para.68.
[445] para.107. Presumably the establishment would be liable in breach of statutory duty for any failure to comply with this duty. It was considered that any reference in the legislation to a VLE or other existing security technology should not be used because it would soon become outdated: para.105.
[446] para.120.

making of reprographic copies of passages from published literary, dramatic or musical works by or on behalf of an educational establishment[447] for the purposes of instruction provided that they are accompanied by a sufficient acknowledgment and the instruction is for a non-commercial purpose.[448] The requirements of sufficient acknowledgment and non-commercial purpose are new. Reprographic copies of passages from published editions may also, to the same limited extent, be made without infringing any copyright in the typographical arrangement of the edition.[449] In this case, no acknowledgment is required and there is no restriction to non-commercial purposes.[450] Copies will be made "on behalf of" an educational establishment if they are made for the purposes of that establishment by any person.[451] The circumstances in which such copying will not amount to an infringement are that not more than 1 per cent of any work may be copied in any quarter, that is, in any period from January 1 to March 31, April 1 to June 30, July 1 to September 30 or October 1 to December 31.[452] However, copying is not permitted by this section if, or to the extent that, licences authorising the copying in question are available and the person making the copies knew or ought to have been aware of that fact.[453] But where the terms of such a licence purport to restrict the proportion of a work which may be copied to less than the above percentage, then such terms are to that extent of no effect.[454] This will be so whether or not the licence imposes terms for payment.[455] The section also contains provisions of the kind already discussed making it an infringement to deal in copies made with the protection of this section.[456] Overall, therefore, the real importance of this section, as with the provisions relating to the copying of broadcasts,[457] is in providing an incentive to owners to ensure that licences are available. In this case, however, there is no requirement that the Secretary of State must approve the scheme, although the specification of a minimum proportion of a work which is to be available for copying, together with the power to refer licences to the Copyright Tribunal, does afford educational establishments some security.[458]

9–108 **Proposed extension.** The Gowers Review[459] recommended that s.36 should be extended to permit passages from works to be made available to students by

---

[447] The Government has rejected a suggestion that for the purposes of CDPA 1988 ss.35 and 36 the definition of educational establishment be extended to museums, galleries, libraries and archives: Taking Forward the Gowers Review of Intellectual Property: Second Stage Consultation on Copyright Exceptions (UKIPO; see http://www.ukipo.org [Accessed November 16, 2010]) para.70.

[448] No acknowledgment is required where this would be impossible for reasons of practicality or otherwise: CDPA 1988 s.36(1A).

[449] s.36(1B).

[450] This is because the copyright in typographical arrangements is not subject to the provisions of the Information Society Directive, and the position of such works has therefore not been altered.

[451] s.174(6).

[452] s.36(2).

[453] s.36(3). Note that there is no equivalent requirement of knowledge in relation to s.35. Presumably this is because it will be easier to determine whether an appropriate scheme has been certified.

[454] s.36(4).

[455] s.36(4).

[456] s.36(5); para.9–102, above. For the purposes of this section, "dealt with" means sold or let for hire, offered or exposed for sale or hire or communicated to the public. Communication to the public was introduced as a further form of dealing on implementation of the Information Society Directive because of the possible commercial nature of such acts. See the Government Conclusions on the Patent Office's Consultation Paper of August 7, 2002, para.5.11.

[457] i.e. under s.35.

[458] It is instructive to compare this provision with the position in the United States where the fair use doctrine will, in certain circumstances, cover the making of multiple copies for classroom use. Guidelines to this effect were agreed upon by authors, publishers and educational establishments. These set out the minimum amount which may be safely copied and were approved by Congress: H.R. Rep. No. 94–1476, 94th Congress, 2d Sess. 66–72 (1976).

[459] Gowers Review of Intellectual Property (HM Treasury, December 2006).

email or VLE without infringing copyright, provided that no licensing scheme was in place for their use.[460] In December 2009, the Government indicated its intention to implement this recommendation by deleting the word "reprographic" from the section altogether and otherwise amending the section in the same way as it proposed to amend s.35.[461] In addition, the Government stated that it intended to extend the exception to cover film and sound recordings.[462] The 1 per cent limit would apply to these works too.[463]

F. LENDING OF COPIES BY EDUCATIONAL ESTABLISHMENTS

Section 36A of the 1988 Act provides that the copyright in a work is not infringed   **9–109** by the lending of copies of the work by an educational establishment. This provision was introduced into the 1988 Act by the Copyright and Related Rights Regulations 1996,[464] implementing the Rental and Related Rights Directive,[465] which was replaced by a codified version in 2006.[466] The provision corresponds to art.6(3) of the codified version of this Directive, which gives Member States the power to exempt entirely certain categories of establishment from the exclusive public lending right of authors and performers.[467] This provision was not affected by the Information Society Directive.[468]

7. LIBRARIES AND ARCHIVES

Background and rationale. Demands are frequently made upon public libraries   **9–110** for copies of articles or parts of periodicals and books in their possession. The fair dealing provisions relating to non-commercial research and private study will often not sufficiently cover this type of situation and, in particular, may not protect the librarian. The 1956 Act introduced provisions dealing with this problem, which in general terms are reproduced in the 1988 Act, together with a number of additional provisions dealing with other situations faced by librarians and archivists.[469] The increasing importance of online sources to the provision of library services was, however, not anticipated by the 1988 Act and the attraction of such sources has been further increased by cuts in library budgets. As a result, librarians are often frustrated by their inability to create databases of particular articles or fulfil library loans electronically.[470] In December 2009 the Government indicated its intention to extend the scope of some of the provisions dealt

---

[460] Recommendation 2; see also para.4.19.

[461] See above, para.9–106.

[462] Taking Forward the Gowers Review of Intellectual Property: Second Stage Consultation on Copyright Exceptions (UK IPO; see *http://www.ukipo.org* [Accessed October 3, 2010]) para.99. The Government considered it unnecessary to extend the section to cover broadcasts because they were already covered by s.35 (para.97) and inappropriate to extend it to artistic works because to permit reproduction of the whole might not satisfy the three-step test while reproduction of small proportions would have little practical value (para.98).

[463] para.102.

[464] SI 1996/2967.

[465] Council Directive 92/100 on rental and lending right and on certain rights related to copyright in the field of intellectual property [1992] OJ L346/61.

[466] Directive 2006/115/EC on rental right and lending right and on certain rights related to copyright in the field of intellectual property [2006] OJ L376/28.

[467] art.6 of the codified Directive also gives Member States a more general discretion to derogate from the exclusive public lending right, "provided that at least authors obtain a remuneration for such lending": art.6(1) and see CDPA 1988 s.40A (para.9–119, below).

[468] See recital 40 and art.1(2)(b) of the Information Society Directive 2001/29.

[469] CDPA 1988 ss.37–44.

[470] As to some of the problems, see Norman, "The Electronic Environment: The Librarian's View". [1996] 2 E.I.P.R. 71.

with in this section below and the proposed changes are indicated where appropriate.[471]

9-111   **The Berne Convention.** The Convention does not contain any specific provision dealing with libraries or archives but presumably the permitted acts under consideration here fall within art.9(2), which allows countries of the Union to permit the reproduction of works in certain special cases, provided that such reproduction does not conflict with normal exploitation of the work and does not unreasonably prejudice the legitimate interests of the owner (i.e. provided the three-step test is satisfied[472]).

9-112   **The Information Society Directive.** Article 5(2)(c) permits Member States to make an exception to the reproduction and distribution rights in respect of specific acts of reproduction made by publicly accessible libraries or museums, or by archives, which are not for direct or indirect economic or commercial advantage.[473] This exception is directed at acts of reproduction by the relevant establishment itself, as opposed to users. The use of the word "specific" no doubt implies that to fall within the exception the copying must not be of a general kind, for example, every issue of a periodical.[474] It is not clear whether the expression "which are not for direct or indirect economic or commercial advantage" refers to the nature of the establishment or the nature of the acts of reproduction, etc. Some indication that it is the former is provided by recital 40, which states that "Member States may provide for an exception or limitation for the benefit of certain non-profit-making establishments, such as publicly accessible libraries and equivalent institutions, as well as archives". Recital 40 also states that the exception in favour of such establishments should not cover uses made in the context of online delivery of protected works or other subject-matter.

In addition, art.5(3)(n) of the Directive permits Member States to make an exception to the reproduction right, to the communication to the public right and to the distribution right in cases where a work is communicated, for the purpose of research or private study, to individual members of the public by dedicated terminals on the premises of establishments of publicly accessible libraries, museums or archives, if the work is contained in their collections and is not subject to purchase or licensing terms. It would seem from the opening words of recital 40 ("Member States may provide for an exception or limitation for the benefit of certain non-profit making establishments...") that the exception is intended to be for the benefit of the establishment.

In October 2009, the European Commission published a Communication[475] in which it indicated its intention to work towards the establishment of "a sustainable system of prior authorisation for a variety of library initiatives" involving "simple and cost-efficient rights clearance systems covering digitisation and on-line dissemination". This would include methods of rights clearance to enable "mass-scale digitisation". It indicated that such methods might include "an extended collective licensing system, whereby a rights manager was deemed to represent "outsiders"—right-holders not formally members of the clearing

---

[471] Taking Forward the Gowers Review of Intellectual Property: Second Stage Consultation on Copyright Exceptions (UK IPO; see *http://www.ukipo.org* [Accessed October 3, 2010]).

[472] See para.9–02, above.

[473] The exception to the distribution right is permitted only to the extent justified by the purpose of the authorised act of reproduction: Information Society Directive art.5(4).

[474] Recital 40 also states that the exception "should be limited to certain special cases covered by the reproduction right".

[475] Copyright in the Knowledge Economy COM (2009) 532 final.

system" or "the possible creation of a statutory exception for such digitisation efforts".[476]

Amendments to the 1988 Act. Only a small number of amendments were made to the 1988 Act on implementation of the Directive, with the aim of ensuring that copies supplied by librarians were only to be used for non-commercial research or private study.   **9–113**

Introductory provisions. The current provisions apply to libraries and archives of descriptions and in conditions prescribed by regulations made by the Secretary of State,[477] which, in the following sections, will be simply referred to as "the Regulations". In the remainder of this section "library" and "archive" will be used in this sense and "librarian" and "archivist" will be used accordingly. In relation to different provisions of the 1988 Act different classes of library are prescribed by the Regulations. These are dealt with in turn, below, as they arise. A number of the provisions require the librarian or archivist to be "satisfied" of certain matters, and in such cases the Regulations provide for cases in which the librarian or archivist may rely on or must require a declaration signed by the person using the library's facilities (referred to here as the "reader") as to those matters.[478] If a reader makes such a declaration which is false in a material particular and is then supplied with a copy which would have been an infringing copy if made by him, then that copy will be treated as an infringing copy and the reader will be liable for infringement as if he had made it himself.[479] In such circumstances it seems clear that the librarian or archivist will not be liable for any infringement. In these provisions, references to a librarian or archivist include a person acting on his behalf.[480]   **9–114**

A. COPYING OF ARTICLES IN PERIODICALS AND PARTS OF PUBLISHED WORKS

Overview. The following two sections of this work should be read in conjunction with one another as they deal with provisions which perform essentially the same function and hence similar comments can be made in relation to both. "Prescribed library" here means those specified in Pt A of Sch.1 to the Regulations. These include the copyright libraries, libraries administered by a library authority, libraries administered by a local authority, school libraries and the libraries of other educational establishments,[481] libraries administered by Parliament or by a Government department and libraries conducted for the purposes of facilitating or encouraging the study of education, religion, philosophy, science (including the social sciences) and the arts. Libraries conducted for profit are, however, specifically excluded.[482] The primary importance of these provisions is in relation to the inter-library loans system and "distance lending", as most libraries now   **9–115**

---

[476] See at p.5.
[477] See the Copyright (Librarians and Archivists) (Copying of Copyright Material) Regulations 1989 (SI 1989/1212) Vol.2 A4.vii, made under ss.37 and 38–43 of the 1988 Act, as amended by the Scotland Act 1998 (Consequential Modifications) (No.1) Order 1999 and the Copyright and Related Rights Regulations 2003 (SI 2003/2498) Sch.1 para.26.
[478] CDPA 1988 s.37(2); regs 4(3), 7(3).
[479] s.37(3).
[480] s.37(6).
[481] As to "educational establishments", see para.9–99, above.
[482] "Conducted for profit" in this context means that the library is established or conducted for profit or forms part of, or is administered by, a body established or conducted for profit: SI 1989/1212 reg.3(5).

provide self-service photocopying facilities for their readers.[483] By permitting limited copying of articles in periodicals and small sections of other works the Act provides the foundations for the above system. These exceptions are, however, subject to a number of complex conditions,[484] compliance with which increases staff costs, whilst arguably doing little to prevent abuses of the system. In practice this may mean that the Regulations are often ignored, as happened with the Regulations which governed the similar provisions of the 1956 Act.[485]

B. ARTICLES IN PERIODICALS

9–116 **Copying by librarians.** Provided certain conditions are met, a librarian may make and supply a copy of an article in a periodical without infringing any copyright in the text, in any illustrations accompanying the text or in the typographical arrangement.[486] For this purpose "article" includes an item of any description in a periodical.[487] The prescribed conditions are (a) that copies are supplied only to persons satisfying the librarian that they require them for the purposes of (i) research for a non-commercial purpose, or (ii) private study, and will not use them for any other purpose; (b) that no person is furnished with more than one copy of the same article or with copies of more than one article contained in the same issue of a periodical; and (c) that persons to whom copies are supplied are required to pay for them a sum not less than the cost (including a contribution to the general expenses of the library) attributable to their production.[488] The production of multiple copies of the same material under this exemption is further restricted by a provision to the effect that a copy shall be supplied only to a person satisfying the librarian that his requirement is not related to any similar requirement of another person.[489] For this purpose the Regulations provide that a reader's requirements are to be regarded as similar to those of another reader if the requirements are for copies of substantially the same material at substantially the same time and for substantially the same purpose. The requirements of readers are to be regarded as related if they receive instructions to which the material is relevant at the same time and place.[490] This can cause problems where a class of students is referred by a lecturer to the same material, as copying by a librarian in these circumstances will clearly not fall within this exception, even though students may be able to copy the material for themselves.[491]

C. PARTS OF PUBLISHED WORKS

9–117 **Copying by librarians.** This section should be read together with the provisions relating to the copying of articles in periodicals (above). If prescribed conditions are complied with, a librarian may make and supply from a published edition a

---

[483] As shown by the decisions in *Moorhouse and Angus and Robertson (Publishers) Pty Ltd v University of New South Wales* [1976] R.P.C. 151 and *CCH Canadian Ltd v Law Society of Upper Canada* [2004] SCC 13, librarians must still be careful as to what and how they allow their readers to copy if they are not to be liable for authorisation of copying. See further paras 7–148 et seq., above.
[484] See para.9–116 and para.9–117, below.
[485] This was discussed by the Whitford Committee: The Report of the Committee to Consider the law on Copyright and Designs, 1977 (Cmnd 6732) paras 242–250.
[486] CDPA 1988 s.38(1).
[487] s.178.
[488] s.38(2), as amended following implementation of the Information Society Directive, and SI 1989/1212 reg.4(2).
[489] s.40(1) and SI 1989/1212 reg.4(2)(b).
[490] s.40(2) and SI 1989/1212 reg.4(2)(b).
[491] Relying on s.29 (fair dealing for the purposes of non-commercial research or private study). See paras 9–29 et seq., above.

copy of part of a literary, dramatic or musical work (other than an article in a periodical) without infringing any copyright in the work, in any illustrations accompanying the work or in the typographical arrangement.[492] The prescribed conditions include restrictions similar in effect to those required for copying of articles in periodicals, save that no person is to be furnished with more than one copy of the same material or with a copy of more than a reasonable proportion of any work.[493] What amounts to a reasonable proportion is not further defined. Again, similar further restrictions are imposed on the production of multiple copies for similar or related uses by different persons as in the case of articles in periodicals.[494] When relying on this section librarians must be careful to avoid inadvertently copying the whole of a work, as might be the case where a photocopy is made of part of a collection of short stories or poems (each story or poem being a separate literary work).

Proposed extension. In tandem with its proposal to extend s.29 (research and private study) to sound recordings, films and broadcasts,[495] the Government has proposed that s.39 be extended to published sound recordings and films on the same terms as presently exist.[496]   **9–118**

D. Lending of Copies by Libraries or Archives

Section 40A(1) of the Act provides that the copyright in a work of any description is not infringed by the lending of a book by a public library if the book is within the public lending right scheme.[497] For this purpose the "public lending right scheme" means the scheme in force under s.1 of the Public Lending Right Act 1979.[498] A book is to be treated as being within the public lending right scheme if it falls within the eligibility criteria laid down by that scheme, irrespective of whether it actually qualifies for payment.[499] The Act further provides that copyright in a work is not infringed by the lending of copies of the work by a prescribed library or archive. For this purpose "prescribed library" means a non-public library which otherwise falls within paras 2 to 6 of Pt A of Sch.1 of the Regulations.[500] These provisions were introduced into the 1988 Act by the Copyright and Related Rights Regulations 1996,[501] implementing the Rental and Related Rights Directive,[502] no doubt with the intention of taking advantage of art.5.[503]   **9–119**

Prospective amendments. In November 2009 the Government indicated its   **9–120**

---

[492] CDPA 1988 s.39(1).

[493] s.39(2)(b).

[494] ss.40(1), (2) and SI 1989/1212 reg.4(2)(b).

[495] Taking Forward the Gowers Review of Intellectual Property: Second Stage Consultation on Copyright Exceptions (UKIPO; see *http://www.ukipo.org* [Accessed November 16, 2010]) para.187.

[496] Taking Forward the Gowers Review of Intellectual Property: Second Stage Consultation on Copyright Exceptions (UKIPO; see *http://www.ukipo.org* [Accessed November 16, 2010]) paras 202 and 226.

[497] CDPA 1988 s.40A(1).

[498] s.40A(1)(a).

[499] See further, para.19–04, below.

[500] Copyright and Related Rights Regulations 1996 (SI 1996/2967) reg.35. In effect "prescribed library" has a slightly narrower meaning in this context (cf. para.9–115, above) in that libraries administered by a library authority and (other) public libraries are excluded from the definition.

[501] SI 1996/2967 reg.11.

[502] Council Directive 92/100 on rental and lending right and on certain rights related to copyright in the field of intellectual property ([1992] OJ L346/61). This has been replaced by the codifying Directive 2006/115/EC on rental right and lending right and on certain rights related to copyright in the field of intellectual property [2006] OJ L376/28.

[503] Now art.6 of the 2006 Directive. Art.6(1) gives Member States the power to derogate from the exclusive lending right in respect of public lending, provided that at least authors obtain a remu-

intention to extend the public lending scheme to cover audio-books and e-books.[504] Accordingly, s.43 of the Digital Economy Act 2010 makes amendments both to s.5 of the Public Lending Right Act 1979 and to s.40A of the 1988 Act. The amendments take effect from a date to be appointed but at the time of writing it is not clear whether they will in fact be implemented.

The new s.5(2) of the 1979 Act extends the meaning of "book" to include an "audio-book" and an "e-book", each of which is separately defined.[505] The new s.40A(1) provides that the lending of "books" so defined will not infringe copyright. As before, a "book" will be treated as being within the scheme if it falls within the eligibility criteria laid down by the scheme, irrespective of whether it actually qualifies for payment.[506]

Libraries are in a position to "lend" audio-books and e-books in at least three different ways: in hard-copy form (e.g. a CD of an audio-book); in the form of a download to the reader's computer or audio player on library premises; and remotely over the internet. The Government's intention was that the scheme should cover the first two of these forms of "lending". However, it was concerned that the third form amounted to a communication to the public which was not permitted by art.6 of the Directive. Accordingly, it concluded that "lending" by remote access should not be included in the scheme.

This seems to have had the following consequences for the drafting of the new provisions. First, the expressions "audio-book" and "e-book" have each been defined not in terms of hard copies but in terms of "works" which have been recorded (as a sound recording or in electronic form as the case may be).[507] Second, as well as permitting "lending", s.40A(1) of the 1988 Act permits copying an audio-book or an e-book as an act incidental to lending it.[508] Third, the definition of the term "lending" in s.18A of the 1988 Act is expressly disapplied, no doubt because this concerns the lending of physical copies of a work (including the original).[509] Instead the term "lending" is to be read in accordance with the definition of "lent out" in s.5 of the 1979 Act.[510] This definition provides that "lent out" means "made available to a member of the public for use away from library premises for a limited time" but expressly does not include "being communicated by means of electronic transmission to a place other than library premises".

E. SUPPLY OF COPIES TO OTHER LIBRARIES

9–121   In addition to the provisions relating to copying by librarians that have already been considered, the Act provides an exception to allow a librarian of a prescribed library to make and supply to another prescribed library a copy of an article in a periodical or the whole or part of a published edition of a literary, dramatic or musical work.[511] Provided that the "prescribed conditions" are complied with, the making and supply of the copy will not infringe copyright in the text of the article or, as the case may be, in the work, in any illustrations accompanying it or in the

---

neration for such lending. However, it seems that CDPA 1988 s.40A may not comply in full with art.6. See further, para.19–02, above.

[504] For background, see Department for Culture Media and Sport's Consultation on the Extension of Public Lending Right to Rights holders of Books in Non-print Formats (July 2009) and its response (November 2009).

[505] See para.19–09, below.

[506] See further, para.19–04, below.

[507] Public Lending Act 1979 s.5(2), read into CDPA 1988 s.40A(1A).

[508] s.40A(1)(b).

[509] s.40A(1A)(d).

[510] s.40A(1A)(d).

[511] CDPA 1988 s.41.

typographical arrangement.[512] Under the Regulations all libraries in the United Kingdom are "prescribed libraries" for the purpose of making and supplying copies under this section,[513] but the receiving library must either fall within the definition of prescribed library set out in Pt A of Sch.1 to the Regulations (see para.9–115, above) or must be a library outside the United Kingdom which is not conducted for profit and which otherwise falls within Pt B of Sch.1.[514] The extent to which copying is permitted under this section depends on the material in question. Where the request is for a single article in an issue of a periodical this may be supplied on condition that only one copy is supplied and that the library receiving the copy pays a sum equivalent to but not exceeding the cost of producing the copy, including a contribution to the general expenses of the library.[515] This provision therefore appears to allow a library to make limited additions to its collection by acquiring for its readers articles from journals to which it does not subscribe. Where the request is for a copy of the whole or part of a published edition, or where the request is for more than one article in a single issue of a periodical then, again, only one copy may be supplied and the library receiving the copy must pay a sum equivalent to but not exceeding the cost of producing the copy.[516] In addition, however, a number of much more restrictive conditions must also be satisfied. Thus the section does not apply if at the time the copy is made the librarian making it knows, or could by reasonable inquiry ascertain, the name and address of a person entitled to authorise the making of the copy.[517] Moreover, the library requesting the copy must provide a written statement to the effect that it is a prescribed library and that it does not know and could not by reasonable inquiry ascertain, the name and address of a person entitled to authorise the making of the copy.[518] It seems that this provision is most likely to be useful in situations where a library wishes to acquire a copy of a book or journal and the publisher has gone out of business, as in these circumstances it can be very difficult to establish who is entitled to grant permission for such a copy to be made.

F. REPLACEMENT COPIES OF WORKS

Recognising that copies of works may become damaged or destroyed in circumstances where it would be difficult or impossible to purchase another original, the Act provides an exception to allow replacement copies to be made, thereby helping to preserve collections of important works.[519] Thus a librarian or archivist of a prescribed library or archive may make a copy from an item in the permanent collection of the library or archive (a) in order to preserve or replace that item by placing the copy in its permanent collection in addition to or in place of it, or (b) in order to replace in the permanent collection of another prescribed library or archive an item which has been lost, destroyed or damaged. In these circumstances the librarian or archivist will not thereby infringe the copyright in any literary, dramatic or musical work, in any illustrations accompanying such a work or, in

9–122

---

[512] s.41(1).
[513] SI 1996/2967 reg.3(2).
[514] reg.3(3). In order to fall within Pt B of Sch.1, a library outside the United Kingdom must be "conducted wholly or mainly for the purpose of facilitating or encouraging the study of bibliography, education, fine arts, history, languages, law, literature, medicine, music, philosophy, religion, science (including natural and social science) or technology".
[515] reg.5(2).
[516] reg.5(2).
[517] CDPA 1988 s.41(2) and SI 1989/1212 reg.5(2)(b).
[518] SI 1989/1212 reg.5(2)(b).
[519] CDPA 1988 s.42.

the case of a published edition, in the typographical arrangement.[520] This exception only applies, however, to reference items; it does not apply to articles available for lending.[521] In addition, the prescribed conditions restrict the making of copies to cases where it is not reasonably practicable to purchase a copy of the item to fulfil the purpose in question.[522] It therefore seems that the operation of this section will be confined to out-of-print books where it would be difficult or disproportionately expensive to purchase a second-hand copy.[523]

9–123   **Proposed extension.** The Gowers Review of Intellectual Property[524] recommended that s.42 should be amended to permit libraries to copy all classes of work in permanent collections for archival purposes and to allow further copies to be made from the archived copy to mitigate against subsequent wear and tear.[525] The Review also proposed a further amendment to enable libraries to "format shift" archival copies to ensure records do not become obsolete.[526] In December 2009 the Government proposed extensive changes to s.42, some of which go beyond those recommended by the Gowers Report.[527] The proposed changes are as follows. First, as recommended in the Gowers Report, to extend the exception to all copyright works. Second, to extend the exception to the contents of the permanent collections of prescribed museums and galleries[528] and to acts of their curators. Third, to permit an item to be copied in order to enable it to be preserved or replaced in the future, should it prove necessary to do so, by placing the copy (or a further copy made from it) in the permanent collection in addition to or in place of the item. Fourth, to permit the making of a copy in a different medium or format from the relevant item, if the librarian, archivist or curator considers the change to be necessary or expedient for the purpose for which the copy is made. This would permit "format shifting". However, the new provisions would not permit the making of further copies from a copy made from the collection of another institution in order to replace a lost, destroyed or damaged item. As before, the exception would be subject to compliance with "prescribed conditions", which would include provision for restricting the making of copies to cases where it was not reasonably practicable to purchase a copy of the item in question to fulfil the purpose for which a copy was required.

G. COPYING OF UNPUBLISHED WORKS

9–124   **Introduction.** In many cases unpublished letters and manuscripts of historical or literary interest have been deposited with libraries or other institutions, and it

---

[520] s.42(1). "Prescribed library" has, in relation to both the library that makes the copy and the receiving library, the same meaning as in s.41 of the 1988 Act (see para.9–115, above). All archives in the United Kingdom are "prescribed archives" for the purpose of making and supplying copies under this section, but the receiving archive must not be conducted for profit. "Conducted for profit" in this context means that the library is established or conducted for profit or forms part of, or is administered by, a body established or conducted for profit: SI 1989/1212 para.3(5).

[521] SI 1989/1212 reg.6(2)(a).

[522] CDPA 1988 s.42(2) and SI 1989/1212 reg.6(2)(b). The library receiving the copy must also pay a sum equivalent to but not exceeding the cost of producing the copy, again including a contribution to the general expenses of the library: reg.6(2)(d).

[523] A similar exception exists in the United States where "the library or archive has, after a reasonable period, determined that an unused replacement cannot be obtained at a fair price": United States Copyright Act 1976, U.S.C. 17, s.108(c).

[524] HM Treasury, December 2006.

[525] Recommendation 10a.

[526] Recommendation 10b.

[527] Taking Forward the Gowers Review of Intellectual Property: Second Stage Consultation on Copyright Exceptions, December 2009. See in particular at p.52.

[528] That is, museums and galleries prescribed by the Secretary of State.

may be in the general public interest that they should eventually be published.[529] Under the 1956 Act the copyright in such unpublished works might have been perpetual[530] and it was often impractical for anyone desiring to publish the material to find out with certainty in whom the copyright was vested. On the other hand, it might often have been difficult to find a publisher prepared to take the risk of publishing when a person might come forward, able to prove good title to the copyright. The 1956 Act therefore made provision to allow such works to be published, provided certain conditions were satisfied.[531]

The 1988 Act, as amended, altered the position relating to the period of copyright in unpublished works, so that perpetual copyright was abolished.[532] The provisions in the 1956 Act dealing with this problem were therefore not repeated. However, in the light of the transitional provisions dealing with the period of copyright in such works,[533] the 1988 Act contains transitional provisions such that the provisions of the 1956 Act continue to apply in modified form to works made before August 1, 1989.

At the same time, the 1988 Act includes a new, more limited, exception to allow copies of unpublished works whether made before or after August 1, 1989 to be made by librarians and archivists and supplied for the purposes of research or private study. This has now been amended to restrict the purposes to non-commercial research and private study.

More generally, these provisions should be viewed alongside the "publication right" which is given to the first person to publish a previously unpublished literary, dramatic, musical or artistic work or a film which is no longer in copyright: the permitted acts now under consideration provide a degree of security for those who copy previously unpublished works (albeit for a limited purpose under the 1988 Act) and the publication right provides a financial incentive for the publication of such works.[534]

Works made before August 1, 1989. As already noted, the provisions of the 1956 Act continue to apply, in modified form,[535] in relation to works made before August 1, 1989.[536] For this purpose, where the making of a work extended over a period it is to be taken as having been made when its making was completed.[537]   **9–125**

The provisions of the 1956 Act (s.7(6)) apply where a manuscript or a copy of an unpublished literary, dramatic or musical work has been kept in a library, museum or other institution at which it is open to public inspection. Provided that more than 50 years have elapsed since the end of the calendar year in which the author died, and more than 100 years have elapsed since the making of the work, the work may be reproduced for purposes of research or private study, or with a view to publication. Although these provisions primarily apply to literary, dramatic or musical works they also apply in respect of artistic works provided for explaining or illustrating the work in question.[538] Where a work is lawfully

---

[529] Similar policy considerations lie behind the publication right, as to which, see Ch.17, below.

[530] Copyright Act 1956 s.2(3) proviso.

[531] ss.7(6)–(9).

[532] See further, paras 6–52 et seq., above.

[533] CDPA 1988 Sch.1 para.12; and see para.6–46, above.

[534] The publication right was introduced by the Copyright and Related Rights Regulations 1996 (SI 1996/2967). See further, Ch.17, below.

[535] The most important modification in that there is no longer a duty to give notice of intended publication: CDPA 1988 Sch.1 para.16. cf. Copyright Act 1956 s.7(7).

[536] CDPA 1988 Sch.1 para.16.

[537] Sch.1 para.1(3).

[538] Copyright Act 1956 s.7(9).

published under these provisions it may also lawfully be broadcast, performed in public or recorded.[539]

9–126 **Provisions of the 1988 Act.** The 1988 Act provides that, if prescribed conditions are complied with, the librarian or archivist of a prescribed library or archive may make and supply a copy of the whole or part of a literary, dramatic or musical work from a document in the library or archive without infringing any copyright in the work or any illustrations accompanying it.[540] This exception applies to works whether they were made before or after August 1, 1989. The prescribed conditions are that this exception only applies if, (a) the copies are supplied only to persons satisfying the librarian or archivist that they require them for the purposes of (i) research for a non-commercial purpose, or (ii) private study, and will not use them for any other purpose; (b) that no person is furnished with more than one copy of the same material; and (c) the person receiving the copy is required to pay for it a sum not less than the cost attributable to its production, including a contribution to the general expenses of the library.[541] Moreover, this exception does not apply if at the time the copy is made the librarian or archivist making it is, or ought to be, aware of the fact that (a) the work had been published before the document was deposited in the library or archive, or (b) the copyright owner has prohibited copying of the work.[542]

9—127 **Proposed extension.** In December 2009 the Government proposed that the scope of the extension be extended to cover unpublished artistic works in general, and unpublished sound recordings and films.[543]

H. LEGAL DEPOSIT LIBRARIES

9–128 **Introduction.** Section 15 of the Copyright Act 1911, which remained in force after that Act's general repeal, required publishers to deliver publications in print form to the British Library for deposit and, on request, to any of five other specified legal deposit libraries.[544] The Legal Deposit Libraries Act 2003 (in this section "the 2003 Act") re-enacted s.15, making certain minor changes and, more significantly, enabled equivalent measures to be made for the increasing volume of non-print material which is published.[545] The aim is to extend the provisions of the Act progressively to cover various non-print media as they develop, including off-line publications such as CD-ROMs and microforms, online publications such as e-journals, and other non-print materials.[546] Section 15 of the 1911 Act was not in fact directly concerned with copyright issues but the 2003 Act necessitated amendments to the 1988 Act to ensure that the various acts required or enabled by the 2003 Act do not infringe copyright.

9–129 **The Information Society Directive.** Article 9 of the Directive provides that the

---

[539] s.7(8).

[540] s.43(1). All libraries and archives in the United Kingdom are prescribed for the purposes of this section: SI 1989/1212 regs 3(2), 3(4).

[541] CDPA 1988 s.43(3) and SI 1989/1212 reg.7, as amended by SI 2003/2498.

[542] s.43(2).

[543] Taking Forward the Gowers Review of Intellectual Property: Second Stage Consultation on Copyright Exceptions (UKIPO; see http://www.ukipo.org [Accessed November 16, 2010]) paras 226 and 228 and pp.49 and 50.

[544] These were the National Libraries of Scotland and Wales, and the University libraries of Oxford, Cambridge and Trinity College Dublin.

[545] The Act came into force on February 1, 2004 (SI 2004/130). The Act is not to apply to works published before this date: s.16(4).

[546] On September 29, 2010 the Government issued a Consultation on the Legal Deposit of Non-Print Works together with a draft statutory instrument. The proposals which are the subject of the Consultation are mentioned where appropriate below.

Directive is to be without prejudice to provisions concerning legal deposit requirements, so that the new provisions of the 1988 Act are permitted by the Directive.

Delivery of works published in print media. Where a copy of a work is delivered to a legal deposit library, in whatever medium, the 2003 Act provides that such delivery is to be taken not to infringe copyright, publication right or database right in relation to any part of the work (or any patent).[547] The 1988 Act has not itself been amended to provide for a defence or permitted act in this respect, but this provision of the 2003 Act presumably falls within the general scope of acts permitted under s.50 as being authorised by Act of Parliament.[548] In the case of works in the form of print media, it is hard to see how the mere act of delivery of a copy of a work to a legal deposit library could constitute an infringement of copyright, unless it were to constitute an issue to the public within the meaning of s.18 of the 1988 Act or unless, where it contained infringing material, it constituted a distribution within the meaning of s.23.   **9–130**

Delivery of works published in non-print media. Section 6 of the 2003 Act enables the Secretary of State to make regulations applying the provisions of that Act to works published in non-print media. Such regulations may make detailed provision regarding the manner of delivery and so on, including delivery by electronic means and as to the medium for delivery of a work published online.[549] The regulations may also require that, with the copy of the work, there is also delivered a copy of any computer program and any information necessary in order to access the work, and a copy of any manual and other material that accompanies the work and is made available to the public.[550] As with delivery of a copy of a work in print media, such delivery is to be taken not to infringe copyright, publication right or database right in relation to any part of the work.[551]   **9–131**

Draft regulations on non-print works. In September 2010 the Government commenced a consultation on draft regulations which make provision for the deposit of "non-print" works in two defined categories.   **9–132**

For these purposes, a "non print work" is defined as an "electronic publication"[552] which is available free or for a charge, which does not consist only of a sound recording or film or both (or only of a sound recording, film or both together with incidental material) and which is published after the date on which the regulations are made.[553] The two defined categories of non-print work with which the draft regulations are concerned are "off line" and "on line" publications, which are separately defined[554] and separately treated.

An "off line publication" is defined as a non-print work which is not accessed or delivered by means of the internet and is recorded in a physical form including

[547] Legal Deposit Libraries Act 2003 s.9(1)(b). Nor is it to constitute breach of any contract relating to any part of the work to which that person is a party: s.9(1)(a).
[548] See para.9–148, below.
[549] See Legal Deposit Libraries Act 2003 s.6(2).
[550] s.6(2)(b).
[551] ss.9(1)(a), (2).
[552] s.14 of the 2003 Act defines an electronic publication as on line or off line publication including any publication in electronic form within the meaning given by s.178 of the 1988 Act. "On line" and "off line" have their own definitions in the draft regulations: see below. As to the definition of "in electronic form", see para.9–168 below. The draft regulations give as examples of publications a book, a sheet of letterpress or music, a map, plan, chart or table or a part of any such work (this is the list of print works to which the 2003 Act applies: see s.1(3) of the Act).
[553] Draft reg.2(3).
[554] Draft reg.2(3).

a CD, DVD or microform.[555] The draft regulations require a copy of every off line publication to be delivered to the British Library Board within one month of the day of publication and to the other deposit libraries on request.[556] The draft regulations make provision for the form and timing of any requests, the medium of delivery and the quality of the delivered material.[557]

An "on line publication" is defined as a non-print work which is accessed[558] or delivered by means of the internet.[559] The definition expressly includes an electronic publication which comprises material packaged and filtered in response to an enquiry from a user.[560] It expressly excludes a "private work", which is defined as an electronic work which is shared by means of the internet using some form of private network such as an intranet or a work which contains personal data and whose circulation is restricted to a defined group of persons.[561] In relation to on line publications, the only obligation is to deliver a copy on request[562] and only to the first requesting deposit library.[563] Again, provision is made as to the form and timing of any requests, the medium of delivery and the quality and nature of the delivered material.[564]

The draft regulations provide that works falling within these categories of "non-print" works are "works of a prescribed description" for the purposes of s.1(4) of the 2003 Act.[565] Accordingly, the delivery of a copy of such a work will not infringe copyright.[566]

9–133   **Web harvesting.** It is clearly contemplated that deposit will not only take place by delivery by publishers but also by deposit libraries themselves taking material directly from the internet ("web harvesting").[567] The 1988 Act has therefore been amended to provide that copyright is not infringed by the copying of a work from the internet by a deposit library or person acting on its behalf if: (a) the work is of a prescribed description, (b) its publication on the internet, or a person publishing it there, is connected with the United Kingdom in a prescribed manner, and (c) the copying is done in accordance with any prescribed conditions.[568] No regulations prescribing such matters have yet been made and the draft regulations[569] do not include such provision. It seems likely that this is because the Government envisages that the process of harvesting will involve the library making an electronic request to the publisher's server which will then transmit a copy of the

---

[555] According to the consultation, "microform" means microfilm or microfiche. It gives as examples of off-line material "an encyclopaedia and a serial of educational and legal material": p.13.

[556] Consultation on the Legal Deposit of Non-Print Works, draft regs 6–13.

[557] See draft regs 5, 8–13.

[558] Irrespective of whether or not there are any restrictions on public access to it, e.g. by means of technical measures such as a password: Consultation p.13.

[559] Draft reg.2(3).

[560] An example given in the Consultation is material compiled from a legal database: see p.13.

[561] Thus, members-only areas within a public site such as Facebook would not be covered by the Regulations: Consultation pp.13–14.

[562] In the case of works which are free of charge and have no access restrictions, deposit must be as soon as reasonably practicable after a written request (draft reg.14), which will normally be sent by a web harvester: Consultation p.15. There is a longer period for works which are subject to a charge or to access restrictions: draft reg.17.

[563] Draft regs 14 and 15. Thus there will only have to be one deposit. It is envisaged that the material will be shared between the deposit libraries: Consultation p.15.

[564] Draft regs 5, 16–22.

[565] reg.3.

[566] Legal Deposit Libraries Act 2003 s.9(1)(b).

[567] See now Consultation pp.15, 16 and 25.

[568] CDPA 1988 s.44A(1), as inserted by the Legal Deposit Libraries Act 2003 s.8(1). Power to prescribe such matters is conferred by s.10 of the 2003 Act.

[569] Consultation on the Legal Deposit of Non-Print Works.

work to the harvesting library.[570] On the face of it therefore the library is not carrying out a restricted act while the publisher will be able to rely on the exemption provided for in s.9 of the 2003 Act.[571]

Acts done in relation to deposited non-print material. The 2003 Act makes   **9–134**
provision for particular acts that may and may not be done in relation to specified copies of a work delivered pursuant to these provisions. These copies are referred to as "relevant material".

"Relevant material" is defined to mean: (i) a copy of a work published in a medium other than print; (ii) a copy of a computer program or a copy of any computer program and any information necessary in order to access the work, and a copy of any manual and other material that accompanies the work and is made available to the public; (iii) a copy of a work which has been published on the internet, where (a) the work is of a prescribed description, (b) the publication of the work on the internet, or a person publishing it there, is connected with the United Kingdom in a prescribed manner, and (c) the copy was made by a deposit library or person acting on its behalf copying the work from the internet in accordance with any prescribed conditions, and (iv) a copy (at any remove) of anything within any of these categories.[572]

As to such material, the 2003 Act starts by stating what a deposit library or person acting on its behalf, or readers,[573] may not do, namely: (a) use the material (whether or not such use necessarily involves the making of a temporary copy of it), (b) copy the material (other than by making a temporary copy where this is necessary for the purpose of using the material), (c) in the case of relevant material comprising or containing a computer program or database, adapt it, (d) lend the material to a third party (other than lending by a deposit library to a reader for use by the reader on library premises controlled by the library), (e) transfer the material to a third party, or (f) dispose of the material.[574] Many such acts will constitute infringements of copyright but they also now constitute breaches of statutory duty.[575]

The 2003 Act then continues by providing that the Secretary of State may nevertheless make provision by regulations permitting a deposit library or a person acting on its behalf, and readers, to do any of these activities in relation to relevant material, subject to such conditions as may be prescribed. Such conditions may deal with: (a) the purposes for which relevant material may be used or copied; (b) the time at which or the circumstances in which readers may first use relevant material; (c) the description of readers who may use relevant material; and (d) the limitations on the number of readers who may use relevant material at any one time (whether by limiting the number of terminals in a deposit library from which readers may at any one time access an electronic publication or otherwise).[576] Finally, to give further effect to these provisions, the 1988 Act has been amended by insertion of a new s.44A(2) to provide that copyright is not infringed by the doing of anything which is so permitted.[577]

Acts in relation to non-print material: the draft regulations. So far as online   **9–135**

---

[570] Consultation on the Legal Deposit of Non-Print Works, paras 11.3 and 11.3.

[571] See the previous paragraph.

[572] Legal Deposit Libraries Act 2003 ss.7(5)(b), 10(6). Power to prescribe such matters is conferred by s.10 of the 2003 Act. No such regulations have yet been made.

[573] A reader is defined as a person who, for the purposes of research or study and with the permission of a deposit library, is on library premises controlled by it: s.7(5)(a).

[574] s.7(1), (2).

[575] s.7(6).

[576] s.7(4).

[577] Inserted by s.8(2).

publications are concerned, the effect of the draft regulations is to limit the permitted act provided for in s.44A(2) to publications published in the United Kingdom by a person who "publishes for an indefinite period using a fixed establishment in the United Kingdom".[578] This is an important limitation in itself and its effects may prove to be broader than expected given that it will not always be easy to identify the publisher of an online publication.[579] The draft regulations set out a number of uses which are permitted for the purposes of s.7 of the 2003 Act and by s.44A(2) of the 1988 Act. The first is that the work may be used by readers but only within certain limits, as follows: the use must be on one display terminal only at any time[580]; use may not commence until seven days have elapsed after the deposit of the work; and use must not be permitted if the publisher has demonstrated on the balance of probabilities that viewing by a reader would conflict with the normal exploitation of the work and unreasonably prejudice the legitimate interests of the publisher.[581] Provision is then made for the making of copies for the purposes of research and private study, the making of accessible copies for visually impaired persons and the copying and adapting of the material for preservation purposes.[582] These provisions are intended to mirror existing or proposed provisions in relation to print works.[583]

9–136   **Excluded activities.** A power has been inserted into the 1988 Act to make regulations to stop one or more of the permitted acts applying, or restrict the way they apply, to non-print material. The stated purpose of such regulations is so that a limit can be put on the application of any of the permitted acts under the 1988 Act to deposited material where, for example, such application gives rise to access that is more generous than that permitted for the same material that other libraries have had to purchase under a contract.[584] The power is nevertheless given in very broad terms. Thus, ss.44A(2) and (3) of the 1988 Act enable the Secretary of State to prescribe certain activities, namely activities: (a) done for a prescribed purpose, (b) done by prescribed descriptions of reader, (c) done in relation to prescribed descriptions of relevant material and (d) done other than in accordance with prescribed conditions. In relation to such activities and in relation to relevant material (see above), the Secretary of State may by regulations exclude the application of such of the provisions of Ch.I of the 1988 Act as are prescribed. No such regulations have yet been made, nor it seems are any planned. This is presumably because the powers which may be imposed under s.7 of the 2003 Act are considered adequate.

9–137   **Regulations.** Draft regulations under the 2003 Act are presently the subject of a consultation.[585] The 2003 Act contains a number of provisions dealing with regulations made under the Act. In general, such regulations may not be made unless the Secretary of State has consulted (a) the deposit libraries, and (b) the publishers appearing to the Secretary of State to be likely to be affected.[586] Regulations dealing with deposit of works in non-print media may not be made

---

[578] regs 35 and 36.

[579] The issues are reviewed in s.8 of the Consultation.

[580] This is intended to mirror the position in relation to print materials: see para.4.3 of the Consultation.

[581] Draft regs 23 to 28. There is also provision about the timing of such "embargos". It is not clear what mechanisms a library will be expected to put in place to determine whether a publisher has so "demonstrated" or how any such determination may be challenged.

[582] Draft regs 29 to 34.

[583] Consultation paras 9.4 to 9.8.

[584] *Hansard*, HL Vol.563 (2003).

[585] See paras 9–132 and 9–135 above.

[586] s.11(2).

so as to apply to works published before the regulations are made[587] or unless the Secretary of State considers that the costs likely to be incurred as a result of the regulations by persons who publish works to which the regulations relate are not disproportionate to the benefit to the public arising from the delivery of copies of such works.[588] Regulations dealing with the deposit of works in non-print media, the permitting of certain acts (i.e. so as to affect the scope of s.44A(2) of the 1988 Act) or the exemption for deposit libraries for "web-harvesting" (i.e. under s.44A(1)), may not be made unless the Secretary of State considers that the regulations do not unreasonably prejudice the interests of persons who publish works to which the regulations relate.[589]

I. COPIES REQUIRED AS CONDITION OF EXPORT

Export licensing for cultural goods: an overview. Most countries seek to ensure **9–138** that articles of cultural and artistic importance remain within their territory.[590] In the United Kingdom, domestic legislation operates alongside EU Regulations.[591] In brief, a licence must be obtained for practically all goods produced or manufactured more than 50 years ago which are worth over certain amounts. Either a UK or European licence may be required depending on the type of object, its value and its intended destination.[592] In either case the application has to be made to the UK authorities.[593]

In many instances the burden of having to obtain a licence is substantially reduced by the existence of the system of Open General Export Licences. However, this system does not apply to goods which require a European licence,[594] nor does such a licence permit exports to an embargoed destination.[595] The Open General Export Licence (Objects of Cultural Interest) allows certain categories of goods to be exported without prior authorisation and in general no licence needs to be presented at the place of export.[596] In all cases where an Open General Export Licence is not available, a specific licence must be applied for.

---

[587] s.11(3).
[588] ss.11(3), (4).
[589] s.11(5).
[590] For further information, see the Museums Libraries and Archives Council's notice, *Export Licensing for Cultural Goods: Procedures and Guidance for Exporters of Works of Art and Other Cultural Goods* which is available at *http://www.culture.gov.uk* [Accessed October 22, 2010].
[591] The Export Control Act 2002 (c.28) empowers the Secretary of State to place restrictions on the export of any class of goods. Current restrictions are to be found in the Export of Objects of Cultural Interest (Control) Order 2003 (SI 2003/2759). European controls are to be found in Council Regulation 116/2009 on the export of cultural goods ([2009] OJ L39/1).
[592] Where the goods are being dispatched to another EU Member State, export restrictions do not apply to certain goods, including goods being exported by, and being the personal property of, their manufacturer or producer, or the spouse, widow or widower of that person; nor do they apply to letters written by or to the exporter or spouse of the exporter: Export of Objects of Cultural Interest (Control) Order 2003 (SI 2003/2759) Sch.1 art.1 reg.1. Where the goods are being dispatched to a destination outside the EU, export restrictions do not apply to certain goods being exported by their "originator": Council Regulation 116/2009 on the export of cultural goods, annex 1, n.1. See *Export Licensing for Cultural Goods: Procedures and Guidance for Exporters of Works of Art and Other Cultural Goods*, p.23.
[593] Council Regulation 116/2009 on the export of cultural goods, art.2(2). See generally *Export Licensing for Cultural Goods: Procedures and Guidance for Exporters of Works of Art and Other Cultural Goods.*
[594] See para.10 of the Open General Export Licence (Objects of Cultural Interest) (hereafter "the OGEL"), May 1, 2004.
[595] See para.1 of the OGEL; an "embargoed destination" is "a destination to which an export ban applies by virtue of a prohibition contained in legislation implementing European Union obligations or United Nations sanctions": see para.7.
[596] There are exceptions: see paras 3 and 4. Works in which copyright may subsist and for which an OGEL is available (irrespective of the intended destination) include photographs more than 50 years old valued at less than £10,000, paintings more than 50 years old in oil or tempera valued at

9–139   **The permitted act.** Where a specific licence is required this will usually be granted.[597] However, in the case of some manuscripts the licence may be made conditional upon a copy of the work being deposited in the British Library, so that it will not be lost to British researchers. Access to the copy will then normally be denied for a period of seven years, unless the owner of the original consents to some lesser restriction.[598] In order to speed up applications for documentary material, Government guidelines recommend that the applicant include a good-quality copy of the original with the licence application.[599] However, the guidelines also recognise that this will not always be possible because the work may still be in copyright and the applicant may well not be the copyright owner.[600] To cover the situation of a copy being required to be deposited as a condition of an export licence, the Act provides that where an article of cultural or historical importance or interest cannot lawfully be exported from the United Kingdom unless a copy of it is made and deposited in an appropriate library or archive,[601] it is not an infringement of copyright to make that copy.[602] The wording of this provision is broad enough to cover conditions contained in both UK and European licences, but it would not protect an applicant who voluntarily enclosed a copy of a work with his application. An applicant who wishes to speed up his application must therefore be diligent in ensuring that he does not infringe copyright.

8. PUBLIC ADMINISTRATION

9–140   **Introduction.** The 1988 Act contains a number of provisions relating to public administration. These provisions rationalise and expand the similar provisions of the 1956 Act and can be divided into four categories. First, there are exceptions relating to Parliamentary and judicial proceedings and to the proceedings of Royal Commissions and statutory inquiries. The Act provides that copyright will not be infringed by anything done for the purpose of such proceedings or for the reporting thereof.[603] Secondly, there are exceptions allowing the copying of public records and material on a statutory register or on a register available for public inspection pursuant to a statutory requirement. Thirdly, there is an exception allowing the Crown to copy and issue to the public copies of previously unpublished works, where these have been communicated to the Crown in the course of public business. Finally, the Act makes it clear that an act done under specific statutory authority will not infringe copyright. The justification for these provisions is the general public interest in permitting the copying of works where this is necessary for effective public administration, in circumstances where the rights of the copyright owner are unlikely to be substantially prejudiced.

less than £180,000, and portraits in any medium more than 50 years old of a British historical personage valued at less than £180,000. See further, *Export Licensing for Cultural Goods: Procedures and Guidance for Exporters of Works of Art and Other Cultural Goods.*

[597] Objections are made to applications relating to between 25 and 50 objects each year out of a total of about 3,000 applications covering about 20,000 objects: *Export Licensing for Cultural Goods: Procedures and Guidance for Exporters of Works of Art and Other Cultural Goods*, para.19.

[598] *Export Licensing for Cultural Goods: Procedures and Guidance for Exporters of Works of Art and Other Cultural Goods*, para.12.

[599] *Export Licensing for Cultural Goods: Procedures and Guidance for Exporters of Works of Art and Other Cultural Goods*, para.12.

[600] *Export Licensing for Cultural Goods: Procedures and Guidance for Exporters of Works of Art and Other Cultural Goods*, para.13.

[601] This is not limited to "prescribed libraries and archives" (cf. para.9–115, above), but in practice the copy will have to be deposited with the British Library: *Export Licensing for Cultural Goods: Procedures and Guidance for Exporters of Works of Art and Other Cultural Goods*, para.12.

[602] CDPA 1988 s.44. This provision was new in 1988. As to the background to its introduction, see Copinger 12th edn, p.204, fn.7.

[603] This provision does not, however, allow a work which is itself a published report of such proceedings to be copied (see para.9–143 and para.9–144, below).

The Berne Convention. The Convention does not contain any specific provision **9–141** dealing with acts of these kinds but presumably they all fall within art.9(2), which allows countries of the Union to permit the reproduction of works in certain special cases, provided that such reproduction does not conflict with normal exploitation of the work and does not unreasonably prejudice the legitimate interests of the owner (i.e. provided the three-step test is satisfied[604]).

The Information Society Directive. No amendments were made to these provi- **9–142** sions of the Act on implementation of the Information Society Directive. Article 5(3)(e) of the Directive permits Member States to make an exception to the reproduction, distribution and communication to the public rights in the case of use for the purposes of public security or to ensure the proper performance or reporting of administrative, parliamentary or judicial proceedings. Article 9 also provides that the Directive is to be without prejudice to provisions concerning access to public documents.

A. Parliamentary and Judicial Proceedings

The copyright in any work is not infringed by anything done for the purposes of **9–143** parliamentary or judicial proceedings.[605] "Parliamentary proceedings" are defined as including proceedings of the Northern Ireland Assembly, the Scottish Parliament or the European Parliament and Assembly proceedings within the meaning of s.1(5) of the Government of Wales Act 2006.[606] "Judicial proceedings" are defined as including proceedings before any court, tribunal or person having authority to decide any matter affecting a person's legal rights or liabilities.[607] This would cover the Copyright Tribunal and seemingly includes arbitration proceedings.[608] In addition, copyright is not infringed by anything done for the purposes of reporting such proceedings, but this is not to be construed as authorising the copying of a work which is itself a published report of the proceedings.[609] Thus it would not be permissible under this section for a journalist to copy a rival's Parliamentary sketch. The reports of *Hansard* and law reports are similarly protected. Whether a use falls within this permitted act is essentially an objective question and the expression "for the purposes of parliamentary or judicial proceedings" should be construed as a whole, rather than focussing on individual words.[610] It has been held in New Zealand that the equivalent provisions of the New Zealand Act applied only to specific proceedings existing at the time the reproduction was made and not to proceedings that were merely contemplated.[611] However, this seems unduly restrictive and in the United Kingdom it has been held at least arguable that under the 1988 Act proceedings need not be in existence.[612] The UK court also left open the question, assuming that proceedings need not yet be in existence, of what the status of copies would be if the proceedings were never in fact brought. It is suggested, however, that

---

[604] See para.9–02, above.

[605] CDPA 1988 s.45(1).

[606] s.178.

[607] s.178.

[608] *London & Leeds Estates v Paribas Ltd (No.2)* [1995] 1 E.G.L.R. 102. In reaching this construction, Mance J. relied upon s.48(1) of the Copyright Act 1956, which defined judicial proceedings as "a proceeding before any court, tribunal or person having by law the power to hear, receive and examine evidence on oath".

[609] CDPA 1988 s.45(2). It must be assumed that "reporting" includes all the acts restricted by copyright including copying, issuing copies to the public and broadcasting.

[610] *A v B* [2000] E.M.L.R. 1006, applying *Pro Sieben Media AG v Carlton UK Television Ltd* [1999] 1 W.L.R. 605; [1999] F.S.R. 610. See also *Vitof Ltd v Altoft* [2006] EWHC 1678 (Ch) at para.175.

[611] *Auckland Medical Aid Trust v Commissioner of Police* [1976] 1 N.Z.L.R. 485.

[612] *A v B* [2000] E.M.L.R. 1006.

the act of copying could not retrospectively become an infringement in this event, and so the copies made would not become infringing copies.

B. ROYAL COMMISSIONS AND STATUTORY INQUIRIES

9–144   The copyright in any work is not infringed by anything done for the purposes of the proceedings of a Royal Commission or statutory inquiry.[613] For this purpose, "Royal Commission" includes a Commission appointed for Northern Ireland by the Secretary of State in pursuance of the prerogative powers of Her Majesty delegated to him under s.7(2) of the Northern Ireland Constitution Act 1973.[614] "Statutory inquiry" means an inquiry held or investigation conducted in pursuance of a duty imposed or power conferred by or under an enactment.[615] Moreover, where a work, or material from it, is contained in a report of a Royal Commission or a statutory inquiry, the copyright in the work is not infringed by issuing copies of the report to the public.[616] Nor is the copyright in any work infringed by anything done for the purposes of reporting any such proceedings held in public, but this is not to be construed as authorising the copying of a work which is itself a published report of the proceedings.[617]

C. MATERIAL OPEN TO PUBLIC INSPECTION OR ON OFFICIAL REGISTER

9–145   The Act provides three related exceptions to allow for the copying of material that is available for public inspection, thus facilitating the use of such material and promoting access to it. The first exception relates to material which is open to public inspection pursuant to a statutory requirement or which is on a statutory register. Any copyright in the material as a literary work is not infringed by the copying of so much of the material as contains factual information, provided this is done by or with the authority of the appropriate person and does not involve the issuing of copies to the public.[618] For these purposes "statutory requirement" means a requirement imposed by a provision made by or under an enactment and "statutory register" means a register maintained in pursuance of a statutory requirement.[619] The "appropriate person" is the person required to make the material open to public inspection or, as the case may be, the person maintaining the register.[620] This provision would presumably, for example, enable copies to be made of records kept for public inspection by the Registrar of Companies.[621] The second exception is confined to material open to public inspection pursuant to a statutory requirement. Provided that the appropriate person has given his authority, copyright in any work will not be infringed by the copying or issuing to the

---

[613] CDPA 1988 s.46(1).

[614] s.46(4).

[615] s.46(4).

[616] s.46(3). Note that there is no exception to allow for the report to be performed in public or to be communicated to the public. It might not, therefore, be possible for the Commission to publish its report on the Internet. See further, Crown, "Copyright and the Internet," (1995) 11(6) Comp. L.&P. 169 at 170.

[617] s.46(2). As to the meaning of "reporting" see the note concerning s.45(2) in para.9–143, above.

[618] CDPA 1988 s.47(1).

[619] s.47(6). An example of a statutory register is the Register of Data Controllers, maintained under the Data Protection Act 1998.

[620] CDPA 1988 s.47(6).

[621] See *Hansard*, HL Vol.501, col.242; Report of the Debates of the House of Commons Standing Committee E in 1988, col.234. In fact, according to the Companies House website, information on the Companies House public register "is made available by virtue of approvals issued by the Registrar in accordance with section 47 of the Copyright, Designs and Patents Act 1988 and Schedule 1 of the Database Regulations (SI 1997/3032). Companies House imposes no rules or requirements on how the information on the public register is used.": see *http://www.companieshouse.gov.uk* [Accessed October 4, 2010].

public of copies if this is for the purpose of enabling the material to be inspected at a more convenient time or place, or if this otherwise facilitates the exercise of any right for the purpose of which the statutory requirement of availability for inspection is imposed.[622] For example, planning documents could be copied for inspection at a more convenient time or place.[623] The third exception, like the first, relates both to material which is open to public inspection pursuant to a statutory requirement and material which is on a statutory register. Where such material contains information about matters of general scientific, technical, commercial or economic interest, copyright is not infringed by the copying or issuing to the public of copies if this is for the purpose of disseminating that information. Again this is dependent upon the authority of the appropriate person being given.[624] An example here would seem to be the copying and publication of a patent specification in so far as this contains material of "general interest". The Secretary of State may provide that these three provisions are only to apply to copies marked in a specified manner,[625] and may extend the provisions to material made open to public inspection by international organisations or under international agreements.[626]

D. MATERIAL COMMUNICATED TO THE CROWN

In certain circumstances the Crown is permitted to make copies of a previously unpublished work and issue these to the public.[627] For these purposes, as well as including the Crown in right of the Scottish Administration, of the Welsh Assembly Government or of Her Majesty's Government in Northern Ireland or in any country outside the United Kingdom to which the copyright Part of the 1988 Act extends,[628] the expression "the Crown" includes a variety of bodies and organisations included in or associated with the National Health Service.[629] The exception applies whenever a literary, dramatic, musical or artistic work has been communicated to the Crown (as so defined) in the course of public business by or with the licence of the copyright owner and a document or other material thing recording or embodying the work is owned by or is in the custody or control of the Crown.[630] In such cases the Crown may, for the purpose for which the work was communicated to it, or any related purpose which could reasonably have been anticipated by the copyright owner, copy the work and issue copies of the work to the public without infringing copyright,[631] subject to any agreement to the contrary.[632] For this purpose "public business" includes any activity carried

9–146

---

[622] CDPA 1988 s.47(2).

[623] *Hansard*, HL Vol.501, col.242.

[624] *Hansard*, HL Vol.501, col.242.

[625] s.47(4). And see the Copyright (Material Open to Public Inspection) (Marking of Copies of Maps) Order 1989 (SI 1989/1099), at Vol.2 A4.vi, which prescribes the marking to be applied to maps, and the Copyright (Material Open to Public Inspection) (Marking of Copies of Plans and Drawings) Order 1990 (SI 1990/1427), at Vol.2 A4.xi, which prescribes the marking to be applied to plans or drawings copied under s.47(2).

[626] s.47(5). As to the definition of "international organisation," see s.178 and the Copyright (Material Open to Public Inspection) (International Organisations) Order 1989 (SI 1989/1098), at Vol.2 A4.v, which extends the provisions to the European Patent Office and the World Intellectual Property Organisation.

[627] CDPA 1988 s.48. "Unpublished" in this context means unpublished otherwise than by virtue of this section: s.48(3). The Crown does not, however, have the right to perform a work in public or communicate a work to the public (see the footnotes to para.9–144, above).

[628] In accordance with the normal definition in CDPA 1988 s.178.

[629] s.48(6).

[630] s.48(1).

[631] s.48(2).

[632] s.48(5).

on by the Crown as defined.[633] It was said during the passage of the Bill that "any related purpose which could reasonably have been anticipated by the copyright owner" might, for example, cover material submitted to a departmental committee which is subsequently included in the committee's report.[634] This can be contrasted with the position of an author who submits a manuscript to the authorities in order to prove that he is engaged in useful employment. The Crown would not be able to publish the work in these circumstances.[635]

These provisions provide the Crown with a remarkably wide exception. There is no restriction, for example, on the Crown using these provisions in order to make a profit at the copyright owner's expense. Making this exception subject to any agreement to the contrary is unlikely to afford much protection to copyright owners, as the communication of the material in question may otherwise be in the owner's interest, so that deciding not to communicate the material unless certain conditions are complied with may not be a viable option. It was suggested during the passage of the Bill that an owner might on occasion be able to rely on an obligation of confidence,[636] but ultimately it seems that the owner will often have to rely on the Crown's good will, a point that was in effect conceded by the Government.[637]

E. PUBLIC RECORDS

9–147   Public records within the meaning of the Public Records Act 1958, the Public Records (Scotland) Act 1937, or the Public Records Act (Northern Ireland) 1923, and Welsh public records (as defined in the Government of Wales Act 2006), which are open to public inspection, may be copied, and a copy may be supplied to any person, provided this is done by or with the authority of an officer appointed under one of those Acts. Once again the justification for such a provision is to facilitate the use of certain material and to promote wider access to it. This exception can therefore be seen as supplementing the provisions relating to statutory registers and material open to public inspection pursuant to a statutory requirement.

F. ACTS DONE UNDER STATUTORY AUTHORITY

9–148   Where the doing of a particular act is specifically authorised by an Act of Parliament, whenever passed, then, unless the Act provides otherwise, the doing of that act does not infringe copyright.[638] This provision was new in the 1988 Act and seems unnecessary, as presumably the defence of statutory authority would always have been available and is in fact expressly preserved by the Act.[639] The reference to a "particular act specifically authorised by an Act of Parliament" is designed to exclude cases where a general activity is authorised by Parliament. Thus it could not be argued that because the Broadcasting Acts authorise broadcasting by independent television this amounts to Parliament having granted a blanket licence to use copyright material.[640] This can be contrasted with the duty placed on companies to provide copies of certain constitution documents to

---

[633] s.48(5).

[634] *Hansard*, HL Vol.495, col.641.

[635] *Hansard*, HL Vol.493, col.1178.

[636] *Hansard*, HL Vol.495, col.641. The permitted acts do not provide a defence to such an action: CDPA 1988 s.28(1) and see para.9–16, above.

[637] *Hansard*, HL Vol.495, col.641.

[638] CDPA 1988 s.50(1) This provision also applies in relation to an enactment contained in Northern Ireland legislation as it applies in relation to an Act of Parliament CDPA 1988 s.50(2).

[639] s.50(3).

[640] *Hansard*, HL Vol.495, col.643.

any member who requires them.[641] It was said during the passage of the Bill that, by virtue of this section, there would be no infringement of copyright in these circumstances, even though the copyright in such documents might not belong to the company concerned.[642]

9. COMPUTER PROGRAMS

Introduction. Amendments to the 1988 Act made by the Copyright (Computer Programs) Regulations 1992[643] included a series of permitted acts relating to computer programs. These amendments implemented Council Directive 91/250/EEC on the legal protection of computer programs[644] (in this section "the Directive"), which when adopted aimed to reconcile the copyright laws of the Member States of the European Union with some of the practical difficulties posed by copyright protection for computer programs. Prior to the implementation of the Directive, the Act only provided a limited exception relating to the transfer of works in electronic form.[645] Further amendment was required on implementation of the Information Society Directive as a result of the change to the fair dealing provisions in s.29 of the 1988 Act but this did not result in any substantial change to the substantive law in this area.[646] In brief, the permitted acts now contained in the Act relate to (a) the right of a "lawful user" of a computer program to make a back-up copy, (b) the right to decompile a program in order to create an independent compatible program, (c) the right of a lawful user to observe, study or test a computer program for certain purposes and (d) a limited right to copy or adapt a program where this is necessary for the lawful use of that program.[647] In conjunction with these permitted acts, s.296A strikes down contractual terms which would frustrate these provisions.[648] It provides that where a person has the use of a computer program under an agreement, any term or condition in the agreement shall be void in so far as it purports to prohibit or restrict the right to make back-up copies, the right to decompile a program or to observe, study or text the functioning of the program in order to determine the ideas and principles which underlie any element of the program. It is worth emphasising that these provisions should be construed consistently with the Directive, as a number of key terms in both the Act and the Directive are left undefined.

9–149

A. BACK-UP COPIES

In the absence of statutory provision, the making of a back-up copy would be an infringement unless the owner had consented to such use. In practice an express right to make back-up copies is often granted and in other cases it may be implied. The Directive, whilst not expressly providing a right to make back-up copies, does so implicitly by providing, under the heading "Exceptions to the restricted acts", that in the absence of contractual provisions the making of a copy of a

9–150

---

[641] Companies Act 2006 s.32.

[642] *Hansard*, HL Vol.495, col.643, concerning the equivalent provision in the Companies Act 1995 (s.19).

[643] SI 1992/3233. As to transitional provisions, see reg.12(2), which provides that the amendments are not to affect any agreement or any term or conditions of an agreement entered into before January 1, 1993. Otherwise, the Regulations apply equally in relation to computer programs created before this date. See also the Software Directive (91/250/EEC) art.9(2).

[644] [1991] OJ L122/42. The Directive has since been consolidated and repealed by Directive 2009/24/EC on the legal protection of computer programs of April 23, 2009 [2009] OJ L111/16.

[645] CDPA 1988 s.56 (see para.9–168, below).

[646] Indeed, it was expressly provided that the Information Society Directive was not to affect the Software Directive: 91/250 art.1(2)(a).

[647] CDPA 1988 ss.50A, 50B, 50BA and 50C.

[648] cf. CDPA 1988 s.28(1) and see para.9–16, above.

program is not to require the authorisation of the right holder where this is necessary for its use by the lawful acquirer in accordance with its intended purpose
and, further, that the making of a back-up copy by a person having a right to use
the program may not be prevented by contract in so far as it is necessary for that
use.[649] Section 50A provides more explicitly that: "It is not an infringement of
copyright for a lawful user of a copy of a computer program to make any back-up
copy of it which is necessary for him to have for the purposes of his lawful use".
A "lawful user" is defined as any person who has a right to use the program,
whether under a licence to do any acts restricted by the copyright in the computer
program or otherwise.[650] Clearly this would extend to a purchaser of a program
who thereby acquires, expressly or impliedly, a licence to use the program and to
any person claiming through the purchaser.[651] But where a term of the purchase
contract expressly limits any licence to the purchaser alone, it seems that any
other user would not be a lawful user, since the use of a program inevitably
involves its reproduction.[652] Examples of cases where a person might have a
"right" to use the program otherwise than under licence would presumably be
where that person was exercising another of the permitted acts, or where that
person had some other defence to an action for infringement. It is worth pointing
out that this permitted act extends only to the making of back-up copies of computer programs. It is not lawful to make a back-up copy of something which
includes works other than computer programs. This will often be the position in
the case of computer games, which will contain other kinds of literary works, as
well as artistic and musical works. The point underlines the importance which
often arises of distinguishing a computer program from other works stored in
digital form.

The Act does not attempt to define "back-up copy," but presumably this refers
to a copy made by the user as a reserve in case of loss of or damage to the
original.[653] The European Commission has stated its opinion that the wording and
objective of art.5(2), under which "a" (i.e. only one) copy is permitted, means
that the purpose may not be other than as a "back-up" to ensure that normal use
of the program can continue in the event of loss or defect of the original.[654] It is
not entirely clear, however, when the making of a back-up copy is to be regarded
as "necessary": the Directive refers merely to acts which are necessary for the
use of the program "in accordance with its intended purpose".[655] While the making of a back-up copy is often no doubt highly desirable, it is arguable that it will
often not be necessary. The provision would be of virtually no application,
however, unless a reasonably liberal construction is given to it, such that the
ordinary and prudent making of a back-up copy is allowed. It has been said that
the section is directed to the situation in which a person who has access to a com-

---

[649] Information Society Directive arts 5(1), (2). The recitals do not deal specifically with back-up
copies. The 18th recital states only: "Whereas [recital 17] means that the acts of loading and running necessary for the use of a copy of a program which has been lawfully acquired, and the act
of correction of its errors, may not be prohibited by contract; whereas, in the absence of specific
contractual provisions, including when a copy of the program has been sold, any other act necessary for the use of the copy of a program may be performed in accordance with its intended
purpose by a lawful acquirer of that copy".

[650] CDPA 1988 s.50A(2).

[651] As to the rights of such persons, see s.56 and para.9–168, below.

[652] s.17(6), "Copying . . . includes the making of copies which are transient or are incidental to
some other use of the work". Also see para.7–20, above.

[653] *The Shorter Oxford English Dictionary* defines a back-up copy in this context as, "a duplicate
copy of a disk, file, program, etc."

[654] See the Commission's communication on the implementation and effect of the original Software
Directive (COM/2000/0199 final).

[655] Information Society Directive art.5(1). See also CDPA 1988 s.296A, which strikes down
contractual terms prohibiting or restricting the making of a back-up copy "which it is necessary
for [the user] to have *for the purposes of the agreed use*".

puter program in the form, for example, of a physical copy such as a CD-ROM also has an express licence to use it, such that the licence will continue even if the original physical copy is lost or damaged. In this situation, the argument continues, the licence can be exercised if access can be had to some other lawful copy, such as a back-up copy, assuming that the licence is not restricted to the original copy. The section is not directed, it is said, to the kind of case in which a person simply buys a computer program, for example a computer game in CD-ROM format, and with it acquires an obviously implied licence to use it. In this situation, if the physical carrier is lost or damaged there is no continuing licence and another copy must be purchased. It would not therefore have been "necessary" to make a back-up copy.[656] While all this may be true, the suggestion does not throw any real light on why it should be "necessary", as opposed to desirable, to make a back-up copy in the first kind of case[657] and the argument appears to depend on the precise nature of any express or implied licence. It would seem particularly difficult to argue that an additional copy was "necessary" if the program is supplied on a physical copy such as a CD-ROM with the intention that it should be copied onto and stored on a hard drive for its normal use. The original physical copy will remain available in case of loss or damage to the hard drive and serves the purpose of a back-up copy. Where the program supplied in physical form is only loaded into RAM or other temporary memory in the course of ordinary use, the case is clearly stronger for arguing that it is "necessary" to make a back-up copy within the spirit of the Directive. In the case of a program supplied via the internet without any accompanying physical copy, again the case is stronger for saying that it is necessary to make a back-up copy.

B. DECOMPILATION

Rationale. Section 50B is designed to meet the "interoperability" requirements   **9–151** of the Software Directive. The final form of this part of the Directive was the result of intense negotiation and lobbying between the various interested parties, in particular major software houses, companies engaged in the production of compatible products and consumers.[658] The fundamental issue at stake was the extent to which designers of computer programs and computer-related products should be entitled to look at and study other programs to enable compatible products to be produced, particularly through knowledge of the program's interfaces. Without such knowledge, communication between two systems is generally impossible, and thus compatible non-infringing products such as application programs and peripheral devices cannot be developed. The nature of computer programs means that determining the nature of the interfaces will inevitably involve reproducing the program at some stage, since the program will normally only be available in machine code, from which these characteristics will not be apparent. The machine code must first be extracted and converted into a higher-level language,[659] a process which would normally involve infringement.[660] Thus, without some form of exception to allow for the decompilation of a program, the copyright owner's monopoly would be extended beyond the boundaries of the "work" and would include the sole right to produce com-

---

[656] *Sony Computer Entertainment v Owen* [2002] EWHC 45 (Ch).

[657] It was not relevant for the purpose of the decision to explore this aspect further.

[658] See T. Dreier, "The Council Directive of 14 May 1991 on the Legal Protection of Computer Programs". [1991] 9 E.I.P.R. 319.

[659] i.e. it must be "decompiled": CDPA 1988 s.50B(1).

[660] s.21(4). It will also usually be necessary to copy the machine code onto some other medium at this stage.

patible products.[661] The EU Court of First Instance considered the meaning of "interoperability" in *Microsoft v Commission* (T–201).[662]

9–152   **The permitted act.** To overcome the problem outlined above, s.50B provides that: "It is not an infringement of copyright for a lawful user of a copy of a computer program expressed in a low-level language to convert it into a version expressed in a higher-level language, or incidentally in the course of so converting it to copy it, (that is, to 'decompile' it)".[663] However, this exception is subject to a number of conditions:

(1) It is only available to a lawful user. "Lawful user" has the same meaning here as in relation to the making of back-up copies.[664]

(2) The decompilation must be necessary in order to obtain the information required to create an independent program which can be operated with the program decompiled or with another program (the "permitted objective").[665]

(3) The information acquired must not be used for any purpose other than that set out above.[666]

The Act goes on to give examples of cases where these conditions will not be satisfied. Thus the Act provides that these conditions will not be satisfied where the information required is "readily available" to the lawful user.[667] Such information will presumably be "readily available" if information regarding a program's interfaces is available from the program's manufacturers. The Act also provides that these conditions will not be satisfied if the user does not confine the decompiling to such acts as are necessary to achieve the permitted objective[668]; nor may the information be supplied to a person who does not require the information for that purpose.[669] Finally, the information must not be used to create a program which is "substantially similar in expression to the program decompiled or be used to do any act restricted by copyright".[670] At first it might appear as though this final restriction imposes two distinct limitations on the right to decompile a program, namely, (1) that the information must not be used to create a program which is substantially similar in expression to the program decompiled; and (2) that the information must not be used to do any act restricted by copyright. However, this last condition should be taken to implement art.6(2)(c) of the Directive, which provides that the information obtained must not be used "for the development, production or marketing of a computer program substantially similar in its expression, or for any other act which infringes copyright". Whilst this

---

[661] In the US the problem of decompilation has been solved not by legislation but by the court's application of the "fair use" doctrine: *Atari Games Corp v Nintendo of America, Inc.* (1992) 975 F.2d 832; *Sega Enterprises v Accolade, Inc.* (1992) 977 F.2d 1510. cf. *Creative Technology Ltd v Aztech Systems PTE Ltd (CA, Singapore)* [1997] F.S.R. 491. In the United Kingdom the defence of fair dealing for the purposes of non-commercial research or private study is specifically excluded in the case of decompilation: CDPA 1988 s.29(4).

[662] See para.24–54.

[663] CDPA 1988 s.50B(1). "Low" and "higher-level" languages are not defined, but machine code, assembly code and object or source code can be taken to represent ascending levels of language.

[664] s.50A(2). cf. art.6(1)(a) of the Software Directive which provides that the right of decompilation may be exercised by "the licensee or by another person having a right to use a copy of the program, or on their behalf by a person authorised to do so".

[665] s.50B(2)(a). It is worth emphasising the latter point, i.e. that decompilation may be carried out with a view to creating a program to be operated with a program other than the one decompiled.

[666] s.50B(2)(b).

[667] s.50B(3)(a).

[668] s.50B(3)(b).

[669] s.50B(3)(c). It seems that this is to act as a condition subsequent, so that if decompilation takes place without infringement (because all the other conditions are met) but the decompiler subsequently supplies this information in contravention of this section, the original decompilation will become, retrospectively, an infringement.

[670] s.50B(3)(d).

seems relatively clear, a degree of uncertainty remains as to what "substantially similar in expression" means. In particular, it is not clear whether this test is the same as the ordinary test of infringement in the United Kingdom, namely, that the defendant's work must not reproduce "a substantial part" of the claimant's work. The potential disparity arises because the Directive seems to have embraced the idea/expression dichotomy,[671] whilst courts in the United Kingdom have proved much more reluctant to do so.[672] It seems likely that courts in the United Kingdom will interpret the words "which is substantially similar in expression" as being equivalent to "which reproduces a substantial part." As with the "back-up" exception, it should be noted that the decompilation exception applies only to computer programs and not to other works which may be embodied in electronic form along with the computer program. This will often restrict the utility of this exception.[673]

Lock and key routines. Section 50B would on its face appear to enable a **9–153** program to be decompiled in order to ascertain any "lock-and-key" routines contained within the program decompiled[674] provided this was done with the objective of creating an independent program which could be operated with the program decompiled or with another program. Whether the independent program could then have been written without infringing copyright would depend on whether the " key" written into it amounted to a substantial part of the target computer program, such that they were substantially similar in expression.[675] However, the lock-and-key routine will constitute a technical device within the meaning of s.296[676] and a person who manufactures for sale, sells, etc. means, the sole intended purpose of which is to facilitate the unauthorised circumvention of the lock-and-key routine will thus infringe the rights conferred by s.296. These issues are dealt with more fully in Ch.15.

C. Observing, Studying and Testing of Computer Programs

Article 5(3) of the Software Directive provides that a person having a right to use **9–154** a copy of a computer program shall be entitled, without the authorisation of the right holder, to observe, study or test the functioning of the program in order to determine the ideas and principles which underlie any element of the program if he does so while performing any of the acts of loading, displaying, running, transmitting or storing the program which he is entitled to do. It was not

---

[671] See further, recital 13 and art.5(3) of the Software Directive.

[672] For example, see *Ibcos Computers Ltd v Barclays Bank Highland Finance Ltd* [1994] F.S.R. 275 at 292, 302. See further, para.7–13, above. Moreover, it should be noted that even in jurisdictions where the idea/expression dichotomy is firmly entrenched, in particular the United States, attempting to distinguish between ideas and expression in the context of computer programs has proved exceptionally difficult. See, for example, *Whelan Associates Inc. v Jaslow Dental Laboratory Inc.* [1987] F.S.R. 1; *Computer Associates v Altai Inc.* (1992) 23 U.S.P.Q. 2d 1241.

[673] Note that in a recent case, *SAS Institute Inc. v World Programming Limited* [2010] EWHC 1829 (Ch); [2010] E.C.D.R. 15, Arnold J. has referred a series of questions to the CJEU on the interpretation of the Software Directive as regards the limits of permitted decompilation: (1) Where a computer program ("the First Program") is protected by copyright as a literary work, is art.1(2) to be interpreted as meaning that it is not an infringement of the copyright in the First Program for a competitor of the right holder without access to the source code of the First Program, either directly or via a process such as decompilation of the object code, to create another program (the Second Program") which replicates the functions of the First Program? Questions 2 to 4 elaborate on the first (for more details, see para.24–57, below).

[674] "Key" routines produce a data stream which, when detected and recognised by a device such as a games console, will "unlock" the device and allow it to be operated.

[675] See paras 7–143 , et seq., above.

[676] In relation to a computer program, a technical device is defined to mean any device intended to prevent or restrict acts that are not authorised by the copyright owner of that computer program and are restricted by copyright: CDPA 1988 s.296(6).

considered necessary to amend the 1988 Act when implementing the Directive because s.29 of the Act already permitted fair dealing with a work, and thus a computer program, for the purposes of research or private study. The effect of the Information Society Directive was, however, to require this general permitted act to be restricted to non-commercial research and also to exclude any private study which is directly or indirectly for a commercial purpose.[677] The result would in many cases have been to exclude the kind of acts covered by art.5(3) of the Software Directive. The provisions of this Directive were expressly not to be affected by the Information Society Directive and so it was necessary for the United Kingdom to deal with the issue on implementation. This was done by the introduction of a new s.50BA, which enacts the provisions of the Software Directive verbatim. It provides that it is not an infringement of copyright for a lawful user[678] of a copy of a computer program to observe, study or test the functioning of the program in order to determine the ideas and principles which underlie any element of the program if he does so while performing any of the acts of loading, displaying, running, transmitting or storing the program which he is entitled to do.[679] At the same time, s.29 has been amended to provide a demarcation between these acts and those permitted under the fair dealing provisions. Thus, s.29(4A) provides that it is not fair dealing under that section to observe, study or test the functioning of a computer program in order to determine the ideas and principles which underlie any element of the program, these acts being acts which are permitted, if at all, if done in accordance with s.50BA. Once again, it should be noted that this exception does not permit the copying of works other than computer programs when observing, etc. computer programs.

D. OTHER ACTS PERMITTED TO LAWFUL USERS

9–155 **Error correction and other lawful acts.** Article 5(1) of the Software Directive provides that, in the absence of specific contractual provisions, authorisation to do any of the acts restricted by copyright will not be necessary where the act in question is necessary for the use of a computer program by its lawful acquirer in accordance with its intended purpose. The article goes on to provide expressly that this is to include the right to correct errors. Section 50C therefore provides that a lawful user[680] may copy or adapt a program where this is necessary for its lawful use and provided that this is not prohibited by a contractual term.[681] Like the Directive, the section then goes on to deal with error correction, by providing that, "It may, in particular, be necessary for the lawful use of a computer program to copy or adapt it for the purpose of correcting errors in it".[682] Although this section appears to implement art.5 of the Directive fairly faithfully, there is a degree of ambiguity in the Directive as to whether it ought to be possible to exclude the right to correct errors by contract. This is because recital 18 of the Directive

---

[677] See para.9–25, above.

[678] "Lawful user" is again defined to mean any person who has a right to use the program, whether under a licence to do any acts restricted by the copyright in the computer program or otherwise: CDPA 1988 s.50A(2).

[679] s.50(BA)(2) goes on to provide that where an act is permitted under this section, it is irrelevant whether or not there exists any term or condition in an agreement which purports to prohibit or restrict the act. Such terms are void under s.296A, as now amended.

[680] "Lawful user" is again defined to mean any person who has a right to use the program, whether under a licence to do any acts restricted by the copyright in the computer program or otherwise: CDPA 1988 s.50A(2).

[681] s.50C(1).

[682] s.50C(2). Note that there is no room for any "right to repair" defence (see paras 5–235 et seq., above) in relation to computer programs, since this is now the subject of a complete statutory code following the implementation of the original Software Directive 91/250: *Mars UK Ltd v Teknowledge Ltd* [2000] E.C.D.R. 99.

provides that "the act of correction of its errors may not be prohibited by contract", whereas art.5 does appear to allow this right to be so restricted. As recitals are considered to be of considerable importance when interpreting European legislation the effect of this inconsistency is uncertain.[683] The 1988 Act does not contain any provision striking down contractual terms prohibiting or restricting such acts.[684]

10. DATABASES

Acts permitted in relation to databases. The Database Regulations 1997[685] introduced a new s.50D into the Act, as required by art.6(1) of the Database Directive.[686] The section provides that it is not an infringement of copyright in a database for a person who has a right to use the database to do, in the exercise of that right, anything which is necessary for the purposes of access to and use of the contents of the database.[687] In this context a "right to use a database" is to include a right to use any part of a database, and the permitted act applies to anything which is necessary to access and use that part.[688] The Act also makes it clear that the exception applies in all circumstances where a person has a right to use a database and not just where the use has been licensed.[689] This provision has to be understood in the context of the dual system of protection for databases introduced by the Database Directive and the Regulations. Except in the case of "existing" databases, copyright will only subsist in a database where the database satisfies the special originality test, that is, where "by reason of the selection or arrangement of the contents of the database the database constitutes the author's own intellectual creation".[690] In contrast, all databases whose production involved a "substantial investment in obtaining, verifying or presenting the contents" will qualify for the sui generis database right,[691] which will subsist alongside any copyright.[692] It should be noted that the permitted act now under consideration only relates to the question of copyright infringement. However, the nature of the database right is such that no equivalent provision is required.[693]

9–156

Avoidance of certain terms relating to databases. As has been seen, in general the permitted acts only relate to the question of infringement of copyright: they do not affect any other right or obligation. Hence it is ordinarily possible to exclude or restrict the operation of the permitted act provisions contractually.

9–157

---

[683] As to the CJEU's approach to the interpretation of Directives and the emphasis placed on "contextual" interpretation, see J. Bengoetxea, *The Legal Reasoning of the European Court of Justice* (Oxford: Clarendon, 1993) pp.233, 240–270.

[684] cf. the provisions of CDPA 1988 s.296A.

[685] Copyright and Rights in Databases Regulations 1997 (SI 1997/3032).

[686] Directive 96/9.

[687] CDPA 1988 s.50D(1). It was said that this permitted act was introduced to protect users of electronic databases who, in order to search a database, may find it necessary to download the whole or a substantial part of the database into the memory of a computer (see House of Commons Standing Committee on Delegated Legislation (Pt 1), December 3, 1997; *Hansard*, HL Vol.584, col.793). However, its general effect is wider than this; the permitted act was introduced to implement art.6(1) of the Database Directive.

[688] s.50D(1). See *Navitaire Inc v Easy Jet Airline Co Ltd (No.3)* [2004] EWHC 1725; [2005] E.C.D.R. 17.

[689] s.50D(1).

[690] See Ch.3, above. Existing databases (i.e. databases created on or before March 27, 1996) will, however, continue to enjoy copyright for the remainder of the copyright term: SI 1997/3032 reg.29.

[691] regs 13, 30.

[692] reg.13(2).

[693] As to the nature of the database right, see Ch.18, below.

However, this was thought to be undesirable in the case of databases.[694] Thus, as with the provisions relating to computer programs (see para.9–149, above), s.296B strikes down contractual terms which would have the effect of nullifying the permitted act. Section 296B thus provides "where under an agreement a person has a right to use a database or part of a database, any term or condition in the agreement shall be void in so far as it purports to prohibit or restrict the performance of any act which would but for s.50D infringe the copyright in the database".[695] This provision was designed to ensure that a contract for the use of an electronic database could not be used so as to stop it being downloaded if that were necessary in order to search it.[696] It should be read alongside reg.19 of the Database Regulations, which provides that "Where under an agreement a person has a right to use a database, or part of a database, which has been made available to the public in any manner, any term or condition in the agreement shall be void in so far as it purports to prevent that person from extracting or reutilising insubstantial parts of the contents of the database, or of that part of the database, for any purpose".[697]

11. DESIGNS

9–158 **Introduction.** Although the permitted acts relating to designs[698] are given extensive treatment elsewhere,[699] they are also briefly outlined below. The aim of these particular provisions is not so much to grant a set of exemptions to a special class of user but to mark out a boundary between copyright and designs law.

9–159 **The Information Society Directive.** Article 9 of the Directive, which deals with the continued application of other legal provisions, states that the Directive is to be without prejudice to provisions relating to designs. No amendment was therefore required to these permitted act sections.

A. DESIGN DOCUMENTS AND MODELS

9–160 The Act provides that it is not an infringement of any copyright in a design document or model recording or embodying a design for anything other than an artistic work or a typeface to make an article to the design or to copy an article made to the design.[700] Design in this context is defined in a very similar way as in relation to the unregistered design right. Thus, design "means the design of any aspect of the shape or configuration (whether internal or external) of the whole or part of an article, other than surface decoration".[701] A design document means any record of a design, whether in the form of a drawing, a written description, a

---

[694] art.8 of the Database Directive prohibits the database right owner from preventing a lawful user carrying out certain acts, but this appears to apply only to sui generis database right, not copyright. Recital 49 appears to be to the same effect. Art.6, which is concerned with copyright, merely states that acts necessary for access or normal use "shall not require the authorisation" of the right holder.

[695] CDPA 1988 s.296B.

[696] *Hansard*, HL Vol.584, col.793.

[697] SI 1997/3032 reg.19(2). Also see para.18–39, below.

[698] CDPA 1988 ss.51–53.

[699] See further, Ch.13, below.

[700] CDPA 1988 s.51(1). Nor is it an infringement of copyright to issue to the public, or include in a film or communicate to the public anything whose making was, by virtue of s.51(1), not an infringement of copyright: s.51(2). Note that copyright in the document or model is not itself removed. See further para.13–169, below. See *Ultra Marketing (UK) Ltd v Universal Components Ltd* [2004] EWHC 468 (Ch).

[701] s.51(3). See *Lambretta Clothing Co Ltd v Teddy Smith (UK) Ltd* [2004] EWCA Civ 886; [2005] R.P.C. 6.

photograph, data stored in a computer or otherwise.[702] This exception was introduced in order to prevent design owners from relying on artistic copyright to protect utilitarian three-dimensional objects. Essentially, the problem arises because copyright subsists in graphic works (which will include a large number of design documents) and sculptures (which may include hand-made design models[703]), irrespective of artistic quality.[704] As copyright may be infringed indirectly as well as directly,[705] and in relation to an artistic work includes the making of a copy in three dimensions of a two-dimensional work,[706] the copying of an end product might well infringe copyright in the design documents or models. This protection was seen as particularly problematic in that purely functional designs were able to enjoy the full copyright term, whereas the copyright in aesthetic (i.e. registrable) designs was restricted to a term of 15 years.[707] It was a desire to remove this anomaly that led Parliament to introduce the section now under consideration[708] which, together with the introduction of the new design right,[709] aims to ensure that functional designs receive a much more appropriate term of protection.

The exclusion from this section of documents or models embodying a design for an artistic work is intended to ensure that artists and sculptors can make preliminary sketches or models without losing copyright in their final work. However, designs for other, functional articles may also fall outside the scope of this section, providing they amount to designs for artistic works.[710] Many of these cases will, however, be caught by s.52 (considered below) with the result that copyright protection will be restricted to a term of 25 years. It should be noted that there is not necessarily a neat demarcation between elements of design which are protected by design right but not copyright (shape, configuration) and those that are protected by copyright but not design right (surface decoration) such that all elements receive some degree of protection.[711]

B. EXPLOITATION OF DESIGNS DERIVED FROM ARTISTIC WORKS

Section 52 was introduced to "truncate copyright where [an artistic] work has been exploited in the mass market".[712] This section applies where an artistic work has been exploited, by or with the copyright owner's consent, by making articles   **9–161**

---

[702] s.51(3).

[703] See *Wham-O Manufacturing v Lincoln* [1985] R.P.C. 127, CA of NZ.

[704] s.4(1)(a).

[705] s.16(3)(b).

[706] s.17(3).

[707] By virtue of the Design Copyright Act 1968 (c.68).

[708] Report of the Debates of the House of Commons Standing Committee E in 1988, cols 238–239.

[709] See Ch.13, below.

[710] For example, engravings for such things as rubber car-floor mats. See *Hi-Tech Autoparts Ltd v Towergate Two Ltd (No.1)* [2002] F.S.R. 15, paras 36 and 39; *Hi-Tech Autoparts Ltd v Towergate Two Ltd (No.2)* [2002] F.S.R. 16, para.16, following *James Arnold & Co Ltd v Miafern Ltd* [1980] R.P.C. 397, at p.403, and *Wham-O Manufacturing Co v Lincoln Industries Ltd* [1985] R.P.C. 127 at 155, CA of NZ (engravings for plastic "frisbees"). Precisely this example was raised during the passage of the Bill by Lord Lucas of Chilworth, who introduced an amendment which would have taken designs for all "functional articles" outside of this exception. Lord Beaverbrook, replying for the Government, stated that in most cases the distinction between an artistic work and a non-artistic work would be "self-evident". Where this is not the case the wording of the section "will allow the courts the freedom they need to reach sensible conclusions": *Hansard*, HL Vol.491, cols 185–186.

[711] See *Lambretta Clothing Co Ltd v Teddy Smith (UK) Ltd* [2004] EWCA Civ 886, and para.13 170, below. See also *Dyson Ltd v Qualtex (UK) Ltd* [2006] EWCA Civ 166, paras 76 et seq. on the meaning of the term "surface decoration".

[712] Hansard, HL Vol.491, col.189.

embodying a copy of the work by means of an industrial process,[713] provided such articles have been marketed (in the United Kingdom or elsewhere).[714] In these circumstances, at the end of 25 years from the end of the calendar year in which such articles were first marketed, copyright will not be infringed by making articles of any description, or by doing anything for the purposes of making articles of any description, or by doing anything in relation to copies so made.[715] Where only part of an artistic work is concerned, this provision only applies in relation to that part.[716]

This section must, however, be read in conjunction with the Copyright (Industrial Process) Order.[717] This Order excludes from the operation of the section certain articles of "a primarily literary or artistic character".[718] As well as books and other printed material, the Order includes sculptures within this definition,[719] thus allowing sculptors to produce and sell their works in potentially large numbers.[720] The difficulty with this is that it is dependent upon being able to say with precision what is and what is not a sculpture and, in particular, being able to distinguish sculptures from other types of artistic works, such as engravings.[721] Under the terms of the Copyright (Industrial Process) Order, the former will gain the full copyright term, the latter will only get protection for 25 years from the end of the year in which articles embodying the work are first marketed.

C. THINGS DONE IN RELIANCE ON REGISTRATION OF DESIGN

9-162   The final permitted act relating to designs gives primacy to the registered design system, so that anyone who relies on the provisions of the Registered Designs Act 1949, or on the accuracy of the register of designs, will not have to be concerned with any potential copyright infringement.[722] It should be noted that this provision is particularly important in relation to commissioned designs, as the owner of the registered design may well not be the owner of the copyright in such cases.[723] The Act thus provides that the copyright in an artistic work is not infringed by anything done (a) in pursuance of an assignment or licence made or granted by a person registered under the Registered Designs Act as the proprietor of a corresponding design, and (b) in good faith in reliance on the registration and without notice of any proceedings for the cancellation or invalidation of the registration or for rectifying the relevant entry into the register of designs.[724] This

---

[713] s.52(4) provides that the Secretary of State may by order make provision as to the circumstances in which an article is to be regarded as made by an industrial process and to exclude from the section such articles of a primarily literary or artistic character as he thinks fit. Thus, pursuant to "The Copyright (Industrial Process and Excluded Articles) (No.2) Order 1989" (SI 1989/1070), (Nr.2) (which entered into force on August 1, 1989 (see Vol.2 B8.ii) an article is to be regarded as made by an industrial process if (a) it is one of more than 50 articles which all fall to be treated as copies of a particular artistic work and which do not together constitute a single set of articles (set of articles was defined in s.44(1) of the Registered Designs Act 1949 and although this section has now been repealed, it is assumed the definition still applies); or (b) it consists of goods manufactured in lengths or pieces, not being handmade goods.

[714] CDPA 1988 s.52(1). "Marketed" here means selling an article or letting an article for hire or offering or exposing an article for sale or hire: s.52(6)(b).

[715] s.52(2).

[716] s.52(3).

[717] The Copyright (Industrial Process and Excluded Articles) (No.2) Order 1989 (1989/1070).

[718] Note that the Act also expressly excludes films from the operation of this section: CDPA 1988 s.52(6)(a).

[719] The Copyright (Industrial Process and excluded Articles) (No.2) Order 1989 r.3(1)(a).

[720] Thus Claes Oldenburg might retain the full term of copyright protection for his "multiples".

[721] See para.3–60, above.

[722] CDPA 1988 s.53.

[723] See further paras 13–001 et seq.

[724] s.53(1).

section applies notwithstanding the fact that the person registered as the proprietor was not entitled to be so registered.[725]

"Corresponding design" here means a design within the meaning of the Registered Designs Act, which, if applied to an article, would produce something which would be treated as a copy of the artistic work.[726]

12. TYPEFACES

Introduction. Designing a typeface is a skilled and time-consuming task, but   **9–163** once the design has been finished it can be copied at a fraction of the cost it originally took to produce. Thus there is real justification for some form of intellectual property protection.[727] While copyright will prima facie subsist in the design for a single letter, copyright will not subsist in sets of lettering as such. The Johnson Committee[728] looked at this problem in 1962 and recommended that the 1956 Act be amended so that copyright protection be extended to cover original sets of lettering,[729] but this recommendation was never implemented. Protection is available under the Registered Designs Act 1949 and the Community Design Regulations for single letters and, it would seem, for a typeface as a whole.[730]

The Vienna Agreement[731] of 1973 was an attempt to set out a minimum international level of protection for typefaces and to provide for their reciprocal protection. Although the United Kingdom signed the Vienna Agreement it never ratified it and, as yet, the Agreement is still not in force. When the Whitford Committee came to look at typefaces it recommended, as had the Johnson Committee before it, that copyright protection be given to sets of lettering and that the United Kingdom should ratify the Vienna Agreement.[732] In the event, this part of the Whitford Committee's recommendations was never implemented, so that copyright still does not subsist in a set of lettering.[733] Nevertheless, it is clear that copyright can subsist in individual letters and characters as graphic works (or sculptures where the pieces are carved) and, as discussed below, the 1988 Act makes special provision in order to restrict the scope of copyright protection in such works.[734]

Whilst the rationale of these sections is relatively clear, it seems that the sec-

---

[725] s.53(1).

[726] s.53(2).

[727] The preamble to the Vienna Agreement for the Protection of Type Faces and their International Deposit (hereafter "the Vienna Agreement") of 1973 states that typefaces play a role in "the dissemination of culture". For a consideration of the ways in which typefaces (and typographical arrangements more generally) can help to convey meaning, see McGann, "Composition as Explanation (of Modern and Postmodern Poetries)" in M. Ezell, J.M. O'Brien and C. O'Keeffe (eds) *Cultural Artifacts and the Production of Meaning* (Ann Arbor: University of Michigan Press, 1994).

[728] Report of the Departmental Committee on Industrial Designs, 1962 (Cmnd. 1808).

[729] Report of the Departmental Committee on Industrial Designs, 1962 (Cmnd. 1808), paras 160–163.

[730] See the Registered Designs Act 1949 s.1(3) as amended, and the Community Design Regulation EC 6/2002, in force on March 6, 2002, and Ch.13, below.

[731] See Vol.2 F9.

[732] The Vienna Agreement is fairly flexible as regards the form protection should take and allows Member States to protect typefaces by means of a sui generis right, or by designs law, or by copyright: Vienna Agreement art.3.

[733] cf. *Plix Products Ltd v Frank M Winstone (Merchants) Ltd* [1986] F.S.R. 63, where Pritchard J. seemed to indicate that copyright subsisted in the "Plix system" or range of products as a whole. Although the New Zealand Court of Appeal referred to this issue, it declined to consider the matter further.

[734] CDPA 1988 ss.54, 55. Note, however, that these sections refer to "copyright in an artistic work consisting of the design of a typeface". As "typeface" is usually taken to refer to "a set of printing type of a particular design" (*Oxford English Dictionary* 2nd edn) the wording of these sections

tions have been designed with mechanical methods of reproduction in mind.[735] Applying these provisions to electronic methods of reproducing a typeface poses a number of difficulties (see para.9–167, below).[736]

9–164 **The Information Society Directive.** Article 9 of the Information Society Directive, which deals with the continued application of other legal provisions, states that the Directive is to be without prejudice to provisions relating to typefaces. No amendment was therefore required to these permitted act sections.

A. TYPEFACES USED IN THE ORDINARY COURSE OF PRINTING

9–165 As has been seen, the design of a typeface will often be an artistic work in which copyright subsists, and the use of such a typeface in, for example, a printer, will involve repeated reproduction of the artistic work. Where the owner of the typeface has licensed its reproduction in an article, such use would usually be the subject of an implied licence, and possibly of the principle of non-derogation from grant.[737] However the Act goes further than this in an attempt to protect a purchaser who purchases an article which incorporates an infringing typeface.[738] Thus the Act provides that it is not an infringement of copyright in an artistic work consisting of the design of a typeface (a) to use the typeface in the ordinary course of typing, composing text, typesetting or printing, (b) to possess an article for the purpose of such use, or (c) to do anything in relation to material produced by such use; and this provision applies notwithstanding the fact that the article which is used, for example a typewriter key, is an infringing copy of the artistic work.[739]

The Act contains various provisions dealing with articles specifically designed or adapted for making copies of a work where they are to be used for making infringing copies. Thus s.24 makes it an infringement of copyright in a work to make, import, sell, etc., an article specifically designed or adapted for making copies of that work, knowing or having reason to believe that it is to be used for making infringing copies[740]; ss.99 and 100 provide for delivery up and seizure of such articles in these circumstances; s.107(2) makes it a criminal offence to make or possess such an article with such knowledge; and s.108 provides for seizure of articles in such an event. These provisions apply whether or not the article is itself an infringing copy. If no further provision were made, these sections would be of no application in, for example, a case where a person dealt with an article incorporating a typeface knowing or having reason to believe that it was to be used without the copyright owner's consent to print material reproducing the typeface. This is because by virtue of s.54(1) infringing copies would not be produced as a result. Although the policy of the Act is to exempt the user of the typeface from liability for infringement in such circumstances, it was clearly thought that this exemption should not be extended to those who deal in typefaces. It is therefore provided by s.54(2) that the above provisions of the Act (ss.24, 99, 100, 107(2) and 108) apply in relation to persons making, importing or dealing

---

seems better suited to describe copyright in a typeface as a whole, rather than protection for individual letters. The fact that copyright subsists in individual characters has to be inferred from general principles relating to artistic works.

[735] See further, *Hansard*, HL Vol.493, col.1181–1182.

[736] For a detailed consideration of these problems see J. Watts and F. Blakemore, "Protection of Software Fonts in UK Law", [1995] 3 E.I.P.R. 133.

[737] See, para.5–236, above.

[738] See *Hansard*, HL Vol.495, col.646. Note that this provision applies even where the purchaser knows that the typeface infringes copyright. However, a person importing or dealing with articles that incorporate an infringing typeface may still be liable for secondary infringement (see below).

[739] CDPA 1988 s.54(1).

[740] See para.8–15, above.

with articles specifically designed or adapted for producing material in a particular typeface as if the production of material as is mentioned in subs.(1) did infringe copyright in the artistic work consisting of the design of the typeface. For this purpose "dealing with" an article means selling, letting for hire, or offering or exposing for sale or hire, exhibiting in public, or distributing the article.[741] A person who makes, imports or deals with such an article will therefore be liable under the above provisions of the Act if he knows or has reason to believe it will be used to make copies of the typeface without the copyright owner's consent. Although simple possession of an article for the purpose of using the typeface is not an infringement,[742] the provisions are to apply in a similar way to the possession of such articles for the purpose of dealing with them.[743]

B. Articles for Producing Material in Particular Typeface

Where articles incorporating the typeface have been marketed by or with the licence of the copyright owner, the Act in effect limits the term of protection, thereby bringing typefaces into line with other artistic works that are industrially exploited.[744] Thus 25 years from the end of the calendar year in which the first such articles are marketed, the artistic work consisting of the design of the typeface may be copied by making further such articles or doing anything for this purpose.[745] Moreover, it will not be an infringement of copyright to do anything in relation to such articles.[746] In this context, "marketed" means sold, let for hire or offered or exposed for sale or hire whether in the United Kingdom or elsewhere.[747] It follows, for example, that after the 25-year period it would be permissible for anyone to make and sell replacement printer keys which reproduce the typeface used on the original printer.[748]

9–166

C. Typefaces in Electronic Form

In the interests of clarity, all the examples that have so far been considered relate to traditional, mechanical, methods of reproducing typefaces. In practice, however, typefaces are now more likely to be copied by means of an electronic process, in particular, as part of the use of a word processing program. It might be thought that there was a difficulty created by this transition to electronic methods of reproduction because of the use of the term "article" in both ss.54 and 55 of the Act, wording which might seem ill-suited to describe the use of software fonts. Where, however, software fonts are recorded or carried in the form of CD-ROMs, etc. or are copied to computer memory in whatever form, these items all constitute "articles".[749] Nevertheless, a difficulty remains in relation to s.55, as the restriction of the term of copyright only applies once articles designed or adapted for producing material in a particular typeface have been marketed. Thus if a font were only to be sold over the internet it might be argued no "articles"

9–167

---

[741] s.54(3).
[742] s.54(1)(b).
[743] s.54(2).
[744] CDPA 1988 s.55.
[745] s.55(2). Note that copyright in the typeface is not itself removed: *Hansard*, HL Vol.493, col.1182. Thus, for example, a sign writer who copies the typeface might still infringe.
[746] s.55(2).
[747] s.55(3).
[748] Note that where such articles have been marketed before August 1, 1989, the 25-year period only runs from December 31, 1989.
[749] *Sony Computer Entertainment Inc v Ball* [2004] EWHC 1738 (Ch); [2005] F.S.R. 9.

would ever be marketed and the term of copyright would remain unaffected.[750] It seems likely, however, that the section would be given a liberal interpretation.

13. WORKS IN ELECTRONIC FORM

9–168   Where a work in electronic form is passed on by the first purchaser, the Act provides an exception to permit the transferee to use the work without infringing copyright.[751] Such a provision is required since, as has already been considered, the use of a work in electronic form will almost invariably involve its reproduction at some stage.[752] Thus the owner of the copyright could argue that in the absence of any legal relationship with the transferee any use of the work would infringe copyright. This provision therefore applies where a copy of a work in electronic form has been purchased on terms which expressly, impliedly or by virtue of any rule of law allow the purchaser to copy the work or to adapt it or to make copies of an adaptation of it, in connection with the purchaser's use of it.[753] Presumably "any rule of law" includes the principle of non-derogation from grant.[754] The provision applies to all works in "electronic form," which means a form usable only by electronic means,[755] and "electronic" itself is defined to mean actuated by electric, magnetic, electro-magnetic, electro-chemical or electro-mechanical energy.[756] In such cases, if there are no express terms (a) prohibiting the transfer of the copy by the purchaser, imposing obligations which continue after a transfer, prohibiting the assignment of any licence or terminating any licence on a transfer, or (b) providing for the terms on which a transferee may do the things which the purchaser was permitted to do, then anything which the purchaser was allowed to do may also be done without infringement of copyright by a transferee.[757] These provisions also apply where the original copy is no longer usable and a further copy used in its place is transferred.[758] Finally, they apply not only on the first transfer, but also on any subsequent transfer.[759]

The Act provides, however, that where the purchaser does not also transfer any copy, adaptation or copy of an adaptation made by him before the transfer, then such a copy is to be treated for all purposes as an infringing copy, as from the time of the transfer.[760] In practice, this means that the purchaser must ensure that he does not retain a back-up copy or a copy on his hard disk.

9–169   **The Information Society Directive.** No amendments were made to this permitted act on implementation of the Directive. The Directive makes no express reference to this kind of act and clearly the saving in art.5(3)(o) for existing minor analogue exceptions does not apply. It would seem that the Government regarded

---

[750] See further, J. Watts and F. Blakemore, "Protection of Software Fonts in UK Law", [1995] 3 E.I.P.R. 133.

[751] CDPA 1988 s.56.

[752] See further, para.7–19, above.

[753] s.56(1).

[754] See, para.5–236, above.

[755] s.178.

[756] s.178.

[757] s.56(2). Also see *Beta Computers (Europe) Ltd v Adobe Systems (Europe) Ltd* [1996] F.S.R. 367 at 372. These provisions do not, however, apply in relation to a copy purchased before August 1, 1989: Sch.1 para.14(6).

[758] s.56(3).

[759] s.56(4).

[760] s.56(2).

this permitted act as an aspect of contract law within the meaning of art.9 of the Directive, although this seems doubtful.[761]

14. MISCELLANEOUS PROVISIONS: LITERARY, DRAMATIC, MUSICAL AND ARTISTIC WORKS

A. ANONYMOUS OR PSEUDONYMOUS WORKS: ACTS PERMITTED ON ASSUMPTIONS AS TO EXPIRY OF COPYRIGHT OR DEATH OF AUTHOR

The permitted acts. Where the identity of the author of a literary, dramatic, musical or artistic work is unknown it will normally be impossible to determine precisely when copyright expires. In recognition of this, the Act provides an exception to allow a work to be freely copied at a time when it is reasonable to assume that copyright has expired.[762] Thus the copyright in a literary, dramatic, musical or artistic work of unknown authorship[763] is not infringed by any act done, or in pursuance of any arrangements made at a time when, it is reasonable to assume either (a) that copyright has expired, or (b) that the author died 70 years or more before the beginning of the calendar year in which the act is done or the arrangements are made.[764] The latter provision does not, however, apply in relation to a work in which Crown copyright subsists, or a work in which copyright originally vested in an international organisation and in which a copyright period longer than 70 years has been specified.[765]

9–170

Transitional provisions. The Act also contains further, transitional, provisions which apply to works made before August 1, 1989. In relation to such works the assumption as to the expiry of copyright does not apply in relation to photographs or in relation to rights conferred on universities and colleges by virtue of the Copyright Act 1775.[766]

9–171

The Information Society Directive. The Directive does not contain any provision expressly covering this permitted act. No doubt, however, s.57 can be regarded as an administrative provision relating to the term of copyright in cases where this is uncertain, rather than as an exemption, exception or limitation to copyright within the ambit of the Directive.

9–172

Orphan Works. The Gowers Review recommended that the Information Soci-

9–173

---

[761] If the permitted act is to be viewed as an aspect of non-derogation from grant, such a principle is not applicable in a field where the position is covered by Community legislation: see para.5–236, above.

[762] CDPA 1988 s.57. Also see s.66A and para.9–198, below.

[763] This phrase is not actually used, but this section virtually repeats the wording of an earlier section of the Act, which provides that, "a work is of unknown authorship if the identity of the author is unknown or, in the case of a work of joint authorship, if the identity of none of the authors is known": s.9(4). The identity of an author is to be regarded as unknown "if it is not possible to ascertain his identity by reasonable inquiry": s.9(5).

[764] s.57(1). In relation to a work of joint authorship the reference to "the author" having died is to be construed as a reference to all the authors having died: s.57(3)(b).

[765] s.57(2). Although these works will have a natural author, the term of copyright in such works is unrelated to the author's death. Whilst this is also true of certain other categories of work (such as works in which Parliamentary copyright subsists), it is only in cases where copyright subsists for longer than 70 years that an honest mistake as to the date of the author's death is likely to result in the reproduction of a work still in copyright. As to the duration of copyright more generally, see Ch.6, above.

[766] CDPA 1988 Sch.1 para.15(2). As to the rights conferred by the 1775 Act, see para.6–84 et seq., above. Note that Sch.1 para.15(3) has been repealed by the Copyright and Related Rights Regulations 2003 (SI 2003/2498), following the amendment to Sch.1 para.12(3), by way of further implementation of the Term Directive.

ety Directive should be amended to introduce an exception for orphan works.[767] In December 2009 the European Commission indicated that it was considering action on orphan works, which it defined as works which are still in copyright but whose owners cannot be identified or located.[768] It indicated that possible approaches included a legally binding standalone instrument on the clearance and mutual recognition of orphan works, an exception to the Directive or guidance on cross-border mutual recognition of orphan works.[769] By May 2010, the Commission had decided on a proposal for the Directive.[770]

B. Use of Notes or Recordings of Spoken Words in Certain Cases

9–174   **Introduction.** The 1988 Act expressly recognises that copyright may subsist in a speaker's words when they are recorded by another person, irrespective of whether the speaker has consented to this "fixation".[771] To alleviate the difficulties this may cause, the Act provides an exception so as to allow the speaker's words to be used by journalists and broadcasters, such that where a person's spoken words are recorded, the subsequent use of that record cannot, in defined circumstances, be prevented by relying on any copyright "in the words as a literary work".[772] Thus, subject to certain conditions, the Act provides that where a record of spoken words is made, in writing[773] or otherwise, for the purpose (a) of reporting current events, or (b) of communicating to the public the whole or part of the work, then it is not an infringement of any copyright in the words as a literary work to use the record or material taken from it (or to copy the record, or any such material, and use the copy) for that purpose.[774]

The conditions which must be complied with are that: (a) the record is a direct record of the spoken words and is not taken from a previous record or from a broadcast; (b) the making of the record was not prohibited by the speaker and, where copyright already subsisted in the work, did not infringe copyright; (c) the use made of the record or material taken from it is not of a kind prohibited by or on behalf of the speaker or copyright owner before the record was made; and (d) the use is by or with the authority of a person who is lawfully in possession of the record.[775]

9–175   **The Information Society Directive.** Although some aspects of this permitted act fall within the exception for the reporting of current events allowed by art.5(3)(c), it is clear that not all of them do, not least because the Act does not contain any requirement to acknowledge the source. The section was not substantively amended on implementation of the Directive. It seems that because the operation of the section depends largely on the absence of prohibition the Government regarded this permitted act as relating to a contractual matter within the spirit of art.9 of the Directive, and thus allowed, but this seems doubtful.

9–176   **Comment.** This section of the Act should be compared with that providing for

---

[767] See para.9–13, above.
[768] Commission Communication Copyright in the Knowledge Economy COM(2009) 532 final.
[769] See at p.6.
[770] See its Communication: A Digital Agenda for Europe COM(2010) 245.
[771] CDPA 1988 ss.3(2), (3) and see para.3–114, above. See below as to the possible existence of a separate reporter's copyright.
[772] s.58.
[773] Writing is defined as including any form of notation or code, whether by hand or otherwise and regardless of the method by which, or the medium in or on which, it is recorded: s.178.
[774] s.58(1).
[775] s.58(2).

fair dealing for the purpose of reporting current events[776] and that for enabling published works to be read in public and then recorded or broadcast.[777] The section presents a number of difficulties of interpretation which are considered below.

The copyright work. The first problem is to identify the copyright work which is not infringed by virtue of the section. The section states that it is not an infringement "of any copyright in the words as a literary work" to use the record or material taken from it.[778] At first sight this provision may seem curiously worded, since no copyright can subsist in words as such, but only in the literary work which comes into existence once the words have been recorded, in writing or otherwise.[779] Presumably, however, the intention is that the provision should apply in the case where a person makes an extemporaneous speech which is recorded by another. In such circumstances two copyright works may come into existence at the same time. The first is the literary work consisting of the speaker's words which are recorded, the copyright in which will normally be owned by the speaker.[780] The permitted act no doubt applies to this work. The second work is the record itself which, if it is in writing, will be a literary work, or, if it is recorded on tape or by a similar method, will be a sound recording. The copyright in this will not normally be owned by the speaker.[781] It seems clear that the permitted act does not apply to this work, even where it is a literary work, since the Act expressly provides that the record must be a direct record of the spoken words and must not be taken from a previous record.[782] The licence of the copyright owner (e.g. the journalist) will therefore be required for the use of the record. There are, however, other works to which the provision applies. In particular, it seems that the provision also applies where copyright subsisted in "the words as a literary work" already, that is, before the words were spoken.[783] An example of this is the case where the speaker writes his speech beforehand, and then delivers it from memory or his prepared text. The speaker will usually be the owner of the copyright in his prepared text. **9–177**

It is also important to consider the position where the speaker recites an extract from some other copyright literary work. Where the licence of the owner of the copyright was not obtained for the making of the record, then it seems the section will not apply, since such a work will not fall within the operation of this section and thus the making of the record will have infringed copyright.[784]

The position of the speaker. It is clear that the section applies whether the words were spoken in public or in private. It is also clear that the section will apply unless the making of the record was expressly prohibited by the speaker, so that it appears that the onus will be on the speaker to prohibit such acts and not upon the maker of the record to seek permission.[785] Nor does it appear that it is necessary that the speaker should even be aware that his words were being recorded. More- **9–178**

---

[776] CDPA 1988 s.30(2) paras 9–49 et seq., above.

[777] s.59, para.9–180, below.

[778] CDPA 1988 s.58(1).

[779] s.3(2).

[780] See further, para.5–06, above.

[781] See para.5–41, above, and CDPA 1988 s.3(3).

[782] s.58(2)(a) and see above; also note that in any event the use of the record must be by or with the authority of a person in lawful possession of the record.

[783] See the wording of s.58(2)(b).

[784] Unless reliance can be placed on another of the permitted acts, for example s.59, para.9–180, below. Also note that the speaker may be the owner of the copyright in such a work.

[785] cf. *Nicols v Pitman* (1884) 26 Ch.3/4: implied understanding between lecturer and audience that notes taken during the course of a lecture delivered to an audience limited and admitted by tickets cannot be published for profit.

over, even if the speaker was aware that his words were being recorded, it does not appear that it is necessary that he knew the use which would be made of the record. This raises the possibility of the speaker being deceived as to the purposes for which the record will be used, although in a case where, for example, a politician makes a statement "off the record" there would no doubt be a strong implication that publication of its contents was prohibited within the meaning of s.58(2)(c). If the making of the record or its use is to be prohibited by the speaker, this must be done before the record is made and any attempt to do so afterwards will apparently be of no effect.

9–179   **The permitted uses.** The purposes for which the record was made may either be the reporting of current events or the broadcasting of the whole or part of the work. The meaning of "reporting current events" has already been considered in the context of the fair dealing exceptions.[786] The advantage of the present exception in this context appears to be that it can be relied upon even if the dealing is not fair (for example because the extract used is too long),[787] or if there is a failure to provide sufficient acknowledgment.[788] As to broadcasting the work, presumably the words "the whole or part of the work" in subs.58(1)(b) must refer to the work whose use is permitted by the section. It is not necessary that there be any element of reporting current events under this limb. The expression "for that purpose" in the concluding words of subs.(1) appears to indicate that if the record is made for one of the defined purposes it may not be used for the other.[789] Yet it may not always be easy to tell for which purpose the record was made and in many cases it will be made for both purposes, for example the broadcasting of a current affairs programme. In this case it would appear permissible to re-use the record for either purpose, so that a record made for the purposes of such a programme could be re-used in order to broadcast "the work" even though the record no longer related to "current events."

The use may be of the record itself or of material taken from it, or a copy of the record.[790] Thus where the record is in the form of a tape recording it appears permissible to transcribe it and print the transcript in a newspaper provided that this is for the purpose of reporting current events. Where the record is in writing it appears permissible to record that material on tape and broadcast the contents of the tape recording. The original "record" must, however, itself be a direct record of the spoken words and must not have been taken, for example, from a broadcast of the spoken words. The express reference to it being permissible to copy the record, and to use the copy, raises the doubt, which might otherwise not have arisen, whether the making of third, fourth and later generation copies is permissible. Were it not for these words it would probably be implicit that the making of such further copies is permissible if for the defined purposes. In many cases a record of an interview will go through several generations of copies before it is printed or broadcast and it would clearly be highly inconvenient if such copying were restricted to the original record and only copies made directly from it. It is thought this cannot have been the intention of the legislature.[791]

---

[786] See paras 9–49 et seq., above.

[787] See paras 9–58 et seq., above.

[788] See para.9–33, above. Note that in any event no acknowledgment is required in connection with the reporting of current events by means of a sound recording, film or broadcast: CDPA 1988 s.30(3).

[789] See further, *Hansard*, HL Vol.501, cols 198–200.

[790] CDPA 1988 s.58(1).

[791] In fact this provision was inserted to allow broadcasters to follow their usual practice of making copies of their original recordings for the purposes of their broadcasts: Report of the Debates of the House of Commons Standing Committee E in 1988 cols 484–5.

C. PUBLIC READING OR RECITATION

The Act provides that the reading or recitation in public by one person of a rea-   **9–180**
sonable extract from a published literary or dramatic work does not infringe any
copyright in the work if it is accompanied by a sufficient acknowledgment.[792] The
definition of "sufficient acknowledgment" has already been considered.[793] In addition, where a reading or recitation does not infringe copyright by virtue of this
provision, the Act provides a limited exception to allow for the reading or recitation to be included in a sound recording or communication to the public.
However, this latter provision only applies where the recording or communication consists mainly of material in relation to which it is not necessary to rely on
this exception.[794] No further guidance is given as to the proportion of the recording or broadcast that may consist of copyright material, but during the passage of
the Bill it was said that the purpose of this exception was to allow the televising
of events such as eisteddfodau, where a speaker might unforeseeably recite an
extract from a literary or dramatic work.[795]

The Information Society Directive. The Directive is not concerned with the   **9–181**
public performing right in works,[796] and thus the acts of reading or recitation in
public permitted by s.59(1) do not come within its ambit. The subsidiary permitted acts of inclusion of the work in a sound recording or broadcast do, however,
and none of the exceptions permitted by the Directive corresponds precisely to
this permitted act, although various permitted exceptions may apply on the facts
of the particular case.[797] It some cases, the general exception in art.5(3)(o) for
existing analogue uses of minor importance may apply. Where this is not the
case, it would seem that the Government relied on art.5(3)(d) to justify not making any amendment to this section. Article 5(3)(d) permits quotations for purposes
such as criticism or review, and so it is arguable that the cases of criticism or
review are illustrative only of the uses which may be made of quotations.

D. ABSTRACTS OF SCIENTIFIC OR TECHNICAL ARTICLES

Before the 1988 Act, it was common practice within the scientific and technical   **9–182**
communities to copy abstracts accompanying an article and to circulate them, but
in the absence of any express provision such copying almost invariably amounted
to an infringement of copyright, as it seems that licences were very seldom
obtained. Nevertheless, it was seen as desirable that such copying be allowed to
continue and put on a proper basis, as databases of abstracts can greatly speed up
research by allowing scientists and researchers to identify papers relevant to their
work without having to look through individual journals.[798] The Act thus provides
that where an article on a scientific or technical subject is published in a periodical accompanied by an abstract indicating the contents of the article, it is not an
infringement of copyright in the abstract, or in the article, to copy the abstract or
issue copies of it to the public.[799] For this purpose "article" includes an item of
any description in a periodical.[800] "Copyright in the abstract or in the article"

---

[792] CDPA 1988 s.59(1).
[793] See para.9–33, above.
[794] s.59(2).
[795] *Hansard*, H.L. Vol. 501, col. 198.
[796] See Information Society Directive 2001/29, recitals 23 and 24.
[797] For example the exceptions under Information Society Directive art.5(3)(c), (f) or (g).
[798] See further, *Hansard*, HL Vol.491, col.106.
[799] CDPA 1988 s.60(1).
[800] s.178.

must be taken to include copyright in the typographical arrangement.[801] Less certain is the meaning of "technical" in this context. The legislative history suggests that a narrow definition should be given to this term, so as only to include engineering subjects and applied sciences,[802] even if as a matter of principle there is no good reason not to extend the exception to a broad range of disciplines.[803]

This provision does not, however, apply if or to the extent that there is a relevant licensing scheme certified under s.143 of the Act.[804] The Act thus provides an incentive to publishers to enter into a licensing agreement and an opportunity for them to receive income for an activity that was previously unregulated,[805] although as yet no such scheme has been certified.

9-183   **The Information Society Directive.** No amendment was made to s.60 on implementation of the Directive. Articles 5(3)(a) and (4) permit Member States to make an exception to the reproduction and distribution rights in the case of non-commercial scientific research, provided a proper acknowledgment is made. Section 60 clearly does not fall within this permitted exception. It would seem that the Government placed reliance on the general saving for existing analogue uses of minor importance permitted by art.5(3)(o), making the assumption that all copying would be "analogue" and that the issue of copies of abstracts to the public could only take place by the issue of hard copies and so again must be analogue use.

E. RECORDINGS OF FOLKSONGS

9-184   **Introduction.** The Act contains provisions, which were new in the 1988 Act, relating to the recording for archival purposes of unpublished songs of unknown authorship,[806] and for the supply by the archivist of copies of such recordings for the purposes of non-commercial research or private study. These provisions should be considered alongside the exception allowing for fair dealing with literary and musical works for the purposes of non-commercial research and private study.[807]

9-185   **The Information Society Directive.** Articles 5(2)(c) and (4) permit Member States to make an exception to the reproduction and distribution rights in respect of specific acts of reproduction made by publicly accessible museums and archives, which are not for direct or indirect economic or commercial advantage. Presumably this extends to enabling copies to be made for such organisations as well as by them. The exception also falls partly within arts 5(2)(b) and 5(3)(a) as regards copying and supplying to the public. An amendment was made to the Act to limit the permitted supply of copies for purposes of *non-commercial* research,[808] with the effect that s.61 now appears to comply with the Directive.

9-186   **Making recordings.** The Act provides that so long as certain conditions are met,

---

[801] This is clear from the legislative history (see the next footnote) and see CDPA 1988 s.28(2) and para.9–16, above.
[802] See *Hansard*, HL Vol.491, cols 106, 110; Vol.495, col.628; HC Vol.138, cols 145–147.
[803] At the very least it is clear that Parliament intended "the humanities" to be excluded from the scope of this provision: HC Vol.138, col.147.
[804] CDPA 1988 s.60(2).
[805] See further, *Hansard*, HL Vol.501, col.252; HC Vol.138, col.147.
[806] The title "folksongs" is merely a signpost: *Hansard*, HC Vol.138, col.110.
[807] See paras 9–29 et seq., above.
[808] At the same time, the definition of private study has been limited to exclude study for commercial purposes: CDPA 1988 s.178.

a sound recording[809] of a performance of a song may be made for the purpose of including it in an archive maintained by a designated body without infringing any copyright in the lyrics or in the accompanying music.[810] For this purpose, a "designated body" is one designated by Order of the Secretary of State,[811] but the Secretary of State is not to designate such a body unless satisfied that it is not established or conducted for profit.[812] There are three conditions to be met:

(1) First, as has been seen, the words of the song must be unpublished and of unknown authorship at the time when the recording is made.[813] For a literary or musical work to be unpublished in this context, copies[814] of the work must not have been issued to the public or made available by means of an electronic retrieval system,[815] but a work is not to be regarded as having been published by its being performed or communicated to the public (other than for the purposes of an electronic retrieval system).[816] Neither will colourable publication, not intended to satisfy the reasonable requirements of the public, amount to publication,[817] nor will any unauthorised publication.[818] For the words to be of "unknown authorship" the identity of the author, or in the case of works of joint authorship,[819] all the authors, must be unknown,[820] and the identity of an author will be regarded as unknown if it is not possible for a person to ascertain his identity by reasonable inquiry, but if his identity is once known it is not to be regarded subsequently as unknown.[821]

(2) Secondly, the making of the recording must not infringe any other copyright.[822] It follows that it will not be possible to copy an existing copyright sound recording by virtue of this section.

(3) Finally, the making of the recording must not be prohibited by any of the performers.[823]

Supply of copies. Once such a recording has been included in a relevant archive, the Act provides that, subject to prescribed conditions, the archivist, or a person acting on his behalf,[824] may make and supply copies without infringing copyright in either the recording or the works included in it.[825] The conditions, prescribed by the Secretary of State, are (a) that copies are only supplied to persons satisfy-

9–187

---

[809] For the definition of a sound recording see CDPA 1988 s.5A(1) and see para.3–77, above.

[810] s.61(1).

[811] s.61(5)(a), (6). As to such designated bodies see the Copyright (Recordings of Folksongs for Archives) (Designated Bodies) Order 1989 (SI 1989/1012); Vol.2 A4.ii. Twelve bodies have so far been designated: The Archive of Traditional Welsh Music; The Centre for English Cultural Tradition and Language; The Charles Parker Archive Trust (1982); The European Centre for Traditional and Regional Cultures; The Folklore Society; The Institute of Folklore Studies in Britain and Canada; The National Museum of Wales, Welsh Folk Museum; The National Sound Archive, the British Library; The North West Sound Archive; The Sound Archives, British Broadcasting Corporation; Ulster Folk and Transport Museum; The Vaughan Williams Memorial Library; and The English Folk Dance and Song Society.

[812] s.61(5)(a).

[813] s.61(2)(a).

[814] For the definition of "copies", see ss.17, 178.

[815] s.175(1).

[816] s.175(4)(a).

[817] s.174(5). As to the meaning of "reasonable requirements of the public", see *Francis, Day and Hunter v Feldman* [1914] 2 Ch.728 and para.3–178, above

[818] s.174(6). For the definition of "unauthorised", see s.178.

[819] For the definition of a work of "joint authorship", see s.10(1) and see paras 4–34 et seq., above.

[820] s.9(4).

[821] s.9(5).

[822] s.61(2)(b).

[823] s.61(2)(c).

[824] CDPA 1988 s.65(1)(c).

[825] s.61(3).

ing the archivist that they require them for purposes of research for a non-commercial purpose or private study and will not use them for any other purpose,[826] and (b) that no person is furnished with more than one copy of the same recording.[827]

F. Representation of Certain Artistic Works on Public Display

9–188   **The permitted acts.** The 1988 Act, as did the 1956 and 1911 Acts, makes provision enabling certain works on public display to be represented without infringing copyright.[828] The provisions of the 1988 Act apply to buildings (irrespective of location), and to models for buildings, sculptures and works of artistic craftsmanship, where these are permanently situated in a public place or in premises open to the public.[829] The Act provides that copyright in such a work is not infringed by making a graphic work representing it, or by making a photograph or film of it, or by making a broadcast of a visual image of it.[830] Furthermore, copyright is not infringed by the issue to the public of copies, or the communication to the public, of anything whose making was, by virtue of this provision, not an infringement of copyright.[831] In relation to anything made before August 1, 1989, it is to be assumed that these provisions were in force at all material times.[832] The expression "open to the public" presumably extends the section to premises to which the public are admitted only on licence or on payment and,[833] if so, there would seem to be nothing to prevent the owner of the premises imposing contractual conditions restricting the copying of the material exhibited.[834]

9–189   **"In such a work."** The words "in such a work" have the potential to limit the scope of this exception quite considerably. For example, someone who takes a photograph of a building might still infringe copyright in the architect's preliminary drawings or plans, since the words "in such a work" would seem to refer only to copyright in the building itself. However, whilst this conclusion may be inevitable given the wording of the Act, it should be noted that Parliament gave this section very little consideration during the passage of the Bill. The wording of this section therefore seems to be the result of the draftsman having paraphrased the wording of the 1956 Act which, it seems, was also not wide enough to cover copyright in preliminary drawings and plans. Yet it is clear that Parliament intended the provisions in the 1956 Act to have the same effect as those in the 1911 Act and these latter provisions were not so limited.[835]

9–190   **The Information Society Directive.** Articles 5(3)(h) and (4) permit Member

---

[826] s.61(4)(a); The Copyright (Recordings of Folksongs for Archives) (Designated Bodies) Order 1989 (SI 1989/1012) reg.3(2)(a). See Vol.2 A4.ii.

[827] s.61(4)(b); The Copyright (Recordings of Folksongs for Archives) (Designated Bodies) Order 1989 (SI 1989/1012) reg.3(2)(b).

[828] CDPA 1988 s.62. cf. Copyright Act 1956 ss.9(3), (4), (6); Copyright Act 1911 s.2(1)(iii).

[829] s.62(1). As to the definition and meaning of "buildings", "sculptures" and "works of artistic craftsmanship", see s.4 and see paras 3–63, 3–60 and 3–67, above, respectively.

[830] s.62(2).

[831] s.62(3).

[832] Sch.1 para.14(4).

[833] In *Cawley v Frost* [1976] 1 W.L.R. 1207 it was held in relation to the Public Order Act 1936, that, where the public have access to premises, those premises should be considered in their entirety, so the fact that the public are denied access to certain areas will not, of itself, stop them being part of a public place.

[834] See CDPA 1988 s.28(1) and *Sports and General Press Agency Ltd v "Our Dogs" Publishing Co Ltd* [1916] 2 K.B. 880; [1917] 2 K.B. 125.

[835] See *Hansard*, HL Vol.195, col.1048; Copyright Act 1956 ss.9(3), 9(4); Copyright Act 1911 s.2(1)(iii) and compare CDPA 1988 s.65(b) (see para.9–195, below).

States to make an exception to the reproduction, distribution and communication to the public rights, in the case of use of works, such as works of architecture or sculpture, made to be located permanently in public places. Section 62 appears to fall squarely within this.

G. ADVERTISEMENT OF SALE OF ARTISTIC WORK

The Act makes special provision to enable copies of artistic works to be made for the purpose of advertising their sale.[836] Thus the Act provides that it is not an infringement of copyright in an artistic work to copy it, or to issue copies of it to the public, for the purpose of advertising the sale of the work.[837] It is therefore permissible in the course of selling a painting to make and publish copies of it in a catalogue. In relation to such copies, however, if they are subsequently dealt with[838] for any other purpose, they are to be treated as infringing copies for the purposes of that dealing and, if that dealing infringes copyright, for all subsequent purposes.[839] Someone who so deals in such copies, and who has the requisite degree of knowledge, will therefore be liable for secondary infringement of copyright.[840] This provision will therefore catch the practice of selling old auction catalogues. The permitted act does not extend to communication to the public; accordingly, placing photographs of artist's works on a website for the purpose of advertising their sale will infringe if unlicensed.

9–191

The Information Society Directive. Articles 5(3)(j) and (4) permit Member States to make an exception to the reproduction, distribution and communication to the public rights in the case of use for the purpose of advertising the public exhibition or sale of artistic works, to the extent necessary to promote the event, excluding any other commercial use. Section 63 appears to fall squarely within this.

9–192

H. MAKING OF SUBSEQUENT WORKS BY SAME ARTIST

Artists often wish to copy aspects of their earlier works when creating a new work, but where the copyright in an earlier work has been assigned (or where the work was made in the course of employment) there is a danger that the artist will infringe copyright by doing so.[841] The Act provides a limited exception to allow artists to copy parts of their earlier works, such that where the author of an artistic work is not the copyright owner, he does not infringe the copyright by copying the work in making another artistic work, provided he does not repeat or imitate the main design of the earlier work.[842] This provision would not, however, affect a claim in contract against an artist who copied part of a work over which he had

9–193

---

[836] CDPA 1988 s.63. This section was new in the 1988 Act.

[837] s.63(1). In *Thurgood v Coyle* [2007] EWHC 2696 (Ch) it was suggested that the reproduction of drawings for a partly completed development for the purposes of advertising the sale of the buildings was within the scope of the permitted act. The facts of the case are not easy to discern from the judgment but if the drawings predated the construction of the buildings this suggestion would seem to be wrong.

[838] For this purpose, "dealt with" means sold or let for hire, offered or exposed for sale or hire, exhibited in public, distributed or communicated to the public. Communication to the public was introduced as a further form of dealing on implementation of the Information Society Directive 2001/29, because of the possible commercial nature of such acts. See the Government Conclusions on the Patent Office's Consultation Paper of August 7, 2002, para.5.11.

[839] s.63(2).

[840] See Ch.8, above, and s.27(6).

[841] cf. *Gross v Seligman, 212 F.930* (2d Cir. 1914) and see Hughes, "The Personality Interest of artists and inventors in Intellectual Property" (1998) 16 Cardozo Arts & Ent. L.J. 81.

[842] CDPA 1988 s.64. The Copyright Acts 1956 s.9(9), and 1911, s.2(1)(ii), contained broadly equivalent provisions.

granted an exclusive licence, since (as has been seen) the exceptions only apply to the question of copyright infringement and the rights of the exclusive licensee against the owner of the copyright lie in contract only.[843] Whether the artist would in fact be liable to the exclusive licensee would depend on the terms of the contract. In the course of Parliamentary debates on this provision two examples of its intended effect were given. First, it was said that this provision would allow an architect to reproduce some part the original design, such as a staircase, in a subsequent building, provided he avoided repeating or imitating the main design. Secondly, it was said that it would allow the painter of a group portrait to re-use sketches to reproduce individual portraits.[844] In addition, it would seem that this section would protect a painter who re-uses a "trade mark" object or motif.[845]

9–194   **The Information Society Directive.** Section 64 was not amended on implementation of the Directive, even though the Directive does not contain any permitted exception which corresponds to this permitted act. It would appear that the Government relied on the general saving for analogue uses of minor importance permitted by art.5(3)(o) and assumed that any digital copying would be de minimis.

I. Reconstruction of Buildings

9–195   The Act provides that anything done for the purposes of reconstructing a building will not infringe two categories of copyright works. First, any copyright in the building; secondly, any copyright in any drawings or plans in accordance with which the building was, by or with the licence of the copyright owner, constructed.[846] For this purpose, in relation to buildings constructed before August 1, 1989, the reference to the owner of the copyright in any drawings or plans is to the person who at the time of construction was the owner of the copyright in the drawings or plans under the 1956 or 1911 Acts, or earlier legislation, as the case may be.[847]

9–196   **The Information Society Directive.** Article 5(3)(m) permits Member States to make an exception to the reproduction, distribution and communication to the public rights, in the case of use of an artistic work in the form of a building or a drawing or plan of a building for the purposes of reconstructing the building. Section 65 appears to fall squarely within this permitted exception.

15. MISCELLANEOUS PROVISIONS: LENDING OF WORKS

9–197   **Section 66 of the Act: compulsory licences for lending.**[848] The public lending

---

[843] See para.5–209, above.

[844] *Hansard*, HL Vol.491, col.191; Vol.493, col.1187.

[845] So, for example, Magritte's *bilboquets* might fall within this section

[846] CDPA 1988 s.65. The Copyright Act 1956 s.9(10) contained a very similar provision. It is perhaps worth contrasting this provision with the "right to repair" established by case law. See paras 5–235 et seq.

[847] Sch.1 para.14(7).

[848] The heading, as amended by the Copyright and Related Rights Regulations 1996 (SI 1996/2967), actually reads, "Miscellaneous: lending of works and playing of sound recordings". However, this is misleading, as the Duration of Copyright and Rights in Performances Regulations (SI 1995/3297), grouped the miscellaneous provisions relating to the playing of sound recordings together with a new section dealing with assumptions as to the expiry of copyright in films (see para.9–198 et seq.,below).

of copies of works is an act restricted by copyright in most types of work,[849] and thus an infringement of copyright unless the licence of the copyright owner has been obtained. By virtue of s.66, however, the Secretary of State has power to order that such lending is to be treated as licensed subject only to payment of a reasonable royalty or other payment.[850] This "permitted act" is thus in reality a compulsory licence and is dealt with in detail elsewhere.[851]

16. MISCELLANEOUS PROVISIONS: FILMS AND SOUND RECORDINGS

A. FILMS: ACTS PERMITTED ON ASSUMPTIONS AS TO EXPIRY OF COPYRIGHT

As has been seen, the term of copyright in films was extended by the Duration of Copyright and Rights in Performances Regulations 1995.[852] The term of copyright is now determined by reference to the date of death of the director, the author of the screen play, the author of the dialogue and the composer of any specially created music: copyright lasts for 70 years from the end of the year in which the last of these persons dies.[853] One effect of this amendment has been to make it more difficult to know precisely when copyright in a film has expired. The Duration of Copyright Regulations therefore introduced a new exception to allow a film to be copied at a time when it is reasonable to assume that copyright has expired.[854] The Act thus provides that copyright in a film is not infringed by an act done, or in pursuance of arrangements made, at a time when it is reasonable to assume either (a) that copyright has expired, or (b) that the last of the persons by reference to whom the copyright period is determined died 70 years or more before the beginning of the calendar year in which the act is done or the arrangements are made.[855] The latter provision does not, however, apply in relation to a film in which Crown copyright subsists, or a film in which copyright originally vested in an international organisation and in which a copyright period longer than 70 years has been specified.[856] These provisions are very similar to those governing the copying of works of unknown authorship,[857] except that there has been no need for complex transitional arrangements.

9–198

The Information Society Directive. The same comment can be made about this permitted act as was made in relation to the provisions governing the copying of works of unknown authorship.[858]

9–199

---

[849] See further, CDPA 1988 s.18A: "the rental or lending of copies of the work to the public is an act restricted by copyright in (a) a literary, dramatic or musical work, (b) an artistic work, other than a work of architecture or a work of applied art, or (c) a film or sound recording." See further, paras 7–97, et seq., above.

[850] s.66(1). S.66 in its present form was introduced by the Copyright and Related Rights Regulations 1996 (SI 1996/2967), which implemented the Rental and Lending Rights Directive (92/100). This new section replaces the original provision. S.66 as originally enacted was similar in operation, but it applied to the rental of works. It is considered elsewhere (see para.28–45 and 28–46, below).

[851] See para.28–45 et seq., below.

[852] SI 1995/3297. See Ch.6, above.

[853] CDPA 1988 s.13B(2), and see para.6–70, above.

[854] s.66A.

[855] s.66A(1).

[856] s.66A(2).

[857] See para.9–170, above.

[858] See para.9–172, above.

B. Playing of Sound Recordings for Purposes of Clubs, etc.

9–200   **The permitted act.** Section 67 of the 1988 Act provides that if certain conditions are met, it is not an infringement of the copyright in a sound recording to play it as part of the activities of, or for the benefit of, a club, society or other organisation.[859] The section is, however, repealed with effect from January 1, 2011.[860]

9–201   **The Information Society Directive.** The public performance right is not one of the rights with which the Directive is directly concerned.[861] However, art.11(1) of the Directive amended the Rental and Related Rights Directive to introduce the Berne three-step test requirement into the exceptions permitted by that Directive.[862] Before this amendment, art.10 of the Rental and Related Rights Directive[863] permitted a Member State to make exceptions or limitations to the rights of phonogram producers, including limitations which are of the same kind as the Member State makes in connection with the protection of copyright in literary and artistic works.[864] Section 67 was not amended on implementation of this Directive, the Government apparently taking the view that its terms were consistent with it.[865] With the amendment of art.10 of the Rental and Related Rights Directive by the Information Society Directive, to require that these limitations comply with the Berne three-step test,[866] amendment was needed to s.67 to narrow the scope of its conditions relating to (a) the motives of the person playing the recording, (b) how the proceeds of any charges made for admission are applied and (c) how the proceeds from the sale of any goods or services made at the time are applied.[867]

9–202   **Organisations to which the section applies.** If s.67 is to apply, the organisation

---

[859] CDPA 1988 s.67(1). Note that the section only applies to sound recordings and not to any musical or literary works embodied in them. The section only comes into play of course if the playing of the recording amounts to the playing of it in public. See s.12(7) of the 1956 Act for the provision made under that Act in this area.

[860] By the Copyright, Designs and Patents Act 1988 (Amendment) Regulations 2010 (SI 2010/2694). See further para.9–205, below.

[861] See Information Society Directive 2001/29, recitals 23 and 24.

[862] The Directive has since been replaced by the codifying Directive 2006/115/EC. As to the Berne three-step test, see paras 9–02, above, and 23–33, below.

[863] Now art.10 of Directive 2006/115.

[864] The other permitted limitations are for (a) private use; (b) use of short excerpts in connection with the reporting of current events; (c) ephemeral fixation by a broadcasting organisation by means of its own facilities and for its own broadcasts; and (d) use solely for the purposes of teaching or scientific research. See now art.10 of Directive 2006/115. All these exceptions correspond to the exceptions permitted by art.15 of the Rome Convention.

[865] This was a view which was apparently shared by the Commission. See the comment in *Phonographic Performance Ltd v Department of Trade and Industry* [2004] EWHC 1795 (Ch); [2004] 1 W.L.R. 2893; [2005] R.P.C. 8, at para.7, a case where proceedings were brought against the Crown alleging failure to implement the Rental and Related Rights Directive. Although it is not particularly clear from the Directive itself, art.8(2) effectively requires Member States to provide protection for owners of the copyright in sound recordings in respect of their public performance, this being a "communication to the public". See also recitals 5 and 11, which respectively state that (a) the protection of the subject matter of related rights protection by communication to the public is to be considered as being of fundamental importance for the Community's economic and cultural development and (b) the Community's legal framework on certain rights related to copyright can be limited to establishing, amongst other things, the right to communication to the public for certain groups of rightholders in the field of related rights protection.

[866] See Information Society Directive art.11(1)(b), amending Rental and Related Rights Directive art.10(3) to provide: "The limitations shall only be applied in certain special cases which do not conflict with a normal exploitation of the subject-matter and do not unreasonably prejudice the legitimate interests of the rightholder".

[867] It was the Government's belief that these changes would prevent organisations seeking to benefit from the CDPA 1988 s.67 exception in relation to activities conducted on a quasi-commercial basis. See the Government Conclusions on the Patent Office's Consulation Paper of August 7, 2002, para.5.15.

in question must be a club, society or other organisation which is not established or conducted for profit and whose main objects are charitable or otherwise concerned with the advancement of religion, education or social welfare.[868] Similar wording also appeared in s.8(1)(a) of the Rating and Valuation (Miscellaneous Provisions) Act 1955 and cases decided under that section are helpful in construing s.67.[869] The following principles apply:

(1) The word "organisation" does not have a wide, unrestricted meaning, since under the *ejusdem generis* rule the reference to clubs and societies colours and cuts down the sort of organisation that falls within the section.[870] The distinguishing characteristic of a club or society is that it consists of individuals who are bound together in some common activity or enterprise.[871]

(2) As to the requirement that the organisation should not be established or conducted for profit, an organisation will not be conducted for profit simply because it makes investments, provided such investments are only a means of achieving other, legitimate, objectives.[872]

(3) The organisation must be one whose main functions, or whose functions when viewed as a whole, are either charitable or otherwise concerned with the advancement of religion, education or social welfare. The fact that one of the main objects of an organisation is, for example, the advancement of education is not enough.[873] In order to fall within the provision, all the main objects of the organisation must satisfy the requirements of s.67(2)(a), although provided each of the main objects satisfies at least one of the requirements (i.e. of charity, religion, education or social welfare), that is enough. If any of the organisation's main objects are held not to be charitable or akin to charitable objects then the organisation will fall outside the protection of this section.[874] However, provided the organisation's main objects satisfy the requirements of this section, the organisation may also have subsidiary objects, such as the benefit of its members.[875]

(4) Whether the objects of an organisation are charitable or not is a question of the general law of charity. Legal charities have to fall into one of four classes, namely, the relief of poverty,[876] the advancement of education,[877] the advancement of religion,[878] and other purposes beneficial to the

---

[868] CDPA 1988 s.67(2)(a). This condition was not altered on amendment.

[869] *Phonographic Performance Ltd v South Tyneside Metropolitan Borough Council* [2001] R.P.C. 594. See also the Miners' Welfare Act 1952 (c.23) s.16, and the Recreational Charities Act 1958 (c.17) s.1.

[870] Unless the words "other organisation" were restricted in some such way, it would be of very wide ambit indeed, including all arms of national government, local government, local authorities, quangos, regional health trusts, etc: *Phonographic Performance Ltd v South Tyneside Metropolitan Borough Council* [2001] R.P.C. 594.

[871] *Phonographic Performance Ltd v South Tyneside Metropolitan Borough Council* [2001] R.P.C. 594. The nature of the organisation is of course further qualified by CDPA 1988 s.67(2).

[872] *National Deposit Friendly Society (Trustees) v Skegness UDC* [1959] A.C. 293, HL per Lord Denning.

[873] *Phonographic Performance Ltd v South Tyneside Metropolitan Borough Council* [2001] R.P.C. 594.

[874] In particular, see *Berry v St Marylebone BC* [1958] Ch.406.

[875] *National Deposit Friendly Society (Trustees) v Skegness UDC*, [1959] A.C. 293, HL per at 310 Lord Denning.

[876] See, e.g. *Re Coulthurst* [1951] Ch.661 at 665.

[877] See further, *Chartered Insurance Institute v London Corporation* [1957] 1 W.I. R. 867; *IRC v McMullen* [1981] A.C. 1.

[878] See further, *United Grand Lodge, etc. v Holborn BC* [1957] 1 W.L.R. 1080; *Berry v St Marylebone BC* [1958] Ch. 406; *Re South Place Ethical Society* [1980] 1 W.L.R. 1565.

community.[879] In addition to this there must be an element of public benefit so that, for example, a trust for the education of employees of a particular company is not a valid legal charity.[880]

(5) The words "or are otherwise concerned with the advancement of religion,
education or social welfare" are intended to include activities which are
quasi-charitable in nature.[881] The words "are otherwise concerned with
the advancement of" impose a limitation on the words "religion, education or social welfare" which follow. They show that the section is
concerned with objects which are of concern to charitable organisations
but which for some reason or other fail to come under the definition of
"charitable purposes" in the strictly legal sense.[882] The nature and effect of
these words is therefore to extend the protection of this section to organisations which are charitable in the popular sense rather than in the strictly
legal sense.[883] In general it has been said that it is impossible to provide a
precise delimitation of organisations which might fall within this definition, so that each case must be considered on its merits.[884] "Social welfare"
means the well-being (whether in the physical, mental or material sense)
of individuals as members of society.[885] Thus the provision of benefits
which tend directly to improve the health or conditions of life comes prima
facie within the expression "social welfare"[886]; there is no need for an el-
eemosynary element.[887] The words "concerned with the advancement of"
require that the organisation does more than enable individuals to advance
their own welfare.[888] By analogy with the law of charities, there must be
an intention to benefit the community.[889] It seems, however, that there is
no need for public benefit in the narrow, technical, sense.[890]

(6) In determining the main objects of an organisation it seems that it may be
permissible to look at the way the organisation's affairs have been
conducted, as well as at its rules.[891] Where the organisation has a written
constitution, however, it is to that and that alone to which the court should
look to ascertain its objects for present purposes[892] and extrinsic evidence
is not admissible to limit the proper meaning of the language used.[893]

Having regard to these principles, a local authority was held not to be an "organisation" within the meaning of s.67, since: (1) As a matter of impression, a
normal user of the English language would not describe all of the main functions
of a local authority, or the functions of a local authority viewed as a whole, as

---

[879] *Income Tax Special Purposes Commissioners v Pemsel* [1891] A.C. 531.

[880] *Oppenheim v Tobacco Securities Trust Co Ltd* [1951] A.C. 297.

[881] *Phonographic Performance Ltd v South Tyneside Metropolitan Borough Council* [2001] R.P.C. 594.

[882] *Phonographic Performance Ltd v South Tyneside Metropolitan Borough Council* [2001] R.P.C. 594.

[883] *National Deposit Friendly Society (Trustees) v Skegness UDC* [1959] A.C. 293, HL per at 311 Lord Keith.

[884] *National Deposit Friendly Society (Trustees) v Skegness UDC* [1959] A.C. 293.

[885] *National Deposit Friendly Society (Trustees) v Skegness UDC* [1959] A.C. 293.

[886] *National Deposit Friendly Society (Trustees) v Skegness UDC* [1957] 2 Q.B. 573.

[887] *Berry v St. Marylebone B.C.* [1958] Ch.406.

[888] *National Deposit Friendly Society (Trustees) v Skegness UDC* [1957] 2 Q.B. 573.

[889] *National Deposit Friendly Society (Trustees) v Skegness UDC* [1957] 2 Q.B. 573; *Independent Order of Oddfellows, etc. v Manchester Corporation* [1957] 1 W.L.R. 1059.

[890] *Skegness UDC v Derbyshire Miners' Welfare Committee* [1959] 2 All E.R. 258; *National Deposit Friendly Society (Trustees) v Skegness UDC* [1959] A.C. 293, per Lord Denning at 321.

[891] *National Deposit Friendly Society (Trustees) v Skegness UDC* [1959] A.C. 293, at 320.

[892] *Phonographic Performance Ltd v South Tyneside Metropolitan Borough Council* [2001] R.P.C. 594.

[893] *Royal College of Nursing v St Marylebone BC* [1958] 1 W.L.R. 95 at 99–100. Also see *Berry v St Marylebone BC* [1958] Ch. 406.

charitable or for the provision of social welfare. Although one of the main objects was undoubtedly the advancement of education, this was not enough; (2) A local authority is something quite different from a club or a society; (3) The objects of a local authority are neither charitable nor quasi-charitable in nature; (4) The function of a local authority is to carry out the administrative and governmental functions in respect of its area, to the extent that these have been devolved from national government; and (5) As to the "main objects" of a local authority, these include education, housing, social and welfare services, control of planning, maintenance of the roads (including pavements and lighting), licensing activities and the raising of money by way of business rates and council tax payments under the provisions of the Local Government Finance Acts 1988 and 1992.[894]

Other conditions, There are three other conditions which have to be satisfied 9–203 before an act is a permitted act:

(1) *The motives of the person playing the recording.* The sound recording must be played by a person who is acting primarily and directly for the benefit of the organisation and who is not acting with a view to gain.[895] This means that the hiring of a DJ or a karaoke operator who is paid a fee will take the playing outside the section.

(2) *Application of charges made for admission.* The proceeds of any charge for admission to the place where the recording is to be heard must be applied solely for the purposes of the organisation.[896]

(3) *Application of proceeds from the sale of any goods or services.* The proceeds from any goods or services sold by, or on behalf of, the organisation (i) in the place where the sound recording is heard, and (ii) on the occasion when the sound recording is played, must be applied solely for the purposes of the organisation.[897]

Comment. The exception applies whether the recording is performed as part of 9–204 the activities of the organisation, for example for the entertainment of those whose education, social welfare, etc. is being advanced, or it is performed for the benefit of the organisation, which would include a performance given to outsiders where the proceeds of the performance are applied solely for the purposes of the organisation. However, it is important to emphasise that these provisions only apply to the playing of sound recordings. They do not apply to any underlying musical or literary work. Thus the practical effect of this section is that organisations falling within this section will not have to seek a licence from Phonographic Performance Ltd ("PPL")[898], but they will still need a licence from the Performing Rights Society Ltd ("PRS"),[899] unless they are diligent in ensuring that they only play recordings of works which are out of copyright.

Repeal. Following a consultation launched in July 2008, in November 2009 the 9–205 Government proposed the repeal of this permitted act.[900] According to the Government, the exception did not appear to be working well and was very

---

[894] *Phonographic Performance Ltd v South Tyneside Metropolitan Borough Council* [2001] R.P.C. 29. Sound recordings were played at aerobics and keep-fit lessons organised by the defendant authority which were open to the public.

[895] CDPA 1988 s.67(2)(b). These, and the succeeding conditions of CDPA 1988 s.67(2), were introduced on amendment, revoking and replacing the previous condition that the proceeds of any charge for admission to the place where the recording is to be heard were to be applied solely for the purposes of the organisation.

[896] s.67(2)(b).

[897] s.67(2)(c).

[898] See para.27–66 below.

[899] See para.27–65 below.

[900] Government Response to the Consultation on changes to exemptions from public performance

complex. Particular difficulties mentioned were the fact that the exemption only applies to copyright in sound recordings and not to musical works so a licence is still required from PRS; disputes as to whether an organisation was within the scope of the permitted act[901]; the fact that the conditions for the operation of this exception differ from those applicable under s.72(1B)(a), which concerns free public showing or playing of broadcasts[902]; and complaints about delays in obtaining a licence, lack of transparency, the levels of fees and the lack of an independent, quick and affordable complaints mechanism when disagreements arose.[903] The Government's other reasons for proposing the repeal of the permitted act included the following: the fact that PPL and PRS had agreed to operate a simplified, joint licensing system for the "Third Sector", if possible with an affordable flat fee; the fact that PPL and PRS were working towards the establishment of a single code of practice and independent ombudsman to deal with Third Sector complaints; and the changes to the Copyright Tribunal rules, which are expected to improve access and reduce costs and delays.[904] The permitted act has now been repealed with effect from January 1, 2011.[905]

17. MISCELLANEOUS PROVISIONS: BROADCASTING

A. INCIDENTAL RECORDING FOR PURPOSES OF BROADCASTING

9–206   **Introduction.** Section 68 of the Act enables a person who is entitled to broadcast a work to make temporary copies of the work for that purpose.[906] In practice the process of broadcasting a work will often involve the making of temporary copies and thus the aim of this section is to allow such copies to be made.[907] In distinction to the other permitted acts, s.68 operates by conferring a licence on the user rather than by stating that copyright is not infringed.

9–207   **The Berne Convention.** This provision directly corresponds to art.11*bis* (3) of the Berne Convention.[908]

9–208   **The Information Society Directive.** Article 5(2)(d) of the Directive permits the making of ephemeral recordings of works by broadcasting organisations by means of their own facilities and for their own broadcasts.[909] No amendment was required to the 1988 Act on implementation of the Directive.

---

rights in sound recordings and performers' rights, November 2009. See *http://www.ipo.gov.uk* [Accessed October 29, 2010].

[901] For example, the Government stated that a dispute had arisen between a user and PPL as to whether the presence of commercial vending machines meant that the proceeds from the sale of any goods and services sold by or on behalf of the organisation were applied solely for the purposes of the organisation as required by s.67(2)(c).

[902] See para.9–218 et seq., below. The Government has repealed this exception so far as it concerns organisations not established or conducted for profit with effect from January 1, 2011. See para.9–235 below.

[903] Government Response to the Consultation on changes to exemptions from public performance rights in sound recordings and performers' rights, November 2009, p.6.

[904] Government Response to the Consultation on changes to exemptions from public performance rights in sound recordings and performers' rights, November 2009, p.11.

[905] See the Copyright, Designs and Patents Act 1988 (Amendment) Regulations 2010 (SI 2010/2694) reg.3(1)

[906] CDPA 1988 s.68. The 1956 Act contained a similar, but more limited provision: Copyright Act 1956 s.6(7). It might be thought that the person having the right to broadcast a work would usually have an implied licence to make copies of the work for that purpose. However, in *Bishop v Stevens* (1990) 72 D.L.R. (4th) 97 the Supreme Court of Canada refused to imply such a term.

[907] These rights may have been assigned to different people. As such, this provision can also be seen as providing a degree of security for the purchaser of the broadcasting rights.

[908] See also United States Copyright Act, 17 U.S.C., s.112.

[909] Note that recital 41 of the Information Society Directive 2001/29, states that "when applying the

The permitted acts. The exception applies in cases where by virtue of a licence   9–209
or assignment of copyright a person is authorised to broadcast (a) a literary,
dramatic or musical work, or an adaptation of such a work, (b) an artistic work,
or (c) a sound recording or film.[910] In such cases that person is to be treated as
licensed by the owner of the copyright in the work to do or authorise certain further acts for the purposes of the broadcast. In the case of a literary, dramatic or
musical work, or an adaptation of such a work, the further acts are the making of
a sound recording or film of the work or adaptation.[911] In the case of an artistic
work the acts are the taking of a photograph or the making of a film of the work.[912]
In the case of a sound recording or film, the acts are the making of a copy of it.[913]
The licence is, however, subject to two conditions, namely, that the recording,
film, photograph or copy in question (a) shall not be used for any other purpose,
and (b) shall be destroyed within 28 days of being first used for broadcasting the
work.[914] Where a recording, film, photograph or copy is made pursuant to the
licence conferred by this section, but is then used for some purpose other than the
broadcast in question, then when used for that other purpose, that article is to be
treated as an infringing copy.[915] Similarly, any such article which is not destroyed
within the specified 28-day period is also to be treated as an infringing copy for
all purposes thereafter.[916] Any person who then deals with such an article with
the requisite degree of knowledge will be liable for secondary infringement.[917]

In practice, broadcasters have found the requirement that they destroy copies
within 28 days to be unduly onerous,[918] in particular, because it would be much
cheaper for broadcasters if they were allowed to retain copies for repeated later
use. This led the operator of a subscription music service transmitted by satellite
to argue that it had a statutory right to make and retain copies for longer than 28
days by virtue of s.135C(1) of the 1988 Act.[919] This argument was rejected on the
grounds that it is clear both as a matter of plain language and from the legislative
history that s.135C(1) "is in nowise concerned with the making by the broadcaster
of copies of sound recordings or the protection of the broadcaster from infringement proceedings in respect of the making of copies".[920]

B. RECORDING FOR PURPOSES OF SUPERVISION OF BROADCASTS, ETC.

The Act makes provision enabling broadcast programmes and programmes   9–210
included in on-demand programme services to be recorded or copied for the
purposes of their supervision and control in a wide range of circumstances. These

---

exception or limitation in respect of ephemeral recordings made by broadcasting organisations it
is understood that a broadcaster's own facilities include those of a person acting on behalf of and
under the responsibility of the broadcasting organisation".

[910] CDPA 1988 s.68(1).
[911] s.68(2)(a).
[912] s.68(2)(b).
[913] s.68(2)(c).
[914] s.68(3).
[915] s.68(4)(a).
[916] s.68(4)(b). See also *Phonographic Performance Ltd v AEI Rediffusion Music Ltd* [1998] Ch. 187;
[1997] R.P.C. 729.
[917] s.27(6) and see Ch.8, above.
[918] It should be noted that the Whitford Committee saw "no absolute need to provide for destruction" (Whitford Committee: The Report of the Committee to Consider the Law on Copyright and
Designs, 1977 (Cmnd. 6732) para.683), but any provision which allowed copies to be retained
indefinitely would place the United Kingdom in breach of the Berne Convention.
[919] *Phonographic Performance Ltd v AEI Rediffusion Music Ltd* [1998] Ch. 187. Sections 135A–
135G were inserted into the 1988 Act by the Broadcasting Act 1990. These sections give
broadcasters a statutory licence to broadcast copyright sound recordings. See further, paras
28–25 et seq., below.
[920] *Phonographic Performance Ltd v AEI Rediffusion Music Ltd* [1998] Ch. 187, at 194.

provisions have frequently been amended to take account of regulatory changes.[921] In their present form they provide as follows.

First, copyright is not infringed by the making or use by the BBC, for the purpose of maintaining supervision and control over programmes broadcast by them or included in any on-demand programme service[922] provided by them, of recordings of those programmes.[923]

Secondly, copyright in a work is not infringed by anything done in pursuance of:

(a) specified statutory provisions,[924] which:

    (i) empower justices of the peace to authorise constables to require persons suspected of committing obscenity or public order offences in respect of programmes included in programme services to allow constables to copy such programmes[925];

    (ii) empower OFCOM when resolving fairness complaints to require recordings of programmes and transcripts of them to be provided, to require arrangements to be made for such recordings to be viewed or heard by complainants and to require copies of correspondence to be provided[926];

    (iii) require broadcasting bodies and the Welsh Authority to retain copies of television and sound programmes they broadcast for specified periods[927];

(b) a condition included in a licence granted under Pt I or Pt III of the Communications Act 2003 or Pt I or II of the Broadcasting Act 1996 by virtue of s.334(1) of the Communications Act 2003, which requires that copies of broadcasts be made and kept[928];

(c) a direction given by OFCOM in accordance with their power to demand scripts and recordings prior to broadcast following a failure by a licence holder to comply with a condition of the licence or with a direction given by them[929];

(d) OFCOM's powers to make and use recordings of programmes for the purpose of maintaining supervision of the programmes included in programme services[930]; or

---

[921] For the details, see the note to s.69 in Vol.2 A1.

[922] This term has the same meaning as in s.368A of the Communications Act 2003: see s.69(6). Pursuant to s.368A a service is an on-demand service if: (a) its principal purpose is the provision of programmes the form and content of which are comparable to the form and content of programmes normally included in television programme services; (b) access to it is on-demand; (c) there is a person who has editorial responsibility for it; (d) it is made available by that person for use by members of the public; and (e) that person is under the jurisdiction of the United Kingdom for the purposes of the Audiovisual Media Services Directive.

[923] CDPA 1988 s.69(1). The reference to on-demand services was inserted by the Audiovisual Media Services Regulations 2009 (SI 2009/2979) with effect from December 29, 2009. SI 2009/2979 implemented the amendments made to Directive 89/552 (the "Television Without Frontiers Directive") by Directive 2007/65 (the "Audiovisual Media Services Directive"). Amongst other things, the amendments required Member States to establish a regulatory system for on-demand programme services. This was effected by the addition of a new Pt 4A to the Communications Act 2003: see SI 2009/2979 reg.2. The Television Without Frontiers Directive and its amendments were subsequently codified in Directive 2010/13 ("the Audiovisual Media Services Directive") [2010] OJ L95/1.

[924] CDPA 1988 s.69(2)(a).

[925] Broadcasting Act 1990 s.167(1).

[926] Broadcasting Act 1996 s.115(4) and (6).

[927] Broadcast Act 1996 s.117; Communications Act 2003 Sch.12 para.20.

[928] s.69(2)(b).

[929] s.69(2)(c); and see Broadcasting Act 1990 s.109(2).

[930] Communications Act 2003 s.334(3).

(e) the powers of the appropriate regulatory authority[931] to require providers of on-demand programme services to supply information about possible contraventions of ss.368BA or 368D of the Communications Act 2003.[932]

Thirdly, copyright is not infringed by the use by OFCOM, in connection with the performance of any of their functions under the Broadcasting Act 1990, the Broadcasting Act 1996 or the Communications Act 2003, of (a) any recording, script or transcript which is provided to them under or by virtue of any provision of those Acts or (b) any existing material which is transferred to them by a scheme made under s.30 of the Communications Act 2003.[933] For this purpose, "existing material" means any recording, script or transcript which was provided to the Independent Television Commission or the Radio Authority in connection with their functions under the 1990 or 1996 Broadcasting Acts, or any recording or transcript which was provided to the Broadcasting Standards Commission under the complaints procedure of the Broadcasting Act 1996.[934]

Finally, copyright is not infringed by the use by an appropriate regulatory authority designated under s.368B of the Communications Act 2003 to regulate on-demand programme services in connection with the performance of their functions under that Act, of any recording, script or transcript which is provided to them under or by virtue of any provision of that Act.[935]

The Information Society Directive. Article 5(3)(d) of the Directive permits Member States to make an exception to the reproduction right for the purpose of "public security". Whether or not s.69 falls within this expression, it no doubt falls within the general spirit, if not the actual wording, of the general saving of art.9.   **9–211**

C. RECORDING FOR PURPOSES OF TIME-SHIFTING

The use of domestic videocassette recorders to make recordings of broadcasts was widespread before the 1998 Act, although unlawful as the law then stood.[936] Section 70 of the 1988 Act legitimised this state of affairs by permitting a recording of a broadcast to be made with a view to enabling it to be listened to or viewed at a later date, such that the copyright in the broadcast and any work included in it will not be infringed.[937]   **9–212**

The Information Society Directive. The Directive does not contain any provision expressly permitting such an exception but art.5(2)(b) allows Member States to make an exception to the reproduction and the distribution rights in respect of reproductions on any medium made by a natural person for private use and for ends that are neither directly nor indirectly commercial, on condition that the rightholders receive fair compensation. Apart from the requirement of compensa-   **9–213**

---

[931] Under Communications Act 2003 s.368O(1) and (3).
[932] CDPA 1988 s.69(2)(d). S.368BA requires the giving of advance notification to the authority before providing an on-demand programme service. S.368D imposes various duties on providers of such services.
[933] CDPA 1988 s.69(3).
[934] s.69(4).
[935] Again, this provision was added by SI 2009/2979 to give effect to the amendments made to Directive 89/552 (the "Television Without Frontiers Directive") by Directive 2007/65 (the "Audiovisual Media Services Directive"). The 1989 Directive and its amendments were codified in Directive 2010/13 [2010] OJ L95/1.
[936] In much the same way as the unlawful act of "home taping" of audio recordings was prevalent.
[937] The same result has been achieved in the United States through an application of the fair-use doctrine. See further, *Sony Corp of America v Universal City Studios* (1984) 464 U.S. 417.

tion, s.70 as enacted fell broadly within the terms of this permitted exception,[938] although some tightening up was required on implementation to limit the permitted act more clearly to private and non-commercial use. No amendment was made, however, to introduce provisions for compensation to rightholders, the Government taking the view that any compensation was likely to be nil or at least of very small amount, and would in any event be swallowed up by the transaction costs of administering any compensation scheme,[939] such that reliance could be placed on recital 35 of the Directive. This states that in "certain situations where the prejudice to the rightholder would be minimal, no obligation for payment may arise".

9–214 **The 1988 Act.** The Act now provides that it is not an infringement of the copyright in a broadcast or in any work included in it to make in domestic premises a recording for private and domestic use if it is solely for the purpose of enabling it to be viewed or listened to at a more convenient time.[940] It has been said that the purpose of the section is to cover the case of an individual who makes a copy of a broadcast and uses it solely for his private and domestic use.[941] It has also been held that the relevant use is that of the copier, so that if the copy is made by one person for the private and domestic use of another, even for the sole purpose of enabling that other person to view it later, this would not fall within the section.[942] But in the same case the court also appears to have conceded that it would not be an infringement for a neighbour to make a copy of a broadcast for a person's private and domestic use. The case was decided on the wording of the Act as it stood before amendment, which was not particularly clear,[943] but now that the provisions have been tightened, it is suggested that there is no reason in principle or on policy grounds why the making of a recording by A, in domestic premises, for the private and domestic use of B, for the sole purpose of enabling B to view or listen to it at a more convenient time, should not fall squarely within the terms of the permitted act. In a case where an individual sets up a business in his own home of making and selling recordings to others, this activity will now be caught by the provisions considered in the next paragraph.

9–215 **Subsequent dealings.** As enacted, recordings made in this way did not become infringing copies under the Act if subsequently dealt with. There was therefore nothing to stop private individuals selling such original copies, provided they had been made in accordance with s.70 and provided also that such acts did not constitute an issue to the public.[944] This possibility was inconsistent with the Directive and so the Act has now been amended to provide that where such a copy is subsequently dealt with it is to be treated as an infringing copy for the purposes

---

[938] This is also the Government's view. See the Transposition Note on implementation of the Directive by the Copyright and Related Rights Regulations 2003 (SI 2003/2498).

[939] See the Analysis of Responses and Government Conclusions on the Patent Office's Consultation Paper of August 7, 2002, para.5.16.

[940] CDPA 1988 s.70(1). Or, apparently, a more convenient place: *Hansard*, HL Vol.501, col.267. The restriction to require the recording to be made in domestic premises was added by amendment on implementation of the Information Society Directive 2001/29. Had this amendment then been in force, it would have prevented any argument by the defendant in *Sony Music Entertainment (UK) Ltd v Easyinternetcafé Ltd* [2003] EWHC 62 (Ch); [2003] F.S.R. 48, that its activities fell within the section. In that case, members of the public were able to download music files from the internet onto the server at the defendant's internet café. The defence failed in any event. See below.

[941] *Sony Music Entertainment (UK) Ltd v Easyinternetcafé Ltd* [2003] EWHC 62; [2003] F.S.R. 48.

[942] *Sony Music Entertainment (UK) Ltd v Easyinternetcafé Ltd* [2003] EWHC 62. The facts were rather extreme, but this seems to be the effect of the judgment.

[943] The section was added at a late stage of the Bill's passage through Parliament, and may not have received the attention it deserved.

[944] See CDPA 1988 s.18.

of that dealing and, if that dealing itself infringes copyright, as an infringing copy for all subsequent purposes.[945]

D. PHOTOGRAPHS OF BROADCASTS

While the 1988 Act provides that in relation to a broadcast, copying includes making a photograph of any image forming part of the broadcast,[946] s.71 of the Act permits the taking of such photographs for private and domestic purposes. As with the time-shifting defence, this permitted act required tightening to make it comply with the Information Society Directive.[947] Thus, the Act now provides that the making in domestic premises for private and domestic purposes of a photograph[948] of the whole or any part of an image forming part of a broadcast, or a copy of such a photograph, does not infringe any copyright in the broadcast or in any film included in it.[949] It should be noted that this exception does not cover the reproduction of an artistic work included in the broadcast. Thus the taking a photograph of a broadcast image which includes an artistic work will infringe copyright in the artistic work, unless the photographer can bring himself within one of the other exceptions, the most likely being incidental inclusion or one of the fair dealing provisions.[950]

9–216

Subsequent dealings. As with the permitted act of time-shifting, the Act has been amended to provide that, in the event of subsequent dealings with such copies, these become infringing copies.[951]

9–217

E. FREE PUBLIC SHOWING OR PLAYING OF BROADCAST

As enacted, s.72 of the 1988 Act provided that the showing or playing of a broadcast in public did not amount to an infringement of the broadcast or of any sound recording or film included in it, if it was not to a paying audience.[952] The permitted act was controversial[953] but in any event was subject to substantial amendment on implementation of the Information Society Directive 2001/29. It has been partially repealed with effect from January 1, 2011.[954]

9–218

The Information Society Directive. The application of the Information Society Directive and the Rental and Related Rights Directive in relation to the public performance of protected subject matter, and of sound recordings in particular, has already been considered in relation to s.67.[955] Much the same considerations apply to s.72, with the result that the section has been amended to cut down its provisions drastically as they apply to the free playing of broadcast sound record-

9–219

---

[945] s.70(2). For this purpose, "dealt with" means sold or let for hire, offered or exposed for sale or hire or communicated to the public": s.70(3).

[946] CDPA 1988 s.17(4). See further, para.7–83, above.

[947] i.e. so that it fell within the provisions of Information Society Directive, 2001/29 art.5(2)(b).

[948] For the definition of "photograph," see. s.4(2) and see para.3–59, above.

[949] s.71.

[950] See paras 9–23 et seq. above.

[951] CDPA 1988 ss.71(2), (3).

[952] The 1956 Act ss.14(8), 14A(9) contained broadly equivalent provisions.

[953] In particular, because of the way the provision permitted the free public performance of broadcast sound recordings in shops, pubs and other places to which the public had access without paying. Separate proceedings have been brought against the United Kingdom by the Commission and Phonographic Performance Ltd alleging a failure to implement the Rental and Related Rights Directive 92/100. See *Phonographic Performance Ltd v Department of Trade and Industry* [2004] EWHC 1795 (Ch); [2004] 1 W.L.R. 2893; [2005] R.P.C. 8 The position is now different following implementation of the Information Society Directive.

[954] See below, para.9–225.

[955] See para.9–201, above.

ings, with the aim of making the permitted act compliant with the three-step test so far as concerns sound recordings.

9–220   The 1988 Act as amended: summary. The basic position is that where a broadcast is without licence shown or played in public to an audience who have not paid for admission to the place where the broadcast is to be seen or heard, this will not infringe any copyright in (a) the broadcast, or (b) any film included in it.[956] As to any copyright in any sound recordings included in the broadcast, the position depends on the nature of the sound recording. Sound recordings have been divided into two categories, namely "excepted" sound recordings and all other sound recordings (which latter category will be referred to here as "non-excepted" sound recordings). As will be seen, virtually all commercially released sound recordings are excepted sound recordings. Subject to two exceptions, the showing or playing of the broadcast will infringe any copyright in an excepted recording[957] but the copyright in any non-excepted sound recording will not be infringed.[958] The exceptional cases in which the showing or playing will not infringe the copyright in an excepted sound recording (the "narrower" permitted acts) are (a) where the playing or showing of the broadcast forms part of the activities of an organisation that is not established or conducted for profit and (b) where the playing or showing of the broadcast is necessary for the purposes of the repair or demonstration of television or radio equipment.[959] These provisions are discussed in detail below.

It is irrelevant for the present purposes if the copyright in the sound recording or film was infringed by the original broadcast, although the fact that the sound recording or film was heard or seen in public by the reception of the broadcast is to be taken into account in assessing the damages for that infringement.[960]

Finally, this exception only applies to the showing and playing of the broadcast and does not extend to any infringing copying which may take place in the course of the showing and playing.[961]

The overall effect of this section is that public houses, cafés, shops and the like need one or more licences to have a television or radio playing for the benefit of customers unless the programme being broadcast does not include any copyright literary, dramatic or musical works[962] or any commercially released sound recordings (i.e. excepted recordings). Thus, for example, it may be possible to show a broadcast sports event by virtue of this exception, although today such programmes usually contain works of the above kinds.[963] It will not be possible under this section to play a radio station which broadcasts popular music,[964] so that a licence from the Performing Rights Society Ltd[965] will be required, nor,

---

[956] CDPA 1988 s.72(1).

[957] s.72(1).

[958] s.72(1) and s.19(3). *Football Association Premier League v QC Leisure* [2009] EWHC 411 (Ch); [2008] F.S.R. 32; [2008] 3 C.M.L.R. 12.

[959] s.72(1B).

[960] s.72(4).

[961] *Football Association Premier League v QC Leisure* [2008] EWHC 1411 (Ch); [2008] F.S.R. 32 at paras 280 to 282 (on the facts there was no copying of a substantial part).

[962] In *Football Association Premier League v QC Leisure* [2008] EWHC 1411 (Ch) at paras 269 to 279, Kitchin J. rejected an argument that if the showing or playing of the broadcast was permitted this prevented any infringement of underlying literary, musical or artistic works.

[963] See, e.g. *Football Association Premier League v QC Leisure* [2008] EWHC 1411 (Ch). See also CDPA 1988 s.31(3) and see para.9–67, above.

[964] cf. *Performing Rights Society Ltd v Camelo* [1936] 3 All E.R. 557.

[965] As to which, see para.27–65, below.

save where one of the narrower permitted acts applies, will it be possible to do so without a licence from Phonographic Performance Ltd.[966]

Excepted sound recordings and the wider permitted act. The underlying aim   **9–221**
is to provide that the public performance by means of broadcasts of ordinary or commercially released sound recordings will require a licence except in cases which fall within the narrower permitted acts. Accordingly, an "excepted sound recording" is defined as a sound recording (a) whose author is not the author of the broadcast in which it is included, and (b) which is a recording of music with or without words spoken or sung.[967] As to (a), the author of a sound recording is the person who undertakes the arrangements necessary for the making of the work ("the producer")[968] and the author of a broadcast is the person who makes the broadcast.[969] Thus, the playing of sound recordings, of whatever kind, produced by the broadcaster itself will fall within the wider permitted act. Otherwise, only if the recording is of the spoken word alone, or of other sounds which do not include any music, can its playing fall within the wider permitted acts. Thus, virtually all commercially released sound recordings will fall outside the wider permitted act.

The narrower permitted acts. A large swathe of sound recordings having been   **9–222**
removed from the ambit of the wider permitted act, the playing of such broadcast recordings is brought back within the ambit of the narrower permitted act in two special situations. In relation to both situations, however, there remains the requirement that the audience should not have paid for admission to the place where the broadcast is to be seen or heard. The first situation is where the playing or showing of the broadcast forms part of the activities of an organisation that is not established or conducted for profit.[970] The nature of such an organisation has already been considered.[971] The second is where the playing or showing of the broadcast is necessary for the purposes of (i) repairing equipment for the reception of broadcasts; (ii) demonstrating that a repair to such equipment has been carried out; or (iii) demonstrating such equipment which is being sold or let for hire or offered or exposed for sale or hire.[972] So the playing of sound recordings in TV or radio repair, retail or hire shops will in general fall within the exception.[973] The intention of both these exceptions is no doubt that, when coupled with the other requirements of the section, they will comply with the three-step test. The second exception appears to be derived from art.5(3)(l) of the Information Society Directive, which permits an exception to be made to the rights prescribed by that Directive in the case of use in connection with the demonstration or repair of equipment. What is relevant for the purposes of s.72,

---

[966] As to which, see para.27–66, below. But see below, as to the notification of such licences.
[967] CDPA 1988 s.72(1A). For an example of the application of this provision, see *Football Association Premier League v QC Leisure* [2008] EWHC 1411 (Ch); [2008] F.S.R. 32 at para.268 (obiter).
[968] ss.9(2)(aa), 178. See para.4–42, above.
[969] s.9(2)(b). See para.4–62, above.
[970] CDPA 1988 s.72(1B)(a).
[971] See para.9–202, above. It should be emphasised that for the purposes of s.72(1B)(a) in contrast to s.67, there is no requirement to show that the organisation's objects are charitable or otherwise concerned with the advancement of religion, education or social welfare. In *Football Association Premier League v QC Leisure* [2008] EWHC 1411 (Ch); [2008] F.S.R. 32 at para.268 the Court stated (obiter) that the defence of s.72(1B) could not be invoked where the playing or showing of the broadcast in public was carried out by pubs which were established and conducted for profit.
[972] s.72(1B)(b).
[973] In *Football Association Premier League v QC Leisure* [2008] EWHC 1411 (Ch) at paras 269 to 279, Kitchin J. rejected an argument that if the showing or playing of a sound recording was permitted under the narrower permitted act this prevented any infringement of an "underlying" musical work.

however, are the exceptions permitted by the Rental and Related Rights Directive, not those permitted by the Information Society Directive. Presumably the Government's thinking was that the exception permitted by art.5(3)(l) must be an example of a case which satisfies the three-step test.[974]

9–223   **Payment for admission.** The Act contains further provision as to the circumstances in which persons are to be treated as having paid for admission. Thus the Act rather cumbersomely provides that an audience is to be treated as having paid for admission to a place if they have paid for admission to a place of which that place forms part.[975] They are also to be treated as having paid for admission to a place if goods or services are supplied at that place (or a place of which it forms part) (a) at prices which are substantially attributable to the facilities afforded for seeing or hearing the broadcast, or (b) at prices exceeding those usually charged there and which are partly attributable to those facilities.[976] On the other hand, persons admitted as residents or inmates of a place are not, for this purpose, to be regarded as having paid for admission to that place,[977] nor are persons admitted as members of a club or society where the payment is only for membership of the club or society and the provision of facilities for seeing or hearing broadcasts is only incidental to the main purposes of the club or society.[978]

9–224   **Notification of licences for excepted recordings.** Given that the circumstances in which broadcasts are heard in commercial situations will vary considerably, and that a public showing may not result from a conscious or deliberate decision (as may be the case where sound recordings are played in public by way of CDs, tapes and the like), the Government introduced a new mechanism for regulating the licensing of the public performance of broadcast sound recordings. Sections 128A and 128B require those collectively licensing the performance of sound recordings via broadcasts to notify the proposed licensing arrangements to the Secretary of State. He will then consider a number of matters, including the extent to which the licensing body has consulted affected parties and whether its proposals take account of factors such as the degree to which potential licensees will be using broadcasts containing recorded music. He then has the power to refer the proposals to the Copyright Tribunal for a determination of whether the arrangements are reasonable.[979] Such a reference has been made and is considered elsewhere.[980]

9–225   **Repeal.** The Government has repealed the narrower permitted act so far as it extends to the activities of organisations not established or conducted for profit together with ss.128A and 128B.[981] The partial repeal of the narrower permitted act will occur in tandem with the repeal of s.67 of the 1988 Act which is

---

[974] Even though the article, as are all the permitted exceptions, is further qualified by the requirement of art.5(5) that the exception conform to the three-step test.

[975] CDPA 1988 s.72(2)(a).

[976] s.72(2)(b).

[977] s.72(3)(a).

[978] s.72(3)(b).

[979] See the Government Conclusions on the Patent Office's Consultation Paper of August 7, 2002, paras 5.20, 5.21. It was expected by the Government that the possibility for referral by this route would largely take the place of referral of proposed licensing arrangements by users to the Tribunal. The Government also concluded that, for the time being at least, no action should be taken in relation to public performance of musical works via broadcasts (which is outside the scope of CDPA 1988 s.72 and was therefore already licensable), but would continue to monitor this aspect: see the Government's conclusion on the Consultation Paper, para.5.22. As to CDPA 1988 ss.128A and 128B, see further paras 28–65 et seq., below.

[980] See below, paras 28–72 et seq.

[981] See the Copyright, Designs and Patents Acts 1988 (Amendment) Regulations 2010 (SI 2010/2694) regs 4(1) and 6. The repeals take effect on January 1, 2011. For background, see the

considered above.[982] The Government's reasons for repealing ss.128A and 128B are considered below.[983]

F. RECEPTION AND RETRANSMISSION OF WIRELESS BROADCAST BY CABLE

Overview. Section 73 of the 1988 Act contains an exception to allow for the reception and immediate retransmission by cable of a wireless broadcast.[984] The original provisions of the 1988 Act dealing with this matter were amended to take into account the changes introduced by the Broadcasting Acts 1990 and 1996.[985] Further amendments were necessary to take account of the changed treatment of broadcasts and cable programme services following implementation of the Information Society Directive. The provisions take effect partly by way of permitted act and partly by way of compulsory licence. The former aspect is dealt with below; the latter aspect is dealt with in detail elsewhere.[986]

9–226

Background. With the passing of the 1956 Act, it became an infringement of copyright in a literary, dramatic, musical or artistic work, or a sound recording or film, to broadcast a work by wireless means or by cable.[987] The 1956 Act also conferred copyright protection on wireless broadcasts themselves.[988] Thereafter difficult questions arose concerning the potential liability of a person who retransmitted a wireless broadcast by including it in a cable broadcast. Although authors and film makers were given a general right to control the cable broadcasting of their works, under s.40(3) of the 1956 Act they were deemed to have freely licensed the cable retransmission of BBC and IBA wireless broadcasts which included their material. Wireless broadcasters also had no right to control further cable transmission of their broadcasts. Consequently, cable operators were able to transmit domestic wireless broadcasts free of charge. Foreign broadcasts were subject to the jurisdiction of the Performing Rights Tribunal so that content owners' claims covered only the additional audience over and above that paid for by the foreign broadcaster.[989]

9–227

The Whitford Committee recommended that wireless broadcasting organisations be granted a cable transmission right, but also that s.40(3) should be extended to cover wireless broadcasts by the BBC or IBA, provided the cable retransmission was of the whole broadcast, was simultaneous and was confined to the area in which the broadcast was intended to be received.[990] Effectively, cable retransmission in the same area was to remain free. However, the Whitford Committee also recommended that the provisions relating to the cable retransmission

---

Government response to the consultation on changes to exemptions from public performance rights in sound recordings and performers' rights at *http://www.ipo.gov.uk* [Accessed October 25, 2010].

[982] para.9–205.

[983] See below, para.28–67.

[984] As did the Copyright Act 1956 s.40.

[985] Broadcasting Act 1996 (c.55) s.138, Sch.9 para.1.

[986] See paras 28–48 et seq., below.

[987] Copyright Act 1956 ss.2(5)(d), 3(5)(c), 2(5)(e) and 3(5)(d). That Act distinguished between broadcasts, which were defined to mean transmissions by wireless telegraphy (s.48(2)), and transmissions by means of a "cable programme service" or, previously, by means of a "diffusion service". See paras 3–86, 3–88 and 7–113, above. Unless otherwise clear from the context, the present discussion uses the expression "broadcast" to include both forms of transmission.

[988] Copyright Act 1956 s.14.

[989] s.28.

[990] The Report of the Committee to Consider the Law on Copyright and Designs, 1977 (Cmnd. 6732) para.446. These recommendations were subsequently adopted by the Government: Green Paper 1981 (Cm. 8302), pp.27–32.

of foreign broadcasts be abandoned.[991] The Cable and Broadcasting Act 1984 gave effect to many of these recommendations.

The 1988 Act originally provided two exceptions as regards cable retransmission, permitting retransmissions under the "must carry" provisions of the Cable and Broadcasting Act 1984 and retransmission within the original broadcast area (the "service area" exception). These exceptions were available both in relation to an action for infringement brought by the owner of the copyright in the wireless broadcast itself and to an action brought by the owners of copyright in works included in the wireless broadcast. However, as regards consent to cable retransmission of the broadcast itself (as opposed to consent to retransmit copyright works included in the broadcast) the service area defence did not apply to cable retransmission of either satellite or encrypted transmissions.

The "must carry" exception was repealed by the Broadcasting Act 1990.[992] This was because cable licences under that Act were no longer subject to "must carry" obligations. The service area exception was maintained. The Broadcasting Act 1996 reimposed "must carry" requirements and hence a "must carry" exception, albeit in a rather different form, was reintroduced. The opportunity was also taken to reform the service area exception.

9–228   **Justification.** A number of countries besides the United Kingdom have made provision to deal with the retransmission of broadcasts by cable.[993] However, the question of whether cable operators should have a right to retransmit broadcasts and the question of whether this should take effect by way of outright exception or by way of compulsory licence has proved controversial.[994] Nevertheless, it is possible to identify at least three reasons why a retransmission right is justifiable in certain circumstances.

First, it can be argued that cable programmes offer better quality services, particularly in areas where reception is poor (so called "shadow zones") and in areas where there are restrictions on the use of individual outdoor aerials.[995] In such cases there would seem to be a general public interest in ensuring that cable services are readily available at an affordable rate. Requiring cable operators to negotiate with both broadcasters and the owners of works included in the broadcasts might impose extraordinarily high transaction costs upon the cable operator, with the result that such services would not be economically viable.

Secondly, it can be argued that such retransmissions do not harm the interests of traditional broadcasters. Indeed, in the case of broadcasters whose income depends upon advertising revenue, such retransmission may even increase profits by allowing the broadcaster to charge more for advertising time, as the advertisements will reach a larger audience. Moreover, in relation to the owners of works

---

[991] The Report of the Committee to Consider the Law on Copyright and Designs, 1977 (Cmnd. 6732) paras 446, 448, 468(v).

[992] Broadcasting Act 1990 s.203(3), Sch.21.

[993] See further, Gendreau, *The Retransmission Right: Copyright and the Rediffusion of Works by Cable* (Oxford: ESC, 1990). A right to retransmit works is recognised under the Berne Convention (art.11bis(1)(ii)), but art.11bis(2) provides, "It shall be a matter for legislation in the countries of the Union to determine the conditions under which the rights mentioned in the previous paragraph [Broadcasting and Related Rights] may be exercised .   .   . but they shall not in any circumstances be prejudicial to the moral rights of the author, nor his right to obtain equitable remuneration". As regards the right to equitable remuneration in relation to retransmission within the original broadcast area (which takes effect by way of exception rather than by way of compulsory licence), it has been said that such remuneration will be obtained from the original broadcaster who will pay fees in respect of the whole audience within that area. See further, the Report of the Committee to Consider the Law on Copyright and Designs, 1977 (Cmnd. 6732) para.430–1.

[994] See the previous note.

[995] See further, Whitford Committee: The Report of the Committee to Consider the Law on Copyright and Designs, 1977 (Cmnd. 6732) para.422.

included in the broadcast, it is possible to view the act of simultaneous retrans-mission as part of the original broadcast and thus not an activity for which they are entitled to claim additional revenue. In particular, it is said that when negotiat-ing a licence with a broadcaster the content owner will assume universal cover-age within the broadcast area and will fix a price accordingly. From this perspec-tive, it could even be said that granting content owners the right to claim additional revenue from cable operators would be unjust, in that the content own-ers would then be paid twice for what is essentially a single use of their work.[996]

Thirdly, it must be noted that in certain circumstances the operators of cable programme services are compelled by a "must carry" obligation to retransmit broadcasts as part of their services. Where cable operators are under such an obligation it might seem unfair to force them to pay for carrying material that they might well have preferred to omit. Moreover, allowing content owners to prevent their works from being retransmitted unless the cable operator agrees to pay royalties might prove to be self-defeating, in that the cable operator might then be able to avoid the "must carry" obligation simply by refusing to pay.

On the other hand, it is possible to identify a number of situations in which the above arguments either do not apply or in which there are other, overriding, policy considerations. For example, allowing cable retransmission of subscrip-tion or pay-per-view broadcasts would have very serious financial repercussions for the operators of such services. Similarly, the above justifications look much less convincing in a case where a cable operator records a transmission with a view to broadcasting it in a modified form at a later date (for example, after hav-ing substituted different advertisements). In such a case the cable operator may well be intending to compete directly with the broadcaster and thus to include such activities within the retransmission right might be to allow the cable opera-tor to make a profit at the broadcaster's expense. Finally, there would seem to be little justification in allowing a cable operator to retransmit works outside the broadcast's normal reception area. Such retransmissions would seem to be particularly unfair on the owners of works included in the broadcasts, as they are more directly deprived of an opportunity to charge for the use of their works.   **9–229**

For these reasons the Act generally confines the retransmission right to the im-mediate retransmission of broadcasts within their normal area of reception. Such a restriction has not proved possible, however, in relation to cable operators operating under a "must carry" obligation who retransmit a broadcast outside of its normal area of reception. In these cases the Act provides that there is still no infringement of copyright in the broadcast, but in relation to works included in the broadcast, the Act provides that these are to be treated as licensed by the owner, subject to the payment of a reasonable royalty by the *broadcaster*. The latter provisions thus take effect by way of compulsory licence and are dealt with in detail elsewhere.[997]

The permitted acts. As the Act now stands, it makes provision for cases where a wireless broadcast[998] is made from a place in the United Kingdom and is received and immediately retransmitted by cable.[999] In such cases the Act provides that copyright is not infringed in two distinct circumstances: **9–230**

---

[996] It should be noted that the Copyright Tribunal has a duty to ensure that copyright owners are not rewarded twice over for the transmission of their works: CDPA 1988 s.134.

[997] See paras 28–48 et seq., below.

[998] A "wireless broadcast" is defined as a broadcast by means of wireless telegraphy: CDPA 1988 s.178, where "wireless telegraphy" is also defined.

[999] s.73(1). The expression "retransmission by cable" is not defined, save that it is to include the transmission of microwave energy between terrestrial fixed points: s.178. Such a transmission is excluded from the definition of wireless telegraphy and thus wireless broadcasts: s.178.

(1) First, the Act provides that copyright in the broadcast, and copyright in any work included in the broadcast, is not infringed if and to the extent that the broadcast is made for reception in the area in which it is retransmitted by cable and forms part of a qualifying service.[1000] "Qualifying service" here means a regional or national Channel 3 service, Channel 4, Channel 5, S4C, the public teletext service, S4C Digital, and the television broadcasting and teletext services of the BBC.[1001] All other services fall outside the operation of this section.[1002]

(2) Secondly, the Act makes provision to deal with the position of cable operators under a "must carry" obligation. To the extent that such an obligation results in works being retransmitted in the original broadcast area, the above provisions apply.[1003] Where a cable operator retransmits a broadcast outside the original broadcast area the Act draws a distinction between the broadcast and any works included in the broadcast. The Act provides that copyright in the broadcast will not be infringed, just as if the retransmission had been confined to the original reception area.[1004] However, any work included in the broadcast is to be treated as licensed by the owner of copyright in the work, subject to the payment of a reasonable royalty.[1005] Thus, as noted above, this later provision takes effect by way of compulsory licence and, accordingly, is dealt with in detail elsewhere.[1006]

9–231   **Retransmission of broadcasts made in other EEA States.** It is important to emphasise that the provisions considered above only apply to cable retransmission of broadcasts made from a place in the United Kingdom.[1007] They do not apply to the retransmission of foreign broadcasts. However, the Cable and Satellite Broadcasting Directive[1008] makes provision so as to facilitate the retransmission of broadcasts made in another EEA Member State. In brief, content owners retain their copyright, but they can only exercise their rights through a collecting society. Moreover, where the content owner has not transferred the management of his rights to a collecting society, the collecting society which manages rights of the same category shall be deemed to be mandated to manage his rights.[1009] This provision was implemented in the United Kingdom by s.144A of the 1988 Act.[1010] These provisions do not, however, affect broadcasters, who retain full control over copyright in their broadcasts and in any work included in the

---

[1000] ss.73(2)(b), 73(3), although where the making of the broadcast was an infringement of the copyright in the work, the fact that the broadcast was retransmitted by cable is to be taken into account in assessing the damages for that infringement: s.178. Note that the Secretary of State is given extensive powers to vary the operation of this subsection (s.73(9)), and may instead order that a compulsory licence is to be available in relation to works which currently fall within this subsection (s.73(10)). The Secretary of State also has power to make appropriate transitional provisions (s.73(11)).

[1001] s.73(6).

[1002] But note that the Secretary of State may by order add any service to, or remove any service from, the definition of "qualifying service" (s.73(8)), and is given further power to make appropriate transitional provisions: s.73(11).

[1003] ss.73(2)(a), (7).

[1004] s.73(2)(a).

[1005] s.73(4).

[1006] See paras 28–48 et seq., below.

[1007] CDPA 1988 s.73(1).

[1008] Council Directive 93/83 on the co-ordination of certain rules concerning copyright and rights related to copyright applicable to satellite broadcasting and cable retransmission; [1993] OJ L248/15.

[1009] Council Directive 93/83 art.9.

[1010] This is considered in detail at paras 28–58 et seq., below.

broadcast which they happen to own.[1011] Thus the operator of a retransmission service will normally have to enter into direct negotiations with the broadcaster in order to get permission to retransmit a foreign broadcast.

G. PROVISION OF MODIFIED COPIES OF BROADCAST

Section 74 of the Act makes provision for the supply of specially modified copies of broadcasts for people who are disabled in some way.[1012] Thus a designated body may make, and issue or lend to the public, copies of television broadcasts which are sub-titled or otherwise modified to meet the special needs of people who are deaf or hard of hearing, or who are otherwise physically or mentally handicapped, without infringing any copyright in the broadcasts or in any work included in them.[1013] For this purpose "designated body" means a body designated by Order of the Secretary of State, who is not to designate a body unless satisfied that it is not established or conducted for profit.[1014] This provision does not apply, however, if, or to the extent that, there is a certified licensing scheme in operation providing for the grant of licences.[1015]

9–232

The Information Society Directive. Articles 5(3)(b) and 4 of the Directive permit Member States to make an exception to the reproduction, distribution and communication to the public rights, in the case of uses, for the benefit of people with a disability, which are directly related to the disability and of a non-commercial nature, to the extent required by the specific disability.[1016] The permitted act of s.74 falls squarely within this.

9–233

H. RECORDING FOR ARCHIVAL PURPOSES

Section 75 of the Act makes provision enabling broadcasts to be recorded for archival purposes.[1017] This section should be read alongside those provisions relating to libraries and archives which are aimed at preserving important works for the nation.[1018] Thus a recording of a broadcast of a designated class,[1019] or a copy of such a recording, may be made for the purpose of being placed in an archive maintained by a designated body without thereby infringing any copyright in the broadcast or in any work included in it.[1020] "Designated" means designated by Order of the Secretary of State, and a body is not to be designated unless it is not established or conducted for profit.[1021]

9–234

The Information Society Directive. Article 5(2)(b) of the Directive permits

9–235

[1011] CDPA 1988 s.144A(6).

[1012] As to the ability to make copies for visually impaired persons, see paras 9–68 et seq., above.

[1013] CDPA 1988 s.74(1).

[1014] s.74(2). The National Sub-titling Library for Deaf People has been designated for this purpose: Copyright (Sub-titling of Broadcasts and Cable Programmes) (Designated Body) Order 1989 (SI 1989/1013). See Vol.2 A4.iii.

[1015] s.74(4). As to such licensing schemes, see Ch.28, below, and, in particular, as to certification, para.28–62, below.

[1016] See now also the provisions of the United Nations Convention on the Rights of Persons with Disabilities mentioned above, para.9–70.

[1017] CDPA 1988 s.75.

[1018] In particular, see ss.42 and 44. See further para.9–122 and para.9–139, above.

[1019] All broadcasts other than encrypted transmissions have been designated for this purpose: The Copyright (Recording for Archives of Designated Class of Broadcasting and Cable Programmes) (Designated Bodies) Order 1993 (SI 1993/74), see Vol.2 A4.xii.

[1020] s.75(1).

[1021] Eight bodies have so far been designated: The British Film Institute, The British Library, The British Medical Association, The British Music Information Centre, The Imperial War Museum, The Music Performance Research Centre, The National Library of Wales and the Scottish Film Council: The Copyright (Recording for Archives of Designated Class of Broadcasting and Cable Programmes) (Designated Bodies) Order 1993 (SI 1993/74). See Vol.2 A4.xii.

Member States to make an exception to the reproduction right in respect of specific acts of reproduction made by publicly accessible archives, which are not for direct or indirect economic or commercial advantage. Section 75 appears to fall squarely within this permitted exception.

Chapter Ten

CROWN RIGHTS, PARLIAMENTARY RIGHTS AND THE RIGHTS OF INTERNATIONAL ORGANISATIONS

1. CROWN RIGHTS

A. Introduction

Introduction. In the absence of special provision, the Crown, like any other legal   **10–01**
person, would no doubt have become entitled to the copyright in many works
under the general rules. Historically, however, the Crown has been entitled under
the royal prerogative to a special form of copyright in a limited number of types
of work. Where this prerogative copyright subsists, the normal rules as to subsistence, title and term do not apply. At the present date, prerogative copyright is
probably of practical importance only to the publishers of copies of the King
James translation of the Bible and the Book of Common Prayer. As well as
preserving prerogative copyright, the 1988 Act contains significant modifications
to the general rules so far as they apply to works created by Her Majesty, her officers and her servants. The effect of these modifications is that copyright subsists
in certain circumstances where it would not otherwise subsist and that copyright
vests in the Crown in certain circumstances where it would otherwise not do so.
Such copyright is called "Crown copyright". With these provisions go special
rules as to the term of Crown copyright in literary, dramatic, musical and artistic
works. The overall effect is to place the Crown in a uniquely privileged position
so far as copyright is concerned.

Rights other than copyright. The limited moral rights in works in which Crown   **10–02**
copyright subsists are dealt with below.[1] The Crown is a qualifying person for the
purposes of design right and rights in semiconductor topographies.[2] The provisions of the 1988 Act dealing with Crown use of designs are dealt with elsewhere.[3]

---

[1] See para.10–76.
[2] CDPA 1988 s.217(2). For the significance of this, see paras 13–85 and 14–08 et seq., below.
[3] See paras 13–34 et seq., below.

The Crown has rights in databases.[4] The circumstances in which the Crown may become entitled to any of the other rights covered in this Work are not the subject of special provision in the 1988 Act.

B. PREROGATIVE COPYRIGHT

10–03   **History.** Printing was originally considered to be a matter of State and accordingly the Crown claimed the right by proclamations, prohibitions, charters of privilege and finally by decrees of Star Chamber, to authorise publications of all types.[5] This right was assumed by Parliament on the abolition of Star Chamber in 1640 but reverted to the Crown at the Restoration. Although the Crown finally lost this right in the 1690s, it nevertheless continued to claim the exclusive right to print and publish a limited number of categories of work. This right resembles copyright in that it is a right to print and publish and to license others to print and publish works of the kinds to which it extends.[6] On the other hand, no specific requirements need to be satisfied before the right subsists in respect of a particular work. Furthermore, the right lasts for an unlimited period and is probably not capable of being lost by non-use.[7] Prerogative copyright was preserved in its entirety by the 1911[8] and 1956 Acts[9] and (except in relation to Acts, Measures and Bills) the 1988 Act.[10] In the following paragraphs, the extent to which the right exists is considered separately in respect of each of the more important categories of work in which it has been claimed to exist.

10–04   **Bibles and prayer books.**[11] The Queen's Printers and the Universities of Oxford and Cambridge hold patents from the Crown under the royal prerogative for the printing of the Bible and other books containing the rites and ceremonies of the Church of England.[12] As long ago as 1828 Lord Lyndhurst L.C. was able to state in relation to a patent extending to Bibles, New Testaments, Psalm Books, the Book of Common Prayer, the Confessions of Faith and the greater and lesser Catechisms that the right of the Crown to grant such patents was a point not admitting of doubt or controversy.[13] A variety of reasons have been offered for the existence of this prerogative power. First, the fact that the Authorised Version of the Bible was commissioned by James I; secondly, the fact that the monarch is head of the Church of England; and thirdly the fact that the monarch, as chief executive officer of the Government, has a duty to superintend the publication of

---

[4] See Ch.18.

[5] See paras 2–09 et seq., above.

[6] *Universities of Oxford and Cambridge v Eyre & Spottiswoode Ltd* [1964] 1 Ch. 736, 748.

[7] There is no generally accepted principle that a prerogative power may be lost by non-use: Maitland, *Constitutional History of England* (1908) p.418; De Smith and Brazier, *Constitutional and Administrative Law*, 8th edn, p.136. See also the discussion in *Attorney-General for New South Wales v Butterworth & Co (Australia) Ltd* (1938) 38 S.R. (N.S.W.) 195, 226 and in Monotti, "Nature and Basis of Crown Copyright in Official Publications" [1992] 9 E.I.P.R. 305.

[8] Copyright Act 1911 s.18.

[9] Copyright Act 1956 s.46(2).

[10] CDPA 1988 s.171(1)(b). Note s.171(5).

[11] For a historical discussion and a review of some of the contemporary issues involved in the enforcement of copyright in religious works, see Syn, "Copyright God: Enforcement of copyright in the Bible and religious works" [2001] 10 E.I.P.R. 454.

[12] The patent relied on by the Queen's Printers in *Universities of Oxford and Cambridge v Eyre & Spottiswoode Ltd* [1964] 1 Ch. 736 covered, in addition to Bibles, "all Books of Common Prayer and Administration of the Sacraments and other Rites and Ceremonies of the Church of England ... and also ... all other Books whatsoever which we have commanded or hereafter shall command to be used in the service of God in the Churches of ... England".

[13] *Manners v Hunter Blair* (1828) 3 Bligh (N.S.) 391, 402. The case concerned a Scottish patent but this dictum was directed at the position in England.

those works upon which the established doctrines of the Church of England are founded.[14]

Bibles: the scope of the prerogative. In the 300 years prior to 1963 no attempt was made to claim that the patents referred to in the previous paragraph extended to translations of the Bible other than the Authorised Version.[15] However, in 1961 a new translation known as the *New English Bible* was published by the Oxford and Cambridge University Presses. Shortly afterwards, the Queen's Printers published an identical version. Proceedings were brought by the University Presses[16] and the Queen's Printers sought to rely on their patent by way of defence. It was common ground that the patents could not grant rights which were more extensive than the prerogative itself.[17] The court held that to permit the Queen's Printers to rely on their patent would amount to an expropriation without compensation of the copyright in the *New English Bible*. In the absence of express statutory authority, such an expropriation in the name of the royal prerogative was not permissible.[18] Accordingly, the royal prerogative did not include the right to print material which infringed copyright. It follows from this decision that in the case of the Bible, prerogative copyright is limited to the Authorised Version and that new translations in which copyright subsists cannot be claimed by the Crown or by persons claiming under it.

10–05

Statutes. Before the 1988 Act came into force, the royal prerogative extended to Acts of Parliament.[19] The rationale for this was usually stated to be the fact that as head of the executive the monarch had the right of promulgating to the people all acts of state and Government and therefore the exclusive privilege of printing legislation.[20] However, s.164 of the 1988 Act abolished the prerogative relating to statutes (whether passed before or after commencement) and made them subject to statutory Crown copyright.[21]

10–06

Judgments. Patents to print law reports were upheld in two seventeenth-century cases,[22] but there is no evidence of any later attempt to assert a royal prerogative in relation to judgments or law reports. It is true that law reporters initially had a practice of seeking judicial sanction before publication.[23] However, by the late eighteenth century this practice had come to be seen as having been without legal

10–07

---

[14] The last of these explanations was preferred by Lord Lyndhurst L.C. in *Manners v Hunter Blair* (1828) 3 Bligh (N.S.) 391, 402, citing Lord Camden in *Donaldson v Beckett* (1774) 4 Burr. 2408, Chief Baron Skinner in *Eyre and Strahan v Carnan* (1781) 6 Bac. Abr. (7th Ed.) 509, 511 and *Universities of Oxford and Cambridge v Richardson* (1802) 6 Ves. 689.

[15] i.e. the King James I Bible of 1611.

[16] *Universities of Oxford and Cambridge v Eyre & Spottiswoode Ltd* [1964] 1 Ch. 736.

[17] *Universities of Oxford and Cambridge v Eyre & Spottiswoode Ltd* [1964] 1 Ch. 736, 749, citing *Basket v University of Cambridge* (1758) 1 Wm. Bl. 105, 121.

[18] Applying *Attorney-General v De Keyser's Royal Hotel Ltd* [1920] A.C. 508.

[19] *Company of Stationers* (1681) 2 Ch. Cas. 76; *Basket v University of Cambridge* (1758) 1 Bl. W. 105; *Baskett v Cunningham* (1762) 1 Bl. W. 370; *Attorney-General for New South Wales v Butterworth & Co. (Australia) Ltd* (1938) 38 S.R. (N.S.W.) 195. The latter case contains a thorough review of the authorities.

[20] See, e.g. *Company of Stationers* (1681) 2 Ch. Cas. 76; Chitty, *A Treatise on the Law of the Prerogatives of the Crown* (1820) p.239.

[21] CDPA 1988 s.164(4) provides that no copyright or right in the nature of copyright other than Crown copyright subsists in an Act or Measure. This provision applies to existing, that is precommencement, Acts of Parliament: CDPA 1988, Sch.1 para.42(1). Although CDPA 1988 s.171(1)(b) contains savings for the royal prerogative, those savings are to have effect subject to s.164(4): see s.171(5).

[22] *Atkins v Company of Stationers* (1666) Carter 89, cited in *Millar v Taylor* (1769) 4 Burr. 2303, 2316; *Roper v Streater* (1685), cited in *Stationers' Company v Parker* (1685) Skinner 233, 234 and in *Millar v Taylor* (1769) 4 Burr. 2303.

[23] Holdsworth, *A History of the English Law*, Vol.12, p.112.

foundation and it was abandoned.[24] It is also true that until the late eighteenth century the House of Lords restrained publication of its decisions, but this was on the ground that such publication was a breach of privilege rather than on the basis of the royal prerogative.[25] Nevertheless, the two seventeenth-century cases have never been overruled and there is no general rule that the prerogative may be lost simply by non-use.[26] On the other hand, it would not be difficult for a court to reach a view that the seventeenth-century cases were decided at a time of "high prerogative" and ought not to be followed.[27] It seems highly unlikely that any prerogative claim will now be asserted by the Crown in respect of judgments or law reports. Even if it was, it would no doubt be met with the contention that to some extent any prerogative copyright has been removed by s.45(2) of the 1988 Act, which provides that copyright is not infringed by anything done for the purposes of reporting judicial proceedings. Nevertheless, the position as to whether copyright in judgments is owned by the judges or by the Crown remains uncertain.[28]

10–08   **The Latin grammar.** In the eighteenth century it was thought that the Crown had a prerogative copyright in the King Edward VI Latin grammar on the grounds that it had been compiled at the King's expense.[29] The reference in the authorities is to the specific publication which was extant at the time and accordingly this right (if any) is highly unlikely to be of any practical importance at the present day.

10–09   **Almanacs.** The control of almanacs was perceived to be of considerable importance to the Crown, since, in addition to astronomical and other information, they might contain copies of the ecclesiastical calendar of the Church of England.[30] In *The Company of Stationers v Seymour*,[31] the Court upheld a grant by the Crown to the Company of Stationers of the exclusive right to print almanacs. However, a century later, in *Stationers' Company v Carnan*[32] the same or a substantially identical grant was held invalid.[33] The report gives no reasons for the decision. However, the successful defendant had contended that Seymour's case ought not to be followed both because it was decided "in the days of high prerogative, soon after the Licensing Act", and because "no solid ground of true prerogative" was stated in the decision. In the unlikely event that an issue as to almanacs were to be raised at the present day, it seems inevitable that Carnan's case would be followed.

---

[24] Holdsworth, *A History of the English Law*, Vol.12, p.113. Subsequently there were, however, occasional instances of judicial pressure being placed on reporters to omit cases from their reports: ibid.

[25] Holdsworth, *A History of the English Law*, Vol.12, p.573.

[26] Maitland, *Constitutional History of England* (1908), p.418; De Smith and Brazier, *Constitutional and Administrative Law*, 8th edn, p.136.

[27] See *Monotti* [1992] 9 E.I.P.R. 305, 309 for a detailed discussion. cf. the judicial history of the prerogative claims over almanacs at para.10–09, below.

[28] See Leith and Fellows "Enabling free on-line access to UK law reports: the copyright problem" [2010] I.J.L. & I.T. 72. It is understood that HMSO has written to the Lord Chancellor seeking his agreement to judgments being freely reproduced subject to acknowledging the source.

[29] *Millar v Taylor* (1769) 4 Burr. 2303, 2329, 2405. These dicta are obiter but of high authority. There seem to be no direct decisions on the point.

[30] The Court in *The Company of Stationers v Seymour* (1677) 1 Mod. 256, 257 stated: "the almanack that is before the common-prayer proceeds from a public constitution; it was first settled by the *Nicene Council*; is established by the canons of the church; and is under the government of the *Archbishop of Canterbury*; so that almanacks may be accounted *prerogative copies*" (reporter's italics). The case is also reported sub nom. *The Corporation of Stationers v Seymour* in 3 Keble 79.

[31] (1677) 1 Mod. 256.

[32] (1775) 2 Wm. Bl. 1004.

[33] Despite the plaintiffs' contention that the regulation of time was a matter of state: report at 1006.

C. STATUTORY CROWN COPYRIGHT

(i) The position under the 1988 Act

(a) *Background*

The Whitford Committee Report. The 1956 Act contained detailed provisions   **10–10**
in relation to Crown copyright.[34] The Whitford Committee was critical of a
number of these provisions. First, it objected to the fact that the Crown obtained
copyright not only in works made by its employees but also in works "made by
or under the direction or control of Her Majesty or a Government department".[35]
The Committee expressed the view that the breadth of this phrase was likely to
lead to difficulty.[36] Secondly, the Committee objected to the fact that the Crown
could obtain copyright in a work simply by virtue of being the first to publish it,
thus extinguishing the author's copyright in it ("the first publication rule").[37] The
Committee considered a number of arguments in favour of retaining Crown copyright, including the difficulty in keeping track of the large number of authors
employed by the Crown, but ultimately concluded that there was no basis for giving the Crown a special status not accorded to other large organisations. Accordingly, the Committee recommended the abolition of statutory Crown copyright.[38]

The 1986 White Paper. The Government, in its 1988 White Paper, did not take   **10–11**
up the Whitford Committee's recommendation that Crown copyright should be
abolished. In fact, it proposed that Crown copyright should continue to subsist in
works made by or under the direction or control of Her Majesty or a Government
department and, on the assumption that the position as to commissioned works
was unclear, should subsist in commissioned works in the absence of agreement
to the contrary.[39] So far as the first publication rule was concerned, the Government stated in the White Paper that it recognised that the rule could work
unfairly.[40] Accordingly, the White Paper contained a proposal for the rule to be
abolished and replaced by a provision allowing the reproduction and publication
by or under the authority of the Crown of unpublished material lawfully acquired
in the course of Crown business.[41] Examples given in the White Paper of the kind
of material the Government had in mind were evidence given to and findings of
committees and statistical or industrial information given to Government
Departments.[42] It was proposed that the new rule would operate subject to any
agreement to the contrary.[43] In fact, as will be seen, only the second of the changes

---

[34] See paras 10–22 et seq., below.
[35] Copyright Act 1956 s.39(1). See para.10–22, below.
[36] Cmnd.6732 para.593. The Committee noted that the uncertainty of the law had enabled Govern-
    ment departments to claim the copyright in computer programs created at their request but without
    any direction or control (see para.596).
[37] Cmnd.6732 paras 595–596. The Committee recognised that this was a somewhat academic
    problem because the policy of HMSO was to obtain copyright clearance in all cases of doubt.
[38] Cmnd.6732 para.600.
[39] *Intellectual Property and Innovation* Cmnd.9712, para.16.6. See also *Hansard*, HL Vol.491,
    col.553–554 and HL Vol. 493, col.1394 for the Government's view that the position as to com-
    missioned works was unclear.
[40] para.16.7.
[41] para.16.8.
[42] para.16.7.
[43] para.16.7.

proposed in the White Paper (the replacement of the first publication rule) was destined to reach the statute book.[44]

10–12   **The policy of the 1988 Act.** The Parliamentary debates indicate that in framing the Bill which became the 1988 Act, the Government accepted the Whitford Committee's objections to the first publication rule, but not its recommendation that Crown copyright be abolished.[45] The Government's view was that statutory Crown copyright had worked well for over 75 years and had given rise to no practical problems. Its abolition would have no discernible public benefit but would necessitate the employment of additional staff at considerable expense in order to keep track of all the authors concerned in the production of Government publications. As had been foreshadowed in the 1986 White Paper,[46] the Bill originally contained express provision to extend Crown copyright to commissioned works. This provision aroused considerable opposition in the House of Lords and was ultimately abandoned after consultations indicated that the Crown would not be seriously inconvenienced if it was not enacted.[47]

(b) *Works made on or after August 1, 1989*

10–13   **Subsistence and ownership.** The general provisions in the 1988 Act relating to subsistence and first ownership of copyright do not apply to works made by Her Majesty or by an officer or servant of the Crown[48] in the course of his duties.[49] Instead, s.163(1) of the 1988 Act provides that where a work[50] is made by Her Majesty or by an officer or servant of the Crown in the course of his duties, the work qualifies for copyright protection even if the ordinary qualification requirements are not satisfied,[51] and that Her Majesty is the owner of any copyright in the work.[52] Thus, for example, if a work is made by an employee of the Crown who is not a qualifying person because he is not domiciled or resident in the United Kingdom or another country to which the provisions of Pt I of the 1988 Act extend, copyright will nevertheless subsist in the work. Of greater practical importance is the fact that Her Majesty becomes the owner of the copyright in all works created by her officers provided the works were made in the course of their duties.[53] It is provided that copyright in a Crown copyright work[54] is referred to in

---

[44] As to the proposal in relation to commissioned works, see *Hansard*, HL Vol.501, col.193.
[45] Hansard, HL Vol. 493, col.1391.
[46] See para.10–11, above.
[47] Hansard, HL Vol.495, col.678; Hansard, H.L Vol.501, cols 193–197. For current official Guidance in relation to commissioned works, together with a draft commissioning agreement, see Guidance Note 5 *Copyright in Works Commissioned by the Crown* (revised March 15, 2008), *http://www.nationalarchives.gov.uk/documents/copyright-in-works-commissioned-by-crown.pdf* [Accessed October 23, 2010].
[48] The expression "the Crown" includes the Crown in right of the Scottish Administration, of the Welsh Assembly Government or of Her Majesty's Government in Northern Ireland or in any country outside the United Kingdom to which the copyright Part of the 1988 Act extends: CDPA 1988 s.178. OPSI has published a list of the bodies it considers to have Crown status: see *http://www.opsi.gov.uk* [Accessed October 12, 2010]. The phrase "officer and servant of the Crown" in s.163(1) means someone engaged in the service of the executive branch of the Government. The Prince of Wales is not such a person: *HRH The Prince of Wales v Associated Newspapers Ltd* [2006] EWHC 522; [2006] E.C.D.R. 20 at para.153 (not challenged on appeal: [2006] EWCA Civ 1776; [2007] 3 W.L.R. 222; [2007] 2 All E.R. 139 at para.75).
[49] CDPA 1988 ss.153(2) (subsistence) and 11(3) (first ownership).
[50] For what may be a copyright work, see CDPA 1988 s.1.
[51] CDPA 1988 s.163(1)(a). For the ordinary qualification requirements, see CDPA 1988 s.153(1) and paras 3–154 et seq., above.
[52] s.163(1)(b).
[53] The rule that an employer is the first owner of the copyright in a work made by his employees is subject to any agreement to the contrary, does not relate to all works, and does not apply to works made by officers: see CDPA 1988 s.11(3).

Pt I of the 1988 Act as "Crown copyright" even if it has been assigned by the Crown.[55]

Term. Section 163(3) of the 1988 Act provides for a special term in respect of   **10–14** Crown copyright in literary, dramatic, musical and artistic works.[56] That term depends on whether the work has been published commercially[57] before the end of the period of 75 years from the end of the calendar year in which it was made. During the Parliamentary debates it was stated that the issue of photocopies to the public by the Public Record Office was excluded from the definition because copies were made on demand.[58] If the work has not been published commercially during this period of 75 years, the term of Crown copyright is 125 years from the end of the calendar year in which the work was made.[59] In the Parliamentary debates on the Bill, the Government gave two reasons for arriving at this term of 125 years.[60] The first was that a term of life of the author plus 50 years was not practical since it would require a large bureaucracy to keep records of the date of death of all the authors of Crown copyright works. The second was that official documents are not in the public domain for the first 30 years of their life (for Royal papers the period is 100 years)[61] and such a term would provide a reasonable period of protection once the documents in question were in the public domain. If, on the other hand, the work has been published commercially before the end of the period of 75 years from the end of the calendar year in which it was made, the term of copyright is 50 years from the end of the calendar year in which it was so published.[62] In relation to works other than literary, dramatic, musical or artistic works, the term is the normal term for the relevant category of work.[63] No publication right arises from the publication of a work in which Crown copyright subsisted.[64]

Works of joint authorship. In the case of works created jointly by Her Majesty   **10–15** or an officer or employee of Her Majesty on the one hand and a third party on the other, s.163 applies only in relation to Her Majesty, her officer or employee and the copyright subsisting by virtue of her or his contribution to the work.[65] Accordingly, in order to establish the subsistence of copyright in that part of the work to which the third party contributed, it is necessary to show that the ordinary

---

[54] i.e. a work made by Her Majesty or by an officer or servant of the Crown in the course of his duties.

[55] CDPA 1988 s.164(2): thus "once Crown copyright always Crown copyright".

[56] The term of Crown copyright was not altered by the Duration of Copyright and Rights in Performances Regulations 1995 (SI 1995/3297).

[57] For a detailed discussion of the meaning of the term "commercial publication", see para.11–11, below.

[58] *Hansard*, H.L Vol.491, col.559.

[59] CDPA 1988 s.163(3)(a).

[60] *Hansard*, HL Vol.491, col.559. As was pointed out for the Government, the period was equivalent to that then proposed for the early works of a long-lived author.

[61] These periods are under review: see *http://www.30yearrulereview.org.uk* [Accessed October 12, 2010].

[62] CDPA 1988 s.163(3)(b). The Parliamentary debates indicate that the Government considered that a term of 125 years from the date of publication would be excessive: *Hansard*, HL Vol.491, col.559.

[63] CDPA 1988 s.163(5) provides that except as provided in s.163 or expressly excluded elsewhere in Pt I of the Act, the provisions of Pt I apply in relation to Crown copyright as to other copyright. For the various terms, see the earlier chapters of this work.

[64] Copyright and Related Rights Regulations 1996 (SI 1996/2967) reg.16(5).

[65] CDPA 1988 s.163(4).

qualifying requirements are satisfied.[66] Furthermore, the term of copyright in that part of the work to which the third party contributed will be the normal term.[67]

10–16 **Application of Part I of the 1988 Act to Crown copyright.** It is provided that with the exception of the special rules outlined above in relation to subsistence, title and term, and subject to any express exclusion elsewhere in Pt I of the 1988 Act, the copyright part of the 1988 Act is to apply to Crown copyright as to other copyright.[68] Accordingly, for example, the ordinary rules will apply to any dealings with Crown copyright[69] and the Crown or its assignee will be entitled to the ordinary remedies for infringement.[70] Moreover, in general, the permitted acts set out in ss28A to 50 of the 1988 Act apply equally to works of Crown copyright.

10–17 **Interrelationship with Parliamentary copyright.** It is provided that s.163 of the 1988 Act does not apply to a work if, or to the extent that, Parliamentary copyright subsists in it.[71]

(c) *Works made before August 1, 1989*

10–18 **Subsistence and ownership.**[72] The provisions of the 1988 Act apply to things existing at commencement as they apply to things coming into existence after commencement, subject to any express provision to the contrary.[73] In the case of Crown copyright, there are a number of express contrary provisions. First, the provisions of s.163 of the 1988 Act apply to works made before commencement only if s.39 of the 1956 Act[74] applied to the work immediately before commencement and the work is not one to which ss.164, 165 or 166 of the 1988 Act applies.[75] Section 164 established a new statutory copyright in Acts and Measures.[76] Section 165 established Parliamentary copyright.[77] Section 166 provided for copyright in Parliamentary Bills.[78] Secondly, every work in which Crown copyright subsisted under the 1956 Act immediately before commencement is to be deemed to satisfy the requirements of the copyright part of the 1988 Act[79] as to qualification for copyright protection.[80] Thirdly, the first owner of copyright in such works is to be determined in accordance with the law in force at the time the work was made.[81] The two latter provisions are of particular importance in view of the nar-

---

[66] As to which see paras 3–154 et seq., above.
[67] A work of joint authorship is a work where the respective contributions of the joint authors are not distinct from each other: CDPA 1988 s.10(1). Difficulties may therefore arise in identifying the respective contributions of the joint authors for the purposes of establishing the term of the copyright in the various parts of the work.
[68] CDPA 1988 s.163(5).
[69] ss.90 to 93A.
[70] ss.96–115.
[71] CDPA 1988 s.163(6). As to Parliamentary copyright, see paras 10–79 et seq., below.
[72] What follows is confined to Crown copyright as defined in CDPA 1988 s.163. For pre-commencement Acts and Measures, Parliamentary copyright and copyright in Parliamentary Bills, see below at paras 10–21, 10–78 and 10–87 respectively.
[73] CDPA 1988 Sch.1 para.3.
[74] See paras 10–22 et seq., below.
[75] CDPA 1988 Sch.1 para.40(1).
[76] See para.10–20, below.
[77] See paras 10–79 et seq., below.
[78] See paras 10–84 et seq., below.
[79] i.e. Pt I.
[80] CDPA 1988 Sch.1 para.35.
[81] Sch.1 para.11(1). Note also para.11(2).

rower scope of Crown copyright under the 1988 Act.[82] The position under the 1956 Act is dealt with later.[83]

Term. The various terms of copyright in pre-commencement works to which   **10–19**
s.163 of the 1988 Act applies are set out in para.41 of Sch.1 to the 1988 Act. In
respect of many works different provisions apply depending on whether or not
the work is a published work. The question which provision applies to a work is
to be determined by reference to the facts immediately before commencement.[84]
Accordingly, the question whether a work is a published work is to be determined
as at the time immediately before commencement.[85] It is further provided that
expressions used in para.41 which were defined for the purposes of the 1956 Act
have the same meaning as in that Act.[86] Copyright continues to subsist in a large
number of categories of work until the date on which it would have expired in accordance with the 1956 Act. Those categories are as follows[87]: published literary,
dramatic and musical works; artistic works other than engravings or photographs;
published engravings; published photographs and photographs taken before June
1, 1957; published sound recordings and sound recordings made before June 1,
1957; and published films and films falling within s.13(3)(a) of the 1956 Act.[88]
Copyright in unpublished literary, dramatic and musical works continues to
subsist until the date on which it expires in accordance with s.163(3)[89] or 50 years
from the end of the calendar year in which the copyright provisions of the 1988
Act came into force,[90] whichever is the later.[91] Copyright in unpublished engravings and unpublished photographs taken on or after June 1, 1957 continues to
subsist until the end of the period of 50 years from the end of the calendar year in
which the 1988 Act came into force.[92] Copyright in films and sound recordings
not falling into any of the above categories continues to subsist until the end of
the period of 50 years from the end of the calendar year in which the 1988 Act
came into force[93] unless the film or sound recording is published before the end
of that period, in which case copyright expires 50 years from the end of the
calendar year in which it was published.[94]

(d) *Acts and Measures*

Acts and Measures passed on or after August 1, 1989. Until the passing of the   **10–20**
1988 Act, the copyright in Acts of Parliament and Measures of the Synod of the
Church of England was vested in the Crown by virtue of the royal prerogative.[95]
The 1988 Act placed the Crown's rights on a statutory footing by providing that
Her Majesty is entitled to copyright in every Act of Parliament and every Mea-

---

[82] As to which see para.10–13, above.
[83] See paras 10–22 et seq., below.
[84] i.e. August 1, 1989.
[85] CDPA 1988 Sch.1 para.41(1).
[86] CDPA 1988 Sch.1 para.41(1).
[87] Sch.1 para.41(2).
[88] i.e. films registered under a former enactment requiring registration of films.
[89] i.e. at the end of the period of 125 years from the end of the calendar year in which the work was
made or, if the work was published commercially before that date, at the end of the period of 50
years from the end of the calendar year in which it was so published.
[90] i.e. 50 years from December 31, 1989.
[91] CDPA 1988 Sch.1 para.41.
[92] Sch.1 para.41(4). The period is therefore 50 years from December 31, 1989.
[93] i.e. 50 years from December 31, 1989.
[94] CDPA 1988 Sch.1 para.40(5).
[95] See para.10–06, above.

sure of the General Synod of the Church of England.[96] The reasons for this change are not clear, although it seems to have been connected with the introduction of the new Parliamentary copyright in respect of Bills.[97] Since May 6 and December 2, 1999 respectively, Her Majesty has been entitled to copyright in Acts of the Scottish Parliament[98] and of the Northern Ireland Assembly.[99] Since May 3, 2007, Her Majesty has been entitled to the copyright in Acts and Measures of the National Assembly for Wales.[100] The copyright subsists from the date of Royal Assent until the end of the period of 50 years from the end of the calendar year in which Royal Assent was given or, in the case of a Measure of the National Assembly for Wales, until the end of the period of 50 years from the end of the calendar year in which the Measure was approved by Her Majesty in Council.[101] No other copyright or right in the nature of copyright subsists in Acts or Measures, and accordingly the prerogative copyright in them is abolished.[102] With the above exceptions, the provisions of Pt I of the 1988 Act apply in relation to copyright in Acts and Measures as they apply to other Crown copyright.[103]

10–21   **Acts and Measures passed before August 1, 1989.** The rules set out in the preceding paragraph apply to pre-commencement Acts and Measures including Church Assembly Measures.[104] This is subject to the general rule that copyright subsists in a pre-commencement work after commencement only if it subsisted in it immediately before commencement.[105] However, as has already been stated, copyright subsisted in Acts of Parliament before the commencement of the 1988 Act by virtue of the royal prerogative.[106]

(ii) The position under the 1956 Act

(a) *Literary, dramatic, musical and artistic works*

10–22   **Subsistence of copyright in works not otherwise protected.**[107] Section 39(1)(a) of the 1956 Act provided that copyright was to subsist in original literary, dramatic, musical and artistic works made by or under the direction or control of Her Majesty or a Government department even if copyright did not subsist in them under the general law.[108] Thus, for example, an unpublished work of which

---

[96] CDPA 1988 s.164(1). The general provisions in the 1988 Act relating to subsistence and duration of copyright do not apply to copyright in Acts and Measures: ss.153(2) (subsistence) and 12(9) (duration).

[97] *Hansard*, HL Vol.501, cols 194–195.

[98] CDPA 1988 s.164(1), as amended by para.25(6) of Sch.8 to the Scotland Act 1998 (c.46). For commencement, see the Scotland Act 1998 (Commencement) Order 1998 (SI 1998/3178) para.2 and Sch.3.

[99] CDPA 1988 s.164(1), as amended by para.8(6) of Sch.13 to the Northern Ireland Act 1998. For commencement, see the Northern Ireland Act 1998 (Commencement No.5) Order 1999 (SI 1999/3209), para.2 and Sch.

[100] CDPA 1988 s.164(1) as amended by para.27(2) of Sch.10 to the Government of Wales Act 2006. By s.161(1) of that Act, the amendment took effect immediately after the ordinary election under s.3 of the Government of Wales Act 1998 held in 2007, which took place on May 3, 2007.

[101] CDPA 1988 s.164(2).

[102] s.164(4).

[103] s.163(3).

[104] CDPA 1988 Sch.1 para.42. The Church Assembly became the General Synod as from November 4, 1970: Synodical Government Measure 1969 (No.2) s.2.

[105] CDPA 1988 Sch.1 para.5.

[106] See para.10–06, above.

[107] For the position under the 1911 Act and before, see the 13th edition of this work.

[108] For an example, see *Secretary of State for Defence v Guardian Newspapers* [1984] Ch. 156, CA.

the author was not a qualified person[109] would nevertheless be protected if made under the direction of a Government department. The expression "made under the direction or control", which derives from the 1911 Act,[110] was not defined.[111] It was probably intended to confer protection beyond works made under a contract of service to works commissioned by the Crown from independent contractors.[112] The term "Government department" was defined as any department of Her Majesty's Government in the United Kingdom or of the Government of Northern Ireland, or any department or agency of any other country to which the section extended.[113]

Ownership of copyright. The 1956 Act contained separate provisions for works   **10–23** made by or under the direction or control[114] of the Crown on the one hand and works first published by or under the direction or control of the Crown on the other. Section 39(1)(b) of the 1956 Act provided that the Crown was entitled to the copyright in every original literary, dramatic, musical or artistic work made by or under the direction or control of Her Majesty or a Government department.[115] Section 39(2) of the 1956 Act provided that the Crown was entitled to the copyright in every original literary, dramatic, musical or artistic work first published in the United Kingdom or another country to which the provisions of the 1956 Act extended if first published by or under the direction of Her Majesty or a Government department.[116] Both these provisions were subject to any agreement made by or on behalf of Her Majesty or a Government department with the author of the work whereby it was agreed that the copyright should vest in the author or in another person designated in the agreement in that behalf.[117]

Term of Crown copyright. As regards literary, dramatic and musical works,   **10–24** s.39(3) of the 1956 Act provided that where the Crown was entitled to copyright by reason of the provisions set out in the preceding paragraph,[118] the term of copyright depended on whether or not the work had been published. Where the work was unpublished, copyright was to continue to subsist so long as it remained unpublished.[119] Where the work was published, copyright was to subsist (or, as the case might be, to continue to subsist) until the end of the period of 50 years

---

[109] As defined in Copyright Act 1956 s.1(5).
[110] Copyright Act 1911 s.18.
[111] Its breadth was the subject of criticism by the Whitford Committee (Cmnd.6731), paras 593 to 600. See para.10–10, above.
[112] In *British Broadcasting Co v Wireless League Gazette Publishing Co* [1926] 1 Ch. 433 it was held on the facts that a list of programmes (the *Radio Times*) published by the BBC was not published under the direction or control of a Government department even though the programmes themselves were broadcast under a revocable licence from the Government and the publication of the list had been approved by the Postmaster-General. In *Land Transport Safety Authority of New Zealand v Glogau* [1999] 1 N.Z.L.R. 261, the New Zealand Court of Appeal held that the fact that log books for taxi drivers had to be in a form approved by the Crown did not mean that log books which were so approved had been made under the Crown's direction or control, even though the power to approve them gave the Crown a degree of direction and control over their content.
[113] Copyright Act 1956 s.39(9).
[114] For the meaning of this term, see para.10–22, above.
[115] For the definition of this expression, see para.10–22, above.
[116] In *Catnic Components v Hill & Smith Ltd* [1981] R.P.C. 407 it was held, presumably on the basis of this provision, that drawings in a patent were Crown copyright. In *Ironside v H.M. Attorney-General* [1988] R.P.C. 197 it was held that the issue by the Chancellor of the Exchequer of a press release containing authorised photographs and descriptions of the new decimal coinage amounted to a publication under the direction or control of a government department.
[117] Copyright Act 1956 s.39(6).
[118] i.e. pursuant to Copyright Act 1956 s.39(1) or (2).
[119] s.39(3)(a).

from the end of the calendar year in which it was first published.[120] As regards artistic works other than engravings or photographs, s.39(4) of the 1956 Act provided that where the Crown was entitled to copyright by reason of the circumstances set out in the preceding paragraph,[121] copyright subsisted until the end of the period of 50 years from the end of the calendar year in which the work was made. For engravings and photographs, it was provided that copyright was to subsist until the end of the period of 50 years from the end of the calendar year in which the work was first published.[122] It would seem that if copyright in a work commissioned by the Crown was vested by agreement in the author rather than the Crown, then the normal term of copyright applied.[123]

(b) *Sound recordings and films*

10–25   **Subsistence, ownership and term.** Section 39(5) of the 1956 Act made similar provision as regards sound recordings and films. First, it provided that copyright was to subsist in sound recordings and films made by or under the direction or control of Her Majesty or a Government department even if copyright did not subsist in them under the general law.[124] Secondly, it provided that in any case where a sound recording or film had been made by or under the direction or control of Her Majesty or a Government department, Her Majesty was to be entitled to the copyright in it.[125] Thirdly, it provided that the copyright should subsist for the same period as if it subsisted and was owned in accordance with the general provisions relating to copyright in sound recordings and films.[126]

(c) *Pre-commencement works*

10–26   **General.** The general transitional provisions applicable under the 1956 Act applied equally to Crown copyright. Accordingly, in general, the provisions discussed above applied in relation to works in existence at the commencement of the 1956 Act[127] as they applied in relation to works which came into existence after its commencement.[128] However, this general position was specifically modified in relation to photographs, sound recordings and films.

10–27   **Photographs, sound recordings and films.** In relation to photographs taken before the commencement of the 1956 Act, Crown copyright was to subsist until the end of the period of 50 years from the end of the calendar year in which they were made.[129] In relation to sound recordings made before commencement, Crown copyright was to subsist for the period of 50 years from the end of the calendar year in which they were made.[130] In relation to films made before commencement, it was provided that no Crown copyright subsisted in them as films. However, in so far as such a film was an original dramatic work as defined in the

---

[120] s.39(3)(b).
[121] i.e. pursuant to Copyright Act 1956 s.39(1) or (2).
[122] s.39(4).
[123] As to which, see Copyright Act 1956 ss.2 and 3.
[124] s.39(5)(a).
[125] s.39(5)(b).
[126] s.39(5)(b). The general provisions were Copyright Act 1956 ss.12 (sound recordings) and 13 (films).
[127] On June 1, 1957.
[128] Copyright Act 1956 Sch.7 para.45(1).
[129] Copyright Act 1956 Sch.7 para.30. Thus, pre-commencement photographs were equated with artistic works other than engravings.
[130] Sch.7 para.31(1). Thus, the normal period of 50 years from first publication (s.12(3) as applied by s.39(5)(b)) was disapplied.

1911 Act,[131] Crown copyright was to subsist in the film to the same extent that it would have subsisted if the film was an original dramatic work.[132] Moreover, in so far as such a film was made up of photographs, they were to be protected in the same way as other Crown copyright photographs made before commencement.[133]

(iii) Enforcement and management of Crown Copyright: general

History. Article 2(4) of the Berne Convention[134] provides that it shall be a matter   **10–28**
for legislation in the countries of the Union to determine the protection to be
granted to official texts of a legislative, administrative and legal nature. In fact,
the United Kingdom Government has long recognised that there is a public interest in members of the public having access to certain types of official information
and Crown copyright has never been fully enforced.[135] In 1989, the European
Commission expressed the view that the public sector should, to the highest
extent possible, make use of the discretion laid down in the Berne Convention to
exempt from copyright texts of a legislative, administrative and legal nature.[136]
The present UK framework originated with the 1999 White Paper *The Future
Management of Crown Copyright*.[137] The general policy is to improve and
encourage access to the broad range of public sector information whilst at the
same time maintaining the integrity and status of works produced within
government.[138] As a result, during the last 15 years, there has been a very
substantial increase in the amount of Crown copyright material which is available for exploitation ("re-use") by members of the public.

Overview. The re-use of Crown copyright and database right material by   **10–29**
members of the public is governed by the United Kingdom Government Licensing Framework for public sector information which was launched in beta form in
October 2010.[139] According to this document: "Government is committed to
opening up access to further sources of information, promoting transparency and
accountability and creating new economic opportunities. It is therefore Government policy to support civil society and the private sector in realising the value
stored in public sector information by enabling it to be re-used and re-
purposed".[140]

    The controller of Her Majesty's Stationery Office ("HMSO"), in her role as
Queen's Printer and Queen's Printer for Scotland, has been appointed by Her
Majesty the Queen by Letters Patent to manage all copyrights and database rights

---

[131] For a discussion of the position under the 1911 Act, see para.3–80, above, and earlier editions of
this work.

[132] Sch.7 para.31(2)(b).

[133] Sch.7 para.31(2)(c).

[134] See Vol.2 F1.

[135] For a brief history of enforcement before the passing of the 1988 Act see the Green Paper *Crown
Copyright in the Information Age: A consultation document on access to public sector information*, Cm. 3819, HMSO, paras 2.2–2.7. See also previous editions of this Work and *Attorney-
General for New South Wales v Butterworth & Co (Australia) Ltd* (1937–38) 38 S.R. N.S.W. 195
at 236.

[136] *Guidelines for improving the synergy between the public and private sectors in the information
market* (European Commission Directorate-General for Telecommunications, Information
Industries and Innovation, 1989, Cat. No.CD-54-88-126-EN-C), para.18.

[137] Cm. 4300.

[138] Cm. 4300, paras 1.3 and 2.2.

[139] "UKGLF". See *http://www.nationalarchives.gov.uk/information-management/uk-gov-licensing-
framework.htm* [Accessed October 21, 2010].

[140] UKGLF para.2.1.

owned by the Crown on Her Majesty's behalf.[141] The Controller is an official in the National Archives,[142] which is a Government department.

Where re-use of Crown copyright material is permitted, the general rules laid down in the Re-use of Public Sector Information Regulations 2005 must be applied.[143] These Regulations are considered in detail below[144] but two points may be noted here. First, they only apply if re-use is permitted: they do not establish any rights to re-use. Second, despite their title, they are not concerned with information as such but rather with the re-use of "documents", defined as "any content whatever its medium".[145] In practice, there is no blanket regime: different categories of material are governed by different published regimes. The various regimes are considered below.[146]

10–30   **Access to Government information.** In parallel with the growth in the amount of *material* available for exploitation there has been a substantial increase in the amount of Government *information* which is accessible to members of the public. This is the result of recent legislation such as the Data Protection Act 1998, the Freedom of Information Act 2000 and the Environmental Information Regulations 2004.[147] Compliance with such legislation may involve the making of copies of Crown copyright material and their supply to the recipient. However, the mere fact of such supply is not considered to imply the grant of any further licence to exploit the material.[148] Accordingly, this legislation is not dealt with further in this Chapter except where it is relevant background to the law relating to the re-use of Crown copyright material. The reader is referred to the specialist texts.[149]

10–31   **Administration of Crown copyright.** General guidance on the management of Crown copyright can be found in *Crown Copyright—an overview for government departments.*[150] In summary:

1. The Controller licenses the re-use of Crown copyright material through The Open Government Licence[151] in accordance with the Regulations on the Re-use of Public Sector Information.[152]

2. Some Government departments have delegated authority from the Controller to license the re-use of the Crown copyright material which they originate. The Controller has also granted limited delegations to parts of government departments which have responsibility for more specialised forms of licensing activity. Delegated activities are monitored by OPSI's Standards Team by means of the Information Fair Trader Scheme.

3. While any department may take initial steps in investigating an alleged in-

---

[141] UKGLF para.3.3.

[142] UKGLF para.3.3.

[143] The Regulations are SI 2005/1515. They are reproduced in Vol. 2 B12.ii. They implement Directive 2003/98/EC of the European Parliament and of the Council of November 17, 2003 on the re-use of public sector information: [2003] OJ L 354/90. The Directive is reproduced in Vol. 2 B12.i.

[144] In paras 10–32 to 10–57.

[145] The definition is considered below, para.10–37. As para.3.1 of the Explanatory Memorandum to the Regulations makes clear, the Directive which they implement "does not affect laws on access but operates alongside them".

[146] In paras 10–58 to 10–75.

[147] SI 2004/3391.

[148] See, e.g. the UK Government Licensing Framework for public sector information *http://www.nationalarchives.gov.uk/documents/uk-government-licensing-framework.pdf* [Accessed October 21, 2010] para.3.4.

[149] See, e.g. Macdonald and others, *The Law of Freedom of Information.*

[150] *http://www.nationalarchives.gov.uk/documents/crown-copyright-an-overview-for-government-departments.pdf* [Accessed October 22, 2010].

[151] See paras 10–59 et seq.

[152] SI 2005/1515. See para.10–32 to 10–57 below.

fringement, the Controller's Information Policy Team should be notified at the earliest opportunity, not least because the Controller would need to be a party to any proceedings.

4. All Government departments have a responsibility for communicating policy and information. They can do this under a central delegation from the Controller, either by publishing the information themselves (including on their websites) or by contracting others to publish official material (in some instances under central contracts managed by HMSO). However, there are restrictions. Private sector publishers must not be granted exclusive publishing rights other than in the official edition because this effectively prevents others from re-using the material. Such publishers must not be granted the right to license the re-use of Crown copyright material except in the context of end-user licensing of electronic products and services.[153]

5. In contractual matters, the Crown is regarded as a single legal entity. Accordingly, a department does not require a formal licence to re-use copyright material originated by another part of government. However, in general departments are obliged to comply with the same rules as any other user.

The National Archives have issued separate guidance in relation to the acquisition of copyright in works commissioned by the Crown.[154]

(iv) The Re-use of Public Sector Information Regulations 2005[155]

Background and statutory framework. On January 20, 1999, the European Commission published a Green Paper: *Public Sector Information: a key resource for Europe*.[156] On June 5, 2002, following a period of consultation, the Commission published a proposal for a Directive on the re-use and commercial exploitation of public sector documents.[157] The Directive was finally adopted on November 17, 2003.[158] Member States were required to implement it by July 1, 2005.[159] The Directive was implemented in the United Kingdom with effect from July 1, 2005 by the Re-use of Public Sector Information Regulations 2005 ("the Regulations").[160] According to the Explanatory Memorandum to the Regulations "The general approach has been to copy out the Directive although in some places provisions have been drafted to use more usual UK legislative language and to tie in with existing definitions".[161] The Commission has carried out a review of the Directive. No specific amendments are recommended but there will be a further review in 2012.[162]

10–32

The objects of the Directive. The recitals to the Directive refer to the significance for individuals of the evolution towards an information and knowledge so-

10–33

---

[153] The National Archives have published guidance as to appropriate notices and acknowledgments: see *http://www.nationalarchives.gov.uk/documents/copyright-and-publishing-guidance.pdf* [Accessed October 22, 2010].

[154] *http://www.nationalarchives.gov.uk/documents/copyright-in-works-commissioned-by-crown.pdf* [Accessed November 15, 2010].

[155] SI 2005/1515. See Vol.2 B12.ii.

[156] COM (1998) 585.

[157] COM(2002) 207 final.

[158] Directive 2003/98/EC of the European Parliament and of the Council of November 17, 2003 on the re-use of public sector information: [2003] OJ L 354/90.

[159] art.12.

[160] SI 2005/1515.

[161] para.4.1

[162] See the Commission's Communications COM(2009) 212 final and COM(2010) 245 final.

ciety and the fact that digital content plays an important role in this evolution.[163] They note that the public sector collects, produces, reproduces and disseminates a wide range of information in many areas of activity and that this information is an increasingly important primary material for the growing market in digital content products and services.[164] According to the recitals, there were considerable differences in the rules and practices relating to the exploitation of such information in the different Member States. These differences constituted barriers to the realisation of the full potential of this primary material, and especially to the development of Community wide digital services. Accordingly, harmonisation in this field was expected to contribute to the achievement of the internal market and to the prevention of distortions of competition in the internal market.[165] It was thought that in the absence of minimum harmonisation at Community level, there was a danger of further divergences between Member States.[166] Accordingly, the Directive establishes a minimum set of rules governing the re-use of existing documents held by public sector bodies of the Member States and the practical means of facilitating such re-use.[167]

10–34   **No obligation to permit re-use.** It should immediately be noted that the Directive does not impose any obligation on public sector bodies to allow the re-use of documents.[168] Rather, it lays down a general framework, based on minimum harmonisation, for the conditions governing re-use of documents where such re-use is permitted by the public sector body in question.[169] Member States are permitted and indeed encouraged to go beyond the minimum standards of the Directive, thus allowing for more extensive re-use.[170] Consistently with this, the Regulations do not impose any obligation to permit re-use. Rather, reg.7(1) simply states: "A public sector body may permit re-use".

10–35   **No effect on intellectual property rights.** The Directive expressly provides that it has no application to documents "for which" third parties hold intellectual property rights.[171] This provision is implemented by reg.5(1)(b), which provides that the Regulations do not apply to a document where a third party owns "relevant intellectual property rights" in the document: reg.5(2). The term "relevant intellectual property rights" means copyright, database right, publication right and rights in performances: see reg.2. It seems that the Regulations are inapplicable whenever a third party owns intellectual property rights in the material in question, even if the public body is entitled to grant sub-licences to end-users.[172]

10–36   **"Public sector body".** The Regulations expressly incorporate the complex defi-

---

[163] Directive 2003/98 recitals 2 and 3.
[164] Recitals 4 and 5.
[165] Recitals 1 and 6.
[166] Recital 7.
[167] art.1(1).
[168] Directive 2003/98, recitals 9, 22 and 24.
[169] Recital 9 and arts 1(1), 1(3) and 3.
[170] Recitals 8, 9, 22.
[171] art.1(2)(b).
[172] See the report of the Advisory Panel on Public Sector Information ("APPSI") on a complaint (SO 42/8/4) by Intelligent Addressing Ltd at paras 2.7 to 2.14. The report is at *http://www.appsi.gov.uk/CategoryView/category/ComplaintsReviewBoard/* [Accessed April 22, 2010] (the role of APPSI is considered below, para.10–51). It seems that OPSI disagreed with APPSI's ruling and intended to issue guidance to explain that "the scope should cover not only documents in which the public sector body owns the IPR but also where the public sector body has acquired the authority to allow re-use through a licence": see the *United Kingdom Report on the Re-use of Public Sector Information 2008*, Cm.7446 at para.3.13. However, it is not clear that any such guidance has been issued.

nition of "public sector body" set out in the Directive.[173] Fortunately, they go on to list a large number of entities which are deemed to be public sector bodies for the purposes of the Regulations.[174] The list includes Ministers of the Crown, Government departments, the House of Commons and the House of Lords, the Northern Ireland Assembly Commissions, Scottish Ministers, the Scottish Parliament and its Corporate Body and the National Assembly for Wales.

"Document". The Directive and Regulations apply to "documents". In the Directive, a document is defined as "any content whatever its medium (written on paper or stored in electronic form or as a sound, visual or audio-visual recording)" or any part of such content.[175] However, recital 9 states that this definition is not intended to cover computer programs. According to recital 11, the definition covers "any representation of acts, facts or information—and any compilation of such acts, facts or information—whatever its medium". Regulation 2 defines "document" in substantially the same terms as the Directive, with an express exclusion for computer programs: "any content, including any part of such content, whether in writing or stored in electronic form or as a sound, visual or audio-visual recording, other than a computer program". The text of recital 11 to the Directive is not incorporated into the definition of "document" in the Regulations, presumably on the basis that it is not considered to limit its scope. However, the Regulations define the word "writing" as including text which is transmitted by electronic means, received in legible form and capable of being used for subsequent reference.[176] The reason for this addition, which is not derived from the terms of the Directive, is unclear. Documents in a number of different categories are excluded from the application of the Directive and Regulations and these are considered in the following paragraphs.

10–37

First exclusion: "public task". The first is documents, the supply of which is an activity falling outside the scope of the public task of the public sector body concerned. For these purposes, the "public task" is "as defined by law or by other binding rules in the Member State, or in the absence of such rules as defined in line with common administrative practice in the Member State in question".[177] Nevertheless, the Directive leaves considerable scope for argument as to whether the supply of a particular document is or is not within the public task. This definition is not expressly incorporated into the Regulations, which simply state that they do not apply to a document where "the activity of supplying the document is one which falls outside the public task of the public sector body". Limited assistance as to the meaning of the expression "public task" may be gained from recital 9, which states that activities falling outside the scope of the public task will typically include the supply of documents which are produced and charged for exclusively on a commercial basis and in competition with others in the market. No doubt it was thought that without such an exclusion, the Directive would effectively make such activities impossible.

10–38

Decisions on "public task". In *The Controller of Her Majesty's Stationery Office v Green Amps Ltd*,[178] a summary judgment application, the court left open the question whether the supply of maps by the Ordnance Survey fell within its

10–39

---

[173] See reg.2.
[174] reg.3(1).
[175] art.2(3).
[176] reg.2.
[177] Directive 2003/98 art.1(2)(a).
[178] [2007] EWHC 2755.

public task.[179] In its report on a complaint[180] by Intelligent Addressing Ltd, APPSI[181] held that the provision by the Ordnance Survey of a commercial product called AddressPoint did not fall within the Ordnance Survey's public task, relying in particular on the terms of recital 9 to the Directive.[182] AddressPoint is described in OPSI's report on the complaint as "a dataset that defines and locates residential, business and public postal addresses in Great Britain. It is created by matching information from Ordnance Survey digital map databases with addresses recorded in the Royal Mail Postal Address File (PAF)".[183]

10–40   **Second exclusion: intellectual property rights.** The Directive does not apply to "documents for which third parties hold intellectual property rights".[184] Recital 22 states that "intellectual property rights" refers to copyright and related rights only, including sui generis forms of protection. Accordingly, the Regulations state that they do not apply to a document where a third party owns relevant intellectual property rights in the document.[185] For these purposes, relevant intellectual property rights are defined as copyright, database right, publication right and rights in performances.[186] Recital 22 also contains the following statement: "This Directive does not apply to documents covered by industrial property rights such as patents, registered designs and trade marks". The precise significance of this statement, which is not reproduced in the text of the Directive or in the Regulations, is unclear. Presumably, however, a public authority would not in practice knowingly permit re-use of a document which would amount to or assist in the infringement of one of these rights.

10–41   **Third exclusion: documents excluded from access by access regimes in the Member States.** The Directive does not apply to documents which are excluded from access by virtue of access regimes in the Member States, including on grounds of the protection of national security, defence or public security or statistical or commercial confidentiality.[187]

10–42   **Implementation of the third exclusion.** According to the Explanatory Memorandum,[188] the third exclusion was taken to mean that the Directive does not apply to documents the information in which is not accessible under specific statutory provision, including access legislation such as the Data Protection Act 1998 and the Freedom of Information Acts.[189] This was thought to create two difficulties.

First, the Freedom of Information Acts exempt from access documents which are reasonably accessible to the applicant otherwise than under their terms. Thus, a literal implementation of the exclusion would exclude a vast number of documents, including, for example, all documents which are publicly available on public authorities' websites. According to the Explanatory Memorandum: "This

---

[179] See para.17.
[180] SO 42/8/4.
[181] For the role of APPSI, see para.10–51, below.
[182] See paras 2.15–2.27.
[183] See para.19, fn.1. For the role of OPSI, see para.10–51, below.
[184] art.1(2)(b).
[185] reg.5(1)(b).
[186] reg.2.
[187] art.1(2)(c). See also art.4(5): such bodies are not required to respond to requests, whether positively or negatively.
[188] para.3.2.
[189] The Freedom of Information Act 2000 and the Freedom of Information (Scotland) Act 2002.

is unacceptable in policy terms and if implemented would render this instrument largely redundant".[190]

Secondly, the Directive only applies to documents which are already accessible. Accordingly, a request to re-use a document which is not already accessible necessarily entails a request under the access legislation. Where the body which receives the re-use request also "holds" the document for the purposes of the access legislation, this does not present a problem. However, the request for re-use will not necessarily be to that person. For example, requests for re-use of Crown copyright documents will be made to HMSO, yet HMSO will be unlikely to "hold" the document. Such a request would place the recipient of the request in the impossible position of having to adjudicate on the access request without actually having the document or even being in receipt of a valid access request.[191]

To deal with these problems, reg.5(2) provides that the Regulations apply to a document if (a) it has been identified by the public sector body as being available for re-use; (b) it has been provided to the applicant; or (c) it is accessible by means other than making a request for it within the meaning of the access legislation.[192]

The practical result is intended to be as follows. If the request for re-use is made to the body which also "holds" the document for access purposes, the request will be treated as an access request as well. If the document is one to which the access legislation applies, then it will be provided to the applicant and it will fall within the scope of the Regulations. If the document is only excluded from the scope of the access legislation because it is reasonably accessible, it will also come within the scope of the Regulations.

If, however, the request is made to a body which does not "hold" the document for access purposes, the Regulations will not apply to it. The applicant will need to identify the body which holds the document for access purposes and make an application for access. If that application succeeds, the applicant will then have to make a fresh request for re-use to the body with the power to grant re-use.

The authors of the Explanatory Memorandum recognise that reg.5(2) involves a "divergence from the approach of the Directive", but consider that in practice its policy intention will still be achieved.

Fourth exclusion: broadcasting, education, research and culture. The Directive does not apply to documents held by public service broadcasters, their subsidiaries and similar bodies,[193] documents held by educational and research establishments[194] or documents held by cultural establishments.[195] These exclusions are substantially reproduced in the Regulations.[196] Where any of them applies,   **10–43**

---

[190] See para.3.4.

[191] para.3.9 identifies other difficulties: such adjudications would not be subject to the jurisdiction of the Information Commissioner; moreover, the implementation of such a system would arguably amount to a change in the national rules for access to documents, something which the Directive is not intended to require (see recital 9).

[192] That is, Data Protection Act 1998, the Freedom of Information Acts or the Environmental Information Regulations

[193] art.1(2)(d). The art.4(5) exclusion applies to these bodies as well.

[194] art.1(2)(e). The art.4(5) exclusion also applies to these bodies. The exclusion expressly applies to organisations established for the transfer of research results where relevant.

[195] 198 art.1(2)(f).

[196] reg.5(3). The only change from the language of the Directive concerns the expression in art.5(2)(d): "documents held by … other bodies or their subsidiaries for the fulfilment of a public service broadcasting remit". This is implemented in the following terms: "documents held by … other bodies or their subsidiaries for the purposes of the provision of programme services or the conduct of any activities which a public service broadcaster is required or empowered to provide or to engage in by or under any enactment or other public instrument". According to the Transposition Note, the purpose of this departure from the language of the Directive is to provide

the public sector body is under no obligation to respond to a request for re-use at all: reg.9(2).[197]

10–44   **"Re-use".** In the Regulations, as in the Directive, "re-use" is defined as the use by a person of a document held by a public sector body for a purpose other than the initial purpose within that public sector body's public task for which the document was produced.[198] The object of this definition is to ensure that public authorities which re-use documents in a manner which is outside the scope of their public task, for example to supply them on a purely commercial basis and in competition with others, can only do so on the same terms (in particular as to payment) as anyone else. This is intended to eliminate cross-subsidies.[199] The Directive goes on to provide that exchange of documents between public sector bodies purely in pursuit of their public tasks does not constitute re-use.[200] This is implemented by reg.4(2)(b), which provides that the transfer from one public sector body to another for the purpose of either body carrying out its public task shall not constitute re-use. In addition, however, reg.4(2)(a) provides that re-use shall not include "the transfer for use of a document *within* a public sector body for the purposes of carrying out its own public task" (italics added). According to the Transposition Note, this is considered to be an elaboration on art.2(4): "it seemed illogical that the transfer of documents between [public sector bodies] would not constitute re-use but those transferred for use within a [public sector body] would". It is not clear why this elaboration was thought necessary given that transfer within a public sector body is likely to be for "the initial purpose within the public task for which the documents were produced".

10–45   **Other limitations.** Three further limitations on the scope of the Directive should be mentioned. First, it does not apply where a person is under a legal obligation to prove an interest in order to gain access to documents.[201] This was expressly implemented in the Regulations.[202] Secondly, the Directive leaves intact and in no way affects existing rules about data protection.[203] Thirdly, the Directive provides that the obligations imposed by it apply only in so far as they are compatible with the provisions of international agreements on the protection of intellectual property rights and in particular the Berne Convention and the TRIPS Agreement.[204] It was thought unnecessary to implement the second and third limitations expressly,[205] but no doubt the Regulations must be construed as so limited.

10–46   **General principle.** Regulation 7 provides that a public sector body may permit re-use and that where it does so, it shall do so in accordance with regs 11 to 16. Regulation 11(2) provides that where possible and appropriate a public sector

---

clarification for UK purposes. While this may be debatable, it seems unlikely that the departure will cause any significant difficulty.

[197] Implementing art.4(5) which, on a literal reading, goes further and provides that there is no need even to "process" the request. But some decision will need to be made before it can be determined that the exclusion applies.

[198] reg.4(1), implementing art.2(4) in substantially the same terms.

[199] Recital 9.

[200] art.2(4).

[201] reg.5(5), implementing art.1 (3).

[202] reg.5(5).

[203] art.1(4). In particular, it does not alter the obligations and rights set out in Directive 95/46/EC.

[204] art.1(5). As has already been stated, recital 22 and art.1(2)(b) preserve third-party intellectual property rights, while recital 24 makes clear that the intellectual property rights of public sector bodies are unaffected. Note also that recital 24 states that the Directive is without prejudice to the Information Society Directive (Directive 2001/29/EC) and the Database Directive (Directive 96/9/EC).

[205] See the Transposition Note.

body shall make a document available for re-use by electronic means. These provisions implement art.3 of the Directive, which sets out the "general principle".[206]

Making of requests. Regulation 6 sets out formal requirements for requests. They must be in writing; state the name of the applicant and an address for correspondence; specify the document requested and state the purpose for which the document is to be re-used. These requirements are not derived from the Directive.

10–47

Processing. Regulation 10[207] provides that where possible and appropriate, a public sector body shall ensure that the procedure for processing a request for re-use is capable of being carried out by electronic means. Regulation 8(1) provides that a public sector body shall respond to a request for re-use (that is, refuse it, make the document available or offer re-use on conditions—see reg.8(4)) promptly and in any event before the end of the 20th working day beginning with the day after receipt. Regulation 8(2) provides that where the documents are extensive in quantity or the request raises complex issues, this time period may be extended by the public sector body for a reasonable time. Regulation 8(3) provides that where time is extended in this way, the public sector body must notify the applicant in writing that no decision on re-use has yet been reached and of an estimated date by which it expects to respond to the request. Such notification must be given before the end of the 20th working day following receipt.[208]

10–48

Refusals. Regulation 9(1)[209] provides that where a public sector body refuses a request, it must notify the applicant in writing of the reason for refusal.[210] The notice must contain a reference to the means of redress available to the applicant: reg.9(3). Regulation 9(4) provides that where the reason for the refusal is that a third party owns relevant intellectual property rights in the document,[211] the reg.9(1) notification must identify, where known, the name of the person who owns the relevant rights or the person from whom the public sector body obtained the document.[212]

10–49

Complaints. The Directive requires an applicant whose request has been refused to be notified of "the means of redress in case the applicant wishes to appeal the decision"[213] but without giving further detail. It also requires applicants to be notified of "the available means of redress relating to decision or practices affect-

10–50

---

[206] The word "appropriate" is an addition but its addition seems to accord with common sense.

[207] Implementing the first part of art.4(1).

[208] With one exception, these provisions reflect the default time limits laid down in art.4(2). The exception is that the default time limits provide that any extension will only be for up to 20 working days whereas the Regulations provide for the extension to be for a reasonable time. Departure from the default position is permitted by the first part of art.4(2). However, recital 12 makes clear that any time limits must be (i) reasonable; (ii) in line with the equivalent time for requests to access the document under the relevant access regime; and (iii) short enough to allow the full economic potential of the documents to be exploited. In the recital it is pointed out that this is particularly important where content (e.g. traffic data) is dynamic and its economic value depends on its immediate availability. The authors of the Transposition Note do not seek to deal with these points, simply asserting that the timescale adopted "is a reasonable approach which is consistent with the time frames laid down for the processing of requests for access to documents".

[209] Implementing the first sentence of art.4(3).

[210] This does not apply where the broadcasting, education, research and culture exception applies: see para.10–43 above.

[211] See above, para.10–40.

[212] This implements the second sentence of art.4(3), which actually requires identification of the rightholder or "the licensor from whom the public sector body has obtained the relevant material". According to the Transposition Note it was thought that where a third party owned intellectual property rights the document might not necessarily have been obtained from the licensor. This is surely right and the terms of the Regulation embody a permissible extension of the applicant's rights.

[213] See art.4(4).

ing them".[214] In the United Kingdom, the means of redress are provided for by regs 17 to 21. As required by the Directive, the complaints procedure must not be limited to refusals to supply documents but must apply where a person "believes that a public sector body has failed to comply with any requirement of these Regulations".[215] It must be made available to the public, where possible and appropriate by electronic means.[216] In summary, the first port of call is the public sector body's internal complaints procedure.[217] Such complaints must be determined within a reasonable time. The complainant must be notified of the determination in writing without delay and reasons must be given.[218]

10–51   **Appeals.** If the internal procedure does not resolve the complaint, the complainant may refer it further. If the original request was to OPSI, HMSO or the Queen's Printer for Scotland,[219] the complaint is considered by APPSI.[220] If the initial request was made to any other public sector body, the complaint may first be referred to OPSI.[221] A complainant who is dissatisfied by OPSI's decision may ask APPSI to review it.[222] No express provision is made for challenging decisions of APPSI, but it is thought that these may be amenable to judicial review.

10–52   **Format of documents.** Public sector bodies may make their documents available in any pre-existing format or language, through electronic means where possible and appropriate. There is no obligation to create or adapt documents in order to comply with a request, nor to provide extracts where this would involve disproportionate effort, nor to continue to produce a certain type of document for the purposes of re-use.[223]

10–53   **Conditions.** Regulation 12(1) provides that a public sector body may impose conditions on re-use. Regulation 12(2) provides that such conditions shall not unnecessarily restrict either "the way in which a document may be re-used" or "competition".[224] Any conditions on re-use shall not discriminate between applicants who make a request for re-use for comparable purposes.[225] If a public sector body which holds a document wishes to re-use it for activities which fall outside the scope of its public task, the same conditions shall apply to that re-use as would apply to re-use by any other applicant for comparable purposes.[226] Article 8(2) of the Directive requires the provision of standard digital licences for

---

[214] art.7.
[215] reg.17(2).
[216] See reg.16(1)(d) and 16(2).
[217] reg.17(1).
[218] reg.17(3) and 4).
[219] For these bodies, see paras 10–29, above.
[220] reg.18(3). APPSI is a Non-Departmental Public Body, established on April 14, 2003 by Douglas Alexander, Minister of State at the Cabinet Office. The complaints procedure is on APPSI's website: *http://www.appsi.gov.uk/complaints-resolution/psi-complaints-procedure.pdf* [Accessed November 15, 2010].
[221] reg.18(1). The complaints procedure is on OPSI's website: *http://www.opsi.gov.uk/about/contact-us/complaints/index* [Accessed November 15, 2010].
[222] reg.20(1).
[223] reg.11, implementing art 5. Recital 13 to the Directive states that to facilitate re-use, public sector bodies should make their documents available in a format which, as far as possible and appropriate, is not dependent on the use of specific software; and that the possible use of documents by and for people with disabilities should be taken into account. These statements are not the subject of express provision in the Regulations, but see para.10–53 (Conditions), below.
[224] These provisions implement art.8(1).
[225] reg.13(1), implementing art.10(1). According to recital 19 to the Directive, this is not intended to prevent two particular types of practice: the exchange of information between public bodies free of charge provided this is for the exercise of public tasks while at the same time charging other parties to re-use the same documents; and the adoption of a differentiated charging policy for commercial and non-commercial re-use.
[226] reg.13(2), implementing art.10(2).

electronic processing. This article is not specifically implemented in the Regulations but standard electronic licences for the re-use of Crown copyright material are available.[227] Any conditions must be published,[228] where possible and appropriate by electronic means.[229]

Charges. Regulation 15(1) permits public sector bodies to charge for re-use. Regulation 15(2) provides that the total income from any charge shall not exceed the sum of (a) the cost of collection, production, reproduction and dissemination of documents;[230] and (b) a reasonable return on investment.[231] Regulation 15(2) provides that any charges shall, so far as reasonably practicable, be calculated in accordance with the accounting principles applicable to the public sector body from time to time and on the basis of a reasonable estimate of the demand for documents over the appropriate accounting period.[232] Where reasonably practicable, standard charges must be established and published,[233] where possible and appropriate by electronic means.[234] On request from an applicant, public sector bodies must specify the basis on which any standard charge has been calculated or, if there is no standard charge, the factors that will be taken into account in calculating the charge.[235]   **10–54**

Decisions on charges. In *The Controller of Her Majesty's Stationery Office v Green Amps Ltd*,[236] the court rejected a submission that charges had to be limited to the cost of reproducing the material together with a reasonable return: the claimants were entitled to base their charges on all the expenditure incurred in the collection of information, mapping and other activities carried out in order to provide the end product, together with a reasonable return on that expenditure, which represented their investment. In the same case[237] it was held that if a public body permitted re-use of copyright material but only at a charge in excess of that permitted by the Regulations, that would not provide a defence to a claim that unlicensed reproduction of the material infringed Crown copyright.   **10–55**

Practical arrangements. The Directive obliges Member States to ensure that practical arrangements are in place to facilitate the search for documents available for re-use.[238] This is implemented by reg.16(1)(c), which requires public sector bodies to make available, where possible and appropriate by electronic means,[239] a list of main documents available for re-use. Such lists must, so far as reasonably practicable, be searchable by electronic means.[240]   **10–56**

Exclusive arrangements. The general principle is that the re-use of documents will be open to all potential actors in the market, even if one or more players al-   **10–57**

---

[227] See below, paras 10–59 et seq.
[228] reg.16(1)(a), implementing the first sentence of art.7 so far as it relates to conditions.
[229] See reg.16(2).
[230] A charge for the costs of these activities may not be made if the same applicant has already been charged for them by the public sector body in respect of access to the same document under information access legislation: reg.15(4).
[231] This implements the first sentence of art.6.
[232] This is intended to implement the second sentence of art.6.
[233] regs 15(5) and 16(1)(b), implementing the first sentence of art.7 so far as it relates to charges.
[234] See reg.16(2).
[235] reg.15(6) and (7), implementing the second and third sentences of art.7.
[236] [2007] EWHC 2755 at para.17.
[237] Also at para.17.
[238] Directive 2003/98 art.9.
[239] See reg.16(2).
[240] reg.16(3).

ready exploits value-added products based on these documents.[241] Exclusive arrangements are dealt with in reg.14, which implements art.11 of the Directive. For these purposes an "exclusive arrangement" means a contract or other arrangement granting an exclusive right to re-use a document. Such arrangements are prohibited except where they are necessary for the provision of a service in the public interest. The validity of the reason for granting any exclusive arrangement shall be reviewed at least once every three years. Any exclusive arrangement entered into after December 31, 2003 shall be published by the public sector body. There are transitional provisions for exclusive arrangements which existed when the Regulations came into force.

(v) Re-use regimes

10–58   General. At the time of writing (October 2010) the system is in a state of flux. Four forms of access can be identified. First, the great majority of publicly available Crown copyright material, including much which was previously re-usable under copyright waivers, may be re-used under a licence called the Open Government Licence.[242] Second, in respect of limited categories of material, reproduction of the whole or part is permitted subject to compliance with conditions (in some cases the copyright is said to have been "waived", albeit conditionally). The categories are as follows[243]: the layout of birth, death, marriage and civil partnership certificates; some Welsh and Scottish national curriculum and similar material; Scottish Administration press notices; and Scottish legislation. Third, provision is made for the obtaining of licences to use material in two further categories, namely ministerial speeches and articles and the front cover of the British passport.[244] Finally the holder of a "PSI licence", the predecessor of the Open Government Licence, may still re-use material under that licence until it expires.[245]

(a) *The Open Government Licence*

10–59   Background. In the 1999 White Paper, the Government undertook to introduce standard terms across government for the reproduction of Crown copyright protected material other than "tradeable information" and to feature the licensing terms on HMSO's website.[246] In accordance with this undertaking, material which the Government wished to allow to be re-used and which was not covered by a specific waiver was divided into "value-added" material,[247] and other material. The use of value-added material had to be paid for. The other material could be re-used if the user had entered into a general licence (called a "Core Licence" and later a "PSI licence").[248] As from December 1, 2009, the concept of "value-added material" was abolished and most material formerly so classified was available for free under a "PSI licence".

10–60   The PSI licence. The PSI licence was granted by the Controller of HMSO and the

---

[241] Directive 2003/98 art.11(1).
[242] Below, paras 10–59 et seq.
[243] See paras 10–66 et seq., below.
[244] See below, paras 10–74 and 10–75.
[245] However, where Government material carries an indication that a PSI licence is required, this is to be taken to mean that the Open Government Licence applies. See *http://www.nationalarchives.gov.uk/information-management/government-licensing/faqs.htm* [Accessed October 21, 2010].
[246] Cm 4300, para.7.3.
[247] The term "tradeable information" was dropped.
[248] See *Copinger* 15th edn and 3rd supp, paras 10–44 to 10–48.

Queen's Printer for Scotland to "users throughout the world" and permitted unlimited use subject to conditions designed amongst other things to ensure accuracy and avoid exploitation of the material for advertising purposes. Application was made online. The licence covered Crown copyright and database right material and other copyright material produced by public sector organisations which the Controller of HMSO and the Queen's Printer for Scotland had been mandated to license. It did not apply where the material was the subject of a specific waiver; where the licensing responsibility had been delegated by HMSO to the originating department; where the licence required a department's approval; where there were security, legal or policy restrictions; where the material contained personal information or comprised photographs, films or computer software; or where other rights were involved. Although this licence has been superseded by the Open Government Licence, it seems likely that many such licences remain in force.

The Open Government Licence: introduction. In October 2010, the Government introduced a new licence, the Open Government Licence, which is designed to be used by all public sector bodies including HMSO.[249] The licence covers material (whether covered by Crown copyright or database right or not) which is expressly made available to the public under its terms or (it seems) which carries an indication that a PSI licence is required.[250] The licence applies not only to material formerly covered by the PSI licence,[251] but also to material which was formerly the subject of a specific waiver. At the time of writing the waivers which had been withdrawn included[252] those in respect of United Kingdom, Wales and Northern Ireland primary and secondary legislation and explanatory notes and Measures of the General Synod of the Church of England[253]; Government press notices for England, Wales and Northern Ireland[254]; scientific, technical and medical articles[255]; unpublished public records[256]; court forms[257]; English National Curriculum and similar material[258]; and a variety of other Government material such as forms, consultative documents, material featured on official websites, headline statistics and typographical arrangements.[259]

10–61

The Open Government Licence: exemptions. The licence contains seven specific exemptions from its scope. They are as follows. First, personal data contained in the material. Second, information that has neither been published

10–62

---

[249] http://www.nationalarchives.gov.uk/doc/open-government-licence/ [Accessed October 21, 2010]. See UK Government Licensing Framework for public sector information ("UKGLF") http:// www.nationalarchives.gov.uk/documents/uk-government-licensing-framework.pdf [Accessed November 15, 2010] paras 1 and 4. The Controller may from time to time issue new versions of the licence and what follows concerns Version 1.0 only.

[250] See http://www.nationalarchives.gov.uk/information-management/government-licensing/ faqs.htm [Accessed October 21, 2010]. In the licence, such material is called "Information".

[251] See UKGLF para.4.1.1.

[252] For a non-exhaustive list, see the National Archives publication "Use of information previously covered by the Crown copyright waiver": http://www.nationalarchives.gov.uk/documents/ waiver-information.pdf [Accessed October 22, 2010].

[253] See Copinger 15th edn paras 10–30 and 10–31. For Scottish legislation, see below paras 10–72 and 10–73.

[254] See Copinger 15th edn para.10–42. For Scottish Administration Press Notices, see para.10–71 below.

[255] See Copinger 14th edn, para.10–30.

[256] See Copinger 15th edn, paras 10–32 to 10–34.

[257] See Copinger 15th edn, paras 10–36 and 10–37.

[258] See Copinger 15th edn, paras 10–39 to 10–41. For equivalent Scottish and Welsh material, see below paras 10–68 to 10–70.

[259] The text of ministerial speeches and articles is also stated to be subject to the Open Government Licence. See Use of information previously covered by the Crown copyright waiver: http:// www.nationalarchives.gov.uk/documents/waiver-information.pdf [Accessed October 22, 2010]. See, however, para.10–74, below.

nor disclosed under information access legislation by or with the consent of the provider of the material. Third, departmental or public sector logos, crests and the Royal Arms, except where they form an integral part of a document or dataset. Fourth, military insignia. Fifth, third-party rights which the provider is not authorised to license. Sixth, information subject to other intellectual property rights, including patents, trade marks and design rights. Seventh, identity documents such as the British passport.[260] Source code and software originated by the Crown is no longer exempted unless it has been developed from a source that is subject to an open source licence.[261] Unlike the PSI licence, the Open Government Licence potentially applies to Crown material that is licensed under a delegation of authority from HMSO.[262]

10–63   **The Open Government Licence: what is permitted.** The licence itself is a worldwide, royalty-free, perpetual, non-exclusive licence to "use" the material subject to certain conditions. The term "use" means to do any act which is restricted by copyright or database right in any medium. The licence contains two illustrative lists of permitted uses.

10–64   **The Open Government Licence: conditions.** The conditions resemble those which applied to the previous waivers and the PSI licence but are shorter. Failure to comply will result in the automatic termination of the licence and any similar licence[263] granted by the provider. First, the source must be acknowledged. This must be done by including any attribution statement specified by the provider of the material and where possible a link to the licence.[264] Second, the user must not use the material in a way that suggests any official status or that the provider endorses the use. Third, the user must not mislead others or misrepresent the material or its source. Fourth, the user must ensure that the use does not breach the Data Protection Act 1988 or the Privacy and Electronic Communications (EC Directive) Regulations 2003.[265] The terms of the Open Government Licence are stated to have been "aligned to be interoperable" with the latest versions of the Creative Commons Attribution Licence.[266] It is not clear what is meant by this. The attribution required by the Creative Commons Attribution Licence appears to extend to authors and therefore to be broader than that required by the Open Government Licence. Moreover, the second, third and fourth conditions mentioned above are not conditions of the Creative Commons licence.[267]

10–65   **The Open Government Licence: other contractual terms.** Use of material which is subject to the licence indicates the user's acceptance of the terms of the licence, thus establishing a contractual licence. Accordingly, there is no longer any need to make a specific application. The material is licensed "as is" and all representations, warranties, obligations and liabilities in relation to the material are excluded to the maximum extent permitted by law. The provider is not liable for any errors or omissions in the material or for any loss, injury or damage of any kind caused by its use. The provider does not guarantee the continued supply

---

[260] As to the British passport, see further below, para.10–75.
[261] See UKGLF para.4.1.1. Software developed from open source software may be released under a licence consistent with the open source software: UKGLF para.5.3.
[262] See UKGLF para.4.1.1.
[263] What amounts to a "similar" licence is left undefined.
[264] In the absence of such an attribution statement or if the material derives from several providers and multiple attributions are not practical, the user "may consider" using the following: "Contains public sector information licensed under the Open Government Licence v1.0".
[265] SI 2003/2426.
[266] See Creative Commons Attribution 2.0 England & Wales: *http://creativecommons.org/licenses/by/2.0/uk/legalcode* [Accessed October 21, 2010].
[267] Although the latter does prohibit derogatory treatment.

of the information. The licence is governed by the law of the jurisdiction in which the provider has its principal place of business unless the provider specifies otherwise.

(b) *Remaining specific waivers*

Birth, death, marriage and civil partnership certificates: background. The extent of the waiver in this field was extensively revised in April 2009.[268] Prior to that date it extended to the form of marriage registers and the completed certificates.[269] The present position is that the Crown asserts copyright in the layout of the certificates, but not in their content.[270] There is no waiver in relation to the form of marriage registers.[271]   **10–66**

Birth, death, marriage and civil partnership certificates: what is permitted. The layout of the form of official birth, death, marriage and civil partnership certificates may be reproduced in any format subject to a number of conditions. It is only the layout of the form which may be reproduced and not the content.[272] The conditions are as follows.[273] First, reproductions of certificates must not be used to provide evidence of birth, death, marriage or civil partnership: instead, an official certificate must be obtained. Secondly, the material must not be used to advertise or promote a particular product or service or in a way which could imply endorsement by the Government. Thirdly, the user must comply with the Data Protection Act 1998 and the Human Rights Act 1998. Fourthly, the Royal Arms and any departmental logo may only be reproduced as an integral part of the certificate.   **10–67**

Welsh National Curriculum and similar material: scope of waiver. At the time of writing, no waiver is in place in respect of English national curriculum and similar material but one remains in place in respect of Welsh material. In Wales, substantial amounts of national curriculum material are created by the National Assembly for Wales and the Qualifications, Curriculum and Assessment Authority for Wales ("ACCAC"). ACCAC has assigned the copyright in some material created by it to the Crown.[274] Copyright is waived subject to conditions in: the National Curriculum Orders,[275] the Programmes of Study[276] and the At-   **10–68**

---

[268] See now Guidance Note 7: Guidance on the Copying of Birth, Death, Marriage and Civil Partnership Certificates, revised April 2009, updated June 5, 2009, *http://www.nationalarchives.gov.uk/documents/copying-bmd-certificates.pdf* [Accessed October 22, 2010].

[269] See Copinger 15th edn and third cumulative supplement, paras 10–37 and 10–38.

[270] Guidance Note 7 para.1.

[271] It is understood that this is not because the Crown does not claim any rights in such registers but because there are few circumstances in which members of the public are likely to obtain access to them. In particular, the certificates issued by General Register Offices do not contain a reproduction of the form of the register (conversation with Mathew Pearce, National Archives, April 27, 2010).

[272] Guidance Note 7, para.2. Accordingly "This guidance does not authorise you to reproduce the contents of any certificate containing personal data about living individuals".

[273] Guidance Note 7, para.2.

[274] Guidance Note 10, Guidance—Reproduction of National Curriculum Material for Wales, revised March 15, 2008. See *http://www.nationalarchives.gov.uk/documents/reproduction-national-curriculum-material-wales.pdf* [Accessed October 21, 2010].

[275] That is, the Statutory Instruments which give the National Curriculum statutory effect.

[276] The Programmes of Study set out for each subject what pupils should be taught. ACCAC has assigned copyright in them to the Crown. Copyright in the explanatory material relating to them has been retained by ACCAC but it has agreed that this material may be reproduced under the same conditions as the Crown protected material provided an appropriate acknowledgment is given: Guidance Note 10, para.11.

tainment Targets.[277] Copyright in the explanatory material relating to the programmes of study is retained by ACCAC but may be reproduced on the same terms as Crown copyright material referred to above.[278] The relevant Guidance Note lists other material the copyright in which is retained by ACCAC but in respect of which a licence may be granted on terms.[279] There is no waiver if copyright in any material is marked as belonging to a person other than the Crown.[280]

10–69   **Welsh National Curriculum and similar material: conditions of waiver.** The conditions are as follows[281]: All reproduction should be made from an official version.[282] The material must be reproduced accurately. In the case of translations into other languages, a competent translator must be used, especially where the translation is to be issued to the public. Care should be taken that material reproduced is from the current or up-to-date version and that out-of-date material is not presented as current. Where out-of-date material is being reproduced for the purposes of drawing comparisons with current material or similar analysis, it should be made clear that the out-of-date material has been superseded, with appropriate cross-references. The material should not be used in a derogatory or misleading manner, nor should it be used for the purposes of advertising or promoting a particular product or service or for promoting particular personal interests or views. The reproduced versions of the material should not be presented in a way which could imply that they have the same authoritative status as the official versions. The Royal Arms and any Assembly or ACCAC logos or similar images should be removed from any copies which are issued or made available to the public, whether in hard copy or in electronic form. Finally, the material must be appropriately acknowledged.[283]

10–70   **Educational material: Scotland.** There is no statutory national curriculum in Scotland. National guidelines are produced by the Scottish Executive Education Department ("SEED") and Learning and Teaching Scotland ("LT Scotland"). Assessment materials are produced by the Scottish Qualifications Agency ("SQA"). Guidelines produced by SEED and LT Scotland are Crown copyright.[284] The SQA has assigned the copyright in some of the material created by it to the Crown,[285] which in turn has been waived, subject to conditions. The material is as follows: the 5–14 Guidelines[286]; the 5–14 National Test Information for Teachers; and the 5–14 National Test Exemplars. The conditions are almost identical to those applicable to the reproduction of legislation.[287]Again, a prescribed acknowledgment must be given.[288] Other paragraphs of the relevant Guidance

---

[277] The Attainment Targets set out the expected standards of pupils' performance for each of the principal subjects studied.

[278] The Attainment Targets set out the expected standards of pupils' performance for each of the principal subjects studied.

[279] Guidance Note 10, paras 12 and 13. See also para.14 which indicates what acknowledgement is considered sufficient when exercising a permitted act in relation to this material.

[280] Guidance Note 10, para.15.

[281] Guidance Note 10, para.8.

[282] The Guidance Note explains what an official version is: see para.8(a).

[283] A form is provided: Guidance Note 10 para.9.

[284] Queen's Printer for Scotland Guidance Note 3, Reproduction of 5–14 Curriculum Documents, January 16, 2002, updated September 20, 2007, para.1. See *http://www.oqps.gov.uk/crown-copyright/guidance/guidance-note-reproduction-of-curriculum-documents* [Accessed November 15, 2010]

[285] Queen's Printer for Scotland Guidance Note 3, paras 6 and 7.

[286] These guidelines are used by schools to describe the curriculum and assessment of pupils from primary 1 to secondary 2. See Queen's Printer for Scotland Guidance Note 3, paras 5, 6 and 8.

[287] See para.10–73.

[288] Queen's Printer for Scotland Guidance Note 3, para.10.

Note set out arrangements for material the copyright in which is retained by the SQA.[289]

Press Notices issued by the Scottish Administration. Government Press Notices for England, Northern Ireland and Wales are now governed by the Open Government Licence.[290] However, a waiver still applies to press notices and releases issued by the Scottish Administration (including their typographical arrangements), which accordingly may be reproduced freely.[291] Where the notice contains a statement that copyright in specific material is not held by the Crown there is no right to reproduce that material.[292] The Crown asks[293] that users ensure that the material is reproduced accurately and not in a way that might confuse or mislead others, that it is correctly acknowledged in the form set out in the Guidance Note and that the Royal Arms are removed when the material is published.[294]

10–71

Scottish legislation: background to and scope of the waiver. Prior to the 1999 White Paper, Crown copyright legislative material could only be reproduced in limited circumstances and subject to stringent conditions.[295] In the White Paper, the Government announced its intention to waive Crown copyright in Acts of Parliament, Measures of the General Synod of the Church of England, Statutory Instruments from England and Wales, and Statutory Rules of Northern Ireland.[296] This was done, and the waiver eventually extended to material in all these categories as well as to Acts of the Northern Ireland Assembly and Scottish Parliament, Explanatory Notes to Acts and to Scottish Statutory Instruments.[297] Since October 2010, all this material apart from Scottish material has been subject to the Open Government Licence.[298] Acts of the Scottish Parliament, Explanatory Notes to such Act and Scottish Statutory Instruments are still covered by a waiver, as are their typographical arrangements.[299]

10–72

Scottish legislation: terms of the waiver. Provided certain conditions are complied with, there are no restrictions whatsoever on how material which is subject to the waiver may be reproduced.[300] However, the waiver is conditional on compliance with those conditions, which are intended to prevent the use of the material in a misleading or derogatory manner.[301] The conditions are as follows[302]: All reproduction should be made from an official version. This means either the authorised versions published by the Queen's Printer for Scotland or the text

10–73

---

[289] Queen's Printer for Scotland Guidance Note 3, paras 12 and 13.

[290] See above, paras 10–61 et seq.

[291] Queen's Printer for Scotland Guidance Note 2: Reproduction of Press Notices Issued by the Scottish Administration, updated September 20, 2007. See *http://www.oqps.gov.uk/crown-copyright/guidance/guidance-note-reproduction-of-scottish-press-notices* [Accessed November 15, 2010].

[292] Guidance Note 2, para.6 .

[293] Sic. It is not clear whether failure to comply with this request will lead to infringement action.

[294] Guidance Note 2, para.7.

[295] See *Copinger* 14th edn, para.10–29.

[296] Cm. 4300, para.5.2.

[297] See *Copinger* 15th edn, paras 10–30 to 10–32.

[298] See paras 10–61 et seq., above.

[299] Queen's Printer for Scotland Guidance Note: Reproduction of Acts of the Scottish Parliament, Explanatory Notes to Acts of the Scottish Parliament and Scottish Statutory Instruments, last updated on September 20, 2007 ("Guidance"), *http://www.oqps.gov.uk/crown-copyright/guidance/guidance-note-reproduction-of-scottish-legislation* [Accessed October 22, 2010], para.6.

[300] Guidance, para.8.

[301] Guidance, para.7.

[302] Guidance, para.10. Some of the conditions are prefaced by "should", others by "must" However, the waiver is expressed to be conditional on their being complied with. Accordingly, it is thought that breach of a condition prefaced by "should" is just as likely to give rise to a termination of the waiver as breach of one prefaced by "must".

featured on the relevant official Scottish Legislation website[303] (users wishing to reproduce the material from any value added legislation product or service provided by the Scottish Administration will need to enter into separate and specific licensing arrangements).[304] The material must be reproduced accurately. In the case of translations into other languages, a competent translator must be used where the translation is to be issued to the public. Care should be taken that material reproduced is from the current or up-to-date version and that out-of-date material is not presented as current. Where out-of-date material is being reproduced for the purposes of drawing comparisons with current material or similar analysis, it should be made clear that the out-of-date material has been superseded, with appropriate cross-references to the current material. The material should not be used in a derogatory or misleading manner, nor should it be used for the purposes of advertising or promoting a particular product or service or for promoting particular personal interests or views.[305] The reproduced versions of the material should not be presented in a way which could imply that they have official status or that they are endorsed by any part of Government. All publisher imprints which are featured on the official versions of the material should be removed from any copies which are issued or made available to the public, whether in hard copy or in electronic form. The Royal Arms may only be reproduced where they form an integral part of the material being reproduced and are used in that context. For example, the cover of an Act of Parliament featuring the Royal Arms may be reproduced in a compendium or database product if the rest of the Act is being reproduced. Finally, the material must be appropriately acknowledged.[306]

(c) *Other schemes*

10–74 **Articles and presentations by Ministers and civil servants.** According to the National Archives publication *Use of information previously covered by the Crown copyright waiver*,[307] re-use of the text of ministerial article and speeches was formerly subject to a waiver but is now governed by the Open Government Licence. In fact, however, this material was formerly subject to a scheme pursuant to which a licence was required,[308] and although the guidance note in relation to this scheme is no longer available, the sample licence agreement which was formerly annexed to the guidance note is on the National Archives website.[309] The agreement is for the grant by the relevant department[310] of a non-exclusive licence to publish the work in question in any format throughout the world; to sub-license customers to access the work in digital products and services; to authorise the inclusion of the article in collective licensing schemes such as that operated by the Copyright Licensing Agency; and to authorise the inclusion of the article as part of document delivery, abstracting or indexing services. The author and the head of department warrant that the work infringes no existing copyright and contains no defamatory or obscene material. They also warrant

---

[303] Guidance Note 6, para.12(a); Scottish guidance para.10(a).
[304] Guidance, para.13.
[305] Presumably a single-interest campaign which is supported by a significant number of other people would not be regarded as a "particular personal interest or view".
[306] See the forms of acknowledgment in the Guidance.
[307] *http://www.nationalarchives.gov.uk/documents/waiver-information.pdf* [Accessed October 22, 2010].
[308] Guidance—Publication of Articles written by Ministers and Civil Servants in Journals and Conference Proceedings, updated December 23, 2008.
[309] *http://www.nationalarchives.gov.uk/documents/articles-ministers-civil-servants-annexa.pdf.* [Accessed November 15, 2010]
[310] To whom the authority to license has been delegated by the Controller.

that the department has obtained permission for the publication of any material which is not Crown copyright. The publisher has five obligations. First, an appropriate acknowledgement must be given (the licence contains a form of words). Second, the author must be identified in a suitably prominent manner. Third, the work must be reproduced accurately and without alteration or amendment except with the author's prior approval. Fourth, the publication must not be for the purpose of advertising or promoting a particular product or service. Finally, a copy of the publication must be provided to the author.

The front cover of the British passport. The front cover of the British passport   **10–75** may be reproduced as part of a work, including promotional and advertising works, provided it is not the main focus of the cover of a work or of an advertisement and there is no alteration.[311] It seems that a specific licence must be sought from the Office of Public Sector Information in each case and that there may be a fee.[312] The Guidance Note gives advice about reproduction of the personal details page of the passport in terms which suggest that the holder may do this and may sub-license others to do it.

D. MORAL RIGHTS

Limited scope in relation to Crown works. The rights created by the 1988 Act   **10–76** to be identified as author or director[313] and to object to derogatory treatment of a work[314] have only limited scope in relation to works in which Crown copyright subsists. The right to be identified as author or director does not apply in relation to a work in which Crown copyright subsists unless the author or director has been identified as such in or on published copies of the work.[315] It follows that the Crown[316] will effectively be able to determine whether this right can ever be asserted in relation to a work in which Crown copyright subsists. The right to object to derogatory treatment of a work in which Crown copyright subsists does not apply to anything done in relation to such a work by or with the authority of the copyright owner unless the author or director is identified at the time of the relevant act or has previously been identified in or on published copies of the work.[317] Even where the right applies, it is not infringed if there is a sufficient disclaimer.[318]

2. PARLIAMENTARY RIGHTS

A. INTRODUCTION

The scheme of the 1988 Act. The 1988 Act created a new species of copyright   **10–77** called parliamentary copyright, which subsists in works made by or under the direction of the House of Commons or the House of Lords.[319] The Act also makes special provision for the copyright in parliamentary bills to belong to one or both

---

[311] Guidance—Reproduction of the Front Cover of the British Passport, revised December 2009, para.4. See *http://www.nationalarchives.gov.uk/documents/reproduction-british-passport.pdf* [Accessed October 22, 2010].
[312] Guidance—Reproduction of the Front Cover of the British Passport, paras 6 and 7.
[313] CDPA 1988 s.77. See Ch.11.
[314] s.80. See Ch.11.
[315] s.79(7)(a). For the meaning of "publication" and related expressions, see s.175(1) and paras 3–174 et seq., above.
[316] Or its assignee: Crown copyright continues to subsist in a work the copyright in which has been assigned by the Crown: CDPA 1988 s.163(2).
[317] s.82(2). For the meaning of "publication" and related expressions, see s.175(1) and paras 3–174 et seq., above.
[318] s.82(2). For the meaning of "sufficient disclaimer", see CDPA 1988 s.178, and Ch.11, below.
[319] CDPA 1988 s.165.

Houses of Parliament.[320] For the purposes of holding, dealing with and enforcing these types of copyright, each House of Parliament is to be treated as a body corporate.[321] These provisions have now been extended to works made by or under the direction of the Scottish Parliament, the Northern Ireland Assembly and the National Assembly for Wales and to bills or (as the case may be) proposed measures introduced into those bodies.[322]

10-78   **The policy of the 1988 Act.** Under the 1956 Act, the Crown was entitled to the copyright in every literary, dramatic, musical or artistic work which was first published under the direction or control of Her Majesty or of a Government department ("the first publication rule").[323] This rule enabled the Crown to obtain the copyright in material produced by Parliament, including perhaps most importantly, in *Hansard*, simply by being the first to publish it. The Whitford Committee criticised the first publication rule on the grounds that it led to potential injustice[324] and the Government proposed its abolition in its 1986 White Paper.[325] However, at the same time it was considered that the abolition of the first publication rule would give rise to uncertainty as to the ownership of the copyright in parliamentary material and in particular in *Hansard*.[326] The Government's original intention was to make such material the subject of Crown copyright.[327] However, following the introduction of the Bill which became the 1988 Act, the Government concluded that to vest such copyright in the Crown would be undesirable, apparently because it would have the effect of vesting the control of parliamentary papers with the controller of HMSO rather than with the House in question.[328] Because the precise legal personalities of the Houses of Parliament were thought to be unclear, it was considered to be necessary to endue them with a statutory legal personality so that they could hold, deal with and enforce their copyright.[329] For Scotland, Northern Ireland and Wales, the equivalent bodies are the Scottish Parliamentary Corporate Body, the Northern Ireland Assembly Commission and the National Assembly for Wales Commission respectively.[330] The structure of the Parliamentary copyright provisions is similar to that of the provisions relating to statutory Crown copyright.[331]

B. PARLIAMENTARY COPYRIGHT

(i) Copyright in works other than Parliamentary Bills

10-79   **Subsistence, ownership and term.** The general provisions of the 1988 Act relating to subsistence, first ownership and duration of copyright do not apply to works made by or under the direction or control of either of the Houses of

---

[320] s.166.
[321] s.167.
[322] See below at paras 10–80 and 10–89, respectively.
[323] Copyright Act 1956 s.39(2).
[324] See para.10–10, above.
[325] *Intellectual Property and Innovation*, Cmnd.9712 para.16.9.
[326] *Intellectual Property and Innovation*, Cmnd.9712 para.16.9.
[327] *Intellectual Property and Innovation*, Cmnd.9712 para.16.9.
[328] *Hansard*, HC, col.93 (S.C.E.); HL Vol.501, col.194.
[329] *Hansard*, H.L., Vol.501, col.194.
[330] See the Parliamentary Copyright (Scottish Parliament) Order 1999 (SI 1999/676), the Parliamentary Copyright (Northern Ireland Assembly) Order 1999 (SI 1999/3146) and the Parliamentary Copyright (National Assembly for Wales) Order 2007 (SI 2007/1116), respectively.
[331] i.e. CDPA 1988 s.163. See paras 10–10 et seq., above.

Parliament.[332] Instead, s.165(1) of the 1988 Act provides that where a work[333] is made by or under the direction or control of either House of Parliament, it qualifies for copyright protection even if the ordinary qualification requirements are not satisfied,[334] and that the House by which, or under the direction or control of which the work is made is the first owner of any copyright in the work.[335] If the work is made by or under the direction or control of both Houses, the two Houses are joint first owners of the copyright.[336] The term "direction and control", which was used in relation to Crown copyright in the 1956 Act,[337] was criticised by the Whitford Committee, which expressed the view that a provision in language of such width was likely to lead to difficulty.[338] Presumably with the object of reducing the likelihood of such difficulties, s.165 of the 1988 Act contains a limited definition of the term. Thus, it is provided that for the purposes of these provisions, works made by or under the direction or control of the House of Commons or House of Lords include any work made by an officer or employee of that House in the course of his duties[339] and any sound recording, film, live broadcast or live cable programme of the proceedings of that House.[340] On the other hand, a work is not to be regarded as made by or under the direction of either House by reason only of its being commissioned by or on behalf of that House.[341] It is provided that copyright in works made under the direction of the Houses of Parliament is referred to in Pt I of the 1988 Act as "Parliamentary copyright" even if it has been assigned to another person.[342] Parliamentary copyright in a literary, dramatic, musical or artistic work continues to subsist until the end of the period of 50 years from the end of the calendar year in which the work was made.[343] In the absence of specific provision, the term of Parliamentary copyright for all other works will be the normal term.[344] No publication right arises from the publication of a work in which Parliamentary copyright subsisted.[345]

Scottish, Welsh and Northern Irish parliamentary copyright. By s.165(7) of the 1988 Act, the provisions of s.165 (which contains provisions as to the subsistence and term of parliamentary copyright) apply, subject to any exceptions or modifications specified by Order in Council,[346] to works made by or under the direction or control of any other legislative body to which the copyright Part of the 1988 Act extends and references to "parliamentary copyright" are to be construed accordingly. By s.157(1), the 1988 Act extends to Wales, Scotland and Northern Ireland. Legislation creating devolved institutions in Scotland, Northern Ireland and Wales has made it necessary to provide for the application of s.165 to works made by or under the direction or control of those bodies. Accordingly,

10–80

---

[332] CDPA 1988 ss.153(2) (subsistence), 11(3) (first ownership) and 12(9) (duration).

[333] For what may be a copyright work, see CDPA 1988 s.1. Note that Parliamentary copyright may subsist in works of all classes.

[334] CDPA 1988 s.165(1)(a). For the ordinary qualification requirements, see CDPA 1988 s.153(1) and paras 3–154 et seq., above.

[335] s.165(1)(b).

[336] s.165(1).

[337] Copyright Act 1956 s.39(1).

[338] Cmnd.6732 para.593.

[339] CDPA 1988 s.165(4)(a).

[340] s.165(4)(b). Note that these definitions are not exhaustive.

[341] s.165(4). Before the passing of the 1988 Act, the Government was of the view that it was unclear whether the words "work made ... under the direction or control of" extended to works which were commissioned: *Hansard*, HL Vol.491, cols 553–554.

[342] CDPA 1988 s.165(2).

[343] CDPA 1988 s.165(3).

[344] As to which, see Ch.6.

[345] Copyright and Related Rights Regulations 1996 (SI 1996/2967) reg.16(5).

[346] A statutory instrument containing an Order in Council under this provision shall be subject to annulment in pursuance of a resolution of either House of Parliament: CDPA 1988 s.165(8).

s.165 of the 1988 Act now applies to works made by or under the direction or control of the Scottish Parliament, the Northern Ireland Assembly and the National Assembly of Wales, with appropriate modifications to make the section applicable to these bodies.[347] The main modifications are that the first owner of Scottish parliamentary copyright is the Scottish Parliamentary Corporate Body,[348] the first owner of Northern Irish parliamentary copyright is the Northern Ireland Assembly Commission[349] and the first owner of Welsh parliamentary copyright is the National Assembly for Wales Commission.[350] In each case there are also appropriate modifications to the definition of the term "under the direction or control".[351]

10–81   **Works of joint authorship.** In the case of works of joint authorship where one or more but not all of the authors are acting on behalf of, or under the direction or control of, one of the legislative bodies in question, s.165 applies only in relation to those authors and the copyright subsisting by virtue of their contribution to the work.[352] Accordingly, in order to establish the subsistence of copyright in that part of the work contributed by a person who was not acting on behalf of or under the direction or control of one of the Houses, it will be necessary to show that the ordinary qualifying requirements are satisfied.[353] Furthermore, the term of copyright in that part of the work to which that person contributed will be the normal term.[354]

10–82   **Application of Part I of the 1988 Act to parliamentary copyright.** It is provided that with the exception of the special rules outlined above in relation to subsistence, title and term, and subject to any express exclusion elsewhere in Pt I of the 1988 Act, the copyright Part of the 1988 Act is to apply to parliamentary copyright as to other copyright.[355] Accordingly, for example, the ordinary rules apply to any dealings with parliamentary copyright[356] and the Houses of Parliament, the Scottish Parliamentary Corporate Body, the Northern Ireland Assembly Commission, the National Assembly for Wales Commission and their assignees are entitled to the ordinary remedies for infringement.[357] It should, however, be noted that copyright is not infringed by anything done for the purposes of

---

[347] For the Scottish Parliament these modifications are effected by the Parliamentary Copyright (Scottish Parliament) Order 1999 (SI 1999/676), with effect from May 6, 1999: ibid., art.1(1). For the Northern Ireland Assembly the modifications are effected by the Parliamentary Copyright (Northern Ireland Assembly) Order 1999 (SI 1999/3146). The latter came into force on the day appointed for the commencement of Pts II and III of the Northern Ireland Act 1998, i.e. December 2, 1999: see the Northern Ireland Act 1998 (Appointed Day) Order 1999 (SI 1999/3208). For the Welsh Assembly, these modifications are effected by the Parliamentary Copyright (National Assembly for Wales) Order 2007 (SI 2007/1116). By art.1(2), the Order came into effect immediately after the ordinary election under s.3 of the Government of Wales Act 1998 held in 2007. That election took place on May 3, 2007.

[348] SI 1999/676 art.2(b).

[349] SI 1999/3146 art.2(b).

[350] SI 2007/1116 art.2(2).

[351] See art.2 of each of the Orders.

[352] CDPA 1988 s.165(5). There is an apparent lacuna in this provision in that it refers only to authors acting on behalf of, or under the direction or control of the House of Commons or Lords. No provision is made in respect of works made jointly by the Houses themselves together with persons not acting on behalf of them or under their direction or control.

[353] As to which see CDPA 1988 s.153(1) and paras 3–154 et seq., above.

[354] A work of joint authorship is a work where the respective contributions of the joint authors are not distinct from each other: CDPA 1988 s.10(1). Difficulties may therefore arise in identifying the respective contributions of the joint authors for the purposes of establishing the term of the copyright in the various parts of the work.

[355] CDPA 1988 s.163(5).

[356] ss.90 to 92.

[357] ss.96–115.

parliamentary proceedings or for the purposes of reporting such proceedings but that copying a published report of those proceedings is an infringement.[358]

Works made before August 1, 1989. The only pre-commencement works to which the provisions of the 1988 Act creating parliamentary copyright apply arc literary, dramatic, musical and artistic works which were created before August 1, 1989 and werc unpublished on that date. Many of the published works created by or under the direction or control of the Houses of Parliament before August 1, 1989 were published by the Crown.[359] Accordingly, the copyright in these works remains vested in the Crown under the first publication rule contained in the 1956 Act.[360]   **10–83**

(ii) Copyright in Parliamentary Bills

Subsistence. Section 166 of the 1988 Act provides that copyright subsists in every Bill introduced into Parliament. In relation to public Bills, copyright subsists from the time when the text of the Bill is handed in to the House in which it is introduced.[361] In relation to private Bills, copyright subsists at the time when a copy of the Bill is first deposited in either House.[362] In relation to personal Bills, copyright subsists from the time when the Bill is given a First Reading in the House of Lords.[363] The copyright status of a Bill before it has been introduced into Parliament is not clear. The ordinary rules as to subsistence of copyright do not apply in relation to copyright under s.166.[364] However, copyright only subsists under s.166 when the Bill has been introduced into Parliament. It would seem to follow that the ordinary rules as to subsistence of copyright in literary works apply before the Bill has been introduced. Furthermore, it may be said that a Bill is not yet in any true sense a Bill until it has been introduced into Parliament. Finally, it is worth noting that although s.166(7) of the 1988 Act expressly provides that no copyright is to subsist in a Bill after it has once subsisted in accordance with s.166, there is no similar provision in relation to the position before such copyright comes into existence. If copyright subsists in Bills before they are introduced into Parliament, that copyright will almost invariably in the case of Government bills be owned by the Crown because they will have been drafted by officers or servants of the Crown in the course of their duties.[365] However, this will not necessarily be true of Bills drafted by or on behalf of private members or the promoters of private bills.   **10–84**

Ownership. The owner of the copyright in a Bill depends on the nature of the Bill itself. Thus, the copyright in a public Bill belongs in the first instance to the House in which it is introduced, but after the Bill has been carried to the second   **10–85**

---

[358] s.45. See para.9–143, above. "Parliamentary proceedings" includes proceedings of the Northern Ireland Assembly or the Scottish Parliament or proceedings of the Welsh Assembly: CDPA 1988 s.178.

[359] *Hansard*, HL Vol.501, col.194.

[360] Copyright Act 1956 s.39.

[361] CDPA 1988 s.166(2).

[362] s.166(3).

[363] s.166(4).

[364] s.153(2) provides that s.153(1) does not apply in relation to parliamentary copyright and contains a cross-reference to s.166. References to parliamentary copyright in Pt I of the 1988 Act (except those in s.165) include references to copyright in Bills: s.166(6).

[365] CDPA 1988 s.163(1). Many draft Bills are created by the Law Commission, which is listcd as a Crown body in OPSI's list of Crown bodies. The Law Commission states that the material on its website is Crown copyright. There is no contrary indication in the draft Bills annexed to its reports. It follows that the Law Commission believes that they are subject to Crown copyright.

House, the copyright belongs to both Houses jointly.[366] The copyright in a private Bill belongs to both Houses jointly.[367] The copyright in a personal Bill belongs in the first instance to the House of Lords,[368] and after it has been carried to the House of Commons it belongs to both Houses jointly.[369]

10–86   **Term.** The time when copyright begins to subsist in a parliamentary Bill is discussed above.[370] So far as concerns the cessation of such copyright, the 1988 Act provides that the copyright automatically ceases on Royal Assent.[371] If the Bill does not receive Royal Assent, the copyright in it ceases on the withdrawal or rejection of the Bill at the end of the Session.[372] However, it is provided that copyright in a Bill which has been rejected in any Session by the House of Lords does not cease to subsist if, by virtue of the Parliament Acts 1911 and 1949, it remains possible for it to be presented for Royal Assent in that Session. It is further provided that no other copyright or right in the nature of copyright subsists in a Bill after parliamentary copyright has once subsisted in it.[373] However, this rule is without prejudice to the subsequent operation of s.166 in relation to a Bill which, having not passed in one session, is reintroduced in a subsequent session.[374] Accordingly, even though copyright will normally cease to subsist in a Bill which has been rejected by Parliament, such copyright will nevertheless come back into existence if the Bill is reintroduced at a later date.

10–87   **Pre-commencement Bills.** The provisions of the 1988 Act relating to parliamentary Bills have only a very limited application to Bills introduced into Parliament before the commencement of the Act on August 1, 1989. The precise extent of the application of these provisions depends on the nature of the Bill. The provisions do not apply to public Bills introduced into Parliament and published before commencement,[375] or to private Bills of which copies were deposited in either House before commencement,[376] or to personal Bills which had been given their First Reading in the House of Lords before commencement.[377] In these instances, the normal provisions of the 1988 Act (including its transitional provisions) will apply.[378] Accordingly, copyright may well subsist in them as literary works.

10–88   **Application of Part I of the 1988 Act to the copyright in parliamentary Bills.** It is provided that with the exception of the special rules outlined above in relation to subsistence, title and term, the copyright Part of the 1988 Act is to apply to copyright in parliamentary Bills as to other parliamentary copyright.[379] The extent to which this Part applies to Parliamentary copyright is dealt with above.[380]

10–89   **Bills of the Scottish Parliament, Northern Ireland Assembly and Welsh**

---

[366] CDPA 1988 s.166(2).
[367] s.166(3).
[368] Such Bills are customarily presented in the House of Lords: 34 *Halsbury's Laws*, 4th edn, reissue), "Parliament", para.907.
[369] CDPA 1988 s.166(4).
[370] See para.10–84.
[371] CDPA 1988 s.166(5)(a).
[372] s.166(5)(b).
[373] s.166(7).
[374] s.166(7).
[375] CDPA 1988 Sch.1 para.43(2)(a).
[376] Sch.1 para.43(2)(b).
[377] Sch.1 para.43(2)(c).
[378] Sch.1 paras 3 and 5.
[379] CDPA 1988 s.166(6).
[380] See para.10–82, above.

Assembly. Section 166A(1) of the 1988 Act[381] provides, with effect from May 6, 1999, that copyright in every Bill introduced into the Scottish Parliament belongs to the Scottish Parliamentary Corporate Body. Copyright under this provision subsists from the time the text of the Bill is handed in to the Parliament for introduction until the Bill receives Royal Assent or, if it does not receive Royal Assent, until it is withdrawn or rejected or no further parliamentary proceedings may be taken in respect of it.[382] With the exception of these special rules in relation to subsistence, title and term, the copyright Part of the 1988 Act is to apply to copyright in Bills of the Scottish Parliament as to other parliamentary copyright.[383] No other copyright or right in the nature of copyright subsists in a Bill after copyright has once subsisted under s.166A. However, this is stated to be without prejudice to the subsequent operation of the section in relation to a Bill which, having not received Royal Assent, is later reintroduced into the Parliament.[384] Section 166B of the 1988 Act makes almost identical provision in relation to Bills introduced into the Northern Ireland Assembly.[385] The copyright in such Bills belongs to the Northern Ireland Assembly Commission.[386] Similar provision is made in respect of proposed Measures and Bills of the National Assembly for Wales by the introduction of new ss.166C and 166D of the 1988 Act.[387] Copyright in such proposed Measures and Bills belongs to the National Assembly for Wales Commission: see ss.166C(1) and 166D(1).

(iii) Position of the Houses of Parliament, the Scottish Parliament, the Northern Ireland Assembly and the National Assembly for Wales

Ownership and legal proceedings. At the time the 1988 Act was being considered in Parliament, the precise legal personality of the Houses of Parliament was thought to be unclear. Accordingly it was considered necessary to provide each House with its own legal personality in order to permit it to hold, deal with and enforce its newly acquired copyright.[388] Thus, for the purposes of holding, dealing with and enforcing copyright, and in connection with all legal proceedings relating to copyright, each House of Parliament is to be treated as having the legal capacities of a body corporate.[389] This status is not to be affected either by a prorogation or by a dissolution.[390] By contrast, Scottish parliamentary copyright is owned by a separate entity, the Scottish Parliamentary Corporate Body, while Northern Irish parliamentary copyright is owned by the Northern

10–90

[381] Introduced by para.25(6) of Sch.8 to the Scotland Act 1998 (c.46) with effect from May 6, 1999: see the Scotland Act 1998 (Commencement) Order 1998 (SI 1998/3178) para.2 and Sch.3.
[382] CDPA 1988 s.166A(2).
[383] s.166A(3).
[384] s.166A(4).
[385] Introduced by para.8(6) of Sch.13 to the Northern Ireland Act 1998 and para.2 of and Schedule to the Northern Ireland Act 1998 (Commencement No. 5) Order 1999 (SI 1999/3209) with effect from December 2, 1999.
[386] CDPA 1988 s.166B(1).
[387] Introduced by para.28 of Sch.10 to the Government of Wales Act 2006. By s.161(1) of that Act, the amendment took effect immediately after the ordinary election under s.3 of the Government of Wales Act 1998 held in 2007, which took place on May 3, 2007, except that so far as relating to the functions of the Welsh Ministers, the Counsel General and the Assembly Commission and in relation to the Auditor General and the Comptroller and Auditor General, it took effect on May 25, 2007 (the date of the end of the "initial period"): see s.161(4) and (5).
[388] *Hansard*, HL Vol.501, col.194.
[389] CDPA 1988 s.167(1).
[390] CDPA 1988 s.167(1).

Ireland Assembly Commission[391] and Welsh parliamentary copyright by the National Assembly for Wales Commission.[392]

10–91   **House of Commons.** The functions of the House of Commons as owner of copyright are exercised by the Speaker on behalf of the House.[393] If so authorised by the Speaker or if there is a vacancy in the office of Speaker, those functions may be discharged by the Chairman of Ways and Means or a Deputy Chairman.[394] On a dissolution of Parliament, a person who on the dissolution was Speaker of the House of Commons, Chairman of Ways and Means or a Deputy Chairman may continue to act until the corresponding appointment is made in the next session of Parliament.[395] Legal proceedings relating to copyright are to be brought by or against the House of Commons in the name of "The Speaker of the House of Commons".[396]

10–92   **House of Lords.** The functions of the House of Lords as owner of copyright are exercised by the Clerk of the Parliaments on behalf of the House.[397] If so authorised by the Clerk of the Parliaments or, in the case of a vacancy in the office of Clerk of the Parliaments, those functions may be discharged by the Clerk Assistant or the Reading Clerk.[398] Legal proceedings relating to copyright are to be brought by or against the House of Lords in the name of "The Clerk of the Parliaments".[399]

(iv) Licensing of parliamentary copyright

10–93   **Administration.** The licensing of UK parliamentary copyright is undertaken by HMSO under the terms of an agreement with the Speaker of the House of Commons and the Clerk of the Parliaments in the House of Lords.[400] Scottish, Welsh and Northern Irish parliamentary copyright is administered by the bodies which own such copyright.[401]

10–94   **Licensing: the parliamentary licence.**[402] United Kingdom parliamentary copyright is licensed under the Parliamentary Licence, which is a non-exclusive non-assignable worldwide licence granted by HMSO on behalf of the Speaker of the House of Commons and the Clerk of the Parliaments to licensees who have applied online to "reproduce" material in a large number of categories.[403] The licence lasts for a period of five years and is free of charge.[404] The licence may be terminated by HMSO for cause and by the licensee without cause.[405] For the House of Commons the categories of material which are licensed include Han-

---

[391] CDPA 1988 ss.166A(1) and 166B(1).
[392] CDPA 1988 ss.166C(1) and 166D(1).
[393] CDPA 1988 s.167(3).
[394] CDPA 1988 s.167(3).
[395] CDPA 1988 s.167(3).
[396] s.167(5)(a).
[397] CDPA 1988 s.167(4).
[398] CDPA 1988 s.167(4).
[399] CDPA 1988 s.167(5)(b).
[400] See the Licence to Reproduce Parliamentary Copyright Information *http://www.nationalarchives.gov.uk/documents/parliamentary-licence-01-00.pdf* [Accessed October 22, 2010].
[401] See para.10–90 above.
[402] For the previous regime, which involved letters and a Guidance Note, see Copinger 15th edn and 2nd supp, paras 10–86 to 10–93.
[403] See Annexes A and B to the licence.
[404] Cll.5, 7, 8.
[405] Cl.14.

sard, Standing Committee Official Reports, public and private bills,[406] registers of interests, Select Committee minutes and reports, and library documents. For the House of Lords the categories include public bills and explanatory notes, private bills, minutes of evidence of select committees and registers of interests. The licence explains how such material may be obtained.[407] The licence does not extend to the broadcasts of proceedings of Parliament[408] or to material in which third parties own copyright.[409] It contains a non-exhaustive list of acts which are deemed to fall within the definition of "reproduce" from which it appears that commercial use is permitted.[410] HMSO and Parliament give no warranty that the licensed material is error free or not defamatory.[411]

The Parliamentary licence: conditions. The licence contains a number of conditions.[412] The reproduction must be accurate and must be from the current official source, that is from material made available by or on behalf of Parliament. If material which has been superseded is to be reproduced, the licensee must make clear that a more up-to-date version is available. The source of the material must be identified and if the material is published, a specified copyright notice must be featured. The material must not be used for the principal purpose of advertising or promoting a particular product or service or in a way which could imply official endorsement or which is otherwise misleading. Official imprints and Parliamentary logos or emblems may not be reproduced (although the Parliamentary portcullis may be reproduced where it forms an integral part of the material and is being reproduced in that context). HMSO must be allowed on request to inspect copies of any works that include licensed material to check that the licensee has kept to the terms of the licence. On request, HMSO and/or Parliament must be granted a complimentary copy of any product or publication which includes licensed material or as the case may be any subscription or end user licence. There are express prohibitions on reproduction for overtly political purposes and use which is knowingly or potentially libellous or slanderous. Finally, the licensee must comply with the Data Protection Act 1998.

10–95

Scottish, Welsh and Northern Irish Parliamentary copyright. Reference should be made to the relevant websites.[413] In general, the terms and conditions imposed by the National Assembly for Wales Commission are similar to those of the Parliamentary Licence while those imposed by the Scottish Parliamentary Corporate Body and the Northern Ireland Assembly Commission are more restrictive.

10–96

---

[406] Explanatory Notes to bills are not mentioned. Presumably this is an oversight. At the time of writing, Guidance Note 14 Reproduction of Bills and Explanatory Notes to Bills of the United Kingdom Parliament (revised May 9, 2005) was available on the National Archives website: (*http://www.nationalarchives.gov.uk/documents/reproduction-bills-uk-parliament.pdf* [Accessed October 23, 2010]) via a link in a list headed "Current Guidance" *http://www.nationalarchives.gov.uk/information-management/our-services/copyright-guidance.htm* [Accessed October 23, 2010]. It is assumed that this too is an oversight given that subject to the omission mentioned above such material is covered by the Parliamentary Licence. However, the literal position appears to be that (i) Explanatory Notes to House of Commons Bills are covered by the waiver in Guidance Note 14 while (ii) Bills in general and Explanatory Notes to House of Lords Bills are governed by the waiver unless the user has a Parliamentary Licence in which case he is bound by its terms. In practice nothing is likely to turn on the point.
[407] Cl.8.
[408] See cl.6.1.
[409] Cl.6.2.
[410] Cl.7.
[411] Cl.16.
[412] Cl.12.
[413] *http://www.scottish.parliament.uk/cnPages/copyright.htm*; *http://www.assemblywales.org/terms.htm*; and *http://www.niassembly.gov.uk/copyright.htm* [Accessed October 23, 2010].

C. MORAL RIGHTS

10–97   **Limited scope in relation to parliamentary copyright works.** The rights created by the 1988 Act to be identified as author or director[414] and to object to derogatory treatment of a work[415] have only limited scope in relation to works in which parliamentary copyright[416] subsists. The right to be identified as author or director does not apply in relation to a work in which parliamentary copyright subsists unless the author or director has been identified as such in or on published copies of the work.[417] It follows that the Houses of Parliament[418] and devolved legislative bodies will effectively be able to determine whether this right can ever be asserted in relation to a work in which parliamentary copyright subsists. The right to object to derogatory treatment of a work in which parliamentary copyright subsists does not apply to anything done in relation to such a work by or with the authority of the copyright owner unless the author or director is identified at the time of the relevant act or has previously been identified in or on published copies of the work.[419] Even where the right applies, it is not infringed if there is a sufficient disclaimer.[420]

3. THE RIGHTS OF INTERNATIONAL ORGANISATIONS

10–98   **Section 168 of the 1988 Act.** This section makes special provision in respect of literary, dramatic, musical or artistic works which have been made by officers or employees of certain international organisations or which have been published by such organisations and which do not qualify for copyright protection under ss.154 or 155 of the Act. The section is considered in paras 3–101 and 3–102, above.

---

[414] CDPA 1988 s.77. See Ch.11.
[415] s.80. See Ch.11.
[416] Which includes Scottish, Northern Irish and Welsh parliamentary copyright: see ss.166A(3), 166B(3), 166C(3) and to 166D(3).
[417] s.79(7)(a). For the meaning of "publication" and related expressions, see s.175(1) and paras 3–174 et seq., above.
[418] Or their assignees: parliamentary copyright continues to subsist in a work the copyright in which has been assigned by the Houses of Parliament: CDPA 1988 s.165(2).
[419] CDPA 1988 s.82(2). For the meaning of "publication" and related expressions, see CDPA 1988 s.175(1), and paras 3–174, above.
[420] CDPA 1988 s.82(2). For what may be a sufficient disclaimer, see CDPA 1988 s.178, and Ch.11, below.

PART II

MORAL RIGHTS

CHAPTER ELEVEN

MORAL RIGHTS

1. INTRODUCTION

Droit moral. The term "moral rights", first introduced into English law by Ch.IV **11–01** of the 1988 Act, has its origins in the "*droit moral*" enjoyed by authors in various countries, notably France, Germany and Italy.[1] It refers collectively to a number of rights which are concerned more with a person's relationship with his creation than the commercial value of them.[2] For, example, an author's moral rights in his work, which in general are regarded as inalienable, are therefore to be distinguished from his economic rights in his work, which in general are alienable. The same is true in respect of performers as regards their performances.

International background. Historically, the protection given to the moral rights **11–02**

---

[1] For a fuller discussion of moral rights and their history, and a comparative study, see G. Davies & K. Garnett, *Moral Rights* (London: Sweet & Maxwell, 2010). For other commentaries on the development of the rights in other countries, see A. Dietz, *Copyright Law in the European Community* (Sijthoff & Noordhoff, 1978), pp.66 et seq.; S. Ricketson and J.C. Ginsburg, *International Copyright and Neighbouring Rights, The Berne Convention and Beyond* 2nd edn (Oxford University Press, 2006), paras 10.01 et seq.; E. Adeney, *The Moral Rights of Authors and Performers—An International and Comparative Analysis* (Oxford University Press, 2006); and L. Nocella, "Copyright and Moral Rights versus Author's Right and Droit Moral: Convergence or Divergence" [2008] Ent. L.R. 19/7, 151.

[2] In *International Copyright and Neighbouring Rights, The Berne Convention and Beyond* 2nd edn (Oxford University Press, 2006), paras 10.02 et seq., Ricketson and Ginsburg note that the adjective "moral" has no precise English equivalent in this context, although the words "spiritual", "non-economic" and "personal" convey something of the intended meaning.

of authors in different countries, particularly those of continental Europe, varied widely. An attempt to bring some cohesion to this situation in the international field was first made in the revisions to the Berne Convention made by the Rome Act of 1928.[3] This required recognition of two rights of authors, first, the right, even after the transfer of copyright, to claim authorship of a work (the "paternity right") and, second, the right to object to any distortion, mutilation or other modification of his work which would be prejudicial to his honour or reputation (the "integrity right").[4] It was left to Contracting States to determine the way in which such protection was afforded. These provisions of the Berne Convention relating to moral rights were extended by the Brussels and Stockholm Acts of 1948 and 1967 respectively, and are now to be found in art.6*bis* of the Paris Act of 1971.[5] Other moral rights, conferred in various jurisdictions, such as the right of an author to choose whether his work should be published or not, the right to modify or withdraw a work (subject to compensation), the right to prevent excessive criticism, and a right to prevent false attribution of authorship, have never found an agreed place internationally.[6]

So far as performers are concerned, in December 1996 the WIPO Performances and Phonograms Treaty 1996 ("WPPT") was adopted at a Diplomatic Conference in Geneva.[7] By wording which is similar to that of art.6*bis* of the Berne Convention, it provides that a performer should, as regards his live, "aural" performances or performances fixed in phonograms (a) have the right to be identified as the performer, except where omission is dictated by the manner of the use of the performance, and (b) to object to any distortion, mutilation or modification of this performance that would be prejudicial to his reputation.[8] These provisions had their origin in a proposal by the International Bureau of WIPO to the first session in 1993 of the Committee of Experts on a possible new instrument on the rights of performers and producers of phonograms.[9] The proposal responded to the concern that technology has made it possible by means of digital technology to manipulate and alter recordings of performances in ways which could easily be very damaging to a performer. During the preparatory work leading to the Diplomatic Conference in 1996 and the adoption of the WPPT, there was general support for the proposals, which were modelled on art.6*bis* of the Berne Convention. At the Diplomatic Conference there was a strong body of opinion in favour of the protection of performers' moral rights from European and Latin American delegates, the national laws of many of whom recognised such rights already.[10]

11–03   **Moral rights in the United Kingdom.** The manner of implementation of the moral rights provisions of the Berne Convention and the WPPT is left to Contracting States. Before the introduction of an express code of moral rights by the 1988 Act, a patchwork of mostly common law rights, such as passing off, defamation and slander of goods,[11] as partly supplemented by statute,[12] was considered sufficient to give effect to art.6*bis* of the Berne Convention in the United Kingdom.

---

[3] As to International Copyright and the Berne Convention, see Chs 23 and 24, below.

[4] art.6*bis* of the Rome Act.

[5] Although parties to the TRIPS agreement must comply with arts 1–21 of the Berne Convention, there is an express exception in the case of the rights conferred by art.6*bis*. See TRIPS art.9.1.

[6] See in more detail, G. Davies & K. Garnett, *Moral Rights* (London: Sweet & Maxwell, 2010), paras 1–02 et seq..

[7] See paras 23–119 et seq., below.

[8] WIPO Performances and Phonograms Treaty art.5(1).

[9] [1993] *Copyright* 142, 148.

[10] S. Ricketson and J.C. Ginsburg, *International Copyright and Neighbouring Rights, the Berne Convention and Beyond* 2nd edn (Oxford University Press, 2006), Vol.II, para.19.52.

[11] See, e.g. G. Davies & K.Garnett, *Moral Rights* (London: Sweet & Maxwell, 2010), para.3–004

Thus when authors' moral rights were first prescribed by the Rome Act, the United Kingdom made no changes to its law and, for example, the Gregory Committee of 1952 felt able to conclude that the Convention as then contained in the Brussels Act imposed no obligations on the United Kingdom to introduce any legislation to alter the law.[13] It became increasingly clear, however, that the law of the United Kingdom did not give effect to the Berne Convention and the Whitford Committee of 1977[14] recommended that proper protection should be introduced. A statutory right of paternity and integrity for authors was therefore introduced by the 1988 Act. At the same time, alterations were made to the existing right of a person to prevent a work being falsely attributed to him as author and a new right of privacy introduced in relation to photographs commissioned for private and domestic purposes, all under the rubric of "moral rights". As regards performers, in theory, as with authors, common law rights have always existed, but a statutory right of paternity and integrity was first introduced in February 2006 by amendment of the 1988 Act[15] in fulfilment of the United Kingdom's obligations under the WPPT.

The rights. The moral rights conferred by the 1988 Act are as follows: **11–04**

Authors' rights

(1) the right of an author of a copyright literary, dramatic, musical or artistic work, or director of a film, to be identified as author or director respectively ("the paternity right");

(2) the right of an author of such a work not to have it subjected to derogatory treatment ("the integrity right");

(3) the right of any person not to have a work or film falsely attributed to him as author or director, respectively; and

(4) the right of any person to privacy in respect of photographs which he commissioned for private and domestic purposes ("the privacy right").

Performers' rights

(1) the right of performer to be identified as such in relation to their performances ("the paternity right");

(2) the right of a performer not to have their performance subjected to derogatory treatment ("the integrity right");

All these rights are collectively referred to in the Act as "moral rights".[16]

Nature of rights. Some general remarks can be made about these rights. First, as **11–05** regards authors' moral rights:

(1) Although all are termed moral rights, only the first two, the paternity and integrity rights, are "authors' rights" as contemplated by the Berne Convention, whereas the other two rights are capable of being enjoyed by

---

and Dworkin, *The Moral Right of the Author, Moral Rights and the Common Law Countries* (Congress of Antwerp, ALAI, 1993), p.81.

[12] Latterly, Copyright Act 1956 s.43, which dealt mainly with the separate right of false attribution of authorship, but which also granted an author rights where an altered version of an artistic work was dealt with as being his unaltered work. The section derived from the Fine Arts Copyright Act 1862 s.7.

[13] Report of the Copyright Committee, Cmnd.8662, paras 219–226. The same view can be found in the Preface to the 7th edn (1936) of this work.

[14] Cmnd.6732, paras 50–57, 80(vi).

[15] The Performances (Moral Rights, etc.) Regulations 2006, which entered into force on February 1, 2006,

[16] See, e.g. the headings of Pt. I Ch.IV and Pt II Ch.III of the 1988 Act and s.94.

any person, author or not. In this context, the term "author" has the same meaning as in the context of copyright, namely the person who creates the work.[17] As will be seen, moral rights are capable of subsisting in works which were made before the commencement of the 1988 Act,[18] and although for the purposes of copyright the author of a work is to be determined in accordance with the law in force at the time when the work was made,[19] in the case of moral rights the author is to be determined in accordance with the current provisions of the 1988 Act, i.e. those in Pt I. This means, for example, that the author of a pre-1988 Act photograph is to be taken for moral rights purposes to be the person who created it and not, as under the 1956 Act, the person who owned the material on which the photograph was taken and thus, possibly, a company.[20] Although as a matter of UK law, the author of a film is now to be taken to be "the principal director", as well as the producer,[21] it is only "the director" who is granted any moral rights in relation to a film. There is no statutory definition of the term "the director" of a film for this purpose; it appears that where there are directors of a film who do not fall within the description of principal director, each will have moral rights, provided the film was jointly directed.[22]

(2) The paternity, integrity and privacy rights only exist in relation to a work which is a copyright work.[23] If, therefore, copyright does not subsist in the work, for example because the qualification conditions are not met[24] or the term of copyright has expired,[25] the author has no such moral rights in respect of it. In contrast, the right of a person not to have a work attributed to him as author applies whatever the copyright status of the work, provided that it at least qualifies as a "work".[26] So, where the work in question is alleged to be a literary work, it must satisfy the requirement that it is a literary work.[27]

(3) Although enjoyment of the paternity, integrity and privacy rights depends upon copyright subsisting in the work, it is important to appreciate that the person who is entitled to exercise these moral rights will often not be the same person as the owner of the copyright. Care must therefore always be taken that exploitation of the work by a copyright owner or his licensees does not infringe any of these moral rights. The rights are in some respects linked, but in others are quite distinct.

(4) The paternity and privacy rights apply in relation to any substantial part of the work as well as in relation to the whole of the work. In contrast, the integrity right and the right to prevent false attribution apply in relation to the whole or *any* part of a work.

(5) Subject to exceptions, the paternity and integrity rights apply to works in

---

[17] CDPA 1988 ss.179, 9(1). As to authorship, see Ch.4. Note that the presumptions as to authorship contained in ss.104 and 105 can be applied.

[18] On August 1, 1989.

[19] CDPA 1988 Sch.1, para.10. See paras 4–09 et seq., above.

[20] See, generally, as to such works, para.4–29, above.

[21] CDPA 1988 s.9(2)(ab). See para.4–48, above.

[22] See para.11–84, below, as to a jointly directed film.

[23] See the wording of CDPA 1988 ss.77(1), 80(1) and 85(1) respectively. A copyright work is a work in which copyright subsists. See ss.178, 1(2).

[24] See Ch.3, above.

[25] See CDPA 1988 s.86(1). As to the term of copyright, see Ch.6, above.

[26] See the wording of CDPA 1988 s.84(1). As to the various types of "work", see Ch.3, above.

[27] *Noah v Shuba* [1991] F.S.R. 14 at 33, applying *Exxon Corporation v Exxon Insurance Consultants International Ltd* [1982] Ch. 119. As to this requirement, see paras 3–11 et seq., above.

existence before the commencement of the 1988 Act,[28] the most important exception being the case of works whose author had died before this date. The privacy right does not apply to photographs taken or films made before this date.

As regards performers' moral rights:
(1) The Act does not in fact define performers as such, only "performance", which is stated to mean: (a) a dramatic performance (which includes dance and mime), (b) a musical performance, (c) a reading or recitation of a literary work, or (d) a performance of a variety act or any similar presentation, which is, or so far as it is, a live performance given by one or more individuals.[29] It follows that for present purposes a performer is the person who "gives" such a performance.
(2) Performers moral rights only exist in relation to qualifying performances. This is a topic which is dealt with elsewhere.[30]
(3) It should be borne in mind that the person entitled to the performers' moral rights may be different from the person entitled to performers' property rights.[31]
(4) The performer's paternity right applies in relation to any substantial part of performance as well as the whole performance, whereas the performers' integrity right applies in relation to any part of the performance.
(5) The performers' moral rights do not apply in relation to performances which took place before February 1, 2006.[32]

As regards all these moral rights, they are personal in nature and are not property rights. They are not, therefore, assignable, in contrast to copyright or performers' property rights.[33] They can, however, be waived and are not infringed if there has been consent to the act in question.[34] Numerous exceptions also exist in relation to the rights.[35] Special provision is made as to exercise of the rights after the death of the person initially entitled to them.[36]

The Information Society Directive. This Directive[37] (as with other European Directives) was not concerned with the moral rights of authors and so did not require any changes to be made to the treatment of moral rights by the 1988 Act. However, other changes to the Act which were made on implementation of the Directive, in particular those relating to broadcasts, cable programme services and on-demand transmissions, required some amendment to the moral rights provisions to bring them into line. **11–06**

EC Commission proposals. The Commission has kept under review the question whether there is a need for harmonisation of moral rights within the European Union. The report of an independent study commissioned by the European Commission concerning moral rights in the context of the exploitation of works **11–07**

---

[28] On August 1, 1989.
[29] CDPA 1988 ss.212, 180(2).
[30] See para.12–24.
[31] As to which, see paras 12–44 et seq.
[32] The Performances (Moral Rights, etc.) Regulations 2006 (SI 2006/18) reg.8, February 1, 2006 being the date the Regulations entered into force.
[33] CDPA 1988 ss. 94, 205L.
[34] See ss. 87(1), 205J.
[35] See paras 11–25 to 11–33 and 11–55, 11–57A and 11–68.
[36] See para.11–72, below.
[37] Directive 2001/29.

through digital technology published in 2000 concluded that there was no need for such harmonisation.[38] The Commission's current view is that there is no need to harmonise moral rights protection in the Community. In its opinion, the international legal framework in practice provides an adequate level playing field for the markets to operate.[39]

2. THE PATERNITY RIGHT

A. THE RIGHT TO BE IDENTIFIED AS AUTHOR OR DIRECTOR

(i) Introduction

11–08   **The right.** In general, the author of a copyright literary, dramatic, musical or artistic work has the right to be identified as the author of the work.[40] A similar right to be identified as the director of a copyright film work is conferred on the director.[41] As has been seen, the right is derived from art.6*bis* of the Berne Convention, which provides that independently of his "economic" rights,[42] and even after any transfer of those rights, an author "shall have the right to claim authorship" of his work.[43] The right belongs to the person who is the author or director of the work in the copyright sense, not the person who, not being such an author, nevertheless contributed ideas, etc. which find expression in the work.[44] The meaning of author in this context has already been discussed.[45] As already noted, the paternity right is only capable of subsisting if at the same time copyright subsists in the work. The right is infringed by the doing of any of the various acts specified in the relevant provisions[46] without the consent of the person entitled to the right.[47] This general statement is, however, subject to important qualifications:

(1) the circumstances in which the right arises vary according to the type of copyright work;

(2) the right is not infringed unless it has been asserted in a specified manner;

(3) the right is subject to numerous exceptions;

(4) the right may be waived or made the subject of consent.

11–09   **Transitional.** The right applies to works made before commencement of the Act (August 1, 1989), except in two cases: first, the case of a film made before this date; secondly, in relation to the other kinds of copyright work, where the author

---

[38] M. Salokannel and A. Strowel with the collaboration of E. Derclaye, Final Report Study Contract No. ETD/99/B5-3000/E 28.

[39] Document SEC(2004) 995 of July 17, 2004, Commission Staff Working Paper on the review of the EC legal framework in the field of copyright and related rights, para.3.5. See, further, para.24–163, below.

[40] CDPA 1988 s.77(1).

[41] s.77(1).

[42] i.e. any copyright vested in him.

[43] Before the implementation of this right by the 1988 Act, the only effective means by which an author could acquire such a right was by contract (see, e.g. *Tolnay v Criterion Film Productions Ltd* [1936] 2 All E.R. 1625) or, where he was also the copyright owner, by making any exploitation of the work conditional upon him being identified (see, e.g. *Miller v Cecil Film Ltd* [1937] 2 All E.R. 464). Note also that since the passing of the 1956 Act, certain acts of fair dealing have only escaped being an infringement if there is a sufficient acknowledgement of the author. See paras 9–40 et seq., above.

[44] *Anya v Wu* [2004] EWHC 386 (Ch).

[45] See para.11–05, above.

[46] CDPA 1988 ss.77(2)–(8).

[47] CDPA 1988 s.87(1).

had died before this date.[48] There are also further transitional provisions limiting the paternity right in respect of works made before commencement, which are considered later.

(ii) The Circumstances in which the Right Exists

As with the other forms of moral rights, the paternity right is a passive right in the sense that it is only capable of being exercised where some form of exploitation of the work takes place, the particular form varying according to the type of copyright work. As will be seen, where the other conditions for infringement are satisfied, it is the person who carries out any of these acts of exploitation who infringes the right.

11–10

(a) *Literary and dramatic works*

The meaning of these expressions is considered elsewhere.[49] In the present context, however, words intended to be sung or spoken with music are treated in the same way as a musical work, not as a literary work.[50] The author of works of these types has the right to be identified whenever any of the following events occur[51]:

11–11

(1) *Commercial publication of the work.* "Commercial publication" is defined as the issue of copies of the work to the public "at a time when copies made in advance of the receipt of orders are generally available to the public."[52] The expression "issue to the public" of copies is itself further defined by a complex set of provisions[53] which are considered in detail elsewhere[54] but it broadly means putting into circulation copies which were not previously in circulation. It therefore refers to the first issue of any particular copy of a work. In the case of literary and dramatic works, "copy" refers to any reproduction of the work in material form,[55] which includes the issue of copies not only in the form of books, newspapers and so on but also in the form of sound recordings, films, etc.[56] Overall, therefore, the expression "commercial publication" contemplates that copies be generally available to the public, whether by way of sale or otherwise, for example in retail outlets, and not simply in response to orders.[57] Commercial publication in this context also includes the making of the work available to the public by means of an electronic retrieval

---

[48] CDPA 1988 Sch.1 para.23(2).

[49] For the meaning of "literary work", see CDPA 1988 s.3(1) and paras 3–08 et seq., above. For the meaning of "dramatic work", see paras 3–32 et seq., above.

[50] CDPA 1988 s.77(2), (3). No doubt one of the reasons for this is because there is no right to be identified as the author of a musical work where it is, e.g., performed in public or broadcast (see below). Given this approach, it would not make sense to have to identify the author of any accompanying lyrics.

[51] s.77(2).

[52] s.175(2)(a).

[53] ss.18(2), (3) & (4).

[54] See paras 7–87 et seq., above. Although the definition of "the issue of copies to the public" is found in the provisions relating to infringement of copyright, it is defined for the purposes of "this Part", i.e. Pt I of the 1988 Act, which includes the moral rights provisions which are contained in Ch.IV of Pt I. See also s.178.

[55] CDPA 1988 s.17(2), which also applies in the case of musical and artistic works. This definition applies to the moral right provisions as well as those relating to copyright. See ss.179, 17(1).

[56] For a detailed discussion, see paras 7–34 et seq., above.

[57] This category of act is not found elsewhere in the Act and the reason for it seems to have been based on a misapprehension. See G. Davies & K. Garnett, *Moral Rights* (London: Sweet & Maxwell, 2010), para.7–023.

system,[58] but it does not include the performance of the work, nor the communication to the public of the work (otherwise than for the purposes of an electronic retrieval system).[59] It should be noted that the paternity right is not exercisable in relation to the rental of copies of the work to the public.[60]

(2) *Performance of the work in public.* Performance in this context has the same meaning as in relation to copyright[61] and is considered in detail in that context.[62] In general it includes any mode of visual or acoustic presentation, including presentation by means of a sound recording, film or broadcast of the work.[63] It also includes delivery in the case of lectures, addresses, speeches and sermons.[64]

(3) *Communication to the public of the work.* Again, this expression has the same meaning as in relation to copyright. It means the communication to the public by electronic transmission, and includes (a) the broadcasting of the work and (b) the making available to the public of the work by electronic transmission in such a way that members of the public may access it from a place and at a time individually chosen by them.[65]

(4) *Inclusion of the work in films and sound recordings issued to public.* The meaning of the expression "issued to the public" has been briefly considered above and in more detail elsewhere.[66] There appears to be an overlap between this category of act and category (1) above, since, as noted there, the meaning of "copy" includes a reproduction of a work in the form of a film or sound recording. Often a work which is included in a film or sound recording and which has been issued to the public will have been commercially published in the sense considered above, but the present category of act is wider in that there is no limiting condition that "copies made in advance of orders be generally available to the public". Again, it should be noted that the paternity right is not exercisable in relation to the rental of copies of the work to the public.[67]

(5) *The doing of any of the above acts in relation to an adaptation of the work.* Adaptation in the context of a literary or dramatic work means (a) a translation of the work, (b) a version of a dramatic work in which it is converted into a non-dramatic work or, in the case of a non-dramatic work, in which it is converted into a dramatic work, or (c) a version of the work in which the story or action is conveyed wholly or mainly by means of pictures in a form suitable for reproduction in a book, or in a newspaper, magazine or similar periodical.[68] In any of these cases, the author of the original work has the right to be identified as the author of that work.[69] If the adaptation is a new copyright work, as it often will be, the author of the adaptation may have a separate right to be identified as its author. The manner in which an author must be identified is considered generally below, but where the author of each work is entitled to be identified, care must be taken to distinguish between the two works and their two authors.

---

[58] CDPA 1988 s.175(2)(b).

[59] s.175(4)(a). As to such acts, see however, the following paragraphs.

[60] i.e. by the doing of any of the acts falling within s.18A.

[61] Again, "performance" is defined in s.19 for the purposes of Pt I of the 1988 Act.

[62] See paras 7–103 et seq., above.

[63] CDPA 1988 s.19(2)(b).

[64] s.19(2)(a).

[65] CDPA 1988 s.20(2). See para.7–121.

[66] See paras 7–87 et seq., above.

[67] i.e. by the doing of any of the acts falling within s.18A.

[68] CDPA 1988 s.21(3)(a).

[69] CDPA 1988 s.77(2) (assuming, of course, that the other conditions for the exercise of the right are satisfied).

(b) *Musical works*

The circumstances in which the author of a musical work, or of a literary work **11–12** consisting of words intended to be sung or spoken with music, has a right of paternity are more restricted.[70] The right is limited to the following cases in which the work is exploited:

(1) *The commercial publication of the work.*[71] This type of exploitation will include the issue of copies not only in the form of sheet music or lyrics in book form but also in the form of sound recordings or film soundtracks.

(2) *The issue to the public of copies of the work in the form of sound recordings.* Again, there appears to be a potential overlap between this category and category (1) above. Although a film whose soundtrack contains a reproduction of the work is a "copy" of the work, the sound-track is now to be treated as part of the film and not a sound recording,[72] and falls within category (4), below.

(3) *The showing in public of a film whose soundtrack includes the work.* The theatrical exhibition of a film whose soundtrack includes the author's music or lyrics is therefore an occasion for the exercise of the paternity right. Where such exhibition occurs by means, for example, of the public showing of a television broadcast of the film, it is not the broadcaster who "shows" the film but the person who is responsible for allowing the public to see the film.[73]

(4) *The issue to the public of copies of a film of which the soundtrack includes the work.* Again, there appears to be an overlap between this category and category (1) above. The common occasion when this category of act will take place is when DVDs are issued to the public.

(5) *The doing of any of the above acts in relation to an adaptation of the work.* The right in such an event is to be identified as the author of the work from which the adaptation was made. An adaptation in the context of a musical work means an arrangement or transcription of the work. The right is therefore to be identified as the author of the original work. Again, the author of the arrangement or transcription, where it is a separate copy-right work, may have a separate right to be identified as the author of that work.

There is therefore no right to be identified as the author of a musical work where the work is performed in public (other than by the public showing of a film which includes it), communicated to the public, or on the rental or lending of copies of the work. The reason for this is that it was thought unrealistic for broadcasters in particular to have to credit every songwriter when any piece of music was used.[74]

(c) *Artistic works*

The author of an artistic work has the right to be identified whenever the work is **11–13** published commercially, or exhibited in public, or a visual image of it is com-

---

[70] CDPA 1988 s.77(3).

[71] See para.11–11, above for the meaning of this expression.

[72] See s.5B(2).

[73] In relation to infringement of copyright by showing a work in public, this is made clear by s.19(4). No equivalent provision applies in relation to moral rights but it is suggested that this is the correct position.

[74] See *Hansard*, HL Vol.493, col.1327.

municated to the public.[75] The right also arises whenever a film including a visual image of the artistic work is shown in public or copies of such a film are issued to the public.[76] The paternity right therefore differs from copyright in an important respect: the owner of the copyright in an artistic work has no control over the public exhibition of the original representation of the work or a non-infringing copy of it.[77]

11–14　　**Works of architecture, sculpture and artistic craftsmanship.** There are further, special provisions relating to these particular classes of artistic work. In the case of a work of architecture in the form of a building[78] or a model for a building, or a sculpture[79] or a work of artistic craftsmanship,[80] the author has the right to be identified whenever copies of a graphic work[81] representing it, or a photograph of it, are issued to the public.[82] Once again, the issue of such copies will often also amount to commercial publication of the work. The author of a work of architecture in the form of a building also has the right to be identified on the building as constructed.[83] Where more than one building is constructed to the design (for example, on a housing estate), the right is to be identified on the first building to be constructed.[84]

(d) *Films*

11–15　　The director of a film[85] has the right to be identified whenever the film is shown in public, or is communicated to the public or copies of the film are issued to the public.[86]

(iii) The Mode of Identification

11–16　　The mode of identification which is required also varies according to the character of the work and the manner of its exploitation:

(1) In the case of commercial exploitation of a work or the issue to the public of copies of a film or sound recording, the author or director, as the case may be, must be identified in or on each copy.[87] The identification must be clear and reasonably prominent,[88] such that it is likely to come to the attention of a person acquiring the copy.[89] Identification in very small print or in a position which will not be apparent will thus not suffice. It would seem that the identification needs be outwardly apparent, for example to a

---

[75] CDPA 1988 s.77(4)(a).

[76] s.77(4)(b). Again, the issue to the public of copies of a film which include the work will often also amount to the commercial publication of the work.

[77] It is an infringement of copyright to exhibit an infringing *copy* of an artistic work in public in the course of a business, knowing or having reason to believe it to be so. See s.23.

[78] A building includes any fixed structure, and a part of a building or fixed structure. See CDPA 1988 s.4(2).

[79] As to the meaning of "sculpture", see para.3–60.

[80] As to works of artistic craftsmanship, see paras 3–65 et seq., above.

[81] A "graphic work" includes any painting, drawing, diagram, map, chart or plan, and any engraving, etching, lithograph, woodcut or similar work. See CDPA 1988 s.4(2).

[82] CDPA 1988 s.77(4)(c).

[83] See further at para.11–16(2), below, as to the way in which the identification must be made.

[84] CDPA 1988 s.77(5).

[85] A "film" means a recording on any medium from which a moving image may by any means be produced. See CDPA 1988 s.5B and para.3–82, above.

[86] CDPA 1988 s.77(6).

[87] CDPA 1988 s.77(7)(a).

[88] See the concluding words of s.77(7).

[89] See the concluding words of s.77(7)(a), considered further, below, "… some *other* manner likely to bring his identity to the notice of a person acquiring a copy".

prospective purchaser inspecting goods which are shrink-wrapped, since the identification must be such as to be likely to come to the attention of a person *acquiring* a copy. If identification "in or on" each copy is not appropriate, identification must be in some other manner which is likely to bring the identity of the author or director to the notice of a person acquiring a copy.[90] If, however, it is correct that the identification must be reasonably apparent before any purchase, it is hard to envisage a case where such identification could be otherwise in or on a copy.

(2) In the case of identification on a building, the author has the right to be identified by appropriate means visible to persons entering or approaching the building.[91] This is clearly satisfied by the common practice of displaying the architect's name in the stonework near the entrance to the building.

(3) In any other case that is public exhibition or performance, the communication to the public or showing of a film in public, the right is to be identified in a manner likely to bring the identity of the author or director to the attention of a person seeing or hearing the performance, exhibition, showing, or communication in question, as the case may be.[92] Thus, for example, in the case of a film which reproduces an author's literary work, the identification will usually take the form of a screen credit along with others involved in the making of the film.[93]

(iv) The Form of Identification

Any reasonable form of identification may be used.[94] This will usually be done **11–17** by stating the ordinary or professional name of the author or director, as the case may be, in words sufficient to indicate that he is the author or director of the work. If, however, the author or director in asserting his right to be identified[95] specifies a pseudonym, initials or some other particular form of identification, that form must be used.[96] It may also be reasonable to employ such a form of identification if it is in fact used by the author or director, even though it has not been specified on assertion of the right. The author must, however, be identified as the author of the work and not simply named.[97] He should thus be named in such a manner that it is clear to all persons who are likely to see the form of identification that he is the author, and it will not be sufficient if inside knowledge is required to work out that this is in fact the case.[98]

(v) Assertion of the Right

An important and controversial hurdle imposed by the 1988 Act as a precondi- **11–18** tion of the exercise of the right of paternity is the requirement that the right must

---

[90] s.77(7)(a).
[91] s.77(7)(b). Again the identification must be clear and reasonably prominent.
[92] s.77(7)(c). Once again, the identification must be clear and reasonably prominent.
[93] See para.27–230, below.
[94] CDPA 1988 s.77(8).
[95] As to this, see below.
[96] CDPA 1988 s.77(8); *Sawkins v Hyperion Records Ltd* [2004] EWHC 1530 (Ch), para.85; [2005] R.P.C. 4, affirmed on appeal: [2005] EWCA Civ 565, paras 66–69; [2005] R.P.C. 32. The claimant had specified "© Copyright 2002 by Lionel Sawkins".
[97] *Sawkins v Hyperion Records Ltd* [2004] EWHC 1530 (Ch), affirmed on appeal: [2005] EWCA Civ 565, para.67 (an acknowledgement in the form "With thanks to Dr Lionel Sawkins for his preparation of performance materials for this recording" held not sufficient since it was unclear and understated what the author had done).
[98] *Sawkins v Hyperion Records Ltd* [2004] EWHC 1530 (Ch), affirmed on appeal: [2005] EWCA Civ 565.

first be formally asserted. Thus an author need not assert the right to be identified if he does not want to, but, if he wishes to enforce the right, he must first have asserted it both in the particular manner required and in such a way as to bind the person whom he subsequently alleges has infringed.[99] Not only is assertion necessary, it is also important that the assertion should be made as soon as possible as, in an action for infringement of the right, the court, in considering remedies, must take into account any delay in doing so.[100] The reason for this requirement is that it was felt that users of copyright material should know where they stood in relation to the right.[101] It is doubtful that this requirement is compliant with the Berne Convention[102] and no other legal system contains such a provision.

11–19 **Mode and effect of assertion of the right.** The right may be asserted in one of two ways: either on an assignment of copyright or by some other instrument in writing which comes to the notice of the person sought to be made liable. Special further provision is made in relation to the public exhibition of an artistic work. These are all considered below. The right may be asserted generally, or in relation to any specified act or description of act.[103] It may thus, for example, be asserted so as to require the author of a literary work to be named on the publication of his work in book form but not in relation to a film which reproduces the work. No particular form of words is required. An "assertion", in ordinary language, is simply an insistence or positive statement of a right or claim. The form of words commonly used is: "[the author] hereby asserts his right to be identified as the author of [the work]".[104] In the case of an assertion by a company,[105] the requirement is satisfied if the assertion is signed on behalf of the company or by the company seal is affixed.[106]

(a) *Assignment of copyright*

11–20 The first method of asserting the right is on an assignment of copyright in the work by the author or director. It is done by including in the instrument effecting the assignment a statement that the author or director asserts, in relation to that work, his right to be identified. It is not necessary that the assignment be the first assignment of the copyright, nor that the author or director be the copyright owner-assignor, nor even, apparently, that he be a party to the assignment, merely that the assignment includes such a statement. It would even seem that such a statement will be effective if it is included without the author's or director's authority or without his knowledge but where he later wishes to rely on it. An assertion made in this manner is binding on the assignee[107] and on anyone claiming through the assignee, whether or not he has notice of the assertion.[108] It is therefore the most effective way of asserting the right, and an author or director who wishes to be as sure as possible of being identified should seek to have such an assertion included in the first assignment of the copyright as a matter of

---

[99] See *Christoffer v Poseidon Film Distributors Ltd.* [2000] E.C.D.R. 487; *Beckingham v Hodgens* [2003] E.C.D.R. 6.

[100] CDPA 1988 s.78(5).

[101] It was considered that the requirement of assertion was not inconsistent with art.6*bis* of the Berne Convention, which only required that an author have the right to *claim* authorship. See *Hansard*, HL Vol.491, col.352.

[102] See G. Davies and K. Garnett, *Moral Rights* (London: Sweet & Maxwell, 2010).

[103] CDPA 1988 s.78(2).

[104] For a precedent, see Vol.2 J1.v.

[105] A company may become entitled by succession to exercise the paternity right after the death of the author or director. See para.11–72, below.

[106] CDPA 1988 s.176(2). See also s.176(1) as it applies to assertion by a licensor under s.78(3)(b).

[107] CDPA 1988 s.78(4)(a).

[108] s.78(4)(a).

course.[109] The possibility of this method of assertion also means that a purchaser of copyright who is concerned by the possible exercise of this right must investigate the entire chain of title if he wishes to be sure of his position.[110] As discussed elsewhere,[111] an assignment of copyright is not effective unless it is in writing signed by or on behalf of the assignor.[112] The assertion may be limited so as to apply to particular acts or part of the copyright term.[113] Where the assertion is included in a partial assignment of copyright, the assertion will be effective in relation to the exercise of the rights assigned, but not other rights.[114]

(b) *Instrument in writing*

An author or director may of course have had no opportunity for stipulating an **11–21** assertion of his right in an assignment of copyright[115] or may not have taken the opportunity to do so.[116] In such a case, or for whatever other reason, the right may also be asserted by an instrument in writing[117] signed by the author or director.[118] An "instrument", in its ordinary meaning, includes any formal or informal document.[119] The assertion must be signed by the author or director himself, and not by someone on his behalf.[120] As with an assertion made on an assignment of copyright, the assertion made by this method may be made either generally or in relation to a specified act or description of acts. Whereas an assertion made on an assignment of copyright may only be made in relation to the work or works which are the subject of the assignment, it seems that an assertion made by this method may be made in relation to a number of the author's works, even future works. The main drawback with an assertion made by this method, however, is that it is binding only on persons to whose notice the assertion is brought.[121]

This method of making an assertion and the requirement that notice of it be brought home to any person before he can be made liable can create problems both for the author or director and for any person dealing with the work. For example, where copies of a work are made on the strength of the fact that no assertion has been made but the author then asserts his right before publication or other distribution of the copies, the publisher is in a difficult position. Commercial publication of the copies which does not include an assertion will amount to an infringement in such circumstances, and the publisher, if he chooses to take the risk of publishing without identifying the author, for example where to do so would cause significant expense or inconvenience, must hope that the author will be denied his remedies on the special ground of the author's delay in making the

---

[109] In practice, where the author or director is the copyright owner-assignor, it will often depend on his relative bargaining position whether the assignment contains an assertion as opposed to a waiver of the right. As to waiver, see para.11–82, below.

[110] Such an assignee or licensee who cannot find out what the position is should therefore seek a warranty from his assignor to the effect that no assertion has been made. The usual warranties relating to title to the copyright will not deal with this issue.

[111] See para.5–85.

[112] CDPA 1988 s.90(3).

[113] s.90(2). See para.5–97, above.

[114] See s.78(2).

[115] For example, because he was not the copyright owner and therefore was not a party to the assignment.

[116] Also of course, he may have assigned his copyright before the provisions of the 1988 Act came into force.

[117] "Writing" includes any form of notation or code, whether by hand or otherwise, and regardless of the method by which, or the medium in or on which, it is recorded:. CDPA 1988 s.178.

[118] CDPA 1988 s.78(2)(b). For a precedent, see Vol.2 J1.v.

[119] *R v Registrar of Companies, ex p. Central Bank of India* [1986] Q.B. 1114 at 1174, 1179.

[120] *Beckingham v Hodgens* [2003] E.C.D.R. 6 (letters and pleadings signed on the author's behalf not sufficient).

[121] CDPA 1988 s.78(4)(b).

assertion.[122] But this may not help the publisher where the author had in fact given notice earlier but to some other person, but only found out later about the assignment or licence under which the publisher is acting. In these circumstances, the special statutory ground for denying the author his remedies appears not to apply since the word "delay" usually implies a measure of fault on the part of the author. The unsatisfactory nature of an assertion which has to be made in this way is further shown by the fact that it may have to be repeatedly made. Thus there is no provision whereby an assertion once made, for example, to the copyright owner, will bind all those claiming under him and there is obviously no guarantee that the copyright owner will bring the assertion to the attention of such persons.

It is not clear whether an assertion once made by either of these methods can be formally withdrawn. In practice, however, the paternity right, once asserted, can be waived.[123]

(c) *Public exhibition of artistic works*

11–22   Special additional provisions deal with the manner of assertion in relation to the public exhibition of an artistic work.[124] These provisions do not affect the validity of an assertion made by either of the two above methods in relation to this category of act but, as already noted, the public exhibition of the original fixation or a non-infringing copy of an artistic work is not a matter which falls within the scope of the copyright in an artistic work. A person who wishes to exhibit an artistic work therefore will have had no cause to investigate the title to the copyright and, since he does not claim "through" the assignee,[125] he will not be bound by an assertion made in an assignment of the copyright. Of course, if he in fact has notice of an assertion made either by this method or in some other instrument he will be bound.

In relation to public exhibition of an artistic work, the right may be asserted by the following additional methods:

(A) First, when the author or other first owner of copyright parts with possession of the original, or of a copy made by him or under his direction or control, by securing that the author is identified on the original or copy, or on a frame, mount or other thing to which it is attached. A number of points can be made about this ill-drafted provision:

(1) It appears to assume that whoever is the first owner of the copyright, whether the author or some other person, will be the first possessor of the original fixation. While this may often be the case (as with a painting made in the artist's studio), it will not necessarily be so.[126] It is only on the parting with possession of it by such first owner that the provision applies. Where the author is not the first owner, but is the first possessor of the work,[127] an identification on the work on parting with possession is apparently of no effect.

(2) The author or first owner may of course part with possession of the work many times before irretrievably parting with possession of it, as where the work is frequently lent. It seems that an identification

---

[122] s.78(4)(b). See para.11–78, below.
[123] See s.87 and para.11–82, below.
[124] CDPA 1988 s.78(3)(a).
[125] See the wording of s.78(4)(a).
[126] See para.5–02, above, as to the distinction between the first owner of the copyright in a work and the first owner of the physical embodiment of it.
[127] As for example, a work made by an employee and kept at his home.

which is on the work on any such occasion will allow the author to exercise his paternity right.

(3) Although this means is characterised as a way in which the right to be identified as author may be asserted, it does not, in fact, require any assertion of the right, only the identification of the author, for example, by his signature. In placing his signature on the work, the author may have had no knowledge that he was doing an act which amounted to an assertion of this aspect of his paternity right.[128] It follows that any person who exhibits an artistic work which bears the name of the artist in one of the relevant places should take the right to have been asserted and ensure that the author's name is apparent to anyone seeing the exhibited work. The transitional provisions of the Act are dealt with separately below, but it should also be noted in this context that even where the relevant parting with possession took place before the commencement of the 1988 Act, an assertion made by this method appears to be sufficient. The presence of the artist's name on any copyright artistic work should therefore be taken as a sufficient assertion unless, for example, it is known that the artist has waived his right.

(4) Again, the identification need not be made by the author himself nor, apparently, with his authority.

(5) In whatever manner such an identification is made, it will bind anyone into whose hands that original or copy comes and remains binding whether or not the identification is still present or visible.[129] This obviously presents a difficulty where the identification was made in a margin which has since been cropped or on a frame which has since been discarded.

(B) Secondly, the right may be asserted by including, in a licence by which the author or other first owner of copyright authorises the making of copies of the work, a statement signed by or on behalf of the person granting the licence that the author asserts his right to be identified in the event of the public exhibition of a copy made in pursuance of the licence.[130] In this case the assertion is binding on the licensee and on anyone into whose hands a copy made in pursuance of the licence comes. The assertion is binding whether or not that person has notice of it.[131] As to this:

(1) Again, it seems that it is only possible to make such an assertion on the granting of a licence by the first owner of the copyright, whether this be the author or another person. It cannot be made on the grant of a licence by a subsequent owner.

(2) For this type of assertion, the mere identification of the author is not sufficient: the assertion must be specific and relate to the public exhibition of the work.[132]

---

[128] An assertion in this form will only amount to an assertion of the right to be identified in relation to the public exhibition of the work.
[129] CDPA 1988 s.78(4)(c).
[130] s.78(3)(b).
[131] s.78(4)(d).
[132] If the licence contains a general assertion but is in fact signed by the author, it will of course satisfy CDPA 1988 s.78(2)(b).

(d) *Joint works*

11–23   In the case of works of joint authorship,[133] the right must be asserted by each joint author in relation to himself.[134] Where only one of two or more joint authors asserts his right, it therefore seems that only he must be identified as author. Where a publisher takes this course, however, he may find himself in as bad a position as if no author is identified at all, since the attribution of one person only as author will clearly be false and he may find himself the subject of a claim in reverse passing off. The prudent course will be to name all authors.[135]

(e) *Assertion and the revived and extended terms of copyright*

11–24   The effect of the revival of copyright[136] on moral rights is considered later.[137] However, any assertion of the paternity right which subsisted immediately before the expiry of copyright is to continue to have effect during the period of revived copyright.[138] Also, any assertion of the paternity right which (a) subsisted immediately before January 1, 1996[139] in relation to an existing copyright work,[140] and (b) is not to expire before the end of the copyright period under the 1988 Act as originally enacted, is to continue to have effect during the period of any extended copyright, subject to any agreement to the contrary.[141]

(vi) Exceptions

11–25   The right to be identified is subject to exceptions of various kinds: (i) as to the description of work, (ii) as to the acts done in relation to a work and (iii) as to the circumstances in which those acts are done.[142]

(a) *Excepted descriptions of work*

11–26   The right does not apply at all in relation to a computer program, the design of a typeface[143] or any computer-generated work. The paternity right was denied to authors of computer programs and typefaces for reasons of practicality, since the right was thought to lead to more problems than benefits for these works,[144] and of course there is no human author of a computer-generated work.[145]

---

[133] A work of joint authorship is one produced by the collaboration of two or more authors in which the contribution of each author is not distinct from that of the other author or authors: CDPA 1988, s.10(1). See para.4–32, above.

[134] CDPA 1988, s.88(1).

[135] The paternity right does not give an author any right *not* to be named as the author of a work of his.

[136] i.e. effected by the Duration of Copyright and Rights in Performances Regulations 1995 (SI 1995/3297).

[137] See para.11–86, below.

[138] See SI 1995/3297 reg.22(2).

[139] i.e the commencement date of SI 1995/3297.

[140] i.e. a work in which copyright subsisted immediately before that date. See SI 1995/3297 reg.14(1).

[141] See SI 1995/3297 reg.21(1).

[142] CDPA 1988 s.79.

[143] The "design of a typeface" includes an ornamental motif used in printing: CDPA 1988 s.178.

[144] *Hansard*, HL 491, col.366. However it is doubtful whether this exclusion is justified under the Berne Convention, since computer programs are fully protected as literary works. See G. Davies & K. Garnett, *Moral Rights* (London: Sweet & Maxwell, 2010), paras 7–083, 7–084.

[145] CDPA 1988 s.79(2). A computer-generated work is defined to be one that is generated by a computer in circumstances such that there is no human author of the work. See s.178.

(b) *Qualified exception of works by reference to nature of copyright*

The right to be identified does not apply in relation to a work in which Crown   **11–27**
copyright or Parliamentary copyright subsists, or a work in which copyright
originally vested in an international organisation by virtue of s.168 of the 1988
Act, unless the author or director has previously been identified as such in or on
published copies of the work.[146] It is not clear whether such previous identification must have been on all published copies: it is suggested that identification on
any published copy will have been enough to preserve the right. Crown copyright
subsists where a work is made by Her Majesty or by an officer or servant of the
Crown in the course of his duties.[147]

Parliamentary copyright subsists when a work is made by or under the direction or control of the House of Commons or the House of Lords.[148] Parliamentary
copyright extends to every Bill introduced into Parliament.[149] An international
organisation is the first owner of copyright in every original literary, dramatic,
musical or artistic work made by an officer or employee of, or published by, an
international organisation as specified in an Order in Council.[150]

(c) *Authority of copyright-owning employer*

The right does not apply to anything done by or with the authority of the copy-   **11–28**
right owner where the copyright in the work originally vested in the author's or
director's employer by virtue of s.11(2) of the 1988 Act.[151] This exception is
clearly of great significance. While an employee-author's right is retained in respect of anything done without the authority of the copyright owner, this is hardly
likely to be of great practical importance since any such act will usually also be
an infringement of copyright.[152] For example, employed journalists or photographers have no right to be identified as the author of their works published in a
newspaper or magazine.[153] There will also clearly be a large number of more general employee-works in respect of which the author has no right to be identified
as author.

(d) *Pre-1988 Act works*

There is a blanket exception to the paternity right in the case of works whose   **11–29**
author died before commencement of the 1988 Act[154] and all pre-commencement
films,[155] but there is a further exception in the case of pre-existing literary,
dramatic, musical and artistic works whose author was alive at this date. Thus,
the right does not apply where (a) copyright first vested in the author and (b) by

---

[146] CDPA 1988 s.79(7).
[147] s.163(1). See para.10–13, above.
[148] s.165(1). See para.10–86, above.
[149] s.166(1).
[150] s.168(1). At present, these are the United Nations, the Specialised Agencies of the United Nations and the Organisation of American States. See the Copyright (International Organisations)
Order 1989 (SI 1989/989), see Vol.2 C1.
[151] The position where the copyright vested in the author's employer by virtue of the earlier Acts is
considered below. A mistake in the earlier drafting of this provision was corrected by the Copyright and Related Rights Regulations 2003 (SI 2003/2498) reg.18(1). See *Copinger* 14th edn,
para.11–31, fn.40.
[152] Although not, for example, in the case of the public exhibition of an artistic work. In such a case
it is not in any event clear why the authority of the copyright owner should be of any relevance.
[153] An even more significant exception which affects journalists, news photographers and other
persons involved with reporting current events is contained in CDPA 1988 s.79(5), considered
below.
[154] August 1, 1989.
[155] CDPA 1988 Sch.1 para.23(2).

virtue of an assignment or licence granted before commencement an act may be done without infringing copyright.[156] Nor does the right apply in relation to such a work where (a) the copyright vested in someone other than the author and (b) an act is done by or with the licence of the copyright owner.[157] These restrictions are clearly likely to affect the exercise of the paternity right in relation to a large number of "old" works.

(e) *Permitted acts*

11–30   The right is not infringed by the doing of various acts which would amount to permitted acts in the context of infringement of copyright.[158] It should be noted that not every act which is permitted for copyright purposes will also escape infringement of the paternity right. On the contrary, the doing of many of the permitted acts will be capable of infringing the paternity right. The permitted acts which do not amount to an infringement of the paternity right are: fair dealing for the purpose of reporting current events by means of a sound recording, film or broadcast[159]; incidental inclusion of the work in an artistic work, sound recording, film or broadcast[160]; anything done for the purposes of an examination[161] by way of setting the questions, communicating the questions to the candidates or answering the questions[162]; anything done for the purposes of parliamentary or judicial proceedings[163] or reporting the same[164]; anything done for the purposes of the proceedings of a Royal Commission or statutory inquiry or for the purpose of reporting any such proceedings held in public[165]; making an article to the design, or copying an article made to the design, in a design document or model recording or embodying a design for anything other than an artistic work or a typeface[166]; copying an artistic work by making articles of any description after the end of the period of 25 years after the end of the calendar year in which the artistic work has been exploited by or with the copyright owner's licence by making articles by industrial process and marketing such articles in the United Kingdom and elsewhere[167]; and those cases where acts are permitted in relation to the copyright in an anonymous or pseudonymous work on the assumption that the copyright has expired or the author has died 70 years or more before the act is done.[168]

11–31   **Reporting current events.** In addition, the right does not apply in relation to any work made for the purpose of reporting current events.[169] The exception which applies to works of employees, and thus employed journalists, photographers and

---

[156] Sch.1 para.23(3)(a).

[157] Sch.1 para.23(3)(b).

[158] CDPA 1988 s.79(4).

[159] s.79(4)(a). But note that fair dealing for the purposes of reporting current events requires a sufficient acknowledgement, except where the reporting is by means of a sound recording, film or broadcast and acknowledgement would be impossible, for reasons of practicality or otherwise. The position here has changed following implementation of the Information Society Directive. See paras 9–40 et seq., above.

[160] CDPA 1988 ss.79(4)(b), and 31. See paras 9–61 et seq., above.

[161] s.32(3). See paras 9–101 et seq., above.

[162] s.79(4)(c).

[163] s.45. See para.9–143, above.

[164] s.79(4)(d).

[165] ss.79(4)(e), 46(1), (2). See para.9–144, above.

[166] ss.79(4)(f), 51. See para.9–156, above.

[167] ss.79(4)(g), 52. See para.9–161, above.

[168] ss.79(4)(h), 57 and 66A. Those are cases in which it is not possible by reasonable inquiry to ascertain the identity of the author. See para.9–170, above.

[169] CDPA 1988 s.79(5). As to the meaning of "reporting current events", see the discussion of s.30(2) at para.9–49, above.

others has already been noted.[170] A further exception which applies in relation to works published in newspapers, etc. is dealt with in the next paragraph. The present exception is wider in scope in that it applies not only to the work of employed and freelance journalists, photographers and film makers, but also to the use of their work in other news-reporting media, such as television and radio. These provisions were included particularly because of the perceived difficulties in attributing authorship in the case of news reporting and the like.[171]

(f) *Non-infringing publications*

The right does not apply in relation to the publication in a newspaper, magazine or similar periodical or in an encyclopaedia, dictionary, yearbook or other collective work[172] of reference, of a literary, dramatic, musical or artistic work made for the purposes of such publication or made available with the consent of the author for the purposes of such publication.[173] Not only will this provision include the work of journalists, etc., but also of advertisers and correspondents.   **11–32**

B. THE RIGHT TO BE IDENTIFIED AS PERFORMER

The right. The right of a performer to be identified as such generally tracks the paternity right of authors and directors. As has been seen, the right is derived from art.5(1) of the WPPT, which specifies that "Independently of a performer's economic rights, and even after the transfer of those rights, the performer shall, as regards his live aural performances or performances fixed in phonograms, have the right to claim to be identified as the performer of his performances, except where the omission is indicated by the manner of the use of the performance, ...".[174] The meaning of performer in this context has already been discussed.[175] Although the rights guaranteed under the Convention extend only to the aural and not to the visual elements of a performance, the rights granted under the 1988 Act are slightly broader in that the performers' paternity right extends to the aural and the visual elements of both a live public performance and a live broadcast of a performance. The right is infringed by the doing of any of the various acts specified in the relevant provisions[176] without the consent of the person entitled to the right.[177] The right is again subject to two important types of limitation: (a) the right is not infringed unless it has previously been asserted; and (b) the right is subject to various exceptions. The right does not apply in relation to any performances which took place before February 1, 2006.[178]   **11–33**

Relevant acts. The right to be identified as the performer arises when a qualify-   **11–34**

---

[170] i.e. that contained in s.79(3).

[171] See *Hansard*, HL Vol.493, cols 1312, 1313; Vol.495, cols 658, 659.

[172] A collective work is a work of joint authorship or a work in which there are distinct contributions by different authors or in which works or parts of works of different authors are incorporated. CDPA 1988 s.178. See para.5–119, above.

[173] s.79(6).

[174] For this purpose. "performers" are defined as actors, singers, musicians, dancers, and other persons who act, sing, deliver, declaim, play in, interpret, or otherwise perform literary or artistic works (or expressions of folklore): art.2(a). The terms "phonogram" and "fixation" are also defined.

[175] See para.11–05, above.

[176] CDPA 1988 s.205(C).

[177] CDPA 1988 s.87(1).

[178] The Performances (Moral Rights, etc.) Regulations 2006 (SI 2006/18) reg.8, February 1, 2006 being the date the Regulations entered into force. This limitation is fully consistent with the WPPT, art.22(2) of which provides that "... a Contracting Party may limit the application of Article 5 of this Treaty [i.e., the article guaranteeing moral rights for performers] to performances which occurred after the entry into force of this Treaty for that Party."

ing performance is given live in public or broadcast live or when a sound recording of such a performance is communicated or issued to the public.[179] The right applies in relation to the whole or any substantial part of a performance.[180]

11–35 **Mode of identification.** The mode of identification which is required varies according to manner of its exploitation[181]:

(i) in the case of a performance given in public, by identification of the performer in a programme accompanying the performance or in some other manner likely to bring his identity to the notice of a person seeing or hearing the performance;

(2) in the case of a broadcast performance, by identification in a manner likely to bring his identity to the notice of a person seeing or hearing the broadcast;

(3) in the case of a sound recording being communicated to the public, by identification in a manner likely to bring his identity to the notice of a person hearing the communication; and

(4) in the case of copies of a recording of a performance being issued to the public,[182] by identification in or on each copy or, if that is not appropriate, in some other manner likely to bring his identity to the notice of a person acquiring a copy.

In all these cases, identification in such other manner as the parties may agree is also permitted.[183] If the performer, when asserting the right,[184] has specified a pseudonym, initials or some other particular form of identification, then this form must be used; otherwise any reasonable form of identification may be used.[185]

11–36 **Group performances.** In relation to a performance given by a group, the right to be identified is not infringed in the case of a performance given in public, a broadcast performance or a sound recording being communicated to the public if the group itself is identified in the above manner.[186] In the case of copies of a recording of a performance by a group being issued to the public where it is not reasonably practicable for each member of the group to be identified, again the right is not infringed provided that the group itself is identified.[187] "Group" means two or more performers who have a particular name by which they may be identified collectively. There is thus no right for performers to be identified individually where a performance is given by a group[188] and indeed, unless the performers have specified a pseudonym or some other particular form of identification, the person liable to identify them has a choice of which form of identification to use.

11–37 **Requirement that right be asserted.** As with the authors' and directors' paternity right, the performers' right is not infringed unless it has been previously asserted in a manner binding on the particular defendant.[189] The right may in the same way be asserted generally, or in relation to any specified act or description

---

[179] CPDA s.205C(1).
[180] CDPA s.205K(1).
[181] CDPA s.205C(2).
[182] It is to be noted that the expression "commercial publication", which is used in relation to the equivalent aspect of the authors' and directors' paternity right, is not repeated here.
[183] CPDA s.205C(2).
[184] See para.11–42, below.
[185] CDPA s.205C(5).
[186] CPDA s.205C(3).
[187] CPDA s.205C(3).
[188] CPDA s.205C(3).
[189] cf. CDPA s.78.

of acts, by instrument in writing signed by or on behalf of the performer,[190] or on an assignment of a performer's property rights, by including in the instrument effecting the assignment a statement that the performer asserts his right to be identified in relation to the performance.[191] The persons bound by an assertion of the right are anyone to whose notice the assertion is brought and, in relation to an assignment of the performer's property rights, the assignee and anyone claiming through him, whether or not he has notice of the assertion.[192] The requirement that an instrument be signed by a person is also satisfied in the case of a body corporate by signature on behalf of the body or by the affixing of its seal.[193]

Exceptions to the right to be identified. The right does not apply where it is not reasonably practicable to identify the performer, or (where identification of a group is permitted) the group.[194] This exception is derived from WPPT art.5(1), which allows identification to be omitted where this "is indicated by the manner of the use of the performance." However, the two expressions do not necessarily mean the same thing. The right is also not infringed in relation to any performance given for the purpose of reporting current events[195] or advertising any goods or services,[196] or in a number of circumstances corresponding to those in which a performer's "Chapter II" rights[197] are not infringed: news reporting; incidental inclusion of a performance or recording; things done for the purpose of examination; parliamentary and judicial proceedings; Royal Commissions and statutory inquiries.[198]   **11–38**

3. THE RIGHT TO OBJECT TO DEROGATORY TREATMENT OF A WORK

A. THE AUTHORS' AND DIRECTORS' RIGHT TO OBJECT TO DEROGATORY TREATMENT

In general, the author[199] of a copyright literary, dramatic, musical or artistic work, and the director of a copyright film, has the right not to have his work subjected to derogatory treatment ("'the integrity right").[200] Again, this right is derived from art.6*bis* of the Berne Convention, which requires that independently of his economic rights, and even after the transfer of any such rights, an author of a work shall have the right to "object to any distortion, mutilation or other modification of, or other derogatory action in relation to, the said work, which would be prejudicial to his honour or reputation". The 1988 Act gives effect to this requirement by first defining a concept of "derogatory treatment" in relation to a work, then providing that the right is infringed by the doing of a number of specified acts in relation to such derogatory treatment, except where such acts have the consent of the person entitled to the right. As with the case of the paternity right, the right only applies in relation to a work in which copyright subsists, and the   **11–39**

---

[190] The possibility of such an assertion being assigned "on behalf of" a performer is thus more generous than in the case of authors and directors. See para.11–21.

[191] CPDA s.205D(2).

[192] CPDA s.205D(3).

[193] CPDA s.210A(2).

[194] CDPA s.205E(2).

[195] CDPA s.205E(3). It seems that it may have been considered that for example the act of a reporter speaking to camera can constitute a performance.

[196] CDPA s.205E(4).

[197] i.e. the rights granted to performers under Pt II Ch.II of the Act. See Ch.12 of this work.

[198] CPDA s.205E(5). As to these exceptions, see paras 12–79 et seq.

[199] As to the meaning of "author", see para.11–05, above.

[200] CDPA 1988 ss.80(1), 1(2). For a form of Statement of Claim, see Vol.2 J2.v.

circumstances in which the integrity right is infringed vary according to the character of the copyright work. The right is also subject to various important exceptions and qualifications. There is, however, no requirement that this right should have been asserted as a prerequisite to liability for infringement. Before the integrity right was introduced by the 1988 Act, the only means by which an author might generally take action in respect of such treatment was under the law of libel.[201]

11–40 **Transitional.** The right applies to works made before commencement of the Act (on August 1, 1989), except in the case of a film made before this date or, in relation to the other kinds of copyright work, where the author had died before this date.[202] The Act contains further provisions limiting the right in relation to pre-commencement works, which are considered below.

11–40A **Works of joint authorship.** In the case of a work of joint authorship, the right is a right of each joint author, his right is satisfied if he consents to the treatment in question.[203]

(i) Derogatory Treatment

11–41 In order to make good a claim of infringement of the integrity right, the author or director must first establish that his work has been subject to a "treatment" and then that such treatment is "derogatory".

11–42 **Treatment.** "Treatment" of a work means, in general, any addition to, deletion from or alteration to or adaptation of the work.[204] As already noted, the integrity right is not limited in its application to a substantial part of a work but applies to any part of it.[205] It is thus a broad, general concept and, *de minimis* acts apart, it covers a spectrum of possible acts carried out on a work, from the addition of a single word to a poem to the destruction of the entire work,[206] so that, towards the latter extreme, it is not necessary that the original work remains recognisable as such.[207] It follows that virtually any change to the work is covered by the expression, subject to the exceptions noted below. The alteration of a single word of a literary or dramatic work, a single note of a musical work, the slightest alteration to an artistic work or the cutting of a single frame from a film therefore amounts to a treatment.[208] Neither is a "treatment" confined to a physical embodiment of the altered work. As will be seen, public performance and broadcasting of a derogatory treatment are among the acts capable of infringing the integrity right.[209] By virtue of a specific exclusion, however, a translation of a literary or dramatic

---

[201] See the cases cited below in relation to the discussion of "derogatory treatment".

[202] CDPA 1988 Sch.1 para.23(2).

[203] s.88(2).

[204] CDPA 1988 s.80(2)(a).

[205] s.89(2).

[206] *Harrison v Harrison* [2010] EWPCC 3, para.60.

[207] *Harrison v Harrison* [2010] EWPCC 3, para.60.

[208] See, e.g. *Confetti Records Ltd v Warner Music UK Ltd* [2003] EWHC 1274 (Ch); [2003] E.M.L.R. 35 ("rap" line added to a song); *Morrison Leahy Music Ltd v Lightbond Ltd* [1993] E.M.L.R. 144 (new recording made by taking short "snatches", lasting from between 10 to 65 seconds, from five songs which lasted from between three to seven minutes, and slight alterations made in the lyrics); *Harrison v Harrison* [2010] EWPCC 3 (changes made on second edition of a work). Where the defendant had scaled down the size of the plaintiff's cartoons, this was conceded to amount to a treatment: *Tidy v Trustees of the Natural History Museum* (1995) 39 I.P.R. 501. The background colour had also been altered to pink and yellow from the original black and white.

[209] This gives effect to art.6*bis* of the Berne Convention, which provides that any "derogatory action" in relation to a work may be objected to by the author.

work does not qualify as a treatment.[210] Therefore, no matter how corrupt or damaging to an author's reputation such a translation may be, he has no remedy by way of infringement of a moral right. Neither does the expression "treatment" extend to an arrangement or transcription of a musical work involving no more than a change of key or register.[211] In both these cases, the justification was said to be that such changes would not affect the basic integrity of the work.[212] The exclusion, however, does not appear to be justified under the Berne Convention and if a translation or change of key or register is so inept or unsuitable as to amount to a derogatory treatment, there seems no good reason why the author should not have a remedy. The definition does, however, include, by its use of the expression "adaptation",[213] the conversion of a dramatic work into a non-dramatic work and of a non-dramatic work into a dramatic work[214] and a version of a literary or dramatic work in which the story or action is conveyed wholly or mainly by means of pictures in a form suitable for reproduction in a book or in a newspaper, magazine or similar periodical.[215]

The right also extends to the treatment of parts of a work resulting from a previous treatment by a person other than the author or director, if those parts are attributed to, or are likely to be regarded as the work of the author or director.[216] This means that if a work is subjected to a treatment by someone other than the author, for example in the course of the editing of a novel by a publisher, further alteration to it, for example by dramatising part of the edited version, will amount to treatment of the original work, but only if the result is seen to be the work of the original author.[217]

"Derogatory" treatment. This expression is at the core of the integrity right. A treatment of a work is "derogatory" if it amounts to distortion or mutilation of the work or is otherwise prejudicial to the honour or reputation of the author or director.[218] In the case of a treatment which is a distortion or mutilation of a work, a concept which is already pejorative, it must also be such as to be prejudicial to the honour or reputation of the author or director: a treatment which is a distortion or a mutilation but which is not prejudicial to the author's honour or reputation is not actionable as an infringement of the integrity right.[219] This follows from the use of the word "otherwise" in relation to the third category of derogatory treatment, indicating that this is a necessary qualification in relation to the first two, and from the wording of art.6*bis* of the Berne Convention, which s.80 was intended to implement.[220] Thus, in art.6*bis*, the words "which would be prejudicial to his honour or reputation" qualify all the derogatory acts referred to. Indeed, unless some such objective qualification is imposed on the words "distortion" and "mutilation", the section would pose great difficulties in its application,

11–43

---

[210] CDPA 1988 s.80(2)(I).

[211] s.80(2)(a).

[212] *Hansard*, HC, SCE, col.388.

[213] CDPA 1988 s.21(3). See paras 7–137 et seq., above.

[214] s.21(3)(a)(ii). See paras 7–140 and 7–141, above.

[215] s.21(3)(a)(iii). See para.7–142, above.

[216] s.80(7).

[217] Although note that in the example given, it could be argued that the dramatisation is itself a "treatment" of the original work. The apparent intention of the provision was to ensure that where A's work was subjected to a treatment by B, and B's work was then subjected to a treatment by C, C's actions could not be the subject of a claim by A, but only by B, if B's contribution was not taken to be the work of A. See *Hansard*, HL Vol.491, col.389.

[218] CDPA 1988 s.80(2)(b). See also A. Waisman, "Rethinking the Moral Right to Integrity" [2008] I.P.Q. 3, 268.

[219] *Confetti Records Ltd v Warner Music UK Ltd* [2003] EWHC 1274 (Ch), para.150; [2003] E.M.L.R. 35; *Pasterfield v Denham* [1999] F.S.R. 168 (County Court).

[220] *Confetti Records Ltd v Warner Music UK Ltd* [2003] 1274 (Ch), para.150; *Pasterfield v Denham* [1999] F.S.R. 168 (County Court).

since the words standing alone are highly subjective. For example, an author's work may be edited in a way which he considers has seriously impaired its worth, and yet to others the alteration may not be significant or may even be thought to be an improvement.[221]

11-44   **Distortion, mutilation, or other prejudicial treatment.** As already noted, these words are pejorative and clearly further cut down the ambit of "treatment" from its defined meaning, namely any "addition to, deletion from or alteration to or adaptation of" a work. A distortion of a work, as a matter of ordinary language, involves some form of twisting or perversion of it.[222] Mutilation of a work involves some form of cutting or destruction so as to render it imperfect. As to the third category of derogatory treatment, the wording covers any addition to, deletion from or alteration to or adaptation of the work which, although not a distortion or mutilation, is nevertheless prejudicial to the honour or reputation of the author or director. It is, however, not easy to conceive of examples of prejudicial treatment which could not also be said to amount to a distortion or mutilation in the general sense of these words.[223]

11-45   **Prejudicial to honour or reputation.** These words are taken from art.6*bis* itself and were intended to give effect to it.[224] In the original proposal for this article, the right was defined as one to object to "any modification of the work which would be prejudicial to [the author's] moral interests". This wording was altered as a result of representations from the British delegation to the effect that the concept of "moral interests" was too vague to have any clear meaning under English law, whereas those of "honour" and "reputation" had a close resemblance to existing personal rights under the laws of defamation and passing off.[225] It is therefore suggested that the words should be interpreted in this light. Thus "reputation" has an objective connotation, referring to what is generally said or believed about a person. "Honour", which is associated with both reputation and good name, is more a matter of respect for a person and his position.[226] Quite clearly, not all additions to, deletions from, alterations to or adaptations of a work will be derogatory in the sense of the Act. Many such alterations can be made, even those with which the author may not agree, which will not amount to derogatory treatment. No doubt the alteration of an author's work so as to make him appear inept, untruthful, bigoted and so on are all examples of derogatory

---

[221] So, in *Pasterfield v Denham* [1999] F.S.R. 168, the fact that the author might have been aggrieved by what had been done was irrelevant. However, in *Tidy v Trustees of the Natural History Museum* (1995) 39 I.P.R. 501, where the plaintiff's cartoons had been reduced in size, the question was treated as being whether this was either a distortion or was otherwise prejudicial to his honour or reputation.

[222] In *Tidy v Trustees of the Natural History Museum* (1995) 39 I.P.R. 501, the question of whether the treatment to which the plaintiff's works had been subjected (reduction in size) amounted to a distortion was held not suitable for summary judgment.

[223] Limited help as to the ambit of this third category is obtained from art.6*bis* of the Berne Convention. The words "distortion" and "mutilation" are used in art.6*bis* itself, so that this category appears to be intended to cover the other acts referred to in art.6*bis*, namely any "other modification of, or other derogatory action in relation to" the work. The original provision of the Berne Convention relating to the integrity right, introduced by the Rome Act of 1928, provided that the author should have the right to object to any "distortion, mutilation or other modification [of his work] which would be prejudicial to his honour or reputation". The present form of the provision was introduced in 1948 by the Brussels Act.

[224] *Confetti Records Ltd v Warner Music UK Ltd* [2003] EWHC 1274 (Ch).

[225] For a full discussion, see G. Davies & K. Garnett, *Moral Rights* (London: Sweet & Maxwell, 2010), para.8–036, and also S. Ricketson and J.C. Ginsburg, *International Copyright and Neighbouring Rights, The Berne Convention and Beyond* 2nd edn (Oxford University Press, 2006), para.10–10.

[226] As regards the concept of "honour" when considering the test for breach of the right of integrity, see E. Adeney, "The moral right of integrity: the past and future of 'honour'" [2005] I.P.Q. 2, 111–134.

treatment. Much will depend on the evidence of the effect which the treatment had on the author's honour or reputation in the eyes of others[227]; it is not enough to assemble a miscellany of trivia and submit, absent relevant evidence, that the vice lies in its cumulative effect.[228] It is not necessary that the treatment should have been carried out with the intention of subjecting the author's or director's work to derogatory treatment. An error which results in important passages of a work being omitted or the colours of an artistic work being poorly printed is capable of amounting to derogatory treatment even though the error was inadvertent. Earlier cases in the related fields of libel, passing off, etc. may serve as useful examples:

(1) Where a work was altered for serial publication by the making of cuts and additions, particularly to heighten interest at the end of each part, and the names of the characters were altered, this was found to be injurious to the author's reputation.[229]

(2) An expert in jade was entitled to refuse to allow publication of an article written by him which had been altered such that its style was no longer considered appropriate by him.[230]

(3) The publication of an author's work in a vulgar and offensive jacket was restrained on the basis that it made the untrue suggestion that the book was just as vulgar and offensive as the cover.[231]

(4) The omission of a few words from a play was arguably sufficient to weaken the whole structure.[232]

Since it is necessary to show that the treatment is prejudicial to the honour or reputation of the author or director, it is normally necessary to adduce evidence to this effect,[233] unless, perhaps, in an extreme case, it is obvious. Evidence should therefore normally be adduced that some members of the public do, or would be likely to, think less of the author or director because of the treatment. It need hardly be said that if the author does not give evidence complaining about the treatment, otherwise than for some good reason, the court is unlikely to find prejudice.[234] Since the issue is whether the treatment is prejudicial, and not whether the author's or director's reputation *has been prejudiced*, or whether the *acts* done in relation to treatment have cause his reputation to suffer, it seems that it does not matter that the witness in fact knows that the treatment was not done by the author, or that the treated work has been published anonymously or with a disclaimer.[235]

Burlesques, parodies, etc. A burlesque or parody may or may not involve a   **11–46** treatment of a claimant's work in the above sense.[236] Where it does not involve a treatment, no question of infringement of the moral right can arise. Where it does so, it will often be plain to all that the work is not actually that of the claimant

---

[227] *Tidy v Trustees of the Natural History Museum* (1995) 39 I.P.R. 501.
[228] *Harrison v Harrison* [2010] EWPCC 3, para.66.
[229] *Humphreys v Thomson & Co Ltd* [1905–1910] Mac.C.C. 148.
[230] *Joseph v National Magazine Co Ltd* [1959] Ch. 14.
[231] *Mosely v Stanley Paul & Co* [1917–1923] Mac.C.C. 341. But *quaere* whether this would amount to a "treatment": see para.11–48.
[232] *Frisby v British Broadcasting Corp* [1967] Ch. 932.
[233] *Confetti Records Ltd v Warner Music UK Ltd* [2003] EWHC 1274 (Ch), para.157; *Harrison v Harrison* [2010] EWPCC 3, para.64 (in the absence of direct evidence, professional honour and reputation categorised as "very modest").
[234] *Confetti Records Ltd v Warner Music UK Ltd* [2003] EWHC 1274 (Ch), para.157.
[235] This conclusion also seems to follow from the provisions in the 1988 Act which provide for the making of a "sufficient disclaimer" (see ss.81(6), 82(2), 103(2)), which suggest that, but for the statutory provision, such a disclaimer would not prevent a treatment from being derogatory.
[236] A burlesque or parody usually involves imitation of the style of another, rather than a particular work.

and so, no matter how critical or contemptuous of the claimant the treatment is, it is suggested that an infringement is unlikely to arise. Perhaps one case in which it might do so is where those who read, hear or see the claimant's work will no longer be able to do so without calling to mind the parody, to the prejudice of his honour or reputation. It is suggested that it is only where the treatment is made out to be the claimant's own work that there can be an infringement.[237] It should be noted that there is no general "fair dealing" exception in relation to parodies.[238]

11–47   **Destruction.** The deliberate and complete destruction of the original embodiment of a work, for example a work of art or an original manuscript, is often a controversial issue. While it almost certainly amounts to a treatment of the work, being a deletion from or alteration to it,[239] the treatment itself can hardly be prejudicial to the author's honour or reputation.[240] Although many systems of law bring such an act within the integrity right, the Berne Convention does not require this.[241]

11–48   **Derogatory use must relate to treatment: work used out of context.** What is the position where a work is used in a context which may be highly injurious to the reputation of the author or director, for example, where a literary work is used in a pornographic film or an artistic work placed in a setting which is entirely inappropriate to it?[242] Is this capable of amounting to a derogatory treatment? As a matter of UK law, the answer seems to be no, since the word derogatory relates to a "treatment" of the work, i.e. the addition, deletion, alteration, etc. and right arises in relation to specified uses of such a treatment and not to a use which is made of the unaltered work. In the above examples, although the use made of the work may be derogatory, the treatment of it itself is not. Although this appears to be the position on the wording of the Act,[243] the fact remains that whether or not a treatment is derogatory may often depend on how that treatment is used. In this respect that Act appears not to be consistent with art.6*bis* of the Berne Convention, which stipulates that the author's right is to object, inter alia, to any derogatory "action" which would be prejudicial to his honour or reputation.[244]

(ii) Circumstances in which the Right is Infringed

11–49   Even when it has been established that a work has been subjected to a derogatory

---

[237] This was the position in *Clark v Associated Newspapers Ltd* [1998] 1 All E.R. 959, but since it was the plaintiff's style which was being parodied rather that a particular work of his, no question of derogatory treatment arose.

[238] See para.9–46.

[239] *Harrison v Harrison* [2010] EWPCC 3, paras 60, 61, citing *Sehgal v the Union of India*, HC (Ind) [2005] F.S.R. 39 (famous bronze mural sculpture, commissioned by the Indian government from an internationally renowned sculptor, but some years later taken down, stored and badly damaged: held, the destruction of a work of art was an extreme form of mutilation).

[240] In *Sehgal v the Union of India*, HC (Ind) [2005] F.S.R. 39 it was held that by reducing the volume of the author's creative corpus it affected his reputation prejudicially, but the reasoning seems unlikely to be followed in the UK.

[241] See further on the point, G. Davies & K. Garnett, *Moral Rights* (London: Sweet & Maxwell, 2010), para.8–23, and also generally for examples of such a right in other jurisdictions.

[242] And consider, e.g. the facts of *Mosely v Stanley Paul & Co* [1917–1923] Mac.C.C. 341 (plaintiff's book published in a vulgar and offensive dust jacket) and *Shostakovich v Twentieth Century Fox Film Corp* (1948) 80 N.Y.S.(2d) 575 (recordings of music used in settings of which the composers did not approve).

[243] In *Morrison Leahy Music Ltd v Lightbond Ltd* [1993] E.M.L.R. 144 short extracts were taken from several recordings of the claimant's songs and compiled, with other material, into one recording. The argument appears to have turned on whether the compilation, rather than the way in which the songs had been cut, was derogatory. In any event, however, the juxtaposition of the short extracts with other material presumably amounted to an addition to or alteration of each work.

[244] For a full discussion on the point, see G. Davies & K. Garnett, *Moral Rights* (London: Sweet & Maxwell, 2000), para.8–022.

treatment, it is only when the treatment is then subjected to one of the specified uses that any question of infringement arises. The specified uses vary with the type of work. As already noted, the word "derogatory" apparently refers to the type of treatment which the work has been subjected to, and not the type of use to which the derogatory treatment is then subjected.

(a) *Literary, dramatic and musical works*

In the case of a literary, dramatic or musical work, the right is infringed by a person who publishes commercially, performs in public or communicates to the public a derogatory treatment of the work.[245] It is also infringed by a person who issues to the public copies of a film or sound recording of, or including, a derogatory treatment of the work.[246] The expressions have already been considered in the context of the paternity right, as has the apparent overlap between them. **11–50**

(b) *Artistic works*

In the case of an artistic work, the right is infringed by a person who publishes commercially or exhibits in public a derogatory treatment of the work or communicates to the public a visual image of a derogatory treatment of the work.[247] The right is also infringed by a person who shows in public a film including a visual image of a derogatory treatment of a work or issues to the public copies of such a film.[248] Again, these expressions have already been considered when dealing with the paternity right. As noted there, public exhibition of an artistic work is an act which is not capable of amounting to infringement of copyright in an artistic work. **11–51**

Works of architecture, sculptures and works of artistic craftsmanship. In the case of works of architecture in the form of a model for a building (but not in the form of a building itself), sculptures and works of artistic craftsmanship, a person infringes the right if he issues to the public copies of a graphic work[249] representing, or of a photograph of,[250] a derogatory treatment of the work.[251] As noted elsewhere in relation to other similar provisions, the issue to the public of such copies will often also amount to commercial publication. Where a work of architecture in the form of a building is the subject of derogatory treatment and its author is identified on the building, his only right is to require the identification to be removed.[252] The subjection of the building to the derogatory treatment is not itself an infringement,[253] so that where the architect is not identified he has no remedy. Neither, it seems, does he have any right to damages whilst his name remains on the building. **11–52**

(c) *Films*

In the case of a film, the right is infringed by a person who shows in public or **11–53**

---

[245] CDPA 1988 s.80(3)(a).
[246] ss.80(3)(a), (b).
[247] CDPA 1988 s.80(4)(a).
[248] s.80(4)(b).
[249] A graphic work includes a painting, drawing, diagram, map, chart or plan, or an engraving, etching, lithograph, woodcut or similar work. See CDPA 1988 s.4(2).
[250] A photograph means a recording of light or other radiation on any medium on which an image is produced or from which an image may by any means be produced, and which is not part of a film. See CDPA 1988 s.4(2).
[251] CDPA 1988 s.80(4)(c).
[252] s.80(5).
[253] Compare the wording of ss.80(4) and (5).

communicates to the public a derogatory treatment of the film or issues to the public copies of a derogatory treatment of the film.[254]

(iii) Other Persons Liable for Infringement

11–54 The integrity right is also infringed by persons possessing or dealing with "infringing" articles. For this purpose, an infringing article is a work or a copy of a work which has been subjected to derogatory treatment within the meaning of the Act and which has been, or is likely to be, the subject of any of the acts referred to above which amount to an infringement of the integrity right.[255] This double requirement means that an article may change in character from a non-infringing to an infringing article, and even back again, depending on the use to which it is intended to be put. In relation to such an article, the right is infringed by a person who, knowing or having reason to believe that it is an infringing article[256]:

(1) possesses it in the course of a business;

(2) sells it or lets it for hire, or offers it or exposes it for sale or hire; or

(3) in the course of a business exhibits it in public or distributes it; or

(4) distributes it otherwise than in the course of a business so as to affect prejudicially the honour or reputation of the author or director.[257]

(iv) Exceptions

11–55 The right is subject to various exceptions depending upon: (a) the character of the work, (b) the acts done in relation to it, (c) the circumstances in which the various acts are done, and (d) whether the work was in existence before the commencement of the 1988 Act.

(A) *Excepted works*. The right does not apply to a computer program.[258] This is so notwithstanding that inept alterations to a computer program which are still likely to be regarded as the work of the original author because, for example, it still carries his name, may be highly damaging to his reputation. As with the paternity right, the exception does not appear to be compatible with the Berne Convention. The right also does not apply to any computer-generated work.[259]

(B) *Reporting current events*. The right does not apply to any work made for the purpose of reporting current events.[260] What is important here is the purpose for which the work was made, not the purpose for which the work is used. The work of a news journalist may therefore be edited, however ineptly, without infringing his integrity right.

(C) *Publications*. The right does not apply in relation to the publication in a newspaper, magazine or similar periodical, or in an encyclopedia, dictionary, yearbook or other collective work of reference, of a literary, dramatic, musical or artistic work made for the purposes of such publication or made available with the consent of the author for the purposes of

---

[254] CDPA 1988 s.80(6).

[255] CDPA 1988 s.83(2).

[256] s.83(1). See paras 8–08 et seq., above.

[257] See paras 8–11 et seq., above, for a discussion of the meaning of these terms in relation to infringement of copyright.

[258] CDPA 1988 s.81(2).

[259] s.81(2). The exception is hardly surprising since a "computer-generated work" is one that is generated by computer in circumstances such that there is no human author of the work: s.178.

[260] s.81(3). See paras 9–40 and 9–49, above.

such publication.[261] The right does not apply in relation to any subsequent exploitation elsewhere of such a work without any modification of the published version.[262]

(D) *Anonymous, pseudonymous works: ss.57 and 66A* . The right is not infringed by an act which, by virtue of ss.57 or 66A, would not infringe copyright in the work.[263] That section refers to anonymous or pseudonymous works and to acts permitted on assumptions as to the expiration of copyright or death of the author.[264]

(E) *Certain purposes.* The right is not infringed by anything done for certain specified purposes, provided that, where the author or director is identified at the time of the relevant act or has previously been identified in or on published copies of the work, there is a "sufficient disclaimer".[265] Those purposes are[266]:

(1) avoiding the commission of an offence;

(2) complying with a duty imposed by or under an enactment; or

(3) in the case of the British Broadcasting Corporation, avoiding the inclusion in a programme broadcast by them of anything which offends against good taste or decency or which is likely to encourage or incite to crime or to lead to disorder or to be offensive to public feeling.

A "sufficient disclaimer" means a clear and reasonably prominent indication given at the time of the act, and if the author or director is then identified, appearing along with the identification, that the work has been subjected to treatment to which the author or director has not consented.[267]

(F) *Existing works.* As with the paternity right, there is a blanket exception to the integrity right in the case of works whose author died before commencement of the 1988 Act[268] and all pre-commencement films,[269] but there are further similar exceptions in the case of then-existing literary, dramatic, musical and artistic works whose author was alive at this date. Thus, the right does not apply where (a) copyright first vested in the author and (b) by virtue of an assignment or licence granted before commencement an act may be done without infringing copyright.[270] Nor does the right apply in relation to such a work where (a) the copyright vested in someone other than the author and (b) an act is done by or with the licence of the copyright owner.[271] These restrictions are clearly likely to affect the exercise of the integrity right in relation to a large number of "old" works.

(v) Qualification of the Right

In the case of certain works, the right is qualified.[272] Those works are: **11–56**

---

[261] s.81(4). As to a collective work, see s.178 and para.5–119, above.
[262] s.81(4).
[263] s.81(5).
[264] s.57, 66A. See para.9–170, above.
[265] s.81(6).
[266] s.81(6).
[267] s.178.
[268] August 1, 1989.
[269] CDPA 1988 Sch.1 para.23(2).
[270] Sch.1 para.23(3)(a).
[271] Sch.1 para.23(3)(b).
[272] CDPA 1988 s.82.

(1) works in which copyright originally vested in the author's or director's employer by virtue of s.11(2)[273];

(2) works in which Crown copyright or Parliamentary copyright subsists; and

(3) works in which copyright originally vested in an international organisation by virtue of s.168.

In all these cases the right does not apply to anything done in relation to such work by or with the authority of the copyright owner, unless the author or director is identified at the time of the relevant act, or has previously been identified in or on published copies of the work. Where, in such cases, the right does apply, it is not infringed if there is a sufficient disclaimer.[274]

This qualification is clearly of substantial significance in so far as it relates to the works of employees where, as will usually be the case, the copyright first vests in the employer.[275] As in the case of the paternity right,[276] this limitation will apply in many cases since exploitation of the derogatory treatment will often have had the consent of the copyright owner: otherwise it will usually also be an infringement of his copyright.[277] The limitation is not, however, quite as wide in scope as that which relates to the paternity right, since the integrity right arises not only in cases where a substantial part of the work has been subjected to derogatory treatment but also where *any* part has been so treated.[278] Exploitation of a derogatory treatment which reproduces or is an adaptation of less than a substantial part of the original will not require the permission of the copyright owner. An author's or director's integrity right in such cases is therefore unaffected by the qualification in s.82. It is suggested that even if in such cases the thing done in relation to the derogatory treatment is done with the permission of the copyright owner, the qualification will still not bite since his *authority* was not required and therefore not given.[279]

Assuming, however, that the thing done in relation to the original work was done with the authority of the copyright owner, then if the employee is not identified as the author or director of the original work, whether at the time or on previously published copies, he has no right to complain even if he can establish derogatory treatment.[280] Even where the author or director has been so identified, he will still be unable to exercise the integrity right where a disclaimer is made.

B. The Performers' Right to Object to Derogatory Treatment

11–57   **Definition of the right.** As with the performers' paternity right, the performers' integrity right tracks the authors' and directors' integrity right. The right to object to derogatory treatment of a performance is thus infringed if a performance is broadcast live, or by means of a sound recording a performance is played in public or communicated to the public, with any distortion, mutilation or other

---

[273] A mistake in the earlier drafting of this provision was corrected by the Copyright and Related Rights Regulations 2003 (SI 2003/2498), reg.18(2). See *Copinger* 14th edn, para.11–56, fn.27.

[274] CDPA 1988 s.82(2). For a definition of sufficient disclaimer, see CDPA 1988 s.178 and para.11–55, above.

[275] It will only not do so where there was an agreement, express or implied, to the contrary. See CDPA 1988 s.11(2) and paras 5–11 et seq., above.

[276] i.e. by virtue of the exception under CDPA 1988 s.79(3). See para.11–28, above.

[277] i.e. the derogatory treatment will usually reproduce or be an adaptation of a substantial part of the original work.

[278] CDPA 1988 s.89(2).

[279] See, e.g. *C.B.S. Songs Ltd v Amstrad Plc* [1988] A.C. 1013, HL; [1988] R.P.C. 567, and paras 7–146 et seq., above.

[280] On the other hand, there is no limitation on the nature of previously published copies which identified the author. Copies long out of print which identified the author will preserve the right.

modification that is prejudicial to the reputation of the performer.[281] The right applies in relation to the whole or any part of a performance.[282] Since there is no concept of a joint performance, the right to object to derogatory treatment applies to all performers individually; there is no separate provision for groups.

Exceptions to right. The right is subject to a number of exceptions, although fewer than in the case of authors and directors. Thus it does not apply in relation to any performance given for the purposes of reporting current events[283] and is not infringed by modifications made to a performance which are consistent with normal editorial or production practice.[284] Furthermore, the right is not infringed by anything done for the purpose of avoiding the commission of an offence, complying with a duty imposed by or under an enactment, or, in the case of the British Broadcasting Corporation, avoiding the inclusion in a programme broadcast by them of anything which offends against good taste or decency or which is likely to encourage or incite crime or lead to disorder or to be offensive to public feeling.[285] In the case of these latter exceptions, where (a) the performer is identified in a manner likely to bring his identity to the notice of a person seeing or hearing the performance as modified by the act in question; or (b) he has previously been identified in or on copies of a sound recording issued to the public, the exceptions are conditional upon a sufficient disclaimer being provided,[286] i.e. a clear and reasonably prominent indication that the modifications did not have the consent of the performer, given at the time of the act and appearing with the identification of the performer, if any.[287]   **11–57A**

Infringement of right by possessing or dealing with infringing article. Possessing or dealing with a sound recording of a performance with modifications prejudicial to the performer's reputation infringes the performer's integrity right.[288] This follows the similar provisions for authors.[289]   **11–57B**

4. FALSE ATTRIBUTION OF AUTHORSHIP OR DIRECTORSHIP

In general, a person has the right not to have a literary, dramatic, musical or artistic work falsely attributed to him as author, or a film falsely attributed to him as director.[290] The right is conferred on authors and non-authors alike,[291] although clearly such statements are most likely to be made in relation to persons who have established reputations, whether as authors, dramatists, composers or artists. There is no equivalent right in relation to performances. The right applies in relation to the whole or any part of the work, not just a substantial part.[292] These provisions of the 1988 Act are largely based upon the equivalent provisions of the   **11–58**

---

[281] CDPA s.205F.
[282] CDPA s.205K(2).
[283] CDPA 205G(2). See para.11–32, fn.00 for the possible reason for this.
[284] CDPA 205G(3).
[285] CDPA 205G(4).
[286] CDPA 205G(5).
[287] CDPA 205G(6).
[288] CDPA s.205H.
[289] CDPA s.83.
[290] CDPA 1988 s.84(1).
[291] This follows from the wording of the Act but see also *Clark v Associated Newspapers Ltd* [1998] 1 All E.R. 959 and *Harrison v Harrison* [2010] EWPCC 3, para.50.
[292] CDPA 1988 s.89(2).

1956 Act.[293] As already pointed out, this right is not prescribed by the Berne Convention. Alongside this statutory right, a person may have a claim in passing off or defamation in relation to such acts.[294]

The section therefore requires that there be an attribution of authorship or directorship and that the attribution be false. "Attribution" in relation to the relevant work means a statement, express or implied, as to who is the author or director of the work.[295] For these purposes, the "work" is the whole work which is attributed to the claimant. So where words are added to the claimant's actual work and the whole attributed to him, the right is infringed.[296] Examples of false attribution include a newspaper article in the first person attributing to a person words which that person did not in fact use,[297] an article which in addition to quoting the actual words of the claimant added to the quote a further 17 words which were not his,[298] a spoof diary column purporting to be by the claimant, a well-known politician, and carrying his photograph, and held to contain a clear statement attributing the column to him[299] and a second edition of work implying that is was by the same author as that of the successful first edition.[300] It does not matter if the claimant is not expressly named as author, provided there is a false attribution which concerns him.[301] In this, in order to succeed, the representation relied on as conveying the message that the claimant was the author of the work must be construed to see what the single correct meaning of it is.[302] In this, the tort is like the tort of defamation[303] but is unlike passing off, where if the same representation may mean different things to different people it is sufficient to establish that one of those meanings at least deceives or causes confusion amongst a substantial number of people.

11–59   **False statement as to adaptation.** The right extends to cases where, contrary to the fact, a literary, dramatic or musical work is falsely represented as being an adaptation[304] of a work of a person.[305] Where, therefore, a play is falsely held out as being based on another's novel, such a statement will amount to a false attribution within the meaning of the Act, even when it is clear that the dramatisation

---

[293] See CDPA 1988 s.43 and *Harrison v Harrison* [2010] EWPCC 3, para.50. The ultimate source of the provisions is s.7 of the Fine Arts Copyright Act 1862 (25 & 26 Vict. c.68), which related only to artistic works.

[294] See, e.g. *Byron v Johnston* (1816) 2 Mer. 29; *Archbold v Sweet* (1832) 1 Moo. & R. 162; *Ridge v The English Illustrated Magazine Ltd* [1911–1916] Mac.C.C. 91 (libel). The precise cause of action in some of the early cases is unclear.

[295] CDPA 1988 s.84(1).

[296] *Noah v Shuba* [1991] F.S.R. 14 at 32.

[297] *Moore v News of the World Ltd* [1972] 1 Q.B. 441.

[298] *Noah v Shuba* [1991] F.S.R. 14 at 32.

[299] *Clark v Associated Newspapers Ltd* [1998] 1 All E.R. 959. This was despite the statement carried in the column that the diary was how the writer imagined the claimant might have recorded certain events. This was held not to neutralise the main impression conveyed by the column as a whole.

[300] *Harrison v Harrison* [2010] EWPCC 3.

[301] *Harrison v Harrison* [2010] EWPCC 3, para.55 (obvious reference in second edition of work to an apparently successful antecedent first edition which must obviously have had an author; irrelevant that a reader of the second edition did not know the name of that author: the message to the reader was that this was the updated second edition of the first edition of the work and was by the author of the first edition).

[302] *Clark v Associated Newspapers Ltd* [1998] 1 W.L.R. 1558; [1998] R.P.C. 261, *Harrison v Harrison* [2010] EWPCC 3, para.55.

[303] See *Charleston v News Group Newspapers Ltd* [1995] 2 A.C. 65 at 71; [1995] E.M.L.R. 129.

[304] For the meaning of adaptation in relation to these works, see CDPA 1988 s.21(3) and paras 7–137 et seq., above.

[305] CDPA 1988 s.84(8).

itself is the work of another. Such a claim could conceivably arise where a play or film is misrepresented, by its title, to be based upon a well-known book.[306]

False statement as to copy of artistic work. A false statement that a copy of an artistic work is a copy made by the author of the artistic work will also amount to a false attribution.[307] The application of this provision appears rather limited today, but clearly could apply where prints are represented as having been made by the artist himself.   **11–60**

False statement as to alterations to artistic work. Where an artistic work has been altered after the author has parted with possession of it, the right of the artist is infringed by a person who, in the course of a business, deals with the altered work as being the unaltered work of the author, or deals with a copy of such work as being a copy of the unaltered work of the author, knowing, or having reason to believe, that this is not the case.[308] Under the similarly worded provisions of the 1862 Act, it was held that the right only applied in the case of a material alteration, not to something which was *de minimis*, and that an alteration was material if it might affect adversely the character or reputation of the artist.[309]   **11–61**

Joint authorship. The right is also infringed by any false statement as to the authorship of a work of joint authorship or by the false attribution of joint authorship in relation to a work of sole authorship.[310] Such a false attribution infringes the right of every person to whom authorship of any description is, whether rightly or wrongly, attributed.[311] If one person only is named as the author of a work of which two persons are the authors, the person who is named has the right to complain of false attribution, not the unnamed author. The right of the unnamed author is to assert his paternity right.[312] Where a work of sole authorship is attributed to two joint authors, the named person who was not the author clearly has the right to complain of false attribution. It seems that the person who was the actual author cannot claim false attribution but can assert a right of paternity, claiming the right to be identified as "the" author of the work, not as a joint author.   **11–62**

Infringing acts. Where a false attribution had been made, a person's rights are infringed by anyone who commits the following acts: **11–63**

(1) *Issue to the public.* This occurs if a person issues to the public copies of a literary, dramatic, musical or artistic work or a film, in or on which there is a false attribution.[313]

(2) *Public exhibition.* This occurs when a person exhibits in public an artistic work, or a copy of an artistic work, in or on which there is a false attribution.[314]

(3) *Public performance.* This occurs if, in the case of a literary, dramatic or musical work, a person performs the work in public or communicates it to the public as being the work of a person or, in the case of a film, shows it in public or communicates it to the public as being directed by a person.

---

[306] Although the section does not in terms refer to a false representation made in relation to a film, a film is capable of being a dramatic work. See para.3–39, above.

[307] CDPA 1988 s.84(8).

[308] CDPA 1988 s.84(6).

[309] *Carlton Illustrators v Coleman & Co Ltd* [1911] 1 K.B. 771 at 780. Evidence was accepted that alterations in the size and colour of a work might so affect the author. An example of a *de minimis* alteration was said to be an alteration to the artist's signature. *Sed quaere.*

[310] CDPA 1988 s.88(4).

[311] s.88(4)

[312] See para.11–23, above, as to the problem where one joint author only asserts his paternity right.

[313] CDPA 1988 s.84(2)(a).

[314] s.84(2)(b).

Infringement only occurs, however, if that person knows or has reason to believe that the attribution is false.[315]

(4) *Associated material.* The right is infringed by the issue to the public, or by the public display of material containing a false attribution in connection with any of the acts mentioned above.[316]

(5) *Indirect infringement.* The right is infringed by a person who, in the course of a business, possesses or deals with a copy of a literary, dramatic, musical or artistic work or a film in or on which there is a false attribution or, in the case of an artistic work, possesses or deals with the work itself when there is a false attribution in or on it. Liability is dependent on that person knowing or having reason to believe that there is such an attribution and that it is false.[317] The references to "dealing" are to selling or letting for hire, offering or exposing for sale or hire, exhibiting in public, or distributing.[318]

The meaning of these various expressions has already been considered.

5. RIGHT TO PRIVACY OF CERTAIN PHOTOGRAPHS AND FILMS

11–64   Limited provisions relating to the use of photographs and films were introduced into the 1988 Act in response to the change in the law which meant that the commissioner of a photograph no longer automatically became entitled to the copyright.[319]

The Act provides that a person who, for private and domestic purposes, commissions the taking of a photograph[320] or the making of a film[321] has, where copyright subsists in the resulting work, a right to "privacy" in such work. The right does not apply in relation to photographs or films taken or made before the commencement of the 1988 Act.[322] In general, such a person has the right[323] not to have:

(1) copies of the work issued to the public;
(2) the work exhibited or shown in public; or
(3) the work communicated to the public.

These rights are infringed by a person who does, or authorises the doing of, any of these acts. The meaning of the various expressions has already been considered. What amounts to commissioning the taking of a photograph has also been considered in detail in relation to the ownership of copyright in pre-1988 Act photographs.[324] Whereas the right of the commissioner to the copyright in such a photograph depends on him not only having commissioned the taking of the photograph but also having paid or agreed to pay for it,[325] the privacy provisions of the 1988 Act do not in terms include a reference to payment. Normally,

---

[315] s.84(3)(a),(b).

[316] s.84(4).

[317] s.84(3).

[318] s.84(7).

[319] As to the old law relating to commissioned photographs, see paras 5–33 et seq., above.

[320] A photograph means a recording of light or other radiation on any medium on which an image is produced or from which an image may by any means be produced, and which is not part of a film. CDPA 1988 s.4(2).

[321] A film means a recording on any medium from which a moving image may by any means be produced. CDPA 1988 s.5(1).

[322] i.e. August 1, 1989. See CDPA 1988 Sch.1 para.24.

[323] CDPA 1988 s.85(1).

[324] See paras 5–33 et seq., above.

[325] See the Copyright Act 1956 s.4(3).

however, a commissioning connotes an obligation to pay.[326] In such circumstances it is clearly possible that the commissioner will not only have rights of privacy under the present provision but also be entitled to the copyright in the photograph or film, in equity at least.[327] The two rights are, however, independent.

Private and domestic purposes. The commissioning must have been for "private and domestic" purposes. This is an expression which is used elsewhere in the Act[328] and envisages ordinary home life or "something close to it".[329] Although the limits of this expression may not be entirely clear, it is important to keep in mind that it qualifies the purposes of the commission and not the subject matter of the photographs.[330] A wedding may to some extent be a public affair and not domestic, but it is suggested that the purposes for which wedding photographs are commissioned are normally both private and domestic, that is the recording of the event for family and friends. The words private and domestic are conjunctive: a photograph which is commissioned for private but not domestic purposes, for example for purposes relating to a person's private business affairs, will not fall within the section.   **11–65**

Infringing acts. Although the photograph or film must have been commissioned for private and domestic purposes, there is no requirement that the infringing act be an invasion of a person's private or domestic affairs. In this sense the right conferred, once the private and domestic purpose test is satisfied in relation to the commissioning, is analogous to a right of copyright: the commissioner can withhold his consent to any of the specified uses for whatever reason. The exploitation for these purposes may therefore become deadlocked where the commissioner and copyright owner are different persons and each declines to consent to its use.[331]   **11–66**

Substantial part. The right only applies in relation to the whole or any substantial part of the work.[332] It is not clear whether these words will be construed in their normal copyright sense[333] or whether they will be judged by the quality or importance of the image in relation to a right of privacy. In theory, a small part of a photograph, for example the image of one person taken from a large group, may not amount to a substantial part of the photograph in the copyright sense, but its use in a newspaper may amount to an invasion of privacy of the kind which the section is designed to prevent. Although in practice a court may have little difficulty in such a case in reaching the conclusion that, even if judged on the copyright test, the section is satisfied, it is suggested that the words should be construed bearing in mind the purpose of the section and therefore, if necessary, in a sense favourable to the protection of a person's privacy in a domestic sphere.   **11–67**

Exceptions. The right is not infringed by an act which, by virtue of various provisions, would not infringe copyright in the work. The provisions are those which   **11–68**

---

[326] *Apple Corps Ltd v Cooper* [1993] F.S.R. 286.
[327] As to the rights in equity of a person who commissions the making of a copyright work, see paras 5–178 et seq., above.
[328] See, e.g. CDPA 1988 s.22 (secondary infringement by importation, if not for "private and domestic" use).
[329] *Mahmood v Galloway* [2006] EWHC 1286, para.19; [2006] E.M.L.R. 26.
[330] So, in *Mahmood v Galloway* [2006] EWHC 1286, the photograph in question was clearly taken for purposes of work: see para.18.
[331] Although this cannot happen in the case of the public exhibition or showing of the work, an act which does not require the consent of the copyright owner (except in the case of an infringing copy).
[332] CDPA 1988 s.89(1).
[333] As to which see paras 7–25 et seq., above.

relate to the incidental inclusion of the work in an artistic work, film or broadcast[334]; parliamentary and judicial proceedings[335]; Royal Commissions and statutory inquiries[336]; acts done under statutory authority[337]; and anonymous or pseudonymous works and acts permitted on assumptions as to the expiry of copyright or death of the author.[338] It is worth noting that no exception exists in relation to any form of fair dealing and in particular any use of a photograph or film for the purpose of reporting current events. As already noted, the right does not apply in relation to photographs or films taken or made before the commencement of the 1988 Act.[339]

11–69 **Joint commissions.** In the case of a work made in pursuance of a joint commission, the right is that of each person who commissions the making of the work.[340] Thus, the right of each is satisfied if he consents to the act in question,[341] and a waiver by one of them under s.87 does not affect the rights of the others.[342] Thus where one of two joint commissioners agrees to the publication of a photograph, the rights of the other to object are not affected.

6. DURATION OF MORAL RIGHTS

11–70 **Authors' rights.** The question of how long authors' moral rights should last has been a matter of controversy in the international treatment of these rights.[343] Article 6*bis* of the Rome revision of the Berne Convention left the period of protection for the paternity and integrity rights unspecified.[344] The Brussels revision of 1948 made it clear that the rights should last for at least the author's lifetime and, to the extent that national legislation permitted,[345] at least until the copyright in the work expired. The Stockholm revision of 1967, now found in the Paris Act, made obligatory a *post mortem* term of 50 years, except for those countries whose legislation did not provide for such protection at the time of their ratification or accession to the Act.[346] Since the rights of paternity and integrity were put on a new, clear statutory basis by the 1988 Act, there was no impediment to the United Kingdom fully implementing art.6*bis*. The 1988 Act therefore provides that the right to be identified as author or director and the right to object to derogatory treatment of a work continues to subsist so long as copyright subsists in the work, as does the right to privacy in commissioned photographs

---

[334] CDPA 1988 ss.5(2)(a) 31. See para.9–61, above.

[335] CDPA 1988 ss.85(2)(b), 45. See para.9–143, above.

[336] CDPA 1988 ss.85(2)(c), 46. See para.9–144, above.

[337] CDPA 1988 ss.85(2)(d), 50. See para.9–148, above.

[338] CDPA 1988 ss.85(2)(e), 57. See para.9–162, above.

[339] i.e. August 1, 1989. See CDPA 1988 Sch.1 para.24.

[340] CDPA 1988 s.88(6).

[341] s.88(6)(a).

[342] s.88(6)(b). See paras 11–82 et seq., below.

[343] The main controversy has been between the "monist" systems, which perceive moral rights and economic rights as being closely linked so that they should be of the same duration, and the "dualist" systems, which perceive them as being separate, so that while the economic rights should be limited in time, moral rights should be perpetual. See further, G. Davies & K. Garnett, *Moral Rights* (London: Sweet & Maxwell, 2010), para.1–015.

[344] The position of the United Kingdom was that since the paternity and integrity rights were adequately protected under the existing common law, and since causes of action such as defamation died with the author, the term of protection prescribed should be no longer than this.

[345] This escape clause was inserted at the insistence particularly of the UK delegation, which opposed any extension of the rights beyond the author's lifetime. See S. Ricketson and J. Ginsburg, *International Copyright and Neighbouring Rights, The Berne Convention and Beyond* (Oxford: OUP, 2006), para.10–11.

[346] The United Kingdom deposited its instrument of ratification of the Paris Act on September 29, 1989, with effect from January 2, 1990. The 1988 Act came into force on August 1, 1989.

and films.[347] The right of a person not to have works falsely attributed to him endures for a different period, namely until 20 years after a person's death.[348] The exercise of these rights after a person's death is considered below.

Extension and revival of copyright term. With the amendments made to the 1988 Act to comply with the EC Directive harmonising the term of copyright to one of life and 70 years after the author's death,[349] provision also had to be made in relation to the period of protection for moral rights. The provisions relating to extension and revival of the term of copyright are considered in detail later.[350] Where the copyright has been extended or revived, the moral rights are exercisable so long as the copyright subsists.[351]   **11–71**

Performers' rights. The statutory performers' moral rights in a performance subsist as long as the performers' economic rights subsist in relation to that performance.[352] This is in conformity with WPPT art.5(2).   **11–71A**

7. TRANSMISSION OF MORAL RIGHTS

Moral rights are not assignable.[353] They are personal, not proprietary, rights. Since, however, they subsist beyond the lifetime of the author or director, and potentially beyond the lifetime of the performer, provision has to be made for the exercise of these rights in the *post mortem* period. Article 6*bis* of the Berne Convention and art.5(2) WPPT leave it to the legislation of each country to provide by whom the *post mortem* paternity and integrity rights should be exercised. As regards these rights, and also in respect of the right of privacy in respect of a photograph or film, the 1988 Act provides that on the death of a person entitled, the right passes to such persons as he may by testamentary disposition specifically direct.[354] Not only may a person appoint more than one person under this provision,[355] but it seems he may also appoint different persons in respect of the different rights. If there is no specific testamentary disposition of the right in this way, but the copyright in the work in question or the performer's property rights (generally, "the property rights") in respect of the performance in question form part of that person's estate, then the right passes to the person to whom the such property rights pass,[356] whether under his will or on intestacy. If and to the extent that the right does not pass in either of these ways, it is exercisable by that person's personal representatives.[357] The right can be similarly transmitted after the death of the person in whom the right becomes vested. Although special pro-   **11–72**

---

[347] CDPA 1988 s.86(1).

[348] s.86(2).

[349] Directive 93/98 of October 29, 1993.

[350] See paras 11–75 et seq., below. The distinction has to be made between cases where the term of UK copyright had not yet expired, in which case the term was in general simply extended from life and 50 years to life and 70 years, and cases in which the UK copyright had expired but had to be revived for the residue of the life and 70-year term.

[351] This follows from the words of CDPA 1988 s.86. Various transitional provisions are considered in the context in which they arise in this chapter.

[352] CDPA 1988 s.205I(1). As to this term, see para.12–30.

[353] CDPA 1988 ss.94, 205L. cf. assignments of copyright and performers' property rights. In relation to the paternity and integrity rights, art.6*bis* of the Berne Convention and art.5 of the WPPT do not state this expressly but it is implicit.

[354] CDPA 1988 ss.95(1)(a), 205M(1)(a).

[355] See ss.95(3), 205M(3) and para.11–76, below.

[356] ss.95(1)(b), 205M(1)(b). See ss.95(3), 205M(3) and para.11–74, below, as to the position where the property rights are split on such a bequest. The provision does not appear very apt in the case of the privacy right (since the point of the section is that the benefit is conferred where the commissioner does *not* own the copyright).

[357] ss.95(1)(c), 205M(1)(c).

vision is made as to the exercise of these rights where there is more than one person entitled,[358] it is not clear whether on the death of one such person his entitlement passes to the survivor or survivors or whether it passes to the persons specified in s.95(1). Since this section is the only mechanism provided for the transmission of the rights, it is suggested that the latter is the correct answer in the case of the death of a person to whom the right has passed by virtue of either testamentary disposition or by following the property right. Where the right has been transmitted to personal representatives under subs.(c), it is suggested that the position is different and that the right becomes exercisable by the survivor or survivors of two or more personal representatives, and then, where the chain of representation continues, by the personal representative of the survivor.[359] Where the chain is broken, the right will be exercisable by whoever obtains a new grant to the original estate. Companies and other bodies corporate may clearly become entitled to moral rights by virtue of these provisions.[360]

Unlike the various forms of property which, after the owner's death, vest in personal representatives and thereafter in beneficiaries or transferees these rights cannot be transferred or divested, even, for example, by personal representatives after administration of the estate is complete. Again, where the right passes to the person entitled to the corresponding property right,[361] the moral right does not become attached to the property right and pass with it on a subsequent assignment. It remains vested in that person until a subsequent transmission under s.95(1) or 205M(1), as the case may be. On normal principles, the production of a grant will be necessary to prove a person's title to these moral rights in an action.[362] Where the moral right passes to the person specifically appointed by testamentary disposition, the right apparently vests in such appointee immediately on death and not, for example, in his executors where he dies testate or in the Public Trustee where he dies intestate. Where the moral right passes with the corresponding property right,[363] the position is more complicated. On the death of the property right owner, the property right will vest first in his executors, or in the Public Trustee and then in his administrators, depending on whether he died testate or intestate.[364] The property right will then be subject to the usual trusts for the administration of the owner's estate and liable to be sold, along with his other assets, to pay his debts and testamentary expenses. Only if it is not sold in the course of administration will the property right pass to the person beneficially entitled to it, whether under the will or under the intestacy rules, by assent or assignment, as the case may be.[365] Presumably the intention is that the corresponding moral right passes to whoever, incidents of administration apart, is or would have been beneficially entitled to the property right.

11–73   **False attribution.** The above provisions affect only the transmission of the paternity, integrity and privacy rights. In the case of the right to prevent false at-

---

[358] See below.

[359] Note the difference in the wording between, on the one hand, paras (a) and (b) ("... the right passes ...") and, on the other, paras (c) ("if or to the extent that the right does not pass under paragraph (a) or (b) it is *exercisable* by his personal representatives".—emphasis added). As to the chain of representation, see Williams, Mortimer and Sunnucks, *Executors, Administrators and Probate* 18th edn (London: Sweet & Maxwell) p.46.

[360] And see ss.176 and 210A, relating to bodies corporate.

[361] i.e. under ss.95(1)(b) or 205M(1)(b).

[362] cf. the position following the death of an owner of copyright, discussed at para.5–127, above.

[363] i.e. under CDPA 1988 ss.95(1)(b) or 205M(1)(b).

[364] See para.5–127, above.

[365] See para.5–130, above.

tribution, which lasts for the shorter period of 20 years after a person's death,[366] the right becomes actionable by a person's personal representatives after his death.[367]

Nature of transmitted right. Although the statute does not say so expressly, the **11–74** rights of paternity, integrity and the right to prevent false attribution which become vested in others by these means remains a right which is referable to the moral rights of the deceased author or performer. Thus, for example, in relation to the authors' paternity right, the right is obviously to have the deceased author or director identified as the author or director of the work, and not the person by whom the right is now exercisable. In the same way, the integrity right which is exercisable after the author's or director's death is a right not to have a derogatory treatment of the deceased author's work exploited. The right of false attribution is a right not to have a work falsely attributed to the deceased person.[368] In contrast, a person who becomes entitled to exercise the privacy right after the commissioner's death simply has the right not to have the relevant photograph or film exploited in any of the specified ways. As already noted, in this respect the privacy right is more analogous to a right of copyright. Any damages recovered by personal representatives by virtue of these provisions in respect of an infringement occurring after a person's death devolve as part of his estate as if the right of action had subsisted and been vested in that person immediately before his death.[369]

Split property rights. During a person's lifetime, any disposition of a property **11–75** right by him, whether partial or total,[370] will not affect the exercise of his corresponding moral rights. The rights remain vested in him. Since, however, on death a person's moral rights may pass to the person entitled to the corresponding property right,[371] a potential difficulty arises when different aspects of the property right become vested in different persons. This may occur, for example, where a bequest is limited so as to apply to one or more, but not all of the things which the property right owner has the exclusive right to do or authorise; or to part, but not the whole, of the period for which the copyright is to subsist.[372] By whom are the moral rights relating to these works to be exercised? The Act provides that where a property right forming part of a person's estate passes in part to one person and in part to another, any right which passes with the property right by virtue of s.95(1) or 205M(2) of the 1988 Act is correspondingly divided.[373] Taking the example of an author who has made a bequest of the right to reproduce his literary works in book form to one person (A) and to reproduce or dramatise them in the form of films to another (B), A but not B is entitled to assert the paternity right in relation to publication of the work in book form and to object to a derogatory treatment which is commercially published in book form, even though, in the latter case, the derogatory treatment may seriously damage the copyright vested in B. As already noted, these moral rights do not pass on any subsequent assignments of these partial rights of corresponding property right. They remain vested in A and B until further transmitted in accordance with ss.95(1) or 205M(1).

---

[366] CDPA 1988 s.86(2). See para.11–70, above.
[367] s.95(5).
[368] Of course the person entitled to exercise this right after the author's or director's death has a quite separate personal right not to have a work or film falsely attributed to *him*.
[369] CDPA 1988 ss.95(6), 205M(5). See, further at para.11–72, below.
[370] As to partial assignments of copyright, see paras 5–97 et seq., above.
[371] i.e. under CDPA 1988 s.95(1)(b) or s.205M(1)(b).
[372] s.95(2)(a), (b) or s.205M(2)(a), (b).
[373] s.95(2).

11–76   Rights jointly exercisable. On transmission of moral rights following death, however, the rights may be transmitted to more than one person jointly. The further transmission of such rights in such circumstances has already been considered, but how are the rights to be exercised in these circumstances? The Act provides that where, by virtue of a succession following testamentary disposition or by virtue of the associated property right passing, a right becomes exercisable by more than one person:

(1) In the case of the right to be identified as author or director, it may be asserted by any of them[374];

(2) In the case of the integrity and privacy rights, the right is exercisable by each of them and is satisfied in relation to any of them if he consents to the treatment or act in question[375];

(3) In any case, any waiver of the right by one of them does not affect the rights of the others.[376]

So, for example, where the paternity right has been passed to A and B, A may assert the right independently of B, and B, it seems, may later bring an action for infringement relying on A's assertion. In the case of the integrity or privacy rights, either A or B may bring an action for infringement and any consent or waiver by B does not affect the exercise of the integrity or privacy right by A.

11–76A   Effect of previous waiver or consent. A consent or waiver previously given or made binds any person to whom the right passes by virtue of these succession provisions.[377]

8. REMEDIES FOR INFRINGEMENT OF MORAL RIGHTS

11–77   An infringement of a moral right is actionable as a breach of statutory duty owed to the person entitled to the right without proof of damage.[378] A person will, in an appropriate case, be entitled to recover general and special damages and an injunction to restrain threatened future breaches of duty. Damages for infringement of the paternity right will no doubt usually be assessed on the basis of the loss of publicity and thus lost opportunity which the omission to name him has caused.[379] In the case of derogatory treatment, damages will, for example, be assessed by reference to the damage which the publicity has done to the person's career and loss of sales. False attribution is likely to lead to damages to an author's reputation and loss of future earnings by the association of his name with a work with which he is unconnected. As with similar cases in the field of passing off, the damage is often likely to be difficult to quantify and the important remedy will usually be an injunction, particularly an interim injunction. No pro-

---

[374] CDPA 1988 ss.95(3)(a). There is no equivalent provision in the case of performers.

[375] ss.95(3)(b), 205M(3)(a).

[376] ss.95(3)(c), 205M(3)(b). See paras 11–80 et seq., below.

[377] ss.95(4), 205M(4).

[378] CDPA 1988 ss.103(1) 205N(1), and *Clark v Associated Newspapers Ltd* [1998] 1 All E.R. 959. See Ch.21, below, as to remedies generally. For forms of Statement of Claim, see Vol.2 J2.iv, v. An interesting discussion of the difficulty of enforcing moral rights in the digital environment, including the potential effect of choice of law on internet disputes, is to be found in C. Waelde and L. de Souza, "Moral Rights and the Internet: Squaring the Circle" [2002] I.P.Q.3, 265–288.

[379] For cases on claims in contract for failure to give credit: see *Marbé v George Edwardes (Daly's Theatre) Ltd* [1929] 1 KB 269; *Tolnay v Criterion Film Productions Ltd* [1936] 2 All E.R. 1625; *Herbert Clayton and Jack Waller Ltd v Oliver* [1930] AC 209; *Joseph v National Magazine Co Ltd* [1959] 1 Ch 14, CA; *Brighton v Jones* [2004] EWHC 1157 (Ch); [2005] F.S.R. 16.

vision is made for any award of additional damages in the case of flagrancy[380] although, presumably, an award of exemplary damages is now obtainable.

Cases where the claim is brought after a person's death raise peculiar difficulties. How, for example, is the measure of damages to be assessed? Infringement of the paternity or integrity rights may affect future sales, but this is a loss which will affect the owner of the property right, who will not necessarily be the person to whom the right has been transmitted. The point is underlined by the fact that it is only where the rights are exercisable by the personal representatives that any damages form part of the deceased's estate.[381] In all other cases, the damages belong beneficially to the person to whom the right has passed, and such person may have no other connection with the author or performer, his estate or his property rights.[382]

Delay. In relation to the paternity right, the court, in considering remedies, is to take into account any delay in asserting the right.[383] This provision was inserted because it was thought it might be unjust to grant an injunction or substantial damages if there was a late assertion of the right after the owner had spent money on exploitation.[384] The provision is clearly intended to go beyond the court's existing discretion to refuse relief on equitable grounds in cases, for example, of acquiescence.　**11–78**

Disclaimer. In proceedings for infringement of the right to object to derogatory treatment, the court may, if it thinks it is an adequate remedy in the circumstances, grant an injunction on terms prohibiting the doing of any act unless a disclaimer is made, in such terms and in such manner as may be approved by the court, dissociating the author, director or performer from the treatment.[385]　**11–79**

9. SUPPLEMENTARY PROVISIONS

A. CONSENT AND WAIVER OF RIGHTS

The Act distinguishes between two types of act which affect the exercise of moral rights, namely consent and waiver. The apparent intention was that a waiver would be appropriate in cases where a release from any claims was required on a long-term or formal basis, while a simple consent would be appropriate in one-off cases when the right might otherwise be infringed.[386]　**11–80**

Consent. It is not an infringement of any moral right to do any act to which the person entitled to the right has consented.[387] Consent may be given orally or in writing, formally or informally, and it may be express or implied from words or conduct. The mere fact that the work or performance was commissioned from the　**11–81**

---

[380] cf. CDPA 1988 s.97(2) in the case of infringement of copyright.
[381] ss.95(6), 205M(5). In such a case, the damages recovered devolve as part of his estate as if the right of action had subsisted and been vested in him immediately before his death. ibid.
[382] Often, a person will have been appointed under CDPA 1988 ss.95(1)(a) or 205M(1)(a) because trust was reposed in him to preserve the author's or performer's good name, not for any personal benefit.
[383] CDPA 1988 s.78(5).
[384] *Hansard*, HL Vol.491, col.365. See para.11–21, above, for a discussion of some of the problems to which this can give rise.
[385] CDPA 1988 ss.103(2), 205N(4). For the definition of "sufficient disclaimer", see CDPA 1988 s.178 and para.11–55, above.
[386] *Hansard* HL Vol.491, col.395; HL Vol.493, col.1336. The distinction is, however, largely illusory. See G. Davies & K. Garnett, *Moral Rights* (London: Sweet & Maxwell, 2010), para.10–048.
[387] CDPA 1988 ss.87(1), 205J(1).

author, setting up an equitable title to the property right in the commissioner, does not mean that consent to do any of the acts within the scope of his moral rights can be inferred.[388]

11–82 **Waiver.** Any of the rights may also be waived by an instrument in writing signed by the person giving up the right.[389] A waiver by one joint author does not affect the rights of the other joint authors.[390] A waiver may relate to a specific work or performance, to works or performances of a specified description or to works or performances generally, and may relate to existing or future works or performances.[391] A waiver may also be conditional or unconditional and may be expressed to be subject to revocation.[392] If a waiver is made in favour of the owner or prospective owner of the related property right, the waiver is presumed to extend to his licensees and successors in title, unless a contrary intention is expressed.[393] The provisions as to formal waiver by instrument in writing do not exclude the operation of the general law of contract or estoppel in relation to an informal waiver or other transaction in relation to the right to be identified, the right to object to derogatory treatment and the privacy right.[394]

11–83 **Waiver and the extended and revived terms.** The effect of the extension and revival of the copyright term on moral rights is considered below. However, any waiver of a moral right which (a) subsisted immediately before January 1, 1996[395] in relation to an existing copyright work,[396] and (b) is not to expire before the end of the copyright period under the 1988 Act as originally enacted, is to continue to have effect during the period of any extended copyright, subject to any agreement to the contrary.[397] Also, any waiver of a moral right which subsisted immediately before the expiry of copyright shall continue to have effect during the period of revived copyright.[398]

B. JOINT DIRECTORS

11–84 The various provisions applicable in relation to joint authorship of a work apply in relation to a film which was, or is alleged to have been, jointly directed.[399] A film is "jointly directed" if it is made by the collaboration of two or more directors, and the contribution of each director is not distinct from that of the other director or directors.[400] As already noted, although for copyright purposes one of the authors of a film is the "principal director",[401] for moral rights purposes the joint directors need not all be principal directors.

---

[388] *Pasterfield v Denham* [1999] F.S.R. 168 (County Court).
[389] CDPA 1988 ss.87(2), 205J(2). For a precedent of a waiver, see Vol.2 J1.vi.
[390] s.88(3).
[391] ss.87(3)(a), 205J(3)(a).
[392] ss.87(3)(b), 205J(3)(b). It is not clear whether a waiver which is expressed to be irrevocable but which is not given for consideration is in fact revocable in the absence of any estoppel. It is suggested that it is not: see G. Davies & K. Garnett, *Moral Rights* (London: Sweet & Maxwell, 2010), para.10–043.
[393] ss.87(3), 205J(3).
[394] ss.87(4), 205J(4).
[395] i.e. the commencement date of SI 1995/3297.
[396] i.e. a work in which copyright subsisted immediately before that date. See SI 1995/3297.
[397] See SI 1995/3297 reg.21(1).
[398] See SI 1995/3297 reg.22(2).
[399] CDPA 1988 s.88(5). As to works of joint authorship, see s.10(1) and paras 4–32 et seq., above.
[400] s.88(5). As to works of joint authorship, see s.10(1) and paras 4–32 et seq., above.
[401] s.9(2)(ab). There is no reason in principle why there should not be joint "principal directors".

10. TRANSITIONAL PROVISIONS

A. AUTHORS' WORKS

(i) Pre-1988 Act Works

Some of the transitional provisions which apply in relation to works in existence **11–85** before the commencement of the 1988 Act[402] have been considered as they arise in the context of the different moral rights but are summarised here.

The authors' paternity and integrity rights apply in relation to works in existence before commencement ("existing works"), but they do not apply in relation to a literary, dramatic, musical or artistic work the author of which died before the commencement, or in relation to a film made before the commencement, of the Act.[403]

In relation to an existing literary, dramatic, musical or artistic work:

(1) Where the copyright first vested in the author, the rights do not apply to anything which by virtue of an assignment of copyright made or licence granted before commencement may be done without infringing copyright.[404] So, for example, where the author was the first owner of the copyright but before commencement granted a licence to publish his work, the licensee may publish it without identifying the author if the licence is silent on the point, for to do so will not infringe the author's copyright. In the same way, if the licence permits the publisher to alter the work,[405] publication of the altered work will not infringe the author's integrity right.

(2) Where the copyright first vested in a person other than the author, the rights in relation to existing works do not apply to anything done by or with the licence of the copyright owner.[406] So where, for example, the copyright first vested in the author's employer, neither the employer nor any successor in title of his need identify the author or concern himself with the integrity right in relation to an act done by him. The same applies to acts done with his licence.

The rights do not apply to anything done in relation to a record made in pursuance of s.8 of the 1956 Act,[407] which provided for a statutory recording licence.

The right to privacy in relation to photographs and films does not apply to photographs taken or films made before the commencement of the 1988 Act.[408]

(ii) Moral Rights and the Revived and Extended Terms of Copyright

The implementation of the Term Directive[409] meant that the term of UK copy- **11–86** right was generally increased from the life of the author of the work and 50 years after his death to life and 70 years. In cases where the work was still in copyright in the United Kingdom, this meant simply extending the period for the new term.

---

[402] August 1, 1989.
[403] CDPA 1988 Sch.1 paras 23(1), (2).
[404] Sch.1 para.23(3)(a).
[405] As to which, see para.5–228, above.
[406] CDPA 1988 Sch.1 para.23(3)(b). In *Morrison Leahy Music Ltd v Lightbond Ltd* [1993] E.M.L.R. 144, the court assumed that where a composer had entered into a publishing agreement whereby the copyright in future compositions was to belong to the publisher, the copyright first vested in the publisher, not the composer. See ibid. s.91, and paras 5–108 et seq., above.
[407] CDPA 1988 Sch.1 para.23(4).
[408] Sch.1 para.24.
[409] Council Directive 93/98 of October 29, 1993, implemented by SI 1995/3297.

In certain other cases, where the UK term had expired but the work was still in copyright in another EEA State, copyright was revived for the remainder of the life and 70-year term.[410] Transitional provisions needed to be made to deal with the moral rights implications of these changes.

11–87   **The extended term.** In general, no special provisions apply. Moral rights are exercisable for the full, extended term in accordance with the provisions of the 1988 Act. However, any assertion of the paternity right or waiver of a moral right which (a) subsisted immediately before January 1, 1996[411] in relation to an existing copyright work,[412] and (b) is not to expire before the end of the copyright period under the 1988 Act as originally enacted, is to continue to have effect during the period of any extended copyright, subject to any agreement to the contrary.[413]

11–88   **The revived term.** In relation to all works which are the subject of revived copyright, the author will have died before the commencement of the 1988 Act. Nothing in the transitional provisions relating to the revived term is to affect the basic transitional provision of the 1988 Act that in such cases the paternity and integrity rights do not apply.[414] It would therefore appear that no paternity or integrity right can exist in relation to the revived term of copyright. Nevertheless, the Regulations make provision for such a case, and also in relation to the privacy right and right to prevent false attribution. Thus it is provided that where the copyright in a work has been revived, moral rights relating to it are also revived or come into being.[415] In such a case, the author or director of a revived copyright work is entitled to exercise the paternity and integrity rights as from its revival on January 1, 1996. Where the author or director had died before this date, the rights are exercisable by his personal representatives.[416] In the case of the privacy right, the draftsman of the Regulations also appears to have overlooked that it is not the author of the photograph or film who is entitled to the right, but the commissioner.[417] In all these cases, any damages recoverable by the personal representatives devolve as part of the author's, director's or commissioner's estate as if the right of action had subsisted and been vested in him immediately before his death.[418] Again, the draftsman appears to have overlooked the fact that in the case of the right to complain of false attribution, the right is that of any person to whom a work has been falsely attributed as author or director, and does not depend on him being an author or director or there being any copyright work. The revival of copyright is therefore of no relevance to such a right.[419]

In addition to these provisions, the Act also provides that the revival of copyright is not to affect the other transitional provisions in the 1988 Act denying or limiting moral rights to works in existence at the commencement of the 1988 Act.[420] Again, this provision is of doubtful application.

Any assertion of the paternity right, and any waiver of any moral right, which

---

[410] For a full discussion, see Ch.6, above.
[411] i.e. the commencement date of SI 1995/3297.
[412] i.e. a work in which copyright subsisted immediately before that date. See SI 1995/3297.
[413] See SI 1995/3297 reg.21(1).
[414] i.e. under CDPA 1988 Sch.1 para.23(2)(a). See SI 1995/3297 reg.22(6).
[415] As where the copyright had expired before August 1, 1989 so that no moral rights ever existed.
[416] This is so even where CDPA 1988 s.95(1)(a) or (b) applied.
[417] See the wording of SI 1995/3297 regs 22(3) and (4): "(3) Moral rights are exercisable after commencement by the author of a work, or as the case may be, the director of a film in which revived copyright subsists … (4) Where the author or director died before commencement—(a) the rights conferred by … CDPA 1988, section 85 … are exercisable after commencement by his personal representatives."
[418] SI 1995/3297 reg.22(5).
[419] cf. the wording of SI 1995/3297 reg.22(4)(b).
[420] i.e. by virtue of CDPA 1988 Sch.1 paras 23 and 24. See para.11–85, above.

subsisted immediately before the expiry of copyright is to continue to have effect during the period of revived copyright.[421]

The Regulations contain various savings for acts done on the basis that the copyright had expired and was thus in the public domain.[422] The provisions relating to savings for infringement of copyright are considered in detail elsewhere,[423] but where by virtue of these provisions an act does not constitute an infringement of copyright, neither does it infringe any moral right.[424]   **11–89**

(iii) Sound Recordings and Films

One of the changes made by the Regulations implementing the Term Directive was to alter the treatment of film soundtracks, which are now to be treated as part of the film.[425] It is not an infringement of any moral right in a film to do anything after January 1, 1996 in pursuance of arrangements made before this date for the exploitation of the sound recording which is now to be treated as the soundtrack.[426]   **11–90**

B. PERFORMERS

The right does not apply in relation to any performances which took place before February 1, 2006.[427]   **11–91**

---

[421] See SI 1995/3297 reg.22(2).

[422] See SI 1995/3297 reg.23.

[423] See paras 5–151 et seq., above.

[424] SI 1995/3297 reg.23(6).

[425] See paras 4–54 et seq., above, for a detailed discussion.

[426] SI 1995/3297 reg.26(4).

[427] The Performances (Moral Rights, etc.) Regulations 2006 (SI 2006/18) reg.8, February 1, 2006 being the date the Regulations entered into force. This limitation is fully consistent with the WPPT art.22(2) of which provides that "… a Contracting Party may limit the application of Article 5 of this Treaty [i.e. the article guaranteeing moral rights for performers] to performances which occurred after the entry into force of this Treaty for that Party."

PART III

RIGHTS IN PERFORMANCES

CHAPTER TWELVE
RIGHTS IN PERFORMANCES

1. INTRODUCTION

A. HISTORICAL

Nature of performers' rights.[1] The performer is the direct intermediary be-   **12–01**
tween the author or composer and the public. A dramatic or musical work may be
read but cannot be fully appreciated unless performed. Authors and other copyright owners are therefore dependent on the talent of performers to interpret their
works and to bring them before the general public. A performance is not a "copyright work" under the 1988 Act, and there has never been a copyright as such in a
performance.[2] Moreover, until certain rights in performances were conferred on
performers by the 1988 Act, as subsequently amended, there was no property
right in the nature of copyright in a performance.

Neither the 1911 Act nor the 1956 Act created any copyright in respect of live

---

[1] For a full treatment of performers' rights, see R. Arnold, *Performers' Rights* 4th edn (London: Sweet & Maxwell, 2008).
[2] CPDA 1988 s.1(1); and see *Apple Corps Ltd v Lingasong Ltd* [1977] F.S.R. 345 at 350.

performances although, as will be seen, some limited statutory protection existed. Following representations from performers' organisations, the extension of copyright or the grant of a similar right in respect of performances had been considered by the Copyright Committee, which reported in 1951 on changes to the copyright law (the Gregory Committee). At that time, such protection was not thought to be justified on two grounds: first, it was considered that the essence of copyright was the protection against the copying of a work reduced to a material form (i.e. fixed in writing or otherwise) and performances, being ephemeral by their nature and never exactly repeated, were too elusive to give rise to a right of property and did not fit into the framework of copyright; second, that such a right would add to the number of licences needed for the exploitation of certain copyright works. The Committee to consider the law on copyright and designs, which reported in 1977 (the Whitford Committee), took the same view, emphasising that to give a performer a copyright in his performance could lead to considerable practical difficulties.[3] The Whitford Committee did, however, recommend making civil remedies such as an injunction and damages available to performers in respect of unauthorised reproduction of live and recorded performances.

In the long legislative process starting with the Whitford Committee report and completed by the adoption of the 1988 Act, the Government indicated its intention to make civil remedies available to performers first in a Green Paper issued in 1981,[4] confirmed later in a White Paper issued in 1986.[5] The 1988 Act duly conferred rights on performers, by requiring their consent to certain acts of exploitation of their performances. Remedies for the enforcement of these rights was conferred by way of a civil action for breach of statutory duty, as well as criminal sanctions. Subsequently, the Act has had to be amended on a number of occasions to comply with EU Directives and to meet other international obligations. Thus, at present, performers benefit from a number of economic rights, according to which their consent is required for certain acts of exploitation of their performances, and which include certain additional property and non-property rights, as well as from moral rights.[6]

12–02   **Origins of performers' rights.** As the copyright system developed for the protection of authors, the question of the protection of performers did not arise for the simple reason that performances could not be reproduced and being ephemeral had no need of protection. Anyone wishing to see or hear a particular performer had to buy a ticket and attend a performance. The position changed early in the twentieth century in response to the increasing possibilities for the exploitation of performances made available as a result of new technical developments, such as sound recording, film production for the cinema and radio and later television broadcasting. In time, the problems faced by performers as a result of these new technologies were raised in various international fora. Performers' organisations (in the United Kingdom, principally the Musicians' Union) were concerned by what they saw as the reduction in employment opportunities which the reproduction and dissemination of their live performances was likely to entail and they therefore sought protection against unauthorised uses of such performances. In due course, the impact of technological change on the performers' professions led to recognition of the need for some form of legal

---

[3] Report of the Committee on the Law of Copyright, Cmd.8662 (1952) paras 170, 172 and 177. See also 1977 Copyright Committee, Cmnd.6732 paras 406 et seq. And see *Groves* in [1990] 6 Ent. L.R. 202 & *Sherrard* in [1992] 6 Ent. L.R. 57.

[4] Cmnd.8302, Ch.6.

[5] Cmnd.9712, Ch.14.

[6] See paras 12–04 et seq. below. The moral rights of performers are discussed in Ch.11, above. On the evolution of performers' rights in the UK, see R. Arnold, *Performers' Rights* 4th edn (London: Sweet and Maxwell, 2008), Ch.1.

protection for performers and their cause was taken up by the International Labour Organisation (ILO) in the 1920s. Thereafter, the ILO continuously promoted an international solution to the problems of performers with a view to safeguarding their employment opportunities. These efforts led to the adoption of the Rome Convention for the Protection of Performers, Producers of Phonograms and Broadcasting Organisations (the Rome Convention) in 1961, which the United Kingdom ratified in 1963.[7]

Dramatic and Musical Performers' Act 1925. It was in the context of the intergovernmental discussions on the protection of performers that some measure of statutory protection came to be afforded to performers in the United Kingdom under the provisions of the Dramatic and Musical Performers' Protection Act 1925, which was modified by the 1956 Act and later repealed and re-enacted by the Dramatic and Musical Performers' Protection Act 1958. That Act was in turn amended by the Performers' Protection Act 1963, in order to give effect to the Rome Convention, and by that of 1972. The nature of the protection afforded by these Acts was to make certain unauthorised acts connected with performances criminal offences punishable by fines and/or imprisonment. Under these Acts, protection was afforded only to performers who performed literary, dramatic, musical or artistic works.[8]   **12–03**

The 1988 Act. All those Acts were repealed in their entirety by the 1988 Act.[9]   **12–04**
Part II of the 1988 Act initially created two separate rights in performances: one for performers, by requiring their consent to the exploitation of their performances, a right which was personal and non-assignable ("performers' rights"); and one for persons having an exclusive recording contract with a performer, which was transferable by contractual assignment ("recording rights").[10] The definition of a performance included a dramatic performance (including dance and mime); a musical performance; a reading or recitation of a literary work, or a performance of a variety act or any similar presentation, to the extent that the performance is a live performance given by one or more individuals. The new Act removed the previous requirement that to be protected a performance had to be of a literary, dramatic, musical or artistic work. This change was introduced in order to protect performances of variety acts, thus affording protection to variety artistes (circus performers and the like) for the first time.[11] The performers' rights were not rights in the nature of copyrights. However, in 1992 the Rental and Related Rights Directive[12] required that performers should be afforded certain transferable property rights. As a result, in 1996 considerable additions and changes were made to the scheme of protection under the 1988 Act in order to implement such legislation in the United Kingdom and to meet other international

---

[7] Ratified by the UK on October 30, 1963, and entered into force on May 18, 1964. See para.12–10, below; see also paras 23–88 et seq., below, concerning the history and progress of the Rome Convention.

[8] See *Copinger*, 12th edn, paras 688 et seq.

[9] CDPA 1988 s.303(2), Sch.8; See Vol.2 E6.i, E6.ii and E6.iii et seq. for the texts of the repealed Acts.

[10] See para.12–20, below.

[11] Parliamentary debates, HC, Standing Committee E, June 9, 1988, col. 54. A variety act is not defined in the 1988 Act. However, the expression was used in the Report of the Whitford Committee to mean performers such as magicians, clowns, jugglers, acrobats and the like (Cmnd. 6732 at para.407) and in the 1986 White Paper (Cmnd. 9712 at para.14.5). See also R. Arnold, *Performers' Rights*, 4th edn (London: Sweet and Maxwell, 2008), paras 2.15–2.17.

[12] Directive 2006/115/EC [2006] OJ L376 (codified version), which repealed and replaced Council Directive 92/100/EEC; see further at paras 12–13 and 24–52, below.

obligations.[13] The result was the creation of a two-tier system of protection; the original rights of the 1988 Act, which granted performers certain non-property rights, and new performers' property rights. Although these new rights were not described as copyright, in effect a new copyright was conferred on performers. Yet further changes were required in 2003 on implementation of the Information Society Directive.[14] Finally, regulations were introduced in February 2006[15] to provide moral rights for performers in fulfilment of the United Kingdom's obligations under the WIPO Performances and Phonograms Treaty 1996 (the WPPT).[16] These are all discussed in further detail below.

B. Summary of the Law Pre-1988 Act—Performers' Protection Acts 1958 to 1972

12–05　**Pre-1988 Act law.** Although these Acts have been repealed it is helpful to an understanding of the law as it now stands to summarise the position before the commencement of the 1988 Act.

(i) Criminal offences

12–06　The main method adopted for the protection of performances was the creation of criminal offences, punishable summarily or on indictment, for knowingly making and exploiting records, films and broadcasts of performances which had been made without the written consent of the performers. Although criminal sanctions remain for making, dealing with and using "illicit recordings" of performances,[17] they are not the main method for the protection of performers' rights today.

(ii) Private rights

12–07　Although the 1958 to 1972 Acts ostensibly provided only for penalties in criminal proceedings against a person found guilty of committing a statutory offence, it was held that those Acts, on their true construction, disclosed an intention to create private rights of action for the benefit of performers. This conclusion was reached because it was apparent from the provisions of the Acts that the obligations and prohibitions were imposed for the benefit or protection of performers as a particular class of individuals. A performer was, therefore, entitled to bring a civil action for breach of statutory duty claiming an injunction and damages.[18]

(iii) Duration of the private right

12–08　It was also held that the private rights thereby conferred did not cease on the death of the performer. The right to consent to the recording and exploitation of a performance vested in the performer's personal representatives when the performer died. The Acts were not limited to the protection of the reputation and future employment prospects of a performer. They also enured for the protection

---

[13] See paras 12–10 et seq., below.

[14] Directive 2001/29/EC of the European Parliament and of the Council, see further at paras 12–16 and 24–79 et seq.

[15] The Performances (Moral Rights, etc.) Regulations 2006.

[16] See paras 12–18 and 23–119, below and Ch.11, above, which deals with the moral rights of performers.

[17] CDPA 1988 s.198. See Ch.22, below.

[18] *Rickless v United Artists* [1988] Q.B. 40; [1987] F.S.R. 362, applying *Lonrho Ltd v Shell Petroleum Ltd (No.2)* [1982] A.C. 173 at 185; *Grower v BBC* [1990] F.S.R. 595. Cf. *Musical Performers' Protection Association Ltd v Lingasong Ltd* [1977] F.S.R. 345.

of the performer's economic interests by ensuring that he was paid for the use of his performances.[19]

The consequence of this construction of the Act was that a performer arguably enjoyed more extensive rights in respect of his performances than an author in respect of his works. The performer enjoyed a quasi-proprietary right akin to copyright, but without any of the safeguards and provisions in the 1956 Act which limited the duration of the right and provided other restrictions on enforcement.

(iv) Persons having exclusive recording rights

The protection of the Acts was, however, confined to performers. It did not extend **12–09** to recording companies or other persons who had obtained exclusive recording contracts in respect of the artists' performances. They had no right of action under those Acts because they did not fall within the class for whose benefit the Acts were passed.[20] They had no cause of action at common law, even though the making and distribution of unauthorised "bootleg" records inflicted serious economic loss on recording companies. They could not claim effective relief for interference with contractual relations of the performers, because the "bootlegger" who made and sold the recording of a live performance of the artist did not interfere with the performance or induce the artist to act in breach of any of his contractual obligations to the recording companies.[21]

This position was remedied by the 1988 Act which creates recording rights in performances for the benefit of producers of sound recordings and other persons having exclusive recording rights.[22]

C. THE INTERNATIONAL PERSPECTIVE

(i) The Rome Convention

On October 26, 1961, the International Convention for the Protection of Perform- **12–10** ers, Producers of Phonograms and Broadcasting Organisations was adopted at Rome.[23] By art.7(1) of the Rome Convention, the United Kingdom, as one of the parties, undertook to protect certain rights of performers. Performers were to have rights which would make it possible for them to prevent the unauthorised broadcasting and communication to the public of a live performance, the fixation of a live performance and the reproduction of a fixation of their performances in certain circumstances.[24] This provision, however, has no further application once the performer has consented to the incorporation of his performance in a visual or audiovisual fixation,[25] so the performer has no right to authorise or prevent the reproduction or secondary use of such a fixation (for example, a film or television programme). The Rome Convention guarantees protection for a term of 20 years, from fixation, performance or broadcasting, as appropriate.[26] The 1963 Performers' Protection Act was passed to enable effect to be given to that Convention.

---

[19] *Rickless v United Artists* [1988] Q.B. 40; [1987] F.S.R. 362, applying *Lonrho Ltd v Shell Petroleum Ltd (No.2)* [1982] A.C. 173 at 185; *Grower v BBC* [1990] F.S.R. 595. Cf. *Musical Performers' Protection Association Ltd v Lingasong Ltd* [1977] F.S.R. 345.
[20] *R.C.A. Corp v Pollard* [1983] Ch.135; [1983] F.S.R. 9.
[21] *R.C.A. Corp v Pollard* [1983] Ch.135.
[22] See paras 12–27 et seq., below.
[23] See paras 23–88 et seq., below, and for the text of the Convention see Vol.2 F5. This Convention is not to be confused with the Rome Act of the Berne Convention.
[24] Rome Convention art.7.
[25] Rome Convention art.19.
[26] Rome Convention art.14.

12–11   Principle of national treatment. Under the terms of the Convention, each Contracting State must apply national treatment in respect of the rights which it accords to performers, producers of sound recordings (phonograms) and broadcasting organisations. In addition, Contracting States are required to offer nationals of other States who are protected by the Convention certain minimum rights. In the case of sound recordings, these include an exclusive right to authorise all reproductions, direct or indirect, and also a right to equitable remuneration (which under national law could alternatively be paid to or shared with performers) for the use of recordings in broadcasts and public performance.[27] Performers acquired only "the possibility of preventing" various specified acts,[28] a distinction which was thought to allow the United Kingdom, in particular, to continue its approach of only protecting performers by criminal sanctions.[29]

(ii) European Union legislation

12–12   There has been considerable legislative activity as a result of the programme to create uniform and improved EU-wide protection for copyright and related rights. Four Directives have necessitated amendments to Pt II of the 1988 Act, and a considerable strengthening of protection for performers has resulted.

12–13   **The Rental and Related Rights Directive.**[30] This provides that performers must have the exclusive right to authorise or prohibit the following acts:

(1) the fixation of their performances[31];

(2) the direct or indirect reproduction of fixations of their performances[32];

(3) the distribution of fixations of their performances[33];

(4) the rental and lending of fixations of their performances[34];

(5) the broadcasting by wireless and the communication to the public of their performances (except where the performance is itself already a broadcast performance or is made from a fixation).[35]

The limitations which Member States might allow to these rights were prescribed[36] and the reproduction, distribution and rental and lending rights were stated to be proprietary, in that they may be transferred, assigned or licensed.[37] As will be seen, the reproduction right has since been enlarged to make it clear that it covers temporary as well as permanent reproduction of fixations of performances.[38]

Performers are thereby ensured a reasonable degree of control over the exploitation of their performances and a share of royalties and other payments (such as "residuals"—fixed amounts payable for particular uses such as

---

[27] Rome Convention arts 5, 10–12. A complete reservation may, however, be made with regard to art.12 (right to equitable remuneration).

[28] Broadcasting, fixation and the reproduction of fixations without consent: art.7(1).

[29] arts 4, 7–9.

[30] Directive 2006/115/EC ([2006] OJ L376 (codified version)), repealing and replacing Council Directive 92/100 on rental right and lending right and on certain rights related to copyright in the field of intellectual property [1992] OJ L346/61.

[31] art.7(1).

[32] art.7, although this has since been repealed and replaced by art.2(a) of the Information Society Directive. See further in the text of this section.

[33] art.9(1).

[34] art.3(1)(b).

[35] art.8.

[36] art.10

[37] As far as the reproduction right is concerned, the original provision of Directive 92/100/EEC has been repealed and replaced by art.2(b) of the Information Society Directive; as regards the other rights, see arts 3(3) and 9(4) of the codified Directive 2006/115/EC.

[38] See para.12–16, below.

rebroadcasts) made for broadcasting or cable-casting sound recordings. There is an unwaivable right to equitable remuneration if the rental right is assigned,[39] and performers must share in a single equitable remuneration paid for the public performance or broadcasting of recordings of their performances.[40]

The Satellite Broadcasting and Cable Retransmission Directive. This requires **12–14** that the rights given to performers under the Rental and Related Rights Directive apply also in relation to broadcasts of their performances by satellite.[41]

The Term Directive. This harmonises the term of protection of copyright and **12–15** certain related rights, including performers' rights.[42] It also introduces a principle of reciprocal treatment for the protection of the performances of non-European Union nationals, in place of the principle of national treatment which previously applied in UK law. See paras 12–30 et seq., below. In July 2008, the Commission of the European Communities published a proposal for a Directive amending the present Term Directive to extend the term of copyright protection for performers (with respect to fixations of their performances in phonograms) from 50 to 95 years. It is proposed that the period of protection of producers of phonograms should also be extended to 95 years (with respect to their recordings) and that producers should set aside 20 per cent of all revenues for a fund for session musicians. For details of the proposals and accompanying measures for the benefit of performers, see paras 12–38 and 24–66, below.[43]

The Information Society Directive.[44] One of the main aims of this Directive, so **12–16** far as performers were concerned, was to implement the 1996 WIPO Performances and Phonograms Treaty (WPPT).[45] In this respect, the Directive did a number of things in the field of performers' rights with the aim of harmonising the rights of reproduction, distribution and communication to the public. First, it replaced the existing reproduction right in the Rental and Related Rights Directive to make it clear that the reproduction right applied in relation to temporary as well as permanent reproductions of performances.[46] Second, it required that performers be granted an on-demand right in relation to fixations of their performances.[47] Finally, it made further provision for the limitations or exceptions which Member States may make to these rights.

(iii) The Trips Agreement

The starting point of the provisions on copyright of the TRIPs Agreement[48] is **12–17** that all Members must comply with the substantive articles (1–21) of the Berne

---

[39] art.5, which applies also to authors. See paras 12–20 et seq., below.
[40] art.8(2), following art.12 Rome Convention. See paras 12–41 and 12–46 et seq., below.
[41] Council Directive 93/83 on the co-ordination of certain rules concerning copyright and rights related to copyright applicable to satellite broadcasting and cable retransmission; [1993] OJ L248/15 art.4.
[42] Directive 2006/116/EC ([2006] OJ L372 (codified version)), repealing and replacing Council Directive 93/98 harmonising the term of protection of copyright and certain related rights [1993] OJ L290/69.
[43] Proposal for a European Parliament and Council Directive amending Directive 2006/116/EC of the European Parliament and of the Council on the term of protection of copyright and certain related rights (COM(2008) 464/3).
[44] Directive 2001/29/EC of the European Parliament and of the Council of May 22, 2001, on the harmonisation of certain aspects of copyright and related rights in the information society.
[45] See para.12–18, below.
[46] Information Society Directive arts 2, 11(1)(a).
[47] Information Society Directive art.3(2)(a).
[48] The Agreement on Trade-Related Aspects of Intellectual Property Rights (TRIPs) is annexed to

Convention, other than the provision on moral rights.[49] By contrast, in the sphere of related rights, there is no equivalent incorporation of the Rome Convention. Instead the TRIPs agreement has its own code of obligations relating to performers and the other beneficiaries of the Rome Convention.

Performers must be provided with exclusive rights covering fixation, reproduction, wireless broadcasting and public communication of live performances (as distinct from recordings thereof). Such rights must last for a minimum of 50 years from the end of the calendar year in which the fixation was made or in which the performance took place.[50]

The TRIPs agreement is of great significance for performers' rights, since the number of countries obliged to offer reciprocal protection is far greater than the number party to the Rome Convention.[51] The level of protection offered by the 1988 Act already exceeds the requirements of the TRIPs Agreement.

(iv) The WIPO Performances and Phonograms Treaty (WPPT)

12–18 The WPPT was adopted at a Diplomatic Conference in Geneva in December 1996.[52] It provides that performers must be accorded inalienable moral rights in respect of live aural performances and performances fixed in phonograms.[53] Audiovisual performances are excluded from protection under the Treaty, like in the Rome Convention.[54] Performers must be given the "exclusive right of authorising" broadcasting (except re-broadcasting), communication to the public (except where the performance is a broadcast performance) and fixation of live performances, direct or indirect reproduction of performances fixed in phonograms, distribution of performances fixed in phonograms, commercial rental of performances fixed in phonograms and making available on demand performances fixed in phonograms.[55] The term of protection for performers is 50 years from the end of the year in which the performance was fixed in a phonogram.[56] Moral rights must last at least until the expiry of a performer's economic rights.[57] There are also provisions concerning copy protection measures, rights management information and enforcement.[58] The Treaty entered into force on March 6, 2002.

2. THE SUBSTANTIVE RIGHTS

A. IMPLEMENTATION OF DIRECTIVES AND OVERVIEW

12–19 **Amendments to the 1988 Act.** The United Kingdom's obligations under the Rome Convention were fully addressed by the 1988 Act. However, the various EU measures referred to above necessitated significant additions and amendments to the Act. Moreover, the introduction of moral rights for the benefit of performers into the law of the United Kingdom was necessary to permit the

---

and forms part of the Marrakesh Agreement Establishing the World Trade Organisation, signed by 124 nations on April 15, 1994.
[49] TRIPs arts 1–21 (omitting art.6bis of the Berne Convention).
[50] TRIPs arts 14(1), (5).
[51] See Ch.25, below.
[52] See paras 23–119 et seq., below.
[53] WIPO Performances and Phonograms Treaty art.5(1).
[54] For a discussion of this exclusion, see paras 23–119 et seq., below.
[55] arts 6–10.
[56] art.17(1).
[57] art.5(2).
[58] arts 18, 19, 23.

United Kingdom to ratify the WPPT 1996.[59] Changes were made by means of four statutory instruments:[60] the Duration of Copyright and Rights in Performances Regulations 1995,[61] the Copyright and Related Rights Regulations 1996,[62] the Copyright and Related Rights Regulations 2003[63] and the Performances (Moral Rights, etc.) Regulations 2006.[64] The latter Regulations came into force on February 1, 2006, and in addition to creating two new rights for performers, the right to be identified as the performer and the right to object to derogatory treatment (so-called moral rights), the Regulations divide up Pt II of the 1988 Act into four chapters and make a number of minor amendments. The four new chapters of Pt II are the following: Ch.1 entitled "Introductory" includes ss.180–181, which give an overview of the various rights granted in Pt II, as amended; Ch.2 entitled "Economic Rights" includes ss.182–205B; Ch.3 entitled "Moral Rights" includes ss.205C–205N (moral rights); and Ch.4 entitled "Qualification for protection, extent and interpretation" includes ss.206–212. These successive alterations have resulted in something of a patchwork of rights, the reason for this being that implementation of these Directives has been effected by statutory instrument using the powers conferred by the European Communities Act 1972. This means that amendments have necessarily been restricted to changes that the Directives have required. Had the Act been amended by primary legislation a more coherent scheme could have been provided for.

Present rights. The new rights required by the Rental and Related Rights Directive and the Performances (Moral Rights, etc.) Regulations were added to the existing scheme, leaving the original rights in place, subject in the case of the latter Regulations to the rearrangement of Pt II of the Act into four chapters. Thus Pt II of the 1988 Act now confers economic rights on a performer and on a person having recording rights in relation to a performance and creates offences in relation to dealing with or using illicit recordings. Performers are also granted certain moral rights, which are discussed in Ch.11, above. The performers' economic rights and rights of persons having recording rights are as follows: **12–20**

    (1) *Rights originally granted by the* 1988 Act

        (a) *Performers' non-property rights*:

            (i) consent is required for making a recording of the whole or any substantial part of a qualifying performance directly from the live performance and for broadcasting live the whole or any substantial part of a qualifying performance or for making a recording of the whole or any substantial part of a qualifying performance directly from a broadcast of the live performance (section 182);[65]

---

[59] Cm.3728.

[60] All three of the Directives relevant to Pt II of the 1988 Act were implemented after the dates required by their provisions. The Rental and Related Rights Directive (Dir.92/100) was due to be implemented by July 1, 1994, but was not implemented in the UK until December 1, 1996. The Duration Directive (Dir.93/98) was due to be implemented by July 1, 1995, but was not implemented in the UK until January 1, 1996. The Information Society Directive was due to be implemented by December 2002, but was not implemented in the UK until October 31, 2003. Potential liability under *Francovich v Italy* ([1991] E.C.R. I–5357) and *Brasserie du Pêcheur SA v Germany* ([1996] Q.B. 404; [1996] 1 C.M.L.R. 889) has been limited by the drafting of the transitional provisions, which are generous to users.

[61] SI 1995/3297.

[62] SI 1996/2967.

[63] SI 2003/2498.

[64] SI 2006/18.

[65] As enacted, the rights were also infringed by the inclusion of the performance in a live cable programme service. The result of the implementation of the Information Society Directive has in ef-

(ii) a performer's rights are infringed by use of a recording made without consent (s.183);[66]

(iii) a performer's rights are infringed by importing, possessing or dealing with an illicit recording (s.184).

(b) *Recording rights* of persons having exclusive recording contracts with performers (s.185).

Under the terms of the 1988 Act as enacted, these rights were intended to be unlike copyright. They differed in various ways, notably in that they could not be assigned, although performers' rights were transmissible on death.[67] These differences have been maintained in the Act as amended.[68] Infringements of these rights were actionable only as breaches of statutory duty, and this too remains the same.[69] An important element of the original scheme of protection was its creation of criminal offences in relation to dealing with or using illicit recordings and certain other related acts, and this too has been retained.

(ii) *Further rights granted on amendment of the* 1988 Act

Performers' property rights. The Rental and Related Rights Directive requires that certain performers' rights be capable of transfer and assignment. The Act as amended therefore confers a category of 'performers' property rights'.[70] This is of particular significance when the rights are infringed, since these are now actionable in the same way as other property rights, including copyright. Performers' property rights are those conferred by ss.182A–CA and 191A and consist of a reproduction right, distribution right, rental right and lending right and finally a making available right.[71] The Rental and Lending Directive also requires that performers have an unwaivable right to equitable remuneration for secondary use (broadcasting and public performance) of sound recordings and with regard to rental of their fixed performances in a sound recording or film. Although these rights are unwaivable, performers may assign them to a collecting society for the purpose of their exercise. These rights are conferred by ss.182D and 191F–H.[72]

Performers' moral rights. The Performances (Moral Rights,

---

fect been to bring cable transmissions within the ambit of broadcasts (see para.7–73, above). In *Bassey v Icon Entertainment Plc* [1995] E.M.L.R. 596, it was held that the term "recording" in s.182 covered a recording and a record of the recording. However, a performer could consent to a recording but their performers' rights were infringed if a record was made from that recording without express or implied consent.

[66] Again, the result of implementation of the Information Society Directive has been to alter the original provisions of the 1988 Act to replace the broadcasting and cable programme rights by a new right (the communication to the public right) which includes broadcasting and on-demand transmissions. See para.12–69, below.

[67] CDPA 1988 s.192 as enacted.

[68] ss.192A, 192B.

[69] See para.12–107, below.

[70] CDPA 1988 s.191.

[71] See para.12–44, below. *Barrett v Universal-Island Records Ltd* ([2006] EWHC 1009 (Ch); [2006] E.M.L.R. 215), where it was held that the rights conferred on a performer by the 1988 Act as amended were rights to authorise or prohibit an act and were sufficiently different rights from those originally conferred by s.182 of the Act as to amount to new rights.

[72] See para.12–49, below.

etc) Regulations 2006[73] have introduced a new Ch.3 of Pt II of the Act, entitled "Moral Rights". This confers the following moral rights on a performer, the right to be identified and the right to object to derogatory treatment of a performance. The rights are granted in respect to any type of live performances, broadcasts of live performances or performances recorded (fixed) in sound recordings and which are communicated or issued to the public. Consistent with the Rome Convention and the WPPT, performers do not enjoy moral rights in relation to their performances recorded in films. These rights are conferred by ss.205C to 205N of the Act as amended, and are described in Ch.11, above.

The rights referred to above as performers' non-property rights and performers' property rights are now laid down in Ch.2 of Pt II of the Act entitled "Economic Rights". The new performers' moral rights are contained in Ch.3 of Pt II of the Act, entitled "Moral Rights". It should be noted that the rights conferred by Pt II on performers are independent of any copyright in, or moral rights relating to, any work performed or any film or sound recording of, or broadcast including, the performance.[74] The rights are also independent of any other right or obligation arising otherwise than under Pt II of the Act,[75] e.g. under another statutory provision or by reason of contractual provisions or as the result of a duty of confidence.   **12–21**

Transitional provisions. The rights conferred by Pt II apply in relation to performances taking place before the commencement of Pt II (August 1, 1989), but no act done before commencement, or in pursuance of arrangements made before commencement, is to be regarded as infringing those rights.[76] The various amendments made to the Act have necessitated a considerable number of further transitional provisions, found in the relevant statutory instruments. The transitional provisions of the Duration of Copyright and Rights in Performances Regulations 1995 are discussed below with the substantive amendments to the provisions affecting the duration of Pt II rights.[77] The Copyright and Related Rights Regulations 1996 apply to performances given before and after commencement, subject to any special transitional provisions and savings.[78] No act done before commencement is to be regarded as an infringement of any new right, or as giving rise to any right to remuneration arising by virtue of the 1996 Regulations.[79] There is a saving for existing agreements made before November 19, 1992, and (unless expressly provided) no act done in pursuance of such an agreement after commencement is to be regarded as an infringement of any new right.[80] Any new right is exercisable as from commencement by the performer or (if he has died) by the person who immediately before commencement was entitled by virtue of s.192(2) to exercise the rights conferred on the performer by Pt II in relation to that performance.[81]   **12–22**

---

[73] SI 2006/18.
[74] CDPA 1988 s.180(4)(a).
[75] s.180(4)(b).
[76] CDPA 1988 s.180(3).
[77] SI 1995/3297 Pt III. See paras 12–33 et seq., below.
[78] SI 1996/2967 reg.26(1). Specific transitional provisions are discussed elsewhere, with the relevant material.
[79] reg.26(2).
[80] reg.27. This is the date of the adoption of Council Directive No.92/100/EEC.
[81] reg.30(1).

As to amendments made by the 2003 Regulations,[82] which implemented the Information Society Directive, the Regulations apply to performances given before as well as after the date the Regulations came into force (October 31, 2003).[83] No act done before commencement is to be regarded as an infringement of any new or extended right arising by virtue of the Regulations.[84] Nothing in the Regulations is to affect any agreement made before December 22, 2002[85] and no act done after commencement, in pursuance of an agreement made before December 22, 2002 is to be regarded as an infringement of any new or extended right arising by virtue of the Regulations.[86] Other transitional provisions are dealt with in this Chapter as they arise. The moral rights conferred by Ch.3 of Pt II of the Copyright, Designs and Patents Act 1988 (as inserted by the Performances (Moral Rights, etc.) Regulations, 2006) do not apply to any performance that took place before the Regulations came into force on February 1, 2006.[87]

B. Protected Performances

(i) Definition of performance

12–23   There is no definition of a performer in the 1988 Act, but the meaning of that term can be gathered from the statutory definition of a performance. In Pt II "performance" refers to live performances of various kinds given by one or more individuals.[88] The relevant kinds of performance are a dramatic performance, which includes dance and mime[89]; a musical performance[90]; a reading or recitation of a literary work[91]; and a performance of a variety act or any similar presentation.[92] In general, sporting performances will not fall within these categories. There is no requirement that the performance be one in public; a performance in a private place such as a recording studio will qualify.[93]

Part II applies to any such performance which is, or so far as it is, a live performance given by one or more individuals.[94] This definition thus excludes from protection under Pt II the use of recorded material or material on film which might form part of, for example, a dramatic or musical presentation. If the performance is given by more than one individual, each performer is entitled to the rights conferred in relation to his or her performance:[95] there is no concept of a joint performance.[96] In most, if not all cases, the performance of each performer is distinct from the performance of the other or others.[97] Note that there is no requirement of originality, so that performers' rights can subsist in each separate performance of, say, the same dramatic work.

---

[82] The Copyright and Related Rights Regulations 2003 (SI 2003/2498).

[83] reg.31(1).

[84] reg.31(2).

[85] reg.32(1). December 22, 2002 is the date when the Information Society Directive should have been implemented. See art.13(1).

[86] Copyright and Related Rights Regulations (SI 2003/2498) reg.32(2).

[87] cf. s.8.

[88] CDPA 1988 s.180(2); Cf. s.19(2) (definition of "performance" in relation to a work).

[89] s.180(2)(a); see s.3(1).

[90] s.180(2)(b); see s.3(1). The relatively simple performance was found to be a musical performance in *Bamgboye v Reed* [2002] EWHC 2922, QBD; [2004] E.M.L.R. 5.

[91] s.180(2)(c), s.211(1).

[92] s.180(2)(d).

[93] *Bamgboye v Reed* [2002] EWHC 2922, QBD.

[94] CDPA 1988 s.180.

[95] *Bamgboye v Reed* [2002] EWHC 2922, QBD.

[96] *Bamgboye v Reed* [2002] EWHC 2922, QBD.

[97] CDPA 1988 s.180. Cf. s.10(1).

(ii) Qualifying performances of performers

No formalities (such as registration, deposit or notice) are required for the subsis- **12–24** tence of performers' rights. However, performers' rights subsist only in relation to a qualifying performance. A performance is a qualifying performance for the purposes of Pt II if it is either:

(1) given by a qualifying individual; or

(2) takes place in a qualifying country.[98]

A qualifying individual means a citizen or subject of, or an individual resident in, a qualifying country.[99] A qualifying country means the United Kingdom[100] or another member of the European Economic Community[101] or, to the extent that any order under s.208 of the 1988 Act so provides, a country designated under that section as enjoying reciprocal protection.[102]

The reference in the definition of a qualifying individual to a person being a citizen or subject of a qualifying country is to be construed, in relation to the United Kingdom, as a reference to his being a British citizen[103] and, in relation to a colony of the United Kingdom, as a reference to his being a British Dependant Territories' citizen by connection with that colony.[104]

(iii) Reciprocal protection

Her Majesty may, by Order in Council,[105] designate as enjoying reciprocal protec- **12–25** tion under Pt II a Convention Country[106] or a country as to which Her Majesty is satisfied that protection has been made or will be made under the law giving adequate protection for British performances.[107] A Convention Country is a country which is a party to a convention relating to performers' rights to which the United Kingdom is also a party.[108] A British performance means a performance given by an individual who is a British citizen or a resident in the United Kingdom, or

---

[98] CDPA 1988 s.181. See Ch.3, above. In this connection, see *Experience Hendrix LLC v Purple Haze Records Ltd* ([2005] EWHC 249 (Ch); [2005] E.M.L.R. 18); *Experience Hendrix LLC v Purple Haze Records Ltd* ([2006] EWHC 968 (Ch)); *Experience Hendrix LLC v Purple Haze Records Ltd* ([2007] EWCA Civ 501; [2007] F.S.R. 31). In a series of decisions concerning the same parties concluding with a decision of the Court of Appeal, it has been held that it was accepted that performances given in the UK prior to the commencement of the Act were qualifying performances due to the specifically retrospective nature of the legislation (cf. s.180(3) of the 1988 Act). The same retrospective effect should be given also to other qualifying countries; no distinction could be drawn between countries who were qualifying members at the commencement of the Act and those that joined subsequently. Swedish and US performances were qualifying performances for the purposes of s.181 at the time the infringement took place. Individual performers who participated in a group performance enjoyed individual rights under the Act, which proceeded on the basis that each individual performer had the rights conferred by the Act so long as the performance was a qualifying performance or the individual was a qualifying individual. For comments on the case, see P. Groves, "Once you are dead, you are made for life", Ent. L.R. 16(7), 196 and P. Gardiner and N. Newing, "Case Comment" [2007] Ent. L.R. 18(1), 34–35.

[99] s.206(1).

[100] s.206(1)(a).

[101] s.206(1)(b).

[102] s.206(1)(c). See para.12–25, below.

[103] s.206(2)(a).

[104] s.206(2)(b).

[105] A statutory instrument containing an Order in Council under s.208 of the 1988 Act is subject to annulment in pursuance of a resolution of either House of Parliament: s.208(6).

[106] CDPA 1988 s.208(1)(a).

[107] s.208(1)(b). This power (i.e. in relation to "non-Convention countries") is exercisable in relation to any of the Channel Islands, the Isle of Man or any colony of the United Kingdom as in relation to a foreign country: CDPA 1988 s.208(5).

[108] CDPA 1988 s.208(2).

which takes place in the United Kingdom.[109] A large number of countries are currently designated as Convention Countries.[110] As the TRIPs agreement continues to take effect, more countries will offer reciprocal protection.

(iv) Territoriality

12–26   Part II of the Copyright, Designs and Patents Act 1988 extends to England and Wales, Scotland and Northern Ireland,[111] but not to the Channel Islands, the Isle of Man or any colony.[112]

For the purposes of Pt II the territorial waters of the United Kingdom are treated as part of the United Kingdom.[113] Part II applies to things done in the UK sector of the continental shelf,[114] on a structure or vessel which is present there for purposes directly connected with the exploration of the sea bed or subsoil or the exploitation of their national resources as it applies to things done in the United Kingdom.[115]

Part II also applies to things done on a British ship, aircraft or hovercraft as it applies to things done in the United Kingdom.[116] A "British ship" means a ship which is a British ship for the purposes of the Merchant Shipping Act 1995 otherwise than by virtue of registration in a country outside the United Kingdom.[117]

C. SUBSISTENCE OF RECORDING RIGHTS

(i) General

12–27   The 1988 Act also creates recording rights in relation to a performance. No right of this kind existed before the 1988 Act. The right is conferred on a person who is a party to and has the benefit of an exclusive recording contract to which the performance is subject[118] or to whom the benefit of the contract has been assigned[119] and who is a qualifying person. Such a person is referred to as a "person having recording rights". That person may be either an individual or a corporate entity.

If a person is subject to an exclusive recording contract, but the person who is a party to or has the benefit of it is not a qualifying person, then the person having the recording rights is any person who is licensed by such a person to make

---

[109] s.208(3).

[110] See The Copyright and Performances (Application to Other Countries) Order 2008 (SI 2008/677), which entered into force on April 6, 2008, as amended in relation to Bermuda by the Copyright and Performances (Application to Other Countries) (Amendment) Order 2009/2745; see Vol.2 C4. The purpose of these Orders is to apply Pt I of the Act to works originating from other countries and to confer on certain countries reciprocal protection under Pt II of the Act in order to satisfy the United Kingdom's international obligations under the Berne Convention, the Universal Copyright Convention, the Rome Convention, the TRIPs Agreement and arising from its membership of the European Community. In particular, in relation to performances, the Order satisfies the obligations imposed by the European Union's membership of TRIPs and also the obligations imposed on member States under Council Decision 2000/278/EC relating to the WIPO Performances and Phonograms Treaty (WPPT) 1996. A consolidated list of the protection afforded to other countries is contained in the 2008 Order and the designated Convention countries are listed in the Schedule to that Order, to which Bermuda should be added.

[111] CDPA 1988 s.207.

[112] s.210(1).

[113] s.109(1).

[114] This is an area designated by order under the Continental Shelf Act 1964 s.1(7): CDPA 1988 s.209(3).

[115] CDPA 1988 s.209(2).

[116] s.210(1).

[117] s.210(2). The Merchant Shipping Act now in force is that of 1995.

[118] CDPA 1988 s.185(2)(a).

[119] s.185(2)(b).

recordings of the performance with a view to their commercial exploitation[120] or any person to whom the benefit of such a licence has been assigned[121] and who is a qualifying person.

No formalities (such as a registration, deposit or notice) are required for the subsistence of recording rights.

(ii) Exclusive recording contract

An "exclusive recording contract" is defined as having certain characteristics[122]: **12–28**

(1) it must be a contract;

(2) it must be between a performer and another person;

(3) it must entitle that other person to make recordings of one of more of the performer's performances with a view to their commercial exploitation. The performances do not have to be qualifying performances within the meaning of the provisions.

(4) it must so entitle him to the exclusion of all other persons, including the performer. The expression "with a view to commercial exploitation" means with a view to the recordings being sold or let for hire, or shown or played in public.[123]

"Recording", in relation to a performance, means a film or sound recording:

(a) made directly from the live performance,

(b) made from a broadcast of the performance,

(c) made directly or indirectly, from another recording of the performance.[124]

(iii) Qualifying person

A "qualifying individual" means a citizen or a subject of, or an individual resident in, a qualifying country; and a "qualifying person" means a qualifying individual or a body corporate or other body having legal personality which is formed under the law of a part of the United Kingdom or another qualifying country[125] and has in any qualifying country a place of business at which substantial business activity is carried on.[126] In determining whether substantial business activity is carried on at a place of business in any country, no account is to be taken of dealings in goods which are at all material times outside that country.[127] **12–29**

D. Duration of Rights

(i) General

As originally enacted, Pt II of the 1988 Act provided simply that performers' rights and recording rights continued to subsist in a performance until the end of the period of 50 years from the end of the calendar year in which the performance **12–30**

---

[120] s.185(3)(a).
[121] s.185(3)(b).
[122] CDPA 1988 s.185(1).
[123] s.185(4).
[124] s.180(2); definitions as for Pt I: s.211(1), s.5A, s.5B.
[125] CDPA 1988 s.206 (1). See para.12–24, above. See also Ch.3, above.
[126] CDPA 1988 s.206(1).
[127] s.206(3).

took place.[128] However, the Duration Directive[129] required significant changes to this rule, and these were implemented by the Duration of Copyright and Rights in Performances Regulations.[130]

First, as the Act now stands, Pt II rights expire at the end of a period of 50 years from the end of the calendar year in which the performance takes place, unless a recording of the performance is released during that period, in which case the rights expire 50 years from the end of the calendar year in which the recording is released.[131] A recording is "released" for these purposes when it is first published, played or shown in public or communicated to the public, and no account is to be taken of any unauthorised act.[132] Thus there is a potential extension of term where release does not take place within the same year as the performance.

12–31   Secondly, the Duration Directive adopts the principle of the "shorter term" to encourage other countries to adopt equivalent standards.[133] The effect of this is to introduce reciprocal treatment for non-EEA nationals. Thus, where a performer is a not a national of an EEA state,[134] the duration of the rights conferred by Pt II is that to which the performer is entitled in the country of which he is a national, provided that this does not exceed the period which would apply if the performer were an EEA national.[135] In relation to performances given before July 1, 1995 the performer is to be treated as an EEA national if he was on July 1, 1995, regarded under the law of the United Kingdom or under the law of another EEA state relating to performers' rights as a national of that State.[136]

There is a derogation from this principle to allow Member States which (at the date of adoption of the Directive) granted a longer term of protection pursuant to their international obligations than would result from reciprocal treatment to continue to do so.[137] The implementing provision is s.191(5), which states that if or to the extent that the application of the reciprocal treatment provision (s.191(4)) would be at variance with an international obligation to which the United Kingdom became subject prior to October 29, 1993, the duration of Pt II rights will be governed by the rules on national treatment.[138]

(ii) Application

12–32   The amended provisions relating to the duration of rights under Pt II of the 1988 Act apply to performances before and after commencement, and may extend or revive performers' rights. Specifically, the new provisions apply to:

(a) performances taking place after commencement (January 1, 1996)[139];

---

[128] CDPA 1988 s.191.

[129] Directive 2006/116/EC [2006] OJ L372 (codified version), repealing and replacing Directive 93/98 harmonising the term of protection of copyright and certain related rights.

[130] SI 1995/3297. See Vol.2 A3.ii.

[131] CDPA 1988 s.191(2).

[132] s.191(3), as amended on implementation of the Information Society Directive to replace the reference to a record being broadcast or included in a cable programme service by its being "communicated to the public". As to the meaning of this expression, see CDPA 1988 ss.211 and 20(2), and para.7–98, above.

[133] Duration Directive 2006/116/EC.

[134] "EEA state" means a state which is a Contracting Party to the Agreement on the European Economic Area 1992 (see para.24–01, below).

[135] CDPA 1988 s.191(4).

[136] Duration of Copyright and Rights in Performances Regulations (hereafter DCRP Regs) (SI 1995/3297) reg.36(2).

[137] Duration Directive art.7(3).

[138] CDPA 1988 ss.191(2), (3).

[139] DCRP Regulations 1995 reg.29(a).

(b) "existing performances",[140] which first qualify for protection under Pt II after commencement[141];

(c) "existing protected performances", subject to the general saving for any longer period applicable under the 1988 provision[142];

(d) "existing performances":

    (i) in which rights under Pt II expired after commencement of that Part (August 1, 1989) and before December 31, 1995, or

    (ii) which were protected by earlier enactments relating to the protection of performers and in which rights under that Part did not arise by reason only that the performance was given at a date such that the rights would have ceased to subsist before the commencement of that part (i.e. more than 50 years before August 1, 1989),

but which on July 1, 1995 were protected in another EEA state under legislation relating to copyright or related rights.[143]

An "existing performance" is one given before commencement (January 1, 1996).[144] An "existing protected performance" is a performance in relation to which rights under Pt II of the 1988 Act subsisted immediately before commencement.[145] A general saving provides that any rights under Pt II of the 1988 Act in an existing protected performance shall continue to subsist until the date on which they would have expired under the 1988 provisions, if that date is later than the date on which the rights would expire under the new provisions.[146]

(iii) Transitional provisions

12–33 Extensive transitional provisions are necessary to deal with rights in relation to performances which are extended or were revived as a result of the amended duration provisions.

12–34 **Extended performance rights.** These are defined as rights under Pt II which subsist by virtue of the amended provisions after the date on which they would have expired under the unamended 1988 provisions.[147] Any extended performance rights are exercisable from commencement by the person who was entitled to exercise those rights immediately before commencement, that is:

(a) in the case of performers' rights, the performer or (if he has died) the person entitled by virtue of s.192(2) of the 1988 Act to exercise those rights[148];

(b) in the case of recording rights, the person who was within the meaning of s.185 of the 1988 Act the person having those rights.[149]

12–35 **Revived performance rights.** These are defined as rights under Pt II which subsist by virtue of the amended provisions either:

(a) after having expired under the unamended 1988 provisions, or

(b) in relation to a performance which was protected by earlier enactments relating to the protection of performers and in which rights under that Part

---

[140] reg.27(1)(a).
[141] reg.29(b).
[142] reg.29(c).
[143] reg.29(d).
[144] reg.27(1)(a).
[145] reg.27(1)(b).
[146] reg.28.
[147] DCRP Regulations 1995 reg.30.
[148] reg.31(1)(a).
[149] reg.31(1)(b).

did not arise because the performance was given at a date such that the rights would have ceased to subsist before the commencement of that Part. These latter are known as "revived pre-1988 rights".[150]

Any revived performance rights are exercisable as from commencement:

(a) in the case of rights which expired after the commencement of the 1988 Act, by the person who was entitled to exercise those rights immediately before they expired[151];

(b) in the case of revived pre-1988 performers' rights, by the performer or his personal representatives[152];

(c) in the case of revived pre-1988 recording rights, by the person who would have been the person having those rights immediately before the death of the performer, applying the provisions of s.185 of the Act to the circumstances then obtaining.[153]

Any remuneration or damages received by a person's personal representatives by virtue of extended or revived performance rights devolves as part of that person's estate as if the right had subsisted and been vested in him immediately before his death.[154]

Existing licences relating to the exploitation of an existing protected performance which subsisted immediately before commencement, and which are not to expire before the end of the period for which rights under Pt II subsist in relation to that performance are automatically extended for the period of any extended performance rights, subject to any agreement to the contrary.[155]

12–36 **Infringement.** There are a number of transitional provisions relating to infringement of revived performance rights, some of which remain potentially relevant. Thus, it is not an infringement of revived performance rights in a performance to do anything after commencement in pursuance of arrangements made before January 1, 1995 at a time when the performance was not protected, nor to issue to the public after commencement a recording of a performance made before July 1, 1995 at a time when the performance was not protected.[156] It is not an infringement of revived performance rights in a performance to do anything after commencement in relation to a sound recording or film made before commencement, or made in pursuance of arrangements made before commencement, which contains a recording of the performance if the recording of the performance was made before July 1, 1995 at a time when the performance was not protected, or the recording of the performance was made in pursuance of arrangements made before July 1, 1995 at a time when the performance was not protected.[157] It is not an infringement of revived performance rights in a performance to do after commencement anything at a time when, or in pursuance of arrangements made at a time when, the name and address of a person entitled to authorise the act cannot by reasonable inquiry be ascertained.[158]

12–37 **Licences of right.** Such licences are available in respect of revived performance rights. The potential licensee will be treated as having the right owner's consent

---

[150] DCRP Regulations 1995 reg.30(b).
[151] reg.31(2)(a).
[152] reg.31(2)(b).
[153] reg.31(2)(c).
[154] reg.31(3).
[155] reg.32.
[156] DCRP Regulations 1995 reg.33(2).
[157] reg.33(3).
[158] reg.33(4). "Arrangements" means arrangements for the exploitation of the performance in question (reg.33(5)).

to acts which require consent, subject only to the payment of such reasonable remuneration as may be agreed or determined in default of agreement by the Copyright Tribunal.[159] The potential licensee must give reasonable notice of his intention to the rights owner, stating when he intends to begin to do the acts.[160] If he
does not give such notice, his acts will not be treated as having consent.[161] If he
does give such notice, his acts will be treated as licensed, and reasonable remuneration will be payable in respect of them even if its amount is not agreed or
determined until later.[162] Either the rights owner or the person claiming to be
treated as having his consent may apply to the Copyright Tribunal to settle the remuneration payable.[163] Either party may subsequently apply to the Tribunal to
vary the order, but only by special leave if the application is within 12 months of
the original order.[164]

Proposals for the extension of the term of protection of sound recordings. On   **12–38**
January 1, 2005, sound recordings published on or before December 31, 1954,
fell into the public domain, making available for exploitation many famous and
still successful recordings without the payment of royalties. This led to calls from
the recording industry and performers to prolong the period of protection afforded to sound recordings to 70 years or more. In May 2007, support for an
increase in the term of protection to at least 70 years came from the House of
Commons Culture, Media and Sport Committee in its report entitled "New Media
and the Creative Industries" (Fifth Report of Session 2006–2007, HC 509–1,
dated May 1, 2007, Recommendation 28 and paras 232–236). The Committee
considered this was necessary to provide reasonable certainty that an artist will
be able to derive benefit from a recording throughout his or her lifetime; it also
considered there was no reason why composers should benefit from a longer term
than performers. However, the Gowers Review of Intellectual Property of
December 2006 recommended against requesting the European Union to consider
such an extension on economic grounds; it concluded that there was little evidence that extension would benefit performers, increase the number of works created or made available, or provide incentives for creativity and it noted a
potentially negative effect on the balance of trade.[165] Subsequently, the Department of Culture, Media and Sport announced on July 27, 2007, that it would not
support extending the term of protection of either producers of sound recordings
or performers.

Meanwhile, as briefly mentioned in para.12–15, above, the Commission of the
European Union has put forward a proposal to the European Parliament and to
the Council to extend the term of protection of certain rights of performers and
producers of sound recordings to 95 years from publication or the first lawful
communication to the public of recorded performances.[166] The proposal aims to
improve the social position of performers, and in particular session musicians,
taking into account that performers are increasingly outliving the existing 50-
year period of protection for their performances. It is proposed that the extension

---

[159] DCRP Regulations 1995 reg.34(1).
[160] reg.34(2).
[161] reg.34(3).
[162] reg.34(4).
[163] reg.35(1).
[164] reg.35(3)(4).
[165] See A. Rahmatian, "The Gowers review on Copyright term Extension" [2007] E.I.P.R. 29(9),
353; P. Groves, "There's nothing new around the sun: everything you think of has been done"
[2007] Ent. L.R. 18(4), 150.
[166] Proposal for a European Parliament and Council Directive amending Directive 2006/116/EC of
the European Council and of the Council on the term of protection of copyright and certain related rights (COM(2008) 464/3). See also N. Dufft et al, "Never Forever: Why Extending the
Term of Protection for Sound Recordings is a Bad Idea" [2008] E.I.P.R. 30(5), 174.

of the period of protection will apply only to fixations of a performance in a phonogram (sound recording). Other fixations of performances will continue to be protected for 50 years. Producers of phonograms will enjoy protection for their recordings also for 95 years. For further details see para.24–90, below. The Commission defends the proposal on the basis that social, cultural and economic measures must be taken to maintain Europe as a prime location for cultural creators in the entertainment and knowledge sectors and to ensure that performers have a decent income and that there will be a European-based music industry in the years to come.[167] Meanwhile, in January 2009, the European Economic and Social Committee (ECOSOC) adopted an opinion on the proposal, recommending inter alia an extension of protection for fixations of performances from 50 to 85 years.[168] Subsequently, in April 2009, the European Parliament approved a text which sets the term at 70 years.[169] The matter is still pending before the Council of the European Union.

The proposal continues to be controversial. While welcomed by the potential beneficiaries, it has also been criticised.[170]

3. OWNERSHIP AND TRANSMISSION OF RIGHTS

A. Ownership

(i) Performers' rights

12–39   The first owner of performers' rights is the performer. There is a single exception to this rule, created by the Copyright and Related Rights Regulations.[171] Where, before commencement (December 1, 1996), the owner or prospective owner of performers' rights in a performance has authorised a person to make a copy of the recording of the performance, any new right (i.e. one created as a result of the 1996 Regulations) in relation to that copy vests in that person on commencement.

It should be noted that the law gives the protection to the individual performer, not, for example, to a group of performers.[172] Where a performer's property rights (or any aspect of them) are owned by more than one person jointly, the consent of all of the rights owners is required.[173]

The performers' rights which are the subject of this chapter are those conferred on performers with regard to their performances. A distinction must be made between rights in performances and any separate copyright which a performer may

---

[167] Commission Press Release, IP/08/1156, July 16, 2008.

[168] Opinion of the European Economic and Social Committee on the "Proposal for a European Parliament and Council Directive amending Directive 2006/116/EC of the European Parliament and of the Council on the term of protection of copyright and related rights, September 4, 2008 (COM (2008) 464final—2008/0157 (COD) OJ 2009/C 182/07).

[169] European Parliament legislative resolution of April 23, 2009, on the proposal for a directive of the European Parliament and of the Council amending Directive 2006/116/EC of the European Parliament and of the Council on the term of protection of copyright and related rights (P6 TA(2009)0282). See also Commission press release IP/09/627 of April 23, 2009.

[170] *The Impact of Copyright Extension for Sound Recordings in the UK*, A Report for the Gowers Review of Intellectual Property prepared by Price Waterhouse Coopers on behalf of the British Phonographic Industry (BPI) (London: PwC Economics, April 28, 2006); B. Hugenholtz, *The Recasting of Copyright and Related Rights for the Knowledge Economy* (University of Amsterdam, 2006); G. Davies, "EU proposes copyright extension from 50 to 95 years", *Copyright World*, September 2008, 20; K. Mullen, "Intellectual Property: Performers' Rights" [2007] E.I.P.R. 29(6), 244; L. Bently, et al, "Creativity stifled? A joint academic statement on the proposed copyright term extension for sound recordings" [2008] E.I.P.R. 30(9), 341; N. Parker, "The fuel of interest: The incentive powers of copyright" [2007] Ent. L.R. 18(1), 7–12.

[171] SI 1996/2967 reg.31(b).

[172] *Bourne v Davis (t/a Brandon Davis Publishing)* 2006 EWHC 1567 (Ch).

[173] ss. 180(1)(a) and 191A(4).

have as the author or co-author of a musical work created through performance. In this regard, in the recent case of *Fisher and Brooker*, it was held, in relation to a musical work which was the product of the collaborative rehearsal process, that under the 1988 Act "provided the contribution of the individual band member to the overall work is both significant (in the sense that it is more than merely trivial) and original (in the sensethat it is the product of skill and labour in its creation) and the resulting work is recorded (whether in writing or otherwise), that band member is entitled to copyright in the work as one of its joint authors and to any composing royalties that follow. This assumes, of course, that there is no contractual arrangement to the contrary".[174] This subject is discussed in Ch.4, 2, C, above.

(ii) Recording rights[175]

The right is conferred on a person who is party to and has the benefit of an exclusive recording contract to which the performance is subject[176] or to whom the benefit of the contract has been assigned[177] and who is a qualifying person. Such a person is referred to as a "person having recording rights". That person may be either an individual or a corporate entity.   **12–40**

If a performance is subject to an exclusive recording contract, but the person who is a party to or has the benefit of it is not a qualifying person, then the person having the recording rights is any person who is licensed by such a person to make recordings of the performance with a view to their commercial exploitation[178] or any person to whom the benefit of such a licence has been assigned[179] and who is a qualifying person.

(iii) Equitable remuneration

A performer is entitled to equitable remuneration in two cases: first, where a sound recording is broadcast or otherwise communicated to the public; secondly, where the performer's rental right in a film or sound recording is transferred to its producer, the performer nevertheless retains a right to equitable remuneration for rental of the film or sound recording.[180]   **12–41**

B. Transmission

(i) Performers' non-property rights

Performers' non-property rights are not assignable, although they are transmissible on death.[181] On the death of a person entitled to any such rights the right passes to such person as the performer may by testamentary disposition specifi-   **12–42**

---

[174] *Fisher v Brooker* [2007] E.M.L.R. 9 at para.46, per Blackburne J. This finding was upheld by the Court of Appeal *Fisher v Brooker* [2008] EWCA Civ 287 and endorsed by the House of Lords [2009] UKHL 41; [2009] 1 W.L.R. 1764; [2009] F.S.R. 25. See also *Sawkins v Hyperion Records Ltd* [2005] EWCA Civ 565 and R. Arnold, "Reflexions on the 'Triumph of Music': copyrights and performers' rights in music", I.P.Q. 2010, 2, 153-164.

[175] See para.12–27, above.

[176] CDPA 1988 s.185(2)(a).

[177] s.185(2)(b).

[178] s.185(3)(a).

[179] s.185(3)(b).

[180] CDPA 1988 s.191G(1), see paras 12–49 ct scq., below.

[181] CDPA 1988 s.192A(1). The Court of Appeal has confirmed that even prior to the enactment of the CDPA 1988 a performer had a civilly enforceable right to protect his economic interests and that right would have devolved on his personal representatives by operation of law. The amended

cally direct, and if or to the extent that there is no such direction, the right is exercisable by the performer's personal representatives.[182] Any damages recovered by personal representatives in respect of an infringement after a person's death devolve as part of his estate as if the right of action had subsisted and been vested in him immediately before his death.[183] Consent which is binding upon the deceased will bind the person or persons to whom the rights pass.[184]

(ii) Recording rights

12-43   As before, recording rights are not assignable or transmissible, even on the death of an individual who is entitled.[185] However, the contractual rights on which they depend are assignable and in such an event the assignee will become the person entitled to the recording rights.[186]

(iii) Performers' property rights

12-44   As has been seen, it was a requirement of the Rental and Related Rights Directive that certain rights should be proprietary, and therefore a category of "performers' property rights" was created on implementation.[187]

A performer's property rights are those conferred by ss.182A–D: namely, the reproduction right, distribution right, rental right and lending right, the making available right, as well as the right to equitable remuneration for exploitation of sound recordings. These are transmissible by assignment, by testamentary disposition or by operation of law, as personal or moveable property.[188] There is a presumption of transfer of the rental right where there is a film production agreement,[189] but also a right to equitable remuneration where the rental right is transferred.[190] There is a similar right to equitable remuneration for exploitation of a sound recording.[191] However, as regards visual or audiovisual performances, once performers have consented to the recording (fixation) of their live performances, they have no further rights as regards the exploitation of any film.

Assignments may be partial, that is, limited to certain acts or to a certain period.[192] An assignment must be in writing signed by or on behalf of the assignor.[193] Specific provision is made for cases where a performer or his agent assigns (or purports to assign) the performer's property rights in relation to a

---

Act did not take away the rights conferred in respect of performers who had died before the Act came into force; see *Experience Hendrix LLC v Purple Haze Records Ltd* [2005] EWHC 249 (Ch); [2005] E.M.L.R. 18; *Experience Hendrix LLC v Purple Haze Records Ltd* [2006] EWHC 968 (Ch); [2008] E.M.L.R. 10 and *Experience Hendrix LLC v Purple Haze Records Ltd* [2007] EWCA Civ 501; [2007] F.S.R. 31.

[182] s.192A(2).
[183] s.192A(5).
[184] s.193(3).
[185] CDPA 1988 s.192B(1).
[186] ss.192B(2), s.185(2)(b), (3)(b).
[187] CDPA 1988 s.191A. Subs.191A(4) provides that where a performer's property rights (or any aspect of them) is owned by more than one person jointly, references in Pt II to the rights owner are to all the owners, so that, in particular, any requirement of the licence of the rights owner requires the licence of all of them. See *Bourne v Davis (t/a Brandon Davis Publishing)* [2006] EWHC 1567, where it was held that a member of a group of musicians had individual performer's property rights in their group performances and any infringement of those rights without his consent or the consent of any assignee was prohibited.
[188] s.191B(1).
[189] s.191F.
[190] s.191G, see para.12–49, below.
[191] s.182D, see para.12–47, below.
[192] s.191B(2). cf. CDPA 1988 s.90(2).
[193] s.191B(3).

future recording of a performance to another person.[194] If on the rights coming into existence the assignee or another person claiming under him would be entitled as against all other persons to require the rights to be vested in him, they vest in the assignee or his successor in title.[195] This ensures that an assignee who would be entitled to specific performance of the agreement becomes the legal owner of the rights as soon as the recording is made. Equally, where the assignee is not entitled to specific performance, a purported assignment would be ineffective.

A licence granted by the owner of a performer's property right is binding on every successor in title to that interest (or prospective interest) in the rights, except a purchaser in good faith for valuable consideration and without notice (actual or constructive) of the licence or a person deriving title from such a purchaser.[196] It is expressly provided that an exclusive licensee of a performer's property rights has the same rights and remedies as if the exclusive licence were a assignment.[197]   **12–45**

There is a presumption that a bequest of any material thing containing an original recording of a performance which was not published before the death of the testator shall include any performer's rights in relation to the recording to which the testator was entitled immediately before his death.[198]

(iv) Equitable remuneration

Two rights to equitable remuneration for performers were introduced as a result of the Rental and Related Rights Directive. The rights have been amended following implementation of the Information Society Directive. In outline, one gives the performer the right to claim equitable remuneration with respect of (a) the communication to the public of sound recordings (other than by way of an on-demand service with respect to which the performer has the right to authorise or prohibit the making available to the public of such recordings) or (b) the public performance of sound recordings (but not films).[199] The other gives an un-waivable right to equitable remuneration where the performer transfers (or is presumed to transfer) his rental right in a film or sound recording to the producer of the film or sound recording.[200]   **12–46**

Right to equitable remuneration for exploitation of a sound recording. The first right arises where a commercially published sound recording of the whole or any substantial part of a qualifying performance is played in public, or included in a communication to the public, other than by way of an on-demand service.[201] The meaning of "commercially published" is not exactly clear; the Performances   **12–47**

---

[194] s.191C(1).
[195] s.191C(2). See para.5–105, above, for a discussion of the equivalent provision in relation to assignments of future copyright.
[196] CDPA 1988 ss.191B(4), 191C(3).
[197] ss.191L(1), 191D(1).
[198] s.191E.
[199] CDPA 1988 s.182D.
[200] ss.191F–H.
[201] CDPA 1988 ss.191F–H. In the present context, what this means in practice is that the right will arise where the recording is broadcast. An on-demand service is used as shorthand in the text for a service whereby the recording is made available to the public by electronic transmission in such a way that members of the public may access it from a place and at a time individually chosen by them. See ss.211 and 20. Broadcast is defined in s.4. Where the recording is made available by way of an on-demand service, the performer has a right to prevent this taking place altogether, not just to equitable remuneration: ss.182(C), 182D(1)(b). See also para.12–67, below. As from October 31, 2003, performers have had no right to any equitable remuneration in respect of such a service. See the Copyright and Related Rights Regulations 2003 (SI 2003/2498) reg.34(1).

(Moral Rights, etc.) Regulations 2006[202] have amended s.182D on this point by the addition of a new subs.1A, which provides: "In subsection 1, the reference to publication of a sound recording includes making it available to the public by electronic transmission in such a way that members of the public may access it from a place and at a time individually chosen by them". As to the statutory definitions in the 1988 Act, for the purposes of Pt II (Rights in Performances) "publication" is to have the same meaning as under Pt I (Copyright), that is, the same meaning as in s.175, where it means, for present purposes, the issue of copies to the public.[203] Excluded from this meaning is any publication which is merely colourable and not intended to satisfy the reasonable requirements of the public, and any unauthorised act. Nothing, however, is said about the meaning of "commercial publication" where it appears in Pt II, although it is defined in s.175 for the purposes of Pt I, where it means either (a) the issuing of copies of the work to the public at a time when copies made in advance of the receipt of orders are generally available to the public; or (b) making the work available to the public by means of an electronic retrieval system.[204]

This definition is not, however, of any relevance for present purposes. In fact, the expression "commercially published" in s.182D is derived from art.8(2) of the Rental and Related Rights Directive, which states that Member States are to provide for equitable remuneration for performers in circumstances where use is made of a phonogram which has been "published for commercial purposes", or of a reproduction of such a phonogram. It is by reference to the wording and purpose of the Directive that the expression must be construed.

12–48   Where the right arises, as described above, the performer is entitled to equitable remuneration from the owner of the copyright in the sound recording.[205] The right may not be assigned except to a collecting society for the purpose of enabling it to enforce the right on the performer's behalf.[206] However, the right is transmissible by testamentary disposition or by operation of law, and it may then be further assigned.[207] The amount payable is as agreed by or on behalf of the persons by and to whom it is payable.[208] In default of such agreement, application may be made to the Copyright Tribunal to determine the amount payable.[209] The Copyright Tribunal may also vary a previous agreement or determination.[210] The Tribunal may order any method of calculation and paying equitable remuneration as it may determine to be reasonable in the circumstances, taking into account the

---

[202] SI 2006/18.

[203] As to the meaning of "issue to the public", see para.7–76, above.

[204] See para.11–12, above, for a discussion of the meaning of the expression "commercially published".

[205] CDPA 1988 s.182D(1).

[206] The Performances (Moral Rights, etc.) Regulations 2006 has inserted a definition of "collecting society" as a new subs.(8) to s.182D. It reads: "In this section "collecting society" means a society or other organisation which has as its main object, or one of its main objects, the exercise of the right to equitable remuneration on behalf of more than one performer". This definition is in line with that contained in s.191G(6). There is no restriction on the nature of the collecting society. cf. CDPA 1988 s.191G(6). As noted above, the right to equitable remuneration in respect of on-demand services was removed as from October 31, 2003. Any assignment made before this date which had effect under CDPA 1988 s.182D(2) is, as from that date, to cease to apply insofar as it relates to this on-demand right. See the Copyright and Related Rights Regulations 2003 reg.34(2).

[207] CDPA 1988 s.182D(2).

[208] s.182D(3).

[209] s.182D(4). As to the basis of assessing such remuneration, see para.28–147, below, and *Stichting ter Exploitatie van Naburige Rechten v Nederlandse Omroep Stichting* E.C.J., (C–245/00) [2003] R.P.C. 42.

[210] CDPA 1988 s.182D(5).

importance of the contribution of the performer to the sound recording.[211] An agreement purporting to exclude or restrict the right to equitable remuneration, or purporting to prevent a person questioning the amount of equitable remuneration or to restrict the powers of the Copyright Tribunal, is of no effect.[212] There is no provision to parallel s.191H(4), which states that in cases where the rental right is transferred, remuneration is not to be considered inequitable merely because it was paid as a single payment, or at the time of transfer of the right.

The right is not subject to any special transitional provisions. However, the general transitional provision under the Copyright and Related Rights Regulations 1996 applies, namely, that no act done before commencement (December 1, 1996) gives rise to any remuneration.[213] Note that the rights to equitable remuneration are not regarded as "new rights" for the purposes of the transitional provisions of the Copyright and Related Rights Regulations 1996, so the saving for agreements made before November 19, 1992, does not apply.[214]

Right to equitable remuneration where rental right transferred. Where a **12–49** performer has transferred his rental right concerning a sound recording or a film to the producer of the sound recording or film, he retains the right to equitable remuneration for the rental.[215] An agreement purporting to exclude or restrict the right to equitable remuneration is of no effect.[216] This right may not be assigned by the performer, except to a collecting society for the purpose of enabling it to enforce the right on his behalf.[217] However, the right is transmissible by testamentary disposition or by operation of law, and it may then be further assigned.[218] The amount payable is as agreed by or on behalf of the persons by and to whom it is payable.[219] In default of such agreement, application may be made to the Copyright Tribunal to determine the amount payable.[220] The Copyright Tribunal may also vary a previous agreement or determination.[221] The Tribunal may order any method of calculation and paying equitable remuneration as it may determine to be reasonable in the circumstances, taking into account the importance of the contribution of the performer to the film or sound recording.[222] Remuneration shall not be considered inequitable merely because it was paid by way of a single payment or at the time of the transfer of the rental right.[223] An agreement is of no effect in so far as it purports to prevent a person questioning the amount of equitable remuneration or to restrict the powers of the Copyright Tribunal.[224]

Where an agreement concerning film production is concluded between a performer and a film producer, the performer shall be presumed, unless the agreement provides to the contrary, to have transferred to the film producer any rental

---

[211] s.182D(6).

[212] s.182D(7).

[213] Copyright and Related Rights Regulations 1996 (SI 1996/2967), reg.26(2).

[214] regs 25(3)(b), 27.

[215] CDPA 1988 s.191G(1).

[216] s.191G(5).

[217] s.191G(2), (6). The collecting society must be an organisation "which has as its main object, or one of its main objects, the exercise of the right to equitable remuneration on behalf of more than one performer".

[218] s.191G(2).

[219] s.191G(3), (4).

[220] s.191H(1). As to the basis of assessing such remuneration, see para.29–134, below, and *Stichting ter Exploitatie van Naburige Rechten v Nederlandse Omroep Stichting* E.C.J. (C–245/00) [2003] R.P.C. 42.

[221] CDPA 1988 s 191H(2).

[222] s.191H(3).

[223] s.191H(4).

[224] s.191H(5).

right in relation to the film arising from the inclusion of a recording of his performance in the film.[225] The right to equitable remuneration under s.191G applies where there is a presumed transfer as in the case of an actual transfer.[226]

12–50 The right is subject to both general and specific transitional provisions, some of which may still be relevant. Thus, the rights to equitable remuneration are not regarded as "new rights" for the purposes of the transitional provisions, so the saving for agreements made before November 19, 1992 does not apply.[227]

There is a specific transitional provision regarding the right to equitable remuneration applicable to rental after April 1, 1997. No right to equitable remuneration under s.191G (right to equitable remuneration where rental right transferred) arises in respect of:

(a) any rental of a sound recording or film before April 1, 1997, or

(b) any rental after that date of a sound recording or film made in pursuance of an agreement entered into before July 1, 1994, unless the performer (or a successor in title of his) before January 1, 1997 notified the person by whom the remuneration would be payable that he intended to exercise that right.[228]

4. CONSENT AND LICENSING

A. GENERAL

12–51 **Consent.** Consent for the purposes of Pt II by a person having performers' non-property rights or by a person having recording rights may be given in relation to a specific performance, a specified description of performances or performances generally. Consent may relate to past or future performances.[229] It is suggested that the same principles apply to performers' property rights.

A person having recording rights in a performance is bound by any consent given by a person through whom he derives his rights under the exclusive recording contract or licence in question, in the same way as if the consent had been given by him.[230]

Where a performer's non-property right passes to another person, any consent binding on the person previously entitled binds the person to whom the right passes in the same way as if the consent had been given by him.[231]

B. POWERS OF THE COPYRIGHT TRIBUNAL

12–52 **The Copyright Tribunal.** The Tribunal has jurisdiction to hear and determine proceedings under various sections of the Act.[232] Its jurisdiction in relation to performers' rights has been expanded considerably since 1988, but it still has no jurisdiction at all in the case of recording rights. Significant changes were made as a result of the Rental and Related Rights Directive, notably the removal of the Tribunal's jurisdiction to consent on behalf of a performer where consent had

---

[225] s.191F(1).

[226] s.191F(4).

[227] Copyright and Related Rights Regulations 1996 (SI 1996/2967) regs 25(3)(b), 27.

[228] reg.33.

[229] CDPA 1988 s.193(1).

[230] s.193(2).

[231] s.193(3).

[232] CDPA 1988 s.205B. See also The Copyright Tribunal Rules 2010 (SI 2010/7910) of March 15, 2010, which came into force on April 6, 2010.

unreasonably been withheld,[233] and by extending the Tribunal's jurisdiction in relation to the rights to equitable remuneration granted by the Rental and Lending Rights Directive.[234] Various statutory licences and licences of right are available.

(i) Compulsory licensing

(1) Power to consent on behalf of a performer. The 1988 Act as enacted gave the Copyright Tribunal power to give consent on behalf of a performer in two types of situation where a person wished to make a recording from a previous recording of a performance, either where the identity or whereabouts of the performer could not be ascertained, or where the performer unreasonably withheld consent. The Rental and Lending Rights Directive did not allow for compulsory licensing in a case where consent was withheld, and this provision was therefore deleted.[235]   **12–53**

Thus, the Tribunal may now give consent only in a case where the identity or whereabouts of the person entitled to the reproduction right cannot be ascertained by reasonable inquiry.[236] The reference to "person entitled to the reproduction right" replaces the original wording of "performer", to deal with cases where the identity and whereabouts of the performer is known, but not the identity or whereabouts of the present owner(s) of the reproduction right.[237] Application must be made by the person wishing to make a copy of a recording of the performance.[238] It is submitted that the explicit reference to the reproduction right is intended to exclude the performers' other economic rights.

(2) Reception and retransmission of a broadcast in a cable programme service. Where a broadcast made from a place in the United Kingdom is, by reception and immediate re-transmission, included in a cable programme service, Part II rights in a performance or recording included in the broadcast are not infringed if and to the extent that the broadcast is made for reception in the area in which the cable programme service is provided.[239] However, where the making of the broadcast was an infringement of those rights, the fact that the broadcast was re-transmitted as a programme in a cable programme service shall be taken into account in assessing the damages for that infringement.   **12–54**

(3) Powers exercisable in consequence of competition report. Licences of right are available in respect of performers' property rights if the Secretary of State, the Competition Commission or the Office of Fair Trading reports that certain specified practices may be expected to operate or have operated against the public interest. The two specified practices are: **12–55**

  (a) the inclusion of conditions in licences granted by the owner of a performer's property rights restricting the use to which a recording may be put by the licensee or the right of the owner to grant other licences;

  (b) the refusal of an owner of a performer's property right to grant licences on reasonable terms.[240]

In such cases the above bodies have powers to cancel or modify such condi-

---

[233] s.205B; paras 12–53 et seq., below.
[234] s.205B; ss.182D, 191H; see para.12–46, above.
[235] Copyright and Rights in Performances Regulations 1996 (SI 1996/2967) reg.23(2), deleting CDPA 1988 s.190(1)(b).
[236] CDPA 1988 s.190(1) as amended by SI 1996/2967 reg.23.
[237] A lacuna highlighted in *Ex p. Sianel Pedwar Cymru* [1993] E.M.L.R. 251.
[238] CDPA 1988 s.190(1).
[239] CDPA 1988 Sch.2 para.19(1) and (2), as amended.
[240] CDPA 1988 Sch.2A para.17(1).

tions or to provide that licences in respect of the performer's property rights shall be available as of right.[241] In default of agreement the terms of such a licence will be settled by the Copyright Tribunal.[242]

12–56   **(4) Lending of certain recordings.** The Secretary of State may by order provide that in the cases specified in the order the lending to the public of copies of films or sound recordings shall be treated as licensed by the performer subject only to the payment of a reasonable royalty or other payment.[243] In default of agreement the amount will be determined by the Copyright Tribunal.[244] The order may make different provision for different cases and may specify cases by reference to any factor relating to the work, the copies lent, the lender or the circumstances of the lending.[245] An application to settle the royalty or other sum payable in pursuance of para.14A of Sch.2 may be made to the Copyright Tribunal by either the owner of a performer's property rights or the person claiming to be treated as licensed by him.[246]

No order may be made under para.14A of Sch.2 if, and to the extent that, there is a licensing scheme certified for this purpose under para.16 of Sch.2A.[247] A person operating or proposing to operate a licensing scheme may apply to the Secretary of State to certify the scheme for the purposes of para.14A.[248] The Secretary of State must certify the scheme by statutory instrument if satisfied that it enables the works to which it relates to be identified with sufficient certainty by persons likely to require licences, and sets out clearly any charges payable and the other terms on which licences will be granted.[249] The order shall be revoked if the scheme ceases to be operated, or may be if it is no longer being operated according to its terms.[250]

(ii) Collective licensing

12–57   Collective licensing bodies (or collecting societies) collect and distribute royalties, and issue licences. They also have an important role in monitoring and enforcement. The economies of scale which result benefit both owners and users, although the market power which can result poses a danger if abused. Part II of the 1988 Act as enacted did not contain any provision dealing with the collective licensing of performers' rights. Such provisions have now been added in relation to performers' property rights by the Copyright and Related Rights Regulations 1996. Schedule 2A now regulates the operation of "licensing schemes" and "licensing bodies" in relation to the licensing of performers' property rights, providing a framework similar to those schemes which already exist in relation to copyright. For a detailed treatment of these provisions and of the powers of the Copyright Tribunal, the reader is referred to Ch.28, below. Details of collecting societies operating in the United Kingdom which represent performers and persons having recording rights may be found in Ch.27, below.

5. INFRINGEMENT

12–58   **New rights.** Under the original scheme of the 1988 Act, infringements of

---

[241] Sch.2A para.17(1A).
[242] Sch.2A para.17(4).
[243] CDPA 1988 Sch.2 para.14A(1). Cf. s.66.
[244] Sch.2 para.14A(1).
[245] Sch.2 para.14A(3).
[246] Sch.2A para.15(1).
[247] Sch.2 para.14A(2).
[248] Sch.2A para.16(1).
[249] Sch.2A para.16(2).
[250] Sch.2A para.16(5).

performers' rights and recording rights were actionable only as breaches of statutory duty.[251] The Rental and Related Rights Directive requires that performers have certain transferable property rights, and the Act was amended accordingly by the 1996 Regulations which introduced the additional performers' property rights of reproduction, distribution (issuing to the public), and rental and lending.[252] A "making available" right as required by the Information Society Directive was subsequently inserted by the Copyright and Related Rights Regulations 2003.[253] Certain remedies are available for infringements of property rights which are not available for breach of statutory duty.[254]

A. INFRINGEMENT OF PERFORMERS' ECONOMIC RIGHTS

Performers' rights in a qualifying performance are infringed by various acts done **12–59** without the consent of the performer. As explained above, these rights are all economic rights but a distinction is made between property and non-property rights, as identified in the treatment which follows, with the different consequences as to the juridical basis of any infringement and as to transmissibility of the right, etc.[255] What amounts to a qualifying recording has already been discussed.[256] Previously, various acts did not constitute an infringement if they were done for a person's private and domestic use.[257] Such encroachments on the rights of performers were in effect an exception or limitation to the right and as such were not consistent with the Information Society Directive unless any such exception was expressly permitted by the Directive. In these cases, therefore, the "private and domestic use" provisions have been deleted and such use is now permitted, if at all, by virtue of the permitted act provisions which apply in relation to these rights.[258] These are considered later.

(i) Recording direct from live performance

It is an infringement for a person to make a recording of the whole or any **12–60** substantial part of a performance directly from the live performance without consent.[259] As the section makes clear, this right refers to the direct recording from a live performance, and makes "bootleggers" infringers. It is a non-property right.[260]

(ii) Live broadcast of performance

It is an infringement of a performer's right to broadcast live the whole or any **12–61** substantial part of a qualifying performance without consent.[261] For this purpose, the following persons are to be regarded as broadcasting a performance: the person transmitting the programme in question if he has responsibility to any extent for its contents; and/or any person providing the programme who makes

---

[251] CDPA 1988 s.194 (as enacted).
[252] Copyright and Related Rights Regulations 1996 (SI 1996/2967).
[253] SI 2003/2498 reg.7, with effect from October 31, 2003.
[254] See paras 12–106 et seq. and Ch.21, below.
[255] See paras 12–42 to 12–45.
[256] See para.12–27, above.
[257] See CDPA 1988 ss.182, 182A and 186. See also art.10 of the Rental and Related Rights Directive.
[258] See paras 12 79 et seq., below.
[259] CDPA 1988 s.182(1)(a).
[260] s.192A.
[261] CDPA 1988 s.182(1)(b).

the arrangements necessary for its transmission with the person transmitting it.[262] This is a non-property right.[263]

(iii) Recording from a broadcast of live performance

12–62 It is an infringement to make a recording of the whole or any substantial part of a performance directly from a broadcast of the live performance without consent.[264] This is also a non-property right.[265]

(iv) Copying a recording of performance without consent (reproduction right)

12–63 It is an infringement to copy a recording of the whole or any substantial part of a qualifying performance without consent.[266] This right is referred to as the "reproduction right".[267] Although it was probably the case that this right, as originally introduced following implementation of the Rental and Related Rights Directive,[268] included transient or incidental copying,[269] the effect of the Information Society Directive was to require this to be made clear.[270] The Act was therefore amended on implementation to provide that copying for this purpose includes the making of a copy which is transient or is incidental to some other use of the original recording.[271] At the same time, a permitted act has been introduced to enable temporary copies to be made to enable transmissions in networks and lawful use.[272] It is immaterial whether the copy is made directly or indirectly.[273] This is a property right.[274]

(v) Issuing copies of recording of a performance to the public

12–64 It is an infringement to issue to the public copies of a recording of the whole or any substantial part of a qualifying performance without consent.[275] This right to authorise or prohibit the issue of copies to the public is referred to as the "distri-

---

[262] s.6(3), which applies to performers' rights expressly by virtue of s.211(2). Certain satellite broadcasts are subject to special rules under s.6A.

[263] s.192A.

[264] CDPA 1988 s.182(1)(c).

[265] s.192A.

[266] CDPA 1988 s.182A.

[267] s.182A(3). Cf. Rental and Lending Rights Directive art.7(1).

[268] See para.12–13, above.

[269] Likewise, the reproduction right in the case of copyright almost certainly included transient copying under the 1956 Act (see para.7–19, above). There was, however, clearly an argument that the Act seemed to make a distinction between copying for the purposes of copyright infringement, which was expressly stated to include copying which was transient or incidental to some other use of the work (CDPA 1988 ss.17(2), (6)) and copying for the purposes of performers' rights, about which the Act was silent.

[270] Art.7 of the Rental and Related Rights Directive was silent on this point but the Information Society Directive repealed art.7 (see art.11(1)(a)). art.2 of the Information Society Directive now takes its place.

[271] CDPA 1988 s.182A(1A).

[272] Sch.2 para.1A.

[273] s.182A(2). In *Mad Hat Music Ltd v Pulse 8 Records* [1993] E.M.L.R. 172 it was held to be arguable that, where a performer had consented to the making of the original recording, no further consent was needed to the making of records from that recording. Such an argument, it is submitted, is inconsistent with the definition of "recording" in s.180(2)(c) since in both the cases of the original and any subsequent recording the alleged offender "makes" a recording of the performance. This case was not followed in *Bassey v Icon Entertainment Plc* [1995] E.M.L.R. 596, and s.182A confirms that further consent is needed to the making of records from an original recording made with consent.

[274] CDPA 1988 s.192A.

[275] CDPA 1988 s.182B(1).

bution right".[276] The word "copies" is expressly defined to include the issue of the original recording of the live performance.[277]

Issue to the public is defined as:

(a) the act of putting into circulation in the EEA copies not previously put into circulation in the EEA by or with the consent of the performer, or

(b) the act of putting into circulation outside the EEA copies not previously put into circulation in the EEA or elsewhere.[278]

Issue to the public does not include:

(a) any subsequent distribution, sale, hiring or loan of copies previously put into circulation (but see s.182C: consent required for rental or lending), or

(b) any subsequent importation of such copies into the United Kingdom or another EEA state,[279] except insofar as para.(a) of subs.(2) applies to putting into circulation in the EEA copies previously put into circulation outside the EEA.[280]

Thus, the distribution right is exhausted by distribution of copies in the EEA: **12–65** once a specific copy has been put into circulation in the EEA, its subsequent importation, distribution or sale will not infringe, except where it is rented or lent to the public in the United Kingdom. However, the distribution right is not exhausted by distribution of copies outside the EEA, so the distribution in the EEA of a copy imported from outside the EEA can be an infringement, even if it was put into circulation with the consent of the performer. This distinction follows from the Rental and Related Rights Directive, which envisages a principle of Community exhaustion, not one of international exhaustion.[281] "Issue to the public" is defined in the same way in relation to the issue of copies of works to the public in Pt I of the 1988 Act (s.18) and the reader is referred to the discussion in Ch.7. A discussion of the principles of Community and international exhaustion is contained in Ch.25, below. This is a property right.[282]

(vi) Renting or lending copies of recording of a performance to the public

It is an infringement to rent or lend to the public copies of a recording of the **12–66** whole or any substantial part of a qualifying performance without consent.[283] The rights to authorise or prohibit such rental and lending are referred to as the "rental right" and "lending right".[284] Again the word "copies" is expressly defined to include the issue of the original recording or the live performance.[285] "Rental" is defined as making a copy of a recording available for use, on terms that it will or may be returned, for direct or indirect economic or commercial advantage.[286] "Lending" is defined as making a copy of a recording available for use, on terms that it will or may be returned, otherwise than for direct or indirect economic or

---

[276] s.182B(5). cf. Rental and Lending Rights Directive art.9(1).

[277] s.182B(4).

[278] s.182B(2).

[279] s.182B(3).

[280] s.182B(3). Cf. s.18, the equivalent provision in Pt I. For a detailed treatment of these definitions, see the discussion on s.18 in paras 7–76 et seq., above.

[281] Rental Directive art.9.

[282] CDPA 1988 s.191A.

[283] CDPA 1988 s.182C. The rental and lending rights do not apply to a copy of a recording of a performance acquired before commencement of the Copyright and Related Rights Regulations 1996 (SI 1996/2967) for the purpose of renting or lending it to the public: reg.34(2).

[284] CDPA 1988 s.182C(7). cf. s.18A, the equivalent provision in Pt I. For a discussion of s.18A, see paras 7–81 et seq., above.

[285] s.182C(6).

[286] s.182C(2)(a).

commercial advantage, through an establishment which is accessible to the public[287] but it does not include making available between establishments which are accessible to the public.[288] For this purpose, where lending by an establishment accessible to the public gives rise to a payment, if the amount of the payment does not go beyond what is necessary to cover the operating costs of the establishment, this is not to be regarded as being for direct or indirect economic or commercial advantage.[289] However, neither "rental" nor "lending" includes:

(a) making available for the purpose of public performance, playing or showing in public or communication to the public;

(b) making available for the purpose of exhibition in public;

(c) making available for on-the-spot-reference use.[290]

Note that where an agreement concerning film production is concluded between a performer and a film producer, the performer is to be presumed, unless the agreement provides to the contrary, to have transferred to the film producer any rental right in relation to the film arising from the inclusion of a recording of his performance in the film.[291] However, the performer retains the right to equitable remuneration for the rental.[292]

(vii) Making available recording of a performance by way of an on-demand service

12–67   In a case where a performance has been recorded, the Rental and Related Rights Directive did not require that performers be given an exclusive right to authorise or prohibit the wireless broadcasting or communication to the public of the performance via that recording, only a right to remuneration with respect to performances recorded on sound recordings.[293] This is reflected in the equitable remuneration right for exploitation of sound recordings in s.182D, which has already been considered.[294] The Information Society Directive does, however, require that performers be given an exclusive right to authorise or prohibit the making available of recordings of their performances by way of an on-demand service.[295] Effect has been given to this by s.182CA, it also being made clear that such acts do not fall within the equitable remuneration provisions.[296]

The Act therefore now provides that a performer's rights are infringed by a person who, without his consent, makes available to the public a recording of the whole or any substantial part of a qualifying performance by electronic transmission in such a way that members of the public may access the recording from a place and at a time individually chosen by them.[297] This is known as the "making available right",[298] and is a property right.[299]

12–68   **Transitional.** This new making available right became exercisable as from

---

[287] s.182C(b).
[288] s.182C(4).
[289] s.182C(5).
[290] s.182C(3). These three exclusions are derived from recital 13 of Dir.92/100.
[291] s.191F(1) See para.12–44, above.
[292] s.191G(1) See para.12–49, above.
[293] Directive 92/100/EEC of November 19, 1992 art. 8(2).
[294] See para.12–46, above.
[295] Information Society Directive art.3(2)(a).
[296] See CDPA 1988 s.182D(1)(b), and para.12–44.
[297] s.182CA(1). See para.7–114, above, for the equivalent right in relation to copyright.
[298] s.182CA(2).
[299] s.191A.

October 31, 2003.[300] The right is exercisable by the performer or, if he had died before then, by the person who immediately before this date was entitled under s.192A(2) to exercise the non-property rights in relation to that performance.[301] Any damages received by a person's personal representatives by virtue of this provision shall devolve as part of that person's estate as if the right had subsisted and been vested in him immediately before his death.[302] Generally, of course, the right is a property right and is transferable and will devolve as such.[303]

(viii) Use of recording made without consent

It is an infringement to show or play in public or communicate to the public the whole or any substantial part of a qualifying performance by means of a recording which was made without the consent of the performer and which the person doing that act knew or had reason to believe was so made.[304] This is a non-property right.[305]   **12–69**

(ix) Dealing with illicit recordings

It is an infringement to import into the United Kingdom, otherwise than for private or domestic use, an "illicit recording".[306] It is also an infringement in the course of a business to possess, sell, let for hire, offer or expose for sale or hire, or distribute a recording which is an "illicit recording".[307] In each of these cases it must also be shown that the person knew or had reason to believe that it was an illicit recording.[308] This is a non-property right.[309]   **12–70**

An "illicit recording" is a recording of the whole or any substantial part of a performance if it is made, otherwise than for private purposes, without the performer's consent.[310] It is immaterial where the recording was made.[311] Certain recordings which were not originally illicit recordings by virtue of the permitted act provisions may become so if subsequently dealt with, by virtue of special provisions under Sch.2.[312] These are: recordings made for purposes of instruction or examination[313]; recordings made by educational establishments for educational purposes[314]; recordings of performances in electronic form retained on transfer of the principal recording[315]; recordings made for the purposes of broadcast[316]; a re-

---

[300] See the Copyright and Related Rights Regulations 2003 (SI 2003/2498) reg.35(1).

[301] See reg.35(1). The Regulations say "if he *has* died", but presumably, given that the right is a property right, the reference is intended to be to his death before commencement.

[302] reg.35(2).

[303] See para.12–67, above.

[304] CDPA 1988 s.183 For the meaning of the expression "in public" see paras 7–95 et seq., above. cf. ss.22, 23, 24, 26 where the same words are used to define secondary infringement of copyright. See Ch.8, above.

[305] s.192A.

[306] CDPA 1988 s.184(1)(a). The provisions are dealt with in more detail in section 6 of this Chapter ("Permitted Acts and Defences"). For Pt I rights cf. s.22 and paras 8–05 et seq., above.

[307] s.184(1)(b).

[308] s.184(1).

[309] s.192A.

[310] s.197(2).

[311] s.197(6).

[312] s.197(5).

[313] Sch.2 para 4(3).

[314] Sch.2 para.6(2).

[315] Sch.2 para.12(2).

[316] Sch.2 para.16(3).

cording made for the purposes of time shifting[317]; and photographs of a broadcast.[318]

B. INFRINGEMENT OF RECORDING RIGHTS

12–71   The rights of the persons having recording rights in relation to a performance may be infringed by various acts done without consent. The provisions as to the relevant consent vary according to the different acts.

(i) Recording

12–72   It is an infringement of the recording right to make a recording of the whole or any substantial part of a performance without the consent of the person having such rights or that of the performer.[319] The performance does not have to be a qualifying performance.

(ii) Use of recording made without consent

12–73   It is an infringement, without the consent of the person having the recording rights, or, in the case of a qualifying performance, that of the performer, to show or play in public the whole or any substantial part of a performance by means of a recording which was made without the appropriate consent.[320] It is also an infringement to communicate to the public the whole or any substantial part of the performance by means of a recording which was made without the appropriate consent.[321] In each of these cases it must also be shown that the person doing the act knew or had reason to believe that it was made without the appropriate consent.[322] The "appropriate consent" is that of the performer or the person who, at the time the consent was given, had recording rights in relation to the performance. If there was more than one such person the consent of all of them is necessary.[323]

(iii) Dealing with illicit recordings

12–74   It is an infringement, without the consent of the person having the recording rights or, in the case of a qualifying performance, that of the performer, to import into the United Kingdom, otherwise than for private and domestic use, a recording of a performance which is an illicit recording.[324] It is also an infringement in the course of business to possess, sell or let for hire, offer or expose for sale or hire, or distribute a recording of the performance which is an illicit recording.[325]

For the purposes of the rights of a person having recording rights, a recording of the whole or any substantial part of a performance subject to the exclusive recording contract is an "illicit recording" if it is made, otherwise than for private

---

[317] Sch.2 para.17A(2).
[318] Sch.2, para.17B(2).
[319] CDPA 1988 s.186(1).
[320] CDPA 1988 s.187(1)(a).
[321] s.187(1)(b).
[322] s.187(1). Cf. ss.22, 23, 24, 26 where the same words are used to define secondary infringement of copyright.
[323] s.187(2).
[324] CDPA 1988 s.188(1)(a).
[325] s.188(1)(b).

purposes, without his consent or that of the performer.[326] In each of these cases it must also be shown that the person knew or had reason to believe that it was an illicit recording.[327]

Where in such an action a defendant shows that the illicit recording was innocently acquired by him or a predecessor in title of his, the only remedy available against him in respect of the infringement is damages not exceeding a reasonable payment in respect of the act complained of. In this context, "innocently acquired" means that the person acquiring the recording did not know and had no reason to believe that it was an illicit recording.[328]

6. PERMITTED ACTS AND DEFENCES

A. GENERAL

Various acts may be done notwithstanding the economic rights conferred by Pt 12–75
II, Ch.2.[329] Such acts correspond broadly to the acts which are permitted notwithstanding copyright.[330] Permitted acts are dealt with in Sch.2 to the 1988 Act.[331] The provisions of the Schedule specify acts which may be done in relation to a performance or a recording. They relate only to the question of infringement of the rights conferred by Ch.2. They do not affect any right or obligation restricting the doing of any of the specified acts.[332] No inference is to be drawn as to the scope of the Ch.2 rights from the description of any of the permitted acts.[333] The provisions of the Schedule are to be construed independently of each other. Thus, the fact that an act does not fall within one provision does not mean that it is not covered by another provision.[334]

The Rental and Related Rights Directive and the Information Society 12–76
Directive. The Rental and Related Rights Directive permitted various exceptions or limitations to be made to the rights of performers.[335] There were four particular permitted exceptions, namely for private use, use of short excerpts in connection with the reporting of current events, ephemeral fixations by broadcasting organisations and use for teaching or scientific research, together with a further general exception which permitted a Member State to make the same kind of exceptions as it did in relation to copyright works protected by the Berne Convention.[336] The permitted act provisions in relation to performers' rights were framed with these permitted exceptions in mind. As with the permitted acts in the copyright field, the provisions relating to performers' rights have been subject to substantial amendment on implementation of the Information Society Directive.[337] The reader is referred to Ch.9 of this Work for a full discussion of the effects of the

---

[326] s.197(3): cf. for performers' rights, s.197(2).
[327] s.188(1).
[328] s.188(2) and (3).
[329] CDPA 1988 s.189, Sch.2.
[330] See CDPA 1988 Ch.III of Pt I. See also Ch.9, above.
[331] Sch. 2 of the Act was amended by the Performances (Moral Rights, etc.) Regulations 2006 (SI 2006/18) Sch. para.9, with effect from February 1, 2006, and the Government of Wales Act 2006 (c.32), Sch.10 para.32, with effect from May 4, 2007.
[332] Sch.2 para.1(1).
[333] Sch.2 para.1(2).
[334] Sch.2 para.1(3).
[335] Rental and Related Rights Directive art.10.
[336] art.10(2).
[337] By the Copyright and Related Rights Regulations 2003 (SI 2003/2498).

Directive on the various permitted acts,[338] since most of what is said there is equally applicable to performer's rights. In the context of performers' rights, as already noted,[339] the Act previously excluded from the scope of infringement certain acts done for a person's private and domestic use.[340] In order to make the Act compliant with the Information Society Directive, these provisions have been deleted and such acts are now only allowed, if at all, to the extent that they come within the permitted acts provisions. The Information Society Directive also amended the Rental and Related Rights Directive to limit the scope of any permitted exceptions or limitations to cases which complied with the "three-step test" laid down by art.9(2) of the Berne Convention, i.e. exceptions must be limited to "certain special cases which do not conflict with a normal exploitation of the subject-matter and do not unreasonably prejudice the legitimate interests of the rightholder."[341] This test is discussed elsewhere.[342] Although the test has not been expressly incorporated into the 1988 Act, a number of the permitted acts have been framed or curtailed with the test in mind.[343]

12–77 **Transitional.** The unamended provisions of Sch.2 of the Act (which set out the permitted acts in relation to performances, etc.) continue to apply to anything done after October 31, 2003, in completion of an act begun before this date which was permitted by those provisions.[344]

12–78 **Circumvention of copy protection devices.** The provisions of art.6(4) of the Information Society Directive, which, in the absence of voluntary measures taken by right owners, deal with measures to resolve the conflict between the interests of beneficiaries of the various permitted exceptions and the rights of right owners in respect of the circumvention of copy-protection devices, are considered elsewhere.[345] These provisions apply in relation to the permitted exceptions to the performers' reproduction and on-demand rights under the Information Society Directive. art.6(4) of the Directive also provides that when art.6 "is applied in the context of" the Rental and Related Rights Directive, "this paragraph" shall apply *mutatis mutandis*. The apparent purpose of this is that in the case of the exceptions which are governed by the Rental and Related Rights Directive, a similar regime as to voluntary or appropriate measures to be taken to ensure that beneficiaries of an exception or limitation can indeed benefit from such exceptions is to apply, although presumably only where there is an equivalent exception as regards performances.

---

[338] See paras 9–07 and 9–08.

[339] See para.12–59, above.

[340] As noted in the text, art.10 of the Rental and Related Rights Directive permitted an exception or limitation from the art.7 reproduction right in respect of private use, so that CDPA 1988 s.182A did not conflict with the Directive. Since art.7 has now been deleted by the Information Society Directive and replaced with art.2 of the latter Directive, this permitted limitation to the reproduction right no longer exists under the Rental and Related Rights Directive. The applicability of the various permitted exceptions under the Information Society Directive is discussed fully in Ch.9, above.

[341] art.11(1)(b) of the Information Society Directive, amending art.10(3) of the Rental and Related Rights Directive. Any exceptions permitted under the Information Society Directive must also comply with this test: art.5(5).

[342] See para.9–02, above.

[343] See, e.g. the Government Conclusions on the Patent Office's Consultation Paper of August 7, 2002, para.5.2.

[344] The Copyright and Related Rights Regulations 2003 reg.33.

[345] See paras 9–10, above, and para.15–23, below.

B. PARTICULAR ACTS

(i) Making of temporary copies

The Directive required the introduction of an entirely new permitted act dealing **12–79**
with the making of temporary copies. This was in reaction to the express right
conferred on performers and owners of rights in recordings to prevent the making
of transient or incidental copies.[346] Thus, it is now provided that the rights
conferred by Ch.2 are not infringed by the making of a temporary copy of a recording of a performance which is transient or incidental, which is an integral
and essential part of a technological process and the sole purpose of which is to
enable either (a) a transmission of the recording in a network between third parties by an intermediary, or (b) a lawful use of the recording, and which has no independent economic significance.[347]

(ii) Criticism, review and news reporting

Rights in performances and recordings are not infringed by fair dealing with a **12–80**
performance or recording:
   (a) for the purpose of criticism or review, of that or another performance or
       recording, or of a work, provided that the performance or recording has
       been made available to the public; or
   (b) for the purpose of reporting current events.[348]

(iii) Incidental inclusion of performance or recording

By virtue of para.3(1) of Sch.2, the rights are not infringed by the incidental **12–81**
inclusion of a performance or recording in a sound recording, film or broadcast.[349]
A performance or recording, so far as it consists of music or words spoken or
sung with music, is not to be regarded as incidentally included in a sound recording or broadcast if it is deliberately included.[350] The rights are not infringed by
anything done in relation to copies of, or the playing, showing or communication
to the public of anything which was, by virtue of para.3(1), not an infringement
of those rights.[351]

(iv) Things done for purposes of instruction or examination

By virtue of para.4(1) of Sch.2 the rights are not infringed by the copying of a re- **12–82**
cording of a performance in the course of instruction, or of preparation for instruction, in the making of films or film sound tracks, provided the copying is done by
a person giving or receiving instruction and the instruction is for a non-
commercial purpose.[352] The rights are not infringed by the copying of a recording
of a performance for the purposes of setting or answering the questions in an ex-

---

[346] See para.9–58, above.
[347] CDPA 1988 Sch.2, para.1A. See paras 9–15 et seq. for the equivalent provision in relation to copyright.
[348] CDPA 1988 Sch.2 para.2. Expressions have the same meaning as in s.30. See paras 9–35 et seq., above.
[349] CDPA 1988 Sch.2 para.3(1). Expressions have the same meaning as in s.31; see paras 9–56 et seq., above.
[350] Sch.2 para.3(3).
[351] Sch.2 para.3(2).
[352] CDPA 1988 Sch.2 para.4(1). Expressions have the same meaning as in s.32: see paras 9–88 et seq., above.

amination or by anything done for the purposes of an examination by way of communicating the questions to the candidates.[353] Where a recording, which would otherwise be an illicit recording is made for the purposes of instruction or examination, but is subsequently dealt with, it is to be treated as an illicit recording for the purposes of that dealing. If that dealing infringes any right conferred by Ch.2 it is to be treated as an illicit recording for all subsequent purposes. For this purpose, "dealt with" means (a) sold or let for hire, offered or exposed for sale or hire, or (b) communicated to the public, unless that communication is itself by virtue of the above provisions,[354] not an infringement of the rights conferred by Ch.2.[355]

(v) Playing or showing sound recording, film or broadcast at educational establishments

12–83   The playing or showing of a sound recording, film or broadcast at an educational establishment for the purposes of instruction before an audience consisting of teachers and pupils at the establishment and other persons directly connected with the activities of the establishment is not a playing or showing of a performance in public for the purposes of infringement of Ch.2 rights.[356] A person is not for this purpose directly connected with the activities of the educational establishment simply because he is the parent of a pupil at the establishment.[357]

(vi) Recording of broadcasts by educational establishments

12–84   A recording of a broadcast, or a copy of such a recording, may be made by or on behalf of an educational establishment for the educational purposes of that establishment without thereby infringing any of the rights conferred by Ch.2 in relation to any performance or recording included in it, provided the education purposes are non-commercial.[358] These rights are also not infringed where a recording of a broadcast or a copy of such a recording, whose making was by virtue of the above provisions not an infringement of such rights, is communicated to the public by a person situated within the premises of an educational establishment provided that the communication cannot be received by any person situated outside the premises of that establishment.[359] However, these provisions do not apply if or to the extent that there is a licensing scheme certified for those purposes under para.16 of Sch.2A providing for the grant of licences.[360] Where a recording of a broadcast which would otherwise be an illicit recording is made by an educational establishment in accordance with this provision, but is subsequently dealt with, it is to be treated as an illicit recording for the purposes of that dealing. If that dealing infringes any right conferred by Ch.2 it is to be treated as an illicit recording for all subsequent purposes. For this purpose, "dealt with" means sold or let for hire, offered or exposed for sale or hire, or communicated from within

---

[353] Sch.2 para.4(2).
[354] i.e. anything done by way of communication of questions to candidates under CDPA 1988 Sch.2 para.4(2)(b)
[355] Sch.2 para.4(3).
[356] CDPA 1988 Sch.2 para.5(1). Expressions have the same meaning as in s.34: see paras 9–96 et seq., above.
[357] Sch.2 para.5(2).
[358] CDPA 1988 Sch.2 para.6(1). Expressions have the same meaning as in s.35: see paras 9–97 et seq., above.
[359] Sch.2 para.6(1A).
[360] Sch.2 para 6(1B).

the premises of an educational establishment to any person situated outside those premises.[361]

(vii) Lending of copies by educational establishments, libraries and archives

The lending of copies of a recording of a performance by an educational establishment does not infringe Ch.2 rights.[362] Similarly, the lending of copies of a recording of a performance by a prescribed library or archive (other than a public library) which is not conducted for profit, does not infringe Ch.2 rights.[363]   **12–85**

(viii) Copy of work required to be made as condition of export

If an article of cultural or historical importance or interest cannot lawfully be exported from the United Kingdom unless a copy of it is made and deposited in an appropriate library or archive, it is not an infringement of any right conferred by Ch.2 to make that copy.[364]   **12–86**

(ix) Parliamentary and judicial proceedings

The rights conferred by Ch.2 are not infringed by anything done for the purposes of parliamentary or judicial proceedings or for the purposes of reporting such proceedings.[365]   **12–87**

(x) Royal Commissions and statutory inquiries

The rights conferred by Ch.2 are not infringed by anything done for the purposes of the proceedings of a Royal Commission or statutory inquiry or for the purposes of reporting any such proceedings held in public.[366]   **12–88**

(xi) Public records

Material which is comprised in public records[367] which are open to public inspection in pursuance of the relevant legislation may be copied and a copy may be supplied to any person, by or with the authority of any officer appointed under the relevant legislation, without infringing Ch.2 rights.[368]   **12–89**

(xii) Acts done under statutory authority

Where the doing of a particular act is specifically authorised by an Act of Parlia-   **12–90**

---

[361] Sch.2 para.6(2).

[362] CDPA 1988 Sch.2 para.6A(1). Expressions have the same meaning as in s.36A; see paras 9–109 et seq., above.

[363] Sch.2 para.6B(1). Expressions have the same meaning as in s.40A(2); and any provision under CDPA 1988 s.37 prescribing libraries or archives for the purposes of that section applies also for the purposes of this paragraph: see paras 9–119 et seq., above.

[364] CDPA 1988 Sch.2 para.7(1). Expressions have the same meaning as in s.44: see paras 9–138 et seq., above.

[365] CDPA 1988 Sch.2 para.8(1). Expressions have the same meaning as in s.45: see paras 9–143 et seq., above.

[366] CDPA 1988 Sch.2 para.9(1). Expressions have the same meaning as in s.46: see paras 9–144 et seq., above.

[367] As defined in the Public Records Act 1958, the Public Records (Scotland) Act 1937, the Public Records Act (Northern Ireland) 1923 or in Welsh public records(as defined by the Government of Wales Act 1998). See CDPA 1988 Sch.2, para.10(1).

[368] CDPA 1988 Sch.2, para.10(1). Expressions have the same meaning as in s.49: see paras 9–147 et seq., above.

ment (including an enactment contained in Northern Ireland legislation),[369] whenever passed, then, unless the Act provides otherwise, the doing of the act does not infringe the rights conferred by Ch.2.[370] This provision is not to be construed as excluding any defence of statutory authority otherwise available under or by virtue of any enactment.[371]

(xiii) Transfer of copies of works in electronic form

12–91 Special provision is made for the case where a recording of a performance in electronic form has been purchased on terms which, expressly or impliedly or by virtue of any rule of law, allow the purchaser to make further recordings in connection with his use of the recording.[372]

If there are no express terms prohibiting the transfer of the recording by the purchaser, imposing obligations which continue after a transfer, prohibiting the assignment of any consent or terminating any consent on a transfer or providing for the terms on which a transferee may do the things which the purchaser was permitted to do, anything which the purchaser was allowed to do may also be done by a transferee without infringing Ch.2 rights. But any recording made by the purchaser which is not also transferred is to be treated as an illicit recording for all purposes after the transfer.[373] The same applies where the original purchased recording is no longer usable for all purposes after the transfer and what is transferred is a further copy used in its place.[374]

These provisions also apply on a subsequent transfer, but do not apply in relation to a recording purchased before the commencement of Ch.2.[375]

(xiv) Use of recordings of spoken words in certain cases

12–92 Where a recording of the reading or the recitation of a literary work is made for the purpose of reporting current events, or of communicating to the public the whole or part of the reading or recitation, it is not an infringement of the Pt II rights to use the recording or to copy the recording and use the copy for that purpose, provided that the following conditions are met[376]:

    (a) the recording is a direct recording of the reading or recitation and is not taken from a previous recording or from a broadcast;

    (b) the making of the recording was not prohibited by or on behalf of the person giving the reading or recitation;

    (c) the use made of the recording is not of a kind prohibited by or on behalf of that person before the recording was made; and

    (d) the use is by or with the authority of a person who is lawfully in possession of the recording.[377]

(xv) Recordings of folk songs

12–93 The recording of a performance of a song may be made for the purpose of includ-

---

[369] CDPA 1988 Sch.2 para.11(2).
[370] Sch.2 para.11(1). Expressions have the same meaning as in s.50: see paras 9–148 et seq., above.
[371] Sch.2 para.11(3).
[372] CDPA 1988 Sch.2 para.12(1). Expressions have the same meaning as in s.56; see paras 9–168 et seq., above.
[373] Sch.2 para.12(2).
[374] Sch.2 para.12(3).
[375] Sch.2 para.12(5).
[376] CDPA 1988 Sch.2 para.13(1). Expressions have the same meaning as in CDPA 1988 s.58: see paras 9–174 et seq., above.
[377] Sch.2 para.13(2).

ing it in an archive maintained by a designated body without infringing any Ch.2 rights. Certain conditions must, however, be met.[378] They are that:

    (a) the words are unpublished and of unknown authorship at the time the recording is made,

    (b) the making of the recording does not infringe any copyright, and

    (c) its making is not prohibited by any performer.[379]

Copies of a recording made in reliance on these provisions and included in an archive maintained by a designated body may, if the prescribed conditions are met, be made and supplied by the archivist without infringing Ch.2 rights.[380] The "prescribed conditions" means the conditions prescribed for the purposes of s.61(3). A designated body means a body designated for the purposes of s.61.[381]

(xvi) Lending of certain recordings

The Secretary of State may by order provide that in specified cases the lending to the public of copies of films or sound recordings shall be treated as licensed by the performer subject only to the payment of such reasonable royalty or other payment as may be agreed or determined in default of agreement by the Copyright Tribunal.[382] No such order shall apply if, or to the extent that there is a licensing scheme certified under para.16 of Sch.2A providing for the grant of licences.[383] This provision does not affect liability under s.184(1)(b) (secondary infringement: possessing or dealing with illicit recording) in respect of the lending of illicit recordings.[384] **12–94**

(xvii) Playing of sound recordings for the purposes of clubs and societies

It is not an infringement of Ch.2 rights to play a sound recording as part of the activities of, or for the benefit of, a club, society or other organisation provided that certain conditions are met.[385] Those conditions are that: **12–95**

    (a) the organisation is not established or conducted for profit and its main objects are charitable or are otherwise concerned with the advancement of religion, education or social welfare,

    (b) that the sound recording is played by a person who is acting primarily and directly for the benefit of the organisation and who is not acting with a view to gain,

    (c) that the proceeds of any charge for admission to the place where the recording is to be heard are applied solely for the purposes of the organisation.[386]

(xviii) Incidental recording for purposes of broadcast

A person who proposes to broadcast a recording of a performance in circum- **12–96**

---

[378] CDPA 1988 Sch.2 para.14(1). Expressions have the same meaning as in s.61: see paras 9–165 et seq., above.

[379] Sch.2 para.14(2).

[380] Sch.2 para.14(3).

[381] Sch.2 para.14(4). See SI 1989/1012; See Vol.2 A4.ii.

[382] CDPA 1988 Sch.2 para.14A(1). Expressions have the same meaning as in s.66: see paras 9–197 et seq., above.

[383] Sch.2 para.14A(2).

[384] Sch.2 para.14A(5).

[385] CDPA 1988 Sch.2 para.15(1). Expressions have the same meaning as in s.67: see paras 9–200 et seq., above.

[386] Sch.2 para.15(2) as amended by SI 2010/2694, The Copyright, Designs and Patents Act 1988 (Amendment) Regulations 2010.

stances not infringing Ch.2 rights is to be treated as having consent for the purpose of Ch.2 for the making of a further recording for the purposes of a broadcast.[387] That consent is subject to certain conditions. They are that the further recording shall not be used for any other purpose and shall be destroyed within 28 days of being first used for broadcasting the performance.[388]

A recording made in accordance with these provisions is to be treated as an illicit recording for the purposes of any use in breach of the condition as to non-use for any other purpose and for all purposes after that condition or the condition as to destruction within 28 days is broken.[389]

(xix) Recordings for the purposes of supervision and control of broadcasts and other services

12–97   The rights conferred by Ch.2 are not infringed by the making or use by the British Broadcasting Corporation, for the purpose of maintaining supervision and control over programmes broadcast by them, or included in any on-demand programme service provided by them, of recordings of those programmes.[390] The rights conferred by Ch.2 are not infringed by anything done in pursuance of:

(a) various provisions of the Broadcasting Acts 1990 and 1996 and Communications Act 2003 (maintenance of supervision and control over programmes and advertisements, etc.); or

(b) a condition which, by virtue of s.334(1) of the Communications Act 2003, is included in a licence granted under Pt I or Pt III of that Act or Pt I or Pt II of the Broadcasting Act 1996; or

(c) a direction given under s.109(2) of the Broadcasting Act 1990 (power of OFCOM to require production of recordings, etc.); or

(d) s.334(3)/ 3680(1) or (3) of the Communications Act 2003.[391]

Further, the rights conferred by Ch.2 are not infringed by:

(a) the use by OFCOM, in connection with the performance of any of their functions under the Broadcasting Act 1990, the Broadcasting Act 1996 or the Communications Act 2003, of any recording, script or transcript which is provided to them under or by virtue of any provision of those Acts; or

(b) any existing material which is transferred to them by a scheme made under s.30 of the Communications Act 2003.[392]

(xx) Recording for the purposes of time-shifting

12–98   The rights conferred by Ch.2 in relation to a performance or recording included in the broadcast are not infringed by the making in domestic premises for private and domestic use of a recording of a broadcast solely for the purpose of enabling

---

[387] CDPA 1988 Sch.2 para.16(1). Expressions have the same meaning as in CDPA 1988 s.68: see paras 9–186 et seq., above.

[388] Sch.2 para.16(2).

[389] Sch.2 para.16(3).

[390] CDPA 1988 Sch.2 para.17(1) as amended by the Audiovisual Media Services Regulations 2009/2979 reg.12(3)(a), December 19, 2009. See para.9–210, above. "On-demand programme service" has the same meaning as in the Communications Act 2003 (for the definition, see para.9–210, above at fn.922).

[391] Sch.2 para.17(2).

[392] Sch.2 para.17(3). Expressions have the same meaning as in s.69: see paras 9–210 et seq., above. For these purposes, "existing material" means (a) any recording, script or transcript which was provided to the Independent Television Commission or the Radio Authority under or by virtue of any provision of the Broadcasting Act 1990 or the Broadcasting Act 1996 and (b) any recording or transcript which was provided to the Broadcasting Standards Commission under s.115(4) or (6) or 116(5) of the Broadcasting Act 1996: CDPA 1988 Sch.2 para.17(4).

it to be viewed or listened to at a more convenient time.[393] Where a recording which would otherwise be an illicit recording is made in accordance with this provision but is subsequently dealt with, it is to be treated as an illicit recording for the purposes of that dealing; and if that dealing infringes any right conferred by Ch.2, it is to be treated as an illicit recording for all subsequent purposes.[394] For this purpose, "dealt with" means sold or let for hire, offered or exposed for sale or hire or communicated to the public.[395]

(xxi) Photographs of broadcasts

The rights conferred by Ch.2 in relation to a performance or recording included **12–99** in the broadcast are not infringed by the making in domestic premises for private and domestic use of a photograph of the whole or any part of an image forming part of a broadcast, or a copy of such a photograph.[396] Where a recording which would otherwise be an illicit recording is made in accordance with this paragraph but is subsequently dealt with, it is to be treated as an illicit recording for the purposes of that dealing, and if that dealing infringes any right conferred by Ch.2, it is to be treated as an illicit recording for all subsequent purposes.[397] For these purposes, "dealt with" means sold or let for hire, offered or exposed for sale or hire or communicated to the public.[398]

(xxii) Free public showing or playing of broadcast

The showing or playing in public of a broadcast to an audience who have not **12–100** paid for admission to the place where the broadcast is to be seen or heard does not infringe any Ch.2 rights in relation to a performance or recording included in the broadcast, or any sound recording (except in so far as it is an "excepted sound recording") or film which is played or shown in public by reception of the broadcast.[399] In addition, in the case of the showing or playing in public of a broadcast to an audience who have not paid for admission to the place where the broadcast is to be seen or heard, the rights in relation to a performance or recording included in any excepted sound recording which is played in public by reception of the broadcast are not infringed if the playing or showing of that broadcast in public is necessary for the purposes of (i) repairing equipment for the reception of broadcasts, (ii) demonstrating that a repair to such equipment has been carried out, or (iii) demonstrating such equipment which is being sold or let for hire or offered or exposed for sale or hire.[400]

The audience is to be treated as having paid for admission to a place in two sets of circumstances; first, if they have paid for admission to a place of which that place forms part and, secondly, if goods or services are supplied at that place (or a place of which it forms part) at prices which are substantially attributable to

---

[393] CDPA 1988 Sch.2 para.17A. Expressions used have the same meaning as in CDPA 1988 s.70: see paras 9–212 et seq., above.

[394] Sch.2 para.17A(2)

[395] Sch.2 para.17A(3).

[396] CDPA 1988 Sch.2 para.17B. Expressions used have the same meaning as in s.71: see paras 9–216 et seq., above.

[397] Sch.2 para.17B(2)

[398] Sch.2 para.17B(3).

[399] CDPA 1988 Sch.2 para.18(1)A, as amended by SI 2010/2694, The Copyright, Designs and Patents Act 1988 (Amendment) Regulation 2010. Expressions have the same meaning as in s.72: see para.9–218, above.

[400] Sch.2 para.18(1B).

the facilities afforded for seeing or hearing the broadcast, or at prices exceeding those usually charged there and which are partly attributable to those facilities.[401]

In two cases persons are not regarded as having paid for admission to a place: first, persons admitted as residents or inmates of the place: secondly, persons admitted as members of a club or society where the payment is only for membership of the club or society and the provision of facilities for seeing or hearing broadcasts is only incidental to the main purposes of the club or society.[402]

Where the making of the broadcast was an infringement of the rights conferred by Ch.2 in relation to a performance or recording, the fact that it was heard or seen in public by the reception of the broadcast is to be taken into account in assessing the damages for that infringement.[403]

(xxiii) Reception and retransmission of wireless broadcast by cable

12–101 Provision is made for the case where a wireless broadcast made from a place in the United Kingdom is received and immediately retransmitted by cable.[404] The rights conferred by Ch.2 in relation to a performance or recording included in the broadcast are not infringed if and to the extent that the broadcast is made for reception in the area in which it is retransmitted by cable; but where the making of the broadcast was an infringement of those rights, the fact that the broadcast was retransmitted by cable shall be taken into account in assessing the damages for that infringement.[405]

Where:

(a) the retransmission by cable is in pursuance of a relevant requirement, but
(b) to any extent, the area in which the retransmission by cable takes place ("the cable area") falls outside the area for reception in which the broadcast is made ("the broadcast area"),

the retransmission by cable (to the extent that it is provided for so much of the cable area as falls outside the broadcast area) of any performance or recording included in the broadcast shall be treated as licensed by the owner of the Ch.2 rights in relation to the performance or recording, subject only to the payment to him by the person making the broadcast of a reasonable royalty or other payment in respect of the retransmission by cable of the broadcast as may be agreed or determined in default of agreement by the Copyright Tribunal.[406] This provision does not apply if, or to the extent that, the retransmission of the performance or recording by cable is (apart from sub-para.19(3)) licensed by the owner of the Ch.2 rights in relation to the performance or recording.[407]

12–102 The Secretary of State may by order provide that in specified cases para.19(2) is to apply in relation to broadcasts of a specified description which are not made as mentioned therein, or may exclude the application of s.19(2) in relation to broadcasts of a specified description made as mentioned therein.[408]

An application to settle the royalty or other sum payable in pursuance of s.19(3)

---

[401] Sch.2 para.18(1).
[402] Sch.2 para.18(3).
[403] Sch. 2 para.18(4).
[404] CDPA 1988 Sch.2 para.19(1). Expressions have the same meaning as in s.73: see paras 9–205 et seq., above.
[405] Sch.2 para.19(2).
[406] Sch.2 para.19(3).
[407] Sch.2 para.19(4).
[408] CDPA 1988 Sch.2 para.19(5).

may be made to the Copyright Tribunal by the owner of the Ch.2 rights or by the person making the broadcast.[409]

(xxiv) Provision of sub-titled copies of broadcast

Certain bodies designated for the purposes of s.74 of the 1988 Act may, for the purpose of providing people who are deaf or hard of hearing, or physically or mentally handicapped in other ways, with copies which are sub-titled or otherwise modified for their special needs, make recordings of such broadcasts and copies of such recordings, and issue or lend copies to the public without infringing Ch.2 rights in relation to a performance or recording included in the broadcast.[410] However, this provision does not apply if, or to the extent that, there is a licensing scheme certified for those purposes under para.16 of Sch.2A providing for the grant of licences.[411]   **12–103**

(xxv) Recording of broadcast for archival purposes

The recording of a broadcast of a designated class[412] or a copy of such a recording may be made for the purpose of being placed in an archive maintained by designated bodies without thereby infringing any right conferred by Ch.2 in relation to a performance or recording included in the broadcast.[413]   **12–104**

7. COPYRIGHT TRIBUNAL CONTROL OVER PERFORMERS' RIGHTS

The Copyright Tribunal exercises control of licensing schemes and licensing bodies dealing with performers' property rights licenses.[414] It thus has control over the amounts payable in respect of the rights to equitable remuneration conferred on performers, namely, the right to equitable remuneration where sound recordings of their performances are played in public or included in a broadcast or cable programme, and the right to such remuneration for rental of sound recordings or films. It also grants consent on behalf of performers who cannot be identified or traced.[415] Finally, the Copyright Tribunal has control over licensing of performers' rights in a number of other specific situations, most of which mirror situations in which the Tribunal exercises control over copyright licensing.[416]   **12–105**

A detailed discussion of the powers of the Copyright Tribunal in relation to performers' rights is given in Ch.28 E, below.

8. REMEDIES AND PENALTIES FOR INFRINGEMENT OF RIGHTS

Performers' rights and recording rights may be enforced by means of an infringe-   **12–106**

---

[409] Sch.2 para.19A(1).
[410] CDPA 1988 Sch.2 para.20(1). Expressions have the same meaning as in s.74: see paras 9–211 et seq., above.
[411] Sch.2 para.20(1A).
[412] See CDPA 1988 s.75, para.9–213, above.
[413] Sch.2 para.21(1). Expressions have the same meaning as in s.75: see paras 9–213, above.
[414] The Tribunal was given control over licensing schemes and licensing bodies concerned with performers' property right licences by CPDA 1988 Sch.2A, inserted into the 1988 Act by the Copyright and Related Rights Regulations 1996 (SI 1996/2697).
[415] CPDA 1988 s.190, as amended by the Copyright and Related Rights Regulations 1966 (SI 1996/2967). See para.27–154, below.
[416] See para.27–155, below.

ment action, including applications for delivery-up and forfeiture, and the right of seizure. The performers' property rights are enforceable by provisions which parallel the relevant copyright infringement provisions.

An infringement of a performer's property rights is actionable by the owner of the performer's property rights[417] or by an exclusive licensee.[418] An exclusive licensee has, except against the owner of the rights, the same rights and remedies in respect of matters occurring after the grant of the licence as if it were an assignment.[419] If the exclusive licensee sues, a defendant may avail himself of any defence which would have been available to him if the action had been brought by the rights owner.[420] Although the rights owner and the exclusive licensee have concurrent rights of action, neither may proceed beyond an application for interim relief without joining the other, except with leave of the court.[421] Where the other party is added as a defendant, he is not liable for any costs in the action unless he takes part in the proceedings.[422]

An infringement of a performer's non-property rights, or of any Ch.2 right conferred on a person having recording rights, is actionable by the person entitled to the right as a breach of statutory duty.[423] An exclusive licensee of performers' non-property rights has no right of action in respect of any breach.

12–107   It is expressly provided that, in an action for infringement of performers' property rights, all such relief by way of damages, injunctions, accounts or otherwise is available to the claimant as is available in respect of the infringement of any other property right.[424] Thus the remedies for infringement of these rights are assimilated to those available for infringement of copyright. Like all property rights, infringement is actionable without proof of damage. The court now has a power to grant an injunction against a service provider in the case of others using its service to infringe a performer's property right.[425]Where in an action for infringement of a performer's property rights it is shown that at the time of the infringement the defendant did not know, and had no reason to believe, that the rights subsisted in the recording to which the action relates, the plaintiff is not entitled to damages against him, but without prejudice to any other remedy. However, the court may in an action for infringement of a performers' property rights having regard to all the circumstances, and in particular to: (a) the flagrancy of the infringement, and (b) any benefit accruing to the defendant by reason of the infringement, award such additional damages as the justice of the case may require.[426]

For performers' non-property rights and recording rights the normal remedies for breach of statutory duty are available.[427] Express provision is made for the remedies of delivery up, seizure and forfeiture of illicit recordings.[428]

A detailed discussion of the remedies and penalties, including criminal sanctions, available for the infringement of performers' rights and recording rights is given in Chs 21 and 22, below.

The remedies for infringement of performers' moral rights are discussed in Ch.11, above.

---

[417] CDPA 1988 s.191I(1).
[418] s.191L(1).
[419] s.191L(2).
[420] s.191L(3).
[421] s.191M(1), (3).
[422] s.191M(2).
[423] s.194.
[424] CDPA 1988 s.191I(2).
[425] s.191JA.
[426] s.191J
[427] s.194.
[428] ss.95–97.

PART IV

DESIGN RIGHT AND THE PROTECTION OF WORKS OF INDUSTRIAL APPLICATION

CHAPTER THIRTEEN

DESIGN RIGHT, UNREGISTERED COMMUNITY DESIGN AND THE PROTECTION OF WORKS OF INDUSTRIAL APPLICATION

Contents　　　　　　　　　　　　　　　　　　　　　　　　　*Para.*

1. THE SCHEME OF PROTECTION

A. INTRODUCTION

This Chapter is mainly concerned with unregistered forms of protection for industrial designs—UK unregistered design right,[1] unregistered Community design and copyright. Forms of registered protection—under the Registered Designs Act 1949 and registered Community design—are dealt with in outline only.   **13–01**

What is "industrial design"? A design is, in broad terms, the plan or scheme for the appearance of an article (or a part of an article). It is concerned with what an article looks like or is intended to look like. It is not concerned with how an article performs its function.[2] The design of an article may be recorded in a drawing, a photograph or a written description or it may be embodied in an actual article. "Industrial" in this context means that the design relates to the appearance of an article intended to fulfil a specific function and, usually, to be mass produced. An industrial design is, therefore, to be distinguished from a work of fine art (such as a painting) which performs no particular function other than to be enjoyed as an object in itself.   **13–02**

Scope of industrial design. Industrial design covers a wide field of activity. Some designs (such as the design of a machine cog) are dictated solely by the functions which the relevant articles are to perform and aesthetic considerations are of no significance. Others (such as the design for a chair), must mix functionality with aesthetic appeal.[3] In yet others (such as a design of soft toy, wallpaper and fabrics), functionality will play very little part but aesthetic appearance will be crucial. Finally, the design of some articles may be derived from a work (such as a painting) which started life as a purely artistic work in its own right and which was not intended to be a design for another article.   **13–03**

B. NATURE OF THE PROBLEM

Conflicting needs. The protection of industrial designs is and has always been   **13–04**

---

[1] References in this chapter to "design right" are references to the UK's design right created by Pt III of the Copyright Designs and Patents Act 1988.

[2] This is the concern of patent law.

[3] A chair must perform the function of a chair so its design will include a leg or legs and a seat but other aspects of its design, such as its elegantly tapering and fluted legs, may be included simply to attract buyers to that particular product.

controversial. At the heart of this controversy is how to balance two conflicting needs. On the one hand, the need to provide protection so as to reward human endeavour and creativity; on the other, the need to allow competition in the production of articles which fulfil a particular function or purpose.

13–05   **The need to protect.** As with any other form of industrial endeavour, there is a need to provide some protection for industrial designs. Protection encourages and rewards innovation and skill; without it, designers may not invest their skill, time or money in a design and, in particular, in a design which is expensive to develop but simple to copy.[4] Moreover, it may be thought that a person who has invested in a design should be entitled to enjoy the benefit of that investment. The design is, in this sense, a form of property.[5] If a work of pure art is to be protected, why not a work of industrial art[6] or a purely functional design which may have involved the same degree of creative effort and probably more investment.[7]

13–06   **The need for competition.** On the other hand, because an industrial design (unlike a work of fine art) determines the shape or appearance of an article which is intended to perform a specific function, there is a need to allow some degree of competition. The greater the extent to which the appearance of an article is dictated by the article's function, the more likely it is that protection of the design will operate to prevent others making articles to fulfil that same function. In such cases, protection would allow the designer to create a monopoly in articles made to fulfil that function. It may also prevent a design idea from being fully developed and exploited, often by someone better suited to the task than its original creator. From this perspective, protection may stultify commercial progress and the development of ideas[8] and may deprive the public of a chance to choose an alternative, possibly cheaper, and possibly better product of the same or a similar design.

13–07   **Forms of protection.** If some protection is thought to be appropriate, then the form of that protection must take into account the need for competition. A monopoly in the use of a design[9] would provide the designer with strong protection and, as questions of copying would be irrelevant, would give competitors some certainty. It would, however, be very restrictive on competitors and public alike, for no one else could produce an article to that design even if they had acted independently. Moreover, monopolies are usually provided under a system of registration which is likely to be time-consuming, expensive and, for many types of design, impractical.[10] An alternative is to protect against copying. In its traditional copyright form, this appears to offer a good balance between protection and competition, in that it arises automatically whilst allowing a competitor to produce the same or a similar design provided he acted independently (without

---

[4] See the Council Regulation 6/2002 on Community design (EC) No. 6/2002 at recital 7.

[5] It was commented in Parliament that nothing could more properly be described as a man's property than the products of his mind, see *Hansard*, H.L. Vol.489, col.1476.

[6] i.e. a design which has features added by way of embellishment in order to make the article to which they are applied more attractive to consumers.

[7] To use the example given in the course of counsel's submissions on behalf of the plaintiff in *British Leyland Motor Corporation Ltd v Armstrong Patents Ltd* [1986] A.C. 577 at 597E; [1986] F.S.R. 221, why should one assume that "there is more merit in creating the shape of Popeye, which attracts copyright protection, than in working out, with great skill and at great expense, the shape of an article of great commercial value and worth which does not 'appeal to the eye' and which is not patentable".

[8] See White Paper "Intellectual Property and Innovation" (Cmnd.9712). April 1986, para.3(b) of the Introduction and para.5 of the Preface to Pt I. See also, the Council Regulation on Community design (EC) No. 6/2002 at recital 10.

[9] i.e. a patent or a registered design type of protection.

[10] e.g. in those areas, such as the fashion industry, where designs change rapidly.

copying). However, such a form of protection requires proof of copying (often by inference) which often gives rise to uncertainty.

The period of protection is also likely to be important. Even if an industrial design is deserving of protection, the need for competition in producing articles to perform the function of the article in question suggests that the period of protection for the design should be both shorter and more easily ascertainable than the period of protection which applies to works of fine art. If protection is to be given to a functional design, then a relatively short period of protection (as in patent law) may be sufficient to allow the designer to make a return on his investment before competitors can enter the market. If, however, the protection relates to the more decorative aspects of the article's appearance, then a longer period of protection should not unduly restrict fair competition.

Given that designs vary from the purely technical to the almost purely artistic, a form and period of protection which is appropriate for one design may be wholly inappropriate for another. As has already been noted, the need to allow competition is much more apparent in the case of functional designs (such as a machine cog) or in the case of the functional aspects of the mixed design (such as a chair) than it is for those designs (such as a child's toy) which are governed largely by aesthetic considerations.[11] Yet, if differing forms or degrees of protection are to be available for different types of design, the need to define clear boundaries between those different types of design becomes vital. The law has long decided that industrial designs should have some form of protection but it is the drawing of these boundaries which has caused difficulties.

C. Bases of Protection

Protection of unregistered designs. An unregistered industrial design may be protected against (broadly speaking) acts of copying under the following bases:

    13–08

  (1) **Design right.** A design which came into existence after August 1, 1989 may be protected by design right—a right introduced by the 1988 Act.

  (2) **(Unregistered) Community design.** A design may be protected as an unregistered Community design under the Community Design Regulation (reg.6/2002).

  (3) **Copyright.** Whilst copyright protection under the 1988 Act is of some very limited importance in relation to designs recorded or embodied in copyright works created after August 1, 1989,[12] it has some greater importance in relation to designs created before that date.[13]

Protection of registered designs. A stronger, monopoly form of protection is also available to industrial designs through registration on the following bases (which are only considered in outline in this work):

    13–09

  (4) **Registered Design.** A design may be protected if registered under the Registered Designs Act 1949.[14]

  (5) **(Registered) Community design.** A design may be protected if registered as a Community design under the Community Design Regulation (reg.6/2002) under a system of registration introduced on April 1, 2003.

---

[11] There is usually little need for anyone else to reproduce aesthetic features, save in so-called "must match" situations, see paras 13–64 et seq., below.

[12] The intention of the 1988 Act (as implemented by CDPA s.51) was, as much as possible, to remove industrial designs from the sphere of copyright protection, see paras 13–302 et seq., below.

[13] The application of the 1988 Act to works created before August 1, 1989 is subject to the transitional provisions contained in Sch.1 of that Act. See paras 13–338 et seq., below.

[14] (c.88) as amended by the CDPA 1988 ss.265–273 and Sch.4, and by the Registered Designs Regulations 2001 (SI 2001/3949).

13–10   **Other bases of protection.** An industrial design may also be protected under the law relating to passing off or breach of confidence, or under patent and registered trade mark law (which are outside the scope of this book).

D. History of Protection of Industrially Applied Works

13–11   The history of protection for industrial designs prior to the 1988 Act shows the difficulties which arise in this area of law.[15] It is also useful to an understanding of the industrial design provisions of the Copyright Designs and Patents Act 1988.

13–12   **Copyright protection before 1911.** Traditionally, copyright law was concerned with the protection of what may broadly be called works of fine art and not with industrial designs. Thus, prior to 1911, there was copyright protection partly under the common law and partly under statute for various categories of works (such as literary works, engravings, sculptures, paintings, drawings and photographs[16]). The form of copyright protection, being automatic and potentially long lasting,[17] was well suited to works of fine art as there was no public interest in allowing "competing" artists to copy each others' works nor to provide them with certainty as to when it would be safe to do so. Whilst there was nothing expressly to exclude copyright from a work which embodied or recorded an industrial design, this was not considered to be a problem; many works of design were two dimensional (e.g. a drawing) and the concept of the infringement of a two dimensional artistic work by its reproduction in three dimensions had yet to be developed.[18]

13–13   **Registered design protection before 1911.** After some initial attempts to extend copyright protection to certain limited categories of design,[19] the first serious attempt to protect designs directly was by statutes passed in 1839 and 1842.[20] Instead of adopting a copyright form of protection, these statutes introduced a system of registration for a wide range of designs and gave the proprietor of a registered design a monopoly in that design lasting up to three years. This period was increased to five years in 1883.[21] Later, the Patents and Designs Act 1907[22] provided for the registration of new or original designs applicable to any article of manufacture by way of pattern, shape, configuration or ornament. It also increased the period of monopoly protection to a maximum of 15 years. Even at this relatively early stage, the needs of competitors in the field of industrial design were recognised by the form of the protection adopted. Thus, the registered design system provided some commercial certainty by giving the proprietor a monopoly in the use of a design, but only where that design had been registered; it also prevented a designer claiming too broad an area of protection for his efforts by requiring him to show that his design was new and by limiting the scope of protec-

---

[15] The history of protection was considered by the House of Lords in *British Leyland Motor Corporation v Armstrong Patents Co Ltd* [1986] A.C. 577; [1986] F.S.R. 221 and by the Whitford Committee Report, Cmnd. 6732 (March 1977), at paras 89–104.

[16] The early history of copyright law has already been considered, see Ch.2, above.

[17] The period of statutory protection was, in general, fixed by reference to the life of the author.

[18] See *Interlego A.G. v Tyco International Inc* [1988] A.C. 217 at 251; [1988] R.P.C. 343, HL and para.13–16, below.

[19] Mostly types of fabric, e.g. the Designing and Printing of Linens Act 1787 (27 Geo.3, c.38) and the Linens Act 1794 (34 Geo. c.23).

[20] The Copyright and Designs Act 1839, repealed and replaced by the Designs Act 1842 (5 & 6 Vict. c.100).

[21] Patents, Trademarks and Designs Act 1883 (46 & 47 Vict. c.57), s.50(1).

[22] Patents and Designs Act 1907 (7 Edw. 7 c.29) s.93 (prior to its amendment by Patents and Designs Act 1919 s.19 as to which, see para.13–15, below).

tion to the use of the design in relation to articles in respect of which it had been registered. It is worth noting, however, that, at this stage, purely functional designs were registrable.[23]

Copyright Act 1911. The Copyright Act 1911 brought all forms of copyright protection under a single statute for the first time and conferred protection for the life of the author plus 50 years[24] on most original literary, dramatic, musical and artistic works.[25] However, s.22 of the 1911 Act provided that no copyright would subsist in designs which were capable of being registered under the Patents and Designs Act 1907[26] unless they were not used or intended to be used as models or patterns for industrial production.[27] The intention behind s.22 seems clear. Works of art were to be protected, if at all, by copyright; industrial designs, if at all, by registration. In the event, s.22 proved less than effective as a means of excluding copyright from the industrial sphere. This was due in part to the fact that it did not restrict or remove copyright protection from artistic works which had not been used and had not been intended to be used industrially at the time that they were made, but which had subsequently been used industrially.[28] It was also due in part to changes in the law of registered designs made after 1911.[29]

13–14

Developments in the law of registered designs. The changes made in the law of registered designs after 1911 meant that fewer designs were capable of registration. As has been seen, when the Copyright Act 1911 was passed, a design was defined in broad terms for the purposes of registration and, it seems, a purely functional design was registrable.[30] However, this changed with the Patents and Designs Act 1919. For the purposes of registration, a design was defined by the 1919 Act as those features of shape, configuration, pattern or ornament which in the finished article appealed to and were judged solely by the eye but not any mode or principle of construction nor anything which was in substance a mere mechanical device.[31] Although the 1919 Act was replaced by the Registered Designs Act 1949,[32] the definition of a design in the 1949 Act (as it then was) remained substantially the same.[33] Designs which were not visually appealing or were functional were therefore excluded from registration.[34] At the other (more artistic) end of the industrial design spectrum, the Registered Design Rules 1949[35] excluded from registration designs for certain articles such as sculptures (other

13–15

---

[23] It was only later that a requirement for "eye appeal" and an exclusion of designs dictated by function became a part of the registered designs legislation, see paras 13–370 to 13–371, below. The requirement for eye appeal has now been dropped by reason of the amendments made by the Registered Designs Regulations 2001. See paras 13–275 et seq., below.

[24] Copyright Act 1911 s.3.

[25] Copyright Act 1911 s.1(1).

[26] The meaning of "capable of being registered" was considered in *Interlego A.G. v Tyco Industries Inc* [1988] R.P.C. 343 at 359, 360, 362 and 364. For the position under the 1907 Act, see para.13–370, below.

[27] Copyright Act 1911 s.22, see para.13–16, below.

[28] See *King Features Syndicate Inc v O & M Kleeman Ltd* [1941] A.C. 417 and para.13–16, below.

[29] See para.13–15, below.

[30] See para.13–13, above.

[31] (9 & 10 Geo. 5, c.80), s.19. It has been suggested that this new wording simply reflected the way in which the old law had been construed by the courts. It seems, however, that this was not the case, see paras 13–13, above and paras 13–370 to 13–371, below.

[32] The Registered Designs Act 1949 s.7 also provided monopoly protection lasting a maximum of 15 years against certain specified dealings in relation to articles in respect of which the design was registered and to which the design or a design not substantially different had been applied.

[33] The Registered Designs Act 1949 s.1(3). The wording of the definition followed the construction of the definition of a "design" under the 1919 Act adopted in *Kestos Ltd v Kempat Ltd* (1935) 53 R.P.C. 139 at 151. See para.13–369, below.

[34] See *Amp Inc v Utilux Proprietary Ltd* [1972] R.P.C. 103 and *British Leyland Motor Corporation v Armstrong Patents Co Ltd* [1986] A.C. 577 at 617H–618E; [1986] F.S.R. 221.

[35] Made under the Registered Designs Act 1949 s.1(4).

than casts or models to be applied industrially), wall plaques and medals, and printed matter primarily of a literary or artistic character (including, for example, book-jackets, dressmaking patterns, greetings cards, maps, plans, postcards, advertisements, cards, etc.).[36] Although these changes were understandable, the narrowing of the definition of a design for the purposes of registration served to reduce the effectiveness of s.22 of the Copyright Act 1911 in excluding copyright from industrial designs.[37]

13–16   **Problems with section 22.** As has been seen,[38] s.22 of the Copyright Act 1911 sought to exclude copyright from works embodying industrial designs by reference to whether the design was registrable. Thus, in so far as the changes in the law of registered designs described above meant that certain designs were not registrable, the works embodying those designs became capable of copyright protection. In practice this was of little significance while the 1911 Act was in force because the copyright works in which most unregistrable industrial designs were recorded were categorised as "plans" which the 1911 Act treated as literary works rather than artistic works.[39] As copyright in a literary work could not be infringed by the making of the article described in that work,[40] designers could not rely on copyright in most cases of industrial copying. It was, however, of significance where the relevant unregistrable industrial design was recorded in an artistic rather than a literary work. This was the case in *King Features Syndicate Inc v O & M Kleeman Ltd*[41] (the Popeye case) where the House of Lords was concerned with copyright in cartoon sketches of Popeye the Sailor. The sketches were drawn for publication in a newspaper but various Popeye dolls and brooches had been made subsequently with the licence of the copyright owner. The defendant had copied these articles without licence and was held thereby to have infringed the copyright in the sketches. The decision established several points of importance; first, various members of the House of Lords commented that s.22 could never have applied to the sketches because the sketches were not designs capable of registration.[42] Secondly, the Lords found that, even if the sketches were designs capable of registration,[43] the question whether s.22 applied to exclude copyright from them was to be determined as at the time that the work was created. If at that time the work was not used nor intended to be used industrially, copyright would subsist and there was nothing in s.22 to remove that copyright if the work was later applied industrially.[44] As there had been no such use or intention at the time that the sketches were created, s.22 did not apply and the sketches retained full copyright protection despite the extensive licensed use which had been made of them.[45] The Lords also accepted that, under the 1911 Act, copyright in the sketches could be infringed by the making of a copy in three

---

[36] Registered Design Rules 1949 r.26.

[37] See para.13–16, below.

[38] See para.13–13, above.

[39] Copyright Act 1911 s.35(1).

[40] See para.7–37, above.

[41] [1941] A.C. 417.

[42] [1941] A.C. 417 at 429–430, 439–440 and 443. The basis for this was that, to be registrable, a design had to be applicable to an article of manufacture. The sketches were not designs for articles but were merely sketches for publication in a newspaper. The defendant did not seek to argue the contrary.

[43] i.e. even if (contrary to the view of the House of Lords) the sketches could be seen as designs applicable to articles of manufacture.

[44] *King Features Syndicate Inc v O & M Kleeman Ltd* [1941] A.C. 417 at 429 and 431, 440–441, 434 and 451–452.

[45] This finding is not entirely easy to justify. Lord Bridge stated in *British Leyland Motor Corporation v Armstrong Patents Ltd* [1986] A.C. 577 at 620B; [1986] F.S.R. 221 that: "The phrase used in s.22 is not used or intended to be used, etc .. . . . It seems to me to be a little difficult to

dimensions[46] and also that it could be infringed indirectly (i.e. by copying articles which had been made to the works).

Copyright Act 1956. The Copyright Act 1911 was replaced by the Copyright Act 1956 under which copyright subsisted in every original literary, dramatic, musical or artistic work.[47] The 1956 Act also restricted the protection given by copyright to industrial designs but, unlike the 1911 Act, did not do so by excluding copyright from the work in question. Instead, ss.9(8) and 10 of the 1956 Act sought to place limits on the type of act which could infringe copyright in the relevant work.[48] As to s.9(8) as has been seen, the 1911 Act had treated many of the works which recorded industrial designs as plans and thus as literary works, the copyright in which would not be infringed by the making of the article so described.[49] However, under the 1956 Act, diagrams, maps, charts and plans were treated as drawings and, therefore, as artistic works.[50] Given the decision in *King Features*,[51] this meant that the copyright in an industrial design drawing could be infringed by the making of articles to the design. It was to counter this that s.9(8) of the 1956 Act provided that the making of an object in three dimensions should not be taken as infringing the copyright in an artistic work in two dimensions if the object would not appear, to the non-expert eye, to be a reproduction of the artistic work. Section 10 was the principal means by which the 1956 Act sought to limit copyright protection for industrial designs. Section 10 applied to an artistic work where a corresponding design[52] had been registered under the Registered Designs Act 1949 or, if it had not been registered, where it had been applied industrially,[53] and articles to which the design had been applied had been marketed.[54] In very broad terms, the nature of the limitation imposed by s.10 was that the copyright in the relevant artistic work would not be infringed to the extent that the Registered Designs Act 1949 provided a remedy or would have provided a remedy had the design been registered.[55] The intention, clearly, was to encourage designers to use the system of registration rather than to rely on copyright.

13–17

Problems with the 1956 Act. In practice, ss.9(8) and 10 of the 1956 Act were

13–18

---

understand what significance the House's decision [in *King Features*] allowed to the words I have emphasised".

[46] Before the Copyright Act 1911, the making of an article was probably not an infringement of the copyright in a two-dimensional artistic work, see *Hanfstaengl v Empire Palace* [1894] 2 Ch. 1. However, the introduction by s.1(2) of the 1911 Act of the words "sole right to produce or reproduce the work ... in any material form whatsoever ..." made it clear that, thereafter, such an act could constitute an infringement, see *Purefoy Engineering Co Ltd v Sykes Boxall & Co Ltd* (1955) 72 R.P.C. 89 at 98, CA.

[47] See Copyright Act 1956 ss.2(1) and 3(2).

[48] These provisions largely adopted the recommendations of the 1952 Gregory Report (Cmnd. 8662).

[49] See para.13–16, above.

[50] Copyright Act 1956 ss.48(1) and 3(1)(a).

[51] See para.13–16, above.

[52] A "corresponding design" in relation to an artistic work was a design which, when applied to an article, resulted in a reproduction of that work, Copyright Act 1956 s.10(7).

[53] The industrial application had to be by or with the consent of the copyright owner, Copyright Act 1956 s.10(2). A design was applied industrially if it was applied to or reproduced on or in more than 50 articles, see the Copyright (Industrial Designs) Rules 1957 (SI 1957/867).

[54] Copyright Act 1956 s.10(2). Marketing in this context meaning that such articles had been sold or let for hire or offered for sale or hire, see Copyright Act 1956 s.10(2)(b).

[55] For the first 15 years, copyright protection was only excluded in relation to those acts covered by the actual registration (see s.10(1)(a)) or those acts which would have been covered had the design been registered for the articles marketed by or with the licence of the copyright owner (s.10(3)(a)). Thereafter, copyright was excluded in relation to all acts which would have been covered by the widest registration which would have been possible in relation to that design. See s.10(1)(b), s.10(3)(b) and s.10(6). See also, *British Leyland Motor Corporation v Armstrong Patents Co Ltd* [1986] A.C. 577 at 620G.

only partly effective in excluding copyright from the industrial sphere. Both provisions were considered in *Dorling v Honnor Marine Ltd*,[56] a case concerning copyright in plans of a sailing dinghy. The defendant had made boats and kits of parts for boats to those plans. It was held that the plans were artistic works and that, unless one of the new defences applied, the copyright in them would have been infringed by the defendant's actions.[57] On the facts, the court found that s.9(8) did not provide a defence in relation to the making of the kits and it suggested, without deciding, that it would not have provided a defence in relation to the making of complete boats either.[58] The court also found that s.10 of the 1956 Act only applied to artistic works whose corresponding designs were either (a) registered,[59] or (b) unregistered but registrable and had been applied industrially.[60] The section, it was found, had no relevance to works whose corresponding designs were unregistrable. As the plans were unregistrable,[61] s.10 did not operate so as to limit copyright protection for them.[62] The decision had wide-ranging implications for it showed that artistic works embodying unregistrable designs (in particular, designs which were unregistrable because they were functional) had full copyright protection lasting for the life of the author plus 50 years.

13–19   **Design Copyright Act 1968.** The attempt to maintain a distinction between industrial design protection and artistic copyright protection was largely abandoned when the Design Copyright Act 1968 was enacted.[63] Notwithstanding the Report of the 1962 Designs Committee,[64] the 1968 Act amended s.10 of the 1956 Act such that an artistic work embodying a design was entitled to full copyright protection. The scope of this protection was only limited where a corresponding design was applied industrially.[65] In such a case, copyright protection for the work was reduced to 15 years.[66] As a result of the 1968 Act, a registrable design recorded in an artistic work became capable of dual protection under both

---

[56] [1965] Ch. 1.

[57] The decision in *Dorling v Honnor Marine Ltd* [1965] Ch. 1; [1964] R.P.C. 160 has been criticised on the basis that a distinction should have been drawn between an act which actually reproduces an artistic work (whether in two or three dimensions), as had been the case in *King Features* [1941] A.C. 417 (see para.13–16, above), and an act which merely amounts to the use of the information contained in an artistic work (such as a drawing) as instructions for making a three-dimensional object. In the latter case, the object, although derived from the information, does not in any real sense reproduce it. The strength of this criticism was accepted in *Canon Kabushiki Kaisha v Green Cartridge Co (Hong Kong) Ltd* [1997] 3 W.L.R. 13 at 17B–E, PC but it was said to be "far too late" to depart from the construction of copyright law taken in Dorling and followed in *L.B. (Plastics) Ltd v Swish Products Ltd* [1979] F.S.R. 145 and *British Leyland Motor Corporation v Armstrong Patents Ltd* [1986] A.C. 577; [1986] F.S.R. 221. Of course, under the 1911 Act, the plans would have been literary rather than artistic works, see para.13–16, above, the law was (and remains) that copyright in a literary work would not, in general, be infringed by the making of an article to that design, see the cases cited at para.7–37, above.

[58] [1965] Ch. 1 at 16–17, 21–22, CA. Defences based on s.9(8) of the Copyright Act 1956 also failed in *L.B. (Plastics) Ltd v Swish Products Ltd* [1979] F.S.R. 145 and *British Leyland Motor Corporation v Armstrong Patents Ltd* [1986] A.C. 577.

[59] Copyright Act 1956 s.10(1).

[60] ss.10(2) and (3). The fact that the limitation placed on copyright protection for unregistered designs by s.10(3) was defined by reference to the protection which would have been available under the registered designs legislation led the Court of Appeal in Dorling to the view that s.10(2) only applied to works whose corresponding designs were registrable see [1965] 1 Ch. 1 at 16 and 19E–F.

[61] [1965] 1 Ch. 1 at 14C–E and at 19F–G.

[62] [1965] 1 Ch. 1 at 13–15 and 19–20.

[63] See *British Leyland Motor Corporation Ltd v Armstrong Patents Ltd* [1986] A.C. 577 at 620H; [1986] F.S.R. 221.

[64] Cmnd. 808. The Committee, by a majority, favoured a continuing limitation on the application of artistic copyright in cases where a design was used industrially.

[65] i.e. applied in the sense set out in Copyright Act 1956 s.10(2)(a) and (b) (as amended).

[66] After the 15-year period, copyright would not be infringed to the extent that the Registered Designs Act 1949 would have provided a remedy had the design been registered at the relevant time, see s.10(2) and (3) as amended.

the Registered Designs Act 1949 and the Copyright Act 1956 (albeit for a reduced period in the latter case in the event that it was applied industrially). However, the 1968 Act did not affect the position as regards unregistrable designs. An unregistrable design recorded in a qualifying work remained entitled to full copyright protection of life plus 50 years in accordance with the decision in *Dorling v Honnor Marine Ltd*.[67]

Further developments in the law of registered designs. Further developments in the law of registered designs increased the significance of copyright protection for unregistrable industrial designs. As has been seen, designs dictated solely by function were excluded from registration under the Registered Designs Act 1949.[68] In *Amp Inc v Utilux Pty Ltd*,[69] this exclusion was construed widely so as to apply to any design which was brought about by, or which was attributable only to, the function of the article. The exclusion would apply even if there could be articles to other designs which would perform that function.[70] On this construction,[71] the test for registration seemed even more stringent and the scope for copyright protection for industrial designs correspondingly greater. More recently, designs which were unregistrable under Registered Designs Rules[72] or because they did not comply with the registered design definition of "design"[73] or because the articles to which they were to be applied did not satisfy the Registered Design definition of an "article"[74] were all held to be entitled to full copyright protection.   **13–20**

Spare parts and *British Leyland v Armstrong Patents*. The law as it stood caused particular problems in relation to spare parts. A spare part for a product will usually be in the same or substantially the same shape as the original part. If, however, the designer of the original part had produced design drawings,[75] copyright in those drawings (however basic and lacking in artistic merit they may be) could often be asserted so as to prevent the manufacture of spare parts by competitors. Further, as such designs were unlikely to be registrable, s.10 did not operate to reduce the period of copyright protection. Accordingly, copyright might allow its owner an effective monopoly in the supply of spare parts for the entire commercial life of the design as well as for the actual life of products with which the design was associated. The point arose directly in *British Leyland Motor Corporation Ltd v Armstrong Patents Ltd*[76] where the defendant was manufacturing spare exhaust pipes to fit the plaintiff's vehicles. The plaintiff claimed that these spares infringed the copyright in its drawings of exhaust pipes for the relevant vehicles. The House of Lords accepted that, as the design drawings were unregistrable, they were not caught by s.10 of the 1956 Act. It also accepted that, because most objects can be recognised from their drawings, s.9(8) of the 1956 Act was incapable of preventing copyright protection extending into   **13–21**

---

[67] [1965] Ch. 1; [1964] R.P.C. 160. See para.13–18, above. For other cases where designs have been found to be unregistrable and, therefore, to enjoy full copyright protection, see para.13–20, below.

[68] s.1(3) of the 1949 Act (prior to its amendment by the CDPA 1988). See para.13–15, above.

[69] [1972] R.P.C. 103.

[70] [1972] R.P.C. 103 at 114–115, 118 and 122, HL. See also *Interlego A.G. v Tyco International Industries Inc* [1989] A.C. 217; [1988] R.P.C. 343 at 355, HL.

[71] Which the House of Lords in *British Leyland Motor Corporation v Armstrong Patents Co Ltd* [1986] A.C. 577 declined to overrule, see at 614D and at 618H–619A.

[72] Rules made under s.1(4) of the Registered Designs Act 1949.

[73] See *Entec (Pollution Control) Ltd v Abacus Mouldings* [1992] F.S.R. 332 following *British Leyland Motor Corporation v Armstrong Patents Co Ltd* [1986] A.C. 577; [1986] F.S.R. 221.

[74] See *Drayton Controls (Engineering) Ltd v Honeywell Control Systems Ltd* [1992] F.S.R. 245.

[75] As was increasingly the case.

[76] [1986] A.C. 577.

areas far beyond its main or originally intended scope.[77] However, in an attempt to allow a measure of competition, the House of Lords accepted that the rights of the copyright owner were subject to an exception which became known as the "spare parts exception". This exception was formulated in various ways but, in essence, it operated to prevent the manufacturer of an article such as a car using his copyrights in a way which would interfere with the right of the owner of that article to have access to a free market for spares to repair it or to keep it in good working order.[78]

13–22   **Semiconductor topographies.** Shortly after the decision in *British Leyland*, there was a further development of significance in the field of industrial design. On December 16, 1986, the Council of the European Communities issued a Directive[79] concerning protection for the design or topography of semiconductor products. This Directive expressly recognised that semiconductor products were capable of being copied at a fraction of the cost which it took to develop them and that their topographies therefore required protection. The Directive was significant in that it included a requirement that the subject matter for protection (the topography) must be original, not only in the sense that it was the product of the creator's own intellectual effort, but also in the sense that it was not commonplace in the semiconductor industry. Further, the protection offered was more limited than that available to normal copyright works. The Directive was implemented in the United Kingdom by the Semiconductor Products (Protection of Topography) Regulations 1987[80] which by reg.9(1) provided that it was not an infringement of the copyright in an artistic work to reproduce a topography.

13–23   **Summary of the law as at 1988.** Thus, as at 1988, the law relating to the protection of industrial designs was in some disarray. Designs which were sufficiently novel were capable of registered design protection lasting 15 years. However, such protection was not proving popular[81] and the exclusion from registrability had, in any event, been construed widely.[82] Save where the uncertain spare parts exception applied,[83] automatic copyright protection, traditionally the preserve of the fine arts, was available to a very wide range of industrial designs provided only that they were recorded in a qualifying copyright work. This copyright protection lasted for the life of the author plus 50 years unless the corresponding design was both registrable under the Registered Designs Act 1949 and had been applied industrially, in which case the term of copyright protection was limited to 15 years.[84] As a result, the full term of copyright protection was available for the least "artistic" of designs[85] whilst the most artistic industrial designs (those which, being visually appealing and not being governed by functionality, were registrable under the Registered Designs Act 1949) had only 15 years' copyright protection. This often led to parties arguing that their designs were not registrable

---

[77] [1986] A.C. 577 at 653C and 639C–D.

[78] The decision in *British Leyland Motor Corporation v Armstrong Patents Co Ltd* [1986] A.C. 577 and its formulation of the spare parts exception has been the subject of much criticism. See, for example, *Canon Kabushiki Kaisha v Green Cartridge Co (Hong Kong) Ltd* [1997] 3 W.L.R. 13.

[79] Council Directive 87/54 EEC.

[80] Now replaced by the Design Right (Semiconductor Topography) Regulations 1989. For the current position, see Ch.14, below.

[81] See paras 102 and 103 of the Whitford Report Cmnd.6732 (March 1977).

[82] See para.13–20, above.

[83] See para.13–21, above.

[84] Under Copyright Act 1956,s.10 (as amended by the 1968 Act), copyright was only limited to 15 years if the design had been industrially applied and was registered or registrable under the Registered Designs Act 1949. The mere fact that a design had been registered did not operate to limit copyright protection to 15 years.

[85] Such as, for example, rivets, screws, a bolt, a block of leather and a washer in *British Northrop Ltd v Texteam Blackburn Ltd* [1974] R.P.C. 57 at 68–69.

even, sometimes, where they had previously registered the design.[86] Finally, a completely separate system of protection was available for semiconductor topographies.

Anomaly concerning three-dimensional works. The use of copyright as a means of protecting industrial designs gave rise to other anomalies. In particular,[87] where an industrial design was recorded in a drawing, the drawing (and indirectly the design) had copyright protection regardless of its artistic merit and regardless of how functional or otherwise the design may be. If, however, the design was only recorded in a three-dimensional article made to the design, then copyright protection was only available if the article itself fell within the definition of an artistic work and, in particular, only if it was a sculpture or a work of artistic craftsmanship—the meaning of the latter being very narrowly construed.[88] This meant that the availability of copyright protection for a design would often depend upon the chance of whether or not a preliminary sketch of the design had been made.					**13–24**

Proposals for reform. Many of the developments in the law which are discussed above were controversial and over the years various proposals for reform were put forward. The contrasting proposals reflected the difference between those who regarded the need for protection as paramount and who saw no need to distinguish between industrial designs and artistic works and those who believed that there was a need to allow more competition in relation to industrial designs than for works of art. Yet, even within the latter category, there was a wide variety of views as to how to meet that need.[89]					**13–25**

The Whitford Report 1977. The Whitford Committee report[90] dealt at length with the law relating to industrial designs[91] and with the differing submissions it had received from various interested parties on how best to balance protection against competition.[92] In its conclusions, the Committee unanimously recommended the repeal of the registered designs monopoly provided by the Registered Designs Act 1949. A majority was in favour of providing copyright protection without the need for registration for so-called "Category A" designs (designs which consisted only of a surface pattern and the shapes of three-dimensional articles of which the aesthetic appearance would influence a purchaser in making a purchase regardless of whether they started life in two or in three dimensions[93]). This protection would, however, be cut to 25 years once the design had been industrially applied. The committee was divided on how to treat designs which it called "Category B" designs (designs of three-dimensional shapes with no such aesthetic appeal). Some felt that no protection was appropriate. Others thought that the protection should be the same as that for Category A designs. Others favoured a limited form of protection under a design deposit copyright system. All, however, were in favour of compulsory licences being available in respect of					**13–26**

---

[86] See, for example, *Interlego A.G. v Tyco International Inc* [1989] A.C. 217; [1988] R.P.C. 343.
[87] See para.197 of the Whitford Report Cmnd.6732 (March 1977).
[88] See *George Hensher Ltd v Restawile Upholstery (Lancs.) Ltd* [1976] A.C. 64; [1974] F.S.R. 173.
[89] This variety of views can be seen in the fact that some countries, such as France, have traditionally followed the so-called doctrine of the "unity of art" (that there should be no distinction between the protection of works or pure art and works of industrial art), whilst others, such as Italy, have traditionally adopted a more restrictive approach to protection, see para.13–36, below.
[90] Cmnd. 6732 (March 1977).
[91] See paras 89–203 of the Report.
[92] See paras 129–164 of the Report .
[93] In order to remove the anomaly referred to in para.13–24, above.

Category B designs, on the ground that the UK market was not being adequately supplied.[94]

13–27   **The 1981 and 1983 Green Papers.** After the Whitford Report, two green papers considered, inter alia, the protection of industrial designs. The 1981 Green Paper[95] favoured the removal of any protection (other than patent protection) from purely functional items, arguing that industrial progress was being hindered by the protection which the law afforded. By contrast, the 1983 Green Paper[96] accepted that novel designs of purely functional items should be given protection. Unlike the Whitford Report, it suggested that all designs could be protected through a system of registration rather than by a form of copyright (although it recommended that the costs of such a proposal be investigated).

13–28   **The 1986 White Paper.**[97] The 1986 White Paper rejected the suggestion in the 1983 Green Paper that all designs be registrable. It proposed, instead, that the Registered Designs Act 1949 be amended to protect only genuinely aesthetic designs but that the period of protection be increased to 25 years. For non-registrable designs, it considered, but rejected as uncertain, protection based on an "unfair copying" law and proposed, instead, a completely new "unregistered design right" based on copyright principles but without the more objectionable features associated with full copyright protection.[98] In particular, it suggested that the new design right provide protection for all original designs, including spare parts,[99] but not including artistic works,[100] and that the term of protection be only 10 years with provision for licences as of right in the last five years of the term.

13–29   **Copyright Designs and Patents Act 1988.** The Copyright Designs and Patents Act 1988 followed, with some important exceptions, the proposals contained in the 1986 White Paper. As with the 1911 and 1956 Acts, the intention behind the 1988 Act is to remove industrial designs from the sphere of copyright and to leave copyright as the preserve of what might properly be called artistic works.[101] The need to provide protection for industrial designs was, however, recognised. To achieve this, the 1988 Act created a wholly new right known as design right. Design right, like copyright, provides automatic protection against copying without any need for formalities such as registration. However, the scope of design right has been carefully limited so as to allow far more competition than the law of copyright allows. Thus, commonplace designs[102] are excluded from design right protection, as are designs which fall within the so-called "must fit" and "must match" exclusions.[103] Moreover, where design right subsists in a design, it only lasts for 15 years or, if articles made to the design are made available for sale or hire within five years from the end of the calendar year when the design was first recorded in a design document or when an article was first made

---

[94] See para.194 of the Report.

[95] Reform of the Law relating to Copyright, Designs and Performers' Protection (Cmnd. 8302). July 1981.

[96] Intellectual Property Rights and Innovation (Cmnd. 9117). December 1983.

[97] Intellectual Property and Innovation (Cmnd. 9712). April 1986.

[98] See para.3.26 of the White Paper.

[99] See paras 3.26 and 3.27 of the White Paper. In *Dyson Ltd v Qualtex (UK) Ltd* [2006] EWCA Civ 166; [2006] R.P.C. 31, the Court of Appeal endorsed the Judge's view that the White Paper clearly rejected both the notion that spare parts should be exempted from any protection regime and the notion that they should be subject to some special regime. They were to be dealt with like all other functional articles.

[100] The United Kingdom having obligations in respect of artistic works under the Berne Convention. See paras 13–36 et seq., below.

[101] See *Hansard*, H.L. Vol.491, cols 185, 186.

[102] CDPA 1988 s.213(4). See paras 13–73 et seq., below.

[103] CDPA 1988 s.213(3). See paras 13–58 et seq., below.

to the design, for 10 years from the end of the calendar year in which that first occurred.[104] Finally, competitors are entitled to seek licences of right in relation to the design in the last five years of its term.[105] The 1988 Act also contained provisions amending the Registered Designs Act 1949[106] and, in particular, increasing the period of protection available to registered designs to 25 years.

The provisions and effect of the 1988 Act are analysed in detail below. However, its effect has been to reduce significantly the role of copyright in the protection of industrial designs. Moreover, although design right has many similarities to copyright, the limitations placed on it by the 1988 Act mean that it should not be regarded as being copyright by another name and that the scope of its protection for industrial designs is much more limited than that previously offered by copyright.[107]

Importantly, it has been stated that, given the terms of the White Paper and the extremely complex economic arguments for and against protection, it is not possible to adopt a purposive approach to the construction of the 1988 Act. Indeed, as regards the vexed subject of spare parts, it must be remembered that although Parliament clearly intended to prevent original equipment manufacturers having absolute control over the supply of spare parts, it chose not to create a general spare parts exclusion. Hence, the design right provisions of the 1988 Act, cannot be construed with some sort of clear purpose in mind as regards spare parts. The courts "must construe [the 1988 Act] as it would be read by a reasonable reader. Here that means taking the language as it stands."[108]

European Community design—the background. The protection of industrial designs has also been the subject of considerable debate within the European Community. The basis of this debate was that the Treaty establishing the European Community provides for the establishment of an internal market, the abolition of obstacles to the free movement of goods in that market and the institution of a system to ensure that competition in that market is not distorted. The fact that the various Member States were providing widely differing levels of protection for industrial designs was seen as being contrary to those aims.[109] As a result, in June 1991, the European Commission produced a Green Paper on the Legal Protection of Industrial Designs.[110] This Paper suggested the creation of a completely new system to protect so-called Community designs and a measure of harmonisation of the Member States' national design laws. The Green Paper was followed by two proposals in December 1993—a proposed Directive on the Legal Protection of Designs[111] and a proposed Regulation for Community designs.[112] After a lengthy process and various amendments, the Directive was finally adopted in 1998 and the Regulation in 2002.   **13–30**

The Directive on the Legal Protection of Designs—further changes to the Registered Designs Act 1949. The Directive on the Legal Protection of De-   **13–31**

[104] CDPA 1988 s.216, see paras 13–103 et seq., below. In contrast, copyright now lasts for the lifetime of the author plus 70 years—see Ch.6, above.
[105] CDPA 1988 s.237. See paras 13–123 et seq., below.
[106] CDPA 1988 ss.265–273 and Sch.4.
[107] See Radcliffe and Caddick "Abbreviating the Scope of Design Right" [1997] E.I.P.R. 534.
[108] *Dyson Ltd v Qualtex (UK) Ltd* [2006] EWCA Civ 166; [2006] R.P.C. 31 at para.11 where Jacob L.J. commented that Parliament had chosen to adopt a "...compromise (some might say fudge) in the form of the language actually chosen in the Act.."
[109] See recitals 1 to 8 of the Regulation on Community designs (EC) No. 6/2002.
[110] III/F.5131/91.
[111] [1993] OJ C345/14; COM. (93) 344 final—SYN 464.
[112] [1994] OJ C29/20; COM. (93) 342 final—SYN 463.

signs[113] required Member States to harmonise their registered design law but did not affect the law of design right.[114] The Directive was implemented in the United Kingdom by the Registered Design Regulations 2001[115] which came into force on December 9, 2001. These Regulations made significant amendments to the Registered Designs Act 1949. In brief,[116] a wider definition of "design" was adopted and requirements were added that a design be new and have individual character. There were also newly drafted exclusions for designs dictated solely by technical function and designs of interconnections. The original draft of the Directive also included a provision excluding protection for the design of any component part of a complex product used for the purpose of repair of that complex product so as to restore its original appearance. However, this wide-ranging exclusion was controversial and was abandoned in favour of a "transitional" arrangement whereby Member States could maintain their existing law (which they could only change for something whose purpose was to liberalise the market for such parts).[117] As a result of these amendments, many of the provisions of the 1949 Act are the same as those contained in the Regulation on Community designs which is considered below. However, these amendments have removed many of the similarities in language that previously existed between the law relating to UK registered design law and UK design right.

13–32   **The Community Design Regulation—protection for Community designs.** Under the Regulation on Community Designs,[118] a Community design can be protected in two ways; first, automatic protection against copying lasting for three years from the date of first marketing and, secondly, upon registration, monopolistic protection lasting for up to 25 years. This two-tier system for the protection of Community designs is intended to operate (for the time being at least) alongside the national laws of the individual Member States. As mentioned above, much of the language governing Community design is the same as that which now applies to UK registered designs. The Regulation came into effect on March 6, 2002 and it became possible to apply for registration of a Community design on April 1, 2003. On September 24, 2007, the European Community acceded (with effect from January 1, 2008) to the Geneva Act of the Hague Agreement concerning the International Registration of Industrial Designs – thereby making the international protection of registered Community designs simpler.[119]

E. PROTECTION REQUIRED BY INTERNATIONAL AGREEMENTS

13–33   In determining the level of protection for industrial designs, the international treaty obligations to which the United Kingdom is subject must be borne in mind.

---

[113] Directive 98/71.

[114] The position regarding the effect of the Directive on the copyright provisions of the CDPA 1988 is more complicated. Art.17 of the Directive provides that a design protected by way of registration must also be eligible for copyright protection under the relevant Member State's law—although the extent of such protection and any conditions under which it is conferred remain a matter for each Member State. No changes have been made to the 1988 Act as a result of the Directive—presumably on the basis that the 1988 Act does not actually exclude the subsistence of copyright in registrable designs albeit that ss.51 and 52 of the 1988 Act effectively remove large swathes of the protection that copyright would otherwise provide for such designs. Given that recital 8 to the Directive states that the principle of cumulation of registered design and copyright protection is important, s.51 and possibly also s.52 may be the subject of future harmonisation.

[115] SI 2001/3949.

[116] The law relating to registered designs is considered in outline at paras 13–251 et seq., below.

[117] This proposed exclusion continues to be the subject of debate. See the Opinion and Reports at COM(2004) 582 final, COD(2004) 0203.

[118] Regulation (EC) No. 6/2002.

[119] For details of the Geneva Act of the Hague Convention (the text of the various Acts of the Convention, a guide to International registration and the current members), see the WIPO website: http://www.wipo.int [Accessed October 20, 2010].

(i) Paris Convention for the Protection of Industrial Property

The Paris Convention for the Protection of Industrial Property,[120] to which the **13–34** United Kingdom is a signatory, provides for the establishment of a Union of countries for the protection of industrial property, a phrase which the Convention provides is to be understood in its broadest sense and which includes industrial designs.[121] Article 2 provides that, in relation to industrial property, nationals of any country of the Union shall enjoy in all other countries the advantages which their respective laws then or thereafter may grant to their own nationals without the imposition of any requirement as to domicile.[122] By art.5*quinquies* of this Convention,[123] industrial designs are required to be protected in all countries of the European Union.

The 1988 Act. As has been seen, the protection of industrial designs under the **13–35** 1988 Act is largely dealt with by way of design right. It would appear that the intention of Parliament was that effect should be given to the United Kingdom's obligations under the Paris Convention by way of Orders in Council made under s.221 of the 1988 Act and providing for designs to qualify for design right in order to fulfil an international obligation.[124] A similar arrangement applies in relation to registered designs.[125]

(ii) Berne Convention

Literary and artistic works—article 2(1). The history and provisions of the **13–36** Berne Convention are considered elsewhere.[126] Under the Convention, the Convention states undertook to adopt measures necessary to protect literary and artistic works as defined by art.2(1) of the Paris Act (1971) thereof. Article 2(1) starts with the general statement that such works include every production in the literary, scientific and artistic domain, whatever may be the mode or form of expression. It then sets out a list of specific types of work to be included. The list is prefaced by the words "such as" and is not, therefore, intended to be exhaustive. However, the type of works covered by the general statement to art.2(1) must, it is suggested, be read in the light of the specific works listed. The listed works include (for present purposes) "... works of drawing, painting, architecture, sculpture, engraving and lithography; ...works of applied art; illustrations, maps, plans, sketches and three-dimensional works relative to geography, topography, architecture or science."

The category comprising "illustrations, maps, sketches and three-dimensional works relative to geography, topography, architecture or science" would not, it is suggested, include most industrial designs.[127] Moreover, the fact that those drafting the Convention saw fit to include this category in the art.2(1) list of works

---

[120] 1883. Revised at Brussels (1900), Washington (1911), the Hague (1925), London (1934), Lisbon (1958) and Stockholm (1967).

[121] Paris Convention arts 1(1)–(3).

[122] i.e. the same protection and the same legal remedies against any infringement—assuming that the conditions and formalities imposed on nationals are complied with, see Paris Convention art.2(1).

[123] i.e. art.5 of the Lisbon (1958) revision of the Paris Convention.

[124] See *Hansard*, H.L. Vol.491, cols 1128–1129. It would seem that Parliament took the view (expressed in the earlier White Paper on Intellectual Property and Innovation (1986, Cmnd. 9712) at paras 2.27 and 3.34) that the Paris Convention applies only as regards aesthetic designs of the kind which are registrable under the Registered Designs Act 1949 and not to the designs of functional articles. This was a view based, presumably, on the terms of arts 4 and 5 of the Paris Convention.

[125] Registered Designs Act 1949 ss.13–15.

[126] See Ch.23, below.

[127] A design sketch for a chair or of a machine cog, for example, would not relate to geography,

suggests that the category of "works of drawing, painting (etc.)" referred to earlier in the list was not intended to encompass all types of drawing or painting but only such of those works which could properly be seen as artistic.[128] On this basis, purely technical "non-artistic" works would be outside the scope of both of these two categories[129] and also, presumably, outside the scope of the general statement referred to above. However, the position is rather different as regards the numerous types of industrial design where some "artistic" element is required to attract buyers and also as regards those works which started their lives as truly artistic works but which were subsequently applied industrially.[130] Initially, the Berne Convention contained no express provision as to such works and different states took differing views of their obligations to protect them as artistic works.[131] These differences in opinion were debated at various conferences called to revise the Convention[132]and led to a provision being added to the Convention at the Berlin Act (1908) to the effect that "works of art applied to industry are protected to the extent permitted by the internal legislation of each country". However, this still left Convention States free to determine whether such works should be treated as works of art on the one hand or as industrial designs or models on the other and to deny protection if they decided on the latter. It was not until the Brussels Act (1948) that the Convention was amended so as to include "works of applied art" within the definition of works for which the Convention (prima facie) requires protection. This is the position maintained by the Stockholm (1967) and also (as appears above) by the Paris (1971) Acts of the Convention.

13–37   **Qualifications on protection—Article 2(7).** Although the definition of literary and artistic works contained in art.2(1) is potentially very wide and would, on its face, cover most industrial designs[133] or works applied industrially, the actual level of protection required by the Convention is significantly qualified by art.2(7) of the Paris Act. This provides that it is for the Convention States to determine the extent of the application of their laws to works of applied art, industrial designs and models, as well as the conditions under which such works, designs and models shall be protected. Article 2(7) also provides that works protected in the country of origin solely as designs and models are entitled in another Convention State only to such special protection as is granted in that country to designs and models, but if no such protection is granted in that country, such works are to be protected as artistic works.[134] Article 2(7) is subject to art.7(4) which provides that, whilst Convention States may determine the term of protection of works of applied art in so far as they are protected as artistic works, that term must be at least 25 years from the making of such a work.

---

topography, architecture or science, see Ricketson, *The Berne Convention for the Protection of Literary and Artistic Works: 1886–1986* at para.6.58.

[128] Ricketson, *The Berne Convention for the Protection of Literary and Artistic Works: 1886–1986*, at paras 6.28 and 6.29.

[129] Unless they related to geography, topography, architecture or science.

[130] Works, for example, such as a painting subsequently used as a pattern for wall paper or cartoon sketches subsequently used as a design for dolls and brooches (see *King Features Syndicate Inc v O. & M. Kleeman Ltd* [1941] A.C. 417—"the Popeye Case", see para.13–16, above.

[131] The differences being between those countries (notably France) which saw no need to distinguish between works or pure art and works of industrial art and those (such as the UK) which either wished to exclude them from the copyright sphere or at least to limit the scope of their copyright protection.

[132] The history of the various debates concerning the protection of industrially applied works is discussed in full in Ricketson, *The Berne Convention for the Protection of Literary and Artistic Works: 1886–1986*, at paras 6.44–6.54.

[133] Assuming they are not purely functional.

[134] art.2(7) of the Stockholm (1967) and Paris (1971) Acts was derived from art.2(5) of the Brussels Act (1900) but with the addition of the phrase commencing with the words "however, if no such protection ... (etc.)". See Ricketson, *The Berne Convention for the Protection of Literary and Artistic Works: 1886–1986*, at para.6.53.

The 1988 Act. It would seem that the 1988 Act complies with the United   **13–38**
Kingdom's obligations under the Berne Convention. Under the 1988 Act, full
copyright is retained in respect of articles which qualify as artistic works in their
own right. Moreover, copyright continues to subsist in artistic works which constitute industrial designs, however, the limitation placed on the scope of protection for such works by s.51 of the 1988 Act is a limitation permitted by art.2(7).
Similarly, the 1988 Act allows copyright to subsist in artistic works which are
industrially applied and the reduction in the period of copyright protection for
such works brought about by s.52 of the 1988 Act—namely to 25 years—is
permitted by arts 2(7) and 7(4).[135]

(iii) Agreement on Trade-Related Aspects of Intellectual Property Rights ("TRIPS")

The history of and background to the Agreement on Trade-Related Aspects   **13–39**
of Intellectual Property Rights ("TRIPS")[136] is considered elsewhere.[137] In
outline, under its provisions, Member States agreed to give effect to the provisions of that Agreement (whilst being free to determine the appropriate method
for so doing). They also agreed to accord the treatment provided for in the Agreement to the nationals of other Member States.[138] Under art.25(1) of TRIPS,
Member States must provide for the protection of independently created industrial
designs that are new or original but they are entitled to provide that designs are
not new or original if they do not significantly differ from known designs or
combinations of known design features and also that protection need not extend
to designs dictated by essentially technical or functional considerations. Article
26 of TRIPS deals with the nature of the protection to be provided; the type of
acts capable of being infringements,[139] limited exceptions from protection,[140] and
a minimum period of protection lasting 10 years.[141] Part III of TRIPS sets out the
way in which the relevant rights may be enforced and the type of remedies which
may be provided.

The 1988 Act. It would seem that the United Kingdom's law of registered designs   **13–40**
complies with TRIPS.[142] If TRIPS applies in relation to the unregistered design
right provisions of the 1988 Act, those too would seem to comply.[143]

---

[135] For detailed discussions of CDPA 1988,ss.51 and 52, see below at paras 13–301 et seq. and 13–
320 et seq. respectively.

[136] Concluded at Geneva on December 15, 1993, GATT document MTN/FA II-AIC.

[137] See Ch.23, below.

[138] TRIPS art.1.

[139] To be an infringement, an act must be undertaken for commercial purposes, TRIPS art.26(1).

[140] art.26(2) which also provides that such exceptions should not unreasonably conflict with the
normal exploitation of protected industrial designs nor unreasonably prejudice the legitimate
interests of the owner of the protected design, taking account of the legitimate interests of third
parties.

[141] TRIPS art.26(3).

[142] For a brief discussion of registered designs see paras 13–272 et seq., below.

[143] In *Re Azrak Hamway International Inc* [1997] R.P.C. 134, it was argued that the design right
licence of right provisions were contrary to TRIPS because they could result in the reduction in
the period of effective protection to less than the 10 years required by art.26(3) and because they
did not constitute limited exceptions within the meaning of art.26(2). This argument was rejected
on the grounds that TRIPS had no application in relation to unregistered design right provisions
of the 1988 Act (as opposed to the registered design provisions of the Registered Designs Act
1949) and that, even if it did, the licence of right provisions (with their provision for licence fees)
would not be contrary to art.26. For a discussion of design right see paras 13–41 et seq., below,
and for licences of right see paras 13–126 et seq., below.

2. INTRODUCTION

13–41   **Nature of design right.** Design right is a property right which subsists in certain original designs.[144] Like copyright, it is not a monopoly right but rather makes copying an infringement. Like copyright, it subsists automatically without the need for any formality such as registration or the deposit of documents. However, the scope of protection for industrial designs under design right is intended to be far narrower than that which copyright often provided before the 1988 Act. Thus, the 1988 Act places wide-ranging limitations on the type of designs which will attract design right protection.[145] Moreover, design right protection where it is available lasts for a maximum of 15 years and, in many cases, for nearer to 10 years.[146] In the last five years of its term, licences of right are available.[147]

13–42   **Interrelationship of design right with copyright.** Design right subsists in certain designs; copyright in (inter alia) certain artistic and literary works. If, therefore, a design is recorded or embodied in such a work, there is a possibility that both design right and copyright will subsist. The 1988 Act does not prevent this but instead seeks to exclude dual protection by both design right and copyright. Thus, s.51 provides that most acts of industrial copying of industrial designs will not infringe any relevant copyright.[148] Such acts are actionable (if at all[149]) as infringements of design right. Where s.51 does not apply, s.236 provides that it is not an infringement of the design right to do anything which is an infringement of copyright. These provisions are considered in more detail later in this Chapter.

13–43   **Interrelationship of design right and registered designs.** There are different definitions of a design for the purposes of design right on the one hand and for the purposes of registration under the Registered Designs Act 1949 on the other.[150] However, many designs will satisfy both definitions. The 1988 Act does nothing to prevent dual protection where this occurs. It should be noted that the proprietor of the registered design and the owner of the design right are not necessarily the same person[151] although, where they are, an assignment of the registered design would carry the design right with it unless the contrary appears.[152]

13–44   **Design right issues.** In approaching a design right case, the following questions may need to be addressed:

    (i) What is the actual design to be relied on—is it a "design" in which design right is capable of subsisting?

    (ii) Does design right actually subsist in the design—i.e. (1) were the necessary conditions for subsistence of design right satisfied when the design was created and, if so, (2) does design right still subsist or has the term expired?

---

[144] CDPA 1988 s.213(1).

[145] The design must be original and not commonplace. Further, any so-called "must fit" and "must match" features are excluded from protection.

[146] For the duration of design right see paras 13–105 et seq., below. Copyright protection is now for the life of the artist plus 70 years.

[147] For the design right licence of right provisions see paras 13–126 et seq., below.

[148] Under CDPA 1988 s.51, the copyright in a design document or model recording or embodying the design for anything other than an artistic work or typeface is not infringed by the making of articles to that design or by the copying of articles made to the design. For a full discussion of s.51, see paras 13–301 et seq., below.

[149] The fact that CDPA 1988 s.51 operates does not mean that there must be a claim in design right; s.51 operates regardless of whether or not design right subsists in the relevant design.

[150] For the design right definition of a design see paras 13–45 et seq., below; for the Registered Design Act 1949 definition, see paras 13–276 et seq., above.

[151] See paras 13–114 et seq., below.

[152] CDPA 1988 s.224, see para.13–121, below.

(iii)   Who owns the design right—this involves asking (1) who was the first owner of the design right and (2) has ownership passed (in law or equity) to some other person?

(iv)   What rights does the design right owner have?

 (v)   In the particular circumstances of the case, are there any reasons why the exclusive rights of the design right owner cannot be asserted—i.e. do any of the usual defences to an action for infringement apply?

(vi)   Are the owner's rights, although exercisable, subject to any form of control?—i.e. are licences of right available?

(vii)   In the case of infringement, what remedies are available?

3. DESIGN RIGHT: SUBJECT MATTER OF PROTECTION

A. Definition of Design

Section 213(2)—definition of design. For design right to subsist, there must be a design within the meaning of s.213(2) of the 1988 Act. This provides: "design" means the design of any aspect of the shape or configuration (whether internal or external) of the whole or part of an article.   **13–45**

The "design". This definition is extremely wide. For example, in the case of a teapot,[153] a claimant may choose to rely on the design of the whole pot but may also rely on the design of one or more of its parts or aspects—such as the spout, the handle, the lid or even a part of the lid.[154] This allows a claimant to define the design relied on in a way that most closely matches what the defendant is alleged to have taken.[155] It also allows the claimant to rely on a number of alternative designs. Thus, a claimant may assert design right in the design of an article as a whole and/or in the design of an article minus certain features and/or in the design of specified aspects of that article.[156] If the article is formed of component parts, the claimant can also rely on the designs of those components as articles in their own right, or as aspects of the design of the whole article.[157]   **13–46**

Given the width of this definition, it is important to identify clearly each separate design being relied upon. As will be seen, the precise identification of the design relied upon is important for a number of reasons. First, it is the design

---

[153] The example used in *Ocular Sciences Ltd v Aspect Vision Care Ltd* [1997] R.P.C. 289 at 422.

[154] See *Farmers Build Ltd v Carier Bulk Materials Handling Ltd* [1999] R.P.C. 461, at 475 and 483–486, where the Court of Appeal upheld claims to design right in the design of the whole of a slurry-separating machine but also in the designs of certain component parts (both as articles in their own right and as parts of the machine). See also *Spraymiser Ltd v Wrightway Marketing Ltd* [2000] E.C.D.R. 349 (design for configurable wooden figure of a man) and *A. Fulton Co Ltd v Grant Barnett & Co Ltd* [2001] R.P.C. 257 at paras 36 and 38 (designs of handles and carrying cases for folding umbrellas).

[155] See *Ocular Sciences Ltd v Aspect Vision Care Ltd* [1997] R.P.C. 289 at 422 and *A Fulton Co Ltd v Totes Isotoner (UK) Ltd* [2004] R.P.C. 16 at para.34 and also at para.23 where Jacob L.J. rejected the idea that this left the law ripe for abuse.

[156] Such as the umbrella case minus part of its cuff in *A Fulton Co Ltd v Totes Isotoner (UK) Ltd* [2004] R.P.C. 16 (a claim based on the design of the whole article failed so that the alternative plea was important) or the umbrella handle minus its protuberant rim in *A Fulton Co Ltd v Grant Barnett & Co Ltd* [2001] R.P.C. 257 at 270.

[157] See *Farmers Build Ltd v Carier Bulk Materials Handling Ltd* [1999] R.P.C. 461, at 475 and 483–486. *Novum (Overseas) Ltd v Iceland Foods Plc* [2002] EWHC 53 shows the importance of pleading alternatives. There a claim based on the design of a freezer as a whole succeeded whereas claims based on the designs of the internal dividers of the freezer and of the gasket between its lid and main body failed (due, respectively, to the "must fit" and commonplace exclusions—see paras 13–57 and 13–58 et.seq., below). For the problems which the choice of design may cause in relation to the "must fit" exclusion, see para.13–60, below).

relied on which is tested for originality.[158] Thus a design which combines a number of features may be original even if some or even all of those component features would not be original if looked at individually.[159] Secondly, one must identify the design in question in order to identify its designer and, hence, the design right owner. In the case of an article on which a team of designers has worked, the design right in the overall design of the whole article may be jointly owned by all of the design team whereas the design rights in the designs of its various parts may be owned by different individuals.[160] Finally, the way in which the design is identified may have serious implications when it comes to proving infringement.[161] A careful pleading of alternative designs is, therefore, advisable. In this regard, it must be borne in mind that design right does not subsist in some underlying abstraction or idea. The claimant's pleading must therefore identify particular aspects of the shape or configuration that are apparent from the physical manifestation of the design (whether that manifestation is on paper or in the product).[162]

13–47   **No requirement of artistic merit or eye appeal.** As with copyright, the relevant design need not have any artistic merit nor need it appeal to the eye. Thus, in principle, design right may subsist in a functional design as well as in one which is intended to be attractive.[163] It is suggested that the design may even be of something which is invisible to the naked eye in normal use.[164] Further, as a design may be described or defined by way of dimensions, very small changes in those dimensions may give rise to a separate design.[165]

13–48   **Any aspect.** It seems that the word "aspect" means something that is discernable or recognisable (although not necessarily visible to the naked eye) in the shape or configuration of an article.[166] As the teapot example shows, an article or even a part of an article may comprise many aspects of shape or configuration. Each of those aspects is capable of being a design for these purposes and, subject to the exclusions discussed below,[167] each is a design in which design right may subsist.

13–49   **Shape or configuration of the whole or part of an article.** The relevant design must be of an aspect of the shape or configuration (whether internal or external) of an article or part of an article. The words "shape" and "configuration" are not

---

[158] CDPA 1988 s.213(1) and s.213(4).
[159] See *Farmers Build Ltd v Carier Bulk Materials Handling Ltd* [1999] R.P.C. 461 at 486 and *Ocular Sciences Ltd v Aspect Vision Care Ltd* [1997] R.P.C. 289 at 429–430. For a full discussion of originality, see paras 13–70 et seq., below. See also *Ultraframe (UK) Ltd v Eurocell Building Plastics Ltd* [2005] EWCA Civ 761; [2005] R.P.C. 36.
[160] See para.13–88, below.
[161] See para.13–152, below. The test for infringement in CDPA 1988 s.226(2) requires a court to ask whether the allegedly infringing article has been made wholly or substantially to the claimant's design. This is relatively straightforward where the claimant's *design* is of a whole article for there the comparison being made is usually of like with like. It is less straightforward where the design in question is of part of an article.
[162] *Rolawn Ltd v Turfmech Machinery Ltd* [2008] EWHC 989 at paras 77–84; [2008] R.P.C. 27 where it was held that the claimant was not entitled to claim design right in "the concept of a mower which has arms folding back ..." nor in "the concept of a tank between two vertical supports."
[163] Subject to the exclusion in relation to surface decoration, see paras 13–69 et seq., below.
[164] Because, for example, it is too small or because it is internal and concealed. See *A Fulton Co Ltd v Totes Isotoner (UK) Ltd* [2004] R.P.C. 16. per Jacob L.J. at para.30. For the position in relation to Community designs, see para.13–205, below.
[165] See *Ocular Sciences Ltd v Aspect Vision Care Ltd* [1997] R.P.C. 289 at 422.
[166] *A Fulton & Co Ltd v Totes Isotoner (UK) Ltd* [2004] R.P.C. 16 per Jacob L.J. at paras 30 and 31. See also *Dyson Ltd v Qualtex (UK) Ltd* [2006] EWCA Civ 166; [2006] R.P.C. 31 at paras 22–26: protection extends to a "mere twiddle" provided it is discernible or recognisable even if considered as part of the whole article it is visually insignificant.
[167] i.e. the exclusions set out in CDPA 1988 s.213(3), see paras 13–54 et seq., below.

defined by the 1988 Act. However, "shape" suggests the outward appearance or external form of an article whilst "configuration" suggests the arrangement of its various interrelating parts. For many years, the same words were included in the definition of a design for registered design purposes,[168] and in that context it was stated that they might for practical purposes be considered as synonymous.[169] However, this may not always be true. Thus, in *Cow & Co Ltd v Cannon Rubber Manufacturers Ltd*, it was stated that the ribbing on a hot water bottle might be configuration but not shape[170] although a better example of a distinction might be the polygonal patches that make up a patchwork quilt.[171] In the design right context, it has been decided that the word configuration may apply to the design of the components present in a circuit board and their interconnection even though a circuit board made to that design could have a wide range of shapes.[172] There is no reason in principle why a simple geometric shape such as a sphere or a spiral or a combination of spirals may not be a "design".[173] Similarly, there is no reason in principle why a very small part or parts of an article should not be the subject of design protection.[174]

As design right is concerned with "any aspect" of the shape or configuration of the whole or part of an article, there is no reason why the relevant design should not be of a two-dimensional aspect of shape (provided it does not fall within the surface decoration exclusion[175]). Thus, the design of a template used in dressmaking or of a stencil may be a design for these purposes.[176] However, the mere use

---

[168] Until it was amended by the Registered Designs Regulations 2001, the Registered Designs Act 1949 s.1 defined a design as "features of shape, configuration, pattern or ornament applied to an article ...".

[169] See *Kestos Ltd v Kempat Ltd* (1936) 53 R.P.C. 139 at 152.

[170] [1959] R.P.C. 240, per Lord Evershed M.R. at 244. It could be argued to the contrary that the ribbing did help define the shape of the bottle. See *Lambretta Clothing Co Ltd v Teddy Smith (UK) Ltd* [2005] R.P.C. 6 at para.20 per Jacob L.J. (with whom Mance L.J. agreed on this point).

[171] The patchwork quilt example was criticised by Jacob L.J. in *Lambretta Clothing Co Ltd v Teddy Smith (UK) Ltd* [2005] R.P.C. 6 at para.28. However, his reasoning is difficult to reconcile with his comments regarding two- or three-dimensional designs (at para.24). Moreover, a quilt is an article, and it is difficult to see why the patches that make up that quilt should not be seen an aspect of its configuration. It is submitted that, in this respect, the views of Sedley L.J. in *Lambretta* (see para.89) are to be preferred.

[172] *Mackie Designs Inc v Behringer Specialised Studio Equipment (UK) Ltd* [1999] R.P.C. 717 at p.721 where Pumfrey J. commented that the configuration of an article includes its relative arrangement of parts or elements. In *Lambretta Clothing Co Ltd v Teddy Smith (UK) Ltd* [2005] R.P.C. 6, Jacob L.J. commented that there may well be force in the criticism of Mackie on the basis that a mere schematic diagram is not the design of an article or part of an article. However, the reasoning in Mackie appears to be consistent with comments made by Laddie J. in *Ocular Sciences Ltd v Aspect Vision Care Ltd* [1997] R.P.C. 289 at p.429 as regards semi-conductor topographies. See also *Vitof Ltd v Altoft* [2006] EWHC 1678 (Ch) in which designs for the positioning of components, the printed copper connecting layers and the holes in the board were held to be protected.

[173] *Sales v Stromberg* [2005] EWHC 1624 (Ch); [2006] F.S.R. 7.

[174] *Red Spider Technology v Omega Completions Technology* [2010] EWHC 59 (Mann J.) at para.127. The court rejected an analogy with copyright (where copyright does not subsist in a single word) and found that the reference to "whole or part of an article" in s.213(2) meant that the design of a 15-degree angle could in principle qualify for protection. It has been pointed out that the ability of a claimant to select small parts of an overall design can give a distorted impression of what a defendant has done and can come close to reversing the burden of proof—see *Virgin Aircraft Airways Ltd v Premium Aircraft Interiors Group Ltd* [2009] EWHC 26; [2009] E.C.D.R. 11 at para.29.

[175] *Dyson Ltd v Qualtex (UK) Ltd* [2006] EWCA Civ 166, [2006] R.P.C. 31 at para.74. For the surface decoration exclusion, see paras 13–69 et seq., below.

[176] It may be argued that a stencil made to the design is itself an artistic work within CDPA 1988 s.4(2)(b) ("engraving, etching, lithograph, woodcut or similar work"). If so, then s.51 would not apply and any design right protection would be excluded in favour of copyright protection, CDPA 1988 s.236. See paras 13–168 et seq., below.

of colour (even if it is not part of the surface decoration) would not be an aspect of configuration.[177]

13–50   An article. The design must be of an aspect of the shape or configuration of the whole or part of an article. Although the word "article" is not defined by the 1988 Act,[178] the fact that the article has to have "shape or configuration" plainly suggests something which has its own separate physical form and which is, in that sense, three dimensional.[179] Thus a contact lens, a mobile phone case, a breast prosthesis are all articles.[180] Similarly, a car or an electrical transformer[181] are articles even though they are made up of various component parts each of which may also be an article in its own right. A chair leg may be an article if it is made separately from the rest of the chair, but not if it is made by shaping the same piece of metal used for the rest of the chair frame. A kitchen unit is an article but the complete fitted kitchen is not.[182] Although the word "article" suggests something in three dimensions, there seems to be no reason why it should exclude objects which are usually regarded as flat but which nevertheless have a physical form such as, for example, a paper template or a stencil.[183] It has been said that the word "article" is not intended to have a restricted meaning, that it could just as well be replaced by the word "thing" and could include a living or formerly living thing.[184]

13–51   Design right is concerned with the design not with the article. Although the design relied upon must be the design of the whole or part of an article, it is important to bear in mind that design right is concerned with the protection of the relevant design and not with the protection of the particular article on which that design happens to be recorded or to which that design happens to be first applied. The design may equally be applied to other articles.[185]

13–52   Design of the whole or part *of* an article. The design must also be of the whole or part *of* an article. In this regard, it is submitted that it is immaterial whether

---

[177] *Lambretta Clothing Co Ltd v Teddy Smith (UK) Ltd* [2004] EWCA Civ 886; [2005] R.P.C. 6 per Jacob L.J. at paras 14–29. On this point, Mance L.J. agreed with Jacob L.J. (para.78) although Sedley L.J. did not (para.88).

[178] By contrast, before it was amended by the Registered Designs Regulations 2001, the Registered Designs Act 1949 s.44(1) defined an "article" (for registered design purposes) as "an article of manufacture and includes any part of an article if that part is made and sold separately." That definition was repealed by Sch.2 of the 2001 Regulations.

[179] The words "shape" and "configuration" by themselves have been said in the registered design context to signify something in three dimensions, see *Kestos Ltd v Kempat Ltd* (1936) 53 R.P.C. 139 at 152.

[180] Such articles being the subject matter of, respectively, *Ocular Sciences Ltd v Aspect Vision Care Ltd* [1997] R.P.C. 289; *Parker & Parker v Tidball* [1997] F.S.R. 680; and *Amoena (UK) Ltd v Trulife Ltd* Unreported, May 23, 1995.

[181] See, respectively, *Ford Motor Co Ltd and Iveco Fiat SpA's Applications* [1993] R.P.C. 399 (Registered Designs Appeal Tribunal) and [1994] R.P.C. 554 (Divisional Court) and *Electronic Techniques (Anglia) Ltd v Critchley Components Ltd* [1997] F.S.R. 401.

[182] See *Mark Wilkinson Furniture Ltd v Woodcraft Designs (Radcliffe) Ltd* [1998] F.S.R. 63 at 73 where the meaning of the word "article" was considered in the context of the "must match" exclusion (see CDPA 1988 s.213(3)(b)(ii) and para.13–64, below).

[183] See para.13–49, above. Further, the word "articles" is used in a copyright context to describe items such as greetings cards, maps, playing cards, etc. which, though flat, have a physical form, see the Copyright (Industrial Process and Excluded Articles) (No.2) Order 1989 (SI 1989/1070) art.3(1)(c).

[184] *Ocular Sciences Ltd v Aspect Vision Care Ltd* [1997] R.P.C. 289 at 425 where the human eye (against which a contact lens must fit) was found to be an article for the purposes of the "must fit" exclusion (see CDPA 1988 s.213(3)(b)(i) and para.13–60, below).

[185] See *Electronic Techniques (Anglia) Ltd v Critchley Components Ltd* [1997] F.S.R. 401 at 418 where the example given was of the design of a spoon with a non-commonplace handle. There was, it was said, no reason why the designer should only be entitled to protection for the application of his design to spoons when it was readily apparent that the same design could be applied to other articles, such as forks.

there is any intention that the design should actually be applied to such an article.[186] A sketch of an imaginary vase is a design *of* a vase even if the artist has no intention of making vases to his design. However, in such a case, the artist may well be able to rely on copyright protection against the copying of his sketch as an artistic work rather than on design right.[187]

Kits. A person who designs or makes a kit of parts cannot necessarily be said to   **13–53**
be designing or making the article which results from the assembly of the kit. Because of this, s.260 of the 1988 Act provides that the design right provisions apply in relation to a kit as they apply in relation to the assembled article; a "kit" being defined as a complete or substantially complete set of components intended to be assembled into an article.[188] However, this does not affect the question whether design right subsists in any of the components of the kit.[189] This provides some flexibility. It allows the designer of a kit of parts to choose whether to assert design right in the design of the completed article or to rely on the designs of the various component parts of the kit. The former may be preferable where it would otherwise be possible to avoid infringing by making complete articles. Conversely, the provision also allows the designer of a whole article to prevent others infringing his design right by the making and selling of kits.[190]

B. EXCLUDED DESIGNS

Introduction. Even if there is a design within the meaning of the definition   **13–54**
discussed above, ss.213(3) and 213(5A) of the 1988 Act contain various exclusions from design right. The exclusions contained in s.213(3) play an important part in the scheme of the 1988 Act, namely to ensure that design right, whilst providing a limited amount of protection for original designs, did not unfairly restrict fair competition.[191]

Section 213(3). This provides that design right does not subsist in: **13–55**
    (a) a method or principle of construction,
    (b) features of shape or configuration of an article which—

        (i) enable the article to be connected to, or placed in, around or against, another article so that either article may perform its function, or

        (ii) are dependent upon the appearance of another article of which the article is intended by the designer to form an integral part, or

    (c) surface decoration.

Before considering these exclusions in detail, it is important to note that these exclusions only operate to exclude design right from the sort of features set out above. Thus, where the design relied upon comprises a number of features only some of which fall within these exclusions, this does not mean that design right

---

[186] It is suggested that it is for this reason that CDPA 1988 s.51, having defined "a design" in virtually identical terms to s.213(2) (i.e. the design ... *of* an article), then refers to such a design being "... *for* anything other than an artistic work or typeface", see para.13–312, below.

[187] Although the sketch is a design *of* an article, it is not a design *for* an article other than an artistic work. Thus, CDPA 1988 s.51 would not exclude copyright protection and s.236 provides that an act will not infringe design right if it would infringe copyright, see paras 13–312 et seq., below.

[188] See CDPA 1988 s.260(1).

[189] CDPA 1988 s.260(?)

[190] See *Hansard*, H.C. SCE, col.592.

[191] See para.13–29, above, and *Hansard*, H.L. Vol.489, col.1479.

cannot subsist in the design as a whole. It simply means that design right cannot be claimed in those excluded features on their own.[192]

(i) A method or principle of construction

13–56   Under s.213(3)(a) of the 1988 Act, design right is excluded from "a method or principle of construction".

It could be argued that this exclusion is unnecessary on the basis that a method or principle of construction is the process by which shape or configuration is imparted to an article, rather than being a design.[193] However, the exclusion (or one similar) was a part of registered design law for many years,[194] and it serves to emphasise that the law of design is only concerned with the appearance of an article (or part of an article) and not with the process by which the article is to be made. It is intended to ensure that designers cannot create an effective monopoly over articles made in a particular way.[195] In essence, protection is not given to a design idea as to the way in which to construct a product—but only to the specific design appearance of that product which has been created by the designer.[196] For the purposes of considering whether a design is excluded on this ground, the notional addressee of the design document is a person familiar with the subject matter of the drawing (as is the case for infringement); and descriptive material referring to part or parts of the drawing may be taken into account.[197]

13–57   **Examples:**

(1) The exclusion means that design right does not subsist in a "design" which requires an article to be made of a particular substance. A pig-slurry-separating machine included as a component part a roller made of laminated rubber of varying degrees of hardness. The shape of the roller was capable of being protected, but the "design" of the type of materials used in constructing it was not because it was a method of construction.[198]

(2) The exclusion can apply where the way in which an article is made has an

---

[192] See *Ultraframe UK Ltd v Fielding* [2003] R.P.C. 23 at paras 69–71 and 78 (a point not challenged on appeal, [2004] R.P.C. 24).

[193] See *Kestos Ltd v Kempat Ltd* (1936) 53 R.P.C. 139 at p.151, a registered design case. See also *Dyson Ltd v Qualtex (UK) Ltd* [2006] EWCA Civ 166; [2006] R.P.C. 31 at para.74.

[194] Although a process of manufacture was not expressly excluded by the Patents, Trademarks and Designs Act 1883 (46 & 47 Vict. c.57) or the Patents and Designs Act 1907 (7 Edw. 7, c.29), it was found to be implicit in the definitions of a design (being a design for the pattern, shape, configuration or ornament of an article) in s.60 of the 1883 Act and s.93 of the 1907 Act), see *Moody v Tree* (1892) R.P.C. 333 and *Bayer's Design* (1907) 24 R.P.C 65. The exclusion was made express when the 1907 Act was amended by the Patents and Designs Act 1919 (9 & 10 Geo. 5, c.80) s.19 and was carried over into the Registered Designs Act 1949, (see s.1(3) prior to its amendment by the CDPA 1988, and s.1(1)(a) thereafter). However, the exclusion has now been removed from registered design law by reason of the amendments to the 1949 Act made by the Registered Designs Regulations 2001. See paras 13–272 et seq., below.

[195] See *Gardex Ltd v Sorata Ltd* [1986] R.P.C. 623 at 638. See also *Landor & Hawa International Ltd v Azure Designs Ltd* [2006] EWCA Civ 1285; [2007] F.S.R. 9 at paras 13 and 14, approving this passage and adopting the following passage from Russell-Clarke, *Copyright in Industrial Design*: "The real meaning is this: that no design shall be construed so widely as to give its proprietor a monopoly in a method or principle of construction. What he gets is a monopoly for one particular individual and specific appearance. If it is possible to get several different appearances, which all embody the general features which he claims, then those features are too general and amount to a method or principle of construction. In other words, any conception which is so general as to allow several different appearances as being made within it, is too broad and will be invalid". See also *Bailey v Haynes* [2006] EWPCC 5; [2007] F.S.R. 10 at paras 51–62 and *Rolawn Ltd v Turfmech Machinery Ltd* [2008] EWHC 989 at paras 92–96.

[196] *Red Spider Technology v Omega Completions Technology* [2010] EWHC 59 (Mann J.) at para.124.

[197] *Landor & Hawa International Ltd v Azure Designs Ltd* [2006] EWCA Civ 1285; [2007] F.S.R. 9 at para.15.

[198] See *Farmers Build Ltd v Carier Bulk Materials Handling Ltd* Unreported March 26, 1997,

impact on its shape or configuration. For example, the "design" for stitching together a mobile phone case with the seams turned in, whilst affecting the appearance of the case, has been held to be a method of construction from which design right was excluded.[199] By contrast, it has also been held that a design for outward pointing seams on a case for a folding umbrella was not a method of construction.[200] On the facts, it is easy to see why the courts reached these differing conclusions. However, if one starts from the assumption that both the inward and outward pointing seams were aspects of the design of their respective articles, it is not easy to define the legal basis on which the exclusion was found to operate in one case but not in the other.[201]

(3) Whilst a claimant was entitled to claim protection for its particular design of windows and cutaways in the housing of a water injection valve, the exclusion meant it could not claim protection for "the concept" or general idea of having rectangular cutaways. Claims relating to the design of the reduction in diameter of the valve and the design of a poppet forming part of the valve were rejected on the same basis.[202]

(4) In the registered designs context, it has been held that the exclusion of a method or principle of construction did not apply to a design whereby the two diagonal hoops on a baby's square activity mat crossed at right angles to each other at the top. What the claimant was seeking to protect was not the method of construction by which the mat was put together, but rather its appearance when put together. It would have been possible for the defendant to design a mat that worked in the same way but that looked different.[203]

(5) Under earlier registered designs legislation, an exclusion of designs amounting to a "mode of construction" was held to apply to a design for the "pattern of a basket consisting of osiers being working in singly with the butt ends being outside",[204] and to a design whereby a corset had "gores or gussets cut horizontally and from the front of the busk towards the back of the corset".[205]

---

transcript at 19 and 29. The point was not raised in the Court of Appeal ([1999] R.P.C. 461). In that case, the exclusion may have been unnecessary in that the "design" for the way in which the roller was made did not define its shape or configuration (thus, design right could never have subsisted in it).

[199] *Parker & Parker v Tidball* [1997] F.S.R. 680 at 696 where it was also doubted whether such a "design" was of an aspect of shape or configuration of an article.

[200] See *A. Fulton Co Ltd v Grant Barnett & Co Ltd* [2001] R.P.C. 257 at para.70.

[201] The distinction between the cases is probably due to the fact that the designer of the umbrella case in *Fulton* [2001] R.P.C. 257 had clearly intended to include the outward pointing seams as a part of his design whereas the designer of the phone case in *Parker & Parker v Tidball* [1997] F.S.R. 680, had probably not consciously "designed" the inward pointing seams or, if he had, that they were simply a "conception of some general characteristic of shape and configuration necessitated by the mode or principle of construction," and therefore excluded from protection (see *Pugh v Riley Cycle Co Ltd* (1912) 29 R.P.C. 196 at para.202 and *Christopher Tasker's Design Right References* [2001] R.P.C. 3 at paras 28 and 33). However, this distinction does not appear clear from the judgments. It may be that the result in *Parker* illustrates the danger of assuming that the claimant's design must include all of the features that appear on an article made to that design.

[202] *Red Spider Technology v Omega Completions Technology* [2010] EWHC 59 (Mann J.) at paras 124-126.

[203] See *Isaac Oren v Red Box Factory* [1999] F.S.R. 785. This exclusion has been removed from the RDA 1949 by the Registered Designs Regulations 2001.

[204] See *Moody v Tree* (1892) 9 R.P.C. 33 at 35, a case decided under the Patents Trademarks and Designs Act 1883, where it was stated that such a "design" was not intended to represent a peculiar shape or pattern of a basket but, rather, the way in which it was to be made.

[205] See *Bayer's Design* (1907) 24 R.P.C 65 at 79, another registered design case decided under the Patents, Trademarks and Designs Act 1883 which cited *Moody v Tree* (1892) 9 R.P.C. 333 and

(ii) The "must fit" and "must match" exclusions

13–58   The "must fit" and the "must match" exclusions reflect Parliament's wish to allow competition where there is no design freedom for either functional or aesthetic reasons.[206] Whilst these exclusions are clearly intended to permit competition in the supply of spare parts and accessories, they are of general application
and for this reason, they cannot be construed with some sort of clear purpose in
mind as regards spare parts but must be construed as they would be read by a reasonable reader using the language as it stands.[207] Whilst these exclusions are a
significant limitation on the scope of design right, it is important to bear in mind
that they only permit copying of those design features which satisfy the terms of
the exclusions. The other features of the design may remain protected.[208] The
scope of these exclusions should not, therefore, be overplayed: they "do not give
a *carte blanche* for pattern spares. Those who wish to make spares during the period of design right must design their own spares and cannot just copy every
detail of the [original equipment manufacturer's] part. To be on the safe side they
will have to make them different as far as possible—for trying to navigate by the
chart provided by this crude statute (i.e. the 1988 Act) is a risky business."[209]

It should also be noted that the terms "must fit" and "must match", whilst convenient, are not terms used in the 1988 Act. It is, therefore, important to look at
the actual wording of the relevant statutory provisions.[210]

(iii) The "must fit" exclusion

13–59   Section 213(3)(b)(i) of the 1988 Act contains the so-called "must fit" or
"interface" exclusion.[211] It provides that design right will not subsist in:"features
of shape or configuration of an article which . . . enable the article to be connected to, or placed in, around or against, another so that either article may
perform its function".

The wording of the exclusion falls into two parts; the first part requires that
there be the requisite relationship between two articles. The second limits the
scope of the exclusion by requiring that that relationship be made so that either
article may perform its function.

13–60   **The relationship between the two articles.** The "must-fit" exclusion is
concerned with the relationship or "interface" between two articles.[212] The nature
of this relationship is broadly defined and there is no reason why the word
"article" should be construed narrowly. Indeed, it has been said that it could have

---

where it was commented that one might as well seek to claim that the bonding together of bricks
using iron bands was a design.

[206] See *Hansard*, H.L. Vol.489, col.1479; H.L. Vol.491, cols 1111–1113; H.L. Vol.494, col.109 and
H.C. Vol.132, cols 597–598. In *Mars UK Ltd v Tecknowledge Ltd* [2000] F.S.R. 138, it was
stated that, given the enactment of the "must fit" and "must match" exclusions, there is no place
in design right cases for any common law spare parts defence. For further background, see paras
13–21 and 13–28, above.

[207] *Dyson Ltd v Qualtex (UK) Ltd* [2006] EWCA Civ 166; [2006] R.P.C. 31 at para.11 where Jacob
L.J. commented that Parliament had chosen to adopt a "...compromise (some might say fudge) in
the form of the language actually chosen in the Act.."

[208] See *Ultraframe UK Ltd v Fielding* [2005] R.P.C. 7 at paras 69–71, 74 and 78. See also *Ultraframe (UK) Ltd v Eurocell Building Plastics Ltd* [2004] EWHC 1785 at para.113.

[209] *Dyson Ltd v Qualtex (UK) Ltd* [2006] EWCA Civ 166; [2006] R.P.C. 31 at para.126 (Jacob L.J.).

[210] See *Dyson Ltd v Qualtex (UK) Ltd* [2006] EWCA Civ 166 at para.27.

[211] In relation to registered designs, there is now an "interconnections" exclusion which appears to
be somewhat more generous to designers than design right's "must fit" exclusion—see s.1C(2) of
the 1949 Act (as amended) and paras 13–278 and 13–223, below.

[212] i.e. the article embodying the design features in issue and the article with which it interfaces—see
Ocular Sciences Ltd v Aspect Vision Care Ltd [1997] R.P.C. 289 at 425.

been replaced by the word "thing"; and that it might include a living or a formerly living thing such as a human eye.[213]

The exclusion is of features of shape or configuration of an article. It is submitted that the "article" for these purposes (i.e. for the purposes of s.213(3)) need not be the same article by reference to which the design right claim is framed (i.e. for the purposes of s.213(2)). Thus, where a claimant relies on design right in a design of an article (the "composite article") made from various component articles, the "must fit" exclusion will apply to those features which allow the composite article to interface with another article. It is, however, unclear whether the exclusion will also apply to those features which allow its various component articles to interface with each other.[214] If it does, then where the claimant relies on the design of a car, the interface exclusion would not only apply to the external interface features of the car (if there are any), but would also apply to the numerous internal interface features of its many component parts.

So that either article may perform its function. The interface must be made so **13–61** that either article may perform its function. In this context, "function" has to be construed widely. Thus, the primary function of a contact lens is to correct the eye's focusing ability, but it is also a part of its function to fit properly and to remain in position in relation to the eyeball and eyelid and to allow oxygen to reach the conjunctiva. The primary function of the human eye is to see but it is also a part of its function to perform that function efficiently by being able to focus light, by being protected and kept clean (e.g. by the operation of the eyelid). Given this, various interface features of contact lenses (i.e. the back radius, diameters and bevelled edges) were found to be present so that both lens and eye could perform their functions. They were, therefore, excluded from protection.[215] By contrast, it was held that the exclusion did not apply to the design of a top cover for a valley assembly for a conservatory roof. Although the cover could be pushed down so that its outer edge touched the window frames, it was not clear

---

[213] See, *Ocular Sciences Ltd v Aspect Vision Care Ltd* [1997] R.P.C. 289 at 425. Not all design features that allow an interface with parts of the human body will be excluded. See para.13–62, below. The term "article" includes a carpet or a floor: *Dyson Ltd v Qualtex (UK) Ltd* [2006] EWCA Civ 166; [2006] R.P.C. 31 at paras 42 and 43.

[214] *Electronic Techniques (Anglia) Ltd v Critchley Components Ltd* [1997] F.S.R. 401 at 416–419 and *Ocular Sciences Ltd v Aspect Vision Care Ltd* [1997] R.P.C. 289 suggest that the exclusion will apply. Whilst this construction is hard to reconcile with the wording of s.213, it does give effect to the intention of the CDPA (to deny protection to spare parts) without doing violence to the infringement provisions in s.226. By contrast, in *Baby Dan AS v Brevi SRL* [1999] F.S.R. 377, at 381–383, it was held that, where a design right claim was framed by reference to a composite article, the "must fit" exclusion only applied to those features which allowed that article to interface with another article and not to those features which allowed its component parts to interface with each other. The difficulty with this is that it may well allow claimants to claim protection against the manufacturers of spare parts. To counter this difficulty, the court in *Baby Dan* suggested that if an alleged infringer was only making component parts, the only design on which the claimant could rely to show an infringement would be the design of the relevant component part. However, it is not clear on what basis the claimant could be prevented from framing his claim by reference to the relevant component part as an aspect of the design of the composite article. There is certainly nothing in s.226 to prevent him doing so. It is submitted that *Electronic Techniques* is to be preferred. However, the reasoning in *Baby Dan* was adopted in *A. Fulton Co Ltd v Grant Barnett & Co Ltd* [2001] R.P.C. 257 at para.73 and, faced with conflicting decisions, the trial judge in *Ultraframe (UK) Ltd v Eurocell Building Plastics Ltd* [2004] EWHC 1785, [2005] R.P.C. 7, at para.21 felt obliged to follow *Baby Dan* (it being the more recent case). The Court of Appeal in *Ultraframe (UK) Ltd v Eurocell* [2005] R.P.C. 36 at para.69 left the point open on the bases that any decision would be obiter and that cases where the point arose were likely to be rare because it was difficult to imagine cases where an overall design of an assembly of parts (e.g. a car) would not be the subject of design right whilst the component parts were.

[215] *Ocular Sciences Ltd v Aspect Vision Care Ltd* [1997] R.P.C. 289, (Laddie J.). That the exclusion can operate where the design feature in question allows an article to perform its function more efficiently is also clear from *Dyson Ltd v Qualtex (UK) Ltd* [2006] EWCA Civ 166 at para.43.

that that interface enabled either the cover or the window frames to perform any particular function.[216]

Several other points arise:

(1) A design feature that meets the interface criteria will be excluded from design right even if it also serves some other function (such as attracting customers).[217]

(2) There is nothing in the wording to suggest that a design feature is only excluded from protection if it is the *only* way in which the necessary interface between the articles could be achieved. Instead, if a number of different design features could permit the interface, the exclusion will apply. It does not matter that a differently designed feature could have performed the same function.[218]

(3) There is some uncertainty as to whether the exclusion would apply only if the designer knew that the relevant features would enable the articles to interface or whether it was sufficient that the features do in fact enable the interface.[219] The latter construction avoids difficult questions of fact as to the designer's intentions. However, it would mean that a design feature may be excluded from protection simply because the defendant is able to show that it permits an interface never contemplated by the designer. The latter construction may also be difficult to reconcile with the words "enable" and "so that" (rather than, for example, the more passive words "allow" or "permit") which arguably suggest that s.213(3)(b)(i) was concerned with where a particular design feature was incorporated with a view to allowing the article to interface with another.

(4) The exclusion may apply even though the articles in question were designed at different times.[220]

(5) For the exclusion to apply, the design feature in question need not be the actual interface feature (i.e. the feature that actually performs the interface with the other article). Instead, it must be a feature that "enables" the interface "*so that either article can perform its function*". Thus, where a vacuum cleaner handle which doubled as a cleaning hose was designed with bleed holes, the exclusion was found to apply. The bleed holes allowed air to pass into the hose even if the hose was pushed hard up against the carpet or floor being cleaned. Accordingly, they were design features which enabled the handle to be placed against a flat surface so as better to perform its function as a cleaning hose.[221] Although this qualitative approach suggests that the exclusion may be of wide application, a design is likely to have other features that are protected. The position of a spare parts manufacturer is, therefore, a risky one.[222]

(6) The fact that one working part of an article is designed so that it does not interfere with the working of another part of that article (or another article)

---

[216] *Ultraframe UK Ltd v Fielding* [2006] EWCA Civ 166 at para.80 (Laddie J.) (a point not raised on appeal, [2004] R.P.C. 24).

[217] *Ocular Sciences Ltd v Aspect Vision Care Ltd* [1997] R.P.C. 289 at para.424. See the trial judge's propositions quoted by the Court of Appeal in *Dyson Ltd v Qualtex (UK) Ltd* [2006] EWCA Civ 166 at para.28.

[218] *Ocular Sciences Ltd v Aspect Vision Care Ltd* [1997] R.P.C. 289 at para.424. See also *Parker & Parker v Tidball* [1997] F.S.R. 680 at para.693 and *Ultraframe (UK) Ltd v Eurocell Building Plastics Ltd* [2005] R.P.C. 7 at para.114. The point was not argued on appeal [2005] R.P.C. 36.

[219] Contrast *A. Fulton Co Ltd v Grant Barnett & Co Ltd* [2001] R.P.C. 257 at para.75 with *Ocular Sciences Ltd v Aspect Vision Care Ltd* [1997] R.P.C. 289 at para.426.

[220] *Dyson Ltd v Qualtex (UK) Ltd* [2006] EWCA Civ 166 at para.46.

[221] *Dyson Ltd v Qualtex (UK) Ltd* [2006] EWCA Civ 166 at paras 40–43.

[222] See para.13–58 above.

does not mean that the space between the parts is a feature that enables function.[223]

Examples. Construing the "must fit" exclusion may plainly give rise to difficul-   **13–62** ties and its operation may best be seen through examples.

(1) **Gasket.** A gasket was designed to fit between the lid and the body of a freezer. The only non-commonplace design feature was an upstanding "ear" which allowed the gasket to fit properly. The must fit exclusion operated. The design of the "ear" (like the design of the gasket as a whole) enabled it to interface with another article (the lid and the body of the freezer) and that interface enabled each of the articles to perform its function—namely to create a draught free and efficient freezer.[224]

(2) **Car exhaust.** The design of a car exhaust must have some design features which enable it to be connected to the engine exhaust manifold and other features which allow it to follow the contours of the car's chassis, to avoid the suspension and rear axle and to be attached at the appropriate points. These design features all satisfy the first part of the wording of the "must fit" exclusion and it seems clear that they also satisfy the second part.[225] For example, the features which allow the exhaust to connect to the engine exhaust manifold are there "so that" the exhaust and the engine may perform their functions, and the features which allow the exhaust to be attached to the chassis do, as a matter of fact, allow the articles to interface even though they may not all be essential or the only possible means of attaching the exhaust to the vehicle. The "must fit" exclusion would, therefore, apply to these design features. By contrast, the design of the internal layout of the exhaust's silencer box does not satisfy the first part of the exclusion, and the design for sporty looking twin exhaust outlets is unlikely to be within the first part of the exclusion and is almost certainly not within the second; these design aspects would not, therefore, fall within the "must fit" exclusion. Thus, if a supplier of spare parts was to copy the whole exhaust, he may be infringing design right in the design of the exhaust as a whole (as well as the designs of some parts of the exhaust) even though design right would have been excluded from the "must fit" aspects of that design.[226]

(3) **Car wheels.** The claimant has designed an attractive alloy spoke wheel for a car. The features which allow the wheel to be fitted to the car and to link with its braking and steering systems will be caught by the "must fit" exclusion. By contrast, the design of the spokes themselves is unlikely to be within the first part of the exclusion and is almost certainly not within the second.[227]

(4) **Table lamp.** A desk lamp must have a socket designed to be fitted with a bulb. The design of the socket would plainly be excluded from design right (as would the design of the bayonet or screw fitting of the bulb itself). If the lamp has an unusually shaped shade, those features of the design which allow that shade to fit around the bulb and to fit against the stand

---

[223] *Dyson Ltd v Qualtex (UK) Ltd* [2006] EWCA Civ 166 at paras 38 and 47.

[224] *Novum Overseas Ltd v Iceland Foods Plc* [2002] EWHC 53 at para.122.

[225] See para.13–61, above.

[226] See, for example, *Novum Overseas Ltd v Iceland Foods Plc* [2002] EWHC 53. There, the "must fit" exclusion operated in respect of the gasket (see Example (1)) and also in respect of certain design features of the internal dividers for the freezers (i.e. the hooks which allowed units to be hung inside the freezer, see para.123). Notwithstanding these exclusions, the design right claim succeeded in relation to the overall design of the freezer (see para.119).

[227] It may, however, be excluded by the "must match" provisions. See paras 13–64 et seq., below.

would be excluded. Other features of the shape of the shade and of the stand would not be.[228]

(5) **Traffic cones.** The design of traffic cones allows them to be placed on a road and to be visible to motorists. However, the design also includes features which allow the cones to be stacked. These features satisfy the first part of the wording of the exclusion. But is this an interface "so that [either of the cones] may perform its function"? The principal function of a traffic cone when in use is to provide a marker to guide or restrict the flow of traffic. However, as traffic cones are often in storage or in transit, an ability to be stacked is likely to be an important factor in their design and in a customer's decision to buy that design of cone in preference to a non-stacking design. In *C & H Engineering v F. Klucznik & Sons Ltd*,[229] the features of the plaintiff's pig fenders which enabled them to be stacked were referred to (in the context of testing for infringement) as "functionally significant".[230] This suggests (as does the approach in *Ocular Sciences Ltd*[231]) that stackability should be treated as part of the cones' function, and that design features which allow stacking should be excluded from design right protection.

13–63
(6) **Plates.** The design of a dinner plate raises interesting questions as regards both parts of the exclusion. Most plates have a feature (their relative flatness) which means that one can be stacked on top of another. Is this, however, a feature which "enables" the plate to be stacked with other plates? The approach in *Ocular Sciences Ltd*[232] suggests that it is. On the other hand, it could be said that it is straining the meaning of the word "enable" to say that it is the design of a plate which "enables" it to be stacked, for the ability to be stacked is something inherent in the nature of a thing which fulfils the function of a plate (unlike traffic markers). Similarly, can it be said that the features which allow plates to be stacked are features which are present so that the plates can perform their function? Possibly; but as the ability to be stacked is something inherent in a plate, the position is much less clear than in the case of the traffic cones. This seems to be why the design of the handle of, say, a teapot, does not fall within the exclusion even though it must interface with the hand of a person holding it.[233]

(7) **Lamp and bracket.** A person designs a lamp with a connecting bracket which allows it to be fitted to a bicycle. Those aspects of the design of the lamp and of the bracket which allow them to fit together are, therefore, excluded from protection. The exclusion of design right is absolute. It does not matter whether a rival uses the design features for the same or for different articles. Thus he is free (so far as design right is concerned) to make his own lamp of another overall design (or other device) to fit on to that bracket or his own bracket to fit that lamp.

(8) **A tow bar.** A "T"-shaped tow bar is designed to allow a recovery vehicle to tow a broken-down vehicle. At the ends of the head of the "T" are slots

---

[228] These may, however, be within the "must match" exclusion. See paras 13–64 et seq., below. In *Ultraframe (UK) Ltd v Eurocell Building Plastics Ltd* [2004] EWHC 1785 (Pat); [2005] R.P.C. 7 at para.113, Lewison J. used the example of the light bulb. The point was not argued on appeal [2005] R.P.C. 36.

[229] [1992] F.S.R. 421.

[230] [1992] F.S.R. 421 at 429.

[231] [1997] R.P.C. 289. See para.13–61, above.

[232] [1997] R.P.C. 289.

[233] See the concession by counsel referred to in *Dyson Ltd v Qualtex (UK) Ltd* [2006] EWCA Civ 166; [2006] R.P.C. 31 at para.28. See also the discussion in *Dyson* at para.52.

into which the wheels of the vehicle being recovered will fit whilst being towed. The design of those slots will be excluded.

(iv) The "must match" exclusion

The third exclusion is the so-called "must match" exclusion contained in s.213(3)(b)(ii) of the 1988 Act. This provides that design right will not subsist in "features of shape or configuration of an article which ... are dependent upon the appearance of another article of which the article is intended by the designer to form an integral part". The wording shows that this exclusion is concerned with a dependency in the design of one article (in whose features the issue of design right arises) upon the appearance of another article of which it is intended to form an integral part. These articles may be referred to as, respectively, the component article and the composite article.[234] The background to this exclusion has already been considered but, in summary, its rationale is to allow a component article to be copied where the circumstances compelled copying for aesthetic reasons. In such a case, the intention of Parliament is that competition in the after-market should prevail.[235] However, the wording of the exclusion is ambiguous and obscure,[236] and various difficulties arise in relation to its construction.   **13–64**

Intention to form an integral part. For the exclusion to operate, the designer of an article must have intended that article to form an integral part of another article. The word "integral" suggests that the article in question must be intended to be incorporated into the other article so that together they form a complete or a whole article. The wording also seems to require that the designer has that other article in mind when creating his design. It is suggested that the exclusion would not apply where the intention was to design an article which could be incorporated into many different other articles for in such a case, the article was not intended to form an integral part of another article. Thus the exclusion would probably apply to the design of a car door for a particular model of car, but not to the design of a removable child's car seat. It is also submitted that the relevant time for determining whether there was the requisite intention is the time when the relevant design is created. Thus, if an article is designed to stand alone as an independent article, the fact that it is subsequently used to form a part of another article will not bring the exclusion into operation. If, for example, a designer designs an all-purpose strut which another person subsequently incorporates together with other matching struts in a design for a protective grill, the exclusion would not operate (assuming, of course, that at the time that the strut was designed, its designer did not intend it to form an integral part of the grill).[237]   **13–65**

Dependent upon the appearance of another article. For the exclusion to operate, the relevant features of shape or configuration of the component article must be dependent upon the appearance of the composite article. This issue of dependency (in contrast to the integral part issue) is not qualified by reference to the designer's intention and requires, it seems, an objective assessment as to whether the relevant design features of the component article had been governed or dictated by the appearance of the composite article. The mere fact that they are compatible with the appearance of the composite article will not be sufficient.   **13–66**

The approach to this issue adopted by the Registered Designs Appeal Tribu-

---

[234] The meaning of "article" has already been considered, see para.13–50, above.
[235] See para.13–58, above.
[236] As commented in *Ford Motor Co Ltd and Iveco Fiat SpA's Applications* [1993] R.P.C. 399 at para.421.
[237] The all-purpose strut was the example used in Parliament, see *Hansard*, H.L. Vol.495, col.700.

nal[238] has been to ask whether the component part, objectively viewed, contributes to the overall shape of the composite article. If so, its design may be said to be dependent upon the design of the whole and to be subject to the exclusion. If, on the other hand, the component part (objectively viewed) could be replaced without substantially altering the appearance or identity of the composite article, then its design is unlikely to be dependent upon the appearance of the other article. The distinction was one which the Tribunal drew by asking whether, if the relevant part was to be replaced, it would have to be replaced, "as a matter of practical commonsense", by a part which is for all practical purposes the same as the original. To the extent that this was so, the Tribunal found that the shape and configuration of the component part was dependent upon the appearance of the composite article, and that the exclusion should apply because a competitor would have no design freedom to produce an alternative design. In applying the test for dependency, the Tribunal considered the appearance of the composite article with the relevant component part or parts in place[239] but where the relevant component article was one of a set of substantially identical parts all intended to form a part of the composite article, the Tribunal considered that the question was whether the design of the set was dependent upon the appearance of the composite article.[240]

Applying this approach in the case of spare parts and accessories for cars, the Registered Designs Appeal Tribunal decided that designs for body panels, doors, bonnet, grille, boot, bumper, instrument panel, spoiler and a windscreen were all designs dependent upon the appearance of the car as a composite article and were all, therefore, excluded by the must match exclusion.[241] By contrast, it found that designs for articles such as a steering wheel, wing mirrors, wheels, wheel covers and seats[242] were not dependent on the appearance of the car as a whole and were not, therefore, covered by the exclusion.[243]

13–67   Summary. The approach of the Tribunal is not entirely easy to reconcile with the actual wording of the "must match" exclusion. However, it appears to achieve broadly what Parliament seems to have intended[244] and the test adopted by the Tribunal, namely whether "substitutions can be made without radically affecting the appearance or identity of the vehicle" has been said by the Court of Appeal to be "essentially the right test".[245] The Court of Appeal has also said the following as regards the "must match" exclusion:

"One has to approach the provision bearing in mind that Parliament did not

---

[238] See *Ford Motor Co Ltd and Iveco Fiat SpA's Design Applications* [1993] R.P.C. 399 at 419–420, a case concerning the substantially identical "must match" exclusion in the Registered Designs Act 1949 s.1(1)(b)(ii) before it was amended by the Registered Designs Regulations 2001. The reasoning of the Tribunal was accepted by the Divisional Court upon judicial review (see [1994] R.P.C. 545 at 554). However, the House of Lords on appeal decided the case solely on the issue of whether the relevant component articles were "articles" within the meaning of s.44 of the 1949 Act and declined to consider the proper construction of the "must match" exclusion, see [1995] R.P.C. 167.

[239] The designer had, after all, intended that part to form an integral part of the composite article. See *Ford and Fiat's Applications* [1993] R.P.C. 399 at 420.

[240] *Ford and Fiat's Applications* [1993] R.P.C. 399 at 420.

[241] *Ford and Fiat's Applications* [1993] R.P.C. 399 at 419–420.

[242] i.e. exactly the sort of articles which, the Tribunal found, were often substituted, often by the original manufacturer itself, in order (for example) to give the vehicle a more sporty appearance.

[243] Although on the facts of that case, the Tribunal found that the designs of wing mirrors and wheel covers were not dependent upon the appearance of the car as a whole, it is not difficult to envisage cases where the designs of such articles would play an important part in defining the overall appearance of the vehicle and where replacement with a matching part would, as a matter of commonsense, be of considerable importance.

[244] A similar approach was adopted in *A. Fulton Co Ltd v Grant Barnett & Co Ltd* [2001] R.P.C. 257 (at para.77).

[245] *Dyson Ltd v Qualtex (UK) Ltd* [2006] EWCA Civ 166; [2006] R.P.C. 31 at para.68 (Jacob L.J.).

intend to exclude all spare parts, or even all externally visible portions of spare parts, ... 'Dependency' must be viewed practically. In some cases the answer is obvious—the paradigm example being body parts of cars. In others it may be necessary to examine the position more carefully. But unless the spare parts dealer can show that as a practical matter there is a real need to copy a feature of shape or configuration because of some design consideration of the whole article, he is not within the exclusion. It is not enough to assert that the public 'prefers' an exact copy for it will always do so .... The more there is design freedom the less is there room for the exclusion. In the end it is a question of degree—the sort of thing where a judge is called upon to make a value judgment."[246]

Examples: 13–68

(1) **A fountain pen cap.** A fountain pen cap is an article and is plainly intended to form an integral part of another article (the fountain pen as a whole). In some cases, certain features of the shape of the cap—for example, the contours—might be dependent upon the appearance of the pen as a whole. These would be excluded from protection. By contrast, other features such as the shape of a distinctive clip may have little to do with the appearance of the rest of the pen and everything to do with the identity of the manufacturer. Such features would not be excluded.

(2) **A chair leg.** A chair leg (assuming it is a separate article) will plainly be intended to form an integral part of another article (namely the chair) and, applying the test adopted in Ford,[247] falls more clearly into the category of being an essential part of the overall shape and appearance of the chair than into the category of accessories.[248] As the features of shape and configuration of the leg are in that sense dependent upon the appearance of the rest of the chair, those features will be excluded from design right. A competitor may, therefore, manufacture a replacement replica leg for that chair.

(3) **A set of chairs.** With a set of chairs, the design of one chair from a matching set of chairs is clearly likely to be dependent upon the appearance of the rest of the set. However, the rest of the set cannot be said to be "an article" of which the single chair can form an integral part. The exclusion would not, therefore, apply and a competitor is not free to make a whole new chair to replace one of the set. A similar point arose in *Mark Wilkinson Furniture Ltd v Woodcraft Designs (Radcliffe) Ltd*[249] where it was held that the exclusion did not apply to exclude design right from the design of one kitchen cupboard albeit that that cupboard had to match the rest of the kitchen. The judge accepted the submission that the complete kitchen was not an article for these purposes but was, instead, a series of matching articles none of which forms an integral part of another.

(v) Surface decoration

Section 213(3) also provides that design right does not subsist in "surface   13–69
decoration".[250]

This exclusion serves to emphasise that what may be seen as a purely artistic

---

[246] *Dyson Ltd v Qualtex (UK) Ltd* [2006] EWCA Civ 166 at para.64 (Jacob L.J.).
[247] [1993] R.P.C. 399. See para.13–66, above.
[248] In other words, the chair legs are closer by analogy to the body panels of a car than to the wheels of a car.
[249] [1998] F.S.R. 62 at 73.
[250] CDPA 1988 s.213(3)(c).

aspect of design should be protected by copyright[251] or registered design[252] rather than by design right. Taken with the exclusion of methods or principles of construction,[253] the surface decoration exclusion shows that design right is concerned with designs for the appearance of the basic form of an article and not with how the article is made or embellished.

Plainly, therefore, the surface decoration exclusion means that design right will not subsist in a pattern or effect created by paint on the surface of an article. However, the exclusion can also apply where that same pattern or effect is created by, for example, a mosaic or by dyeing the material (even where the material is dyed right through).[254] The surface decoration exclusion might, therefore, apply to a three-dimensional design feature. However, the article would have to be one which could notionally be perceived as one with a surface provided with decoration—albeit that that decoration could be either two- or three-dimensional.[255]

Of course, not everything that is on a surface will be surface decoration and, as many articles are designed with a view to their aesthetic appeal, it is not always easy to determine the point at which a three-dimensional design feature ceases to be merely an aspect of the shape of that article and becomes part of its surface decoration.[256] Ultimately, determining whether a design feature is or is not surface decoration involves a value judgment. In exercising that value judgment, the court will consider whether that feature is a significant part of the essential shape or configuration of an article[257] (i.e. whether it helps define the shape or whether it would be perceived as merely decorating a surface which is already there[258]) and whether the feature serves a function. If a surface feature has a significant function it cannot be surface decoration; if it has no function or a merely trivial function, it will be.[259]

13–70   Examples:

---

[251] In broad terms, surface decoration is excluded from design right but, as an artistic work within CDPA 1988 s.4, will, have copyright protection—see *Dyson Ltd v Qualtex (UK) Ltd* [2006] EWCA Civ 166; [2006] R.P.C. 31 at para.76. There may be circumstances in which CDPA 1988 s.51 operates to exclude copyright protection. For a full discussion of s.51 and of the difficulties arising from *Lambretta Clothing Co Ltd v Teddy Smith (UK) Ltd*, see paras 13–301 et seq., below. In *Dyson*, Jacob L.J. commented (at para.76) that *Lambretta* was "an exceptional case" where what was sought to be protected fell between copyright protection and design right protection and had neither, see para.13–311, below.

[252] Being a feature of "...the lines, contours, colours, shape, texture or materials of the product or its ornamentation" within Registered Designs Act 1949 s.1(2) (as amended by the Registered Designs Regulations 2001.

[253] See paras 13–56 et seq., above.

[254] *Lambretta Clothing Co Ltd v Teddy Smith (UK) Ltd* [2005] R.P.C. 6 at para.30. In *Dyson Ltd v Qualtex (UK) Ltd* [2006] EWCA Civ 166; [2006] R.P.C. 31 at para.76, Jacob L.J. commented that *Lambretta* was "an exceptional case" where what was sought to be protected fell between copyright protection and design right protection and had neither. See para.13–311, below. In that case, the "design" consisted of a combination of coloured fabrics for a track top. Even if this was a design within the meaning of s.213 (contrary to the views of Jacob and Mance L.J.J. although not of Sedley L.J., see para.13–49, above), the surface decoration exclusion would operate to exclude design right from the design. Jacob L.J. (using the example of a stick of Brighton Rock) commented that it made no difference that the dye went right through the fabric.

[255] *Dyson Ltd v Qualtex (UK) Ltd* [2006] EWCA Civ 166 at paras 73–84 (Jacob L.J.).

[256] See, for example, *Mark Wilkinson Furniture Ltd v Woodcraft Designs (Radcliffe) Ltd* [1998] F.S.R. 62 at para.73, discussed in example (3), below.

[257] *A. Fulton Co Ltd v Grant Barnett & Co Ltd* [2001] R.P.C. 257 at para.79. In *Hi-Tech Autoparts Ltd v Towergate Two Ltd* [2002] F.S.R. 270, the small projections on the underside of rubber floor mats for a car were held not to be surface decoration but to be important parts of the configuration of the mats as a whole. They were functional features giving the mats a non-slip quality. They were not merely decorative features having an incidental functional quality.

[258] *Dyson Ltd v Qualtex (UK) Ltd* [2006] EWCA Civ 166; [2006] R.P.C. 31 at paras 79–80.

[259] *Dyson Ltd v Qualtex (UK) Ltd* [2006] EWCA Civ 166 at paras 73–84. The exclusion applied to the beading in the *Mark Wilkinson* case ([1998] F.S.R. 62) which merely served to cover over cracks in the surface of the kitchen cupboards. In *Helmet Integrated Systems Ltd v Tunnard* [2006] F.S.R. 41, the scallop design on a fire-fighter's helmet was found to be surface decoration

(1) **Plates and vases.** The exclusion will apply to the willow pattern on a plate, or the painted surface of a vase.[260]

(2) **Desk top.** The design for a decorative pattern on a tooled leather desk top would constitute surface decoration.[261]

(3) **Relief carving.** Despite the use of the word "surface", the surface decoration exclusion applies not only to two-dimensional decoration but also to any aspect of design which may properly be seen as decorating the surface of an article. Thus relief carving on church choir stalls would be excluded as would a three-dimensional pattern on the surface of a plate. If however, the carving or pattern ceases merely to decorate the surface of an article and, instead, becomes part of or defines the form or substance of the article then the exclusion will not operate.

(4) **Kitchen cupboards.** Certain aspects of the design of kitchen cupboard units have been held to constitute surface decoration. Thus, the painted finish, the cockbeading on the door frame and "V" grooves used to decorate the main frame were all excluded from protection. On the other hand, the cornice for the top of the cupboard, the rounded quadrant design for the corners of the cupboard and the recessed panels for its doors and sides were not treated as surface decoration. Rather than being surface decoration, they were features which were themselves liable to surface decoration.[262]

(5) **Pattern of holes, doilies and stencils.** In *Jo y Jo v Matalan Retail Ltd*[263] an issue arose as to whether the pattern of holes on the front of a garment was surface decoration. Although the judge did not decide this issue, he commented that it was arguable that it was not surface decoration because the holes were (by definition) devoid of surface. It is submitted that such argument was incorrect. The surface being decorated was the surface of the substance from which the holes were cut. If it were otherwise, a pattern on a desk created by tooled leather or by relief carving would be surface decoration whilst the same pattern created by holes would not be. There could be no logic in such a distinction. Thus, a pattern for a doily would be surface decoration. By contrast, the same pattern for a stencil would not be surface decoration for, in such a case, the pattern would not (and would not be intended to) decorate the stencil as such. It would, instead, be an inherent part of the shape of the stencil the application of which is intended to put decoration on something else (i.e. a wall).[264]

(6) **Fabrics.** Embroidery on the front of a garment was surface decoration (being the result of the application of stitches to the garment after it had otherwise been made). By contrast, the edging and welt of the garment were not surface decoration but were parts of the essential garment.[265]

---

because its primary purpose was as surface decoration. Any functional effect was incidental (the point was not argued on appeal [2007] F.S.R. 16).

[260] See *Dyson Ltd v Qualtex (UK) Ltd* [2006] EWCA Civ 166; [2006] R.P.C. 31 at para.75.

[261] See the reference to painting on the flat surface of a three-dimensional article in *Dyson Ltd v Qualtex (UK) Ltd* [2006] EWCA Civ 166 at para.75.

[262] *Mark Wilkinson Furniture Ltd v Woodcraft Designs (Radcliffe) Ltd* [1998] F.S.R. 62 at para.73.

[263] [2000] E.C.D.R. 178.

[264] See also the perforated drum that was a part of the slurry machine in *Farmers Build Ltd v Carier Bulk Material Handling Ltd* [1999] R.P.C. 461 at 485 and in which design right subsisted.

[265] *Jo-y-Jo v Matalan Retail Ltd* [2000] E.C.D.R. 178, where the judge was influenced by the fact that the stitching was done after the garment was made, i.e. it was applied to a pre-existing surface. It is submitted that the time of application may sometimes be of assistance but it is by no means conclusive as to whether a design feature is surface decoration.

(vi) Olympic symbols, etc.

13–71 **Section 213(5A)—Olympic and Paralympic symbols.** Under this provision,[266] design right does not subsist in a design which consists of or contains a controlled representation within the meaning of the Olympic Symbol, etc. (Protection) Act 1995. This applies only to designs created on or after September 20, 1995.[267] A controlled representation for these purposes means (a) a representation of the Olympic or Paralympic symbol, the Olympic or Paralympic motto or a protected word or (b) a representation of something so similar to the Olympic or Paralympic symbol or motto as to be likely to create in the public mind an association with it or a word so similar to a protected word as to be likely to create in the public mind an association with the Olympic or Paralympic Games or movement.[268]

4. CONDITIONS FOR SUBSISTENCE

A. SUMMARY OF REQUIREMENTS

13–72 Assuming that design right is capable of subsisting in a design, the question then arises whether on the facts design right actually does subsist. For these purposes, the following conditions must be satisfied:

(i) The design must be original both in the copyright sense of the word and also in the sense that it is not commonplace in the relevant design field (see ss.213(1) and 213(4) of the 1988 Act).

(ii) The design must have been recorded in a design document or an article must have been made to the design (see s.213(6) of the 1988 Act).

(iii) The design must have been recorded in a design document or an article must have been made to the design after August 1, 1989 (see s.213(7) of the 1988 Act).

(iv) The design must qualify for design right under the territorial qualification conditions (see s.213(5) of the 1988 Act).

B. ORIGINALITY

13–73 **Section 213.** By s.213(1) of the 1988 Act, design right subsists in "an original design". Further, s.213(4) provides that "[a] design is not 'original' for the purposes of this Part if it is commonplace in the design field in question at the time of its creation."

The effect of these provisions is that originality must be considered in two stages. First, the design must be original in the copyright sense of the word. Secondly, the design must not be commonplace within s.213(4).[269] The use of the word "original" in relation to design right (a form of protection based on copy-

---

[266] Added to CDPA 1988 by the Olympic Symbol, etc. (Protection) Act 1995 s.14(1). The 1995 Act created a quasi-property right called "the Olympic Association Right" (see s.1). This right has been vested in the British Olympic Association.

[267] Olympic Symbol, etc. (Protection) Act 1995 s.14(2). For these purposes, a design is created on the first day on which (a) it is recorded in a design document or (b) an article is made to it; ibid., s.14(3).

[268] Olympic Symbol, etc. (Protection) Act 1995 ss.3(1) and 5A. By s.18(1), the Olympic symbol is the symbol of five interlocking rings, the Olympic Motto is " *Citius, altius, fortius*". The following are protected words, namely Olympiad, Olympiads, Olympian, Olympians, Olympic, and Olympics, ibid., and their Paralympic equivalents—s.18(2). References to the Olympic Motto or to a protected word include the motto or word in translation into any language, ibid., s.18(3).

[269] *Farmers Build Ltd v Carier Bulk Material Handling Ltd* [1999] R.P.C. 461 at 475 and 482.

right) plainly suggests that it is intended to bear its copyright meaning.[270] More-over, the negative form of wording used in s.213(4) suggests that that subsection was not intended to be an exhaustive definition as regards originality but, rather, to be an attempt to exclude some (commonplace) designs which would otherwise be treated as original.[271] As a result of the two-stage test, a design may qualify as original for copyright purposes yet may fail to qualify for design right for being commonplace. The commonplace exclusion is therefore a significant departure from the law of copyright and many designs recorded or embodied in copyright works will be excluded from design right protection as a result.

Originality and commonplace tests relate to *the design* relied on. It is important to note that it is the design relied on by the claimant (rather than the design document or article in which it is recorded or embodied) which must be original and which must not be commonplace.[272] Thus, if the design is of a single feature (i.e. a part of an article) then it must be ascertained whether that isolated design is original and if so, whether or not it is commonplace. If, however, the design comprises a combination of features then the originality and commonplace tests relate to that combination of features. In this latter case, the fact that some or even all of the constituent features taken individually would not be original or would be commonplace does not necessarily mean that the overall design must also be.
13–74

Originality in the copyright sense. The test for originality in copyright is considered in detail earlier in this work.[273] In summary, the test is "concerned not with any originality of ideas but with their form of expression, and it is in that expression that originality is requisite. That expression need not be original or novel in form but it must originate from the author and not be copied from another work ...A drawing which is simply traced from another drawing is not an original artistic work: a drawing which is made without any copying from anything originates from the artist."[274] More recently, the European Court of Justice has stated that the test is whether the material comprises the author's own intellectual creation.[275] Thus, in the design right context, all that is meant by an "original design" is that "the design for which protection is claimed must have originated from the designer in the sense that it is not simply a copy by him of a previous design made by someone else."[276] On this basis, the fact that a design looks like or even is identical to another design or article does not mean that it is
13–75

---

[270] As to which, see para.13–75, below.

[271] Given that the copyright test of originality is in no way concerned with whether or not a work is "commonplace", it seems strange that the 1988 Act decided to remove design right from commonplace designs by providing that such designs were not original rather than simply providing that design right should not subsist in them as it does with, for example, "must fit" and "must match" designs (as to which, see paras 13–58 et seq., above).

[272] *Farmers Build Ltd v Carier Bulk Material Handling Ltd* [1999] R.P.C. 461 at para.483.

[273] See Ch.3, above and *Interlego AG v Tyco Industries Inc* [1989] A.C. 217 at paras 262F–263E; [1988] R.P.C. 343, (PC). See also the discussion in *Dyson Ltd v Qualtex (UK) Ltd* [2006] EWCA Civ 166; [2006] R.P.C. 31 at paras 85–90.

[274] *British Northrop Ltd v Texteam Blackburn Ltd* [1974] R.P.C. 57 at para.68, a passage quoted with approval in *Interlego A.G. v Tyco Industries Inc* [1989] A.C. 217 at para.261E; [1988] R.P.C. 343. It has been held that where a design feature originated in a mistake, the decision to adopt that mistake may well involve a sufficient exercise of skill to constitute originality: see *Guild v Eskandar* [2003] F.S.R. 3.

[275] *Infopaq International A/S v Danske Dagblades Forening* (C–5/08) [2009] E.C.D.R. 16.

[276] *Farmers Build Ltd v Carier Bulk Material Handling Ltd* [1999] R.P.C. 461 at para.481.

not original; the issue is whether the designer used his own independent skill to create it as opposed to merely copying from another design.[277]

Further, provided design as a whole can properly be said to embody the independent work of its designer, it will be original in the required sense even if substantial parts of it have been copied from an earlier design. Thus, a design for a pig slurry separating machine which included some features copied from earlier machines and some other features was original because the designer had expended his own time, labour and skill in creating it.[278] This does not mean, however, that every combination of old design features will be original. To add an old design feature to another existing design does not necessarily result in an *original* new design—for the decision to add that feature does not involve originality in the copyright sense; all that has been done is to create a "mere collocation".[279]

13–76 **Commonplace in the design field at the time of its creation.** Even if a design is original in a copyright sense, s.213(4) provides that it will not be original for design right purposes if it is "commonplace in the design field in question at the time of its creation".

It was stated in Parliament that this provision was intended to prevent mundane, routine and well-known designs from acquiring design right,[280] and it has been said that its effect is to exclude designs which are "trite, trivial, common-or-garden, hackneyed or of the type which would excite no peculiar attention in those in the relevant art".[281] As set out below, the commonplace exclusion requires the court to compare the design in issue with other designs in the relevant design field. Logically, therefore, the first issue is to identify the relevant design field.[282]

13–77 **Design field.** There is no statutory definition of "design field". However, the expression is clearly intended to set sensible limits to the scope of the inquiry into whether a design is commonplace.[283] In some cases, the design field identified by the courts has been extremely narrow—such as the design field of long-necked beer bottles[284] or of wooden configurable figures of the human form.[285] In *Mark Wilkinson Furniture Ltd v Woodcraft Designs (Radcliffe) Ltd*,[286] it was held that the design field was not "cabinetry generally" (even though the design features in question may have been better known in that wider field) but was instead fitted kitchen furniture as that was a discrete design field with its own particular problems and characteristics. However, it now seems clear that these cases adopted too narrow a view of the design field.

---

[277] *C & H Engineering Ltd v F. Klucznick & Sons Ltd* [1992] F.S.R. 421 at 427 and *Dyson Ltd v Qualtex (UK) Ltd* [2006] EWCA Civ 166; [2006] R.P.C. 31 paras 89–90.

[278] *Farmers Build Ltd v Carier Bulk Material Handling Ltd* [1999] R.P.C. 461 at paras 475 and 486.

[279] *Dyson Ltd v Qualtex (UK) Ltd* [2006] EWCA Civ 166; [2006] R.P.C. 31 at paras 95–96 (Jacob L.J.).

[280] See *Hansard*, S.C.E. col.575.

[281] See *Ocular Sciences Ltd v Aspect Vision Care Ltd* [1997] R.P.C. 289 at para.429. See also *Parker & Parker v Tidball* [1997] F.S.R. 680 at 693. See also *Dyson Ltd v Qualtex (UK) Ltd* [2006] EWCA Civ 166; [2006] R.P.C. 31 at para.109, where the court commented that the claimant's redesign "was no trivial operation—there was nothing trite about it."

[282] *Lambretta Clothing Co Ltd v Teddy Smith (UK) Ltd* [2005] R.P.C. 6 at para.43.

[283] *Scholes Windows Ltd v Magnet Ltd* [2002] F.S.R. 10 at para.31. In practice, a considerable amount of time and money is spent looking for and considering examples of similar designs in an effort to show that a particular design is or is not commonplace.

[284] *Round Imports v PLM Redfearn Ltd* (1999) 22(7) I.P.D. 22071.

[285] *Spraymiser Ltd v Wrightway Marketing Ltd* [2000] E.C.D.R. 349.

[286] [1998] F.S.R. 62 at 74.

In *Scholes Windows Ltd v Magnet Ltd*,[287] a case concerning a design feature for a U-PVC window, the Court of Appeal found that the relevant design field was that of window design generally—including the designs of traditional wooden "sash" windows. This was so even though the driving forces and design constraints that operate in relation to U-PVC windows were said to be quite different from those that operate for other types of window. Subsequently, in *Lambretta Clothing Co Ltd v Teddy Smith (UK) Ltd*,[288] the Court of Appeal stated that a "reasonably broad" approach is called for when identifying the relevant design field and that what matters are the sort of designs with which a notional designer of the article in question would be familiar. In that case, the design was of a "multi-purpose" garment—a tracktop intended for leisurewear but with a "sporty" image. Jacob L.J. commented that the designer would naturally look to and have as part of his background knowledge and experience, the design of sportswear. Accordingly, for the purposes of the commonplace provision, the relevant design field encompassed the design of well-known actual sportswear and the trial judge had been wrong to narrow the design field to that of "casual wear as distinct from sportswear". The position would have been different if the design had been for a "sportswear-only" garment (such as a wet suit).[289]

Although the 1988 Act does not make it clear, the fact that the 1988 Act is a territorial Act suggests that the relevant design field is limited to the United Kingdom.[290] However, this does not mean that the court must ignore the international position when determining what is or is not commonplace in the relevant design field. The issue is whether "the design" is commonplace and not whether an article made to that design is commonplace. Accordingly (and consistent with the approach in *Lambretta*), it may well be that a design for an article only marketed abroad has become sufficiently well known to designers and the informed public in the United Kingdom to become commonplace.

Commonplace. Having identified the relevant design field, the court must decide **13–78** whether the design in issue was commonplace in that design field. In deciding this, it is important to bear in mind that the issue is whether the design rather than the article is commonplace. For example, doors may be commonplace articles but a design for a door need not be a commonplace design.[291]

The "commonplace" provision was considered in detail in *Farmers Build Ltd v Carier Bulk Material Handling Ltd*.[292] In that case, the Court of Appeal noted that the commonplace provision was not intended to be a means of limiting protection for spare parts (if it was, there would have been no need for the "must fit" and "must match" provisions in s.213(3)(b)[293]). The Court of Appeal also stated that the relatively short period, the narrow scope of design right protection and the fact that design right could extend to designs of functional articles sug-

---

[287] *Scholes Windows Ltd v Magnet Ltd* [2002] F.S.R. 10 at paras 31–38.

[288] [2005] R.P.C. 6 at paras 43–47. *Lambretta* was followed in *Ultraframe (UK) Ltd v Eurocell Building Plastics Ltd* [2005] R.P.C. 36.

[289] In such a case, the designer would not naturally look to designs from the leisurewear design field. Thus, the design field could properly be narrowed to that of wet suits or, at the very least, to water sportswear only. In the light of *Lambretta*, it was accepted at trial in *Rolawn Ltd v Turfmech Machinery Ltd* (a case concerning the design of wide area mowers) that the correct design field was that of garden machinery generally rather than the narrower field of mower design (see [2008] EWHC 989 at para.87).

[290] Or, perhaps, to the United Kingdom and any country to which the design right provisions have been extended under CDPA 1988 s.255.

[291] See *Hansard*, S.C.E. col.575. See also, *Farmers Build Ltd v Carier Bulk Material Handling Ltd* [1999] R.P.C. 461at para.483 and *A. Fulton Co Ltd v Grant Barnett & Co Ltd* [2001] R.P.C. 257 at para.54.

[292] [1999] R.P.C. 461 at para.483.

[293] [1999] R.P.C. 461 at para.480.

gested that the commonplace provision should be construed narrowly for, if it were construed broadly it would remove protection from many designs of functional articles. The rationale for the provision was to prevent claims arising where the functional nature of the design meant that there was bound to be a substantial similarity between designs. Accordingly, to have design right protection, a design must in some respects be different from other designs so that it could fairly and reasonably be described as not commonplace. However, the Court of Appeal emphasised that this was not to be equated with a requirement of novelty for to do so would remove the protection that design right had been intended to confer on functional designs.

With these comments in mind, the Court of Appeal laid down guidelines as to the approach which the court should adopt when faced with the argument that a design was not original because it was commonplace.[294] These guidelines were, in summary:

(1) To compare the design of the article in which design right is claimed with other designs of other articles in the same design field as at the time of its creation (and also with the defendant's article).

(2) To ensure that the claimant's design had not been copied from another design, i.e. to ensure that it was original in the copyright sense.

(3) Assuming the claimant's design had not been copied, to compare it with other designs for similar articles in the same design field in order to assess how similar it is to them, i.e. the "commonplace" test.[295]

(4) This comparison is to be conducted objectively and will depend on all of the circumstances. Assuming the claimant had not copied another design, then the closer the similarity, the more probable it is that there is only one way of designing the article and that the design can reasonably be called commonplace.

(5) If the claimant's design has aspects not found in any other design in the field in question, the court is entitled to conclude that the design is not commonplace.

In another case, the Court of Appeal has commented that "what really matters is what prior designs the experts are able to identify and how much those designs are shown to be current in the thinking of designers in the field at the time of creation of the design."[296]

It should be noted that whilst expert evidence is admissible to assist the court in appreciating the differences and similarities in the designs compared, ultimately it is for the court and not for experts to decide objectively on the available evidence whether a design is commonplace.[297] For these purposes, as has been indicated, the test is not one of novelty. Instead, it is whether the design is commonplace (i.e. "trite, trivial, common-or-garden, hackneyed or of the type which would excite no peculiar attention in those in the relevant art"[298]) in the relevant design field. In this context, it should be borne in mind that that which is

---

[294] [1999] R.P.C. 461 at paras 482–483. See also *Scholes Windows Ltd v Magnet Ltd* [2002] F.S.R. 10(CA) at paras 27 et seq.

[295] In the report of *Farmers Build*, these other articles were said to be those made by persons other than the parties or persons unconnected with the parties. It appears that "unconnected" should read "connected", see *Ultraframe (UK) Ltd v Eurocell Building Plastics Ltd* [2005] R.P.C. 7. at para.111. The point was not argued on appeal ([2005] R.P.C. 36).

[296] *Lambretta Clothing Co Ltd v Teddy Smith (UK) Ltd* [2004] EWCA Civ 886; [2005] R.P.C. 6 at para.56.

[297] *Scholes Windows Ltd v Magnet Ltd* [2002] F.S.R. 10, at para.49. For this reason, the Court of Appeal will only interfere with the trial judge's conclusion in cases of misdirection or an error in principle—see *Lambretta Clothing Co Ltd v Teddy Smith (UK) Ltd* [2004] EWCA Civ 886 at para.49.

[298] See para.13–76 above.

commonplace in a design field will be ready to hand; it will not be matter that has to be hunted for and found at the last minute.[299] Further, the fact that some or even all of the constituent parts of a design are commonplace when looked at individually, does not mean that the overall design will also be commonplace—although plainly, in many cases, a run-of-the-mill combination of well-known features will produce a commonplace combination of features.[300]

At the time of its creation. To decide whether the design in issue is commonplace, that design must be compared with other designs in the relevant design field as at the time when it was created. For these purposes it does not matter whether those other designs were created many years before provided they can fairly and reasonably be said to be in the design field when the design in issue is created. Thus, in *Scholes Windows Ltd v Magnet Ltd*, the claimant's design (created in 1994) for an "S" shaped horn feature on its window frames was found to be commonplace when compared with pre-1915 designs for such features which, although no longer on the market, could still be seen by designers and interested members of the public on many houses and which were, therefore, still common in the built environment in 1994.[301]   **13–79**

Examples. Various decisions show how the courts have dealt with the commonplace exclusion.   **13–80**

(1) The addition of a metal roll bar to an otherwise commonplace pig fender distinguished that design for a pig fender design from other designs of pig fenders. It took that design outside the ordinary. The overall design was not, therefore commonplace.[302]

(2) The design for a new pig-slurry-separating machine had certain aspects which had been copied from earlier machines but also included features which differed in significant respects from any previous design. Thus the design of the new machine (as well as the designs of many of those additional features individually) was original in the copyright sense and was not commonplace.[303]

(3) The designs for various contact lenses included nothing "out of the ordinary" and all of the features were well known (save one which was more related to the lens' manufacture than to its design). Whether taken individually or in combination, the design features relied upon were commonplace.[304]

(4) Although it was commonplace for folding umbrellas to have rectangular handles, that did not mean that every design of a rectangular handle for such an umbrella would be commonplace. There was still considerable scope for detailed design work to create a handle with its own qualities, as the examples of so-called "prior part" showed.[305]

(5) Conical liners were not unusual in the "very specialised design field" of shaped charge warheads for missiles". However, small variations in shape could make a large difference in performance. The fact that the perfor-

---

[299] *Ultraframe (UK) Ltd v Eurocell Building Plastics Ltd* [2005] EWCA Civ 761; [2005] R.P.C. 36 at para.60 (Jacob L.J.).
[300] *Farmers Build Ltd v Carier Bulk Material Handling Ltd* [1999] R.P.C. 461 at para.486. See also *Ocular Sciences Ltd v Aspect Vision Care Ltd* [1997] R.P.C. 289 at paras 429–430.
[301] See *Scholes Windows Ltd v Magnet Ltd* [2002] F.S.R. 10 at paras 39–44.
[302] *C & H Engineering Ltd v F. Klucznick & Sons Ltd* [1992] F.S.R.
[303] *Farmers Build Ltd v Carier Bulk Materials Handling Ltd* [1999] R.P.C. 461 at 485 to 486.
[304] *Ocular Sciences Ltd v Aspect Vision Care Ltd* [1997] R.P.C. 289 at paras 428 430.
[305] *A Fulton Co Ltd v Grant Barnett & Co Ltd* [2001] R.P.C. 257 at paras 49–60, where it was also commented (at para.52) that the existence of one or two examples of reasonably obscure prior art does not necessarily mean that that design was commonplace.

mance of the warhead in question was, at the time, unmatched, suggested that its design was not commonplace.[306]

C. RECORDED IN A DESIGN DOCUMENT OR ARTICLE MADE

13–81   **Section 213(6).** Under s.213(6) of the 1988 Act, design right does not subsist "... unless and until the design has been recorded in a design document or an article has been made to the design". As will be seen, ascertaining when a design has been recorded in a design document or when an article has been made to the design is important not only as regards the subsistence of design right but also in order to determine when the design right will expire[307] and the date upon which licenses as of right will become available.[308]

13–82   **Design document.** Design right may subsist where the design has been recorded in a design document. For these purposes, a "design document" is defined as being "any record of a design, whether in the form of a drawing, a written description, a photograph, data stored on a computer or otherwise."[309] The words "any record of a design" and "otherwise" suggest that this definition should be construed widely and it has been held that the other words are not intended to be limiting but are rather examples of possible ways in which the record of an aspect of design can be made.[310] In particular, although no express reference is made to diagrams and plans (as opposed to drawings) there seems to be no reason why they should not constitute a sufficient record of a design. A list of the dimensions by which a design is defined or described can be a sufficient record,[311] so too could a digital record by way of data stored on a computer. As with copyright, there is no requirement that the design document should be of any particular artistic quality or aesthetic merit. As design right may subsist in the design of even a single aspect of the shape or configuration of a part of an article, it seems likely that the most simple or basic sketch will suffice.[312]

13–83   **An article made to the design.** Design right may also subsist where an article has been made to the design. This wording is slightly awkward. As has already been discussed, the word "article" is not defined but is clearly a reference to something having its own physical form.[313] However, as the relevant design could be the design of any aspect of the shape or configuration of an article, it would have been preferable had the 1988 Act referred to the making of an article to the design or incorporating the design. Again, there is no requirement that the article made to the design be of any particular quality. In this respect, the 1988 Act has sensibly avoided one of the anomalies of the old law. Prior to the 1988 Act, where a design was recorded in a drawing it could have copyright protection regardless of the artistic merit of the drawing. Where however, the design was only recorded in the form of an article made to the design, there was only copy-

---

[306] In *Societa Esplosivi Industriali SpA v Ordnance Technologies (UK) Ltd* [2007] EWHC 2875, [2008] R.P.C. 12 at paras 44–45.

[307] For the duration of design right, see paras 13–103 et seq., below.

[308] For licences of right see paras 13–126 et seq., below.

[309] CDPA 1988 s.263(1). See *Societa Esplosivi Industriali SpA v Ordnance Technologies (UK) Ltd* [2007] EWHC 2875; [2008] R.P.C. 12 at para.46 where it was commented that the design was recorded by way of being data stored in a computer and by the making of articles to the design.

[310] See *Mackie Designs Inc v Behringer Specialised Studio Equipment (UK) Ltd* [1999] R.P.C. 717 at 721.

[311] See *Ocular Sciences Ltd v Aspect Vision Care Ltd* [1997] R.P.C. 289 at 422–423.

[312] In *Sales v Stromberg* [2005] EWHC 1624 (Ch); [2006] F.S.R. 7, the apparent lack of artistic merit in the design drawings was held to be irrelevant because there had been no difficulty in making a prototype to the design.

[313] See para.13–50, above.

right protection if that article was itself an artistic work (i.e. either a sculpture or a work of artistic craftsmanship). As these terms had been restrictively construed, such designs were rarely protected.[314]

D. RECORDED OR MADE ON OR AFTER AUGUST 1, 1989

By s.213(7) of the 1988 Act, design right will not subsist in a design unless the design was recorded in a design document or an article was made to the design after the commencement of the 1988 Act, which was on August 1, 1989.[315] **13–84**

E. QUALIFYING CONDITIONS

Design right, like copyright, will only subsist if certain territorial conditions are satisfied. In order to determine whether a design satisfies these conditions, it may be necessary to establish the identity of the designer; whether the design was created in pursuance of a commission; and whether it was created in the course of employment. These matters will be considered before turning to the actual qualification provisions. **13–85**

(i) The designer

The identity of the designer of a design is of importance in order to determine whether the design qualifies for design right[316] and also, if it does so qualify, in order to determine who is the first owner of that design right.[317] **13–86**

Section 214(1). In the case of a design which is not a computer-generated design,[318] s.214(1) of the 1988 Act provides that "the 'designer', in relation to a design, means the person who created it". It is not wholly clear from this wording whether the person who created a design is the person who had the design idea or the person who first recorded it in a design document or made an article to it.[319] The word "created" may suggest the latter.[320] However, the design right provisions taken as a whole show that the creator for these purposes is the person who had the design idea and this is, it is submitted, the correct construction.[321] A design has a separate existence from the tangible form in which it is represented (i.e. the design document recording it or the article made to it)[322] and the definition of the designer clearly refers to the creator of the design rather than to the creator of the design document or of the article made to the design. As there is no requirement that the recording of the design need be done by or at the behest of the designer, it may happen that the designer and the person who records it are completely different persons. It will not, of course, always be easy to determine (as a matter of fact) whose idea a particular design was (particularly if a design **13–87**

---

[314] See *George Hensher Ltd v Restawile Upholstery (Lancs.) Ltd* [1976] A.C. 64; [1974] F.S.R. 173 and para.13–24, above.

[315] Although design right cannot subsist in a design document or article created before August 1, 1989 such document or article may be entitled to copyright protection as an artistic or literary work as to which, see paras 13–338 et seq. and 13–364 et seq., below.

[316] Whether by reference to the designer himself under CDPA 1988 s.218 (see para.13–94, below) or by reference to his commissioner or employer under CDPA 1988 s.219 (see para.13–93, below).

[317] See CDPA 1988 s.215(1) and paras 13–109 et seq., below.

[318] For the designer of computer-generated designs, see para.13–89, below.

[319] The same issue as to "creation" arises in relation to whether a design was commonplace in the field of design in question at the time of its creation—see para.13–79, above.

[320] It suggests the production of something tangible (a creation) which records the design.

[321] This was the approach adopted in *C & H Engineering Ltd v F. Klucznick & Sons Ltd* [1992] F.S.R. 421 at 428 where it was stated that "the creator is not necessarily the person who records the design but usually will be".

[322] See CDPA 1988 s.213(6) and paras 13–81 et seq., above.

has been through various stages of development and discussion), and a distinction must be drawn between persons whose contributions related to the design of the shape or configuration of the article (who are designers) and those whose contributions were, for example, in relation to matters of construction (who are not).[323]

13–88   **Designers of joint designs.** In the case of a joint design, any reference to the designer is a reference to all the designers of the design.[324] A joint design is defined by s.259(1) of the 1988 Act as "a design produced by the collaboration of two or more designers in which the contribution of each is not distinct from that of the other or others". This provision is substantially the same as that relating to copyright works of joint authorship and its meaning is considered in that context.[325] The collaboration must be in relation to the production of the relevant design rather than the production of an article to the design. Accordingly a court should ask who, as a matter of fact and degree, has made a significant contribution to the creation of the design and should disregard contributions which are more concerned with matters of construction than with design appearance.[326] Again, it is important to identify precisely the design with which one is concerned. Where an article is designed by a group, the design of the overall article may be a joint design. However, the design of individual parts or aspects of the article may be the work of a single designer and, therefore, not joint designs.

13–89   **Designer of a computer-generated design.** A computer-generated design is defined by s.263(1) of the 1988 Act as a design "generated by computer in circumstances that there is no human designer". If the design is a computer-generated design, s.214(2) provides that "the person by whom the arrangements necessary for the creation of the design are undertaken shall be taken to be the designer". Substantially the same words are used in the copyright provisions of the 1988 Act in relation to computer-generated literary, dramatic, musical and artistic works,[327] and are considered in that context.[328]

(ii) Design created in pursuance of a commission

13–90   In order to determine whether the design qualifies for design right[329] and, if so, who is its first owner,[330] it may also be necessary to ascertain whether a design was created "in pursuance of a commission".

The 1988 Act does not expressly state what the thing is which is being commissioned. Nor does the 1988 Act define the word "commission" save to say that it means a commission for money or money's worth.[331] The meaning of the word "commission" has already been considered in relation to the Copyright Act

---

[323] See *Parker & Parker v Tidball* [1997] F.S.R. 680 at 701. See also *A. Fulton Co Ltd v Grant Barnett & Co Ltd* [2001] R.P.C. 257 at para.81.

[324] CDPA 1988 s.259(2).

[325] s.10(1); see Ch.4, above.

[326] See *Parker & Parker v Tidball* [1997] F.S.R. 680 at 701.

[327] CDPA 1988 s.9(3).

[328] See para.4–13.

[329] See CDPA 1988 s.219 and paras 13–93 et seq., below.

[330] s.215(2). See paras 13–109 et seq., below.

[331] s.263(1). The Registered Designs Act 1949 s.2(1A) now contains the same definition. It seems that there is no requirement for the court to assess the adequacy of the consideration paid by way of commission. Thus, at first instance in *Farmers Build Ltd v Carier Bulk Materials Handling Ltd* Unreported, March 26, 1997, transcript at 29, it was held that it was irrelevant that the designer was not fully compensated for his design costs (the point was not raised on appeal, [1999] R.P.C. 461). Further, a designer who was not paid for his design work but who expected to recover his costs through being able to mass-produce articles to the design (and who would have charged for his design work if that production work had been given to someone) was held to have been com-

1956 and the Copyright Act 1911.[332] However, some care is required when relying on copyright commissioning cases because the wording used in those earlier Acts was somewhat different to that used in the 1988 Act.[333] In the design right context, it has been decided that, for a design to have been created pursuant to a commission, there must have been a contract prior to the creation of the relevant design. This contract must involve mutual obligations; namely the obligation of the designer to create the design and the obligation of the commissioner to pay for it.[334] It seems clear, therefore, that the contract must be for the creation of a *design* and not merely for the supply of some product. Having said this, there are cases where the former can be inferred from the latter. For example, a contract for the supply of custom-made office desks may well involve impliedly commissioning the design of those desks whereas a contract to be supplied with the manufacturer's standard range desks would not. Ultimately, the approach to any commissioning case under the 1988 Act is to identify the relevant commission and to ask whether the design in question was created "in pursuance" of it.[335]

(iii) Design created in the course of employment

The question whether a design was created in the course of employment is also **13–91** relevant both as regards qualification for design right[336] and first ownership of such design right.[337] In this context, s.263(1) of the 1988 Act provides that "'employee', 'employment' and 'employer' refer to employment under a contract of service or of apprenticeship". Substantially the same wording appears in those provisions of the 1988 Act which deal with copyright works created by an employee in the course of his employment[338] and have been considered in detail in that context.[339] However, in summary, the first issue is whether the designer was employed under a contract of service or apprenticeship. In this regard, a contract of service will exist where (i) the servant has agreed that, in consideration of a wage or other remuneration, he will provide his own work and skill in the performance of some service for his master; and (ii) the servant has agreed, expressly or impliedly, that in performing that service he will be subject to the other's control in a sufficient degree to make that other the master; and (iii) the other terms of the agreement are not inconsistent with the contract being a contract of service.[340] If there is such a contract, then the second issue is whether the design was created in the course of the designer's employment under that contract.[341]

---

missioned to create the relevant design, see *Spraymiser Ltd v Wrightway Marketing Ltd* [2000] E.C.D.R. 349.

[332] See paras 5–32 et seq., above.

[333] In particular, the 1988 Act may be more favourable to commissioners than the 1956 Act in that it covers any design made pursuant to the commission (clearly covering, for example, preparatory design sketches). The wording of the 1956 Act is somewhat more equivocal in that "the work" there may refer only to the actual commissioned work.

[334] *Ultraframe UK Ltd v Fielding* [2003] EWCA Civ 1805; [2004] RPC 24 at paras 30–33.

[335] In *Farmers Build Ltd v Carier Bulk Materials Handling Ltd*, a commission to produce a machine was held to give the commissioner the design rights in the design. (Unreported, March 26, 1997, transcript p.29. Not challenged on appeal, [1999] R.P.C. 461). Similarly in *Apps v Weldtite Products Ltd* [2001] F.S.R. 39, the defendant had commissioned the claimant to produce a report on its bicycle stabilisers and to make recommendations as to any new stabiliser (if required). It was held that the claimant's designs for a new stabiliser were made pursuant to a commission in that it was inevitable that he would have to indicate at least the general configuration for a replacement stabiliser in order to fulfil the tasks he had been set. The defendant was, therefore, held to be the design right owner.

[336] CDPA 1988 s.219 (see para.13–93, below).

[337] s.215(3), see paras 13–109 et seq., below.

[338] ss.11(2) and 178.

[339] See paras 5–11 et seq., above.

[340] This being the "well understood" meaning of "a contract of service", see *Ultraframe UK Ltd v*

(iv) Qualification provisions

13–92 The provisions which govern whether a design qualifies for design right are contained in s.213(5) of the 1988 Act.[342] In summary, a design may qualify for design right protection by reference to:

(i) the person by whom the design was commissioned or with whom its designer was employed; or

(ii) its designer;

(iii) the person by whom and the country in which articles made to the design were first marketed; or

(iv) the provisions of any Order made under s.221 of the 1988 Act.

(v) Qualification by reference to commissioning or employment

13–93 Under s.219, a design qualifies for design right if it is created in pursuance of a commission from or in the course of employment with a qualifying person.[343] In the case of a joint commission or joint employment,[344] the design will qualify for design right protection if any of the commissioners or employers is a qualifying person.[345] The meaning of the term "a qualifying person" is considered below.[346] Whilst it is not entirely clear from the wording of s.219, it is submitted that for the design to qualify for design right by reference to employment, the employer must be a qualifying person at the time when the design is created otherwise the design could not be said to have been created "in the course of employment ... with a qualifying person". The position is less clear in relation to a commissioned design, but it is submitted that a commissioner too would have to be a qualifying person at the time that the design was created if the design is to qualify under this head. It should be noted that if a design was created in pursuance of a commission or in the course of employment, but the commissioner or employer is not a qualifying person, then that design cannot qualify by reference to its designer.[347] The two methods of qualification are mutually exclusive. However, such a design may still qualify by reference to first marketing or under s.221.[348]

(vi) Qualification by reference to the designer

13–94 If a design was not created in pursuance of a commission or in the course of employment, then it will qualify for design right protection under s.218 of the 1988 Act if the designer is a qualifying individual or, in the case of a computer-

---

Fielding [2003] EWCA Civ 1805; [2004] R.P.C. 24 at para.21, where a director and 100% shareholder was held not to be an employee. Contrast *A. Fulton Co Ltd v Grant Barnett & Co Ltd* [2001] R.P.C. 257 at para.83 where the designer was the chairman, chief executive and a director, and where it was stated in the company's account that no director had a service contract but where, because he was taxed under PAYE and worked for no-one else, he was held to be an employee.

[341] For a case in which this issue was considered at length, see *Intercase UK Ltd v Time Computers Ltd* [2003] EWHC 2988 (Ch); [2004] E.C.D.R. 8 at paras 9–18.

[342] For a case where the court was forced to conclude ("not ... with any great enthusiasm") that a design created by a US citizen did not qualify for design right protection, see *Mackie Designs Inc. v Behringer Specialised Studio Equipment (UK) Ltd* [1999] R.P.C. 717.

[343] CDPA 1988 s.219(1).

[344] Unlike "joint design", the words "joint commission" and "joint employment" are not defined.

[345] CDPA 1988 s.219(2).

[346] See para.13–101, below.

[347] For qualification of a design by reference to its designer, see para.13–94, below.

[348] See, respectively, paras 13–95 et seq. and 13–98, below.

generated design, if the designer is a qualifying person.[349] If such a design was a joint design, it will qualify for design right protection provided one of the designers is a qualifying individual or (as the case may be) a qualifying person. The meaning of "a qualifying individual" and "a qualifying person" are considered below.[350]

(vii) Qualification by reference to first marketing

If a design does not qualify by reference to the designer, or the commissioner or employer, it may nevertheless qualify under s.220 if the first marketing of articles made to the design is by a qualifying person[351] who is exclusively authorised to put such articles on the market in the United Kingdom, and such first marketing takes place in the United Kingdom or in another country to which the design right provisions extend by virtue of an Order made under s.255,[352] or in another Member State of the European Economic Community. **13–95**

Marketing. The reference to the marketing of articles is to their being sold or let for hire, or offered or exposed for sale or hire in the course of a business.[353] In order to prevent abuses, no account is taken of marketing "which is merely colourable and not intended to satisfy the reasonable requirements of the public".[354] **13–96**

Exclusively authorised. Not only must the person who first markets the relevant articles be a qualifying person, he must also show that he was exclusively authorised to put the articles on the market in the United Kingdom. For these purposes, this means that he was authorised by the person who would have been the first owner of design right (whether as designer, commissioner or employer) if he had been a qualifying person or by a person lawfully claiming under such a person and that that authorisation was exclusive in the sense that its exclusivity is capable of being enforced by legal proceedings in the United Kingdom.[355] It will be noted that the requirement that the exclusivity be capable of enforcement in the United Kingdom may raise difficult issues on the choice and conflict of laws. It may also give rise to questions of enforceability under European competition law. Where the first marketing is done jointly by two or more persons, then the design will qualify for design right if any one of those persons is a qualifying person who is exclusively authorised to put the articles on the market in the United Kingdom.[356] **13–97**

(viii) Qualification by Order made under section 221

Section 221 of the 1988 Act provides that Her Majesty may, with a view to fulfilling an international obligation, by Order in Council provide that a design qualifies for design right protection if such requirements as are specified in the Order are met. It was indicated in the course of Parliamentary debate[357] that this Order would be used to ensure that the United Kingdom complied with its obligations **13–98**

---

[349] CDPA 1988 s.218(1) and (2).
[350] See, respectively, paras 13–100 and 13–101, below.
[351] For the meaning of "qualifying person" see para.13–101, below.
[352] See para.13–102, below.
[353] CDPA 1988 s.263(2).
[354] s.263(2). The meaning of "colourable" is considered in detail in relation to the meaning of publication and commercial publication for copyright purposes; see para.3–178, above, and CDPA 1988 s.175(5).
[355] CDPA 1988 s.220(4).
[356] s.220(2). For the meaning of "qualifying person" see para.13–101, below.
[357] By Lord Beaverbrook—see *Hansard*, H.L. Vol.491, cols 1128–1129.

under, for example, the Paris Convention for the protection of industrial property.[358] To date, however, no such Order has been made.

(ix) Qualifying individuals, person and countries

13–99   As appears above, in order to ascertain whether a design qualifies for design right, it may be necessary to determine whether there is a qualifying individual, a qualifying person or a qualifying country.

13–100   **Qualifying individual.** A qualifying individual is defined by s.217(1) of the 1988 Act as "a citizen or subject of, or an individual habitually resident in, a qualifying country". The requirement that an individual be "a citizen or subject of a qualifying country" is construed, in relation to the United Kingdom, as a reference to the individual being a British citizen. In relation to a UK colony, it is construed as a reference to his being a British Dependent Territories citizen by his connection with that colony.[359] The phrase "habitual residence" is not defined by the 1988 Act. However, it suggests a more stringent test than the simple residence test necessary to qualify for copyright protection.[360]

13–101   **Qualifying person.** A qualifying person is defined by s.217(1) of the 1988 Act as "a qualifying individual or a body corporate or other body having legal personality which (a) is formed under the law of a part of the United Kingdom or another qualifying country, and (b) has in any qualifying country a place of business at which substantial business activity is carried on." The word "business" includes a trade or profession,[361] and in determining whether substantial business activity is being carried on at a place of business in any country, no account is to be taken of dealings in goods which are at all times outside that country.[362] By requiring a body corporate to have a substantial business activity in a qualifying country, design right has again adopted a more stringent qualification test than that which applies in copyright.[363] However, it should be noted that there is no requirement that the relevant activity be in respect of any particular type of article. References to a qualifying person also include the Crown or the government of any other qualifying country.[364]

13–102   **Qualifying country.** A qualifying country is defined by s.217(3) of the 1988 Act as "(a) the United Kingdom,[365] (b) a country to which this Part extends by virtue of an Order made under s.255, (c) another Member State of the European Economic Community, or (d) to the extent that an Order under s.256 so provides, a country designated under that section as enjoying reciprocal protection". Under s.255 of the 1988 Act, an Order in Council may be made to extend the application of the design right provisions of the 1988 Act (subject to such exceptions and modifications as may be specified) to any of the Channel Islands, the Isle of Man or any colony. The legislature of any country to which the design right provisions are so extended may modify or add to those provisions so as to adapt the design right protection to the circumstances of that country, but not so as to deny

---

[358] (1883). See para.13–34, above.
[359] CDPA 1988 s.217(4).
[360] s.154(1)(b) and see Ch.3, above.
[361] CDPA 1988 s.263(1).
[362] s.217(5).
[363] s.154(1)(c).
[364] s.217(2).
[365] i.e. England and Wales, Scotland and Northern Ireland.

design right protection in a case where it would otherwise exist.[366] If a country ceases to be a colony of the United Kingdom, it shall continue to be treated as such a country until an Order in Council is made designating it as a country enjoying reciprocal protection or an Order in Council is made declaring that it will cease to be so treated because the design right provisions as part of the law of that country have been amended or repealed.[367]

As yet, no Order has been made under s.255 of the 1988 Act. By s.256, where the law of a country provides adequate protection for British designs, an Order in Council may be made designating that country as one enjoying reciprocal protection under the design right provisions of the 1988 Act. If that other country provides adequate protection for only certain classes of British design or only for designs applied to a certain class of article, then any Order made shall contain limiting provisions, limiting to a corresponding extent the protection afforded by the design right provisions of the 1988 Act to designs connected with that country. At present, 16 countries (including the Channel Islands, the Isle of Man and various colonies) have been recognised as providing adequate protection for British designs and so have been designated as enjoying reciprocal protection under the design right provisions of the 1988 Act.[368]

5. DURATION

The position before the 1988 Act. One of the least satisfactory features of the law prior to the 1988 Act[369] was that a design which was unregistrable under the registered designs legislation (often because it was purely functional) was entitled to full copyright protection lasting for the lifetime of the author plus 50 years. This often allowed the designer an effective monopoly lasting for a considerable time and contrasted strangely with the protection for registrable designs which was then generally limited to a maximum of 15 years.[370]   **13–103**

The 1988 Act. Design right offers two alternative periods of protection.   **13–104**

(i) **The 15-year rule.** By s.216(1)(a) of the 1988 Act, design right in a design will expire 15 years from the end of the calendar year in which that design document or that article came into existence (whichever first occurred).[371]

(ii) **The 10-year rule.** However, by ss.216(1)(b) and 216(2) of the 1988 Act, if articles made to the design are made available for sale or hire anywhere in the world by or with the licence of the design right owner within five years from the end of the calendar year in which the design was recorded in a design document or in which an article is made to the design, then the design right will expire 10 years from the end of the calendar year in which the articles were first made available for sale or hire.

Under these provisions, a design can never have protection for longer than 15

---

[366] CDPA 1988 s.255(4).

[367] s.255(5).

[368] Design Right (Reciprocal Protection) (No.2) Order (1989) (SI 1989/1294) see Vol.2 C2.

[369] See generally para.13–23, above.

[370] Under the registered design legislation before its amendment by the CDPA 1988, a design which was registered had protection for up to 15 years, see Registered Designs Act 1949 s.8. Under the Copyright Act 1956 s.10 (as amended by the Design Copyright Act 1968), a registrable design which was applied industrially had copyright protection limited to 15 years. Since the CDPA 1988, the maximum period of protection available to registered designs has been increased to 25 years, see Registered Designs Act 1949 s.8 as amended.

[371] As has been seen, design right does not subsist in a design unless and until the design is recorded in a design document or until an article is made to the design, see CDPA 1988 s.213(6) and paras 13–81 et seq., above, and unless the design qualifies in accordance with s.213(5), see paras 13–92 et seq., above. However, it is the former event that is important as regards the operation of the 15-year rule.

years from the end of the calendar year in which it was recorded in a design document or in which an article was made to the design, and will in most cases be reduced by the 10-year rule. If, of course, articles are made available for sale or hire almost immediately after design right starts to subsist, the period of design right may last only 10 years.

13–105 **Example.** On June 1, 2000, a designer created a design document recording his design for a revolutionary new aircraft wing. Design right subsisted in his design from that date. Whilst the 15-year rule applies, design right will expire at the end of 2015.[372] If, however, aircraft wings made to the design are made available for sale or hire at any time up to and including December 31, 2005, then the 10-year rule will operate. Thus, if wings were sold on (for example), October 1, 2002, then design right would expire at the end of 2012.[373] By contrast, if aircraft wings are first made available for sale or hire *after* December 31, 2005, then the 10-year rule will never operate and the 15-year period will continue.

13–106 **Articles made to the design made available for sale or hire.** In the context of the 10-year rule, the time when "articles made to the design are [first] made available for sale or hire" is not further defined.[374] However, it has been decided that the expression "made available" means the date when the public could first actually obtain the articles. It connotes something that is actually in existence. The mere taking of advance orders will not suffice.[375] Although s.216(1)(b) refers to "articles" being made available, it is submitted that the section will operate as soon as a single article is made available in the required sense.[376]

6. TITLE TO AND DEALINGS WITH DESIGN RIGHT

A. INTRODUCTION

13–107 **Property right.** Design right is a property right[377] and, subject to the provisions of 1988 Act, the usual principles of property law govern questions of title and how it may be transmitted. Design right (like copyright[378]) may have separate legal and equitable owners, and it may be co-owned either by joint tenants or by tenants in common in equal or other shares. The title to design right may also be divided so that different people own different aspects of it.[379]

As design right is a form of property in its own right, ownership of the design right must be distinguished from ownership of the design document which records the design or ownership of an article made to the design. A similar point has already been made in relation to copyright.[380] As with other forms of property, dealings which transfer title to design right must be distinguished from dealings which merely give another person the right (a licence) to do something in re-

---

[372] i.e. 15 years from the end of the calendar year in which the design document was created.

[373] i.e. 10 years from the end of the calendar year in which articles made to the design were first made available for sale or hire.

[374] By contrast, in the case of copyright, some guidance as to when a work is "made available to the public" is given by CDPA 1988 s.12. See para.6–48, above.

[375] *Dyson Ltd v Qualtex (UK) Ltd* [2006] EWCA Civ 166; [2006] R.P.C. 31 at paras 115–119.

[376] This seems consistent with the fact that the section is concerned when the making available "first occurred". It also makes more sense of the provision. See also para.13–149 below.

[377] CDPA 1988 s.213(1).

[378] See para.5–01, above.

[379] Because, for example, of an assignment limited by way of time or of some only of the exclusive rights given by the CDPA 1988.

[380] See para.5–02, above.

lation to the property which would otherwise be an actionable wrong. The latter form of dealing does not affect title to design right.[381]

Scheme of this section. This section will consider, first, who is the first owner of design right; secondly, ownership in other circumstances, in particular whether the first owner holds the design right on trust or subject to the rights of any other person; thirdly, the transmission of title to design right; fourthly, the grant of licences relating to design right; fifthly, the availability of licences of right and, finally, Crown use.   **13–108**

B. FIRST OWNER OF DESIGN RIGHT

Definition of "first owner". Section 215 determines who is the first owner of the design right in a design. It provides that: **13–109**

"(1) The designer is the first owner of any design right in a design which is not created in pursuance of a commission or in the course of employment.

(2) Where a design is created in pursuance of a commission, the person commissioning the design is the first owner of any design right in it.

(3) Where, in a case not falling within subs.(2) above, a design is created by an employee in the course of employment, his employer is the first owner of any design right in the design.

(4) If a design qualifies for design right protection by virtue of s.220 (qualification by reference to first marketing of articles made to the design), the above rules do not apply and the person by whom the articles in question are marketed is the first owner of the design right."

It is clear from this definition that the issue of the identity of the first owner of design right is closely linked to the question whether the design satisfies the qualification conditions and many of the relevant terms are considered in that context.[382] It should be noted, however, that the first owner of design right as defined by s.215 is the first legal owner of design right but is not necessarily the first owner in equity.[383]

Designer as first owner. Subject to s.215(4),[384] the designer is the first owner of design right in a design provided it was not created in pursuance of a commission or in the course of employment.[385] If the design was a joint design, then the first owners will be only those designers who are qualifying individuals or, as the case may be, qualifying persons.[386] The fact that a group of designers has together designed an article does not mean that they must all be joint first owners of any design rights which arise in relation to that article. As has been seen,[387] the design of component parts of the article may be attributable to different individuals. If so, those individuals are the designers of those parts and each will be the first owner of the design right in the design of each respective part. Each individual may (depending on the circumstances) hold the design right on trust for, or subject   **13–110**

---

[381] Save that the CDPA 1988 s.222(4). provides that any licence granted by a design right owner will bind some of his successors in title (see para.13–123, below) and CDPA 1988 s.225 also confers certain exceptional rights on exclusive licensees (see para.13–124, below).

[382] See paras 13–92 et seq., above.

[383] For equitable ownership see para.13–115, below.

[384] i.e. unless the design in question qualifies for design right under CDPA 1988 s.220, i.e. by reference to first marketing, as to which, see paras 13–95 et seq., above.

[385] CDPA 1988, s.215(1). For the meaning of "designer", "commission" and "employment", see paras 13–86 et seq., above.

[386] s.218(4). As to joint designs, see para.13–88, above.

[387] See para.13–88, above.

to the express or implied terms of a contract between himself and the other designers.[388]

13–111   **Commissioner as first owner.** Subject, again, to s.215(4),[389] the first owner of design right in a design created in pursuance of a commission will be the person who commissioned it.[390] The circumstances when a design may be said to have been created in pursuance of a commission have already been discussed.[391] Where a design was jointly commissioned, only those commissioners who are qualifying persons are first owners of the design right.[392] In providing that the commissioner is the first owner of design right, the 1988 Act has followed the approach which has long been adopted in the registered designs legislation rather than the approach adopted in relation to copyright.[393]

13–112   **Employer as first owner.** Subject again to s.215(4),[394] the first owner of design right in a design which was not created in pursuance of a commission,[395] but which was created by an employee in the course of his employment will be the employer.[396] The test for determining whether a person was acting in the course of his employment has already been considered.[397] In the case of joint employers, only those employers who are qualifying persons are first owners of that design right.[398]

13–113   **Person who first markets as first owner.** If a design qualifies for design right under s.220 of the 1988 Act (i.e. by reference to the first marketing of articles made to the design[399]) then, notwithstanding the other provisions as to first ownership, the first owner will be the person by whom those articles are marketed.[400] Where articles made to the design are first marketed by more than one person, only those who are qualifying persons and who are exclusively authorised to put the articles on the market in the United Kingdom will be first owners of the design right.[401] This first marketing provision contrasts with the other provisions as to first ownership. In linking first ownership to marketing rather than to the creation of the design, it means that the first owner may be someone wholly unconnected

---

[388] See para.13–115, below.

[389] i.e. unless the design qualifies under s.220 by reference to first marketing (see paras 13–95 et seq., above).

[390] CDPA 1988 s.215(2). For a case where the commissioner was the first owner of design right in a design, see *Farmers Build Ltd v Carier Bulk Materials Handling Ltd* Unreported, March 26, 1997, transcript at 29. It has been said that it is arguable that the application of s.215(2) is impliedly subject to any agreement between the parties to the contrary and so legal title could still vest in the designer—see *Vitof Ltd v Altoft* [2006] EWHC 1678 at para.170. Given the existence of s.223 (assignment of future design right where there is a signed agreement—see para.13–120 below) such an argument might fail. But, even if it did, s.215(2) only regulates the legal ownership and if there was a contrary agreement, equitable title could lie elsewhere.

[391] See para.13–90, above.

[392] CDPA 1988 s.219(3). As to the meaning of "qualifying person" see para.13–101, above.

[393] It was stated in Parliament that it was important that the ownership provisions for design right and for registered designs were the same because both rights can apply in respect of the same design—see *Hansard*, H.L. Vol.491, col.1116. The reason for this distinction was that design right (and, presumably registered designs) "... concerns the designs of articles, which are the very essence of industry. Consequently, it seems to us that he who pays the piper should call the tune", see *Hansard*, H.L. Vol.494, col.114.

[394] i.e. unless the design qualifies under s.220 by reference to first marketing (see paras 13–95 et seq., above).

[395] See para.13–90, above.

[396] CDPA 1988 s.215(3).

[397] See para.13–91, above.

[398] CDPA 1988 s.219(3). As to the meaning of "qualifying person" see para.13–101, above.

[399] See paras 13–95 et seq., above.

[400] CDPA 1988 s.215(4).

[401] s.220(3). As to the meaning of "qualifying person", "market" and "exclusive authorisation" see paras 13–101 and 13–96 et seq., above.

with the design idea. Accordingly, if foreign designers or, as the case may be, foreign commissioners or employers[402] wish their designs to have design right protection in the United Kingdom, they must not only take steps to ensure that the first marketing complies with all of the qualification requirements of s.220[403] but should also be aware that the first owner of the design right will be the person whom they exclusively authorise to market articles made to the design. They may, therefore, wish to provide by way of contract for an assignment of design right to themselves or for some form of trust so as to limit the first marketer's right to deal with and control the relevant design right.

Differing first owners of design right, registered design and copyright. As **13–114** has already been seen,[404] there remains some overlap in the protection which may be afforded to a design by design right, by registration under the Registered Designs Act 1949 and by copyright. However, it should not be assumed that the first owner of the design right is the same person as the original proprietor for registered design purposes or the first owner of the copyright. The provisions for first ownership of design right are similar to those governing the original proprietorship of a registered design under the Registered Designs Act 1949.[405] In particular, similar provisions govern ownership of designs made in pursuance of a commission or created in the course of employment,[406] and there will be no difference between the identity of the "author" of a design for registered design purposes and of its "designer" for design right purposes. Both are defined as the person who creates the design in question.[407]

However, the first ownership provisions for design right diverge from the original proprietor provisions for registered designs where a design qualifies for design right protection by virtue of the first marketing provisions in s.220 of the 1988 Act. In such a case, the first marketer will be the first owner of the design right[408] but, as there is no equivalent provision in respect of registered designs, a different person may be the original proprietor of the design for registered design purposes. As s.3(3) of the Registered Designs Act 1949 (as amended) states that an application for the registration of a design in which design right subsists must be made by the person claiming to be the owner of the design right, this would mean that there could be no registration of such a design until ownership of the two rights is in common hands (for example, after an assignment).

There are also circumstances in which copyright and design right co-exist but where there will be different first owners. In particular, the designer (the person who creates the design idea) may not be the person who records that idea in a design document or who makes an article to the design. In such a case, the first owner of the design right will not necessarily be the first owner of the copyright which subsists in the design document or (if the article is an artistic work) in the article. Further, the owner of design right in a design created pursuant to a commission is the commissioner; yet as there are now no commissioning provisions in relation to copyright,[409] the legal owner of copyright in a design drawing recording that design will be the author of the drawing. Accordingly, if the design right owner does not also own the copyright in the corresponding copyright work,

---

[402] i.e. a designer, a commissioner or an employer who is not himself a qualifying individual or (as the case may be) a qualifying person.
[403] See paras 13–95 et seq., above.
[404] See para.13–43, above.
[405] Registered Designs Act 1949 s.2 as amended by the CDPA 1988.
[406] See CDPA 1988 s.215(2) and (3) and Registered Designs Act 1949 s.2(1A) and (1B) (as amended).
[407] See Registered Designs Act 1949 s.2(3) and CDPA 1988 s.214(1).
[408] See paras 13–95 et seq., above.
[409] See para.5–32, above.

then care must be taken not to use the design in a way which would infringe that copyright. In particular, care will be required when acting outside the scope of the exclusion in s.51.[410]

C. OWNERSHIP IN OTHER CIRCUMSTANCES

13–115   **Equitable ownership.** The first ownership provisions of the 1988 Act determine who is the first legal owner of design right. However, that person may not be the first beneficial or equitable owner. Equitable title may vest in another person by virtue of a contract or by reason of a fiduciary relationship.[411] Such situations have already been considered in relation to equitable title to copyright at paras 5–168 and 5–171 et seq., above.

D. TRANSMISSION OF TITLE

13–116   As design right is a property right, ownership of it (whether legal or equitable) may pass or be transmitted from one person to another. The law on the transmission of title to design right mirrors that which relates to copyright and has already been considered fully in that context.[412]

13–117   **Section 222(1).** Section 222(1) of the 1988 Act provides that design right is "transmissible by assignment, by testamentary disposition, or by operation of law, as personal or moveable property". This wording is identical to that used in relation to copyright, and the meaning of the phrases "transmission by operation of law" and "transmission by testamentary disposition" and the general nature of assignments have already been considered in that context.[413]

13–118   **Assignments in writing and equitable assignments.** Section 222(3) provides that an assignment of design right is not effective unless it is in writing and signed[414] by or on behalf of the assignor. The same wording is used in relation to copyright and its meaning has already been considered in that context.[415]

13–119   **Partial assignments of design right.** As with copyright, an assignment may be of the whole or of a part of the design right. By s.222(2), a partial assignment is an assignment limited so as to apply "(a) to one or more, but not all, of the things the design right owner has the exclusive right to do; (b) to part, but not the whole, of the period for which the right is to subsist".[416] A design right owner has the exclusive right to reproduce the design for commercial purposes by making articles to that design or by making a design document recording the design for the purpose of enabling such articles to be made.[417] Thus, an assignment of the right to reproduce the design by making one particular type of article would be a partial assignment. In the event of partial assignment, the different aspects of

---

[410] CDPA 1988 s.51 provides that it is not an infringement of any copyright in a design document or model recording or embodying a design for anything other than an artistic work to make an article to the design, or copy an article made to a design, see paras 13–301 et seq., below.

[411] The equitable ownership of designs created by the director of and 100% shareholder in a company was considered in *Ultraframe UK Ltd v Fielding* [2003] EWCA Civ 1805; [2004] R.P.C. 24.

[412] See, generally, Ch.5 and, in particular, paras 5–66 et seq. (legal title) and paras 5–189 et seq. (equitable title).

[413] CDPA 1988 s.90(1). For the meaning of "transmission by testamentary disposition", see para.5–125, above. For the meaning of "transmission by operation of law" see paras 5–135 et seq., above.

[414] In the case of a body corporate, the requirement for a signature is also satisfied by the affixing of its seal. CDPA 1988 s.261.

[415] CDPA 1988 s.90(3), see para.5–85, above.

[416] The period for which the design right subsists is discussed at paras 13–103 et seq., above.

[417] CDPA 1988 s.226(1), see paras 13–148, below.

design right will have different design right owners.[418] Again, these provisions mirror those relating to copyright.[419]

Assignment of future design right. As a general rule, a person cannot legally   **13–120**
assign future property,[420] and an attempt to do so amounts, at best, to an equitable assignment.[421] However, s.223 of the 1988 Act creates an exception to this rule in the case of future design right. It provides that where, under an agreement signed[422] by or on behalf of the prospective owner of a future design right, the prospective owner purports to assign the future design right (wholly or partially) then, upon the right coming into existence, title to it will vest in the purported assignee (or in a person claiming under him) provided he would be entitled as against all other persons to require the design right to be vested in him. It will be noted that under s.223 the assignee of a prospective owner may himself further assign the future design right.[423] The equivalent provisions in relation to copyright have already been considered.[424]

Assignment of registered design carries with it the design right. The 1988 Act   **13–121**
seeks to minimise instances of separate ownership of design right and a corresponding registered design. Thus, s.224 provides that "where a design consisting of a design in which design right subsists is registered under the Registered Designs Act 1949 and the proprietor of the registered design is also the design right owner, an assignment of the right in the registered design shall be taken to be also an assignment of the design right, unless a contrary intention appears". This provision only applies where the same person owns the registered design and the design right.[425] Further, it appears to apply only where the design which has been registered is the same as the design in which design right subsists. Because of the differences in the definitions of a design for registered design purposes and for design right purposes, the two designs may not be the same.[426] This, again, emphasises the need for care in determining precisely the design with which one is concerned. It also means that care must be taken with an assignment to ensure that it covers all such rights as are required in order to allow the exploitation of a design.

E. LICENCES

Nature of a licence. A licence must be distinguished from an assignment. In its   **13–122**
widest sense, a licence is merely a permission to do something in relation to property which would otherwise be an actionable wrong. The 1988 Act does not

---

[418] s.258(1).

[419] ss.90(2) and 173(1). See paras 5–97 et seq., above.

[420] i.e. property which had not come into existence at the time of the purported assignment.

[421] On the basis that there was a promise to assign which if supported by consideration was enforceable by specific performance—see *Snell's Principles of Equity* 31st edn at paras 5–25 to 5–26.

[422] In the case of a body corporate, the requirement for a signature is also satisfied by the affixing of its seal. CDPA 1988 s.261.

[423] s.223(2).

[424] s.91. See paras 5–110 et seq., above. Where the section applies, the assignee will acquire (when the design right comes into existence) the full legal (and beneficial) title rather than the equitable title that he would have acquired under the general rule. He is, therefore, able to bring proceedings in his own name without the need to join the assignor.

[425] By reason of Registered Designs Act 1949 s.3(3) (as amended), the initial proprietor of a registered design should generally be the design right owner.

[426] See Registered Designs Act 1949 s.1(1) discussed at paras 13–276 et seq., below and CDPA 1988 s.213(2), discussed at paras 13–45 et seq., above. The changes in the definition of a design for registered design purposes have reduced the similarity in the wording of the definitions but have probably increased the similarity in their meaning.

require that a licence relating to design right be in writing.[427] The licence may be in writing or oral. It may be granted expressly or be implied from the circumstances, or arise by way of estoppel. Further, it may be gratuitous in which case it is prima facie revocable (subject to any issue of estoppel). It may be granted under a contract, in which case its extent is a matter of construction of that contract. Finally, it may arise as a result of the licence of right provisions of the 1988 Act. Save as regards licences of right, the law as regards licences of design right is substantially the same as that which relates to licences of copyright. This has already been considered in detail.[428]

13–123   **Successors in title.** The 1988 Act creates various design right exceptions to the general rule of law that a licence only binds the person who grants it. Thus s.222(4) provides that a licence granted by the owner of design right is binding on every successor in title of the title of the grantor except a purchaser in good faith for valuable consideration and without notice (actual or constructive) of the licences, or a person deriving title from such a purchaser. Under s.223(3), a licence granted by a prospective owner of design right will be similarly binding. Finally, s.225(2) provides that an exclusive licensee has the same rights against any successor in title who is bound by the licence as he has against the person granting the licence. The similar provision relating to licences granted under copyright are considered elsewhere.[429]

13–124   **Exclusive licences.** Design right, like copyright, may be the subject of an exclusive licence. Under s.225(1) of the 1988 Act, an exclusive licence is "a licence in writing signed[430] by or on behalf of the design right owner authorising the licensee to the exclusion of all other persons, including the person granting the licence, to exercise a right which would otherwise be exercisable exclusively by the design right owner".[431] The significance of an exclusive licence lies in the special rights which s.234 of the 1988 Act confers upon exclusive licensees and, in particular, the right to bring an action for infringement and to recover damages in his or her own name.[432] The definition of an exclusive licence and the nature of the special rights granted to an exclusive licensee are the same as those which apply in copyright and have already been considered in that context.[433]

13–125   **Other licences.** Save as is mentioned above, the 1988 Act contains no special provisions as regards gratuitous or contractual licences and the law regarding implied or informal licenses is as discussed in relation to licences of copyright.[434]

F. LICENCES OF RIGHT

13–126   **The 1986 White Paper.** When the 1986 White Paper on Intellectual Property[435] proposed the introduction of design right, it also made recommendations intended to ensure that design right did not create unfair monopolies. Thus it recommended

---

[427] However, to qualify as an exclusive licence, the licence would have to be in writing and signed by or on behalf of the design right owner. See para.13–124, below.

[428] See paras 5–198 et seq., above.

[429] See para.5–201, above.

[430] For a body corporate, the requirement for a signature is also satisfied by affixing the seal, CDPA 1988 s.261.

[431] i.e. any part of the right to reproduce the design for commercial purposes (a) by making articles to that design or (b) by making a design document recording the design for the purpose of enabling such articles to be made. See CDPA 1988 s.226.

[432] See para.13–172, below.

[433] CDPA 1988 ss.92 and 101. See paras 5–207 et seq., above.

[434] See paras 5–217 et seq., above.

[435] Intellectual Property and Innovation (Cmnd. 9712). April 1986 at paras 3.26–3.39.

that there should be a limited right for owners of equipment to repair that equipment. It also recommended that licences of right should be available in the last five years of the term of design right. This would, it was suggested, allow competition from other manufacturers reasonably early in the life of a design whilst allowing the original designer sufficient time to gain a market lead and to make a return on his design expenses. The White Paper also proposed that licences of right should be available at any time in the life of a design if the Monopolies and Mergers Commission found that design right was being exercised in a manner contrary to the public interest. In the event, the 1988 Act introduced the "must fit" and "must match" exclusions which were of much wider significance than the limited right to repair suggested by the White Paper[436] but nevertheless adopted in full the White Paper's proposals for licences of right.

Section 237—licence of right in the last five years of design right. The most important licence of right provision is s.237 of the 1988 Act. This provides that any person is entitled as of right to a licence in the last five years of the term of a design right.[437] This appears simple enough, but various difficulties are likely to arise. In particular, in order to determine when a licence of right becomes available, one must first ascertain whether the relevant design is subject to the 15-year term of protection or to the 10-year term. As has been seen,[438] the 10-year term applies when articles made to the design have been made available for sale or hire less than five years from the date when design right first subsisted in the design. Where it applies, the 10-year term runs from the end of the calendar year in which such articles were first made available.[439] A prospective licensee would, therefore, have to ascertain not only when design right came into subsistence[440] but also whether and, if so, when, articles made to the design were first made available for sale or hire. Without the co-operation of the design right owner, these matters may be difficult or impossible to establish. If the prospective licensee and the design right owner cannot agree as to subsistence of design right or as to its term or as to the identity of the person in whom it first vested, then such issues may be referred to the Comptroller for his decision.[441] The Secretary of State has power by Order to exclude the operation of s.237(1) if it appears to him to be necessary in order to comply with an international obligation or to secure or maintain reciprocal protection for British designs in other countries.[442]

13–127

Section 238—licence of right in the public interest. If, following a reference to the Competition Commission, whatever needs to be remedied, mitigated or prevented by the Secretary of State, or by the Competition Commission or by the Office of Fair Trading includes (a) conditions in licences granted by a design right owner restricting the use of the design by the licensee or the right of the design right owner to grant other licences or (b) a refusal by the design right owner to grant licences on reasonable terms, then s.238 of the 1988 Act (as modified by the Competition Act 2002) provides that the powers conferred by Sch.8 of the Competition Act 2002 shall include the power to cancel or modify those

13–128

---

[436] See paras 13–28 and 13–29, above.

[437] CDPA 1988, s.237(1). It was stated in the course of debate in Committee that a period of five years exclusive rights is sufficient; "... it gives the original designer a lead in the market ... together with all the inherent advantages which the originator will have ...", see *Hansard*, H.C. SCE, col.596.

[438] For a discussion of the alternative periods of duration, see paras 13–103 et seq., above.

[439] See para.13–104, above.

[440] i.e. when the design was recorded in a design document or when an article was first made to the design, see paras 13–81 et seq., above.

[441] CDPA 1988 s.246(1). See para.13–192, below.

[442] s.237(3). As yet, no such Order has been made.

conditions and instead, or in addition to, provide that a licence shall be available as of right. The terms of such licence would, in default of agreement, be fixed by the Comptroller[443] and it seems that such a licence may be made available at any time during the term of design right. However, the procedure is complicated and likely to be time consuming and costly. Further, it is submitted that it would require some very substantial abuse in order to justify the grant of such a licence earlier than in the last five years of the life of the design right.

13–129   **Terms of a licence of right.** Where s.237 applies, a person is entitled to a licence of right to do anything which would otherwise infringe the design right.[444] Where s.238 applies, he is entitled to a licence to do the things in respect of which the relevant Order of the Secretary of State requires a licence to be made available.[445] Although such a licence cannot be denied,[446] it may, nevertheless be granted on terms. The relevant terms should be agreed by the parties or, in default of agreement, settled by the Comptroller-General of Patents, Designs and Trade Marks.[447] The Secretary of State has power to prescribe by order factors to which the Comptroller must have regard in settling the terms of any licence.[448] However, no such order has yet been made and, in the absence of express guidance, the Comptroller has adopted the patent-licence-of-right test, namely that the terms should be those which protect the interests of the parties in a manner which is fair and reasonable and which would have been agreed in free negotiation by a willing licensor and a willing licensee.[449] It is submitted that this is the correct test. However, as the Patents Act 1977 contains various provisions governing the grounds upon which a patent licence of right may be granted and matters to which the Comptroller must have regard when exercising his powers,[450] which provisions were not adopted by the 1988 Act for design right licences of right, it is also submitted that some care must be exercised when relying on patent-licence-of-right cases and principles in design right cases.[451]

Because the licence of right to which a person is entitled under s.237 is a licence to do anything which would otherwise infringe the design right, neither the design right owner nor the Comptroller can refuse to grant a licence of right under that section, which permits sub-licensing (if that is what the prospective li-

---

[443] CDPA 1988 s.238(3).

[444] CDPA 1988 ss.237(1) and 247(3)(a). This would not include, for example, the right to make articles to a design outside the United Kingdom. For the acts capable of infringing design right, see paras 13–152 et seq., below.

[445] s.247(3)(b).

[446] By either the design right owner or by the Comptroller, s.247(3).

[447] ss.237(2), 238(3) and 263(1). Where a decision of the Comptroller is reported in the Reports of Patent Cases (R.P.C.s), a copy of the licence granted is also set out in full. These provide useful guidance as to the sort of terms which have been accepted by parties or imposed by the Comptroller.

[448] s.247(4).

[449] See *Roger Bance and Anor's Licence of Right (Copyright) Application* [1996] R.P.C. 667 at 672; *Pioneer Oil Tools Ltd Licence of Right (Copyright) Application* [1997] R.P.C. 573 at 580; and *Sterling Fluid Systems Ltd's Licence of Right (Copyright) Application* [2000] R.P.C. 775 at 780. All these cases concerned copyright in a design document recording a design which was created before the commencement of the CDPA 1988. However, by reason of the transitional provisions (CDPA 1988 Sch.1 paras 19(2) and (3)), the design-right-licence-of-right provisions applied. In *NIC Instruments Ltd's Licence of Right (Design Right) Application* [2005] R.P.C. 1 at para.18, the Comptroller adopted the willing licensor and licensee approach and rejected the argument that the correct approach was that which would be adopted by a court assessing damages. He also held that the licence fee should not reflect any adverse effect on the right owner's business arising from the sale by the applicant of articles made to the design.

[450] Patents Act 1977 ss.48–50 (inclusive).

[451] See *Pioneer Oil Tools Ltd's Application* [1997] R.P.C. 573 at 580 and (in relation to the appropriate royalty rate) at 581.

censee seeks).[452] They may, however, impose such terms on the right to grant sub-licences as may be fair and reasonable to protect the interests of the parties. Such terms may include, for example, the obligation to provide the licensor with details of the persons to whom sub-licences are to be granted, of the articles which the sub-licensees are authorised to make and of any changes in the sub-licence arrangements.[453]

Other terms imposed on licensees of right under s.237 have included a provision that, in view of the fact that the parties were competitors, certain sensitive information need not be disclosed to the licensor but to an independent accountant,[454] a provision for the termination of the licence in the event of the licensee being in breach of the terms of the licence or being insolvent, and an obligation on the licensee to keep full and accurate records for inspection by the licensor (and to retain such records for three years after the licensor's right to inspect had expired). By contrast, in another case, the Comptroller refused to include a provision allowing termination for breach by the licensee and refused a provision for an annual audit but instead ordered interest on late payments at 2.5 per cent above base rate.[455] In that same case, the Comptroller also found that, as a matter of principle, a licence of right could contain a provision which required the applicant to mark goods as his rather than those of the design right owner—although such a provision was refused on the facts.[456] He also refused to include a warranty as to title but adopted the design right owner's concession that the licence should contain a recital that the design right owner had represented that it owned the design right.[457]

The licence fee. The most important term in most licences of right is likely to be   **13–130** the fee payable by the licensee to the licensor. Again, this should be such sum as would be agreed between a willing licensor and licensee. This will plainly depend upon the nature of the proposed use. Where only limited use is intended, the payment may be by way of a lump sum but if the licensee proposes to manufacture articles to the design, the fee is more likely to be a royalty based on a percentage of the sale price of each such article sold. The level of investment made by the original designer in the design is also likely to be important.[458] So too is the amount that it would cost the licensee to re-design his products so as to avoid the need to take a licence[459] and the fact that the designs were for articles competing with a number of similar products and that a large proportion of their value lay in the materials used rather than in their design.[460] By contrast, the fact that a designer had had to use particular skill in creating the design or that the licensor

---

[452] See *Roger Bance's Application* [1996] R.P.C. 667 at 672, 682–683 where the licensee wished for such a licence and *Pioneer Oil Tools Ltd's Application* [1997] R.P.C. 573 at 602 where it did not. It is, presumably, for the proposed licensee to ensure that the terms of the licence actually granted cover its anticipated activities. See also *NIC Instruments Ltd's Licence of Right (Design Right) Application* [2005] R.P.C. 1 at para.48.

[453] See *Roger Bance's Application* [1996] R.P.C. 667 at 672 and 682–683.

[454] *Sterling Fluid Systems Ltd's Application* [2000] R.P.C. 775 at 797.

[455] *NIC Instruments Ltd's Licence of Right (Design Right) Application* [2005] R.P.C. 1 at paras 59–60. The Comptroller commented that a provision permitting termination was pointless as the licensee could apply for and obtain a new licence immediately following termination. He held that the licensor's remedy for breach was an action for what was in effect a breach of contract. He refused the provision for an annual audit on the basis that the cost would be out all proportion to the sums involved.

[456] *NIC Instruments Ltd's Licence of Right (Design Right) Application* [2005] R.P.C. 1 at paras 50–53.

[457] *NIC Instruments Ltd's Licence of Right (Design Right) Application* [2005] R.P.C. 1 at para.56.

[458] See *Hansard*, H.C. SCE, col.596.

[459] *Sterling Fluid Systems Ltd's Application* [2000] R.P.C. 775 at 790–792. See also *NIC Instruments Ltd's Licence of Right (Design Right) Application* [2005] R.P.C. 1 at para.42.

[460] *Stafford Engineering Services Ltd's Licence of Right (Copyright) Application* [2000] R.P.C. 797 at 811–812 where this fact suggested that a low royalty of 4% was justified.

might lose sales in his capacity as a manufacturer have been held to be irrelevant.[461]

Ultimately, the question is one of market forces; of how much, when it comes down to commercial realities, a person would be prepared to pay for a licence to use the design.[462] In assessing this, the amount paid under comparable licences (if sufficiently similar licences exist[463]) or the amount agreed by the parties in other dealings may well be relevant.[464] There is no reason why the sum which would be payable under a patent licence[465] should be the starting point for a design right licence.[466] In particular, it appears that the "profits available" approach (i.e. to determine the licence fee by reference to the profits available to the licensee)[467] is reasonably firmly established in design right cases.[468] The profits available approach involves determining the net profit available to the licensee, and then deciding in what proportions a willing licensor and licensee would divide that profit. Thus, in one design right case where the licensee's anticipated available profit was 32 per cent of its anticipated sale price,[469] it was held that the licensor should get 25 per cent of that profit, i.e. 8 per cent of the sale price.[470] This 8 per cent was then uplifted to 9 per cent to take account of the fact that the licensee had access to special markets not open to the licensor and could, therefore, sell goods made to the design at a premium.[471] The idea of dividing the available profit such that the licensee would receive its usual net profit margin on past trading—namely 3.3 per cent—was rejected on the ground that a willing licensee was unlikely to settle for so low a return.[472] In another case, the royalty rate fixed was 6.5 per cent of the invoiced price excluding VAT and transport costs.[473] In

---

[461] See *Stafford Engineering Services Ltd's Application* [2000] R.P.C. 797 at 810 and *E-UK Controls Ltd's Licence of Right (Copyright) Application* [1998] R.P.C. 833 at 840. See also *NIC Instruments Ltd's Licence of Right (Design Right) Application* [2005] R.P.C. 1 at para.18.

[462] See *Roger Bance's Application* [1996] R.P.C. 667 at pp.678–679 and *Pioneer Oil Tools Ltd's Application* [1997] R.P.C. 573 at 589.

[463] See *Pioneer Oil Tools Ltd's Application* [1997] R.P.C. 573 at 591 and *Sterling Fluid Systems Ltd's Application* [2000] R.P.C. 77 5 at 789.

[464] See *Roger Bance's Application* [1996] R.P.C. 667 at p. 674.

[465] Such royalty generally being 5 to 7% of the sale price of articles made using the relevant mechanical invention.

[466] See *Roger Bance's Application* [1996] R.P.C. 667 at 676 where the Comptroller commented that there was no clear justification (other than as "a certain gut reaction") for accepting the sum which would be payable under a patent licence of right as a starting point.

[467] In patent cases, there has been some reluctance to adopt the "available profits" approach—see, for example, *Smith Kline & French Laboratories Ltd's (Cimetidine) Patent* [1990] F.S.R. 203 and *Gerber Garment Technology Inc v Lectra Systems Ltd & Anor* [1995] R.P.C. 383 at 418 to 419, where the approach was nevertheless adopted because both parties suggested it and because there was no evidence of any sufficiently similar comparable licences, ibid. at 418–419.

[468] See *Sterling Fluid Systems Ltd's Application* [2000] R.P.C. 775 at 785 (where it was stated that this approach better reflected commercial reality), *E-UK Controls Ltd's Application* [1998] R.P.C. 833 and *Stafford Engineering Services Ltd's Application* [2000] R.P.C. 797 at 809. In *Pioneer Oil Tools Ltd's Application* [1997] R.P.C. 573 at 581, the Comptroller commented that one of the arguments against the use of the "profits available" approach in patent cases was the wording of Patents Act 1977 (c.37) s.50(1)(b) which requires that the royalty be fixed by reference to the licensor's remuneration rather than the licensee's. He pointed out that there is no comparable provision in the CDPA 1988 in relation to design right. In *Roger Bance's Application* [1996] R.P.C. 667, the "profits available" approach was used as a means to cross-check other figures. See also *NIC Instruments Ltd's Licence of Right (Design Right) Application* [2005] R.P.C. 1. On the facts, the Comptroller allowed the applicant half its normal overhead rate in calculating the available profits para.38.

[469] *Pioneer Oil Tool Ltd's Application* [1997] R.P.C. 573 at 588.

[470] *Pioneer Oil Tool Ltd's Application* [1997] R.P.C. 573 at 589. The same percentage split was applied in *NIC Instruments Ltd's Licence of Right (Design Right) Application* [2005] R.P.C. 1 at para.40.

[471] *Pioneer Oil Tool Ltd's Application* [1997] R.P.C. 573 at 590.

[472] *Pioneer Oil Tool Ltd's Application* [1997] R.P.C. 573 at 589.

[473] *Stafford's Engineering Service Ltd's Application* [2000] R.P.C. 797 at 809.

yet another, it was 4 per cent of that price less VAT, packaging and transport costs.[474]

In *NIC Instruments Ltd's Licence of Right (Design Right) Application*, the applicant sold articles made to the design as components of a kit. On the evidence the vast majority of its sales of these kits would not have been made if the articles had not been included. The Comptroller held that a willing licensor and licensee would have taken this into account in one of two ways. They could have based the royalty rate on the value of the kit, but if so they would have discounted it to reflect the fact that the kit contained other components on which the applicant would expect to make a reasonable margin. Alternatively, they could have based the rate on the components alone but would have increased it to take account of the fact that the components were allowing a higher-value product to be sold. The Comptroller concluded that the actual royalty would end up the same whichever approach was adopted and that the question whether the royalty should be based on the kit or the components was therefore more one of convenience than of fundamental principle. He decided to calculate the royalty as a percentage of the price of the kits.[475] Further, as the applicant sold the articles through middlemen (whereas the design right owner sold them through its own distribution network), the Comptroller adopted a "half way house" between a royalty based on the price at which the applicant sold the articles to the middlemen (which royalty would only take account of the applicant's profit) and the price paid by the end-user (which would also take into account the profit made by the middlemen).[476]

Application to Comptroller to settle terms. In default of agreement by the parties,[477] the prospective licensee can apply to the Comptroller to settle the terms of the licence.[478] Such an application cannot be made earlier than one year before the licence of right first becomes available under that section.[479] The basis on which the Comptroller settles the terms of a licence has already been discussed above. Where the Comptroller settles the terms, the date on which the licence takes effect is either, in the case of an application made under s.237 and made before the earliest date on which a licence of right could take effect under that section, that date[480] or, in all other cases, the date of the application to the Comptroller.[481] An appeal against a decision of the Comptroller lies to the Registered Designs Appeal Tribunal.[482] No appeal lies against the decision of the Tribunal, the only remedy being judicial review by the Divisional Court.   **13–131**

Terms of licence when design right owner is unknown. If the identity of the design right owner cannot be discovered on reasonable inquiry, a person may still apply to the Comptroller to settle the terms of a licence and the Comptroller may   **13–132**

---

[474] *Sterling Fluid Systems Ltd's Application* [2000] R.P.C. 775.

[475] [2005] R.P.C. 1 at paras 23–24.

[476] [2005] R.P.C. 1 at para.31.

[477] CDPA 1988 ss.237(2) and 238(3). Despite the wording of these sections, it is not thought that it is essential to be able to prove such default before making an application to the Comptroller—see *Roussel-Uclaf (Clemence & Le Martret's) Patent* [1987] R.P.C. 109 (a patent case) per Falconer J. at 117.

[478] CDPA 1988 s.247(1). An application may be made for a licence in respect of more than just one design, see *Split Roller Bearing Co Ltd's Licence of Right (Copyright) Application* [1996] R.P.C. 225 at 231. The prospective licensor has, it appears, no right to apply to the Comptroller under s.247.

[479] CDPA 1988 s.247(2).

[480] i.e. the date five years from the end of the term of design right, see para.13–127, above.

[481] CDPA 1988 s.247(6).

[482] s.249.

order that the licence be free of any obligation to make any payment.[483] If such an order is made, the design right owner may apply to vary the terms of that licence but only with effect from the date when the application to vary is made.[484] Further, even if it emerges that a licence had not been available as of right,[485] the licensee is not liable for damages or an account of profits in respect of anything done at a time before the licensee was aware of any claim by the design right owner that a licence was not available. These limitations on the subsequent rights and remedies of the design right owner suggest that the Comptroller should examine with care the evidence adduced by the prospective licensee as to his attempts to identify the design right owner.

13–133　**Prohibition on the licensee claiming a connection with the owner.** The 1988 Act provides that a licensee under a licence of right shall not, without the consent of the design right owner, apply to goods marketed or to be marketed under the licence a trade description which indicates that he is a licensee of the design right owner nor use such a trade description in any advertisement in relation to such goods.[486] A breach of this prohibition is actionable by the design right owner.[487]

Section 240 of the 1988 Act permits a government department or a person authorised in writing by a government department to do anything for the purpose of supplying articles for the services of the Crown or to dispose of articles no longer required for the services of the Crown. Such use of a design is called "Crown use". A person does not have to be authorised by a government department before he makes Crown use of a design on behalf of that department; the authorisation may be given before or after the use and whether or not the person is authorised (directly or indirectly) by the design right owner. Furthermore, any person acquiring anything sold as a result of the exercise of the Crown use powers, is entitled to deal with it in the same manner as if the design right were held on behalf of the Crown.

G. CROWN USE

13–134　**Crown use not an infringement.** Under s.240 of the 1988 Act, certain uses of a design by the Crown will not constitute an infringement of that design right even though such use was without the licence of the design right owner. Similar provisions exist under the Registered Designs Act 1949 and the Patents Act 1977.[488]

Section 240 of the 1988 Act permits a government department[489] or a person authorised in writing by a government department to do anything for the purpose of supplying articles for the services of the Crown or to dispose of articles no longer required for the services of the Crown. Such use of a design is called "Crown

---

[483] CDPA 1988 s.248(1) and (2).

[484] s.248(3).

[485] Because, for example, the design was not in the last five years of its term of protection.

[486] CDPA 1988 s.254. "Trade description" and "advertisement" have the same meaning as in the Trade Descriptions Act 1968 (c.29).

[487] CDPA 1988 s.245(2): actionable as a breach of statutory duty.

[488] Registered Designs Act 1949 (c.88) s.12 and Patents Act 1977 (c.37) ss.55–59.

[489] "Government department" is defined as including a Northern Ireland department and any part of the Scottish Administration; see CDPA 1988 s.263(1) (as amended by the Scotland Act 1998 (Consequential Modifications) (No.2) Order 1999 (SI 1999/1820)). Since June 23, 1999, the power conferred by s.240(1) on a government department is also exercisable for the purposes of a visiting force or headquarters to the extent that it would have been exercisable if that visiting force or headquarters were a part of the home forces and references to "Crown use" in ss.240(5) to (7) shall be construed accordingly. This provision does not, however, authorise the doing of anything in relation to design right which is for foreign defence purposes or health service purposes within the meaning of ss.240(3) and (4). See The Visiting Forces and International Headquarters (Application of Law) Order 1999 (SI 1999/1736) art.3.

use".[490] A person does not have to be authorised by a government department *before* he makes Crown use of a design on behalf of that department; the authorisation may be given before or after the use and whether or not the person is authorised (directly or indirectly) by the design right owner.[491] Furthermore, any person acquiring anything sold as a result of the exercise of the Crown use powers, is entitled to deal with it in the same manner as if the design right were held on behalf of the Crown.[492]

"Crown use"—services of the Crown. To be permitted, the relevant use must relate to "services of the Crown". This does not cover every area of Crown activity but only use for (a) the defence of the realm, (b) foreign defence purposes and (c) health service purposes.[493]   **13–135**

The supply of articles for foreign defence purposes means their supply for the defence of a country outside the realm in pursuance of an agreement or arrangement between the government of that country and the British Government; or their supply for use by armed forces in pursuance of a resolution of the United Nations.[494] The supply of articles for "health service purposes" includes their supply for the purpose of providing various medical, dental and pharmaceutical services.[495]

Crown use during emergency. Section 244 of the 1988 Act contains special provisions which apply during a period of emergency[496] and which extend the scope of Crown use. They permit any act which would otherwise be an infringement of design right for any purpose which appears to the government department concerned necessary or expedient: **13–136**

(a) for the efficient prosecution of any war in which the government is engaged;

(b) for the maintenance of supplies and services essential to the life of the community;

(c) for securing a sufficiency of supplies and services essential for the well-being of the community;

(d) for promoting the productivity of industry, commerce and agriculture;

(e) for fostering and directing export and reducing imports and generally redressing the balance of trade;

(f) generally for ensuring that the whole resources of the community are available for use; or

---

[490] CDPA 1988 s.240(5).

[491] s.240(6).

[492] i.e. where an article no longer required for the services of the crown is disposed of by sale, ss.240(1)(a) and 240(7).

[493] CDPA 1988 s.240(2). It appears that this definition is narrower than the equivalent Crown use provisions in the Registered Designs Act 1949 where "Crown use" is not defined save that is "deemed to include" certain defence and United Nations uses (see RDA 1949 Sch.1 para.1).

[494] CDPA 1988 s.240(3).

[495] CDPA 1988 s.240(4). Such services are "(za) primary medical services or primary dental services under the National Health Service Act 2006 or the National Health Service (Wales) Act 2006 or primary medical services under Part I of the National Health Service (Scotland) Act 1978. (a) pharmaceutical services, general medical services or general dental services under (i) Chapter 1 of Part 7 of the National Health Service Act 2006, or Chapter 1 of part 7 of the National Health Service (Wales) Act 2006 (in the case of pharmaceutical services), (ii) Part II of the National Health Service (Scotland) Act 1978 (in the case of pharmaceutical services or general dental services), or the corresponding provisions of the law in force in Northern Ireland, or (b) personal medical or personal dental services in accordance with arrangements made under ... (ii) section 17C of the 1978 Act (in the case of personal dental services), (iii) the corresponding provisions of the law in force in Northern Ireland, or (c) local pharmaceutical services provided under the National Health Service Act 2006 or the National Health Service (Wales) Act 2006."

[496] The period of emergency being a period declared by Order in Council to be a period of emergency, see CDPA 1988 s.244(3).

(g) for assisting the relief of suffering and the restoration and distribution of essential supplies and services in any country outside the United Kingdom which is in grave distress as a result of war.

13–137 **Notification of Crown use to design right owner.** Section 241(1) of the 1988 Act provides that, where Crown use is made, the government department concerned must (unless it is contrary to the public interest, or unless the identity of the design right owner cannot be ascertained) notify the design right owner of the Crown use and give the design right owner such information as to the extent of the Crown use as the design right owner may from time to time require.[497]

13–138 **Terms of Crown use.** Although Crown use will not constitute an infringement of the design right, s.241(2) of the 1988 Act provides that the use must be on terms to be agreed by the government department concerned and the design right owner with the approval of the Treasury. Such agreement may be made before or after the relevant use. In default of agreement, any party may refer the matter to the court for its determination of the terms for the Crown use.[498]

In determining a dispute as to the terms for Crown use, a court must have regard to any remuneration which the design right owner is entitled to receive, directly or indirectly, from any government department in respect of the design and to whether the design right owner or the design right owner's predecessor in title has, in the court's opinion, without reasonable cause failed to comply with the department's request for the use of the design on reasonable terms.[499] This plainly suggests that the terms to be agreed by the parties or to be imposed by the court should be "reasonable" terms. It is submitted that the terms should be those which protect the interests of the parties in a manner which is fair and reasonable and which would be agreed by a willing licensor and a willing government department. Whilst this test resembles that for licences of right, it seems likely that the terms which a willing licensor might agree with a willing government department may well be rather different to those which would be agreed with a rival manufacturer. The terms may include provision for payment in addition to any sum which may be payable by way of compensation for loss of profit under s.243.[500] Where the identity of the design right owner cannot be ascertained on reasonable enquiry, the government department concerned may apply to the court which may order that no royalty or other sum should be payable in respect of the Crown use of the design until the owner agrees terms with the department or refers the matter to the court for determination.[501] It is, therefore, in the design right owner's interests to refer the matter to court as soon as possible once he becomes aware of the Crown use.

13–139 **Compensation for loss of profit.** In addition to any other terms which may be agreed or imposed by the court,[502] s.243 of the 1988 Act provides that, where Crown use is made of a design, the government department should pay compensation for any loss suffered by the design right owner or (if there is an exclusive licence in force in respect of the design) the exclusive licensee resulting from

---

[497] CDPA 1988 s.241(1). For the position where there is an exclusive licence in force in respect of the design, see para.13–141, below.

[498] CDPA 1988 ss.241(2) and 252(1). The relevant court with jurisdiction to determine disputes as to the terms for Crown use are defined by s.252(6) as being (a) in England and Wales, the High Court or any patents county court having jurisdiction under s.287; (b) in Scotland the Court of Session and (c) in Northern Ireland, the High Court. For jurisdiction generally, see paras 13–191 et seq., below.

[499] s.252(2).

[500] s.243(5), see para.13–139, below.

[501] s.241(3).

[502] i.e. under CDPA 1988 s.241.

such person not being awarded a contract to supply the articles made to the design. Compensation is not payable for losses due to any failure to secure contracts for the supply of articles otherwise than for the services of the Crown.[503] However, although compensation is only payable to the extent that the design right owner or exclusive licensee could have met the contract from his existing manufacturing capacity, it is nevertheless payable even if there were circumstances which would have rendered the design right owner or the exclusive licensee ineligible to be awarded that contract.[504] In determining the level of compensation, regard must be had to the actual profit which would have been made on such a contract and to the extent to which any manufacturing capacity was under-used.[505] The actual level of compensation should be agreed between the design right owner or the exclusive licensee and the government department concerned, with the approval of the Treasury.[506] In the absence of agreement, any of the parties may refer the matter to the court for its determination.[507]

Rights of third parties in relation to Crown use. In many cases, third parties will have an interest in or in relation to the relevant design right. Accordingly, the 1988 Act provides that the provisions of any licence, assignment or agreement made between the design right owner (or his predecessors or successors in title) and any other person[508] are of no effect in relation to Crown use or any act incidental to Crown use insofar as they seek to restrict or regulate anything done in relation to the design or the use of any model, document or other information relating to the design or seek to provide for the making of payment in respect of, or calculated by reference to such use. Furthermore, the copying or issuing to the public of copies of any such model or document, or any such use, is deemed not to be an infringement of any copyright in the model or document.[509] However, this is not to be construed as authorising the disclosure of any model, document or information in contravention of the licence, assignment or agreement.[510]   **13–140**

Exclusive licences. Special provisions apply where an exclusive licence[511] has been granted in respect of the relevant design right. The provisions applicable depend upon whether or not the exclusive licence was granted for royalties.[512]   **13–141**

Where the exclusive licence was granted for royalties, the licensee is plainly directly interested in the determination of the sum payable by the Crown in respect of Crown use. Accordingly, where such a licence is in force in respect of the relevant design, (i) any agreement between the design right owner and a government department settling the terms for Crown use[513] will require the consent of the exclusive licensee.[514] Further, (ii) the exclusive licensee is entitled to recover from the design right owner such part of the payment for Crown use as may be agreed between the design right owner and the licensee. In default of such agreement, any party may refer the matter to the court for its

---

[503] s.243(4).
[504] s.243(2).
[505] ss.243(2) and 243(3).
[506] Unless the government department is any part of the Scottish Administration, see the Scotland Act 1998 (Consequential Modifications) (No.2) Order 1999 (SI 1999/1820) art.4, Sch.2 para.93(3).
[507] CDPA 1988 ss.243(5) and 252(1).
[508] Other than a government department, CDPA 1988 s.242(1). See para.13–134, above.
[509] s.242(1).
[510] s.242(2).
[511] For the meaning of "exclusive licence", see para.13–124, above.
[512] See CDPA 1988 s.242(3). "Royalties" include any benefit determined by reference to the use of the design, see s.242(6).
[513] i.e. an agreement under CDPA 1988 s.241(2).
[514] s.242(3)(a).

determination.[515] The interest of a licensee under an exclusive licence granted for royalties is also apparent from the fact that a determination by the court of the amount of *any payment* to be made for Crown use is of no effect unless that licensee had been notified of the reference to the court and had been given an opportunity to be heard.[516] If the court is asked to determine the proportion payable to the exclusive licensee, the court is required to determine what would be just having regard to any expenditure incurred by the licensee in developing the design or in making payments to the design right owner in consideration of the licence (other than royalties or other payments determined by reference to the use of the design).[517]

Where the exclusive licence was not granted for royalties, (i) the exclusive licensee takes the place of the design right owner for the purposes of being notified of the Crown use and in settling the terms for Crown use under s. 241 of the 1988 Act.[518] However, (ii) s.241 will not apply in relation to the actions of the licensee by virtue of being authorised by a government department in respect of Crown use.[519]

13–142   **Assignments for royalties.** Special provisions also apply where the design right has been assigned to the design right owner in consideration of royalties. In these circumstances, the settlement of terms for Crown use under s. 241 of the 1988 Act has to take into account both the design right owner and the assignor, and any payment for Crown use is to be divided between them in such proportion as may be agreed. In default of agreement, any party may refer the matter to the court for its determination.[520] In these circumstances, the provisions of s.241 do apply in relation to any act incidental to Crown use as they apply in relation to Crown use of the design.[521]

13–143   **Use of model, document or other information.** As mentioned above,[522] the provisions of any licence, assignment or agreement between the design right owner and any person other than a government department are of no effect in relation to Crown use of a design so far as they restrict or regulate anything done in relation to the design, or the use of any model, document or other information relating to it. However, the person entitled to the benefit of such a provision which is thereby rendered inoperative is placed in the position of the design right owner as regards settlement of terms for Crown use.[523]

7. THE RIGHTS OF THE DESIGN RIGHT OWNER AND INFRINGEMENT

A. INTRODUCTION

13–144   This section deals with the rights that the 1988 Act confers upon a design right owner (i.e. the rights to exploit or to deal with the design in a non-litigious context) and with the infringement of those rights. As with copyright, the rights and forms of infringement fall into two categories—primary and secondary. The

---

[515] ss.242(3)(a)(ii) and 252(1).
[516] s.252(4).
[517] s.252(5).
[518] s.242(3)(b)(i). For s.241, see para.13–138, above.
[519] s.242(3)(b)(ii).
[520] CDPA 1988, ss.242(4) and 252(1).
[521] s.242(4)(b).
[522] CDPA 1988 s.242(1) and see para.13–140, above.
[523] s.242(5).

former are concerned largely with the copying of a design for commercial purposes; the latter with commercial dealings in such copies.

B. Exclusive Rights and Primary Infringements

Exclusive rights of design right owner. Primary infringements of design right are defined by reference to the exclusive rights of the design right owner. Those exclusive rights are set out in s.226(1) of the 1988 Act which provides that:

> "The owner of the design right in a design has the exclusive right to reproduce the design for commercial purposes—
> (a) by making articles to that design, or
> (b) by making a design document recording the design for the purpose of enabling such articles to be made."

13–145

Primary infringement. Subject to certain statutory exceptions,[524] it is an infringement of design right for a person without the licence of the design right owner to do or to authorise another to do anything which is the exclusive right of the design right owner.[525] Whether a person has the necessary licence is, of course, a matter of fact to be determined in each case.[526] The meaning of the word "authorise" has already been considered in relation to infringements of copyright.[527]

13–146

Commercial purposes. The design right owner's exclusive rights (and therefore the scope of infringement) are limited to the right to reproduce the design for commercial purposes. An act done in relation to an article is only done for commercial purposes if it is done with a view to that article being sold or hired in the course of business.[528] Although this definition does not fit entirely easily with the way in which s.226(1) is phrased, it seems clear enough that its inclusion means that a person who (for example) makes articles to a design intending to use those articles domestically does not thereby infringe design right. Even if such a person subsequently decides to sell or hire out the relevant articles in the course of business, that person would not be liable for infringement.[529] This result seems, at first sight, strange. However, as a person is unlikely to make many articles with a view to non-commercial purposes, it should in practice create few problems.

13–147

(i) Making articles to the design

Scope of exclusive right. Under s.226(1)(a), the design right owner has the exclusive right to reproduce the design for commercial purposes by making articles to the design. The scope of this exclusive right and, therefore, the area of potential primary infringement is defined by s.226(2). This provides that "reproduction of a design by making articles to the design means copying the design so as to produce articles exactly or substantially to that design."

It is clear from this that design right is concerned with an exclusive right to copy the design. In this it is like copyright. However, the scope of the exclusive

13–148

---

[524] CDPA 1988, s.226(5) and ss.236–245, see paras 13–166 et seq., below.

[525] s.226(3).

[526] For a discussion of design right licences, see paras 13–122 et seq., above.

[527] See paras 7–146 et seq., above. For a case on authorisation in the context of infringement of industrial copyright under the transitional provisions of the 1988 Act, see *Pensher Security Door Co Ltd v Sunderland City Council* [2000] R.P.C. 249 at 276–279 (CA).

[528] CDPA 1988 s.263(3).

[529] The fact that the copying was not an infringement means that the copy cannot be an infringing article within CDPA 1988 s.228. Accordingly, dealings with the article will not constitute secondary infringements. As to secondary infringements, see paras 13–160 et seq., below.

right for design right is significantly different to that for copyright in two respects. First, to infringe design right, the relevant act must have been done for "commercial purposes" (the meaning of which is considered above[530]); in general, copyright law has no such requirement. Second, in copyright cases, the exclusive right is to copy the copyright work or a substantial part of that work.[531] By contrast, in design right cases, the exclusive right is to copy the design so as to produce articles exactly or substantially to that design. As the scope of the exclusive rights conferred by copyright and by design right are different, so too are the tests for infringement. In particular, for design right, it may not be enough that the defendant has copied a part (even a substantial part) of the claimant's design. Instead, one must look at the whole of that design and ask if the defendant's article is made to or substantially to that design.[532]

13–149   **Reproducing the design by "making articles".** The exclusive right relates to the making of articles. As design right is concerned with the protection of a design (i.e. with shape or configuration) and not with the particular substrate on which it is recorded nor with the article to which it is first applied, the exclusive right extends to the making of any article provided that article can be said to have been made exactly or substantially to the relevant design.[533] Thus, a person who designs a doll will (assuming design right subsists in the design) have the exclusive right to produce toothbrush holders exactly or substantially to that design.[534] Similarly, there is no reason why the designer of a spoon with a novel handle should not have the exclusive right to apply that design of handle to other articles.[535] On the wording of the 1988 Act, it appears that, provided design right subsists in a design (i.e. it was not commonplace in the design field in which it was created), then the design right owner can claim exclusive rights in other areas even if the design would be commonplace in those other areas. Thus, in the example given above, if design right subsisted in the design of the doll, the exclusive rights of the owner would extend to its use in relation to a toothbrush holder even if the design would have been commonplace had it originated in that design field.

---

[530] See para.13–147 above.

[531] CDPA 1988 s.16, see para.7–05 above. For substantial part, see paras 7–25 et seq., above.

[532] See *L. Woolley Jewellers Ltd v A & A Jewellery Ltd* [2003] F.S.R. 15 at paras 15 and 19 (CA). See also *Guild v Eskandar Ltd* [2003] F.S.R. 23 at paras 11 and 58 (CA). This is why careful pleading of the design relied on is essential and why claimants define that design or designs to reflect what the defendant has taken, see para.13–45, above.

[533] See *Electronic Techniques (Anglia) Ltd v Critchley Components Ltd* [1997] F.S.R. 401 at 418. As to whether the relevant article has been made "exactly or substantially" to the relevant design, see paras 13–152 et seq., below. In *Societa Esplosivi Industriali SpA v Ordnance Technologies (UK) Ltd* [2007] EWHC 2875; [2008] R.P.C. 12 at para.53, Lindsay J. queried (but did not decide) whether the words "so as to produce" in s.226(2) meant that a defendant could also be a primary infringer if he had, with *a view* to making infringing articles, copied a design without actually ever making an offending article (which would be an infringement under s.226(1)(a)) and without creating a design document (which would be an infringement under s.226(1)(b)). On this construction, a person who takes preparatory steps for making an infringing article might infringe design right. However, such a construction requires the words "so as to produce" to be read as a reference to the intention of the alleged infringer. Whilst it is possible to read s.226(2) in this way, it is submitted that it would not be correct to do so and that the better view is that the words "so as to produce" in s.226(2) should be read in a causative sense—i.e. as meaning that the copying has produced (or has resulted in) articles which have been made exactly or substantially to the design (contrast the words "for the purpose of enabling" in s.226(1)(b), see para.13–159, below). Thus, the acts of primary infringement are the making of articles exactly or substantially to the design or the making of a design document recording the design for the purpose of enabling such articles to be made; nothing else.

[534] This was the example used in the course of Parliamentary debate—see *Hansard*, H.L. Vol.491, cols 1131–1132 and H.L. Vol.495, col.703.

[535] See *Electronic Techniques (Anglia) Ltd v Critchley Components Ltd* [1997] F.S.R. 401 at 418. Whether the making of the other article is covered by the exclusive right will, of course, depend upon whether it has been made exactly or substantially to the relevant design.

Although s.226 refers to the exclusive right to make "articles", it is submitted, both as a matter of statutory construction[536] and as a matter of common sense, that this exclusive right extends to and can be infringed by the making of just a single article to the design.[537] The meaning of the word "article" has already been considered; an article may be a simple article (such as a mug), it may be a composite article (such as a teapot or a car) which is made up of various component articles, or it may be one of those component articles (such as a teapot lid or an exhaust pipe).[538]

The test for infringement. Given the nature of the exclusive rights conferred on the design rights owner, the question of infringement of design right by the making of articles must be approached in two stages; the first is to determine whether there has in fact been copying; the second is to determine whether an article has been made by the alleged infringer either exactly or substantially to the claimant's design.[539]   **13–150**

Copying the design. Design right is not infringed by a person who makes an article or articles to a design which was created independently.[540] Copying must have occurred. Such copying may have been direct or indirect, and it is immaterial whether any intervening acts themselves infringe the design right.[541] Copying may also be established by direct evidence or, more often, by inference from the surrounding circumstances including the extent of the similarities and the differences between the claimant's design and the defendant's article.[542] However, it is important to bear in mind that substantial similarities may be the inevitable consequence of the functional nature of the design in issue.[543] Further, the fact that a component article was "bought in" (off the shelf) by the defendant may defeat an   **13–151**

---

[536] Under the Interpretation Act 1978 s.6(c).

[537] See *C & H Engineering Ltd v F. Klucznik & Sons Ltd* [1992] F.S.R. 421 at 428 ("allegedly infringing article or articles"). It might be argued to the contrary that the equivalent provision in the Registered Designs Act 1949 s.7(1) (as amended by the CDPA 1988) and also CDPA 1988 s.51 both refer to "an article" (i.e. in the singular) and that this suggests that the use of the plural in the design right provisions of the CDPA 1988 was deliberate. However, it seems unlikely that the exclusive rights of a design right owner were not intended to cover cases where a "one-off" article was made to a design. Significantly, the acts of secondary infringement are defined by reference to dealings with "an infringing article", see paras 13–160 et seq., below.

[538] See para.13–50, above.

[539] See *C & H Engineering Ltd v F. Klucznik & Sons Ltd* [1992] F.S.R. 421 at 428. It has been said that although there is in theory a two-step test, in reality, it is hard to imagine a case where it is proved that a design has been copied without the copy being made exactly or substantially to the claimant's design—see *Virgin Aircraft Airways Ltd v Premium Aircraft Interiors Group Ltd* [2009] EWHC 26, [2009] E.C.D.R. 11 at para.33 (the design issues were not argued on appeal ([2010] EWCA Civ 1062).

[540] CDPA 1988 s.226(2) was added by amendment to the original Bill with the specific purpose of clarifying that the use of the term "reproduction" in design right meant (as it does in copyright) that proof of copying was essential to proving infringement, see *Hansard*, H.L. Vol.495, col.703. For other Parliamentary discussion on this point, see *Hansard*, H.L. Vol.491, cols 1132, 1133; and H.L. Vol.494, cols 125, 126.

[541] CDPA 1988 s.226(4). For a discussion of direct and indirect copying, see paras 7–15 et seq., above.

[542] See para.13–153, below. See *Virgin Aircraft Airways Ltd v Premium Aircraft Interiors Group Ltd* [2009] EWHC 26; [2009] E.C.D.R. 11 at para.37 where it was commented that the role of experts in this regard is not to evaluate the evidence but to point out both similarities and differences and to deal with their significance so that the court can come to a view as to whether there is a rebuttable inference of copying. The extent and nature of the similarities may raise the inference of copying and may shift the onus on to the defendant to prove that he did not copy (see *A. Fulton Co Ltd v Grant Barnett & Co Ltd* [2001] R.P.C. 257 at para.96). In *C & H Engineering Ltd v F. Klucznick & Sons Ltd* [1992] F.S.R. 421 at p.429, the court was satisfied on the evidence that there had been copying whereas in *Ocular Sciences Ltd v Aspect Vision Care Ltd* [1997] R.P.C. 289 at 423–424, the alleged infringer was able to rebut the inference of copying by showing that it had gone through its own independent design process. The meaning of "copying" is also discussed in detail in relation to copyright at paras 7–17 et seq., above.

[543] *Farmers Build Ltd v Carier Bulk Material Handling Ltd* [1999] R.P.C. 461 at 481–482.

inference of copying that might otherwise arise from such a similarity.[544] In the absence of proof that actual design features have been copied, a person who merely draws inspiration from a design, in the sense of getting ideas by looking at it, is not copying the *design*.[545]

13–152 **Infringement by making articles exactly or substantially to the design.** Proof of copying by itself is not enough. To establish an infringement, the claimant must also show that the alleged infringer has copied the design "so as to produce articles exactly or substantially to that design".[546]

This plainly requires a comparison to be made. However, it is important to note that on the wording of s.226(2), the comparison to be made is between the allegedly infringing article on the one hand and the claimant's design on the other, and the issue is whether the former has been made exactly or substantially to the latter. The allegedly infringing article does not have to be of the same type as that with which the relevant design was concerned.[547] However, it does have to be an article. The design, on the other hand, may be of the whole or of any part of an article.[548] Where the design is of a whole article, the required comparison should be relatively straightforward—particularly where the design is for the same type of article as the allegedly infringing article—for then the comparison is of like for like.[549] However, where the design relied on is the design of a part of an article, the comparison is likely to be more difficult. Taking the example of the teapot, it seems strange to argue that the defendant's allegedly infringing teapot can have been produced exactly or substantially to the claimant's design for the spout of a teapot. Nevertheless, the fact that the definition of "design" in s.213 allows a claimant to assert design right in a part of an article[550] suggests that s.226 should be construed as allowing such a design (the design of a part of an article) to be infringed by the making of an article, and this conclusion would appear to be supported by the authorities.[551] It also seems in keeping with the intention of Parliament.[552]

13–153 **Exactly or substantially.** Where the copying does not produce an article made exactly to the claimant's design, the question whether it has been made *substan-*

---

[544] *Baby Dan AS v Brevi SRL* [1999] F.S.R. 377 at 388.

[545] *Red Spider Technology v Omega Completions Technology* [2010] EWHC 59 (Mann J.) at paras 132 and 147.

[546] CDPA 1988 s.226(2).

[547] See para.13–149, above.

[548] See paras 13–45 et seq., above.

[549] As in *C & H Engineering Ltd v F. Klucznik & Sons Ltd* [1992] F.S.R. 421 where the allegedly infringing pig fenders were compared with the claimant's design for a pig fender (see para.13–155, below). These were the sort of cases referred to in the course of Parliamentary debate—see *Hansard*, H.L. Vol.495, col.703.

[550] See para.13–46, above.

[551] See for example, *Scholes Windows Ltd v Magnet Ltd* [2002] F.S.R. 10, a case concerning a design for a small "S" shaped horn extension to the upper casement of a window which the defendant had copied in its windows. The trial judge stated that, if the design had not been commonplace, the defendant would have been liable for infringement of design right in the design. It would seem, therefore, that he accepted that the defendant's window had been produced exactly or substantially to that design (see [2000] F.S.R. 432 at 446–447). The Court of Appeal stated that it did not need to express any concluded view on the question of infringement but commented that it would have been reluctant to interfere with his conclusion (see [2002] F.S.R. 172 at para.51). See also *Electronic Techniques (Anglia) Ltd v Critchley Components Ltd* [1997] F.S.R. 401 at 418, *Lambretta Clothing Co Ltd v Teddy Smith (UK) Ltd* [2005] R.P.C. 6. at para.75 and *Virgin Aircraft Airways Ltd v Premium Aircraft Interiors Group Ltd* [2009] EWHC 26; [2009] E.C.D.R. 11 at para.31 (the design issues were not argued on appeal ([2010] EWCA Civ 1062).

[552] In the course of Parliamentary debate, the example used was of fins at the end of an aircraft wing—see *Hansard* H.L. Vol.494, col.124. It is submitted that Parliament clearly envisaged that a person who produced aircraft wings which incorporated the design of such fins would be an infringer.

tially to that design is to be determined objectively through the eyes of those persons to whom the claimant's design is directed.[553]

On the one hand, any similarities, in particular similarities in respect of unusual or attractive design features, may lead to the conclusion that, despite any other differences, the allegedly infringing article has been made substantially to the claimant's design. It is submitted that an objective observer may form the view that an article has been made substantially to a design even though that design forms only a small part of the article in quantitative terms, provided it plays an important role in qualitative terms.[554] On the other hand, similarities in respect of features whose design is dictated solely or largely by the function which the article is to perform are likely to be of little assistance to a claimant.[555]

If the alleged infringer has used the design in making a different type of article, it may be that the impact of the design in that article is very different—particularly where the other features of shape and configuration of the article cause the whole article to seem very different to the design relied on.[556] In such a case, an objective observer may take the view that the article as a whole has not been made substantially to the design and the claim for infringement would, therefore, fail.

Where the design is defined by reference to the most detailed and specific dimensions, then the mere fact that the allegedly infringing articles cannot be distinguished from the claimant's design by visual inspection is not enough; the claimant would have to show that the defendant had produced an extremely similar design in order to prove infringement.[557] By contrast, a circuit board made to a design recorded in a circuit diagram could take a number of forms. Thus visual similarities may not always be required in order to establish an infringement of design right.[558]

Treatment of commonplace and excluded features. Section 226 of the 1988 Act does not make clear how the court should approach the question of infringement of a design which includes features which taken individually would be commonplace or features from which design right is excluded.[559]   **13–154**

Given that design right subsists in the whole of a design and not just in its non-commonplace features,[560] it is submitted that commonplace features should not be ignored for the purposes of making the comparison between the allegedly infringing article and the claimant's design, although a court would be unlikely to find that an allegedly infringing article has been made exactly or substantially to the claimant's design unless there are other more striking similarities than in respect of commonplace features.[561]

The position is less clear where the design includes features from which design

[553] See *C & H Engineering Ltd v F. Klucznik & Sons Ltd* [1992] F.S.R. 421 at 428 and *Baby Dan AS v Brevi SRL* [1999] F.S.R. 377 at 385.

[554] Using the example referred to in Parliament of fins at the end of an aircraft wing (see *Hansard* H.L. Vol.494, col.124); such fins, whilst small, would plainly of great significance and should be capable of protection. It is submitted that an alleged infringer whose aircraft wings incorporated the design of such fins would, therefore, be producing articles (i.e. the wings) *substantially* to the claimant's design (i.e. of the fin).

[555] As was the case in *C & H Engineering Ltd v F. Klucznik & Sons Ltd* [1992] F.S.R. 421 and para.13–155, below. See also *Baby Dan SA v Brevi SRL* [1999] F.S.R. 377 at 390, where similarities in relation to features as simple as a hinge support and a hook were insufficient to show that the articles had been made substantially to the claimant's design.

[556] See *Electronic Techniques (Anglia) Ltd v Critchley Components Ltd* [1997] F.S.R. 401 at 418.

[557] See *Ocular Sciences Ltd v Aspect Vision Care Ltd* [1997] R.P.C. 289 at 424.

[558] See *Mackie Designs Inc v Behringer Specialised Studio Equipment (UK) Ltd* [1999] R.P.C. 717 at 719. See also *Ocular Sciences Ltd v Aspect Vision Care Ltd* [1997] R.P.C. 289 at 429.

[559] i.e. by the exclusions contained in CDPA 1988 s.213(3).

[560] See para.13–74, above.

[561] This appears to have been the approach adopted in *C & H Engineering Ltd v F. Klucznik & Sons Ltd* [1992] F.S.R. 421 where the court, when determining whether there had been an infringe-

right is excluded (e.g. for being a method of construction, "must fit", "must match" or surface decoration). Again, there seems to be no reason why those features should be ignored when considering whether an allegedly infringing article has been made exactly or substantially to the claimant's design. Such features are a part of the overall design within the meaning of s. 213(2) of the 1988 Act even though s.213(3) provides that design right will not subsist in them. If, of course, the only features of the design which have been copied are excluded features, then there can be no infringement of any design right.

Given the nature of the test for infringement, a claimant should pay careful attention to the type of articles which the alleged infringer has made and would be well advised to frame his design right claim in the way which produces the most favourable comparison between his design and what he believes the alleged infringer has taken.[562]

13–155 *C & H Engineering v F. Klucznick & Sons.* The different ways in which the test for infringement may be applied can be seen from the decision in *C & H Engineering Ltd v Klucznik & Sons Ltd*.[563] There, the relevant design was of a whole article—namely a whole pig fender.[564] The design was not commonplace because it had incorporated a two-inch pipe acting as a roll bar on the top of an otherwise commonplace pig fender. The alleged infringer had also produced pig fenders with a roll bar and its incorporation of the roll bar had been the result of copying. Objectively viewed, however, the allegedly infringing fender was not made exactly or substantially to the design of the claimant's fender. Whilst there were similarities between the fenders, those similarities were in respect of features which pig fenders must have in order to perform their function as pig fenders. Further, an objective observer would be struck by the differences in the designs of the fenders and, in particular, by design features unique to the allegedly infringing fenders which allowed them to be stacked. Thus, despite the evidence of copying, the claimant's case failed.

C & H Engineering Ltd might (depending upon the precise facts) have been argued in other ways (although it is unlikely that this would have produced a different result in that case). A discussion of these other ways shows how s.226 works and how claimants may be able to strengthen their position by framing their design right claims in the way which produces the closest comparison between their designs and the articles which the alleged infringer has made. Thus, instead of relying on the design of the whole fender, the claimant could have relied on the design of just the roll bar,[565] making it the claimant's design for the purposes of the comparison. This would have allowed the claimant to argue that other parts of its fender[566] were irrelevant for the purposes of the comparison. Instead, the comparison would have been between the claimant's design of the roll bar on the one hand and the alleged infringer's article (either the alleged infringer's fender or the alleged infringer's roll bar, assuming it was itself a separate article) on the other. However, on the facts of *C & H Engineering Ltd*, it is

---

ment, had regard to the whole of the claimant's fender despite having found that pig fenders without a roll bar were commonplace. For a detailed discussion of the decision in *C & H Engineering*, see para.13–155, below.

[562] See *Ocular Sciences Ltd v Aspect Vision Care Ltd* [1997] R.P.C. 289 at 422.

[563] [1992] F.S.R. 421.

[564] i.e. the relevant design was of the entire pig fender and not of any individual part of it. As to the contrary view (i.e. that the relevant design was of the roll bar only), see *Parker & Parker v Tidball* [1997] F.S.R. 680 at 691 and see para.13–156, below.

[565] On the basis that its design was the design of a part of an article (i.e. as part of the fender) or, if as appears to have been the case, the roll bar had its own separate form, as the design of an article in its own right. For the meaning of "an article", see para.13–50, above.

[566] Including those, such as the stacking features, which the court found to be significant when looking at the whole article.

submitted that the claimant's case would still have failed. If the claimant's design of a roll bar was compared with the alleged infringer's fender, then that fender was plainly not an article made exactly to that design and was unlikely to have been an article made substantially to it.[567] Similarly, if the claimant's design of a roll bar was compared with the alleged infringer's roll bar, then it seems unlikely that the claimant could have persuaded the court that so functional a feature as a roll bar had been made exactly or substantially to that design.

Parker & Parker v Tidball. The difficulties which may arise in applying the test for infringement can be seen in *Parker & Parker v Tidball*[568] where the court was concerned with various design features of leather cases for mobile phones. Some of these were found to be commonplace and others were excluded by the must fit exclusion. However, each of the remainder (each being the design of a part of an article) was treated as a separate design in which design right subsisted. In approaching the question of infringement of each of these designs, the court first asked whether the relevant design feature had been copied. It then compared the whole of the defendant's allegedly infringing mobile phone case with the whole of the plaintiff's mobile phone case in order to determine whether the defendant had made articles exactly or substantially to the plaintiff's design.[569] It is submitted that this approach was incorrect. First, the approach seems contrary to s.226 of the 1988 Act. The references in that section to "a design" and to "that design" are plainly references to the design relied upon by the claimant, and the issue is whether the alleged act of copying has produced an article exactly or substantially "to that design". If the relevant design is the design of a part of an article then it is against that design—the design of the part of an article—that the allegedly infringing article must be compared. The wording of the section does not require and, indeed does not justify, any comparison being made with the article of which the claimant's design is a part. Moreover, whilst the judge in *Parker & Parker v Tidball* plainly considered himself to be following the approach in *C & H Engineering Ltd*, it is submitted that he misconstrued the decision in that case. The judge took the view that the relevant design in *C & H Engineering Ltd* had been the design of a part of an article rather than of a whole article—namely the design of just the roll bar rather than the design of a pig fender.[570] In fact, whilst the point is never expressly addressed, it would appear that the claimant in *C & H Engineering Ltd* was asserting design right in the whole of its drawing of a fender and not just in any part,[571] and that is why the court in that case compared the allegedly infringing fender with the whole of the claimant's fender.[572] On this basis, it is submitted that whilst a comparison with the whole of the plaintiff's mobile phone case would have been justified had the plaintiff been relying upon the design of the whole case, it was not justified when the plaintiff was relying on designs of parts of the case. It was suggested in *Parker & Parker v Tidball*[573] that the justification for testing for infringement of design right in the design of a part of an article by reference to the whole article is that there could otherwise be no

13–156

---

[567] Even on the basis that the word "substantial" has a qualitative meaning, see para.13–153, above.
[568] [1997] F.S.R. 680.
[569] [1997] F.S.R. 680 at 691 and 702–706.
[570] [1997] F.S.R. 680 at 691.
[571] [1992] F.S.R. 421, see the drawing reproduced at 422, the issue numbered (3) at 425 and the words of Aldous J. at 425.
[572] As the designs for the leather cases had some non-commonplace features, it is submitted that *Parker & Parker v Tidball* [1997] F.S.R. 680, above, could have been argued on the basis that the relevant design was the design of the whole case—albeit that design right was excluded from certain "must fit" features. However, it appears that this would have made no difference to the result.
[573] [1997] F.S.R. 680 at 691.

infringement of the design of part of an article. However, it is submitted that this is not the case; whilst it may well be correct to say that a whole article cannot be made exactly to the design of a part of an article, an article may still be made substantially to the design of a part such that it would satisfy the test for infringement.[574] In any event, given the wide meaning of "article",[575] a claimant may, in those cases where an article is made up of various component parts which themselves qualify as articles, be able to tailor his design right claim so as to rely on the design right subsisting in one of those component parts.

13–157 *A. Fulton v Totes Isotoner.* The way in which a design right claim can be tailored can be seen in *A. Fulton Co Ltd v Totes Isotoner (UK) Ltd.*[576] There the claimant had designed an umbrella case. The defendant's umbrella case was copied from that design but had a section cut out from its top cuff (where the umbrella was inserted). The claimant accordingly relied not only on the design of the whole case but also on the design of the whole case minus a cut-out section—thereby matching what the defendant had taken. The claim based on the design of the whole case failed but the claim based on the design minus the cut-out succeeded.

(ii) Making a design document

13–158 **Scope of the exclusive right.** Under s.226(1)(b), the design right owner has the exclusive right to reproduce the design for commercial purposes by making a design document recording the design for the purpose of enabling "such articles" to be made. In this context, the reference to "such articles" is a reference back to articles made to the design which are the subject of s.226(1)(a).[577] A person who does this or who authorises another to do this, without the licence of the design right owner, is liable for infringement of design right.

The meaning of "commercial purposes", of "authorises" and of "design document" have already been considered.[578] It is not clear whether the words "recording the design" mean that the design document in question must have recorded the whole of the claimant's design or whether the recording of some part of the design would be sufficient. On the one hand, the wording of s.226(1)(b) suggests that the record should be of the whole design and as s.226(1)(b) (unlike s.216(1)(a)) is not qualified by the words "exactly or substantially" in s.226(2), it could be argued that the "*expressio unius*" argument means that it cannot be construed as applying where the design document only records a part of the design.[579] On the other hand, the court in *C & H Engineering Ltd*[580] seems to have accepted that there had been "copying [of] the design" for the purposes of s.226(1)(a) even though the evidence was only of the copying of a part of the design.[581] If the copying of a part was sufficient for these purposes, then why would the recording of a part of a design for the purposes of s.226(1)(b) not also be so? Given that the relevant design document must be created by the alleged

---

[574] See para.13–153, above.
[575] See para.13–50, above.
[576] [2004] R.P.C. 16.
[577] For the meaning of "making articles to the design" under CDPA 1988 s.226(1)(a), see para.13–152, above.
[578] See paras 13–147, 13–146 and 13–82, above and CDPA 1988 s.263(1).
[579] See *Societa Esplosivi Industriali SpA v Ordnance Technologies (UK) Ltd* [2007] EWHC 2875 at para.55; [2008] R.P.C. 12.
[580] [1992] F.S.R. 421.
[581] [1992] F.S.R. 421 at 429. It was only after making a finding of copying that the court in C & H Engineering Ltd then went on to consider whether the articles had been made exactly or substantially to the claimant's design. The finding of copying does not, therefore, appear to have been influenced by the reference later in s.226(2) to articles being made "substantially" to the design.

infringer for the purpose of enabling articles to be made exactly or substantially to the claimant's design,[582] the latter interpretation would appear to be preferable.

For the purpose of enabling articles to be made to the design. Under s.226(1)(b), the making of the relevant design document must have been "for the purpose of enabling" articles to be made to the design right owner's design. **13–159**

This, it is submitted, would operate where a person makes or authorises another to make the relevant design document knowing or intending it to be used in the production process of the article in question. It would not, however, operate where at the time of creation, there was no intention so to use the document.[583] Whilst it is not clear, it would seem that the words "for the purpose" govern the word "making" so that a person who makes a design document at the request of another but without having any knowledge as to that other person's purpose would not be liable for infringement, although this would mean that the person making that request could not be liable for authorising.[584] Whether the relevant purpose is present must, it seems, be judged as at the time that the design document was created. If at that time there was no intention to make articles to the design, then there could be no infringement under this head even if the document was subsequently used for that purpose.[585]

As a result, a person who prints off copies of the design of a famous article (such as an engine or a gun) with a view to those prints being used as wall posters is not infringing under s.226(1)(b). Although such a person has made a design document for commercial purposes, he or she has not done so for the purpose of enabling such articles (i.e. the engine or gun) to be made.[586] Of course, if another person (for commercial purposes) makes such articles using the prints as a design, that person would be infringing under s.226(1)(a).[587]

C. Secondary Infringements

Acts of secondary infringement. The acts of secondary infringement are defined by s.227(1) of the 1988 Act which provides that design right is infringed[588] by a person who, without the licence of the design right owner— **13–160**

"(a) imports into the United Kingdom for commercial purposes,[589] or

(b) has in his possession for commercial purposes, or

(c) sells, lets for hire, or offers or exposes for sale or hire, in the course of a business,[590]

an article which is, and which he knows or has reason to believe is, an infringing article."

In summary, therefore, secondary infringements of design right involve some

---

582 See para.13–159, below.

583 Because, for example, it was created as an artistic work in its own right or even because it was created for a brochure.

584 It is likely to be rare in industrial design cases that the maker of a design document would not realise that the document is to be used in the process of making articles to the design.

585 See *Societa Esplosivi Industriali SpA v Ordnance Technologies (UK) Ltd* [2007] EWHC 2875 at paras 56–62; [2008] R.P.C. 12.

586 Such a person may, however, infringe copyright in an artistic work recording the design unless the s.52 defence operates—see para.13–170 below.

587 See *Societa Esplosivi Industriali SpA v Ordnance Technologies (UK) Ltd* [2007] EWHC 2875 at para.60.

588 Unless one of the exceptions applies, see paras 13–166 et seq., below.

589 In *Baby Dan AS v Brevi SRL* [1999] F.S.R. 377 at 391, it was stated that a foreign manufacturer which arranged and charged for transporting its goods to its UK distributor, would be jointly liable for importation of infringing articles.

590 In *Baby Dan AS v Brevi SRL* [1999] F.S.R. 377, it was also held that a foreign manufacturer whose goods and catalogue were displayed at a UK trade fair and which supplied UK retailers through a UK corporate vehicle was liable for offering infringing articles for sale.

form of dealing with an infringing article by a person who has the requisite knowledge. This is very similar to the position in relation to copyright and many of the required elements have already been dealt with that context.[591] The words "commercial purposes" have already been considered in the context of primary infringement of design right.[592]

(i) An infringing article

13–161   A person is not liable for a secondary infringement of design right unless he knows or has reason to believe that the article with which he is dealing is an infringing article. An article is an infringing article in relation to a design either if its making to that design was an infringement of the design right in that design,[593] or if it has been or if it is proposed to be imported into the United Kingdom and its making to that design in the United Kingdom would have been an infringement of design right in the design or a breach of an exclusive licence agreement relating to the design.[594] On the other hand, a design document is not an infringing article even if the making of the design document was or would have constituted an infringement of design right.[595] Whilst this means that a person who imports or deals with[596] a design document will not be liable for a secondary infringement, that person's activities may justify the design right owner in seeking a quia timet injunction if there is evidence to suggest that the design document is to be used to make articles to the design.

13–162   **Presumption as to time of making article.** If it is shown that an article has been made to a design in which design right subsists or in which design right has subsisted at any time, then there is a presumption until the contrary is proved that the article was made at a time when design right subsisted.[597] The onus is, therefore, on the alleged infringer to show that the article was made at a time either before design right subsisted[598] or at a time after design right had expired.[599]

13–163   **Importation from European Community.** If an article may be lawfully imported into the United Kingdom under any enforceable European Community right within the meaning of s.2(1) of the European Communities Act 1972,[600] then that article is not an infringing article.[601]

(ii) Treatment of territorial waters and continental shelf

13–164   When considering whether there has been a secondary infringement and whether an article is an infringing article, the provisions of s.257 of the 1988 Act should be borne in mind and, in particular, the provision which treats the territorial waters of the United Kingdom as a part of the United Kingdom. The only act of

---

[591] CDPA 1988 ss.22 and 23, as to which see Ch.8, above.

[592] See para.13–144, above. See also CDPA 1988 ss.23(a), (c) and (d).

[593] CDPA 1988 s.228(2). As to whether the making of the article was an infringement, see paras 13–146 et seq., above.

[594] s.228(3).

[595] s.228(6).

[596] i.e. possesses the design document or sells, lets for hire or offers it for sale or hire.

[597] CDPA 1988 s.228(4).

[598] i.e. before the design was recorded in a design document, see para.13–81, above, or at a time before the design qualified for design right, see para.13–84, above.

[599] See paras 13–103 et seq., above.

[600] c.68.

[601] CDPA 1988 s.228(5).

infringement defined by reference to the United Kingdom is importation.[602] Whether bringing goods into the territorial waters can constitute importation has already been considered in relation to infringements of copyright.[603]

(iii) Knowledge or reason to believe

To establish a secondary infringement of design right, the claimant must prove that the person importing or dealing with the infringing article knew or had reason to believe that the article in question was an infringing article. The same requirement of knowledge or of reason to believe also forms a part of the definition of secondary infringements of copyright and has been discussed in detail in that context.[604]

13–165

8. EXCEPTIONS TO RIGHTS

A. Introduction

The rights of design right owners and the provisions as to infringement of design right are subject to the various exceptions set out in ss.236 to 245 of the 1988 Act.[605] These exceptions include the provisions relating to licences of right[606] and to Crown use of designs,[607] both of which have already been considered.[608] The other exceptions are (1) where there is parallel copyright protection (s.236) and (2) where the Secretary of State makes an appropriate Order under s.245.

13–166

B. Parallel copyright protection — sections 236 and 51

Sections 236 and 51. As has been seen, the intention behind the 1988 Act was, as far as possible, to remove industrial design from the sphere of copyright.[609] Sections 236 and 51 are the means by which the 1988 Act attempts to draw the boundary between copyright protection for artistic works and design right protection for industrial designs and to make the two forms of protection mutually exclusive.[610] The need for these provisions arises from the fact that many designs are recorded in works in which copyright may subsist.

13–167

Statement of section 236 of the 1988 Act. Section 236 of the 1988 Act provides that "[w]here copyright subsists in a work which consists of or includes a design in which design right subsists, it is not an infringement of design right in the design to do anything which is an infringement of copyright in that work". In other words, the prospect of dual protection against any particular act is excluded. If that act infringes copyright, it will not also infringe design right. This would apply even in those cases where the copyright owner and the design right owner are different persons.[611]

13–168

Effect of section 51. The significance of the s.236 exception to design right

13–169

---

[602] CDPA 1988 s.227(1)(a).
[603] See para.8–14, above.
[604] See Ch.8, above.
[605] CDPA 1988 ss.226(5) and 227(2).
[606] ss.237–239.
[607] ss.240–244.
[608] For licences of right see paras 13–126 et seq., above. For Crown use, see paras 13–134 et seq., above.
[609] See para.13–29, above.
[610] See *Hansard*, H.L. Vol.491, col.1136.
[611] See para.13–114, above.

protection is much more limited than may at first appear. This is because s.51 provides that "[i]t is not an infringement of any copyright in a design document or model recording or embodying a design for anything other than an artistic work or typeface to make an article to the design or to copy an article made to the design". Thus, where s.51 operates, the relevant acts cannot be infringements of copyright, accordingly s.36 would not prevent a person suing for infringement of such design right may subsist in the design.

13–170 **Examples.** The effect of s.51 is considered in detail later in this Chapter. For present purposes, the operation of ss.236 and 51 is best seen by way of examples.[612] In these examples, it is to be assumed that both copyright and design right subsist:

(1) A painting of an imaginary chair is an artistic work. It also records the painter's design of a chair. However, the painting is not a design document or model for anything. It is a thing in itself. Accordingly s.51 would not operate to exclude copyright protection and, by reason of s.236, there is no design right protection in respect of acts that would infringe copyright.

(2) A preliminary drawing of an imaginary chair produced by the artist prior to painting the picture referred to in (1) above would be an artistic work and would in one sense be recording the design of a chair.[613] However, the drawing is not a design for a chair. It is the design for an artistic work (the painting) so, again, s.51 would have no application. Again, by reason of s.236, there is no design right protection in respect of acts that would infringe copyright.

(3) A craftsman draws a design for a new style of chair which he intends to make by hand. The drawing would be an artistic work. It also records the design both of and also for a chair. However, it is likely that the chair depicted would itself be an artistic work—being a work of artistic craftsmanship. If so, s.51 would not operate. Once again, by reason of s.236, there is no design right protection in respect of acts that would infringe copyright.

(4) An employee of a furniture warehouse draws a design for a chair which is to be mass-produced on a production line. The drawing is both the design of and for a chair but in this case that chair is unlikely to be a work of artistic craftsmanship.[614] Section 51 would apply and a person who makes a chair to that design or who copies a chair made to the design would not infringe the copyright in that drawing. Accordingly, s.236 would not exclude an action for infringement of design right by the design right owner in respect of those acts.

(5) The photocopying of the drawing referred to in (4) above would not be one of the acts to which s.51 applies. Thus, a person who makes such a photocopy would still infringe copyright and s.236 would defeat any action by the design right owner for infringement of design right.[615]

(6) By contrast, a person who photographs a chair made to the design draw-

---

[612] CDPA 1988 s.51 is considered in more detail at paras 13–301 et seq., below.

[613] A similar example was used in the course of debate in Parliament, see *Hansard*, H.L. Vol.491, col.1136.

[614] See *George Hensher Ltd v Restawile Upholstery (Lancs.) Ltd* [1975] R.P.C. 454 and para.13–24, above.

[615] This is the situation envisaged by Mance L.J. in *Lambretta Clothing Co Ltd v Teddy Smith (UK) Ltd* [2004] EWCA Civ 886; [2005] R.P.C. 6 at para.84. But for ss.51 and 236, making the photocopy would (assuming it was done for commercial purposes and with the purpose of enabling articles to be made to the design) amount to an infringement within CDPA 1988

ing referred to in (4) above would probably be copying an article made to the design. Section 51 would, therefore, operate. However, if there was no infringement of copyright, s.236 would not operate to prevent the design right owner suing for infringement of design right.[616]

C. Order of Secretary of State—Section 245

Under s.245, the Secretary of State may, if it appears to him to be necessary in order to comply with an international obligation or to secure reciprocal protection for British designs in other countries, make an Order providing that acts of a description specified in the Order do not infringe design right.[617] The Order may make different provision for different descriptions of design or article.[618] To date, no such Order has been made. **13–171**

9. PARTIES TO ACTION AND REMEDIES FOR INFRINGEMENT

A. Those Entitled to Sue for Infringement

The persons who may sue for infringement of design right have already been considered in Ch.21 of this work. In summary, they include the following: namely, the legal owner of design right,[619] the equitable owner[620] an exclusive licensee[621] and a joint owner.[622] **13–172**

B. Those Who May Be Sued

The position as regards those who may be sued is similar to that which applies in copyright.[623] They include the person who actually does the relevant act (including employees of companies) and, in the case of the primary infringements, a person who authorises that act (including, although depending upon their level of personal involvement, directors of companies). There may be one infringer or a number of joint tortfeasors. **13–173**

C. Remedies

Section 229(2). Section 229(2) of the 1988 Act provides that, in an action for infringement: **13–174**

> "… all such relief by way of damages, injunctions, accounts or otherwise is available to the plaintiff as is available in respect of the infringement of any other property right."

This provision is identically worded to s.96(2) which applies in respect of remedies for infringement of copyright. The nature of these remedies has already

---

ss.226(1)(b) and 263(1), i.e. the making of a design document recording the design (see paras 13–158 et seq., above).

[616] Again, assuming the photograph was taken for commercial purposes and with the purpose of enabling chairs to be made to the design, its taking would amount to an infringement within CDPA 1988 ss.226(1)(b) and 263(1).

[617] CDPA 1988 s.245(1).

[618] s.245(2).

[619] See para.21–22, below.

[620] See paras 21–24 et seq., below. The legal owner must be joined (or an assignment of legal title obtained) before an equitable owner can obtain final relief.

[621] See paras 21–27 et seq., below. The rights of an exclusive licensee are concurrent with those of the design right owner.

[622] See para.21–36, below.

[623] As to which, see paras 21–39 et seq., below.

been fully considered in Ch.21.[624] In this chapter, reference is made only to the particular sections of the 1988 Act relating to design right.

13–175　**Damages.** A design right owner or an exclusive licensee is entitled to claim damages for any infringement of design right, and s.229(3) provides that a court may, having regard to all the circumstances and in particular to the flagrancy of the infringement and any benefit accruing to the defendant by reason of the infringement, award such additional damages as the justice of the case may require.[625] The way in which the courts approach the question of damages has already been considered in detail in relation to copyright.[626] As with copyright, the damages recoverable for a primary infringement of design right may be limited where the defendant is an innocent infringer as defined in s.233(1).[627] Unlike copyright, there is also a provision limiting damages for secondary infringements where the defendant establishes that the infringing article in question was innocently acquired by him or his predecessor in title.[628] In such a case, s.233(2) provides that the only remedy available against that defendant for that infringement is damages not exceeding a reasonable royalty in respect of the act in respect of which complaint is made.[629] As with copyright, in a case where a design right owner has concurrent rights with an exclusive licensee, the court in assessing damages must take into account the terms of the licence and any pecuniary remedy already awarded or available to either in respect of the infringement.[630]

13–176　**Limitation on damages—where design right owner unknown.** As has been seen,[631] a person may seek a licence of right in respect of a design where the design right owner is unknown. Where such a licence is granted but it is subsequently discovered that the licence had not been available, the licensee will not be liable for damages (or an account of profits) for the period for which he was unaware that a licence was not available.

13–177　**Injunctions.** The principles upon which a court may grant final and interlocutory injunctions are dealt with elsewhere.[632] There are, however, various situations in which a court will not grant an injunction in a design right case. First, as has already been noted, an injunction may not be granted in an action for secondary infringement where the defendant can show that the infringing article in question had been acquired innocently.[633] Secondly, an injunction will not be granted in

---

[624] See paras 21–123 et seq., below.

[625] For the identically worded provisions as to additional damages in copyright, see CDPA 1988 s.97(2).

[626] See Ch.21, below. In *Novum (Overseas) Ltd v Iceland Foods Plc* [2002] EWHC 53 at paras 125–128, a design right case, it was stated that for the additional damages to be awarded, there must be some additional measure of turpitude in the actions of the defendant.

[627] See para.21–75, below.

[628] "Innocently acquired" means that the person acquiring the article did not know and had no reason to believe that the article in question was an infringing article, see CDPA 1988 s.233(3). The test for innocent acquisition is an objective one, see *Badge Sales v PSM International* [2006] F.S.R. 1. In that case it was also held that the standard of proof is the balance of probabilities and the test is objective.

[629] CDPA 1988 s.233(2) (which has no copyright equivalent). The burden of proof is on the defendant who seeks to rely on s.233(2), the standard of proof is the balance of probabilities and the test is objective, see *Badge Sales v PSM International* [2006] F.S.R. 1.

[630] s.235(4)(a). This applies whether or not the design right owner and the exclusive licensee are both parties to the action. These provisions and their copyright equivalent, s.102(4), are discussed at para.21–222, below.

[631] See para.13–132, above.

[632] For the interlocutory relief available (including interlocutory injunctions, *Anton Piller* orders, orders to disclose the identity of infringers and *Mareva* injunctions), see paras 21–131 et seq., below. For final injunctions, see paras 21–168 et seq., below.

[633] See CDPA 1988 s.233(2) and see para.13–175, above.

any action for infringement of design right in a design[634] where a licence of right is available under ss.237 or 238 of the 1988 Act[635] and where the defendant undertakes to take such a licence on terms to be agreed or, in default of agreement, settled by the Comptroller.[636] This limitation will not, however, preclude the grant of an injunction covering the period between the date of the Order and the time when the licence of right becomes available.

Accounts. As with cases of infringement of copyright, a claimant may opt for an account of profits instead of damages.[637] As has been seen,[638] an account is not available in a case of secondary infringement where the defendant establishes that the infringing article in question was innocently acquired by him or his predecessor in title. Further, where the defendant undertakes to take a licence of right or where the design right owner is unknown, the right to an account is limited in the same way that the right to damages was limited.[639] Where an action relates to an infringement where an exclusive licence has concurrent rights with the design right owner, no account of profits may be directed if an award of damages has been made or an account of profits directed in favour of the other person with concurrent rights. If an account of profits is ordered, then (subject to any other agreement) the court must apportion the profits as between the owners of the concurrent rights in such manner as it thinks just.[640] Again, this applies whether or not both the design right owner and the exclusive licensee were parties to the action.[641]   **13–178**

Effect of undertaking by defendant to take a licence of right. A defendant in proceedings for infringement of design right may restrict the remedies available against him by giving an undertaking to take a licence of right (assuming one is available) on terms to be agreed or to be settled by the Comptroller. If the defendant gives such an undertaking, s.239(1) of the 1988 Act provides that no injunction shall be granted against him, no order for delivery up shall be made under s.230, and that the amount recoverable against him by way of damages or on an account of profits shall not exceed double the amount which would have been payable by him as licensee if such a licence on those terms had been granted before the earliest infringement.[642] It should be noted, however, that this limitation only applies to remedies otherwise available against the defendant in respect of an infringement committed after licences of right became available in respect of the relevant designs.[643]   **13–179**

The defendant may give such an undertaking at any time before a final order in the proceedings without any admission of liability.[644] Thus, despite giving an undertaking, the defendant may still contest matters at issue in the infringement

---

[634] i.e. whether primary or secondary infringement.

[635] For licences of right, see paras 13–126 et seq., above.

[636] See CDPA 1988 s.239. See para.13–179, below.

[637] For a full discussion of the principles upon which a court may order an account of profits, see para.21–192 and paras 21–209 et seq., below.

[638] See CDPA 1988 s.233(2) discussed in para.13–175, above.

[639] See paras 13–176 and 13–179, below.

[640] See CDPA 1988 s.235(4)(b) and (c).

[641] CDPA 1988 s.235(4).

[642] CDPA 1988 s.239(1)(c). As damages are usually calculated on the basis of the sum which would have been payable in return for a licence to do the wrongful act, this provision is unlikely to be of much significance to a defendant where the claimant is claiming damages. It might, however, be of some importance where the claimant seeks an account of profits.

[643] s.239(3).

[644] s.239(2).

proceedings[645] including, for example, whether design right subsists in the claimant's design and whether the defendant's activities constitute an infringement. This raises the question of the status of the licence if the proceedings are subsequently determined against the claimant. Clearly a term may be included in the licence making it clear that the licence will determine in the event that the defendant's actions were found not to infringe design right. The position is less clear as regards such money as may have already have been paid under such a licence. In Roger Bance and Anor's Licence of Right (Copyright) Application,[646] the Comptroller took the view that if a defendant chooses to take the potential benefits which s.239 gives those who undertake to take a licence,[647] then the defendant should not be entitled to recover sums paid under the licence if the claimant's action subsequently fails.[648] However, given the wording of s.239, it may be that this view is only partially correct. Section 239 refers to an undertaking given in "proceedings for infringement of design right in a design in respect of which a licence is available as of right ...". Whilst the Comptroller's view seems to be correct where the proceedings fail only because the claimant is unable to prove an act of infringement,[649] it seems harder to justify where the claimant's action fails because he was unable to prove any design right subsisted in his alleged design.[650] An undertaking may be given even though the design right has expired by the time it is offered.[651]

13–180   **Delivery up.** Under s.230 of the 1988 Act, a design right owner[652] may apply to the court for an order for delivery up of certain articles. Very similar provisions apply as regards copyright.[653]

13–181   **Order for forfeiture, destruction, etc.** Under s.231(1) of the 1988 Act, an application may be made to the court[654] for an order that the infringing article or other thing delivered up under s.230 be forfeited to the design right owner, or destroyed, or otherwise dealt with as the court thinks fit, or for a decision that no such order should be made. This power and the corresponding powers relating to copyright and performers' rights (ss.114 and 204) have already been considered.[655]

13–182   **Privilege for professional designs representatives.** The privilege which applies to communications between a person and his solicitor can now extend to communications between a person and his professional designs representative as to any matter relating to the protection of any design.[656] It appears that this privilege

---

[645] That this was the intention of Parliament was made clear in the course of debate, see *Hansard*, H.L. Vol.491, col.1156.

[646] [1996] R.P.C. 667.

[647] i.e. the limitation on the remedies available against him if the claimant succeeded.

[648] [1996] R.P.C. 667 at 686.

[649] In such a case, the proceedings would still have been "proceedings for the infringement of design right in a design in respect of which a licence is available as of right ..." notwithstanding the claimant's failure to show an actual act of infringement.

[650] In such a case, the proceedings were never "proceedings for infringement of design right in a design in respect of which a licence is available as of right ..." (emphasis added). If no design right subsisted, then no licence was ever available of right.

[651] *Ultraframe (UK) Ltd v Eurocell Building Plastics Ltd* [2005] EWCA Civ 761; [2005] R.P.C. 36.

[652] Where there are concurrent rights, the term "design right owner" includes the exclusive licensee, see CDPA 1988 s.234(2).

[653] Delivery up is dealt with in Ch.21, below.

[654] As with CDPA 1988 s.230, the application under CDPA 1988 s.231 may be made in the County Court or, in Scotland, the sheriff court, see CDPA 1988 s.232(1) and (2).

[655] See paras 21–218 et seq., below.

[656] Community Design Regulations 2005 (SI 2005/2339) reg.4 .

extends to UK unregistered design right cases.[657] The privilege covers two types of communication; the first is any communication which passes between a person and his "professional designs representative", the second is any communication made for the purposes of obtaining information which a person is seeking for the purpose of instructing his professional designs representative or in response to a request for such information.[658] For these purposes, a professional designs representative is a person on the special list of professional representatives in design matters established under art.78 of the Community Design Regulation.[659] The effect of this is to place such persons on the same footing as patent agents.[660]

10. THREATS

Introduction. In the commercial world, making a threat to bring infringement proceedings against another person may cause serious damage; the alleged infringer may feel obliged to stop making the article in question and, more importantly, if the threat is made known more widely, his customers may be reluctant to deal with him. The potential for such damage led to provisions being included in the Patents Act 1977[661] and in the Registered Designs Act 1949[662] allowing a person aggrieved by such a threat to bring an action seeking a declaration that the threat was unjustifiable, an injunction against further such threats, and an award of damages. However, one of the anomalies in the use of copyright to protect industrial designs prior to the 1988 Act was that there was no similar protection against groundless threats of copyright proceedings. The 1988 Act, therefore, includes provisions against the making of groundless threats of design right proceedings.[663]   **13–183**

Section 253—threat of proceedings for infringement. Section 253(1) of the 1988 Act provides that: **13–184**

> "Where a person threatens another person with proceedings for infringement of design right, a person aggrieved by the threats may bring an action against him claiming—
>> (a) a declaration to the effect that the threats are unjustifiable;
>> (b) an injunction against the continuance of the threats;
>> (c) damages in respect of any loss which he has sustained by the threats."

Form of threat. The 1988 Act does not require that the threat be in any particular form and there is no reason why it may not be oral as well as written; implied as   **13–185**

---

[657] Although the privilege arises under the so-called Community Design Regulations 2005, those Regulations extend beyond Community design (see regs 6 and 6A which deal with UK Registered Designs). Further, reg.4 refers to "any design" and does not (unlike regs 1 to 3 and 5) refer to "Community design". Moreover, other provisions included in the Regulations (e.g. the inclusion of a threats and a Crown use provision for Community designs) appear to be intended to reduce the differences between Community design proceedings and design right proceedings. It would, therefore, be strange if the privilege under reg.4 only applied to professional design representatives in Community design claims and not in design right claims—particularly as such claims are often brought in the same proceedings.

[658] Community Design Regulations 2005 (SI 2005/2339) reg.4(2).

[659] Community Design Regulations 2005 (SI 2005/2339) reg.4(3) . The list is of those people who are entitled to represent clients in design matters at OHIM.

[660] Communications with whom are privileged under CDPA 1988 s.220.

[661] (c.37) s.70.

[662] s.26.

[663] There are still no such provisions in relation to copyright. It was stated in Parliament that a change was unnecessary in the case of copyright because, it was considered, the position as regards ownership of copyright was usually clear—see *Hansard*, H.L. Vol.501, col.338. It is worth noting that the draft Civil Copyright and Unregistered Design Right Pre-Action Protocol contains a provision that states that a departure from the Pre-Action Protocol might be justified if the fact that the sending of a letter before action would expose the claimant to a threats action.

well as express.[664] A threat may be made in a private letter.[665] However, a threat made in the course of without prejudice communications or without prejudice meetings cannot found a threats action.[666] To be actionable, the material relied on as being a threat must be such that the recipient would reasonably see it[667] as being a threat of legal proceedings for infringement of design right (however innocently phrased that threat may have been made[668]). The threat must also, it would seem, be for the bringing of proceedings in the United Kingdom.[669]

In determining whether something constitutes a threat, it must be seen in context; thus a document which is not threatening when read in isolation may well be when read in the context of the correspondence as a whole.[670] However, mere notification that a design is protected by design right is not sufficient for these purposes.[671] This would, it seems, allow a design right owner to say sufficient to put someone on notice of the design right owner's rights for the purposes of subsequently proving secondary infringement if the recipient ignores those rights. However, the borderline between a threat of proceedings and mere notification of the existence of design right is often very fine, and design right claimants and their professional advisers must clearly exercise care in the way in which they assert claims if they wish to avoid the risk of a threats action being brought against them.

13–186   **Excluded threats.** It is specifically provided[672] that an action cannot be brought under s.253 where the threat was to bring proceedings for the making of something or for the importation of something. This provision recognises that the real evil at which the "threats" provision is aimed is the making of threats to customers and traders.[673] It is, however, important to bear in mind that the exclusion is defined not by reference to the identity of the person receiving the threat

---

[664] The Patents Act 1977 s.70(1) and the Registered Designs Act 1949 s.26(1) both refer to the threats being "by circulars, advertisements or otherwise ...". These words have been widely construed, see *Speedcranes Ltd v Thomson* [1978] R.P.C. 221. For a design right threats case, see *Grimme Landmaschinefabrik GmbH & Co KG v Scott* [2009] EWHC 2691; [2010] F.S.R. 11 (the point was not raised in the appeal [2010] EWCA Civ. 1110).

[665] *Skinner v Perry* (1893) 10 R.P.C. 1.

[666] See *Unilever Plc v The Procter & Gamble Co* [2000] 1 W.L.R. 2436, [2000] F.S.R. 344 (CA). To remain privileged, the threat must have been made in the context of a genuine attempt to resolve or negotiate a settlement of a dispute. In *Kooltrade Ltd v XTS Ltd* [2001] F.S.R. 158, a letter purporting to be without prejudice was sent at a time when there were no negotiations taking place. Pumfrey J. found that the letter constituted a threat. He commented (at p.164) that the letter had not been "nothing whatever to do with negotiation and everything to do with making the claimant's position with [its customer] as difficult as possible". On the other hand, if a document is part of a bona fide attempt to reach a negotiated settlement, the privilege will apply even though the document is not expressly said to be "without prejudice"—see *Best Buy Co. Inc v Worldwide Sales Corp.* [2010] EWHC 1666 at paras 28 and 38–42; [2010] F.S.R. 35.

[667] See *C and P Development Co (London) Ltd v Sisabro Novelty Co Ltd* (1953) 70 R.P.C. 277 at 280 (a patent case). See also *Brain v Ingledew Brown Bennison & Garrett* [1997] F.S.R. 511 at 521 (another patent case) where it was stated that, in applying this test, the court must guard against being led down a path of forensic analysis to a meaning which is narrower or broader than would occur to an ordinary recipient.

[668] See *Hansard*, H.L. Vol.494, col.142.

[669] *Prince Plc v Prince Sports Group Inc* [1998] F.S.R. 21 at 27, a trade mark case. However, the same reasoning would apply given that design right arises under UK law.

[670] See *Brain v Ingledew Brown Bennison & Garrett* [1997] F.S.R. 511 at 521. See also *L'Oreal (UK) Ltd v John & Johnson* [2000] F.S.R. 686—a case brought under s.21 Trade Marks Act 1994—where it was found to be at least arguable that a solicitor's letter (said to be the work of a master of Delphic utterances) constituted a threat because, although it disclaimed making any threat, its thrust could reasonably be taken to be a warning of possible future infringement proceedings and this was how its recipient understood it. The threat might have been veiled and muffled but it remained sufficient to unsettle the recipient.

[671] CDPA 1988 s.253(4).

[672] CDPA 1988 s.253(3).

[673] See *Hansard*, H.L. Vol.491, col.1162 and H.L. Vol.494, cols 142–143. The exclusion (which also appears in the Patents Act 1977 s.70(4)) was added to the CDPA 1988 during the course of

but only by reference to the nature of the act in relation to which proceedings are threatened (i.e. manufacturing or importing). These excluded threats will usually (although not invariably) be made to the manufacturer or the importer, and their exclusion means that a design right owner may notify such persons of his claim[674] without running the risk of a threats action. It may be that he could even notify others of that threat but clearly very great care would be required in case this was construed as a threat of proceedings against persons in relation to acts other than the manufacture or importation of anything.[675]

Person aggrieved. The person entitled to bring an action under s.253 is "a person aggrieved by the threats". To be a person aggrieved, the claimant must personally have had a real as opposed to a fanciful, commercial interest which has been interfered with.[676] This does not, however, mean that he must have suffered actual damage; he may, for example, have been able to avert damage from the threat on that occasion but wish to prevent (by a declaration and injunction) any future recurrences of the threat which might cause actual damage.[677] Thus, a retailer of allegedly infringing articles who receives a threat of proceedings for infringement will clearly be a person aggrieved but so too would be the person who had supplied him with the relevant articles.[678] It may be that a director, an executive or a shareholder of a company may have sufficient personal interest in threats made to that company to make him a person aggrieved in respect of threats directed at that company. However, such a finding would require a close degree of identity between the fortunes of the company and of the individual concerned.[679]   **13–187**

Person issuing threats. The person against whom a threats action is brought is the person who makes the threat even if that person has no interest in the design right in question. Thus where a solicitor makes such a threat on his client's behalf, both the client and the solicitor himself could be sued for the threat.[680]   **13–188**

Defences. Once the claimant in a threats action proves that threats have been made and that he is a person aggrieved by them, then the onus is on the defendant to show that the threat had been justified, i.e. that the acts in respect of which the threat of proceedings was made did constitute (or if done would have constituted) an infringement of the design right concerned.   **13–189**

Available relief. If the threats action is successful, then s.253 makes clear that a court may make a declaration that the threat was unjustifiable, grant an injunction   **13–190**

---

debate. The CDPA 1988 also amended the Registered Designs Act 1949 so as to add the same exclusion to s.26 of the 1949 Act, see s.26(2A).

[674] According to Lord Beaverbrook, such notification may be in "strong and unambiguous terms", *Hansard*, H.L. Vol.494, col.143.

[675] See *Neild v Rockley* [1986] F.S.R. 3. See also *Cavity Trays Ltd v RMC Panel Products Ltd* [1996] R.P.C. 361 (a patent case) where Aldous L.J. stated that a person could safely threaten a person for manufacturing products but not for disposing of those products when manufactured.

[676] See *Brain v Ingledew Brown Bennison & Garrett* [1997] F.S.R. 511 at 519, a case decided under the Patents Act 1977 s.70 but where much of the reasoning was based on provisions (e.g. s.70(3) and (4)) which are in substantially similar terms to those relating to design right threats (see CDPA 1988 s.253(2) and (3)).

[677] *Brain v Ingledew Brown Bennison & Garrett* [1997] F.S.R. 511 at 516–521.

[678] As was the case in *Carflow Products (UK) Ltd v Linwood Securities (Birmingham) Ltd* [1996] F.S.R. 424, a case brought under Registered Designs Act 1949 s.26 and CDPA 1988 s.253(1).

[679] See *Brain v Ingledew Brown Bennison & Garrett* [1997] F.S.R. 511 at 524.

[680] However, in *Earles Utilities Ltd v Harrison* (1934) 52 R.P.C. 77, a statement by a solicitor that he would advise his client to commence proceedings was held not to be a threat. In *Reckitt Benckiser UK v Home Pairfum Ltd* [2004] EWHC Pat 302; [2004] F.S.R. 37 the court refused permission to join a firm of solicitors as defendants to a threats action because one of the reasons for the joinder was to make the solicitors and their relationship with the claimant uncomfortable. The claim would therefore be an abuse of process.

against the continuance of such threats and award damages in respect of any loss which has been caused by the threats. To recover damages, a claimant must show that it is more likely than not that the threat in fact resulted in the alleged damage. It must have been an effective or dominant cause of that damage.[681] Thus, if the matters said to constitute damage occurred because of the issue of proceedings against the recipient rather than as a result of the threat, then it was not the threat which caused that damage.[682]

11. JURISDICTION

13–191   Under the 1988 Act, the Comptroller-General of Patents, Designs and Trade Marks, the High Court, the Patents County Court and other county courts have varying degrees of jurisdiction in relation to certain design right issues.

A. COMPTROLLER-GENERAL OF PATENTS, DESIGNS AND TRADE MARKS

13–192   **Section 246—disputes as to subsistence, term and first owner of design right.** Section 246(1) of the 1988 Act provides that where there is a dispute as to (a) the subsistence of design right, (b) the term of design right or (c) the identity of the first owner of design right, a party to that dispute may refer the matter to the Comptroller-General of Patents, Designs and Trade Marks for his decision.[683] Moreover, under s.246(2), no other court shall decide such matters except (a) on a reference or appeal from the Comptroller, or (b) in infringement or other proceedings in which the issue arises incidentally,[684] or (c) in proceedings brought with the agreement of the parties or with the leave of the Comptroller. The Comptroller's decision on the matter referred to him is binding on the parties to the dispute,[685] but he also has jurisdiction to determine any incidental question of fact or law arising in the course of the reference.[686] The Comptroller may order (or, if both parties agree, must order) that the proceedings brought before him under s.246 or any question or issue (whether of fact or law) be referred to the High Court[687] on such terms as he may direct.[688] Where such a reference is made, the court may exercise the power otherwise conferred on the Comptroller and may, after its determination, refer any matter back to the Comptroller.[689] Under s.251(4), an appeal from any decision of the Comptroller in s.246 proceedings lies to the High Court.[690]

13–193   **Section 247—terms of licence of right.** Under s.247 of the 1988 Act, the

---

[681] *Carflow Products (UK) Ltd v Linwood Securities (Birmingham) Ltd & others* [1996] F.S.R. 424. Although the judgment mentions the need to establish a "prima facie connection" between the threat and the alleged damage, the judgment as a whole shows that the burden is on the claimant to establish his claim according to the normal civil standard of proof (the balance of probabilities).

[682] *Carflow Products (UK) Ltd v Linwood Securities (Birmingham) Ltd & others* [1996] F.S.R. 424.

[683] The only reported case under s.246 is *Christopher Tasker's Design Right References* [2001] R.P.C. 3 where the Comptroller determined issues concerning the subsistence, duration and ownership of design right in various design features relating to a wardrobe system.

[684] e.g. a "threats" action brought under CDPA 1988 s.253.

[685] s.246(1).

[686] s.246(3).

[687] In Scotland, the Court of Session.

[688] CDPA 1988, s.251(1) and (2).

[689] s.251(3).

[690] In Scotland, the appeal is to the Court of Session. The extended jurisdiction of the Patents County Court does not include appeals from the Comptroller, see Patents County Court (Designation and Jurisdiction) Order 1994 (SI 1994/1609) art.4 (see para.13–199, below). As s.246 proceedings concern substantive matters in relation to design right, an appeal to the High Court was thought appropriate. By contrast, an appeal from the Comptroller in relation to the settlement of the terms of a licence of right (see s.247) is to the Appeal Tribunal constituted under Registered Designs Act 1949 s.28, a procedure thought to be less expensive and more appropriate for licensing matters, see *Hansard*, H.C. SCE, col.610.

Comptroller is also given jurisdiction to hear an application to settle the terms of a design right licence of right. The nature of such an application and the appeals process from the Comptroller's decision have already been considered.[691]

Rules of procedure before the Comptroller. The procedure before the Comptroller is regulated by rules.[692] These allow the Comptroller to give such directions as to the conduct of the proceedings as he considers appropriate— including giving directions for a case management conference or a pre-hearing review, for witness statements and (in certain circumstances) witnesses and the variation of time limits. They also provide for the procedure and evidence at hearings before the Comptroller, for representation and rights of audience, and for costs. Finally, they allow for the Comptroller to appoint an adviser to assist in any proceedings before him. **13–194**

B. THE COURT

References and appeals from the Comptroller. As has already been seen,[693] the High Court[694] has jurisdiction to hear references and appeals from the Comptroller in relation to the issues of subsistence, term and first ownership of design right. **13–195**

Crown use. The High Court and a designated patents county court[695] have jurisdiction to determine any reference made to resolve disputes concerning Crown use of a design. These may include disputes as to the terms for Crown use, the rights of third parties in the case of Crown use, and compensation for Crown use. **13–196**

Delivery up, disposal, etc. Any county court has jurisdiction[696] to hear proceedings seeking an order for delivery up in the circumstances provided for in s.230 of the 1988 Act, and also for an order under s.231 as to how an article delivered up should be dealt with.[697] **13–197**

Actions for infringement—High Court. The High Court has unlimited jurisdiction to hear an action relating to infringement of design right.[698] **13–198**

Actions for infringement—patents county courts. A designated patents county court[699] has special jurisdiction to hear and determine any action or matter relating to patents or designs over which the High Court would have jurisdiction, together with any claims or matters ancillary to, or arising from, such **13–199**

---

[691] See paras 13–131 and 13–192, above.

[692] See the Design Right (Proceedings before Comptroller) Rules 1989 (SI 1989/1130), made under CDPA 1988 s.250. For the text of these Rules (as variously amended), see Vol.2 B8.iii.

[693] CDPA 1988 s.251 and para.13–192, above.

[694] In Scotland, the Court of Session.

[695] CDPA 1988 s.252(6). In Scotland, the relevant court is the Court of Session. The only county court presently designated as a patents county court under s.287 is the Central London County Court, see Patents County Court (Designation and Jurisdiction) Order 1994 (SI 1994/1609). See para.13–199, below.

[696] CDPA 1988 s.232, in Scotland, the sheriff's court. In Northern Ireland, a county court only has jurisdiction where the value of the relevant article does not exceed the county court's limit for actions in tort.

[697] For a discussion of ss.230 and 231, see Ch.21, below.

[698] Such actions are assigned to the Chancery Division, see Senior Courts Act 1981 Sch.1 para.1(i) (as amended by the CDPA 1988 Sch.7 para.28(3)).

[699] The only county court presently designated as a patents county court is the Central London County Court, see para.13–192, above. The practice and procedure of a patents county court is governed by Pt 63 of the Civil Procedure Rules (see rr.63.17 et seq.). As from October 1, 2010, a simpler route for lower value claims in the Patents County Court was introduced. This features scale costs for each stage of the process with a cap on costs of £50,000 for a claim involving liability and £25,000 for an inquiry as to damages or an account of profits.

proceedings.[700] In these respects, therefore, its jurisdiction is not limited in any of the ways in which that of an ordinary county court is limited.[701] The reference to "designs" shows that the jurisdiction of a patent county court extends to actions relating to infringement of design right;[702] it has also been held to include actions for infringement of copyright in design documents created before the 1988 Act came into force and in respect of which copyright protection may still be available because of the postponement of the operation of s.51 effected by the transitional provisions of that Act.[703]

13–200   **Actions for infringement—other county courts.** The position as regards the jurisdiction of ordinary county courts to hear design right cases is less clear. Because s.287 expressly provides for a designated patent county court to have jurisdiction over proceedings relating to "patents and designs", and s.232 expressly provides that an ordinary county court may make orders for delivery up and disposal, etc. of certain infringing articles, it has sometimes been argued that the ordinary county courts have no jurisdiction to hear design right claims. It is submitted that this argument is wrong and that design right claims, like copyright claims, fall within the county court's tortious jurisdiction.[704] The need for s.287 arose from the fact that a county court would otherwise have no jurisdiction in relation to patents and registered designs.[705] The need for s.232 (and its copyright equivalent, s.115) arose from the fact that an order for delivery up or disposal of certain infringing articles would not have fallen within any of the powers conferred on the county court by the County Courts Act 1984. Accordingly, the inclusion of these provisions in the 1988 Act should not be taken as support for the proposition that the county court has no jurisdiction to hear design right claims.

12. UNREGISTERED COMMUNITY DESIGNS: INTRODUCTION

13–201   A design may qualify for protection as a Community design under the European

---

[700] Patents County Court (Designation and Jurisdiction) Order 1994 (SI 1994/1609) art.3.

[701] Since the High Court and County Courts Jurisdiction Order 1991 (SI 1991/724) art.2(1)(l), the jurisdiction of a county court in tort claims has not been limited by reference to the value of such claims. However, a limitation remains on a county court's jurisdiction in relation to the making of freezing and search orders, see County Court Remedies Regulations 1991 (SI 1991/1222) regs 2 and 3. This limitation does not apply to a patents county court acting within its special jurisdiction, see *McDonald v Graham* [1994] R.P.C. 407 at 435 (which concerned the predecessor to Patents County Court (Designation and Jurisdiction) Order 1994 (SI 1994/1609) art.3).

[702] See *PSM International Plc v Specialised Fastener Products (Southern) Ltd* [1993] F.S.R. 113 at 117. See also *McDonald v Graham* [1994] R.P.C. 407 at 435 where Ralph Gibson L.J. stated that, whilst it was unnecessary to make a finding on the point, he was inclined to the view that the word "designs" in relation to the jurisdiction of the patents county court was limited to rights arising under legislation dealing with designs; plainly this would include design right.

[703] See *PSM International Plc v Specialised Fastener Products (Southern) Ltd* [1993] F.S.R. 113 at 116–117. It is submitted that this decision is correct and is not inconsistent with the comments of Ralph Gibson L.J. in *McDonald v Graham* [1994] R.P.C. 407 at 435. For example, the 1988 Act referred to the relevant transitional provisions relating to copyright in such works under the heading " designs". For the effect of the transitional provisions on CDPA 1988, s.51, see paras 13–340 et seq., below.

[704] See *PSM International Plc v Specialised Fastener Products (Southern) Ltd* [1993] F.S.R. 113 at 116. In *McDonald v Graham* [1994] R.P.C. 407 at 435–436, the Court of Appeal rejected the claim that an ordinary county court had jurisdiction to grant freezing and search orders in a copyright action but did not question that court's jurisdiction to hear the action itself. For the jurisdiction of a county court in relation to claims in tort, see County Courts Act 1984 s.15.

[705] The Patents Act 1977 s.130(1) and the Registered Designs Act 1949 s.27(1), unlike the CDPA 1988, expressly confer jurisdiction on the High Court only. Special provision was, therefore, required to confer jurisdiction on a patent county court in relation to such rights.

Council Regulation on Community designs.[706] As has already been seen,[707] this Regulation created two forms of protection:

(a) a short three-year period of protection for unregistered Community designs (which is considered below); and

(b) a longer period of protection (up to 25 years) for registered Community designs (which will be considered in outline later in this Chapter).

The two types of protection created by the Regulation are intended to meet the differing needs of different sectors of industry in the Community. The unregistered form of protection is aimed at those sectors of industry where a requirement of registration would be burdensome and impractical and where the need for long-term protection may be less important, e.g. industries that produce large numbers of designs for products with (often) a short market life. By contrast, the registered form of protection is intended to meet the needs of those sectors of industry where the longer life of the products requires a longer period of protection and where registration provides greater certainty.[708] The Regulation came into force on March 6, 2002. However, the Regulation does not (unlike the 1988 Act[709]) provide that its provisions only apply to designs created after it came into force. It would seem, therefore, that Community design protection may well be available for a design which predates March 6, 2002—although this will be of far greater significance as regards the registration of a Community design (where the maximum period of protection is 25 years) than in the case of an unregistered Community design (where the period of protection is only three years).

A Community design is enforceable in all Member States of the European Community. As such, there needs to be some degree of consistency of interpretation across all member states. For these purposes, decisions of the Office for Harmonisation of the Internal Market (OHIM) and of the courts of other Member States provide useful guidance.[710]

Nature of unregistered Community design. As with copyright and design right, unregistered Community design is a property right which subsists automatically and provides protection against the copying of the design.[711] As with national law, monopoly protection of a design is only available where the design is registered.   **13–202**

Interrelation with design right. As has also been seen, the protection for Community designs under the Regulation was not intended to replace UK design right. Thus, an unregistered design may be protected both as a Community design and also under design right.[712]   **13–203**

13. UNREGISTERED COMMUNITY DESIGNS: DEFINITION OF A COMMUNITY DESIGN

Definition of design. Under the Regulation, protection is provided for designs   **13–204**

---

[706] Regulation (EC) No. 6/2002.

[707] See paras 13–30 et seq., above.

[708] See recitals 15 to 17 of the Directive by which the national laws of Member States relating to registered designs were harmonised (91/71/EC).

[709] CDPA 1988 s.213(7).

[710] *The Procter & Gamble Co v Reckitt Benckiser (UK) Ltd* [2006] EWHC 3154; [2007] F.S.R. 13 at para.24.

[711] See, respectively, arts 27, 11(1) and 19(2) of Regulation (EC) No. 6/2002.

[712] See art.96(2) of Regulation (EC) No. 6/2002 . The claimant would, of course, have to establish that he owns both rights.

which meet the criteria of novelty and individual character and which are not otherwise excluded. For these purposes, a "design" is very widely defined[713] as:

"... the appearance of the whole or a part of a product resulting from the features of, in particular, the lines, contours, colours, shape, texture and/or materials of the product itself and/or its ornamentation"

"product" for these purposes means:

"...any industrial or handicraft item, including inter alia parts intended to be assembled into a complex product, packaging, get-up, graphic symbols and typographic typefaces, but excluding computer programs"

and a "complex product" is:

"...a product which is composed of multiple components which can be replaced permitting disassembly and re-assembly of the product."

13–205   **Scope of definition of design.** The Community definition of a "design" is, therefore, concerned with the appearance of a product or of a part of a product.[714] The fact that the definition refers to a part of a product means that, like UK design right, a claimant need not rely on the design of the whole product but may rely on the design of one or more of its parts. In this way, the holder of a Community design right can improve his prospects of success in an infringement action by pleading alternative designs and by relying on designs that are as close as possible to the design of the defendant's product.[715]

The Community definition of design does not contain an express requirement of aesthetic quality or eye appeal.[716] However, the fact that the Regulation requires a design to have "individual character"[717] and excludes protection from component parts that are not visible in normal use[718] and from features of appearance that are dictated solely by function,[719] means that purely functional designs are unlikely to be protected.

The definition of a Community design is significantly wider than that for UK design right.[720] This is apparent not only from the list of relevant design features (lines, contours, colours, etc.) but also from the definition of a "product" and, in particular, the inclusion in that definition of get-up, graphic symbols and

---

[713] art.3 of Regulation (EC) No. 6/2002. The limitation on the protection offered by Community design is achieved through the requirements of novelty and individual character, and through specific exclusions (as discussed below) rather than by narrowing the definition of a design.

[714] For an interesting argument that in context of the Design Directive (91/71/EC), the word "appearance" is not necessarily limited to appearance to the eye but may include appearance to the touch, see David Musker, *Community Design Law* (London: Sweet & Maxwell, 2002) at para.1–012. The argument may be slightly stronger in relation to unregistered Community design under the Regulation (EC) No. 6/2002 because the recitals to the Regulation do not include an equivalent to recital 11 to the Directive). The fact that the definition of design refers to appearance resulting from the features of texture and materials may lend some support to this argument for, if those words were to be construed as applying only where the texture or material had a visible effect, those words would otherwise appear to add little to the other words included in the definition (such as "lines", "contours" "shape", etc.).

[715] See the discussion of this point in relation to design right at para.13–46, above. The closer the designs are, the more likely it is that they would produce the same overall impression on an informed user (i.e. constitute an infringement—see paras 13–245 et seq., below). However, if too simple a design is chosen or if the design relied on has only a few features, a court may be inclined to find that such design is not novel or that it lacks individual character. It may also be difficult to establish copying.

[716] See recital 14 to the Directive (91/71/EC). There is no reason to think that the position would be different under the Regulation (EC) No. 6/2002 even though the Regulation does not have an equivalent recital.

[717] See Regulation arts 4(1) and 6 and paras 13–210 et seq., below.

[718] See Regulation art.4(2) and paras 13–218 et seq.below.

[719] See Regulation art.8(1) and paras 13–221 et seq., below.

[720] It is also much wider than the former definition of a design in the Registered Designs Act 1949. However, since the 1949 Act was amended by the Registered Designs Regulations 2001, its definition of "design" is almost identical to that in the Regulation.

typographical typefaces. Clearly, therefore, the design can be two dimensional as well as three dimensional. Further, in contrast to the position under design right, the definition of a design for the purposes of Community design expressly includes appearance resulting from the ornamentation of the product. Accordingly, decorative features of design (whether surface or otherwise) may qualify for protection. Indeed, the definition also refers to colours.[721] In this regard, it is unclear whether a single colour would be treated as a design—particularly where it is the only design feature relied upon.[722] Moreover, the fact that the definition refers to texture and materials shows that the appearance of a product as imparted by the substances from which that product is made can be a design.[723]

Internal design features. It has been held that the definition of a design in the European Directive 98/71 (the same as that in the Regulation) is concerned only with features that can be visually perceived and would not, therefore, extend to the internal features of a non-complex product such an ice cream.[724]There is some force in this conclusion given that, in the case of complex products, component parts that are not visible during normal use are deprived of protection.[725] It would seem strange to deprive these features of protection whilst allowing protection for the internal features of non-complex products.[726] **13–206**

Product. This word is also broadly defined and, given the references to packaging, get-up, graphic symbols and typographical typefaces, will clearly cover areas which, in English law, have generally been a matter for copyright[727] or trade mark law.[728] As is clear from the above definitions, the product may itself be a complex product, i.e. a product which is comprised of multiple components (each **13–207**

---

[721] In *Lambretta Clothing Co Ltd v Teddy Smith (UK) Ltd* [2004] EWCA Civ 886; [2005] R.P.C. 6, it was commented that the Community definition of design would "clearly" have covered the claimant's choice of colours for its track top (red of the body panels, blue with white stripes for the sleeves, and white for the zip). However, it appears that the claimant's design claim had to be based on UK design right—which claim failed as the design (i.e. a choice of colours) was not an aspect of "shape or configuration" of the top. See para.13–49, above.

[722] It is likely to be difficult to establish that a defendant has copied a design when that design is simply a choice of colour without any other design features. A claimant may choose whether or not to rely on his designs for the colour or colours of a product in addition to other features. If he wishes to do so, it may be easier to establish individual character (see the two *Bumag v Procter & Gamble* decisions given by OHIM on May 15, 2006—ICD 1741 and ICD 1758) but the scope of protection is narrower. For the significance of colour in relation to registered Community designs, see para.13–283.

[723] This appears to differ from the position as it was under the Registered Designs Act 1949 before it was amended in 2001, see the old registered design cases discussed at para.13–57, above, where such design features were excluded from protection for being modes of construction.

[724] *Re Cancellation of Registered Design for "Chocolate Interior"* [2007] E.D.C.R. 3 (District Administrative Court in Warsaw). In this respect, the protection offered by Community design may be narrower than that under UK design right (see para.13–47 above).

[725] See art.4(2) which provides that such features are not novel and have no individual character— see para.13–218, below.

[726] The need for a specific exclusion in the case of a component part is that that part has its own separate identity at least until it is incorporated into the complex product of which it is intended to be a part. The interior of, say, an ice cream, has no such separate identity.

[727] It may be that some "handicraft" items would also qualify for copyright protection in the UK as works of artistic craftsmanship, see para.13–313, below. Where copyright protection is available, the availability of unregistered Community design is of little benefit. However, the same definition of design applies to a registered Community design, and the protection offered to registered Community designs (being monopolistic) may well be of significant value to a designer.

[728] Community design protection may offer a useful alternative to a trade mark. Unlike the law of trade marks, there is no need to prove that the design denotes the trade origin of goods, nor that it is distinctive (provided it is novel and has individual character). Nor does it matter whether or not the design results from the nature of the goods (provided it is not dictated solely by the technical function of the product). Further, the protection of an unregistered Community design is not by reference to a class of product for which it is registered. For the different purposes behind trade mark protection and designs protection, see *The Procter & Gamble Company v Reckitt Benckiser (UK) Ltd* [2007] EWCA Civ 936; [2008] F.S.R. 8 at paras 27 and 28.

of which might also be a product) which can be replaced permitting assembly and re-assembly. An obvious example of a complex product would be a car.[729]

14. UNREGISTERED COMMUNITY DESIGNS: REQUIREMENTS OF NOVELTY AND INDIVIDUAL CHARACTER

13–208   **Requirements that a design be new and have individual character.** Whilst "design" is defined in wide terms, by reason of art.4(1) of the Regulation, a design will only be protected by a Community design to the extent that it is new and has individual character.[730] This provision and art.4(2) (which lays down additional criteria by which the novelty and individual character of designs for component parts of complex products are assessed and which is considered below[731]) significantly limit the scope of Community design protection. There are three important preliminary points that arise in relation to these requirements:

First, it is the *design* in issue that is tested for novelty and individual character rather than the product to which the design has been applied or in which it is incorporated.

Second, the novelty and individual character of an unregistered design are tested as at the time that that design was made available to the public. It does not, therefore, matter when that design was created. The issue is whether it was new and had individual character compared with other designs on the date when it was made available to the public.[732]

Third, whilst the tests for novelty and individual character overlap to an extent, there are significant differences.[733] It is, therefore, possible that a design will pass one test but fail the other.[734]

A. NOVELTY

13–209   **Meaning of "new".** To be protected as a Community design, a design must be "new". Under art.5(1)(a) of the Regulation, an unregistered Community design will be considered new if no identical design has been made available to the pub-

---

[729] At first sight this appears to mirror the position under design right (see para.13–50, above). However, in relation to design right, it was stated that whilst a kitchen unit was an article, the whole kitchen was not. There is a suggestion that the position may be different in relation to Community designs and that a complete kitchen may be treated as a complex product (see David Musker, *Community Design Law* (London: Sweet & Maxwell, 2002) at paras 1–019 and 1–1027).

[730] In *Bailey v Haynes* [2006] EWPCC 5; [2007] F.S.R. 10 at para.54, H.H. Judge Fysh QC held that the onus was on the person seeking to challenge the subsistence of the Community Design to prove that it was not new and did not have original character. However, no reference was made to art.85(2) of the Designs Regulation, which provides that the Community Design Court shall treat the Community design as valid if the right holder produces proof that the conditions laid down in art.11 have been met and indicates what constitutes the original character of his Community design. In *Karen Millen Ltd v Dunnes Stores Ltd* [2009] E.C.C. 4 at para.55 the Irish High Court held that the effect of art.85(2) was that once the claimant had shown that the design had been made available within 3 years prior to the alleged infringement and had identified the elements relied on to establish individual character, the burden shifted to the defendant to establish one or more grounds of invalidity on the balance of probabilities.

[731] See para.13–218, below.

[732] arts 5(1)(a) and 6(1)(a). For registered designs, the relevant date is the filing date of the application or, if priority is claimed, the priority date (see arts 5(1)(b) and 6(1)(b)).

[733] *Normann Copenhagen ApS v Paton Calvert Housewares Ltd* [2010] E.C.D.R. 3 at para.16 (OHIM's Third Board of Appeal).

[734] See *The Procter & Gamble Co v Reckitt Benckiser (UK) Ltd* [2006] EWHC 3154; [2007] F.S.R. 13 at para.25.

lic before the date on which the design for which protection is claimed was first made available to the public.[735]

This provision means that the design in question must be compared with any other designs that have been made available to the public. For these purposes, art.5(2) provides that the designs shall be deemed to be identical if their features differ only in immaterial details. Thus, to be "new", a design need only differ from any other design in some material respect and, as with UK design right, it seems clear that a design may be new even though some or even all of its component design features taken by themselves would not be.[736] The novelty test is not, therefore, a particularly onerous test.[737] However, art.5 gives no guidance as to what material and immaterial details are. Nor does art.5 state by whose eyes the designs must be compared. One possibility is that it is by the eyes of persons in the "circles specialising in the sector concerned, operating within the Community" (the test under art.7); another possibility is that it is the eyes of the "informed user" (the test under art.6).[738] However, as the issue appears to be essentially one of fact (i.e. are the designs identical or not), it is submitted that the issue is probably one for the judge to determine objectively, albeit that the judge might (as in design right cases) hear expert evidence to assist in determining whether any differences are or are not material.[739]

B. INDIVIDUAL CHARACTER

Requirement to have individual character. To be protected as a Community design, a design must have individual character. For these purposes, art.6(1) of the Regulation provides that: **13–210**

"A design shall be considered to have individual character if the overall impression it produces on the informed user differs from the overall impression produced on such a user by any design which has been made available to the public (a) in the case of an unregistered Community design, before the date on which the design for which protection is claimed was first made available to the public..."[740]

and art.6(2) that:

"In assessing individual character, the degree of design freedom of the designer in developing the design shall be taken into consideration."

Recital 14 to the Regulation provides the following guidance as to the test for individual character:

---

[735] For a discussion of the date when a design is first made available to the public, see para.13–215, below.

[736] See para.13–74, above.

[737] In this respect, the test resembles that which the courts undertake in assessing whether a design is commonplace for the purposes of design right—see *Farmers Build Ltd v Carier Bulk Material Handling Ltd* [1999] R.P.C. 461, discussed at paras 13–78 et seq., above.

[738] When determining whether a design has been made available to the public, the test in art.7 requires one to look to the knowledge of people in the circles specialised in the sector concerned operating within the Community (i.e. experts) (see para.13–215, below). By contrast, the test for overall impression under art.6 is by reference to the eye of the "informed user". It is not clear that either of these tests would be appropriate for art.5 purposes. The art.7 test would be difficult to apply if the relevant designs were from different sectors and it is difficult to see what the art.6 test would add if applied for art.5 purposes as well as for art.6 purposes. For the argument in favour of the art.7 test applying to art.5, see David Musker *Community Design Law* (London: Sweet & Maxwell, 2002) at para.1–045.

[739] This was also the view adopted by OHIM's Third Board of Appeal in *Normann Copenhagen ApS v Paton Calvert Housewares Ltd* [2010] E.C.D.R. 3 at para.25.

[740] For a discussion of the date when a design is first made available to the public, see para.13–215, below. For registered Community designs, the relevant date is the date when the application for registration was filed or, if priority is claimed, the priority date—see art.6(1)(b).

"The assessment as to whether a design has individual character should be based on whether the overall impression produced on an informed user viewing the design clearly differs from the overall impression produced on him by the existing design corpus, taking into consideration the nature of the product to which the design is applied or in which it is incorporated, and in particular the industrial sector to which it belongs and the degree of freedom which the designer had in developing the design."

In essence, as appears from the decision of the General Court of the European Court of Justice in *Grupo Promer Mon Graphic SA v Office for Harmonisation in the Internal Market*, in assessing the overall impression, the court must identify similarities and differences between the competing designs and determine whether they would have been of significance to the informed user.[741]

The test for individual character therefore requires one to identify the relevant "informed user", to identify the designs to be compared and to compare the overall impressions produced by those designs on the informed user.

13–211   **The informed user.** The test for individual character is conducted through the eyes of the "informed user". This hypothetical person is a "user", not a designer or a manufacturer.[742] The person is a user (even a habitual user) of the type of product to which the design being tested for individual character has been applied.[743] Importantly, this hypothetical user, being "informed", is not the "average consumer" known to trade mark law[744] but is (as the words of art.6(1) and recital 14 show) taken to be aware of other similar designs which form part of the "design corpus", aware of design issues arising from the nature of the product[745] and aware of the degree of freedom available to the designer. In an appropriate case, the informed user could be a child of 5 to 10 years of age or in the case of promotional goods, a marketing manager in a company using that type of goods in order to promote its own products.[746]

On this basis, the informed user must be "reasonably discriminatory", "able to appreciate enough detail to decide whether a design creates an overall impression which has individual character", taken to know where shapes are, to some extent, required to be the way they are by reason of function, alert to design issues and "fairly familiar" with them.[747] It seems clear, therefore, that the informed user is someone who would approach the task of determining individual character with

---

[741] [2010] E.D.C.R. 7 at paras 76–84 (a registered Community design case). See also *J. Choo (Jersey) Ltd v Towerstone Ltd* [2008] F.S.R. 19.

[742] *Woodhouse UK Plc v Architectural Lighting Systems* [2005] EWPCC (Des) 25; [2006] R.P.C. 1, where H.H. Judge Fysh QC commented that the informed user must be a regular user of articles of the sort which is the subject of the design; that he could be a consumer or buyer or be otherwise familiar with the subject matter, for example, through use at work. The relevant passage from the judgment of H.H. Judge Fysh QC was quoted with apparent approval by Jacob L.J. in *The Procter & Gamble Company v Reckitt Benckiser (UK) Ltd* [2007] EWCA Civ 936 at para.32; [2007] F.S.R. 13.

[743] *Normann Copenhagen ApS v Paton Calvert Housewares Ltd* [2010] E.C.D.R. 3 at para.26 (OHIM's Third Board of Appeal). In registered Community design cases, the identity of the informed user might be affected by the scope of the definition provided in the application for registration of the product(s) in which the design is to be incorporated or applied—see *Grupo Promer Mon Graphic SA v Office for Harmonisation in the Internal Market* [2010] E.D.C.R. 7 at para.56.

[744] *The Procter & Gamble Company v Reckitt Benckiser (UK) Ltd* [2007] EWCA Civ 936 (a case concerning a registered community design) per Jacob LJ at paras 16 and 24.

[745] See *Arrmet, S.R.L.'s Design* [2004] E.C.D.R. 24 (OHIM) at paras 16–18 where it was held that the informed user is familiar with the basic features of the product in question and with the prior art known in the normal course of business to the circles specialised in the sector concerned.

[746] *Grupo Promer Mon Graphic SA v Office for Harmonisation in the Internal Market* [2010] E.D.C.R. 7 (a registered community design case) at para.64.

[747] *The Procter & Gamble Company v Reckitt Benckiser (UK) Ltd* [2007] EWCA Civ 936 at paras 23–28 and 35(ii). In *Procter & Gamble* (which concern the design of spray cans for air fresheners), it was found that the informed user would take into account the fact that there were design

some degree of method and with more rigour than would an ordinary consumer.[748] Having said this, being a user rather than a designer or an expert, the informed user is unlikely to pay undue attention to technical design details but would instead take an overall view including a view of the attractiveness and practicability of the design.[749]

What is to be compared? The test for individual character requires the court to compare the overall impressions which different designs produce on the informed user. On the one hand is the design being tested for individual character[750]; on the other is any other design which has been made available to the public—i.e. any design within the "existing design corpus"—the meaning of which is considered below.[751]

    13–212

It is important to be clear as to what it is that is being compared—namely the designs. The court is not concerned with other features of any product to which those designs may have been applied.[752] Further, the comparison is between the claimant's design on the one hand and the corresponding part of the other design(s) on the other.[753] One must, in effect, compare like with like. This emphasises the importance of defining the design to be protected with care. If the design for which protection is sought is defined too generally, it may be invalidated by other designs in the design corpus. If, however, it is defined too narrowly, it may be difficult to establish infringement.[754] The fact that the comparison is of the "overall" impressions produced by the relevant designs suggests that it would be wrong to look solely at the various component elements of those designs. The issue, instead, is whether an informed user looking at those designs as a whole would see the overall designs as different or, taking the words of recital 14, as clearly different.[755]

Overall impression. To have individual character, the overall impression which a design produces on the informed user must differ from the overall impression produced by other designs in the design corpus.

    13–213

---

constraints arising from the fact that the spray canisters in question had to be "grippable so that the index finger could pull the trigger, the trigger had to be shaped to fit the finger and had to have sufficient space behind it for it to be pulled"—per Jacob LJ at para.29.

[748] In *Atria Yhtyma Oyj v HK Ruokatalo Group Oyj* [2008] E.C.D.R. 6, the Third Board of Appeal at OHIM stated the informed user was a user of the product in question and was not an industry specialist. See also the Invalidity Division's decision in *Holey Soles Holdings v Crocs Inc* [2008] E.C.D.R. 8 at paras 35–36. In *Bailey v Haynes* [2006] EWPCC 5; [2007] F.S.R. 10, H.H. Judge Fysh Q.C. stated at para.55 that when considering individual character, the enquiry focuses on those having a practical interest in the use to which the product incorporating the design is to be put.

[749] *Wuxi Kipor Power Co Ltd v Honda Giken Kogyo Kabushiki Kaisha* [2009] E.C.D.R. 4 (OHIM Third Board of Appeal).

[750] Where validity is the issue, the claimant's design will be defined by the statements of case in unregistered design cases and by the registration in registered design cases.

[751] See para.13–215 below.

[752] See *J. Choo (Jersey) Ltd v Towerstone Ltd* [2008] F.S.R. 19 (Floyd J.) where features such as the fabric from which the different bags were made and the presence or absence of the claimant's logo on the defendants' bags did not affect the question of whether the overall impression was the same as these were not features of the design in issue.

[753] *The Procter & Gamble* at first instance (Lewison J.) [2006] EWHC 3154; [2007] F.S.R. 13 at paras 44–49. As the issue was whether the claimant's registered design had been infringed, the comparison was between the claimant's and defendant's designs.

[754] *The Procter & Gamble* at first instance (Lewison J.) [2006] EWHC 3154; [2007] F.S.R. 13 at para.48.

[755] In *Prodir SA v Dariusz Liberia* [2008] E.C.D.R. 7, the Invalidity Division of OHIM suggested at para.12 that the comparison involves looking at both the individual features and the weight of those features taken as a whole. In Arrmet, S.R.L.'s Design [2004] E.C.D.R. 24 (OHIM) at para.19 it was held that the designs must be compared both on their various features taken individually and "on the weight of the various features according to their influence on the overall impression". For a similar approach to the "overall impression" test for infringement, see *Dyson Limited v Vax Limited* [2010] EWHC 1923 at paras 64–94.

Although art.6(1) simply refers to "differs", recital 14 uses the words "clearly differs". On this basis, it has been held that the word "clearly" is "plainly ... relevant" to the issue whether a design qualifies for protection and that it should, in effect, be read into art.6(1).[756] This would mean that there is a significant difference between the "overall impression" test when used to determine whether a design qualifies for protection under art.6(1) and the "overall impression" test when used to determine whether there has been an infringement under art.10(1).[757] In the latter context, the word "clearly" is not read into art.10(1). It was said that the reason for this distinction is that "[d]ifferent policies are involved. It is one thing to restrict the grant of a monopoly right to designs which are shown 'clearly' to differ from the existing design corpus. That makes sense—you need clear blue water between the registered design and the 'prior art', otherwise there is a real risk that design monopolies will or may interfere with routine, ordinary, minor everyday design modifications—what patent lawyers call 'mere workshop modifications'. But no such policy applies to the scope of protection. It is sufficient to avoid infringement if the accused product is of a design which produces a 'different overall impression'. There is no policy requirement that the difference be 'clear'. If a design differs, that is enough—an informed user can discriminate."[758] In applying the overall impression test, the court will look at both similarities and differences between the respective designs. However, what matters is the overall impression produced on the informed user by both.[759] It is what strikes the mind of the informed user looking at the relevant design as a design. Further, it is what strikes the mind when carefully viewing the design. The possibility of imperfect recollection (i.e. that which sticks in the mind after looking) has only a limited part to play.[760]

In making the comparison, the court must have regard to the appropriate level of generality. This is the level of generality at which the informed user would make the comparison. As was pointed out in one case, at a high level of generality, a Ford Focus would create the same overall impression as a Renault Clio. However, that is clearly not the level of generality at which the informed user would compare the respective designs. A lower degree of generality (i.e. a higher degree of particularity) would be required.[761] Thus, in *The Procter & Gamble v Reckitt Benckiser (UK) Ltd*, a "canister fitted with a trigger spray device on top" was too general a description of the design in issue and in *Rolawn Ltd v Turfmech Machinery Ltd*, the comparison between two designs of lawn mowers had to be made when viewed close up where the relevant detail of the differences between the two could be observed and not from "across a field or two".[762]

The relevant impressions are those produced on the informed user who is, according to recital 14, "viewing the design". This suggests that the test for individual character may involve considerations similar to those that arose under the test

---

[756] *The Procter & Gamble v Reckitt Benckiser (UK) Ltd* [2007] EWCA Civ 936 per Jacob L.J. at para.18.

[757] As to which see paras 13–245 et seq., below.

[758] *The Procter & Gamble* per Jacob LJ at para.19. The General Court of the ECJ did not refer to this issue in *Grupo Promer Mon Graphic SA v Office for Harmonisation in the Internal Market* [2010] E.D.C.R. 7 (although, strictly, the point did not arise in that case).

[759] *Dyson Limited v Vax Limited* [2010] EWHC 1923 (Pat) at para.46—a case concerning the "overall impression" test for infringement.

[760] *The Procter & Gamble* per Jacob L.J. at paras 25 to 27 and 35(v).

[761] *Rolawn Ltd v Turfmech Machinery Ltd* [2008] EWHC 989 (Pat); [2008] R.P.C. 27 (Mann J.) at para.112.

[762] *Rolawn Ltd v Turfmech Machinery Ltd* [2008] EWHC 989 (Pat) (Mann J.) at para.125. Although these comments were made in the context of the test for infringement, they should apply equally to assessments of validity, save for the need for the design to be "clearly" different to the prior art (see above).

of eye appeal that used to be a part of UK registered design law.[763] Under that test, a design had eye appeal if there was something peculiar, distinctive, significant or striking about its appearance—something which would catch the eye of a customer and distinguish that design from any other.[764] It has been suggested that when assessing the overall impression of a design, an informed user would focus his or her attention mainly on the features which are essential or characteristic of the product in question, at least where those features are the ones with the largest surface area and "the most important visibility". Where the most important visual parts of the design do not give a different overall impression and the other parts of the design are not sufficiently different in appearance or importance to change the impression given by the main elements, then the overall impression produced by the design is not different from that produced by the prior design.[765] However, the fact that two designs both include features that are banal or common to all examples of the type of products in issue, is unlikely to mean that they will create the same overall impression on the informed user.[766]

Significance of design freedom. In making the comparison between designs in order to see whether a design has individual character, art.6(2) requires the informed user to have regard to "the degree of design freedom of the designer in developing the design".[767] For these purposes (although not for other purposes), the court may have regard to evidence of design freedom derived from designs produced after the design in issue—if a wide variety of designs was produced after the design in issue, that would be evidence that the designer had not been constrained to design the product in the way that he had.[768]

13–214

In the absence of specific restrictions imposed on a designer, similarities are likely to attract the attention of the informed user[769] and may lead to the conclusion that the designs do not produce different overall impressions.[770] By contrast, where design freedom is limited, smaller differences may lead the informed user to the opposite conclusion.[771] However, the relevant restrictions must be design restrictions arising from the technical function of the product (or an element thereof) or from statutory requirements which result in a standardisation of certain

---

[763] In *Woodhouse UK Plc v Architectural Lighting Systems* [2005] EWPCC (Des) 25; [2006] R.P.C. 1, H.H. Judge Fysh QC commented that, since the territory is designs and not patents, what matters most is the appearance of things; accordingly, focus on eye-appeal is more pertinent than familiarity with the underlying operational or manufacturing technology (if any).

[764] For the old law (before the 1949 Act was amended by the Registered Design Regulations 2001), see *Amp Inc v Utilux Proprietary Ltd* [1972] R.P.C. 103 at 108, 112–113 and 121 and paras 13–290 and 13–353 below.

[765] In *Arrmet, S.R.L.'s Design* [2004] E.C.D.R. 24 (OHIM) at paras 22–26.

[766] *Normann Copenhagen ApS v Paton Calvert Housewares Ltd* [2010] E.C.D.R. 3 at para.32 (OHIM's Third Board of Appeal)—a case concerning the design of a colander.

[767] The same requirement applies as regards the test for infringement—see art.10(2).

[768] *Dyson Ltd v Vax Ltd* [2010] EWHC 1923 (Pat) at para.37 (a case concerning "overall impression" test in the context of infringement). For other purposes, the comparison is with designs that were in the design corpus at the date that the design in issue was made available to the public—see para.13–215 below.

[769] *Grupo Promer Mon Graphic SA v Office for Harmonisation in the Internal Market* [2010] E.C.D.R. 7 (General Court (Fifth Chamber) of the ECJ. See also *Atria Thtyma* [2008] E.C.D.R. 6, where the Third Board of Appeal adopted a wide view of the design freedom available to the designer of a hamburger.

[770] *Normann Copenhagen ApS v Paton Calvert Housewares Ltd* [2010] E.C.D.R. 3 at paras 38–39 where OHIM's Third Board of Appeal commented that a designer of a colander had a variety of design options.

[771] *The Procter & Gamble*, per Jacob L.J. at para.30. See also *Arrmet, S.R.L.'s Design* [2004] E.C.D.R. 24 (OHIM) at para.17. A somewhat similar concern to allow competition where the functional nature of the product permits no real design freedom is clearly apparent in UK design right decisions such as *Farmers Build Ltd v Carier Bulk Handling Ltd* [1999] R.P.C. 461, see paras 13–78 et seq., above.

features which will be common to designs applied to the product concerned.[772] They may include economic considerations (e.g. the need for the item to be inexpensive)[773] but they will not include the designer's own internal constraints (e.g. his own limited financial or production resources). The "test must be an objective one which applies to all designers".[774]

C. DESIGNS MADE AVAILABLE TO THE PUBLIC

13–215 **Designs made available to the public; the "existing design corpus".** As appears from the above, in order to determine whether a design is new and whether it has individual character, it is necessary to look at other designs which have been "made available to the public" at the time that the design in question was made available to the public[775]—or, to use the words of recital 14, the "existing design corpus". For these purposes, art.7(1) of the Regulation provides:

"... a design shall be deemed to have been made available to the public if it has been published following registration or otherwise, or exhibited, used in trade or otherwise disclosed, before the [relevant date[776]] except where these events could not reasonably have become known in the normal course of business to the circles specialised in the sector concerned, operating within the Community. The design shall not, however, be deemed to have been made available to the public for the sole reason that it has been disclosed to a third person under explicit or implicit conditions of confidentiality."

Article 7(1) therefore contains two qualifications which significantly limit the scope of the enquiry.

13–216 **Event not becoming known in the sector concerned.** The first qualification is that the mere fact that a design has been published, exhibited, used in trade or otherwise disclosed is not sufficient to establish that that design is part of the design corpus, if the event relied on was not such as would reasonably have become known in the normal course of business to the circles specialised in the sector concerned, operating within the Community.

The language of art.7(1) shows that the "sector concerned" is the sector of the alleged prior art (i.e. of the design said to have been made available to the public) and not the sector of the design in issue (i.e. the design being tested for individual

---

[772] In *Dyson Ltd v Vax Ltd* [2010] EWHC 1923 (Pat) it was held, inter alia, (at paras 72–75) that the design freedom of a designer of a vacuum cleaner was constrained by the need to have large rear wheels to carry the weight of the motor and to enable the cleaner to be dragged over obstacles but that, in any event, the informed user would notice considerable differences between the designs in question. In *Grupo Promer Mon Graphic SA v Office for Harmonisation in the Internal Market* [2010] E.D.C.R. 7 at para.67 (a registered community design case) the General Court (Fifth Chamber) of the ECJ found (at paras 68–70) that the designer of a "rapper" or "tazo" had a severely restricted design freedom given that the paradigm for that type of product is a small flat or nearly flat disc on which coloured images could be printed with, often, a curve towards the centre so that a noise is made if pressed by a child's finger. The General Court also commented (at para.56) that the court's assessment of the degree of design freedom in a registered Community design case could be affected by the definition given in the application for registration of the product(s) in which the design is intended to be incorporated or applied.

[773] *Dyson Ltd v Vax Ltd* [2010] EWHC 1923 (Pat) at para.34.

[774] *The Procter & Gamble*, per Jacob L.J. at para.31 agreeing with the approach of Lewison J. at first instance ([2006] EWHC 3154; [2007] F.S.R. 13 at para.43).

[775] For registered Community designs, the relevant date is the date of filing of the application for registration of the design for which protection is claimed or, if priority is claimed, the date of priority. As mentioned above, in considering the degree of design freedom enjoyed by a designer, the court may have regard to designs produced after the design in issue, see para.13–214 above.

[776] For unregistered designs, the relevant date is the date that the design being tested for novelty and individual character was made available to the public—see arts 5(1)(a) and 6(1)(a). For registered designs, it is the date of filing of the application for registration or, if priority is claimed, the date of priority—see arts 5(1)(b) and 6(1)(b).

character).[777] In principle, the persons in the circles specialising in the sector concerned would comprise all individuals who conduct trade in relation to products in that sector (including those who design, make, advertise, distribute and sell such products in the course of trade). However, in some cases, the circles would be more restricted than that.[770] If such persons could not reasonably have been aware of the design, then that design will not be taken to have been made available to the public.

A design has been held to have been made available to the public where it has been published in an application for a three-dimensional trade mark,[779] where it was filed and published as a community design,[780] and where it had been the subject of a European Patent Application.[781] Further, as art.7(1) does not require that the design should have been made available "within the Community", an event taking place outside the Community might amount to publication provided it meant that the design had become known to those operating within the relevant circles within the Community. Thus a design published in the United States could form part of the relevant design corpus.[782]

It is worth noting that the reference in recital 14 is to the "existing design corpus". It has been said that the word "existing" shows that the court is not concerned with the whole history of product development and that the word "corpus" is indicative of the general body of design rather than each and every example of it.[783] The concept imports the notion of "what's about in the market?" and "what has been about in the recent past?" It does not require an archival mind or a more than average memory but does demand some awareness of product trend and availability and some knowledge of basic technical considerations (if any).[784]

Disclosure in confidence. The second qualification is that a design will not be deemed to have been made available to the public on the sole ground that it had been disclosed to a third person under explicit or implicit conditions of confidentiality.   **13–217**

D. Additional Criteria for Complex Products

Component parts of complex products—must be visible in normal use. As mentioned above, art.4(2) of the Regulation lays down additional criteria by which the novelty and individual character are assessed in the case of a design for a component part of a complex product.[785]   **13–218**

Article 4(2) provides that:

"A design applied to or incorporated in a product which constitutes a

---

[777] *Green Lane Products Ltd v PMS International Group Ltd.* [2007] EWHC 1712; [2008] F.S.R. 1 (Lewison J.) upheld on appeal [2008] EWCA Civ 358; [2008] F.S.R. 28. This does beg the question why the informed user of the latter product should be taken to be aware of such other designs.

[778] *Green Lane Products Ltd v PMS International Group Ltd* [2007] EWHC 1712; [2008] F.S.R. 1.

[779] *Mafin SpA's Design* [2005] E.C.D.R. 29 (OHIM).

[780] *Central Vista (M) Sdn Bhd. v Pemi Trade Sro* [2009] E.D.C.R. 21 (Designs Registry)—where the issue was whether a UK registered design had individual character when compared with an earlier registered Community design. In *Central Vista*, the Registry also expressed the view that displaying a prototype made to a design at a trade exhibition would amount to disclosure to the public.

[781] *Normann Copenhagen ApS v Paton Calvert Housewares Ltd* [2010] E.C.D.R. 3 at paras 13–14 where OHIM's Third Board of Appeal commented that such publication meant that the design was deemed to have been made available to the public for the purposes of art.7(1).

[782] *Thane International Group's application* [2006] E.C.D.R. 8 (Landsgericht Frankfurt am Main).

[783] *The Procter & Gamble* at first instance (Lewison J.) [2006] EWHC 3154; [2007] F.S.R. 13.

[784] *Woodhouse UK Plc v Architectural Lighting Systems* [2005] EWPCC (Des) 25; [2006] R.P.C. 1.

[785] See art.3 and para.13–208, above.

component part of a complex product shall only be considered to be new and to have individual character (a) if the component part, once it has been incorporated into the complex product, remains visible during normal use of the latter and (b) to the extent that those visible features fulfil in themselves the requirements as to novelty and individual character."

This provision (together with the technical function and interconnections exclusions considered below) was clearly intended to address concerns relating to "spare parts" and, in particular, automotive "spare parts". Thus, the exclusion of protection for the design of any component that is not visible in normal use will clearly mean that Community design protection is not available for the designs of "under the bonnet" car components. However, the provision is of general application. In this respect, art.4(2) goes much further in limiting the scope of Community design than the 1988 Act goes in limiting UK design right.[786]

13–219   **Visible in normal use.** The requirement that a component part remains visible during normal use does not, it seems, mean that it should *always* be visible during normal use. It seems that it is sufficient that the whole of the part can be seen for some of the time and in such a way that all of its essential features can be apprehended.[787] "Normal use" for these purposes is defined by art.4(3) as meaning use by the end user, excluding maintenance, servicing or repair work. This test may not always be easy to apply. For example, it seems clear that the exclusion is intended to apply to "under the bonnet" parts of a car that would be visible when (for example) the windscreen washer water reservoir or the engine oil are topped up. But what about parts of the car that are only visible when the petrol cap is opened to fill up with petrol? What about the parts of a fountain pen that are only visible when the pen is being refilled with ink? These would not appear to be acts of "maintenance". Yet it is not easy to see how those acts differ from the act of filling up with water or oil—each affects the ability of the product to perform its function.[788]

15. UNREGISTERED COMMUNITY DESIGNS: OTHER EXCLUSIONS FROM PROTECTION

13–220   As well as excluding Community design from designs that are not novel or that do not have individual character, the Regulation has exclusions that apply in respect of features of appearance solely dictated by the technical function of the product, and features allowing the interconnection of products and designs that are contrary to public policy or to accepted principles of morality. These exclusions are considered below.

---

[786] For design right, the definition of a design expressly refers to internal features, and the main limitations on protection are the "must fit" and "must match" exclusions. See paras 13–45 et seq., and paras 13–58 et seq., above.

[787] *Lindner Recyclingtech GmbH v Franssons Verkstader AB* [2010] E.C.D.R. 1, where a cutting rotor forming part of a shredding machine was held to be visible for these purposes even though it remained covered for much of the time whilst material was being shredded and even though the spinning of the rotor limited the extent to which its features could be perceived. The Third Board of Appeal of OHIM accepted that the rotor needed to be open for observation during shredding and that the user had shown various methods of carrying out such observation (mirrors, cameras or an observation platform).

[788] In *Honda Motor Co Ltd v Kwang Yang Motor Co Ltd* [2008] E.C.D.R. 5 the Third Board of Appeal at OHIM held that where the appearance of an internal combustion engine was registered as a Community design, the only details of the design that could contribute to the overall impression of the design were those details that could be seen during use of the product in which that engine was installed (e.g. a lawn mower). Unfortunately the Board did not directly address the relevance of further features of the design that might be seen by the informed user during, for example, routine maintenance.

A. EXCLUSION OF DESIGNS DICTATED SOLELY BY THEIR TECHNICAL FUNCTION

Article 8(1) of the Regulation provides that: **13–221**

"A Community design shall not subsist in features of appearance of a product which are solely dictated by its technical function".

As appears from recital 10, where this exclusion applies, the relevant features should not be taken into consideration for the purpose of determining whether the other features of the design fulfil the requirements for protection as a Community design.

The extent of the exclusion under art.8(1) is controversial. In particular, it is   **13–222** unclear whether the exclusion should be construed as applying only where the design in question is the only design by which the product in question could perform its function (i.e. where the function could not be performed by any other design) or whether it applies whenever a design was as a matter of fact dictated solely by the function of the product even though it was not the only design that was capable of allowing that function to be performed. The former (narrower) construction could be said to be consistent with recital 10 of the Regulation as it does less to restrict the protection of non-aesthetic (i.e. functional) designs.[789] However, this narrower construction can be criticised on the basis that it means that "it is not easy to think of concrete examples where this exclusion would apply. A table tennis ball must be a sphere, perhaps".[790] Indeed, construed in this way, the exclusion would do little to promote what many perceive to be a policy behind the design legislation—namely to limit monopolies outside the sphere of patent law. Further, the wording of art.8(1) taken by itself seems to point more naturally to the latter (wider) construction.[791]

As indicated, the point is a controversial one. In *Landor & Hawa International Ltd v Azure Designs Ltd*, the Court of Appeal said that the narrower construction of art.8(1) is the correct one.[792] However, the High Court in *Dyson Limited v Vax Limited*[793] has ruled that the Court of Appeal's decision on this point was strictly obiter and has concluded that the wider construction favoured by the Third Board of Appeal of OHIM in *Lindner Recyclingtech GmbH v Franssons Verkstader AB*[794] was to be preferred. Significantly, the House of Lords in construing the similarly worded exclusion in s.1(3) of the Registered Designs Act 1949 (before its amendment by the CDPA 1988) had adopted the wider construction.[795]

As regards the meaning of "technical function" for the purposes of art.8(1); there seems to be no reason why the function of a product should be narrowly

---

[789] Recital 10 states that "[t]echnological innovation should not be hampered by granting design protection to features dictated solely by a technical function", but goes on to provide that "[i]t is understood that this does not entail that a design must have an aesthetic quality". The narrower construction is also supported by the comments of the Advocate General in *Philips v Remington* [2001] E.T.M.R. 509 and is consistent with the comments of the European Economic & Social Committee, [1995] OJ C110/12 (May 2, 1995).

[790] See *The Procter & Gamble Co v. Reckitt Benckiser (UK) Ltd* [2006] EWHC 3154; [2007] F.S.R. 13 at para.28.

[791] The criticisms of the narrow construction and the arguments in favour of the wider construction are persuasively set out by the Third Board of Appeal of OHIM in *Lindner Recyclingtech GmbH v Franssons Verkstader AB* [2010] E.C.D.R. 1 at paras 28–37.

[792] [2006] EWCA Civ 1285; [2007] F.S.R. 9. *Bailey v Haynes* [2006] EWPCC 5; [2007] F.S.R. 10 is to the same effect.

[793] [2010] EWHC 1923 (Pat) (Arnold J.) at paras 23–31.

[794] [2010] E.C.D.R. 1.

[795] See *Amp Inc v Utilux Pty Ltd* [1972] R.P.C. 103.

construed.[796] However, the exclusion will only operate where the feature is dictated solely by function and it has been said that, as most designers are concerned with both functionality and eye appeal, their designs are unlikely to be solely functional. So long as functionality is not the only relevant factor, a design will be eligible for protection.[797] Whether a design is or is not functional in the sense required by art.8(1) is a matter to be judged objectively—whereby the reasonable observer asks himself whether purely functional considerations could have been relevant when a specific feature was chosen.

B. THE "INTERCONNECTIONS" EXCLUSION

13–223   Under art.8(2) of the Regulation:

> "A Community design will not subsist in features of appearance of a product which must necessarily be reproduced in their exact form and dimensions in order to permit the product in which the design is incorporated or to which it is applied to be mechanically connected to or placed in, around or against another product so that either product may perform its function".

Although this exclusion is called the "interconnections" exclusion, much of its wording mirrors that of the United Kingdom "must fit" exclusion for design right.[798] As with the "must fit" exclusion, art.8(2) does not apply only to spare parts and, as the wording of recital 14 makes clear, it will also apply where there is a need to allow the interoperability of products of different makes. However, the words "must necessarily be reproduced in their exact form and dimensions" suggests that this interconnections exclusion may be somewhat narrower in scope than the "must fit" exclusion.[799]

13–224   **Modular products.** The application of art.8(2) is subject to art.8(3) which provides that notwithstanding art.8(2) (and subject to satisfying the requirements of novelty and of having individual character):

> ". . . a Community design shall . . . subsist in a design serving the purpose of allowing multiple assembly or connection of mutually interchangeable products within a modular system".

In this regard, recital 11 states that:

> "The mechanical fittings of modular products may nevertheless constitute an important element of the innovative characteristics of modular products and present a major marketing asset, and therefore should be eligible for protection".

The interconnections exclusion will not, therefore, remove protection from "mutually interchangeable" products—such as children's building blocks.

C. EXCLUSIONS DUE TO PUBLIC POLICY OR MORALITY

13–225   Article 9 of the Regulation provides that Community design shall not subsist in a design which is contrary to public policy or to accepted principles of morality.

---

[796] See, for example, the comments in *Ocular Sciences Ltd v Aspect Vision Care Ltd* [1999] R.P.C. 289 at 425, regarding the function of contact lenses for the purposes of the must fit exclusion contained in s.213(3)(b)(i) of the 1988 Act. See para.13–61, above.

[797] *Lindner Recyclingtech GmbH v Franssons Verkstader AB* [2010] E.C.D.R. 1 at paras 33–35 where it was said that aspects of the design of an industrial shredder were pleasing to the eye and enhanced the working environment of those operating it. Similarly in *Dyson Limited v Vax Limited* [2010] EWHC 1923 (Pat) at para.59, the design of the transparent bin for the Claimant's vacuum cleaner was found to be influenced by a mixture of both technical and aesthetic factors so that the exclusion did not operate.

[798] CDPA 1988 s.213(3)(b)(i) which is considered in detail at paras 13–58 et seq., above.

[799] Contrast the position under design right, see para.13–61, above.

This differs from the position under copyright and design right where the balance of authority suggests that a contravention of public policy or morality does not prevent copyright or design right subsisting, but only prevents its being enforced by the courts.[800]

The European Directive on the legal protection of designs[801] contains the same exclusion. However, the Directive also contains a recital (recital 16) which is not in the Regulation and which makes it clear that it was not the intention to harmonise national concepts of public policy or morality. This was, presumably, because the Directive was dealing with national laws whereas the Regulation was creating a Community wide right. It is, therefore, unclear whose law resolves the issue of public policy or morality in the context of a Community design. It seems unlikely that it is the law of the country that is hearing the dispute, as that country may take a very different view to these issues than the country where the alleged infringement of the design occurred. The most likely meaning is that the design must not offend against any Member State's public policy or principles of morality.

16. UNREGISTERED COMMUNITY DESIGNS: GROUNDS FOR INVALIDITY

Introduction. A design will be invalid if it does not satisfy the definition of a design in art.3(a), or if it falls within one of the limitations and exclusions in arts 4 to 9. There are, however, other grounds on which a Community design may be declared invalid. Articles 24 to 26 of the Regulation deal with invalidity, setting out the various grounds of invalidity, the manner in which these grounds can be raised and the consequences of invalidity.   **13–226**

Declaration of invalidity. In the case of an unregistered Community design, art.24(3) provides that a declaration of invalidity can be made by a Community design court on application or on the basis of a counterclaim in infringement proceedings.[802] Article 24(2) provides that such a declaration can be made even after the Community design has lapsed.   **13–227**

Grounds of invalidity. Article 25 lists the only grounds[803] on which a Community design can be declared invalid. They are: **13–228**

  (a) That the design does not correspond with the definition (of design) in Article 3.
  (b) That the design does not fulfil the requirements of Articles 4 to 9, i.e. the provisions relating to novelty, individual character, technical function, interconnections and public policy or morality.[804]
  (c) That the (alleged) right-holder is not entitled under Article 14 [see paras 13–217 et seq., below]. Only the person who is entitled under Article 14 can rely on this ground.[805]

---

[800] See paras 3–304 et seq., above.
[801] Directive 98/71/EC.
[802] For the meaning of Community design courts, see Regulation (EC) No. 6/2002, art.80 and para.13–260, below.
[803] In *Grupo Promer Mon Graphic SA v Office for Harmonisation in the Internal Market* [2010] E.D.C.R. 7 (a registered community design case) (at paras 30 to 33), the General Court (Fifth Chamber) of the ECJ ruled that the list of grounds set out in art.25 is exhaustive and rejected an argument that a design may be invalid on the ground that the proprietor had acted in bad faith.
[804] See, for example, *Lindner Recyclingtech GmbH v Franssons Verkstader AB* [2010] E.C.D.R. 1.
[805] See Regulation (EC) No. 6/2002, art.25(2). Ground (b) is by far the most popular ground for challenging the validity of a design.

(d) —[806]

(e) That the design has used an already existing distinctive sign in circumstances where Community or national law (e.g. the law of passing off or trade mark law) would permit the right-holder of that sign to prohibit such use.[807] Only the holder of that right can rely on this ground.[808]

(f) That the design constitutes an unauthorised use of a work protected under the copyright law of a Member State. Again, only the owner of that copyright can rely on this ground.[809]

(g) That the design constitutes an improper use of any of the items listed in Article 6ter of the Paris Convention for the Protection of Industrial Property or are badges, emblems and escutcheons other than those covered by Article 6 and which are of particular public interest in a Member State. Only the person or entity concerned by such use can rely on this ground.[810]

17. UNREGISTERED COMMUNITY DESIGNS: DURATION

13–229 **Duration—three years only.** Under art.11(1), an unregistered community design is only entitled to a very short period of protection—namely three years from the date when the design is first made available to the public within the Community. This contrasts with the much longer periods of protection for a design under design right (15 years from when the design is first recorded or, where articles made to the design are marketed, 10 years from the date of first marketing) and for where a design is registered (up to 25 years). Another potentially important difference between Community design and design right is that, under art.11(1), a design will not have Community design protection before it is first made available to the public. If, therefore, the defendant obtains details of and copies the design *before* that event, some other remedy would have to be found—such as copyright or design right.

13–230 **Date when design made available to the public.** The three-year protection for an unregistered Community design starts on the date when the design is first made available to the public within the Community. For these purposes, art.11(2) provides that:

"... a design shall be deemed to have been made available to the public within the Community if it has been published, exhibited, used in trade or otherwise disclosed in such a way that, in the normal course of business, these events could reasonably have become known to the circles specialising in the sector concerned, operating within the Community. The design shall not,

---

[806] This ground (that the registered Community design was in conflict with an earlier registered design, or an earlier application for registration) relates solely to registered Community designs. It was considered in *Grupo Promer Mon Graphic SA v Office for Harmonisation in the Internal Market* [2010] E.D.C.R. 7 where the General Court (Fifth Chamber) of the ECJ decided that the registered Community design in issue was "in conflict" because it did not create a different overall impression from the earlier design. In other words, it applied the infringement test from art.10(2)—see paras 13–245 et seq. below.

[807] For examples of this provision in operation, see *Beifa Group Co. Ltd v Office for Harmonisation in the Internal Market* [2010] E.T.M.R. 42 at paras 50–55 where the General Court of the ECJ found that art.25(1)(e) did not require the design to reproduce the earlier sign in full or in detail but that it was sufficient if it made use of a sign so similar to the earlier sign that there was a likelihood of confusion on the part of the relevant public. See also *Zellweger Analytic's Design* [2006] E.C.D.R. 17 and *OOO Business-Aliance v VITEC Global Ltd* [2009] E.C.D.R.7 (Invalidity Division of OHIM) where it was stated that a trade mark registered in a member state is presumed to be a "distinctive sign" for the purposes of art.25(1)(e).

[808] art.25(3)

[809] See art.25(3).

[810] See art.25(4).

however, be deemed to have been made available to the public for the sole reason that it has been disclosed to a third person under explicit or implicit conditions of confidentiality".

This is the same definition that applies under art.7 and has been considered in that context.[811] Accordingly, it would seem that a design might be found to have been made available in the Community even though it had only been published (etc.) outside the Community. The only criteria is whether its publication (etc.) was such as to have become known in the relevant circles within the Community.[812]

18. UNREGISTERED COMMUNITY DESIGNS: OWNERSHIP AND DEALINGS

A. Ownership of a Community Design Right to the Community Design

Ownership of a Community design is governed by art.14 of the Regulation. Article 14(1) provides that:

13–231

"The right to the Community design shall vest in the designer or his successor in title."

However, art.14(3) provides that:

".   .   . where a design is developed by an employee in the execution of his duties or following the instructions given by his employer, the right to the Community design shall vest in the employer, unless otherwise agreed or specified under national law."

Who is the designer. The starting point, therefore, is to identify the designer. For these purposes, terms such as "designer" and "successor in title" are to be given an autonomous and uniform interpretation throughout the Community.[813] Although art.14 talks in terms of the designer being the person who developed the design rather than the person who created it, there is no reason to think that the identity of the designer for these purposes will differ from the identity of the designer for the purposes of UK design right.[814]

13–232

Where the designer is an employee. If the designer was an employee and developed the design in the execution of his duties or following instructions given by his employer then, under art.14(3), Community design will vest in the employer unless otherwise agreed or specified under national law. This provision envisages the existence of an employment relationship and will not apply to other forms of relationship such as, for example, principal and agent.

13–233

It would seem that any issue as to whether the designer was an employee, whether he had been acting in the execution of his duties or under instructions from his employer and whether there had been some contrary agreement or specification would be governed by the national law that governed the relationship between the relevant parties. The issue whether the designer had been acting in the execution of his duties would seem to correspond with the test under UK

---

[811] See para.13–215, above.

[812] For the meaning of "circles specialising in the sector concerned", see para.13–216 above and *Green Lane Products Ltd v PMS International Group Ltd* [2007] EWHC 1712; [2008] F.S.R. 1.

[813] *Foundacion Espanola Para La Innovacion de la Artesania v Cul de Sac Espacio Creativo SL* [2010] R.P.C. 13 at paras 63–67.

[814] See para.13–86, above.

design right where the issue is whether the designer was an employee acting in the course of his employment.[815]

13–234 **Where the designer was not an employee.** If art.14(3) does not apply (because, for example, the designer was not an employee or because he was not acting in execution of his duties or under the instructions of his employer or because the parties or national law had specified otherwise), then the Community design will vest in the designer or his successor in title pursuant to art.14(1).

13–235 **Ownership by agreement.** The reference in art.14(1) to "successors in title" clearly envisages that title to a Community design can pass.[816] What is less clear is whether an agreement made before the creation of the design can affect the identity of the first owner. Article 14(3) provides for such a situation in the case of an employee. However, there is no equivalent provision dealing with such a case for non-employees. In the absence of a specific provision such as s.223 of the 1988 Act (which applies to UK design rights), it would seem that where English law governs,[817] such an agreement would take effect as, at best, an equitable assignment and would not affect the issue of the vesting of legal title.[818]

13–236 **Commissioned designs.** The position set out in the previous paragraph would seem to apply to cases where the designer created the design pursuant to a commission for it is now clear that art.14(3) does not extend to such cases but is limited (as mentioned above) to relationships that can properly be characterised as employment relationships.[819] On this basis, the best that a commissioner could hope for is to be entitled in equity to the Community design.[820]

13–237 **Joint developed designs.** Where two or more people jointly develop a design, art.14(2) provides that the right to the Community design will vest in them jointly. These provisions appear similar to those that apply in UK design right.

13–238 **Disputes over entitlement to a Community design.** If a person who is not entitled to an unregistered Community design in the sense set out above discloses or claims an unregistered Community design, then arts 15(1) and 15(2) of the Regulation provide that the person properly entitled to the Community design or jointly entitled to that design, may (without prejudice to any other remedy that may be open to him) claim to be recognised as the legitimate holder of the design or, as the case may be, the joint holder. There is, however, a significant difference to UK national law in that art.15(3) of the Regulation also provides that legal proceedings to be recognised as the legitimate holder (but not, it seems any other rights) will be barred three years after the other person disclosed the unregistered design or after the publication of the registered design (unless the other person had acted in bad faith).[821] It seems clear that this limitation period is against the commencement of proceedings seeking recognition as the legitimate holder of the Community design after the relevant three-year period (rather than the continuation of existing proceedings).

---

[815] See para.13–91, above.

[816] See *Foundacion Espanola Para La Innovacion de la Artesania v Cul de Sac Espacio Creativo SL* [2010] R.P.C. 13 at paras 69–77 and 80–81. See also, "Dealings with a Community Design" at paras 13–239 et seq., below

[817] i.e. where England is where on the relevant date, the holder of the Community design has his seat or domicile or (if that does not apply) an establishment—see art.27(1) of the Regulation.

[818] For the position as regards s.223, see para.13–120, above.

[819] *Foundacion Espanola Para La Innovacion de la Artesania v Cul de Sac Espacio Creativo SL* [2010] R.P.C. 13 at paras 43–55.

[820] See the previous paragraph.

[821] For unregistered Community design, which only lasts three years from the date when the design was disclosed, this limitation is of little significance. However, the same restriction also applies to registered Community designs which can last for up to 25 years.

B. DEALINGS WITH A COMMUNITY DESIGN

Community design as a property right. Articles 27 to 34 of the Regulation deal   **13–239**
with the status of Community designs as objects of property.

Dealing with a Community design—the governing law. Article 27 of the   **13–240**
Regulation lays down a code regarding dealings with a Community design and
the law that will govern those dealings. Article 27(1) provides that:

> "Unless Articles 28, 29, 30, 31 and 32 provide otherwise, a Community
> design as an object of property shall be dealt with in its entirety, and for the
> whole area of the Community, as a national design right of the Member
> State in which:
>
> (a) the holder has his seat or his domicile on the relevant date; or
>
> (b) where point (a) does not apply, the holder has an establishment on the
> relevant date".

Article 27(3) provides that:

> "In the case of joint holders, if two or more of them fulfil the condition
> under paragraph 1, the Member State referred to in that paragraph shall be
> determined:
>
> (a) (a) in the case of an unregistered Community design, by reference to
> the relevant joint holder designated by them by common
> agreement.   . ."[822]

Finally, art.27(4) provides that where the previous paragraphs of Article 27 do
not apply, "the Member State referred to in paragraph 1 shall be the Member
State in which the seat of the Office is situated", i.e. Spain.

A number of points arise out of this. First, (unless one of arts 28 to 32 applies)
the Community design must be dealt with in its entirety and for the whole area of
the Community.[823] This is an important restriction on the normal right of a property owner to deal with his property as he thinks fit, and it is clearly intended to
help prevent Community designs becoming fragmented by having different owners in different countries. Second, although Community design is a Community
wide property right, a single national law will govern dealings with that right.[824]
The applicable national law is ascertained in accordance with art.27 (unless arts
28 to 32 provide otherwise[825]). Third, as is clear from art.27, the applicable
national law may change depending on the circumstances of the holder or holders.

Where English law governs, it would seem that the principles set out by the
Court of Appeal in *Ifejika v Ifejika*[826] will apply, namely that the right (as a chose
in action) may be assigned in law or in equity. Whilst a written legal assignment
is usual, an assignment may be effected in equity provided there is a sufficient
expression of an intention to assign in the context of a transaction—i.e. an expression from which it can be inferred that the property was intended to pass. Of
course, an enforceable contract to assign will also be effective to effect an assignment in equity.

---

[822] It is not clear which law applies where only one of the joint holders has a seat or domicile or
establishment in a Member State although common sense suggests that the law of that Member
State will apply.

[823] See also Regulation (EC) No. 6/2002, art.1(3) which states that a Community design "shall have
a unitary character. It shall have equal effect throughout the Community. It shall not be registered,
transferred or surrendered or be the subject of a decision declaring it invalid, nor shall its use be
prohibited, save in respect of the whole Community. This principle and its implications shall apply unless otherwise provided in this Regulation".

[824] *Foundacion Espanola Para La Innovacion de la Artesania v Cul de Sac Espacio Creativo SL*
[2010] R.P.C. 13 at para.80.

[825] art.28 only applies to registered Community designs. For the position regarding arts 29 and 30
see para.13–241, below. For arts 31 and 32 see below at paras 13–242 and 13–243, respectively.

[826] [2010] EWCA Civ. 563; [2010] F.S.R. 29—a registered designs case.

13–241   **Security, rights in rem, execution.** Articles 29 and 30 of the Regulation provide that a registered Community design may be given as security or be the subject of rights in rem and may be levied in execution; on request, such dealings can be entered on the register. There are, however, no equivalent provisions in the case of unregistered Community designs. Given this, it seems probable that the general provision in art.27(1) would operate so that any such dealing in relation to an unregistered Community design would only be permitted if it was a dealing for the design in its entirety and for the whole area of the Community. Again, the rationale for this would seem to be to prevent possible uncertainty arising from there being different property interests in a Community design in different Member States.

13–242   **Insolvency proceedings.** Under art.31 of the Regulation, insolvency proceedings in which a Community design may be involved can only be opened in the Member State within the territory in which the centre of the debtor's main interests is situated. Where the debtor is a joint proprietor, this applies only to his share. By reason of art.33(4), the effect of insolvency proceedings on any third parties shall be governed by the national law of the Member State in which those proceedings are first brought.

13–243   **Licensing.** As an exception to the general provision in art.27 requiring Community designs to be dealt with in their entirety, art.32(1) provides that a Community design may be licensed for the whole or part of the Community. Article 33(1) provides that the effects of a licence granted under art.32 shall be governed by the law of the Member State determined in accordance with art.27.[827] However, art.32(1) provides that a licence may be exclusive or non-exclusive and, under arts 32(3) and (4), exclusive and non-exclusive licensees have somewhat wider rights to sue for infringement than would be the case for licensees under UK design right. These wider rights are considered later in this chapter.[828]

Under English law, a licence is merely a permission to do that which would otherwise infringe some property right. Thus, a licensee who goes beyond the scope of his licence would be infringing the relevant property right. Article 32(2) adopts the same approach, providing that a licensee who contravenes any provision in his licence contract with regard to duration, or the form in which the design can be used, or the range of products for which the licence is granted, or the quality of products manufactured by the licensee is liable to be sued by the holder of the Community design.

19. UNREGISTERED COMMUNITY DESIGNS: RIGHTS CONFERRED, INFRINGEMENT, PERMITTED ACTS

13–244   **Introduction.** An unregistered Community design, like copyright and design right, confers on its holder certain exclusive rights. These exclusive rights are to use the relevant design in any of the ways set out in art.19(1) of the Regulation, provided such use results from copying of the protected design (see art.19(2)).

Significantly, by reason of art.10, the scope of the protection offered by Community design is not limited to such use of just the protected design. Instead, it extends to such use of any other design that does not produce a different overall impression on the informed user. A person who, without the holder's consent, does one of the acts specified in art.19 in respect of a design which falls within the scope of protection laid down in art.10 may be infringing the Community design.

---

[827] See para.13–240, above.
[828] See para.13–256, below.

The exclusive rights conferred by Community design and, therefore, the scope of infringement are subject to the limitations set out in arts 20 to 23 (referred to below as "permitted acts"). In contrast to the position under copyright and design right, there are no categories of secondary infringement of Community design.

A. RIGHTS CONFERRED BY AND INFRINGEMENT OF UNREGISTERED COMMUNITY DESIGN

Rights conferred by a Community design. Article 19 of the Regulation sets out the rights conferred by a Community design on its holder and, therefore, defines the acts that are capable of infringing that Community design.   **13–245**

Article 19(1) deals with the position regarding registered Community designs. It states that:

"A registered Community design shall confer on its holder the exclusive right to use it and to prevent any third party not having his consent from using it. The aforementioned use shall cover, in particular, the making, offering, putting on the market, importing, exporting or using of a product in which the design is incorporated or to which it has been applied, or stocking such a product for those purposes."

In relation to unregistered Community designs, art.19(2) provides that:

"An unregistered Community design shall, however, confer on its holder the right to prevent the acts referred to in paragraph 1 only if the contested use results from copying the protected design.

The contested use shall not be deemed to result from copying the protected design if it results from an independent work of creation by a designer who may be reasonably thought not to be familiar with the design made available to the public by the holder".

Article 19 must be read in the light of art.10 which provides that:

"(1) The scope of protection conferred by a Community design shall include any design which does not produce on the informed user a different overall impression.

(2) In assessing the scope of protection, the degree of freedom of the designer in developing his design shall be taken into consideration."

Scope of protection. A number of points arise from these provisions.   **13–246**

First, the types of use that fall within the exclusive rights and which are therefore capable of being infringements are very broadly defined by art.19. They include even "using of" a product to which the design has been applied or in which the design is incorporated and "stocking" such product for any reason other than the stated purposes.

Secondly, as has been noted above, under art.10 the exclusive right is not just to use the design in the ways specified in art.19, it extends to the use of any design that does not produce on the informed user a different overall impression. On this basis, the holder of a Community design in the design for a handle of a spoon would have the exclusive right to apply that design to a fork or even to a vase. If someone else were to copy that design (without permission) by using it as the handle for a fork, they would making a product (the fork) to which the design (of a handle) had been applied and would be infringing unless they fell within one of the limitations contained in arts 20 to 23.[829] For these purposes, the mean-

---

[829] In this respect, the approach to infringement for the purposes of art.19 appears to be somewhat closer to the approach in copyright than to that in design right. As has been seen, for copyright the test is whether the defendant has copied the work or a substantial part of it. For design right, it

ing of "informed user" and of "overall impression" have already been considered in the context of whether a design has individual character.[830]

Thirdly, in assessing the scope of protection for a design, art.10(2) requires that the degree of freedom of the designer in developing his design must be taken into account. This is an important provision. If the designer had little design freedom (as is often the case with designs for more functional products), then two similar designs are less likely to produce the same overall impression on an informed user. Instead, that user would be likely to be influenced by small differences. Equally, where the designer has a greater degree of design freedom (as is the case with more aesthetic designs, e.g. of a toy) similarities are more likely to produce the same overall impression on the informed user.[831] Again, the meaning of this requirement has already been considered in the context of whether a design has individual character.[832]

Fourthly, to establish an infringement of an unregistered Community design, proof of copying is required. In this respect, the law reflects that for copyright and design right, and there is no reason to think that what has already been said in relation to those rights would not apply equally in an unregistered Community design case.[833] In fact, the second part of art.19(2) clearly assumes that a presumption of copying can arise as a result of similarities between the designs. Further, the possibility of indirect copying of an unregistered Community design is recognised in art.19(2) which provides that the presumption of copying can be rebutted by proof that the contested use was the result of an independent work of creation by a designer who may be reasonably thought not to be familiar with the protected design.

13–247   Judicial guidance. As appears from the decision of the General Court of the European Court of Justice in *Grupo Promer Mon Graphic SA v Office for Harmonisation in the Internal Market*,[834] the "overall impression" test requires the court to identify similarities and differences between the competing designs and to determine whether they would have been of significance to the informed user. There is further guidance as to the scope of protection for Community designs in *The Procter & Gamble Co v Reckitt Benckiser (UK) Ltd*.[835] There the Court of Appeal commented that the test whether the accused design creates a different overall impression on the informed user is "inherently rather imprecise" as it needs to cover not only exact imitations but also things which come too close. For this reason it leaves a considerable margin for the judgment of the trial judge just as the "substantial part" test does in copyright cases.[836] The Court of Appeal

---

is whether the defendant has made an article to or substantially to the design—see para.13–149, above. Consistently with this, it has been commented that the design of an aerosol can, in principle, be infringed by, say, a vase. See *Procter & Gamble Co v Reckitt Benckiser (UK) Ltd* [2006] EWHC 3154; [2007] F.S.R. 13 at para.27.

[830] See paras 13–210 et seq., above. For the application of these concepts in the context of infringement, see *Dyson Ltd v Vax Ltd* [2010] EWHC 1923 (Pat).

[831] See, for example, *Grupo Promer Mon Graphic SA v Office for Harmonisation in the Internal Market* [2010] E.D.C.R. 7 at para.82 (a registered community design case decided by the General Court of the ECJ).

[832] See paras 13–210 et seq., above. For an infringement case where the limited degree of design freedom played an important part in leading the court to conclude that the parties' designs would not create the same overall impression, see *Dyson Ltd v Vax Ltd* [2010] EWHC 1923 (Pat).

[833] See para.13–151, above.

[834] [2010] E.D.C.R. 7 at paras 76–84 (a registered community design case). See also *J. Choo (Jersey) Ltd v Towerstone Ltd* [2008] F.S.R. 19.

[835] [2007] EWCA Civ 936; [2008] F.S.R. 8.

[836] *The Procter & Gamble Co v Reckitt Benckiser (UK) Ltd* [2007] EWCA Civ 936; [2008] F.S.R. 8 at para.34 where Jacob L.J. left open whether the sort of margin was the same in both types of case.

also made a number of general observations as to the test for infringement. These were, in summary[837]:

(1) The defendant's product will infringe if its design does not produce a different overall impression on the informed user. As has already been seen, the word "clearly" is not read into this test.[838] Thus, to defeat a claim of infringement, a defendant need not show that his design produces a clearly different overall impression; it is enough that it produces a different overall impression.

(2) The informed user is taken to be fairly familiar with design issues.[839]

(3) If the protected design is markedly different to the general design corpus, its overall impression would be more significant and the room for differences which do not create a substantially different overall impression will be greater. In effect, the scope of protection for such a design is greater. In this regard, the informed user is taken to be aware of the existing design corpus.

(4) Despite this, the test remains "is the overall impression different"? It is not sufficient to ask whether the defendant's product is closer to the protected design than to the general design corpus.

(5) The comparison between the protected design and the defendant's design is conducted with a reasonable degree of care. The possibility of imperfect recollection plays only a limited role.[840]

(6) The court must identify the overall impression of the protected design with care. It is helpful to use pictures as part of the identification.

(7) The court must descend to the level of generality that the notional informed user would use. On the facts of *Procter & Gamble*, it would be too general to say that the overall impression was of a canister fitter with a trigger device on the top.

(8) The court must then identify the overall impression of the defendant's product.

(9) Finally, the court must ask whether the two overall impressions are different. This is "almost the equivalent to asking whether they are the same—the difference is nuanced, probably, involving a question of onus and no more".

Treatment of excluded features. In determining whether a design creates the same overall impression as the protected design, it is important to bear in mind that it is the designs that are being compared rather than the products to which they have been applied or in which they are incorporated. Further, although recital 10 indicates that features which are excluded from protection should not be taken into account in determining whether other features fulfil the requirements for protection, the fact remains that such features remain part of the design (albeit that they are excluded from protection), there seems to be no reason why they should not be taken into account in deciding whether the protected design and any other design produce different overall impressions for the purposes of art.10. However, the nature of the exclusions means that such features are unlikely to be of great significance to an informed user.   **13–248**

B. Permitted Acts

Permitted acts. Articles 20, 21, 23 and, importantly, 110 of the Regulation lay   **13–249**

---

[837] *The Procter & Gamble Co v Reckitt Benckiser (UK) Ltd* [2007] EWCA Civ 936 at para.35.
[838] See para.13–213, above
[839] For more on the identity and characteristics of the informed user, see para.13–211, above.
[840] See para.13–213, above.

down a number of limitations on the rights conferred on the holder of an unregistered Community design.

13–250   **Non-commercial acts.** Article 20(1) of the Regulation provides that:

"The rights conferred by a Community design shall not be exercised in respect of

    (a) acts done privately and for non-commercial purposes;

    (b) acts done for experimental purposes;

    (c) acts of reproduction for the purpose of making citations or of teaching, provided that such acts are compatible with fair trade practices and do not unduly prejudice the normal exploitation of the design, and that mention is made of the source".

These are plainly important limitations on the rights under a Community design. Many of the concepts are familiar from copyright and/or design right.

13–251   **Ships and aircraft temporarily entering the Community.** Article 20(2) of the Regulation provides that the rights conferred by a Community design shall not be exercised in respect of (a) the equipment on aircraft and ships registered in a third (i.e. non-Community) country when these temporarily enter Community territory; (b) the importation into the Community of spare parts and accessories for the purpose of repairing such craft; and (c) the execution of repairs to such craft.

13–252   **Exhaustion of rights.** Under art.21 of the Regulation, the rights conferred by a Community design do not extend to acts relating to a product in which a design within the scope of protection is incorporated or to which it has been applied, when the product has been put on the market in the Community by the holder of the Community design or with his consent.

13–253   **Government use.** Under art.23 of the Regulation, a provision in the law of a Member State allowing use of national designs by or for the Government, will apply to Community designs but only to the extent that the use is necessary for essential defence or security needs. Article 23 of the Regulation as implemented in the United Kingdom[841] makes provision for Crown use of Community designs (both unregistered and registered) in terms that are substantially identical to those for unregistered UK design right.[842] However, in view of the terms of art.23, the definition of "services of the Crown" is different. For the purposes of unregistered UK design right "services of the Crown" include defence of the realm; foreign defence purposes; and health service purposes.[843] By contrast, for the purposes of Community designs, "services of the Crown" are limited to those which are necessary for essential defence and security needs. Not surprisingly, there is no attempt to define the expression "essential defence or security needs".

13–254   **Spare parts—transitional provision.** Another important limitation on Community design protection is the transitional provision contained in art.110 of the Regulation. This deals with spare parts. It provides that protection as a Community design shall not exist for a design which constitutes a component part of a complex product used within the meaning of art.19(1) for the purpose of the repair of that complex product so as to restore its original appearance.

This provision has similarities to the "must match" exclusion that applies in design right, and that formerly applied in UK registered designs—particularly in

---

[841] With effect from October 1, 2005 by reg.5 of and the Schedule to the Community Design Regulations 2005 (SI 2005/2339).

[842] See paras 13–134 et seq. above

[843] See para.13–135 above

its concept of restoring the original design appearance of a product.[844] However, there are also important differences in wording. For example, the definition of a design to which the exclusion in art.110 might apply is much wider than the definition of a design for the purposes of the "must match" exclusion. However, under the Regulation, the exclusion only applies to designs which may be used for the purpose of repair.

As mentioned above, art.110 is a transitional provision, for it states that it shall only operate until the Regulation is amended following a proposal from the Commission. The background to this is that there is still considerable controversy as to whether the designs of spare parts should be afforded protection. Because of this controversy, the Directive on the legal protection of designs presently permits Member States to retain any existing protection for spare parts under national law (although not to increase such protection), but provides that, within three years of implementation, the Commission should submit an analysis of the consequences that this has had on consumers, on competition, and on the internal market, and is to consider harmonisation of the law in this area and the possibility of introducing a remuneration system and a more limited period of protection.[845] However, the Commission is clearly keen to remove such protection and, pending any proposal following such review, the Regulation excludes such spare parts from any protection under Community design (see recital 13 of the Regulation).

20. UNREGISTERED COMMUNITY DESIGNS: ACTIONS AND REMEDIES

A. WHO CAN SUE

The Holder. By reason of art.19 of the Regulation, the person primarily entitled to sue for infringement of unregistered Community design is the holder, i.e. the person in whom Community right is vested. This is the person identified under art.14 of the Regulation or that person's successor in title. **13–255**

Licensees—the rights of exclusive and non-exclusive licensees to sue. **13–256**
However, special provisions govern the position in respect of licensees. In this regard, art.32(3) of the Regulation provides that:

> "Without prejudice to the provisions of the licensing contract, the licensee may bring proceedings for infringement of a Community design only if the right holder consents thereto. However, the holder of an exclusive licence may bring such proceedings if the right holder in the Community design, having been given notice to do so, does not himself bring infringement proceedings within an appropriate period".

And art.32(4) that:

> "A licensee shall, for the purpose of obtaining compensation for damage suffered by him, be entitled to intervene in an infringement action brought by the right holder in a Community design".

The position is, therefore, both similar and dissimilar to the position under

---

[844] See s.213(3)(b)(ii) of the 1988 Act and s.1(1)(b)(ii) of the Registered Designs Act 1949 (before its amendment by the Registered Designs Regulations 2001) and, in particular, *Ford Motor Co Ltd and Iveco Fiat SpA's Registered Design Applications* [1993] R.P.C. 339 (discussed at para.13–66, above). The 1949 Act now has an exclusion in substantially the same terms as art.110 of the Regulation—see s.7A(5) of the 1949 Act (as amended).

[845] See art.14 and recital 19 of the Design Directive (98/71/EC). This analysis should have been submitted in October 2004.

copyright and design right.[846] It is similar in that the primary party entitled to sue remains the holder of the right, although an exclusive licensee may bring an action. It is dissimilar in that a non-exclusive licensee of a Community design may sue (provided he has the holder's permission to do so), and in that the holder need not, it seems be joined as a party when a licensee of a Community design sues. However, the underlying rationale is clearly the same as in English law—namely to prevent an infringer being exposed to a claim by both the holder and the licensee.

B. Jurisdiction and Remedies

13–257　**Introduction.** Articles 79 to 94 of the Regulation contain extensive provisions dealing with issues of jurisdiction and enforcement in relation to Community designs.

13–258　**Application of the Judgments Regulation.**[847] First, art.79 of the Regulation confirms that, as a general rule and subject to the provisions of the Regulation, the Judgments Regulation[848] shall apply to proceedings relating to Community designs, as well as to proceedings relating to actions on the basis of Community designs and national designs enjoying simultaneous protection. Thus, the general rule is that a person must be sued in his country of domicile—although there are other bases on which jurisdiction may be founded under the Convention.

13–259　**Jurisdiction under article 82.** In essence, the approach of the Regulation is consistent with this general rule. Thus, under arts 82(1), (2) and (3) of the Regulation, any action or claim for (a) infringement and threatened infringement of Community design, (b) a declaration of non-infringement of Community designs, (c) a declaration of invalidity of a Community design, and (d) counterclaims seeking a declaration of invalidity raised in connection with an action under (a) above, must be brought in:

    (1) the courts of the Member State in which the defendant is domiciled or (if there is no such State) in which he has an establishment; or

    (2) if the defendant has no such domicile or establishment, the courts of the Member State in which the claimant is domiciled or (if there is no such State), where the claimant has an establishment; or

    (c) if the claimant also has no such domicile or establishment, the courts of the State where the Office has its seat (i.e. Spain).

Article 82(4) provides that the parties may agree or accept the jurisdiction of the courts of another Member State. Finally, art.82(5) provides that actions for infringement or threatened infringement and for a counterclaim for a declaration of invalidity brought within such actions may be brought in the courts of the Member State where an act of infringement has been committed or threatened, although, as set out below, where jurisdiction is based on this ground, it is limited to infringements occurring in that Member State.

13–260　**Community design courts.** For the purposes of art.82 of the Regulation, the courts to which jurisdiction is given are the Community design courts of the

---

[846] See, respectively, paras 21–27 et seq., below and para.13–172, above.

[847] Council Regulation 44/2001 on jurisdiction and the recognition and enforcement of judgments in civil and commercial matters [2001] OJ L 12/1-23.

[848] art.79 actually refers to the Brussels Convention. However, this is to be construed as a reference to the Judgments Regulation: see art.68(2) of that Regulation.

Member State in question.[849] Community design courts are those national courts which the relevant Member State has designated under art.80 of the Regulation.[850] Article 81 of the Regulation provides that these courts have exclusive jurisdiction in respect of the actions referred to in para.13–244, above. In exercising their exclusive jurisdiction, the Community design court must apply the provisions of the Regulation, but in matters not covered by the Regulation shall apply its national law and rules of procedure.[851]

Jurisdiction—infringement. Article 83 of the Regulation deals with the extent of the jurisdiction conferred on a Community design court by art.82 in respect of acts of infringement or threatened infringement. It provides that where jurisdiction is based on any of arts 82(1), (2), (3) or (4), the relevant court has jurisdiction in respect of any acts or infringement committed or threatened within the territory of any of the Member States. However, where jurisdiction is based on art.82(5), the relevant court only has jurisdiction in respect of acts of infringement committed or threatened in the Member State where that court is situated. **13–261**

In an action in respect of an infringement or threatened infringement of Community design, art.85(2) provides that, if the right-holder proves that the conditions laid down in art.11 have been met and indicates what constitutes the individual character of his Community design, the Community design court must treat the design as valid unless the defendant contests validity by way of a plea or with a counterclaim for a declaration of invalidity. It would seem that the reference to the "conditions laid down in Article 11" is a reference to proving that the design has been made available to the public in accordance with art.11(2).[852]

Where actions for infringement or threatened infringement involving the same cause of action and same parties are brought in the courts of different Member States, one seized on the basis of Community design, the other on the basis of a national design providing simultaneous protection, the court other than that first seized of the matter shall of its own motion decline jurisdiction in favour of that court. A Community design court should also reject an action if a final judgment on the merits has been given on the same cause of action and between the same parties on the basis of a design right providing simultaneous protection—and vice versa.[853]

Jurisdiction—claims or counterclaims for a declaration of invalidity. Article 84 of the Regulation deals with issues arising from a claim for invalidity. It provides that (1) an action or counterclaim for invalidity may only be based on the grounds set out in art.25 of the Regulation[854]; (2) in the cases referred to in arts 25(2), (3), (4) and (5), the action or counterclaim could only be brought by **13–262**

---

[849] Non-Community design courts may hear actions relating to Community designs other than those referred to in Regulation, art.81 if the law of the relevant Member State permits. Otherwise, the courts of the State where the Office has its seat (Spain) have jurisdiction to hear such actions— see Regulation, art.93.

[850] These are as follows. In England and Wales, the High Court and any county court designated as a Patents County Court under s.287(1) of the CDPA 1988 and (for the purposes of hearing appeals from judgments of the courts so designated) the Court of Appeal; in Scotland, the Court of Session (at first instance and also for appeals); and in Northern Ireland, the High Court and (for appeals) the Court of Appeal. See the Community Designs (Designation of Community Design Courts) Regulations 2005 (SI 2005/696).

[851] Regulation art.88.

[852] If Regulation art.85(2) also required the holder to prove that the conditions in s.1 (i.e. arts 3 to 9) were satisfied, then the requirement that he indicate what constitutes individual character would be otiose.

[853] Regulation art.95.

[854] See paras 13–226 et seq., above.

the person named in those provisions[855]; (3) if the counterclaim is brought in an action to which the holder of the Community design in question was not a party (because, for example, it was an action by the licensee), the holder must be informed and may be joined as a party; and (4) the validity of a Community design cannot be put in issue in an action for a declaration of non-infringement. Where a court declares that a Community design is invalid, that declaration is effective in all Member States.[856]

13–263 **Remedies.** Where a Community design court finds that a defendant has infringed or threatened to infringe a Community design, it must (unless there are special reasons for not doing so) order the following[857]:

  (a) an order prohibiting the defendant proceeding with the acts that constituted or would constitute an infringement (i.e. an injunction).[858]
  (b) an order to seize the infringing products (delivery up).
  (c) an order to seize materials and implements predominantly used in order to manufacture the infringing products (if their owner knew the effect for which such use was intended or if such effect would have been obvious).
  (d) any other sanctions appropriate under the circumstances and permitted by the national law of the Member State in which the acts of infringement or threatened infringement took place.

Without prejudice to the court's duty to make such orders in appropriate cases, the remedies available in respect of infringement of Community design have been brought into line with those in UK unregistered design right.[859] In particular, it has been provided that in proceedings for infringement of a Community design, all such relief by way of damages, injunctions, accounts or otherwise will be available to the holder of the Community design as would be available in respect of the infringement of any other property right[860] and express provision has been made for delivery up and disposal of an infringing article.[861] However, unlike UK design right, there is no partial defence for "innocent" infringers.[862]

13–264 **Interim relief.** Article 90 of the Regulation provides that application may be made to a Community design court for such provisional measures (i.e. interim relief) as may be available under national law, even if a Community design court of another Member State has jurisdiction as to the substance of the case. Where such an application is made, the defendant is permitted to raise the issue of the validity of the Community design although not by way of a counterclaim seeking a declaration of invalidity. This is clearly because that is an issue for the court hearing the substance of the case.

---

[855] See para.13–228, above.
[856] Regulation art.87.
[857] Regulation, art.89.
[858] In the context of Community trade marks. Advocate General Cruz Villalon expressed the view in *DHL Express (France) SAS v Chronopost SA* (C–235/09) that an order of a competent national court prohibiting an infringer from using a Community trade mark would, in principle, have effect throughout the EU. This would seem to be equally applicable to a similar order relating to a Community design.
[859] Community Design Regulations 2005 (SI 2005/2339) regs 1A to 1D.
[860] Community Design Regulations 2005 (SI 2005/2339) reg.1A(2). The same provision has been added to the UK's Registered Designs Act 1949 at s.24A. This mirrors the design right position as set out in CDPA 1988 s.229(2)—see para.13–174, above.
[861] Community Design Regulations 2005 (SI 2005/2339) regs 1B and 1C. These are in substantially the same terms as the UK design right provisions in CDPA 1988 ss.230 and 231 (as to which see paras 13–180 and 13–181, above). The definition of "infringing article" (reg.1D) is substantially the same as that contained in CDPA 1988 s.228 (see para.13–161 above).
[862] In *J Choo (Jersey) Ltd v Towerstone Ltd* [2008] F.S.R. 19, Floyd J. confirmed that there was no defence of innocence available to defendants for infringement of registered Community designs. The same must apply to unregistered Community designs. For the position in UK design right, see CDPA 1988 s.233 and para.13–175, above.

Appeals. Appeals from a Community design court of first instance lies to a Community design court of second instance on such conditions as the national law of the Member State should provide. The national rules would also govern any further appeal from the court of second instance.[863]

13–265

Privilege for professional designs representatives. A privilege has been introduced covering communications with professional design representatives.[864]

13–266

21. UNREGISTERED COMMUNITY DESIGNS: THREATS

Background. Provisions making groundless threats to sue for infringement actionable have been part of UK registered design and patent law for many years and were introduced for United Kingdom unregistered design right by s.253 of the CDPA 1988.[865] Similar provision has now been made in relation to Community designs.

13–267

In the case of registered Community designs, the threats provisions are significant because a person cannot as claimant (as opposed to a counterclaiming defendant) challenge the validity of a registered Community design other than in revocation proceedings through the Office for Harmonization in the Internal Market. A claimant cannot, therefore, rely on invalidity of a registered Community design as a ground for a declaration of non-infringement. However, a claimant in a threats action can challenge the validity of a registered community design.[866]

The threats. As from October 1, 2005, where any person (whether entitled to or interested in a Community design or not) by circulars, advertisements or otherwise threatens any other person with proceedings for infringement of a Community design, any person aggrieved thereby may bring an action against him.[867] The words "by circulars, advertisements or otherwise" have been widely construed and it has been held that the words "or otherwise"[868] are not to be construed ejusdem generis with the words "circulars, advertisements".[869] As with UK unregistered design right, mere notification that a design is a Community design does not constitute a threat and there is no liability for threats to bring proceedings for an infringement alleged to consist in the making or importing of anything.[870] In *Quads 4 Kids*, the defendant (the holder of various registered Community designs) had used eBay's "VeRO" (Verified Rights Owner) procedure to complain about a listing that he claimed infringed his rights. This led to the listing being removed by eBay. It was held that the complaint was arguably an actionable threat.[871]

13–268

Although a Community design is a Community wide right, it seems likely that to be actionable, the threat in issue must be of proceedings to be brought in the United Kingdom.[872]

---

[863] Regulation, art.92.

[864] See para.13–182, above.

[865] See paras 13–183 et seq., above.

[866] *Quads 4 Kids v Campbell* [2006] EWHC 2482 and Community Design Regulations 2005 (SI 2005/2339) reg.2(3).

[867] Community Design Regulations 2005 (SI 2005/2339) reg.2(1).

[868] These words do not appear in CDPA 1988 s.253 and are borrowed from the Patents Act 1977 s.70 and Registered Designs Act 1949 s.26.

[869] *Speedcranes Ltd v Thomson* [1978] R.P.C. 221.

[870] Community Design Regulations 2005 (SI 2005/2339) reg.2(6) and 2(5), respectively. For the rationale behind the latter provision, see para.13–186, above.

[871] [2006] EWHC 2482 at paras 23–31 (Pumfrey J.).

[872] See *Best Buy Co. Inc v Worldwide Sales Corp.* [2010] EWHC 1666 at paras 13–16 (a Community trade mark case).

13–269   **Person aggrieved.** It is anticipated that this term will be interpreted in the same way as for unregistered UK design right.[873]

13–270   **The defence.** Where the defendant proves that the acts in respect of which the proceedings were threatened constitute or (if done) would constitute an infringement of an unregistered Community design right, the claimant shall not be entitled to relief.[874] Where the defendant proves that the acts constitute or would constitute an infringement of a registered Community design, the claimant will only be entitled to relief if he shows that the registration was invalid.[875] In each case the onus is on the defendant. It seems that either defence is available irrespective of whether the threat concerns a registered or an unregistered Community design.

13–271   **Remedies.** The remedies available are a declaration, an injunction and damages.[876]

22. REGISTERED DESIGNS AND REGISTERED COMMUNITY DESIGNS

A. INTRODUCTION

13–272   An industrial design may qualify for protection by way of registration under either the Registered Designs Act 1949 or under the Council Regulation on Community designs.[877] A detailed discussion of the law of registered designs is outside the scope of this work and the following is merely an outline of some of the relevant law.[878] For a detailed discussion and, in particular a discussion as to process of registration and dealings involving the register, readers are referred to specialist works on the subject.[879]

The international protection of registered designs became simpler on January 1, 2008 when the European Community's accession to the Geneva Act of the Hague Agreement concerning the International Registration of Industrial Designs became effective.[880]

13–273   **Background.** The history of registered protection for industrial designs and of the Registered Designs Act 1949 has already been described.[881] As has been seen, when the Copyright, Designs and Patents Act 1988 introduced design right, it also made amendments to the 1949 Act in an effort to rationalise the scheme of protection for industrial designs. However, further and more substantial amendments were made to the 1949 Act on December 9, 2001 when the Registered

---

[873] See para.13–187 above.

[874] Community Design Regulations 2005 (SI 2005/2339) reg.2(4).

[875] Community Design Regulations 2005 (SI 2005/2339) reg.2(3).

[876] Community Design Regulations 2005 (SI 2005/2339) reg.2(2). See para.13–190 above. In *Quads 4 Kids* [2006] EWHC 2482, Pumfrey J. granted an interim injunction to restrain threats made by way of eBay's "VeRO" (Verified Rights Owner) procedure.

[877] Regulation (EC) No. 6/2002.

[878] i.e. under the RDA 1949, since its amendment by the Registered Design Regulations 2001, and under the Regulation.

[879] Such as *Russell-Clarke & Howe on Industrial Design* 8th edn (London: Sweet & Maxwell, 2010). See also Izquierdo Peris, "Registered Community Design: First Two-Year Balance from an Insider's Perspective" [2006] E.I.P.R. 146.

[880] For details of the Geneva Act of the Hague Convention (the text of the various Acts of the Convention, a guide to International registration and the current members), see the WIPO website: *http://www.wipo.int* [Accessed October 21, 2010].

[881] See paras 13–11 et seq, above.

Design Regulations 2001[882] came into force. These amendments were made to implement the terms of the Directive on the Legal Protection of Designs[883] which required Member States of the European Union to harmonise their national laws on registered designs. Shortly thereafter, the Council Regulation on Community design was adopted[884] introducing a short (three-year) period of protection for unregistered Community designs[885] and a system of protection for registered Community designs. This protection for Community designs has not replaced national law. As a result, protection by registration is now available under both the 1949 Act and the Regulation. Further, as set out below, much of the law governing registered designs is common to both the 1949 Act (as amended) and the Council Regulation.

Transitional provisions for the 1949 Act. The amendments to the Registered Designs Act 1949 came into effect on December 9, 2001 but are subject to transitional provisions.[886] In essence, the old law will continue to apply only in relation to (a) the determination of applications for registration that were pending on the date when the Regulations came into effect; (b) the cancellation or invalidation of registrations made in respect of any application made before that date; and (c) infringements occurring before that date. In all other respects, the new law applies.[887]   **13–274**

B. THE NEW LAW

Summary of the new law. The Registered Designs Act 1949 in its amended (post-December 6, 2001) form and the Regulation on Community design (Reg.6/2002) share many provisions in common. In particular, they share the same wide definition of a design, the same requirements for novelty and for individual character, and the same exclusions in respect of designs dictated solely by technical function, of designs of interconnections, and of designs which are contrary to public policy or morality. The scope of protection under the 1949 Act and under the Regulation is also the same—covering both the registered design itself and any other design that does not create a different overall impression on an informer user.   **13–275**

Definition of design. The Registered Designs Act 1949 (as amended) and the Regulation contain the same definition of a "design" for the purposes of registration.[888] That definition is also the same as that which applies for the purposes of unregistered Community design and has been considered in that context.[889] Importantly, although the definition of a design is the same as for unregistered community designs, the monopolistic protection provided by registration cannot extend beyond the design depicted in the application for registration.[890]   **13–276**

Requirements of novelty and individual character; the period of grace. The   **13–277**

---

[882] SI 2001/3949.

[883] Directive 98/71/EC.

[884] Regulation (EC) No. 6/2002.

[885] The protection of unregistered Community designs has been considered in detail at paras 13–201 et seq., above.

[886] Registered Design Regulations 2001 (SI 2001/3949), regs 11–14.

[887] An attack on the validity of the transitional provisions in reg.12 failed in *Oakley Inc v Animal Ltd* [2005] EWCA Civ 1191; [2006] Ch. 337; [2006] R.P.C. 9.

[888] RDA 1949 s.1(2) and (3) and Regulation, art.3.

[889] See paras 13–204 et seq., above. For the significance of the inclusion of "colour" in the definition of design, see para.13–283, below.

[890] *The Procter & Gamble Co v Reckitt Benckiser (UK) Ltd* [2006] EWHC 3154; [2007] F.S.R. 13 at para.27.

Registered Designs Act 1949 (as amended) and the Regulation also share substantively the same requirements that the design be new and have individual character.[891] Much the same provisions apply to unregistered Community designs and have been considered in that context.[892] There are, however, the following important differences:

(1) In the case of a registered design, in assessing whether a design is novel and also whether it has individual character, the required comparisons are between the design in question[893] and other designs that have been made available to the public before the date of filing the application for registration of the design in question (or, if a priority is claimed, before the date of priority). Again, therefore, the issue is not when the design was created, but whether it was new and had individual character when compared with other designs that had been made available to the public as at that date.

(2) The 12-month so-called "period of grace".[894] By reason of this period of grace, certain disclosures of the design for which protection is claimed will not be treated as disclosures so as to deprive that design of novelty or individual character. This period of grace applies to any disclosure made during the 12 months immediately preceding the date of filing of the application for registration of that design provided that disclosure was made by (a) the designer, (b) his successor in title, or (c) a third person in consequence of information provided or action taken by the designer, or his successor in title.

13–278   **Exclusions.** The 1949 Act (as amended) and the Regulation contain the same exclusions from protection—namely designs solely dictated by the technical function of the product, the designs for interconnections and designs that are contrary to public policy or morality.[895] These exclusions have already been considered in relation to unregistered Community designs.[896] As has been mentioned,[897] there is an on-going debate as to whether there should also be an exclusion for designs of component parts of a complex product used to repair that complex product so as to restore its original appearance (the equivalent of the "must match" exclusion in UK design right). For the present, there is no such exclusion.

13–279   **Duration.** The duration of registered design protection is the same as it was under the Registered Designs Act 1949 before it was amended, i.e. a maximum of 25 years. This is made up of an initial five years from registration and four further five-year periods for which the holder can apply (subject to the payment of the appropriate fee).[898]

13–280   **Ownership and assignment.**
The provisions governing proprietorship of a design and of a registered design for the purposes of the Registered Designs Act 1949 differ in some respects from those which apply under the EC Regulation.

---

[891] RDA 1949 s.1B and Regulation (EC) No. 6/2002, arts 4–6.

[892] See paras 13–208 et seq., above.

[893] In *Piotrowski v Compagnie Gervais Danone* [2008] E.T.M.R. 27, the Third Board of Appeal of OHIM held that the design constitutes all the features contained in the representation of the design unless some kind of disclaimer is used.

[894] RDA 1949 s.1B(6)(c) and (d) and Regulation, art.7(2).

[895] RDA 1949 ss.1B, 1C and 1D (as amended) and Regulation, arts 8 and 9.

[896] See paras 13–220 et seq., above.

[897] See para.13–31, above.

[898] RDA 1949 s.8 (as amended) and Regulation, art.12. Renewals of Community design are governed by Regulation, art.13.

UK registered designs. Under the 1949 Act, the person who creates a design is **13–281** its author. This person is the original proprietor of that design unless he was acting in pursuance of a commission or in the course of employment in which cases, his commissioner or employer is, respectively, the original proprietor. Where the design was generated by computer in circumstances where there is no human author, the author is taken to be the person who made the arrangements necessary for the creation of the design.[899]

When a design is registered on the application of a person claiming to be the proprietor of the design, that person is registered as the proprietor of the registered design.[900]

A registered design and an application for registration are forms of property[901] and title to them may pass by assignment, transmission or operation of law[902] in which case the person who becomes entitled to them may apply to have notice of his interest entered on the register.[903] Title to a registered design (being a chose in action) may be assigned in law or in equity. A legal assignment has to be in writing signed by the assignor.[904] However, an assignment may be effected in equity provided there is a sufficient expression of an intention to assign in the context of a transaction from which it can be inferred that the property was intended to pass. Of course, an enforceable contract to assign will also be effective to effect an assignment in equity.[905]

Community design. Under the Regulation, the provisions governing ownership **13–282** are somewhat different.[906] In brief, title will vest in the designer or (if the designer was an employee acting in execution of his duties or under instructions from his employer) in his employer. The position as regards a commissioned work and to a work generated by computer are not dealt with expressly. The person in whose name the registered Community design is registered, or prior to registration, the person in whose name the application was filed is deemed to be the person entitled in any proceedings.[907] The Regulation confers on the designer (even if he is not the owner of the design), the right to be cited as such before the Office and in the register.[908]

Title to a registered Community design and to an application for registration of a Community design are forms of property and can be transferred and the transferee's name entered on the register. The principles that apply under English national law as regards dealings with UK registered designs will also apply to dealings with Community designs in those cases where England is the Member state in which the holder of the right has his seat or domicile or (if that does not apply) has an establishment on the relevant date.[909]

Monopoly rights conferred by registration, infringement and permitted acts. **13–283** The provisions of the Registered Designs Act 1949 (as amended) and of the Regulation defining the exclusive rights that registration confers on the proprietor

---

[899] RDA 1949 s.2(1), (1A), (3) and (4).
[900] RDA 1949 ss.1(2) and 17. "Claiming to be the proprietor" for these purposes means rightfully claiming to be the proprietor. Save for commissioned works, the proprietor of a new design is its author. See *Woodhouse UK Plc v Architectural Lighting Systems* [2006] R.P.C. 1 at para.25.
[901] RDA 1949 s.15A.
[902] RDA 1949 ss.2(2) and 15B. See also Regulation 6/2002 arts 27(1) and 34(1). A registered Community design must be dealt with in its entirety for the whole of the Community.
[903] RDA 1949 s.19.
[904] RDA 1949 s.15B(3).
[905] *Ifejika v Ifejika* [2010] EWCA Civ.563, [2010] F.S.R. 29 at para.25.
[906] For the ownership of an unregistered Community designs, see paras 13–231 et seq., above.
[907] Regulation art.17.
[908] Regulation art.18.
[909] EC Regulation 6/2002 arts 27(1) and 34(1).

(and, therefore, defining the acts capable of constituting an infringement) are in substance, the same. So too are the provisions relating to permitted acts[910] and remedies.[911] Subject to the differences discussed below, these provisions are also the same as those which apply to unregistered Community designs and have been considered in that context.[912]

In summary, the registered proprietor has a monopoly on the use of the design and of any design which does not produce a different overall impression on the informed user. Permitted acts include non-commercial acts and Government use. Infringement actions can be brought by the proprietor, by an exclusive licensee or (with the consent of the proprietor) by a non-exclusive licensee.[913]

The first (and crucial) difference is that for a registered design, the exclusive rights of the proprietor are monopolistic in nature. Thus, unlike copyright, UK design right and unregistered Community design, the issue of copying does not arise; if another person does an act covered by the proprietor's exclusive rights, that person may be infringing the registered design or registered Community design regardless of whether or not that person had copied that design.

The second difference is that, under the Regulation, a right of prior use shall exist for any third person who can establish that, before the date of filing of the application, he had in good faith commenced use in the Community (or has made serious and effective preparations to that end) of a design included within the scope of protection of a registered Community design, which had not been copied from the latter.[914]

Third, as has been mentioned,[915] the protection conferred by registration will depend on what was depicted in the application for registration. If only a part of an article was depicted, that part alone will be protected. However, although an applicant is required to identify the products to which his design will be applied, the scope of protection is not limited to such products.[916] Instead, as has been seen, it extends to any product and a defendant who has made a different product may still infringe if his design does not create a different overall impression on the informed user.[917]

Fourth, with regard to the protection of colour as part of a design, it has been said that if an applicant wishes to have protection for his design of colours, those colours must be depicted.[918] This is clearly correct. However, in the case of a monochrome line drawing, what is protected is likely to be the shape or contours of the product and colours will not be protected if they are not depicted. 'In this

---

[910] RDA 1949 ss.7 and 7A; Regulation arts 10, 19–23 and 110.

[911] RDA 1949 s.24A and the Community Design Regulations 2005 (SI 2005/2339) reg.1A(2).

[912] See paras 13–244 et seq., above. The nature of the rights conferred is considered at para.13–245 above; the scope of protection at 13–246; the judicial guidance at para.13–247; the treatment of excluded features at para.13–248; permitted acts at paras 13–249 et seq.; and remedies at paras 13–263 et seq., above.

[913] See para.13–249, above.

[914] Regulation, art.22.

[915] See para.13–276, above.

[916] EC Regulation 6/2002 art.36(6).

[917] See paras 13–245 et seq., above. In *Casio Keisanki Kabushiki Kaisha, Re* [2007] E.C.D.R. 13 at para.20, the Third Board of Appeal at OHIM stated that the breadth of the definition of the product for the purposes of registration might have implications for the extent of the exclusive right. One of the reasons given for this statement was that the exclusive right covers the sale etc. of products "in which the design is incorporated" with the meaning of art.19. However, given the clear terms of art.36(6) it is not clear that this can be correct. Other reasons given were more credible—namely that the definition of the product might affect the determination of prior art and the identification of the informed user. This is consistent with the statement of the General Court in *Grupo Promer Mon Graphic SA v OHIM* [2010] E.C.D.R. 7 at para.56 that the definition might affect both the identity of the informed user and the court's assessment of the degree of freedom of the designer.

[918] *The Procter & Gamble Co v Reckett Benckiser (UK) Ltd* [2006] EWHC 3154; [2007] F.S.R. 13 at para.29 (Lewison J.).

regard, it is important to bear in mind that registration of a design depicted in black and white provides protection for the depicted shape and configuration whatever the colour used. Thus, a defendant cannot rely on the different overall impression created by its use of colours in relation to its product.[919] Of course, for the same reason, it may be more difficult to establish the validity of a design depicted in black and white than one depicting colours.[920]

Fifth, it appears that in the case of UK registered design, an infringement action may be brought by the proprietor or by an exclusive licensee.[921] In contrast, in the case of Community registered design (like unregistered Community designs), an action may be also be brought (with the consent of the proprietor) by a non-exclusive licensee.[922]

Interrelation with design right. A design capable of registration will often, but will not invariably, also be a design for design right purposes. This is because of the different definitions of design, the different exclusions and the difference between the tests of novelty and individual character that apply to registered designs and the test of originality (including whether the design is commonplace) that applies in design right. Subject to this, a design may be entitled to both forms of protection. Indeed, s.224 of the 1988 Act recognises that the owner of the registered design may also be the owner of the design right and, in such a case, an assignment of the registered design will carry the design right with it unless the contrary appears.　**13–284**

Interrelation with copyright. The interrelation of registered designs with copyright has become much less complicated since the 1988 Act because the level of copyright protection for a work is no longer defined expressly by reference to the registration or registrability of any corresponding design.[923] However, ss.51 and 52 of the 1988 Act will in practice remove or limit the copyright protection for many registered or registrable designs. Moreover, under s.53, the copyright in an artistic work is not infringed by anything done in pursuance of an assignment or licence granted by the registered proprietor of a design corresponding to the copyright work and done in good faith in reliance upon the registration and without notice of any proceedings to cancel or rectify the registration. Thus where a person acts pursuant to rights granted by the registered design proprietor, he has a defence to any action brought against him but a different person claiming to own the copyright in a corresponding artistic work.[924]　**13–285**

C. THE OLD LAW

Summary of the old law under the 1949 Act. As set out above, the old law (i.e. the Registered Designs Act 1949 in its pre-December 9, 2001 form) still governs (a) the determination of applications for registration that were pending on the date when the Regulations came into effect; (b) the cancellation or invalidation of registrations made in respect of any application made before that date; and (c) infringements occurring before that date. Under that old law, there had to be a　**13–286**

---

[919] As was the case in *The Procter & Gamble Co v Reckett Benckiser*.

[920] See the two *Bumag v Procter & Gamble* decisions given by OHIM on 15 May 2006—ICD 1741 and ICD 1758.

[921] RDA 1949 ss.15C and 24F. This is the same position as applies in UK unregistered design right (see para.13–172, above).

[922] See para.13–256, above.

[923] For the problems that arose before 1988, see paras 13–11 et seq., above.

[924] Assuming that he acts in good faith and without knowledge of any proceedings for the cancellation or rectification of the registration.

design (which was more narrowly defined) applied to an article.[925] That design had to have eye appeal[926] and not be dictated solely by the function of the article nor dependent upon the appearance of another article of which it was intended to form an integral part.[927] The design had to be new.[928] Designs were registered in respect of articles or sets of articles. In contrast to design right and copyright, a designer need not satisfy any territorial qualification requirements in order to register his design.

13–287   **Former meaning of "design".** Under the old law, a design was defined by s.1(1) of the Registered Designs Act 1949 (before its amendment) as:

"... features of shape, configuration, pattern or ornament applied to an article by any industrial process, being features which in the finished article appeal to and are judged by the eye, but does not include—

(a) a method or principle of construction, or

(b) features of shape or configuration of an article which—

(i) are dictated solely by the function which the article has to perform, or

(ii) are dependent upon the appearance of another article of which the article is intended by the author of the design to form an integral part".

The relevant design has, therefore, to be distinguished from the article to which it was applied. It did not even need to be the design of an entire article. The registrable design comprised only those features which appealed to and were judged by the eye and which were not within the specified exclusions.

13–288   **Shape, configuration, pattern or ornament.** The meaning of the words "shape" and "configuration" has already been considered,[929] and it has been said that the words "pattern" and "ornament" are practically synonymous, being substantially in two as opposed to three dimensions[930]; an article can exist without any pattern or ornament upon it, whereas it can have no existence at all apart from its shape and configuration.

13–289   **Applied to an article.** The relevant features of shape, configuration, pattern or ornament were to be applied to an article by any industrial process. For these purposes, an article meant an article of manufacture, and included any part of an article, provided that part was made and sold separately.[931] The relevant design feature had to be applied to such an article, i.e. added to the article by making it to the shape or configuration, or with that feature of pattern or ornament.[932] The reference to the application of the design to an article being by any industrial process simply suggested the capability of the mass production of such articles whether by a machine or by a hand process.

13–290   **Appeal to and be judged by the eye.** Under the old law, the relevant design features had to be such that in the finished article they appealed to, and were judged by the eye. Before it was amended by the 1988 Act, the Registered Designs Act 1949 had referred to features which appeal to, and are judged solely

---

[925] i.e. features of shape, configuration, pattern or ornament applied to an article by any industrial process—see RDA 1949 s.1(1).

[926] s.1(1).

[927] s.1(1)(b).

[928] s.1(2).

[929] See para.13–48, above.

[930] See *Kestos Ltd v Kempat Ltd* (1936) 53 R.P.C. 139 at 152.

[931] RDA 1949 s.44(1).

[932] See *Amp Inc v Utilux Proprietary Ltd* 1972 R.P.C. 103 at 108.

by the eye,[933] but even after the 1988 Act, it seems that the test remained whether or not the feature in question was such as to cause a customer to prefer the appearance of the article to which it is applied over the appearance of another article.[934] There had to be something special, peculiar, distinctive, significant or striking about its appearance; something which caught and in that sense appealed to the eye.[935] This was determined according to the eye of the customer at whom the article was aimed. It did not appear to matter whether or not it was the object of the designer to achieve eye appeal nor that the design feature related to the article's function.[936] The relevant feature did not need to be immediately visible. Thus, a design for the interior of a chocolate egg had eye appeal; whilst it was not immediately visible, it would become apparent to a consumer, when the egg was being eaten and would, presumably, be attractive.[937]

Excluded designs. Various designs were specifically excluded from registration under the old law. Thus, a method or principle of construction was excluded as were design features that were dependent upon the appearance of another article of which the article was intended by the author of the design to form an integral part.[938] These exclusions mirrored those which apply in relation to design right and have been considered in that context.[939] The other exclusion under the old law for registered design was of features dictated solely by the function which the article had to perform. This not only excluded those features which allowed and which alone would allow the article to perform its function but also excluded any feature which the designer included solely to make the article work regardless of whether there were other ways in which the article could have been designed in order to perform that function.[940]   **13–291**

Exclusion of designs for articles of primarily literary or artistic character.   **13–292**
Section 1(5) of the 1949 Act (in its pre-2001 form) provided for the making of rules to exclude from registration designs for articles of a primarily literary or artistic nature which, it was considered, more properly fell within the field of copyright.[941] The application of the Rules made under this section was not always easy to justify. As has been seen,[942] plans for the assembly of a kit of parts for a sailing dinghy were treated as plans within the Rules and, therefore, fell outside the scope of registration.

Materiality. Under s.1(3) of the 1949 Act (in its pre-2001 form), a design could not be registered in respect of an article, if the appearance of the article was not   **13–293**

---

[933] See RDA 1949 s.1(3) (prior to amendment).

[934] See *Amp Inc v Utilux Proprietary Ltd* [1972] R.P.C. 103 at 108, 112–113 and 121.

[935] *Amp Inc v Utilux Proprietary Ltd* [1972] R.P.C. 103 at 121.

[936] As with the design features of "Lego" bricks in *Interlego A.G. v Tyco Industries Inc* [1989] A.C. 217; [1988] R.P.C. 343. If, however, the only reason why the particular feature was attractive to the observer was that it made the article look best suited for its purpose, then despite having eye appeal, the design was excluded under the functionality exclusion discussed, below—see, for example, *Amp Inc v Utilux Proprietary Ltd* [1971] R.P.C. 103 at 118–119.

[937] See *Ferrero's Design* [1978] R.P.C. 473.

[938] See *Isaac Oren v Red Box Factory* [1998] F.S.R. 676.

[939] See paras 13–56 et seq., above (method or principle of construction) and paras 13–64 et seq., above (must match).

[940] *Amp Inc v Utilux Proprietary Ltd* [1972] R.P.C. 103 at 109–110, 113, 117–118 and 122.

[941] Under the Registered Design Rules 1995 r.26, designs for works of sculpture (other than casts or models used or intended to be used as models or patterns to be multiplied industrially), wall plaques, medals, medallions and printed matter primarily of a literary or artistic character, including (by way of example) book jackets, calendars, dress-making patterns, greeting cards, maps, plans, etc , are excluded from registration. The Registered Designs Rules 1995 were revoked, subject to transitional provisions, with effect from October 1, 2006: see the Registered Designs Rules 2006 (SI 2006/1975).

[942] *Dorling v Honor Marine Ltd* [1965] Ch. 1; [1964] R.P.C. 160, see para.13–18, above.

material, i.e. if aesthetic considerations were not normally taken into account to a material extent by persons acquiring or using such an article and would not be taken into account if the design were applied to the article.[943]

13–294   **The design had to be "new".** In order to be registered under the old law, the design in question had to be new.[944] In this context, it is important to remember that it was the relevant design features relied upon that had to be new and not necessarily the design of the whole of the article to which they were to be applied.[945] Moreover, when testing for novelty, the question was not whether the particular design (i.e. the particular features of shape (etc.)) was novel in itself but whether its application to that particular kind of article was novel.[946]

Under s.1(4) of the 1949 Act (in its pre-2001 form), a design was not to be regarded as new if it was the same as a design registered in respect of the same or any other article in pursuance of a prior application,[947] or the same as a design published in the United Kingdom in respect of the same or any other article before the date of the application.[948] Nor would a design be regarded as new if it differed from such a design only in immaterial details or in features which were variants commonly used in the trade. Whether the differences were in more than just immaterial details was to be judged objectively and by eye by asking whether the design imparted a different appearance.

13–295   **Duration.** Under the 1949 Act (in its pre-2001 form), the initial period of protection provided by registration lasted for five years from registration. This could, however, be extended by four further periods each of five years by application to the registrar. The maximum period of protection was, therefore, 25 years from registration.[949]

13–296   **Ownership.** The ownership of design under the old law was the same as under the new law and has already been considered.[950]

13–297   **Infringements.** Under the old law, a registered design was infringed by a person who, without licence of the registered proprietor of the design, (a) made or imported either for sale or hire or for use for the purposes of a trade or business or (b) sold, hired, or offered or exposed for sale or hire an article in respect of which the design was registered and to which that design or a design not substantially different from it had been applied.[951] It was also an infringement to make, without licence, anything for enabling such an article to be made in the

---

[943] RDA 1949 s.1(3).

[944] RDA 1949 s.1(2).

[945] Thus, if the design relied on was the pattern to be applied to the seat of a chair, it was that design and not the design of the chair which was tested for novelty.

[946] i.e. the kind of article having regard to its general character and use rather than to the strict categories of articles as set out in the schedule to the design rules—see *Saunder v Wiel* (1892) 10 R.P.C. 29 at 33 and *Re Clarke's Design* (1896) 13 R.P.C. 351.

[947] Under RDA 1949 s.4, an owner of a prior registered design could add to the articles in respect of which that design was registered. He could also apply to modify or vary the registered design provided he did not alter its character or substantially affect its identity.

[948] Under RDA 1949 s.6, certain forms of disclosure (disclosure in confidence or by a third party, etc.) did not, by themselves, prevent registration of the design. For example, where a copyright artistic work had a corresponding design, use of the artistic work (other than its industrial application through the marketing of articles made to the design) would not of itself mean that the design could not be "new" for the purposes of registration under the old law—see RDA 1949 ss.6(4) and (5).

[949] RDA 1949 s.8.

[950] See para.13–280, above.

[951] RDA 1949 s.7(1) and (2).

United Kingdom or elsewhere.[952] Section 7(4) (in its pre-2001 form) dealt with the question of infringement in relation to a kit.[953]

23. COPYRIGHT AND WORKS OF INDUSTRIAL APPLICATION

As has been seen,[954] the Copyright, Designs and Patents Act 1988 contains provisions intended to prevent copyright being used to protect works which fall more properly within the industrial than the artistic field. Despite this, copyright remains of some importance in relation to works of industrial application which were created after the 1988 Act came into force[955] and of considerable importance where such works were created before that date.   **13–298**

The nature of copyright protection for works of industrial application is best approached by reference to the date when the work in question was created. For these purposes, works fall into the following categories:

(1) Those created on or after August 1, 1989 (after the 1988 Act came into force);

(2) Those created on or after June 1, 1957 but before August 1, 1989 (i.e. whilst the Copyright Act 1956 was in force); or

(3) Those created before June 1, 1957 (i.e. at any time before the Copyright Act 1956 came into force).

The general law of copyright applicable to works created in each of these periods has already been considered in the main Copyright chapters of this work. This section is concerned only with aspects of copyright law which particularly affect copyright works of industrial application.

24. COPYRIGHT WORKS OF INDUSTRIAL APPLICATION MADE ON OR AFTER AUGUST 1, 1989

A. INTRODUCTION

Copyright in works of industrial application. A copyright work of industrial application is likely to be an artistic work.[956] The subsistence of copyright in such a work is considered in the main Copyright section of this book.[957] In brief, the work would have to be original in the copyright sense of the word[958] and the relevant qualification requirements would have to have been satisfied.[959] The acts which (unless they fall within the categories of permitted acts discussed below[960]) constitute infringements of copyright under the 1988 Act have also already been considered in detail.[961]   **13–299**

Permitted acts. The 1988 Act provides for various permitted acts—acts which   **13–300**

---

[952] RDA 1949 s.7(3).
[953] i.e. a complete or substantially complete set of components intended to be assembled into a kit.
[954] See paras 13–29 et seq., above.
[955] August 1, 1989.
[956] i.e. (a) a graphic work, photograph, sculpture or collage irrespective of artistic quality; (b) a work of architecture being a building or a model for a building or (c) a work of artistic craftsmanship—CDPA 1988 s.4.
[957] See Ch.3, above.
[958] CDPA 1988 s.1(1)(a)
[959] s.1(3).
[960] See para.13–300, below.
[961] See Chs 7 and 8, above.

do not constitute infringements of copyright.[962] Many are of little or no relevance to works of industrial application. The following, however, are of particular importance and will be considered in detail below.

(1) Section 51—which provides that any copyright in a design document or a model recording or embodying a design for anything other than an artistic work will not be infringed by certain design-right-type acts of infringements. However, other acts may still infringe the copyright in such a work.

(2) Section 52—which provides that where an artistic work is exploited by or with the licence of the copyright owner through the making and marketing of articles which constitute copies of the work, then the period of copyright protection for the work is reduced in respect of a wide range of activities to a period of 25 years from the date of first marketing.

(3) Section 53—which provides that copyright in an artistic work is not infringed by anything done in pursuance of an assignment or licence by a person registered under the Registered Designs Act 1949 as the proprietor of a corresponding design and which is done in good faith in reliance upon that registration.

B. SECTION 51

(i) Statement of section 51(1)

13–301   **Section 51.** Section 51(1) of the 1988 Act provides that:

"It is not an infringement of any copyright in a design document or model recording or embodying a design for anything other than an artistic work or a typeface to make an article to the design or to copy an article made to the design".

(ii) Preliminary points

13–302   **Scheme of 1988 Act.** Section 51 is crucial to the 1988 Act scheme of protection for industrial designs under the 1988 Act. Broadly speaking, its aim is to remove industrial designs from the sphere of copyright protection[963] and to address the problems identified by the House of Lords in *British Leyland Motor Corp Ltd v Armstrong Patents Co. Ltd.*[964] To do this, s.51 distinguishes between works that record designs for artistic works or typefaces on the one hand, and works that record designs for anything else on the other. Section 51 has no effect on the scope of copyright protection for the former but radically reduces the scope of copyright protection for the latter. The rationale for this is that where the work in question is the design for an end product which is itself an artistic work (or typeface) protected by copyright, then the work should also be protected by copyright. If, however, the end product is not an artistic work (or typeface) and thus has no copyright protection, then there is no reason why a document recording the design of that product should have such protection.

13–303   **Partial exclusion.** Although s.51 was intended to take industrial designs out of

---

[962] The permitted acts are set out in Ch.III of the CDPA 1988 and are discussed in the main copyright section of this book—see Ch.9, above.

[963] This was made clear in the course of Parliamentary debate—see *Hansard*, H.L. Vol.490, col.1175; H.L. Vol.491, col.185 and H.C., SCE, col.244. However, the difficulty in achieving this aim is apparent from cases such as *Hi-Tech Autoparts Ltd v Towergate Two Ltd (No.2)* [2002] F.S.R. 270, see para.13–313, example (11), below.

[964] [1986] AC 577—see para.13–21, above and *Lucasfilm Ltd v Ainsworth* [2009] EWCA Civ 1328, [2010] F.S.R. 10 at para.83.

copyright,[965] it does not do this by providing that no copyright can subsist in a work which records or embodies an industrial design. Instead, it provides that certain acts[966] will not infringe copyright. Other acts may still infringe copyright.[967] It should be noted, however, that if the work is an artistic work which has been exploited industrially then even if copyright protection was not excluded by s.51, the term of copyright protection may be reduced to 25 years by s.52.[968]

No correlation between the operation of section 51 and the availability of   **13–304**
design right protection. The wording of s.51 plainly shows that it is intended to exclude copyright protection from those areas in which design right is to operate. However, the fact that an act does not infringe copyright because of the operation of s.51 does not necessarily mean that that act must infringe design right instead. The limitation upon the copyright protection imposed by s.51 is not co-extensive with the existence of design right protection. There may well be cases where the copyright subsisting in a work recording an industrial design is unenforceable under s.51 but no design right subsists in the design. It may be, for example, that the design right does not subsist because the design is commonplace,[969] or because it is excluded by the must fit or must match provisions of s.213(3)(b),[970] or because the design right qualification requirements are not satisfied.[971] Similarly, the fact that the copying of a design document does not infringe design right does not necessarily mean that it must have infringed copyright in that document.[972]

Examples: **13–305**
  (1) A drawing of a contact lens is original in the sense that the drawing is the designer's own work. Copyright will, therefore, subsist in the drawing. However, the design embodied in the drawing may not be original for design purposes because it is commonplace. If (as seems probable) the design drawing was created for the making of lenses, then s.51 will apply to limit copyright protection even though the design has no design right protection. The designer, therefore, can rely on neither copyright nor design right to prevent others making lenses to his design.[973]

  (2) Copyright may subsist in design drawings of a car exhaust pipe. Section 51 will prevent the designer relying on that copyright to prevent others making exhausts to his design. However, the design right requirement of originality and its "must fit" exclusion may well mean that the design (or some of its features) has no design right protection.

(iii) Conditions for application of section 51

As indicated above, s.51 only operates to exclude copyright protection in respect   **13–306**

---

[965] See para.13–302, above.
[966] i.e. the making of an article to the relevant design or the copying of an article made to that design. Broadly speaking, these are the design-right-type acts of infringement.
[967] In this respect, CDPA 1988 s.51 is similar to Copyright Act 1956 s.10—see para.13–17, above.
[968] For a discussion of CDPA 1988 s.52, see paras 13–320 et seq., below.
[969] See paras 13–76 et seq., above.
[970] CDPA 1988 s.213(3) excludes design right from methods of construction, "must fit" and "must match" designs and surface decoration, see paras 13–58 et seq., above. Copyright has no equivalent exclusions.
[971] See, for example, *Mackie Designs Inc v Behringer Specialised Studio Equipment (UK) Ltd* [1999] R.P.C. 717 where the claimant (a US company) sought (unsuccessfully) to rely on copyright in its drawings of circuit boards because it did not qualify for design right protection. For the differing qualification provisions for copyright and design right, see Ch.3 and paras 13–85 et seq., above, respectively.
[972] It is not the case that if you do not have design right you must have copyright—see *Lambretta Clothing Co Ltd v Teddy Smith (UK) Ltd* [2004] EWCA Civ 886; [2005] R.P.C. 6 at paras 35–38.
[973] See *Ocular Sciences Ltd v Aspect Vision Care Ltd* [1997] R.P.C. 289.

of "a design document or model recording or embodying a design for anything other than an artistic work or a typeface."

13–307   **Design document.** For these purposes, a design document is defined by s.51(3) as "any record of a design, whether stored in the form of a drawing, a written description, a photograph, data stored on a computer or otherwise." The meaning of these words has already been considered in the context of design right.[974] In brief, the principal definition requires that it be any record of a design. There is no reason why this should be construed narrowly. For example, the definition refers expressly to a design being recorded in a drawing but there is no reason why it may not be recorded in a diagram or plan. The reference to "a written description" is curious,[975] but serves to emphasise the width of the definition of a "design document". The meaning of "a design" for these purposes is considered below.[976]

13–308   **Model.** The word "model" is not defined by the 1988 Act but in ordinary usage can mean a three-dimensional representation of either a proposed or an existing structure or object.[977] Of course, s.51 is only concerned with models in which copyright is capable of subsisting—for example, a model which qualifies as a copyright work in its own right as a sculpture.[978]

13–309   **Illustrations**

(1) A model for an aircraft wing may be a sculpture or, possibly, a work of artistic craftsmanship. If so, it would be an artistic work in which copyright subsists. However, such a model would also be a design for a non-artistic work, namely an aircraft wing. Section 51 would, therefore, operate to limit its copyright protection.

(2) A plaster cast model for a marble carving of a head would probably be an artistic work[979] in which copyright subsists. As the marble carving would also be an artistic work, the plaster model embodies the design for an artistic work and s.51 would not operate to limit copyright in the model.

(3) Copyright subsists in the model for a building.[980] As the building itself is also an artistic work in its own right,[981] the model would be a model for an artistic work. Again, s.51 would not operate in relation to the model.

13–310   Recording or embodying a design. For s.51(1) to operate, the relevant design document or model must be one "recording or embodying a design".[982] Reading into this the definition of "design" contained in s.51(3), this means that for s.51(1) to operate, the relevant design document or model must be one:

"recording or embodying a [design of any aspect of the shape or configuration (whether internal or external) of the whole or part of an article, other than surface decoration]"

The definition of "design" is very similar to that which applies in relation to design right.[983] Clearly, therefore, as a general rule, s.51 is intended to operate to limit copyright protection for designs of the shape and configuration of articles,

---

[974] CDPA 1988 s.263(1) and para.13–82, above.
[975] See para.13–318, below.
[976] See para.13–310, below.
[977] See the Shorter Oxford English Dictionary.
[978] See para.3–60, above.
[979] i.e. a sculpture or a work of artistic craftsmanship within CDPA 1988 s.4(1).
[980] s.4(1)(b).
[981] s.4(1)(b).
[982] CDPA 1988 s.51(1).
[983] s.213(2). See paras 13–45 et seq., above.

i.e. for industrial designs.[984] There is, however, an important difference between s.51 and the design right provisions relating to a design. This is that s.51 has no equivalent to ss.213(3)(a) or (b) of the 1988 Act. This difference ensures that methods of construction and "must fit" and "must match" design features are not only excluded from design right protection (by reason of s.213(3)(a) and (b)), but that they are also excluded from the copyright protection that might otherwise be available to them when recorded in a design document.[985]

Another difference between s.51 and the design right provisions is that "surface decoration" is expressly excluded from the definition of a "design" for the purposes of s.51. By contrast, it is not excluded from the definition of a "design" for design right purposes. Instead, a separate subsection, s.213(3)(c), provides that design right does not subsist in surface decoration. This difference would not appear to be particularly significant and, subject to difficulties arising from *Lambretta Clothing Co Ltd v Teddy Smith (UK) Ltd*,[986] it seems clear that Parliament intended that where a design document records surface decoration, the designer should be able to claim copyright protection but not design right protection.[987]

Lambretta Clothing Co Ltd v Teddy Smith (UK) Ltd. As indicated above, certain   **13–311**
difficulties have arisen in relation to s.51 as a result of the difference of views in the Court of Appeal in *Lambretta Clothing Co Ltd v Teddy Smith (UK) Ltd*[988] *Lambretta* concerned a design drawing showing a track top made up of red body panels, blue sleeves with white stripes and a white zip. The shape of the garment was not original (being based on an existing sample). However, the claimant claimed design right in the choice of colours, and copyright in the whole of the design drawing as an artistic work. The design right claim was rejected (by a majority of the Court) on the basis that the choice of colours was not an aspect of shape or configuration and (unanimously) on the basis that, even if it was, it was commonplace as well as being surface decoration. There was, however, a difference of opinion regarding the application of s.51.

Jacob L.J. found that s.51 did operate. In his judgment, the drawing was a design document and the fact that "surface decoration" was excluded from the definition of a design made no difference. This was because the colours had no existence (either physically or conceptually) apart from the shape of the top. It was not as if that surface decoration could exist on other substrates in the way that a picture or logo could. Thus, if the claimant could assert artistic copyright in respect of the colours it would, in effect, be asserting copyright in the shape of the garment which was what s.51 was intended to prevent.[989]

---

[984] See *Jo-y-Jo v Matalan Retail Ltd* [2000] E.D.C.R. 178, where it was held that CDPA 1988 s.51 did not apply in relation to the design of the edging and welt of a garment because they were not aspects of the shape or configuration of the garment.

[985] See paras 13–304 and 13–305, example (2), above, and see *Lambretta Clothing Co Ltd v Teddy Smith (UK) Ltd* [2004] EWCA Civ 886; [2005] R.P.C. 6 at para.80.

[986] [2004] EWCA Civ 886, [2005] R.P.C. 6. See paras 13–311 et seq., below.

[987] The reference to surface decoration was added to s.51(3) during Parliamentary debate. It was intended to ensure that surface decoration, such as relief carving, which might in one sense be said to be an aspect of shape or configuration, was not excluded from copyright protection. See *Hansard*, H.L. Vol.493, cols 1179–1180. In *Jo-y-Jo v Matalan Retail Ltd* [2000] E.D.C.R. 178, it was held that s.51 did not exclude protection for the embroidery on the front of a garment because it was surface decoration. In *The Flashing Badge Company Ltd v Groves* [2007] EWHC 1372; [2007] F.S.R. 36, the claimant relied on the copyright in design drawings of badges. Insofar as the drawings recorded the shape of the badges, s.51 applied because the drawing was a design for something that was not in itself an artistic work. However, insofar as the drawings recorded the surface decoration for such badges, s.51 did not operate.

[988] [2004] EWCA Civ 886; [2005] R.P.C. 6.

[989] [2004] EWCA Civ 886 at para.39.

Mance L.J. disagreed.[990] In his judgment, for s.51 to operate, it was necessary for the court to conclude "that the article was made, or was a copy of an article made, to the design meaning "the design [as embodied in the drawing] of any aspect of the shape or configuration . . . of the whole or part of an article, other than surface decoration.'" Even if this was satisfied, s.51 only operated to the extent that the article had been made or was copied from an article made to the design in the limited sense as defined by s.51(3). To the extent that the design in issue went beyond the design in that limited sense, copyright in the design document would remain enforceable. On this basis, because it was improbable that the defendant had copied the shape and configuration shown in the drawing but had at most copied the colours (which the Court of Appeal had found were not aspects of shape or configuration), s.51 could not operate. Mance L.J. went on to comment that he believed that his conclusions were consistent with the position regarding surface decoration which is excluded from design right by s.213(3)(c) but which is excluded by s.51(3) from the concept of a design for the purposes of s.51(1). Thus, copyright in a design document showing an article with surface decoration could still be infringed. In his judgment, the wording of s.51 did not provide any basis for limiting copyright protection for surface decoration to a situation where the surface decoration could be said itself to constitute a separate drawing.

Sedley L.J. said he agreed with Jacob L.J. However, he also stated that in his view, the colours were more than just surface decoration and were, in fact, part of the configuration of the top.[991] On that basis, s.51 would clearly apply and the issue of the colours having no existence apart from the shape of the top would be irrelevant.

It is difficult to determine what exactly (if any) is the ratio of *Lambretta* in relation to s.51 and, as Sedley L.J. commented, neither the approach of Jacob L.J. nor that of Mance L.J. is unproblematical. However, it is submitted that there is much to be said for the view of Mance L.J. The difficulty with the approach of Jacob L.J. is that the claimant was not asserting that the defendant had made an article to the design as defined by s.51(3). Instead, it was asserting that the defendant had copied the colours shown on its drawing—which colours were not part of the "design of any aspect of the shape or configuration ... of . . . an article other than surface decoration".[992] To that extent, it is difficult to see why s.51(1) should operate to limit copyright protection for the drawing. Indeed, it seems strange that a claimant should be deprived of copyright protection for its design for the colouring of an article simply because its record of that design was recorded in a design document that depicted the whole article. Equally, it seems a strange result that colours found to be surface decoration for the purposes of design right were not treated as being surface decoration for the purposes of s.51. Whilst it might be correct to say that the colours in *Lambretta* were somehow limited by the shape of the top, there is nothing obvious in the wording of s.51 to suggest that they could not therefore still be treated as surface decoration for the purposes of s.51. Indeed, it could be argued that the colours were no more limited by the shape of the top than any other form of decoration would be when such decoration is designed to fit the shape of the surface to which it is to be applied (e.g. a face designed to cover the surface on a mug).

The Court of Appeal has since commented that *Lambretta* was an exceptional case where "the shape of the article was unoriginal and so not within [UK

---

[990] [2004] EWCA Civ 886 at paras 79–85.

[991] [2004] EWCA Civ 886 at paras 88–89. If they were an aspect of the configuration, CDPA 1988 s.51 would clearly operate.

[992] As Jacob L.J. (and Mance L.J.) accepted for the purposes of the design right claim (at para.29).

unregistered design right] and the colourways had no independent notional existence from the article and were not surface decoration". It concluded that such
cases would be rare.[993] Indeed, in *The Flashing Badge Company Ltd v Groves*[994]—
which concerned the surface decoration of badges—it was held that, although the
designs for the surface decoration had to follow the design of the shape of the
badges, they were not designs that could only exist as part of the shape of the
badges. They could be applied to any other substrate. Section 51 did not,
therefore, operate to exclude copyright protection from the design of the surface
decoration.

A design *for* anything other than an artistic work. For s.51 to operate, the rel-   **13–312**
evant design document or model must not only record or embody a design, it
must also be a design document or model "*for* anything other than an artistic
work or typeface".

It is important to note that s.51 requires that the relevant design must be both
the design of an article in the sense set out above, and also the design *for* an
article (other than an artistic work or a typeface). The use of the word *for* suggests that the design document or model was produced as part of the process of
producing something else; that it was a design[995] created as a precursor to an
article rather than being created as an end in itself. The words "artistic work"
will, presumably, bear their usual meaning as set out in s.4 of the 1988 Act.[996]
Clearly, if the end product is an artistic work capable of protection by copyright,
then it makes sense for any design documents for, and models of that product, to
be similarly protected.[997] As appears from the examples set out below, it seems
likely that one effect of s.51 will be an increase in the importance of the category
of works of artistic craftsmanship as a type of artistic work.[998] However, as
example (11) below shows, it is possible that the designs for some very functional
and mass-produced articles may still qualify for copyright protection on the
ground that the articles are engravings and, hence, artistic works. This is plainly a
serious limitation on the effectiveness of s.51 as a means of excluding copyright
from the sphere of industrial designs.

The question whether the design was *for* anything other than an artistic work
or typeface turns, it is submitted, on the intentions of the designer. If the work
was intended to be used as the design document or model *for* a product which is
neither artistic nor a typeface, then the section will operate; otherwise, it does
not. Although the section does not expressly say so, it seems that this state of
mind must be determined as at the time that the design document or model was
created.[999] Thus, s.51 would not apply to a work which started life as a purely
artistic work even if that work was subsequently used as the design basis for

---

[993] *Dyson Ltd v Qualtex (UK) Ltd* [2006] EWCA Civ 166; [2006] R.P.C. 31, Jacob L.J.
[994] [2007] EWHC 1372; [2007] F.S.R. 36; [2007] E.C.D.R. 17 (Rimer J.).
[995] As recorded or embodied in the relevant design document or model.
[996] See Ch.3, above.
[997] See, generally, the explanation of CDPA 1988 s.51 given in the course of debate by Lord Beaverbrook, *Hansard*, H.L. Vol.491, cols 185–186. See also *Guild v Eskandar Ltd* [2001] F.S.R. 645
where certain items of designer ladies' clothing were found not to be artistic works or works of
artistic craftsmanship. Accordingly, s.51 operated to limit copyright protection for the designs for
such items. This finding was not challenged on appeal ([2002] EWCA Civ 316, [2003] F.S.R. 3).
[998] For a full discussion of the meaning of works of artistic craftsmanship see paras 3–65 et seq.,
above.
[999] This would be consistent with the approach of the House of Lords in construing Copyright Act
1911 s.22 in *King Features Syndicate Ltd v O & M Kleeman Ltd* [1941] A.C. 417, see para.13–
16, above. This point was argued at first instance in *Lucasfilm Ltd v Ainsworth* [2008] EWHC
1878 at paras 139–141. However, it was found that the point did not arise because, on the facts,
the drawings in question had been created as designs for costumes/props. As those costumes/
props (the helmets and armour to be worn by storm troopers in the *Star Wars* films) were not
artistic works, s.51 was held to operate.

industrially exploited articles. In such a case, the only limitation on the copyright protection would be that provided by s.52, which is considered below.[1000]

13–313   **Examples.** The way in which s.51 operates is best understood by way of examples.

(1) A craftsman potter produces a one-off vase without producing any prior design documents or models. The vase is not a design document nor is it a model. It is the intended end product. Section 51 will not operate to limit any copyright which subsists in the vase as a work of artistic craftsmanship. Design right may also subsist in the design of the vase.[1001] However, design right protection is excluded in favour of the copyright protection.[1002]

(2) A craftsman potter produces a prototype vase with a view to mass producing vases to that design. Copyright may subsist in the prototype as a work of artistic craftsmanship. However, in contrast to example (1) above, this prototype is a model in that it records a design for future vases. Whether s.51 operates will depend upon whether or not those future vases are themselves artistic works (i.e. works of artistic craftsmanship). If they are not (because, for example, they are mass produced with no element of craftsmanship), s.51 will operate to limit copyright protection. It seems that this would also be so even if the design was rejected and never used. Another person may, therefore, make vases to this design without infringing copyright, although he may of course be infringing such design right as may subsist in the design.[1003]

(3) A famous painter paints a picture featuring a rustic kitchen chair. Copyright will subsist in the painting as an artistic work. It might be argued that the painting is a design document in that it records the design of the shape and configuration *of* a chair.[1004] However, the artist did not create the painting with a view to making chairs to that design. Accordingly the painting, whilst recording (arguably) the design *of* a chair, is not a design document *for* a chair. Section 51 will not operate and the painting will retain full copyright protection. If a manufacturer subsequently obtains the artist's permission to make chairs to the design shown in the painting, s.51 will still not apply (although s.52 would[1005]). The painting was not a design document *for* a chair at the time that it was created.

(4) If the same artist had produced a sketch depicting a chair prior to producing his painting, then copyright would also subsist in that sketch as an artistic work. As in illustration (3) above, the sketch is the design document *of* a chair but it is plainly not the design document *for* a chair because it is not preparatory to the production of a chair. If the sketch can be said

---

[1000] See paras 13–320 et seq., below.

[1001] The vase being an article made to the design, CDPA 1988 s.213(6), see para.13–83, above. This assumes that the design right conditions for subsistence are satisfied.

[1002] s.236.

[1003] See the note to Example (1), above.

[1004] On the other hand, it might be said that the whole essence of a design is that it is something which is preparatory to the creation of something else. Accordingly, as most artists create a painting intending it to be an end in itself, a painting cannot be said to be a design either of or for an object depicted in the painting. On this basis, as with illustration (1), above, CDPA 1988 s.51 would never be relevant. The difficulty with such a construction is that it begs the question why the word "for" (as opposed to the word "of") was then used in s.51. The fact is that the painting does depict the artist's idea of a chair, or it may record the shape or configuration of an actual chair (depending upon whether or not the artist is painting from real life). The painting records, in that sense, the design of a chair even though it is not the design for a chair.

[1005] See paras 13–320 et seq., below.

to be a design document *for* anything, it is *for* the painting which is an artistic work. Accordingly, s.51 would not operate to limit copyright.[1006]

(5) Copyright may subsist in a painting or sketch created by a furniture designer of a chair intended for mass production. However, the work is not only a design document recording the design of a chair but is also a design document *for* a chair. As the chair is unlikely to be an artistic work in its own right,[1007] s.51 would operate. Accordingly, another person who makes a chair to that design would not infringe copyright but may, of course, be infringing any design right which subsists in the design.[1008]

(6) If the same furniture designer had sketched only a chair leg, the result would be the same as in (5) above. If the chair leg was an article in its own right, the sketch would be a design document recording the design *of* a chair leg and would also be a design document *for* a chair leg.[1009] If the chair leg was not an "article" in its own right but is merely a part of a larger article,[1010] then the sketch would be a design document recording the design of a chair leg but it would still be a design document *for* the chair to which the leg is to be fitted. In either event, as the chair for which the design was created is unlikely to be an artistic work,[1011] s.51 would operate.

(7) An artist draws cartoon sketches of a futuristic car for a comic strip in a child's magazine. Copyright will subsist in these sketches as artistic works. Further, although the works are design documents in the sense that they record a design *of* a car, they are not design documents *for* anything other than an artistic work. There is no intention to apply them to a car. Section 51 does not, therefore, operate.[1012]

(8) The same artist is asked to design a futuristic car which is to be built for and used in a new science fiction film. The artist's sketches will be design documents recording the design of a car and, as the futuristic car when made for the film may well be an artistic work,[1013] they would also be design documents *for* a thing which is an artistic work. If so, s.51 would not operate.

(9) An artist draws cartoon sketches of an imaginary character to be used in a newspaper.[1014] Copyright will subsist in the sketches as artistic works but, as with the vase in illustration (1) above, the sketches are not designs *for* anything other than an artistic work. Section 51 does not, therefore, operate.

[1006] It could also be argued that the design is for the surface decoration of an article (i.e. the painting) and, therefore, that CDPA 1988 s.51 would not operate because surface decoration is excluded from the definition of a design by s.51(3) For the problems relating to surface decoration, see para.13–311, above.

[1007] Unless, which seems unlikely, the chair qualifies as a work of artistic craftsmanship—but see *George Hensher Ltd v Restawile Upholstery (Lancs) Ltd* [1976] A.C. 64; [1974] F.S.R. 173 and para.13–24, above.

[1008] See the note to Example (1), above.

[1009] Which is probably not an artistic work—see para.13–24, above.

[1010] i.e. a chair leg which is made separately from the rest of the chair rather than merely being a part of a larger article—see para.13–50, above.

[1011] See para.13–24, above.

[1012] See *BBC Worldwide Ltd v Pally Screen Printing Ltd* [1998] F.S.R. 665 at 672 where it was stated that if the relevant drawings had from the outset been intended to be used to decide the shape and appearance of three-dimensional children's television characters (the Teletubbies), s.51 would arguably operate whereas if they had been intended to be used as prototypes for a comic strip it would not.

[1013] i.e. a work of artistic craftsmanship—see by way of analogy, *Shelley Film Ltd v Rex Features Ltd* [1994] E.M.L.R. 134.

[1014] For example, sketches such as those of *Popeye in King Features Syndicate Ltd v O & M Kleeman Ltd* [1941] A.C. 417.

(10) An interior designer makes a drawing of the proposed pattern to be applied to a stencil. Copyright will subsist in the drawing as an artistic work. The drawing is not of surface decoration but is the design document recording the design of the actual shape or configuration *of* the stencil.[1015] Further, it is also the design document *for* a stencil. However, as a stencil made to the design would probably be an artistic work,[1016] s.51 would not operate.

(11) A designer creates drawings and an engraved metal plate to produce rubber floor mats for cars. The drawings and plate are, respectively, a design document and a model recording the design for the rubber mats. However, as the mats themselves were (strangely) artistic works (being engravings), s.51 did not operate to limit copyright protection for the designs.[1017]

(12) Drawings of the helmets and armour to be worn by storm troopers in the *Star Wars* films were not sculptures because their primary purpose was utilitarian and they lacked the necessary quality of artistic creation. Nor were they works of artistic craftsmanship because their purpose was not to appeal to the aesthetic at all but was, rather, to give an impression in a film. Thus, s.51 operated to limit copyright protection for the drawings.[1018]

13–314   **Or a typeface.** Typefaces are also expressly excluded from the operation of s.51. The distinct copyright regime which applies to typefaces has already been considered.[1019]

(iv) Permitted acts under section 51

13–315   Where s.51(1) applies, it is not an infringement of any copyright in the relevant design document or model to make an article to the design or to copy an article made to the design. However, these are only permitted acts in relation to the copyright in the work. A person who so acts may nevertheless infringe any design right which may subsist in the relevant design. Further, as has been pointed out,[1020] other acts may still constitute infringements of copyright.

13–316   **To make an article to the design.** The phrase "to make an article to the design" is not defined for the purposes of s.51,[1021] however, it clearly refers to the making of a three dimensional object to the design. Accordingly, using the examples set out in para.13–282, above, the making of contact lenses in accordance with the drawings would amount to making articles to the design and would not infringe copyright by reason of s.51. Similarly, making exhausts to the drawings would not infringe copyright in the drawings. By contrast, the making of a photocopy of the drawings would remain an infringement of copyright. Whether or not the

---

[1015] See para.13–70 (example 5), above.
[1016] Being either an "engraving, etching, lithograph, woodcut or similar work" within CDPA 1988 s.4(2)(b) or, possibly, a work of artistic craftsmanship.
[1017] See *Hi-Tech Autoparts Ltd v Towergate Two Ltd (No.2)* [2002] F.S.R. 270. See para.3–55, above.
[1018] See *Lucasfilm Ltd v Ainsworth* [2009] EWCA Civ.1328; [2010] F.S.R. 10 at paras 70–72, 75–77 and 80 approving the decision at first instance ([2008] EWHC 1878; [2009] F.S.R. 103 at paras 94–141). The same reasoning applied to clay models of a storm trooper's head and the original clay armour. See at para.81 (on appeal) and para.142 (at first instance).
[1019] See paras 9–163 et seq., above.
[1020] See para.13–300, above.
[1021] The same words are used in relation to primary infringements of design right—see CDPA 1988 s.226(1) and are, not entirely helpfully, defined in that context as "copying the design so as to produce articles exactly or substantially to that design"—see CDPA 1988 s.226(2) and paras 13–152 et seq., above.

making of such a photocopy constituted the making of an article,[1022] this would not be making an article to the design but would, instead, be copying the design document.

To copy an article made to the design. At first sight, this provision appears to add little to the previous provision which allows the making of an article to the design. However, the words "to copy" in s.51 are wider than the words "to make an article". They mean that, where s.51 operates, a competitor is not only permitted (for copyright purposes) to make an article by copying articles which the designer has made to his design[1023] but also to produce his own design drawings[1024] provided they have been copied from articles made to the design document rather than being copied direct from the designer's drawings.

13–317

In effect, this part of s.51(1) operates to exclude a copyright claim in respect of any act of copying of an article made to the design, whatever the result of that copying. It was on this basis that it was held to be arguable that s.51 excluded a copyright claim in *BBC Worldwide Ltd v PallyScreen Printing Ltd*.[1025] In that case, the defendants had made garments featuring pictures of the characters from the BBC television series "The Teletubbies". The picture on one group of garments had clearly been copied from a photograph of the Teletubby characters and it was arguable that the picture on the other group of garments had been copied from the Teletubby characters as they had appeared on television. In both cases, there had been indirect copying of the claimant's copyright drawings.[1026] However, on the assumption that the drawings had been the design for the characters (and not, therefore, the designs for something that was an artistic work or typeface[1027]), then what the defendants had done was to copy an article made to the design (i.e. the Teletubby shown in the photograph or on television). On this basis, it was arguable that s.51 operated.[1028] Strangely, the result would have been different if the defendant had copied the drawings directly, for in such a case, the defendant would not have been copying an article made to the design nor would it have been making an article to the design within s.51.[1029]

Making an article where the design document is a written description. As has been seen, the definition of a design document expressly includes a design recorded in the form of a "written description".[1030] This inclusion is curious. As the

13–318

[1022] There are good reasons for suggesting that a photocopy is not an article for these purposes. In this context, as in the design right context, an article should be seen as something with shape and configuration—i.e. a positive physical form—see para.13–50, above. This conclusion is supported by *BBC Worldwide Ltd v Pally Screen Printing Ltd* [1998] F.S.R. 665 where the copying of a design by printing it on a T-shirt did not constitute the making of an article to the design.

[1023] Such an action would also be covered by the right to make an article to the design.

[1024] Which, as stated in para.13–316, above, would not be covered by the permission to "make an article to the design".

[1025] [1998] F.S.R. 665.

[1026] In accordance with the decision in *King Features Syndicate Inc v O and M Kleeman Ltd* [1941] A.C. 417. See para.13–16, above.

[1027] See para.13–313 (example 7), above.

[1028] In *Mackie Designs Inc v Behringer Specialised Studio Equipment (UK) Ltd* [1999] R.P.C. 717 at 723 it was said that the reasoning in *BBC Worldwide Ltd v Pally Screen Printing Ltd* [1998] F.S.R. 665 was said to be not just "arguable" but "compelling". In Mackie it was held that a defendant who had copied a circuit board made to the claimant's circuit diagram was indirectly copying the claimant's design but was doing so by copying an article made to that design. Hence, a copyright claim would be excluded by CDPA 1998 s.51.

[1029] See *BBC Worldwide Ltd v Pally Screen Printing Ltd* [1998] F S R 665, where it was commented that, with any attempt to draw a boundary between copyright and design right protection, there would inevitably be hard cases near the borderline.

[1030] CDPA 1988 s.51(3).

making of a three-dimensional article cannot infringe the copyright in a literary work,[1031] it would seem that s.51 had no need to provide for such a design.[1032]

13–319 **Section 51(2).** Finally, under s.51(2),[1033] it is not an infringement of the copyright to issue to the public, or include in the film or communicate to the public, anything the making of which was, by virtue of s.51(1), not an infringement of that copyright. The reason for this provision is that, where s.51(1) applies, the article made to the design or a copy of an article made to the design is not an infringing copy. Thus, most dealings with that article or copy could not amount to infringements of copyright.[1034] However, as has been seen, the issue to the public of copies not previously in circulation would usually constitute a primary infringement of copyright even though the copies in question are not infringing copies. Accordingly, these and the other acts referred to in s.51(2) are expressly made permitted acts so far as copyright is concerned.

C. SECTION 52

(i) Introduction

13–320 Although s.51 of the 1988 Act will operate to limit the copyright protection available for many industrial designs, it does not deal with the problem of copyright protection for artistic works properly so-called (such as sculptures or paintings) or designs for such works which are subsequently exploited industrially. This is the purpose of s.52.

13–321 **Rationale.** What lies behind s.52 is the feeling that full copyright protection, whilst justified in the case of artistic works which remain in the artistic field, is not justified where the copyright owner chooses to exploit his work industrially. In such a case, there is no reason why the period of protection to which the copyright owner is entitled should be any longer than the period of protection available to the proprietor of a registered design. To achieve this, s.52 (where it applies) reduces the period of copyright protection in respect of most but not all acts of infringement to a period of 25 years from the end of the year in which the work in question was first exploited.[1035]

13–322 **Interrelationship with section 51.** The operation of s.52 is not dependent upon, nor is it mutually exclusive with the operation of s.51. Where an artistic work is exploited industrially, s.52 may operate to reduce the period of whatever copyright protection is available for the work regardless of whether or not the types of acts capable of infringing that copyright have been limited by reason of s.51.

(ii) Statement of section 52

13–323 Section 52 provides:

(1) This section applies where an artistic work has been exploited by or with the licence of the copyright owner, by—

[1031] See para.7–37, above.
[1032] It may be that the words were intended to cover cases where the design comprises a drawing supplemented by a written description.
[1033] Since October 31, 2003 when it was amended by the Copyright and Related Rights Regulations 2003 (SI 2003/2498).
[1034] See Ch.8, above.
[1035] In this sense, CDPA 1988 s.52 is similar in approach to Copyright Act 1956 s.10(2) and (3) (as amended by the Design Copyright Act 1968). However, in contrast to s.10, the operation of s.52 is not in any way dependent upon whether or not the design in question was registrable.

(a) making by an industrial process articles falling to be treated for the purposes of this Part as copies of the work, and

(b) marketing such articles in the United Kingdom or elsewhere.

(2) After the end of the period of 25 years from the end of the calendar year in which such articles are first marketed, the work may be copied by making articles of any description, or doing anything for the purpose of making articles of any description, and anything may be done in relation to articles so made, without infringing copyright in the work".

(iii) Conditions for application of section 52

Industrial process. For s.52 to operate, the relevant artistic work must have been exploited by the making of articles by an industrial process.[1036] Under s.52(4), the Secretary of State may, by Order, provide for the circumstances in which an article, or any description of an article, is to be regarded for the purposes of s.52 as made by an industrial process. The relevant Order[1037] provides that:

13–324

> "An article is to be regarded for the purposes of section 52 ... as made by an industrial process if—
>
>   (a) it is one of more than fifty articles which—
>   (i) all fall to be treated for the purposes of Part I of this Act as copies of a particular artistic work, but
>   (ii) do not all together constitute a single set of articles as defined in section 44 of the Registered Designs Act 1949; or
>   (b) it consists of goods manufactured in lengths or pieces, not being hand-made goods".

Despite the reference to an industrial process, the wording of the Order makes it clear that s.52 may apply whether the relevant articles have been made by hand or by some mechanical process. The reference to "industrial" for these purposes is a reference to the scale rather than the precise means of production. There is, however, an exception in that s.52 will not apply to goods which are manufactured in lengths or pieces and which are hand-made. This exception may save full-term copyright in the case of, say, lengths of hand-shaped architrave or pieces of a hand-made jigsaw.[1038] It would seem that there is no reason why each of the 51 or more articles made need be identical provided they are all copies of the relevant work.

It has been held that the relevant industrial process could have occurred anywhere and not necessarily in the United Kingdom.[1039] Although this seems perfectly sensible, it is not immediately clear why (given the principle of the territoriality of copyright) UK copyright should be restricted as a result of events that take place entirely outside the United Kingdom. It also remains unclear why s.52(1)(b) includes the words "whether in the United Kingdom or elsewhere" whereas s.52(1)(a) does not. Nor is it clear why, when those same words were added to s.10(2)(b) of the 1956 Act (by an amendment made by the Design Copy-

---

[1036] CDPA 1988 s.52(1)(a).

[1037] The Copyright (Industrial Process and Excluded Articles) (No.2) Order 1989 (SI 1989/1070), para.2—Vol.2 B8.ii,

[1038] The architrave and the jigsaw may also qualify as "sculptures". If so, they would in any event be excluded from the operation of s.52 by the Copyright (Industrial Process and Excluded Articles) (No.2) Order 1989 (SI1989/1070) para.3(1)(a), see below.

[1039] See *Lucasfilm Ltd v Ainsworth* [2008] EWHC 1878; [2009] F.S.R. 103 (at first instance) where Mann J. commented at paras 158–164 that, given that the purpose of s.52 was to restrict copyright where there had been industrial exploitation of a copyright work, he could "detect no point of principle which would indicate that it should matter whether the articles were manufactured in the UK as opposed to elsewhere. Such a distinction would be arbitrary".

right Act 1968), they were not also added to s.10(2)(a). It has been argued that the words may have been inserted to put beyond doubt that for the purposes of the section it did not matter where sales (etc.) took place.[1040] However, a similar doubt could equally arise as to whether the manufacture needed to be in the United Kingdom before reliance could be placed on the section. The fact is that Parliament chose to add the words to one condition but not to the other. Having said this, if Parliament had intended to link the restriction on copyright to some act of exploitation in the United Kingdom, a more obvious course might have been for the words "whether in the United Kingdom or elsewhere" to qualify s.52(1)(a) rather than s.52(1)(b)—i.e. to provide that the act of manufacture (rather than the marketing) could take place anywhere provided the marketing was in the United Kingdom.

13–325 **Articles.** For s.52 to operate, articles must have been made. The meaning of "article" has been considered in relation to design right[1041] and there is no reason to believe that a different meaning should be adopted here. However, the making of certain articles will not trigger the operation of s.52. First, s.52(6) provides that references in s.52 to articles do not include films. Thus, the making of multiple copies of a film of an artistic work will not amount to the making of articles for the purposes of s.52. Accordingly, copyright protection for the artistic work will not be reduced as a result of the making of such films.[1042] Secondly, under s.52(4), the Secretary of State is empowered to exclude from the operation of s.52 such articles of a primarily artistic or literary nature as he may think fit. The following articles are excluded by the relevant Order[1043]:

(a) works of sculpture, other than casts or models used or intended to be used as models or patterns to be multiplied by any industrial process;

(b) wall plaques, medals and medallions; and

(c) printed matter primarily of a literary or artistic character, including book jackets, calendars, certificates, coupons, dress-making patterns, greetings cards, labels, leaflets, maps, plans, playing cards, postcards, stamps, trade advertisements, trade forms and cards, transfers and similar articles".

Thus, even if a work is industrially exploited by the making of any of these articles, s.52 will not operate. The same articles are also excluded from registration under the registered designs legislation[1044] in which context it has been said that their protection was more naturally a matter for copyright than for registered design.[1045] The meaning of the words "works of sculpture" and of "models" have already been considered.[1046] In the last category—"printed matter of a literary or artistic character"—the list of items is not intended to be exclusive[1047] but the category does give rise to some difficulties. Thus, although wallpaper may be said to be an article of printed matter of an artistic nature, it has always been treated as

---

[1040] See *Lucasfilm Ltd v Ainsworth* [2008] EWHC 1878; [2009] F.S.R. 103 (Mann J.).

[1041] CDPA 1988 s.213(2). See para.13–50, above.

[1042] See *Hansard*, H.L. Vol.501, cols 245–246.

[1043] The Copyright (Industrial Process and Excluded Articles) (No.2) Order 1989 (SI 1989/1070) para.3(1)—see Vol.2B8.ii.

[1044] Registered Designs Rules 1995 (SI 1995/2912) reg.26.

[1045] See *Lamson Industries Ltd's Application* [1978] R.P.C. 1 at 7. See also *Hansard*, H.L. Vol.501, cols 245–246 and H.C., SCE, cols 249 and 250 where it was made clear that the intention was that s.52 should operate where the owner of the copyright in a painting chose to exploit that work by, say, reproducing it on tin trays but not where he reproduced it in the form of prints. The situation envisaged in *Hansard* arose in *Fearns v Anglo-Dutch Paint and Chemical Company Ltd* [2007] EWHC 955 (Ch) where Christopher Floyd QC decided that s.52 operated to restrict copyright protection for the claimant's design and logo which had been applied to paint tins (this finding was not challenged on appeal— [2008] EWCA Civ.99).

[1046] See, respectively, paras 3–60 and 13–308, above.

[1047] See *Lamson Industries Ltd's Application* [1978] R.P.C. 1 at 6.

otherwise in the context of the equivalent registered designs rule on the ground that it is not a similar article to the other articles listed in the rule.[1048]

Which are to be treated as copies of the work. Section 52 only applies where the relevant articles fall to be treated as copies of the relevant artistic work for the purposes of Pt I of the 1988 Act.[1049] This is determined by reference to what constitutes copying for the purposes of s.17 of the 1988 Act.[1050] Thus, where the artistic work is reproduced on only part of an article (for example, as a pattern on one side of a plate) the article would, nevertheless be treated as a copy for these purposes. Further, it would seem that an article will be treated as a copy of an artistic work when the copier has reproduced a substantial part of the work.[1051] If this were otherwise, the value of s.52 in limiting the scope of copyright protection in the industrial field would be severely reduced.

13–326

Marketing of such articles. Before s.52 can operate, it must be shown that the relevant articles have been marketed in the United Kingdom or elsewhere.[1052] References to the marketing of an article are defined[1053] as being references to its being sold or let for hire or offered or exposed for sale or hire. The meaning of this has already been considered in the context of secondary infringements of copyright.[1054] It should be noted, however, that s.52 operates whether or not the relevant act was done in the United Kingdom.

13–327

Exploitation of part only. It is clear from the terms of s.52(3) that a copyright owner may choose to exploit part only of his copyright work by making and marketing articles falling to be treated as copies of that part of the work. The significance of this is considered below.[1055]

13–328

(iv) Consequences of section 52 applying

Section 52(2). If an artistic work has been exploited within the meaning of s.52(1), then s.52(2) provides that "[a]fter the end of the period of 25 years from the end of the calendar year in which such articles are first marketed, the work may be copied by making articles of any description, or doing anything for the purpose of making articles of any description, and anything may be done in relation to articles so made, without infringing copyright in the work". Thus, s.52(2) only operates to reduce the period of copyright protection against certain specified acts. Copyright protection remains otherwise unaffected. If a rival steps outside the permitted areas, he may still infringe copyright over its full term. The period of 25 years is plainly intended to be analogous to the period of protection available to a registered design, the latter being 25 years from the date of application for registration. In effect, the act of marketing is treated as being the moment when the copyright owner takes his work out of the purely artistic sphere and into the industrial.

13–329

Work may be copied by making an article of any description. Where s.52 applies, s.52(2) allows a person, after the 25-year period, to copy the work by mak-

13–330

[1048] A wallpaper design may, therefore, be registered under the RDA 1949, see *Lamson Industries Ltd's Application* [1978] R.P.C. 1 at 6 and 8.

[1049] i.e. the copyright provisions of the CDPA 1988.

[1050] CDPA 1988 s.179 refers to CDPA 1988 s.17 for the definition of "copy and copying". For a detailed discussion of s.17 reference should be made to Ch.7, above.

[1051] See paras 7–25 et seq., above.

[1052] CDPA 1988 s.52(1)(b).

[1053] s.52(6)(b).

[1054] s.23(b), considered in Ch.8, above.

[1055] See para.13–334, below.

ing an article[1056] of any description without infringing copyright. Accordingly, subject to the specific exclusion discussed below, a person may copy the work in the form of whatever type of article he chooses. He is not limited to the type of articles by which the copyright owner had chosen to exploit his work. However, because s.52(6)(a) states that references to articles in s.52 do not include films, a person cannot copy the work in the form of a film after the 25-year period.

What is less clear is whether, when s.52 applies, it allows a person to make articles of the types which are specified by the Order of the Secretary of State made under s.52(4)(b).[1057] In *Jules Rimet Cup Ltd v Football Association* it was decided that it did not.[1058] In that case, the Football Association had exploited the World Cup Willie design drawings in a way that had brought into operation s.10 of the 1956 Act and (under the transitional provisions) s.52 of the 1988 Act.[1059] Nevertheless, it was held that the permission which s.52(2) gave to copy the work "by making article of any description" did not extend to articles of the type specified in the Order made by the Secretary of State. A contrary argument would be that s.52(4)(b) provides that the relevant Order may be made "excluding [such articles] from the operation of this section". This suggests that the exclusion is intended to apply in relation to subs.(1), i.e .in determining the type of articles whose making and marketing would trigger the operation of s.52. It seems more difficult to argue that s.52 "operates" in relation to the articles the making of which is not to be an infringement by reason of subs.(2). It could also be said that if the intention had been to exclude articles of a primarily literary or artistic nature wherever a reference was made to "articles" in s.52, then the exclusion could and perhaps should have been contained in s.52(6) together with the exclusion of films.[1060] Finally, as s.52(2) allows others to copy the work by making articles which are themselves artistic works, there seems to be no reason why others should be excluded from copying the work by making articles which are primarily of a literary or artistic character.

13–331   Illustrations.

(1) Where a painting has been exploited by the copyright owner within the meaning of s.52(1) in the form of making table mats, then 25 years after the end of the calendar year of first marketing of such mats, other persons will be able to copy the work as a design on crockery as well as on table mats. It seems, however, that the work could not be copied by use on wallpaper or on material fabric (or any other articles excluded pursuant to s.52(4))—although the contrary may be arguable.[1061]

(2) An artist draws cartoon sketches of a futuristic car for a comic strip in a science fiction magazine. Copyright will subsist in these sketches as artistic works. As has been seen, s.51 does not operate in relation to such works. But if the artist subsequently allows toy cars of that design to be made and marketed in sufficient quantities, then s.52 will operate. After 25 years from first marketing, a rival manufacturer may make toy or real cars to the same design or make pencil erasers to the design.

[1056] The meaning of an "article" has already been considered, see para.13–50, above.

[1057] i.e. the articles of a primarily literary or artistic nature specified in the Copyright (Industrial Process and Excluded Articles) (No.2) Order 1989 (SI 1989/1070), see para.13–325, above.

[1058] [2007] EWHC 2376; [2008] F.S.R. 10 at paras 23–25 (R.Wyand QC).

[1059] See paras 13–344 et seq., below.

[1060] Interestingly, the debate in Parliament shows that CDPA 1988 s.52(6)(a) was enacted because a film could not be called an article primarily of literary or artistic character within what is now s.52(4)(b). Thus, s.52(6)(a) was enacted to ensure that the making of multiple films did not trigger the operation of s.52. There was no reference to the significance of either provision as regards articles it was permitted to make under s.52(2). See *Hansard*, H.L. Vol.501, cols 245–246 and H.C., SCE, cols 249–250.

[1061] See para.13–330, above.

Doing anything for the purpose of making articles of any description. Where   **13–332**
s.52 applies, s.52(2) also permits the doing of anything for the purpose of making
articles of any description.[1062] This would, for example, allow a rival to prepare
manufacturing drawings for an article, such drawings not themselves being
"articles". However, it is important to note that the drawings would have to have
been produced for the purpose of making the articles.

Anything may be done with articles so made. Section 52(2) also permits deal-   **13–333**
ings with the articles of any description so made. The words "so made" are plainly
a reference to articles which it is permissible to make after the 25-year period has
expired.[1063] Such articles may, therefore, be issued to the public without infringing copyright or included in a film or communicated to the public. The section
does not permit dealings with articles made before the 25-year period has expired.

Exploitation of part only. As has been seen, a copyright owner may choose to   **13–334**
exploit or to allow the exploitation of his work in part only. In such event, s.52(2)
only applies in relation to that part. Any act in relation to the unexploited part
will remain an infringement of copyright.

D. SECTION 53

Section 53 of the 1988 Act provides that: **13–335**

    (1) The copyright in an artistic work is not infringed by anything done—

        (a) in pursuance of an assignment or licence made or granted by a person
            registered under the Registered Designs Act 1949 as the proprietor of
            a corresponding design, and

        (b) in good faith in reliance on the registration and without notice of any
            proceedings for the cancellation of the registration or for rectifying
            the relevant entry in the register of designs;

  and this is so notwithstanding that the person registered as the proprietor was
not the proprietor of the design for the purposes of the 1949 Act.

    (2) In subsection (1) a 'corresponding design', in relation to an artistic
work means a design within the meaning of the 1949 Act which, if applied
to an article would produce something which would be treated for the
purposes of this Part as a copy of the artistic work".

Rationale. This provision was intended to deal with those cases where a design   **13–336**
is covered by both copyright and by registration under the Registered Designs
Act 1949 and where a person acts under an assignment or licence from the proprietor of the registered design. Normally, this will present no problem in that the
owner of the copyright in a work will usually also be the proprietor of its corresponding registered design. In giving his permission as registered proprietor, he
can hardly complain about the infringement of copyright. The difficulties arise
where the owner and the proprietor are different. Previously this was dealt with
by Sch.1 to the Copyright Act 1956. Section 53 is intended to re-enact that
provision.[1064]

Conditions for application of section 53. The wording of s.53 is largely self-   **13–337**
explanatory. To take advantage of the section, the relevant act must have been in
pursuance of an assignment or licence. An act outside the scope of such assignment or licence may still infringe copyright in the relevant work. The assignment

---

[1062] See para.13–330, above.
[1063] See para.13–330, above.
[1064] See *Hansard*, H.C. SCE, col.251.

or licence must have been made by someone who was registered as the proprietor of the corresponding design even if he was not truly the proprietor for the purposes of the Registered Designs Act 1949.

25. COPYRIGHT WORKS OF INDUSTRIAL APPLICATION MADE ON OR AFTER JUNE 1, 1957 BUT BEFORE AUGUST 1989

A. INTRODUCTION

13–338 **Copyright in existing works of industrial application.** Any work created before August 1, 1989 is referred to by the 1988 Act as an existing work.[1065] This Part of this Chapter is concerned only with the issues which arise where such works are of industrial application and were created during the period that the Copyright Act 1956 Act was in force, i.e. on or after June 1, 1957 but before August 1, 1989.

13–339 **Permitted acts.** Certain acts which would otherwise infringe the copyright in an existing work will, provided they occur after August 1, 1989, be permitted acts under the 1988 Act. For copyright works of industrial application, the most significant provisions are ss.51 to 53. Section 53 applies without any qualification in relation to works created before commencement of the 1988 Act.[1066] However, the application of s.51 and of s.52 in the case of existing works is subject to the transitional provisions of the 1988 Act which are discussed below.

B. PERMITTED ACTS—POSTPONEMENT OF THE OPERATION OF SECTION 51

13–340 **Limitation of protection for industrial designs—the transitional provisions.** In the case of an existing work, the transitional provisions of the 1988 Act provided that s.51 would not apply for a period of 10 years after commencement, i.e. until August 1, 1999.[1067] Thus, any existing copyright work which is a design document or model recording or embodying a design for anything other than an artistic work or typeface[1068] retained its copyright protection against the full range of possible acts of infringement until that date.[1069] This protection was, however, subject to the operation of any rule of law preventing or restricting the enforcement of copyright in relation to a design.[1070]

13–341 **Licences of right during the period of postponement.** The transitional provisions also provided that, during the 10-year period for which s.51 did not apply, the design right licence of right provisions would apply (subject to certain modifications) to any relevant copyright as they applied in relation to design right.[1071] Under these provisions, any person was entitled to a licence of right in respect of any relevant copyright for the last five years of the ten-year period of

---

[1065] CDPA 1988 Sch.1 para.1(3).

[1066] As to CDPA 1988 s.53, see paras 13–335 et seq., above.

[1067] CDPA 1988 Sch.1 para.19(1).

[1068] For the meaning of "design document" and "model" see paras 13–307 et seq., above.

[1069] Assuming, of course, that copyright in the relevant work does not expire before then.

[1070] Sch.1 para.19(9). Such rules of law will include the "spare parts" exception, see *British Leyland Motor Corporation v Armstrong Patents Co Ltd* [1986] A.C. 577; [1986] F.S.R. 221, see paras 5–235 et seq. and 13–21, above.

[1071] See CDPA 1988 Sch.1 paras 19(2)–(7). The design right licence of right provisions are discussed at paras 13–126 et seq., above.

postponement (i.e. after August 1, 1994[1072]) until August 1, 1999,[1073] the licence being to do those acts which would have been permitted by section 51 had the relevant work been a new work rather than an existing work.[1074]

After the period of postponement. Since August 1, 1999, s.51 has applied to existing works just as it does to new works.[1075]   **13–342**

Rationale for transitional provisions. The intention behind the transitional pro-   **13–343**
visions relating to s.51 was plainly to ensure that, in general terms, the scope of protection for existing works[1076] of industrial design was broadly the same as that for new works of that type. Before the 1988 Act, such works were entitled to copyright protection.[1077] In the case of new works of the same type, copyright protection is effectively denied by s.51 and any protection is a matter for design right with its more limited duration, its licences of right and wide-ranging "must fit" and "must match" exclusions. However, design right cannot subsist in designs recorded or embodied in existing works.[1078] Thus, if s.51 had applied to existing works of industrial design, many designs would have been left without protection. To avoid so drastic a change, the transitional provisions postponed the operation of s.51 for the 10 years to August 1, 1999[1079] whilst providing for licences of right and the continuation of rules of law such as those in *British Leyland Motor Corporation v Armstrong Patents Co Ltd*[1080] to ensure that this residual copyright did not result in the effective monopolies which copyright protection had previously created.

C. PERMITTED ACTS—THE APPLICATION OF SECTION 52

(i) Industrial application of artistic works—the transitional provisions

Schedule 1 paragraph 20. In the case of existing works created whilst the 1956   **13–344**
Act was in force, the application of s.52 was subject to the transitional provisions contained in Sch.1 para.20 to the 1988 Act.[1081] These provided that:

(1) Where section 10 of the 1956 Act[1082] (effect of industrial application of design corresponding to artistic work) applied in relation to an artistic work at any time before commencement, section 52(2) of this Act applies with the substitution for the period of 25 years mentioned there of the relevant period of 15 years as defined in section 10(3) of the 1956 Act" and

(2) Except as provided in sub-paragraph (1), section 52 applies only

---

[1072] Sch.1 para.19(2), (3) and s.237.

[1073] Since August 1, 1999, a licence to do the things permitted by s.51 has not been necessary

[1074] Sch.1 para.19(7). Thus, the terms of a s.238 licence of right arising in relation to an existing work may differ to those of a licence arising under the design right provisions. In the latter, the licence may be in respect of anything which the Order of the Secretary of State requires.

[1075] For the application of CDPA 1988 s.51 to new works, see paras 13–301 et seq., above.

[1076] Again, "existing works" in this context means works which existed as at August 1, 1989 when the CDPA 1988 came into force.

[1077] Assuming they were recorded in copyright works. Such copyright protection was subject to the largely ineffective s.9(8) of the 1956 Act, the "spare parts" exception put forward in *British Leyland Motor Corporation v Armstrong Patents Co Ltd* [1986] A.C. 577; [1986] F.S.R. 221 and to a reduction in term to 15 years where s.10 of the 1956 Act (as amended by the Design Copyright Act 1968) applied.

[1078] Design right only applies to designs created after August 1, 1989.

[1079] i.e. a period roughly similar to the 10-year period of design right protection, see paras 13–103 et seq., above.

[1080] CDPA 1988 Sch.1 para.19(a) and [1986] A.C. 577.

[1081] *Lucasfilm Ltd v Ainsworth* [2009] EWCA Civ.1328; [2010] F.S.R. 10 is a case concerning the application of these transitional provisions, see paras 89–98.

[1082] i.e. the Copyright Act 1956.

where articles are marketed as mentioned in subsection (1)(b) after commencement".

The need for para.20(1) arose from the repeal of the whole of the Copyright Act 1956. Where s.10 of the 1956 Act had applied to an artistic work, it reduced the period of copyright protection to 15 years.[1083] The transitional provisions of the 1988 Act effectively maintained that period of protection for those works by providing that s.52(2) would apply to them but with a 15-year period of protection. Thus, no copyright can now subsist in such works—the very latest date for such protection having expired being July 31, 2004. If, however, s.10 did not apply to a work at any time (i.e. before August 1, 1989), then para.20(2) ensures that s.52 will not operate retrospectively and that it will only apply if articles are marketed within the meaning of s.52(1)(b) on or after August 1, 1989.[1084] In such cases, s.52 will apply to the existing work just as it does to new works.

13–345   **The application of section 52 to existing works.** Under the transitional provisions, the following questions arise when considering the application of s.52 to a work of industrial application created whilst the 1956 Act was in force:

(1) Did s.10 of the 1956 Act apply to the work at any time prior to August 1, 1989?

(2) If so, what acts are now permitted by reason of s.52(2) as modified by para.20(1)? and

(3) If s.10 did not apply to the work before August 1, 1989, have articles been marketed on or after August 1, 1989 within the meaning of para.20(2)?

These questions remain important, for if s.10 of the 1956 Act did not apply to the work and there has been no marketing of articles within the meaning of s.52(1)(b) since July 31, 1989, the work would remain entitled to copyright for its full term and copyright may still subsist.

(ii) Did section 10 of the 1956 Act apply to the work at any time?

13–346   **History of section 10 of the Copyright Act 1956.** The first question is whether s.10 of the 1956 Act had applied to the work at any time. Before this question can be answered, it is necessary to consider the history of s.10 and its amendment by the Design Copyright Act 1968.[1085] Prior to its amendment, s.10 applied to two types of work; (i) a work whose corresponding design had been registered under the Registered Designs Act 1949[1086]; and (ii) a work whose corresponding design was not registered but had been applied industrially through the making and marketing of articles to the designs.[1087] It did not, however, apply to a work whose corresponding design was unregistrable.[1088] Where s.10 applied, it excluded copyright protection in so far as protection was or would have been available through registration of the corresponding design.[1089] The 1968 Act made substantial amendments to s.10 as a result of which s.10 only applied to one type of a work,

---

[1083] See s.10(3) as amended by the Design Copyright Act 1968 (the 15-year period ran from the date when articles made to the design were first marketed, see para.13–346, below). For the reasons discussed at para.13–347, below, it is submitted that the question whether s.10 in its unamended form ever applied to a work does not arise.

[1084] See para.13–327, above.

[1085] See paras 13–17 et seq., above. The 1968 Act came into force on October 25, 1968.

[1086] Copyright Act 1956 s.10(1).

[1087] Copyright Act 1956 s.10(2).

[1088] See *Dorling v Honnor Marine Ltd* [1965] Ch. 1 at 16 and 19E-F; [1964] R.P.C. 160. This was due to the nature of the limitations on the copyright protection (s.10(6)), see para.13–18, above.

[1089] The provisions limiting copyright protection were complicated. In essence, where s.10(1) applied, copyright protection was excluded in the 15 years after registration to the extent that the

i.e. one whose corresponding design had been applied industrially through the making and marketing of articles to the design.[1090] Where the amended s.10 applied, the relevant artistic work retained its copyright protection for a period of 15 years from the date on which articles made to the design were first marketed.[1091] After that period, copyright in the work would not be infringed to the extent that registration would have provided a remedy had the corresponding design been registered at the relevant time.[1092] Despite these amendments, s.10 still only applied to an artistic work whose corresponding design was capable of registration.[1093]

The amended or unamended form of section 10. As has been seen, para.20(1)   **13–347**
of the transitional provisions of the 1988 Act applies to an existing artistic work if s.10 of the 1956 Act had applied to that work "at any time" before August 1, 1989.[1094] This presents no difficulty in the case of an artistic work which was created after s.10 was amended by the Design Copyright Act 1968. In such a case, the reference to s.10 in para.20(1) must clearly be a reference to s.10 in its amended form. The question arises, however, how to treat a work created before the amendment of s.10.[1095] It is submitted that, notwithstanding the words "at any time", the transitional provisions are only concerned with whether s.10 applied in its amended (post-1968 Act) form.[1096] Paragraph 20(1) states that it applies "[w]here section 10 ... (effect of industrial application of design corresponding to artistic work) applied to an artistic work ...". The words in parentheses suggest that s.10 is being referred to in its amended form. As has been seen,[1097] prior to its amendment, s.10 could apply to two types of work; a work whose corresponding design was registered, and a work whose corresponding design was not registered but had been applied industrially. The words in parentheses are not particularly appropriate as regards the first type of work. By contrast, after s.10 was amended,

---

actual registration provided protection. Thereafter it was excluded to the extent that registration of the design in the widest possible terms would have provided protection. Where s.10(2) applied, copyright protection was excluded in the 15 years after articles made to the design were first marketed to the extent that registration in relation to that type of article would have provided protection. Thereafter, it was excluded to the extent that registration of the design in the widest possible terms would have provided protection. See Copyright Act 1956 s.10(1), (2), (3) and (6). One of the advantages of CDPA 1988 s.52 is the abandonment of this approach.

[1090] Copyright Act 1956 s.10(2)(b) (as amended).

[1091] Copyright Act 1956 s.10(3) (as amended).

[1092] Copyright Act 1956 s.10(3) (as amended). Again, it was to be presumed that the widest possible registration was in place as at the time of the act of alleged infringement, see Copyright Act 1956 s.10(3) and (6).

[1093] The definition of a "corresponding design" in Copyright Act 1956 s.10(7) was not amended by the 1988 Act and remained the same as that contained in the Registered Designs Act 1949 s.44(1) (which has now been repealed by the Registered Design Regulations 2001). Similarly, s.10(4) of the 1956 Act was not amended by the 1988 Act. Had the 1968 Act intended s.10 to apply to unregistrable designs as well as registrable designs, s.10(4) would have been deprived of any meaning or operation. For these reasons it has been held that s.10 as amended only applied to works whose corresponding designs were capable of registration, see *British Leyland Motor Corporation v Armstrong Patents Co Ltd* [1986] A.C. 577; [1986] F.S.R. 221; [1986] R.P.C. 279 at 308–309 and 314–316, CA and *Entec (Pollution Control) Ltd v Abacus Mouldings* [1992] F.S.R. 332 at 336. Further, as s.10(3) (as amended) still limited the scope of copyright (after the 15-year period) by reference to potential protection under the Registered Designs Act 1949, the reasoning in *Dorling v Honor Marine Ltd* [1965] Ch. 1 remained applicable, see *British Leyland Motor Corporation v Armstrong Patents Co Ltd* at 316.

[1094] CDPA 1988 Sch.1 para.20(1), see para.13–344, above.

[1095] i.e. do the transitional provisions require one to ask whether s.10 of the 1956 Act applied in its unamended form to the work at any time before that date and in its amended form at any time after that date; or to ask simply whether s.10 applied in its amended form at any time.

[1096] This was the approach in *Drayton Controls (Engineering) Ltd v Honeywell Control Systems Ltd* [1992] F.S.R. 245 at 256 where, in determining the application of the transitional provisions to drawings one of which proceeded the 1968 Act, the court only had regard to s.10 in its amended form.

[1097] See para.13–346, below.

it only applied to a work whose corresponding design had been applied industrially. The words in parenthesis, therefore, describe accurately the only situation in which section 10 applied after its amendment. Further, para.20(1) provides that if s. 10 had applied, s.52(2) of the 1988 Act applies "with the substitution for the period of 25 years ... of the relevant period of 15-years as defined in section 10(3) of the 1956 Act". This again suggests that reference is being made to s.10 in its amended form. The 15-year period "as defined by section 10(3)" runs from the date on which relevant articles were first sold, let for hire or offered for sale or hire. There may have been no such date under s.10 in its unamended form because s.10 could then have applied simply because the corresponding design had been registered. Finally, such a construction is more consistent with the approach of the 1988 Act in relation to new works where copyright and registration may co-exist and where s.52 only applies if a design has been applied industrially.[1098]

13–348   **Section 10 (as amended).** Accordingly, it is submitted that for the purposes of the transitional provisions relating to s.52 of the 1988 Act, the question whether s.10 of the 1956 Act applied to an existing work at any time prior to August 1, 1989, must be answered by reference to s.10 as amended by the Design Copyright Act 1968. Section 10 (as so amended) applied:

Where copyright subsists in an artistic work, and—

> (a) a corresponding design is applied industrially by or with the licence of the owner of the copyright in the work, and
> (b) articles to which the design has been so applied are sold, let for hire, or offered for sale or hire whether in the United Kingdom or elsewhere".

There must, therefore, have been (1) an artistic work, (2) a corresponding design, (3) industrial application of the corresponding design and (4) relevant marketing of articles. In the absence of any of these factors, s.10 would not have applied and, therefore, the modified version of s.52 would not apply either.[1099]

13–349   **A corresponding design.** For s.10 of the 1956 Act to have applied to an artistic work, that work had to have a "corresponding design". A corresponding design was defined by s.10(7) as a design which, when applied to an article, resulted in a reproduction of the relevant artistic work. For these purposes, a "reproduction" included a version produced by converting the work into a three-dimensional form or, if it were in three dimensions, by converting it into a two-dimensional form.[1100] Thus, the novel design of a chair depicted in a drawing could be a corresponding design[1101] because a chair made to that design would reproduce the drawing.

13–350   **Limitations on the meaning of "corresponding design".** The scope of the definition of a corresponding design and, therefore, the application of s.10 was, however, subject to limitations. The most important of these, namely that the design in question be one capable of registration under the Registered Designs Act 1949, is considered in more detail below. Another was that the definition only applied to those designs embodied in an artistic work which, when applied to an article, would result in a reproduction of that work. Thus, in a case where the relevant artistic work was a drawing of a thermostatic radiator valve, a design consisting of the shape of one part of the valve (such as a bezel) was not a corre-

---

[1098] See, generally, paras 13–320 et seq., above.
[1099] i.e. CDPA 1988 s.52 as modified by Sch.1 para.20(1), see para.13–344, above.
[1100] Copyright Act 1956 s.48.
[1101] Assuming that it was capable of registration, see para.13–351, below.

sponding design because an article made to it would not be a reproduction of the drawing of the complete valve.[1102] Finally, it would seem that the question whether a design was a corresponding design was subject to the effect of s.9(8) of the 1956 Act. Section 9(8) provided that the making of a three-dimensional object should not be taken to infringe copyright in an artistic work in two dimensions if the object would not have appeared, to persons who were not experts in relation to objects of that description, to be a reproduction of that work. Although s.9(8) did not in terms qualify the meaning of a "reproduction", it effectively placed a limit on what would be regarded as a reproduction. Accordingly, it seems probable that if s.9(8) applied to a work, then the relevant design would not be a corresponding design because an article made to that design would not have been treated as a reproduction of that work.

Corresponding design must be capable of registration. The most important limitation on the application of s.10 was that a design, to be a corresponding design, must be a design capable of registration under the Registered Designs Act 1949. Although this was not a requirement expressly stated in s.10(7), it was clearly established by the authorities.[1103] At the relevant time,[1104] a "design" was defined by the 1949 Act as: **13–351**

> "... features of shape, configuration, pattern or ornament applied to an article by any industrial process or means being features which in the finished article appeal to and are judged solely by the eye but does not include a method or principle of construction[1105] or features of shape or configuration which are dictated solely by the function which the article to be made in that shape or configuration has to perform."[1106]

Corresponding design—features of shape, configuration, pattern or ornament applied to an article. It was said in one case,[1107] that the words "shape" and "configuration" were, for practical purposes, synonymous as were the words "pattern" and "ornament". Shape and configuration both signified something in three dimensions; the form in which the article itself was fashioned. Pattern and ornament were substantially in two as opposed to three dimensions; an article could exist without any pattern or ornament upon it, whereas it could have no existence at all apart from its shape and configuration. Whilst there were also cases which suggested that "shape" and "configuration" should not always be regarded as synonymous,[1108] this remains a convenient summary of the definition of a design for registered design purposes at the relevant time (i.e. before the 1988 Act). If the design did not satisfy this definition, s.10 of the 1956 Act would not   **13–352**

[1102] See *Drayton Controls (Engineering) Ltd v Honeywell Control Systems Ltd* [1992] F.S.R. 245, per Knox J. at 258 following the result in *Sifam Electrical Instrument v Sangamo Weston* [1973] R.P.C. 899 where the point was not argued.

[1103] See, for example, *Drayton Controls Engineering Ltd v Honeywell Control Systems Ltd* [1992] F.S.R. 245, above, and *Entec (Pollution Control) Ltd v Abacus Mouldings* [1992] F.S.R. 332 at 336.

[1104] For these purposes, the definition is that which applied before the 1949 Act was amended by the CDPA 1988 and by the Registered Design Regulations 2001 (SI 2001/3949).

[1105] The meaning of "methods or principles of construction" is considered in the context of design right, see paras 13–56 et seq., above.

[1106] Registered Designs Act 1949 s.1(3) (prior to its amendment by the 1988 Act).

[1107] *Kestos Ltd v Kempat Ltd* (1936) 53 R.P.C. 139 at 152.

[1108] See *Amp Inc v Utilux Proprietary Ltd* [1972] R.P.C. 103 at 108, *Gramophone Co Ltd v Magazine Holder Co* (1910) 27 R.P.C. 152 at 159, *P.B. Cow & Co Ltd v Cannon Rubber Manufacturers Ltd* [1959] R.P.C. 347 (where ribs on a hot-water bottle (designed to prevent a user being scalded) were held to be features of configuration but not shape) and *Somner Allibert (UK) Ltd v Flair Plastics Ltd* [1987] R.P.C. 599 (where grooves applied in the manufacturing process to the backs of plastic chairs were found to be features of configuration but not of shape). See also the debate in *Lambretta Clothing Co Ltd v Teddy Smith (UK) Ltd* [2004] EWCA Civ 886; [2005] R.P.C. 6 and para.13–49, above).

have applied to the relevant work. Because an "article" was defined as any article of manufacture including any part of an article if that part was made and sold separately, the design of a part of an article would not have been registrable if that part was not intended to be sold separately from the rest of the article.[1109]

13–353   **Corresponding design—eye appeal.** At the relevant time, to be capable of registration, the design had to "appeal to and [be] judged solely by the eye".[1110] This meant that, when judged by the eye of the customer, the design had to have an appeal created by a distinctiveness of shape, pattern or ornament calculated to influence a customer choice. The appeal need not have been aesthetic or artistic although, if it was, it would presumably have satisfied the requirement.[1111] It did not necessarily matter that the designer did not consciously intend his design to have eye appeal[1112] but plainly, his intention may be relevant. Thus, a design for a toy was likely by its very nature to have eye appeal[1113] whereas the design for washer or a nut was unlikely to. It has been said that, in applying the test of eye appeal, the court should look at the design of the entire finished article and if some of its features had eye appeal, then the design of the whole article has eye appeal.[1114] However, it is not clear that this approach is consistent with the definition of a design for the purposes of registration at that time. Under that definition, the relevant registrable design may not be of the whole article. What was registrable was only those features of shape, configuration (etc.) to be applied to an article which had eye appeal (and which were not dictated solely by function).[1115]

13–354   **Corresponding design—dictated solely by function.** At the relevant time, a design was not capable of registration if it was dictated solely by the function which the relevant article was to perform. This exclusion operated separately from the requirement of eye appeal, thus a design may have eye appeal yet nevertheless not be registrable because it was dictated solely by function.[1116] It has been stated that, for the exclusion to have operated, each and every feature of the design must have been dictated solely by function so that, if some of its features were not dictated by function, the design as a whole would have been registrable even though the majority of features were so dictated.[1117] It is submitted that this was wrong. As stated above, at the relevant time, the registrable design was of those features of shape or configuration (etc.) applied to an article which have eye appeal and which were not dictated solely by function. It was not the design

---

[1109] See *Drayton Controls (Engineering) Ltd v Honeywell Control Systems Ltd* [1992] F.S.R. 245 at 257–258 following *Sifam Electrical Instrument v Sangamo Weston* [1973] R.P.C. 899 at 913.

[1110] The need for a design to appeal to the eye was introduced by the Patents and Designs Act 1919 (see para.13–15, above and para.13–369, below). The CDPA 1988 removed the word "solely" from the Registered Design Act 1949 definition of a design. For new designs (i.e. designs created after December 9, 2001), the requirement of eye appeal has been removed altogether by reason of amendments made by the Registered Designs Regulations 2001, see paras 13–275 et seq., above.

[1111] See *Interlego A.G. v Tyco International Inc* [1989] A.C. 217; [1988] R.P.C. 343 at 355, PC. See also, *Amp Inc v Utilux Pty Ltd* [1972] R.P.C. 103, *British Leyland Motor Corporation v Armstrong Patents Co Ltd* [1986] A.C. 577; [1986] R.P.C. 279; *Interlego A.G. v Alex Folley, etc. Ltd* [1987] F.S.R. 283 and *Gardex Ltd v Sorata Ltd* [1986] R.P.C. 623. See para.13–290, above.

[1112] See *Amp Inc v Utilux Pty Ltd* [1972] R.P.C. 103 at 110.

[1113] See *Interlego A.G. v Tyco International Inc* [1989] A.C. 217; [1988] R.P.C. 343 at 357–358, PC.

[1114] See *Interlego A.G. v Tyco International Inc* [1989] A.C. 217; [1988] R.P.C. 343 at 353.

[1115] It appears that neither party in Interlego put forward this construction of the definition of a design in *Interlego A.G. v Tyco International Inc* [1989] A.C. 217; [1988] R.P.C. 343 (see pp.353–354). However, it is submitted that this was not because this construction is wrong but because, on the facts of that case, it was not in the interests of either party to rely on it.

[1116] *Interlego A.G. v Tyco International Inc* [1989] A.C. 217; [1988] R.P.C. 343 at 355–356.

[1117] *Interlego A.G. v Tyco International Inc* [1989] A.C. 217; [1988] R.P.C. 343 at 353–356, especially at 354. This construction of RDA 1949 s.1(3) (in its unamended form) has been much criticised—see *Fellner on Industrial Design Law* at paras 2.040–2.045.

of the whole article, even though the design is registered in respect of an article.[1118] In determining whether a design was dictated solely by function, it was not necessary to show that the design in question was the only design by which the article could have performed its function. The exclusion could have applied in any case where the relevant features of shape were brought about by, or were attributable only to the function of the article even if that same function could be performed by an article of a different shape.[1119]

Corresponding design—excluded designs. In addition to those designs which failed to meet the definition of "a design",[1120] certain other categories of design were expressly excluded from registration at the relevant time. Section 10(4) of the 1956 Act provided that, for the purposes of s.10(2) and (3), no account should be taken of articles (primarily literary or artistic in character) in respect of which the design in question was excluded from registration by rules made under s.1(4) of the Registered Designs Act 1949. Under the relevant rules (since repealed), designs for the following articles were excluded from registration[1121]:

    (1) works of sculpture other than casts or models used or intended to be used as models or patterns to be multiplied by any industrial process.

    (2) wall plaques and medals.

    (3) printed matter primarily of a literary or artistic character, including book jackets, calendars, certificates, coupons, dressmaking patterns, greetings cards, leaflets, maps, plans, postcards, stamps, trade advertisements, trade forms, and cards, transfers, and the like"

As the designs for such articles were excluded from registration, s.10 of the 1956 could not have applied to them, nor, therefore, can the modified version of s.52(2) of the 1988 Act.[1122]

13–355

Corresponding design—no requirement of novelty. The question also arises whether s.10 could have applied to a work where the design in question, whilst being a design as defined above and not being within a category of excluded designs, was not registrable because it failed to satisfy the registered design requirement of novelty.[1123] It is submitted that s.10 would have applied to such a work.[1124]

13–356

Applied industrially. For s.10 of the 1956 to have applied to an artistic work, a

13–357

[1118] See RDA 1949 s.1(1) (before its amendment by the 1988 Act) and s.1(2) after its amendment by that Act but before its amendment by the Registered Designs Regulations 2001.

[1119] See *Interlego A.G. v Tyco International Industries Inc* [1989] A.C. 217; [1988] R.P.C. 343 at 355 and *Amp Inc v Utilux Pty Ltd* [1972] R.P.C. 103 at 114–115, 118 and 122.

[1120] See paras 13–352 et seq., above.

[1121] See r.26 of Designs Rules 1949 (SI 1949/2368), subsequently replaced by, in turn the Designs Rules 1984 (SI 1984/1989), the Registered Designs Rules 1989 (SI 1989/1105) and the Registered Designs Rules 1995 (SI 1995/2912) (as amended SI 1999/3196). Rule 26 has now been repealed by the Registered Designs (Amendment) Rules 2001 (SI 2001/3950). Claims that the relevant design had been applied industrially but only in relation to articles that were excluded from registration (and therefore that s.10 of the 1956 Act did not apply) were rejected in *Jules Rimet Cup Ltd v Football Association* [2007] EWHC 2376; [2008] F.S.R. 10 (at para.22) and in *Lucas-film Ltd v Ainsworth* [2009] EWCA Civ.1328; [2010] F.S.R. 10 at para.99 confirming the decision at first instance [2008] EWHC 1878 (at paras 155–156). See also *Fearns v Anglo-Dutch Paint and Chemical Company Ltd* [2007] EWCA 955 and para.13–325, above.

[1122] For the modified version of CDPA 1988 s.52(2) see para.13–344, above.

[1123] See Registered Designs Act 1949 s.1(2) (in pre-1988 unamended form).

[1124] As has been seen, the authorities had established that the test for these purposes was whether there was a design "capable of registration" (see, for example, *Entec (Pollution Control) Ltd v Abacus Mouldings* [1992] F.S.R. 332 at 336). Although such words were not contained in s.10 itself, they had been used in Copyright Act 1911 s.22 in which context they were found to require only that the design in question possess the essential features of a "design" within the meaning of the Registered Designs Act 1949 s.1(3) and not to exclude designs which were denied protection for want of novelty or originality, see *Interlego A.G. v Tyco International Industries Inc* [1988] R.P.C. 343 at 361–364.

corresponding design had to have been applied industrially prior to August 1, 1989[1125] by or with the licence of the copyright owner. By rules made under s.10(5),[1126] a design would have been applied industrially where it was applied by any process to or was reproduced on or in, more than 50 articles not together constituting a single set, or in goods manufactured in lengths or pieces other than hand-made goods. These rules were similar to those which now apply in relation to s.52 of the 1988 Act and have been considered in that context.[1127] In brief, the word "industrially" merely suggested quantity rather than any particular method of production.

At first instance in *Lucasfilm Ltd v Ainsworth*[1128] it was held that the process of industrial application could have occurred anywhere in the world. Mann J. commented that, given that the purpose of s.10 of the 1956 Act (and now of s.52 of the 1988 Act) was to restrict copyright where there had been industrial exploitation of a copyright work, he could "detect no point of principle which would indicate that it should matter whether the articles were manufactured in the United Kingdom as opposed to elsewhere. Such a distinction would be arbitrary."[1129]

13–358   **Articles marketed in the UK or elsewhere.** Finally, for s.10 of the 1956 Act to have applied, articles to which the corresponding design had been applied[1130] had to have been sold, let for hire, or offered for sale or hire whether in the United Kingdom or elsewhere and prior to August 1, 1989. Under s.10(2) (as amended by the Design Copyright Act 1968),[1131] the relevant marketing of articles might have taken place anywhere. However, s.10(2) contemplates that the relevant articles have been made available to the public. It does not apply to the sale by a manufacturer, manufacturing to the copyright owner's design and instructions, for the purpose of sale to the owner.[1132]

(iii) Consequences of section 10 having applied

13–359   **Application of modified section 52(2).** If s.10 of the 1956 Act had applied at any time to an existing artistic work prior to August 1, 1989, then under the transitional provisions, s.52 of the 1988 Act applied to that work thereafter but with a period of 15 years (as defined in s.10(3) of the 1956 Act[1133]) instead of the period of 25 years that applies to new works.

Section 52(2), with the substitution of the appropriate words from s.10(3) of the 1956 Act, provides that:

> "After the end of the period of [15 years beginning with the date on which articles to which the design has been applied industrially were first sold, let for hire or offered for sale or hire in the United Kingdom or elsewhere[1134]], the work may be copied by making articles of any description, or doing anything for the purpose of making articles of any description, and anything may be done in relation to articles so made, without infringing copyright in the work".

13–360   **15-year period of full copyright protection.** Thus, where the modified version

---

[1125] i.e. before the Copyright Act 1956 was repealed.

[1126] Copyright (Industrial Designs) Rules 1957 (SI 1957/867) (see *Copinger* 12th edn, para.1742).

[1127] See para.13–324, above.

[1128] [2008] EWHC 1878 at paras 158–164, Mann J.

[1129] For the contrary view, see para.13–324, above.

[1130] i.e. applied industrially by or with the consent of the copyright owner—see above.

[1131] See para.13–357, above.

[1132] *Lucasfilm Ltd v Ainsworth* [2008] EWHC 1878; [2009] F.S.R. 2 at para.157.

[1133] CDPA 1988 Sch.1 para.20(1). See para.13–344, above.

[1134] The words in brackets are derived from Copyright Act 1956 ss.10(3) and 10(2).

of s.52(2) of the 1988 Act applied, it limited the period of full copyright protection for an existing work to the relevant 15-year period. As has already been noted, the substitution of the 15-year period was plainly intended to ensure that the works to which s.10 of the 1956 Act had previously applied continued to receive the same period of protection. It should also be noted that the 15-year period ran from the actual date of first marketing and not from the end of the calendar year in which the first marketing occurred[1135]—something which it was not always be easy for competitors to ascertain. As mentioned above, the very latest date on which this 15-year period could have expired in relation to existing works was July 31, 2004.[1136]

Permitted acts after the 15-year period. The 15-year period of protection has now expired for all works to which the modified version of s.52(2) applied. Accordingly, under s.52(2) any person may copy any such work by making articles of any description and do anything for the purpose of making articles of any description and do anything in relation to articles so made, without infringing copyright in such work. The nature of these permitted acts has already been considered in relation to the application of s.52(2) to new works.[1137] In essence, most acts of industrial copying of the work are permitted. In other respects, the copyright remains unaffected and may be enforced for the rest of its usual term.[1138]   **13–361**

Interrelation with section 51. The operation of the modified s.52(2) of the 1988 Act is neither dependent upon nor mutually exclusive with the operation of s.51 of that Act after the end of the ten-year period of postponement which applies in relation to s.51 under the transitional provisions of the 1988 Act.[1139]   **13–362**

(iv) Marketing of articles within paragraph 20(2)

If s.10 of the 1956 Act had not applied to an existing artistic work,[1140] then s.52 of the 1988 Act will not apply to that work unless articles are marketed as mentioned in s.52(1)(b) after commencement.[1141] At first sight, this appears to suggest that s.52 in its unmodified form will apply to any existing work (other than those to which s.10 of the 1956 Act applied) where relevant articles are marketed on or after August 1, 1989. However, if this were the case, an existing work which had been applied industrially before August 1, 1989 but to which s.10 had not applied[1142] would become subject to s.52 merely because its marketing continued after August 1, 1989. It is submitted that this is not the effect of para.20(2)[1143] and that para.20(2) only allows s.52 to operate in those cases where an existing work is first marketed within the meaning of s.52 after the commencement of the 1988   **13–363**

[1135] This contrasts with the position under the unmodified version of CDPA 1988 s.52(2) but is consistent with the position as it had been under Copyright Act 1956 s.10.

[1136] For Copyright Act 1956 s.10 to have applied to an existing work, the relevant act of first marketing must have occurred prior to August 1989. Thus, no existing work to which s.10 of the 1956 Act applied could retain full copyright protection after 15 years from that date.

[1137] See paras 13–329 et seq., above.

[1138] i.e. for the life of the author plus 70 years—see Ch.6, above.

[1139] See para.13–322, above.

[1140] As to which see paras 13–346 et seq., above.

[1141] CDPA 1988 Sch.1 para.20(2), see para.13–344, above.

[1142] Because, for example, its corresponding design had not been registrable.

[1143] In *Entec (Pollution Control) Ltd v Abacus Mouldings* [1992] F.S.R. 332, an existing work had been industrially applied prior to August 1, 1989 but Copyright Act 1956 s.10 (and, therefore, CDPA 1988 Sch.1 para.20(1)) had not applied because its corresponding design was unregistrable. It was not suggested that CDPA 1988 Sch.1 para.20(2) might apply if there was any further marketing of goods after that date. In any event, as 10 years have passed since the commencement of the CDPA 1988 s.51 would operate effectively to remove copyright protection from many works of industrial design, see para.13–340, above.

Act and, possibly, in those cases where the marketing of articles had commenced before that date but the requisite 50 articles required for s.10 of the 1956 Act to apply[1144] had not yet been made when the 1988 came into force. Where articles are so marketed, then s.52 will apply to the existing work just as it does to new works.[1145]

26. COPYRIGHT WORKS OF INDUSTRIAL APPLICATION CREATED BEFORE JUNE 1, 1957

A. INTRODUCTION

13–364   All works created before August 1, 1989 are referred to by the 1988 Act as existing works.[1146] This Part of this Chapter is concerned only with works of industrial application created before the Copyright Act 1956 Act came into force, i.e. before June 1, 1957.

B. SUBSISTENCE OF COPYRIGHT

(i) An additional provision as to subsistence

13–365   **Schedule 1 paragraph 6(1) of the transitional provisions.** In addition to the general provisions as to subsistence of copyright in existing works, the 1988 Act contains an additional provision which excludes copyright from certain works of industrial design created before June 1, 1957.[1147] Thus, para.6(1) of Sch.1 to the 1988 Act provides that:

> "Copyright shall not subsist by virtue of this Act in an artistic work made before 1st June 1957 which at the time when the work was made constituted a design capable of registration under the Registered Designs Act 1949 or under the enactments repealed by that Act, and was used, or intended to be used, as a model or pattern to be multiplied by an industrial process".[1148]

In summary, therefore, no copyright will subsist in a work created before June 1, 1957 if: (1) the work in question was an artistic work; and (2) the work, at the time that it was created, constituted a design capable of registration; and (3) at the time that the work was created, the design was used or was intended to be used, as a model or pattern to be multiplied by an industrial process. These criteria are considered below. As the relevant provisions of paras 6(1) and 6(2) are in substantially the same terms as their equivalents in the 1911 and 1956 Acts,[1149] they will, presumably, be construed in the same way.[1150]

(ii) Background to the additional provision

13–366   The need for this additional provision arose from similar provisions whereby the Copyright Acts of 1911 and 1956 had excluded copyright from such works cre-

---

[1144] See para.13–357, above.
[1145] See paras 13–329 et seq., above.
[1146] CDPA 1988 Sch.1 para.1(3).
[1147] CDPA 1988 Sch.1 para.6(1).
[1148] Sch.1 para.6(2) of the 1988 Act provides for when a design is to be deemed to have been used as a model or pattern to be multiplied by any industrial process.
[1149] See paras 13–366 et seq., below.
[1150] CDPA 1988 s.172.

ated before June 1, 1957. Thus, s.22 of the Copyright Act 1911[1151] had expressly excluded copyright from designs capable of being registered under the Patents and Designs Act 1907, except those which, though capable of being so registered, are not used or intended to be used as models or patterns to be multiplied by any industrial process.[1152] When the 1911 Act was repealed by the Copyright Act 1956, the 1956 Act[1153] provided that "[c]opyright shall not subsist by virtue of this Act in any artistic work made before the commencement of section 10[1154] which, at the time when the work was made, constituted a design capable of registration under the Registered Designs Act, 1949, or under the enactments repealed by the Act, and was used, or intended to be used, as a model or pattern to be multiplied by any industrial process".[1155] This provision thereby ensured that works from which the 1911 Act had excluded copyright did not acquire copyright under the 1956 Act,[1156] although the draftsman took the opportunity to bring the wording of the exclusion up to date by replacing the reference to the Patents and Designs Act 1907 with a reference to the 1949 Act or enactments repealed by that Act. It also removed the awkward double negative and the uncertainty as to the time at which the court should determine whether copyright was excluded, which had been features of s.22 of the 1911 Act.[1157]

(iii) Design capable of registration

For the additional provision to exclude copyright from a work, the relevant artistic work[1158] must constitute a design which, at the time that it was created, was capable of being registered under the Registered Designs Act 1949 or the Acts repealed by that Act. For these purposes, works fall into the following categories: (1) those created between 1950 and June 1, 1957; (2) those created between 1919 and before 1950; (3) those created between 1907 and before 1919 and, finally, (4) those created before 1907.   **13–367**

Work created between 1950 and 1957. In the case of a work created on or after January 1, 1950[1159] and before June 1, 1957, the question is whether that work constituted a design capable of registration under the Registered Designs Act 1949. The test for whether a design should be treated for these purposes as being capable of registration under the 1949 Act has already been considered in detail.[1160]   **13–368**

Work created between 1919 and 1950. In the case of works created between   **13–369**

1151 See para.13–14, above.
1152 Under s.22(2) of the 1911 Act, r.89 of the rules made under the Patents and Designs Act 1907 applied for the purpose of determining when a design was deemed to be used or intended to have been used for these purposes. Rule 89 was in substantially the same form as CDPA 1988 Sch.1 para.6(2), see para.13–372, below.
1153 Copyright Act 1956 Sch.7 para.8(2).
1154 Copyright Act 1956 s.10 was one of the means by which the 1956 Act sought to limit copyright protection for industrial designs. However it did not apply to works created before the 1956 Act came into force, see Sch., para.8(1) of that Act.
1155 Copyright Act 1956 Sch.7 para.8(3) again provided for rules by which a design was deemed to be used as a model or pattern to be multiplied by any industrial process.
1156 Such an express exclusion was required, as the 1956 Act permitted copyright to subsist in all original literary, dramatic, musical and artistic works including those created before June 1, 1957 (see ss.2(1), 3(2) and Sch.7 para.1 and *Interlego A.G. v Tyco International Inc* [1989] A.C. 217; [1988] R.P.C. 343 at 361).
1157 In this respect, Copyright Act 1956 Sch.7 para.8(2) effectively followed Copyright Act 1911 s.22 as construed in *King Features Syndicate v O. & M. Kleeman Ltd* [1941] A.C. 417 at 427, see *Interlego A.G. v Tyco International Industries Inc* [1988] R.P.C. 343 at 361. As regards *King Features*, see para.13–16, above.
1158 "Artistic work" would clearly bear its usual copyright meaning.
1159 The date on which the 1949 Act came into force—see s.49(2) of the 1949 Act.
1160 See paras 13–351 et seq., above.

1919 and before 1950, the relevant definition of a design capable of registration is that contained in s.93 of the Patents and Designs Act 1907 as amended by s.19 of the Patents and Designs Act 1919.[1161] This amended definition provided that:

> "Design means only the features of shape, configuration, pattern, or ornament applied to any article by any industrial process or means, whether manual, mechanical or chemical, separate or combined, which in the finished article appeal to and are judged solely by the eye; but which does not include any mode or principle of construction or anything which is in substance a mere mechanical device".

As the wording of the 1949 Act was derived from judicial pronouncements as to the meaning of s.19 of the 1919 Act, the test whether a design was a design capable of registration under the 1919 Act is the same as under the 1949 Act (before its amendment by the 1988 Act).[1162]

13–370   **Work created between 1907 and 1919.** In the case of a work created between 1907 and 1919, the question whether the design in question was registrable at the time that it was created is governed by the definition of a design contained in s.93 of the Patents and Designs Act 1907 as it was prior to its amendment by the Patents and Designs Act 1919.[1163] Section 93 of the 1907 Act (in its unamended form) provided that:

> "Design means any design ... applicable to any article, whether the design is applicable for the pattern, or for the shape or configuration, or for the ornament thereof, or for any two or more of such purposes, and by whatever means it is applicable, whether by printing, painting, embroidering, weaving, sewing, modelling, casting, embossing, engraving, staining, or any other means whatever, manual or mechanical, or chemical, separate or combined."

This definition[1164] does not expressly refer to any requirement of eye appeal nor does it expressly exclude functional designs. It has been stated[1165] that the wording of each of the 1919 and 1949 Acts was based on judicial decisions as to its predecessors. If so, the meaning of a design capable of registration under the 1907 Act would be substantially the same as that under the 1949 and 1919 Acts which have already been considered.[1166] However, it is by no means clear that this was the case.[1167] There were certainly cases decided prior to the 1907 Act in which no objection was taken to the registrability of the relevant design on the

---

[1161] It would appear that the amendment was effective from the date of the Act—December 23, 1919.

[1162] See *Amp Inc v Utilux Pty Ltd* [1972] R.P.C. 103 at 113–114 referring to *Kestos Ltd v Kempat Ltd* (1936) 53 R.P.C. 139 and *Tecalemot Ltd v Ewarts Ltd (No.2)* (1927) 44 R.P.C. 503. For the meaning of a design under the 1949 Act before its amendment, see paras 13–351 et seq., above

[1163] It has been suggested (see para.209 and para.20–08, respectively, of the 12th and 13th editions of this book) that *Pytram Ltd v Models (Leicester) Ltd* [1930] 1 Ch. 639 is authority for the proposition that the amended version of Patents and Designs Act 1907 s.93 applied to pre-amendment (i.e. pre-1919 works). It is submitted that this is not correct. In *Pytram*, Clauson J. had regard to the amended version of s.93 because he was concerned with a work created after 1919. There is nothing in his judgment (and in particular at p.646 of his judgment) to suggest that the unamended version of s.93 would not apply in the case of a work created between 1911 and 1919. The question was left open by Whitford J. in *Weir Pumps Ltd v CML Pumps Ltd* [1984] F.S.R. 33 at 37.

[1164] Described as "somewhat unhelpful" by Lord Oliver in *Interlego A.G. v Tyco International Inc* [1989] A.C. 217; [1988] R.P.C. 343 at 353.

[1165] See *Fellner on Industrial Design Law* at para.1.012.

[1166] See paras 13–368 and 13–369 respectively, above.

[1167] This claim was raised in argument in *British Leyland Motor Corporation v Armstrong Patents Co Ltd* [1986] A.C. 577; [1986] R.P.C. 279 but was expressly left open by Lord Bridge. The confusion appears to derive from the use of the words "eye appeal" in some of the earlier cases. However, such use appears to have been in the context that it was the eye that was appealed to in order to determine whether the allegedly infringing article was the same as or was an obvious imitation of the registered design—see *Amp Inc v Utilux Pty Ltd* [1972] R.P.C. 103 at 119–121.

grounds of their very obvious functionality,[1168] and there was nothing in the 1907 Act to suggest that that Act changed this.

Work created before 1907. It seems that the definition of a design contained in the 1907 Act will also govern whether a work created before the 1907 Act came into force should be treated as capable of registration for these purposes. Paragraph 6(1) of Sch.1 to the 1988 Act refers to those Acts repealed by the 1949 Act, i.e. only the 1907 and the 1919 Acts and not the earlier registered design acts which those Acts had replaced. In any event, the 1907 Act was intended to be a consolidating Act and it would seem, therefore, that the meaning of registrability before it was passed should have been largely the same as that under the 1907 Act itself.[1169]

13–371

(iv) Used or intended to be used as a model or pattern

Finally, for the additional provision to exclude the subsistence of copyright, it would have to be shown that, at the time that the work in question was made, the relevant design was either used or intended to be used as a model or pattern to be multiplied by an industrial process. Paragraph 6(2) of Sch.1 to the 1988 Act provides that:

13–372

"... a design shall be deemed to be used or intended to be used as a model or pattern to be multiplied by any industrial process—

(a) when the design is reproduced or is intended to be reproduced on more than 50 single articles, unless all the articles in which the design is reproduced or is intended to be reproduced together form only a single set of articles as defined in section 44(1) of the Registered Designs Act 1949, or

(b) when the design is to be applied to—

(i) printed paper hangings,

(ii) carpets, floor cloths or oil cloths, manufactured or sold in lengths or pieces,

(iii) textile piece goods, or textile goods manufactured or sold in lengths or pieces, or

(iv) lace, not made by hand".

As is clear from the wording of para.6(1), the design must be used or there must be an intention to make use of the design in the relevant way at the time that the relevant artistic work was created. In this respect, the 1988 Act (like the 1956 Act[1170]) has adopted the construction of s.22 of the 1911 Act applied by the House of Lords in *King Features Syndicate Inc v O & M Kleeman Ltd* .[1171]

C. PERMITTED ACTS

Section 51. Section 51 of the 1988 Act operates in the same way for any work created before August 1, 1989. Its application in relation to works created before

13–373

[1168] See *Leatheries Ltd v Lycett Saddle and Motor Accessories Co Ltd* (1909) 26 R.P.C. 166, where the design was of the base springs of a bicycle saddle; *Gillard v Worrall* (1905) 22 R.P.C. 76, where the design was of a gas jet for a baker's oven and *Werner Motors Ltd v A.W. Gamage Ltd* (1904) 21 R.P.C. 621, where the design was of a motorcycle frame. In none of these cases was any point taken as to the obvious functionality of the design. Instead, the main line of defence was a lack of novelty in the design or the denial of any act of infringement. In fact, in *Gillard*, Hall V.C. expressly ignored the utility of the design—see at para.79.

[1169] See, the comments of Lord Oliver in relation to the substantially identical Sch.7 para.8(2) of the 1956 Act in *Interlego A.G. v Tyco International Inc* [1989] A.C. 217; [1988] R.P.C. 343 at 359–363.

[1170] See para.13–366, above.

[1171] [1941] A.C. 417. See para.13–16, above.

June 1, 1957 will, therefore, be no different to its application to works created while the 1956 Act was in force, which has already been considered above.[1172]

13–374   **Section 52.** As has been seen,[1173] the application of s.52 to existing works is subject to the transitional provisions contained in para.20 of Sch.1 to the 1988 Act. However, the modified version of s.52 which may apply to 1956 Act works[1174] cannot apply to any work created before June 1, 1957.[1175] Thus, s.52 will only be of relevance to a work created before that date if para.20(2) applies to that work, i.e. if there has been relevant marketing of articles after the commencement of the 1988 Act. What constitutes marketing for these purposes has already been considered in relation to 1956 Act works.[1176] If s.52 applies in such a case, it applies in its unmodified form.[1177]

13–375   **Section 53.** Section 53 applies to permit certain acts occurring on or after August 1, 1989 to a work created whilst the 1911 Act was in force without any qualification.

[1172] i.e. those works created between June 1, 1957 and August 1, 1989—see paras 13–340 et seq., above.

[1173] See para.13–344, above.

[1174] Under CDPA 1988 para.20(1) s.52 applied with a modified (shorter) 15-year period in those cases where s.10 of the 1956 Act had applied to the work in question at any time prior to commencement of the 1988 Act—see paras 13–344 et seq., above.

[1175] Copyright Act 1956 s.10 did not apply to any work created before that Act came into force—see para.8(1) of Sch.7—thus, CDPA 1988 Sch.1 para.20(1) and its modified version of s.52 cannot apply to such a work.

[1176] See para.13–363, above.

[1177] i.e. with its usual 25-year period rather than the modified 15-year period which applies where para.20(1) operates.

PART V

MISCELLANEOUS RIGHTS

CHAPTER FOURTEEN

SEMICONDUCTOR TOPOGRAPHIES

1. INTRODUCTION

Background. Many modern goods, such as computers, televisions, aircraft engines, medical equipment and machine tools contain electronic integrated circuits, usually called "chips". Such chips are physically tiny yet may contain many hundreds of thousands of electronic components (e.g. transistors) and connections. Their appearance, when viewed from above under a microscope, may be likened to a complex city street plan. Most chips contain broadly similar components and operate in broadly similar ways. However, the designer of a chip must plan the layout (or topography) of its various components and connections in a way which not only allows it to perform its particular intended function efficiently but which also minimises its size and allows for ease of manufacture; a process which may involve considerable skill and investment. This Chapter is concerned with the protection of such designs.   **14–01**

A chip consists of a sandwich of materials including semiconducting material (usually called a "wafer"),[1] insulating material[2] and conductive material.[3] The chip is formed by coating the wafer of semiconductor material with an insulator. The desired layout of the components for the chip is then imparted by a process of etching through the insulator into the semiconductor material and by depositing other materials into the holes thus created so as to form the relevant components.[4] The pattern for this process of etching and depositing is determined by using a mask or a series of masks which record the desired design layout of the components.[5] The connections between these components are provided by the addition of conductive material and the layout of these connections is determined by another mask or series of masks.   **14–02**

---

[1] For example, silicon, germanium or gallium arsenide. A semiconducting material, as its name suggests, is a material whose ability to conduct electricity falls somewhere between that of a conductor such as metal on the one hand and that of an insulator on the other.

[2] e.g. silicon dioxide.

[3] e.g. aluminium.

[4] These other materials (often called "dopants") change the electrical conductivity of the part of the semiconductor wafer to which they are applied and thereby create the desired components (e.g. the transistors).

[5] The design of the overall layout is three-dimensional but has to be broken down into its individual separate layers. A separate mask (i.e. a template) is made (usually photographically) record-

14–03   **Summary of protection.** The Copyright Act 1956 made no special provision for the protection of chips. Instead, protection depended upon whether the design was recorded in something characterised as an artistic work, i.e. a design drawing or mask[6] recording the layout. However, in 1987, the Council of the European Communities issued a Directive[7] requiring all Member States to provide protection for the designs for semiconductor products in accordance with the terms of the Directive.[8] The United Kingdom initially sought to implement this Directive through the Semiconductor Products (Protection of Topography) Regulations 1987[9] which came into force on November 7, 1987[10] and which introduced something called a "topography right". However, the 1987 Regulations were revoked by the Design Right (Semiconductor Topographies) Regulations 1989[11] which came into force on August 1, 1989.[12] The 1989 Regulations provide that the design right provisions in Pt III of the 1988 Act have effect, with certain important modifications, in relation to a design which is a semiconductor topography.[13] The modifications were required because the provisions of Pt III are in some respects different to the terms of the Council Directive[14] and of later Council Decisions.[15]

2. PROTECTION OF SEMICONDUCTOR TOPOGRAPHIES

14–04   If a design is a semiconductor topography then, under the Design Right (Semiconductor Topographies) Regulations 1989,[16] the design right provisions contained in Pt III of the 1988 Act apply subject to the modifications made by regs 4 to 9 of the Regulations. The provisions of Pt III have already been considered in the design right chapter of this work. This present chapter is concerned only with issues which specifically concern semiconductor topographies and, in particular, with the modifications made to Pt III by the 1989 Regulations.

A. A DESIGN WHICH IS A SEMICONDUCTOR TOPOGRAPHY

14–05   **A design.** For the 1989 Regulations to apply, there must be a design which is a semiconductor topography. This means[17]:

"... a design within the meaning of section 213(2) of the Act which is a design of either of the following:

---

ing each layer of the design. The more complicated the chip, the greater the number of layers and, therefore, of masks is likely to be.

[6] Which is usually a photograph.

[7] Council Directive 87/54/EEC [1987] OJ L24/36. See Vol.2 H1.

[8] The need to provide for such protection arose from the fact that the United States' Semiconductor Chip Protection Act 1984 s.902 contains reciprocity provisions whereby works of semiconductor topography from other countries were only given protection in the US if those other countries provided equivalent protection for US works.

[9] SI 1987/1497.

[10] SI 1987/1497 reg.1.

[11] SI 1989/1100; see Vol.2 B9.i. As the 1989 Regulations and the 1987 Regulations (SI 1987/1497) were both intended to implement the Semiconductor Directive, the nature of their protection is, broadly speaking, the same. There are, however, slight differences in relation to, for example, the qualification provisions contained in reg.3 of the 1987 Regulations and reg.4 of the 1989 Regulations.

[12] SI 1989/1100 reg.1. For the position in relation to topographies created before this date, see paras 14–23 and 14–24, below.

[13] SI 1989/1100 reg.3.

[14] SI 1989/1100.

[15] Council Decisions 87/532/EEC [1987] OJ 313/22 and 88/311/EEC [1988] OJ 140/13.

[16] SI 1989/100 reg.3.

[17] SI 1989/1100 reg.2(1).

(a) the pattern fixed, or intended to be fixed, in or upon—

    (i) a layer of semiconductor product, or

    (ii) a layer of material in the course of and for the purpose of the manufacture of a semiconductor product, or

(b) the arrangement of the patterns fixed, or intended to be fixed, in or upon the layers of a semiconductor product in relation to one another".

For these purposes, a semiconductor product is an article the purpose, or one of the purposes of which, is the performance of an electronic function and which consists of two or more layers, at least one of which is composed of a semiconducting material and in or upon one or more of which is fixed a pattern appertaining to that or another function.[18]

Whether a design is a design within s.213(2) is considered in the design right chapter of this work.[19] A design which is a semiconductor topography is clearly a design of the shape or configuration of an article (i.e. of a semiconductor product). Under Pt III, the design relied upon may be of any aspect of the whole or part of that product.

Excluded designs. Although s.213(3) of the 1988 Act applies to a design which is a semiconductor topography as to any other design, the so-called "must match" and surface decoration exclusions are unlikely to be of any significance in relation to a design for a semiconductor topography.[20]   **14–06**

B. Subsistence of Design Right

Originality. To qualify for design right, a design which is a semiconductor topography must, like any other design, be original and not be commonplace in the design field in question at the time of its creation.[21] The meaning of these requirements has already been considered in relation to design right generally.[22] In this context, the relevant design field is that of the semiconductor industry generally.[23]   **14–07**

Qualification for design right. As has been seen,[24] design right only subsists if the relevant design qualifies for protection. Qualification may be by reference to the designer or the person by whom he was commissioned or employed. It may also be by reference to the person by whom and the country in which articles made to the design were first marketed. Finally, a design may qualify in accordance with any Order made under s.221 of the 1988 Act. These provisions as to qualification are considered in the design right chapter of this work. However, in the case of semiconductor topographies, they are subject to various modifications.   **14–08**

Qualifying person. The first modification is in the definition of a "qualifying person". With effect from August 1, 2006, the definition of a "qualifying person"   **14–09**

---

[18] reg.2(1).

[19] See paras 13–45 et seq., above.

[20] For a full discussion of the exclusions contained in CDPA 1988 s.213(3), see paras 13–54 et seq., above.

[21] CDPA 1988 ss.213(1) and 213(4).

[22] See paras 13–73 et seq., above.

[23] Council Directive 87/54/EEC art.2(2) expressly stated that the design must not be commonplace in the semiconductor industry. The 1987 Regulations (SI 1987/1497) reg.3(3) stated that a design was not original if it was commonplace among creators of topographies or manufacturers of semiconductor products.

[24] See paras 13–85 et seq., above.

is the same as for design right except that the definition of "qualifying country" is different (see below).[25]

Accordingly, since August 1, 2006 under s.217 as modified, the following are qualifying persons in relation to semiconductor topographies:

(a) a qualifying individual, meaning a citizen or subject of or an individual habitually resident in a qualifying country: CDPA 1988 s.217(1)[26];

(b) a body corporate or other body having legal personality which (i) is formed under the law of a part of the United Kingdom or of another qualifying country and (ii) has in any qualifying country a place of business at which substantial business activity is carried on: CDPA 1988 s.217(1)[27];

(c) the Crown and the government of any other qualifying country: CDPA 1988 s.217(2).

The term "qualifying country" now means the United Kingdom, another Member State of the European Community, the Isle of Man, Gibraltar, the Channel Islands, any colony and any country listed in the Schedule to the 1989 Regulations as modified.[28] The object of the changes made with effect from August 1, 2006 was to give effect to the Council Decision of December 22, 1994 on the extension of the legal protection of topographies of semiconductor products to persons from a member of the World Trade Organization.[29] Accordingly, the Schedule to the 1989 Regulations has been substituted by a list of parties to the Agreement establishing the World Trade Organisation (other than Member States who are already within the definition of "qualifying country").

The position for semiconductor topographies created before August 1, 2006 is not entirely clear. It is possible that the provisions set out above apply and that semiconductor topographies that meet the new criteria for qualification but did not meet the old qualification criteria will acquire protection.[30] However, it seems equally arguable that the old criteria should continue to govern subsistence for such topographies.[31] Under the old criteria, the following were qualifying persons under s.217(1) as modified by the 1989 Regulations:[32]

(a) A qualifying individual, meaning a citizen or subject of or an individual habitually resident in a qualifying country. For these purposes, "a qualifying country" included only the United Kingdom[33] or another Member State of the European Economic Community.[34]

(b) A body corporate or other body having legal personality which had in any qualifying country or in Gibraltar a place of business at which substantial

---

[25] See the amendments to the Design Right (Semiconductor Topographies) Regulations 1989 (SI 1989/1100) effected by the Design Right (Semiconductor Topographies) (Amendment) Regulations 2006 (SI 2006/1833) which came into force on August 1, 2006.

[26] For the term "qualifying country", see below. For the terms "citizen or subject of" and "habitually resident", see para.13–100, above.

[27] For the term "qualifying country", see below. For the other terms in this definition, see para.13–101, above.

[28] See the modifications made by SI 2006/1833 and SI 2008/1434.

[29] See 94/824/EC; [1994] OJ L 349/210

[30] In this regard it is noted that the "savings" provisions in Statutory Instruments such as the Copyright and Performances (Application to Other Countries) Order 2008 (SI 2008/677) art.7 assume that existing works can acquire protection as a result of such changes in qualifications provisions.

[31] See for example, ss.16(1)(b) and 23(1) of the Interpretation Act 1978 which provide that a repeal would not "affect the previous operation of the enactment repealed or anything duly done or suffered under that enactment".

[32] SI 1989/1100 reg.4(2).

[33] The reference to a person being a citizen of the UK is to be construed as a reference to that person being a British citizen; see CDPA 1988 s.217(4) as modified by SI 1989/1100 reg.4(2).

[34] CDPA 1988 s.217(3), as modified by SI 1989/1100 reg.4(2). Thus, for the purposes of semiconductor topography, a country will not be a qualifying country merely because it has been the subject of an Order under CDPA 1988 s.255 or 256.

business activity was carried on.[35] As noted in (a) above, the definition of a "qualifying country" was somewhat narrower than for design right cases.

(c) A person who fell within one of the additional classes set out in Pt I of the Schedule to the 1989 Regulations.[36] These classes included (1) British Dependent Territory Citizens; (2) citizens and subjects of any country specified in Pt II of the Regulations[37]; (3) habitual residents of any country specified in Pt II of the Regulations[38] or the Isle of Man, the Channel Islands or any colony; and (4) firms and bodies corporate formed under the law of, or any part of, the United Kingdom, Gibraltar, another Member State of the European Economic Community of any country specified in Pt II of the Regulations[39] with a place of business within any country so specified at which substantial business activity is carried on.[40]

Semiconductor topographies created under a commission or during employment. The second modification to the qualification provisions is where a semiconductor topography is created in pursuance of a commission or in the course of employment. In such a case, s.215 is modified[41] to allow for an agreement in writing to override the normal rule whereby the commissioner or the employer is automatically the first owner of design right. If, as a result of such an agreement, it is the designer who is the first owner of design right in a semiconductor topography, then s.217(3) as modified[42] provides that the relevant topography cannot qualify by reference to the commissioner or employer and, that the provisions governing qualification by reference to its designer[43] will apply as if the topography had not been created in pursuance of a commission or in the course of employment.

14–10

First marketing. The next modification is to s.220. As has been seen, where a design does not qualify by reference to the designer, commissioner or employer, it may nevertheless qualify by reference to the first marketing of articles made to the design.[44] In its unmodified form, s.220(1) requires: (a) that such first marketing be by a qualifying person who is exclusively authorised to put such articles on the market in the United Kingdom and (b) that such first marketing takes place in the United Kingdom, or in a country to which the 1988 Act extends by Order made under s.255, or in another Member State of the European Economic Community. In the case of semiconductor topographies, these requirements are modified so that (a) the qualifying person must be exclusively authorised to put such articles on the market in every Member State of the European Economic Community and (b) the first marketing must take place within the territory of any Member State.[45] Further, the definition of "exclusively authorised" as modified[46] refers only to "exclusivity capable of being enforced by legal proceedings" rather

14–11

---

[35] In determining whether substantial business activity is carried on at a place of business in any country, no account is taken of dealings in goods which are at all material times outside that country; CDPA 1988 s.217(5), as modified by SI 1989/1100 reg.4(2).

[36] As amended by the Design Right (Semiconductor Topographies) (Amendment) Regulations 1993 (SI 1993/ 2497). For earlier amendments, see SI 1989/2147, SI 1990/1003, SI 1991/2237 and SI 1992/400.

[37] i.e. Australia, Austria, Finland, French overseas territories, Iceland, Japan, Liechtenstein, Norway, Sweden, Switzerland, and the USA. See Vol.2 B9i of the previous edition of this work.

[38] See the countries listed above.

[39] See the countries listed above.

[40] See para.14–09(b), above.

[41] SI 1989/1100 reg.5. See also para.14–13, below.

[42] SI 1989/1100 reg.4(3).

[43] i.e. CDPA 1988 s.218(2) to (4).

[44] See paras 13–95 et seq., above.

[45] See CDPA 1988 s.220(1) as modified by SI 1989/1100 reg.4(4).

than to "exclusivity capable of being enforced by legal proceedings in the United Kingdom".

14–12   **Meaning of marketing.** The definition of marketing has already been considered.[47] However, in the case of semiconductor topographies, the Regulations also provide that, in determining whether there has been any marketing (or whether anything has been made available for sale of hire), no account shall be taken of any sale or hire, or any offer or exposure for sale or hire, which is subject to an obligation of confidence in respect of information about the topography in question. There are, however, two exceptions to this; namely, (a) where the article or topography sold or hired or offered or exposed for sale or hire has been sold or hired on a previous occasion (whether or not subject to an obligation of confidence), or (b) where the obligation is imposed at the behest of the Crown, or of the Government of any country outside the United Kingdom, for the protection of security in connection with the production of arms, munitions or war material.[48]

C. Ownership

14–13   **The first owner of design right is defined by s.215 of the 1988 Act.** As has already been seen, where a topography is created pursuant to a commission or in the course of employment, s.215 is modified by the 1989 Regulations[49] so as to allow for an agreement in writing to override the normal rule whereby the commissioner or the employer is automatically the first owner of design right. The agreement may provide for any other person to be the first owner.

D. Duration

14–14   Section 216 of the 1988 Act is modified by the 1989 Regulations so that the rules concerning the duration of design right in a semiconductor topography are somewhat different to those for other design rights.[50] Thus, the expiry of design right in a semiconductor topography is either: (a) 10 years from the end of the calendar year in which the topography or articles made to the topography were first made available for sale or hire anywhere in the world by or with the licence of the design right owner[51]; or (b) if neither the topography nor articles made to it are made available as mentioned above within a period of 15 years commencing with the earlier of the time when the topography was first recorded in a design document or the time when an article was first made to the topography, at the end of that 15-year period.

14–15   Thus, the period of protection for a semiconductor topography may be considerably longer than that for other designs. As has been seen, the normal position is that protection is subject to a maximum period of 15 years.[52] It would seem that, for semiconductor topographies, the maximum period of protection may be up to 25 years in a case where the topography or articles made to it were first marketed just before the end of the 10-year period.

---

[46] CDPA 1988 s.220(4) as modified by SI 1989/1100 reg.4(4).

[47] See para.13–96, above.

[48] SI 1989/1100 reg.7. This provision is included to give effect to the requirements of the Council Directive, 87/54/EEC art.1(c).

[49] SI 1989/1100 reg.5.

[50] This modification presumably being so as to comply with the requirements of Council Directive 87/54/EEC arts 7(3) and (4).

[51] In determining whether there has been any relevant sale or hire for these purposes, the 1989 Regulations provide that no account shall be taken of certain sales or hire which are subject to an obligation of confidence, see para.14–12, above.

[52] See para.13–104, above.

E. INFRINGEMENT

One of the most important areas of difference between the provisions for semiconductor topographies and those for other designs lies in what does and does not constitute an infringement of design right.   **14–16**

Primary infringement: private non-commercial acts and acts of analysis and evaluation. To be liable for primary infringement of design right, a person must have reproduced the relevant design by (a) making articles to that design or (b) making a design document recording that design for the purpose of enabling such articles to be made. In normal design right cases, such acts will only infringe design right if done "for commercial purposes".[53] There is no such requirement for semiconductor topographies.[54] However, s.226(1A) as added by the 1989 Regulations[55] provides for two situations where such acts will not infringe design right. The first is where the reproduction of the topography was done privately for non-commercial aims.[56] The second is where the reproduction of the topography is for the purpose of analysing or evaluating the design or analysing, evaluating or teaching the concepts, processes, systems or techniques embodied in it. This ties in with the reverse engineering provisions contained in reg.8(4) of the 1989 Regulations which are discussed below.   **14–17**

Primary infringement: reverse engineering. Probably the most significant difference between the treatment of semiconductor topographies and the treatment of other designs is that the 1989 Regulations expressly provide that it is not an infringement of design right in a semiconductor topography (a) to create another original semiconductor topography as a result of an analysis or evaluation of the first topography or of the concepts, processes, systems or techniques embodied in it or (b) to reproduce that other topography.[57] Thus, a person may obtain another's semiconductor product embodying a semiconductor topography in which design right subsists. He may analyse it (in effect decompile it) to determine its design layout (and, as appears from the preceding paragraph, may even copy the topography for this purpose). He may then use the concepts, processes, systems and techniques embodied in that layout in creating his own original topography which he can then use in the manufacture of chips. The aim of this provision appears to be to ensure that the copying of ideas embodied in another's topography is permitted but that the copying of the topography itself is not[58] and reg.8(4) expressly provides that the topography which a person creates as a result of this process of reverse engineering must itself be original.   **14–18**

Infringements in relation to the whole or a substantial part of a design. The test for infringement of design right is considered in detail in the design right chapter of this work. However, the Regulations also provide that anything which would be an infringement of design right in a topography if done to a topography   **14–19**

---

[53] i.e. with a view to the relevant article being sold or hired in the course of a business; CDPA 1988 s.263(3). See para.13–147, above.

[54] CDPA 1988 s.226(1) as substituted by SI 1989/1100 reg.8(1).

[55] SI 1989/1100 reg.8(1). The wording of reg.8(1) follows that of Council Directive 87/54/EEC arts 5(2) and 5(3).

[56] i.e. this is more favourable to the owners of topography design right than the normal design right requirement that the reproduction be for commercial purposes (as to which see para.13–147, above).

[57] SI 1989/1100 reg.8(4) following Council Directive 87/54/EEC art.5(4).

[58] This is consistent with Council Directive 87/54/EEC art.8, which states that "The protection granted to the topographies of semiconductor products . . . . shall not extend to any concept, process, system technique or encoded information embodied in the topography other than the topography itself".

as a whole is an infringement of the design right in the topography if done to a significant part of the topography. It would seem, therefore, that in order to prove infringement of design right in a semiconductor topography, one may either show that the allegedly infringing topography is made exactly or substantially to the topography replied upon or that it is made exactly or substantially to a substantial part of that topography.[59]

14–20   Secondary infringement: general. Acts of secondary infringements are defined by s.227 of the 1988 Act. They comprise certain dealings with articles which the infringer knows or has reason to believe are infringing articles. The general nature of secondary infringement and the meaning of an "infringing article" have already been considered in the main design right chapter of this work.[60] For present purposes, however, it should be noted that the changes in the definition of primary infringement referred to above will affect whether or not the making of a particular article was an infringement and, therefore, whether that article is an infringing article for the purposes of s.237. Further, the 1989 Regulations alter the definition of an "infringing article" for the purposes of semiconductor topographies so that it may include a design document.[61] Thus, a mask recording the design of a part of the topography would, it is submitted, be a design document and (assuming its making was an infringement) dealings with it may constitute secondary infringements.

14–21   Secondary infringement: previous sale or hire. The 1989 Regulations also provide that s.227 does not apply (i.e. there is no act of secondary infringement) if the article in question has previously been sold or hired within (a) the United Kingdom by or with the licence of the owner of the design right in the topography in question, or within (b) the territory of any other Member State of the European Economic Community or of Gibraltar by or with the consent of the person for the time being entitled to import it into or sell or hire it within that territory.[62]

F. LICENCES OF RIGHT

14–22   Licences of right. The 1989 Regulations provide that s.237 of the 1988 Act does not apply in the case of a semiconductor topography.[63] Thus, licences of right are not available automatically in the last five years of the term of design right in a semiconductor topography.[64] The Regulations do not, however, exclude the possibility of licences of right arising under s.238.[65]

---

[59] SI 1989/1100 reg.8(5). This, it seems, brings the test for infringement for semiconductor topographies closer to the test for infringement of copyright. In other design right cases, the making of an article infringes design right in a design if that article has been made exactly or substantially to the design whereas in copyright cases, the making of a thing infringes copyright in a work if the thing in question reproduces the copyright work or a substantial part thereof. It may be, therefore, that a claimant in semiconductor topography does not face the sort of difficulties in framing his case which face claimants in other design right cases. See, generally, paras 13–148, 13–152 and 13–154, above.

[60] See paras 13–160 et seq., above.

[61] SI 1989/1100 reg.8(3) provides that CDPA 1988 s.228(6) (which provides that, in the case of other designs, the expression "infringing articles" does not include design documents) does not apply to semiconductor topographies.

[62] SI 1989/1100 reg.8(2).

[63] SI 1989/1100 reg.9.

[64] In this, the 1989 Regulations follow the requirements of Council Directive 87/54/EEC art.6, which provides that the exclusive rights protecting semiconductor topographies should not be subject to the grant of automatic licences for the sole reason that a certain period of time had elapsed.

[65] For a full discussion of licences of right (including those arising under CDPA 1988 s.238), see paras 13–126 et seq., above.

G. TRANSITIONAL PROVISIONS

Semiconductor topographies created before November 7, 1987. As mentioned above, prior to November 7, 1987,[66] the protection of semiconductor topographies was a matter (if at all) for copyright law. The application of copyright to works existing at the commencement of the 1988 Act is governed by the transitional provisions of that Act and is considered in the copyright section of this work. Under those transitional provisions, the application of s.51 to existing works was postponed until August 1, 1999.[67] In the case of copyright in topographies created before November 7, 1987, the 1989 Regulations do nothing to alter this[68]; such topographies retained full copyright protection until August 1, 1999.[69] However the 1989 Regulations did modify para.19(2) of those transitional provisions so that no licences of right were available under s.237 of the 1988 Act in respect of such topographies although they may have been under s.238.[70]

14–23

Semiconductor topographies created on or after November 7, 1987 and before August 1, 1989. Some difficulty arises in relation to semiconductor topographies created on or after November 7, 1987 but before August 1, 1989, i.e. whilst the 1987 Regulations were in force. Although copyright may still subsist in artistic works recording such topographies, this will provide little protection because in respect of such topographies s.51 of the 1988 Act operated with no period of postponement.[71] Further, as the 1987 Regulations were unequivocally revoked by the 1989 Regulations, it seems clear that the 1987 Regulations also provide no protection in respect of events occurring after their revocation. Finally, it may be argued that the 1989 Regulations themselves provide no protection. This would seem to follow from the fact that, under the 1989 Regulations, protection for topographies is merely a modified form of the design right protection available under Pt III of the 1988 Act and from the fact that, under s.213(7) of Pt III, there is no design right in a design created before commencement.[72] Notwithstanding this, it is submitted that the 1989 Regulations should be construed as having conferred design right protection on topographies created between November 7, 1987 and July 31, 1989. The 1989 Regulations were plainly not intended to remove protection from all topographies created before commencement, otherwise they would also have removed copyright protection from those created before November 7, 1987. Further, there is no logical reason why protection should have been excluded only for those topographies which were created between November 7, 1987 and July 31, 1989, particularly given that such an exclusion would place the United Kingdom in breach of its obligation to comply with the EEC Council Directive.[73] The clear intention to exclude copyright protection suggests that protection was intended to be available under either the 1987 or the 1989 Regulations. As the 1987 Regulations are

14–24

---

[66] i.e. the commencement date of the Semiconductor (Protection of Topography) Regulations 1987 (SI 1987/1497). See para.14–03, above.

[67] CDPA 1988 Sch.1 para.19(1).

[68] This contrasts with the position in relation to topographies created between November 7, 1987 and August 1, 1989 as to which see para.14–24, below.

[69] Since that date it has not been an infringement of the copyright in the relevant work to make an article to the design nor to copy an article made to the design. See para.13–340, above.

[70] SI 1989/1100 reg.10(3).

[71] See SI 1989/1100 reg.10(2), which provided that para.19(1) of the transitional provisions of the 1988 Act (Sch.1) did not apply to topographies created between November 7, 1987 and July 31, 1989. Thus, since August 1, 1989, it has not been an infringement of the copyright in the relevant work to make an article to the design or to copy an article made to the design. This contrasts with the position in relation to works recording topographies created before November 7, 1987; see para.14–23, above.

[72] CDPA 1988 s.213(7).

[73] 87/54/EEC. See Vol.2 H1.

expressly revoked without any savings, it is submitted that the 1989 Regulations must have been intended to apply.

Given the duration provisions,[74] a semiconductor topography created in this period cannot retain its protection beyond August 1, 2014 and many will, depending on their date of first marketing, have lost their protection before that date.

---

[74] See paras 14–14 and 14–15 above.

CHAPTER FIFTEEN

CIRCUMVENTION OF PROTECTION MEASURES AND RIGHTS MANAGEMENT INFORMATION

Contents

1. INTRODUCTION

Protection measures. The first part of this chapter is concerned with remedies against the circumvention of "protection measures", a term which derives from the 1988 Act as amended to give effect to the Information Society Directive. In very general terms, a protection measure is a device or technological measure which is applied to a copyright work and which prevents or restricts acts which are not authorised by the owner of the copyright. In the 1988 Act, the term is also applied to the subject matter of rights in performances, publication right and database right. At the time of writing, the technology is in a state of development. However, it may be said that in very general terms, such devices tend to fall into one of two categories. The first is "access control", where access to the work is controlled, usually by encrypting it. The second is "copy control", where the extent or nature of copying of the work is controlled, for example by a "copy management system" like those embodied in eBook readers.[1] Protection measures have been applied in many fields, but mainly where copies are issued to the public in digital form, such as computer games, electronic books, recorded music and DVD films. Such measures are frequently circumvented, often by the application of computer programs which are distributed on the internet.[2] Accordingly, it has been considered necessary to provide specific legislative protection for them. The second, third and fourth parts of this chapter deal with that protection. The law relating to unauthorised decoders is dealt with elsewhere.[3]

15–01

Rights management information. The fifth part of this chapter deals with the related topic of rights management information. Works that appear in digital form are at particular risk of being altered, mutilated, misappropriated, copied or

15–02

---

[1] See para.26–80, below.

[2] For accounts of the technology and attempts to circumvent it, see Koempel, "Digital Rights Management" [2005] C.T.L.R. 239; Akester, "Digital Rights Management in the 21st Century" [2006] 3 E.I.P.R. 159; Stromdale, "The Problems with DRM" [2006] 1 Ent. L.R. 1; Stromdale, "Public and Private Sectors Focus on DRM and Copy Protection" [2006] 3 Ent. L.R. 101; and Fox, "Another Nail in the Coffin for Copy-protection Technologies? Sony BMG's XCP and MediaMax Debacle" [2006] 7 Ent. L.R. 214.

[3] See Ch.16, below.

otherwise distributed without the consent of the rights holder. To combat such activities, rights holders have developed "rights management information". Such information, which is often contained in an electronic "watermark" embedded in the protected material, may identify the content of the work and the author and owner of the rights and may also set out the terms and conditions associated with the use of the work (e.g. details of any licence which has already been granted or the conditions under which licences may be obtained). The availability of such information obviously benefits rights holders. It also enables users to have confidence in the authenticity of the material and to be clear as to the terms and conditions under which it may be used. As is the case with any technological measure, rights management information is vulnerable to manipulation or removal (e.g. by so-called "watermark washing") by infringers who may go on to distribute copies of the protected material which no longer have any or any accurate rights-management information attached to them.

2. PROTECTION MEASURES: HISTORY OF PROTECTION

15–03   **Background to the 1988 Act.** At the time when the Bill which became the 1988 Act was being debated, there were growing concerns about the potential for piracy of audio and video recordings which had been created by the introduction of the new digital technology. Particular anxiety was expressed about the fact that the reproduction of a digital recording, in contrast to reproduction of an analogue recording, does not result in any deterioration in quality. Possible solutions to the problem of private copying or "home taping" of analogue and digital sound recordings and audiovisual material, including the introduction of a levy payable on the sale of blank recording tape and the use of spoiler or copy protection systems, were also under discussion. Although the film and recording industries, as well as software manufacturers, had by that time succeeded in developing devices which could be built into their recordings to prevent or limit copying or at least to spoil the quality of copies made,[4] it was feared (correctly as it turned out) that pirates would be equally ingenious in creating other devices to circumvent such devices. At the same time, considerable concern was expressed by the computer industry about the growth of software packages which had the effect of by-passing the copy protection embodied in computer programmes.[5] In response to these concerns, limited rights and remedies in relation to such "circumvention devices" were introduced in s.296 of the 1988 Act. Those remedies extended to various acts of making and dealing with such devices, but did not apply to their possession. They were limited to cases where copies of the work in question were issued to the public in electronic form. No rights or remedies were introduced in respect of the act of circumvention itself.

15–04   **The Software Directive and the 1992 amendment.** On May 14, 1991 the Council of the European Communities adopted a Directive on the legal protection of computer programs ("the Software Directive").[6] This Directive required Member States to provide appropriate remedies against any act of putting into circulation or possessing for commercial purposes "any means the sole intended purpose of which is to facilitate the unauthorised removal or circumvention of

---

[4] Examples cited in Standing Committee E included the provision on digital tapes of a second inaudible signal which was of such high frequency that special equipment was needed to copy it; and the provision of encoding on video recordings: *Hansard*, HC, cols 733–734 (June 21, 1988) (S.C.E.).

[5] *Hansard*, HC, cols 733–734 (June 21, 1988) (S.C.E.).

[6] [1991] OJ L122/42. See Vol.2 H14.

any technical device which may have been applied to protect a computer program".[7] In order to give effect to the Directive, s.296 was extended to cover the possession in the course of a business of a device which was designed or adapted to circumvent copy protection which had been applied to copies of a computer program.[8] That version of s.296 is considered in the 14th edition of this work.[9]

The WIPO Copyright Treaty and the WIPO Performances and Phonograms Treaty. In the meantime, digital technology had provided the impetus for an explosion in the use of copy protection devices. The need to provide protection for such devices was recognised at an international level with the inclusion of provisions to that effect in the WIPO Copyright Treaty (WCT) and the WIPO Performances and Phonograms Treaty (WPPT), both adopted in December 1996.[10] Thus, art.11 WCT and art.18 WPPT oblige Contracting Parties to provide adequate legal protection and effective legal remedies against the circumvention of effective technological measures used by rights owners in connection with the exercise of their rights and that restrict acts, in respect of their works, performances or phonograms, respectively, which are not authorised by the respective right owner or permitted by law. These provisions are expressed in broad terms and leave considerable scope to individual states in deciding how they are to be implemented.[11]

15–05

The Information Society Directive. On January 21, 1998, the European Commission submitted a proposal for a Directive on the harmonisation of certain aspects of copyright and related rights.[12] The proposal contained detailed provision for the protection of "effective technological measures". "Technological measures" were defined as "any device, product or component incorporated into a process, device or product designed to prevent or inhibit the infringement of any" copyright, related rights or database right.[13] Such measures were only deemed to be effective where "the work or other subject matter is rendered accessible to the user only through application of an access code or process, including by decryption, descrambling or other transformation of the work or other subject matter, with the authority of the rightholders".[14] On May 22, 2001, such a Directive was adopted ("the Information Society Directive").[15] Detailed provisions in relation to "technological measures" remain, but their form is significantly altered from that of the draft. "Technological measures" are defined as "any technology,

15–06

---

[7] Software Directive 91/250 art.7(1).

[8] CDPA 1988 s.296(2A), inserted by the Copyright (Computer Programs) Regulations 1992 (SI 1992/3233), para.10, with effect from January 1, 1993. In *Kabushiki Kaisha Sony Computer Entertainment Inc v Ball* [2004] EWHC 1738 (Ch); [2005] F.S.R. 9 at para.21, Laddie J. rejected arguments as to the construction of s.296 based on the construction of the Software Directive because the 1988 Act was passed before this came into force and does not purport to give effect to it. However, this appears to overlook the fact that the object of amending s.296 was "in order to properly align its provisions with those of the Software Directive": see the Explanatory Note to the Regulations. Increasingly, however, this point will become academic as the version of s.296 as amended by the Regulations ceases to apply.

[9] At paras 15–02 to 15–05. In *Kabushiki Kaisha Sony Computer Entertainment Inc v Ball* [2004] EWHC 1738 (Ch) at para.21, Laddie J. rejected an argument that under this version of s.296 it was sufficient to prove that the defendant knew or had reason to believe that the device would be used to overcome copy protection and thus that it was not necessary to show that the defendant knew or had reason to believe that it would be used to making infringing copies.

[10] See Vol.2 F13 and F14.

[11] See, generally, Barczewski, "International Framework for Legal Protection of Digital Rights Management Systems" [2005] E.I.P.R. 165.

[12] [1998] O.J. C108/6.

[13] art.6(2).

[14] art.6(2).

[15] [2001] OJ L167/10. See Vol.2 H7.

device or component that, in the normal course of its operation, is designed to prevent or restrict acts, in respect of works or other subject matter, which are not authorised by the rightholder ...". Such measures are deemed "effective" where the use of the work or other subject matter "is controlled by the rightholders through application of an access control or protection process, such as encryption, scrambling or other transformation of the work or other subject-matter or a copy control mechanism, which achieves the protection objective".[16] In contrast to the draft, the Directive as adopted contains detailed provision about the inter-relationship between effective technological measures and permitted acts.[17] Article 1(2)(a) expressly provides that it leaves intact and shall in no way affect the Software Directive, which is discussed above.[18] During the negotiations on the Information Society Directive, the UK Government expressed concern about the difficulties which might arise from the existence of separate regimes for computer programs and other works, not only because it is not always clear whether a work is a computer program, but also because computer programs may be used as technological protection measures for other works.[19] However, neither the Commission, nor the majority of other Member States, felt it appropriate to seek a unified approach to protection measures, although the Commission committed itself to an early review of the issue.[20] Thus, although there are amendments to s.296, their main object is simply to ensure that the section conforms in style with the new sections which follow it, so as to lend coherence to this Part of the Act overall.[21]

15–07   **Implementation of the Information Society Directive.** The Information Society Directive was implemented in the United Kingdom by the Copyright and Related Rights Regulations 2003.[22] These Regulations substituted a new s.296 of the 1988 Act and added six new sections (296ZA to 296ZF), all under the new heading "Circumvention of protection measures". In accordance with art.1(2)(a) of the Information Society Directive,[23] there are now two separate schemes, the first relating to protection measures for computer programs only and the second relating to protection measures for all other works. In relation to computer programs only, the revised s.296 provides for civil remedies in respect of the circumvention of "technical devices", which are defined as devices "intended to prevent or restrict acts that are not authorised by the copyright owner of that computer program and are restricted by copyright".[24] These remedies apply not only against those who make or deal with the means to circumvent such devices but also against those who publish information which is intended to enable or assist the removal or circumvention of such devices.[25] There are no criminal remedies. In relation to works other than computer programs, there are now both civil and criminal remedies. Section 296ZA provides civil remedies in respect of

---

[16] art.6(3). It has apparently been argued that this definition does not include "access control" technology because such technology does not necessarily prevent acts restricted by copyright. However, this argument seems to be precluded by the express reference to "an access control ... process". See *Braun* [2003] 11 E.I.P.R. 496.

[17] art.6(4).

[18] See para.15–04.

[19] Consultation on UK Implementation of Directive 2001/29: Analysis of Responses and Government Conclusions, para.6.3.

[20] Analysis of Responses and Government Conclusions, para.6.3.

[21] See the Patent Office's Transposition Note in relation to the Regulations and see, generally, Barczewski, "International Framework for Legal Protection of Digital Rights Management Systems" [2005] E.I.P.R. 165.

[22] SI 2003/2498. The Regulations came into force on October 31, 2003.

[23] See para.15–06, above.

[24] CDPA 1988 s.296(6). See paras 15–08 et seq., below.

[25] s.296(1)(b). See para.15–11, below.

acts of circumvention of "technological measures", which are defined as "any technology, device or component which is designed, in the normal course of its operation, to protect a copyright work".[26] At the same time, s.296ZD provides civil remedies in respect of devices and services designed to circumvent technological measures.[27] These civil remedies also apply to technological measures designed to protect the subject matter of rights in performances, publication right and database right.[28] Section 296ZB provides for criminal offences in respect of devices and services designed to circumvent technological measures,[29] while s.296ZC contains provisions in relation to search warrants and forfeiture.[30] These criminal remedies are limited to measures to protect copyright. Finally, s.296ZE makes specific provision for the position where effective technological measures prevent permitted acts[31] or analogous acts in relation to the subject matter of rights in performances, database right and publication right.[32] The previous version of s.296 continues to apply to acts done before October 31, 2003, while the new provisions apply to acts done on or after that date.[33]

3. PROTECTION MEASURES: COMPUTER PROGRAMS

"Technical device". Section 296 applies where a "technical device" has been "applied" to a computer program. A "technical device" is defined as "any device intended to prevent or restrict acts that are not authorised by the copyright owner of that computer program and are restricted by copyright".[34] This definition is arguably rather narrower than that contained in the Software Directive: "any technical device which may have been applied to protect a computer program".[35] However, it may be that there is little practical distinction. The definition is arguably also narrower than that of "copy protection" in the previous version of s.296: "any device or means intended to prevent or restrict copying of a work or impair the quality of copies made". The following points should also be noted. First, it is not necessary to prove that the device is actually effective: all that need be proved is that it is intended to prevent or restrict infringements. Secondly, the definition does not make clear whose intention is in issue, but this is presumably the intention of the manufacturer or (if the manufacture is commissioned) of the person who commissions the manufacture. Thirdly, although it is necessary to show that the device was intended to prevent acts which are restricted by copyright, this is unlikely to be difficult in the case of a computer program, since any access to the work will involve copying.

15–08

Examples of technical devices. *Sony v Owen* and *Sony v Ball*,[36] the only reported cases on the previous version of s.296, concerned codes embedded into CD or

15–09

---

[26] s.296ZF(1). See para.15–19, below.
[27] See para.15–28, below.
[28] ss.296ZA(6), 296ZD(8).
[29] See paras 15–29 et seq., below.
[30] See para.15–34, below.
[31] See paras 15–35 et seq., below.
[32] s.296ZE(11).
[33] Copyright and Related Rights Regulations 2003 (SI 2003/2498) regs 1 and 40. Further, no act done after October 1, 2003 in pursuance of an agreement made before December 22, 2002 shall be regarded as an infringement of any new or extended right arising by virtue of the Regulations reg.32(2).
[34] CDPA 1988 s.296(6).
[35] Software Directive art.7(1)(c).
[36] *Sony Computer Entertainment v Owen* [2002] EWHC 45 (Ch); [2002] E.C.D.R. 27 and *Kabushiki Kaisha Sony Computer Entertainment Inc v Ball* [2004] EWHC 1738 (Ch); [2005] F.S.R. 9 (the latter also involved the new version of s.296 as well as s.296ZD). See MacCulloch, "Game Over: The Region Lock in Video Games" [2005] 5 E.I.P.R. 176.

DVD versions of computer games for playing on Sony's Playstation consoles. On the facts of those cases, if such a CD or DVD was copied by an ordinary member of the public (e.g. using a CD burner), the code would not be read by the copying machine and the resulting copy would not run on the console because the console's computer program would fail to find the code. If, on the other hand, the console's process of finding the code could be by-passed (in those cases by chips known as "the Messiah" and "the Messiah 2"), the game could be run on the console. When the game was loaded onto the console, a copy was made. In *Sony v Owen* it was held under the previous version of the section that Sony's arrangements[37] were a device or means intended to prevent the making of such further copies and therefore amounted to "copy protection". In *Sony v Ball* it was held that the same applied both under the new version of the section and under the previous version. In the latter case, it was argued that Sony's copy protection system did not amount to a technical device because it was applied primarily to the hardware (the console) rather than to the copies of the copyright works (the versions of the games). This argument was rejected for four reasons.[38] First, the court held that under the pre-amendment version of s.296 this did not matter because there was no reference to the protection being applied to a copyright work. Secondly, there was nothing in the new version of s.296 or in s.296ZD to require the protection to be "on" the software rather than in the hardware: a protection device may be "applied" to a program either by being put on the program or on the software which reads it, or both. Thirdly, there was no reason why the legislature should have been concerned as to where the copy protection system resides. Finally, in any event, as with most copy protection systems which operate on a lock-and-key basis with the hardware decrypting or unscrambling encrypted or scrambled software, the copy protection was located partly in the software and partly in the hardware. In *Nintendo v Playables*,[39] which also concerned computer game consoles, the claimants relied on the shape of the connector arrangement of the slot on the console and the corresponding shape of the game cards; the boot-up software on the console which checked for the presence of certain data files on the card and prevented execution of the program on the card if the files were not found; and the use of shared key encryption technology and scrambling to enable the console to detect whether the card was authentic. The judge was satisfied that the boot-up software and the use of encryption and scrambling amounted to "effective technical measures" for the purposes of s.296ZD because they were intended to prevent the game being copied across to the console. However, he doubted whether the physical shape and electrical characteristics of the connector were "effective technical measures", suggesting that it was at least arguable that the section had in mind something which acts as a barrier to copying once such a connection has been made or at least that the question was one of degree. It seems that he applied the same reasoning to the claim under s.296.[40]

15–10   **Persons with rights.** The new s.296 grants rights to three categories of person.[41] First, the person issuing the copies of the computer program to the public or com-

---

[37] The judge stated that "the codes" amounted to copy protection. Presumably what was actually meant was Sony's arrangements including the codes.

[38] *Kabushiki Kaisha Sony Computer Entertainment Inc v Ball* [2004] EWHC 1738 (Ch) at para.40.

[39] *Nintendo Company Ltd v Playables Ltd* [2010] EWHC 1932 (Ch); [2010] F.S.R. 36.

[40] See at paras 23, 24 and 37.

[41] Contrast the previous CDPA 1988 s.296, under which the only person with a remedy was the person issuing copies to the public: s.296(2).

municating the program to the public.[42] Issuing to the public of copies of a work means the act of putting into circulation in the EEA copies not previously put into circulation in the EEA by or with the consent of the copyright owner, or the act of putting into circulation outside the EEA, copies not previously put into circulation in the EEA or elsewhere.[43] Communication to the public means communication to the public by electronic transmission, including making the work available in such a way that members of the public may access it from a place and at a time individually chosen by them ("on demand").[44] It is worth emphasising that these provisions potentially give rights to non-exclusive licensees as well as to copyright owners and exclusive licensees. The language of this part of s.296 could be read as confining the existence of the rights to the period during which the person seeking to exercise them is actually issuing the copies or communicating the program to the public[45]; however, it seems unlikely that this is what was intended. In practice it is likely that a person who had ceased to issue the copies to the public would remain interested in preventing their further reproduction. The second category of person with rights is the copyright owner or his exclusive licensee (if this person does not fall within the first category).[46] It is not clear from the wording of this paragraph whether the rights of the copyright owner and his exclusive licensee are intended to be concurrent or alternative. On the one hand, subs.296(2)(b) refers to "the copyright owner or his exclusive licensee". On the other, subs.296(3) states that the rights conferred by the section are concurrent and this provision arguably applies as much to the rights conferred on the copyright owner and his exclusive licensee as to the other rights conferred by the section. Presumably, although this is not stated, it is necessary that the claimant should be the copyright owner or exclusive licensee at the time of the act complained of rather than (for example) at the time when the program was issued to the public. The third category is the owner or exclusive licensee of any intellectual property right in the technical device itself.[47] This would no doubt extend to the owners of patents and design rights as well as of copyright. Again, although on the face of it these rights are stated to be alternative, the effect of subs.296(3) may be that they are concurrent. Once more, it seems likely that it is necessary for the claimant to have such rights at the time of the act complained of, although again this is not made clear.

Making or dealing with means. The primary targets of s.296 are those who   **15–11**
manufacture and deal with the means to circumvent such technical devices. Accordingly, the section creates rights which are exercisable against persons who, with a specified state of mind, manufacture for sale or hire, import, distribute, sell, let for hire, offer or expose for sale or hire, advertise for sale or hire or possess for commercial purposes[48] any means the sole intended purpose of which is to facilitate the unauthorised removal or circumvention of the technical device.[49] The state of mind in question is knowledge or reason to believe that the means in

---

[42] s.296(2)(a).

[43] s.18(2), applied by s.296(8). For a full discussion of the meaning of the term "issue to the public", see paras 3–176 et seq., above.

[44] s.20, applied by s.296(8). For a full discussion of the meaning of the term "communication to the public", see paras 7–112 et seq., above.

[45] s.296(2) states that the person who has the rights is the person *issuing* the copies or *communicating* the work (rather than the person who *has issued them* or *has communicated* it).

[46] This fills an obvious *lacuna* in the previous law.

[47] Again, persons in this category had no remedy under the previous law. However, it remains to be seen to what extent such persons will be interested in enforcing their rights.

[48] art.7(1)(c) of the Software Directive 91/250 envisaged that possession for commercial purposes would attract liability. A new subs.(2A) was added to the old CDPA 1988 s.296 in order to give effect to this: see para.15–04, above.

[49] CDPA 1988 s.296(1)(b)(i).

question will be used to make infringing copies in the United Kingdom.[50] It is not necessary to show that the defendant knew or had reason to believe that any particular program was to be copied or that the means would only be used for making infringing copies.[51] Article 7(1)(c) of the Software Directive, which requires Member States to provide appropriate remedies against those committing "any act of putting into circulation, or the possession for commercial purposes, of any means", does not make such a state of mind a condition of liability. Since s.296 makes the presence of such a state of mind a condition of establishing liability for such acts, it has been argued that art.7(1)(c) has not been correctly implemented.[52]

15–12   **"Means".** The expression "means the sole intended purpose of which is to facilitate the unauthorised removal of any technical device" derives directly from the Software Directive,[53] where it is not further defined. The use of the extremely broad term "means" is no doubt intended to protect these provisions from technological obsolescence. It is not clear whether the use of the phrase "sole intended purpose" involves a subjective or objective test. If the test is subjective, difficult questions may arise as to whose intention is meant. Where the manufacturer is sued, no doubt the relevant intention will be that of the manufacturer. Where, however, the person being sued is further down the chain of supply, the requirement that the intended purpose is "the sole intended purpose" will arguably mean that it is necessary to prove that this purpose was intended both by the manufacturer and the person sued. It seems more likely, therefore, that the test is in fact objective. The previous version of s.296 used the words "any device or means specifically designed or adapted to circumvent the form of copy-protection employed". In *Sony v Owen*,[54] which was decided under that previous version, it was argued that the Messiah had potential uses other than the making of infringing copies, for example to run software which had not been designed by Sony. This argument was rejected: the codes amounted to copy protection and the Messiah was specifically designed to circumvent them. In *Sony v Ball*[55] a similar argument on the new version of s.296 failed because all the intended purposes relied on by the defendant were unauthorised. More recently, in *Nintendo v Playables*,[56] the judge emphasised that the fact that a device may be used for a purpose which does not involve infringement of copyright does not mean that the sole intended purpose is not the unauthorised circumvention of a technical device.

15–13   **"Unauthorised".** The term "unauthorised" is not defined in s.296. Section 296(8) provides that expressions which are defined for the purposes of the copyright part of the 1988 Act have the same meaning in s.296. The word "unauthorised" is

---

[50] *Nintendo Company Ltd v Playables Ltd* [2010] EWHC 1932 (Ch); [2010] F.S.R. 36 at para.40. For a discussion of the meaning of these terms in the copyright context, see paras 8–03 et seq., above. In *Kabushiki Kaisha Sony Computer Entertainment Inc v Ball* [2004] EWHC 1738 (Ch); [2005] F.S.R. 9 at para.27, Laddie J. rejected an argument that it was sufficient to prove that the defendant knew or had reason to believe that the device would be used to overcome copy-protection.

[51] *Nintendo Company Ltd v Playables Ltd* [2010] EWHC 1932 (Ch) at para.35. The defendants' defence that they did not know or have reason to believe that the devices would be used to make infringing copies failed on the facts: see para.38.

[52] The point was taken in *Nintendo Company Ltd v Playables Ltd* [2010] EWHC 1932 (Ch). Since the defendants did not put forward any argument Floyd J. did not decide the point but applied the language of the statute, observing that the Directive only requires that there be "appropriate" remedies. See para.31.

[53] Software Directive art.7(1)(c).

[54] *Sony Computer Entertainment v Owen* [2002] EWHC 45 (Ch); [2002] E.M.L.R. 34; [2002] E.C.D.R. 27.

[55] *Kabushiki Kaisha Sony Computer Entertainment Inc v Ball* [2004] EWHC 1738 (Ch); [2005] F.S.R. 9. There does not appear to have been argument about whether "purpose" was objective or subjective in this case.

[56] *Nintendo Company Ltd v Playables Ltd* [2010] EWHC 1932 (Ch); [2010] F.S.R. 36 at para.34.

defined in the copyright part of the 1988 Act.[57] However, the definition only applies where the word is used "as regards anything done in relation to a work" and would therefore appear to be inapplicable to the removal or circumvention of a technical device. The word "unauthorised" did not appear in the original version of s.296, nor was it added when the section was amended to give effect to the Software Directive.[58] The question therefore arises as to whether its introduction into the section makes any substantive difference. In principle it would seem to be clearly arguable that an act can only be unauthorised if there is someone who is capable of granting the authority to do it. Section 296 does not itself create a right to authorise the removal or circumvention of technical devices. It would follow that the question of authorisation would have to be considered apart from the section itself. If so, an act of removal or circumvention would only be unauthorised if done in breach of UK law, for example in breach of an effective contractual prohibition, by infringing an intellectual or other property right, by the misuse of confidential information or by otherwise acting in breach of a prohibition which exists independently of s.296. However, it is far from clear that the insertion of the word "unauthorised" was intended to effect a change in the law.[59] Furthermore, this interpretation would deprive s.296 of much of its effect.[60] Moreover, it seems doubtful that those who framed the Software Directive intended that the question whether an act of removal or circumvention was unauthorised should depend on the vagaries of national law.[61] Finally, in *Sony v Ball*,[62] Laddie J. stated that the purpose of the revised version of s.296 was to prohibit trade in devices which overcome copy protection without regard to whether that assisted copyright infringement.[63] It would seem to follow that the better view is that the term "unauthorised" means without the authority of a person with rights under the section.

Inter-relationship with permitted acts. Under ss.50A to 50C of the 1988 Act, a   **15–14**

---

[57] CDPA 1988 s.178 provides that it means "done otherwise than" (a) by or with the licence of the copyright owner; or (b) where copyright does not subsist in the work, by or with the licence of the author or (where s.11(2) of the 1988 Act would have applied) his employer or persons lawfully claiming under them; or (c) pursuant to s.48.

[58] As to which, see para.15–04, above.

[59] The Government's exact words in para.6.4 of its *Analysis of Responses and Government Conclusions* are as follows: "The consultation paper proposed to retain s.296, as amended on implementation of Directive 91/250, but in relation to computer programs only ... This remains the intention, but in the light of comments made by parties with particular interests in computer programs, the Government has concluded that it is desirable to make some further adjustments to s.296 in order to bring its wording into closer alignment with that of Article 7(1)(c) of Directive 91/250, which it is now the sole function of s.296 to implement. These changes do not, however, alter the basic approach in s.296, and the Government has concluded that it would not be appropriate to make more substantial changes, such as the introduction of criminal sanctions ...". See also the Patent Office's Transposition Note: "Section 296 has been amended principally so that it conforms in style with the new sections directly resulting from transposing Article 6 which follow it, so as to lend coherence to this Part of the Act overall. Also, this section has been expanded so that the right to bring a civil action is vested in more people than previously. Again, this conforms with the new sections. This aspect of the amendment has been made by means of further implementing Directive 91/250/EEC (Article 7)".

[60] In *BBC Enterprises Ltd v Hi-Tech Xtravision Ltd* [1991] 2 A.C. 327; [1992] R.P.C. 167, a similar argument in relation to the term "not entitled" in s.298(2) of the 1988 Act succeeded at first instance but not in the Court of Appeal or the House of Lords.

[61] It seems improbable that the term might mean "unauthorised under European law".

[62] [2004] EWHC 1738 (Ch); [2005] F.S.R. 9; [2004] E.C.D.R. 33.

[63] In that case, the defendant argued that the intended purposes of the device included acts which would be authorised by the claimant (presumably it was contended that it was implicit that if those acts were indeed authorised, the removal or circumvention would also be authorised, but this is not clear from the judgment). The judge noted that this argument could only succeed if the acts in question were authorised by Sony but held that they were not because they would infringe its copyright: see paras 28 to 33. Since this part of the argument failed, it was not necessary for the judge to consider whether the actual removal or circumvention for the purposes of these acts was authorised. Accordingly, the decision appears to leave open the question of the meaning of "unauthorised".

lawful user of a computer program is entitled to carry out certain acts in relation to a computer program which would otherwise infringe copyright. Those acts include, for example, the making of back up copies.[64] In some cases, under s.296A of the 1988 Act, contractual terms which purport to prohibit or restrict such acts are void.[65] The question arises as to what happens where the existence of a technical device prevents the operation of one of these permitted acts, for example where a copy protection device prevents the making of back-ups.[66] Unlike in the case of protection measures in respect of other rights,[67] the Government did not introduce a statutory procedure aimed at resolving the tension between technical devices on the one hand and the permitted acts on the other. In theory, of course, there is no such tension. The act of circumvention is not an infringement of the section and a supplier of means or information is only liable if he can be shown to have known or had reason to believe that it will be used to make infringing copies. In practice, however, it is impossible for a supplier to know exactly what will be done with the means or information he supplies. This may well deter suppliers from supplying those who genuinely wish only to carry out permitted acts. It is doubtful whether this is consistent with the requirement of art.7(1) of the Software Directive that the rights in respect of technical devices should be "without prejudice to" the permitted acts.

15–15   **Publication of information.** The rights under s.296 are also available against those who, again with the specified state of mind, publish information intended to enable or assist persons to remove or circumvent the technical device.[68] This category of persons is not specifically mentioned in the Software Directive, but derives from the previous version of s.296. The state of mind in question is knowledge or reason to believe that the information in question will be used to make infringing copies.[69] In this case, there is no requirement that the removal or circumvention in question should be unauthorised.

15–16   **The rights and remedies.** The person with rights under s.296 has the same "rights" against the persons defined in the previous paragraphs as a copyright owner has in respect of an infringement of copyright. The absence of any reference to "remedies" in the section has given rise to some uncertainty as to the meaning of this provision, since rights are of little use without remedies.[70] However, if the point were raised, it seems inevitable that a court would conclude that the intention was that the person with rights should be entitled to the normal remedies for copyright infringement, that is, an injunction, together with damages or an account of profits.[71] In addition, it seems that the person with rights will not be entitled to damages if the defendant can show that he did not know and had no reason to believe that copyright subsisted in the work to which the action relates[72]; while on the other hand he will be entitled to additional damages in the same circumstances in which such damages are available for copyright

---

[64] See, generally, paras 9–149 et seq., above.

[65] See, generally, para.9–149, above.

[66] It is obvious, for example, that a technical device cannot simply be declared "void" like a term in an agreement.

[67] See below at paras 15–35 to 15–39.

[68] CDPA 1988 s.296(1)(b)(ii).

[69] s.296(1)(b). This was the position under the previous version of s.296. For a detailed discussion of the terms "knowledge" and "reason to believe", see paras 8–08 et seq., above.

[70] CDPA 1988 s.298, which is structured in a similar way to s.296, refers to "rights and remedies".

[71] Under s.96(2). See Ch.21. This interpretation is supported by the statement of the minister (Mr Butcher) in Standing Committee E (*Hansard*, HC, col.737 (June 21, 1988) (S.C.E.): "The remedies are to be the same as those available to a copyright owner in respect of infringement. That is analogous to the provisions of clause 277 relating to fraudulent reception of broadcasts".

[72] s.97(1). See paras 21–75 et seq., below.

infringement.[73] Section 296(4) expressly provides that a person with rights may obtain an order for delivery up of or seize without a court order means the sole intended purpose of which is to facilitate the unauthorised removal or circumvention of a technical device. These rights are the same rights as a copyright owner has in relation to infringing copies under ss.99 and 100 of the 1988 Act.[74] The rights exist where a person has the means in question in his possession, custody or control with the intention that they should be used to facilitate the unauthorised removal or circumvention of any technical device which has been applied to a computer program.[75] Where goods have been delivered up or seized under these provisions, the normal copyright provisions apply in relation to the making of disposal orders with the necessary modifications.[76]

Concurrent nature of the rights and remedies. The rights under s.296 are   **15–17**
expressed to be concurrent and it is provided that certain other provisions of the copyright Part of the 1988 Act apply to proceedings under s.296 in relation to persons with concurrent rights as they apply in proceedings under those provisions in relation to a copyright owner and exclusive licensee with concurrent rights.[77] The first provision is s.101(3), which provides that in an action brought by an exclusive licensee a defendant may avail himself of any defence which would have been available to him if the action had been brought by the copyright owner.[78] Thus, for example, a defendant to an action brought by an exclusive licensee may rely on a licence granted by the copyright owner. The purpose of applying s.101(3) would appear to be to provide that if a defendant has a defence against one of the persons with rights, for example because he has a licence, he may rely on that defence in proceedings brought by another of the persons with rights against whom he would not otherwise have a defence. Presumably this also means that where a defendant would be able to raise a defence of estoppel against one person with rights, he would also be able to set up that estoppel against any other person with rights who sought to rely on the section. The other provisions of the copyright Part of the 1988 Act which are applied to s.296 are subss.102(1) to (5), which contain provisions as to proceedings brought by a copyright owner or exclusive licensee alone.[79] The effect of the application of subss.102(1) to (3) is that if an action is brought by a person with rights in relation to an infringement in respect of which other persons with rights have concurrent rights of action, the action may not be proceeded with (except for the purposes of obtaining interim relief) without joining the others or obtaining the leave of the court. A person joined in accordance with this provision will not be liable for any costs in the action unless he takes part in the proceedings. Given the number and variety of persons who may have concurrent rights, this provision may well cause considerable practical difficulties for a claimant who wishes to proceed to trial. Of course, such a claimant will be able to obtain the court's permission to proceed without joining others. However, the purpose of subs.102(1) is to protect defendants from being sued by more than one claimant in separate actions. It seems likely, therefore, that a court will expect claimants to take considerable steps to identify other persons with rights before it will grant permission to proceed without their being joined. Such steps may be time-consuming and

---

[73] s.97(2). See paras 21–202 et seq., below.
[74] See para.21–216 (delivery up) and paras 21–57 et seq. (seizure without a court order).
[75] s.296(4).
[76] s.296(7). As to these, see s.114 and paras 21–218 et seq., below.
[77] CDPA 1988 s.296(3), (5).
[78] See para.21–27, below.
[79] For the operation of these provisions, see para.21–27, below.

expensive. The effect of the application of subs.102(4) is as follows.[80] First, when assessing damages the court is obliged to take into account the terms of any[81] licence between two or more persons with rights and any pecuniary remedy already awarded to or available to other persons with rights. Secondly, no account of profits shall be directed in favour of one person with rights if an award of damages has already been made or an account of profits has already been directed in favour of another person with rights. Thirdly, if an account of profits is directed, the court is obliged to apportion the profits between the persons with rights as it considers just, subject to any agreement between them. The effect of the application of subs.102(5)[82] is that before one person with rights applies for an order for delivery up or exercises the right of seizure without a court order, he must notify any other person having rights. That person may then apply for such order for delivery up or (as the case may be) prohibiting or permitting the exercise of the right of seizure without a court order as the court thinks fit, having regard to the terms of any licence between the parties.

15–18   **Other provisions about proceedings.** The presumptions contained in ss.104 to 106 of the 1988 Act[83] and the withdrawal of the privilege against self-incrimination effected by s.72 of the Senior Courts Act 1981[84] apply in relation to proceedings under s.296 as they apply in relation to proceedings under the copyright Part of the 1988 Act.[85]

4. PROTECTION MEASURES: WORKS OTHER THAN COMPUTER PROGRAMS

A. CIVIL REMEDIES

15–19   **"Technological measures".** As has been explained above,[86] the separate Community schemes for protection measures in respect of computer programs on the one hand and protection measures in respect of all other rights on the other have been implemented by creating two separate schemes in the 1988 Act. Accordingly, the new ss.296ZA and 296ZC apply where effective technological measures have been applied to a copyright work other than a computer program.[87] They also apply (with any necessary adaptations) where such measures have been applied to the subject matter of rights in performances, publication right or database right.[88] In what follows, for ease of exposition, the new provisions of the 1988 Act will be considered as they apply to copyright. "Technological measures" are defined as any technology, device or component which is designed, in the normal course of its operation, to protect a copyright work other than a computer program.[89] This definition is reproduced verbatim from the Information

---

[80] See para.21–222, below, for an account of the operation of s.102(4) in the copyright context.

[81] There seems no reason to limit the application of s.102(4) to any licence between a copyright owner with rights and an exclusive licensee with rights, although this is normally the only licence which is likely to be relevant under s.296.

[82] See para.21–222, below.

[83] As to which, see paras 21–260 et seq., below.

[84] Together with its Scottish and Northern Irish equivalents, s.15 of the Law Reform (Miscellaneous Provisions) (Scotland) Act 1985 and s.94A of the Judicature (Northern Ireland) Act 1978. See para.21–163, below.

[85] CDPA 1988 s.296(7).

[86] See para.15–07, above.

[87] CDPA 1988 ss.296ZA(1)(a) and 296ZD(1)(a).

[88] ss.296ZA(6) and 296ZD(8).

[89] s.296ZF(1).

Society Directive.[90] The use of the broad term "technology" is presumably designed to deal with future developments in the field of copy protection. The term "protection" means the prevention or restriction of acts that are not authorised by the copyright owner of that work and are restricted by copyright.[91] It has been said that the main purpose of the copy protection system must be to protect a copyright work so as to prevent infringements of copyright.[92] However, it is suggested that in fact it is sufficient if such protection is one of the purposes for which the measures were designed. In *Sony v Ball*[93] (discussed above)[94] the court rejected an argument that Sony's copy protection system did not amount to a technological measure because it was directed at the hardware rather than the copyright material.[95]

"Effective". Section 296ZF(2) contains what appears at first sight to be an exhaustive definition of what technological measures are effective. However, the terms of the Information Society Directive make clear that the definition is not in fact exhaustive.[96] In accordance with the definition, measures will be effective if the "use" of the work is controlled by the copyright owner through one of two alternative methods which achieves "the intended protection". For these purposes, the "use" of the work is limited to use of the work which is within the scope of the acts restricted by copyright.[97] It is not, however, sufficient that the measures have the general effect of preventing or restricting infringement: they must physically prevent it.[98] The alternative methods of control are, first, an access control or protection process such as encryption, scrambling or other transformation of the work; and, secondly, a copy control mechanism.[99] The "intended protection" is presumably the prevention or restriction of acts that are not authorised by the copyright owner and are restricted by copyright.[100] By contrast with the position under the previous and current versions of s.296, it is not sufficient for the claimant to show that the measures are intended to achieve their object; rather, they must actually achieve it. On the other hand, it is not necessary to prove that they are completely effective: if that were the case there would be no need for the section in the first place.[101]

15–20

---

[90] Directive 2001/29 on the harmonisation of certain aspects of copyright and related rights in the information society, [2001] OJ L167/10, art.6(3).

[91] s.296ZF(3)(a).

[92] *Kabushiki Kaisha Sony Computer Entertainment Inc v Ball* [2004] EWHC 1738 (Ch); [2005] F.S.R. 9 at para.39.

[93] *Kabushiki Kaisha Sony Computer Entertainment Inc v Ball* [2004] EWHC 1738 (Ch) at para.43.

[94] See paras 15–09, 15–11 and 15–12.

[95] *Kabushiki Kaisha Sony Computer Entertainment Inc v Ball* [2004] EWHC 1738 (Ch) at para.43. For a more detailed account, see para.15–09, above.

[96] *Nintendo Company Ltd v Playables Ltd* [2010] EWHC 1932 (Ch); [2010] F.S.R. 36 at para.14. The point seems to be that the Directive states that the measures will be "deemed" effective if the conditions set out in subs.(2) are met, not that they will *only* be deemed effective in such circumstances.

[97] s.296ZF(3)(b).

[98] Thus, in order to establish liability in respect of acts relating to chips of the type involved in the *Sony v Owen* and *Sony v Ball* cases, it is necessary to prove to the requisite standard that the playing of the CD or DVD version involves copying within the meaning of s.17 of the 1988 Act. In *R. v Higgs* [2008] EWCA Crim 1324; [2009] 1 W.L.R. 73; [2008] F.S.R. 34, a prosecution under s.296ZB, the Crown did not set out to do this, relying on the fact that the technological measures discouraged the making of infringing copies by preventing their use. The defendant's appeal against conviction was allowed. The problem identified in *Higgs* was surmounted in *R. v Gilham* [2009] EWCA Crim 2293; [2010] E.C.D.R. 5.

[99] s.296ZF(2).

[100] See s.296ZF(3)(a) and see para.15–19, above.

[101] *R. v Higgs* [2008] EWCA Crim 1324; [2009] 1 W.L.R. 73; [2008] F.S.R. 34; *Nintendo Company Ltd v Playables Ltd* [2010] EWHC 1932 (Ch); [2010] F.S.R. 36 at para.17.

15–21   **Effective technological measures: cases under the 1988 Act.**[102] *Sony v Ball*
concerned chips which circumvented technological measures relating to the playing of computer games on Sony's Playstation consoles. The facts are set out
above.[103] Sony's arrangements were held to amount to "effective technological
measures".[104] The criminal cases of *R. v Higgs*[105] and *R. v Gilham*[106] concerned
games consoles made by Sony, Microsoft and Nintendo, but were not concerned
with the detail of the technological measures. *Nintendo v Playables*[107] also
concerned games consoles. The facts and decision are discussed above.[108] Finally,
in *UEFA v Euroview Sport*[109] the High Court referred to the Court of Justice the
question whether encryption of broadcasts amounts to an effective technological
measure.

15–22   **Measures in other jurisdictions.** A number of other types of technological measure have been the subject of reported litigation elsewhere, especially in the
United States. The US legislation in this field[110] is significantly different to that
contained in the 1988 Act. Accordingly, while the reported decisions provide
useful illustrations of the technology, they are of little or no use in interpreting
the European and United Kingdom legislation.

Considerable litigation has resulted from the application of the Content
Scramble System or "CSS" to DVD films. According to the reported cases, CSS
employs an algorithm configured by a set of "keys" to encrypt a DVD's contents.
Decryption requires a set of "player keys" as well as an understanding of the CSS
encryption algorithm. Without the player keys and the algorithm, a DVD player
cannot access the contents of the DVD. With the player keys and the algorithm,
the player can display the film on a screen, but the viewer cannot copy the film
using the copy function. The film studios distributed the CSS technology to the
manufacturers of DVD players under a licensing scheme pursuant to which the
manufacturers were obliged to keep the player keys confidential and prevent the
transmission of CSS data from a DVD drive. Not long after DVDs began to be
distributed on a wide scale, decryption programs were developed and soon
became widely available on the Internet. In one case, film studios obtained injunctions against a defendant who had posted a copy of a decryption program called
"DeCSS" on a website.[111] In another, film studios obtained an injunction against
a company which marketed decryption programs for the purposes of making
backup copies of DVDs.[112] In Norway a teenager was acquitted of charges relating to offences allegedly committed while developing and publishing DeCSS.[113]

Another measure which has been the subject of litigation in the United States

---

[102] For a general survey of the position in relation to digital works, see *Current Developments in Digital Rights Management*, a report prepared for the 10th session of WIPO's Standing Commit-tee on Copyright and Related Rights by Jeffrey Cunard, Keith Hill and Chris Barlas. See also Morrison and Gillies [2002] 2 E.I.P.R. 74 (webcast content) and Marks and Turnbull [2000] 5 E.I.P.R. 198. See also Stromdale, "The Problems with DRM" [2006] Ent. L.R. 1.

[103] para.15–09.

[104] *Kabushiki Kaisha Sony Computer Entertainment Inc v Ball* [2004] EWHC 1738 (Ch); [2005] F.S.R. 9 at para.39.

[105] [2008] EWCA Crim 1324; [2009] 1 W.L.R. 73; [2008] F.S.R. 34.

[106] [2009] EWCA Crim 2293; [2010] E.C.D.R. 5.

[107] *Nintendo Company Ltd v Playables Ltd* [2010] EWHC 1932 (Ch); [2010] F.S.R. 36.

[108] para.15–09.

[109] *Union of European Football Associations v Euroview Sport Ltd* [2010] EWHC 1066 (Ch,); [2010] E.U.L.R. 583 at paras 31 and 44.

[110] That is, the Digital Millennium Copyright Act, 17 U.S.C. §§ 1201 et seq.

[111] *Universal City Studios, Inc v Reimerdes*, 111 F.Supp.2d 346 (S.D.N.Y. 2000); affirmed on appeal in *Universal City Studios, Inc v Corley* 273 F.3d 429 (2d Cir. 2001).

[112] *321 Studios v Metro Goldwyn Mayer Studios Inc* No.C 02-1955 (N.D.Cal.).

[113] The acquittal was upheld on appeal: *Public Prosecutor v Johansen* [2004] E.C.D.R 17 (Borgart-ing Appellate Court).

is Adobe's Acrobat eBook format. According to the reported cases, where an electronic book in this format is downloaded from a publisher's website, it is accompanied by an electronic "voucher" which is recognised and read by the copy of Adobe's eBook Reader program which is on the purchaser's computer. The book can then only be read on the computer onto which it has been downloaded. Furthermore, the publisher is able to restrict the purchaser's use of the book, for example to prevent it being copied, printed or distributed electronically. In one reported case the defendant sold a software program which converted eBook Reader formatted books into "naked PDF" format, thus making them easy to copy, print and distribute in electronic form.[114]

A third form of measure which has been litigated in the United States is the encoding and security measures developed by RealNetworks to enable audio and video content to be "streamed" to consumers without permitting them to download it. According to the reported cases, this has been achieved by the operation of two security devices: the "Secret Handshake", an authentication sequence which ensures that all files encoded in RealNetworks' RealMedia format will only be sent to a RealPlayer software program, and the "Copy Switch", a piece of data in all RealMedia files which contains the content owner's preference regarding whether the stream may be copied by the consumer. The RealPlayer program reads the Copy Switch and obeys the content owner's wishes. In one reported case the defendant distributed and marketed a software product which circumvented the Secret Handshake by mimicing a RealPlayer and bypassed the Copy Switch, thus enabling streamed content to be downloaded. The court granted an interim injunction.[115]

Other measures which have been the subject of litigation in other jurisdictions include: a user identity and password granted to secure access to internet services,[116] a "secret handshake" which enabled the server run by the provider of a 24-hour online gaming service for purchasers of games software on CD to check the authenticity of the purchaser's product code,[117] a dongle which prevented access to a computer program,[118] technology embedded in a classified listing website which was designed to avoid automatic postings[119] and measures which prevented the unauthorised "unlocking" of mobile phones.[120]

Acts of circumvention which attract liability. Where effective technological measures have been applied to a copyright work other than a computer program, s.296ZA creates rights and remedies against a person who does anything which circumvents those measures. However, that person is only liable if he knew or   **15–23**

---

[114] *United States of America v Elcom Ltd* 203 F. Supp. 2d 1111, a criminal case. This report concerns the denial of the defendant's motion to dismiss the indictment on constitutional grounds.

[115] *RealNetworks Inc v Streambox, Inc* 2000 U.S. Dist. Lexis 1889. This case settled in September 2000: see *Current Developments in Digital Rights Management*, a report prepared for the 10th session of WIPO's Standing Committee on Copyright and Related Rights by Jeffrey Cunard, Keith Hill and Chris Barlas.

[116] *IMS Inquiry Management Systems Ltd v Berkshire Information Inc* 307 F. Supp. 2d 521—this was held to be an effective technological protection measure, but not to have been circumvented by the improper use of someone else's validly issued user identity and password to gain access. On the question of whether such use amounted to circumvention this decision was not followed in *Actuate Corp v International Business Machines Corp* (N.D. Cal.) 2010 WL 1340519.

[117] *Davidson & Associates, Inc v Internet Gateway* 334 F. Supp. 2d 1164, affirmed in *Davidson & Associates v Jung* 422 F. 3d 630.

[118] *MGE UPS Systems Inc v GE Consumer and Industrial Inc* U.S.C.A. (5th Cir. 2010).

[119] *Craigslist Inc v Naturemarket Inc* (N.D. Cal.) 694 F. Supp. 2d 1039.

[120] See e.g. *Tracfone Wireless Inc v Tropical Export Inc* (S.D. Florida) 2009 WL 3055386.

had reasonable grounds to know that he was "pursuing that objective", that is, presumably, the circumvention of the measures in question.[121]

15–24   **Acts of circumvention: cryptography exception.** There is a limited exception in the case of research into cryptography. Where a person, for the purposes of research into cryptography, does anything which circumvents effective technological measures, he is only liable if in so doing, or in issuing information derived from that research, he affects prejudicially the rights of the copyright owner.[122] In itself, the act of decrypting a technological measure for the purposes of genuine cryptographical research is unlikely to prejudice the copyright owner. The difficulty arises where the results of that research are published. In such circumstances, the rights of the copyright owner are likely to have been prejudiced so that the researcher will not be able to rely on the exception.[123]

15–25   **Acts of circumvention: persons with rights and the exercise of those rights.** In the case of acts of circumvention, s.296ZA gives rights to a person issuing to the public copies of the work to which the measures have been applied or communicating that work to the public and to the copyright owner or his exclusive licensee if he is not the person issuing copies of the work or communicating the work.[124] This terminology is identical to that contained in s.296 and is discussed above.[125] As is the case under s.296, these rights are the same as the rights of a copyright owner in respect of an infringement of copyright and are concurrent.[126] This too is discussed above.[127] In contrast to the position under s.296, no rights are granted to the owner or exclusive licensee of any intellectual property right in the technological measures themselves. The presumptions contained in ss.104 to 106 of the 1988 Act,[128] the presumptions contained in reg.22 of the Copyright and Rights in Databases Regulations[129] and the withdrawal of the privilege against self-incrimination effected by s.2 of the Senior Courts Act 1981[130] apply in relation to proceedings under s.296ZA as they apply in relation to proceedings under the copyright Part of the 1988 Act.[131]

15–26   **Devices and services: acts attracting liability.** Where effective technological measures have been applied to a copyright work other than a computer program, s.296ZD creates rights and remedies against persons who make or deal with certain devices, products or components or provide certain services.[132] The acts which attract liability are expressed in terms which are substantially identical to

---

[121] CDPA 1988 s.296ZA(1)(b). This limitation derives from art.6(1) of the Information Society Directive 2001/29.

[122] CDPA 1988 s.296ZA(2) (this derives from recital 48 to the Information Society Directive 2001/29, which states that the protection accorded to technical devices by the Directive should not hinder research into cryptography: see *Analysis of Responses and Government Conclusions* para.6.6). Even if the liability arises because of the prejudicial effect of the publication, it remains liability for the act of circumvention itself rather than for the act of publication.

[123] Note, further, that the publication may attract criminal liability under s.296ZB(2) or civil liability under s.296ZD(1)(b) if it can be said to amount to the provision of a service and the other conditions for liability under those provisions are satisfied. There is no cryptography defence in s.296ZB(2) or s.296ZD(1)(b).

[124] CDPA 1988 s.296ZA(3).

[125] See para.15–10.

[126] s.296ZA(3), (4).

[127] See para.15–17.

[128] See paras 21–260, below.

[129] SI 1997/3032.

[130] Together with its Scottish and Northern Irish equivalents, s.15 of the Law Reform (Miscellaneous Provisions) (Scotland) Act 1985 and s.94A of the Judicature (Northern Ireland) Act 1978. See para.21–163, below.

[131] s.296ZA(5) and (6).

[132] CDPA 1988 s.296ZD(1).

those contained in the Information Society Directive.[133] In relation to devices, products or components, the relevant acts are: manufacturing, importing, distributing, selling or letting for hire, advertising for sale or hire or possessing for commercial purposes. It is clear that even some non-commercial activities, such as importation for personal use and distributions which are not made in the course of a business, will attract liability. In respect of services, liability occurs when the service is provided. There is no liability for offering or advertising the service. There is no "knowledge" or "reason to believe" defence; accordingly, s.296ZD creates "a tort of strict liability".[134]

Devices and services: conditions for liability. In either case, liability only arises   **15–27**
if one of three alternative conditions is satisfied. The first is that the goods or services are promoted, advertised or marketed for the purpose of the circumvention of the measures in question.[135] It is presumably not necessary to prove that the person making or dealing with the goods or providing the services has himself engaged in any such promotion, advertising or marketing.

The second alternative condition is that the goods or services have only a limited commercially significant purpose or use other than to circumvent the measures in question.[136] Recital 48 to the Information Society Directive states that the Directive is not intended to prevent the normal operation of electronic equipment and its technological development, nor is it intended to imply an obligation to design devices, products or services to correspond to technological measures (e.g., to design computers to respond to "copy control flags"). Accordingly, the object of this second condition is to "respect proportionality" and to avoid prohibiting "those devices or activities which have a commercially significant purpose or use other than to circumvent the technical protection".[137] The question appears to be one of the purpose for which the device is sold.[138] The question of whether commercial significance is or is not "limited" will be one of fact or degree. The practical effect of this second condition will no doubt be to prevent defendants from relying on the fact that even though the goods or services can be used to circumvent the measures in question, they have another, "innocent" use, unless that use can be shown to be "commercially significant". In *Nintendo v Playables* the court held that the fact that the goods could be used to enable non-infringing uses of Nintendo's consoles (e.g. to play home-made games on them) was irrelevant: such uses still involved circumvention of the measures.[139]

The third alternative condition is that the goods or services are primarily designed, produced, adapted or performed for the purpose of enabling or facilitating the circumvention of the measures in question.[140] There are differing decisions as to whether this refers to circumvention within the United Kingdom.[141] In the case of goods, this condition clearly focuses on the intention of the designer

---

[133] Directive 2001/29 on the harmonisation of certain aspects of copyright and related rights in the information society [2001] O.J. L167/10 art.6(1).

[134] *Kabushiki Kaisha Sony Computer Entertainment Inc v Ball* [2004] EWHC 1738 (Ch); [2005] F.S.R. 9 at para.39.

[135] CDPA 1988 s.296ZD(1)(b)(i).

[136] s.296ZD(1)(b)(ii).

[137] See recital 48 to the Information Society Directive 2001/29.

[138] *Nintendo Company Ltd v Playables Ltd* [2010] EWHC 1932 (Ch); [2010] F.S.R. 36 at para.41.

[139] *Nintendo Company Ltd v Playables Ltd* [2010] EWHC 1932 (Ch) at para.21(ii). It is debatable whether Floyd J.'s interpretation pays sufficient regard to the fact that the measures must be designed to control the use of "a copyright work", that is a work in which copyright subsists under the 1988 Act: s.1(2), and to the defence under s.296ZD(7).

[140] s.296ZD(1)(b)(iii).

[141] In *Kabushiki Kaisha Sony Computer Entertainment Inc v Ball* [2004] EWHC 1738 (Ch); [2005] F.S.R. 9 at para.40, Laddie J. held that it did. However, in *Nintendo Company Ltd v Playables*

or manufacturer. In the case of services, however, the focus is also on the intention of the person who is performing them. This will raise questions of fact and degree.[142]

15–28   **Devices and services: persons with rights and the exercise of those rights.** In this case, the categories of persons with rights are identical to those under s.296.[143] These categories are discussed above.[144] Again, the rights are the same as the rights of a copyright owner in respect of an infringement of copyright and are concurrent.[145] The effect of this is considered above.[146] It is expressly provided that a person with rights under s.296ZD may obtain an order for delivery up or seize without a court order any device, product or component which offends the section.[147] These rights are the same rights as a copyright owner has in relation to infringing copies under ss.99 and 100 of the 1988 Act.[148] The rights exist where a person has the device, product or component in his possession, custody or control with the intention that it should be used to circumvent effective technological measures. Where goods have been delivered up or seized under these provisions, the normal copyright provisions apply in relation to the making of disposal orders, with the necessary modifications.[149] These rights as to delivery up and seizure without a court order are also concurrent.[150] Again, the effect of this is considered above.[151] Again, the presumptions contained in ss.104 to 106 of the 1988 Act,[152] the presumptions in reg.22 of the Copyright and Rights in Databases Regulations[153] and the withdrawal of the privilege against self-incrimination effected by s.72 of the Senior Courts Act 1981[154] apply in relation to proceedings under s.296ZD as they apply in relation to proceedings under the copyright Part of the 1988 Act.[155] Finally, it is expressly provided that s.97(1) of the 1988 Act, which provides a limited defence to a claim for damages in proceedings for infringement of copyright,[156] applies to proceedings under s.296ZD so that a defendant has a defence to a claim for damages under that section (but without prejudice to any other remedy) if he did not know or have reason to believe that his acts enabled or facilitated an infringement of copyright.[157]

B. CRIMINAL REMEDIES

15–29   **Introduction.** There were no criminal offences under the previous version of

---

Ltd [2010] EWHC 1932 (Ch); [2010] F.S.R. 36 at para.42, Floyd J. disagreed on the basis that in contrast to s.296 there is no requirement to prove knowledge or reason to believe that the device will be used to infringe. It is debatable whether Floyd J.'s interpretation pays sufficient regard to the fact that the measures must be designed to control the use of "a copyright work", that is a work in which copyright subsists under the 1988 Act: s.1(2), or to the defence under s.296ZD(7).

[142] See, e.g. *Kabushiki Kaisha Sony Computer Entertainment Inc v Ball* [2004] EWHC 1738 (Ch) at para.40.
[143] CDPA 1988 s.296ZD(2).
[144] See para.15–10.
[145] s.296ZD(3).
[146] See para.15–17.
[147] s.296ZD(4).
[148] See para.21–216 (delivery up) and paras 21–57 et seq. (seizure without a court order).
[149] s.296ZD(6).
[150] s.296ZD(5).
[151] See para.15–17.
[152] See paras 21–260 et seq., below.
[153] SI 1997/3032.
[154] Together with its Scottish and Northern Irish equivalents, s.15 of the Law Reform (Miscellaneous Provisions) (Scotland) Act 1985 and s.94A of the Judicature (Northern Ireland) Act 1978. See para.21–163, below.
[155] CDPA 1988 s.296ZD(6), (9).
[156] See paras 21–75 et seq., below.
[157] s.296ZD(7).

s.296, presumably because the Software Directive provides for "remedies" but not "sanctions" in respect of circumvention devices.[158] The Information Society Directive requires Member States to provide "adequate legal protection" both against the act of circumvention itself and against devices and services designed to assist such circumvention.[159] It also requires Member States to provide appropriate sanctions and remedies and requires sanctions to be "effective, proportionate and dissuasive".[160] Against that background, criminal offences have been introduced in this field. However, their scope is limited.[161] First, consistently with the terms of the Software Directive and the previous position, there are no criminal offences in relation to the circumvention of technical devices applied to computer programs. Secondly, the act of circumvention itself is not a criminal offence. The criminal sanctions are limited to activities in relation to devices and services which are designed to circumvent technological measures. Thirdly, as in the case of the copyright offences, almost all the offences consist of some form of commercial activity. The only exception is activity which has a prejudicial effect on the copyright owner. Fourthly, the criminal provisions cover a more limited range of devices, products or components than are the subject of civil liability. Fifthly, there is a defence that the defendant did not know and had no reasonable grounds for believing that the device or service enabled or facilitated circumvention. Sixthly, the criminal provisions are limited to technological measures designed to protect copyright works (other than computer programs) and do not, as in the case of the civil provisions, extend to measures designed to protect the subject matter of rights in performances, database right or publication right. Finally, the penalties are relatively low. Any acts which took place prior to October 31, 2003 cannot be the subject of a prosecution under s.296ZB.[162]

Offences in relation to devices, products or components.[163] Section 296ZB(1) **15–30** criminalises certain acts if committed in relation to any device, product or component which is primarily designed, produced or adapted for the purpose of enabling or facilitating the circumvention of effective technological measures. The meaning of these expressions is considered elsewhere.[164] It should be emphasised that acts of making or dealing with devices which are promoted, advertised or marketed for the purpose of circumvention or which have only a limited commercially significant purpose or use other than to circumvent may attract civil liability but will not attract criminal liability. The acts which are made criminal are as follows: manufacturing for sale or hire; importing otherwise than for private and domestic use; selling or letting for hire in the course of a business; offering, exposing or advertising for sale or hire in the course of a business; possessing in the course of a business; distributing in the course of a business; and distributing otherwise than in the course of a business to such an extent as to affect prejudicially the copyright owner.[165] The wording of subs.296ZB(1) is similar to that of subs.107(1), which provides for offences in relation to the making of and dealing with infringing copies of copyright works. The provisions of

---

[158] Software Directive 91/250 art.7(1).
[159] Information Society Directive 2001/29 arts 6(1) and (2).
[160] Information Society Directive 2001/29 art.8(1).
[161] This is because the Government took the view that the language of the Information Society Directive art.6(2) was not sufficiently clear to be used to formulate criminal offences: *Analysis of Responses and Government Conclusions*, para.6.8.
[162] See Copyright and Related Rights Regulations 2003 (SI 2003/2498) regs 1 and 40.
[163] See *R. v Higgs* [2008] EWCA Crim 1324; [2009] 1 W.L.R. 73; [2008] F.S.R. 34 and *R. v Gilham* [2010] EWCA Crim 2293; [2010] E.C.D.R. 5.
[164] para.15–27.
[165] CDPA 1988 s.296ZB(1).

subs.107(1) are discussed elsewhere.[166] There appear to be only two significant differences in the range of acts which are caught. First, advertising for sale or hire is an offence under s.296ZB but not under s.107. This is no doubt because advertising for sale or hire is specifically referred to in the Information Society Directive.[167] Secondly, possession in the course of a business is only an offence under s.107 if the article is possessed with a view to committing an act infringing copyright.[168] Again, this difference is probably dictated by the terms of the Directive, which simply refers to possession for commercial purposes.[169]

15–31   **Offences in relation to services.** Again, the language of the criminal provisions is derived from the civil provisions. It is an offence to provide, promote, advertise or market in the course of a business or otherwise than in the course of a business to such an extent as to affect prejudicially the copyright owner a service the purpose of which is to enable or facilitate the circumvention of effective technological measures.[170] This provision differs from subs.296ZD(1) because there is no civil liability for promoting, advertising or marketing such services although there is civil liability for providing services which are promoted, advertised or marketed for the purpose of circumvention. It seems unlikely that this distinction will be of any practical importance.

15–32   **Defences to criminal liability.** There are two statutory defences, which apply both to the offences in relation to devices and to those in relation to services. First, it is provided that s.296ZB does not make unlawful anything done by, or on behalf of, law enforcement agencies or any of the intelligence services[171] in the interests of national security or for the purposes of the prevention or detection of crime, the investigation of an offence or the conduct of a prosecution.[172] It is thought that on general principles the burden of proving that the defendant falls within the scope of this exception may lie on the defendant (the standard being to the balance of probabilities).[173] It is also a defence for the defendant to prove that he did not know and had no reasonable ground for believing that the device, product or component or (as the case may be) the service enabled or facilitated the circumvention of effective technological measures.[174] In this case, the burden of proof clearly lies on the defendant. Again, applying general principles, the standard will be to the balance of probabilities.

15–33   **Penalties.** A person guilty of any offence under s.296ZB is liable on summary conviction to imprisonment for a term not exceeding three months or a fine not exceeding the statutory maximum[175] or both; or on conviction on indictment to an unlimited fine or to imprisonment for a term not exceeding two years, or both.[176] These penalties are the maximum permitted in respect of offences created (as these offences were) by subordinate legislation made under the European Com-

---

[166] See para.22–14, below.

[167] Information Society Directive 2001/29 art.6(2).

[168] CDPA 1988 s.107(1)(c).

[169] Information Society Directive art.6(2).

[170] CDPA 1988 s.296ZB(2).

[171] As defined in s.81 of the Regulation of Investigatory Powers Act 2000.

[172] CDPA 1988 s.296ZB(3). This defence is expressly sanctioned by recital 51 to the Information Society Directive.

[173] For a discussion of the application of these general principles to s.107, see paras 22–62 et seq., below.

[174] s.296ZB(5). For a discussion of the terms "knowledge" and "reason to believe", see paras 8–08 et seq., above.

[175] Currently £5,000: Interpretation Act 1978 Sch.1, applying Magistrates Courts Act 1980 s.32(9) as amended by Criminal Justice Act 1991 s.17(2)(c).

[176] CDPA 1988 s.296ZB(4).

munities Act 1972.[177] As a result, they are considerably lower than those for most other offences under the 1988 Act.

Search warrants and forfeiture. Section 296ZC provides that certain provisions of the 1988 Act which concern search warrants and forfeiture apply to offences under s.296ZB with specified modifications. The sections are s.297B, which makes provision for the issue of search warrants where offences in relation to unauthorised decoders are suspected; and ss.297C and 297D, which make provision for the forfeiture of unauthorised decoders. The effect is as follows. First, where a justice of the peace is satisfied that there are reasonable grounds to believe that an offence under s.296ZB has been or is about to be committed in any premises or that evidence that such an offence has been or is about to be committed is in those premises, he may issue a warrant authorising a constable to enter and search the premises, using such reasonable force as is necessary.[178] The limitations on and manner of execution of such a warrant contained in s.297B will apply. These are considered elsewhere.[179] Secondly, where devices, products or components for the purpose of circumventing effective technological measures have come into the possession of any person in connection with the investigation or prosecution of an offence under subs.297ZB(1) of the 1988 Act, that person may apply under s.297C for an order for forfeiture of such devices, products or components.[180] The procedure on such an application will be governed by s.297C, which is considered elsewhere.[181] There are equivalent provisions for Scotland.[182]

15–34

C. REMEDY WHERE MEASURES PREVENT PERMITTED ACTS

Introduction. With a view to resolving the obvious tension between the protection it grants to technological measures on the one hand and the existence of a wide range of permitted acts on the other, the Information Society Directive requires Member States to take appropriate measures to ensure that right holders allow the exercise of the permitted acts derived from arts 5(2)(a), (2)(b), (2)(c), (2)(d), (2)(e), (3)(a), (3)(b) or (3)(e) to take place.[183] Such measures need only be taken if there are no voluntary measures taken by rightholders, including agreements between rightholders and other parties concerned.[184] The background to these provisions is considered elsewhere.[185] Section 296ZE of the 1988 Act contains a scheme for dealing with such cases. Under the scheme a complainant may make a complaint to the Secretary of State who will investigate certain matters. Depending on the outcome of that investigation the Secretary of State may give a direction requiring the owner of the rights in the work to which the measure has been applied to ensure that the complainant can benefit from the

15–35

---

[177] See s.2(2) and Sch.2 para.1(1)(d). The offences were created by the Copyright and Related Rights Regulations 2003 (SI 2003/2498).

[178] CDPA 1988 s.297B(1), as modified by s.296ZC(2).

[179] See para.16–26, below, and the paragraphs referred to there.

[180] s.297C(1), (2), as modified by s.296ZC(3), (4).

[181] See para.16–26, below, and the paragraphs referred to there.

[182] For search warrants, see s.297B, as modified by s.296ZC(1), (2); for forfeiture, see s.297D, as modified by s.296ZC(3), (4).

[183] Information Society Directive 2001/29 art.6(4). For an account of how this provision has been implemented in a variety of European countries, see *Braun* [2003] 11 E.I.P.R. 496. The author discerns a trend towards the use of mediation and arbitration provisions. See also Akester, "The impact of digital rights management on freedom of expression—the first empirical assessment" [2010] 41(1) I.I.C. 31–58 and *Automated Rights Management Systems and Copyright Limitations and Exceptions*, a report dated April 27, 2006 by Nic Garnett for WIPO's Standing Committee on Copyright and Related Rights, concentrating on visually impaired persons and distance education.

[184] art.6(4).

[185] See paras 9–10 and 9–11, above.

permitted act. Failure to comply with a direction will amount to a breach of statutory duty, which will be actionable by the complainant or a representative of a body of complainants.[186] It appears that as at February 2009 these provisions had not been used.[187]

15–36   **Scope of the scheme.** Section 296ZE has a number of limitations. First, it has no application in the case of computer programs.[188] This is because the Information Society Directive expressly leaves the law as to computer programs, as contained in the Software Directive, unchanged.[189] Secondly, it does not apply to copyright works made available to the public on agreed contractual terms in such a way that members of the public may access them from a place and at a time individually chosen by them.[190] This exclusion would apply, for example, to pay-per-use and video-on-demand services but not to non-interactive forms of online use.[191] Thirdly, in accordance with the Directive, s.296ZE only applies to the permitted acts listed in Pt 1 of Sch.5A to the 1988 Act. Fourthly, the section only applies where the complainant, or the class of persons represented by the complainant, has lawful access to the protected copyright work.[192] On the other hand, the section applies (with any necessary adaptations) to rights in performances, database right and publication right.[193]

15–37   **Notice of complaint.** The operation of the scheme is triggered by the issue of a notice of complaint to the Secretary of State.[194] A notice of complaint may be issued by a person on his own account or as a representative of a class of persons. In each case the basis of the complaint is that the application of an effective technological measure[195] to a copyright work[196] prevents the person or class of persons from carrying out a permitted act in relation to that work.[197] The Secretary of State may give directions as to the form and manner in which a notice of complaint may be delivered to him.[198]

15–38   **Action on receipt of notice: is there a voluntary measure or agreement?** The Secretary of State may give directions generally as to the procedure to be fol-

---

[186] This summary derives from the Patent Office's *Transposition Note*. During the consultation process, rightholders argued that some time should elapse before these provisions took effect in order to enable voluntary measures to be put in place. This argument gains some support from the terms of recital 51 ("in the absence of such voluntary measures or agreements within a reasonable period of time, Member States should take appropriate measures") but less so from art.6(4), which contains no reference to a reasonable period to elapse before measures are taken. See *Analysis of Responses and Government Conclusions*, para.6.13.

[187] See Akester, "The impact of digital rights management on freedom of expression—the first empirical assessment" [2010] 41(1) IIC 31–58. This article contains a useful summary of detailed research into the practical aspects of the interrelationship between DRM and the permitted acts.

[188] This follows from the definition of technological measures in CDPA 1988 s.296ZF(1).

[189] See para.15–06, above.

[190] s.296ZE(10), applying art.7(4) of the Information Society Directive. Presumably it is thought that where matters are already regulated by contract, there are adequate other remedies.

[191] See recital 53 to the Information Society Directive 2001/29.

[192] s.296ZE(10).

[193] s.296ZE(11). The relevant exceptions to rights in performances and database right are listed in Sch.5A Pts 2 and 3.

[194] This is a reference to the Secretary of State for Trade and Industry.

[195] For the meaning of this term, see paras 15–19 and 15–20, above.

[196] The scheme does not apply to computer programs: see CDPA 1988 s.296ZE(2). On the other hand, it does apply with any necessary adaptations to the subject matter of rights in performances, database right and publication right: s.296ZE(11).

[197] s.296ZE(2).

[198] s.296ZE(4)(a). Such directions must be published in such manner as in the Secretary of State's opinion will secure adequate publicity for them: s.296ZE(4). No such directions had been published at the time of writing.

lowed in relation to a complaint made under this section.[199] The section provides for the following procedure, which is designed to ensure, in accordance with the Directive, that measures are only taken by the Secretary of State if there are no existing voluntary or contractual arrangements.[200] Following receipt of the notice, the Secretary of State may give the owner of the copyright work or an exclusive licensee such directions[201] as appear to him to be requisite or expedient for the purpose of establishing whether there is any relevant subsisting voluntary measure or agreement.[202] For these purposes, a voluntary measure is a measure taken voluntarily by the copyright owner, his exclusive licensee or a person issuing copies of or communicating the work to the public the effect of which is to enable a person to carry out a permitted act.[203] An agreement is an agreement between the copyright owner, his exclusive licensee or a person issuing copies of or communicating the work to the public and another party which has the same effect.[204] The Secretary of State may give directions as to the form and manner in which evidence of any voluntary measure or agreement may be delivered to him.[205] It is the duty of a person to whom a direction has been given under this provision to give effect to that direction.[206] By contrast with the duty to comply with a direction of the type referred to in the next paragraph, this duty is not expressed to be owed to the complainant or those whom he represents. It appears, therefore, that it is owed to the Secretary of State, who can presumably enforce it by injunctive relief (although this not stated expressly in the section). There is no express provision for an appeal against the making or refusal to make such a direction. Presumably, however, the decision to make or not to make a direction will be amenable to judicial review. It may also be possible for a person to whom a direction is addressed to challenge its validity by way of a defence to enforcement proceedings, but this is not clear.

Action in the absence of a voluntary measure or agreement. Where it is established that there is no subsisting voluntary measure or agreement, the Secretary of State may give such directions[207] as appear to him to be requisite or expedient for the purpose of ensuring that the copyright owner or his exclusive licensee makes available to the complainant the means of carrying out the permitted act "to the extent necessary to so benefit from the permitted act".[208] The Government's view is that a refusal by the Secretary of State to exercise his discretion to take action in a proper case would be subject to judicial review.[209] The need for the phrase "to the extent necessary to so benefit from the permitted act", which derives from the Information Society Directive, is unclear. Presumably it is intended to emphasise that any direction will be limited to the provision of the means necessary to carry out the permitted act and no further. However,

15–39

---

[199] CDPA 1988 s.296ZE(3)(a). Such directions must be published in such manner as in the Secretary of State's opinion will secure adequate publicity for them: s.296ZE(4). No such directions had been published at the time of writing.

[200] See para.15–35, above.

[201] Which must be in writing and which may be varied or revoked by a subsequent direction under s.296ZE: see s.296ZE(7), (8).

[202] s.296ZE(3)(a).

[203] s.296ZE(1)(a).

[204] s.296ZE(1)(b).

[205] s.296ZE(4)(b). Such directions must be published in such manner as in the Secretary of State's opinion will secure adequate publicity for them: s.296ZE(4). No such directions had been published at the time of writing.

[206] s.296ZE(5).

[207] Which must be in writing and which may be varied or revoked by a subsequent direction under CDPA 1988 s.296ZE: see s.296ZE(7), (8).

[208] s.296ZE(3)(b).

[209] *Analysis of Responses and Government Conclusions*, para.6.15.

this appears to be evident from the other words of the subsection. More importantly, perhaps, it is far from clear how this will work in practice. A software patch which allows a user access in order to carry out one of the permitted acts is likely to enable access for all purposes.

The effect of such a direction is that the copyright owner (or exclusive licensee as the case may be) owes a statutory duty to the complainant or, in the case of a representative complaint, to the representative and each person in the class represented. A breach of that duty is actionable as a breach of statutory duty, subject to the defences and other incidents applying to actions for breach of statutory duty.[210] Typically, such a duty is likely to be enforced by a claim for injunctive relief. There seems no reason in principle why a representative action could not be brought where the duty is owed to a class. Again, there is no express provision for an appeal against the making or refusal to make such a direction. Presumably, again, the decision to make or not to make a direction will be amenable to judicial review. It seems unlikely that a copyright owner or exclusive licensee to whom a direction is addressed will be able to challenge its validity by way of a defence to enforcement proceedings, but the existing of pending judicial review proceedings might be grounds for an adjournment of such proceedings until the outcome of the judicial review.

5. RIGHTS MANAGEMENT INFORMATION

15–40 **The WIPO Copyright Treaty.** Article 12 of the WIPO Copyright Treaty ("WCT") requires contracting parties to provide adequate and effective legal remedies against any person who knowingly removes or alters electronic rights management information[211] without authority. The same article requires Contracting Parties to provide adequate and effective legal remedies against any person who knowingly distributes, imports for distribution, broadcasts or communicates to the public without authority works or copies of works knowing that electronic rights management information has been removed without authority. In both cases the remedies only need be provided against persons who know or (with respect to civil remedies) have reasonable grounds to believe that the act in question will induce, enable, facilitate or conceal an infringement of any right covered by the Treaty or the Berne Convention.[212] For these purposes, "rights management information" is defined as "information which identifies the work, the author of the work, the owner of any right in the work, or information about the terms and conditions of use of the work, and any numbers or codes that represent such information, when any of these items of information is attached to a copy of a work or appears in connection with the communication of a work to the public".[213] The Agreed Statement provides that Contracting Parties will not rely on art.12 to devise or implement rights management systems that would have the effect of imposing formalities which are not permitted under the Berne Convention or the WCT itself, prohibiting the free movement of goods or impeding the enjoyment of rights under the WCT.[214]

15–41 **The WIPO Performances and Phonograms Treaty.** Article 19 of the WIPO

---

[210] s.296ZE(6).
[211] See Vol.2 F13. For background information as to the nature of rights management information, see para.15–02, above.
[212] WCT art.12(1). For the rights covered, see paras 23–04 et seq. (Berne) and 23–66 et seq. (WCT). The Agreed Statement makes clear that the reference to "any right covered by this Treaty or by the Berne Convention" includes both exclusive rights and rights of remuneration. See Vol.2 F13.
[213] WCT art.12(2).
[214] See Vol.2 F13.

Performances and Phonograms Treaty ("WPPT") requires Contracting Parties to provide substantially the same remedies in the field of performances and phonograms. For the purposes of art.19, the relevant state of mind is knowing or (with respect to civil remedies) having reasonable grounds to believe that the act in question will induce, enable, facilitate or conceal an infringement of any right covered by the WPPT[215]; the offending acts other than removal or alteration of the information must be directed at copies of fixed performances or phonograms[216]; while rights management information is defined as "information which identifies the performer, the performance of the performer, the producer of the phonogram, the phonogram, the owner of any right in the performance or phonogram, or information about the terms and conditions of use of the performance or phonogram, and any numbers or codes that represent such information, when any of these items of information is attached to a copy of a fixed performance or a phonogram or appears in connection with the communication or making available of a fixed performance or a phonogram to the public".[217] As in the case of art.12 of the WCT, the Agreed Statement provides that Contracting Parties will not rely on art.19 to devise or implement rights management systems that would have the effect of imposing formalities which are not permitted under the Berne Convention or the WCT itself, prohibiting the free movement of goods or impeding the enjoyment of rights under the WCT.[218]

Provisions of the Information Society Directive.[219] Article 7 of the Directive   **15–42**
contains provisions which are intended to implement the WIPO and WPPT Treaties. Thus, art.7(1) sets out a list of offending acts in terms which are substantially the same as those of the Treaties, while art.7(2) adopts the definitions of rights management information contained in the Treaties.

Provisions of the 1988 Act. The Directive was implemented by adding a new   **15–43**
s.296ZG to the 1988 Act.[220] In general, the terms of the section follow closely those of the Directive and thus of the WCT and WPPT. Thus, the new section creates civil (but not criminal) remedies against those who tamper with electronic rights management information or deal with copies of works from which such information has been removed or in respect of which it has been altered. The terms of the section apply with the necessary adaptations to rights in performances, publication right and database right,[221] but for ease of exposition they are considered below as they apply to copyright.[222]

"Rights management information".[223] There are three elements to the   **15–44**
definition. First, the information must have been "provided" by the copyright owner or the holder of "any right under copyright". The latter expression is

---

[215] WPPT art.19(1). See Vol.2 F14. For the rights covered, see paras 23–119 et seq. The Agreed Statement makes clear that the reference to "any right covered by this Treaty" includes both exclusive rights and rights of remuneration. See Vol.2 F14.

[216] art.19(1)(ii).

[217] art.19(2).

[218] See Vol.2 H8.

[219] Directive 2001/29 [2001] OJ L167/10. See Vol.2 H8.

[220] This was effected by the Copyright and Related Rights Regulations 2003 (SI 2003/2498) reg.25, with effect from October 31, 2003 (SI 2003/2498 reg.1).

[221] CDPA 1988 s.296ZG(8).

[222] No act done before October 31, 2003 and no act done after October 31, 2003 in pursuance of an agreement made before December 22, 2002 is to be regarded as an infringement of the provisions: Copyright and Related Rights Regulations 2003 (SI 2003/2498) regs 31(2) and 32(2).

[223] CDPA 1988 s.296ZG(7)(b).

intended to transpose the Directive's term "rightholders" into English law.[224] This is a broad term, the exact scope of which is debatable. It obviously includes the copyright owner. It presumably also includes an exclusive licensee. Arguably it might be said to include non-exclusive licensees as well, but this is not clear. Secondly, the information must fall within one of two categories. Either it must identify the work, the author, the copyright owner or the holder of any intellectual property rights (whether in the work or not is not stated); or it must be information about the terms and conditions of use of the work. Thirdly, "rights management information" includes any numbers or codes which represent such information.[225]

15–45 **Persons with rights.** Two categories of persons have rights. First, a person issuing copies of the work to the public or communicating the work to the public. Secondly, the copyright owner or his exclusive licensee if he is not the person issuing copies of the work to the public or communicating the work to the public.[226]

15–46 **Persons against whom rights are exercisable: D and E.** The rights are exercisable against two categories of person, named in the section as "D" and "E". D is a person who knowingly and without authority removes or alters electronic rights management information which is associated with a copy of a copyright work or appears in connection with the communication to the public of a copyright work. D is only liable if at the time he commits the act in question, he knows or has reason to believe that by doing so he is inducing, enabling, facilitating or concealing an infringement of copyright.[227] E is a person who knowingly and without authority distributes, imports for distribution or communicates to the public copies of a copyright work from which electronic rights management information associated with the copies or appearing in connection with the communication to the public of copies of the work has been altered or removed without authority. As in D's case, E is only liable if at the time he commits the act in question he knows or has reason to believe that by so doing he is inducing, enabling, facilitating or concealing an infringement of copyright.[228] The phrase "without authority" derives from the WCT and WPPT treaties via the Information Society Directive and is not further defined in any of these documents. It is not wholly clear whose authority is relevant. On the one hand, it might be argued that since the section does not expressly create a right to prevent the removal or tampering of electronic rights management information, the relevant authority must be sought elsewhere than in the section, for example in contract. On the other hand, it is quite possible that what is intended is that any person with rights under the section may give the relevant authority.

---

[224] The Government originally intended to limit the remedies to information provided by copyright owners, but eventually conceded that the terms of the Information Society Directive 2001/29 required a broader term: *Analysis of Responses and Government Conclusions*, para.7.2.

[225] In the United States case of *The IQ Group Ltd v Wiesner Publishing LLC* 409 F. Supp. 2d 587 (US DC NJ January 10, 2006), it was held that a logo and a hyperlink which appeared on copies of emails advertising insurance services to agents did not amount to "copyright management information" for the purposes of 17 U.S.C. § 1202 both because the logo was a service mark and because 17 U.S.C. § 1202 only protected information which functioned as a component of an automated copyright protection or management system. This decision was not followed in *McClatchey v The Associated Press* 2007 W.L. 776103 (US DC W.D. Pa March 9, 2007). The claimant claimed that, using a computer, she had made a print of a photograph taken by her. On the print appeared the title, her name and a copyright notice. A photograph of the print was taken by a photographer employed by the defendant news agency, and the claimant claimed that the defendant then cropped the title, her name and the copyright notice and replaced them with other material before distributing the revised version. On the defendant's summary judgment application the court held that 17 U.S.S. § 1202 protects information which is not in digital form.

[226] CDPA 1988 s.296ZG(3), (4).

[227] CDPA 1988 s.296ZG(1).

[228] s.296ZG(2).

The rights. In the case of a person issuing copies of the work to the public or **15–47** communicating the work to the public, the rights are the same rights as the owner of copyright has in respect of an infringement of copyright. In the case of an exclusive licensee of the copyright, the rights are the same as he has in respect of an infringement of copyright.[229] The effect of similar provisions in respect of the circumvention of technical devices is discussed above.[230] The rights are expressed to be concurrent and ss.101(3) and 102(1) to (4) of the 1988 Act apply in proceedings under s.296ZG in relation to persons with concurrent rights as they apply, in proceedings mentioned in those provisions, in relation to a copyright owner and exclusive licensee with concurrent rights.[231] The effect of an analogous provision in relation to the circumvention of technical devices is discussed above.[232] The presumptions contained in ss.104 to 106 of the 1988 Act,[233] the presumptions in reg.22 of the Copyright and Rights in Databases Regulations[234] and the withdrawal of the privilege against self-incrimination effected by s.72of the Senior Courts Act 1981[235] apply in relation to proceedings under s.296ZG as they apply in relation to proceedings under the copyright Part of the 1988 Act.[236]

---

[229] CDPA 1988 s.296ZG(3).

[230] para.15–16.

[231] 231 s.296ZG(5).

[232] para.15–17.

[233] See paras 21–260 et seq., below.

[234] SI 1997/3032.

[235] Together with its Scottish and Northern Irish equivalents, s.15 of the Law Reform (Miscellaneous Provisions) (Scotland) Act 1985 and s.94A of the Judicature (Northern Ireland) Act 1978. See para.21–163, below.

[236] CDPA 1988 s.296ZG(6) and (9).

FRAUDULENT RECEPTION OF TRANSMISSIONS

1. HISTORICAL INTRODUCTION

Position before 1984. The increase in cable and satellite broadcasting inevitably brought with it attempts to gain access to transmissions without paying the fees demanded by those who broadcast them. Satellite broadcasters attempted to limit reception to those who had paid for it by transmitting their signals in encrypted form and charging the viewer for the use of a decoding device. Pirates responded by making and distributing unauthorised decoding devices which enabled viewers to watch the programmes without paying for them. Pirates also discovered methods of "re-enabling" legitimate decoding devices which had been "disabled" because the viewer had failed to keep up the requisite subscription. In 1996 it was estimated that between five and 20 per cent of the decoding devices in circulation in the European Community were unauthorised.[1] The widespread use of such devices clearly has adverse effects both for the broadcaster, which loses subscription revenue, and for the owners of the rights in the programmes, whose income may be reduced. Before the passing of the Cable and Broadcasting Act 1984,[2] the law was thought to provide very limited protection to broadcasters in relation to such activities,[3] and the Government was concerned that those who were taking a large commercial risk in relation to the provision of cable and satellite programmes should have the reassurance that a solid legal framework was in place to prevent people enjoying the benefits of those services without paying for them.[4]   **16–01**

Cable and Broadcasting Act 1984. The Cable and Broadcasting Act 1984[5] cre-   **16–02**

---

[1] See the European Commission's *Green Paper on the legal protection for encrypted services in the internal market*, COM (96) 76 final, March 6, 1996, p.5.

[2] (c.46).

[3] It seems that there was no legal basis on which non-subscribers could be prevented from receiving satellite broadcasts: *BBC Enterprises v Hi-Tech Xtravision Ltd* [1990] 1 Ch. 609, 614 (Staughton L.J.). The position of cable broadcasters was stronger because the recipient of a cable programme needs to make a physical connection with the cable and an unauthorised connection would be a trespass: *BBC Enterprises v Hi-Tech Xtravision Ltd* [1990] F.S.R. 217, 229 (Scott J.). That this was the view of the Government seems clear from the parliamentary debates on the bill: *Hansard*, HC Vol.59, col./48.

[4] *Hansard*, HC Vol.59, col.748.

[5] (c.46).

ated both a new summary offence[6] and a new set of proprietary rights.[7] The provisions of the Act applied to broadcasting services in three categories: first, cable programme services; secondly, television or sound broadcasting services provided by the BBC or the IBA; and thirdly services which consisted in the sending, by means of a telecommunications system, of sounds or visual images which were provided for a person providing a service within one of the two former categories.[8] In broad terms, the new summary offence was committed by dishonestly receiving a programme included in such a service with the intention of avoiding payment of any charge applicable to its reception.[9] The new proprietary rights were infringed (again in broad terms) by the manufacture of or dealing with any apparatus or device designed or adapted to enable or assist persons to receive programmes without payment; and by the publication of any information calculated to enable or assist persons to receive programmes without payment.[10]

16–03　　**The 1988 Act and the Broadcasting Acts 1990 and 1996.** These provisions of the 1984 Act were repealed by the 1988 Act,[11] and replaced by similar, but not identical, provisions.[12] However, by 1989 the judgment of Scott J. in *BBC Enterprises Ltd v Hi-Tech Xtravision Ltd*[13] had cast serious doubts on the effectiveness of the new rights. Moreover, the BBC and others were concerned about the absence of a criminal remedy for the creation and use of unauthorised decoders.[14] Accordingly, a new summary offence of possessing and dealing with unauthorised decoders was inserted into the 1988 Act by the Broadcasting Act 1990.[15] The Broadcasting Act 1996 increased the scope of this offence, made it triable either way,[16] and increased the maximum penalties for it.[17]

16–04　　**The Conditional Access Directive.** On November 20, 1998, the European Parliament and Council adopted a Directive on the legal protection of services based on, or consisting of, conditional access.[18] The Directive required Member States both to take measures to prohibit, and to provide sanctions and remedies against a long list of commercial activities in relation to "illicit devices".[19] In the Directive, the term "illicit device" means any equipment or software designed or adapted to give access to a "protected service" in an intelligible form without the authorisation of the service provider.[20] For these purposes, "protected services" are: television broadcasting, radio broadcasting and information society services; provided in each case that they are provided against remuneration and on the basis of

---

[6] s.53.
[7] s.54.
[8] s.53(2).
[9] s.53.
[10] s.54(2).
[11] CDPA 1988 s.303(2) and Sch.8.
[12] ss.297–299.
[13] [1990] F.S.R. 217. The decision was in fact overturned by the Court of Appeal [1990] 1 Ch. 609 and the Court of Appeal's decision was upheld by the House of Lords [1991] 2 A.C. 327.
[14] *Hansard*, HL Vol.521, cols 1696 et seq. The example was given of a person who made an unauthorised decoder available on a housing estate, thus giving rise to a large number of relatively small infringements of a type which would not warrant civil proceedings, but might be deterred by a criminal conviction: *Hansard*, HL Vol.521, col.1697.
[15] CDPA 1988 s.297A, inserted by the Broadcasting Act 1990 s.179.
[16] i.e. either in the Magistrates' Court or in the Crown Court.
[17] Broadcasting Act 1996 s.140(1), amending CDPA 1988 s.297A(1).
[18] [1998] OJ L320/54. See Vol.2 H6.
[19] arts 3 to 5.
[20] art.2(e).

"conditional access".[21] The term "conditional access" means any technical measure or arrangement whereby access to the protected service in an intelligible form is made conditional upon prior individual authorisation.[22] In order to comply with the Conditional Access Directive, substantial changes were made to the 1988 Act with effect from May 28, 2000.[23] Both the criminal provisions as to unauthorised decoders contained in s.297A and the scope of the right conferred by s.298 were substantially reworded. Section 297A was extended to cover information society services as well as broadcasts so as to make express reference to the circumvention of conditional access technology. Section 298 now expressly grants rights to providers of conditional access services (whether from the United Kingdom or another Member State). It also now grants rights to those who broadcast and send encrypted transmissions from Member States other than the United Kingdom. Finally, the range of infringing activities covered by the two sections has been substantially increased.

The Copyright etc. Act 2002. This Act dramatically increased the maximum penalties for the unauthorised decoder offences,[24] while at the same time making provision as to search warrants and forfeiture.[25]   **16–05**

2. POSITION UNDER THE 1988 ACT

A. THE SCHEME OF THE ACT

The scheme of the 1988 Act. The 1988 Act in its present form contains a combination of civil and criminal remedies. First, the dishonest receiver of programmes may be proceeded against in the Magistrates' Court.[26] Secondly, a person who makes, imports, distributes or carries out any of a range of commercial activities in relation to an unauthorised decoder may be proceeded against either in the Magistrates' Court or by way of trial on indictment.[27] Thirdly, there are provisions as to search warrants in relation to the unauthorised decoder offences and as to forfeiture of unauthorised decoders.[28] Finally, broadcasters and others have civil remedies both against those who make, import, distribute or carry out any of a range of commercial activities in relation to unauthorised decoders or similar devices, and against those who publish information which assists access to their programmes or transmissions without permission.[29] There are no civil remedies against the dishonest receiver of programmes, presumably because such remedies would be unlikely to be exercised. There are a number of minor differences between the activities which constitute offences in relation to unauthorised decoders on the one hand, and the matters which may be the subject of civil proceedings on the other. It remains to be seen whether these differences will prove to be significant in practice.   **16–06**

B. OFFENCE OF FRAUDULENTLY RECEIVING PROGRAMMES

Offence under section 297. This section of the 1988 Act is aimed at those who   **16–07**

---

[21] art.2(a). The term "information society services" is considered in more detail below: see paras 16–16 et seq..

[22] art.2(b).

[23] This was effected by substituting new CDPA 1988 ss.297A and 298: see the Conditional Access (Unauthorised Decoders) Regulations 2000 (SI 2000/1175) reg.1.

[24] s.1(4)(a).

[25] ss.2(4) and 5.

[26] s.297.

[27] s.297A.

[28] ss.297B to 297D.

[29] s.298.

knowingly receive broadcasts which they are not entitled to receive. The section makes it an offence dishonestly[30] to receive a programme included in a broadcasting service provided from a place in the United Kingdom[31] with intent to avoid payment of any charge applicable to the reception of the programme. For this purpose, "programme", "broadcasting" and related expressions have the same meanings as in the copyright Part of the 1988 Act.[32] The 1988 Act provides that, where s.297 applies in relation to a broadcasting service, it also applies to any service run for the person providing that service, or a person providing programmes for that service, which consists wholly or mainly in the sending by means of a telecommunications system of sound or visual images, or both.[33] The offence under s.297 of the 1988 Act is entirely different to that committed by a person who installs or uses a television without a licence.[34]

16–08   **"A programme included in a broadcasting service provided from a place in the United Kingdom".** Murphy v Media Protection Services Ltd[35] concerned the application of s.297 to the reception by means of decoder cards purchased in Greece of broadcasts containing material which originated in the United Kingdom but had been "repackaged" in Greece. The case concerned the showing of broadcasts of English Premier League football matches transmitted by a Greek television programme provider (NOVA) by a satellite, the footprint of which extended to the appellant's public house in Portsmouth. The appellant obtained access to the programmes using a viewing card supplied by NOVA, which was cheaper than subscribing to the service provided by the Premier League's English licensee BSkyB. The card was not "pirate" in the sense of having been manufactured and marketed without NOVA's authorisation but NOVA had not authorised its use outside Greece and was contractually prohibited from exporting the card from Greece.

The visual images and ambient sound of the matches were recorded at the ground by BSkyB. They were then sent to the BT Tower from where feeds were sent to BSkyB and to the Premier League at Chiswick. BSkyB added material and the resulting feed was uploaded to a satellite and transmitted to BSkyB's subscribers. At Chiswick, the Premier League added an English commentary to the feed. The result was then encrypted and sent to NOVA in Greece by a satellite link. NOVA added material including an optional Greek commentary, a logo and advertisements. The material was then uplinked to NOVA's satellite from where it was transmitted in encrypted form to subscribers.

Subsection 299(5) of the 1988 Act provides that in s.297 the term "broadcasting" and related expressions have the same meaning as in the copyright part of the Act. The term "broadcast" is defined in subss.6(1) and (1A). Subsection 6(4) defines "the place from which a broadcast is made" as the place where, under the control and responsibility of the person making the broadcast, the programme-carrying signals are introduced into an uninterrupted chain of communication.

The appellant argued (in summary) that the definition in subs.6(4) should also

---

[30] Whether an accused acted dishonestly is a question of fact. The tribunal of fact must first decide whether, according to the ordinary standards of reasonable and honest people, what was done was dishonest and, if so, whether the defendant must have realised that what he was doing was dishonest by those standards: R. v Ghosh [1982] Q.B. 1053. It is difficult to see what the requirement of dishonesty adds to the offence given that it is only committed if the accused intended to avoid payment of the charge.

[31] For the meaning of this phrase, see the next paragraph.

[32] CDPA 1988 s.299(5). See ibid., s.6.

[33] s.299(4).

[34] This is a summary offence under the Communications Act 2003 (c.21) s.363(1).

[35] [2007] EWHC 3091(Admin); [2008] 1 W.L.R. 1869; [2008] F.S.R. 15; [2008] E.C.D.R. 9 and [2008] EWHC 1666; [2008] F.S.R. 33.

be applied to s.297 and accordingly the NOVA transmissions were not "broadcasts" and even if they had been they were made from Greece, not the United Kingdom. Thus, the appellant contended, s.297 was limited to the use of unauthorised decoders and cards to decode encrypted transmissions for which legitimate decoders and cards were available on the domestic market, for example the use of fake decoder cards to view BSkyB's transmissions in the United Kingdom.[36]

The Court rejected this argument, holding that the words of subs.299(5) only imported subss.6(1) and probably 6(1A) into s.297. The other elements of s.6 were irrelevant to s.297, being directed at the location of a broadcast for the purposes of subsistence of copyright and the description of the restricted act of broadcasting.[37]

The court held that s.297 requires the court first to identify the "programme" received, then to decide whether it was included in a "broadcasting service" and finally to determine where that service was provided from. Applying the definitions in s.6, a "programme" is any item included in a "broadcast", which itself is "an electronic transmission of visual images, sounds or other information" which is capable of being lawfully received by members of the public. A "broadcasting service" is no more than a succession of such transmissions. The place from which a broadcasting service is provided is the point at which the initial transmission of the programme for ultimate reception by the public takes place. Given that subs.6(4) has no application to s.297, the manner of transmission of the programme between its origin and the public is irrelevant, provided its identity is not affected.[38]

On the facts, the "programme" comprised the visuals and ambient sound transmitted from the football ground in the United Kingdom. The addition of other material by BSkyB and NOVA did not change the identity of the programme as received by the appellant. The "broadcasting service" was the supply of such programmes for simultaneous lawful reception from BSkyB by members of the public in the United Kingdom. The initial transmission of the programme for ultimate reception by the public took place in the United Kingdom.[39]

If it had been relevant the court would have held that both the Premier League and BSkyB were broadcasters for these purposes since they had editorial responsibility for the composition of schedules of television programmes so far as the transmitted match was concerned.[40]

The Court did not appear to take the view that the expression "broadcasting service" should be construed in accordance with the Conditional Access Directive. It is true that s.297 was not passed to implement the Conditional Access Directive. However, subs.299(5) of the 1988 Act makes clear that the term "broadcasting" and related expressions in s.297 are intended to have the same meaning as in ss.297A and 298. Sections 297A and 298 are intended to implement that Directive—and in both these sections the expression "broadcasting service" is intended to represent two out of the three elements (television and radio broadcasting) of the definition of "protected service" in the Directive (the other element is an information society service).

"With intent to avoid the payment of any charge". In *Murphy* it was also contended that because the appellant had paid a charge for the NOVA decoder   **16–09**

---

[36] *Murphy v Media Protection Services Ltd* [2007] EWHC 3091 (Admin) at paras 17–21.
[37] *Murphy v Media Protection Services Ltd* [2007] EWHC 3091 (Admin) at para.35.
[38] *Murphy v Media Protection Services Ltd* [2007] EWHC 3091 (Admin) at paras 36–38, 41.
[39] *Murphy v Media Protection Services Ltd* [2007] EWHC 3091 (Admin) at paras 36–38.
[40] *Murphy v Media Protection Services Ltd* [2007] EWHC 3091 (Admin) at para.39.

and card she did not have the requisite intent to avoid the charge. The court rejected this argument. The appellant knew that BSkyB had an exclusive licence to broadcast in the United Kingdom and had made arrangements to receive its broadcasts without paying its charge.[41] This result appears to follow from the factual finding that the "programme" in question was the material transmitted from the ground in the United Kingdom by BSkyB.

16–10   **Users of "genuine" decoder cards purchased in the Community.** In the light of the reference to the Court of Justice in *FAPL v QC Leisure*[42] the Administrative Court referred a number of issues to the European Court of Justice.[43] They are as follows:

First, whether the term "illicit device" in the Conditional Access Directive refers to a device which is "pirated" in the sense that it has not been manufactured and marketed by or on behalf of the relevant service provider, and that its inherent physical nature has been adapted or designed to bypass the charging arrangements put in place by the service provider. The relevance of this issue to s.297 was stated to be that if the term extends to devices which are not "pirated" then a prosecution under s.297(1) in relation to the reception of programmes by means of such a device might offend against art.3(2) of the Conditional Access Directive, which prohibits Member States from restricting the free provision of conditional access services and the free movement of such devices. It might also offend against the free movement principles of the Treaty itself. The Court stated that it shared Kitchin J.'s provisional view in *FAPL* that the term was limited to "pirated" devices.[44]

Second, whether the prosecution of the appellant under s.297(1) was a measure having equivalent effect to a quantitative restriction on imports of decoder cards under art.28 EC or on the appellant's ability to receive a service from another Member State within the meaning of art.49 EC.[45]

Third, whether s.297(1) is discriminatory in that it explicitly confers protection on broadcasting services provided from the United Kingdom but denies equivalent protection to such services provided from other Member States.[46]

Fourth, whether the contractual ban on the export of decoder cards from Greece infringed art.81 EC,[47] it being argued for the appellant that if that was the case, the exclusive right claimed by BSkyB to broadcast in the United Kingdom did not exist such that BSkyB's charge was not "applicable". In this context, the court expressed unease about the bringing of a prosecution under s.297(1) in circumstances where the establishment of an essential element of the offence depended upon the compatibility with EC law of an export ban imposed in a licence agreement between two companies who were legally strangers to the appellant.[48]

The court emphasised that s.297 remains enforceable save to the extent that it may be disapplied in order to give effect to EC law. Accordingly, in cases where EC law is not engaged (for example where the card is "pirate" or counterfeit or

[41] *Murphy v Media Protection Services Ltd* [2007] EWHC 3091 at para.42.
[42] *Football Association Premier League Ltd v QC Leisure* [2008] EWHC (Ch) 1411; [2008] F.S.R. 32; [2008] 3 C.M.L.R. 12, discussed in para.16–30 (below).
[43] *Murphy v Media Protection Services Ltd* [2008] EWHC (Admin) 1666.
[44] *Murphy v Media Protection Services Ltd* [2008] EWHC (Admin) 1666 at paras 26–34.
[45] *Murphy v Media Protection Services Ltd* [2008] EWHC (Admin) 1666 at paras 37–45. See now arts 34 and 56 of the TFEU.
[46] *Murphy v Media Protection Services Ltd* [2008] EWHC (Admin) 1666 at paras 46–50.
[47] Now art.101 of the TFEU. See Vol.2 G1.
[48] *Murphy v Media Protection Services Ltd* [2008] EWHC (Admin) 1666 at paras 51–60.

has been stolen) there is no impediment to prosecutions and convictions under s.297.[49]

Penalty and liability of corporate officers. A person who commits an offence   **16–11**
under s.297 is liable on summary conviction to a fine not exceeding level 5 on the standard scale.[50] If such an offence is committed by a body corporate and is proved to have been committed with the consent or connivance[51] of a director, manager, secretary or other similar officer of the body, or a person purporting to act in any such capacity, he, as well as the body corporate, will be guilty of the offence and liable to be proceeded against and punished accordingly.[52] In relation to a body corporate whose affairs are managed by its members, "director" means a member of the body corporate.[53]

C. Offences Relating to Unauthorised Decoders

Development of section 297A. This section of the 1988 Act is aimed at those   **16–12**
who carry out any of a wide array of activities in relation to unauthorised decoders. It was inserted in the 1988 Act by the Broadcasting Act 1990.[54] In its original form it created offences of making, importing, selling or letting for hire any unauthorised decoder. Section 140(1) of the Broadcasting Act 1996 extended the ambit of the section to the activities of offering or exposing for sale or hire and of advertising for sale or hire any unauthorised decoder.[55] The section was amended again with effect from May 28, 2000 to further extend the range of activities covered and to extend protection to information society services as well as broadcasts.[56]

Interpretation of section 297A: the problem. The present version of s.297A   **16–13**
was inserted by a statutory instrument made under the European Communities Act. The Explanatory Notes state that the instrument is intended to implement the Conditional Access Directive and that the new version of s.297A is intended to cover the activities prohibited by the Conditional Access Directive.[57] The Conditional Access Directive does not require Member States to introduce criminal sanctions but does require them to introduce effective, dissuasive and proportionate sanctions.[58] The question arises as to whether s.297A should be interpreted in accordance with the 1988 Act[59] or whether the terms of the Directive should be incorporated into it.[60] This may be a somewhat academic question. There are only two obvious differences between the terms of the section and the relevant terms of the Directive and it is doubtful whether either is of much significance. First, the definitions of "broadcasting" are different. However, in the

---

[49] *Murphy v Media Protection Services Ltd* [2008] EWHC (Admin) 1666 at paras 63–65.
[50] CDPA 1988 s.297(1). Level 5 on the standard scale is currently £5,000: Criminal Justice Act 1982 s.37(2) as substituted by Criminal Justice Act 1991 s.17(1).
[51] For the meaning of the terms "consent" and "connivance", see para.22–23, below.
[52] CDPA 1988 s.297(2). For case law relevant to the equivalent provisions in s.110 of the Act, see para.22–23 below.
[53] s.297(2).
[54] s.179(1) with effect from January 1, 1991: see the Broadcasting Act 1990 (Commencement No.1 and Transitional Provisions) Order 1990 (SI 1990/2347).
[55] With effect from October 1, 1996: Broadcasting Act 1996 (Commencement No.1 and Transitional Provisions) Order 1996 (SI 1996/2120).
[56] This was effected by reg.1 of the Conditional Access (Unauthorised Decoders) Regulations 2000 (SI 2000/1175), which substitutes a new CDPA 1988 s.297A.
[57] See previous fn.
[58] Recital 23 and arts 3 and 5.
[59] As is the case for s.297: see paras 16–07 to 16–10
[60] As is the case for s.298: see *Football Association Premier League Ltd v QC Leisure* [2008] EWHC 1411 (Ch); [2008] F.S.R. 32; [2008] 3 C.M.L.R. 12 ("the *FAPL* case") at para.56.

FAPL case the judge reached the same provisional view on the basis of the Directive as had been reached by the Divisional Court in *Murphy* on the basis of the Act. Of course the Court of Justice in the *FAPL* case may disagree with the judge's preliminary view. Second, the section requires the infringing device to be designed or adapted to access the service in question without payment of a fee whereas the Directive speaks simply of unauthorised access. In practice, however, unauthorised access will avoid payment of a fee.

16–14 **Interpretation of section 297A: the arguments.** In favour of the application of the terms of the Directive are the terms of the Explanatory Notes referred to in the previous paragraph, together with the fact that many of the definitions in s.297A are read over into s.298. Against are the following. First, the Directive does not require the imposition of criminal sanctions. Secondly, in *Murphy*[61] the Divisional Court appeared to suggest that the definitions of "programme", "broadcast" and related expressions in s.297A should be construed as one with s.297,[62] that is by reference to the terms of the 1988 Act. Thirdly, the decision to apply the terms of the Directive in *FAPL* resulted from an agreement between the parties. Given the uncertainty, in what follows, the terminology of the Act will be adopted but references to the Directive's provisions will be made where relevant.

16–15 **"Transmission".** The section applies to apparatus designed or adapted to enable encrypted transmissions to be decoded. There are now two types of transmission: first, any programme included in a broadcasting service which is provided from a place in the United Kingdom or any other Member State.[63] For these purposes, "programme", "broadcasting" and related expressions have the same meanings as in the copyright Part of the 1988 Act.[64] The second type of transmission is an "information society service" which is provided from a place in the United Kingdom or any other Member State.[65] The meaning of the term "information society service" is considered in the following paragraphs. In the Directive the equivalent term to "transmission" is "protected service", which is defined as including television broadcasting as defined in a different European Directive, radio broadcasting, information society services and the provision of conditional access considered as a service in its own right.[66]

16–16 **"Information society service": the basic definition.** Section 297A incorporates by reference the definition of information society service contained in Directive 98/34/EC[67] (as amended by Directive 98/48/EC).[68] Article 1(2) of Directive 98/34/EC contains a complex and lengthy definition of the term "information society service" which in general terms is intended to include services provided over the internet while excluding traditional broadcasting activities. Obvious examples of "information society services" are the provision of music and video files for downloading; the supply of information to subscribers via the internet; and the provision of internet access and email services.[69] In other fields it has been held that the provision of the Google Adwords service is an information society ser-

---

[61] *Murphy v Media Protection Services Ltd* [2008] EWHC 1666 (Admin); [2008] F.S.R. 33.
[62] See paras 31–33.
[63] CDPA 1988 s.297A(4).
[64] s.299(5).
[65] s.297A(4).
[66] See paras 16–28 et seq., below.
[67] [1998] OJ L204/37.
[68] [1998] OJ L217/18.
[69] See recital 18 to the E-Commerce Directive 2000/31/EC, which refers to "services consisting of the transmission of information via a communication network, in providing access to a communication network or in hosting information provided by a recipient of the service" as being within the definition.

vice[70], as is the provision of search engine services[71] and the operation of a website on which blog postings might be made.[72] The question of whether the service provided by eBay is such a service has been referred to the Court of Justice.[73]

The basic definition is as follows: "any service normally provided for remuneration, at a distance, by electronic means and at the individual request of a recipient of services". There are then three sub-definitions of this basic definition and Annex V to Directive 98/34 EC contains an indicative list of services not covered by the definition. Since the list in Annex V is divided into categories which correspond to the three sub-definitions, the Annex V items are listed here immediately after the sub-definitions.

"For remuneration". The use of email or similar communications by natural persons acting outside their trade, business or profession is not within the definition even if it is used to complete a contract.[74]   **16–17**

The remuneration need not come directly from the recipient.[75] Consistently with this, in an English case it has been stated that a service which involved the provision of internet access would be "for remuneration" provided the provider obtained remuneration from some source, for example from advertising or commission on telephone charges.[76]

"At a distance". This means that the service is provided without the parties being simultaneously present. According to Annex V, the following services are not information society services: medical examinations or treatment at a doctor's surgery using electronic equipment where the patient is physically present; consultation of an electronic catalogue in a shop with a customer on site; plane ticket reservations at a travel agency in the physical presence of the customer by means of a network of computers; and electronic games made available in a video-arcade where the customer is physically present. The same applies to other activities which by their very nature cannot be carried out at a distance and by electronic means, such as the statutory auditing of company accounts.[77]   **16–18**

"By electronic means". This means that the service is sent initially and received at its destination by means of electronic equipment for the processing (including digital compression) and storage of data and entirely transmitted, conveyed and received by wire, radio, optical means or by other electromagnetic means. Annex V states that services having material content even though provided via electronic devices are not provided "by electronic means". Examples are: automatic cash or ticket machines; and the provision of access to road networks or car parks which charge for use even where there are electronic devices at the entrance or exit to control access or ensure that payment is made. Other examples of services not provided "by electronic means" are the off-line provision of CD-Roms or software on disk; and services which are not provided via electronic processing or inventory systems, such as voice telephony services, fax or telex services, services provided via voice telephony or fax, telephone or fax consultation of doctors or lawyers, and telephone or fax direct marketing.   **16–19**

---

[70] Joined Cases C–236/08, C–237/08 and C–238/08, [2010] E.T.M.R. 30.
[71] *Metropolitan International Schools Ltd v Designtechnica Corp* [2009] EWHC 1765 (QB); [2009] E.M.L.R. 27 at para.84.
[72] *Kaschke v Gray* [2010] EWHC 690 (QB) at para.43.
[73] *L'Oreal SA v eBay International AG* [2009] EWHC 1094; [2009] R.P.C. 21. In this context it may be noted that the online sale of goods is within the definition but that their delivery is not: see recital 18 to the E-Commerce Directive 2000/31/EC.
[74] See recital 18 to the E-Commerce Directive 2000/31/EC.
[75] See recital 18 to the E-Commerce Directive 2000/31/EC.
[76] *Bunt v Tilley* [2006] EWHC 407; [2007] 1 W.L.R. 1243; [2006] E.M.L.R. 18, Eady J. (obiter).
[77] See recital 18 to the E-Commerce Directive 2000/31/EC.

16–20   **"At the individual request of a recipient of services".** This means that the service is provided through the transmission of data on individual request. Thus, for example, services which are transmitted "point to point", such as video on demand or the provision of commercial services by email are within the definition.[78] Annex V states that the following are not within this definition: services provided by transmitting data without individual demand for simultaneous reception by an unlimited number of individual receivers ("point to multipoint transmission"); television broadcasting services including near-video on demand services covered by point (a) of art.1 of Directive 89/552/EEC[79]; radio broadcasting services; and teletext where it is televised.

16–21   **"Unauthorised decoder".** All the offences under s.297A concern activities in relation to unauthorised decoders. The equivalent term in the Directive is "illicit device".[80] Relevant definitions appear in s.297A(4). The term "decoder" means any apparatus which is designed or adapted to enable (whether on its own or with any other apparatus) an encrypted transmission to be decoded. "Apparatus" includes any device, component or electronic data, including software. "Encrypted" includes subjected to scrambling or the operation of cryptographic envelopes, electronic locks, passwords or any other analogous applications. A decoder is "unauthorised" if it is designed or adapted to enable an encrypted transmission, or any service of which it forms part, to be accessed in an intelligible form without payment of the fee (however imposed) which the person making the transmission, or on whose behalf it is made, charges for accessing the transmission or service (whether by the circumvention of any conditional access technology related to the transmission or service or by any other means).[81] "Conditional access technology" means any technical measure or arrangement whereby access to encrypted transmissions in an intelligible form is made conditional on prior individual authorisation.[82]

16–22   **Offending acts.** The section embraces almost all the commercial activities which might conceivably be carried out in relation to an unauthorised decoder. Thus, an offence is committed by making, importing, distributing, selling, letting for hire or offering or exposing for sale or hire[83] any unauthorised decoder.[84] An offence is committed by possessing such a decoder for commercial purposes.[85] A further offence is committed by installing, maintaining or replacing such a decoder for commercial purposes.[86] Yet further offences are committed by advertising such a decoder for sale or hire and otherwise promoting such a decoder by means of commercial communications.[87] It will be noted that some non-commercial activities are in fact caught by the section. Thus, the offences of making and importing are not qualified by the requirement that the act in question be for commercial

---

[78] See recital 18 to the E-Commerce Directive 2000/31/EC.

[79] This is considered below, para.16–29. On near video on demand, see *Mediakabel BV v Commissariaat voor de Media* (C–89/04) [2005] E.C.R. I–4891.

[80] See para.16–31, below.

[81] In *R. v Mainwaring* [2002] F.S.R. 20, it was held that a decoder which had been advertised and sold in the United Kingdom but was designed for decoding programmes broadcast from the Netherlands was "unauthorised" even though the broadcaster had no rights to charge a fee in the United Kingdom and did not seek to do so: the decoder enabled the transmission to be accessed without payment of a fee.

[82] s.297A(4).

[83] In using the words "offering or exposing for sale or hire", the Act goes beyond the terms of the Directive.

[84] s.297(1)(a).

[85] s.297(1)(b). The expression "for commercial purposes" derives from the Directive and is the subject of a reference in the *FAPL* case. See below para.16–32.

[86] s.297(1)(c).

[87] s.297(1)(d).

purposes. In practice, however, it seems unlikely that such non-commercial activity would ever be the subject of a prosecution.

Enforcement regime. Contraventions of s.297A which are carried out in the course of a business and which harm the collective interests of consumers in the United Kingdom are subject to the enforcement regime laid down by Pt 8 of the Enterprise Act 2002.[88] This is discussed elsewhere.[89] Furthermore, the procedural requirements contained in s.230 of the Enterprise Act 2002 must be complied with before a weights and measures authority commences a prosecution under s.297A.[90] Again, these requirements are discussed elsewhere.[91] **16–23**

Defences. It is a defence to any prosecution for an offence under the section for the defendant to prove that he did not know, and had no reasonable ground for believing, that the decoder was an unauthorised decoder.[92] Depending on the facts, the competition and implied authorisation defences canvassed in the *FAPL* case may also be relevant.[93] **16–24**

Penalties and sentencing. A person who commits an offence under the section is liable on summary conviction to imprisonment for up to six months or to a fine not exceeding the statutory maximum and on conviction on indictment to imprisonment for a term not exceeding 10 years or to an unlimited fine or both.[94] **16–25**

Search warrants and forfeiture. Section 297B contains provisions as to search warrants in respect of offences under s.297A. Sections 297C and 297D contain provisions as to the forfeiture of unauthorised decoders. These sections mirror their equivalents in the copyright field, which are discussed elsewhere.[95] **16–26**

D. APPARATUS, ETC., FOR UNAUTHORISED RECEPTION OF TRANSMISSIONS

Section 298: general. Section 298 of the 1988 Act creates what has been described as a "transmission right".[96] Its purpose has been stated to be to enable providers of broadcasting and other services to obtain recompense by giving them the right to supply apparatus designed or adapted to receive their **16–27**

---

[88] Enterprise Act 2002 (Pt 8 Domestic Infringements) Order 2003 (SI 2003/1593), which came into force on June 20, 2003.

[89] See para.22–45, below.

[90] Enterprise Act 2002 s.230(2), applied by the Enterprise Act 2002 (Pt 8 Notice to OFT of Intended Prosecution Specified Enactments, Revocation and Transitional Provision) Order 2003 (SI 2003/1376), with effect from June 20, 2003.

[91] See para.22–44, below.

[92] CDPA 1988 s.297A(3). In accordance with general principles, the standard of proof will be the balance of probabilities.

[93] See paras 16–33 and 16–34, below.

[94] CDPA 1988 s.297A(2). These penalties were increased by the Broadcasting Act 1996 s.140(1) with effect from October 1, 1996: Broadcasting Act 1996 (Commencement No.1 and Transitional Provisions) Order 1996 (SI 1996/2120) and again by the Copyright, etc. and Trade Marks (Offences and Enforcement) Act 2002 s.1(4)(a) in relation to offences committed after November 20, 2002. The statutory maximum is currently £5,000: Interpretation Act 1978 Sch.1, applying Magistrates' Courts Act 1980 s.32(9) as amended by Criminal Justice Act 1991 s.17(2)(c). In *R. v Bakker* [2001] EWCA Crim 2354, which predates the significant increase in penalties with effect from November 20, 2002, the appellants were a police officer and a computer engineer. They had illegally sold and distributed between 20 and 30 cable television decoder boxes, with a putative loss to cable companies of £55 per box per month. For this they were indicted for conspiracy to defraud. They had also made and sold counterfeit software causing a loss to software companies of up to £15,000. On appeal their sentences were reduced to eight and six months respectively.

[95] See paras 22–49 et seq. (search warrants) and 22–56 et seq. (forfeiture).

[96] *British Sky Broadcasting Group Ltd v Lyons* [1995] F.S.R. 357, 362. It has been held in a criminal context that CDPA 1988 s.298 creates a right not to have others making apparatus and devices designed to be of use to persons who are not authorised to receive programmes and accord-

transmissions.[97] The section gives rights and remedies in civil proceedings to broadcasters, senders of encrypted transmissions and providers of conditional access services against those who make or deal with unauthorised decoders and similar apparatus and against those who publish information to enable others to receive programmes which they are not entitled to receive.[98] By contrast with the position under s.297A there seems no real doubt that the terms of s.298 are to be interpreted in accordance with those of the Conditional Access Directive and those terms will be used in what follows.[99]

16–28 **Protected services.** The Directive requires rights to be granted to providers of "protected services" whose interests are affected by an infringing activity.[100] In order to be protected a service must be "provided against remuneration"[101] and "on the basis of conditional access".[102] "Conditional access" means "any technical measure and/or arrangement whereby access to the protected service in an intelligible form is made conditional upon prior individual authorisation".[103] There are four types of protected service: television broadcasting, radio broadcasting, information society services and the provision of conditional access to such services considered as a service in its own right. The definition of television broadcasting has given rise to difficulties and is dealt with at length below.[104] "Radio broadcasting" is defined as "any transmission by wire or over the air, including by satellite, of radio programmes intended for reception by the public".[105] The definition of "information society services" is dealt with above.[106] The provision of conditional access in its own right is not further defined.

16–29 **Television broadcasting: the definition.** The Directive incorporates the definition in art.1(a) of the Television Without Frontiers Directive,[107] which is as follows: "the initial transmission by wire or over the air, including that by satellite, in unencoded or encoded form, of television programmes intended for reception by the public. It includes the communication of programmes between undertakings with a view to their being relayed to the public. It does not include communication services providing items of information or other messages on individual demand such as telecopying, electronic data banks and other similar services". The following points have been established in the case law.[108] First, the expression is not defined by opposition to the concept of "information society service" and therefore does not necessarily cover services not covered by that

---

ingly that a conspiracy to injure that right amounts to a conspiracy to defraud: *R. v Bridgeman and Butt* [1996] F.S.R. 538 (Crown Ct).

[97] *British Sky Broadcasting Group Ltd v Lyons* [1995] F.S.R. 357, 361.

[98] For a case on the equivalent Hong Kong provisions, see *Satellite Television Asian Region Ltd v Alpha Communications Ltd* [2003] H.K.L.R.D. 282.

[99] The point was agreed by the parties in *Football Association Premier League Ltd v QC Leisure* [2008] EWHC 1411; [2008] F.S.R. 32; [2008] 3 C.M.L.R. 12.

[100] art.5(2).

[101] See para.16–17 above as to the meaning of this in the context of the definition of information society services. In the *FAPL* case, Kitchin J. expressed the view that the remuneration comprised the subscriptions and fees paid by final consumers which were passed on to FAPL by its licensees (at para.131). For the facts, see para.16–30, below.

[102] art.2(a).

[103] art.2(b).

[104] paras 16–29 et seq.

[105] art.2(a) second indent.

[106] paras 16–16 to 16–20.

[107] 89/552/EEC.

[108] Principally *Mediakabel BV v Commissariaat voor de Media* (C–89/04) [2005] E.C.R. I–4891. See also *Kabel Deutschland Vertrieb und Service GmbH & Co KG v Niedersächsische Landesmedienanstalt für privaten Rundfunk* (C–336/07) [2008] E.C.R. I–10889; [2009] 2 C.M..L.R. 6 ("telemedia" services including "teleshopping").

concept.[109] Secondly, the important question is whether the service is intended for an indeterminate number of potential television viewers to whom the same images are transmitted simultaneously. Thirdly, the manner in which the images are disseminated is not a determining factor.

The *FAPL*[110] and *UEFA*[111] cases. In these cases, the facts were similar to those   **16–30**
in *Murphy*[112] with the additional element that some of the decoder cards had been issued by the Middle East and North Africa sub-licensee ("ART"). Civil proceedings were brought for copyright infringement and under s.298 against suppliers of equipment and decoder cards to pubs and bars and against the operators and licensees of four pubs. The claimants were the Football Association Premier League Ltd ("FAPL"), which organised the filming of the matches, and FAPL's Greek sub-licensee ("NOVA"). FAPL's Middle East and North Africa sub-licensee ("ART") was not a party. It was not in dispute that NOVA was a provider of a protected service, but FAPL's standing to sue was in dispute because it was not the immediate broadcaster.

Kitchin J. referred the question of the immediate broadcaster's standing to sue to the European Court of Justice, but expressed the provisional view that FAPL was providing a television broadcasting service and as such had standing. FAPL did transmit television programmes for reception by the public, namely the visual coverage, ambient sound and English language commentary of the matches. It did not matter that that transmission was indirect because art.1(a) of the Television Without Frontiers Directive extends to the communication of programmes between undertakings with a view to their being relayed to the public. Nor did it matter that the licensees added logos and, on occasion, commentary nor that they cut to and from FAPL's feed, depending on their own schedules, but without interrupting the coverage. These steps did not change the essential identity of the programmes.[113]

The defendants argued that the definition of "television broadcasting" in art.1(a) should be qualified by reference to the definition of "broadcaster" in art.1(b) as "the natural or legal person who has editorial responsibility for the composition of schedules of television programmes within the meaning of (a) and who transmits them or has them transmitted by third parties". Kitchin J. acknowledged that if that argument was correct, there would be considerable force in the submission that FAPL was not engaged in television broadcasting: it did not provide whole schedules of programmes which were simply relayed over the network of others nor did it have editorial responsibility for the schedule of programmes broadcast by its licensees. However, Kitchin J.'s provisional view was that it was not appropriate to import art.1(b) into art.1(a) for these purposes. Article 2(a) of the Conditional Access Directive was clear in only referring to art.1(a). That was a sensible scheme given that the purposes of the Directives are different. The Television Without Frontiers Directive is concerned with regulation and naturally identifies the broadcaster as the person with editorial responsibility for the composition of whole schedules of programmes. The result was a definition of television broadcasting which was consistent with the defini-

---

[109] That said, television broadcasting services within the definition are excluded from the definition of information society services. See above para.16–20.
[110] *Football Association Premier League Ltd v QC Leisure* [2008] EWHC 1411 (Ch); [2008] F.S.R. 32; [2008] 3 C.M.L.R. 12.
[111] *Union of European Football Associations v Euroview Sport Ltd* [2010] EWHC (Ch) 1066. So far as relevant to this chapter the questions in the *UEFA* case are substantially the same as those in the *FAPL* case. For the reasons why there are two separate cases, and therefore two separate references, see [2010] EWHC 1066 at paras 17–32.
[112] para.16–08, above.
[113] paras 121–127.

tion of "radio broadcasting" in art.2(a). There was nothing inconsistent in having more than one protected service in a single transmission.[114]

It seems that the Commission takes a different view to that of Kitchin J., but intends to initiate work to assess the need for additional measures to close this "loophole".[115]

16–31   **"Illicit device".** The forms of infringing activity which the Directive requires Member States to prohibit all concern "illicit devices", which are defined as "any equipment or software designed or adapted to give access to a protected service in an intelligible form without the authorisation of the service provider".[116] In *FAPL* and *UEFA*, Kitchin J. referred to the Court of Justice the question whether the expression "illicit device" is limited to "pirate" devices, that is to say cards made and issued by third parties without the authorisation of the protected service provider, or whether it extends to cards which are used to give access to the protected service without authorisation, even if they have been issued by the service provider.

Kitchin J. expressed the provisional view that the expression was limited to "pirate" devices. His reasons were as follows.[117] First, recitals 13 and 15 suggest that the Directive is concerned with the production and placing on the market of devices which do not originate with a legitimate service provider rather than the unauthorised use of devices which do originate from a legitimate provider. Secondly, if (as the claimants contended) the Directive was only concerned with the effect of the devices, there would be no need to limit its scope to "illicit" devices. Rather it would have been directed at all devices which are used to give unauthorised access. Thirdly, the presence in the definitions of "conditional access device" and "illicit device" of the phrase "designed or adapted" suggest a focus on the physical or inherent nature of the device. Fourthly, any reading of the definition which means that a device is "illicit" or "not illicit" depending on where it is intended to be used would be "wholly unworkable" given the scope of the infringing activities listed in art.4. Fifthly, if the expression extended to non-"pirated" devices, it was hard to see what substance there could be in art.3(2)(b) (which prohibits Member States from restricting the free movement of conditional access devices). Sixthly, the Green Paper of March 6, 1996, which is referred to in recital 4, appeared to contain the view that any restriction on parallel imports of "non-pirate" decoders would be disproportionate. Finally, the Commission had expressed the view that the proposal for the Directive concerned "commercial piracy activities against protected services". The Commission has since endorsed Kitchin J.'s provisional view.[118]

16–32   **Infringing activities.** The Directive, like s.297A, embraces almost all the commercial activities which might conceivably be carried out in relation to an illicit device.[119] Thus, an infringement is committed by manufacturing, importing, distributing, selling or renting an illicit device. An infringement is also committed by possessing such a device for commercial purposes.[120] A further infringement is committed by installing, maintaining or replacing such a device for commercial purposes. Yet further infringements are committed by the use of

---

[114] paras 128–130.
[115] Second report on the implementation of the Directive: (COM (2008) 593 final) at para.3.3.1.
[116] art.2(e).
[117] *Football Association Premier League Ltd v QC Leisure* [2008] EWHC 1411 (Ch); [2008] F.S.R. 32; [2008] 3 C.M.L.R. 12 at paras 81–99.
[118] See its second report on the implementation of the Directive (COM (2008) 593 final) at para.3.3.1.
[119] art.4.
[120] s.297(1)(b).

commercial communications to promote illicit devices. In the *FAPL* case Kitchin J. referred to the Court of Justice the question whether a person who possesses devices in the course of a business but not with a view to dealing with them commercially infringes. He expressed the provisional view that such possession would infringe.[121]

Competition defences. In *FAPL*,[122] the defendant suppliers contended that if the Conditional Access Directive extends to non-"pirated" devices, its provisions amount to an unlawful restriction on the free movement of goods or services. Kitchin J. referred this question to the Court of Justice but expressed the provisional view that the defendants' arguments were no more than a re-run of their arguments as to the meaning of the expression "illicit device" and amounted to an attack on the validity of the Directive itself, which was unlikely to succeed.[123] The defendants also argued that FAPL's contractual prohibition on the export by its licensees of decoder cards infringed art.81 of the Treaty.[124] If the prohibition was void this would have given them a defence to the claims for injunctions to restrain them from arranging the supply into the United Kingdom of domestic NOVA decoder cards for domestic use and commercial NOVA cards for commercial use. Kitchin J. referred the question of what legal test the national court should apply and what circumstances it should take into consideration in deciding whether the export restriction engaged art.81.[125]   **16–33**

Defence of implied authorisation. Another question which arose in the *FAPL* case was whether a defence of implied authorisation might arise on the basis of *Betts v Wilmott*[126] in circumstances where the decoder cards had been sold without any restriction on their use. The factual basis for the defence was not established. However, Kitchin J. stated that he had "considerable sympathy" with the claimants' submission that the principles laid down in the trade mark case of *Zino Davidoff v A&G Imports Ltd*[127] were applicable so that "consent must be so expressed that an intention to renounce [the claimants'] rights is unequivocally demonstrated".[128]   **16–34**

Rights and remedies. The Directive requires Member States to take the necessary measures to ensure that providers of protected services whose interests are affected by infringing activity have access to appropriate remedies. These must include actions for damages, injunctions and other preventative measures and, where appropriate, applications for disposal of illicit devices outside commercial channels.[129] The rights and remedies conferred by s.298 are the same rights and remedies as a copyright owner has in respect of an infringement of copyright.[130] It is expressly provided that the person entitled to rights under the section is entitled to the same rights to an order for delivery up or to seize items which would offend under the terms of the section as a copyright owner has in relation   **16–35**

---

[121] *Football Association Premier League Ltd v QC Leisure* [2008] EWHC 1411 (Ch); [2008] F.S.R. 32; [2008] 3 C.M.L.R. 12 at para.137.
[122] *Football Association Premier League Ltd v QC Leisure* [2008] EWHC 1411 (Ch); [2008] F.S.R. 32; [2008] 3 C.M.L.R. 12.
[123] *Football Association Premier League Ltd v QC Leisure* [2008] EWHC 1411 (Ch) at paras 316, 333.
[124] Now art.101 of the TFEU. See Vol.2 G1.
[125] *Football Association Premier League Ltd v QC Leisure* [2008] EWHC 1411 (Ch) at paras 344 and 368.
[126] (1871) L.C. 6 Ch. App. 239 (see para 5–221, above).
[127] Joined cases C–414/99; C–415/99 and C–416/99 [2002] R.P.C. 20.
[128] *Football Association Premier League Ltd v QC Leisure* [2008] EWHC 1411 (Ch) at paras 174–175.
[129] art.5(2).
[130] CDPA 1988 s.298(2). As to these rights and remedies, see ss.96 and 97 and Ch.22 below.

to an infringing copy.[131] In addition, the withdrawal of the privilege against self-incrimination effected by s.72 of the Senior Courts Act 1981 applies to proceedings under s.298 as to proceedings for infringement of copyright.[132] Finally, it is provided that s.97(1) of the 1988 Act, which prevents an award of damages being made in the case of an innocent infringement of copyright, applies to proceedings under s.298 with the modification that the reference in s.97(1) to the defendant not knowing or having reason to believe that copyright subsisted in the work is to be construed as a reference to his not knowing or having reason to believe that his acts infringed the rights conferred by s.298.[133]

E. Extent and Application of Sections 297 to 299

16–36 **Extent.** Sections 297 to 299 of the 1988 Act extend to England, Wales, Scotland and Northern Ireland.[134] They may be extended to the Isle of Man or to any of the Channel Islands by Order in Council with such exceptions and modifications as may be specified in the Order.[135] An Order in Council has been made in respect of Guernsey under s.304(5) of the 1988 Act.[136] It extends the sections to Guernsey in modified form.[137] No other such orders have been made.

16–37 **Application.** Under s.299(1) of the 1988 Act, s.297 may be applied by Order in Council in relation to programmes included in services provided from a country or territory outside the United Kingdom.[138] Section 299(1) of the 1988 Act also provides that s.298 of the Act[139] may be applied by Order in Council in relation to such programmes and to encrypted[140] transmissions sent from such a country or territory. A statutory instrument containing such an Order in Council is subject to annulment in pursuance of a resolution of either House of Parliament.[141] An Order in Council has been made in respect of Guernsey under s.299(1) of the 1988 Act relating to ss.297 and 298 of the 1988 Act.[142]

---

[131] s.298(3). For the remedies of a copyright owner, see para.21–216 (delivery up) and paras 21–57 et seq. (seizure). CDPA 1988 s.114, which deals with the disposal of infringing items which have been delivered up or seized, applies with the necessary modifications to items delivered up or seized under this section: s.298(6). For a discussion of s.114, see paras 21–218 et seq., below.

[132] s.298(4). The same applies to the Scottish and Northern Irish equivalents of the Senior Courts Act 1981 s.72.

[133] s.298(5).

[134] CDPA 1988 s.304(2).

[135] ss.304(4)(d) (Isle of Man) and 304(5) (Channel Islands).

[136] The Copyright, Designs and Patents Act 1988 (Guernsey) Order 1989 (SI 1989/1997). See Vol.2 A4.viii. Although referring to CDPA 1988 ss.297 to 299, this Order was made on November 1, 1989, before ss.297A to 297D were inserted in the 1988 Act.

[137] Copyright, Designs and Patents Act 1988 (Guernsey) Order 1989 Sch.

[138] CDPA 1988 s.299(5) provides that the words "programme", "broadcasting" and related expressions in s.299 are to have the same meaning as in the copyright Part of the 1988 Act.

[139] As to which see paras 16–27 et seq., above.

[140] For the meaning of "encrypted", see para.16–21, above.

[141] s.299(3).

[142] The Fraudulent Reception of Transmissions (Guernsey) Order 1989 (SI 1989/2003): see Vol.2 A4.ix.

PUBLICATION RIGHT

1. INTRODUCTION

The Copyright and Related Rights Regulations 1996[1] introduced (from December **17–01** 1, 1996) a new property right equivalent to copyright, called a "publication right".[2] The right is granted without formality to any person who, after the expiry of copyright protection, publishes for the first time a previously unpublished literary, dramatic, musical or artistic work or a film. The new right therefore supplements existing rights given to publishers in their typographical arrangement of published editions.[3] However, publication right differs considerably from the right of publishers in their typographical arrangements: first, the publication right is only available in respect of previously unpublished works whereas the typographical right applies to published editions of previously published works; and, second, the rights granted by the publication right are much more extensive than the mere right to prevent facsimile copying of a typographical arrangement.[4] This new right lasts for 25 years from the end of the year in which the work was first published.

---

[1] SI 1996/2967, in this Chapter "the Regulations". References to particular regulations are to the Regulations unless otherwise stated. The Electronic Commerce (EC Directive) Regulations 2002 (SI 2002/2013) apply to these Regulations: see the Electronic Commerce (EC Directive) (Extension) (No.2) Regulations 2003 (SI 2003/2500) reg.2, Sch. Pt 1. SI 2002/2013 is considered in Ch.21.

[2] regs 16 and 17.

[3] CDPA 1988 ss.1(1)(c), 8.

[4] Something of an analogue to the publication right may have existed by virtue of s.3 of the Literary Property Act 1842 (c.45): "the copyright in every book which shall be published after the death of its author shall endure for the term of forty-two years from the first publication thereof, and shall be the property of the proprietor of the author's manuscript from which such book shall be first published, and his assigns." For an illustration of the operation of that provision, see *MacMillan v Dent* [1907] 1 Ch. 107, 114 (in which copyright was held to exist on publication of letters written by Charles Lamb (who had died in 1834)).

2. BACKGROUND

17–02   The Regulations implemented art.4 of the original Term Directive.[5] Harmonisation in this area was considered necessary because some countries had a publication right (most notably the so-called *editio princeps* in Germany on which the
Directive is mainly based[6]) and others did not. These differences presented a
potential barrier to completion of the internal market. However, no proposal for
harmonisation of a publication right was included in the first version of the Term
Directive. This was said to be because the Commission did not feel compelled to
harmonise rights which "up until now have hardly affected the internal market or
that only exist in one or two Member States."[7] However, the Commission had a
change of heart prior to its publication of the amended proposal.[8]

3. WHEN THE PUBLICATION RIGHT IS AVAILABLE

17–03   **Overview.** The publication right arises when a person publishes for the first time
a previously unpublished work in which copyright has expired. In order to have
the right, a publisher must (a) publish (b) a relevant work (c) which has not previously been published (d) in which copyright has expired and (e) which qualifies
for the right.

A. PUBLISH

17–04   The right arises on publication of a previously unpublished work. The concept of
publication therefore has a dual role: previous publication will defeat the right,
whereas first publication after expiry of the copyright term gives rise to the right.
Publication has the same meaning in both contexts,[9] subject to one important
qualification. While it is clear that publication must take place in the EEA for the
publication right to arise, the regulations and Directive leave it unclear whether
publication outside the EEA will defeat the right (see para.17–10, below)

Publication in this context includes any making available to the public and, in
particular, includes the issue of copies to the public; making the work available
by means of an electronic retrieval system; the rental or lending of copies of the
work to the public; the performance, exhibition or showing of the work in public;
or communicating the work to the public by electric transmission.[10] A number of
questions relating to this definition are considered below (see paras 17–07 et seq.,
below).

---

[5] Council Directive 93/98 harmonising the term of protection of copyright and certain related
rights. This directive and its amendments were codified in a new Term Directive (2006/116/EC):
[2006] OJ L372/12. Art.4 of the new Term Directive is in the same terms as art.4 of the original
Term Directive and states that "[a]ny person who, after the expiry of copyright protection, for the
first time lawfully publishes or lawfully communicates to the public a previously unpublished
work, shall benefit from a protection equivalent to the economic rights of the author. The term of
protection of such rights shall be 25 years from the time when the work was first lawfully
published or lawfully communicated to the public." In what follows, references to the Term
Directive are to the codified directive unless otherwise stated.

[6] Law on Copyright and Neighbouring Rights (Copyright Law) 1965 art.71.

[7] Von Lewinski, "EC Proposal for a Council Directive Harmonizing the Term of Protection of
Copyright and Certain Related Rights" (1992) 23 I.I.C. 785 at 805.

[8] It seems strange that the Commission chose to harmonise the publication right but left typographical arrangement provisions unharmonised, given that typographical arrangements were protected
in the United Kingdom: CDPA 1988 ss.1(1)(c), 8; Ireland: Copyright Act 1963 (c.10) s.20; and
Greece: Copyright Related Rights and Cultural Matters Law (No.2121/1993) art.51.

[9] cf. art.4 of the Term Directive, which provides that the right arises either where a person "lawfully publishes" or "lawfully communicates to the public" a "previously *unpublished* work",
potentially suggesting that a "communication to the public" , not amounting to publication, during the copyright term will not prevent the publication right from arising on some later act.

[10] reg.16(2), as amended by the Copyright and Related Rights Regulations 2003 (SI 2003/2498).
The amendments were made as part of the implementation of the Information Society Directive

B. Relevant works

General. The publication right arises when a person publishes for the first time a previously unpublished work. Regulation 16(7) states that in this context a "work" means a literary, dramatic, musical or artistic work or a film.   **17–05**

Exclusions. No publication right arises from the publication of a work in which Crown copyright or Parliamentary copyright subsisted.[11] This limitation seems to have little basis in the Directive. However, it may be that since art.4 refers to works, a term which is assumed to have the same meaning as in the Berne Convention, the limitation can be supported indirectly. This is because under art.2(4) of the Berne Convention: "It shall be a matter for legislation in the countries of the Union to determine the protection to be granted to official texts of a legislative, administrative and legal nature". Under existing UK law, such works are treated differently from other literary and artistic works as regards ownership and duration, and it may be assumed that insofar as these provisions do not require modification in order to comply with art.1 of the Term Directive, it is also legitimate to exempt such works when implementing art.4.[12] The policy behind such an exemption is less obvious: it could be argued that Crown copyright works should be administered for the benefit of the public as a whole, and it would therefore be inappropriate to allow a private individual to obtain a property right over such a work.[13]   **17–06**

C. The requirement that the work be previously unpublished

Introduction. The right is acquired only where the work is previously unpublished. As has been seen, publication in this context includes any making available to the public and, in particular, includes the issue of copies to the public; making the work available by means of an electronic retrieval system; the rental or lending of copies of the work to the public; the performance, exhibition or showing of the work in public; or communicating the work to the public by electronic transmission.[14] This definition of publication is broader than that under existing UK copyright law, most obviously in its inclusion of performance, exhibition, showing and communicating to the public by electronic transmission.[15] This presents the possibility that a work could be unpublished for copyright purposes, but published for publication right purposes.   **17–07**

Sale or lending of the original. It is notable that a work is published by the issue, rental or lending of copies of a work, but not, it seems, by the sale or lending   **17–08**

(2001/29/EC), and replaced the previous reference to the acts of broadcasting a work or including a work in a cable programme service with the single act of "communicating the work to the public" and introduced a new generic description of "any making available to the public" in place of "any communication to the public." Communicating a work to the public, however, has an extended meaning, covering any communication to the public by electronic transmission, and includes wireless or cable broadcasts and any electronic transmission by way of an "on-demand" service. See further, CDPA 1988 s.20 and para.7–121, above.

[11] reg.16(5).

[12] See further, as to Crown and Parliamentary copyright, Ch.10, above.

[13] Alternatively, the justification for the exclusion may be that after a number of years such works will almost invariably have been made available to the public, for example by being placed in the Public Record Office, and this, it may have been assumed, was sufficient to publish the work so that no publication right could later arise. However, the placing of a single copy of a work in a public library is probably insufficient to prevent the publication right from coming into existence: see para.17–09, below.

[14] reg.16(2).

[15] Compare CDPA 1988 s.175(4) and Berne Convention for the Protection of Literary and Artistic Works art.3(3).

of the original.[16] This follows from the wording of regs 16(2)(a) and (c), which refer to the issue and rental or lending of "copies".[17] If doubt existed about this interpretation because of the non-exhaustive nature of the definition of publication, it is removed by the fact that the act of sale or lending of the original to a person would not itself amount to a communication to the public. Although the term "public" has been given a wide meaning in the context of "public performance" and "publication", so that in one case the exposure of six copies was held to be a publication,[18] even this wide meaning would probably not encompass the simple sale or loan of the original even if the purchaser or borrower was a "member of the public".[19]

17–09 **Single copies in public libraries**. One difficult question which the Regulations do not address is whether the placing of an original manuscript or a single copy of a work with a public library is sufficient to amount to "making available" to the public. While the words "any making available to the public" might appear broad enough to cover this situation, the better view, given the specific examples of "making available" in reg.16(2), is that such an act does not of itself constitute publication.

17–10 **Place of first publication**. The right will presumably not arise if the work has been made available to the public at any time during the term of copyright. As mentioned, it is left unclear whether there is any geographical limitation on publication which operates to prevent the publication right arising, and, in particular, whether previous publication outside the EEA prevents the publication right arising when the work is later first published in the EEA.

The failure to specify any such geographical limitation might be taken to imply that none is to operate, so that prior publication anywhere in the world prevents the right from arising.[20] Such a view would be reinforced by the fact that reg.16(4)(a) expressly states that "a work qualifies for publication right only if first publication is in the European Economic Area".[21]

Nevertheless, it might be possible to argue that only prior publication in the EEA will operate to prevent the right arising.[22] At a general level, it might be argued that because the Directive is concerned only with the EEA, no significance is to be attached to any publication outside the EEA. Since it is only publication in the EEA that gives rise to the right, it is only prior publication in the EEA that prevents the right from arising. Such a view has the advantage that dif-

---

[16] There is no parallel to s.175(5) of the 1988 Act, which excludes from the definition of publication "publication which is merely colourable and not intended to satisfy the reasonable requirements of the public".

[17] In *Microsoft Corporation v Electro-wide Ltd* [1997] F.S.R. 580 it was argued that s.18 of the 1988 Act excluded the act of issuing a single copy, and Laddie J. proceeded on the basis that this submission was correct. The view that the term "copies" in the Regulations does not include the original is reinforced by the fact that it has been thought necessary, in order to implement the Rental Right Directive 92/100, to state explicitly in s.18(4) of the Act that issuing of copies includes issuing of the original.

[18] *Francis Day and Hunter v Feldman* [1914] 2 Ch. 728.

[19] See below as to the position where a single copy of a work is placed in a public library.

[20] In the context of contracts in restraint of trade, courts have treated a failure to specify the geographical limits of a restriction as indicating that the restriction is to operate on a worldwide basis: see, for example, *Mont v Mills* [1993] F.S.R. 577.

[21] The right therefore would not operate to provide an incentive to introduce works published outside the EEA into the EEA (as for example used to be the case with patents of importation), but only to induce first publication in the EEA.

[22] In the context of the Registered Designs Act 1949, the failure of the statute to specify where a divesting act must take place was interpreted as requiring the act to have occurred in the United Kingdom. See *Bissell AG's Design* [1964] R.P.C. 125: applicant could not rely on s.6(4) where artwork had been "applied industrially" to an article and one such article had been "sold"; held by Registrar to require sale of the article in the United Kingdom.

ficult questions will be avoided concerning virtually simultaneous publication inside and outside the EEA. In this respect, the fact that there is no explicit provision on virtually simultaneous publication outside the EEA (in contrast with the normal 30-day rule) might be taken to indicate that such publication is of no significance.[23] However, no matter how desirable this conclusion may be, the symmetry upon which this argument depends can only be sustained if reg.16(4) is read as if it said "a work qualifies for publication right only on (a) first publication in the European Economic Area, and (b) if the publisher of the work is at the time of first publication a national of an EEA state." In other words, the reference to first publication in reg.16(4) must be explained as indicating that no publication right arises as regards further publication in the EEA,[24] rather than that no publication right arises if the work has been previously published outside the EEA. Not only does this seem to be a highly artificial construction, it would render the word "first" in reg.16(4) superfluous, since it is already clear from the wording of reg.16(1) that no publication right arises as regards further publication in the EEA.

Publication of part. If part of a work has previously been published, there does 17–11 not seem to be any reason why the publication right should not arise in relation to the remainder. There is authority to suggest that publication of a small part of a work will not amount to publication of a work as a whole. Thus, for example, the printing of the voice parts of a musical score contained in an arrangement for the voice and the piano would not amount to a publication of the musical composition as a whole.[25] Presumably, however, only the unpublished parts of such a work would attract the protection of the new right, so that it would not be possible to rely on publication right in the unpublished part to prevent further publication of the previously published (presumably now public domain) aspects.

Publication in a different medium. A related question arises as to whether pub- 17–12 lication of a work in one medium prevents the right arising in relation to publication in a different medium. For example, is an unpublished musical score to be treated as previously published as a result of publication of a phonogram which embodies a performance of the score? Since publication occurs where "copies" of the work have been issued to the public, the answer appears to depend on whether what has been already published amounts to a copy. Regulation 17(4) states that provisions contained in Ch.1 of Pt I of the 1988 Act defining expressions used generally in Pt I, "apply, with any necessary adaptations, for the purpose of supplementing the substantive provisions of that Part as applied by this regulation." Hence, it might be appropriate to employ the meaning of copy from Pt I. For the purposes of Pt I of the 1988 Act, a copy of a musical work means a reproduction of it in any material form.[26]

This approach is also consistent with authorities which suggest that publication by sale of an article embodying a design is effective to publish the drawings on which the design was based.[27] Thus, it was held that a claimant was likely to be able to establish copyright in drawings as a result of first publication in the

---

[23] reg.16(4). cf. Berne Convention for the Protection of Literary and Artistic Works art.3(4).

[24] This is how the word "first" is used in art. 4 of the Term Directive, in the phrase "for the first time lawfully publishes".

[25] *Fairlie v Boosey* (1878–9) 4 A.C. 711 at 730.

[26] CDPA 1988 ss.17(1), (2).

[27] *Merchant Adventurers Ltd v M. Grew & Co Ltd* [1973] R.P.C. 1 at 10 (Graham J.); *British Northrop v Texteam Blackburn Ltd* [1972] Ch. 242; [1973] F.S.R. 241 (Megarry J.). It should be noted, however, that these authorities were decided in the context of qualification for copyright so that the decision that the work was published operated in favour of the plaintiff copyright

United Kingdom of three-dimensional light fittings.[28] If these authorities are sound, and they are applied in the context of publication right, it would seem that no publication right will be available for publication of an artist's preliminary drawings for a sculpture, if the sculpture which faithfully reproduces the preliminary drawings, has itself been published.

A preferable interpretation of the Directive would have been that such acts do not amount to publication, and that "publication" in the context of publication right means publication of a work or a reproduction of it in the (notational and dimensional) form in which the work was brought into existence. The differences which exist between a drawing and a sculpture, or a sound recording and a score, are potentially of value to the public, and there is therefore a justification for the law providing an incentive to disclose these unpublished embodiments. In order to achieve such a construction of the publication right under the existing implementing Regulations, it would be necessary to define the term "copies" in a different way from that in the 1988 Act. This, in turn, would require a restrictive construction of reg.17(4) as not relating to issues of acquisition of publication right but only to the limited purpose of "supplementing the substantive provisions" of Pt I, that is, when defining the scope and attributes of the publication right.

17–13   **Unauthorised publication.** When determining whether the work was previously unpublished, no account is to be taken of any unauthorised act.[29] Thus, unauthorised publications are neither sufficient to give rise to publication right, nor to prevent the right arising in the case of a later authorised publication. However, a number of problems exist in defining and applying the notion of "unauthorised".

17–14   **Unauthorised publication where copyright subsists.** Where copyright subsists in a work, the term "unauthorised" is left undefined by the Regulations. However, as has been seen, reg.17(4) states that provisions contained in Ch.1 of Pt I of the 1988 Act defining expressions used generally in Pt I, "apply, with any necessary adaptations, for the purpose of supplementing the substantive provisions of that Part as applied by this regulation." The term "unauthorised" is, in turn, defined in the Act, as done without the licence of the copyright owner.[30] A work, therefore, is not to be treated as having been previously published where that publication was unlicensed. For example, if the owner of copyright in unpublished letters or diaries allowed a biographer access to the letters solely for research purposes, but the biographer published the letters, it would remain open for a person, once copyright had expired, to publish the letters and gain the publication right. Whether this would be so if the biographer's act of publishing was deemed a fair dealing or in the public interest is less clear. In those circumstances the publication would be "unauthorised" in the sense of "otherwise than with the licence of the copyright owner", even though such a licence would be unnecessary for the act to be legal. Similarly, the question arises whether publication occurs where a painting is placed on public display without the licence of the copyright owner, since such an act is "unauthorised" even though the copyright owner does not have the exclusive right to control such exhibition.

---

owner and against a defendant who was making "technical points" (per Graham J., *Merchant Adventurers Ltd v M. Grew & Co. Ltd* at [1972] Ch. 242).

[28] *Merchant Adventurers Ltd v M. Grew & Co. Ltd* [1972] Ch. 242.

[29] reg.16(3). See also CDPA 1988 s.175(6).

[30] CDPA 1988 s.178. The term is relevant when determining whether protection arises in relation to a typographical arrangement, whether the exceptions contained in ss.33, 46, 59, 60 operate, and to the s.105 presumptions. As to the application of this provision in relation to the publication right, see reg.17(4) and see below. Para.46 of Sch.1 to the 1988 Act defines "unauthorised" in a slightly different way for things done before June 1, 1957 as acts done otherwise than with the "consent or acquiescence" of the copyright owner.

An alternative interpretation is that the notion of an "unauthorised act" might suggest that no account should be taken of any act which required authorisation.[31] While such an interpretation seems difficult to reconcile with the terms of s.178, it would be more consistent with the Directive which employs the word "lawful".[32] Moreover, reg.17(4) may be read as not requiring application of the defining expressions used in the 1988 Act, when (as here) considering whether publication right arises, because the regulation requires their application only when construing "the substantive provisions of that Part as applied by this regulation"—matters such as infringement or assignment of the publication right.

Unauthorised publication when copyright does not subsist. If publication takes place either before copyright subsists, or after its expiry, the statutory definition of "unauthorised" in the 1988 Act is (and could be) of no assistance, because there is no copyright owner. The Regulation therefore explains that in relation to a time when there is no copyright in the work, an unauthorised act "means an act done without the consent of the owner of the physical medium in which the work is embodied or on which it is recorded".[33] So, for example, a thief who publishes a manuscript will not obtain the new publication right.   **17–15**

Anonymous works. An added difficulty may arise in relation to anonymous works. Elsewhere it is explained that exceptions exist to an action for infringement of copyright where it is reasonable to assume that copyright in such a work has expired.[34] What would happen if, at this stage, a person publishes a previously unpublished work? It seems that the publisher would not benefit from the publication right if it was later shown that copyright had in fact subsisted because of the requirement of "expiry of copyright" (see paras 17–18 et seq., below). However, once the copyright had expired, would the earlier publication prevent the acquisition of the publication right? Since there was no authorisation of the earlier publication, it seems it can be ignored even though it was not unlawful, because it was otherwise than with the licence of the copyright owner (see para.17–14, above).   **17–16**

First publication in another EEA State. Consideration also needs to be given to the question of whether the absence of authorisation must be assessed according to the law of the United Kingdom or the country of first publication. In the absence of any express provision dealing with this issue, the most convenient interpretation of the Regulations would seem to be to apply the same notion of "unauthorised", irrespective of the place of first publication, whenever publication right is claimed in the United Kingdom. As will be seen, it appears likely that publishers will be able to obtain publication right in one Member State over a work that is still protected by copyright in another Member State. Logically, therefore, it would seem to make most sense to define "unauthorised" according to the law of the country where publication right is being claimed. This would mean, for example, that a publisher in France of a previously unpublished work, in which copyright has expired, with the consent of the owner of the physical medium, would acquire the new publication right in the United Kingdom, even if the publication was in breach of the French law of *droit de divulgation*. This conclusion may, however, be in conflict with the Directive, since the Directive   **17–17**

---

[31] This might even mean that prior publication of a work by another should also be ignored if it constituted a breach of confidence or contract.
[32] Term Directive art.4.
[33] reg.16(3).
[34] CDPA 1988 ss.57, 66A and see above at para.9–170 and para.9–198, respectively.

requires that the work be "lawfully published".[35] Whilst it could be replied that the publication would have been lawful in the United Kingdom, the fact remains that so long as the work is only published in France there has not been a "lawful" publication.

D. THE REQUIREMENT OF EXPIRY OF COPYRIGHT

17–18   The right is only available "after the expiry of copyright protection".[36] Expiry in this context presumably means expiry in the United Kingdom as, despite harmonisation, copyright and related rights remain essentially national rights. The purpose of limiting the publication right may be presumed to have been to avoid duplication of rights in the same work, but would seem to have a number of additional consequences. These are considered below. However, the question of when copyright will expire is largely beyond the scope of this chapter.[37]

17–19   **Works in which copyright has never subsisted.** One consequence of limiting the availability of the right to cases where copyright "has expired" may be to exclude from the operation of the right works in which copyright has never subsisted,[38] as it would seem highly artificial to say that copyright in such a work has "expired". Copyright may not have "subsisted" in an unpublished work for two reasons: first, the work might have been created at a time when no statutory copyright existed; secondly, the work might have failed to attract copyright because of the author's nationality. In order fully to understand both scenarios, the history of the protection of unpublished works needs to be considered. Comments will be confined initially to a consideration of works produced by British authors.

17–20   **Lack of statutory copyright at the time of creation: common law copyright.** The requirement that copyright "subsisted" might, at first, appear to exclude all works created at a time before copyright protection existed for that category of work. Statutory copyrights were recognised in books from 1710,[39] in engravings from 1735,[40] in sculptures from 1798,[41] and in paintings, drawings and photographs from 1862.[42] Thus, for example, Shakespeare's plays were written long before the passage of the Statute of Anne, and Van Dyck's paintings were created before the passage of the Fine Arts Copyright Act. However, with the exception of the latter Act, the copyright statutes only protected published works, with unpublished works falling to be protected by what was called "common law copyright", a form of protection that was potentially perpetual. With the Copyright Act 1911, statutory copyright protection arose on creation rather than publication in relation to all classes of work and common law copyright was abolished.[43]

A publisher claiming "publication right" could argue that the reference to

---

[35] art.4.

[36] reg.16(1).

[37] See Ch.6.

[38] The limitation is consistent with the terms of the Term Directive, but other countries, most notably Germany, have taken different approaches. This is considered in more detail at para.17–27, below.

[39] Statute of Anne 1709 (8 Anne c.19).

[40] Engraving Copyright Act 1734 (8 Geo. 2 c.13).

[41] Copyright Act 1798 (38 Geo. 3 c.71).

[42] Fine Arts Copyright Act 1862 (25 & 26 Vict. c.68).

[43] This change in approach followed from the United Kingdom's ratification of the Berne Convention, which required Member States to provide protection for "Authors who are subjects or citizens of any of the countries of the Union .   .   . whether unpublished or first published in the country of the Union." Although common law copyright probably in any event extended to protect foreign authors, simply by equating protection for published and unpublished works the Berne Convention seemed to require a change in the United Kingdom's approach.

"copyright" having "expired" includes a reference to common law copyright which existed in unpublished works prior to July 1, 1912. However, it is doubtful whether such a construction is likely to be accepted. One reason for this lies in the fact that when, in the past, the legislature has intended to include the common law right within the definition of "copyright" it has said so expressly, but no such express reference is to be found in the Regulations.[44] Although the common law right was sometimes referred to as "common law copyright", it was also referred to as "the right to restrain publication at common law";[45] "quasi-copyright"; a "right analogous to copyright;"[46] and an "inchoate copyright",[47] again suggesting that "copyright" should only be taken to include the common law right where the legislation concerned says so expressly.

Moreover, whilst the common law right clearly existed with respect to unpublished literary manuscripts,[48] the exact nature, coverage and content of the common law right was never clearly established. In particular, a degree of doubt remains as to whether the common law right subsisted in unpublished artistic works, where most of the problems we are concerned with arise.[49]

On the assumption that the term "copyright" in the Regulations refers to statutory copyright only, it is necessary to see which unpublished works have been granted statutory protection. As has already been noted, prior to the Copyright Act 1911, statutory copyright applied in relation only to published works, with the exception of works covered by the Fine Art Copyright Act 1862. An important initial distinction must therefore be drawn between those unpublished works in which statutory rights were first granted in 1911, and paintings, drawings and photographs.   **17–21**

Retrospective vesting of statutory copyright in most unpublished works under the Copyright Act 1911. The Copyright Act 1911 abolished common law copyright, and conferred statutory protection automatically from creation. The transitional provisions contained in the first schedule of the 1911 Act were such that this applied to pre-existing works as well as to works created after July 1, 1912.[50] As a result, all literary, dramatic and musical works and engravings which remain unpublished will have enjoyed statutory copyright protection.   **17–22**

Sculptures. A different rule applied to unpublished sculptures created prior to July 1, 1912. These works were protected as if the Act had been in force at the date of their creation. Thus, unpublished sculptures were given a term of the life of the author and 50 years thereafter, with the result that sculptures would only come into copyright under the 1911 Act if the author died after July 1, 1862 (i.e.   **17–23**

---

[44] cf. Copyright Act 1911 Sch.1.

[45] Copyright Act 1911 Sch.1.

[46] See Robertson, The Law of Copyright (Oxford: Clarendon, 1912), pp.v, 42.

[47] See Macgillivray, *The Copyright Act 1911* (London: Stevens and Sons, 1912), p.122. The notion of an "inchoate" copyright may be particularly significant since it seems difficult to argue that an inchoate right can, in the normal sense, have expired.

[48] See *Donaldson v Beckett* 1 E.R. 837; (1774) 2 Bro. P.C. 129; 4 Burr. 2408.

[49] The leading case which is said to establish the existence of common law copyright in unpublished artistic works is *Prince Albert v Strange* 41 E.R. 1171; (1849) 18 L.J. Eq. 120, but it should be noted that this case was also decided on the grounds of breach of confidence. Furthermore, if common law copyright did subsist in unpublished artistic works this creates a difficult question as to when this copyright expired, bearing in mind that the Fine Arts Copyright Act 1862 also applied to unpublished works. The dominant view seems to have been that the common law right did subsist, but that it expired at the same time as statutory copyright (for example, see Scrutton, *The Law of Copyright* (London: John Murray, 1883), p.230), but little support for this view can be gained from the 1862 Act. Indeed, the preamble to the 1862 Act states "whereas by law, as now established, the authors of paintings, drawings and photographs have no copyrights in such their works."

[50] i.e. the date the 1911 Act came into force.

50 years before the 1911 Act came into force). Sculptures not retrospectively protected by the 1911 Act, i.e. sculptures created by an author who died more than 50 years before, could only have enjoyed copyright on publication.

17–24   **New subject matter.**The Copyright Act 1911 also extended statutory protection to a variety of subject matter for the first time. Of such subject matter, only works of artistic craftsmanship constitute works that might now be the subject of publication right.[51] The transitional provisions of the 1911 Act did not operate so as to give unpublished works of artistic craftsmanship retrospective protection, so there was no statutory copyright protection for such works prior to July 1, 1912.[52]

17–25   **The problem of unpublished drawings, paintings and photographs.** The Fine Arts Copyright Act 1862[53] granted statutory copyright in a painting, drawing or photograph from the moment of its creation rather than publication.[54] Consequently, unpublished paintings, drawings and photographs created after the coming into force of the 1862 Act will be works in which copyright has "subsisted" for the purposes of the publication right.[55] However, the transitional provisions of the 1862 Act as regards previously created unpublished works were not as generous as those of the 1911 Act for other works. An unpublished painting, drawing or photograph, created before the coming into force of the 1862 Act received protection if it had not been "sold or disposed of before the commencement of the Act"[56] and if the term of protection under the 1862 Act had already not expired. Since the term was seven years post-mortem auctoris, this meant that no statutory copyright existed for any such work created by an artist or photographer who had died prior to 1855.[57]

From the above, it will be seen that the following works by British authors will have enjoyed statutory copyright protection and will thus (at some point) be eligible for publication right protection:

(a) All unpublished literary, dramatic and musical works and engravings irrespective of the date of their creation.

(b) Unpublished paintings, drawings and photographs created after the coming into force of the 1862 Act.

(c) Unpublished sculptures on which copyright was conferred by the 1911 Act, i.e. sculptures created by an author who died within the 50 years immediately prior to the coming into force of the 1911 Act.

---

[51] See para.17–05, above.

[52] Copyright Act 1911 Sch.1.

[53] (25 & 26 Vict. c.68).

[54] *Tuck v Priester* (1887) 19 Q.B.D. 629; *Bowden Bros. v Amalgamated Pictorials* [1911] 1 Ch. 386. Also see *Copinger* 4th edn, p.369.

[55] Registration under that Act was only a pre-condition to bringing an action for infringement, it did not affect the question of whether copyright subsisted in the work, but it should be noted that it would be possible to argue that some forms of registration under the 1862 Act were in any event sufficient to communicate the work to the public. In particular, it should be noted that the 1862 Act provided that in addition to a written description, the registration could include "if the Person registering shall so desire a Sketch, Outline, or Photograph of the said works" (s.4). Whilst a sketch of a painting could probably not be said to communicate the final work to the public, it is less clear whether providing a photograph of a work would be sufficient. In part this question is connected with the issue of whether depositing a single copy of a work with a library is sufficient to communicate a work to the public (see para.17–09, above). The argument that at least some forms of registration would be sufficient to communicate the work to the public would seem stronger in this case, however, because the registration of a work seems to carry with it some notion of public accessibility.

[56] Fine Arts Copyright Act 1862 s.1.

[57] It might be possible to argue that the effect of the 1862 Act was retrospectively to vest copyright in all unpublished works covered by the Act, even though on such a retrospective vesting copyright had already lapsed in many cases. However, such an argument would be highly artificial and sits uneasily with the wording of that Act: Fine Arts Copyright Act 1862 s.1. Similarly, it could be argued that the 1911 Act retrospectively vested copyright in all unpublished sculptures.

(d) In addition, all "British" films will have enjoyed copyright protection at some point in time. Films created before June 1, 1957 will have been protected as a series of photographs under the 1862 or 1911 Acts.[58] Films created after that date will have received express statutory protection.

Works by British authors which may never have enjoyed copyright and which may not, therefore, be eligible for publication right protection are as follows:

(a) Unpublished paintings, drawings or photographs created by an author who died before 1855.

(b) Unpublished paintings, drawings or photographs created before 1862 which had been "sold or disposed of before the commencement of the Act".[59]

(c) Unpublished sculptures that were created by an author who died more than 50 years prior to the coming into force of the 1911 Act, i.e. before July 1, 1862.

(d) Unpublished works of artistic craftsmanship created before July 1, 1912.

Foreign works which may never have enjoyed copyright. So far consideration has been restricted to works created by British authors, but consideration also needs to be given to the position of foreign works, again in order to try and determine whether there are any unpublished works which have never enjoyed copyright in the United Kingdom, with the result that they may not be eligible for publication right. In order to determine whether an unpublished foreign work has ever enjoyed copyright in the United Kingdom attention should be paid to the following principles:

17–26

(a) If the work is of a type which would not have enjoyed copyright protection if made by a British author (see above), then it is safe to assume that the work has never been in copyright in the United Kingdom.

(b) If the work was made after the 1911 Act came into force then the following additional principles can be applied:

(i) If the work was created by a resident or citizen of a country which has never had copyright relations with the United Kingdom then copyright will not have subsisted in the work. In this case it seems that the publication right may not be available.

(ii) If the work was created by a citizen or resident of a Berne or Universal Copyright Convention country, or a country which has entered into a bilateral treaty with the United Kingdom after reciprocal protection was extended to that country by Order in Council, then the work will have enjoyed copyright protection in the United Kingdom.

(iii) Even if the work was created by a citizen or resident of a Berne or Universal Copyright Convention country before reciprocal protection was extended to that country, then the work may still have been in copyright. This is because both Conventions require retrospective protection for unpublished works.[60] Thus such a work will have enjoyed copyright protection in the United Kingdom, unless the

---

[58] See *Barker v Hulton* (1912) 28 T.L.R. 496 and *Nordisk Films Co. Ltd v Onda* [1917–1923] Macg. C.C. 337, respectively.

[59] Fine Arts Copyright Act 1862 s.1.

[60] Berne Convention for the Protection of Literary and Artistic Works art.18(1); Universal Copyright Convention art.VII. It would, of course, be possible for the United Kingdom to enter into a bilateral treaty which did not extend retrospective protection to unpublished works.

term of copyright had already expired.[61] In the latter case no copyright will ever have subsisted in the work and it seems that the publication right may not be available.

(c) If the work was created *before* the 1911 Act came into force then attention should be paid to the following:

(i) If the work was a literary work created by a foreign author then it seems that the work enjoyed copyright under the 1911 Act, irrespective of whether the country of origin enjoyed copyright relations with the United Kingdom. This conclusion follows from the effect of s.24 and Sch.1 of the 1911 Act. The effect of these provisions was to give statutory copyright to any work which enjoyed "common law copyright" protection and which could have obtained statutory copyright on publication. As common law copyright probably subsisted in foreign works, and foreign authors could probably obtain copyright protection under the 1842 Act by first publishing the work in the United Kingdom (even if resident outside the United Kingdom),[62] it seems that the effect of the 1911 Act was to grant statutory copyright protection to such works.[63]

(ii) The above rule probably also applies to dramatic and musical works and engravings created before July 1, 1912, and to sculptures created between July 1, 1862 and July 1, 1912.

(iii) The rule in (i), above, has no application to paintings, drawings and photographs. These works will therefore not have been able to enjoy copyright protection in the United Kingdom, except by virtue of an international agreement.

---

[61] This is most likely to have occurred in relation to artistic works. In addition, however, it should be noted that the Berne and Universal Copyright Conventions allow Member States to restrict the term of protection to that granted in the work's country of origin: Berne Convention for the protection of literary and artistic works art.7(8); Universal Copyright Convention (UCC) art.IV(4). The Berne provision was implemented in the United Kingdom by the Copyright Act 1911 s.29(1)(ii) and by the Order in Council made on June 24, 1912 (S.R. & O. 1912/913) and by the subsequent Order dated March 16, 1933 (S.R. & O. 1933/253). It was maintained under the 1956 Act by the Copyright (International Conventions) Order 1957 (SI 1957/1523), but was cancelled by the Copyright (International Conventions) (Amendment) Order 1958 (SI 1958/1254) so that the normal copyright term applied thereafter to all works. However, the 1958 Order did not revive copyrights. At first sight this might seem to have important implications for foreign works created prior to the country of origin entering into copyright relations with the United Kingdom, where that country entered into such relations prior to the 1958 Order's coming into force as, for example, foreign unpublished literary, dramatic and musical works and engravings may not have enjoyed perpetual protection. However, it seems that all pre-existing foreign literary, dramatic and musical works and engravings were brought into copyright by the 1911 Act. Thus the above Orders could only have excluded from copyright works made between the coming into force of the 1911 Act and the coming into force of the 1958 Order. As the period between these two pieces of legislation is less than 50 years, these Orders will only act in such a way as to prevent copyright from having subsisted in a work in the United Kingdom where the country of origin provided a term of protection less than that required by the Berne Convention. This is most likely to have occurred in relation to those Universal Copyright Convention Countries which entered into copyright relations with the United Kingdom on September 27, 1957 (for example, Cuba), as a signatory to the UCC. These can provide protection for as short a period as 25 years from registration: UCC art.4. Therefore, to take a hypothetical example, if a Cuban author registered (but never published) a literary work in 1920 and at that time Cuba provided a period of protection for 25 years from first registration, it is probable that this work will never have been in copyright in the United Kingdom. However, even this conclusion is open to doubt since both the 1957 and 1958 Orders were repealed in 1964 (Copyright (International Conventions) Order 1964 (SI 1964/690)), and it can be argued that this Order, unlike the 1958 Order, did revive copyrights. Also see *Copinger* 10th edn, paras 1167–1171, pp.428–430.

[62] See, in particular, the speeches of Lord Westbury and Lord Cairns in *Routledge v Low* (1868) L.R. 3 H.L. 100. It should also be noted that Lord Salisbury gave the President of the United States an assurance in a despatch of June 16, 1891 that a citizen of the United Sates did not have to be resident in the United Kingdom in order to obtain statutory copyright. Also see *Copinger* 4th edn, pp.91–97. cf. *Jeffreys v Boosey* 10 E.R. 681; (1854) 4 H.L.C. 815.

[63] cf. Copyright Act 1911 s.1.

(iv) Where the work in question is a painting, drawing or photograph created by a foreign author the following questions should be asked: first, would the work have been eligible for protection had it been created by a British author? (see point (a), above); secondly did the country of origin enjoy copyright relations with the United Kingdom on July 1, 1912? If the answers to these questions are yes, then prima facie the work will have enjoyed copyright protection. However, even if these conditions are satisfied, it is still possible that the work will never have been in copyright, either because the term of copyright in the country of origin had expired, or because there was no copyright protection in the country of origin because of a failure to comply with formalities required by the law in that country.[64]

An alternative way to have implemented the Directive. The preceding paragraphs demonstrate that the requirement of "expiry" of copyright often makes determining whether a work qualifies for the publication right a complex task. It would have been simpler, and might have accorded with the presumed purpose of the new right (that is, to provide an incentive for the publication of works to which the public has not had access) to have made the publication right available irrespective of whether the work has ever enjoyed copyright protection. This might have been achieved simply by saying that unpublished works could benefit from the publication right if the author of the work had died 70 or more years previously.[65]   **17–27**

Expiry of copyright in unpublished works. Although copyright has subsisted in most unpublished works, the publication right is only available on "expiry" thereof. One effect of the requirement of the expiry of copyright is that the publication right is unlikely to be of great significance in the United Kingdom for some time to come.[66] This is because of the dual effect of the changes made as regards unpublished works in the 1988 Act and the other changes to the copyright term introduced to give effect to the Term Directive. Again, a distinction must be drawn between three classes of works: literary, dramatic, musical works and engravings; paintings, drawings and photographs; and sculptures.   **17–28**

Expiry of copyright in unpublished literary, dramatic, musical works and engravings. Section 17 of the Copyright Act 1911 conferred protection on unpublished literary, dramatic and musical works and engravings for 50 years from the date of any eventual publication. This term for unpublished literary, dramatic and musical works and engravings was retained in 1956 and extended to photographs made on or after June 1, 1957.[67] This meant that there was potential perpetual copyright in these works until publication.[68] The 1988 Act ended this situation by providing that copyright in such unpublished works (unpublished as   **17–29**

---

[64] See International Copyright Act 1886 (49 & 50 Vict. c.33) s.2(3).

[65] The German Law on Copyright and Neighbouring Rights (Copyright Law) 1965 expressly provides that the publication right applies "to works which have not previously been published and which were never protected within the jurisdiction of this Act, but whose authors have been dead for longer than 70 years": Copyright Act 1965 art.71(1). The question of whether a work ever enjoyed copyright protection in Germany is therefore irrelevant. Also see Te Deum Urteil des Bundesgerichtshofs vom 21 März 1975 Aktz.: I ZR 109/73 (Kammergericht) noted at (1975) GRUR Heft 8 at 447 and see Burrell & Haslam, "The Publication Right: Europe's First Decision" [1998] E.I.P.R. 210.

[66] Also see Williams, "Publication Right" (1997) 15 *International Media Law* 15 at 15–16.

[67] Copyright Act 1956 ss.2(3), 3(4). Under the 1911 Act copyright subsisted in photographs for a term of 50 years from the making of the original negative: Copyright Act 1911 s.21. This term was retained in 1956 for photographs made before June 1, 1957, irrespective of whether the photographs had been published by that date: Copyright Act 1956 Sch.7(2).

[68] See further, para.6–38, above.

of August 1, 1989) was to be limited to a fixed period of 50 years from January 1, 1990, i.e. until December 31, 2039.[69] For some works unpublished on August 1, 1989 the relevant copyright will have been extended by the increase in the term of copyright to life and 70 years.[70] For example, if an author died in 1985 leaving unpublished copyright manuscripts (which remained unpublished on August 1, 1989), the effect of the changes made by the 1988 Act was that copyright was to last until the end of 2039. However, as a result of the increase in the duration of copyright to life plus 70 years, copyright will be extended to 2055. However, if an author died in 1940 and his works were unpublished on August 1, 1989, the extension would have no effect and the relevant date remains December 31, 2039.[71] The effect of these transitional provisions is, therefore, such that the operation of the publication right is currently restricted to unpublished artistic works (other than engravings).

17–30 **Expiry of copyright in unpublished paintings, drawings and photographs.** As indicated, paintings, drawings and photographs, in contrast, may well be the subject of the publication right immediately. If such a work was protected under the 1862 Act, it would have received no additional protection under the 1911 Act if copyright under the 1862 Act had expired (that is, if the author died before July 1, 1905).[72] If copyright under the 1862 Act had not expired then such works were protected as if the 1911 Act had been in force at the date of their creation.[73] In relation to unpublished artistic works (including sculptures) created after the coming into force of the 1911 Act, the term of copyright was to be the same as for published works, i.e. the life of the author and 50 years thereafter.

17–31 **Expiry of copyright in unpublished sculptures and works of artistic craftsmanship.** Unpublished sculptures and works of artistic craftsmanship were protected under the Copyright Act 1911 for an author's life plus 50 years. These periods were extended under the Duration of Copyright and Rights in Performances Regulations 1995. It will therefore be possible to establish publication right where a sculpture is first published after December 1, 1996 and that sculpture was created by a sculptor who died after July 1, 1862 but more than 70 years prior to publication. Similarly, publication right will exist where an unpublished work of artistic craftsmanship created after July 1, 1912 is first published after December 1, 1996 and that work was created by a craftsman who died more than 70 years prior to publication.

17–32 **Examples of application of the publication right.** The above points are perhaps best illustrated by examples:

First, an unpublished literary, dramatic or musical work created by a British author after the 1911 Act came into force. In these cases it is clear that the publication right can arise as soon as copyright expires. Thus if someone were to discover an unpublished literary work created in 1915 by T.E. Lawrence (who died in 1935), he could communicate this to the public and gain the benefit of the publication right as soon as copyright expires. However, because of the

---

[69] CDPA 1988 Sch.1 para.12(4).

[70] See further, para.6–44, above.

[71] This appears to be the effect of reg.16(c) of the Duration of Copyright and Rights in Performances Regulations 1995, although Sch.1 para.12 of the 1988 Act has not been amended.

[72] The term of protection under the Fine Arts Copyright Act 1862 was the life of the author and seven years thereafter. Thus copyright would have expired under the 1862 Act if the author died before July 1, 1905. It should also be noted that copyright could lapse under the 1862 Act prior to the expiry of the full copyright term. In particular, copyright would lapse on transfer of the property in the physical embodiment of the work, unless copyright was expressly reserved to one of the parties: ibid., s.1. A different rule applied in relation to commissioned works.

[73] Copyright Act 1911 s.24, Sch.1.

transitional provisions relating to the term of copyright in unpublished works, copyright in such a work will not expire until December 31, 2039.

Secondly, an unpublished literary, dramatic or musical work created by a British author before July 1, 1912. Such a work may or may not have been eligible for statutory copyright protection at the time of its creation. This might, therefore, seem to require the complex examination of the history of any particular work to be undertaken. However, as has been seen, the effect of s.24 of the Copyright Act 1911 would seem to be such that copyright was vested in all unpublished literary, dramatic and musical works, irrespective of the date of their creation.[74] Thus if someone were to discover an unpublished play by Shakespeare (who died in 1616), it seems that they could potentially gain the benefit of the publication right, but again because of the effect of the transitional provisions of the 1988 Act, not until December 31, 2039.

Thirdly, an unpublished artistic work (other than an engraving) produced in 1913 by Welsh painter Gwen John (who died in 1939). As the copyright in this work will have expired at the end of 1989, but then will have been revived for a further 20 years, the publication right would have been available from the end of 2009.   **17–33**

Fourthly, an unpublished drawing made in 1875 by Dante Gabriel Rosetti (who died in 1882). Such a work attracted copyright under the 1862 Act, and copyright expired in 1889. Therefore, publication right would arise were the drawing to have been published after December 1, 1996.[75]

Fifthly, an unpublished painting created by J.M.W. Turner in 1840. Since Turner died in 1851, such a painting never attracted copyright under the Fine Arts Copyright Act 1862. It therefore seems that no publication right will arise on publication of this work.[76]

Sixthly, unpublished scores created by Austrian composer, Wolfgang Amadeus Mozart (who died in 1791). These attracted common law copyright, and, as a result of s.17 of the 1911 Act, this was converted into a copyright for 50 years from publication. In turn, the 1988 Act imposed a fixed period of 50 years from January 1, 1990. Publication right will therefore be available if the scores are first published after December 31, 2039.[77]   **17–34**

Seventhly, a painting by Edward Degas (a Frenchman) who died in 1917. The work will have been protected by copyright as a result of France being a signatory to the Berne Convention.[78] Copyright will have lapsed in 1967, and publication after December 1, 1996 would give rise to the publication right.[79]

Eighthly, an unpublished painting by Spanish artist Francisco Jose de Goya y Lucientes (who died in 1828). Since such a work would not have received copyright protection in the United Kingdom,[80] it seems that publication would not give rise to the publication right.

Ninthly, an unpublished painting by American artist John Singer Sargent (who

---

[74] Copyright Act 1911 s.24, Sch.1.

[75] However, had the unpublished drawing been registered under the Fine Arts Copyright Act 1862, the question of whether registration amounted to publication would arise, see para.17–25, fn.55, above.

[76] But see para.17–20, above.

[77] See para.17–29, above.

[78] But also, prior to that, under bilateral arrangements made under the International Copyright Act 1844 (7 & 8 Vict. c.12).

[79] Just such a scenario appeared to have occurred when it was revealed that Degas' Danseuses had been located. However, that work had been previously exhibited in 1924 so that the work was not "previously unpublished". See *Guardian*, August 23, 1997.

[80] See para.17–26, above, and see the example referring to J.M.W. Turner in para.17–33, above.

died in 1925). Since the United States had a specific arrangement with the United Kingdom, this attracted copyright which expired in 1975.[81]

17–35   **Additional consequences.** The requirement of expiry of copyright, considered above, may also act as a disincentive to publish works in the last 25 years of the copyright term. This is because a publisher will be able to obtain a longer period of protection by waiting until copyright has lapsed and relying on the publication right.[82] This effect seems to undermine the assumed purpose of the publication right, which is to encourage and reward the bringing into the public sphere of works not as yet available.[83]

Moreover, the transitional provisions may have important implications for the European single market. It seems that far from helping to create a single market for copyright works, in the short term the publication right may actually serve to create barriers to trade within Europe. This is because different countries have different transitional provisions relating to the term of copyright. As a result, it might be possible for a publisher to acquire UK publication right protection for a work which is still protected by copyright in another Member State. Bearing in mind the underlying rationale of the Term Directive, this seems to be a highly undesirable result.[84]

E. Qualification

17–36   A work qualifies for publication right protection only if first publication is in the European Economic Area and the publisher of the work is at the time of first publication a national of an EEA State.[85] The meaning of publication has already been considered.[86] Where two or more persons jointly publish the work, it is sufficient if any of them is a national of an EEA State.[87] In contrast with arts 1 and 3 of the Term Directive, details as to qualification are not explicitly provided in relation to the publication right.[88] It is therefore possible that some Member States might make the right available in broader circumstances. That would clearly be undesirable. Interestingly, no provision is made to allow for the possible extension of the terms of reg.16(4) allowing recognition of the rights of foreign publishers, where the country of publication provides reciprocal rights to publishers in the EEA.[89]

4. OWNERSHIP

17–37   As noted above, the first publisher of a previously unpublished work will be the

---

[81] See further, paras 3–239 et seq., above.

[82] It is a strange consequence of the Directive that provisions in German law designed to avoid such an undesirable situation have had to be repealed in order to implement the Directive. See, as originally enacted, German Law on Copyright and Neighbouring Rights (Copyright Law) 1965 art.64(2). This provision was repealed by the Amendment of June 23, 1995, BGBl. I of June 29, 1995, p.842. See further, Nimmer and Geller (eds), *International Copyright Law and Practice* (New York: Matthew Bender & Co, 1996), pp.GER36, GER128-GER129.

[83] Indirectly, the right might also encourage and reward researchers who locate valuable works in archives.

[84] See Council Directive 2006/116/EC harmonising the term of protection of copyright and certain related rights, recital3.

[85] reg.16(4). As to which states, see reg.2.

[86] See para.17–04, above.

[87] reg.16(4). Compare CDPA 1988 s.154(3).

[88] Contrast Directive 2006/116/EC harmonising the term of protection of copyright and certain related rights art.7.

[89] Contrast CDPA 1988 s.159. Council Directive on the legal protection of databases art.11(3).

first owner of the publication right.[90] In line with the extended definition given to "publication" in this context, the first publisher of the work will be the person who first makes the work available to the public and, in particular, will include the person who first issues copies to the public; makes the work available by means of an electronic retrieval system; rents or lends copies to the public; performs, exhibits or shows the work in public; or communicates the work to the public.

The effect of these provisions would seem to be that the owner of unpublished material in which copyright has expired must think carefully before allowing others to make use of the work. For example, if the owner of an unpublished painting were to lend the work to a museum or gallery in order that it might be exhibited, then prima facie it will be the museum or gallery which will be the first owner of the publication right.[91]

5. THE NATURE OF THE RIGHT

Introduction. The publication right is a property right equivalent to copyright.[92] The publisher, however, does not get the benefit of any moral rights.[93] Otherwise, the substantive provisions of Pt I of the 1988 Act relating to copyright (that is, rights of the copyright owner, acts permitted in relation to copyright works, dealings with rights in copyright works, remedies for infringement, and licensing) apply in relation to the publication right as in relation to copyright.[94] Moreover, except where the context otherwise requires, any other enactment relating to copyright, whether made before or after the Regulations, applies in relation to publication right as in relation to copyright.[95]   **17–38**

However, there are a number of exceptions and modifications.

Permitted acts. As regards permitted acts, while Ch.III of Pt I of the 1988 Act applies in general, reg.17(2) declares that four sections have no application to the publication right. The first is s.57 which concerns acts permitted in relation to anonymous works. This exclusion may affect the publication right in two ways. First, in assessing whether copyright has expired for the purposes of acquisition of the publication right, a publisher is unable to rely on the assumption that copyright has expired. Secondly, and more significantly, a person cannot rely on the assumption that copyright has lapsed in an underlying work to justify infringement of the publisher's right. To permit the use of such a defence in relation to the publisher's right would clearly undermine the whole effect of the publication right. The exception provided by s.66A (acts permitted on assumption as to expiry of copyright in films) is excluded for the same reason.   **17–39**

The other permitted acts excluded by reg.17 appear to be of no great significance and are excluded as a housekeeping exercise. Thus s.64 (which allows an artist to repeat aspects of his or her earlier work) is excluded, as this section could have no application since the artist will in all cases have been dead for a considerable number of years. Similarly, s.67 (which permits the playing of sound recordings at clubs) is excluded because the publication right does not arise in relation to sound recordings.

Civil remedies. The provisions of Ch.VI of the 1988 Act apply, so that the stan-   **17–40**

---

[90] reg.16(1).
[91] Also see Williams, "Publication Right" (1997) 15 *International Media Law* 15 at 15-16.
[92] reg.16(1).
[93] reg.17(1).
[94] reg.17(1).
[95] reg.17(5). In this context "enactment" is defined as including an enactment contained in subordinate legislation within the meaning of the Interpretation Act 1978.

dard remedies for copyright infringement are available for infringement of publication right,[96] including the provisions relating to additional damages.[97] The presumptions contained in ss.104 to 106 of the 1988 Act[98] do not apply: see reg.17(2)(b) of the Regulations. However, where copies of a work as issued to the public bear a statement that a named person was the owner of publication right in the work at the date of issue of the copies, that statement shall be admissible as evidence of the fact stated and shall be presumed to be correct until the contrary is proved.[99] Like the presumptions in ss.104 to 106 of the 1988 Act, the presumption does not apply in criminal proceedings for an offence, but does apply in proceedings in the criminal courts for delivery up under CDPA 1988 s.108 (as applied to publication right by reg.17): see reg.17B.

17–41   **Criminal liability.** Sections 107(4) and (5) of the 1988 Act, which concern criminal penalties, are modified in certain circumstances, so that the severity of the punishments is reduced. More specifically, a person convicted of an offence in relation to the publication right faces a maximum punishment on summary conviction of imprisonment for a term not exceeding three months, or a fine not exceeding level 5 on the standard scale, or both.[100] This can be contrasted with the usual criminal penalties, which on summary conviction, are imprisonment for a term not exceeding six months and a variable fine (depending on the precise nature of the offence).[101] The maximum penalty on indictment is imprisonment for a term not exceeding ten years, or a fine, or both.[102]

17–42   **Licensing and the Copyright Tribunal**. In general the provisions of Chs VII and VIII concerning the licensing and the Copyright Tribunal apply. Consequently, the exploitation of publication right is subject to the same controls as the exploitation of copyright, and thus the actions of licensing bodies are open to possible review. However a number of minor modifications have been made to these provisions. Thus s.116(4) is expressly removed. That provision, which is considered in detail elsewhere,[103] excludes certain situations from the general provisions applying to licensing schemes, so that collective works and works made by employees of a single company do not fall within references to licences or licensing schemes covering works of more than one author. Further modifications are made to ss.116(2), 117 and 124, which relate to review by the Copyright Tribunal of licensing schemes, so that in relation to the publication right, the words "works of more than one author" are substituted by "works of more than one publisher".

17–43   **Miscellaneous modifications**. Regulation 17(4) further provides that other relevant provisions of Pt I apply, with any necessary adaptations, for the purposes of "supplementing the substantive provisions of that part as applied by the Regulations." The provisions are those:

---

[96] In particular, note CDPA 1988 s.96(2), "In an action for infringement of copyright all such relief by way of damages, injunctions, accounts or otherwise is available to the plaintiff as in respect of any other property right." More generally, see ss.96–102 and see paras 21–123 et seq., below.

[97] See s.97(2).

[98] As to which see paras 21–271, below.

[99] reg.17A, inserted with effect from April 29, 2006 by the Intellectual Property (Enforcement etc.) Regulations 2006 (SI 2006/1028).

[100] reg.17(3)(a).

[101] See further, para.22–24, below. The reason for the difference is that the offence was created by a provision made under the European Communities Act 1972 Sch.2 para.1(1)(d) of which provides that this is the maximum penalty on summary trial for offences created this way.

[102] CDPA 1988 s.107, as amended by the Copyright, etc. and Trade Marks (Offences and Enforcement) Act 2002.

[103] See para.28–131, below.

(a) in Ch.I, defining expressions used in Pt I,
(b) in Ch.IX, ss.161 (territorial waters and the continental shelf) and 162 (British ships aircraft and hovercraft), and
(c) in Ch.X, ss.171(1) and (3) (savings for other rules of law, etc.), and ss.172 to 179 (general interpretation provisions).

Duration. Publication right expires at the end of the period of 25 years from the end of the calendar year in which the work was first published.[104]   **17–44**

6. TRANSITIONAL PROVISION AND PRE-EXISTING COPIES

Pre-existing copies. Neither the Regulations nor the Directive deals with the question of pre-existing copies, that is to say, they do not deal with the issue of whether the publication right extends to control the use of copies made prior to the publication right coming into existence. Once the publication right arises, is the issue of pre-existing copies to the public an infringement? There are, in fact, two related issues here: first, what is the position where a copy of a work has been made prior to December 1, 1996 (i.e. before the Regulations came into force) and second, what is the position where a person makes a copy of an unpublished work which is subsequently communicated to the public by someone else. The first issue is essentially a matter for transitional arrangements, the second is a matter of policy.   **17–45**

Transitional provisions. Regulation 25 defines "new right" as a "right arising by virtue of these Regulations, in relation to a copyright work . . . to authorise or prohibit an act", and probably therefore includes the publication right. Regulation 27(2) explains that no act done in pursuance of an agreement made before November 19, 1992 shall be regarded as an infringement of any new right. Regulation 34 states that "any new right in relation to a copyright work does not apply to a copy of the work acquired by a person before commencement for the purpose of renting or lending it to the public". Apart from these two provisions, there is no saving for pre-existing copies analogous to the provisions protecting vested interests where copyright is revived by virtue of the Duration Regulations[105] or when copyright "springs" into existence when a country becomes a party to the Berne Union.[106] This may be an oversight on the part of the Government, but not one that a court is likely to rectify. Consequently, it seems that any copies made prior to December 1, 1996 may not be issued to the public without the consent of the owner of the publication right.   **17–46**

Pre-existing copies made after December 1, 1996 but prior to publication of the work. In Germany it has been held that copies that have been produced prior to the publication of the work may still be used in the course of a public performance without infringing the publication right.[107] The court's reasoning was that as a purely economic right, the publication right did not extend to control the use of copies produced in good faith prior to the right coming into existence. Whilst the goal of harmonisation might suggest that this approach be adopted in the United Kingdom, the Regulations do not appear to allow for such a solution.   **17–47**

---

[104] reg.16(6). Contrast arts 4 and 8 of the Term Directive.
[105] reg.23.
[106] See the Copyright and Performances (Application to Other Countries) Order 2008 (SI 2008/677).
[107] T *E DEUM* Urteil des Bundesgerichtshofs vom 21 März 1975 Aktz.: I ZR 109/73 (Kammergericht) noted at (1975) GRUR Heft 8 at 447 and see Burrell & Haslam, "The Publication Right: Europe's First Decision" [1998] E.I.P.R. 210.

CHAPTER EIGHTEEN

DATABASE RIGHT

1. INTRODUCTION

Overview. The Copyright and Rights in Databases Regulations 1997[1] ("the **18–01** Regulations") implemented in the United Kingdom the provisions of the EC Directive on the legal protection of databases[2] ("the Directive"). The Regulations created a sui generis database right that arises where there has been a "substantial investment in obtaining, verifying or presenting of the contents of the database".[3] At the same time, a new class of literary work, namely a database, was created, but having a different test of originality than for other works.[4] Thus a database will only be eligible for copyright protection if it is "original" in the sense that "by reason of the selection or arrangement of [its] contents" it constitutes the "author's own intellectual creation".[5] Previously a database would have been eligible for copyright protection as a table or compilation, provided that the relatively low test of originality applied to literary works in general, the skill and labour criterion, was satisfied.[6] Now, however, databases are excluded from the

---

[1] SI 1997/3032, which entered into force January 1, 1998. The Copyright and Rights in Databases (Amendment) Regulations 2003 (SI 2003/ 2501) extend database right protection to include databases whose maker is connected with the Isle of Man.

[2] Directive 96/9/EC of March 11, 1996.

[3] Copyright and Rights in Databases Regulations 1997 reg.13(1), implementing part of art.7(1) of the Directive. See further para.18–15, below.

[4] Note, however, that in *Infopaq International v Danske Dagblades Forening* (C–5/08) [2010] F.S.R. 20, the ECJ held that the author's own intellectual creation was relevant to assessing whether reproduction in part of a newspaper article had taken place. See further the discussion of originality for literary works in general at para.3–131 above.

[5] CDPA 1988 s.3A(2) (cf. reg.6 of the Regulations and art.3(1) of the Directive, which continue "No other criteria shall be applied to determine their eligibility for that protection."). See para.3–148 and the judgment of Floyd J. in *Football Dataco Ltd v Britten Pools Ltd* [2010] EWHC 841 (Ch); [2010] RPC 17 (sub. nom. *Football Datco Ltd v Britten Pools Ltd*), in which he concluded that the selection or arrangement required is not confined to selection or arrangement performed after the data is finally created.

[6] As to which, see paras 3–147 et seq., above.

category of literary works consisting of tables or compilations, and are treated as a separate category of literary works.[7]

18–02   **What is a database in fact?** In general, a database is an organised collection of information or data, often stored in digital form on computer disk, and is arguably comprised of two parts: the structure and the contents.[8] It is important to note that this fundamental distinction between structure and contents can be somewhat artificial—given a large amount of properly indexed but otherwise unstructured data, it is possible to achieve very similar functionality to a database in which the data stored is more systematically structured; it is nevertheless a distinction which underpins the Directive.[9]

18–03   **The Directive.** The recitals to the final form of the Directive explain that the Commission considered databases not to be "sufficiently protected in all Member States by existing legislation" and stated that "such protection, where it exists, has different attributes".[10] The Commission was concerned about the effects of the differing attributes in the legislation of Member States and the negative effect this would have on the functioning of the internal market.[11] It is notable that the final form of the Directive represents a significant widening of the rights originally proposed in the Green Paper. The Directive, which has been largely incorporated into the Regulations, seeks to remedy the problems outlined by the Commission in the Green Paper through the creation of a two-tier protection for databases.

18–04   **The Commission's 1988 Green Paper.** In June 1988, the European Commission produced a Green Paper on copyright and the challenge of technology.[12] One of the issues identified by the Commission as requiring immediate action was the legal protection afforded to databases, defined in that paper as collections of information stored and accessed by electronic means. The Commission solicited views as to whether the selection and arrangement of the compilation within a database composed of works should itself be protected by copyright and whether a database containing material not then protected by copyright should be protected by copyright or a new sui generis right. However, it was not until four

---

[7] CDPA 1988 s.3(1) as amended by reg.5(a) of the Copyright and Rights in Databases Regulations 1997. See paras 3–148 et seq.

[8] The vast majority of computer databases are "relational" following the set of 12 rules for database design originally proposed by Edgar Codd of IBM in the late 1960s. Relational databases usually consist of a series of interrelated tables of data. For example, a database containing information about a company's current customers may contain one table of data consisting of unique customer numbers and the name of each customer and a separate table consisting of the unique customer numbers and each customer's telephone number. By combining information from the two tables by using the common customer numbers it is thus possible to relate each telephone number to each customer name. It is also possible, by running "queries" usually written in "Structured Query Language", to obtain selections and arrangements of the raw data that correspond to a particular request. A major benefit of relational databases is their separation between logical design and physical implementation (i.e. the computer servers upon which the database is run and the disks on which the data are stored) and consequently it is usually possible to change the physical implementation without significant software re-coding.

[9] In this context, note recital 23 of Directive 96/9 which denies protection to the computer programs "used in the making or operation of a database", such programs being otherwise protectable as literary works. Recently there has been development of so-called post-relational database models which operate on the basis of categorisation of data rather than relying upon relationships within it.

[10] Directive 96/9, recital 1.

[11] Directive 96/9, recital 2, similar points are made in recitals 3 and 4. See also the discussion in the decision of the Court of Appeal on the rationale for the Directive in *British Horseracing Board Ltd v William Hill Organisation Ltd* [2001] EWCA Civ 1268; [2002] E.C.D.R. 4. Following the reference in this case to the European Court of Justice, the Court of Appeal issued a further decision on appeal: [2005] EWCA Civ 863; [2005] R.P.C. 35.

[12] COM(88) 172 final, June 7, 1988.

years later that the Commission published its proposal for a Directive on the legal protection of databases throughout the European Union, with the aim of conferring full copyright protection on databases meeting an originality test and a short term sui generis "right to prevent unfair extraction" for databases, whether or not they also qualified for copyright protection.[13]

Definition of "database" in the Directive. A database is defined for the purposes of the Directive, the 1988 Act and the Regulation as a "collection of independent works, data or other materials arranged in a systematic or methodical way and individually accessible by electronic or other means".[14] At the outset it is important to note that this definition, unlike that in the initial Green Paper, is not limited to electronic databases and purportedly applies to any such collection whatever its form.[15] On January 1, 1998, the Copyright and Rights in Databases Regulations 1997[16] came into force, altering the copyright protection given to databases by the 1988 Act by incorporating into UK law the criterion of originality defined in the Directive for databases protected as literary copyright works, and creating the new sui generis right called "database" right.

18–05

Operation of the two forms of protection. It was an objective of the Directive to give copyright protection to the structure of the database and database right protection both to the contents and the structure of the database.[17] The Commission has tried to meet this objective through separating the rights that can subsist in a database and applying two types of protection to the two parts of a database.[18] However, it is not clear whether the Regulations actually achieve those objectives. The Regulations enable a database to gain protection either through copyright or a database right, or both, although they fail to state that any copyright subsisting in the structure will not extend to the contents and is without prejudice to any other rights subsisting in the contents. The definition of "a database" was adopted from the Directive verbatim in the Regulations.[19] This definition in the Regulations may lead to problems because a situation could arise where the contents will not be protected by copyright, not being "original", but the structure will be, by being "original". The Regulations do not appear to provide for this but such a distinction between the contents of a database and the selection or arrangement of the contents of a database is made in the Directive.[20] This distinction was discussed in the Consultative Paper on United Kingdom Implementation[21] but was not carried over into the Regulations, although the Regulations state that they "make provision for the purpose of implementing" the Directive.[22]

18–06

---

[13] [1992] OJ C156/4. The original proposal was for a right with a duration of 10 years. This was extended to the period of 15 years following a request from the European Parliament and the scope of a protectable database extended to include collections of data—Amended Proposal for a Council Directive on the Legal Protection of Databases COM(93) 464 final, October 4, 1993.

[14] CDPA 1988 s.3A(1), as amended by reg.6 of SI 1997/3032, implementing art.1(2) of Directive 96/9.

[15] Directive 96/9 art.1(1).

[16] SI 1997/3032, note that the Regulations have been amended by the Copyright and Rights in Databases (Amendment) Regulations 2003 (SI 2003/2501), which, among other things, extend database right protection to include databases whose maker is connected with the Isle of Man.

[17] Directive 96/9, recitals 15 and 58 and arts 3(2) and 7(1).

[18] Whilst not being inconsistent with the other objectives of the Directive as well.

[19] CDPA 1988 s.3A(1) and Directive 96/9 art.1.

[20] Directive 96/9 art.3(2).

[21] "Consultative Paper on United Kingdom Implementation" dated August 1997, para.4.2.

[22] Copyright and Rights in Databases Regulations 1997 reg.2. It is nevertheless well established that domestic legislation which was intended to enact a directive must be construed so far as is

2. DATABASES AS LITERARY COPYRIGHT WORKS

18–07   **Application of copyright principles.** The protection of original databases which are literary works is governed by the copyright law as laid down in the 1988 Act.

> *Football Dataco Ltd v Britten Pools Ltd.* In this case, Floyd J. identified a four-step approach to database copyright: (i) identify the data which is collected and arranged in the database; (ii) analyse the work which goes into the creation of the database by collecting and arranging the data so identified, to isolate that work which was properly to be regarded as selection and arrangement; (iii) ask whether the work of selection and arrangement was the author's own intellectual creation and in particular whether it involved the author's judgment, taste or discretion; and finally (iv) ask whether the work is quantitatively sufficient to attract copyright protection.[23] The key question in determining whether the work is original is the extent to which the author can be shown to have exercised judgment, taste or discretion in selecting and arranging the data but without having regard to a subjective assessment of whether the work in question is good, bad or indifferent.

18–08   **Originality.** Copyright databases are treated in detail elsewhere in this work.[24] Generally, however, the criterion of originality for copyright databases set out in the 1988 Act means that a literary work consisting of a database is original, if, and only if, by reason of the selection or arrangement of the contents of the database, it constitutes the author's own intellectual creation.[25] This definition should be read alongside the Directive, which provides that no criterion other than originality in the sense of the author's intellectual creation shall be applied to determine the eligibility of a database for copyright protection, and in particular, no aesthetic or qualitative criteria shall be applied.[26] This is almost certainly a different standard of originality to that adopted for other literary works under the 1988 Act and is consistent with other EU harmonisation measures on the criterion of originality.[27] This conclusion is supported by the facts that the Commission felt it necessary to introduce the sui generis right in the first place, and that the Commission considered that it had increased the threshold for copyright protection in the Directive.[28]

18–09   **Author of a copyright database.** The author of such an original database is the

---

possible in conformity with that directive. See, for example, *Lister v Forth Dry Dock & Engineering Co Ltd* [1990] 1 A.C. 546; [1989] 2 C.M.L.R. 194.

[23] [2010] R.P.C. 17. This decision is, however, understood to be subject to an appeal to the Court of Appeal.

[24] See 3–146 et seq., above.

[25] CDPA 1988 s.3A(2); see also recital 39 of Directive 96/9.

[26] Directive 96/9, recital 15.

[27] No doubt the origin of this approach is art.2(5) of the Berne Convention, which provides that "collections of literary or artistic works such as encyclopaedias and anthologies which, by reason of the selection and arrangement of their contents, constitute intellectual creations shall be protected as such, without prejudice to the copyright in each of the works forming part of such collections". The same approach was adopted in Directive 91/250/EEC on the legal protection of computer programs, art.1(3) of which provides that "A computer program shall be protected if it is original in the sense that it is the author's own intellectual creation. No other criteria shall be applied to determine its eligibility for protection". See also *Infopaq International v Danske Dagblades Forening* (C–5/08) [2010] F.S.R. 20 in which the ECJ held that the author's own intellectual creation was relevant to assessing whether reproduction in part of a newspaper article had taken place.

[28] Recital 60 of Directive 96/9 states that "some Member States currently protect under copyright arrangements databases which do not meet the criteria for eligibility for copyright protection laid down in this Directive ...".

person who creates it, and a natural person.[29] However, many databases are probably computer-generated works, in which case under the 1988 Act the author would be the person by whom the arrangements necessary for the creation of the work are undertaken.[30] The question arises as to whether this is consistent with the requirement that the database constitutes the author's own intellectual creation.[31]

3. THE SUI GENERIS DATABASE RIGHT

A. INTRODUCTION

The Regulations create a sui generis property right called "database right". The **18–10** right can subsist whether or not the database or its contents is a copyright work,[32] and was apparently created to fill the gap created by raising, or at least changing, the threshold for copyright protection with the different criterion of originality for databases. Since the Directive was implemented into national law, there has been some litigation in the national courts of Member States in which the scope of the sui generis rights has been considered.[33] In particular, six of these cases have resulted in decisions being made by the European Court of Justice under art.234 EC (now art.267 TFEU).[34]

---

[29] CDPA 1988 s.9(1).

[30] CDPA 1988 s.9(3).

[31] On this point it should be noted that, given the exclusively economic focus behind the harmonisation of the rights in Directive 96/9, it is strongly arguable that the provisions in the 1988 Act which automatically vest ownership in the hands of the person making the arrangements are compatible. See also *Fixtures Marketing Limited v Organismos Prognostikon agonon Podosfairou AE (OPAP)* (C–5/08) [2004] E.C.R. I–10549, para.26 which notes that there is no requirement that a database be its maker's own intellectual creation to be classified as such—the question of originality is only relevant to assessing whether the database qualifies for copyright protection. A related issue is the extent to which computer-generated databases satisfy the requirement for originality. In *Football Dataco v Britten Pools Ltd* [2010] EWHC 841 (Ch); [2010] R.P.C. 17, Floyd J. formed the view that this requirement excluded computer generated databases from protection on the basis that they lacked sufficient originality. It is submitted that although many computer-generated databases are unlikely to be sufficiently original, the question should be whether the programmer has exercised sufficient judgement, taste and discretion in setting up the computer-generated work.

[32] Copyright and Rights in Databases Regulations 1997 reg.13(2).

[33] Some caution is required in distilling principles from this case law because it pre-dates the authoritative rulings of the ECJ on the scope of the Directive. Notable cases include *British Horseracing Board Ltd v William Hill Organisation Ltd* [2001] R.P.C. 31 in which Laddie J. dealt at some length with the nature of the right. On appeal the Court of Appeal ([2002] E.C.D.R. 4), without determining the appeal itself or dealing substantively with the points raised, referred the case to European Court of Justice under art.234 EC. Other notable cases include *Royal Mail Group Plc (formerly Consignia Plc) v i-CD Publishing (UK) Ltd* [2004] EWHC 286; [2004] E.C.D.R. 18, which concerned the licensing of mailing list databases; *France Telecom MA v MA Editions Sarl* [2001] E.C.C. 4, and *Re Unauthorised Reproduction of Telephone Directories on CD ROM* [2002] E.C.D.R. 3, in both of which it was held that unauthorised extraction from electronic telephone directory databases was prohibited; *Sietech Hearing Ltd v Borland* [2003] E.C.D.R. 26; *Danske Dagblades Forening (DDF) v Newsbooster* [2003] E.C.D.R. 5, and *Algemeen Dagblad BV v Eureka Internetdiensten* [2002] E.C.D.R. 1, both of which concerned alleged database rights in connection with internet news headlines; *Noir d'Irvoire SPRL v Home Boutiques Private Ltd Co SPRL* [2003] E.C.D.R. 29, in which palettes of colours were held not to constitute databases; *Hit Bit Software GmbH v AOL Bertelsmann Online GmbH* [2001] E.C.D.R. 18, in which MIDI music files on AOL's website were held not to constitute databases; *Societeé Tigrest Sarl v Société Reed Expositions France* [2002] E.C.C. 29, [2003] E.C.D.R. 20, in which a catalogue of trade exhibitors was held to constitute a database; and *Nederlandse Omroep Stichting v Holdingmaatschappij de Telegraaf NV* [2002] E.C.D.R. 8, in which a compilation of television programme schedules in a newspaper was held not to entail any substantial investment and was thus held not to constitute a protectable database.

[34] *The British Horseracing Board Ltd v William Hill Organisation Ltd* (C–203/02) [2005] E.C.D.R. 1; [2005] R.P.C 13; *Fixtures Marketing v Oy Veikkaus AB* (C–46/02) [2005] E.C.D.R. 2, *Fixtures Marketing v Organismos Prognostikon Agonon Podosfairou (OPAP)* [2005] 1 C.M.L.R. 16 and

B. "DATABASE"

18–11   **Definition of database: general.** The Regulations define a database as a collection of independent works, data or other materials which are arranged in a systematic or methodical way, and are individually accessible by electronic or other means.[35] As already noted, this definition should be considered alongside the Directive and its recitals, which provide[36] that a database should be understood to include literary, artistic, musical or other collections of works, or collections of other material such as texts, sound, images, numbers, facts, and data and to cover also collections of independent works, data or other materials which are systematically or methodically arranged and can be individually accessed. The Directive and recitals also make it clear that certain types of works were specifically excluded from protection as a database; for example, computer programs used in the making or operation of databases accessible by electronic means, and recordings or audiovisual, cinematographic, literary or musical works as such, do not fall within the scope of the Directive.[37] It is also stated that "as a rule, the compilation of several recordings of musical performances on a CD[38] does not come within the scope of the Directive, both because, as a compilation, it does not meet the conditions for copyright protection and because it does not represent a substantial enough investment to be eligible under the *sui generis* right".[39]

The ECJ in *Fixtures Marketing v OPAP*[40] explicitly noted that the fact that the information in a database related to sporting fixtures does not preclude the database from gaining sui generis protection.[41] Furthermore, "it is irrelevant whether the collection is made up of materials from a source or sources other than the person who constitutes that collection, materials created by that person himself or materials falling within both those categories."[42] The materials in question must be "independent" materials which are "separable from one another" and it is for this reason that it is not possible for an audiovisual, cinematographic, literary or musical work to constitute a database.[43] However, there is nothing in the Directive which requires a database to be its maker's own intellectual creation as such and the criterion of originality is only relevant to the question of whether copyright protection applies.[44]

18–12   **Arrangement and accessibility.** Classification of a collection as a protectable database requires systematic or methodological arrangement and individual accessibility. The ECJ noted that "While it is not necessary for the systematic or

---

[2005] E.C.D.R. 3; *Fixtures Marketing Ltd v Svenska SpelAB* [2005] E.C.D.R. 4; *Directmedia Publishing GmbH v Albert-Ludwigs-Universität Freiburg* (C–304/07) [2009] RPC 10, [2009] E.M.L.R. 6, [2009] E.C.D.R. 3; and *Apis-Hristovich EOOD v Lakorda AD* (C–545/07) [2009] 3 C.M.L.R. 3, [2009] E.C.D.R. 13.

[35] Copyright and Rights in Databases Regulations 1997 reg.6. This definition is taken directly from art.1 of Directive 96/9.

[36] Recital 17.

[37] Directive 96/9 art.1(3) and recitals 17 and 23.

[38] Despite compilations of musical performances on CD being excluded from protection, electronic databases may include devices such as CD-ROM, CD-I and presumably DVD, pursuant to recital 22 of Directive 96/9.

[39] Recital 19.

[40] *Fixtures Marketing Ltd v Organismos prognostikon agonon podosfairou* (C–444/02) [2005] 1 C.M.L.R. 16; [2005] E.C.D.R. 3.

[41] *Fixtures Marketing Ltd v Organismos prognostikon agonon podosfairou AE(OPAP)* (C–444/02) [2005] 1 C.M.L.R. 16 and [2005] E.C.D.R. 3 para.23.

[42] *Fixtures Marketing Limited v Organismos prognostikon agonon podosfairou AE(OPAP)* (C–444/02) [2005] 1 C.M.L.R. 16 and [2005] E.C.D.R. 3 para.25.

[43] Directive, 17th recital. See also *Fixtures Marketing Limited v Organismos prognostikon agonon podosfairou AE(OPAP)* (C–444/02) [2005] 1 C.M.L.R. 16; [2005] E.C.D.R. 3, para.29.

[44] *Fixtures Marketing Limited v Organismos prognostikon agonon podosfairou AE(OPAP)* (C–444/02) [2004] E.C.R. I–10549, para.26.

methodological arrangement to be physically apparent… that condition implies that the collection should be maintained in a fixed base, of some sort, and include technical means such as electronic, electromagnetic or electro-optical processes…, or other means, such as an index, a table of contents, or a particular plan or method of classification, to allow the retrieval of any independent material contained within it."[45] In short, what makes a protectable database different from a mere collection of materials is a means of retrieving each of its constituent materials individually from the collection. The arrangement of those data in the form of a fixtures list of the dates, times and names of teams in various football matches meets the conditions as to systematic or methodological arrangement and individual accessibility. The fact that lots are drawn to decide the pairing of teams was held not diminish that conclusion.[46]

Independent materials. In the *Fixtures Marketing* cases, the date, time of, and identity of the two teams playing in football matches were held by the ECJ to constitute independent materials "in that they have autonomous informative value".[47] Indeed the ECJ noted that "although it is true that the interest of a football league lies in the overall result of the various matches in that league, the fact remains that the data concerning the date, the time and the identity of the teams in a particular match have an independent value in that they provide interested third parties with relevant information."[48] Consequently the compilation of dates, times and names of teams relating to various fixtures in a football league is a collection of independent materials.[49] It would thus appear that the ECJ has adopted a very wide approach to what may constitute a database and that, aside from compilations in which the individual elements are related such as a film, establishing the required individual accessibility is a relatively low hurdle for the owner of the database to establish.   **18–13**

Storage medium. One question that arises from the definition in the Regulations is whether databases other than electronic databases are covered, despite the clear guidance in the Directive that they should be. This issue turns on the meaning of "or other means". If the meaning is confined to "or other analogous means", then the Regulations cover electronic databases only and other databases such as paper databases will only be eligible for protection under copyright as a table or compilation.[50] If "or other means" is not so confined, then other databases such as paper databases will be eligible for database right. The Regulations themselves make no mention of the scope of databases that are intended to be covered and no definition is given for the meaning of "other means". Recital 14 of the Directive states that "the Directive should be extended to cover non-electronic databases" and thus it seems clear that it was the express intention of the Directive that databases other than electronic ones should be eligible for database right. It is submitted that the Regulations, therefore, cover non-electronic databases. However, if this interpretation is correct, then the requirement that the works or data be individually accessible becomes difficult to interpret.   **18–14**

This difficulty can be illustrated as follows: an indexed newspaper will argu-

---

[45] *Fixtures Marketing Limited v Organismos prognostikon agonon podosfairou AE(OPAP)* (C–444/02) [2004] E.C.R. I–10549.

[46] *Fixtures Marketing Limited v Organismos prognostikon agonon podosfairou AE(OPAP)* (C–444/02) [2004] E.C.R. I–10549.

[47] *Fixtures Marketing Limited v Organismos prognostikon agonon podosfairou AE(OPAP)* (C–444/02) [2004] E.C.R. I–10549.

[48] *Fixtures Marketing Limited v Organismos prognostikon agonon podosfairou AE(OPAP)* (C–444/02) [2004] E.C.R. I 10549.

[49] *Fixtures Marketing Limited v Organismos prognostikon agonon podosfairou AE(OPAP)* (C–444/02) [2004] E.C.R. I–10549.

[50] See para.3–146, above.

ably satisfy the requirements for a non-electronic database by being a collection of independent works arranged in a systematic way. Each independent work will be individually accessible by the reader as he is able to discern and discriminate with his eye one work over any other work. If this sort of individual accessibility is sufficient to yield a database right, then the threshold of this part of the criteria will be easily crossed.

It can be seen from the above illustration that problems could arise if newspapers were paper databases and therefore only eligible for copyright protection if they met the alternative test for originality. It is submitted that, if the Regulations do include non-electronic databases, the new test for originality will have a much wider application than could have been intended.

C. SUBSISTENCE

18–15 **Substantial Investment.** Database right will subsist in a database "if there has been a substantial investment in obtaining, verifying or presenting the contents of the database".[51] "Substantial" in relation to any investment, means substantial in terms of quantity or quality, or a combination of both.[52] The investment required for a database to be eligible for database right is defined as "any investment, whether of financial, human or technical resources"[53]; this definition in the Regulations is in line with recital 7 of the Directive which states also that the making of the database requires "investment of considerable human, technical and financial resources".

The substantial investment requirement was considered by the Dutch Appeal Court in a case in 2006.[54] In this case an assertion that sui generis rights existed in an estate agent's property database failed. However, it would appear that in the *Directmedia* case,[55] an investment of €34,900 was considered to be a substantial investment by the referring German court in relation to the creation of a database of poetry even though it seems that at least some of this sum was expended on the collation of the data itself.[56]

The ECJ considered the meaning of the term "substantial investment" in the *British Horseracing Board* case.[57] It was noted that the purpose of the Directive was to promote and protect investment in data storage and processing systems and it therefore follows that the investment protected refers to that "in the creation of that database as such." Expanding on what that investment relates to, the ECJ concluded that it refers to the resources used to seek out pre-existing independent materials and collate them into the database, but crucially did not extend to the resources used for the primary creation of the independent materials themselves[58]. According to Mme Stix-Hackl, the Advocate General in the case, relevant factors in assessing substantiality include the scale, nature and contents

---

[51] reg.13(1), implementing art.7 of the Directive.

[52] reg.12(1).

[53] reg.12(1).

[54] *Nederlandse Vereniging van Makelaars in Onroerende Goederen en Vastgoeddeskundigen NVM v Zoekallehuizen.nl* Unreported, July 4, 2006, noted at [2007] E.I.P.R. N73–4.

[55] *Directmedia Publishing GmbH v Albert-Ludwigs-Universität Freiburg* ECJ (C–304/07) [2008] E.C.R. I–7565.

[56] para.24.

[57] *The British Horseracing Board Limited v William Hill Organisation Limited* (C–203/02) [2005] R.P.C 13.

[58] *The British Horseracing Board Limited v William Hill Organisation Limited* (C–203/02) [2005] R.P.C 13, paras 30–31. See also the comments of Jacob L.J. when the case came back before the Court of Appeal following the ECJ judgment [2005] R.P.C. 25. Jacob L.J. held that the ECJ's analysis of investments in paras 37–41 of its decision is dependant on a finding that the database of runners and riders was not one consisting of "existing independent materials" but that the

of the database and the commercial sector to which it relates.[59] The ECJ noted that "investment in the creation of a database may consist in the deployment of human, financial or technical resources… the quantitative assessment refers to quantifiable resources and the qualitative assessment to efforts which cannot be quantified, such as intellectual effort or energy"[60]

Obtaining, verifying or presenting. As noted above, the sui generis right 18–16 subsists where there has been investment in "obtaining", "verifying" or "presenting" a database. "Verification" must be understood, according to the ECJ, as referring to the resources used with a view to ensuring the accuracy of the information contained in a database by monitoring the accuracy of the materials collected when the database was created and during its operation.[61] Given that the investment relating to the creation of the materials themselves is not protectable under the sui generis right, "verification" activities relating to the "stage of creation of data or other materials which are subsequently collected in a database" may not therefore be taken into account.[62] "Obtaining", on the other hand, relates to the resources used to seek out existing independent materials and collecting them into the database. It does not cover the resources used for the creation of the materials making up the contents of a database.[63] The investment in "presenting" the contents of a database relates to the resources used for the purpose of giving the database its function of processing information: "those used for the systematic or methodological arrangement of the materials contained in that database and the organisation of their individual accessibility."[64]

Distinction between "pre-existent data" and creation: general. It is submitted 18–17 that this theoretical distinction between "pre-existent" data and acts relating to the creation of a database may be difficult to apply in practice.[65] Indeed in the *British Horseracing Board* case the ECJ itself noted that, where the creation of a database is linked to the creation of the materials in the database, there is nothing to preclude the sui generis right where it can be shown that there was substantial investment in the creation of the database which "was independent of the resources used to create those materials".[66] Further it noted in a rather Delphic conclusion that, although the creator of the data in a database may not require particular resources to verify data because they were created by him, "the fact remains that the collection of those data, their systematic or methodological arrangement in the database, the organisation of their individual accessibility and

---

nature of the information contained within it changed once the data had the stamp of official approval—see further below.

[59] Also relevant is recital 40 to the Directive ("such investment may consist of the implementation of financial resources and/or the expending of time, effort and energy"). See *Fixtures Marketing Limited v Svenska Spel AB* (C–338/02) [2004] E.C.R. I–10497, AG Opinion unreported, paras 34–46.

[60] *Fixtures Marketing v Oy Veikkaus AB* at [2004] E.C.R. I–10365, *Fixtures Marketing v Organismos Prognostikon Agonon Podosfairou (OPAP)* at [2004] E.C.R. I–10549 and *Fixtures Marketing Ltd v Svenska SpelAB* at [2004] E.C.R. I–10365.

[61] *The British Horseracing Board Limited v William Hill Organisation Limited* (C–203/02) [2005] R.P.C 13.

[62] *The British Horseracing Board Limited v William Hill Organisation Limited* (C–203/02) [2005] R.P.C 13, paras. 34, 42.

[63] *The British Horseracing Board Limited v William Hill Organisation Limited* (C–203/02) [2005] R.P.C 13.

[64] *Fixtures Marketing Limited v Svenska Spel AB* (C–338/02) [2004] E.C.R. I–10497.

[65] Indeed it is likely that the distinction adopted by the ECJ will lead to wide variations in the scope of protection afforded to databases in different member states as national courts grapple with the problem of determining principles guiding the assessment of which data is pre-existent.

[66] *The British Horseracing Board Limited v William Hill Organisation Limited* (C–203/02) [2005] R.P.C 13, para.35.

the verification of their accuracy throughout the operation of the database may require substantial investment"[67]

The distinction: the *British Horseracing Board* case. Thankfully the ECJ went on to consider the facts of the case (a questionable extension of their jurisdiction under art.234 EC now art.267 TFEU)[68] and concluded that certain aspects of the British Horseracing Board's investment were not protectable under the sui generis right. In particular, investment relating to the selection of the horses admitted to run in a race was held to concern the creation of the data which made up the lists in the database and thus could not be taken into account.[69] Similarly, checking the credentials of a potential entrant in a race (including checks on the identity of the person making the entry, the characteristics of the horse, its owner and the jockey) was also considered investment in the creation of the data and not the verification of the contents of the database.[70] These factual conclusions are important, even though they are only provisional, because the theoretical distinction relied upon by the ECJ appears to be applied robustly with the result that the ambit of the sui generis right is significantly narrower than was previously assumed in litigation before the national courts of the EU member states.

The findings of the European Court of Justice in the *British Horseracing Board* case were subsequently considered by the Court of Appeal. The Board submitted that the European Court had proceeded on a misunderstanding of the facts concerning the investment that had been made in the database and detailed a series of seven steps that led to the database being created. Jacob L.J. held that the European Court had not misunderstood the primary facts, nor had it indulged in an illegitimate fact-finding exercise. The principal flaw in the Board's submissions was held to be that the Court of Justice had implicitly rejected an approach permitting a deconstruction of the database—it focused solely on the final database that was eventually published. Consequently, when the question was asked whether the British Horseracing Board published database was one consisting of "existing *independent* materials" the answer was held to be no. The British Horseracing Board database contained unique information—the official list of runners and riders—but the nature of the information changed as a result of the British Horseracing Board's imprimatur and it thus became something different from a mere database of existing material. The European Court had concluded that the "... investment in the selection, for the purpose of organising horse racing, of the horses admitted to run in the race concerned relates to the creation of the data which make up the lists for those races which appear in the BHB database." In considering this sentence, Jacob and Pill L.JJ. in the Court of Appeal noted that "selection might, out of context, be taken to denote something like a creative choice but in context it clearly does not have that meaning." This finding is supported by the French version of the European Court's judgment (the court's working language) which employs the term *determination* which does not imply a requirement for creativity.

The distinction: the *Fixtures Marketing* cases. A similar result was reached in

---

[67] *The British Horseracing Board Limited v William Hill Organisation Limited* (C–203/02) [2005] R.P.C 13, para.36.

[68] See, for example, the decision of Laddie J. in *Arsenal Football Club v Reed (No.2)* [2003] EWCA Civ 696; [2003] E.T.M.R. 36). It is notable that the ECJ's findings of fact in these cases are often expressed to be provisional and determined from the facts supplied by the national court in the order for a reference under art.234 EC. This acknowledgment arguably addresses some of the criticisms levied by Laddie J. in the *Arsenal* case. The Court of Appeal in *British Horseracing Board v William Hill Organisation Ltd* [2005] EWCA Civ 863; [2005] R.P.C. 35 nevertheless upheld the findings of the ECJ in the face of submissions on the basis of the *Arsenal* case.

[69] *The British Horseracing Board Limited v William Hill Organisation Limited* (C–203/02) [2005] R.P.C. 13, para.38.

[70] *The British Horseracing Board Limited v William Hill Organisation Limited* (C–203/02) [2005] R.P.C. 13.

the *Fixtures Marketing* cases which concerned the exploitation of English and Scottish football fixtures lists. Here it was concluded that the resources deployed for arranging the dates and times and identities of home and away teams were an investment in the creation of the fixtures list itself and, as they were related to the original data, could not be taken into account in assessing the scope of protection under the sui generis right.[71] Furthermore the ECJ stated that the collection of the data making up a football fixtures list did not require any particular effort on the part of the professional leagues, and thus no independent investment was provided which led to a protectable database right.[72] Nor was any particular effort expended in verifying the accuracy of data on league matches when the list was drawn up since the leagues were directly involved in the creation of the relevant data. Finally, no substantial investment occurred in the presentation of a football fixtures list as it was too closely linked to the creation of the data as such.[73]

Conclusion on sporting fixtures and similar material. In the light of these   **18–18**
robust judgments it might appear that sporting fixtures are unprotectable by means of sui generis database right on the basis that no sufficient investment will be made in the database per se. It would be wrong, however, to conclude that sporting fixtures databases (or, for example, television listings) can no longer be protected in principle. The consequence of the ECJ's decision in those cases is that some unusual element of investment must be provided when the pre-existing data is assembled into a database in order for it to be protectable. It may well be possible, therefore, for enhanced investment in more sophisticated presentation of the data in the database by means of the compilation of enhanced indexing, for example, to satisfy the requirements for protection.

Effect on the "spin-off theory". One interesting argument that has been   **18–19**
advanced in connection with the scope of the sui generis right concerns the so-called "spin-off theory". The argument essentially runs as follows: the purpose of harmonising the law of databases through the Directive was to provide European incentives for investment by protecting investments made in connection with preparing commercial databases; the purpose of protecting those investments was to ensure that the profits might be repaid from the principal activity for which the money was invested. Thus it is arguable that the Directive should not protect "spin-off" uses of a database which were not related to the investment creating it. This argument was made in several of the *Fixtures Marketing* cases at the European Court of Justice on the basis that the investment in the databases in issue in the proceedings was necessary for the organisation of sporting bets and not for the protection of the database per se—the investment would have been made in any event and the database was merely a by-product on another market. This argument was largely, and it is submitted correctly, rejected by A.G. Stix-Hackl on the grounds that there is no suggestion from the Directive that the protection for a database depends on its purpose.[74] Although not addressed explicitly by the ECJ in its judgments, the approach adopted to narrowing the scope of the invest-

---

[71] *Fixtures Marketing v Oy Veikkaus AB* (C–338/02) [2004] E.C.R. I–10365. A similar result was reached by Floyd J. in *Football Datco Ltd* (above).
[72] *Fixtures Marketing v Oy Veikkaus AB* (C–338/02) [2004] E.C.R. I–10365.
[73] *Fixtures Marketing Limited v Svenska Spel AB* (C–338/02) [2004] E.C.R. I–10497. *Fixtures Marketing Limited v Organismos prognostikon agonon podosfairou AE(OPAP)* (C–444/02) [2004] E.C.R. I–10549. *Fixtures Marketing v Oy Veikkaus AB* (C–46/02) [2004] E.C.R. I–10365.
[74] *Fixtures Marketing Ltd v Svenska Spel AB* (C–338/02), Opinion of A.G.Stix-Hakl Unreported, paras 42 46. See also E. Derclaye, "Databases *Sui Generis* Right: should we adopt the spin-off theory" [2004] E.I.P.R. 402. See also *Nederlandse Vereniging van Makelaars in Onroerende Goederen en Vastgoeddeskundigen NVM v Zoekallehuizen.nl* Unreported, July 4, 2006 (Arnheim Appeal Court) noted at [2007] E.I.P.R. 29(5), N73–4.

ment that can be taken into consideration would appear to support a rejection of the spin-off theory.[75]

D. QUALIFICATION

18–20 **General.** Regulation 18(1) provides that database right does not subsist in a database unless, at the material time, its maker, or if jointly, one or more of its makers, was:

(a) an individual who was a national of an EEA state or habitually resident within the EEA state;

(b) a body incorporated under the law of an EEA state and which, at that time, satisfied one of the conditions in reg.18(2);

(c) a partnership or other unincorporated body which was formed under the law of an EEA state and which, at that time, satisfied the condition in reg.18(2)(a); or

(d) the analogous persons (an individual, body, partnership or unincorporated body) within the Isle of Man.[76]

The conditions in reg.18(2) that are required to be satisfied are:

(a) that the body has its central administration or principal place of business within the EEA; or

(b) that the body has its registered office within the EEA and the body's operations are linked on an ongoing basis with the economy of an EEA state.[77]

18–21 **"Foreign" databases.** As to "foreign" databases, recital 56 to the Directive states in effect that the maker of a database will not qualify for a database right in situations other than those provided for under reg.18 unless the country of which the maker of the database is a national or where the maker is habitually resident "offers comparable protection to nationals of a Member State or those who have their habitual residence in the territory of the Community", i.e. the Directive is based in this regard on the principle of material reciprocity and protection will only be given to non-EEA nationals on a reciprocal basis. It follows that a foreign database may qualify for copyright protection but not for database right protection. This may prove to be an important distinction in relation, for example, to US databases.[78]

E. TITLE

18–22 **First ownership.** The maker of a database is the first owner of the database right in it.[79] Pursuant to reg.14(1), the "person who takes the initiative in obtaining, verifying or presenting the contents of a database and assumes the risks of investing in that obtaining, verification or presentation shall be regarded as the maker of, and as having made, the database". Under reg.14(2) where "the database is made by an employee in the course of his employment, his employer shall be regarded as the maker of, and has having made, the database, subject to any agreement to the contrary". The provision for databases created in the course of employment is similar in effect, if not in form, to the provisions for copyright

---

[75] See para.18–00, above. See also *Re Musical Hits Database*, Bundesgerichtshof (Germany), decision of July 21, 2005 [2006] E.C.C. 31.

[76] Copyright and Rights in Databases Regulations 1997 reg.18(1)(d)–(f) introduced by the Copyright and Rights in Databases (Amendment) Regulations 2003 (SI 2003/2501) reg.5.

[77] reg.18(2A) applies similar requirements to qualification by connection with the Isle of Man, although notably the link is made to the economy of the Isle of Man.

[78] In the long run, this problem is likely to be solved by an international instrument on the protection of databases by means of a system of sui generis protection.

[79] Copyright and Rights in Databases Regulations 1997 reg.15.

works as provided for in the 1988 Act[80] and so presumably the case law on the corresponding provision in the 1988 Act applies.[81] Accordingly, whether an individual is an employee as opposed to an independent contractor and, if the individual is an employee, whether the database was made in the course of his employment, will be determined in much the same way as with copyright works.[82] While the Regulations make no provision for joint ownership, they do provide for joint makers of a database. Regulation 14(5) states that "a database is made jointly if two or more persons acting together in collaboration take the initiative in obtaining, verifying or presenting the contents of the database and assume the risk of investing in that obtaining, verification or presentation". Clearly, therefore, there may be joint first owners of database right. These ownership provisions were considered in *Pennwell Publishing (UK) Limited v Onstein*.[83] The case concerned a departing employee from Pennwell who had added his various non-work related contact details to the Microsoft Outlook email system maintained by his employer. The key question was whether the relevant database was prepared in the course of employment. The court held that where an address list is maintained on Outlook or a similar program which is part of an employer's email system, the rights in question will usually belong to the employer regardless of whether it also contains personal contacts of the employee.[84]

Where a database is made by Her Majesty or by an officer or servant of the Crown in the course of his duties, Her Majesty is to be regarded as the maker of the database.[85] Where the database is made by, or under the direction or control of the House of Commons or the House of Lords, the House by whom, or under whose direction or control, the database is made is to be regarded as the maker of the database.[86] If made by or under the direction or control of both Houses, then the two Houses are to be regarded as joint makers of the database.[87] Where a database is made by or under the direction or control of the Scottish Parliament, the Scottish Parliamentary Corporate Body is to be regarded as the maker of the database.[88]

Transmission. The provisions in the 1988 Act governing transmission of copyright are incorporated into the Regulations.[89]   **18–23**

F. DURATION

General. Prima facie, database right subsists until the end of the period of 15   **18–24**
years from the end of the calendar year in which the making of the database was completed.[90] If, however, the database is made available to the public within that 15-year period, the term of database right will expire 15 years from the date when it was first so made available.[91] It follows that making a database available to the public within the original 15-year term will result in the clock being re-set and a 15–year term starting again.

---

[80] CDPA 1988 s.11(2).
[81] See paras 5–08 et seq., above.
[82] See paras 5–12 et seq., above.
[83] [2007] EWHC 1570 (QB); [2008] 2 B.C.L.C. 246.
[84] See also *Cureton v Mark Insulations Ltd* [2006] EWHC 2279 (Admin), in which a submission that database right in a database created by an agent for his principal was owned by the principal was rejected.
[85] reg.14(3).
[86] reg.14(4).
[87] reg.14(4)(6).
[88] reg.14(4A), introduced into the Regulations by SI 1999/1042.
[89] Copyright and Rights in Databases Regulations 1997 reg.23 states that CDPA 1988 ss.90–93 apply; see also paras 5–00 et seq., above.
[90] Copyright and Rights in Databases Regulations 1997 reg.17(1). Cf. Directive 96/9 art.10.
[91] reg.17(2).

18–25   **Effect of changes.** If any substantial change is made to the contents of a database, including a substantial change resulting from the accumulation of successive additions, deletions or alterations, which results in the database being considered to be a substantial new investment, this will lead to the database resulting from that investment having its own, new term of protection. Regulation 12 defines "investment" as including any investment, whether of financial, human or technical resources. Article 10(3) of the Directive indicates that "substantial change" should be evaluated "qualitatively and quantitatively". Some further guidance is provided in the recitals to the Directive. Recital 54 states that the "burden of proof that the criteria exist for concluding that a substantial modification of the contents of a database is to be regarded as a substantial new investment lies with the maker of the database resulting from such investment". Furthermore, recital 55 states that a substantial new investment "may include a substantial verification of the contents of the database".

18–26   **The *British Horseracing Board* case.** In this case the question arose as to whether every "substantial change" made to a database resulted in a new protectable database. This issue was not considered by the ECJ in its judgment. However, A.G. Stix-Hackl noted that databases which are constantly updated are "dynamic" in the sense that there is only ever one database and that previous versions "disappear" as new data is added to it. She stated that the basic principle to be applied in determining whether the term of protection had been extended was to consider the objective of the changes, that is, to ask whether they had been done to bring the database up to date with the aim that the whole database was the object of the new investment concerned. The consequence of this would be, as A.G. Stix-Hackl termed it, that dynamic databases enjoy a "rolling sui generis right" in which the whole database, and not just the changes as such, enjoy a new term of protection. Moreover, given that changes may be made to a database which, although insubstantial when taken individually, may be sufficient to amount to a substantial change when taken together, it will not be difficult to secure effectively unlimited protection on a rolling right.[92] This approach is broadly consistent with that adopted by Laddie J. at first instance.[93]

Given that the approach adopted by the ECJ was to distinguish investment in the constituent data of the database from that of creating the database per se,[94] it is arguable that substantial reorganisations of the presentation of a database will be sufficient to afford an extended term of protection. To obtain a "rolling right" the investment must relate to the database per se rather than merely acquiring more data.

---

[92] The *British Horseracing Board Ltd v William Hill Organisation Ltd* (C–203/02) [2004] E.C.R. I–10415, Opinion of A.G. Stix-Hackl, paras 149–155.

[93] See *The British Horseracing Board Ltd v William Hill Organisation Ltd* [2001] R.P.C. 31. This approach it is submitted, fails to give proper effect to art.10(3) of Directive 96/9 which refers to any "substantial" change, including any which would result in the database being considered to be a "substantial new investment". In *British Horseracing Board* itself, the database was considered as a single database by all the witnesses, and it would have been impossible and unreal to split it into a number of discrete units. Laddie J. dealt with this problem by concluding that "This does not render Art 10(3) meaningless. First it emphasises that the term keeps being renewed as the database is renewed. Secondly it makes clear that if someone takes an existing database and adds significantly to it, he obtains protection for the database incorporating his additions. This would be so even if the new author is not the same as the author of the original database." Nevertheless, this does not deal with the core point. It is suggested that the right approach, which is essentially the one that Laddie J. took, is to give the repeated extraction provisions of art.7(5) of the Directive a purposive construction and treat them as applying to a dynamic database as much as to a static one. See also the decision of HHJ Birss QC in *Beechwood House Publishing v Guardian Products and others* [2010] EWPCC 012, unreported.

[94] See para.18–17, above.

G. INFRINGEMENT AND PERMITTED ACTS

General. A person will be held to infringe database right in a database if, without **18–27**
the consent of the owner of the right, he extracts or re-utilises all or a substantial
part of its contents.[95] An additional form of infringement occurs where the
repeated and systematic extraction or re-utilisation of insubstantial parts of the
contents of a database amounts to the extraction or re-utilisation of a substantial
part of those contents. An example of a situation where permission should be
sought from the rightholder is given in recital 44 of the Directive. It states: "when
on-screen display of the contents of a database necessitates the permanent or
temporary transfer of all or a substantial part of such contents to another medium,
that act should be subject to authorisation by the rightholder."[96]

Extraction and re-utilisation. The restricted acts are "extraction and re- **18–28**
utilisation". In relation to the contents of a database, "extraction" means the permanent or temporary[97] transfer of those contents to another medium by any means
or in any form, and "re-utilisation" means making those contents available to the
public by any means.[98] This definition should be read in the context of art.7 of the
Directive which provides that "re-utilisation" means any form of making available to the public "all or a substantial part of the contents of the database by the
distribution of copies, by renting, by on-line or other forms of transmission". The
making available of a database was considered by Floyd J. in *Football Dataco v
Sportradar*[99]. This case concerned a database called "Sports Live Data" which
was compiled from publicly accessible data and stored on servers in Germany
and Austria. In the context of a dispute over jurisdiction, the court considered the
issue of where "making available" occurred in relation to those servers. Floyd J.
held that the act of making available to the public by online transmission is committed and committed only where the transmission takes place. He concluded
that, although the placing of data on a server in one country can result in it being
accessed by those in another country, that does not mean that the party who made
the data available has performed the act of making available in the country of
reception. In relation to the various infringing acts, A.G. Stix-Hackl legitimately
notes that there is potentially an error in the drafting of the Directive—the definition of "extraction" in art.7(2)(a) requires "all or a substantial part" and yet
art.7(5) refers to the "repeated and systematic extraction and/or re-utilization of
insubstantial parts…".

Proof of infringement. In the *Apis-Hristovich* case,[100] the ECJ noted that the fact **18–29**
that materials obtained by the maker from sources not accessible to the public appear in allegedly infringing database is not in itself proof of an infringement.
However, it does amount to relevant circumstantial evidence from which an
inference of extraction can be made.

Purpose of extraction or re-utilisation. One of the issues which arose in the **18–30**

---

[95] The acts that infringe a database right are provided for in reg.16 of the Copyright and Rights in
Databases Regulations 1997.
[96] See also *Directmedia Publishing GmbH v Albert-Ludwigs-Universität Freiburg* (C–304/07)
[2009] RPC 10, which concerned on-screen consulation of a database.
[97] In *Apis-Hristovich EOOD v Lakorda AD* (C–545/07) [2009] 3 C.M.L.R. 3, [2009] E.C.D.R. 13
the ECJ made clear that the difference between permanent and temporary transfer is based on the
length of time during which the extracted materials are stored in a medium other than the original
database.
[98] reg.12 of the Copyright and Rights in Databases Regulations 1997.
[99] *Football Dataco Limited and others v Sportradar GmbH and others* [2010] EWHC 2911 (Ch),
unreported decision of November 17, 2010.
[100] *Apis-Hristovich EOOD v Lakorda AD* (C–545/07) [2009] 3 C.M.L.R. 3, [2009] E.C.D.R. 13.

British Horseracing Board case was whether William Hill's activities constituted acts of extraction or re-utilisation under art.7 of the Directive. The ECJ emphasised that the rights to prevent extraction and re-utilisation must be construed in the context of the wider objectives of the sui generis right, namely the protection of the investment of the maker of the database.[101] Consequently it concluded that the fact (if it be the case) that the act of extraction or re-utilisation is for the purpose of creating another database (whether in competition with the original database or not, of a different size, or part of wider activities) is irrelevant.[102] Moreover, given that the term "for commercial purposes" which had been included in the original proposal for the Directive had been dropped, the ECJ concluded that it was irrelevant whether the act in question was done for a commercial or non-commercial purpose.[103]

18–31 **Indirect use.** In connection with the question of whether it was possible to infringe by means of using derived works, the ECJ concluded in the same case that there is no requirement for extraction and re-utilisation to be taken directly from the original database. Unauthorised extraction and re-utilisation by a third party from a source other than the database are capable of prejudicing the maker's protected investment. Imposing such a requirement would leave the maker of the database with no reasonable protection from unauthorised copying.[104] This would appear significantly to widen the scope of protection to include down-stream derived works.

18–32 **"Mere consultation".** Unfortunately in the *British Horseracing Board* case the ECJ did not proffer an explanation of the circumstances where "consultation" drifts into "extraction". It would appear that "consultation" is intimately related to controlling access to a database. The maker of a database can reserve access to himself or specific people. However, if the owner makes the database or part of it accessible to the public the sui generis right does not prevent third parties from "consulting" that database.[105] The same limitation applies where the owner of a database authorises a third party to re-utilise the contents of the database "in other words, to distribute it to the public."[106] The ECJ reiterated that, according to the definition of re-utilisation in art.7(2)(b) of the Directive, when read in conjunction with the 41st recital, the grant of authorisation for the re-utilisation of the database or a substantial part thereof implies consent to the database being made accessible to the public by the third party to whom that authorisation was given.[107] However, the fact that a database can be consulted by third parties through someone who was given authorisation to re-utilise does not prevent the maker from recovering the costs of his investment. The ECJ concluded that "it is legitimate for the maker to charge a fee for the re-utilisation of the whole or a part of his database which reflects, inter alia, the prospect of subsequent consulta-

[101] *The British Horseracing Board Ltd v William Hill Organisation Ltd* (C–203/02) [2005] R.P.C. 13, para.45.
[102] *The British Horseracing Board Ltd v William Hill Organisation Ltd* (C–203/02) [2005] R.P.C. 13, para.47
[103] *The British Horseracing Board Ltd v William Hill Organisation Ltd* (C–203/02) [2005] R.P.C. 13, para.48.
[104] *The British Horseracing Board Ltd v William Hill Organisation Ltd* (C–203/02) [2005] R.P.C. 13, para.52.
[105] *The British Horseracing Board Ltd v William Hill Organisation Ltd* (C–203/02) [2005] R.P.C. 13, paras 54–5. See also *Finn No AS v Supersok AS* [2007] E.C.D.R. 12, which concerned the repeated consultation of estate agent databases.
[106] *The British Horseracing Board Ltd v William Hill Organisation Ltd* (C–203/02) [2005] R.P.C. 13, para.56.
[107] *The British Horseracing Board Ltd v William Hill Organisation Ltd* (C–203/02) [2005] R.P.C. 13, para.56.

tion and thus guarantees him a sufficient return".[108] Of course, the sui generis right does not, however, prevent a lawful user from extracting and re-utilising insubstantial parts of the contents of a database. In summary, any acts of extraction ("the transfer of the contents of the database to another medium") and acts of re-utilisation ("the making available to the public of the contents of a database") which affect the whole or a substantial part of the protected database require the authorisation of the maker, even where the database has been made accessible to public either directly or through a third-party intermediary.[109]

The *British Horseracing Board* case. In this case the information displayed by   **18–33**
William Hill was derived first from newspapers published before the races and subsequently from the "raw data feed" supplied by a third party. Both of these sources had their ultimate origin in the British Horseracing Board's database and the ECJ concluded in another potentially questionable finding of fact that William Hill carried out acts of extraction and re-utilisation which potentially constituted infringements subject to the requirement of substantiality.[110] Data which originated in the British Horseracing Board database was extracted by being transferred from one medium to another, and William Hill re-utilised data by making it available to the public on its internet site to enable its clients to bet on horses.[111]

Repeated acts. As far as the prohibition on repeated acts of "extraction" or "re-   **18–34**
utilisation" in art.7(5) of the Directive is concerned, A.G. Stix-Hackl considered the provisions of art.9 of the Berne Convention and art.13 of the TRIPs agreement and concluded that they could not be applied as a guide to understanding the scope of art.7(5).[112] In relation to "repeated and systematic extraction", A.G. Stix-Hackl noted that it is not entirely clear whether the two requirements are alternative or cumulative, as some language versions of the Directive link the requirements with "and" and others with "or". The majority of the language versions link the requirement with "and", which led her to conclude that they are to be understood cumulatively, as in the English text.[113] The conclusion she reached was that there was a repeated and systematic act when it is carried out at regular intervals, for example, weekly or monthly.

The ECJ reiterated that the general rule set out in art.8(1) and the 42nd recital to the Directive is that the maker of a database cannot prevent a lawful user of that database from extracting or re-utilising insubstantial parts of the database. Article 7(5) should therefore be properly construed as an exception to that general rule.[114] "The provision therefore prohibits acts of extraction made by users of the database which, because of their repeated and systematic character, would lead to the reconstitution of the database as a whole or, at the very least, of a

---

[108] *The British Horseracing Board Ltd v William Hill Organisation Ltd* (C–203/02) [2005] R.P.C. 13, para.56.
[109] *The British Horseracing Board Ltd v William Hill Organisation Ltd* (C–203/02) [2005] R.P.C. 13, para.61.
[110] See para.18–36, below.
[111] *The British Horseracing Board Ltd v William Hill Organisation Ltd* (C–203/02) [2005] R.P.C. 13, paras 65–67.
[112] Case C–338/02, *Fixtures Marketing Ltd v Svenska Spel AB*, Advocate General's Opinion, [2004] E.C.R. I–10487, paras 111–116.
[113] *The British Horseracing Board Ltd v William Hill Organisation Ltd* (C–203/02) [2005] R.P.C. 13, para.39.
[114] *The British Horseracing Board Ltd v William Hill Organisation Ltd* (C–203/02) [2005] R.P.C. 13, para.84.

substantial part of it…"[115] Similarly, the expression "acts which conflict with the normal exploitation of [a] database or which unreasonably prejudice the legitimate interests of the maker of the database" refer to unauthorised actions "for the purpose of reconstituting, through the cumulative effect of acts of extraction, the whole or a substantial part of the contents of a database…".[116] The ECJ held that William Hill's acts took place on the occasion of each race held and were therefore repeated and systematic but only concerned insubstantial parts of the protected database. However, because William Hill's acts were not intended to circumvent the prohibition laid down in art.7(1), there is no possibility that William Hill might reconstitute the whole or a substantial part of the protected database and thus no infringement.[117]

18–35   ***Directmedia.***[118] This case concerned a database of poetry which had been compiled as part of the "Klassikerwortschatz" ("vocabulary of the classics") project at Freiburg University. The task of compiling the database took two years and cost EUR 34,900 and was undertaken on behalf of the University. Directmedia marketed a CD ROM entitled *1000 Gedichte, die jeder haben muss* ("1000 poems everyone should have") and of the poems included in the CD ROM, 856 were chosen on the basis of the Klassikerwortschatz database. The University sought an injunction and damages against Directmedia and on appeal the Bundesgerichtshof referred a question to the ECJ asking whether, on the basis of a finding that Directmedia had used the list of verse titles drawn up in the University's database as a guide to select the poems that were to appear on its CD ROM, there had been an "extraction" within the meaning of art.7(2)(a). This question raised the issue of whether the approach set out in the ECJ's decision in *British Horseracing Board v William Hill* was limited to "extraction" in which there was a direct transfer of the contents of a database or whether it also included use of a database for the purposes of consultation and critical inquiry. The ECJ held that what was decisive was whether there was an act of "transfer" of all or part of the contents of the database to another medium[119] and such transfer was not limited to acts transferring all or a substantial part of the contents of the database.[120] Accordingly the ECJ found that transfer of material from one database to another following an on-screen consultation of the first database is capable of constituting an "extraction" within the meaning of art.7(2)(a). The ECJ thereby reached a conclusion consistent with that of AG Sharpston.[121]

18–36   **Substantiality.** If a database right subsists in an electronic database, then downloading a substantial part of that database without authorisation from the owner of database right will amount to an infringement. Furthermore, even if a single item or value is not in itself of sufficient qualitative importance, such that its isolated downloading will not amount to infringement, its repeated and systematic downloading may be an infringement. "Substantial", in relation to any

---

[115] *The British Horseracing Board Ltd v William Hill Organisation Ltd* (C–203/02) [2005] R.P.C. 13, para.87.

[116] *The British Horseracing Board Ltd v William Hill Organisation Ltd* (C–203/02) [2005] R.P.C. 13, para.89.

[117] *The British Horseracing Board Ltd v William Hill Organisation Ltd* (C–203/02) [2005] R.P.C. 13, paras 91–92.

[118] *Directmedia Publishing GmbH v Albert-Ludwigs-Universität Freiburg* (C–304/07) [2008] E.C.R. I–7565.

[119] para.36.

[120] paras 42–44.

[121] Whose opinion is reported at [2008] E.C.D.R. 16.

extraction or re-utilisation, means substantial in terms of quantity or quality or a combination of both.[122]

The *British Horseracing Board* case. In this case, in connection with the mean-   **18–37**
ings of the terms "substantial part" and "insubstantial part", the ECJ confirmed
that a quantitative assessment is made by comparing the volume of data extracted
from the database and/or re-utilised with the volume of the contents of the whole
of the database.[123] The qualitative assessment refers to the scale of the investment
in the obtaining, verification or presentation of the contents forming the subject
of the extraction and/or reutilisation regardless of whether those contents are
quantitatively significant relative to the whole.[124] The ECJ noted that "a
quantitatively negligible part of the contents of a database may in fact represent,
in terms of obtaining, verification or presentation, significant human, technical or
financial investment."[125] However, since the sui generis right does not affect the
works, data or materials in the database, the intrinsic value of the data concerned
is not a relevant criterion for making the qualitative assessment.[126]

Again, in a provisional finding of fact, the ECJ noted that the acts related to
only a very small proportion of the whole of the database and consequently did
not constitute a substantial part when evaluated quantitatively.[127] William Hill
had only used the names of the horses in the relevant race, the date, time and
name of the race and the name of the racecourse. The correct test for assessing
whether this was a substantial part evaluated qualitatively was to examine
whether the human, technical and financial efforts put in by the maker of the
database in obtaining, verifying and presenting those data constituted a
substantial investment. Despite the argument that without the lists of horses running in races those races could not take place and the data were thus vital to the
organisation of horse races, the ECJ reiterated that the intrinsic value of the data
affected is not a relevant criterion in the assessment.[128] Moreover, given that the
resources used for the creation of the data as such are also irrelevant to the assessment,[129] the materials extracted and re-utilised by William Hill were held not
to require an investment which was independent of that required for their creation and consequently did not constitute a substantial part in qualitative terms.[130]

Apis-Hristovich.[131] In this case the ECJ held that where there was a body of   **18–38**
materials which comprised various separate modules, the volume of the materials
that were extracted or re-utilised must be compared with the total contents of the
module from which it was taken if the module satisfies the requirements for
protection as a database. In the event that the various modules did not qualify for
protection in their own right, the comparison was to be made between the collection of materials as a whole and the material extracted or re-utilised. This ap-

---

[122] reg.12(1) of the Copyright and Rights in Databases Regulations 1997.
[123] *The British Horseracing Board Ltd v William Hill Organisation Ltd* (C–203/02) [2005] R.P.C. 13, para.70.
[124] *The British Horseracing Board Ltd v William Hill Organisation Ltd* (C–203/02) [2005] R.P.C. 13, para.82.
[125] *The British Horseracing Board Ltd v William Hill Organisation Ltd* (C–203/02) [2005] R.P.C. 13, para.71.
[126] *The British Horseracing Board Ltd v William Hill Organisation Ltd* (C–203/02) [2005] R.P.C. 13, para.72.
[127] *The British Horseracing Board Ltd v William Hill Organisation Ltd* (C–203/02) [2005] R.P.C. 13, para.74.
[128] *The British Horseracing Board Ltd v William Hill Organisation Ltd* (C–203/02) [2005] R.P.C. 13, para.77–78.
[129] *The British Horseracing Board Ltd v William Hill Organisation Ltd* (C–203/02) [2005] R.P.C. 13, paras 31–33, 79.
[130] *The British Horseracing Board Ltd v William Hill Organisation Ltd* [2005] R.P.C. 13, para.80.
[131] *Apis-Hristovich EOOD v Lakorda AD* (C–545/07) [2009] 3 C.M.L.R. 3.

proach suggests that it is generally desirable for a claimant to identify the smallest modules or parts of a database in which database right subsists in order to increase the likelihood that what is taken will be found to have been a substantial part.[132]

18–39   **Restrictions on contractual terms affecting lawful users.** Any contractual term that purports to narrow or exclude the rights of extraction and re-utilisation of a lawful user of a database or a part of a database will be void.[133] "Lawful user", in relation to a database, means any person who (whether under a licence to do any of the acts restricted by any database right in the database or otherwise) has a right to use the database.[134]

18–40   **Permitted acts.** The Regulations permit a number of acts which would otherwise be an infringement of database right.[135] Regulation 20(1) contains a fair dealing defence,[136] which provides that database right in a database which has been made available to the public in any manner is not infringed by fair dealing with a substantial part of its contents if:

(a) that part is extracted from the database by a person who is, apart from this provision, a "lawful user of the database";

(b) it is extracted for the purpose of illustration for teaching or research and not for any commercial purpose; and

(c) the source is indicated.

This exception relates to the restricted act of "extraction" only. "Re-utilisation" for these purposes is not permitted, presumably because the permitted act does not encompass making the database available to the public.

Schedule 1 to the Regulations provides for further exceptions to database right,[137] these exceptions relating generally to public administration. Regulation 20A(1) also provides that database right is not infringed by the copying of a work from the internet by a deposit library[138] or a person acting on its behalf where its publication on the internet, or a person publishing it there, is connected with the United Kingdom.[139] There are no exceptions to infringement relating to criticism, review and news reporting,[140] and no other exceptions for libraries and archives.[141] Generally, the Directive, and thus reg.20, provide for far fewer exceptions to infringement of database right than the equivalent provisions of the 1988 Act relating to copyright works, and the exceptions which are created are narrower.

18–41   **Permitted acts on assumption of expiry of the right.** Database right is not infringed by the extraction or re-utilisation of a substantial part of the contents of a database at a time when, or in pursuance of arrangements made at a time when:

(a) it is not possible by reasonable inquiry to ascertain the identity of the maker; and

---

[132] The ECJ also held that the fact that part of the materials contained in a database (in that case a database of case law) were official and publicly accessible did not absolve the national court of having to make an assessment of whether a substantial part of the data had been extracted or re-utilised: para.73

[133] reg.19(2) of the Copyright and Rights in Databases Regulations 1997.

[134] reg.12(1).

[135] These are permitted by art. 6 of Directive 96/9.

[136] For the permitted acts of fair dealing in relation to copyright works, see paras 9–00 et seq.

[137] See reg.20(2) of the Copyright and Rights in Databases Regulations 1997.

[138] "Deposit libraries" have the same meaning as in s.7 of the Legal Deposit Libraries Act 2003, see reg.20(4)(b). For permitted acts in relation to copyright and Deposit Libraries, see paras 9–00 et seq. For Deposit Libraries generally, see paras 26–00 et seq.

[139] reg.20A(1)(b) inserted by the Legal Deposit Libraries Act 2003 s.8(2) in force from February, 2004. Further provisions, including reg.20A(2), provide that no database infringement occurs in relation to any of the permitted activities under s.7 of the 2003 Act.

[140] Cf. CDPA 1988 s.30.

[141] Cf. CDPA 1998 ss.37–44.

(b) it is reasonable to assume that database right has expired.[142]

H. PROCEEDINGS

Statutory presumptions. The Regulations contain two presumptions which are   **18–42**
relevant in proceedings to determine who is the maker of a database. First, where
the name purporting to be that of the maker appears on copies of the database as
published, or on the database when it was made, the person whose name appears
is to be presumed, until the contrary is proved[143]:

(a) to be the maker of the database; and

(b) to have made it in circumstances not falling within regs 14(2) to (4).[144]

Consequently, if this presumption applies, the named person shall be presumed
to be the maker of it and thus the first owner.

Secondly, where copies of the database as published bear a label or a mark
stating:

(a) that a named person was the maker of the database; or

(b) that the database was first published in a specified year,

the label or mark shall be admissible as evidence of the facts stated and shall be
presumed to be correct until the contrary is proved.[145] The above presumptions
apply in relation to each person alleged to be one of the makers.[146]

Remedies. The remedies available to a database owner for infringement of   **18–43**
database right are the same as the civil remedies as provided under the 1988 Act
for infringement of copyright.[147] It should be noted that flagrancy damages are
therefore available for infringement of database right, and that rights and remedies equivalent to those available to exclusive licensees under copyright are
available to exclusive licensees of database right.[148] There are no criminal offences created under the Regulations.

I. COPYRIGHT TRIBUNAL

Regulations 24 and 25 refer to Sch.2 to the Regulations give the Copyright   **18–44**
Tribunal a parallel jurisdiction to that for copyright.[149]

J. TRANSITIONAL PROVISIONS

Transitional provisions and the retrospective effect of database right. It   **18–45**
should be noted that nothing in the Regulations affects any agreement made
before the commencement of the Regulations on January 1, 1998.[150] No act done
before commencement, or, after commencement in pursuance of an agreement
made before commencement, shall be regarded as an infringement of database

---

[142] reg.21 of the Copyright and Rights in Databases Regulations 1997.

[143] reg.22(2) of the Copyright and Rights in Databases Regulations 1997.

[144] regs 14(2) and 14(4) refer to situations where the database was made by an employee, or by Her
Majesty or by an officer or servant of the Crown, or under the direction or control of the House of
Commons or the House of Lords.

[145] reg.22(3).

[146] reg.22(4).

[147] See reg.23. For these remedies, see Ch.21, below.

[148] See reg.23 applying CPDA 1988 ss.121 and 102. CDPA 1988 s.97(2) which applies by virtue of
reg.23.

[149] See generally Ch.28.

[150] reg.28(1) of the Copyright and Rights in Databases Regulations 1997 reg.28 was amended by the
Copyright and Rights in Databases (Amendment) Regulations 2003 (SI 2003/2501) reg.8.

right in a database.[151] The Regulations also deal with databases in existence prior to commencement of the Regulations. Regulation 29(1) provides that, where a database was created on or before March 27, 1996, and was a copyright work immediately before commencement, copyright shall continue to subsist in the database for the remainder of its copyright term under the 1988 Act.[152] Databases up to 15 years old also qualify for database right: reg.30 provides that, where the making of a database was completed on or after January 1, 1983, and on commencement of the Regulations database right began to subsist in the database, then database right shall subsist in the database for the period of 15 years beginning on January 1, 1998.[153]

---

[151] regs 28(3), 28(4) provide similar savings in respect of those acts relating to Isle of Man databases protected from November 1, 2003.

[152] Note also the provisions of recital60 to Directive 96/9 which relate to the higher standard of originality for the copyright protection of databases and provide that "[the] harmonisation of the criteria for determining whether a database is to be protected by copyright may not have the effect of reducing the term of protection currently enjoyed by the rightholders concerned".

[153] There are equivalent provisions in relation to the Isle of Man: see reg.30(b)(ii).

PUBLIC LENDING RIGHT

1. INTRODUCTION

Public lending right. After a long and chequered career a public lending right 　　**19–01**
Bill became law in 1979. The Public Lending Right Act 1979[1] was, however,
something of a misnomer. That is to say, although the object of the Act is to enable the creation of a Scheme[2] under which payments are provided to authors out
of a central fund, the "right" was not part of the author's copyright. Instead, the
Act created a right to remuneration in accordance with a statutory scheme, with
such remuneration only conferred on authors if their books are registered under
the Act and then lent to the public by local library authorities in the United
Kingdom.[3] A book is only eligible for the Scheme if it is a "printed and bound
publication" whilst certain categories of books, e.g. books of music are excluded.
Further, books which are not lent do not qualify under the public lending right
scheme; this will, no doubt, effectively exclude many books of reference.

This underlying position changed as a result of the implementation of Council
Directive 92/100,[4] which requires Member States to provide a right to authorise
or prohibit the rental and lending of copies of copyright works, whilst allowing
for derogation from that exclusive right in respect of public lending if authors
receive remuneration for such lending.

As a consequence of amendments introduced by s.43 of the Digital Economy
Act 2010, but which, as of August 31, 2010, appeared unlikely to be brought into
force in the near future[5], certain definitions are to be added to the Public Lending
Right Act with the intention of extending its scope to audio books and e-books,
as well as including the producers and narrators of books recorded as sound
recordings within the class of authors. As these changes only appear to apply to
the Act[6], they will have no effect on the eligibility requirements unless and until
equivalent amendments are made to the Scheme. As of August 31, 2010, there
had been no proposals for such amendments. Similar amendments are made to
the 1988 Act, again with the intention of making equivalent extension to the

---

[1] See Vol.2 B3.i. The Act extends to Northern Ireland and came into force on March 1, 1980 (SI
1980/83); and see the Transfer of Functions (Acts, Libraries and National Heritage) Order 1986
(SI 1986/600).

[2] Contained in the appendix to The Public Lending Right Scheme 1982 (Commencement) Order
1982 (SI 1982/719) as amended. See Vol.2 B3.ii for the present Scheme.

[3] Public Lending Right Act 1979 s.1(1).

[4] This Directive has been repealed by Council Directive 2006/115/EC on rental and lending right
and on certain rights related to copyright in the field of intellectual property ([2006] OJ L376/28),
which codifies a number of amendments to it. See Vol.2 H12. In the rest of this Chapter, references to "the Directive" and "the Rental Rights Directive" are to Directive 2006/115/EC unless
otherwise stated.

[5] See para.19–09, below.

[6] See para.19–09, below.

scope of the Public Lending Right, but which again will have no effect unless and until amendments are made to the Scheme.

2. THE RIGHT TO CONTROL LENDING

19–02   **The exclusive right to rent and lend to the public.** The implementation of Directive 2006/115/EC gave copyright owners, for the first time, the exclusive right to rent and lend their works to the public in the United Kingdom. Article 1 of the Directive requires Member States to provide a right to authorise or prohibit the rental and lending of copies of copyright works, whilst provision is made in art.6 for derogation from that exclusive right in respect of public lending, provided that authors receive remuneration for such lending. These provisions were implemented by ss.18A and 40A of the 1988 Act respectively.[7] Section 18A sets out the general principle applicable to most categories of copyright works, namely that lending copies of a work is an act restricted by the copyright in that work.[8] The exception to that general rule permitted by art.6 of the Directive is provided by the creation of a permitted act by s.40A.[9] Thus, subs.40A(1) provides that copyright in a work of any description is not infringed by the lending of a book by a public library if the book is within the public lending right scheme. Subsection 40A(1)(a) confirms that the reference to "the public lending right scheme" means the scheme in force under the Public Lending Right Act 1979.[10] Subsection 40A(1)(b) seeks to define those books which are within the public lending right scheme for the purpose of s.40A(1), as "a book within the meaning of the provisions of the scheme relating to eligibility, whether or not it is in fact eligible". The most natural meaning of this elliptical phrase is that the book must be a book of the type described in arts 6 or 6A of the Scheme, but need not be a book whose author is or whose authors are eligible authors within the meaning of arts 5 or 5A of the Scheme.[11] Alternatively, the definition may be intended to re- fer to books which would be eligible for registration, in terms of both the nature of the book and the eligibility of the author, but which have not been registered.[12] This latter construction is unlikely to be correct because whether or not the book is registered does not have any obvious effect on "whether or not it is in fact eligible" for registration. The difficulty with either construction of the subsection is that certain classes of author do not obtain a remuneration for lending their books: on the former construction, books written or illustrated by non-eligible authors lose the protection of s.18A without the potential compensation of receiv- ing income under the public lending right scheme. On the latter construction, authors of books that could be registered under the Scheme but which have not been would also lose the protection of s.18A without potential compensation under the Scheme. If this is right, s.40A(1) does not comply in full with the pro- visions of art.6(1) of the Directive.

A possible route to avoid this implementation failure, but one that relies, at best, on a strained construction of subs.40A(1)(b), is to interpret it to mean that a book is "within the public lending right scheme" if it is entered on the Register of the public lending right Scheme, and that there shall be no enquiry as to "whether or not it is in fact eligible" for such entry. This would make the permitted act cre-

---

[7] Added by The Copyright and Related Rights Regulations 1996 (SI 1996/2967), regs 10(2) and 11(2), respectively.

[8] See para.7–97, above, for a detailed discussion of CDPA 1988 s.18A.

[9] See, similarly, the provisions of CDPA 1988 s.66 relating to the compulsory licensing of lending of literary, dramatic, musical, or artistic works, sound recordings or films and see Ch.29, below.

[10] See para.19–04, below.

[11] See para.19–12, below.

[12] See para.19–16, below.

ated by s.40A of the 1988 Act and the right to remuneration under the Scheme coextensive and would thus comply with art.6 of the Directive. It would also be consistent with subss.1(7) and 4(3) of the Act which stipulate that the Scheme shall require, respectively, that the Public Lending Right is created by registration, and that the Register is conclusive as to its subsistence. If, however, this was the intention of subs.40A(1)(b), it is difficult to imagine why it was not simply drafted by reference to the Register.

Pending Amendments. As noted above, s.43 of the Digital Economy Act 2010 **19–03** will introduce certain amendments to the 1988 Act with the intention of broadening the scope of the public lending right and of the exception to infringement under s.40A. If and when those amendments come into force, subs.40A(1) will be amended and a new subs.40A(1A) introduced. These subsections will read as follows:

(1) Copyright in a work of any description is not infringed by the following acts by a public library in relation to a book within the public lending right scheme—

(a) lending the book;

(b) in relation to an audio-book or e-book, copying or issuing a copy of the book as an act incidental to lending it.

(1A) In subsection (1)—

(a) 'book', 'audio-book' and 'e-book' have the meanings given in section 5 of the Public Lending Right Act 1979[13],

(b) 'the public lending right scheme' means the scheme in force under section 1 of that Act,

(c) a book is within the public lending right scheme if it is a book within the meaning of the provisions of the scheme relating to eligibility, whether or not it is in fact eligible, and

(d) 'lending' is to be read in accordance with the definition of "lent out" in section 5 of that Act (and section 18A of this Act does not apply)."

As can be seen, the difficult wording of the current subs.40A(1)(b) will be retained as the new subs.40A(1A)(c) and the problems of construction discussed above remain. The main change is to permit, by the new subs.40A(1)(b), acts of copying of audio-books and e-books that are incidental to them being lent. This will protect libraries from allegations of infringement when, for example, authorising borrowers to copy e-books from the library's system onto their own devices.

In addition, as these amendments are intended to permit the lending of audio-books that will contain a performance by a narrator, the permitted acts in relation to rights in performances, contained in para.6B of Sch.2 to the 1988 Act, will also be extended.

3. THE PUBLIC LENDING RIGHT ACT 1979

The Scheme. To become eligible for a payment under the public lending right **19–04** scheme, the book must be registered.[14] It is only when the Registrar of Public Lending Right has determined, in accordance with the Scheme, the sum (if any) due by way of public lending right in the case of any registered book, that the author obtains an effective right since only then is he able to recover such sums

---

[13] For the amendments to s. 5 of the Public Lending Right Act 1979, see para.19–09, below
[14] Public Lending Right Act 1979 ss.1(7) and s.4.

from the Registrar as a debt due.[15] The basic fund is a fixed sum for each financial year, which has from time to time been increased and decreased, and from which administration expenses and so on are to be paid,[16] so that the annual sum received by any one author is always likely to be small, as has proved to be the case in the past. Further, as such sums are dependent upon the number of times a book is lent,[17] popular authors benefit more than the less popular, although as a consequence of the method of calculation the amount per author is capped.[18] Another factor which could reduce the sum per author is the fact that the Act applies to all authors, not just UK authors, so that foreign authors are also entitled to benefit under the Act unless excluded by the Scheme.[19] The right under the Scheme is to last from the date of the book's first publication (or, if later, the beginning of the year in which application is made for it to be registered) until 70 years have elapsed since the end of the year in which the author died.[20]

19–05 **Administration of public lending right.** Most of the important matters relating to the administration of the public lending right are not contained in the 1979 Act but are provided for by a scheme[21] which may be varied from time to time.[22]

Matters to be covered by the Scheme are:

(a) Classes, descriptions and categories of books in respect of which public lending right subsists.[23]

(b) Scales of payments to be made from the central fund in respect of public lending right.[24]

(c) The establishment and maintenance of a register of books in respect of which public lending right subsists and the persons entitled to the right in respect of any registered book, the register to be conclusive as to subsistence of and entitlement to public lending right.[25]

(d) The making and amendment of entries in the register.[26]

(e) Public lending right is:

 (i) to be established by registration,

 (ii) to be transmissible by assignment or assignation, by testamentary disposition or by operation of law, as personal or movable property,

 (iii) to be claimed by or on behalf of the person for the time being entitled, and

 (iv) to be renounced (either in whole or in part, and either temporarily or

---

[15] s.1(5).

[16] s.2. The current fixed sum is £8m: see the Public Lending Right (Increase of Limit) Order 2003 (SI 2003/839). The sum for the financial year beginning April 1, 2003 was £14.252m.

[17] s.3(3)

[18] See para.19–18, below. The current capped sum per author is £6,600. A March 2009 report on the Public Lending Right by the Registrar available at *http://www.plr.uk.com/mediaCentre/publications/pdfPublications/plrInTheUk.pdf* [Accessed August 31, 2010] recorded that 232 authors receive the maximum payment and many of these are not bestsellers.

[19] Such rights are currently limited: see para.19–12, below.

[20] s.1(6): and see para.19–17, below. The right initially granted by the Act (as specified in s.1(6)) lasted only 50 years from the author's death but this is expressly subject to any provision made in the Scheme. The term in the Scheme was extended to 70 years by SI 1997/1576 with effect from July 15, 1997 to bring the term of protection into line with the extended term of copyright brought about by the Duration of Copyright and Rights in Performances Regulations 1995. See Ch.6, above.

[21] Public Lending Right Act 1979 s.3(1). See Vol.2 B3.ii for the present Scheme.

[22] Public Lending Right Act 1979 s.3(7).

[23] Public Lending Right Act 1979 s.1(2).

[24] Public Lending Right Act s.1(2).

[25] Public Lending Right Act 1979 ss.1(4) and s.4(3).

[26] Public Lending Right Act 1979 s.4(4).

for all time) on notice being given to the Registrar of Public Lending Right to that effect.[27]

(f) Public lending right is to be dependent on, and its extent is ascertainable
by reference to, the number of occasions on which books are lent out from
particular libraries, to be specified by the Scheme or identified in accordance with provision made by it.[28]

(g) Local library authorities are to be required:

   (i) to give information as to loans made by them to the public of books
        in respect of which public lending right subsists, or of other books,
        and

   (ii) to arrange for books to be numbered, or otherwise marked or coded,
        with a view to facilitating the maintenance of the register and the
        ascertainment and administration of public lending right.[29]

(h) Local authorities will be reimbursed their expenses in giving effect to the
Scheme. The amount of such expenditure is to be ascertained in accordance with such calculations as the Scheme may prescribe.[30]

The register. Only books which fall within a class, description or category of   **19–06**
books prescribed by the Scheme as one in respect of which public lending right
subsists can be registered.[31] An entry on the register is conclusive both as to subsistence of and entitlement to public lending right.[32] Entries on the register are to
be made or amended on application made in the manner prescribed by the Scheme
and supported by particulars so as to indicate, in the case of any book, who (if
anyone) is for the time being entitled to public lending right in respect of it.[33] The
Registrar of Public Lending Right may direct the removal from the register of
every entry relating to a book in whose case no sum has become due by way of
public lending right for a period of at least 10 years, but without prejudice to a
subsequent application for the entries to be restored to the register.[34] The Registrar may require the payment of fees, according to scales and rates prescribed by
the Scheme, for supplying copies of entries in the register; and a copy of an entry,
certified under the hand of the Registrar or one of his officers with authority in
that behalf (which authority it is not necessary to prove) is to be admissible in evidence in all legal proceedings as of equal validity with the original.[35]

Registrar of public lending right. Public lending right is to be administered by   **19–07**
the Registrar of Public Lending Right and his staff,[36] the Registrar being under a
duty to establish and maintain the register in accordance with the Scheme and to
determine the sums due by way of public lending right.[37] The central fund out of
which sums will be paid in respect of public lending right will be under the control
of the Registrar.[38]

Offences. The 1979 Act makes it an offence for any person, in connection with   **19–08**
the entry of any matter whatsoever in the register, to make any statement which

---

[27] Public Lending Right Act 1979 s.1(7).
[28] Public Lending Right Act 1979 s.3(3).
[29] Public Lending Right Act 1979 s.3(5).
[30] Public Lending Right Act 1979 s.3(6).
[31] Public Lending Right Act 1979 s.4(2).
[32] Public Lending Right Act 1979 s.4(3).
[33] Public Lending Right Act 1979 s.4(4).
[34] Public Lending Right Act 1979 s.4(5).
[35] Public Lending Right Act 1979 s.4(6).
[36] Public Lending Right Act 1979 s.1(3). The Public Lending Right Office is in Stockton-on-Tees.
[37] Public Lending Right Act 1979 s.1(4), (5).
[38] Public Lending Right Act 1979 s.2.

he knows to be false in a material particular or recklessly to make any statement which is false in a material particular. A person who commits such an offence is liable on summary conviction to a fine of not more than level 5 on the standard scale.[39] Where such an offence has been committed by a body corporate and is proved to have been committed with the consent or connivance of, or to be attributable to any neglect on the part of, a director, manager, secretary or other similar officer of the body corporate, or any person who was purporting to act in such capacity, he (as well as the body corporate) will be guilty of that offence and be liable to be proceeded against accordingly. Where the affairs of a body corporate are managed by its members, this provision applies in relation to the acts and defaults of a member in connection with his functions of management as if he were a director of the body corporate.[40]

19–09 **Pending Amendments.** As noted above, s.43 of the Digital Economy Act 2010 will introduce a number of changes to the Public Lending Right Act 1979. These changes are intended to broaden the scope of the Public Lending Right so that it also applies to works that are recorded as sound recordings, and to works recorded electronically, so long as they consist mainly of written or spoken words or still pictures, rather than being restricted to printed and bound volumes.

The changes will introduce new definitions to s.5 of the Public Lending Right Act. If and when it comes into force, the new s.5(2) will read as follows:

"In this Act any reference to 'the scheme' is to the scheme prepared and brought into force by the Secretary of State in accordance with sections 1 and 3 of this Act (including the scheme as varied from time to time under section 3(7)[41]; and:-

'author', in relation to a work recorded as a sound recording, includes a producer or narrator;

'book' includes—

(a) a work recorded as a sound recording and consisting mainly of spoken words (an 'audio-book'), and

(b) a work, other than an audio-book, recorded in electronic form and consisting mainly of (or of any combination of) written or spoken words or still pictures (an 'e-book');

'lent out'—

(a) means made available to a member of the public for use away from library premises for a limited time, but

does not include being communicated by means of electronic transmission to a place other than library premises,

and 'loan' and 'borrowed' are to be read accordingly;

'library premises' has the meaning given in section 8(7) of the Public Libraries and Museums Act 1964;

'local library authority' means—

(a) a library authority under the Public Libraries and Museums Act 1964,

(b) a statutory library authority within the Public Libraries (Scotland) Act 1955, and

(c) an Education and Library Board within the Education and Libraries (Northern Ireland) Order 1972;

---

[39] Public Lending Right Act 1979 s.4(7).
[40] Public Lending Right Act 1979 s.4(8).
[41] Sic: the Act omits the second closing parenthesis which should presumably appear here.

'prescribed' means prescribed by the scheme;

'producer' has the meaning given in section 178 of the Copyright, Designs and Patents Act 1988;

'the register' means the register required by section 1(4) to be established and maintained by the Registrar;

'the Registrar' means the Registrar of Public Lending Right.

'sound recording' has the meaning given in section 5A(1) of the Copyright, Designs and Patents Act 1988."

The scope of these amendments is, regrettably, another area that lacks complete clarity. Section 5 appears on its face to only include definitions of terms used "in this Act", that is, within the Public Lending Right Act itself. However, the Act itself merely enables the creation of a Scheme, and the Scheme is contained in the annex to a separate statutory instrument[42] with its own set of definitions.[43] On occasion those definitions refer back to the Act to adopt a definition from it, but the definitions of the Act are not adopted wholesale. As a consequence, mere changes to the definitions of the Public Lending Right Act have no effect on the operation of the Scheme, and the definitions, in particular, of an "eligible book", and an "eligible person" in relation to an author remain unchanged. Even once the amendments of s.43 of the Digital Economy Act are brought into force, therefore, the Scheme will have to be amended in a way that broadens its eligibility requirements before those amendments will have any effect.

On June 17, 2010, a press release from UK Government's Department of Culture Media and Sport noted that the non-print format extension of the Public Lending Right had been suspended, to be considered as part of a spending review in the autumn of that year[44]. As of August 31, 2010, no further statements on the fate of this extension had been issued.

4. THE SCHEME

History of the Scheme. The present Scheme is now found in the appendix to The Public Lending Right Scheme 1982 (Commencement) Order 1982, as amended from time to time.   **19–10**

Registration required: eligible books and posthumously eligible books. To be eligible for public lending right, a book must first be a printed and bound publication (this includes a paperback edition) and an application must be made for registration.[45] But not all books are registrable.[46] Thus, for instance, books bearing the name of a body corporate or an unincorporated association as author do not qualify, nor do serial publications such as newspapers, magazines, journals and periodicals, or books which are or are mainly musical scores.[47] No book will now qualify unless it has an ISBN number.[48]   **19–11**

A posthumously eligible book is a book qualifying under art.6 whose author, or one of whose authors, is a posthumously eligible person, and the book is either published within one year before his death or within 10 years after his death, and

---

[42] The Scheme, as amended, is set out in Vol.2 B3.ii.

[43] Public Lending Right Scheme 1982 art. 2.

[44] http://www.culture.gov.uk/news/media_releases/7191.aspx [Accessed August 31, 2010].

[45] Public Lending Right Scheme 1982 arts 9, 10, 14, 14A, 17, 17B and Sch.1 .

[46] arts 6 and 6A.

[47] art.6(2).

[48] art.6(2)(g). See the variation made to the Scheme by the Public Lending Right Scheme 1982 (Commencement of Variations) Order 1999 (SI 1999/420).

that person had successfully applied to register for Public Lending right during his lifetime, or the book consists of or incorporates a previously registered work.[49]

19–12 **Eligible persons and posthumously eligible persons.** To qualify for registration, the author, or at least one of the authors, must be an eligible person, or a posthumously eligible person. An eligible person must be an author of the book who at the date of the application has his only or principal home in any member State of the European Economic Area, or, if he has no home, has been present in a member State for not less than 12 months out of the preceding 24 months.[50] Under art.5A of the Scheme, in relation to an application relating to a posthumously eligible book, an author who is dead is a posthumously eligible person if, had he been an applicant for first registration of public lending right in relation to that book at the date of his death, he would have been an eligible person in accordance with art.5 of the Scheme.

19–13 **Authors.** Authors are also defined by the Scheme and include writers and translators, as well as editors and compilers who have made a sufficient contribution to the book, and illustrators.[51] Applications after an author's death are possible.[52] Books published up to 10 years after the author's death are also included.[53]

19–14 **The register.** The register has to contain particulars of the title of the book, the name or names of the persons appearing on the title page as the authors thereof, the true identity of an author if different from such name, the number given to the book by the Registrar, the name and address of each person entitled to the right in respect of the book and, if more than one, the share of each such person in such right.[54] Where a book has two or more authors, including any who are not eligible persons, the share of any non-eligible person will not be registered until he becomes and remains an eligible person and makes an application for registration.[55] Only registered owners are entitled to payment.[56] So, where only one of two authors is eligible, he will be paid 50 per cent of the share, with the balance being paid back into the Fund.

19–15 **Inspection of the register.** The right depends on registration,[57] and the register is conclusive as to whether public lending right subsists in a particular book and also as to the persons (if any) who are for the time being entitled to the right.[58] However, the Scheme gives no automatic right for the public to inspect the register.[59] On the contrary, it is provided[60] that the Registrar shall not supply a copy of any entry in the register otherwise than to a registered owner, as regards any entry which relates to his registered interest, or to such other person as the registered owner may direct, but if the entry also relates to other registered own-

---

[49] art.6A.
[50] Public Lending Right Scheme 1982 arts 5 and 5A: see art.5 (which defines "principal home") and Sch.5, as amended by the Public Lending Right Scheme 1982 (Commencement of Variations) Order 2000 (SI 2000/933) and Public Lending Right Scheme 1982 (Commencement of Variations) Order 2004 (SI 2004/1258).
[51] Public Lending Right Scheme 1982 art.4(1), but subject to art.4(2).
[52] arts 5A, 6A, 14A and 17B.
[53] arts 6 and 6A.
[54] Public Lending Right Scheme 1982 arts 7 and 8 and see art.9A. The register may be amended: arts 12 and 13.
[55] arts 2(1) "eligible author", 9(2), (3), 9A, 14 and 17. As to posthumously eligible persons see arts 9(4), 9A, 14A and 17B.
[56] art.47.
[57] Public Lending Right Scheme 1982 art.10: see art.2(1) as to "registered interest".
[58] art.11.
[59] See Public Lending Right Act 1979 s.4(3), (6).
[60] art.11.

ers, only with the consent of all such owners. There is provision for a fee to be made payable for a copy entry, but in practice none is charged by the Registrar to registered owners. The provisions of the Scheme as to production of copy entries are intended to protect the privacy of owners, as the register includes a number of personal details, such as, for instance, the real names of those who write under a *nom de plume*, as well as details of the amounts of payments made under the Scheme, which some owners prefer to keep confidential. However, the Registrar is happy to pass on to owners requests for information from members of the public or press.

Procedure for registration. The Scheme sets out the procedures to be followed **19–16** for registration of public lending right, or of an eligible author's share of the right, or of a posthumously eligible person's share of the right, for the transfer of a registered interest and for the renunciation of a registered interest.[61] The Registrar may require evidence to be submitted to satisfy him that a book is an eligible book, that a person applying as author for the first registration of public lending right, or the registration of a share of the right, is in fact the author of that book and is an eligible person, that any co-author who is not a party to an application for first registration of public lending right is dead or cannot be traced despite all reasonable steps having been taken to do so, and (where an application under art.17(1)(c)(iv) has been made) that there is such an agreement or arrangement as is mentioned therein and that the share of public lending right of the person making the application is as specified in that agreement or arrangement. For these purposes the Registrar may require a statutory declaration to be made.[62] The Registrar has power to treat applications as abandoned when information requested has not been given.[63] Also, under s.4(5) of the 1979 Act, the Registrar has power to remove entries from the register where no sum has become due by way of public lending right for a period of at least 10 years, although application for restoration to the register can subsequently be made.[64]

Transmission and duration of public lending right. The Scheme provides that **19–17** a registered interest is transmissible by assignment or assignation, by testamentary disposition or by operation of law, as personal or movable property, so long, as regards a particular book, as the right in respect of that book is capable of subsisting.[65] Under the Scheme the duration of public lending right in respect of a book and the period during which there may be dealings therein is from the date of the book's first publication (or, if later, the beginning of the sampling year in which application is made for it to be registered) until 70 years have elapsed since the end of the sampling year in which the author died,[66] or, if the book is registered as the work of more than one author, as regards dealings in the share of the right attributable to that author, the end of the year in which that author died. "Sampling year" means the period of 12 months ending on June 30.[67]

The procedure for transfer is dealt with in the Scheme,[68] including provision for the transfer to an author on attaining full age, since only adults can be

---

[61] Public Lending Right Scheme 1982 arts 3, 14, 14A, 15, 16, 17, 17A and 17B and Sch.1.
[62] art.18.
[63] art.33.
[64] art.34.
[65] Public Lending Right Scheme 1982 art.19.
[66] art.20 as amended with effect from July 15, 1997; previously the right lasted for 50 years from the end of the relevant year.
[67] art.36.
[68] arts 14, 21, 22, 23 and 24 and Sch.1.

registered.[69] Procedure following death is also dealt with by the Scheme.[70] The Scheme also deals with transfer on bankruptcy, liquidation or sequestration.[71] Finally, the Scheme provides a procedure to be followed for renunciation of a registered interest.[72]

19–18   **Calculation of public lending right.** Public lending right is calculated by means of two complex formulae set out in the Scheme.[73] The first formula determines the number of notional loans of a book in each sampling year. The second formula is used to calculate the sum due by way of public lending right using the number of notional loans. The basic element of the first formula in respect of any book is the number of loans of that book recorded during the sampling year at the operative sampling points in the various groups of service points. Service points which are to be operative sampling points or which are to be included in operative sampling points are designated yearly for the prescribed period by the Registrar from lists of service points (libraries and mobile libraries) supplied to the Registrar by local library authorities, with power for the Registrar to discontinue designation and designate a new sampling point. No operative sampling point is to remain an operative sampling point for more than four years. Loans are defined as loans whereby books are lent out from a service point to individual borrowers, and includes loans of books not normally held at that service point.[74] It would seem, therefore, that a book available in some libraries, but which might not be held at any of the current operative sampling points, would not qualify for public lending right. Further, even if a book was available in an operative sampling point and was used, but was not lent (the case for most reference books), it would not qualify for public lending right.

19–19   **Payment in respect of public lending right.** Any sum due in respect of public lending right is to be paid without interest to the relevant registered owner as at June 30 in any financial year, and will be paid on the last day of that year unless paid earlier.[75] However, payment will not be made unless the right has been claimed by or on behalf of the person for the time being entitled, as to which the Registrar may require evidence.[76] At the end of each financial year the Registrar is to give notice to every registered owner, to whom a sum is payable by way of public lending right in respect of that year, of the notional number of lendings for that year of each book in respect of which he is a registered owner and the amount of such sum. Where no sum is payable, notice will not be given of the number of notional loans unless requested by the registered owner not later than six months after the end of the relevant financial year.[77]

---

[69] arts 14, 17(3) and 25 and Sch.1.

[70] arts 26 and 27.

[71] arts 28, 29, 30 and 31.

[72] arts 14 and 32 and Sch.1.

[73] Public Lending Right Scheme 1982 arts 36– 44 and 46 and Sch.2.

[74] art.36, and see art.42(3)(c) entitling the Registrar to disregard any loan where an International Standard Book Number is not specified in respect of that book in the report of a local library authority.

[75] Public Lending Right Scheme 1982 arts 47, 49 and 51 and Sch.4.

[76] arts 48 and 50.

[77] arts 49(3), (5).

CHAPTER TWENTY

ARTIST'S RESALE RIGHT

1. INTRODUCTION

Artist's resale right. On February 14, 2006, an entirely new and controversial intellectual property right, the Artist's Resale Right, was introduced into the law of the United Kingdom when "The Artist's Resale Right Regulations 2006"[1] entered into force, giving living British artists the right to receive a royalty on the resale of their works.[2] The Regulations implemented the much-debated EC Directive on the resale right for the benefit of the author of an original work of art, which came into force on October 13, 2001, after 10 years of negotiation, hereafter the EC Directive.[3] The United Kingdom had strongly opposed the EC Directive and voted against it on the ground that it posed risks to the UK art market, the largest in the European Union.[4] The artist's resale right is a Continental import more commonly known as the *"droit de suite"*, the expression used in France, where the right was first introduced in 1920. The Regulations also amount to the implementation by the United Kingdom of the option to introduce such a right given by art.14 *ter* of the Berne Convention for the Protection of Literary and Artistic Works (Paris Act 1971, hereafter the Berne Convention). The new intellectual property right "artist's resale right" (ARR) is to be enjoyed by the creator of a work of art for as long as copyright continues to subsist in the work, which is normally for 70 years after the death of the artist; it may accordingly be inherited by the artist's successors.[5] The right consists in the entitlement to claim a royalty on the resale of the work following its first transfer by the artist. The amount of the royalty is calculated on the basis of the sale price and not on any increase in the value of the work.

20–01

---

[1] SI 2006/346. For a commentary on the law and practice of ARR, see S. Stokes, *Artists' Resale Right (Droit de suite)* (Leicester: Institute of Art and Law Ltd, 2006).

[2] ARR applies only to living British artists until January 1, 2012. On its introduction in 2006, the UK Government negotiated a delay in the application of the royalty to works by deceased artists (which represent the most valuable sector of the UK art market) until 2010, a derogation which was extended to 2012 with effect from December 1, 2009 (see para.20–23, below).

[3] Directive 2001/84/EC of the European Parliament and of the Council ([2001] OJ L272/32). See also paras 24–101 et seq., below.

[4] See para.20–04, below.

[5] Note that art.8(2) of Directive 2001/84/EC provides for a special derogation which is limited to those Member States which did not previously have ARR in their national law (e.g. the United Kingdom). Such a State was permitted to prevent successors of deceased artists from exercising their resale right until January 1, 2010 and reg.17 of the 2006 Regulations took advantage of that derogation. Article 8(3) allowed the derogation to be extended until January 1, 2012, subject to certain conditions (see para.20–23, below).

20–02   **History of the artist's resale right.** The origin of the *droit de suite* is to be found in legislation adopted in France in 1920.[6] The concept of the right for visual artists had been first promoted by Albert Vaunois in an article in the *Chronique de Paris* in 1893,[7] which resulted in a successful campaign for legislation on the subject in France. The idea behind the right is to look after the interests of artists and other creators of artistic works. It is a well-known feature of the art market, past and present, that artists at an early stage of their career may be obliged to sell work cheaply to earn a living. Thereafter, the work may be resold a number of times, passing through different hands and in the process the work may increase considerably in value, benefiting the successive owners of the work, as well as dealers and the art market. The only person who fails to benefit in such a scenario is the original artist who created the work and to whose talent and growing fame increases in value are largely attributable. The resale right aims to redress this imbalance by allowing the artist to follow (hence the expression *droit de suite*, or right to follow) the fortunes of his work and to participate in the profit made from the increase in value each time the work changes hands. The justification for the right, according to the EC Directive, is "to ensure that authors of graphic and plastic works of art share in the economic success of their original works of art. It helps to redress the balance between the economic situation of authors of graphic and plastic works of art and that of other creators who benefit from successive exploitations of their works".[8]

20–03   **Artist's Resale Right in the Berne Convention.** The example of the new French law on *droit de suite* was followed by Belgium in 1921; subsequently, these two countries, supported by the ALAI (*Association littéraire et artistique internationale*), an international association representing the interests of authors, raised the issue at the Revision Conference for the Berne Convention, which took place in Rome in 1928. The Rome Conference adopted the following "voeu" (or resolution) on the subject:

"The Conference expresses the desire that those countries of the Union which have not yet adopted legislative provisions guaranteeing to the benefit of artists an inalienable right to a share in the proceeds of successive public sales of their original works should take into account the possibility of considering such provisions".[9]

The United Kingdom, together with a number of other countries, abstained from the vote.

However, the example set by France and Belgium gradually attracted support and after the Second World War the number of States recognising resale right grew steadily. Thus, at the Brussels Revision Conference in 1948, the principle of the *droit de suite* was introduced into the Berne Convention, thereby gaining acceptance as the subject-matter of copyright protection as opposed to that of related rights. Since a number of delegations, including that of the United Kingdom, still raised objections to the inclusion of the right in the Berne Convention, it was made optional, so that Union members were not obliged to introduce it, and subject to material reciprocity.

Article 14 *ter* of the present text of the Berne Convention is substantially the same as the original text and reads as follows[10]:

---

[6] Law of May 20, 1920.

[7] *Chronique de Paris*, February 25, 1893.

[8] Directive, recital3.

[9] *Actes de la Conférence de Rome* 1928, 283.

[10] Originally it was art.14*bis* and very minor amendments were made at the Paris Revision Confer-

"Article 14ter, paragraph (1). Scope of the right

The author, or after his death the persons or institutions authorized by national legislation, shall, with respect to original works of art and original manuscripts of writers and composers, enjoy the inalienable right to an interest in any sale of the work subsequent to the first transfer by the author of the work.

Article 14ter, paragraph (2). Applicable Law

The protection provided by the preceding paragraph may be claimed in a country of the Union only if legislation in the country to which the author belongs so permits, and to the extent permitted by the country where this protection is claimed.

Article 14ter, paragraph (3). Procedure

The procedure for collection and the amounts shall be matters for determination by national legislation."

It should be noted that art.14 *ter* covers not only works of art but also original manuscripts of authors and composers. However, this option has not been taken up in either the EC Directive or in the UK 2006 Regulations. The right does not apply to works of architecture or to applied art. The right is not assignable; this is to prevent the artist, in order to make a living, being forced to part with it. However, it is transmissible on death. The right is optional in that Union members are not obliged to introduce it and it can only be claimed in a Union country if, and to the extent that, it forms part of the law there. Thus, contrary to the general principle of national treatment on which the Berne Convention is based, this right is subject to material reciprocity and can only be claimed by a national of a country which grants the right in another country which also grants the right and to the extent of the protection granted in the latter country.[11]

The position of the United Kingdom. As discussed above, the United Kingdom   **20–04**
opposed the inclusion of ARR in the Berne Convention and was instrumental in ensuring that the right was made optional and not obligatory. It was also opposed to the EC Directive. The reason for this long-standing opposition was simply that successive UK governments did not believe the introduction of the right was in the national interest. At present, the United Kingdom has the largest art market within the European Union[12] and a pre-eminent position in the international art market.[13] It has always been the Government's position that the introduction of the resale right into the United Kingdom would pose the risk of sales being

---

ence in 1971, the word "transfer" being substituted for "disposal" in para.(1) and "extent" for "degree" in para.(2).

[11] See further on art.14 *ter* C. Masouyé, *Guide to the Berne Convention* (WIPO Geneva, 1978), and S. Ricketson and J.C. Ginsburg, *International Copyright and Neighbouring Rights, The Berne Convention and Beyond* 2nd edn (Oxford University Press, 2006), paras 11–53 et seq. There is extensive literature on resale right; the following references give a general overview on its origins and status under the Berne Convention and in a few major countries: F. Hepp, "Royalties from Works of the Fine Arts: Origin of the concept of *droit de suite* in Copyright Law" (1959) 6 Bull Cop Soc USA 91; R. Plaisant, " *Droit de suite*" [1969] Copyright 157; E. Ulmer, "The *'Droit de Suite'* in International Copyright Law" (1975) 6 IIC 12; W. Nordemann, "The *'Droit de Suite'* in Art.14 *ter* of the Berne Convention and in the Copyright Law of the Federal Republic of Germany" [1977] *Copyright* 337; US Copyright Office, *Droit de suite: The Artist's Resale Royalty* (1992 report), summarised at 16 *Columbia—VLA Journal of Law & the Arts* 318 (1992); K. Graddy and S. Szymanski, "Scoping Study: Artist's Resale Right" (report prepared by the Intellectual Property Institute on behalf of the UK Patent office, October 2005, Ref. CT/CONS/016); U. Klement, "Resale Royalties for Visual Artists: An Analysis of International Developments and the Implications for New Zealand", *New Zealand Intellectual Property Journal*, September 2006, 215; P. Valentin " *Droit de suite*" [2006] E.I.P.R. 28(5), 268; N. Kawashima, "The *Droit de suite* Controversy Revisited: Context, Effects and the Price of Art" [2006] I.P.Q. 3, 223.

[12] In 2008, the UK's share of the EU art market was 69%. See C. McAndrew, *The International Art Market 2007-2009 – Trends in the Art Trade during Global Recession*, TEFAF Study 2010. See also, C. McAndrew, *The International Art Market-A Study of Europe in a Global Context*, TEFAF 2008, and *Emerging Economies and the Art Trade in 2008 – Globalisaion and the Art Market*, TEFAF 2009.

[13] The USA and the UK dominated the global art and antiques market in 2008, with a combined

diverted from the United Kingdom to countries which do not apply a resale right, thus putting the London art market at a competitive disadvantage compared to its main competitors in the art trade, primarily Switzerland (Geneva) and the United States of America (New York). The British perspective prior to the introduction of the right was described as follows:

"Put simply, the London art market dwarfs that of any other Member State, accounting for 60–70 per cent of the total EU turnover. There is no true EU 'internal market' when it comes to art sales. Furthermore, London's dominance in this area is not attributable solely—or even mainly—to the absence of a resale right. Other factors such as the reputation and expertise of London dealers must come into account. Finally, the logical conclusion of the single market argument is bizarre, because even if London's success was a direct consequence of the absence of an artists' resale right, then displacement of art business outside the EU to the United States or Switzerland (who do not have a resale right) must be at least a likely consequence of the Directive".[14]

Following the adoption of the EC Directive, the UK Government accepted its obligation to legislate on resale right but approached the task of implementing the EC Directive with a view to minimising the risk of sales being diverted from the United Kingdom, while taking account of the needs of artists.

"The Directive is largely prescriptive although there are a number of options available to Member States. As made clear in consultations with interest groups both before and after adoption of the Directive, it has always been the Government's intention to minimize the diversion of trade and to allow the gradual adaptation of the art market in the United Kingdom to this new right".[15]

The Government also took the view that a number of the requirements within the EC Directive itself, namely the sliding scale of royalties and the cap on any one royalty payment, would provide significant protection to the UK art market by reducing the number of dealers electing not to sell in Member States.[16]

At the time of the adoption of the 2006 Regulations, the Government announced that "the regulations ensure a just reward for living British artists' creativity while protecting the valuable UK art market. . . The balanced Government approach will benefit struggling artists without placing a heavy administrative burden on the art market and will minimize the risk that sales would be driven offshore."[17]

The fears of the UK Government that the new artists' resale right might have a negative impact on the UK art market have not been realised so far. Since the implementation of the Regulations, the art market has continued to prosper in spite of a drop of 12 per cent from its peak in 2007 resulting from the global recession.[18] A 2008 study, commissioned by the Intellectual Property Office (IPO) from the Intellectual Property Institute (IPI) and published in January 2008 (IPI Study), provided inter alia an assessment of the impact on the UK art market of the introduction of artist's resale right. It concluded that there was no evidence that the right had diverted business away from the United Kingdom, where the size of the art market had grown as fast, if not faster, than the art market in

---

share of over two-thirds of the value of all transactions. China is gaining share in the global market. In 2007, it achieved the third largest sales worldwide, and in 2008 maintained that position with a share of 9% (ahead of France's 6%). See C. McAndrew, *The International Art Market 2007-2009 – Trends in the Art Trade during Global Recession*, TEFAF Study 2010.

[14] G. Tritton, *Intellectual Property in Europe* 3rd edn (London: Sweet and Maxwell, 2008), para.4–129.

[15] *Patent Office Regulatory Impact Assessment*, February 14, 2006, para.2.4.

[16] The Artist's Resale Right Regulations 2006 Sch.1 para.2.

[17] DTI Press Release, February 14, 2006.

[18] See C. McAndrew, *The International Art Market 2007-2009 – Trends in the Art Trade during Global Recession*, TEFAF Study 2010, p.15.

jurisdictions where the right is not currently payable. It expressed the view also that there was no evidence that ARR had led to a reduction in art market prices; on the contrary, prices had appreciated substantially for art eligible for the right and faster than in markets where ARR was not currently payable.[19] Nevertheless, ARR remains controversial and its impact and value to artists is disputed.[20]

2. THE SUBSTANTIVE RIGHT

Artist's Resale Right. The Artist's Resale Right Regulations 2006[21] create a new intellectual property right (resale right) to be enjoyed by the author of a work in which copyright subsists. The right entitles the author to claim a royalty on any sale of his work which is a resale subsequent to the first transfer of ownership by the author (resale royalty) for as long as copyright continues to subsist in the work.[22] The author, in relation to a work, means the person who creates it (and that artist's successors in title).[23] The amount of the royalty is based on the sale price, i.e. the price obtained for the sale, net of the tax payable on the sale, and converted into euro at the European Central Bank reference rate prevailing at the contract date (for the calculation of the resale royalty, see Regulations Sch.I, and para.20–17, below).[24]

20–05

The following analysis takes into account the Regulations themselves and the explanatory memorandum to the Regulations prepared by the Department of Trade and Industry and laid before Parliament on December 14, 2005, as well as the consultation documents published by the UK Patent Office.

Resale. The resale right applies to a royalty on any sale of the work which is a resale subsequent to the first transfer of ownership by the author ("resale royalty"[25]). Regulation 12 defines when a sale is to be regarded as a resale, thereby attracting the obligation to pay resale royalty. The sale of a work may be regarded as a resale notwithstanding that the first transfer of ownership was not made for a monetary (or any) consideration. Thus, a resale following a gift by the artist would also qualify.

20–06

(a) the buyer or the seller, or (where the sale takes place through an agent) the agent of the buyer or the seller, is acting in the course of a business of dealing in works of art; and

(b) the sale price is not less than 1,000 euro.

Thus, an art-market professional must be involved in the sale, either as principal or agent, and a minimum price threshold of 1,000 euro is imposed. In setting this threshold, the Government took into account that 88 per cent of works by living artists sold in the United Kingdom in the 1,000–3,000 euro price range in 2003–2004 were by British artists. Another concern was that a higher threshold could have excluded some forms of art, such as photographs, from benefitting from the right.

Furthermore, there is an exemption for certain sales where the work was recently acquired from the artist, namely, where:

(a) the seller previously acquired the work directly from the author less than three years before the sale; and

---

[19] K. Graddy, N. Horowitz and S. Szymanski, "A Study into the effect on the UK art market of the introduction of the artist's resale right", Intellectual Property Institute (IPI), January 2008, p.38.

[20] See para.20–23, below.

[21] SI 2006/346.

[22] reg.3(1) and (2).

[23] regs 3(2) and 9.

[24] reg.3(4).

[25] reg.3(1).

(b) the sale price does not exceed 10,000 euro.

This provision aims to encourage galleries to support new talent by buying works, secure in the knowledge that, if a work is sold relatively quickly, and for less than 10,000 euros, no further payment will be due to the artist.

3. WORKS COVERED

20–07   **Definition of works.** The Regulations define the works of art covered by them as meaning any work of graphic or plastic art such as a picture, a collage, a painting, a drawing, an engraving, a print, a lithograph, a sculpture, a tapestry, a ceramic, an item of glassware or a photograph. A copy of a work is not to be regarded as a work unless the copy is one of a limited number which have been made by the author or under his authority.[26] This definition follows closely that of the EC Directive.[27] It should be noted, however, that the definition is not exhaustive, due to the inclusion of the words "such as". Accordingly, the sale, for example, of original pieces of jewellery and furniture is not necessarily excluded from the scope of the resale right.[28]

4. OWNERSHIP AND TRANSMISSION OF RIGHTS

20–08   **The owner of the right.** ARR vests in the individual artist who creates the work and is the author of the work.[29] At present, in the United Kingdom, the resale right only applies to living artists and will not apply to the beneficiaries of deceased artists until 2012 at the earliest.[30] The right is personal to the author and is inalienable, which means that it may neither be assigned nor waived.[31] The right may be transferred only in limited circumstances. "Transfer of ownership by the author" includes, in particular; (a) transmission of the work from the author by testamentary disposition, or in accordance with the rules of intestate succession; (b) disposal of the work by the author's personal representatives for the purpose of the administration of his estate; and (c) disposal of the work by an official receiver or a trustee in bankruptcy, for the purpose of the realisation of the author's estate.[32]

20–09   **Joint authorship.** Regulation 5 makes provision for works which are the joint product of two or more artists. In the case of a work of joint authorship, the resale right belongs to the authors as owners in common and the right is held in equal shares or in such other shares as may be agreed. Any such agreement must be in writing signed by or on behalf of each party to the agreement. A work of joint authorship means a work created by two or more authors.

20–10   **Proof of authorship.** Regulation 6 lays down a rebuttable presumption that a signatory of the work is its creator. Thus, where a name purporting to be that of the author appeared on the work when it was made, the person whose name appeared, shall, unless the contrary is proved, be presumed to be the author of the work. The same applies, in the case of a work alleged to be a work of joint authorship, in relation to each person alleged to be one of the authors.

---

[26] reg.4(1) and (2).

[27] art.2(1)

[28] Art market professionals consider this ambiguity to be a problem in that they could be found to be in breach of their obligations if they fail to identify a work which is liable for ARR or conversely if they mistakenly apply ARR to a work where none is due.

[29] reg.3(1).

[30] reg.17; see also para.20–23, below.

[31] reg.7(1).

[32] reg.3(5).

Inalienability of the right. In conformity with the Berne Convention and the EC   **20–11**
Directive, the resale right is not assignable and any charge on a resale right is
void.[33] However, the transfer of a resale right where it has been transmitted to a
qualifying charitable body is permitted, provided that the transfer is to another
such charitable body.[34] A resale right may also be transferred to a trustee for the
person who would otherwise be entitled to exercise the right (the beneficiary), or
from the trustee to the beneficiary.[35]

No waiver of the right. Resale right may not be waived and any agreement to   **20–12**
share or repay resale royalties is precluded. This, does not, however, prevent a
collecting society from collecting resale right royalties on the right holder's
behalf in return for a percentage of the royalty.[36]

Persons entitled on succession. On the death of its holder, a resale right may be   **20–13**
transmitted as personal or moveable property by testamentary disposition or in
accordance with the rules of intestate succession and it may be further so transmitted by any person into whose hands it passes. It may be so transmitted to a natural
person or to a qualifying charitable body. If it is transmitted to more than one
person, it shall belong to them as owners in common. It is also made clear that in
the absence of any heirs it may pass to the Crown as *bona vacantia* ("ownerless
property").[37]

Qualified persons. Regulation 10 lays down certain nationality requirements for   **20–14**
the enjoyment of the resale right. Resale right is a right based on reciprocity and,
therefore, may be exercised only by a qualifying individual or body and may only
be transmitted by a person who, at the time of his death, is a qualifying individual.
A qualifying individual is one who is a national of a State of the European Economic Area (EEA)[38] or of a State according reciprocal protection under the Berne
Convention and listed in Sch.2 of the Regulations. The EC Directive provides the
option to additionally confer the right upon artists habitually resident in the
United Kingdom,[39] but this was not taken up by the Government.[40] It follows that
an individual who does not satisfy these requirements may nevertheless inherit
resale right, but such an individual may not exercise it or further pass it on while
the requirements remain unsatisfied. However, there is nothing to prevent a resale
right from being exercised after it has been transmitted as *bona vacantia*.

Vesting of right by operation of law. ARR may vest by operation of law in a   **20–15**
personal representative of a deceased person; or by an official receiver or a trustee
in bankruptcy and there is nothing to prevent the right from being exercised by
any person acting in that capacity.

5. EXERCISE OF THE RIGHT

Liability to pay resale royalty. Under reg.13, a specified art-market professional   **20–16**

---

[33] reg.7(1) and (2).
[34] reg.7(3),(4) and (5).
[35] reg.11.
[36] regs 8 and 14.
[37] reg.9.
[38] The resale right will not apply in Austria, Ireland, the Netherlands and the United Kingdom on
sales of works by deceased artists until 2012 at the earliest.
[39] art.7(3).
[40] Countries outside the EEA whose nationals may enjoy resale right are the following: Algeria,
Brazil, Bulgaria, Burkina Faso, Chile, Congo, Costa Rica, Croatia, Ecuador, Guinea, Iraq, Ivory
Coast, Laos, Madagascar, Mali, Monaco, Morocco, Peru, Philippines, Romania, Russian Federation, Senegal, Serbia and Montenegro, Tunisia, Turkey and Uruguay.

involved with the sale is made jointly and severally liable with the seller to pay the resale royalty. This was done to simplify and reduce the cost of collecting the payments, since otherwise artists and collecting societies would have been left with the tasks of obtaining details about sellers from the art dealer or gallery, tracking down the seller and extracting payment from him. The art-market professional who is so liable (the so-called relevant person) is the agent of the seller, or where there is no such agent, the agent of the buyer, or (again if there is no such agent) the buyer. Thus, where the agent of the seller is a professional, that agent will be liable; and a buyer who is a professional will be liable only if no professional is involved, whether as an agent of the seller or the buyer. The expression "art-market professional" comes from the EC Directive.[41] It encompasses galleries, auctioneers and generally any dealers in works of art.

20–17   **Calculation of resale royalty.** The resale royalty payable on the sale of a work is the sum of the following amounts, being percentage amounts of consecutive portions of the sale price on a sliding scale:

Portion of the sale price	Percentage amount
From 0 to 50,000 euro	4%
From 50,000.01 to 200,000 euro	3%
From 200,000.01 to 350,000 euro	1%
From 350,000.01 to 500,000 euro	0.5%
Exceeding 500,000 euro	0.25%

Thus, as from February 14, 2006, when an artist's work is resold on the UK art market for the equivalent of 1,000 euro or more, he will receive a royalty of 4 per cent of the sale price. The rates were largely determined by the EC Directive,[42] but, in so far as the Directive allows a choice of percentage for the lowest price band, the lowest figure of 4 per cent was chosen.[43]

However, the total amount of the royalty payable on any sale shall not in any event exceed €12,500.

20–18   **Collective management.** Compulsory collective management is imposed by reg.14 so that the resale right may not be claimed by artists directly but can be exercised only through a collecting society. This applies even where the holder of the resale right has not transferred the management of his right to a collecting society. In such case, the collecting society which manages copyright on behalf of artists shall be deemed to be mandated to manage his right. Where there is more than one such collecting society, the right holder may choose which of them to give his mandate to. The Government took the view that compulsory collective management would be the most efficient and reliable method of ensuring artists received their royalties. This will become of even greater importance once the right is applied to the works of deceased artists in due course.[44] Evidence from collecting societies in other countries, which are already managing resale rights, shows that the right can be managed effectively and at reasonable cost even when dealing with small amounts.

At present, August 2010, there are three collecting societies in the United Kingdom with the mandate to administer the resale right, namely, the Artists'

---

[41] art.1(2).
[42] art.4.
[43] Artist's Resale Rights Regulations 2006 Sch.1.
[44] See para.20–23, below.

Collecting Society (A©S),[45] set up with the sole object of collecting resale right royalties, Artists' Rights Administration Ltd ("ARA") (which represents principally Russian artists) and the Design and Artists Copyright Society Ltd ("DACS").[46] As mentioned above, if an artist has not mandated any particular society to collect resale royalties on his or her behalf then the collecting society which manages both copyright, in general, for all artists and artists' resale right will be deemed to be mandated. Currently DACS is the only society which meets this criterion. Therefore any artist who has not mandated another society will be deemed to have mandated DACS to collect on his behalf. Following the introduction of the resale right in February 2006, DACS started to distribute royalties to artists as early as July 2006. In the meantime, DACS has collected £7.5 million in resale rights royalties due to artists. In 2008, £3.4 million was paid out to over 1,100.[47]

The IPI Study[48] drew on feedback from all sectors of the art market, including dealers, collecting societies, auction houses and artists. It assessed the costs of administering the right and concluded that, while the administrative burden of the resale right does not seem to have been excessive for most businesses, there have been a number of problems associated with difficulties in establishing the nationality of artists and the requirement to calculate ARR royalties in euros. The study noted that a significant minority of art market professionals, including the major auction houses, deem the administration of the right to be intrusive and burdensome. The cost of administering the right by collecting societies (15 per cent) appeared reasonable to the authors of the report.

Meanwhile, a particular concern of dealers and auction houses is reported to be the perceived inadequacy and lack of reliability of the artist databases maintained by the collecting societies; this is associated with difficulties and consequential costs[49] in establishing the nationality of artists and whether they qualify to receive the royalty (i.e. whether an artist is a citizen of the EEA or other reciprocating country).[50] In this connection, it is important to note that the liability to pay ARR rests with the parties privy to the transaction and not the collecting societies; thus, auction houses must ensure that all artists entitled are identified prior to a sale being advertised in order to enable them to raise a complete invoice at point of sale. In cases where an eligible artist has been misidentified by a collecting society, the auctioneer is unable to pass on the royalty to the vendor or the purchaser, and becomes liable for the royalty payments.[51] It has been suggested that the central problem of identifying qualifying artists could be solved by introducing a requirement that artists must register on a publicly available database if they wish to exercise their right to receive ARR royalties.[52]

---

[45] For further information about A©S, see its website: *http://www.artistscollectingsociety.org.uk* [Accessed September 13, 2010]. See also para.27–54, below.

[46] For further information about DACS, see its website: *http://www.dacs.org.uk* [Accessed September 13, 2010]. See also para.27–60.

[47] DACS Royalties Report 2008, p.2.

[48] See para.20–04 and fn.19, above, at p.2.

[49] Prior to the introduction of ARR, the UK Government estimated that the administrative costs for auction houses would be £1 per lot. However, both the Froshauer report (fn.51, below, at p.10) and the Graddy report (fn.19, above, at p.35) state that these costs are significantly higher and the UKIPO's Impact Assessment of the possible extension of the derogation for deceased artists estimated the costs per transaction for business from less than £10 per transaction to over £40 per transaction; Explanatory Memorandum to the Artist Resale Right (Amendment) Regulations 2009 (SI 2009/2792), p.13.

[50] See para.20–14, above.

[51] I. Froshauer, *The Impact of the Artist Resale Rights on the Art Market in the United Kingdom*, an independent study sponsored by the *Antiques Trade Gazette* (London: January 2008) p.13.

[52] T. Froshauer, fn.51, above, p.15.

6. ENFORCEMENT

20–19   **Right to information.** Holders of a resale right are empowered to obtain the information necessary to enable them to enforce their rights. These powers are laid down in reg.15 and enable the holder of the right in respect of a sale, or a person acting on his behalf, to have the right to obtain information by making a request from any art-market professional involved in the sale. Such requests must, however, be made within three years of the sale in question. The information that may be so requested is any that may be necessary in order to secure payment of the resale royalty, and, in particular, to ascertain the amount of the royalty that is due and, where the royalty is not paid by the person to whom the request is made, the name and address of any person who is liable. Information supplied is to be treated as confidential.

20–20   **Sanctions.** If the requested information is not supplied within 90 days of the receipt of the request, the person making the request may, in accordance with the rules of the court, apply to the county court for an order requiring the person to whom the request is made to supply the information.[53]

7. TRANSITIONAL PROVISIONS

20–21   **Date of application.** The Regulations do not apply to sales where the date of the relevant contract for sale preceded the commencement of the Regulations, February 14, 2006. However, they do apply notwithstanding that the work sold was made before that commencement.[54] Resale right will, of course, only exist if the work is still in copyright.[55]

20–22   **Transitional rules of succession.** Regulation 16(2) deals with the situation where the author of a work (or a person to whom the resale right in that work is deemed to have been transmitted) died before the commencement of the Regulations, and was at his death a qualifying individual. In such circumstances, resale right cannot at the time have been transmitted to the artist's successors under reg.9.[56] Accordingly, a rule is provided to determine who should then be regarded as the artist's successors for the purpose of holding resale right. Under this rule, the right is deemed to have passed with copyright in the work, if the copyright formed part of the artist's estate; or failing that, to have passed with the work itself. If the artist owned neither the work nor the copyright in it, or if neither passed to a specific beneficiary, resale right in the work is deemed to have been transmitted to the person(s) beneficially entitled to his residuary estate. The same rule applies where the deemed successor in turn died before the commencement of the Regulations.

Where the deceased author of the work was one of a number of joint authors, the right deemed to have been transmitted by the author under reg.16 is one of that number of equal shares in the resale right. Where a resale right is deemed to have been transmitted to more than one person, the right shall be deemed to have been transmitted to them in equal shares as owners in common.

---

[53] In Scotland, such an application shall be made by way of summary application to the sheriff, and the procedure for breach of an order shall proceed in like manner as for a contempt of court.
[54] reg.16(1).
[55] reg.3(1) and (2).
[56] See para.20–13, above.

8. DEROGATION FOR DECEASED ARTISTS

Postponement of application of the resale right to sales of deceased artists. When **20–23** ARR was introduced in 2006, reg.17 laid down that those to whom a resale right is transmitted (or deemed to be transmitted) after the death of the artist, in accordance with the Regulations, could not exercise the right until January 1, 2010. The provision was introduced in the exercise of an option open under the Directive to Member States such as the United Kingdom which did not have resale right at the date of entry into force of the Directive (October 13, 2001).[57] The UK Government declared at the time the Regulations entered into force that it had exercised this option to protect the most valuable sector of the UK art market, namely works by deceased artists. The Directive[58] made provision for the delay in the application of the right to this market to be extended until January 1, 2012, but only "if necessary to enable the economic operators in that Member State to adapt gradually to the resale right system while maintaining their economic viability".[59]

Meanwhile, in June 2008, the Government launched a consultation[60] to assess the likely impact of the resale right and the derogation for deceased artists on the UK art market, seeking views on whether to maintain the existing derogation for a further two years until January 1, 2012, or to allow the derogation to lapse so that works by deceased artists still in copyright would become eligible for the resale right. The consultation provoked 400 responses of which 90 per cent (mostly from artists and artists' estates) were in favour of allowing the derogation to lapse. The art trade, represented by dealers and auction houses, however, supported extending the derogation to 2012.[61]

Following the consultation, the UK Government concluded that the economic climate had affected the UK art market's ability to cope with the application of resale right to the works of deceased artists and announced its intention to prolong the derogation. According to the Explanatory Memorandum accompanying the ensuing Regulations laid before Parliament:

"It was estimated that there would be a four-fold increase in the number of transactions subject to resale right which would add to the administrative burden of the art market and require a change in working practices. It was considered doubtful that the UK art market could deal with these changes during such a difficult economic climate and continue to remain viable especially if, at the same time, they also had to deal with a reduction in volume of sales and a possible diversion of sales to other markets outside the EU which are not subject to resale right obligations."[62]

In December 2008, the UK Government notified the European Commission that it intended to maintain its existing derogation from resale rights for the works

---

[57] Directive art.8(2).

[58] art.8(3).

[59] art.8(3).

[60] The consultation closed on September 29, 2008; see UKIPO document, "Resale Right: the Derogation for Deceased Artists", available at http://www.ipo.gov.uk [Accessed September 13, 2010]; and DACS' "Submission to the Government Consultation on Artist's Resale Right", September 2008, http://www.dacs.org.uk [Accessed September 13, 2010].

[61] Press Release, UKIPO, November 11, 2008. The British Art Market Federation, in its response to the consultation expressed the view that " Droit de suite is a very inefficient way of benefiting artists in financial need. In the UK, the largest art market in Europe, only about 1,500 artists living in the EU and other qualifying countries have received any payment. Artists would appear therefore to have less than a one per cent chance of receiving anything at all, and the majority of payments that are made go to those who are already commercially successful." BAMF, Response to the IPO Consultation on the Artist's Resale Right, September 2008, p.4.

[62] Explanatory Memorandum to the Artist's Resale Right (Amendment) Regulations 2009 (SI 2009/2792) para.7.1.

of deceased artists for a further two years until January 1, 2010,[63] and, in December 2009, the United Kingdom amended the 2006 Regulations accordingly.[64] In the Explanatory Memorandum to the Regulations, the Government stated that the derogation will not be reviewed again before January 1, 2012, when it will expire.

---

[63] Letter to the Commission dated December 18, 2008, from J. Denham, Secretary of State for Innovation, Universities and Skills (Press Release, UKIPO, December 18, 2008).
[64] The Artist's Resale Right (Amendment) Regulations 2009 (SI 2009/2792), which entered into force on December 1, 2009.

PART VI

REMEDIES

CHAPTER TWENTY ONE

CIVIL REMEDIES

1. INTRODUCTION

A. Scope of this Chapter

Scope of this Chapter. This Chapter covers the non-criminal remedies and procedure in respect of infringements of all the rights covered in this work with the following exceptions and qualifications. First, a detailed treatment of the procedure and remedies in unregistered designs cases can be found in Ch.13. Second, this work only deals in outline with registered designs and Community registered designs. Accordingly, remedies and procedure for infringement of those rights do not feature in this Chapter. Finally, it should be emphasised that this Chapter is not intended to be anything like a comprehensive treatise on the subject of civil procedure. Rather it is intended to highlight and discuss those aspects of civil procedure which are specifically relevant to the enforcement of the rights covered in this work.   **21–01**

Other remedies. Where the infringement also constitutes a criminal offence, a potential claimant should always consider whether or not the expense of civil litigation might be avoided by reporting the infringement to the appropriate authority or even by commencing a private prosecution.[1] For criminal remedies, reference should be made to Chs 15 and 16, above and Ch.22, below. Consideration should also be given, where relevant, to reporting the matter to the Commissioners of Customs and Excise. Customs seizure is dealt with in Ch.22.   **21–02**

B. International Obligations

The Berne Convention.[2] Article 36 of the Paris Act provides that each party to the Convention undertakes to adopt, in accordance with its constitution, the measures necessary to ensure the application of the Convention. Article 2(6) provides that the protection conferred by the Convention shall operate for the benefit of the author and his successors in title and art.15(1) provides that the author shall be entitled to institute infringement proceedings. However, art.5(2) provides that apart from the provisions of the Convention, the extent of protection, as well as the means of redress afforded to the author to protect his rights, shall be governed exclusively by the laws of the country where protection is   **21–03**

---

[1] For a discussion of the advantages and disadvantages of criminal proceedings, see paras 22–47 and 22–48, below.
[2] See paras 23–04 et seq., below. The text is in Vol.2 F1.

claimed. The only specific provision as to enforcement is contained in art.16, which provides that infringing copies shall be liable to seizure in any country of the Union where the work enjoys legal protection and that this protection shall also apply to reproductions coming from a country where the work is not protected or has ceased to be protected. The article goes on to state that the seizure shall take place in accordance with the legislation of each country. With this exception, the Convention leaves the question of enforcement to the law of the protecting country.[3]

21–04   **TRIPS and the WIPO treaties.**[4] In contrast to the Berne Convention, the TRIPS agreement contains extensive provisions about enforcement, many of them at a very general level. They are discussed in para.23–136, below. Most of the more specific provisions are mirrored in the European Enforcement Directive[5] and are mentioned below where relevant. The WIPO Treaties[6] each contain a single provision, borrowed from art.41(1) of TRIPS, in the following form: "Contracting Parties shall ensure that enforcement procedures are available under their law so as to permit effective action against any act of infringement of rights covered by this Treaty, including expeditious remedies to prevent infringement and remedies which constitute a deterrent to further infringements". Neither the signature of the TRIPS agreement nor the entry into the WIPO treaties provoked any changes to English procedural law.

21–05   **ACTA.** The draft of the Anti-Counterfeiting Trade Agreement which was current at the time of writing[7] contained extensive provisions in relation to civil enforcement,[8] covering injunctions, financial remedies, the destruction of infringing material, the disclosure of information by alleged infringers and interim ("provisional") measures. It is not thought that any of the provisions of this draft impose any greater requirements on signatories than those contained in the Enforcement Directive.[9]

C. COMMUNITY LAW

21–06   **Introduction.** Until relatively recently, the enforcement of intellectual property rights was generally regarded as a matter for individual Member States. However, Community legislation in this area has recently become more extensive.

21–07   **The E-Commerce Directive.**[10] This Directive creates no new remedies but rather establishes limited defences for intermediary service providers who are "mere conduits" or engaged in the activities of "caching" or "hosting" ("the E-Commerce defences"). These defences are considered below.[11] The Directive also states the important principle that intermediaries are under no general obligation to monitor the information which they transmit or store nor any obligation

---

[3] For a discussion of the reasons for and limitations of this, see Ricketson & Ginsburg, *International Copyright and Neighbouring Rights The Berne Convention and Beyond* (2006) para.4.08.

[4] See paras 23–136, 23–66 and 23–119 et seq., respectively. The texts are in Vol.2 F11, F13 and F14.

[5] As to which see paras 21–09 et seq.

[6] The WIPO Copyright Treaty art.14(2) and the WIPO Performances and Phonograms Treaty art.23(2). For these treaties generally, see paras 23–66 et seq. and 23–119 et seq. The texts of the treaties are in Vol.2 F13 and F14.

[7] Consolidated text dated November 15, 2010.

[8] See s.2.

[9] As to which, see paras 21–09 et seq., below.

[10] Directive 2000/31/EC of the European Parliament and of the Council of June 9, 2000 on certain legal aspects of information society services, in particular electronic commerce, in the Internal Market. Relevant extracts are at Vol.2 H7.

[11] paras 21–100 et seq.

actively to seek facts or circumstances indicating illegal activity.[12] The Directive expressly provides that the E-Commerce defences do not affect the possibility for a court or administrative authority, in accordance with Member States' legal systems, of requiring the service provider to terminate or prevent an infringement.[13] The E-Commerce Directive has been implemented in the United Kingdom by Regulations.[14] The European Commission recently issued a consultation on the future of the Directive.[15]

The Information Society Directive.[16] Article 8 of this Directive contains three requirements under the heading "Sanctions and remedies". First, Member States are obliged to provide appropriate sanctions and remedies in respect of infringement of the rights and obligations set out in the Directive and to take all the measures necessary to ensure that those sanctions and remedies are applied. The sanctions are to be effective, proportionate and dissuasive.[17] No specific legislation was introduced to implement this requirement, no doubt because no implementation was considered necessary. Second, Member States are obliged to take the measures necessary to ensure that right-holders whose interests are affected by an infringing activity carried out in their territories can bring an action for damages and an injunction and for the seizure of infringing material as well as devices, products or components promoted or intended to circumvent technical measures.[18] This requirement resulted in the introduction of s.101A of the 1988 Act, which is considered below,[19] and in new provisions relating to circumvention devices which are dealt with in Ch.15. Third, Member States are obliged to ensure that rightholders are in a position to apply for an injunction against intermediaries whose services are used by a third party to infringe copyright or a related right.[20] This requirement was implemented by the introduction of s.97A into the 1988 Act. This is dealt with below.[21]

21–08

The Enforcement Directive. On April 29, 2004, the European Parliament and the Council adopted a Directive on the enforcement of intellectual property rights.[22] Member States were obliged to implement the Directive by April 28, 2006.[23] The declared object of the Directive was to reduce or eliminate the prejudice to the functioning of the single market and to substantive intellectual property laws which was perceived to be caused by the disparities between national procedural regimes.[24] This was to be achieved by the approximation of national enforcement systems so as to ensure a "high, equivalent and homogeneous level

21–09

---

[12] art.15.

[13] arts 12(3), 13(3) and 14(3).

[14] The Electronic Commerce (EC Directive) Regulations 2002 (SI 2002 No. 2013). See Vol.2 B10.i.

[15] http://ec.europa.eu/internal_market/consultations/2010/e-commerce_en.htm [Accessed October 12, 2010].

[16] Directive 2001/29/EC of the European Parliament and of the Council of May 22, 2001 on the harmonisation of certain aspects of copyright and related rights in the information society.See Vol.2 H8.

[17] art.8(1).

[18] art.8(2).

[19] paras 21–30 et seq.

[20] art.8(3).

[21] paras 21–179 et seq.

[22] [2004] OJ L157/45. For background, see the Green Paper on combating counterfeiting and piracy in the single market, COM(98) 569 final; the follow-up to the Green Paper, COM (2000) 789 final; and the proposal for the Directive, COM(2003) 46 final.

[23] art.20(1).

[24] Recitals 7–9. For criticism, see Cornish et al. [2003] E.I.P.R. 447.

of protection in the Internal Market",[25] building on but going beyond TRIPs.[26] However, the Directive does not prevent individual Member States from introducing provisions which are more favourable to rightholders than those of the Directive.[27] The Directive is expressed to apply to all intellectual property rights.[28] The Commission has published a list of intellectual property rights to which it believes the Directive applies.[29] The list appears to include all the rights covered in this Chapter. Member States were obliged to report to the Commission on the implementation of the Directive by April 29, 2009; on the basis of these reports, the Commission is obliged to report on the Directive's application.[30] The specific provisions of the Directive are referred to below where relevant.

21–10   **Implementation of the Enforcement Directive.** Few of the Directive's numerous provisions were thought to require a change in English law. Those that were, were implemented by the Intellectual Property (Enforcement etc.) Regulations 2006 which came into force on April 29, 2006 ("the Enforcement Regulations"),[31] and by certain changes to the Civil Procedure Rules and Practice Directions.[32] These changes are mentioned below where appropriate.

21–11   **Representative actions.** Article 4(c) of the Enforcement Directive requires Member States to recognise as persons entitled to seek application of the measure, procedures and remedies referred to in Ch.II of the Directive "intellectual property collective rights-management bodies which are regularly recognised as having a right to represent holders of intellectual property rights, in so far as permitted by and in accordance with the provisions of the applicable law". In the previous edition of the work, it was suggested that this would require to be implemented by legislation.[33] However, the Government concluded that art.4 of the Directive did not impose any obligations on Member States to create any new classes of persons entitled to sue.[34] Nevertheless, on September 26, 2006 the Government launched a consultation in relation to three legislative options which would enable actions to be undertaken by a representative or representative organisation on behalf of a group of intellectual property rights holders who might, or might not be individually named in a situation where an individual would have a direct cause of action.[35] The consultation closed on December 18, 2006. There have been no further developments in respect of the introduction of representative actions in the intellectual property field. However, the introduction of new Civil Procedure Rules in relation to "collective proceedings" remains under discussion.[36]

---

[25] Recital 10.

[26] For this "TRIPS-plus" approach, see para.24–151, below.

[27] art.2(1).

[28] art.1.

[29] [2005] OJ L94/37.

[30] art.18(1). The European Parliament has recently called on the Commission to produce the report: Resolution of September 22, 2010 on enforcement of intellectual property rights in the internal market (2009/2178(INI)), paras 8 to 10.

[31] SI 2006/1028.

[32] See CPR Update 41, published on April 6, 2006.

[33] *Copinger* 15th edn, para.22–03.

[34] See the Transposition Note attached to the original consultation on implementation.

[35] The consultation document is on the UK IPO website. The definition of "representative action" is at para.2 on p.3. The options are summarised at para.17 on p.6.

[36] See most recently the Draft Court Rules for Collective Proceedings published by the Civil Justice Council on February 2, 2010: *http://www.civiljusticecouncil.gov.uk/files/ CJC__Draft__Rules__for__Collective__Actions__Feb__2010.pdf* [Accessed October 12, 2010]. The draft rules define "collective proceedings" as "proceedings which by virtue of any enactment

D. OVERVIEW OF THE REMEDIES FOR THE VARIOUS RIGHTS

Copyright and publication right. Copyright is a property right and an infringe-   **21–12**
ment is actionable by the copyright owner.[37] An infringement occurring after the
grant of an exclusive licence is also actionable by the exclusive licensee.[38] Certain
infringements are also actionable by a non-exclusive licensee.[39]

In an action for infringement all such relief, by way of damages, injunctions,
accounts or otherwise, is available to the claimant as is available in respect of the
infringement of any other property right.[40] However, that general rule is subject
to a number of qualifications. Three relate to damages. First, there is a defence to
a damages claim in the very limited number of cases where the defendant did not
know and had no reason to believe that copyright subsisted in the work in
question.[41] Secondly, the court may award a species of damages called "additional
damages" which is peculiar to this field.[42] Third, specific provision is made in
regulations as to the basis of the assessment of damages where a defendant knew
or had reason to believe that he was infringing.[43]

Further qualifications concern injunctions. First, there is a defence to claims
for an injunction and for an order for delivery up where the defendant undertakes
to take a licence of right which is available under s.144 of the 1988 Act.[44]
Secondly, as well as granting an injunction against the infringer, the court may
also grant an injunction against a service provider who has actual knowledge that
another person is using its service to infringe copyright.[45] Thirdly, provisions in
the Digital Economy Act 2010 (if implemented) include the imposition of obligations on internet service providers to limit infringers' internet access and provision to enable the courts to grant injunctions to block access to sites used for
infringement.[46] The court's equitable power to order delivery up of infringing
articles is amplified by an express statutory power, which extends to articles
specifically designed or adapted for making copies of a particular copyright
work.[47] Finally, in certain limited circumstances, a copyright owner can seize
infringing copies without the need to obtain a court order.[48]

The Digital Economy Act 2010 introduced substantial new provisions concerning unlicensed file sharing of copyright material. These provisions are covered in
s.9 of this Chapter.

Publication right is a property right equivalent to copyright and the same pro-

---

may be brought by a representative on behalf of persons whose claims raise common issues and
in respect of those common issues": draft r.19.16(2)(b).

[37] CDPA 1988 s.96(1).

[38] s.101.

[39] s.101A.

[40] s.96(2).

[41] s.97(1).

[42] s.97(2). The Government has proposed the abolition of additional damages by replacing references in s.97(2) to "additional damages" with references to "aggravated and restitutionary
damages". The amending legislation would confirm that such damages would be available to
corporate as well as individual claimants. The Government intended that the explanatory notes to
the amending legislation would state that aggravated and restitutionary damages were intended to
cover all the aspects set out in art.13(1) of the Enforcement Directive, including both damages
and an account of profits. See *The Law on Damages Response to Consultation* CP(R) 9/07,
Ministry of Justice, July 1, 2009, pp.55 and 56.

[43] See para.21–194, below. The effect of these provisions remains to be worked out.

[44] s.98. For a discussion of s.144, see paras 28–325 et seq., below. If this provision operates there is
also a limit on the financial remedies available: s.98(1)(c).

[45] s.97A.

[46] See para.21–57, below.

[47] s.99.

[48] s.100.

visions as to remedies apply as apply to copyright.[49] In the remainder of this Chapter, statements about copyright apply to publication right unless otherwise stated.

21–13   **Moral rights and performers' moral rights.** Unlike copyright, moral rights are not property rights. Infringements of moral rights and performers' moral rights are actionable as a breach of statutory duty owed to the person entitled to the right.[50] In proceedings for infringement of the right to object to derogatory treatment the court may grant an injunction prohibiting the doing of an act unless a disclaimer is made, dissociating the author, director or performer (as the case may be) from the treatment of the work or performance.[51] The provisions of the Digital Economy Act 2010 concerning online infringement of copyright[52] do not extenD to moral rights.

21–14   **Performers' property rights.** Like copyright, performers' property rights (as their name suggests) are property rights.[53] An infringement is actionable by the rights owner.[54] An infringement occurring after the grant of an exclusive licence is also actionable by the exclusive licensee.[55] There is no provision for an action by a non-exclusive licensee. As in the case of copyright, in an action for infringement all such relief, by way of damages, injunctions, accounts or otherwise, is available to the claimant as is available in respect of the infringement of any other property right.[56] By analogy with the copyright position, there is a defence to a damages claim where the defendant did not know and had no reason to believe that the rights subsisted in the recording to which the action relates[57]; the court has the power to award additional damages[58]; there is a defence to claims for an injunction and delivery up where the defendant undertakes to take a licence of right which is available under para.17 of Sch.2A to the 1988 Act[59]; and the court may grant an injunction against a service provider who has actual knowledge that another person is using its service to infringe a performer's property right.[60] Again, by analogy with the position in relation to copyright, there is a statutory right to an order for delivery up of illicit recordings (although not of articles specifically designed or adapted for making copies of a particular recording).[61] There is also a right in limited circumstances to seize illicit recordings without a court order.[62] The provisions of the Digital Economy Act 2010 concerning online infringement of copyright[63] do not extend to rights in performances.

---

[49] Copyright and Related Rights Regulations 1996 (SI 1996/2967) regs.16(1) and 17(1). Note also reg.17(5), which provides that except where the context requires otherwise, any other enactment relating to copyright, whether passed or made before or after the Regulations, applies in relation to publication right as in relation to copyright. It follows that the provisions in the Digital Economy Act 2010 which relate to online infringement and which take effect as amendments to the Communications Act 2003 (ss.3 to 16) or as free-standing sections (ss.17 and 18) apply to publication right even though they only refer to "copyright".
[50] CDPA 1988 s.103(1) and 205N.
[51] s.103(2) and 205N(4).
[52] See paras 21–288 et seq.
[53] CDPA 1988 s.191A.
[54] s.191I(1).
[55] s.191L.
[56] s.191I(2).
[57] s.191J(1).
[58] s.191J(2). See, however, para.21–12 fn.42, above.
[59] s.191K.
[60] s.191JA.
[61] s.195.
[62] s.196.
[63] See paras 21–288 et seq.

Performers' non-property rights and recording rights. In contrast to perform-   **21–15**
ers' property rights, these rights are not property rights and, like moral rights, are
actionable by the person entitled to the right as a breach of statutory duty.[64] A
person having performers' non-property rights or recording rights can, however,
apply for an order for delivery up of illicit recordings[65] or (in limited circumstances) seize such recordings without a court order.[66]

Unregistered design right and semi-conductor topographies. Unregistered   **21–16**
design right is a property right.[67] An infringement is actionable by the design
right owner.[68] An infringement occurring after the grant of an exclusive licence is
also actionable by the exclusive licensee.[69] There is no provision for an action by
a non-exclusive licensee. As in the case of copyright, in an action for infringement all such relief, by way of damages, injunctions, accounts or otherwise, is
available to the claimant as is available in respect of the infringement of any
other property right.[70] By analogy with the copyright position, there is a defence
to a damages claim where the defendant did not know and had no reason to
believe that design right subsisted in the design to which the action relates.[71]
Uniquely to design right, where in an action for secondary infringement, the defendant shows that the infringing article was innocently acquired by him or a predecessor in title, the only remedy is a reasonable royalty.[72] In other respects, the
provisions of the 1988 Act are similar to those for copyright. Thus, the court has
the power to award additional damages[73]; there is a defence to claims for an
injunction and delivery up where the defendant undertakes to take a licence of
right under s.237 or 238 of the 1988 Act[74]; and there is a statutory right to an order for delivery up.[75] On the other hand, there is no right to seize infringing
articles without a court order. Certain uses of unregistered designs by the Crown
are not infringements but give rise to a right to compensation which, in the
absence of agreement, may be determined on a reference to the court.[76]

Rights in respect of semiconductor topographies are governed by the design
right provisions of the 1988 Act with the modifications set out in Ch.14, above.[77]
In the remainder of this Chapter, statements about design right apply to rights in
respect of semiconductor topographies unless otherwise stated.

Community designs. To some extent, rights under Community designs raise dif-   **21–17**
ferent issues to the other rights covered in this work and reference should be
made to Ch.13, above.[78] The Community Designs Regulation provides that where
a Community design court[79] finds that a defendant has infringed or threatened to
infringe a Community design, it is obliged, in the absence of special reasons, to

---

[64] CDPA 1988 s.194.
[65] s.195.
[66] s.196.
[67] CDPA 1988 s.213(1).
[68] s.229(1).
[69] s.234.
[70] s.229(2).
[71] s.233(1).
[72] s.233(2).
[73] s.229(3). See, however, para.21–12 fn.42 above.
[74] s.239.
[75] s.230.
[76] ss.240–252.
[77] See the Design Right (Semiconductor Topographies) Regulations 1989 (SI 1989/1100) reg.3.
[78] See paras 13–255 et seq., above
[79] That is, in England and Wales, the High Court, any county court designated as a Patents County
    Court under s.287(1) CDPA 1988 (at present only Central London County Court) and the Court
    of Appeal: Community Designs (Designation of Community Design Courts) Regulations 2005

grant an injunction; to order the seizure of the infringing products and materials and implements predominantly used to manufacture the infringing goods[80]; and to make an order imposing "other sanctions appropriate under the circumstances which are provided by the law of the Member State in which the acts of infringement or threatened infringement are committed".[81] The court is also obliged to take such measures in accordance with its national law as are aimed at ensuring that such orders are complied with.[82] United Kingdom law provides that in an action for infringement of a Community design, all such relief by way of damages, injunctions, accounts or otherwise is available as is available in respect of the infringement of any other property right.[83] In appropriate circumstances, the court may now also make orders for the delivery up and disposal of infringing articles and of things specifically designed or adapted for making infringing articles.[84] There is no defence to a damages claim for "innocent" infringers of Community designs.[85]

21–18   **Rights in respect of protection measures, rights management information and unauthorised decoders.** In each of these cases, the person with rights has the same rights and remedies in respect of an infringement as a copyright owner has in respect of an infringement of copyright.[86] Thus, in an action for infringement all such relief, by way of damages, injunctions, accounts or otherwise, is available to the claimant as is available in respect of the infringement of any other property right.[87] In addition, a person with rights in respect of protection measures (whether in relation to computer programs or otherwise) has the same right to apply for an order for delivery up of circumvention devices or to seize them without a court order as a copyright owner has in relation to infringing copies.[88] Finally, in the case of protection measures other than those relating to computer programs, there is a defence to a damages claim where the defendant did not know and had no reason to believe that his acts enabled or facilitated an infringement of the right in question.[89]

21–19   **Database right.** Database right is a property right.[90] Since April 29, 2006 the remedies available to the owner and an exclusive licensee of database right have been the same as those for infringement of copyright.[91]

21–20   **Equitable remuneration.** The appropriate remedy for an author or performer wishing to fix the amount of the equitable remuneration or dissatisfied with the

---

(SI 2005/696) reg.2. Proceedings in the High Court must be brought in the Chancery Division: see CPR 63.13(1)(a).

[80] Provided their owner knew the effect for which such use was intended or if such effect would have been obvious in the circumstances.

[81] See art.89(1) of Council Regulation No.6/2002 on Community designs: [2002] OJ L3/1.

[82] See art.89(2) of Council Regulation No.6/2002 on Community designs [2002] OJ L3/1.

[83] See reg.1A(2) of the Community Design Regulations 2005 (SI 2005/2339) introduced by reg.2(3) of and para.9 of Sch.3 to the Enforcement Regulations with effect from April 29, 2006.

[84] See regs 1B to 1D of the Community Design Regulations.

[85] *J Choo Jersey Ltd v Towerstone Ltd* [2008] EWHC 346 (Ch); [2008] F.S.R. 19.

[86] CDPA 1988 ss.296(2) (circumvention of technical devices applied to computer programs); 296ZA(3) (circumvention of technological measures applied to works other than computer programs); 296ZD(3) (devices and services designed to circumvent technological measures applied to works other than computer programs); 296ZG(3) (rights management information); and 298(2) (apparatus, etc. for unauthorised reception of transmissions).

[87] s.96(2).

[88] s.296(4) (computer programs) and s.296ZD(4) (other works).

[89] s.296ZD(7). See para.21–85, below.

[90] Copyright and Rights in Databases Regulations 1997 (SI 1997/3032) reg.13.

[91] Copyright and Rights in Databases Regulations 1997 (SI 1997/3032) reg.23; Enforcement Regulations (SI 2006/1028) reg.2(3) and Sch.3 para.6.

amount payable is an application to the Copyright Tribunal. This is discussed elsewhere.[92]

Terminology in this Chapter. In the remainder of this Chapter, the term "non-property rights" means: moral rights, performers' moral rights, performers' non-property rights, recording rights, and rights in respect of protection measures, rights management information and unauthorised decoders.

21–21

2. WHO MAY SUE OR TAKE ACTION

A. Legal Owner or Person With Rights

Copyright, performers' property rights, unregistered UK design right and database right. These rights are property rights and accordingly the remedies are given to the owner, that is to say, the original owner, or a person deriving title under him by a valid assignment or otherwise. Where different persons are (whether in consequence of a partial assignment or otherwise) entitled to different aspects of the right, the owner for this purpose is the person who is entitled to the relevant aspect of the right.[93]

21–22

Non-property rights. In the case of the non-property rights, the remedies are given to the person entitled to the right, whose identity is specified in the relevant legislation, or a person to whom that right has been lawfully transmitted.

21–23

B. Equitable Owner

Copyright. As to equitable ownership generally, see paras 5–174 et seq., above. A person entitled to the copyright in equity may start an action and seek interim relief relying on his equitable title. In general, however, he will not be entitled to final relief unless he has either joined the legal owner as a party (co-claimant or defendant) or obtained an assignment of the legal title.[94] The purpose of the rule is to protect the defendant from the possibility of being sued again by the legal

21–24

---

[92] See paras 28–128 and 28–147, below.

[93] CDPA 1988 s.173(1) for copyright and database right, s.191A(3) for performers' property rights and s.258(1) for design right.

[94] *Merchant Adventurers Ltd v Grew & Co Ltd* [1972] Ch. 242 at 252, [1971] F.S.R. 233; *Performing Right Society Ltd v London Theatre of Varieties Ltd* [1924] A.C. 1 at 14, 15 and 35; *EM Bowden's Patents Syndicate Ltd v Herbert Smith & Co* [1904] 2 Ch. 86 at 91; *Ward Lock & Co Ltd v Long* [1906] 2 Ch. 550; *University of London Press Ltd v University Tutorial* [1916] 2 Ch. 601; *Hexagon Pty Ltd v Australian Broadcasting Commission* [1976] R.P.C. 628; *Roban Jig & Tool Co Ltd v Taylor* [1979] F.S.R. 130 at 135; *Wah Sang Industrial Co v Takmay Industrial Co Ltd* [1980] F.S.R. 303; *John Richardson Computers Limited v Flanders* [1993] F.S.R. 497; *Bookmakers' Afternoon Greyhound Services Ltd v Wilf Gilbert (Staffordshire) Ltd* [1994] F.S.R. 723; *Batjac Productions Inc v Simitar Entertainment (UK) Limited & Another* [1996] F.S.R. 139; *Orwin v Attorney-General* [1998] F.S.R. 415 at 423, CA; *Comprop Ltd v Moran* Unreported, March 20, 2002 (Royal Court of Jersey); cf. *Roland Corporation v Lorenzo & Sons Pty Ltd* (1991) 22 I.P.R. 245 (Fed Ct of Australia) where it was said that a plaintiff could obtain declaratory and injunctive relief, even though he had no title, legal or equitable, at the date of issue of the writ. In *Orwin v Attorney-General* [1998] F.S.R. 415 the claimant in copyright infringement proceedings claimed to be the legal, alternatively the equitable owner of various copyrights. In support of his claim to equitable ownership, he relied on an agreement between him and a company of which he had been a director. The company had been struck off the Register. He brought separate proceedings against the Attorney-General (representing the Crown) for an order pursuant to s.51 of the Trustee Act 1925, vesting the copyrights in him, claiming that the Crown held the copyrights on trust for him. The order was refused on the basis that (a) it was not at all clear from the evidence that the legal estate was vested in the Crown on trust for the claimant (in which case there would be no jurisdiction to make the order) and (b) the order should not be made in the absence of the defendant in the copyright proceedings, who was entitled to adduce evidence, cross-examine and make representations. The Court of Appeal made an order consolidating the Trustee Act proceedings with the copyright proceedings.

owner, in particular a bona fide assignee of the copyright for value without notice of the equitable owner's rights. It follows that there may be cases where the Court can be satisfied that there is no real possibility of a claim by the legal owner or for some other reason the rule, which is a rule of practice, not law, can be relaxed.[95] It is thought that such cases will rarely arise.

If the equitable owner chooses to get in the legal title, as opposed to joining the legal owner, a mere assignment of copyright is insufficient. The assignment must include accrued rights of action in order to perfect the equitable owner's title to sue,[96] although in a quia timet action where the only remedy sought is a permanent injunction, a mere assignment of copyright without accrued causes of action should be sufficient. It appears that, if the defendant wishes to take the point, he can apply for the action to be stayed until the claimant perfects his title or joins the legal owner.[97] It also appears that an equitable owner is entitled to the remedies available under the 1988 Act as against the bare legal owner.[98]

The rights so far provided for under the online infringement provisions of the Digital Economy Act 2010[99] are granted to the "copyright owner", which term is defined as a copyright owner within the meaning of the copyright Part of the 1988 Act or someone authorised to act on that person's behalf.[100] An equitable owner does not appear to fall within the definition of "copyright owner". Whether an equitable owner will be entitled to apply for a "blocking injunction" under s.17 of the Digital Economy Act will depend on the terms of any regulations made under that section.

21–25   **Performers' property rights, unregistered UK design right and database right.** It seems that an equitable owner of a performer's property right, design right, or database right will have the same rights to sue as an equitable owner of copyright. The classic situation in which an equitable title arises is where a person commissions another to create a work and there is an express or implied term of the contract of commission that the intellectual property rights in the work will belong to the commissioner. In the case of design right, of course, such a situation will not normally arise because the 1988 Act provides that where a design right is created in pursuance of a commission, the person commissioning the design is the first owner of any design right.[101] A similar provision applies to database right.[102]

21–26   **Non-property rights.** There can be no "equitable owner" of these rights. They are not assignable, but only capable of transmission, if at all, on death.[103] Recording rights do not pass even on death.[104]

---

[95] See *Performing Right Society Ltd v London Theatre of Varieties Ltd* [1924] A.C. 1, at 18; *William Brandt's Sons & Co v Dunlop Rubber Co Ltd* [1905] A.C. 454 at 462; *Weddell v Pearce & Major* [1988] Ch. 26 at 43; *Batjac Productions Inc v Simitar Entertainment (UK) Ltd* [1996] F.S.R. 139; *Musical Fidelity Ltd v Vickers* [2002] EWHC 1000 (Ch): final relief granted to equitable owner after legal owners, a firm of solicitors, undertook to assign the copyright to the claimant (not challenged on appeal: [2002] EWCA Civ 1989; [2003] F.S.R. 50).

[96] *Batjac Productions Inc v Simitar Entertainment (UK) Ltd & Another* [1996] F.S.R. 139.

[97] *Weddell v Pearce & Major* [1988] Ch. 26 at 41. However, in *E.M. Bowden's Patents Syndicate Ltd v Herbert Smith & Co* [1904] 2 Ch. 86 and 122, the authority relied upon by Scott J. in the *Weddell* case, the action was not stayed in terms; the trial, which had commenced before the point was taken, was adjourned to enable the legal owner as at the date of the Writ to be joined.

[98] *Cableship Ltd v Williams* [1991] I.P.D. 14205, Hoffmann J.; *Vitof Ltd v Altoft* [2006] EWHC 1678 (Ch) at para.174.

[99] That is, new ss.124A to 124N of the Communications Act 2003.

[100] Communications Act 2003 s.124N.

[101] CDPA 1988 s.215(2) and see para.13–11, above.

[102] Copyright and Rights in Databases Regulations 1997 (SI 1997/3032) reg.14(1).

[103] CDPA 1988 ss.94 and 205L (moral rights and performers' moral rights not assignable), 95 and

C. EXCLUSIVE LICENSEE

Copyright. For the definition of "exclusive licensee" (which includes an   **21–27**
exclusive importer or distributor[105]) see paras 5–208 et seq., above. Section 101
of the 1988 Act provides that an exclusive licensee has the same rights and remedies, except against the copyright owner, in respect of matters occurring after the
grant of the licence as if the licence had been an assignment.[106] This right is
purely procedural—the exclusive licensee has no property right. Presumably the
words "except against the copyright owner" are there to ensure that the exclusive
licensee cannot sue the copyright owner for infringement of copyright, but is
restricted to his contractual remedies under the exclusive licence. Without these
words, the copyright owner would be treated as an assignor of the copyright and
any act of infringement by him would be "without the licence of the copyright
owner", in the words of s.16(2).

The rights and remedies of an exclusive licensee are concurrent with those of
the copyright owner and references in Pt I of the 1988 Act to the copyright owner
are to be construed accordingly.[107] In an action brought by an exclusive licensee,
a defendant may avail himself of any defence which would have been available
to him if the action had been brought by the copyright owner.[108] Where a copyright owner and an exclusive licensee have concurrent rights of action, the one
may not proceed with the action without the permission of the court,[109] unless the
other is joined as a claimant or added as a defendant.[110] A copyright owner or
exclusive licensee may apply for an interim injunction without joining the other
or obtaining the leave of the court.[111]

The rights so far provided for under the online infringement provisions of the
Digital Economy Act 2010[112] are granted to the "copyright owner", which term is
defined as a copyright owner within the meaning of the copyright Part of the
1988 Act or someone authorised to act on that person's behalf.[113] An exclusive licensee does not appear to fall within the definition of "copyright owner" but may
of course be authorised to act on the copyright owner's behalf. Whether an
exclusive licensee will be entitled to apply for a "blocking injunction" under s.17
of the Digital Economy Act will depend on the terms of any regulations made
under that section. For a fuller discussion of the position of statutory exclusive
licensees, see paras 5–208 et seq., above.

Performers' property rights, design right and database right. There are cor-   **21–28**

205M (when moral rights and performers' moral right pass on death), 192A (performers' non-
property rights only pass on death) and 192B (rights of persons having recording rights are not
assignable or transmissible at all).

[104] CDPA 1988 s.192B.

[105] *Biotrading & Financing Oy v Biohit Ltd* [1998] F.S.R. 109.

[106] CDPA 1988 s.101(1).

[107] s.101(2).

[108] s.101(3). See, e.g. *JHP Ltd v BBC Worldwide Ltd* [2008] EWHC 757 (Ch); [2008] F.S.R. 29, in
which the defendant successfully defended an exclusive licensee's claim on the basis of a "licence
by estoppel" from the copyright owner.

[109] For an example of where permission was given by consent, see *Bodley Head Ltd v Flegon* [1972]
R.P.C. 587. See para.5–210, above.

[110] s.102(1). A copyright owner or exclusive licensee who is joined as a defendant in pursuance of
this provision is not liable for any costs of the action unless he takes part in the proceedings:
s.102(2). For special provisions which apply where a copyright owner and exclusive licensee
have concurrent rights of action, see para.21–222, below.

[111] s.102(3).

[112] That is, new ss.124A to 124N of the Communications Act 2003.

[113] Communications Act 2003 s.124N.

responding provisions giving the same remedies to exclusive licensees of performers' property rights,[114] design right[115] and database right.[116]

21–29   **Non-property rights.** There are no provisions in respect of statutory exclusive licences for these rights. A non-statutory exclusive licensee will have no right to bring proceedings.

D. NON-EXCLUSIVE LICENSEES AND AGENTS

21–30   **Section 101A of the 1988 Act: background.** The essence of a licence is a contractual or personal relationship whereby the licensee is permitted to do an act or acts which would, but for the licence, be an infringement. A non-exclusive licensee is not the owner of the copyright or any interest in it. For these reasons, prior to October 31, 2003, non-exclusive licensees had no right to bring proceedings for infringement.[117] Since October 31, 2003, however, some non-exclusive licensees have had the right to bring proceedings under s.101A of the 1988 Act.[118]

This provision was introduced as a result of representations made by broadcasters during the consultation in relation to the implementation of the Information Society Directive. Prior to the implementation of the Directive, broadcasts and cable programmes (including programmes transmitted in "on-demand" services) were protected under ss.6 and 7 of the 1988 Act respectively. The Government's draft implementing regulations proposed the complete removal of the term "cable programme service" from the 1988 Act and the alteration of the definition of "broadcast" so as to include internet transmissions of a broadcast character. In their representations on the draft regulations,[119] many broadcasters expressed the concern that this would reduce the amount of protection for on-demand services. They argued that where (as, for example, in the case of acquired programming such as films), the broadcaster was not the owner or exclusive licensee of the rights in the underlying works, it would be unable to take action against infringers. Licensors might become reluctant to grant licences or they might charge higher fees. Licensors might be reluctant to take action themselves or not have the funds to do so. Where the on-demand service consisted of a large number of clips, it might not be feasible for the numerous owners in the rights to take action but it would be vital for them to be able to do so.

The Government did not accept that the existing law protected the service as such rather than the programmes provided in it, which were protected in other ways.[120] Nevertheless, it considered that it would be reasonable for service providers to be able to act against infringements connected to their activities in circumstances where they were neither the owner nor the exclusive licensee but the owner of the copyright in the content wished them to act.[121]

Accordingly, the Government considered it appropriate to introduce such provision, but applying to non-exclusive licensees in general.[122] The Patent Office's Transposition Note states that the purpose of s.101A is to ensure that all right

---

[114] CDPA 1988 ss.191L and 191M.

[115] ss.234 and 235.

[116] Copyright and Rights in Databases Regulations 1997 (SI 1997/3032) reg.23.

[117] *Nicol v Barranger* [1917–1923] Mac.C.C. 219.

[118] CDPA 1988 s.101A, inserted by reg.28 of the Copyright and Related Rights Regulations 2003 (SI 2003/2498). For a discussion of the transitional provisions, see Copinger 15th edn para.22–23, fn.82.

[119] In particular the BBC's representations, which were supported by the Producers' Rights Agency, ITC, Channel 4 and Channel 5.

[120] Consultation: Analysis of Responses and Government Conclusions, para.8.5.

[121] Consultation: Analysis of Responses and Government Conclusions, para.8.6.

[122] Consultation: Analysis of Responses and Government Conclusions, para.8.6.

holders are able to protect their rights, in line with art.8(2) of the Information Society Directive.[123]

The rights so far provided for under the online infringement provisions of the Digital Economy Act 2010[124] are granted to the "copyright owner", which term is defined as a copyright owner within the meaning of the copyright Part of the 1988 Act or someone authorised to act on that person's behalf.[125] A non-exclusive licensee does not fall within the definition of "copyright owner" but may of course be so authorised. Whether a non-exclusive licensee will be entitled to apply for a "blocking injunction" under s.17 of the Digital Economy Act will depend on the terms of any regulations made under that section.

Non-exclusive licensees with a right of action. For the purposes of the section, the expression "non-exclusive licensee" means the holder of a licence authorising the licensee to exercise a right which remains exercisable by the copyright owner.[126] However, not every such licensee has a right of action. First, it is necessary for the non-exclusive licence to be in writing and signed by or on behalf of the copyright owner.[127] Secondly, it is necessary that the licence should expressly grant the licensee a right of action under s.101A of the 1988 Act.[128] **21–31**

Infringing acts in respect of which there is a right of action. Even if these two requirements are met, the licensee only has a right of action if the infringing act was "directly connected to a prior licensed act of the licensee".[129] This formulation clearly gives broadcasters the rights they sought in the course of the consultation.[130] However, as the Government intended, the right is not restricted to broadcasters. Accordingly, for example, it would seem that a record company which pressed a CD under a non-exclusive licence from MCPS would be able to sue a person who made further copies from that CD but not otherwise. **21–32**

Rights concurrent. As in the case of an exclusive licensee, the rights of the non-exclusive licensee and the copyright owner are concurrent and the statutory consequences of this are the same.[131] **21–33**

Agents. In general, a mere agent acting on behalf of the copyright owner does not have an interest in the work such as to entitle him to claim relief.[132] For example, the Mechanical Copyright Protection Society Ltd (MCPS), unlike the Performing Right Society Ltd (PRS), does not take assignments of copyright from its members and cannot, therefore, bring proceedings in its own name for infringement of its members' rights.[133] However, where a body exists to represent copyright owners who are its members, representative proceedings for copyright infringement may be brought by a limited selection of those members.[134] Moreover, the rights so far provided for under the online infringement provisions of **21–34**

---

[123] This provides that Member States shall provide "appropriate" sanctions and remedies in respect of infringements of the rights and obligations set out in the Directive. See Vol.2 H7.

[124] That is, new ss.124A to 124N of the Communications Act 2003.

[125] Communications Act 2003 s.124N.

[126] CDPA 1988 s.101A(6).

[127] s.101A(1)(b)(i).

[128] s.101A(1)(b)(ii).

[129] CDPA 1988 s.101A(1)(a).

[130] See para.21–30, above.

[131] CDPA 1988 s.101A(2) to (5). For the position in relation to exclusive licensees, see para.21–222, below.

[132] *Nicol v Stockdale* (1818) 3 Swans.687; *Petty v Taylor* [1897] 1 Ch. 465.

[133] For MCPS and the PRS, see below at paras 27–63 and 27–65 respectively.

[134] See, e.g. *Independiente Ltd and others v Music Trading On-Line (HK) Ltd* [2003] EWHC 470 (Ch); [2007] F.S.R. 21, which concerned members of the British Phonographic Industry Ltd.

the Digital Economy Act 2010[135] are granted to a copyright owner within the meaning of the copyright Part of the 1988 Act or someone authorised to act on that person's behalf.[136] It follows that those rights may be exercised by an agent whose authority extends to the enforcement of the rights in question. Whether an agent will be entitled to apply for a "blocking injunction" under s.17 of the Digital Economy Act will depend on the terms of any regulations made under that section.

21–35   **Other rights.** Non-exclusive licensees in respect of other rights have no rights to sue for infringement. Again, presumably, a mere agent acting on behalf of an owner of such a right cannot bring an action in his own name.

E. JOINT OWNERS

21–36   **Copyright, performers' property rights, design right and database right.** Where copyright (or any aspect of copyright) is owned by more than one person jointly, references to the copyright owner are to all the owners.[137] There are similar provisions for performers' property rights and design right.[138] The effect of these provisions is that one joint owner can sue to prevent a third party[139] or even another joint owner[140] from carrying out a restricted act without his licence. There are numerous authorities for the proposition that where a third party is sued for copyright infringement, there is no requirement to join the other joint owner.[141] However, some doubt has been cast on this by the introduction of CPR 19.3, which provides that where a claimant claims to be entitled to a remedy jointly with another person that person must be joined as a party unless the court otherwise orders, together with certain obiter remarks made in a case on rights in performances.[142] Although the point is not free of doubt, it is thought that the better view is that one joint owner can still sue.[143] It seems that one joint owner can only obtain damages for the injury done to his share.[144] Although there is provision for joint ownership of database right,[145] the Database Regulations do not contain any equivalent provisions to those for copyright, performers' property rights and design right. Nevertheless, it is thought that the position is the same.

21–37   **Non-property rights.** There is no provision for joint ownership of these rights.

---

[135] That is, new ss.124A to 124N of the Communications Act 2003.

[136] Communications Act 2003 s.124N.

[137] CDPA 1988 s.173(2). This definition applies for the purposes of the online infringement provisions of the Communications Act (see s.124N) and s.17 of the Digital Economy Act 2010, which provides for "blocking injunctions".

[138] ss.191A(4) and 258(2).

[139] See para.5–173, above.

[140] See para.5–173, above.

[141] See para.5–173 above.

[142] *Experience Hendrix LLC v Purple Haze Records Ltd* [2005] EWHC 249 (Ch); [2005] E.M.L.R. 18. In this case the Judge declined to express a view on the question whether one co-owner of a performer's rights may sue in respect of them without joining his co-owners. The Judge noted that "a respectable body of authority" in the field of copyright allowed such an action by a co-owner and stated that it would be surprising if CPR 19.3 had altered this. The Judge then stated that ss.191I and 191A(4) of the 1988 Act appeared to contemplate all joint owners being parties to the action (para.23). Section 191I provides that an infringement of a performer's property rights is actionable by "the rights owner". Subsection 191A(4) provides that where a performer's property rights (or any aspect of them) is (sic) owned jointly, references in the Act to the rights owner are to all the owners.

[143] As to CPR 19.3, in view of the previous practice there would seem to be no reason why a court should not grant permission so far as necessary. As to *Experience Hendrix*, the Judge did not say why he thought that ss.191I and 191A(4) were any different to ss.96(1) and 173(2) of the 1988 Act, which are in substantially identical terms and it is suggested that there is no material distinction.

[144] See para.5–173, above.

[145] Copyright and Rights in Databases Regulations 1997 (SI 1997/3032) regs.14(6) and 15.

3. RELEVANT DATE OF TITLE

Before the introduction of the Civil Procedure Rules, it was essential that, at the **21–38** date of the issue of the writ, the claimant had a legal or equitable title to the relevant right.[146] A claimant might commence proceedings relying on his equitable title to the copyright and get in the legal title afterwards or join the legal owner; but a claimant with no title at all could not sue, acquire a title by written assignment subsequently and then obtain the permission of the court to amend so as to validate the claim form ex post facto.[147] Accordingly, a writ which was issued before the claimant had acquired any title was incurably bad.[148] The claimant's proper course in such a case was to issue a new writ founded on his new cause of action.[149] Since the introduction of the Civil Procedure Rules, it has been held that the court has a discretion as to whether to allow an amendment which makes good a defect in the claimant's title to sue even though the event relied on as correcting the defect did not arise until after the proceedings were issued, so that in strict law the claimant did not have a cause of action at the time he issued his process. That discretion is to be exercised in accordance with the justice of the case.[150] Where the limitation period has expired before the application to amend, and the amendment involves a "new claim", the claimant will additionally have to satisfy the court that the new claim arises out of the same or substantially the same facts as an existing claim: CPR 17.4(2). In one case (not involving intellectual property rights) a claimant originally relied on an oral assignment of his cause of action but after the limitation period had expired sought to amend to rely on a written assignment which post-dated the issue of the claim form. Permission was granted. It was held that this was a "new claim" but that it arose out of substantially the same facts as the original claim.[151] However, where at the date the proceedings are issued the claimant knows that he has no title, the proceedings are liable to be struck out as an abuse of process and permission to amend will not be granted.[152]

4. WHO MAY BE SUED?

A. COPYRIGHT AND DESIGN RIGHT: PRIMARY INFRINGERS

For copyright and design right purposes, the persons who are primarily liable to **21–39** be sued are individuals and companies who, without the licence of the owner of the right in question, do, or authorise others to do, any one or more of the separate and distinct acts which are restricted by the right in question.[153] Thus, for example, in relation to a published book which is alleged to infringe copyright,

---

[146] *Beloff v Pressdram Ltd* [1973] F.S.R. 33; *Arrowin Ltd v Trimguard (UK) Ltd* [1984] R.P.C. 581.

[147] *Roban Jig & Tool Co Ltd & Elkadart Ltd v Taylor & Others* [1979] F.S.R. 130; *Acorn Computers v MCS Micro Computer Systems* (1984–1985) 57 A.L.R. 389; see also *Nicol v Barranger* [1912–1923] Mac.C.C. 219.

[148] *Belegging-en Exploitatiemaatschappij Lavender BV v Witten Industrial Diamonds Ltd* [1979] F.S.R. 59.

[149] *Form Tubes Ltd v Guinness Brothers Plc* [1989] F.S.R. 41.

[150] See most recently *Pictkthall v Hill Dickinson LLP* [2009] EWCA Civ 943 at para.26 and *Finlan v Eyton Morris Winfield* [2007] EWHC 914 (Ch) at para.46, applying *Hendry v Chartsearch Ltd* [1998] C.L.C. 1382, *Maridive & Oil Services (SAE) v CAN Insurance Company (Europe) Ltd* [2002] EWCA Civ 369 and *Smith v Henniker-Major* [2002] B.C.C. 544 (on appeal [2002] EWCA Civ 762; [2003] Ch. 182).

[151] See *Finlan v Eyton Morris Winfield* [2007] EWHC 914 (Ch) at paras 59 and 66.

[152] *Pickthall v Hill Dickinson LLP* [2009] EWCA Civ 943.

[153] CDPA 1988 ss.16(1) and (2) and 226(1) and (3); doing and authorising the doing are separate acts of infringement: *Ash v Hutchinson* [1936] Ch. 489; *MCA Records Ltd v Charly Records Ltd* [2000] E.M.L.R. 743 at 807.

the author, printer and publisher are all liable to be sued for infringement of copyright, regardless of whether they knew or had reason to believe that the book infringed copyright. A person who has personally committed primary infringements of copyright (and presumably design right) cannot escape personal liability simply because he has committed them in the course of carrying out his duties as an employee or agent or as the director of a company.[154] It is not essential to be able to identify the infringer by name.[155]

B. COPYRIGHT AND DESIGN RIGHT: SECONDARY INFRINGERS

21–40 Persons may also be liable for secondary acts of infringement such as importation and sale of infringing copies.[156] Liability depends on proof of the requisite knowledge or reason to believe. Thus, for example, in order to establish that a retailer of books or records is liable for infringement of copyright by selling or offering for sale books or records, it must be proved that the retailer knew at the relevant time or had reason to believe that the book or record was an infringing copy of the work.[157] The most common way of fixing the retailer with the requisite knowledge is by giving him express notice by letter of the claimant's allegation of infringement.[158] A reasonable time should be allowed for the prospective defendant to investigate the claim.[159] It is thought that as in the case of primary infringements, a person who has personally committed a secondary infringement cannot escape personal liability simply because he has committed it in the course of carrying out his duties as an employee or agent or as the director of a company. Although it is not possible to "authorise" a secondary infringement, a person authorising such an act may be liable as a joint tortfeasor.[160]

C. OTHER RIGHTS: DIRECT INFRINGERS

21–41 For other rights, there is no distinction between primary and secondary infringements and whether it is necessary to prove that the defendant had a particular state of mind depends on the right in question. Some infringements of moral rights depend on a particular state of mind while others do not.[161] For performers' property and non-property rights and the rights of persons having recording rights, the Act sets out various acts which, if committed without the licence of the person entitled to enforce the right, are infringements irrespective of the question of whether the person committing the act knew or had reason to believe that he was infringing.[162] Some infringements of rights in respect of protection measures, rights management information and unauthorised decoders depend on a particu-

---

[154] *C Evans & Sons Ltd v Spritebrand Ltd* [1985] F.S.R. 267 at 271. For when a director may be jointly liable with his company see para.21–52, below.

[155] In *Bloomsbury Publishing Group Ltd v News Group Newspapers Ltd* [2003] 1 W.L.R. 1633; [2003] F.S.R. 45, the claimant knew that copies of a book which it proposed to publish had been offered to the press but had been unable to identify the person concerned. The Court granted an interim injunction against "the person or persons who have offered the publishers of the *Sun*, the *Daily Mail*, and the *Daily Mirror* newspapers a copy of the book *Harry Potter and the Order of the Phoenix* by J.K. Rowling or any part thereof and the person or persons who has or have physical possession of a copy of the said book or any part thereof without the consent of the claimants". See also *Hampshire Waste Services Ltd v Persons Unknown* [2003] EWHC 1738 (Ch) (injunction restraining unnamed persons from entering or remaining without the claimant's consent on named incinerator sites).

[156] See Ch.8, above.

[157] CDPA 1988 s.23.

[158] See para.8–10, above.

[159] See para.8–10, above.

[160] See paras 21–42 et seq., below.

[161] See Ch.11, above.

[162] See Ch.12, above.

lar state or mind and others do not.[163] Again, it is thought that a person who has personally committed an infringement cannot escape personal liability simply because he has committed it in the course of carrying out his duties as an employee or agent or as the director of a company.

D. Joint Tortfeasors

General. In certain circumstances a person may be liable for infringement of copyright by reason of having been a joint tortfeasor. It is often said that this will be the case in two situations. The first is where an infringing act has been committed pursuant to a common design between the actual infringer (who is primarily liable) and some other person, who is therefore liable as a joint infringer. The second is where the infringing act has been procured by another person, who is likewise liable as a joint infringer. It is an open question whether these are distinct torts, or whether they are simply different examples of the kind of factual circumstances which will give rise to joint liability.[164] In *Sabaf SPA v MFI Furniture Centres*,[165] the Court of Appeal stated as follows:

21–42

> "The underlying concept for joint tortfeasance must be that the joint tortfeasor has been so involved in the commission of the tort as to make himself liable for the tort. Unless he has made the infringing act his own, he has not himself committed the tort. That notion seems to us what underlies all the decisions to which we were referred. If there is a common design or concerted action or otherwise a combination to secure the doing of the infringing acts, then each of the combiners has made the act his own and will be liable."[166]

However, in *Fabio Perini SPA v LPC Group Plc*[167] the Court of Appeal stated that it preferred to apply an earlier statement of the law in *Unilever Plc v Gillette (UK) Ltd*[168] to the effect that it was "enough if the parties combined to secure the doing of acts which in the event prove to be infringements".

Common design.[169] If there is a concerted design by two persons to sell goods which they know or have reason to believe infringe copyright, then the parties, who have such a design and execute it, are joint tortfeasors and are both liable for infringement.[170] It is suggested that where the infringement alleged is secondary, so that the claimant has to establish "guilty knowledge", a person without such knowledge cannot be a joint tortfeasor, whether he is the person committing the

21–43

---

[163] See Chs 15 and 16, above.

[164] *MCA Records Inc v Charly Records Ltd* [2002] F.S.R. 26 at para.36.

[165] [2002] EWCA Civ 976; [2003] R.P.C. 14 at para.59.

[166] The issue was not appealed further but Lord Hoffmann approved a test for joint tortfeasance as being whether the acts were done pursuant to a common design so that the secondary party has made the act his own: [2004] UKHL 45; [2005] R.P.C. 10 at para.39 as analysed in *Handi-Craft Company v B Free World Ltd* [2007] EWHC 10 (Pat); [2007] E.C.D.R. 21 at para.188, on appeal but not on this point [2008] EWCA Civ 868.

[167] [2010] EWCA Civ 525 at para.105.

[168] [1989] R.P.C. 583, CA.

[169] In *Unilever Plc v Gillette (UK) Ltd* [1989] R.P.C. 583, where the development of the law is analysed, Mustill L.J. said that the phrases "concerted action" or "agreed on common action" would serve just as well.

[170] *Morton-Norwich Products Inc v Intercen Ltd* [1978] R.P.C. 501; *Ash v Hutchinson* [1936] Ch. 489; *PRS Ltd v Mitchell, etc. Ltd* [1924] 1 K.B. 762; *Ravenscroft v Herbert & Another* [1980] R.P.C. 193; *Cadbury Ltd v Ulmer GmbH.* [1988] F.S.R. 385, *Crystal Glass Industries Ltd v Alwince Products Ltd* [1986] R.P.C. 259 (CA of New Zealand); *CBS Songs Ltd v Amstrad Consumer Electronics Plc* [1988] A.C. 1013; [1988] R.P.C. 567; *Grower v BBC* [1990] F.S.R. 595 at 607–612; *MCA Records Inc v Charly Records Ltd* [2002] F.S.R. 26.

secondary act (in which case there is, of course, no tort) or the other party to the common design. Both must have the requisite degree of knowledge.[171]

In relation to patents, the law was reviewed in *Unilever Plc v Chefaro Proprietaries Ltd*.[172] There must be shown some act in furtherance of the design, not a mere agreement. It is not necessary to show a design to infringe deliberately. It is sufficient to show that the design related to acts which constitute infringement.[173] The mere capacity of a parent company to control a subsidiary does not make the two companies joint tortfeasors. What matters is the extent of control actually exercised by one over the other.[174] The same principles presumably apply to primary infringements of copyright. Provided that an act of infringement is in fact committed in the United Kingdom and it is proved that the defendants had a common design to commit that act, it does not matter whether the agreement which is the basis of such design was made within or outside the jurisdiction, nor does it matter that the defendant himself has not done any act within the jurisdiction which, taken by itself, could be said to amount to a several infringement.[175] It is a case of one tort committed by one of them on behalf of and in concert with the other. If, however, the claimant is suing in respect of the infringement of his foreign copyrights (as he now can in some cases[176]), the court will apply the relevant foreign law of joint tortfeasorship.[177]

21–44   **Procurement.** A person who procures a particular infringement by inducement, incitement or persuasion[178] is jointly and severally liable with the infringer for the damage suffered by the person entitled to sue. This is a form of liability which derives from the general law of tort and is distinct from authorisation, although they are often pleaded in the alternative. Procuring must be distinguished from merely facilitating or assisting, which does not give rise to liability even if the facilitator or assister knows that the acts in question are infringing (see the next paragraph).[179] Nor is there a general duty on a person under the 1988 Act, or at common law, actionable by the copyright owner, to prevent or discourage or warn others against infringement, giving rise to an action in negligence for failing to do so.[180] In general, a claimant needs to prove that an identifiable individual was procured to commit an identifiable infringement.[181] However, the absence of such evidence does not preclude a finding of liability for procuring.[182]

21–45   **Supply of equipment which may be used to infringe.** A person who sells and

---

[171] *Mattel Inc v Tonka Corp.* [1992] F.S.R. 28.

[172] [1994] F.S.R. 135, applying *Mölnycke AB v Procter-Gamble Ltd (No.6)* [1992] 1 W.L.R. 1112; [1992] R.P.C. 21, CA and *Unilever plc v Gillette (UK) Ltd* [1989] R.P.C. 583, CA.

[173] See, to the same effect *Societa Esplosivi Industriali SpA v Ordnance Technologies (UK) Ltd* [2007] EWHC 2875 (Ch); [2008] R.P.C. 12 at paras 83 and 85 (UK unregistered design right).

[174] *Intel Corporation v General Instrument Corporation & Others (No.2)* [1991] R.P.C. 235. See also the summary of the law in *Football Dataco Ltd v Sportradar GmbH* [2010] EWHC 2911(Ch) at para.38.

[175] See *Morton-Norwich Products Inc v Intercen Ltd* [1978] R.P.C. 501 and *Football Dataco Ltd v Sportradar GmbH* [2010] EWHC 2911(Ch) at para.37.

[176] See paras 21–123 et seq., below.

[177] *Coin Controls Ltd v Suzo International (UK) Ltd* [1997] F.S.R. 660.

[178] See *CBS Songs Ltd v Amstrad Comsumer Electronics Plc* [1988] A.C. 1013, per Lord Templeman at 1058.

[179] *Belegging-En Exploitatiemaatschappij Lavender BV v Witten Industrial Diamonds Ltd* [1979] F.S.R. 59; *CBS Songs Ltd v Amstrad Comsumer Electronics Plc* [1988] A.C. 1013; *PLG Research Ltd v Ardon International Ltd* [1993] F.S.R. 197; *Twentieth Century Fox Film Corp v Newzbin Ltd* [2010] EWHC 608(Ch); [2010] E.C.D.R. 8 at para.108. See, also, *Credit Lyonnais Bank Nederland NV v Export Credit Guarantee Dept.* [1998] 1 Lloyd's Rep.19.

[180] *CBS Songs Ltd v Amstrad Comsumer Electronics Plc* [1988] A.C. 1013; [1988] R.P.C. 567; *Paterson Zochonis Ltd v Merfarken Packaging* [1983] F.S.R. 273.

[181] *CBS Songs Ltd v Amstrad Comsumer Electronics Plc* [1988] A.C. 1012; *L'Oréal SA v eBay International AG* [2009] EWHC 1094 (Ch); [2009] R.P.C. 21 at para.359

[182] *Twentieth Century Fox Film Corp v Newzbin Ltd* [2010] EWHC 608 (Ch); [2010] F.S.R. 21 at

advertises to the public a product, such as a tape recorder, which might be used for either lawful or unlawful purposes, does not procure an infringement of copyright by the purchaser or user who makes the decision as to use.[183] He may persuade the person to purchase the product, but does not procure him to use it to infringe copyright. Each must act with the other in the commission of the tort as where two or more persons are closely involved in the design, production and manufacture of the infringing article. There is no common design and, therefore, no joint liability between a manufacturer and purchaser of recording equipment capable of being used to make infringing tapes. The manufacturer has no control over or interest in the equipment after sale.[184] The same applies where a foreign supplier supplies a machine which is used to infringe a patent, even if the supplier helps to install the machine.[185] In the analogous case of *L'Oreal v eBay*[186] the operator of eBay was held not to be liable as a joint tortfeasor for trade mark infringements by sellers: it was not under a duty to prevent infringement; the site had no relevant inbuilt bias towards infringement; and at worst it was guilty of facilitation.

However, a foreign supplier of machines to a UK purchaser which used them to infringe a patent was held to have crossed the line when the supplier's employees, acting under the supply agreement, supervised the assembly and start-up of the machines and the training of the purchaser's staff in their use.[187] Moreover, in the *Newzbin* case, a website operator which indexed and reported on what it knew were infringing copies of large numbers of films so as to enable them to be located, assembled and downloaded in return for a fee was held liable as a joint tortfeasor.[188] The defendant was providing a sophisticated search and indexing facility containing a considerable body of useful information about the films together with a facility for assembling each infringing copy from thousands of smaller files. The facility provided the means of infringement, was created by the defendant and was entirely within its control. A large proportion of the material in question was very likely to be protected by copyright, as the defendant knew. No filtering system had been installed although on the evidence this could easily have been done. The defendant had actively encouraged the making of reports on copyright films. It knowingly guided users toward infringing material and then provided the means to download them. It assisted users to infringe by giving advice in forums. It profited from the infringement. It kept no records of the infringement.[189]

Exceptionally, where copyright is infringed by a public performance of the work or by the playing or showing of the work in public by means of apparatus for playing sound recordings, showing films or receiving visual images by electronic means, those who supplied the apparatus may, if they can be shown to have the appropriate state of mind, be liable as secondary infringers.[190]

Supply of infringing goods, software or infringing material. The mere supply   **21–46**

---

para.110. In that case, however, the claimants were only unable to point to specific infringements because the defendants had not kept records.

[183] *CBS Songs Ltd v Amstrad Consumer Electronics Plc* [1988] A.C. 1013.

[184] *CBS Songs Ltd v Amstrad Consumer Electronics Plc* [1988] A.C. 1013.

[185] *Fabio Perini SPA v LPC Group Plc* [2010] EWCA Civ 525 at para.105.

[186] *L'Oreal SA v eBay International AG* [2009] EWHC 1094(Ch), [2009] E.T.M.R. 53 at paras 346–352.

[187] *Fabio Perini SPA v LPC Group Plc* [2010] EWCA Civ 525 at paras 107–109.

[188] *Twentieth Century Fox Film Corp v Newzbin Ltd* [2010] EWHC 608 (Ch) at paras 110 to 112. Authorisation was also found on the same facts. See para.7–149, above.

[189] See paras 98–101, 111 and 112.

[190] CDPA 1988, s.26(2). An occupier of the premises and the supplier of the sound recording or film may also be liable: ss.26(3) and (4). See above, paras 8–16 et seq., above.

from abroad of infringing goods or software may well not give rise to liability as a joint tortfeasor. Thus in a patent case,[191] a supplier which merely supplied infringing goods to a purchaser which was free to do what it wanted with them was not a joint tortfeasor even though the supplier knew that the goods would be imported into and sold in the United Kingdom and in supplying the goods facilitated the commission of the tort. In another case, software had been supplied by a company located outside the jurisdiction to a company within the jurisdiction which then used it. The supplier had consulted closely with the person to whom it was supplied and incorporated what were held to be infringing copies of code and graphic works. The supplier had no say in whether the software was used or not. It was held that the supplier was not jointly liable for the infringing use of the software within the jurisdiction.[192] By contrast, where material hosted on foreign servers which was alleged to infringe UK copyright and database right was made available to UK customers via hyperlinks in the form of pop-up windows on their computers, there was a "good arguable case" for jurisdiction purposes that the operator of the foreign servers, which had complete control over the content of the pop-up windows, was jointly liable for acts of procuring copying, extraction and re-utilisation by customers.[193]

21–47   **File sharing: accessory liability of the uploader.** It has been held that the individual uploader is primarily liable for the communication of the work in question to the public.[194] An individual downloader is no doubt primarily liable for copying. In addition, however, file sharing can give rise to a number of potential accessory liabilities. It has been suggested that the uploader is liable for "authorising the performance of the infringement" (sic) by the downloader.[195] However, it is a prerequisite of liability for authorisation that the alleged "authoriser" should have or purport to have authority to license the act in question[196] and it seems unlikely that this will be the case. Depending on the facts, the better view may be that the uploader will be liable for the downloader's infringement as a joint tortfeasor. Given the difficulties of enforcing copyright against such individuals, the focus in the United Kingdom is now on the enforcement methods introduced in the Digital Economy Act 2010. This is dealt with elsewhere.[197]

21–48   **File sharing: accessory liability of software providers.** There are no reported UK decisions in relation to claims against the providers of conventional file sharing software. If such claims come to be determined, the courts will no doubt apply the principles which were applied in the *Newzbin* case.[198] The following cases from other jurisdictions are mentioned by way of illustration only. They all concerned "second generation" networks involving a decentralised indexing system where the provider of the software did not host any files or indexes of infringing files and did not regulate or provide access.

In *Buma/Stemra v KaZaA*[199] the Dutch Supreme Court upheld a decision of the Court of Appeals to refuse an injunction to prevent the distribution of KaZaA file-sharing software. The primary grounds for the decision included the fact that

---

[191] *Sabaf SPA v MFI Furniture Centres* [2002] EWCA Civ 976; [2003] R.P.C. 14.
[192] *Navitaire Inc v easyJet Airline Co Ltd (No.2)* [2005] EWHC 282 (Ch); [2006] R.P.C. 4, para.99.
[193] *Football Dataco Ltd v Sportradar GmbH* [2010] EWHC 2911(Ch) at paras 41 and 82. There was also a good arguable case of authorisation. For the "making available" element of this decision, see para.7–135, above.
[194] *Polydor Ltd v Brown* [2005] EWHC 3191(Ch).
[195] *Polydor Ltd v Brown* [2005] EWHC 3191(Ch), para.9.
[196] See para.7–148, above.
[197] See paras 21–301 et seq., below.
[198] See para.21–46, above.
[199] [2004] E.C.D.R. 16.

the use of the software did not depend on any intervention by the provider[200] and that providing the means to infringe did not itself amount to an infringement.[201] It does not appear that there was any evidence that the provider had encouraged any infringement.

By contrast, in *Universal Music Australia Pty Ltd and Others v Sharman License Holdings Ltd and Others*[202] the Federal Court of Australia held providers of the KaZaA software liable for authorising the infringements which resulted from its use. This decision was based on the Australian law of authorising, which is different to that of the United Kingdom. The court took account of findings that the defendants could have reduced the amount of infringement by filtering but had not done so; increasing amounts of file sharing was in the defendants' interest; the defendants knew that copyright infringement was the predominant use of the software; and that the defendants had exhorted or encouraged users of the software to infringe copyright.[203]

In *Metro-Goldwyn-Mayer Studios Inc v Grokster Ltd*[204] the US Supreme Court held that a person who induces an infringement is contributorily liable for it. One who distributes a device with the object of promoting its use to infringe copyright, as shown by clear expression or other affirmative steps taken to foster infringement, is liable for the resulting acts of infringement by third parties. Mere knowledge of potential or actual infringing uses is not enough. Nor are ordinary acts incidental to product distribution (technical support, product updates). The inducement rule premises liability on purposeful, culpable expression and conduct. On the facts, there was clear evidence of unlawful intent: at a time when providers of a previous form of file-sharing was under threat in the courts, the defendant had invited its users to take up the defendant's software by way of replacement; there was no filtering; and revenue depended on advertising which in turn depended on high volume infringing use.[205]

File sharing: position of ISPs. The position of ISPs whose services are used for file-sharing depends in large part on the E-Commerce defences. These are considered below.　　　　　**21–49**

Choice of defendant. The claimant can choose which tortfeasor to sue. He does not have to sue all of them. The defendant cannot dictate whom a claimant shall sue or make the choice for him. The claimant can also choose which joint tortfeasor to enforce his judgment against. It is not an abuse of process to sue the directors of a company personally for copyright infringements in respect of which a judgement has already been obtained against the company.[206] It is permissible to join an alleged joint tortfeasor for the purpose of obtaining disclosure against him.[207]　　　　　**21–50**

E. CONSPIRACY

Parties to a conspiracy to infringe copyright or the other rights covered by this　　**21–51**

---

[200] para.34.

[201] para.41.

[202] [2005] FCA 1242; (2005) 65 I.P.R. 289.

[203] See paras 404 to 411.

[204] 125 S Ct. 2764 (2005).

[205] After Grokster announced that it was closing down, the claimants obtained summary judgment against Streamcast: *Metro-Goldwyn-Mayer Studios Inc v Grokster Ltd* 454F. Supp. 2d. 966 C.D. Cal., 2006.

[206] *Ashley Wilde Group Ltd v Kocak* [2010] EWHC 2284 (Ch) at paras 11–12. For the personal liability of company directors, see para.21–52, below.

[207] *Mölnlycke AB v Procter & Gamble Ltd* [1992] 1 W.L.R. 1112; [1992] R.P.C. 21, CA.

Chapter may also be liable to be sued.[208] A conspiracy to injure by unlawful means is actionable where the claimant proves that he has suffered loss or damage as a result of unlawful action taken pursuant to a combination or agreement between the defendant and another person or persons to injure him by unlawful means. The "unlawful means" must be shown to have caused the loss.[209] The tort is committed if the defendant intends to cause harm to the claimant as an end in itself but also if he intends to inflict harm on the claimant as a means to protect or promote his own economic interests. The fact that the defendant may not wish to harm the claimant is irrelevant. On the other hand, mere foresight that the acts in question may or will probably damage the claimant is not sufficient: the defendant must intend to injure the claimant.[210] Damages for injury to reputation or feelings are not recoverable in an action for conspiracy.[211]

F. Directors and Controlling Shareholders of Companies

21–52   **Basis for liability.** If a company has committed an act of infringement, the directors and controlling shareholders may in certain circumstances be personally liable. Of course, if the director or shareholder himself has actually committed an infringing act (albeit on behalf of the company) he is liable. For example, a director of a music publishing company would be liable if he were to photocopy sheet music without the licence of the copyright owner and it would be no defence to say that he did it on behalf of the company. Also, a director may be liable for having authorised an act of infringement.[212] However, directors of a company are not liable simply because they are directors.[213] Furthermore, in general, a director will not be liable if he does no more than carry out his constitutional role in the governance of the company, that is to say by voting at board meetings.[214] By the same token, a shareholder who does no more than exercise his power of control through the constitutional organs of the company by, for example, voting at general meetings or exercising his power to appoint directors, will not be liable either.[215]

It has been said that a director who has participated in corporate decisions by voting at board meetings and who then carries out the duties entrusted to him by the board should not except in rare circumstances find himself liable as a joint tortfeasor merely on the basis of a common design but that if he commits a tort personally the position is different.[216]

The position is also different if the director or shareholder is exercising control

---

[208] See generally *Clerk & Lindsell on Torts*. What follows is only the barest outline.

[209] *Total Network SL v Her Majesty's Revenue and Customs* [2008] UKHL 19; [2008] 1 A.C. 1174; paras 95–96 and 119.

[210] *OBG Ltd v Allan* [2007] UKHL 21; [2008] 1 A.C. 1 at paras 42–43, 62 and 164–166. These statements were applied to the tort of unlawful means conspiracy by the Court of Appeal in *Meretz Investments NV v ACP Ltd* [2007] EWCA Civ 1303; [2008] Ch. 244. See also *Bank of Tokyo-Mitsubishi UFJ Ltd v Baskan Gida Sanayi Ve Pazarlama AS* [2009] EWHC 1276 (Ch); [2010] Bus. L.R. D1 at para.833.

[211] *Lonhro Plc v Fayed (No.5)* [1993] 1 W.L.R. 1489.

[212] See paras 7–146 et seq., above, for the meaning of "authorise".

[213] *Cropper, etc. Ltd v Cropper* (1906) 23 R.P.C. 388; *Rainham Chemical Works v Belvedere Fish Guano Co Ltd* [1921] 2 A.C. 465 at 488; *Prichard & Constance (Wholesale) Co Ltd v Amata Ltd* (1924) 42 R.P.C. 63; *Evans & Sons Ltd v Spritebrand Ltd* [1985] F.S.R. 267.

[214] *MCA Records Inc v Charly Records Ltd* [2002] F.S.R. 26, para.49. There may be exceptions to this rule, but they will be "rare indeed": ibid. In *Societa Esplosivi Industriali SpA v Ordnance Technologies (UK) Ltd* [2007] EWHC 2875 (Ch); [2008] R.P.C. 12, Lindsay J. referred to doubts about the correctness of *MCA v Charly* (para.78) but ultimately decided that he was bound by it (para.79).

[215] *MCA Records Inc v Charly Records Ltd* [2002] F.S.R. 26, para.49. Again, exceptions will be "rare indeed": ibid.

[216] *Aqua-Aid Incorporated v Growing Technologies Inc* [2009] EWHC 450 (Ch) para.14. If this is intended to mean that a director who procures or authorises an employee to commit an act of in-

otherwise than through the company's constitutional organs. If that is the case, he will be liable as a joint tortfeasor if the circumstances are such that he would be so liable if he were not a director or controlling shareholder.[217] It will not be a defence for him to contend that he could have procured the same acts through the exercise of constitutional control.[218] Thus, for example, if a director exercising control otherwise than through the company's constitutional organs personally orders or procures the commission of an infringing act, he is liable.[219] So too if in some other way he and the company join together in a concerted action to secure that the infringing act is done.[220] It is not essential to establish a knowing, deliberate, wilful participation in the alleged tort. Each case depends on its own particular facts.[221] However, if the company's infringing act is a secondary act of infringement so that so-called "guilty knowledge" is an essential ingredient of the tort, it is likely that the director will only be liable for having ordered or procured that act if he himself had the same "guilty knowledge".[222] Finally, if a company is formed for the express purpose of committing infringing acts, the individuals promoting the company will be personally responsible for the consequences.[223] Similarly, where exceptionally the company is a mere tool or "cat's paw" of the director or other officer.[224]

Procedural issues. The fact that an application to join a director is made because it is feared that damages and costs may be irrecoverable against a corporate defendant is not, by itself, considered a mere tactical ruse, putting unfair pressure on the defendant to settle.[225] As to joinder of directors, see also para.21–50, above.

21–53

---

fringement is not personally liable if he is acting in accordance with the directions of the board, this appears to go beyond what was said in *MCA Records Inc v Charly Records Ltd* [2002] F.S.R. 26.

[217] *MCA Records Inc v Charly Records Ltd* [2002] F.S.R. 26, para.50. See also *Australasian Performing Right Association Ltd v Valamo Pty Ltd* (1990) 18 I.P.R. 216 (Fed. Ct. of Australia) and *Experience Hendrix LLC v Purple Haze Records Ltd* [2005] EWHC 249 (Ch); [2005] E.M.L.R. 18, a case involving rights in performances, where summary judgment was granted against a director who was alleged to have personally arranged for the making and issuing to the public of infringing material.

[218] *MCA Records Inc v Charly Records Ltd* [2002] F.S.R. 26, para.50.

[219] *MCA Records Inc v Charly Records Ltd* [2002] F.S.R. 26, para.50; *British Thomson-Houston Co Ltd v Sterling Accessories Ltd* [1924] 2 Ch. 33; *Betts v De Vitre* 3 Ch. App.441; *Mentmore Manufacturing Co Ltd v National Merchandising Manufacturing Co Inc* (1978) 89 D.L.R. (3d) 195 (Can.).

[220] *MCA Records Inc v Charly Records Ltd* [2002] F.S.R. 26 paras 52 and 53.

[221] *Evans & Sons Ltd v Spritebrand Ltd* [1985] F.S.R. 267; *White Horse Distillers Ltd v Gregson Associates Ltd* [1984] R.P.C. 61 at 90, 91; *A.P. Besson Ltd v Fulleon Ltd* [1986] F.S.R. 319; *Canon Kabushiki Kaisha v Green Cartridge Co Ltd* [1996] F.S.R. 874. In *Societa Esplosivi Industriali SpA v Ordnance Technologies (UK) Ltd* [2007] EWHC 2875 (Ch); [2008] R.P.C. 12; [2008] 2 All E.R. 622, Lindsay J. suggested that in the case of a tort of strict liability (such as primary infringement of copyright or design right) it was sufficient to prove that the defendant intended the acts alleged to comprise the infringement and it was not necessary to prove that the defendant knew that those acts would amount to infringements (paras 83–85). He went on to hold liable for design right infringement the sole shareholder and director of a company who had known and intended that his employees would commit the acts of infringement, had told them that the design right owner did not object to the infringing activity and had taken no steps to prevent the infringement. According to the judge, this amounted to "a facilitation of the breach with a view to there being a breach". The defendant therefore shared a common design with the company that the acts complained of should take place and was personally involved in the infringement to an extent sufficient to render him jointly liable (para.104).

[222] *Evans & Sons Ltd v Spritebrand Ltd* [1985] F.S.R. 267; *MCA Records Inc v Charly Records Ltd* [2002] F.S.R. 26, para.51; and see, by analogy, *Mattel Inc v Tonka Corp.* [1992] F.S.R. 28.

[223] *Rainham Chemical Works v Belvedere Fish Guano Co* [1921] 2 A.C. 465 at 475; *P.S. Johnson & Associates Ltd v Bucko Enterprises Ltd* [1975] 1 N.Z.L.R. 311; *Prichard, etc. Ltd v Amata Ltd* (1925) 42 R.P.C. 63.

[224] *Townsend v Haworth*, reported as a note to *Sykes v Haworth* (1875) 48 L.J. Ch. (NS) 770, at 772.

[225] *PLG Research Ltd v Ardon International Ltd* [1992] F.S.R. 59.

G. VICARIOUS LIABILITY

21–54 Where an employee of a person, firm or company personally commits an act of infringement in the course of his employment, the employer will usually be vicariously liable.[226]

H. PERSONS IN POSSESSION OF INFRINGING COPIES, INFRINGING ARTICLES OR ILLICIT RECORDINGS

21–55 The court has power in certain circumstances,[227] on application by any of the following, namely, a copyright owner, a person having performers' rights (whether property or non-property), a person having recording rights, a design right owner, or an exclusive licensee within the meaning of the Act, to make an order for the delivery up to the applicant or to such other person as the court may direct of infringing copies, illicit recordings or infringing articles (as the case may be). As will be seen,[228] the power is only exercisable against a person who has infringing copies or illicit recordings in his possession, custody or control in the course of a business or infringing articles in his possession, custody or control for commercial purposes. Of course, if such a person knows or has reason to believe that an article in his possession in the course of a business (or, for design right, in his possession for commercial purposes) is an infringing copy, illicit recording or infringing article (as the case may be) he is liable to be sued as a secondary infringer in any event. Even if such a person did not have "guilty knowledge" at the time he acquired the article, it is usually easy to notify him of the relevant facts so that, after a reasonable time to make inquiries, continued possession will amount to a secondary act of infringement. However, it is not a necessary ingredient of the right to apply for an order for delivery up of infringing copies, illicit recordings or infringing articles that the person in possession of the item in question has the "guilty knowledge" necessary to make him a secondary infringer.[229] There is analogous provision in relation to articles specifically designed or adapted for making copies of a particular copyright work, or articles to a particular design (but not copies of a particular illicit recording). In these cases, however, it is necessary to show "guilty knowledge" and, accordingly, that the defendant has infringed the copyright or design right as the case may be. There are analogous provisions in relation to unauthorised decoders and circumvention devices (although in the latter case it must be shown that the defendant intended that the device should be used for the purposes of circumvention).[230] There is no provision of this kind in relation to database right or moral rights. Relevant provisions of the Enforcement Directive and the court's powers to make orders for delivery up in infringement proceedings are dealt with below.[231]

I. SERVICE PROVIDERS

21–56 Specific provision is made for the grant of injunctions against service providers. This is dealt with below.[232]

---

[226] See *Clerk & Lindsell on Torts* 19th edn, Ch.6. See generally *Majrowski v Guy's and St. Thomas' NHS Trust* [2006] UKHL 34; [2007] 1 A.C. 224.

[227] For the detail of these provisions see para.21–216, below.

[228] See para.21–216, below.

[229] *Lagenes Ltd v It's At (UK) Ltd* [1991] F.S.R. 492.

[230] See above at paras 16–35 (decoders) and 15–16 and 15–28 (circumvention devices).

[231] paras 21–214 et seq.

[232] See paras 21–179 et seq., below.

5. RIGHT OF SEIZURE WITHOUT COURT ORDER

Introduction. The 1988 Act confers on the following persons, namely, copyright   **21–57**
owners (including exclusive licensees), persons having performers' rights
(including exclusive licensees in the case of performers' property rights) and
persons having recording rights, the right to seize infringing copies[233] and illicit
recordings[234] without the need for a court order,[235] such as a search order.[236] As to
the exercise of this remedy where an exclusive licensee has concurrent rights, see
para.21–222, below. This remedy was introduced at the instigation of popular
music groups and record companies to deal with, for example, persons selling
infringing T-shirts on the street outside a pop concert venue. In such cases, a
search order is of no use because the trader may well have disappeared by the
time the order has been obtained. Because of the restricted circumstances in
which and the stringent conditions under which this right may be exercised, the
search order will continue to be an important judicial remedy. There is no right of
seizure without a court order in relation to design right, database right or moral
rights. However, the copyright provisions are applied to unauthorised decoders
and circumvention devices (although in the latter case it must be shown that the
defendant intended that the device should be used for the purposes of
circumvention).[237] In what follows, the infringing copy, illicit recording, decoder
or device as the case may be is referred to as an "offending article".

Circumstances in which the right may be exercised. A person having such a   **21–58**
right, or a person authorised by him, may seize an offending article in specified
circumstances. First, the offending article must be found exposed or otherwise
immediately available for sale or hire.[238] Second, the offending article must be
one in respect of which the person entitled to the right would be entitled to apply
for an order for delivery up under s.99 or s.195.[239] Broadly speaking, this means
that the person from whom the article is to be seized must have it in his possession, custody or control in the course of a business and it must have been made
less than six years prior to the seizure. In the case of copyright, performers'
rights, design right and unauthorised decoders, such a person need not be an
infringer himself, as where he does not possess the necessary "guilty knowledge".
In the case of circumvention devices, "guilty knowledge" must be shown. For a
full discussion of the entitlement to an order under s.99 or s.195, see para.21–
216, below.

Conditions for exercise of the right. The right to seize and detain is exercisable   **21–59**
subject to certain conditions:
  (1) Before anything is seized, notice of the time and place of the proposed
       seizure must be given to a local police station.[240]
  (2) Although a person may, for the purpose of exercising the right, enter
       premises to which the public have access, he may not seize anything in
       the possession, custody or control of a person at a permanent or regular

---

[233] For the definition of infringing copy, see para.8–03, above.
[234] For the definition of illicit recording, see para.12–70, above.
[235] CDPA 1988 ss.100 and 196.
[236] See para.21–156, below.
[237] CDPA 1988 ss.298(3) (decoders); 296(4) (circumvention devices in respect of computer
    programs); 296ZD(4) (other circumvention devices).
[238] CDPA 1988 ss.100(1) and 196(1).
[239] ss.100(1) and 196(1).
[240] CDPA 1988 ss.100(2) and 196(2).

place of business of his.[241] "Premises" includes land, buildings, moveable structures, vehicles, vessels, aircraft and hovercraft.[242] This is an important condition which precludes "self help" seizure of goods from shops, offices, warehouses and other similar business premises.

(3) A person exercising the right may not use any force.[243] Like the requirement of prior notification to a local police station, this requirement has been imposed in the interests of maintaining public order.

(4) At the time when anything is seized there must be left at the place where it was seized a notice in the prescribed form containing the prescribed particulars as to the person by whom or on whose authority the seizure is made and the grounds on which it is made.[244] The forms and particulars are prescribed by order of the Secretary of State made by statutory instrument subject to annulment in pursuance of a resolution of either House of Parliament.[245]

(5) The exercise of the right to seize and detain is subject to any decision of the court in the exercise of its jurisdiction to make an order as to the disposal of an offending article.[246] Under that jurisdiction, the court may make an order that offending articles seized or detained shall be forfeited to the copyright owner or destroyed or otherwise dealt with as the court may think fit.[247]

21–60　　**Practical considerations.** It can be seen at once that it might be difficult for a person wanting to exercise this right to know whether or not the conditions were satisfied. For example, whilst in some cases it might be obvious that the articles he intends to seize were made less than six years ago,[248] in others it may well not be. What is meant by the expression "a permanent or regular place of business"? It is suggested that a market trader who runs a market stall every week in the same location has a regular (albeit not permanent) place of business. What if he has no right to a particular location for his stall within the market, but sets up his stall each week according to whatever space is available? Does "place of business" refer to the market generally or to a particular site within the market? It is suggested that the former is more likely to be correct, because the right is designed to catch the fly-by-night trader who disappears off the scene and cannot easily be traced. A market-stall holder can be served with a seizure order if he regularly uses the same market, albeit that the precise location of his stall may change from week to week. Furthermore, what is the position in respect of record fairs, which are held annually at each of three or four different locations around the country? It is suggested that a person who regularly attends each such venue year on year has many "regular places of business" and that the right cannot be exercised at any of those places. Presumably a trader just starting out in business and operating his stall at any such record fair for the first time has no "permanent or regular place of business". In many cases it must be difficult for a person wishing to exercise the right of seizure to know whether or not the trader is trading from his regular place of business. Because of these difficulties and, no doubt, other difficulties which could arise on the particular facts of each individual case, this right is, in practice, used sparingly and only in the most obvious of cases.

---

[241] ss.100(3) and 196(3).
[242] ss.100(5) and 196(5).
[243] ss.100(3) and 196(3).
[244] ss.100(5), (6) and 196(5), (6). See SI 1989/1006, Vol.2.
[245] ibid.
[246] ss.100(1) and 196(1).
[247] Under s.114 or 204 as the case may be; see paras 21–218 et seq., below.
[248] For example, an illicit recording of a performance only given within the previous six years.

The risk of an action for unlawful interference with goods and the possibility of aggravated or exemplary damages in such an action is a deterrent to those contemplating the self-help powers in ss.100 and 196.

6. DEFENCES

It is, of course, always an answer to a claim of infringement that the claimant has failed to establish an essential ingredient of his cause of action. Defendants frequently put in issue (by non-admission) and sometimes deny subsistence and ownership of the relevant right. Copying is often denied or, if the defendant admits to having copied, he sometimes pleads that the part taken was not substantial. General equitable defences such as waiver, estoppel, acquiescence and "clean hands" are often raised.[249] There are, however, several specific points worth noting relevant to defences.

21–61

A. LICENCES AND PERMITTED ACTS

Copyright. Copyright is not infringed if the person who does, or authorises another to do, acts restricted by the copyright has the licence of the copyright owner to do the act in question.[250] A licence from the copyright owner is also a defence to acts which would otherwise be secondary acts of infringement.[251] If the copyright is owned by more than one person jointly, there will be an infringement unless the licence has been obtained from all the joint owners.[252]

21–62

Moral rights. Similarly, moral rights and performers' moral rights are not infringed if the person entitled to the right has consented to the act in question[253] or if the right has been waived.[254]

21–63

Performers' rights. Again, consent is a defence to a claim for infringement of performers' property and non-property rights and of the rights of persons having recording rights.[255] If a performer's property right is owned by more than one person jointly, there will be an infringement unless the consent has been obtained from all the joint owners.[256]

21–64

Design right. Design right is not infringed if the person who does, or authorises another to do, any act which would otherwise be a primary infringement has the licence of the owner to do the act in question[257] or if the owner has licensed an act which would otherwise be a secondary infringement.[258]

21–65

Circumvention of protection measures. Licence or consent is not a specific defence to liability in respect of the circumvention of protection measures. However, it is a defence to an allegation of making or dealing with the means of

21–66

---

[249] Recent cases on acquiescence or estoppel in this field include *Dyson Ltd v Qualtex (UK) Ltd* [2004] EWHC 2981 (Ch); [2005] R.P.C. 19 (defence failed); *Navitaire Inc v easyJet Airline Company* [2004] EWHC 1725 (Ch); [2006] R.P.C. 3 (see para.148—defence failed because there was no reliance on any representation or on the claimant's failure to take steps to enforce copyright); *Brooker v Fisher*(see para.5–220 above); and *JHP Ltd v BBC Worldwide Ltd* [2008] EWHC 757 (Ch); [2008] F.S.R. 29 at para.21 ("licence by estoppel").

[250] CDPA 1988 s.16(2) and see paras 5–198 et seq., above.

[251] ss.22–24 and see para.8–02, above.

[252] s.173(2).

[253] CDPA 1988 ss.87(1) and 205J(1) and see para.11–81, above.

[254] ss.87(2) and 205J(2) and see para.11–82, above.

[255] See para.12–51, above.

[256] CDPA 1988 s.191A(4).

[257] CDPA 1988 s.226(3) and see para.13–122 et seq., above.

[258] s.227(1) and see para.13–122 et seq., above.

circumventing a technical device applied to a computer program or publishing information intended to enable or assist such circumvention that the defendant did not know or have reasonable grounds to believe that it was to be used to make infringing copies.[259] It would seem to follow that it will also be a defence to show that the copies which were intended to be made would not in fact have been infringing, for example because there was a licence to make them. It is also a defence to an allegation of making or dealing with such means to show that any intended removal or circumvention of the technical device was authorised.[260] It is a defence to an allegation of circumvention of technical measures applied to a work other than a computer program to show that the device prevents or restricts acts which are in fact not an infringement of copyright, for example because they are licensed.[261] The same applies to the acts of making or dealing with devices aimed at circumventing such measures.[262]

21–67 **Rights management information.** The existence of authority is a defence to liability for removing or altering rights management information.[263]

21–68 **Unauthorised decoders.** As with liability for the circumvention of protection measures, there is no specific defence of licence or consent to liability in respect of unauthorised decoders. However, it is a defence to an allegation of making or dealing with an unauthorised decoder that the access which it is designed to achieve will in fact be access to which the person in question is entitled.[264]

21–69 **Database right.** The consent of the owner of the right is a defence.[265]

21–70 **Permitted acts.** There are also many acts which may be done without the licence of the rights owner and without infringing his rights. For copyright, they are dealt with in Ch.III of Pt I of the 1988 Act and are described as "Acts Permitted in relation to Copyright Works". For moral rights and performers' moral rights they are set out in the main body of the section of the Act dealing with those rights. For rights in performances they are dealt with in Sch.2 to the 1988 Act. For design right, they are set out Ch.III of Pt III of the 1988 Act. These are not strictly speaking defences, since the Act provides that these acts can be done without infringing the right in question. There are no specific "permitted acts" in respect of the circumvention of protection measures, rights management information or unauthorised decoders apart from a limited exception for liability in respect of the circumvention of protection measures for acts done for the purposes of research into cryptography.[266] A small number of acts may be done without infringing database right. These are set out in the Regulations.[267]

B. Ignorance not Necessarily a Defence

21–71 **Copyright and design right.** Ignorance is no excuse for primary infringement of copyright,[268] and the same is no doubt true of design right. If the defendant has in fact derived his work, either directly or indirectly, from the work in which the

---

[259] CDPA 1988 s.296(1)(b). See paras 15–11 and 15–15, above.

[260] s.296(1)(b)(i). See para.15–13, above.

[261] This follows from the definition of "effective technical measure" in s.296ZF.

[262] See previous fn.

[263] CDPA 1988 s.296ZG(1). See para.15–46, above.

[264] CDPA 1988 s.298(2). See para.16–31, above.

[265] Copyright and Rights in Databases Regulations 1997 (SI 1997/3032) reg.16(1). See para.18–27, above.

[266] CDPA 1988 s.296ZA(2). See para.15–24, above.

[267] Copyright and Rights in Databases Regulations 1997 (SI 1997/3032).

[268] *Mansell v Valley Printing Co* [1908] 2 Ch. 441; *Lee v Simpson* (1847) 3 C.B. 871; *Wittman v Op-*

claimant has rights, the fact that the defendant was unaware that the work he has copied existed (for instance, where he made copies of a play which, unknown to him, had been copied from a novel of which he had no knowledge), or was the claimant's, or was the subject of copyright, affords no defence to the action for primary infringement, although it may affect the remedy.[269] Similarly, it is no defence to liability for primary infringement of copyright or design right that the defendant has relied upon a licence or assignment, which he believed had been granted by the owner of the right, if this is not the case; though, again, it may affect the remedy. Liability for secondary infringement, such as by importation or sale, is, of course, dependent on proof that the defendant knew or had reason to believe that he was dealing in infringing or illicit copies or infringing articles. Plainly "ignorance" is a defence for secondary infringement.

Acts permitted on assumption of expiry of rights. In certain cases, acts which would otherwise infringe the copyright in anonymous or pseudonymous works, films and database right are permitted where it is reasonable to assume that the right has expired. These permitted acts are considered elsewhere.[270]   **21–72**

Other rights. For the other rights covered in this Chapter, there is no distinction between primary and secondary infringements. Whether ignorance will amount to a defence will depend on the provisions establishing the right in question and the facts of the individual case.   **21–73**

C. DEFENCES TO DAMAGES CLAIMS

Introduction. There are a number of different types of defence to claims for damages in respect of the rights covered in this Chapter. In the case of copyright, performers' property rights, design right and database right, a defendant will have such a defence if he can show that he did not know or have reasonable grounds to believe that the relevant right subsisted ("the subsistence defence"). This defence is dealt with in paras 21–75 to 21–82, below. There are then certain specific defences to claims for damages in respect of certain infringements of performers' non-property rights and recording rights (para.21–83, below), design right (para.21–84, below), and rights in respect of protection measures, rights management information and unauthorised decoders (paras 21–85 to 21–86, below). In most cases, these defences are of limited application, both because of their expressed scope and because they are without prejudice to other remedies.   **21–74**

Scope of the subsistence defence. A claimant is not entitled to damages in respect of an infringement of copyright if it is shown that, at the time of the infringement, the defendant did not know, and had no reason to believe, that copyright subsisted in the work to which the action relates.[271] There are similar provisions for performers' property rights,[272] design right[273] and database right.[274]   **21–75**

---

penheim (1884) 27 Ch. D. 260; *Byrne v Statist Co* [1914] 1 K.B. 622; *Sony Music Entertainment (UK) Ltd v Easyinternetcafe Ltd* [2003] F.S.R. 48.

[269] For example, an injunction might well not be granted against an innocent infringer who makes it clear, once he knows the true position, that he does not intend to continue infringing; also, there will be no grounds for an award of additional damages against an innocent infringer and the court may refuse to order an account of profits.

[270] See above at paras 9–170 et seq. (literary, dramatic, musical and artistic works), 9–198 (films) and 18–41 (databases).

[271] CDPA 1988 s.97(1).

[272] s.191J(1).

[273] s.233(1).

[274] The Copyright and Rights in Databases Regulations 1997 (SI 1997/3032) reg.23.

In each case, the onus is on the defendant to establish these matters by evidence.[275] This defence to the damages claim is, however, without prejudice to any other remedy, such as delivery up or an account of profits.[276] This defence to damages claims in copyright cases has existed in similar form since the 1911 Act[277] and the authorities are all under the old law.

21–76   **The subsistence defence: application to secondary infringers of copyright and design right.** It is difficult to see how this defence could apply to a secondary infringer. Anyone who knows or has reason to believe that he is dealing in infringing copies must know or have reason to believe that copyright subsists, because that is an essential part of the meaning of "infringing copies". He cannot, therefore, be said to have no reason to believe that copyright subsists in the work.

21–77   **The subsistence defence: direct infringers.** When can a direct infringer have no reason to believe that the relevant rights subsisted? It is suggested that a defendant can only have no reason to believe that the relevant rights subsist if he has grounds for thinking that (a) the term of protection has run out; or (b) the work, recording, design or database is of such a character that it ought not to be a subject of protection; or (c) possibly, because the work, recording, design or database is a foreign work.

21–78   **The subsistence defence: belief that term has run out.** In a copyright case, if an infringer were to ascertain that the author of the original work was born 170 years ago but, after due inquiry, he could not discover the date of the author's death, he might have reason to believe that the copyright had run out. Or, again, if a copyright work bearing no author's or publisher's name, is pronounced by experts to be the work of A, who died 80 years ago, whereas it is, in fact, the work of B, who died only 60 years ago, this, perhaps, is another case in which this section might be successfully pleaded.[278] Different considerations apply in the case of performers' property rights, design right and database right because the term of these rights does not depend on when the author died but on the date when the protected material came into being or was publicly released. Where such a date appears on what reasonably appears to be a legitimate version, a defendant will presumably be able to rely on that date as a basis for a reasonable belief that the rights had run out. Where, however, no such date appears, a defendant will be expected to have made all reasonable enquiries as to the date the protected material came into being or was released. Whether he has done so will be a question of fact. It is suggested that no person has a right to assume, without inquiry, that a copyright work published anonymously is not the subject of rights.

21–79   **The subsistence defence: belief that material not entitled to protection.** If the defendant contends that he did not think the material in question was of a character which ought to be entitled to protection, upon the court holding the contrary, the defendant may have some difficulty in convincing the court that he had no reason for anticipating the court's decision.[279] Of course, it might be different if the defendant's belief was based upon a decision of the court which was subsequently overruled.

---

[275] *James Arnold & Co Ltd v Miafern Ltd* [1980] R.P.C. 397 at 410.

[276] s.97(1).

[277] 1911 Act s.8 and 1956 Act s.17(2).

[278] See *J Whitaker & Sons Ltd v Publishers' Circular Ltd* [1946–1947] Mac.C.C. 10.

[279] See *Pytram Ltd v Models, etc. Ltd* [1930] 1 Ch. 639, where a mistaken view of the construction of s.22 of the 1911 Act was stated by Clauson J. not to afford a defence under s.8 of that Act; he later held that, in fact, the view was not mistaken so that it was unnecessary to rely upon s.8 of that Act. See also *Field v Lemaire* (1939) 4 D.L.R. 561.

The subsistence defence: foreign works, performances, designs and databases. In respect of copyright, if the work was a foreign work, it is likely that it would be entitled to protection in this country, either because the 1988 Act had been extended or applied to the works of such countries by Order in Council, or because the work was simultaneously published in this country. It is thought that, while a defendant would not be able to rely on ignorance of an Order in Council, he might, depending on the precise facts, be able to say that he was unaware of simultaneous publication. Similarly, it is likely that a foreign performance would be entitled to protection in this country, either because it took place in another Member State or another country designated by Order in Council as enjoying reciprocal protection or because the performer was a citizen or subject of or resident in another Member State or another such country. A defendant is more likely to be able to rely on the defence in respect of foreign designs and databases, in respect of which there is less reciprocal protection.

21–80

The subsistence defence: mistake as to identity of owner of right or existence of the protected material. The defence does not apply if the defendant publishes a copyright work under a wrong impression as to who is the copyright owner.[280] In one case a publisher published the work of X which, unknown to the publisher, contained large extracts from the work of Y, whose identity was well known to the publisher. The publisher was unable to contend successfully that he did not know and had no reason to believe copyright did not subsist in Y's work. All he could urge was that he did not believe that X had copied from Y's work, and that was held not to bring him within the section.[281] Nor, it is suggested, is ignorance of the existence of the copyright work (in a case of indirect copying),[282] a good basis for alleging ignorance that copyright subsisted in the work.

21–81

The subsistence defence: other considerations. In deciding whether a defendant did not know and had no reason to believe that copyright subsisted in a work, the court will take into account all the relevant circumstances, for example: the nature of the claimant's work, the fact that the claimant's name was or was not printed on it, the fact that the work bore or did not bear a claim to copyright in it,[283] any legal advice which the defendant received[284] and the fact that there may have been a long-standing practice of copying works of the character of the claimant's work without complaint. A general practice of copying would not, however, provide a defence to liability,[285] as distinct from a defence to damages.

21–82

Defence to damages for infringement of performers' non-property rights and recording rights. A totally separate defence to a claim for damages is available to a person charged with contravening s.182(1) (recording or broadcasting a live performance without the consent of the performer) or s.186(1) (making a recording of a performance without the consent of the performer or person having

21–83

---

[280] *Byrne v Statist Co* [1914] 1 K.B. 622. See also *Gribble v Manitoba Free Press Ltd* [1932] 1 D.L.R. 169.
[281] *John Lane The Bodley Head Ltd v Associated Newspapers Ltd* [1936] 1 K.B. 715.
[282] See para.7–15, above.
[283] *Swinstead v R. Underwood & Sons* [1923–1928] Mac.C.C. 39 (copyright in a tombstone; defendant not liable for infringement damages).
[284] A defence based on erroneous advice allegedly given by a patent agent failed in *AP Besson v Fulleon Ltd* [1986] F.S.R. 319 because the defendant's evidence as to the question which was asked and the advice given was insufficiently specific.
[285] *Walter v Steinkopff* [1892] 3 Ch. 489; *Banier v News Group Newspapers Limited* [1997] F.S.R. 812 (this case is irrelevant for the purposes of a s.97(1) defence, but mentioned here as it establishes the proposition that the apparent wide-spread practice amongst newspapers of publishing photographs without a licence and then seeking to obtain a licence retrospectively, provides no defence to liability).

recording rights) of the 1988 Act.[286] No damages shall be awarded against a defendant who shows that at the time of the infringement he believed on reasonable grounds that consent had been given.

21-84   Defence to damages for infringement of unregistered United Kingdom design right. Where a person obtains a licence of right in circumstances where the identity of the design right owner is unknown and it is subsequently established that a licence was not available as of right, the licensee is not liable in damages for, or for an account of profits in respect of, anything done before he was aware of any claim by the design right owner that a licence was not available.[287] Although "innocent" infringers of registered designs have a defence to a claim for damages,[288] this defence is not available to infringers of registered or unregistered Community designs.[289]

21-85   Defence to damages: protection measures and rights management information. In general, the persons with these rights have the same rights against those who breach their rights as a copyright owner has in respect of infringement of copyright.[290] It follows that s.97(1) of the 1988 Act should apply so that a defendant would have a defence to a claim for damages where he could show that he did not know and had no reason to believe that the relevant right (copyright, publication right, rights in performances or database right as the case might be) subsisted in the work, performance or database which was protected by the protection measure or with which the rights management information was associated (as the case might be).[291] This appears to be the case in relation to claims to enforce rights in respect of protection measures for computer programs, claims in respect of the acts of circumventing protection measures for works or protected material other than computer programs and all claims in respect of rights management information. However, where proceedings are brought in respect of devices and services designed to circumvent protection measures other than those applied to computer programs, the defence is made out if the defendant shows that he did not know or have reason to believe that his acts enabled or facilitated an infringement of the copyright or other protected material in question.[292] This is likely to be a much easier test to satisfy than that applicable to the other claims mentioned in this paragraph.

21-86   Defence to damages: unauthorised decoders. In proceedings in respect of unauthorised decoders, it is a defence to a claim for damages that the defendant did not know or have reason to believe that his acts infringed the rights conferred by s.298 of the 1988 Act.[293]

D. WHEN ABSENCE OF DAMAGE IS A DEFENCE

21-87   In a copyright case, the fact that the infringement has not caused the claimant copyright owner any damage is irrelevant to liability for infringement. Copyright is a right of property and a copyright owner is entitled to take legal proceedings for the protection of that property, even though he has not suffered or cannot

---

[286] CDPA 1988 ss.182(3) and 186(2).
[287] CDPA 1988 s.248(4).
[288] Under Registered Designs Act 1949 s.24B.
[289] *J Choo Jersey Ltd v Towerstone Ltd* [2008] EWHC 346 (Ch); [2008] F.S.R. 19 at para.37.
[290] CDPA 1988 ss.296(2), 296ZA(3), 296ZD(2) and 296ZG(3).
[291] If this were not the intention s.296ZD(7) would not refer to "section 97(1) ... as it applies to proceedings for infringement of the rights conferred by this section".
[292] s.296ZD(7).
[293] CDPA 1988 s.298(5).

prove actual loss or damage.[294] The same is presumably true of performers' property rights, design right and database right. Furthermore, damage does not appear to be essential to the causes of action under the provisions as to protection measures, rights management information and unauthorised decoders. Nevertheless, a claimant who commences proceedings without having suffered damage does so at his own risk as to costs. By contrast, infringements of moral rights, performers' non-property rights and the rights of persons having recording rights are treated as breaches of statutory duty,[295] where damage is usually an essential ingredient of the tort.[296]

E. UNDERTAKING TO TAKE LICENCE OF RIGHT

Introduction. The 1988 Act imposes restrictions on the availability of certain   **21–88** remedies in cases where an undertaking is given by a defendant to infringement proceedings to take a licence of right in respect of copyright, performers' property rights, design right and database right.[297]

When the restrictions apply. The restrictions apply where[298]:   **21–89**
  (1) There are in existence proceedings for infringement of copyright, performers' property rights, design right or database right, as the case may be;
  (2) In respect of that copyright, performer's property right, design right or database right a licence is available as of right under s.144 or para.19 of Sch.1 to the 1988 Act (copyright),[299] para.17 of Sch.2A to the 1988 Act (performers' property rights),[300] ss.237 or 238 of the 1988 Act (design right),[301] or para.15(1) of Sch.2 to the Copyright and Rights in Databases Regulations 1996[302]; and
  (3) The defendant to the proceedings undertakes to take a licence on such terms as may be agreed or, in default of agreement, settled by the Copyright Tribunal (in the case of copyright, performers' property rights or database right) or comptroller (in the case of design right).

Procedure. The defendant may give the undertaking at any time before final or-   **21–90** der in the proceedings and he may give it without any admission of liability.[303] The defendant is therefore entitled to continue to contest the action both on grounds of liability for infringement and quantum. The effect of the defendant giving the undertaking is as follows: first, the statutory provisions provide that no injunction shall be granted against him.[304] However, it has been held that where there are doubts as to the financial ability of the party giving the undertaking to comply with its terms, it is necessary for that party to show that the undertaking is one which he can reasonably be expected to honour.[305] Second, no order for delivery up shall be made under ss.99, 195 or 230 of the 1988 Act (as the case

---

[294] *Weatherby & Sons v International Horse Agency and Exchange Ltd* [1910] 2 Ch. 297; *Hawkes & Son (London) Ltd v Paramount Film Service Ltd* [1934] Ch. 593, at 603, 608.
[295] CDPA 1988 ss.103(1) and 194.
[296] See generally, *Clerk & Lindsell on Torts*.
[297] CDPA 1988 ss.98, 191K and 239. Copyright and Rights in Databases Regulations 1997 (SI 1997/3032) reg.23, applying s.98 to database right.
[298] CDPA 1988 ss.98(1), 191K(1) and 239(1).
[299] See para.28–54, below.
[300] See para.28–54, below.
[301] See paras 13–127 and 13–128 et seq., above.
[302] SI 1997/3032. See para.28–54, below.
[303] CDPA 1988 ss.98(2), 191K(2) and 239(2).
[304] ss.98(1)(a), 191K(1)(a) and 239(1)(a).
[305] *Dyrlund Smith A/S v Turverville Smith Ltd* [1998] F.S.R. 774, CA. It is not clear how this approach can be reconciled with the clear terms of the sections.

may be).[306] Third, the amount recoverable against the defendant by way of damages or on an account of profits shall not exceed double the amount which would have been payable by him as licensee if such a licence on those terms had been granted before the earliest infringement.[307] The giving of the undertaking thus operates to provide a ceiling to the amount of payment which the defendant is liable to make to the claimant for infringement. In a design right case, an undertaking may be given even though the design right has expired by the time it is offered.[308]

21–91   **Prior infringements.** These provisions do not affect the remedies available in respect of an infringement committed before the relevant licence of right was available.[309]

F. INNOCENTLY ACQUIRED ILLICIT RECORDINGS AND INFRINGING ARTICLES

21–92   There is a "remedy" defence to the secondary acts of infringement contained in s.184(1) (infringement of performers' rights by importing, possessing or dealing with illicit recordings) and s.188(1) (infringement of recording rights by importing, possessing or dealing with illicit recordings). In subs.(2) of those sections it is provided that, where the defendant shows that the illicit recording was innocently acquired by him or by a predecessor in title of his, the only remedy available against him in respect of the infringement is damages not exceeding a reasonable payment in respect of the act complained of. "Innocently acquired" means that the person acquiring the recording did not know and had no reason to believe that it was an illicit recording.[310] There is a similar provision in the case of secondary infringement of design right.[311]

G. PUBLIC INTEREST

21–93   **Introduction.** There has long been recognised a defence to a claim for copyright infringement based on the fact that the immorality or similar impropriety of the claimant's work itself is such as to prevent its enforcement. That defence is dealt with elsewhere.[312] Further, since 1972, the courts have also recognised a more general defence of public interest to claims for copyright infringement.[313] Although this defence was not expressly referred to in the 1956 Act, subs.171(3) of

---

[306] ss.98(1)(b), 191K(1)(b) and 239(1)(b). There is no provision for statutory delivery up in respect of database right.

[307] ss.98(1)(c), 191K(1)(c) and 239(1)(c).

[308] *Ultraframe (UK) Ltd v Eurocell Building Plastics Ltd* [2005] EWCA Civ 761; [2005] R.P.C. 36.

[309] CDPA 1988 ss.98(3), 191K(3) and 239(3).

[310] CDPA 1988 ss.184(3) and 188(3).

[311] s.233(2)—the expression used in this sub-section is "not exceeding a reasonable royalty in respect of the act complained of". Because s.233(2) refers to reason to believe and not to the defendant's actual belief, the test is objective: *Badge Sales v PMS International Group Ltd* [2006] F.S.R. 1.

[312] See paras 3–304 et seq., above.

[313] See *Beloff v Pressdram Ltd* [1973] F.S.R. 33; *Lion Laboratories Ltd v Evans* [1985] Q.B. 526; *Church of Scientology of California v Miller, The Times*, October 23, 1987; *Attorney-General v Guardian Newspapers (No.2)* [1990] 1 A.C. 109; [1989] 2 F.S.R. 181; *Beggars Banquet Records Ltd v Carlton Television Ltd* [1993] E.M.L.R. 349; *ZYX Music Gmbh v King* [1995] E.M.L.R. 281; [1995] F.S.R. 566; *PCR Ltd v Dow Jones Telerate Ltd* [1998] F.S.R. 170; *Service Corp. International Plc v Channel Four Television Corp., The Independent* [1999] E.M.L.R. 83; *Ashdown v Telegraph Group Ltd* [2001] EWCA Civ 1142; [2002] Ch. 149; [2002] R.P.C. 5 (the leading case); and *HRH The Prince of Wales v Associated Newspapers Ltd* [2006] EWHC 522(Ch); [2006] E.C.D.R. 20 . The defence has been recognised in Australia: *Acohs v RA Bashford* (1997) 37 I.P.R. 542. See also *Aztech Systems Pte Ltd v Creative Technology Ltd* [1996] F.S.R. 54 (High Ct of Singapore), where the public interest was a factor taken into account in considering a fair dealing defence and the Dutch case *Church of Spiritual Technology, Religious*

the 1988 Act provides that nothing in Pt I of the Act (which concerns copyright) affects any rule of law preventing or restricting the enforcement of copyright on grounds of public interest or otherwise. Even before the Human Rights Act 1998 came into force, this more general defence was held to extend not only to cases where the defendant had infringed the claimant's copyright in order to reveal some form of impropriety on the part of the claimant, but also to cases where disclosure was otherwise in the public interest.[314] The passing of the Human Rights Act 1998 has given the defence new definition and accordingly, the authorities decided before it came into force must be approached with caution.[315] There is no equivalent to subs.171(3) for the other rights considered in this Chapter. Nevertheless, the existence of a public interest in disclosure may well give rise to a defence to injunctive relief in respect of such claims.[316]

Tension between copyright and freedom of expression. Copyright is a prop- **21–94** erty right and it has been held that in general a copyright owner is not obliged to justify its exercise. Accordingly, a copyright owner does not need to demonstrate an intention to exploit the work in question as a condition of obtaining relief and is entitled to assert copyright in order to maintain privacy in the work.[317] Never- theless, where the infringement at issue involves a disclosure of information which was not previously in the public domain, a fundamental tension may arise between the copyright owner's right to peaceful enjoyment of his property on the one hand and the defendant's right to free expression on the other. Both these rights are enshrined in the European Convention on Human Rights.[318]

In *Ashdown v Telegraph Group Ltd*,[319] the Court of Appeal held that the right to free expression will only "trump" the copyright owner's right to peaceful enjoyment of his property where the infringement in question is actually neces- sary in the public interest.[320] As the Court of Appeal pointed out, this will not usually be the case.[321] For example, the information conveyed by a literary work may well be capable of being disclosed without there being any need to reproduce the actual words in which that information was expressed.[322] On the other hand, in some cases some verbatim reproduction will be necessary, for example in or- der to demonstrate the authenticity of the document in question.[323] Accordingly, the court must look closely at the facts of each case.[324]

First solution: refusal of injunction. It will usually be sufficient in order to give **21–95**

Technology Center, New Era Publications International APS v Dataweb B.V. [2004] E.C.D.R. 25 (publication of extracts from texts on the internet in order to warn people about alleged dangers of Scientology: no copyright infringement).

[314] See *Lion Laboratories Ltd v Evans* [1985] Q.B. 526, as explained in *Ashdown v Telegraph Group Ltd* [2001] EWCA Civ 1142; [2000] R.P.C. 604, para.58, not following dicta of the majority in *Hyde Park Residence Ltd v Yelland* [2001] Ch. 143; and *PCR Ltd v Dow Jones Telerate Ltd* [1998] F.S.R. 170 at 187 (Lloyd J.).

[315] For a discussion, see *Copinger* 14th edn (para.22–48).

[316] See para.21–172, below.

[317] *HRH The Prince of Wales v Associated Newspapers Ltd* [2006] EWHC 522 (Ch) at para.183. The issue did not arise on appeal, but the contrary argument was described as "interesting and novel": [2006] EWCA Civ 1776; [2008] Ch. 57 at para.82.

[318] See art.1 of the First Protocol and art.10 respectively.

[319] [2001] EWCA Civ 1142; [2002] Ch. 149; [2002] R.P.C. 5.

[320] *Ashdown* paras 43, 59, 81.

[321] *Ashdown* paras 39 and 59.

[322] In *HRH The Prince of Wales v Associated Newspapers Ltd* [2006] EWHC 522 (Ch), Blackburne J. accepted a submission that the public interest must be greater to justify the use of the form of the words appearing in the copyright work than to justify the use of the information contained in the work. This point did not arise on the appeal: [2006] EWCA Civ 1776.

[323] On the facts of *Ashdown*, the Court of Appeal held that the extensive reproduction of an 8-page minute was unjustified because the publication of "one or two extracts" would have sufficed to demonstrate the authenticity of the minute in question: see para.59.

[324] *Ashdown* para.45.

effect to the right of freedom of expression for the court to refuse as a matter of discretion to grant the claimant copyright owner injunctive relief, leaving the copyright owner to his remedies by way of damages or an account of profits.[325] This is not an application of the public interest defence, but rather an application of the 1988 Act in a way which accommodates the right of freedom of expression.[326] As the Court of Appeal put it: "freedom of expression should not normally carry with it the right to make free use of another's work".[327]

21–96   **Second solution: public interest defence.** In *Ashdown*, the Court of Appeal went on to hold that in the rare case where it is in the public interest that the copyright work should be reproduced without any sanction, this is permissible under the public interest defence provided by subs.171(3).[328] This follows from the fact that this defence is not limited to cases where the defendant has infringed the claimant's copyright in order to reveal some form of impropriety and in fact "the circumstances in which public interest may override copyright are not capable of precise categorisation or definition".[329] The Court of Appeal stated that a refusal to grant an injunction would "usually" be sufficient, because where a newspaper considered it necessary to copy the exact words of another there was no reason in principle why it should not indemnify the author for any financial loss suffered or account to him for any profit made.[330] However, where the defendant is not a newspaper, it is not at all clear from the Ashdown decision in what circumstances the court is likely to consider it sufficient for the claimant to be refused injunctive relief as opposed to being deprived of his other remedies by the application of the public interest defence. Presumably much will depend on the nature of the work in question and the defendant's financial circumstances. For example, where a notional royalty is likely to be very high and the defendant is a person of limited means, it may be appropriate to apply the full public interest defence and deprive the claimant of his right to financial compensation. The opposite result may occur where a notional royalty would be low but the defendant, however impoverished, stands to make a considerable profit from the disclosure.

21–97   **Other cases involving claims of public interest.** In *Grisbrook v MGN Ltd*[331] it was alleged that the defendant newspaper publisher had infringed a freelance photographer's copyright in photographs by making them available on back number websites. The defendant sought to rely on art.10 on the basis that it was making the back numbers available to the public. This argument was rejected on the grounds that Parliament had already made extensive provision for such material to be made available to the public in prescribed libraries and that the back numbers were available at the British Library and other deposit libraries.[332] In *Unilever Plc v Griffin*,[333] the claimant sought to restrain the defendant from using a picture of a jar of Marmite in a party political election political broadcast to be broadcast by the British National Party. On an application for an interim injunction, the Judge suggested that the public interest test was too narrow to assist

---

[325] *Ashdown v Telegraph Group Ltd* [2001] EWCA Civ 1142; [2002] Ch. 149; [2002] R.P.C. 5, para.46. For these remedies, see below at paras 21–193 et seq. and 21–209 et seq., respectively.
[326] *Ashdown* paras 45–47.
[327] *Ashdown* para.46.
[328] *Ashdown v Telegraph Group Ltd* [2001] EWCA Civ 1142; [2002] Ch. 149; [2002] R.P.C. 5, para.47.
[329] *Ashdown* para.58, not following dicta of the majority in *Hyde Park Residence Ltd v Yelland* [2001] Ch. 143; [2000] R.P.C. 604.
[330] *Ashdown* para.58.
[331] [2009] EWHC 2520 (Ch).
[332] See at para.71.
[333] [2010] EWHC 899 (Ch); [2010] F.S.R. 33 at para.18.

defendants in a case of that type but that there might be scope for further development, particularly in a political context of that type.

Related defences. Where public interest issues arise, defendants frequently seek   **21–98**
to rely on one of the permitted acts. In particular, in a freedom of expression case,
a defendant may, depending on the facts, be able to rely on the defence of fair
dealing for the purposes of reporting current events or (although this is less likely)
for the purposes of criticism or review.[334] Even if these defences are not available, a defendant may be able to resist injunctive relief on the grounds that the
claimant does not come to the court with clean hands.

Interim relief. The principles governing the grant of interim injunctions where   **21–99**
the right to freedom of expression is engaged are discussed below (para.21–139).

H. Use in Electronic Networks: Mere Conduit, Caching and Hosting

(i) Introduction

Introduction.[335] The Electronic Commerce, or E-Commerce, Directive[336]   **21–100**
provides, amongst other things, for "horizontal" exclusions of the liabilities of
service providers which may arise out of the transmission and storage of information in their electronic networks. The exclusions are horizontal in the sense
that they apply to liabilities of all kinds and thus not just in respect of infringements of copyright or other intellectual property rights. The underlying rationale
is that exposure to such claims would have a chilling effect on the functioning of
networks. The effect of the Directive is that, subject to various safeguards, any
"liability" of a service provider in respect of the activities of "mere conduit",
"caching" or "hosting" of information is to be exempted, while retaining the possibility of their being subject to injunctive relief. All these acts may involve the
transient or permanent reproduction of material in computer memory. Where
copies made in this way are temporary, they may come within the exception
provided for by s.28A of the 1988 Act, provided they are "transient or incidental",
and their making is "an integral and essential part of a technological process" and
for the sole purpose of enabling "a transmission of a work in a network between
third parties by an intermediary". This provision is discussed elsewhere.[337]
Otherwise, however, service providers will have to rely on the E-Commerce
Directive, which was implemented in the United Kingdom with effect from
August 21, 2002, by the Electronic Commerce (EC Directive) Regulations
2002.[338]

The aim of the E-Commerce Directive. Recital 42 to the E-Commerce Direc-   **21–101**
tive provides that:

> "The exemptions from liability ... cover only cases where the activity of the
> service provider is limited to the technical process of operating and giving
> access to a communication network over which information made available
> by third parties is transmitted or temporarily stored, for the sole purpose of

---

[334] See above at paras 9–49 et seq. and 9–40 et seq., respectively.
[335] See, generally, Strachan: "The Internet of Tomorrow: The New-Old Communications Tool of
Control" [2004] E.I.P.R. 123.
[336] Directive 2000/31/EC [2000] OJ L178/1. See Vol.2 H7.
[337] See para.9–20, above.
[338] SI 2002/2013. See Vol.2 B10.i. Reg.16, which concerns "Stop Now Orders" came into force on
October 23, 2002.

making the transmission more efficient; this activity is of a mere technical, automatic and passive nature, which implies that the information society service provider has neither knowledge of nor control over the information which is transmitted or stored".

On its face this appears to be a general statement in relation to all three defences. However, it has been pointed out that if this is so, the recital does not sit easily with the hosting defence, not only because the defence is not confined to cases where the storage is merely temporary but also because the defence can be relied on even if the service provider has knowledge of the information (provided he does not know that the information is "unlawful").[339]

21–102 **Review.** The Directive required the Commission to review its application by July 17, 2003.[340] That review took place.[341] The Commission concluded that in general this part of the Directive had been satisfactorily implemented. It proposed to continue to monitor and analyse new developments and to examine any future need to adapt the present framework, including whether there was a need for further exemptions from liability, for example in relation to hyperlinks and search engines.[342]

21–103 **The Regulations: general.** The Regulations closely follow the provisions of the Directive. Their effect is to provide a defence to claims for damages or any other kind of pecuniary remedy in defined situations. Technically the acts in question remain infringements and so any copies made in the process which, the regulations apart, would be infringing copies, remain so. The consequences so far as criminal proceedings are concerned are dealt with elsewhere.[343] Nothing in the regulations is to prevent a person agreeing contractual terms which differ from the terms of the regulations.[344] Neither the Directive nor the Regulations specifically deal with the position of providers of such services as hyperlinks, location tools or content aggregation. On June 8, 2005, the Government published a consultation on whether the exemptions should be extended to such providers. The Government concluded that there was insufficient evidence to justify such an extension.[345]

21–104 **Key definitions.** The Regulations and Directive contain certain key definitions, namely a "service provider", "information society services" and a "recipient of the service." A "service provider" means any person providing an information society service.[346] The term "information society service" is defined in the same way as in s.297A of the 1988 Act (which concerns unauthorised decoders) and is considered elsewhere.[347] "Recipient of the service" is defined to mean any person who, for professional ends or otherwise, uses an information society service, in particular for the purposes of seeking information or making it accessible.[348] This effectively repeats the wording of the Directive,[349] which also makes it clear that a "person" includes any natural or legal person. This definition emphasises that "recipient" means a recipient of the service provider's service, not just of the in-

---

[339] *Kaschke v Gray* [2010] EWHC 690 (QB) paras 44 to 46 in which, however, no solution is suggested to this conundrum.
[340] E-Commerce Directive 2000/31 art.21(1).
[341] COM 2003 (702) final.
[342] COM 2003(702), para.4.6.
[343] See para.22–25, below.
[344] SI 2002/2013 reg.20(1).
[345] See *http://www.berr.gov.uk/files/file35905.pdf* [Accessed October 14, 2010].
[346] reg.2(1), repeating art.2(b) of the Directive.
[347] See paras 16–16 et seq., above.
[348] SI 2002/2013, reg.2(1).
[349] E-Commerce Directive 2000/31 art.2(d).

formation supplied, and it thus includes the third parties who provide the information.

(ii) The defence of mere conduit

The defence of mere conduit. Regulation 17(1) provides that where an informa- **21–105**
tion society service is provided which consists of the transmission in a communication network of information provided by a recipient of the service or the provision of access to a communication network, the service provider shall not be liable for damages or for any other pecuniary remedy or for any criminal sanction as a result of that transmission where the service provider (a) did not initiate the transmission; (b) did not select the receiver of the transmission; and (c) did not select or modify the information contained in the transmission. This follows the wording of art.12(1). These acts of transmission and of provision of access are to include the automatic, intermediate and transient storage of the information transmitted where: (a) this takes place for the sole purpose of carrying out the transmission in the communication network, and (b) the information is not stored for any period longer than is reasonably necessary for the transmission (see reg.17(2)). Again, this follows the wording of art.12(2).

The Directive. Regulation 17 and art.12 must be read in conjunction with the **21–106**
recitals to the Directive. Recital 43 states that a service provider can benefit from the exemptions for "mere conduit" (and for "caching") when it is "in no way involved" with the information transmitted. The recital adds that this is conditional, among other things, on the service provider not modifying the information that it transmits, although this does not include manipulations of a technical nature which take place in the course of the transmission, since they do not alter the "integrity" of the information contained in the transmission. Recital 44 adds that a service provider who deliberately collaborates with one of the recipients of its service in order to undertake illegal acts goes beyond the activities of "mere conduit" (or "caching") and as a result cannot benefit from the liability exemptions. This provision is not repeated in the Regulations but no doubt they must be interpreted consistently with this recital.

The operation of the defence. The intention is therefore to provide a defence to **21–107**
any pecuniary claim (or to any criminal charge) in the case of such passive and intermediate acts of a service provider. The defence extends to all acts of the service provider which would otherwise be infringing, and thus not only to the transient reproduction of works in the service provider's servers but also to possession of infringing copies of the information on its servers and acts of transmission of works by it (for example by acts which would infringe the communication and making available to the public rights). As already noted, a service provider may be liable as a joint tortfeasor where it has deliberately collaborated with a third party to commit infringing acts but otherwise, provided the conditions in the regulation are satisfied, any pecuniary liability of the service provider which might otherwise arise in respect of the infringing acts of a third party is excluded. It appears that a service provider is not liable if it suspects or even knows that its networks are being used as a conduit for infringing material, unless perhaps the making available of its networks in such circumstances could be construed as deliberate collaboration. As to the possibility of injunctive relief, however, see paras 21–119 et seq., below.

  The requirement that the information should not be stored for any period longer than is reasonably necessary for the transmission makes it clear that storage, even transient storage, for some longer period will take the activity outside the defence. To the extent that storage takes place for caching purposes, this is dealt with by reg.18 and art.13. The element of passivity required of the service provider is also underlined by the references to the "automatic", "intermediate" and "transient" storage of information, and the requirement that such storage is only to be for the sole purpose of carrying out the transmission. "Automatic" is intended to refer to the requirement that the act of storage occurs through the ordinary operation of the technology, "intermediate" to the fact that the storage takes place in the course of transmission and "transient" to the fact that it is for a limited time. The element of intermediacy is further underlined by the fact that the regulation applies only in relation to information provided by a recipient of the service. This means that to the extent that any infringing material is provided by the service provider itself there will be no defence. Further emphasis as to both these matters is given by the three conditions in reg.17(1). As to these:

(a) No initiation of the transmission by the service provider. The reference to initiation shows that although the service provider may be the transmitter of the information, or the first in line in an integrated network transmission, provided it does not take the decision to start off the process its actions will fall within the defence. This will include an automatic transmission in response to a request.

(b) No selection of the receiver of the transmission. A service provider may well carry out the process of directing the information to the recipient, but if this is done as an automated response to a request from the provider of the information it will not have "selected" the recipient.

(c) No selection or modification of the information contained in the transmission. This speaks for itself although, as seen, manipulations of a technical nature which take place in the course of the transmission can take place without losing the benefit of the defence (recital 43).

According to evidence accepted in *Bunt v Tilley*,[350] internet service providers (ISPs) normally delete emails automatically on initial transmission to the subscriber. The Judge appeared to accept a submission that an ISP which had done no more than provide internet access to individuals who had allegedly used such access to post defamatory material on a Usenet message board would be able to rely on the "mere conduit" defence. By contrast, the Judge appeared to accept the suggestion that an ISP which provides web-based email services is unlikely to be considered a mere conduit in relation to the messages because they are retained on its server until deleted by the recipient. Such an ISP is likely to be held to have "hosted" the messages.

The mere conduit defence was also considered in *Metropolitan International Schools Ltd v Designtechnica Corporation*,[351] which concerned Google's liability if any for publication of allegedly defamatory "snippets" produced in response to searches. The Judge decided that this did not amount to publication and accordingly the E-Commerce defences were of no relevance.[352] However, he doubted (obiter) whether the defence would extend to a cached index created automatically in relation to the operation of the search engine.[353]

(iii) The defence of caching

21–108   **The defence of caching.** "Caching" is the local storing of information in a network that is in frequent demand by users, such that users may access the infor-

---

[350] The defamation case of *Bunt v Tilley* [2006] EWHC 407; [2007] 1 W.L.R. 1243; [2006] E.M.L.R. 18, (Eady J.).
[351] [2009] EWHC 1765 (QB).
[352] para.113.
[353] para.89.

mation more quickly so as to avoid the network being slowed up by repeated access to the source of the information.[354] Caching may take place in the user's own system or locally in the network. In practice, it is a technical and automatic process.

Regulation 18 provides that where an information society service is provided which consists of the transmission in a communication network of information provided by a recipient of the service, the service provider shall not be liable for damages or for any other pecuniary remedy or for any criminal sanction as a result of that transmission where: (a) the information is the subject of automatic, intermediate and temporary storage where that storage is for the sole purpose of making more efficient onward transmission of the information to other recipients of the service upon their request; and where (b) the service provider: (i) does not modify the information; (ii) complies with conditions on access to the information; (iii) complies with any rules regarding the updating of the information, specified in a manner widely recognised and used by industry; (iv) does not interfere with the lawful use of technology, widely recognised and used by industry, to obtain data on the use of the information; and (v) acts expeditiously to remove or to disable access to the information he has stored upon obtaining actual knowledge of the fact that the information at the initial source of the transmission has been removed from the network, or access to it has been disabled, or that a court or an administrative authority has ordered such removal or disablement.[355]

The wording closely follows that of the Directive.[356] For an account of the process of caching, see *Bunt v Tilley*.[357] In that case it was conceded that the "caching" defence would not be available where an ISP had hosted the Usenet message board on its servers, stored postings for a few weeks to enable the users to access them and, while not operating the newsgroups, had the ability to remove postings from its news group server (albeit they might still be viewed via other servers).

In *Metropolitan International Schools Ltd v Designtechnica Corporation*,[358] the Judge pointed out that the automatic process which produces snippets for web users often involves a process of selection and "editing", albeit automatic, in order to provide a brief summary of the primary content on the relevant web page and suggested (obiter) that this might be classified as "modification of the content", thus removing the defence.[359]

Additional guidance and condition (i). Recital 43 to the Directive states that a **21–109** service provider can benefit from the exemptions for "caching" when it is "in no way involved" with the information transmitted. The recital adds that this is conditional, among other things, on the service provider not modifying the information that it transmits. The recital goes on to say that the condition that the information is not modified does not include manipulations of a technical nature which take place in the course of the transmission, since they do not alter the "integrity" of the information contained in the transmission. Recital 44 adds that a service provider who deliberately collaborates with one of the recipients of its service in order to undertake illegal acts goes beyond the activities of "caching" and as a result cannot benefit from the liability exemptions. These provisions

---

[354] See generally, Hugenholtz, "Caching and Copyright: The Right of Temporary Copying" [2000] E.I.P.R. 482 and Julia-Barceló, "On-line intermediary liability issues: comparing EU and US frameworks" [2000] E.I.P.R. 106.

[355] SI 2002/2013 reg.18.

[356] E-Commerce Directive 2000/31 art.13.

[357] [2006] EWHC 407; [2006] E.M.L.R. 18.

[358] [2009] EWHC 1765 (QB). For the facts, see above, para.21–107.

[359] para.92.

(apart from the condition that the information is not modified) are not repeated in the Regulations but no doubt the latter must be interpreted consistently with this recital. As to the possibility of an injunction, see paras 21–119 et seq., below.

21–110   **Condition (ii): compliance with conditions on access to the information.** This is not further defined, either in the Directive or the Regulations. It is thought that it means conditions imposed by the provider of the information, for example a requirement to pay a fee before the information may be accessed. If service providers were to permit users to access information supplied as part of a conditional access service from a cache without paying the fee, this would obviously undermine the business of the provider of the information.

21–111   **Condition (iii): compliance with industry rules regarding updating of information.** The object of this condition is evidently to ensure that the caching does not result in the provision of "stale" information. However, the references to industry rules and practice may clearly lead to uncertainty as to whether or not a provider has complied with them and has therefore infringed. The Directive expressly encourages the drawing up of relevant codes of conduct.[360]

21–112   **Condition (iv): non-interference with technology to obtain data on use of the information.** The reason for this condition is that web-pages which are delivered directly from caches do not register "hits". As a result, where advertising income or royalties are paid on a "per-hit" basis, the provider of the information will lose out unless it is able to obtain data on the use of the information in the cache.

21–113   **Condition (v): acting to remove or disable access.** The requirement to act expeditiously to remove or disable access to the information arises where the service provider has knowledge of any one of three alternative matters. It must be emphasised that what is relevant for this purpose is not knowledge or reasonable grounds to believe that the cached material is infringing or otherwise unlawful, or even that it is so, with the result that any such knowledge would be immaterial (compare the test in relation to hosting, below). Indeed, as will be seen, the Directive makes it clear that a general obligation is not to be imposed on providers, when providing caching services, to monitor the information which they transmit, nor a general obligation actively to seek facts or circumstances indicating illegal activity.[361] As to whether a service provider has the knowledge relevant for the purposes of the caching defence, it might have been thought better to leave matters as they stood in the regulation, which merely repeats the wording of the Directive,[362] and seems reasonably clear.

21–114   **Caching: knowledge: Regulation 22: background.** In its response to the consultation process, however, the Government said:

> "The limitations on liability for caches and hosts apply if an intermediary does not have actual knowledge of illegal activity or information. In line with the Directive, the draft Regulations did not propose specifying how actual knowledge is obtained. A number of comments sought further detail on what constitutes actual knowledge and what type of notice would give rise to it. Others recognised the inherent difficulties of providing a definition of actual knowledge but requested that some attention instead be given to what would *not* constitute actual knowledge. The Government remains of the view that providing a positive definition would risk creating loopholes

---

[360] E-Commerce Directive 2000/31 art.16.
[361] See E-Commerce Directive 2000/31 art.15(1).
[362] art.13(1)(e).

that could be exploited to avoid liability inappropriately. Being too prescriptive about what does not constitute actual knowledge raises similar concerns. However, it recognises that intermediaries face difficulties in assessing whether they are likely to be deemed to have actual knowledge. Given that the courts will ultimately decide individual cases, the Government believes it appropriate for them to have regard at least to whether a notice has been sent to the intermediary in question and, if so, whether it contains key information about the sender, where the relevant information is stored and why it is considered unlawful ...".

There appears to be some confusion in this response between the different types of knowledge required for the caching and hosting defences, and to what extent each requires "actual" or "deemed" knowledge. As already pointed out, the knowledge, whether actual or deemed, of unlawful activity is irrelevant for the purposes of the caching defence. Actual knowledge of one of the three specified matters is all that is relevant.

Caching: terms of reg.22. Despite this, therefore, the Government added reg.22, **21–115** which provides that in determining whether a service provider has actual knowledge for the purposes of reg.18(b)(v) (and also of reg.19(a)(i)—the hosting defence), a court shall take into account all matters which appear to it in the particular circumstances to be relevant and, among other things, shall have regard to whether a service provider has received a notice through a means of contact made available in accordance with reg.6(1)(c). This regulation provides that a person providing an information society service shall make available to the recipient of the service and any relevant enforcement authority, in a form and manner which is easily, directly and permanently accessible, the details of the service provider, including his electronic mail address, which make it possible to contact him rapidly and communicate with him in a direct and effective manner. Further, under reg.22, a court is to have regard to the extent to which any such notice includes: (i) the full name and address of the sender of the notice; (ii) details of the location of the information in question; and (iii) details of the unlawful nature of the activity or information in question. As will be seen, this provision, particularly (iii), seems relevant only to the hosting defence. Information about the location of the information might be relevant to whether or not the service provider had acted expeditiously to remove the information from cache memory, but this is not to what the regulation is directed. It is suggested that reg.22 adds nothing to the caching defence and should not construed as doing so since otherwise it would go beyond the terms of the Directive.

(iv) Hosting

The defence of hosting. "Hosting" is the provision of space to users for content, **21–116** such as web sites, news groups or bulletin boards. Regulation 19 provides that where an information society service is provided which consists of the storage of information provided by a recipient of the service, the service provider shall not be liable for damages or for any other pecuniary remedy or for any criminal sanction as a result of that storage where: (a) the service provider: (i) does not have actual knowledge of unlawful activity or information and, where a claim for damages is made, is not aware of facts or circumstances from which it would have been apparent to the service provider that the activity or information was unlawful; or (ii) upon obtaining such knowledge or awareness, acts expeditiously to remove or to disable access to the information, and (b) the recipient of the service was not acting under the authority or the control of the service provider. The wording closely follows that of the Directive.[363]

In *Bunt v Tilley*[364] the Judge appeared to accept (obiter) the suggestion that an ISP which provided web-based email services is likely to be held to have "hosted" the messages. In respect of the defendant ISP which had hosted the Usenet message board on its servers, stored postings for a few weeks to enable the users to access them and, while not operating the newsgroups, had the ability to remove postings from its news group server (albeit they might still be viewed via other servers), the Judge held (obiter) that the hosting defence was satisfied on the facts because the claimant had no prospect of proving actual knowledge within the meaning of reg.19(1)(a)(i). In particular, the claimant had failed to comply with the notice provisions of reg.22.

In *Kaschke v Gray*,[365] it was held that when considering whether a defendant was providing a service that consisted of the storage of information provided by a recipient, the courts should focus on the allegedly unlawful information (and not, for example, on the totality of any website on which it might be displayed) and ask whether so far as that information was concerned the service provided consisted only of and was limited to the storage of information.[366]

In *Google France*,[367] which concerned the Google Adwords service, the Court of Justice held that the critical question was whether the party seeking to rely on the hosting defence played an active role of such a kind as to give it knowledge of or control over the data stored or whether its role was neutral in the sense of being merely technical, automatic and passive, pointing to a lack of knowledge or control. If it had not played an active role it could only be liable if having obtained knowledge of the infringement it failed to act expeditiously to remove or disable access to the data.[368] The Court of Justice went on to say that the hosting defence was not precluded by the fact that Google was paid for the service on terms it set; the fact that Google provided "general information" to the advertiser; or the "concordance between the keyword selected and the search term entered by an internet user". However, the following factual considerations were relevant: (i) Google processed the data entered by the advertiser; (ii) the resulting display was made under conditions Google controlled—Google determined the order of display according to inter alia the remuneration paid by the advertisers; and (iii) Google's role (if any) in drafting the advertisement and in the establishment or selection of keywords.

In *Metropolitan International Schools Ltd v Designtechnica Corp*,[369] the Judge expressed the view (obiter) that in order for Google to be able to rely on the hosting defence in relation to the snippets, specific legislation would be required.[370]

In *Kaschke v Gray*,[371] the court suggested (obiter) that the hosting defence would not apply to material displayed on the homepage of a website in circumstances where the defendant had solicited and written copy; conducted polls and interviews which were then placed on the site; and personally intervened in the priority accorded to material in lists of "recommended" and "recent blogs" which

---

[363] E-Commerce Directive 2000/31 art.14(1).

[364] [2006] EWHC 407; [2006] E.M.L.R. 18.

[365] [2010] EWHC 690 (QB)

[366] paras 47–76.

[367] Joined Cases C–236/08, C–237/08 and C–238/08, *Google France SARL v Viaticum SA* [2010] R.P.C. 19.

[368] See at para.120.

[369] [2009] EWHC 1765 (QB). See para.21–107 above.

[370] See at para.112.

[371] [2010] EWHC 690 (QB).

were otherwise generated automatically or by input from readers.[372] So far as each individual blog was concerned, it was stated (obiter) to be arguable that the making by the site operator of spelling and grammatical corrections or the removal of offensive postings would take him outside the scope of the defence because his activities would not be limited to storage.[373] In addition, it was suggested, such activity would give rise to an issue for trial as to whether the recipient was acting under the control of the site operator.[374]

The question whether eBay can rely on the hosting defence remains open, having been referred to the Court of Justice.[375]

"Unlawful information". Presumably, this term in the present context means information whose storage would involve the infringement of an intellectual property right.[376]

21–117

Knowledge. The regulation, like the Directive, makes a distinction between different kinds of knowledge in relation to different kinds of liability. In relation to civil claims for damages (which presumably should be read as including claims for other civil pecuniary remedies), the fact that there are grounds on which the unlawfulness might be apparent to the service provider will be enough to remove the defence, irrespective of the service provider's actual knowledge. In relation to criminal liability, however, actual knowledge is required before the defence is removed. The same provision is made for the purposes of determining whether a service provider has actual knowledge for these purposes as for the caching defence.[377] This provision only relates to the issue of actual knowledge in the first limb of reg.19(a)(i), and not the "reasonable grounds" issue in the second limb. Again, it is suggested that it adds nothing to the defence. Presumably the issue of actual knowledge and knowledge on the "reasonable grounds" basis will be approached in the same way as the issue of knowledge for the purposes of secondary infringement of copyright.[378] The Directive enables Member States to establish procedures governing the removal or disabling of access to information, i.e. notice-and-take-down procedures.[379] Following consultation, the Government has decided that in the first place this should be a matter for industry codes of conduct rather than statutory regulation, something which in turn is encouraged by the Directive.[380] It is difficult to see, however, how such codes could affect the question of knowledge or whether the service provider had acted expeditiously to remove or disable access to cached material, both being primarily issues of fact.

21–118

(v) Powers to require service providers to prevent or terminate infringement

General. In the case of all acts of conduit, caching and hosting, the Directive provides that it is not to affect the possibility for a court or administrative authority, in accordance with Member States' legal systems, requiring the service provider to terminate or prevent an infringement.[381] This is supplemented by recital 45 which states that the Directive does not affect the possibility of injunc-

21–119

---

[372] paras 77–80.
[373] para.86.
[374] para.110.
[375] *L'Oreal SA v eBay International AG* [2009] EWHC 1094 (Ch), [2009] E.T.M.R. 53 at para.443.
[376] E-Commerce Directive 2000/31 art.14(1)(a) speaks of "illegal" information.
[377] See para.21–115, above.
[378] See paras 8–08 et seq., above.
[379] E-Commerce Directive 2000/31 art.14(3).
[380] art.16(1).
[381] E-Commerce Directive 2000/31 arts 12(3), 13(2) and 14(3).

tions of different kinds, in particular ones requiring the termination or prevention of any infringement, including the removal of illegal information or the disabling of access to it. The regulations provide that nothing in regs 17, 18 and 19 shall affect the rights of any party to apply to a court for relief to prevent or stop infringement of any rights.[382] The Regulations also provide that any power of an administrative authority to prevent or stop infringement of any rights shall continue to apply notwithstanding regs 17, 18 and 19.[383]

21–120   **The powers in the context of the E-Commerce defences.** No doubt these provisions were included as a matter of caution but it is not clear what they added to the general law. As already noted, the general effect of the Regulations is not to make the acts of service providers permitted acts of the kind referred to in Ch.III of the 1988 Act. They remain infringements but there is now a defence in relation to pecuniary claims and criminal proceedings. If an infringement is being committed because the service provider is acting outside the scope of any defence granted by the Regulations, then an injunction can be granted on normal principles. If a service provider is acting within the Regulations in relation to its hosting activities but it is subsequently given sufficient notice of a likely infringement, then unless it acts to remove or to disable access to the information the defences will not apply and the service provider will be liable to the normal remedies, including the grant of an injunction, in respect of any infringement which is continuing or which is likely to be committed in the future. As has been seen, in relation to the caching defence the relevant kind of notice required is rather different, and perhaps an injunction might be justified where the service provider unreasonably refused to co-operate in disabling the activities of a known and persistent infringer. Again as already noted, it appears that in the case of mere conduit a service provider is not liable in respect of any pecuniary remedy even if it knows or suspects that a third party is using its networks to transmit infringing material, provided no deliberate collaboration has occurred, and it is a prerequisite of the defence that any storage ends once it is no longer reasonably necessary for the transmission. In such a case, it may be that an injunction might be appropriate against an uncooperative service provider so as to prevent access to its network by a third party where it was likely that infringing material was to be transmitted.[384]

21–121   **The powers in other contexts.** The saving for powers to require service providers to prevent or terminate infringement has acquired new significance in the light of subsequent legislation. Article 8(3) of the Information Society Directive[385] requires Member States to ensure that rightholders are in a position to apply for an injunction against intermediaries whose services are used by a third party to infringe a copyright or related right. This provision, which has been implemented by s.97A of the 1988 Act, is considered below.[386] In addition, the Digital Economy Act 2010 contains provisions which (if implemented) will

---

[382] SI 2002/2013 reg.20(1)(a).
[383] reg.20(2).
[384] In *Bunt v Tilley* [2006] EWHC 407; [2007] 1 W.L.R. 1243; [2006] E.M.L.R. 18, Eady J. suggested (obiter) that ISPs which had done no more than provide internet access to individuals who had allegedly used such access to post defamatory material on a Usenet message board would be able to rely on the "mere conduit" defence. He also suggested that the grant of an injunction against such ISPs to restrain the publication of the same or similar words defamatory of the claimant would be "unworkable and disproportionate". The ISPs in question did not host any of the material about which the claimant complained, nor did they have the power to amend or modify any Usenet content. The grant of an injunction in respect of a defendant which had no way of ensuring compliance with its terms would be pointless.
[385] 2001/29, [2001] OJ L167/6. See Vol.2 H7.
[386] See paras 21–179 et seq.

permit OFCOM to require service providers to restrict subscribers' internet access with a view to preventing unlicensed peer-to-peer file sharing and to block access to particular sites. These powers too are dealt with below.[387]

Monitoring of information. Although the caching and hosting exemptions in particular may be affected by the service provider's knowledge of any infringement, the Directive makes it clear that a general obligation is not to be imposed on providers, when providing conduit, caching and hosting services, to monitor the information which they transmit or store, nor a general obligation actively to seek facts or circumstances indicating illegal activity.[388] This is not repeated in the Regulations since there is no such obligation under UK law in the first place. Nevertheless, it should be noted that recital 44 provides that the Directive does not affect the possibility of Member States requiring service providers who host information provided by recipients of their service to apply such duties of care as can reasonably be expected from them and which are specified by national law, in order to detect and prevent certain types of illegal activities. **21-122**

7. REMEDIES AND PROCEDURE

A. JURISDICTION

Extent of the 1988 Act. Parts I (copyright and moral rights), II (rights in performances), III (design right) and VII (which includes the provisions as to protection measures, rights management information and decoders) all extend (so far as relevant) to England and Wales, Scotland and Northern Ireland.[389] The Database Regulations extend to the United Kingdom.[390] For the purposes of Pts I to III, the territorial waters of the United Kingdom are treated as part of the United Kingdom.[391] These Parts apply to things done in the UK sector of the continental shelf on a structure or vessel which is present there for purposes directly connected with the exploration of the sea bed or subsoil or the exploitation of their natural resources as they apply to things done in the United Kingdom.[392] The UK sector of the continental shelf means the areas designated by order under s.1(7) of the Continental Shelf Act 1964.[393] Parts I and II of the 1988 Act apply to things done on a British ship, aircraft or hovercraft as they apply to things done in the United Kingdom.[394] Curiously, there is no equivalent provision for design right. However, the courts have jurisdiction over torts committed on British ships[395] and statutes normally extend thereto.[396] **21-123**

Extent of the 1988 Act may be increased. Parts I and III of the Act may be extended to any of the Channel Islands, the Isle of Man or any colony.[397] Similarly, the provisions in respect of fraudulent reception of transmissions may **21-124**

---

[387] See paras 21–186 et seq
[388] E-Commerce Directive 2000/31 art.15(1).
[389] See, respectively, CDPA 1988 ss.157, 207, 255 and 304.
[390] SI 1997/3032 reg.1(3).
[391] CDPA 1988 ss.161(1), 209(1) and 257(1).
[392] ss.161(2), 209(2) and 257(2).
[393] ss.161(3), 209(3) and 257(3).
[394] ss.162(1) and 210(1). For definitions of British ship, aircraft and hovercraft see subss.(2) of those sections.
[395] *Lloyd v Guibert* (1865) L.R. 1 Q.B. 115; *Davidson v Hill* [1901] 2 K.B. 606.
[396] *Schwartz v The India Rubber, etc. Co Ltd* [1912] 2 K.B. 299.
[397] CDPA 1988 ss.157(2) and 255(2).

be extended to the Isle of Man and any of the Channel Islands.[398] These provisions have scarcely been used.[399] Otherwise, there is no provision for extending the provisions in respect of the other rights covered in this Chapter.

21–125   **Acts committed outside the United Kingdom.** In addition to the provisions mentioned in para.21–123, above, various provisions of the 1988 Act make it clear that acts committed outside the United Kingdom cannot be infringements of copyright under the 1988 Act. For example, copyright is defined in territorial terms, as the exclusive right to do the restricted acts "in the United Kingdom".[400] The distribution right, which is expressed (in s.18(2) of the 1988 Act) in terms of the act of putting copies into circulation in the EEA, might appear to constitute an exception to this rule. However, it is thought that this does not give any rights in respect of activities outside the United Kingdom as defined in the 1988 Act.[401] By contrast, a person who, when outside the United Kingdom, authorises the commission of a restricted act in the United Kingdom will infringe.[402] It is thought that similar principles apply to the other rights covered in this work.

21–126   **Claims relating to foreign rights: scope of the following paragraphs.** The following paragraphs relate to the unregistered rights covered in this work other than unregistered community designs, which have their own regime which is considered elsewhere.[403] Since registered designs are only touched on in this work and are subject to different considerations, they are not covered here.

21–127   **Claims relating to foreign rights: general.** After a considerable period of uncertainty, the Court of Appeal has now provided welcome clarification in this field.[404] According to the Court of Appeal, the position depends entirely on the location of the allegedly infringing act. If that act took place in the European Union or (it appears) in a state which is party to the Lugano Convention ("a Lugano state"),[405] questions of jurisdiction are governed by the Judgments Regulation or the Lugano Convention as the case may be.[406] These are in materially identical terms. If, on the other hand, the act took place outside the European Union or a Lugano state, it is simply not "justiciable" in the English courts or (in the terms used by the Court of Appeal) there is no "subject-matter" jurisdiction.

21–128   **Acts committed in the EU or in a Lugano state.** It is necessary at the outset to distinguish between "personal" jurisdiction and "subject matter" jurisdiction or "justiciability". A court may have personal jurisdiction over a defendant yet may still refuse to hear the case because it will not accept "subject-matter" jurisdic-

---

[398] s.304(4) and (5).

[399] See paras 3–272 et seq., above.

[400] CDPA 1988 s.16(1). *Def Lepp Music v Stuart-Brown* [1986] R.P.C. 273; *Jonathan Cape Ltd v Consolidated Press Ltd* [1954] 1 W.L.R. 1313; *Pearce v Ove Arup Ltd* [2000] Ch. 403 at 438; [1999] F.S.R. 525 (obiter).

[401] See para.7–91, above. The same applies to the distribution right in respect of performers' rights: see s.182B(2).

[402] *ABKCO Music & Records Inc v Music Collection International Ltd* [1995] R.P.C. 657.

[403] See paras 13–255 et seq., above.

[404] *Pearce v Ove Arup Partnership Ltd* [2000] Ch. 403; [1999] F.S.R. 525; *Lucasfilm Ltd v Ainsworth* [2009] EWCA Civ 1328; [2010] F.S.R. 10. However, it is understood that the latter case is under appeal to the House of Lords.

[405] i.e. Switzerland, Norway and Iceland.

[406] Council Regulation (EC) No. 44/2001 on jurisdiction and the recognition and enforcement of judgments in civil and commercial matters [2000] OJ L12/1 (which, so far as relevant, governs actions against defendants domiciled in EU Member States, including, since July 1, 2007, Denmark—see the Civil Jurisdiction and Judgments Regulations 2007 (SI 2007/1655) reg.3(3)) and the Lugano Convention on jurisdiction and the recognition and enforcement of judgments in civil and commercial matters (which, so far as relevant, governs actions against defendants domiciled in Switzerland, Norway and Iceland). The position as between different parts of the United Kingdom is governed by the Civil Jurisdiction and Judgments Act 1982 (c.27) Sch.4.

tion, usually as a result of a rule derived from considerations of public policy. According to the Court of Appeal, where the acts complained of took place in the European Union (or, it seems, a Lugano state) and the Regulation (or the Convention) confers personal jurisdiction over the defendant (typically because of his domicile[407]), then there is no additional requirement that the English courts should have "subject-matter jurisdiction".[408] Nor is there any scope for applying the doctrine of forum non conveniens, that is the court will not entertain an argument that another EU or Lugano court would be a more appropriate venue for the action.[409] Nevertheless, regard must also be had to the provisions of the Regulation as to related pending actions in other EU courts: see arts 27 to 30.

Position in other cases. In actions which are not subject to the Judgments Regulation or the Conventions, the Court of Appeal has now decided that issues as to the validity or infringement of foreign intellectual property rights are simply not justiciable in the English courts. The fact that the court may have personal jurisdiction over the defendant is irrelevant. This is the result of the application of the *Moçambique* rule[410] to intellectual property rights. This rule, which originated in a case about trespass to land in South Africa, provided that the English court had no jurisdiction to entertain an action for (1) the determination of the title to, or the right to the possession of, any immovable situate out of England (foreign land); or (2) the recovery of damages for trespass to such immovable.[411] Despite the fact that doubts had been expressed about this in other cases,[412] and that the rule has been partially abrogated in relation to land[413] the Court of Appeal held that the rule is not limited to land, nor is it limited to claims about title or validity.[414] The Court of Appeal set out a series of policy reasons for its decision and noted that there was no international convention for the international litigation of copyrights in a single state.[415] **21–129**

The court's *in personam* jurisdiction. Even though the *Moçambique* rule applies to copyright, the court nevertheless has jurisdiction by way of exception to the *Moçambique* rule to make orders *in personam* which would result in the transfer from one party to another of foreign intellectual property.[416] Such orders may be made where the claim is based on a contract or equity between the parties but the precise extent of the jurisdiction is unclear.[417] It has been held that where a defendant legal owner of copyright has assigned the UK copyright together with all foreign copyrights to a third party with notice of the equitable owner's title, the court has jurisdiction to order the assignee to assign to the equitable owner not only the UK copyrights but also the foreign copyrights even though the assignee has not assumed any express personal obligation to do so.[418] Likewise, the UK court has jurisdiction to determine issues of title to worldwide **21–130**

---

[407] See art.2.

[408] *Pearce v Ove Arup Partnership Ltd* [2000] Ch. 403; [1999] F.S.R. 525 as analysed in *Lucasfilm Ltd v Ainsworth* [2009] EWCA Civ 1328; [2010] F.S.R. 10 at para.128.

[409] *Owusu v Jackson* (C–281/02) [2005] E.C.R. I–1383 as analysed in *Lucasfilm Ltd v Ainsworth* [2009] EWCA Civ 1328 at para.127.

[410] i.e. the rule in *British South Africa v Companhia de Moçambique* [1893] A.C. 602.

[411] This is the formulation of the rule which was adopted by the House of Lords in *Hesperides Hotels v Muftizade* [1979] A.C. 508.

[412] *Pearce v Ove Arup Ltd* [2000] Ch. 403 at 439–40; [1999] F.S.R. 525 and *R. Griggs Group Ltd v Evans* [2004] EWHC 1088 (Ch); [2005] Ch. 153 and [2004] F.S.R. 48 at paras 135–139.

[413] Civil Jurisdiction and Judgments Act 1982 (c.27) s.30(1).

[414] *Lucasfilm Ltd v Ainsworth* [2009] EWCA Civ 1328; [2010] F.S.R. 10 at para.175.

[415] See at paras 176—186.

[416] Dicey & Morris, *The Conflict of Laws* 14th edn, r.122(3)(a).

[417] See Dicey & Morris, *The Conflict of Laws* 14th edn, paras 23–041 to 23–050.

[418] *R. Griggs Group Ltd v Evans* [2005] Ch. 153 and [2004] F.S.R. 48. It should be noted that because of the way the issue developed in this case, the court assumed (unless and to the extent that it

copyrights which arise out of a contract containing English choice of law and jurisdiction clauses.[419]

B. INTERIM RELIEF

(i) Injunction

21–131   **General.** In many cases, the most important remedy for infringement of the rights covered in this Chapter is an injunction. An injunction may be either interim, that is one granted prior to the trial and only until after judgment or further order, or it may be final and permanent. Most injunctions sought are of a negative or prohibitory nature. However, an interim mandatory injunction may also be granted, to require a person to do something. The criteria for the grant of such injunctions are considered below.[420] Applications for interim injunctions are frequently made in actions for infringement of copyright and similar rights, since damages are often not an adequate remedy for the injury suffered by the claimant.[421] A quia timet injunction may be granted before any infringement has taken place. In order to obtain one, a claimant does not necessarily have to show a real threat of future infringement. Prevarication by the defendant may be enough.[422] The enforcement of injunctions is considered below.[423]

21–132   **The Enforcement Directive: interim injunctions.** Article 9(1)(a) of the Directive requires Member States to ensure that the judicial authorities may issue an "interlocutory" injunction to prevent any imminent infringement of an intellectual property right or to forbid the continuation of alleged infringements on a provisional basis.[424] Similar provision is made in art.50(1)(a) of TRIPS. Article 9(3) of the Directive (which is based on art.50(3) of TRIPS) provides that the judicial authorities shall have the authority to require the applicant to provide any reasonably available evidence in order to satisfy themselves with a sufficient degree of certainty that the applicant is the rightholder and that the applicant's rights are being infringed, or that such infringement is imminent. There was no need to take specific measures to implement these requirements, which were already provided for in the court procedures and case law. The Directive also provides for an alternative remedy to an interim injunction, namely an order that

---

would be unreasonable to do so) in favour of the equitable owner both that all relevant local laws as to the equitable owner's entitlement to an order transferring the copyright to him were the same as English law and that no relevant local courts would consider it a breach of comity to make the order sought: see paras 25, 114 and 141. However, it seems that a similar order was upheld in *Lucasfilm Ltd v Ainsworth* [2009] EWCA Civ 1328; [2010] F.S.R. 10: see at paras 196 and 208.

[419] *Crosstown Music Co 1 LLC v Rive Droite Music Ltd* [2010] EWCA Civ 1222.

[420] See para.21–148, below.

[421] *Coral Index Ltd v Regent Index Ltd* [1970] R.P.C. 147; *Annabel's (Berkeley Square) Ltd v G Schock* [1972] R.P.C. 838 at 845; *Slick Brands (Clothing) Ltd v Jollybird Ltd* [1975] F.S.R. 470; *Foseco International Ltd v Fordath Ltd* [1975] F.S.R. 507; *Combe International Ltd v Scholl (UK) Ltd* [1980] R.P.C. 1; *Monet of London Ltd v Sybil Richards Ltd* [1978] F.S.R. 368 at 375; cf. *Aljose Fashions Ltd v Alfred Young & Co Ltd* [1978] F.S.R. 364; *Foster v Mountford and Rigby Ltd* [1978] F.S.R. 582 (breach of confidence—Supreme Court of Northern Territory, Australia).

[422] *Linpac Mouldings Ltd v Eagleton Direct Export Ltd* [1994] F.S.R. 545, CA. Arguably a rather more stringent test was applied in *Burrows v Smith* [2010] EWHC 22 (Ch) at 50: "a strong case of probability that the apprehended mischief will, in fact, arise".

[423] para.21–178.

[424] For a discussion of the implementation of this provision in the various Member States, see Evidence and Right of Information in Intellectual Property Rights, a Report of the legal sub-group of the European Observatory on Counterfeiting and Piracy: http://ec.europa.eu/internal__market/iprenforcement/observatory/index__en.htm [Accessed October 12, 2010].

the infringement continue subject to guarantees. This was specifically implemented, and is considered below.[425]

The Enforcement Directive: without notice applications. Article 50(2) of   **21–133**
TRIPS provides that the judicial authorities must have authority to adopt provisional measures *inaudita altera parte* where appropriate, in particular where any delay is likely to cause irreparable harm to the right holder, or where there is a demonstrable risk of evidence being destroyed. Consistently with this, art.9(4) of the Directive permits interim injunctions to be obtained without the defendant having been heard in appropriate cases, in particular where any delay would cause irreparable harm to the rightholder. In such circumstances, consistently with art.50(4) of TRIPS, (a) "the parties shall be so informed without delay after the execution of the measures at the latest" and (b) a review, including a right to be heard, shall take place upon request of the defendant with a view to deciding, within a reasonable time after notification of the measures, whether the measures should be modified, revoked or confirmed. Article 9(5) of the Directive makes provision (consistent with art.50(6) of TRIPS) as to interim injunctions which are obtained before the commencement of proceedings. Member States are obliged to ensure that such injunctions are revoked or otherwise cease to have effect upon request of the defendant if the applicant does not start proceedings within a reasonable period, which period is to be determined by the judicial authority making the order where the law of a Member State so permits or (in the absence of such a determination) 20 working days or 31 calendar days, whichever is the longer. The procedure for without notice applications is considered below.[426]

Interim injunctions: general considerations.[427] The object of an interim injunc-   **21–134**
tion is to give the claimant temporary protection against injury by the continuing violation of his rights between the grant of the injunction and the trial for which he cannot be adequately compensated in damages in the action. This need to protect the claimant must be weighed against the corresponding need of the defendant to be protected against injury resulting from his being prevented from exercising his legal rights and for which injury he could not be adequately compensated under the claimant's cross-undertaking in damages. An interim injunction is thus a temporary, discretionary remedy. In general, it is not part of the court's function at this early stage in the litigation to try to resolve conflicts of evidence or difficult questions of law which call for detailed argument and mature consideration. In brief, at the interim stage the court usually has to make a decision when the existence of the right or the violation of it or both is uncertain and will remain uncertain until final judgment is given in the action. The court seeks to achieve a balance of justice, rather than of convenience. While the court disregards fanciful claims, it must contemplate that either party may succeed and do its best to ensure that nothing occurs pending trial which will prejudice their rights. This is difficult because both parties are often asserting wholly inconsistent claims.[428] Nevertheless the court should attempt to hold the ring until a just decision on the validity of the claim can be made.[429]

American Cyanamid v Ethicon.[430] In this, the leading case, the House of Lords   **21–135**
set out certain general principles to be applied on applications for interim

---

[425] paras 21–152 and 21–153.
[426] para.21–150.
[427] See, generally, *American Cyanamid Co v Ethicon Ltd* [1975] A.C. 396.
[428] *Francome v Mirror Group Newspapers Ltd* [1984] 1 W.L.R. 892.
[429] *Att.-Gen. v Guardian Newspapers Ltd* [1987] 1 W.L.R. 1248.
[430] [1975] A.C. 396.

injunctions. Those principles may be summarised as follows. The first question is whether the claimant has shown that there is a serious question to be tried. If there is not, the application will be refused.[431] If there is, the next question is whether, if the claimant were to obtain a permanent injunction at trial, he would be adequately compensated by an award of damages for the loss he had sustained before the trial as a result of the continuing acts of the defendant. If damages would be an adequate remedy, the court will normally refuse to grant an interim injunction, however strong the claimant's claim appears to be.[432] If damages would not be an adequate remedy for the claimant, the court goes on to consider whether the defendant, if he were to succeed at the trial, would be adequately compensated under the claimant's cross-undertaking in damages for the loss which he had sustained before the trial by being prevented from doing the acts sought to be restrained. If damages in the measure recoverable under the undertaking would be an adequate remedy and the claimant would be in a financial position to pay them, there would be no reason upon that ground for re-fusing an interim injunction. If the court is in doubt as to the adequacy of the re-spective remedies in damages available to either the claimant or the defendant or both, the question of the balance of convenience arises. The expression "balance of justice" may be better.[433] At this stage, the court considers the potential injustice to the claimant if the injunction is withheld and the potential injustice to the defendant if the injunction is granted. The course to be taken is that which would involve the least risk of ultimate injustice, having regard to the actual and potential rights and liabilities of the parties on both sides.[434] Many factors may be relevant, including the extent to which the disadvantages to each party would be incapable of being compensated in damages in the event of his succeeding at trial. If the extent of such uncompensatable damage would not differ widely, it is relevant to consider the strength of the parties' respective cases, at least if it is ap-parent on undisputed evidence that the strength of one party's case is disproportionate. In the last resort, where other factors appear to be evenly bal-anced, it is the prudent course to take such measures as are calculated to preserve the status quo.[435]

21–136   *Series 5 Software v Ltd v Clarke.*[436] In this case, Laddie J. sought to reformulate the principles applicable to the grant of interim injunctions, as follows: (1) The grant of an interim injunction is a matter of discretion and depends on all the facts of the case; (2) There are no fixed rules as to when an injunction should or should not be granted. The relief must be kept flexible; (3) Because of the practice adopted on the hearing of applications for interim relief, the court should rarely attempt to resolve complex issues of disputed fact or law; (4) Major factors to bear in mind are (a) the extent to which damages are likely to be an adequate remedy for each party and the ability of the other party to pay, (b) the balance of

---

[431] This is consistent with art.50(3) of TRIPS which requires judicial authorities to have the author-ity to require the applicant to provide any reasonably available evidence in order to satisfy them with a sufficient degree of certainty that the applicant is the right holder and that the applicant's right is being infringed or that such infringement is imminent.

[432] *American Cyanamid Co v Ethicon Ltd* [1975] A.C. 396; [1975] F.S.R. 101; *British Association of Aesthetic Plastic Surgeons v Cambright Ltd* [1987] R.P.C. 549; *Baltimore Aircoil Co Inc & Oth-ers v Evapco & Another* (1994) I.P.D. 17081. There is nothing to stop a claimant who is confident about the merits of his case seeking summary judgment and an interim injunction in the alterna-tive although permission may need to be sought under CPR 24.4 for the summary judgment ap-plication to be heard before the defendant has acknowledged service and served a defence.

[433] *Francome v Mirror Group Newspapers Ltd* [1984] 1 W.L.R. 892 at 899.

[434] *Fleming Fabrications Ltd v Albion Cylinders Ltd* [1989] R.P.C. 47; *Mail Newspapers Plc v Express Newspapers Plc* [1987] F.S.R. 90; *Shelley Films Ltd v Rex Features Ltd* [1994] E.M.L.R. 134.

[435] *American Cyanamid Co v Ethicon Ltd* [1975] A.C. 396.

[436] [1996] F.S.R. 273.

convenience, (c) the maintenance of the status quo, and (d) any clear view the court may reach as to the relative strength of the parties' cases.[437] This decision is frequently cited.[438] In a passing off case[439] the Court of Appeal left open the question whether or not *Series 5* was correct, but stated that the *American Cyanamid* rules had a "degree of flexibility" and did not prevent the court from giving proper weight to any clear view of the merits, where this could be reached without the need for a mini-trial. It was particularly important to give "proper weight" to the merits when the grant or refusal of an injunction would affect the commercial outcome of the case.

Application of the *American Cyanamid* principles: general. The paragraphs immediately following deal with certain cases where the *American Cyanamid* principles do not apply to the grant of interim injunctions or apply in modified form. Thereafter, an attempt is made to discuss the application of the *American Cyanamid* principles so far as they are relevant to the rights covered in this work.   **21–137**

Where decision will determine the case. Where the case will in effect be decided on the application for interim relief, the principles in *American Cyanamid* do not apply.[440] This is frequently the case when the court is considering a contractual provision which restrains certain activity (e.g. the use of confidential information) for a short period. Depending on the facts, the same may apply in a copyright case. The precise significance of the fact that the grant or refusal of an injunction will determine the case appears to depend on the facts. In *NWL Ltd v Woods*,[441] Lord Diplock stated that in such a case the degree of likelihood that the claimant will succeed is a factor to be brought into the balance when weighing the risks that injustice will result from deciding the application one way or the other. In some cases this has been held to mean that the court should attempt to reach a view on the merits.[442] In others, however, where the court has not been able to reach such a view, the fact that the grant of an injunction would be determinative of the case has led it to refuse one altogether.[443] In *Play It Ltd v Digital Bridges Ltd*,[444] Morritt V.-C. stated that in most cases involving intellectual property not only were damages an inadequate remedy to both sides, but the decision whether or not to grant an injunction was likely to be determinative because there was little incentive to an unsuccessful applicant to continue to trial   **21–138**

---

[437] [1996] F.S.R. 273 at 286.

[438] See, e.g. *Antec International Ltd v South Western Chicks (Warren) Ltd* [1997] F.S.R. 278 (passing off, Laddie J.: *Series 5* contains the reasons why the merits may be taken into account); *Barnsley Brewery Company Ltd v RBNB* [1997] F.S.R. 462 (passing off, Walker J.: *Series 5* a valuable reminder of the background and context of *American Cyanamid Co v Ethicon Ltd* [1975] A.C. 396 and its basic message—avoidance of mini-trials and doing least injustice); *Intelsec Systems Ltd v Grech-Cini* [2001] 1 W.L.R. 1190 (Nicholas Warren QC: as a result of *Series 5* it may be that the court can consider the strength of the parties' cases "more widely" in relation to the balance of convenience); *Wyeth Holdings Corp v Alpharma* [2003] EWHC 3196 (Pat) (patents; Laddie J. stated that he did not resile from anything he said in *Series 5*, but was unable to form a clear view on the merits). See also *O2 Ltd v Hutchison 3G UK Ltd* [2004] EWHC 2571 (Ch); [2005] E.T.M.R. 61, where the Judge took account of the weakness of the claim in a trade mark case where the defendant wished to rely on the comparative advertising defence.

[439] *Guardian Media Group Plc v Associated Newspapers Ltd* Unreported, January 20, 2000, para.18.

[440] *NWL Ltd v Woods* [1979] 1 W.L.R. 1294; *Cayne v Global Natural Resources Plc* [1984] 1 All E.R. 225; *Lawrence David Ltd v Ashton* [1989] F.S.R. 87; *Lansing Linde v Kerr* [1991] 1 W.L.R. 251; *Entec Pollution Control Ltd v Abacus Mouldings* [1992] F.S.R. 332; *Instance v Denny Bros Printing Ltd* [2000] F.S.R. 869.

[441] [1979] 1 W.L.R. 1294.

[442] See, e.g. *Lansing Linde v Kerr* [1991] 1 W.L.R. 251; *Sun Valley Foods Ltd v Vincent* [2000] F.S.R. 825; *Instance v Denny Bros Printing Ltd* [2000] F.S.R. 869; *BBC v Talksport Ltd* [2001] F.S.R. 6.

[443] *Cayne v Global Natural Resources Plc* [1984] 1 All E.R. 225; *Entec Pollution Control Ltd v Abacus Mouldings* [1992] F.S.R. 332.

[444] [2005] EWHC 1001 (Ch).

and little point in an unsuccessful respondent going to trial because of the difficulty, even if he won, of reverting commercially to the position he occupied before the injunction was wrongly granted. For that reason, Morritt V.-C. held that if in such a case the pecuniary remedy of the parties was inadequate to each of them, it was appropriate to consider the strength of their respective cases.[445]

21–139 **Cases involving freedom of expression.** Section 12 of the Human Rights Act 1998[446] applies where a court is considering whether to grant any relief which, if granted, might affect the exercise of the right to freedom of expression.[447] Where this is the case, no such relief is to be granted so as to restrain publication before trial unless the court is satisfied that the applicant is likely to establish that publication should not be allowed.[448] The effect of this is that the *American Cyanamid* test does not apply. After considerable uncertainty as to the correct test,[449] the House of Lords has now held that "likely" has an extended meaning which sets the normal standard higher than the *Cyanamid* standard but which permits the court to dispense with that higher standard where particular circumstances make this necessary.[450] In general, therefore, the standard is one of "probably" or more likely than not. However, there will be cases where a lesser degree of likelihood will suffice. Examples include cases where the potential adverse consequences of disclosure would be particularly grave[451] and where a short-lived injunction is necessary in order to enable the court to hear and give proper consideration to an application for interim relief.[452] Section 12(3) goes on to provide that the court must have particular regard to the importance of the Convention right of freedom of expression.[453] It then provides that where the proceedings relate to material which the respondent claims, or which appears to the court, to be journalistic, literary or artistic material (or to conduct connected with such material), the court must have particular regard to the following three matters: the extent to which the material has, or is about to become available to the public; the extent to which it

---

[445] In *Red Bull GmbH v Mean Fiddler Music Group Plc* [2004] EWHC 991 (Ch) (passing off), the Judge held that the grant of an injunction would effectively determine the action but that the correct test was whether there was a serious issue to be tried, albeit that he should scrutinise the evidence with particular care. However, it seems the defendant did not argue that the court should give a judgment on the merits, but rather that the correct test was whether there was a "prima facie case". It is not clear what authorities were cited to the Judge.

[446] c.42.

[447] That is, the right to free expression laid down by art.10 of the European Convention on Human Rights: see Human Rights Act 1998 s.12(1).

[448] Human Rights Act 1998 s.12(3). Section 12(2) provides that where the respondent is neither present nor represented, no such relief is to be granted unless the court is satisfied that the applicant has taken all practical steps to notify the respondent or there are compelling reasons why the respondent should not be notified.

[449] In *Imutran Ltd v Uncaged Campaigns Ltd* [2002] F.S.R. 2, Morritt V.-C. noted that the word "likely" suggested a higher standard than the ordinary *Cyanamid* standard but doubted whether the difference would be significant in most cases. In *Cream Holdings Ltd v Banerjee* [2003] EWCA Civ 103; [2003] Ch.650; [2003] E.M.L.R. 16, paras 61 and 121, the Court of Appeal held that the phrase "is likely to establish" meant "has a real prospect of establishing" rather than "is more likely than not to establish".

[450] *Cream Holdings Ltd v Banerjee* [2005] 1 A.C. 253; [2005] E.M.L.R. 1.

[451] Such as a case where the claimant's claim depended on a question of fact on which he had an arguable but distinctly poor case, but where the disclosure of the information would lead to a grave risk of personal injury: *Cream Holdings Ltd v Bannerjee* [2004] UKHL 44 [2005] 1 A.C. 253 at para.19.

[452] *Cream Holdings Ltd v Banerjee* [2004] UKHL 44 at para.22. The lower threshold was contended for in *Unilever Plc v Grifffin* [2010] EWHC 899 (Ch); [2010] F.S.R. 33 in which a 7-day injunction was sought: para.8. In fact it was held that the higher threshold was crossed on two out of three causes of action: para.23.

[453] For an example of an application of this subsection, see *Psychology Press Ltd v Flanagan* [2002] EWHC 1205, QBD.

is or would be in the public interest for the material to be published; and any relevant privacy code.[454]

***American Cyanamid*: adequacy of damages.** In actions in respect of the rights covered in this work, damages are often not an adequate remedy since there are difficulties both in ascertaining and in quantifying such damage as injury to the claimant's property, business, commercial opportunity, reputation and goodwill.[455] The court will take into account the fact that the defendant might not be in a financial position to meet a claim for substantial damages against him.[456] Conversely, the court will take into account the ability or otherwise of the claimant to compensate the defendant on the cross-undertaking in damages.[457] The mere fact that a party is of slender means is not, however, conclusive.[458] **21–140**

***American Cyanamid*: balance of convenience.** There are many factors varying from case to case which will influence the court's decision on the balance of convenience. For example, in some cases the court has held it against a defendant, in granting an injunction, that the defendant has walked into an existing situation with his eyes open and taken a calculated risk.[459] The court will discount obligations incurred by the claimant with a view to bolstering up his case on the balance of convenience.[460] On the other hand, it has been held against a claimant that the effect of the injunction would be disastrous to the defendant and disrupt his business,[461] even though it appears that the defendant has acted in a surreptitious way in the manner that he has gone about establishing his business.[462] **21–141**

The relevance of the merits to the balance of convenience. In *American Cyanamid*, it was held that if the extent of the uncompensatable damage would not differ widely as between the two respective parties, it is relevant to consider the **21–142**

---

[454] Human Rights Act 1998 s.12(4)(a), (b).

[455] Examples include: *Elanco Products Ltd v Mandops (Agrochemical Specialists) Ltd* [1979] F.S.R. 46 (copyright); *Rolls Royce Motors Ltd & Another v Zanelli & Others* [1979] R.P.C. 148 (copyright and trade mark); *P.G. Mavros (Private) Ltd v Ponter* Unreported, Laurence Collins QC, July 7, 1999 (copyright); and *Play It Ltd v Digital Bridges Ltd* [2005] EWHC 1001 (Ch). See, however, *IBS Technologies (PVT) Ltd v APM Technologies SA*, Michael Briggs QC, April 7, 2003, *Audi Performance Racing v Revo Technick Ltd* [2003] EWHC 1668, Ch. D. and *Vollers Corsets Company Ltd v Cook* [2003] EWHC 2693 (Ch); [2004] E.C.D.R. 28, all copyright cases in which it was held that damages would be an adequate remedy for the claimant but not the defendant. Damages were also held to be an adequate remedy in the database case *Planet Ace Ltd v Hendon Mob*, Evans-Lombe J., February 4, 2005, Lawtel document no. AC9100604.

[456] *Missing Link Software v Magee* [1989] F.S.R. 361 at 368; *Mirage Studios v Counter-Feat Clothing Company Ltd* [1991] F.S.R. 145 at 152; *Dyrlund-Smith A/S v Turberville Smith Ltd* [1998] F.S.R. 774.

[457] *Morning Star Co-operative Society Ltd v Express Newspapers Ltd* [1979] F.S.R. 113. In some cases, the court may require the provision of a bond (*Anton Piller KG v Manufacturing Processes Ltd* [1976] R.P.C. 719; *JC Penney Co Inc v Penneys Ltd* [1975] R.P.C. 367; *Harman Pictures NV v Osborne* [1967] 1 W.L.R. 723; *Globelgance BV v Sarkissian* [1974] R.P.C. 603) or a payment into court (*Vernon & Co (Pulp Products) Ltd v Universal Pulp Containers Ltd* [1980] F.S.R. 179 at 191; *CPC (United Kingdom) Inc v Keenan* [1986] F.S.R. 527 at 536; *Brupat Ltd v Sandford Marine Products Ltd* [1983] R.P.C. 61 at 67).

[458] *Apple Corps Ltd v Lingasong Ltd* [1977] F.S.R. 345; *Allen v Jambo Holdings Ltd* [1980] 1 W.L.R. 1252; [1980] 2 All E.R. 502 CA.

[459] *Hymac v Priestman Bros.Ltd* [1978] R.P.C. 495; *Netlon v Bridport* [1979] F.S.R. 530; *News Group Newspapers Ltd v The Rocket Record Co Ltd* [1981] F.S.R. 89 at 107; *BBC v Talbot Motor Co Ltd* [1981] F.S.R. 228; *Elida Gibbs Ltd v Colgate-Palmolive Ltd* [1983] F.S.R. 95; *Elan Digital Systems Ltd v Elan Computers Ltd* [1984] F.S.R. 373; *Reckitt & Colman Products Inc v Borden Inc* [1987] F.S.R. 228 at 240; *Consorzio del Prosciutio di Parma v Marks & Spencer Plc* [1990] F.S.R. 530 at 541.

[460] *Raindrop Data Systems Ltd v Systemics Ltd* [1988] F.S.R. 354.

[461] *Fison Ltd v E J Godwin (Peat) Industries Ltd* [1976] R.P.C. 653; *Baskin Robbins Ice Cream Co v Gutman* [1976] F.S.R. 545; *IVS Technologies (PVT) Ltd v APM Technologies S.A.*, Michael Briggs QC, April 7, 2003; *Audi Performance Racing v Revo Technick Ltd* [2003] EWHC 1668 (Ch) and *Vollers Corsets Company Ltd v Cook* [2003] EWHC 2693 (Ch).

[462] *Potters-Ballotini v Weston Baker* [1977] R.P.C. 202.

strength of their respective cases, provided that it is apparent on undisputed evidence that the strength of one party's case is disproportionate. In practice, the strength of the parties' respective cases is often taken into account on the balance of convenience because it affects the likelihood that they will suffer damage between the grant or refusal of the interim injunction and the trial.[463]

21–143   *American Cyanamid*: **the status quo.** Where other factors appear to be evenly balanced, the court will often take such measures as are calculated to preserve the status quo. If, on the one hand, the defendant is enjoined temporarily from doing something which he has not done before, the only effect of the interim injunction in the event of his succeeding at the trial may be to postpone the date at which he is able to embark on a course of action which he has not previously found it necessary to undertake. If, on the other hand, the defendant is interrupted in the conduct of an established enterprise, the injunction would cause much greater inconvenience to him since he would have to start again to establish it in the event of his succeeding at the trial.[464] The preservation of the status quo particularly favours the grant of an injunction in those cases where the defendant has only just begun to do the act complained of and where he has no established business or his sales and capital investment have been small, while the claimant has an established business.[465] In such cases it is often easier to calculate the damage which the defendant will suffer by reason of the injunction than it is to calculate the damage which will be done to the claimant if the defendant is not restrained. For example, it may be easier to calculate the expenditure thrown away by a defendant in printing and promoting a book, the publication of which is restrained by injunction, than it is to calculate the injury which will be done to the sales and goodwill of the claimant's existing book if publication by the defendant is not restrained.[466] The courts will generally, as a temporary measure, protect a long-established business against the activities of an interloper.[467]

There are, however, some cases in which the courts will take the view that the damage to the claimant can be readily calculated by reference to the sales made by the defendant and that the damage which would be done to the defendant by preventing him from getting a foot in the market as soon as possible is not easily quantifiable.[468] The defendant may undertake to keep an account of his sales.[469] Where there is only a risk of unquantifiable damage to the claimant and a certainty of unquantifiable damage to the defendant the court will often refuse to maintain

---

[463] See the cases referred to in para.21–136, above; *CMI Centres for Medical Innovation GmbH v Phytopharm Plc* [1999] F.S.R. 235 (confidence); and *Quad International Inc v Goldstar Publications Ltd* [2003] EWHC 2081 (passing off).

[464] *American Cyanamid Co v Ethicon Ltd* [1975] A.C. 396; [1975] F.S.R. 101.

[465] *Elanco Products Ltd v Mandops (Agrochemical Specialists) Ltd* [1979] F.S.R. 46; *Polydor Ltd v Harlequin Record Shop Ltd* [1980] 1 C.M.L.R. 669 at 676; [1980] F.S.R. 194; *Sodastream Ltd v Thorn Cascade Co Ltd* [1982] R.P.C. 459; *Biba Group Ltd v Biba Boutique* [1980] R.P.C. 413; *Esanda Ltd v Esanda Finance Ltd* [1984] F.S.R. 96 (High Ct. of New Zealand); *Mail Newspapers Plc v Insert Media Ltd* [1987] R.P.C. 521; *Fleming Fabrications Ltd v Albion Cylinders Ltd* [1989] R.P.C. 47; *Missing Link Software v Magee* [1989] F.S.R. 361 at 368; *Alfa Laval Cheese Systems Ltd v Wincanton Engineering Ltd* [1990] F.S.R. 583 at 594; *Wyeth Holdings Corp v Alpharma* [2003] EWHC 3196.

[466] *Mothercare Ltd v Robson Books Ltd* [1979] F.S.R. 466.

[467] *Chill Foods (Scotland) Ltd v Cool Foods Ltd* [1977] R.P.C. 522.

[468] *Catnic Components Ltd v Stressline Ltd* [1976] F.S.R. 157; *Kwik Lok Corp v WBW Engineers Ltd* [1975] F.S.R. 237; *Belfast Ropework Co Ltd v Pixdane Ltd* [1976] F.S.R. 337; *Temple Instruments Ltd v Hollis Heels Ltd* [1973] R.P.C. 15; *Polaroid Corp v Eastman Kodak Co* [1976] F.S.R. 530; [1977] F.S.R. 25, CA; *Netlon v Bridport-Gundry* [1979] F.S.R. 530; *Hunter v Fitzroy Robinson & Partners* [1978] F.S.R. 167; *Potters-Ballotini Ltd v Weston Baker* [1977] R.P.C. 202; *Corruplast Ltd v George Harrison (Agencies) Ltd* [1978] R.P.C. 761; *Taverner Rutledge Ltd v Trexapalm Ltd* [1977] R.P.C. 275; *The Boots Co Ltd v Approved Prescription Services Ltd* [1988] F.S.R. 45; *John Wyeth & Bro. Ltd v M & A Pharmachem* [1988] F.S.R. 26.

[469] *Catnic Components Ltd v Stressline Ltd* [1976] F.S.R. 157 at 160, 163; *Concrete Systems v Devon Symonds Holdings* [1978] S.A.S.R. 79.

the status quo and dismiss a claim for an injunction.[470] One course taken by the court in such cases is to grant or refuse an injunction and order a speedy trial of the action.[471]

The time factor. One problem which has arisen in determining the status quo is **21–144** the fixing of the relevant time. It has been suggested[472] that the relevant date for determining the status quo may variously be the date on which the defendant first did the offending act, or the date on which the claimant first learned of that act, or the date on which the claimant first ought to have been aware of the defendant's act, or the date when the claimant first complained to the defendant, or the date when the claimant sent his letter before action or the date when the claimant issued his claim form. There is much to be said in favour of the view that the status quo to be preserved by an injunction is that state of affairs which existed before the defendant first began to do the act which the claimant seeks to restrain by injunction.[473] However, in *Garden House Foods Ltd v Milk Marketing Board*,[474] Lord Diplock said (obiter[475]):

> "In my opinion, the relevant *status quo* to which reference was made in *American Cyanamid* is the state of affairs existing during the period immediately preceding the issue of the Writ claiming the permanent injunction, or if there be unreasonable delay between the issue of the Writ and the motion for an interlocutory injunction, the period immediately preceding motion. The duration of that period since the state of affairs last changed must be more than minimal, having regard to the total length of the relationship between the parties in respect of which the injunction is granted; otherwise the state of affairs before the last change would be the relevant *status quo*".

In two recent cases,[476] the claimants had discovered the infringements at about the time they commenced and began proceedings expeditiously. In each case, the status quo was taken to be the period immediately before the commencement of the infringement.

It may be very difficult to identify the status quo in a rapidly changing commercial situation; for example, at the outset of a character merchandising operation.[477] Where there is no letter before action and there is delay after the issue of the claim form before service, the date of service of the claim form may be the relevant date for deciding what represents the status quo.[478]

Although a defendant who chooses to continue with a course of action after a dispute arises cannot gain any benefit thereby, if the defendant was substantially committed to a course of action when the dispute arose and continued along that

---

[470] *John Walker & Sons Ltd v Rothmans International Ltd* [1978] F.S.R. 357; *Unider Ltd v Marks & Spencer Plc* [1988] R.P.C. 275.

[471] *Lawrence David Ltd v Ashton* [1989] F.S.R. 87; *Johnson & Bloy (Holdings) Ltd v Wolstenholme Rink Plc* [1989] F.S.R. 135. (both cases where an injunction was granted to enforce a restrictive covenant or obligation of confidence by ex-employees, pending a speedy trial); *Alfa Laval Cheese Systems Ltd v Wincanton Engineering Ltd* [1990] F.S.R. 583 at 594.

[472] *Alfred Dunhill Ltd v Sunoptic SA* [1979] F.S.R. 337; see *Alfa Laval Cheese Systems Ltd v Wincanton Engineering Ltd* [1990] F.S.R. 583 at 594.

[473] *Metric Resources Corp v Leasemetric Ltd* [1979] F.S.R. 571; *John Walker & Sons Ltd v Rothmans International Ltd* [1978] F.S.R. 357; *Consorzio del Prosciutto di Parma v Marks & Spencer Plc* [1990] F.S.R. 530 at 541; *The British Diabetic Association v The Diabetic Society* noted at [1992] I.P.D. 15103.

[474] [1984] 1 A.C. 130 at 140; [1984] F.S.R. 23; see also *Jian Tools for Sales Inc v Roderick Manhattan Group Ltd* [1995] F.S.R. 924.

[475] See *The British Diabetic Association v The Diabetic Society* noted at [1992] I.P.D. 15103.

[476] *Play It Ltd v Digital Bridges Ltd* [2005] EWHC 1001 (Ch) and *Global Coal Ltd v ICAP Energy Ltd* [2006] EWCA Civ 167.

[477] *Mirage Studios v Counter-Feat Clothing Company Ltd* [1991] F.S.R. 145 at 153.

[478] *Graham v Delderfield* [1992] F.S.R. 313.

course, the status quo is represented by the defendant being committed to that course of action. The position is not analogous to the building cases where the defendant builder presses ahead as quickly as possible with construction after complaint is made so as to present a court with a fait accompli. That type of situation represents a change of course.[479]

21-145   **Other relevant considerations.** As well as the interests of freedom of speech (as to which, see above), the interests of the public in general may also be taken into account in the exercise of the court's discretion.[480] Unexplained delay in applying for interim relief will weigh heavily against the claimant and is often fatal.[481] However, the court will take into account whether or not the defendant has been led into expense, or lulled into security, or misled by the inaction of the claimant.[482] The question is whether the delay is culpable or unreasonable so as to make it unjust to grant the injunction sought. Delay is not prejudicial, for example, if it is explicable by attempts to settle the dispute.[483] A claimant is not precluded from asserting his rights, even by way of interim injunction, merely because he has tolerated some acts which have infringed his rights.[484] Section 239 of the 1988 Act provides that where, in a design right case, a defendant undertakes to take a licence of right, no injunction shall be granted against him. However, this does not mean that no injunction may be granted in any case where the defendant offers immediately to take a licence of right. Where a question can reasonably be raised as to the financial ability of the defendant to comply with the financial obligations that would be imposed by the licence, it is incumbent on him to show that the undertaking is one which he can reasonably be expected to honour.[485] Furthermore, if the offer is to enter into a licence of right at the end of the trial if the defendant loses, the application for an injunction should be decided on *American Cyanamid* principles.[486]

21-146   **Cross-undertaking in damages: the Enforcement Directive.** Article 9(7) of the Enforcement Directive provides (consistently with art.50(7) of TRIPS) that where provisional measures are revoked or lapse due to any act or omission by the applicant, or where it is subsequently found that there has been no infringement, the judicial authorities shall have the authority to order the applicant, upon

---

[479] *Management Publications Ltd v Blenheim Exhibitions Group Plc* [1991] F.S.R. 550.

[480] *R. v Secretary of State for Transport, ex p. Factortame Ltd (No.2)* [1991] A.C. 603; [1990] 3 C.M.L.R. 375; *Cambridge Nutrition Ltd v BBC* [1990] 3 All E.R. 523; *Beggars Banquet Records Ltd v Carlton Television Ltd* [1993] E.M.L.R. 349.

[481] *Southey v Sherwood* (1817) 2 Mer. 435; *Mawman v Tegg* (1826) 2 Russ. 385, 393; *Lewis v Chapman* (1840) 3 Beav. 133; *Kenitex Chemicals Inc v Kenitex Textured Coating Ltd* [1965] 2 F.S.R. 109 (3 months' delay—no injunction); *Bravington Ltd v Barrington Tennant* [1957] R.P.C. 183 (3 months' unexplained delay); *Park Court Hotel Ltd v Trans-World Hotels Ltd* [1970] F.S.R. 89; *Celanese Corp v Akzo Chemie UK Ltd* [1976] F.S.R. 273 (no injunction—6 months' delay between launching of motion and hearing of motion); *Radley Gowns Ltd v Costas Spyrou* [1975] F.S.R. 445; *Russel-Uclaf v G. P. Searle & Co Ltd* [1977] F.S.R. 125; *Foseco International Ltd v Fordath Ltd* [1975] F.S.R. 507; *Nichols Advanced Vehicle Systems Inc & Others v Rees, Oliver & Others* [1979] R.P.C. 127; *My Kinda Town v Soll* [1983] R.P.C. 407 at 418; *Century Electronics Ltd v CVS Enterprises Ltd* [1983] F.S.R. 1 (4 months' delay after becoming aware of defendant's activities); *The Quaker Oats Company v Alltrades Distributors Ltd* [1981] F.S.R. 9 (2 months' delay after learning of imports of infringing goods); *Hoover Plc v George Hulme Ltd* [1982] F.S.R. 565 at 587, 588; *Dalgety Spillers Foods Ltd v Food Brokers Ltd* [1994] F.S.R. 504; *Baltimore Aircoil Co Inc & Others v Evapco & Another* (1994) I.P.D. 17081; *BASF Plc v CEP (UK) Plc* (1996) I.P.D. 19030.

[482] See previous note and *Byford v Rainbow Communications Ltd* (1995) I.P.D. 18132; *Express Newspapers Plc v Liverpool Daily Post & Echo Plc* [1985] 3 All E.R. 680.

[483] *CPC (United Kingdom) Ltd v Keenan* [1986] F.S.R. 527.

[484] *News Group Newspapers Ltd v The Mirror Group Newspapers (1986) Ltd* [1989] F.S.R. 126; *Raychem Corp v Thermon (UK) Ltd* [1989] R.P.C. 423.

[485] *Dyrlund Smith A/S v Turberville Smith Ltd* [1998] F.S.R. 774.

[486] *Dyrlund Smith A/S v Turberville Smith Ltd* [1998] F.S.R. 774

request of the defendant, to provide the defendant appropriate compensation for any injury caused by the injunction. Article 9(6) of the Directive provides that the competent judicial authorities may make the grant of an interim injunction conditional on the lodging by the applicant of adequate security or an equivalent assurance intended to ensure compensation for any prejudice suffered by the defendant.

Cross-undertaking in damages: practice. Consistently with the Directive, the   **21–147**
court will normally refuse to grant an interim injunction unless the claimant is willing to furnish an undertaking by himself or by some other willing and responsible person to compensate the defendant for any loss which the defendant (or any other person served with or notified of the order) sustain and which the court considers the claimant should pay.[487] A claimant should specifically give evidence as to his ability to meet his liability on the cross-undertaking.[488]

The court retains a discretion as to whether and when to enforce the undertaking[489] and may not do so if it considers that the conduct of the defendant makes it inequitable to do so. It has been said that if the undertaking is enforced, damages are assessed on the same basis as if the undertaking had been a contract between the claimant and the defendant that the claimant would not prevent the defendant from doing that which he was restrained from doing by the terms of the injunction.[490] However, in *Lilly Icos LLC v 8PM Chemists Ltd*,[491] after a full review of the authorities, it was held that the remedy awarded under a cross-undertaking is one of equitable compensation rather than common law damages.[492] As to causation, it was held that the correct test was the "but for" test; the defendant is not obliged to show that the injunction was the sole cause of the loss, but the test is not satisfied if the loss was caused as much by the existence of the litigation as by the injunction.[493] Since the defendant is normally being compensated for being prevented from carrying on its business in the way it would normally have done, compensation is to be assessed not as if the injunction deprived the defendant of a contractual benefit but with the benefit of hindsight.[494] No compensation will be awarded for loss sustained by an unlawful business or where the beneficiary of the cross-undertaking has to rely to a substantial extent on his own illegality in order to establish the loss.[495] It seems that a claimant may be estopped by convention or representation or prevented by

---

[487] *Hoffmann-La Roche & Co AG v Secretary of State for Trade and Industry* [1975] A.C. 295. Practice Direction—Interim Injunctions, para.5.1.

[488] *Brigid Foley Ltd v Elliott* [1982] R.P.C. 433.

[489] *Cheltenham & Gloucester Building Society v Ricketts* [1993] 1 W.L.R. 1545; *Balkanbank v Taher & Others* [1995] 1 W.L.R. 1056.

[490] *Hoffmann-La Roche & Co AG v Secretary of State for Trade and Industry* [1975] A.C. 295; *Novello v James* (1854) 24 L.J. Ch. 111; *Air Express Ltd v Ansett Transport Industries (Operations) Pty* (1979) 146 C.L.R. 249 at 267 (High Ct of Australia); *Finansiera Avenida SA v Shiblaq, The Times*, January 14, 1991. See, also, *Helitune Ltd v Stewart Hughes Ltd* [1994] F.S.R. 422. See, however, *R v The Medicines Control Agency, ex p. Smith & Nephew Pharmaceuticals Ltd (Primecrown Ltd Intervening)* [1999] R.P.C. 705 at 714 and *Les Laboratoires Servier v Apotex Inc* [2008] EWHC 2347 (Ch) at para.7; [2009] F.S.R. 3, suggesting that the measure of damages based on a notional breach of contract might be too narrow. In *Iman Said Abdul Aziz Al-Rawas v Pegasus Energy Ltd* [2008] EWHC 617 (QB), Jack J. held that damages were to be assessed on a contractual basis: para.15.

[491] [2010] EWHC 1905 (Ch); [2010] F.S.R. 4.

[492] See at para.20. The Judge held that on the facts he did not need to consider questions of remoteness of mitigation: see at paras 42 and 43.

[493] See at paras 32–37.

[494] See at para.40.

[495] para.287. It does not matter whether the acts in question are unlawful under English law or under foreign law: ibid.

the principle of "approbation and reprobation" from relying on a defence of illegality.[496]

Even if the claimant chooses not to pursue his action at trial, the defendant is not entitled to an inquiry on the cross-undertaking as of right and no such inquiry will be ordered if the court is satisfied that the defendant did in fact infringe copyright.[497] However, if the interim order restrains the defendant in wider terms than prove at trial to have been justifiable, then the court will normally order an inquiry on the claimant's cross-undertaking even though he has been successful in proving infringement.[498] The cross-undertaking is automatically implied, both in cases of the grant of an injunction and also on the giving of an undertaking to the court by the defendant,[499] whether by consent or otherwise.

The benefit of the cross-undertaking may as a matter of discretion be expressly extended to third parties unconnected with the dispute who may incur expenditure in complying with the order or may otherwise be affected by it. However, in the absence of such express provision, such a third party has no claim in restitution against a claimant who has been enriched at the third party's expense by reason of the existence of the injunction. There is also no basis on which the party who has been "wrongfully" injuncted can claim damages on behalf of such a third party, nor can the benefit of the cross-undertaking be extended to such a third party by an estoppel.[500]

21–148   **Interim mandatory injunctions.** Different principles govern the court's discretion to grant interim mandatory injunctions which are usually more drastic in their effects. According to Phillips L.J. in *Zockoll Group Ltd v Mercury Communications Ltd*,[501] the following passage from the judgment of Chadwick J. in *Nottingham Building Society v Eurodynamics Systems*[502] is all the citation that should be necessary on the question of mandatory injunctions:

> "In my view the principles to be applied are these. First, this being an interlocutory matter, the overriding consideration is which course is likely to involve the least risk of injustice if it turns out to be 'wrong' in the sense described by Hoffman J.[503]
>
> Secondly, in considering whether to grant a mandatory injunction, the court must keep in mind that an order which requires a party to take some positive step at an interlocutory stage, may well carry a greater risk of injustice if it turns out to have been wrongly made than an order which merely prohibits action, thereby preserving the *status quo*.
>
> Thirdly, it is legitimate, where a mandatory injunction is sought, to consider whether the court does feel a high degree of assurance that the claimant will be able to establish this right at a trial. That is because the greater the degree of assurance the claimant will ultimately establish his right, the less will be the risk of injustice if the injunction is granted.
>
> But, finally, even where the court is unable to feel any high degree of assurance that the claimant will establish his right, there may still be circumstances in which it is appropriate to grant a mandatory injunction at an interlocutory stage. Those circumstances will exist where the risk of injustice if

---

[496] paras 296–300, 307.

[497] *Waterlow Publishers Ltd v Rose & Another* [1995] F.S.R. 207.

[498] *John Richardson Computers Limited v Flanders (No.2)* [1994] F.S.R. 144.

[499] *Catnic Components Ltd v Bainbridge Bros (Engineers) Ltd* [1976] F.S.R. 112.

[500] See *Smithkline Beecham Plc v Apotex Europe Ltd* [2006] EWCA Civ 658; [2007] Ch. 71; [2007] F.S.R. 6.

[501] [1998] F.S.R. 360 at 366.

[502] [1993] F.S.R. 468 at 474.

[503] A reference to *Films Rover Ltd v Cannon Film Sales Ltd* [1987] 1 W.L.R. 670.

this injunction is refused sufficiently outweigh the risk of injustice if it is granted".[504]

Subsequently, in *National Commercial Bank Jamaica Ltd v Olint Corp Ltd*[505] the Privy Council stated that the *American Cyanamid* principles applied to all interim injunctions and accordingly any attempt to classify them as prohibitory or mandatory was "barren".[506] In both cases, the underlying principle was the same, namely, that the court should take whichever course seemed likely to cause the least irremediable prejudice to one party or the other. It was true that the features which ordinarily justified describing an injunction as mandatory were often more likely to cause irremediable prejudice than in cases in which a defendant was merely prevented from taking or continuing with some course of action, but this was no more than a generalisation. What was required in each case was to examine what on the particular facts of the case the consequences of granting or withholding of the injunction was likely to be. If it appeared that the injunction was likely to cause irremediable prejudice to the defendant, a court might be reluctant to grant it unless satisfied that the chances that it would turn out to have been wrongly granted were low; that is to say, that the court would feel a high degree of assurance that at the trial it would appear that the injunction was rightly granted.[507]

An interim mandatory injunction may be granted to require a defendant to take all practical steps to recover allegedly infringing items which have been distributed. Where title has passed, the court may order the defendant to ask for them back.[508]

Procedure. The application is made under CPR Pt 23.[509] The following points **21–149** may be made in relation to the rights covered in this work. First, on any application, whether with or without notice, a party is not entitled to rely on confidential evidence which has not been or will not be revealed to the other side.[510] Thus a defendant against whom a without notice injunction has been granted is entitled to see all the evidence on which the injunction was granted, so that he can comment on it and adduce contrary evidence. Secondly, the evidence should deal with questions as to what damage the claimant would suffer if the injunction is refused and what damage the defendant will suffer if the injunction is granted[511] and it is common for evidence to be filed as to the respective financial means of the claimant and the defendant.[512] Thirdly, it is desirable that an interim injunction is expressed in words which the person restrained can readily understand, particularly if he is not in court when it is granted, and that the terms of the injunction should be clear.[513] Finally, it is also desirable that an interim injunction is not expressed in terms such as the "claimant's copyright", since it has been held that this means that in order to succeed on an application to commit the de-

---

[504] These principles were applied in *Psychometric Services Ltd v Merant International Ltd* [2002] F.S.R. 8 (If source code was not delivered up claimant likely to go into liquidation; delivery up ordered).

[505] [2009] UKPC 16; [2009] 1 W.L.R. 1405.

[506] para.20.

[507] para.19.

[508] *British Broadcasting Corp v Precord Ltd* noted at [1991] I.P.D. 15023.

[509] For draft entries for the application notice, see Vol.2 J2.vi. See, generally, CPR Pt 25: Practice Direction 25A—Interim Injunctions; and Ch.5 of the *Chancery Guide*.

[510] *VNU Business Publications BV v Ziff Davies (UK) Ltd* [1992] R.P.C. 269, following *Re K* [1963] Ch. 381 CA, and *WEA Records v Visions Channel 4* [1983] 1 W.L.R. 721 CA.

[511] *Antec International Ltd v South Western Chicks (Warren) Ltd* [1997] F.S.R. 278.

[512] *Standex International Ltd v CB Blades* [1976] F.S.R. 114.

[513] *Staver Co Inc v Digitext Display Ltd* [1985] F.S.R. 512; *Video Arts Limited v Paget Industries Ltd* [1988] F.S.R. 501; *Khorasandrijan v Bush* [1993] Q.B. 727; *Hunter Kane Ltd v Watkins*, Ch. D., February 12, 2003 (Bernard Livesey QC).

fendant for contempt, the claimant is obliged to prove the very things which are in issue in the action.[514] As to enforcement of injunctions, see para.21–178, below.

21–150   **Without notice applications: practice.** Consistently with the provisions of the Enforcement Directive,[515] an application for an injunction may be made without notifying the party against whom relief is sought.[516] The grant of such an injunction involves making an order against a defendant before he has had an opportunity to put his case. Accordingly, the authorities make clear that such applications should only be made where there is grave urgency, possible risk of irreparable damage or some other particular circumstances which would justify the grant of relief at this early stage, e.g. that the purpose of the injunction would be frustrated if the defendant was warned.[517] Except where secrecy is essential, an applicant must put the respondent on informal notice.[518] There are two additional safeguards for a respondent. First, the applicant is under a duty to make full and frank disclosure of all relevant facts. Breach of this duty may lead to the discharge of the order.[519] Second, the applicant's advocate should draw to the court's attention any defence (whether of fact or law or mixed fact and law) which could be advanced on behalf of the respondent in opposition to the application.

The requirement of the Directive that "the parties[520] shall be so informed without delay" appears to be satisfied by PD25 para.5.1(2), which requires that where an application is made without notice, unless the court orders otherwise, the applicant must undertake to serve on the respondent the application notice, evidence in support and any order made as soon as practicable. The requirement that there should be a review of the orders "within a reasonable time after notification of the measures" is satisfied by PD25 para.5.1(3) which requires that where an application is made without notice, unless the court orders otherwise, the order must contain a return date for a further hearing at which the other party can be present. As to the requirement that the order lapses or is revoked unless proceedings are started within a reasonable time, the combined effect of CPR 25.2 and PD25 para.4.4 is that where the court grants an interim remedy before the start of proceedings the court will either require an undertaking that a claim will be commenced or it will give a direction to that effect. No doubt a failure without very good reason to comply with such an undertaking or direction can be expected to result in the discharge of any interim injunction.

21–151   **Costs of applications.** Where the application is determined on the balance of convenience, the normal order is that costs are reserved to the trial judge.[521] However, the court may depart from that principle, for example where the

---

[514] *The Staver Company Inc v Digitext Display Ltd* [1985] F.S.R. 512; *Video Arts Ltd v Paget Industries Ltd* [1988] F.S.R. 501; *Grisbrook v MGN Ltd* [2009] EWHC 2520 (Ch) at para.75 (a case involving a consent order). See, however, *Spectravest Inc v Aperknit Ltd* [1988] F.S.R. 161, in which the first of these authorities was not followed, although the point was academic (see at 170).

[515] See para.21–133, above.

[516] CPR 25.3.

[517] *Hoffmann-La Roche & Co AG v Secretary of State for Trade and Industry* [1975] A.C. 295; *American Cyanamid Co v Ethicon Ltd* [1975] A.C. 396; [1975] F.S.R. 101; *Morning Star Co-operative Society Ltd v Express Newspapers Ltd* [1979] F.S.R. 113; *Whitbread v Calder Valley Inns*, unreported, cited in *Square Moves Ltd v Moorcroft* [1992] I.P.D. 15122; *TRP v Thorley*, CA (1993) noted in the *Supreme Court Practice 1999*, para.29/1A/21 and [1993] 8 SCP News. *Mayne Pharma (UK) v Teva UK Ltd* [2004] EWHC 3248 (Ch); *Cinpres Gas Injection Ltd v Melea Ltd* [2005] EWHC 3180 (Pat); [2006] F.S.R. 36.

[518] *Practice Direction 25A—Interim Injunctions*, para.4.3(3); *Chancery Guide*, para.5.4.

[519] *Civil Procedure 2010* para.25.3.5.

[520] In an adversarial system this must presumably be taken to mean "the defendant".

[521] *Desquenne et Giral UK Ltd v Richardson* [2001] F.S.R. 1.

outcome of the hearing of the application was so plain that the court should conclude that a party had wasted time and money in fighting the issue[522] or where the court forms a realistic view that the case is not likely to go to trial and the substantive merits are very plain.[523]

(ii) Continuation subject to guarantees

The Enforcement Directive. The Directive requires Member States to ensure that the judicial authorities have the power to make the continuation of the infringement subject to the lodging of guarantees intended to ensure the compensation of the rightholder.[524] Article 9(1)(a) makes clear that the order is intended to be an alternative to the grant of an interim injunction and that the guarantees are intended to ensure that the rightholder is compensated in the event that it emerges at trial that there was in fact an infringement. Article 9(4) of the Directive requires such orders to be available without the defendant having been heard in appropriate cases, in particular where any delay would cause irreparable harm to the rightholder. It is not easy to see when this will be the case. As is the case for without notice applications for injunctions, four procedural safeguards apply: first, the defendant[525] must be notified without delay after execution of the measures at the latest[526]; secondly there must be a return date[527]; thirdly, there must be provision that any order granted prior to the commencement of proceedings will lapse or be revoked if proceedings are not commenced within a specified period[528]; and fourthly there must be a power to require a cross-undertaking as to damages and to enforce it.[529]

21–152

The CPR. This part of art.9(1)(a) was expressly implemented by the introduction of CPR 25.1(p), which is stated to apply in "intellectual property proceedings". This term is not defined in CPR 25.1(p). However, CPR 25.1(p) expressly refers to art.9(1)(a) of the Directive and the Commission has expressed the view that the Directive covers a wide range of rights, including all the rights covered in this Chapter.[530] In general, as will be seen, where damages would be an adequate remedy and the defendant would be in a position to pay them an interim injunction is likely to be refused. It would clearly be open to a claimant to argue in such a case that guarantees should be lodged instead. No doubt a defendant would riposte that guarantees are unnecessary. As to the Directive's requirement that such relief be available on a without notice application, CPR 25.3(1) enables the court to grant interim remedies without notice if there was good reason for not giving notice. Although the procedural safeguards required by the Directive[531] are not expressly provided for in the CPR in relation to such interim orders it seems inevitable that they would be applied as a matter of discretion.

21–153

---

[522] As in the pre-CPR case of *Bushbury Land Rover v Bushbury Ltd* [1997] F.S.R. 709, referred to in *Picnic at Ascot v Derigs* [2001] F.S.R. 2.

[523] As in the pre-CPR case of *Direct Line Group Ltd v Direct Line Estate Agency Ltd* [1997] F.S.R. 374, also referred to in *Picnic at Ascot v Derigs* [2001] F.S.R. 8.

[524] art.9(3) provides that the judicial authorities shall have the authority to require the applicant to provide any reasonably available evidence in order to satisfy themselves with a sufficient degree of certainty that the applicant is the rightholder and that the applicant's rights are being infringed, or that such infringement is imminent. There is no express provision in the CPR to this effect, but it is implicit in the rules of practice as to the strength of the case required before interim relief will be granted.

[525] The Directive says "the parties", but it is presumably the defendant who is meant.

[526] See para.21–133, above.

[527] See para.21–133, above.

[528] art.9(5). See para.21–150, above.

[529] art.9(6) and (7). See para.21–146, above.

[530] See 2005/295/EC, [2005] OJ L94/37.

[531] See the previous paragraph.

(iii) Preservation of evidence and interim delivery up

21–154   **The Enforcement Directive.** Consistently with art.50(1)(b) of TRIPS, art.7(1) of the Directive provides that Member States must ensure that even before the commencement of proceedings the judicial authorities may order prompt and effective provisional measures to preserve relevant evidence, subject to the protection of confidential information. Such measures may be ordered without the other party being heard. The Directive provides for safeguards analogous to those applicable in the case of interim injunctions.[532] Article 9(2) of the Directive requires Member States to ensure that the judicial authorities have the power to order the seizure or delivery up of goods suspected of infringing an intellectual property right[533] so as to prevent their entry into or movement within the channels of commerce. Article 9(4) of the Directive requires interim delivery up orders to be available without the defendant having been heard in appropriate cases, in particular where any delay would cause irreparable harm to the rightholder. The same four procedural safeguards apply as for without notice applications for injunctions.[534]

21–155   **The CPR.** No specific provision was made to implement arts 7(1) or 9(2), presumably because CPR 25.1(c)(i) gives the court broad powers to order on an interim basis the detention, custody or preservation of "relevant property", that is property which is the subject of a claim or as to which any question may arise on a claim[535]; and the court has a statutory power to make a search order.[536] CPR 25.3(1) enables the court to grant interim remedies without notice if there was good reason for not giving notice. Although the procedural safeguards required by the Directive[537] are not expressly provided for in the CPR in relation to such interim orders it again seems inevitable that they would be applied as a matter of discretion.

(iv) Search and seizure orders

21–156   **Search orders.** The High Court has jurisdiction, on an application made to the court by a claimant without notice and in private, to make a mandatory order requiring a defendant to permit or allow the claimant and his representatives to enter the defendant's premises, as specified in the order, so as to inspect articles and documents relevant to the proceedings and to remove them or take copies of them[538] and even to take the proceeds of infringing articles.[539] A draft form of or-

---

[532] See para.21–152, above.

[533] art.9(3) provides that the judicial authorities shall have the authority to require the applicant to provide any reasonably available evidence in order to satisfy themselves with a sufficient degree of certainty that the applicant is the rightholder and that the applicant's rights are being infringed, or that such infringement is imminent. There is no express provision in the CPR to this effect, but it is implicit in the rules of practice as to the strength of the case required before interim relief will be granted.

[534] See para.21–152, above.

[535] CPR 25.1(2).

[536] See below, para.21–156.

[537] See the previous paragraph.

[538] Civil Procedure Act 1997 s.7; CPR 25.1(1)(h); *Anton Piller KG v Manufacturing Processes Ltd & Others* [1976] Ch. 55; [1976] F.S.R. 129; *EMI Ltd v Pandit* [1976] R.P.C. 333; *Pall Europe Ltd v Microfiltrex Ltd* [1976] R.P.C. 326; *Rank Film Distributors Ltd & Others v Video Information Centre & Others* [1982] A.C. 380; [1981] F.S.R. 363; *International Electronics Ltd v Weigh Data Ltd*, *The Times*, March 13, 1980; *Gates v Swift* [1981] F.S.R. 57; *Booker McConnell Plc v Plascow* [1985] R.P.C. 425; *Columbia Picture Industries Inc v Robinson* [1987] Ch. 38; [1986] F.S.R. 367; *Manor Electronics Ltd v Dickson* [1988] R.P.C. 618; *Swedac Ltd v Magnet & Southern Plc* [1989] F.S.R. 243; *Universal Thermosensors Ltd v Hibben* [1992] 1 W.L.R. 840.

[539] *CBS United Kingdom Ltd v Lambert* [1983] Ch. 37.

der is annexed to *Practice Direction 25A—Interim Injunctions.*[540] There are many decided cases on seizure orders and reference should be made to the relevant specialist works. However, the following points can be made. First, this form of order has, in many copyright, confidence and passing-off cases, proved to be one of great efficacy, because the defendant is taken completely by surprise before he is able to deal further with the documents and articles relating to the offending acts. The defendant knows nothing of the proceedings until he is required by the order to admit the claimant and his representatives to the premises. Secondly, three conditions must be satisfied before the court will make an order: first, the claimant must show that he has an extremely strong prima facie case; secondly, the claimant must show that he has suffered, or is likely to suffer, very serious and irreparable damage if an order is not made; and, thirdly, there must be clear evidence that the defendant has in his possession incriminating documents or things and that there is a real possibility that he may destroy such material before any application can be made on notice.[541] Thirdly, the order must be served and carried out in the presence of a supervising solicitor, who is experienced in the workings of search orders and who is wholly independent of the claimant and his solicitors.[542] The introduction of this requirement has considerably increased the cost and complexity of such applications. Fourthly, if the defendant wishes to apply to the court to discharge the order as having been improperly obtained, he is allowed to do so.[543] Fifthly, the order will only normally be made in respect of precisely defined premises.[544] Sixthly, as a matter of the law of evidence, information derived or obtained as a result of a search order which ought never have to have been obtained is admissible.[545] The court, however, has a jurisdiction *in personam* to restrain the use made of such information where it would be inequitable for the claimant to do so.[546] Seventhly, the applicant is under a duty to make full disclosure to the court and to act in the utmost good faith.[547] The court may discharge a search order on the grounds of non-disclosure and order costs to be awarded on an indemnity basis, with immediate assessment. For the operation of the privilege against self-incrimination in these applications, see below.[548]

(v) Identity of infringers

The Enforcement Directive. Article 8(1) of the Directive (headed "Right of information") requires Member States to ensure that in response to a justified and   **21–157**

---

[540] The standard form makes specific reference to the privilege against self-incrimination. Para.7.9 of PD25A refers to the fact that s.72 of the Senior Courts Act 1981 (see para.21–163, below) and other provisions remove the privilege against self-incrimination in certain cases, but makes clear that the privilege may still be claimed in relation to potential criminal proceedings outside those provisions. The scope of any such privilege is limited: *C Plc v P* [2007] EWCA Civ 493; [2008] Ch. 1; *Civil Procedure 2010*, para.31.3.31.

[541] *Anton Piller K.G. v Manufacturing Processes Ltd* [1976] Ch. 55.

[542] *Practice Direction—Interim Injunctions* para.7.2.

[543] Standard form order, paras 10 and 27.

[544] *Protector Alarms Ltd v Maxim Alarms Ltd* [1978] F.S.R. 442; *Cook Industries Inc v Galliher* [1979] Ch. 439; *Universal City Studios Inc v Mukhtar & Sons Ltd* [1976] 2 All E.R. 330.

[545] *Helliwell v Piggot-Sims* [1980] F.S.R. 356.

[546] *Lord Ashburton v Pape* [1913] 2 Ch. 469. *Guess? Inc v Lee Seck Mon* [1987] F.S.R. 125 (CA of Hong Kong); *English & American Insurance Co Ltd v Herbert Smith* [1988] F.S.R. 232; *Naf Naf SA v Dickens (London) Ltd* [1993] F.S.R. 424.

[547] *Booker McConnell Plc v Plascow* [1985] R.P.C. 425; see also *Dormeuil Frères SA v Nicolian International (Textiles) Ltd* [1989] F.S.R. 255. This duty includes a duty to point out to the judge any differences between the order sought and the standard order annexed to *Practice Direction—Interim Injunctions* (see *The Gadget Shop Ltd v The Bug.com Ltd* [2001] F.S.R. 26) and to inform a judge of the Queen's Bench Division in a copyright and breach of confidence case that the natural forum is the Chancery Division (see *Elvee Ltd v Taylor* [2002] F.S.R. 48). See generally *Civil Procedure 2010*, para.25.3.5.

[548] See para.21–163, below.

proportionate request of the claimant the judicial authorities may order that information on the origin and distribution networks of infringing goods or services to be provided by the infringer and/or any other person who (a) was found in possession of the infringing goods on a commercial scale; (b) was found using the infringing services on a commercial scale; (c) was found to be providing on a commercial scale services used in infringing activities; or (d) was indicated by a person within (a) to (c) as being involved in the production, manufacture or distribution of the goods or the provision of the services.[549] Article 8(2) provides that the information so ordered shall, as appropriate, comprise (a) the names and addresses of the producers, manufacturers, distributers, suppliers and other previous holders of the goods or services, as well as the intended wholesalers and retailers and (b) information on the quantities produced, manufactured, delivered, received or ordered, as well as the price obtained. These provisions are expressed to be without prejudice to provisions allowing rights holders to receive fuller information, provisions governing the use of the material disclosed and its misuse, provisions as to the right of silence and confidentiality and provisions as to confidentiality and data protection. They go considerably beyond art.47 of TRIPS.

21–158   **General.** Consistently with these provisions, in an action for infringement of copyright or related rights, the court frequently exercises its jurisdiction, on an interim application, to make an order requiring a defendant to make a witness statement setting out the names and addresses of the suppliers and purchasers of infringing material and articles known to him.[550] He is also required to state the dates and quantities supplied, and to exhibit documents relating to supplies and purchases.[551] This is a valuable form of order because it enables the claimant in a copyright action, for example, to obtain from retailers of infringing goods details as to the wholesale or manufacturing sources of supply. The basis of the jurisdiction is that a person, whether he is himself an infringer, or has become innocently involved without personal liability in the wrongdoing[552] of others, is under a duty to assist those injured by those acts to give full information by way of disclosure of documents and of the identity of the wrongdoers.[553] It matters not if the or the wrongdoers are out of the jurisdiction.[554] The application should be made promptly.[555] It seems that if a respondent which is out of the jurisdiction indicates

---

[549] For a discussion of the implementation of this provision in the various Member States, see Evidence and Right of Information in Intellectual Property Rights, a Report of the legal sub-group of the European Observatory on Counterfeiting and Piracy: *http://ec.europa.eu/internal_market/iprenforcement/observatory/index_en.htm* [Accessed October 12, 2010].

[550] Such orders are not included in the list of interim remedies in CPR 25.1(1). However, the list is not intended to be exhaustive: CPR 25.1(3).

[551] *Radio Corp of America v Reddington's Rare Records* [1974] 1 W.L.R. 1445; *Harry Freedman v Hillingdon Shirts Co Ltd* [1975] F.S.R. 449; *EMI Ltd & Another v Sarwar* [1977] F.S.R. 146; *Loose v Williamson* [1978] 1 W.L.R. 639; *EMI Ltd & Others v Pandit* [1976] R.P.C. 333.

[552] In *Ashworth Hospital Authority v MGN Ltd* [2002] 1 W.L.R. 2033; [2003] F.S.R. 17, the Court of Appeal held that the jurisdiction applied in breach of confidence cases. In the House of Lords (*Ashworth Hospital Authority v MGN Ltd* [2002] UKHL 29; [1973] F.S.R. 365), it was held (obiter) that it did not matter whether the wrongdoing was tortious, in breach of contract, a civil wrong or a crime (paras 34, 53). In *Financial Times Ltd v Interbrew SA* [2002] E.M.L.R. 24; [2002] 2 Ll. Rep. 229, the Court of Appeal held that the jurisdiction applies in relation to equitable as well as common law wrongs, in particular in breach of confidence cases.

[553] *Norwich Pharmacal Co v Customs and Excise Commissioners* [1974] A.C. 133; [1973] F.S.R. 365; *British Steel Corp v Granada Television Ltd* [1981] A.C. 1096; *X Ltd v Morgan-Grampian Plc* [1990] 2 W.L.R. 1000.

[554] *Smith Kline & French Laboratories Ltd v Global Pharmaceutics Ltd* [1986] R.P.C. 394 and *Jade Engineering Ltd v Antiference Window Systems* [1996] F.S.R. 461.

[555] *Wilmot Breeden Ltd v Woodcock Ltd* [1981] F.S.R. 15.

that it will comply with such an order, permission will be granted to serve the application out of the jurisdiction.[556]

The procedure has recently been used to discover the identity of unlicensed file-sharers. It was considered by the Court of Justice in *Productores de Música de España (Promusicae) v Telefónica de España SAU* C–275/06.[557] The Court held that Directive 2002/58/EC on privacy and electronic communications did not prohibit Member States from providing for such orders[558] but that there was nothing in the Information Society Directive, the E-Commerce Directive or the Enforcement Directive which obliged Member States to provide for them.[559] The Court went on to say that Community law requires that, when transposing those Directives, care must be taken to rely on an interpretation of them which allows a fair balance to be struck between the various fundamental rights protected by the Community legal order (in particular the right to property and the right to privacy). In addition, the Court said, when implementing the measures transposing those Directives, the authorities and courts of the Member States must not only interpret their national law in a manner consistent with those Directives but also make sure that they do not rely on an interpretation of them which would be in conflict with those fundamental rights or with the other general principles of Community law, such as the principle of proportionality.[560] Subsequently, in *Bonnier Audio AB v Perfect Communication Sweden AB*,[561] the Hogsta Domstolen—Sweden referred to the Court of Justice the question whether such orders were precluded by Directive 2006/24 on the retention of data.[562]

Conditions. The jurisdiction to order disclosure exists if three conditions are satisfied: first, the third party has become mixed up in the transactions of which disclosure is required.[563] It is sufficient if it can be shown that there is "a good indication" of wrongdoing but not every piece of a pleaded case is in position.[564] Secondly, the order for disclosure must be for a legitimate purpose. It is not necessary for the applicant to show that he intends to sue the person so identified. It is sufficient that (for example) he intends to dismiss a wrongdoer who is an employee.[565] However, it is necessary for the applicant to identify the purpose for which the information is sought and the use of the material will then be restricted

21–159

---

[556] See *Lockton Companies International v Persons Unknown* [2010] EWHC 3423 (QB) in which permission was granted to serve out of the jurisdiction.

[557] [2008] 2 C.M.L.R. 17.

[558] See at para.54.

[559] paras 57–60.

[560] para.70.

[561] Case C–461/10.

[562] [2006] OJ L105/54.

[563] In *The Coca-Cola Company v British Telecommunications Plc* [1999] F.S.R. 518, the claimant wished to sue a third party who had been involved in the delivery of infringing goods. The court was satisfied that it was very probable that a mobile telephone had been used by the third party in connection with the delivery. The respondent service provider was ordered to disclose the address of the third party. See also *Totalise Plc v The Motley Fool Ltd* [2001] 4 E.M.L.R. 750 (order made against operators of website on whose discussion boards defamatory material had been posted anonymously).

[564] *Carlton Film Distributors Ltd v VCI Plc* [2003] F.S.R. 47. See to the same effect *Mitsui & Co Ltd v Nexen Petroleum UK Ltd* [2005] EWHC 625 (Ch); at para.21 "a wrong must have been carried out, or arguably carried out" and *Eli Lilly and Company Ltd v Neopharma Ltd* [2008] EWHC 415 (Ch); [2008] F.S.R. 25 at para.28 (names of customers who were arguably wrongdoers).

[565] Note however that in its judgment in *Financial Times Ltd v United Kingdom* [2010] E.M.L.R. 21 at para.58, a case where freedom of expression was engaged, the European Court of Human Rights appeared to disapprove the obtaining of such orders by private litigants in order to prevent crime.

to that purpose unless the court orders otherwise.[566] Thirdly, where the respondent is innocent of any participation in the wrongdoing, the remedy is one of last resort, only to be exercised if there is no other practicable means of obtaining the information.[567]

21–160   **Scope of order.** The jurisdiction is not confined to cases of identifying wrongdoers.[568] It has been used to discover the names and addresses of persons to whom the defendant had sent a letter which the claimant alleged contained false statements.[569] It may be exercised to discover what has happened to property and in aid of a freezing order, where it is just and convenient to make the order.[570] The jurisdiction to order disclosure against a person who has become mixed up in the torts of others applies a fortiori against the wrongdoer himself.[571] Disclosure may therefore be ordered against a defendant if there is a reasonable cause of action pleaded against him.[572]

In *Roberts v Jump Knitwear*[573] it was held that no disclosure order would be made to reveal the names of innocent third parties who had been supplied with allegedly infringing articles. It is doubtful whether that decision was correct.[574] Under s.99(1) of the 1988 Act there is a right to apply for an order for delivery up and under that jurisdiction an order for delivery up may be made regardless of the existence of any knowledge of the defendant that the copy is an infringing copy. In those circumstances the court has jurisdiction to make an order against the person who has allegedly put infringing copies into circulation requiring him to disclose the identity of the persons to whom such copies have been supplied. The fact that it has not yet been established that the copies are infringing copies is not a bar to this jurisdiction. The issue will not be decided between the claimant and the third party until proceedings under s.99 have been brought and determined.[575]

In appropriate cases, however, the disclosure of names of the defendant's customers may be refused or limited to the claimant's advisers so as to protect the defendant from approaches to his customers by the claimant which might damage his goodwill or might amount to a misuse of confidential information.[576]

Where the claimant's intention is to sue, the obligation to give information extends to all information necessary to enable the claimant to decide whether it is

---

[566] *Ashworth Hospital Authority v MGN Ltd* [2002] 1 W.L.R. 2033; [2003] F.S.R. 17, at paras 45 to 53, overruling *Financial Times Ltd v Interbrew SA* [2002] E.M.L.R. 24; [2002] 2 Ll. Rep. 229.

[567] *Mitsui & Co Ltd v Nexen Petroleum UK Ltd* [2005] EWHC 625 (Ch) at para.24.

[568] *Jade Engineering Ltd v Antiference Window Systems* [1996] F.S.R. 461; cf. *Arab Monetary Fund v Hashim* [1992] 2 All E.R. 911, suggesting that the jurisdiction in *Norwich Pharmacal Co v Customs and Excise Commissioners* [1974] A.C. 133; [1973] F.S.R. 365 extends only to identifying the wrongdoers and no further.

[569] *CHC Software Care Ltd v Hopkins & Wood* [1993] F.S.R. 241.

[570] *Mercantile Credit (Europe) AG v Aiyela* [1994] Q.B. 366; [1993] F.S.R. 745 (Hobhouse J.); cf. *Arab Monetary Fund v Hashim* [1992] 2 All E.R. 911, suggesting that the *Norwich Pharmacal* jurisdiction extends only to identifying the wrongdoers and no further.

[571] *Norwich Pharmacal Co v Customs and Excise Commissioners* [1974] A.C. 133 at pp.175C–D.

[572] *CFC Software Care Ltd v Hopkins & Wood* [1993] F.S.R. 241.

[573] [1981] F.S.R. 527.

[574] *Lagenes Ltd v It's At (UK) Ltd* [1991] F.S.R. 492; it was not followed in *Jade Engineering Ltd v Antiference Window Systems* [1996] F.S.R. 461. In *Eli Lilly and Company Ltd v Neopharma Ltd* [2008] EWHC 41 (Ch); [2008] F.S.R. 25, the Judge stated that on the basis of *Sega Enterprises Ltd v Alca Electronics Ltd* [1982] F.S.R. 516 he should approach the question of whether to grant disclosure of customers' names in a similar way to the question whether to grant an interim injunction para.32.

[575] *Lagenes Ltd v It's At (UK) Ltd* [1991] F.S.R. 492.

[576] *Kentron Properties Pty Ltd v Jimmy's Co Ltd* [1979] F.S.R. 86 at 96; *Sega Enterprises Ltd v Alca Electronics & Others* [1982] F.S.R. 516; *Moore & Craven* [1871] 7 L.R. Ch. App. 94; *Jade Engineering Ltd v Antiference Window Systems* [1996] F.S.R. 461.

worth suing the wrongdoer or not.[577] In principle, a defendant may be ordered to state whether the order for goods has been solicited by the manufacturer or whether the defendant has initiated the order, and to give disclosure of all relevant documents. In *Société Romanaise de la Chaussure SA v British Shoe Corp Ltd*,[578] the defendant was ordered to state the grounds of its belief that it was the only customer for the goods and that the manufacturer held no other stocks. The defendant was also ordered to give disclosure of all documents relevant to the grounds of belief. It was pointed out that the information was disclosable in due course in any case. It was not harmful to the defendant to order the information to be produced now, but it was harmful to the claimant if left to speculate in the absence of the information.

Costs. Normally, where the respondent is in no way implicated with the unlawful act in question, the applicant will be ordered to pay the respondent's costs, including the costs of complying with the order. There may be exceptions to this rule, but not where the respondent had a genuine doubt as to whether the applicant was entitled to the order; the respondent was under a legal obligation not to reveal the information (or the legal position was not clear and the respondent had a reasonable doubt as to his obligations); the respondent might be subject to proceedings if disclosure was given voluntarily; the respondent would or might suffer damage by giving the disclosure; or the disclosure would or might infringe a legitimate interest of another.[579]   **21–161**

Section 10 of the Contempt of Court Act 1981.[580] Section 10 provides that no Court may require a person to disclose, nor is any person guilty of contempt of court for refusing to disclose, the source of information contained in a publication for which he is responsible, unless it be established to the satisfaction of the court that disclosure is necessary in the interests of justice or national security or for the prevention of disorder or crime. It is "in the interests of justice", in the sense in which the phrase is used in s.10, that persons should be enabled to exercise important legal rights and to protect themselves from serious legal wrongs whether or not resort to legal proceedings in a court of law will be necessary to attain those objectives.[581]   **21–162**

Section 10 must now be applied in accordance with the jurisprudence of art.10 of the European Convention on Human Rights.[582]

The applicable principles have recently been restated by the European Court of Human Rights.[583] Accordingly, the court must start from the proposition that freedom of expression constitutes one of the essential foundations of a democratic society and that the safeguards guaranteed to the press are of particular importance. Protection of journalistic sources is one of the basic conditions for press freedom since without such protection sources may be deterred from assisting the press in informing the public on matters of public interest. As a result, the vital watchdog role of the press may be undermined and the ability of the press to provide accurate and reliable reporting may be adversely affected.[584] Disclosure orders have a detrimental effect not only on the source in question (whose identity

---

[577] *Société Romanaise de la Chaussure SA v British Shoe Corporation Ltd* [1991] F.S.R. 1.
[578] [1991] F.S.R. 1.
[579] *Totalise Plc v The Motley Fool Ltd* [2001] 4 E.M.L.R. 750.
[580] c.49.
[581] *Ashworth Hospital Authority v MGN Ltd* [2002] UKHL 29; [2002] 1 W.L.R. 2033; [2003] F.S.R. 17, para.39.
[582] *Ashworth Hospital Authority v MGN Ltd* [2002] UKHL 29.
[583] *Financial Times Ltd v United Kingdom*, Application 821/03, [2010] E.M.L.R. 21. The decision draws heavily on *Goodwin v United Kingdom* (1996) 22 E.H.R.R. 123.
[584] *Financial Times Ltd v United Kingdom* [2010] E.M.L.R. 21 at para.59.

may be revealed) but also on the newspaper (whose reputation may be negatively affected in the eyes of future potential sources by the disclosure) and on the public (who have an interest in receiving information imparted through anonymous sources and who are also potential sources themselves).[585] Accordingly, an order for source disclosure cannot be compatible with art.10 unless it is justified by an overriding requirement in the public interest.[586] As a matter of general principle, the "necessity" of any restriction on freedom of expression must be convincingly established. It is for the national authorities to assess in the first place whether there is a "pressing social need" for the restriction and in making that assessment they enjoy a certain margin of appreciation. However, in the context of orders to disclose the identity of sources the national margin of appreciation is circumscribed by the interest of democratic society in ensuring and maintaining a free press. This interest will weigh heavily in the balance in determining whether the restriction is proportionate to the legitimate aim pursued.

Accordingly, limitations on the confidentiality of journalists' sources call for the most careful scrutiny by the European Court of Human Rights.[587] The Court must look at the interference and determine whether the reasons adduced by the national authorities to justify it are "relevant and sufficient".[588]

On the other hand, the exercise of freedom of expression carries with it duties and responsibilities which also apply to the press. Article 10 protects a journalist's right—and duty—to impart information on matters of public interest provided he is acting in good faith in order to provide accurate and reliable information in accordance with the ethics of journalism.[589]

It may be that the public perception of the principle of non-disclosure of sources would suffer no real damage where it was overridden in circumstances where a source was clearly acting in bad faith with harmful purposes and disclosed intentionally falsified information. However, courts should be slow to assume, in the absence of compelling evidence, that these factors are present in any particular case. In any event, given the multiple interests in play, the conduct of the source can never be decisive in determining whether a disclosure order ought to be made but will merely operate as one, albeit important, factor in the balancing exercise.[590]

Ashworth Hospital Authority v MGN Ltd[591] concerned the publication by a newspaper of medical records which appeared to have come from a hospital's confidential computer database and to have been provided to the newspaper by an employee at the hospital in exchange for a cash payment. The hospital wished to identify the employee for the purposes of dismissing him. The House of Lords upheld an order that the newspaper disclose its source.

In *Financial Times Ltd v United Kingdom*,[592] a document suggesting that the claimant company might be about to buy another company had been leaked to the press. The publication resulted in a significant decline in the claimant's share price and a significant rise in the target company's share price. A disclosure order which had been made on an interim application was upheld by the Court of Appeal, which described the leak as "relatively modest", albeit this did not diminish

---

[585] *Financial Times Ltd v United Kingdom* [2010] E.M.L.R. 21 at para.63.
[586] *Financial Times Ltd v United Kingdom* [2010] E.M.L.R. 21 at para.59.
[587] *Financial Times Ltd v United Kingdom* [2010] E.M.L.R. 21 at para.60.
[588] *Financial Times Ltd v United Kingdom* [2010] E.M.L.R. 21 at para.61.
[589] *Financial Times Ltd v United Kingdom* [2010] E.M.L.R. 21 at para.62.
[590] *Financial Times Ltd v United Kingdom* [2010] E.M.L.R. 21 at para.63.
[591] [2002] UKHL 29.
[592] [2010] E.M.L.R. 21 at paras 64–73

the prospective seriousness of its repetition.[593] The European Court of Human Rights held that the claimant's interests in eliminating the threat of damage through future leaks and in obtaining damages for past breaches of confidence had been insufficient to outweigh the public interest in the protection of journalists' sources. The Court of Appeal had considered it critical that the source's motives were maleficent but the evidence of this was insufficient[594]; the claimant had not sought urgent injunctive relief for breach of confidence when informed of the leak[595]; the conclusion that there were no less invasive means of identifying the source was based on inference; and the claimant had not given full details of the enquiries it had made.[596]

This decision suggests that it will seldom (if ever) be appropriate to make an order on an interim basis. In *Ackroyd v Mersey Care NHS Trust*,[597] the Court of Appeal held that in most cases where a source disclosure order was sought against a journalist, it would not be appropriate to make the order on a summary judgment application.[598]

Self-incrimination. The frequent use of search orders in proceedings for infringement of copyright coupled with orders to give disclosure of names and addresses of suppliers and related documents used to give rise to problems with the privilege against self-incrimination. The circumstances in which infringement takes place frequently involve the commission of criminal offences or subject the defendant to penalties. The infringement may even involve a criminal conspiracy to defraud. In such cases, the defendant used to be able to claim the privilege against self-incrimination to set aside an order for disclosure or production of documents or information.[599]   **21–163**

In order to meet that situation the position as to the privilege against self-incrimination was altered by the provisions of s.72 of the Senior Courts Act 1981 (as amended by Sch.7 to the 1988 Act).[600] The privilege has been withdrawn from a party and his or her spouse in the proceedings and circumstances specified in s.72. A person is not excused from answering questions put to him or from complying with an order by reason that to do so would tend to expose him or his or her spouse to proceedings for a related offence or the recovery of a related penalty. The withdrawal of the privilege applies to civil proceedings in the High Court for infringement of rights pertaining to any "intellectual property"—i.e. "patent, trademark, copyright, design right, registered design, technical or commercial information or other intellectual property"—or for passing off. It also applies to proceedings to obtain disclosure of information relating to the infringement of such a right.

The defendant is, however, given the safeguard that no statement or admission by a person in answering a question or complying with an order is, in proceed-

---

[593] *Interbrew SA v Financial Times Ltd* [2002] EWCA Civ 274; [2002] E.M.L.R. 446 at para.54.
[594] para.66.
[595] para.69.
[596] para.69.
[597] [2003] E.M.L.R. 36 at para.68.
[598] In compliance with the disclosure order made in *Ashworth Hospital Authority v MGN Ltd* [2002] UKHL 29, the newspaper disclosed that the intermediary was a freelance journalist. That disclosure did not, however, reveal the identity of the original source in the hospital. The journalist resisted disclosure of his source on the grounds that his position was distinguishable from that of the newspaper. Disclosure was refused at trial: *Mersey Care NHS Trust v Ackroyd* [2006] EWHC 107 (QB); [2006] E.M.L.R. 12. This decision was upheld on appeal: *Mersey Care NHS Trust v Ackroyd* [2007] EWCA Civ 101; [2007] H.R.L.R. 19.
[599] *Rank Film Distributors Ltd v Video Information Centre* [1982] A.C. 380; [1981] F.S.R. 363.
[600] *Crest Homes Plc v Marks* [1987] A.C. 829; [1988] R.P.C. 21.

ings for a related offence, admissible against the person or his spouse.[601] It is admissible in proceedings for perjury or contempt of court. A "related offence" is one which is committed by or in the course of the infringement or passing off to which the proceedings relate or "any offence" revealed by the facts on which the claimant relies in the proceedings. The effect of the definition of "related offence" is that it is only where there is a risk of further damage to the claimant that the defendant is denied the right to claim the privilege in respect of self-incrimination for offences not committed by or in connection with the alleged infringement. The "related offence" is defined in different and much wider terms in the case of proceedings to prevent future torts than in the case of proceedings for past or present infringements.[602]

The privilege has also been abrogated in proceedings for the recovery or administration of any property, for the execution of a trust or for an account of any property or dealings with property in relation to offences under the Theft Act 1968, the Fraud Act 2006, other offences of fraud and certain proceedings under the Children Act 1989.[603]

It has been suggested that these exclusions require review in the light of the Human Rights Act 1998.[604]

In cases where these exclusions do not apply, the privilege against self-incrimination still applies. It is not necessary for the defendant to claim the privilege: an order whereby the defendant may be incriminated should never be made. However, such an order can usually be made against a foreign corporation because there is no risk of prosecution. The defendant is not entitled to claim the privilege if he is adequately protected against prejudice.[605] Thus, an order may properly be made whose execution is conditional (a) upon the defendant being advised of his right to claim privilege and (b) upon his expressly declining the right.[606] The privilege should be claimed by the defendant himself on oath.[607] A defendant served with a search order is entitled to supply all documents which he claims may be incriminating to the supervising solicitor. If the latter decides that they are incriminating they will be excluded from the search.[608]

21–164   **Position of intermediaries.** The E-Commerce Directive[609] enables Member States to "establish" obligations whereby service providers must provide information about infringing activities of users of their services.[610] Presumably *Norwich Pharmacal*[611] orders fall within the scope of this, so that nothing in the Regulations affords a defence in relation to the exercise of this jurisdiction.

(vi) Freezing injunctions

21–165   **The Enforcement Directive.** Article 9(2) of the Directive requires Member States to ensure that in the case of infringement on a commercial scale, where the

---

[601] The court may, however, permit the claimant, upon application, to inform the police of any alleged theft of his property or of any admissions made by the defendant—see *Process Development Ltd v Hogg* [1996] F.S.R. 45.

[602] *Universal City Studios Inc v Hubbard* [1984] Ch. 225; [1984] R.P.C. 43.

[603] See Theft Act 1968 s.31; Fraud Act 2006 s.13; Children Act 1989 s.98.

[604] See *Civil Procedure 2010*, para.31.3.32.

[605] *AT&T Istel v Tully* [1993] A.C. 45 HL.

[606] *IBM United Kingdom Ltd v Prima Data International Ltd* [1994] 1 W.L.R. 719.

[607] *Downie & Others v Coe & Others*, The Times, November 28, 1997.

[608] See the standard order annexed to *Practice Direction 25A—Interim Injunctions*, para.11.

[609] Directive 2000/31/EC of the European Parliament and of the Council of June 9, 2000 on certain legal aspects of information society services, in particular electronic commerce, in the Internal Market (Directive on electronic commerce). Relevant extracts are at Vol.2 H7.

[610] art.15(2).

[611] See paras 21–158 et seq., above.

injured party[612] demonstrates circumstances likely to endanger the recovery of damages, the judicial authorities have the power to order the precautionary seizure of the alleged infringer's movable and immovable property, including the blocking of his or her bank accounts and other assets. The article continues: "To that end, the competent authorities may order the communication of bank, financial or commercial documents, or appropriate access to the relevant information".

Freezing injunctions. No steps needed to be taken to implement art.9(2) because the court has a wide discretionary jurisdiction to make restraint and disclosure orders in respect of a defendant's assets both in and outside England and Wales and both before and after judgment, in order to prevent a defendant from taking action, such as disposal of assets, designed to frustrate subsequent orders of the court in favour of a claimant. The power extends to the grant of disclosure in aid of the injunction. Many cases continue to be reported on the grant and discharge of freezing injunctions and reference should be made to more specialised works for a full account of this jurisdiction. As in the case of search orders, there are now standard forms of freezing injunctions.[613]   **21–166**

C. FINAL RELIEF

(i) Declaratory judgment

The court has the power to make binding declarations whether or not any other remedy is claimed.[614] Declaratory relief may be sought by a right holder against an alleged infringer or by a potential defendant who wishes to establish that he is not infringing.[615]   **21–167**

The grant of a declaration is discretionary[616] and the court will be concerned to establish that the declaration will have some utility before granting it.[617] Accordingly, the court will not make a declaratory order to the effect that copyright will subsist in documents not yet in existence, but which it is anticipated will be brought into existence. There must be before the court specific documents, the character of which can be established.[618] Nor will the court make declarations of right amounting to conclusions of fact from hypothetical or assumed states of fact.[619] There must be put before the court evidence of an actual or intended infringement of copyright and the court will not attempt an exhaustive enunciation

---

[612] art.9(3) provides that the judicial authorities shall have the authority to require the applicant to provide any reasonably available evidence in order to satisfy themselves with a sufficient degree of certainty that the applicant is the rightholder and that the applicant's rights are being infringed, or that such infringement is imminent. There is no express provision in the CPR to this effect, but it is implicit in the rules of practice as to the strength of the case required before interim relief will be granted.

[613] See *Practice Direction 25A—Interim Injunctions*.

[614] CPR 40.20. As to interim declarations, see CPR 25.1(1)(b) and *Civil Procedure 2010* para.25.1.15.

[615] art.44(2) of TRIPS permits the making of a declaration where the remedies provided by Pt III are inconsistent with a Member's law but this appears to have no application to the UK. No specific provision is made in the Enforcement Directive.

[616] See generally *Civil Procedure 2010*, paras 40.20.1 et seq. and *Rolls-Royce Plc v Unite the Union* [2009] EWCA Civ 387; [2010] 1 W.L.R. 318.

[617] See, e.g. *Nokia Corp v InterDigital Technology Corp* [2007] EWHC 3077 (Pat) at para.5: would the declaration if granted be the equivalent of shouting in an empty room or is there some point in it?

[618] *Odhams Press Ltd v London and Provincial Sporting News Agency, etc. Ltd* [1936] Ch. 357.

[619] *Wyke Group Plc v Cooper Roller Bearings Co Ltd* [1996] F.S.R. 126.

of the factual circumstances in which infringement has or has not occurred.[620] The court may grant a declaration by consent where it is essential to do justice between the parties.[621]

A declaration as to non-infringement is, like other forms of declaration, discretionary.[622] Declarations as to non-infringement should be regarded as an unusual remedy and caution exercised in extending the circumstances in which they are granted.[623] In general, the court will not grant declaratory relief against a person who has not asserted any right but may do so if the claimant has a genuine commercial reason for seeking the declaration.[624]

The court will not normally grant a declaration of non-infringement on an application for summary judgment. Nevertheless, a declaration may be granted where a judgment is obtained without a trial (e.g. a default judgment), when full justice cannot otherwise be done. For example, a declaration may be granted that a publishing agreement is at an end, so facilitating an author in his efforts to sell his work elsewhere. It is important that the declaration in question should not affect the rights of anyone other than the defendants or the persons claiming through them.[625]

In *Point Solutions Ltd v Focus Business Solutions Ltd*,[626] Focus had alleged that Point had infringed its copyright in computer software. Point commenced proceedings for a declaration of non-infringement, claiming independent design. Focus did not raise a positive case of copying, simply putting Point to proof of its case. No evidence (expert or otherwise) was adduced as to the software in issue. The claim was dismissed, primarily because the Judge found that Point had failed to prove independent design, but also because there was no evidence that the allegations had caused damage and because a declaration would prevent Focus from alleging infringement in proceedings where all the evidence was available. On appeal no criticism was made of the Judge's failure to address copying and her decision as to independent design was upheld. The Court of Appeal also stated (obiter) that it was not persuaded that the Judge had been wrong to hold that there was no need for a declaration in the absence of damage but criticised the suggestion that a declaration would shut Focus out of proceedings—Focus had chosen not to adduce further evidence. The Court of Appeal canvassed two possible approaches a Court might take in such cases in future. First, it might put the party in Focus's position to an election, requiring it either to make a positive case as to infringement or to limit the issue at trial to the question whether an allegation of infringement had been made (described as a "put up or shut up" order).[627] Alternatively, it was suggested that a Judge should be slow to allow a

---

[620] *Moorehouse & Angus Robertson (Publishers) Pty Ltd v University of New South Wales* [1976] R.P.C. 51.

[621] For example, to give effect to a compromise agreement which provided that if certain conditions were not fulfilled a party should be at liberty to obtain judgment in the terms of the declarations sought: *Animatrix v O'Kelly* [2008] EWCA Civ 1415.

[622] *Della Reed Ltd v Delkim Developments* [1988] F.S.R. 329.

[623] *Messier Dowty Ltd v Sabena SA* [2001] 1 All E.R. 275.

[624] *Wyke Group Plc v Cooper Roller Bearings Co Ltd* [1996] F.S.R. 126. *Nokia Corp v InterDigital Technology Corp* [2006] EWCA Civ 1618; [2007] F.S.R. 23 at para.15. In the latter case the Court of Appeal upheld the trial Judge's refusal to grant reverse summary judgment on a claim for a declaration. Although no right had been asserted, the claimant had a real commercial interest in the declaration sought because it would determine (at least in the United Kingdom) whether the defendant's patents were essential to use for complying with an industry standard.

[625] *Patten v Burke Publishing Co Ltd* [1991] 1 W.L.R. 541; [1991] F.S.R. 483, followed in *Aitbelaid v Nima, The Times*, July 19, 1991.

[626] [2005] EWHC 3096; [2006] F.S.R. 31; on appeal [2007] EWCA Civ 14.

[627] para.34.

case to come to trial where the parties had failed to adduce the evidence necessary to resolve the real issue between them.[628]

(ii) Permanent injunction

General. Article 44(1) of TRIPS requires Members to authorise judicial authorities to grant injunctions. It also provides that members are not obliged to authorise the grant of injunctions where protected subject matter was acquired or ordered without knowledge or reason to believe that dealing with it would infringe.[629] Article 11 of the Enforcement Directive requires Member States to ensure that where a finding of infringement is made the judicial authorities may issue an injunction.

21–168

Consistently with this, if a claimant succeeds at the trial in establishing infringement of copyright, he will normally be entitled to a permanent injunction to restrain future infringements.[630] An injunction is a discretionary remedy, and general equitable principles will apply, for example, the "clean hands" principle.[631]

The question whether an injunction ought to be granted permanently is determined by reference to the circumstances and state of the law existing at the date when the question falls to be determined and the court's consideration is not confined to those circumstances existing at the date of the claim form. Accordingly, where undertakings had been offered before the commencement of proceedings but after their commencement the defendant denied liability and withdrew the undertakings, the Court of Appeal upheld the grant of an injunction.[632]

In the past it has been said that there is no need for the claimant to prove actual damage before an injunction will be granted.[633] However, the current practice is that the court will not grant an injunction where the infringement is technical or unlikely to cause real damage if it recurs.[634] Where the prima facie position is that the infringement has occurred once and for all and is finished and done with, the

---

[628] para.47.

[629] The latter provision would permit the "innocent acquisition" defence in injunction claims in unregistered UK design right cases: see CDPA 1988 s.233(2). However, there is no equivalent provision in the Enforcement Directive (art.12 does not go so far) and it is therefore debatable whether s.233(2) is actually consistent with the Directive.

[630] *Weatherby & Sons v International Horse Agency and Exchange Ltd* [1910] 2 Ch. 297; *Performing Right Society Ltd v Ciryl Theatrical Syndicate Ltd* [1923] 2 K.B. 146; *Samuelson v Producers Distributing Co Ltd* (1931) 48 R.P.C. 580 at 593; *Performing Right Society Ltd v Mitchell and Booker (Palais de Danse) Ltd* [1924] 1 K.B. 762, 774; *Pride of Derby and Derbyshire Angling Association Ltd v British Celanese Ltd* [1953] Ch. 149, 181, 194; *Morris v Redland Bricks Ltd* [1970] A.C. 652 at 664D, 665F; *Colgate Palmolive Ltd v Markwell Finance Ltd* [1990] R.P.C. 197 at 200; *Performing Right Society Ltd v Berman* [1975] F.S.R. 400 at 403; *Phonographic Performance Ltd v Maitra* [1998] 1 W.L.R. 870 CA; *Ludlow Music Inc v Williams* [2002] F.S.R 57; [2002] E.M.L.R. 29. One of the reasons for granting an injunction after a dispute as to whether the acts complained of infringe is that the defendant will have maintained at trial that he has the right to do them and will have expressly or implicitly threatened to continue to infringe: *Cantor Gaming Ltd v Gameaccount Global Ltd* [2007] EWHC 1914 (Ch); [2008] F.S.R. 4 at para.101. For an exceptional case where the court refused an injunction, see *Banks v EMI Songs Ltd (No.2)* [1996] E.M.L.R. 452 discussed in the next paragraph.

[631] *Ocular Sciences Ltd v Aspect Vision Care Ltd* [1997] R.P.C. 289.

[632] *Landor and Hawa International Ltd v Azure Designs Ltd* [2006] EWCA Civ 1285; [2007] F.S.R. 9.

[633] *Smith v Johnson* (1863) 33 L.J.Ch. 137; *Campbell v Scott* (1842) 11 Sim. 31; *Weatherby & Sons v International Horse Agency and Exchange Ltd* [1910] 2 Ch. 297 at 305; *Hawkes & Son (London) Ltd v Paramount Film Service Ltd* [1934] Ch. 593 at 608.

[634] The concept of proportionality has been given greater status in recent times, reinforcing the fact that the court should not encourage costly litigation over very little by granting relief even in trivial cases: *Cantor Gaming Ltd v Gameaccount Global Ltd* [2007] EWHC 1914 (Ch); [2008] F.S.R. 4 at para.112. However, a claimant does not need to go so far as to show that the grant of an injunction is "really necessary" to ensure that its rights are protected: *Cantor Gaming Ltd v*

claimant will be required to show positively that the defendant is likely to continue his infringement.[635] If, in addition, the defendant had given a bona fide undertaking not to repeat the infringement, that is an important factor which would influence the court in refusing an injunction. In the majority of such cases, it would be very difficult for a claimant, whose rights had been infringed, to prove positively a definite likelihood of a repetition of the infringement. On the other hand, if the letter containing the undertaking contains a false justification of the infringement and the defendant persists in putting the claimant's rights in issue and maintaining "a quite hopeless justification of its reprehensible conduct", justice requires that the claimant be protected by an injunction.[636] The same may be true if the court considers it appropriate for those undertakings to be backed by court sanction, e.g. because previous contractual undertakings have been breached or because there is a dispute about their scope or because the defendant's approach to ensuring compliance is more casual than necessary to guarantee protection of the claimant's rights.[637] In *Performing Right Society Ltd v Berman*[638] infringement was alleged by the playing by a band of music at a club operated by the defendants. No undertaking had been given not to repeat the infringement. An injunction was granted notwithstanding that the club had subsequently closed down.

21–169   **Damages in lieu.** Article 12 of the Enforcement Directive permits Member States to provide that in an appropriate case and at the request of the person liable to an injunction, the court may award pecuniary relief but only if (a) the infringer acted unintentionally and without negligence, (b) the execution of the measures in question would cause him or her disproportionate harm and (c) pecuniary compensation to the injured party appears reasonably satisfactory. Recital 25 makes clear that this power is not intended to be used where the commercial use of counterfeit goods or the supply of services would infringe laws other than intellectual property laws or would be likely to harm consumers.

Article 12 has not been specifically implemented in the United Kingdom. It is not clear whether art.12 is an exhaustive statement of the circumstances in which damages are to be available in lieu of an injunction or whether a power to grant damages in lieu in a broader set of circumstances is inherent in the general discretion pursuant to art.11. Clearly, if art.12 is exhaustive, the case law referred to below will cease to be of much relevance in intellectual property cases.

In *Shelfer v City of London Electric Lighting Co*,[639] it was stated to be a "good working rule" that if the injury to the claimant's rights was small and capable of being estimated in money and could be adequately compensated by a small money payment and the case was one in which it would be oppressive to grant an injunction, the court might award damages in substitution for an injunction. In *Jaggard v Sawyer*, the Court of Appeal emphasised that the test is one of oppression and not merely the balance of convenience.[640] In *Banks v CBS Songs Ltd*

Gameaccount Global Ltd [2007] EWHC 1914 at para.125. See also para.129, where the Judge emphasised that the mere fact that a person is held entitled to relief of a given kind does not automatically entitle that person to the costs of obtaining it, if the breach is of minimal importance or the proceedings pointless.

[635] *Performing Right Society Ltd v Berman* [1975] F.S.R. 400 (High Ct of Rhodesia); *P.R.S. v Butcher* [1975] F.S.R. 405 (High Ct of Rhodesia).

[636] *Banier v News Group Newspapers Ltd* [1997] F.S.R. 812 at 816.

[637] *Cantor Gaming Ltd v Gameaccount Global Ltd* [2007] EWHC 1914 (Ch); [2008] F.S.R. 4 at paras 107–109.

[638] [1975] F.S.R. 400 (High Ct of Rhodesia).

[639] [1895] 1 Ch. 287.

[640] [1995] 1 W.L.R. 269. In *Navitaire Inc v easyJet Airline Co Ltd (No.2)* [2005] EWHC 0282 (Ch);

(No.2),[641] a record company argued that a songwriter's claim to an injunction should be refused on the basis of *Shelfer*. The court rejected this submission on the grounds that since the copyright might last another century it was impossible to say that the claimant could be adequately compensated by a small money payment.[642] The court nevertheless refused an injunction because although the case was outside the working rule set out in *Shelfer*, it was "wholly exceptional": the defendants had been exploiting the lyrics for some 11 years; it was accepted that most of the commercial use had probably already occurred; and the claimant had made plain that what she really wanted was money—the claim for an injunction was made not because she wanted to stop the commercial exploitation but in order to negotiate a price.

In *Regan v Paul Properties Ltd*,[643] Mummery L.J. (with whom Tuckey L.J. and Wilson L.J. agreed) summarised the effect of Shelfer in the following propositions:

(1) A claimant is prima facie entitled to an injunction against a person committing a wrongful act which invades the claimant's legal right.

(2) The wrongdoer is not entitled to ask the court to sanction his wrongdoing by purchasing the claimant's rights on payment of damages assessed by the court.

(3) The court has jurisdiction to award damages instead of an injunction, but the jurisdiction does not mean that the court is "a tribunal for legalising wrongful acts" by a defendant who is able and willing to pay damages.

(4) The judicial discretion to award damages in lieu should pay attention to well-settled principles and should not be exercised to deprive a claimant of his prima facie right except under very exceptional circumstances.

(5) Although it is not possible to specify all the circumstances relevant to the exercise of the discretion or to lay down rules for its exercise, it is relevant to consider the following factors: whether the injury to the claimant's legal rights is small; whether the injury can be estimated in money; whether it can be adequately compensated by a small money payment; whether it would be oppressive to the defendant to grant an injunction; whether the claimant has shown that he only wants money; whether the conduct of the claimant renders it unjust to give him more than pecuniary relief; and whether there are any other circumstances which justified the refusal of an injunction.

The observations of Mummery L.J. should be compared with those of Lloyd L.J. (with whom Buxton L.J. and Rix L.J. agreed) in *Jacklin v Chief Constable of West Yorkshire*[644]:

"the *Shelfer* principles are only a working rule, although a long hallowed and reliable working rule, but it is clear that the four elements ... are cumulative and that it is necessary for a defendant to satisfy the first three, but that it is by no means sufficient for it to do so. There has to be some additional factor, characterised in *Shelfer* and in *Jaggard v Sawyer* as oppression, to justify withholding the injunctive remedy, which is the claimant's prima facie right as ancillary to his property rights."

This statement has been interpreted as importing a requirement that in order to

---

[2006] R.P.C. 4 at para.104, Pumfrey J. held that the grant of an injunction would be "oppressive" if it would be "grossly disproportionate to the right protected".

[641] [1996] E.M.L.R. 452.

[642] See, to the same effect, *Ludlow Music Inc v Williams* [2002] EWHC 638 (Ch); [2002] F.S.R. 57, where an attempt to invoke the *Shelfer* principle failed.

[643] [2006] EWCA Civ 1319; [2007] Ch. 135 at para.36.

[644] [2007] EWCA Civ 181 at para.48.

avoid the grant of an injunction, a defendant must show that all four of the *Shelfer* criteria have been satisfied.[645]

21–170   **Statutory limits on grant of injunction.** In proceedings for infringement of the right to object to derogatory treatment of a work,[646] the Court may, if it thinks it is an adequate remedy in the circumstances, grant an injunction on terms prohibiting the doing of any act unless a disclaimer is made, dissociating the author or director from the treatment of the work.[647] Analogous provision is made in relation to the live broadcast, playing in public or communication to the public of a qualifying performance which has been subjected to derogatory treatment.[648] In other specified circumstances, the 1988 Act provides that an injunction should not be granted.[649]

21–171   **Delay in taking proceedings.** The tendency of the court is not to refuse an injunction at the hearing of the action merely on account of delay in instituting proceedings,[650] subject to the provisions of the Limitation Act 1980. Of course, such delay may be a factor in establishing general equitable defences such as laches, acquiescence, waiver and estoppel.[651] Under certain circumstances delay might be held to amount to a tacit permission to reproduce the work.[652]

21–172   **Public policy and public interest cases.** An injunction may be refused on the grounds of public policy or public interest. These defences are considered elsewhere.[653]

21–173   **Scope of injunction: future and other works.** It has been held that an injunction will not be granted to restrain infringements of future numbers of a periodical, although the defendants have systematically copied from numbers already published[654] and that no injunction will be granted against copying a future football fixture list.[655] However, these cases do not represent the current state of the law. The critical question is whether the defendant will be in a position to know what he can and cannot do. Accordingly, injunctions have been granted to restrain infringement of copyright in future television schedules[656] and in Microsoft's operating software, whether existing or future.[657] Likewise, in a representative action for infringement of sound recording copyrights brought by some

---

[645] *HKruk II (CHC) Ltd v Heaney* [2010] EWHC 2245 (Ch).

[646] CDPA 1988 s.80.

[647] s.103(2).

[648] CDPA 1988 s.205N(4).

[649] See "undertaking to take licence of right", paras 21–88 et seq., above and "innocently acquired illicit recordings and infringing articles", para.21–92, above.

[650] *Hogg v Scott* (1874) L.R. Eq. 444; *Morris v Ashbee* (1868) L.R. 7 Eq. 34; *Fullwood v Fullwood* (1878) 9 Ch. D. 176; *Reliance Rubber Co Ltd v Reliance Tyre Co Ltd* (1925) 42 R.P.C. 91; *Aktiebologet Manusv R.J. Fullwood & Bland Ltd* (1948) 65 R.P.C. 329.

[651] See, generally, *Fisher v Brooker* [2009] UKHL 41; [2009] 1 W.L.R. 1764; [2009] F.S.R. 25; and para.5–220, above.

[652] *Rundell v Murray* (1821) Jac. 311; *Saunders v Smith* (1838) 3 My. & Cr. 711. See also *Ludlow Music Inc v Williams* [2001] F.S.R. 271 (summary judgment): arguable acquiescence defence and *Ludlow Music Inc v Williams* [2002] EWHC 638, Ch. D.; [2002] F.S.R. 57 (trial): if injunction had been sought in respect of existing pressings of infringing CDs it would have been refused on grounds of acquiescence.

[653] See paras 3–304 et seq. and 21–93 et seq., above.

[654] *Cate v Devon, etc. Newspaper Co* (1889) 40 Ch. D. 500 at 507; *Sweet v GW Bromley & Co* [1905–1910] Mac.C.C. 203; but see *Bradbury v Sharp* [1891] W.N. 123 and *TM Hall & Co v Whittington & Co* [1892] 18 V.L.R. 525.

[655] *Football League Ltd v Littlewoods Pools Ltd* [1959] Ch. 637.

[656] *Independent Television Publications Ltd v Time Out Ltd* [1984] F.S.R. 64. The report is unclear but the injunction must have applied to future works.

[657] *Microsoft Corp v Electro-Wide Ltd* [1997] F.S.R. 580: injunction in respect of any operating system software in which the claimant owned copyright.

members of the British Phonographic Industry on behalf of all its members the court held that it would have power to grant an injunction extending to the copyrights of all the members because their recordings were issued under labels or marks giving rise to the presumption of ownership provided for by s.105(1) of the 1988 Act and this would be readily apparent to the defendants.[658] On the other hand, an injunction will not be granted in relation to copyright in future films where it is difficult to identify the owner or exclusive licensee of film copyright[659] nor will an injunction be granted to restrain infringement generally.[660]

Scope of injunction: injunction post expiry of right. In *Dyson Appliances Ltd v Hoover Ltd (No.2)*,[661] the defendant had infringed the claimant's patent by various forms of development activity, thus obtaining a "springboard" in the market which the court assessed at 12 months. Because of this, the claimant would have been entitled to "springboard" damages in respect of the period of 12 months after the expiry of the patent.[662] Because those damages would be very difficult to quantify, the claimant was granted an injunction to restrain acts which would otherwise have infringed the patent for a period of 12 months after its expiry. It is not yet clear whether this decision will be applied to the rights covered in this work.[663]   **21–174**

Scope of injunction: acts in respect of existing rights. In general, where the claimant has established an infringement of his rights, and subject to the points made above, he is entitled to an injunction to restrain any future infringement of those rights.[664] Exceptionally, the court may grant relief in a narrower form. Thus, for example, in one passing-off and trade mark case, the Court of Appeal upheld an injunction limited to dealing with software which the defendant knew or had reason to believe to be counterfeit.[665] The court emphasised that this decision was confined to its facts. In another case involving passing off and trade marks, the court rejected undertakings which were qualified so that the defendant would not be in breach of them if it had at all times maintained in force a regulatory procedure to the satisfaction of the court and if it dealt expeditiously with any complaints from the claimant.[666]   **21–175**

Where portion only of the defendant's work is copied. Where only part of a   **21–176**

---

[658] *Independiente Ltd v Music Trading Online (HK) Ltd* [2003] EWHC 470 (Ch) at para.27. For these presumptions, see paras 21–260 et seq., below.

[659] *Columbia Picture Industries v Robinson* [1987] Ch. 38; [1986] F.S.R. 367.

[660] *Twentieth Century Fox Film Corp v Newzbin Limited* [2010] EWHC 608 (Ch); [2010] E.C.D.R. 8; [2010] E.M.L.R. 17; [2010] F.S.R. 21.

[661] [2001] R.P.C. 27.

[662] See *Gerber Garment Technology v Lectra Systems Ltd* [1997] R.P.C. 443.

[663] The injunction was granted under s.61(1) of the Patents Act 1977 (c.37), which is in rather different terms ss.96, 191I and 229 of the 1988 Act and the decision was based in part on European patents jurisprudence.

[664] *Microsoft Corp v Plato Technology Ltd*, CA, Unreported, July 15, 1999. In *Coflexip SA v Stolt Comex Seaways MS Ltd* [1999] F.S.R. 483, a patent case, Laddie J. had held that where the defendant was an honest trader, the injunction should generally be limited to the acts found to infringe rather than to any acts of infringement of the whole patent. This decision was distinguished in *Aktiebolget Volvo v Heritage (Leicester) Ltd* [2000] F.S.R. 253 (trade marks; defendant had not acted in accordance with honest commercial practices) but followed in *Beautimatic International Ltd v Mitchell International Pharmaceuticals Ltd* [2000] F.S.R. 267 (trade marks). However, Laddie J.'s decision was overruled by the Court of Appeal: *Coflexip S.A. v Stolt Comex Seaways MS Ltd* [2001] 1 All E.R. 952. Accordingly, the authority of the *Beautimatic* decision is doubtful.

[665] *Microsoft Corp v Plato Technology Ltd*, CA, Unreported, July 15, 1999. See also *Sun Microsystems Inc v Amtec Computer Corp Ltd* [2006] EWHC 62 (Ch); [2006] F.S.R. 35 (trade marks; injunction limited to parallel imports and including provisions exonerating defendant if it had checked with the claimant first and had no knowledge or belief that it was infringing).

[666] *British Telecommunications Plc v Nextcall Telecom Plc* [2000] F.S.R. 679: the proposed undertakings would have involved the court descending into the commercial arena in order to decide whether there had been a breach.

work has been copied, and the part which has been copied from the claimant's work can be separated from that which has not been copied, an injunction will be granted only against the objectionable part or parts.[667] But even where a very large proportion of a work of a piratical nature is unquestionably non-infringing, if the parts which have been copied cannot be separated from those which are non-infringing without destroying the use and value of the original matter, he who has made an improper use of that which did not belong to him must suffer the consequences of so doing, and an injunction will be granted against the whole.[668] He has only himself to blame for the consequences of mixing another person's work with his own in such a way that they cannot be separated. Where the claim is for a permanent injunction, as distinct from an interim injunction, it will not usually be appropriate to weigh the damage which the defendant will suffer by reason of the injunction (for example, through the loss of non-infringing material), against the damage which the claimant will suffer if the injunction is refused.[669]

21–177　**Form of injunction.** The modern form of interim injunction contains provisions that:

1. A defendant who is an individual who is ordered not to do something must not do it himself or in any other way; he must not do it through others acting on his behalf or on his instructions or with his encouragement.
2. A defendant which is a corporation and which is ordered not to do something must not do it itself or by its directors officers employees or agents or in any other way".

Final injunctions are often expressed in similar terms.

The terms of the injunction must be clear, otherwise the court will not grant it. The defendant is entitled to know precisely what acts he is prohibited from committing.[670] If there is a dispute as to whether the defendant's conduct is a breach of an order or undertaking the defendant can apply to the court for guidance.[671]

21–178　**Enforcement of injunctions.** Articles 9 and 12 of the Enforcement Directive provide that where provided for by national law, non-compliance with an injunction shall, where appropriate, be subject to a recurring penalty payment, with a view to ensuring compliance, but otherwise leave the enforcement of injunctions to national courts. The general rule in England and Wales is that injunctions may be enforced against a defendant who is an individual by committal and sequestration; and against a defendant which is a body corporate, by sequestration; and also by committal and sequestration against its directors and other officers.[672] In less serious cases the court may, instead of these penalties, impose a fine and payment of costs,[673] or merely the payment of costs.[674] Breach of an undertaking to the court is punishable in the same way as breach of an injunction.[675]

---

[667] *Jarrold v Houlston* (1857) 3 K. & J. 708; *Lamb v Evans* [1892] 3 Ch. 462.

[668] *Advanced Vehicle Systems Inc & Others v Rees, Oliver & Others* [1979] R.P.C. 127 at 141.

[669] *Macmillan Publishers Ltd v Thomas Reed Publications Ltd* [1993] F.S.R. 455 at 366, 467. But see the law about awarding damages in lieu of an injunction: para.21–169, above.

[670] *Staver Co Inc v Digitext Display Ltd* [1985] F.S.R. 512; *Columbia Picture Industries v Robinson* [1987] Ch. 38; [1986] F.S.R. 367; *Video Arts Ltd v Paget Industries Ltd* [1988] F.S.R. 501; *Khorasandrijan v Bush* [1993] Q.B. 727.

[671] *Spectravest Inc v Aperknit Ltd* [1988] F.S.R. 161.

[672] RSC Ord.45 r.5, Ord.46 r.5 and Ord.52, preserved by the CPR. *Att-Gen for Tuvalu v Philatelic Distribution Corp Ltd* [1990] 1 W.L.R. 926. See generally *Arlidge, Eady & Smith on Contempt.*

[673] RSC Ord.52 r.9; *Phonographic Performance Ltd v Amusement Caterers (Peckham) Ltd* [1964]

To establish contempt of court it is sufficient to prove that the defendant's conduct was intentional and that he knew all the facts which made it a breach of the order. It is not necessary to prove that the defendant knew it was a breach.[676] However, it is not a contempt of court to fail to carry out the impossible.[677] The court has to decide what the defendant has done, even if the injunction is an interim one and that involves deciding issues in the action.[678] The court has a discretion to decline to hear a litigant's appeal where he has wilfully and contumaciously failed to comply with an order of the court.[679] Where, on an application to commit for contempt of court, the court is satisfied that the breach of the undertaking to the court is also a breach of contract by the contemnor, in respect of which there is no defence to a claim for damages, the court may make a summary award of damages in addition to an order for costs on an indemnity basis.[680]

(iii) Injunctions against service providers[681]

(a) *European legislation*

Article 8(3) of the Information Society Directive.[682] This provision requires Member States to ensure that holders of copyright and rights in performances are in a position to apply for an injunction against intermediaries whose services are used by a third party to infringe their rights. The reason for this provision appears from recital 59, which notes that in a digital environment the services of intermediaries may increasingly be used by third parties and that in many cases such intermediaries are best placed to bring such infringing activities to an end. Accordingly, the recital continues, rightholders should have the possibility of applying for an injunction against an intermediary who carries a third party's infringement in a network, even when the intermediary's acts are exempted under art.5 (that is, because they constitute a permitted act).   **21–179**

Article 11 of the Enforcement Directive. The final sentence of this article, which is expressed to be without prejudice to art.8(3), is in identical terms to it except that it applies to all intellectual property rights and (most relevantly) to database right.   **21–180**

Reference to the Court of Justice. Questions as to the scope of the obligation placed on Member States by the final sentence of art.11, and in particular the   **21–181**

Ch. 195; *Steiner Products Ltd v Willy Steiner Ltd* [1966] 1 W.L.R. 986; *Ronson Products Ltd v Ronson Furniture Ltd* [1966] R.P.C. 497; *Re Mileage Conference Group, etc. Ltd's Agreement* [1966] 1 W.L.R. 1137; *Re W. (B.) (An Infant)* [1969] 2 Ch. 50; *GCT (Management) Ltd v The Laurie Marsh Group Ltd* [1973] R.P.C. 432; in *Re Grantham Wholesale, etc. Ltd* [1972] 1 W.L.R. 559; *Jennison v Baker* [1972] 2 Q.B. 52.

[674] *Ronson Products Ltd v Ronson Furniture Ltd* [1966] R.P.C. 497. In contempt proceedings costs are usually awarded on an indemnity basis.

[675] *Re Mileage Conference Group, etc. Ltd's Agreement* [1966] 1 W.L.R. 1137; *Biba Ltd v Stratford Investments Ltd* [1973] R.P.C. 799.

[676] *British Telecommunications Plc v Nextcall Telecom Plc* [2000] F.S.R. 679.

[677] *Sectorguard Plc v Dienne Plc* [2009] EWHC 2693 (Ch) at para.33.

[678] *Spectravest Inc v Aperknit Ltd* [1988] F.S.R. 161. Note, however, that it is desirable to avoid this by phrasing interim injunctions in terms which refer to specific acts rather than, for example, to "the claimant's copyright". See para.21–149, above.

[679] *X Ltd v Morgan Grampian Ltd* [1991] 1 A.C. 1 HL. However, this is a jurisdiction which should be exercised only exceptionally: *Atlantic Capital Corp v Johnson, Independent*, July 15, 1994.

[680] *Midland Marts Ltd v Hobday* [1989] 1 W.L.R. 1143; additional damages may be awarded: *Phonographic Performance Ltd v Reader* [2005] F.S.R. 42.

[681] For the obligations imposed on service providers by the Communications Act 2003 with a view to reducing unlicensed peer to peer file sharing, see paras 21–288 et seq.

[682] 2001/29, [2001] OJ L 167/6. See Vol.2 H7.

scope of the injunction which it requires to be available against intermediaries, were referred to the Court of Justice in *L'Oréal v eBay*.[683] In the subsequent case of *Twentieth Century Fox Film Corp v Newzbin Ltd*,[684] the Judge applied s.97A of the 1988 Act (which implements art.8(3)) without making a reference. In *Newzbin* the service provider was found to be infringing anyway, so s.97A added nothing to the claim. However, it seems inevitable that if relief under s.97A is sought against a non-infringing service provider before the determination of the reference in *L'Oréal v eBay* a reference will have to be made in relation to art.8(3).

(b) *The 1988 Act*

21–182   **General.** The Government's initial view was that there was no need for specific legislative implementation of art.8(3) because injunctions would be available at common law (it is no doubt for this reason that the third sentence of art.11 has never been formally implemented).[685] However, during the consultation on the implementation of the Information Society Directive, right owner organisations generally expressed concern that unless specific provision was made to implement art.8(3), there would be uncertainty as to their rights to apply for injunctions, particularly where intermediaries themselves were not infringing because of the art.5(1) exemption, which permits temporary acts of copying.[686] Accordingly, in order to avoid uncertainty, the Government decided to implement art.8(3) specifically.

21–183   **Sections 97A and 191JA.** These sections were therefore introduced into the 1988 Act by the Copyright and Related Rights Regulations 2003.[687] They give the High Court[688] power to grant an injunction against a service provider[689] where that service provider has actual knowledge of another person using its service to infringe copyright or (as the case may be) a performer's property right. Section 97A applies to database right.[690]

21–184   **Actual knowledge.** In determining whether a service provider has actual knowledge for these purposes, the court is obliged to take into account: first, all matters which appear to it in the particular circumstances to be relevant; secondly, whether a service provider has received a notice through a means of contact made available in accordance with reg.6(1)(c) of the E-Commerce Regulations; and thirdly, the extent to which any such notice includes (i) the full name and address of the sender and (ii) details of the infringement in question.[691] Given the breadth of the factors which the court must take into account, the absence of a

---

[683] *L'Oréal SA v eBay International AG* [2009] EWHC 1094 (Ch); [2009] R.P.C. 21 at paras 455–465.

[684] *Twentieth Century Fox Film Corp v Newzbin Ltd* [2010] EWHC 608 (Ch); [2010] F.S.R. 21.

[685] In *L'Oréal SA v eBay International AG* [2009] EWHC 1094 (Ch); [2009] R.P.C. 21 at para.454, Arnold J. held that if art.11 required the grant of an injunction against an intermediary who is not an infringer, then that fact provided a sufficient reason for a court of equity to exercise its power to grant such an injunction to protect an intellectual property right which had been infringed. In saying this, he was not treating art.11 as having direct effect; but as providing a principled basis for the exercise of an existing jurisdiction in a new way. As has been stated, he went on to refer questions to the Court of Justice.

[686] See the Analysis of Responses and Government Conclusions, para.8.3

[687] SI 2003/2498, Vol.2 A3.v, with effect from October 31, 2003.

[688] In Scotland, the Court of Session.

[689] For these purposes, service provider has the same meaning as in the Electronic Commerce Regulations (SI 2002/2013), as to which see para.21–104, above.

[690] The Copyright and Rights in Databases regulations 1997 (SI 1997/3032) reg.23.

[691] CDPA 1988 ss.97A(2) and 191JA(2).

reg.6(1)(c) notice is in no way conclusive.[692] In general, it seems that the question of whether a service provider has actual knowledge for these purposes will be determined in the same way as for secondary infringement of copyright.[693]

Practice. Sections 97A and 191JA have seldom been used. It appears that this is at least in part because of concerns by right holders that they will have to pay service providers' costs even if an injunction is granted. *Twentieth Century Fox Film Corp v Newzbin Ltd*[694] is the only reported case in which either section has been applied. The court found that the service provider was itself infringing and accordingly the relief (under s.97A) added nothing to what the claimant was already entitled to.[695]   **21–185**

(c) Section 17 Digital Economy Act 2010: blocking injunctions

Background. In its original form, the Digital Economy Bill contained a clause (cl.17) which would have permitted the Secretary of State by Order to amend the copyright Part of the 1988 Act for the purpose of preventing or reducing the infringement of copyright if it appeared to him appropriate to do so having regard to technological developments that had occurred or were likely to occur. This clause met fierce opposition and was replaced in the House of Lords by a Liberal Democrat amendment which forms the origin of s.17. That clause was revised by the Government and it is the revised clause which became law. The new section permits the Secretary of State to introduce a power to require internet service providers to block access to certain websites which are used for or in connection with the infringement of copyright. It is primarily directed at websites outside the jurisdiction which host or link to substantial amounts of infringing content.[696]   **21–186**

Implementation. Section 17(1) enables the Secretary of State to introduce this power by regulations.[697] Such regulations may not be made unless the Secretary of State is satisfied that the use of the internet for activities that infringe copyright is having a serious adverse effect on business or consumers; that making the regulations is a proportionate may to address that effect; and that making the regulations would not prejudice national security or the prevention or detection of crime.[698] Section 18 sets out an elaborate process, analogous to the "super-affirmative resolution" procedure[699] which must be followed before such regulations may be made.   **21–187**

Blocking injunctions: general. The regulations may make provision about the granting by a court of a "blocking injunction" in respect of location on the internet which a court is satisfied has been, is being or is likely to be used for or in   **21–188**

---

[692] *Twentieth Century Fox Film Corp v Newzbin Ltd* [2010] EWHC 608 (Ch); [2010] F.S.R. 21; at para.135.
[693] See paras 8–09 et seq., above.
[694] *Twentieth Century Fox Film Corp v Newzbin Ltd* [2010] EWHC 608 (Ch); [2010] E.C.D.R. 8; [2010] F.S.R. 21.
[695] For the court's decision as to the scope of the injunction, see para.21–173.
[696] See *Hansard* H.L. Vol. 717 Col. 1456, 1468.
[697] Any regulations must be made by statutory instrument (subs.(10)) and with the Lord Chancellor's consent (subs. (9)). There is broad discretion as to the content of such regulations (subs.(7)(d) and (e)) and they may modify the copyright Part of the 1988 Act and make consequential modifications to other legislation (subs.(8)).
[698] It seems that the Government was concerned that the introduction of a site blocking provision might cause an increase in the use of encrypted sites: *Hansard* H.L. Vol. 717 Col. 1457, 1461, 1469.
[699] As to which, see Legislative and Regulatory Reform Act 2006 s.18.

connection with any activity that infringes copyright.[700] A "blocking injunction" is an injunction that requires a service provider to prevent its service being used to gain access to the location.[701] The term "service provider" has the same meaning as in s.97A of the 1988 Act.[702] It will readily be seen that this is an extremely wide power. Its exercise does not depend on any complicity of the service provider in the infringement; it applies even where a site is no longer being used for infringement; and it applies to sites being used "in connection with" infringement. The term "copyright" appears to be limited to UK copyright.[703]

21–189 **Conditions for grant of injunction.**[704] The regulations must provide that a court may not grant an injunction unless satisfied that the location in question satisfies one of three alternative criteria. The first is that it is one from which a substantial amount of material has been, is being or is likely to be obtained in infringement of copyright. The term "substantial" is not defined. The second is that it is one at which a substantial amount of material has been, is being or is likely to be made available in infringement of copyright. The third is that it is being or is likely to be used to facilitate access to a location which satisfies one of the first two criteria. It follows that the operator of the site which is the subject of the application need not itself either be committing an infringement or be secondarily liable for an infringement. Even a search engine operator might fall within the third condition. However, it seems unlikely that a court which has regard to the criteria for the grant of an injunction (see the next paragraph) would subject an ordinary search engine operator's site to a blocking order. In any event, the regulations may contain provision about when a location is or is not to be treated as being used to facilitate access to another location.[705] Such provision could be used to provide an express exclusion of search engines or indeed hyperlinkers or content aggregators.[706]

21–190 **Criteria for grant of an injunction.** The regulations must provide that in determining whether to grant an injunction the court is obliged to take account of five matters.[707] They are as follows. First, any evidence of steps taken by the service provider or by an operator to prevent infringement of copyright in "qualifying material" (that is, material obtained or made available in infringement of copyright).[708] So far as it is directed at service providers, this provision is clearly designed to encourage service providers to take their own measures to prevent infringements by means of their services. However, it must be construed in the context of the E-Commerce Directive, which prevents the imposition of a general obligation on providers to monitor the information they transmit or store or actively to seek facts or circumstances seeking illegal activity.[709] So far as it is directed at site operators, it will clearly be relevant to consider what measures (if any) have been taken to filter infringing material. The second matter is any evidence of steps taken by the copyright owner or by a licensee of copyright in the

---

[700] s.17(1).

[701] s.17(2).

[702] See para.21–104, above.

[703] First, it is expressly provided that the Act extends to the United Kingdom: s.46(1) (subs.(2) is irrelevant for these purposes because s.17 does not operate by way of amendment to the 1988 Act). Second, there is a reference in s.17(5)(b) to "the copyright owner" and this is defined as having the same meaning as in the copyright Part of the 1988 Act: see s.17(12).

[704] s.17(4).

[705] s.17(7)(a).

[706] The Government's intention is that search engines should not be liable to these measures if they inadvertently feature infringing material: *Hansard* H.L. Vol. 718 Col. 480.

[707] s.17(5)(a)–(e).

[708] s.17(12).

[709] Directive 2000/31 art.15(1). See Vol.2 H7.

qualifying material to facilitate lawful access to the qualifying material. This provision is no doubt designed to encourage content owners to make material available to the public on reasonable terms. However, it would be surprising (and might raise serious human rights issues[710]) if a court were to refuse a blocking injunction because (for example) a content owner had refused to make its works available electronically. The third matter is "any representations made by a Minister of the Crown". The purpose of this is obscure. Presumably it will mean that the Crown will have to be given notice of any application. The fourth matter is whether the injunction would be likely to have a disproportionate effect on any person's legitimate interests. No doubt a court would be reluctant to block a site the content of which was predominantly lawful.[711] The final matter is the importance of freedom of expression. Presumably this is not intended to extend existing defences to infringement (either by way of permitted acts or as a matter of public interest). If so, however, it is not clear what it adds to the previous one.

Procedure and costs. The regulations must provide that no injunction may be granted unless notice of the application has been given in a form and by such means as are specified in the regulations, to the service provider and to operators of the location.[712] The term "operator" is not the proprietor of the location but is "a person who has editorial control over material available at the location".[713] The regulations may provide that notice of an application may be given to operators of a location by being published in accordance with regulations.[714] This provision is no doubt designed to avoid the difficulties which will inevitably arise of identifying the operators of the site and (where relevant) serving them out of the jurisdiction. The court is not to be required to be satisfied that the application has come to an operator's notice. It follows that access to a site may be blocked without any operator having any knowledge of the application. However, given the potential seriousness of the consequences which may result from this (particularly if all the large internet service providers are subject to the order) it seems unlikely that a court would be willing to grant a blocking injunction in circumstances where it was not satisfied that an operator had notice of the application except in the most obvious case. As to costs, the regulations may provide that a court is not to make an order for costs against the service provider.[715] Indeed, it is certainly possible that a court would order an applicant to pay a blameless service provider's costs of responding to an application. If the location to be blocked is out of the jurisdiction or its operators cannot be found it seems likely in practice that the applicant will have to pay its own costs as well.[716]

21–191

(iv) Election between damages and account of profits

A successful claimant is usually entitled to an inquiry as to damages[717] or, at his election, an account of profits.[718] He is not entitled to both, since the principle which lies behind the equitable remedy of an account of profits is that the claim-

21–192

---

[710] See in particular art.1 of the First Protocol to the European Convention on Human Rights.

[711] It is not intended that the provision should disproportionately affect sites such as YouTube: *Hansard* H.L. Vol. 718 Col. 472.

[712] s.17(6). Curiously, the Act says "operators", not "the operators". It may be sufficient therefore for one of several operators to have notice.

[713] s.17(12). The Act refers to control over "material", not "all the material" nor the relevant material.

[714] s.17(7)(b).

[715] s.17(7)(c).

[716] It is the Government's view that "Essentially ... the costs should be borne, not by the ISPs but by those seeking a court order": *Hansard* H.C. Vol. 508 Col. 1135.

[717] See paras 21–193 et seq., below.

[718] See paras 21–209 et seq., below.

ant condones the infringement and takes the profits made by the infringer for the use of his property.[719] The remedies are, therefore, mutually inconsistent and the claimant must elect between the two.[720] Furthermore, a claimant who has chosen to sue more than one member of a chain of distribution may not elect for damages against one defendant and profits against another.[721] Once a clear, unequivocal election has been made, for example the entering of judgment for one or the other,[722] the claimant cannot change his mind and opt for the other remedy. A claim form claiming only damages does not amount to such an election and the claimant will usually be permitted to amend at any time before judgment to include a claim for an account.[723] The election should be made at the latest when infringement is established,[724] but the claimant cannot be forced to make an election before then.[725] Prior to making his election, the claimant is entitled to disclosure and inspection of such documents and an order for the provision of such information as may be necessary to enable him to make an informed choice.[726] This should not be an over-lengthy or unnecessarily sophisticated exercise. The claimant is not entitled to know exactly the amount of any damage or profits, but only to such information as the court considers to be a fair basis in the circumstances of the particular case for an election.[727]

(v) Damages

21–193   **General.** Subject to any special defence as to damages,[728] a successful claimant is entitled to recover damages for the infringement of his right. Actions for infringement of moral rights, performers' non-property rights and the rights of persons having recording rights are treated as breaches of statutory duty[729] and, presumably, damages are assessed using the same principles as those applicable to the commission of any other breach of statutory duty.[730] For actions for infringement of copyright, design right and performers' property rights, the 1988 Act provides that all such relief by way of, inter alia, damages is available to the claimant as is available in respect of the infringement of any other property

---

[719] *Caxton Publishing Co Ltd v Sutherland Publishing Co Ltd* [1939] A.C. 178 at 198; *De Vitre (JD) v Betts (W)* (1873) L.R. 6, HL 319; *Island Records Ltd v Tring International Plc* [1995] F.S.R. 560. But see Laddie J.'s rejection of this justification in *Cala Homes (South) Ltd v Alfred McAlpine Homes East Ltd* [1996] F.S.R. 36; according to Laddie J. there is no need for the legal fiction of condoning the infringement—the claimant has to elect for the simple reason that the two remedies are inconsistent.

[720] Note, however, that the view has been expressed that the effect of the implementation of the Enforcement Directive is that this requirement to elect has been abolished. See para.21–194, below.

[721] *Spring Form Inc v Toy Brokers Ltd* [2002] F.S.R. 276. This is because once the claimant has elected to be compensated in damages for the appearance in commerce of the infringing article, the compensation which he receives reflects all the commercial stages through which the article goes: see *Gerber Garment Technology v Lectra Systems Ltd* [1997] R.P.C. 443.

[722] *Island Records Ltd v Tring International Plc* [1995] F.S.R. 560, 563 (Lightman J.); *Led Builders Pty Ltd v Eagle Homes Pty Ltd (No.3)* (1996) 36 I.P.R. 293.

[723] *Thornton Hall Manufacturing Ltd v Shanton Apparel Ltd* (1988) 12 I.P.R. 48 (High Ct of NZ).

[724] *Redrow Homes Ltd v Betts Bros Plc* [1997] F.S.R. 828 at 831 (Court of Session (Inner House)); *Led Builders Pty Ltd v Eagle Homes Pty Ltd (No.3)* (1996) 36 I.P.R. 293.

[725] *Dr Martens Australia Pty Ltd v Bata Shoes Co of Australia Pty Ltd* (1997) I.P.R. 163; but see *Zupanovich Pty Ltd v Beale Nominees Pty Ltd* (1995) 32 I.P.R. 339 at 355 (Carr J.); however, it seems that Carr J. was contemplating cases where liability was not in issue. See also *Gentry Homes Pty Ltd v Diamond Homes Pty Ltd* (1993) A.I.P.C. 91–008.

[726] *Minnesota Mining & Manufacturing Co v C Jeffries Pty Ltd* [1993] F.S.R. 189(Fed. Ct of NSW); *Island Records Ltd v Tring International Plc* [1995] F.S.R. 560; *Led Builders Pty Ltd v Eagle Homes Pty Ltd (No.3)* (1996) 36 I.P.R. 293.

[727] *Island Records v Tring International Plc* (above); *Brugge v Medicaid* [1996] F.S.R. 362; *Vestergaard Frandsen A/S v Bestnet Europe Ltd* [2009] EWHC 1456 (Ch) at para.116.

[728] See paras 21–74 et seq., above.

[729] CDPA 1988 ss.103(1) and 194.

[730] Reference should be made to the standard textbooks on torts such as *Clerk & Lindsell*.

right.[731] It is often said that the measure of damage for copyright infringement is the depreciation caused by the infringement to the value of the copyright as a chose in action.[732] It has now been held that the principles set out in the patent case of *General Tire and Rubber Co v Firestone Tyre and Rubber Co Ltd* are applicable in copyright cases.[733] Accordingly, the general rule, as in the case of any other "economic" tort, is that the measure of damages is to be, so far as possible, that sum of money which will put the injured party in the same position as he would have been in if he had not sustained the wrong.[734] It seems, therefore, that damages for all the rights covered in this work are now to be assessed on the same footing. However, it is necessary to consider the impact of the Enforcement Directive on these general principles.

Article 13(1) of the Enforcement Directive and the Enforcement Regulations.[735] Regulation 3 of the Enforcement Regulations, implementing art.13(1) of the Enforcement Directive,[736] provides as follows: **21–194**

"(1) Where in an action for infringement of an intellectual property right the defendant knew, or had reasonable grounds to know, that he engaged in infringing activity, the damages awarded to the claimant shall be appropriate to the actual prejudice he suffered as a result of the infringement.[737]

(2) When awarding such damages—

(a) all appropriate aspects shall be taken into account, including in particular—

(i) the negative economic consequences, including any lost profits, which the claimant has suffered, and any unfair profits made by the defendant; and

(ii) elements other than economic factors, including the moral prejudice caused to the claimant by the infringement; or

(b) where appropriate, they may be awarded on the basis of the royalties or fees which would have been due had the defendant obtained a licence.

(3) This regulation does not affect the operation of any enactment or rule of law relating to remedies for the infringement of intellectual property rights except to the extent that it is inconsistent with the provisions of this regulation."

Regulation 3 reproduces art.13(1) in substantially identical terms. According to the Explanatory Memorandum to the Enforcement Regulations, because art.13(1) contains a number of terms the meaning of which is unclear, such as "actual prejudice" and "moral prejudice", the Government decided to adopt a "copy out approach". The purpose of reg.3(3) was:

"to avoid the implication that art.13(1) provides a complete code that displaces the national law of damages (in particular any suggestion that it introduces punitive damages)".

---

[731] CDPA 1988 ss.96(2), 229(2) and 191I(2).

[732] *Sutherland Publishing Co Ltd v Caxton Publishing Co Ltd* [1936] Ch. 323 per Lord Wright M.R., at 336; *Prior v Landsdowne Press Pty Ltd* [1977] R.P.C. 511 (Sup.Ct. of Victoria); *Interfirm Comparison (Australia) Pty Ltd v Law Society of New South Wales* [1977] R.P.C. 137; *Infabrics Ltd v Jaytex Shirt Co Ltd* [1984] R.P.C. 405 at 457; *Paterson Zochonis Ltd v Merfarken Packaging Ltd* [1983] F.S.R. 273 at 281, 287, 294; *International Writing School Inc v Rimila Pty Ltd* (1994) 30 I.P.R. 250 (Fed Ct of Aus); *Claydon Architectural Metalwork v D.J. Higgins & Sons* [1997] F.S.R. 475.

[733] [1976] R.P.C. 197, applied in *Blayney v Clogau St David's Gold Mines Ltd* [2003] F.S.R. 19.

[734] Applying *Livingstone v Rawyards Coal Co* (1880) 5 A.C. 25 at 39.

[735] The Intellectual Property (Enforcement, etc.) Regulations 2006 (SI 2006/1028).

[736] For a discussion of the implementation of this provision in the various Member States, see Civil Damages in Intellectual Property Rights Cases, a Report of the legal sub-group of the European Observatory on Counterfeiting and Piracy: *http://ec.europa.eu/internal_market/iprenforcement/observatory/index_en.htm* [Accessed October 12, 2010].

[737] See also art.45(1) of TRIPS: damages must be available and be "adequate to compensate for the injury the right holder has suffered".

In *Experience Hendrix LLC v The Times Newspapers Ltd*[738] the defendant relied on a chain of title which was later found to be unsustainable. Shortly before the infringement commenced the claimants had set out their claim to title in correspondence. Although the court accepted that this left the defendant in a quandary, it held that it was nevertheless sufficient to fix it with reasonable grounds to know that it engaged in infringing activity.[739]

Regulation 3(2) involves two alternative measures of damages. The first takes "all appropriate aspects" into account. The second involves the assessment of damages "where appropriate" on the user principle.[740] There is no guidance in the Regulations as to where it would be appropriate for damages to be assessed on the alternative basis. However, recital 24 to the Enforcement Directive suggests that the alternative measure would be appropriate "for example where it would be difficult to determine the amount of actual prejudice suffered". In *Experience Hendrix LLC v The Times Newspapers Ltd*[741] the court assessed damages on the first basis (which it described as the "loss sustained approach"). This was for two reasons. First, the infringement had caused the claimants to suspend a film and CD project relating to the infringed material and thus to suffer loss. Second, there were formidable difficulties in assessing the appropriate notional licence fee.[742] Presumably, the existence of alternative measures of damages would not invalidate a result like that in the *Blayney* case[743] in which in effect the terms of reg.3(2)(a) were applied to some parts of the loss while those of reg.3(2)(b) were applied to the rest.

Obvious difficulties arise from the phrase "any unfair profits made by the defendant". It is not immediately clear why "unfair profits" should be relevant to an assessment of the "damages" which will be "appropriate" to "the actual prejudice suffered by the claimant" and which, according to recital 26 to the Directive, are intended to be compensatory. Under the previous law a claimant could recover lost profits on sales made by the defendant which the claimant could show he would have made but for the infringement. However, such loss would seem to be included in the phrase "lost profits which the claimant has suffered". Some have argued that if, despite the fact that the award is intended to be compensatory, this part of reg.3(2) is in fact directed at the award of an account of profits, the effect of the provision is to eliminate the obligation to elect between damages and an account of profits. However, it seems unlikely that an English court would consider it "appropriate" to take into account both damages and an account of profits: they have always been considered to be alternative remedies.[744]

Other difficulties may arise from the term "moral prejudice", which is undefined. However, given the availability depending on the circumstances of aggravated and additional damages, it is not obvious that it will add a great deal to the existing law. In its Response to its Consultation on Damages,[745] the Government stated its intention to replace the reference to additional damages in the 1988 Act with a reference to "aggravated and restitutionary damages". The term "restitutionary damages" means an account of profits.[746] The Government intends to make clear in an accompanying Explanatory Note that this (together presum-

---

[738] [2010] EWHC 1986 (Ch).
[739] paras 69–72.
[740] As to which see paras 21–196 et seq., below.
[741] [2010] EWHC 1986 (Ch).
[742] See at para.137.
[743] *Blayney v Clogau St David's Gold Mines Ltd* [2003] F.S.R. 19. See para.21–197, below.
[744] See para.21–192, above.
[745] *http://www.justice.gov.uk/consultations/docs/law-damages-response.pdf* [Accessed October 16, 2010].
[746] See the Government's Consultation Paper *The law on Damages* CP9/07, *http://*

ably with the claimant's entitlement to ordinary damages) is intended "to cover all the aspects set out in [art.13(1)] including both damages and an account of profits".[747]

In conclusion, the impact of this provision on the existing law of damages remains unclear.

Article 13(2) of the Enforcement Directive. This provision, which mirrors part of art.45(2) of TRIPS, provides that Member States may provide for recovery of profits or the payment of damages, which may be pre-established, in the cases where the infringer did not know or have reasonable grounds to know that he was infringing. Article 13(2) has not been specifically implemented in the United Kingdom,[748] and accordingly UK domestic law applies.[749] As has already been seen,[750] "innocence" is not generally a defence but may be relied on as a defence to a claim for damages in certain limited circumstances. Moreover, there is authority to suggest that innocence may be a ground for contending that an account of profits should not be ordered as a matter of discretion.[751]   **21–195**

General Tire. According to the House of Lords in this case, there are two essential principles in valuing the claim: first, that the claimant has the burden of showing his loss; and secondly, that the defendant being a wrongdoer, damages should be liberally assessed within the constraint that the object is to compensate the claimant and not punish the defendant.[752] There are three main groups of reported cases which exemplify the court's approach to typical situations.   **21–196**

The first is where the claimant is a manufacturer, who exploits his right to make articles or products which he sells at a profit. The benefit of the right is realised through the sale of the article or product. In such a case, the infringement diverts sales from the right owner to the infringer. The measure of damages is then normally the profit which would have been realised by the owner of the right if the sales had been made by him.[753] The assessment of damages for lost profits should take account of the fact that the lost sales are of "extra production" and that only certain specific extra costs (marginal costs) would have been incurred in making the additional sales. Nevertheless, in practice, costs go up and so it may be appropriate to temper this approach in making the assessment.[754]

The second group of cases is where the right is exploited by the grant of licences for royalty payments. If the infringer uses the right without a licence, the

---

webarchive.nationalarchives.gov.uk/+/http://www.dca.gov.uk/consult/damages/cp0907.pdf [Accessed October 16, 2010], para.195; and Pt III of the Law Commission's report Aggravated, Exemplary and Restitutionary damages; *http://www.lawcom.gov.uk/docs/lc247.pdf* [Accessed October 16, 2010].

[747] See *http://www.justice.gov.uk/consultations/docs/law-damages-response.pdf* [Accessed October 16, 2010] pp.55–56.

[748] The Government is opposed to a system of pre-established damages on the grounds that they are not be compensatory. See *http://www.justice.gov.uk/consultations/docs/law-damages-response.pdf* [Accessed October 16, 2010] p.56.

[749] *Experience Hendrix LLC v The Times Newspapers Ltd* [2010] EWHC 1986 (Ch) para.68.

[750] See above, paras 21–74 et seq.

[751] See below, para.21–209.

[752] Applying *Pneumatic Tyre Co Ltd v Puncture Proof Pneumatic Tyre Co Ltd* (1899) 16 R.P.C. 209 at 215.

[753] Examples in copyright cases being *Birn Bros Ltd v Keene & Co Ltd* [1918] 2 Ch. 281 and *Columbia Pictures Industries v Robinson* [1988] F.S.R. 531. Note, however, that these are both cases under the 1956 Act pursuant to which conversion damages were also available. In *Ultraframe (UK) Ltd v Eurocell Building Plastics Ltd* [2006] EWHC 1344 (Pat) the defendant had been a distributor of the claimant's products before it began to make and sell its own infringing products instead. The Judge rejected (at para.3) an argument that the claimant was not entitled to recover lost profits on sales which it was able to prove it would have made to the defendant but for the infringement.

[754] *Ultraframe (UK) Ltd v Eurocell Building Plastics Ltd* [2006] EWHC 1344 (Pat) at para.47.

measure of damages is the amount he would have had to pay by way of royalty instead of acting illegally.[755] The amount of such a royalty is a matter of evidence. However, before a "going rate" can be taken as the basis on which the infringer ought to pay damages, it must be shown that the circumstances in which the going rate was paid are the same as or comparable with those in which the rightholder and infringer are assumed to strike their bargain.

In the third group of cases, there is no normal rate of profit and no normal royalty. In such a case it is for the claimant to adduce evidence to guide the court. The evidence may consist of the practice in the trade or other trades, expert opinion, evidence as to the profitability of the right and any other factor on which the judge can decide the measure of loss. The ultimate process is one of judicial estimation of the available indications. In this third group of cases, the court is seeking to assess the price which could reasonably have been charged for a licence.[756] The hypothesis is that the actual licensor and the actual infringer are willing to negotiate with each other as they are, with their strengths and weaknesses, in the market as it exists.[757] In a case within this group, the court may have to call into play "inference, conjecture and the like", and apply "a sound imagination and the practice of the broad axe".[758] In some cases it may be appropriate to award as damages the cost of producing or commissioning the material in a form which did not infringe copyright.[759]

21–197 *General Tire* **groups not exhaustive.** The three groups of case referred to in *General Tire* were not expressed to be exhaustive.[760] Accordingly, for example, where the claimant is in competition with the defendant, there is no reason why he cannot recover lost profits on sales made by the defendant which he can show he would have made but for the infringement (*General Tire* group 1) and a notional licence fee (calculated in accordance with *General Tire* group 2 or 3 as appropriate) in respect of all other sales made by the defendant.[761] Moreover, the fact that the pirated work may have injured the reputation of and vulgarised the original may be taken into consideration in assessing the amount of damages.[762]

---

[755] Examples in copyright cases being *Performing Right Society Ltd v Bradford Corp* [1917–1923] Mac.C.C. 309; *Chabot v Davies* [1936] 2 All E.R. 221; *Stovin-Bradford v Volpoint Ltd* [1971] Ch. 1007 at 1016, 1020; *Lewis Trusts v Bambers Stores Ltd* [1983] F.S.R. 453 at 469; *Devefi Pty Ltd v Mateffy Perl Nagy Pty Ltd* [1993] R.P.C. 193 (Fed. Ct. of Australia); and *Nottinghamshire Healthcare National Health Service Trust v News Group Newspapers Ltd* [2002] EWHC 409; [2002] R.P.C. 49.

[756] See *Meters Ltd v Metropolitan Gas Meters Ltd* (1911) 28 R.P.C. 157 at 164–165.

[757] *General Tire and Rubber Co v Firestone Tyre and Rubber Co Ltd* [1976] R.P.C. 197 at 221. However, any impecuniosity on the part of the licensee is disregarded: *Irvine v Talksport Ltd* [2002] EWHC 367 (Ch); [2002] 1 W.L.R. 2355; [2002] F.S.R. 60, para.74.

[758] *Watson, Laidlaw & Co Ltd v Pott, Cassells and Williamson* (1914) 31 R.P.C. 104 at 118 per Lord Shaw (a patent case). For the application of this approach in copyright cases, see *SPE International Ltd v Professional Preparation Contractors (UK) Ltd* [2002] EWHC 881, Ch. D.; *Ludlow Music Inc v Williams* [2002] F.S.R. 868 and *Blayney v Clogau St David's Gold Mines Ltd* [2003] F.S.R. 19. See also *Brown v Mcasso Music Production Ltd* [2005] EWCC Cpwt 1 at para.66; [2005] F.S.R. 40; [2006] E.M.L.R. 3 (permission to appeal refused: [2005] EWCA Civ 621; [2006] F.S.R. 24) and *London General Holdings Ltd v USP Plc* [2005] EWCA Civ 931; [2006] F.S.R. 6 at para.43.

[759] *Peninsular Business Services Ltd v Citation Plc* [2004] F.S.R. 17 (H.H. Judge Maddocks). See also *Pollock v Williamson* [1923] V.L.R. 225 (court awarded the cost of obtaining a non-infringing translation by a person of the highest competence).

[760] *General Tire and Rubber Company v Firestone Tyre and Rubber Company Ltd* [1976] R.P.C. 197 at 212; see *Blayney v Clogau St David's Gold Mines Ltd* [2003] F.S.R. 19 at para.12.

[761] *Blayney v Clogau St David's Gold Mines Ltd* [2003] F.S.R. 19 at para.20.

[762] *Hanfstaengl v W. H. Smith & Sons* [1905] 1 Ch. 519; *Lewis Trusts v Bambers Stores Ltd* [1983] F.S.R. 453 at 469; *Allibert S.A. v O'Connor* [1982] F.S.R. 317 (High Ct of Ireland) and see *Milpurrurru v Indofurn Pty Ltd* (1994) 30 I.P.R. 209 (Fed. Ct of Aus.).

In *Mansell (V.) & Co Ltd v Wesley (H.) Ltd*,[763] it was held that the claimant was justified in withdrawing his stock, the design of which had been vulgarised, and adding to his claim for damages the loss so suffered. In *Experience Hendrix LLC v The Times Newspapers Ltd*[764] the infringement had caused the claimants to suspend a film and CD project relating to the infringed material and they were held entitled to recover damages representing the delayed receipt of income from the project. By the same token, if the claimant has been forced to keep down or even reduce its prices as a result of the infringement, any resulting loss of profit is a recoverable head of damage.[765] The fact that the defendant could have achieved the same result without using the claimant's work is not relevant when assessing the claimant's loss.[766] In a patent case, a claimant has recovered damages to represent lost profits on sales of associated non-patented goods, spare parts and servicing and profits lost in the period after the expiry of the patent as a result of the competitive "bridgehead" built up by the defendant's infringements during the subsistence of the patent.[767] It is possible in an appropriate case to recover as damages the costs of employing inquiry agents[768]; internal staff costs incurred as a result of the infringement[769]; and the costs of "policing" an injunction where the breaches of the injunction also amounted to infringements of copyright.[770]

Limits on amount of damages. The ordinary rules as to causation, foreseeability and remoteness will be applied.[771] If it was reasonably foreseeable that the defendant's acts of infringement would cause a particular head of damage to the claimant, damages under that head ought to be recoverable. But the infringement must be an effective cause of the damage. Where a defendant copied the claimant's technical brochure and used the infringing copy for the purpose of selling a competing product, it was held that the claimant's loss of sales was due to lawful competition and was not caused by the infringement.[772] The damages will not include loss suffered because of the commission by a third party of an-   **21–198**

---

[763] [1936–1945] Mac.C.C. 288.

[764] [2010] EWHC 1986 (Ch).

[765] *Ultraframe (UK) Ltd v Eurocell Building Plastics Ltd* [2005] EWHC 2111 (Ch) at para.9(5); *Ultraframe (UK) Ltd v Eurocell Building Plastics Ltd* [2006] EWHC 1344 (Pat) at paras 47 and 183–185.

[766] See, e.g. *Work Model Enterprises Ltd v Ecosystem Ltd* [1996] F.S.R. 356.

[767] *Gerber Garment Technology Inc v Lectra Systems Ltd* [1995] R.P.C. 383; [1997] R.P.C. 443 CA. See also *Ultraframe (UK) Ltd v Eurocell Building Plastics Ltd* [2005] EWHC 2111 (Ch) at para.9(6) and *Retail Systems Technology v McGuire* [2007] IEHC 13.

[768] *British Motor Trade Association v Salvadori* [1949] Ch. 556; *South African Music Rights Organisation Ltd v Trust Butchers (Pty) Ltd* (1978) 1 S.A.L.R. 1052.

[769] See *Aerospace Publishing Ltd v Thames Water Utilities Ltd* [2007] EWCA Civ 3; [2007] Bus. L.R. 726 at para.86. The fact and extent of the diversion of staff time have to be properly established. The claimant has to establish that the diversion caused significant disruption to its business. In the ordinary case, it is reasonable for the court to infer that if their time had not been diverted, staff would have applied it to activities which would have generated revenue to the claimant in an amount at least equal to the costs of employing them during that time.

[770] *Phonographic Performance Ltd v Reader* [2005] EWHC 416 (Ch); [2005] F.S.R. 42.

[771] *Gerber Garment Technology Inc v Lectra Systems Ltd* [1995] R.P.C. 383; [1997] R.P.C. 443, CA (a patent case); *Claydon Architectural Metalwork v DJ Higgins & Sons* [1997] F.S.R. 475.

[772] *Work Model Enterprises Ltd v Ecosystem Ltd & Clix Interiors Ltd* [1996] F.S.R. 356; see also *Peninsular Business Services Ltd v Citation Plc* [2004] F.S.R. 17 (manuals not used in sales process) and *A-One Accessory Imports Pty Ltd v Off Road Imports Pty Ltd* (1996) 34 I.P.R. 332: infringing brochure was the key to sales; defendant would have taken six months to make non-infringing version; claimant entitled to lost profits for six months. See also *London General Holdings Ltd v USP Plc* [2005] EWCA Civ 931; [2006] F.S.R. 6: no damages where all the loss results from use of the ideas contained in a document rather than any unauthorised deployment of its text. In the Australian case of *Eagle Rock Entertainment Ltd v Caisley* [2005] FCA 1238 the defendant had made infringing master copies and provided them to third parties for manufacture of infringing copies in Brazil and Spain. The acts of making and providing the masters took place in Australia. The court granted damages for the claimant's loss of sales in these countries which (it held) was caused by the infringements in Australia. See also *Experience Hendrix LLC v The Times Newspapers Ltd* [2010] EWHC 1986 (Ch) at para.142: damages were recoverable for the

other tort, such as passing off,[773] which has been facilitated by the defendant's infringement of copyright.

21–199   **Practice.** Damages are usually assessed on an inquiry before the Master after liability for infringement has been established at the trial of the action, with costs of the inquiry reserved. It does not follow automatically that, because a claimant has succeeded on liability, he should be entitled to an inquiry as to damages. If the court is satisfied that an inquiry would be fruitless, it may refuse an order one. The burden is on the claimant to prove damage, but not to a degree of certainty. Once it is shown that pirate marketing has taken place, some loss of sales will be assumed.[774] Moreover, an inquiry will be ordered even if the claimant can only show a prima facie or arguable case that he will recover damages.[775] If the court thinks the damages are likely to be negligible or small, it can use its case management powers to stop the case getting out of hand.[776] Furthermore, because the remedy of an inquiry is discretionary,[777] the court may decide to assess the damages in a very simple case at trial in order to save costs.[778] For that reason, and notwithstanding the fact that it is the court's practice to try intellectual property cases on liability alone, leaving damages to be assessed on an inquiry if the claimant is successful, it is prudent for a claimant to apply at the Case Management Conference for an order for a split trial so that there is no possibility of his being caught by surprise at trial should the judge subsequently decide to assess damages on the spot.[779] Other than in simple cases, it is usually prudent to have formal statements of case in the inquiry.[780] An application to dismiss an inquiry as to damages for want of prosecution is not governed by the same considerations as on an application to strike out proceedings before an order has been made.[781]

21–200   **Special cases.** For special provisions in the case where the copyright owner has granted an exclusive licence which encompasses the defendant's infringing acts, see para.21–222, below. For the right to information from the defendant before electing between an inquiry as to damages and an account of profits, see para.21–192, above. Where performers' rights or the rights of persons having recording rights are infringed by the making of a broadcast of a performance or recording, then, if the broadcast is made from a place in the United Kingdom and is received

---

delayed receipt of income from worldwide exploitation of the rights infringed because the delay was caused by the UK infringement.

[773] *Paterson Zochonis Ltd v Merfarken Packaging Ltd* [1983] F.S.R. 273.

[774] *Columbia Pictures Industries v Robinson* [1988] F.S.R. 531.

[775] *McDonald's Hamburgers Ltd v Burger King (UK) Ltd* [1987] F.S.R. 112 (inquiry ordered even though quantum "speculative"); *Brain v Ingledew Brown Bennison & Garret (a firm)* [1997] F.S.R. 511 (inquiry ordered although prospects of recovery "weak" on current evidence); *Prince Plc v Prince Sports Group Inc* [1998] F.S.R. 21 (application adjourned to enable claimant to adduce evidence); *Reed Executive Plc v Reed Business Information Ltd* [2004] EWCA Civ 887; [2004] 1 W.L.R. 3026; [2005] F.S.R. 3, para.164 (criteria unchanged by introduction of the CPR).

[776] *Reed Executive Plc v Reed Business Information Ltd* [2004] EWCA Civ 887, para.164. For example, the court can require the claimant to put in a statement of case and supporting evidence without requiring the defendant to do anything with a view to encouraging a claimant who has little to gain to think twice; it can order the trial to be on paper unless a case for cross-examination is made out; disclosure can be restricted or done away with; a time-limit for the hearing can be imposed: ibid.

[777] *Allied Maples Group Ltd v Simmons & Simmons* [1995] 1 W.L.R. 1602 at 1622; *Brain v Ingledew Brown Bennison & Garret (a firm)* [1997] F.S.R. 511.

[778] See, e.g. *Michael O'Mara Books Ltd v Express Newspapers Plc* [1999] F.S.R. 49 (an application for summary judgment).

[779] This also has the advantage of ensuring that disclosure is limited to the issues relating to liability, as opposed to quantum—see para.21–282, below.

[780] *Gerber Garment Technology Inc v Lectra Systems Ltd & Another* [1994] F.S.R. 471 (a patent case).

[781] *Nichols Advanced Vehicle Systems Inc v Rees, Oliver & Others (No.2)* [1985] R.P.C. 445.

and immediately retransmitted by cable, the fact of such retransmission is to be taken into account in assessing damages for the infringement.[782] Any damages recovered by a personal representative in respect of infringement of performers' rights in respect of an infringement after a person's death devolve as part of his estate as if the right (or right of action) had subsisted and been vested in him immediately before his death.[783]

(vi) Aggravated, exemplary and additional damages

Aggravated and exemplary damages. There is nothing to stop the court awarding an additional sum in respect of aggravated damages to take account of injury to the claimant's proper feelings of pride and dignity, humiliation, distress, insult or pain caused by the circumstances of the defendant's conduct.[784] In addition, following the overruling of *AB v South West Water Services*[785] it appears that the court now has power to award exemplary damages in cases involving copyright and the other rights covered in this work, provided the case falls into one of the three categories identified by Lord Devlin in *Rookes v Barnard*.[786]

21–201

Additional damages: general. In actions for infringement of copyright, design right and performers' property rights, the court has power, having regard to all the circumstances, and in particular to the flagrancy of the infringement and any benefit accruing to the defendant by reason of the infringement, to award such additional damages as the justice of the case may require.[787] The remedy is discretionary.[788] Additional damages cannot be awarded to a claimant who has elected for an account of profits.[789] The Government intends to replace the term "additional damages" in the 1988 Act with the term "aggravated and restitution-

21–202

---

[782] CDPA 1988 Sch.2 para.19(2).

[783] s.192A(5); Duration of Copyright & Rights in Performances Regulations (SI 1995/3297) reg.31(3); Copyrights and Related Rights Regulations (SI 1996/2967) reg.30(2).

[784] *Nottinghamshire Healthcare National Health Service Trust v News Group Newspapers Ltd* [2002] EWHC 409; [2002] R.P.C. 49, para.51. As to aggravated damages generally, see *Clerk & Lindsell on Torts*.

[785] [1993] Q.B. 507. In this case it was held that exemplary damages were not available in respect of torts in respect of which such damages had not been awarded before 1964. It was thought that there was no such award in a copyright case. However, *AB v South West Water Services* was overruled by the House of Lords in *Kuddus v Chief Constable of Leicestershire* [2001] UKHL 29; [2002] 2 A.C. 122. Accordingly, there seems to be no reason why exemplary damages cannot be awarded in a copyright case.

[786] [1964] A.C. 1129. The two relevant categories are: first, oppressive, arbitrary or unconstitutional action by government servants; and second, where the defendant's conduct has been calculated by him to make a profit which may well exceed the compensation payable to the claimant. See, generally, *Clerk & Lindsell on Torts*.

[787] CDPA 1988 ss.97(2), 229(3) and 191J(2). The provisions of the 1988 Act are wider than s.17(3) of the 1956 Act. For a summary of the principles for awarding damages under s.17(3), see *Noah v Shuba* [1991] F.S.R. 14 at 29–31. The 1988 Act has removed that part of s.17(3) which required the court to be satisfied that "effective relief was not otherwise available to the plaintiff" before an award of additional damages could be made. Under s.17(3), if, for example, effective relief was available to the plaintiff in respect of another cause of action, such as libel or breach of confidence, or because conversion damages, as well as infringement damages, were available, relief might not be given by an award of additional damages for infringement of copyright—see *Beloff v Pressdram Ltd* [1973] F.S.R. 38; *Prior v Landsdowne Press (Pty) Ltd* [1977] R.P.C. 511; *Ravenscroft v Herbert & Another* [1980] R.P.C. 193. See also para.704 of the report of the Whitford Committee (Cmnd.6732) as explained in *Nottinghamshire Healthcare National Health Service Trust v News Group Newspapers Ltd* [2002] EWHC 409; [2002] R.P.C. 49.

[788] *Raben Footwear Pty Ltd v Polygram Records Inc* [1997] I.P.R. 417; *Pro Sieben Media AG v Carlton UK Television Ltd* [1998] F.S.R. 43. For a summary of the law in Australia, see *Sullivan v FNH Investments Pty Ltd* [2003] F.C.A. 323; (2003) 57 I.P.R. 6, but note that the statutory power to award additional damages (s.115(4) of the Copyright Act 1968) is in very different terms from s.97(2).

[789] *Redrow Homes Ltd v Betts Brothers Plc* [1998] F.S.R. 345.

ary damages".[790] Given that the Court's power to award additional damages permits an "aggravation" of an award on a far wider basis than common law aggravated damages (see para.21–206, below.), the effect of such a change would be to reduce the scope of damages under s.97(2).

21–203   **Flagrancy.** Flagrancy implies scandalous conduct or deceit, including deliberate and calculated infringement where a defendant reaps a pecuniary advantage in excess of the damages he would otherwise have to pay.[791] Where the infringement has been carried out in breach of a court order, it is fairly to be described as flagrant.[792] Flagrancy is not a necessary ingredient of additional damages. It is merely a factor to take into account if it is present.[793]

21–204   **Benefit to the defendant.** It has been held that the presence of this factor permits the court to include an element of restitution in its award, having regard to the benefit gained by the defendant, for example where the normal compensation awarded to the claimant leaves the defendant still enjoying the fruit of his infringement.[794] Such an award overlaps to a certain extent with the remedy of an account of profits,[795] but is not co-extensive with it because it permits the court to take account of benefit which is not profit, for example where a defendant has established himself in the market and generated a goodwill by a flagrant infringement.[796] It has been suggested (obiter) that the inclusion of a restitutionary element in an award of additional damages might be appropriate in two specific circumstances. The first was where a defendant who had declined the claimant's offer of a licence went on and deliberately infringed. In such a case, an award of additional damages might be made to bring the total of damages up to the fee originally sought by the claimant or even to enable the claimant to participate in the profits made by the defendant while also recovering damages for the invasion of his right. The second was where the copyright owner was not in the business of granting licences. In those circumstances, an award of strictly compensatory damages might be accompanied by an award of additional damages reflecting the benefit derived by the defendant. Thus, if the correct approach to infringement damages was to calculate a royalty on a "profits available" basis, then in a case of flagrant infringement it might be right to take a larger share of the available profits for the claimant's account than might otherwise be taken.[797]

---

[790] See above, para.21–194.

[791] *Ravenscroft v Herbert & Another* [1980] R.P.C. 193, at 206; *ZYX Muisc Ltd v King* [1995] F.S.R. 566.

[792] *Sony Computer Entertainment Inc v Owen* [2002] EWHC 45; [2002] E.C.D.R. 27 at para.28. *Phonographic Performance Ltd v Reader* [2005] EWHC 416 (Ch); [2005] F.S.R. 42. Where a defendant's contempt is also an infringement of copyright, the court may well award damages (including additional damages) at the same time as it deals with the contempt. See the *Reader* case. Unless there has been a full trial, the court is likely to impose the summary judgment burden on the claimant in respect of such a damages claim: *Independiente Ltd v Music Trading On-Line (HK) Ltd* [2007] EWHC 533 (Ch); [2007] F.S.R. 21; at para.38.

[793] *Cala Homes (South) Ltd v Alfred McAlpine Homes East Ltd* [1995] F.S.R. 818 at 838; *ZYX Music Ltd v King* [1995] F.S.R. 566.

[794] *Nottinghamshire Healthcare National Health Service Trust v News Group Newspapers Ltd* [2002] EWHC 409; [2002] R.P.C. 49, at para.51 (Pumfrey, J.).

[795] cf. *ZYX Music Ltd v King* [1995] F.S.R. 566, in which the Judge ordered that the award of additional damages should include a sum representing the extent to which ordinary damages would not adequately reflect inter alia the defendant's profit.

[796] cf. *ZYX Music Ltd v King* [1995] F.S.R. 566; see also the observations of Lord Clyde in *Redrow Homes Ltd v Betts Brothers Plc* [1998] F.S.R. 345 at 353 and cf. the 1956 Act case of *Nichols Advanced Vehicle Systems Inc & Others v Rees Oliver & Others* [1979] R.P.C. 127.

[797] See *Ludlow Music Inc v Williams* [2002] EWHC 638, Ch; [2002] F.S.R. 57, Pumfrey, J.

Again, the benefit to the defendant is not a necessary ingredient of a claim for flagrancy damages. It is merely a factor to take into account.[798]

Can the award include a punitive element? After much uncertainty, it has been held at first instance that an award of additional damages may not contain a purely punitive element.[799] The reasons for this include the existence of a relevant statutory offence (under s.107 of the 1988 Act[800]) and the risk that an infringer might in a case of concurrent copyrights be exposed to successive actions by the owners of the different copyrights, each seeking punishment in respect of his own interest.[801] It should be noted, however, that exemplary damages, which may include a punitive element, are probably now available for infringement of copyright and the other rights covered in this work.[802]

21–205

Other relevant considerations. Section 97(2) is drafted in the widest terms. The court is clearly permitted to take account of the factors admitted as aggravation at common law, that is any injury to the claimant's proper feelings of pride and dignity, humiliation, distress, insult or pain caused by the circumstances of the defendant's conduct.[803] However, the section permits an aggravation of the award on a basis far wider than that.[804] Thus, for example, the courts have taken into account, sometimes under the heading of flagrancy and sometimes not: the fact that the material reproduced was obviously stolen from the claimant[805]; the destruction of evidence by the defendant[806]; the fact that the infringement continued in the face of a warning[807]; attempts to conceal the infringement by disingenuous correspondence[808]; the absence of an apology[809]; and upset caused to the claimant's employees.[810] On the other hand, it appears that the court may take account of any "mitigating circumstances"[811]; the defendant's means[812]; reasonable doubts about the claimant's title[813]; provocation by the claimant[814]; and whether the defendant reasonably believed that the claimant would grant him a licence.[815]

21–206

---

[798] *Cala Homes (South) Ltd v Alfred McAlpine Homes East Ltd* [1995] F.S.R. 818 at 838; *ZYX Music Ltd v King* [1995] F.S.R. 566.

[799] *Nottinghamshire Healthcare National Health Service Trust v News Group Newspapers Ltd* [2002] EWHC 409; [2002] R.P.C. 49, para.51. Put another way, an award of additional damages may contain a punitive element provided its purpose is not solely to punish the defendant: *Phonographic Performance Ltd v Reader* [2005] EWHC 416 (Ch); [2005] F.S.R. 42.

[800] See Ch.22, below.

[801] *Nottinghamshire Healthcare National Health Service Trust v News Group Newspapers Ltd* [2002] EWHC 409; [2002] R.P.C. 49, para.51.

[802] See para.21–201, above.

[803] *Nottinghamshire Healthcare National Service Trust v News Group Newspapers Ltd* [2002] EWHC 409; [2002] R.P.C. 49; cf. the 1956 Act cases of *Nichols Advanced Vehicle Systems Inc & Others v Rees Oliver & Others* [1979] F.S.R. 33 and *Beloff v Pressdram Ltd* [1973] F.S.R. 33.

[804] See the previous note.

[805] *Nottinghamshire Healthcare National Health Service Trust v News Group Newspapers Ltd* [2002] EWHC 409, para.60. The way the defendant obtained the copied material was also held to be relevant (under the heading of flagrancy) in the 1956 Act case of *Beloff v Pressdram Ltd* [1973] F.S.R. 33.

[806] *Nottinghamshire Healthcare National Health Service Trust v News Group Newspapers Ltd* [2002] EWHC 409.

[807] *Peninsular Business Services Ltd v Citation Plc* [2004] F.S.R. 17 (H.H. Judge Maddocks).

[808] ibid.

[809] *Nottinghamshire Healthcare National Health Service Trust v News Group Newspapers Ltd* [2002] EWHC 409, at para.51; cf. the 1956 Act case of *Beloff v Pressdram Ltd* [1973] F.S.R. 33—lack of regret.

[810] *Nottinghamshire Healthcare National Health Service Trust v News Group Newspapers Ltd* [2002] EWHC 409, para.51.

[811] *Michael O'Mara Books Ltd v Express Newspapers Plc* [1999] F.S.R. 49; *Sony Computer Entertainment Inc v Owen* [2002] EWHC 45, [2002] E.M.L.R. 34 at para.28.

[812] *Michael O'Mara Books Ltd v Express Newspapers Plc* [1999] F.S.R. 49.

[813] *MCA Records Inc v Charly Records Ltd* [2000] E.M.L.R. 743 at 814: "It may be that the difficul-

21-207   **Quantum.** Each case obviously depends on its own facts. However, the reader may be assisted by some examples of actual awards. Additional damages have been awarded in a number of reported cases under the 1988 Act.[816] In one case, which concerned the manufacture and sale of infringing CDs, and the infringement had not been particularly beneficial to the defendants, the court had in mind a sum of £1 per infringing CD produced and not sold and £5 per infringing CD sold.[817] In another, when a newspaper had published a stolen photograph of an inmate of a mental hospital, ordinary damages were assessed at £450 and additional damages were assessed at £9,550.[818] In a third, a consultant in employment law and other fields had deliberately infringed copyright in the manuals of a competitor. Ordinary and additional damages were assessed at £9,000 each. The amount of the additional damages was described as a "premium" or "mark-up".[819] In another case where sound recordings had been played in public without a licence in breach of a court order, a 100 per cent mark-up was applied.[820] Two awards are reported in cases under the 1956 Act[821]: a sum of £2,000 where the conduct of the defendant had been deceitful and treacherous, thereby obtaining benefits for himself and inflicting on the claimant humiliation for which it was difficult to compensate[822]; and an award of £1,000 against a photographer, who sold to the Press photographs taken by him for a client in circumstances in which the copyright vested in the client.[823]

21-208   **Procedure.** Where a claim is made for additional damages under the 1988 Act, the particulars of claim must include a statement to that effect and the grounds for claiming them.[824] There is no set rule as to whether the question of flagrancy should be dealt with at trial or on an inquiry as to damages; accordingly it is for the court to lay down a sensible procedure in each case.[825] The assessment of additional damages will usually be made by the Master in the course of the conduct of the inquiry as to damages for infringement of copyright.[826] However, where the trial judge has made a finding as to flagrancy, he should direct the court taking the inquiry to have particular regard to the findings as to the flagrancy of the in-

---

ties about MCA's title are at least part of the circumstances to which I am required to have regard; but in my view they rank low on the list".

[814] *Beloff v Pressdram Ltd* [1973] F.S.R. 33 (a 1956 Act case).

[815] *Ludlow Music Inc v Williams* [2002] F.S.R 57 and [2002] E.M.L.R. 29.

[816] Note, however, that the *quantum* of additional damages is often left to the Master and that such decisions are not usually reported.

[817] *Springsteen v Flute International Ltd* [1999] E.M.L.R. 180.

[818] *Nottinghamshire Healthcare National Health Service Trust v News Group Newspapers Ltd* [2002] EWHC 409; [2002] R.P.C. 49, para.60. The court observed that if this exceeded the sum which was appropriate under s.97(2) having regard to the benefit to the defendant, no further infringements of that kind would take place; but that if further such infringements took place it would show that the advantage to the newspaper still exceeded the award of damages.

[819] *Peninsular Business Services Ltd v Citation Plc* [2004] F.S.R. 17 (H.H. Judge Maddocks). The judge used as a yardstick s.1 of the Landlord and Tenant Act 1730, pursuant to which a landlord may recover "double value" against a tenant who wilfully holds over after the termination of a lease. However, this section is a penal provision (see the terms of the section and e.g. *Lloyd v Rosbee* (1810) 2 Camp. 453); accordingly it is not clear how far the reasoning is consistent with *Nottinghamshire Healthcare National Health Service Trust v News Group Newspapers Ltd* [2002] R.P.C. 49; [2002] R.P.C. 49, which is not referred to in the judgment. See also *Microsoft Corp v Able System Development Ltd* [2002] 3 H.K.L.R.D. 515 (High Court of Hong Kong): additional damages representing 10 per cent of ordinary damages.

[820] *Phonographic Performance Ltd v Reader* [2005] EWHC 416 (Ch); [2005] F.S.R. 42, The *Peninsular* case was analysed as one where a "broad brush" approach had been adopted.

[821] Note, however, that the criteria were different: see the notes to para.21–202, above.

[822] *Nichols Advanced Vehicle Systems Inc v Rees (No.3)* [1988] R.P.C. 71.

[823] *Williams v Settle* [1960] 1 W.L.R. 1072.

[824] CPR PD63 para.22.1.

[825] *Condé Nast Publications Ltd v MGN Ltd* [1998] F.S.R. 427.

[826] *The Lady Anne Tennant v Associated Newspapers Group Ltd* [1979] F.S.R. 298; *Microsoft Corp v Electro-Wide Ltd & Another* [1997] F.S.R. 580.

fringement made in the judgment.[827] In general, the trial judge may indicate in his judgment that additional damages should be awarded and the considerations which are relevant to their assessment.[828]

(vii) Account of profits

General. An alternative remedy to damages is an account of profits, which was originally an equitable remedy incidental to the right to an injunction.[829] The account is of net profit[830]; for example, the sale price of the infringing article, less manufacturing and delivery costs.[831] As an account is an equitable remedy, it is liable to be defeated by the usual equitable defences such as acquiescence, unclean hands and laches. It is desirable that the court should consider the practical consequences of ordering the remedy of profits in the particular case.[832] The court will readily grant an account where there has been deliberate, knowing infringement, but it appears that it may refuse an account if the infringement has been entirely innocent.[833] The court will not refuse to grant an account merely because damages might be an adequate remedy (such that the claimant may benefit from a "windfall").[834]

21–209

The principles upon which such an account is granted were thus stated by Wigram V.C. in *Colburn v Simms*.[835]

> "It is true that the court does not, by an account, accurately measure the damage sustained by the proprietor of an expensive work from the invasion of his copyright by the publication of a cheaper book. It is impossible to know how many copies of the dearer book are excluded from sale by the interposition of the cheaper one. The court, by the account, as the nearest approximation which it can make to justice, takes from the wrongdoer all the profits he has made by his piracy, and gives them to the party who has been wronged. In doing this the court may often give the injured party more, in fact, than he is entitled to, for *non constat* that a single additional copy of the more expensive book would have been sold, if the injury by the sale of the cheaper book had not been committed. The court of equity, however, does not give anything beyond the account".

---

[827] *MCA Records Inc v Charly Records Ltd* [2001] EWCA Civ 1441; [2002] F.S.R. 26.

[828] *ZYX Music GmbH v Chris King & Others* [1995] F.S.R. 566.

[829] CDPA 1988 s.96(2); *Hogg v Kirby* (1803) 8 Ves.215; *Grimson v Eyre* (1804) 9 Ves. 341 at 346; *Baily v Taylor* (1830) 1 R. & M. 73; *Sheriff v Coates* (1830) 1 R. & M. 159; *Kelly v Hooper* (1840) 4 Jur. 21. For a review of the principles involved in taking an account of profits see Kirby in [1991] 10 E.I.P.R. 367 and Bently in [1991] 1 E.I.P.R. 5. See also Bently in [1990] 3 E.I.P.R. 106 on *Potton Ltd v Yorkclose Ltd* [1990] F.S.R. 11.

[830] *Delfe v Delamotte* (1857) 3 K. & J. 581; cf. *Pike v Nicholas* (1869) L.R. 5 Ch. 251. If the claimant has paid tax on the profits, the profits will be net of tax, subject to an obligation to account for any tax reclaim or tax credit which may subsequently arise: *Celanese International Corp v BP Chemicals Ltd* [1999] R.P.C. 203, para.137.

[831] *My Kinda Town v Soll* [1983] R.P.C. 15 at 49. *House of Spring Gardens Ltd v Point Blank Ltd* [1985] F.S.R. 327 (Supreme Ct. of Ireland); *Potton Ltd v Yorkclose Ltd* [1990] F.S.R. 11; *Van Camp Chocolates Ltd v Milsbrooks Ltd* [1984] 1 N.Z.L.R. 354. Where the claimant sues two or more defendants in a chain of distribution, a defendant who is obliged to indemnify another defendant who is further down the chain may deduct the amount of the indemnity from his profits: *Spring Form Inc v Toy Brokers Ltd* [2002] F.S.R. 276.

[832] *Allied Signal Inc v Du Pont Canada Inc* (1995) 33 I.P.R. 511 at 531–532.

[833] *Sir Terence Orby Conran v Mean Fiddler Holdings Ltd* [1997] F.S.R. 856 at 861 (Robert Walker J.); an account was refused in that case (which concerned infringement of trade marks), the infringement having been initially innocent and ceased upon commencement of proceedings, and where discussions between the parties might have made proceedings unnecessary. It was held that whether to grant an account lay within the discretion of the court. However, the fact that the defendant's infringement was done innocently will not necessarily preclude the granting of an account: see *Wienerworld Ltd v Vision Video Ltd* [1998] F.S.R. 832, a copyright case.

[834] *Wienerworld Ltd v Vision Video Ltd* [1998] F.S.R. 832.

[835] (1843) 2 Ha. 543, 560; see *Pike v Nicholas* (1870) L.R. 5 Ch. 251 and *International Credit Control Ltd v Axelion* [1974] 1 N.Z.L.R. 695.

The basis on which an account is ordered is that there should not be any unjust enrichment on the part of the defendant, and that the defendant should be deprived of any profit (even including an unrealised profit) attributable to wrongful acts committed in breach of the claimant's rights.[836] Accordingly, an account of profits will not extend to matters not quantifiable as "profits", such as the acquisition of an enhanced position in the market.[837] For these purposes, the accounting defendant is treated as if he had carried on his business on behalf of the claimant.[838] It is not the purpose of the account to identify what saving the defendant has made by adopting the infringing activity instead of a non-infringing activity.[839] By the same token, a claimant cannot increase his claim by arguing that the defendant could or should have generated higher profits.[840] It is no answer to a claim for an account that the defendant could have made the same profits by following an alternative, non-infringing course.[841]

21–210 **Non-proprietary rights.** It has been held that in general an account of profits is not available for the invasion of a non-proprietary right.[842] This creates a difficulty in respect of claims for an account for infringement of moral rights, performers' non-property rights and recording rights, all of which are actionable as breach of statutory duty. Where the infringement was with knowledge or reasonable grounds to believe, the claimant may be able to rely on reg.3 of the Enforcement Regulations[843] to the extent that the profits are found to be "unfair". In respect of innocent infringements, however, it does nor appear that the remedy is available, nor does art.13(2) of the Enforcement Directive require there to be one.

21–211 **Where defendant has mixed infringing and non-infringing material.** While an account of profits may be a useful remedy in a simple case, it is very difficult to take where part only of the defendant's material infringes the claimant's copyright. In such a case an attempt must be made to apportion profits according to the relative value of the infringing and non-infringing material. For example, in a case of infringement of copyright in architectural drawings by the construction of houses, there would be excluded from the account profits attributable to the purchase, landscaping and sale of the land on which the houses were built, any increase in the value of the houses during the interval between the completion of the houses and sale, and profits attributable to the advertising, marketing and selling of the houses.[844] In the absence of some special reason to the contrary, the profits of a single project should be apportioned to different parts or aspects of the project in the same proportions as the costs and expenses are attributed to

---

[836] See, e.g. *Celanese International Corp v BP Chemicals Ltd* [1999] R.P.C. 203 (a patent case) at para.37: the court is trying to determine what profits have been caused, in the legal sense, by the defendant's wrongful acts.

[837] *Redrow Homes Ltd v Betts Brothers Plc* [1999] 1 A.C. 197 at p.209D–E; [1988] F.S.R. 345 at 353 (Lord Clyde).

[838] *Celanese International Corp v BP Chemicals Ltd* [1999] R.P.C. 203, para.36.

[839] *Celanese International Corp v BP Chemicals Ltd* [1999] R.P.C. 203, paras 39–40 and 63–72, following *Peter Pan Manufacturing Corp v Corsets Silhouette* [1963] R.P.C. 45, *Baker Energy Resources Corp v Reading & Bates Construction* (1998) 58 C.P.R. (3d) 359 and *Potton Ltd v Yorkclose Ltd* [1990] F.S.R. 11.

[840] *Celanese International Corp v BP Chemicals Ltd* [1999] R.P.C. 203, para.42, following *Dart Industries Inc v Decor Corp Pty Ltd* (1993) 26 I.P.R. 193.

[841] *Celanese International Corp v BP Chemicals Ltd* [1999] R.P.C. 203, para.39.

[842] *Devenish Nutrition Ltd v Sanofi-Adventis SA (France)* [2008] EWCA Civ 1086 at paras 75 and 155; [2009] Ch. 390.

[843] The Intellectual Property (Enforcement etc.) Regulations 2006 (SI 2006/1028).

[844] *Potton Ltd v Yorkclose Ltd* [1990] F.S.R. 11.

them.[845] However, the court may depart from this rule if, for example, the costs and expenses of a particular part are not an accurate reflection of the contribution made by that part to the whole.[846]

Infringement part of a larger enterprise. Where the infringement was only part of a larger enterprise which generated profits, it is for the defendant to show that it is inequitable to order an account of the whole profits, by demonstrating that only a proportion of the profits were made by means of the infringement.[847] If the defendant cannot establish that not all of the profits made were attributable to the infringement, the result will be that it must account for the whole of the profit made by the enterprise.[848] However, once the need for an apportionment has been established, there is no onus on either party in relation to the question of what apportionment should take place.[849]   **21–212**

In *Dart Industries Inc v Decor Corp Pty Ltd*[850] it was held on the facts of that case that the proportion of overhead costs which were attributable to the obtaining of the relevant profit might be deducted in arriving at a profit figure. It was pointed out that where the manufacture of a product constituted a side line of the defendant's business and made use of spare capacity, it would not be right to deduct a proportion of overhead costs since these would have been incurred in any event. Where, however, the product was an integral part of the defendant's range, such that if the product in question had not been manufactured, some alternative product would have been, it would be wrong in principle to deny the defendant a deduction of a proportion of his overheads. Otherwise the defendant would be in a worse position than if he had never manufactured the infringing article. Again, if it is shown that overheads were increased by the production of the infringing article, or would have been reduced had it not been produced, it may be appropriate to attribute the difference to the infringing product.

In the patent case of *Celanese International Corp v BP Chemicals Ltd*,[851] the defendant divided its business into units. The infringing process was used in two plants which were both included in one of the units, the BPC Acetyls Business Unit. Each plant used a different mix of starting materials to produce different final product mixes in differently designed hardware with different overall capital and running costs and different overall profitabilities. Some of the overheads of the BPC Acetyls Business Unit were attributable to the two plants; others were

---

[845] *Potton Ltd v Yorkclose Ltd* [1990] F.S.R. 11 at 19.

[846] *Celanese International Corp v BP Chemicals Ltd* [1999] R.P.C. 203, para.55. A particular part or process may be very cheap but add a lot of value (ibid.), as in *The Wellcome Foundation Ltd v Apotex Inc*, Fed Court of Canada, August 26, 1998 (MacKay, J.) where the court (at para.57) rejected an apportionment based on the relative costs of infringing and non-infringing ingredients of a combination drug because the infringing ingredient was "the major potentiating ingredient". See also *Dart Industries Inc v Decor Corp Pty Ltd* (1993) 26 I.P.R. 193 (High Ct of Aus) (a patent action), where the defendant was held liable to account for the profits made from the manufacture and sale of plastic canisters where only the lids infringed. The sales were attributable to the lid, without which the canisters would never have been made. Another situation where the court may wish to depart from the general rule is where there is a standard process involving a number of steps and where one step is replaced by an infringing process which results in an increase in profits: *Celanese International Corp v BP Chemicals Ltd* [1999] R.P.C. 203, para.58. If the court is able to depart from the general rule, it is released from mathematical constraints and has a wide discretion to pick whatever figure it thinks is fair (ibid., para.57).

[847] *Zupanovich Pty Ltd v Beale Nominees Pty Ltd* (1995) 32 I.P.R. 339; *Warman International Ltd v Dwyer* (1995) 128 A.L.R. 201 at 211–212; *Celanese International Corp v BP Chemicals Ltd* [1999] R.P.C. 203, para.73.

[848] *Zupanovich Pty Ltd v Beale Nominees Pty Ltd* (1995) 32 I.P.R. 339 at pp.358–359 (Carr J.).

[849] *My Kinda Town v Soll* [1983] R.P.C. 15 at 57; *Celanese International Corp v BP Chemicals Ltd* [1999] R.P.C. 203, para.73.

[850] (1993) 26 I.P.R. 193 (High Ct of Aus.) (a patent action). See also *LED Builders Pty Ltd v Eagle Homes Pty Ltd* (1999) 44 I.P.R. 24 (F.C.A., Lindgren J.) where a building company was permitted an allowance for general overheads.

[851] [1999] R.P.C. 203.

not. Three major issues arose. First, whether the plants should be treated separately or whether a loss made on one could be set off against a profit made on another. The court held that the plants should be treated as separate businesses which happened to be run on the same site and shared some common upstream and downstream plant and services.[852] Secondly, how overheads should be apportioned. The claimant contended that the defendant should not be allowed to deduct any overheads which would have been incurred if the infringement had not taken place. However, the judge accepted the defendant's submission that the proportion of overheads which were attributable to the plants should be deducted.[853] Thirdly, the defendant's overheads included research and development costs. The claimant contended that the defendant was only entitled to deduct such costs if they were useful and were used during the period of infringement. This argument was rejected.[854]

21–213 **Procedure.** A claimant is obliged to elect between the alternative remedies of damages and an account and is entitled to disclosure before doing so.[855] An account will be refused if it is clear that there are no profits.[856] Where a claimant is awarded an account of profits, he cannot also be awarded additional damages.[857] The account is normally taken by the Master. Where an account is sought against two or more defendants in a chain of distribution who may be obliged to indemnify each other, the accounts must be taken together and no order must be made for payment in respect of any infringing article until the claimant undertakes not to make a claim in respect of that article against any other defendant.[858] A claimant is entitled to disclosure for the purposes of the account. In general, the defendant will be obliged to give full particulars, in a witness statement, of the number of copies printed and sold, and the cost of publication and distribution, verified by the production of all proper vouchers and receipts.[859] For special provisions in the case where the copyright owner has granted an exclusive licence which encompasses the defendant's infringing acts, see para.21–222 below.

(viii) Delivery up and disposal

(a) *The Enforcement Directive*

21–214 **Corrective measures.** Article 10 of the Enforcement Directive (headed "corrective measures") requires Member States to ensure that the competent judicial authorities may order, at the request of the applicant, appropriate measures to be taken with regard to infringing goods and implements principally used in the creation or manufacture of such goods.[860] The measures are to include recall from the channels of commerce, definitive removal from the channels of commerce[861] or destruction and are to be carried out at the expense of the infringer unless par-

---

[852] paras 78 and 87.

[853] paras 88–94.

[854] paras 96–101.

[855] See above, para.21–192, above.

[856] *Lee v Alston* (1789) 1 Ves. 78; *Colburn v Simms* (1843) 2 Ha. 543; *Powell v Aiken* (1857) 4 K. & J. 343.

[857] *Redrow Homes Ltd v Betts Brothers Plc* [1999] 1 A.C. 197; [1998] F.S.R. 345; see para.21–202, above.

[858] *Spring Form Inc v Toy Brokers Ltd* [2002] F.S.R. 276.

[859] *Stevens v Brett* (1863) 12 W.R. 572.

[860] art.10(1). For a critique of the operation of art.10, see *Corrective Measures in Intellectual Property Rights*, a report of the Legal Sub-group of the European Counterfeiting and Piracy Observatory.

[861] The Legal Sub-group of the European Counterfeiting and Piracy Observatory considers it to be

ticular reasons are invoked for not doing so.[862] The authorities are obliged to take into account the need for proportionality between the seriousness of the infringement and the remedies ordered as well as the interests of third parties.[863] This provision mirrors art.46 of TRIPS so far as it is relevant to the rights covered in this Chapter.

Alternative measures. As is the case in relation to injunctions, art.12 of the Directive permits Member States to provide that in an appropriate case and at the request of the person liable to corrective measures, the court may award pecuniary relief only. Such an order may only be awarded if (a) the infringer acted unintentionally and without negligence; (b) the execution of the measures in question would cause him or her disproportionate harm; and (c) pecuniary compensation to the injured party appears reasonably satisfactory. Recital 25 makes clear that this power is not intended to be used where the commercial use of counterfeit goods or the supply of services would infringe laws other than intellectual property laws or would be likely to harm consumers. This provision has not been expressly implemented in the United Kingdom. However, as will be seen, both the statutory and equitable powers to order delivery up are discretionary and accordingly a pecuniary remedy could no doubt be awarded against an innocent infringer if an order for delivery up were thought to be oppressive. **21–215**

(b) *Delivery up*

Statutory power to make an order for delivery up. A copyright owner (or exclusive licensee[864]) may apply for an order for delivery up to him or to such other person as the Court may direct of (a) infringing copies[865] in a person's possession, custody or control in the course of a business and (b) articles in a person's possession, custody or control specifically designed or adapted for making copies of a copyright work which that person knows or has to reason to believe have been used or are to be used to make infringing copies.[866] Note that there is no "guilty knowledge" provision under (a).[867] An example of (b) would be a mould or template. A person having performers' rights (including an exclusive licensee of a performer's property right[868]) or having recording rights in relation to a performance may apply to the Court for an order that an illicit recording[869] in another person's possession, custody or control in the course of a business be **21–216**

---

unclear whether this relates only to situations where the goods are still in the possession of the infringer or whether it extends to goods in the distribution chain: Corrective Measures in Intellectual Property Rights, p.3.

[862] art.10(2).

[863] art.10(3). Recital 24 gives as particular examples of third parties whose interests are to be taken into account consumers and private parties acting in good faith.

[864] CDPA 1988 s.101(1) and (2).

[865] As to which see CDPA 1988 s.27 and para.8–03, above.

[866] CDPA 1988 s.99(1). In relation to means for facilitating the unauthorised removal or circumvention of technical devices applied to computer programs which a person has in his possession, custody or control with the intention that they should be used to facilitate the unauthorised removal of any technical device which has been applied to a computer program, a person with rights under CDPA 1988 s.296(2) has the same rights as a copyright owner has under s.99(1) in respect of infringing copies: see CDPA 1988 s.296(4). In relation to a device, product or component which a person has in his possession, custody or control with the intention that it should be used to circumvent effective technological measures, a person with rights under CDPA 1988 s.296ZD(2) has the same rights as a copyright owner has under s.99(1) in respect of infringing copies: see CDPA 1988 s.296ZD(4).

[867] *Lagenes Ltd v It's At (UK) Ltd* [1991] F.S.R. 492.

[868] CDPA 1988 s.191L(1) & (2).

[869] As to which see CDPA 1988 s.197 and para.12–70, above.

delivered up to him or to such other person as the court may direct.[870] A UK unregistered design right owner (or exclusive licensee[871]) may apply for an order for delivery up to him or to such other person as the court may direct of (a) infringing articles[872] in a person's possession, custody or control for commercial purposes[873] and (b) anything in a person's possession, custody or control specifically designed or adapted for making articles to a particular design which that person knows or has to reason to believe has been used or is to be used to make infringing articles.[874] Similar provision is made in relation to community designs.[875] The court has jurisdiction to make a mandatory order for delivery up on an interim application, if there is a high degree of assurance that the claimant will establish his entitlement at trial and the risk of injustice, if the injunction were refused, sufficiently outweighs the risk of injustice if it were granted.[876]

This power does not affect any other power of the court[877]; for example, its equitable jurisdiction (which is considered in the next paragraph). The power is not available where a defendant in infringement proceedings undertakes to take a licence of right where such a licence is available,[878] nor when the defendant shows that an illicit recording was "innocently acquired" by him.[879]

A person to whom an infringing copy or other article, illicit recording or infringing article or other thing is delivered in pursuance of an order must retain it pending the making of an order, or the decision not to make an order, as to its disposal under ss.114, 204 or 231 of the 1988 Act, as the case may be.[880]

An order for delivery up must not be made unless the court also makes, or it appears to the court that there are grounds for making, an order for the disposal of the infringing copy or other article under ss.114, 204 or 231 of the 1988 Act, as the case may be.[881] Delivery up is a discretionary remedy and consistently with art.10 of the Enforcement Directive will not be ordered in cases where its effect is disproportionate and would cause greater harm than is necessary in order to safeguard the legitimate interests of the claimant.[882]

In general,[883] an application for an order for delivery up may not be made after the end of the period of six years from the date on which the infringing copy or article, illicit recording or infringing article or thing in question was made.[884]

21–217 **Equitable jurisdiction to order delivery up.** The court still has an equitable[885] jurisdiction to order delivery up of articles which have been created in violation

---

[870] CDPA 1988 s.195(1).

[871] CDPA 1988 s.234(1) and (2).

[872] As to which see CDPA 1988 s.228 and para.13–161, above.

[873] For the definition of "commercial purposes" see para.13–147, above.

[874] CDPA 1988 s.230(1).

[875] See the Community Design Regulations 2005 (SI 2005/339) reg.1A(2).

[876] *Nottingham Building Society v Eurodynamics Systems Plc* [1993] F.S.R. 468 at 474, and see para.21–148, above.

[877] CDPA 1988 ss.99(4), 195(4) and 230(7).

[878] CDPA 1988 ss.98, 191K and 239.

[879] See para.21–148, above.

[880] CDPA 1988 ss.99(3), 195(3) and 230(6). See para.21–218 below.

[881] CDPA 1988 ss.99(2), 195(2) and 230(2).

[882] *Ocular Sciences Ltd v Aspect Vision Care Ltd (No.2)* [1997] R.P.C. 289; see also, *Valeo Vision SA v Flexible Lamps Ltd* [1995] R.P.C. 205, where delivery up was refused on the grounds that it was a commercial nonsense and not in the interests of justice—a licence of right was available to the defendant very soon and any advantage to the defendant in being able to retain infringing copies could be reflected in the inquiry.

[883] For exceptions, which are (broadly) similar to ss.28 and 32 of the Limitation Act 1980, see CDPA 1988 ss.113(2), (3), 203(2), (3) and 230(4), (5).

[884] CDPA 1988 ss.99(2) and 113, 195(2) and 203 and 230(2).

[885] And therefore discretionary: *Ocular Sciences Ltd v Aspect Vision Care Ltd (No.2)* [1997] R.P.C. 289 at 410 and 420.

of a claimant's right, but only for the purposes of destruction.[886] This principle could be used, for example, to support an order for delivery up of a derogatory treatment of a work where there was reason to believe that the defendant might not obey the terms of an injunction or, perhaps, where the defendant intended to make use of the derogatory treatment without infringing the moral right. In fact, it is frequently used in copyright cases generally. The jurisdiction extends to articles which are not in themselves infringing copies, if they were brought into being as the result of the use of infringing copies.[887]

The basis of the equitable jurisdiction is not that the infringing copies belong to the claimant, but the protection of the claimant's rights by preventing their use by the defendant.[888] The relief should therefore be limited to what is necessary for the protection of the claimant's rights, not the punishment of the defendant.[889] Thus the relief will not be granted if the articles can be rendered non-infringing,[890] nor if the articles have been taken out of the jurisdiction and there is no evidence of an intention to reimport them.[891]

Where a defendant has mixed the claimant's work with work of his own, then, if it is physically possible to sever one from the other, the order for delivery up will apply only to the infringing material,[892] but where the parts are physically inseparable the order for delivery up may extend to the whole of the article.[893]

The exercise of the jurisdiction to make an order for delivery up, particularly at the interim stage, may be affected by the provisions of the Contempt of Court Act 1981 relating to disclosure of sources of information.[894]

For special provisions in the case where the copyright owner has granted an exclusive licence which encompasses the defendant's infringing acts, see para.21–222, below.

(c) Disposal

The power. The court has power[895] to make orders as to the disposal of infringing copies and other articles, illicit recordings, and infringing articles and other things which have been delivered up in pursuance of an order,[896] or which have been seized or detained by the owner of the relevant right or a person authorised   **21–218**

---

[886] *Hole v Bradbury* (1879) L.R. 12 Ch. D. 886; cf. *Delfe v Delamotte* (1857) 3 K. & J. 581; *Stannard v Harrison* (1871) 11 W.R. 811. The statutory provisions as to delivery up are stated not to affect any other power of the court: CDPA 1988 ss.99(4), 195(4) and 230(7).

[887] *Chappell & Co Ltd v Columbia Graphophone Co* [1914] 2 Ch. 124.

[888] It is in substance a species of injunction: *Ocular Sciences Ltd v Aspect Vision Care Ltd* [1997] R.P.C. 289 at 410 and 420. See also *Cantor Gaming Ltd v Gameaccount Global Ltd* [2007] EWHC 1914 (Ch); [2008] F.S.R. 4 at para.126: delivery up is usually undertaken in aid of an injunction, to ensure that there is no stray use.

[889] *Vavasseur v Krupp* (1879) 9 Ch. D. 351 at 360; *Mergenthaler Limotype Co Ltd v Intertype Co Ltd* (1926) 43 R.P.C. 381 (both patent cases).

[890] *Electrical & Musical Industries Ltd v Lissen Ltd* (1936) 54 R.P.C. 5 at 35; *British United Shoe Machinery Co Ltd v Gimson Shoes Machinery Co Ltd* (1928) 45 R.P.C. 85 at 105; *Geodesic Constructions Pty Ltd v Gatson* (1976) S.A.S.R. 453 at 471.

[891] *Roussel Uclaf v Pan Laboratories Pty Ltd* (1994) 29 I.P.R. 556 (Fed. Ct. of Aus.).

[892] *Warne & Co v Seebohm* (1888) 39 Ch. D. 73; *Nichols Advanced Vehicle Systems Inc v Rees* [1979] R.P.C. 127.

[893] *Stevens v Wildy* (1850) 11 L.J. Ch. 190; *Secretary of State for Defence v Guardian Newspapers* [1985] A.C. 339.

[894] Contempt of Court Act 1981 (c.49) s.10; see above, para.21–162, above.

[895] ss.114, 204 and 231 of the 1988 Act. S.114 applies with the necessary modifications to means for facilitating the unauthorised removal or circumvention of technical devices applied to computer programs (see CDPA 1988 s.296(7)) and to devices designed to circumvent technical measures in relation to other works (CDPA 1988 s.296ZD(6)).

[896] i.e. an Order under ss.99 or 118, 195 or 199 or 230 of the 1988 Act, as the case may be.

by him.[897] The application may be brought in the High Court or a county court.[898] Where there is no pending action, the application is by claim form.[899] Where there is a pending action, it is thought that the application should be made by notice under Pt 23.[900]

The application may be for an order that the material in question shall be:

(1) forfeited to the owner of the relevant right; or

(2) destroyed; or

(3) otherwise dealt with as the court may think fit.[901]

An application may also be made (for example, by a defendant) for a decision that no such order should be made.[902] If the court decides that no order should be made, the person in whose possession, custody or control the material was before being delivered up or seized is entitled to its return.[903]

21–219   **Procedure and decision.** In considering what order (if any) should be made, the court is to consider whether other remedies available in an action for infringement of copyright, infringement of the rights conferred by Ch.2 of Pt II of the 1988 Act (that is, the Chapter conferring economic rights in performances) or infringement of design right would be adequate to compensate the owner of the relevant right and to protect his interests.[904] Provision is made for the protection of the interests of third parties. The procedure for making an order includes service of notice on persons having an interest in the material.[905] Any such person is entitled to appear in proceedings for such an order, whether or not he was served with notice, and to appeal against any order made, whether or not he appeared.[906] An order is not to take effect until the end of the period within which notice of an appeal may be given or, if before the end of that period, notice of appeal is duly given, until the final determination or abandonment of the proceedings on the appeal.[907] For special provisions in the case where the copyright owner has granted an exclusive licence which encompasses the defendant's infringing acts, see para.21–222, below.

21–220   **Where more than one person interested.** Where there is more than one person interested in the material, the court is to make such order as it thinks just and may, in particular, direct that the material be sold, or otherwise dealt with, and the proceeds divided.[908] A person has an interest for the purposes of these provisions if an order could be made in his favour in respect of it under certain other

---

[897] i.e. seized or detained under ss.100 or 196 of the 1988 Act, as the case may be. Note the absence of a seizure provision in respect of design right.

[898] ss.115(1), 205(1) and 232(1) of the 1988 Act. There is no financial limit on the county court jurisdiction: High Court and County Courts Jurisdiction Order 1991 (SI 1991/724) art.2(1)(n). It is provided that the provisions giving jurisdiction to county courts are not to affect the High Court's jurisdiction: CDPA 1988 ss.115(3), 205(3) and 232(3).

[899] There is now no requirement that the proceedings be brought by Pt 8 claim form. Accordingly, the usual principles will apply as to the choice of originating process.

[900] Following the repeal of RSC Ord.93 r.24 and CCR Ord.49 r.4A, there does not seem to be any specific provision about such claims. However, prior to the introduction of the CPR, applications in pending actions were made by summons or motion in the action: RSC Ord.93 r.24(2). Moreover, PD63 para.23.1 (discussed below,) makes provision for service of "the claim form, *or application notice*, where appropriate" (emphasis added).

[901] CDPA 1988 ss.114(1), 204(1) and 231(1).

[902] CDPA 1988 ss.114(1), 204(1) and 231(1).

[903] ss.114(5), 204(5) and 231(5).

[904] CDPA 1988 ss.114(2), 204(2) and 231(2).

[905] PD63 para.23.1.

[906] CDPA 1988 ss.114(3), 204(3) and 231(3).

[907] CDPA 1988 ss.114(3), 204(3) and 231(3).

[908] CDPA 1988 ss.114(4), 204(4) and 231(4).

provisions.[909] Apart from that express provision, the 1988 Act does not define what is meant by "an interest" or a "person interested". The expressions would obviously embrace a person who has a legal or equitable title to or interest in the material, or to rights in it or an exclusive licence but are not necessarily so confined and may extend to persons who have "commercial interests" which would be damaged or prejudiced by orders for forfeiture, destruction or disposal.

(d) *Costs*

Article 10(2) of the Enforcement Directive provides that the courts shall order the measures of delivery up and destruction to be taken at the infringer's expense unless "particular reasons are invoked for not doing so". Paragraph 26.1 of the Practice Direction to Pt 63 of the Civil Procedure Rules states that where a delivery up or destruction order has been made in an intellectual property case, the defendant will pay the costs of compliance unless the court orders otherwise. According to the Government, this provision was introduced in the interests of clarity and because the Directive stipulates that the Court "shall order". It is difficult to conceive of a situation in which someone other than the defendant would have been ordered to pay the costs of such an exercise prior to the introduction of the new paragraph. Accordingly, it seems unlikely that it will involve any change in practice.

21–221

(ix) The position of exclusive licensees

In cases where an exclusive licensee has concurrent rights with a copyright owner, owner of a performer's property right or design right, special considerations apply to the remedies of delivery up, seizure without a court order, damages and account of profits.

21–222

First, the owner of the right must notify the exclusive licensee before applying for an order for delivery up under ss.99, 195 or 230 and (in the case of copyright and performer's property rights) before exercising the right of seizure under ss.100 or 196, as the case may be.[910] The exclusive licensee can then apply to the court and the court may make such order for delivery up under ss.99, 195 or 230 as it thinks fit having regard to the terms of the licence. In the case of copyright and performer's property rights, the court may also make such order as it thinks fit, having regard to the terms of the licence, prohibiting or permitting the exercise by the rights owner of the right of seizure under ss.100 or 196, as the case may be.[911]

Secondly, in an action for infringement of copyright, performer's property rights or design right which relates wholly or partly to an infringement in respect of which the owner of the right and an exclusive licensee have or had concurrent rights of action:

(a) the court is directed to take into account, when assessing damages, the terms of the licence and any pecuniary remedy already awarded or available to either of them in respect of the infringement;

(b) the court may not direct an account of profits if an award of damages has

---

[909] In the case of each of the three types of right being described here, (i.e. (1) copyright, (2) performer's rights and recording rights and (3) design right), the other provisions being referred to are the equivalent provisions for the other two types of right together with s.19 of the Trade Marks Act 1994 (c.26) (including that section as applied by reg.4 of the Community Trade Mark Regulations 2006 (SI 2006/1027)); s.24D of the Registered Designs Act 1949; and reg.1C of the Community Design Regulations 2005 (SI 2005/2339).

[910] CDPA 1988 ss.102(5), 191M(5) and 235(5).

[911] CDPA 1988 ss.102(5), 191M(5) and 235(5).

been made, or an account of profits has been directed in favour of the other of them in respect of the infringement;

(c) if an account of profits is directed the court must apportion the profits between them as the court considers just, subject to any agreement between them.

These provisions apply whether or not the owner of the right and the exclusive licensee are both parties to the action.[912]

(x) Publicity orders

21–223   Article 15 of the Enforcement Directive requires Member States to ensure that in proceedings for infringement of an intellectual property right the judicial authorities may order at the request of the rights holder and at the expense of the infringer appropriate measures for the dissemination of the information concerning the decision, including displaying it and publishing it in full or in part. Member States are also given a discretion to provide for other additional publicity measures which are appropriate to the particular circumstances, including prominent advertising. According to recital 27 the object of this provision is "to act as a supplementary deterrent to future infringers and to contribute to the awareness of the public at large".

With a view to giving effect to the mandatory part of art.15, para.29.2 of PD63 provides as follows: "Where the court finds that an intellectual property right has been infringed, the court may, at the request of the applicant, order appropriate measures for the dissemination and publication of the judgment to be taken at the defendant's expense." In Scotland, equivalent legislative provision has been made.[913] Such orders are now relatively frequently made but seldom reported. In one case the parties agreed (without apparent disapproval from the Judge) that the defendant which had been found liable would display on the homepage of its website for a period of one year or further order of the court a short statement to that effect together with a hyperlink to the judgment on the British and Irish Legal Information Institute (BAILLI) website. The Judge said that it would be open to the defendant to add a statement that it was seeking to appeal the judgment.[914]

The discretionary part of art.15 has not been implemented.

(xi) Points as to costs

21–224   **Scope.** There are no specific rules as to costs in actions concerning the rights covered in this work, and the reader is referred to the relevant Civil Procedure Rules and specialist works. The following paragraphs cover certain specific applications of those rules to actions concerning the rights covered in this work.

21–225   **Pre-action behaviour.** Pre-action behaviour may be crucial to the final costs order.[915] Pre-action behaviour in relation to the enforcement of the rights covered in this work is discussed below.[916]

21–226   **Defendants' pre-action offers.** In a previous edition of this work, it was stated that as a general rule a claimant in a copyright case was not obliged to rest satis-

---

[912] CDPA 1988 ss.102(4), 191M(4) and 235(4).
[913] See reg.5 of the Intellectual Property (Enforcement, etc.) Regulations 2006 (SI 2006/1028).
[914] *Vestergaard Frandsen A/S v Bestnet Europe Ltd* [2009] EWHC 1456 (Ch) at para.114; [2010] F.S.R. 2.
[915] CPR 44.3(5)(a).
[916] See paras 21–232 et seq., below.

fied with the defendant's promise not to infringe and was entitled to go to court to vindicate his right.[917] The introduction of the Civil Procedure Rules has swept away the old rules as to costs and it seems unlikely that this proposition remains correct as a general rule. Much will depend on the nature of the infringement and the infringer. If a respectable and financially strong defendant, who has been guilty of innocent infringement, offers suitable contractual undertakings together with such other relief as the claimant may reasonably expect to recover at trial (such as delivery up, *Tring*-type disclosure and a money offer), a claimant who nevertheless commences proceedings may well do so at his own risk as to costs. By contrast, where the defendant's offer can be shown to be worthless, for example because the infringement was deliberate and flagrant, a claimant may well be considered to be justified in commencing proceedings (after complying with such requirements as to pre-action behaviour as may be applicable). In one recent case,[918] it was held that where a defendant offered a contractual undertaking, to be backed by a court undertaking if there was a breach and the claimant pressed ahead and obtained an injunction, it was difficult to say that the claimant had been the wholly successful party for the purposes of costs: rather the claimant had obtained a "marginal advance".[919] The Judge stated[920] that if a defendant has admitted some infringement but given a claimant some cause for distrust as to the scope of the admission, there is a case for awarding the claimant its reasonable and proportionate costs of establishing that the defendant has not in fact committed greater infringements even if the claimant is unsuccessful in establishing any further infringement.[921]

Part 36 offers. It is important to offer everything which the claimant can reasonably claim in order to obtain proper protection on costs. Thus in one case,[922] an offer to destroy infringing material and undertake not to exploit it further was insufficient to protect a defendant where there was also a claim for a declaration and delivery up.   **21–227**

Costs of split trials. Where there is an order for a split trial and the only relief the claimant obtains is an enquiry as to damages or an account of profits, but it is uncertain whether the claimant will recover more than nominal damages, the trial judge may well be justified in deferring any order as to costs until the final outcome is known.[923] Where there has been a Pt 36 offer or a payment into court, the issue of costs will normally be reserved until after the value of the financial claim has been assessed.[924]   **21–228**

---

[917] *Copinger* 14th edn, para.22–101.
[918] *Cantor Gaming Ltd v Gameaccount Global Ltd* [2007] EWHC 2381 (Ch); [2008] F.S.R. 4.
[919] para.21.
[920] Following *Cantor Fitzgerald International v Tradition (UK) Ltd* [2001] EWCA Civ 942.
[921] para.67.
[922] *Experience Hendrix LLC v Times Newspapers Ltd* [2008] EWHC 458 (Ch).
[923] *Weill v Mean Fiddler Holdings Ltd* [2003] EWCA Civ 1058 at para.34. But note *Alan Williams Entertainments Ltd v Hurd* [2006] EWCA Civ 1637 at para.39, in which the court emphasised that the policy of CPR 1.4(2)(i) and the need to promote settlement might justify a different order. See also *Shepherds Investments Ltd v Walters* [2007] EWCA Civ 292 (where the authorities are listed) and *Hampshire County Council v Supportways Community Services Ltd* [2006] EWCA Civ 1170: enquiry made conditional on payment of percentage of adverse costs order on trial of liability; incidence of balance to be determined by court making enquiry. In *Experience Hendrix LLC v The Times Newspapers Ltd* [2008] EWHC 458 (Ch), Warren J. noted that where it is clear on the evidence that the claimant is only interested in money, it may be appropriate for the costs of establishing liability to be reserved, but that even then the position may not be clear since the claimant might need *Tring* disclosure before being able to make his election and to make an informed decision as to whether to accept the defendant's money offer para.10.
[924] *Tulett Prebon Plc v BGC Brokers LP* [2010] EWHC 989 (QB) at para.6.

21–229   **Costs of internal experts.** In the patent case of *Re Nossen's Patent*,[925] the court permitted the claimant to recover, by way of costs, a sum in respect of experiments conducted by its employees for the purposes of the proceedings. It has been held that this principle applies generally in intellectual property proceedings.[926] Thus, a corporate claimant may in principle recover a reasonable sum in respect of expert services performed by its own staff in investigating, formulating and presenting its claim. Non-expert staff costs may also be recovered as damages.[927]

21–230   **Joinder pursuant to s.102(1) of the 1988 Act.** A copyright owner or exclusive licensee added as a defendant pursuant to s.102(1) of the 1988 Act is not liable for any costs unless he takes part in the proceedings.[928] There are similar provisions in respect of performers' property rights and design right.[929]

8. PROCEDURAL AND RELATED MATTERS

A. INFRINGEMENT OF EACH RIGHT A SEPARATE TORT

21–231   The various rights conferred upon a copyright owner, including the right to authorise any of the restricted acts, are separate and distinct rights, and the infringement of each is a distinct and separate tort. The same is true of moral rights, rights in performances and design right. Consequently, for example, judgment against the author of an infringing work for having authorised its printing is no bar to an action against the printer.

B. PRE-ACTION CONDUCT

21–232   **General.** There are no pre-action protocols in respect of claims involving the rights covered in this Chapter.[930] The position is therefore governed by Practice Direction—Pre-Action Conduct, which provides amongst other things that parties to a potential dispute should exchange sufficient information to enable them to understand each other's position and make informed decisions about settlement and how to proceed; and make appropriate attempts to resolve the matter without starting proceedings.[931] Where the claim is for breach of statutory duty (e.g. for infringement of moral rights or performers' non-property rights) s.2 of the Compensation Act 2006 applies. Thus, an apology or other redress does not of itself amount to an admission of breach of statutory duty.

21–233   **The draft pre-action Code of Practice.** An Intellectual Property Pre-Action Protocol Committee was established by the Law Society some time ago to develop pre-action protocols for intellectual property cases. However, before the final drafts were published, the Committee was informed that no such protocols were now required.[932] Nevertheless, the Committee published its drafts in the

---

[925] [1969] 1 W.L.R. 638.
[926] *Admiral Management Services Ltd v Para Protect Europe Ltd* [2002] EWHC 233 (Ch); [2002] 1 W.L.R. 2722 and [2002] F.S.R. 59.
[927] See para.21–197 above.
[928] CDPA 1988 s.102(2).
[929] ss.191M(2) and 235(2).
[930] See, however, *Practice Direction—Competition Law—Claims Relating to the Application of Articles 81 and 82 of the EC Treaty and Chapters I and II of Part I of the Competition Act 1998.*
[931] para.6.1.
[932] See the Introduction to the Code of Practice referred to in the next note.

form of a Code of Practice.[933] The Code does not have the force of law[934] and does not appear to have been relied on by the court in any reported case. However, it contains useful guidance and so is dealt with here. It should be noted that one of the recommendations made by Jackson L.J. in his Review of Civil Litigation Costs was that there be consultation with court users, practitioners and judges in order to ascertain whether there is support either for an intellectual property pre-action protocol or for the Patents Court and Patents County Court Guide to give guidance as to pre-action conduct.[935]

General. The Code applies to all intellectual property disputes.[936] The aim of the Code is to ensure that the parties inform each other about their cases before proceedings commence with a view to avoiding litigation and (if litigation is unavoidable) keeping costs to a proportionate level.[937] Accordingly, the Code sets out certain prescribed information which a prospective claimant must include in a letter of claim and which a prospective defendant must include in a letter of response. This information is described in the following paragraphs. The Code first sets out general requirements which all such letters should conform to. It then sets out specific requirements for certain types of claim. The Code also requires the parties to show that they have considered alternative methods of resolving their dispute.[938] In the Code, a person making a claim is referred to as a claimant and a person responding to a claim as a defendant.   **21–234**

When the Code may be departed from. There are a number of such circumstances.[939] The examples given in the Code are: where it is reasonable for the claimant to apply for interim relief in a manner and timescale which is inconsistent with the Code; where there is a reasonable and urgent need to issue proceedings in order to found jurisdiction; where the limitation period is about to expire; where a claim for threats might arise; and where it would not be reasonable to expect compliance with the Code having regard to the parties' previous dealings. Since a threats claim might arise in many cases of alleged design right infringement, it seems likely that the Code will seldom be used in this field.   **21–235**

Letters of claim under the Code: general.[940] A letter of claim under the Code should state that it follows the Code and the defendant should also do so; should enclose a copy of the Code where the defendant is unrepresented; should identify the claimant; should list the remedies the claimant seeks; and should give details of any funding arrangements entered into.[941]   **21–236**

Letters of response under the Code: general. The letter of response should be   **21–237**

---

[933] *Code of Practice for pre-action conduct in intellectual property disputes*, January 2004. See *http://www.reedsmith.com/__db/__documents/code__of__practice__booklet.pdf* [Accessed October 16, 2010].

[934] Although it was published with the support of Sir Hugh Laddie who was a member of the Committee.

[935] Pt 5 para.5.3.

[936] para.2.1. In the case of a mixed claim (e.g. infringement of copyright and breach of contract) it provides that the parties should follow the requirements of any applicable pre-action protocols and codes of practice as far as possible.

[937] para.1.2.

[938] The examples given in the Code (para.6) are: without prejudice discussion, determination by an independent expert, mediation and arbitration.

[939] para.2.2. Para.2.1 also provides that in more complex cases it may be reasonable to extend the time limits provided for in the Code.

[940] These documents are not intended to have the same status as a statement of case. They should be sufficiently detailed to enable each party to understand the other's case, but their preparation should not place an unreasonable or disproportionate cost burden on either party: para.2.3.

[941] para.3.2.

sent within 14 days or any shorter time specified by the claimant.[942] If this cannot be done, the defendant should contact the claimant and supply an alternative date.[943] The letter of response should state whether and to what extent the claim is accepted or rejected.[944] If the claim or any part of it is accepted, the defendant should state what remedies the defendant is prepared to offer, including whether he is prepared to stop the acts complained of and offer undertakings.[945] If the defendant is prepared to offer a financial remedy, the letter should provide the claimant with the relevant information to enable the claimant to know the basis on which the sum offered has been calculated.[946] If the defendant requires more information the letter should identify the information required and state why it is needed.[947] If the claim is rejected, the letter should explain why, giving a sufficient indication of any facts on which the defendant currently relies in support of any substantive defence.[948] Where the defendant is considering making a counterclaim, it should give the same details of the counterclaim as would be required if it were a claimant.[949] Finally, the letter should give details of any funding arrangements entered into.[950]

21–238   **Letters of claim: additional provisions for copyright, moral rights, database right and unregistered design right.** As well as the matters referred to in the para.21–236, above, a letter of claim in relation to claims for infringement of these rights should also contain the following where appropriate.[951] First, sufficient information to identify the work or design in question,[952] including where possible a copy. Secondly, the date of creation (in the case of copyright) or the year of first marketing (in the case of UK unregistered design right). Thirdly, an explanation of how and by whom the claimant's work was created; in the case of a moral right, the letter should identify the author or director as appropriate and how any paternity right relied on was asserted. Fourthly, details of the claimant's title. Fifthly, details of any other person with an interest in the work and of the interest itself. Sixthly, details of the infringing actions or threatened infringing actions and why that activity has infringed or will infringe. Seventhly, in cases of alleged infringement by copying, sufficient details to enable the defendant to identify the infringing work. Eighthly, the relevant parts of the infringing work which are or will be copied. Ninthly, the relevant parts of the claimant's work which have been or will be copied. Tenthly, how the defendant obtained access to the claimant's work. Finally, whether there is to be a claim for additional damages and if so what acts are relied on.

21–239   **Letters of response: additional provisions for copyright, moral rights, database right and unregistered design right.** A letter of response in relation to these claims should, where appropriate, explain why the defendant disputes that the right in issue subsists, that the work is original, is owned by the claimant or has been copied and why the work which is claimed to be an infringement is not

---

[942] para.4.2.

[943] para.4.2. In almost all cases the defendant will be expected to have responded within 28 days of receipt of the letter of claim: ibid.

[944] para.4.2(a).

[945] para.4.2(b).

[946] para.4.2(c). In some cases, it will be reasonable for the respondent to require the claimant and its advisers to keep this material confidential: ibid.

[947] para.4.2(d).

[948] para.4.2(e).

[949] para.4.2(f).

[950] para.4.2(g).

[951] App.B.

[952] In a copyright case the letter should identify the type of work in accordance with the descriptions set out in ss.1(1) and 3 to 8 of the 1988 Act.

an infringement; should state whether the defendant is prepared to enter into a licence agreement; and should inform the claimant, in accordance with the Code, whether the defendant intends to make a claim for unjustified threats.[953]

Letters of claim and response: additional provisions for threats claims. In these cases, the letter of claim should additionally where appropriate identify the correspondence or other activities of the defendant complained of, where possible enclosing copies and identify the relevant statutory provision relied on.[954] Where the defendant does not agree with the claimant's characterisation of the meaning of any words complained of, the letter of response should state the defendant's reasons for so disagreeing.[955]

21–240

C. Commencement of Proceedings and Transfer

(i) The High Court

Jurisdiction limits? Prior to the introduction of the Civil Procedure Rules, claims in relation to the rights covered in this work were usually commenced in the High Court because of the availability there of specialist judges and facilities for swift interlocutory relief.

21–241

Paragraph 2.1 of PD7 provides that proceedings (whether for damages or for a specified sum) may not be started in the High Court unless the value of the claim is more than £25,000.[956] CPR 16.3(5) (so far as it relates to matters other than personal injuries) states that where a claim form is to be issued in the High Court it must state either that the claimant expects to recover more than £25,000; or that some other enactment provides that the claim may only be commenced in the High Court; or that the claim is to be in one or more of the specialist High Court lists. However, in many cases involving the rights covered in this work, it cannot be said that the claimant expects to recover more than £25,000. Examples include: where only quia timet relief is sought; where the alleged infringement has only just begun; and where the claimant is unclear as to the extent of the damage. There are no relevant enactments which require ordinary actions concerning the rights dealt with in this work to be commenced in the High Court, nor is there a relevant specialist list. Accordingly, the effect of PD7 para.2.1 and CPR 16.3(5) would appear to be that cases where the claimant does not expect to recover over £25,000 must be commenced in a County Court.

However, para.2.5 of PD7 provides that a claim relating to Chancery business may, subject to any enactment, rule or practice direction, be dealt with in the High Court or a County Court. Both copyright and design right are Chancery business for these purposes.[957] Although this paragraph is expressed to be subject to any enactment, rule or practice direction, it is certainly arguable as a matter of construction that is not intended to be read subject to para.2.1.[958] If this analysis is correct, copyright and design right claims will be correctly brought in the High Court whatever the value of the action. Claims in respect of the other rights covered in this Chapter are not stated to be Chancery business in Sch.1 to the Supreme Court Act 1981. However, the list in Sch.1 is not exhaustive and CPR 63.13(1) makes clear that claims in relation to almost all intellectual property rights must be heard in the Chancery Division, the Patents County Court or (with

---

[953] App.B.
[954] App.F.
[955] App. F.
[956] CPR PD7 para.2.1.
[957] CPR PD7 para.2.1.
[958] In particular, unlike para.2.4, para.2.5 is not expressly stated to be subject to para.2.1.

exceptions) a county court where there is also a Chancery District Registry.[959] One potential difficulty with this argument is that none of the matters set out in CPR 16.3(5) (above) is the fact that the claim concerns Chancery business.

21–242 **Argument based on the value of the claim.** A further argument which can be used by claimants is that the value of the claim is not the amount of damages or profits sought but the value to the claimant of an injunction. The value to the claimant of an injunction can be said to be the amount of loss which its existence can be expected to prevent. This will often exceed £25,000. PD7 para.2.1 speaks of the "value" of the claim. However, this argument is also inconsistent with CPR 16.3(5), which requires a High Court claim form to state that the claimant expects to "recover" more than £25,000.

21–243 **Conclusion.** It seems therefore that there is a risk that a technical objection may be made where the claimant is unable to say that he expects to recover more than £25,000. However, there is no reported case in which this has occurred. CPR 3.10 provides that errors of procedure such as a failure to comply with a rule or practice direction do not invalidate any step taken in the proceedings unless the court so orders and that the court may make an order to remedy the error. If a point as to jurisdiction were successfully taken against a claimant after a claim form had been issued it is likely that the court would simply transfer the case to a County Court (most likely the Patents County Court)[960] with appropriate directions in the meantime.

21–244 **Division.** CPR 63.13 when read in conjunction with para.18.1 of PD 63 provides that claims in respect of the rights covered in this Chapter must be brought in the Chancery Division of the High Court.

(ii) The Patents County Court

21–245 **The Patents County Court.** Section 287 of the 1988 Act permits the Lord Chancellor by order to designate any county court as a patents county court and to confer on it jurisdiction to hear and determine such descriptions of proceedings concerning patents and designs and related proceedings as may be specified in the order. The special jurisdiction of a patents county court is exercisable throughout England and Wales: s.287(2). The Central London County Court has been designated a patents county court pursuant to this section.[961] So far as relevant to the rights covered by this work, the jurisdiction conferred is to hear and determine any action or matter relating to designs over which the High Court would have jurisdiction (except over appeals from the Comptroller), together with any claims or matters ancillary to, or arising from, such proceedings.[962] In addition, however, the Patents County Court has jurisdiction to hear copyright claims under the ordinary county court tort jurisdiction provided for in s.15 of the County Courts Act 1984.[963] Accordingly copyright claims are sometimes commenced in and frequently transferred to the "Patents County Court" (in reality the

---

[959] See para.21–248, below.

[960] See paras 21–245 et seq., below.

[961] By the Patents County Court (Designation and Jurisdiction) Order 1994 (SI 1994/1609).

[962] SI 1994/1609 art.3. The jurisdiction also extends to trade mark cases.

[963] See para.21–248 below. This was assumed in *PSM International Plc v Specialised Fastener Products (Southern) Ltd* [1993] F.S.R. 113 and *McDonald v Graham* [1994] R.P.C. 407 at 416 and 435, and so held in *National Guild of Removers & Storers v Silveria* [2010] EWPCC 015 (trade marks and passing off).

Central London County Court since copyright is not within the special jurisdiction of the Patents County Court.[964]

Reform of the Patents County Court. The Patents County Court was created to serve the interests of small- and medium-sized enterprises by providing an affordable forum for intellectual property litigation.[965] However, it did not succeed in providing this.[966] As a result, the system was arguably defective when measured against the standards set by art.41 of TRIPS and art.3 of the Enforcement Directive.[967] Following proposals for reform from several quarters,[968] in April 2009 the Intellectual Property Users' Committee established a Working Group to formulate proposals for reform. The Working Group produced draft proposals for consultation on June 15, 2009[969] and final proposals on July 31, 2009.[970] Jackson L.J. in the Review of Civil Litigation costs recommended that these proposals be adopted with the addition of a fast and small claims track and that one or more district judges, deputy district judges or recorders with specialist experience should be available to deal with such cases.[971] **21–246**

The reforms and their implementation. Many of the proposed reforms have been implemented by amendments to CPR 63 and 45 which came into force on October 1, 2010.[972] In *Technical Fibre Products Ltd v Bell*[973] it was held (without the benefit of contrary argument) that the new procedures do not apply to cases pending in the Patents County Court before October 1, 2010. By contrast, the new provisions about transfer of cases between the High Court and the Patents County Court[974] apply to all cases whenever commenced.[975] The new procedural rules apply to cases transferred to the Patents County Court on or after October 1, 2010.[976] The new rules include provision that proceedings in a Patents County Court will be dealt with by the patents judge of that court or another judge with appropriate specialist expertise nominated by the Lord Chancellor.[977] Other changes are dealt with in this chapter where appropriate. **21–247**

A number of the reforms have not yet been implemented for a variety of reasons. The proposal that the Patents County Court should be renamed the Intellectual Property County Court and that its special jurisdiction should be extended

---

[964] It is however proposed that the special jurisdiction should be extended to cover all intellectual property rights: see the Intellectual Property Users' Committee Working Group's *Final Report on proposals for Reform of the Patents County Court*, July 31, 2009, p.14.

[965] See Intellectual Property Users' Committee Working Group's *Consultation on Proposals for Reform of the Patents County Court*, June 2009 ("IPUC Consultation"), pp.5–7.

[966] See IPUC Consultation pp.7–8 and the Intellectual Property Users' Committee Working Group's *Final Report on Proposals for Reform of the Patents County Court*, July 31, 2009 ("IPUC Report"), Executive Summary.

[967] IPUC Consultation, p.10.

[968] IPUC Consultation, pp.8–9.

[969] IPUC Consultation.

[970] IPUC Report.

[971] Part 5 paras 4.5 and 4.6.

[972] See the Civil Procedure (Amendment No. 2) Rules 2010 (SI 2010/1953).

[973] [2010] EWPCC 011 at para.9.

[974] As to which , see para.21–257, below.

[975] *Technical Fibre Products Ltd v Bell* [2010] EWPCC 011 at paras 10 and 11 (obiter). In *Alk-Abello Ltd v Meridian Medical Technologies* [2010] EWPCC 014 this was assumed to be correct: para.13.

[976] *Westwood v Knight* [2010] EWPCC 016, para.9. In that case, certain amendments to the High Court statements of case were found to be necessary following the transfer. In particular, it was necessary to add a point on the pre-action protocol, to obtain a statement of truth signed by the appropriate person (see para.21–254, below) and to provide more detail of an allegation: paras 19–21.

[977] CPR 63.19, inserted by the Civil Procedure (Amendment No. 2) Rules 2010 (SI 2010/1953).

to include all forms of intellectual property would require primary legislation.[978] The proposal that there should be a financial limit of £500,000 (excluding interest) on the damages or profits recoverable on a claim in the Patents County Court would require an Order in Council under s.288 of the 1988 Act. It is expected that this will be implemented in April 2011.[979] Whether Jackson L.J.'s proposals for small claims and a fast track are implemented depends on the Government's response to the report.

(iii) Other county courts

21–248   **Jurisdiction.** The county courts have jurisdiction under their general jurisdiction in tort to hear and determine cases of infringement of copyright.[980] It is suggested that the same can be said of cases of infringement of the other rights covered in this Chapter. Special jurisdiction is given to the county courts to make orders for the delivery up and final disposal of infringing copies, illicit recordings and infringing articles.[981] This jurisdiction also extends to means of circumventing protection measures for computer programs, devices for circumventing protection measures for other works and unauthorised decoders.[982] With the exception of the Patents County Court, County Courts do not have jurisdiction to grant seizure orders,[983] while except in the case of a nominated Judge of the Mercantile List of the Central London County Court, their jurisdiction to grant freezing orders is limited (relevantly) to circumstances where the property to be frozen forms or may form the subject-matter of proceedings or where the order is sought in aid of execution.[984]

21–249   CPR 63.13 when read in conjunction with para.18.1 of PD 63 provides that claims in respect of the rights covered in this Chapter must be brought in a county court where there is also a Chancery District Registry. There are Chancery district registries at Birmingham, Bristol, Caernarfon, Cardiff, Leeds, Liverpool, Manchester, Mold, Newcastle upon Tyne and Preston.[985] The jurisdiction of the Patents County Court is discussed above.[986]

(iv) Commencement: the claim form

21–250   **The draft pre-action Code of Practice.** This provides that a claimant should not issue proceedings until either he has received a letter of response from the defen-

---

[978] See the Government's Consultation on the amount of the financial limit to the Patents County Court's jurisdiction *http://www.ipo.gov.uk/consult_pcc.pdf* at para.31 [Accessed November 11, 2010].

[979] The Government is presently consulting as to the amount of the financial limits, see *http://www.ipo.gov.uk/consult_pcc.pdf* [Accessed November 11, 2010].

[980] See *PSM International Plc v Specialised Fastener Products (Southern) Ltd* [1993] F.S.R. 113 and *McDonald & Another v Graham* [1994] R.P.C. 407 at 435; *Gerber Garment Technology Inc v Lectro Systems Ltd* [1997] R.P.C. 443 (infringement of a patent a statutory tort).

[981] CDPA 1988 ss.115, 205 and 232. This jurisdiction has no financial limit: High Court and County Courts Jurisdiction Order 1991 (SI 1991/724) art.2.

[982] This is because CDPA 1988 ss.99 and 114 are applied to such articles by ss.296(4) and (7) (means of circumventing protection measures for computer programs), 296ZD(4) and (6) (devices for circumventing protection measures for other works) and 298(3) and (6) (decoders). S.115 simply gives County Courts jurisdiction to make orders under ss.99 and 114.

[983] County Court Remedies Regulations 1991 (SI 1991/1222) reg.3(1), (2).

[984] County Court Remedies Regulations 1991 (SI 1991/1222) reg.3(3).

[985] See PD 63 para.16.2.

[986] para.24–246.

dant or 14 days have elapsed since the letter of claim was sent and the defendant has not responded, nor given a reasonable explanation for his failure to respond.[987]

The claim form. Claims will almost always be brought as Pt 7 claims. The claim form must contain a concise statement of the nature of the claim, specify the remedy which the claimant seeks and, where money is claimed, contain a statement of value.[988] A claim which is expressed in such general terms as "infringement of unregistered design right" would be unlikely to comply with this rule, and claimants will have to be more precise. What is required is a brief statement of the right in question and of the remedies sought. A claim form must be marked "Intellectual Property" in the top right-hand corner below the title of the court in which it has been issued.[989]

21–251

(v) The particulars of claim

General. A claimant who seeks additional damages must so state in the particulars of claim form and state the grounds for claiming them.[990] Otherwise, with the exception of cases in the Patents County Court, as to which, see para.21–254, below, there are no specific provisions relating to the rights covered in this Chapter. However, it is worth noting that para.7.3(1) of PD16 provides that where a claim is based on a written agreement, a copy of the contract or documents constituting the agreement should be attached to or served with the particulars of claim. It is thought that this provision does not require a claimant to attach copies of his or her documents of title to the particulars of claim. The reference to "claims based upon a written agreement" is almost certainly a reference to claims brought to enforce a contract or to recover damages for its breach. Appendix 1 to the Chancery Guide contains guidelines on statements of case.

21–252

In a pre-CPR edition of this work it was stated that a claimant in a copyright action was expected to indicate in particulars to a statement of claim, by reference to parallel passages or otherwise, the parts he mainly relied upon as constituting an infringement, but that he might well reserve the right, at the trial, to rely upon general similarities as further evidence of piracy.[991] Following the introduction of the Civil Procedure Rules, it seems unlikely that such an approach would be considered acceptable. In a nineteenth-century case, it was held that if a claimant brings an action to protect a work, being only entitled to copyright in a small part of such work, he ought to tell the defendant, in his claim, what that part is, otherwise costs unnecessarily incurred must be borne by the claimant.[992] It seems inevitable that the same principle would be applied today.

Design right cases. In design right cases it is important that the claimant should identify in the particulars of claim with precision each and every "design" relied on. Well-advised claimants will confine themselves to their best case "designs".[993] In such cases, all points of similarity (whether they form important parts of the work alleged to have been copied, unimportant parts or even something which strictly does not form part of the work sued upon) should be disclosed well in advance of trial, normally in the statements of case but at least in the witness

21–253

---

[987] para.5.
[988] CPR 16.2(1). The statement of value must be in accordance with CPR 16.2(3).
[989] PD 63 para.17.1.
[990] PD 63 para.22.1.
[991] *Copinger on Copyright* 14th edn, para.22–120.
[992] *Page v Wisden* (1869) 17 W.R. 483.
[993] *Dyson Ltd v Qualtex (UK) Ltd* [2006] EWCA Civ 166; [2006] R.P.C. 31, at para.122.

statements.[994] No doubt these principles apply equally where appropriate in cases involving the other rights covered in this work.

21–254   **The Patents County Court.** With effect from October 1, 2010, the particulars of claim must state whether the claimant has complied with para.7.1(1) of and Annex A (para.2) to the Practice Direction—Pre-Action Conduct,[995] which require a claimant to serve a pre-action letter of claim and set out detailed requirements as to its contents.

With effect from the same date there are two new requirements as to statements of case in the Patents County Court:

First, a statement of case must set out concisely all the facts and arguments upon which the party serving it relies.[996] According to the Intellectual Property Court Users' Committee Working Group's Consultation, this is the logical development of the modern "cards on the table" approach to litigation but is also essential to put the court in the position where it knows enough about the case and the issues to exercise robust case management. It is expected that the content of statements of case will be the subject of specific guidance which may include model statements of case. The Working Group's Consultation sets out in detail what this requirement is intended to mean in patents cases and states that this guidance is intended to apply mutatis mutandis to claims involving rights other than patents. It is clear from this that statements of case must now include any arguments of law.[997] As will become apparent, the objective is that the statements of case should be the primary basis on which the case will go to trial. They will stand as evidence in themselves (hence the new requirement as to statements of truth—see below). On the other hand, there will be no obligation on the claimant to rebut potential arguments by the defendant in advance: these will still be dealt with in the reply.[998]

Second, the statement of truth verifying a statement of case must be signed by a person with knowledge of the facts alleged or, if no one person has knowledge of all the facts, by persons who between them have knowledge of all the facts alleged.[999] The purpose of this requirement is to allow statements of case to stand as evidence. Where more than one person signs a statement of truth they should indicate in some suitable way which parts of the statement of case they are confirming.[1000]

D. Form of Defence

21–255   **Defence: general.** In his defence a defendant must state which of the allegations he denies, which he is unable to admit and which he admits. Where he denies an allegation he must state his reasons for so doing and if he intends to put forward a different version of events from that given by the claimant, he must state his own

---

[994] *Lambretta Clothing Co Ltd v Teddy Smith (UK) Ltd* [2004] EWCA Civ 886; [2005] R.P.C. 6.

[995] CPR 63.20(2), inserted by SI 2010/1953.

[996] CPR 63.20(1), inserted by SI 2010/1953.

[997] IPUC Consultation, p.13. However, at the pleading stage it may well be unnecessary to do more than state concisely what the argument is rather than take up space setting it out in elaborate detail. This is because a concise statement will suffice to enable the court to deal with the matter at the CMC and because skeleton arguments can be directed: *Westwood v Knight* [2010] EWPCC 016, para.59.

[998] IPUC Consultation, p.13.

[999] CPR 63.21, inserted by SI 2010/1953.

[1000] *Westwood v Knight* [2010] EWPCC 016 paras 24, 26. In that case, which had been transferred to the Patents County Court, the claimant obtained permission to amend her High Court particulars of claim because the statement of truth had been signed by her solicitor pursuant to PD22 para.3.7.

version.[1001] Where a defendant fails to deal with an allegation in his defence, he shall be taken to admit it unless either he has set out in his defence the nature of his case in relation to the issue to which that allegation is relevant or the allegation relates to the amount of money claimed.[1002]

Accordingly, the defendant to an action for infringement of the rights covered in this chapter should, if he desires to dispute the subsistence of the right or the claimant's title to the right or both, specifically raise the point in his defence. He may do this by non-admission, leaving the claimant to prove his case at trial, or by denial. Any positive case (for example, an assertion that the right belongs to a third party and not to the claimant) should be specifically pleaded. Any other specific defence should be pleaded with supporting facts.[1003]

In principle a defendant to a design right claim will plead to each alleged design, raising challenges to originality or alleging commonplace or identifying any of the exclusions which are alleged to apply. It may be possible to limit the issues to sample issues by application even before service of the defence. If not, sample issues should be identified at a case management conference. The samples should be such as will in principle determine the whole case.[1004] Following identification of the sample issues, the parties should produce a sort of Scott schedule identifying each design relied on and the defences relied on in relation to each such design.[1005]

Defence: Patents County Court. In the Patents County Court the general requirements as to statements of case apply to the defence.[1006] However, the time limits in the CPR do not apply. It seems clear that the prescribed time limits are primarily designed for patents claims but they apply to all claims in the Patents County Court. They are as follows. First, where the particulars of claim contain a confirmation that the claimant has served a letter of claim which complies with Practice Direction—Pre-Action Conduct, the period for filing a defence is 42 days after service of the particulars of claim. Otherwise the period is 70 days.[1007] The difference derives from the fact that in the former case the defendant will have had more prior notice of the claimant's claim.[1008] In either case a reply to the defence is to be served within 28 days of service of the defence and a reply to a defence to counterclaim within 14 days of service of the defence to counterclaim.[1009] These time periods may only be extended by order of the court (and not by consent) and for good reason.[1010]   **21–256**

Transfer between High Court and Patents County Court. Prior to the reforms of the Patents County Court, CPR 30 and PD 30 set out the criteria for transfer   **21–257**

[1001] CPR 16.5(1) and (2).
[1002] CPR 16.5(3) to (6).
[1003] As to pleading of "Euro defences" see *Ransburg-Gema AG v Electrostatic Plant Systems Ltd* [1990] F.S.R. 287.
[1004] As in *Sweeney v MacMillan* [2002] R.P.C. 35.
[1005] *Dyson Ltd v Qualtex (UK) Ltd* [2006] EWCA Civ 166; [2006] R.P.C. 31, at paras 122–24.
[1006] See para.21–254, above.
[1007] CPR 63.22(2) and (3). This period does not apply if CPR 15.4(2) provides for a longer period. CPR 15.4(2) provides for special time limits for the defence where the claim form is served outside the jurisdiction, the defendant is disputing the court's jurisdiction, the claimant has applied for summary judgment before service of the defence or the claim has been served on an agent whose principal is outside the jurisdiction.
[1008] IPUC Consultation p.14.
[1009] CPR 63.22(4), (5).
[1010] CPR 63.22(6).

between the High Court and a county court.[1011] CPR 63.18 now provides that when considering whether to transfer proceedings to or from a patents county court the court will have regard to the provisions of PD 30.

PD 30 has been amended to introduce a number of criteria in addition to those in CPR 30 (which still apply). They are: whether a party can only afford to bring or defend the claim in a patents county court[1012]; and whether the claim is appropriate to be determined by a patents county court having regard in particular to the value of the claim (including the value of an injunction), the complexity of the issues and the estimated length of trial.[1013] The primary criterion should be whether the case is one in respect of which an SME requires the forum to be the Patents County Court in order to achieve access to justice. The secondary criterion should be proportionality and in considering proportionality the value of the claim and the complexity of the issues will be relevant but not determinative factors. It is expected that guidelines will be published. Questions of transfer are to be determined quickly and with the minimum of formality.[1014]

In addition, PD 30 contains a new para.9.2 which provides that where there is an order for transfer the court may specify terms for the transfer and award reduced or no costs where it allows the claimant to withdraw the claim. Presumably it is thought that a claimant might wish to withdraw a claim which is to be transferred to the Patents County Court because the likely shortfall on recoverable costs as a result of the application of scale costs[1015] would be disproportionate to the end to be achieved; by the same token, a claimant in the Patents County Court might wish to withdraw a claim which was to be transferred to the High Court because of the loss of costs protection that would entail in the event that it were to lose.

CPR 63.25(4) and (5) provide that applications in the Patents County Court for transfer to the High Court must be made before or at the case management conference and that applications to transfer the claim later in the proceedings will only be considered where there are exceptional circumstances.

21–258   **Case management, applications and trial.** Where the proceedings are not in the Patents County Court the normal rules apply.

In the Patents County Court, CPR 63.23(1) provides that at the first case management conference after those defendants who intend to file and serve a defence have done so,[1016] the court will identify the issues and decide whether to make an order in accordance with para.29.1 of PD 63.[1017] This paragraph (which was introduced with effect from October 1, 2010) provides the court may order

---

[1011] The High Court has no power under s.41 of the County Courts Act 1984 to order the transfer from the Patents County Court to the High Court of a case within the Patents County Court's special jurisdiction: CDPA 1988 s.289(1). The IPUC Working Group proposed that this prohibition be repealed on the grounds that it encourages forum shopping and makes it more difficult to ensure the correct distribution of business between the two courts: IPUC Consultation p.16; IPUC Report p.15.

[1012] The critical question will presumably be whether the party can afford to pay more than the maximum scale costs if it loses. See para.21–287, below.

[1013] See PD30 para.9.1. The reference to the estimated length of trial is because it is envisaged that trials in the Patents County Court will take no more than 2 days: PD 63 para.31.2.

[1014] Report pp.15–16. See generally, *Alk-Abello Ltd v Meridian Medical Technologies* [2010] EW-PCC 0149. In *Westwood v Knight* [2010] EWPCC 016 at para.10, the Judge commended a provision in an order for transfer from the High Court to the Patents County Court which directed a case management conference on the first open date after a date three weeks after the transfer.

[1015] para.21–287.

[1016] It is envisaged that the first case management conference will take place approximately 2–4 weeks after completion of the statements of case and (it appears) will be an oral hearing: IPUC Report p.14.

[1017] There is no need to file a skeleton argument at an interim stage if it would simply duplicate a witness statement: *Westwood v Knight* [2010] EWPCC 016 at para.15.

any of the following (so far as relevant to the rights covered in this Chapter): specific disclosure, witness statements, experts' reports, cross-examination at trial or written submissions or skeleton arguments. Paragraph 29.2 provides that the court will only make such an order in relation to specific and identified issues and if it is satisfied that the benefit of the further material in terms of its value in resolving those issues appears likely to justify the cost of producing and dealing with it. This provides a marked contrast to the position in the High Court, where most of these things (and indeed standard disclosure) are the norm. The object is that where possible the claim will go to trial on the statements of case.[1018] The CPR 63.23(2) provides that the court will not consider an application by a party to submit material additional to that ordered under para.(1) save in exceptional circumstances.

As to applications in the Patents County Court, CPR 63.25 provides that except at a case management conference a respondent to an application must file and serve a response within five days of service of the application notice and the application will be dealt with without a hearing unless the court thinks a hearing necessary. Practice Direction 63 para.30.1 provides that where a hearing is considered necessary it will be conducted by telephone or video conference[1019] unless the court considers that a hearing in person would be more cost effective for the parties or is otherwise necessary in the interests of justice. CPR 63.26 provides that costs will be reserved to the conclusion of the trial when they will be subject to summary assessment[1020] but that where a party has behaved unreasonably the court will made an order for costs at the conclusion of the hearing.[1021]

CPR 63.23(3) provides that the court may determine the claim on the papers when all parties consent. Where there is a hearing, PD 63 para.31.2 provides that where possible the court will determine the claim solely on the basis of the parties' statements of case and oral submissions. PD63 para.31.2 provides that the court will set the timetable at trial and will, so far as appropriate, allocate equal time to the parties. Cross-examination will be strictly controlled by the court. The court will endeavour to ensure that the trial lasts no more than two days.

E. SUMMARY JUDGMENT

The general principles which are applicable in summary judgment applications are set out in CPR Pt 24 and the numerous authorities under that Part.[1022] The following specific points can be made as to summary judgment applications in respect of claims involving the rights covered in this Chapter. First, if the relief sought on the application for summary judgment includes an injunction (as it usually will in intellectual property cases) the application should be made directly

21–259

[1018] Report p.14. For an example of the kind of directions which might be given following a transfer from the High Court, see *Westwood v Knight* [2010] EWPCC 016, paras 19 et seq. The Judge went though the issues (paras 39 et seq.), giving permission to file evidence as to the originality of an alleged copyright work (which was in issue on the statements of case) and as to the detail of the alleged infringements, but in most instances leaving the parties to rely on their statements of case. The Judge noted (at para.41) that it may well not be necessary to adduce evidence in order to establish that the cost of filing evidence is justified by its benefit. No directions were given for disclosure, expert evidence or cross-examination (paras 56–58). The Judge pointed out that it may well be necessary for the parties to consider the question of the application of the costs cap to transferred cases when the case is transferred (para.28).

[1019] In accordance with PD 23A paras 6.2 to 7.

[1020] Pursuant to s.VII of CPR 45.

[1021] Such an order will be in addition to any scale costs recoverable from that party: CPR 45.43.

[1022] See the current edition of *Civil Procedure*.

to the Judge instead of the Master.[1023] Secondly, where the issue is whether a substantial part of the claimant's work has been taken, that should normally go to trial since it is a matter of fact and degree.[1024] However, this will not be the case where the court is satisfied on the application for summary judgment that no further evidence is likely to emerge and, therefore, that there is no point in the matter going to trial.[1025] Thirdly, where a claimant alleges infringement of copyright in a number of works, he is entitled to apply for summary judgment in respect of some of them, leaving the others to a trial.[1026] Fourthly, where on an application under CPR Pt 24, a claimant succeeds in establishing that there is no triable issue that part of the defendant's work infringes, it will not normally be correct to deny the claimant a permanent injunction against that part because the defendant argues that such an injunction may not be granted after a full trial.[1027] Fifthly, if a claimant in his supporting evidence claims to be the owner of the copyright without giving full details of each and every fact underlying the claim to subsistence and ownership, and if there is no reason to believe, from the defendant's evidence or otherwise, that the claimant's claim is not true, the court will not give the defendant permission to defend on the basis that something may turn up during the course of disclosure or Pt 18 Answers.[1028] The judgment will usually contain a permanent injunction and an order for an inquiry as to damages, including, if appropriate, additional damages. The inquiry will normally be conducted before a Master.

F. PRESUMPTIONS

(i) International obligations and the Enforcement Directive

21–260   **The Berne Convention.**[1029] Some of the provisions of the Berne Convention as to presumptions are closely followed in the 1988 Act but in other cases there is significant divergence.

Article 15(1) provides that in order that the author of a literary or artistic work protected by the Convention shall in the absence of proof to the contrary be regarded as such and consequently entitled to institute infringement proceedings, it shall be sufficient for his name to appear on the work in "the usual manner". This applies even if this name is a pseudonym provided the pseudonym leaves no doubt as to the author's identity. There is no definition of what is "the usual manner". Article 15(2) provides an analogous presumption in relation to the makers of cinematographic works. Articles 15(1) and (2) are closely followed in the 1988 Act.

Article 15(3) provides that in the case of anonymous and pseudonymous works

---

[1023] *Chancery Guide* para.6.26.

[1024] *Total Information Processing Systems Ltd v Daman Ltd* [1992] F.S.R. 171, applying *Leco Instruments UK Ltd v Land Pyrometers Ltd* [1982] R.P.C. 133.

[1025] *Ludlow Music Inc v Williams* [2001] F.S.R. 271. In *J Choo Jersey Ltd v Towerstone Ltd* [2008] EWHC 346 (Ch); [2008] F.S.R. 19 (designs), the judge was prepared to grant summary judgment not only on the issue of whether the defendant's articles gave the same overall impression as the claimant's design, but also on the issue of whether the fact that they did was the result of copying. The evidence appears to have been limited to a comparison of the design and the infringing article but it was conceded that no other evidence relevant to the issue of copying was likely to be forthcoming at trial: para.22.

[1026] *Macmillan Publishers Ltd v Thomas Reed Publications Ltd* [1993] F.S.R. 455. This case predates the CPR but the principle should still hold good.

[1027] *Macmillan Publishers Ltd v Thomas Reed Publications Ltd* [1993] F.S.R. 455, applying *Mawman v Tegg* (1826) 2 Russ.385. Again, this case predates the CPR but the principle should still hold good.

[1028] *Microsoft Corp v Electro-Wide Ltd & Another* [1997] F.S.R. 580.

[1029] See generally paras 23–04 et seq., below.

other than those referred to in art.15(1), i.e. where there is no name on the work or the pseudonym leaves doubt as to the author's identity, the publisher shall be deemed unless the contrary is proved to "represent" the author and in such capacity he shall be entitled to protect and enforce the author's rights. The implementation of this provision would have involved the adoption of a concept of a copyright owner's agent having a right to sue on behalf of his principal which is foreign to UK law.[1030] Accordingly, as will be seen, the CDPA 1988 provides that in such a case the publisher is presumed to be the copyright owner. Article 15(3) goes on to provide that the presumption which it creates ceases when the author reveals his identity and establishes his claim to authorship. Given the manner in which art.15(3) has been implemented in the United Kingdom, the adoption of such a provision would have been inappropriate.

The Universal Copyright Convention[1031] and the Rome Convention.[1032] These Conventions both provide that where a Contracting State requires compliance with formalities as a condition of copyright protection, compliance with such formalities will be deemed in some instances to be satisfied if copies of the work bear the appropriate copyright notice. No reference is made to these notices in the 1988 Act because in accordance with the Berne Convention no formalities are required as a condition of UK copyright protection. Nevertheless, the copyright notices required by these Conventions are frequently used, not only because they may afford protection in countries which are not parties to the Berne Convention but also because they provide notice of a claim to copyright. In addition, such a notice may assist in establishing at least two of the presumptions in the 1988 Act.[1033] For the purposes of the Universal Copyright Convention, the notice is the symbol © accompanied by the name of the copyright proprietor and the year of first publication placed in such manner and location as to give reasonable notice of a claim of copyright.[1034] For the purposes of the Phonograms Convention, the notice is the symbol P accompanied by the year of first publication placed in such a manner as to give reasonable notice of the claim of protection.[1035]   **21–261**

The Enforcement Directive. Article 5(1) of the Directive provides that for the purposes of applying the measures, procedure and remedies provided for in the Directive, for the author of a literary or artistic work in the absence of proof to the contrary to be regarded as such, and consequently to be entitled to institute infringement proceedings, it shall be sufficient for his/her name to appear on the work in the usual manner. This provision is intended to adopt art.15 of the Berne Convention.[1036] Article 5(2) provides that this provision applies mutatis mutandis to the holders of rights related to copyright.   **21–262**

(ii) The 1988 Act

Introduction. The 1988 Act contains a series of presumptions designed to assist a claimant in a copyright action whether on an application for interim relief, or at the trial.[1037] These presumptions apply in proceedings for infringement of copyright. They also apply in proceedings under ss.296 (circumvention of techni-   **21–263**

[1030] Although see now the amendments to the Communications Act 2003 by the Digital Economy Act 2010.
[1031] See generally para.23–79 et seq., below.
[1032] See generally para.23–88 et seq., below.
[1033] See below.
[1034] art.II(1).
[1035] art.11.
[1036] See recital 19.
[1037] CDPA 1988 ss.104–106.

cal devices applied to computer programs), 296ZA and 296ZD (circumvention of technological measures applied to other works and devices and services designed to circumvent such measures) and 296ZG (rights management information).[1038] More limited presumptions apply in proceedings for infringement of publication right and rights in performances. Presumptions similar to those applicable in copyright proceedings apply in relation to database right. These presumptions do not apply in criminal proceedings for an offence but they do apply to proceedings for delivery up orders in criminal proceedings.[1039] There are no analogous presumptions in relation to design right or moral rights. A number of other presumptions are dealt with elsewhere in this work. They concern the time an infringing article was made,[1040] the validity of unregistered community designs[1041] and the transfer of rental rights in the case of a film production agreement.[1042]

(a) Proceedings for infringement of copyright

21–264   **Presumption of authorship where author's name on copies or work.** Where a name purporting to be that of the author appeared on copies of a literary, dramatic, musical or artistic work as published or appeared on the work when it was made, the person whose name so appeared is to be presumed, until the contrary is proved, to be the author of the work.[1043] If, however, the name purports to be that of an "arranger", the only presumption is that the "name" in question did some work of arrangement.[1044] It is further to be presumed, until the contrary is proved, that the work was made in circumstances not falling within the provisions relating to works produced in the course of employment, or the provisions relating to Crown copyright, parliamentary copyright or copyright of certain international organisations.[1045] The effect of this provision is that, where an author's name appears in the circumstances indicated, it will not be necessary for the claimant to prove that the person so named as author actually wrote, composed or created the work. It will be sufficient for the claimant to establish a documentary title commencing from such author. Where the work is alleged to be a work of joint authorship, a similar presumption is made in relation to each person alleged to be one of the authors of the work.[1046]

In the equivalent provision in the 1956 Act, it was expressly provided that the "name" must be either the true name of the person whose name so appeared, or a name by which he was commonly known.[1047] It is suggested that the absence of these words in the 1988 Act is a change of expression and not a change of substance[1048] and that if a name by which a person is commonly known appears on copies of the work as author, then the presumption will still apply. The whole purpose of the presumption is to identify "a person" who is to be presumed to be the author. Such a person could not be identified except by reference to his actual name or a name by which he was commonly known. The situation of a person who is commonly known by some name other than his real name falls, it is suggested, within the natural meaning of the presumption, even without the words

---

[1038] See, respectively, CDPA 1988 ss.296(7)(a), 296ZA(5)(a), 296ZD(6)(a) and 296ZG(6)(a).
[1039] See CDPA 1988 ss.107(6) and 197A(2); Copyright and Related Rights Regulations 1996 (SI 1996/2967) reg.17A. There are no database right offences.
[1040] CDPA 1988 ss.27(4) and 228(4). See paras 8–03 and 13–162, above.
[1041] Regulation 6/2002, art.85. See para.13–261, above.
[1042] CDPA 1988 ss.93A and 191F. See paras 5–107 and 12–44, above.
[1043] CDPA 1988 s.104(2)(a).
[1044] per Cross J. in *Roberton v Lewis* [1976] R.P.C. 169.
[1045] CDPA 1988 s.104(2)(b).
[1046] s.104(3).
[1047] s.20(2) of the 1956 Act. s
[1048] See s.172(2).

which appeared in the equivalent provision of the 1956 Act. To take a fictitious example, it is suggested that the court would not refuse to apply the presumption in the case of a book entitled *My Early Life by ABCD*, merely because ABCD is not the author's real name. Clearly there is a name purporting to be that of the author on the book, so the first part of the presumption is satisfied. All that is left to do is to identify the actual person to whom that name refers. That must be the author known as ABCD, because it could not be anyone else. Such an interpretation would be broadly consistent with art.15(1) of the Berne Convention, which is purportedly adopted in art.5 of the Enforcement Directive,[1049] although it should be noted that the Convention makes it a condition that the pseudonym should leave no doubt as to the author's identity.

Presumption of ownership where publisher's name on copies of work. Where an author's name does not appear on a literary, dramatic, musical or artistic work but the work qualifies for copyright protection by virtue of first publication in the United Kingdom, or in another country to which the relevant provision of the 1988 Act extends, and a name purporting to be that of the publisher appeared on copies of the work as first published, the person whose name so appeared is presumed to have been the owner of the copyright at the time of publication.[1050] Again, this presumption applies until the contrary is proved.[1051] If the publisher is to be presumed to have been the owner of the copyright at the time of publication, it follows that it is to be presumed that the author did not own the copyright at that time. The onus is on the person challenging the publisher's presumed ownership of the copyright to prove affirmatively that the person named as publisher did not own the copyright when the work was published.[1052] It may be arguable that the copyright notice stipulated for in the Universal Copyright Convention (the symbol © accompanied by the name of the copyright proprietor and the year of first publication) gives rise to a presumption as to ownership at the time of first publication but such an argument will only succeed if the name of the proprietor is capable of being construed as the name of the publisher.

21–265

Presumption of originality and first publication where author dead or unknown. In the case of a literary, dramatic, musical or artistic work, if the author of the work is dead, or the identity of the author cannot be ascertained by reasonable inquiry, the work is to be presumed to be an original work in the absence of evidence to the contrary.[1053] Furthermore, in such cases, it is to be presumed, in the absence of evidence to the contrary, that the claimant's allegations as to what was the first publication of the work and as to the country of first publication are correct.[1054]

21–266

Sound recordings: ownership and first publication. Where copies of a sound recording as issued to the public bear a label or other mark stating (a) that a named person was the owner of copyright in the recording at the date of issue of the copies; or (b) that the recording was first published in a specified year or in a specified country, the label or mark shall be admissible as evidence of the facts so

21–267

[1049] See recital 19 of the Directive but note, however, that unlike art.15(1) of Berne art.5 contains no express provision as to pseudonyms.
[1050] See CDPA 1988 s.104(4).
[1051] See CDPA 1988 s.104(4).
[1052] *Warwick Film Productions Ltd v Eisinger* [1969] 1 Ch. 508.
[1053] CDPA 1988 s.104(5)(a).
[1054] s.104(5)(b).

stated and shall be presumed to be correct until the contrary is proved.[1055] This presumption applies equally in proceedings relating to an infringement alleged to have occurred before the date on which the copies were issued to the public.[1056] It is arguable that the effect of this provision is that the copyright notice stipulated for in the Rome Convention (the symbol P accompanied by the year of first publication) gives rise to a presumption as to the year of first publication but only if the symbol P is construed as meaning "first published".

21–268   **Films: presumption arising from issue of copies to the public.** In proceedings brought with respect to a film, where copies of the film as issued to the public bear a statement containing specified facts, that statement is admissible as evidence of the facts stated and is presumed to be correct until the contrary is proved.[1057] The facts in question are, first, that a named person was the director or producer of the film[1058]; secondly, that a named person was the principal director, the author of the screenplay, the author of the dialogue or the composer of music specifically created for and used in the film[1059]; thirdly, that a named person was the owner of the copyright in the film at the date of issue of the copies[1060]; or fourthly, that the film was first published in a specified year or in a specified country.[1061] As in the case of the presumption in relation to sound recordings, this presumption applies equally in proceedings relating to an infringement alleged to have occurred before the date on which the copies were issued to the public.[1062] For the purpose of this presumption, a statement that a person was the director of a film shall be taken, unless a contrary indication appears, as meaning that he was the principal director of the film.[1063]

21–269   **Films: presumption arising from showing in public or communication to the public.** A presumption also applies to proceedings with respect to a film where the film as shown in public or communicated to the public bears a statement that a named person was the director or producer of the film, that a named person was the principal director, the author of the screenplay, the author of the dialogue or the composer of music specifically created for and used in the film or that a named person was the owner of the copyright in the film immediately after it was made.[1064] This presumption equally applies in proceedings relating to an infringement alleged to have occurred before the date on which the film was shown in public, or communicated to the public.[1065] Again, a statement that a person was the director of a film shall be taken, unless a contrary indication appears, as meaning that he was the principal director of the film.[1066]

21–270   **Computer programs.** A similar provision applies in the case of a computer program where copies of the program are issued to the public in electronic form bearing a statement that a named person was the owner of the copyright in the program at the date of issue of the copies or that the program was first published

---

[1055] CDPA 1988 s.105(1). For an example of the use of this presumption, see *Independiente Ltd v Music Trading Online (HK) Ltd* [2003] EWHC 470 (Ch).
[1056] s.105(4).
[1057] CDPA 1988 s.105(2).
[1058] s.105(2)(a).
[1059] s.105(2)(aa).
[1060] s.105(2)(b).
[1061] s.105(2)(c).
[1062] s.105(4).
[1063] s.105(6).
[1064] CDPA 1988 s.105(5).
[1065] s.105(4) and 105(5).
[1066] s.105(6).

in a specified country or that copies of it were first issued to the public in electronic form in a specified year.[1067]

(b) *Proceedings for infringement of publication right*

The presumptions contained in ss.104 to 106 of the 1988 Act[1068] do not apply in proceedings for infringement of publication right.[1069] However, in such proceedings, where copies of a work as issued to the public bear a statement that a named person was the owner of publication right in the work at the date of issue of the copies, the statement is to be admissible as evidence of the fact stated and to be presumed to be correct until the contrary is proved.[1070]   **21–271**

(c) *Proceedings for infringement of rights in performances*

With effect from April 29, 2006, in proceedings with respect to the rights in a performance, where copies of a recording of the performance as issued to the public bear a statement that a named person was the performer, the statement is to be admissible as evidence of the fact stated and is to be presumed to be correct until the contrary is proved.[1071] Where the performer is not the owner of the rights, no presumptions arise. Moreover, there is no presumption in favour of the holders of recording rights.   **21–272**

(d) *Proceedings for infringement of database right*

Where proceedings are brought in respect of database right, similar presumptions apply. First, where a name purporting to be that of the maker appeared on copies of the database as published, or on the database when it was made, the person whose name appeared shall be presumed, until the contrary is proved, to be the maker of the database and to have made it in circumstances not falling within regs 14(2) to (4), that is not to have made it in the course of employment, in the course of duties as an officer or servant of the Crown or under the direction or control of the House of Commons or House of Lords.[1072] Secondly, where copies of a database as published bear a label or mark stating that a named person was the maker of the database or that the database was first published in a specified year, that label or mark shall be admissible as evidence of the facts stated unless the contrary is proved.[1073] In the case of a database alleged to have been made jointly, these provisions apply in relation to each person alleged to be one of the makers.[1074]   **21–273**

(e) *Proceedings for infringement of Crown copyright*

Special provision is made for presumptions relating to works subject to Crown copyright. In proceedings brought with respect to a literary, dramatic or musical   **21–274**

[1067] CDPA 1988 s.105(3).
[1068] See paras 21–264 to 21–270, above.
[1069] Copyright and Related Rights Regulations 1996 (SI 1996/2967) reg.17(2)(b).
[1070] Copyright and Related Rights Regulations 1996 (SI 1996/2967) reg.17A introduced with effect from April 29, 2006 by reg.2(3) and Sch.3 para.5 to the Intellectual Property (Enforcement etc.) Regulations 2006 (SI 2006/1028) in order to implement art.5 of the Enforcement Directive.
[1071] CDPA 1988 s.197A(1), introduced by regs 2(2) and 10 of Sch.2 para.10 to the Intellectual Property (Enforcement etc.) Regulations 2006 (SI 2006/1028) in order to implement art.5 of the Enforcement Directive.
[1072] Copyright and Rights in Databases Regulations (SI 1997/3032) reg.22(2).
[1073] Copyright and Rights in Databases Regulations (SI 1997/3032) reg.22(2).
[1074] Copyright and Rights in Databases Regulations (SI 1997/3032) reg.22(4).

work in which Crown copyright subsists, where there appears on printed copies of the work a statement of the year in which the work was first published commercially, that statement shall be admissible in evidence of the fact stated and shall be presumed to be correct in the absence of evidence to the contrary.[1075]

G. PROOF OF COPYING

21–275 **Whether copying has occurred or not is a matter of fact.**[1076] Direct evidence of copying is rarely available and reliance frequently has to be placed on inference drawn from circumstantial evidence.[1077] The basis of secondary proof of copying normally lies in the establishment of similarities between the claimant's work and the defendant's work, combined with proof of the possibility of access by the author of the defendant's work to the claimant's work. Inferences may properly be drawn from the surrounding circumstances and from the nature of the similarities themselves.[1078] It is good practice for the claimant to particularise at an early stage in an action the alleged points of similarity between his work and the defendant's work.[1079] The existence of a striking general similarity coupled with evidence of the opportunity to copy will establish a prima facie case of copying which the defendant then has to answer.[1080] The evidential burden shifts to the defendant who may then seek to adduce evidence of some alternative explanation for the similarities between the two works, for example, evidence of independent creation or common source.[1081] In a pre-CPR case, the Court declined to order interrogatories seeking evidence of the detailed history of the defendant's development of its copyright work on the grounds that they were "fishing" for information which would be the subject of evidence at the trial.[1082] However, a different view might now be taken. The task of the judge is to consider the evidence as a whole and decide whether there has been copying or not.[1083] An appellate court will not normally interfere with the judge's findings of fact.[1084]

21–276 **Similar fact evidence.** In a civil case a court faced with a question as to the admissibility of similar fact evidence must first decide whether the evidence (if true) would be logically probative or disprobative of some matter which requires proof in the action. If so, the court must decide whether the admission of the evidence would accord with the overriding objective of deciding cases justly.[1085] Thus, where the issue in a copyright case is whether the similarity between the

---

[1075] CDPA 1988 s.106.

[1076] For the admissibility of expert evidence on this issue, see para.21–277, below.

[1077] *Sifam Electrical Instrument Co Ltd v Sangamo Western Ltd* [1973] R.P.C. 899.

[1078] *John Richardson Computers Ltd v Flanders* [1993] F.S.R. 497 at 543.

[1079] *N&P Windows Ltd v Cego Ltd* [1989] F.S.R. 56.

[1080] In *Francis Day & Hunter Ltd v Bron* [1963] 1 Ch. 587 at 614, Willmer L.J. (with whom Upjohn L.J. agreed) stated that where there is a substantial degree of objective similarity between C's and D's work, that of itself will afford prima facie evidence of a causal connection between C's and Ds' work, or at least is a circumstance from which such an inference can be drawn. See also *Cadieux v Beauchimin* [1901–1904] Mac.C.C. 4 (Sup of Canada) and *Mathieson v Universal Stock Exchange* [1901–1904] Mac.C.C. 4 (Buckley J.).

[1081] For a fuller discussion, see para.7–17, above.

[1082] *Rockwell International Corp v Serck Industries Ltd* [1988] F.S.R. 187.

[1083] *L. B. (Plastics) Ltd v Swish Products Ltd* [1979] R.P.C. 551 HL; *Antocks Lairn Ltd v I. Bloohn Ltd* [1971] F.S.R. 490 at 493; *Catnic Components Ltd & Another v Hill and Smith Ltd* [1979] F.S.R. 619 at 626; *The Duriron Co Inc v Hugh Jennings & Co Ltd* [1984] F.S.R. 1; *Wham-O Manufacturing Co v Lincoln Industries Ltd* [1985] R.P.C. 127 (Court of Appeal of New Zealand); and see *Francis Day & Hunter Ltd v Bron* [1963] Ch. 587 (proof of copying from memory).

[1084] *L.B. (Plastics) Ltd v Swish Products Ltd* [1979] R.P.C. 551 HL; *Designers Guild Ltd v Russell Williams (Textiles) Ltd* [2001] 1 W.L.R 2416 (substantial part).

[1085] *O'Brien v Chief Constable of South Wales Police* [2005] UKHL 26; [2005] 2 A.C. 534. See also *Mood Music Publishing Co Ltd v De Wolfe Ltd* [1976] Ch. 119; [1976] F.S.R. 149; *R. v Scarrott* [1978] Q.B. 1016; *Omega v Africio Textile* [1982] 1 S.A.L.R. 951; *Berger v Raymond Sun Ltd*

claimant's work and the defendant's work is due to copying or is a coincidence, it is relevant to know that the defendant has produced works which bear a close resemblance to works other than the work in question which are the subject of copyright. Whereas similarity between two works might be mere coincidence in one case, it is unlikely that there could be coincidental similarity in, say, four cases. The probative force of several resemblances together is much better than one alone. It does not matter in such cases that the claimant has not alleged that infringement of copyright has occurred in the other cases. It is sufficient to allege that copying has occurred. Depending on the circumstances, such evidence may be just as probative, especially if it is likely that copyright subsists in the other works and the defendant would have known of or was reckless as to this.[1086] It seems that the similar facts do not need to be pleaded in the claimant's reply, provided that the defendant is not taken by surprise at the trial.[1087] Although similar fact evidence is admissible to establish the possibility or probability of infringement, the court will not, in the absence of an allegation that the defendant has made a practice of copying others' work, order disclosure of documents which are directed solely towards the credit of the defendant.[1088]

H. Expert Evidence

Copying. Expert evidence may be called (with the permission of the court[1089]) to point out coincidences, similarities or identical omissions with a view to establishing copying,[1090] but it is not proper, unless the expert is suitably qualified,[1091] for an expert witness to state, as a matter of opinion, that the work was copied from another.[1092] That is a question for the judge.[1093] In a patent case it has been said that:

> "the primary function of the expert witnesses is to educate the court in the technology—they come as teachers, as makers of the mantle for the court to don. What matters is how good they are at explaining things. It is permis-

21–277

[1984] 1 W.L.R. 625; *Perrin v Drennan* [1991] F.S.R. 81; and *Designers Guild Ltd v Russell Williams (Textiles) Ltd* [1998] F.S.R. 275, where the learned judge held that it was prima facie oppressive to seek, at least to a limited extent, to turn a case about infringement of copyright in one design to a case concerning copying (even if not copyright infringement) of two other designs. If by that the learned judge meant no more than that the prima facie oppressiveness consisted of an extension of the length (and therefore the costs) of the trial, which would have to be balanced against the probative value of the evidence, then that is in line with the previous cases. If, however, he meant more, it is difficult to see what he had in mind. All attempts to introduce similar fact evidence involve an allegation of copying other works. The particular instances of similar fact which the learned judge disallowed on this ground could have been (and indeed were) disallowed on other grounds (the claimants disclaimed any infringement of copyright and never satisfactorily put their case in a clear and comprehensible way). See also *Stoddard International Plc v William Lomas Carpets Ltd* [2001] F.S.R. 44: similar fact evidence must be clear in order to be probative; and *Mattel Inc v Woolbro (Distributors) Ltd* [2003] EWHC 2412 (Ch); [2004] F.S.R. 12: showing that various products of the defendant are very similar to earlier products of the claimant may only show that the defendant gets inspiration from the claimant or that both get inspiration from current fashion trends. To prove a habit of copying may involve a very detailed analysis of the precise degree of similarity and surrounding fashion trends which may justify its exclusion on grounds of proportionality.

[1086] *Perrin v Drennan* [1991] F.S.R. 81, where leave was given to amend pleadings to allege similar facts.

[1087] *Designers Guild Ltd v Russell Williams (Textiles) Ltd* [1998] F.S.R. 275.

[1088] *EG Music & Another v SF (Films) Distributors Ltd & Another* [1978] F.S.R. 121.

[1089] See, generally, CPR Pt 35 and PD 35. The question of expert evidence should be raised at the Case Management Conference.

[1090] *LB (Plastics) Ltd v Swish Products Ltd* [1979] R.P.C. 551 HL at 619; *Billhofer Maschinen Fabrik GmbH v Dixon & Co Ltd* [1990] F.S.R. 105. *Barrett v Universal-Island Records Ltd* [2006] EWHC 1009 (Ch); [2006] E.M.L.R. 21.

[1091] Civil Evidence Act 1972 s.3; *Mölnlycke AB v Proctor & Gamble (No.5)* [1994] R.P.C. 49 at 113; *Gluverbel SA v British Coal Corp & Another* [1995] F.S.R. 254 at 271.

[1092] *Deeks v Wells* [1928–1935] Mac.C.C. 353 (PC); *Bauman v Fussell* [1978] R.P.C. 485.

[1093] *Monsoon Ltd v India Imports of Rhode Island Ltd* [1993] F.S.R. 486. See also para.7–18, above.

sible for the expert to opine on the 'ultimate question' ie whether or not the invention is obvious. However such conclusions in themselves are of little value. What matters are the reasons for the opinion."[1094]

21–278 **Design right cases.** It has been said[1095] that many of the points which arise in relation to subsistence of unregistered UK design right do not really need expert evidence at all. Even technical points are likely to be uncontroversial and amenable to the single joint expert procedure. Early firm case management is called for. Normally this would best be done by a judge, moreover one who has some experience of this sort of case.

21–279 **Artistic craftsmanship.** Expert witnesses may also be called with permission to give evidence on the question whether a particular work is a work of artistic craftsmanship. The experts should be persons with special capabilities and qualifications for forming an opinion on the matter in question, although it will still be a question for the decision of the judge at the end of the day.[1096]

21–280 **Patents County Court.** Expert evidence will only be permitted in relation to specific and identified issues and if the court is satisfied that the benefit of the further material in terms of its value in resolving those issues appears likely to justify the cost of producing and dealing with it.[1097]

I. DISCLOSURE AND INSPECTION

21–281 **The Enforcement Directive.** Article 6(1) of the Directive, which mirrors art.43(1) of TRIPS,[1098] requires Member States to ensure that on application by a party which (a) has presented "reasonably available evidence[1099] sufficient to support its claims" and (b) in substantiating those claims has specified evidence which lies in the control of the opposing party, the judicial authorities have the power to order the opposing party to "present" such evidence, subject to the protection of confidential information.[1100] In the case of an infringement committed on a commercial scale, the judicial authorities must be able to order disclosure of banking, financial or commercial documents.

21–282 **Practice in England and Wales.** The general principles which are applicable to disclosure are set out in CPR Pt 31 and the numerous authorities under that Part.[1101] The following specific points can be made as to disclosure in cases involving the rights covered in this Chapter.

First, if, as is common, there is a split trial as to liability and quantum of dam-

---

[1094] *Actavis UK Ltd v Novartis AG* [2009] EWHC 41 (Ch) at para.139, applying *Technip France SA's Patent* [2004] EWCA Civ 381; [2004] R.P.C. 46; at paras 12–16.

[1095] See *Dyson Ltd v Qualtex (UK) Ltd* [2006] EWCA Civ 166; [2006] R.P.C. 31, at para.125.

[1096] *George Hensher Ltd v Restawile Upholstery (Lancs.) Ltd* [1976] A.C. 64 at 82; [1974] F.S.R. 173.

[1097] PD63 para.29.2, for cases commenced on or after October 1, 2010.

[1098] art.43(2) of TRIPS provides that where a party refuses to provide information or impedes a procedure relating to an enforcement action, Members may empower judicial authorities to proceed on the basis of the information before them, including the complaint, subject to providing the parties an opportunity to be heard. This provision, which does not seem to add anything to procedure in England and Wales, is not reproduced in the Enforcement Directive.

[1099] Member States may provide that a reasonable sample of a substantial number of copies of a work or other protected object may be considered by the judicial authorities to constitute reasonable evidence. No such provision has been made in the United Kingdom. If an issue arises the parties will usually be expected to agree a representative sample.

[1100] For a discussion of the implementation of this provision in the various Member States, see Evidence and Right of Information in Intellectual Property Rights, a Report of the legal sub-group of the European Observatory on Counterfeiting and Piracy: *http://ec.europa.eu/internal_market/iprenforcement/observatory/index_en.htm* [Accessed October 12, 2010].

[1101] See, generally, the current edition of *Civil Procedure*.

ages, the court will not normally require disclosure of documents relating only to quantum before liability has been established. Thus, where there is to be a split trial, disclosure will not be ordered before liability is established merely to enable a party to form an estimate of the amount in issue or (in the past, when Legal Aid was available) to enable information to be given to the Legal Services Commission.[1102] Special circumstances must be shown,[1103] such as, possibly, a genuine wish by the defendant to make a bona fide offer to settle.[1104]

Secondly, if confidential documents are relevant the court may, in its discretion, require the defendant to give an undertaking not to make use of the information disclosed thereby and limit the right to take away documents or make copies of them.[1105] Inspection of documents relating to trade secrets may be ordered subject to safeguards as to where and by whom the documents may be inspected. A fair balance has to be struck between the natural wish of a party to have his confidential documents adequately protected and the natural wish of the other party to see any documents which may support his case.[1106] Irrelevant but confidential material may be redacted from documents before they are disclosed, although this can lead to controversy.

Thirdly, in intellectual property cases, the defendant is not entitled to privilege from giving disclosure on the ground that he would tend to incriminate himself. This privilege was withdrawn by s.72 of the Supreme Court Act 1981, as amended.[1107]

Finally, it has been held that a claimant may confine his claim in copyright to part of an unpublished work and, in that case, he will not be required, on disclosure, to disclose the remainder.[1108]

For disclosure for the purpose of making an informed election between an inquiry as to damages and an account of profits, see para.21–192, above. For an example of the adverse costs consequences which may result from a failure to carry out a reasonable search at the proper time, see *Anglia Autoflow Ltd v Wrightfield Ltd*.[1109]

Patents County Court. The rules as to standard disclosure do not apply.[1110] **21–283**
Specific disclosure may be ordered but only in relation to specific and identified issues and if the court is satisfied that the benefit of the further material in terms of its value in resolving those issues appears likely to justify the cost of producing and dealing with it.[1111]

[1102] *Baldock v Addison* [1995] 1 W.L.R. 158; [1994] F.S.R. 665 and *Kapur v JW Francis & Co & Another, The Times*, March 4, 1998, not following *Hazeltine Corp v British Broadcasting Corp* [1979] F.S.R. 523. See also *De La Rue v Dickinson* 3 K. & J. 388; *Fennessy v Clark* [1887] 37 Ch. D. 184; *Lea v Saxby* 32 L.T.R. 731 and *William Gaynor & Son Ltd v HP Bulmer Ltd, The Times*, January 19, 1984.

[1103] See previous note.

[1104] *Kapur v JW Francis & Co, The Times*, March 4, 1998, CA.

[1105] *Centri-Spray v Cera International Ltd & Others* [1979] F.S.R. 175; see also on confidentiality *R. v NSPCC* [1978] A.C. 171; *Science Research Council v Nasse* [1980] A.C. 1028; and *Porton Capital Technology Funds v 3M UK Holdings Ltd* [2010] EWHC 114 (Comm) (confidentiality club).

[1106] *Format Communications Mfg Ltd v ITT (UK) Ltd* [1983] F.S.R. 473; *Zink (John) and Co Ltd v Wilkinson* [1973] R.P.C. 717; *Roussel Uclaf v ICI* [1989] R.P.C. 59; *Atari v Philips Electronics and Associated Industries Ltd* [1988] 5 F.S.R. 416; *Roussel Uclaf v ICI (No.2)* [1990] R.P.C. 45; *Ixora Trading v Jones* [1990] F.S.R. 251.

[1107] See paras 21–163 et seq., above.

[1108] *Sitwell v Sun Engraving Co Ltd* (1938) 107 L.J. Ch. 68.

[1109] [2008] EWPCC 3 (computer software).

[1110] CPR 63.24(2), for cases commenced on or after October 1, 2010.

[1111] PD63 para.29.2.

J. PRODUCTION OF ORIGINAL WORK

21–284   In an action for infringement of copyright in a work it is not necessary to produce the original from which the alleged copy has been derived[1112] if it can be proved by other satisfactory evidence.[1113] Indeed, in many cases, the original work has disappeared or been destroyed before the action is commenced or comes to trial.[1114]

K. PERIOD OF LIMITATION

21–285   The 1988 Act provides no special limitation period (except in respect of applications for delivery up[1115]), so that the six-year period provided in the Limitation Act 1980[1116] for actions for tort operates in respect of actions for infringement of all the rights covered in this Chapter. It is important to note that each act of infringement is a separate tort. The fact that the claimant's remedy for one act of infringement is barred does not extinguish the claimant's copyright: he may sue for subsequent or continuing infringements committed within the limitation period. The effect of *Giles v Rhind*,[1117] would appear to be that s.32(1)(b) of the Limitation Act, which provides for the postponement of the limitation period in the event of deliberate concealment of any fact relevant to the claimant's cause of action, applies to proceedings for the infringement of the rights covered in this Work.

L. COSTS

21–286   **General.** Article 14 of the Enforcement Directive requires Member States to ensure that reasonable and proportionate legal costs and other expenses incurred by the successful party shall, as a general rule, be borne by the unsuccessful party, unless equity does not allow this.[1118] CPR 44.3 and the rules about the recovery as damages of the costs of investigation[1119] are consistent with this.

21–287   **Patents County Court.** Specific rules apply unless (relevantly) the court considers that a party has behaved in a manner which amounts to an abuse of the court's process.[1120] It seems that this is a more stringent test than that recommended by the Working Party which proposed that off-scale costs should be available "in exceptional cases" where a party "has behaved unreasonably, and in particular in a manner which amounts to an abuse of the Court's procedures".[1121] It appears that it will not be sufficient to show that the party has behaved in such a way as would justify an assessment of costs on the indemnity basis.

[1112] *Lucas v Williams & Sons* [1892] 2 Q.B. 113.

[1113] *Wham-O Manufacturing Co v Lincoln Industries Ltd* [1985] R.P.C. 127. In *ABB Ltd v New Zealand Insulators Ltd* [2006] NZHC 1072 at para.164 it was held that this principle is equally applicable to the loss of the original drawing when considering whether the creation of a work which was derived from it had involved sufficient skill and labour to confer protection on the new work. It is suggested that the same principle would apply in England and Wales.

[1114] *George Hensher Ltd v Restawile Upholstery (Lancs) Ltd* [1976] A.C. 64 at 79H; [1974] F.S.R. 173; *James Arnold & Co Ltd v Miafern Ltd* [1980] R.P.C. 397 at 402; *Allibert SA v O'Connor* [1981] F.S.R. 613 at 621; *Wham-O Manufacturing Co v Lincoln Industries Ltd* [1985] R.P.C. 127 at 142; *Plix Products Ltd v Frank M. Winstone (Merchants) Ltd* [1986] F.S.R. 608.

[1115] See para.21–216 et seq., above.

[1116] (c.58) s.2.

[1117] [2008] EWCA Civ 118; [2009] Ch. 191.

[1118] This provision goes further than art.45(2) of TRIPS, which simply provides that the judicial authorities shall have the authority to order the infringer to pay the right holder expenses, which may include appropriate attorneys' fees.

[1119] See para.21–197, above.

[1120] CPR 45.41(2), in respect of cases commenced on or after October 1, 2010.

[1121] Report p.15.

The rules are as follows. First, costs will be summarily assessed and there will be no detailed assessment.[1122] Second, the court will not order a party to pay total costs of more than £50,000 on the final determination of a claim in relation to liability and £25,000 on an inquiry as to damages or an account of profits. These figures are intended to include disbursements, any success fee and any insurance premium.[1123]

There are four qualifications to this.[1124] First, maximum amounts of scale costs are applicable to each stage in the action in accordance with the Costs Practice Direction. Secondly, these amounts apply after the court has applied the provisions on set off in accordance with CPR 44.3(9)(a), which provides for the set off of costs orders against each other. Thirdly, where a party has been ordered to pay the costs of an application because it has acted unreasonably,[1125] the amount of such an order will not count for the purposes of these figures. Fourthly, where appropriate, VAT can be recovered in addition to the amount of the scale costs.

The amount of the scale costs to be awarded will depend on the nature and complexity of the claim.[1126] There are different maxima depending whether the stages are up to determination of liability or are stages in an inquiry or account. The maxima for stages up to determination of liability are (relevantly) as follows: for the particulars of claim, defence and counterclaim and reply and defence to counterclaim: £6,125 each; for a reply to defence to counterclaim: £3,000; for attendance at a case management conference: £2,500; for making or responding to an application: £2,500; for providing or inspecting disclosure: £5,000; for preparing witness statements: £5,000; for preparing experts' reports: £7,500; for preparing for and attending trial and judgment: £15,000; and for preparing for determination on the papers: £5,000. The maxima for stages in an inquiry or account are in most cases significantly less. They are: for points of claim or defence: £2,500; for attendance at a case management conference: £2,500; for making or responding to an application: £2,500; for providing or inspecting disclosure: £2,500; for preparing experts' reports: £5,000; for preparing for and attending trial and judgment: £7,500; and for preparing for determination on the papers: £2,500.

9. ONLINE INFRINGEMENT: ENFORCEMENT OF RIGHTS

A. INTRODUCTION

Nature of the Digital Economy Act provisions. This section covers the provisions of the Digital Economy Act 2010 which are directed at the reduction of unlicensed peer to peer file sharing. It is important to note at the outset that these provisions do not alter the substantive law of copyright, nor do they detract from the rights of copyright owners and others to bring court proceedings in respect of such infringements. Rather, they are intended to prevent or deter such infringements by a three-stage process which is intended to take place in conjunction with the continuing development by rights holders of easily available legitimate sources of digital material and a campaign to educate infringers about the unlawfulness of their activities and the damage which is believed to result from them.   **21–288**

[1122] CPR 45.41(3). Accordingly, various rules are disapplied by CPR 45.41(3). They are: CPR 44.3(8) which provides for payments of costs on account prior to assessment; and CPR 44.3A(2)(b) and (c), 44.7(b) and Pt 47, all of which concern detailed assessment.

[1123] IPUC Report p.15. See also CPR 45.41 importing the definition of "costs" in CPR 43.2, which includes "disbursement" and "any additional liability incurred under a funding arrangement".

[1124] CPR 45.42(2), (3), (5); CPR 45.43.

[1125] para.21–258.

[1126] CPR 45.42(4).

21–289   **The three-stage process.** The three stages of the process are as follows. First, at the request of right holders, internet service providers will be required to send warning letters to subscribers whose access is being used to infringe. Second, providers will be required to supply right holders with anonymised lists of the most serious infringers as a prelude to their identification pursuant to court orders followed by legal action. The obligations imposed on providers by the first two stages of the process are called the "initial obligations". If the initial obligations do not result in a substantial reduction in the amount of infringement, the third stage of the process will be implemented. This will impose "technical obligations" on internet service providers requiring them to impose "technical measures" to prevent or hinder the use of particular subscribers' internet access for such infringement.

21–290   **Outline of section.** This section details the background to the new legislation[1127] before covering the initial obligations,[1128] the provisions for subscriber appeals relating to the initial obligations,[1129] the "technical obligations",[1130] and finally the provisions as to costs, administration and enforcement.[1131]

B. BACKGROUND

(i)   General consideration

21–291   **Position before the Digital Economy Act 2010.** The development of peer-to-peer file-sharing systems is dealt with elsewhere.[1132] In *Polydor v Brown*[1133] it was held that connecting a computer to the internet, where the computer is running peer-to-peer software, and where music files containing copies of copyright works are present in a shared directory, amounts to communication to the public of those works by the person in control of the computer. An individual who downloads a copy of such a file is also liable for making a copy if it is in copyright and he or she is not licensed to download it. In practice, it is easier for rights holders to identify those who make the works available than those who download them.[1134] This has generally been achieved by downloading and running the file sharing software in question, searching for a particular work and identifying the Internet Protocol ("IP") addresses of computers which contain copies of infringing material in their shared folders. It is possible to identify the internet service provider who allocated a particular IP address in Europe by using tables of IP address allocations which are available from regional internet registries.[1135] Rights holders then apply to the court under the *Norwich Pharmacal* jurisdiction for orders that the service providers disclose the identity of the account holder.[1136] Service providers do not generally oppose such applications provided they are reimbursed their costs of compliance. However, the obtaining of a *Norwich Pharmacal* order is expensive and only a limited number of infringers can be identified under any particular order. While enforcement action against a limited number of individuals may have some deterrent effect, the number of people

---

[1127] paras 21–291 to 21–300, below.
[1128] paras 21–303 to 21–340, below.
[1129] paras 21–341 to 21–352, below.
[1130] para.21–353 to 21–360, below
[1131] paras 21–361 to 21–367.
[1132] See para.26–200, below.
[1133] [2005] EWHC 3191.
[1134] See, e.g. *Hansard* H.L. Vol. 716 Col. 447.
[1135] Such as RIPE NCC.
[1136] See paras 21–158 et seq., above..

involved in unlicensed file sharing is so large that effective enforcement in this way is not considered to be practicable.[1137]

Difficulties any enforcement regime must confront.[1138] The enforcement of 　**21–292** copyright against unlicensed peer-to-peer file sharers has thrown up a host of practical and legal issues the extent of which goes some way to explain the complexity of the legislation which has now been introduced. Those issues include the following. First, how to identify infringers. There are a number of practical problems. One is that while it is possible to identify the subscriber, he or she may not in fact be the actual infringer, who may be a minor or an unauthorised third party who is unknown to the subscriber. Another is that the IP address used for the infringement may well be "dynamic", that is a different IP address may be allocated to a subscriber each time he or she accesses the internet. If the exact time of the infringement is not properly recorded or the service provider does not keep detailed records, it may not be possible to deduce who the address was allocated to at the relevant time.[1139] In addition, internet traffic can be disguised by the use of technologies such as proxy servers, encryption or anonymous proxies. There are particular problems in matching IP addresses to mobile users.[1140] The second issue is how to identify infringers without an unwarranted interference with their rights to privacy and under data protection legislation.[1141] The third issue is how any enforcement regime which does not simply involve legal action by rights holders is to be paid for and in particular how costs are to be shared between copyright owners and service providers.[1142] For example, the solution chosen by the Government will require service providers to respond to infringement reports supplied by rights holders and some will have to upgrade their computer systems as a result[1143]; at the same time, OFCOM will have to introduce codes of practice, carry out extensive investigations, supply detailed reports, administer the system and create and oversee an appeals body. All these things will have to be paid for. The fourth issue is how to ensure that any legislative solution conforms with Community legislation, notably the E-Commerce Directive (in particular that part of it which prohibits any requirement that service providers monitor the information they transmit or store),[1144] but also Community technical standards and telecoms legislation. The fifth issue is how to ensure that any solution does not leave individual subscribers without access to the internet, which even if not yet considered to be a right[1145] is certainly akin to a necessity for most people. The sixth issue is how to effect a change in culture amongst those who share files unlawfully issue rather than (for example) simply diverting infringers to unregulated or anonymous service providers. The final is-

---

[1137] For a discussion of the difficulties, see the BERR Consultation of July 2008, referred to in para., 21–296 below, at para.7.5, and *EMI Records (Ireland) Ltd v UPC Communications Ireland Ltd* Irish High Court, Charleton J., October 11, 2010, at para.62. This decision contains a clear general discussion of the issues and technology. However, it was decided on legislation which was held not to comply with the requirements of the European legislation, and is therefore of limited legal value in the United Kingdom.

[1138] See generally the BERR Consultation of July 2008.

[1139] This applies to the addresses allocated to most residential subscribers: see p.3 of the Mott MacDonald Report on the costs of the implementation of the Digital Economy Bill, February 2010. This report can be found on the BIS website.

[1140] See p.12 of the Mott MacDonald Report, *http://interactive.bis.gov.uk/digitalbritain/wp-content/uploads/2010/04/Mott-MacDonald-P2P-Final-Report.pdf* [Accessed November 11, 2010].

[1141] See generally the *Promusicae* case discussed at para.21–158, above.

[1142] See generally the Mott MacDonald Report.

[1143] See, generally, the Mott MacDonald Report.

[1144] See art.15(1) and para 21–122, above.

[1145] See the opinion of Mr Richard Spearman QC, which is available at *http://www.publications.parliament.uk/pa/jt200910/jtselect/jtrights/44/4414.htm* [Accessed November 11, 2010].

sue is how to deal with circumstances in which subscribers make their service available to others, whether in the home or in a business context, and have little or no control over how those others use it.

(ii) Reports and consultation documents

21–293 **The Gowers Report (November 2006).** In this report, Andrew Gowers noted that legal action by rights holders against individuals had not led to a significant reduction in unlicensed peer to peer use.[1146] He also noted that service providers had limited liability as a result of the E-Commerce Directive,[1147] but had generally been cooperative in attempts to reduce large-scale infringement by providing details of large-scale infringers.[1148] He referred to the fact that the Internet Service Providers' Association was undertaking work to encourage service providers and rights owners to collaborate.[1149] The report's Recommendation 39 was in these terms: "Observe the industry agreement of protocols for sharing data between service providers and rights holders to remove and disbar users engaged in 'piracy'. If this has not proved operationally successful by the end of 2007, Government should consider whether to legislate".

21–294 **Creative Britain (February 2008).** In this report, the Government stated that in accordance with the Gowers Report it preferred that there should be voluntary solutions between content owners and network operators rather than regulation[1150] and that it recognised the value of the current discussions between service providers and rights owners.[1151] However, it went on to make clear that it intended to consult on the form and content of legislation that would require service providers and rights holders to cooperate in taking action on file sharing with a view to implementing legislation by April 2009.[1152]

21–195 **The MOU (July 2008).** On July 24, 2008, a number of major service providers signed an agreement with a number of content owners and representatives of content owners.[1153] The Government and OFCOM were also parties. The stated objective of the MOU was to achieve a significant reduction in unlawful file sharing and a change in popular attitude towards infringement within a period of two to three years.[1154] In short, the signatories agreed to work together and with OFCOM to develop voluntary codes of practice covering standards of evidence, actions against alleged infringers, indemnities in respect of incorrect allegations of file sharing and routes of appeal for consumers. During 2008 and 2009 OFCOM and the British Phonographic Industry operated a trial of a notification system. 50,000 notifications were sent to six service providers at a rate of about 1,000 per week.[1155]

[1146] http://www.official-documents.gov.uk/document/other/0118404830/0118404830.pdf, at para.5.93 [Accessed November 11, 2010].

[1147] http://webarchive.nationalarchives.gov.uk/+/http://www.culture.gov.uk/reference_library/publications/3572.aspx, at para 5.94 [Accessed November 11, 010].

[1148] para.5.98.

[1149] para.5.99.

[1150] para.5.1.

[1151] para.5.9.

[1152] Commitment 15.

[1153] Joint memorandum of understanding on an approach to reduce unlawful file-sharing. http://www.bpi.co.uk/our-work/protecting-uk-music/article/joint-memorandum-of-understanding-on-an-approach-to-reduce-unlawful-file-sharing.aspx [Accessed November 11, 2010].

[1154] "Objective".

[1155] See the Mott MacDonald Report pp.1 and 23.

The BERR[1156] Consultation (July 2008). On the same date as the MOU was   **21–296**
signed, BERR issued a consultation on regulatory action. The stated aim was to
take forward Gowers Recommendation 39 and the commitments made in the
Creative Britain report.[1157] According to the consultation document, legislation
was necessary because it had not been possible to arrive quickly at an agreement
in which all service providers would participate.[1158] The Government stated that
its preferred option was a "co-regulatory"[1159] approach comprising three
elements. First, the introduction of codes of practice applied by OFCOM relating
to (a) education and awareness, (b) the making of lawful content available in a
choice of formats and at a range of prices and (c) notifications to repeat infringers.
Second, the development by OFCOM of a code of practice on mechanisms to
deal with repeat infringers, including technical solutions (such as traffic management, filtering and marking of legitimate content) and ways in which rights holders could take action against repeat infringers. Third, an obligation on service
providers to take action against infringing subscribers.[1160] Other options
canvassed included the imposition of a legislative requirement on service providers to take action against individuals identified by rights holders as unlawfully
file-sharing.[1161]

Government response to the BERR consultation (January 2009). By the time   **21–297**
it responded to the consultation the Government had concluded that its preferred
approach was not satisfactory for a number of reasons.[1162] First, although rights
holders favoured the approach, it was not supported by service providers or
consumers.[1163] Second, according to the Government, the approach "would have
a significant disadvantage in terms of substantial regulatory uncertainty, rendering it impossible for service providers to understand the nature and the extend
[sic] of the obligation to be imposed on them".[1164] Third, it was thought that the
approach would give rise to significant concerns about consumer protection and
about how to accommodate rights holders and smaller service providers who
were not involved in the MOU.[1165] At the same time, the Government noted that
recent evidence had suggested that where service providers had notified subscribers that their accounts were being used for infringement this had had excellent
results. Accordingly, the Government had decided to adopt one of the alternative
options canvassed in the consultation: the imposition of an obligation on service
providers to take action against infringers. However, this was to have additional
elements.[1166] First, subject to receipt of reasonable levels of proof from rights
holders, service providers would be obliged to notify alleged infringers that their
conduct was unlawful (the "notification obligation"). Second, service providers
would be obliged to collect anonymised information on serious repeat infringers
which would be made available to rights holders ("the information collection
obligation"). The Government made clear that such information would be derived
from rights holders' notifications and that it was not intending to require service

---

[1156] The then Department for Business, Enterprise and Regulatory Reform.
[1157] *http://www.berr.gov.uk/files/file47139.pdf* [Accessed November 11, 2010]. See para.2.2. For the
      Gowers and Creative Britain reports, see paras 21–293 and 21–294, above respectively.
[1158] See para.1.2.
[1159] i.e. "a self-regulatory approach that is backed up in some way by a regulatory requirement": see
      para.8.7.
[1160] para.1.4.
[1161] "Option A2", paras 9.7 and 9.8.
[1162] *http://bis.gov.uk/files/file49907.pdf* [Accessed November 11, 2010.]
[1163] p.3.
[1164] p.4.
[1165] p.4. For the MOU, see para.21–195, above.
[1166] p.5.

providers to monitor their subscribers' activities.[1167] This revised option became "Action 13" of the Digital Britain Report which was published in June 2009[1168] and is the root of the "initial obligations" contained in the Digital Economy Act.

21–298   **The BIS[1169] Consultation (June 2009).** These recommendations were given more specific form in a consultation issued by BIS on June 16, 2009.[1170] The proposal was for OFCOM to enforce service providers' notification and information collection obligations by a code of practice.[1171] In addition, OFCOM would have the power to impose other conditions on service providers in the event that the notification process did not result in a significant reduction of unlawful activity. Those conditions would require providers to impose "technical measures" such as blocking (of sites, IP addresses or URLs), protocol blocking, port blocking, bandwidth capping, bandwidth shaping and content identification and filtering.[1172] On August 25, 2009, the Government published a statement[1173] elaborating on this in three respects. First, the power to direct the introduction of technical measures (which would now be vested in the Secretary of State rather than OF-COM) would only be implemented once OFCOM had carried out preparatory work on the mechanics of introducing them. Second, a power to suspend subscribers' accounts should be added to the list of possible technical measures. Third, costs should be borne by the party which incurred them except that the operating costs of sending notifications should be divided equally between service providers and right holders.

21–299   **BIS response to the consultation (November 2009).** In its response, the Government indicated its intention to implement the notification and information collection obligations together with the proposal on technical measures set out in the consultation document as modified by the August 2009 statement.[1174] As to costs, the Government stated that it proposed to adopt the proposal in that statement except that right holders would now be charged a flat fee per notification.[1175] Finally, the Government proposed the introduction of a threshold level of infringement before any obligations would apply to a particular service provider.[1176]

21–300   **European proposals.** In May 2010, after the passage of the Digital Economy Act, the European Commission indicated that it intended, following "extensive stakeholder dialogue" to report by 2012 on the need for additional measures to reinforce the protection against persistent violations of intellectual property rights in the online environment consistently with the guarantees provided in the Telecoms framework and fundamental rights on data protection and privacy.[1177]

[1167] Cf. art.15 of the E-Commerce Directive (discussed at para.21–122, above).
[1168] http://webarchive.nationalarchives.gov.uk/uk+/http://www.culture.gov.uk/reference_library/media_releases/5783.aspx [Accessed November 11, 2010].
[1169] The Department for Business, Innovation and Skills, the successor to BERR.
[1170] http://www.berr.gov.uk/files/files51703.pdf [Accessed November 11, 2010].
[1171] para.4.2.
[1172] para.4.3.
[1173] http://www.ppa.co.uk/legal-and-public-affairs/ppa-responses-and-evidence/~/media/Documents/Legal/Consultations/BIS%20Announcement%20Mid%20august%2009.ashx [Accessed November 11, 2010].
[1174] http://www.berr.gov.uk/files/file53648.pdf, p.11 [Accessed November 11, 2010].
[1175] p.12.
[1176] p.12.
[1177] Communication from the Commission A Digital Agenda for Europe COM(2010) 245 p.10.

C. THE LEGISLATION

(i) Introduction

Overview. Legislation was introduced by way of amendments to the Communications Act 2003 ("the 2003 Act") which were made by the Digital Economy Act 2010.[1178] As foreshadowed in the BIS consultation, the legislation is to be implemented in two phases the second of which may not in fact be necessary. In the first phase providers will be obliged to notify subscribers that copyright owners have reported that they are infringing and to provide rights owners with anonymised lists of subscribers whose accounts are being frequently used for infringement (the "initial obligations"), thus (it is believed) enabling copyright owners to concentrate their use of existing remedies against the most serious infringers.[1179] If the combination of initial obligations and existing remedies does not effect a change of culture and act as a sufficient deterrent to unlawful file-sharing, the second phase of the legislation will be implemented. In this phase the Secretary of State will be able to direct service providers to limit or suspend infringers' access to the internet by "technical measures". The legislation is expressed in very general terms, its detailed implementation being left to codes of practice to be developed or approved by OFCOM. At the time of writing, OFCOM had produced a draft code for consultation.[1180] The Act also contains elaborate provisions requiring OFCOM to report on the effectiveness or otherwise of the legislation.[1181]

21–301

Commencement. The Digital Economy Act received Royal Assent on April 8, 2010. However, the "initial obligations" only come into effect once a code for regulating them is in force.[1182] The Act obliges OFCOM either to have approved such a code or to have made one themselves by January 8, 2011 or such later date as the Secretary of State may specify.[1183] The Government expressed the hope that service providers, copyright owners and consumers would contribute to an industry code.[1184] However, in anticipation of having to make their own code, on May 28, 2010, just over seven weeks after the Act was passed, OFCOM published a Draft Initial Obligations Code for consultation ("the draft code").[1185] The closing date for responses was July 30, 2010. In September 2010 the Government announced its intention to grant OFCOM an extension of three months to approve

21–302

[1178] The text of the new provisions is in Vol.2 B11.ii. A table of parliamentary debates is in Vol.2 D8.

[1179] During the parliamentary debates the Government suggested that a court might refuse to grant a *Norwich Pharmacal* order in respect of a subscriber whose account had not been used for sufficient infringements to justify his or her inclusion on a copyright infringement list: *Hansard* H.L. Vol. 716 Col. 1043. See also Vol. 717 Col. 1260. However, the legislation does not seek to circumscribe the *Norwich Pharmacal* jurisdiction in any way.

[1180] *http://stakeholders.ofcom.org.uk/consultations/copyright-infringement/* [Accessed November 11, 2010].

[1181] s.124F.

[1182] s.124C(2).

[1183] s.124C, 124D. The date January 8, 2011 is calculated as follows. S.124D(2) provides that OFCOM may but need not make such a code for a time before the end of "the period of six months beginning with the day on which sections 124A and 124B come into force". Those sections were inserted by ss.3 and 4 of the Digital Economy Act 2010, which came into force on June 8, 2010, two months after Royal Assent: see s.47(1).

[1184] Digital Economy Act 2010, Explanatory Notes para.48.

[1185] *http://stakeholders.ofcom.org.uk/consultations/copyright-infringement/* [Accessed November 11, 2010].

or make its code.[1186] No order imposing technical measures may be made within the period of 12 months beginning with the date on which there is an initial obligations code in force.[1187] It follows that no measures to limit infringers' access to the internet can be taken before April 8, 2012. The validity of the Act is presently the subject of judicial review proceedings.

(ii) The initial obligations

(a) *Rights and right holders covered*

21–303   **Rights covered.** The legislation is limited to online infringement of copyright and has no application to infringement of rights in performances.[1188]

21–304   **Copyright owner.** The operation of the legislation is triggered by a report by a "copyright owner" to an "internet service provider" about an infringement of copyright by means of a "subscriber's" "internet access service". The expression "copyright owner" is defined as a copyright owner within the meaning of the copyright Part of the 1988 Act or someone authorised by that person to act on his behalf.[1189] The definition makes specific reference to s.173 of the 1988 Act, which contains two provisions. The first is that where different persons are entitled to different aspects of copyright in a work, the copyright owner is the person entitled to the relevant aspect. Unlicensed peer-to-peer file sharing involves (at least) infringement of the making available right and of the reproduction right. Arguably in each case the infringement is carried out "by means of" a subscriber's internet access service. It follows that if these rights are in different ownership, either copyright owner will be able to take advantage of the provisions of the Act. The second provision in s.173 is that where copyright or an aspect of copyright is owned jointly, references to the copyright owner are to all the owners. It seems therefore that any report would have to be made by all joint owners (or their agent). Subsections 101(2) and 101A(2) of the 1988 Act provide that where a licensee has remedies for infringement which are concurrent with those of the copyright owner, references to the copyright owner are to be construed accordingly. It is thought that that these provisions are confined to the exercise of court remedies for infringement and will not apply for the purposes of the 2003 Act; accordingly, licensees who have not been appointed as agents for the purposes of 2003 Act will not be able to exercise any rights under that Act.

21–305   **Agent of copyright owner.** There are no formal requirements in the 2003 Act for the grant of such authorisation.[1190] The inclusion of a copyright owner's agent is presumably directed in particular at permitting reports to be made by representa-

---

[1186] *Online Infringement of Copyright (Initial Obligations) Cost Sharing HM Government Response* (BIS, September 2010). *http://www.bis.gov.uk/assets/biscore/business-sectors/docs/o/10–1131–online-copyright-infringement-government-response.pdf* [Accessed November 11, 2010].

[1187] s.124H(2).

[1188] ss.124A(1), 124G(2).

[1189] s.124N. Although this is not stated expressly, the authority must presumably relate to the act in question. In its Outline of the Initial Obligations Code (January 2010: *http://interactive.bis.gov.uk/digitalbritain/wp-content/uploads/2010/01/Online-Infringement-Copyright.pdf* [Accessed November 11, 2010]) BIS suggested that the code might allow reports to be issued by "the copyright owner, their authorised legal representatives or the authorised copyright licence owner". In fact, however, OFCOM's draft code simply adopts the definition in the 2003 Act (para.1). The BIS document went on to suggest the inclusion of a provision that only one party would be entitled to issue a report per alleged infringement so as to avoid multiple reports. No such provision is contained in the draft code, perhaps because the probability of multiple reports was considered to be low.

[1190] However, the draft code requires a copyright infringement report to include evidence of authorisation. Difficulties are therefore likely to arise if the authority has only been given orally.

tive bodies (such as the British Phonographic Industry) and collecting societies which do not take an assignment of the relevant copyright but rather act as their members' agent for the purposes of enforcement. Although the legislation is primarily directed at file-sharing, it is not intended to be so limited.[1191] In one sense it can be said that any online infringement has been committed "by means of" an internet access service. However, a report can only be made if the rights holder knows the IP address which is being used for the infringement, which will not normally be the case in circumstances other than peer-to-peer file sharing.

Terminology. The use of the term "copyright owner" to refer both to the actual owner of the copyright and to his or her authorised agent is confusing. For example, the service provider's obligation to notify a subscriber of an apparent infringement is triggered by the sending by a "copyright owner" of a "copyright infringement report" to the provider. A "copyright infringement report" is a report that "states that there has been an infringement of the owner's copyright".[1192] However, if the report is made by an agent of the copyright owner, it will not be the agent's copyright which will appear to have been infringed. For clarity, in what follows, the expression "copyright owner" will only be used to refer to the actual copyright owner.

21–306

Persons qualified to report: the legislation. The 2003 Act provides that any initial obligations code may specify conditions that must be met for rights under the file sharing provisions to apply and may require copyright owners or their agents to provide information or assistance which is reasonably required to determine whether such a condition is met.[1193] Such provision may specify that a right or obligation does not apply in relation to a copyright owner or his agent unless he has made arrangements with a service provider regarding the number of copyright infringement reports he may make to the service provider within a particular period and regarding payment in advance of a contribution towards meeting costs incurred by the service provider.[1194] The purpose of this latter provision is to ensure that service providers have some advance warning of the number of copyright infringement reports they may expect to receive and some advance payment of their costs of processing those reports.

21–307

Qualifying copyright owners: the draft code. A copyright owner or his agent only has rights under the draft code[1195] if he has given an estimate of the number of copyright infringement reports ("reports") he intends to make in a "notification period" and has met his obligations as to the payment of costs in each case in accordance with a statutory instrument made under the 2003 Act.[1196] The "notification period" will be laid down by that statutory instrument.[1197] The estimate must

21–308

[1191] At the time of the House of Lords Committee Stage, the Government had not identified a "non peer-to-peer application" for the Act but expressed itself to be conscious of the speed of technological change: *Hansard* H.L. Vol. 716 Col.446.

[1192] s.124A(3)(a).

[1193] s.124C(3)(a).

[1194] s.124C(4).

[1195] As a "qualifying copyright owner".

[1196] The draft code refers to the draft statutory instrument set out in Annex C to BIS's *Consultation document on cost sharing* published on March 30, 2010 *http:;//www.bis.gov.uk/assets/biscore/ business-sectors/docs/10–915–consultation-online-infringement-of-copyright.pdf* [Accessed November 11, 2010]: the Online Infringement of Copyright (Initial Obligations) (Sharing of Costs) Order.

[1197] s.124M. See generally para.21–363, below. The draft instrument provides that the first notification period will be the period between a date determined by OFCOM and the following March 31 and that subsequent notification periods will be each year commencing April 1: art.2.

be sent at least two months before the start of the notification period.[1198] Obligations as to the payment of costs are dealt with in more detail below.[1199]

21–309   **Quality assurance.** The draft code makes it a pre-condition for being able to
send a report that the maker has provided OFCOM with a Quality Assurance
report.[1200] Such a report must be submitted before the first report is sent and then
annually.[1201] It must detail the evidence gathering processes and systems to be
used (and certify their robustness and accuracy), the steps taken to ensure the integrity and accuracy of the evidence and the processes for auditing the systems. It
must also identify examples of quality assurance issues which have occurred in
the past year and measures taken to assure their resolution, certify compliance
with data protection laws and include any other information directed by OFCOM.
The draft code provides that copyright owners must comply with the procedures
set out in such a report[1202] and effect any changes directed by OFCOM.[1203]

(b) *Internet service providers: definitions*

21–310   **"Internet service providers".** As has already been made clear, the legislation
imposes obligations on "internet service providers" where there are alleged to
have been infringements by means of internet access services provided to
"subscribers". An "internet service provider" is a person who provides an "internet access service".[1204] An "internet access service" is "an electronic communications service that—(a) is provided to a subscriber, (b) consists entirely or mainly
of the provision of access to the internet and (c) includes the allocation of an IP
address[1205] or IP addresses to the subscriber to enable that access".[1206] A "subscriber" is a person who receives an internet access service under an agreement
with the provider of the service and does not receive it as a communications
provider.[1207]

21–311   **"Communications provider", "electronic communications service" and
"electronic communications network".** A communications provider is a person
who (within the meaning of s.32(4) of the 2003 Act) provides an electronic communications network or an electronic communications service. An "electronic
communications network" is "a transmission system for the conveyance, by the
use of electrical, magnetic or electro-magnetic energy, of signals of any description", together with "such of the following as are used, by the person providing
the system and in association with it, for the conveyance of the signals—(i) apparatus comprised in the system; (ii) apparatus used for the switching or routing of
the signals; and (iii) software and stored data".[1208] References to the provision of
an electronic communications network include references to its establishment,

---

[1198] Draft code para.2.2.
[1199] paras 21–361 et seq.
[1200] Draft code para.3.5, presumably made under s.124D(5)(h) of the 2003 Act.
[1201] para.3.5.
[1202] para.3.7.
[1203] para.3.6.
[1204] Communications Act 2003 s.124N.
[1205] That is, an internet protocol address: see s.124N.
[1206] s.124N.
[1207] s.124N.
[1208] s.32(1), implementing art.2(a) of Directive 2002/21/EC on a common regulatory framework for
electronic communications, [2002] OJ L108/33. See Vol.2 D8. The definition in art.2(a) is
amended by art.1(2)(a) of Directive 2009/140/EC, which must be implemented by May 25, 2011,
by the addition of the phrase "including network elements which are not active". The revised definition (with the added words in italics) reads: "'electronic communications network' means
transmission systems and, where applicable, switching or routing equipment and other resources,
including network elements which are not active, which permit the conveyance of signals by

maintenance or operation.[1209] An "electronic communications service" means "a service consisting in, or having as its principal feature, the conveyance by means of an electronic communications network of signals, except in so far as it is a content service".[1210] A "content service" means "so much of any service as consists in one or both of the following—(a) the provision of material with a view to its being comprised in signals conveyed by means of an electronic communications network; (b) the exercise of editorial control over the contents of signals conveyed by means of such a network".[1211] The Act contains a number of other provisions which supplement these definitions.[1212]

Application of the definitions: general. It is clear that an ordinary individual user of an ordinary internet service provider's services to access the internet is a "subscriber". It is also clear that the effect of the exclusion of persons who receive access "as a communications provider" from the definition of "subscriber" is that someone who purchases "wholesale" internet access from a service provider is not a subscriber.[1213] In such circumstances, OFCOM consider that the wholesale provider is not a service provider but that the retail provider may be.[1214] Where the retail provider does not have direct control over or access to the allocation of IP addresses to its subscribers, and so does not possess enough information to process the reports, OFCOM state that it will be required to ensure that it is able to do so, for example by entering into a contract for processing services from the wholesale provider.[1215] However, between these two categories there are a number of users whose position is far less clear.[1216]   **21–312**

Wi-Fi network operators. This paragraph deals solely with Wi-Fi network operators who do not use the service for their own purposes. In their introduction to the draft code, OFCOM express the view that operators of Wi-Fi networks fall within the definition of "internet service provider" where the service is provided by means of an agreement with the subscriber even where the agreement is oral or "implicit".[1217] Where a Wi-Fi network is provided in conjunction with other goods or services to a customer, such as a coffee shop or a hotel, OFCOM presume that the provider is an internet service provider.[1218] This seems correct so long as the provider allocates an IP address to users: the 2003 Act contains no requirement that the agreement should be in writing or even contractual. OFCOM recognise, however, that there may be circumstances where there is an issue as to whether the agreement for goods or services extends to the use of the in-   **21–313**

---

wire, radio, optical or other electromagnetic means, including satellite networks, fixed (circuit- and packet-switched, including Internet) and mobile terrestrial networks, electricity cable systems, to the extent that they are used for the purpose of transmitting signals, networks used for radio and television broadcasting, and cable television networks, irrespective of the type of information conveyed".

[1209] s.32(4)(a).
[1210] s.32(2), implementing art.2(c) of Directive 2002/21/EC.
[1211] s.32(7). The Act in fact states "by means of a such a network" but presumably this is an error.
[1212] See generally s.32.
[1213] See the BIS publication *Online Infringement of Copyright: detail regarding clauses 4-16*, January 2010, *http://interactive.bis.gov.uk/digitalbritain/wp-content/uploads/2009/11/Online-infringement-Copyright-clauses-4–16.pdf*, p.1 [Accessed November 11, 2010].
[1214] para.3.26.
[1215] para.3.27.
[1216] See, generally, the BIS publications *Online Infringement of Copyright: Detail Regarding Clauses 4-16*, January 2010, pp.1 to 3 and *Online Infringement of Copyright: Libraries, Universities and Wi-Fi Providers*, February 2010, *http://interactive.bis.gov.uk/digitalbritain/wp-content/uploads/2010/02/Example-infringement-notifications.pdf* [Accessed November 11, 2010].
[1217] para.3.22.
[1218] para.3.23.

ternet access service.[1219] OFCOM go on to suggest that the position may be different in the case of open access Wi-Fi networks where there is no payment or agreement.[1220] In those circumstances, OFCOM's view is that the person making the service available would be a "subscriber".[1221] The basis for this view is not clear. First, it is perfectly possible depending on the facts that there is an agreement between an open access Wi-Fi operator and a user. Second, however, depending on the facts, it seems strongly arguable that the person making the service available receives it as a communications provider. The parliamentary debates and material prepared during the passage of the Act provide little assistance on this point.[1222]

21–314   Subscribers who both use the service and make it available to others. Where a person receives internet access for his or her own purposes but also allows other persons to use the service on the recipient's own computer, the recipient will remain a subscriber for the purposes of any infringements committed by such other persons. This is because the recipient is not providing an electronic communications service to the other persons and cannot therefore be said to be receiving the service as a communications provider. However, the recipient may also make the service available to third parties on other computers or terminals in domestic, business, academic or library premises controlled by the recipient. OFCOM's view appears to be that such a recipient is a "subscriber" for the purposes of the third parties' use as well as for the purposes of its own use.[1223] Given the terms of s.124N of the 2003 Act, that is a surprising interpretation. To the extent that the recipient is making the service available to third parties, he or she receives the service as communications provider. A person who receives a service as a communications provider cannot be a "subscriber". It is certainly arguable therefore that the recipient is not a subscriber for any purposes, but this would leave a large lacuna in the application of the Act. It is suggested that a more likely interpretation is that the recipient is a subscriber in respect of his or her own use but not in respect of the third party's use. If the recipient has an agreement with and allocates an IP address to the third party, the recipient will be an internet service provider. However, the recipient is unlikely to be covered by the draft code because it only applies to service providers with over 400,000 subscribers.[1224] As a result, however, there will be no one to send a copyright infringement report to in respect of infringements carried out by the third party. It is not clear that this is what the Government intended.

(c) *Internet service providers covered*

21–315   Infringement thresholds. The 2003 Act provides that any initial obligations code may specify conditions that must be met for obligations under the file shar-

---

[1219] para.3.23.
[1220] para.3.22.
[1221] paras 3–22 and 3–30.
[1222] In House of Lords Committee, Lord Young of Norwood Green stated: "We recognise that libraries, other wi-fi operators and open-access providers such as universities serve an important function, not least in helping the less advantaged in getting access online. We do not think that they are caught as individual service providers [sic], which we think they are not, or as consumers [sic]": *Hansard* H.L. Vol. 716 Col. 447. Subsequently, however, the Government referred to the precautions universities could take to prevent infringement via wireless networks, thus suggesting that they might be subscribers: see, e.g. *Hansard* H.L. Vol. 717 Col. 1303. In its publication *Online Infringement of Copyright: Libraries, Universities and Wi-Fi Providers* (February 2010), BIS stated that the question whether universities were ISPs, subscribers or neither was one of fact as was the question whether Wi-Fi network operators were ISPs or subscribers.
[1223] See para.3.31 of the introduction to the draft code, apparently referring to the need for such persons to take steps to protect their networks against use for infringement.
[1224] para.2.4.2, discussed at para.21–318, below.

ing provisions to apply and may require service providers to provide information or assistance which is reasonably required to determine whether such conditions are met.[1225] Such provision may provide that except as provided by the code, rights and obligations do not apply in relation to a service provider unless the number of copyright infringement reports the service provider receives within a particular period reaches a threshold set out in the code and that if the threshold is reached, rights or obligations apply with effect from the date when it is reached or from a later time.[1226] The Government's intention was that the initial obligations would fall on all service providers except those which were demonstrated to have a very low level of online infringement (in respect of which it was considered that the costs of compliance would be disproportionate to the end to be achieved). The Government anticipated that most small- and medium-sized service providers and possibly the mobile networks would fall under the threshold. Exemption would be subject to continual review. Once a service provider had crossed the threshold, it would remain subject to the initial obligations.[1227]

Infringement thresholds: the draft code. OFCOM decided not to introduce thresholds based on the number of reports for the simple reason that no reports had been issued to date and accordingly OFCOM was unable to set a threshold based on reports which was objectively justifiable, non-discriminatory and proportionate.[1228] However, OFCOM have a more general power under the Act to make "other provision for the purpose of regulating the initial obligations".[1229] OFCOM consider that in circumstances where it is not possible to determine an appropriate threshold based on the number of reports, they may set a threshold based on other criteria.[1230] **21–316**

The draft code: exclusion of mobile service providers. Pursuant to this provision, OFCOM have decided to exclude mobile service providers altogether. This is for two reasons. First, mobile networks are technically less conducive to online infringement.[1231] Second, because of the way mobile operators assign public IP addresses, an IP address identified as related to copyright infringement may be in use by multiple individual mobile subscribers at the time of the alleged infringement.[1232] Accordingly, the draft code only applies to service providers which provide a "fixed internet access service",[1233] which means "an internet access service provided from one or more fixed locations and, for the avoidance of doubt, does not include an internet access service provided by means of a licensed mobile network".[1234] A service provider which provides both a fixed service and a service by other means is only subject to the draft code where a copyright infringement report received by it relates to a subscriber receiving a fixed service.[1235] **21–317**

[1225] s.124C(3)(a).

[1226] s.124C(5).

[1227] Digital Economy Act 2010, Explanatory Notes para.51.

[1228] Introduction to draft code, para.3.8. The requirements of objective justification etc. are imposed by Communications Act 2003 s.124E(1)(i) to (k). Codes must also be transparent: s.124E(1)(l).

[1229] s.124D(5)(h).

[1230] Introduction to draft code, para.3.9.

[1231] Introduction to draft code, para.3.11, referring to recent evidence that more than 95% of infringements took place on fixed networks. During the parliamentary debates the Government expressed the view that file sharing on mobile networks was not as yet a significant problem: *Hansard* H.L. Vol. 716 Col. 448.

[1232] para.3.12.

[1233] para.2.4.

[1234] para.1.

[1235] para.2.6. Presumably what is meant is that the code only applies where the material in question has been made available using a fixed internet service.

The draft code makes clear that the criteria for inclusion of service providers will be kept under review.[1236]

21–318   **The draft code: subscriber threshold.** Also under their general power to make provision for regulating the initial obligations, OFCOM have decided to exclude fixed service providers with 400,000 or fewer subscribers from the initial obligations.[1237] Their reasons for this include the fact that even if this exclusion is applied, the seven service providers who (at the time of publication of the draft code) provide 96.5 per cent of the residential and SME business broadband market would be covered by the code[1238] and that the result is consistent with the Government's expectation that most small and medium-sized service providers would be excluded.[1239] Again, this criterion will be kept under review, and will be altered if there is widespread evasion by infringers migrating to providers who are not covered.[1240]

21–319   **The draft code: quality assurance.** Before issuing its first notification and annually thereafter each service provider covered by the code will be obliged to provide OFCOM with a quality assurance report.[1241] The report will have to detail the processes and systems used to match information provided in copyright infringement reports to subscriber accounts; certify that the provider has done what is reasonably practical to ensure that such processes and systems are robust and accurate; detail steps taken to ensure the integrity and accuracy of such processes; detail the processes the provider has put in place to audit its systems; identify any examples of quality assurance issues which have occurred during the year and the measures taken to resolve them; provide a statement of compliance with relevant data protection laws; and include any other information as directed by OFCOM.[1242] Providers must also make such changes to their processes and systems as are directed by OFCOM, which may require the provider's processes and systems to be audited by an independent third party.[1243] Finally, the draft code provides that the provider must comply with the procedures set out in such documentation.[1244]

(d)   *Content of the initial obligations: general*

21–320   The initial obligations are set out in ss.124A and 124B of the 2003 Act.[1245] In summary, once an initial obligations code is in place, an internet service provider who has received a report from a copyright owner or his agent that a subscriber or someone whom a subscriber has allowed to use his service has infringed the owner's copyright, the provider will be obliged to notify the subscriber in question. The notification will include explanatory material about copyright infringement. The hope is that the subscriber will thus be deterred from infringing further or will take the steps necessary to prevent the account from being used by others to infringe. On request from a copyright owner (or agent), a provider must supply the owner with a list of infringements reported against accounts used for more persistent infringement. The list will not disclose the ac-

---

[1236] para.2.7.
[1237] Draft code para.2.4.2.
[1238] Introduction to draft code para.3.15.1.
[1239] Introduction to draft code para.3.15.
[1240] Draft code para.2.7. Introduction to draft code paras 3.16 to 3.18.
[1241] For OFCOM's thinking about such reports, see the introduction to the draft code paras 5.6 to 5.8.
[1242] para.4.5.
[1243] para.4.6.
[1244] para.4.7.
[1245] See s.124C(1).

count holder's identity. The owner will then be able to apply to the court for an order disclosing that identity as a prelude to legal action. It is considered that this will enable copyright owners to concentrate their attention on the most persistent infringers.

(e) *Copyright infringement reports*

When a copyright infringement report may be made. Subject to compliance with the preconditions set out above,[1246] and provided an initial obligations code is in force, a copyright owner or his agent may make a report if it "appears" to him that a subscriber has infringed the owner's copyright by means of the service or that another person whom the subscriber has allowed to use the service has so infringed.[1247] The terms of the draft code in relation to quality assurance[1248] and the contents of reports[1249] together with the requirement that in the event of an appeal the burden will be on the maker of the report to establish that there has been an infringement[1250] suggest that it would be unwise to base a report on anything other than a firm evidential foundation. The word "allowed" is not defined. It is presumably intended to cover a spectrum from express permission to someone who leaves a Wi-Fi network unsecured. In this context it should be noted that an appeal against a report will succeed where a subscriber shows that he or she took reasonable steps to prevent others infringing copyright by means of the internet access service.[1251]

21–321

Content of copyright infringement reports: the Act. A copyright infringement report is defined as a report which states that there appears to have been an infringement of the owner's copyright, includes a description of the apparent infringement, includes evidence of the apparent infringement that shows the subscriber's IP address and the time at which the evidence was gathered and complies with any other requirement of the initial obligations code.[1252] The code must specify requirements as to the means of obtaining evidence of infringement of copyright for inclusion in a report, the standard of evidence that must be included and the form of the report.[1253]

21–322

Content of copyright infringement reports: the draft code. The report must be in the maker's standard form[1254] and must comply with any directions OFCOM may give from time to time.[1255] The draft code requires it to contain the following information[1256]: the maker's name and registered[1257] address; where relevant, the name and registered[1258] address of the actual copyright owner, together with evidence of authorisation; an identification of the relevant work in which UK copyright is said to subsist, including its title and a description of its nature; a statement that there appears to have been an infringement of the copyright owner's

21–323

[1246] paras 21–307 to 21–309.
[1247] s.124A(1)(a) and (b). Draft Code para.3.1.
[1248] See para.21–309, above.
[1249] See para.21–323, below.
[1250] Discussed further at para.21–346, below.
[1251] s.124K(6)(b).
[1252] Communications Act 2003 s.124A(3)(a) to (c) and (e).
[1253] Communications Act 2003 s.124E(2).
[1254] Draft code para.3.4.
[1255] para.3.4. OFCOM believe that there are costs benefits in having a standard form for reports. They propose that industry pursue agreement on the format in the first instance. In default of agreement they may impose one: Introduction to draft code para.4.9.
[1256] paras 3.3(a) to (k).
[1257] It is not clear what the term "registered" means so far as concerns individuals.
[1258] See previous footnote.

copyright in the work; a description of the apparent infringement, including the filename, a description of the content of the file and (where appropriate) the hash code[1259] of the infringing content; a statement that to the best of the maker's knowledge, no consent has been given; the date and time on which the evidence was gathered[1260]; the IP address associated with the apparent infringement; the port number used; the website or protocol via which the apparent infringement occurred; a "unique infringement identifier" allocated by the maker; and the date and time of issue of the report. According to OFCOM this formidable list is based on information currently produced by agents working on behalf of copyright owners and is believed to match the standard of evidence required by the courts in relation to civil proceedings for copyright infringement.[1261]

21–324   **Retention of evidence.** The draft code requires the maker of the report to retain any evidence which is additional to that which supports the contents of the report and on which it may seek to rely in the event of a subscriber appeal.[1262] This evidence must be made available to a subscriber on request in an electronic format free of charge and within 10 working days of a request for it being received.[1263]

21–325   **Timing and delivery of copyright infringement reports.** The 2003 Act provides that a report must be sent within the period of one month beginning with the day on which the evidence was gathered.[1264] However, this was intended to be an "outer limit"[1265] and the draft code reduces the period to 10 working days.[1266] This is because in OFCOM's view the longer the period between evidence being gathered and subscribers receiving a notification the less effective the notifications programme will be.[1267] The draft code provides that reports "will" be sent by electronic means in a standardised format.[1268]

21–326   **Service provider's obligations on receipt of a report.** The draft code provides that on receipt of a report the service provider must acknowledge receipt to the maker and that this may be by automated response.[1269] As soon as practically possible and in any event within 10 working days of receipt of a report the service provider must notify the maker of the report if the information contained in it does not relate to one of its subscribers, the report does not comply with the requirements of the code or there are grounds for not processing the report.[1270] The grounds for not processing the report (which must be stated in the notice)[1271] include the following: the IP address was not allocated to the service provider at the time of the alleged infringement; the IP address was not used by one of the service provider's subscribers at the relevant time; the subscriber using the IP address at the relevant time cannot reliably be identified; the report refers to an account which is no longer active; the service provider does not hold an electronic

---

[1259] Described by OFCOM as "a unique identifier, attached to a digital content file. A hash code is created when a digital content file is created and new hash code is allocated if the content file is edited or modified. Hash code matching can also be used as part of the process of verifying the identify of a content asset": Introduction to the draft code para.4.3 note 12.

[1260] This is to be done using Universal Coordinated Time and must include both the start time and end time of the session.

[1261] Introduction to the draft code para.4.3.

[1262] para.3.9.

[1263] para.3.9.

[1264] s.124A(3)(d).

[1265] See para.50 of the Explanatory Notes to the Digital Economy Act.

[1266] para.3.2. Presumably it is thought that this requirement may be imposed under s.124D(5)(h).

[1267] Introduction to draft code para.4.7.

[1268] para.3.8.

[1269] para.4.1.

[1270] para.4.2.

[1271] para.4.4.

or postal address for the subscriber and it is not reasonably practicable for the service provider to obtain this information; the IP address relates to a subscriber who does not receive a fixed internet access service from the service provider; there is some other reason why, in the service provider's reasonable opinion, the report should not be processed.[1272] The draft code provides that if a rejection notice has been sent, the provider is not obliged to send a notification relating to the report.[1273] OFCOM have proposed the agreement of a standard set of rejection codes.[1274]

No scope for inaccuracy. The draft code emphasises that any failure by the maker of a report to comply with the obligations set out in the code in respect of the issue of a report will render the report invalid and that the service provider will not be subject to the requirements of the code in relation to the report.[1275] On the face of it, it seems that any non-compliance, however small, will invalidate the report. Moreover, as is made clear in the previous paragraph, there is no obligation on a service provider to notify the maker of the report that it is being rejected in sufficient time to enable any defects to be remedied. On the face of it therefore copyright owners and their agents must get it exactly right first time. However, as discussed below[1276] the draft code may provide scope for curing such defects on appeal.

21–327

(f) Notification and copyright infringement lists

Notification: the 2003 Act. The Act provides that a service provider which has received a copyright infringement report must notify[1277] the subscriber of the report within one month of its receipt if the initial obligations code requires it to do so.[1278] The Act requires the initial obligations code to specify the following in relation to a subscriber in relation to whom the provider receives one or more reports: requirements as to the means by which the provider identifies the subscriber; which of the reports the provider must notify the subscriber of; and requirements as to the form, contents and means of notification in each case.[1279]

21–328

Notification: overall approach of the draft code. The draft code's overall approach must be seen in the context of the other initial obligation imposed on internet service providers, which is the provision of copyright infringement lists. The 2003 Act obliges providers to supply copyright owners or their agents on request with anonymised lists of infringements carried out by means of accounts in respect of which a threshold set by the code has been reached.[1280] This threshold may be set by reference to any matter, including one or more of: the number of reports, the time within which the reports are made and the time of the apparent infringement to which they relate.[1281] However, the threshold must operate in such a way that a report received more than 12 months before a particular date

21–329

[1272] para.4.3. Other grounds for not processing a report might include that it was issued too late or is incomplete or that the maker has not paid the service provider in accordance with the requirements of the costs order: Introduction to draft code, para.5.4.
[1273] Draft code, para.5.3.
[1274] Introduction to draft code para.5.5.
[1275] para.2.3.
[1276] para.21–350.
[1277] That is, send a notification to the electronic or postal address held by the provider for the subscriber: s.124A(9). It is expressly provided that the special notification provisions contained in ss.394 to 396 of the 2003 Act do not apply.
[1278] s.124A(4), (5).
[1279] s.124E(3).
[1280] Pursuant to s.124E(1)(c).
[1281] s.124E(5).

does not affect whether the threshold is met on that date.[1282] OFCOM have concluded that the Act describes a notification process that involves an escalation leading to the provider putting the subscriber on a copyright infringement list.[1283] Strictly speaking, that is not correct. There is no obligation on the provider to "put" a subscriber on to a list: the obligation is to supply the owner or agent with a list if asked. Moreover, the Act envisages that the threshold for supplying a list will be defined by reference to the number and timing of reports or infringements rather than the number of notifications.[1284] Nevertheless, the Government's clearly expressed intention during the passage of the Bill was that subscribers should receive a number of warnings before being placed on a "serious infringer list".[1285]

21–330   **Copyright infringement lists: the threshold.** OFCOM considered three main options for "escalation": by reference to the volume of reports,[1286] to the subscriber's behaviour over time and to the value of infringements (some infringements being more serious than others).[1287] Ultimately, OFCOM decided to adopt a time-based process, on the grounds that[1288]: it would be relatively straightforward and pragmatic to implement; it would be consistent with the objective of the legislation (allowing time for the subscriber to come into compliance); it would avoid disputes over subjective evaluations of the value of copyright infringements; it would ensure that each report counted; and it would allow for the fact that different types of content might have different patterns of copyright infringement. Accordingly, the draft code requires providers to maintain a database of subscribers who have received a third notification in the past 12 months.[1289] It is only if a subscriber is on such a database that the provider is obliged to provide a copyright infringement list.[1290]

21–331   **Does the threshold comply with the Act?** The Act expressly requires the provision of copyright infringement lists once *copyright infringement reports* have reached the threshold set by the code.[1291] However, the threshold in the draft code is based on the number of *notifications*. This means that many reports will not in fact count because they will have been submitted during periods (such as the calendar month after the first report) when they do not trigger a notification.[1292] No doubt this approach can be justified on the basis that reports which do not count do not count for a good reason, namely that they concern infringements which took place during a period when the subscriber was supposed to be coming into compliance. An additional problem with the draft code is that the Act requires the provision of a list to a copyright owner (or his agent) when reports *made by that owner (or agent)* in relation to the subscriber have reached the threshold.[1293] Yet a copyright owner (or agent) will be entitled to a list as soon as a third

---

[1282] s.124E(6).
[1283] Introduction to draft code, para.5.9.
[1284] See s.124B(3) and 124E(5). See also per Lord Young of Norwood Green HL Vol. 716 Col. 467: "we would expect the threshold to be based on the number of CIRs received over a period of time".
[1285] BIS/DCMS *Outline of Initial Obligations Code*, January 2010 paras 2(b) and 3(a).
[1286] As envisaged in the BIS/DCMS *Outline of Initial Obligations Code*, January 2010 paras 2(b) and 3(c).
[1287] Introduction to draft code para.5.10. Infringements in relation to pre-release material or a major software release might be more serious: ibid.
[1288] Introduction to draft code, para.5.13.
[1289] para.6.1.
[1290] para.6.4.
[1291] Communications Act 2003 s.124B(3).
[1292] For which reports will and will not trigger a notification, see para.21–334, below.
[1293] s.124B(3).

notification has been sent even if the list only refers to a single report from that owner or agent.[1294]

Obligatory contents of notification: the 2003 Act. The Act lists what must be included in a notification, which is as follows: a statement that the notification is sent under s.124A in response to a copyright infringement report; the name of the maker of the report; a description of the apparent infringement; evidence of the apparent infringement showing the subscriber's IP address and the time the evidence was gathered; information about subscriber appeals and the grounds on which they may be made; information about copyright and its purpose; advice (or information enabling the subscriber to obtain advice) about how to obtain lawful access to copyright works; advice appropriate to the subscriber[1295] or information enabling the subscriber to obtain advice about the steps the subscriber may take to protect an internet access service from unauthorised use; and anything else required by the initial obligations code.[1296]   **21–332**

Discretionary contents of notification: the 2003 Act. The Act expressly lists the things which the code may additionally require notices to include. They are as follows: a statement that information about the apparent infringement may be kept by the provider; a statement that the maker of the report[1297] may require the provider to disclose which reports made by the maker to the provider relate to the subscriber; a statement that following such disclosure the copyright owner[1298] may apply to court to learn the subscriber's identity and bring proceedings for infringement; and where the requirement to send the notification arises partly because of a report which has previously been notified, a statement that the number of reports relating to the subscriber may be taken into account for the purposes of any technical measures.[1299]   **21–333**

Notification: timing and mechanics. The draft code provides for the sending of a first, second and third notification followed by an update notification. The structure is as follows. The first copyright infringement report will trigger a first notification, which may be sent electronically or by post.[1300] If a further report is received more than one calendar month but less than six months after the first notification,[1301] this will trigger a second notification, which again may be sent electronically or by post.[1302] It should be noted that it is not necessary that the further report should be received from the same owner or agent as the first one.[1303] If a further report is received more than one calendar month after the posting[1304] of the second notification but not more than 12 months after the receipt of the report which triggered the first notification, this will trigger a third notification which   **21–334**

[1294] Draft code paras 6.3 and 6.4.

[1295] s.124A(7).

[1296] s.124A(6).

[1297] The expression "the copyright owner" is used. Where an agent has made a report, this expression may be construed to extend to the actual copyright owner.

[1298] Again, the expression "the copyright owner" is used. Presumably here it cannot refer to an agent because such an agent would not necessarily have standing to bring proceedings for infringement.

[1299] s.124A(8). For "technical measures", see paras 21–353 et seq., below.

[1300] Draft code, para.5.5.

[1301] The purpose of waiting a month is to allow the subscriber to stop infringing or to take steps to prevent infringement, e.g. by securing a wireless connection or adding parental controls: BIS/DCMS *Outline of Initial Obligations Code*, January 2010 para.2(b).

[1302] Draft code, para.5.6.

[1303] Draft code para.5.6.2.

[1304] Sic. This presumably should read "sending".

must be sent by recorded delivery.[1305] Again, it is not necessary that the further report should be received from the same owner or agent as either of the previous reports.[1306] At this point, the subscriber must be placed on the copyright infringement list.[1307] Once a subscriber is on a list, any further reports will trigger update notifications (which may be sent electronically or by post) no more than once every three calendar months.[1308] Each notification must be sent within 10 working days beginning on the date the provider receives the report.[1309]

21–335   **Content of all notifications.** The draft code requires all notifications to include all the matters they are required by the Act to include.[1310] It also requires them to include all the matters which the Act expressly gives OFCOM a discretion to require them to include.[1311] In addition, the draft code requires all notifications to include the following[1312]: the registered address of the actual copyright owner and (where relevant) his agent, together (where relevant) with evidence of the agent's authorisation; a statement that providers must hold other reports associated with the subscriber and that these are available on request; details of the start and end time of the period during which evidence of infringement was gathered; a statement that the IP address allocated to the subscriber has been identified as being used for online infringement; a statement that the subscriber has a right under data protection legislation to any information, including copyright infringement reports, held on him or her; a statement that the provider will so far as reasonably practicable destroy information it holds in relation to the notification 12 months after receipt; and a note of the copyright owner's statement that no express or implied licence has been granted and of the ability of the owner to bring a legal action for damages in relation to the infringement.[1313]

21–336   **Additional content of notifications.** Each type of notification is required to contain additional material appropriate to the stage at which it is made. The first notification must state that information about further reported infringements will also be retained for 12 months from receipt, that such information may lead to further notifications and potentially legal action and that such information is available from the provider on request.[1314] The second notification must state that it is the second notification in the last six months; that a further notification within 12 months of the first will result in the disclosure at the request of a copyright owner or his agent in anonymised form of the content of reports made by that owner or agent; and that such material may be used to obtain a court order for disclosure of the subscriber's identity with a view to proceedings.[1315] The third notification must state that it is the third notification in the last 12 months and will result in the disclosure at the request of a copyright owner or his agent in anonymised form of the content of reports made by that owner or agent, which mate-

---

[1305] Draft code, paras 5.7 and 5.8. The notice need not be sent by recorded delivery if the provider does not have and cannot reasonably obtain the subscriber's postal address.

[1306] Draft code para.5.7.2.

[1307] Draft code para.6.1. See below para.21–338.

[1308] Draft code para.5.9.

[1309] Draft code para.5.4. This period represents a reduction of the "outer limit" of one month set by s.124A(5) of the Act: see para.50 of the Explanatory Notes to the Digital Economy Act 2010.

[1310] See para.21–332, above.

[1311] Introduction to the draft code, para.5.17. For the discretionary matters, see para.21–333, above.

[1312] Draft code, paras 5.17 to 5.19.

[1313] No mention is made of an injunction.

[1314] Draft code, para.5.13. The Government envisages that the first notification will be "expressed in sympathetic terms. ... We expect that the approach will be one of concern for the individual who has carried out an infringement": see per Lord Davies of Oldham during the second reading: Hansard Vol. 715 Col. 794.

[1315] Draft code para.5.14.

rial may be used to obtain a court order for disclosure of the subscriber's identity with a view to proceedings.[1316] The update notification must state that it is an update notification sent as a result of reports being received in the period since the previous notification and give the same information about disclosure and proceedings as the third notification.[1317] OFCOM have provided illustrative draft notifications[1318] and are considering the possibility of imposing a standard approach to notifications.[1319]

Retention of records by service providers. The Act requires the code to contain provision about how providers are to keep information about subscribers and to limit the time for which they may keep the information.[1320] The draft code provides that unless a rejection notice has been sent, the service provider must keep for 12 months after receipt of a report a record of it and its contents and a record of any notification sent, including the identity of the subscriber and the date.[1321] As far as reasonably practicable the provider must retain this information for no longer than 12 months.[1322] When it deletes such a record in relation to a third notification, the provider must also delete the information from the database of subscribers who have received a third notification.[1323] **21–337**

Copyright infringement lists: the 2003 Act. The Act requires a provider to supply a copyright owner or his agent with a copyright infringement list for a period if the owner requests the list for that period and the code requires it.[1324] A copyright infringement list is a list which sets out in relation to each "relevant subscriber" (but in anonymised form) which of the copyright infringement reports made by the owner or agent to the provider relate to the subscriber.[1325] A subscriber is a "relevant subscriber" if copyright infringement reports made by the owner (or agent) to the provider in relation to that subscriber have reached the threshold set out in the code.[1326] **21–338**

Copyright infringement lists: practical considerations. It is clear that a subscriber may be placed on a copyright infringement list even though he or she has not personally committed an act of copyright infringement: it is sufficient that others have used his or her service to infringe and the subscriber has not appealed the resulting reports. Even if the subscriber appeals, then provided the act of infringement is shown to have occurred by means of the subscriber's service, the appeal will not succeed unless the subscriber shows both that he or she did not commit the infringement and that he or she took reasonable steps to prevent the use of the service for infringement. It follows that a subscriber may be placed on a list even though he or she has merely facilitated infringements, and has not therefore committed an actionable wrong. Since being placed on a copyright infringement list may result in legal action, the threat of being placed on one may well have a deterrent effect on those who facilitate infringement in this way. On the other hand, copyright owners will not be able to assume that all those on a copyright infringement list are in fact liable for copyright infringement. **21–339**

[1316] Draft code para.5.15.
[1317] Draft code para.5.16.
[1318] Annex 6 to the draft code.
[1319] Introduction to draft code, para.5.24.
[1320] s.124E(1)(d) and (e).
[1321] Draft code para.5.1.
[1322] Draft code para.5.2.
[1323] para.6.1. For this database, see para.21–340, below.
[1324] s.124B(1).
[1325] s.124B(2).
[1326] s.124B(3).

21–340 **Copyright infringement lists: procedure in the draft code.** On request by an owner or agent,[1327] the provider must supply[1328] a copyright infringement list for a period of time specified by the owner or agent, which may be up to a maximum of 12 months prior to the date of the request.[1329] Only one request may be made every three months.[1330] A copyright infringement list is a list setting out which of the copyright infringement reports made by the owner or agent relate to a subscriber in respect of whom the owner or agent has made at least one report during the 12 months prior to the request.[1331] The list must be supplied within five days of the request.[1332] A subscriber is entitled at any time to request information about alleged infringements relating to their account in accordance with applicable laws and regulations, including the Data Protection Act.[1333] Two observations may be made. First, depending on the dates of any copyright infringement reports, it is possible that if the owner or agent specifies a period of less than 12 months, he may receive a list but it will be empty. Second, even if the owner or agent specifies a period of 12 months, it is possible that the list will only mention a single report (because the other notifications which have caused the threshold to be crossed relate to others' copyrights). It is not clear what (if anything) a copyright owner or agent will be able to conclude from such a list.

(g) *Subscriber appeals*

21–341 **General.** The 2003 Act requires the initial obligations code to confer on subscribers the right to appeal to an independent person identified by the code.[1334] The term "independent" means for practical purposes independent, so far as determining subscriber appeals is concerned, of providers, copyright owners and their agents and OFCOM.[1335] There is no right of a further appeal[1336] except presumably by way of judicial review.

21–342 **The appeals body.** The draft code states that OFCOM shall appoint an independent person ("the appeals body") to determine appeals.[1337] The appeals body is required to establish procedures ("appeal procedures") which are to be subject to OFCOM's approval.[1338] OFCOM is entitled to require the appeals body to provide it with such information as it considers necessary for carrying out its functions under the 2003 Act.[1339] The appeals body may request such information and as-

---

[1327] Who must of course be qualified to report, as to which see paras 21–307 to 21–309, above.
[1328] In electronic form if so requested: draft code para.6.5.
[1329] para.6.2.
[1330] para.6.6.
[1331] paras 6.3 and 6.4.
[1332] Draft code para.6.6.
[1333] Draft code para.6.7.
[1334] Communications Act 2003 s.124E(1)(h).
[1335] Communications Act 2003 s.124K(2)(c). For these purposes, providers, copyright owners and agents are not limited to those to whom the code applies: see s.124N. The phrase "for all practical purposes" was included because the appeals body will be funded by copyright owners and internet service providers: see the BIS document "Online Infringement of Copyright: Other issues covered by Government amendments tabled at report", February 2010. Presumably the term "so far as determining subscriber appeals is concerned" has been inserted because few people do not have a contract with an internet service provider and do not own some copyrights, however insignificant.
[1336] By contrast, any technical obligations code must provide a right of a further appeal to the First-tier Tribunal: see para.21–359, below. The Government's view was that in respect of the initial obligations a right of further appeal would be disproportionate: *Hansard* H.L. Vol. 716 Col. 1024.
[1337] para.7.1.
[1338] para.7.4.
[1339] para.7.5.

sistance from OFCOM as it considers appropriate.[1340] The appeals body and the provider to whom the appeal relates are obliged to ensure, to the greatest extent possible, that the appealing subscriber's identity is not disclosed, directly or indirectly, to the copyright owner or agent without the subscriber's express written consent.[1341] This requirement is not required by the 2003 Act but is consistent with the statutory requirement that a copyright infringement list must not enable the subscriber to be identified. However, in some instances the disclosure of the subscriber's identity to the rights holder may be thought necessary, for example to enable the rights holder to check the factual basis for the grounds of appeal or (in the case of a successful appeal) to enable the rights holder to discharge its liability for costs (although the latter could still be achieved anonymously).

Procedure for appealing. The draft code requires the appeal procedures to set out the form and service requirements of any necessary notices or other communications.[1342] The appeal procedures must include a standard form of appeal notice which enables the subscriber to set out in particular: details of the act or omission under appeal; the grounds of appeal; any steps taken by the subscriber to prevent others from infringing copyright by means of the relevant service; and such additional information as the appeals body considers appropriate. This must be supported by a statement of truth confirming that the information in the notice and any evidence submitted with it is true to the best of the subscriber's knowledge and belief.[1343] The appeal procedures must set out time limits for any notices or communications. Any such time limit may be extended by the appeals body where it considers it appropriate, taking into account all relevant circumstances.[1344] At the time of writing there is to be no fee for appealing but the Government may impose a fee if there is a significant number of vexatious appeals.[1345]   **21–343**

What may be appealed. In accordance with the 2003 Act,[1346] the draft code provides that an appeal may relate to a copyright infringement report, a notification, the inclusion or proposed inclusion of an entry on a copyright infringement list or any other act or omission under the code by a provider, copyright owner or agent.[1347]   **21–344**

Grounds of appeal.[1348] The draft code provides that the grounds of appeal may include the following: first, that the apparent infringement to which a copyright infringement report relates was not an infringement; second, that the report does not relate to the subscriber's IP address at the time of the apparent infringement; third, that the act constituting the apparent infringement was not done by the subscriber and the subscriber took reasonable steps to prevent other persons infringing copyright by means of his or her service[1349]; fourth, that an act or omission by a provider, owner or agent amounts to a contravention of the code or of an obliga-   **21–345**

[1340] para.7.6.
[1341] para.7.7.
[1342] para.7.8.
[1343] para.7.9. No provision is made as to the form of any evidence and there are no express sanctions for making a false statement of truth.
[1344] para.7.10.
[1345] *Online Infringement of Copyright (Initial Obligations) Cost Sharing HM Government Response* (BIS, September 2010) *http://www.bis.gov.uk/assets/biscore/business-sectors/docs/o/10–1131–online-copyright-infringement-government-response* [Accessed November 11, 2010].
[1346] s.123N.
[1347] para.7.11.
[1348] See Communications Act 2003 ss.124K(3)–(6).
[1349] Communications Act 2003 s.124K(6) provides that where the appeal is based on a contention that the act was not an infringement or does not relate to the subscriber's IP address, the appeal

tion regulated by it; fifth "any other ground on which a subscriber chooses to rely as to why the act or omission should not have occurred".[1350] These grounds are considered in turn.

21–346 **Not an infringement; wrong IP address.** The Act requires the code to provide that irrespective of the grounds raised by the subscriber the appeal must be allowed unless the owner, agent or provider shows that the act was an infringement and relates to the subscriber's address at the time of the infringement.[1351] Accordingly, pursuant to the draft code, the appeals body must be "satisfied that there is sufficient evidence to show" that there was an infringement and that the IP address was the subscriber's.[1352] Neither the Act nor the code specifies the applicable standard of proof, which is presumably on the balance of probabilities.[1353]

21–347 **Not the subscriber and reasonable steps taken.** Here, the burden of proof lies on the subscriber.[1354] Whether the subscriber did or did not do the act in question is a simple question of fact although the evidence may be complex. The question whether the subscriber took reasonable steps is less straightforward. The following points may tentatively be made. First, the requirement is not to have taken all reasonable steps. It follows that a subscriber will not be expected to have left no stone unturned. Second, the subscriber must show that he or she took steps to prevent other persons from infringing copyright by means of the service. It seems therefore that the enquiry is not limited to the steps (if any) taken in relation to the particular infringement. Third, the draft code (but not the Act) provides that the appeal body must take "due account" of the subscriber's technical knowledge and the extent to which he or she may have been aware of his or her ability to control access to the service.[1355] It follows that at least to this extent the subscriber's personal characteristics and circumstances are relevant. What is not clear is whether this is only the case in relation to the subscriber's state of mind or whether it goes further to include such considerations as (for example) the subscriber's ability in practice to control the actions of another family member. Finally, during the Parliamentary debates the Government stated its view that in a case where a connection had been hacked into, a subscriber who proved that he or she had complied with the security measures set out in a notification letter would be likely succeed on appeal.[1356]

21–348 **Contravention by owner, agent or provider.** It seems unlikely that this category will be much used, at least as a free-standing ground. However, it is conceivable that a breach of the code may cause damage and the appeals body will have the power to award compensation.[1357] This ground might also apply where some part of the investigative process had involved the commission of an unlawful act by or on behalf of a copyright owner or agent.

---

must be allowed if the subscriber shows that he did not do the act and took reasonable steps to prevent others using his service to infringe. This apparent non sequitur is avoided in the draft code by making the latter grounds freestanding.

[1350] para.7.12.

[1351] Communications Act 2003 s.124K(5); draft code para.7.23. This is the case in relation to any copyright infringement report to which the appeal relates and to any copyright infringement report "by reference to which anything to which the appeal relates was done".

[1352] para.7.23.

[1353] See below for the provisions of the draft code in relation to evidence.

[1354] Communications Act 2003 s.124K(6); draft code para.7.24.

[1355] para.7.21. Clearly any notifications will have a critical role to play.

[1356] *Hansard* H.L. Vol. 716 Cols 859, 1031 and 1336; Vol. 717 Col. 1304.

[1357] Draft code para.7.27.2.

Any other ground as to why the act or omission should not have occurred.   **21–349**
The nature of this ground of appeal, which is not derived from the Act, is obscure.
The "act or omission" referred to appears to be an act or omission of the owner,
agent or provider. The expression "should not have occurred" is presumably
intended to introduce a requirement of breach of duty (contractual or otherwise)
but is expressed in the vaguest of terms. Presumably this ground would cover
cases in which evidence of infringement had been gathered unlawfully.

Submissions and evidence. Within five days of receiving an appeal, the appeals   **21–350**
body must send a copy to the provider or to any relevant owner or agent (in the
latter case ensuring the subscriber's anonymity) or to both provider and owner or
agent.[1358] Where appropriate, the provider or copyright owner or agent must be
given the opportunity to make "written submissions" on the grounds of appeal.[1359]
The draft code goes on to provide that an owner, agent or provider may be invited
to make "additional submissions".[1360] The circumstances in which such additional
submissions may be invited are not explained but they are to be made with the
written submissions.[1361] Specific provision is made as to the content of the information or evidence which the additional submissions may comprise. If the information or evidence is sought from an owner or agent it may include the following[1362]: evidence of subsistence, title, infringement and absence of licence; where
relevant, evidence of an agent's authority; reasons why this information or evidence was not included in the copyright infringement report[1363]; and any additional information which may be specified in the appeal procedures. If additional submissions are sought from the provider, they may include information
or evidence as to the measures taken by the provider to determine that the report
related to an IP address used by the subscriber at the time of the alleged infringement, together with any additional information which may be specified in the appeal procedures.[1364] In all cases the information or evidence must include a statement sworn by an authorised individual confirming that the information is true to
the best of his or her knowledge or belief.[1365] If the appeals body decides to take
additional submissions into account it must afford the subscriber the opportunity
to make additional written submissions in response.[1366] As well as inviting additional submissions, the appeals body may require an owner, agent or provider
to supply such information as it may require for the purposes of determining the
appeal.[1367] The code provides that oral submissions and hearings will only occur
in exceptional circumstances.[1368]

Determination of appeals. In accordance with the 2003 Act,[1369] the draft code   **21–351**
provides that an appeal may only be rejected if the appeals body is satisfied as
respects any relevant copyright infringement report that the apparent infringe-

---

[1358] Draft code para.7.13.
[1359] Draft code para.7.14.
[1360] paras 7.15 and 7.16.
[1361] See previous footnote.
[1362] Draft code para.7.15.
[1363] This is a curious provision. The code does not require copyright infringement reports to contain
"evidence". As to "information", the absence of crucial information of this type ought presumably to have resulted in the rejection of the report by the provider. It seems therefore that the
purpose of this provision may be to enable an owner or agent to validate a defective report which
has been wrongly acted upon by the provider. There is no such provision in the Act and it would
be surprising if there were: it is bound to act as a disincentive to proper compliance with the code.
[1364] Draft code para.7.16.
[1365] Draft code paras 7.15 and 7.16. Presumably this "statement", being required to be "sworn", must
be either an affidavit or a statutory declaration.
[1366] Draft code para.7.18.
[1367] Draft code para.7.17.
[1368] Draft code para.7.19.
[1369] s.124K(5).

ment was an infringement of copyright and that the report relates to the subscriber's IP address at the time of that infringement.[1370] The draft code goes on to provide that irrespective of the grounds of the appeal, it must be upheld if the appeals body is satisfied that the subscriber has shown that in relation to a relevant copyright infringement report the act constituting the apparent infringement was not done by the subscriber and the subscriber took reasonable steps to prevent others infringing copyright by means of the service.[1371] The determination must be in writing and contain reasons.[1372] It must be sent to the subscriber, owner or agent and provider in accordance with the appeal procedures, subject to the requirement that the subscriber's identity must not be disclosed to the owner or agent.[1373]

21–352   **Remedies.** The 2003 Act requires the code to confer a number of powers on the appeals body. These are set out almost verbatim in the draft code. The first is a power to secure as far as practicable that a subscriber is not prejudiced for the purposes of the Act by an act or omission in respect of which an appeal is determined in his favour.[1374] The obvious application of this power would be to direct that a groundless copyright infringement report must be disregarded for the purposes of a copyright infringement list. Second, the power to award compensation to be paid by an owner or agent or a provider to a subscriber affected by such an act or omission.[1375] Third, to direct the owner, agent or provider to reimburse the subscriber's reasonable costs.[1376] This last power must be exercised in favour of a subscriber whose appeal succeeds unless the appeals body is satisfied that it would be unjust to exercise it having regard to all the circumstances, including the parties' conduct before and during the proceedings.[1377]

(iii) Technical obligations

(a) *Introduction and definitions*

21–353   **Overview.** The Government's aim is for the initial obligations to effect a significant reduction in the amount of online infringement by file sharing. In case that does not occur, the Act gives the Secretary of State powers to introduce further "technical" obligations.[1378] In summary, the technical obligations will require providers to reduce, limit or suspend access to the internet for subscribers who have been placed on a copyright infringement list. Such measures are intended to be "exceptional and a last resort", directed only at the most serious infringers.[1379]

21–354   **Definitions.** A "technical obligation" in relation to a provider is an obligation to take a technical measure against some or all "relevant subscribers" for the

---

[1370] para.7.23.
[1371] As has already been mentioned, s.124K(6) provides that if a subscriber proves these matters the appeal must be allowed where the grounds are that there was no infringement or the address was not the subscriber's. This extends this provision to appeals on all grounds.
[1372] Draft code para.7.25.
[1373] Draft code para.7.26.
[1374] s.124K(7)(a); draft code para.7.27.1.
[1375] s.124K(7)(b); draft code para.7.27.2. Compensation is to be payable within the time indicated by the appeals body: draft code para.7.28.
[1376] s.124K(7)(c); draft code, para.7.27.3. How these are to be assessed is not made clear.
[1377] s.124K(8); draft code para.7.28.
[1378] Explanatory Notes para.62.
[1379] Lord Mandelson, during the second reading of the Digital Economy Bill, *Hansard* H.L. Vol. 715 Col. 745. Note, however, that a person may potentially become subject to technical measures once a single provider has received three reports in respect of his or her account over a twelve month period and (as is made clear above), he or she may not have infringed at all.

purposes of preventing or reducing infringement by means of the internet.[1380] A "relevant subscriber" is a subscriber in respect of whom the threshold for being placed on a copyright infringement list has been crossed.[1381] A "technical measure" is a measure that limits the speed or other capacity of the service provided to a subscriber, prevents a subscriber from using the service to gain access to particular material or limits such use, suspends the service provided to the subscriber or limits the service provided to the subscriber in another way.[1382] Permanent disconnection is not a possibility, but there is no limit on the length of period a suspension may last.

(b) *Implementation*

OFCOM's reporting, assessment and preparation duties. In order to enable the Government to monitor the effectiveness of the initial obligations, the 2003 Act obliges OFCOM to prepare and publish[1383] reports for the Secretary of State about the infringement of copyright by subscribers to internet access services.[1384] The reports are intended to provide a source of information for the Secretary of State to take into account when taking decisions as to whether to impose technical obligations on providers. In addition, the 2003 Act empowers the Secretary of State to direct[1385] OFCOM to assess whether one or more technical obligations should be imposed, to take steps to prepare for such obligations and to provide and publish[1386] a report on the assessment or steps to the Secretary of State.[1387] Providers and copyright owners and their agents are obliged to give OFCOM any assistance which they reasonably require for the purposes of complying with such a direction.[1388]

21–355

Criteria for and timing of imposition of technical obligations. The Act provides that the Secretary of State may by order[1389] impose a technical obligation on providers if OFCOM have assessed whether technical obligations should be imposed and taking into account that assessment, reports prepared by OFCOM and any other matter which appears to the Secretary of State to be relevant, he or she considers it appropriate to make the order.[1390] Consistently with the Government's stated hope that the initial obligations will be sufficient to produce a substantial reduction in infringement, no order may be made within the period of 12 months beginning with the first day on which there is an initial obligations code in force.[1391] It seems likely therefore that no such order will be made before April 8, 2012.[1392]

21–356

Content of order imposing technical obligations. The Act provides that the order must specify the date from which the technical obligation is to have effect or

21–357

[1380] s.124G(2).
[1381] s.124G(4).
[1382] s.124G(3).
[1383] OFCOM may however exclude from the published version information which OFCOM could refuse to disclose under the Freedom of Information Act 2000.
[1384] Communications Act 2003 s.124F.
[1385] Any direction must be laid before Parliament: s.124G(7).
[1386] s.124G(8). Again, OFCOM may exclude from the published version information which they could refuse to disclose under the Freedom of Information Act 2000: s.124G(9).
[1387] s.124G(1). For the details of the assessment and steps, see s.124G(5).
[1388] s.124G(6).
[1389] Made pursuant to a procedure analogous to the "super-affirmative resolution procedure": see s.124H(5)–(10).
[1390] s.124H(1).
[1391] s.124H(2).
[1392] See para.21–302, above.

provide for that date to be specified.[1393] The order may also specify the criteria for taking the technical measure concerned against a subscriber together with the steps to be taken as part of the measure and when they are to be taken.[1394] No doubt if these matters are not specified they will be stated in the technical obligations code.[1395]

21–358   **The technical obligations code.** As was the case in relation to the initial obligations, the Act leaves much of the detail to be fleshed out by a code of practice. In this instance, however, there is no provision for OFCOM to approve a voluntary code: rather, OFCOM are obliged to make one.[1396] As was the case in respect of the initial obligations, the code may: specify conditions which must be met for rights and obligations under it to apply; require owners, their agents and providers to provide information and assistance; confer extensive powers on OFCOM themselves; and make other provision for the purpose of regulating the technical obligations.[1397] Again, the code must satisfy numerous requirements in relation to enforcement, subscriber appeals, contributions to costs, objective justification, non-discrimination, proportionality and transparency.[1398]

(c) *Subscriber appeals*

21–359   **The right to appeal.** The provisions in the 2003 Act concerning subscriber appeals[1399] are equally applicable to the technical obligations. However, in the case of technical obligations, the subscriber's position is to be stronger in two respects. First, the subscriber is to have a further right of appeal to the First-tier Tribunal,[1400] including on grounds that the subscriber appeal was based on an error of fact, wrong in law or unreasonable.[1401] Second, the code must secure that unless the subscriber waives the right to appeal, a technical measure is not taken against a subscriber until the period for bringing an appeal or further appeal has ended and any appeal or further appeal has been disposed of.[1402]

21–360   **Determination of appeals.** The 2003 Act makes specific provision as to the determination of appeals in relation to technical measures or proposed technical measures. The person determining the appeal must have the power to confirm the measure, to require the measure not to be taken or withdrawn or to substitute any other measure that the provider has power to take.[1403] The powers to order the measure not to be taken or withdrawn and the power to substitute another measure may both be exercised even if the appeal is not upheld, but only in exceptional circumstances.[1404] The person determining the appeal must also have the power to take any steps OFCOM could take in relation to the act or omission giving rise to the technical measure and to remit the decision whether to confirm the technical measure or any matter relating to that decision to OFCOM.[1405]

[1393] s.124H(3).
[1394] s.124H(4).
[1395] See next paragraph.
[1396] s.124I(1). The code must be made by order subject to annulment in pursuance of a resolution of either House of Parliament: s.124I(8).
[1397] s.124I(3)(a).
[1398] s.124I(4).
[1399] s.124K. See above, paras 21–341 et seq.
[1400] s.124K(2)(a).
[1401] s.124K(10)(a).
[1402] s.124K(11).
[1403] s.124K(9)(a).
[1404] s.124K(9)(b). What may amount to exceptional circumstances is not stated.
[1405] s.124K(9)(c) and (d). The purpose of these provisions is obscure.

(iv) Costs, administration and enforcement

(a) *Costs sharing*

The 2003 Act. The Act provides that the Secretary of State may by order[1406]   **21–361**
specify provisions that must be included in an initial obligations code or a technical obligations code about payment of contributions towards costs incurred under
the Act.[1407] Any such provision must be limited to payment by copyright owners
and their agents, providers and (in relation to subscriber appeals) subscribers.[1408]
The provision may relate, in particular, to payment by a copyright owner or agent
of a contribution towards a provider's costs or to payment by an owner or agent
or provider towards OFCOM's costs.[1409] Such provision may also include provision about costs incurred before the provision is included in a code; provision for
payment in advance and reimbursement of overpayments; provision about the
calculation of costs; and provision about when and how contributions must be
paid.[1410] The Act also requires the code to make any provision about contributions that the order requires it to include.[1411]

Sharing of costs of initial obligations: the draft code. In its present form, the   **21–362**
draft code provides that costs must be shared in accordance with any order made
by the Secretary of State and that in the absence of an order costs will lie where
they fall.[1412] However, OFCOM expect to issue a further consultation on costs
sharing once an order is in place.[1413]

Sharing of costs of initial obligations: the draft statutory instrument. On   **21–363**
March 30, 2010, BIS published a consultation on costs sharing which included a
draft statutory instrument.[1414] The consultation closed on May 25, 2010. In summary, the draft provided for copyright owners and their agents to contribute to
service providers' costs of carrying out the initial obligations and to OFCOM's
costs of carrying out their functions under the Act.[1415] The amount of such
contributions was to be set by OFCOM. The draft order required OFCOM to
"have regard to the desirability of ensuring" that the notification costs of all copyright owners or their agents amounted to 75 per cent of the costs incurred by service providers in carrying out the initial obligations.[1416] At the same time, OF-
COM were obliged to fix the contributions to their own costs "with a view to
securing" that 75 per cent of such costs are paid by copyright owners or their
agents while service providers pay the rest.[1417] The Government recognised that
there was a strong argument that copyright owners or their agents should bear all
the costs of the scheme. However it decided to require service providers to bear
some of the costs on the grounds that this would give them an incentive to minimise the costs of sending notifications, to take voluntary measures to reduce online infringement and "to participate in commercial offers under which a bilateral

---

[1406] A draft of which must be approved by a resolution of each house: s.124L(5).
[1407] s.124M(1).
[1408] s.124M(2).
[1409] s.124M(3).
[1410] s.124M(4).
[1411] s.124E(1)(f).
[1412] para.8.
[1413] Introduction to the draft code para.2.18.
[1414] *http://www.bis.gov.uk/assets/biscore/business-sectors/docs/10–915–consultation-online-
infringement-of-copyright.pdf* [Accessed November 11, 2010].
[1415] arts 4 and 5.
[1416] art.4(4)(b).
[1417] art.5(2)(c) and (d).

agreement could reduce the numbers of notifications they receive".[1418] In its response to the consultation, the Government indicated that the 75/25 per cent split would ultimately be adopted.[1419] Provision was also made in the draft order for the time for payment of such costs.[1420]

(b) Administration, enforcement and information collection

21–364   **Administration.** The Act requires the codes (in effect) to require OFCOM to administer and enforce them.[1421] The draft initial obligations code empowers OFCOM to make such directions as they consider necessary to give effect to the requirements under the code.[1422]

21–365   **Enforcement of the obligations and penalties.** The Act applies the enforcement procedures applicable to providers of electronic communications networks and services.[1423] In broad terms, the process involves OFCOM notifying the owner, agent or provider that it has grounds to believe there has been a contravention followed by civil enforcement of financial penalties.[1424] The Act provides that penalties may be such an amount not exceeding £250,000 as OFCOM determine to be appropriate and proportionate.[1425] The draft initial obligations code contains detailed provisions about enforcement[1426] and penalties.[1427]

21–366   **Information collection.** The Act requires the code (in effect) to contain adequate arrangements for OFCOM to obtain information or assistance from owners, agents and providers.[1428] In accordance with this, the draft initial obligations code expressly requires owners, agents and providers to provide OFCOM with such information, assistance or both as OFCOM reasonably request for the purposes of administering and enforcing the code within such period as OFCOM may specify.[1429]

21–367   **Indemnities and dispute resolution.** The Act provides that the codes may make provision requiring a copyright owner or agent to indemnify a provider for loss or damage resulting from the owner or agent's failure to comply with the code or the copyright infringement provisions.[1430] It also requires (in effect) that the code contain adequate arrangements for resolving disputes between owners and their agents on the one hand and providers on the other in relation to acts or omissions in relation to an initial obligation or an initial obligations code.[1431] The draft initial obligations code empowers OFCOM to determine such disputes,[1432] but only in limited circumstances. In particular, the following criteria must be met:

[1418] BIS Consultation on cost sharing, p.15.

[1419] *Online Infringement of Copyright (Initial Obligations) Cost Sharing HM Government Response* (BIS, September 2010) *http://www.bis.gov.uk/assets/biscore/business-sectors/docs/o/10–1131–online-copyright-infringement-government-response* [Accessed November 11, 2010].

[1420] arts 6 and 7.

[1421] ss.124D(6), 124E(7)(a) and (c), 124E(8), 124J.

[1422] para.9.1.

[1423] s.124L(1), applying ss.94 to 96.

[1424] See generally ss.94 to 96 of the Act.

[1425] s.124L(2). OFCOM must take account of any representations by the party being penalised and any steps taken towards compliance or for remedying the contravention. The sum may be amended by the Secretary of State by order: s.124L(4) and (5).

[1426] paras 9.21 to 9.27.

[1427] paras 9.3 to 9.12.

[1428] ss.124D(6) and 124E(7)(b).

[1429] para.9.2.

[1430] ss.124E(8)(b) and 124J(3)(b).

[1431] ss.124D(6), 124E(7)(a), (9) and 124J(2)(a).

[1432] para.9.13.

one of the parties must have referred the dispute to OFCOM; the parties must have made reasonable attempts to resolve the issue themselves; there are no alternative means to resolve it[1433]; and there is evidence of breach of the code by one party to the dispute.[1434] The draft code sets out a procedure for determining such disputes[1435] and outlines OFCOM's powers, which are extensive.[1436]

[1433] Given the court's wide powers to grant declaratory relief, it is not in fact easy to envisage when this criterion will be met.

[1434] para.9.14.

[1435] paras 9.15 to 9.18.

[1436] para.9.19.

CHAPTER TWENTY TWO

CRIMINAL REMEDIES AND CUSTOMS SEIZURE

Contents   *Para.*

1. CRIMINAL REMEDIES

A. HISTORICAL INTRODUCTION

Early history. From the Copyright Act of 1709[1] to the end of the nineteenth   **22–01**
century, infringers were not liable to be imprisoned. However, under many of the
Copyright Acts in force during this period,[2] infringers were liable in summary
proceedings brought by the copyright owner to financial penalties and infringing
copies were liable to be forfeited. These remedies were in addition to any liability
for damages. The extent to which these provisions created criminal offences
varied. For example, s.6 of the Fine Arts Copyright Act 1862[3] was held to create
a criminal offence[4] while the Dramatic Copyright Act 1833[5] was held not to do
so.[6] Criminal remedies similar to those of the present day were first introduced in
the Musical (Summary Proceedings) Copyright Act 1902 as amended by the
Musical Copyright Act 1906.[7]

The Musical Copyright Act 1906. The origins of the Musical Copyright Act   **22–02**
1906[8] are to be found in the Musical (Summary Proceedings) Copyright Act
1902,[9] which was directed at pirated copies of musical works, and in particular at
preventing what was perceived to be a growing practice of selling pirated sheet

---

[1] 8 Anne c.19.

[2] As to which see paras 2–18 et seq., above.

[3] 25 & 26 Vict. c.68. See Vol.2 E5.ix.

[4] *Ex p. Graves* (1868) L.R. 3 Ch. App.642. See however *Re Johnson* (1866) 15 W.R. 160 where a
Commissioner in Bankruptcy held that a penalty recoverable under this Act was analogous to
damages for assault.

[5] Vol.2 E5.v.

[6] *Adams v Batley* (1887) 18 Q.B.D. 625. See also *R. v Willets* (1906) 70 J.P. 127 where the Common Sergeant observed, apparently on the basis of a concession by the prosecution, that the
Copyright Act 1842 (5 & 6 Vict. c.45) did not create criminal offences.

[7] 2 Edw. 7 c.15. See *Copinger* 5th edn, p.212 and Alexander *Criminalising copyright: a story of
publishers, pirates and pieces of eight* C.L.J. 2007, 66(3), 625–656.

[8] 6 Edw. 7 c.36.

[9] 2 Edw. 7 c.15.

music in the streets at very low prices.[10] The main point of concern was that the pirated copies did not carry the name of their printer and accordingly copyright owners experienced difficulties in finding a substantial person to proceed against.[11] The 1902 Act provided for the seizure of such copies by constables and for their destruction, forfeiture or delivery up by order of a court of summary jurisdiction. However, it did not create criminal offences. For a variety of reasons,[12] the Act was a failure. Under the 1906 Act, making or dealing with pirated copies of sheet music became punishable on summary conviction by a fine.[13] Second offenders were liable to imprisonment for up to two months.[14] The burden of proving lack of guilty knowledge was on the defendant.[15] Constables were given powers to arrest street hawkers.[16] Provision was made for courts of summary jurisdiction to issue search warrants and to order the forfeiture or destruction of pirated copies so seized.[17]

22–03   **The 1911 and 1956 Acts.** The framers of the 1911 Act originally intended that all the provisions of the 1902 and 1906 Acts should be extended, in consolidated form, to all categories of copyright work.[18] However, this provoked considerable opposition in Parliament and substantial modification proved necessary.[19] As a result, new criminal provisions were introduced in respect of infringements of the copyright in all categories of work.[20] Making or dealing with an infringing copy, making or possessing a plate for the purposes of making infringing copies, and causing works to be performed in public without a licence were all made offences punishable in the case of a first offender by a fine and in the case of a second offender by imprisonment for up to two months.[21] The burden of proving guilty knowledge on the prosecutor and the powers of arrest, search and seizure contained in the 1902 and 1906 Acts were not applied more generally. Meanwhile, the 1902 and 1906 Acts were left in place.[22] The provisions of the 1911 Act were substantially reproduced in the 1956 Act,[23] but the 1902 and 1906 Acts were repealed by it.[24]

22–04   **The Whitford Committee and amendments to the 1956 Act.** In 1977 the Whitford Committee heard evidence that because of the difficulties of proving guilty knowledge and the small size of the penalties, the criminal provisions of the 1956

---

[10] For the background to this provision, see *Copinger* 5th edn, pp.214–216. It seems that at that time copyright sheet music sold at 2s. per sheet but infringing copies were being sold at 2d. per sheet: see the speech of Lord Monkswell introducing what was to become the 1902 Act: *Hansard*, Vol.106, col.456.

[11] See *Copinger* 4th edn, p.331. It seems that copyright owners ultimately decided to take the law into their own hands by seizing copies of pirated sheet music from the street hawkers. It was only when this led to fights in the streets that the 1902 Act was passed, in the face of considerable opposition: Scrutton, *The Law of Copyright* 4th edn, pp.v and 107.

[12] Which are summarised in *Copinger* 5th edn, pp.215–216. For detailed analysis of the causes of the Act's failure, see the debate on the abortive Copyright Bill of 1904, in particular at *Hansard*, Vol.130, cols 1158–59, 1167–68 and 1191–93. In the course of the debate it was claimed that the sale of pirated copies of sheet music had actually increased since the 1902 Act had been passed.

[13] 1906 Act (c.36) s.1(1).

[14] See previous fn.

[15] See fn.13.

[16] s.1(2).

[17] s.2.

[18] See *Copinger* 5th edn, p.212.

[19] See *Copinger* 5th edn, p.212. See also MacGillivray, *The Copyright Act 1911, Annotated* (1912), p.94.

[20] Copyright Act 1911 s.11, Vol.2 E3.

[21] Copyright Act 1911 s.11(1) and (2).

[22] Copyright Act 1911 s.11(4).

[23] Copyright Act 1956 s.21.

[24] Copyright Act 1956 s.50 and Sch.9.

Act were seldom used.[25] The Committee recommended that there be a new offence of possessing an infringing copy in the course of trade;[26] that the burden of
proof on the issue of knowledge should be placed on the defendant;[27] and that
fines for copyright infringement should "at least be kept in line with penalties
under the Performers' Protection Acts and offences against property generally".[28]
The Committee also recommended that the public performance of sound recordings and films should be made an offence.[29] By 1981, none of these recommendations had been implemented and concerns about sound recording and video piracy
were mounting. In 1982 and 1983, two statutes were passed with a view to deter-
ring these activities. The Copyright Act 1956 (Amendment) Act 1982[30] made
possession by way of trade of an infringing copy of a sound recording or a film an
offence. The Copyright (Amendment) Act 1983[31] made the offences of making
for sale or hire, importing and distributing infringing copies of films or sound
recordings triable either way[32] with a maximum penalty of two years'
imprisonment.[33] Both the 1982 and the 1983 Acts were presented[34] as interim
measures pending the full revision of the law of copyright which was ultimately
to be effected by the 1988 Act.[35] During the debates that led to the 1983 Act, it
was acknowledged by the Government[36] that video piracy was spreading rapidly,[37]
that it was under the control of substantial criminals,[38] and that London had
become the world centre of pirate video production.[39] In 1985, the increased
penalties for sound recordings and films contained in the 1983 Act were extended
to offences in relation to computer programs.[40]

The Performers' Protection Acts. The criminal offences of making recordings   **22–05**
of a performance without the performer's consent and dealing with such recordings were created by the Dramatic and Musical Performers' Protection Act 1925
(15 & 16 Geo. 5 c.46). This Act was introduced to deter what was perceived to be
a growing practice of making recordings of radio broadcasts of performances for
further reproduction and sale. Parliament's main concern was that this was deter-
ring good performers from appearing on radio; but anxiety was also expressed
about the effect on the artistes' reputations of the poor quality of such recordings.[41]
There was some opposition to the introduction of criminal sanctions in this area.[42]
However, the Bill's supporters pointed out that there were criminal sanctions in
the Copyright Act 1911 and that there was a defence where the copying was not

---

[25] Cmnd. 6732, paras 708 et seq.

[26] Cmnd. 6732, para.711.

[27] The Committee appears to have intended that it should be for the accused to prove both that he
did not know and that he had no reasonable grounds to suspect that the copy in question was
infringing: Cmnd. 6732, para.711.

[28] Cmnd. 6732, para.711.

[29] Cmnd. 6732, para.713.

[30] (c.35).

[31] (c.42).

[32] i.e. either in the Magistrates' Court or the Crown Court.

[33] This was effected by the introduction of new subss.21(7A) and (7B) into the 1956 Act.

[34] In both cases, the Bills were sponsored by private members.

[35] See, as to the 1982 Act, *Hansard*, HC Vol.27, col.590 and, as to the 1983 Act, *Hansard*, HC
Vol.35, col.605.

[36] Which ultimately supported both Bills, albeit in limited form.

[37] *Hansard*, HC Vol.35, col.619.

[38] *Hansard*, HC Vol.41, col.1137.

[39] *Hansard*, HC Vol.41, cols 1114–1115.

[40] By the Copyright (Computer Software) Amendment Act 1985 (c.41) (see Vol.2 E7). Like the
1982 and 1983 Acts, this statute originated as a private member's bill but was supported by the
Government as an interim measure pending the introduction of what was to become the 1988
Act. See *Hansard*, HC Vol.73, col.1371.

[41] See *Hansard*, HC Vol.185, cols 1970–71 and HL Vol.62, cols 18–19.

[42] See, e.g. *Hansard*, HC Vol.185, col.1971.

for the purpose of trade, and the opposition was overcome.[43] The 1925 Act was later modified and then replaced by the Performers' Protection Acts 1958–1972.[44] By 1972, a conviction on indictment for making a recording of a performance without the performer's consent or for dealing with such a recording carried a maximum penalty of two years' imprisonment.[45] On their face, these Acts created criminal sanctions only, but the civil courts were able to hold that their breach was actionable as a breach of statutory duty.[46]

22–06   **Background to the 1988 Act.** In its 1986 White Paper[47] the Government asserted that the deterrent effect of the increased penalties for offences in relation to sound recordings, films and computer programs had been very successful, particularly in relation to video piracy, and that it therefore proposed to extend the increased penalties to all categories of copyright material.[48] The Government also proposed, in accordance with the Whitford Committee report, to make unauthorised public performance of sound recordings and films an offence,[49] and to make possession in the course of trade of infringing copies of any type of work an offence.[50] In addition, the Government observed that establishing guilty knowledge could be a major and costly obstacle for the prosecution, as for a civil plaintiff, and that this could discourage the initiation of proceedings. It accordingly proposed a "relaxation" of the requirements of guilty knowledge in criminal proceedings in identical terms to that proposed in respect of civil proceedings for secondary infringements.[51] Finally, it proposed that offences in relation to rights in performances should be brought into line with those in relation to copyright both in terms of the types of activities which would be offences and in relation to penalties.[52] As will be seen, all these proposals were implemented in the 1988 Act.

22–07   **The policy of the 1988 Act.** The parliamentary debates on the criminal provisions of the 1988 Act demonstrate that when drafting the new s.107 the Government was concerned both to increase protection for the rights of the copyright owner and to protect consumers from poor quality counterfeit goods. Thus, Government spokesmen in both Houses of Parliament made it clear that they regarded copyright infringement as equivalent to theft.[53] However, the point was also made that pirate or counterfeit goods were seldom of the same quality as the originals and in the case of counterfeit goods such as electrical appliances or brake shoes "there is a very real safety problem".[54] The consumer protection aspects of s.107 were emphasised by new ss.107A and 198A of the 1988 Act[55] which impose a duty on local weights and measures authorities to enforce the criminal provisions in their area and apply certain sections of the Trade Descrip-

---

[43] See, e.g. *Hansard*, HC Vol.185, cols 1971, 1974 to 1975.

[44] See Vol.2 E6.

[45] Dramatic and Musical Performers' Protection Act 1958 (6 & 7 Eliz. 2 c.44) s.1, as amended by the Performers' Protection Act 1972 (c.32). See Vol.2 E6.i and E6.iii.

[46] See the discussion at para.12–07, above.

[47] *Intellectual Property and Innovation*, Cmnd. 9712.

[48] para.12.8.

[49] para.12.10.

[50] para.12.11.

[51] For what is a secondary infringement, see Ch.8, above.

[52] *Intellectual Property and Innovation*, Cmnd. 9712, para.14.3.

[53] See, e.g. *Hansard*, HL Vol.491, col.420, per Lord Beaverbrook.

[54] *Hansard*, HL Vol.491, col.420. Note, however, that the creation of criminal offences for design right infringement was not being considered.

[55] Added by Criminal Justice and Public Order Act 1994 (c.33) s.165, with effect from April 6, 2007. See the Criminal Justice and Public Order Act 1994 (Commencement No. 14) Order 2007 (SI 2007/621).

tions Act 1968[56] to such enforcement. This aspect of Government policy is also emphasised by the fact that the penalties under s.107, while in most cases greater than before, were originally commensurate with those found in consumer protection statutes such as the Trade Descriptions Act 1968[57] and the Food Safety Act 1990[58] rather than with those for offences against property generally.[59] The first of the Government's concerns ("infringement is equivalent to theft") has been echoed by the Court of Criminal Appeal in a statement that the making and distribution of counterfeit video films is a serious offence amounting in effect to theft of the copyright owner's intellectual property.[60] Furthermore, it has been held that s.107 of the 1988 Act is not confined to cases of "piracy"[61] and that the section may therefore be used by a collecting society against a person who is alleged to have distributed infringing copies of copyright works belonging to one of the society's members even though there has been a pre-existing commercial relationship between the society and the alleged infringer.[62]

The Copyright, etc. and Trade Marks (Offences and Enforcement) Act   **22–08**
2002.[63] This Act came into force on November 20, 2002.[64] The bill which later became the Act was introduced as a private member's bill but at all times had Government support. It emerged in the context of a perception that the existing penalties for the offences under the 1988 Act were insufficient, as a result of which organised criminals had entered the field. There were also concerns about inconsistencies between the copyright and trade mark regimes. Accordingly, the penalties for the either-way offences under the 1988 Act were brought into line with those under the Trade Marks Act 1994; search warrants were made available in respect of all the main 1988 Act offences rather than only a selection; and the forfeiture provisions in force in respect of trade marks were applied to the offences under the 1988 Act. It should be noted that the intended harmonisation between the copyright and trade marks regimes was only partially achieved. All offences under the Trade Marks Act 1994, including those of selling goods bearing a sign identical to a registered trade mark, are triable either way (that is, in the Magistrates' Court or in the Crown Court) and carry a maximum penalty of ten years' imprisonment. By contrast, even taking account of the effect of the 2002 Act, many offences under the 1988 Act, including the offence of selling an infringing copy of a copyright work, remain triable only summarily (that is, in the Magistrates' Court) and carry a maximum penalty of three months' imprisonment.[65] Perhaps the most significant effect of the 2002 Act is that because of the increase in penalties, the more serious offences under the 1988 Act are now "arrestable offences" as defined in the Police and Criminal Evidence Act 1984.[66] As a result, in respect of those who commit such offences, ordinary citizens and police officers have extensive powers of arrest without warrant.[67]

---

[56] (c.29).
[57] (c.29).
[58] (c.16).
[59] This is no longer the case. See para.22–21, below.
[60] *R. v Carter* [1993] F.S.R. 303.
[61] i.e. for these purposes cases where the alleged infringement is carried out by persons who have and have had no previous commercial relationship with the copyright owner.
[62] *Thames and Hudson Ltd v Design and Artists Copyright Society Ltd* [1995] F.S.R. 153.
[63] (c.25.)
[64] See the Copyright, etc. and Trade Marks (Offences and Enforcement) Act 2002 (Commencement) Order 2002 (SI 2002/2749).
[65] See para.22–21, below. The maximum term of imprisonment for such offences was recently reduced from six months to three months: SI 2010/2694.
[66] (c.60) s.24(1)(b).
[67] Police and Criminal Evidence Act 1984 s.24(4) to 24(7).

22–09   **The Copyright and Related Rights Regulations 2003.**[68] These Regulations came into force on October 31, 2003. As well as introducing new offences in relation to the circumvention of protection measures, which are dealt with elsewhere,[69] they also introduced new offences of infringing copyright by communicating a work to the public and of infringing a performer's making available right.[70] Since there was no previous offence which covered these activities, a loophole has been closed. Initially, however, the penalties for these offences were low[71]. In accordance with general principles, these provisions do not apply to pre-commencement acts.[72]

22–10   **The Digital Economy Act 2010 and the 2010 Regulations.** The Gowers Review on Intellectual Property noted the disparity between the maximum sentences for "online" and "physical" infringement and recommended that they be matched.[73] However, the Government decided not to implement this recommendation on the grounds that "prison should be used mainly for serious and dangerous offenders and that sentences should only be as long as necessary for punishment and public protection".[74] Instead of implementing Recommendation 36, the Government decided following a consultation[75] to introduce exceptional statutory maximum fines for all either way copyright and rights in performances offences (including communication to the public offences) tried in the Magistrates Courts. This was effected by s.42 of the Digital Economy Act. The result is that the disparity in maximum sentences identified in the Gowers Report remains.

More recently, by reg.5 of the Copyright, Designs and Patents Act 1988 (Amendment) Regulations 2010,[76] the maximum term of imprisonment for the summary offences in s.107 was reduced from six months to three months with effect from January 1, 2011. This change was not referred to in the consultation and does not apply to offences in relation to rights in performances. In fact it appears to be no more than a by-product of the main provisions of the Regulations, which remove the permitted acts provided for in ss.67, 72(1B)(a) and Sch.2 para.15 to the 1988 Act.[77] The removal of the permitted acts means that some acts of playing in public which had previously been permitted are now summary offences under s.107(3). Since the 2010 Regulations were made under s.2 of the European Communities Act, the maximum penalties which may be imposed in respect of any summary offences which they create are imprisonment for up to three months or a fine of up to the statutory maximum (£5,000).[78] However, the reduction in the maximum sentence from six months to three months has not been limited to summary offences which had previously been permitted acts, nor to sub.(3), but extends to all summary offences under s.107: see the amended subs.(5). While it is obvious that limiting the reduction to acts which had previ-

---

[68] SI 2003/2498.

[69] See paras 15–29 et seq.

[70] New CDPA 1988 ss.107(2A) and 198(1A), introduced by reg.26.

[71] On summary conviction: imprisonment for up to three months or a fine of up to the statutory maximum of £5,000; on conviction on indictment: imprisonment for up to two years or an unlimited fine. The offences were created by subordinate legislation made under the European Communities Act 1972 (i.e. SI 2003/2498) and these are the maximum penalties available for such offences: see Sch.2 para.1 to that Act.

[72] reg.40(3).

[73] Recommendation 36.

[74] See the Government's Consultation *http://www.ipo.gov.uk/response-gowers36.pdf* [Accessed November 16, 2010] in which it is also noted that the more serious copyright offences are being indicted under the general law, such as the Fraud Act 2006.

[75] See previous fn.

[76] SI 2010/2694

[77] For these permitted acts, see paras 9–200 et seq., 9–218 et seq., and 12–95 respectively, above.

[78] See Sch.2 para.1 to that Act

ously been permitted would have created difficulties for Magistrates' Courts, it is not clear why it was thought necessary to impose a reduction across the board.[79]

B. INTERNATIONAL OBLIGATIONS

Position prior to TRIPS. In general, international conventions prior to TRIPS did not impose any requirement for the imposition of criminal sanctions, leaving the question of remedies to individual states. Thus, for example, art.7(1) of the Rome Convention (1961) provided that the protection provided for performers by the Convention should "include the possibility of preventing" certain acts of broadcasting, fixation and reproduction of fixations of their performances when committed without their consent. This was interpreted as leaving it open to the United Kingdom to retain its existing legislation which provided for protection by means of the criminal law.[80]   **22–11**

TRIPS. The first international instrument in the field to require the imposition of criminal sanctions was the TRIPS agreement.[81] Article 61 requires members to provide for criminal procedures and penalties to be applied at least in cases of wilful trademark counterfeiting or copyright piracy on a commercial scale. It states that remedies available shall include imprisonment or monetary fines or both sufficient to provide a deterrent, consistently with the level of penalties applied for crimes of a corresponding gravity. It goes on to provide that in appropriate cases remedies available shall include the seizure, forfeiture and destruction of the infringing goods and of any materials and implements the predominant use of which has been in the commission of the offence. Finally, the article permits Members to provide for criminal procedures and penalties to be applied in other cases of infringement of intellectual property rights, in particular where they are committed wilfully and on a commercial scale. This last provision would no doubt permit the creation of criminal offences in relation to rights in performances.   **22–12**

Community legislation. Although there have previously been proposals for legislation requiring the imposition of criminal remedies, there is presently no such legislation. Article 16 of the Enforcement Directive simply states that without prejudice to the civil and administrative measures, procedures and remedies laid down by that Directive, Member States may apply other appropriate sanctions in cases where intellectual property rights have been infringed.   **22–13**

C. CRIMINAL OFFENCES AND PENALTIES

(i) Copyright offences

Section 107(1): offences involving making, possessing or dealing with infringing copies. A person commits an offence who, without the licence of the copyright owner,[82] does any of a number of acts in relation to an article which is, and which he knows or has reason to believe is, an infringing copy[83] of a copyright work. The acts in question are making for sale or hire[84]; importing into the United   **22–14**

---

[79] The Explanatory Memorandum to SI 2010/2694 does not explain this: see para.4.7, which deals with the background to the amendment to s.107(5).

[80] See the *WIPO Guide to the Rome Convention* para.7.5.

[81] See generally paras 23 136 et seq.

[82] As to which, see CDPA 1988 ss.173 and 101(2), and paras 5–198 et seq., above.

[83] See CDPA 1988 s.27 and paras 8–03 et seq., above for the meaning of infringing copy.

[84] CDPA 1988 s.107(1)(a).

Kingdom otherwise than for his private and domestic use[85]; possessing in the course of a business[86] with a view to committing any act infringing the copyright[87]; in the course of a business selling or letting for hire, offering or exposing for sale or hire, exhibiting in public or distributing[88]; and distributing otherwise than in the course of a business to such an extent as to affect prejudicially the owner of the copyright.[89] The wording of s.107(1) of the 1988 Act is similar to that of the sections of the Act which create civil liability and the reader is referred to the relevant chapters for a detailed discussion of those provisions. The following points may be made. First, with one exception,[90] the only types of infringement which are made criminal offences are infringements with obvious commercial purposes. Thus, for example, in contrast to the position in civil proceedings, no liability attaches to the making of an infringing copy unless the copy has been made for sale or hire.[91] Secondly, no offence is committed by doing any act unless the accused has the requisite state of mind. This applies as much to "primary" as to "secondary" infringements.[92] Thirdly, the state of mind required to be proved by the prosecution is expressed in identical terms to that required to be proved by a claimant in a civil action for secondary infringement, namely knowledge or reason to believe that the copy is an infringing one.[93] The test for "reason to believe" is an entirely objective one.[94]

22–15   **"With a view".** The offence of possession in the course of a business is limited to possession "with a view to committing any act infringing the copyright". It is not clear whether "with a view" means "with the intention of" or something less. In *R. v Zaman*,[95] which concerned criminal offences under the Trade Marks Act 1994,[96] it was held that the words "with a view" in the expression "with a view to gain" were not to be equated with the words "with intent to". The Court of Appeal therefore upheld the trial judge's direction that the prosecution had to satisfy the jury that gain "was [the defendant's] idea, ... was in his mind as a real pos-

---

[85] CDPA 1988 s.107(1)(b).

[86] In *R v Kousar* [2009] EWCA Crim 139, [2009] 2 Cr. App. R. 5, a trade mark case, it was held that a wife who had not objected to the presence in the loft of the jointly owned matrimonial home of substantial quantities of counterfeit goods intended by her husband for sale in the course of a market trading business in which she was not involved was not in possession of such goods, whether in the course of a business or otherwise. The case was not however put in terms of secondary liability.

[87] CDPA 1988 s.107(1)(c).

[88] CDPA 1988 s.107(1)(d).

[89] CDPA 1988 s.107(1)(e). In the Hong Kong case of *Hksar v Chan Nai Ming* (TMCC 1268/2005) it was held that the transmission of a film to 30 or 40 downloaders using BitTorrent sofware would have prejudicially affected the owner of the copyright. See Tofalides and Fearn, "BitTorrent Copyright Infringement" [2006] 2 Ent. L.R. 81 and Low, "Tackling Online Copyright Infringers in Hong Kong" [2006] 4 Ent. L.R. 122. The issue of whether the copyright owner had been prejudiced did not arise on the defendant's appeals, which were dismissed: HCMA 1221/2005, Beeson J. and Final Appeal No.3 of 2007 (Criminal).

[90] The offence of distributing infringing copies to such an extent as to affect prejudicially the owner of the copyright.

[91] CDPA 1988 s.107(1)(a).

[92] As to the distinction, see para.7–02, above.

[93] Compare CDPA 1988 ss.22 and 23. Note also that despite the recommendations of the Whitford Committee (referred to in para.22–04, above), there was no reversal of the burden of proof on this issue and accordingly it lies on the prosecution. See *Stockton-on-Tees BC v Frost* [2010] EWHC 1304 (Admin) para.4 ("no reason to believe" should presumably read "reason to believe").

[94] See the civil case of *LA Gear Inc v Hi-Tec Sports Plc* [1992] F.S.R. 121; the view expressed in the text was upheld by Mr Recorder Harman in *R. v Mudd* Unreported, September 20, 1995, Crown Court at Middlesex Guildhall), who ruled that the prosecution had to prove that a reasonable man with the defendant's background and experience of the field in which he was operating would have had reason to believe that the article was infringing.

[95] [2002] EWCA Crim 1862; [2003] F.S.R. 13.

[96] See s.92(1) of the Trade Marks Act 1994 (c.26).

sibility, something that might realistically happen". The Court's reasoning derives from a close reading of the Trade Marks Act 1994. Nevertheless, some of that reasoning may yet apply by analogy to s.107. In particular, it is clearly arguable that the choice of the phrase "with a view to committing" rather than "with intent to commit" was deliberate and that therefore something less than intention was envisaged. See also *R v Dooley*[97]: a person possesses something "with a view to" X if X is one of his objectives. The case concerned possession of indecent photographs of children but the Court of Appeal expressed itself in general terms.

Section 107(2): offences in relation to articles designed for making copies of copyright works. Other offences are committed by a person who makes an article specifically designed or adapted for making copies of a particular copyright work,[98] or has such an article in his possession,[99] if in either case he knows or has reason to believe that the article is to be used to make infringing copies for sale or hire in the course of a business. Section 107(2) is similar to s.24 of the 1988 Act,[100] but contains several differences. First, *dealing* with articles designed for making copies of copyright works is not a criminal offence. It is doubtful whether this difference is of any practical importance since anyone dealing with an article is likely to have had it in his possession. Secondly, s.24 requires possession to have been in the course of a business while s.107(2) merely requires the possessor to know or have reason to believe that the article is to be used to make infringing copies for sale, hire or use in the course of a business. The criminal provision will therefore apply to a person who is merely looking after the article for the real infringer if the former has the requisite state of mind. Thirdly, s.107(2) requires the possessor to know or have reason to believe that the infringing copies to be made with the article are to have a commercial purpose whereas s.24 simply requires the possessor to know or have reason to believe that infringing copies are to be made. Finally, the terms of s.107(2) make clear beyond doubt that the only articles to which the subsection applies are articles designed or adapted for making copies of a particular copyright work. It follows that articles such as photocopiers, video recorders and cassette recorders are excluded from its ambit. On the other hand, a computer onto which a file or program has been loaded so as to copy it may fall within the section.[101]

22–16

Section 107(2A): communicating to the public. Article 3 of the Information Society Directive[102] makes provision in respect of the communication of copyright works to the public ("communication right"). Article 8(1) provides that Member States shall provide appropriate sanctions and remedies in respect of infringements of the rights and obligations set out in the Directive and that sanctions thus provided for must be effective, proportionate and dissuasive. The Government decided that in order properly to implement the Directive it was necessary to create a new criminal offence. Accordingly, the Copyright and Related Rights Regulations[103] introduced a new subs.107(2A) which makes it an offence to infringe the copyright in a work by communicating that work to the public either in the course of a business or to such an extent as to affect prejudicially the copyright owner. The offence is only committed if the accused knew or had reason to believe that copyright in the work would thereby be infringed. The term

22–17

---

[97] [2005] EWCA Crim 3093; [2006] 1 Cr. App. R. 21.
[98] CDPA 1988, s.107(2)(a).
[99] CDPA 1988, s.107(2)(b).
[100] See para.8–15, above.
[101] cf. the wording of CDPA 1988 s.24(1), although the effect is almost certainly the same. See para.8–15, above.
[102] Directive 2001/29/EC, [2001] OJ L167/10.
[103] SI 2003/2498.

"communication to the public" is defined in s.20 of the 1988 Act as "communication to the public by electronic transmission" and is stated to include broadcasting and "the making available to the public of the work by electronic communication in such a way that members of the public may access it from a place and at a time individually chosen by them", that is "on-demand" services. These terms are the same in civil and criminal proceedings and reference should be made to the discussion of them in the civil context.[104] Section 107(2A) does not apply to acts committed before October 31, 2003.[105]

22–18   **Section 107(3): offences in relation to public performances.** Criminal offences may also be committed in relation to the public performance of works. Where copyright is infringed (otherwise than by reception of a communication to the public[106]) by the public performance of a literary, dramatic or musical work or by the playing or showing in public of a sound recording or film, any person who caused the work to be so performed, played or shown is guilty of an offence if he knew or had reason to believe that copyright would be infringed.[107] Section 107(3) differs from s.19 of the 1988 Act[108] in that liability falls on a person who has "caused" the work to be performed, played or shown.[109] Questions as to the meaning of "causing" arose in a number of reported cases under the Dramatic Copyright Act 1833[110] as extended by the Copyright Act 1842.[111] These statutes imposed liability on a person who caused a musical or dramatic work to be represented without the licence of the copyright owner, and accordingly these authorities are relevant to the interpretation of s.107(3). In general, as might be expected, a person was not liable for causing a work to be represented unless he was actually responsible for bringing the representation about. Thus, a company which made and supplied film versions of a dramatic work to music halls and theatres which were then shown to the public did not cause the dramatic work to be represented, even though the supplier knew (and presumably intended) that the films would be so shown.[112] This decision (if correct) would no doubt be of equal application to those who supply sound recordings to discos and night clubs.[113] Similarly, where the landlord of a tavern hired a room to S who put on a series of infringing performances of a musical work, the landlord was held not to have caused the performances to be represented even though he had supplied S with equipment, had advertised and sold tickets in the bar, and had been put on notice of the copyright owner's rights after the performances began.[114] Again, where the owner of a theatre let it out to D who put on an infringing production of a play, the owner was held not to have caused the performance to be represented even though he had supplied equipment and scene shifters, had paid for printing and advertising, and was paid by a share of the gross receipts.[115] A different result was reached where the performer was an agent of the owner of the premises. Thus, where the owner of a theatre who also employed its company, including his son, who was the stage manager, let out the theatre and the company

---

[104] See paras 7–112 et seq., above.

[105] See reg.40(3) of the Copyright and Related Rights Regulations (SI 2003/2498).

[106] For the meaning of this term, see the previous paragraph.

[107] CDPA 1988 s.107(3)(a), (b).

[108] As to which see paras 7–103 et seq., above.

[109] A person who caused a performance would no doubt be liable in civil proceedings as a joint tortfeasor. See paras 21–42 et seq., above.

[110] (3 Wm. 4 c.15). See Vol.2 E5.v.

[111] (5 & 6 Vict. c.45). See Vol.2 E5.vii.

[112] *Karno v Pathé Frères* (1908) 99 L.T. 114. The decision is obiter on this point: ibid. at 119.

[113] This is treated as a special case for the purposes of civil liability: CDPA 1988 s.26.

[114] *Russell v Briant*, 137 E.R. 737; (1849) 8 C.B. 836.

[115] *Lyon v Knowles* (1863) B. & S. 556; affirmed 122 E.R. 209; (1863) B. & S. 566.

to his son, who put on an infringing production of a play, the owner was held to have caused the play to be represented because he retained control and because what was done by his son was done with his permission.[116] Similarly, where the owner of a music hall engaged a singer to sing whatever songs the singer wished and the singer performed a song without a licence to do so, the owner was held liable on the grounds that the singer sang as his agent.[117] In *French v Day, Gregory and others*[118] it was held that the general manager of a theatre who had no power to engage or dismiss its artistes, who acted at all times in accordance with the proprietors' instructions, and who obtained no financial benefit from the production did not cause a work to be represented even though he had authority to stop it: he was merely the "mouthpiece" of the proprietor. If this decision is correct, it would seem to follow that a cinema projectionist or disc jockey who was an employee would not be liable if, following his employer's instructions, he projected a film or played a sound recording without the licence of the copyright owner, even though he actually caused the film to be shown or the sound recording to be played. It seems unlikely that this result was intended by Parliament. The brief report in *French's* case does not make clear to what extent the defendant was actually involved in or knew about the infringing performance.[119] Moreover, in the earlier case of *Parsons v Chapman*,[120] which was not cited in *French's* case, it was held that the acting manager of a theatre, who paid the actors' salaries and dismissed them, caused a play to be performed, and that it made no difference that he did so as agent of the proprietor. For these reasons, it seems unlikely that *French's* case would be followed today.

Sound recordings and wireless broadcasts: limitations. No offence can be committed in relation to a work which does not qualify for copyright protection in the first place.[121] There are specific limitations on the scope of s.107 when a sound recording or a wireless broadcast only qualifies for protection by reason of a connection with certain countries.[122] Those limitations derive from the limitations on the protection granted by those countries to works connected with the United Kingdom.[123] For the purposes of sound recordings, the countries fall into two categories. If the connection is with a country in the first category,[124] then no offence is committed by communicating it to the public or playing it in public. If the connection is with a country in the second category,[125] no offence is committed by playing it in public or communicating it to the public by broadcasting it. When a wireless broadcast qualifies for protection only by reason of a connection with certain countries, no offence is committed by communicating it to the public except if it is broadcast by wireless telegraphy.[126]   **22–19**

Trap purchases. An offence is only committed if the relevant act is done without   **22–20**

---

[116] *Marsh v Conquest* (1864) 17 C.B.N.S. 418.

[117] *Monaghan v Taylor* (1886) 2 T.L.R. 685.

[118] *French v Day, Gregory and others* (1893) 9 T.L.R. 548.

[119] Reference is made to the "introduction" of the piece in question, but it is not clear what this means.

[120] (1831) 5 C. & P. 33, a case under 10 Geo. 2, c.28.

[121] See, generally, paras 3–154 et seq.

[122] Copyright and Performances (Application to Other Countries) Order 2008 (SI 2008/677) art.3 and Sch. See Vol.2 C4.

[123] See generally para.3–211 above.

[124] These countries are not marked with a "hash" (#) or asterisk in the third column of the table in the Schedule to SI 2008/677.

[125] These countries are marked with a "hash" (#) in the third column of the table in the Schedule to SI 2008/677. They include the United States of America.

[126] Copyright and Performances (Application to Other Countries) Order 2008 (SI 2008/677) art.3 and Sch. The countries are those not marked by an asterisk in the fourth column of the table in the Schedule.

the licence of the copyright owner. Many prosecutions are likely to be commenced as a result of a trap purchase by the copyright owner or some person acting on his behalf or with his licence. The question arises whether a defendant to an allegation of selling an infringing copy would be able to rely on these facts to argue that no offence had been committed. It is well established that entrapment is not a defence to a criminal charge.[127] It also seems unlikely in normal circumstances that evidence of a trap purchase would be excluded under s.78 of the Police and Criminal Evidence Act 1984.[128] However, it might be argued that the sale took place with the licence of the copyright owner and therefore did not constitute an offence.[129] It seems that by analogy with authorities on consent under the Patents Acts this is likely to be treated as a question of fact turning in particular on the authority given to the actual purchaser and what he does. In one case, the plaintiff was the proprietor of a patent in a telescopic ladder which consisted of two ladders combined with each other, the inner being raised or lowered by means of an endless cord. In order to obtain evidence of infringement, the plaintiff sent his agent to order such a ladder from the defendant. The defendant initially made a telescopic ladder without a cord but the plaintiff's agent refused to accept it without the cord and the defendant ultimately added a cord. It was held that the plaintiff by his agent had consented to the infringement.[130] On the other hand, where the proprietor of a patent in a particular type of tyre sent his agent to the defendant to repair a worn-out version of the tyre and the defendant repaired it in infringement of the patent, it was held that no consent had been given. On the facts, the plaintiff's agent's authority was limited to seeing whether the defendant was infringing the patent[131] and did not extend to ordering an infringing repair.[132] It is worth noting[133] that in this case there was no evidence that the plaintiff's agent had specified any particular method of repair.

22–21   **Mode of trial and penalties.** The more serious offences of making for sale or hire, importation, distribution (whether or not in the course of a business) and communication to the public (however committed) are triable both summarily (i.e. in the Magistrates' Court) and on indictment (i.e. in the Crown Court). On summary conviction for any of these offences the maximum penalty is imprisonment for a period of six months (three in the case of communication to the public) or a fine of £50,000[134] or both. On conviction on indictment these offences carry a maximum penalty of imprisonment for ten years (two for communication to the public) or an unlimited fine or both.[135] All the other offences under section are triable only summarily and carry a maximum penalty of six months' imprisonment[136] or a fine not exceeding level 5 on the standard scale[137] or both.[138]

22–22   **Sentencing.** Prior to the increase in the maximum term of imprisonment to 10

---

[127] *R. v Sang* [1980] A.C. 402.

[128] See *R. v Loosely* [2002] 1 W.L.R. 2060 and *Blackstone's Criminal Practice* 2010 at para.F2.26.

[129] This issue will not usually arise in civil proceedings because evidence of a trap purchase is likely to be sufficient to persuade a court to grant an injunction and an enquiry or an account. The prosecution can prevent the issue arising in criminal proceedings by charging the defendant with offences other than sale in relation to the goods sold in the trap purchase, e.g. possession in the course of a business, or offering or exposing for sale.

[130] *Kelly v Batchelar* (1893) 10 R.P.C. 289.

[131] " ... it was employment of an agent for the purpose of seeing what the defendant would do under given circumstances", per North J. at 250.

[132] *Dunlop Pneumatic Tyre Company Ltd v Neal* [1899] 1 Ch. 807; (1899) 16 R.P.C. 247.

[133] Although this was not part of North J.'s decision.

[134] With effect from June 8, 2010.

[135] CDPA 1988 s.107(4) and (4A). These penalties have varied over the years. See paras 22–07 and 22–10, above.

[136] With effect from January 1, 2011, this is reduced to three months' imprisonment. See para.22–10 above.

years in 2002, the Court of Appeal made clear its view that counterfeiting is equivalent to theft[139] and that counterfeiting offences should "normally attract at least a short sentence of imprisonment".[140] There are few reported cases in which defendants have been sentenced for copyright offences since 2002. However, since the maximum penalties for the either way offences are the same as for the trade mark offences and since many trade mark offences could (subject to evidential considerations) equally have been prosecuted as copyright offences, sentencing decisions in relation to such cases may well have relevance in the copyright field.[141] In one case, the defendant, a man of good character, had operated a rather unsophisticated but profitable business from home producing infringing copies of games, DVDs, VCDs and videos over a period of two years. His turnover was about £27,000 per year. A total sentence of 21 months' imprisonment was upheld by the Court of Appeal.[142] In another, the defendant had a business producing high-quality CD counterfeits. He admitted to having produced between 3,000 and 4,000 and stated that he was intending to produce 2,000 per week. He had no relevant previous convictions. He claimed that initially he had thought he was exploiting a loophole in the law, but admitted that he had come to realise that this was not so. A sentence of 30 months' imprisonment was upheld.[143] In a third, the Court of Appeal upheld a sentence of 12 months' imprisonment for a teacher who was of good character who had pleaded guilty to the wholesale sale of mobile phone accessories including counterfeit covers. The sentence was in the context of a confiscation order of £84,548 and an order that the defendant pay prosecution costs of £25,000. The defendant would have to sell his house to pay these sums.[144] In a fourth, the defendant had made, decorated and supplied counterfeit pottery making a profit of £4,000 over a period of 10 months. He was charged with trade mark offences. A sentence of nine months' immediate imprisonment was upheld on the grounds (amongst others) that a sentence for trade mark offences has to contain some element of deterrence especially because such crimes are difficult, time consuming and expensive to detect.[145] In a fifth, the 54-year-old appellant who was of good character pleaded guilty to trade mark offences after a search of his home which had yielded computer equipment, at least three working DVD writers, about 20,000 discs and about 11,000 individual music albums on computer hard drives. The retail value of the music seized, if it had been genuine, would have been £530,000. In addition, over 5,000 DVDs were seized together with hundreds of computer games. There was evidence of wholesale sales. The appellant had profited in the sum of about £10,000 over four

---

[137] Currently £5,000: Criminal Justice Act 1982 (c.48) s.37(2) as substituted by Criminal Justice Act 1991 (c.53) s.17(1).

[138] CDPA 1988 s.107(5).

[139] *R. v Carter* [1993] F.S.R. 303. See also *R. v DuKett* [1998] 2 Cr.App.R. (S.) 59: "Infringement of copyright is widespread. It does, in an ethical sense, involve stealing other men's property, and in its cumulative effect is able to cause serious damage to legitimate commercial and proprietary interests .... A serious view is to be taken of the distribution by way of business and the recording for such distribution of pirated material which, if bought legitimately, would cost substantial sums of money" (Jowitt J.).

[140] *R. v Kemp* (1995) 16 Cr. App.R. (S.) 941. Note, however, that this case also involved trade mark offences in respect of which the maximum sentence was 10 years' imprisonment and the Court of Criminal Appeal may well have had this in mind when making this observation (see however the first paragraph of Hooper J.'s judgment in which he appears to suggest that all the offences were under CDPA 1988 s.107 and carried a maximum of two years).

[141] Note, however, that the sentencing guidelines applicable to Trade Mark Offences have not been extended to copyright offences.

[142] *R. v Passley* [2003] EWCA Crim 2727; [2004] 1 Cr.App.R. (S.) 70. The Court considered the cases of *R. v Carter* and *R. v Kemp* (above). A similar sentence resulted on similar facts in *R v Lee* [2010] EWCA Crim 268, in which a substantial confiscation order was made.

[143] *R. v Gleeson* [2001] EWCA Crim 2023; [2002] 1 Cr.App.R. (S.) 112.

[144] *R. v Sheikh* [2006] EWCA Crim 3692.

[145] *R. v Wooldridge* [2005] EWCA Crim 1086; [2006] 1 Cr .App. R. (S.) 13.

or five years. Most if not all of the purchasers were aware of the counterfeit nature of the goods. Sentences of 18 months concurrent on each count were upheld.[146] By contrast with these cases, offenders convicted of a small number of sales on eBay may well escape imprisonment.[147]

22–23 **Criminal liability of company officers and others.** Where an offence under s.107 of the 1988 Act committed by a body corporate is proved to have been committed with the consent or connivance of a director, manager,[148] secretary or other similar officer of the body, or a person purporting to act in such a capacity, that person is guilty of the offence and liable to be proceeded against and punished accordingly.[149] The effect of this provision is that the consenting or conniving officer is deemed to be guilty of the same offence as the company and is subject to the same penalties. A director consents to the commission of an offence where he knows the material facts which constitute the offence and has agreed to the company's conduct of the business on the basis of such facts. Consent can be established by inference as well as by proof of an express agreement.[150] It has been said that an officer connives in the commission of an offence where "he is equally well aware of what is going on but his agreement is tacit, not actively encouraging what happens but letting it continue and saying nothing about it".[151] Connivance too may be proved by inference, the strength of which will depend on the extent to which the matters in question were under the officer's direction or control.[152]

22–24 **Publication right.** Section 107 applies equally to publication right[153] with the single modification that on summary conviction the maximum penalty is three months' imprisonment or a fine not exceeding level 5[154] on the standard scale or both.[155]

22–25 **The "mere conduit", "caching" and "hosting" defences.** These defences, which were introduced in order to implement the E-Commerce Directive, apply to criminal proceedings as much as to civil proceedings.[156] Their substantive provisions are considered elsewhere.[157] The Regulations which implement the Directive provide that where a service provider relies on one of these defences, it bears an evidential burden of proof in relation to the defence. Accordingly, where evi-

---

[146] *R. v Hatton* [2007] EWCA Crim 1860; [2008] 1 Cr .App. R. (S.) 74. The court referred to *R. v Kirkwood* [2005] EWCA Crim 3534; [2006] 2 Cr. App. R. (S.) 39 in which a total sentence of 21 months was upheld on similar facts.

[147] See, e.g. *R v Pettit* [2009] EWCA Crim 2573.

[148] It seems that Parliament intended that this expression would continue to be interpreted by the courts to mean a senior manager who did not have a seat on the board of directors: *Hansard*, HL Vol.493, col.1370. The earlier case law is summarised in *R. v Boal* [1992] 1 Q.B. 591 where it was held in relation to a provision similar to CDPA 1988 s.110 that the word "manager" referred only to a person who was in a position of real authority in the company with both the power and the responsibility to decide corporate policy and strategy.

[149] CDPA 1988 s.110(1).

[150] *R. v Chargot Ltd* [2008] UKHL 73; [2009] 1 W.L.R. 1 at para.34.

[151] *Huckerby v Elliott* [1970] 1 All E.R. 189 at 194 (obiter).

[152] *R. v Chargot Ltd* [2008] UKHL 73, para.34.

[153] See the Copyright and Related Rights Regulations 1996 (SI 1996/2967) reg.17(1), Vol.2 A3.iii.

[154] Currently £5,000: Criminal Justice Act 1982 (c.48) s.37(2) as substituted by Criminal Justice Act 1991 (c.53) s.17(1).

[155] Copyright and Related Rights Regulations 1996 (SI 1996/2967) reg.17(3). This offence was created by statutory instrument under the European Communities Act 1972 and these are the maximum penalties available when offences are created in this way: European Communities Act 1972 (c.68) Sch.2 para.1(1)(d). No attempt was made to increase these penalties in the Copyright, etc. and Trade Marks (Offences and Enforcement) Act 2002 (c.25) or the Digital Economy Act 2010. They will cease to be anomalous as from January 1, 2011: see para.22–10, above.

[156] See the Electronic Commerce (EC Directive) Regulations 2002 (SI 2002/2013) regs 17 to 19.

[157] See paras 21–100 et seq., above.

dence is adduced which is sufficient to raise an issue with respect to the defence, the court or jury is to assume that the defence is satisfied unless the prosecution proves beyond reasonable doubt that it is not.[158] It is thought that this "reverse burden" does not offend the presumption of innocence enshrined in art.6(2) of the European Convention on Human Rights and is accordingly valid.[159]

(ii) Offences in relation to rights in performances under the 1988 Act

Offences of making, dealing with and using illicit recordings under section 198 of the 1988 Act. These offences fall into three broad categories. First, a person commits an offence if, without sufficient consent,[160] he does one of a number of acts in relation to a recording which is, and which he knows or has reason to believe is, an illicit recording.[161] Those acts are as follows: making for sale or hire[162]; importing into the United Kingdom otherwise than for his private and domestic use[163]; possessing in the course of a business with a view to infringing any of the rights conferred by Ch.2 of Pt II of the 1988 Act (that is, the Chapter conferring economic rights in performances)[164]; and in the course of a business selling or letting for hire, offering or exposing for sale or hire, or distributing.[165] Secondly, a person who infringes a performer's making available right after October 31, 2003 in the course of a business or otherwise so as to affect prejudicially the owner of the making available right, commits an offence if he knows or has reason to believe that by doing so he is infringing the making available right in the recording.[166] Thirdly, a person also commits an offence who causes a recording of a performance made without sufficient consent to be shown or played in public or communicated to the public, thereby infringing any of the rights under the Chapter of the 1988 Act conferring economic rights in performances) if he knows or has reason to know that those rights are thereby infringed.[167]

22–26

Comparison with civil provisions. Subsections 198(1)–(3) of the 1988 Act have the effect of making most civil infringements of rights in performances criminal offences, albeit using different terminology to that used in the civil provisions.[168] The main differences are as follows.[169] First, all the criminal offences require "guilty knowledge". Many civil infringements do not.[170] Secondly, the civil infringement of broadcasting live a qualifying performance without consent[171] is not made a criminal offence. Thirdly, rights at civil law are infringed by the pos-

22–27

---

[158] Electronic Commerce (EC Directive) Regulations 2002 (SI 2002/2013) reg.21(2).

[159] Note, however, that the law is in a state of development: see para.22–63 et seq., below.

[160] As to which see para.22–29, below.

[161] As to which, see para.22–28, below.

[162] CDPA 1988 s.198(1)(a).

[163] CDPA 1988 s.198(1)(b).

[164] Pt II of CDPA 1988 is the part headed "Rights in Performances". For a discussion of the term "with a view", see para.22–15, above.

[165] CDPA 1988 s.198(1)(d)(i) to (iii).

[166] CDPA 1988 s.198(1A), inserted by the Copyright and Related Rights Regulations 2003 (SI 2003/2498) reg.26 (for commencement, see ibid., reg.40(3)). The "making available right" is the right to authorise or prohibit the making available of a recording by electronic transmission in such a way that members of the public may access it from a place and at a time individually chosen by them (i.e. "on demand"): see CDPA 1988 s.182CA and para.12–67, above.

[167] CDPA 1988 s.198(2)(a), (b).

[168] For discussion of the civil provisions, see Ch.12, above.

[169] There are others, but they are unlikely to be of any practical effect.

[170] See, e.g. CDPA 1988 ss.182(1)(a) and 186(1).

[171] CDPA 1988 s.182(1)(b).

session of an illicit recording in the course of a business;[172] a criminal offence is only committed by a person who possesses an illicit recording in the course of a business if that possession is with a view to infringing any economic rights in performances.[173] Fourthly, there are no criminal provisions in relation to performers' property rights.[174] Finally, the offences in the first broad category referred to in the previous paragraph are committed by making and dealing with "illicit recordings" without "sufficient consent". The offence in the third broad category referred to in that paragraph is committed in relation to recordings made without "sufficient consent". The term "illicit recording" is defined differently for the purposes of criminal and civil proceedings.[175] The term "sufficient consent" is not relevant to civil proceedings. The two terms are dealt with in the next two paragraphs.

22–28   **"Illicit recording".** A recording is only illicit if it is a recording of the whole or a substantial part of a performance[176] and has been made otherwise than for private purposes.[177] If those pre-conditions are satisfied, then so far as concerns criminal proceedings, the recording is illicit whether it is illicit "for the purposes of" a performer's rights or "for the purposes of" a person having recording rights in the performance.[178] A performer will only have rights in a qualifying performance,[179] i.e. a performance which is given by a qualifying individual or takes place in a qualifying country.[180] "For the purposes of" the performer's rights, the recording is illicit if made without the performer's consent.[181] A person will have recording rights in a performance (whether or not it is a qualifying one) if he is a qualifying person and is a party to and has the benefit of an exclusive recording contract in relation to the performance or he is an assignee of such a person.[182] If the recording is subject to an exclusive recording contract but the person with the benefit of the contract or his assignee is not a qualifying person, then a licensee of that person or an assignee of such a licence will have the recording rights provided the licensee or assignee is a qualifying person.[183] "For the purposes of" the rights of the person having recording rights, the recording is illicit if it was made without the consent of the person having recording rights or of the performer.[184] It seems that the consent of one will suffice. The extended definition of "illicit recording" contained in s.197(5) of the 1988 Act applies to criminal proceedings.[185] It is provided[186] that for the purposes of determining whether a recording is an illicit one it is immaterial where it was made. This cannot have been intended to make it a criminal offence to make for sale or hire an illicit recording outside the United Kingdom: there is a rule of construction that in the absence of express words to the contrary the conduct prohibited by a criminal statute shall be an offence under English law only if it took place within the jurisdiction.[187] Rather, the intention appears to be that it should be an offence both to import into the United Kingdom

---

[172] CDPA 1988 ss.184(1)(b) and 188(1)(b).
[173] CDPA 1988 s.198(1)(c).
[174] i.e. under ss.182A to 182C.
[175] Compare CDPA 1988 s.197(4) with CDPA 1988 s.197(2) and (3).
[176] The term "performance" is defined in CDPA 1988 s.180(2). See para.12–23, above.
[177] CDPA 1988 s.197(2) and (3), applied by s.197(4).
[178] CDPA 1988 s.197(4).
[179] CDPA 1988 ss.182–184.
[180] CDPA 1988 s.18. Qualifying individual and country are defined in s.206. See para.12–24, above.
[181] CDPA 1988 s.197(2).
[182] CDPA 1988 s.185(2).
[183] CDPA 1988 s.185(3).
[184] CDPA 1988 s.197(3).
[185] See para.12–70, above, for a full discussion.
[186] By CDPA 1988 s.197(6).
[187] *Blackstone's Criminal Practice* 2010, para.A8.2.

an illicit recording which has been made abroad and to deal with such a recording within the United Kingdom.

"Sufficient consent". In the case of a qualifying performance (i.e. a performance which is given by a qualifying individual or takes place in a qualifying country),[188] sufficient consent means the consent of the performer.[189] In the case of a non-qualifying performance subject to an exclusive recording contract,[190] the meaning of sufficient consent depends on the offence charged. In the case of an offence of making an illicit recording, sufficient consent means the consent of the performer or of the person having recording rights at the time the consent is given.[191] If there is more than one person with recording rights the consent must be the consent of both or all of them.[192] In the case of all the other offences under s.198(1) (possessing or dealing with a recording) and the offences under s.198(2) (showing, playing or communicating the recording), sufficient consent means the consent of the person having recording rights or, if there is more than one such person, of both or all of them.[193]

22–29

Penalties for offences under section 198. The offences of making for sale or hire, importing and distributing are triable either way (i.e. both summarily and on indictment). They carry a maximum penalty on summary conviction of imprisonment for a term not exceeding six months or a fine not exceeding £50,000[194] or both; but on conviction on indictment they carry a maximum penalty of imprisonment for ten years or an unlimited fine or both.[195] The "making available" offence is also triable either way. The maximum penalty on summary conviction is imprisonment for a term not exceeding three months or a fine not exceeding £50,000[196] or both; on conviction on indictment, the maximum penalty is imprisonment for two years or an unlimited fine or both.[197] The other offences under s.198 are triable only summarily and carry a maximum penalty on summary conviction of six months' imprisonment or a fine not exceeding level 5 on the standard scale[198] or both.[199]

22–30

Liability of officers. Where an offence under s.198 of the 1988 Act committed by a body corporate is proved to have been committed with the consent or connivance of a director, manager, secretary or other similar officer of the body, or a person purporting to act in such a capacity, that person is guilty of the offence and

22–31

---

[188] CDPA 1988 s.181. Qualifying individual and country are defined in s.206. See para.12–24, above.

[189] CDPA 1988 s.198(3)(a).

[190] Defined in CDPA 1988 s.185. See para.12–28, above.

[191] CDPA 1988 s.198(3)(b)(i). The consent of one of them will suffice.

[192] CDPA 1988 s.198(3)(b).

[193] CDPA 1988 s.198(3)(b)(ii).

[194] This figure was increased from the statutory maximum (£5,000: Interpretation Act 1978 (c.30) Sch.1, applying Magistrates' Courts Act 1980 (c.43) s.32(9) as amended by Criminal Justice Act 1991 (c.53) s.17(2)(c)) by Digital Economy Act 2010 s.42(3) with effect from June 8, 2010. For background, see para.22–10, above

[195] CDPA 1988 s.198(5), as amended by the Copyright, etc. and Trade Marks (Offences and Enforcement) Act 2002 s.1(3), in respect of offences committed on or after November 20, 2002: see the Copyright, etc. and Trade Marks (Offences and Enforcement) Act 2002 (Commencement) Order 2002 (SI 2002/2749).

[196] This too was increased from the statutory maximum by Digital Economy Act 2010 s.42(3) with effect from June 8, 2010.

[197] CDPA 1988 s.198(5A). This offence was created by statutory instrument under the European Communities Act 1972 (the new Copyright and Related Rights Regulations 2002, SI 2003/2498) and this is the maximum period of imprisonment which may be provided for when offences are created in this way: European Communities Act 1972 (c.68) Sch.2 para.1(1)(d).

[198] Also currently £5,000: Criminal Justice Act 1982 (c.48) s.37(2) as substituted by Criminal Justice Act 1991 (c.53) s.17(1).

[199] CDPA 1988 s.198(6).

liable to be proceeded against and punished accordingly.[200] The effect of this provision is that the consenting or conniving officer is deemed to be guilty of the same offence as the company and is subject to the same penalties. The equivalent copyright provision is considered above.[201]

22–32   **False representations of authorisation.** It is an offence for a person (such as an artiste's agent) to represent falsely that he is authorised by any person to give consent for the purposes of Ch.2 of Pt II of the 1988 Act (that is, the Chapter conferring economic rights in performances) in relation to a performance, unless he believes on reasonable grounds that he is so authorised.[202] The maximum penalty on summary conviction is six months' imprisonment or a fine not exceeding level 5 on the standard scale[203] or both.[204] Company officers who consent to or connive at the commission of offences by their companies under this section may also be personally liable (see the previous paragraph).

22–33   **Defences.** No offence is committed by the doing of an act which by virtue of any provision in Sch.2 to the 1988 Act (which sets out various "permitted acts") may be done without infringing any of the rights under Ch.2 of Pt II of the 1988 Act (that is, the Chapter conferring economic rights in performances).[205] Furthermore, the "mere conduit", "caching" and "hosting" defences provided for by the E-Commerce Directive apply to these offences.[206] Their substantive provisions are considered elsewhere.[207] The burden of proof in relation to these defences is considered above.[208]

(iii) Some other relevant offences

22–34   **Aiding, abetting, counselling and procuring.** The terms of the 1988 Act do not expressly exclude criminal liability as an accessory for the offences contained in the statute. It follows that a person may be criminally liable for an offence under the 1988 Act on the basis that he has aided, abetted, counselled or procured its commission.[209] Aiding, abetting, counselling or procuring a summary offence is triable summarily, while aiding, abetting, counselling or procuring an offence triable either way[210] is itself triable either way.[211]

22–35   **Encouraging or assisting crime.**[212] The common law offence of incitement has been replaced by three statutory offences under ss.44, 45 and 46 of the Serious Crime Act 2007. They are as follows: intentionally encouraging or assisting an offence; encouraging or assisting an offence, believing it will be committed; and encouraging or assisting offences, believing one or more will be committed. There is a defence of acting reasonably. Mode of trial for the first two of these of-

---

[200] CDPA 1988 s.202(1).

[201] See, para.22–23.

[202] CDPA 1988 s.201(1).

[203] £5,000: see Criminal Justice Act 1982 (c.48) s.37(2) as substituted by Criminal Justice Act 1991 (c.53) s.17(1).

[204] CDPA 1988 s.201(2).

[205] CDPA 1988 s.198(4). See paras 12–75 et seq., above, for permitted acts.

[206] See the Electronic Commerce (EC Directive) Regulations 2002 (SI 2002/2013) regs 17–19.

[207] See paras 21–100 et seq., above.

[208] See para.22–25, above.

[209] *R. v Jefferson* [1994] 1 All E.R. 270; Accessories and Abettors Act 1861 (24 & 25 Vict. c.94) s.8; Magistrates' Courts Act 1980 (c.43) s.44(1).

[210] i.e. triable either summarily (in the Magistrates' Court) or on indictment (in the Crown Court).

[211] Magistrates' Courts Act 1980 (c.43) s.44(2). Whether an offence under CDPA 1988 is triable only summarily or is triable either way is stated in the relevant paragraph above.

[212] What follows is the briefest outline. See *Blackstone's Criminal Practice 2010* section A6.

fences is to be determined as if the defendant had committed the anticipated offence. The third of these offences is triable only on indictment. Penalties are related to those for the anticipated offences.

Attempts. It is an offence to do an act which is more than preparatory to the commission of a relevant substantive offence with intent to commit that offence.[213] However, there can be no attempt to commit an offence which is triable only summarily,[214] as are many of the offences under the 1988 Act.[215] In general, the maximum penalties on conviction of attempting to commit an offence are the same as those on conviction of the offence attempted.[216]   **22–36**

Statutory conspiracy. With the exceptions of conspiracy to defraud,[217] conspiracy to outrage public decency and conspiracy to corrupt public morals, the offence of conspiracy at common law was abolished by the Criminal Law Act 1977[218] and replaced by the offence of statutory conspiracy. If a person agrees with another that a course of conduct shall be pursued which, if the agreement is carried out in accordance with their intentions, will necessarily involve the commission of an offence (or would do so but for a factual impossibility), he is guilty of the offence of statutory conspiracy.[219] The offence is triable only on indictment.[220] The consent of the Director of Public Prosecutions is required before proceedings can be brought in respect of a conspiracy to commit a summary offence.[221] The maximum penalty on conviction of conspiracy to commit an offence under the 1988 Act is the same as that for the offence itself.[222]   **22–37**

Conspiracy to defraud. The offence is constituted by an agreement, by two or more, by dishonesty to deprive a person of something which is his, or to which he is or would be or might be entitled; or an agreement by two or more by dishonesty to injure some proprietary right of that person.[223] Such rights include copyright,[224] and no doubt also design right and the rights in a performance. It is permissible to charge a person with conspiracy to defraud even though the conspiracy alleged was also a conspiracy to commit a substantive offence.[225] The offence is triable on indictment only.[226] The maximum sentence is 10 years' imprisonment or a fine or both.[227]   **22–38**

Theft and fraud. Theft is defined as the dishonest appropriation of property   **22–39**

---

[213] Criminal Attempts Act 1981 (c.47) s.1.
[214] s.1(4) and Interpretation Act 1978 (c.30) Sch.1.
[215] Whether an offence is triable summarily or is triable either way is stated in the relevant paragraph above.
[216] Criminal Attempts Act 1981 s.4(1)(c).
[217] As to which see para.22–38, below.
[218] Criminal Law Act 1977(c.45), s.5.
[219] Criminal Law Act 1977 s.1(1).
[220] Criminal Law Act 1977 s.3(1).
[221] Criminal Law Act 1977 s.4.
[222] Criminal Law Act 1977 s.3(1).
[223] *Scott v Metropolitan Police Commissioner* [1975] A.C. 819.
[224] In *Rank Film Distributors v Video Information Centre* [1982] A.C. 380; [1981] F.S.R. 363, a majority of the House of Lords held that "the risk of those who deal in or manufacture illicit films being prosecuted for [conspiracy to defraud]" was "by no means remote or fanciful". There have been a number of reported prosecutions of conspiracy to defraud copyright owners. See, in particular, *R. v Willetts* (1906) 70 J.P. 127; *R. v Whiteley* (1907) 148 C.C.C. Sessions Papers 267; *R. v Bokenham* [1905–1910] Mac.C.C. 290; and *Scott v Metropolitan Police Commissioner* [1975] A.C. 819. In *R. v Bridgeman and Butt* [1996] F.S.R. 538 (H.H. Judge Halbert, Chester County Court), it was held that a conspiracy to re-enable disabled smartcards for the reception of satellite transmissions amounted to a conspiracy to defraud the transmitting company because it would prejudice its rights under CDPA 1988 s.298(2).
[225] Criminal Justice Act 1987 (c.38) s.12(1).
[226] Criminal Justice Act 1987 (c.38) s.12(3).
[227] Criminal Justice Act 1987 (c.38) s.12(3).

belonging to another with the intention of permanently depriving that other of it.[228] An assumption by a person of any of the rights of an owner amounts to an appropriation.[229] For these purposes, "property"[230] includes "money and all other property, real or personal, including things in action and other intangible property". By s.1(1) of the 1988 Act, copyright is defined as a "property right" and by s.90(1) it is transmissible as personal or moveable property. At first sight it would seem that a person who dishonestly dealt with the copyright in a work as if it were his own would commit the offence of theft because he had assumed one of the rights of the copyright owner.[231] However, the House of Lords has held that the definition of property in the Theft Act 1968[232] does not appear to include copyright[233] and it might be difficult to persuade a court to depart from this, even though it does not appear to have been based on full argument.[234] Theft carries a maximum sentence of imprisonment following trial on indictment of seven years' imprisonment.[235] The offence of obtaining by deception was repealed with effect from January 15, 2007 and replaced by a new offence of fraud by false representation.[236] This offence is committed by dishonestly making a false representation with an intention to make a gain or to cause loss or expose another to a risk of loss. "Gain" and "loss" extend only to gain or loss in money or property (whether temporary or permanent) and "property" is defined in the same way as for theft.[237] It follows that the House of Lords holding referred to above may well present a difficulty in prosecuting someone who has obtained an assignment of copyright by means of a false representation. The maximum penalty for fraud on trial by indictment is 10 years' imprisonment.[238]

22–40   **Design right.** The 1988 Act creates no offences in relation to design right. However, design right, like copyright, is a property right[239] and it might therefore be open to a prosecutor to charge a defendant with theft of design right or with fraud in relation to a design right.[240] It would also seem likely that the offence of conspiracy to defraud[241] would be committed by the parties to a conspiracy to deprive a person of his design right.

22–41   **Other offences under the 1988 Act.** The 1988 Act also creates criminal liability

---

[228] Theft Act 1968 (c.60) s.1(1).

[229] Theft Act 1968 (c.60) s.3(1) as interpreted by the House of Lords in *DPP v Gomez* [1993] A.C. 442.

[230] Theft Act 1968 (c.60) s.4(1).

[231] In Ormerod, D. and Williams, D. (eds), *Smith's Law of Theft* (Oxford: Oxford University Press, 2007) 9th edn at para.2.158, the editors express the view that copyright amounts to "property" for these purposes.

[232] Theft Act 1968 (c.60).

[233] *Rank Film Distributors v Video Information Centre* [1982] A.C. 380 at 445; [1981] F.S.R. 363 .

[234] A further potential difficulty arises from the fact that a theft is only committed if the accused has the intention *permanently* to deprive the true owner of the property. A person who purports to assign a copyright belonging to another may well know that such assignment will be of no legal effect and thus not intend any permanent deprivation of the copyright (he will of course intend permanently to deprive the purported assignee of his money). In those circumstances, the prosecution would need to rely on Theft Act 1968 s.6(1) which provides so far as relevant: "A person appropriating property belonging to another without meaning the other permanently to lose the thing itself is nevertheless to be regarded as having the intention of permanently depriving the other of it if his intention is to treat the thing as his own to dispose of regardless of the other's rights; … ". See *Blackstone's Criminal Practice* 2010, paras B4.42 et seq. for the relevant case law.

[235] Theft Act 1968 (c.60) s.7.

[236] Fraud Act 2006 s.2. See *Blackstone's Criminal Practice* 2010 at paras B5.1 et seq.

[237] Fraud Act 2006 s.5.

[238] Fraud Act 2006 s.1(3).

[239] CDPA 1988 s.213(1).

[240] But note the points made in the previous paragraph.

[241] As to which see para.22–38, above.

in respect of devices and services designed to circumvent technological measures and in respect of unauthorised decoders. These offences are dealt with elsewhere.[242]

The "mere conduit", "caching" and "hosting" defences. These defences, which are considered above,[243] apply in all criminal proceedings. **22–42**

D. SOME PROCEDURAL MATTERS

(i) Introduction

This section of this work is only intended to deal with procedural matters which are specifically relevant to the offences under the 1988 Act. For a comprehensive account of criminal procedure and evidence, the reader is referred to the standard texts.[244] **22–43**

(ii) Enforcement methods[245]

Enforcement by local authorities. In 1994, it was intended that it should become the duty of every local weights and measures authority to enforce the provisions of ss.107 and 198 of the 1988 Act within its area and new sections (107A and 198A) were introduced into the 1988 Act accordingly.[246] The new sections were only in fact introduced with effect from April 6, 2007.[247] To assist authorities in fulfilling these new duties, Parliament provided that various sections of the Trade Descriptions Act 1968[248] were to apply in relation to the enforcement of ss.107 and 198 as they apply in relation to the enforcement of that Act.[249] Those sections give officers the power to make test purchases,[250] inspect goods, enter premises, require the production of documents, seize and detain goods and break open containers.[251] Various types of obstruction of officers are made an offence.[252] There is provision for an owner of goods who has suffered loss by reason of their seizure or detention to obtain compensation[253] if he is not convicted of an offence committed in relation to the goods.[254] If proceedings are to be brought by a local authority under these sections, it is obliged to give the OFT notice of its intention to commence them and to inform it of their outcome.[255] When local authorities do prosecute, they must have regard to their own public protection enforcement **22–44**

---

[242] See paras 15–20 et seq. and 16–12 et seq., respectively.

[243] See para.22–25, above.

[244] See, e.g. *Blackstone's Criminal Practice, Archbold Criminal Pleading, Evidence and Practice, Stones' Justices Manual, Andrews and Hirst on Criminal Evidence.*

[245] For the Government's strategy on IP crime, see *http://www.ipo.gov.uk* [Accessed September 30, 2010].

[246] CDPA 1988 ss.107A and 198A, introduced by Criminal Justice and Public Order Act 1994 (c.33) s.165.

[247] See the Criminal Justice and Public Order Act 1994 (Commencement No. 14) Order 2007 (SI 2007/621).

[248] Trade Descriptions Act 1968 (c.29).

[249] CDPA 1988 ss.107A(2) and 198A(2).

[250] Trade Descriptions Act 1968 (c.29) s.27.

[251] Trade Descriptions Act 1968 (c.29) s.28(1).

[252] Trade Descriptions Act 1968 (c.29) s.29.

[253] The right to and amount of which is to be determined by arbitration: Trade Descriptions Act 1968 (c.29) s.33(2).

[254] Trade Descriptions Act 1968 (c.29) s.33.

[255] Enterprise Act 2002 s.230(2), applied by the Enterprise Act 2002 (Part 8 Notice to OFT of Intended Prosecution Specified Enactments, Revocation and Transitional Provision) Order 2003 (SI 2003/1376). The purpose of these provisions is to reinforce the OFT's co-ordination role in respect of the legislation to which Pt 8 of the Enterprise Act 2002 applies. For example, the OFT

policies. Failure to comply with such a policy may lead to a stay of the proceedings on the grounds of abuse of process,[256] but only in an exceptional case.[257] In very exceptional cases, a local authority's decision to prosecute may also be the subject of a judicial review.[258]

22–45   Civil enforcement under the Enterprise Act 2002. Contraventions of ss.107 and 198 of the 1988 Act which are carried out in the course of a business and which harm the collective interests of consumers in the United Kingdom are subject to the enforcement regime laid down by Pt 8 of the Enterprise Act 2002.[259] Part 8 permits certain bodies ("enforcers") to apply to the court for "enforcement orders", which are similar to injunctions.[260] As well as prohibiting further contraventions, such orders may also require the person against whom they are made to publish their terms and a corrective statement.[261] An undertaking may be accepted instead.[262] A "consultation" machinery, which is designed to prevent further infringement without the need for an application to the court, must be gone through before an application is made.[263] The OFT[264] and all local weights and measures authorities are "general enforcers" for the purposes of Pt 8.[265] Other bodies may be designated as enforcers by the Secretary of State.[266] At the time of writing, certain statutory regulators had been so designated, as had the Consumers Association (Which?).[267] In future, other private organisations may also be so designated if they satisfy certain criteria.[268]

22–46   Private prosecution.[269] There are no restrictions on who may prosecute an of-

---

would be able to inform one authority that another was already prosecuting or that an enforcement order had been granted. This might lead the first authority to decide that it was not necessary to prosecute: see Explanatory Notes to the Enterprise Act 2002, para.576. On October 14, 2010, the Government announced that the OFT's responsibilities in this field were under review. See *http://www.bis.gov.uk/policies/consumer-issues* [Accessed November 16, 2010].

[256] *R. v Adaway* [2004] EWCA Crim 2831; (2004) 168 J.P. 645.

[257] *Wandsworth LBC v Rashid* [2009] EWHC 1844 (Admin); [2010] Env. L.R. 22.

[258] *R. (Butler) v Wychavon District Council* [2006] EWHC 2977 (Admin).

[259] Enterprise Act 2002 (Pt 8 Domestic Infringements) Order 2003 (SI 2003/1593) art.2 and Schedule, applying to infringements committed on or after June 20, 2003.

[260] Enterprise Act 2002 s.217.

[261] Enterprise Act 2002 s.217(8).

[262] Enterprise Act 2002 s.217(9).

[263] Enterprise Act 2002 s.214.

[264] See para.28–287, below. Note, however, that the OFT's consumer role is under review: see *http://www.bis.gov.uk/policies/consumer-issues* [Accessed November 16, 2010].

[265] Enterprise Act 2002 s.213(1)(b).

[266] s.213.

[267] The full list is on the Department of Business Innovation and Skills website: *http://www.bis.gov.uk* [Accessed September 30, 2010]. Relevant statutory instruments include the Enterprise Act 2002 (Part 8 Designated Enforcers: Criteria for Designation, Designation of Public Bodies as Designated Enforcers and Transitional Provisions) Order 2003 (SI 2003/1399) and the Enterprise Act 2002 (Part 8) (Designation of the Consumers' Association) Order 2005 (SI 2005/917).

[268] i.e. the criteria set out in SI 2003/1399.

[269] See generally on private prosecutions *Scopelight Ltd v Chief Constable of Northumbria Police Force* [2009] EWCA Civ 1156; [2010] 2 W.L.R. 1138. Police had investigated an offence but the Crown Prosecution Service ("CPS") had decided not to prosecute. The point in issue was whether the police were permitted to pass on material gathered in the investigation to a potential private prosecutor. The Court of Appeal held that they could do so in appropriate circumstances. The question in each case was whether it was necessary in all the circumstances that the property seized should be retained for forensic examination or for investigation in connection with an offence or for use as evidence at a trial for an offence. In determining that question at least the following circumstances would be relevant: the identity and motive of the potential prosecutor; the gravity of the allegation together with the reasoning behind the negative decision of the CPS and thus the extent to which, in the particular case, the public had a legitimate interest in the criminal prosecution of the conduct in question; the police's view of the significance of what has been retained; and any material fact concerning the proposed defendant. See para.53.

fender for an offence under the 1988 Act[270] and there have been many private prosecutions under the Act since it was introduced. Most private prosecutions are brought by local authorities, but some have been brought by private individuals. The right to bring a private prosecution is of considerable antiquity and has been stated to be a valuable safeguard against inertia or partiality on the part of the authorities.[271] However, the right is capable of being abused.[272] Accordingly, there are constraints on its exercise. First, the Magistrates' Court before which it is sought to commence the proceedings by the issue of a summons may refuse to do so on the grounds that the proceedings are an abuse of the process of the court or other impropriety is involved.[273] Secondly, the Director of Public Prosecutions is given statutory powers to take over the conduct of private prosecutions[274] and this power may be used to effect the discontinuance of a prosecution which is considered to be contrary to the public interest.[275] Thirdly, the court has the power to stay the proceedings on the ground that they amount to an abuse of its process. This power is generally exercised on one of two grounds: either because the defendant has been or will be prejudiced in the preparation or conduct of his defence by delay on the part of the prosecution, or because the prosecution has manipulated or misused the process of the court so as to deprive the defendant of a protection provided by the law or to take advantage of a technicality.[276] Finally, a vexa-

---

[270] In its Consultation Paper No.149: *Consents to Prosecution* (The Stationery Office, 1997), the Law Commission invited discussion as to whether the consent of the DPP ought to be required before a private prosecution for copyright infringement could be commenced (see in particular paras 6.47–6.51). In its final report (*Consents to Prosecution*, Law Commission 255), the Commission concluded that it would not be appropriate to impose a consent requirement in copyright cases: see at para.5–51. See *R. v Rollins* [2010] UKSC 39; [2010] 1 W.L.R. 1922 at para.9, for the general proposition that anyone can prosecute an offence under a public general act provided in the case of a body corporate that it is empowered to do so by the instrument that gives it the power to act.

[271] *Gouriet v Union of Post Office Workers* [1978] A.C. 435 at 477 and 497.

[272] *Jones v Whalley* [2006] UKHL 41; [2007] 1 A.C. 63; [2006] 4 All E.R. 113 at para.16. See also *Scopelight Ltd v Chief Constable of Northumbria Police Force* [2009] EWCA Civ 1156; [2010] 2 W.L.R. 1138 at para.43.

[273] This power is rarely used. See, generally, *Blackstone's Criminal Practice 2010*, para.D5.5 and *R. (Michael Craik, Chief Constable of Northumbria Police) v Newcastle upon Tyne Magistrates Court* [2010] EWHC 935 (Admin), where the issue of a summons was successfully challenged in judicial review proceedings. Where the CPS has brought and discontinued proceedings in respect of an alleged offence, no special rules apply to the Magistrates' decision whether to issue a summons in respect of the same allegations at the behest of a private prosecutor. By contrast, if a CPS prosecution is already on foot, the Magistrates should be slow to issue such a summons. See *R. (Charlson) v Guildford Magistrates' Court* [2006] EWHC 2318 (Admin); [2006] 1 W.L.R. 3494; (2006) 170 J.P. 739; [2007] R.T.R. 1 at para.36.

[274] Prosecution of Offences Act 1985 (c.23) s.6(2).

[275] In *R. v Tower Bridge Magistrates' Court* [1994] Q.B. 340 it was observed that this power could be used if there was insufficient evidence, or the prosecution would be contrary to the public interest, or to avoid duplication, or for "any other good reason". The power was used by the DPP under earlier legislation (which was in similar terms) to bring an end to a private prosecution of a defendant who had been given an undertaking by the DPP that he would not be prosecuted in exchange for giving evidence for the Crown (*Turner v DPP* (1979) 68 Cr. App.R. 70); and also where the defendant to pending criminal proceedings brought a private prosecution against one of the Crown's witnesses and the DPP was satisfied that the proceedings were a vexatious attempt to discredit that witness (*R. v DPP, Ex p. Raymond* (1980) 70 Cr. App.R. 233; *Raymond v Attorney-General* [1982] Q.B. 839). The DPP's current policy is only to intervene on evidential grounds if there is clearly no case to answer: see *R. v DPP, Ex p. Duckenfield* [2000] 1 W.L.R. 55, where the Divisional Court refused to interfere with this policy.

[276] See the detailed discussion in *Archbold Criminal Pleading Evidence and Practice* 2010 at paras 4–48 et seq. and note *R. v Leominster Magistrates' Court and Another Ex p. Aston Manor Brewery Co* (1997) 94(5) L.S.G. 32 DC as to the difficulties which may arise where there are concurrent civil and criminal proceedings. See para.22–44, above as to local authorities' obligations to comply with their own policies. See also *Dacre v City of Westminster Magistrates Court* [2008] EWHC 1667 (Admin); [2009] 1 W.L.R. 2241: a private prosecution may be stayed as an abuse of process where the prosecutor has encouraged the crime or created the same mischief as that about which he or she complains.

tious prosecutor may be made the subject of a criminal proceedings order under s.42 of the Senior Courts Act 1981.[277]

(iii) Choice of remedy

22–47   **Advantages of criminal proceedings.** Criminal proceedings have two obvious advantages to a copyright owner faced with an infringement.[278] First, for some defendants, a criminal conviction may be more of a deterrent to future infringement than an injunction limited to a particular work or works. It is recognised that penalties for second and further offences are generally greater than those for first offences. Second, the rules as to costs in respect of indictable offences (i.e. offences which are triable either way,[279] thus including the more serious copyright and rights in performances offences) are generally quite favourable to a prosecutor who is not a public authority. In any case the court may order the defendant to pay a successful prosecutor's costs. On the other hand, in determining the amount of any costs order, the court is obliged to take account of a number of factors (including the defendant's means) which would not be relevant in a civil case.[280] However, in proceedings for an indictable offence, the court has the power[281] to make an award of prosecution costs out of Central (i.e. government[282]) Funds whether the defendant is convicted or acquitted. The practice is that such an order should be made save where there is good reason for not doing so, for example, where proceedings have been instituted or continued without good cause.[283]

22–48   **Disadvantages of criminal proceedings.** First, there is no entitlement to an injunction or to an inquiry as to damages or an account of profits.[284] Secondly, subject to what is said below about the burden of proof, the prosecution must establish guilt beyond reasonable doubt rather than merely on the balance of probabilities. Thirdly, it is necessary in criminal proceedings for copyright offences to prove knowledge or reason to believe even in respect of primary infringements.[285] Fourthly, the presumptions contained in ss.104 and 105 of the 1988 Act do not apply in criminal proceedings.[286] Fifthly, all persons charged with the duty of investigating offences,[287] whether before or after proceedings have been begun, are obliged to have regard to the Code of Practice under the

---

[277] *Scopelight Ltd v Chief Constable of Northumbria Police Force* [2009] EWCA Civ 1156; [2010] 2 W.L.R. 1138 at para.45.

[278] A possible further advantage, i.e. that the prosecution may not have to prove the absence of a licence or consent, is dealt with in detail in paras 22–62 et seq., below.

[279] See Interpretation Act 1978 (c.30) Sch.1.

[280] For an example in this field, see *R. v Bow Street Magistrates' Court, Ex p. Mitchell* [2001] F.S.R. 267.

[281] Under Prosecution of Offences Act 1985 (c.23) s.17(1).

[282] Interpretation Act 1978 (c.30) Sch.1.

[283] *Practice Direction on Costs in Criminal Proceedings* [2004] 2 All E.R. 1070, para.III.1.1.

[284] It is true that the criminal court may make an order for compensation under the Powers of Criminal Courts (Sentencing) Act 2000 (c.6) s.130: see *Blackstone's Criminal Practice*, 2010 paras E16.1 et seq. However, such an award is only to be made in a clear case and copyright cases seldom are. Moreover, any award will be confined to the matters proved or admitted by the defendant. On a fully contested trial, it would be usual to seek to prove a small number of offences only, while on a guilty plea the number of matters admitted by the defendant may well be small. Note also the availability of deprivation orders under Powers of Criminal Courts (Sentencing) Act 2000 s.143 and confiscation orders under the Proceeds of Crime Act 2002 (c.29).

[285] See para.22–14, above.

[286] By CDPA 1988 s.107(6). Note however, that the presumption contained in s.27(4) does apply.

[287] It was held on the similar wording in the Police and Criminal Evidence Act 1984 (c.60) s.67(9), that the question whether a person was "charged with the duty of investigating offences or charging offenders" was one of fact: *R. v Seelig* [1992] 1 W.L.R. 148; (1992) 94 Cr. App.R. 17 at 26. In that case, the Court of Appeal was not prepared to interfere with a finding that DTI inspectors

Criminal Procedure and Investigations Act 1996.[288] The Code contains detailed requirements as to the conduct of investigations. Among its provisions are a duty to pursue all reasonable lines of inquiry, whether they point towards or away from the suspect[289]; a duty to record and retain all information, including negative information, which has a bearing on the offence being investigated[290]; a duty to retain draft witness statements where their content differs from the final version[291]; and a duty to retain communications with experts.[292] Sixthly, the prosecution in criminal proceedings have extensive duties of disclosure.[293] In the main these are not significantly different in scope from a claimant's obligations as to disclosure in civil proceedings.[294] However, having applied the Code of Practice, the prosecution may well have in their possession more disclosable material of a damaging nature than would a claimant in civil proceedings.[295] Seventhly, the defence duties of disclosure remain limited. Where the case is to be tried summarily, the defence is not obliged to provide a defence statement;[296] accordingly, the basis of the defence may not become apparent until late in the trial, leaving

---

were not within s.67(9). It has subsequently been held that store detectives (*R. v Bayliss* (1994) 98 Cr. App.R. 235) and commercial investigators employed by a betting shop (*R. v Twaites* (1991) 92 Cr. App.R. 106) may be within the subsection while the officers of the Federation Against Copyright Theft are within it (*Joy v Federation Against Copyright Theft* [1993] Crim. L.R. 588). It is clear from these cases that the "duty" may arise simply from an ordinary contract. It follows that officers of a collecting society charged with investigating cases of criminal infringement or solicitors instructed to prepare criminal proceedings in respect of an infringement may well (depending on the facts) be subject to the Code of Practice. See *Blackstone's Criminal Practice 2010* para.D1.1

[288] Criminal Procedure and Investigations Act 1996 (c.25). See s.26(1) of the Act. The Code of Practice is reproduced in App.4 to *Blackstone's Criminal Practice*, 2010. Persons charged with a duty of investigating offences are also obliged to have regard to the Codes of Practice under the Police and Criminal Evidence Act 1984 (c.60): see s.67(9) of that Act. The 1984 Act Codes concern, inter alia, searches, seizure of property, detention and questioning, identification and tape recording of interviews. They are reproduced in App.1 to *Blackstone's Criminal Practice*, 2010. It has been held that the provisions of the Codes concerning the interviewing of detained persons or persons attending police stations voluntarily do not apply to interviews conducted by persons other than police officers elsewhere than in police stations: see *R. v South Central Division Magistrates' Court, Ex p. Secretary of State for Social Security Daily Telegraph* November 28, 2000. Administrative Court, (interview with officers of benefits agency at their premises) and *R. v South East Wiltshire Magistrates, Ex p. Beale* Unreported, December 11, 2002 DC (interview with trading standards officers at their office). In such circumstances the suspect has no right to free legal advice but may be entitled to advice under the Green Form scheme, which is means tested. The limit of a trading standards officer's obligations in such circumstances is to give the suspect the opportunity to consult a solicitor. It would be wholly inappropriate to advise on the availability of legal assistance: see *Ex p. Beale*.

[289] Code of Practice, para.3.5.

[290] paras 4.1–4.4.

[291] para.5.4.

[292] para.5.4.

[293] This applies whether or not the prosecutor is charged with the investigation of offences: *Scopelight Ltd v Chief Constable of Northumbria Police Force* [2009] EWCA Civ 1156; [2010] 2 W.L.R. 1138 at para.46.

[294] The extensive prosecution disclosure obligations which formerly existed at common law were replaced in limited form by the Criminal Procedure and Investigations Act 1996 (c.25). S.3 provides that any material which in the prosecutor's opinion might undermine the case for the prosecution against the accused must be disclosed. If the accused gives a defence statement (which is obligatory in the case of trial on indictment but voluntary in summary proceedings), the prosecution must also disclose any material which might reasonably be expected to assist the accused's defence: Criminal Procedure and Investigations Act 1996 s.7. For the definition of "criminal investigation", see Criminal Procedure and Investigations Act 1996 s.1(4). See also the Attorney-General's Guidelines on Disclosure in Criminal Proceedings, *Blackstone's Criminal Practice*, 2010, App.4.

[295] This is of course only correct since the interests of justice outweigh those of the parties in criminal proceedings. In practice, the CPS and other prosecuting agencies often give wider disclosure than is required by the terms of the Criminal Procedure and Investigations Act 1996 and the Attorney-General's Guidelines.

[296] They may however supply a voluntary statement under Criminal Procedure and Investigations Act 1996 (c.25) s.6. Such a statement is only likely to be served where the defence are seeking further disclosure from the prosecution pursuant to s.7 of the Act.

the prosecution little or no time to prepare cross-examination or evidence in rebuttal. Where the case is to be tried on indictment, the defence duties of disclosure are more extensive. A written statement must be provided, setting out the nature of the defence, including any particular defences on which the defendant intends to rely, indicating the matters of fact on which the defendant takes issue with the prosecutor and the reasons for so taking issue, particulars of the matters of fact to be relied on for the purpose of the defence (including details of any alibi) and any points of law together with authorities.[297] However, there is no requirement on the defence to give disclosure of documents. Eighthly, the time limit for commencing summary proceedings[298] is only six months.[299] This may cause difficulties if a lengthy investigation is necessary before proceedings can be commenced. Ninth, the Divisional Court has emphasised that a private prosecutor is "still a prosecutor and subject to the same obligations as a minister of justice as are the public prosecuting authorities".[300] Finally, it has recently been emphasised that the criminal courts are not an appropriate forum for cases of any complexity, not least because of the difficulty a prosecutor is likely to face in rectifying technical slip ups.[301]

(iv) Search warrants under the 1988 Act

22–49 **Background.** Search warrants in this field were first introduced in the Musical Copyright Act 1906, which empowered justices to issue them in respect of pirated sheet music.[302] Specific provision for the issue of search warrants in relation to other copyright offences was first made by the Copyright (Amendment) Act 1983,[303] which provided for the issue of warrants in respect of the offences of making, importing and distributing infringing copies of sound recordings and films.[304] Sections 109 and 200 of the 1988 Act extended these powers to offences of making, importing and distributing infringing copies of copyright works of all types and illicit recordings.[305] By the Copyright, etc. and Trade Marks (Offences and Enforcement) Act 2002 these powers were extended to all offences of making or dealing with infringing copies, all offences in relation to articles specifically designed for making copies of a copyright work and all offences of making or dealing with illicit recordings.[306] At the same time as the new offences of infringement of copyright by communication to the public and infringement of the performers' making available right were introduced, these powers were again extended to cover these offences.[307] Since January 1, 2006, the general provisions as to the obtaining of search warrants contained in s.8 of the Police and Criminal

---

[297] Criminal Procedure and Investigations Act 1996 (c.25) s.6A.

[298] As to which offences are triable only summarily, see the relevant paragraphs above.

[299] Magistrates' Court Act 1980 (c.43) s.127. There is no time limit for commencing proceedings for an either-way offence,but prosecution delay may justify a stay on grounds of abuse of process.

[300] See *R. v Belmarsh Magistrates Court ex p. Watts* [1999] 2 Cr. App. R. 188.

[301] *R. v. Gilham* [2009] EWCA Crim 2293; [2010] E.C.D.R. 5 at para.30, referring to *R. v. Higgs* [2008] EWCA Crim 1324; [2009] 1 W.L.R. 73; [2009] F.S.R. 34 at para.36.

[302] See para.22–02, above.

[303] Copyright (Amendment) Act 1983 (c.42).

[304] A new s.21A was added to the Copyright Act 1956.

[305] CDPA 1988 ss.109(1)(a) and 200(1)(a)..

[306] Copyright, etc. and Trade Marks (Offences and Enforcement) Act 2002 (c.25) s.2. The powers do not apply to the offences under s.107(3) (public performance of works, sound recordings or films) or 198(2) (causing a recording made without consent to be show or played in public or communicated to the public).

[307] Copyright and Related Rights Regulations 2003 (SI 2003/2498), reg.26, with effect from October 31, 2003.

Evidence Act 1984[308] apply to all indictable offences[309] and thus to the either way offences under ss.107 and 198. It follows that the provisions as to search warrants under the 1988 Act will be of diminished importance.

When a warrant under the 1988 Act may be issued. Sections 109 and 200 **22–50** provide that where a justice of the peace is satisfied by information on oath given by a constable that there are reasonable grounds for believing that an offence of making, importing or distributing an infringing copy, communication to the public, making, importing or distributing an illicit recording or making available has been or is about to be committed in any premises and that evidence that such an offence has been or is about to be committed is in the premises, he may issue a search warrant.[310] The word "premises" is defined as including land, buildings, fixed or moveable structures, vehicles, vessels, aircraft and hovercraft.[311]

Effect of warrants under the 1988 Act. The effect of the warrant is to authorise **22–51** a constable to enter and search the premises, using such reasonable force as is necessary.[312] However, the warrant may not authorise the constable to search for items which are subject to legal privilege[313] or which constitute "excluded" or "special procedure" material consisting of documents or records as defined in the Police and Criminal Evidence Act 1984.[314] The definitions of "excluded" and "special procedure" material are lengthy and complex.[315] In broad terms, so far as is likely to be relevant to the field of copyright and rights in performances, the effect of this limitation is that the warrant may not authorise a search for journalistic material[316] consisting of documents or records; or for documents or records which are in the possession of a person who acquired or created them in the course of a trade, business, profession or other occupation or for the purposes of any office and who holds them subject to any express or implied undertaking to hold them in confidence[317] or subject to any statutory restriction on disclosure or obligation as to secrecy. The warrant may authorise persons (such, no doubt, as the right owner or his representative) to accompany any constable who is executing it. Warrants remain in force for three months from the date of their issue.[318] In executing a warrant issued on the basis that there are grounds that a copyright offence has been or is about to be committed, the constable may seize an article if he reasonably believes that it is evidence that *any* offence under s.107(1), (2) or (2A) of the 1988 Act has been or is about to be committed, i.e. not merely an of-

---

[308] See the standard criminal procedure texts.

[309] Police and Criminal Evidence Act 1984 s.8(1)(a), as amended by the Serious Organised Crime and Police Act 2005 (c.15) Sch.7(3) para.43(3).

[310] CDPA 1988 ss.109(1) and 200(1).

[311] CDPA 1988 ss.109(5) and 200(4).

[312] CDPA 1988 ss.109(1) and 200(1).

[313] As defined in Police and Criminal Evidence Act 1984 (c.60) s.10. Note that items held with the intention of furthering a criminal purpose are not within the definition of items subject to legal privilege: ibid. s.10(2).

[314] See CDPA 1988 ss.109(2) and 200(2).

[315] See Police and Criminal Evidence Act 1984 ss.11 to 14.

[316] Defined by Police and Criminal Evidence Act 1984 s.13 as material acquired or created for the purposes of journalism if it is in the possession of the person who acquired it or created it for the purposes of journalism.

[317] Except in the case of personal records (i.e. records concerning an individual and relating to his physical or mental health or to certain types of counselling or assistance which have been given to him: Police and Criminal Evidence Act 1984 s.12), an undertaking to hold documents or records in confidence is of no effect for these purposes if it arises as between employer and employee or between a company and an associated company: Police and Criminal Evidence Act 1984 s.14(3)–(6).

[318] CDPA 1988 ss.109(3)(b) and 200(3)(b) as amended by the Serious and Organised Crime and Police Act 2005 (c.15) Sch.16 para.6.

fence on the basis of which the warrant was obtained.[319] Where the warrant has been issued on the basis of an offence in relation to rights in performances, the constable may seize an article if he reasonably believes that it is evidence that any offence under s.198(1) or (1A) has been or is about to be committed.[320]

(v) Delivery up under the 1988 Act

22–52   **Delivery up under section 108 of the 1988 Act: copyright.**[321] The court before which proceedings are brought against a person for an offence under s.107 of the 1988 Act may, if satisfied that at the time of his arrest or charge he had in his possession, custody or control in the course of a business an infringing copy of a copyright work, order the infringing copy to be delivered up to the copyright owner or to such other person as the court may direct.[322] A conviction is not a pre-condition for the making of an order for delivery up. The same provision applies to articles specifically designed or adapted for making copies of a particular copyright work, provided the person knew or had reason to believe that the article had been or was to be used to make infringing copies.[323] The presumptions contained in ss.104 to 106 of the 1988 Act apply on an application for delivery up.[324] For the purposes of these provisions a person is treated as charged with an offence when he is orally charged or is served with a summons or indictment.[325] An order may be made by the court of its own motion or on the application of the prosecutor.[326] However, no order may be made after the time limited for the making of a delivery up order in civil proceedings[327] or if it appears unlikely that a disposal order will be made.[328] An appeal against a delivery up order made by a Magistrates' Court lies to the Crown Court.[329] A person to whom an article is delivered up pursuant to the section is obliged to retain it pending the making of a disposal order or the decision not to make one.[330] The powers to order delivery up under s.108 of the 1988 Act are expressly without prejudice to the powers of the court under s.143 of the Powers of Criminal Courts (Sentencing) Act 2000,[331] which gives the court extensive powers to make an order depriving a person of his rights in property which has been or was intended to be used for the purpose of committing or facilitating[332] the commission of an offence and is discussed below.[333]

22–53   **Delivery up under section 199 of the 1988 Act: rights in performances.** The court's powers to order delivery up of illicit recordings in criminal proceedings

---

[319] CDPA 1988 s.109(4). This covers all the offences under s.107 except those involving the public performance of works, sound recordings or films.

[320] CDPA 1988 s.200(3A), inserted by the Copyright, etc. and Trade Marks (Offences and Enforcement) Act 2002 (c.25) s.2. This covers all the offences under s.198 except that of causing a recording made without consent to be played or shown in public or communicated to the public.

[321] For delivery up in civil proceedings, see paras 21–214 et seq, above.

[322] CDPA 1988 s.108(1). Compare the similar provisions in civil proceedings under ibid. s.99.

[323] CDPA 1988 s.108(1).

[324] CDPA 1988 s.107(6). As to these presumptions, see paras 21–260 et seq., above.

[325] CDPA 1988 s.108(2).

[326] CDPA 1988 s.108(3).

[327] CDPA 1988 s.108(3)(a); for the time limit see CDPA 1988 s.113 and para.21–216, above.

[328] CDPA 1988 s.108(3)(b); for disposal orders see s.114.

[329] CDPA 1988 s.108(4).

[330] CDPA 1988 s.108(5); as to disposal orders see s.114.

[331] c.6. See CDPA 1988 s.108(6), as amended by the Powers of Criminal Courts (Sentencing) Act 2000 Sch.9 para.115.

[332] Which expression includes steps taken after the offence to dispose of property or to avoid apprehension or detection: Powers of Criminal Courts (Sentencing) Act 2000 s.143(8).

[333] See paras 22–54 et seq., below.

are substantially the same as those relating to infringing copies of copyright works.[334]

(vi) Deprivation, forfeiture and confiscation

General provisions as to deprivation. Statutory provisions as to deprivation apply generally to all criminal cases. These provisions are now contained in s.143 of the Powers of Criminal Courts (Sentencing) Act 2000.[335] There are two regimes which are relevant to the offences under the 1988 Act. The first (s.143(1)) applies where a person has been convicted of an offence. In such a case the court may order the deprivation of any property which it is satisfied has been lawfully seized from that person or was in his possession or control at the time when he was apprehended for the offence or when a summons was issued in respect of it. Before an order may be made under this provision, the court must be satisfied that the property in question has been used for the purpose of committing or facilitating the commission of an offence or was intended by the defendant to be used for that purpose. The second regime (s.143(2)) applies where a person has been convicted of an offence and that offence, or another offence which has been taken into consideration on sentence, consists of the unlawful possession of property which has been lawfully seized from the defendant or was in his possession at the time of arrest or the issue of a summons. In that case, the court may make a deprivation order irrespective of whether the property had been or was intended to be used for the commission or to facilitate the commission of an offence. Under each regime, the deprivation power is discretionary and the court is obliged to have regard to the value of the property and to the likely effect of a deprivation order on the offender.[336] The former provision would theoretically permit the court to order the deprivation of equipment (e.g. a computer or photocopier) which had been used to manufacture infringing copies. However, it seems unlikely that a court would make such an order if the defendant's livelihood depended on his keeping the equipment for legitimate uses.[337]

22–54

Extension of these powers in other contexts. It will be apparent that these general provisions, although extensive, have their limitations. First, it is necessary that the defendant should have been convicted of an offence. Thus, no application may be made where the investigation does not lead to a prosecution or where the defendant is acquitted. Secondly, the property must have been lawfully seized or have been in the defendant's possession at the time of his arrest or of the issue of the summons. No application may be made where the property has come into an investigator's possession by other means. Thirdly, there is no provision which expressly enables the court in a case where a large number of items have been seized to draw inferences from samples. For reasons of this type, specific forfeiture provisions were introduced in a variety of fields, including most relevantly in the field of trade marks,[338] which sought to remove each of the three limitations set out above.

22–55

Forfeiture under the 1998 Act: general. The Copyright, etc. and Trade Marks (Offences and Enforcement) Act 2002[339] introduced new provisions in respect of the forfeiture of infringing copies, articles specifically designed for making cop-

22–56

---

[334] As to which see the previous paragraph.
[335] c.6.
[336] Powers of Criminal Courts (Sentencing) Act 2000 s.143(4).
[337] See, e.g. *Blackstone's Criminal Practice*, 2010, para.E18.2.
[338] Trade Marks Act 1994 (c.26) s.97.
[339] c.25.

ies, illicit recordings and unauthorised decoders. These provisions, which came into force on November 20, 2002, are modelled on s.97 of the Trade Marks Act 1994 and their introduction was intended to further the aim of harmonising the criminal provisions in respect of copyright, performers' rights and decoders with those in respect of trade marks.[340]

22–57 **Forfeiture proceedings: threshold conditions and venue.** Section 114A of the 1988 Act[341] applies where infringing copies or articles specifically adapted or designed for making copies of a particular copyright work have come into the possession of any person in connection with the investigation or prosecution of a "relevant" offence.[342] Thus they apply not only where a police officer has seized an infringing copy in the course of an arrest but also, for example, where a private investigator has been handed an infringing copy by an informer. The application for forfeiture must be made by the person into whose possession the copies or articles have come.[343] The definition of "relevant offence" extends beyond offences under s.107(1), (2) or (2A) of the 1988 Act to offences under the Trade Descriptions Act 1968, the Business Protection from Misleading Marketing Regulations 2008[344] and the Consumer Protection from Unfair Trading Regulations 2008[345] and to offences involving dishonesty or deception.[346] Therefore, forfeiture may take place even if there is in fact no intellectual property content to the investigation or prosecution, for example if it is really concerned with a burglary or the handling of stolen goods. Furthermore, an application for forfeiture may be made whether or not proceedings have been brought. Thus, for example, where an authority accumulates a large number of infringing articles as a result of a raid but is unable to prosecute because the offender has absconded or given a false name, forfeiture can nevertheless be sought.[347] If proceedings have been brought for a relevant offence relating to some or all of the infringing articles, the application must be made to the court where those proceedings are taking place.[348] Otherwise, the application must be brought by way of complaint to a Magistrates' Court.[349]

22–58 **Forfeiture proceedings: the decision.** The court may only make a forfeiture order if it is satisfied (presumably to the civil rather than the criminal standard, although this is not stated) that a relevant offence has been committed in relation to the infringing copies or articles.[350] In reaching its decision, the court is expressly permitted to infer that a relevant offence has been committed in relation to any infringing copies or articles if it is satisfied that such an offence has been committed in relation to infringing copies or articles of which the infringing copies or articles in question are representative (whether by reason of being of the same design or part of the same consignment or batch or otherwise).[351] It is not clear what this subsection is intended to achieve, since even in the absence of such a provision there would be no obstacle to the court reaching its conclusions from inference. Moreover, the subsection fails to make clear exactly what type of

---

[340] See *Hansard* HC Vol.375 cols 628-9 (second reading).
[341] The equivalent provision for Scotland is in s.114B.
[342] CDPA 1988 s.114A(1).
[343] CDPA 1988 s.114A(1).
[344] SI 2008/1276.
[345] SI 2008/1277.
[346] s.114A(2).
[347] *Hansard* HC, Standing Committee C, January 9, 2002, col.9.
[348] CDPA 1988 s.114A(3)(a).
[349] CDPA 1988 s.114A(3)(b).
[350] CDPA 1988 s.114A(4).
[351] CDPA 1988 s.114A(4).

inferences may be drawn. Take, for example, a consignment of 1,000 counterfeit music CDs which is found in a defendant's possession. Suppose that the consignment is made up of 100 batches, each of which consists of 10 identical CDs. In this case, for practical reasons, the prosecution may be forced to limit the charges to possession of one CD from each of (say) 15 of the 100 batches. On conviction, it will certainly be open to the court to order forfeiture of the whole contents of those 15 batches. However, does the mere fact that the court has found that the contents of those batches are counterfeit entitle it to infer that the contents of the other 85 batches (which may include copies of entirely different copyright works) are also counterfeit? Much will depend on the facts. In practice, defendants in this position are seldom unduly concerned to retain possession of the goods in question and can frequently be persuaded to sign a disclaimer in respect of any rights they may have in them.

Forfeiture proceedings: form of order and appeals. The court's powers as to the terms of the order are very wide: it may order the copies or articles to be destroyed in accordance with such directions as it may give; alternatively it may direct that the copies or articles shall be forfeited to the owner of the copyright in question or dealt with in such way as it considers appropriate.[352] Any person aggrieved by the grant or refusal of an order by a Magistrates' court will be permitted to appeal to the Crown Court.[353] In the Crown Court the position as to appeals is less clear. Where the defendant has been convicted, an appeal by him will presumably lie to the Court of Criminal Appeal under s.9(1) of the Criminal Appeal Act 1968.[354] However, where the defendant has been acquitted but a forfeiture order has nevertheless been made, or where someone other than a defendant to criminal proceedings wishes to appeal, it is less clear what jurisdiction the Court of Criminal Appeal would have to hear the appeal. The court will be permitted to delay implementation of the order pending an appeal or an appeal by case stated.[355]   **22–59**

Forfeiture of illicit recordings and unauthorised decoders. The copyright provisions discussed above are mirrored by provisions in respect of illicit recordings (s.204A of the 1988 Act)[356] and unauthorised decoders (s.279C of the 1988 Act).[357] In the case of unauthorised decoders, if the court does not order the destruction of the decoders, it may direct that they shall be forfeited to the person with rights and remedies under s.298 of the 1988 Act.[358]   **22–60**

Confiscation. A conviction for an offence under ss.107(1) or (2), 198(1) or 297A of the 1988 Act means that the defendant is deemed to have a "criminal lifestyle" for the purposes of the Proceeds of Crime Act 2002.[359] This automatically triggers "an unlimited review of all property that [the defendant] holds at the time of the order or has received or expended in the previous six years, in which the court is required to make assumptions that the property stems from his 'general criminal conduct' unless he proves otherwise or it is not in the interest of justice to make the assumption".[360] Conviction for other offences under the 1988 Act may lead to the same result, depending on the facts. The Act works in such a way that   **22–61**

---

[352] CDPA 1988 s.114A(8), (9).
[353] CDPA 1988 s.114A(6).
[354] c.19.
[355] CDPA 1988 s.114A(7).
[356] In Scotland, s.204B.
[357] In Scotland, s.297D.
[358] For s.298, see para.22–38, above.
[359] See Sch. 2 para.7.
[360] *Blackstone's Criminal Practice*, 2010, para. E19.1.

the amounts ordered to be payable under it can vastly exceed the amount of financial relief which would be awarded (but not, of course, to the victim) in civil proceedings in respect of the equivalent acts.

(vii) The burden of proof

22–62 **Introduction.** In criminal proceedings, the burden generally lies on the prosecution to prove every element of the offence beyond reasonable doubt. Juries are often directed that they must not convict unless they are "sure" or "satisfied so that they feel sure" of the defendant's guilt.[361] On the other hand, where the defendant relies for his defence on any "exception, exemption, proviso, excuse or qualification", the burden of proving such exception, etc. on the balance of probabilities is on him.[362] Thus, for example, in the case of driving without a licence, it has been held that the prosecution must prove that the accused was driving, but the burden is on the accused to prove that he had a driving licence.[363] This "reverse burden" is a "legal" burden rather than an "evidential" burden: the defendant is required to prove the facts necessary to establish the defence on the balance of probabilities, rather than merely to raise an issue with respect to the defence.[364] The question arises whether any of the ingredients of the criminal offences under the 1988 Act fall into this category and if so whether this is compatible with the right to a fair trial enshrined in the Human Rights Act 1998. After a review of the general law, the following paragraphs will consider first phrases such as "without the licence of the copyright owner" in s.107 and "without sufficient consent" in s.198, together with the term "a person who infringes" in ss.107(2A) and 198(1A)[365]; secondly the provision in s.198 that no offence is committed by the commission of a "permitted act"[366]; and finally the terms "infringing copy" in s.107 and "illicit recording" in s.198.[367] The burden of proof in relation to the "mere conduit", "caching" and "hosting" defences is considered above.[368]

22–63 **General legal propositions.** It seems that there are two separate questions in each case. First, irrespective of the Human Rights Act, does the provision in question, as a matter of construction, impose a burden of proof on the defendant? Secondly, if it does, what is the impact of the Human Rights Act on the provision?[369] The first question is one of construction, but if the "linguistic construction" is unclear, the court may take account of policy considerations including in particular the parties' respective abilities to discharge the burden in question.[370] As to the second question, the Convention jurisprudence has been summarised as follows[371]:

> "The overriding concern is that a trial should be fair, and the presumption of innocence is a fundamental right directed to that end. The Convention does

---

[361] For the authorities, see *Blackstone's Criminal Practice*, 2010, para.F3.38.

[362] Magistrates' Courts Act 1980 (c.43) s.101 (summary proceedings); *R. v Hunt* [1987] A.C. 352 (trial on indictment).

[363] *John v Humphreys* [1955] 1 W.L.R. 325. See also *DPP v Hay* [2005] EWHC Admin 1395.

[364] *The Queen on the application of Grundy & Co Excavations Ltd* [2003] EWHC Admin 272 (QB).

[365] See para.22–66, below.

[366] See para.22–67, below.

[367] See para.22–68, below.

[368] See para.22–25, above.

[369] This was the approach adopted in *The Queen on the application of Grundy & Co Excavations Ltd* [2003] EWHC Admin 272 (QB).

[370] *R. v Hunt* [1987] A.C. 352.

[371] *Attorney General's Reference No. 4 of 2002* [2004] UKHL 43; [2005] 1 A.C. 264 at para.21. This is now the leading case.

not outlaw presumptions of fact or law but requires that these should be kept within reasonable limits and should not be arbitrary. It is open to states to define the constituent elements of a criminal offence, excluding the requirement of mens rea. But the substance and effect of any presumption adverse to a defendant must be examined, and must be reasonable. Relevant to any judgment on reasonableness or proportionality will be the opportunity given to the defendant to rebut the presumption, maintenance of the rights of the defence, flexibility in application of the presumption, retention by the court of a power to assess the evidence, the importance of what is at stake and the difficulty which a prosecutor may face in the absence of a presumption. ... The justifiability of any infringement of the presumption of innocence cannot be resolved by any rule of thumb, but on examination of all the facts and circumstances of the particular provision as applied in the particular case."

In *R. v Johnstone*[372] the House of Lords upheld a provision which imposed a legal burden on a defendant under s.92 of the Trade Marks Act 1994, which creates various offences in relation to the use of signs identical or similar to trade marks with a view to gain and without consent. Section 92(5) provides that it is a defence to a charge under s.92 for the defendant to prove that he believed on reasonable grounds that the use of the sign in the manner in which it was used, or was to be used, was not an infringement of the registered trade mark. The reasons given for the decision in *R. v Johnstone* were: the urgent international pressure, in the interest of consumers and traders alike, to restrain fraudulent trading in counterfeit goods; the framing of offences against s.92 as offences of "near absolute liability"; the dependence of the defence on facts within the defendant's own knowledge; the fact that those who trade in brand products are aware of the need to be on guard against counterfeit goods, to deal with reputable suppliers and keep records and of the risks they take if they do not; and the fact that it is to be expected that those who supply traders with counterfeit products, if traceable at all by outside investigators, are unlikely to be co-operative so that, in practice, if the prosecution were obliged to prove that a trader acted dishonestly, fewer investigations would be undertaken and fewer prosecutions would take place.[373]

Decisions since *R v. Johnstone*. In subsequent cases, at least where offences are not of a merely regulatory nature, the courts have placed a single consideration at the forefront of their reasoning, namely whether the reverse burden is necessary to the effective operation of the provision in question.[374] It seems clear that whatever the position under previous statues and although one of the mischiefs which the offences under the 1988 Act aim to prevent is harm to consumers,[375] the severity of the penalties for these offences is such that they cannot in any sense be considered to be merely "regulatory". Accordingly, the recent cases on official secrets and fox hunting are of direct relevance.   **22–64**

Authorities. In the leading case on the criminal copyright provisions of the 1956 Act,[376] it was conceded by the prosecution that the burden of proving that the copies were infringing copies lay on them, while there was no issue as to whether the defendant had a licence to possess them. There are no reported cases on the   **22–65**

---

[372] *R. v Johnstone* [2003] UKHL 28; [2003] 1 W.L.R. 1736.
[373] *R. v Johnstone* [2003] UKHL 28; [2003] 1 W.L.R. 1736 at paras 52 and 53. See the analysis of this decision in *Attorney General's Reference No. 4 of 2002* [2004] UKHL 43; [2005] 1 A.C. 264 at para.27.
[374] See in particular *R v Keogh* [2007] EWCA Crim 528; [2007] 1 W.L.R. 1500, at para.26 (official secrets) and *DPP v Wright* [2009] EWHC 105 (Admin); [2010] Q.B. 224 at paras 85 and 87 (fox hunting).
[375] See para.22–07 above.
[376] *Musa v Le Maitre* [1987] F.S.R. 272.

incidence of the burden of proof in relation to offences relating to performers' rights. Accordingly, in each case, the question remains open.

22-66   **Licence or consent.** In the previous edition of this work it was suggested that in prosecutions under ss.107(1) and (2A) and 198(1) and (1A) the burden lay on the defendant to prove that he had a licence or sufficient consent.[377] This was because in each case, the defendant alleging a licence or consent would be raising an "exception, exemption, proviso, excuse or qualification". Thus, the provision could be said to create an offence plus an exception. The defendant would have no difficulty proving the existence of the licence or consent, whereas the prosecution might have considerable difficulties proving its absence. The policy reasons for reversing the burden which were outlined in *R. v Johnstone* applied as much to copyright offences as to trade mark offences. However, it is debatable whether these views accord with the more recent trend which is to consider the matter as one of necessity. In particular, although there may be practical difficulties in identifying the rights holder and obtaining a statement that no licence or consent has been granted, it would be an unusual case where such difficulties proved insuperable in practice. It would seem to follow that the imposition of a reverse burden is not necessary in such cases. It would therefore be open to a court to hold that in relation to the offences under ss.107(2A) and 198(1A) the requirement that the communication be shown to infringe is part of the definition of the offence itself and did not involve an exception, etc. while in the case of the other provisions the burden on the issue of licence or consent lay on the prosecution.

22-67   **Permitted acts.** If the provision in s.198 that no offence is committed by the commission of a "permitted act" is construed as an "exception, exemption, proviso, excuse or qualification", then the arguments for the imposition of a reverse burden in relation to this issue are stronger. However, it is possible that a court would conclude that the extent of the permitted acts is such that this is not an exception etc. but instead is part of the scope of the offence itself.[378] If so, there would be no case for reversing the burden. Even if the provision were construed as an exception etc., a court might well take account of the fact that it would not be necessary for the prosecution to negative each permitted act in each case: rather it would be for the defendant to discharge an evidential burden that the act was permitted in some particular way and for the prosecution to rebut it. In a recent Divisional Court case that was considered a decisive reason for refusing to impose a reverse burden.[379]

22-68   **"Infringing copy" and "illicit recording".** An infringing copy of a copyright work is in effect a copy made without the licence of the copyright owner,[380] while an illicit recording is a recording made without the consent of the performer or a person having recording rights or both.[381] It follows that a "dealing" offence will not occur if the article dealt with has been made with a licence or with consent. It is clearly arguable therefore that the wording of both ss.107 and 198 contains a hidden "exception, exemption, proviso, excuse or qualification". The same point arises where a defendant seeks to contend that an allegedly infringing copy with which he has dealt was not in fact infringing because its making was a permitted

---

[377] *Copinger* 15th edn, paras 23–61 to 23–62.
[378] Compare *DPP v Wright* [2009] EWHC 105 (Admin); [2010] Q.B. 224 at para.84.
[379] *DPP v Wright* [2009] EWHC 105 (Admin) at para.87.
[380] By CDPA 1988 s.27(2), an article is an infringing copy if its making constituted an infringement of the copyright in question. By s.16(2), copyright in a work is infringed by a person who does a restricted act without the licence of the copyright owner. By s.17(1), the copying of a work is a restricted act.
[381] See the definition in CDPA 1988 s.197(4).

act (e.g. fair dealing)[382]; or that an allegedly illicit recording with which he has dealt was not in fact illicit because its making was a permitted act.[383]

It is thought that these provisions are not likely to be construed as imposing a burden on the defendant, for the following reasons. First, the effect of placing the burden on the defendant would be far-reaching. In a case where dealing with an infringing copy was alleged, the prosecution would not need to prove who owned the copyright infringed either at the time the infringing copy was made or at the time of the act of dealing complained of.[384] In a case where dealing with an illicit recording was alleged, the prosecution would not be obliged to prove who owned any of the rights in the performance either at the time the recording was made or at the time it was dealt with. It would follow that in some cases it would be easier to establish criminal than civil liability. Secondly, there is clearly scope for unfairness if a defendant charged with selling an infringing or illicit article is obliged to prove that the article, which he may have purchased through a long chain of suppliers, was made by licence or with consent, or indeed that its making was a permitted act. It is thought that a criminal court would be likely to wish to avoid such unfairness. Finally, the terms of the Act are such that the prosecution have to prove in all cases that the defendant knew or had reason to believe that the article was infringing or illicit.[385] It is difficult to see how this could be done without also proving that the article was indeed infringing or illicit.

2. SEIZURE BY CUSTOMS OF IMPORTED COPIES

A. OVERVIEW AND HISTORICAL INTRODUCTION

Overview. Since its original (1886) Act, the Berne Convention has always contained provision for the seizure of imported infringing copies, leaving the manner of seizure to domestic law.[386] Before the adoption of the Convention, provision already existed for a copyright owner to notify Customs of his interest with a view to prohibiting the importation of infringing books.[387] The 1911 Act extended this to copies of all copyright works.[388] Similar provision was made by the 1956 Act,[389] but this was expressly limited to infringing copies of published literary, dramatic and musical works. Section 111 of the 1988 Act re-enacted these provisions of the 1956 Act and extended them to infringing copies of sound recordings and films. However, these provisions were seldom used.[390] Since July 1, 1995, a new regime has been in force under European legislation, although this has been subject to frequent amendment. It covers goods which infringe most of the rights covered in this work, but does not apply to parallel imports or overruns. For reasons which will become apparent, many more rights owners have taken advantage of this scheme than that under the 1988 Act. Nevertheless, s.111 remains in force, although its scope remains limited to printed copies of published literary dramatic and musical works, and copies of sound recordings and films,

22–69

---

[382] For permitted acts, see Ch.9, above.

[383] Under CDPA 1988 Sch.2. This is unlikely in practice.

[384] Of course, the prosecution would still have to prove that copyright subsisted; and this might depend on identifying a qualifying author who might also have been the owner of the copyright at the time the infringing copy was made.

[385] See *Stockton-on-Tees BC v Frost* [2010] EWHC 1304 (Admin) at para.4 (obiter).

[386] See art.12 of the 1886 Act and art.16 of the Paris Act (Vol.2 F1).

[387] Customs Consolidation Act 1876 s.42; Table of Prohibitions.

[388] Copyright Act 1911 s.14. See Vol.2 E3.

[389] Copyright Act 1956 s.22. See Vol.2 E1.

[390] It seems that no more than 10 or 12 notifications were made each year under the 1988 Act before July 1995. This and some of the other information which follows was very kindly provided by Mr Ronald Bann of HM Customs and Excise.

and it only applies where the EC legislation does not apply. Neither regime applies to goods imported for genuine private or domestic use. It should be emphasised that this part of this chapter deals only with the seizure of imported copies. A copyright owner's rights to seize infringing copies which are exposed or immediately available for sale or hire are dealt with elsewhere.[391]

22–70   **The 1986 Regulation.** The first Community legislation of this type was the Council Regulation of 1986,[392] which was aimed at preventing the importation into the Community of goods which infringed a trade mark registered in a Member State.[393] This Regulation permitted a trade mark owner to notify the customs authorities of his interest; if an attempt was made to import goods which infringed the trade mark, the customs authorities could seize and destroy or otherwise dispose of them. There were perceived to be a number of defects in the system.[394] First, it applied only to trade marks and not to other intellectual property rights. Secondly, it made no provision for the customs authorities to act on their own initiative, as opposed to at the request of the rights owner. Thirdly, it did not apply to goods which were entered for export or re-export from the Community, or to goods otherwise under customs control in the Community.

22–71   **TRIPS obligations.** Section 4 of the TRIPS agreement[395] contains "special requirements related to border measures", which may be briefly summarised as follows. First, Members are obliged to enable right-holders who have valid grounds for suspecting that the importation of counterfeit trade mark or pirated copyright goods may take place, to apply for the suspension of the release into free circulation of such goods.[396] Such measures may be applied to other intellectual property rights and to exports.[397] Right-holders are to be obliged to provide prima facie evidence of infringement[398] and may be obliged to provide security.[399] If the applicant has not commenced proceedings within 10 working days of receiving notice of the suspension, or any extended period of 10 days, the goods must be released.[400] Provision is to be made for affording the right-holder an opportunity to inspect the goods.[401] The mechanics to be applied where action is taken by customs authorities on their own initiative ("ex officio") are laid down.[402] Competent authorities are to have power to order the destruction or disposal of infringing goods.[403] Finally, provision may be made to exclude from the applica-

---

[391] See CDPA 1988 s.100 and paras 21–57 et seq., above.

[392] Council Regulation 3842/86 laying down measures to prohibit the release for free circulation of counterfeit goods, [1986] OJ L375/1.

[393] Council Regulation 3842/86 arts 1(2)(a) and 2.

[394] See, in particular, the recitals to reg.3295/94 laying down measures to prohibit the release for free circulation, export and re-export from the Community of goods infringing certain intellectual property rights, [1994] OJ L 341/8 and the Opinion of the Economic and Social Committee on the less extensive proposed Regulation, [1994] OJ C52/37, para.2.6 and para.3.2.

[395] See Vol.2 F11.

[396] art.51.

[397] art.51.

[398] art.52.

[399] art.53. They may be required to indemnify the importer, consignee and owner for injury caused by wrongful detention of the goods: art.56.

[400] art.55.

[401] art.57. The competent authorities may be allowed to inform the right-holder of the names and addresses of the consignor, importer and consignee and the quantity of the goods where a positive determination has been made as to the merits: art.57.

[402] art.58.

[403] art.59.

tion of these provisions small quantities of goods of a non-commercial nature contained in travellers' personal luggage or sent in small consignments.[404]

The 1994 Regulation. The 1986 Regulation was repealed by Council Regulation   **22–72**
3295/94 ("the 1994 Regulation"), which was directly applicable in all Member States from July 1, 1995.[405] The 1994 Regulation was intended to address the defects referred to above and to take account of TRIPS.[406] Thus, the general structure of the Regulation was based on the TRIPS provisions referred to above, customs authorities were permitted to act on their own initiative, the number of categories of rights protected was increased and the range of circumstances in which goods might be seized was extended. In 1995, the 1994 Regulation was supplemented by Commission Regulation 1367/95 ("the 1995 Implementing Regulation").[407] The Counterfeit and Pirated Goods (Customs) Regulations 1995[408] ("the 1995 Customs Regulations") and the Counterfeit and Pirated Goods (Consequential Provisions) Regulations 1995[409] ("the 1995 Consequential Regulations") contained provisions designed to implement the Council and Commission Regulations in the United Kingdom. In 1999, the 1994 Regulation was amended in order to increase the range of circumstances in which goods might be seized.[410] In order the give effect to this, the 1995 Customs Regulations and the 1995 Consequential Regulations were revoked and replaced by new regulations ("the 1999 Customs Regulations" and "the 1999 Consequential Provisions Regulations").[411] The 1999 Customs Regulations were amended by further Regulations in 2003, which abolished fees for applications to the Commissioners ("the 2003 Regulations") with effect from October 1, 2003.[412]

The Council Regulation and the Domestic Regulations. Against a background   **22–73**
of mounting concerns about the extent of the trade in counterfeit and pirated goods,[413] the 1994 Regulation was in turn replaced by a new Council Regulation ("the Council Regulation") with effect from July 1, 2004.[414] The Council Regulation retained the structure of its predecessor, but introduced certain changes. The main changes which are relevant to the rights covered by this work are as follows. First, a standard application form was introduced. Secondly, application fees

---

[404] art.60.

[405] art.17.

[406] See the sixth recital. Art..6(2)(b) of this Regulation is the subject of a reference to the Court of Justice in *Koninklijke Philips Electronics N.V. v Lucheng Meijing Industrial Company Ltd, Far East Sourcing Ltd, Röhlig Hing Kong Ltd and Rohlig Belgium N.V.* (C–446/09)

[407] Commission Regulation 1367/95 laying down provisions for the implementation of Council Regulation (EC) No.3295/94 laying down measures to prohibit the release for free circulation, export, re-export or entry for a suspensive procedure of counterfeit and pirated goods, [1995] OJ L133/2.

[408] SI 1995/1430.

[409] SI 1995/1447.

[410] By Council Regulation 241/99 [1999] OJ L27/1.

[411] SI 1999/1601 and 1618, respectively.

[412] SI 2003/2316. These Regulations were introduced in anticipation of the 2004 Council Regulation, which is dealt with below.

[413] According to the Explanatory Memorandum to the draft regulation (COM (2003) 20 final), there was a ninefold increase in the number of infringing items intercepted at the EU's external frontiers over the four years from 1998 to 2001 (from 10 million to 100 million). Counterfeiters had become more interested in quantity than quality, concentrating less on items with a high value added, and more on household objects produced on a commercial scale. There had been particular increases in seizures of foodstuffs and CDs. Organised crime was increasingly active in the field.

[414] Council Regulation 1383/2003 concerning customs action against goods suspected of infringing certain intellectual property rights and the measures to be taken against goods found to have infringed such rights, [2003] OJ L196/7 (see Vol.2 B7.ai). See generally Daele: " Regulation 1383/2003: A New Step in the Fight against Counterfeit and Pirated Goods at the Borders of the European Union" [2004] E.I.P.R. 214.

were abolished (although this had already occurred in the United Kingdom). Thirdly, provision was introduced for supplying additional information to the right-holder at an earlier stage. Finally, sanctions were introduced for the misuse of information so supplied. Although it is directly applicable, the Council Regulation envisaged that a further, implementing regulation would be introduced by the Commission.[415] On October 21, 2004 an implementing regulation ("the 2004 Implementing Regulation") was adopted.[416] The 2004 Implementing Regulation is directly applicable. It repealed the 1995 Implementing Regulation.[417] In 2004 the Government introduced new regulations which implemented parts of the Council Regulation in the United Kingdom ("the Domestic Regulations").[418] With effect from July 1, 2004, the Domestic Regulations revoked the 1999 Customs Regulations, the 1999 Consequential Regulations and the 2003 Regulations. Those parts of the Council Regulation which had not been implemented by the Domestic Regulations were directly applicable, and in most cases guidance as to their application had been given by the Commissioners of Customs and Excise ("the Commissioners").[419] The Implementing Regulation was amended in 2007.[420] The amendments took account of the accession to the Community of Bulgaria and Romania,[421] provided a new form for applications for Community action[422] and removed the list of competent authorities to which applications for action must be submitted, which is now published in the Official Journal instead.[423]

22–74 **The *Penbrook* case and the amendments to the Domestic Regulations.** The Domestic Regulations introduced two different regimes depending on the rights in issue. In respect of goods which were alleged to infringe copyright, rights in performances, publication right, database right and trade marks, the normal customs condemnation regime was applied by reg.7.[424] A different regime was applied by reg.9 to goods which were alleged to infringe designs, patents and similar rights.[425] In *HMRC v Penbrook Enterprises Ltd*[426] it was held in effect that the reg.7 regime was inconsistent with art.13 of the Council Regulation because it did not result in the commencement of court proceedings within 10 working days of receipt of the notification of suspension of release or detention. As a result, HMRC notified right holders of its intention to apply the reg.9 scheme to all types of goods.[427] Subsequently, the Domestic Regulations were substantially amended[428] to delete both the reg.7 and the reg.9 regimes, leaving the question of the commencement of court proceedings to be governed entirely by art.13 of the

---

[415] See arts 20, 21.

[416] Commission Regulation (EC) No. 1891/2004 of October 21, 2004 laying down provisions for the implementation of Council Regulation (EC) No. 1383/2003 concerning customs action against goods suspected of infringing certain intellectual property rights and the measures to be taken against goods found to have infringed such rights [2004] OJ L328/16. See Vol.2 B7.aii.

[417] art.10. For transitional provisions, see *Copinger* 15th edn, para.23–69, fn.91.

[418] The Goods Infringing Intellectual Property Right (Customs) Regulations 2004 (SI 2004/1473). See Vol.2 B7.bii.

[419] Customs Notice 34 Intellectual Property Rights, July 2004 ("Customs Notice 34").

[420] By Commission Regulation (EC) No 1172/2007 [2007] OJ L261/12.

[421] With effect from October 6, 2007 (art.2).

[422] With effect from January 1, 2007 (art.2).

[423] With effect from October 6, 2007 (art.2).

[424] See *Copinger* 15th edn, paras 23–86 and 23–88.

[425] For the full list of the rights to which this scheme applied, see *Copinger* 15th edn, para.23–86.

[426] [2008] NIMag 2, Deputy District Judge (Magistrates' Courts) Rafferty.

[427] Letter from Her Majesty's Revenue & Customs' Customs & International Supply Chain Integrity & Facilitation unit dated June 22, 2009, which may be found on the IPKat website, *http://ipkitten.blogspot.com/2009/06/uk-customs-procedures-and-burden-of.html* [Accessed November 16, 2010]. For the full list of rights in this category, see *Copinger* 15th edn, para.23–86.

[428] By the Goods Infringing Intellectual Property Rights (Customs) (Amendment) Regulations 2010

Council Regulation. At the same time, the opportunity was taken to implement art.11 of the Council Regulation, which provides for destruction by consent.

B. THE COUNCIL REGULATION AND THE DOMESTIC REGULATIONS

The types of goods to which the Council Regulation applies. The Council Regulation applies both to "counterfeit" and to "pirated" goods. Broadly speaking, "counterfeit goods" are defined as goods which infringe a registered trade mark.[429] "Pirated goods" are defined as goods "which are or contain copies made without the consent of the holder of a copyright or related right[430] or design right, regardless of whether it is registered in national law, or of a person duly authorised by the right-holder in the country of production, in cases where the making of those copies would constitute an infringement of that right under the Community Design Regulation[431] or the law of the Member State in which the application for action by the customs authorities is made".[432] The term "pirated goods" also includes goods which infringe patents, supplementary protection certificates, plant variety rights, designations of origin or geographical indication and geographical designations.[433] Moulds or matrices specifically designed or adapted for making pirated goods are treated as pirated goods if the use of such moulds or matrices infringes the right-holder's rights under Community law or the law of the Member State in which the application for action by the customs authorities is made.[434] The discussion which follows is confined to those categories of goods which infringe the rights covered in this work. **22–75**

The "right-holder". For the purposes of the Council Regulation, this term is broadly defined as meaning (relevantly): the holder of a copyright, related right or design right; any other person authorised to use the right; or "a representative of the right-holder or authorised user".[435] The 2004 Implementing Regulation provides that the latter term includes a collecting society which has as its sole or principal purpose the management or administration of copyrights or related rights.[436] **22–76**

Excepted goods. Goods which are protected by a copyright, related right or design right and have been manufactured with the consent of the right-holder are not within the definition of "pirated goods".[437] Accordingly, the Council Regulation has no application to parallel imports. Goods "which have been manufactured or are protected by another intellectual property right [to which the Council Regulation applies] under conditions other than those agreed with the right-holder" are also excluded.[438] This appears to exclude over-runs and similar goods. Finally, as permitted under TRIPS,[439] the Council Regulation does not apply to goods of a non-commercial nature contained in travellers' personal luggage **22–77**

(SI 2010/324) and the Goods Infringing Intellectual Property Rights (Customs) (Amendment) (No. 2) Regulations 2010 (SI 2010/992).

[429] The full definition is in art.2 (1)(a). See Vol.2 B7.ai.

[430] By reg.2(2) of the Goods Infringing Intellectual Property Rights (Customs) Regulations 2004 (SI 2004/1473) (Vol.2 B7.bii), the term "copyright or related right" is to be construed as a reference to "copyright, rights in performances, publication rights or database rights".

[431] Council Regulation 6/2002 on Community designs [2002] OJ 3/1.

[432] Regulation 1383/2003 art.2 (1)(b). See Vol.2 B7.ai.

[433] art.2(1)(c).

[434] art.2(3).

[435] Regulation 1383/2003 art.2(2).

[436] art.1(2).

[437] art.3(1).

[438] art.3(1).

[439] See art.60.

within the limits laid down in respect of relief from customs duty, provided there are no material indications to suggest the goods are part of commercial traffic.[440]

22–78   **When the Council Regulation applies to goods.** The Council Regulation applies when goods have been "entered for release for free circulation, export or re-export"[441]; or have been "found during checks on goods entering or leaving the Community customs territory[442] ..., placed under a suspensive procedure[443] ..., in the process of being re-exported subject to notification",[444] or placed in a free zone or free warehouse[445] ("an Article 1(1) situation"). These terms are derived from Council Regulation (EC) No.2913/92 which established the Community Customs Code.[446] Broadly speaking, goods "entered for release for free circulation" are non-Community goods which it is intended to import into the Community but which have not yet been released by Customs.[447] Goods "entered for export" are goods which are intended to be exported from the Community, but which have not yet cleared Customs.[448] Goods "entered for re-export" are non-Community goods[449] which it is intended to re-export from the Community but which have not yet cleared customs.[450] Checks may be made on goods when they enter or leave the Community Customs territory.[451] The relevant categories of "suspensive procedure" under which goods may be placed are as follows.[452] First, the "external transit" procedure, which permits the movement from one point to another within the customs territory of the Community of non-Community goods without such goods being subject to import duties or commercial policy measures; and of Community goods subject to a Community measure involving their export to third countries and in respect of which the corresponding customs formalities for export have been carried out.[453] Secondly, the "customs warehousing" procedure, which permits the storage in a customs warehouse of non-Community goods without such goods being subject to import duties or commercial policy measures; and of Community goods where Community legislation provides that their being placed in a customs warehouse shall attract the application of measures normally attaching to the export of such goods.[454] Thirdly, the "inward processing" procedure, which permits non-Community goods which are intended to be re-exported from the Community in processed form to be used without their being subject to import duties or commercial policy measures; and permits goods released for free circulation to be used with repayment or remission of the import duties chargeable on them if they are exported from the customs territory of the Community in processed form.[455] Fourthly, the procedure for "processing under customs control", which permits non-Community goods to be used in the customs territory of the Community in operations which alter their

---

[440] art.3(2). According to the Commission's website, the purpose of the proviso was to allow for checks on travellers to make sure that the use of couriers or "mules" does not conceal a large flow of goods.

[441] In accordance with art.61 of Council Regulation (EC) No.2913/92 establishing the Community Customs Code, as amended [1992] OJ L302/1 ("Regulation 2913/92").

[442] In accordance with arts 37 and 183 of Reg.2913/92.

[443] Within the meaning of art.84(1)(a) of Reg.2913/92.

[444] Under art.182(2) of Reg.2913/92.

[445] Within the meaning of art.166 of Reg.2913/92. See art.1(1) of Reg.1383/2003.

[446] [1992] OJ L302/1.

[447] arts 37(1), 59(1) and 79.

[448] arts 161 and 162.

[449] As defined in art.4(8).

[450] art.182(1).

[451] arts 37 and 183.

[452] art.84(1)(a).

[453] art.91(1).

[454] art.98(1).

[455] art.114.

nature or state and allows the products of such operations to be released for free circulation.[456] Finally, the "temporary importation" procedure, which allows the use in the customs territory of the Community of non-Community goods intended for re-export without having undergone any change except normal depreciation with total or partial relief from import duties and without their being subject to commercial policy measures.[457]

Action by customs authorities on their own initiative: Article 4: general. **22–79**
Article 4 contains two provisions. The first (art.4(1)) enables customs authorities who have come across goods which they suspect to be pirated to notify right-holders who have not made an application for action under art.5 (or who have made an application which has not yet been granted) and to hold the goods in order to enable such an application to be made.[458] The second (art.4(2)) enables customs authorities to seek information from the right-holder in order to "confirm" their suspicions.

Article 4(2): confirming suspicions. It seems logical to consider art.4(2) first. **22–80**
This provides that the customs authorities may, in accordance with the rules in force in the Member State concerned, without divulging any information other than the actual or supposed number of items and their nature, and before informing the right-holder of the possible infringement, ask the right-holder to provide them with any information they may need to confirm their suspicions. Two difficulties arise. First, it is not clear how this is to work in practice: giving the prescribed information to the right-holder is virtually bound to alert him to the possible infringement. Secondly, the phrase "confirm their suspicions" is ambiguous. It could refer to strengthening existing suspicions. On the other hand, it could refer to making those suspicions definitively valid. It seems likely that the object of the art.4(2) procedure is to provide sufficient support for the authorities' suspicions to justify invoking the art.4(1) procedure (it is not clear what other purpose there might be). Given that art.4(2) appears to apply where there is thought to be a "possible infringement", it seems likely that the phrase refers to strengthening existing suspicions.

Article 4(1): action. Article 4(1) provides that where, before an application has **22–81**
been made by a right-holder (or, if one has been made, before it has been granted), in the course of checks carried out on goods in an art.1(1) situation,[459] the customs authorities have "sufficient grounds for suspecting" that goods are pirated goods, they are permitted to take certain action. The Regulation does not state what grounds are "sufficient". However, art.4(1) appears to be intended to reflect art.58 of TRIPS, which sets out the procedure which is to be applicable if Members require competent authorities to act on their own initiative and suspend the release of goods in respect of which they have acquired prima facie evidence that an intellectual property right is being infringed. This would suggest a test of whether there is a prima facie case. Such a test would be consistent with the wording of art.4 for two reasons. First, it would seem to follow from the interpretation of art.4(2) suggested above that the standard is more than a mere possibility. Secondly, however, the use of the words "grounds for suspecting" suggests that it is not necessary to establish a belief that it is more probable than not that the

---

[456] art.130.
[457] art. 137.
[458] art.6 of the 2004 Implementing Regulation provides that in the case of perishable goods the procedure for suspension of release or detention shall be initiated primarily in respect of products for which an application has already been lodged. This is presumably because of the practical difficulties involved in operating this procedure quickly enough to prevent damage to the goods.
[459] For the art.1(1) of Regulation 1383/2003 situations, see para.22–78, above.

goods are pirated. If there are sufficient grounds, art.4(1) permits the customs authorities to suspend the release of the goods or detain them for three working days "from the moment of receipt of the notification by the right-holder and by the declarant or holder of the goods, if the latter are known" in order to enable the right-holder to make an application under art.5(1).[460] This appears to envisage that both the right-holder on the one hand and the declarant or holder of the goods on the other will be notified by the customs authorities that the goods have been suspended or detained. Curiously, however, the Regulation does not lay down any express power to do this. The purpose of taking the action is stated to be to enable the right-holder to submit an application for action in accordance with art.5.

22–82   **Article 4: the Customs Notice.** Regulations 3 and 4 of the Domestic Regulations, which were intended to implement art.4, have been revoked.[461] The practice is set out in HMRC's Notice 34 (June 2010).[462] The Notice follows closely the form of art.4. It states that HMRC will act if they "suspect" that the goods infringe (without stating how strong any suspicion needs to be). As permitted by the Regulation, HMRC state that they may disclose to the right holder the number of items and their nature. In the absence of any application for action within the three working day period, the goods will be released. If there is an application within that period, the ten working day period (during which consent to destruction must be obtained or proceedings commenced) will begin on the day following the acceptance of the application for action[463] (this appears to mean the grant of the application). Finally, the Notice provides that ex officio action is not permitted in respect of perishable goods.

22–83   **Application for action: Articles 5 and 6.** The Council Regulation provides that a right-holder may apply in writing to the competent customs department for action to be taken when goods are found in an art.1(1) situation.[464] It also provides that Member States are to designate the customs department competent to receive and process applications and to encourage right-holders to lodge applications electronically where electronic data interchange systems exist.[465] It goes on to provide that where the applicant is the right-holder of a Community design right, the application may, as well as requesting action in the Member State in which it is lodged, also request action by the customs authorities of one or more other Member States.[466] It then states that the application must be made out on a form established in accordance with the procedure set out in art.21(2) and which contains all the information needed to enable the goods in question to be readily recognised by the customs authorities and in particular three types of mandatory information: an accurate and detailed technical description of the goods; any

---

[460] art.5 of the 2004 Implementing Regulation apparently seeks to clarify this provision by stating that if the customs service informs the declarant or holder of the goods that they have been detained or their release suspended pursuant to art.4(1) of the Council Regulation, the time limit of 3 working days is to be counted only from the time the right-holder is notified. As to art.5(1) applications, see para.22–83, below.

[461] By the Goods Infringing Intellectual Property Rights (Customs) (Amendment) (No. 2) Regulations 2010 (SI 2010/992).

[462] Vol.2 B7.biii.

[463] para.5.2.2.

[464] art.5(1). For the art.1(1) situations, see para.22–78, above.

[465] arts 5(2) and (3). See also art.8(1) of the 2004 Implementing Regulation, which provides that Member States must inform the Commission as soon as possible of the competent customs department, and art.8(6) which provides for publication of a list of such departments in the Official Journal. The remainder of art.8 makes provision for the exchange of information between the Commission and competent customs departments.

[466] art.5(4). If action is sought in other Member States, the application form must indicate them and the contact details of the right-holder in each Member State so indicated: art.5(5).

specific information the right-holder may have concerning the type or pattern of fraud; and the name and address of the right-holder's contact person.[467] Article 21(2) envisages that the Commission will introduce an implementing Regulation to deal with this. This has been done.[468] The Council Regulation goes on to say that the application must also include the declaration required by art.6.[469] This is a declaration accepting: (i) liability to the persons involved in the art.1(1) situation if a procedure to determine whether the goods are pirated is discontinued owing to an act or omission by the right-holder or the goods are found not to be pirated;[470] (ii) liability for costs incurred in keeping the goods under customs control;[471] and (iii) liability for the costs of translations where the application is for action in more than one Member State.[472] Next, the Council Regulation provides that the application must contain proof that the applicant holds the right for the goods in question.[473] Right-holders are also encouraged to forward other information, such as the value of the "original"[474] goods on the legitimate market; the location of the goods or their intended destination; particulars identifying the consignment or packages; the scheduled arrival or departure date; the means of transport; the identity of the importer, exporter or holder; the country of production and the routes used by traffickers; and the technical differences between the authentic and suspect goods.[475] The Regulation states that details may be required which are specific to the type of intellectual property right referred to in the application for action.[476]

Articles 5 and 6: the Customs Notice. These articles are not covered in the Domestic Regulations, but are referred to in Customs Notice 34.[477] There is no formal designation of a customs department to receive and process applications, but this role clearly devolves on HMRC. Applicants are directed to the forms an-   **22–84**

---

[467] art.5(5). Compare the requirements of art.52 of TRIPS, which states that the application must provide adequate evidence to satisfy the competent authorities that there is a prima facie case of infringement and a detailed description of the goods to make them readily recognisable.

[468] reg.1891/2004 [2004] OJ L328/16 ("the 2004 Implementing Regulation"). The relevant forms are at Annexes I and II. The forms contain detailed notes as to their completion and submission, as to which see also the requirements of art.3 of the 2004 Implementing Regulation. The form for application for community action (Annex II) has been amended by Commission Regulation (EC) No 1172/2007 [2007] OJ L261/12 with effect from January 1, 2007.

[469] art.5(5). A representative applicant must produce such a declaration signed by the right-holder or person authorised to use the right; or a document authorising him to bear any costs arising from customs action on their behalf in accordance with art.6 of the Council Regulation: see art.2(3) of the 2004 Implementing Regulation. Presumably what is meant is a document pursuant to which the representative undertakes to be liable for such costs.

[470] art.6(1).

[471] art.6(1).

[472] art.6(2). The relevant forms are at Annexes I-A and II-A to the 2004 Implementing Regulation. In each case, the undertaking to pay costs extends to the costs occasioned by the destruction of infringing goods pursuant to art.17.

[473] As to this, the 2004 Implementing Regulation provides as follows. First, where the application is lodged by the holder of a copyright, related right or unregistered design right, the proof required is evidence of authorship or of the applicant's status as right-holder: art.2(1)(a). Presumably what is meant is that if the applicant is the right-holder because he is the author, then he must provide proof of authorship; whereas if he is the right-holder as a result of transmission of title, then he must provide some document of title. It is not clear in either case precisely what will suffice. Secondly, where the application is lodged by any other person authorised to use the right, the proof required is that which is required of a right-holder together with the document by which the applicant is authorised to use the right in question: art.2(1)(b). Thirdly, where the application is lodged by a representative of the right-holder or person authorised to use the right, the proof required is that required of a right-holder together with the representative's authorisation to act: art.2(1)(c).

[474] The forms at Annexes I and II to the 2004 Implementing Regulation, refer to "authentic" goods.

[475] reg.1383/2003 art.5(5).

[476] art.5(6). The 2004 Implementing Regulation provides that such details may include the place of manufacture or production, the distribution network and the names of licensees: see art.4.

[477] See para.22–82, above.

nexed to the Implementing Regulation, which can also be found on the Commission's website.[478] The Notice gives the address to which the form should be sent[479] and provides that wherever possible the applicant should submit the completed application form 30 working days before he or she expects the infringing goods to be imported or exported, or before he or she wants the monitoring period to commence.[480]

22–85   **Decision on an application: Articles 5(7), 5(8) and 8.** The Council Regulation provides that the application must be processed and the applicant must be notified of the decision within 30 working days of its receipt.[481] The right-holder may not be charged a fee.[482] Where the application does not contain the mandatory information which it is required to include, the competent customs department may decide not to process it. If so, it must provide reasons for its refusal and include information on the appeal procedure.[483] If an application is granted, the department is obliged to specify the period during which the authorities are to take action. The period must not exceed one year from the date of adoption of the decision.[484] On expiry of that period and if all liabilities under the Regulation have been paid, the period may be extended.[485] The right-holder is obliged to notify the department if his right ceases to be validly registered or expires.[486] A decision granting the application is to be forwarded to those customs offices of the Member State or States likely to be concerned by the relevant goods.[487] If asked, the applicant is obliged to provide any additional information necessary to the implementation of the decision.[488]

22–86   **Articles 5(7), 5(8) and 8: the Customs Notice.** Again, these provisions are not dealt with in the Domestic Regulations but are covered in Customs Notice 34, which closely follows the provisions of the Regulation. The Notice provides that applications, if granted, are valid for up to 12 months. The period of an application may be extended by further 12–month periods by applying to HMRC prior to the expiry date. The validity period of an application cannot extend beyond the expiry period of any intellectual property right protection in force when the application (or request for extension) is made. For applications covering multiple rights, the validity of the application will end on the expiry of the first right to expire, if this is less than 12 months from the date of the application.[489]

22–87   **Immediate action when goods are found following a decision: Article 9. Use of information: Article 12.** Article 9 provides that where a customs office which

---

[478] *http://ec.europa.eu* [Accessed September 30, 2010].

[479] para.3.5.

[480] para.3.4.

[481] art.5(7). The form of the decision is prescribed by the Implementing Regulation: see Annex I Box 14 and Annex II Box 15.

[482] reg.1383/2003 art.5(7).

[483] art.5(8). The application may only be resubmitted when duly completed.

[484] art.8(1), (2), (3).

[485] art.8(1), (2). The same rules apply *mutatis mutandis* to an extension as apply to an initial application: art.7.

[486] art.8(1). The art.6 undertakings at Annexes I-A and II-A to the 2004 Implementing Regulation include an undertaking to notify the designated customs department of any "alteration to or loss of" the relevant rights.

[487] art.8(2). It seems that the primary obligation to do this (and to forward any translations) lies on the applicant, but that with his consent it may be forwarded directly by the department which has taken the decision. The 2004 Implementing Regulation provides that on receipt of "the extract of a decision", the Member State shall complete without delay the "acknowledgement of receipt" section of the form and return a copy of the extract to the designated customs department: see art.3.

[488] art.8(2).

[489] para.3.6.

has received the decision granting an application is satisfied, after consulting the applicant if necessary, that goods in an art.1(1) situation are suspected of being pirated, it is obliged to suspend their release or detain them.[490] The customs office is obliged immediately to inform the department which processed the application.[491] The office or department must inform the right-holder and the declarant of its action and may inform them of the actual or estimated quantity and the actual or supposed nature of the goods.[492] With a view to establishing whether an intellectual property right has been infringed, and in accordance with national provisions on the protection of personal data, commercial and industrial secrecy and professional and administrative confidentiality, the office or department is obliged to inform the right-holder of the names and addresses of the consignor, consignee, declarant or holder of the goods and their origin and provenance.[493] Information supplied under this provision (art.9(3)) may be used only for the purposes of art.10 (which states that national law shall apply when deciding whether the goods are pirated), art.11 (agreed disposal) and art.13(1) (which refers to release of the goods if proceedings have not been commenced).[494] It is thought that the references to art.10 and art.13(1) mean that the information may be used by the right-holder in proceedings to decide whether the goods are pirated, but the wording is not entirely clear. Any other use of such information, unless permitted by national law, may, on the basis of national law, result in civil liability and lead to the suspension of the application for the remaining period of its validity (it is assumed that the word "application" should read "decision").[495] In the event of any further misuse, the department may refuse to renew the application (again, it is thought that "application" should read "decision"). The right-holder and the consignor, consignee, declarant or holder must be allowed to inspect the goods.[496] The office may take samples and, according to the rules of the Member State concerned, hand them over to the right-holder at his express request, strictly for the purposes of analysis and to facilitate the subsequent procedure.[497]

Articles 9 and 12: Domestic Regulations and Customs Notice. Customs Notice 34 provides that if the Commissioners detect goods suspected of infringing intellectual property rights they will detain them and notify the application and the declarant, providing details of the actual or estimated quantity and the nature of the goods.[498] The Notice goes on to state that if the applicant has a valid application in force (it is thought that this should be a reference to a valid decision), at the applicant's request the Commissioners will (where known) supply the name and address of the declarant, consignee, consignor, importer or exporter

22–88

---

[490] art.9(1). A refusal to detain goods may be challenged by way of judicial review: see, e.g. *Nokia Corporation v Her Majesty's Commissioners of Revenue & Customs* [2009] EWHC 1903 (Ch); [2010] F.S.R. 5.

[491] art.9(1)

[492] art.9(2).

[493] art.9(3).

[494] art.12. It has been said that the purpose of this restriction is to prevent right-holders from contacting the holder of the goods and authorising their release on payment of a fee, thus permitting counterfeit goods to come on to the market and providing a disincentive to customs officers to exercise their powers: see Daele: "Regulation 1383/2003: A New Step in the Fight against Counterfeit and Pirated Goods at the Borders of the European Union" [2004] E.I.P.R. 214.

[495] art.12.

[496] art.9(3).

[497] art.9(3). Where circumstances allow, samples must be returned on completion of analysis and, where applicable, before the goods are released or their detention ended. Any analysis is to be carried out under the sole responsibility of the right-holder.

[498] para.3.8.

and manufacturer.[499] The Domestic Regulations make provision as to the misuse of information, as follows.

"Misuse of information" is defined as use of information supplied under art.9(3) otherwise than for the purposes specified in arts 10, 11 and 13(1) of the Council Regulation or pursuant to an enactment or order of the court.[500] Insofar as it refers to an enactment or an order of the court, this provision goes beyond the terms of art.12. Regulation 11(1) provides that where the Commissioners have reasonable grounds for believing that there has been a misuse of information by the right-holder, they may suspend the decision in force at the time of the misuse in relation to a relevant intellectual property right for the remainder of the period of its validity. Three points may be noted. First, suspension may occur where the Commissioners have reasonable grounds to believe that misuse has taken place rather than when it has actually taken place. Arguably this goes beyond what is permitted by the Council Regulation. Secondly, the suspension is limited to a "relevant intellectual property right", that is a right in relation to which information was supplied under art.9(3) and in relation to which the Commissioners have reasonable grounds to believe that a misuse has taken place.[501] Where a decision involves more than one intellectual property right but the misuse involves only one right, the suspension will be limited to that right. This appears to be a limitation on the scope of the remedy (which is, of course, permitted by the terms of the Council Regulation). Thirdly, the reference in the definition of misuse to orders of the court appears to be a further limitation on the scope of the remedy. The Domestic Regulations go on to provide that where the Commissioners have reasonable grounds for believing that there has been a further misuse of information within three years of a previous misuse, they may suspend the decision in force at the time of the misuse in relation to a relevant intellectual property right for the remainder of the period of its validity and refuse to renew it or accept a new application in relation to a relevant intellectual property right for a period of up to one year from its expiry.[502] No provision is made for civil liability for the misuse of information. The Domestic Regulations also provide for the making available of samples in accordance with the Council Regulation.[503]

22–89   **Destruction by consent: Article 11.** The Council Regulation permits Member States to provide that rather than undergoing the legal process of determining whether the goods are infringing,[504] it should be open to the parties to agree that the goods are simply destroyed. The process is to comply with the following conditions. First, within 10[505] working days of receipt of notification that release of the goods has been suspended or the goods have been detained, the right-holder is to inform the authorities that the goods infringe.[506] At the same time, he must supply the written agreement of the declarant, holder or owner of the goods to abandon them for destruction. If the authorities agree, this agreement may be supplied directly. Secondly, agreement is to be presumed if the declarant, holder or owner has not specifically opposed destruction within "the prescribed period", that is, presumably, the period of 10 days from receipt of notification and any

---

[499] para.3.8.

[500] reg.11(3)(a).

[501] reg.11(3)(b).

[502] reg.11(2).

[503] reg.6.

[504] As to which, see paras 22–91 et seq., above.

[505] Three working days if the goods are perishable.

[506] The 2004 Implementing Regulation provides that where an application for action is lodged in accordance with art.4(1) of the Council Regulation before the expiry of the time limit of three working days and that application has been accepted, the period of 10 (or three, as the case may be) working days runs from the day after the application is received: see art.5.

extension thereof.[507] Thirdly, destruction is to be carried out, unless national legislation provides otherwise, at the expense and under the responsibility of the right-holder. It is to be "systematically preceded" by the taking of samples for keeping by the customs authorities in such conditions that they constitute evidence admissible in legal proceedings in the Member State in which they might be needed. The conclusion of an art.11 procedure is not a defence to proceedings for an offence under art.18.[508]

Article 11: the Domestic Regulations. Regulation 7 provides that the Commis-   **22–90**
sioners may treat as abandoned for destruction goods which have been suspended or detailed by virtue of art.9 of the Council Regulation in the following circumstances. First, the right-holder must have informed the Commissioners within the "specified period" that the goods infringe.[509] The "specified period" is the period of 10 working days from receipt of the notification to the right-holder provided for in art.9 or in the case of perishable goods, three working days. The specified period may be extended for up to 10 working days.[510] If the right holder has done this, the goods will be treated as abandoned if either the right-holder has provided the Commissioners with the written agreement of the declarant, the holder or the owner of the goods (described as "interested parties") that the goods may be destroyed[511] or no interested party has specifically opposed the destruction of the goods within the specified period.[512] Where one interested party has given its written agreement but another interested party has opposed the destruction of the goods within the specified period, the Commissioners may not treat the goods as abandoned.[513] Where the goods are treated as abandoned under this procedure, the right-holder must bear the expense of and responsibility for destruction unless otherwise specified by the Commissioners and the Commissioners must retain a sample of the goods in such a condition that that it can be used if required as evidence in legal proceedings.[514]

Court determination as to whether goods are pirated: Articles 10 and 13. If   **22–91**
the goods are not destroyed by consent, it is necessary to determine whether they are pirated. Article 10 of the Council Regulation provides simply that the law in force in the Member State within the territory of which the goods are placed in the art.1(1) situation shall apply to this determination. However, art.13 provides that if within 10 working days of receipt of the notification of suspension of release or detention, the customs office has not been notified that proceedings have been initiated to determine whether the goods are pirated or an art.11 agreement has not been received, release of the goods shall be granted or their detention shall be ended as appropriate.[515] The period may be extended by up to 10

---

[507] Or, as the case may be, receipt of the art.4(1) application (see art.5 of the 2004 Implementing Regulation), together with any extension of the period (as to which, see previous note).

[508] *Schenker SIA v Valsts ieņēmumu dienests* (C–93/08) [2009] E.C.R. I–903.

[509] reg.7(1).

[510] reg.7(5).

[511] The Commissioners may accept the written agreement directly from the interested party: reg.7(3).

[512] reg.7(1).

[513] reg.7(2).

[514] reg.7(4).

[515] Subject to completion of all customs formalities: art.13. In the case of perishable goods, this period is three days: ibid. The 2004 Implementing Regulation provides that where an application for action is lodged in accordance with art.4(1) of the Council Regulation before the expiry of the time limit of three working days and that application has been accepted, the period of 10 (or three, as the case may be) working days runs from the day after the application is received: see art.5. See also art.7(1) of the 2004 Implementing Regulation.

working days.[516] It follows that proceedings must be implemented within this time limit in order to prevent the release of the goods.

22–92   **Articles 10 and 13: Customs Notice.** The former provisions of the Domestic Regulations as to the commencement of proceedings have now been revoked.[517] The Notice simply identifies the appropriate courts and observes that if detention beyond the 10-day period (or any extension thereof) is required the applicant should "seek the permission of the court", presumably by way of injunctive relief.

22–93   **Interim release of the goods: Article 14 of the Council Regulation.** This article provides (relevantly) that the declarant, owner, importer, holder or consignee of goods suspected of infringing design rights shall be able to obtain their release or an end to their detention on provision of security. There are three pre-conditions: first, the customs office or department must have been notified that a procedure has been initiated within the prescribed period to determine whether the goods are pirated goods; secondly, the authority "empowered for this purpose" must not have authorised precautionary measures before expiry of that time limit; and thirdly, all customs formalities must have been completed.[518] The security must be sufficient to protect the interests of the right-holder and its payment is not to affect his other remedies.[519] Article 14 goes on to provide that where the procedure to determine whether the goods are pirated has been commenced otherwise than by the right-holder, the security shall be released if the person initiating "the said procedure" does not exercise his right to institute legal proceedings within 20 working days of the date on which he receives notification of the suspension of release or the detention. Finally, art.14 provides that where the second subparagraph of art.13(1) applies, that is, where the time for the right-holder to initiate proceedings has been extended from 10 to 20 working days, the 20-day period may be extended to 30 working days.[520] It is not easy to understand how the latter provisions are intended to interact with those of art.13.

22–94   **Article 14: Customs Notice.** The Domestic Regulations do not deal with art.14. Customs Notice 34 states that the owner, importer or consignee has the right to take delivery of the goods against a security, provided that the matter has been referred to the court within the required period, the court has not issued an injunction or imposed any other interim measure and all customs formalities have been completed. It goes on to say that the security must be sufficient to protect the right-holder's interests and that it is customary for this matter to be dealt with as part of the Court procedure. The Commissioners will not hold the security and the arrangements will be a private matter between the parties.[521]

22–95   **Storage of the goods.** Article 15 of the Council Regulation provides that the conditions of storage of the goods are for Member States to decide but that they shall not give rise to costs for the customs administration. The Domestic Regula-

---

[516] art.13. In the case of perishable goods, no extension is permitted: ibid. See also arts 7(1) and (2) of the 2004 Implementing Regulation, which provide respectively that if there is insufficient time to apply for such proceedings, an extension may be deemed to be appropriate and that where an extension has already been granted under art.11 of the Council Regulation, no further extension may be granted under art.13(1).

[517] By SI 2010/324. See *Copinger* 15th edn, paras 23–86 to 23–88.

[518] art.14(1).

[519] art.14(2).

[520] art.14(2).

[521] Customs Notice 34, para.5.2.4.

tions make no provision for storage or storage costs, but Customs Notice 34 makes clear that storage will be at the expense of the applicant.[522]

Final disposal of the goods. Article 16 of the Council Regulation provides that goods found to be pirated shall not be allowed to enter the Community customs territory, released for free circulation, removed from the Community customs territory, exported, re-exported, placed under a suspensive procedure or placed in a free zone or free warehouse. Article 17(1) provides that without prejudice to the other legal remedies open to the right-holder, Member States shall adopt the measures necessary (a) to allow the competent authorities to destroy the goods or dispose of them outside commercial channels in such a way as to preclude injury to the right-holder, without compensation and, unless otherwise specified in national legislation, at no cost to the exchequer; and (b) to take any other measures effectively depriving the persons concerned of any economic gains from the transaction. No specific provision is made in the Domestic Regulations. However, this does not appear to be necessary: these matters will either be dealt with by consent or by the court. If the right-holder then wishes to seek an account of profits in accordance with art.17(1)(b), then he can no doubt bring a separate action claiming such an account.   **22–96**

Article 18: penalties. Article 18 requires member states to introduce penalties to apply in the cases of violation of the Regulation. It provides that the penalties must be effective, proportionate and dissuasive. Recital 10 to the Regulation provides that it is necessary to lay down the measures applicable to goods which have been found to be counterfeit, pirated or generally to infringe certain intellectual property rights and that such measures "should not only deprive those responsible for trading in such goods of the economic benefits of the transaction and penalise them but also constitute an effective deterrent to further transactions of the same kind". The Court of Justice has proceeded[523] on the basis that a fine imposed following a conviction in national proceedings for infringement by a declarant of goods of arts 9 and 16 of the Regulation was imposed pursuant to a measure implementing art.18. The reference to art.9 is curious, since that article provides for customs offices to take action (and for subsequent procedures) and does not impose any prohibition on the declarant.[524] Article 16, on the other hand, does prohibit (amongst other things) the release for free circulation of infringing material, and that is what the declarant had done.   **22–97**

Article 18: implementation. No specific provision has been introduced to implement art.18 in the United Kingdom. So far as copyright is concerned, importation of infringing articles otherwise than for the importer's private and domestic use is an offence provided the importer knew or had reason to believe that the article was an infringing copy.[525] However, there is no equivalent offence for design right, which is also covered by the Regulation.[526] Presumably it is thought that such cases are covered by the existing Customs legislation.[527]   **22–98**

Article 19: liability of customs authorities and right-holder. This article provides that except as provided by national laws, the customs authorities shall not be liable to (i) a right-holder for failing to detect pirated goods or to suspend their release or to detain them or (ii) to the persons involved in the art.1(1) situa-   **22–99**

---

[522] Customs Notice 34, para.3.7.
[523] In *Schenker SIA v Valsts ieņēmumu dienests* (C–93/08) [2009] E.C.R. I–903.
[524] See para.22–96, above.
[525] CDPA 1988 s.107(1)(b).
[526] See art.2(1)(b).
[527] In particular, Customs & Excise Management Act 1979 s. 50.

tion for the exercise of their powers.[528] Article 19 goes on to provide that the right-holder's civil liability shall be governed by the law of the Member State in which the goods in question were placed in the art.1(1) situation.[529] Depending on the facts, such liability might arise under the English law of malicious falsehood.

C. SECTION 111 OF THE 1988 ACT

22–100   **The scope of section 111 of the 1988 Act.** Section 111, which contains similar provisions to those in the Council Regulation, originally applied to all infringing printed copies of published literary, dramatic or musical works and to all infringing copies of sound recordings or films which were imported into the United Kingdom (there was an exception for goods imported for private or domestic use). However, in 1995, at the same time as the Council Regulation came into force, the scope of the section was severely curtailed in order to give effect to the Community obligation to establish the internal market.[530] The section as amended does not apply to goods placed or expected to be placed in an art.1(1) situation in respect of which an application may be made under the Council Regulation,[531] nor does it apply to infringing copies which arrive in the United Kingdom from within the European Economic Area unless they have not been entered for free circulation.[532] The section remains restricted to infringing printed copies of published literary dramatic and musical works, and to copies of sound recordings and films.[533] The exception for goods imported for private or domestic use also remains. Unlike the Council Regulation, the section applies to all "infringing copies", including parallel imports and over-runs, and it seems likely that this is in fact the only area in which the section is now of any practical effect.

22–101   **Notice procedure under section 111 of the 1988 Act.**[534] The owner of the copyright in any published literary, dramatic or musical work may give notice[535] to the Commissioners of Customs and Excise requesting them to treat as prohibited goods printed copies of the work which are infringing copies.[536] The notice must state that the person giving it is the owner of the copyright in the work and must specify the period during which the goods are to be treated as prohibited. The period must not exceed five years, and shall not extend beyond the period for which copyright is to subsist.[537] The owner of the copyright in a sound recording or film may also give notice[538] in writing to the Commissioners with a view to preventing the importation of infringing copies. The notice must state that he is the

---

[528] art.19(1).

[529] art.19(2).

[530] The amendments were effected by the Copyright (EC Measures Relating to Pirated Goods and Abolition of Restrictions on the Import of Goods) Regulations 1995 (SI 1995/1445).

[531] CDPA 1988 s.111(3B), added with effect from July 1, 1995 by The Copyright (EC Measures Relating to Pirated Goods and Abolition of Restrictions on the Import of Goods) Regulations 1995 (SI 1995/1445), reg.2 and amended by the Goods Infringing Intellectual Property Rights (Customs) Regulations 2004 (SI 2004/1473), reg.12. For the meaning of the term art.1(1) situation, see para.29–78, below.

[532] CDPA 1988 s.111(3A), added with effect from July 1, 1995 by The Copyright (EC Measures Relating to Pirated Goods and Abolition of Restrictions on the Import of Goods) Regulations 1995 (SI 1995/1445) reg.2.

[533] CDPA 1988 s.111(1) and (3).

[534] See generally HM Customs Notice 34: *Intellectual Property Rights*, June 2010 (Vol.2 B7.biii).

[535] In the form contained in Sch.1 to the Copyright (Customs) Regulations (SI 1989/1178) (Vol.2 B7.bi). A separate notice must be given in respect of each work: ibid. reg.2(1). There is a fee of £30 plus VAT per notice: ibid., reg.4.

[536] CDPA 1988 s.111(1); see ibid. s.27 for the definition of an infringing copy.

[537] CDPA 1988 s.111(2).

[538] In the form contained in Sch.2 to the Copyright (Customs) Regulations (SI 1989/1178). A sepa-

owner of the copyright in the work, that infringing copies of the work are expected to arrive in the United Kingdom at a time and place specified in the notice,[539] and that he requests the Commissioners to treat the copies as prohibited goods.[540] In all cases, a copy of the copyright work must be supplied to the Com missioners with the notice.[541] At the same time, or at the time the goods to which the notice relates are imported, the person giving the notice must provide the Commissioners with such evidence as they may reasonably require to enable them to establish that he is the owner of the copyright in the work and that any goods detained are infringing copies.[542] The person giving the notice must give the Commissioners such security as they may require against liability and expense they may suffer as a result of the notice,[543] and must keep them indemnified against such liability and expense.[544] The person giving the notice must inform the Commissioners of any change in the ownership of the copyright and of any other change affecting the notice within 14 days of such change.[545] The notice is deemed to have been withdrawn within 14 days of any change in the ownership of the copyright or if the person giving the notice fails to comply with any requirement of the Regulations.[546] There is a right of appeal against a refusal by the Commissioners to accept a notice.[547]

Effect of a notice under section 111. When a notice under s.111 of the 1988 Act   **22–102** is in force, the importation of goods to which it applies (otherwise than for the private and domestic use of the importer) is prohibited.[548] The prohibition does not, however, render the importer liable to any penalty other than the forfeiture of the goods.[549] The normal Customs law will apply. Accordingly, the owner of the goods must be notified of the seizure.[550] Any person claiming that the goods were not liable to seizure then has one month to give notice of a claim to the Commissioners.[551] In the absence of such a notice, the goods will be treated as condemned.[552] If such a notice is given, the Commissioners are obliged to take proceedings for condemnation of the goods.[553] If the goods are condemned, or deemed to be condemned, the Commissioners have a discretion as to how to dispose of them[554] but they will normally be destroyed.[555]

---

rate notice must be given in respect of each work and in respect of each expected importation: ibid. reg.2(2). There is a fee of £30 plus VAT per notice: ibid. reg.4.
[539] In this respect the requirements are much more onerous than those relating to published literary, dramatic or musical works.
[540] CDPA 1988 s.111(3); see ibid. s.27 for the definition of an infringing copy.
[541] The Copyright (Customs) Regulations 1989 (SI 1989/1178) reg.5.
[542] SI 1989/1178 reg.5.
[543] SI 1989/1178 reg.6.
[544] SI 1989/1178 reg.7.
[545] SI 1989/1178 reg.8.
[546] SI 1989/1178 reg.9.
[547] The appeal process is via the Excise and Customs appeal procedure laid down by HM Customs and Excise Notice 990.
[548] CDPA 1988 s.111(4).
[549] CDPA 1988 s.111(4).
[550] Customs and Excise Management Act 1979 (c.2) Sch.3 para.1(2). There is no obligation to notify the owner if he or his servant oragent was present at the seizure or if the seizure was in a ship or aircraft and took place in the presence of the master or commander: ibid.
[551] Customs and Excise Management Act 1979 (c.2) Sch.3 para.3. The month runs from the date of service of notice of seizure or (in the absence of such service) from the date of the seizure itself.
[552] Under Customs and Excise Management Act 1979 (c.2) Sch.3 para.5.
[553] Under Customs and Excise Management Act 1979 (c.2) Sch.3 para.8. The proceedings may be in the Magistrates' Court or the High Court: ibid. para.8(1)(a).
[554] Customs and Excise Management Act 1979 (c.2) s.139(5).
[555] HM Customs Notice 34: *Customs: Intellectual Property Rights*, July 2004, p.7. This is not expressly stated in the current version of the Notice.

PART VII

INTERNATIONAL ASPECTS

Chapter Twenty Three

INTERNATIONAL TREATIES

Contents   *Para.*

1. INTRODUCTION—SCOPE OF INTERNATIONAL COPYRIGHT

23–01   **Relationship between international conventions, treaties and agreements, and domestic law.** International copyright is concerned with treaties, conventions or agreements between nations requiring their Contracting States to respect, in their own countries, the copyright of nationals of other Contracting States. There is no general principle of international law requiring such protection[1] and, before the making of international agreements regarding the matter, a book written by a foreigner and published abroad could obtain no protection in this country.[2] Similarly, no protection was afforded abroad to the works of British nationals.

In some countries, such conventions, treaties or agreements are regarded as self-executing, becoming automatically part of the law of the land following adherence to the convention in question, and are so regarded by the courts. However, in the United Kingdom, since 1911, this is not the case, and domestic legislation is required to give effect to the treaty obligations undertaken. The courts are not concerned, therefore, except in very limited circumstances (such as where an Act is ambiguous and the Parliamentary record shows the intention was to implement the Convention),[3] to interpret such treaties, conventions or agree-

---

[1] See *Def Lepp Music v Stuart-Brown* [1986] R.P.C. 273.
[2] *Guichard v Mori* (1831) 9 L.J.Ch. 227. The question of how far under the Acts of Anne and of 1842 an alien could obtain copyright at all in England (apart from the International Copyright Acts) was discussed in *Jefferys (C) v Boosey (T)* (1854) 4 H.L.C. 815, and *Routledge v Low* [1868] L.R. 3 H.L. 100.
[3] See Ch.3 as regards the protection of works of foreign origin.

ments, but only the Acts of Parliament and Orders in Council made for the purpose of giving effect thereto.[4]

As regards the international scope of copyright, there are a number of different aspects to be taken into consideration. In this Chapter, the general body of conventions, treaties and agreements regulating the copyright and related rights relations between different countries at the universal and regional levels are discussed. The protection afforded to copyright and related rights under the law of the European Union is dealt with in Ch.24, below. The protection of works of United Kingdom origin in foreign countries is covered in Ch.25, below. Finally, the protection actually afforded to foreign works by the law of the United Kingdom is explained elsewhere in Ch.3, above.

Major copyright Conventions. The two major copyright Conventions are the Berne Convention for the Protection of Literary and Artistic Works, first adopted in 1886, and the Universal Copyright Convention of 1952. Other Conventions and Agreements to which this country is a party and which have taken on increasing importance in international copyright and related rights relations over the years include the Rome Convention for the Protection of Performers, Producers of Phonograms and Broadcasting Organisations 1961 (the Rome Convention), the Convention for the Protection of Producers of Phonograms against the Unauthorised Duplication of their Phonograms 1971 (the Phonograms Convention), and the Agreement on Trade-Related Aspects of Intellectual Property Rights 1994 (the TRIPs Agreement).   **23–02**

In December 1996, the Berne and Rome Conventions were supplemented and updated by the adoption of two new important international instruments, the WIPO Copyright Treaty and the WIPO Performances and Phonograms Treaty. The United Kingdom ratified these treaties on March 14, 2010.

All these treaties are discussed in this Chapter.[5]

Other conventions of relevance to copyright and related rights. There are a number of other Conventions of lesser importance because of either their limited membership and scope, or their regional character. These are briefly discussed in Pts 9 and 10 of this Chapter and include the Convention Relating to the Distribution of Programme-Carrying Signals Transmitted by Satellite (Brussels, 1974),[6] the Vienna Typefaces Convention,[7] the Madrid Double Taxation Convention,[8] the UNESCO Convention on Cultural Diversity,[9] the Pan-American Conventions,[10] and a number of Council of Europe Conventions and Recommendations.[11] Other potential agreements currently under discussion at intergovernmental level are also discussed in Pt 9.[12]   **23–03**

There are also a series of European Union Directives on the subject of copyright and related rights, all of which have already been implemented in the United Kingdom. More European Union legislation may be expected in the future. Current European Union legislation and the programme of the Commission concerning copyright and related rights is dealt with in Ch.24, below.

---

[4] *The Jade* [1976] 1 W.L.R. 430. See also *Smith Kline & French Laboratories Ltd v RD Harbottle (Mercantile) Ltd* [1979] F.S.R. 555 and *E's Applications* [1983] R.P.C. 231.
[5] The full texts of these Conventions are reproduced in Vol.2 of this work.
[6] See paras 23–156 et seq., below.
[7] See paras 23–160 et seq., below.
[8] See paras 23–162 et seq., below.
[9] See paras 23–164 et seq., below.
[10] See paras 23–178 et seq., below.
[11] See paras 23–181 et seq., below.
[12] See paras 23–168 et seq., below.

2. THE BERNE CONVENTION AND ITS REVISIONS

A. HISTORY

23–04   **Early treaties.** Prior to 1886, international copyright was regulated to a limited extent by bilateral treaties between a number of European nations.[13] During the nineteenth century, international copyright relations developed gradually as the need was perceived to prevent international piracy of copyright works.[14] In England, the Crown was authorised, by the International Copyright Act 1844,[15] and various amending Acts,[16] by Order in Council, to direct that works first published in foreign countries should be entitled to copyright in the United Kingdom, and, between 1846 and 1886, the United Kingdom entered into a series of bilateral treaties with other European countries providing for reciprocal protection to authors of the respective countries. A large number of Orders in Council were promulgated under the 1844 Act to give effect to these treaties. The general purpose of the treaties entered into by the United Kingdom was to give the authors of works first published in one of the States party thereto the same privileges in the other States as would have been enjoyed if the work had been first published there. By the mid-nineteenth century, the United Kingdom had entered into bilateral agreements on copyright with Belgium, France, Hanover, Prussia, Sardinia-Italy and Spain.[17]

23–05   **Berne Convention.** These early treaties gave rise to a complicated situation, for the rights of a foreign author in the United Kingdom and of a British national elsewhere varied according to the particular treaty or Order in Council concerned and it was difficult for an author to establish the extent to which he was protected in a country other than his own. In 1884 and 1885, at the initiative of the Swiss Government, conferences were held in an attempt to draw up an international copyright treaty.[18] The United Kingdom was a party to these Conferences, which resulted at the Diplomatic Conference held at Berne in 1886 in the framing of a Convention, known as the Berne Convention, whereby the Contracting States were "constituted into a Union for the protection of the rights of authors over their literary and artistic works".[19] To enable the United Kingdom to give effect to this Convention by Orders in Council, the International Copyright Act 1886[20] was passed.

---

[13] S. Ricketson and J.C. Ginsburg, *International Copyright and Neighbouring Rights, The Berne Convention and Beyond* 2nd edn (Oxford: Oxford University Press, 2006), paras 1.29 et seq.

[14] S. Ricketson and J.C. Ginsburg, *International Copyright and Neighbouring Rights, The Berne Convention and Beyond* 2nd edn (Oxford: Oxford University Press, 2006), paras 1.30 et seq.

[15] 7 & 8 Vict. c.12. See also I. Davis, "A Century of Copyright: the United Kingdom and the Berne Convention", [1986] *Copyright* 177.

[16] 15 & 16 Vict. c.12; 25 & 26 Vict. c.68; 38 & 39 Vict.c.12.

[17] S. Ricketson and J.C. Ginsburg, *International Copyright and Neighbouring Rights, The Berne Convention and Beyond* 2nd edn (Oxford: Oxford University Press, 2006), paras 1.30 et seq.

[18] S. Ricketson and J.C. Ginsburg, *International Copyright and Neighbouring Rights, The Berne Convention and Beyond* 2nd edn (Oxford: Oxford University Press, 2006), paras 2.19 et seq. and paras 2.38 et seq.

[19] Berne Convention 1886 art.1. The UK adhered to this Convention on November 28, 1887. The new Convention entered into force on December 5, 1887, with the following membership: Belgium, France, Germany, Haiti, Italy, Spain, Switzerland, Tunisia and the UK. The UK ratified the Convention on behalf also of its colonial possessions and principal self-governing dominions. As to the history and development of the Berne Convention, see: C. Masouyé, *Guide to the Berne Convention for the Protection of Literary and Artistic Works (Paris Act, 1971)* (Geneva: WIPO, 1978); A. Bogsch, "The First Hundred Years of the Berne Convention for the Protection of Literary and Artistic Works", [1986] *Copyright* 291, and S. Ricketson and J.C. Ginsburg, *International Copyright and Neighbouring Rights, The Berne Convention and Beyond* 2nd edn (Oxford: Oxford University Press, 2006).

[20] 49 & 50 Vict. c.33.

The Berne Convention has been revised[21] periodically to take account of new technologies, the development of which in turn gave rise to new uses of copyright protected works, and of political, economic and social changes. Over the years, new rights for copyright owners have been recognised, raising the level of protection and increasing the uniformity of treatment of rights owners in the Contracting States. These revisions are discussed below.

Additional Act of Paris 1896. In 1896, a further Diplomatic Conference was held in Paris[22] to consider certain modifications aimed at clarifying and consolidating the original Convention and which experience had shown to be necessary or expedient. For example, it was made clear that the expression "published" meant "published for the first time" and that authors being nationals of countries not party to the Berne Convention but whose works were first published in a Berne country were protected under the Convention. Posthumous works were expressly protected. This Conference resulted in what was called the "Additional Act of Paris 1896", which was adopted by the United Kingdom on March 7, 1898. The revision took the form of a separate instrument, the Additional Act, as opposed to a revised Berne Convention, because a number of the proposed amendments were unacceptable to some Contracting States. A major and lasting consequence of this for the future of the Berne Union was the replacement of one single treaty by several different Acts of the Convention, each with restricted membership as various countries became bound by slightly different texts.[23] A further Interpretative Declaration[24] was also adopted, containing certain authentic interpretations of the Act agreed by the majority of the States present. These included that protection should depend only on compliance with formalities in the country of origin and a definition of "published", limiting the concept to the making available of copies and making it clear that "performance" of a work did not constitute publication. The United Kingdom did not accept the Declaration, its contents being at variance with its domestic law at the time.

23–06

The revised Berne Convention of Berlin 1908. In 1908, a further Diplomatic Conference was held in Berlin,[25] the object of which was "to secure, if possible, a general agreement to such a revision of the Berne Convention and the Additional Act of Paris as would enable the Contracting States to sign a single new instrument containing stipulations of a more complete and simple character, with a view, not only to affording a more effectual protection to the author, but also to removing the more salient difficulties which had been encountered in the working

23–07

---

[21] Art.17 of the 1886 Act provided for periodic revisions. The history of the various Acts of the Berne Convention is as follows: September 9, 1886: Berne Convention (entry into force December 5, 1887); May 4, 1896: Additional Act of Paris (entry into force on December 9, 1897); November 13, 1908: Berlin Act (entry into force September 9, 1910); March 20, 1914: Additional Protocol of Berne (entry into force on April 20, 1915); June 2, 1928: Rome Act (entry into force August 1, 1931); June 26, 1948: Brussels Act (entry into force August 1, 1951); June 14, 1967: Stockholm Act (revised substantive provisions never entered into force; they were themselves revised in 1971; administrative provisions entered into force in 1970); July 24, 1971: Paris Act (entry into force October 10, 1974). The WIPO Copyright Treaty adopted by the Diplomatic Conference on December 20, 1996, is not a revised Act of the Berne Convention but a new treaty, which is a special agreement within the meaning of art.20 of the Berne Convention.
[22] S. Ricketson and J.C. Ginsburg, *International Copyright and Neighbouring Rights, The Berne Convention and Beyond* 2nd edn (Oxford University Press, 2006), paras 3.02 to 3.07 et seq.
[23] See paras 23–61 to 23–65, below, and "General Table of Copyright and Related Rights Conventions and National Laws", Ch.25, below.
[24] *The Berne Convention for the Protection of Literary and Artistic Works from 1886 to 1986* (Geneva: WIPO, 1986) texts, p.229.
[25] S. Ricketson and J.C. Ginsburg, *International Copyright and Neighbouring Rights, The Berne Convention and Beyond* 2nd edn (Oxford: Oxford University Press, 2006), paras 3.08 to 3.20 et seq.

of the existing arrangements".[26] The result of the Conference was the Revised Berne Convention or Berlin Act 1908, which replaced the original Convention of 1887, and the Additional Act of Paris 1896, except that States who were signatories to the original Convention and the Additional Act of Paris could still elect to be bound by the provisions of these Conventions in preference to those of the Revised Convention.[27] Among the most important changes agreed were the inclusion of architectural, choreographic and pantomime works; the grant of a translation right for the full term of the copyright in the original work,[28] adaptations, musical arrangements and other reproductions in altered form of a literary or artistic work, as well as collections of works, as original works, without prejudice to the rights of the authors of the original works. Authors of musical works were protected with regard to mechanical reproduction by the new recording techniques and cinematographic works of sufficient originality were also accorded protection for the first time. It further embodied three basic principles which have been regarded as pillars of the Convention ever since: the principle of national treatment, which entitles authors of one Union country to the same rights in other Union countries as those accorded by the laws of those countries to their own nationals; the principle of the absence of formalities, according to which the enjoyment and exercise of rights were not to be subject to any formality, such as registration; and the principle of independence of protection, according to which the enjoyment and exercise of rights, as well as their enforcement, was to be governed exclusively by the laws of the country in which protection was claimed. For the first time, the term of protection was fixed at the life of the author plus 50 years; however, this term was not obligatory and it was open to Union countries to adopt a different term. The United Kingdom ratified the Berlin text in 1912.[29]

An additional Protocol was agreed to on March 20, 1914. The 1896 Paris Act had admitted to the benefits of the Convention authors from non-Union countries who first published their works in a Union country. However, this presented a problem because often authors from Union countries did not receive adequate reciprocal protection for their works in non-Union countries. The most notorious case was that of the United States of America, whose nationals benefited from the Berne Convention by first publishing over the border in Canada. However, nationals of Union countries were generally not afforded protection in the United States. The 1914 additional Protocol was promoted by the United Kingdom at the instigation of Canada (at the time a self-governing Dominion) and permitted the government of a Union country to restrict protection in the case of authors from non-Union countries which failed to protect the authors from the Union country in an adequate manner. Only Canada availed itself of this facility.

23–08   **Rome and Brussels Acts.** The Berne Convention was revised at Rome in 1928[30] and again at Brussels in 1948.[31] Two important modifications were adopted at Rome: the recognition for the first time of moral rights (specifically, the right to claim authorship of a work and the right to claim respect for its integrity) and the right of authors to control the use of their works in broadcasting (the exclusive

---

[26] Report of British Commissioners, Blue Book 1909, Miscellaneous (No.2) Cd.4467, p.5.

[27] Berlin Act art.27.

[28] See art.VI of the original Berne Convention of 1886, which provided for a translation right of 10 years following publication of the work in the original language in a country of the Union. See I. Davis, "A Century of Copyright: the United Kingdom and the Berne Convention" [1986] *Copyright* 177, p.179.

[29] [1912] *Le Droit d'Auteur*, 90. The new Act had entered into force on September 9, 1910.

[30] The Rome Act came into force on August 1, 1931. S. Ricketson and J.C. Ginsburg, *International Copyright and Neighbouring Rights, The Berne Convention and Beyond* 2nd edn (Oxford: Oxford University Press, 2006), paras 3.22 to 3.32.

[31] The Brussels Act came into force on August 1, 1951.

right of radiodiffusion). The copyright protection available to films was extended to cover films which did not possess an original character, protection being afforded to such films under the new text as photographic works rather than as cinematographic works. As regards moral rights, Contracting States were left free to determine the way in which these rights should be protected and it was not mandatory for such rights to be protected through the copyright law. Thus the United Kingdom was able to continue to protect such rights by other means, such as passing off, defamation and slander of goods.[32] The Rome Act was considered to have achieved relatively little to advance the cause of authors. Work on a further revision started early in the 1930s but was interrupted by the Second World War.

After the war, work resumed and the Brussels Act was adopted at a conference in 1948.[33] The latter revision was limited to refining and consolidating the changes made by the Berlin and Rome Acts; among other changes, cinematographic works (without qualification) and photographic works were included in the primary list of works protected, along with works of applied art. Perhaps the most significant change related to the term of protection; the option to derogate from the standard minimum term of life plus 50 years was removed. No fundamental extensions to authors' rights were introduced but a number of other important changes were made. These included: modification of the definition of publication, so that publication within 30 days was considered as being simultaneous; assimilation of rebroadcasting, relaying and public playing of broadcasts to the basic broadcasting right introduced in the Rome Act, extension of the author's right in relation to the filming of his work to cover distribution and public performance of the film; and the guarantee of an author's right to equitable remuneration in respect of the mechanical recording of his work, in countries which did not recognise an exclusive recording right. These various amendments involved alterations to which effect could only be given in the United Kingdom by new legislation. Thus, one of the reasons for the passing of the 1956 Act was to enable the United Kingdom to ratify the Brussels Act.[34] During the Brussels Conference, motions were adopted calling for protection (without prejudice to the rights of authors) to be included in the Convention for sound recordings, broadcasts and performers.[35] These led in due course to the adoption of the Rome Convention in 1961.[36]

It should also be noted that, at the Rome Conference in 1928, a resolution had been adopted calling for world unification of authors' rights through an accommodation between the Berne Convention and the two most important inter-American Conventions, the Buenos Aires and Havana Conventions[37] and to discuss the formation of an international copyright convention of wider geographical scope, the Berne Convention membership being limited at that time to European countries and their colonies and dominions in other parts of the world. Although this idea was not taken up at the Brussels Conference, it was not abandoned, and, under the auspices of the United Nations Educational, Scientific

---

[32] See Ch.11, above.

[33] S. Ricketson and J.C. Ginsburg, *International Copyright and Neighbouring Rights, The Berne Convention and Beyond* 2nd edn (Oxford: Oxford University Press, 2006), paras 3.33 et seq.

[34] For text see *Copinger* 10th edn, paras 1681 et seq .

[35] *Actes de la Conférence de Bruxelles*, 587 (votes VI, VII and VIII).

[36] See paras 23–88 et seq., below.

[37] *Actes de la Conférence de Rome*, 350. S. Ricketson and J.C. Ginsburg, *International Copyright and Neighbouring Rights, The Berne Convention and Beyond* 2nd edn (Oxford: Oxford University Press, 2006), para.3.31. The Buenos Aires and Havana Conventions are discussed at paras 23–178 et seq., below.

and Cultural Organisation (UNESCO), the Universal Copyright Convention was later concluded in Paris in 1952.[38]

23–09   **Stockholm Act.** The Berne Convention was again revised at Stockholm in 1967.[39] This introduced the controversial Protocol Regarding Developing Countries[40] designed to meet the wishes of certain developing countries which considered the extent of protection provided by the Berne Convention too great in the light of the particular domestic circumstances of such countries. The Protocol therefore provided that any such country which ratified or acceded to the Convention could make reservations in respect of certain matters, particularly in relation to reproduction and translation rights, broadcasting for non-profit making purposes and compulsory licensing of protected works for educational purposes, which would have the effect of giving less protection in that country than was afforded in other countries of the Berne Union.

The adoption of the Protocol, despite opposition from the developed nations, led to a serious situation in the international copyright community. Thus, although art.21 of the Stockholm Convention made the Protocol an integral part of the Convention, art.28 provided that any country ratifying or acceding to the Convention could declare that its ratification or accession was not to apply to the substantive provisions of the Convention and the Protocol. As a result, by 1970, none of the major developed countries had ratified or acceded to the substantive provisions of these instruments. The United Kingdom, for instance, acceded only to the administrative provisions and final clauses, namely arts 22 to 38, linked to the new Convention establishing the World Intellectual Property Organisation (WIPO).[41]

Article 26 of the Stockholm Act provided the possibility of amending the administrative clauses, including art.26 itself, by the Assembly of the Union. The entry into force of any such amendment required that three-fourths of the countries' members of the Assembly had notified their acceptance of it to the Director General of WIPO.

23–10   **Paris Act.** This situation was particularly unfortunate since it had been hoped that one of the results of the Stockholm revision would have been that the United States of America would eventually join the Berne Union after revising its domestic law. However, such hopes faded as a result of what transpired at Stockholm. Serious attempts were therefore made, following Stockholm, to try to resolve this situation, including proposals to revise the Universal Copyright Convention and to revise further the Berne Convention. In fact both Conventions were revised in Paris in 1971, arts 22 and 23 of the Paris revision of Berne being amended later in October 1979, in accordance with the procedure provided for by art.26. The main change, in 1971, as regards the Berne Convention, was the dropping of art.21 relating to the Protocol Regarding Developing Countries and the

---

[38] Regarding the UCC, see paras 23–79 et seq.

[39] Cmnd.4412. For text see *Copinger* 11th edn, paras 1681 et seq. See *Records of the Intellectual Property Conference of Stockholm* (Geneva: WIPO, 1971) and S. Ricketson, *The Berne Convention for the Protection of Literary and Artistic Works: 1886–1896* (Queen Mary College, University of London, 1987), paras 3.49–3.65. See also S. Ricketson and J.C. Ginsburg, *International Copyright and Neighbouring Rights, The Berne Convention and Beyond* 2nd edn (Oxford: Oxford University Press, 2006), paras 3.49–3.67.

[40] See R.F. Whale, *The Stockholm Act of the Berne Copyright Union*. Protocol Regarding the Developing Countries, (British Copyright Council, London, 1968); and D.M. Schrader, "Analysis of the Protocol Regarding Developing Countries", [1970] 17 *Bulletin of the Copyright Society of the USA* 160.

[41] The UK ratified the Stockholm Act on February 26, 1970, and made a declaration to the effect that its ratification did not apply to arts 1 to 21 and to the Protocol Regarding Developing Countries.

Protocol itself and, instead, the inclusion of acceptable special provisions in favour of developing countries in art.21 and an Appendix in the Paris revision of Berne. As a result, many countries, among them some of the major countries (including the United Kingdom) subsequently adhered to the Paris Act. So far as the United States of America is concerned, that country acceded to the Paris Act with effect from March 1, 1989.[42] Some of the changes to the Paris Act required amendments to the 1956 Act before the United Kingdom could ratify it.[43] The necessary changes to the law were made in the 1988 Act (the copyright provisions of which came into force on August 1, 1989) and this country eventually ratified the Paris Act on September 29, 1989, with effect from January 2, 1990.[44] The substantive provisions of the Paris Act,[45] which remain in force today, are examined below.[46]

WIPO Copyright Treaty. The substantive provisions of the Paris Act have been supplemented by the WIPO Copyright Treaty, adopted on December 20, 1996. The Treaty is a special agreement within the meaning of art.20 of the Berne Convention and does not derogate in any way from the existing obligations that Contracting States of the Berne Convention have to each other under the Paris Act.[47] The new Treaty and the circumstances in which it was adopted are discussed below.[48] At the time, the negotiation of a new revised Act of the Berne Convention itself was ruled out as the Member States took the view that the required unanimity for the adoption of such a revised Act was not politically possible. Nevertheless, since the adoption of the Paris Act in 1971, a consensus had arisen on the need for new international regulations on copyright to address technical developments and enforcement of rights.   **23–11**

B. SUBSTANTIVE PROVISIONS OF PARIS ACT

Principles underlying the Convention. Two systems are possible for an international copyright convention. Theoretically, the most satisfactory system would be a complete copyright code to be applied in each country of the Union both for nationals and subjects of other countries of the Union.   **23–12**

A less satisfactory system is one which merely requires each Member State to give to the nationals of other Member States the same protection as it gives to its own nationals, so-called national treatment, with the result that the measure of protection will vary from state to state. The system in fact adopted in the Berne Convention represented a compromise of the two systems and the revisions of the Convention referred to above have tended to extend the principle of the common code. In fact the Paris Act embodies a reasonably complete code but, as will

---

[42] [1988] *Copyright* 444.
[43] See Report of the 1977 Copyright Committee, Cmnd.6732, paras 50–60 and 85 and *Intellectual Property and Innovation* (White Paper) 1986 Cmnd.9712.
[44] [1989] *Copyright* 287.
[45] For text see Vol.2 at F1 et seq. For an examination of the equivalent provisions of the Brussels Convention, see *Copinger* 10th edn, Ch.24, and of the Stockholm Convention see *Copinger* 11th edn, Ch.24.
[46] See paras 23–12 et seq., below.
[47] WIPO Copyright Treaty art.1. Art.20 Berne Convention provides: "The Governments of the countries of the Union reserve the right to enter into special agreements among themselves, in so far as such agreements grant to authors more extensive rights than those granted by the Convention, or contain other provisions not contrary to this Convention. The provisions of existing agreements which satisfy these conditions shall remain applicable".
[48] See paras 23–66 et seq., below.

be seen, specifically reserves to members the right to deal with certain matters according to their own legislation.[49]

23–13   **Eligibility for protection.** Articles 4, 5 and 6 of the Berlin, Rome and Brussels Conventions contained the fundamental dual principle of mutual protection, by means of national treatment, and code protection. Articles 4, 5 and 6(1) of the Brussels Convention have been redrafted and rearranged to form arts 3, 4 and 5 of the Paris Act.[50]

Article 3 contains the general criteria for eligibility for protection and provides as follows:

> "(1) The protection of this Convention shall apply to:
>
> (a) authors who are nationals of one of the countries of the Union, for their works, whether published or not;
>
> (b) authors who are not nationals of one of the countries of the Union, for their works first published in one of those countries, or simultaneously in a country outside the Union and in a country of the Union.
>
> (2) Authors who are not nationals of one of the countries of the Union but who have their habitual residence in one of them shall, for the purposes of this Convention, be assimilated to nationals of that country".

This article is broader in scope than the Brussels Act, since works of nationals of Union countries are to be protected, even if first publication takes place in a non-Union country. The previous position was that first publication in a non-Union country would have meant loss of protection: art.4 of Brussels. Further, protection is to be afforded to nationals of non-Union countries habitually resident in a Union country.[51] It is to be noted that the Paris Act provides, in a similar way to the Brussels Act, that it is open to any country of the Union to restrict protection to works whose authors are nationals of a non-Union country which does not give reciprocal rights and are not habitually resident in a country of the Union: art.6.[52]

The Paris Act (art.4) contains special criteria of eligibility for protection in respect of cinematographic works and works of architecture (new in Stockholm). This article provides:

> "The protection of this Convention shall apply, even if the conditions of Article 3 are not fulfilled, to:
>
> (a) authors of cinematographic works the maker of which has his headquarters or habitual residence in one of the countries of the Union;
>
> (b) authors of works of architecture erected in a country of the Union or of other artistic works incorporated in a building or other structure located in a country of the Union".

23–14   **What is "publication"?** As has been seen, under art.3 of the Paris Act, protection, in the case of authors who are not nationals of one of the countries of the Union, depends upon first publication of the work in a Union country, or publication simultaneously in a non-Union country and in a Union country. Article 3(3) defines the expression "published works" as follows:

> "works published with the consent of their authors, whatever may be the means of manufacture of the copies, provided that the availability of such

---

[49] See paras 24–16, et seq., below.

[50] See C. Masouyé, *Guide to the Berne Convention for the Protection of Literary and Artistic Works (Paris Act, 1971)* (WIPO, Geneva, 1978), pp.26–38.

[51] See CDPA 1988 s.154.

[52] See C. Masouyé, *Guide to the Berne Convention for the Protection of Literary and Artistic Works (Paris Act, 1971)* (WIPO, Geneva, 1978), pp.39–40.

copies has been such as to satisfy the reasonable requirements of the public, having regard to the nature of the work. The performance of a dramatic, dramatico-musical, cinematographic or musical work, the public recitation of a literary work, the communication by wire or the broadcasting of literary or artistic works, the exhibition of a work of art and the construction of a work of architecture is not to constitute publication".

This definition has been changed in certain respects from that in art.4(4) of the Brussels Act. Thus the present definition is to apply generally whereas, under art.4(4), the definition was only to apply for the purposes of arts 4, 5 and 6 of the Brussels Act. Again, whereas previously it had been understood that there could be no publication unless it was authorised, the new definition expressly limits publication to works published with the consent of the authors. Finally, the language used is now more suitable to cover various kinds of works, in that publication depends, to some extent, on the nature of the work.[53] The concept of publication in the Paris Act is, therefore, similar to that adopted by the 1988 Act,[54] and all that is required to constitute publication in a particular country is that copies should be made available for sale in that country, with the consent of the copyright owner, in sufficient quantity to satisfy the reasonable requirements of the public there, having regard to the nature of the work.

It will have been noted that, under the Paris Act, the construction of a work of architecture does not constitute publication. However, the 1988 Act provides that the construction of a work of architecture in the form of a building is to be the equivalent of publication of the work.[55]

Simultaneous publication. The alternative to first publication in a Union country, to entitle authors who are nationals of non-Union countries to the protection of the Paris Act, is simultaneous publication in a non-Union country and in a Union country: art.3(1). Prior to the Brussels Act the only provision dealing with "simultaneous publication" was art.4 in connection with country of origin. As there was no definition of this term, "simultaneous" prima facie appeared to involve publication on the same day. However, art.4(3) of the Brussels Act added a definition which is substantially repeated in art.3(4) of the Paris Act. According to this definition, a work is to be considered as having been published simultaneously in several countries, if it has been published in two or more countries within 30 days of its first publication.[56]   **23–15**

Extent of protection. The extent of protection is dealt with in art.5 of the Paris Act which lays down the principle of national treatment and provides as follows: **23–16**

"(1) Authors shall enjoy, in respect of works for which they are protected under this Convention, in countries of the Union other than the country of origin, the rights which their respective laws do now or may hereafter grant to their nationals, as well as the rights specially granted by this Convention.

...

(3) Protection in the country of origin is governed by domestic law. However, when the author is not a national of the country of origin of the work for which he is protected under this Convention, he shall enjoy in that country the same rights as national authors".

A distinction is made between the extent of protection in the country of origin and in other countries of the Union, since protection in the country of origin is

---

[53] See C. Masouyé, *Guide to the Berne Convention for the Protection of Literary and Artistic Works (Paris Act, 1971)* (WIPO, Geneva, 1978), pp.27–28.
[54] See CDPA 1988 s.175.
[55] Compare s.175(3) and Copyright Act 1956 s.49(2)(a). See para.3–178, above.
[56] See CDPA 1988 s.155(3).

governed by the domestic law but, in countries other than the country of origin, the author is given not only the rights which are given under their domestic laws, but also the rights granted by the Convention. In theory, therefore, an author can be worse off in the country of origin than in other countries of the Union.[57]

23–17 **Country of origin.** It will be noted that, under art.5 of the Paris Act, authors are protected in countries other than the country of origin, and that a distinction is made as to the type of protection afforded in the country of origin and in other countries.[58] Country of origin is defined in art.5(4) as follows:

"The country of origin shall be considered to be:

(a) in the case of works first published in a country of the Union, that country; in the case of works published simultaneously in several countries of the Union which grant different terms of protection, the country whose legislation grants the shortest term of protection;

(b) in the case of works published simultaneously in a country outside the Union and in a country of the Union, the latter country;

(c) in the case of unpublished works or of works first published in a country outside the Union, without simultaneous publication in a country of the Union, the country of the Union of which the author is a national provided that:

(i) when these are cinematographic works the maker of which has his headquarters or his habitual residence in a country of the Union, the country of origin shall be that country, and

(ii) when these are works of architecture erected in a country of the Union or other artistic works incorporated in a building or other structure located in a country of the Union, the country of origin shall be that country".

23–18 **Rights of nationals of a Union country.** The result of the above articles is that nationals of a Union country are to be accorded protection in every Union country for: (a) unpublished works, (b) works published in the Union country in which protection is sought, (c) works published in another Union country, and (d) works published in a non-Union country. This last is a change from the Brussels Act under which, subject to simultaneous publication, protection was lost if a work was first published in a non-Union country: art.4(1) of Brussels. Thus, a British subject can claim in, say, France, national treatment both for his unpublished works and for his published works wherever published.

It has been mentioned above (para.23–13) that nationals of non-Union countries, but who are habitually resident in one of them, are to be assimilated to nationals of that country (art.3(2) of Paris); also that cinematographic works and works of architecture may be protected in certain circumstances irrespective of the nationality of their authors.

23–19 **Rights of nationals of a non-Union country.** Nationals of a non-Union country, other than those habitually resident in a Union country, are to be accorded protection for their works first published in a Union country, or simultaneously published in a non-Union country and in a Union country. No protection is, therefore, given to unpublished works of nationals of non-Union countries unless

---

[57] See C. Masouyé, *Guide to the Berne Convention for the Protection of Literary and Artistic Works (Paris Act, 1971)* (WIPO, Geneva, 1978), pp.32–34.
[58] See C. Masouyé, *Guide to the Berne Convention for the Protection of Literary and Artistic Works (Paris Act, 1971)* (WIPO, Geneva, 1978), pp.35 et seq.

they are habitually resident in a Union country.[59] This means that an author, being a national of a non-Union country, habitually resident in, say, France, is protected in France under the Convention for his unpublished works, which would not be the case if he were habitually resident in his own country. However, it has been mentioned above (para.23–17) that cinematographic works and works of architecture may be protected, in certain circumstances, irrespective of the nationality of their authors.

No formalities. It was provided by art.2 of the original Berne Convention that enjoyment of the rights conferred by the Convention should be "subject to the accomplishment of the conditions and formalities prescribed by the law of the country of origin of the work", and, in order to make it clear that the formalities of the country in which protection was sought need not be complied with, the Interpretative Declaration of Paris provided that the copyright should depend upon these conditions and formalities "solely". It followed from these provisions that it was always necessary, where a foreigner sought protection in a country other than that in which he first published his work, to inquire as to what formalities were prescribed by the country of origin of the work. Moreover, the question was raised whether, if a work was totally unprotected in its country of origin, it could claim any protection in other Union countries. Obviously, such a question might involve inquiries into difficult points of foreign law upon which the local tribunal might find it hard to pronounce a correct decision.[60] The Berlin Act, however, marked a considerable advance in principle by providing, in art.4,[61] that "the enjoyment and exercise of" copyright in the various countries "shall not be subject to the performance of any formality", and that "such enjoyment and such exercise are independent of the existence of protection in the country of origin of the work"—that is to say, there are not to be any formalities precedent to obtaining copyright, for instance, reservation of copyright, nor any formalities precedent to the bringing of an action for infringement, such as the registration which was necessary under the repealed English legislation—prior to the commencement of proceedings to enforce copyright in a literary work. "Consequently"—as the paragraph proceeded—"apart from the express stipulations of the present Convention, the extent of protection, as well as the means of redress secured to the author to safeguard his rights, shall be governed exclusively by the laws of the country where protection is claimed".

  However, it is to be noted that this paragraph, now art.5(2) of Paris, only applies to the rights conferred in art.5(1) of Paris, that is to say, to the rights enjoyed in countries other than the country of origin of the work. The equivalent art.4(2) of the Brussels Act only applied to the rights in art.4(1) of that Act which was concerned with the rights of nationals of a Union country. Article 5(1) of the Paris Act, however, applies both to the rights of nationals of non-Union countries as well as to the rights of nationals of Union countries.

The term of protection. Article 7(1) of the Paris Act lays down a minimum term of protection granted by the Convention and binding on all countries of the Union

23–20

23–21

---

[59] See CDPA 1988 ss.154 and 155. As to the meaning of "publication", and "simultaneous publication", see paras 23–14 and 23–15, above.

[60] For instance, the point was raised in the German courts as to whether Oscar Wilde's work *Salome* would have been debarred from copyright in England upon the ground that the work was blasphemous. In England it was provided by s.2(3) of the International Copyright Act 1886 (now repealed), that "the International Copyright Acts and an Order made thereunder shall not confer on any person any greater right or longer term of copyright in any work than that enjoyed in the foreign country in which such work was first published". As to the difficulties that arose upon the words "any greater right", see *Hanfstaengl v Empire Palace* [1894] 3 Ch. 109; and as to compliance with the conditions of the country of origin, *Sarpy v Holland* [1908] 2 Ch. 198.

[61] Equivalent provisions are contained in the Rome, Brussels, Stockholm and Paris Acts.

for the life of the author and 50 years after his death with respect to literary and artistic works. This term was introduced at the Berlin Revision (1908) but only became an obligation under the Brussels Act 1948.[62] By art.2, para.(2), of the original Convention it was provided that copyright "must not exceed, in the other countries, the duration of the protection granted in the said country of origin". At the Diplomatic Conference at Berlin in 1908, an effort was made to induce the States represented there to agree to a uniform term of protection as a condition of membership of the Union. This effort did not, however, entirely succeed, and art.7 (subsequently revised and made obligatory in the Brussels Act) of the Berlin Convention was agreed to as a compromise.

Article 7 was again revised in the Stockholm Act, repeated in the Paris Act, and contains some new provisions. The basic term of protection is still to be the life of the author and 50 years after his death: art.7(1). However, unlike the Brussels Act, minimum terms of protection have now been laid down for cinematographic works, photographic works and works of applied art. Thus, in the case of cinematographic works, the countries of the Union may provide that the term of protection is to expire 50 years after the work has been made available to the public with the consent of the author,[63] or, failing such an event within 50 years from the making of such a work, 50 years after the making: art.7(2).[64] In the case of photographic works and works of applied art in so far as they are protected as artistic works, it is to be a matter for legislation in the countries of the Union to determine the term of protection thereof; however, this term is to last at least until the end of a period of 25 years from the making of such a work: art.7(4). In the case of anonymous or pseudonymous works where the identity of the author remains undisclosed, the period is 50 years after the work has been lawfully made available to the public: art.7(3). Article 7(4) of the Brussels Act referred to 50 years from the date of publication. However, the Paris Act (like Stockholm) now provides that countries of the Union are not required to protect anonymous or pseudonymous works in respect of which it is reasonable to presume that their author has been dead for 50 years: art.7(3).[65]

Article 7(5) of the Paris Act provides that the term of protection subsequent to the death of the author and the terms provided by paras (2) (cinematographic works), (3) (anonymous and pseudonymous works), and (4) (photographic works and works of applied art) are to run from the date of death or of the event referred to in those paragraphs, but such terms are to be deemed to begin on January 1 of the year following the death or such event.

As stated above, the Brussels Act omitted the provisions of art.7(2) of the Rome Act which entitled countries of the Union to provide a shorter period of protection than those laid down in art.7, and this necessitated the abolition in the United Kingdom, by the 1956 Act, of the proviso to s.3 of the 1911 Act allowing works to be published under a compulsory licence at the expiration of 25 years from the death of the author. On the other hand, a provision of the Paris Act (new in Stockholm) permits those countries of the Union bound by the Rome Act of the Convention, which grant in their domestic legislation shorter terms of protection than those in art.7, to maintain such terms when ratifying or acceding to the Paris Act: art.7(7).

23–22   The Paris Act further provides that the countries of the Union may grant a term of protection in excess of those provided by art.7: art.7(6). Again, the Paris Act

---

[62] See C. Masouyé, *Guide to the Berne Convention for the Protection of Literary and Artistic Works (Paris Act, 1971)* (WIPO, Geneva, 1978), pp.45 et seq.
[63] See para.23–23, below.
[64] See CDPA 1988 s.13.
[65] See ss.9(4) and 12(2).

provides that in any case the term is to be governed by the legislation of the country where protection is claimed, but unless the legislation of that country otherwise provides, the term is not to exceed the term fixed in the country of origin of the work: art.7(8).

It will be noted that the Paris Act does not, in respect of the basic term of protection, draw any distinction between published and unpublished works.

The Rome Act added, for the first time, provisions with regard to the minimum term of copyright in works of joint authorship, namely one expiring with the death of the author who dies last. However, the Brussels Act dropped this provision and, instead, provided that, in the case of a work of joint authorship, the term of protection was to be calculated from the date of the death of the last surviving author: art.7*bis*. As a result, the maximum term of 50 years from the death of the last surviving author became obligatory and this again resulted in an alteration in English law under the provisions of the 1956 Act, continued by the 1988 Act. The Paris Act contains an equivalent provision: art.7*bis*.

Protected works. What are the works which must be protected? Article 1 of the Paris Act[66] states that the countries to which the Convention applies are constituted into a Union for the protection of the rights of authors in their "literary and artistic works". Article 2(1) then provides that: **23–23**

"The expression 'literary and artistic works' shall include every production in the literary, scientific, and artistic domain, whatever may be the mode or form of its expression, such as books, pamphlets, and other writings; lectures, addresses, sermons and other works of the same nature; dramatic or dramatico-musical works, choreographic works and entertainments in dumb show, musical compositions with or without words; cinematographic works to which are assimilated works expressed by a process analogous to cinematography; works of drawing, painting, architecture, sculpture, engraving and lithography; photographic works to which are assimilated works expressed by a process analogous to photography; works of applied art, illustrations; maps, plans, sketches, and three-dimensional works relative to geography, topography, architecture or science".

This definition presents something of a trap to the English lawyer accustomed to the general words "literary, dramatic, musical and artistic works" in the English Copyright Acts who may therefore think, mistakenly, that the words "literary and artistic works" appearing in the Convention do not include dramatic or musical works. Prior to the Berlin Act, there was no obligation to protect choreographic works or works of architecture, but, in countries where such works received protection, the other Union countries were entitled to the benefit of such protection. Photographic and cinematographic works were included in the definition of "literary and artistic works" for the first time by the Brussels Act. Photographic works were previously protected under art.3 which was not repeated in the Brussels Act. Prior to the Brussels Act, cinematographic productions were protected under art.14, but only as literary or artistic works if the author had given the work an original character: in the absence of such an original character, they were protected as photographic works. This qualification was adopted in this country by the 1911 Act, and the change brought about by the Brussels Act of the Convention was followed here in the 1956 Act by the introduction of a special section dealing with the copyright in cinematograph

---

[66] See C. Masouyé, *Guide to the Berne Convention for the Protection of Literary and Artistic Works (Paris Act, 1971)* (WIPO, Geneva, 1978), pp.12 et seq.

films.[67] This definition differed slightly from that in the Brussels Act, in particular the deletion of the words "the acting form of which is fixed in writing or otherwise" after the reference to "entertainments in dumb show". This is because art.2(2) of the Paris Act provides that it shall be a matter for legislation in the countries of the Union to prescribe that works in general, or any specified categories of works, shall not be protected unless they have been fixed in some material form.[68]

The Paris Act expressly provides, however, that the protection of the Convention is not to apply to news of the day, nor to miscellaneous facts having the character of mere items of press information: art.2(8). Article 9(3) of the Brussels Act was slightly differently worded in that it provided that the protection of the Convention was not to apply to news of the day nor to miscellaneous information having the character of mere items of news. Thus, no copyright protection is afforded by the Convention to news or facts constituting press information. There are no equivalent provisions of English law, and material published in the press is afforded the same protection as other literary material, subject only to the qualification that information is not protected as such by copyright law, but only the form in which the information is expressed.

23–24   **Translations, adaptations and arrangements, collections, works of applied art.** Article 2(3) of the Paris Act[69] then goes on to provide that "Translations, adaptations, arrangements of music and other alterations of a literary or artistic work shall be protected as original works without prejudice to the copyright in the original work". The countries of the Union are therefore bound to make provision for the protection of the above-mentioned works and also for collections such as encyclopedias and anthologies: art.2(5). On the other hand, it is a matter for legislation in the countries of the Union to determine the protection to be granted to official texts of a legislative, administrative and legal nature, and to official translations of such texts: art.2(4).

The provisions of art.2 as to adaptations must be read in conjunction with art.12, which declares that authors of literary or artistic works are to enjoy the exclusive right of authorising adaptations, arrangements and other alterations of their works. Article 2(7) provides that it is a matter of domestic legislation as to how far works of applied art and industrial designs and models are protected, subject to art.7(4), which provides for a minimum term of protection of 25 years from the making of a work of applied art.[70]

23–25   **Speeches.** Lectures and speeches first received protection, as such, under the Rome Act; previously, unless constituting literary works, they would not have fallen within the protection of the existing Convention. As a consequence, it is provided (art.2*bis*)[71] that the domestic legislation of any country may limit protection in respect of political speeches and speeches delivered in the course of legal proceedings and may determine the conditions under which lectures and addresses delivered in public may be reproduced by the press, broadcast, communicated to the public by wire and made the subject of public communication

---

[67] Copyright Act 1956 s.13, and see CDPA 1988 s.1(1)(b).
[68] See CDPA 1988 s.3(2) and (3).
[69] See C. Masouyé, *Guide to the Berne Convention for the Protection of Literary and Artistic Works (Paris Act, 1971)* (WIPO, Geneva, 1978), pp.19 et seq.
[70] See para.23–21, above.
[71] See C. Masouyé, *Guide to the Berne Convention for the Protection of Literary and Artistic Works (Paris Act, 1971)* (WIPO, Geneva, 1978), p.24.

as envisaged in art.11*bis*(1),[72] when such use is justified by the informatory purpose. Article 2 bis of the Brussels Act was limited to reproduction by the press. On the other hand, such article was not restricted to public lectures and addresses, nor did it contain a reference to the use being justified by the informatory purpose.

Translation rights. It will be noted that translations are to be protected, and this is so, apparently, whether or not they are authorised translations, subject to the rights of the author of the original work: art.2(3). Article 8[73] deals with the rights of the author of the original work, stipulating that:

> "Authors of literary and artistic works protected by this Convention shall enjoy the exclusive right of making and of authorising the translation of their works throughout the term of protection of their rights in the original works".

23–26

The question of translations is of prime importance from the international point of view, for it is only by means of translations that an author of a literary or scientific work can practically make his work known in a country speaking another language than his own. Complete rights in respect of authorising translations were only gained for the first time under the Berlin Act. The original Convention only gave the exclusive right of translation for a period of 10 years from publication of the original work, and this only to authors who were subjects of a Union country. The Additional Act of Paris gave to such authors the exclusive right of translation during the whole period of copyright in the original work, subject, however, to the condition that an authorised translation, in the language for which protection was claimed, should be published in a Union country within 10 years from the first publication of the original work. Under the Berlin, Rome, Brussels, Stockholm and Paris Acts, authors—whether citizens of a Union country or not—who first published in a Union country, enjoy the exclusive right of authorising a translation during the entire period of copyright in the original work, free from any such conditions as to publication of an authorised translation. Under the Stockholm, and now Paris, Acts authors of a Union country would enjoy this right even if they had published in a non-Union country. Citizens of non-Union countries, however, have no right to protection against translations of their unpublished works. The exclusive right of translation is, however, limited in so far as compulsory licences for developing countries are foreseen in art.II of the Appendix to the Paris Act.[74]

Reproduction rights. Prior to Stockholm the Convention did not contain a provision expressly recognising a right of reproduction, notwithstanding that such a right was commonplace in the legislation of many countries of the Union.[75] To correct this anomaly the Stockholm Act provided, and that of Paris now provides, that authors of literary and artistic works protected by the Convention are to have the exclusive right of authorising the reproduction of these works in any manner or form: art.9(1). All methods of reproduction and processes known or yet to be discovered are envisaged. Further, any sound or visual recording is to be considered as a reproduction for the purposes of the Convention: art.9(3). Because of the introduction of art.9(3), it has not been necessary to repeat art.13(1) of Brussels giving authors of musical works the right to authorise the recording of such works.

23–27

---

[72] See paras 9–174 et seq., above, and para.23–31, below.
[73] See C. Masouyé, *Guide to the Berne Convention for the Protection of Literary and Artistic Works (Paris Act, 1971)* (WIPO, Geneva, 1978), p.53.
[74] See para.23–53 below.
[75] See C. Masouyé, *Guide to the Berne Convention for the Protection of Literary and Artistic Works (Paris Act, 1971)* (WIPO, Geneva, 1978), pp.54 et seq.

However, both the Stockholm and Paris Acts go on to provide that the countries of the Union may permit the reproduction of such works in certain special cases, provided that such reproduction does not conflict with a normal exploitation of the work and does not unreasonably prejudice the legitimate interests of the author: art.9(2).[76] This provision has become of great importance in international copyright and the same principle, now known as "the three-step test of the Berne Convention" has been incorporated also into the TRIPs Agreement and the World Copyright Treaty (WCT), where the scope of the principle has been extended from the reproduction right to all exclusive rights in the case of TRIPs and the exclusive rights of authors in the case of the WCT. The principle has also been included in the World Performances and Phonograms Treaty (WPPT) so far as the rights provided for in that Treaty are concerned.[77] The three-step test is discussed below.

23–28   **Exceptions.** The Paris Act of the Berne Convention contains, in arts 10 and 10*bis*, provisions giving limited freedom to use works by means of exceptions to the rights granted by the Convention.[78] These specific exceptions and limitations sanctioned by the Paris Act concern quotations, the use of works by way of illustration for teaching, reproduction by the media for information purposes and reporting current events, as well as non-voluntary (compulsory) licensing systems.

(i) Quotations

23–29   Article 10(1) provides:
> "It shall be permissible to make quotations from a work which has already been lawfully made available to the public, provided that their making is compatible with fair practice, and their extent does not exceed that justified by the purpose, including quotations from newspaper articles and periodicals in the form of press summaries".

In this provision, "quotation" means including one or more passages from someone else's work in one's own. Quotation consists of reproducing extracts from a work either to illustrate a theme or defend some proposition or to describe or criticise the work quoted from. The use of quotations is not confined to literature: it may be from a book, a newspaper, a review, a cinematographic film, a recording or a radio or television programme.[79] This is wider than art.10(1) of the Brussels Act, which was new and only permitted quotations from newspaper articles and periodicals, and "short" quotations at that. However, when a work is quoted, the source and name of the author, if given, must be mentioned: art.10(3).[80]

There are three limits on these licences to quote. In the first place, the work from which the extract is taken must have been lawfully made available to the public. Secondly, the quotation must be "compatible with fair practice", implying an objective appreciation of what is normally considered acceptable. The fairness or otherwise of the quotation is ultimately a matter for the courts to decide. Thirdly, the quotation must only be to the extent justified by the purpose, which again is a matter for the courts.

---

[76] See CDPA 1988 ss.28–76.

[77] WPPT art.16.

[78] See C. Masouyé, *Guide to the Berne Convention for the Protection of Literary and Artistic Works (Paris Act, 1971)* (WIPO, Geneva, 1978), pp.58 et seq.

[79] See C. Masouyé, *Guide to the Berne Convention for the Protection of Library and Artistic Works (Paris Act, 1971)* (WIPO, Geneva, 1978), p.58.

[80] See CDPA 1988 ss.29 and 30.

(ii) Use of Works by Way of Illustration for Teaching

The right to use a work for teaching purposes is laid down in art.10(2), which   **23–30**
revises art.10(2) of the Brussels Act. This right is subject to the same conditions
as exist for quotations. It provides that it is to be a matter for legislation in the
countries of the Union and for special agreements existing or to be concluded between them, to permit the utilisation, to the extent justified by the purpose, of literary or artistic works by way of illustration in publications, broadcasts or sound
or visual recordings for teaching, provided such utilisation is compatible with fair
practice. Again this is subject to mention being made of the source and name of
the author, if given: art.10(3).[81]

It should be noted that since the Stockholm Act the word "extracts" no longer
appears, so that the utilisation is not limited to extracts as before. It would seem,
therefore, that entire works can be used for teaching purposes, assuming fair
practice and no greater use than is justified by the purpose. The word "teaching"
includes teaching at all levels, in educational institutions generally but excludes
scientific research.[82]

(iii) Use by the Media and Reporting Current Events

Article 10*bis* and (2)[83] provide for certain exceptions for the benefit of the media.   **23–31**
Under art.10*bis*(1) it is to be a matter for legislation in the countries of the Union
to permit the reproduction by the press, the broadcasting or the communication to
the public by wire of articles published in newspapers or periodicals on current
economic, political or religious topics, and of broadcast works of the same
character, in cases in which the reproduction, broadcasting or such communication thereof is not expressly reserved, providing the source is indicated. The legal
consequences of a breach of this obligation are to be determined by the legislation of the country where protection is claimed. Article 9(2) of the Brussels Act
contained a similar provision except that it was confined to reproduction by the
press.

Article 10*bis*(2) provides further that it is also to be a matter for such legislation to determine the conditions under which, for the purpose of reporting current
events by means of photography, cinematography, broadcasting or communication to the public by wire, literary or artistic works seen or heard in the course of
the event may, to the extent justified by the informatory purpose, be reproduced
and made available to the public. This provision is wider than art.10*bis* of the
Brussels Act, which was new and which it replaces, and, in particular, is no longer limited to "short extracts" from literary and artistic works. However, the use
is limited to the extent justified by the informatory purpose and the works must
have been seen or heard in the course of the event.[84] Under this provision the
conditions prescribed may dispense with the need to seek prior permission and,
in some cases, the payment of a fair remuneration.[85]

---

[81] CDPA 1988 ss.23–36.

[82] See C. Masouyé, *Guide to the Berne Convention for the Protection of Literary and Artistic
Works (Paris Act, 1971)* (WIPO, Geneva, 1978), p.60.

[83] See C. Masouyé, *Guide to the Berne Convention for the Protection of Literary and Artistic
Works (Paris Act, 1971)* (WIPO, Geneva, 1978), p.61.

[84] See CDPA 1988 s.30: and see paras 9–44 et seq., above.

[85] See C. Masouyé, *Guide to the Berne Convention for the Protection of Literary and Artistic
Works (Paris Act, 1971)* (WIPO, Geneva, 1978), pp.62 et seq.

(iv) Compulsory licences to record

23–32   Article 13(1)[86] of the Brussels Act, which provided that the authors of musical works were to have the exclusive rights of recording such works and the public performance by means of mechanical instruments of the work thus recorded, was not repeated in the Stockholm Act as the first right was covered by art.9 of the Stockholm Act, repeated in Paris, and the second right by art.11 of the Stockholm Act, repeated in Paris. However, the Stockholm Act, like that of Brussels, contained provisions, repeated in Paris, permitting the countries of the Union to impose reservations and conditions on the rights of authors of musical works to record their works, so as to permit compulsory licences to record such music: art.13(1). However, such article makes clear that compulsory licences may also extend to words accompanying the music, whereas, under art.13 of the Brussels Act, this was not clear. But such reservations and conditions are not to be prejudicial to the rights of the authors of the music and words to obtain equitable remuneration. The 1911 Act gave the right to record on royalty terms in respect of any work which had previously been recorded, and this right was repeated in the 1956 Act, but abolished by the 1988 Act.[87]

23–33   **The three-step test of the Berne Convention**. As mentioned above in para.23–27, art.9(2) of the Berne Convention permits other exceptions to the principle of the exclusive right of reproduction in certain special cases, provided that the permitted reproduction does not conflict with a normal exploitation of the work and does not unreasonably prejudice the legitimate interests of the author. It is the assessment whether any given exception satisfies the criteria laid down in art.9(2) that has come to be known as the "three-step test": first, the reproduction must be for a specific purpose and is allowed only in certain special cases; secondly, the reproduction should not conflict with a normal exploitation of the work; and thirdly, the use must not unreasonably prejudice the legitimate interests of the author. These three conditions are cumulative, all three having to be satisfied before reproduction is allowed and each condition raises problems of interpretation.

As regards the first condition, the words "in certain special cases" indicate that the circumstances justifying the making of an exception must, in themselves, be special or exceptional. The use must be for a specific, designated purpose: a broadly framed exemption, for example, for private or personal use, generally, would not be justified here. Secondly, there must be something "special" about this purpose; "special" here meaning that the use is justified by some clear reason of public policy or other exceptional circumstance.[88]

However, even where a special case is established, if the contemplated reproduction would be such as to conflict with a normal exploitation of the work, it is not permitted at all under art.9(2). No guidance is given in the Convention as to the meaning of the expression "normal exploitation" of a work, but in the records of the Stockholm Diplomatic Conference leading to the adoption of art.9(2)

---

[86] See C. Masouyé, *Guide to the Berne Convention for the Protection of Literary and Artistic Works (Paris Act, 1971)* (WIPO, Geneva, 1978), p.79.

[87] See CDPA 1988 Sch.1 para.21.

[88] See S. Ricketson, *The Berne Convention for the protection of literary and artistic works: 1886–1896* (Queen Mary College, University of London, 1987), pp.482 et seq. But see also: S. Ricketson and J.C. Ginsburg, *International Copyright and Neighbouring Rights, The Berne Convention and Beyond* 2nd edn (Oxford: Oxford University Press, 2006), paras 13.12 et seq. See also M. Senftleben, *An Analysis of the Three-Step Test in International and EC Copyright Law* (Kluwer, 2004); K.J. Koelman, "Fixing the Three-Step Test" [2006] E.I.P.R. 28(8), 407–412 and *Declaration of a group of academics* "A Balanced Interpretation of the 'Three-Step Test' in Copyright Law", Geiger, Hilty, Griffiths, Suthersanen, et al, July 24, 2008; J. Griffiths, "The 'Three-Step Test' in European Copyright Law—problems and solutions", [2009] I.P.Q. 428.

an example is given of a use which would conflict with such normal exploitation, namely the photocopying of a "very large number of copies" for a particular purpose.[89] Masouyé gives another example: "Novels, schoolbooks, etc. are normally exploited by being printed and sold to the public. This Article does not permit member countries to allow this, *e.g.* under compulsory licences, even if payment is made to the copyright owner".[90]

If there is no such conflict, then the next step is to consider whether there is un- **23–34**
reasonable prejudice to the legitimate interests of the author. "In cases where there would be serious loss of profit for the copyright owner, the law should provide him with some compensation", such as, for example, a system of compulsory licensing with equitable remuneration.[91]

The three-step test provides the legislator with certain guidelines to follow when shaping exceptions to the copyright law. However, it provides a rather flimsy basis for legislation in the light of all the new digital, high-speed and global reproduction techniques available to the public in the world of the internet.[92]

Performing rights and recitation rights. The performing rights of authors of **23–35**
dramatic, dramatico-musical and musical works are required to be protected by art.11 of the Paris Act.[93] Under the original Convention these rights had to be specially reserved by notice on the title page, if the work was published, but the Berlin, Rome and Brussels Acts provided that authors, to enjoy protection, should not be bound to forbid the public presentation or performance thereof. This provision was deleted in the Stockholm Act as being superfluous and is not repeated in the Paris Act. The Stockholm Act, and now the Paris Act, makes clear that the public performance of a work by sound recordings is included so that the part of art.13(1) of the Brussels Act relating thereto was not repeated in Stockholm, nor is it repeated in the Paris Act. Apart from public performance, the article also covers any communication to the public of the performance of such works. By the same article, authors of dramatic or dramatico-musical works are required to be protected, during the existence of their rights in the original works, against the unauthorised public performance or communication of translations of their works: art.11(2).

Rights relating to the recitation of literary works were given to the authors thereof by art.11 *ter* of the Stockholm Act, repeated in Paris, which expanded art.11 *ter* of the Brussels Act to equate recitation rights to performing rights under art.11. Thus art.11 *ter* covers the public recitation of literary works and also any communication to the public of the recitation of such works. Also, by the same article, authors of literary works are required to be protected, during the existence of their rights in the original works, against the unauthorised public recitation or communication of translations of their works.

Copyright Tribunal. In connection with art.11 of the Brussels Act, the United **23–36**
Kingdom delegation at Brussels declared that they accepted the provisions of art.11 on the understanding that HM Government remained free to enact such

---

[89] *Records of the Intellectual Property Conference of Stockholm (1967)*, WIPO Geneva, 1971, Main Committee I-Report, at 1145 et seq.
[90] See C. Masouyé, *Guide to the Berne Convention for the Protection of Literary and Artistic Works (Paris Act, 1971)* (WIPO, Geneva, 1978), p.55.
[91] See C. Masouyé, *Guide to the Berne Convention for the Protection of Literary and Artistic Works (Paris Act, 1971)* (WIPO, Geneva, 1978), p 56.
[92] See also paras *23*–72, 23–127 and 23–142, below.
[93] See C. Masouyé, *Guide to the Berne Convention for the Protection of Literary and Artistic Works (Paris Act, 1971)* (WIPO, Geneva, 1978), pp.64 et seq.

legislation as they might consider necessary, in the public interest, to prevent or deal with any abuse of the monopoly rights conferred upon owners of copyright by the law of the United Kingdom.[94] It was in reliance upon this declaration that the 1956 Act introduced a Performing Right Tribunal with powers to modify and enforce licences granted by licensing bodies for the public performance of works controlled by such bodies.[95] This declaration was not repeated at Stockholm (or Paris), but it was agreed that countries were free to enact measures to restrict possible abuses of monopoly.[96] The Performing Right Tribunal has now been renamed as the Copyright Tribunal with a much wider jurisdiction.[97]

23–37   **Broadcasting rights.** The Rome Act first introduced provisions with regard to radio communication, but these were substantially amplified by the Brussels Act and repeated in the Stockholm and Paris Acts. Article 11*bis* of the Paris Act provides that authors of literary and artistic works are to have the exclusive right of authorising the broadcasting of their works and communication of their works to the public by wireless, the communication of their works to the public by wire or by rebroadcasting of the broadcast of the work when the communication is made by an organisation other than the original one, and the communication of their works to the public by loudspeaker or other instrument transmitting the broadcast of the work. The conditions for the exercise of these rights are left to the legislation of individual countries, provided that such legislation does not affect the right of the author to obtain equitable remuneration. Thus, Member States may substitute for the authors' exclusive rights a system of compulsory licences.[98]

The Paris Act, therefore, confers upon authors three distinct rights in respect of broadcast performances of their works: namely, first, the right to restrict the original broadcast, secondly, the right to restrict any diffusion of the broadcast by an independent receiving authority, and thirdly, the right to restrict the public performance of the broadcast at the receiving end. The first two rights were clearly conferred by the 1956 Act,[99] but, after much discussion during the passing of that Act, the right to restrict the operation of a diffusion service was considerably qualified by s.40(3) of that Act.[100]

23–38   **Recordings of broadcasts.** It is further provided, by art.11*bis*(3) of the Paris Act, that a permission to broadcast is not to imply permission to record the broadcast. But there then follows a somewhat ambiguous paragraph as follows:

"It shall, however, be a matter for legislation in the countries of the Union to determine the regulations for ephemeral recordings made by a broadcasting organisation by means of its own facilities and used for its own broadcasts. The preservation of these recordings in official archives may, on the ground

---

[94] *Actes de la Conference de Bruxelles* (1951), p.82.

[95] Copyright Act 1956 ss.23–30.

[96] *Records of the Intellectual Property Conference of Stockholm (1967)*, (Geneva: WIPO, 1971), Vol.II, Report of Main Committee I,para.263. See also Summary Minutes (Main Committee I),paras 1407–1427 and see C. Masouyé, *Guide to the Berne Convention for the Protection of Literary and Artistic Works (Paris Act, 1971)* (Geneva: WIPO, 1978), p.99.

[97] CDPA 1988 ss.116–152: and see paras 28–81 et seq., below. This jurisdiction now covers the compulsory licence to include sound recordings (but not the music on the sound recordings) in broadcasts and cable programme services created by an amendment of the CDPA 1988 introduced by s.175 of the Broadcasting Act 1990 (c.42), and the compulsory licence to provide information about broadcast programmes introduced by s.176 of and Sch.17 to the 1990 Act. As to the coming into force of these provisions, see the Broadcasting Act 1990 (Commencement No.1 and Transitional Provisions) Order 1990 (SI 1990/2347), Vol.2 A2.ii.

[98] See C. Masouyé, *Guide to the Berne Convention for the Protection of Literary and Artistic Works (Paris Act, 1971)* (Geneva: WIPO, 1978), p.70.

[99] Copyright Act 1956 ss.2(5)(d) and (e) and 3(5)(c) and (d).

[100] ss.2, 3 and 40, Copyright Act 1956, were amended by the Cable and Broadcasting Act 1984 (c.46). See now CDPA 1988 ss.16(1), 72 and 73.

of their exceptional documentary character, be authorised by such legislation".

Section 6(7) of the 1956 Act was designed to give effect to the provisions of the article as to ephemeral recordings, but there was no provision for the preservation of recordings in official archives.[101]

Cinematographic rights. As has already been pointed out,[102] cinematographic works are now treated as of the class of literary and artistic works receiving general protection under art.2 of the Paris Act. But the rights of authors of literary or artistic works, whose material may be included in a cinematograph film, are dealt with in art.14 of the Paris Act,[103] and it is expressly stated, by art.14*bis*(1) thereof, previously art.14(2) of the Brussels Act, that the protection of a cinematographic work as an original work is without prejudice to the rights of the author of the work adapted or reproduced. The author is required to be given the exclusive right of authorising, first, the cinematographic adaptation and reproduction of his works, and the distribution of the works thus adapted or reproduced and, secondly, the right of public performance and communication to the public by wire of the works thus adapted or reproduced. The latter right was new in the Stockholm Act. Article 14 further provides that the adaptation into any other artistic form of a cinematographic production derived from literary or artistic works is, without prejudice to the authorisation of the author of the cinematographic production, to remain subject to the authorisation of the authors of the original works. Section 13(7) of the 1956 Act provided that, where the copyright in a cinematograph film had expired, a person who caused the film to be seen, or to be seen and heard, in public did not thereby infringe any copyright subsisting in any literary, dramatic, musical or artistic work. Since the film copyright may well have expired before that in the works included in them, it is difficult to see how this provision accorded with art.14 of the Paris Act. The 1988 Act contains no such provision.   **23–39**

Soundtracks of films. Article 14(3) of the Paris Act provides that the provisions of art.13(1) are not to apply with respect to films, so no compulsory licences for musical works and associated words to be incorporated in films are permitted. Article 14(3), therefore, was designed to prevent countries restricting in any manner the rights of authors of musical works to have these works included in the soundtracks of cinematograph films. While there was some doubt whether, under s.19(2) of the 1911 Act, the compulsory licence provisions thereby enacted could be utilised for the purpose of cinematograph films, it is clear that the similar provisions of s.8 of the 1956 Act did not apply, since they applied only where a manufacturer intended to sell a record by retail. Section 8 of the 1956 Act has been repealed by the 1988 Act, which contains no equivalent provision.   **23–40**

Cinematograph films. It has been mentioned above[104] that cinematographic works are included in the class of works protected under art.2, and that art.14 *bis*(1) provides that such protection is without prejudice to the copyright in any work adapted or reproduced.[105] Article 14*bis*(1) goes on to make clear what was previously understood to be the position, namely that the owner of the copyright   **23–41**

---

[101] See now CDPA 1988 ss.68 and 75, which latter section provides for recording for archival purposes. See para.9–234, above.

[102] See para.23–23, above.

[103] See C. Masouyé, *Guide to the Berne Convention for the Protection of Literary and Artistic Works (Paris Act, 1971)* (Geneva: WIPO, 1978), pp.82 et seq

[104] See paras 23–23 and 23–39, above.

[105] See C. Masouyé, *Guide to the Berne Convention for the Protection of Literary and Artistic Works (Paris Act, 1971)* (Geneva: WIPO, 1978), p.85.

in a cinematographic work is to have the same rights as the author of an original work, including the rights under art.14.[106]

Article 14*bis*(2)(a), which was new to Stockholm, leaves the question of ownership of the copyright in a cinematographic work to the legislation of the country where protection is claimed. However, the rest of art.14*bis*(2) and art.14*bis*(3), which also were new to Stockholm, contain provisions dealing with the rights of authors of contributions to a cinematographic work in countries where they are included among the owners of the copyright in such a work. Section 13(4) and (10) of the 1956 Act, however, provided that the maker of a cinematograph film, that is the person by whom the arrangements necessary for the making of the film are undertaken, was the initial owner of the copyright in the film. Section 9(2) and (11) of the 1988 Act contained the same definition until amended by the Copyright and Related Rights Regulations 1996[107]; the law now provides that such owner is the author, which in the case of a film shall be taken to be the producer and the principal director.

23–42   **"Moral rights".** The Rome Act, for the first time, introduced provisions intended to extend an author's rights beyond those generally understood in common law countries to be included in the term "copyright". These provisions cover what is known in Continental law countries as the author's "*droit moral*" or moral right.[108] These provisions were extended by the Brussels Act,[109] art.6*bis*, and provided, first, that, even after the assignment of his copyright, the author should have the right during his lifetime to claim authorship of the work, and to object to any "distortion, mutilation or other alteration thereof or any other action in relation to the said work which would be prejudicial to his honour or reputation". Secondly, it was provided that the rights granted to the author as aforesaid should, after his death, be maintained at least until the expiry of the copyright. Thirdly, the means of redress for safeguarding the rights granted by this article was left to the national law. These provisions were, with amendments, repeated in the Stockholm and Paris Acts.

Thus, the Stockholm Act, in art.6*bis*, whilst preserving the author's right to claim authorship of the work (the right of paternity), has made slight changes in the wording, repeated in the Paris Act, of the right to object to mutilation (the right of integrity) which now covers the right of the author to object to any "distortion, mutilation or other modification of, or other derogatory action in relation to, the said work, which would be prejudicial to his honour or reputation". A further amendment, introduced by art.6*bis* of the Stockholm Act and repeated in the Paris Act, is to make the grant of such rights compulsory at least until the expiration of the copyright, rather than during the author's lifetime and optional thereafter until the expiration of copyright as under art.6*bis* of the Brussels Act.

23–43   **Obligation to safeguard moral rights by legislation.** It will be observed, first, that the Brussels, Stockholm and Paris Acts make the grant of such rights compulsory for the period prescribed and, secondly, that the Convention requires the rights to be safeguarded by the legislation of the country where protection is claimed. It would seem to follow from this that, not only are countries of the Union bound to grant such rights, but that they must be granted by statute law. So

---

[106] See para.23–39, above.

[107] SI 1996/2967.

[108] See as to moral rights generally Ch.11, below, G. Davies and K. Garnett QC, *Moral Rights* (London: Sweet and Maxwell, 2010) and E. Adeney, *The Moral Rights of Authors and Performers—An International and Comparative Analysis* (Oxford: Oxford University Press, 2006).

[109] See C. Masouyé, *Guide to the Berne Convention for the Protection of Literary and Artistic Works (Paris Act, 1971)* (Geneva: WIPO, 1978), pp.41 et seq.

far as this country is concerned, prior to the 1988 Act the only statute law at all concerned with either of these rights was s.43 of the 1956 Act. But even this section, whilst going some way to grant a right of integrity, only did so in respect of artistic works. Further, not only did such section not grant a right of paternity to authors but, instead, made it an offence to ascribe paternity to a non-author. Other than this, and actions for passing off, defamation and slander of goods, English law did not, before the 1988 Act, afford protection for the rights provided for in art.6*bis*.[110]

It has been argued, therefore, that, prior to the 1988 Act, this country had not complied with the obligations of art.6*bis*; it is interesting to note, in this regard, that the 1952 Copyright Committee stated that, in the 20 years since the Rome Act had been accepted, no other Union country had complained that this country had failed to discharge its obligations under art.6*bis*.[111] However, the 1977 Copyright Committee, after having considered the matter in detail, in particular the question whether this country had failed to discharge such obligations,[112] recommended that the Copyright Act should be amended to make proper provision for moral rights under copyright law.[113] It is to be noted that art.36 of the Paris Act provides that it is understood that, at the time a country becomes bound by that Act, it will be in a position under its domestic law, to give effect to the provisions thereof, and the 1988 Act now, for the first time in this country, provides statutory protection for moral rights, by granting a paternity right, an integrity right and a right to privacy of certain photographs and films, as well as providing for false attribution of authorship.[114] This was done as from August 1, 1989, just before the United Kingdom deposited its instrument of ratification of the Paris Act on September 29, 1989, with effect from January 2, 1990.

"Droit de suite" (Artists' Resale Right). A further new right, which was   **23–44** introduced for the first time in the Brussels Act, deals with what is known in Continental-law countries, as the "*droit de suite*", the so-called "artists' resale right". Article 14 *ter* of the Stockholm Act, replacing art.14*bis* of the Brussels Act, provided, and now art.14 *ter* of the Paris Act provides,[115] that the author or, after his death, the persons or institutions authorised by national legislation are, with respect to original works of art and original manuscripts, to enjoy the inalienable right to an interest in any sale of the work subsequent to the first transfer thereof by the author. This matter, however, is left to the legislation of individual members[116] and enjoyment of the right depends on reciprocity. It cannot be claimed in any country introducing such legislation by an author belonging to a country which does not have such legislation. The 1977 Copyright Committee recommended that "*droit de suite*" should not be introduced in the United Kingdom,[117] and the 1988 Act made no provision for such a right. However, the situation has changed following the adoption on September 27, 2001, of the Directive of the European Parliament and of the Council on the resale right for the benefit of the author of an original work of art by the European Parliament and Council

---

[110] See Ch.11.

[111] Cmnd.8662, para.220.

[112] Cmnd.6732, paras 50–57.

[113] Cmnd.6732, para.85(vi).

[114] CDPA 1988 ss.2(2), 77–89, 94, 95, 103, and Sch.1 paras 22, 23 and 24; and see Ch.11.

[115] See C. Masouyé, *Guide to the Berne Convention for the Protection of Literary and Artistic Works (Paris Act, 1971)* (Geneva: WIPO, 1978), p.90.

[116] See as to "*droit de suite*" in the European Union, C. Doutrelepont, "*Le Droit et l'objet d'art: le droit de suite des artistes plasticiens dans l'Union européenne*" (Brussels: Bruylant, 1996); in France and certain other countries, R. Plaisant, "The '*droit de suite*'" [1969] *Copyright* 157; in Germany, A. Dietz, "Letter from the Federal Republic of Germany" [1980] *Copyright* 85. See also W. Duchemin, "The Community Directive on the Resale Right" [2002] 191 *RIDA* 3.

[117] Cmnd.6732, para.805.

of the European Communities after many years of negotiation.[118] According to the Directive, Member States were obliged to bring their domestic laws into conformity by January 1, 2006. Accordingly, the UK Government implemented the Directive by the introduction of The Artist's Resale Right Regulations 2006.[119]

23–45   **Protection of rights.** The remedy of a person whose work has been pirated is to be governed by the local law. Article 4(2) of Brussels, replaced by art.5(2) of Stockholm, and now by art.5(2) of Paris provides that, "apart from the provisions of this Convention, the extent of protection, as well as the means of redress afforded to the author to protect his rights, shall be governed exclusively by the laws of the country where protection is claimed".[120]

However, seizure of the pirated copies is a remedy which ought to be secured to authors by the legislation of every Union country, for art.16[121] provides as follows:

"(1) Infringing copies of a work shall be liable to seizure in any country of the Union where the work enjoys legal protection.

(2) The provisions of the preceding paragraph shall also apply to reproductions coming from a country where the work is not protected, or has ceased to be protected.

(3) The seizure shall take place in accordance with the legislation of each country".

Notwithstanding the provisions of the Convention, each Union country is to be at liberty "to permit, to control, or to prohibit, by legislation or regulation, the circulation, presentation, or exhibition of any work or production in regard to which the competent authority may find it necessary to exercise that right"; art.17 of the Paris Act.

23–46   **Presumptions.** Article 15 of the Paris Act,[122] as did art.15 of the Brussels Act and art.15 of the Stockholm Act, provides for certain presumptions as to authorship.[123] Thus, art.15(1) provides that, in order that the author of a literary or artistic work protected by the Convention shall, in the absence of proof to the contrary, be regarded as such and consequently entitled to institute infringement proceedings in the countries of the Union, it is to be sufficient for his name to appear on the work in the usual manner.

Article 15(1) is to be applicable even if the name is a pseudonym, where the pseudonym adopted by the author leaves no doubt as to his identity. Article 15(3), however, provides that, in the case of anonymous and pseudonymous works, other than those referred to in art.15(1), the publisher whose name appears on the work, in the absence of proof to the contrary, is to be deemed to represent the author, and in that capacity he is to be entitled to protect and enforce the author's rights. These provisions are to cease to apply when the author reveals his identity and establishes his claim to authorship of the work.

Article 15 of the Stockholm Act, now art.15 of the Paris Act, also contained

---

[118] Directive 2001/84/EC.

[119] SI 2006/346 of February 13, 2006. See Ch.20, below.

[120] An important and instructive case came before the Paris Court of Appeal which, affirming the decision of the Seine Civil Tribunal, held that the manager of the Paris branch and representative in Paris of an Argentine newspaper was liable in damages for putting on sale in France copies of the newspaper printed in Buenos Aires, and containing pirated portions of a novel written by a French author. This liability, the court stated, would exist "even if the legislation of the country of publication accorded no protection to copyright": *Foley v Cazaux*, [1913] *Le Droit d'Auteur* 100.

[121] See also Brussels Act art.13(3) as to seizure of recordings: and see CDPA 1988 ss.100 and 114.

[122] See C. Masouyé, *Guide to the Berne Convention for the Protection of Literary and Artistic Works (Paris Act, 1971)* (Geneva: WIPO, 1978), p.93.

[123] See CDPA 1988 ss.104–106.

certain new provisions. Thus, art.15(2) provides that the person or body corporate whose name appears on a cinematographic work "in the usual manner" shall, in the absence of proof to the contrary, be presumed to be the maker of such work.[124]

Again, art.15(4) provides that, in the case of unpublished works where the identity of the author is unknown, but where there is every ground to presume that he is a national of a country of the Union, it is to be a matter for legislation in that country to designate the competent authority who shall represent the author and shall be entitled to protect and enforce his rights in the countries of the Union.[125]

Retrospective effect. An alteration was made as regards retrospective effect in the Berlin Act, and is repeated in the Rome, Brussels, Stockholm and Paris Acts. Under the original Convention it was provided that its provisions should apply to all works which, at the time of its coming into force, had "not yet fallen into the public domain in their country of origin". The Berlin, Rome, Brussels, Stockholm and Paris Acts (art.18(1)) only except works which have, at the moment of their coming into force, fallen into the public domain in their country of origin "through the expiry of the term of protection". Works, therefore, which have, in the country of their origin, lost their protection owing to failure to comply with formalities, such as registration and so forth, are intended to be protected under the Convention, as also, apparently, are works which were previously entitled to no protection whatsoever, for instance (in some countries), works of architecture and photographs.[126] On the other hand, art.18(2) provides that if, through the expiry of the term of protection which was previously granted, a work has fallen into the public domain of the country where protection is claimed, that work is not to be protected anew. These provisions are to apply also in the case of new accessions to the Union, and to cases in which protection is extended by the application of art.7 or by the abandonment of reservations: art.18(4). **23–47**

Article 18(3), however, provides that the application of the principle laid down in art.18(1) and (2) is to take effect subject to any provisions contained in special conventions to that effect existing or to be concluded between countries of the Union, and that, in the absence of such provisions, the respective countries are to determine, so far as they are respectively concerned, the conditions of application of such principle.

Convention not to limit wider protection. Article 19 of the Paris Act[127] expressly states that the Convention is not to preclude authors from the benefit of any greater protection granted by the local law, and art.20 thereof preserves the right of Member States to make special agreements with other Member States giving greater protection to their respective nationals than is required under the Convention.[128] The various Directives adopted by the European Union on the subject of copyright and the new WIPO Copyright Treaty[129] are examples of such special agreements. **23–48**

---

[124] See s.105.

[125] See s.169.

[126] The 1911 Act did not comply with the provisions as to retrospective effect and, in adhering to the Berlin Act, the UK made a reservation upon the point. This reservation was not maintained when the UK ratified the Rome Act, presumably on the ground that it was not necessary to do so in view of the fact that the Convention did not make necessary any alteration of English law previously in force. The Acts of 1956 and 1988 appear, in substance, to comply with this article.

[127] See C. Masouyé, *Guide to the Berne Convention for the Protection of Literary and Artistic Works (Paris Act, 1971)* (WIPO, Geneva, 1978), p 103.

[128] See C. Masouyé, *Guide to the Berne Convention for the Protection of Literary and Artistic Works (Paris Act, 1971)* (WIPO, Geneva, 1978), p.104.

[129] See Ch.25 and paras 23–66 et seq.

C. ADMINISTRATIVE PROVISIONS AND FINAL CLAUSES OF PARIS ACT

23–49 **Administrative provisions and final clauses.** Articles 22 to 26 of the Stockholm Act, now arts 22 to 26 of the Paris Act,[130] contain the administrative provisions, and arts 27 to 38,[131] the final clauses of the Convention, contain certain general provisions. Articles 22 and 23 of the Paris Act providing for the Assembly of the Union and its Executive Committee were amended in October 1979.[132] Article 24 of the Paris Act provides that the administrative tasks with respect to the Union are to be performed by the International Bureau, being the International Bureau of Intellectual Property referred to in the Convention establishing the World Intellectual Property Organisation[133]: art.22(2)(ii).

This latter Convention was framed at Stockholm in 1967 and was signed by the United Kingdom on July 14, 1967. The objects of the Organisation established by the Convention are stated to be to promote the protection of intellectual property throughout the world through co-operation among States and, where appropriate, in collaboration with any other international organisation, and to ensure administrative co-operation among the various Unions, including the Berne Union: art.3. Article 12(1) of this Convention provides that the Organisation is to enjoy on the territory of each Member State, in conformity with the laws of that State, such legal capacity as may be necessary for the fulfilment of the Organisation's objectives and for the exercise of its functions. Accordingly the United Kingdom has provided by statutory instrument,[134] which came into operation on the date on which the Convention entered into force with respect to this country, that the Organisation is to have the legal capacities of a body corporate. The Convention was ratified by the United Kingdom on February 26, 1969, and entered into force on April 26, 1970.

D. STOCKHOLM PROTOCOL REGARDING DEVELOPING COUNTRIES

23–50 **Protocol.** As has been mentioned,[135] the Stockholm revision of the Berne Convention introduced the controversial Protocol Regarding Developing Countries[136] which provided that any developing country which ratified or acceded to the Stockholm Act could make reservations in respect of certain matters, which would have the effect of giving less protection in that country than was afforded in other countries of the Union. Because of this controversy, however, although art.21 of Stockholm made the Protocol an integral part of the Convention, this was subject to the provisions of art.28 of Stockholm which enabled any country ratifying or acceding to the Act to declare that its ratification or accession was not to apply to the substantive provisions of the Act and the Protocol. Since today no

---

[130] See C. Masouyé, *Guide to the Berne Convention for the Protection of Literary and Artistic Works (Paris Act, 1971)* (WIPO, Geneva, 1978), pp.106–120.

[131] See C. Masouyé, *Guide to the Berne Convention for the Protection of Literary and Artistic Works (Paris Act, 1971)* (WIPO, Geneva, 1978), pp.121–145.

[132] Amendments to arts 22 and 23 were adopted in 1979 by the Assembly of the Berne Union, when it decided to adopt biennial, instead of triennial, budgets and to hold its ordinary sessions every two years. These amendments entered into force on November 19, 1984. See A. Bogsch, "The First Hundred Years of the Berne Convention for the Protection of Literary and Artistic Works", [1986] *Copyright* 291 at 314. See also S. Ricketson and J.C. Ginsburg, *International Copyright and Neighbouring Rights, The Berne Convention and Beyond* 2nd edn (Oxford: Oxford University Press, 2006), paras 16.12 and 16.49.

[133] For text see Vol.2 F7.

[134] The World Intellectual Property Organisation (Immunities and Privileges) Order 1968 (SI 1968/890).

[135] See para.23–09, above.

[136] See also S. Ricketson and J.C. Ginsburg, *International Copyright and Neighbouring Rights, The Berne Convention and Beyond* 2nd edn (Oxford: Oxford University Press, 2006),paras 14.18 et seq.

country of the Union remains bound by the substantive provisions of the Stockholm Act and its Protocol, the Protocol has become of historical interest only and for that reason its substantive provisions are not considered further here. For a detailed account of these provisions of the Protocol, the reader is referred to paras 24–52 to 24–58 of the 14th edition of the present work.

E. APPENDIX TO PARIS ACT

Appendix. As has been mentioned,[137] the Paris Act has dropped art.21 relating to the Protocol Regarding Developing Countries and the Protocol itself, and substituted another art.21 and an Appendix containing provisions dealing with developing countries, such article providing that the Appendix forms an integral part of the Paris Act. However, this is subject to art.28 under which any country may declare that its ratification or accession shall not apply to the substantive provisions of the Paris Act and the Appendix.   **23–51**

Mode of operation of Appendix. Article I of the Appendix provides that any country regarded as a developing country in conformity with the established practice of the General Assembly of the United Nations which ratifies or accedes to the Paris Act and which, having regard to its economic situation and its social or cultural needs, does not consider itself immediately in a position to make provision for the protection of all the rights as provided for in the Paris Act, may declare that it avails itself of one or both faculties in arts II and III; or instead of availing itself of the faculty in art.II may make a declaration according to art.V(1)(a) relating to art.30 of the Paris Act. Any such declaration notified before the expiration of the first 10 years from the entry into force of the substantive provisions of the Paris Act and the Appendix lasts until the expiration of such period. Any notification after the expiration of that period lasts for 10 years. Any such declarations may be renewed in whole or in part for further periods of 10 years.   **23–52**

Any country which has ceased to be regarded as a developing country cannot renew its declaration and, whether or not it withdraws its declaration, it is precluded from availing itself of such faculties after the expiration of the 10-year period then running, or from the expiration of a period of three years after it has ceased to be regarded as a developing country, whichever period expires later. Notwithstanding a declaration ceases to be effective, copies in stock made under a licence granted by virtue of the Appendix may be disposed of. Further, where a country avails itself of any of such faculties, no country may give less protection to works originating in the former country than it is obliged to give under the substantive provisions of the Paris Act.

The faculty under Article II; translation rights.[138] This enables a developing country, in relation to works published in printed or analogous form of reproduction, to substitute for the exclusive right of translation provided for in art.8 of the Paris Act, a system of non-exclusive and non-transferable licences, granted by the competent authority, subject to certain conditions and the provisions of art.IV. As the latter largely apply also to art.III licences, they are dealt with below after the faculty under art.III.   **23–53**

The first condition is one of time. Thus, if after the expiration of a period of three years, or any longer period determined by the national legislation of such country, commencing on the date of first publication of the work, a translation of the work has not been published in a language in general use in that country by

---

[137] See para.23–10, above.
[138] See para.23–26, above.

the owner of the translation rights, or with his authorisation, any national of such country may obtain a licence to make a translation of the work in the said language and publish the translation in printed or analogous forms of reproduction. Alternatively a licence may be granted if all the editions of the translation published in the language concerned are out of print. A further alternative arises in the case of translations into a language which is not in general use in one or more developed countries who are Union members; in which case one year is to be substituted for the period of three years above mentioned. But any developing country availing itself of this faculty may, with the unanimous agreement of the developed countries which are Union members and in which the same language is in general use, substitute, in the case of translations into that language for the said period of three years an agreed shorter period of not less than one year; this provision will not apply where the language in question is English, French or Spanish. However, these time limits only bring the faculty into operation. That is to say, no licence obtainable after a three-year period is to be granted until a further period of six months has elapsed or nine months in the case of a one-year period, in each case from the date the applicant complies with the requirements of art.IV(1), or, where the identity or address of the owner of the translation rights is unknown, from the date on which the applicant sends copies of his application submitted to the competent authority as provided by art.IV(2).

Apart from the condition as to time, art.II imposes other conditions. Thus, if during such six- or nine-month period a translation in the language in respect of which the application was made is published by the owner of the translation rights or with his authorisation, no licence can be granted. Any licence in fact granted can only be for the purpose of teaching, scholarship or research. If a licence is granted, but a translation of the work is published by the owner of the translation rights or with his authorisation at a price reasonably related to that normally charged in the country for comparable works, the licence will terminate if such translation is in the same language and with substantially the same content as the translation published under the licence. However, existing stocks may be disposed of. No licence may be granted when the author has withdrawn all copies of the work from circulation.

Article II also contains provisions dealing with licences in respect of works with illustrations as well as text, and translations for the purposes of use in broadcasts.

23–54   **The faculty under Article III; reproduction rights.**[139] This enables a developing country to substitute for the exclusive right of reproduction provided for in art.9 of the Paris Act a system of non-exclusive and non-transferable licences, granted by the competent authority, subject to certain conditions and the provisions of art.IV dealt with below. The works to which this faculty applies are works published in printed or analogous forms of reproduction and to the reproduction in audiovisual form of certain lawfully made audiovisual fixations and to the translation of any incorporated text.

As with art.2, the first condition is one of time. Thus, a licence may be obtained by a national of such country to reproduce and publish a particular edition of a work at a price reasonably related to that normally charged in the country for comparable works or a lower price for use in connection with systematic instructional activities if, after the expiration of the prescribed period, copies of such edition have not been distributed in that country to the general public or in connection with systematic instructional activities, by the owner of the reproduc-

---

[139] See para.23–27, above.

tion rights or with his authorisation, at such first-mentioned price. A licence may also be obtained to reproduce and publish an edition of the work which has been so distributed if, after the expiration of the applicable period, no authorised copies of the edition have been on sale for a period of six months in such country to the general public or in connection with systematic instructional activities at a price reasonably related to that normally charged in that country for comparable works.

The commencing date for the various prescribed periods is the date of first publication of the edition in question and the periods are, subject to any longer periods determined by the legislation of the country in question: for works of the natural and physical sciences, including mathematics, and of technology, three years; for works of fiction, poetry, drama and music, and for art books, seven years; for all other works, five years. Again, these periods only bring the faculty into operation. Thus no licence obtainable after a three-year period is to be granted until six months from the date the applicant complies with the requirements of art.IV(1) or, where the identity or the address of the owner of the reproduction rights is unknown, from the date on which the applicant sends, as provided by art.IV(2), copies of his application submitted to the competent authority. In respect of other periods there appears to be no extra time-factor unless the owner of the rights cannot be found and art.IV(2) applies. In such case no licence is to be granted until three months from the date of the dispatch of the copies of the application.

Article III imposes other conditions apart from time. Thus, if during the extra periods of six or three months above mentioned a distribution of copies of the edition in question has taken place in the country of the kind mentioned above, no licence is to be granted. Further, no licence is to be granted if the author has withdrawn from circulation all copies of the edition in question. Again, a licence to reproduce and publish a translation of a work is not to be granted if, either the translation was not published by the owner of the translation rights or with his authorisation, or the translation is not in a language in general use in the country concerned. Also if a distribution of copies of the edition in question has taken place in the country of the kind mentioned above, any licence granted is to terminate if such edition is in the same language and with substantially the same content as the edition which was published under the licence. However, existing stocks may be disposed of.

The provisions of Article IV. The provisions of arts II and III are subject to   **23–55** art.IV which contains certain provisions relating to procedural matters and licence terms.

As to procedure, art.IV provides that a licence under arts II or III may only be granted if the applicant, in accordance with the procedure of the country concerned, establishes, either that he has requested, and been denied, the necessary authorisation by the owner of the relevant rights, or that, after due diligence, he was unable to find such owner. He must also, when making his request, inform any designated national or international information centre. If the owner cannot be found, then art.IV requires the applicant to send copies of his application to the competent authority for a licence to various persons.

As to licence terms, art.IV contains certain provisions which, it would seem, would have to be contained in a licence or, at least, taken into account when the licence is granted. Thus, it is provided that the name of the author is to be indicated in all copies of the translation or reproduction published under the licence. The title of the work and, in the case of a translation, the original title of the work is to appear on all such copies. Further, licences to export are not permitted and all such copies are to bear a notice in the appropriate language stating that the copies are available for distribution only in the country or territory to which the licence applies. Also, the licence must provide for just compensation of the owner of the relevant rights and for payment and transmittal of such compensation. Finally, national legislation must ensure a correct translation of the work, or an accurate reproduction of the particular edition, as the case may be.

F. Entry into Force of Stockholm Act

23–56   **Ratification or accession.** Because of the controversy over the introduction into the Stockholm revision of the Berne Convention of the Protocol Regarding Developing Countries,[140] which was made an integral part of the Stockholm Act (art.21), the Act permitted any country of the Union ratifying or acceding thereto to declare that its ratification or accession was not to apply to the substantive provisions of the Convention (arts 1–21) and the Protocol: art.21(1)(b)(i). Alternatively, such a country might declare that its ratification or accession was not to apply to the administrative provisions of the Act (arts 22–26): art.28(1)(b)(ii). Ratification or accession in either way carried with it the final clauses of the Stockholm Act (arts 27–38): art.28(3). There were, therefore, two distinct ways in which a country of the Union might have become a party to the Stockholm Act but, as a result, none of the major developed countries ratified or acceded to the substantive provisions of the Stockholm Act.

23–57   **The substantive provisions of the Stockholm Act and its Protocol.** Articles 1 to 21 and the Protocol were to come into force with respect to the first five countries which had ratified or acceded to it without declaring that their ratification or accession should not apply to such Articles and Protocol, and without making the declaration permitted by para.(1)(b)(i) of the Protocol, three months after the deposit of the fifth instrument of ratification or accession: art.28(2)(a). As arts 1–21 and the Appendix 3 to the Paris Act came into force on October 10, 1974, no country may now ratify or accede to Stockholm; art.34(1) Paris. However, the previous Acts remain in force in relations with countries of the Union which do not ratify or accede to the Paris Act; art.32(1) Paris.

23–58   **The Protocol..** However, the Protocol could be applied before the entry into force of the Stockholm Act (art.28(2)(d)) and, therefore, art.28(2)(a) was made subject to the provisions of art.5 of the Protocol. Article 5 provided that any country of the Union might declare, at any time before becoming bound by arts 1–21 and the Protocol, either: (a) in the case of a developing country, that it intended to apply the provisions of the Protocol to works whose country of origin is a country of the Union which admits the application of the reservations under the Protocol; or (b) that it admitted the application of the provisions of the Protocol to works of which it is the country of origin by countries which, on becoming bound by arts 1 to 21 and by the Protocol, or on making a declaration of application of the Protocol by virtue of the provision of (a), have made reservations permitted by the Protocol. If a country had already separately accepted the Protocol in accordance with art.5 thereof, its declaration under art.28(1)(b)(i) might only relate to arts 1–20: art.28(1)(c).

23–59   **The administrative provisions.** The administrative provisions of the Stockholm Act arts 22 to 26, were to come into force with respect to the first seven countries that had ratified or acceded without declaring that their ratification or accession did not apply to such articles, three months after the deposit of the seventh instrument of ratification or accession: art.28(2)(b).

---

[140] See para.23–50, above.

Declarations and notifications. The Stockholm Act provided for various decla-			**23–60**
rations or notifications. For instance, art.7(7) provided that any country of the
Union bound by the Rome Act, which grants shorter terms of protection than
those provided for in art.7 of the Stockholm Act, might maintain such terms
when ratifying or acceding to the Stockholm Act. Again, art.33, which provided,
in para.(1), for the settling of disputes about the interpretation or application of
the Stockholm Act, provided, in para.(2), that a country, when ratifying or acceding to the Stockholm Act, might declare that it did not consider itself bound by
para.(1). Further, art.38(2) provided that countries of the Union not bound by arts
22–26 (the administrative provisions of the Stockholm Act) might, until five
years after the entry into force of the Convention establishing the World Intellectual Property Organisation[141] exercise, if they so desired, the rights provided
under such articles as if they were bound by such articles, by giving written
notification thereof as prescribed by art.38(2).

State of ratifications or accessions. The only countries which adhered to the			**23–61**
substantive provisions of the Stockholm Act and the Protocol in due time, i.e.
prior to October 10, 1974, were Chad, the former East Germany, Mauritania,
Pakistan, Romania and Senegal. Notwithstanding that this was more than five
countries, the substantive provisions never entered into force in view of the declarations made by Pakistan and Mauritania.[142]

On the other hand, the administrative provisions of the Stockholm Act did
come into force, the following countries having adhered thereto: Australia,
Austria, Belgium, Canada, Chad, Denmark, Fiji, Finland, Germany,[143] Ireland,
Israel, Liechtenstein, Morocco, Pakistan, Romania, Senegal, Spain, Sweden,
Switzerland and the United Kingdom.

Romania's ratification was accompanied by declarations under arts 7(7) and
33(2). Pakistan and Senegal made declarations under art.5(1)(a) of the Protocol.
Bulgaria and Sweden made declarations under art.5(1)(b) of the Protocol.
Pakistan's accession was accompanied by a declaration that Pakistan availed
itself of the reservations in art.1 of the Protocol other than that in art.1(a): Mauritania's accession was accompanied by a declaration that Mauritania availed itself
of the reservations in art.1 of the Protocol. Finally, the following countries availed
themselves of the provisions of art.38(2): Argentina, Belgium, Brazil, Bulgaria,
Cameroon, Chile, the then Czechoslovakia, Dahomey (now the Republic of Benin), France, Gabon, Greece, the Holy See, Hungary, Italy, the then Ivory Coast,
Japan, Luxembourg, Malta, Monaco, the Netherlands, Niger, Norway, Portugal,
South Africa, Tunisia, Turkey and Yugoslavia.

G. ENTRY INTO FORCE OF PARIS ACT

Ratification or accession. The method of entry into force of the Paris Act was			**23–62**
complicated. Thus, under art.28(2)(a), arts 1 to 21 (the substantive provisions)
and the Appendix were to come into force three months after both the following
conditions had been fulfilled. First, at least five countries of the Union must have
ratified or acceded to the Paris Act without making a declaration under para.(1)(b)
of art.28. Secondly, France, Spain, the United Kingdom and the United States of
America must have become bound by the Paris revision of the Universal Copyright Convention. Such entry into force applied to those countries of the Union
which, at least three months before the coming into force, had deposited instru-

---

[141] See para.23–49, above.
[142] See para.23–59, above.
[143] Both Germany (Democratic Republic) and Germany (Federal Republic) adhered to the
administrative provisions of the Stockholm Act.

ments of ratification or accession not containing a declaration under para.(1)(b) of art.28. With regard to any other Union country which ratifies or accedes to the Paris Act without making such a declaration, arts 1 to 21 and the Appendix are to come into force three months after the date on which the Director General of the World Intellectual Property Organisation (WIPO) has notified the deposit of the relevant instrument of ratification or accession, unless a subsequent date has been indicated in the instrument deposited, in which case entry into force takes place on the date indicated.

The declaration under art.28(1)(b) is to the effect that the ratification or accession of the country concerned is not to apply to arts 1 to 21 and the Appendix. However, if such country has previously made a declaration under art.6(1) of the Appendix, then it may declare only that its ratification or accession is not to apply to arts 1 to 20. Any country which has made such a declaration may at a later time declare that it extends the effects of its ratification or accession to those provisions.

So far as arts 22 to 38 (the administrative and final provisions) are concerned, art.28(3) provides that, as regards any country which ratifies or accedes to the Paris Act with or without a declaration under art.28(1)(d), arts 22 to 38 are to come into force three months after the date on which the Director General has notified the deposit of the relevant instrument of ratification or accession, unless a subsequent date has been indicated in the instrument deposited, in which case entry into force takes place on the date indicated.

Articles 29 and 30(2)(b) contain provisions for accession by non-Union countries.

Article 29*bis* provides that the ratification or accession to the Paris Act by any country not bound by arts 22 to 38 of the Stockholm Act is, for the sole purposes of art.14(2) of the Convention establishing the World Intellectual Property Organisation, to amount to ratification of or accession to the Stockholm Act with the limitation set forth in art.28(1)(b)(i) thereof.

Article 30(2)(a) enables any country ratifying or acceding to the Paris Act, subject to art.5(2) of the Appendix, to retain the benefit of the reservations it has previously formulated.

23–63 Finally, art.6(1) of the Appendix (relating to developing countries) provides that any Union country may declare, as from the date of the Paris Act, and at any time before becoming bound by arts 1 to 21 and the Appendix, as follows: (i) if it is a country which, were it bound by arts 1 to 21 and the Appendix, would be entitled to avail itself of the faculties referred to in art.1(1) of the Appendix, that it will apply the provisions of art.2 or of art.3 of the Appendix or of both to works whose country of origin is a country which, pursuant to (ii), admits the application of those articles to such works, or which is bound by arts 1 to 21 and this Appendix; such declaration may, instead of referring to art.2, refer to art.5 of the Appendix; (ii) that it admits the application of the Appendix to works of which it is the country of origin by countries which have made a declaration under (i) or a notification under art.1 of the Appendix.

Articles 1 to 21 and the Appendix entered into force on October 10, 1974, by which time the requirements of art.28(2)(a) had been complied with. Articles 22 to 38 are also now in force. The United Kingdom ratified the Paris Act with effect from January 2, 1990.

23–64 As of August 31, 2010, the following countries have ratified or acceded to the whole of the Paris Act including the Appendix: Albania, Algeria, Andorra, Antigua and Barbuda, Argentina, Armenia, Australia, Austria, Azerbaijan, Bahrain, Bangladesh, Barbados, Belarus, Belgium, Belize, Benin, Bhutan, Bolivia, Bosnia and Herzegovina, Botswana, Brazil, Brunei Darussalam, Bulgaria, Burkina Faso,

Cameroon, Canada, Cape Verde, Central African Republic, Chile, China,[144] Colombia, Comoros, Congo, Costa Rica, Côte d'Ivoire, Croatia, Cuba, Cyprus, Czech Republic, Democratic People's Republic of Korea, Democratic Republic of the Congo, Denmark, Djibouti, Dominica, Dominican Republic, Ecuador, Egypt, El Salvador, Equatorial Guinea, Estonia, Finland, France, Gabon, Gambia, Georgia, Germany, Ghana, Greece, Grenada, Guatemala, Guinea, Guinea-Bissau, Guyana, Haiti, Holy See, Honduras, Hungary, Iceland, India, Indonesia, Ireland, Israel, Italy, Jamaica, Japan, Jordan, Kazakhstan, Kenya, Kyrgyzstan, Latvia, Lesotho, Liberia, Libyan Arab Jamahiriya, Liechtenstein, Lithuania, Luxembourg, Malawi, Malaysia, Mali, Mauritania, Mauritius, Mexico, Micronesia (Federated States of), Monaco, Mongolia, Montenegro, Morocco, Namibia, Nepal, Netherlands (for the Kingdom in Europe only), Nicaragua, Niger, Nigeria, Norway, Oman, Panama, Paraguay, Peru, Philippines, Poland, Portugal, Qatar, Republic of Korea, Republic of Moldova, Romania, Russian Federation, Rwanda, Saint Kitts and Nevis, Saint Lucia, Saint Vincent and the Grenadines, Samoa, Saudi Arabia, Senegal, Serbia (Republic of), Singapore, Slovakia (Slovak Republic), Slovenia, Spain, Sri Lanka, Sudan, Suriname, Swaziland, Sweden, Switzerland, Syrian Arab Republic, Tajikistan, Thailand, the former Yugoslav Republic of Macedonia, Togo, Tonga, Trinidad and Tobago, Tunisia, Turkey, Ukraine, United Arab Emirates, United Kingdom (with the Isle of Man), United Republic of Tanzania, United States of America, Uruguay, Uzbekistan, Venezuela (Bolivarian Republic of), Viet Nam, Yemen and Zambia.

The following countries have now ratified or acceded to the Paris Act, other than arts 1 to 21 and the Appendix, by reason of having made a declaration under art.28(1)(b): Bahamas, Malta, South Africa and Zimbabwe. Articles 22 to 38 of the Paris Act apply also to the Netherlands Antilles and Aruba.

Algeria, Bahamas, Cuba, Democratic People's Republic of Korea, Egypt, Guatemala, India, Indonesia, Israel, Italy, Jordan, Lesotho, Liberia, Libyan Arab Jamahiriya, Lithuania, Malta, Mauritius, Mongolia, Nepal, Oman, Saint Lucia, South Africa, Thailand, Tunisia, Turkey, United Republic of Tanzania, Venezuela (Bolivarian Republic of) and Viet Nam have made declarations that they do not consider themselves bound by art.33(1) concerning the settlement of disputes by the International Court of Justice. Bosnia and Herzegovina, Cyprus, Montenegro, Serbia and Slovenia have made reservations concerning the right of translation. Portugal has declared that its ratification shall not apply to art.14*bis*(2)(c) to the effect that the undertaking by authors to bring contributions to the making of a cinematographic work must be in a written agreement. India has made a declaration under art.14bis (2)(b) (presumption of legitimation for some authors who have brought contributions to the making of the cinematographic work). Algeria, Bahrain, Bangladesh, Cuba, Democratic People's Republic of Korea, Jordan, Mongolia and Singapore availed themselves of one or both of the faculties provided for in arts II and III of the Appendix until October 10, 2004. Bangladesh, Cuba, Jordan, Mongolia, Oman, Philippines, Samoa, Sri Lanka, Sudan, Syrian Arab Republic, Thailand, United Arab Emirates, Uzbekistan, Viet Nam and Yemen have availed themselves of one or both of the faculties provided for in arts II and III of the Appendix until October 10, 2014. Germany, Norway and the United Kingdom have declared that they admit the application of the Appendix of the Paris Act to works of which they are the State of origin by States which have made a declaration under art.VI(1)(i) of the Appendix or a notification under art.1 of the Appendix.

---

[144] The Paris Act applies also to the Hong Kong and Macau Special Administrative Regions.

H. PRESENT MEMBERS OF THE COPYRIGHT UNION

23–65   **Countries forming the Copyright Union.** As of August 31, 2010,[145] the following 164 countries form the Copyright Union: Albania, Algeria, Andorra, Antigua and Barbuda, Argentina, Armenia, Australia, Austria, Azerbaijan, Bahamas, Bahrain, Bangladesh, Barbados, Belarus, Belgium, Belize, Benin, Bhutan, Bolivia, Bosnia and Herzegovina, Botswana, Brazil, Brunei Darussalam, Bulgaria, Burkina Faso, Cameroon, Canada, Cape Verde, Central African Republic, Chad, Chile, China (China extended the application of the Paris Act of the Berne Convention to Hong Kong from July 1, 1997, and to Macao from December 20, 1999), Colombia, Comoros, Congo, Costa Rica, Côte d'Ivoire, Croatia, Cuba, Cyprus, Czech Republic, Democratic People's Republic of Korea, Democratic Republic of the Congo, Denmark, Djibouti, Dominica, Dominican Republic, Ecuador, Egypt, El Salvador, Equatorial Guinea, Estonia, Fiji, Finland, France (including overseas territories and the territorial entity of Mayotte), Gabon, Gambia, Georgia, Germany,[146] Ghana, Greece, Grenada, Guatemala, Guinea, Guinea-Bissau, Guyana, Haiti, Holy See, Honduras, Hungary, Iceland, India, Indonesia, Ireland, Israel, Italy, Jamaica, Japan, Jordan, Kazakhstan, Kenya, Kyrgyzstan (Kyrgyz Republic), Latvia, Lebanon (Lebanese Republic), Lesotho, Liberia, Libyan Arab Jamahiriya, Liechtenstein, Lithuania, Luxembourg, Madagascar, Malawi, Malaysia, Mali, Malta, Mauritania, Mauritius, Mexico, Micronesia (Federated States of), Monaco, Mongolia, Montenegro, Morocco, Namibia, Nepal, Netherlands, New Zealand, Nicaragua, Niger, Nigeria, Norway, Oman, Pakistan, Panama, Paraguay, Peru, Philippines, Poland, Portugal, Qatar, Republic of Korea, Republic of Moldova, Romania, Russian Federation, Rwanda, Saint Kitts and Nevis, Saint Lucia, Saint Vincent and the Grenadines, Samoa, Saudi Arabia, Senegal, Serbia, Singapore, Slovakia (Slovak Republic), Slovenia, South Africa, Spain, Sri Lanka, Sudan, Suriname, Swaziland, Sweden, Switzerland, Syrian Arab Republic, Tajikistan, Thailand, the former Yugoslav Republic of Macedonia, Togo, Tonga, Trinidad and Tobago, Tunisia, Turkey, Ukraine, United Arab Emirates, United Kingdom,[147] United Republic of Tanzania, United States of America (including the territories of American Samoa, Guam, the Northern Mariana Islands, Puerto Rico and the US Virgin Islands), Uruguay, Uzbekistan, Venezuela (Bolivarian Republic of), Viet Nam, Yemen, Zambia and Zimbabwe.

3. THE WIPO COPYRIGHT TREATY 1996

A. HISTORY

23–66   **Need for new international regulations.** In the course of the 1980s, a consensus developed that there was a need for new international regulations concerning the application of the Berne Convention. There were two main reasons for this. The first was the need to update the level of protection afforded by the Convention to deal with the technical developments which had emerged since the adoption of

---

[145] The situation is constantly changing and the current position can be obtained by consulting the World Intellectual Property Organization website: *http://www.wipo.int/treaties* [Accessed September 13, 2010].

[146] The Treaty of Union of August 31, 1990 (BGBL, 1990, Pt II, 885 et seq.) between the former Federal Republic of Germany and the former German Democratic Republic, which effected the reunification of Germany, provided that, in the case of copyright, the law of the former Federal Republic of Germany (i.e. the Copyright Law of September 9, 1965, as amended), was to apply in the territory of the former German Democratic Republic with effect from October 3, 1990.

[147] The UK extended the application of the Paris Act of the Berne Convention to the Isle of Man with effect from March 18, 1996.

the Paris Act 1971. Secondly, the shortcomings of the Convention with respect to standards of protection and the lack of any mechanism therein for enforcing the obligations of Member States or for the settlement of disputes between them were brought into focus in the context of the GATT Multilateral Trade Negotiations (the Uruguay Round). The deliberations of the GATT Working Group on Trade-Related Aspects of Intellectual Property (TRIPs) resulted, in December 1993, in agreement on the text of a new international instrument which, following the successful outcome of the Uruguay Round, was formally adopted at Marrakesh in April 1994. The TRIPs Agreement contains enforceable copyright treaty obligations, which include the requirements of the Paris Act of the Berne Convention and impose additional standards of protection exceeding those of the Berne Convention.[148]

A new substantive revision of the Berne Convention was ruled out, however. A formal revision would require unanimity among the Member States. At the time, such unanimity was perceived to be politically impossible in view of the widely differing standards and objects of protection in the then more than 100 Member States (on January 1, 1997, the Berne Union comprised 121 States). Thus, work proceeded on the basis that any new instrument would be an independent multilateral treaty, possibly in the form of a Protocol to the Convention, and that such an instrument would be likely to take the form of a special agreement under art.20 of the Convention.

Work on a possible Protocol to the Convention began in 1991. According to the relevant WIPO programme items for the years 1990–1991 and 1992–1993,[149] the purpose of the Protocol would be to clarify the existing or establish new international standards where, under the Paris Act of the Berne Convention, doubts may exist as to the extent to which the Convention applies. It was considered that such clarification was required because governments interpret their obligations under the Convention differently. Discrepancies had arisen in respect of certain subject-matters of protection (e.g. computer programs, sound recordings, computer-generated works); certain rights (e.g. rental right, public lending right, right of distribution of copies of any kind of works, right of display); the applicability of the conventional minima (no formalities, term of protection, etc.); and the obligation of granting national treatment (without reciprocity) to foreigners. The desirability of covering the rights of producers of sound recordings in the protocol was also to be examined.

Terms of reference of possible Protocol. Following two sessions of the Committee of Experts responsible for the preparation of the possible Protocol, held in 1991 and 1992 respectively,[150] its terms of reference were modified,[151] due mainly to the fact that agreement could not be reached on the inclusion of the protection of producers of sound recordings in the possible Protocol, as had been proposed by WIPO.[152] According to the modified terms of reference, the issues agreed to be discussed in connection with the possible Protocol were the following: (1) computer programs, (2) databases, (3) rental right, (4) non-voluntary licences for

23–67

---

[148] See paras 23–136 et seq., below.
[149] Programmes adopted by the Assembly and Conference of Representatives of the Berne Union, October 1989 and October 1991 (see WIPO documents AB/XX/2, item PRG. 02(2) and AB/XX/20, paras 152 and 199, for the 1990/1991 biennium, and document AB/XXII/22, para.197, for the 1992/1993 biennium).
[150] For the reports of these sessions, see *Copyright* 1992: First Session at 30 and Second Session at 66 and 93.
[151] The terms of reference of the Committee of Experts were modified by the Assembly and the Conference of Representatives of the Berne Union in September 1992 (see WIPO document B/A/XIII/2, para.22).
[152] WIPO Programme 1992/3 (document AB/XXII/2, item 03(2)).

the sound recording of musical works, (5) non-voluntary licences for primary broadcasting and satellite communication, (6) distribution right, including importation right, (7) duration of the protection of photographic works, (8) communication to the public by satellite broadcasting, (9) enforcement of rights, and (10) national treatment. A separate Committee of Experts on a Possible Instrument for the Protection of the Rights of Performers and Producers of Phonograms (sound recordings) was established to discuss all questions concerning the effective international protection of the rights of performers and producers of sound recordings. A third session of the Committee of Experts on the possible Protocol to the Berne Convention[153] and a first session of the Committee of Experts on the possible Instrument[154] were held in 1993. The nature of the relationship, if any, between the possible Protocol and the possible Instrument, when and if adopted, and between the latter and the Rome Convention for the Protection of Performers, Producers of Phonograms and Broadcasting Organisations 1961, and the Convention for the Protection of Producers of Phonograms Against Unauthorised Duplication of Their Phonograms 1971, were also the subject of discussion.

23–68   **The digital agenda.** Further sessions of the Committees of Experts were convened in 1994 and 1995[155] in the course of which the need to address also issues connected with the exploitation of works in the digital environment of the so-called Global Information Infrastructure was recognised (the Digital Agenda). Following the publication in September 1996 by WIPO of "basic proposals" for the substantive provisions of three treaties dealing respectively with authors' rights, the rights of phonogram producers and performers and sui generis intellectual property protection of databases (i.e. non-copyright protection), a Diplomatic Conference on Certain Copyright and Neighbouring Rights Questions was held in Geneva from December 2 to 20, 1996; the "basic proposals" formed the basis for negotiation. On December 20, 1996, two new international instruments were adopted and opened for signature: the WIPO Copyright Treaty and the WIPO Performances and Phonograms Treaty.[156] The issue of sui generis protection for databases was postponed. The Conference also adopted a number of agreed statements concerning the WIPO Copyright Treaty[157] and the WIPO Performances and Phonograms Treaty,[158] a Resolution concerning audiovisual performances[159] and a Recommendation concerning databases calling for further discussion of the issue.[160]

There follows in this chapter a summary of the WIPO Copyright Treaty and its related statements in view of the close relationship of the new Treaty with the Paris Act of the Berne Convention. The WIPO Performances and Phonograms

---

[153] See Report of the third session, (Geneva, June 1993), Copyright 1993, 179.

[154] See Report of the first session (Geneva, June/July, 1993), Copyright 1993, 196.

[155] See Copyright 1994, 44, and Industrial Property and Copyright 1995, 107, 110 and 427.

[156] The Final Act of the Diplomatic Conference (CRNR/DC/98) was signed by the following 57 states on December 20, 1996: Angola, Argentina, Australia, Austria, Azerbaijan, Belgium, Bolivia, Brazil, Burkina Faso, Canada, Chile, China, Colombia, Croatia, Cuba, Denmark, Ecuador, El Salvador, Finland, Germany, Honduras, Hungary, Indonesia, Ireland, Italy, Jamaica, Japan, Kazakhstan, Kenya, Mexico, Mongolia, Namibia, the Netherlands, New Zealand, Nicaragua, Norway, Peru, Philippines, Republic of Korea, Republic of Moldova, Romania, Russian Federation, Singapore, Slovakia, Slovenia, Spain, Sudan, Sweden, Switzerland, Togo, Trinidad and Tobago, UK, USA, Uzbekistan, Venezuela, Zimbabwe. The European Communities also signed the Final Act. The following also signed the WIPO Copyright Treaty and the WIPO Performances and Phonograms Treaty: Bolivia, Burkina Faso, Chile, Germany, Indonesia, Italy, Kenya, Mongolia, Namibia, Spain, Togo, Venezuela, European Communities.

[157] Document CRNR/DC/96 of December 20, 1996.

[158] Document CRNR/DC/97 of December 20, 1996.

[159] Document CRNR/DC/99 of December 20, 1996.

[160] CRNR/DC/100 of December 20, 1996, and see para.23–78, below.

Treaty and its related statements are discussed below, in s.7 of this Chapter, following the discussion of the Rome and Phonograms Conventions in ss.5 and 6.[161] The status of the related statements in relation to interpreting the Treaties may be evaluated in the light of the Vienna Convention on the Law of Treaties and, in particular, s.3 thereof concerning interpretation of treaties.[162]

B. SUBSTANTIVE PROVISIONS OF THE WIPO COPYRIGHT TREATY

The Treaty and its explanatory statements. The Diplomatic Conference **23–69** adopted the Treaty and a series of explanatory statements, representing the agreed interpretation to be given to certain provisions of the Treaty. With one exception, the explanatory statements were adopted by consensus. The exception was that relating to the reproduction right. In the following discussion, these statements are taken into account. As already stated, the Treaty is a special agreement within the meaning of art.20 of the Berne Convention[163] and does not derogate from existing obligations that Contracting Parties have to each other under that Convention (art.1). Parties shall comply with arts 1 to 21 and the Appendix of the Paris Act of the Convention (art.1(4)). The statement concerning art.1(4) makes it clear that the reproduction right as provided for in art.9 of the Berne Convention, and the exceptions permitted thereunder, fully apply in the digital environment, in particular to the use of works in digital form. Moreover, the storage of a protected work in digital form in an electronic medium constitutes a reproduction within the meaning of art.9 of the Berne Convention.

Article 2 defines the scope of copyright protection as extending to expressions and not to ideas, procedures, methods of operation or mathematical concepts as such.

Article 3 provides that Contracting Parties shall apply mutatis mutandis the provisions of arts 2 to 6 of the Berne Convention, concerning protected works, conditions of protection, including criteria of eligibility, national treatment and the possibility of restricting protection in the case of works made by nationals of certain non-Union countries, respectively, in respect of the protection provided for in the Treaty. According to the related statement, the expressions "country of the Union" and "country outside the Union" in the Berne Convention are to be read as references to countries that are respectively members or non-members of the Treaty.

New protected works. Computer programs are protected as literary works within **23–70** the meaning of art.2 of the Berne Convention (art.4); this provision is of a declaratory nature since it confirms the existing understanding that such programs were

---

[161] See J. Reinbothe and S. von Lewinski, *The WIPO Treaties 1996* (London: Butterworths/LexisNexis, 2002), M. Ficsor, *The Law of Copyright and the Internet: the 1966 WIPO Treaties, their interpretation and implementation* (Oxford: Oxford University Press, 2002) and the following accounts of the results of the Diplomatic Conference: "WIPO Diplomatic Conference on Certain Copyright and Neighbouring Rights Questions", [1997] *Copyright* 97; J. Reinbothe, M. Martin-Prat and S. von Lewinski, "The New WIPO Treaties: A First Résumé" [1997] 4 E.I.P.R. 171; T.C. Vinje, "The New WIPO Copyright Treaty: A Happy Result in Geneva" [1997] 5 E.I.P.R. 230; M. Fabiani, "The Geneva Diplomatic Conference on Copyright and the Rights of Performers and Phonogram Producers" [1997] 3 Ent. L.R. 98. See also J. Reinbothe and S. von Lewinski, "The WIPO Treaties 1996: Ready to Come into Force" [2002] E.I.P.R. 199.

[162] See arts 31 to 33. Art.31(2) and (4) are of particular relevance: "2. The context for the purpose of the interpretation of a treaty shall comprise, in addition to the text, including its preamble and annexes: (a) any agreement relating to the treaty which was made between all the parties in connection with the conclusion of the treaty; (b) any instrument which was made by one or more parties in connection with the conclusion of the treaty and accepted by the other parties as an instrument related to the treaty. 4. A special meaning shall be given to a term if it is established that the parties so intended".

[163] In the Treaty, reference to the Berne Convention means the Paris Act thereof (art.1(3)).

already protected under Berne. Compilations of data or other material, in any form, which by reason of the selection or arrangement of their contents constitute intellectual creations are protected as such. This protection does not extend to the data or material itself and is without prejudice to any copyright subsisting in the data or material contained in the compilation (art.5). The accompanying statements to these two articles assert that the scope of protection provided is consistent with art.2 of the Berne Convention and on a par with the relevant provisions of the TRIPs Agreement.[164]

23–71   Newly recognised rights. An express right of distribution is recognised giving authors the exclusive right to authorise or prohibit the making available to the public of the original and copies of their works through sale or other transfer of ownership (art.6). According to the accompanying statement, the expressions "original" and "copies" refer exclusively to fixed copies that can be put into circulation as tangible objects. The right may be made subject to exhaustion after the first sale or other transfer of ownership (art.6(2)). This right is new to the Berne Convention and is also not recognised in the TRIPs Agreement, although it is provided for in a number of national laws and considered in some jurisdictions as a component of the reproduction right.

Subject to certain limitations, a right to authorise commercial rental is recognised in favour of authors of computer programs, cinematographic works and works embodied in phonograms (sound recordings (art.7)). The accompanying statement explains that Contracting Parties are not required under this article to provide an exclusive right of commercial rental to authors who, under the domestic law of that country, are not granted such rights with respect of sound recordings and that the obligation is consistent with art.14(4) of the TRIPs Agreement. As regards computer programs, the right is excluded where the program itself is not the essential object of the rental. As for films, the right only applies where commercial rental has led to widespread copying which has materially impaired the exclusive right of reproduction. However, Contracting Parties which on April 15, 1994, had and continue to have a system of equitable remuneration of authors for rental may maintain that system unless the reproduction right is being materially impaired (art.7(3)).[165]

Finally, to deal with new means of communication over services such as the internet, art.8 provides authors with the exclusive right to authorise any communication to the public of their works, by wire or wireless means, including the making available to the public of their works in such a way that members of the public may access these works from a place and at a time individually chosen by them, i.e. online transmissions over interactive services. Thus authors have obtained a valuable right to authorise on-demand transmissions. However, to allay the fears of mere electronic communication systems service providers, who feared that they would be made responsible for clearing copyright in programs sent over their networks, the accompanying statement explains that it is understood that the mere provision of physical facilities for enabling or making a communication does not in itself amount to communication within the meaning of the Treaty or the Berne Convention. It is also pointed out that Contracting Parties may apply art.11bis(2) of the Berne Convention and provide for compulsory licensing.

In respect of photographic works, the possibility provided by art.7(4) of the Berne Convention to limit the term of protection to 25 years shall no longer apply (art.9), the general term of protection of 50 years *post mortem auctoris* being applicable instead.

---

[164] art.10 (1) and (2) of the TRIPs Agreement.
[165] cf. art.11 of the TRIPs Agreement, which has a parallel provision.

Limitations and exceptions: Extension of the three-step test of the Berne   **23–72**
Convention. As regards limitations and exceptions to authors' rights, the limitation of art.9(2) of the Berne Convention to the effect that limitations and exceptions to the reproduction right must not conflict with a normal exploitation of the
work nor unreasonably prejudice the legitimate interests of the author (the so-
called three-step test of the Berne Convention) is extended to apply not merely to
the reproduction right but also to all authors' rights (art.10).[166] According to the
accompanying statement, this provision neither reduces nor extends the scope of
art.9(2) of the Berne Convention, but permits Contracting Parties to carry forward
and appropriately extend into the digital environment limitations and exceptions
in their national laws, which have been considered acceptable under the Berne
Convention. Similarly, it is to be understood as permitting them to devise new
exceptions and limitations appropriate in the digital network environment.[167]

Technical protection. The importance of the use of technical anti-copying de-   **23–73**
vices in the fight against piracy of works of all kinds is recognised in art.11,
which provides for the Contracting Parties to provide adequate legal protection
and effective legal remedies against the circumvention of effective technological
measures used by authors to prevent unauthorised use of their works. Certain
obligations concerning electronic rights management information are included
with the same aim; thus Contracting Parties must provide adequate and effective
legal remedies against acts which may induce, enable, facilitate or conceal an infringement of any right protected under the Treaty or the Berne Convention, both
exclusive rights and rights of remuneration,[168] and including acts such as the removal or alteration of electronic rights management information without authority; the distribution, importation for distribution, broadcast or communication to
the public, without authority, of works or copies of works knowing that electronic
rights management information has been removed or altered without authority.
"Rights management information" is defined as information that "identifies the
work, the author of the work, the owner of any right in the work, or information
about the terms and conditions of use of the work, and any numbers or codes that
represent such information, when any of these items of information is attached to
a copy of a work or appears in connection with the communication of a work to
the public" (art.12). Contracting Parties may not rely on this article to devise or
implement rights management systems that would have the effect of imposing
formalities, which are not permitted under the Berne Convention or the Treaty,
prohibiting the free movement of goods or impeding the enjoyment of rights
under the Treaty (accompanying statement concerning art.12).

Retroactive effect and enforcement. Article 13 of the Treaty provides that the   **23–74**
rules of art.18 of the Berne Convention concerning retroactive effect, or the way
in which the Convention applies to works already in existence when their country
of origin first joins the Convention, shall apply to the protection provided for
under the Treaty. Thus the Treaty applies to all works which, at the moment of its
coming into force, have not yet fallen into the public domain in the country of
origin through the expiry of the term of protection.

   Article 14 deals with enforcement of rights, obliging the Contracting Parties to
ensure that enforcement procedures are available to permit effective action against
infringement, including remedies to prevent infringements and remedies which
constitute a deterrent to further infringements. This provision is of a very general

---

[166] cf. art.13 of the TRIPs Agreement and see para.23–33, above.
[167] This statement was adopted not by consensus but by majority vote. It is therefore of more limited
   value than the other statements to which all present agreed.
[168] See the accompanying statement concerning art.12 of the Treaty.

nature and does not include any reference to the more effective enforcement provisions contained in arts 41 to 61 of the TRIPs Agreement. The Diplomatic Conference specifically rejected a "basic proposal" to either include the TRIPs enforcement provisions in an annex or by reference (which would have simply required Contracting Parties to apply the relevant provisions of the TRIPs Agreement).

C. SIGNATORIES AND ENTRY INTO FORCE

23–75   **Parties to the** Treaty. Any Member State of the World Intellectual Property Organisation (WIPO) may become party to the Treaty, as well as any intergovernmental organisation competent in respect of, and having legislation binding on its Member States on, matters dealt with by the Treaty. The European Union has signed the Treaty on this basis (art.17). The Treaty entered into force three months after the deposit of 30 instruments of ratification or accession by states with the Director General of WIPO (art.20). Thereafter, new parties are bound by the Treaty three months from the date on which they deposit their instruments (art.21). No reservations to the Treaty are permitted (art.22), although it may be denounced on giving one year's notice (art.23). The Treaty is administered by the International Bureau of WIPO[169] (art.16) and supervised by an Assembly, which deals with matters concerning the maintenance and development of the Treaty and its application and operation.[170]

The Treaty was open for signature until December 31, 1997, at which date 51 States had signed the Treaty as well as the European Community.[171]

As of August 31, 2010, the following 87 countries and the European Union had ratified or acceded to the Treaty: Albania, Argentina, Armenia, Australia, Austria, Azerbaijan, Bahrain, Belarus, Belgium, Benin, Bosnia and Herzegovina, Botswana, Bulgaria, Burkina Faso, Chile, China, Colombia, Costa Rica, Croatia, Cyprus, Czech Republic, Denmark, Dominican Republic, Ecuador, El Salvador, Estonia, Finland, France, Gabon, Germany, Georgia, Ghana, Greece, Guatemala, Guinea, Honduras, Hungary, Indonesia, Ireland, Italy, Jamaica, Japan, Jordan, Kazakhstan, Kyrgyzstan (Kyrgyz Republic), Latvia, Liechtenstein, Lithuania, Luxembourg, Mali, Malta, Mexico, Mongolia, Montenegro, Netherlands, Nicaragua, Oman, Panama, Paraguay, Peru, Philippines, Poland, Portugal, Qatar, Republic of Korea, Republic of Moldova, Romania, Russian Federation, Saint Lucia, Senegal, Serbia (Republic of), Singapore, Slovakia (Slovak Republic), Slovenia, Spain, Sweden, Switzerland, Tajikistan, the former Yugoslav Republic of Macedonia, Togo, Trinidad and Tobago, Turkey, Ukraine, United Arab Emirates, United Kingdom, United States of America and Uruguay.

The Council of the European Community approved the Treaty with regard to matters within its competence by decision dated March 16, 2000 and the European Union ratified the Convention with effect from March 14, 2010.[172]

---

[169] The Director General of WIPO is the depository of the Treaty (art.25).

[170] WCT art.15(2)(a).

[171] Argentina, Austria, Belarus, Belgium, Bolivia, Burkina Faso, Canada, Chile, Colombia, Costa Rica, Croatia, Denmark, Ecuador, Estonia, Finland, France, Germany, Ghana, Greece, Hungary, Indonesia, Ireland, Israel, Italy, Kazakhstan, Kenya, Kyrgyzstan, Luxembourg, Mexico, Moldova (Republic of), Monaco, Mongolia, Namibia, the Netherlands, Nigeria, Panama, Portugal, Romania, Senegal, Slovakia, Slovenia, South Africa, Spain, Sweden, Switzerland, Togo, United Kingdom, United States of America, Uruguay, Venezuela, European Community.

[172] Council Decision of March 16, 2000, on the approval, on behalf of the European Community, of the WIPO Copyright Treaty and the WIPO Performances and Phonograms Treaty ([2000] OJ L89/6). See Vol.2 11. The decision authorised the President of the Council to deposit the instrument of ratification as from the date by which Member States are obliged to implement the Directive; the deposit took place on December 14, 2009 and took effect on March 14, 2010.

D. PENDING ISSUES NOT ADDRESSED BY THE TREATY

Problems left unresolved. It will be noted that of the list of matters considered   **23–76**
by the Committees of Experts on a possible Protocol to the Berne Convention,
some did not find solutions in the Treaty. For example, the proposal to include an
additional specific right to authorise or prohibit importation in the context of the
new distribution right was rejected. Likewise, agreement could not be reached on
a rule concerning the international exhaustion of the distribution right, leaving
the question of national or international exhaustion to national law. The proposals to abolish the non-voluntary licences for broadcasting of literary and artistic
works and for the sound recording of musical works, permitted respectively by
art.11*bis*(2) and art.13 of the Berne Convention, were also abandoned.

The digital agenda. As regards the digital agenda, two important issues for   **23–77**
which solutions were proposed in the "basic proposals" were not resolved. First,
agreement could not be reached on the proposal to make it clear that acts such as
temporary storage in electronic communications media constitute acts of
reproduction.[173] Similarly, the proposal to clarify the concept of "publication", by
specifically providing that making a work available to the public through on
demand interactive systems should be treated as publication, was not followed.[174]

Databases. In particular, the Conference was unable to reach a sufficient   **23–78**
consensus on the subject of the sui generis protection of databases, which require
significant investment but do not necessarily qualify for protection as a literary
work (non-original databases), to be able to adopt an international instrument on
the subject. Instead, a recommendation was adopted by the Conference in which
the participants expressed interest in examining further the possible implications
and benefits of a sui generis system of protection of databases at the international
level and recommended that the competent authorities of WIPO should, in the
first quarter of 1997, decide on a schedule for further preparatory work on a
Treaty on Intellectual Property in Respect of Databases.[175] In doing so, the recommendation recognised that databases are a vital element in the development of
a global information infrastructure and the need to strike a balance in relation
thereto between the interests of the producers of databases in protection from
unfair copying and the interests of users in having appropriate access to the
benefits of a global information infrastructure. Meanwhile, the issue has been
discussed repeatedly under the auspices of WIPO, but to date no consensus on
the need for or contents of a new international instrument on the subject has
emerged and in 2005 it was decided to drop the matter for the time being.

4. THE UNIVERSAL COPYRIGHT CONVENTION AND ITS REVISION

A. HISTORY

Object of Convention. Largely with the object of creating a bridge between the   **23–79**
Berne Convention countries on the one hand and the Pan-American Convention
countries on the other hand,[176] and particularly in the hope that the United States
of America might be persuaded to enter into copyright relations with the Berne

---

[173] See Basic Proposal 7.
[174] See Basic Proposal 3.
[175] WIPO Document CRNR/DC/100 of December 20, 1996.
[176] See paras 23–178 et seq., below.

Union countries, a draft International Convention was prepared under the auspices of the United Nations Organisation for Education, Science and Culture (UNESCO), which resulted in the Universal Copyright Convention (UCC), signed at Geneva on September 6, 1952.[177] The Convention entered into force on September 16, 1955.

At the time, the Convention represented a turning point in intergovernmental copyright relations and was hailed by many scholars and experts in the copyright field as one of the most significant milestones in the entire history of copyright.[178] For the United States of America it "marked the culmination of a seven years' effort ... to improve its copyright relations with the rest of the world".[179]

The great advantage of the Convention was that it established a set of minimum standards for copyright throughout the world, which could be accepted by countries with very different copyright systems: those which conformed to the principle of the Berne Convention requiring the granting of copyright protection without formalities and those countries with copyright laws which made protection dependent on compliance with formalities such as notice, deposit, registration or other formal requirements.

23–80   The Convention was a success and has attracted many members, for many years outstripping the membership of the Berne Convention, its lower level of protection being of particular interest to developing countries. Administered by UNESCO, the progress of the Convention is monitored by the Intergovernmental Committee established thereunder.[180] The latter co-operates closely with the Executive Committee of the Berne Union in copyright matters.

In due course, in parallel with moves to revise the Berne Convention, recommendations were made for the holding of a revision Conference in mid-1971 for the purpose of revising this Convention in an attempt to resolve the unfortunate situation which had arisen over the Protocol Regarding Developing Countries to the Stockholm revision of the Berne Convention. The Universal Copyright Convention, like the Berne Convention, was revised in Paris in 1971.[181]

Following the accession of the United States of America to the Paris Act of the Berne Convention with effect from March 1, 1989, as well as those of large numbers of developing countries over the past 25 years, including many in Latin America, the Universal Copyright Convention has lost part of its raison d'être and importance. The accession of the Russian Federation in 1995 to the Paris Act of the Berne Convention has further reduced its importance in providing copyright links between major countries. It is of interest to note that, in 1971, at the time of the adoption of the Paris Acts of the Berne Convention and the Universal Copyright Convention, both Conventions had 59 Member States. As of January 15, 2009, by contrast, the Berne Union comprises 164 Member States as compared with the 100 Member States of the UCC (Geneva and Paris Acts). Since the publication of the Main Work, Montenegro has adhered to the Paris Act of the UCC.

---

[177] As a result the Convention is variously referred to as the Universal, Geneva or UNESCO Convention. As regards the 1952 text of the UCC, see *Records of the Intergovernmental Conference*, Geneva, 1952, UNESCO, Paris, 1954; see also T.R. Kupferman and M. Foner (eds.), *Universal Copyright Convention Analysed* (New York: Federal Legal Publications, Inc., 1955).

[178] cf. C.B. Seton in Kupferman and Foner, xi.

[179] per the Hon. Arthur Fisher, US Register of Copyrights, in Kupferman and Foner, Universal Copyright Convention Analysed (New York: Federal Legal Publications, Inc., 1955).

[180] UCC art.XI.

[181] *Records of the Conference for Revision of the Universal Copyright Convention*, Paris, July 5–24, 1971, UNESCO, Paris 1973. See also A. Bogsch, *The Law of Copyright Under the Universal Copyright Convention* 3rd rev. edn (New York: Sijthoff, Leyden and Bowker, 1972).

B. SUBSTANTIVE PROVISIONS

Main provisions. Basically, the effect of the revised Universal Copyright Convention[182] is that each Contracting State undertakes to give to the unpublished works of the nationals of all other Contracting States the same protection as it gives to the unpublished works of its own nationals as well as the protection specially granted by the Convention, and further undertakes to give to the published works of nationals of the other Contracting States wherever first published, and to published works of the nationals of any country if first published in one of the other Contracting States, the same rights as it gives to works first published in its own territory as well as the protection specially granted by the Convention. Furthermore, such published works, if first published outside the territory of the Contracting State in question and not being the work of a national author, are to enjoy such protection without formality, such as registration or the deposit of copies, provided only that from the time of first publication all copies published bear the symbol © accompanied by the name of the copyright proprietor and the year of first publication, placed in such manner and location as to give reasonable notice of claim of copyright.[183] The Convention is not to apply to works which, at the effective date of the Convention in a Contracting State where protection is claimed, are permanently in the public domain in that State.

23–81

Term of copyright. The Convention provides for a minimum term of protection, namely, the life of the author and 25 years after his death. It is, however, provided that any Contracting State which, upon the effective date of the Convention in that State, does not compute the term of protection upon the basis of the life of the author, shall be entitled to compute the term of protection from the date of first publication of the work or from its registration prior to publication, provided that the term of protection is not to be less than 25 years from the date of first publication or registration. "Publication" is defined in the Convention as meaning the reproduction in tangible form and the general distribution to the public of copies of a work from which it can be read or otherwise visually perceived.

23–82

Minimum protection required. As to the nature of the protection to be afforded, the Convention provides that each Contracting State shall give adequate and effective protection to the rights of authors and other copyright proprietors in literary, scientific and artistic works, including writings, musical, dramatic and cinematographic works, and paintings, engravings and sculpture. It is further provided that these rights are to include the basic rights ensuring the author's economic interests, including the exclusive right to authorise reproduction by any means, public performance and broadcasting, and are to extend to the work either in its original form or in any form recognisably derived from the original. Any Contracting State may make exceptions to such rights, provided these do not conflict with the spirit and provisions of the Convention, but shall nevertheless accord a reasonable degree of effective protection to each of the rights to which exception has been made. It is also provided that such rights include the exclusive right to make, publish and authorise the making and publication of translations of works, but the Contracting State may make provision for compulsory licences to translate if, after the expiration of a period of seven years from the date of first publication, a translation has not been published in a language in general use in that state.

23–83

While promising protection on the general lines above indicated, this Conven-

---

[182] For the text of the 1971 Convention see Vol.2 F2.
[183] The positioning of such notice on various types of works is considered in the UNESCO Copyright Bulletin, 1957, Vol.X, No.2, pp.225 and 247.

tion does not describe the details of protection which are to be afforded by the Contracting States and substantially leaves the mode and extent of protection to the separate legislation of each state. It only extended further than the Berne Convention in requiring protection to be given to published works, not only if first published in a Contracting State, but if first published anywhere, if the author is a national of a Contracting State.[184] To meet this requirement of the Convention, and in order to enable the United Kingdom to ratify the Convention, the 1956 Act altered the law of the United Kingdom so as to protect the published works of nationals of Contracting States although first published outside the United Kingdom and the Convention area.[185] The most important amendment in the Paris revision of this Convention was to provide for various forms of compulsory licence in favour of developing countries similar to those in the Appendix to the Paris revision of the Berne Convention.[186] This did not call for any revision of this country's law and the United Kingdom has, in fact, ratified the Paris revision of this Convention.

C. RELATIONSHIP WITH THE BERNE CONVENTION

23–84 **Safeguards for the** Berne Convention. The relationship between the Universal Copyright Convention and the Berne Convention is expressed in the text of the UCC itself, which provides:

"This Convention shall not in any way affect the provisions of the Berne Convention for the Protection of Literary and Artistic Works or membership in the Union created by that Convention".[187]

To that article in both the 1952 and 1971 texts is annexed a Declaration, which is an integral part of the Convention for the States bound by the Berne Convention. According to the 1952 text, works which, according to the Berne Convention, have as their country of origin a country which has withdrawn from the Berne Union, shall not be protected by the Universal Copyright Convention in the countries of the Berne Union. Moreover, as between members of the Berne Union, only the Berne Convention will apply. In the 1971 text, these rules are relaxed in favour of countries which at the time of withdrawal from the Berne Union are recognised as developing countries availing themselves of the provisions of Article 5*bis* of the 1971 text concerning compulsory licences to translate.

These provisions, the aim of which was to deter withdrawal from the Berne Union and to exclude the application of the Universal Copyright Convention between Berne Member States, responded to the fear of certain members of the Berne Union that the existence of the UCC might encourage defections by Berne Union Member States seeking to downgrade the level of protection of their international copyright obligations.[188]

D. ENTRY INTO FORCE OF THE 1952 AND 1971 CONVENTIONS

23–85 **Ratification or accession.** Countries, may ratify, accept or accede to this Convention which originally came into force three months after the deposit of 12 instruments of ratification, acceptance or accession, including such deposit by four

---

[184] But see now art.3(1) of the Paris Act of Berne, para.23–13, above.

[185] Copyright Act 1956 ss.2(2) and 3(3) and see CDPA 1988 ss.154 and 155.

[186] See paras 23–51 et seq., above.

[187] UCC, 1952 and 1971 texts, art.XVII and see also Declaration annexed to that article.

[188] cf. A. Bogsch, "Co-existence of the Universal Copyright Convention with the Berne Conventions", in Kupferman and Foner, *Universal Copyright Convention Analysed* (New York: Federal Legal Publications, Inc., 1995), p.141 and S. Ricketson, *The Berne Convention for the Protection of Literary and Artistic Works: 1886–1896* (Queen Mary College, University of London, 1987), paras 15.27 et seq.

non-Berne Union members, on September 16, 1955.[189] Subsequently, the Convention came into force in respect of any state three months after that state deposited its instrument of ratification, acceptance or accession.

Accession to the 1971 Convention by a state not party to the 1952 Convention also constitutes accession to that Convention; but, if its instrument of accession was deposited before the 1971 Convention came into force, such state could make its accession to the 1952 Convention conditional upon the coming into force of the 1971 Convention. After the coming into force of the 1971 Convention, no state may accede solely to the 1952 Convention. Relations between states party to the 1971 Convention and states that are party only to the 1952 Convention are governed by the 1952 Convention. However, any state party only to the 1952 Convention may, by a notification deposited with the Director General, declare that it will admit the application of the 1971 Convention to works of its nationals or works first published in its territory by all states party to the 1971 Convention.

The 1971 Convention in fact came into force on July 10, 1974, three months after the deposit of 12 instruments of ratification, acceptance or accession.

The following 65 countries have now ratified or acceded to the 1971 Convention as of August 31, 2010. Albania, Algeria, Australia, Austria, Bahamas, Bangladesh, Barbados, Bolivia, Bosnia and Herzogovina, Brazil, Bulgaria, Cameroon, China, Colombia, Costa Rica, Croatia, Cyprus, Czech Republic, Denmark, Dominican Republic, Ecuador, El Salvador, Finland, France, Germany, Guinea, the Holy See, Hungary, India, Italy, Japan, Kenya, Liechtenstein, Macedonia (the former Yugoslav Republic of), Mexico, Monaco, Montenegro, Morocco, the Netherlands, Niger, Norway, Panama, Peru, Poland, Portugal, Republic of Korea, Russian Federation, Rwanda, Saint Vincent and the Grenadines, Saudi Arabia, Senegal, Serbia (Republic of), Slovakia (Slovak Republic), Slovenia, Spain, Sri Lanka, Sweden, Switzerland, Togo, Trinidad and Tobago, Tunisia, United Kingdom, United States of America, Uruguay and Venezuela (Bolivarian Republic of).

23–86

The following countries have availed themselves of the exceptions in favour of developing countries: Algeria, Bangladesh, Bolivia, China, Mexico, Republic of Korea and Tunisia.

E. Parties to the Universal Copyright Convention

Convention countries.[190] As of August 31, 2010, the following 100 countries are party to the Universal Copyright Convention 1952 (Geneva or Paris Acts). Albania, Algeria, Andorra, Argentina, Australia, Austria, Azerbaijan, Bahamas, Bangladesh, Barbados, Belarus, Belgium, Belize, Bolivia, Bosnia and Herzegovina, Brazil, Bulgaria, Cambodia, Cameroon, Canada, Chile, China, Colombia, Costa Rica, Croatia, Cuba, Cyprus, Czech Republic, Denmark, Dominican Republic, Ecuador, El Salvador, Fiji, Finland, France, Germany,[191] Ghana, Greece, Guatemala, Guinea, Haiti, the Holy See, Hungary, Iceland, India, Ireland, Israel, Italy, Japan, Kazakhstan, Kenya, Lao People's Democratic Republic, Lebanon, Liberia, Liechtenstein, Luxembourg, Macedonia (the former Yugoslav Republic of), Mexico, Monaco, Montenegro, Morocco, the Netherlands, New Zealand, Nicaragua, Niger, Nigeria, Norway, Pakistan, Panama, Paraguay, Peru, Poland, Portugal, Republic of Korea, Republic of Moldova, Russian Federation, Rwanda,

23–87

---

[189] UCC 1952 text, art.IX.
[190] The situation is constantly changing and the current position can be obtained by consulting the UNESCO website: *http://www.unesco.org* [Accessed September 13, 2010].
[191] See fn.143, above.

Saint Vincent and the Grenadines, Saudi Arabia, Senegal, Serbia (Republic of), Slovakia (Slovak Republic), Slovenia, Spain, Sri Lanka, Sweden, Switzerland, Tajikistan, Togo, Trinidad and Tobago, Tunisia, Ukraine, United Kingdom[192] (extended to British Virgin Islands, Gibraltar, Isle of Man and Saint Helena), United States of America (extended to American Samoa, Guam, the Northern Mariana Islands, Puerto Rico, the US Virgin Islands), Uruguay and Venezuela (Bolivarian Republic of).

5. THE ROME CONVENTION

A. HISTORY

23–88   **The Convention for the Protection of Performers, Producers of Phonograms and Broadcasting Organisations** (the Rome Convention) was adopted in Rome on October 26, 1961,[193] at a Diplomatic Conference convened by the International Labour Organisation (ILO), the United Nations Organisation for Education, Science and Culture (UNESCO) and the United International Bureaux for the Protection of Intellectual Property (BIRPI), the predecessor organisation of WIPO. These three organisations constitute the Secretariat of the Intergovernmental Committee set up under the Convention to monitor its application and operation.[194]

23–89   **Neighbouring rights.** The rights of the beneficiaries of the Rome Convention are widely referred to as "neighbouring rights", although the term appears nowhere in the Convention. This expression is often used for ease of reference and is the term favoured by the World Intellectual Property Organisation (WIPO) to describe the rights. The term appears to have been coined during the many years work leading to the adoption of the Convention, and derives from the French expression *"droits voisins du droit d'auteur"*. In 1956, already, a study group of the Berne Union considered the question and concluded:

> "Although most participants felt that '"neighbouring rights"' was probably not an entirely correct term, no agreement was possible on any other term. It was therefore decided that the term '"neighbouring rights"' which, because of its long use has the advantage of having become a generally known expression may, at least for the time being, be retained in the form of '"so-called neighbouring rights"'.[195]

The expression is inappropriate as regards the rights granted in the United Kingdom and other common law countries. Such rights are generally a property right, which may vest in individuals or in a legal entity, and are described as copyright. For example, in such countries the rights of producers of phonograms and broadcasters are invariably described as copyrights. However, in civil law countries it serves the purpose of defining rights, such as those of the beneficiaries of the Rome Convention, which have a close connection with authors' rights, but relate to works, productions and other subject-matter which are considered

---

[192] The effective date for the UK was September 27, 1957, and, as regards the 1971 Convention, it was July 10, 1974.

[193] The Final Act of the Conference and the Convention were signed by the following States: Argentina, Austria, Belgium, Brazil, Cambodia, Chile, Denmark, France, Federal Republic of Germany, the Holy See, Iceland, India, Italy, Mexico, Spain, Sweden, UK and Yugoslavia. See *Records of the Diplomatic Conference on the International Protection of Performers, Producers of Phonograms and Broadcasting Organisations*, ILO, UNESCO, BIRPI, 1968. For text of the Convention, see Vol.2 F5.

[194] Rome Convention art.32(1) and (5).

[195] Report of the Study Group on so-called "neighbouring rights" (intermediate intellectual rights), Paris, May 1956, para.I.

not to qualify for authors' rights because such rights are linked to the personality of the creator, and thus may only be granted to a natural person.

Related rights. In recent years, there has been a growing consensus that the term   **23–90**
"related rights" is to be preferred. This is the term used by the Commission of the European Union to describe the rights of the beneficiaries of the Rome Convention and it is the term used throughout this book.

Preparation of the Convention. The Rome Convention was the result of many   **23–91**
years of discussion and preparation, the work of several inter-governmental committees and the involvement of the three inter-governmental organisations mentioned above, the ILO, UNESCO and BIRPI.[196] The ILO had first become involved with the problems faced by performers as a result of technological change in the 1920s. Traditionally, a performance had been ephemeral, perishing "in the very instant of its production".[197] With the development of recording techniques, cinema, radio and television, performances could be recorded in permanent form and the performances repeated and distributed by broadcast and gramophone records to a wider audience. The performers claimed that these developments deprived them of employment opportunities as their physical presence and live performances could be and were being replaced by the exploitation of their recorded performances. The subject of performers' rights was considered at the Berne Convention Revision Conference, which took place at Rome in 1928. That Conference considered that an international convention on the subject was premature, but called on governments to consider measures to protect performers. The subject of protecting sound recordings under the Berne Convention was first advocated by the United Kingdom at the Berlin Revision Conference of 1908, and at each such Conference thereafter, in 1928 at Rome and 1948 at Brussels. For their part, representatives of producers and broadcasters, both of whom sought protection for their productions against unauthorised use, continued to press for international action. A meeting of experts was convened in Samadan, Switzerland in 1939 by the Secretariat of the Berne Union and the International Institute for the Unification of Private Law. Two draft treaties resulted, one for the protection of performers and producers of phonograms and the second for broadcasting organisations. After the Second World War, the issues were raised again at the Berne Convention Revision Conference held in Brussels in 1948, which adopted a series of separate *voeux* (resolutions) calling on governments to consider means for providing protection for performers, producers of phonograms and broadcasting organisations, in each case without prejudice to the rights of authors.[198] At that stage, the issues were still seen as separate problems:

"The Convention was based from the outset on social objectives. The origins

---

[196] For a detailed review of the history of the Convention, see C. Masouyé, *Guide to the Rome Convention and to the Phonograms Convention* (WIPO, Geneva, 1981), pp.7 et seq. (hereafter "WIPO RC and PC Guide"); see also C. Masouyé, "Performers' Rights in the Rome Convention", XXXXVI RIDA (1965) 162; Stewart, *International Copyright and Neighbouring Rights* (Butterworths, London, 1983) Ch.8, and S. Ricketson, *The Berne Convention for the protection of literary and artistic works: 1886–1896* (Queen Mary College, University of London, 1987), paras 15.45 et seq., and H.H. von Rauscher auf Weeg, "The Rome Convention Rights: a Comparative Review of Legislation and International Developments over Twelve Years" [1974] *Bulletin of the Copyright Society of the USA* 237.

[197] per Adam Smith, *The Wealth of Nations*, quoted by E. Thompson in: "Twenty Years of the Rome Convention: Some Personal Reflections" [1981] *Copyright* 270 at 274.

[198] *Voeux VI (Protection des fabricants des phonogrammes), VII (Protection des radioémissions) and VIII (Droits voisins du droit d'auteur et notamment protection des artistes exécutants): Documents de la Conférence réunie à Bruxelles du 5 au 26 juin 1948, Bureau de l'Union Internationale pour la protection des oeuvres littéraires et artistiques* (Berne, 1951), p.428. For Resolutions concerning the protection of performers, phonograms and broadcasts between 1927 and 1935, see pp.455 et seq. and 477 et seq.; for Resolutions on the subject adopted between 1936 and 1948, see pp.493, 505 and 509.

of the Convention in the 1920s and 1930s were based on a need recognised, not only by performers but also by certain governments, to protect performers' rights in the light of the increased use of recording devices. The decision to protect all three beneficiaries in a single Convention was taken many years later".[199]

Following a series of conferences during the 1950s, which produced various drafts of a convention,[200] in 1960, a committee of experts convened jointly by the ILO, UNESCO and BIRPI, met at the Hague and drew up a draft convention (the Hague draft), which brought together provisions for the protection of the three future beneficiaries of the Rome Convention in one instrument and served as a basis for the work of the Diplomatic Conference in Rome the following year.

23–92　**A pioneer Convention.** The Rome Convention has often been referred to as a pioneer Convention in that, at the time of its adoption, it was not a Convention that merely reflected existing national legislation but it broke new ground and there were very few countries whose legislation was compatible with it. In this sense, it was ahead of its time and set minimum standards of protection for the three beneficiaries which governments were obliged to incorporate in their national legislation before they could adhere to it.[201] Its pioneer character, however, had the necessary corollary that, to obtain a consensus, the level of protection provided for was low.

23–93　**Reasons for slow growth of membership.** The Rome Convention, after its difficult birth, remained controversial. It was, and still is to some extent, opposed by organisations representing the authors and broadcasting organisations. The former opposed the granting of exclusive rights to other categories of right owners both for reasons of principle and on practical grounds. The authors have argued that the beneficiaries are not truly creative and that they should not therefore benefit from the same kind of protection as authors do. It has also been suggested that performance rights in sound recordings compete with and diminish the value of authors' performance rights.[202] The broadcasters have taken the view that the rights they enjoy under the Rome Convention are of no great benefit and have been opposed to certain of the rights of the other beneficiaries provided for in the Convention, in particular, those of performers and the concept of the payment of equitable remuneration to performers and producers for the broadcasting of sound recordings.[203]

As a result, the membership of the Convention grew slowly. Fifteen years after its adoption, in 1976, it had only 17 Member States. However, in the 1970s the

---

[199] "Recommendations Concerning the Protection of Performers, Producers of Phonograms and Broadcasting Organisations", adopted in February 1979 by a Sub-committee of the Intergovernmental Committee of the Rome Convention, [1979] *Copyright* 105.

[200] Draft Conventions adopted by Committees of Experts of the ILO in 1951, [1951] *Le Droit d'Auteur*, 137 and 1956, [1956] *Le Droit d'Auteur* 93; draft prepared by a Committee of Governmental experts convened by UNESCO and the Secretariat of the Berne Union, [1957] *Le Droit d'Auteur* 72 and Supplement April 1957.

[201] The Rome Convention art.26.

[202] This assertion has been rejected by the Intergovernmental Committee of the Rome Convention following a study of the matter: "It is therefore clear that there is no evidence to support the proposition that authors' revenue has decreased as a result of neighbouring rights ... In addition, the Sub-committee believes that a possible adverse effect on authors' royalties would not in any event constitute a sufficient reason for opposing the rights provided for in the Rome Convention since justice demands that performers and producers of phonograms should enjoy secondary rights in phonograms". Recommendations Concerning the Protection of Performers, Producers of Phonograms and Broadcasting Organisations, para.28, fn.199, above.

[203] cf. J.F. da Costa, "Some Reflexions on the Rome Convention", [1976] *Copyright* 80; G. Davies, "The Rome Convention 1961—A Brief Summary of its Development and Prospects", [1979] E.I.P.R. 154; E. Thompson, "Twenty years of the Rome Convention: Some Personal Reflections" [1981] *Copyright* 270, fn.197, above.

Intergovernmental Committee of the Rome Convention acted as a catalyst for the promotion of the Convention by undertaking a series of initiatives with a view to promoting adherence to the Convention. In 1974, a model law for the implementation of the Rome Convention in national legislation was agreed by the Intergovernmental Committee[204] and endorsed by the representative organisations of the three beneficiaries of the Convention, who pledged themselves to support any legislation which might be introduced in the future based on the provisions of the model law. The European Broadcasting Union formally withdrew its opposition to the Convention, in general terms, but maintained its opposition to the provisions thereof relating to performance rights in sound recordings. Subsequently, in 1979, following an enquiry into the practical implementation of the Convention undertaken by its Intergovernmental Committee between 1975 and 1978, a series of conclusions and recommendations were adopted with the aim of promoting wider acceptance of the Convention and of providing guidance to States as to how the Convention may be applied in practice.[205]

The work undertaken to promote the Convention in the 1970s bore fruit. By its twentieth anniversary in October 1981, its membership had grown to 32 and, as of August 31, 2010, the Convention had 91 Member States.

Present relevance of the Convention. Although the possibility of revision of the   **23–94**
Convention is foreseen,[206] no revision has taken place in spite of the fact that technical developments have greatly reduced the value of its protection to the three beneficiaries. The main reason for a reluctance to revise the Convention in the past was the fear that the compromise it represented between conflicting interests would be reopened and that the balance achieved therein between those interests risked being upset in any revision. However this may be, the Rome Convention is now outdated in many respects. The extent of the protection provided for in the Convention and the balance of interests among the three beneficiaries reflected in the Convention were determined in the light of the technology existing and foreseen in 1961. "… Technological development in the past two decades in the areas of concern to the beneficiaries has occurred at an unprecedented pace and has introduced new techniques (especially satellites, cable television, videograms) none of which could have been foreseen at the time of the drafting of the Convention".[207] Three further decades have passed since the Intergovernmental Committee of the Rome Convention made that statement in 1979 and the proliferation of new technologies affecting the rights of the three beneficiaries of the Rome Convention have grown exponentially. Some of these problems were addressed in the context of the WIPO Performances and Phonograms Treaty 1996, discussed below in s.7 of this Chapter. However, that instrument did not cover either the protection of audiovisual performances or the protection of broadcasting organisations, the third beneficiary of the Rome Convention. Efforts to adopt new instruments on these topics have been the subject of more recent, but so far unsuccessful negotiations (see paras 23–135 and 23–175, below).

---

[204] Model Law Concerning the Protection of Performers, Producers of Phonograms and Broadcasting Organisations, published by ILO, UNESCO and WIPO in 1974; for text see [1974] *Copyright* 163.

[205] Recommendations, Concerning the Protection of Performers, Producers of Phonograms and Broadcasting Organisations, cf. fn.199, above.

[206] Rome Convention art.32(1)(b).

[207] cf. Recommendations Concerning the Protection of Performers, Producers of Phonograms and Broadcasting Organisations, cf. fn.199, above.

B. SUBSTANTIVE PROVISIONS

23–95   **Definition of the beneficiaries of the Rome Convention.** As mentioned above, the Convention deals with the rights of three beneficiaries: performers, producers of phonograms and broadcasting organisations.

Performers are defined as: "actors, singers, musicians, dancers, and other persons who act, sing, deliver, declaim, play in, or otherwise perform literary or artistic works".[208] The limitation to artists who perform literary and artistic works results in the exclusion of variety and circus artists but the Convention specifically provides that a state may extend protection to such artists.[209]

The term *producer of phonograms* requires explanation. A phonogram, in plain terms, is an original sound recording. Traditionally, phonograms have been reproduced and made available to the public in physical formats, e.g. LPs, CDs, minidiscs, cassettes or other media. Today, sound recordings are made available to the public also in digital form and are not embodied in any physical carrier; thus, they can be accessed over the internet. The traditional markets for them have been transformed by the technical developments of the past twenty years. The Convention defines a phonogram as follows: "'phonogram' means any exclusively aural fixation of sounds of a performance or of other sounds".[210] This means mainly recordings of performances of music or the spoken word but also covers recordings of other sounds such as bird song, wildlife sounds and sound effects. The "producer of phonograms" means "the person who, or the legal entity which, first fixes the sounds of a performance or other sounds".[211] In practice, this is usually a record company although there are also many independent producers who produce original recordings and then sell or license them to record companies.

Broadcasting organisations needs no explanation but the definition of broadcasting has given rise to some difficulty. It is defined in the Convention as meaning "the transmission by wireless means for public reception of sound or of images and sounds".[212] Technical developments since 1961 have rendered the definition restrictive in that, for example, cable distribution of broadcasts is excluded. It has also been argued that transmission of broadcast programmes by satellite is not covered,[213] although a majority of the members of the Intergovernmental Committee of the Rome Convention has expressed the view that the definition of the Convention does include satellite transmissions.[214]

23–96   **National treatment.** The protection given by the Convention is based on the principle of national treatment, which means the treatment accorded by the domestic law of the Contracting State in which protection is claimed. Thus, each

---

[208] Rome Convention art.3(a).

[209] art.9.

[210] art.3(b).

[211] art.3(c).

[212] art.3(f).

[213] According to the European Broadcasting Union: " Article 13 does not protect broadcasters against distribution by cable, and this is so serious a deficiency that, in Europe, at least, the broadcasting organisations have had to seek a remedy from the Council of Europe under the aegis of which an intergovernmental agreement [European Agreement on the Protection of Television Broadcasts, see para.23–182, below] has come into existence whose main object is to protect television broadcasts against cable distribution. Nor is the Rome Convention applicable to the transport of programmes by satellite, and a separate convention concluded in 1974 was needed to shore up this gap in protection" [Convention Relating to the Distribution of Programme-Carrying Signals Transmitted by Satellite, see paras 23–156 et seq., below]. (See "EBU Observations on the Implementation of the Rome Convention", Annex II of doc. ILO/UNESCO/WIPO/ICR/SC.1/IMP/2, 1979.)

[214] See Report of the Fourth Ordinary Session of the Intergovernmental Committee of the Rome Convention, [1974] *Copyright* 41, paras 19 et seq.

Contracting State extends the same protection to beneficiaries from other Contracting States as it does to its own nationals.[215] National treatment is that accorded by the Contracting State (i) to performers who are its nationals, as regards performances taking place, broadcast, or first fixed on its territory; to producers of phonograms who are its nationals, as regards phonograms first fixed or first published on its territory; to broadcasting organisations which have their headquarters on its territory, as regards broadcasts transmitted from transmitters situated on its territory. Contracting States shall grant national treatment to performers if any of the following conditions are met: the performance takes place in another Contracting State; the performance is incorporated in a phonogram which is protected under the Convention; the performance, not being fixed on a phonogram, is carried by a broadcast protected by the Convention.[216] The points of attachment for the protection of producers of phonograms are the following: the producer is a national of another Contracting State (criterion of nationality); the first fixation of the sound was made in another Contracting State (criterion of fixation)[217]; the phonogram was first published in another Contracting State (criterion of publication).[218] The criterion of publication includes simultaneous publication in a Contracting State within 30 days of first publication.[219] The points of attachment for national treatment for broadcasters are either that the headquarters of the broadcasting organisation is situated in another Contracting State or that the broadcast was transmitted from a transmitter situated in another Contracting State.[220]

The general rule of national treatment may be modified, however, by principles of reciprocity with regard to the performance rights in phonograms provided for under art.12, since according to art.16 of the Convention States are permitted to make various reservations concerning these rights and the rights of broadcasters under art.13 with respect to the performance in public of their television broadcasts, and these reservations include limiting protection by insisting on material reciprocity. This also applies to the duration of art.12 rights.[221]

Performers' rights. The principal protection provided for performers in the Convention is contained in art.7, which gives performers the possibility of preventing certain acts done without their consent: for example, the broadcasting and communication to the public of their live performance; the fixation of their unfixed performance; the reproduction of a fixation of their performance, subject to certain conditions. However, once a performer has consented to the incorporation of his performance in a visual or audiovisual fixation, art.7 has no further application.[222] These rights are not exclusive rights to authorise or prohibit the acts in question. The protection is defined as giving performers "the possibility of preventing" the acts in question; this means that Member States are free to protect performers not only by means of specific rights, but also by the application of the   **23–97**

---

[215] Rome Convention art.2.

[216] art.4.

[217] art.17 provides that any state that, on the date of the adoption of the Convention on October 26, 1961, granted protection to producers of phonograms solely on the basis of the criterion of fixation may declare that it will apply the criterion of fixation alone.

[218] art.5.

[219] art.5(2). However, a Contracting State may declare that it will not apply the criterion of publication or, alternatively, the criterion of fixation (art.5(3)).

[220] art.6. However, a Contracting State may declare that it will protect broadcasters only if the headquarters of the broadcasting organisation is situated in another Contracting State and the broadcast was transmitted from a transmitter situated in the same Contracting State (art.6(2)).

[221] Art.16(1)(a)(iv) and (b). The reservations made by the Contracting States to the Rome Convention are listed in note 8 to the General Table of Copyright and Related Rights Conventions in Ch.25, below.

[222] Rome Convention art.19.

laws of unfair competition or the imposition of criminal sanctions. Indeed, prior to the 1988 Act, the United Kingdom protected performers by means of criminal sanctions.[223]

23–98   **Rights of producers of phonograms.** The exclusive rights of producers of phonograms are dealt with in art.10, which gives them the right to authorise or prohibit the direct or indirect reproduction of their phonograms. This is the right that enables producers to combat piracy, counterfeiting and the like.

23–99   **Performance rights in phonograms.** Article 12 provides for performance rights in phonograms and concerns both performers and producers of phonograms. Article 12 provides a right to a single equitable remuneration in favour of producers of phonograms, or performers, or both, if a phonogram published for commercial purposes, or a reproduction of such phonogram, is used directly for broadcasting or for any communication to the public. This applies therefore to the secondary use of phonograms both for public performances (such as at cafés, hotels, theatres, in juke boxes and other public places) and in broadcasting, by sound or television services. States are free to reserve art.12 altogether or in respect of certain uses[224] or to give the right to producers alone, to performers alone, or to give the right to one with the obligation to share the single remuneration with the other or to both with the obligation to share the remuneration equally. States, therefore, have a great deal of freedom as to how they apply art.12. It should also be noted that unlike the performance rights of authors under the copyright conventions, art.12 does not give performers and producers of phonograms the right to authorise or prohibit the communication to the public or the broadcasting of their phonograms, but gives a mere right to receive equitable remuneration. This differs from the position in the United Kingdom where, since 1934, the producers' right to authorise or prohibit such use has been recognised.[225]

23–100   **Exclusive rights of broadcasting organisations.** Article 13 deals with the rights of broadcasting organisations which are granted the right to authorise or prohibit: the rebroadcasting of their broadcasts; the fixation of their broadcasts; the reproduction of fixations of their broadcasts made without their consent; the reproduction of ephemeral fixations of their broadcasts, made in accordance with art.15, if the reproduction is made for purposes different from those referred to in that article;[226] and the communication to the public of their television broadcasts, if such communication is made in places accessible to the public against payment of an entrance fee. It is a matter for the domestic law of the State where protection of this right is claimed to determine the conditions under which it may be exercised.[227]

---

[223] See Ch.12, above.

[224] art.16(1)(a)(i) and (ii). As regards art.12, the following reservations are also permitted: as regards phonograms the producer of which is not a national of another Contracting State, the article will not apply; as regards phonograms the producer of which is a national of another Contracting State, it will limit the protection provided for by that article to the extent to which and, and to the term for which, the latter State grants protection to phonograms first fixed by a national of the State making the declaration; however, the fact that the Contracting State of which the producer is a national does not grant the protection to the same beneficiary or beneficiaries as the State making the declaration shall not be considered as a difference in the extent of the protection (arts 16(1)(a)(iii) and (iv)).

[225] See Ch.3, above.

[226] Rome Convention art.13 (a), (b) and (c).

[227] Rome Convention art.13(d). However, a Contracting State may make a reservation as regards art.13(d) to the effect it will not apply that article (art.16((1)(b)).

Duration. The minimum term of protection provided for by the Convention[228] is 20 years computed from the end of the year in which:

    (a) the fixation was made, for phonograms and performances incorporated therein;

    (b) the performance took place, for performances not incorporated in phonograms;

    (c) the broadcast took place, for broadcasts.

23–101

Common provisions. Certain exceptions to the protection granted by the Convention are permitted as regards private use; use of short excerpts in connection with the reporting of current events; ephemeral fixations made by broadcasting organisations, by means of their own facilities and for their own broadcasts; use solely for the purposes of teaching or scientific research. Moreover, a Contracting State may provide for the same kinds of limitations with regard to the beneficiaries of the Convention as are permitted in connection with copyright in literary or artistic works.[229]

23–102

Formalities. Where Contracting States require compliance with formalities as a condition of protection in relation to phonograms, these shall be considered as fulfilled if all authorised duplicates of the phonogram or their containers bear a notice consisting of the symbol Ⓟ, accompanied by the year date of the first publication. The container or notice must also identify the producer, his successor in title or his exclusive licensee.[230]

23–103

No retroactivity. The Convention has no retroactive effect; rights acquired before the date it comes into force for any state are not prejudiced and no state is obliged to apply its provisions before that date.[231]

23–104

C. Relationship with the Berne Convention

Safeguard for authors' rights. The relationship of the Rome Convention with that of Berne is dealt with in art.1 of the Convention which contains a safeguard for copyright proper, providing that the:

> "Protection granted under this Convention shall leave intact and shall in no way affect the protection of copyright in literary and artistic works. Consequently, no provision of this Convention may be interpreted as prejudicing such protection".

23–105

This is a key provision of the Rome Convention. Throughout the long negotiations leading to the adoption of the Convention, the authors' societies had:

> "looked with some fear and suspicion on the proposals to protect the neighbouring rights. They claimed that a convention on this subject was useless or at least superfluous; most problems could be dealt with by contract; and in any case it was premature since the function of international treaties was to follow, and not to precede, national legislation, and, on this subject, few countries had passed laws. This being so, these bodies were determined to maintain the integrity of copyright, fearing the impact the creation of these new rights would have on the rights authors already enjoyed".[232]

Two examples of the kind of situation which the authors had in mind and in which conflict may arise will illustrate the problem. The first is where, as a result

---

[228] Rome Convention art.14.
[229] Rome Convention art.15.
[230] Rome Convention art.11.
[231] Rome Convention art.20.
[232] WIPO RC and PC Guide, para.1.4.

of the beneficiaries of the Rome Convention having rights, more than one authorisation becomes necessary for the use of a work, for example, where both the author of a work and the producer of a phonogram incorporating the work have the right to authorise a use such as broadcasting or rental. It has been argued that, if the author wishes to authorise the use but the producer refuses, this "affects" the rights of the author because the exercise of the right is prevented. Secondly, users may require two licences in respect of performance rights, one from the authors' society and one from the society representing producers and/or performers; here the authors feared that their income from this source would therefore be diminished.

Thus, art.1 was introduced as a preliminary provision to make it clear that the legal situation of the copyright owner is unaffected by the rights of the beneficiaries of the Rome Convention. However, the possible effects of the Convention on the economic interests of authors is another matter.[233] Article 1 does not mean that the rights of the beneficiaries of the Rome Convention must be subordinated to the exercise of the rights of authors. As Masouyé stated:

> "It does not proclaim [copyright's] superiority by laying down that neighbouring rights may never be stronger in content or scope than those enjoyed by authors ... Whenever, by virtue of the copyright law, the authorization of the author is necessary for the reproduction or other use of his work, the need for this authorisation is not affected by the Convention. Conversely, when, by virtue of this Convention, the consent of the performer, recorder or broadcaster is necessary, the need for his consent does not disappear because authorisation by the author is also necessary".[234]

It is clear that this does not altogether solve the authors' problem, since the *existence* of other rights may have an impact on the *exercise* of their rights. It would hardly be equitable, however, if they had won the argument on this point and succeeded in preventing the present beneficiaries of the Rome Convention from obtaining any protection.

23–106 **Closed Convention.** A further safeguard for authors is built into the Rome Convention. Only states which are members of either the Berne Convention or of the Universal Copyright Convention may adhere to it; it is thus a so-called closed convention, the aim of the relevant provisions being to ensure that no state will protect the beneficiaries of the Rome Convention without already having in place legislation for the protection of authors.[235] Thus so-called neighbouring rights may not be given precedence over copyright.

D. Parties to the Rome Convention

23–107 **States which may adhere to the Convention.** The Convention is open to adherence by any state member of the United Nations, which is also a member of the Berne Convention or the Universal Copyright Convention. It entered into force three months after the date of deposit of the sixth instrument of ratification, acceptance or accession on May 18, 1964.

23–108 **Present membership.** As of August 31, 2010, the following 91 States were party to the Convention: Albania, Algeria, Andorra, Argentina, Armenia, Australia, Austria, Azerbaijan, Bahrain, Barbados, Belarus, Belgium, Bolivia, Bosnia and Herzegovina, Brazil, Bulgaria, Burkina Faso, Canada, Cape Verde, Chile, Colombia, Congo, Costa Rica, Croatia, Cyprus, Czech Republic, Denmark, Do-

---

[233] Records of the Rome Conference, p.38; WIPO RC and PC Guide, para.1.5.

[234] WIPO RC and PC Guide, paras 1.10 and 1.12. See also Records of the Rome Conference, p.38.

[235] Rome Convention art.23 (on signature and deposit) and art.24 (on ratification and accession).

minica, Dominican Republic, Ecuador, El Salvador, Estonia, Fiji, Finland, France, Georgia, Germany, Greece, Guatemala, Honduras, Hungary, Iceland, Ireland, Israel, Italy, Jamaica, Japan, Kyrgyzstan (Kyrgyz Republic), Latvia, Lebanon, Lesotho, Liechtenstein, Lithuania, Luxembourg, Mexico, Monaco, Montenegro, Netherlands (for the Kingdom in Europe), Nicaragua, Niger, Nigeria, Norway, Panama, Paraguay, Peru, Philippines, Poland, Portugal, Republic of Korea, Republic of Moldova, Romania, Russian Federation, Saint Lucia, Serbia (Republic of), Slovakia (Slovak Republic), Slovenia, Spain, Sweden, Switzerland, Syrian Arab Republic, Tajikistan, the former Yugoslav Republic of Macedonia, Togo, Turkey, Ukraine, United Arab Emirates, United Kingdom, Uruguay, Venezuela (Bolivarian Republic of) and Viet Nam.

6. THE PHONOGRAMS CONVENTION

A. HISTORY

The Convention for the Protection of Producers of Phonograms Against Un- **23–109**
authorised Duplication of their Phonograms (the Phonograms Convention) was adopted on October 29, 1971, in Geneva, at a Diplomatic Conference convened jointly by the United Nations Organisation for Education, Science and Culture (UNESCO) and the World Intellectual Property Organisation (WIPO).[236] The purpose of the Convention was limited and specific: to provide international protection against what had become during the late 1960s the widespread and increasing problem of piracy of phonograms.[237] Piracy may be defined as the manufacture of duplicates of legitimately produced phonograms without the authorisation of the original producer of the phonogram and the importation, distribution, or sale to the public of such unlawful duplicates for commercial gain.[238] It was generally recognised that piracy damages the interests not only of the producers of phonograms but also those of the authors and performers whose works and performances are incorporated in phonograms, since the pirate who copies phonograms pays nothing to the authors and composers whose music and lyrics are copied, nothing to the recording artists and musicians and, nothing, of course, to the producer of the legitimate recording. Better protection against piracy would, therefore, be in the long-term interests of all these categories of right owners.

---

[236] *Records of the International Conference of States on the Protection of Phonograms*, Geneva, October 18 to 29, 1971, UNESCO, WIPO, 1975. See also A.L. Kaminstein, "Convention for the Protection of Producers of Phonograms Against Unauthorised Duplication of their Phonograms" 19 *Bulletin of the Copyright Society of the USA* [1972] 175; E. Ulmer, "The Convention for the Protection of Producers of Phonograms Against Unauthorised Duplication of their Phonograms" [1972] 3 I.I.C. 317; S. Ricketson, *The Berne Convention for the protection of literary and artistic works: 1886–1896* (Queen Mary College, University of London, 1987), paras 15.55 et seq.; Stewart, *International Copyright and Neighbouring Rights*, (London: Butterworths, 1983), Ch.9.

[237] Film and video piracy was excluded from the outset. Cinematographic works are protected under the Berne and Universal Copyright Conventions and governments took the view that authors of such works, including film producers as copyright owners or successors in title to the authors of such works, were adequately protected against piracy under national legislation and the copyright conventions.

[238] Two different kinds of piracy of phonograms should be distinguished: "Piracy"— *stricto sensu*—is the unauthorised duplication of an original phonogram distributed to the public with labels, artwork, trade marks and packaging different from, although often similar to, those of the original legitimate phonogram; the legitimate producer's trade mark is not used. "Counterfeiting" is the unauthorised duplication and distribution of an original phonogram and its packaging as a whole. The legitimate producer's original label, artwork, trade marks and packaging are copied as well as the sounds contained in the original legitimate recording. A third illegal activity is also described as piracy, namely "bootlegging", which means the unauthorised recording of an artist's performance. Bootlegging is not covered by the Phonograms Convention. cf. G. Davies, *Piracy of Phonograms* 2nd edn (Oxford: ESC Publishing Ltd, 1986) pp.4 et seq., and generally.

23–110   **The need for the Convention.** International action to combat piracy was first called for at a meeting of experts, which had gathered in 1970 to prepare for the revision of the Berne and Universal Copyright Conventions, due to take place the following year. In view of the urgency of the piracy problem, a committee of governmental experts convened by UNESCO and WIPO met in March 1971 and prepared a draft convention, which served as the basis for the Diplomatic Conference held later that same year. The speed with which agreement was reached on this international instrument was unprecedented, reflecting the serious nature of the problem. While authors and composers had legal protection against piracy of their works incorporated in phonograms under national laws and the Berne and Universal Copyright Conventions, Governments recognised that the existing international conventions did not provide those most affected, the producers of phonograms themselves, with adequate legal tools to deal with the widespread piracy which was destroying their markets. The Rome Convention provided producers of phonograms with the right to authorise or prohibit the direct or indirect reproduction of their phonograms, but did not provide any protection in respect of importation or distribution of unauthorised copies, unless these acts were linked with the act of reproduction itself. Moreover, the Rome Convention was open only to Member States of the Berne and Universal Copyright Conventions and had a very limited membership at the time, only 11 Member States in 1971, whereas piracy was and remains an international problem requiring the co-operation of as many countries as possible worldwide.

Furthermore, national legislation protecting phonograms varied greatly. Some countries protected them by means of specific rights: copyright or related rights; others protected them under the law of unfair competition or by means of penal sanctions. International protection was afforded in common law countries under the Berne and Universal Copyright Conventions on the basis of national treatment under these conventions, while elsewhere the only international protection available to producers was afforded by the Rome Convention. The proponents of the Phonograms Convention, therefore, sought an urgent solution by means of a new, simple international instrument, which as many countries as possible would be able to join. Such an instrument with a broad membership would create "a kind of *cordon sanitaire*... by providing that in case of an unauthorised duplication the importation and distribution in the Contracting States can also be prohibited".[239]

B. Substantive Provisions

23–111   **Obligations of Member States.** The heart of the Convention is art.2 which establishes the obligations of Member States as to whom they must protect and against what:

> "Each Contracting State shall protect producers of phonograms who are nationals of other Contracting States against the making of duplicates without the consent of the producer and against the importation of such duplicates, provided that any such making or importation is for the purpose of distribution to the public, and against the distribution of such duplicates to the public".

The terms "producers of phonograms" and "phonograms" are defined in the

---

[239] E. Ulmer, "The Convention for the Protection of Producers of Phonograms Against Unauthorised Duplication of their Phonograms" [1972] 3.I.I.C., 317, para.4.

same way as in the Rome Convention,[240] and the only criterion for protection is the producers' nationality. Unlike the Rome Convention, the Phonograms Convention is not based on national treatment. Contracting States are obliged to provide the required protection to nationals of other Contracting States regardless of their domestic law. This obligation may have the result that foreign repertoire from another Contracting State of the Phonograms Convention enjoys a higher standard of protection than national repertoire. The means by which the Phonograms Convention is to be implemented is left by its art.3 to the domestic law of each Contracting State and shall include one or more of the following: protection by means of the grant of a copyright or other specific right, which secure an exclusive right to the producer; protection by means of the law relating to unfair competition; protection by penal sanctions. The term "other specific right" refers to rights in the nature of copyright or authors' rights but known as "neighbouring" or "related" rights. Unfair competition is defined in the Paris Convention for the Protection of Industrial Property as meaning "any act of competition contrary to honest practices in industrial or commercial matters".[241] As far as penal sanctions are concerned, any state choosing this method of protection must make it a criminal offence to do any of the acts referred to in art.2 punishable by fines and imprisonment.

Duration of the protection. Like in the Rome Convention, the minimum term of protection under the Convention is 20 years. This may be computed either from the end of the year of first fixation, as in the Rome Convention, or of the year in which the phonogram was first published.[242] However, the 20-year minimum only applies if the national law prescribes a specific term. Thus, the Convention recognised the fact that under the law of unfair competition, for example, protection may not be limited in time. The Convention does not provide for material reciprocity with regard to term.   **23–112**

Formalities and exceptions. Where Contracting States require compliance with formalities as a condition of protection in relation to phonograms, as in the Rome Convention, these shall be considered as fulfilled if all authorised duplicates of the phonogram or their containers bear a notice consisting of the symbol P in a circle; similar to ©, accompanied by the year date of first publication. The container or notice must also identify the producer, his successor in title or his exclusive licensee.[243] The Convention also provides that Contracting States may make the same kinds of limitations as are permitted with respect to the protection of authors of literary and artistic works. However, no compulsory licences are allowed, except in the following circumstances: the duplication is for use solely for the purpose of teaching or scientific research; the licence is valid only within the territory of the Contracting State whose competent authority has granted the licence and shall not extend to the export of duplicates; and finally any such licence must give rise to equitable remuneration.[244]   **23–113**

No retroactivity. Like the Rome Convention, there is no obligation to afford the protection of the Convention retroactively to phonograms fixed before the   **23–114**

---

[240] Phonograms Convention art.1, Rome Convention art.3. For the text of the Convention, see Vol.2 F8.
[241] Paris Convention art.10 *bis*.
[242] Phonograms Convention art.4.
[243] Phonograms Convention art.5.
[244] Phonograms Convention art.6.

Convention entered into force with respect to them, although Contracting States are free to do so, if they so wish.[245]

C. RELATIONSHIP WITH THE COPYRIGHT CONVENTIONS AND THE ROME CONVENTION

23–115   **Safeguard for copyright and related rights.** The Convention contains a clause for the safeguard of copyright and related rights, providing that the Convention shall in no way be interpreted to limit or prejudice the protection otherwise secured to authors, to performers, to producers of phonograms or to broadcasting organisations under any domestic law or international agreement.[246] The relevant international agreements are the Berne Convention, the Universal Copyright Convention, the Rome Convention and the Paris Convention. A further link with these agreements is provided by the fact that WIPO provides the administration for all services relating to the Convention and its Secretariat.[247]

23–116   **Relationship to the Rome Convention.** The reasons why it was considered necessary to adopt a special Convention to deal with piracy have been noted in para.23–110, above. The Convention is not a special agreement concluded under art.22 of the Rome Convention; such a special agreement would have been limited to the existing Member States of the Rome Convention and, as seen above, the Phonograms Convention was intended to be open to adherence by as many states as possible. The Convention may be seen, therefore, as complementary to that of Rome. It contains no provision which is contrary thereto. So far as states which are party to both Conventions are concerned, the relations between them will be governed by both Conventions. Article 21 of Rome provides that the protection provided by that Convention shall not prejudice any protection otherwise secured to performers, producers of phonograms and broadcasting organisations. This being so, countries party to both conventions must each accord the other the benefits of both cumulatively, applying whichever gives the greater protection.[248] There is also a safeguard clause for performers, confirming that Contracting States are free to legislate as they see fit for the protection of performers whose performances are recorded on phonograms.[249]

D. PARTIES TO THE PHONOGRAMS CONVENTION

23–117   **States which may adhere to the Convention.** Unlike the Rome Convention whose membership is limited to states members of one or other of the two copyright conventions, and in order to secure the greatest possible number of Contracting States so as to put an end to international piracy, the Convention is open to adherence by any state member of the United Nations, or of any of its Specialised Agencies, or of the International Atomic Energy Agency, or any state party to the Statute of the International Court of Justice. Any state joining the Convention must be in a position to give effect to its obligations under the Convention in accordance with its domestic law.[250]

23–118   **Entry into force and membership.** The Convention came into force following the deposit of the fifth instrument of ratification or accession on April 18, 1973.

---

[245] Phonograms Convention art.7(3).
[246] Phonograms Convention art.7(1).
[247] Phonograms Convention art.8.
[248] cf. *WIPO RC and PC Guide*, para.7.5.
[249] Phonograms Convention art.7(2).
[250] Phonograms Convention art.9(4).

Membership of the Convention grew relatively quickly and, as of August 31, 2010, the following 77 States were party to the Convention: Albania, Algeria, Argentina, Armenia, Australia, Austria, Azerbaijan, Barbados, Belarus, Bosnia and Herzegovina, Brazil, Bulgaria, Burkina Faso, Chile, China,[251] Colombia, Costa Rica, Croatia, Cyprus, Czech Republic, Democratic Republic of the Congo, Denmark, Ecuador, Egypt, El Salvador, Estonia, Fiji, Finland,[252] France, Germany, Greece, Guatemala, Holy See, Honduras, Hungary, India, Israel, Italy,[253] Jamaica, Japan, Kazakhstan, Kenya, Kyrgyzstan (Kyrgyz Republic), Latvia, Liberia, Liechtenstein, Lithuania, Luxembourg, Mexico, Monaco, Montenegro, Netherlands (for the Kingdom in Europe), New Zealand, Nicaragua, Norway, Panama, Paraguay, Peru, Republic of Korea, Republic of Moldova, Romania, Russian Federation, Saint Lucia, Serbia (Republic of), Slovakia (Slovak Republic), Slovenia, Spain, Sweden, Switzerland, the former Yugoslav Republic of Macedonia, Togo, Trinidad and Tobago, Ukraine, United Kingdom, United States of America, Ukraine, Uruguay, Venezuela (Bolivarian Republic of) and Viet Nam.

7. WIPO PERFORMANCES AND PHONOGRAMS TREATY 1996

A. History

Background. The advances in technology of recent years have revolutionised the media and the means of exploitation of works protected by copyright and the subject-matter of related rights. The events leading to the adoption of the new WIPO Treaties on Copyright and Performances and Phonograms have been described in s.3 of this Chapter. As there mentioned, in 1992, a separate Committee of Experts on a Possible Instrument for the Protection of the Rights of Performers and Producers of Phonograms was established to discuss all questions concerning the effective international protection of the rights of performers and producers of phonograms.[254] The first session of the Committee of Experts on the Possible Instrument was held in 1993[255] and altogether six sessions were held.[256] The WIPO Performances and Phonograms Treaty was adopted by the Diplomatic Conference on Certain Copyright and Neighbouring Rights Questions, held in Geneva in December 1996, which also adopted the WIPO Copyright Treaty.

    The question of the protection of producers of phonograms was removed from the terms of reference of the Committee of Experts on a Possible Protocol to the

23–119

---

[251] The Phonograms Convention applies also to the Hong Kong Special Administrative Region of China with effect from July 1, 1997 and to the Macao Special Administrative Region of China with effect from December 20, 1999.

[252] Finland has declared, in accordance with art.7(4) of the Convention, that it will apply the criterion according to which it affords protection to producers of phonograms solely on the basis of the place of first fixation instead of the criterion of the nationality of the producer.

[253] Italy has declared, in accordance with art.7(4) of the Convention, that it will apply the criterion according to which it affords protection to producers of phonograms solely on the basis of the place of first fixation instead of the criterion of the nationality of the producer.

[254] Terms of Reference of the Committee of Experts on a Possible Instrument on the Protection of the Rights of Performers and Producers of Phonograms, see "Questions Concerning a Possible Instrument for the Protection of the Rights of Performers and Producers of Phonograms", para.5 (WIPO Memorandum, [1993] *Copyright* 142).

[255] Report of the First Session, Geneva, June 28 to July 2, 1993, [1993] *Copyright* 196.

[256] November 1993, [1994] *Copyright* 44; December 1994, [1995] *Industrial Property and Copyright* 110; September 1995, [1995] *Industrial Property and Copyright* 425; February 1996, [1996] *Industrial Property and Copyright* 118; and May 1996, [1996] *Industrial Property and Copyright* 236.

Berne Convention because agreement could not be reached on including such rights in the Protocol. Civil law countries which protect producers of phonograms by means of related rights objected, in principle, to producers' rights being dealt with in the context of the Berne Convention. At the same time, there was agreement that it would not be appropriate to discuss questions related to the protection of producers of phonograms without also discussing the protection of performers, whose performances are embodied in phonograms.[257] Thus, the decision not to consider the rights of producers of phonograms and performers in the context of the Protocol to the Berne Convention was influenced by the international classification of the rights of producers and performers as related rights protected by the Rome Convention, rather than authors' rights or copyrights, protected by the Berne Convention.

The most important issues to be discussed in relation to the new instrument were the following: of specific interest to performers, moral rights, the economic rights of performers in their unfixed (live) performances; of interest to both categories of right owners were, rights of reproduction, modification, rights of distribution and importation, rights to make available phonograms and performances to the public for interactive and on-demand access systems, rental rights, rights to remuneration for broadcasting or communication to the public, term of protection and enforcement of rights. There was broad agreement that the level of protection provided for producers and performers under the Rome and Phonograms Conventions was in need of improvement to bring the protection into line with the realities of contemporary technology, which had created new means for creating, storing, performing and disseminating phonograms and performances. However, the question whether the rights of performers in respect of audiovisual fixations, i.e. in film, television broadcasts and video, should be covered by the new instrument was and remained controversial until the closing stages of the Diplomatic Conference in 1996; in the event, as a result of the sustained opposition of the film and broadcasting industries, the decision was made to confine the Treaty to performances fixed in phonograms.

23–120   **Relation to the WIPO Copyright Treaty.** The Performances and Phonograms Treaty parallels many of the provisions of the WIPO Copyright Treaty. The Preamble of the new Treaty reflects the concern to update and strengthen the protection of producers and performers by recognising the need to introduce new international rules to provide adequate solutions to the questions raised by economic, social, cultural and technological developments, and the profound impact of the development and convergence of information and communication technologies on the production and use of performances and phonograms.

As in the case of the WIPO Copyright Treaty, a series of agreed statements were adopted at the same time as the WIPO Performances and Phonograms Treaty concerning the interpretation of the various articles of the Treaty. The following analysis of the Treaty takes account of these statements.[258]

---

[257] WIPO memorandum, [1993] *Copyright* 142.

[258] See J. Reinbothe and S. von Lewinski, *The WIPO Treaties 1996* (London: Butterworths/ LexisNexis, 2002), M. Ficsor, *The Law of Copyright and the Internet: the 1966 WIPO Treaties, their interpretation and implementation,* (Oxford: Oxford University Press, 2002); see also the following accounts of the results of the Diplomatic Conference: "WIPO Diplomatic Conference on Certain Copyright and Neighbouring Rights Questions" [1997] *Copyright* 97; J. Reinbothe, M. Martin-Prat and S. von Lewinski, "The New WIPO Treaties: A First Résumé" [1997] 4 E.I.P.R. 171; T.C. Vinje, "The New WIPO Copyright Treaty: A Happy Result in Geneva, [1997] 5 E.I.P.R. 230, M. Fabiani, "The Geneva Diplomatic Conference on Copyright and the Rights of Performers and Phonogram Producers" [1997] 3 Ent. L.R. 98; V. A. Espinel, "Harmony on the Internet: The WIPO Performances and Phonograms Treaty and United Kingdom Copyright Law"

B. Substantive Provisions

Definitions of the beneficiaries of the Convention and its subject-matter. The **23–121**
beneficiaries of protection under the Treaty are performers and producers of phonograms, as defined in the Treaty. These definitions differ from those of the Rome
Convention. That of performers is expanded to include those who perform expressions of folklore in addition to literary or artistic works. The new definition of
"producer of phonograms" does not appear to involve any substantive change.
The definition reads: "'Producer of a phonogram' means the person, or the legal
entity, who or which takes the initiative and has the responsibility for the first fixation of the sounds of a performance or other sounds, or the representations of
sounds". The words "or the representations of sounds" are new.

The definition of phonogram is also new. In the Rome and Phonograms
Conventions, "'phonogram' means any exclusively aural fixation of sounds of a
performance or of other sounds"; the words "exclusively aural" have been deleted
and the following words added at the end of the definition instead: "other than in
the form of a fixation incorporated in a cinematographic or other audiovisual
work". This is clarified by an agreed statement according to which this definition
"does not suggest that rights in the phonogram are in any way affected through
their incorporation into a cinematographic or other audiovisual work". Thus,
phonograms are protected independently and separately even where they are later
included as part of a film or other audiovisual work. As in the Rome Convention,
the term "performance" is not defined but may be assumed to mean any performance of expressions of folklore or of a literary or artistic work.

The performers and producers protected are nationals of the Contracting Parties, who would meet the criteria for eligibility for protection provided for by the
Rome Convention (see para.23–96, above). In relation to these criteria, which
include the criteria of nationality, fixation and publication, definitions are
provided of fixation[259] and publication. Fixation is not defined in either the Rome
or Phonograms Conventions. Here it is defined as "the embodiment of sounds, or
of the representations thereof, from which they can be perceived, reproduced or
communicated through a device"[260] and an agreed statement provides a further
explanation of the term: "it is understood that fixation means the finalisation of
the master tape ('*bande-mère*')".[261] Publication of a fixed performance or a phonogram means the offering of copies of the fixed performance or the phonogram
to the public, *with the consent of the right holder*, and provided that copies are offered to the public in reasonable quantity.[262] The words in italics are new as
compared to the definition of the Rome and Phonograms Conventions.

National treatment. Protection under the Treaty is based on the principle of **23–122**
national treatment, defined as meaning Contracting Parties shall accord to nationals of other Contracting Parties the treatment it accords to its own nationals with
regard to the exclusive rights specifically granted in the Treaty, subject to certain
permitted reservations concerning performance rights in phonograms.[263]

Performers' rights. Moral rights are recognised in favour of performers for the **23–123**
first time at international level, as regards a performer'live aural performances

---

[1998] Ent. L.R. 21. See also J. Reinbothe and S. von Lewinski, "The WIPO Treaties 1996:
Ready to Come into Force" [2002] E.I.P.R. 199.

[259] The possibility of applying only the criterion of fixation in accordance with art.17 of the Rome
Convention is maintained (Treaty art.3(3)).

[260] Treaty art.2(c).

[261] Statement concerning art.3(2).

[262] Treaty art.3(e).

[263] Treaty art.4.

fixed in phonograms.[264] A performer has the right to be identified as the performer of his performances, except where omission is dictated by the manner of the use of the performance, and to object to any distortion, mutilation or other modification of his performances that would be prejudicial to his reputation. If the legislation of the Contracting Party permits, such rights may also be maintained after the performer's death.

Performers are also guaranteed certain exclusive rights for the first time by international treaty. These are the exclusive right of authorising:

  (i) the broadcasting and communication to the public of their unfixed performances (except where the performance is already a broadcast performance) and the fixation of their unfixed performances[265];

  (ii) the direct or indirect reproduction of their performances fixed in phonograms in any manner or form[266];

  (iii) subject to national rules relating to exhaustion of rights, the making available to the public of the original and copies of their performances fixed in phonograms through sale or other transfer of ownership[267];

  (iv) the commercial rental to the public of the original and copies of their performances fixed in phonograms, except that a Contracting Party that has a system of equitable remuneration of performers for the rental of copies of their performances may maintain such a system, provided that the commercial rental of phonograms is not giving rise to the material impairment of the exclusive right of reproduction of performers[268];

  (v) the making available to the public of their performances fixed in phonograms, by wire or wireless means, in such a way that members of the public may access them from a place and at a time individually chosen by them.[269]

23–124   **Rights of producers of phonograms.** Producers of phonograms are guaranteed the following exclusive rights to authorise:

  (i) the direct or indirect reproduction of their phonograms, in any manner or form[270];

  (ii) subject to national rules of exhaustion of rights, the making available to the public of the original and copies of their phonograms through sale or other transfer of ownership (right of distribution)[271];

  (iii) subject to the same proviso mentioned above in relation to performers, the commercial rental to the public of the original and copies of their phonograms[272];

  (iv) the making available to the public of their phonograms, by wire or wireless means, in such a way that members of the public may access them from a place and at a time individually chosen by them.[273]

23–125   **Scope of these rights.** For the first time, performers are granted an exclusive right to reproduction of their performances by international convention. Under the Rome Convention art.7, the rights afforded to performers were not exclusive

---

[264] Treaty art.5.
[265] Treaty art.6.
[266] Treaty art.7.
[267] Treaty art.8.
[268] Treaty art.9.
[269] Treaty art.10.
[270] Treaty art.11.
[271] Treaty art.12.
[272] Treaty art.13.
[273] Treaty art.14.

rights but the possibility of preventing the doing of certain acts without their consent. The reason for this was to leave complete freedom of choice as to the means used to implement the Convention to the Member States.

The words "in any manner or form" in the reproduction rights of both performers and producers are new as compared with the Rome and Phonograms Conventions.[274] This expression is already found in art.9(1) of the Berne Convention concerning the right of reproduction enjoyed by authors. It has been included to make it clear that there is no difference between the rights of the beneficiaries and those of authors in this respect.[275] An agreed statement clarifies the extent of the reproduction rights granted to the beneficiaries, as follows: "The reproduction right, as set out in Articles 7 and 11, and the exceptions permitted thereunder through Article 16, fully apply in the digital environment, in particular to the use of performances and phonograms in digital form. It is understood that the storage of a protected performance or phonogram in digital form in an electronic medium constitutes a reproduction within the meaning of these articles".

As regards the new exclusive right to "make available" performances and phonograms to the public, this right is not the equivalent of the right of communication to the public established in art.8 of the WIPO Copyright Treaty for authors of literary and artistic works.[276] There is no agreed statement concerning this new right but the preparatory documents for the Diplomatic Conference make it clear that the intention behind the provision is to provide performers and producers with exclusive rights to authorise the use of their performances and phonograms in situations where, in the electronic marketplace, retail sales of phonograms are replaced by a database open to the public for the direct delivery of music via communication networks to home computers, and members of the public are able to access such phonograms from a place and at a time individually chosen by them, in the context of online, on-demand interactive services.[277] The right is intended to cover both directly interactive ways of making available and subscription services with similar effects.[278]

Common provisions. Both performers and producers of phonograms shall enjoy the right to a single equitable remuneration for the direct or indirect use of phonograms published for commercial purposes for broadcasting or for any communication to the public.[279] Such remuneration may be claimed from the user by the performer or the producer or by both. In the absence of agreement between the parties, national legislation may set the terms according to which such remuneration shall be shared. However, reservations may be made with regard to these provisions, in respect of certain uses or other limitations, and the provisions may be excluded altogether, as in the Rome Convention. It had been proposed that the various rights of reservation given by art.16(1)(a) of the Rome Convention should not apply in the case of broadcasting or communication to the public by wire or wireless means when the broadcasts or communication can only be

23–126

---

[274] art.7 of the Rome Convention gives performers the possibility of preventing "the fixation, without their consent, of their unfixed performances"; art.10 thereof gives producers "the right to authorise or prohibit the direct or indirect reproduction of their phonograms". Under the Phonograms Convention, producers are protected "against the making of duplicates without the consent of the producer" (art.2).

[275] Basic Proposal for the Substantive Provisions of the Treaty for the Protection of the Rights of Performers and Producers of Phonograms to be considered by the Diplomatic Conference (hereinafter "Basic Proposal"), WIPO document CRNR/DC/5, Notes on art.14 para.14.06.

[276] See para.23–71, above.

[277] Basic Proposal for the Substantive Provisions of the Treaty for the Protection of the Rights of Performers and Producers of Phonograms to be considered by the Diplomatic Conference (hereinafter "Basic Proposal"), WIPO document CRNR/DC/5, notes on art.18 paras 18.01–18.12.

[278] Basic Proposal, paras 18.06 and 18.08.

[279] Treaty art.15.

received on subscription and payment.[280] This proposal was rejected and the situation under the Rome Convention has been perpetuated so that unlike in the case of the performance rights of authors under the copyright conventions, performers and producers of phonograms do not benefit from a right to authorise or prohibit the communication to the public or the broadcasting of phonograms but have a mere right to receive equitable remuneration for such use; and even the right to equitable remuneration may be denied or limited by the Contracting States.[281] An agreed statement gives some recognition to the problem, providing that it is understood that nothing precludes a Contracting Party from providing exclusive rights to a performer or producer of phonograms beyond those required to be provided under this Treaty,[282] as indeed the United Kingdom does.[283] Nevertheless, in the digital age to leave performers and producers of phonograms without effective international protection in this area leaves them vulnerable to exploitation and without the means to control or obtain adequate remuneration for these uses.

The term "published for commercial purposes" includes phonograms made available to the public by wire or wireless means in such a way that members of the public may access them from a place and at a time individually chosen by them.[284]

"Broadcasting" is defined with a wider meaning than in the Rome Convention, as follows:

> " 'broadcasting' means the transmission by wireless means for public reception of sounds or of images and sounds *or of the representations thereof; such transmission by satellite is also 'broadcasting' transmission of encrypted signals is 'broadcasting' where the means for decrypting are provided to the public by the broadcasting organisation or with its consent".*[285]

(The words in italics are new). The Treaty also includes the following definition of communication to the public of a performance or a phonogram:

> "the transmission to the public by any medium, otherwise than by broadcasting, of sounds of a performance or the sounds or the representations of sounds fixed in a phonogram ... communication to the public includes making the sounds or representations of sounds fixed in a phonogram audible to the public".[286]

An agreed statement regarding these rights to equitable remuneration reads as follows:

> "It is understood that Article 15 does not represent a complete resolution of the level of rights of broadcasting and communication to the public that should be enjoyed by performers and phonogram producers in the digital age. Delegations were unable to achieve consensus on differing proposals for aspects of exclusivity to be provided in certain circumstances or for rights to be provided without the possibility of reservations, and have therefore left the issue to future resolution".[287]

A further agreed statement states that rights to equitable remuneration may

---

[280] Basic Proposal, paras 12.04 and 19.04.
[281] Treaty art.15(3).
[282] Agreed Statement Concerning Art.1.
[283] CDPA 1988 s.16(c) and (d).
[284] Treaty art.15(4).
[285] Art.2(f).
[286] Art.2(g).
[287] Agreed Statement Concerning Art.15.

also be granted to performers of folklore and producers of phonograms recording folklore where such phonograms have not been published for commercial gain.[288]

Limitations and exceptions: Application of the three-step test of the Berne Convention. The same kinds of limitations may be made by Contracting Parties with respect to the rights of performers and producers of phonograms as are provided for in their national legislation in connection with the protection of literary and artistic works.[289] Such limitations shall be subject to the principle of the three-step test of the Berne Convention and are, therefore, confined to certain special cases which do not conflict with a normal exploitation of the performance or phonogram and do not unreasonably prejudice the legitimate interests of the performer or of the producer of the phonogram.[290] According to an agreed statement,[291] this means that, as with respect to the WIPO Copyright Treaty, Contracting Parties may carry forward and appropriately extend into the digital environment limitations and exceptions in their national laws which have been considered acceptable under the Berne Convention and that they may devise new exceptions and limitations that are appropriate in the digital network environment.   **23–127**

Term of protection. The duration of the protection shall last, in the case of performers, for 50 years computed from the end of the year in which the performance was fixed in a phonogram. With respect to producers, who are also afforded a 50-year term of protection, the term is computed from the end of the year in which the phonogram was published, or, failing such publication within 50 years from fixation of the phonogram, 50 years from the end of the year in which the fixation was made.[292] This provision represents progress in comparison with the Rome and Phonograms Conventions, both of which provide for a minimum period of protection of only 20 years.[293]   **23–128**

Obligations concerning technological measures and rights management information. As in the WIPO Copyright Treaty,[294] Contracting Parties undertake certain obligations to provide adequate legal protection and effective legal remedies against: **23–129**

(a) the circumvention of effective technological measures that are used by performers or producers of phonograms in connection with the exercise of their rights under the Treaty and that restrict acts, in respect of their performances or phonograms, which are not authorised by the performers or the producers of phonograms concerned or permitted by law[295];

(b) any person knowingly performing any of the following acts knowing, or with respect to civil remedies having reasonable grounds to know, that it will induce, enable, facilitate or conceal an infringement of any right covered by the Treaty:

(i) to remove or alter any electronic rights management information[296] without authority;

---

[288] Agreed Statement Concerning Art.15.

[289] cf. Berne Convention arts 10 and 11.

[290] Berne Convention art.9(2); cf. para.23–33, above.

[291] Agreed Statement Concerning Art.16: "The agreed statement concerning Art.10 (on Limitations and Exceptions) of the WIPO Copyright Treaty is applicable *mutatis mutandis* also to Art.16 (on Limitations and Exceptions) of the WIPO Performances and Phonograms Treaty".

[292] Treaty art.17.

[293] Rome Convention art.14; Phonograms Convention art.4.

[294] See discussion of the equivalent provisions concerning the WIPO Copyright Treaty para.23–73, above.

[295] Treaty art.18.

[296] Rights management information is defined as meaning: "information which identifies the performer, the performance of the performer, the producer of the phonogram, the phonogram, the

(ii) to distribute, import for distribution, broadcast, communicate or make available to the public, without authority, performances, copies of fixed performances or phonograms knowing that electronic rights management information has been removed or altered without authority.[297]

23–130   **Formalities and reservations.** The enjoyment and exercise of the rights provided for by the Treaty may not be made subject to any formality.[298] No reservations may be made under the Treaty except in relation to performance rights in phonograms.[299]

23–131   **Retroactive effect and enforcement.** The Treaty provides that the provisions of art.18 of the Berne Convention concerning retroactive effect, shall apply *mutatis mutandis* to the protection provided for under the Treaty.[300] Thus, the Treaty applies to all performances and phonograms which, at the moment of its coming into force, have not yet fallen into the public domain in the country of origin through the expiry of the term of protection.

The Treaty also contains identical provisions concerning enforcement to those of the WIPO Copyright Treaty.[301] Thus, Contracting Parties are obliged to ensure that enforcement procedures are available to permit effective action against infringement, including remedies to prevent infringements and remedies which constitute a deterrent to further infringements. This provision is of a very general nature and does not include any reference to the more effective enforcement provisions contained in arts 41 to 61 of the TRIPs Agreement. The Diplomatic Conference specifically rejected a "basic proposal" to either include the TRIPs enforcement provisions in an annex or by reference (which would have simply required Contracting Parties to apply the relevant provisions of the TRIPs Agreement).[302]

C. Relationship to Copyright Conventions and the Rome and Phonograms Conventions

23–132   **No derogation from existing obligations.** The relation of the Treaty to the copyright and related rights conventions is laid down in art.1. This provides that nothing in the Treaty shall derogate from existing obligations that Contracting Parties have to each other under the Rome Convention[303] or prejudice any rights and obligations under any other treaties.[304] The protection granted shall also leave intact and in no way affect the protection of copyright in literary and artistic works; nor may any provision of the Treaty be interpreted as prejudicing such protection.[305]

An agreed statement concerning art.1 seeks to clarify the provisions on the relationship between rights in phonograms under the Treaty and copyright in works embodied in the phonograms. In cases where authorisation is needed from both

---

owner of any right in the performance or phonogram, any numbers or codes that represent such information, when any of these items of information is attached to a copy of a fixed performance or a phonogram or appears in connection with the communication or making available of a fixed performance or a phonogram to the public" (art.19).

[297] Art.19.
[298] Art.20.
[299] Art.21.
[300] Treaty art.22.
[301] Treaty art.23.
[302] Basic Proposal, Notes on art.27, paras 27.01 to 27.03.
[303] Treaty art.1(1).
[304] Art.1(3).
[305] Art.1(2).

the author of a work embodied in the phonogram and a performer or producer owning rights in the phonogram, the need for the authorisation of the author does not cease to exist because the authorisation of the performer or producer is also required, and vice versa.

As already mentioned,[306] the statement also makes it clear that nothing in the copyright safeguard provisions precludes a Contracting State from providing exclusive rights to a performer or producer of phonograms beyond those required to be provided under the Treaty.

D. SIGNATORIES AND ENTRY INTO FORCE

Parties to the Treaty. Any Member State of the World Intellectual Property Organisation (WIPO) may become party to the Treaty, as well as any intergovernmental organisation competent in respect of, and having legislation binding on its Member States on, matters dealt with by the Treaty.[307] The European Union signed and ratified the Treaty on this basis. The Treaty entered into force three months after the deposit of 30 instruments of ratification or accession by States with the Director General of WIPO.[308] Thereafter, new parties are bound by the Treaty three months from the date on which they deposit their instruments.[309] The Treaty may be denounced on giving one year's notice.[310]

23–133

The Treaty is administered by the International Bureau of WIPO[311] and supervised by an Assembly, which deals with matters concerning the maintenance and development of the Treaty and its application and operation.[312]

The Treaty was open for signature until December 31, 1997, at which date 50 states had signed it as well as the then European Community.[313]

By February 20, 2002, instruments of ratification of or accession to the Treaty had been deposited by 30 states. Accordingly, the Treaty entered into force on May 20, 2002.

23–134

As of August 31, 2010, the following 85 States and the European Union were parties to the Treaty:

Albania, Argentina, Armenia, Australia, Austria, Azerbaijan, Bahrain, Belarus, Belgium, Benin, Bosnia and Herzegovina, Botswana, Bulgaria, Burkina Faso, Chile, China, Colombia, Costa Rica, Croatia, Cyprus, Czech Republic, Denmark, Dominican Republic, Ecuador, El Salvador, Estonia, Finland, France, Gabon, Germany, Georgia, Greece, Guatemala, Guinea, Honduras, Hungary, Indonesia, Ireland, Italy, Jamaica, Japan, Jordan, Kazakhstan, Kyrgyzstan (Kyrgyz Republic), Latvia, Liechtenstein, Lithuania, Luxembourg, Mali, Malta, Mexico, Mongolia, Montenegro, Netherlands, Nicaragua, Oman, Panama, Paraguay, Peru, Philippines, Poland, Portugal, Qatar, Republic of Korea, Republic of Moldova, Romania, Russian Federation, Saint Lucia, Senegal, Serbia (Republic of), Singapore, Slovakia (Slovak Republic), Slovenia, Spain, Sweden,

---

[306] See para.23–125, above.
[307] Treaty art.26.
[308] Art.29.
[309] Art.30.
[310] Art.31.
[311] Art.25.
[312] Art.24.
[313] Argentina, Austria, Belarus, Belgium, Bolivia, Burkina Faso, Canada, Chile, Colombia, Costa Rica, Croatia, Denmark, Ecuador, European Communities, Estonia, Finland, France, Germany, Ghana, Greece, Hungary, Indonesia, Ireland, Israel, Italy, Kazakhstan, Kenya, Luxembourg, Mexico, Monaco, Mongolia, Namibia, the Netherlands, Nigeria, Panama, Portugal, Republic of Moldova, Romania, Senegal, Slovakia, Slovenia, South Africa, Spain, Sweden, Switzerland, Togo, United Kingdom, United States of America, Uruguay, Venezuela.

Switzerland, the former Yugoslav Republic of Macedonia, Togo, Trinidad and Tobago, Turkey, Ukraine, United Arab Emirates, United Kingdom, United States of America and Uruguay.[314] The Council of the European Community approved the Treaty with regard to matters within its competence by decision dated March 16, 2000 and the European Union ratified it with effect from March 14, 2010.[315]

E. PENDING ISSUES NOT ADDRESSED BY THE TREATY

23–135   **Problems left unresolved.** A major drawback of the Treaty is the failure to cover the rights of performers in the audiovisual fixations of their performances. This was recognised in the resolution adopted by the Diplomatic Conference, which noted "that the development of technologies will allow for a rapid growth of audiovisual services and that this will increase the opportunities for performing artists to exploit their audiovisual performances that will be transmitted by these services" and drew attention to the need to ensure an adequate level of protection for audiovisual performances, in particular in the new digital environment. To that end, the resolution called for work to be started on a protocol to the Treaty concerning audiovisual performances, with a view to the adoption of such a protocol not later than in 1998.[316] The issue proved too controversial for the 1998 deadline for a new instrument to be met. It was not until December 2000[317] that a Diplomatic Conference on the Protection of Audiovisual Performances convened by WIPO took place but the Conference ended in failure.[318] Provisional agreement was reached on a number of issues including national treatment, economic rights of performers in their unfixed performances, the exclusive rights of reproduction, distribution and rental, the right of making available of fixed performances, the right of broadcasting and communication to the public and protection against the circumvention of technological protection measures. It was also agreed that audiovisual performers would be granted moral rights protection, including the right to be identified as the performer of their performances and to object to any distortion, mutilation or other modification of their performances which would be prejudicial to their reputations, taking due account of the nature of audiovisual fixations. The issue which led to the breakdown of the negotiations was the law applicable to a transfer of economic rights from the performer to the film producer or others. The United States insisted on the US concept of "work made for hire" being explicitly recognised in the new instrument by the inclusion of a mandatory although rebuttable presumption of transfer of all exclusive economic rights to the producer, once the performer had consented to the audiovisual fixation of his performance. In the interests of the powerful US film industry, the United States also argued that the statutory transfer provisions

---

[314] Under the WPPT, Member States may make certain reservations. All such reservations are listed in the footnotes to the General Table of Copyright and Related Rights Conventions in Ch.25.

[315] See para.23–75, above. The Council decision authorised its President to deposit the instrument of ratification as from the date by which Member States are obliged to implement the Directive ([2001] O.J. L89, p.6); see Vol.2 I1.

[316] Resolution Concerning Audiovisual Performances, adopted by the Diplomatic Conference on December 20, 1996. In March 1997, the Governing Bodies of WIPO established a Committee of Experts on the protocol concerning audiovisual performances.

[317] The Committee of Experts on a Protocol concerning Audiovisual Performances met twice in September 1997 and June 1998. Subsequently, the matter was considered by the WIPO Standing Committee on Copyright and Related Rights, which met in November 1998, May 1999, November 1999 and April 2000 (see WIPO docs. SCCR/1/9, SCCR/2/11, SCCR/3/11 and SCCR/4/6).

[318] The Diplomatic Conference on the Protection of Audiovisual Performances met in Geneva from December 7 to 20, 2000. See also S. von Lewinski, "The WIPO Diplomatic Conference on Audiovisual Performances: A First Resume" [2001] E.I.P.R. 333 and "International protection for audiovisual performers: a never-ending story? A résumé of the WIPO Diplomatic Conference 200" [2001] 189 RIDA 3.

of the law of the country where a film is produced should have extraterritorial application in the country of exploitation. This was opposed by many countries with a civil law approach, including the European Community and its Member States; the latter defended the position that contractual transfer provisions should be given only limited recognition in the country of exploitation and that in any case the law in the country of exploitation should be respected.

The Diplomatic Conference concluded by recommending to the Assemblies of Member States of WIPO, in their September 2001 session, that they reconvene the Diplomatic Conference for the purpose of reaching agreement on outstanding issues.[319] At that meeting, the Assemblies of Member States of WIPO noted the Chairman's observations that a great deal of work needed to be done before agreement could be reached on this question. The Assemblies decided that the matter would remain on the agenda for their future meetings in September 2002, at which the Chairman would report on progress.[320] At the Assemblies' 2002 meeting it was decided to convene an ad hoc informal meeting relating to this issue in 2003 to assess possible ways of resolving the outstanding issues. The informal meeting took place in November 2003, but no results thereof were published. Since then, informal consultations among Member States and key stakeholders in the private sector have continued under the auspices of WIPO, in order to identify ways and means for making progress on outstanding issues and the issue of the protection of audiovisual performances has remained on the agenda of the General Assembly of WIPO and of that of WIPO's Standing Committee on Copyright and Related Rights (SCCR).

At its most recent meeting in June 2010, the SCCR reviewed the status of discussions on this subject and called for concrete proposals to advance negotiations.[321]

Other questions of importance which were not dealt with in the Treaty contrary to expectations were: the proposal to include an additional specific right to authorise or prohibit importation in the context of the new distribution right; exhaustion of the distribution right (a question left to national law); the proposed exclusive right to authorise modification of performances and phonograms (this right was proposed in order to cover any possible situation in which digital or other technological manipulation might be used to circumvent traditional notions of reproduction)[322]; proposals to afford exclusive rights of broadcasting and public performance of phonograms, at least in the digital environment.

As regards the digital agenda, as in the WIPO Copyright Treaty, two important issues for which solutions were proposed in the "basic proposals" were not resolved. First, agreement could not be reached on the proposal to clarify that acts such as temporary storage in electronic communications media constitute acts of reproduction.[323] Similarly, the proposal to clarify the concept of "publication", by specifically providing that making a work available to the public through on demand interactive systems should be treated as publication, was not followed.[324]

---

[319] Summary Minutes (Plenary) of the Diplomatic Conference on the Protection of Audiovisual Performances, Geneva, December 7–20, 2000.

[320] WIPO doc. A/36/15, para.186.

[321] WIPO Press Release PR/2010/648; see also SCCR, Twentieth Session, June 21-24, 2010, Draft Report (SCCR/20/13 PROV).

[322] Basic Proposal, Notes on art.8, para.8.04.

[323] Notes on art.7, para.7.07.

[324] Notes on art.2, para.2.20.

8. THE TRIPS AGREEMENT

A. HISTORY

23–136   **The Uruguay Round of the GATT General Agreement on Tariffs and Trade** (the GATT Agreement) was concluded on December 15, 1993, after seven years of negotiations, and the final act was signed in Marrakesh, Morocco, on April 15, 1994. Thus, the Round had a successful outcome, adopting the Agreement establishing the World Trade Organisation (WTO) to replace the GATT Agreement administration, and Annex 1C thereto, the Agreement on Trade-Related Aspects of Intellectual Property Rights, (the TRIPs Agreement): see below, Vol.2 F11.

23–137   **Scope of the Agreement.** The TRIPs Agreement is concerned, inter alia, with copyright and related rights. It sets standards for the Member States of the WTO ("Members") concerning the availability, scope and use of intellectual property rights generally, covering not only copyright and related rights but also trade marks, geographical indications, industrial designs, patents, layout designs (topographies) of integrated circuits, the protection of know-how (undisclosed information) and control of anti-competitive practices in contractual licences. It includes also provisions for the enforcement of intellectual property rights and dispute prevention and settlement measures.[325]

According to the Agreement, WTO Members are obliged to legislate to provide the standards of protection laid down therein for the various categories of intellectual property right owners covered by the Agreement. Members are free to determine the appropriate method of implementing the provisions of the Agreement within their own legal system and practice.[326] They are obliged to accord the treatment provided for in the Agreement to the nationals of other Members[327] and to accord most categories of intellectual property rights owners treatment no less favourable than it accords to its own nationals with regard to the protection of intellectual property (national treatment).[328] As regards performers, producers of phonograms (sound recordings), and broadcasting organisations, however, the latter obligation (national treatment) only applies in respect of the rights provided

---

[325] On the TRIPs Agreement generally, see D. Gervais, *The TRIPS Agreement—Drafting History and Analysis* 2nd edn (London: Sweet and Maxwell, 2003); M. Blakeney, *Trade Related Aspects of Intellectual Property Rights: A Concise Guide to the TRIPs Agreement* (London: Sweet and Maxwell, 1996); as regards the relationship between the TRIPs Agreement and the copyright and related rights conventions, see "Implications of the TRIPs Agreement on Treaties Administered by WIPO", memorandum prepared by the International Bureau of WIPO, [1996] *Copyright* 164. For further reading, see: F.K. Beier and G. Schricker, *From GATT to TRIPs—The Agreement on Trade-Related Aspects of Intellectual Property Rights* (1996); J.H.J. Bourgois, "The EC in the WTO and Advisory Opinion 1/94: An Echternach Procession."; C.M. Correa, "TRIPs Agreement: Copyright and Related Rights", [1992] 25 I.I.C. 543; P.E. Geller, "Intellectual Property in the Global Marketplace: Impact of TRIPs Dispute Settlements?" (1995) 29 *The International Lawyer*" 99; N. Khlestov, "WTO-WIPO Co-operation: Does it have a Future" [1997] 10 E.I.P.R. 560; P. Samuelson, "Challenges for the WIPO and the Trade-related Aspects of IP Rights Council in Regulating IP Rights in the Information Age" [1999] E.I.P.R. 578; S.K. Verma "TRIPs--Development and Transfer of Technology", IIC, vol.27, N.31, 1996, 331; A. Otten, "The Fundamental Importance of the TRIPs Agreement for a Better Enforcement of Copyright", records of the ALAI Berlin Congress, June 16–19, 1999, 41.

[326] TRIPs Agreement art.1(1).

[327] TRIPs Agreement art.1(3). In respect of the relevant intellectual property right, the nationals of other Members shall be understood as those natural or legal persons that would meet the criteria for eligibility for protection provided for in the Paris Convention (1967), the Berne Convention (1971), the Rome Convention and the Treaty on Intellectual Property in Respect of Integrated Circuits, if all Members of the WTO were members of those conventions.

[328] TRIPs Agreement art.3. (This provision is subject to the exceptions provided for in the international, intellectual property conventions, including the Berne Convention and the Rome Convention.)

under the Agreement. The Agreement also provides for most-favoured-nation treatment, according to which, subject to certain defined exceptions, any advantage, favour, privilege or immunity granted by a Member to the nationals of any other country shall be accorded immediately and unconditionally to the nationals of all other Members.[329] This is a principle not recognised by the copyright and related rights conventions.

B. Substantive Provisions

The standards of protection to be afforded in relation to copyright and related rights may be summarised as follows: Members shall comply with arts 1–21 of, and also the Appendix to, the Paris Act 1971 of the Berne Convention,[330] with the one exception of the provisions of the Convention concerning moral rights, which were expressly excluded from the scope of the Agreement.[331] Copyright protection under the Agreement extends to expressions and not to ideas, procedures, methods of operation or mathematical concepts as such.[332]   **23–138**

Computer programs shall be protected as literary works under the Berne Convention and compilations of data or other material (databases), which by reason of the selection or arrangement of their contents constitute intellectual creations, shall be protected as such,[333] without prejudice to any copyright subsisting in the data or material itself.

Rental rights. In principle, the right to authorise or prohibit the commercial rental to the public of originals or copies of their works are to be provided for authors and their successors in title in respect of at least computer programs and cinematographic works. However, as regards cinematographic works, Members are excepted from this obligation unless such rental has led to widespread copying of such works which is materially impairing the exclusive right of reproduction conferred in that Member's territory on authors and their successors in title. In respect of computer programs, this obligation does not apply to rentals where the program itself is not the essential object of the rental.[334]   **23–139**

Terms of protection calculated on a basis other than the life of a natural person, shall be no less than 50 years from authorised publication, or in the absence of such publication, from making.[335] Limitations shall not conflict with a normal exploitation of the work or unreasonably prejudice the legitimate interests of the right holder.[336]   **23–140**

Performers, producers of phonograms (sound recordings) and broadcasting organisations are specifically protected. Performers shall have the following rights: the possibility of preventing the unauthorised fixation of their unfixed performance and the reproduction of such fixation as well as the unauthorised broadcasting and communication of their live performances. Producers of phonograms shall enjoy the right to authorise or prohibit the direct or indirect reproduction, and the rental of, their phonograms. Other right holders in phonograms may   **23–141**

---

[329] TRIPs Agreement art.4.
[330] See paras 23–10, et seq., above.
[331] TRIPs Agreement art.9.
[332] TRIPs Agreement art.9(2).
[333] TRIPs Agreement art.10.
[334] TRIPs Agreement art.11.
[335] TRIPs Agreement art.12. (This does not apply to photographic works or works of applied art.)
[336] art.13. (cf. the Berne Convention art.9(2).)

also enjoy a rental right therein under national law.[337] The term of protection of performers and producers shall be not less than 50 years computed from the end of the year in which the fixation was made or the performance took place. The TRIPs Agreement contains no provisions relating to the broadcasting and public performance rights of producers and performers.[338]

Broadcasting organisations shall have the right to prohibit the fixation, the reproduction of fixations, and the rebroadcasting by wireless means of broadcasts, as well as the communication to the public of television broadcasts of the same. The term of protection shall be 20 years from the end of the calendar year in which the broadcast took place.[339]

23–142　　**Limitations and exceptions.** The Agreement provides that, with respect to literary and artistic works, Members shall confine limitations or exceptions to exclusive rights to certain special cases which do not conflict with a normal exploitation of the work and do not unreasonably prejudice the legitimate interests of the right holder. This provision is in line with art.9(2) of the Berne Convention ("the three-step test"), which is expressed in similar terms.[340]

In relation to the rights of performers, producers of phonograms and broadcasting organisations guaranteed by the TRIPs Agreement, any member may provide for conditions, limitations, exceptions and reservations to the extent permitted by the Rome Convention.[341] However, this is qualified by the application of the three-step test of the Berne Convention also to limitations on related rights.[342] The rule of retroactivity of art.18 of the Berne Convention shall also apply, *mutatis mutandis*, to the rights of performers and producers of phonograms in phonograms, so that all phonograms not in the public domain at the date of entry into force of the Agreement with respect to any Member will be protected.[343] This provision goes further than the Rome Convention which does not require retroactive application of its provisions.

23–143　　**The Application of the three-step test by a WTO Panel.** Of particular interest in connection with limitations under the TRIPs Agreement, is the application of the "three-step test" of the Berne Convention by a World Trade Organisation Panel in its report on a complaint brought against the United States of America by the European Union[344] under the TRIPs dispute prevention and settlement procedure.[345] This report would appear to be the first judicial interpretation of the three-step test. The panel found that the term "special cases" in the first condition requires that a limitation or exception in national legislation should be clearly defined and should be narrow in its scope and reach. However, a limitation or exception may be compatible with the first condition even if it pursues a special purpose whose underlying legitimacy in a normative sense cannot be discerned.

---

[337] If on April 15, 1994, a Member had in force a system of equitable remuneration of right holders in respect of the rental of phonograms, it may maintain such system provided that the commercial rental of phonograms is not giving rise to the material impairment of the exclusive rights of reproduction of right holders (TRIPs Agreement art.14(4)).

[338] cf. The Rome Convention art.12.

[339] TRIPs Agreement art.14.

[340] TRIPs Agreement art.13.

[341] cf. the Rome Convention art.15, which permits exceptions for: private use; use of short excerpts in connection with the reporting of current events; ephemeral recordings by broadcasting organisations; use solely for purposes of teaching or scientific research. Moreover, the same kinds of limitations are permitted as are provided for in respect of literary and artistic works. Compulsory licenses are only permitted to the extent they are compatible with the Convention.

[342] TRIPs Agreement art.14(6); cf. para.23–33, above.

[343] art.14(6).

[344] Panel Report WT/DS160/R of June 15, 2000: United States—s.110(5) of the Copyright Act.

[345] See para.23–148, below.

Thus, the first condition does not imply passing a judgment on the legitimacy of the exceptions in dispute (as had been argued by the European Union).[346] As regards the second condition, that an exception should not conflict with the normal exploitation of a work, the panel considered that a conflict arises when the exception or limitation enters into economic competition with the ways that right holders normally extract economic value from that right to the work (i.e. the copyright) and thereby deprives them of significant or tangible commercial gain.[347] The panel finally gave its opinion on the third condition of the three-step test, that the exception or limitation must not unreasonably prejudice the legitimate interests of the right holder, finding that there is unreasonable prejudice where an exception or limitation causes or has the potential to cause an unreasonable loss of income to the copyright holder.[348]

Anti-competitive practices. The Agreement also permits Members to provide in their national legislation for control of anti-competitive practices in contractual licences.[349] This is of particular relevance in the copyright and related rights field to the practices of collecting societies.   **23–144**

General obligations concerning enforcement measures. As regards enforcement, Members are obliged to ensure that enforcement procedures are available under their national laws to permit effective action against any act of infringement of the intellectual property rights covered by the agreement, including remedies to prevent infringements, which are expeditious and constitute a deterrent to further infringements but without creating barriers to legitimate trade or allowing abuse.[350] Such procedures shall be fair and equitable, simple, cheap and timely.[351] Parties to a proceeding shall have an opportunity for review by a judicial authority of final administrative decisions and, subject to national jurisdictional rules, of at least the legal aspects of initial judicial decisions on the merits of a case. However, there is no obligation to provide for review of acquittals in criminal cases.[352]   **23–145**

Standards of procedure and remedies. The Agreement also lays down standards with regard to civil and administrative procedures and remedies,[353] in order to guarantee fair and equitable procedures for the enforcement of intellectual property rights. Included are inter alia rules concerning evidence, injunctions, damages, disposal of infringing goods and right of information concerning the identity of those engaged in infringing practices.[354] The adoption of provisional measures by Members is foreseen to prevent infringements, and in particular to   **23–146**

---

[346] Panel Report, para.6.112.

[347] ibid., para.6.183.

[348] Concerning the Panel Report, see J.C. Ginsburg, "Toward Supranational Copyright Law? The WTO Panel Decision and the "Three-Step Test" for Copyright Exceptions", (2001) 187 RIDA 3; D.J. Brennan, "The Three-Step Test Frenzy—Why the TRIPs Panel Decision might be considered Per Incuriam", [2002] IPQ 2, 212; Y.Gaubic, "Les exceptions au droit d'auteur: un nouvel avenir", [2001] *Communicaion Commerce électronique*, no.6, 12; B.C. Goldmann, "Victory for Songwriters in WTO Music Royalties Dispute between U.S. and E.U.—Background of the Conflict Over the Extension of Homestyle Exemption", (2001) 32 IIC 412; M. Ficsor, "How much of What? The "Three-Step Test" and its application in two recent WTO dispute settlement cases", (2002) 192 RIDA 110; and J. Bornkamm, "Copyright and the Public Interest—The Three-Step Test in International Copyright", paper delivered at the Fordham University School of Law 10th Annual Conference on International Intellectual Property Law and Policy, New York, April 4–5, 2002. See also K.J. Koelman, "Fixing the Three-Step Test" [2006] E.I.P.R. 28(8), 407–412.

[349] TRIPs Agreement art.40.

[350] TRIPs Agreement art.41(1).

[351] art.41(2).

[352] art.41(4).

[353] TRIPs Agreement ss.2–5, arts 42–61.

[354] Arts 42 to 49.

prevent the entry into the channels of commerce in their jurisdiction of goods, including imported goods immediately after customs clearance.[355] There are also special requirements related to border controls to enable a right holder, who has valid grounds for suspecting that the importation of counterfeit trademark or pirated copyright goods may take place, subject to various conditions, to lodge an application in writing with the competent authorities, administrative or judicial, for the suspension by the customs authorities of the release into free circulation of such goods.[356]

23–147   Criminal procedures. Members are obliged also to provide for criminal procedures and penalties to be applied at least in cases of wilful trademark counterfeiting or copyright piracy on a commercial scale. Remedies available shall include imprisonment and/or monetary fines sufficient to provide a deterrent, consistently with the level of penalties applied for crimes of a corresponding gravity. Where appropriate, remedies shall also include the seizure, forfeiture and destruction of the infringing goods and of any materials and implements the predominant use of which has been in the commission of the offence.[357]

23–148   Dispute prevention and settlement. The Agreement provides for a dispute settlement procedure under the WTO,[358] according to which, should a dispute arise regarding the obligations of a Member, there is the possibility of taking action under the GATT Understanding on Rules and Procedures Governing the Settlement of Disputes. This aspect of the agreement is of particular importance in view of the sanctions which may be imposed under that procedure on a Member which fails to comply with its obligations under the TRIPs Agreement. The fact that under the Berne Convention there are no sanctions whatsoever should a Member State thereof be in breach of its obligations thereunder was an important reason for the GATT TRIPs negotiations.[359] This difference is one of the strengths of the TRIPs Agreement. Under the Berne Convention, disputes between countries of the Union may be brought by one of the countries in question before the International Court of Justice.[360] The provision is not obligatory and there are no sanctions. "An adverse decision of the International Court carries no condemnation; the Court merely makes a finding as to the law and it is then a matter for the countries in question to solve by diplomatic or legislative means, as they wish".[361]

The TRIPs dispute settlement mechanism may be invoked both in the areas of

---

[355] art.50.

[356] arts 51–60.

[357] TRIPs Agreement art.61.

[358] TRIPs Agreement art.64. The settlement of disputes under the Agreement will be subject to the provisions of arts XXII and XXIII of the General Agreement on Tariffs and Trade 1994 as elaborated and applied by the understanding on Rules and Procedures Governing the Settlement of Disputes.

[359] It should be noted, however, that, under the auspices of WIPO, a Committee of Experts on the Settlement of Intellectual Property Disputes Between States held eight sessions to discuss a draft Treaty on the subject in the mid–1990s. The aim of the Treaty, to be administered by WIPO, was to establish procedures for the amicable settlement of disputes. However, disagreement about the need for such a Treaty led to a Diplomatic Conference scheduled to take place in the biennium 1994/1995 being shelved. For a report of the 8th Committee of Experts see [1996] *Industrial Property and Copyright* 319. For the draft Treaty and proposed Regulations, see [1995] *Copyright* 168 and 205. Meanwhile, the WIPO Arbitration and Mediation Center was established in 1994 to offer arbitration and mediation services for the resolution of international commercial disputes between private parties in the field of intellectual property. The Center has focused on establishing an operational and legal framework for the administration of disputes relating to the internet and electronic commerce (for further information see *http://arbiter.wipo.int/center* [Accessed September 14, 2010]).

[360] Berne Convention art.33.

[361] See C. Masouyé, *Guide to the Berne Convention for the Protection of Literary and Artistic Works (Paris Act, 1971)* (Geneva: WIPO, 1978), para.33.5.

minimum standards of protection and of enforcement. To date, it has been invoked in a number of cases concerning copyright and related rights (inter alia the complaints by the United States of America and European Communities filed against Japan in 1996 concerning the protection of sound recordings under TRIPs[362]; the complaints filed by the United States of America in 1998 against the European Communities and Greece in respect of the lack of effective remedies against copyright infringement in Greece[363]; a complaint by the European Communities filed in 1999 against the United States of America concerning exemptions in the US Copyright Act permitting communication to the public of broadcast works by certain commercial establishments without the authorisation of right-holders or payment of royalties.[364] The United States also filed complaints against Denmark and Sweden concerning the lack of provisional measures in the context of civil proceedings in TRIPs matters[365] and against Ireland for failure to comply with TRIPs provisions on copyright and related rights.[366] Some of these cases have been the subject of consultations; on some, mutually agreed solutions have been found, and others have led to WTO dispute settlement panel or Appellate Body reports upholding the complaints and determining that the copyright legislation of the country in question should be amended.[367]

In 2009, a WTO panel issued a ruling in a dispute settlement procedure initiated by the United States of America against China for breach of intellectual property obligations under the TRIPs Agreement.[368] The dispute included two copyright aspects: first the panel held that Chinese censorship rules, which bar copyright protection from works that fail content review, are in breach of art.5(1) of the Berne Convention (incorporated into TRIPs under art.9 thereof), which entitles authors to enjoy copyright protection in all WTO countries, and of art.41(1) of TRIPs, which requires enforcement procedures to be available to right owners. Second the panel considered whether China's quantitative and financial thresholds for criminal liability (for example, the rule limiting criminal liability to cases where the unauthorised reproduction involved more than 500 infringing copies), are compatible with the obligation laid down in art.61 TRIPs to provide criminal sanctions for copyright infringement "on a commercial scale". The panel held that there was insufficient evidence to conclude that the thresholds in China's law indeed violate TRIPs. It observed that the meaning of "commercial scale" would depend on the particular circumstances of each case and can vary depending on the product, commerce or type of piracy involved. It defined "commercial scale" as "the magnitude or extent at which engagement in commerce, or activities pertaining to or bearing on commerce, are typically or usually carried on, in other words, the magnitude or extent of typical or usual commercial activity".

Exhaustion. It should be noted that, for the purposes of dispute settlement under the TRIPs Agreement, nothing in the Agreement "shall be used to address the issue of the exhaustion of intellectual property rights".[369] Thus, like the copyright and related rights conventions, the TRIPs Agreement leaves the question of exhaustion of rights to national law.   **23–149**

---

[362] WT/DS28 and WT/DS42.

[363] WT/DS/124/1 and WT/DS/125/1.

[364] WT/DS/160/1.

[365] WT/DS/83 and WT/DS/86.

[366] WT/DS/82.

[367] An overview of the state of play of WTO disputes is available on the WTO website, *http://www.wto.org* [Accessed September 14, 2010]. As of August 31, 2010, 29 TRIPs-related disputes had been settled, mutually agreed solutions having been notified to the WTO, or were still pending, of which 10 concerned copyright or related rights issues.

[368] The panel report is available from: *http://www.wto.org/english/news e/news09 e/362r e.htm*.

[369] TRIPs Agreement art.6.

23–150   **Transitional arrangements** are provided for to give Members time to bring their legislation into line with the Agreement. In particular, the least-developed-country Members are not obliged to apply the provisions of the Agreement with regard, inter alia, to copyright and related rights for a period of 10 years, which may be extended on motivated request.[370]

23–151   **The TRIPs Council.** Finally, the Agreement establishes a Council for Trade-Related Aspects of Intellectual Property Rights to monitor the operation of the Agreement and, in particular, Members' compliance with their obligations thereunder. In carrying out its functions, the Council is required to establish, within one year of its first meeting, appropriate arrangements for co-operation with the World Intellectual Property Organisation (WIPO).TRIPs Agreement art.68. To that end, an Agreement between WIPO and WTO was reached in December 1995.[371]

It should also be noted that the TRIPs Agreement is due to be reviewed in the context of the Doha Trade Negotiations launched under the auspices of the World Trade Organisation in 2001. The issues which are under review at present concern industrial property.

C. DIRECT EFFECT OF TRIPs IN TRIPs MEMBER STATES

23–152   Reference is made in Ch.24 to decisions of the European Court of Justice in which the question whether the TRIPs Agreement can have direct effect in the European Union is discussed.[372] The question has also arisen at the national level where, within the European Union, there are diverging views on the direct applicability of TRIPs, depending on the legal order of the individual Member States. Direct effect is only possible in States whose constitutions accord domestic legal effect to international agreements. The different approaches may be illustrated by the following examples. Germany: The German Government takes the view that TRIPs may have direct effect in Germany. In the memorandum introducing the German Draft Act for the Ratification of the WTO Agreement, it said the following: "Domestic law by and large is in conformity with the results of the negotiations; in addition some of the provisions, at least those of the Agreement on Trade-Related Aspects of Intellectual Property Rights, are directly applicable".[373] Ireland: The Irish High Court has given direct effect to TRIPs in a patent case. It based its judgement not on Community law but on the domestic law according to which any treaty supersedes domestic law in relation to certain patents.[374] United Kingdom: The High Court has held that TRIPs could not have direct effect in the United Kingdom for several reasons: the language of art.1(1) of TRIPs was not that of a treaty intended by the signatories to have direct effect; the fundamental character of the WTO and TRIPs was merely an agreement among nations and thus was not self-executing by way of conferring private rights on citizens. WTO and TRIPs were not capable of having direct effect and, even if some provisions of TRIPs were capable of having such effect, art.32 at is-

---

[370] TRIPs Agreement arts 65 and 66.
[371] For text, see [1996] *Industrial Property and Copyright, Bilateral Treaties, Text 03*, 001.
[372] cf. Ch.24, para.24–173.
[373] *Entwurf eines Gesetzes zu dem Übereinkommen vom 15. April 1994 zur Errichtung der Welthandelsorganisation, Denkschrift,* para.6, Bundestagdrucksache 12/7655(neu).
[374] *Allen & Hanbury's Ltd v Controller of Patents, Designs, and Trademarks,* [1997] 1N.Ir. 416 (High Ct 1996).

sue was not sufficiently clear and precise to do so; the Court found these points so self-evident as to fall within the *acte claire* doctrine.[375]

D. Parties to the TRIPs Agreement

All Member Countries of the Agreement establishing the World Trade Organiza-   **23–153**
tion (WTO) are automatically Members of the TRIPs Agreement, which as mentioned above is Annex C1 to that Agreement. As of August 31, 2010, there were 153 Members of the WTO and 30 Observer governments; the latter must start accession negotiations within five years of becoming observers.

E. WIPO/WTO Agreement

This agreement, signed on December 22, 1995, entered into force on January 1,   **23–154**
1996. It provides inter alia for WTO Members and their nationals to have access to copies of laws and regulations in the WIPO collection, and copies of translations thereof, on the same terms as apply to Member States of WIPO and nationals of those states. Access is also guaranteed on the same terms to any computerised database of the International Bureau of WIPO containing laws and regulations. The WTO Secretariat is also given access free of charge to any such database.[376] Provision is further made for the WTO Secretariat and the Council for TRIPs to have access to the laws and regulations of WTO members in the WIPO collection. The International Bureau shall not put any restrictions on the use that the WTO Secretariat may make of the copies of laws, regulations and translations transmitted accordingly.[377] Reciprocal arrangements are made for WTO to transmit laws and regulations received by them to WIPO, under the same conditions.[378] WIPO will give WTO Members which are developing countries but not Member States of WIPO the same assistance for translation of laws and regulations as it provides to its own Members which are developing countries.[379]

Similar arrangements are provided for developing countries which are Members of WTO but not of WIPO as regards legal-technical assistance relating to the TRIPs Agreement.[380] Finally, the WTO Secretariat and the International Bureau of WIPO are to enhance co-operation in their legal-technical assistance and technical co-operation activities relating to the TRIPs Agreement for developing countries, keep in regular contact and exchange non-confidential information.[381]

9. OTHER CONVENTIONS OF RELEVANCE TO THE COPYRIGHT AND RELATED RIGHTS CONVENTIONS

A. Introduction

There are a number of other Conventions of relevance to the copyright and re-   **23–155**
lated rights conventions. For the sake of completeness, these are briefly discussed below in sections B to E of this Chapter. A number of potential agreements currently under discussion but not yet adopted are mentioned below in section F.

---

[375] In *Lenzing AG's European Patent (UK)* [1997] R.P.C. 235.
[376] WIPO-WTO Agreement art.2(1) and (2).
[377] art.2(3).
[378] art.2(4).
[379] art.2(5).
[380] art.4(1).
[381] art.4(2) and (3).

B. THE SATELLITE CONVENTION

23–156   **The Convention relating to the distribution of programme-carrying signals transmitted by satellite**, known as the Satellite Convention, was adopted on May 21, 1974, in Brussels.[382] The Convention differs from the copyright and related rights conventions in that it is an international *public* law Convention as opposed to an international *private* law convention and thus grants no private rights, imposing instead certain obligations on States. The reason for this approach was that many governments took the view that "if affirmative rights were to be accorded to originating broadcasting organisations as a matter of private law under a new international convention, these should be counterbalanced by granting correlative rights to contributors to programmes, particularly authors and other copyright owners". Moreover, there was concern that any new convention should not prejudice the Rome Convention.[383] Granting further private rights to broadcasters would have upset the balance between the three beneficiaries of the Rome Convention.[384]

The aim of the Convention was to regulate potential legal problems raised by intercontinental transmissions of television programmes by satellite. It provides measures to prevent ground stations belonging to broadcasters and cable distribution companies within the satellite footprint from poaching and distributing programme-carrying signals transmitted by satellite which were not intended for them.[385] The problem arose during the late 1960s when the European Broadcasting Union sought protection of its members' programmes transmitted by point-to-point and distribution satellites to ground stations. In the main, the programmes transmitted were not copyright material but live sporting events, news items, etc. transmitted between broadcasting organisations and not designed for reception by the public. Such transmissions were vulnerable to poaching, or piracy, and the question arose whether the rights of broadcasters under the Rome Convention gave the broadcasters protection with respect to satellite distribution. The Rome Convention defines broadcasting as the transmission by wireless means *for public reception* of sounds or of images and sounds[386] and the transmitted broadcasts concerned were not necessarily for direct reception by the public. There was general agreement that broadcasts transmitted to the public by means of direct broadcasting satellites were covered by the Convention and many took the view that, since point-to-point and distribution satellite broadcasts were ultimately destined for reception by the public, these were also protected.[387] However, sufficient doubt remained for the broadcasters to seek specific protection against piracy of their programmes transmitted by point-to-point and distribution

---

[382] For text, see [1974] *Copyright* 151 and Vol.2 F10. See also *Records of the International Conference of States on the Distribution of Programme-Carrying Signals Transmitted by Satellite*, UNESCO/WIPO, 1977; S.M. Stewart, "International Copyright and Neighbouring Rights" (London: Butterworths, 1983), Ch.10; S. Ricketson, *The Berne Convention for the protection of Literary and Artistic Works: 1886–1896* (Queen Mary College, University of London, 1987), paras 15.57, et seq.; E. Ulmer, "Protection of authors in relation to the transmission via satellite of broadcast programmes" LXXXXII RIDA 4 (1977).

[383] See Report of the General Rapporteur, B. Ringer, in the *Records of the Diplomatic Conference*, para.10.

[384] *Records of the Diplomatic Conference*, para.11.

[385] Preamble to the Convention, para.4: "Convinced that an international system should be established under which measures would be provided to prevent distributors from distributing programme-carrying signals transmitted by satellite which were not intended for those distributors".

[386] Rome Convention art.3(f).

[387] B. Ringer, *Records of the Diplomatic Conference*, para.37.

satellites. Following a series of meetings starting in 1968,[388] the Convention was adopted in 1974.[389]

Substantive provisions. The scope of the Convention is limited; it provides that   **23–157**
each Contracting State undertakes to take adequate measures to prevent the distribution on or from its territory of any programme-carrying signal by any distributor for whom the signal emitted to or passing through the satellite is not
intended. The obligation applies where the originating organisation is a national
of another Contracting State and where the signal distributed is a derived signal
(i.e. a signal obtained by modifying the technical characteristics of the emitted
signal).[390] The term "take adequate measures" leaves Contracting States free to
decide on the kind of protection to be provided; it may be by a specific right, but
may also be by means of administrative measures, penal sanctions or telecommunications laws or regulation[391]; the duration of the protection is also left to domestic legislation.[392] Exceptions are provided for news reporting, quotations and
educational use.[393]

The Convention specifically does not apply where the signals emitted by or on
behalf of the originating organisation are intended for direct reception from the
satellite by the general public.[394] The Convention does not have retrospective
effect.[395]

Relationship to the Berne and Rome Conventions. The Satellite Convention   **23–158**
itself stipulates that its provisions are in no way to be interpreted to limit or prejudice the protection secured to authors, performers, producers of phonograms, or
broadcasting organisations, under any domestic or international agreement.[396]
Furthermore, the Preamble to the Convention refers to the need not to impair or
prejudice in any way wider acceptance of the Rome Convention.[397] In practice,
problems in this connection do not appear to have arisen, the number of Member
States of the Rome Convention having increased from 14 at the time of the adoption of the Satellite Convention in May 1974[398] to 91 States on August 31, 2010.
The progress of the Satellite Convention is monitored by the Assembly and Executive Committee of the Berne Union, in the absence of any intergovernmental
committee of its own.

Entry into force and parties to the Satellite Convention. The Convention   **23–159**
entered into force on August 25, 1979, following the deposit of the fifth instrument of ratification or accession. As of August 31, 2010, the following 34 States
were party thereto: Armenia, Australia, Austria, Bahrain, Bosnia and Herzegovina, Costa Rica, Croatia, El Salvador, Germany, Greece, Honduras, Italy,

---

[388] Working Group on Copyright Problems of Satellite Communications (Geneva, October 14–16, 1968), [1968] *Copyright* 230; UNESCO/BIRPI Committee of Governmental Experts on Problems in the Field of Copyright and of the Protection of Performers, Producers of Phonograms and Broadcasting Organisations Raised by Transmission via Space Satellites, which met on the fol-lowing occasions: Lausanne/Ouchy, April 21–30, 1971 [1971] *Copyright* 102; Paris, May 9–11, 1972 [1972] *Copyright* 142; and Nairobi, July 2–11, 1973 [1973] *Copyright* 147.

[389] The Convention was signed on May 21, 1974, the date of its adoption, by the following States: Belgium, Brazil, Cyprus, Germany (Federal Republic), Israel, Italy, the then Ivory Coast, Kenya, Lebanon, Mexico, Morocco, Senegal, Spain, Switzerland, United States.

[390] The Satellite Convention art.2(1).

[391] B. Ringer, *Records of the Diplomatic Conference*, para.79.

[392] The Satellite Convention art.2(2).

[393] Art.4.

[394] Art.3.

[395] Art.5.

[396] Satellite Convention art.7.

[397] Preamble, para.5.

[398] [1975] *Copyright* 32.

Jamaica, Kenya, Mexico, Montenegro, Morocco, Nicaragua, Oman, Panama, Peru, Portugal, Republic of Moldova, Rwanda, Russian Federation, Serbia, Singapore, Slovenia, Switzerland, the former Yugoslav Republic of Macedonia, Togo, Trinidad and Tobago, United States of America and Viet Nam.

C. THE VIENNA TYPEFACES AGREEMENT

23–160   **The Vienna Agreement for the Protection of Typefaces and their International Deposit** (the Vienna Agreement), was adopted on June 12, 1973, in Vienna. A Protocol to the Agreement was also adopted on that day concerning the term of protection to be accorded to typefaces. The Agreement constituted a Union for the protection of typefaces,[399] which are defined as sets of designs, intended to provide means for composing texts by any graphic technique, of the following: letters and alphabets as such with their accessories such as accents and punctuation marks; numerals and other figurative signs such as conventional signs, symbols and scientific signs; ornaments such as borders, fleurons and vignettes. The term "typefaces" does not include typefaces of a form dictated by purely technical requirements.[400]

According to the Agreement, the Contracting States undertake to ensure the protection of typefaces, by establishing a special national deposit, or by adapting the deposit provided for in their national industrial design laws, or by their national copyright provisions. These kinds of protection may be cumulative.[401] The Agreement is based on the principle of national treatment.[402] To qualify for protection, typefaces must be novel, or original, or both.[403] The protection afforded by the Agreement confers on the owner, who may be a natural person or legal entity,[404] the right to prohibit the making without consent of any reproduction of the typeface as well as the commercial distribution and importation of such reproductions.[405] The term of protection provided for in the Agreement is a minimum of 15 years.[406] However, according to the Protocol to the Agreement, States party to the Protocol shall provide a minimum of 25 years instead.[407] The Agreement also provides for a system of international deposit and recording thereof in an international register to be administered by the International Bureau of the World Intellectual Property Organisation (WIPO).[408]

Detailed Regulations concerning the international deposit of typefaces are annexed to the Agreement.[409]

23–161   **Entry into force and parties to the Convention.** The Agreement has never entered into force. For it to do so would require that five states had deposited their instruments of ratification or accession. To date, only France and Germany

---

[399] Vienna Agreement art.1. Report of the Diplomatic Conference and text, see [1973] *Copyright* 122 and 132. For text see Vol.2 F9. See also S. Ricketson, *The Berne Convention for the protection of literary and artistic works: 1886–1896* (Queen Mary College, University of London, 1987), para.15.62.
[400] Vienna Agreement art.2.
[401] art.3.
[402] art.5.
[403] art.7.
[404] art.4.
[405] art.8.
[406] art.9.
[407] Protocol art.1.
[408] Ch.II, arts 12–25.
[409] Art.29 and Regulations Under the Vienna Agreement for the Protection of Typefaces and their International Deposit.

have done so.[410] It is a closed Convention; only states party to either the Paris Union for the Protection of Industrial Property, the Berne Convention or the Universal Copyright Convention may become party to the Agreement. Although the United Kingdom signed the Agreement on the date of its adoption, it has not ratified it.

D. The Madrid Double Taxation Convention

The Convention for the Avoidance of Double Taxation of Copyright Royalties (the Madrid Convention) was adopted in Madrid on December 13, 1979, under the auspices of the United Nations Organisation for Education, Science and Culture (UNESCO) and the World Intellectual Property Organisation (WIPO).[411] The subject-matter of the Convention is of importance to authors who earn royalties from the exploitation of their works and are liable to pay tax thereon in more than one country. However, the Convention has no impact on the creation and subsistence of authors' rights.   **23–162**

Under the Convention, each Contracting State undertakes to make every possible effort, in accordance with its Constitution and certain guiding principles laid down in the Convention: "to avoid double taxation of copyright royalties, where possible, and, should it subsist, to eliminate it or to reduce its effect ... by means of bilateral agreements or by way of domestic measures".[412] The guiding principles relate to matters such as fiscal sovereignty and equality of rights of states to tax copyright royalties and fiscal non-discrimination.[413]

A model of a bilateral agreement, comprising several alternative provisions, is attached to the Convention but does not form an integral part thereof.

The administration of the Convention is entrusted to UNESCO and WIPO jointly.

An additional Protocol was adopted at the same time as the Convention, providing for its provisions to apply also to the taxation of royalties paid to performers, producers of phonograms and broadcasting organisations in respect of rights related to copyright or "neighbouring rights".   **23–163**

In order to enter into force, the Convention requires the adherence of 10 states.[414] To date, only seven have done so and the Convention remains a dead letter.[415] The United Kingdom did not sign the Convention, its delegate declaring that, while endorsing the aims of the Convention, it objected to the method employed—a multilateral Convention—which was unrealistic and risked being ineffective.[416] For these reasons, the United Kingdom could not accept the texts, at that time,[417] and has not since changed its attitude.

---

[410] As of August 31, 2010.

[411] For the report of the Diplomatic Conference and text of the Convention and its Protocol, see [1980] *Copyright* 12. See also S. Ricketson, *The Berne Convention for the Protection of Literary and Artistic Works: 1886–1896* (Queen Mary College, University of London, 1987), para.15.60.

[412] The Madrid Convention art.8.

[413] arts 5–7.

[414] Madrid Convention art.13.

[415] The Convention was signed by: Cameroon, the then Czechoslovakia, the Holy See and Israel. As of August 31, 2010, the following states have adhered to the Convention: Czech Republic (1993); Ecuador (1994); Egypt (1982); India (1983); Iraq (1981); Peru (1988); Slovakia (1993). The Protocol was signed by Cameroon, the Holy See and Israel. As of August 2004 the following states have adhered to it: Czech Republic and Slovakia. Information received from WIPO.

[416] General Report of the Diplomatic Conference on the Double Taxation of Copyright Royalties, Madrid, November 26 to December 13, 1979, [1980] *Copyright* 12 et seq., at para.175.

[417] General Report of the Diplomatic Conference on the Double Taxation of Copyright Royalties, Madrid, November 26 to December 13, 1979, [1980] *Copyright* 12, et seq., at para.179.

E. THE UNESCO CONVENTION ON CULTURAL DIVERSITY

23–164   **The Convention on the Protection and Promotion of the Diversity of Cultural Expressions**, commonly referred to as the Convention on Cultural Diversity, was adopted by the General Conference of the United Nations Educational, Scientific and Cultural Organisation (UNESCO) on October 20, 2005, in Paris. The Convention does not directly deal with copyright matters. However, it concerns measures to protect and promote the diversity of cultural expressions and, therefore, its implementation at national level could affect the production, distribution, importation and exportation of copyright works such as films, music, books and other cultural products. The convention was approved by 148 UNESCO Member States, against strong opposition from the United States of America.[418]

The aim of the Convention was to confirm the right of countries to adopt and implement policies on the protection of local culture and domestic creative industries against competition from foreign goods and services. The Convention recognises the ability of governments to adopt measures to safeguard local culture and increase the diversity of artistic expressions. In this regard, the Convention allows countries to take steps to foster and encourage local creative activity, production and dissemination of local cultural works.[419] It also states the need to incorporate culture as a strategic element in national and international development policies.[420] The Convention was seen as a needed response to the growing dominance of a small number of multinational players in the cultural field, in particular in the audiovisual sector, and the parallel decrease in the range of available cultural goods to choose from.

23–165   **Substantive provisions.** The convention recognises countries' "sovereign right" to protect and promote the diversity of cultural expressions within their territory.[421] This includes the ability to introduce regulatory measures, provide financial assistance and take other steps to support domestic cultural industries and individual artists and creators. The convention also confirms countries' right to take "all appropriate measures" to protect and preserve cultural expressions that are under threat, at risk of extinction or otherwise in need of urgent safeguarding.[422] These rights confirm the ability of signatory countries to introduce measures such as competition rules or tax duties on foreign imports, aimed at promoting domestic production of cultural goods; establish quotas to block imports of foreign products; and grant funds or offer subsidies to local industries and creators.

23–166   **Relationship to other copyright conventions.** A major issue during the negotiation process was the relationship of the Convention with other international agreements, including copyright treaties and trade agreements that address copyright issues. The concern was that the Convention will be seen as overriding existing obligations to protect foreign works, or undermining commitments under bilateral or multilateral trade agreements. The final text recognised the "'mutual supportiveness'" of the Convention and other treaties, and stated that in interpreting other treaties or entering into new ones, countries shall take into account the pro-

---

[418] For the text of the Convention and meeting protocols see: *http://www.unesco.org* [Accessed September 14, 2010]
[419] art.7 of the Convention.
[420] art.13 of the Convention.
[421] art.6(1) of the Convention.
[422] art.8 of the Convention.

visions of the Convention.[423] It is also stated that the Convention should not be interpreted as modifying rights and obligations under other treaties ratified by signatories.[424] This confirms that while the Convention on Cultural Diversity is not subordinated to other treaties, international obligations relating to copyright may not be undermined by its provisions.

Entry into force and parties to the UNESCO Convention on Cultural Diversity. The Convention entered into force on March 18, 2007. As of August 31, 2010, 112 countries have joined the Convention, including: Afghanistan, Albania, Andorra, Argentina, Armenia, Australia, Austria, Azerbaijan, Bangladesh, Barbados, Belarus, Benin, Bolivia, Bosnia and Herzegovina, Brazil, Bulgaria, Burkina Faso, Burundi, Cambodia, Cameroon, Canada, Chad, Chile, China, Congo, Côte d'Ivoire, Croatia, Cuba, Cyprus, Denmark, Djibouti, Dominican Republic, Ecuador, Egypt, Equatorial Guinea, Estonia, Ethiopia, Finland, France, Gabon, Georgia, Germany, Greece, Grenada, Guatemala, Guinea, Guyana, Haiti, Hungary, Iceland, India, Ireland, Italy, Jamaica, Jordan, Kenya, Kuwait, Lao People's Democratic Republic, Latvia, Lesotho, Lithuania, Luxembourg, Madagascar, Malawi, Mali, Malta, Mauritius, Mexico, Monaco, Mongolia, Montenegro, Mozambique, Namibia, Netherlands, New Zealand, Nicaragua, Niger, Nigeria, Norway, Oman, Panama, Paraguay, Peru, Poland, Portugal, Qatar, Republic of Korea, Republic of Moldova, Romania, Saint Lucia, Saint Vincent and the Grenadines, Senegal, Serbia, Seychelles, Slovakia, Slovenia, South Africa, Spain, Sudan, Sweden, Switzerland, Syrian Arab Republic, Tajikistan, The former Yugoslav Republic of Macedonia, Togo, Trinidad and Tobago, Tunisia, Ukraine, the United Kingdom, Uruguay, Viet Nam, and Zimbabwe.

23–167

F. OTHER AGREEMENTS UNDER DISCUSSION

WIPO instrument on the protection of traditional cultural expressions/ expressions of folklore

23–168

    Overview. Discussions on a new form of legal protection for folklore and traditional cultural expressions have been ongoing at the World Intellectual Property Organisation (WIPO) for over ten years. These discussions are part of a broader process that also considers the legal protection of genetic resources and traditional knowledge. In respect of folklore and traditional cultural expressions, the proposed protection currently under review will be complementary to other intellectual property rights. It will also preclude the grant and exercise of intellectual property rights in works based on traditional expressions by unauthorised parties.

Process and state-of-play. Negotiations are held by an Intergovernmental Committee established by WIPO's General Assembly in October 2000. In 2009, following years of deliberations that have resulted in no meaningful progress, the Intergovernmental Committee was instructed by WIPO's General Assembly to undertake "text-based negotiations" and to reach agreement on the text of an international legal instrument.[425] Although it is yet unclear whether this instrument will be a new treaty, a declaration, or a non-binding document, a draft text

23–169

---

[423] art.20(1).
[424] art.20(2).
[425] See *http://www.wipo.int/tk/en/* [Accessed September 14, 2010] and, in particular, the decision of WIPO's thirty-eighth session of the General Assembly (Agenda Item 29).

on the protection of folklore prepared by WIPO's secretariat is currently being debated by Member States.[426]

23–170   **Scope of protection.** The text under discussion outlines elements of protection that resemble traditional copyright in many respects, but also go beyond copyright law on a number of substantive points. It is aimed at providing a new layer of protection which will complement available copyright and other intellectual property rights.[427] According to the most recent version of the text, folklore expressions will generally be protected against acts of misappropriation or misuse. Three categories of folklore expressions are identified and different levels of protection are afforded to each category. Expressions which have been notified or registered with the responsible authority as having particular cultural or spiritual value will entitle their beneficiaries to protection resembling the exclusive rights recognised under conventional copyright, including the right to prevent unauthorised use by means of reproduction, distribution, communication and other forms of exploitation. Use of registered expressions will require prior and informed consent from the beneficiary community. Registered expressions will also be protected in a manner similar to that afforded under conventional moral rights. This will include rights against distortion or mutilation and a right of acknowledgement of the beneficiary. The second category of expressions includes those that have not been registered as having a particular value. These expressions will benefit from protection that is similar to conventional moral rights, but their use will not require prior authorisation from the beneficiary community. Accordingly, protection for non-registered folklore expressions will extend only to the manner in which these expressions are used, with rights to prevent distortion or other derogatory treatment, to require identification of the source or beneficiary and to prevent false indication or allegation. The third category of protected expressions includes cultural expressions that are secret. These expressions are protected against unauthorised disclosure and any subsequent use or acquisition of intellectual property rights in respect of such expressions.

Protection against misappropriation or misuse of all three categories of cultural expressions will continue for as long as the expression continues to meet the criteria for protected subject-matter (i.e. in the case of secret expressions, as long as they remain secret, and in the case of registered expressions, as long as they remain registered).[428]

23–171   **Protected subject-matter.** Although still under negotiation and subject to different proposed amendments, the draft list of protected subject-matter is extensive and covers any form of tangible or intangible traditional cultural expression. This includes verbal expressions, music, dance, plays and forms of art such as drawings, designs, sculptures, jewellery, textiles and many others.[429] It is proposed that protection will extend to any expression which is the product of a creative intellectual activity that is indicative of a particular community or indigenous peoples and is maintained by them.[430] The beneficiaries of protection will be the indigenous peoples or community, but some countries seek to expressly include the nation in the definition of beneficiaries.[431] Protection will be subject to certain limitations, and proposed provisions on exceptions will allow exploitation within

---

[426] Most recently, this text was included as part of document WIPO/GRTKF/IC/17/4 PROV. Available from *http://www.wipo.int/tk/en/igc/index.html* [Accessed September 14, 2010].

[427] Draft art.10.

[428] Draft art.6.

[429] Draft art.1(1).

[430] Draft art.1(2).

[431] Draft art.2.

the community and certain other uses such as in teaching, research, private study, criticism and incidental use. Non-excepted use that breaches the rights of communities recognised by the new instrument may be subject to civil and criminal remedies.[432]

Anti-Counterfeiting Trade Agreement (ACTA)   **23–172**
    Overview. The Anti-Counterfeiting Trade Agreement (ACTA) is a new plurilateral agreement on intellectual property enforcement. It seeks to create a new international framework on enforcement and harmonise intellectual property enforcement standards and best practices. The Agreement also aims at enhancing cooperation between enforcement agencies in investigating and tackling domestic and cross-border infringement of intellectual property rights, including copyright. The ACTA does not address substantive rights or liability rules, and does not attempt to change existing obligations under international intellectual property law. To a large extent ACTA can be seen as an attempt to fill a gap in international law on the issue of enforcement, because no other international agreement deals with enforcement measures in detail. The TRIPs agreement includes some provisions on enforcement and identifies minimum enforcement standards, but these are relatively general and unlike ACTA do not specifically address digital issues.[433]

Process and state-of-play. ACTA was an initiative of the United States of America and Japan. Following initial talks, an official announcement of negotiations towards a new anti-counterfeiting trade agreement was made jointly by the United States, the European Union, Japan and Switzerland in October 2007.[434] Negotiations opened in June 2008 and eleven rounds of talks have taken place, each time in a different location in a participating country. The eleventh and final round of ACTA negotiations was held in Japan in September 2010, following which an official announcement of the conclusion of negotiations was made.[435] The text was not finalised in the last negotiating round due to a number of unresolved issues. However, following further talks outside official negotiations, on November 15, 2010 a press release announced that agreement has been reached on the final text.   **23–173**

ACTA negotiating countries included Australia, Canada, the European Union (on behalf of its 27 member States), Japan, Korea, Mexico, Morocco, New Zealand, Singapore, Switzerland and the United States. A number of other countries reportedly attended the negotiations as observers and may sign the agreement at a later stage. The declared aim of negotiators is to leave the agreement open for other countries to join.[436]

ACTA negotiations took place outside international institutions such as the WTO or WIPO. The meetings were held behind closed doors and limited information was disclosed to the public. This has led to strong criticism and vocal calls for transparency, in particular from civil society and consumer groups. To respond to the growing criticism and following online leaks of draft texts and other confidential documents, negotiators released a first draft of the agreement in April 2010.[437] A near-final version of the text was made available in October

---

[432] Draft art.8.
[433] See above paras 24–145 to 24–147.
[434] Available from *http:////www.ustr.gov* [Accessed September 14, 2010].
[435] *http://www.ustr.gov/about-us/press-office/press-releases/2010/october/statement-ambassador-ron-kirk-regarding-acta-negot* [Accessed November 16, 2010].
[436] See *http://www.ustr.gov/*.
[437] Available from: *http://trade.ec.europa.eu/doclib/docs/2010/april/tradoc_146029.pdf* [Accessed September 14, 2010].

2010 following the last negotiating meeting.[438] The finalised text of the Agreement was made public in mid-November.[439]

23–174   **Substantive provisions.** According to the final text of November 2010,[440] ACTA is comprised of six chapters, with the main chapter addressing rules on civil and criminal enforcement, border measures and enforcement on the internet. The preamble to the agreement acknowledges the critical need for effective enforcement of rights to sustaining economic growth, and notes the proliferation of services that distribute infringing content. It expresses the desire to address the problem of infringement, including online, in a manner that balances the rights and interests of users, right holders and service providers, and to promote cooperation between right holders and service providers with respect to infringements that take place in the digital environment.

The main text includes a general obligation on signatories to make available enforcement procedures that permit effective action against any acts of infringement, including expeditious remedies to prevent infringement and remedies which constitute a deterrent to further infringement. Signatories also undertake to apply enforcement procedures in a manner that avoids the creation of barriers to legitimate trade.[441]

Obligations concerning civil enforcement address the availability of injunctions, orders to obtain relevant information on the infringement that the alleged infringer possesses, and provisional measures.[442] A provision on damages requires countries to make available at least one of the following: pre-established damages, presumptions for determining the amount of damages sufficient to compensate the right holder for the harm caused by the infringement or (at least in the case of copyright infringement) additional damages.[443]

On border measures, ACTA provides that countries shall establish procedures for dealing with imports and exports, and may establish procedures for dealing with goods in transit, suspected of infringing rights.[444] These procedures apply in respect of goods of a commercial nature, even where they are sent in small consignments, but a de-minimis provision allows the exclusion of small quantities of goods of a non-commercial nature imported or exported in travellers' luggage.

ACTA's criminal enforcement rules require countries to provide for criminal sanctions in at least cases of wilful piracy on a commercial scale.[445] The text further clarifies that 'commercial scale' includes at least those acts carried out as commercial activities for direct or indirect economic or commercial advantage. Other provisions on criminal procedures address an obligation to provide penalties that include imprisonment as well as monetary fines sufficiently high to provide a deterrent to future infringement; seizure, forfeiture and destruction of infringing goods by competent authorities; and an obligation to empower enforcement authorities to take ex officio action in appropriate cases.[446]

As regards online enforcement, the text requires countries to make available enforcement procedures that permit effective action against acts of infringement committed "in the digital environment", including expeditious remedies to

---

[438] *http:www.ustr.gov/webfm__send/2338* [Accessed November 16,2010].

[439] *http://ustr.gov/webfm__send/2379* [Accessed November 25, 2010].

[440] At the time of writing this chapter, the agreement is yet to be signed by negotiating countries.

[441] Chapter Two, Section 1.

[442] Chapter Two, Section 2.

[443] Chapter Two, Section 2, art.2.3.

[444] Chapter Two, Section 3.

[445] Chapter Two, Section 4, art. 2.14.

[446] Chapter Two, Section 4.

prevent infringement and remedies which constitute a deterrent to future infringement.[447] ACTA also recognises the ability of countries to establish disclosure procedures, whereby rights owners can seek an injunction against an online service provider to reveal the details of a subscriber whose account has been used for infringement; ACTA does not, however, oblige countries to make available such disclosure procedures.[448] The chapter dealing with enforcement in the digital environment also establishes detailed obligations on the protection of technological protection measures against circumvention, including a prohibition against the manufacture, importation or distribution of circumvention devices, and protection against the removal or alteration of electronic rights management information.[449]

Other ACTA chapters deal with international cooperation between enforcement agencies, information sharing, capacity building and technical assistance in the areas of enforcement, public awareness, training and the implementation of enforcement legislation.[450] A chapter on institutional arrangements establishes a new committee responsible for reviewing the implementation of the agreement, dealing with future amendments and approving the accession of new countries as parties.[451]

WIPO treaty on the protection of broadcasters   23–175
Overview. The protection of broadcasters under a new international treaty has been on WIPO's agenda since 1998, so far leading to no meaningful outcome. Ongoing discussions consider the need to update and modernise the level of protection afforded to broadcasters under the 1961 Rome Convention,[452] in particular in light of technological developments that have taken place in recent years. A draft treaty was prepared by WIPO's Standing Committee on Copyright and Related Rights (SCCR), but due to the diverging positions of Member States as regards the scope of rights that should be recognised, no consensus could be reached. There are differing approaches to the type and level of protection that should be established under the new treaty. Some countries favour a rights-based treaty that will establish a set of exclusive rights for broadcasters over their programme-carrying signal, in addition to any copyright subsisting in the underlying broadcast works. Other countries limit their support to protection against signal theft, without granting broadcasters exclusive rights over their signals. Another contentious issue during the negotiations was whether the treaty's protection will extend to internet transmissions such as webcasting (internet-only broadcasts) and simulcasting (simultaneous internet and traditional over-the-air broadcasts); eventually, in 2006, countries agreed to exclude these transmissions from the scope of the agreement and focus on "traditional"' broadcasts in their negotiations.

Process and state of play. WIPO continues to consider the protection of   23–176
broadcasting organisations under its agenda. Following a recommendation made by the SCCR, in October 2006 WIPO's General Assembly decided to convene a diplomatic conference on this topic, on the condition that the SCCR could come up with a streamlined text for a basic proposal for a treaty. Special sessions of the SCCR were held for this purpose in the course of 2007, but no consensus could be achieved and negotiations eventually broke down. Consequently, the SCCR

---

[447] Chapter Two, Section 5, art.2.18 (1).
[448] Chapter Two, Section 5, art..2.18 (4).
[449] Chapter Two, Section 5, art.2.18(5), (6) and (7).
[450] Chapters Three and Four.
[451] Chapter Five.
[452] See para.23–100, above.

recommended to the General Assembly to continue with discussions before a diplomatic conference is convened, and the Assembly approved this recommendation. Discussions continued within the SCCR and in 2010, in order to facilitate progress and promote consensus, WIPO arranged a series of regional meetings and consultations to consider this topic with stakeholders from different countries. The SCCR continues to keep this issue on its agenda for future meetings.[453]

23–177   WIPO treaty on minimum exceptions and limitations

As discussed earlier,[454] international copyright law allows countries to introduce exceptions and limitations to the rights granted to authors, performers and producers to the extent that these exceptions meet certain criteria established under the so-called "three-step test'". International law does not, however, oblige countries to introduce exceptions and leaves this issue open for countries to decide at national level. In recent years, a number of calls have been made to introduce mandatory exceptions at international level and under a new legal instrument, in particular to benefit certain groups of beneficiaries. During the May 2009 session of WIPO's Standing Committee on Copyright and Related Rights (SCCR), a group of countries, namely Brazil, Ecuador and Paraguay, submitted a proposal for a treaty on minimum exceptions for the benefit of visually impaired and reading-disabled persons. The treaty, originally prepared by the World Blind Union, proposed mandatory obligations to enable and facilitate improved access to copyright works on formats or copies accessible by the visually impaired.[455] The draft proposal also expressly recognises the need in certain circumstances to circumvent technological measures to render the copyright work accessible or to make copies of the work on formats which may be accessed by visually impaired persons. The issue continued to be on the agenda of the SCCR in its December 2009 and June 2010 meetings.[456]

10. REGIONAL CONVENTIONS

A. PAN-AMERICAN CONVENTIONS

23–178   As seen above at paras 23–79 et seq., the principal purpose of the Universal Copyright Convention (UCC) was to provide a conventional link to govern copyright relations between the countries of the Berne Union, on the one hand, and the Member States of the various multilateral copyright conventions which had been adopted between 1889 and 1928 by certain of the States on the American continent, including in some cases the United States of America, on the other.[457] These include the Montevideo Convention and the so-called Pan-American

---

[453] WIPO paper SCCR/17/INF/1. Further information on the process and past meetings available from *http://www.wipo.int/copyright/en/* [Accessed September 14, 2010].

[454] See paras 23–72, 23–127 and 23–142, above.

[455] The proposal is available from *http://www.wipo.int/edocs/mdocs/copyright/en/sccr__18/ sccr__18__5.pdf* [Accessed September 14, 2010].

[456] WIPO paper SCCR/20/13 Prov.

[457] "The Conference [for the adoption of the UCC] was the logical development of the desire expressed by many nations for many years and on many different occasions for some international agreement on the rights of authors which would be acceptable to the Member States of the Berne Union for the Protection of Literary and Artistic Works, and to the members of the Organisation of American States, and, if possible, also to other States which were not members of either." Report of the Rapporteur-General (Sir John Blake) of the Intergovernmental Conference of States for the adoption of the Universal Copyright Convention, Geneva, August 18 to September 6, 1952, in T.R. Kupferman and M. Foner (eds), *Universal Copyright Convention Analysed* (New York: Federal Legal Publications Inc., 1955), p.214.

Conventions.[458] The Universal Copyright Convention provides specifically that the Convention shall not abrogate any copyright relations in effect exclusively between two or more American Republics and that in the event of any difference between the provisions of the UCC and any Pan-American Convention the most recently formulated shall prevail.[459]

The Pan-American Conventions were all influenced by the Berne Convention and reflected the aim of their signatories to obtain a copyright treaty which would attract all the States of the Americas.[460] However, all the Conventions differed fundamentally from the Berne Convention in that they provided that copyright protection, at least for published works, be subject to compliance with formalities.[461] With the passage of time, and the adherence of many of the Latin-American States as well as the United States of America to the Berne Convention and the UCC, these conventions are no longer of more than historical interest. The United Kingdom was never party to any of them.

The Montevideo Convention[462] (January 11, 1889) was influenced by and largely modelled on the Berne Convention. However, it rejected the principle of national treatment and adopted a wholly different principle to that of the Berne Convention, conferring upon an author belonging to one country of the Union in the other countries of the Union the rights which he enjoys in the country where he first publishes, not the rights which authors enjoy in the country where the infringement takes place. Thus, under this Convention, the law of the country of origin follows the work into the other countries of the Union. Membership was limited to signatory states which ratified the Convention; as far as non-signatory states were concerned, these could accede to the Convention but only benefited from conventional relations with signatory states which accepted their accession. This limited the value of the Convention, since of the five signatory states that ratified it (Argentina, Bolivia, Paraguay, Peru and Uruguay), Peru and Uruguay refused to recognise accessions by non-Latin American states.[463] **23–179**

The Pan-American Conventions are those of Mexico City[464] (1902), Rio de Janeiro[465] (1906), Buenos Aires[466] (1910), Caracas[467] (1911), Havana[468] (1928) and **23–180**

---

[458] The full text of these Conventions, and information concerning the states to which they apply, will be found in "Copyright Laws and Treaties of the World", published by UNESCO. They are also reproduced in T.R. Kupferman and M. Foner, *Universal Copyright Convention Analysed* (New York: Federal Legal Publications Inc., 1995), 614 et seq. See also H.G. Henn, "Interrelation Between the UCC and the Pan-American Copyright Conventions" in T.R. Kupferman and M. Foner, 125; S. Ricketson, *The Berne Convention for the protection of literary and artistic works: 1886–1896* (Queen Mary College, University of London, 1987), paras 15.3 et seq. and S.P. Ladas, "Patents, Trademarks, and Related Rights; National and International Protection" (Cambridge: Harvard University Press, 1975). See also "Les Conventions pan-américaines concernant la protection de la propriété intellectuelle: Mexico (1902), Rio de Janeiro 1906, Buenos Aires 1910" [1911] *Le Droit d'Auteur*, 58.

[459] Art.XVIII of the 1952 and 1971 texts.

[460] With the exception of the Montevideo Convention, the Pan-American Conventions were open to adherence only by countries of the Western Hemisphere, i.e. American States.

[461] See H.G. Henn, "Interrelation Between the UCC and the Pan-American Copyright Conventions" in T.R. Kupferman and M. Foner, p.137.

[462] Convention of Montevideo on Literary and Artistic Property, January 11, 1889.

[463] [1889] *Le Droit d'Auteur* 52.

[464] Convention for the Protection of Literary and Artistic Property, January 27, 1902.

[465] Convention for the Protection of Patents of Invention, Drawings and Industrial Models, Trade-Marks and Literary and Artistic Property, August 23, 1906.

[466] Convention Concerning Literary and Artistic Copyright, August 11, 1910.

[467] Agreement on Literary and Artistic Property, July 17, 1911.

[468] Revision of the Conference of Buenos Aires Regarding Literary and Artistic Copyright, February 18, 1928.

Washington[469] (1946). These all had the aim of attracting the adherence of all American States, an aim in which none of them succeeded. The later of these Conventions are all modifications of the original Convention of 1902, and all adopt the Berne principle of according national protection to works published in any of the countries of the Union (principle of national treatment). But under the Convention of 1902, in order to obtain copyright in another country, it was an "indispensable" condition that the author or his representatives should address a petition to the official department of each government, claiming the recognition of the right. This was modified by the later Conventions, and, under the Convention of 1910, it simply provided that "the acknowledgment of a copyright obtained in one state, in conformity with its laws, shall produce its effects of full right, in all the other states, without the necessity of complying with any other formality, provided always there shall appear in the work a statement that indicates the reservation of the property right".[470] The Convention of 1902 was ratified by Costa Rica, the Dominican Republic, El Salvador, Guatemala, Honduras, Nicaragua and the United States of America. The Convention of 1906 was ratified by Brazil, Chile, Costa Rica, Ecuador, El Salvador, Guatemala, Honduras, Nicaragua and Panama. The Convention of 1910 was ratified by 14 states, making it the most successful of these conventions; namely, Argentina, Bolivia, Brazil, Chile Colombia, Costa Rica, the Dominican Republic, Ecuador, Haiti, Guatemala, Honduras, Mexico, Nicaragua, Panama, Peru, Paraguay, Uruguay and the United States of America. The 1911 Convention, which was modelled on the Montevideo Convention, was signed by Bolivia, Colombia, Ecuador, Peru and Venezuela but ratified only by the last three of these.[471] Finally, the Convention of 1928, which was a revision of the Buenos Aires Convention, was ratified by only Costa Rica, Ecuador, Guatemala, Nicaragua and Panama.

Many years later, a further Convention was concluded at Washington in 1946 under the auspices of the Pan-American Union, according to which rights of copyright set out in some detail are to be conferred as between the signatory countries without formality or restriction. This Convention replaced, in relations between the Contracting States, the Conventions of Buenos Aires (1910), Havana (1928) and all earlier inter-American Conventions on copyright but did not affect rights acquired under those Conventions.Washington Convention, art.XVII. The Washington Convention was ratified by Argentina, Bolivia, Brazil, Chile, Colombia, Costa Rica, Cuba, Dominica, Ecuador, Guatemala, Haiti, Honduras, Mexico, Nicaragua and Paraguay.

B. COUNCIL OF EUROPE CONVENTIONS AND RECOMMENDATIONS

23–181   **Interest of the Council of Europe in Copyright and Related Rights.** A table showing the parties to the Council of Europe Copyright and Related Rights Conventions as of October 15, 2008, follows para.23–186 (see also the Council of Europe's website at *http://www.coe.int* for updated information). More recently, it has also undertaken studies of a number of copyright and related rights law questions, which have resulted in the adoption by the Council of Ministers of a series of recommendations and declarations.[472] The United Kingdom is a member of the Council of Europe and party or signatory to these instruments.

---

[469] Inter-American Convention on the Rights of the Author in Literary, Scientific and Artistic Works, 1946.
[470] Buenos Aires Convention art.3.
[471] "L'Union bolivienne et la protection de la propriété intellectuelle", [1912] *Le Droit d'Auteur* 58.
[472] Doc. DH–MM (96) 4, for an account of Council of Europe activities to 1996. In May 2005 the Council of Europe Steering Committee on the Mass Media (CDMM) was renamed the Steering Committee on the Media and New Communications Services (CDMC) and its terms of reference

The Council of Europe's policy in these matters has been expressed as follows: "copyright and neighbouring rights are at the basis of the creation, production and circulation of audiovisual works in Europe and…it is necessary to provide for a minimum harmonisation of national rules in the area of copyright and neighbouring rights so as to guarantee adequate protection of rights holders, while facilitating the public's access to audiovisual creations through the new opportunities offered by technical developments".[473] The value to the international community of the Council of Europe's involvement in these matters lies in its efforts to promote copyright and related rights throughout its 47 Member States in Western and Eastern Europe. The Agreements are also open to signature and ratification by non-signatory States which participate in their elaboration and to accession by other non-Member States.

European agreements on broadcasting. The European Agreement concerning   **23–182**
Programme Exchanges by means of Television Films, 1958, aims to facilitate the exchange of television films, inter alia, in the framework of the European Broadcasting Union.[474]

The European Agreement on the Protection of Television Broadcasts, 1960, with its Protocol, 1965, and three additional Protocols (1974, 1983 and 1989),[475] was adopted as a temporary, regional arrangement with limited objectives. It was foreseen that it would remain in force only until such time as an international convention on related rights, including the protection of television broadcasts, was established.[476] Broadcasting organisations have the right to authorise the following acts in relation to their television broadcasts: re-broadcasting, cable distribution, communication to the public and audiovisual recording in another country. The parties can make protected utilisations subject to given reservations, and, in particular, can withhold completely the protection of cable distribution. The adoption of the Rome Convention in 1961 led to the adoption of the 1965 Protocol to the Agreement, which urged Contracting Parties to accede to the Rome Convention; the slow pace of adherence to the Rome Convention subsequently resulted in the adoption of the three Additional Protocols of 1974, 1983 and 1989, which had the same aim. They all provided that, after a prescribed date, no state could remain or become a party to the Agreement unless it had become a party to the Rome Convention. The date prescribed by the second Protocol was January 1, 1990 and, since the third Protocol (aimed at postponing the deadline once more) had not entered into force on that date, four states then ceased to be members.

The European Agreement for the Prevention of Broadcasts transmitted from Stations outside National Territories 1965, reinforces, within Europe, compliance

---

were redefined. These no longer include matters of intellectual property. The new Committee will continue to monitor questions of copyright in the context of its work and, in particular, the impact of copyright on the exercise of the right to freedom of and access to information. The reports of the CDMC are available on the Council of Europe website. The Agreements, Resolutions and Declarations mentioned are all available from the Publications Section, Council of Europe, F-67075 Strasbourg Cedex, France.

[473] Resolution No.1 on media economics and political and cultural pluralism, 3rd. European Ministerial Conference on Mass Media Policy (October 1991).

[474] Adopted in Paris on December 15, 1958, this Agreement entered into force on July 1, 1961. As of August 31, 2010, the following 14 members of the Council of Europe were party to the European Agreement Concerning Programme Exchanges by means of Television Films: Belgium, Croatia, Cyprus, Denmark, France, Greece, Ireland, Luxembourg, the Netherlands, Norway, Spain, Sweden, Turkey and the United Kingdom. Non-Member States Israel and Tunisia have also ratified the Agreement.

[475] Adopted in Strasbourg on June 22, 1960, this Agreement entered into force on July 1, 1961. As of August 31, 2010, the following seven members of the Council of Europe were party thereto: Croatia, Denmark, France, Germany, Norway, Sweden and the United Kingdom.

[476] Agreement art.13.

with the International Telecommunication Union (ITU) Radio Regulations. The Agreement aims to prevent the establishment of broadcasting stations on board ships, aircraft or other objects, such as platforms and artificial islands outside national territories (pirate stations) , which transmit broadcasts intended for reception within the territory of one of the parties and requires all broadcasting to be licensed.[477]

The European Convention relating to Questions of Copyright Law and Neighbouring Rights in the Framework of Transfrontier Broadcasting by Satellite was adopted on May 11, 1994, but as of October 15, 2008, it had not yet entered into force. The Convention indicates the criteria for identifying the applicable national law governing relations between broadcasters and rights holders in respect of the transmission of works and other contributions by direct broadcasting satellite (DBS) or by fixed satellite services (FSS) under conditions which are comparable to direct broadcasting by satellite. The Convention also deals with ways and means of acquiring rights in works which are used for broadcasting by satellite. Furthermore, it establishes a minimum harmonisation of the level of protection of the various categories of rights holders (authors, composers, audiovisual producers, performers, phonogram producers, broadcasting organisations).[478] The Council of Europe is currently considering whether a new Council of Europe instrument designed to reinforce the protection of the related rights of broadcasting organisations should be prepared.[479]

23–183   **Convention on Cybercrime.**[480] This is the first international treaty to address criminal law and procedural aspects of various types of behaviour directed against computer systems, networks and data. It contains provisions concerning offences related to infringements of copyright and neighbouring rights (art.10). It was opened for signature on November 23, 2001, and has been signed by 32 Member States of the Council of Europe as well as by Canada, Japan, South Africa and the United States of America. It entered into force on July 1, 2004, following ratification by five countries, including at least three Member States of the Council of Europe. As of August 31, 2010, the Convention had been ratified by 29 Member States: Albania, Armenia, Azerbaijan, Bosnia and Herzegovina, Bulgaria, Croatia, Cyprus, Denmark, Estonia, Finland, France, Germany, Hungary, Iceland, Italy, Latvia, Lithuania, Moldova, Montenegro, Netherlands, Norway, Portugal, Romania, Serbia, Slovakia, Slovenia, Spain, the former Yugoslav Republic of Macedonia and Ukraine. One non-Member State, the United States of America, has also ratified the convention.

An additional Protocol to the Convention on Cybercrime, concerning the criminalisation of acts of a racist and xenophobic nature committed through computer systems,[481] was adopted on January 28, 2003. The Protocol entered into force on March 1, 2006, and as of August 31, 2010, it had been ratified by 18 Member States: Albania, Armenia, Bosnia and Herzegovina, Croatia, Cyprus, Denmark, France, Latvia, Lithuania, Montenegro, Netherlands, Norway, Portugal, Romania, Serbia, Slovenia, the former Yugoslav Republic of Macedonia and Ukraine.

---

[477] Adopted in Strasbourg on January 22, 1965, this Agreement entered into force on October 19, 1967. As of August 31, 2010, the following 19 members of the Council of Europe were party thereto: Belgium, Croatia, Cyprus, Denmark, France, Germany, Greece, Ireland, Italy, Liechtenstein, the Netherlands (including the Netherlands' Antilles and Aruba), Norway, Poland, Portugal, Spain, Sweden, Switzerland, Turkey and the United Kingdom.

[478] Council of Europe activities concerning the protection of copyright and neighbouring rights in the media sector (doc.DH—MM(94)(4), paras 18 et seq.

[479] Decision No. CM/875/20022008 adopted by the Committee of Ministers of February 20, 2008, at the 1,018th meeting of the Ministers' Deputies.

[480] Convention on Cybercrime (CETS No.185).

[481] CETS No.189.

Recommendations and Declarations. These identify key issues for priority ac-   **23–184**
tion and lay down principles designed to guide Member States in improving the
level of protection provided by their national laws and relate to copyright law
questions in the following fields: copyright law principles to be respected in the
field of television broadcasting by satellite and cable,[482] the protection of related
rights,[483] the legal protection of encrypted television services,[484] sound and audiovisual private copying,[485] measures to combat piracy in the field of copyright and
neighbouring rights,[486] measures against sound and audiovisual piracy,[487]
principles relating to copyright law questions in the field of reprography,[488] the
promotion of education and awareness in the area of copyright and neighbouring
rights concerning creativity,[489] copyright and cultural policy,[490] and on measures
to protect copyright and neighbouring rights and combat piracy, especially in the
digital environment.[491]

Subsequently, a Recommendation was adopted in 2002 on measures to
enhance the protection of the neighbouring rights of broadcasting organisations.[492]
Two further Parliamentary Assembly Recommendations have been adopted on
the subject of counterfeiting; the first, adopted in 2004, entitled "Counterfeiting:
Problems and Solutions", recommended inter alia that Member States further
tighten national laws and measures against counterfeiting and seek their harmonisation at European level as exemplified by European Union legislation.[493] A
further recommendation adopted in 2007, on the need for a Council of Europe
Convention on the suppression of counterfeiting and trafficking in counterfeit
goods, called on the Member States to tackle the problem of counterfeiting in a
more comprehensive manner, and suggested the preparation of a European
convention on the suppression of counterfeiting as well as information campaigns
on its dangers and better protection of intellectual property. It recognised that
counterfeiting can endanger consumers' health and safety, seriously damage the
economy and nurture criminal networks.[494]

European agreements on related topics, including the information society. A   **23–185**
number of European Conventions on topics having an impact on copyright and
related rights have been adopted in the past twenty years. These do not deal
directly with copyright and related rights but concern aspects of the information
society and broadcasting.

The European Convention on Transfrontier Television,[495] adopted on May 5,
1989, and which entered into force on May 1, 1993, creates a legal framework for
the free circulation of trans-frontier television programmes in Europe, through
minimum common rules, in fields such as programming, advertising, sponsorship
and the protection of certain individual rights, such as the right to exercise the

---

[482] Recommendation No.R (86) 2 of February 14, 1986.
[483] Declaration on the protection of neighbouring rights (adopted by the Committee of Ministers of the Council of Europe on February 17, 1994).
[484] Recommendation No.R (91) 14 of September 27, 1991.
[485] Recommendation No.R (88) 1 of January 18, 1988.
[486] Recommendation No.R (88) 2 of January 18, 1988.
[487] Recommendation No.R (95) 1 of January 11, 1995.
[488] Recommendation No.R (90) 11 of April 25, 1990.
[489] Recommendation No.R (94) 3 of April 5, 1994.
[490] Recommendation No.R (86) 9 of May 1986.
[491] Recommendation No.R (2001) 7 of September 5, 2001.
[492] Recommendation No.R (2002) 7 of September 11, 2002.
[493] Recommendation 1673 (2004) of September 4, 2004.
[494] Recommendation 1793 (2007) of April 20, 2007. The Committee of Ministers issued a reply to these recommendations on November 28, 2008 (Doc. 11458).
[495] CETS No.132.

right to reply to TV programmes. The Convention has been amended by a Protocol,[496] which entered into force on March 1, 2002.

The Convention on Information and Legal Cooperation concerning "Information Society Services"[497] was adopted on October 4, 2001. The aim of the Convention, which was prepared in close co-operation between the Council of Europe and the Commission of the European Union is to set up a legal information and co-operation system in the area of new communication services, following the example of Directive 98/34/EC[498] and extending it beyond the borders of the European Union. According to the Council of Europe, it will enable it to act as a clearing house for draft legislation in the field of "Information Society Services", in order to provide a harmonised approach to the regulation of online services at the pan-European level. The Convention will enter into force after the expression of their consent to be bound by five signatories of which at least one is not a Member State of the European Economic Area. As of August 31, 2010, the Convention had not entered into force.

23–186   The European Convention for the Protection of the Audiovisual Heritage and its Protocol on the Protection of Television Productions[499] were adopted on November 8, 2001. On January 1, 2008, the Convention entered into force, following ratification by five countries (of which at least four had to be Member States of the Council of Europe), namely: Croatia, Hungary, Lithuania, Monaco and Slovakia. The Convention concerns the principle of compulsory legal deposit and conservation in film archives of all moving-image material produced or co-produced and made available to the public in each signatory state. The material has to be available for consultation for academic or research purposes, subject to the international or national rules on copyright. As of August 31, 2010, the Protocol had not entered into force.

The European Convention on the Legal Protection of Services Based on, or Consisting of, Conditional Access,[500] was adopted on January 23, 2001, and entered into force on July 1, 2003. The Convention seeks to protect operators and providers of paid radio, TV and online services against unlawful reception of such services. It supplements a European Community Directive[501] on the same subject by extending protection throughout Europe. Under the Convention, it is a criminal offence to manufacture, import, distribute, sell, offer for hire, possess or install decoders or smart cards enabling access to be obtained unlawfully to the above-mentioned services. The promotion, marketing or advertising of illicit devices are also prohibited. Penalties include seizure and confiscation of devices or material and of any profits or financial gain resulting from the unlawful activity. The aim of the Convention is to help European providers of audiovisual and online services to reduce financial losses sustained as a result of electronic and computer piracy, in the interest of both service operators and the public. As of August

---

[496] CETS No.171.

[497] CETS No.180.

[498] Directive 98/34/EC of the European Parliament and of the Council of June 22, 1998, laying down a procedure for the provision of information in the field of technical standards and regulations and of rules on Information Society services ([1998] OJ L204, July 21, 1998, p.37). Directive as amended by Directive 98/48/EC of the European Parliament and of the Council ([1998] OJ L217, of August 5, 1988, p.18).

[499] CETS Nos 183 and 184.

[500] CETS No.178.

[501] Directive 98/84/EC of the European Parliament and of the Council of November 20, 1998, on the legal protection of services based on, or consisting of, conditional access (cf. para.24–144 below and Vol.2 H6).

31, 2010, the Convention had the following nine Member States: Bosnia and Herzegovina, Bulgaria, Croatia, Cyprus, France, Moldova, Netherlands, Romania and Switzerland.

TABLE OF COUNCIL OF EUROPE COPYRIGHT AND RELATED RIGHTS CONVENTIONS[1]

Member States of the Council of Europe	European Agreement Concerning Programme Exchanges by Means of Television Films 1958[2]	Agreement on the Protection of Television Broadcasts 1960[3]	European Agreement for the Prevention of Broadcasts Transmitted from Stations Outside National Territories 1965[4]	European Convention Relating to Questions of Copyright Law and Neighbouring Rights in the Framework of Transfrontier Broadcasting by Satellite 1994[5]	Convention on Cybercrime 2001[6] Additional Protocol 2003[7]
	Date of entry into force	(e) Date of entry into force (d) Date denunciation took effect	Date of entry into force	(a) Date of signature (b) Date of ratification	Date of entry into force of (a) Convention (b) Protocol
Albania					(a) July 1, 2004 (b) March 1, 2006
Andorra					
Armenia					(a) and (b) February 1, 2007
Austria					
Azerbaijan					(a) July 1, 2010
Belgium	April 8, 1962	(e) March 8, 1968 (d) January 1, 1990	October 19, 1967	(a) August 6, 1998	

Member States of the Council of Europe	European Agreement Concerning Programme Exchanges by Means of Television Films 1958[2]	Agreement on the Protection of Television Broadcasts 1960[3]	European Agreement for the Prevention of Broadcasts Transmitted from Stations Outside National Territories 1965[4]	European Convention Relating to Questions of Copyright Law and Neighbouring Rights in the Framework of Transfrontier Broadcasting by Satellite 1994[5]	Convention on Cybercrime 2001[6] Additional Protocol 2003[7]
Bosnia and Herzegovina				(a) February 21, 2005	(a) & (b) September 1, 2006
Bulgaria					(a) August 1, 2005
Croatia	December 31, 2004	(e) December 31, 2004	December 31, 2004		(a) July 1, 2004 (b) November 1, 2008
Cyprus	February 20, 1970	(e) February 22, 1970 (d) January 1, 1990	October 2, 1971	(a) February 10, 1995 (b) December 21, 1998	(a) May 1, 2005 (b) March 1, 2006
Czech Republic					
Denmark	November 25, 1961	(e) November 27, 1961	October 19, 1967		(a) October 1, 2005 (b) March 1, 2006.

Member States of the Council of Europe	European Agreement Concerning Programme Exchanges by Means of Television Films 1958[2]	Agreement on the Protection of Television Broadcasts 1960[3]	European Agreement for the Prevention of Broadcasts Transmitted from Stations Outside National Territories 1965[4]	European Convention Relating to Questions of Copyright Law and Neighbouring Rights in the Framework of Transfrontier Broadcasting by Satellite 1994[5]	Convention on Cybercrime 2001[6] Additional Protocol 2003[7]
Estonia					(a) July 1, 2004
Finland					(a) September 1, 2007
France	July 1, 1961	(e) July 1, 1961	April 6, 1968		(a) May 1, 2006 (b) May 1, 2006
Georgia					
Germany		(e) October 9, 1967	February 28, 1970	(a) April 18, 1997	(a) July 1, 2009
Greece	February 9, 1962		August 14, 1979		
Hungary					(a) July 1, 2004
Iceland					(a) May 1, 2007
Ireland	April 4, 1965		February 23, 1969		
Italy			March 19, 1983		(a) October 1, 2008

Member States of the Council of Europe	European Agreement Concerning Programme Exchanges by Means of Television Films 1958[2]	Agreement on the Protection of Television Broadcasts 1960[3]	European Agreement for the Prevention of Broadcasts Transmitted from Stations Outside National Territories 1965[4]	European Convention Relating to Questions of Copyright Law and Neighbouring Rights in the Framework of Transfrontier Broadcasting by Satellite 1994[5]	Convention on Cybercrime 2001[6] Additional Protocol 2003[7]
Latvia					(a) June 1, 2007 (b) June 1, 2007
Liechtenstein			February 14, 1977		
Lithuania					(a) July 1, 2004 (b) February 1, 2007
Luxembourg	October 31, 1963			(a) May 11, 1994	
Malta					
Moldova					(a) September 1, 2009
Monaco					
Montenegro					(a) & (b) July 1, 2010
Netherlands	March 5, 1967		September 27, 1974		(a) March 1, 2007

Member States of the Council of Europe	European Agreement Concerning Programme Exchanges by Means of Television Films 1958[2]	Agreement on the Protection of Television Broadcasts 1960[3]	European Agreement for the Prevention of Broadcasts Transmitted from Stations Outside National Territories 1965[4]	European Convention Relating to Questions of Copyright Law and Neighbouring Rights in the Framework of Transfrontier Broadcasting by Satellite 1994[5]	Convention on Cybercrime 2001[6] Additional Protocol 2003[7]
Norway	March 15, 1963	(e) August 10, 1968	October 17, 1971	(a) May 11, 1994 (b) June 19, 1998	(a) October 1, 2006 (b) August 1, 2008
Poland			November 11, 1994		
Portugal			September 7, 1969		(a) & (b) July 1, 2010
Romania					(a) September 1, 2004 (b) November 1, 2009
Russian Federation					
San Marino				(a) May 11, 1994	
Serbia					(a) & (b) August 1, 2009
Slovakia					(a) May 1, 2008

Member States of the Council of Europe	European Agreement Concerning Programme Exchanges by Means of Television Films 1958[2]	Agreement on the Protection of Television Broadcasts 1960[3]	European Agreement for the Prevention of Broadcasts Transmitted from Stations Outside National Territories 1965[4]	European Convention Relating to Questions of Copyright Law and Neighbouring Rights in the Framework of Trans-frontier Broadcasting by Satellite 1994[5]	Convention on Cyber-crime 2001[6] Additional Protocol 2003[7]
Slovenia					(a) January 1, 2005 (b) March 1, 2006
Spain	January 4, 1974	(e) October 23, 1971 (d) January 1, 1990	March 11, 1988	(a) May 11, 1994	(a) October 1, 2010
Sweden	July 1, 1961	(e) July 1, 1961	October 19, 1967		
Switzerland			September 19, 1976	(a) May 11, 1994	
The former Yugoslav Republic of Macedonia					(a) January 1, 2005 (b) March 1, 2006
Turkey	March 28, 1964	(e) January 20, 1976 (d) January 1, 1990	February 17, 1975		

Member States of the Council of Europe	European Agreement Concerning Programme Exchanges by Means of Television Films 1958[2]	Agreement on the Protection of Television Broadcasts 1960[3]	European Agreement for the Prevention of Broadcasts Transmitted from Stations Outside National Territories 1965[4]	European Convention Relating to Questions of Copyright Law and Neighbouring Rights in the Framework of Transfrontier Broadcasting by Satellite 1994[5]	Convention on Cybercrime 2001[6] Additional Protocol 2003[7]
Ukraine					(a) July 1, 2006 (b) April 1, 2007
United Kingdom	July 1, 1961	(e) July 1, 1961	December 3, 1967	(a) October 2, 1996	
EC				(a) June 26, 1996	
Non-Member States[8]					
Belarus					
Canada					
Holy See					
Israel	February 15, 1978				
Japan					
Morocco					
South Africa					
Tunisia	February 22, 1969				
USA					(a) January 1, 2007

[1] See Ch.23(10)(B). This Table is up to date as of August 31, 2010.

[2] CETS No. 027. The Agreement is open for accession by the following non-Member States: Israel, Morocco and Tunisia.

[3] CETS No. 034. As regards the Protocol to this Agreement (CETS No. 054, 1965) and the three additional Protocols thereto (CETS No. 081, 1974; CETS No. 113, 1983 and CETS No. 131, 1989), see para.24–182, above.

[4] CETS No. 053. The Agreement is open for accession by Morocco.

[5] CETS No. 153. This Convention is open for signature and ratification by the Member States, the other States party to the European Cultural Convention (Belarus and the Holy See), and on behalf of the European Community. (Monaco, previously a non-member, joined the Council of Europe on October 5, 2004.)

[6] CETS No. 185. This Convention entered into force on July 1, 2004. It is open for signature and ratification by the Member States of the Council of Europe and by non-Member States which participated in its elaboration, namely, Canada, Japan, South Africa and the United States of America. To date it has been signed by the following Member States: Albania, Azerbaijan, Armenia, Austria, Belgium, Bosnia and Herzegovina, Bulgaria, Croatia, Cyprus, Czech Republic, Denmark, Estonia, Finland, France, Germany, Greece, Hungary, Iceland, Ireland, Italy, Latvia, Lithuania, Luxembourg, Malta, Moldova, Montenegro, Netherlands, Norway, Poland, Portugal, Romania, Serbia, Slovakia, Slovenia, Spain, Sweden, Switzerland, the former Yugoslav Republic of Macedonia, Ukraine and the United Kingdom and the following Non-Member States: Canada, Japan, South Africa and the United States of America.

[7] An Additional Protocol to the Convention on Cybercrime, concerning the criminalisation of acts of a racist and xenophobic nature committed through computer systems (CETS No: 189) was adopted on January 28, 2003,and entered into force on March 1, 2005. To date it has been signed by the following Member States: Albania, Armenia, Austria, Belgium, Bosnia and Herzegovina, Croatia, Cyprus, Denmark, Estonia, Finland, France, Germany, Greece, Iceland, Latvia, Lithuania, Luxembourg, Malta, Moldova, Montenegro, Netherlands, Poland, Portugal, Romania, Serbia, Slovenia, Sweden, Switzerland, the former Yugoslav Republic of Macedonia and the Ukraine and the following Non-Member States: Canada and South Africa.

[8] Note that some of the treaties listed are open for signature and ratification by one or more States not party to the Council of Europe (cf. nn. 2, 4, 5, 6 and 7, above).

CHAPTER TWENTY FOUR

EUROPEAN UNION LAW

1. INTRODUCTION

24–01   **Overview of the creation and enlargement of the European Union.** On March 24, 1957, the Treaty establishing the European Economic Community (the EEC Treaty) was adopted at Rome.[1] Together with the Treaties creating the European Coal and Steel Community (ECSC) and the European Atomic Energy Community (EURATOM), the Treaty set up a framework for economic and political co-operation among the original six founding Member States,[2] leading to the development of a Common Market. In 1967, the institutions of the three European Communities, ECSC, EURATOM and the EEC, were merged and a single European Commission, Council of Ministers and European Parliament were created. The United Kingdom of Great Britain and Northern Ireland, Denmark and the Republic of Ireland acceded to the European Communities on January 1, 1973. The United Kingdom's accession to the Treaty was implemented in the UK legal system by the European Communities Act 1972,[3] under which, as since amended, much of the legislation required to implement the European Union Directives and Regulations has been introduced.

Subsequently, the Maastricht Treaty on European Union (TEU),[4] which came into force on November 1, 1993,[5] created a new structure, the European Union, with separate legal powers, but within which the existing communities, including the European Economic Community (EEC), continued to operate. The EEC Treaty was renamed the Treaty establishing the European Community (the EC Treaty). The TEU enlarged the aims of the EEC Treaty and substantially amended its provisions, principally in the areas concerned with economic and monetary union. In 1999, the Treaty of Amsterdam entered into force, placing greater emphasis on the rights of the European citizen and extending the powers of the

---

[1] The EEC Treaty was subsequently amended on a number of occasions and renamed the Treaty establishing the European Community in 1993. Meantime, as seen below, the Treaty of Rome has been superseded, following the entry into force of the Lisbon Treaty on December 1, 2009, by the Treaty on European Union (TEU) and the Treaty on the Functioning of the European Union (TFEU).

[2] Belgium, France, Federal Republic of Germany, Italy, Luxembourg and the Netherlands.

[3] c.68; the combined effect of ss.2(1) and 3(1) of the Act is that the law of the European Union, as a body of provisions of the Treaties and their implementing measures and judicial decisions interpreting and applying those provisions, is fully integrated into the laws of the United Kingdom and, since January 1, 1973, has formed part of the national legal order.

[4] The Maastricht Treaty, negotiated at Maastricht in December 1991 and formally signed by the Member States on February 7, 1992.

[5] The changes to the European Communities Act 1972 consequent on the UK's accession to the TEU were effected by the European Communities (Amendment) Act 1993 (c.32).

European Parliament. The Treaty of Amsterdam further amended the TEU and the EC Treaty and it should be noted that the EC Treaty was very substantially amended at Amsterdam and its provisions renumbered. The Treaties were revised once more at Nice in 2000 with the aim of adapting the way in which the European institutions operate in order to facilitate the entry into the European Union of twelve new Member States, mainly from Eastern Europe. The Treaty of Nice entered into force on February 1, 2003, after being ratified by the then 15 Member States of the European Union according to their respective constitutional rules.[6] The institutional reforms achieved by the Treaty of Nice did not drastically change the institutional balance, but made some adjustments to the functions and composition of the institutions and further enhanced co-operation.

Most recently, on December 1, 2009, the Treaty of Lisbon entered into force bringing about sweeping changes to the TEU and the EC Treaty, involving amendments to all of the articles in the former and to 216 provisions in the latter, thus transforming and replacing the previous EU framework.[7] The familiar terminology of the European institutions and EU law has also been changed. The European Community has ceased to exist and has been replaced by the European Union, which has succeeded it and taken over all its rights and obligations. The "Treaty on European Union" keeps the same name but the Treaty establishing the European Community (the EC Treaty) has become the "Treaty on the Functioning of the European Union". The articles, titles and sections of the Treaty on European Union (TEU) and of the Treaty on the Functioning of the European Union (TFEU), as amended by the Treaty of Lisbon, have been renumbered in accordance with tables of equivalences annexed to the Treaty of Lisbon and forming an integral part thereof.[8] While the articles relevant to this Chapter have all been renumbered in the TFEU, the various provisions as such have not been substantially modified and are reproduced with their new numbering (and earlier equivalents) in Vol.2 G1. All references in this Chapter to the articles of the TFEU are to the consolidated version of the Treaty, incorporating the changes made by the Treaty of Lisbon.[9] The designations of the European courts have also been changed. The European Court of Justice (ECJ) has been renamed the Court of Justice of the European Union (CJEU) and the court of first instance has been designated as the "General Court".[10] In this Chapter, these courts are referred to as the "Court of Justice" and the "General Court".

In this Chapter, references to the Treaty establishing the European Economic Community, adopted at Rome, and as amended prior to 1993, is referred to as "the EEC Treaty". The Treaty establishing the European Community, adopted at Maastricht in 1993 and amended at Amsterdam and Nice in 1999 and 2003 respectively, is referred to as "the EC Treaty". The most recent treaties, the Treaty on European Union and the Treaty on the Functioning of the European Union are referred to hereafter as "the TEU" and "the TFEU", respectively.

Since the United Kingdom acceded to the European Union in 1973, its

---

[6] Signed at Nice on December 11, 2000, [2001] OJ C80/1, March 10, 2001.

[7] Signed at Lisbon on December 13, 2007, [2007] OJ C306/01 of December 17, 2007. The legislation necessary to give domestic legal effect to the Treaty in the United Kingdom is contained in the European Communities (Amendment) Act 2008 (c.7). See consolidated versions of the Lisbon texts of the TEU and TFEU [2010] OJ C83/01, March 30, 2010. The consolidated version is available on-line at *http://europa.eu.int/eur-lex/en/treaties*. Articles of the Lisbon text of the TFEU relevant to this Chapter are reproduced in Vol.2 G1.

[8] Treaty of Lisbon art.5. See Vol.2 G2.

[9] Until the entry into force of the Treaty of Lisbon, strictly speaking, all of the legislative measures taken by the former European Community were in terms of EEC (or, after Maastricht, EC) law; in this work the term EU law is used to describe both the past body of EEC and EC measures and law, as well as those resulting from the Treaty of Lisbon.

[10] See Treaty of Lisbon s.5 on the Court of Justice of the European Union (arts 251–281 (ex arts 221 to 245 TEC)). The jurisdiction of the General Court is laid down in art.256 (ex art.225 TEC).

membership has expanded to 27. First came the accession of Greece on January 1, 1981, followed by those of Spain and Portugal on January 1, 1986, and those of Austria, Sweden and Finland on January 1, 1995. More recently, on May 1, 2004, the following 10 new Member States acceded to what has meanwhile become the European Union: Czech Republic, Estonia, Cyprus, Latvia, Lithuania, Hungary, Malta, Poland, Slovenia and Slovakia. Finally on January 1, 2007, Bulgaria and Romania acceded to the European Union. With the accession of these 12 new Member States, the overall "EU-27" population has increased to nearly half a billion.[11] In addition, Croatia, Iceland, the former Yugoslav Republic of Macedonia and Turkey have been recognised as official candidates for membership.[12] The Accession Treaties provided that the twelve new Member States had to have complied with EU law by the respective dates of their accession, including the *acquis communautaire* (existing body of the then Community law) with regard to copyright and related rights.

24–02   **The European Economic Area (EEA).** The EEA was created by the EEA Agreement,[13] which came into force on January 1, 1994.[14] It included Austria, Finland and Sweden, before their accession to the European Union,[15] and thus now comprises all the Member States of the European Union together with Iceland, Liechtenstein and Norway.[16]

The new EU Member States were obliged by the Accession Treaty to become members of the EEA with effect from May 1, 2004. The Enlargement Agreement providing for the participation of Bulgaria and Romania in the European Economic Area was signed on July 24, 2007.[17]

24–03   **Scope of this section.** It is the purpose of this chapter to consider the effect of EU law on the various rights enjoyed under the 1988 Act by the owners of copyright and related rights subsisting under that Act. It is beyond the scope of this chapter to describe in any detail the functions and workings of the European Union and its institutions, or of the relationship between EU law and the national law of Member States.[18]

The application of EU competition law to copyright and related rights, is not the subject of the present chapter but is dealt with at Ch.28, paras 28–221 et seq., below. However, it should be noted that the interface between intellectual property rights and EU competition law (arts 101 and 102 of the Treaty dealing respectively with prohibited anti-competitive agreements and practices and abuse of dominant positions (ex arts 81 and 82)) has become a topic of increasing importance in the last fifteen years and the impact of this interface needs to be borne in mind when considering the scope of the exclusive rights granted by the

---

[11] G. Lanzieri, "Population and social conditions", eurostat Statistics in focus 81/2008.

[12] Other potential candidates for membership are Albania, Bosnia and Herzegovina, Kosovo, Montenegro and Serbia.

[13] The Agreement on the European Economic Area, signed at Oporto on May 2, 1992, as adjusted by the Protocol signed at Brussels on March 17, 1993.

[14] The legislation necessary to give domestic legal effect in the UK to the Agreement is contained in the European Economic Area Act 1993 (c.51).

[15] Of the EFTA countries, only Switzerland opted not to join the EEA.

[16] With effect from January 1, 1994, therefore, most EU law (including all the copyright and related rights measures discussed in this Chapter) extends to the EFTA countries (except Switzerland, and, for the time being, Liechtenstein).

[17] Press release 182 of the Council of the European Union.

[18] The reader is referred to specialist works on these subjects, see, e.g. K.P.E. Lasok and D. Lasok, *Law and Institutions of the European Union* 6th edn (Butterworths, 1994); D. Wyatt and A. Dashwood, *European Community Law* 3rd edn (London: Sweet & Maxwell,1993); A.G. Toth, *The Oxford Encyclopaedia of European Community Law* (OUP). V. Korah, *Intellectual Property Rights and the EC Competition Rules* (Sweet and Maxwell, 2007). D. Chalmers, G. Davies and G. Monti, *European Union Law*, 2nd edn (Cambridge University Press, 2010).

1988 Act. Efforts to balance these rights have resulted in a body of case law of the Court of Justice of the European Union (CJEU) affecting the exercise of copyright and related rights. For many years such case law was mainly concerned with the control of the activities of collecting societies, which by their nature normally occupy a dominant position on the market (see Ch.28, paras 28–237 et seq., below). More recently, the court has developed its case law to deal with conflicts arising when the exercise of an intellectual property right threatens to thwart competition on a given market. In such cases, it has put curbs on the exploitation of exclusive rights where, in the view of the court, a particular exercise of copyright by its owner conflicts with art.102 of the Treaty, amounting to abuse of a dominant position. The court does not question the extent and terms of intellectual property rights granted by Member States but reserves the right "in exceptional circumstances" to limit the owner's freedom to exercise the right as he sees fit and to force him to grant a licence to competitors (compulsory licence).[19]

Before dealing with the impact of EU law on the exercise of copyright and related rights in the United Kingdom, it is necessary first to give a brief description of the relevant principles upon which the European Union is based and which affect intellectual property rights.

2. THE FREE MOVEMENT OF GOODS AND SERVICES WITHIN THE EUROPEAN UNION

Principal aims of the European Union: realisation of an internal market.   **24–04**
Article 2 of the now superseded EEC Treaty establishing the original European Community provided that the Community's task included the promotion throughout the Community of: a harmonious development of economic activities; a high degree of convergence of economic performance; the raising of the standard of living and quality of life; and economic and social cohesion and solidarity among Member States. This task was to be achieved by the establishment of a common market and an economic and monetary union. The establishment of a common market was therefore expressed as a means to an end, rather than an end in itself, but it was this preliminary aim which implied before all else the removal of all obstacles to the free movement of goods, persons, services and capital within the territory of the common market, and therefore across the boundaries of the Member States. These aims have been restated in art.3 TEU, as follows:

1. The union shall offer its citizens an area of freedom, security and justice without internal frontiers, in which the *free movement of persons* is ensured in conjunction with appropriate measures with respect to external border controls, asylum, immigration and the prevention and combating of crime.

3. The Union shall establish an *internal market*. ...
   It shall promote *economic, social and territorial cohesion...*

4. The Union shall establish an *economic* and monetary *union...*" [Emphasis added]

The TFEU establishes that the Union has exclusive competence inter alia in

---

[19] *Radio Telefis Eireann and Independent Television Publications Ltd v Commission of the European Communities (Magill)* (C–241/91P) [1995] E.C.R. I–743; *IMS Health GmbH & Co OHG v NOC Health GmbH & Co KG* (C–418/01) [2004] 4 C.M.L.R. 28; *Microsoft Corp. v Commission of the European Communities* (T–201/04), CFI (Grand Chamber), September 17, 2007 [2007] EUECJ. See also S. Anderman (ed.), *The Interface between Intellectual Property Rights and Competition Policy* (Cambridge University Press, 2007).

the areas of customs union, the establishing of competition rules necessary for the functioning of the internal market and a common commercial policy (art.3). Further, the Union shall share competence between the Union and the Member States inter alia in the following principal areas relevant to this Work: internal market, economic, social and territorial cohesion and consumer protection (art.4). Other relevant areas of Union competence include that of supporting the actions of Member States in the areas of, inter alia, culture and industry (art.6).

24–05 **Measures to remove obstacles to the common market.** Obstacles to the free movement of goods between Member States may be found in a variety of measures adopted by national governments, for example in customs duties, import quotas and subsidies for a particular national industry. Obstacles to the creation of an internal market may also be found in practices adopted by private bodies trading within the internal market, which are aimed at restricting competition and isolating national markets. It is with these obstacles in mind that the original aims of the European Economic Community (EEC) included:

    (a) the elimination, as between Member States, of customs duties and of quantitative restrictions on the import and export of goods, and of all other measures of equivalent effect;

    (c) an internal market characterised by the abolition, as between Member States, of obstacles to the free movement of goods, persons, services and capital; and

    (g) the institution of a system ensuring that competition in the Common Market is not distorted.[20]

These objectives find more detailed expression in later parts of the TFEU.

24–06 **Free movement of goods.** This objective is the subject of arts 28 and 29 of the TFEU (ex arts 23 and 24 EC Treaty), forming the title Free Movement of Goods, which is Title II of Pt Three of the TFEU, devoted to EU policies and internal actions. The position of this title reflects the fundamental importance attributed to this objective in the framework of the TFEU, although the objective of free movement of goods was not itself expressed as a principle in any article of the EEC Treaty in its original form.[21] The principle is now expressly referred to in arts 119 and 26 TFEU (ex arts 4 and 14 of the EC Treaty).[22] Nevertheless, well before this amendment to the EC Treaty, the Court of Justice, in its judgments in cases which came before it raising the issue of free movement of goods, stressed the importance of this principle, which was to be deduced from the wording, spirit and structure of this title. By such case law, the court established this principle as a rule of EU law as firmly as if it had from the beginning been expressly set out as such in an article of the EEC Treaty.[23]

24–07 **Free movement of services.** The general provisions governing the freedom to provide services are contained in arts 56 to 62 TFEU (ex arts 49 to 55 EC Treaty). Where, however, the principle of free movement of services touches on the field of transport or the liberalisation of banking and insurance services, the general provisions are subject to the particular provisions of the titles governing transport and the free movement of capital respectively. As seen above, the principle of

---

[20] art.3 EC Treaty (previously art.2 EEC). These provisions have been replaced in substance by arts 3 to 6 TFEU.

[21] art.3(c), as originally worded, referred only to the removal of obstacles to the free movement of persons, services and capital.

[22] Inserted (originally as art.8a) by the Single European Act, which came into force on July 1, 1987; later arts 3(a) and 7(a) of the EC Treaty.

[23] For a full treatment of the subject of the free movement of goods, see P. Oliver, *Free Movement of Goods in the European Community* 5th edn (London: Sweet & Maxwell, 2010).

free movement of goods was not expressly contained in any article of the original EEC Treaty, and yet was the area in which the European Union experienced the fastest development. In contrast, the principle of free movement of services was, from the beginning, contained in art.3 EC Treaty, but it is only in recent years that the European Union has begun to focus its attention on the development of an effective regime for the free movement of services, in particular in relation to economic rather than professional services.

In essence, the framework of the provisions on services requires the abolition of restrictions imposed on nationals established in one Member State who provide services to persons established in another Member State. The basic principles are set out in arts 56 and 57 TFEU (ex arts 49 and 50 EC Treaty), both of which are directly effective Treaty provisions. Article 57 TFEU (ex art.50 EC Treaty) defines services as including, in particular, activities of an industrial or commercial character, as well as the activities of craftsmen and of the professions. The Court of Justice has further stated that the restrictions to be abolished pursuant to arts 56 and 57 TFEU include all requirements imposed on the person providing the service by reason, in particular, of his nationality, or the fact that he does not habitually reside in the state where the service is provided, and which do not apply to persons established within the national territory, or which may prevent or otherwise obstruct the activities of the person providing the service.[24]

3. CONFLICT BETWEEN COPYRIGHT AND RELATED RIGHTS AND THE FREE MOVEMENT OF GOODS AND SERVICES

Copyright as an intellectual property right. The preferred term in early "Community" law for what are more usually now called intellectual property rights was intellectual and commercial property rights. This was the term used in the original art.36 of the EEC Treaty[25] and in reg.17.[26] The term copyright is nowhere mentioned in the EEC Treaty or indeed in the TFEU. Despite the absence of any express reference to copyright, there was little doubt that copyright was to be considered as an intellectual property right for the purposes of the Treaty and its implementing measures.[27] This was confirmed by the Court of Justice in the case of *Musik-Vertrieb Membran v GEMA*,[28] in which the court rejected the argument that its case law on intellectual property rights could not extend to copyright because copyright was aimed at protecting the author's moral rights as much as his economic rights. The court, while recognising the presence of both economic and moral rights behind the protection of copyright in national legislation, stated that the questions before it concerned the economic aspect of copyright and that the commercial exploitation of copyright raised the same issues as any other form of intellectual and commercial property right in relation to the control of

24–08

---

[24] *Van Binsbergen v Bedrijfsvereniging Metaalnijverheid* (Case 33/74) [1974] E.C.R. 1299 at 1309, para.10.

[25] See further para.24–24, below.

[26] reg.17/62; [1962] OJ 13/204, providing the procedure for enforcement of the competition rules (see further para.28–215, below); see art.4(2)(b), where the reference to intellectual and commercial property is followed by the description "in particular, patents, utility models, designs or trade marks".

[27] See the discussion in A. Dietz, *Copyright Law in the European Community*, (Alphen aan den Rijn, Sijthoff & Noordhoff, 1978), p.13, paras 27–31. See also the submissions of Advocate General Roemer in *Deutsche Grammophon GmbH v Metro-SB-Grossmarkte GmbH* (Case 78/70) [1971] E.C.R. 487; Lord Denning M.R. in *Application des Gaz S.A. v Falks Veritas Ltd* [1974] Ch. 381; [1974] 2 C.M.L.R. 75 at 82, para 23; *Yate Security Products Ltd v Newman* [1990] F.S.R. 320.

[28] Cases 55 & 57/80, [1981] E.C.R. 147; see also *Basset v SACEM* (Case 402/85) [1987] E.C.R. 1747 at para.11.

markets by the author and those acting under him. Subsequently, the court has applied the principles laid down in *Musik-Vertrieb Membran v GEMA* to related rights, and in particular performers' rights.[29]

As between the different intellectual property rights it has been pointed out that copyright is closer in nature to a patent than a trade mark.[30] It has been suggested that as between patents and trade marks, the underlying justification for the protection is stronger in the case of the former than the latter, and to the extent that this is correct, the same may apply to copyright.[31] However, one important difference between patents and copyright is that whereas the exercise of a patent right will necessarily involve the creation of a material object either itself the subject of the patent, or made by a process the subject of the patent, the exercise of copyright will not always do so, since copyright gives not only the right to control the production of products reproducing the copyright work, but also, for instance, the right to control performance of the copyright work. The same applies to related rights. Unlike the right to control production, which is exhausted once a product is produced, the right to control performance is not exhausted upon the occasion of the first performance of the work. It is a right that will accrue in respect of each performance of the work, allowing an author to exercise a continuing control over the performance of his work.[32]

24–09   **Territoriality.** However, it is a common characteristic of all intellectual property rights that they confer some degree of monopoly or exclusivity, and that the extent in content, time and territory of that monopoly or exclusivity is in the first instance a matter for the national law of the state granting the right in question.[33] The fact that an intellectual property right is the creature of the national laws of the state granting the right necessarily places limits on the territory within which such a right is effective. This has been referred to as the "territoriality principle" of intellectual property rights,[34] but it is really no more than a necessary reflection of the territorial limit to the sovereignty of the state concerned. In the present context, an act which is complained of as being an infringement of an intellectual property right, but which was committed in France, must be judged by French law.[35] Such an act is not an infringement of any rights granted under the 1988 Act.

International conventions in the field of copyright and related rights have helped to increase the protection available for the foreign owner of copyright and related rights in the states adhering to such conventions, but this is achieved by each state according copyright to the works of foreign authors under its own national laws.[36] It is not the aim (or effect) of such conventions to create a unitary right recognised throughout the combined territories of the signatories.

24–10   **Non-discrimination on the grounds of nationality.** The principle that copyright

---

[29] *Phil Collins v Imtrat HandelsGmbH and Verwaltungesellschaft mbH v EMI Electrola GmbH* (Joined Cases C92–326/92) [1993] E.C.R. I–05145; [1993] 3 C.M.L.R. 773.

[30] Advocate General Roemer in Case 78/70, *Deutsche Grammophon GmbH v Metro-SB-Grossmarkte GmbH* [1971] E.C.R. 487. See also *Sirena S.R.L. v Eda S.R.L.* (Case 40/70) [1971] E.C.R. 69.

[31] See the views expressed by Advocate General Dutheillet de Lamothe in *Sirena S.R.L. v Eda S.R.L.* [1971] E.C.R. 69 at 87.

[32] See further, as to the importance of this distinction, para.24–29, below.

[33] See *Keurkoop B.V. v Nancy Kean Gifts B.V.* (Case 144/81) [1982] E.C.R. 2853; *EMI Electrola GmbH v Patricia Im- und Export Verwaltungsgesellschaft GmbH* (Case 341/87) [1989] E.C.R. 79; *Maxicar v Renault* (Case 53/87) [1988] E.C.R. 6039.

[34] Advocate General Roemer in *Deutsche Grammophon GmbH v Metro-SB-Grossmarkte GmbH* (Case 78/70) [1971] E.C.R. 487; C.M.L.R. 631 at 647–648.

[35] This is a separate issue from whether such a complaint is justiciable in the courts of a territory other than that in which the alleged infringement was committed; see, as to the position in England: para.21–125, above.

[36] See Ch.23, above.

and related rights, which because of their effects on the free movement of goods and services fall within the scope of the TFEU, are also subject to the general principle of non-discrimination by reason of nationality laid down by art.18 TFEU (ex art.12 EC Treaty) has long been established by the Court of Justice.[37] This principle prohibits not only overt discrimination by reason of nationality but also all covert forms of discrimination which, by the application of other distinguishing criteria, lead to the same result.[38] In a 2005 case, *Société Tod's SPA & Another v Heyraud SA*, the Court, applying this principle, has confirmed that the right of an author from one Member State to claim the copyright protection afforded by the law of another Member State may not be subject to a distinguishing criterion based on the country of origin of the work.[39] At issue was whether the proprietor of a design produced in Italy, where designs are not protected as artistic works but under a special law, could claim copyright protection in France. The Berne Convention for the Protection of Literary and Artistic Works (the Berne Convention)[40] provides in such circumstances that "works protected in the country of origin solely as designs .   .   . shall be entitled in another country of the Union only to such special protection as is granted in that country to designs .   .   . ", thereby subjecting the level of protection afforded to designs to the principle of reciprocity (art.2(7) Berne Convention). The Court held that application of this provision of the Berne Convention in a Member State of the European Union led to a distinction based on the criterion of the country of origin of the work and to an indirect discrimination on grounds of nationality. No obligations imposed on Member States by the EU Treaties or secondary legislation may be made subject to a condition of reciprocity.[41]

Monopoly or exclusivity. Whilst international conventions have achieved a measure of harmonisation in certain aspects of the extent of the exclusivity granted by the laws of each state to the owner of copyright and related rights, and notably, in the case of copyright, in the duration of such exclusivity, the extent, particularly of the content, of such exclusivity remains a matter for the laws of each state. It should be noted, however, that the extensive EU programme of harmonisation of the law of copyright and related rights has set standards in relation also to the extent of certain rights.[42] In the present context, the exclusive rights granted to the owner of copyright under the 1988 Act as amended to date generally include the right to copy the work the subject of copyright, issue copies thereof to the public, rent or lend it, perform, show or play the work in public, communicate it to the public and adapt it, all in the manner and forms appropriate to the type of work in question, and also the right to authorise others to exercise such rights, or any one or more of the acts which the copyright owner has the exclusive right to do, and for part or all of the life of the copyright.

24–11

Justification for monopoly or exclusivity: "exhaustion of rights". The justification for the monopoly or exclusivity accorded to the owner of an intellectual property right is that it gives him the protection necessary to allow him to obtain just recompense for his expenditure of time, effort and money in the cre-

24–12

---

[37] *Phil Collins* (Joined Cases C–92/92 and C–326/92) [1993] E.C.R. I–5145 and *Ricordi* (C–360/00) [2002] E.C.R. I–5089.

[38] *Pastoors and Trans-Cap* (C–29/95) [1997] E.C.R. I–285 and *Commission v Italy* (C–224/00) [2002] E.C.R. I–2965.

[39] Case C–28/04 *Tod's SpA and Tod's France SARL v Heyrand S.A.*; reference for a preliminary ruling by the *Tribunal de Grande Instance de Paris*, December 5, 2003. Judgment of the Court, June 30, 2005 [2005] E.C.R. I–5781.

[40] See Ch.23, above.

[41] *Colegio de Oficiales de la Marina Mercante Espanola* (C–405/01) [2003] E.C.R. I–10391; [2005] 2 C.M.L.R. 13.

[42] See paras 24–43 et seq., below.

ation or invention of the matter the subject of the right. Thus, where the exercise of the right can result in the production of a material object which will then be the subject of commerce, as is the case with a patent and, to a large extent with copyright, the owner of the right is able, in the territory of the state according such right, to control the production of such material objects, either by producing them himself, or by licensing another to do so, and in either case he is able to extract his recompense on the occasion of the first sale with his consent of such products in that territory. Thereafter, in principle, as a general rule, such products can be freely sold by way of trade within the territory of that state (apart from any enforceable contractual terms preventing such resale) and the owner of the right cannot assert his monopoly or exclusivity to prevent such resale.[43] This is a characteristic common to all intellectual property rights. In terminology developed in continental jurisdictions, the owner of the right has "exhausted his rights" by such authorised first sale.

24–13   **Territorial monopoly or exclusivity and the prevention of imports.** The right of first sale accorded to the owner of an intellectual property right under the national laws of state A usually carries with it the right to prevent the importation into the territory of state A of products protected in state A by the right in question, which have been manufactured in state B without the authority of the owner of the right in state A. Without this additional protection the monopoly or exclusivity could be rendered valueless as a result of such international trade, and the whole purpose of the monopoly or exclusivity would be defeated.

Whether this protection, for the owner's home market in state A can also be invoked against imports of products in respect of the manufacture of which in state B the owner could not complain, either because they were manufactured by him under an equivalent right accorded to him by the laws of state B, or by someone deriving title to such equivalent right from him, or by a licensee under such right, either of himself or of his successor in title, is a question which depends on the intellectual property right concerned and on the national laws of state A under which such right is enforced. The question may be put in continental terms as whether such a sale, or disposition of the right of sale, abroad can properly be said to exhaust the owner's rights under the laws of the home market. In the United Kingdom the question turns, apart from considerations of EU law, entirely on the precise terms in which the right to prevent imports is given by the relevant statute to the owner of the intellectual property right.

24–14   **Imports into the United Kingdom.** Under the Copyright Act 1956,[44] the position appeared to turn on the answer to the hypothetical question whether the product being imported was manufactured in the foreign country by a person who, had he manufactured the product in the United Kingdom, would not thereby have infringed copyright. If this question was answered affirmatively, then importation of the product could not be prevented, but if this question was answered in the negative, then importation could be prevented, even though the manufacture was in fact not an infringement of copyright under the copyright laws of the country where the product was actually manufactured.[45]

---

[43] It should be noted here, however, that not all rights are exhausted on first sale (see paras 24–29 et seq., below).

[44] Copyright Act 1956 ss.5(2) and 16(2).

[45] *Polydor Ltd and R.S.O. Records Inc v Harlequin Record Shop Ltd and Simons Records Ltd* [1980] F.S.R. 194; (for the decision of the CJEU on the effect of Community law, see [1982] E.C.R. 329; [1982] F.S.R. 358); *CBS United Kingdom Ltd v Charmdale Record Distributors Ltd* [1981] Ch. 91; [1980] F.S.R. 289; *The Who Group Ltd and Polydor Ltd v Stage One (Records) Ltd* [1980] F.S.R. 268.

The 1988 Act maintained and tightened this rule.[46] Under the 1956 Act, the contractual nature of an exclusive licence prevented an exclusive licensee of the copyright in the United Kingdom from restraining the importation into the United Kingdom of products manufactured abroad by the copyright owner or by anyone under licence from him or his successor in title.[47] Importation of such products into the United Kingdom might have rendered the copyright owner in breach of his contract with the licensee, but it was not an infringement of the copyright, and consequently the restrictions on importation under the 1956 Act did not apply. The 1988 Act amended this prohibition on importation to include, in its definition of an infringing copy of a work, imported products the manufacture of which in the United Kingdom would have been a breach of an exclusive licence agreement in relation to that work.[48]

However, the 1988 Act also makes express provision for imports which are subject to EU law.[49] The definition of an infringing copy of a work in s.27(3) of the Act is not to be construed as applying to an article which may be lawfully imported into the United Kingdom by virtue of any enforceable EU right.[50]

The prevention of imports: conflict with the aims of the European Union.   **24–15**
The exercise of copyright, and other intellectual property rights to prevent imports into a state has so far been considered only in a national context, where the boundaries of the state define the limits for the purposes both of the enforcement of the right in question and of the state's control of its trade with other countries. In the context of the European Union, copyright continues to be accorded by the separate national laws of each of the Member States,[51] with the consequence that national boundaries continue to determine the limits to the enforcement of each of these copyrights, but, as has been explained above,[52] the national boundaries are no longer allowed to present an obstacle to the free movement of goods and services within the EU. However, it should readily be appreciated, from the discussion above, that nationally held intellectual property rights such as copyright, by the very combination of their twin characteristics of territoriality and exclusivity, are capable of being used to prevent imports into one Member State of copies of a work lawfully on the market in another Member State, and thus constituting in themselves an obstacle to the free movement of goods and services within the EU.[53]

4. RESOLUTION OF THE CONFLICT BETWEEN INTELLECTUAL PROPERTY RIGHTS AND THE AIMS OF THE EUROPEAN UNION

A. CREATION OF EU INTELLECTUAL PROPERTY RIGHTS

Creation of unitary rights. One solution to the problem of ensuring that intel-   **24–16**
lectual property rights do not present an obstacle to the realisation of the Internal

---

[46] CDPA 1988 ss.22, 27(1) and 27(3).

[47] Copyright Act 1956 s.19(4).

[48] CDPA 1988 s.27(3)(b).

[49] CDPA 1988 s.27(5). Similar provisions exist in relation to design right, see CDPA 1988 s.228(3) and (5).

[50] As defined by the European Communities Act 1972 (as amended), s.2(1); see para.24–01, above.

[51] References in this chapter to Member States are effectively references to EEA States, see para.24–01, above.

[52] See paras 24–04 et seq., above.

[53] As was stated in relation to patents by the Court of Justice in Parke, *Davis v Probel* (Case 24/67) [1968] E.C.R. 81; and in relation to copyright in *Musik-Vertrieb Membran v GEMA* (Cases 55 & 57/80) [1981] E.C.R. 147 at para.13.

Market is to create a unitary right covering the combined territories of the Member States,[54] the content of which is determined by EU law, not by the national laws of the separate Member States, and to which effect is given in identical manner in the national courts of each Member State.

24–17   **Community Patent Convention.** Such was the objective in relation to patents of the Community Patent Convention, signed by the nine Member States of the then EEC on December 15, 1975.[55] The Convention applied, by its arts 32 and 81, the principle of exhaustion of rights to patents, in that a Community patent could not be asserted to prevent the importation into one Member State of a product marketed in another Member State by the patentee or with his express consent. The Convention was subject to ratification by the then nine Member States, but ratification did not take place.[56] Subsequent enlargement of the Community caused further difficulties which prevented the Convention being ratified, and has, in effect, long ago removed any chance of the Convention entering into force. The concept of a unitary Community patent was seen in the 1970s as a means of preventing patents being used to restrict intra-Community trade. The considerable progress which has been made since then in the harmonisation of national patent laws and the success of the 38-Member State European Patent Convention (EPC) removed any urgent need to establish a unitary patent in the European Union.[57] However, on August 1, 2000, the European Commission put forward a proposal for a "Regulation on the Community Patent" (now the EU patent under the Lisbon Treaty).[58] Under the proposal, upon grant, EU patents would be single patents legally valid throughout the European Union and the Regulation would be the applicable framework. It is proposed that EU patents would be granted by the European Patent Office and therefore a revision of the European Patent Convention (EPC) is required. Thus, the effective establishment of the EU patent does not depend solely on the adoption of the Regulation on the EU Patent, but also requires the convening of a Diplomatic Conference to revise the EPC to accommodate it. However, negotiations stalled subsequently on the question of languages and the jurisdiction of the proposed EU Patent Courts of first and second instance.

Meanwhile, in December 2009, Member States unanimously adopted Council Conclusions and a general approach on a Regulation for an EU Patent to bring about an enhanced patent system in Europe.[59] The package agreed covered the key elements to bring about a single EU Patent and establish a new patent court in the European Union but excluded translation arrangements. On the new patent court, an opinion from the Court of Justice is awaited later this year.[60] As regards translations, Member States agreed that the translations for the EU Patent would

---

[54] See fn.51, above.

[55] [1976] OJ L17/1.

[56] Denmark was unable to ratify the Convention.

[57] For the subsequent difficulties experienced by the EU in progressing the Community Patent Convention, see G. Tritton, et al., *Intellectual Property in Europe* 3rd edn (London: Sweet & Maxwell, 2008), paras 2–205 et seq.

[58] Proposal for a Council Regulation on the Community Patent (presented by the Commission), COM (2000) 412 final, August 1, 2000. On April 10, 2002, the European Parliament voted in favour of a resolution approving the Commission's then proposal. Meanwhile, on February 20, 2002, the Commission put forward a proposal for a Directive on the Patentability of Computer-Implemented Inventions (COM (2000) 92 final). A common position concerning the latest proposal on this subject (IP/04/659) was adopted by the Council in May 2004 and is now before the Parliament.

[59] IP/09/1880. See also COM (2000) 412, "Proposal for a Council Regulation on the Community Patent".

[60] The Opinion of the Advocates General (Opinion 1/09) in the case was delivered on July 2, 2010. It concluded that "As its stands at present, the envisaged Agreement creating a unified patent litigation system is incompatible with the treaties".

form part of a separate Regulation. On July 1, 2010, therefore, the Commission put forward a proposal for a Council Regulation on translation arrangements for the future EU patent.[61] The proposal builds on the existing language regime of the EPO, so that EU patents would be examined and granted in one of the official languages of the EPO, English, French or German. As in the EPO, the granted patent will be published in the language of the proceedings and this will be the legally binding text. The publication will include translations of the claims into the other two EPO official languages. It is proposed that no further translations into other languages will be required from the patent proprietor except in the case of a legal dispute concerning the EU patent.

Community Trade Mark. A proposed Regulation on a Community Trade Mark   **24–18**
was put forward in 1980 and amended in 1984.[62] A Regulation was finally adopted by the Council of Ministers on January 14, 1994.[63] Once registered, a Community trade mark is valid for the entire European Union. The Regulation applies exhaustion of rights to the Community trade mark, in that a Community trade mark cannot be used to prohibit its use in relation to goods marketed in the Community under that mark by the proprietor of the mark or with his consent.[64]

Copyright. So far as copyright is concerned, to date there has been no formal   **24–19**
proposal from the Commission for a full codification of EU copyright law. Such codification has not been considered justified in the past because copyright enjoys the special position that no registration system is required in any of the laws of the Member States for the subsistence of copyright under national laws, and also because a certain degree of harmonisation as to the content of the right in the Member States has already been achieved as a result of a succession of international conventions to which the Member States are party. Until recently, it was therefore argued that there was no need for a special agreement between Member States (such as the Community Patent Convention) but that the further harmonisation necessary to allow for the realisation of the Internal Market could be achieved by appropriate directives issued by the Council.[65] Thus, in spite of the programme of harmonisation undertaken in recent years, the *acquis commu-nautaire* in the field of copyright remains limited in its scope and does not cover the whole field of copyright and related rights.

Nevertheless, in the past year suggestions have been made that the time for a codification of copyright law has come in documents published by the Commission of the European Union.[66] The prospects for success of such a codification have been enhanced by the new art.118(1) TFEU,[67] which provides for intellectual property legislation to be adopted in accordance with the ordinary legisla-

---

[61] IP/10/870. COM (2010) 350 final of June 30, 2010, "Proposal for a Council Regulation (EU) on the translation arrangements for the European Union patent".

[62] [1980] OJ C351/1; [1984] OJ C230/1; [1981] 1 C.M.L.R. 365 (original text).

[63] Council Reg.40/94/EC; [1994] OJ L11/1. The Regulation came into force on April 14, 1994.

[64] Council Reg.40/94/EC; [1994] OJ L11/1, art.13(1). The principle of exhaustion does not apply where there are legitimate reasons for the proprietor to oppose further commercial exploitation of the goods: Council Reg.40/94/EC; [1994] OJ L11/1, art.13(2).

[65] Under what are now arts 114 and 115 of the Treaty (ex arts 94 and 95 TEC). As to the considerable progress that has been made in recent years in harmonising national copyright and related rights laws of the Member States through this means, see the discussion at paras 24–43 et seq., below.

[66] "A new strategy for the single market: at the service of Europe's economy and society", Report to the President of the European Commission by Mario Monti, May 9, 2010; "A Digital Agenda for Europe", Communication from the Commission to the European Parliament, the Council, the European Economic and Social Committee and the Committee of the Regions (Brussels, COM(2010)245), May 19, 2010. For details, see paras 24–169 and 24–170, below.

[67] art.118(1) reads as follows: "In the context of the establishment and functioning of the internal market, the European Parliament and the Council, acting in accordance with the ordinary legisla-

tive procedure, meaning that unanimity would not be required for the adoption of a Regulation on copyright. The procedure was no doubt introduced to facilitate the adoption of the EU Patent but could also be used for copyright.

B. Case Law of the Court of Justice Developing the Principle of Exhaustion of Rights and the Specific Object of the Intellectual Property Right

24–20   **Role of the Court of Justice of the European Union (CJEU).** In the absence of a unitary system of intellectual property rights, it was left to the Court of Justice to resolve the conflict between the national intellectual property rights and the aims of the European Union. The court's solution had to take account of the protection afforded to national property rights, in particular to intellectual and commercial property rights, under arts 345 and 36 TFEU (ex arts 295 and 30 EC Treaty).

24–21   **Article 345 TFEU.** Article 345 (ex art.295 EC Treaty), which is found in Pt 7 of the Treaty, devoted to general and final provisions, provides that the Treaty shall in no way prejudice the rules in Member States governing the system of property ownership.[68] However, the object of this article is to guarantee, in a general manner, the freedom of the Member States to organise their own systems of property, but not to guarantee that the EU institutions may not intervene in the subjective right of property, as was affirmed by the Court of Justice by its judgment in *Consten & Grundig v EC Commission*.[69]

24–22   **Article 36 TFEU.** Article 36 TFEU (ex art.30 EC Treaty) allows for exceptions to the principle of free movement of goods, in that the provisions of arts 34 and 35 TFEU (ex arts 28 and 29 EC Treaty) are not to preclude prohibitions on imports and exports justified on specified grounds, which include the protection of industrial and commercial property, provided that such measures do not constitute a means of arbitrary discrimination or a disguised restriction on trade between Member States.[70] The Court of Justice has stated that, in so far as art.36 TFEU provides exceptions to the fundamental rule of free movement of goods between Member States, the exceptions are to be interpreted strictly.[71]

24–23   **Distinction between the existence or substance of intellectual property rights and their exercise.** The solution adopted by the Court of Justice was to draw from the interpretation of these articles a distinction between the existence of nationally held intellectual property rights and their exercise. This distinction was first drawn in *Consten & Grundig v Commission*,[72] in which the court was considering an appeal against a decision of the Commission which prohibited,

---

tive procedure, shall establish measures for the creation of European intellectual property rights to provide uniform protection of intellectual property rights throughout the Union and for the setting up of centralised Union-wide authorisation, coordination and supervision arrangements", see Vol.2 G1.

[68] For the text of art.345 (ex art.295 TEC), see Vol.2 G1.

[69] *Consten & Grundig v EC Commission* (Cases 56 & 58/64) [1966] E.C.R. 299; and see the Opinion of Advocate General Roemer at [1966] C.M.L.R. 443. See also *RTE and ITP v Commission* (Cases C–241 & 242/GIP) [1995] E.C.R. I–743.

[70] For the text of art.36, see Vol. 2 G1.

[71] *Re Export Tax on Art Treasures* (Case 7/68) [1968] E.C.R. 423; *Simmenthal SpA v Amministrazione delle Finanze dello Stato* (Case 35/76) [1976] E.C.R. 1871; *Commission v Ireland* (Case 113/80) [1981] E.C.R. 1624; *Commission v Italy* (Case 95/81) [1982] E.C.R. 2187.

[72] For a commentary on subsequent developments, see G. Friden, "Recent Developments in EEC Intellectual Property Law: The distinction between Existence and Exercise revisited." [1989] C.M.L.Rev.193. For criticism of the distinction, see F.K. Beier, "Industrial Property and Internal Market" (1990) 2 I.I.C. 131 and A. Reindl, "The Magic of Magill: TV Program Guides as a Limit

under art.101(1) TFEU (ex art.81(1) EC Treaty), an agreement relating to the exercise of trade marks. The distinction was then developed in a number of cases, in relation to trade marks,[73] copyright,[74] and similar rights of protection under German law,[75] design rights,[76] patents[77] and performers' rights.[78] The essence of the distinction is that EU law does not affect the grant, substance or existence of such rights, which remain a matter for the respective national laws of the Member States.[79] However, EU law may interfere with the exercise of such rights to the extent that such exercise is contrary to a fundamental rule of EU law.

Development of distinction into principle of EU law. Although the distinction   **24–24** was primarily developed by reference to art.36 TFEU (ex art.30 EC Treaty) and the derogation in that article for the protection of industrial and commercial property, the extension of the distinction to the free movement of services and to the application of competition policy required the court to develop the doctrine as a principle of EU law, of which art.36 TFEU is an express example relating to the free movement of goods. This was a progression from *Consten & Grundig v Commission*,[80] where the Court of Justice pointed out that art.36 had, by its very terms and position in the Treaty, no application to the rules on competition.[81] The foundation for this extension by the Court of Justice of the distinction between the exercise of the rights of intellectual property to fields beyond the free movement of goods was not fully explained in its reasoning,[82] and there are no parallel exceptions in the chapters of the Treaty on the freedom to provide services or the application of the competition rules. Nevertheless, in *Coditel S.A. v Cine Vog Films S.A.*[83] the Court of Justice stated that whilst art.56 TFEU (ex art.49 EC Treaty) prohibits restrictions upon the freedom to provide services, it does not thereby mean restrictions upon the exercise of certain economic activities which have their origin in the application of national legislation for the protection of intellectual property, save where such application constitutes a means of arbitrary discrimination or disguised restriction on trade between Member States. The explanation for this teleological interpretation of the TFEU may simply be the

---

of Copyright Law?" (1993) 1 I.I.C. 60. See also T.C.Vinje, "The Final Word on Magill" [1995] 6 EIPR 297.

[73] *Sirena S.R.L. v Eda S.R.L.* (Case 40/70) [1971] E.C.R. 69; *Centrafarm B.V. v Winthrop B.V.* (Case 16/74) [1974] E.C.R. 1183; *EMI Records Ltd v CBS United Kingdom Ltd* (Case 51/75) [1976] E.C.R. 811; *Dansk Supermarked A/S v A/S Imerco* (Case 58/80) [1981] E.C.R. 181.

[74] *Coditel S.A. v Cine Vog Films S.A.* (Case 62/79) [1980] E.C.R. 881; *Coditel S.A. v Cine Vog Films S.A. (No. 2)* (Case 262/81) [1982] E.C.R. 3381; *Polydor Ltd and R.S.O. Records Inc v Harlequin Record Shop Ltd and Simons Records Ltd* (Case 270/80) [1982] E.C.R. 329; *Radio Telefis Éireann v Commission* (T–69/89) [1991] 4 C.M.L.R. 586 at 617 para.71 and *Radio Telefis Éireann and ITP v Commission* (C–241 & 242/91P) [1995] E.C.R. I–743.

[75] *Deutsche Grammophon GmbH v Metro-SB-Grossmarkte GmbH* (Case 78/70) [1971] E.C.R. 487.

[76] *Keurkoop B.V. v Nancy Kean Gifts B.V.* (Case 144/81) [1982] E.C.R. 2853.

[77] *Parke, Davis v Probel* (Case 24/67) [1968] E.C.R. 55; *Centrafarm B.V.v Sterling Drug Inc* (Cases 15 & 16/74) [1974] E.C.R. 1147 at 1183; *Thetford Corporation v Fiamma SpA* (Case 35/87) [1988] E.C.R. 3585.

[78] *Phil Collins v Imtrat HandelsGmbH and Verwaltungsgesellschaft mbH v EMI Electrola GmbH (Joined Cases C 92–326/92)* .

[79] As stated by the CJEU in: *Thetford Corporation v Fiamma SpA* (Case 35/87) [1988] E.C.R. 3585; *Keurkoop B.V.v Nancy Kean Gifts B.V.* (Case 144/81) [1982] E.C.R. 2853; [1983] 2 C.M.L.R. 47; *EMI Electrola GmbH v Patricia Im- und Export Verwaltungsgesellschaft GmbH* (Case 341/87) [1989] E.C.R. 79; *Commission v United Kingdom and Italy* (Cases C–30/90 and 235/89) [1992] E.C.R. I–777; *Deutsche Renault AG v Audi AG* (C–317/91) [1993] E.C.R. I–6277; *IHT Internazionale Heiztechnik GmbH v Ideal-Standard GmbH* (C–9/93) [1994] E.C.R. I–2789; *Phil Collins v Imtrat HandelsGmbH* and *Verwaltungsgesellschaft GmbH v EMI Electrola GmbH* (Joined Cases C92–326/92) [1993] E.C.R. I–5145.

[80] Cases 56 & 58/64 [1966] E.C.R. 299; [1966] C.M.L.R. 418.

[81] Cases 56 & 58/64 [1966] C.M.L.R. 418 at 476

[82] See, e.g. *Sirena S.R.L. v Eda S.R.L.* (Case 40/70) [1971] E.C.R. 69.

[83] (Case 62/79) [1980] E.C.R. 881 at para.15; [1981] 2 C.M.L.R. 362 at 400 para.15; see also *Coditel S.A. v Cine Vog Films S.A. (No. 2)* (Case 262/81) [1982] E.C.R. 3381.

willingness of the Court of Justice to develop principles for the application of EU law to ensure uniformity in its sectors of influence. Moreover, the Court of Justice has stressed repeatedly that the goal of the European Union is a single market. To the extent that the Court of Justice develops limits on the ability of national intellectual property laws to derogate from that goal, it would be illogical for the Court to apply different rules in respect of the market in goods to those applied in respect of the market in services.

24–25   **Development of the concept of the specific object of an intellectual property right.** The case law of the Court of Justice has made it clear that the existence of intellectual property rights is not affected by the TJEU. Only the exercise of those rights requires justification as a derogation from the principle of free movement of goods or services, in that such derogation must not constitute a means of arbitrary discrimination or a disguised restriction on trade between Member States. In *Deutsche Grammophon GmbH v Metro-SB-Grossmärkte GmbH & Co K.G.*,[84] the court gave detailed consideration to the terms of art.36 TFEU and held that the article only permits restrictions on the freedom of trade to the extent that they are justified for the protection of the rights that form the specific object of that property.[85] The court thereby further developed the concept of the distinction between the existence or substance and the exercise of the right, by introducing the concept of the specific object of the intellectual property right. The specific object of the right is a matter of its substance, and the exercise by the owner of the right of what is no more than the specific object of the right will be protected by the derogation from the principle of free movement in art.36. Anything further done by the owner of the right which restricts the free movement of goods or services between Member States will be struck down as incompatible with EU law.

Since its judgment in the *Deutsche Grammophon* case, the court has affirmed the concept of the specific object of the intellectual property right as governing the limits of the exceptions in art.36 TFEU in favour of intellectual property rights, in relation to patents,[86] trade marks,[87] copyright,[88] and registered designs.[89]

24–26   **The *Deutsche Grammophon* Case.** Whilst the position was therefore quickly clarified in relation to patents and trade marks, the Court of Justice was not so clear, in its earlier judgment in the *Deutsche Grammophon* case, in relation to a right under German law similar to copyright. The court merely stated that it conflicted with the provisions regarding the free movement of goods in the Internal Market if a producer of sound recordings so exercises the exclusive right granted to him by the legislation of a Member State to market protected goods (in

---

[84] Case 78/70 [1971] E.C.R. 487.

[85] *Case 78/70* [1971] C.M.L.R. 631 at 657para.11; repeated by the court in a later trade mark case: Case 119/75, *Terrapin (Overseas) Ltd v Terranova Industrie* [1976] E.C.R. 1039; [1976] 2 C.M.L.R. 482 at 505 para.5.

[86] *Centrafarm B.V. v Sterling Drug Inc.* (Case 15/74) [1974] E.C.R. 1147 at 1183; *Merck & Co Inc v Stephar B.V.* (Case 187/80) [1981] E.C.R. 2063; *Pharmon B.V. v Hoechst AG* (Case 19/84) [1985] E.C.R. 2281; *Windsurfing International Inc v EC Commission* (Case 193/83) [1986] E.C.R. 611; *Allen & Hanburys v Generics UK* [1988] E.C.R. 1245; *Commission v United Kingdom and Italy* (Cases C–30/90 and 235/89) [1992] E.C.R. I–777.

[87] *Centrafarm B.V. v Winthrop B.V.* (Case 16/74) [1974] E.C.R. 1183; *Centrafarm B.V. v American Home Products Inc* (Case 3/78) [1978] E.C.R. 1823; *S.A. CNL-Sucal NV v Hag GF AG.* (Case C–10/89) [1990] 3 C.M.L.R. 571 at 608, para.14.

[88] *Coditel S.A. v Cine Vog Films S.A.* (Case 62/79) [1980] E.C.R. 881; *Musik-Vertrieb Membran GmbH v GEMA* (Cases 55 & 57/80) [1981] E.C.R. 146; *Coditel S.A. v Cine Vog Films S.A. (No. 2)* (Case 262/81) [1982] E.C.R. 3381; *Basset v SACEM* (Case 402/85) [1987] E.C.R. 1747; see also the Opinion of Advocate General Jacobs in *Ministère Public v Tournier* (Case 395/87) [1989] E.C.R. 25; and *Lucazeau v SACEM* (Cases 110/88 241/88 and 242/88) [1989] E.C.R. 2811.

[89] *Keurkoop B.V. v Nancy Kean Gifts B.V.* (Case 144/81) [1982] E.C.R. 2853; *Volvo AB v Eric Veng (UK) Ltd* (Case 238/87) [1988] E.C.R. 6211.

this case records) so as to prohibit the marketing in that Member State of products that have been sold by himself or with his consent in another Member State, solely because this marketing has not occurred in the territory of the first Member State.[90] The court did not take the opportunity of defining in more precise terms the specific object of copyright,[91] yet clearly accepted that in the case before it the attempt by Deutsche Grammophon to prevent the re-importation of the products into Germany went beyond the specific object of the right in question.

When the case came back before the German court, issues arose on the facts as to whether there had been a marketing of the records in France by Polydor S.A. (a wholly owned subsidiary of Deutsche Grammophon) and as to whether Deutsche Grammophon was responsible for, and had therefore consented to, that marketing. The German court decided against Deutsche Grammophon on these issues, and applied the ruling of the Court of Justice to prevent Deutsche Grammophon from asserting its exclusive distribution rights in Germany, under the German Copyright Act, to prevent the re-importation of the records in question from France.[92]

Subsequent development by national courts. After the *Deutsche Grammophon* case,[93] it was left to the national courts to define what they considered to be the specific object of copyright under their laws, guided by the rulings of the Court of Justice in that case and the *Centrafarm/Sterling*[94] and *Centrafarm/Winthrop*[95] cases. In *Time Limit S.A. v SABAM*[96] the Belgian Court of Appeal was called on to consider the validity of certain royalties levied by the Belgian performing right society SABAM. Following the guidance laid down by the Court of Justice in the above cases, the Belgian Court defined the specific object of copyright in a musical work as including the right of reproduction, but not the right to lay down the territorial limits within which the product embodying the reproduction may be marketed.

24–27

Further development by the Court of Justice. The first case concerning the right of reproduction and the exercise of copyright to come before the Court of Justice after the *Deutsche Grammophon* case was *Musik-Vertrieb Membran v GEMA*.[97] This case raised the question of the compatibility with EU law of the practice of the German authors' and composers' collecting society by which it collected the difference between the royalty fees paid to authors in the exporting Member State and the royalty fees payable in Germany when records were imported into Germany from another Member State. The court, after rejecting the argument that the moral rights aspect of copyright required it to be treated differently to other intellectual property rights,[98] stated that the right involved in the case was the right to exploit commercially the marketing of the protected work, particularly in the form of licences granted in return for payment of royalties. In respect of the exercise of such an economic right, the court reaffirmed, in accordance with its development of the doctrine of exhaustion of rights for other forms

24–28

---

[90] *Deutsche Grammophon GmbH v Metro-SB-Grossmärkte GmbH* (Case 78/70) [1971] E.C.R. 487.
[91] *Deutsche Grammophon GmbH v Metro-SB-Grossmärkte GmbH* (Case 78/70) [1971] E.C.R. 487; [1971] C.M.L.R. 631 at 657–658 at para.13.
[92] See also the Opinion of Advocate General Roemer, *Deutsche Grammophon GmbH v Metro-SB-Grossmärkte GmbH (Case 78/70)* [1971] E.C.R. 487
[93] *Deutsche Grammophon GmbH v Metro-SB-Grossmärkte GmbH* [1972] C.M.L.R. 107.
[94] *Centrafarm B.V. v Sterling Drug Inc.* (Case 15/74) [1974] E.C.R. 1147 at 1183.
[95] *Centrafarm B.V. v Winthrop B.V.* (Case 16/74) [1974] E.C.R. 1183.
[96] [1979] 2 C.M.L.R. 578 at 582, para.9].
[97] Cases 55 & 57/80 [1981] F.C.R. 147.
[98] In *Radio Telefís Éireann v Commission* the court stressed that the specific object of copyright is to protect both the economic and moral rights of the copyright owner (T–69/89) [1991] E.C.R. II–00485; [1991] 4 C.M.L.R. 586 at 617, para.71.

of intellectual property, and without therefore needing to define further the specific object of copyright, that the copyright owner could not rely on the exclusive exploitation right conferred by copyright to restrict the importation of the sound recordings which had been lawfully marketed in another Member State by the copyright owner or with his consent. In *Parfums Christian Dior*,[99] the court held that the rights of a copyright holder to restrain the reproduction of a protected work in a reseller's advertising could not be greater than those conferred on a trade mark proprietor in similar circumstances.[100]

24–29 **Divisibility of copyright: reproduction right and performance right.** As has already been stated,[101] copyright, unlike other forms of intellectual property, is a divisible right, in that copyright in a work gives a bundle of rights including separate rights to control the reproduction and performance of the work. The Court of Justice has acknowledged that these two separate rights form divisible elements of the specific subject-matter of copyright, and that exhaustion of the right to control reproduction will not necessarily exhaust the right to control performance.[102] The two *Coditel* cases[103] raised the question of whether the owner of a copyright work could rely on that copyright to prevent the transmission in one Member State of the work lawfully broadcast in another Member State. In the first *Coditel* case, the court was asked to consider the question in relation to former arts 30, 36, 59 and 60 (new TFEU arts 36, 42, 66 and 75). The court held that films differ from those literary and artistic works for which the placing of the work at the disposal of the public is inseparable from the circulation of the material object in which the work is reproduced, such as a book or a record. Rather, films belong to that category of literary and artistic works which are made available to the public by performance which can be infinitely repeated. The commercial exploitation of such works falls within the domain of movement of services. In these circumstances, the court held that it is part of the essential function of copyright that the owner of the copyright in a film and his assigns may require fees for any showing of that film.[104] Consequently, the court decided that the provisions of the Treaty relating to the freedom to provide services would not prevent the assignee of the performing right in a film from exercising his right to prohibit exhibition of the film in a Member State without his authority, if the film was picked up and transmitted after being broadcast in another Member State by a third party with the consent of the original owner.[105]

In *Football Association Premier League Limited v QC Leisure*,[106] ten questions were referred to the Court of Justice.[107] These questions concerned the interpretation of Directive 98/84/EC (the Conditional Access Directive—see

---

[99] *Parfums Christian Dior S.A. v Evora B.V.* (C–337/95) [1997] E.C.R. I–6013; [1998] 1 C.M.L.R. 737.

[100] *Parfums Christian Dior S.A. v Evora B.V.* (C–337/95) [1997] E.C.R. I–6013; [1998] 1 C.M.L.R. 737, paras 55–59. Further consideration was given to the issue by the court in the *Magill* case; see para.28–57, below.

[101] See para.24–08, above.

[102] *Coditel S.A. v Cine Vog Films S.A.* (Case 62/79) [1980] E.C.R. 881; *Coditel S.A. v Cine Vog Films S.A. (No. 2)* (Case 262/81) [1982] E.C.R. 3381; *Basset v SACEM* (Case 402/85) [1987] E.C.R. 1747; *Warner Brothers Inc v Erik Christiansen* (Case 158/86) [1988] E.C.R. 2605; *Ministère Public v Tournier* (Case 395/87) [1989] E.C.R. 2521.

[103] *Coditel S.A. v Cine Vog Films S.A.* (Case 62/79) [1980] E.C.R. 881; *Coditel S.A. v Cine Vog Films S.A. (No. 2)* (Case 262/81) [1982] E.C.R. 3381.

[104] *Coditel S.A. v Cine Vog Films S.A.* (Case 62/79) [1980] E.C.R. 881.

[105] *Coditel S.A. v Cine Vog Films S.A.* (Case 62/79) [1980] E.C.R. 881.

[106] [2008] EWHC 1411 (Ch)

[107] Case C–403/08 referred for a preliminary ruling from the High Court of Justice (Chancery Division) lodged on September 17, 2008. This case has been joined with *Karen Murphy v Media Protection Services Ltd* (C–429/08). Applications to participate in the proceedings, submitted respectively by the Union of European Football Associations (UEFA), British Sky Broadcasting

para.16–04, above and para.24–144, below), of Directive 2001/29/EC (the Information Society Directive—see paras 24–109 to 24–142, below) and of Directive 93/83/EC (the Satellite and Cable Directive—see paras 24–75 to 24–83) and included questions regarding defences under arts 34 and 36, 56 and 101 TFEU to allegations that (a) satellite decoder cards, issued for use in Greece and subject to a contractual restriction that limited their use to that Member State, became "illicit devices" within the meaning of Directive 98/84/EC upon their use in the United Kingdom, and (b) that the public showing of the broadcasts to which those decoder cards gave access in the United Kingdom infringed the copyright in various works included in those broadcasts. These questions will require consideration of the specific subject-matter by reference to the essential function of the conditional access right given by Directive 98/84/EC, and whether, when exploited by means of tangible items such as decoder cards, the right falls within the category of intellectual property rights, like the showing of a film, for which a fee can be charged for each separate act of exploitation, or whether it is a right like the reproduction of a book that is "exhausted" once it has been placed on the market in the Community. Further, the questions will require the consideration of whether the decision in *Coditel* remains good law in light of the legislative developments that have occurred since it was decided[108] and which are aimed at developing a single audiovisual area covering the whole of the European Union.

Distinction applied to records and video cassettes. Since the *Coditel* cases, the   **24–30**
Court of Justice has further considered the specific subject-matter of copyright in the context of performances of sound recordings on records and of films on video cassettes. Both records and video cassettes are media where the commercial exploitation of the performance right in the copyright work cannot be separated from the distribution of the material product, subject to the right of reproduction. For both forms of reproduction of the copyright work, the court has upheld the right of the copyright owner to continue to exploit the commercial performance of his work despite the exhaustion of the right of reproduction in the material form of the copyright work.[109] In *Ministère Public v Tournier*,[110] the Court of Justice held that national copyright legislation which prevented the public performance of sound recordings from records, without the payment of royalties in respect of such performance, even when royalties have already been paid for the reproduction of the work in the form of such records in another Member State, is not incompatible with former arts 30 and 59 (arts 36 and 66 TFEU).

The Court of Justice adopted a similar approach in *Warner Brothers Inc v Erik Christiansen*[111] to Danish legislation which allowed the owner of the Danish copyright to prevent the rental on the Danish market, without his consent, of video cassettes purchased in another Member State, where there was no legislation governing the exercise of copyright upon the rental of the cassettes and where they had been marketed with the consent of the owner of the copyright in that Member State. The Danish legislation was not, the court held, incompatible with former arts 30 and 36 (arts 36 and 42 TFEU).

Ltd., Setanta Sports, SARL and the Motion Picture Association were rejected by the Court on December 16, 2009 ((2010) OJ C100/15).

[108] i.e. the passage of Directive 89/552/EEC (the Television Without Frontiers Directive, which primarily deals with the regulation of broadcasters), Directive 93/83/EEC, Directive 98/84/EEC and Directive 2001/29/EC.

[109] *Basset v SACEM* (Case 402/85) [1987] E.C.R. 1747 and per Advocate General Lenz at 180 para.26; *Warner Brothers Inc v Erik Christiansen* (Case 158/86) [1988] E.C.R. 2605; see also paras 24 and 24 of the Opinion of Advocate General Jacobs in *Ministère Public v Tournier* [1989] E.C.R. 2421 and *Lucazeau v SACEM* (Cases 110/88, 241/88 and 242/88) [1989] E.C.R. 2811.

[110] *Ministère Public v Tournier* (Case 395/87) [1989] E.C.R. 2421. Contrast the court's decision in *Musik-Vertrieb Membran v GEMA* (Cases 55 & 57/80) [1981] E.C.R. 147.

[111] Case 158/86 [1988] E.C.R. 2605.

Nevertheless this case provided greater difficulty in defining the border between the continuous right of exploitation in the performance of a work and the right of reproduction and first distribution of a work. In reaching its decision in the *Warner Brothers* case, the court avoided expressly classifying the protection of the rental right under Danish law as falling either under the continuing right of exploitation in the performance of the copyright work, or as being a departure from the principle that the right of reproduction and first marketing of a work is exhausted with respect to a product reproducing that work following the first placing of that product on the market by or with the consent of the copyright owner.

However, in *Metronome Musik GmbH v Music Point Hokam GmbH*,[112] the Court of Justice confirmed that the release into circulation of a sound recording on disc or cassette cannot render lawful other forms of exploitation of the protected work, such as rental, that are of a different nature from sale or any other lawful form of distribution.

Thus, while the first marketing of a copyright work in a material form by or with the consent of the copyright owner within the European Union will exhaust, in relation to that product, the right of exploitation in the reproduction of the copyright work, the right of exploitation in relation to the performance or rental of the work thereby remains unaffected, even in respect of performance by means of, or rental of, that product. Meanwhile, in *Foreningen af Danske Videogramdistributorer v Laserdisken*,[113] the Court of Justice has held that it is not contrary to former arts 30 and 36 of the Treaty or to the Council Directive on rental right and lending right and on certain rights related to copyright in the field of intellectual property[114] for the holder of an exclusive rental right to prohibit copies of a film from being offered for rental in a Member State, even where the offering of those copies for rental has been authorised in the territory of another Member State, Thus, the court has made it clear that the exclusive right to authorise or prohibit the rental of a film is comparable to the right of public performance and, unlike the right of distribution, is not exhausted as soon as it has been exercised.

C. LIMITATIONS ON THE PRINCIPLE OF EXHAUSTION OF RIGHTS

(i) Goods originating outside the European Union

24–31   **International exhaustion: goods originating outside the European Union.** The question has arisen whether the principle of exhaustion of rights applies to prevent a right owner in a Member State from asserting his right against the importation into that Member State of goods which were marketed by him or with his consent outside the European Union.[115] In *EMI Records Ltd v CBS United*

---

[112] Case C–200/96 [1998] E.C.R. I–1953.

[113] Case C–61/97, judgment of September 22, 1998 [1998] E.C.R. I–05171; [2000] E.C.D.R. 139.

[114] Council Directive 92/100/EEC of November 19, 1992 [1992] OJ L346/61.

[115] The territory of the European Union comprises the national territories of the 27 Member States of the EU. The EEA Agreement contains equivalent provisions to former arts 28 to 30 of the Treaty (arts 34 to 36 TFEU), and it is thought that the principle of exhaustion will be applied throughout the EEA, that is, in addition, to the territories of the three EEA States who are not members of the EU, i.e. Iceland, Norway and Liechtenstein (although not applying to Liechtenstein for the time being); see para.24–01, above. As to whether this assumption is correct, see, however, the discussion in G. Tritton et al., *Intellectual Property in Europe* 3rd edn (London: Sweet & Maxwell, 2008) paras 7.555 et seq. Note that the EFTA Court, in an advisory opinion in *Mag Instrument Inc v California Trading Company Norway* (E–2/97) (judgment of December 3, 1997 [1998] E.T.M.R. 85), held that it is for the EFTA States to decide whether they wish to introduce or maintain the principle of international exhaustion of rights conferred by a trade mark with regard to goods originating outside the EEA.

Kingdom Ltd,[116] CBS, who owned the mark "Columbia" in the United States and other non-Member States, imported goods under the mark into the European Union, and EMI, who owned the mark in various Member States, sought to prevent such imports. The mark had once been in common ownership. The Court of Justice held that the principle of exhaustion of rights had no application to goods originating from outside the Union. The court explained this limitation to the principle on the ground that it is the free movement of goods within the Union which is the aim of the Internal Market, and the exercise of intellectual property rights to prevent the importation into a Member State of goods manufactured or first marketed outside the Union in no way jeopardises the unity of the Internal Market which former arts 28 to 30 (arts 34, 35 and 36 TFEU) and the principle embodied in them are intended to ensure.[117]

The court adopted a similar approach in *Silhouette International Schmied GmbH & Co KG v Harlauer Handels GmbH*,[118] in which it confirmed that art.7 of the Trade Marks Directive[119] precluded Member States from providing that trade mark rights become exhausted in a Member State by virtue of the marketing of the goods in a non-Member State with the proprietor's consent. The *Silhouette* judgment established the absolute principle of EEA-wide exhaustion, finding that Member States are precluded from extending the principle of EEA-wide exhaustion by means of national rules providing for international exhaustion.[120] Although the judgment related to the exhaustion of trade mark rights, the principle applies also to other intellectual property rights, including copyright. The *Silhouette* judgment was confirmed by the Court of Justice in *Sebago and Another v GB-Unic*, the court adding that the legal consequence of exhaustion can arise only if the consent extends to every individual item of the goods in respect of which exhaustion is pleaded.[121]

The issue of exhaustion of trade mark rights and, in particular, of the implications of a change from the existing EU/EEA exhaustion régime, as confirmed by *Silhouette* and *Sebago*, to that of international exhaustion, was much debated for many years. Following discussions in the Internal Market Council, the Commission announced in May 2000 that it had decided not to propose a change to the current EEA-wide exhaustion approach.[122] Subsequently, on October 3, 2001, the European Parliament called on the Commission to produce by December 31, 2002, a report including a detailed study of the implications of a possible transition to the principle of international exhaustion for European manufacturers and consumers, as well as jobs.[123] The report in the form of a Commission Staff Work-

---

[116] *EMI Records Ltd v CBS United Kingdom Ltd* (Case 51/75) [1976] E.C.R. 811. N.B. Ex arts 31 to 33 and 35 have been repealed.

[117] *EMI Records Ltd v CBS United Kingdom Ltd* (Case 51/75) [1976] E.C.R. 811.

[118] (C–355/96) [1998] E.C.R. I–4799: (The opinion of Advocate General Jacobs, which was followed by the court, is reported at [1998] F.S.R. 474).

[119] Directive 89/100/EEC of December 21, 1988, to approximate the laws of the Member States relating to trade marks; [1989] OJ L40/1.

[120] As regards the EEA, see paras 24–01 and 24–103, below.

[121] *Sebago and Maison Dubois* (C–173/98) [1999] E.C.R. I–4103.

[122] See "Exhaustion of Trade Mark Rights—Working document from the Commission services on exhaustion of trade mark rights" submitted to the Council and the European Parliament on December 9, 1999, and communiqué from Commissioner Bolkestein on the issue of exhaustion of trade mark rights, June 2, 2000. See also NERA Study "The Economic Consequences of the Choice of Regime of Exhaustion in the Area of Trade Marks", published by the Commission on February 8, 1999, and House of Commons Select Committee on Trade and Industry Report on "Trade Marks, Fakes and Consumers", Eighth Report, Session 1998–99, June 29, 1999, H.C. 380. See also A. Carboni, "Cases about Spectacles and Torches: Now Can We See the Light" [1998] E.I.P.R. 470; W.R. Cornish,"Silhouette"—Through a Glass Darkly", in *Festschrift Till Gunnar Karnell*, (Stockholm: Gotab AB, 1999) 99.

[123] Document A5-0311/2001.

ing Paper was duly published on May 21, 2003,[124] and concluded that there were no "deficiencies in current legal provision relating to possible abuses of trade marks within the EU".

In a recent case, the Court of Justice has held on a reference from the *Hoge Raad* (Netherlands) that the consent of the proprietor of a trade mark to the marketing of goods bearing that mark carried out directly in the EEA by a third party who has no economic link to that proprietor may be implied, in so far as such consent is to be inferred from facts and circumstances prior to, simultaneous with or subsequent to the placing of the goods on the market in that area which, in the view of the national court, unequivocally demonstrates that the proprietor has renounced his exclusive rights.[125]

24–32   **Goods in free circulation in the European Union.** In the *EMI* case, above, the Court of Justice had to consider the further problem of the exercise of an intellectual property right in Member State A, against the importation into that state of goods from Member State B but which had been manufactured outside the European Union. It was argued that the combined effect of arts 28(2) TFEU (ex art.23(2) EC Treaty) and art.29(1) TFEU (ex art.24(1) EC Treaty) was to place such goods for all purposes on an equal footing with goods manufactured in Member State B. Article 28(2) TFEU (ex art.23(2) EC Treaty) provides that the provisions, inter alia, of arts 34 to 37 (ex arts 28 to 31) shall apply to products originating from non-Member States which are in free circulation in Member States. Article 29(1) provides that products originating from a non-Member State shall be considered in free circulation in a Member State if all import formalities and customs duties have been complied with and paid. The Court of Justice held, however, that neither the rules of the Treaty on the free movement of goods, nor those on the putting into free circulation of products from third countries, nor the principles governing the common commercial policy,[126] prohibit the proprietor of a mark in all Member States of the Community from exercising his right in order to prevent the importation of similar products bearing the same mark and coming from a non-Member State.[127] However, in the case of trade marks, art.7 of the Trade Marks Directive does apply to prevent the proprietor from exercising his rights where goods manufactured in a non-Member State have been marketed in a Member State with his consent (or the consent of a person with whom he has economic links, such as a member of the same corporate group).[128]

24–33   **The CDPA 1988.** Applying the *EMI* decision to copyright, therefore, the owner of copyright in the United Kingdom may exercise his right under the 1988 Act to prevent the unlicensed importation into the United Kingdom of products manufactured outside the EEA, for example in the United States of America, where such manufacture may have been lawful, but was not by or with the consent of such owner of the UK copyright within the meaning of the relevant provisions

---

[124] Document SEC(2003) 575, entitled: "Possible abuses of trade mark rights within the EU in the context of Community exhaustion".

[125] Case C–324/01, Judgment of the Court (First Chamber) October 15, 2009—Makro Zelfbedieningsgroothandel C.V., Metro Cash and Carry B.V., *Remo Zaandam B.V. v Diesel S.P.A.* OJ C297/14, December 5, 2009.

[126] Found in arts 206 and 207 of the Treaty (ex arts 131 and 133; (ex arts 132 and 134 have been repealed)), under which agreements have been concluded between the Community and certain third countries; see further paras 24–34 et seq., below.

[127] *EMI Records Ltd v CBS United Kingdom Ltd* (Case 51/75) [1976] 2 C.M.L.R. 235 at 266 at para.21.

[128] *Phytheron International S.A. v Jean Bourdon S.A.* (C–352/95) [1997] E.C.R. I–1729; [1997] 3 C.M.L.R. 199.

of the 1988 Act.[129] This remains so, even if importation is being effected via another Member State, at least where the rights in that other Member State are owned by the same person.[130]

(ii) Goods originating in the territory of States associated with the European Union

Agreements between third countries and the European Union. The European   24–34
Union has entered into agreements with a number of third countries, in some
cases with a view to such third countries becoming members of the Union,[131] in
other cases with a view to developing trade and other links between the Union
and such third countries.[132] The form of such agreements varies depending on the
closeness of the commercial, political and economic links which the agreement is
intended to create between the Union and the third country in question. However,
nearly all such agreements seek to improve the flow of trade between the Union
and such third country, and to this end include provisions similar to those in arts
34 to 37 (ex arts 28 to 31) of the TFEU.[133]

The question therefore arises in the case of each third country which has
entered into such an agreement with the European Union, whether the provisions
of the agreement in question are such as to give rise to a principle of free movement of goods between the Union and such third country which can be invoked
as being of directly applicable effect to prevent the exercise of intellectual property rights affecting that trade, in the same way as the principle has been applied
to trade between Member States of the Union, as discussed above.[134]

Association Agreement between Portugal and the European Union. This   24–35
question came before the Court of Justice in *Polydor Ltd v Harlequin Record
Shop Ltd*,[135] on a request by the Court of Appeal for a preliminary ruling as to the
interpretation and effect of the Agreement of July 22, 1972 between Portugal (at
the time not a member of the Union) and the Union. Article 4(2) of the Agreement, which came into force on January 1, 1973, provided for the abolition of
measures having an effect on imports equivalent to quantitative restrictions by

---

[129] See para.24–12, above. See also CDPA 1988 s.18(2), discussed at paras 7–90 et seq., above.

[130] As to where this is not the case, see para.24–38, below.

[131] As in the case of the original treaties with Greece and Turkey, of July 9, 1961 and September 12, 1963, respectively.

[132] For example, the Treaties concluded with the EFTA countries, setting up a free trade area between the Community and those countries: Austria, Iceland, Sweden, Switzerland, all of July 22,
1972; Norway, May 14, 1973; and Finland, October 5, 1973. Others include: Malta, December 5,
1970; Cyprus, December 19, 1972; Israel, May 11, 1975; Mexico, July 15, 1975; Tunisia, April
24, 1977; Algeria, April 26, 1977; Morocco, April 27, 1976; Jordan, Syria and Egypt, January
18, 1977; Lebanese Republic, May 3, 1977; and Lomé Convention, December 15, 1989. There
are also a number of agreements concluded with European states, some of which are now EU
Member States: Poland and Hungary, December 16, 1991; Romania, July 28, 1980; Albania,
October 26, 1992; Bulgaria, March 8, 1993; Czech Republic and Slovakia, October 4, 1993; and
Slovenia, April 5, 1993. Free Trade Agreements have also been entered into with Latvia, Lithuania and Estonia, July 18, 1994; and Faroe Islands, December 6, 1996.

[133] As in the case of the original treaties with Greece and Turkey, of July 9, 1961 and September 12,
1963, respectively. As to the EEA Agreement, see para.24–29, above.

[134] See para.24–03, above and see paras 28–181 et seq., below. See also D. Roth QC and V. Rose,
Bellamy and Child, European Community Law of Competition 6th edn (London: Sweet &
Maxwell, 2008), paras 1–096 to 1–104. See also Arts: N. March Hunnings, "Enforceability of the
EEC-EFTA Free Trade Agreements" (1977) 2 E.L.Rev. 163; M. Waelbrook "A Reply", (1978) 3
E.L.Rev 27 and N. March Hunnings, "A Rejoinder" (1978) 3 E.L.Rev 278.

[135] *Polydor Ltd and R.S.O. Ltd v Harlequin Record Shop Ltd and Simons Records Ltd* (Case 270/80)
[1982] E.C.R. 329; and see *Adams v Public Prosecutor, Canton Basle* [1978] 3 C.M.L.R. 480 in
which the Swiss Supreme Court decided that art.23 of the EEC-Switzerland Treaty (in terms similar to art.101 of the Treaty, ex art.81) does not create any right of action for private persons in
the Swiss courts; see also, in respect of the EEC-Austria Treaty, *Austro-Mechana Gesellschaft v
Gramola Winter & Co* [1984] 2 C.M.L.R. 626 (decision of the Austrian Supreme Court).

January 1, 1975. Article 23 of the Agreement provided in terms identical to art.36 (ex art.30) of the TFEU that the Agreement should not preclude prohibitions or restrictions on imports or exports justified on grounds of the protection of intellectual property.

The plaintiffs, who were the owners of the exclusive right to manufacture records of certain sound recordings in the United Kingdom, sought to prevent the importation into the United Kingdom by the defendants of records embodying such sound recordings manufactured lawfully in Portugal under licence from a company associated with the plaintiffs, which was the holder of the exclusive right to manufacture records of the sound recordings in Portugal. It was argued, on an application for interlocutory relief, that art.14(2) of the Agreement provided the defendants with a complete defence to the action. Reversing the decision at first instance, the Court of Appeal refused the grant of an interlocutory injunction and referred the issues of interpretation and effect of arts 14(2) and 23 of the Agreement to the Court of Justice.

To reach its decision, the Court of Justice returned to first principles and examined the objectives of the Agreement of July 22, 1972, in comparison with the Treaty of Rome. The court noted that the Agreement with Portugal was a Free Trade Agreement, the aims of which were different to those of the Treaty, which were to unite the national markets into a single market reproducing the conditions of a domestic market by establishing a common market and progressively approximating the economic policies of the Member States. The court held that in the circumstances of the Agreement of July 22, 1972, restrictions on trade in goods might be justifiable on the grounds of protection of intellectual property within the European Union. Consequently in the framework of the free trade arrangement, a prohibition on the importation into the Union of products from a non-Member State based on copyright could be justified. Article 14(2) of the Agreement could not therefore be relied on to prohibit the enforcement of that right as a restriction on trade.

24–36   **Direct effect of such agreements.** Although the Court of Justice did not consider the question of direct effect in this case, the court has subsequently held in relation to other treaties, for example art.2(1) of the Yaoundé Convention of 1963, that directly effective rights may arise within the Member States from a treaty with associated states.[136] The Court of Justice has made it clear that all agreements with third countries may be capable of giving rise to directly effective provisions. Further, the court has rejected the argument that the question of direct effect is linked to the question of reciprocity. Failure by a third state to accord direct effect to the provisions of an agreement will not prevent those provisions having direct effect within the European Union.[137]

(iii) Spurious goods

24–37   **Right to oppose infringement of the specific object of an intellectual property right.** The limits introduced to the exercise of intellectual property rights by the principle of free movement of goods, as set by the test of exhaustion of rights, have no application to the exercise of an intellectual property right by the owner of that right against merely spurious goods, and this is so whatever the country of origin of such spurious goods. The reason for this is that it is part of the substance,

---

[136] *Conceria Daniele Bresciani v Amministrazione delle Finanze* (Case 87/75) [1976] E.C.R. 129; cf. *EMI Records Ltd v CBS United Kingdom Ltd* and *EMI Records Ltd v CBS Grammofon A/s* (Cases 518, 86/75) [1976] E.C.R. 811 at 871.
[137] *Hauptzollamt Mainz v Kupferberg* (Case 104/81) [1982] E.C.R. 3641.

or specific object, of an intellectual property right to be able to prevent others making unauthorised use of the subject-matter protected by the intellectual property right, in a manner which directly usurps the primary exclusive rights granted to the owner of the intellectual property right. This was expressly confirmed by the Court of Justice in the *Centrafarm/Sterling* and *Centrafarm/Winthrop* cases,[138] in which it stated that the right to oppose infringement was part of the specific object of patents[139] and the right to prevent others taking advantage of a mark by selling goods improperly bearing the mark was part of the specific object of trade marks.[140] There has been no case before the Court of Justice expressly raising the protection of copyright works against spurious infringement. However, presumably a similar protection will be afforded to copyright works where the rights sought to be asserted against the spurious goods are part of the specific subject of copyright, whether relating to the right of reproduction or the right of performance.

Imported spurious goods. This right of protection arises both when the owner 24–38
of an intellectual property right in Member State A seeks to assert that right in state A against goods produced in state A, and when he seeks to assert that right in state A against goods manufactured in state B being imported into state A. In the latter case it does not matter whether state B is a Member State of the European Union or not. So long as the goods have not been brought into existence with the consent of the owner in state A of the intellectual property right, he has not, in connection with the creation of the goods, exercised that intellectual property right, or any equivalent intellectual property right he may enjoy in state B, so that the question of having exhausted either right cannot arise.[141] Thus, the owner of copyright under the CDPA 1988 may still assert his rights under that Act to prevent the importation into the United Kingdom of goods which reproduce his copyright work and which have been manufactured without his consent abroad, whether in the territory of a Member State of the European Union or not.[142]

D. EXHAUSTION OF RIGHTS: ASSOCIATED PROBLEMS

The principle of exhaustion of rights, consent and associated problems. For 24–39
copyright works legitimately marketed within the European Union the essential problem remains the determination of the degree of connection required between the marketing of the work in Member State B and the person who seeks to exercise an intellectual property right in Member State A to prevent the importation of that work, before the principle of the exhaustion of rights applies to preclude him from doing so. In its development of the theory of the specific object of the various intellectual property rights,[143] the court has emphasised that the owner of such a right will be considered to have exhausted his rights when they have been exercised within the European Union by the owner himself or with his consent, or by a person connected with him by ties of legal or economic dependence. Nevertheless the use of the notion of consent to determine the exhaustion of the rights by their owner does not provide a clear solution to all the problems that arise in seeking to resolve the conflict between the principles of

---

[138] (Cases 15 & 16/74) [1974] E.C.R. 1147 at 1183.
[139] (Case 15/74) [1974] 2 C.M.L.R. 503.
[140] *(Case 16/74)* [1974] 2 C.M.L.R. 508; see also *Centrafarm v American Home Products Corporation* [1978] E.C.R. 1823.
[141] See para.24–37, below.
[142] Principally under CDPA 1988 ss.22 and 27; previously under ss.5(2) and 16(2) of the 1956 Act.
[143] See para.24–23, above.

free movement and the territorial nature of national intellectual property regimes. In connection with copyright, three particular problems may be mentioned which arise:

  (a) where copyright protection afforded by the various national laws of the Member States differs in some material respect[144];

  (b) where the owner of exclusive rights held in each Member State has dealt with them in some states so as to lose his exclusivity in those states[145]; and

  (c) where the exclusive rights in different Member States are held by different persons, but were once held by the same person.[146]

(i) Differing protection among Member States

24–40   The absence of complete harmonisation among the Member States in the field of intellectual and commercial property rights causes some uncertainty as to the position of the owner of a right in one Member State seeking to prevent the import of the protected work from another Member State which provides for a lesser degree of protection for that right. Initially the question arose in connection with attempts to prevent the import of products from countries which either provided no equivalent intellectual property right[147] or provided for such a right but subject to a system of compulsory licensing.[148] More recently the division of the specific object of copyright into two elements, the right of reproduction and the right of performance, has generated further complexities that have had to be resolved.

   The importance of the notion of consent in addressing the dilemma of differing levels of protection appeared early in the court's case law. In *Parke, Davis & Co v Probel*,[149] the Court of Justice was asked for its preliminary ruling on a number of questions concerning the proposed exercise by the patentee in the Netherlands of his patent rights in that country to prevent the import into and sale in the Netherlands of medicine manufactured in Italy. At that time, no patent protection was available in Italy in respect of the medicine. The Dutch patentee had no connection with and had not consented to the manufacture of the medicine in Italy. The answer given by the Court of Justice was that the principle of free movement of goods had no application to such a case, and the Dutch patentee was not prohibited by such principle from exercising his patent rights in the Netherlands to prevent the import and sale of such medicine.

   Later, in *Merck & Co Inc v Stephar B.V.*,[150] the Court of Justice considered the position where a Dutch patentee was seeking to prevent the import into and sale in the Netherlands by an importer of pharmaceutical products which the Dutch patentee had himself marketed in Italy. The Court of Justice, reaffirming its previous definition of the specific object of a patent right, refused to allow the principle of free movement of goods to be restricted so as to uphold the prohibition under national law of the importation of the goods. The crucial factor was that the patentee had chosen to market the product on the Italian market. Once he had made this choice, he had exhausted his patent rights in all territories of the European Union in respect of those products so marketed. The court stated that it is for the proprietor of the patent to decide, in the light of all the circumstances, which

---

[144] See para.24–38, below.
[145] See para.24–39, below.
[146] See para.24–40, below.
[147] Such as in *Parke, Davis & Co v Probel* (Case 24/67) [1968] E.C.R. 55.
[148] Such as in *Musik-Vertrieb Membran GmbH v GEMA* (Cases 55 & 57/80) [1981 E.C.R. 146; and *Pharmon B.V. v Hoechst A.G.* (Case 19/84) [1985] E.C.R. 2281 and see also *Ramsberg-Gema A.G. v Electrostatic Plant Systems Ltd* [1990] F.S.R. 287.
[149] (Case 24/67) [1968] E.C.R. 55.
[150] (Case 187/80) [1981] E.C.R. 2063.

include the absence of patent protection in a given Member State, under what conditions he will market his product. If he chooses to do so in a Member State which does not provide patent protection, then he must accept the consequences of his choice as regards the free movement of those goods within the Common Market.[151] The Court of Justice viewed this as the logical extension of the principle established through its developing case law that the proprietor of an intellectual property right protected by a national law cannot rely on that law to protect the importation of a product which has been lawfully marketed in another Member State by the proprietor himself or with his consent.[152] This position was confirmed in *Merck & Co Inc v Primecrown Limited*.[153]

Part of the developing case law to which the court was referring in *Merck v Stephar* is the case of *Musik-Vertrieb Membran GmbH v GEMA*.[154] GEMA, a German management collecting society, had brought separate actions in the German courts against Membran and against K-Tel International on the grounds that they had infringed the distribution rights of the authors represented by GEMA by importing into Germany sound recordings of musical works protected under German copyright. The sound recordings were already in free circulation in other Member States, inter alia, in the United Kingdom, but GEMA claimed damages equivalent to the difference between the licence fees already paid in another Member State and the royalty in force in Germany. On a request by the German Federal Court of Justice for a preliminary ruling, the Court of Justice ruled that arts 34 and 36 (ex arts 28 and 30) of the TFEU precluded the exercise of rights granted under national legislation which enabled a copyright management society, empowered to exercise the copyright of composers of musical works reproduced on sound recordings in other Member States, to invoke those rights on the distribution of the sound recordings in the national market following their circulation in that other Member State by or with the consent of the owners of those copyrights, in order to claim the payment of a fee equal to the royalties ordinarily paid for the marketing on the national market less the lower royalties already paid in the Member State of manufacture.[155]

It is to be noted that part of the factual background in the *Musik-Vertrieb* case, above, was that the UK legislation enforced a statutory licensing scheme, taking effect after records of the work had been made with a view to sale by or with the licence of the author. This scheme included a fixed rate of royalty payment as a consequence of which contractual royalties tended to be agreed at the same level as the statutory rate. The Court of Justice refused to allow this statutory restriction on the freedom of the copyright owner to affect its decision. The court's reasoning for this was twofold. First, the existence of a disparity between national laws which is capable of distorting competition between Member States cannot justify a Member State giving legal protection to practices of a private body which are incompatible with the rules concerning the free movement of goods. Second, within the Internal Market an author has the right to choose the place in which, in the light of all the circumstances, he wishes to put the work into circulation. In making that choice, the author looks to his best interests, which may include not only the level of remuneration but other factors such as opportunities for distributing his work and the marketing facilities.[156]

In both the *Merck v Stephar* and *Musik-Vertrieb* cases, above, the court refused

---

[151] (Case 187/80) [1981] E.C.R. 2063 at 2081.
[152] (Case 187/80) [1981] E.C.R. 2063 at 2082.
[153] (C–267/95) [1996] E.C.R. I–6285 .
[154] (Cases 55 & 57/80) [1981] E.C.R. 146 .
[155] (Cases 55 & 57/80) [1981] E.C.R. 146 at 166.
[156] (Cases 55 & 57/80) [1981] E.C.R. 146 at 165.

to allow the exercise of national legislation to protect the owner of a right in one Member State from the effects of differing levels of protection under the laws of another Member State because the circulation of that work in that other Member State had been by, or with the consent of, the owner of the right. The importance of the existence of such consent is reinforced by the decision of the Court of Justice in *Pharmon B.V. v Hoechst A.G.*[157] Under the UK patent legislation, the holder of the patent for the drug "frusemide" was required to grant a compulsory licence for the manufacture, importation and sale of "frusemide" within the territory of the United Kingdom to a local undertaking. The licence contained a prohibition upon the exportation of the drugs manufactured under the licence. The licensee sold the drug to a Dutch undertaking which sought to market the drug in Holland; in response, the patentee, Hoechst, instituted proceedings for an injunction. The Court of Justice, on a request for a preliminary ruling as to the compatibility of the Dutch patent legislation with arts 34 and 36 (ex arts 28 and 30) of the Treaty, upheld the right of the patentee on the ground that, when a patentee is required by the legislation of a Member State to grant a compulsory licence for the manufacture and marketing of the patented product, the patentee cannot be deemed to have consented to the operation of that third party, as he has been deprived of the right freely to determine the conditions under which he markets his products. Only in this way did the court feel that the patentee would be able to protect the substance of his exclusive rights under the patent. However, where the patentee was under no legal obligation to market his product in a particular Member State, but did so because he felt ethically obliged to, his rights were thereby exhausted: *Merck & Co Inc v Primecrown Limited.*[158]

The Court of Justice returned to the doctrine of consent in the case of *EMI Electrola GmbH v Patricia Im-und Export Verwaltungsgesellschaft GmbH.*[159] At issue was whether EMI Electrola, the copyright holder in Germany for a particular sound recording still protected by German copyright, could prevent the import of copies of the sound recording marketed in Denmark. Although the copies of the sound recording had been marketed in Denmark without the consent of the holder of the Danish rights of reproduction and distribution for the sound recording, the marketing was lawful as the period of copyright protection in Denmark had expired. The defendants argued that since the works were lawfully marketed in Denmark, they were entitled to export them to Germany. In this instance, the court upheld the right of EMI Electrola to rely on their exclusive rights of reproduction and distribution of the work in Germany. The expiry of the copyright protection in Denmark did not alter the absence of consent by the German right-holder to the marketing of the work in another Member State.

It would therefore seem that disparities between national legal systems for the protection of intellectual property will not affect the court's decision that the primary factor for deciding whether the principles of free movement override national protection for copyright works is the absence or presence of the consent of the right-holder to the marketing of the work in the other Member State.[160]

Nevertheless, the application of the test of consent can be complicated. As the

---

[157] (Case 19/84) [1985] E.C.R. 2281.

[158] (C–267/95) [1996] E.C.R. I–6285. See also W. Alexander, "Intellectual Property and the Free Movement of Goods—1996 Case Law of the European Court of Justice", [1998] 28 IIC 16.

[159] (Case 341/87) [1989] E.C.R. 79.

[160] See the Opinion of Advocate General Darmon, (Case 341/87) [1989] E.C.R. 79 at 418 et seq. Such disparities have, of course, led to measures being taken at Community level to harmonise the content of national copyright and related rights laws; see paras 24–41 et seq., below.

Court of Justice observed in the *EMI Electrola v Patricia* case,[161] the state of EU law at the time was characterised by a lack of harmonisation or approximation of legislation on the protection of literary and artistic property. It was, and still is for the national legislatures to specify the conditions and rules of that protection.

Leaving the determination of conditions and rules of protection to the national legislatures raised two separate problems. First, apart from differing periods of protection, differences in the nature of that protection lead to a variance between the rights protected in the different Member States.[162] Second, it might not be straightforward to determine whether the right being invoked is part of the existence and exercise of the right of reproduction in a copyright work, or whether the right is part of the existence and exercise of the right of performance in a copyright work. If it is the latter, the right may not be exhausted by a single exercise, but would appear to be capable of repeated exploitation.[163] The degree of harmonisation of national legislation in the field of copyright and related rights achieved in recent years has in some measure solved these problems.[164]

The present state of the case law of the Court of Justice suggests not only that consent will be the dominant factor in determining whether the holder of copyright has exhausted his rights, but also that the copyright owner will remain free to decide when to exercise that consent. The proviso to this remains the second sentence of art.36 (ex art.30), namely: the prohibitions or restrictions allowed or imposed by the national legislation must not be such as to constitute a means of arbitrary discrimination or a disguised measure for restricting trade between Member States.

So far, the Court of Justice has not been asked to consider the situation where the proprietor of an intellectual property right in one Member State, either by deliberate choice or otherwise, has not obtained equivalent protection in other Member States where such rights are available. In such a case, would the principles of free movement permit the owner of the right to prevent the import of products marketed by another, when it was his failure to obtain equivalent right protection which allowed that other to market the products in another Member State? Applying the test of consent as developed in the Court of Justice's case law as discussed above, this question would be answered in the negative. But, in the case of patents, if the failure to obtain such a parallel patent were due to a deliberate choice, then could it be said that the exercise of the rights under the patent laws of one Member State, where patent protection had been obtained, amounted, in the circumstances, to an arbitrary discrimination or a disguised restriction on trade between Member States?

Similarly, if the holder of copyright in, say the Netherlands, does not act to assert his rights against manufacture and sale of goods in the Netherlands known to him to be taking place in infringement of his rights, it cannot be said that he has consented in a positive sense to such manufacture and sale, but the question arises whether it can be said that in such circumstances the exercise of his rights under the CDPA 1988 to prevent importation of those goods into the United Kingdom amounts to arbitrary discrimination or disguised restriction on such trade.[165]

Whether the proviso to art.36 (ex art.30) is satisfied, it is suggested, is in any

---

[161] *EMI Electrola GmbH v Patricia Im- und Export Verwaltungsgesellschaft GmbH* (Case 341/87) [1989] E.C.R. 79.

[162] See, for example, the decision of the Court in *Warner Brothers Inc v Erik Christiansen* (Case 158/86) [1988] E.C.R. 2605, which leaves unclear the nature of the right protected by the Danish copyright laws relating to the rental of video cassettes, referred to at para.24–28, above.

[163] See para.24–27, above.

[164] See paras 24–41 et seq., below.

[165] See the arguments raised in *British Leyland Motor Corporation Ltd v Wyatt Interpart Company*

case a matter for the consideration of the national court which is asked to enforce the intellectual property right in question.[166] There may be sound commercial reasons why, in the first example, the owner of the patent right in the Netherlands does not wish to take out patent protection in a particular country, and, in the second example, the owner of the copyright in the United Kingdom does not wish to exercise his parallel rights in the Netherlands to prevent the infringement at source. If so, then it is difficult to see how such action could be found to be arbitrary or, indeed, to be aimed at trade between Member States at all.[167]

Although no direct answer to these problems has been given by the Court of Justice, recent developments, as discussed above, would suggest that, in such a situation, the court would uphold the prohibition on the imports. The Court of Justice has repeatedly stressed, that in the absence of harmonisation, it will not interfere with the existence or structure of national intellectual property rights. Thus, in *Keurkoop B.V. v Nancy Kean Gifts B.V.*,[168] the Court of Justice was asked to pronounce on the compatibility of Dutch design rights with arts 34 and 36 (ex arts 28 and 30). The design rights in question could be acquired by the first person to register them, without inquiry as to whether that person was also the author of the design or a person claiming title under the author. The only right of challenge to that registration vested in the author of the design or the person commissioning the design from the author. No creative or artistic activity was therefore required as a condition for a person to register a design. The question was raised for the Court of Justice's preliminary ruling by the Dutch Regional Court of Appeal, in proceedings in the Dutch courts in which the proprietor of the Dutch design right sought to prevent the importation into Holland of products manufactured in another Member State lawfully but, without his authority, and which were identical to the registered design. The Court of Justice held that the design legislation in issue fell within the scope of the provisions of art.36 (ex art.30) on the protection of industrial and commercial property, and that the proprietor of the Dutch design right could prevent the importation into Holland from another Member State of products identical in appearance to the protected design, provided that they had not been marketed by him or with his consent, and that the rights of the respective proprietors of the designs had been created independently of one another.

The problem of exhaustion of the rights conferred by a trade mark was referred once again to the Court of Justice in *Zino Davidoff SA v A & G Imports Ltd*.[169] The context again concerned so-called "grey re-imports", i.e. goods which have been marketed for the first time by the right-holder, or with his consent, outside the EEA and are then imported into the EEA. In its judgment, the court characterised the issue before it as the determination of the circumstances in which the proprietor of a trade mark may be regarded as having consented, directly or indirectly, to the importation and marketing within the EEA by third parties who currently own them of products bearing that mark, which have been placed on the market outside the EEA by the proprietor of the mark or with his consent. The

---

Ltd [1979] F.S.R. 39 and [1979] F.S.R. 583 CA; see also *Maxicar v Renault* (Case 53/87) [1988] E.C.R. 6039.

[166] As was confirmed by the Court of Justice in *Centrafarm B.V. v American Home Products Corporation* (Case 3/78) [1978] E.C.R. 1823. See also *British Leyland Motor Corporation Ltd v T.I. Silencers Ltd* [1979] F.S.R. 591.

[167] See *Lerose Ltd v Hawick Jersey International Ltd* [1973] F.S.R. 15; *Lowenbrau Munchen v Grunhalle Lager International Ltd* [1974] F.S.R. 1.

[168] Case 144/81 [1982] E.C.R. 2853; see also *Maxicar v Renault* (Case 53/87) [1988] E.C.R. 6039.

[169] *Zino Davidoff SA v A & G Imports Ltd; Levi Strauss and Co, Levi Strauss (UK) Ltd v Tesco Stores; Tesco plc and Costco Wholesale UK Ltd* (Joined Cases C–414/99, C–415/99 and C–416/99) (references for a preliminary ruling from the High Court of Justice of England and Wales, Chancery Division (Patent Court)). Judgment of November 20, 2001: [2000] 2 W.L.R. 321.

court observed that consent, which was tantamount to the renunciation by the proprietor of his exclusive right to prevent imports into the EEA, was the decisive factor in the extinction of that right. It went on to reject a suggestion that questions of consent should be a matter for the national laws of Member States, since if that were so, protection for trade mark proprietors would vary according to the legal system concerned. Accordingly, it concluded, it was for the court to supply a uniform interpretation of the concept of consent. In view of its serious consequences, the court held that consent must be so expressed that an intention to renounce the rights of the trade mark proprietor is unequivocally demonstrated. Such an intention will normally be gathered from an express statement of consent. However, it is conceivable that consent might be inferred from facts and circumstances before, during or after the placing of the goods on the market outside the EEA which unequivocally demonstrate that the trade mark proprietor has renounced his rights. It is for the trader alleging consent to prove it and not for the trade mark proprietor to prove its absence. Accordingly, implied consent cannot be inferred from mere silence on the part of the proprietor; from the fact that the proprietor has not communicated his opposition to marketing within the EEA; from the fact that the goods do not carry a warning that placing them on the market in the EEA is prohibited; from the fact that the proprietor transferred title to them without imposing contractual restrictions on the transferee; or from the fact that, according to the law governing that contract, in the absence of such restrictions, the property right transferred includes an unlimited right of resale or at least a right to market the goods in the EEA. It is irrelevant that the importer of the goods is not aware that the proprietor does not consent to their being placed on the market in the EEA or being sold there by traders other than authorised retailers. It is also irrelevant that the authorised retailers or wholesalers in the EEA have not imposed contractual restrictions on their own purchasers setting out such opposition, even if they have been informed of it by the trade mark proprietor.

Subsequently, in *Levi Strauss & Co v Tesco Stores Ltd*, before the UK Patents Court, Pumfrey J. stated that the clear thrust of the Court of Justice's decision was that only express consent to the subsequent marketing within the EEA would suffice.[170] He went on to accept that the effect of the decision was to create a presumption of infringement; to require that presumption to be rebutted by evidence which in most cases the defendant would not be able to provide, that is, evidence of unambiguous consent; and to condemn genuine goods of the proprietor to the status of counterfeit goods. In his view, these consequences were "certainly striking but they are inevitable".[171]

The Court of Justice dealt subsequently in the case *Van Doren v Lifestyle Sports*[172] with the question of the extent to which national courts may decide the question whether goods have been placed on the market in the EEA with the trade mark owner's consent by reference to national rules as to the allocation of the burden of proof, since the case turned on where the goods in question "had been put on the market by the trade mark owner or with his consent". As the court established in *Zino Davidoff and Levi Strauss*, it is the trader who relies on consent to prove it. In its judgment, however, the court held that a national rule of evidence according to which a defendant relying on a plea of exhaustion of the trade mark had to prove the existence of the conditions for such exhaustion was consistent with EU law. Nevertheless, such a rule of evidence might have to be

---

[170] [2002] EWHC 1556 (Ch).
[171] [2002] EWHC 1556 (Ch) at paras 17 and 19.
[172] *Van Doren and Q. GmbH v Lifestyle Sports—Sportswear Handelsgesellschaft GmbH* (C–244/00) [2003] E.C.R. I–3051

qualified in the light of the EU principles on the protection of the free movement of goods. Where a party succeeded in establishing that there was a "real risk of partitioning national markets" if he bore that burden of proof, particularly where the proprietor marketed his products in the EEA under an exclusive distribution system, it was for the proprietor to establish that the products were initially placed on the market outside the EEA by him or with his consent. If such evidence was adduced, it was for the defendant to prove the proprietor's consent to subsequent marketing of the products in the EEA.

(ii) Loss of exclusivity in some Member States

24–41   It has not been unusual for the owner of copyright in a work in the various countries of the world which recognise his right, to divide the world into primary and secondary markets. Such has often been the case, for example, with literary works, where language has a greater importance in determining markets than national boundaries. Thus, an English author, or more usually the British publisher who has acquired the rights to the work, might exploit the copyright by licensing the exclusive right of publication in the English language in North America to a North American publisher, reserving to himself the exclusive right of publication in the English language in the United Kingdom, whilst allowing either party to sell their copies of the work in the English language in other secondary markets such as the rest of Europe. What if the North American publisher, or someone else, then imports into Holland a large quantity of copies of the work in the English language, which were lawfully produced in North America, and someone then seeks to import these into the United Kingdom? Is the British publisher entitled to assert his exclusive rights against such imports? It may be that the copies in question were first sold in North America, in which case the British publisher would have received royalties calculated on the higher rate appropriate to a primary, exclusive, market, but even so, on the principle in *EMI Records Ltd v CBS United Kingdom Ltd*,[173] why should a first sale in a non-Member State have any effect on exclusive rights enjoyed in a Member State? On the other hand, the copies in question may have been the subject of a first sale by the North American publisher in Holland, from which the British publisher would have received royalties calculated on the lower rate appropriate to a secondary, non-exclusive, market. In such a case, the first marketing of the works in Holland took place with the consent of the British publisher, and applying the test of consent, as currently developed, he could be considered to have exhausted his exclusive rights within the European Union by such first marketing, notwithstanding that he received only the lower royalty.[174] Should this be the correct analysis of the application of the principle of the exhaustion of rights and the notion of consent to the division between primary and secondary markets, the distinction between markets, when both are within the European Union, becomes one that is difficult, if not impossible, to protect through the use of exclusive national copyright.

The case law of the Court of Justice has shown a growing awareness of the commercial difficulties inherent in the use of the notion of consent within a market lacking harmonisation. However, the concept of exhaustion of rights, in its present state of development does not provide ready answers to the problems which may arise from the complex manner in which copyright is capable of

---

[173] Case 51/75 [1976] E.C.R. 811; [1976] 2 C.M.L.R. 235.
[174] *Musik-Vertrieb Membran GmbH v GEMA* (Cases 55 & 57/80) [1981] E.C.R. 146; *Dansk Supermarked A/S v Imerco A/S* (Case 58/80) [1981] E.C.R. 181; *Merck & Co Inc v Stephar B.V.* (Case 187/80) [1981] E.C.R. 2063 .

exploitation in different countries, for what, in the past, have been considered justifiable commercial reasons.[175] The concept requires a good deal more definition before these questions can be answered with any confidence.[176]

(iii) Common origin of rights

The divisibility of copyright and related rights geographically by reference to national boundaries, or even in areas which cut across national boundaries, allows owners of such rights in various Member States to dispose of their rights in relation to particular territories to different persons by way of outright assignments or by licences. Once this has occurred, the question arises of whether EU law prevents the assignee or licensee of the owner of the copyright under the CDPA 1988 from asserting his right to prevent imports into the United Kingdom of products made in, e.g. France, by the assignee or licensee from the same person of the French copyright?[177]

    In relation to trade marks, the "common origin" principle was developed early in the case law of the European Union.[178] No distinction was made between direct and indirect sales, nor did the application of the principle depend on a previous marketing. It was sufficient in the case of trade marks for the principle of free movement of goods within the Community to apply in order to prevent the exercise of a trade mark in Member State A against goods bearing that mark and lawfully originating in Member State B, that the two marks should have had a common origin. This left it unclear how far this principle extended to other intellectual property rights. The Court of Justice's decision, to the effect that the principle did not apply to patents granted under compulsory licence,[179] allowed the premise that by analogy it did not apply to other intellectual property rights such as copyright and designs.[180] The Court of Justice has now clarified the position and reconsidered the "common origin" principle. The principle no longer has a role to play in the resolution of the conflict between the free movement of goods and national intellectual property rights. In its ruling in *S.A. CNL-Sucal N.v v Hag GF A.G ("Hag II")*,[181] the court rejected the principle of common origin, and confirmed its doctrine that exceptions to the principle of free movement of goods in the Common Market will be allowed only in so far as the excep-

24–42

---

[175] See, for example, the concern expressed in relation to these problems by the 1977 Copyright Committee, Cmnd. 6732, paras 83–84.

[176] See, for example, the discussion on Distribution Right, Exhaustion and Rental Right, in Ch.4 of the Commission's Green Paper on Copyright and the Challenge of Technology, Commission (COM (88) 172 final).

[177] i.e. under CDPA 1988 s.27(5).

[178] *Sirena S.R.L. v Eda S.R.L.* (Case 40/70) [1971] E.C.R. 69; *Van Zuylen Freres v Hag* (Case 192/73) [1974] E.C.R. 731; *Terrapin (Overseas) Ltd v Terranova Industrie* (Case 119/75) [1976] E.C.R. 1039. See also *Re the Persil Trade Mark* [1978] F.S.R. 348; *Centrafarm B.V. v American Home Products Corporation* (Case 3/78) [1978] E.C.R. 1823. See also D. Roth QC and V. Rose, *Bellamy and Child, European Community Law of Competition* 6th edn (London: Sweet & Maxwell, 2008), paras 8–036—8–041.

[179] See D. Roth QC and V. Rose, *Bellamy and Child, European Community Law of Competition* 6th edn (London: Sweet & Maxwell, 2008), para.8–023; *Pharmon B.V. v Hoechst A.G.* (Case 19/84) [1985] E.C.R. 2281.

[180] In *Terrapin (Overseas) Ltd v Terranova Industrie* (Case 119/75) [1976] E.C.R. 1039, the Court of Justice justified the application of the common origin doctrine to trade marks on the ground that the basic function of a trade mark, that is to guarantee to consumers that the product has the same origin, is already undermined where the original right has been subdivided (at 506, para.6). Such reasoning would not appear to be applicable to the subdivision of copyrights or patents. See also the remarks of Advocate General Roemer, *Deutsche Grammophon GmbH v Metro-SB-Grossmärkte GmbH & Co K.G.* (Case 78/70) [1971] E.C.R. 487, to the effect that copyright is more closely related to patent rights than to the trade mark right. This was later reaffirmed by Advocate General Darmon in *EMI Electrola GmbH v Patricia Im- und Export Verwaltungsgesellschaft GmbH* (Case 341/87) [1989] E.C.R. 79.

[181] (Case C–10/89) [1990] E.C.R. I–03711; [1990] 3 C.M.L.R. 571.

tions are justified for safeguarding rights which are the specific subject-matter of that property.[182] This ruling does not resolve all the unanswered problems raised by the court's notion of exhaustion of rights, but it does remove the uncertainty that was caused by the parallel existence of the independent doctrine of common origin.

In *IHT Internazionale Heiztechnik GmbH v Ideal-Standard GmbH*,[183] the Court of Justice held that the effect of *Hag II* was that, where the unitary control of the mark in different Member States had been lost by a voluntary assignment, the assignee in one Member State cannot be said to have consented to another economically independent undertaking having placed the products on the market in another Member State. In such a case, the assignee had no power to determine the products to which the mark might be affixed in the other Member State nor to control their quality. This reasoning appears to be equally applicable to the assignment of copyright in a work for one Member State by the person who holds the copyright in that work in other Member States.

5. HARMONISATION OF NATIONAL COPYRIGHT AND RELATED RIGHTS

A. Background and History of the Commission's Harmonisation Programme

24–43 **Introduction.** Prior to the accession of the United Kingdom to the European Economic Community[184] on January 1, 1973,[185] the Commission of the then European Communities (the Commission) had not initiated any measures for the harmonisation of national laws in the field of copyright. However, in the 1990s, following a period of studies and consultations over the previous ten years, the Commission embarked on a programme of harmonisation of national copyright laws by means of Directives which is still continuing. Meanwhile as a result of the implementation of the Directives adopted to date in the United Kingdom, this programme has led to a number of far-reaching changes to the UK copyright law, similar in impact to the changes brought about in UK legislation following the United Kingdom's participation in the work leading to the adoption of the Berne Convention,[186] and subsequent membership thereof.[187] This EU harmonisation programme had little impact on the 1988 Act, but in the intervening years that Act has been amended on a number of occasions to bring the law of the United Kingdom into conformity with the series of EC Directives adopted in the field of copyright and related rights since 1991, and described below in paras 24–46, et seq.

Directives for the harmonisation of national laws adopted by the Council of Ministers under arts 114 and 115 (ex arts 94 and 95) of the TFEU are addressed to the Member States, which are obliged to modify their national laws so as to

---

[182] (Case C–10/89) [1990] E.C.R. I–03711; [1990] 3 C.M.L.R. 571 at 607.
[183] (Case C–9/93) [1993] E.C.R. I–2789 at para.43ff.
[184] As to the terminology used in this work, see para.24–01 and fn.13, above.
[185] For a discussion of the effect of the accession of the UK to the Treaty, in the light of the subsequent development of EU law, on the exercise of various rights enjoyed under the Copyright, Designs and Patents Act 1988 by the owner of copyright subsisting under that Act, see paras 24–03 et seq., above.
[186] The Convention for the Protection of Literary and Artistic Works signed at Berne on September 9, 1886, as subsequently amended.
[187] See paras 23–04 et seq., above. See also *Guide to the Berne Convention*, (Geneva: World Intellectual Property Organisation (WIPO), 1978) and S. Ricketson, *The Berne Convention for the Protection of Literary and Artistic Works: 1886–1986*, (London: Centre for Commercial Law, Queen Mary College; Kluwer, 1987).

bring into force such laws, regulations and administrative provisions as may be necessary to comply with the particular directive by a certain date. Thus, the existing and future EU legislation on copyright has exerted considerable influence on the copyright law of the United Kingdom already, and future legislation will continue to do so. Since the United Kingdom and Ireland are the only two countries in the European Union whose copyright laws follow the Anglo-American copyright tradition, the United Kingdom has already been obliged to incorporate certain concepts of the Continental-European *le droit d'auteur* (author's right) approach to copyright into its law on the subject, and this trend is likely to continue. The character of the copyright law of the United Kingdom has already undergone some change with the introduction of moral rights, a continental law import not yet harmonised in the European Union, and the artist's resale right, as the direct result of a Directive on the subject, as well as in other respects referred to later in this chapter.[188] The influence of the case law of the Court of Justice on the interpretation of the existing copyright Directives will also be felt. As discussed below, the Court of Justice is building up a European copyright law and this will only develop in the light of the increasing number of references being made by national courts to the Court of Justice for preliminary opinions, which are then binding on the national courts.

Distinction between *copyright* and *authors' rights*. For newcomers to the field of copyright, it should be explained that within the European Union there are two basic approaches to the protection of the categories of right owners afforded protection in the United Kingdom under the Copyright, Designs and Patents Act 1988. The Continental-European or civil law approach to author's right (*le droit d'auteur*) is based on the protection of the individual author. A work is considered to be an expression of the author's personality and it follows, therefore, that only individual, natural persons may be accorded an author's right. The Anglo-American or common law approach of *copyright* admits protection both of individuals and of corporate bodies, and thus permits a wide variety of creative endeavour to benefit from copyright protection. Thus, in EU countries with a civil law tradition, as a general rule legal entities, as opposed to natural persons, are not accorded authors' rights under the *droit d'auteur* system so that, for example, neither producers of films and sound recordings, nor broadcasting organisations are considered to be authors. To the extent that the beneficiaries of the Rome Convention[189] and film producers are afforded protection in *droit d'auteur* countries, they are protected by means of rights related to copyright, known as related or neighbouring rights (*droits voisins du droit d'auteur*).

24-44

A further distinction between *copyright* and *droit d'auteur* systems concerns the requirement, common to both, that only original works may be protected. The requirement of originality is defined differently in the various Member States. In civil law countries, originality requires a degree of creativity reflecting the individuality of the author's personality, whereas in the United Kingdom, original means only that the work originates with the author and is not copied. The interpretation of the notion of originality has traditionally been reserved to the courts in both systems.[190] As discussed below, a number of the Directives specify that to benefit from protection a work must be original in the sense that it is the

---

[188] See, e.g. paras 24–163, 24–101 et seq., 24–44 and 24–62, below.
[189] The International Convention for the Protection of Performers, Producers of Phonograms and Broadcasting Organisations, signed at Rome on October 26, 1961. The Convention entered into force on May 18, 1964 (see paras 23–88 et seq., above). The Rome Convention is not to be confused with the Rome Act revising the Berne Convention 1928. See also *Guide to the Rome Convention and the Phonograms Convention* (Geneva: World Intellectual Property Organisation (WIPO), 1981).
[190] On the question of originality and other distinctions (formalities, ownership and assignability of

author's own intellectual creation. This definition of originality has been confirmed by the Court of Justice but it would seem to be compatible with the present position in the United Kingdom.[191]

The copyright harmonisation programme of the Commission thus has to steer a difficult course between the copyright and author's right approaches. The task is facilitated, however, by the existing common ground between the Member States in the field of copyright resulting from their common membership of the Berne Union.[192]

24–45 **History of EU interest in copyright and related rights.** In the following, the history of the interest of the European Union in copyright and related rights is reviewed and attention is drawn to the impact that Union legislation has already had and is likely to have in the future on the law of the United Kingdom.

Detailed analyses of the manner in which those Directives which have already been adopted, have been implemented or in UK law, are to be found in the relevant chapters of this work.[193]

The first call for action by the Commission in relation to copyright came from the European Parliament in a Resolution on the Preservation of the European Cultural Heritage in 1974. This asked the Commission "to propose measures to be adopted by the Council to approximate the national laws on the protection of the cultural heritage, royalties and other related intellectual property rights".[194] In response to this Resolution, the Commission put forward a series of policy documents on the subject of EU action in the cultural sector,[195] including some aspects of copyright law, and commissioned a number of comparative law studies[196] to

---

rights, moral rights and related rights) between copyright and *droit d'auteur*, see G. Davies, "The Convergence of Copyright and Authors' Rights-Reality or Chimera?" (1995) 26 I.I.C. 964; see also T.K. Dreier, "Authorship and New Technologies from the Point of View of the Civil Law Traditions" (1995) 26 I.I.C. 989; D.M. Rose, "Copyright in Stage Production Elements: Requirements of Originality and Record under English Law" [1998] Ent. L.R. 30.

[191] See para.3–128, above, as to the definition of originality in the UK. See also *Infopaq International A/S v Danske Dagblades Forening* (C–5/08) [2009] ECR 1–0000 at para.35.

[192] The Berne Union consists of those States which are signatories to the various Acts of the Berne Convention, which was adopted in 1886 and revised at Berlin (1908), Rome (1928), Brussels (1948), Stockholm (1967) and Paris (1971). Each revised text of the Convention is known as an Act, e.g. the Paris Act, etc. "The creation of a single Union, based on the principle of the assimilation of foreigner to national, with certain minimum standards of protection, and capable, by means of revision, of meeting world changes, allows recently joined countries to have international relationships with all the Union countries including those not yet bound by the most recently revised text of the Convention." *Guide to the Rome Convention and the Phonograms Convention* (Geneva: World Intellectual Property Organisation (WIPO), 1981), above, para.1.7, fn.52, above. See also paras 23–04 et seq., above.

[193] See Chs 3, 6, 7, 12, 14, 17 and 18.

[194] Resolution of May 13, 1974, para.11: [1974] OJ C62/6 and [1974] 5 EC Bull., point 2406.

[195] *Community Action in the Cultural Sector*, Commission Communication to the Council: [1977] 6 EC Bull. Supp.; *Stronger Community Action in the Cultural Sector*, Commission Communication to the Council, 1982, COM (82) 590 final, October 16, 1982.

[196] See the following in the Cultural Studies Series: A. Dietz, *Copyright Law in the European Community: A comparative investigation of national copyright legislation with special reference to the provisions of the Treaty establishing the European Economic Community*, document COM. XII/125/76 (published in English by Sijthoff and Noordhoff, 1978). A. Dietz, *Le droit primaire des contrats d'auteur dans les États membres de la Communauté européenne*, document COM. SG-Culture/4/81FR (1981); also published in German: *Das primäre Urhebervertragsrecht in der Bundesrepublik Deutschland und in den anderen Mitgliedsstaaten der EG* (Schweitzer Verlag, 1984). F. Gotzen, *Performers' Rights in the European Economic Community*, document COM. XII/52/78. F. Gotzen, *Performing Rights Contracts*, document COM. XII/47/80. G. Davies, *Piracy of Phonograms*, document COM. XII/235/80, (published for the Commission by ESC Publishing Ltd, 1981; rev 2nd edn, 1986). G. Davies, *Piracy of Phonograms*, document COM. XII/235/80, (published for the Commission by ESC Publishing Ltd, 1981; rev 2nd edn, 1986). G. Davies, *The Private Copying of Sound and Audiovisual Recordings*, document COM. SG-Culture/39/83 (published for the Commission by ESC Publishing Ltd, 1984). See also W. Duchemin, *Copyright Protection for Photographs in the European Economic Community* (1977) and

examine various aspects of the protection of authors of literary and artistic works, producers of phonograms and performers[197] within the European Union.

The need for a degree of harmonisation of the copyright laws of Member States came into focus during the late 1970s and the 1980s in the context of litigation which opposed the directly applicable provisions of the Treaty concerning the free movement of goods and freedom to provide services within the European Union and the exclusive rights granted by national copyright laws, which were territorial in nature.[198] The need for such harmonisation became more urgent following the political decision to complete the internal market (defined by the Single European Act of July 1, 1987, as being "an area without frontiers in which the free movement of goods, persons, services and capital is ensured in accordance with the provisions of the Treaty") by January 1, 1993.[199]

Subsequently, beginning with the Commission's action plan entitled "Europe's Way to the Information Society", published in 1994,[200] the Commission identified intellectual property protection as a key issue given the critical role creative content and innovation were likely to play in the further development of the so-called "Information Society", and addressed the challenges to copyright and related rights brought about by new technologies such as digitisation and multimedia.

The action plan resulted in a proposal for further harmonisation of copyright and related rights, in the form of a draft Directive on the harmonisation of certain aspects of copyright and related rights in the information society (Information Society Directive) published in December 1997,[201] which also had the aim of bringing EU legislation into conformity with the new WIPO Treaties, the WIPO Copyright Treaty (WCT) and the WIPO Performances and Phonograms Treaty (WPPT).[202] These two Treaties, adopted in 1996, had established new international standards for the protection of authors, performers and producers of phonograms and imposed fresh obligations on Member States of the European Union. Meanwhile, the Information Society Directive came into force in May 2002[203] and was supposed to be implemented in the national laws of EU Member States before December 22, 2001.[204] The deadline was not met by the United Kingdom whose necessary implementing legislation only entered into force on October 31, 2003.[205]

The European Council also formally approved the WCT and WPPT and authorised the President of the Council to ratify the Treaties on behalf of the European Union, as from the deadline for implementation by the Member States.[206]

W. Duchemin, "Suggestions with a view to improving the protection of photographs within the European Economic Community" [1980] 105 RIDA 2 and 25.

[197] See also, with particular reference to the rights of producers of phonograms and performers, G. Davies and H.H. von Rauscher auf Weeg, *Challenges to Copyright and Related Rights in the European Community* (ESC Publishing Ltd, 1983).

[198] See paras 24–07 et seq., above.

[199] art.8A: for the text see Vol.2 G1 et seq. See also the Commission's White Paper, *Completing the Internal Market*, COM (85) 310 final.

[200] COM (94) 347 final of July 19, 1994.

[201] *Proposal for a Directive on the Harmonisation of Certain Aspects of Copyright and Related Rights in the Information Society* (COM(97) 628 final) of December 10, 1997, see paras 24–79 et seq, below.

[202] See paras 23–72 et seq. and 23–115 et seq., above.

[203] Directive 2001/29/EC of the European Parliament and of the Council ([2001] OJ L167/10); see Vol.2 H8 and paras 24–96 et seq., below.

[204] Directive 2001/29/EC of the European Parliament and of the Council art.13.

[205] Copyright and Related Rights Regs 2003 (SI 2003/2498).

[206] Council Decision of March 16, 2000, on the approval, on behalf of the European Community, of the WIPO Copyright Treaty and the WIPO Performances and Phonograms Treaty ([2000] OJ EC 189/6); see Vol.2 I1. The EU Member States ratified the treaties with effect from March 14, 2010.

B. THE CHALLENGE OF TECHNOLOGY: THE ACQUIS COMMUNAUTAIRE 1991–1996

24–46   The following account of the Commission's past and present programme for harmonisation of copyright and related rights is presented for convenience in three parts: first, the original harmonisation programme put in motion by the Commission's first Green Paper, published in 1988, entitled "Copyright and the Challenge of Technology: Copyright Issues Requiring Immediate Action"[207] and its follow-up, most of which has now been implemented by a first generation of Community legislation, which now represents the *acquis communautaire*; second, the new generation of Community legislation which had its origins in the Commission's Green Paper "Copyright and Related Rights in the Information Society", issued in 1995 and is still in the course of implementation[208]; and, finally, the latest proposals of the Commission for further action in the field of copyright and related rights in the future.[209]

24–47   **The 1988 Green Paper and its follow-up.** The Commission's first major step towards harmonisation was the Green Paper published in 1988, entitled "Copyright and the Challenge of Technology: Copyright Issues Requiring Immediate Action".[210] In it the Commission suggested a minimalist approach, taking the view that many issues of copyright law did not need to be the subject of action at Community level. Since all Member States were party to the Berne Convention and to the Universal Copyright Convention, a fundamental convergence of many areas of their copyright laws had already been achieved.[211] The Community's approach, therefore, should be marked by a need to address Community problems, and any temptation to engage in law reform for its own sake should be resisted.[212] The Green Paper therefore focused attention on six issues which it considered required immediate action. These were: piracy (unauthorised reproduction of works and related subject-matter for commercial gain); private copying (home taping) of sound and audiovisual recordings; the distribution right, its exhaustion and rental rights; the legal protection of computer programs; legal problems relating to the operation of databases; and the role of the European Union in multilateral and bilateral external relations affecting these matters. In the Commission's view, legislative solutions to these issues would promote, at EU level, the protection, the increased status and the stimulation of intellectual and artistic creativity which it considered a precious asset, the source of Europe's cultural identity and that of each individual state.[213]

Of particular interest were the general comments of the Commission, in the introduction to the Green Paper, as to the overall objectives which the then EEC should seek to achieve in its legislative programme for copyright protection. These were described as four-fold. First, to ensure the proper functioning of the then Common Market, so that creators and providers of copyright goods and services should be able to treat the EEC as a single internal market. Secondly, to

---

Due to the Association Agreements that the European Union has concluded with third countries, ratification by the European Community and its Member States will trigger ratification in due course by as many as 42 countries.

[207] COM(88) 172 final. [1988] 6 EC Bull, points 1.2.1 et seq.

[208] *Green Paper on Copyright and Related Rights in the Information Society* (hereinafter "Green Paper"), COM(95) 382 final of July 19, 1995: see also *Follow-up to the Green Paper on Copyright and Related Rights in the Information Society* (hereinafter "Follow-up to the Green Paper"), COM(96) 568 final of November 20, 1996.

[209] See paras 24–158 et seq., below.

[210] See para.24–46, above.

[211] Green Paper, fn.207, above, para.1.4.9, and see, paras 23–04 et seq. and 23–79 et seq., above.

[212] Green Paper, fn.207, above, para.1.4.10.

[213] Green Paper, para.24–46, above, para.1.4.4.

improve the competitiveness of the EEC economy in relation to its trading partners, particularly in areas such as the media and information. Thirdly, the intellectual property of EEC nationals, which represented considerable investment in terms of finance and effort, should not be misappropriated by others outside its external frontiers.[214] Fourthly, in developing EEC rules on copyright, due regard should be had to ensuring that copyright was not used to create monopolies of undue scope and duration, and, therefore, to the limitations to be imposed on the rights granted in the interests of third parties and the public at large.[215] The central theme of these concerns, that of using copyright to create a favourable environment to stimulate and protect the creativity and investment of individuals for the benefit of the EEC economy, balanced against the potential danger, inherent in copyright, of creating anti-competitive monopolies, is one that mirrors the conflicts with which the Court of Justice has been faced in developing its case law in the field of industrial property rights.[216]

The Green Paper was a consultative document, intended to provide a basis for discussion. It was not a definitive statement of the Commission's position, nor an exhaustive study of all the problems requiring attention. The views of governments and interested parties (authors, performers, the film, recording and broadcasting industries, and consumers) were sought and a series of hearings held.[217] The Green Paper was generally welcomed but gave rise to criticism in some quarters for concentrating on issues, such as piracy, home taping and computer programs, said to be of more concern to industry than to authors.[218] It should be noted, however, that the legal basis for any action by the EEC was restricted under the Treaty of Rome, as revised, prior to the adoption of the Lisbon Treaty. Harmonisation of the laws of Member States could only be undertaken to the extent required for the proper functioning of the internal market (art.3(1)(h).[219] Thus, the then Community could only legislate where differences in the legal protection provided by the laws and practices of Member States represented sources of barriers to trade and distortions of competition which impeded the achievement and proper functioning of the internal market, and to prevent such differences becoming greater. It could not, therefore, harmonise legislation for the sake of it, but only to eliminate differences with the objective of introducing the single internal market and ensuring that competition in that market is not distorted). The harmonisation programme of the Commission to date has been based on this rule.

The differences in the level of protection afforded to related rights within the Community were very much greater than any differences in the protection of

---

[214] See, in respect of one possible method of challenging misappropriation of intellectual property by others outside the EU, "Re Unauthorised Reproduction of Sound Recordings in Indonesia " [1988] 1 C.M.L.R. 387, concerning the use of the New Commercial Policy Instrument, Regulation 2641/84: [1984] OJ L252/1, against illicit commercial practices.

[215] *Green Paper*, fn.207, above, paras 1.3.1 to 1.3.6.

[216] See para.24–07, above.

[217] (1) Hearing on the Legal Protection of Computer Programs (October 1988). (2) Hearing on Audiovisual Home Copying (December 1988). (3) Hearing on Rental Rights and Certain Aspects of Piracy (September 1989). (4) Hearing on the Protection of Databases (April 1990). (5) Hearing on Moral Rights (November/December 1993). Further hearings and consultations have been held in connection with the Commission's later proposals for directives on the artist's resale right, copyright and related rights in the information society and enforcement, discussed later in this Chapter.

[218] See M. Möller, "Author's Right or Copyright?" in F. Gotzen (ed.), *Copyright and the European Community* (1989); G. Schricker, "Harmonisation of Copyright in the European Economic Community " (1989) 20 I.I.C. 466. See also on the *Green Paper* generally, T. Dreier, and S. von Lewinski, "The European Commission's Activities in the Field of Copyright" (1991) *Journal of the Copyright Society of the U.S.A.*, 96.

[219] art.3(1) of the Treaty was repealed by the Lisbon Treaty and replaced, in substance (but not to the letter and not mentioning harmonisation of laws), by arts 3 to 6 TFEU.

authors' rights and there was, therefore, at that time a correspondingly greater need for action by the Community in the field of related rights.

24–48   **Follow-up to the Green Paper.** In January 1991, the Commission issued a document, entitled *Follow-up to the Green Paper*,[220] which put forward a comprehensive working programme in the field of copyright (in the sense of author's rights) and so-called "related" or "neighbouring" rights.[221] In it, the Commission stressed the need to harmonise copyright and related rights at a high level of protection, arguing that such rights are fundamental to intellectual creation, their protection ensuring the maintenance and development of creativity in the interest of authors, cultural industries, consumers and society as a whole. It was proposed that the following legislative action be taken by December 31, 1991:

(i)   A decision that the Member States should adhere to the 1971 Paris Act of the Berne Convention and to the Rome Convention.[222]

(ii) Proposals for directives on the following subjects to be laid before the Council:

(1) rental right, lending right and certain related rights;

(2) home copying of sound and audiovisual recordings;

(3) harmonisation of the legal protection of databases;

(4) harmonisation of the term of protection for copyright and certain related rights;

(5) harmonisation of copyright rules applicable to satellite broadcasting and cable transmission.[223]

Of these six proposals, one, private copying of sound and audiovisual recordings, remained outstanding until the adoption of the Information Society Directive. This proved a controversial issue to which solutions were hard to find. The Commission's position shifted more than once and the issue is not yet fully resolved.[224]

The Commission also announced its intention to study the need for action on the following issues before the end of 1992: moral rights, reprography, artist's resale right, as well as the collective management of copyright and related rights and collecting societies. In the meantime, the Commission has legislated on all these issues, with the exception of moral rights.[225] Reprography was covered by the Directive on the harmonisation of certain aspects of copyright and related rights in the information society of May 22, 2001.[226] Artist's resale right was dealt with by the Directive on the resale right for the benefit of the author of an original work of art.[227] The collective management of copyright and related rights and collecting societies has been the subject not of a Directive, but of a Commission Recommendation of October 18, 2005, on collective cross-border manage-

---

[220] *Follow-up to the Green Paper: Working Programme of the Commission in the Field of Copyright and Neighbouring Rights* (hereinafter "Follow-up to the Green Paper"), Commission Communication to the Council, document COM(584) 90 final, January 17, 1991.

[221] Terms applied to the rights of the beneficiaries of the Rome Convention for the Protection of Performers, Producers of Phonograms and Broadcasting Organisations 1961. Hereinafter, the term "related rights", also used by the Commission in recent directives, is used.

[222] All Member States are party to the Berne Convention (Paris Act 1971).

[223] *Follow-up to the Green Paper*, p.39.

[224] The present position is discussed in paras 24–115 and 24–159 et seq., below. See also J. Reinbothe, "Private Copying, Levies and DRMs against the Background of the EU Copyright Framework", speech delivered at the DRM Levies Conference, September 8, 2003.

[225] See para.24–163, below.

[226] Directive 2001/29/EC ([2001] OJ L 167/10). See Vol.2 H8 and para.24–109 et seq., below.

[227] Directive 2001/84/EC ([2001] OJ L 272/32 of October 13, 2001); see also Ch.20, above, and Vol.2 H9 (see paras 24–101 et seq., below).

ment of copyright and related rights for legitimate online music services.[228] The recommendation puts forward measures for improving the EU-wide licensing of copyright for online services.[229] To date, the Commission proposes to take no action with regard to moral rights.[230] The Commission stated that, in its work, it would be guided by two principles: the need to strengthen the protection of copyright and related rights, and the need for a comprehensive approach, aiming at a basic level of harmonisation, common to all Member States, of those aspects of copyright and related rights which might have implications for the creation of the internal market.

Legislative measures adopted to date. Eight legislative texts have been adopted so far by the Council of Ministers and one proposed text rejected. Of these texts, six represent the first generation of measures adopted to harmonise the copyright laws of the Member States, originating as they do from the original 1988 Green Paper. These six first-generation Directives are the following: (1) the Directive on the legal protection of computer programs of May 14, 1991[231]; (2) the Directive on rental right and lending right and on certain rights related to copyright in the field of intellectual property, of November 19, 1992[232]; (3) the Directive on the co-ordination of certain rules concerning copyright and rights related to copyright applicable to satellite broadcasting and cable re-transmission of September 27, 1993[233]; (4) the Directive harmonising the term of protection of copyright and certain related rights of October 29, 1993[234]; (5) the Directive on the legal protection of databases of March 11, 1996[235]; and (6) the Directive on the resale right for the benefit of the author of an original work of art adopted on June 6, 2001.[236] Two Directives of the second generation following on the Green Paper on the Information Society have been adopted subsequently: first, the Directive on the harmonisation of certain aspects of copyright and related rights in the information society of May 22, 2001[237] and, second, the Directive on the enforcement of intellectual property rights of April 19, 2004.[238] Together, these eight directives represent the EU legal framework, known as the "*aquis communautaire*" in the field of copyright and related rights.

24–49

The state of implementation of these Directives by the Member States as of October 15, 2010, is set out in the Table showing the implementation of the EU Directives on copyright and related rights in the Member States of the European Union, EEA and Switzerland at para.25–175, below (referred to in this section as the Directive Implementation Table).

---

[228] 2005/737/EC [2005] OJ L276/54. This edition of the Official Journal, of October 21, 2005, mistakenly records the date of the Recommendation as May 18, 2005. Shortly thereafter a corrigendum was issued, correcting the date to October 18, 2005: OJ L284/10.

[229] See paras 24–160 and Ch.28, para.27–22, below. On February 7, 2008, the Commission published the results of the first Monitoring of the Recommendation. It concluded that the Recommendation had produced an impact on the licensing marketplace and had been endorsed by a number of collective rights managers, music publishers and users. The Commission will follow further developments and repeat the monitoring should a clear need to do so arise.

[230] See para.24–163, below.

[231] Directive 91/240 [1991] OJ L122/4246. See Vol.2 H2 et seq. On February 2, 2008, the European Commission put forward a proposal for a Directive of the European Parliament and of the Council on the legal protection of computer programs (codified version).

[232] Directive 92/100 [1992] OJ L346/61. Repealed and replaced with effect from January 16, 2007, by Directive 2006/115/EC [2006] OJ L376. See Vol.2 H12 et seq.

[233] Directive 93/83 [1993] OJ L248/15. See Vol.2 H2 et seq.

[234] Directive 93/98 [1993] OJ L290/9. Repealed and replaced with effect from January 16, 2007 by Directive 2006/116/EC [2006] OJ L372. See Vol.2 H13 et seq.

[235] Directive of the Parliament and Council 96/9/EC [1996] OJ L77/20. See Vol.2 H3 et seq.

[236] Directive 2001/84/EC [2001] OJ L272/32. See Vol.2 H9.

[237] Directive 2001/29/EC [2001] OJ L167/10. See Vol.2 H8.

[238] Directive 2004/48/EC [2004] OJ L195/16. See Vol.2 H11.

The proposal which did not obtain the support of the Council of Ministers was that concerning the adherence of Member States to the Paris Act 1971 of the Berne Convention and the Rome Convention. For the sake of completeness, it should also be noted that, in a separate, but related field, the Council of Ministers adopted a Directive on the legal protection of semi-conductor products as long ago as 1986.[239]

24–50 **Proposed Decision Concerning Adherence to the Berne and Rome Conventions.** This was the first proposal for Community legislation in this field and was put forward to the Council in December 1990. It would have required all Member States to adhere to and comply with the Paris Act 1971 of the Berne Convention and the Rome Convention before the end of 1992. The proposal was rejected for political reasons in December 1991.

The Commission made the proposal, considering that adherence of all the Member States to the Conventions would provide a harmonised basis on which rules for copyright and related rights could be built. It would also have represented a step forward in the fight against piracy of sound recordings and audiovisual works. At the time, Belgium and Ireland were not parties to the Paris Act of the Berne Convention, while Belgium, Greece, the Netherlands, Portugal and Spain had not ratified the Rome Convention.[240] Since the standard of protection, therefore, varied considerably among the Member States, the Commission's proposal aimed at eliminating the consequent distortions and at clearing the way for the internal market.

The proposal was rejected by the Council of Ministers, having been opposed by the Member States. It would have incorporated the Conventions into EU law, thus bringing them under EU responsibility. This would have given the Commission negotiating authority on behalf of the Member States in the administrative bodies of the Conventions, at a time when there was no EU legislation on the subject-matter of the Conventions, and would have subjected the latter to surveillance by the Court of Justice. At the time, the EU Member States were reluctant to relinquish responsibility on these issues to the Community and considered that other measures could be adopted to achieve the goal of copyright harmonisation and to ensure that all Member States adhered to the Conventions. The Council, therefore, in May 1992 adopted a Resolution instead, in which the Member States concerned undertook to adhere to the Paris Act of the Berne Convention and the Rome Convention by January 1, 1995, and to introduce national legislation to ensure effective compliance therewith.[241] Given the problem of piracy, this Resolution also invited the Commission, when negotiating agreements with third countries on behalf of the Community, to pay particular attention to encouraging such third countries to adhere to the Conventions and to comply effectively with the standards of protection provided for therein.

(i) Council Directive on the Legal Protection of Computer Programs (the Software Directive).[242]

24–51 The final text of the Directive was adopted on May 14, 1991, following a two-

---

[239] Directive 87/54: [1986] OJ L24/36. See Vol.2 H1 et seq. and, as to the position in the United Kingdom, Ch.14, above.

[240] Belgium, Greece and the Netherlands had no legislation at that time on related rights. Now, all three have legislated on the subject and all have meanwhile ratified the Rome Convention.

[241] Council Resolution on increased protection for copyright and neighbouring rights of May 14, 1992; [1992] OJ C138/01.

[242] Directive 91/240/EEC; [1991] OJ L122/42, consolidated and repealed by Directive 2009/24/EC on the legal protection of computer programs of April 23, 2009 which took effect on May 25, 2009.

year legislative process[243] and the deadline for its implementation by the Member States was set at January 1, 1993, the date of the establishment of the internal market.[244] This Directive, which had been amended by subsequent EC directives, was repealed and replaced by Directive 2009/24/EC of April 23, 2009. Directive 2009/24/EC is a consolidating measure only, being a codified text taking into account amendments already made to Directive 92/100 by other EC Directives. However, it should be noted that the numbering of the recitals and articles of the two directives differ somewhat. References in this chapter are to the new codified directive, unless otherwise indicated.

Background. The Directive had been foreshadowed in the Green Paper, in which the Commission had announced its intention to submit a proposal for a Directive for the protection of computer programs within the framework of copyright and related rights.   **24–52**

Terms of the Directive. The Directive establishes that computer programs are to be protected under copyright law as literary works within the meaning of the Berne Convention,[245] thus following an international trend.[246] The aim was to secure clear and effective copyright protection for computer programs in all Member States, to remove differences in protection which had negative effects on the functioning of the common market and to avoid any such differences arising in the future by harmonising such issues as the beneficiaries and subject-matter of protection, the exclusive rights on which protected persons should be able to rely in order to authorise or prohibit certain acts, and the duration of protection.   **24–53**

By specifying that computer programs were to be protected as literary works within the meaning of the Berne Convention, the Directive effectively achieved an equally important aim for the Member States: that of integrating programs into an established system of international protection, bringing with it the advantages of certain minimum standards of protection and national treatment for Community software in the Contracting States of the Berne Convention.

On the question of authorship, the Directive defines the author of a computer program as the natural person or group of natural persons who created the program or, where the legislation of the Member State permits, the legal person designated as the right-holder by that legislation. The restricted acts include reproduction, translation, adaptation, arrangement and any form of distribution to the public, including rental.[247] During the legislative process, the draft Directive gave rise to considerable controversy.[248] It opposed the interests of the major manufacturers of computer software on the one hand, and companies specialising in developing computer products compatible with those of the market leaders and software users on the other. The major manufacturers sought a high level of copyright protection, whereas the developers wanted to be able to analyse exist-

---

[243] The first draft of the Directive was published in January 1989: *Proposal for a Council Directive on the legal protection of computer programs*, COM(88) 816 final-SYN 183: [1989] OJ C91/4, submitted by the Commission on January 5, 1989.

[244] See the Directive Implementation Table, para.24–175, below.

[245] Directive 2009/24/EC art.1(1).

[246] See para.23–70, above.

[247] Directive 2009/24/EC art.4.

[248] See, inter alia, W.R. Cornish, "Interoperable Systems and Copyright" [1989] 11 E.I.P.R. 391 and "Computer Program Copyright and the Berne Convention" [1990] 4 E.I.P.R. 129; W.T. Lake, et al, "Seeking Compatibility or Avoiding Development Costs? A Reply on Software Copyright in the EC" [1989] 12 E.I.P.R. 431; M. Colombe, and C. Meyer, "Interoperability Still Threatened by EC Software Directive: A Status Report" [1990] 9 E.I.P.R. 324; C.G. Miller, "The Proposal for an EC Council Directive on the Legal Protection of Computer Programs" [1990] 10 E.I.P.R. 347; T. Dreier, "The Council Directive of 14 May 1991 on the Legal Protection of Computer Programs" [1991] 9 E.I.P.R. 319.

ing programs by means of reverse engineering, and software users were concerned that the protection afforded would hinder the use and maintenance of software. The final text is a compromise which permits exceptions to the restricted acts in certain limited circumstances, inter alia, where necessary for the use of the computer program by the lawful acquirer in accordance with its intended purpose, including error correction, and to make it possible to connect all components of a computer system, including those of different manufacturers, so that they can work together.[249]

On April 10, 2000, the Commission submitted a report on the implementation of the Directive to the other Community institutions. According to the report, the objectives of the Directive have been achieved and the effects on the software industry are satisfactory (as demonstrated for example by industry growth and a decrease in software piracy). It concluded that no substantive amendment of the Directive was appropriate or necessary.[250]

Case Law of the European Court.

24–54   **Decided Cases.** The decompilation exception permitted by art.6 of the Directive has been the subject of dispute in the case *Microsoft Corporation v Commission*.[251] The exception permits reproduction of computer code when it is indispensable to obtain the information necessary to achieve the interoperability of an independently created computer program with other programs, subject to certain conditions. In the *Microsoft* case, the concept and definition of "interoperability" was at issue. Microsoft and the Commission disagreed as to whether the concept of interoperability employed in the contested decision of the Commission is or is not compatible with that envisaged by the Software Directive. The then Court of First Instance in its decision found that the Commission's concept of interoperability, according to which interoperability between two software products means the capacity for them to exchange information and to use that information mutually in order to allow each of those software products to function in all the ways envisaged, is consistent with that envisaged by the Software Directive. The Court held also inter alia that what was at issue in the case was a decision adopted in application of art.102 of the TFEU, a provision of higher rank than the Software Directive; thus, in the present case, the question was not so much whether the concept of interoperability in the contested decision was consistent with that directive as whether the Commission correctly determined the degree of interoperability that should be attainable in the light of the objectives of art.102 EC.[252]

24–55   **Pending References to the Court of Justice.** A number of questions have been referred to the European Court for a preliminary ruling. These are reproduced below.

24–56   *Case C–393/09*[253]

(1) Should Article 1(2) of Council Directive 91/250/EEC of 14 May 1991 on the legal protection of computer programs be interpreted as meaning that,

---

[249] Directive 2009/24/EC arts 5 and 6.

[250] COM(2000) 199 final, April 10, 2000.

[251] *Microsoft v Commission of the European Communities* (T–201/04R), CFI (Grand Chamber), September 17, 2007, [2007] EUECJ; [2007] 5 C.M.L.R. 11. See also (T–167/08R) [2009] 4 C.M.L.R. 16.

[252] Judgment, paras 225–227.

[253] *Bezpecnostni Softwarova Asociace (Security software association) v Svav Softwarove Ochrany* (C–393/09), reference from the Ministry of Culture of the Czech Republic lodged on October 5, 2009; [2010] OJ C11/24.

for the purposes of the copyright protection of a computer program as a work under that directive, the phrase "the expression in any form of a computer program" also includes the graphic user interface of the computer programme of part thereof?

(2) If the answer to the first question is in the affirmative, does television broadcasting, whereby the public is enabled to have sensory perception of the graphic user interface of a computer program or part thereof, albeit without the possibility of exercising control over the program, constitute making work or part thereof available to the public within the meaning of Article 3(1) of European Parliament and Council Directive 2001/29/EC of 22 May 2001 on the harmonisation of certain aspects of copyright and related rights in the information society?

Case 406/10[254]   **24–57**

1. Where a computer program ("the First Program") is protected by copyright as a literary work, is Article 1(2) to be interpreted as meaning that it is not an infringement of the copyright in the First Program for a competitor of the rightholder without access to the source code of the First Program, either directly or via a process such as decompilation of the object code, to create another program ("the Second Program") which replicates the functions of the First Program?

2. Is the answer to question 1 affected by any of the following factors:

(a) the nature and/or extent of the functionality of the First Program;

(b) the nature and/or extent of the skill, judgment and labour which has been expended by the author of the First Program in devising the functionality of the First Program;

(c) the level of detail to which the functionality of the First Program has been reproduced in the Second Program;

(d) if the source code for the Second Program reproduces aspects of the source code of the First Program to an extent which goes beyond that which was strictly necessary in order to produce the same functionality as the First Program?

3. Where the First Program interprets and executes application programs written by users of the First Program in a programming language devised by the author of the First Program which comprises keywords devised or selected by the author of the First Program and a syntax devised by the author of the First Program, is Article 1(2) to be interpreted as meaning that it is not an infringement of the copyright in the First Program for the Second Program to be written so as to interpret and execute such application programs using the same keywords and the same syntax?

4. Where the First Program reads from and writes to data files in a particular format devised by the author of the First Program, is Article 1(2) to be interpreted as meaning that it is not an infringement of the copyright in the First Program for the Second Program to be written so as to read from and write to data files in the same format?

5. Does it make any difference to the answer to questions 1, 3 and 4 if the author of the Second Program created the Second Program by:

(a) observing, studying and testing the functioning of the First Program; or

(b) reading a manual created and published by the author of the First Program which describes the functions of the First Program ("the Manual"); or

---

[254] *SAS Institute Inc. v World Programming Limited*, reference from the UK High Court of Justice (Chancery Division) (Arnold J.) [2010] EWHC 1829 (Ch).

(c) both (a) and (b)?

6. Where a person has the right to use a copy of the First Program under a licence, is Article 5(3) to be interpreting as meaning that the licensee is entitled, without the authorisation of the rightholder, to perform acts of loading, running and storing the program in order to observe, test or study the functioning of the First Program so as to determine the ideas and principles which underlie any element of the program, if the licence permits the licensee to perform acts of loading, running and storing the First Program when using it for the particular purpose permitted by the licence, but the acts done in order to observe, study or test the First Program extend outside the scope of the purpose permitted by the licence?

7. Is Article 5(3) to be interpreted as meaning that acts of observing, testing or studying of the functioning of the First Program are to be regarded as being done in order to determine the ideas or principles which underlie any element of the First Program where they are done:

(a) to ascertain the way in which the First Program functions, in particular details which are not described in the Manual, for the purpose of writing the Second Program in the manner referred to in question 1 above;

(b) to ascertain how the First Program interprets and executes statements written in the programming language which it interprets and executes (see question 3 above);

(c) to ascertain the formats of data files which are written to or read by the First Program (see question 4 above);

(d) to compare the performance of the Second Program with the First Program for the purpose of investigating reasons why their performances differ and to improve the performance of the Second Program;

(e) to conduct parallel tests of the First Program and the Second Program in order to compare their outputs in the course of developing the Second Program, in particular by running the same test scripts through both the First Program and the Second Program;

(f) to ascertain the output of the log file generated by the First Program in order to produce a log file which is identical or similar in appearance;

(g) to cause the First Program to output data (in fact, data correlating zip codes to States of the USA) for the purpose of ascertaining whether or not it corresponds with official databases of such data, and if it does not so correspond, to program the Second Program so that it will respond in the same way as the First Program to the same input data.

24–58   **Implementation in the United Kingdom.** The Directive has been implemented in the United Kingdom by the Copyright (Computer Programs) Regulations 1992, which entered into force on January 1, 1993.[255]

(ii) Directive on Rental Right and Lending Right and on Certain Rights Related to Copyright in the Field of Intellectual Property (the Rental and Related Rights Directive).[256]

24–59   This Directive was adopted on November 19, 1992, having first been proposed

---

[255] SI 1992/3233. For a detailed analysis of the implementation of the Directive in UK law, see paras 3–27 et seq., above.

[256] Council Directive 92/100/EEC; [1992] OJ L346/61 consolidated and repealed by Directive 2006/115/EC with effect from January 16, 2007, OJ L 376 of December 27, 2006. See also A. Mosawi, "Some Implications of the New Regulations Regarding Rental Rights" [1995] 8 Ent. L.R. 307; R. Fry, "Rental Rights Derailed: Performers and Authors Lose Out on Rental Income for Old Productions" [1997] 2 Ent. L.R. 31 and P. Kamina, "British Film Copyright and the Incorrect Implementation of the EC Copyright Directives" [1998] E.I.P.R. 109.

by the Commission to the Council in December 1990. Member States were given until July 1, 1994, to bring their laws into line with it.[257] This Directive, which had been amended by subsequent EC directives, was repealed and replaced by Directive 2006/115/EC with effect from January 16, 2007, without prejudice to the obligations of the Member States relating to the time-limits for transposition into national law of the Directives, and their application. Directive 2006/115/EC is a consolidating measure only, being a codified text taking into account amendments already made to Directive 92/100 by other EC Directives. However, it should be noted that the numbering of the recitals and articles of the two directives differ somewhat. References in this chapter are to the new codified directive, unless otherwise indicated.

Background. The Directive deals with two major topics which were already addressed in the Green Paper, the threat of piracy, and rental and lending of, inter alia, books, films and sound recordings.[258] However, it goes much further by providing for a harmonised legal framework for the protection of performers, producers of phonograms and broadcasting organisations throughout the European Union. **24–60**

One of the major areas where differences existed hitherto between Member States is in the nature and level of protection afforded to performers, producers of phonograms and broadcasting organisations. In the United Kingdom and Ireland, producers of phonograms and broadcasting organisations were protected under the copyright law, while performers enjoyed related rights protection. In the other Member States, the situation varied widely; some countries afforded a high level of protection under related rights legislation to these categories of right owners while others afforded them little or no specific protection. Likewise, the term of protection for related rights varied between 20 and 50 years[259] and it was not until 2002 that the last of the then 15 EC Member States adhered to the Rome Convention of which related rights owners are the beneficiaries.[260] The aim of the Directive, therefore, was twofold: to eliminate the differences which existed between the various Member States as regards the legal protection afforded to authors and owners of related rights with respect to rental and lending rights by providing a harmonised level of legal protection for all right owners; and to strengthen the position of right owners in the fight against piracy by establishing a minimum standard of rights of fixation, reproduction, distribution, broadcasting and communication to the public for owners of related rights.

Terms of the Directive. As regards rental and lending, exclusive rights to authorise or prohibit rental and lending are granted to authors, performers, film and phonogram producers in respect of their works, performances, films and sound recordings.[261] The Court of Justice has held that the exclusive rental rights guaranteed by the Directive are not exhausted in a Member State even where the **24–61**

---

[257] Directive 92/100 art.15. In 1998, the EC Commission referred Ireland to the Court of Justice for failure to communicate national measures for transposing the Directive into national law. Meanwhile, Ireland has adopted a new law, the Copyright and Related Rights Act 2000 (No.28/2000), which entered into force on January 1, 2001 and complies with the Directive. See the Directive Implementation Table, para.24–175, below.

[258] See Chs 2 and 4 of the Green Paper.

[259] See paras 24–84 et seq., below. On the Directive, see also J. Reinbothe, and S. von Lewinski, *The EC Directive on Lending Rights and on Piracy* (London: Sweet & Maxwell, 1993).

[260] Portugal became party to the Rome Convention on July 17, 2002.

[261] Directive 2006/115/EC art.3.

offering of those copies for rental has been authorised in the territory of another Member State.[262]

However, Member States are free to derogate from the exclusive right in respect of public lending, provided that authors at least obtain remuneration for such lending.[263] The Directive also seeks to protect authors and performers from signing away their rights by providing that, where they have transferred or assigned their rental right in a film or sound recording, they retain an inalienable right to obtain an equitable remuneration for the rental.[264]

Chapter II of Directive 92/100 concerned related rights and afforded the basic rights of the Rome Convention to its beneficiaries (performers, producers of phonograms and broadcasting organisations) in relation to rights of fixation,[265] reproduction[266] and broadcasting and communication to the public.[267] The new Directive 2006/115/EC no longer includes provisions concerning the reproduction right because these have been replaced with similar, but somewhat broader provisions, in the Information Society Directive.[268]

Article 8 of the Directive provides for the payment of equitable remuneration to performers and producers when a sound recording published for commercial purposes or a reproduction of such a recording is used for broadcasting or other communication to the public. There is no definition of the term "equitable remuneration" in the Directive. The Court of Justice has held that the Directive requires Member States to lay down rules ensuring that users pay equitable remuneration and that Member States are not bound by any particular criteria in the way this is done, although it stressed that the concept of equitable remuneration in the Directive must be interpreted uniformly in all EU Member States.[269] In the absence of any EU definition of the term "equitable remuneration", there is no objective reason to justify the court in laying down such criteria. To do so would necessarily entail its acting in the place of Member States. Accordingly, it is for Member States alone to determine, in their own territories, the most appropriate criteria for assuring, within the limits imposed by EU law and the Directive, adherence to that EU concept. Such a conclusion is consistent with art.12 of the Rome Convention for the Protection of Performers, Producers of Phonograms and Broadcasting Organisations, 1961 (as to which, see para.23–109, above). The court concluded that art.8 did not preclude the application by the Dutch Courts of a model for calculating the amount of equitable remuneration which operated by reference to variable and fixed factors, such as the number of hours of phonograms broadcast, viewing and listening densities achieved, the tariffs fixed by agreement in the field, the tariffs set by public broadcasting organisations in bordering Member States and the amounts paid by commercial stations. Moreover, whether the remuneration was equitable was to be assessed, in particular, in the light of the value of the use of a commercial phonogram in trade.

In addition, the Directive provides for an exclusive distribution right which is without prejudice to the rental and lending right and which may only be exhausted within the European Union where the first sale in the European Union is made by

---

[262] See para.24–29, above.
[263] Directive 2006/115/EC art.6.
[264] art.4.
[265] art.7.
[266] Directive 92/100 art.7, repealed and replaced by art.2(b)(c)(d)(e) of Directive 2001/29/EC (see paras 24–112, et. seq., below).
[267] art.8.
[268] Directive 2001/29/EC; see paras 24–109 et seq., below.
[269] In *Stichting ter Exploitatie van Naburige Rechten (SENA) v Nederlandse Omroep Stichting (NOS)* (C–245/00) [2003] E.C.R. I–1251; [2003] R.P.C. 120 (22), 757–768.

the right-holder or with his consent.[270] The Directive also provides a related right to authorise or prohibit distribution for film producers with respect to their films.

Authorship of cinematographic or audiovisual works. The Directive also tackled the issue of the authorship of cinematographic or audiovisual works in the European Union by providing that the director of such a work is to be regarded as a co-author in addition to other possible co-authors, including the producer. According to art.2(2) of Directive 92/100: "For the purposes of the Directive", the principal director of a cinematographic or audiovisual work shall be considered as its author or one of its authors. Member States may provide for others to be considered as its "co-authors". Those Member States which did not provide for author's rights for film directors were fundamentally opposed to this provision due to concern that it would cause difficulties for the exploitation of films in their territories. Accordingly, on the occasion of the adoption of the Directive, the Commission made a political commitment to produce a report on the question of authorship of cinematographic or audiovisual works in the European Union. That report was published on December 6, 2002.[271]

24–62

In the meantime, the limited effect of art.2(2) has been significantly extended. The original text of art.2(2) was limited to "the purposes of this Directive", that is the harmonisation of the rental and lending right and related rights. However, art.1(5) of Directive 93/83/EEC on the co-ordination of certain rules concerning copyright and rights related to copyright to satellite broadcasting and cable re-transmission extended the effect of art.2(2) to the right to authorise the communication to the public by satellite. Soon after, art.2(1) of Directive 93/98/EEC Harmonising the Term of Protection of Copyright and Certain Related Rights applied art.2(2) to all rights in cinematographic and audiovisual works.

In its report, the Commission concludes that there is no evidence that the vesting of original authorship in the principal director has caused difficulties in the exploitation or distribution of films or in the effective tackling of piracy or other unauthorised use. In practice, relevant exploitation rights are transferred to the producer, either by operation of law or by contract. Potential difficulties resulting from disparities in national legislation are "levelled" by contractual arrangements. Nevertheless, the Commission announced its intention to keep under review not only the issue of first ownership of rights but also the contractual arrangements between producers and other right-holders together with the increasingly complex area of rights administration in this field.

Public Lending Right. The public lending right provisions of Directive 2006/ 115/EC are contained in arts 1, 3 and 6 (previous arts 1, 2 and 5). Article 1 provides for a right to authorise or prohibit the rental and lending of originals and copies of copyright works, and other subject-matter, namely, performances, sound recordings and films (art.3). Member States may, however, derogate from the exclusive right in respect of public lending, provided that at least authors obtain remuneration for such lending (art.6). Member States have discretion to determine the level of remuneration to be paid to right-holders, and also are entitled to exempt completely some types of lending establishments from both the exclusive lending right and the remuneration right. Article 5(4) of the Directive called for the Commission to draw up a Report on public lending in the Community before July 1, 1997. Because of delays in the implementation of the

24–63

---

[270] Directive 2006/115/EC art.9. On February 4, 2002, the Commission announced that it intended to pursue infringement proceedings against Denmark for a partial failure to implement these provisions of the Directive: *http://europa.eu.int/comm/internal_market/en/intprop/news/02-191.htm*. Press Release IP/02/191 of that date. These proceedings have since been closed.
[271] COM (2002) 691 final.

Directive, this was postponed and published finally in September 2002.[272] The Commission considers harmonisation of the PLR to be important for the internal market because the lending activities of public institutions can have a significant and negative effect on the commercial rental market, particularly for music and films. The report assessed the implementation of the PLR provisions under the Directive and concluded, inter alia, that, although there has been an improvement compared to the situation prior to the adoption of the Directive, the public lending right (PLR) is being applied differently in the various EU Member States and in some cases is not being applied properly.[273] Moreover, there had been serious delays in the implementation of the Directive on this subject. It reiterated the Commission's commitment to ensuring that the PLR is effective in all Member States and to monitoring the way increasing use of new technologies is affecting the application of PLR.

Case Law of the Court of Justice

24–64   **Decided cases.**
    PLR Cases. Infringement proceedings under art.226 of the Treaty were taken against a number of Member States for failure to implement the PLR provisions of the Directive in due time. In particular, the Commission pursued infringement proceedings against a number of Member States on this issue, referring several to the Court of Justice on the ground that they had failed to implement PLR fully or adequately into national legislation.[274] The Commission took action against Ireland, Italy, Portugal and Spain asking the Court to declare that by exempting all, or in the case of Spain almost all, categories of public lending establishments, including educational and academic institutions, from paying the public lending right remuneration these countries were in breach of their obligations under the Directive.[275] These cases resulted in court judgments declaring that these States had failed to fulfil their obligations under the Directive in these respects.[276]

24–65   ***Rental Right.*** On a different issue concerning the rental right, the Commission laid a complaint before the Court because Portugal had created in its national law a rental right in favour of producers of videograms. The Court held that creating such a right was contrary to Portugal's obligations under the Directive. Moreover, creating the right in national legislation led to some doubt as to who is responsible for paying the remuneration owed to performers on assignment of the rental right.[277]

24–66   ***Rental Right and Satellite and Cable Directives.*** The Court of Justice handed down a decision in 2006 in a case which raised questions arising out of both the Rental Right Directive and the Satellite and Cable Directive (the *Lagardère* case).[278] The French *Cour de Cassation* had referred the following questions to the European Court:

---

[272] COM(2002) 502 final of September 9, 2002, "Report from the Commission to the Council, the European Parliament and the Economic and Social Committee on the public lending right in the European Union."

[273] COM(2002) 502 final, paras 4, 4.2, 5.1 and 5.2.

[274] See Press releases IP/04/60 (January 16, 2004), IP/04 891 (July 13, 2004), IP/04/1519 (December 21, 2004), IP/05/347 (March 21, 2005), IP/05/921 (July 13, 2005).

[275] Cases C–175/05, *Commission v Ireland* [2007] E.C.R. I–100003; [2007] E.C.D.R. 8; C–198/05, *Commission v Italy* [2006] E.C.R. I–107; C–53/05, *Commission v Portugal* [2006] E.C.R. I–6215; and C–36/05, *Commission v Spain* [2006] E.C.R. I–10313.

[276] Judgments of the Court dated January 11, 2007 (Ireland), July 6, 2006 (Portugal) and October 26, 2006 (Italy and Spain).

[277] Case C–61/05, *Commission v Portugal* [2006] E.C.R. I–6779, judgment of July 13, 2006.

[278] Case C–192/04 [2005] *Lagardère Active Broadcast v Société pour la perception de la rémunéra-*

(1) Where a broadcasting company transmitting from the territory of one Member state uses, in order to extend the transmission of its programmes to a part of its national audience, a transmitter situated nearby on the territory of another Member State, of which its majority-held subsidiary is the licence holder, does the legislation of the latter State govern the single equitable remuneration which is required by Article 8(2) of Directive 92/100 (the Rental Right Directive) … and Article 4 of Directive 93/83 (the Satellite and Cable Directive) … and is payable in respect of the phonograms published for commercial purposes included in the programmes retransmitted?

(2) If so, is the original broadcasting company entitled to deduct the sums paid by its subsidiary from the remuneration claimed from it in respect of all the transmissions received within national territory?

The Court held that:

(1) In the case of a broadcast of the kind at issue in this case, Council Directive 93/83 (the Satellite and Cable Directive) does not preclude the fee for phonogram use being governed not only by the law of the Member State in whose territory the broadcasting company is established but also by the legislation of the Member State in which, for technical reasons, the terrestrial transmitter broadcasting to the first State is located.

(2) Article 8(2) of Council Directive 92/100 (the Rental Right Directive) must be interpreted as meaning that, for determination of the equitable remuneration mentioned in that provision, the broadcasting company is not entitled unilaterally to deduct from the amount of the royalty paid or claimed in the Member State in whose territory the terrestrial transmitter broadcasting to the first State is located.

Compatibility of national technical standard with EU Law. The Court of Justice has also considered a reference from the *Tribunale di Forli*, Italy, for a preliminary ruling on the question whether a national law imposing the obligation to affix to all recordings of cinematographic or audiovisual works put on sale the sign (stamp) of the national body responsible for collecting royalties was compatible with EU law, including the Rental Right Directive. The Court held, on the basis of EU law on the subject of procedures for the provision of information in the field of technical standards and regulations and of rules on Information Society Services, that the obligation to affix the distinctive sign "SIAE" to compact discs of works of figurative art, for the purposes of marketing them in the Member State concerned, constitutes a technical regulation which must be notified to the Commission; if not, it cannot be invoked against an individual.[279]   **24–67**

Pending References to the Court for a Preliminary Ruling

The following questions have been referred to the Court for a preliminary ruling and are reproduced below.   **24–68**

C–98/08[280]   **24–69**

Question referred (concerning the compatibility of exclusive rights of phonogram producers with the Directive):

tion équitable (SPRE), Gesellschaft zur Verwertung von Leistungsschutzrechten mbh (GVL); Compagnie européenne de radiodiffusion et de télévision Europe 1 SA (CERT) (Third Party) [2005] E.C.R. 1–07199.

[279] Case C–20/05 Judgment of November 8, 2007 [2007] OJ C315/4 December 12, 2007 (Party: Karl Josef Wilhelma Schwibbert).

[280] Case C–98/08 [2008] OJ C128/39, reference for a preliminary ruling from the Juzgado de Lo Mercantil no.7 in Madrid lodged on March 4, 2008— Asociación de Gestión de Derechos In-

Does Community law, and in particular, Council Directive 92/100/EEC of 19 November 1992 on rental right and lending right and on certain rights related to copyright in the field of intellectual property permit the Member States to adopt a provision like Article 109.1 of Law 22/1987 of 11 November on Intellectual Property, which recognises the exclusive right of producers and phonograms published for commercial purposes to authorise the public communication of those phonograms and copies thereof?

24–70   *C–135/10*[281]

Question referred (concerning the direct applicability of the Rome Convention, the TRIPs Agreement and the WPPT). This case also concerns the Information Society Directive (see questions (c) (d) and para.24–126, below).

(a) Are the Rome Convention for the Protection of Performers, Producers of Phonograms and Broadcasting Organisations of 26 October 1961, the TRIPs Agreement (Agreement on Trade-Related Aspects of Intellectual Property Rights) and the WIPO (World Intellectual Property Organisation) Treaty on Performances and Phonograms (WPPT) directly applicable within the Community legal order?

(b) Are the abovementioned sources of uniform international law also directly effective within the context of private-law relationships?

(c) Do the concepts of "communication to the public" contained in the abovementioned treaty-law texts mirror the Community concepts contained in Directives 92/100/EEC and 2001/29/EC and, if not, which source should take precedence?

(d) Does the broadcasting, free of charge, of phonograms within private dental practices engaged in professional economic activity, for the benefit of patients of those practices and enjoyed by them without any active choice on their part, constitute "communication to the public" or "making available to the public" for the purposes of the application of Article 3(2)(b) of Directive 2001/29/EC?

(e) Does such an act of transmission entitle the phonogram producers to the payment of remuneration?

24–71   *C–228/10*[282]

Questions referred (concerning the interpretation of art.7 of the Directive):

Q.7 Fixation Right

Where sequential fragments of a broadcast (in this case frames of digital video and audio) are created (i) within the memory of a decoder or (ii) on a television screen and an extensive section of the broadcast is reproduced if the sequential fragments are considered together but only a limited number of fragments exist at any point in time:

(a) Is the question of whether those sequential fragments are a fixation of the broadcast to be determined by the rule of national copyright law relating to what constitutes an infringing reproduction of a copyright work or is it a matter of interpretation of Article 7 of Directive 2006/115?

(b) If it is a matter of interpretation of Article 7 of Directive 2006/115, can such transient copies be considered a "fixation" at all, and if so should the

---

telectuales (AGEDI) and *Asociación de Artistas Intérpretes o Ejecutantes—Sociedad de Gestión de España (AIE) v Sogecable S.A. and Canal Satélite Digital S.L.*

[281] Case C–135/10 *SCF-Consorio Foografici v Marco del Corso* , reference for a preliminary ruling from the Corte di Appello di Torino (Italy) lodged on March 15, 2010.

[282] *Union of European Football Associations (UEFA) and British Sky Broadcasting Limited v Euroview Sport Ltd* (C–228/10) reference for a preliminary ruling from the High Court of Justice (Chancery Division) (United Kingdom) made on May 10, 2010.

national court consider all of the fragments of each work as a whole or only the limited number of fragments which exist at any point in time? If the latter, what test should the national court apply to the question of whether the a fixation of the broadcast has been made within the meaning of that Article? (c) Does the fixation right in Article 7 of Directive 2006/115 extend to the creation of transient images on a television screen?

C–271/10[283]   **24–72**

Question referred (concerning the interpretation of art.5(1) of the Directive): Does Article 5(1) of Council Directive 92/100/EEC of 19 November 1992 on rental right and lending right and on certain rights related to copyright in the field of intellectual property, now Article 6(1) of Directive 2006/115/EC of the European Parliament and of the Council of 12 December 2006 on rental right and lending right and on certain rights related to copyright in the field of intellectual property, according to which at least authors should obtain a remuneration for public lending, preclude a national provision which sets the remuneration at a flat rate of EUR 1 per adult per year and of EUR 0.5 per minor per year?

C–277/10[284]   **24–73**

Questions referred (concerning the rights of film producers in the European Union):

1. Must the provisions of European Union law concerning copyright and related rights, and in particular Article 2(2), (5) and (6) of Directive 92/100, Article 1(5) of Directive 93/83 and Article 2(1) of Directive 93/98, in conjunction with Article 4 of Directive 92/100, Article 2 of Directive 93/83 and Articles 2 and 3 and Article 5(2)(b) of Directive 2001/29, be interpreted as meaning that the principal director of a cinematographic or audiovisual work or other authors of films designated by the legislatures of the Member States are directly (primarily) entitled in all events, by law, to the exploitation rights in respect of reproduction, satellite broadcasting and other communication to the public through the making available to the public and that the film-maker is not entitled thereto directly (primarily) and exclusively;

Are laws of the Member States which assign the exploitation rights by law directly (primarily) and exclusively to the film-maker inconsistent with European Union law?

If the answer to Question 1 is in the affirmative:

2a. Does European Union law grant the legislatures of the Member States the option of providing for a legal presumption in favour of a transfer to the filmmaker of the exploitation rights within the meaning of paragraph 1 to which the principal director of a cinematographic or audiovisual work or other authors of films designated by the legislatures of the Member States are entitled, even in respect of rights other than rental and lending rights, and if so, must the conditions laid down in Article 2(5) and (6) of Directive 92/100, in conjunction with Article 4 of that directive, be satisfied?

2b. Must the primary ownership of rights of the principal director of a cinematographic or audiovisual work, or of other authors of films designated by the legislature of a Member State also be applied to the rights granted by the legislature of a Member State to equitable remuneration, such as 'empty

---

[283] *Cvba Vereniging van Educatieve en Wetenschappelijke Auteurs v Belgische Staat* (C–271/10), reference for a preliminary ruling from the *Raad van State* (Belgium), lodged on May 21, 2010.
[284] *Luksan v Petrus van der Let* (C–277/10) reference for a preliminary ruling from the *Handelsgericht* Vienna (Austria), lodged on June 3, 2010.

cassette remuneration' pursuant to Paragraph 42b of the Austrian Urheberge-setz (Copyright law, 'UrhG'), or to rights to fair compensation within the meaning of Article 5(2)(b) of Directive 2001/29?

If the answer to Question 2b is in the affirmative:

3. Does European Union law grant the legislatures of the Member States the option of providing for a legal presumption in favour of a transfer to the filmmaker of the rights to remuneration within the meaning of paragraph 2 to which the principal director of a cinematographic or audiovisual work or other authors of films designated by the legislatures of the Member States are entitled, and if so, must the conditions laid down in Article 2(5) and (6) of Directive 92/100, III conjunction with Article 4 of that directive, be satisfied?

If the answer to Question 3 is in the affirmative:

4. If a legal provision of a Member State accords to the principal director of a cinematographic or audiovisual work or other authors of films designated by the legislatures of the Member States a right to half of the statutory rights to remuneration, but provides that that right is capable of alteration and not therefore unwaivable, is that provision consistent with the aforementioned provisions of European Union law in the area of copyright and related rights?

24-74 **Implementation in the United Kingdom.** The United Kingdom implemented the Directive by the Copyright and Related Rights Regulations 1996,[285] which entered into force on December 1, 1996, and implemented also the Satellite and Cable Directive as well as certain provisions of the Duration Directive, which were not covered by the Duration of Copyright and Rights in Performances Regulations 1995.[286] The latter entered into force on January 1, 1996.

The majority of the rights provided for in the Directive were already provided for by UK law, but a number of changes to domestic legislation were needed to comply with it. For example, the 1988 Act did not give authors exclusive rental and lending rights in respect of all literary, musical and dramatic works and artistic works or provide for similar rights for performers. Under the Directive, the principal director of a film must be treated as an author in addition to the producer thereof, who alone was considered the author under the 1988 Act. Performers were also given a statutory right to claim from producers of phonograms a share in the remuneration paid for the broadcasting or other communication to the public of commercially published phonograms of their performances, whereas previously such remuneration was shared with performers on a voluntary basis; performers were also granted exclusive rights in respect of distribution of recordings of their performances.

On July 26, 2001, the European Commission decided to refer the United Kingdom to the Court of Justice for incomplete implementation of this Directive. According to the Commission, the United Kingdom was not respecting art.8(2) thereof, which entitles performers and producers of phonograms to equitable remuneration each time their music is broadcast in a place accessible to the public. The United Kingdom has argued that it is possible to set aside these rights in the

[285] SI 1996/2967. The UK missed the deadline under art.15 of the Directive, according to which implementing legislation should have been in place by July 1, 1994. For a detailed analysis of the implementation of the Directive in UK law, see Chs 3, 6, 7 and 12, above. See also A. Sutcliffe, "Equitable Remuneration for Rental: Areas of Uncertainty Analysed" [1998] Ent. L.R. 59.
[286] SI 1995/3297.

case of broadcasting free of charge to the public, as is the case, for example, with background music in shops.[287]

(iii) Directive on the Co-ordination of Certain Rights Concerning Copyright and Rights Related to Copyright Applicable to Satellite Broadcasting and Cable Re-transmission (the Satellite and Cable Directive).[288]

This Directive was adopted on September 27, 1993, having first been proposed by the Commission to the Council in October 1991. Member States were given until January 1, 1995, to bring their laws into line with it.[289]   **24–75**

Background. The problem of harmonising EU copyright and related rights legislation in the field of cable re-transmission had first been addressed by the Commission in its Green Paper on the establishment of a common market in the field of broadcasting, published in 1984 and known as "Television Without Frontiers".[290] There, the Commission had proposed that, in order to eliminate obstacles to the free flow of radio and television programmes by cable throughout the European Union, once a programme had been broadcast in one of the Member States, the exclusive rights of authors and other rights owners to authorise or prohibit cable re-transmission should be replaced by a system of compulsory licences. Right owners would have had a right to receive equitable remuneration for such cable re-transmission but would have been obliged to exercise the right through collecting societies. A system of compulsory arbitration in the event that the parties failed to agree was also envisaged. Thus, once a right owner had consented to the broadcasting of his work in one Member State, it could have been rebroadcast throughout the Community. This proposal, the aim of which was to overturn the *Coditel* decisions of the Court of Justice,[291] found almost no support. The court had ruled that the owner of a copyright work could rely on his right to prohibit transmission of the work without his authority in one Member State, even where the work had been lawfully broadcast in another Member State with the consent of the right owner in that State. As a result of the strong opposition to the copyright chapter manifested during the consultation process, it was dropped from the final Directive "Television Without Frontiers", as adopted in October 1989.[292] The Commission subsequently returned to the subject in 1990 in its Communication on Audiovisual Policy[293] and in a discussion paper "Broadcasting and Copyright in the Internal Market".[294] The first draft of the Satellite and Cable Directive followed in October 1991.[295] As discussed in para.24–27, above, the questions referred to the Court of Justice following *Football Association Premier League Limited v QC Leisure* may result in a review of the *Coditel* decision in light of the subsequent legislative developments that have since affected broadcasting within the community (see below, para.24–79, for   **24–76**

---

[287] *Commission v UK* (Case 458/2002). On January 11, 2005, the Commission withdrew its action and on March 22, 2005, the Court of Justice ordered the case removed from the Register.

[288] Council Directive 93/83/EEC; [1993] OJ L248.

[289] Directive 93/83 art.14(1). See the Directive Implementation Table, para.24–175, below.

[290] *Television Without Frontiers*, Commission Communication to the Council, COM(84) 300 final, June 14, 1984.

[291] *Coditel S.A. v Ciné-Vog Films S.A.* (Case 62/79) [1980] E.C.R. 881 and *Coditel S.A. v Ciné-Vog Films S.A. (No. 2)* (Case 262/81) [1982] E.C.R. 3381.

[292] Directive 89/552, on the co-ordination of certain provisions laid down by law, regulation or administrative action in Member States concerning the pursuit of television broadcasting activities; [1989] OJ L298/23.

[293] COM(90) 78 final, February 21, 1990.

[294] SEC. (90) 2194, November 8, 1990.

[295] [1991] OJ C255/3.

questions referred to the court in that and another case which are relevant to this
Directive).

24-77   **Terms of the Directive.** The principal feature of the Directive is that, in the case
of communication to the public by satellite, it requires the broadcaster to obtain,
by agreement, the authorisation of all the copyright and related rights' owners
concerned in the Member State where the broadcast originates, i.e. the law applicable to the communication to the public is that of the country of origin.[296]
Thus, the broadcaster is obliged to clear the rights for the whole footprint in one
negotiation, so avoiding the cumulative application of several national laws to
one single act of broadcasting. In such negotiations, however, the Directive
provides that, in arriving at the amount of the payment to be made for the rights
acquired, the parties should take account of all aspects of the broadcast, such as
the actual audience, the potential audience and the language version.[297] With
regard to cable re-transmission of simultaneous, unaltered and unabridged programmes, the Directive provides for compulsory, collective administration of
rights.[298] These proposals were not foreseen in the Green Paper.

The Directive provides for a common minimum standard of protection to be
afforded to authors and owners of related rights in all the Member States in order
to remove existing obstacles to cross-border broadcasting by satellite (whether
by direct satellite or communications satellite) and cable re-transmission caused
by the differences between national laws. According to its preamble, the Directive sets out to harmonise legislation so as to ensure a high level of protection for
authors, performers, phonogram producers and broadcasting organisations and to
prevent a broadcasting organisation taking advantage of differences in levels of
protection by relocating their activities.[299] As regards protection for the beneficiaries of related rights, the Directive provides for it to be aligned with the rights
accorded to them under the Directive on rental right and lending right and certain
rights related to copyright in the field of intellectual property, referred to above.[300]
This guarantees performers and phonogram producers remuneration for satellite
broadcasting of sound recordings, but not a right to authorise or prohibit such
broadcasting, rights which producers enjoy at present under the national laws of
certain Member States, including the United Kingdom.[301]

The Directive guarantees authors the exclusive right to authorise satellite
broadcasting and to exercise that right by agreement; owners of related rights are
entitled to equitable remuneration.[302] Except in the case of cinematographic and
audiovisual works, however, collective agreements may be extended in certain
circumstances to right-holders not represented by the collecting society.[303] Existing agreements concerning satellite broadcasting were permitted to remain in
force until January 1, 2000.

As regards re-transmission by cable of broadcasts, the applicable copyright
and related rights are to be observed, and authorisation obtained, on the basis of

---

[296] Directive 93/83/EEC see para.24–75, above. Recital 14 and arts 2(b) and (3). It should be noted
that the majority of Member States grant producers of phonograms and performers only rights to
equitable remuneration for the broadcasting of their phonograms and recorded performances, as
opposed to exclusive rights to authorise or prohibit use thereof, in line with the minimum standards of the Rome Convention (art.12) and the Rental Rights Directive (art.8(2)).
[297] Directive, recital 17.
[298] Directive, art.8.
[299] Directive 93/83, recital 24.
[300] Directive 93/83, recital 25.
[301] Producers of phonograms enjoy the right to authorise or prohibit the satellite broadcasting of
sound recordings in Portugal, Spain and the UK.
[302] Directive 93/83 arts 2 and 4.
[303] art.3.

individual or collective contractual agreements between authors, holders of related rights and cable operators. Existing statutory licence systems were to be
phased out by December 31, 1997.[304] However, such rights are only to be
exercised through a collecting society and, where a right-holder has not
transferred the management of his rights to a collecting society, the collecting society which manages rights of the same category shall be deemed to be mandated
to manage his rights. If there is more than one such society, the right owner shall
have a choice. In the case of failure to agree, the Directive provides for either
party to seek the assistance of mediators.[305]

The Court of Justice has handed down a decision in response to a referral asking whether a system for the reception of television programmes broadcast ter-
restrially or by satellite and their exclusive distribution to the guests occupying
the rooms of a hotel constitutes an "act of communication to the public" or
"reception by the public" for copyright infringement purposes. The court
concluded that the issue in question was not governed by the Directive and must
consequently be decided in accordance with national law.[306]

Finally, the Commission undertook to submit a report, not later than January 1,
2000, on the application of the Directive and, if necessary, to make further
proposals to adapt it to developments in the audio and audiovisual sector.[307] This
provision originated in an amendment of the European Parliament, which was
concerned that the Directive should keep pace with developments in digital
broadcasting technology. In the future, digital broadcasting by satellite and cable
will be increasingly used to operate new electronic delivery systems direct to
consumers, becoming in fact a new means of distribution. Phonogram producers
and performers argue that such electronic delivery systems will displace sales of
recordings in the form of hard copies (pre-recorded discs and cassette tapes), thus
undermining revenues and leading to a reduction in investment in recorded music.
To enable them adequately to control this future market and preserve their
reproduction and distribution rights, they seek the right to authorise communication to the public of sound recordings by satellite and cable instead of a mere
right to remuneration.

The report was published on July 26, 2002.[308] The Commission has identified
two important areas of action. First, citizens have increasingly been encountering
difficulties in accessing satellite channels transmitted outside the Member State
in which they are resident, for example, because the programmes transmitted by
the channel are encrypted so as to prevent reception beyond national borders. The
Commission considers that this is contrary to the principle of the Directive, which
involves moving beyond a purely national approach. It therefore intends to carry
out a study with a view to resolving this problem. Second, the Commission
intends to assess the existing methods of managing the rights to cable retransmission before considering whether or not to revise the Directive. In this context, the
Commission identifies a number of issues which it considers may require resolution, including: difficulties in resolving disputes as to payment for rights linked to
retransmission by mediation; difficulties in negotiating those rights in the first
place; the possible establishment of a "one-stop shop" for cable retransmission;
and the possible rationalisation of the management of rights relating to the installation of shared antennas, for example, in blocks of flats. The Commission has

---

[304] art.8.
[305] art.9.
[306] *Entidad de Gestion de Derechos de los Productores Audiovisuales (Egeda) v Hosteleria Asturi-
ana SA (Hoasa)* (C–293/98) [2000] E.C.R. I–629; [2000] E.C.D.R. 231.
[307] Directive 93/83/EEC, para.24–75, above.
[308] COM(2002) 430 final of July 26, 2002.

also considered whether it is necessary to extend the scope of the Directive to take account of ongoing technological developments (including digital television and the internet) but has concluded that it is too early to gauge the impact and content of these changes and therefore too early to determine whether such an extension is necessary. The report has been followed by two working sessions of interested parties and the revision process is ongoing.[309]

Case Law of the European Court

24–78   **Decided cases.** On June 1, 2006, the Court of Justice held, on a reference from the Belgian Cour de Cassation for a preliminary ruling, that art.9(2) of the Satellite and Cable Directive is to be interpreted as meaning that, where a collecting society is deemed to be mandated to manage the rights of a copyright owner or holder of related rights who has not transferred the management of his rights to a collecting society, that society has the power to exercise that right holder's right to grant or refuse authorisation to a cable operator for cable retransmission and, consequently, its mandate is not limited to management of the pecuniary aspects of those rights.[310] Another case decided by the Court relating to the Satellite and Cable Directive as well as the Rental Right Directive is described in para.24–66, above.

24–79   **Pending References to the Court of Justice.**
   Cases C–403/08[311] *and C–228/10*[312]

   These cases, *Football Association Premier League Limited v QC Leisure* (see para.24–29), *Union of European Football Associations (UEFA)* and *British Sky Broadcasting Limited v Euroview Sport Ltd*, are concerned with the import into the United Kingdom of decoder cards acquired overseas and which enable access to non-UK transmissions of Premier League and European Football Association's (UEFA) matches. The questions referred include questions on the interpretation of the Satellite and Cable Directive but it should be noted that in these cases questions have also been referred for a preliminary ruling on the interpretation of the following additional Directives and provisions of the TFEU: arts 2, 3, 5 and 6 of the Information Society Directive; Directive 98/84/EC (conditional access); Directive 2006/115/EC (rental right, etc, as codified); arts 34, 36 and 54 TFEU in the context of Directive 98/84/EC (conditional access) and of art.6 of Directive 2001/29/EC (Information Society) and finally on the interpretation of the treaty rules on competition under art.101 TFEU, see paras 24–71, above and 24–80 and 24–81, below. Since case C–429/08 has been joined with case C–403/08, only the questions referred in the latter case are reproduced here. The questions referred in C–403/08 and C–228/10 are in identical terms for the most part. One of the three questions related to the present Directive is common to both cases whereas each has submitted one additional question on this subject.

---

[309] See document SEC (2004) 995 of July 19, 2004 "Commission Working Paper on the review of the EC legal framework in the field of copyright and related rights", para.1.2.

[310] *Uradex SCRL v Union Professionnelle de la Radio et de la Télédistribution (RTD) and Société Intercommunale pour la Diffusion de la Télévision (BRUTELE)* (C–169/05) [2006] OJ C143; [2006] E.C.R. I–4973.

[311] *Football Association Premier League Ltd, NetMed Hellas SA, Multichoice Hellas SA v Q.C. Leisure, et al* (C–403/08) reference for a preliminary ruling from the High Court of Justice (Chancery Division) lodged on September 17, 2008. This case has been joined with, *Karen Murphy v Media Protection Services Ltd* (C–429/08). Applications to participate in the proceedings, submitted respectively by the Union of European Football Associations (UEFA), British Sky Broadcasting Ltd, Setanta Sports SARL and the Motion Picture Association were rejected by the Court on December 16, 2009 ((2010) OJ C100/15).

[312] *Union of European Football Associations (UEFA) and British Sky Broadcasting Limited v Euroview Sport Ltd* (C–228/10) for a preliminary ruling reference from the High Court of Justice (Chancery Division) (United Kingdom) made on May 10, 2010.

C–403/08 Q.7 and C–228/10 Q.8: Defence under Directive 93/83 **24–80**

Questions referred:

Is it compatible with Directive 93/83/EEC or with Articles 34 and 36 or 56 TFEU if national copyright law provides that when transient copies of works included in a satellite broadcast or of the broadcast itself are created inside a decoder box or on a television screen, there is an infringement of copyright under the law of the country of reception of the broadcast?

Does it affect the position if the broadcast is decoded using a satellite decoder card which has been issued by the provider of a satellite broadcasting service in another Member State on the condition that the satellite decoder card is only authorised for use in that other Member State?

C–228/10 Q.9: Whether UEFA is a broadcaster under Directive 93/83 **24–81**

Where an organisation ("the First Organisation") either transmits or has transmitted on its behalf, signals carrying visual images and audio feed from a live sporting event via an encrypted satellite multilateral feed to an authorised group of broadcasters in different countries, and those broadcasters then transmit (either by terrestrial TV signals or by satellite) programmes of the live sporting event containing the visual images and audio feed but also their own station identifying logo and (according to their own editorial discretion) their own audio commentaries and their own materials during before and after match play and during half-time breaks ("the Downstream Programmes"):—

(a) Does the encrypted multilateral feed constitute a "to the public by satellite" within Article 1(2)(a) and 1(2)(c) of Directive 93/83, where decryption means for the feed itself are not made available to the public, but decryption means are made available to decrypt the signals carrying the Downstream Programmes where they are carried by satellite and the Downstream Programmes are unencrypted where they are transmitted from terrestrial transmitters?

(b) Is the First Organisation introducing into its multilateral feed "the programme-carrying signals intended for reception by the public into an uninterrupted chain of communication leading to the satellite and down towards the earth"?

(c) Where Article 1(2)(a) refers to the act of introducing being "under the control and responsibility of the broadcasting organisation", is the First Organisation the or a relevant broadcasting organisation for this purpose, or alternatively can the signals be regarded as being introduced into the multilateral feed under the control and responsibility of the downstream broadcasters?

C–431/09 and C–432/09[313] **24–82**

Questions referred (concerning the interpretation of the Directive):

(1) Does the Satellite and Cable Directive preclude the requirement that a supplier of digital satellite television must obtain the consent of the copyright holders in the case where a broadcasting organisation transmits its programme carrying signals, either by a fixed link or by an encrypted satellite signal, to a supplier of digital satellite television which is independent of the broadcasting organisation, and that supplier has those signals encrypted and beamed to a satellite by a company associated with it, after which those

---

[313] *Airfield NV and Canal Digitaal BV v Belgische Vereniging van Auteurs, Componisten en Uitgevers CVBA (Sabam)* (C–431/09 and C–432/09); reference for a preliminary ruling from the *Hof van Beroep te Brussel* (Belgium).

signals are beamed down, with the consent of the broadcasting organisation, as part of a package of television programmes and therefore bundled, to the satellite television supplier's subscribers, who are able to view the programmes simultaneously and unaltered by means of a decryption card or a smart card provided by the satellite television supplier?

(2) Does the Directive preclude the requirement that a supplier of digital satellite television must obtain the consent of the copyright holders in the case where a broadcasting organisation transmits its programme-carrying signals to a satellite in accordance with the instructions of a digital television supplier which is independent of the broadcasting organisation, after which those signals are beamed down, with the consent of the broadcasting organisation, as part of a package of television programmes and therefore bundled, to the satellite television supplier's subscribers, who are able to view the programmes simultaneously and unaltered by means of a decryption card or smart card provided by the satellite television supplier?

24–83   **Implementation in the United Kingdom.** The Directive has been implemented in the United Kingdom by the Copyright and Related Rights Regulations 1996, which entered into force on December 1, 1996.[314] However, under the 1988 Act, the United Kingdom granted rights to holders of related rights which went beyond the minimum standards of the Directive. For example, producers of films and sound recordings are protected as authors and enjoy the right to authorise or prohibit satellite broadcasting and cable distribution. Moreover, whereas most right owners are represented by and exercise their rights through collecting societies, this is done voluntarily and they are under no obligation to do so.

(iv) Directive Harmonising the Term of Protection of Copyright and Related Rights (the Term Directive).

24–84   The Directive was adopted on October 29, 1993, and the deadline for implementation by Member States was July 1, 1995.[315] This Directive, which had been amended by subsequent EC Directives, was repealed and replaced by a new codified text by means of Directive 2006/116/EC with effect from January 16, 2007.[316] Directive 2006/116/EC is a consolidating measure only, being a codified text taking into account amendments already made to Directive 93/98 by other EC Directives. However, it should be noted that the numbering of the recitals and articles of the two directives differ somewhat. References in this Supplement are to the new codified directive unless otherwise indicated.

24–85   **Background.** The subject of term of protection was not discussed in the Green Paper. This was surprising since, at the time, the periods of protection for authors and, particularly, for holders of related rights varied widely in the Community. Minimum periods of protection are laid down in the Berne Convention (50 years after the death of the author (*post mortem auctoris*, hereinafter pma)) and the Rome Convention (20 years), but Contracting States were free to provide longer periods of protection and some Community Member States had done so. A majority granted authors 50 years pma, but France (for musical works only) and Germany granted 70 years pma and Spain 60 years pma. As regards related rights,

---

[314] SI 1996/2967. For an analysis of the implementation of the Directive in UK law, see Ch.7, above.
[315] See Directive 93/98 art.13. See the Directive Implementation Table, para.24–175, below.
[316] [2006] OJ L372.

no less than five different durations applied across the Member States ranging from 20 to 50 years from publication and/or fixation.[317]

These disparities clearly created obstacles to the free movement of goods and services and led to distortions of competition, since the same work could at the same time be protected in one Member State and not in another. Commission action on this subject was precipitated by the European Court of Justice, which in the *Patricia* case[318] ruled that, in the absence of harmonisation of national laws, it was for the national legislature to determine the conditions of such protection, including its duration. In so far as disparities between national laws might lead to restrictions on intra-Community trade, those restrictions were justified under art.36 of the Treaty as long as they were due to the disparity between the rules concerning the period of protection and this was inseparably linked to the existence of the exclusive right.

In its Follow-up to the Green Paper, therefore, the Commission announced its intention of drawing up a directive on this subject,[319] and a proposal was put forward to the Council in March 1992.[320]

Terms of the Directive. The Directive provides for a uniform period of protec- **24–86** tion for authors of 70 years pma, thus harmonising upwards to the longest period of protection in any Member State. The main justification for this prolongation was stated[321] to be that, under the Berne Convention, 50 years pma had been intended to provide protection for the author and the first two generations of his descendants. Since the average lifespan in Member States had increased, 50 years was no longer sufficient to cover two generations. Moreover, due regard to established rights was a general principle of law established by the Community legal order and, therefore, harmonisation of the terms of copyright and related rights could not have the effect of reducing the protection then enjoyed by any right-holders in the Community.[322] The Directive does not apply to moral rights, presumably because in some Member States, for example, France,[323] such rights are perpetual. As regards related rights, the Directive set the period of protection at 50 years after lawful publication or communication to the public. This was also the period advocated by the Commission for related rights in the Uruguay Round negotiations under the General Agreement on Tariffs and Trade (GATT), which resulted, inter alia, in the Agreement on Trade-Related Aspects of Intellectual Property Rights, Including Trade in Counterfeit Goods (the TRIPs Agreement).[324]

In order to ensure full harmonisation, the date from which each term of protection is to be calculated was fixed, in conformity with the Berne and Rome Conventions, at the first day of January of the year following the death of the

---

[317] At the end of 1993, the periods in force were: 50 years in Denmark (from fixation), France (from fixation), Greece (from fixation), Ireland (from publication), Netherlands (from fixation), Portugal (from publication) and the UK (from publication); 40 years in Spain (from publication); 30 years in Italy (from deposit); 24 years in Germany (from publication or fixation) and 20 years in Luxembourg (from fixation).

[318] *EMI Electrola v Patricia and Others* (Case 341/87) [1989] E.C.R. 79; [1989] 2 C.M.L.R. 413.

[319] *Follow-up to the Green Paper*, see para.24–48, above.

[320] COM(92) 33 final-SYn.395: [1992] OJ C92/6.

[321] Directive 2006/116/EC, recital 6.

[322] Directive 2006/116/EC, recital 10.

[323] Law on the Intellectual Property Code (Legislative Part), No. 92597 of July 1, 1992, as last amended by Law No.921336 of December 16, 1992, art.L.1211: "An author shall enjoy the right to respect for his name, his authorship and his work. This right shall attach to his person.It shall be perpetual, inalienable and imprescriptible. It may be transmitted *mortis causa* to the heirs of the author."

[324] See paras 23–136 et seq. and specifically para.23–140, above.

author or other relevant event, such as publication.[325] The relevant event so far as related rights are concerned is the performance, fixation, transmission, lawful publication or communication to the public.

The preceding directives on copyright and related rights made provision for minimum terms of protection only, subject to further harmonisation. The Directive therefore repealed the provisions of those Directives as regards term and substituted its own rules.

The new terms applied to all works and other subject-matter of protection still protected in at least one Member State on July 1, 1995.

It is to be noted that film producers are treated, like in the Directive on rental and related rights,[326] as owners of related rights in this Directive, being granted a period of protection of 50 years calculated from first fixation or, if published, from publication or communication to the public. The Directive provides that the 70 years pma of protection for authors of cinematographic or audiovisual works will begin with the death of the last survivor of the following persons: the director, the screen writer (i.e. the author of the scenario), the scriptwriter (i.e. the author of the dialogue), and the composer of the music. This does not include the producer, previously considered the sole author under the laws of the United Kingdom. Photographs are to be protected for 70 years as works, if they are original in the sense that they are the author's own intellectual creation.[327] The Directive represents a departure from the standards of the Berne Convention which provides for a minimum of 50 years pma for works (maintained in the new WIPO Copyright Treaty[328]) but only 24 years for photographs.[329]

The trend towards extending the term of protection of authors from 50 to 70 years pma has not met with unanimous approval. It has been pointed out that it is seldom the descendants of an author who benefit from copyright after his death, but rather his publisher, and that no adequate debate has taken place in recent years on the justifications for longer terms in the light of the public interest.[330]

Case Law of the Court of Justice

24–87   ***Butterfly Music v Caroselli Edizione.*** In this case, the Court of Justice addressed transitional provisions for the introduction of a harmonised 50-year term of protection for rights of performers and of producers of phonograms pursuant to the Directive in Italy, where the period of protection was increased from 30 to 50 years.[331] As a result, rights in a sound recording which had fallen into the public domain were revived and enforced against Butterfly Music. The latter contended that, even if the rights had revived, the Italian law did not comply with the obligation on Member States to "adopt the necessary provisions to protect in particular acquired rights of third parties" as laid down in the Directive. The Italian law

---

[325] Directive 2006/116/EC art.8.

[326] See para.24–62, above.

[327] Directive 2006/116/EC art.6.

[328] At the time Directive 93/98 was adopted, there was a movement towards prolonging the period of protection under the Berne Convention to 70 years pma. See "Memorandum of the International Bureau of WIPO on Questions concerning a possible Protocol to the Berne Convention", (BCP/CE/I/3), October 1991. In the event, however, the WIPO Copyright Treaty did not alter the term of protection of literary and artistic works.

[329] The WIPO Copyright Treaty (see paras 23–66 et seq., above) extended the minimum term of protection for photographic works to 50 years pma.

[330] See, for example, S. Ricketson, "The Copyright Term" (1992) 6 I.I.C. 755; S. von Lewinski, in (1992) 6 I.I.C. 785; G. Dworkin, "Authorship of Films and the European Commission Proposals for Harmonising the Term of Copyright" [1993] 5 E.I.P.R. 151; G. Davies, *Copyright and the Public Interest* 2nd edn (London: Sweet & Maxwell, 2002).

[331] *Butterfly Music Srl v Carosello Edizioni Musicale Discografiche SRL (Federazione Industria Musicale Italiana Intervening)* (C–60/98) [1999] E.C.R. I–3939.

provided, in the event of revival of rights, for a three-month period in which previously legally made copies could be distributed after the entry into force of the new period of protection. The court held that the three-month period for distribution was reasonable having regard to the objective pursued, namely to provide transitional measures which would not frustrate the application of the new term of protection. The judgment has been criticised on the ground that three months is a short period for third parties who have legally acquired rights which they have exercised in good faith.

Land Hessen v Ricordi.[332] The Court addressed the term of copyright protection **24–88**
also in a case concerning the term of protection granted by German law to Puccini's "La Bohème". The court held that it was contrary to the prohibition of discrimination on grounds of nationality in former art.12 of the EC Treaty (art.25 TFEU) for the term of protection granted by the legislation of one Member State to the works of an author who was a national of another Member State to be shorter than the term granted to the works of its own nationals. Thus, the full 70 years, copyright protection of the German law applied to "La Bohème" in Germany .

Sony Music Entertainment (Germany).[333] In this case the Court considered the **24–89**
question whether the terms of protection provided for by the Directive, art.10(2) of which gives protection throughout the European Union to all works and subject-matter which were protected in at least one of the Member States on July 1, 1995, apply also in the case of subject-matter that has not at any time been protected in the Member State in which protection is sought. The Court held that the term of protection is also applicable, pursuant to art.10(2) of the Directive, where the subject-matter at issue has at no time been protected in the Member State in which the protection is sought. Thus, the terms of protection apply in a situation where the work or subject-matter at issue was, on July 1, 1995, protected as such in at least one Member State under that Member State's national legislation on copyright and related rights and where the holder of such rights in respect of that work or subject-matter, who is a national of a non-Member State, benefited, at that date, from the protection provided for by those national provisions.

Proposal to extend the term of protection of performances. In July 2008, the **24–90**
Commission published a proposal for a Directive amending the present Term Directive in two main respects.[334]

Firstly, it proposes to extend the term of copyright protection for performers (with respect to their fixed performances) and for producers of sound recordings (with respect to their recordings) from 50 to 95 years. This is said to be justified because the current employment status and conditions for the average European performer are not very rewarding, and few make a living from their profession. As regards producers of sound recordings, the principal challenges they face are

---

[332] *Land Hessen v G. Ricordi & Co Buhnen-und Musikverlag GmbH* (C–360/00) [2002] E.C.R. I–5089; [2003] E.C.D.R. 1.
[333] *Sony Music Entertainment (Germany) GmbH v Falcon Neue Medien Vertrieb GmbH*, Judgment of the Court (Grand Chamber) of January 20, 2009 (reference for a preliminary ruling from the *Bundesgerichtshof* (Germany) lodged on May 16, 2007 OJ C69 21.3.2009, p.6–6; [2009] E.C.D.R. 12.
[334] COM(2008) 464 final, July 16, 2008, Proposal for a European Parliament and Council Directive amending Directive 2006/116/EC of the European Parliament and of the Council on the term of protection of copyright and related rights. See also Commission Staff Working Document dated April 23, 2008, "Impact Assessment on the Legal and Economic Situation of Performers and Record Producers in the European Union" (COM(2008) 464 final) (SEC(2008) 2287). See also the Opinion of the European Economic and Social Committee, January 14, 2009, OJ C182/36 of August 4, 2009. The Committee proposed extending the term of protection to 85 years.

the evaporation of the CD markets and the insufficient replacement revenue from online sales. Since 2001, the total European market for recorded music has lost 22 per cent of its value and physical sales of recordings have declined by 30 per cent in the past five years. It is argued that a longer term of protection would generate additional income to help finance new talent and would enable record companies to better spread the risk in developing new talent. The proposal also contains accompanying measures for the benefit of performers, including the establishment of a fund for session musicians to which producers of phonograms will have to contribute 20 per cent of revenues generated from the exclusive rights of distribution, reproduction and making available of phonograms containing performances by session musicians during the extended term.[335] Revenue derived from broadcasting and communication to the public as well as private copying and rental will not be affected. The fund will be administered by collecting societies and musicians will be entitled to an annual payment. Performers will also benefit from a so-called "use it or lose it" clause. If a phonogram producer does not publish a phonogram, which, but for the term extension, would be in the public domain, the rights in the fixation of the performance shall revert to the performer, at his request, and the producer's rights shall expire. Further, if after one year subsequent to the term extension, neither the producer nor the performer has made the phonogram available to the public, the rights in the phonogram and in the performance shall expire. The term extension will apply to phonograms and performances fixed thereon whose initial term of protection of 50 years has not expired at the date of adoption of the proposed Directive.

Second, the proposed Directive aims to introduce a uniform means of calculating the term of protection applying to a musical composition with words, which contains the contributions of several authors. This is required because, in different Member States, musical compositions comprising a musical score and lyrics (or a libretto) written by more than one author are protected for different terms. In some Member States, such co-written musical compositions are classified as a single work of joint authorship with a unitary term of protection, running from the death of the last surviving co-author, while in others these are protected as separate works with separate terms running from the death of each contributing author. This means that, in some Member States, a musical composition with words will be protected for 70 years after the death of the last surviving, contributing author, whereas in others each contribution will lose protection 70 years after the death of its author. These discrepancies in term applying to one musical composition lead to difficulties in administering copyright in co-written works across the Community. They also lead to difficulties in cross-border distribution of royalties. It is proposed therefore to provide that, only for the purpose of calculating its term of protection, a musical composition with words would be treated as if it were a work of joint authorship, whether or not this composition with words would qualify otherwise as a work of joint authorship.[336]

The European Parliament (EP) approved the Commission's proposal, subject to some amendments. In particular, it proposed extending the period of protection for producers and performers from 50 to 70 years. It proposed also that phonogram producers should be under an obligation to set aside, at least once a year,

---

[335] Member States may exempt phonogram producers whose total annual revenue does not exceed a threshold of EUR 2 million from this obligation.

[336] The IPO issued a press release recalling that the Gowers Review of Intellectual Property, which reported in 2006, recommended against an extension of copyright term for producers of phonograms and performers and stated "Because copyright represents a monopoly we need to be very clear that the circumstances justify an extension". In December 2008, however, the UK Government unexpectedly announced that it was now willing to support the Commission's proposal (statement by the UK Culture Secretary, December 11, 2008).

a sum corresponding to 20 per cent of the revenues from the exclusive rights of distribution, reproduction and making available of phonograms for the benefit of non-featured performers (session musicians). "Revenues" means the revenues derived by the phonogram producer before deducting costs. The EP also proposed that performers should be able to recover their copyright after 50 years, should the producer fail to market the sound recording. Finally, it proposed that a newly introduced "clean slate" would prevent record producers from making deductions from the royalties they pay to featured performers.[337] The EP also requested the Commission to carry out an assessment of the possible need for an extension of the term of protection of rights to performers and producers in the audiovisual sector in 2010.[338]

Implementation in the United Kingdom. The Directive has been implemented   **24–91**
in the United Kingdom by the Duration of Copyright and Rights in Performances Regulations 1995, which entered into force on January 1, 1996,[339] and by the Copyright and Related Rights Regulations 1996, which entered into force on December 1, 1996.[340] The Directive obliged the United Kingdom to extend the period of protection of literary, dramatic, musical and artistic works in the United Kingdom to 70 years pma and to change the manner in which the duration of copyright in films is calculated to 70 years, based on the life not of the author of a film under the 1988 Act, (the producer), but of certain persons connected with the film.

The Copyright and Related Rights Regulations 1996 introduced a further provision of the Duration Directive into the law of the United Kingdom, the new 24-year protection for works in which the copyright has expired but which have never before been published (the so-called "publication right").[341]

(v) Directive on the Legal Protection of Databases (the Database Directive).[342]

The Directive was adopted on March 11, 1996, having originally been put   **24–92**
forward in 1992.[343] Member States were given until January 1, 1998, to implement the Directive.[344] The Directive is to be distinguished from the Directive on Data Protection adopted on October 23, 1995, which harmonises the treatment in the Member States of the protection of personal data (defined as any data relating to an identifiable natural person) held on individuals.[345]

Background. The 1988 Green Paper contained a chapter on databases and in it   **24–93**

---

[337] EP legislative resolution of April 23, 2009 (COM(2008) 9464-C6-0281/2008-2008/0157 (COD)).

[338] art.3, proposed Directive, as amended. For the Commission's response, see Press Release IP/09/627, April 23, 2009.

[339] SI 1995/3297.

[340] SI 1996/2967. For a detailed analysis of the implementation of the Directive in UK law, see Chs 6 and 12, above. See also P. Kamina, "Authorship of Films and Implementation of the Term Directive: The Dramatic Tale of Two Copyrights" [1994] 8 E.I.P.R. 319; D. Bradshaw, "The EC Copyright Duration Directive: Its Main Highlights and Some of its Ramifications for Businesses in the UK Entertainment Industry", [1995] 5 Ent. L.R. 171; J.N. Adams, "The Duration of Copyright in the United Kingdom after the Regulations", [1997] 1 Ent. L.R. 23; A. Robinson, "The Life and Terms of UK Copyright in Original Works" [1997] 2 Ent. L.R. 60.

[341] See Ch.17, above.

[342] Directive 96/9/EC of the European Parliament and of the Council; [1996] OJ L77/20.

[343] Original proposal: [1992] OJ C156/4.

[344] Directive 96/9 art.16. The Commission referred Luxembourg to the European Court for failure to implement the Directive in time, cf. *The Commission of the European Communities v Luxembourg* [2000] E.C.D.R. 246. See the Directive Implementation Table, para.24–175, below.

[345] Directive 95/46/EC on the protection of individuals with regard to the processing of personal data and on the free movement of such data, [1995] OJ L281/31.

the Commission, without reaching any firm conclusions itself on these issues, requested comments on the following questions:

(a) whether the mode of compilation within a database of works should be protected by copyright; and

(b) whether that right to protect the mode of compilation, in addition to possible contractual arrangements to that effect, should be extended to databases containing material not protected by copyright and whether this protection should be copyright or a right sui generis.[346]

The response indicated strong interest in the harmonisation of the protection of databases and, at a hearing held in April 1990, right owners expressed overwhelming support for protection of databases by means of copyright. There was no support for a sui generis or related rights approach.

In its *Follow-up to the Green Paper*, therefore, the Commission concluded that a uniform and stable legal environment for the creation of databases within the Community should be established without further delay, given the economic importance of the sector and the risk of distortions arising within the internal market.[347] The Commission recognised also the danger that, without such a uniform legal environment, investment in modern information storage and retrieval systems would not take place within the Community.

24–94   **Terms of the Directive.** The Directive defines the term "database" as "a collection of independent works, data or other materials arranged in a systematic or methodical way and individually accessible by electronic or other means".[348] The databases protected under the Directive are collections or compilations of data, works or other materials, arranged, stored and accessed by electronic means or analogous processes. The Directive adopts a two-tier approach to the protection of such databases. Copyright protection will apply if the database is *original*, in the sense that, by reason of the selection or arrangement of its contents, it constitutes the author's own intellectual creation. No other criteria are to be applied to determine their eligibility for protection,[349] aesthetic or qualitative criteria being expressly excluded.[350] In such cases, the database will be considered a collection within the meaning of art.2(5) of the Berne Convention. However, the Commission, recognising that many databases are unlikely to meet this requirement of originality, has sought to safeguard also the position of makers of such *non-original* databases against misappropriation by providing for a sui generis right to protect against unauthorised extraction or re-utilisation of the whole or of a substantial part of the contents of a database. This right depends on the maker of the database showing that there has been qualitatively and/or quantitatively a substantial investment in either the obtaining, verification or presentation of its contents.[351]

The copyright in existing works incorporated into the database is not affected by the Directive, the owners of copyright therein retaining their exclusive

---

[346] *Green Paper*, para.24–47, above.

[347] *Follow-up to the Green Paper*, para.24–48, above.

[348] Directive 96/9 art.1. However, this definition is expanded by recital 17, which states: "Whereas the term 'database' should be understood to include literary, artistic, musical or other collections of works or collections of other material such as texts, sound, images, numbers, facts, and data; whereas it should cover collections of independent works, data or other materials which are systematically or methodically arranged and can be individually accessed; whereas this means that a recording or an audiovisual, cinematographic, literary or musical work as such does not fall within the scope of this Directive".

[349] Directive 96/9 art.3(1).

[350] Recital 16.

[351] art.7.

rights.[352] Moral rights remain outside the scope of the Directive also, this aspect of protection being left to national laws.[353] The author of a database protected by copyright is defined as being the natural person or group of natural persons who created the database, or, where national legislation permits, the legal person designated as the right-holder by that legislation. Where collective works are recognised by the legislation of a Member State, the economic rights shall be owned by the person holding the copyright.[354] Arrangements applicable to the copyright ownership of databases created by employees are left to national legislation.[355]

The duration of protection for original databases protected by copyright is covered by the Duration Directive and thus the same as that afforded to literary works, i.e. 70 years pma. As regards the sui generis right to prevent unauthorised extraction or re-utilisation, the period of protection runs from the date of completion of the non-original database and lasts for 15 years from January 1 of the year following the date of completion. Any substantial change to the contents of a database, which would result in the database being considered to be a substantial new investment, will give rise to a new period of protection.[356]

The usual exceptions to copyright protection permitted by the Berne Convention, including private use of a non-electronic database, use for teaching or scientific research and other non-profit making purposes, are foreseen, subject, in the case of databases protected by copyright, to the safeguards of art.9(2) of the Berne Convention.[357] Moreover, a person having the right to use a database will not infringe copyright by the performance of any act necessary for the purposes of access to and normal use of the contents of the database.[358]

The beneficiaries of the sui generis right are the makers of non-original databases, who are nationals of, or have their habitual residence in, a Member State.[359] As regards the extension of the sui generis right to databases produced in third countries, the Directive provides for the conclusion by the Council of agreements on the subject. The term of protection extended to databases produced in third countries shall not exceed 15 years.[360]

While the objective of the Directive to provide a harmonised system of protection for databases has been generally welcomed, certain of its provisions have been the subject of controversy.[361] Perhaps the most difficult question in the preparatory work was the proposal that a database shall be protected by copyright

---

[352] art.3(2).
[353] Recital 28.
[354] art.4.
[355] Recital 29.
[356] art.10.
[357] Re: art.9(2) Berne Convention, see paras 23–04 et seq. and specifically paras 23–33 et seq., above.
[358] Directive 96/9 arts 6 & 9.
[359] art.11(1).
[360] art.11(3).
[361] See, inter alia, M. Pattison, "The European Commission's Proposal on the Protection of Computer Databases" [1992] 4 E.I.P.R. 113; J. Hughes, and E. Weightman, "EC Database Protection: Fine Tuning the Commission's Proposal" [1992] 5 E.I.P.R. 147; P. Cerina, "The Originality Requirement in the Protection of Databases in Europe and the United States " (1993) 5 I.I.C. 579. See also L. Kaye, "The Proposed EU Directive for the Legal Protection of Databases: A Cornerstone of the Information Society?" [1995] 17 E.I.P.R. 583; S. Chalton, "The Amended Database Directive Proposal: A Commentary and Synopsis" [1994] 3 E.I.P.R. 94 and "The Effect of the EC Database Directive on United Kingdom Copyright Law in Relation to Databases: A Comparison of Features" [1997] 6 E.I.P.R. 278; W.R. Cornish, "1996 European Community Directive on Database Protection" (1996) 21 *Columbia-VLA Journal of Law and the Arts* 1; S. Beutler, "The Protection of Multimedia Products through the European Community's Directive on the Legal Protection of Databases" [1996] 8 Ent. L.R. 317; S. Smith, "Legal Protection of Factual Compilations and Databases in England—How will the Database Directive Change the Law in this Area?" [1997] I.P.Q. No. 4, 450; S. Lai, "Database Protection in the United

if it is original, in the sense that it is a collection of works or materials which, by reason of the selection or arrangement of their contents, constitutes the author's own intellectual creation (art.3). Although originality is a common requirement for copyright protection of works in all Member States, the standards for original-ity vary.[362] In the United Kingdom, originality means only that the database is not copied and that it originates or emanates from the author, whereas under the Mainland-European approach originality means something more: the work must show some creativity. Originality was formerly defined in Germany, for example, in relation to computer programs:

> "The minimum requirements of copyrightability are met only at a somewhat higher level; they presuppose a significant amount of creativity with respect to selection, accumulation, arrangement and organisation, as compared to the general, average ability."[363]

The phrase *author's own intellectual creation* is the same as that used in the Directive on the protection of computer programs (art.1(3)) which was appar-ently adopted to indicate that the UK concept of originality was intended.[364] Re-cital 16 indicates this is also the case in this Directive, stating that no aesthetic or qualitative criteria should be applied to determine eligibility for protection. However, even if this is the intention, originality of content, according to the present UK concept, will not be sufficient to provide protection to a database. The author will have to show originality in the selection or arrangement of the content of the database. The selection or arrangement criteria derive from art.2(5) of the Berne Convention relating to collections and compilations but appear to pose problems in the context of databases.

It has been pointed out that many databases are of value for the very reason that they are complete collections of the relevant materials, being comprehensive rather than selective in their contents. Likewise the arrangement requirement needs clarification, since the arrangement of material in a database is normally dictated by the computer program running the database and by the operating system being used on the computer and is not controlled by the author of the database.

Now that the criterion of originality in the selection or arrangement has been retained in the final Directive as the basis for copyright protection, many com-mercially valuable databases will fall outside the protection of the copyright law and will benefit only from the new sui generis right to prevent unauthorised extraction or re-utilisation of a database for a period of 15 years.

In December 2005, the European Commission published an evaluation report on database protection in the European Union.[365] The aim of the evaluation was to assess the extent to which the policy goals of the Database Directive had been achieved and, in particular, whether the introduction of the sui generis right led to an increase in the European database industry's rate of growth and in database production. The Commission noted that the vague terms used in the Directive to define the sui generis right have caused considerable uncertainty and pointed out

---

Kingdom—The New deal and its Effect on Software Protection" [1998] 1 E.I.P.R. 32. N. Thakur, "Database Protection in the European Union and the United States : The European Database Directive as an Optimum Global Model?" [2001] I.P.Q. 100.

[362] See P. Cerina, *The Originality Requirement in the Protection of Databases in Europe and the United States* (1993) 1.1.C. 579.

[363] This definition of the Federal Supreme Court of May 9, 1985, (Case No.1 ZR52/83), was handed down prior to the adoption of the computer programs Directive (Directive 91/ 250). See English text in [1986] I.I.C. 688.

[364] See B. Czarnota and R.J. Hart, *Legal Protection of Computer Programs in Europe: A Guide to the EC Directive* (London: Butterworths, 1991) p.44.

[365] DG Internal Market and Services Working paper, First evaluation of Directive 96/9/EC on the legal protection of databases, December 12, 2005.

that the scope of the sui generis right had been severely curtailed in a series of judgments rendered by the European Court of Justice (ECJ) in November 2004.[366] The evaluation concluded that the economic impact of the sui generis right on database production is unproven. However, the European publishing industry argued that this protection is crucial to the continued success of their activities. In addition, most of those consulted believe that the sui generis right has brought about greater legal certainty, reduced the costs associated with the protection of databases, created more business opportunities and facilitated the marketing of databases. The evaluation is ongoing and stakeholders have been invited to submit their views and comments and to provide further evidence of the economic impact of the sui generis protection.

Case Law of the Court of Justice

Magill. Databases have been the subject of two decisions by the Court of Justice in cases concerning the balance to be struck between intellectual property rights and EC competition law.[367] These cases are discussed more fully in Ch.28. They establish that the exclusive right of reproduction forms part of the owner's rights, so that refusal to grant a licence, even if it is the act of an undertaking holding a dominant position, cannot in itself constitute abuse of a dominant position. This principle applies to all intellectual property rights.[368] Nevertheless, exercise of an exclusive right by the owner may, in exceptional circumstances, involve abusive conduct and justify compulsory licences being imposed by the European Commission pursuant to art.82 of the Treaty.[369] In *Magill*, Radio Telefís Éireann and ITP (as agent for the ITV companies) refused on the basis of copyright protection to grant licences to third parties to reproduce their programme listings (recognised as protected databases). The court found that this amounted to an abuse of their dominant positions and that exceptional circumstances were present. These were that the refusal concerned a product the supply of which was indispensable for carrying on the new business (the publishing of a general weekly television guide); without the information it would be impossible to publish and sell the guide; the refusal prevented the emergence of a new product for which there was a potential consumer demand and was not justified by objective considerations; it was also likely to exclude all competition in the secondary market.[370]

24–95

IMS Health and NDC Health. More recently, in *IMS Health v NDC Health*, the court was concerned with the refusal to license data on regional sales of pharmaceutical products in Germany contained in a particular database within the meaning of the German copyright law. In finding the refusal abusive, the court identified three cumulative conditions which are sufficient to determine the existence of exceptional circumstances: that the refusal is preventing the emergence of a new product for which there is a potential consumer demand; that it is unjustified; and that it is such as to exclude any competition on a secondary

24–96

---

[366] See para.24–97, below.

[367] *Volvo AB v Erik Veng (UK) Ltd, Case 238/87* [1988] E.C.R. 6211; *RTÉ and ITP v Commission (Magill)* (C–241 & 242/91P) [1995] E.C.R. I–734; *IMS Health GmbH & Co OHG v NDC Health GmbH & Co KG* (C–418/01) [2004] E.C.R. I–5039; [2004] E.C.D.R. 9. See also T.C. Vinje, "The Final Word on Magill", [1995] 6 E.I.P.R. 297; T. Ramsauer, "Just Another Brick?—The European Court of Justice on the Interface between European Competition Law and Intellectual Property", e.Copyright Bulletin, Paris, Unesco, April-June 2004.

[368] *Volvo AB v Erik Veng (UK)* (Case 238/87) [1988] E.C.R. 6211 and *RTE and ITP v Commission (Magill)* (C–241 & 242/91P) [1995] E.C.R. I 734.

[369] *Volvo AB v Erik Veng (UK)* (Case 238/87) [1988] E.C.R. 6211 and *RTE and ITP v Commission (Magill)* (C–241 & 242/91P) [1995] E.C.R. I–734.

[370] *RTE and ITP v Commission (Magill)* (C–241 & 242/91P) [1995] E.C.R. I–734.

market.[371] The secondary market may be a potential market or even a hypothetical market.[372]

24–97   ***Fixtures Marketing Ltd and British Horseracing Board.*** The November 2004 judgments of the Court of Justice relating to the interpretation of the sui generis protection afforded by the Database Directive in a series of cases referred by national courts and considered together are also of particular interest.[373]

The four judgments concern the scope of the sui generis protection of the Directive in the context of sporting databases (football fixture lists and a database containing a register of thoroughbred horses and information on horseracing). Fixtures Marketing Ltd and the British Horseracing Board (BHB) alleged that other companies had infringed their rights in their databases. The Court held that the Directive reserves the protection of the sui generis right for databases which show that there has been, qualitatively or quantitatively, a substantial investment in the obtaining, verification or presentation of their contents. It then decided that the expression "investment" in the obtaining of the contents of a database refers to the resources used to seek out existing materials and collect them in the database. It does not cover the resources used for the creation of materials which make up the contents of the database. The fact that the maker of a database is also the creator of the materials contained in it does not exclude that database from the protection of the sui generis right, provided that he establishes that the obtaining of those materials, their verification or their presentation required substantial investment in quantitative or qualitative terms, which was independent of the resources used to create those materials. Applying these principles, the Court then found that neither the obtaining, verification nor presentation of the contents of a football fixture list or a schedule of horse races constitutes substantial investment giving rise to protection against the use of the data by third parties. In the BHB case, the Court found also that the expression "substantial part", in quantitative terms, must be assessed in relation to the total volume of the contents of the database. In qualitative terms, it refers to the scale of the investment in the obtaining, verification or presentation of the contents extracted or re-utilised. It concluded that, since the materials extracted and re-utilised by William Hill did not require investment by BHB which was independent of the resources required for their creation, those materials did not constitute a substantial part of the contents of the BHB database.

As the Commission points out in its evaluation of the Database Directive,[374] the scope of the sui generis right was severely curtailed by these judgments. The protection for non-original databases has been decreased at least with respect to producers of databases that "create" the data and information that comprises their databases, as opposed to obtaining the information from others.

24–98   ***Directmedia Publishing GmbH.*** On October 9, 2008, the Court of Justice handed down its judgment on a reference for a preliminary ruling from the *Bundesgerichtshof* (Germany) on the question of whether the adoption of data from a database protected under the Database Directive and its incorporation in a different

---

[371] *IMS Health GmbH & Co OHG v NDC Health GmbH & Co KG* (C–418/01) [2004] E.C.R. 9 at para.38.

[372] *IMS Health GmbH & Co OHG v NDC Health GmbH & Co KG* (C–418/01) [2004] E.C.R. 9 at para.44. See also H. Meinberg, "From Magill to IMS Health: the new product requirement and the diversity of intellectual property rights" [2006] EIPR 398.

[373] Judgments of the Court in *Fixtures Marketing Ltd v Oy Veikkaus Ab*, *The British Horseracing Board Ltd v William Hill Organisation Ltd*, *Fixtures Marketing Ltd v Svenska Spel AB*, *Fixtures Marketing Ltd v Organismos prognostikon agonon podosfairou (OPAP)* (C–46/02 [2004] E.C.R. I–10365; [2005] E.C.D.R. 2; C–203/02 [2004] E.C.R. I–10415; [2005] E.C.D.R. 28; C–338/02 [2005] E.C.D.R. 4; and C–444/02 [2004] E.C.R. I–10549; [2005] E.C.D.R. 3).

[374] See para.24–94, above, and the conclusions to para.4.1 of the evaluation.

database constitute an extraction within the meaning of art.7(2)(a) of that Directive, even in the case where that adoption follows individual assessments resulting from consultation of the database, or does extraction within the meaning of that provision presuppose the (physical) copying of data.[375] Advocate General Sharpston delivered an opinion on the case on July 10, 2008. The reference was made in the course of proceedings between Directmedia Publishing GmbH and the Albert-Ludwigs-Universität Freiburg following the marketing by Directmedia of a collection of verse compiled from a list of German verse titles drawn up by a professor at the University, Mr Knoop. The University had published an anthology of poems selected by Knoop as well as a list of verse titles compiled by him on the Internet under the title "The 1100 most important poems in German literature between 1730 and 1900". Directmedia published a CD-ROM "1000 poems everyone should have". Of the poems on that CD-ROM, 876 date from the period between 1720 and 1900, and 856 of these are also mentioned in the Knoop list. In selecting the poems for inclusion on its CD-ROM, Directmedia used the Knoop list as a guide. It omitted certain poems on the list, added others and, in respect of each poem, critically examined the selection made by Mr Knoop. Directmedia took the actual texts of each poem from its own digital resources. The question arose in proceedings brought by the University against Directmedia for infringement of copyright, cessation and damages.

Article 7(2)(a) defines the concept of extraction as "the permanent or temporary transfer of all or a substantial part of the contents of a database to another medium by any means or in any form". The ECJ's answer to the question referred was that "The transfer of material from a protected database to another database following an on-screen consultation of the first database and an individual assessment of the material contained in that first database is capable of constituting an 'extraction', within the meaning of art.7 to the extent that—which it is for the referring court to ascertain—that operation amounts to the transfer of a substantial part, evaluated qualitatively or quantitatively, of the content of the protected database, or to transfers of insubstantial parts, which by their repeated or systematic nature, would have resulted in the reconstruction of a substantial part of those contents".

Apis-Hristovich EOOD v Lakorda AD.[376] In this case, the Court was asked a **24–99** series of questions as to how the terms "permanent transfer" and "temporary transfer" are to be interpreted and delimited in relation to each other for the purpose of determining if "extraction" has taken place in interpreting art.7(2)(a) of the Directive. The Court held that the delimitation of these terms is based on the length of time during which materials extracted from a protected database are stored in a medium other than that database. An extraction takes place is when the materials are stored in a medium other than that database. The judgment gives a number of examples of when extraction takes place in response to subsidiary questions posed in the reference.

Implementation in the United Kingdom. The Directive has been implemented **24–100** in the United Kingdom by means of the Copyright and Rights in Databases Regulation 1997, which entered into force on January 1, 1998.[377]

The 1988 Act made no specific provision for databases, but made provision for

---

[375] Case C–304/07, Judgment of October 9, 2008. Reference lodged on July 2, 2007— *Directmedia Publishing GmbH v 1. Albert-Ludwigs-Universität Freiburg, 2. Professor Ulrich Knoop* [2007] OJ C211/40; [2008] E.C.R. I–07565 .

[376] *Apis-Hristovivh EOOD v Lakorda AD* (C–545/07) ([2008] OJ C51/57). Reference for a preliminary ruling from the *Sofiyski gradski sad* (Bulgaria) lodged on December 4, 2007 .

[377] SI 1997/3032; see Ch.18, above.

protection of copyright in compilations and a database may be considered to be a type of compilation. The Regulations bring the law into line with the Directive, by defining databases and providing that copyright protection should only be accorded to a database which, by virtue of the selection or arrangement of the contents, constitutes the author's own intellectual creation. Thus, the definition of literary work has been modified to include a database, as defined in the Directive; and the meaning of "original" has been defined in relation to databases in accordance with the Directive.[378] Provision is also made as required for the sui generis database right.[379]

(vi) Directive 2001/84/EC on the resale right for the benefit of the author of an original work of art (the Artists' Resale Right or *Droit de Suite* Directive).[380]

24–101   The Directive was adopted on September 27, 2001, and the deadline for implementation by Member States was January 1, 2006. Meanwhile, all Member States have brought their national legislation into conformity with the Directive with the exception of Spain. The ECJ issued a declaration on January 31, 2007, to the effect that Spain had failed to fulfil its obligations under the Directive by failing to adopt the necessary national legislation.[381] However, those Member States, including the United Kingdom, which did not provide for artists' resale rights when the Directive came into force (on the day of its publication in the *Office Journal* of the European Communities)[382] will be able to restrict its application to living artists only, for a further four years until January 1, 2010. Thereafter, at the request of a Member State it will be possible to extend that period for a further two years subject to certain conditions. These unprecedented rules reflect the fact that the Directive was strongly resisted by some Member States, including the United Kingdom, and the result represents a hard-fought compromise.[383]

24–102   **Background.** Community action on this subject was first put forward in the Commission's follow-up to the 1988 Green Paper. In that document, the Commission announced its intention of carrying out a study on artist's resale right (often referred to as "*droit de suite*"). Following a number of consultation exercises based on questionnaires and public hearings,[384] and after having conducted studies[385] into the legal and economic aspects of the matter, in 1996 a first proposal for a Parliament and Council Directive on this subject was put forward by the Commission.[386] Due to the controversy surrounding the proposal, the draft Directive went through a number of drafts between 1996 and 2001.[387]

24–103   **Terms of the Directive.** The Directive introduces harmonised legal arrange-

---

[378] regs 5 and 6.

[379] regs 12–25; and see Ch.18, above.

[380] Directive 2001/84/EC, on the resale right for the benefit of the author of an original work of art [2001] OJ L272/32 of October 13, 2001; see also Ch.20, above and Vol.2 H9.

[381] *Commission of the European Communities v Kingdom of Spain* (C–32/07), OJ C79, 29.3.2008, p.6–7.

[382] Directive 2001/84/EC, art.13

[383] Austria, Ireland, the Netherlands and Luxembourg also opposed the introduction of artists' resale rights.

[384] Hearings were held in July and November 1991, August 1994 and February 1995.

[385] *Le droit de suite dans l'Union européenne, Analyse juridique, Eléments économiques*, Brussels 1995, study carried out by the Commission. See also, *Das Folgerecht der bildenden Kunstler*, ifo Institut für Wirtschaftsforschung, Munich, 1994.

[386] Original Proposal and Explanatory Memorandum: COM(96) 97 final [1996] OJ C178/16.

[387] See Opinion of the Economic and Social Committee, [1997] OJ C75/17, March 10, 1997; Opinion of the European Parliament, [1997] OJ C132/88, April 28, 1997; see also S. Hughes, "Droit de Suite: A Critical Analysis of the Approved Directive" [1997] 12 E.I.P.R., 694; amended Proposal of the Commission, COM(98) 78 final, March 12, 1998 ([1998] OJ C125/8, April 23, 1998);

ments for the artist's resale right Community wide. The *raison d'être* of the artist's resale right is essentially to provide authors of original works of art with financial support linked to the value of their works on the market. This is achieved on the basis of price bands focusing on the resale price of works with declining royalty scales. The right is defined as "an unassignable and inalienable right, enjoyed by the author of an original work of graphic or plastic art, to an economic interest in successive sales of the work concerned" i.e. a right to receive a royalty based on the sale price obtained for any resale of protected works of the visual arts, subsequent to the first transfer of the work by the author.[388] The right applies to all acts of resale involving art market professionals such as sellers, buyers, dealers or intermediaries, and covers sales in salesrooms and art galleries and, in general, any dealing in works of art. Transactions effected by individuals acting in their private capacity without the participation of an art market professional, as well as acts of resale by such individuals to museums, which are not for profit and open to the public, are excepted.[389]

The artist's resale right is recognised by the Berne Convention, pursuant to which countries of the Union are free to decide whether or not to introduce the right into their domestic law. The right is therefore not governed by the rule of national treatment, but subject to reciprocity; thus countries of the Berne Union may only claim protection for their nationals in other such countries when they themselves have national legislation providing for such a right for nationals of other Union countries.[390] However, it is pointed out in the Directive that it follows from the case law of the Court of Justice of the European Communities that reciprocity clauses in the Community context run counter to the principle of equal treatment resulting from the prohibition of any discrimination on grounds of nationality.[391] At the time of the adoption of the Directive, 11[392] of the then 15 Member States of the European Union recognised the artist's resale right in principle and nine applied it in practice.[393] In each of these Member States, the right is included as a property right in the legislation on copyright and is limited in duration.[394] There are substantial differences in these laws as regards the works covered by the right, the holders of the right, the transactions giving rise to payment of a royalty, the rates applied and the basis on which these are calculated.[395] The Commission concluded, therefore, that, in relation to the free movement of

---

Council Common Position of June 19, 2000 ([2000] OJ C300/1, of October 20, 2000 and Decision of the European Parliament of December 13, 2000 ([2000] OJ C232/173), Decision of the European Parliament of July 3, 2001 and Decision of the Council of July 19, 2001.

[388] Directive 2001/84/EC, recital 1 and art.1(1).

[389] Recital 18 and art.1(2).

[390] art.14 *ter*, Berne Convention. However, recital 7 of the Directive proposes that the EC take action in the external sphere to make art.14 *ter* compulsory in order to introduce obligatory resale rights at international level. For this reason, art.7.1 of the Directive states that "Member States shall provide that authors who are nationals of third countries, and . . . their successors in title, shall enjoy the resale right in accordance with this Directive and the legislation of the Member State concerned only if legislation in the country of which the author or his/her successor in title is a national permits resale right protection in that country for authors from the Member States and their successors in title". Art.7.2 states that "On the basis of information provided by the Member States, the Commission shall publish as soon as possible an indicative list of those third countries which fulfil the condition set out in para.(1)". Meanwhile the Member States have agreed that, for a third country to appear on the list, there should be legislation in place and that evidence of its application should also be provided. To date the Commission has not been supplied with evidence for any third country which demonstrates that they qualify for inclusion on such a list.

[391] Resale Right Directive, recital 6.

[392] Belgium, Denmark, Finland, France, Germany, Greece, Italy, Luxembourg, Spain, Portugal, Sweden (cf. Explanatory memorandum, Table 5).

[393] Italy and Luxembourg recognised the artists' resale right but did not yet apply it in practice. Austria, Ireland, the Netherlands and the United Kingdom did not recognise the right.

[394] Explanatory memorandum, para.1(6), p.2.

[395] para.1(7), p.3.

goods and distortions of competition, the substantial differences between the various laws of the Member States and the uncertainty about the application of the artist's resale right in the various provisions of the Member States have a direct negative impact on the proper functioning of the internal market in works of art[396] and that, therefore, Community legislation was required under the then art.95 of the Treaty (now art.114 TFEU).[397]

The resale right royalty shall be payable by the seller. The right shall not apply to acts of resale where the seller has acquired the work directly from the author less than three years before the resale and where the resale price does not exceed €10,000.[398]

The aim of the Directive is to ensure that artists share in the economic success of their works and, to this end, the right is to be inalienable so that it is impossible to waive it or assign it to another party. The original works of art to which the artist's resale right relates are: works of graphic or plastic art such as pictures, collages, paintings, drawings, engravings, prints, lithographics, sculptures, tapestries, ceramics, glassware and photographs, provided they are made by the artist himself or are copies considered to be original works of art.[399] Copies are to be considered original works of art if they have been made in limited numbers by the artist himself or under his authority. Such copies will normally have been numbered, signed or otherwise duly authorised by the artist.[400] Original manuscripts of writers and composers are excluded.[401]

The minimum threshold for the payment of royalties in application of the right is to be set by the Member States, but may not exceed €3,000.[402] Royalties are payable to the author of the work, and, after his death to his legal heirs,[403] on the sales price net of taxes.[404] The royalty rates to be paid by the seller[405] are set at the following rates for the various sale price bands: 4 per cent for the portion of the sale price up to €50,000; 3 per cent for the portion of the sale price from €50,001 to 200,000; 1 per cent for the portion of the sale price from €200,001 to 350,000; 0.5 per cent for the portion of the sale price from €350,001 to 500,000; 0.25 per cent for the portion of the sale price exceeding €500.[406] However, the total amount of the royalty may not exceed €12,500. Member States are also free to apply a rate of 5 per cent for the portion of the sale price up to €50,000.[407] If the minimum sale price set is lower than €3,000, the Member State shall also determine the rate applicable to the portion of the sale price up to €3,000, but this may not be lower than 4 per cent.[408] Member States may provide for compulsory or optional collective management of royalties paid over by virtue of the artist's resale right.[409] They are also under an obligation to make arrangements for payment to be made to nationals of third countries, provided that authors from EU Member States enjoy reciprocal treatment in the third countries

---

[396] para.1(7), p.3.
[397] Resale Right Directive, recital 10.
[398] art.1(3).
[399] art.2(1).
[400] art.2(2).
[401] Recital 19.
[402] art.3.
[403] art.6(1).
[404] art.5.
[405] art.1(4).
[406] art.4(1).
[407] art.4(2).
[408] art.4(3).
[409] art.6(2).

concerned.[410] For three years from the date of any transaction in the work, any dealer and commercial agent, sales director or organiser of public sales is obliged to supply right owners with all necessary information in order to enable them to secure payment of royalties in respect of the sale of works.[411]

The Directive also makes provision for adjusting the minimum threshold and the rates of royalties, including the maximum rate; the Commission is obliged to present a report on the implementation of the Directive by January 1, 2009, and every four years thereafter, in order that account can be taken of its impact on the competitiveness of the European market in modern and contemporary art and adjustments made, where appropriate.[412]

The duration of the right is 70 years pma as provided for in the Term Directive.[413]

Case Law of the Court of Justice. The Court has issued one ruling on the subject   **24–104** of the Directive on a reference from the Tribunal de Grande Instance in France.[414] The court interpreted art.6(1) as not precluding a provision of national law which reserves the benefit of the resale right to the artist's heirs at law alone, to the exclusion of testamentary legatees. That being so, it is for the referring court, for the purposes of applying the national provision transposing art.6(1) to take due account of all the relevant rules for the resolution of conflicts of laws relating to the transfer on succession of the resale right.

Implementation in the United Kingdom. Throughout the negotiations leading   **24–105** to the adoption of the Directive, the proposal was much criticised in the United Kingdom because of London 's pre-eminence in the international art market. It is feared that, once the artists' resale right is introduced, the result will be that art sales will be conducted in non-EU countries, in particular, Switzerland (Geneva) and the United States of America (New York), thus putting London in an unfair competitive position in relation to Geneva and New York, damaging the UK art market and leading to a loss of art works, revenue and jobs. The UK Government also argued that the administrative burden of collecting the royalty would outweigh by far any benefit to artists.[415]

The Directive has been implemented in the United Kingdom by means of the Artist's Resale Right Regulations 2006, which entered into force on February 14, 2006.[416]

C. THE INFORMATION SOCIETY

The 1995 Green Paper on Copyright and Related Rights in the Information   **24–106** **Society and its Follow-up.** The Bangemann report on "Europe and the Information Society"[417] led to the adoption of an action plan[418] by the Commission, which identified intellectual property protection as a key issue, given the critical role

---

[410] art.7.

[411] art.9.

[412] art.11.

[413] art.8; cf. paras 24–84 et seq.

[414] *Fundación Gala- Salvador Dali and Visual Entidad de Gestión de Artistas Plásticos (VEGAP) v Société des auteurs dans les arts graphiques et plastiques (ADAGP) and Others* (C–518/08) Judgment of the Court (Third Chamber, April 15, 2010) OJ C148, 5.6.2010, p.7–7; [2010] E.C.R. I–0.

[415] See, e.g. *The Times*, leading article, June 8, 1998; *The Times*, "Artists gain but markets lose", Supplement, p.3, July 17, 2001.

[416] SI 2006/346; see Ch.20.

[417] *Europe and the Global Information Society. Recommendations to the European Council*, by the High-Level Group on the Information Society, May 26, 1994.

[418] *Europe's Way to the Information Society-An Action Plan*, COM(94) 347 final July 19, 1994.

creative content and innovation was likely to play in the development of the information society. The Green Paper on Copyright and Related Rights in the Information Society[419] was essentially a further step in a process of consultation, seeking the views of interested parties and Member States on the extent to which there was a need to adapt the legal environment for intellectual property within the Single Market in order to respond to the developing information society. The information society is nowhere defined but is described as being the result of technological progress, which by combining information technology, high-speed telecommunications and television has made it possible "to process, store, retrieve and communicate information in whatever form it may take, whether oral, written or visual, unconstrained by distance, time and volume".[420] The Green Paper saw the information society as a reality, in that, thanks to digital communications technology, the information superhighways (publicly accessible networks capable of transferring large amounts of information at high speed between users) had already begun to transmit works and other subject-matter protected by copyright and related rights in interactive services. The Green Paper was concerned, therefore, to describe how the information society was expected to develop, and with the implications of the development of these new technologies for the system of copyright and related rights. According to the Commission, while respecting the principle of subsidiarity, the Community has an obligation to take measures in respect of copyright and related rights in order to guarantee the free movement of goods, the freedom to provide services and to avoid creating distortions of competition.[421]

The Commission identified nine areas in which it considered harmonisation of the laws of Member States on copyright and related rights should be given priority in order to ensure that the information society could operate properly. These were: the applicable law when a work is exploited; the question of exhaustion of rights (Community wide exhaustion is part of the *acquis communautaire*; the question arises whether the Community should apply international exhaustion); the reproduction right, and the exceptions to it, particularly for private copying; the definition of the right of communication to the public; the possible introduction of a new exclusive right to digital dissemination or transmission; the introduction of a new exclusive right to authorise digital broadcasting for holders of related rights (as opposed to a right to equitable remuneration); moral rights; the acquisition and management of rights so as to facilitate access to works and related matter; and technical systems of identification and protection of works and other protected matter.

Following publication of the Green Paper, many submissions were received from, and hearings held with, interested parties.[422] Thereafter, the Commission drew up its Single Market policy in the area of copyright and related rights in the information society, which was published as a follow-up to the Green Paper in November 1996.[423]

24–107   **Follow-up to the 1995 Green Paper.** The Commission concluded from the pro-

---

[419] COM(95) 382 final of July 19, 1995. See also T. Hoeren, "The Green Paper on Copyright and Related Rights in the Information Society" [1995] 10 E.I.P.R. 511 and M. Pullen, "The Green Paper on Copyright and Related Rights in the Information Society (Is it all a Question of Binary Numbers)" [1996] 2 Ent. L.R. 80.

[420] Bangemann report, n.1.

[421] *Green Paper*, para.12.

[422] Hearings were held in January 1996 and the consultation process was concluded by a conference "Copyright and Related Rights on the Threshold of the 21st Century", held in June 1996 in Florence.

[423] *Follow-up to the Green Paper on Copyright and Related Rights in the Information Society*, COM(96) 568 final of November 20, 1996.

cess of consultation referred to, that there was a need for further harmonisation of copyright and related rights, pointing out that "The use of computer technology, digitisation and the convergence of communication and telecommunication networks are already having an enormous impact on the transborder-wide exploitation of literary, musical or audio-visual works and other protected subject-matter such as phonograms or fixed performances".[424] In proposing readjustment of the existing legal framework, it asserted that the traditionally high level of copyright protection should be maintained and further developed to meet the needs and practices of copyright markets. Four issues were identified for priority action, the reproduction right (including exceptions thereto), the right of communication to the public, the legal protection of the integrity of technical identification and protection schemes and the distribution right (including the principle of exhaustion), and, indeed, these issues are dealt with in the subsequently adopted European Parliament and Council Directive on the harmonisation of certain aspects of copyright and related rights in the Information Society, discussed below.[425]

Issues requiring further evaluation. Several other issues discussed in the 1995 Green Paper were identified as requiring further evaluation before any action could be taken. As regards the proposal to strengthen the right of certain holders of related rights (producers of phonograms and performers) to control broadcasting, notably in its new form of multichannel broadcasting, by the grant of exclusive rights to replace the present right at Community level to equitable remuneration, the Commission took the view at the time that the case for such new rights had not yet been made out.[426] It put forward two reasons why such rights might need strengthening at a future date: the fact that more Member States might wish to grant such exclusive rights in the future to particular holders of related rights; and that multichannel broadcasting might become a primary market for the exploitation of phonograms and fixed performances. However, since digital broadcasting and multichannel broadcasting were only in their infancy at the time, the Commission expressed its intention to continue to evaluate developments in the market and to take the necessary legislative action, should it prove necessary at a future date.[427] The Commission's decision not to legislate for these new rights was much criticised by the rights owners concerned, who argued that exclusive rights to authorise or prohibit broadcasting are essential in the digital environment.

24–108

Another issue on which no action was recommended was that of the applicable law and law enforcement in the digital environment, i.e. the question as to which country's law applies to transnational acts of exploitation. The consultation process had indicated that the majority of interested parties took the view that the problems which might be created by the transfrontier nature of acts of digital transmission could be taken care of through contractual freedom and the application of existing private international law; nevertheless, in view of the complex legal situation, it was indicated that guidance on existing rules rather than outright harmonisation would be welcomed. The Commission, therefore, stated that it was considering issuing a clarifying Communication on the subject, which would

---

[424] *Follow-up to the Green Paper on Copyright and Related Rights in the Information Society*, Chs 1, 3.

[425] COM(97) 628 final of December 10, 1997 (see paras 24–109 et seq., below).

[426] It should be noted that the majority of Member States grant producers of phonograms and performers only rights to equitable remuneration for the broadcasting of their phonograms and recorded performances, as opposed to exclusive rights to authorise or prohibit such, in line with the minimum standards of the Rome Convention (art.12) and the Rental Rights Directive (art.8(2)).

[427] *Follow-up to the Green Paper*, Ch.3, 1.

address the applicable-law issues as well as the enforcement of rights. The Commission also expressed its intention to study the enforcement-related issue of liability for copyright infringements to evaluate the need for an initiative at EU level.[428] In the Green Paper of 1995, the Commission had appeared to favour the applicable law being defined as the country of origin.[429] After consultation, the Commission's view changed; in the Explanatory memorandum to the Proposal for the Information Society Directive,[430] the Commission stated that potential infringements were governed by the national laws under which the right had been granted and where protection was sought. Thus, in the case of transnational acts of exploitation, several national laws might apply in parallel.[431]

A further issue on which no action was recommended at the time was management of rights. The consultation process had indicated that the majority of interested parties took the view that management of rights should in principle be left to the market, irrespective of the introduction of digitisation. The usefulness of collective management is not called into question. Some parties, however, were calling for harmonised measures to adequately control the behaviour of collecting societies, both in terms of licensing and competition rules. Others had requested a clarification of the application of Community competition rules to collecting societies and collective management, through a code of conduct or voluntary guidelines. The Commission intended, therefore, to continue to study the issue in the light of the development of the market with particular regard to the Single Market. A future Community initiative was envisaged to define, both under the Single Market and the competition rules of the EC Treaty, the rights and obligations of collecting societies, in particular with respect to the methods of collection. Issues to be tackled would include the calculation of tariffs, supervision mechanisms, and the application of the rules on competition to collecting societies and collective management.[432]

Finally, the Commission took the view that the time was not yet ripe for Community action on moral rights, although it was recognised that moral rights had an economic impact and would be affected by the exploitation of works and other protected subject-matter by digital technology. However, at that time, consultations had shown that moral rights were not posing any real problem so far as the Single Market was concerned. The situation might change with the emergence of the digital environment and, therefore, the Commission proposed to further study the development of the market and see whether existing disparities in legislation constituted significant obstacles to the exploitation of protected subject-matter, which might require action at Community level.[433]

The Commission also drew attention to the international dimension of the information society and to the negotiations underway at that time under the auspices of WIPO to set minimum standards of protection at the international level in the context of the work which led to the subsequent adoption in December 1996 of the WIPO Copyright Treaty (hereafter referred to as WCT) and the WIPO Performances and Phonograms Treaty (hereafter referred to as WPPT).[434]

In relation to moral rights, it should be noted that the WPPT provides that performers should enjoy moral rights with respect to their live audio perfor-

---

[428] *Follow-up to the Green Paper*, Ch.3, 2.
[429] cf. arts 2 & 3 of the Cable and Satellite Directive 93/83, see para.24–106, above.
[430] See para.24–109, below.
[431] Explanatory memorandum, Ch.2, 8.
[432] Ch.3, 3 and see para.24–160, below.
[433] Ch.3, 4 and see para.24–163, below.
[434] Ch.4.

mances fixed in phonograms and this is, therefore, an issue the Commission will have to address sooner or later.[435]

(i) Directive on the harmonisation of certain aspects of copyright and related rights in the information society (the Information Society Directive).

The Directive was adopted on May 22, 2001,[436] having first been proposed by the Commission in December 1997.[437] Member States were given until December 22, 2002, to comply with the Directive.[438] Only Greece and Denmark met the deadline. Italy and Austria implemented the Directive in April and June 2003, respectively. In July 2003, the Commission sent reasoned opinions to the other 11 Member States which were in the course of implementation. In the meantime, the Directive has been transposed into domestic law by Germany, Luxembourg and the United Kingdom, but the Commission has referred Belgium, Spain, France, the Netherlands, Portugal, Finland and Sweden to the Court of Justice for failure to implement. In the meantime, the Directive has been transposed into domestic law by all the Member States of the enlarged European Union, including the latest new Members, Bulgaria and Romania.

24–109

Background. In its original proposal, the Commission announced that its aim was not only to ensure a level playing field within the Community for goods and services containing material protected by copyright in the digital environment, but also to implement a significant number of the obligations set out in the two new Treaties already referred to, the WCT and WPPT.[439] The legal basis for the Directive rests on arts 47(2), 55 and 95 of the Treaty of Rome, as amended.[440] As is the case with other Directives in the field of copyright and related rights, the Directive does not aim at a general harmonisation of laws but at harmonising those matters which are necessary for the smooth functioning of the internal market. The Directive recognises that liability for activities in the network environment concerns not only copyright and related rights but other areas of the law, such as defamation, misleading advertising, or infringement of trademarks. These matters are addressed in another Directive on certain legal aspects of information society services, in particular electronic commerce, which clarifies and harmonises various legal issues on this subject.[441] At the time of the adoption of the Directive, the Commission announced: "Not only is this Directive the most important measure ever to be adopted by Europe in the copyright field but it brings European copyright rules into the digital age. The Directive will stimulate creativity and innovation by ensuring that all material protected by copyright, including books, films, music are adequately protected by copyright. It provides a secure environment for cross-border trade in copyright protected goods and services, and will facilitate the development of electronic commerce in the field of

24–110

---

[435] WPPT art.5

[436] Directive 2001/29/EC of the European Parliament and of the Council ([2001] OJ L167/10); see Vol.2 H8.

[437] COM(97) 628 final, December 10, 1997; [1998] OJ C108/6.

[438] Information Society Directive art.13. See the Directive Implementation Table, para.24–175, below.

[439] Both Treaties have been signed on behalf of the European Community (cf. Decision of the Council authorising accession of the EC to the WCT and WPPT, April 24, 1998 [1998] OJ C165/8), Vol.2 I1. For a full treatment of both Treaties, see Ch.23, above.

[440] Preamble to the Information Society Directive, para.1.

[441] Information Society Directive, recital 16; see Directive 2000/31/EC of the European Parliament and of the Council of June 8, 2000, on certain legal aspects of information society services, in particular electronic commerce, in the internal market (Directive on electronic commerce, [2000] OJ L178/1, July 17, 2000). See para.24–144, below, and Vol.2 H7.

new and multimedia products and services (both online and offline via, e.g.CDs)."[442]

24-111 **Terms of the Directive.** The Information Society Directive focuses on the four issues for which Community legislation was forecast in the Follow-up to the Green Paper, the reproduction right, the right of communication to the public of works and right of making available to the public other subject-matter, the distribution right, exceptions and limitations to these rights and the legal protection of technological measures and rights-management information.[443]

24-112 **The reproduction right.** The Directive defines the scope of the acts covered by the reproduction right with regard to the different beneficiaries in conformity with the *acquis communautaire*.[444] It seeks to provide all right owners with the exclusive right to authorise or prohibit direct or indirect,[445] temporary or permanent reproduction by any means and in any form, in whole or in part,[446] of their works, fixed performances, phonograms, films and broadcasts, respectively.[447] This provision aims at ensuring that all authors, performers, phonogram and film producers and broadcasting organisations benefit from the same level of protection for their works or other subject-matter as regards the acts protected by the reproduction right.[448] The definition aims at covering all relevant acts of reproduction, whether online or offline, in material or immaterial form and is in line with the WCT and the WPPT.[449] In *Football Association Premier League Limited v QC Leisure* discussed at para.24-29, above, one of the questions referred to the ECJ concerned the interpretation of the reproduction right in cases where a work is said to have been reproduced by copying small sequential fragments of the work (in this case frames of digital video and audio) but where only a small number of those fragments exist at any one time. The question first asks whether this is a question for the national court or for the ECJ, and if the latter, it asks the ECJ to rule on whether all of those fragments, or only those which simultaneously exist, should be considered when assessing the reproduction. Finally, the ECJ is asked to rule on whether the reproduction right in art.2 of the Directive extends to the creation of transient images on a television screen.

24-113 **Right of communication to the public of works and right of making available to the public other subject-matter.** The Directive provides authors with the exclusive right to authorise or prohibit any communication to the public of their works, by wire or wireless means, including the making available to the public thereof in such a way that members of the public may access them from a

---

[442] Commission Press Release, April 9, 2001.

[443] On the Proposed Directive, see: S. von Lewinski, "A Successful Step towards Copyright and Related Rights in the Information Age: The New EC Proposal for a Harmonisation Directive" [1998] E.I.P.R. 135; M. Hart, "The Proposed Directive for Copyright in the Information Society: Nice Rights, Shame about the Exceptions" [1998] E.I.P.R. 169; G.P. Cornish, "Libraries and the Harmonisation of Copyright" [1998] E.I.P.R. 241; T. Heide, "The Berne Three-step Test and the Proposed Copyright Directive" [1999] E.I.P.R. 103; M. Doherty and I. Griffiths, "The Harmonisation of European Union; Copyright Law for the Digital Age" [2000] E.I.P.R. 17; B. Hugenholtz, "Why the Copyright Directive is Unimportant and Possibly Invalid" [2000] E.I.P.R. 499; T.C. Vinje, "Should we Begin Digging Copyright's Grave" [2000] E.I.P.R. 551

[444] Information Society Directive, recital 21.

[445] cf. art.7, Rental and Related Rights Directive 92/100 (see para.24-59, above).

[446] cf. art.4a, Software Directive 91/250 (see para.24-51, above) and art.5a of the Database Directive 96/9 (see para.24-92, above).

[447] Information Society Directive art.2.

[448] Explanatory memorandum, comments on art.1 para.1 (now art.2).

[449] As regards the harmonisation of exceptions to the reproduction right, see para.24-115, below.

place and at a time individually chosen by them.[450] The other right owners, performers, phonogram producers, film producers and broadcasting organisations, are provided with the exclusive right to authorise or prohibit the making available to the public, by wire or wireless means, in such a way that members of the public may access them from a place and at a time individually chosen by them.[451] These rights are not to be exhausted by any act of communication to the public or making available to the public[452] as defined in the Directive. The authors' right of communication to the public is to be understood in a broad sense as covering all communication to the public not present at the place where the communication originates. It covers any transmission or retransmission of a work to the public by wire or wireless means, including broadcasting.[453] The right of the other right owners to make subject-matter available to the public should be also understood as covering all acts of making available such subject-matter to members of the public not present at the place where the act of making available originates.[454] Thus the interactive environment is addressed, implementing the relevant provisions of the WCT and WPPT at Community level,[455] all right-holders being given an exclusive right to make available to the public copyright works or any other subject-matter by way of interactive on-demand transmissions. Such interactive on-demand transmissions are characterised by the fact that members of the public may access them from a place and at a time individually chosen by them. The right applies also in circumstances where several unrelated members of the public may have individual access, from different places and at different times, to a work which is on a publicly accessible site. It is irrelevant whether any individual member of the public has actually retrieved it or not. Since the provision of services, and online services in particular, does not give rise to exhaustion of rights, every online service is an act which will always require authorisation.[456] In *Football Association Premier League Limited v QC Leisure* discussed at para.24–29, above, one of the questions referred to the ECJ concerned the interpretation of this right and in particular whether the showing of a satellite broadcast to patrons via a single television screen within a public house, the signal having been received by a satellite dish or aerial on or adjacent to that public house, amounted to an act of communication to the public. Expressing his preliminary view in the UK Court, Kitchin J. thought that this was not an act of communication to the public.

Distribution right. The Directive provides authors, in respect of the original of their works or of copies thereof, with the exclusive right to authorise or prohibit any form of distribution to the public by sale or otherwise, thus harmonising the distribution right for authors of all categories of works.[457] The first sale in the Community of the original of a work or copies thereof by the right-holder or with his consent exhausts the right to control resale of that object in the Community but it should not be exhausted outside the Community.[458] This reflects the established case law of the European Court of Justice and excludes the possibility of Member States applying international exhaustion. In *Silhouette International*   **24–114**

---

[450] Information Society Directive art.3(1).
[451] art.3(2).
[452] art.3(3).
[453] Recital 23.
[454] Recital 24.
[455] cf. art.8 WCT and arts 10 and 14 WPPT.
[456] Confirmed by *Laserdisken v Kulturministeriet* (C–479/04) OJ C281, 18.11.2006, p.10–10, [2006] E.C.R. I–8089. ECJ judgment of September 12, 2006. See para.24–122, below.
[457] cf. art.6(1) WCT.
[458] Information Society Directive art.4.

Schmied GmbH & Co KG v Hartlauer Handelsgesellschaft Gmbh,[459] the European Court of Justice decided that there is no international exhaustion of trade mark rights as a result of products being put on the market by the proprietor or with his consent in the EEA. It should be noted in this connection that the Rental and Related Rights Directive[460] has already harmonised the distribution right for four groups of rights owners (performers, broadcasters, phonogram producers and film producers).

24–115   **Exceptions.** The exceptions and limitations to the reproduction right and the communication to the public right, including the right of making available to the public by interactive means have been harmonised and reassessed in the light of the new electronic environment. This was considered important to avoid divergent interpretations in Member States and the risk of obstacles to trade within the Community as well as to safeguard a fair balance of rights between right-holders themselves and between right-holders and users of protected subject-matter.[461] The Directive also seeks to promote learning and culture by protecting works and other subject-matter, while permitting exceptions or limitations in the public interest for the purpose of education and teaching.[462] The Directive contains, first, mandatory exceptions with respect to temporary, transient or incidental acts of reproduction, which are an integral and essential part of a technological process, such as transmissions between networks, where such acts have no economic importance. This exception includes acts which enable browsing as well as acts of caching, including those which enable transmission systems to function efficiently, provided that the intermediary does not modify the information and does not interfere with the lawful use of technology to obtain data on the use of the information.[463] In *Football Association Premier League Limited v QC Leisure* discussed at para.24–29, above, one of the questions referred to the ECJ concerned the interpretation of the term "independent economic significance" in art.5(1), and in particular asked whether transient copies had independent economic significance if those transient copies were the only basis upon which a rights holder could extract remuneration for the use of his rights. In the judgment of the UK court, Kitchin J. indicated that his preliminary view was that they would not give them independent economic significance if they were not inherently possessed of it.

Second, the Directive provides for an exhaustive, closed list of permitted exceptions and limitations to the reproduction right and the right of communication to the public. These exceptions are optional and Member States will be free to keep or introduce them at national level or not to do so; however, no further exceptions will be permitted. It is understood that all these exceptions are subject to the "three-step test" laid down in art.9(2) of the Berne Convention, i.e. limitations to the reproduction right are only permitted in "certain special cases", which do not "conflict with a normal exploitation of the work" and do not "unreasonably prejudice the legitimate interests of the author".[464]

As regards the reproduction right, Member States may provide for exceptions or limitations to the right: "in respect of reprography (except in the case of sheet music, the paper reproduction of which remains prohibited), provided that the right-holders receive fair compensation; in respect of reproductions on any

---

[459] cf. *Silhouette International Schmied GmbH & Co KG v Hartlauer Handelsgesellschaft Gmbh* (C–355/96) "Silhouette/Hartlauer" [1999] 3 C.M.L.R. 267, see para.24–29.
[460] cf. The Rental and Related Rights Directive art.9, and see para.24–59, above.
[461] Information Society Directive, recital 31.
[462] Recital 14.
[463] Recital 33.
[464] On the "three-step test" see paras 23–33 et seq., above.

medium made by a natural person for private use and for ends that are neither directly nor indirectly commercial, on condition that the right-holders receive fair compensation, which takes account of the application or non-application of technological measures".[465]

Member States may provide for fair compensation for right-holders also when applying the optional provisions on exceptions and limitations, which do not require such compensation.[466] As regards the reproduction right, Member States may also provide for limitations with respect to: acts of reproduction made by publicly accessible libraries, educational establishments, museums or archives, which are not for direct or indirect economic or commercial advantage; ephemeral recordings made by broadcasting organisations by means of their own facilities and for their own broadcasts; reproductions of broadcasts made by social institutions pursuing non-commercial purposes, such as hospitals or prisons, subject, in the latter case, to the payment of fair compensation to the right-holders.

The exceptions permitting reprography and private copying are not manda-tory; where such exceptions are provided for, then the right-holders are to be entitled to fair compensation, which, in the case of private copying, is to take ac-count of the application or non-application of technological protection measures. However, the Directive does not impose harmonisation of remuneration schemes. As regards reprography, the existing remuneration schemes, where they exist, are not considered to create major barriers to the internal market, and are to be permit-ted to continue.[467] As regards private copying, no distinction is made in the articles of the Directive between analogue and digital technology, contrary to expectations.[468] However, private copying may not be permitted without fair compensation being paid, and Member States are to be free to introduce or continue remuneration schemes to compensate for the prejudice to right-holders. A recital acknowledges that differences between those remuneration schemes af-fect the functioning of the internal market but asserts that, with regard to analogue private reproduction, those differences should not have a significant impact on the development of the information society. By contrast, digital private copying is recognised in the Recital as likely to be more widespread and to have a greater economic impact. It is suggested, therefore, that due account should be taken of the differences between digital and analogue private copying and it is stated that a distinction should be made in certain respects between them.[469] Thus, when ap-plying the exception or limitation on private copying, Member States are called on to take due account of technological and economic developments, in particu-lar with respect to digital private copying and remuneration schemes, when effec-tive technological protection measures are available. At the same time, such

---

[465] Information Society Directive art.5(2).

[466] Recital 35.

[467] Recital 37.

[468] In the *Green Paper*, the Commission had pointed out that a situation in which private copying is legal in some Member States and not in others would create serious difficulty and place barriers in the way of trade. It had stated that a degree of harmonisation would be required to resolve the problems, suggesting that "Where the technology does not allow copying to be prevented, a valid response may continue to be that levies should be charged on the equipment and recording medium, and private copying declared permissible. But where there is the technical means to limit or prevent private copying, there is no further justification for what amounts to a system of statutory licensing and equitable remuneration." *Green Paper*, s.III, reproduction right, paras 1 and 3. Likewise, in the *Follow-up to the Green Paper*, the Commission outlined its intention to make private copying a fully restricted act, with respect to certain acts of exploitation in the digital environment, whereas in other situations, such as analogue copying, private copying might be permitted Community-wide, be it with or without remuneration. *Follow-up*, p.12.

[469] Information Society Directive, recital 38.

exceptions or limitations should not inhibit the use of technological measures or their enforcement against circumvention.[470]

So far as determining the form, detailed arrangements and possible level of fair compensation, account is to be taken of the particular circumstances of each case. When evaluating these circumstances, it is suggested in a recital that a valuable criterion would be the possible harm to the right-holders resulting from the act in question. In cases where right-holders have already received payment in some other form, for instance as part of a licence fee, no specific or separate payment may be due. The level of fair compensation should take full account of the degree of use of technological protection measures referred to in the Directive. In certain cases where the prejudice to the right-holder would be minimal, no obligation for payment may arise.[471]

Further limitations to both the right of reproduction and the right of communication to the public are provided for, all of which are commonly to be found in the present legislation of Member States and are also envisaged by the international copyright and related rights conventions. These include standard exceptions concerning, for example, use for teaching or scientific research, use by persons with disabilities and the use of quotations for the purpose of criticism or review, etc.[472] A far-reaching exception is included permitting reproduction by the press, the communication to the public or making available of published articles on current economic, political or religious topics or of broadcast works or other subject-matter of the same character, in cases where such use is not expressly reserved, and as long as the source, including the author's name is indicated. Similarly, it is permissible to use works or other subject-matter in connection with the reporting of current events, to the extent justified by the informatory purpose and as long as the source and author's name are given, where possible. This is a far-reaching exception in that it is not restricted to the reproduction of short extracts but appears to allow reproduction of complete works.[473]

The Directive further provides a long list of other optional, permitted exceptions and limitations to the reproduction right, and rights of communication and making available to the public. This list represents, in practice, all the specific exceptions presently to be found in the copyright laws of the Member States, including some common to many Member States, such as incidental use and use for the purpose of caricature, parody or pastiche, as well as some more unusual exceptions, peculiar to particular Member States, for example, use of works, such as works of architecture or sculpture, made to be located permanently in public places[474] and use for the purpose of advertising the public exhibition or sale of artistic works.[475]

24–116   **Obligations concerning technological measures.** As forecast in the Green Paper and its follow-up, and in order to comply with the WCT and WPPT, right-holders are to be permitted to make use of technological measures designed to prevent or restrict acts not authorised by them.[476] Thus, Member States are to provide adequate legal protection against illegal activities which enable or facilitate the circumvention of any effective technological measures, which the person concerned carries out in the knowledge or with reasonable grounds to know that

---

[470] Recital 39.
[471] Recital 35.
[472] art.5(3).
[473] art.5(3)(c).
[474] cf. art.59, German Copyright Act 1965 (as amended in 1998).
[475] cf. art.L122-5(3)(d) of the French Intellectual Property Code (1992).
[476] Information Society Directive 2001/29, recital 47.

he or she is pursuing that objective.[477] The obligation on States is to protect against any of the following activities: manufacture, import, distribution, sale, rental, advertisement for sale or rental, or possession for commercial purposes of devices, products or components or the provision of services which are promoted, advertised or marketed for the purpose of circumvention of, or which have only limited commercially significant purpose or use other than to circumvent,[478] or are primarily designed, produced, adapted or performed for the purpose of enabling or facilitating the circumvention of any effective technological measures.[479] The term technological measure is defined as meaning any technology, device, product or component incorporated into a process, device or component that, in the normal course of its operation, is designed to prevent or restrict acts, in respect of works or other subject-matter, which are not authorised by the right-holder.[480] Technological measures are deemed effective where the use of a protected work or other subject-matter is controlled by the right-holders through application of an access control or protection process, such as encryption, scrambling or other transformation of the work or other subject-matter or a copy control mechanism, which achieves the protection objective.[481]

Notwithstanding the legal protection of technological measures apparently guaranteed by the Directive, the normal operation of electronic equipment and its technological development should not be prevented.[482] Moreover, the legal protection of such measures is to apply without prejudice to public policy, as reflected by the provisions of the Directive concerning exceptions and limitations. Thus, it is provided that, in the absence of voluntary measures taken by right-holders, including agreements between right-holders and other parties concerned, Member States shall take appropriate measures to ensure that right-holders make available to beneficiaries of certain exceptions or limitations the means of benefiting from that exception or limitation. This applies, inter alia, to reprography, non-commercial reproduction by libraries, the making of ephemeral recordings by broadcasting organisations and non-commercial reproductions of broadcasts in hospitals and prisons. In this respect, an obligation is imposed on Member States to take such measures.[483]

In the case of private copying, the Directive is more cautious. Voluntary measures to facilitate private copying are to be promoted by Member States but, in their absence, Member States are permitted to take measures to enable beneficiaries of a private use exception to take advantage thereof but are not obliged to do so. At the same time, it is also stipulated that right-holders are not to be prevented from using technological measures in order to control the number of reproductions made.[484]

It is also specifically provided that the technological measures applied voluntarily by right-holders, including those applied in implementation of voluntary agreements, and those applied in implementation of measures taken by Member States, shall be protected.[485]

Finally, it is recognised that the protection of technological measures should ensure a secure environment for the provision of interactive on-demand services.

---

[477] art.6(1).
[478] Thus, circumvention equipment which is an accessory function of a multipurpose machine is not covered. This lacuna has been criticised.
[479] art.6(2).
[480] art.6(3).
[481] art.6(3).
[482] Information Society Directive recital 48
[483] art.6(4) para.1 and recital 51.
[484] art.6(4) para.2 and recital 52.
[485] art.6(4) para.3.

Thus, it is made clear that the provisions enabling Member States to take measures to give beneficiaries of exceptions access to works do not apply to works or other subject-matter made available to the public on agreed contractual terms in such a way that members of the public may access them from a place and at a time individually chosen by them.[486]

The apparent guarantee in the proposed Directive that exceptions permitting private copying should not inhibit the use of technological measures or their enforcement against circumvention is welcome.[487] However, it is open to doubt whether the legal protection of technological measures prevails over the exceptions permitted under the proposed Directive or not. Moreover, Member States are to be free to set their own rules on this issue; this will inevitably lead to the various industries involved being obliged to adapt their protection systems to comply with differing national definitions of what private copying is and how much should be allowed.

According to the statement of the Council's reasons for its amendments to the Commission's earlier, amended proposal,[488] the European Parliament had suggested that it be stipulated in art.5(4) (current art.5(5)) that the legal protection of technological measures prevailed over the exceptions listed in art.5. The Commission had disagreed and, in its amended proposal,[489] the exceptions provided for in art.5 prevailed over the legal protection of technological measures. The Council, however, has stated that its version of art.6(1) makes it "clear that Art.6(1) protects against circumvention of all technological measures designed to prevent or restrict acts not authorised by the right-holder, regardless of whether the person performing the circumvention is a beneficiary of one of the exceptions provided for in Art.5".[490] Thus, it seems the intention is to allow technological measures to prevail over, inter alia, the exception permitting private use. But this rule has been qualified by the introduction of so-called "safeguards for the protection of the legitimate interests of beneficiaries of exceptions" in art.6(4)[491]; these appear to be contradictory provisions obliging right-holders to make available to beneficiaries of exceptions and limitations, including reproduction for private use, the means of benefiting therefrom, thus precluding the use of technological measures to stop private copying altogether. As noted above, only agreed contractual terms for on-demand supply of works or other subject-matter are to prevail over these provisions.[492]

The recitals shed some light on these provisions. As stated in recital 47, technological development will allow right-holders to make use of technological measures designed to prevent or restrict acts not authorised by the right-holders. Harmonised legal protection against circumvention of effective technological measures and against provision of devices and products or services to this effect is therefore required. However, recital 51 lays down the principle that the legal protection of technological measures applies without prejudice to public policy and that Member States should promote voluntary measures by right-holders to accommodate achieving the objectives of certain exceptions and limitations. In the absence of such voluntary measures within a reasonable period of time,

---

[486] art.6(4) para.5.

[487] Recital 39, last sentence: "Such exceptions or limitations should not inhibit the use of technological measures or their enforcement against circumvention."

[488] Council Common Position (EC) No. 48/2000 adopted by the Council on September 28, 2000. Statement of the Council's Reasons ([2000] OJ C344/1, December 1, 2000).

[489] COM(1999) 250 final ([1999] OJ C180/6, June 25, 1999).

[490] Council Common Position, see above, para.43.

[491] Council Common Position, see above, para.44 and see also Information Society Directive, para.24–109, above, recitals 51 and 52.

[492] Council Common Position, see above, para.44 and see also Directive art.6(4) para.4.1.

Member States are under an obligation to take appropriate measures to ensure that right-holders provide beneficiaries of such exceptions or limitations with appropriate means of benefiting from them, *by modifying an implemented technological measure or by other means* [emphasis added].[493]

With specific reference to private copying, however, recital 52 calls for voluntary measures to make reproduction for private use possible and provides that, in the absence of such voluntary measures, Member States may impose solutions "to enable beneficiaries of the exception or limitation concerned to benefit from it" but they are not obliged to do so. Both voluntary measures and measures imposed by Member States:

"do not prevent right-holders from using technological measures which are consistent with the exceptions or limitations on private copying in national law in accordance with Art.5(2)(b), taking account of the condition of fair compensation under that provision and the possible differentiation between various conditions of use in accordance with Art.5(5), such as controlling the number of reproductions. In order to prevent abuse of such measures, any technological measures applied in their implementation should enjoy legal protection."[494]

The upshot of these confused and confusing provisions appears to be that the use of technological measures to prevent private copying altogether is allowed in principle but not in practice. Where a Member State provides for a private use exception, the public must be allowed to make copies for private use, "*on condition that the right-holders receive fair compensation which takes account of the application or non-application of technological measures*".[495] Presumably, the suggestion here is that the right-holders would get more compensation if no technological controls are used and less if, say, as hinted at in recital 52, the number of reproductions is controlled. However, these proposals beg a number of questions. How can electronic distribution of works be controlled, if a right to private use overrides exclusive reproduction rights and prevents right-holders from using technological measures to stop consumers making copies from the new online digital multimedia services which dominate the internet? If technological measures must permit private use, and must be adapted to differing national legal requirements, what will be the impact on commercial piracy? Where is the technology that can handle these situations? Furthermore, is it compatible with the three-step test of the Berne Convention embodied in the Directive: "The exceptions and limitations … shall only be applied in certain special cases which do not conflict with a normal exploitation of the work or other subject-matter and do not unreasonably prejudice the legitimate interests of the right-holders"[496] and with the WIPO Treaties of 1996[497] to prevent the use of technological measures to stop private copying?

Obligations concerning rights management information. On this subject, the   **24–117**
Directive follows the structure of the relevant articles of the WCT and WPPT.[498] It recognises that important progress has been made in the international standardisation of technical systems of identification of works and protected subject-matter in digital format. It aims at encouraging the use of compatible systems of identification of works, which provide information about the terms and conditions of use of works so as to facilitate the management of rights, as well as at the

---

[493] Directive, recital 51.
[494] The Directive, recital 52.
[495] art.5(2)(b).
[496] art.5(5).
[497] art.10(2) WIPO Copyright Treaty (WCT) and art.16(2) WIPO Performers and Phonograms Treaty (WPPT) 1996.
[498] art.13 WCT and art.19 WPPT.

protection of such systems in the networked environment.[499] It therefore imposes an obligation on Member States to provide adequate legal protection against any person knowingly performing without authority any of the following acts: the removal or alteration of any electronic rights-management information; the distribution, importation for distribution, broadcasting, communication or making available to the public of works or other protected subject-matter from which electronic rights-management information has been removed or altered without authority. The qualification "knowingly performing" an act means knowing, or having reasonable grounds to know, that by so doing the person concerned is inducing, enabling, facilitating or concealing an infringement of any copyright or related right (including the sui generis database right).[500] Rights-management is defined as information provided by right-holders which identifies the work or other subject-matter, the author or other right-holder, or information about the terms and conditions of the use of the work or other subject-matter, and any numbers or codes that represent such information.[501]

24–118   **Sanctions and remedies.** The provisions of the Directive are to be backed up by Member States with effective sanctions and remedies in respect of infringements of the rights and obligations set out in the Directive. Member States are to take all measures necessary to ensure that the sanctions and remedies are applied and they are effective, proportionate and dissuasive.[502] Among the remedies to be provided must be an action for damages, the possibility to apply for an injunction and, where appropriate, the seizure of infringing material and circumvention devices.[503] Furthermore, Member States are to ensure that right-holders are in a position to apply for an injunction against intermediaries whose services are used by a third party to infringe a copyright or related right.[504] This possibility is necessary because in the digital environment the services of intermediaries may increasingly be used by third parties for infringing activities and in many cases such intermediaries are best placed to bring such infringing activities to an end.[505]

24–119   **Continued application of other legal provisions.** The protection provided under the Directive is without prejudice to national or Community legal provisions in other areas, such as industrial property, data protection, etc.[506]

Case Law of the Court of Justice.

24–120   Since the 15th edition of this Work was published in 2005, the first decisions of the Court of Justice on issues arising from the Directive have been handed down and a substantial number of references have been made to the Court for a preliminary ruling.

24–121   **Decided cases.**

Concept of communication to the public. A reference for a preliminary ruling was made to the Court of Justice by a Spanish court in the context of litigation between the Spanish authors' society and a hotel chain. The question posed was whether the communication of protected copyright works by means of television sets installed in hotel rooms was a "communication to the public" within the

---

[499] Information Society Directive, recitals 54–57.
[500] art.7(1).
[501] art.7(2).
[502] Information Society Directive art.8(1) and recital 58.
[503] art.8(2).
[504] art.8(3).
[505] Recital 59.
[506] Information Society Directive art.9 and recital 60.

meaning of the Directive. The Court ruled that, while the mere provision of physical facilities does not as such amount to communication within the meaning of the Directive, the distribution of a signal by means of television sets by a hotel to customers staying in its rooms, whatever technique is used to transmit the signal, constitutes communication to the public within the meaning of art.3(1) of the Directive.[507]

Exhaustion of the distribution right. In *Laserdisken v Kulturministeriet* the Court of Justice had to consider whether the Directive permitted Member States to legislate for an international exhaustion of rights régime or to retain domestic law providing that the distribution right was exhausted when the first sale or other transfer of ownership was made anywhere in the world. The Court held that art.4(2) of the Directive, in conjunction with recital 28 in the preamble to the Directive, provides that it is not open to the Member States to provide for a rule of exhaustion other than the EU-wide exhaustion rule. The Directive is, therefore, to be interpreted as precluding national rules providing for exhaustion of the distribution right in respect of the original or copies of a work placed on the market outside the European Union by the right holder or with his consent.[508]   **24–122**

The distribution right. On April 17, 2008, the Court of Justice handed down its judgment on a reference for a preliminary ruling from the *Bundesgerichtshof* (Germany) in the case of *Peek & Cloppenburg KG v Cassina SpA*.[509]   **24–123**

The case concerned the use, without the consent of the copyright holder, of reproductions of copyright-protected items of furniture as furnishings arranged in a sales area and for decorative display. The question in summary was whether such use, which does not involve any form of transfer of ownership or possession, does or does not constitute a form of distribution to the public. The Court held that the concept of distribution to the public, otherwise than through sale, of the original of a work or a copy thereof, for the purpose of art.4(1) of the Directive, applies only where there is a transfer of the ownership of that object. As a result, neither granting to the public the right to use reproductions of a work protected by copyright nor exhibiting to the public those reproductions without actually granting a right to use them can constitute such a form of distribution.[510]

Data-capture process. On July 16, 2009, the Court of Justice handed down its   **24–124**

---

[507] *Sociedad General de Autores y Editores de España (SGAE) v Rafael Hoteles SA* (C–306/05), judgment of December 7, 2006 [2007] E.C.R. I–11519; [2007] E.C.D.R. 2. See also, A. Bateman, "The Use of Televisions in Hotel Rooms" [2007] EIPR 22. Confirmed in C–136/09, (reference for a preliminary ruling from the Arios Pagos (Greece)), where the court held that "The hotelier, by installing televisions in his hotel rooms and by connecting them to the central antenna of his hotel, thereby, and without more, carries out an act of communication to the public within the meaning of Article 391 of Directive 2001/29/EC".

[508] (C–479/04), judgment of the Court (Grand Chamber) of September 12, 2006 (reference for a preliminary ruling from the Østre Landsret (Denmark)), OJ C281, 18.11.2006, p.10–10; [2006] E.C.R. I–8089; see also Case Comment, "The ECJ has no Doubts Over Community Exhaustion" [2007] Ent. L.R. 70.

[509] (C–456/06) Judgment of April 17, 2008, reference for a preliminary ruling from the *Bundesgerichtshof* (Germany), *Peek & Cloppenburg KG v Cassina SpA* OJ C142, 7.6.2008, p.7–8; [2008] E.C.R. I–2731.

[510] The ECJ interpreted the Directive in the light of World Copyright Treaty 1996 art.6, which defines the right of distribution as the "right of authorizing the making available to the public of the original and copies of their works through sale or other transfer of ownership". This interpretation is somewhat at odds with the traditional interpretation of the distribution right under national laws, where it has normally referred to the right to offer to the public or to place in circulation the original work or copies thereof. See, for example, the UK right which means the issue to the public of copies of a work.

judgment on a reference for a preliminary ruling from the *Hogesteret* (Denmark) in the case of *Infopaq International A/S v Danske Dagblades Forening*.[511]

The case concerned the scope of various terms defined in art.5(1) of the Information Society Directive in relation to a technological process which consisted in scanning articles followed by conversion into text file, electronic processing of the reproduction, storage of part of that reproduction and printing it out. The court held:

1. An act occurring during a data capture process, which consists of storing an extract of a protected work comprising 11 words and printing out that extract, is such as to come within the concept of reproduction in part within the meaning of Article 2 of Directive 2001/29/EC ..., if the elements thus reproduced are the expression of the intellectual creation of their author; it is for the national court to make this determination;

2. The act of printing out an extract of 11 words, during a data capture process such as that at issue in the main proceedings, does not fulfil the condition of being transient in nature as required by Article 5(1) of Directive 2001/29 and, therefore, that process cannot be carried out without the consent of the relevant rightholders.

Subsequently, a further reference has been made from the same court in a case concerning the same parties for a preliminary ruling on various questions posed in the first reference to which the Court did not reply. This is mentioned in para.24–131, below.

24–125   *Case C–467/08.*[512]

On October 21, 2010, the Court handed down its decision in the case of *Padawan SL v Sociedad General de Autores y Editores de España (SGAE) et al.* The reference for a preliminary ruling concerns the interpretation of the concept of "fair compensation" in art.5(2)(b) of the Information Society Directive (2001/29/EC) paid to copyright holders in respect of the exception for private copying. The reference was made in the course of proceedings between Padawan and SGAE concerning the so-called "private copying levy" allegedly owed by Padawan in respect of CD-R, CD-RW, DVD-R and MP3 players marketed by it and posed five questions to the Court.

First, the Court decided that the concept of "fair compensation" is an autonomous concept of European Union law which must be interpreted uniformly in all the Member States where a private copying exception has been introduced, irrespective of the power conferred on them to determine, within the limits imposed by EU law and in particular by the directive, the form, detailed arrangements for financing and collection, and the level of that fair compensation. Second, it held that the "fair balance" between the persons concerned means that fair compensation must be calculated on the basis of the criterion of the harm caused to authors of protected works by the introduction of the private copying exception. It is consistent with the requirements of that "fair balance" to provide that persons who have digital reproduction equipment, devices and media and who, on that basis, in law or in fact, make that equipment available to private users or provide them with copying services are the persons liable to finance the fair compensation,

---

[511] (C–5/08) OJ C220/7 of September 12, 2009.

[512] Case C–467/08, *Padawan SL v Sociedad General de Autores y Editores de España (SGAE) and Intervening Parties*: *Entidad de Gestión de Derechos de los Productores Audiovisuales (EDEDA), Asociación de Artistas Intérpretes o Ejecutantes – Sociedad de Gestión de España (AIE), Asociación de Gestión de Derechos Intelectuales (AGEDI), Centro Español de Derechos Reprográficos (CEDRO)*, judgment of the CJEU (Third Chamber) of October 21, 2010 (as yet unreported) in reply to a reference for a preliminary ruling from the *Audiencia Provincial de Barcelona* (Spain) lodged on October 31, 2008 (OJ C19, 21.1.2009, p.12).

inasmuch as they are able to pass on to private users the actual burden of financing it. Third, in response to the third and fourth questions, the Court found that art.5(2)(b) of Directive 2001/29 must be interpreted as meaning that a link is necessary between the application of the levy intended to finance fair compensation with respect to digital reproduction equipment, devices and media and the deemed use of them for the purposes of private copying. It held that the fact that equipment or devices are able to make copies is sufficient in itself to justify the application of the private copying levy, provided that the equipment or devices have been made available to natural persons as private users. Nevertheless, the indiscriminate application of the private copying levy, in particular with respect to digital reproduction equipment, devices and media not made available to private users and clearly reserved for uses other than private copying, is incompatible with the Directive. In response to the last question, which asked whether the system adopted in Spain is compatible with the Directive, the Court held that it is for the national court to determine the answer to that question in the light of the answers provided to the first four questions.

Pending references to the Court of Justice

A number of referrals have been made to the Court of Justice for a preliminary ruling. These are reproduced below (see also para.24–70, above).   **24–126**

Case C–557/07.[513]   **24–127**

Questions referred (concerning the definition of intermediary):

(1) Is the term "intermediary" in Article 5(1)(a) and Article 8(3) of the Directive to be interpreted as including an access provider who merely provides a user with access to the network by allocating him a dynamic IP address but does not himself provide him with any services such as email, FTP or file-sharing services and does not exercise any control, either in law or in fact, over the services which the user makes use of?

(2) If the first question is answered in the affirmative: is Article 8(3) of Directive 2004/48/EC (the enforcement Directive),[514] having regard to Article 6 and Article 15 of Directive 2002/58/EC concerning the processing of personal data and the protection of privacy in the electronic communications sector, to be interpreted (restrictively) as not permitting the disclosure of personal traffic data to private third parties for the purpose of civil proceedings for alleged infringements of exclusive rights protected by copyright (rights of exploitation and use)?

C–387/09.[515]   **24–128**

Questions referred (concerning the interpretation of "fair compensation" for private copying):

1. Is the concept of "fair compensation" in Article 5(2)(b) of Directive 2001/29/EC (1) a new Community concept which must be interpreted in the same way in all the Member States of the European Community?

2. If the reply to the first question is in the affirmative:

2.1. If a national system of equitable remuneration for private copying existed before the entry into force of Directive 2001/29/EC, must the national provisions

---

[513] Case C–557/07. Reference for a preliminary ruling from the *Oberster Gerichtshof* (Austria) lodged on December 14, 2007— *LSG-Gesellschaft zur Wahrnehmung von Leistungsschutzrechten GmbH v Tele2 Telecommunication GmbH* OJ C113, 16.5.2009, p.14–14.

[514] [2004] OJ L157/45.

[515] *Entidad de Gestión de Derechos de los Productores Audiovisuales (EGEDA) v Magnatrading S.L*, reference from the *Juzgado Mercantil No 1 de Santa Cruz de Tenerife* OJ C312/19 of December 19, 2009.

be interpreted "in conformity" with the new concept of "fair compensation" for private copying following the entry into force of Directive 29/2001?

2.2. Must the scope of the private copying exception in Article 5(2)(b) of Directive 2001/29, and the criteria set out in recital 35 in the preamble to the directive, be taken into account in order to determine which devices are subject to the payment of fair compensation and the amount thereof?

If that is the case, would it be compatible with the Community concept of "fair compensation for private copying" (a) to establish a liability to pay that compensation in respect of devices intended for personal and professional use other than "private copying" and/or (b) to set a flat-rate payment which does not take account of whether the devices are used for the purposes of private copying and the harm which is liable to result from such use, thereby making situations where there is no harm or where the harm is negligible also subject to the payment of compensation? 2.3. Is a system which, by setting a private copying limit, establishes a general liability to pay fair compensation on a certain category of equipment or media (for example, recordable CD-R and DVD-R data computer disks), irrespective of whether they are purchased by natural persons for private use or by natural persons for professional use, in order to generate and store their own data or in compliance with legal obligations, or by legal persons who do not benefit from the private copying exception in any circumstances, compatible with Article 5(2)(b) of Directive 2001/29?

3. If the reply to the first question is in the negative:

3.1. Does that mean that Member States have complete freedom to lay down the criteria and mechanisms for determining which devices are subject to the payment of fair compensation for private copying and the amounts thereof, or are there certain limits on that freedom and, if so, what are they?

3.2. Does that mean that Member States are entitled to permit private third parties to collect compensation in respect of works which authors have assigned voluntarily and free of charge to a society by means of licences or are there certain limits on that right and, if so, what are they?

3.3. Does that mean that Member States are entitled to permit private third parties to collect compensation from users where such users lawfully comply with a provision which is public and binding or are there certain limits on that right and, if so, what are they?

24–129   *Case C–462/09.*[516]

Questions referred (liability to pay "fair compensation"):

1. Does Directive 2001/29/EC, (1) in particular Article 5(2)(b) and (5) thereof, provide any assistance in determining who should be regarded under national law as owing the 'fair compensation' referred to in Article 5(2)(b)? If so, what assistance does it provide?

2. In a case of distance selling in which the buyer is established in a different Member State to that of the seller, does Article 5(5) of Directive 2001/29/EC require national law to be interpreted so broadly that a person owing the 'fair compensation' referred to in Article 5(2)(b) of the directive who is acting on a commercial basis owes such compensation in at least one of the Member States involved in the distance selling?

---

[516] *Stichting de Thuiskopie v Mijndert van der Lee, Hananja van der Lee, Opus Supplies Deutschland GmbH*, referral from the Hoge Raad (Supreme Court) of the Netherlands. OJ C–24/38 of January 30, 2010.

C–283/10.[517]   **24–130**

Questions referred (concerning communication of musical works to the public and collective management):

Is Article 3(1) of Directive 2001/29/EC of the European Parliament and of the Council of 22 May 2001 to be interpreted to the effect that "communication to the public" means:

- exclusively communication to the public where the public is not present at the place where the communication originates, or
- also any other communication of a work which is carried out directly in a place open to the public using any means of public performance or direct presentation of the work?

In the event that point (a) represents the correct meaning, does that mean that the acts, referred to in point (b), by which works are communicated directly to the public do not fall within the scope of that directive or that they do not constitute communication of a work to the public, but rather the public performance of a work, within the meaning of Article 11(1)(i) of the Berne Convention?

In the event that point (b) represents the correct meaning, does Article 3(1) of the directive permit Member States to make statutory provision for the compulsory collective management of the right to communicate musical works to the public, irrespective of the means of communication used, even though that right can be and is managed individually by authors, no provision being made for authors to be able to exclude their works from collective management?

C–302/10.[518]   **24–131**

Questions referred (concerning a data-capture process for use in the drawing up of summaries of selected articles in daily newspapers and peridodicals and the interpretation of Article 5(1) of the Information Society Directive; cf. the decision in case C–5/08 of July 16, 2009, referred to in para.24–124, above):

1. Is the stage of the technological process at which temporary acts of reproduction take place relevant to whether they constitute "an integral and essential part of a technological process" (see Article 5(1) of the Infosoc Directive (1))?

2. Can temporary acts of reproduction be an "integral and essential part of a technological process" if they consist of manual scanning of entire newspaper articles whereby the latter are transformed from a printed medium into a digital medium?

3. Does "lawful use" (see Article 5(1) of the Infosoc Directive) include any form of use which does not require the copyright holder's consent?

4. Does "lawful use" (see Article 5(1) of the Infosoc Directive) include the scanning by a commercial business of entire newspaper articles and subsequent processing of the reproduction, for use in the business's summary writing, even where the rightholder has not given consent to those acts, if the other requirements in the provision are satisfied?

Is it relevant to the answer to the question whether the 11 words are stored after the data capture process is terminated?

5. What criteria should be used to assess whether temporary acts of reproduction have "independent economic significance" (see Article 5(1) of the Infosoc Directive) if the other requirements in the provision are satisfied?

---

[517] *Circ & Variete Globus Bucureşti v Uniunea Compozitorilor şi Muzicologilor din România—Asociaţia pentru Drepturi de Autor—U.C.M.R—A.D.A.* (C–283/10) referred by *Inalta curte de Casatie si Justitie* (Court of Cassation), Romania, lodged on June 7, 2010, OJ C234, 28.8.2010, p.25–25.

[518] *Infopaq International A/S v Danske Dagblades Forening* (C–302/10) reference for a preliminary ruling from the Hojesteret (Denmark) lodged on June 18, 2010 (see para.24–124, above, for a previous judgment of the Court on this case).

6. Can the user's efficiency gains from temporary acts of reproduction be taken into account in assessing whether the acts have independent economic significance (see Article 5(1) of the Infosoc Directive)?

7. Can the scanning by a commercial business of entire newspaper articles and the subsequent processing of the reproduction be regarded as constituting "certain special cases which do not conflict with a normal exploitation" of the newspaper articles and "not unreasonably [prejudicing] the legitimate interests of the right-holder" (see Article 5(5)), if the requirements in Article 5(1) of the directive are satisfied?

Is it relevant to the answer to the question whether the 11 words are stored after the data capture process is terminated?

24–132   *C–406/10.*[519]

Questions referred (on the interpretation of Article 2(a) of the Directive). Other questions in this case have also been referred as regards the interpretation of the Software Directive and are referred to above in para.24–57. The questions regarding the Information Society Directive are the following (retaining the numbering of the reference as a whole):

8. Where the Manual is protected by copyright as a literary work, is Article 2(a) to be interpreted as meaning that it is an infringement of the copyright in the Manual for the author of the Second Program to reproduce or substantially reproduce in the Second Program any of the following matters described in the Manual:

(a) the selection of statistical operations which have been implemented in the First Program;

(b) the mathematical formulae used in the Manual to describe those operations;

(c) the particular commands or combinations of commands by which those operations may be invoked;

(d) the options which the author of the First Program has provided in respect of various commands;

(e) the keywords and syntax recognised by the First Program;

(f) the defaults which the author of the First Program has chosen to implement in the event that a particular command or option is not specified by the user;

(g) the number of iterations which the First Program will perform in certain circumstances?

9. Is Article 2(a) to be interpreted as meaning that it is an infringement of the copyright in the Manual for the author of the Second Program to reproduce or substantially reproduce in a manual describing the Second Program the keywords and syntax recognised by the First Program?

24–133   *C–70/10.*[520]

Questions referred (concerning an injunction to stop Internet users sharing files):

Do Directives 2001/29 (Infosoc) and 2004/48 (Enforcement), in conjunction with Directives 95/46, 2000/31 (e-commerce) and 2002/58 (protection of privacy in the electronic communications sector), construed in particular in the light of Articles 8 and 10 of the European Convention on the Protection of Human Rights

---

[519] *SAS Institute Inc. v World Programming Limited*, reference from the High Court of Justice (Case 406/10) (Chancery Division) (Arnold, J.) [2010] EWHC 1829 (Ch).

[520] *Scarlet Extended v Société Belge des auteurs, compositeurs et éditeurs* (C–70/10) reference for a preliminary ruling from the *Cour d'Appel de Bruxelles* (Belgium) lodged on February 5, 2010, OJ C113, 1.5.2010, p.20–20.

and Fundamental Freedoms, permit Member States to authorise a national court before which substantive proceedings have been brought and on the basis merely of a statutory provision stating that: "They [the national courts] may also issue an injunction against intermediaries whose services are used by a third party to infringe a copyright or related right", to order an Internet Service Provider (ISP) to introduce, for all its customers, *in abstracto* and as a preventive measure, exclusively at the cost of that ISP and for an unlimited period, a system for filtering all electronic communications, both incoming and outgoing, passing via its services, in particular those involving the use of peer-to-peer software, in order to identify on its network the sharing of electronic files containing a musical, cinematographic or audio-visual work in respect of which the applicant claims to hold rights, and subsequently to block the transfer of such files, either at the point at which they are requested or at which they are sent?

2. If the answer to the question in paragraph 1 is in the affirmative, do those directives require a national court, called upon to give a ruling on an application for an injunction against an intermediary whose services are used by a third party to infringe a copyright, to apply the principle of proportionality when deciding on the effectiveness and dissuasive effect of the measure sought?

Note that in another case, C–360/10,[521] the same questions have been referred by the Belgian court in relation to the identification and blocking of electronic files containing musical, cinematographic or audio-visual works.

C–135/10 (concerning the direct applicability of the Rome Convention, the TRIPs Agreement and the WPPT). This case also concerns Directive 92/100/EEC (Rental Right, etc) (see questions (c) (d) and (e), above).[522]   **24–134**

(c) Do the concepts of "communication to the public" contained in the above-mentioned treaty-law texts mirror the Community concepts contained in Directives 92/100/EEC and 2001/29/EC and, if not, which source should take precedence?

(d) Does the broadcasting, free of charge, of phonograms within private dental practices engaged in professional economic activity, for the benefit of patients of those practices and enjoyed by them without any active choice on their part, constitute "communication to the public" or "making available to the public" for the purposes of the application of Article 3(2)(b) of Directive 2001/29/EC?

(e) Does such an act of transmission entitle the phonogram producers to the payment of remuneration?

C–145/10.[523]   **24–135**

Questions referred (concerning the interpretation of Article 5(3) (d) and (e) of the Directive):

1. Is Article 6(1) of Council Regulation (EC) No 44/2001 of 22 December 2000 on jurisdiction and the recognition and enforcement of judgments in civil and commercial matters to be interpreted as meaning that its application and therefore joint legal proceedings are not precluded where actions brought against several defendants for copyright infringements identical in substance are based on differing national legal grounds the essential elements of which are neverthe-

---

[521] *Belgische Vereniging van Auteurs, Componisten en Uitgevers (SABAM) v N.V. Netlog* (C–360/10) reference for a preliminary ruling lodged on January 28, 2010 by the *Rechtbank van Eerste Aanleg*, Brussels (Belgium), January 28, 2010.

[522] Case *SCF-Consorzio Fonografici v Marco del Corso*, reference for a preliminary ruling from the Corte di Appello di Torino (Italy) lodged on March 15, 2010, OJ C134/27.

[523] *Eva-Maria Painer v Standard Verlags GmbH, Axel Springer AG, Suddeutsche Zeitung GmbH, Spiegel-Verlag Rudolf Augstein GmbH & Co KG and verlag M. DuMont Schauberg Expedition der Kölnischen Zeitung GmbH & Co KG* (C–145/10) reference for a preliminary ruling by the *Handelsgericht*, Vienna (Austria), lodged on March 22, 2010, OJ C148, 5.6.2010, p.17–18.

less identical in substance—such as applies to all European States in proceedings for a prohibitory injunction, not based on fault, in claims for reasonable remuneration for copyright infringements and in claims in damages for unlawful exploitation?

2. (a) Is Article 5(3)(d) of Directive 2001/29/EC of the European Parliament and of the Council of 22 May 2001 on the harmonisation of certain aspects of copyright and related rights in the information society, in the light of Article 5(5) of that directive, to be interpreted as meaning that its application is not precluded where a press report quoting a work or other protected matter is not a literary work protected by copyright?

(b) Is Article 5(3)(d) of the directive, in the light of Article 5(5) thereof, to be interpreted as meaning that its application is not precluded where the name of the author or performer is not attached to the work or other protected matter quoted?

3. (a) Is Article 5(3)(e) of Directive 2001/29, in the light of Article 5(5) thereof, to be interpreted as meaning that in the interests of criminal justice in the context of public security its application requires a specific, current and express appeal for publication of the image on the part of the security authorities, i.e. that publication of the image must be officially ordered for search purposes, or otherwise an offence is committed?

(b) If the answer to question 3a should be in the negative: are the media permitted to rely on Article 5(3)(e) of the directive even if, without such a search request being made by the authorities, they should decide, of their own volition, whether images should be published "in the interests of public security"?

(c) If the answer to question 3b should be in the affirmative: is it then sufficient for the media to assert after the event that publication of an image served to trace a person or is it always necessary for there to be a specific appeal to readers to assist in a search in the investigation of an offence, which must be directly linked to the publication of the photograph?

4. Are Article 1(1) of Directive 2001/29 in conjunction with Article 5(5) thereof and Article 12 of the Berne Convention for the Protection of Literary and Artistic Works (Paris Act of 24 July 1971), as revised on 28 September 1979, particularly in the light of Article 1 of the First Additional Protocol to the European Convention for the Protection of Human Rights and Fundamental Freedoms (ECHR) of 20 March 1952 and Article 17 of the Charter of Fundamental Rights of the European Union, to be interpreted as meaning that photographic works and/or photographs, particularly portrait photos, are afforded "weaker" copyright protection or no copyright protection at all against adaptations because, in view of their "realistic image", the degree of formative freedom is too minor?

24–136　　*C–162/10.*[524]

Questions referred (concerning whether phonogram producers should receive payment from hotels playing TV/radio in guest bedrooms):

(i) Is a hotel operator which provides in guest bedrooms televisions and/or radios to which it distributes a broadcast signal a "user" making a "communication to the public" of a phonogram which may be played in a broadcast for the purposes of Article 8(2) of Codified Directive 2006/115/EC of the European Parliament and the Council of 12 December, 2006?

(ii) If the answer to paragraph (i) is in the affirmative, does Article 8(2) of Directive 2006/115/EC oblige Member States to provide a right to payment of

---

[524] *Phonographic Performance (Ireland) Ltd v Ireland* (C–162/10) reference for a preliminary ruling from the High Court of Ireland made on April 7, 2010, OJ C161, 19.6.2010, p.28–28.

equitable remuneration from the hotel operator in addition to equitable remuneration from the broadcaster for the playing of the phonogram?

(iii) If the answer to paragraph (i) is in the affirmative, does Article 10 of Directive 2006/115/EC permit Member States to exempt hotel operators from the obligation to pay "a single equitable remuneration" on the grounds of "private use" within the meaning of Article 10(1)(a)?

(iv) Is a hotel operator which provides in a guest bedroom apparatus (other than a television or radio) and phonograms in physical or digital form which may be played on or heard from such apparatus a "user" making a "communication to the public" of the phonograms within the meaning of Article 8(2) of Directive 2006/115/EC?

(v) If the answer to paragraph (iv) is in the affirmative, does Article 10 of Directive 2006/115/EC permit Member States to exempt hotel operators from the obligation to pay "a single equitable remuneration" on the grounds of "private use" within the meaning of Article 10(1)(a) of Directive 2006/115/EC?

Cases C–403/08,[525] *C–429/08*[526] *and C–228/10.*[527]   24–137

These cases are concerned with the import into the United Kingdom of decoder cards acquired overseas and which enable access to non-UK transmissions of Premier League and European Football Association's (UEFA) matches. The questions referred include questions on the interpretation of arts 2, 3, 5 and 6 of the Information Society Directive but it should be noted that in these cases questions have also been referred for a preliminary ruling on the interpretation of the following additional Directives and provisions of the TFEU: Directive 98/84/EC (conditional access); Directive 2006/115/EC (rental right, etc, as codified), Directive 93/83/EEC (Satellite and Cable); arts 34, 36 and 54 TFEU in the content of Directive 98/84/EC (conditional access) and of art.6 of Directive 2001/29/EC) and finally on the interpretation of the treaty rules on competition under art.101 TFEU. Since Case C–429/08 has been joined with Case C–403/08, only the questions referred in the latter case are reproduced here. The questions referred in C–403/08 and C–228/10 are in identical terms except insofar as each has submitted one or more additional questions. Where this is the case, it is noted below.

Case C–228/10 only: Article 6 Directive 2001/29/EC—Technological Measures.   24–138
Questions referred:

In circumstances where:

(i) copyright works are included in a satellite broadcast

(ii) the broadcast is transmitted in encrypted form

(iii) only for access to the satellite broadcaster's subscribers

(iv) subscribers are provided with a decoder card which allows them to access the broadcast

(a) Does encryption constitute "technological measures" within the meaning of Article 6(3) of Directive 2001/29/EC? If so, is it also "effective" within the meaning of Article 6(3) of Directive 2001/29/EC?

---

[525] *Football Association Premier League Ltd, NetMed Hellas SA, Multichoice Hellas SA v Q.C. Leisure, et al* (C–403/08) reference for a preliminary ruling from the High Court of Justice (Chancery Division) lodged on September 17, 2008 OJ C301, 22.11.2008, p.19–22. This case has been joined with Case C–429/08.

[526] *Karen Murphy v Media Protection Services Ltd* (C–429/08) reference for a preliminary ruling from the High Court of Justice, Queen's Bench Division (Administrative Court) lodged on September 29, 2008 OJ C301, 22.11.2008, p.26–28. This case has been joined with case C–403/08.

[527] *Union of European Football Associations (UEFA) and British Sky Broadcasting Limited v Euroview Sport Ltd* (C–228/10) reference from the High Court of Justice (Chancery Division) reference for a preliminary ruling from the High Court of Justice (Chancery Division) (United Kingdom) made on May 10, 2010, OJ C209, 31.7.2010, p.16–21.

(b) Does the use of a decoder card, which has been issued by the organisation making the satellite broadcast to a customer pursuant to a subscription agreement in a first Member State in order to obtain access in a second Member State to the broadcast and the copyright works included in the broadcast, amount to "circumvention" of such technological measures in circumstances where the broadcasting organisation does not consent to such use of the decoder card?

(c) Is a trader who imports decoder cards into the second Member State and advertises them for sale and use there to be regarded as importing or advertising devices, or providing services, which:—

(i) are promoted, advertised or marketed for the purpose of circumvention within Article 6(2)(a) of the Directive?

(ii) have only a limited commercially significant purpose or use other than to circumvent within Article 6(2)(b) of the Directive?

(iii) are primarily designed, produced, adapted or performed for the purpose of enabling or facilitating circumvention within Article 6(2)(c) of the Directive?

(d) Are the above circumstances excluded from the scope of Article 6 of Directive 2001/29/EC by reason of the fact that they are more specifically covered by Directive 98/84/EC?

24–139   *Cases C–403/08 and C–228/10.*

Q.4 Reproduction Right

Where sequential fragments of a film, broadcast, literary work, musical work or sound recording (in this case frames of digital video and audio) are created (i) within the memory of a decoder or (ii) in the case of a film, broadcast and literary work on a television screen and the whole work is reproduced if the sequential fragments are considered together but only a limited number of fragments exist at any point in time:

(a) Is the question of whether those works have been reproduced in whole or in part to be determined by the rule of national copyright law relating to what constitutes an infringing reproduction of a copyright work or is it a matter of interpretation of Article 2 of Directive 2001/29/EC?

(b) If it is a matter of interpretation of Article 2 of Directive 2001/29/EC, should the national court consider all of the fragments of each work as a whole or only the limited number of fragments which exist at any point in time? If the latter, what test should the national court apply to the question of whether the works have been reproduced in substantial part within the meaning of that Article?

(c) Does the reproduction right in Article 2 of Directive 2001/29/EC extend to the creation of transient images on a television screen?

Q.5 Independent Economic Significance

(a) Are transient copies of a work created within a satellite television decoder box or on a television screen linked to the decoder box whose sole purpose is to enable a use of the work not otherwise restricted by law to be regarded as having "independent economic significance" within the meaning of Article 5(1) of Directive 2001/29/EC by reason of the fact that such copies provide the only basis upon which the rights holder can extract remuneration for the use of his rights?

(b) Is the answer to Question 5(a) affected by (i) whether the transient copies have any inherent value or (ii) whether the transient copies comprise a small part of a collection of works and/or other subject matter which otherwise may be used without infringement of copyright or (iii) whether the exclusive licensee of the rights holder in another Member State has already received remuneration for use of the work in that Member State?

Q.6 Communication to public by wire or wireless means

(a) Is a copyright work communicated to the public by wire or wireless means within the meaning of Article 3 of Directive 2001/29/EC where a satellite broadcast is received at a commercial premises for example a bar and communicated or shown at those premises via a single television screen and speakers to members of the public present?

(b) Is the answer to Question 6(a) affected if:

(i) the members of the pubic present constitute a new public not contemplated by the broadcaster (in this case because a domestic decoder card for use in one Member State is used for a commercial audience in another Member State)?

(ii) The members of the public are not a paying audience according to national law?

C–403/08 only: (iii) the television broadcast signal is received by an aerial or satellite dish on the roof of or adjacent to the premises where the television is situated?

(c) If the answer to any part of (b) is Yes, what factors should be taken into account in determining whether there is a communication of the work which has originated from a place where members of the audience are not present.

Implementation in the United Kingdom. The Directive was implemented in the United Kingdom by the Copyright and Related Rights Regulations 2003, which came into force on October 31, 2003[528] and amended the 1988 Act substantially. These amendments are discussed in the relevant chapters of this work, in particular, in Chs 4, 7, 9, 12, 15, 22 and 23. **24–140**

Study on the implementation and effect of the Directive. In 2006, the European Commission commissioned a major study carried out by the Institute for Information Law at the University of Amsterdam in cooperation with the Queen Mary Intellectual Property Research Centre of the University of London which examined the implementation and effect of the Information Society Directive in Member States' laws in the light of the development of the digital market.[529] The study is in two parts: Pt I provides an early and tentative assessment of the Directive on the development of on-line business models; Pt II offers a comprehensive inventory of the actual implementation of the Directive in the 24 Member States covered. Part II also gives a summary of disparities and specific problems arising from the implementation of the Directive. **24–141**

The purpose of the study was to assist the Commission in evaluating whether the Directive remains the appropriate response to the continuing challenges faced by the stakeholders concerned, such as rights holders, commercial users, consumers, educational and scientific users.

Further report on the application of the Directive. The Commission published a staff working document reporting on the application of the Directive on November 30, 2007.[530] The report contains an assessment of how arts 5 (exceptions and limitations), 6 (obligations as to technical measures) and 8 (sanctions **24–142**

---

[528] M. Hart and S. Holmes, "Implementation of the Copyright Directive in the UK " [2004] E.I.P.R. 254.

[529] L. Guibault and G. Westkamp et al., "Study on the Implementation and Effect in Member States' Laws of Directive 2001/29/EC on the Harmonisation of Certain Aspects of Copyright and Related Rights in the Information Society", Institute for Information Law, University of Amsterdam, and Queen Mary Intellectual Property Research Institute, Centre for Commercial Law Studies, University of London, February 2007.

[530] Report to the Council, the European Parliament and the Economic and Social Committee on the application of Directive 2001/29/EC on the harmonisation of certain aspects of copyright and related rights in the information society (SEC(2007) 1556), November 30, 2007.

and remedies) of the Directive have been transposed by the Member States and applied by the national courts.[531]

24–143   **Green Paper "Copyright in the Knowledge Economy".** According to the Commission, this new Green Paper published in July 2008 is an attempt to structure the copyright debate as it relates to scientific publishing, the digital preservation of Europe's cultural heritage, orphan works, consumer access to protected works and the special needs of the disabled to participate in the information society. It focuses not only on the dissemination of knowledge for research, science and education but also on the current legal framework in the area of copyright and the possibilities it can currently offer to a variety of users (social institutions, museums, search engines, disabled people and teaching establishments).[532] Its purpose is to foster a debate on how knowledge for research, science and education can best be disseminated in an online environment. It deals principally with general issues regarding exceptions to exclusive rights introduced in the Information Society Directive but also addresses the exceptions and limitations permitted under the Database Directive.[533] It considers also specific issues related to the exceptions and limitations which are most relevant for the dissemination of knowledge and whether these exceptions should evolve in the era of digital dissemination.[534]

(ii) Other EU Initiatives Relevant to the Information Society.

24–144   Two further EU non-intellectual property initiatives associated with the information society are relevant in the context of copyright: The EC Directive on the legal protection of conditional access services[535] and the EC Directive on Electronic Commerce (the E-Commerce Directive).[536]

   The Conditional Access Directive aims to create a uniform legal environment for the protection of television and radio broadcasting and conditional access services, that is, services offered to the public where access is subject to payment of subscriptions, such as pay-television. It provides protection against illicit devices which enable or facilitate the circumvention of technological measures designed to protect legally provided services. Specifically prohibited are: the manufacture, import, distribution, sale, rental or possession for commercial purposes of illicit devices such as pirate decoders, their installation, maintenance or replacement for commercial purposes, and also the use of commercial services to promote such devices. Member States were given until May 28, 2000, to implement the Directive.[537]

   E-Commerce Directive. The second initiative is the E-Commerce Directive. which seeks to establish specific harmonised rules only where strictly necessary to ensure that businesses and citizens can supply and receive information society services throughout the European Union regardless of frontiers. These areas

---

[531] See also the Green Paper "Copyright in the Knowledge Economy", July 16, 2008, (COM(2008) 466/3) and para.24–141, above.

[532] Commission Press release IP/08/1156, July 16, 2008 and Green Paper "Copyright in the Knowledge Economy", July 16, 2008, (COM(2008) 466/3).

[533] See paras 24–94 et seq., above.

[534] Green Paper, fn.532, above, para.1.1.

[535] Directive 98/84/EC of the European Parliament and of the Council on the legal protection of services based on, or consisting of, conditional access (The Conditional Access Directive [1998] OJ L320/54 November 28, 1998). See Vol.2 H6.

[536] Directive 2000/31/EC of the European Parliament and of the Council of June 8, 2000, on certain legal aspects of information society services, in particular electronic commerce, in the Internal Market (the E-Commerce Directive [2001] OJ L178/1, July 17, 2000). See Vol.2 H7.

[537] Directive 98/84/EC art.6. For implementation in the United Kingdom, see above, para.16–04, above.

include definition of where operators are established, transparency obligations for operators, transparency requirements for commercial communications, conclusion and validity of electronic contracts, liability of internet intermediaries, online dispute settlement and the role of national authorities. Member States are required to provide for fast, efficient legal redress appropriate to the online environment and to ensure that sanctions for violations of the rules established under the Directive are effective, proportionate and dissuasive. Most importantly, the Directive lays down that information society services should be supervised at the source of the activity and that such services should therefore be subject to the law of the Member State in which the service provider is established, i.e. the country of origin principle applies. Member States were given until January 17, 2002, to implement the Directive.[538] In April 2003, the Commission issued a report on the Implementation of the Directive[539] as part of the Commission's comprehensive Internal Market strategy to remove barriers to services. The report stressed that enforcement at national level had to be consolidated and that joint efforts were required to fight piracy effectively. Issues that deserved further reflection included the need to create a balanced and coherent enforcement framework applicable to all kinds of piracy and counterfeiting and the distribution of keys and illicit devices via the internet.

In November 2003, the Commission published a first report on the application of the Directive.[540] The report concluded that the Internal Market objectives of the Directive had been met and that it had provided a sound legal framework for information society services in the Internal Market. It had also led to modernisation of existing national legislation, for example in contract law, to ensure the full validity of online transactions. The Commission concluded that revision of the Directive would be premature. Instead, it intended to focus on ensuring that the Directive is correctly applied and on collecting feedback from business and consumers alike. It proposed action to improve administrative co-operation between the Member States; to raise awareness amongst business and citizens of the European Union; to collect information from businesses and citizens on their experience of the Directive in practice and to strengthen international cooperation.

Meanwhile, the Commission has published a second report based on a 2007 study of the impact of the Directive.[541] It concludes that the efficiency of the Directive's implementation occasionally seems questionable, thus reducing the legal security of audiovisual service providers. It is proposed to establish a group of experts with the specific mandate to take action to bolster and facilitate administrative cooperation between Member States as well as between the Member States and the Commission.

In 2002, the Commission commenced proceedings in the Court of Justice against Spain and Greece for failure to notify implementing legislation.[542] On July 10, 2003, Advocate General Geelhoed expressed the opinion that Spain had failed properly to implement the Directive. As at April 24, 2003, the Commission remained unclear as to whether the Directive had been completely implemented in a compatible form in several other Member States. A report on the implementation of the Directive contains a detailed summary of developments in the field and sets out the action which the Commission intends to take to strengthen the ef-

---

[538] Directive 2000/31/EC art.22.
[539] COM(2003)198 final, of April 24, 2003; see also press release IP/03/583 of April 29, 2003.
[540] COM (2003) 702 final of November 21, 2003; see also press release IP/03/1580 of the same date.
[541] COM (2008) 593 final of September 30, 2008.
[542] Cases C–58/02 and C–219/02 respectively

fect of the Directive.[543] First, the Commission intends to make vigorous efforts to ensure that the Directive is fully implemented. Second, it intends to consult with Member States on the practical difficulties they have encountered when enforcing the Directive. Third, it intends to encourage industry and national authorities to work together to combat piracy. Fourth, it intends to continue to co-operate with other European countries and international organisations in order to enforce the coherent application of European rules against piracy. In this context, the Commission notes that the Commission's proposal for a Council Framework Decision on attacks against information systems,[544] if implemented in accordance with the Commission's intentions, would create a new offence of illegal access to information systems. This offence would be committed by any person who unlawfully accessed a conditional access service.[545] The Commission also intends to work towards the ratification of European Convention ETS No.178 on the legal protection of services based on, or consisting of, conditional access.[546] Finally, the Commission notes that much piracy in the field derives from the fact that providers often limit access to their services to subscribers in a particular Member State, thus preventing access to residents of other states even though they are willing to pay.[547] The Commission recommends that right-holders and service providers seek contractual solutions to this problem.[548]

Case Law of the Court of Justice

24–145   **Decided cases.** In the case *Productores de MÚsica de España (Promusicae) v Telefónica de España SAU*,[549] on a reference for a preliminary ruling from the *Juzgado de lo Mercantil* No. 5 of Madrid (Spain), the Court had occasion to rule on questions concerning the interpretation of the E-Commerce Directive, the Infosoc Directive, the Enforcement Directive and the Directive on privacy and electronic communications in January 2008.[550] The case concerned *Telefónica's* refusal to disclose to *Promusicae*, acting on behalf of its members who are owners of intellectual property rights, personal data relating to the use of the internet by means of connections provided by *Telefónica*. The Court held that the directives do not require the Member States to lay down, in a situation such as that in the main proceedings, an obligation to communicate personal data in order to ensure effective protection of copyright in the context of civil proceedings. However, Community law requires that, when transposing those directives, the Member States take care to rely on an interpretation of them which allows a fair balance to be struck between the various fundamental rights protected by the Community legal order. Further, when implementing the measures transposing those directives, the authorities and courts of the Member States must not only interpret their national law in a manner consistent with those directives but also make sure that they do not rely on an interpretation of them which would be in conflict with those fundamental rights or with the other general principles of Community law, such as the principle of proportionality.

---

[543] COM (2003) 198 final, paras 3.2 and 7.2.
[544] COM 2002 (173) final of April 19, 2002
[545] COM 2002 (173), para.5.4.
[546] COM 2002 (173), para.6.2.
[547] COM 2002 (173), para.4.4.
[548] COM 2002 (173), para.7.2.
[549] Case C–275/06, Judgment of January 29, 2008. Reference for a preliminary ruling from the Juzgado de lo Mercantil No. 5 of Madrid (Spain), *Productores de MÚsica de España (Promusicae) v Telefónica de España SAU* [2008] E.C.R. I–271; [2008] 2 C.M.L.R. 17.
[550] Directive 2002/58/EC of the European Parliament and the of the Council of July 12, 2002, concerning the processing of personal data and the protection of privacy in the electronic communications sector ([2002] OJ L201/37).

In another case, *LSG-Gesellschaft zur Wahrnehmung von Leistungshutzrechtten GmbH v Tele2 Telecommunication GmbH*,[551] in a case concerning the protection of the confidentiality of electronic communication, the Court held that when transposing the E-commerce Directive and the Information Society Directive into national law Member States must ensure that they allow a fair balance to be struck between the various fundamental rights involved. Moreover, they must not only interpret their national law in a manner consistent with the directives but also make sure that they do not rely on an interpretation of those directives which would conflict with those fundamental rights or with the other general principles of EU law, such as the principle of proportionality. In the same case, the court held that access providers which merely provide users with Internet access, without offering other services such as email, FTP or filesharing services or exercising any control, whether de iure or de facto, over the services which users make sue of, must be regarded as "intermediaries" within the meaning of art.8(3) of the Information Society Directive.

Pending references to the Court of Justice. In *Football Association Premier*   **24–146**
League Limited v QC Leisure (discussed at para.24–27, above), three questions on the interpretation of this directive were referred to the Court of Justice. The first of these questions concerned the interpretation of the term "illicit device". That term is defined within the directive as "any equipment or software designed or adapted to give access to a protected service in an intelligible form without the authorisation of the service provider". It was the claimant's case that satellite decoder cards that were sold by foreign broadcasters to enable access to their encrypted television channels but which were sold on the condition that they would only be used in that broadcaster's home territory became such illicit devices when they were used in the United Kingdom to access that broadcaster's television channels. Kitchin J., assisted by the *travaux préparatoires* of the Directive indicated that, in his opinion, the definition only applies to counterfeit or pirate cards because of the words "designed or adapted", but held that this was not acte clair. As a consequence, a question asking whether those foreign cards were illicit devices, and what the words "designed or adapted" meant was referred. The second question was concerned with who has a cause of action under Directive 98/84/EC. This asks a number of sub-questions. First, does a cause of action only accrue to parties that fall within the definition of "broadcaster" in the TV without Frontiers Directive 89/552/EEC? This question arose because the definition of "television broadcasting" in Directive 98/84/EC is made by reference to the definition of that term in art.1(a) of Directive 89/552/EEC. The Defendants argued that incorporating this definition by reference was not merely a convenient shorthand, incorporating the text of art.1(a) of Directive 89/552/EEC into 98/84/EC stripped of the context in which it appears in the earlier Directive, but instead that the meaning and scope of "television broadcasting", could only be properly understood by considering it in light of the whole of Directive 89/552/EEC. In particular, they argued, a Claimant must also fall within the definition of "broadcaster" that appears in its art.1(b). Kitchin J. indicated that, in his opinion, this was not the correct approach, but considered that the question should be referred.

The second sub-questions concerned where in the chain of communication the party claiming that their rights under Directive 98/84/EC had to lie. In this case, the main claimant provided an encrypted service that was accessed by the over-

---

[551] *LSG-Gesellschaft zur Wahrnehmung von Leistungshutzrechtten GmbH v Tele2 Telecommunication GmbH* (C–557/07), referred by the *Oberster Gerichtshof*, Austria, Judgment of February 19, 2009 [2009] E.C.R. I–1227.

seas broadcasters. Those broadcasters decrypted this first signal, added their own logos, commentary and adverts, then multiplexed that altered signal with their other channel offerings, re-encrypted that channel package with their choice of encryption technology (in each case different from that of the main claimant's encryption technology) and then broadcast it. The questions referred ask whether: (i) the use of devices that enable the decryption of the downstream provider's channel package are to be regarded as giving access to the first undertakings service, or (ii) whether that first undertaking has a right of action under the directive because its interests are affected by the access to the downstream provider's service. Kitchin J.'s preliminary view was that both these approaches were valid. There was no reason, he thought, why a downstream broadcaster could not act as a gate-keeper for numerous protected services, including his own service, and further would have found that the interests of the first undertaking were sufficiently affected to bring it within Directive 98/84/EC.

The third question concerned the meaning of "commercial purposes" and whether this applied only to dealings in the allegedly illicit devices, or whether it also applied to the use of such illicit devices in the course of a business. Kitchin J. indicated that, in his opinion, both types of activity fell within the definition of "commercial purposes". Meanwhile, similar questions have been referred in two further pending cases: *Karen Murphy v Media Protection Services Ltd*[552] in 2008 which has since been joined with the *Football Association Premier League v QC Leisure* case by the Court of Justice[553] and *Union of European Football Associations (UEFA) and British Sky Broadcasting Limited v Euroview Sport Ltd* in 2010.[554] The first two questions relating to the conditional access Directive referred in the UEFA case are identical to the questions referred in the *Football Premier League* case.

(iii) Directive on the enforcement of intellectual property rights (the Enforcement Directive).

24–147   The Directive was adopted on April 29, 2004,[555] having been first proposed by the Commission in January 2003.[556] Member States were given until April 29, 2006, to comply with the Directive.[557] As of October 15, 2008, all the Member States except Luxembourg[558] and Sweden[559] had implemented the Directive.

24–148   **Background.** The Commission had first signalled its intention to legislate on

---

[552] *Karen Murphy v Media Protection Services Ltd* (C–429/08) lodged on September 28 2008 on a reference for a preliminary ruling from the High Court of Justice (England and Wales), Queen's Bench Division (Administrative Court), OJ C301, 22.11.2008, pp.26–28.

[553] Order of the President of the Court in Case C–403/08 and Case C–429/08 dated December 3, 2008.

[554] *Union of European Football Associations (UEFA) and British Sky Broadcasting Limited v Euroview Sport Ltd* (C–228/10) lodged on May 10, 2010, on a reference from the High Court of Justice (England and Wales), Chancery Division, OJ C209, 31.7.2010, p.16–21.

[555] Directive 2004/48/EC of the European Parliament and of the Council of April 29, 2004, on the enforcement of intellectual property rights [2004] OJ L157 of April 30, 2004, as corrected in [2004] OJ L195/16 of June 2, 2004.

[556] COM(2003) 46 final of January 30, 2003, entitled "Proposal for a Directive of the European Parliament and of the Council on measures and procedures to ensure the enforcement of intellectual property rights". See C.H. Massa and A. Strowel, "The Scope of the Proposed IP Enforcement Directive: Torn between the Desire to Harmonise Remedies and the Need to Combat Piracy" [2004] E.I.P.R. 244.

[557] Directive 2004/48 art. 20.

[558] The CJEU in a judgment dated February 21, 2008, declared that Luxembourg had failed to fulfil its obligations under the Directive by failing to introduce the necessary legislation (C–328/07).

[559] The CJEU in a judgment dated May 15, 2008, declared that Sweden had failed to fulfil its obligations under the Directive by failing to introduce the necessary legislation (C–341/07). A similar judgment declaring Germany to have failed to comply with the Directive was issued on June 5, 2008. Germany notified its implementation of the Directive on July 11, 2008.

enforcement in the *Follow-up to the 1995 Green Paper*.[560] Thereafter, in October 1998, the Commission adopted a Green Paper on Combating Counterfeiting and Piracy in the Single Market.[561] It considered that these practices jeopardised the proper functioning of the Single Market, deflected trade and distorted competition, and were prejudicial to the development of all forms of creativity and to the growth and competitiveness of European industry. The aim of the *Green Paper* was to evaluate the economic impact of counterfeiting and piracy in the Single Market, to assess the effectiveness of legislation, in the field and to examine possible initiatives to improve the situation. Initiatives envisaged included: monitoring by the private sector, technical devices for safety and authentification, sanctions and other means of enforcing intellectual property rights, as well as improved administrative co-operation between the competent authorities. The publication of the *Green Paper* marked the start of a wide-ranging consultation of all the interested parties concerned, the Member States and the institutions of the European Union. A hearing of interested parties was held in March 1999 and a report on the responses to the *Green Paper* was published in June 1999.[562]

Follow-up to the Green Paper. As a result of the responses to the *Green Paper*, in November 2000 the Commission published a follow-up to the *Green Paper*,[563] announcing that counterfeiting and piracy were major problems in most economic and industrial sectors in the Single Market and that the European Community should take steps to strengthen and improve the fight against counterfeiting and piracy. It estimated that EU businesses which operate internationally were losing between €400 million and €800 million in the Single Market and €2,000 million in non-member countries. It concluded also that, in addition to its economic and social consequences, the phenomenon seemed to be increasingly linked to organised crime and was continuing to spread via the internet. The *Follow-up* contained an action plan, identifying actions that should be carried out as a matter of urgency, medium-term actions and other initiatives. In particular, it was proposed to introduce a Directive as a matter of urgency aimed at strengthening the means for enforcing intellectual property rights.

24–149

Medium-term actions planned included: the setting up of administrative co-operation mechanisms, particularly between the competent national authorities, but also between these authorities and the Commission; examination of the need to submit proposals to harmonise the maximum thresholds for criminal sanctions, extending Europol's powers to include combating counterfeiting and piracy, and improving access to information by establishing a structure permitting access—via an internet site, for example—to judgments of national courts.

Other proposed long-term initiatives aimed at making better use of existing information systems, strengthening co-operation and exchange of information between the private sector and public authorities and promoting European judicial co-operation. In regard to the latter, the Commission proposed to address the problem of counterfeiting and piracy enforcement in connection with work in progress on civil and criminal judicial co-operation.[564] Consideration was also to

---

[560] cf. 24–106, above.

[561] COM(98) 569 final of October 15, 1998.

[562] *Final Report on responses to the European Commission Green Paper on Counterfeiting and Piracy*, June 1999, by Amédée Turner QC and Christopher Jackson.

[563] Communication from the Commission to the Council, the European Parliament and the Economic and Social Committee, *Follow-up to the Green Paper on Combating Counterfeiting and Piracy in the Single Market*, COM(2000) 789 of November 17, 2000.

[564] *Follow-up to the Green Paper*, para.25; cf. COM(2000) 495, July 26, 2000.

be given to establishing a specialised intellectual property rights tribunal with jurisdiction over cases concerning the validity and infringement of such rights.[565]

24–150   **Objectives of the Directive.** As emphasised in its Preamble, the Directive seeks to create a level playing field for the enforcement of intellectual property rights in the EU Member States by eliminating existing disparities in national legislations and by ensuring a high, equivalent and homogeneous level of protection in the internal market.[566] It covers infringement of all intellectual property rights, including both copyright and industrial property rights, which have been the subject of harmonisation within the European Union. It aims to build on Member States' international obligations,[567] and notably on the TRIPs Agreement,[568] and concentrates on infringements carried out for commercial purposes or which cause significant harm to right-holders. In addition to helping to combat illegal practices, the Directive is designed to foster legitimate trade and the development of the information society. In proposing the Directive, the Commission suggested that ever-increasing harm was being done to business (lower investments, closure of SMEs), society (job losses, consumer safety, threat to creativity) and governments (loss of tax revenue) because of increasing counterfeiting and piracy. The Directive does not aim to establish harmonised rules for judicial co-operation, jurisdiction, the recognition and enforcement of decisions in civil and commercial matters, or deal with applicable law.[569]

24–151   **Terms of the Directive.** The Directive is without prejudice to the specific provisions on the enforcement of rights and on exceptions contained in existing Community legislation.[570] It is based on best practice in the legislation of the Member States and requires all Member States to provide for the measures, procedures and remedies necessary to ensure the enforcement of intellectual property rights; such measures shall be effective, proportionate and dissuasive.[571] The Directive provides, inter alia, for provisional and precautionary measures, including interlocutory injunctions intended to prevent any imminent infringement of rights[572]; for measures for preserving evidence giving powers to judicial authorities to order discovery of documents[573] as well as provisional measures to preserve evidence, and to order the seizure and delivery up of infringing goods and, in appropriate cases, the materials and implements used in the production and/or distribution of the goods and documents relating thereto; these measures may be taken, if necessary, without the other party having been heard[574]; and for powers to force offenders to pay damages appropriate to the actual prejudice suffered by the right-holders to compensate for lost income.[575]

The Directive follows a "TRIPs plus" approach (cf. paras 23–145 et seq., above). The TRIPs Agreement provides for minimum common standards on enforcement of rights to be applicable at international level and implemented in all the EU Member States. The Directive supplements TRIPs by the following: it establishes the right for collective rights-management bodies and professional defence bodies, such as trade associations, as well as right-holders and their

---

[565] *Follow-up to the Green Paper.* cf. also doc. COM(2000) 109 final, March 1, 2000.
[566] Enforcement Directive, recitals 7 and 10.
[567] Recital 6.
[568] Recitals 4 and 5.
[569] Recital 11.
[570] Enforcement Directive 2004/48 art.2 .
[571] art.3.
[572] art.9.
[573] art.6.
[574] art.7.
[575] art.11.

licensees directly, to initiate legal proceedings[576]; it provides for presumptions of authorship or ownership of rights for the benefiaries of copyright and related rights[577]; it gives judicial authorities the power to force those selling pirated or counterfeit goods to disclose information on where the goods come from, on quantities ordered, produced and delivered and on prices, as well as to identify people involved in production and distribution networks[578]; the publication of judgments for deterrent purposes; and corrective measures including the withdrawal at the offender's expense of goods found to be infringing from channels of commerce.[579]

The implementation of the Directive is to be kept under review. Member States are to report to the Commission on its implementation three years from its entry into force (May 20, 2006) on the basis of which the Commission is to assess the effectiveness of the measures taken and evaluate the need for amendments to the Directive.[580] On September 11, 2009, the Commission published a communication stating that it plans to complement the existing regulatory framework with non-legislative measures to make for more collaborative and focused enforcement across the Internal Market, in particular, by: supporting enforcement through an EU Counterfeiting and Piracy Observatory; fostering administrative cooperation throughout the Internal Market and facilitatingvoluntary arrangements between stakeholders.[581]

Case Law of the Court of Justice

To date there have been no decisions of the Court of Justice in relation to the Enforcement Directive. There has, however, been one reference to the Court for a preliminary ruling. **24–152**

C–406/09.[582]   **24–153**

Questions referred:

(1) Is the phrase "civil and commercial matters" in Article 1 of Regulation (EC) No 44/2001 on jurisdiction and the recognition and enforcement of judgments in civil and commercial matters to be interpreted in such a way that this regulation applies also to the recognition and enforcement of an order for payment of "Ordnungsgeld" (an administrative fine) pursuant to Paragraph 890 of the German Code of Civil Procedure (Zivilprozessordnung)?

(2) Is Article 14 of the Directive 2004/48 on the enforcement of intellectual property rights to be interpreted as applying also to enforcement proceedings relating to

(i) an order made in another Member State concerning an infringement of intellectual property rights;

(ii) an order made in another Member State imposing a penalty or fine for breach of an injunction against infringement of intellectual property rights;

(iii) costs determination orders made in another Member State on the basis of the orders referred to at (i) and (ii) above?

---

[576] art.4.

[577] art.5.

[578] art.8.

[579] art.10.

[580] art.18.

[581] Communication from the Commission to the Council, the European Parliament and the European Economic and Social Committee: "Enhancing the enforcement of intellectual property rights in the internal market COM(2009) 467 final.

[582] *Realchemie Nederland BV v Bayer CropScience AG* (C–406/09), referred by the *Hoge Raad* (Supreme Court) of the Netherlands and lodged on October 21, 2009, OJ C312 19.12.2009, p.25–26.

24–154 **Implementation of the Directive in the United Kingdom.** The Directive has
been implemented in the United Kingdom by means of The Intellectual Property
(Enforcement, etc.) Regulations 2006,[583] which entered into force on April 29,
2006. In addition, changes to the court rules to implement the Directive were
introduced by the 41st update to the Civil Procedure Rules, which came into
force on April 6, 2006.

**(iv) Other EU Initiatives Relevant to the Enforcement of Intellectual
Property Rights.**

24–155 **Council Regulation concerning customs action against goods suspected of
infringing certain intellectual property rights and the measures to be taken
against goods found to have infringed such rights.**[584] The Regulation enables
customs authorities, in cooperation with right holders to improve controls at
external borders. It simplifies the procedure for the lodging of applications for action with the customs authorities, in particular for small- and medium-sized
enterprises (SMEs), and for the destruction of fraudulent goods. The Regulation
lays down the conditions for customs action where goods are suspected of infringing intellectual property rights, and on the other hand the measures to be taken
against goods that have been found to infringe such rights.

24–156 **Commission Regulation laying down provisions for the implementation of
Council Regulation (EC) No 1383/2003** concerning customs action against
goods suspected of infringing certain intellectual property rights and the measures
to be taken against goods found to have infringed such rights.[585] This regulation
clarifies the provisions for the implementation of the above Council Regulation
concerning customs action. It defines the natural and legal persons who may represent the holder of a right or any other persons who may represent the holder of
a right or any other person authorised to use the right. It is also necessary to
specify the nature of the proof of ownership of intellectual property. The Regulation also lays down inter alia the procedures for the exchange of information between Member States and the Commission, so that it is possible for the Commission to monitor the effective application of the procedure and recognise patterns
of fraud, and for the Member States to introduce appropriate risk analysis. The
Regulation applied with effect from July 1, 2004.

In October 2005, a Communication from the Commission to the Council, the
European Parliament and the European Economic and Social Committee on a
customs response to latest trends in counterfeiting and piracy was published. The
Commission proposes a series of customs measures aimed at protecting the
European Union more effectively against counterfeiting and piracy. These
measures include improving legislation, strengthening partnership between
customs and business and increasing international cooperation. The measures in
question will be implemented by customs.[586]

24–157 **Proposal for a directive on criminal measures.** A further draft directive to harmonise national criminal measures aimed at ensuring the enforcement of intellectual property rights other than patents was put forward by the European Com-

---

[583] SI 2006/1028.

[584] (EC) No.1383/2003 of July 22, 2003 OJ L196/7 August 2, 2003. The Regulation was applied
with effect from July 1, 2004 and repealed Regulation (EC) No.3295/94 from that date. See references for a preliminary ruling in Cases C–132/07 of March 5, 2007 (*Beecham Group v Andacon
NV*) and C–93/08 of February 28, 2008 (*Schenker SIA v Valstsienemumu dienests*).

[585] (EC) No. 1891/2004, OJ L328 October 30, 2004 as amended by Commission Regulation (EC)
No. 1172/2007 of October 5, 2007.

[586] COM (2005) 479 final of October 11, 2005, not published in the OJ.

mission in April 2007. It took the view that a sufficiently dissuasive set of penalties applicable throughout the Community was needed to make the provisions laid down in the Enforcement Directive complete. The proposed new directive reflected the Commission's opinion that the Community legislature has the power to take the criminal law measures that are necessary where these are required for the effective implementation of Community law.[587] The draft directive was considered and adopted by the European Parliament on April 25 2007.[588] Since then the proposal has been pending in the Council and appears to have been shelved for the time being.

Instead, in September 2008, the Council adopted a Resolution on a comprehensive European anti-counterfeiting and anti-piracy plan dealing with the enforcement of all intellectual property rights, including patents. The Resolution invites the Commission to set up a European counterfeiting and piracy observatory to enable a regular assessment to be made of the extent of these problems, to disseminate information about them and to raise awareness of the dangers posed by them. It also invites the Commission and the Member States to use all appropriate means to combat counterfeiting and piracy effectively, and inter alia to submit an anti-counterfeiting customs plan for the years 2009 to 2012; and, finally, to step up the protection of intellectual property rights internationally.[589]

As proposed by the Resolution, the European Observatory on Counterfeiting and Piracy was set up by the Commission on April 2, 2009. The Observatory is coordinated by the Commission and brings together representatives from Member States administrations, private industry and consumer organisations to improve enforcement of intellectual property rights. The Observatory will serve as the central resource for gathering, monitoring and reporting information and data related to all intellectual property rights infringements. It will be a platform for representatives from national authorities and stakeholders to exchange ideas and expertise on best practices, to develop joint enforcement strategies and to make recommendations to policy makers.[590] In this connection, on October 11, 2009, the Commission issued a Communication "Enhancing the enforcement of intellectual property rights in the internal market".[591]

D. FORECAST FOR FUTURE COMMUNITY INITIATIVES

Outstanding issues. The Community legislative framework in the field of copyright and related rights remains under review by the Commission, which is continuing to evaluate the need for further legislation on a number of subjects. As   **24–158**

---

[587] This opinion is based on the judgment of the Court of Justice in Case C–176/03 (*Commission v Council*) which confirmed that the Commission has power to propose a harmonised approach to criminal sanctions if such measures are essential for the completion of the internal market.

[588] Proposal for a directive of the European Parliament and of the Council on criminal measures aimed at ensuring the enforcement of intellectual property rights (COM(2006)0168); see also European Parliament legislative resolution and position adopted on April 24, 2007, concerning the amended proposal for the directive. ECOSOC delivered its opinion on the draft on October 27, 2007.

[589] Council Resolution of September 24, 2008, on a comprehensive European anti-counterfeiting and anti-piracy plan [2008] OJ C243/01.

[590] See Speech of Charlie McGreevy, European Commissioner for Internal Market and Services, April 2, 2009 (SPEECH/09/169). For information about the Observatory, see markt-iprobservatory@ec.europa.eu.

[591] COM(2009) 467 final, October 11, 2009: "Enhancing the enforcement of intellectual property rights in the internal market", Communication from the Commission to the Council, the European Parliament and the European Economic and Social Committee. DG Trade has recently launched an EU IPR survey 2010 on IPR protection and enforcement in third countries in order to enable it to review its priorities in its strategy for the enforcement of IPRs.

mentioned above,[592] a number of other future Community initiatives in the field of copyright were forecast in the 1988 Green Paper and the Follow-up thereto published in 1990 as well as in the 1995 Green Paper on Copyright in the Information Society and its Follow-up. In the Follow-up to the 1988 Green Paper, the Commission announced that legislative action was to be taken on six issues by the end of 1991.[593] Although the Commission's timetable slipped somewhat, as seen in paras 24–48 et seq., above, action has been taken in the meantime on all of these issues.

The last outstanding issue, private copying, was tackled rather half-heartedly in the Information Society Directive (see paras 24–115 and 24–116, above) but no attempt has been made to date to harmonise existing national legislation providing for remuneration schemes for private copying. Since art.12 of the Information Society Directive calls for regular review of the application of the Directive in general and, in particular, of its provisions concerning exceptions in the light of the development of the digital market, further legislation on this subject cannot be excluded because 20 Member States have legislated at national level on the subject. For this reason, the history of Commission activities on this matter remains relevant and is summarised in para.24–159, below.[594]

As already noted,[595] the Commission, in the *Follow-up to the 1995 Green Paper*, discussed the desirability of harmonisation in some other areas and announced its intention of continuing to evaluate the need for Community legislation on the following issues: the introduction of exclusive rights for the benefit of holders of related rights (performers and producers) to control broadcasting; applicable law and law enforcement; the collective management of copyright and related rights and collecting societies; and moral rights.[596] On two of these issues, exclusive broadcasting rights and applicable law, no proposal for action has been published by the Commission to date. The exclusive broadcasting right was discussed at the International Conference on Intellectual Property Rights, "Creativity and Intellectual Property Rights: Evolving Scenarios and Perspectives", Vienna, July 12–14, 1998, where divergent views were expressed as to the need to update the current legal framework for the protection of works and other subject matter.[597] However, the Commission has been active in the other areas. The issue of law enforcement has been dealt with by the Enforcement Directive[598] as described in paras 24–147 et seq., above, and recent developments on the subject of the collective management of rights and moral rights are discussed below in paras 24–160 and 24–162 to 24–163, respectively.

24–159   **Private copying of sound and audiovisual recordings.** The issue of private copying[599] has proved one of the most difficult to resolve, and the Commission's position on the subject has shifted more than once. Because of the importance of

---

[592] See paras 24–47, 24–48 and 24–106 to 24–108, above.

[593] See para.24–48, above.

[594] See also Ch.13, above, for European Community Protection for Designs.

[595] See para.24–106, above.

[596] See *Follow-up to the Green Paper*, Chs 8.3, 8.4 and 8.5 and p.39.

[597] See records of the Conference published by the European Commission, DG Internal Market, conclusions of the first panel. On the subject of applicable law, see S. Plenter, "Choice of Law Rules for Copyright Infringements in the Global Information Infrastructure: A Never-ending Story?" [2001] E.I.P.R. 313.

[598] Enforcement Directive, see paras 24–147 et seq., above.

[599] Private copying (sometimes called home taping) is the non-commercial copying of sound and audiovisual recordings for personal domestic use; in other words, it is the act of recording, in the home, the music from a pre-recorded record or tape, the film from a pre-recorded video cassette tape or video disc, or a radio or television programme as broadcast. For an international comparative study of this practice, see G. Davies, and M. Hung, *Music and Video Private Copying: An International Survey of the Problem and the Law* (London: Sweet & Maxwell, 1993).

the topic, for both legal and economic reasons, the Commission's changing response to the issue is briefly discussed here.

In the 1988 Green Paper, the Commission pointed out that the topic of audiovisual private copying was ripe for discussion at the Community level for three principal reasons[600]:

(1) The industries most concerned claimed that private copying was causing them economic harm and had negative effects on right owners generally and sought greater protection.[601] These interests were opposed by interests favouring freedom for the public to engage in home copying, including manufacturers of blank tape and recording equipment and consumer organisations.[602]

(2) Measures had been introduced at the national level by some, but not all, Member States,[603] and by a number of trading partners among non-Member States[604] to compensate right owners, thus creating new divergencies in intellectual property law among Member States. That situation gave rise to concern that "the divergencies may have significant, negative effects on the functioning of the internal market".[605]

(3) "New technical developments are increasing the ease and attractiveness of home copying of audiovisual material: high-speed copying, improvements in the quality of home made copies, and now the arrival of digital audio tape (DAT) with its capacity for making perfect copies both rapidly and cheaply, have raised new questions as to how copyright laws should deal with the matter." The question also arose how to secure the investment in time, effort and money needed for the creation of audiovisual works if technical developments make it possible to produce perfect, rapid and cheap copies on machines accessible to almost anyone.[606]

In its conclusions, the Commission recognised that the practice of home copying might cause losses to right-holders to the extent that it could be a substitute for sales of pre-recorded material.[607] It concluded, however, that while royalty or "levy" schemes in existence should be retained where they already existed, if Member States considered such schemes the best way to remunerate right owners,[608] there was no need for action by the Commission at that time to make such schemes mandatory by harmonising existing schemes with respect to audio analogue products, taking the view that analogue products were becoming obsolete.[609] As regards video home taping, the Commission also considered that any initiative to generalise levy schemes would not be justified. It undertook to

---

[600] COM(88) 172 final, paras 3.1.3 to 3.1.6.

[601] The main argument put forward by right owners today is that the practice of private copying is a new and widespread method of exploitation of works with respect to which they should enjoy protection. Moreover, private copying combined with the perfect-quality reproduction made possible by digital technology, has given the problem a completely new dimension so that it is no longer equitable for the practice to be permitted as an exception to the reproduction right.

[602] These interests deny that any prejudice is caused to right owners by private copying. See, for example, publication of the Home Taping Rights Campaign Office, London, 1987; D.G. Jerrard, "The Case for Digital Audio Tape: an Opportunity, not a Problem" [1987] 10 E.I.P.R. 279.

[603] The following Member States have introduced private copying legislation providing for remuneration to be paid to right owners: Austria, Belgium, Denmark, Finland, France, Germany, Greece, Italy, the Netherlands, Portugal and Spain.

[604] See G. Davies and M. Hung, *Music and Video Private Copying: An International Survey of the Problem and the Law* (London: Sweet & Maxwell, 1993), Ch.7.

[605] *Green Paper*, para.3.1.5.

[606] para 3.1.6.

[607] para.3.12.1.

[608] para.3.12.3.

[609] para.3.10.22.

keep national legislation and technical developments under review to ensure that "appropriate action is taken if it becomes necessary".[610]

The Commission, however, did conclude that, with regard to digital audio tape, DAT, "Community measures to require a degree of technical protection would be desirable provided that they are technically feasible and properly balanced in respect of all the interests concerned".[611] Accordingly, the Commission invited comments on the desirability of technical solutions in general and, in particular, as regards digital audio recordings.[612]

The Commission also asked for the views of interested parties "as to whether it is accepted that levies should remain in those Member States which have introduced them, and could be introduced if Member States so wish in those countries which have not yet introduced them".[613]

Subsequently, the Commission continued to study the matter and to consult with interested parties. A hearing was held in December 1988,[614] and a further meeting with interested parties took place in November 1989. During those consultations, the Commission's conclusion that there was no need to harmonise legislation on remuneration for private copying was much criticised. In its 1990 document, *Follow-up to the Green Paper*, the Commission announced that, given the need to complete the internal market, it intended to lay a proposal for a Directive before the Council on private copying in 1991. It stated also that it was favourably disposed to the general use of a technical system, known as SCMS (the serial copying management system),[615] which limits the copying capabilities of consumer DAT recording equipment, saying:

"New technology is to be encouraged, but not where it would damage the interests of right-holders and consumers. The SCMS satisfies these requirements by allowing copies to be made while at the same time limiting the practice; the user thus has the full benefit of technical progress. It also allows right-holders to keep at least partial control of the exploitation of their works by preventing the making of the unlimited series of copies permitted by DAT technology."[616]

Thereafter, the Commission has continued to waver, continuing to consider the issue and to consult thereon. It submitted a working document to the Council in 1992, on which no consensus was reached, and a consultation paper was issued to interested parties in 1993.[617] Meanwhile, the Commission again addressed the issue in its 1995 Green Paper on the Information Society and the Follow-up thereto. There it indicated that it would legislate on private copying in the context

---

[610] para.3.12.4.

[611] para.3.10.5.

[612] para.3.13.1.

[613] para.3.13.2.

[614] Record of the hearing on Audio-Visual Home Copying, Brussels, December 12, 1988 (Document 11/D/5069/89).

[615] SCMS operates by codes embedded into the digital information received by a DAT recorder and circuitry controlling the functions of the recorder. Based on the nature of the codes, the DAT recorder either permits unrestricted copying, or permits copying while labelling the copy with codes to restrict further copying, or prevents copying altogether. The technical standards for DAT systems, the Digital Audio Interface Standard (IEC958) and the DAT Standard (IEC60A124), were modified in 1991 to incorporate the system. In May 1990, the Japanese Government introduced administrative measures to implement SCMS with regard to DAT recorders. In October 1992, America adopted the Audio Home Recording Act which makes the incorporation of a technical control mechanism to prevent unauthorised serial copying of protected works in digital recording equipment and interface devices obligatory. The legislation applies not only to SCMS but to any other future system with the same functional characteristics certified by the Secretary of Commerce. See also G. Davies and M. Hung, *Music and Video Private Copying: An International Survey of the Problem and the Law* (London: Sweet & Maxwell, 1993), ss.5.1.4.3. and 5.2.3.

[616] *Follow-up to the Green Paper*, para.3.4.

[617] *Consultation Paper on Private Copying*, Directorate General XV of the European Commission 1993, para.2.2.

of harmonising the exceptions permitted in Member States to the reproduction right and that it would be necessary to distinguish between "digital" and "analogue" private copying. Proposed action was that, with respect to certain acts of exploitation of copyright (in the digital environment), private copying would become a fully restricted act, in other situations (analogue) it would be permitted Community-wide, be it with or without remuneration.[618] However, as described above,[619] in the Information Society Directive, the Commission came down against legislating on the subject, leaving Member States free to maintain or introduce exceptions for private copying, with or without remuneration schemes.

In the meantime, the Commission has continued to seek solutions to the private copying problem. In October 2004, the Commission consulted Member States on the scope of the private copying exception and existing systems of remuneration. Replies from Member States were due in March 2006. The UK Government in reply stated inter alia that the private copying exceptions in UK law are so limited in their nature, scope and application that minimal prejudice to the right holder arises and no compensation is deemed necessary. Following the consultation, copyright levy reform was included in the Commission Work Program for 2006, with the aim of adopting a proposal for reform in the autumn of that year and in June 2006 the Commission launched a "Stakeholder Consultation on Copyright Levies in a Converging World", with the intention of consulting the public to ensure that any proposals for change were technically viable, practically workable and based on a "bottom-up" approach. These consultations did not result in any new proposals.

Subsequently, in February 2008, the Commission launched a fresh look at copyright levies with a new round of consultations "in order to deepen the Commission's understanding on the functioning of private copying levy schemes set up at national level". A questionnaire, together with a background document, was issued and all stakeholders were invited to submit views and comments under the following main headings: main characteristics of the private copying levy systems; economic, social and cultural dimension of private copying levies; cross-border trade and e-commerce issues; professional users of ICT equipment; grey market; consumer issues; double payment; alternative licensing; distribution issues. The consultation was followed by a public hearing on the subject in May 2008. No firm conclusions or proposals for action have yet been published.[620] Nevertheless, since 20 Member States apply levies which vary with respect to the media or equipment on which levies are imposed and the rates applied it would seem that the matter is ripe for EU intervention and in May 2010 the Monti Report, referred to in para.24–169, below, has recommended legislation on the subject.

In another context, that of cross-border E-commerce, the Commission has noted recently that practical solutions to the management of existing copyright levies is required to solve cross-border management of such levies. It points out that, at present, cross-border traders may end up paying and reporting copyright levies in several countries for the same goods. It is suggested, therefore, that the current system of reporting, paying and refunding the levies is an impediment to cross-border commerce.[621]

Collective Management of Copyright and Related Rights. To date the Com-   **24–160**

---

[618] *Follow-up to the Green Paper*, pp.11 and 12.

[619] See para.24–115, above.

[620] See Commission Press Release IP/08/238, Questionnaire Second call for comments entitled "Fair compensation for acts of private copying" and Background document with the same title dated February 14, 2008; "Public Hearing on Private Copying Levies", Brussels, May 27, 2008.

[621] COM(2009) 557 final, October 22, 2009, Communication from the Commission to the European

mission has not legislated on this subject; instead, in 2005, it issued a Recommendation limited to the question of collective cross-border management of copyright and related rights for legitimate online music services (see para.24–161, below). This was the result of years of inconclusive consultations but it has not stopped continuing discussions about the need for EU legislation on the subject, described briefly below.

As foreseen in the *Follow-up to the 1995 Green Paper on Copyright and Related Rights in the Information Society*, the issue of the management of rights continued to be addressed by the Commission. A study on certain aspects of collective management was carried out by a private consultant at the Commission's request and completed in early 2000.[622] The subject was also on the agenda of two Conferences organised by the Commission in 1998[623] and 2000[624] respectively. Subsequently, a public hearing on collective management of rights was held in November 2000.[625] These discussions showed broad support for the dominant position of collecting societies and general agreement on the essential place of collective management in the administration of rights but were inconclusive on the need for Community legislation.

In April 2004, the Commission brought the consultation process to an end with the publication of a communication entitled "The Management of Copyright and Related Rights in the Internal Market"[626] in which it argued in favour of the need for Community legislation in the field of collective management of rights, explaining that following the harmonisation brought about by the various Directives in the field of intellectual property, it was crucial to ensure a level playing field at EU level of rules and conditions for effective rights management in the internal market. The communication addressed issues such as EU-wide licensing, the need for the large-scale introduction of Digital Rights Management systems acceptable to all stakeholders, and the establishment and status of collecting societies. In relation to individual rights management, the Commission found that there was sufficient common ground in the Member States so that differences in national laws did not give rise to concern with respect to the functioning of the internal market and that immediate action at EU level was not called for. On the subject of the collective management of rights, by contrast, the Commission had concluded that the efficiency, transparency and accountability of collecting societies were crucial for the functioning of the Internal Market; thus, as regards the cross-border marketing of goods and provision of services based on copyright and related rights, legislative action was in its view required to harmonise those aspects of collective management which affect cross-border trade and which had been identified as impeding the full potential of the Internal Market. Surprisingly, however, following consultations with interested parties, the Commission decided not to legislate for the time being on this controversial subject, instead issuing the Recommendation already referred to.

---

parliament, the Council, the Economic and Social Committee: Cross-Border Business to Consumer e-Commerce in the EU.

[622] *"Étude sur la gestion collective des droits d'auteur dans l'Union Européenne"*, (Study on collective management of copyright in the European Union), (Deloitte and Touche, ITEC Group 2000).

[623] Vienna Conference on Creativity and Intellectual Property Rights: Evolving Scenarios and Perspectives, July 12–14, 1998 (Conclusions, Panel 5).

[624] Strasbourg Conference on Management and Legitimate Use of Intellectual Property, July 9–11, 2000 (Conclusions, Panel 3).

[625] Hearing on Collective Management, Brussels, November 13–14, 2000. Issues discussed in the context of the internal market included: rules relating to the establishment of collecting societies and freedom to provide services; appropriate exercise of collective management; supervision and settlement of disputes; new forms of collective licensing models and the need for a level playing field for collective management.

[626] Document COM (2004) 261 final of April 16, 2004, "Communication from the Commission to the Council, the European Parliament and the European Economic and Social Committee".

Commission recommendation on collective cross-border management of   **24–161**
copyright and related rights for legitimate online music services.[627] The recommendation puts forward measures for improving the EU-wide licensing of online rights in musical works. The aim of the Recommendation is to foster a
climate where EU-wide licences are more readily available for online music service providers.[628] The recommendation sets out to promote multi-territorial
licensing "in order to enhance greater legal certainty to commercial users in relation to their activity and to foster the development of legitimate online services,
increasing, in turn, the revenue for right holders".[629] Up to now, collecting societies have operated on a territorial basis, entering into reciprocal agreements with
collecting societies in other countries for mutual representation. Thus, users have
been able to obtain licences for European or worldwide repertoire from any
national collecting society. The Recommendation accepts this system and
proposes that cooperation between collecting societies allowing each society in
the European Union to grant an EU-wide licence covering the other societies'
repertoires should be improved. However, as an alternative, it provides that right
holders should have the choice of appointing a collective rights manager
anywhere in the European Union for the online use of their musical works across
the entire European Union ("EU-wide direct licensing"). The Commission is
seeking to promote collective management services which operate across national
borders. Thus, right holders would be able to freely choose the collective rights
manager or collecting society for the management of the rights necessary to operate legitimate online music services across the Community, irrespective of the
Member State of residence or the nationality of either the collective rights
manager or the rights holder.[630] For example, an Italian right holder seeking to
licence his repertoire for online music services would be encouraged to entrust
his rights to the UK Performing Rights Society (PRS), or another society within
the European Union, rather than to leave them with the Italian authors' society,
SGAE. The aim clearly is to encourage competition between collecting societies.

According to the Commission, the recommendation reflects its view as to how
the market should develop. In October 2005 it announced it would take tougher
action if insufficient progress was made.[631]

In the meantime, on January 17, 2007, the Commission announced its intention to assess the development of Europe's online music sector in the light of the
Recommendation. It therefore invited stakeholders to submit views and comments on their initial experience with the recommendation and, in general, on
their views on how the online music sector has developed since its adoption. In
this respect, the Commission identified several policy areas where views and
opinions by the market players appeared essential to it and posed a series of questions to interested parties relating to the nature of the instrument, EU-wide licensing issues, the scope of the recommendation and governance and transparency.[632]
The Commission received a large number of replies from a wide variety of
stakeholders, including collecting societies, publishers, users and eight Member
States. On February 7, 2008, it published a summary report of the results of the
monitoring process. The monitoring revealed that at that stage there was a nascent
market for EU-wide licensing of music for online services and that the recom-

---

[627] 2005/737/EC of May 18, 2005.
[628] For a more detailed discussion of the Commission's proposals and the Recommendation, see
paras 27–20 et seq., below.
[629] Recommendation, recital 8.
[630] Directive, recital 9.
[631] Announcement of Internal Market and Services Commissioner, Charlie McCreavy, IP/05/1261,
October 12, 2005.
[632] Call for comments, January 17, 2007.

mendation appeared to have had an impact on the licensing marketplace. The Commission announced it would follow further developments and repeat the monitoring, should a clear need to do so arise.[633]

24–162	**Proposed framework Directive on collective management**. Subsequently, in March 2007, the Legal Affairs Committee of the European Parliament (EP) adopted an own-initiative report which was critical of the recommendation. The EP regards the Commission's choice of a soft law instrument as inappropriate and called for it to consult publicly and thereafter present a proposal for a flexible framework directive designed to regulate the collective management of copyright and related rights in cross-border online music services.

Thus, the subject of collective management of rights in the digital online environment has continued to be the subject of discussion within the Commission, as will be seen from the accounts given below of recent Green Papers and other consultation documents issued by the Commission. A public hearing on the governance of collective rights management in the European Union was held in April 2010 and the Commission has announced that it will put forward a proposal for a framework Directive on collective rights management in the course of 2010.[634]

24–163	**Moral rights.** Moral rights is another subject which the Commission has been keeping under review and holding consultations about in order to determine whether or not there is a need for Community action on the subject.[635] In this connection it should be noted that in its judgment in the *Phil Collins* case as long ago as 1993 the Court of Justice defined the specific subject-matter of copyright and performers' rights, as follows:

"The specific subject-matter of those rights, as governed by national legislation, is to ensure the protection of the *moral* and economic rights of their holders. The protection of moral rights enables authors and performers, in particular, to object to any distortion, mutilation or other modification of a work which would be prejudicial to their honour or reputation". It went on to hold that "the exclusive rights conferred by literary and artistic property are by their nature such as to affect trade in goods and services and also competitive relationships within the Community. For that reason, and as the Court has consistently held, those rights, although governed by national legislation, are subject to the requirements of the Treaty and therefore fall within its scope of application" [emphasis added].[636]

Nonetheless, the Commission has not so far come up with any proposal for harmonisation of moral rights in view of its sensitive character and the fact that opinions on the subject vary widely.

The subject was discussed at the Vienna and Strasbourg Conferences held in 1998 and 2000, respectively, and referred to in the previous paragraph. In 1998, divergent views were expressed as regards further harmonisation at Community level and it was agreed to continue to study the matter. Meanwhile, a comparative study on the subject was supported by the Commission and published in April 2000.[637] The study concluded that Community wide harmonisation of moral rights is not necessary or desirable at present for a number of reasons. Firstly,

---

[633] Monitoring of the 2005 Music Online Recommendation, Brussels February 7, 2008.

[634] COM(2010) 245, "A Digital Agenda for Europe", p.9.

[635] See on this subject, G. Davies and K. Garnett, *Moral Rights* (London: Sweet and Maxwell, 2010), Chs 5 and 31B.

[636] Joined cases *Phil Collins v Imtrat Handelsgesellschaft mbH and Patricia Im-und Export Verhandlungsgesellschaft mbH* and *Leif Emanuel Kraul v EMI Electrola GmbH*, C–92/92 and C–326/92, judgment of the Court, October 20, 1993, paras 20 and 22.

[637] A. Strowel and M. Salokannel, with the assistance of E. Derclaye, "Moral rights in the context of

most interested parties are very cautious about any initiative to harmonise moral rights; this results from fears that any agreed text would be such a compromise that the level of protection of moral rights would be lower than is the case at present and could lead, for example, to waivable moral rights Community-wide. Secondly, there is a general perception among the interested parties that the present differences in national legislations on the subject of moral rights have no impact on the functioning of the internal market. Thirdly, governments do not appear to consider it necessary to harmonise moral rights. Instead, it was proposed that the European Community should promote collective agreements dealing with "good practices" in the field of moral rights, either at national or Community level.[638]

In 2004, the Commission confirmed its view that there is no apparent need to harmonise moral rights protection in the Community. It stated that, in its opinion, in practice, the international legal framework seemed to provide an adequate level playing field for the markets to operate, taking into account the protection for moral rights both in the analogue and digital environments.[639] Meanwhile, there has been no further action on the subject. In the long run, however, in the light of the Court of Justice's decision in the *Phil Collins* case, referred to above, harmonisation of moral rights cannot be put off indefinitely.[640]

Ongoing Review of the EU Legal Framework in the Field of Copyright and Related Rights. On July 19, 2004, the Commission published a staff working paper on the review of the EC legal framework in the field of copyright and related rights.[641] The objective of the review was twofold: first, to improve the operation of the *acquis communautaire* in the field of copyright and its coherence; and second to safeguard the good functioning of the internal market.   **24–164**

As regards the first objective, the paper assessed whether any inconsistencies in the definitions or on rules on exceptions and limitations between the different Directives hamper the operation of the *acquis communautaire* or have a harmful impact on the fair balance of rights and other interests, including those of users and consumers. The various Directives were reviewed and compared with the standard set by the Information Society Directive with a view to approximation but only minor adjustments were considered necessary. The Commission is committed to updating and simplifying the *acquis communautaire* as anounced in its Annual Policy Strategy for 2004 and in the Better Regulation Action Plan.[642] In this connection, the Commission announced in the paper that it was working on the objective of codifying the *acquis communautaire*. At the time it was working on the codification of the Software Directive, the Rental Right Directive and the Term Directive.[643] Meanwhile, all three directives have been repealed and

---

the exploitation of works through digital technology", Final Report, April 2000 (Study contract No. ETD/99/B5-3000/E 28).

[638] A. Strowel and M. Salokannel, with the assistance of E. Derclaye, "Moral rights in the context of the exploitation of works through digital technology", VI Conclusion, pp.225 et seq.

[639] Document SEC (2004) 995 of July 17, 2004, Commission Staff Working Paper on the review of the EC legal framework in the field of copyright and related rights, para.3.5.

[640] Note also that moral rights are treated by the EU as a trade and investment issue externally. EU Commission, *Report on United States Barriers to trade and Investment 2000* (Brussels, July 2000), para.6.1.

[641] Document SEC (2004) 995 of July 17, 2004, Commission Staff Working Paper on the review of the EC legal framework in the field of copyright and related rights, para.3.5.

[642] COM (2002) 278 final, of June 5, 2002.

[643] Detailed information and documentation on this subject is available on the EU Internal Market Intellectual Property website.

replaced by codified texts.[644] On December 12, 2005, the Commission published an evaluation of the protection EU law gives to databases.[645] The second objective was addressed by an analysis of whether the Community legislative framework in this area still contained shortcomings having a negative impact on the functioning of the internal market. It concluded that for the time being there was only a need to harmonise the criteria used to determine the beneficiaries of protection in the field of related rights (the so-called "points of attachment"). It considered that these criteria have an impact on the internal market and are also relevant to the adherance of the Community and its Member States to the WIPO Performances and Phonograms Treaty (WPPT).[646]

The Commission subsequently consulted on these issues and two major studies were commissioned and published: The first by the Institute for Information Law at the University of Amsterdam[647] examined the *acquis communautaire* with special focus on inconsistencies and lack of clarity, as well as a series of priority issues identified by the Commission as meriting special attention, including: the possible extension of the term of protection of phonograms; possible alignment of the term of protection of co-written musical works, the problems connected to multiple copyright ownership, including the issue of "orphan works", and copyright awareness among consumers. A second study carried out by the same institution in cooperation with the Queen Mary Intellectual Property Research Centre of the University of London examined the implementation and effect of the Information Society Directive in Member States' laws in the light of the development of the digital market[648] A focal point of the study is the development of online business models. Its purpose was to assist the Commission in evaluating whether the Directive remains the appropriate response to the continuing challenges faced by the stakeholders concerned, such as rights holders, commercial users, consumers, educational and scientific users.

24–165   **Green Paper on Copyright in the Knowledge Economy.** In July 2008, the Commission published a new Green Paper "Copyright in the Knowledge Economy".[649] The purpose of the Green Paper was to foster a debate on how knowledge for research, science and education can best be disseminated in the online environment and set out a number of issues connected with copyright in the "knowledge economy". These issues included exceptions to exclusive rights introduced in the Information Society Directive[650] and exceptions and limitations under the Database Directive,[651] as well as specific issues related to exceptions and limitations in the era of digital dissemination. It addressed these issues taking into account the perspectives of publishers, libraries, educational establishments, museums, archives, researchers, people with a disability and the public at large. The Green Paper was described as the basis of an ongoing consultation with

---

[644] Directive 2009/24/EC (Software), Directive 2006/115/EC (Rental Right Directive) and, Directive 2006/116/EC (Term Directive).

[645] DG Internal Market and Services Working paper, First Evaluation of Directive 96/9/EC on the legal protection of databases; see also para.24–94, above.

[646] Document SEC (2004) 995, para.3.4. In the meantime, no proposal for legislation on points of attachment has been published but the EU and its Member States have ratified the WCT and WPPT with effect from March 14, 2010.

[647] B. Hugenholtz, et al., "The Recasting of Copyright and Related Rights for the Knowledge Economy", November 2006.

[648] L. Guibault et al. and G. Westkamp, "Study on the Implementation and Effect in Member States' Laws of Directive 2001/29/EC on the Harmonisation of Certain Aspects of Copyright and Related Rights in the Information Society", Institute for Information Law, University of Amsterdam, and Queen Mary Intellectual Property Research Institute, Centre for Commercial Law Studies, University of London, February 2007.

[649] COM(2008) 466/3, July 16, 2008.

[650] See para.24–115, above.

[651] See para.24–94, above.

Member States and stakeholders on the issues, which the Commission planned as a structured debate on the long-term future of copyright policy as it relates inter alia to scientific publishing, the digital preservation of Europe's cultural heritage, orphan works, consumer access to protected works and the special needs for the disabled to participate in the information society.[652]

Subsequently, in October 2009, in response to the consultation, the Commission published a Communication[653] presenting its main findings with respect to the issues of digital preservation and dissemination of scholarly, cultural and educational material by libraries, the use of orphan works, access to knowledge for persons with disabilities, and user-created content. It also highlighted actions which the Commission intends to launch in order to find suitable solutions to the problems identified. Thus, the following further action was proposed: to consider whether the creation of a statutory exception covering digitisation and dissemination of copyright works by libraries is required; to consider possible solutions to the orphan works problem (including a legally binding standalone instrument on the clearance and mutual recognition of orphan works, a new exception to the 2001 Directive, or guidance on cross border mutual recognition of orphan works); to continue to monitor the evolution of an integrated European space for cross-border distance learning; and to encourage publishers to make more works in accessible formats available to disabled persons on the basis that TPM should not prevent the conversion of legally acquired works into accessible formats. No action was proposed on user-created works, but the Commission intends to further investigate the specific needs of non-professionals who rely on protected works to create their own works [sic].

A public hearing on orphan works was held shortly after the publication of the Communication and the Commission has since announced its intention to legislate on the subject.[654]

Latest Initiatives. Since then, the Commission has published a number of reports which touch on the future of copyright in Europe to a greater or lesser extent: a reflection document on creative content in a European Digital Single Market (October 2009)[655]; a new Green Paper on the future of the cultural and creative industries (April 2010); a report by former Commissioner Mario Monti on a new strategy for the single market (May 2010); and a Communication setting out a digital agenda for Europe (May 2010). The proposals relevant to copyright are briefly described below.   **24–166**

Creative Content in a European Digital Single Market, October 2009.[656] This document acknowledges that copyright is the basis for creativity and that it is a cornerstone of Europe's cultural heritage and recognises that the creative sectors contribute 2.6 per cent of the European Union's GDP as well as employing more than 3 per cent of the EU work force. However, the starting point of the paper is the objective of creating in the European Union a "modern, pro-competitive, and   **24–167**

---

[652] Press release IP/08/1156, July 16, 2008.

[653] Communication from the Commission, " Copyright in the Knowledge Economy", October 19, 2009. Press release IP/09/1544.

[654] See paras 24–170 and 24–171, below.

[655] "Creative Content in a European Single Market: Challenges for the Future", A Reflection Document of DG INFSO and DG MARKT, October 22, 2009; Green Paper "Unlocking the potential of cultural and creative industries" (Brussels, COM(2010) 183); "A new strategy for the single market: at the service of Europe's economy and society", Report to the President of the European Commission by Mario Monti, May 9, 2010; "A Digital Agenda for Europe", Communication from the Commission to the European Parliament, the Council, the European Economic and Social Committee and the Committee of the Regions (Brussels, COM(2010) 245), May 19, 2010.

[656] "Creative Content in a European Digital Single Market: Challenges for the Future", a reflection document of DG INFSO and DG Markt, October 2009.

consumer friendly legal framework" for what it describes as a "genuine single market for creative content online".[657] It suggests that new online services require a more dynamic and flexible framework in which they can legally offer "diverse, attractive and affordable content to consumers" and states that "consumer confusion and frustration is compounded by the fact that business models, statutory rules and contractual relations between the parties differ fundamentally between content sectors and across the 27 EU Member States...". While recognising that copyright law is territorial and subject to the national legal order of the Member States, it regards territorial licensing of music as an obstacle, blocking access by commercial users, and appears to regret that the principle of exhaustion only applies to tangible goods sold in the EEA and not to performance rights.[658] The paper puts forward a number of possible EU actions to facilitate a single market for creative content online: extending collective licensing to embrace "orphan works" and out-of-print works; further harmonisation of limitations and exceptions; and more rapid development of cross-border internet services by means of the creation of a streamlined pan-European and/or multi-territory licensing process, by means in the case of music of single licensing of rights in a "one-stop-shop". Options suggested include online databases providing freely accessible ownership and licence information on world repertoire; extending the 1993 Satellite and Cable Directive to online delivery of audiovisual content with a view to making possible licences covering the entire European Union. A more radical solution attributed to stakeholders which it is suggested would "create a more coherent licensing framework at European level" would be to establish a "European Copyright Law" by means of an EU Regulation with EU-wide effect, creating a single market for copyright and related rights and streamlining rights management across the Single Market.[659]

24–168   **Green Paper on Unlocking the potential of cultural and creative industries (CCIs), April 2010.**[660] Issued half a year later, the Commission's Green Paper is less concerned with consumer access and creating a Single Market for the licensing of works protected by copyright and related rights in the European Union than with unlocking the potential of the cultural and creative industries (CCIs being a dynamic and highly innovative sector with great economic potential). It recognises that to remain competitive in the new digital economy and changing global environment, it is necessary to put in place the right conditions for creativity and innovation to flourish.[661] The Commission will therefore work:

"to create a true single market for online content and services (i.e. borderless and safe EU web services and digital content markets,with high levels of trust and confidence, a balanced regulatory framework governing the management of intellectual property rights, measures to facilitate cross-border online content services, the fostering of multi-territorial licences, adequate protection and remuneration for rights holders and active support for the digitisation of Europe's rich cultural heritage).

The focus of the Commission's strategy on intellectual property:

"is clearly on the use and management of rights, looking for a balance between

---

[657] "Creative Content", para.1.
[658] "Creative Content", para.4.2.
[659] "Creative Content", para.5.
[660] COM(2010) 183, Green paper entitled "Unlocking the potential of cultural and creative industries", Brussels, April 27, 2010.
[661] COM(2010) 183, pp.1 to 3.

the necessary protection and sustainability of creation and the need to foster the development of new services and business modesl".[662]

The Commission intends to propose measures following the results of the consultation on the Green Paper by 2012.[663]

The Monti Report, May 2010. The Monti report was prepared at the request of **24–169** the President of the European Commission, J.M. Barroso, who with a view to relaunching the single market asked Mr Monti for a fresh look at how the market and the social dimensions of an integrated European economy can be mutually strengthened. Chapter 2.3 entitled "Shaping Europe's digital single market" is relevant here. Mr Monti calculates that the lack of such a market costs the European Union a potential gain of 4 per cent of GDP thus providing huge opportunities for EU Cultural and Creative Industries (CCIs). Among the goals of an EU digital market are the following: a seamless regulatory space for telecommunications services and infrastructures and a Pan-European online E-commerce retail market. To achieve these goals a single market for online digital content is required as:

> "European markets for online digital content are still underdeveloped as the complexity and lack of transparency of the copyright regime creates an unfavourable business environment. It is urgent to simplify copyright clearance and management by facilitating pan-European content licensing, by developing EU-wide copyright rules, including a framework for digital rights management".[664]

The report suggests that licensing and copyright levies on blank media and equipment need to be addressed and that a clear and predictable EU framework for orphan works is required.

A key recommendation of the report is the creation of an EU copyright title, by means of an EU copyright law, including an EU framework for copyright clearance and management. A legal framework for EU-wide online broadcasting is also proposed.[665] Thus, the idea of an EU-wide copyright code first mooted in the 'Creative Content' document referred to above appears to be gathering force.[666]

A Digital Agenda for Europe, May 2010. The various reports and consultation **24–170** documents referred to above have been followed up by a communication from the Commission published in May 2010.[667] It states that "[T]he overall aim of the digital agenda is to deliver sustainable economic and social benefits from a digital single market based on fast and ultra fast internet and interoperable applications". The Europe 2020 Strategy has been launched to prepare the EU economy for the challenges of the next decade and the digital agenda for Europe is one of seven flagship initiatives of that Strategy.[668] Seven obstacles to a digital single market are identified: fragmented digital markets (there is a patchwork of national online markets); lack of interoperability; rising cybercrime and risk of low trust in networks; lack of investment; insufficient research and innovation efforts; lack of

---

[662] COM(2010) 183, p.8.

[663] COM (2010) 245 (A Digital Agenda for Europe), p.31.

[664] Monti Report, p.45.

[665] Monti Report, p.46.

[666] See also the *European Copyright Code* developed by the "Wittem Project" established in 2002 as a collaboration between copyright scholars in the EU concerned with the development of EU copyright law. For more information, see *http://www.copyrightcode.eu* [Accessed October 27, 2010].

[667] COM(2010) 245, Brussels, May 19, 2010, "A Digital Agenda for Europe", Communication from the Commission to the European Parliament, the Council, the Economic and Social Committee and the Committee of the Regions.

[668] COM(2010) 245, p.1.

digital literacy and skills and missed opportunities in addressing societal challenges.[669] The fragmentation of digital markets is the area where copyright and related rights are affected.

The Commission proposes to simplify copyright clearance, management and cross-border licensing by:

1. Enhancing the governance, transparency and pan European licensing for (online) rights management by proposing a framework Directive on collective rights management by 2010.

2. Creating a legal framework to facilitate the digitisation and dissemination of cultural works in Europe by proposing a Directive on orphan works by 2010.[670]

Other actions proposed include: issuing a Green Paper addressing the opportunities and challenges of online distribution of audiovisual works and other creative content in the course of 2010; issuing a report by 2012 on the need for measures beyond collective rights management allowing EU citizens, online content services providers and right holders to benefit from the full potential of the digital internal market, including measures to promote cross-border and pan-European licences, without excluding or favouring any particular option; following a review of the Directive on the enforcement of intellectual property rights, reporting by 2012 on the need for additional measures to reinforce the protection against persistent violations of intellectual property rights in the online environment.[671]

The document also states that in the area of digital services and intellectual property technological progress will need to be further reflected in international trade agreements. It proposes therefore to work with third countries to improve international trade conditions for digital goods and services, including with regard to intellectual property rights.[672]

24–171   It is to be expected, therefore, that new proposals for legislation on collective licensing and orphan works will be put forward by the Commission in the course of 2010.

E. EXTERNAL RELATIONS OF THE EUROPEAN UNION

24–172   The 1995 Follow-up document also drew attention to the international dimension of the information society and the corresponding need for a truly international level playing field as regards the protection of copyright and related rights. For some years now, the European Union, represented by the Commission, has played an active role in multilateral external relations in this field, for example, in the negotiations leading to the adoption of the TRIPs Agreement in the context of the Uruguay Round of GATT, and now in the Doha Round of negotiations under the auspices of the WTO. The European Union also claims competence to represent the views of the Member States, through the Commission, so far as it concerns matters upon which the European Union has legislated, in inter-governmental meetings on the subject of copyright and related rights convened by the World Intellectual Property Organisation (WIPO), which administers the Berne and Rome Conventions.[673] Thus, the Commission played an active role in the negoti-

---

[669] COM(2010) 245, pp.5 and 6.
[670] COM(2010) 245, p.9.
[671] COM(2010) 245, p.10.
[672] COM(2010) 245, p.34.
[673] The administration of the Rome Convention is tripartite and shared between WIPO, the

ations which led to the adoption of the WCT and WPPT under the auspices of WIPO in December 1997.[674]

In the meantime, a Council Decision was adopted in March 2000 on the approval, on behalf of the European Community, of the WIPO Copyright Treaty and the WIPO Performances and Phonograms Treaty.[675] The decision gave the President of the Council the authority to deposit the instruments of conclusion with the Director General of WIPO as from the date by which the Member States were to bring into force the Information Society Directive, referred to above.[676]

In so far as intellectual property matters upon which the European Union has legislated are concerned, the Commission claims competence to represent the Member States at the inter-governmental level.[677] Thus, the Commission has continued to represent the Member States in inter-governmental meetings on the subject of copyright and related rights and has actively participated, inter alia, in the negotiations concerning the draft WIPO Treaty on the Protection of Audiovisual Performances and the draft WIPO Treaty on the Protection of the Rights of Broadcasting Organisations.[678]

Furthermore, as a result of the establishment of the European Economic Area, which entered into force on January 1, 1994, embracing the European Community and its then Member States on the one hand; and Austria, Finland, Iceland, Norway and Sweden and, under the conditions laid down in art.1(2) of the Protocol Adjusting the Agreement on the European Economic Area, Liechtenstein[679] on the other, the EEA States undertook to accept the relevant *acquis communautaire*, that is, the general principles of the European Union Treaties and other legislation, including the existing and future directives on copyright and related rights, as interpreted by the Court of Justice of the European Union.[680]

Community competence with respect to the TRIPs Agreement. The Court of Justice has had occasion to consider the question of the competence of the European Union and the jurisdiction of the court in respect of TRIPs, as well as the question whether TRIPs has direct effect in the Member States. In 1994, the court delivered an Opinion, holding that the EU and the Member States shared competence to conclude the TRIPs Agreement, except with respect to its provisions on the release into free circulation of counterfeit goods.[681] In *Hermès International v FHT Marketing Choice BV*,[682] the jurisdiction of the court to interpret TRIPs was questioned by a group of Member States on the ground that, as the European Union had still not adopted any harmonising measures in the area in question (TRIPs art.50, which deals with provisional measures against intellectual property infringement), that provision of the TRIPs Agreement did

24–173

International Labour Organisation (ILO) and the United Nations Educational, Scientific and Cultural Organisation, (UNESCO).

[674] See paras 23–66 et seq. and 23–119 et seq., above.

[675] Council Decision 2000/278/EC of April 11, 2000 ([2000] OJ L89/6).

[676] Council Decision 2000/278, art.2, and see para.24–106, above.

[677] K.H. Pilny and B.R. Eagle, "The Significance of Intellectual Property at the Community Level *vis-à-vis* Non-EU Trading Nations" [1998] E.I.P.R. 4.

[678] See paras 23–135 and 23–175, above, respectively.

[679] In relation to the EEA Agreement, these countries are referred to as the "EFTA States". At present, following the accession of Austria, Finland and Sweden to the EU, the following EFTA States are parties to the Agreement: Iceland, Liechtenstein and Norway. Switzerland, which is a Member State of the European Free Trade Association (EFTA), is not a Contracting State to the EEA Agreement and is not in a position to become a party to it, following the negative outcome of a referendum on the subject, which took place on December 6, 1992. For details of the various EC Directives adopted and implemented by the EFTA States, see the Directive Implementation Table, para.24–175, below.

[680] See *Follow-up to the Green Paper*, Ch.7.5.

[681] Opinion 1/94 of November 15, 1994 [1994] E.C.R. I–5267

[682] *Hermès International v FHT Marketing Choice BV* (C–53/96) [1998] E.C.R. I–3603

not fall within the scope of application of EU law. The court held that it did have jurisdiction on two grounds: first, the European Union had concluded and the Member States had ratified the WTO without distinction as to competence vis-à-vis other contracting parties. Second, since the European Union is a party to the TRIPs Agreement and since that agreement applies to the EU trade mark (and national trade marks), the courts when called upon to apply national rules with a view to ordering provisional measures for the protection of rights arising under a trade mark, are required to do so, as far as possible, in the light of the wording and purpose of art.50 of the TRIPs Agreement. Jurisdiction was based, therefore, to some extent, on the internal harmonisation of trade mark law.

In joined cases *Parfums Christian Dior SA and Assco Geruste GmbH*,[683] the court held that its jurisdiction to interpret art.50 of TRIPs is not restricted solely to situations covered by trade mark law but extends to intellectual property rights falling within the scope of the TRIPs Agreement; the judicial bodies of the Member States and the European Union are obliged for practical and legal reasons to give the TRIPs Agreement a uniform interpretation.

On the question of the direct effect of TRIPs, the court held that the provisions of TRIPs, an annex to the WTO Agreement, are not such as to create rights upon which individuals may rely directly before the courts of the Member States by virtue of EU law. The court then drew a distinction between fields to which TRIPs applies in respect of which there is EU legislation and areas where there is none. In the first case, the judicial authorities of both the Member States and the European Union must apply national rules as far as possible in conformity with the relevant provisions of TRIPs. Where the European Union has not legislated, competence for the protection of intellectual property remains with the Member States and does not fall within the scope of EU law. In this latter case, EU law neither requires nor forbids that the legal order of a Member State should accord to individuals the right to rely directly on a rule laid down by TRIPs or that it should oblige the courts to apply that rule of its own motion.[684] In the case *Léon Van Parys NV v Belgisch Interventie- en Restitutiebureau*, the Court of Justice once again considered whether the WTO agreements, including the TRIPs Agreement, give EU nationals a right to rely on those agreements in legal proceedings challenging the validity of EU legislation.[685] It pointed out that the WTO agreements are not in principle among the rules which the Court must take into account when reviewing the legality of measures adopted by the EU institutions. It is only where the European Union has intended to implement a particular obligation assumed in the context of the WTO, or where the EU measure refers expressly to particular provisions of the WTO agreements, that it is for the Court to review the legality of a EU measure in light of the WTO rules. Finding that these conditions were not met in this case, the Court went on to hold that a legal person cannot plead before a national court the incompatibility of EU legislation with certain rules of the WTO. That principle is not affected by the fact that the Dispute Settlement Body of the WTO has declared there to be such incompatibil-

---

[683] *Parfums Christian Dior SA v TUK Consultancy BV* and *Assco Gerüste GmbH and Rob van Dijk v Wilhelm Layher GmbH & Co KG and Layher BV* (Joined Cases C–300/98 and C–392/98) [2000] E.C.R. I–11307; [2001] E.C.D.R. 159.

[684] *Parfums Christian Dior SA v TUK Consultancy BV* and *Assco Gerüste GmbH and Rob van Dijk v Wilhelm Layher GmbH & Co KG and Layher BV* (Joined Cases C–300/98 and C–392/98) [2000] E.C.R. I–11307; [2001] ECD.R. 159, para.49.

[685] *Léon van Parys NV v Belgisch Interventie-en Restitutiebureau (BIRB)*, Case C–377/02, Judgment of March 1, 2005 [2005]E.C.R.I–1465.

ity, given the Commission's discretion to remedy the situation, for example, by means of a negotiated settlement.[686]

In its bilateral relations, the European Union has also been active in the field of copyright and related rights. For example, in the trade and co-operation agreements concluded in 1989 and 1990 between the European Union and most of the countries of central and eastern Europe, the question of intellectual, industrial and commercial property was given particular attention, especially because of its implications for direct investment in those countries by EU businesses and for the transfer of technology.[687] In its accession negotiations with candidate countries, including the 10 new Member States, the European Union has treated the internal market as an important area for the accession process and insisted on full implementation of the *acquis communautaire* Directives over the whole field of intellectual property by the candidate countries.

The relationship between EU law and the TRIPs Agreement was considered by the then Court of First Instance in the case of *Microsoft Corporation v Commission* in its judgment of September 2007.[688] In this case, Microsoft had criticised the Commission for having interpreted art.102 TFEU (ex art.82) in a way that it considered inconsistent with art.13 of the TRIPs Agreement, which confines limitations or exceptions to exclusive rights to certain special cases which do not conflict with a normal exploitation of the work and do not unreasonably prejudice the legitimate interests of the right holder.[689] The CFI recognised the principle laid down by the Court of Justice, according to which international agreements concluded by the European Union take primacy over provisions of secondary EU legislation, which means that such provisions must, so far as is possible, be interpreted in a manner which is consistent with those agreements, but held that the principle applies only where the international agreement at issue prevails over the provision of EU law concerned.[690] It held that the TRIPs Agreement does not prevail over primary EU law and, therefore, does not apply to the interpretation of art.102 TFEU.[691] Referring to the Court of Justice decision in *Portugal v Council*,[692] it relied on the case law referred to in para.24–173, above, and held, therefore, that Microsoft could not rely on art.13 TRIPs.

24–174

---

[686] *Léon van Parys NV v Belgisch Interventie-en Restitutiebureau (BIRB)*, Case C–377/02, Judgment of March 1, 2005.

[687] Follow up to the Green Paper, Ch.7.6.

[688] Case T–201/04R, CFI (Grand Chamber) September 17, 2007

[689] art.13 TRIPs embodies the principles of art.9(2) of the Berne Convention and its so-called "three-step test" for permissible limitations; see paras 9–02 to 9–04 and paras 25–33 and 25–34 of the Main Work.

[690] Judgment, para.797.

[691] Judgment, para.798.

[692] [1999] ECRI–8395.

24–175

Table Showing the Implementation of EC Directives on Copyright and Related Rights in the Member States of the EU, EEA and Switzerland on October 15, 2010

Member States	Computer Programs Directive 2009/24/EC	Rental and Lending Right Directive 2006/115/EC)	Satellite Broadcasting & Cable Retransmission Directive 93/83/EEC (01.01.1995)	Term of Copyright Protection Directive 2006/116/EC)	Protection of Databases Directive 96/9/EC (31.12.1997)	Information Society Directive Directive 2001/29/EC (22.12.2002)	Artists' Resale Right Directive 2001/84/EC (01.01.2006)	Enforcement of Intellectual Property Rights Directive 2004/48/EC (29.04.2006)
EU Countries[1]								
Austria	01.11.1993	11.02.1993	02.05.1996	29.03.1996	09.01.1998	06.06.2003	16.02.2006	21.06.2006
Belgium	27.07.1994	27.07.1994 14.05.2004	27.07.1994	27.07.1994	14.11.1998	27.05.2005	23.01.2007 10.09.2007	10.05.2007
Bulgaria	09.12.2005	09.12.2005	09.12.2005	09.12.2005	09.12.2005	09.12.2005	09.12.2005	05.09.2006
Cyprus*	19.07.2002	19.07.2002 18.10.2002	19.07.2002	19.07.2002	19.07.2002	30.04.2004	28.07.2006	28.07.2006
Czech Republic*	12.05.2000	12.05.2000	12.05.2000	12.05.200	08.12.1961 05.03.1964 18.05.1990 18.12.1991 12.05.2000	08.12.1961 18.05.1990 01.12.1993 12.05.2000 23.02.2005 22.05.2006	12.05.2000 22.05.2006 22.05.2006	26.05.2006
Denmark*	19.12.1992	13.06.1995 14.06.1995 17.12.2002	13.06.1995 12.03.2003	14.06.1995	26.06.1998	17.12.2002	21.12.2005	15.12.2005 05.04.2006

Estonia*	18.11.2002	18.11.2002 10.04.2004	18.11.2002	18.11.2002	18.11.2002	25.10.2004 13.02.2006 24.03.2006	20.06.2006	(01.01.2006) 29.05.2006
Finland	07.05.1993 22.12.1993	24.03.1995 05.11.1997 27.12.2006	24.03.1995	22.12.1995	03.04.1998 22.10.2003	20.10.2005 20.12.2005	12.05.2006	04.08.2006
France	11.05.1994	01.07.1992 18.06.2003	28.03.1997	28.03.1997	01.07.1998	03.08.2006	03.08.2006 10.05.2007	30.10.2007 29.06.2008
Germany	23.06.1993	29.06.1995	20.05.1998	23.06.1995	28.07.1997	10.09.2003	15.11.2006	11.07.2008
Greece	04.03.1993	04.03.1993	04.03.1993 24.12.1997	04.03.1993 24.12.1997	15.03.2000	10.10.2002	26.01.2007	26.01.2007
Hungary*	06.07.1999 27.11.2003	06.07.1999 27.11.2003	06.07.1999 27.11.2003	06.07.1999 27.11.2003	17.11.2001 27.11.2003	06.07.1999 27.11.2003	19.10.2005	08.05.2006
Ireland	02.02.1993	01.03.2001	01.03.2001	01.07.1995	01.03.2001	19.01.2004	23.06.2006	11.07.2006
Italy	31.12.1992	16.12.1994 28.11.2006	18.11.1996	27.02.1996 13.06.1997	30.04.1999 06.05.1999	14.04.2003	25.03.2006	07.04.2006
Latvia*	27.04.2000 01.05.2004	27.04.2000 01.05.2004	27.04.2000 01.05.2004	27.04.2000 01.05.2004	27.04.2000 01.05.2004	27.04.2000 01.05.2004	27.04.2000 01.05.2004	27.02.2007
Lithuania*	21.03.2003	21.03.2003	21.03.2003	21.03.2003	21.03.2003	21.03.2003	21.03.2003 31.10.2006	04.11.2006
Luxembourg	28.04.1995	16.09.1997 25.01.2007	16.09.1997 30.04.2001	16.09.1997	30.04.2001	29.04.2004	30.04.2001 29.04.2004 22.09.2006	28.05.2009
Malta*	01.01.2001	01.01.2001	24.04.2000	01.01.2001	01.01.2001 10.01.2003	23.12.2003	14.08.2006	12.12.2006

Netherlands	07.07.1994	28.12.1995	18.07.1996	28.12.1995	08.07.1999	06.07.2004 18.08.2004 24.08.2004	16.02.2006 02.03.2006	22.03.2007
Poland*	23.05.1994 07.07.2000	23.05.1994 27.11.2002	23.05.1994 07.07.2000 27.11.2002	23.05.1994 07.07.2000 27.11.2002	23.05.1994 26.09.2000 09.11.2001	26.09.2000 30.04.2004	21.04.2006	09.05.2007
Portugal	17.06.1994 20.10.1994	03.09.1997 27.11.1997 30.06.2006	03.09.1997 27.11.1997	03.09.1997 27.11.1997	04.07.2000	24.08.2004	29.06.2006	01.04.2008
Romania	26.03.1996 30.06.2004 19.09.2005 31.07.2006	26.03.1996 30.06.2004 19.09.2005 31.07.2006	26.03.1996 30.06.2004 19.09.2005 31.07.2006	26.03.1996 30.06.2004 19.09.2005 31.07.2006	26.03.1996 30.06.2004 19.09.2005 31.07.2006	26.03.1996 30.06.2004 19.09.2005 31.07.2006	26.03.1996 30.06.2004 19.09.2005 31.07.2006	31.07.2006
Slovakia*	31.12.2003	31.12.2003	31.12.2003 05.05.2007	31.12.2003	31.12.2003	31.12.2003 01.03.2007	31.12.2003 01.03.2007	01.03.2007
Slovenia	14.04.1995	14.04.1995	14.04.1995 26.04.2004 26.08.2004	14.04.1995 09.02.2001	14.04.1995 09.02.2001 26.08.2004	14.04.1995 09.02.2001 26.08.2004	14.04.1995 17.02.2006	09.06.2006
Spain[2]	24.12.1993	31.12.1994	13.10.1995 22.04.1996 07.03.1998	13.10.1995	07.03.1998	08.07.2006	16.12.1992 22.04.1996	06.06.2006
Sweden	01.01.1993	01.06.1995	07.12.1995	07.12.1995	01.01.1998	08.06.2005	25.06.2007	01.04.2009
United Kingdom	01.01.1993	01.12.1996	01.12.1996	19.12.1995	01.01.1998	31.10.2003 22.03.2005 (Gibraltar)	13.02.2006 01.06.2006 (Gibraltar)	29.04.2006
EFTA Countries[3]								

Iceland	Fully implemented	Fully implemented	Fully implemented	Fully implemented	Fully implemented	Fully implemented	Fully implemented	—
Liechten-stein	Fully implemented	Fully implemented	Fully implemented	Fully implemented	Fully implemented	Fully implemented	Fully implemented	—
Norway	Fully implemented	Fully implemented	Fully implemented	Fully implemented	Fully implemented	Fully implemented	Fully implemented	—
Switzer-land[4]	Compatible law	Partially implemented[5]	Compatible law	Compatible law	No intention to implement	Partially implemented[6]	No intention to implement	Intention to implement partially

[1] The date refers to the date of publication in a State's official journal or, failing that, to the date of adoption or the date of entry into force (where the law so provides)—Concerning the new Member States (*), the implementing measures notified to the Commission have not yet been accepted as complete or in conformity with the respective Directive.

[2] The CJEU has declared in a judgment of January 31, 2007, that Spain has failed to adopt, within the period prescribed, the laws, etc. necessary to comply with the Artist's Resale Right Directive, thus failing to fulfil its obligations under that Directive (Case C–32/07 (OJ C82 of April 14, 2007 and C–79/7 of March 29, 2008).

[3] See EFTA website: *http://www.efta.int.* As regards the EEA Agreement, see paras 24–01 and 24–172, above.

[4] The revision of the Swiss national copyright law in 1994 contained provisions to make the law compatible with E.C. copyright directives in force at that time. In June 2006, the Swiss Federal Government launched the legislative process for the revision of the current Copyright Law with a new draft to bring it into line with international standards and to enable Switzerland to ratify the WCT and WPPT, which occurred on October 5, 2007. Amendments were made to arts 10, 33, 33a, 36, 37, 39 as well as arts 39a to 39c, 62, 67, 69, 69a.

[5] The rental right applies to date only to computer programs.

[6] There is, for example, a divergence in relation to the scope of the private copying exception in art.5(2)(b) which in Switzerland refers to the "private Kreis/ private circle" ("any use in the personal sphere or within a circle of persons closely connected to each other, such as relations or friends") rather than to copies made "by the individual for his or her own private use and for no direct or indirect economic or commercial gain".

CHAPTER TWENTY FIVE

THE PROTECTION OF COPYRIGHT WORKS ABROAD

General Table of Copyright and Related Rights Conventions and National   25–01
Laws. The following Table shows the extent to which copyright works protected
under the 1988 Act are protected in other countries in accordance with the
principal international treaties to which the United Kingdom is party, and which
have entered into force with respect to those countries on August 31, 2010. The
substantive provisions of each of these treaties are discussed in detail in Ch.23,
above. The aim of this Table is to present in a readily accessible form the basic
information the reader requires to establish whether a work is protected in the
188 countries listed. The information provided by the Table is explained below.

Berne Convention for the Protection of Literary and Artistic Works, 1886.   25–02
The Table shows the membership, if any, of the Berne Union and the latest Act(s)
of the Berne Convention to which the country in question is party; the Table also
shows which countries have made declarations with regard to certain provisions
of the Convention affecting the protection they afford to nationals of other
Member States; these declarations are explained in the footnotes to the Table.
This column of the Table is up to date to August 31, 2010.

Universal Copyright Convention, 1952. The Table shows the membership, if   25–03
any, of the Universal Copyright Convention and whether the country in question
is party to the 1952 Geneva Act of the Convention or to the 1971 Paris Act.
Countries which availed themselves of the exceptions to protection in favour of
developing countries are also indicated. This column of the Table is up to date to
August 31, 2010.

Other treaties. The Table also gives the dates of the adherences of each country   25–04
(where appropriate) to the following additional treaties:

    The Agreement on Trade Related Aspects of Intellectual Property (TRIPs)
    1994. This column of the Table is up to date to August 31, 2010.

    The Rome Convention for the Protection of Performers, Producers of
    Phonograms and Broadcasting Organisations (the Rome Convention)
    1961. This column of the Table is up to date to August 31, 2010.

    The Convention for the Protection of Producers of Phonograms against
    the Unauthorised Duplication of their Phonograms (the Phonograms
    Convention) 1971. This column of the Table is up to date to August 31,
    2010.

    The Convention Relating to the Distribution of Programme-Carrying
    Signals Transmitted by Satellite (the Satellite Convention) 1974. This col-
    umn of the Table is up to date to August 31, 2010.

    The WIPO Copyright Treaty (WCT) 1996. This column of the Table is up
    to date to August 31, 2010.

    The WIPO Performances and Phonograms Treaty (WPPT) 1996. This
    column of the Table is up to date to August 31, 2010.

National laws. The international treaties included in the Table oblige the Member   25–05
States to provide nationals of other Member States with the minimum standards
of protection guaranteed by the treaties and, in the case of the Berne Convention,

the UCC, the TRIPs Agreement, the Rome Convention, the WIPO Copyright Treaty and the WIPO Performances and Phonograms Treaty, with so-called national treatment.[1] This means that a Member State gives to nationals of other Member States not only the minimum standards of protection provided for by the international treaty in question but also the same protection as it gives to its own nationals under its domestic law.[2] To establish whether any given work is protected in a particular country, it is necessary, therefore, to know not only which international treaties the country in question is party to but also to be able to identify the copyright law in force in that country.

The Table gives the date of the principal copyright laws in force in the countries listed, with the date of the most recent amendments to the laws in brackets. Since the 15th Edition of this Work was written in late 2004, it is of interest to note that, although only ten entirely new laws on copyright and related rights have been adopted, no less than 67 national laws have been amended.

The period of protection for literary and artistic works (as defined in the Berne Convention art.2(1)) is shown also in the Table.[3] Here it may be noted that the number of countries which now grant literary and artistic works a period of protection of 70 years pma or more has increased since the 15th Edition from 53 to 79.

Where a given country has adhered to one or other of the treaties listed, it is included in the Table, even if it has no domestic copyright law or no information is available about such law. In these cases, under the heading "Date of the principal law", the remark "No legislation" or "Unknown" is made, as the case may be, and the period of protection shown corresponds to the minimum period required by the treaty to which the country is party. In principle, rights owners are guaranteed all the rights which the treaty in question expressly gives them and, where the treaty to which the country is party provides for a specific, minimum period of protection for nationals of other Member States, that period will apply in accordance with the provisions of the treaty in question.

25–06　　**Sources.** The information given about the membership of the various conventions and treaties listed above is based on their current status as published on August 31, 2010, on the websites of WIPO (World Intellectual Property Organisation), Unesco (United Nations Organisation for Science, Education and Culture) and the WTO (World Trade Organisation), as well as, in some cases, on additional more up to date information from the organisations themselves or from the editors' own sources. The date of the latest law applicable in the countries in question and the term of protection is based mainly on the most recently available information in the following collections of laws: WIPO's "Collection of Laws for Electronic Access" (CLEA); WIPO's Cumulative Index of Copyright and Related Rights Laws and Treaties; and Unesco's "Collection of National Copyright Laws".

---

[1] See Ch.23, above, regarding the national treatment provisions of the various Conventions.
[2] The United Kingdom implements its obligations under these international agreements by extending protection to the works of nationals of other countries by means of statutory instruments issued pursuant to the CDPA 1988 ss.159 and 208; see Part C, below.
[3] See also Table n.6.

GENERAL TABLE OF COPYRIGHT AND RELATED RIGHTS CONVENTIONS[1]

Signatories	Berne Convention[2] September 9, 1886 and Subsequent Acts	UCC[3] September 6, 1952 revised in Paris, July 24, 1971	TRIPS April 15, 1994	Rome Convention October 26, 1961	Geneva Phonograms Convention October 29, 1971	Satellite Convention May 21, 1974	WIPO Copyright Treaty[4]	WIPO Performances and Phonograms Treaty[5]	Date of Principal Law (most recent amendment)[6]	Period of Protection[6]
Afghanistan			Observer[7]						No legislation	
Albania	Paris A	Paris	September 8, 2000	September 1, 2000	June 26, 2001		August 6, 2005	May 20, 2002	20058	70 years pma
Algeria	Paris A, C, H	Paris*	Observer[7]	April 22, 2007[8]					2003	50 years from January 1 pma
Andorra	Paris A	Geneva	Observer[7]	May 25, 2004					1999	70 years pma
Angola			November 23, 1996						1990	50 years pma (from end of year)
Antigua and Barbuda	Paris A		January 1, 1995						2002	50 years pma
Argentina	Paris A	Geneva	January 1, 1995	March 2, 1992	June 30, 1973		March 6, 2002	May 20, 2002	1933 (2009)	70 years pma
Armenia	Paris A		February 5, 2003	January 31, 2003	January 31, 2003	December 13, 1993	March 6, 2005	March 6, 2005	2006 (2009)	70 years from January 1, pma

Signatories	Berne Convention[2] September 9, 1886 and Subsequent Acts	UCC[3] September 6, 1952 revised in Paris, July 24, 1971	TRIPS April 15, 1994	Rome Convention October 26, 1961	Geneva Phonograms Convention October 29, 1971	Satellite Convention May 21, 1974	WIPO Copyright Treaty[4]	WIPO Performances and Phonograms Treaty[5]	Date of Principal Law (most recent amendment)[6]	Period of Protection[6]
Australia	Paris A	Paris	January 1, 1995	September 30, 1992[8]	June 22, 1974	October 26, 1990	July 26, 2007	July 26, 2007[14]	1968 (2010)	70 years pma (from end of year)
Austria	Paris A	Paris	January 1, 1995	June 9, 1973[8]	August 21, 1982	August 6, 1982	March 14, 2010	March 14, 2010	1936 (2006)	70 years pma
Azerbaijan	Paris A	Geneva	Observer[7]	October 8, 2005	September 1, 2001		April 11, 2006	April 11, 2006	1996	50 years pma
Bahamas	Paris B,H Brussels	Paris	Observer[7]						1998	70 years pma (from end of year)
Bahrain, Kingdom of	Paris A, C		January 1, 1995	January 18, 2006		May 1, 2007	December 15, 2005	December 15, 2005	1993 (2008)	70 years pma
Bangladesh	Paris A, C, D	Paris*	January 1, 1995						2000 (2006)	60 years from January 1, pma
Barbados	Paris A	Paris	January 1, 1995	September 18, 1983	July 29, 1983				1998	50 years pma
Belarus	Paris A	Geneva	Observer[8]	May 27, 2003	April 17, 2003		March 6, 2002	May 20, 2002	1996 (2008)	50 years pma

Signatories	Berne Convention[2] September 9, 1886 and Subsequent Acts	UCC[3] September 6, 1952 revised in Paris, July 24, 1971	TRIPS April 15, 1994	Rome Convention October 26, 1961	Geneva Phonograms Convention October 29, 1971	Satellite Convention May 21, 1974	WIPO Copyright Treaty[4]	WIPO Performances and Phonograms Treaty[5]	Date of Principal Law (most recent amendment)[6]	Period of Protection[6]
Belgium	Paris A	Geneva	January 1, 1995	October 2, 1999[8]			August 30, 2006	August 30, 2006[14]	1994 (2006)	70 years from January 1, pma
Belize	Paris A	Geneva	January 1, 1995						2000 (2001)	50 years pma (from end of year)
Benin	Paris A		February 22, 1996				April 16, 2006	April 16, 2006	1984 (2006)	70 years pma (from end of year)
Bhutan	Paris A		Observer[7]						2001	50 years pma (from end of year)
Bolivia	Paris A	Paris*	September 12, 1995	November 24, 1993					1992 (1997)	50 years pma (from end of year)

Signatories	Berne Convention[2] September 9, 1886 and Subsequent Acts	UCC[3] September 6, 1952 revised in Paris, July 24, 1971	TRIPS April 15, 1994	Rome Convention October 26, 1961	Geneva Phonograms Convention October 29, 1971	Satellite Convention May 21, 1974	WIPO Copyright Treaty[4]	WIPO Performances and Phonograms Treaty[5]	Date of Principal Law (most recent amendment)[6]	Period of Protection[6]
Bosnia and Herzegovina	Paris A, E	Paris	Observer[7]	May 19, 2009[9]	May 25, 2009[10]	March 6, 1992	November 25, 2009	November 25, 2009	2002 (2006)	70 years from January 1, pma
Botswana	Paris A		May 31, 1995				January 27, 2005	January 27, 2005	2000 (2005)	50 years pma
Brazil	Paris A	Paris	January 1, 1995	September 29, 1965	November 28, 1975				1998 (2003)	70 years from January 1, pma
Brunei Darussalam	Paris A		January 1, 1995						1999	50 years pma (from end of year)
Bulgaria	Paris A	Paris	December 1, 1996	August 31, 1995[8]	September 6, 1995		March 6, 2002	May 20, 2002	1993 (2002)	70 years pma
Burkina Faso	Paris A		June 3, 1995	January 14, 1988	January 30, 1988		March 6, 2002	May 20, 2002	1997 (2001)	70 years pma (from end of year)
Burundi			June 23, 1995						1978 (2005)	50 years pma (from end of year)

Signatories	Berne Convention[2] September 9, 1886 and Subsequent Acts	UCC[3] September 6, 1952 revised in Paris, July 24, 1971	TRIPS April 15, 1994	Rome Convention October 26, 1961	Geneva Phonograms Convention October 29, 1971	Satellite Convention May 21, 1974	WIPO Copyright Treaty[4]	WIPO Performances and Phonograms Treaty[5]	Date of Principal Law (most recent amendment)[6]	Period of Protection[6]
Cambodia		Geneva	October 13, 2004						2003	50 years pma
Cameroon	Paris A	Paris	December 13, 1995						2000 (2001)	50 years pma (from end of year)
Canada	Paris A	Geneva	January 1, 1995	June 4, 1998[8]					1985 (2007)[15]	50 years pma (from end of year)
Cape Verde	Paris A		July 23, 2008	July 3, 1997					1990	50 years from January 1, pma
Central African Republic	Paris A		May 31, 1995						1985	50 years pma (from end of year)
Chad	Stockholm B Brussels		October 19, 1995						2003	50 years pma minimum of BC

Signatories	Berne Convention[2] September 9, 1886 and Subsequent Acts	UCC[3] September 6, 1952 revised in Paris, July 24, 1971	TRIPS April 15, 1994	Rome Convention October 26, 1961	Geneva Phonograms Convention October 29, 1971	Satellite Convention May 21, 1974	WIPO Copyright Treaty[4]	WIPO Performances and Phonograms Treaty[5]	Date of Principal Law (most recent amendment)[6]	Period of Protection[6]
Chile	Paris A[3]	Geneva	January 1, 1995	September 5, 1974	March 24, 1977		March 6, 2002	May 20, 2002[14]	1970 (2003)	50 years pma
China	Paris A[11]	Paris*	December 11, 2001		April 30, 1993[11]		June 9, 2007[12]	June 9, 2007[14]	1990 (2010)	50 years pma
Colombia	Paris A	Paris	April 30, 1995	September 17, 1976	May 16, 1994		March 6, 2002	May 20, 2002	1982 (2002)	80 years pma
Comoros	Paris A		Observer[7]						1957	50 years pma minimum of BC
Congo	Paris A		March 27, 1997	May 18, 1964[8]					1982 (1999)	70 years pma
Costa Rica	Paris A	Paris	January 1, 1995	September 9, 1971	June 17, 1982	June 25, 1999	March 6, 2002	May 20, 2002[14]	1982 (2000)	70 years pma
Côte d'Ivoire	Paris A		January 1, 1995						1996	99 years pma (from end of year)
Croatia	Paris A	Paris	November 30, 2000	April 20, 2000	April 20, 2000	October 8, 1991	March 6, 2002	May 20, 2002	2003 (2007)	70 years from January 1, pma

Signatories	Berne Convention[2] September 9, 1886 and Subsequent Acts	UCC[3] September 6, 1952 revised in Paris, July 24, 1971	TRIPS April 15, 1994	Rome Convention October 26, 1961	Geneva Phonograms Convention October 29, 1971	Satellite Convention May 21, 1974	WIPO Copyright Treaty[4]	WIPO Performances and Phonograms Treaty[5]	Date of Principal Law (most recent amendment)[6]	Period of Protection[6]
Cuba	Paris A, C, D, H	Geneva	April 20, 1995						1977 (1991)	50 years from January 1, pma
Cyprus	Paris A, E	Paris	July 30, 1995	June 17, 2009	September 30, 1993		November 4, 2003	December 2, 2005	1976 (2004)	50 years pma (from end of year)
Czech Republic	Paris A	Paris	January 1, 1995	January 1, 1993[8]	January 1, 1993		March 6, 2002	May 20, 2002	2000 (2006)	70 years pma (from January 1 pma)
Democratic People's Republic of Korea	Paris A, C, H								2001	50 years pma minimum of BC
Democratic Republic of the Congo	Paris A		January 1, 1997		November 29, 1977				1986	50 years pma (from end of year)
Denmark	Paris A	Paris	January 1, 1995	September 23, 1965[8]	March 24, 1977		March 14, 2010	March 14, 2010[14]	1995 (2006)	70 years pma

Signatories	Berne Convention[2] September 9, 1886 and Subsequent Acts	UCC[3] September 6, 1952 revised in Paris, July 24, 1971	TRIPS April 15, 1994	Rome Convention October 26, 1961	Geneva Phonograms Convention October 29, 1971	Satellite Convention May 21, 1974	WIPO Copyright Treaty[4]	WIPO Performances and Phonograms Treaty[5]	Date of Principal Law (most recent amendment)[6]	Period of Protection[6]
Djibouti	Paris A		May 31, 1995						1996 (2006)	50 years pma
Dominica	Paris A		January 1, 1995	November 9, 1999					2003	70 years pma
Dominican Republic	Paris A	Paris	March 9, 1995	January 27, 1987			January 10, 2006	January 10, 2006	2000 (2006)	70 years from January 1 pma
Ecuador	Paris A	Paris	January 21, 1996	May 18, 1964	September 14, 1974		March 6, 2002	May 20, 2002	1998	70 years pma
Egypt	Paris A, H		June 30, 1995		April 23, 1978				2002 (2005)	50 years pma
El Salvador	Paris A	Paris	May 7, 1995	June 29, 1979	February 9, 1979	July 22, 2008	March 6, 2002	May 20, 2002	1993 (2005)	70 years pma
Equatorial Guinea	Paris A		Observer[5]						1980	50 years pma minimum of BC
Estonia	Paris A		November 13, 1999	April 28, 2000[8]	May 28, 2000		March 14, 2010	March 14, 2010	1992 (2004)	70 years pma
Ethiopia			Observer[7]						1960 (2004)	50 years pma (from end of year)

Signatories	Berne Convention[2] September 9, 1886 and Subsequent Acts	UCC[3] September 6, 1952 revised in Paris, July 24, 1971	TRIPS April 15, 1994	Rome Convention October 26, 1961	Geneva Phonograms Convention October 29, 1971	Satellite Convention May 21, 1974	WIPO Copyright Treaty[4]	WIPO Performances and Phonograms Treaty[5]	Date of Principal Law (most recent amendment)[6]	Period of Protection[6]
European Union			January 1, 1995				March 14, 2010	March 14, 2010	Directives cf. Ch.24, above	70 years pma Dir. 2006/116/EC
Fiji	Stockholm B Brussels	Geneva	January 14, 1996	April 11, 1972[8]	April 18, 1973				1999 (2003)	50 years pma
Finland	Paris A	Paris	January 1, 1995	October 21, 1983[8]	April 18, 1973		March 14, 2010	March 14, 2010[14]	1961 (1998)	70 years pma (from end of year)
France	Paris A	Paris	January 1, 1995	July 3, 1987[8]	April 18, 1973		March 14, 2010	March 14, 2010[14]	1992 (2010)	70 years pma (from end of year)
Gabon	Paris A		January 1, 1995				March 6, 2002	May 20, 2002	1987	50 years pma minimum of BC
Gambia	Paris A		October 23, 1996						No legislation	50 years pma minimum of BC

Signatories	Berne Convention[2] September 9, 1886 and Subsequent Acts	UCC[3] September 6, 1952 revised in Paris, July 24, 1971	TRIPS April 15, 1994	Rome Convention October 26, 1961	Geneva Phonograms Convention October 29, 1971	Satellite Convention May 21, 1974	WIPO Copyright Treaty[4]	WIPO Performances and Phonograms Treaty[5]	Date of Principal Law (most recent amendment)[6]	Period of Protection[6]
Georgia	Paris A		June 14, 2000	August 14, 2004			March 6, 2002	May 20, 2002	1999 (2000)	70 years pma from January 1, pma
Germany	Paris A, I	Paris	January 1, 1995	October 21, 1966[8]	May 18, 1974	August 25, 1979	March 14, 2010	March 14, 2010[14]	1965 (2008)	70 years pma (from end of year)
Ghana	Paris A	Geneva	January 1, 1995				November 18, 2006		20055	70 years pma
Greece	Paris A	Geneva	January 1, 1995	January 6, 1993	February 9, 1994	October 22, 1991	Marrch 14, 2010	March 14, 2010	1993 (2007)	70 years pma (from end of year)
Grenada	Paris A		February 22, 1996						1989	50 years pma
Guatemala	Paris A, H	Geneva	July 21, 1995	January 14, 1977	February 1, 1977		February 4, 2003	January 8, 2003	1998 (2003)	75 years pma

Signatories	Berne Convention[2] September 9, 1886 and Subsequent Acts	UCC[3] September 6, 1952 revised in Paris, July 24, 1971	TRIPS April 15, 1994	Rome Convention October 26, 1961	Geneva Phonograms Convention October 29, 1971	Satellite Convention May 21, 1974	WIPO Copyright Treaty[4]	WIPO Performances and Phonograms Treaty[5]	Date of Principal Law (most recent amendment)[6]	Period of Protection[6]
Guinea	Paris A	Paris	October 25, 1995				May 25, 2002	May 25, 2002	1980	80 years pma (from end of year), thereafter paying public domain
Guinea-Bissau	Paris A		May 31, 1995						Un-known	50 years pma minimum of BC
Guyana	Paris A		January 1, 1995						1999	50 years pma
Haiti	Paris A	Geneva	January 30, 1996						1968 (2005)	25 years pma (50 years pma minimum of BC)

Signatories	Berne Convention[2] September 9, 1886 and Subsequent Acts	UCC[3] September 6, 1952 revised in Paris, July 24, 1971	TRIPS April 15, 1994	Rome Convention October 26, 1961	Geneva Phonograms Convention October 29, 1971	Satellite Convention May 21, 1974	WIPO Copyright Treaty[4]	WIPO Performances and Phonograms Treaty[5]	Date of Principal Law (most recent amendment)[6]	Period of Protection[6]
Holy See (Vatican)	Paris A	Paris	Observer[7]		July 18, 1977				1960 (2005)	70 years pma (from end of year)
Honduras	Paris A		January 1, 1995	February 16, 1990	March 6, 1990	April 7, 2008	May 20, 2002	May 20, 2002	1999	75 years pma
Hong Kong (SAR of China)[10]	Paris A	Paris	January 1, 1995		July 1, 1997				1997 (2007)	50 years pma
Hungary	Paris A	Paris	January 1, 1995	February 10, 1995	May 28, 1975		March 6, 2002	May 20, 2002	1999 (2009)	70 years from January 1, pma
Iceland	Paris A	Geneva	January 1, 1995	June 15, 1994[8]					1972 (2006)	70 years pma (from end of year)
India	Paris A, F, H	Paris	January 1, 1995		February 12, 1975				1957 (2000)	60 years from January 1, pma

Signatories	Berne Convention[2] September 9, 1886 and Subsequent Acts	UCC[3] September 6, 1952 revised in Paris, July 24, 1971	TRIPS April 15, 1994	Rome Convention October 26, 1961	Geneva Phonograms Convention October 29, 1971	Satellite Convention May 21, 1974	WIPO Copyright Treaty[4]	WIPO Performances and Phonograms Treaty[5]	Date of Principal Law (most recent amendment)[6]	Period of Protection[6]
Indonesia	Paris A, H		January 1, 1995				March 6, 2002	February 15, 2005	2000	50 years pma from January 1, pma
Iran (Islamic Republic of)			Observer[7]						1970	50 years pma
Iraq			Observer[7]						1971 (200	50 years pma
Ireland	Paris A	Geneva	January 1, 1995	September 19, 1979[8]			March 14, 2010	March 14, 2010	2000 (2004)	70 years pma
Israel	Paris A, H	Geneva	April 21, 1995	December 20, 2002[8]	May 1, 1978				2007	70 years, from January 1, pma
Italy	Paris A, H	Paris	January 1, 1995	April 8, 1975	March 24, 1977	July 7, 1981	March 14, 2010	March 14, 2010	1941 (2003)	70 years, from January 1, pma
Jamaica	Paris A		March 9, 1995	January 27, 1994	January 11, 1994	January 12, 2000	June 12, 2002	June 12, 2002	1993 (1999)	50 years pma
Japan	Paris A	Paris	January 1, 1995	October 26, 1989[8]	October 14, 1978		March 6, 2002	October 9, 2002[14]	1970 (2009)	50 years, from January 1, pma

Signatories	Berne Convention[2] September 9, 1886 and Subsequent Acts	UCC[3] September 6, 1952 revised in Paris, July 24, 1971	TRIPS April 15, 1994	Rome Convention October 26, 1961	Geneva Phonograms Convention October 29, 1971	Satellite Convention May 21, 1974	WIPO Copyright Treaty[4]	WIPO Performances and Phonograms Treaty[5]	Date of Principal Law (most recent amendment)[6]	Period of Protection[6]
Jordan	Paris A, C, D, H		April 11, 2000				April 27, 2004	May 24, 2004	1992 (2005)	50 years from January 1, pma
Kazakhstan	Paris A	Geneva	Observer[7]		August 3, 2001		November 12, 2004	November 12, 2004	1996 (2007)	50 years pma
Kenya	Paris A	Paris	January 1, 1995		April 21, 1976	August 25, 1979			2001	50 years pma (from end of year)
Kuwait			January 1, 1995						1999	50 years pma
(Kyrgyz Republic)	Paris A		December 20, 1998	August 13, 2003	October 12, 2002		March 6, 2002	August 15, 2002	1998 (2006)	50 years from January 1, pma
Lao People's Democratic Republic		Geneva	Observer[7]						2007 (2008)	50 years pma
Latvia	Paris A		February 10, 1999	August 20, 1999	August 23, 1997		March 6, 2002	May 20, 2002	2000 (2007)	70 years from January 1, pma

Signatories	Berne Convention[2] September 9, 1886 and Subsequent Acts	UCC[3] September 6, 1952 revised in Paris, July 24, 1971	TRIPS April 15, 1994	Rome Convention October 26, 1961	Geneva Phonograms Convention October 29, 1971	Satellite Convention May 21, 1974	WIPO Copyright Treaty[4]	WIPO Performances and Phonograms Treaty[5]	Date of Principal Law (most recent amendment)[6]	Period of Protection[6]
Lebanon (Lebanese Republic)	Rome	Geneva	Observer[7]	August 12, 1997					1999 (2002)	50 years pma (from end of year)
Lesotho	Paris A, H		May 31, 1995	January 26, 1990[8]					1989	50 years pma (from end of year)
Liberia, Republic of	Paris A, H	Geneva	Observer[7]						1972 (1997)	25 years pma (50 years under BC)
Libya	Paris A,H		Observer[7]						1968 (1984)	50 years pma (from end of year)
Liechtenstein	Paris A	Paris	September 1, 1995	October 12, 1999[8]	October 12, 1999		April 30, 2007	April 30, 2007	1999	70 years pma
Lithuania	Paris A,H		May 31, 2001	July 22, 1999	January 27, 2000		March 6, 2002	May 20, 2002	1999 (2008)	70 years pma

Signatories	Berne Convention[2] September 9, 1886 and Subsequent Acts	UCC[3] September 6, 1952 revised in Paris, July 24, 1971	TRIPS April 15, 1994	Rome Convention October 26, 1961	Geneva Phonograms Convention October 29, 1971	Satellite Convention May 21, 1974	WIPO Copyright Treaty[4]	WIPO Performances and Phonograms Treaty[5]	Date of Principal Law (most recent amendment)[6]	Period of Protection[6]
Luxembourg	Paris A	Geneva	January 1, 1995	February 25, 1976[8]	March 8, 1976		March 14, 2010	March 14, 2010	2001 (2004)	70 years from January 1, pma
Macau (SAR of China)[10]	Paris A	Paris	January 1, 1995		December 20, 1999				1999 (2000)	50 years pma
Madagascar	Brussels		November 17, 1995						1995 (2006)	70 years pma (from end of year)
Malawi	Paris A	Geneva	May 31, 1995						1989	50 years pma (from end of year)
Malaysia	Paris A		January 1, 1995						1987 (2003)	50 years pma
Maldives			May 31, 1995						No legislation	50 years pma minimum of TRIPs
Mali	Paris A		May 31, 1995				April 24, 2002	May 20, 2002	1977 (1999)	50 years pma

Signatories	Berne Convention[2] September 9, 1886 and Subsequent Acts	UCC[3] September 6, 1952 revised in Paris, July 24, 1971	TRIPS April 15, 1994	Rome Convention October 26, 1961	Geneva Phonograms Convention October 29, 1971	Satellite Convention May 21, 1974	WIPO Copyright Treaty[4]	WIPO Performances and Phonograms Treaty[5]	Date of Principal Law (most recent amendment)[6]	Period of Protection[6]
Malta	Paris B, H Rome	Geneva	January 1, 1995				March 14, 2010	March 14, 2010	2000 (2004)	70 years pma (from end of year)
Mauritania	Paris A		May 31, 1995						1957	50 years pma minimum of BC
Mauritius	Paris A, H	Geneva	January 1, 1995						1997	50 years pma
Mexico	Paris A	Paris*	January 1, 1995	May 18, 1964	December 21, 1973	August 25, 1979	March 6, 2002	May 20, 2002	1997 (2005)	75 years pma
Micronesia (Federated States of)	Paris A								1982 (2003)	50 years pma
Monaco	Paris A	Paris		December 6, 1985[8]	December 2, 1974				1948 (1949)	50 years pma
Mongolia	Paris A, C, D, H		January 29, 1997				October 25, 2002	October 25, 2002	1993 (2001)	50 years pma
Montenegro	Paris A	Paris	Observer[7]	June 3, 2006	June 3, 2006	June 3, 2006	June 3, 2006	June 3, 2006	2005 (2008)	70 years pma

Signatories	Berne Convention[2] September 9, 1886 and Subsequent Acts	UCC[3] September 6, 1952 revised in Paris, July 24, 1971	TRIPS April 15, 1994	Rome Convention October 26, 1961	Geneva Phonograms Convention October 29, 1971	Satellite Convention May 21, 1974	WIPO Copyright Treaty[4]	WIPO Performances and Phonograms Treaty[5]	Date of Principal Law (most recent amendment)[6]	Period of Protection[6]
Morocco	Paris A	Paris	January 1, 1995			June 30, 1983			2000 (2006)	50 years pma (from end of year)
Mozambique			August 26, 1995						2001 (2003)	70 years pma
Myanmar			January 1, 1995						1914 (2001)	50 years pma
Namibia	Paris A		January 1, 1995						1978 (1997)	50 years pma (from end of year)
Nauru									1956 (1971)	50 years pma
Nepal	Paris A, H		April 23, 2004						2002	50 years pma
Netherlands	Paris A[13]	Paris	January 1, 1995[13]	October 7, 1993[13] &[8]	October 12, 1993[13]		March 14, 2010	March 14, 2010	1912 (2006)	70 years pma (from end of year)

Signatories	Berne Convention[2] September 9, 1886 and Subsequent Acts	UCC[3] September 6, 1952 revised in Paris, July 24, 1971	TRIPS April 15, 1994	Rome Convention October 26, 1961	Geneva Phonograms Convention October 29, 1971	Satellite Convention May 21, 1974	WIPO Copyright Treaty[4]	WIPO Performances and Phonograms Treaty[5]	Date of Principal Law (most recent amendment)[6]	Period of Protection[6]
New Zealand	Rome	Geneva	January 1, 1995		August 13, 1976				1994 (2008)[16]	50 years pma (from end of year)
Nicaragua	Paris A	Geneva	September 3, 1995	August 10, 2000	August 10, 2000	August 25, 1979	March 6, 2003	March 6, 2003	1999 (2006)	70 years from January 1, pma
Niger	Paris A	Paris	December 13, 1996	May 18, 1964[8]					1993	50 years pma (from end of year)
Nigeria	Paris A	Geneva	January 1, 1995	October 29, 1993[8]					1988 (2006)	70 years pma (from the end of the year)
Norway	Paris A, I	Paris	January 1, 1995	July 10, 1978[8]	August 1, 1978				1961 (2005)	70 years pma (from end of year); 50 years for certain works

Signatories	Berne Convention[2] September 9, 1886 and Subsequent Acts	UCC[3] September 6, 1952 revised in Paris, July 24, 1971	TRIPS April 15, 1994	Rome Convention October 26, 1961	Geneva Phonograms Convention October 29, 1971	Satellite Convention May 21, 1974	WIPO Copyright Treaty[4]	WIPO Performances and Phonograms Treaty[5]	Date of Principal Law (most recent amendment)[6]	Period of Protection[6]
Oman	Paris A, D, H		November 9, 2000			March 18, 2008	September 20, 2005	September 20, 2005	2008	70 years from January 1, pma
Pakistan	Stockholm B Rome	Geneva	January 1, 1995						1962 (2000)	50 years from January 1, pma
Panama	Paris A	Paris	September 6, 1997	September 2, 1983	June 29, 1974	September 25, 1985	March 6, 2002	May 20, 2002	1994 (2000)	50 years pma
Papua New Guinea			June 9, 1996						2000	50 years pma
Paraguay	Paris A	Geneva	January 1, 1995	February 26, 1970	February 13, 1979		March 6, 2002	May 20, 2002	1998 (1999)	70 years pma
Peru	Paris A	Paris	January 1, 1995	August 7, 1985	August 24, 1985	August 7, 1985	March 6, 2002	July 18, 2002	1996 (2009)	70 years pma
Philippines	Paris A, D	Geneva	January 1, 1995	September 25, 1984			October 4, 2002	October 4, 2002	1998	50 years pma
Poland	Paris A	Paris	July 1, 1995	June 13, 1997			March 23, 2004	October 21, 2003	1994 (2005)	70 years pma
Portugal	Paris A, G	Paris	January 1, 1995	July 17, 2002		March 11, 1996	March 14, 2010	March 14, 2010	1985 (2008)	70 years pma
Qatar	Paris A		January 13, 1996			October 28, 2005	October 28, 2005		2002	50 years pma

Signatories	Berne Convention[2] September 9, 1886 and Subsequent Acts	UCC[3] September 6, 1952 revised in Paris, July 24, 1971	TRIPS April 15, 1994	Rome Convention October 26, 1961	Geneva Phonograms Convention October 29, 1971	Satellite Convention May 21, 1974	WIPO Copyright Treaty[4]	WIPO Performances and Phonograms Treaty[5]	Date of Principal Law (most recent amendment)[6]	Period of Protection[6]
Republic of Korea	Paris A	Paris*	January 1, 1995	March 18, 2009[8]	October 10, 1987		June 24, 2004	March 18, 2009[14]	1986 (2006)	50 years from January 1, pma
Republic of Moldova	Paris A	Geneva	July 26, 2001	December 5, 1995	July 17, 2000	October 28, 2008	March 6, 2002	May 20, 2002	1994 (2004)	50 years from January 1, pma
Romania	Paris A		January 1, 1995	October 22, 1998	October 1, 1998		March 6, 2002	May 20, 2002	1996	70 years pma
Russian Federation	Paris A	Paris	observer[7]	May 26, 2003[8]	March 13, 1995	January 20, 1989	February 5, 2009	February 5, 2009[14]	1993 (2004)	70 years from January 1, pma
Rwanda	Paris A	Paris	May 22, 1996			July 25, 2001			1983	50 years pma
Saint Kitts and Nevis	Paris A		February 21, 1996						2000	50 years pma
Saint Lucia	Paris A, H		January 1, 1995	August 17, 1996[8]	April 2, 2001		March 6, 2002	May 20, 2002	1995 (2000)	50 years pma
Saint Vincent and the Grenadines	Paris A	Paris	January 1, 1995						2003 (2005)	70 years pma (from end of year)

Signatories	Berne Convention[2] September 9, 1886 and Subsequent Acts	UCC[3] September 6, 1952 revised in Paris, July 24, 1971	TRIPS April 15, 1994	Rome Convention October 26, 1961	Geneva Phonograms Convention October 29, 1971	Satellite Convention May 21, 1974	WIPO Copyright Treaty[4]	WIPO Performances and Phonograms Treaty[5]	Date of Principal Law (most recent amendment)[6]	Period of Protection[6]
Samoa	Paris A, D		Observer[7]						1998	75 years pma
San Marino									1991	50 years pma (from end of year)
Sao Tome and Principe			Observer[7]						Unknown	
Saudi Arabia	Paris A	Paris	December 11, 2005						2004 (2005)	50 years pma
Senegal	Paris A	Paris	January 1, 1995				May 18, 2002	May 20, 2002	1973 (2008)	50 years pma (from end of year)
Serbia (Republic of)	Paris A, E	Paris	Observer[7]	June 10, 2003	June 10, 2003	April 27, 1992	June 13, 2003	June 13, 2003	2005	70 years pma
Seychelles			Observer[7]						1984 (1991)	25 years pma (from end of year)

Signatories	Berne Convention[2] September 9, 1886 and Subsequent Acts	UCC[3] September 6, 1952 revised in Paris, July 24, 1971	TRIPS April 15, 1994	Rome Convention October 26, 1961	Geneva Phonograms Convention October 29, 1971	Satellite Convention May 21, 1974	WIPO Copyright Treaty[4]	WIPO Performances and Phonograms Treaty[5]	Date of Principal Law (most recent amendment)[6]	Period of Protection[6]
Sierra Leone			July 23, 1995						1965	50 years pma (from end of the year)
Singapore	Paris A, C		January 1, 1995			April 27, 2005	April 17, 2005	April 17, 2005[14]	1987 (2008)	70 years pma (from end of year)
Slovakia (Slovak Republic)	Paris A	Paris	January 1, 1995	January 1, 1993[8]	January 1, 1993		March 6, 2002	May 2002	2003	70 years, from January 1 pma
Slovenia	Paris A, E	Paris	July 30, 1995	October 9, 1996[8]	October 15, 1996	June 25, 1991	March 6, 2002	May 20, 2002	1995 (2006)	70 years pma
Solomon Islands			July 26, 1996						1987 (1996)	50 years pma (from end of year)
South Africa	Paris B, H Brussels		January 1, 1995						1978 (2002)	50 years pma (from end of year)

Signatories	Berne Convention[2] September 9, 1886 and Subsequent Acts	UCC[3] September 6, 1952 revised in Paris, July 24, 1971	TRIPS April 15, 1994	Rome Convention October 26, 1961	Geneva Phonograms Convention October 29, 1971	Satellite Convention May 21, 1974	WIPO Copyright Treaty[4]	WIPO Performances and Phonograms Treaty[5]	Date of Principal Law (most recent amendment)[6]	Period of Protection[6]
Spain	Paris A	Paris	January 1, 1995	November 14, 1991[8]	August 24, 1974		March 14, 2010	March 14, 2010	1996 (2006)	70 years pma
Sri Lanka	A, D	Paris	January 1, 1995						2000 (2005)	70 years pma
Sudan	Paris A, D		Observer[7]						1996	50 years pma; 25 years pma for certain works
Suriname	Paris A		January 1, 1995						1913 (1984)	50 years pma
Swaziland	Paris A		January 1, 1995						1912	50 years pma minimum of BC
Sweden	Paris A	Paris	January 1, 1995	May 18, 1964	April 18, 1973		March 14, 2010	March 14, 2010[14]	1960 (2009)	70 years pma

Signatories	Berne Convention[2] September 9, 1886 and Subsequent Acts	UCC[3] September 6, 1952 revised in Paris, July 24, 1971	TRIPS April 15, 1994	Rome Convention October 26, 1961	Geneva Phonograms Convention October 29, 1971	Satellite Convention May 21, 1974	WIPO Copyright Treaty[4]	WIPO Performances and Phonograms Treaty[5]	Date of Principal Law (most recent amendment)[6]	Period of Protection[6]
Switzerland	Paris A	Paris	July 1, 1995	September 24, 1993	September 30, 1993	September 24, 1993	July 1, 2008	July 1, 2008[14]	1992 (2008)	70 years pma, 50 years for certain works (both from end of year)
Syrian Arab Republic	Paris A, D			May 13, 2006					2001	50 years pma
Taiwan			January 1, 2002						1928 (2009)	50 years pma
Tajikistan	Paris A	Geneva	Observer[7]	May 19, 2008			April 5, 2009		1998 (2003)	50 years pma
Thailand	Paris A, D, H,		January 1, 1995						1994 (1995)	50 years pma
The former Yugoslav Republic of Macedonia	Paris A	Paris	April 4, 2003	March 2, 1998[8]	March 2, 1998	November 17, 1991	February 4, 2004	March 20, 2005[14]	1996 (2005)	70 years pma
Togo	Paris A	Paris	May 31, 1995	June 10, 2003	June 10, 2003	June 10, 2003	May 21, 2003	May 21, 2003	1991	50 years pma (from end of year)

Signatories	Berne Convention[2] September 9, 1886 and Subsequent Acts	UCC[3] September 6, 1952 revised in Paris, July 24, 1971	TRIPS April 15, 1994	Rome Convention October 26, 1961	Geneva Phono-grams Convention October 29, 1971	Satellite Conven-tion May 21, 1974	WIPO Copy-right Treaty[4]	WIPO Perfor-mances and Phono-grams Treaty[5]	Date of Principal Law (most recent amend-ment)[6]	Period of Protec-tion[6]
Tonga	Paris A		July 27, 2007						2002	50 years pma (from end of year)
Trinidad and Tobago	Paris A	Paris	March 1, 1995		October 1, 1988	November 1, 1996	November 28, 2008	November 28, 2008	1997 (2008)	50 years pma; 75 years from publica-tion for certain works
Tunisia	Paris A, H	Paris	March 29, 1995						1994	50 years from January 1, pma
Turkey	Paris A, H		March 26, 1995	April 8, 2004			November 28, 2008	November 28, 2008	1951 (2008)	70 years pma
Uganda			January 1, 1995						1964 (2006)	50 years pma or from publica-tion, which-ever lat-est

Signatories	Berne Convention[2] September 9, 1886 and Subsequent Acts	UCC[3] September 6, 1952 revised in Paris, July 24, 1971	TRIPS April 15, 1994	Rome Convention October 26, 1961	Geneva Phonograms Convention October 29, 1971	Satellite Convention May 21, 1974	WIPO Copyright Treaty[4]	WIPO Performances and Phonograms Treaty[5]	Date of Principal Law (most recent amendment)[6]	Period of Protection[6]
Ukraine	Paris A	Geneva	May 16, 2008	June 12, 2002	February 18, 2000		March 6, 2002	May 20, 2002	2001 (2003)	70 years pma
United Arab Emirates	Paris A, D		April 10, 1996	January 14, 2005			July 14, 2004	June 9, 2005	2002	50 years from January 1, pma
United Kingdom	Paris A, I (extended to Isle of Man from March 18, 1996)	Paris	January 1, 1995	May 18, 1964 (extended to Isle of Man from July 28, 1999)[8]	April 18, 1973		March 14, 2010	March 14, 2010	1988 (2009)	70 years pma
United Republic of Tanzania	Paris A, H		January 1, 1995						1999 (2003)	50 years pma (from end of year)

Signatories	Berne Convention[2] September 9, 1886 and Subsequent Acts	UCC[3] September 6, 1952 revised in Paris, July 24, 1971	TRIPS April 15, 1994	Rome Convention October 26, 1961	Geneva Phonograms Convention October 29, 1971	Satellite Convention May 21, 1974	WIPO Copyright Treaty[4]	WIPO Performances and Phonograms Treaty[5]	Date of Principal Law (most recent amendment)[6]	Period of Protection[6]
United States of America	Paris A	Paris	January 1, 1995		March 10, 1974	March 7, 1985	March 6, 2002	May 20, 2002[14]	1976 (2009)	70 years pma; for works made for hire 95 years from first publication or 120 years from creation, whichever expires first
Uruguay	Paris A	Paris	January 1, 1995	July 4, 1977	January 18, 1983		June 5, 2009	August 28, 2008	1937 (2003)	50 years pma
Uzbekistan	Paris A, D		Observer[7]						2006	50 years from January 1, pma
Vanuatu			Observer[7]						2000	50 years pma

Signatories	Berne Convention[2] September 9, 1886 and Subsequent Acts	UCC[3] September 6, 1952 revised in Paris, July 24, 1971	TRIPS April 15, 1994	Rome Convention October 26, 1961	Geneva Phonograms Convention October 29, 1971	Satellite Convention May 21, 1974	WIPO Copyright Treaty[4]	WIPO Performances and Phonograms Treaty[5]	Date of Principal Law (most recent amendment)[6]	Period of Protection[6]
Venezuela (Bolivian Republic of)	Paris A, H	Paris	January 1, 1995	January 30, 1996	November 18, 1982				1993 (1999)	60 years from January 1, pma
Viet Nam	Paris A, D, H		January 11, 2007	March 1, 2007[8]	July 6, 2005	January 12, 2006			2005 (2009)	50 years pma (from end of year)
Yemen	Paris A, D		Observer[7]						1994 (2006)	30 years from January 1, pma or 25 years from January 1, of year of production for certain works
Zambia	Paris A	Geneva	January 1, 1995						1994	50 years pma (from end of year)

Signatories	Berne Convention[2] September 9, 1886 and Subsequent Acts	UCC[3] September 6, 1952 revised in Paris, July 24, 1971	TRIPS April 15, 1994	Rome Convention October 26, 1961	Geneva Phonograms Convention October 29, 1971	Satellite Convention May 21, 1974	WIPO Copyright Treaty[4]	WIPO Performances and Phonograms Treaty[5]	Date of Principal Law (most recent amendment)[6]	Period of Protection[6]
Zimbabwe	Paris B Rome		March 5, 1995						1967 (1982)	50 years pma (from end of year)
Total number of Member States	164	Paris 65 Geneva 35 Total 100	Member States 153 Observers 30	91	77	34	88	86	184 laws 2 unknown 3 no legislation	

¹ This table reflects the status of ratifications and accessions to the Conventions as of August 31, 2010. The authors are indebted to WIPO, Unesco and the WTO for the information used in compiling this table. For more up to date information, see the following web pages: *http://www.wipo.org* [Accessed September 23, 2010]; *http://www.portal.unesco.org/culture* [Accessed September 23, 2010]; and *http://www.wto.org* [Accessed September 23, 2010].

² Berne Convention: "Paris" means the Berne Convention as revised at Paris on July 24, 1971 (Paris Act); "Stockholm" means the said Convention as revised at Stockholm on July 14, 1967 (Stockholm Act); "Brussels" means the said Convention as revised at Brussels on June 26, 1948 (Brussels Act); "Rome" means the said Convention as revised at Rome on June 2, 1928 (Rome Act). Paris Revision Countries which have ratified or acceded to the entire Paris Act of the Berne Convention, including the Appendix, are indicated as "Paris A". Countries which have declared that their ratification or accession does not apply to arts 1–21 and the Appendix are indicated as "Paris B". Countries which availed themselves of one or both of the faculties provided for in arts II and III of the Appendix until October 10, 2004, are indicated as "Paris C". Countries which have availed themselves of one or both of the faculties provided for in arts II and III of the Appendix until October 10, 2014, are indicated as "Paris D". Countries which made a declaration concerning the right of translation under Art. V of the Appendix are indicated as "Paris E". Countries which made a declaration under art.14*bis*(2)(b) are indicated as "Paris F" (presumption of legitimation for some authors who have brought contributions to the making of the cinematographic work). Countries which have made a declaration under art.14*bis*(2)(c) are indicated as "Paris G" (undertaking by authors to bring contributions to the making of a cinematographic work must be in writing). Countries which made a declaration under art.33(2) relating to the International Court of Justice are indicated as "Paris H". Countries which made a declaration that they admit the application of the Appendix of the Paris Act to works of which it is the State of origin are indicated as Paris I.

Stockholm Revision: The substantive provisions of the Stockholm revision did not, and now cannot, come into force. However, previous Acts remain in force in relations with those countries of the Union which have not ratified or acceded to the Paris Act. For countries which have ratified or acceded to the whole of the Paris Act and the Appendix, no reference is made to either Stockholm or earlier revisions. Countries which declared that their ratification or accession does not apply to arts 1–21 of the Stockholm Act and the Protocol Regarding Developing Countries are indicated as "Stockholm B". This also indicates countries which ratified or acceded to the entire Stockholm Act, the substantive provisions of which have not come into force.

³ UCC: Countries which have ratified or acceded to the 1971 Paris revised Convention are indicated as "Paris" (most of these are party also to the Geneva Convention); others are shown as "Geneva". Countries which have availed themselves of the exceptions in favour of developing countries are indicated as "Paris*".

⁴ The WIPO Copyright Treaty entered into force on March 6, 2002. See para.23–75, above.

⁵The WIPO Performances and Phonograms Treaty entered into force on May 20, 2002. See para.23–133, above.

⁶ The date of the principal law is given, with the date of the most recent amendment in brackets. The period of protection is for literary and artistic works (as defined in art.2(1) of the Berne Convention), and is indicated as either *post mortem auctoris* (pma), pma from the end of the calendar year, or pma from January 1 of the following year. Many countries have different periods of protection for

different works, e.g. for photographs, computer programs, collective works, works where the author is a legal entity and for the subject-matter of related rights. For some works the period of protection runs from the date of publication. In some countries the period of protection is less than that required by international convention. In such cases the indicated period does not apply to foreign works.

[7] An "observer" State must start accession negotiations within five years of becoming an observer (except Holy See).

[8] The instruments of ratification or accession to the Rome Convention, or subsequent notifications, deposited with the Secretary-General of the United Nations by the following States contain declarations made under the articles mentioned hereafter (with reference to publication in *Le Droit d'auteur* (Copyright) for the years 1962 to 1964, in *Copyright* for the years 1965 to 1994, in *Industrial Property and Copyright* until May 1998 and, in *Intellectual Property Laws and Treaties* from June 1998 until December 2001). Thereafter, notifications may be consulted on the WIPO website: *http://www.wipo.int/treaties* [Accessed September 23, 2010].

> Algeria, arts 5(3) (concerning art.5(1)(c), art.6(2) and art.16(1)(a)(iii) and (iv));
>
> Australia, arts 5(3) (concerning art.5(1)(c)), 6(2), 16(1)(a)(i) and 16(1)(b) [1992, p.301];
>
> Austria, art.16(1)(a)(iii) and (iv) and 1(b) [1973, p.67];
>
> Belarus, arts 5(3) (concerning art.5(1)(b)), 6(2), 16(1)(a)(iii) and (iv);
>
> Belgium, arts 5(3) (concerning art.5(1)(c)), 6(2), 16(1)(a)(iii) and (iv) [1999, p.119];
>
> Bulgaria, art.16(1)(a)(iii) and (iv) [1995, p.262];
>
> Canada, art.5(3) (concerning arts 5(1)(b) and (c)), 6(2) (concerning arts 6(1)) and 16(1)(a)(iv) [1998, p.42];
>
> Congo, arts 5(3) (concerning art.5(1)(c)) and 16(1)(a)(i) [1964, p.127];
>
> Croatia, arts 5(3) (concerning art.5(1)(b)) and 16(1)(a)(iii) and (iv) [2000, p.14];
>
> Czech Republic, art.16(1)(a)(iii) and (iv) [1964, p.110];
>
> Denmark, arts 5(3) (concerning art.5(1)(c)), 6(2), 16(1)(a)(ii) and (iv) [1965, p.214];
>
> Estonia, arts 5(3) (concerning arts 5(1) (c)), and 6(2), and as from October 9, 2003, art.16(1)(a)(iv);
>
> Fiji, arts 5(3) (concerning art.5(1)(b)), 6(2) and 16(1) (a)(i) [1972, pp.88 and 178];
>
> Finland, arts 16(1)(a)(i), (ii) and (iv) and 17 [1983, p.287 and 1994, p.152];
>
> France, arts 5(3) (concerning art.5(1)(c)) and 16(1)(a)(iii) and (iv) [1987, p.184];
>
> Germany, arts 5(3) (concerning art.5(1)(b)) and 16(1)(a)(iv) [1966, p.237];
>
> Iceland, arts 5(3) (concerning art.5(1)(b)), 6(2) and 16(1)(a)(i), (ii), (iii) and (iv) [1994, p.152];
>
> Ireland, arts 5(3) (concerning art.5(1)(b)), 6(2) and 16(1)(a)(ii) [1979, p.218];
>
> Israel, arts 5(3) (concerning art.5(1)(b)), 6(2) (concerning art.6(1)) and 16(1)(a)(iii), (iv) and 16(1)(b);
>
> Italy, arts 6(2), 16(1)(a)(ii), (iii) and (iv), 16(1)(b) and 17 [1975, p 44];
>
> Japan, arts 5(3) (concerning art.5(1)(c)) and 16(1)(a)(ii) and (iv) [1989, p.288];

Latvia, art.16(1)(a)(iii) [1999, p.76];

Lesotho, art.16(1)(a)(ii) and (1)(b) [1990, p.95];

Liechtenstein, art.5(3) (concerning art.5(1)(b)) and art.16(1)(a)(iii) and (iv) [1999, p.119];

Lithuania, art.16(1)(a)(iii) [1999, p.76];

Luxembourg, arts 5(3) (concerning art.5(1)(c)), 16(1)(a)(i) and 16(1)(b) [1976, p.24];

Monaco, arts 5(3) (concerning art.5(1)(c)), 16(1)(a)(i) and 16(1)(b) [1985, p.422];

Netherlands, art.16(1)(a)(iii) and (iv) [1993, p.253];

Niger, arts 5(3) (concerning art.5(1)(c)) and 16(1)(a)(i) [1963, p.155];

Nigeria, arts 5(3) (concerning art.5(1)(c)), 6(2) and 16(1)(a)(ii), (iii) and (iv) [1993, p.253];

Norway, arts 6(2) and 16(1)(a)(iii) and (iv) [1978, p.133; in respect of 16(1)(a)(ii) modified: 1989, p.288];

Poland, arts 5(3) (concerning art.5(1) (c)), 6(2), and 16(1)(a)(ii), (iii) and (iv) and 16(1)(b) [1997, p.170];

Republic of Korea, arts 5(3), 6(2), 16(1)(a)(ii), (iii) and (iv) and 16(1)(b).

Republic of Moldova, arts 5(3) (concerning art.5(1)(b)), 6(2), 16(1)(a)(iii), (iii) and (iv) [1996, p.40];

Romania, arts 5(3), 6(2), 16(1)(a)(iii) and (iv) [1998, p.54];

Russian Federation, arts 5(3) (concerning art.5(1)(b)), 6(2) and 16(1)(a)(iii) and (iv);

Saint Lucia, arts 5(3) (concerning art.5(1)(c)) and 16(1)(a)(iii);

Slovakia, art.16(1)(a)(iii) and (iv) [1964, p.110];

Slovenia, arts 5(3) (concerning art.5(1)(c)) and 16(1)(a)(i) [1996, p.318];

Spain, arts 5(3) (concerning art.5(1)(c)), 6(2) and 16(1)(a)(iii) and (iv) [1991, p.221];

Sweden, art.16(1)(a)(iv) [1962, p.211; 1986, p.382];

Switzerland, arts 5(3) (concerning art.5(1)(b)) and 16(1)(a)(iii) and (iv) [1993, p.254];

The former Yugoslav Republic of Macedonia, arts 5(3) (concerning art.5(1)(c)) and 16(1)(a)(i) [1998, p.42];

United Kingdom, arts 5(3) (concerning art.5(1)(b)), 6(2) and 16(1)(a)(ii), (iii) and (iv) [1963, p.244]; the same declarations were made for Gibraltar and Bermuda [1967, p.36; 1970, p.108];

Viet Nam, arts 16(1)(a)(i) and 16(1)(b) concerning arts 12 and 13(d).

[9] Bosnia and Herzegovina: Signature by Yugoslavia. Succession to signature by Bosnia and Herzegovina: Date of Deposit: January 12, 1994, with effect from March 6, 1992.

[10] Bosnia and Herzegovina: on January 12, 1994, this country deposited its instrument of succession to signature with effect from March 1, 1992. This followed the signature by the Socialist Federal Republic of Yugoslavia on October 29, 1971.

[11] China: The Paris Act of the Berne Convention and the Geneva Phonograms Convention have applied to Hong Kong from July 1, 1997 and to Macao from December 20, 1999

[12] China has declared that the WCT shall not apply to the Macao Special Administrative Region of the People's Republic of China. The Treaty has applied to the Hong Kong Special Administrative Region of China with effect from October 1, 2008.

[13] Netherlands: accession for the Kingdom in Europe. Arts 22–38 of the Paris Act of the Berne Convention apply also to the Netherlands Antilles and Aruba.

[14] The instruments of ratification or accession to the WPPT, or subsequent notifications, deposited with the Director-General of WIPO by the following States contain declarations made under the articles mentioned hereafter. Notifications may be consulted on the WIPO website: *http://www.wipo.int/treaties* [Accessed September 23, 2010].

Australia: Pursuant to art.3(3) of the WPPT, Australia will not apply the criterion of publication concerning the protection of producers of phonograms. Further, it will not apply the provisions of art.15(1) in respect of: (a) the use of phonograms for (i) radio broadcasting, and (ii) communication to the public within the meaning of the first sentence of art.2(g), and (b) the communication to the public of phonograms by way of making the sounds of the phonograms available to the public by means of the operation of equipment to receive a broadcast or other transmission of the phonograms.

Belgium: Pursuant to art.3(3) of the WPPT, Belgium will not apply the criterion of publication with effect from August 30, 2006.

Chile: Pursuant to art.15(3) of the WPPT, the Republic of Chile will apply the provisions of art.15(1) of the Treaty only in respect of direct uses of phonograms published for commercial purposes for broadcasting or for any communication to the public. Pursuant to art.15(3) of the Treaty, as regards phonograms the producer or performer of which is a national of another Contracting Party which has made a declaration under art.15(3) of the Treaty, the Republic of Chile will apply, notwithstanding the provisions of the preceding declaration, the provisions of art.15(1) of the Treaty to the extent that Party grants the protection provided for by the provisions of art.15(1) of the Treaty.

China: The WPPT shall not apply to the Macao Special Administrative Region of the People's Republic of China. The Treaty has applied to the Hong Kong Special Administrative Region of China with effect from October 1, 2008. With respect to the right of producers of phonograms stipulated in art.15(1) of the Treaty, relevant laws of Hong Kong shall apply. Hong Kong does not consider itself bound by art.15(1) WPPT with regard to the right of performers.

Costa Rica: Pursuant to art.15(3) WPPT, Costa Rica shall only apply art.15(1) in respect of broadcasting or communication to the public for commercial purposes and shall not apply the said provisions to traditional free non-interactive over-the-air broadcasting.

Denmark: In accordance with art.3(3) of the Treaty, Denmark has declared that it will not apply the criterion of publication concerning the protection of phonograms.

Finland: Pursuant to art.3(3) of the WPPT, Finland avails itself of the possibilities provided in art.17 of the International Convention for the Protection of Performers, Producers of Phonograms and Broadcasting Organisations (Rome Convention) and refers to the notification made at the time of ratification by Finland of the Rome Convention, stating that it will apply, for the purposes of art.5 of the said Convention, the criterion of fixation alone and, for the purposes of art.16(1)(a)(iv), the criterion of fixation instead of the criterion of nationality.

France: In accordance with art.3(3) of the Treaty, France has declared that it will not apply the criterion of publication concerning the protection of phonograms.

Germany: In accordance with art.3(3) of the Treaty, Germany has declared that it will not apply the criterion of fixation concerning the protection of phonograms.

Japan: Pursuant to art.3(3) WPPT, Japan will not apply the criterion of publication concerning the protection of producers of phonograms. Pursuant to art.15(3), as regards phonograms the producer of which is a national of another Contracting Party which has made a declaration under art.15(3) of the Treaty, the Government of Japan will apply art.15(1) to the extent that the Party grants the protection provided for by the provisions of art.15(1). Further, Japan will apply the provisions of art.15(1) in respect of the direct or indirect use of the phonograms published for commercial purposes for broadcasting, cable casting (wire diffusion) or "automatic public transmission of unfixed information". For purposes of this declaration, "automatic public transmission of unfixed information" shall mean transmission by means of inputting information into an automatic public transmission server (as defined in art. 2(1)(9*quinquies*)(i) of the Copyright Law of Japan) already connected with a telecommunication line that is provided for use by the public, which is carried out automatically in response to a request from the public and which is intended for direct receipt by the public. Japan will also apply the provisions of art.15(1) in respect of the direct or indirect use of the phonograms made available to the public, by wire or wireless means, in such a way that members of the public may access them from a place and at a time individually chosen by them for "automatic public transmission of unfixed information".

Republic of Korea: In accordance with art.15(3) of the WPPT, the Republic of Korea will apply the provision of art.15(1) thereof in respect of the use of phonograms published for commercial purposes for broadcasting or transmission by wire. Transmission by wire does not include transmission over the internet. In accordance with art.3(3) of the Treaty, this State has declared that it will not apply the criterion of publication concerning the protection of phonograms. In accordance with art.15(3) of the Treaty, as regards phonograms the producer or performer of which is a national of another Contracting Party which has made a declaration under art.15(3) thereof, the Republic of Korea will apply the provisions of art.15(1) thereof to the extent to which, and to the term for which, the other Contracting Party grants protection to phonograms the producer or performer of which is a national of the Republic of Korea under the provisions of art.15(1) thereof.

Russian Federation: In accordance with art.15(3) of the WPPT, the Russian Federation shall not apply the provisions of art.15(1) of the said Treaty in relation to phonograms, the producer of which is not a citizen or legal person of another Contracting Party; shall limit the protection granted, in accordance with art.15(1) of the WPPT, in relation to phonograms, the producer of which is a citizen or legal person of another Contracting Party, within the scope and on the conditions provided for by this Contracting Party for phonograms first recorded by a citizen or legal person of the Russian Federation. In accordance with art.3(3) of the WPPT, the Russian Federation notifies that when it acceded to the International Convention for the Protection of Performers, Producers of Phonograms and Broadcasting Organisations (Rome Convention) of October 26, 1961, the Russian Federation in accordance with art.5(3) of the Rome Convention, declared that it shall not apply the fixation criterion provided for in art.5(1)(b) of the Rome Convention.

Singapore: Pursuant to art.15(3) WPPT, Singapore will limit the provisions of art.15(1) in the following ways: (i) Producers of phonograms have the exclusive right to make available to the public a sound recording by means of, or as part of, a digital audio transmission; and (ii) Perform-

ers can bring an action of unauthorised communication of a live performance to the public (on a network or otherwise) in such a way that the recording may be accessed by any person from a place and at a time chosen
by him. In this context, "communication" includes broadcasting, inclusion in a cable programme service and the making available of the live
performance in such a way that the performance may be accessed by any
person from a place and at a time chosen by him.

Sweden: In accordance with art.3(3) of WPPT, the Kingdom of Sweden
has declared that it will not apply the criterion of publication, with the
exception of the reproduction right for phonogram producers.

Switzerland: In accordance with art.3(3) of WPPT, the Kingdom of Sweden has declared that it will not apply the criterion of fixation, applying
therefore the criterion of publication.

The FYRM: Pursuant to art.3(3) of the WPPT, the FYRM shall not apply
the provision on the criterion of publication in respect of the national
treatment on protection of phonogram producers in relation to the
expressed reservation of the FRYM on art.5(3) of the International
Convention for the Protection of Performers, Phonogram Producers and
Broadcasting Organizations (Rome Convention). Pursuant to art.15(3) of
the WPPT, the FRYM shall also not apply the provision on single equitable remuneration for the performers and for the phonogram producers for
direct or indirect use of phonograms published for commercial purposes
for broadcasting or for any other communication to the public, in relation
to the expressed reservation of the FYRM on art.16(1)(a)(i) of the Rome
Convention.

United States of America: Pursuant to art.15(3) of the WPPT, the USA
will apply the provisions of art.15(1) of the WIPO Performances and Phonograms Treaty only in respect of certain acts of broadcasting and communication to the public by digital means for which a direct or indirect fee
is charged for reception, and for other retransmissions and digital phono-
record deliveries, as provided under the US law.

[15] Canada: It should be noted that the Copyright Act Amendment Bill C–32
was tabled on June 2, 2010 and is a successor to Bill C-61. Bill C-32 updates Canadian copyright law in particular regarding internet-related issues, including
international standards in this regard. It however also delineates certain exceptions and mandates a review by Parliament every five year.

[16] New Zealand: A bill that was introduced and has to date passed its first reading, aims to repeal s.92a and replace it with a three-strikes notice regime to deter
illegal file sharing. It is due to be returned with a report to Parliament by the
Commerce Select Committee on October 22, 2010.

PART VIII

EXPLOITATION AND CONTROL OF RIGHTS

CHAPTER TWENTY SIX

EXPLOITATION OF RIGHTS IN PARTICULAR INDUSTRIES

Contents   *Para.*

1. THE PUBLISHING INDUSTRY

A. THE GENERAL NATURE OF THE PUBLISHING INDUSTRY

The publishing industry in the United Kingdom is a vibrant and diverse industry, producing a wide variety of material both in conventional printed form and in various electronic forms, such as CD-ROMs, online journals and material published over the internet. The principal sectors of the publishing industry, are: book publishing, magazine publishing, journal publishing, electronic publishing and newspaper publishing. Electronic publishing is an aspect of all the other areas of publishing, and can involve offline (e.g. CD-ROM) or online publishing (including internet) and will be dealt with briefly in the context of book publishing, magazine publishing and journal publishing. Newspaper publishing is considered in depth in a separate section.[1]

26–01

Book publishing. Book publishing is big business. In 2009, the sales of books by the UK publishing industry amounted to approximately £3,053 million.[2] Books are published in hardback and paperback form in a wide variety of shapes and sizes. Some (particularly works of fiction) consist only of text; others are illustrated. Of those that are illustrated, the illustrations range from simple line drawings or tables through to complex hand-drawn full colour artwork, colour and black-and-white photographs, and "pop-up" illustrations. The book publishing industry has for a long time generally been considered to consist of two principal sectors, namely "trade publishers" (i.e. those who publish books for the general public, and whose books are primarily made available through retail bookshops) on the one hand and those who publish for the professions (e.g. legal, accountancy, medical, engineering, etc.), academic works (e.g. for schools, colleges and universities) and encyclopaedias on the other. Of course, within each of these two broad divisions, various publishers specialise in particular subject areas. Whilst it is still fair to describe the industry as consisting of these two principal sectors, electronic publishers are increasingly becoming a significant sector in their own right, as well as forming part of the above two sectors. The Publishers' Association has established the Digital Publishing Forum, with its aim being to brief publishers on technical developments, market trends and legal issues in the area of digital publishing. The distinction between "trade publishers" and other publishers is important, since it affects the rights which are generally acquired by these different groups of publishers.

26–02

Over the last 20 years or so there has been a marked tendency towards so-called "vertical publishing", whereby the hardback and paperback editions of a particular book are published by the same publisher. Hardback books generally command a higher selling price (and usually also a higher profit margin) than paperback books, as they have a much higher perceived value in the eyes of the purchaser. Many books are published originally in hardback, with a paperback edition usually being published from six months to a year or so later, once the demand for the hardback edition has fallen off. In the past, publishers tended to specialise either in publishing in hardback or in paperback. It is now far more common for publishers to have the facility to publish both hardback and paperback editions, perhaps under different imprints but within the same corporate group.

A further tendency within the last 20 years or so has been towards the

---

[1] See paras 26–109 et seq., below.
[2] For up-to-date statistics of the UK book publishing industry, see the website of The Publishers' Association at *http://www.publishers.org.uk* [Accessed October 29, 2010].

concentration of book publishing within the hands of a few multinational corporations, often having interests not only in book publishing but also in other media such as television, music and film production and distribution. Notwithstanding the dominance of the multinational publishers, there is still a wide range of small- to medium-sized independent publishers, often concentrating on specialised sectors of the book market. In addition, there are a number of "book packagers", who create books for publication under publishers' imprints, and oversee the whole process from concept through to delivery of the finished books to the publisher or to the publisher's distributor. Very often the books in question will have been conceived by the packager and the idea "sold" to publishers both in English-language markets and in foreign-language markets, and the development and production of the books is financed by stage payments from the publishers. This process is particularly suited to highly illustrated works, where the surrounding text can be produced in a number of different languages.

With developments in computer and printing technology, it is now feasible for books to be created using desktop publishing software, and small print runs can be economically viable. This makes it possible for even an individual to carry out every aspect of the publishing process, from writing the book to designing the page layout and printing and publishing.

There are also so-called "vanity publishers", who will publish a work provided that the author pays all or a substantial part of the cost of producing and publishing the book. In general, this does not represent a good deal for the author, and authors will usually only resort to this if they cannot get a conventional publisher to publish the book at the publisher's own risk and expense.

Developments in print-on-demand technology and the internet have led to a growth in self-publishing opportunities. Websites such as Lulu.com and Author-House offer authors the opportunity to publish their works at minimal cost to themselves, but with the opportunity of wide availability, including through internet booksellers, such as Amazon and Barnes & Noble, and through conventional bookshops. These websites allow authors to retain full control over their work, including design, ownership of rights and pricing. Books are printed only when orders are received, so there is no inventory.

A significant development in this area is the launch by Amazon, through its US website Amazon.com, of its self-publishing service branded "CreateSpace". Authors upload their work in PDF form, the files are checked to ensure that they comply with the CreateSpace technical submission requirements, and once that hurdle has been successfully cleared, a proof is ordered so that the author can check and be satisfied with the book. Once the book is finished, it can be available for sale on Amazon.com within 15 business days. Authors can choose the sales channels through which the book is available, which could be just the author's own CreateSpace E-Store, or can also include Amazon.com and can also include what Amazon refers to as the "Expanded Distribution Channel", which comprises CreateSpace Direct (Amazon's wholesale website, where resellers purchase books), bookstores and online retailers and US libraries and academic institutions. However, the books cannot at present be listed for sale on any of Amazon's other international websites. This can have implications for the amount which the author receives from each sale, because CreateSpace charges a percentage of the list price (20 per cent on sales through the author's CreateSpace E-Store, 40 per cent on sales through Amazon.com and 60 per cent on sales through the Expanded Distribution Channel) plus a fixed charge and a charge per page, which vary according to whether the book is in black and white or in colour, and also according to the number of pages.

26–03   **Book distribution.** Books may reach the ultimate purchaser by a number of different routes, the most common of which are as follows:

(a) *Retailers*

Many bookshops purchase direct from the publishers, often ordering through an electronic ordering system, which enables bookshops to order precisely the number of books which they expect to be able to sell or for which they have actual requests from customers. In general, bookshops purchase on a "sale-or-return" basis, but where large quantities of any particular title are involved, some publishers are prepared to offer booksellers a higher discount off the "published price" or "recommended retail price" in return for the transaction being on a "firm sale" basis. Booksellers in the United Kingdom are now free to sell books to the ultimate purchaser at whatever price they choose, since the abolition of the Net Book Agreement. In practice, relatively few titles are sold at a discount from the publisher's recommended retail price, and those that are sold at a discount from the recommended price tend to be best-sellers or special promotions at the largest chain booksellers.

(b) *Wholesalers*

Many bookshops are supplied largely by wholesalers. If wholesalers purchase books from publishers in bulk and supply bookshops they need to obtain a substantial discount from the publishers in order to enable them to supply bookshops at a price which enables the bookshop in turn to make a profit on those books.

(c) *Distributors*

Distributors provide warehousing and distribution services for publishers, including invoicing and collection of payment from bookshops, in return for commission.

(d) *Book clubs*

There are a number of general and special interest book clubs which operate throughout the United Kingdom, whereby members of the public can obtain books by mail order, many of them being at prices lower than are available through bookshops. Book clubs attract new members by means of an introductory special offer, with a number of books at very cheap prices, in return for which the purchaser generally makes a commitment to buy a minimum number of books over a given period of time. The books sold by book clubs may, if quantities are small, be the publisher's original editions or, in the case of larger quantities, will be the book clubs' own editions with their own imprint. The book clubs' own editions may either be produced for them by the publisher at the same time as it arranges the printing of its own edition (in which case the longer print run thereby made possible will reduce unit costs) or they may be manufactured by the book club itself. This will affect the terms on which the book club deals with the publisher and will also affect the amount which the author receives from the sale of copies through the book club.

(e) *Direct sales*

There are a number of organisations that sell books direct to individual members of the public, particularly at people's offices. The books sold in this way may be the publishers' regular editions or they may be editions specifically produced for and with the imprint of the direct seller. This method of sale has become increasingly popular and now constitutes a significant part of the market for some books. However, there is considerable concern amongst authors and their representatives that publishers are selling books to direct sellers (including book clubs) too soon after first publication and at very reduced prices, which damages bookshop sales and therefore reduces the royalties authors can expect to receive.

(f) *Internet sales*

Increasingly, books are being sold through online booksellers such as *Amazon.co.uk* and *WHSmith.co.uk*, as well as supermarket websites, such as *Tesco.com*. Although online booksellers currently represent less than one-fifth of the total retail market for books,[3] they are increasing their share, and they also supply other products, such as computer games, software and music. *Amazon.co.uk* is the dominant online UK-based bookseller. Other significant UK online booksellers include Waterstone's. Many independent booksellers, publishers and individuals also use *Amazon.co.uk* to reach new markets by listing stock and selling books on the *Amazon.co.uk* Marketplace platform, which can also provide an opportunity to buy rare and out-of-print books. *Amazon.co.uk*'s Associates scheme enables third-party websites to link to *Amazon.co.uk* and be paid a proportion of any sales that are made as a result of the link. This option has been popular with individual booksellers, publishers and other organisations, such as schools, fan sites and charities, as well as private individuals. Waterstone's has a similar scheme on its website. AbeBooks, based in Canada and with a European office in Germany, is now a subsidiary of Amazon.com, Inc. It describes itself as "an online marketplace for books" and through its various international websites it offers a search facility for over 100 million (it claims) new, second-hand, rare and out-of-print books from more than 13,500 booksellers.

A UK website The Book Depository (*http://www.bookdepository.co.uk* [Accessed October 29, 2010]) has the aim of "making 'All books available to All' through pioneering supply chain initiatives, republishing and digitising of content", and is both a book distributor and also a publisher in that it reprints a substantial (and increasing) number of titles that are out of print and can supply them within a few days. The Book Depository claims to be the fastest-growing book distributor in Europe.

A relatively new development sees major publishers competing with retailers in selling books direct from their own revamped websites. Random House UK, Penguin and Pan Macmillan are all now selling books directly to consumers. Some of the Hachette Livre group of UK publishers (which includes Headline, Hodder & Stoughton, John Murray, Little, Brown, Octopus and Orion) offer books direct to consumers from their own respective websites and others via a link to Amazon.co.uk. Harper-Collins offers books direct to consumers via a link from its website to Amazon.co.uk. How all of this affects booksellers is not clear, but the Booksellers Association has expressed concern. Publishers have endeavoured to reassure the industry that they are not intending to take sales away from booksellers, but rather add some extra value, for example in terms of additional content. But unless publishers are actually generating new business by their direct-to-consumer sales, it is hard to see how this can do anything but harm to booksellers' sales. Concern has also been expressed by the Booksellers Association that consumers might be confused by the multiplicity of places to buy books online, and that their response may be simply to default to purchasing from Amazon, rather than, for example, independent booksellers' websites.

---

[3] In 2009 internet sales amounted to 17.1% of total UK book sales (source: Books & The Consumer (BML/TNS)— *http://www.bookmarketing.co.uk* [Accessed October 29, 2010]). In 2007 Amazon.co.uk's market share was 16% (source: Books & The Consumer (BML/TNS)— *http://www.bookmarketing.co.uk* [Accessed October 29, 2010]. For the most recent statistics on UK book sales, see the website of The Booksellers Association at *http://www.booksellers.org.uk* [Accessed October 29, 2010]. In the US, Amazon.com outsells bricks and mortar chain stores for combined sales of books, DVDs and CDs (source: *http://www.fonerbooks.com* [Accessed October 29, 2010]).

Magazine publishing. There are varying estimates of the number of magazine   **26–04**
titles published in the United Kingdom, but BRAD (British Rate and Data) and
the Periodical Publishers Association ("PPA") respectively indicate the numbers
at 4,811 "business" titles and 3,212 "consumer" titles, although the numbers will
change from year to year. According to BRAD, 224 new business titles entered
the UK market in 2008, an increase of 10.3 per cent since 2007. PPA reports that
UK consumers are expected to spend £2.5 billion on magazines in 2010. It says
that "magazines reach 87 per cent of the total adult population (compared with
only 74 per cent of the adult population accessing the Internet)", with the 15–24-
year-old age group being the most likely to read magazines. As well as the distinction between "business" titles on the one hand and "consumer" titles on the other,
in recent years there has emerged the so-called "customer publishing" sector,
comprising publications produced under contract for companies and distributed
either free of charge or offered for sale to customers. This sector has enjoyed
rapid growth. The customer publishing industry was worth £904 million in 2007
and is projected to be worth £1 billion by 2010. The industry saw a 12 per cent
growth in 2007, with around 120 new brands coming into the market.[4]

The UK magazine publishing industry is dominated by a small number of major companies who publish a large and often diverse range of titles. Some titles
are produced in different versions for different markets, either in the same
language (e.g. separate English-language editions for the American and UK
markets) or in different languages for various different countries, while retaining
the same overall identity and brand, notwithstanding differences in content. The
UK magazine publishing industry also has a large number of small independent
publishers, often producing magazines for special interests, and there are a large
number of new titles published on a regular basis.

Magazine distribution. The vast majority of consumer magazines are sold in the   **26–05**
United Kingdom through retail outlets. In general, magazines tend to be
distributed through a number of large or independent distributors. The distributors make arrangements with the printers of the magazines for the magazines to
be shipped to wholesalers who in turn distribute to individual newsagents. There
are 55,000 retail outlets in the United Kingdom. There are approximately 2,600
regular frequency consumer magazines distributed through the retail supply
chain, which generate around £1.9 billion in retail revenue. At present, 16 per
cent of consumer magazines are sold in the United Kingdom on subscription by
mail order, either by the publisher directly or through subscription agents, but
often at a substantial discount from the cover price charged in newsagents.
However, the proportion of magazines sold in this way is likely to increase.
Some magazines are *only* available on subscription. About 24 per cent of business and professional magazines are sold through subscriptions, and as much as
90 per cent of so-called "business-to-business" magazines are sold by
subscription. In addition, a number of magazine publishers are making all or
parts of their magazines available, in some cases at a charge, over the internet.
Sometimes this is to enable them to present information in a way which cannot
be done on the printed page; sometimes this is to enable additional background
information to be published; often it also enables the publishers to present up-to-
the-minute news, which cannot be done in a printed monthly magazine. The
more comprehensive the material available on the internet, the more likely the
publisher will charge to access it. Even if there is a charge to access all of the material, some of it will usually be available free of charge as a "taster".

---

[4] For the latest available statistics of the UK magazine publishing industry, see the website of The
Periodical Publishers' Association at *http://www.ppa.co.uk* [Accessed October 29, 2010]. The
Association of Publishing Agencies ("APA") is the representative body for the customer publish-
ing industry (*http://www.apa.co.uk* [Accessed October 29, 2010]).

26–06   **Journal publishing.** This sector mainly comprises the publication of professional (including scientific) and academic journals. It is difficult to obtain clear
and up-to-date statistics of the scale of the journal publishing sector.[5] The total
turnover of all journals for the years 1999 and 2000 was £554.29 million. Of this,
£286.3 million represented UK-only publishers and £267.99 million represented
the turnover of international publishers. As with book and magazine publishing,
there are a number of major players in this market sector, as well as independent
publishers. Journals tend to be sold on subscription, either by direct arrangement
between the publisher and the subscriber or through subscription agents acting on
behalf of the publisher. Something under 50 per cent of revenue is earned from
subscriptions in this way.[6] Traditionally, journals have been made available only
in printed form, but now most journals are available online, either in addition to
or instead of the printed version.[7] A number of major journal publishers are
involved in arrangements with academic institutions to provide their journals online pursuant to a "site licence", permitting unlimited access to the journals in
question for all students and staff of the licensed academic institutions.[8] For the
latest available statistics of the UK journal publishing industry, see the website of
The Association of Learned and Professional Society Publishers at *http://
www.alpsp.org* [Accessed October 29, 2010]. However, the statistics available
here are not up-to-date.

B. SOURCES OF COPYRIGHT WORKS

26–07   (a) All sections of the publishing industry involve the creation of literary works.
These are created by "authors",[9] including journalists. While authors of books are
generally unlikely to be employees of the publisher (although there are some
exceptions to this), it is common for journalists to be employees of magazine and
newspaper publishers, although there are substantial numbers of freelance
journalists. Where an author (including a journalist) is an employee, then the
copyright in works created in the course of his or her employment are owned by
the employer, subject to any agreement to the contrary.[10] Many authors are
represented by literary agents, who will negotiate contracts with book, newspaper
and magazine publishers on behalf of their client authors. Authors' agents do not
usually have authority to sign contracts on behalf of their authors.

26–08   (b) In the case of illustrated works, specialist illustrators, artists and photographers
are the primary sources of the illustrations. Depending on the publishers in question, some illustrators may be in-house employees, in which case the employer
will own the copyright in their work, but in general illustrators, artists and
photographers are more likely to be freelance. Many specialist illustrators and
photographers are represented by agents, who provide the link between the illustrator or photographer on the one hand and the publisher on the other hand and

---

[5] Some statistics for UK Journal publishing for 1999 and 2000 are contained in a survey conducted
in 2001 and published in August 2002 by TFPL Ltd on behalf, and amongst the membership, of
the Publishers' Association ("PA") and the Association of Learned and Professional Society
Publishers ("ALPSP"). The TFPL survey is available on the ALPSP website *http://
www.alpsp.org/ngen__public/default.asp?ID=245* [Accessed October 18, 2010] and many other
useful resources are also available on the ALPSP web site.

[6] See the TFPL survey.

[7] In the TFPL surveys for 1999 and 2000, 91 of the 169 respondents published some, or all, of their
journals electronically, and those electronic journals represented 70 per cent of the total number
of titles covered in the survey. Some of the respondents published all of their journals electronically; some publish some, but not all, of their journals electronically; and some publish only in
print.

[8] See para.26–77, below.

[9] In the technical sense as used in CDPA 1988 s.9 and in the colloquial sense.

[10] See CDPA 1988 s.11(2), and paras 5–08 et seq., above.

who can provide the right person for the particular task in hand. The agent will also negotiate on behalf of the illustrator/photographer the terms upon which the work will be created specifically for the publisher or otherwise made available to the publisher. In the case of photographs, many photographers place their existing work with photographic libraries, some of which specialise in particular subject areas, and publishers use picture researchers to find the required images from these libraries, who are authorised to grant copyright licences as agent for the photographers.

(c) All sections of the publishing industry use editors to a greater or lesser extent, and an editor may contribute to the overall copyright in a literary work, depending on the nature of the work and the extent of the editor's contribution. Where the work consists of contributions from a number of different authors, under the general editorship of one person, the editor's contribution is likely to be substantial and result in the creation of a new copyright work, of which the editor will be the author.[11] Where, on the other hand, the editor's function is more of a copy-editing role, then the editor's work may not be sufficient to make him an "author".[12] Editing and copy-editing is frequently carried out by in-house employees, so that the copyright in any work created by them will be owned by the publisher, but copy-editing is often outsourced to freelancers, and so publishers should be made aware that they need to acquire an assignment of copyright in such cases. Even where the amount of copy-editing is sufficient to result in the creation of a new copyright work, the publisher is unlikely to assert copyright in it (quite apart from the effect of any assignment by the "true" author).   **26–09**

(d) Designers and typesetters are responsible for creating the overall "look" of a publication. Design work is normally done in-house, particularly with the desktop publishing software which is now widely used, and much of the work previously done by typesetters is also carried out in-house, so that the work created on computer by the publisher is sent to the repro-house (if applicable) and printer to produce the finished product. To the extent that any copyrights are created in this process, they should be owned by the publisher, although publishers should check the standard terms and conditions of business of the repro-houses and printers with whom they deal. The publisher is the "author" of the typographical arrangement of the published edition of a work and hence the first owner of the copyright in it.[13]   **26–10**

C. Works Created and Main Rights Required for Exploitation

(i) Books

The end product in the book publishing process is a book written by one or more authors and edited either in-house or by an independent editor or panel of editors. The rights required by the publisher will depend on the nature of the book in question, and may differ according to whether the book is a "trade" publication or a professional, academic or encyclopaedia publication: **26–11**

(a) *"Trade" publications*

The publisher will require the following rights to be granted by each author and   **26–12**

---

[11] See para.4–20, above.
[12] See *Fylde Microsystems Ltd v Key Radio Systems Ltd* [1998] F.S.R. 449, by analogy.
[13] CDPA 1988 ss.9(2)(d), 11(1). See paras 4–67 and 5–64, above.

any other individual who has contributed copyright material to the work (e.g. by way of editing) by way of exclusive licence and usually for the full period of copyright. The publisher may also seek a complete or partial waiver of moral rights, particularly for the purpose of exercising electronic-form publication rights and licensing serial rights and subsidiary rights. Authors may well resist such a request, if professionally advised.

26–13   **(1) Volume form publication rights.** i.e. the right to publish the work as a printed book. For the purposes of calculating the royalties payable to the author, this right is often sub-divided into very specific types of volume form, e.g. trade hardback, trade paperback, mass market paperback, book club, etc. and different royalty rates will apply to the different types of volume form publication and according to whether particular copies are sold in the "home" territory or in "export" markets.

26–14   **(2) Electronic form publication rights.** i.e. the right to publish the work in any electronic form (whether online or offline) whether in conjunction with any other works or not, and by means of any technology now known or subsequently developed.

26–15   **(3) Serialisation rights.** These are commonly divided into first serial rights and second serial rights, meaning the right to publish a serialisation commencing before and after publication of the book respectively.

26–16   **(4) Translation rights.** i.e. the right to translate the work into foreign languages and to publish the foreign language editions. Traditionally, this has involved publication in printed form only, but nowadays when granting translation rights, the parties should at least *consider* electronic publishing rights too.

26–17   **(5) Various "subsidiary rights".** These are rights which the publisher will usually license to third parties, including:

> electronic publishing rights (insofar as not directly exercised by the publisher);
>
> the mechanical reproduction of the work (i.e. audio tapes of undramatised readings of the work);
>
> quotation and extract rights (i.e. the right to authorise others to publish quotations or extracts from the work in other works);
>
> reprographic reproduction rights (these are often granted by the publishers to the Copyright Licensing Agency (CLA)[14] to authorise photocopying and other forms of reprographic reproduction under various blanket licensing schemes and individual licences);
>
> condensation rights (i.e. the right to produce and publish a condensed version of the work—this right might be expressly subject to the author's prior written consent, as a condensation might, unless expressly authorised, infringe an author's integrity right)[15];
>
> film, television and live stage dramatisation rights (i.e. the right to dramatise the work and present that dramatisation by means of film, television or live stage although these rights are more commonly reserved by authors and negotiated on the author's behalf through specialist agents);

---

[14] As to the CLA, see para.27–59, below.
[15] i.e. under CDPA 1988 s.80. See paras 11–34 et seq., above.

database right where the work in question constitutes a database for the purposes of the Copyright and Rights in Databases Regulations 1997[16];

Braille rights[17] have for many years been granted to UK publishers. In anticipation of the Copyright (Visually Impaired Persons) Act 2002, which is dealt with elsewhere,[18] the Publishers' Association and other representatives of rights holders produced a set of guidelines on access to books, magazines and journals for visually impaired persons.[19] In addition, the CLA has introduced a Visually Impaired Persons Licence designed specifically for not-for-profit organisations wishing to make and to circulate copies of copyright works in a format accessible to visually impaired persons. The CLA has also made alternative provision for educational establishments wishing to make similar copies available for their own staff and students.[20]

(b) *Professional, academic and encyclopaedia works*

The publisher will require an assignment of the entire copyright in the work for the full period of copyright together with a waiver of all moral rights. This is particularly so in relation to works which have several authors or editors and works which are expected to go into a number of editions in the future, so that the material can freely be used in future editions, whatever the form those editions may take. In addition, in relation to professional or academic works, the publisher will require the express right (but probably without a corresponding obligation) to continue using the author's name on and in relation to any number of future editions. This is because this type of work often comes to be known by the author's name (*Copinger and Skone James* being an example).   **26–18**

With this type of work, the publisher will also require an obligation on the part of the author to revise the work when the publisher considers it necessary, in order to keep the work up to date. This is particularly important where a work has already been associated with a particular author, but if the original author is unable or fails to revise the work, the publisher invariably retains the right to engage someone else to do so. This illustrates why the publisher requires to have the complete copyright in the work and a waiver of all of the author's moral rights: a new author brought in to revise the work must have the freedom to reuse and amend all or any of the work as thought fit, without the new author or the publisher being exposed to a claim by the original author for infringement of copyright or of moral rights or passing off.

(ii) Magazines

Employed writers and editors and regular contributors to magazines will normally be expected to assign the full copyright in their work to the publisher. With regard to occasional articles, the publisher will probably require no more than first British publication rights (although the period of exclusivity should be spelt out) unless the magazine circulates elsewhere or the publisher requires to syndicate the   **26–19**

---

[16] See Ch.18, above.

[17] i.e. the right to convert the work in question into Braille or to record the work for the sole use of the blind and print-handicapped, on a free-of-charge basis, where the author receives no payment.

[18] See paras 9–68 et seq., above.

[19] These guidelines are available on the Publishers' Association website at *http://www.publishers.org.uk/images/stories/AboutPA/Copyright__and__Visual__Impairment.pdf* [Accessed October 18, 2010].

[20] Details are available on the CLA web site, *http://www.cla.co.uk/.licences/licences__available/visual__impaired/* [Accessed October 18, 2010].

article to other magazines (e.g. foreign editions of the same magazine, possibly involving translation into foreign languages), in which case wider rights will be required. Furthermore, if the magazine is available electronically, e.g. over the internet, then the publisher might insist on a full assignment of copyright in relation to all material which it publishes (perhaps on the basis that it would license the author to reuse the material elsewhere after a certain period).

(iii) Journals

26–20   Journals vary in the rights that they require. Academic and scientific journals tend to require a full assignment of copyright from all contributors, albeit that they authorise contributors to reuse their material, e.g. in books written or co-written by or with contributions from the authors, subject to giving credit to the journal where the work is first published. This gives the publisher the ability to publish the material in all media without further consultation with the authors of the articles. Journals aimed at other professions, however, tend to require no more than the simple non-exclusive right to publish—this assumes that there is limited opportunity for the reuse of material in competing journals. Assuming that the journals in question are currently published in printed form only, then, unless wider rights were explicitly acquired by the publisher, a licence to publish in printed form is all that is likely to be implied. Accordingly, if, for example, the publisher then wanted to publish back issues over the internet, it would need further consents from all the authors.

(iv) Electronic publishers

26–21   Because of the rapid developments in technology, which make new forms of electronic delivery available, electronic publishers require maximum flexibility to exploit works in whatever way they can. Works which are published electronically will often be updated very regularly (ranging from daily to quarterly), and this again requires maximum flexibility. For this reason, and because works published electronically frequently have many authors, electronic publishers usually require a complete assignment of copyright in all material which they publish. It is particularly important for them to obtain a world-wide assignment of copyright, consisting of the equivalent rights throughout the world. With the advent of satellite broadcasting and further exploration of outer space, one can imagine rights being required even beyond the world.

Where a full assignment of copyright is, for any reason, not obtainable, an electronic publisher will require an exclusive licence of "electronic publication rights". The rights should be defined widely, giving as many examples as possible, stipulating that these are by way of example only and not by way of limitation and are to include all media and means of exploitation now known or subsequently developed. If the licence is governed by English law, this should be effective.[21]

D. TRADE UNIONS AND TRADE ASSOCIATIONS WHICH REPRESENT SOURCES OF WORKS AND ORGANISATIONS THAT EXPLOIT THEM

26–22   **Authors.** There are two main bodies representing authors: the Society of Authors ("SoA")[22] and the Writers Guild of Great Britain ("WGGB").[23] The SoA tends to represent authors of books, whereas the WGGB tends to represent authors of ma-

---

[21] As to the construction of agreements in relation to new technologies, see para.5–229, above.
[22] *http://www.societyofauthors.org* [Accessed October 29, 2010].

terial intended primarily for film and television exploitation. The SoA has entered into so-called "Minimum Terms Agreements" with a number of book publishers, specifying the minimum terms that the publisher will offer to members of the SoA. The WGGB has entered into agreements with broadcasters and unions representing film producers, specifying minimum terms that would be offered to WGGB members.

Author's agents. Quite apart from being entitled to join the SoA or the WGGB, many authors are represented by an agent, who will negotiate terms with publishers and others who exploit the author's material. The author's agents themselves have a body called the Authors' Agents Association,[24] through which they discuss matters of interest to authors' agents generally and develop policies to recommend to their members.   **26–23**

Illustrators. Illustrators are represented by the Association of Illustrators.[25]   **26–24**

Publishers. The following organisations represent various types of publishers[26]:   **26–25**

> the Publishers Association represents book publishers (the major book publishers, and some smaller publishers, are members);
>
> the Independent Publishers Guild represents an increasing number of small to medium-sized, independent book publishers;
>
> the Scottish Publishers Association represents independent Scottish book publishers;
>
> the Periodical Publishers Association represents magazine publishers; and
>
> the Association of Learned and Professional Society Publishers represents the publishers of professional and academic journals.

Printers. Printers are represented by the British Printing Industries Federation.[27]   **26–26**

Booksellers. Booksellers are represented by the Booksellers Association.[28]   **26–27**

Actors. Actors (e.g. in relation to sound recordings of works on tape) are represented by British Actors Equity (commonly known as "Equity").[29] Although Equity has agreements with most organisations that use its members' talent, specifying minimum terms, it does not have any such arrangements with publishers of sound recordings.   **26–28**

---

[23] *http://www.writersguild.org.uk* [Accessed October 29, 2010].

[24] For more information about the Association of Authors' Agents, including a copy of their Code of Practice, see its website at *http://www.agentsassoc.co.uk* [Accessed October 29, 2010].

[25] For more information about the Association of Illustrators, see its website at *http://www.aoi.co.uk* [Accessed October 29, 2010].

[26] For more information about the organisations representing publishers, and for useful links, see their respective websites: The Publishers' Association: *http://www.publishers.org.uk* [Accessed October 29, 2010]; The Independent Publishers' Guild: *http://www.ipg.uk.com* [Accessed October 29, 2010]; The Scottish Publishers' Association: *http://www.scottishbooks.org*; The Periodical Publishers Association: *http://www.ppa.co.uk* [Accessed October 29, 2010]; The Association of Learned and Professional Society Publishers: *http://www.alpsp.org* [Accessed October 29, 2010].

[27] For more information about the British Printing Industries Federation, see its website at *http://www.bpif.org.uk* [Accessed October 29, 2010].

[28] For more information about the Booksellers Association, see its website at *http://www.booksellers.org.uk* [Accessed October 29, 2010].

[29] For more information about British Actors Equity, see its website at *http://www.equity.org.uk* [Accessed October 29, 2010].

E. COLLECTING SOCIETIES AND LICENSING AGENCIES RESPONSIBLE FOR ADMINISTERING RIGHTS

26–29   **Authors' societies.** The Authors Licensing and Collecting Society ("ALCS")[30] administers a number of rights on behalf of authors, primarily the reprographic reproduction right (which it grants to the Copyright Licensing Agency ("CLA"),[31] and it distributes income received from the CLA amongst its author members. ALCS also administers the foreign lending right, cable and satellite retransmission right, private recording right, off-air recording right, rental right, public reception of broadcasts right and a limited performance right on behalf of its members.[32]

26–30   **Artists' and illustrators' societies.** Design and Artists' Copyright Society ("DACS")[33] administers the right to make copies of artistic works on behalf of its members (which include the estates of deceased artists) and also administers the Artist's Resale Right on behalf of artists in the United Kingdom.[34]

26–31   **Publishers' societies.** The members of Publishers Licensing Society ("PLS")[35] are the Publishers Association, the Periodical Publishers Association and the Association of Learned and Professional Society Publishers. PLS administers the reprographic reproduction right and digital copying rights on behalf of publishers, and grants them to the CLA, so that the CLA is able to administer such rights on behalf of both publishers and authors. The CLA has established various blanket licensing schemes, e.g. for educational establishments and for business, and also licenses larger-scale photocopying (with the prior consent of the rights owners) through its CLARCS (rapid clearing system) system. The CLA has reciprocal arrangements with similar organisations outside the United Kingdom.[36] PLS distributes income received from CLA amongst its publisher members.

26–32   **Educational users.** There are two licensing schemes for the purposes of s.35 of the 1988 Act which have been certified pursuant to s.143 of the Act. The scheme operated by Educational Recording Agency Limited allows the recording of certain broadcasts and cable programmes by educational establishments for the educational purposes of such establishments in return for specified payments. The scheme operated by Open University Educational Enterprises Limited allows the recording off air of Open University television programmes by schools and further and higher education establishments in return for specified fees.[37] The Educational Recording Agency Ltd scheme has been superseded a number of times.[38]

---

[30] For more information about the Authors' Licensing and Collecting Society, and for useful links, see its website at *http://www.alcs.co.uk* [Accessed October 29, 2010].

[31] For more information about the Copyright Licensing Agency, see its website at *http://www.cla.co.uk* [Accessed October 29, 2010]

[32] See, further, as to the CLA, para.27–59, below.

[33] For more information about Design and Artists' Copyright Society, see its website at *http://www.dacs.co.uk* [Accessed October 29, 2010].

[34] See, further as to DACS, para.27–60, below. As to the Artist's Resale Right, see Ch. 20 above.

[35] For more information about Publishers Licensing Society, see its website at *http://www.pls.org.uk* [Accessed October 29, 2010].

[36] See, further, as to CLA, para.27–59, below.

[37] As to licensing schemes, see paras 28–62 et seq., below. For the schemes themselves, see Vol.2 B2.

[38] The present scheme is set out in SI 2007/266. See Vol.2 B2.i.

F. Publishing Agreements

(i) Formalities of publishing arrangements

No formalities required. In the United Kingdom, contracts between authors and   **26-33**
publishers are not, as in some countries, regulated by any special law, but their
validity, construction and enforcement depend upon the ordinary rules of law
governing contracts relating to dealings with personal property. Such contracts
do not even have to be in writing, unless they are to effect an assignment of copyright or are to constitute an exclusive licence.[39] In practice, publishing arrangements vary from the most informal, for example an oral or an implied licence to
publish a single article, to a formal, full-length publishing agreement. It is with
the informal agreement, where many (or perhaps all) of the essential terms are
left to implication, that it is often most difficult to determine the respective rights
of the parties.[40] Some guidance may be found in the Publishers' Association
Code of Practice (the major book publishers in the United Kingdom are members
of the Association) which seeks to establish general principles for its members to
follow, rather than uniformity of contract.[41]

(ii) Formal agreements: common forms of publishing arrangements

Questions which may arise on the construction of assignments and licences are   **26-34**
dealt with elsewhere.[42] This section is concerned with problems peculiar to the
publishing industry. Agreements between authors and publishers fall commonly
into two principal classes:

(a) outright disposals of copyright, whether for a fixed sum or on royalty
terms; and

(b) licences for a period on royalty terms.

More rarely, such agreements may take the form of profit-sharing agreements.

Agreement for outright disposal of copyright. The consequences for the author   **26-35**
of making an outright disposal of his copyright in consideration of receiving
royalties are discussed elsewhere.[43] Where copyright is sold for a single payment,
the matter is relatively simple, because the rights of the parties are concluded at
once. If the copyright in the work is to belong to the publisher (whether upon
payment of a fixed sum or royalties), an assignment in writing of the copyright by
the author to the publisher should be made even though the work has been written to the order of the publisher, since the copyright will vest, in the first instance,
in the author unless the author is an employee of the publisher.[44] If no assignment
has been executed, however, the publisher may none the less have acquired
certain equitable rights in the commissioned work.[45]

Under the 1988 Act, an assignment in writing of the copyright in a work not
yet created will operate to vest the copyright in the work in the assignee as soon
as the work comes into existence and without further assurance.[46] Consequently,
if an author has made an agreement with one publisher to assign the copyright in

---

[39] See CDPA 1988 ss.90(3) and 92(1) and paras 5–85 and 5–208, above, respectively.
[40] See, e.g. *Ray v Classic FM* [1998] F.S.R. 622.
[41] See para.26–39, below.
[42] See Ch.5.
[43] See paras 5–83 et seq., above.
[44] CDPA 1988 s.11(1) and (2). As to what would amount to an assignment, see paras 5–87 et seq.
and 5–204 et seq., above.
[45] See paras 5–174 et seq., above.
[46] CDPA 1988 s.91. As to assignment of future copyright, see para.5–108 et seq., above.

his next book to that publisher, and subsequently, when about to write that book, he agrees to assign the copyright in it to a second publisher, the copyright will, upon the book being written, vest in the first publisher and not in the second publisher. Both agreements will operate as agreements only until the work is in fact created, so that their priority will depend merely upon the dates of the respective agreements and be unaffected by any question of notice.[47]

After an author has parted with the copyright in a book he is not at liberty to reproduce substantially the same matter in another work. In the absence of any special agreement, the second publication would be an infringement of the copyright in the first.[48]

26–36   **Agreements conferring licences.** In the case of a royalty agreement, the advisability (from the author's point of view) of securing that a licence only is granted to the publisher is discussed elsewhere.[49] If the royalty payable to the author is a certain proportion of the published or recommended retail price of the work, the agreement may specify a minimum price at which the book is to be published, but with the abolition of the Net Book Agreement in the 1990s, a publisher can no longer guarantee that the book will be sold in retail shops at no less than that price. Whilst the Net Book Agreement was in force, it was common for authors' royalties on copies sold in the "home" market to be calculated upon the retail price at which books were sold in shops. However, since the abolition of the Net Book Agreement, some publishers calculate royalties on the recommended retail price, while others calculate all royalties on the publisher's net receipts.

The industry continues to debate whether or not recommended retail prices should continue to be shown on book covers. There is considerable opposition amongst authors to their abolition, mainly because it is feared that calculation of royalties would then have to move entirely to the "net receipts" basis and that authors would lose out. Their removal could also result in an increase in costs to independent booksellers, putting them at a further disadvantage compared with the large chains and supermarkets. At the annual Booksellers' Association Conference in May 2006 it was decided to continue with the practice of printing prices on books, but the debate looks likely to go on. Whether the practice of stipulating recommended retail prices could infringe competition law, given that in the vast majority of cases books will be sold in retail shops at the recommended retail prices specified by publishers, especially if printed on the book covers, is yet to be decided.

26–37   **Profit-sharing agreement.** Nowadays, profit-sharing is not a very common arrangement between author and publisher, although it has been suggested that it might be a suitable way of providing appropriate compensation to a very successful author. In such an agreement, generally the publisher takes the whole risk of the costs of publication,[50] and the net profits are divided between the parties. This may create a partnership, and the right to publish the work will be a partnership asset; whether an assignment or licence of the copyright will be granted will depend upon the express or implied terms of the agreement. A profit-sharing agreement between an author and a publisher may establish a fiduciary relation-

---

[47] See, as to the position under an option to publish an author's next work, *Macdonald (E) Ltd v Eyles* [1921] 1 Ch. 631.
[48] *Colburn v Simms* (1843) 2 Hare 543; see, as to artistic works, CDPA 1988 s.64.
[49] See paras 5–78 and 5–80, above.
[50] *Reade v Bentley* (1858) 4 K. & J. 656 where an argument that the publisher was merely an agent was rejected because he had taken those risks.

ship between the parties, and the author will then be entitled to an account from the publisher.[51]

Whether a joint venture is terminable by notice. The author's right to determine the profit-sharing agreement will depend upon the express or implied terms of the agreement. If the agreement grants no more than a licence, then the author may be able to determine it on giving reasonable notice.[52]   **26–38**

G. Matters to be Considered in Drafting Publishing Agreements

(i) The Publishers Association Code of Practice.

In 1982 the Publishers Association first issued its Code of Practice to its members, who include the major book publishers in the United Kingdom. The Code, revised and reissued subsequently (most recently in 2010), is intended as a guide to good publishing practice which the Publishers Association recommends to its members in their dealings with authors. Since it cannot deal with every possible situation that can arise in the course of dealings between publishers and authors (and as so much depends on the type of work involved, the market it is aimed at, the standing of the author, and so on), the Publishers' Association stresses the importance of following the general principles of the Code. It adds that it is impractical to expect "total uniformity of contract or practice". The purpose of the Code is to assist in developing and preserving a constructive and co-operative relationship between authors (and the agents and the representatives acting for them) and their publishers, this being vital to successful publishing.   **26–39**

The Code sets out 20 principles (which apply only to agreements whereby an author assigns or licenses an interest in the copyright of a work to a publisher) with explanatory comment by way of example (which is not intended to be an exhaustive explanation). These principles serve as guidance only, and do not have any contractual effect, except to the extent that publishers embody them in their contracts with authors. The principles are as follows (the commentary here is not taken verbatim from the Code):

(a) *The publishing contract must be clear, unambiguous and comprehensive, and must be honoured in both the letter and the spirit*

The contract should in particular define: the work by its title or, where it is not yet completed, the nature, agreed length and scope of the work; the nature of the rights granted, the ownership of the copyright (an assignment or an exclusive licence), whether publication in digital form is included in the rights granted, and the formats, territories and languages covered by the agreement; the time scale for delivery and publication; payments to the author; provisions for sub-licensing; responsibility for index, etc. and for clearing and paying for third-party copyright permissions; and termination and reversion of rights.   **26–40**

(b) *The contract should be clear about ownership of the copyright*

An exclusive licence is normally sufficient for a publisher, but with some works (e.g. encyclopedias and reference works, certain types of academic works,

---

[51] See *Barry v Stevens* (1862) 31 Beav. 258 as to the creation and consequences of such a fiduciary relationship generally.

[52] See *Reade v Bentley* (1858) 4 K. & J. 656, where notice was validly given at a time when the publisher had not incurred expenses on a new edition; approved in *Abrahams v Herbert Reiach Ltd* [1922] 1 K.B. 477 at 480. Contrast *Holland v Methuen & Co Ltd* [1928–35] Mac.C.C. 247: no right to determine on notice (otherwise than for breach of contract) where the agreement was to pay royalties rather than for profit-sharing.

publishers' compilations edited from many outside contributions, some translations and works particularly vulnerable to copyright infringement because of their extensive international sale) there may be good reason for the publisher to acquire the copyright, to make it easier for the publisher to protect the work as a whole.

(c) *The publisher should be aware of the author's moral rights*

This applies in particular to the paternity right and to the integrity right. A publisher drafting a publishing contract should be aware of these rights. In addition, the paternity right may require to be asserted by the author, which is most conveniently done by the publisher on the book or menu page itself, on the author's behalf. The publisher should also be aware that the paternity right and integrity right do not apply in certain circumstances, and that there are circumstances where a waiver of the author's moral rights may be appropriate, and the publisher should allow sufficient time to permit discussion of this and to make alternative arrangements if necessary.

(d) *The publisher should be willing and take any opportunity to explain the terms of the contract and the reasons for each provision, particularly to an author who is not professionally represented.*

(e) *Where appropriate, the publisher must give the author a proper opportunity to share in the success of the work*

For example, royalty rates might escalate after sales reach certain specified levels.

(f) *The publisher must handle manuscripts promptly, and keep the author informed of progress*

26–41   Manuscripts and synopses should be acknowledged promptly on receipt by the publisher (unless the publisher makes it clear on its website that it does not acknowledge unsolicited materials), and authors should get at least a progress report within six weeks. It is important, however, for the publisher to know if the manuscript or synopsis is being simultaneously submitted to any other publisher.

(g) *The publisher must not cancel a contract without good and proper reason*

This includes the situation where the author fails to deliver on time or fails to deliver a work of sufficient standard and quality to be suitable for publication, or if the publisher has reason to believe that the work is defamatory or otherwise illegal. If the publisher rejects the book on grounds of quality, the publisher must give the author sufficiently detailed reasons for rejection. If there is a change in the publisher's circumstances or policies such that it no longer wishes to publish the work (however good it may be), the publisher must compensate the author. Depending on the grounds for rejection of the book, the publisher may be liable for further advances and an additional sum to compensate the author, but if the grounds for rejection are reasonable, the author may be liable to repay advances received. The Publishers Association provides an Informal Arbitration Procedure for the resolution of disputes.

(h) *The contract must set out the anticipated timetable for publication*

The contract should make clear the time scale within which the author undertakes to deliver the completed manuscript and within which the publisher undertakes to publish it.

(i) *The publisher should be willing to share precautions against legal risks not arising from carelessness by the author*

This refers primarily to the risks of libel, breach of privacy, confidentiality and data protection. It is primarily the author's responsibility to ensure that the work does not contain any illegal content, but the publisher may also be liable, and so legal vetting requires very close cooperation between author and publisher, and sharing the costs of libel reading and/or libel insurance may be desirable.

(j) *The publisher should consider assisting the author by funding additional costs involved in preparing the work for publication*

This would cover, e.g. cost of indexing and costs of third-party copyright permissions, which could be recouped out of royalties payable subsequently to the author.

(k) *The publisher must ensure that the author receives a regular and clear account of sales made and money due*

Accounts should be rendered at least annually, and more commonly twice yearly. **26–42** The contract should specify the accounting periods, and stipulate when royalty statements should be delivered and royalties paid. Publishers should always observe these dates and obligations scrupulously. The publisher may be prepared to disclose details of the number of copies printed, provided this is not disclosed other than to the author's professional advisers. Publishers should also be prepared to give authors indications of sales to date, which must be realistic, having regard to frequency of accounting, unsold stock which may be returned by booksellers or stock supplied on consignment.

(l) *The publisher must ensure that the author can clearly ascertain how any payments due from sub-licensed agreements will be calculated*

(m) *The publisher should keep the author informed of all important design, promotion, marketing and sub-licensing decisions*

There should be full consultation with the author on these matters, including, e.g. the jacket design, jacket text, promotional and review activities and sale of major subsidiary rights.

(n) *The publisher should inform the author clearly about opportunities for amendment of the work in the course of production*

It is much more expensive to alter a work that has been typeset than one which has not yet been typeset. The contract should make clear whether proofs will be provided, whose responsibility it is to check them, and what scale of author's revisions to proofs will be acceptable.

(o) *It is essential that both the publisher and the author have a clear common understanding of the significance attaching to the option clause in a publishing contract*

The option for the publisher to acquire rights over the author's next work or works is important. It should be carefully negotiated and fully understood by both parties. It is not usually desirable for an option to cover more than one work.

(p) *The publisher should recognise that the remaindering of stock may effectively end the author's expectations of earnings*

Before remaindering a work, the publisher should inform the author and give him the opportunity to purchase all or part of the stock at the remainder price. Whether the author should receive a royalty on such copies is to be determined by the contract. In appropriate areas of publishing, the question of whether remaindering of stock should trigger a full or partial reversion of rights to the author should be carefully thought out, particularly if the title might subsequently be considered for a print-on-demand programme or be available as an e-book.

(q) *The contract must set out reasonable and precise terms for the reversion* **26–43** *of rights*

When a publisher has invested in the development of an author's work on the market, and the work is a contribution to the store of literature and knowledge, and the publisher expects to market the work for many years, it is reasonable for the publisher to acquire publication rights for the full term of copyright, on condition that there are safeguards providing for reversion of rights in appropriate circumstances, e.g. fundamental breach of contract by the publisher, or when the work has been out of print and not available on the market for a stipulated time, or (in some cases) if sales fall below an agreed low level—and these should be specified in the contract itself. The availability of titles via print-on-demand and e-book technology reduce the likelihood of books going out of print, and the parties need to consider whether rights should or should not revert in such circumstances. Reversion of rights should not normally apply where the copyright has been purchased outright, nor to multi-authored or edited works, particularly where these go through multiple editions.

    (r) *The publisher should endeavour to keep the author informed of changes in the ownership of the publishing rights and of any changes in the imprint under which a work appears*

Most publishers expect to sign a contract on behalf of their successors and assigns (although an author may seek to restrict the right to assign), and if changes in rights ownership or of publishing imprint subsequently occur, the publisher should certainly inform and, if at all possible, do what it reasonably can to ensure publishing continuity for an author in these new circumstances.

    (s) *The publisher should be willing to help the author and the author's estate in the administration of literary affairs*

By way of example, the publisher should agree to act as an expert witness on questions of the valuation of a literary estate.

    (t) *Above all, the publisher must recognise the importance of co-operation with the author in an enterprise in which both are essential*

This relationship can only be fulfilled in an atmosphere of confidence, in which authors get the fullest possible credit for their work and achievements.

(ii) Minimum Terms Agreements

26–44   Quite a few years ago, the Society of Authors and the Writers' Guild of Great Britain negotiated Minimum Terms Agreements ("MTAs") with a number of book publishers, whereby the publishers agreed that the terms and conditions which they would offer to authors who are members of the Society or Guild would be no less favourable to the author than those specified in the MTA to which they are a party. In practice, all the MTAs vary a little, but they have many provisions in common. These MTAs continue to exist and to provide some benefit to members who are not represented by agents, but they have been somewhat dormant in recent years and the Society of Authors has not attempted to renegotiate them. This is partly because contracts with trade publishers have improved, as a result of pressure from agents as well as from the Society of Authors and the Writers' Guild. In addition, the Society of Authors puts out guidance on its website for its members on new developments as and when they occur, and issues its "Guide to Publishing Contracts", containing detailed advice on royalty rates and on all of the commonly found clauses in publishing contracts, and this is free to members of the Society and available to non-members for a charge.

    The following is a summary of the main terms covered by the MTAs. Naturally, they are drafted to take account of an author's concerns, and so can be contrasted with the principles set out in the Publishers Association Code of Practice.

26–45   **Term granted and review.** Traditionally, publishers expected to be granted a licence for the full period of copyright, subject to reversion of rights to the author in certain circumstances. This is reflected in some of the MTAs. However, one form of MTA provides that the duration of the licence granted to the publisher is a matter for negotiation (although in practice the licence is likely to be for the full period of copyright). Another MTA, however, provides for an initial term not

exceeding 30 years from first publication of the book, with a right to initiate negotiations for (but not an absolute right to acquire) a further period.

MTAs generally also provide for a review of the terms of the agreement on
every tenth anniversary of the publication date. This review may be limited in
some cases to terms relating to royalties or subsidiary rights. When the review
has been initiated, the terms involved are to be considered in the light of comparable terms prevailing in the trade and altered to the extent that may be just and
equitable. In the absence of agreement on what is just and equitable, the matter is
to be referred to arbitration.

Consultation. MTAs may provide for the author to have a contractual right to all   **26–46**
or any of the following:

- (a) consultation on and approval of copy editing and the final number and
     type of illustrations (such approval not to be unreasonably withheld);
- (b) consultation on publication date;
- (c) sight of roughs or proofs of the jacket and of the jacket blurb;
- (d) no change in the title or text to be made by the publisher without the
     author's consent (except, in some cases, in order to conform with house
     style);
- (e) information, on request, as to the number of copies printed in the first and
     subsequent print-runs;
- (f) an opportunity to see and approve the edited typescript before it is sent to
     the printers;
- (g) two complete sets of the proofs of the work (one to be corrected and
     returned to the publisher within a specified period);
- (h) to make corrections to the proofs up to 15 per cent of the cost of
     composition.

Royalties. MTAs vary, and the following is a guide, but is regarded as reason-   **26–47**
ably typical. Different considerations may apply according to the nature of the
book (for example, the royalty rates will be lower for heavily illustrated works
and for children's books).

(a) *The advance*

This is usually not less than 65 per cent of the author's estimated receipts from   **26–48**
the sale of the projected first printing if the work is to be published by the
publisher only in hardback or only in paperback, or 55 per cent if it is to be
published by the publisher both in hardback and in paperback.

If the work is commissioned by the publisher, then the advance is usually payable as to one third on signature of contract; one third on delivery of final and
revised typescript; and one third within one year of delivery or on publication,
whichever is the sooner.

If the work is not commissioned, the advance is usually paid half on signature
of contract and the other half within one year of signature of contract or on publication, whichever is the sooner.

(b) *Hardback royalties*

The basic scale of royalties may be as follows, but there may be situations where   **26–49**
other rates of royalty will apply (and many publishers have now ceased to
calculate royalties on published price, and instead use only the "net receipts"
basis"):

Home market.

> On the first 2,500 copies: 10 per cent of published price
> On the next 2,500 copies: 12.5 per cent of published price
> On all further copies sold: 15 per cent of published price

Export market.

> On the first 2,500 copies: 10 per cent of price received
> On the next 2.500 copies: 12.5 per cent of price received
> On all further copies sold: 15 per cent of price received

(c) Paperback royalties

26–50   A typical royalty scale is as follows:

Home market.

> On the first 40,000 copies: 7.5 per cent of published price
> On all further copies sold: 10 per cent of published price

Export market.

> On the first 50,000 copies: 6 per cent of published price
> On all further copies sold: 8 per cent of published price

(d) United States rights

26–51   If the publisher arranges publication of an American edition on a royalty basis, the publisher retains a maximum of 15 per cent of the proceeds, inclusive of any sub-agent's commission.

(e) Translation rights

26–52   The publisher retains not more than 20 per cent of the proceeds from any foreign language edition, inclusive of any sub-agent's commission.

(f) Subsidiary rights

26–53   Receipts from sale or licensing of some of the major subsidiary rights are often divided as follows:

	Author	*Publisher*
First Serial	90 per cent	10 per cent
Second Serial	75 per cent	25 per cent
Merchandising	80 per cent	20 per cent
TV and radio readings	75 per cent	25 per cent

26–54   **General matters.** MTAs also deal with issues such as payment of copyright fees for agreed illustrations, sharing the cost of an index, the number of free copies of each edition that the author should receive from the publisher, requirements as to rendering statements of account, and the situations in which rights will revert to the author (such as failure by the publisher to comply with the terms of the contract, liquidation or receivership of the publisher, the work being out of print, and in some cases, where annual sales of the work fall below specified levels).

H. TERMS FOUND IN PUBLISHING AGREEMENTS

(i) Effect of submission of manuscript

The simplest form of contract is where a manuscript is sent to a publisher without anything being said about terms. A non-exclusive licence may be made orally or implied by conduct from the circumstances of the case. For example, if a person writes a letter to the editor of a newspaper, there is an implied licence to publish the letter in the absence of any express indication to the contrary (e.g. where the letter is marked "Not for Publication"). Similarly, if an author submits an article to the editor of a journal or periodical, the submission of the manuscript may by custom, or necessary implication, be treated as an offer of a licence to publish in consideration of payment on the usual terms for that publication. Such an offer can at once be accepted by the editor or publisher of that journal or periodical without further communication with the author.[53]

26–55

On the other hand, if an author submits the typescript of a book to a publisher without anything more, then it will probably amount to no more than an offer to enter into negotiations for a publishing contract, and would not constitute an offer capable of immediate acceptance so as to form a binding contract. Accordingly, in that situation, the publisher would not be entitled simply to accept the book and publish it without reaching agreement with the author on terms. What, short of actual publication, amounts to an acceptance of an author's manuscript will depend upon the circumstances of the case. In *Malcolm v Chancellor, Masters and Scholars of the University of Oxford*,[54] it was held that an oral agreement had been reached on the telephone between the author and the publisher for the publication of the book at a fair royalty. The Court of Appeal held that the fact that the parties had not agreed on matters such as the print run, the price of the book or the format for publication did not mean that no contract existed. The Court considered, after receiving expert evidence on the plaintiff's behalf that was not contradicted, that these matters would either be agreed later between the parties or would be decided by the publishers.[55] If, however, before publication, there are detailed discussions about the form of publication and these never come to fruition, no licence to publish will be implied.[56] In *Myers v Macmillan Press Ltd*[57] the plaintiff author sued for failure to publish. There was no written contract between the parties for the work in question, but the defendant, having considered a specimen part of the work, had instructed the plaintiff to "go ahead" with the work. By the date of the trial the defendant had conceded that there was a contract: the parties had previously entered into two written contracts for other books and it was accepted by both parties at trial that the same terms would govern the work in question.

(ii) Obligations as to manuscript

In the absence of agreement to the contrary, where a manuscript submitted to a publisher is lost or destroyed through his negligence, or that of his employees,

26–56

---

[53] As to such a trade custom, see *Hall-Brown v Iliffe & Sons* [1928–1935] Mac.C.C. 88 (where the custom was found not to apply, as the parties were negotiating terms).

[54] Court of Appeal, December 18, 1990; reported at [1994] E.M.L.R. 17.

[55] The decision relies on the assumption underlying *Abrahams v Herbert Reiach Ltd*, [1922] 1. K.B. 477, that an agreement between a publisher and an author for the publication of a book for a stated consideration and no more is a complete and enforceable contract. For commentary on *Malcolm* see *Nyman* in [1991] 3 Ent.L.R.84.

[56] *Hall-Brown v Iliffe & Sons Ltd* [1928–1935] Mac. C.C. 88.

[57] Unreported, March 3, 1998.

the author may recover its value.[58] Once there is an agreement to publish, whether ownership of the manuscript itself passes to the publisher depends on the terms of any contract between the publisher and the author, but the grant of a licence to publish alone does not confer ownership of the manuscript upon the publisher. Whether an author who is willing to leave his manuscript in the hands of the publisher for a substantial period after its initial publication will, where the publishing agreement is silent as to its ownership, be treated as abandoning it, is an open question.[59] In practice, a book publishing agreement will often stipulate whether or not the manuscript is to be returned to the author when no longer required for production purposes. In addition, the agreement will usually provide expressly that the publisher is not liable to the author for any loss of or damage to the manuscript (and any accompanying materials) while in the possession of the publishers, and authors should keep copies of everything that they submit to a publisher.

26–57   **Whether obligation to publish.** Where the copyright in a work is sold outright, the publisher is under no obligation to publish, unless there is an express or implied term to that effect in the agreement.[60] However, if the author is tied to the publisher for a period of time or a number of works, the absence of an obligation to publish may be an indication that the agreement is in restraint of trade or may indicate such inequality of bargaining power as to render the agreement unenforceable.[61] But where there is an agreement to publish, without stating any date of publication, an undertaking to publish within a reasonable time will be implied.[62] If publication is delayed beyond that period, the author is entitled to damages resulting from that delay and possibly also to damages for loss of publicity or opportunity to enhance his reputation.[63] In *Moorhead v Paul Brennan*[64] the author granted the publisher an exclusive worldwide publishing contract for her book for the legal term of copyright. The publisher had an obligation to publish the work within a stated time but had no resources to publish abroad. It was held that although no term was to be implied into the contract that the publisher should himself publish abroad, a term was to be implied that the publisher would not impede or obstruct opportunities to receive royalties from persons willing to publish under licence abroad. The publisher was in breach by refusing to grant a licence to the only likely sub-publisher abroad except on unreasonable terms.

(iii) Meaning of "edition"

26–58   In current publishing practice, the word "edition" is used to denote all the copies

---

[58] *Stone v Long* [1901–1904] Mac.C.C. 66. But contrast *Howard v Harris* (1884) Cababé & Ellis 253 in which the defendant was held to owe no duty of any sort to the plaintiff to preserve the manuscript.

[59] In *Moorhouse v Angus & Robertson (No.1) Pty* [1981] 1 N.S.W.L.R. 700, the Court of Appeal of New Zealand reversed a finding of abandonment at first instance ([1980] F.S.R. 231), leaving the question of law open. See also *Copyright*, No.5, May 1966, p.144; as to letters, see para.5–224, above.

[60] The absence of such an express or implied term means that the publisher need not publish and the author may have no remedy. However, the court would clearly wish to imply such a term, to avoid an unreasonable result: contrast *Nichols v The Amalgamated Press* [1905–1910] Mac.C.C. 166 with *Hole v Bradbury* (1897) 12 Ch. D. 886 at 895.

[61] *AS Schroeder Music Publishing Co Ltd v Macaulay* [1974] W.L.R. 1308; [1974] 3 All E.R. 616; *Clifford Davis Management Ltd v WEA Records Ltd* [1975] 1 All E.R. 237. For a full discussion of the restraint of trade doctrine see paras 28–330 et seq., below.

[62] *Crane v C Arthur Pearson Ltd* [1936–1945] Mac.C.C. 125; *Barrow v Chappell & Co Ltd* [1976] R.P.C. 355.

[63] *Crane v C Arthur Pearson Ltd* [1936–1945] Mac.C.C. 125; *Barrow v Chappell & Co Ltd* [1976] R.P.C. 355; and *Abrahams v Herbert Reiach Ltd* [1922] 1 K.B. 477.

[64] [1991] 20 I.P.R. 161 (Sup Ct of NSW).

of a work that are published in exactly the same form, both as to the content and the medium of publication. Copies of a work are frequently issued in batches according to demand, and copies are frequently supplied in small quantities to meet specific orders from members of the general public. Where a work is reprinted, with no alterations, the reprint is sometimes referred to as a new "impression". Where, however, any substantive change is made, e.g. in updating a work or adding a new preface, this is now regarded as a new "edition".[65]

The number of copies. Where the agreement is for the exclusive publication of a specified number of copies, that number only can be printed and sold, and, until their sale, the author cannot revoke the authority given to the publishers, or himself publish the work.[66] A term that the publisher shall publish a second edition, if demanded by the public, and print as many copies as he can sell, gives the publisher the right, when such demand arises, to publish and sell as many copies as can properly be considered to belong to that edition, and to prevent the author, or any other person, from publishing until such copies have been sold. If the agreement is silent as to the number of copies to be published, the publisher must publish as many as is reasonable in all the circumstances.[67]

26–59

Number of editions. When the number of editions or copies to be published is not specified, the publisher is not bound to publish more than one edition. The further rights of the parties depend upon the provisions, express or implied, of the contract. In principle, where no term of the contract is specified, the parties may determine the agreement upon giving reasonable notice.[68]

26–60

(iv) The meaning of "volume form"

A publishing agreement will traditionally grant to the publisher the right to publish the work in "volume form". The expression "volume form" is generally understood in the book publishing industry to connote publication in the form of a printed book. It would not generally be understood to include publication in any electronic format.[69] The expression "volume form" also distinguishes between publication of a work as a whole and publication by instalments in "serial form", so that the exclusive right to publish in volume form would be infringed by publication of substantially the whole of the work in a single issue of a magazine.[70] A grant of the exclusive right to produce, print, publish and sell a work in "volume" form has been held to give the grantee sufficient title to sue for infringement where the defendant merely had in his possession an infringing copy of a proof of

26–61

---

[65] It is unlikely that *Reade v Bentley* (1858) 4 K. & J. 656, where the meaning of "edition" was extensively discussed, has any application today. In another old case, *Blackwood v Brewster* [1860] 23 Sess.Cas. (2nd Ser.) 142, it was held that an editor, who was to be paid for preparation of every new edition of a work, was not entitled to superintend, or to claim payment for, reprinting the work to replace copies destroyed by fire. The copies reprinted did not form a new edition, but replaced the part of the edition destroyed.

[66] He may be entitled to publish a second edition: see *Warne v Routledge* (1874) L.R. 1 8 Eq. 497.

[67] *Abrahams v Herbert Reiach Ltd*, above; and see *Malcolm v Chancellor, Masters & Scholars of the University of Oxford* [1994] E.M.L.R. 17, above, where failure to specify the number of copies to be printed did not prevent there being a binding contract to publish the work.

[68] See, e.g. *Reade v Bentley*, above; contrast *Holland v Methuen & Co Ltd*, [1928–1935] Mac.C.C. 247, where there was no right to determine until the publisher was in breach of contract.

[69] Although this has been disputed by Random House, Inc. in its long-running saga over ownership of electronic rights in important backlist titles that long pre-dated the notion of electronic publication. See below.

[70] *Jonathan Cape Ltd v Consolidated Press Ltd* [1954] 1 W.L.R. 1313; [1954] 3 All E.R. 253.

the book, and had offered it for sale to a newspaper: the copies were copies of the work in volume form.[71]

(v) "Electronic" form

26–62   Many publishers have for a number of years been careful to acquire (where the authors or their agents would agree) electronic rights alongside traditional print publication rights, even if they did not have any immediate intention of publishing in an electronic form. Where the contract contains no express clause dealing with publication in this form, it will be a question of construction whether the rights granted extend this far.[72] Clearly, and as cases in the United States have shown,[73] old-style contracts which merely grant rights limited, for example, to publication "in book form" may well not extend to publication in electronic form.

(vi) Price and style of publication

26–63   The contract may provide for the manner and style of the publication and the price at which it is to be issued to the public, but if the price at which the work is to be sold is not fixed by agreement, or otherwise arranged by the author and publisher, the publisher is the proper person to fix it.[74] At the same time, he would not be permitted to fix upon a style, or sell at a price, which would be clearly injurious either to the literary reputation or the pecuniary interests of the author without the author's consent.

26–64   **Right to alter.** Whether a publisher has the right to alter an author's work will depend upon whether the agreement amounts to an assignment or a licence, the terms of that assignment or licence, and on the extent to which the author's moral right of integrity is affected, or has been waived. These are points discussed elsewhere.[75] Subject to the terms of the contract, the writer of a signed article is entitled to complain of alterations in the text made without his consent.[76] On the other hand, if an author is employed to write a work of a particular description, and does so, the employer may have no right to complain if the result is unsatisfactory where he has agreed to accept the product of the skill and taste of the author.[77]

(vii) Whether benefit assignable.

26–65   A publishing contract is usually regarded as a personal contract, and thus unassignable unless the contract specifically provides for assignment by the publisher. Publishers' contracts with authors often provide that the publisher contracts for

---

[71] *Michael O'Mara Books Ltd v Express Newspapers plc* [1999] F.S.R. 49.

[72] See para.5–229 as to construction of licences in the face of new technologies.

[73] See, e.g. *Random House Inc v Rosetta Books* (July 11, 2001), where "the right to print, publish and sell the work[s] in book form" was held not to include the right to publish the books in electronic form; *Tasini v New York Times* (June 25, 2001) where work of freelancers which was originally produced for printed publications was infringed by being included in various electronic databases. For a review of the US cases affecting this issue, see Radcliffe, "New Media Convergence: Acquiring Rights to Existing Works for the Internet under U.S. Law" [2001] E.I.P.R. 172.

[74] *Benning v Dove* (1831) 5 C. & P. 427; and see *Abrahams v Herbert Reiach Ltd*, [1922] 1 K.B. 477, and also *Malcolm v Chancellor, Masters and Scholars of the University of Oxford* [1994] E.M.L.R.17, where it was held that the failure to agree upon the format of publication (i.e. hardback or paperback, or both) and/or the price at which the book would be published did not, of itself, prevent the existence of a binding contract to publish the work.

[75] See paras 5–206 and 5–228, above, but see also *Barrow v Chappell & Co Ltd* [1976] R.P.C. 355.

[76] *Joseph v National Magazine Co Ltd* [1959] Ch.14.

[77] *Ellis v British Filmcraft Productions Ltd* [1928–1935] Mac.C.C. 51.

itself, its assignees and its successors in business, and would no doubt argue that this is sufficient to give it absolute freedom to assign the benefit of the contract without needing the consent of the author. This is debatable, but of course it is preferable that the contract wording should make it clear one way or the other. The point is discussed elsewhere.[78]

(viii) Stock in hand

It is a common situation that, after the end of the term of a publishing agreement, **26–66** a publisher has a remaining stock of the work lawfully made during the term. The position under the older cases was that since copies printed during the term of the agreement would not have been infringing copies, they could be sold without infringing copyright, although the author might have had a remedy in breach of contract if excessive printing had taken place towards the end of the term of the agreement with a view to stockpiling. Today, the sale of such copies will almost certainly amount to an issue of copies to the public within the meaning of s.18 of the 1988 Act,[79] and thus will be an infringement, unless licensed. Whether such an act is licensed will depend upon the terms, express or implied, of the contract.

(ix) Non-compete clause

Publishing contracts frequently contain a clause stipulating that the author should **26–67** not write or have published a work that, in the publisher's opinion, would compete with or affect prejudicially the sales of the work that is the subject of the contract. Assuming that no question of restraint of trade arises,[80] such clauses will usually be enforced by way of injunction.[81] Although they are arguably not appropriate in a contract for a novel, they are today a standard clause, inserted by the publisher in its standard form of publishing contract, and intended solely for the benefit of the publisher. These clauses are seldom questioned by the author (unless the author is represented by a literary agent or lawyer) and are therefore almost invariably not specifically negotiated. What is at issue, of course, is whether the author is entitled to write a new but competing work, not whether the author is entitled to write a work which reproduces a substantial part of the work which is subject to the publishing contract, this being a breach of the exclusive rights likely to be granted to the publisher.

I. CONSEQUENCES OF BREACH OF A PUBLISHING AGREEMENT

(i) Failure to supply the work

Specific performance. The court will not order specific performance of an agree- **26–68** ment to create a work. Such an agreement is a contract to provide personal ser-

---

[78] See para.5–227, above.
[79] See para.7–87, above.
[80] See para.28–330, below.
[81] See, e.g. *Psychology Press Ltd v Flanagan* [2002] EWHC 1205 (QB). The public policy exemplified in the law of contract whereby the court regularly enforces provisions for the restriction of unfair competition (provided always that they are reasonable and proportionate) outweighed any freedom of expression considerations under art.10 of the European Convention on Human Rights. It is not clear whether it was argued on behalf of the defendants that the "competing works" clause of the contract was an unjustifiable restraint of trade, on the basis that it might unfairly restrict the extent to which the author could earn a living from writing books on her specialist subject.

vices and there would be no means of enforcing such an order.[82] However, the court can order specific performance of an agreement to assign copyright, or can order an author to deliver a completed manuscript to the publisher.[83]

If the author undertakes to write a work and dies before completing it, his executors or administrators will usually be discharged from the contract, for the undertaking was merely personal in its nature, and has become impossible to perform[84] but it may be that if the author has assigned the copyright in the work, the copyright in any completed part may pass to the publisher, depending on the wording of the contract.

26–69   Damages. Problems arise where the agreement does not make express provision for failure to deliver the manuscript. In practice, publishing agreements will nowadays provide that if the author fails to supply the work by the agreed date, or by any mutually agreed subsequent date, the publisher will have the right to terminate the contract and obtain repayment of any advance previously paid to the author. It is sometimes also a condition that the author will not arrange for the publication of the work in question by any other publisher, without first offering it to the original publisher upon the terms set out in the original publishing contract. If, however, the author delivers part, but not all, of the work, the agreement will usually give the publisher the express right to engage someone else to complete the work, and to pay the cost of doing so out of monies otherwise payable to the author under the agreement.

If the author fails or refuses to supply the manuscript, in breach of contract, the publisher will have a remedy in damages.[85] Where the author fails to supply the manuscript, the publisher can recover as damages any outlay made in reliance on the contract and the estimated loss of profit, or any other consequential loss.[86]

(ii) Failure to publish a work

26–70   Specific performance. While a publishing agreement remains completely unperformed, it may be impracticable for the court to order specific performance by the publisher of his agreement to publish, although where the order could be enforced without practical difficulty, such an order may be made. This may depend upon how far the exact terms of publication have been agreed. The court cannot order specific performance of an agreement to publish where it would require supervision of the editing process.[87] In *Malcolm v Chancellor, Masters and Scholars of the University of Oxford*,[88] where the judge at first instance would not have ordered specific performance of the contract (had he found one to exist, which he did not), the Court of Appeal (which, by a majority, held that a contract

---

[82] *Clarke v Price* (1819) Wils. 157; see *Page One Records Ltd v Britton* [1968] 1 W.L.R. 157 where an injunction was refused when it would have amounted to a decree of specific performance.

[83] *Thombleson v Black* (1837) 1 Jur. 198; and see *Macdonald (E) Ltd v Eyles* [1921] 1 Ch. 631 at 638, where Peterson J. construed the agreement as a contract to sell the products of the author's labour or industry, and granted an injunction requiring the author to deliver the completed manuscript to the publisher and restraining her from disposing of the work in breach of the agreement; see also *Transatlantic Records Ltd v Bulltown Ltd* [1980] CA transcript 164.

[84] *Marshall v Broadhurst* (1831) 1 Tyrwh. 348 at 350.

[85] *Gale v Leckie* (1817) 2 Stark. N.P. 107.

[86] See general principles formulated in *Anglia TV v Reed* [1972] 1 Q.B. 60. For an example of such a claim, see *Times Newspapers Ltd v George Weidenfeld & Nicholson Ltd* [2002] F.S.R. 29.

[87] *See Joseph v National Magazine Co Ltd* [1959] Ch.14, above, in which specific performance was refused, as editing of the article was necessary, distinguishing *Barrow v Chappell & Co Ltd*, [1976] R.P.C. 355 (decided in 1951) where the score of the musical work was ready for publication and the judge found that the publisher was not entitled to edit it without the composer's consent, and the publisher had offered an undertaking to publish if found to be bound by the agreement.

[88] [1994] E.M.L.R. 17.

did exist) approved the judge's decision on this point, and ordered an inquiry as to damages. Whether it would ever be in an author's interest to obtain an order for specific performance of a contract to publish his work, is a moot point. If the parties have fallen out to the extent that the author has had to litigate in order to establish that the publisher is in breach of a contract to publish, it may not be sensible for the author to have that publisher publish his work (in particular, presumably, under the terms of an exclusive licence).

Damages. Damages may be awarded against publishers in respect of delay in publication, amounting to a breach of contract, a failure to publish by an agreed date or within a reasonable time thereafter[89] or a refusal to publish amounting to a repudiatory breach of contract. Damages for failure to publish by an agreed date or a refusal to publish at all may be based upon an estimate of what the claimant would have got if the defendant had carried out its bargain.[90] In *Joseph v National Magazine Co Ltd*,[91] damages were assessed on the loss to the plaintiff as an expert in jade of the enhancement of his reputation which would have resulted from the publication. In *Malcolm v Chancellor, Masters and Scholars of the University of Oxford*, an inquiry as to damages was ordered both to recompense the author for loss of the opportunity for him to enhance his reputation by securing the imprimatur of the Oxford University Press on his work[92] and to compensate the author for loss of royalties. An author may also claim remuneration on a *quantum meruit* basis for work done on a publication which is abandoned,[93] as an alternative to damages for loss of royalties.

26–71

Where the time of publication, number of copies and price and form of the book are left to the discretion of the publisher, the damages for failure to publish are based on a reasonable estimate of the amount that the author would have earned if the publisher had complied with his contract to publish. This will require consideration of everything likely to affect the amount of the profit, such as the nature and popularity of the subject matter, the reputation of the author, the cost of producing a book on that subject, the price of such a book, the business capacity of the publishers and the chances of earning profits by sales of the book.[94] It will involve examining the publishing history of books deemed to be comparable to the one in suit and estimating how many copies would have been sold in each format, in each applicable language, at what prices and at what times. The courts are able to consider the conflicting evidence adduced by each party and form their own view, which they did in *Malcolm*[95] and in *Myers v Macmillan Press Ltd*.[96] In *Myers*, it was accepted by both parties that if the plaintiff succeeded on liability, he could elect between two alternative bases for assessing damages. The first is the loss of profits which, on the court's assessment, he would have made had the defendant performed its obligations under the publishing agreement. The second basis is a *quantum meruit*. The judge said that the second basis is less satisfactory, as it involves carrying out an exercise which does not reflect what happens in practice, i.e. assessing what would have been a reasonable number of

---

[89] See *White v Constable & Co* [1901–1904] Mac.C.C. 2.

[90] See *Abrahams v Herbert Reiach Ltd* [1922] 1 K.B. 477.

[91] See [1959] Ch.14. See also *Tedesco v Bosa* (1993) 10 O.R. (3d) 799, noted at [1993] 3 Ent.L.R. 58 (Ontario Ct Gen Div).

[92] On the inquiry as to damages ordered by the Court of Appeal, a substantial sum was awarded under this head. The findings are reported at *http://www.akme.btinternet.co.uk* [Accessed October 29, 2010]. The entire history of the litigation is the subject of Andrew Malcolm's book *The Remedy* (AKME Publications).

[93] *Planché v Colburn* (1831) 8 Bing. 14

[94] *Abrahams v Herbert Reiach Ltd* [1922] 1 K.B. 477.

[95] *Malcolm v Chancellor, Masters and Scholars of the University of Oxford* [1994] E.M.L.R. 17.

[96] Unreported, March 3, 1988.

hours for the plaintiff to have spent in writing the work and what would have been a reasonable hourly rate to pay for that work. In the event, the first basis of assessment would clearly have resulted in a higher award, and so damages for loss of profits were awarded. If the author has incurred specific expenses in connection with the agreement, such as preparing illustrations for the text, these can be claimed as special damages.[97] Where a publishing agreement requires the defendant to publish the first edition of the claimant's book, and the agreement also contemplates that further editions will be published, the failure by the defendant to publish the first edition of the book will entitle the claimant to damages both for failure to publish the first edition and also for the loss of the chance to establish the title, by the success of the first edition, which would lead to repeat editions in the future, and hence generate royalties on those further editions.[98] Where the breach by the publisher is something other than a failure to publish, the measure of damages will be the loss sustained by the author by reason of the publisher's breach.

26–72   **Account of profits.** In limited circumstances an account of profits can be awarded as a remedy for breach of contract.[99]

26–73   **Damages for breach of obligation to "use all reasonable endeavours" to obtain right of first negotiation.** An obligation to use all reasonable endeavours to obtain a right of first negotiation from any assignee of the purchaser for the author to do specified work, in good faith, may be legally binding[100]. Such an obligation, if clear and certain, does not become any less clear or certain because of the wide range of routes by which the obligation can be discharged.

(iii) Breach of contract to ghost-write an autobiography

26–74   In *Sadler v Reynolds*,[101] it was held that Reynolds had breached a contract with Sadler under which Sadler was to write Reynolds' autobiography and to share the proceeds equally. The breach consisted of entering into a contract with another ghost-writer for the same purpose. The publisher with whom Sadler had negotiated a contract for publication of Reynolds' autobiography gave evidence that the advance agreed (£70,000 to be shared equally between Sadler and Reynolds) was intended to represent their likely royalties from the book, and the judge accordingly awarded Sadler £35,000 for loss of royalties and a further sum of £1,000 for loss of the opportunity to enhance his reputation by publication of the book.

J. PARTICULAR PROBLEMS OR POINTS WHICH CONFRONT THE PUBLISHING INDUSTRY

(i) Territorial issues

26–75   **Territorial rights.** The question of territorial rights is one that particularly concerns UK book publishers, because English language books are read in many countries around the world, and exclusivity of publishing rights is an essential factor in the economics of publishing any particular work. In relation to works which are suitable for sale in the English language both in the United Kingdom and in the United States of America, rights are generally shared between UK and

---

[97] As in *Joseph v National Magazine Co Ltd* [1959] Ch.14.
[98] *Thornton v Tulett* Unreported, March 2, 2000, CA.
[99] *Attorney-General v Blake* [2001] 1 A.C. 268; [2000] E.M.L.R. 949.
[100] *Lambert v HTV Cymru (Wales) Ltd* [1998] F.S.R. 874.
[101] [2005] EWHC (QB) 309.

American publishers as follows: the UK publisher will have the exclusive rights to publish in the United Kingdom and the Republic of Ireland, Australia, New Zealand, South Africa, the Middle East and Commonwealth countries (other than Canada); the American publisher will have the exclusive right to publish in the United States, its territories and dependencies, Canada and the Philippines; the rest of the world is treated as an "open market", where both the UK publisher and the American publisher have the non-exclusive right to publish. It is particularly important to note that, in general, the countries of the EEA, other than the United Kingdom and the Republic of Ireland, form part of the "open market", and so copies of a work placed on sale in any of those countries by or with the consent of the copyright owner can be imported into the United Kingdom, against the wishes of the UK publisher who has exclusive rights for the United Kingdom territory. American editions of books tend to be significantly cheaper than the corresponding UK editions[102] and can therefore undercut the corresponding UK editions if they can find their way into the UK market. United Kingdom publishers could avoid this potential problem if they were able to secure exclusive publishing rights throughout the EEA but this does not seem to happen in practice.

Internet bookshops (including supermarket websites and websites that sell other media, such as CDs and DVDs) are now a well-established and substantial part of the distribution chain for books. These offer the opportunity to anyone in the world to order books (often American editions) via the internet at discounted prices, which may be substantially lower than those applying, for example, in the United Kingdom. However, if an internet bookshop were to sell copies of an American edition to someone in the United Kingdom, in circumstances where a UK publisher has exclusive rights to publish that work in the United Kingdom, then this may amount to infringement of copyright,[103] depending on where the sale takes place and who is the importer.

United Kingdom trade publishers face a number of difficulties, including:

- increasing parallel importation of US "open market" editions entering the United Kingdom via Europe;
- the value of UK English language rights being diminished by parallel importation of US editions via other European countries;
- the growth of internet bookselling facilitating parallel importation; and
- parallel importation of "open market" editions facilitating the trade in illegal (infringing) editions which have not entered the EU lawfully.

In response, UK publishers are increasingly seeking from authors and agents Exclusive English Language Rights to Europe as a practical way of protecting their home market, where previously they had held exclusive UK territorial rights. It is anticipated that with more countries joining the European Union, the incentive for UK publishers, authors and authors' agents to acquire and sell Exclusive European Rights, which can be operated effectively within the Community regime of Exhaustion of Rights, is likely to increase.

Following discussions between representatives of The Publishers Association and Amazon.co.uk, a new notice-and-take-down procedure has been introduced to deal with territorial (or other) rights infringements both for main catalogue items and items being resold on Marketplace on Amazon.co.uk. Details of the procedure are on the Publishers Association website, with links to the appropriate sections of the Amazon.co.uk website. This should help UK publishers protect

---

[102] This may in part be explained by the fact that the larger American territory enables American publishers to print larger quantities and hence have lower unit costs, although this advantage of the American publishers can be affected by the exchange rate between the US dollar, sterling and the euro.

[103] See CDPA 1988 ss.18(1), (2), 22, 23.

their UK exclusivity from being infringed by the importation of American editions via the internet.

26–76   **Territory: are worldwide rights enough?** With satellite broadcasting now commonplace and with the establishment of a base on the moon becoming a real possibility, the question arises whether it is still sufficient for publishers and other users of copyright material to acquire rights on no more than a worldwide basis. For many years the American film and television industries have routinely acquired rights "throughout the universe". Precisely what the legal effect of this is, bearing in mind that rights of copyright do not at present extend beyond the earth, may be open to debate, but such a grant should at least be binding as a matter of contract as between the grantor and the grantee, if not as against third parties. Perhaps it is now also time for UK publishers (particularly electronic publishers) to acquire rights in copyright works on a universe-wide basis.

(ii) Site licensing of journals.

26–77   The publishing of journals electronically and making them available to educational establishments throughout the United Kingdom on the basis of a site licence represents a major step forward in educational publishing. Previously, site licensing had been adopted on an individual basis between higher education institutions ("HEIs") and publishers, but never before on a national basis. Trials of site licensing on a national basis were initially carried out by a few publishers, with government assistance. The initial scheme (known as the Higher Education Funding Councils United Kingdom Pilot Site Licence Initiative ("PSLI"), ran from 1995 to 1997, aiming to offer greater access to research and teaching materials through a combination of reduced prices and the lifting of restrictions on the use of materials (such as photocopying for course packs). The scheme also sought to assess different site licence models (as each of the publishers involved used a slightly different arrangement) and whether this is a way forward for the future, and also to evaluate the use of different media (e.g. paper and electronic).

The PSLI was followed by the United Kingdom National Electronic Site Licence Initiative ("NESLI"), for a period of three years from January 1, 1999. In contrast with the PSLI, the NESLI was run by a managing agent, which carried out negotiations with publishers, managed delivery of the electronic material and oversaw the day-to-day operation of the programme. NESLI has now been followed by NESLi2, initially for the period 2003–2006, building on the experience of the earlier initiatives.[104] Content from 17 leading scholarly publishers is covered by NESLi2 agreements, which typically span one to three years in duration, and over 7,000 online journals are available to authorised users in this way. The content itself is made accessible directly from publishers' bespoke web platforms. By way of example, Oxford University Press makes available under NESLi2 its online collection of journals from arts, social science, scientific, technical, medical and professional and humanities disciplines, covering law, life sciences, mathematics, medicine and social sciences, for undergraduate, postgraduate and research level users.

The electronic distribution of journals via a site licence arrangement raises a number of important copyright issues. First, it involves the digitisation of the works in question. The publisher therefore has to ensure that it owns the necessary right to do this, or to authorise others to do so, in relation to all of the mate-

---

[104] For up-to-date information on various licensing initiatives, see the website of the Association of Learned and Professional Society Publishers: *http://www.alpsp.org.uk* [Accessed October 29, 2010].

rial in question before it proceeds, since digitisation without consent of the copy-right owner could amount to infringement. The publisher will also want to ensure that the site licence specifies very particularly the limitations of the rights granted to the educational establishments that are being licensed and the users who are entitled to use the material pursuant to the site licence. The site licence should also specify what rights are to be granted to print any of the material that is made available electronically. The site licence should also contain provisions for the protection of the intellectual property in the material, particularly given that the digitisation and electronic communication of the material renders it vulnerable to piracy. The site licence may authorise some people to access the material off-site, e.g. at home, and this has particular implications for the security of the intel-lectual property. This raises a question for academic institutions to consider whether the abuse of electronically available copyright material should, in the case of a student, lead to expulsion from the course, and in the case of a member of staff, to dismissal. A series of model licences has been developed for the acquisition of electronic journals and other electronic resources by libraries of various types: single academic institutions; academic consortia; public libraries; and corporate and other special libraries. They are available free of charge from *http://www.licensingmodels.com* [Accessed October 29, 2010].

A group made up of publishers and members of the Pharmaceutical Documen-tation Ring (which comprises companies in the pharmaceutical industry) has produced a new Model Licence for the licensing of digital journal content to the pharmaceutical industry. The Model Licence, along with a background document outlining the history of the Model Licence and explanations of the rationale behind some of the clauses, can be downloaded from the ALPSP website.

The Model NESLi2 Licence for Journals continues to be used and brought up-to-date with latest developments in the delivery of teaching and learning and the dissemination of research activity in the academic community.

The changes made in October 2006 relate to the more recent developments of wireless networks, Shibboleth (a standards-based, open source software package for web single sign-on across or within organisational boundaries, allowing sites to make informed authorisation decisions for individual access of protected on-line resources in a privacy-preserving manner), electronic repositories and self-archiving.

Further changes were made to the Model NESLi2 Licence in May 2007 relat-ing to an expansion of the Authorised Users and Secure Authentication defini-tions, dark archives used by the publisher ("dark archives" is generally taken to mean a collection of materials preserved for future use but with no current ac-cess, and is principally associated with collections of online serial publications and databases that are held by an organisation *other than* the publisher; these materials are kept in escrow for future use in case they are no longer available from the publisher) and an indication of compliance with Project Transfer. In September 2008, the dark archives clause was strengthened and some minor changes were made to the Schedules to tighten-up the wording regarding subscription periods and fees.

In 2007 JISC Collections launched NESLi2 SMP (NESLi2 for Small- and Medium-sized Publishers). This facilitates access for staff and students in universities, colleges and research councils in the United Kingdom to a wider range of online journals from small and medium-sized publishers. Twenty-two publishers currently participate in this initiative, with some 904 journal titles be-ing made available to academic libraries.

As the number of digital resources in library collections grows, libraries have increasing difficulty in managing, and ensuring that they comply with, the ever-growing number of different licences that they hold. JISC Collections tries to minimise this work by using the JISC model licence as the basis for all of its agreements and trying to minimise the variations that it introduces into those licences.

Increasingly, librarians are looking for technology to help them manage their licences and let their users know what they can and cannot do with electronic resources. One such technology involves machine-readable licences that allow licence terms to be stored and communicated electronically between library systems that should ultimately be able to provide licence information to library staff and to end users at the point of use.

JISC Collections has been working with the international standards body EDItEUR on the "ONIX for Licensing Terms" project to develop the tools and formats required to express the full range and complexity of licensing terms in a structured machine-readable form that can be communicated between systems using a standard XML-based schema.

ONIX for Publications Licenses (ONIX-PL) is intended to support the licensing of electronic resources—such as online journals and e-books—to academic and corporate libraries. It will enable libraries to:

- express licenses in a machine-readable format
- load them into electronic resource management systems
- link them to digital resources
- compare different licenses with each other
- easily see what users can and cannot do with different electronic resources and communicate key usage terms to users

Publishers will also benefit from the ability to maintain their licenses in a standard machine-readable form.

So far about 40 licence expressions have been created in the ONIX-PL format for machine readable licences and the interface is scheduled to be ready for testing by the end of October 2010.

(iii) Electronic publishing

26–78   **Electronic publishing generally.** The issues currently being tackled in relation to the site licensing of electronically published journals are also being dealt with in relation to the digitisation of other works required by libraries in academic institutions. Publishers are increasingly being met with requests for the right to digitise all or parts of various works. This involves the publishers in checking that they either have the rights or can clear the necessary rights. It also involves consideration of how the digitisation takes place and by whom it is carried out. For example, an increasing number of "photocopiers" are now, in fact, digital copiers, although this may not be widely realised by rights owners. It is assumed that these "digital copiers" are generally being used to prepare materials for the production of printed materials, although they could be used as a delivery mechanism for on-screen display. The way in which these copiers work does not, however, constitute true "digitisation", and would not allow the flexibility of usage that true digitisation can afford.

The making available of materials in digital form raises issues as to how the material should be paid for. This in turn depends on a number of elements, including the degree of risk to the publisher or other rights owner in terms of protection of intellectual property and possible loss of direct sales which might otherwise have been made.

26–79   In March 1998 it was announced that agreement had been reached between the Joint Information Systems Committee of the United Kingdom Higher Education Funding Councils and the Publishers Association, making it possible for HEIs to have ready access to digital versions of academic publications. This involves the creation of a model licence to enable HEIs to disseminate digital versions of publications within agreed sites; agreement on the charging formula to be applied by publishers when HEIs digitise existing printed material; and publishing guidelines on what is meant by the concept of "fair dealing" in a digital environment. The Copyright Licensing Agency ("CLA") offers a licence to HEIs to digitise extracts from books, journals and periodicals and to make them available to students and staff over a network. Charges are set by the rightsholders, either on a per-student basis (particularly suitable for textbooks) or on a flat-fee basis of a fee per page multiplied by the number of pages.

A further and complementary development is the HERON scheme. HERON offers a national service to the UK academic community for copyright clearance, digitisation and delivery of book extracts and journal articles. In addition, HERON has also developed a resource bank of digitised materials for rapid reuse (subject to copyright permissions). HERON's status as a designated Trusted Repository means that it is entitled to hold copies of CLA-cleared digitised texts. These texts form the basis of HERON's resource bank of archived pre-digitised material. The remaining content comprises copies of material requested through HERON, where the rightsholder has given permission for a master copy to be stored. The HERON charging structure has a number of elements:

Institutional Subscription: Each institution pays an annual subscription fee to HERON in order to use the service.

Copyright clearance: This payment is dictated by the rightsholder. The majority of requests are calculated on a "per-student-per-page" basis for use by students on a specific course. Only those students on the specified course can be directed to the material (although other students may use the material should they come across it during their own private study or research. 5p is the most common rate but charges can still vary quite a lot. Some requests (especially for journal articles) are charged on a flat-fee basis which allows any student registered at the institution to be directed to the material.

Supply fee: This fee will vary depending on whether or not the document is a resupply from HERON's existing archive or a new document, requiring digitisation.

Completion fee: HERON adds a completion charge on extracts for carrying out this work and to cover the development of the HERON service.

HERON currently has 50 subscribing institutions across the British Isles and in Norway and Japan.

A Trial Scanning Licence for Further Education was introduced by the Copyright Licensing Agency ("CLA") in 2003 and a Trial Photocopying and Scanning Licence for Higher Education was introduced by CLA in 2005. In September 2006 the CLA announced that it has extended its standard licence for independent Higher Education Institutions ("HEIs") to permit them and their registered students to make digital copies of documents, as well as physical photocopies. This brings the licence into line with the standard licence for the HEIs which are members of Universities UK or the Standing Conference of Principals. The new licences ran for an initial two-year trial period until August 31, 2008 and have been extended for a further three years. Details and copies of these licences and associated documents (such as a User Guide) can be obtained from the CLA website *http://www.cla.co.uk* [Accessed October 29, 2010].

In March 2007 the CLA announced that following lengthy negotiations, it had agreed a central photocopying and scanning licence for the NHS in England.

In April 2007 the CLA clarified the distinction between the photocopying and scanning licences granted to HEIs and to the NHS in England, Wales, Scotland and Northern Ireland. The CLA stated that it recognised that there is a significant degree of co-operation, collaboration and partnership between HEIs and NHS Trusts—especially in respect of Teaching Hospitals, joint library facilities and staff engaged in delivering teaching and/or participating in courses of study in one or both sectors, and made clear that the principles underpinning the making of licensed copies are that:

- copies made by, for or on behalf of staff and students of a university or College of Higher Education are subject to the terms of the HE Licence;
- copies made by, for, or on behalf of, staff employed by the NHS are subject to the terms and conditions of the NHS Licence;
- all copying activity should retain an intimate link between the collection of printed books, journals and magazines owned by the respective HEI or NHS Trust and its delivery to an authorised user contracted to/enrolled with that HEI or contracted to that NHS Trust.

CLA announced on October 15, 2007 that it had introduced a new for to the Adult Education sector: the enhanced Trial Scanning Licence. This is the first licence of its type to include digital uses such as scanning and retyping of print resources. The licence came into effect from November 1, 2007 and is running on a trial basis and. It is available to all Adult and Community Education and Learning providers. The enhanced licence permits the creation of digital copies made from print originals owned by the licensee and for those digital copies to be used with technologies such as digital whiteboards, within Virtual Learning Environments, including email and fax.

26–80   **e-books.** For a number of years now, electronic books (or "e-books") have been a commercial reality, available in a variety of formats for reading either on a dedicated e-book reader or on a hand-held palmtop computer, a mobile phone, a laptop computer, a netbook computer or a desktop computer. Unfortunately, at present there is no common standard used by producers and manufacturers and none of the e-book readers support all of the formats. In an effort to correct this situation, many of the major software companies and device manufacturers in the e-book market are backing new common standards that are being drafted by the International Digital Publishing Forum ("IDPF"), which address how e-books are produced and read. The IDPF is the trade and standards association for the digital publishing industry. Its members consist of academic, trade and professional publishers, hardware and software companies, digital content retailers, libraries, educational institutions, accessibility advocates and related organisations whose common goals are to advance the competitiveness and exposure of digital publishing.

The IDPF released on September 11, 2007 a new technical standard to facilitate digital content creation, distribution and use by consumers. Known as "ePub", the new standard is composed of three open standards, namely the Open Publication Structure (OPS), the Open Packaging Format (OPF) and the Open Container Format (OCF). ePub allows publishers to release a single standard file into their sales and distribution channels and also enables consumers to exchange unencrypted e-books and other digital publications between reading systems that support the new standard. But Digital Rights Management ("DRM"), which limits the number of devices on which an e-book can be installed (generally varying between three and five devices), will remain an issue on which there is unlikely to be a common solution.

BookDROP version 1.0 was published on December 8, 2008. It is a standard jointly developed by the Book Industry Study Group and the Association of American Publishers, with the intention of supporting the search and discovery of digital book content on the Internet, while allowing publishers to manage the quality and availability of their content.

Some figures will illustrate what is happening with e-books. According to the Publishers Association, total sales by publishers in the United Kingdom of digital products amounted to £150 million in 2009. Of this, £5 million consisted of general consumer titles; £8 million consisted of consumer reference titles; £8 to £9 million consisted of school/English Language Teaching titles; and £130 million consisted of academic and professional titles. In the United States, in 2009 e-book sales (trade only) amounted to $169.5 million, and 2010 has to date seen the growth of 204 per cent.[105] A report published by Forrester Research on November 5, 2010 found that US e-book sales in 2010 were expected to reach US$966 million, and that by 2015 US e-book sales were expected to reach US$2.8 billion.

The international scientific and professional publisher Springer claims to have the largest collection of STM (scientific, technical and medical) books online, consisting of nearly 40,000 e-books, with more than 4,000 new e-books and so-called "eReferences" being added each year. Springer is also selling digital versions of its yearly copyrighted collections dating from 2004. Further, it is moving to a more open business model that allows libraries and institutions to make e-books available to all users simultaneously at all times and permits remote access, as well as providing sophisticated management tools for librarians. Springer eBooks, eReferences and eBook Series are offered as an annual package, whereas libraries and institutions can either purchase the entire annual collection or may purchase any number of Subject Collections (Subject Collections include Architecture, Design and Arts; Behavioural Sciences; Biomedical & Life Sciences; Business & Economics; Chemistry & Material Science; Computer Science; Earth and Environmental Science; Medicine; and Physics & Astronomy). Full archiving rights with continuous access to purchased content are free as long as the subscribing institution's account remains active with Springer.

Palgrave Macmillan launched its own ebook platform, Palgrave Connect, in January 2009. More than 4,500 ebooks are available in the collections organised by year of publication and by discipline, with 2009 and backlist collections available to purchase on the basis of a one-time fee granting perpetual access. The platform is being shared with Palgrave Macmillan's sister company, Nature Publishing Group, offering both ebooks and journals through a single administration system and is said by Palgrave Macmillan to be "an important first step towards offering integrated collections of content in the future".

Sony launched its eBook Store on the internet at the end of September 2006: *http://www.ebookstore.sony.com* [Accessed October 29, 2010]. It carries thousands of bestselling titles from leading publishers, including HarperCollins, Simon & Schuster and Random House. In addition, Sony has launched and continues to update its range of Reader devices to go with the eBook Store.

There are now quite a large number of dedicated e-book readers on the market. The best-known are the Sony Reader range and the Amazon Kindle. However, the latest entrant on the market is not, strictly speaking, a dedicated e-book reader: it is the Apple iPad (launched in April 2010), which is far more than just an e-book reader. It is, in effect, a so-called tablet computer. The iPad works in conjunction with the iBooks app, which is downloadable free from the Apple App Store. Using the iBooks app, one can access the iBookstore to download e-books to the iPad. An iTunes Store account is required for this purpose. The iBooks app can also be used on the Apple iPhone and iPod Touch, so long as they have the operating system iOS 4 or later. iBooks uses books published in the ePub format. It is possible to add ePub files to iBooks, provided that they are DRM-free and synchronised to an iPad (or iPhone or iPod Touch with the ap-

[105] Source: IDPF/AAP.

propriate operating system) using iTunes. Six months after the launch of the iPad and the simultaneous launch of the iBookstore, it is not easy to assess its impact, but it is fair to say that, at this stage, there is far less content available through the iBookstore than through its major rival, the Kindle store. Having said that, Kindle e-books can now be used on the iPad, courtesy of the Kindle app for the iPad. This gives iPad users access to more than 450,000 Kindle titles.

The Amazon Kindle became available in the United Kingdom only quite some time after its launch in the United States, but has now proved popular in the United Kingdom. There is now a dedicated UK Kindle Store, with the biggest selection of any e-bookstore in the United Kingdom—more than 450,000 ebooks, including bestsellers and new releases. United Kingdom and international newspapers, magazines, and blogs, plus more than 1 million free e-books, are also available. The Kindle is available in two versions—one with Wi-Fi and one with Wi-Fi plus 3G. Prices of the new Kindles are very competitive. Unlike the iPad, the Kindle uses an E-Ink screen, which provides high contrast and is easy to read in all lighting conditions, even in bright sunlight. E-books can be downloaded direct to the Kindle over Wi-Fi or 3G, and the Kindle has capacity for up to 3,500 books.

It is not difficult to see how convenient it would be to be able to carry hundreds of books on a small, lightweight device that will not give you eye strain—those in professions such as engineers, doctors, lawyers could all benefit, as would schoolchildren. Already some newspapers and magazines are available on e-book readers. The iPad has a vivid full-colour display. The Kindle and other dedicated e-book readers can currently only display black and white, but it is hoped that that will soon change—in fact, the first full-colour E-Ink e-book reader was launched in November 2010 and is due to be on sale in early 2011. In the meantime, publishers and booksellers (including, of course, internet booksellers) are all gearing up for massively increased sales of e-books. Unlike the other e-book readers available in the United Kingdom, the Amazon Kindle (currently) cannot use the EPUB format.

The increasing importance of e-books brings its own problems that the publishing industry is beginning to grapple with, including the following:

26–81   **Pricing of e-books.** One aspect of the debate centres on the contrast between the "retail model" and the "agency model" of pricing. Under the "retail model" of selling e-books, publishers sell to retailers, who then sell to readers at a price that the retailer determines. Under the "agency model", publishers set the price, and retailers take a commission on the sale to readers. In the United States, Macmillan moved to the agency model of pricing with all of its retailers simultaneously around the end of March 2010. Other US publishers have adopted the same pricing model: Hachette, HarperCollins, Penguin and Simon & Schuster. If a publisher is able to ensure that all retailers acquire its e-books on the agency pricing model, then all retailers will be selling the particular book at the same price. In the United Kingdom, Hachette announced that it will switch some booksellers to the agency pricing model, and this resulted in certain retailers removing its e-books from sale. Amazon.co.uk continued to set its own prices and to sell Hachette UK titles. It is understood that other major UK publishers plan to follow Hachette in switching to the agency pricing model. In October 2010 Amazon.co.uk issued a statement saying that it would "continue to fight against higher prices for e-books" and confirming that Hachette "will require Amazon and other UK booksellers to accept an agency model for e-books" and that they anticipated that Hachette would then raise prices on e-books for consumers almost across the board. They pointed out the experience in the United States that switching to the agency pricing model was followed by an increase in digital book prices almost across the board, not just on new books.

Another aspect of the debate on e-book pricing concerns whether e-books should be priced at the same price as the corresponding printed book, or lower (or indeed higher) than that. After all, with e-books there are no manufacturing costs, no warehousing costs and very little in terms of distribution costs. These factors would suggest that e-books should be priced lower than their corresponding printed version. On the other hand, an e-book might be considered to be more convenient and actually worth more than a printed book. In the printed book sector, an individual book could have three distinct editions priced at considerably different levels—the hardback being the most expensive, then the trade paperback, and the mass-market paperback being the cheapest. With e-books, there is generally no difference in the format—although there is scope for value-added versions to be sold alongside a standard e-book version. For example, the value-added (or "enhanced") version might contain interviews with the author or material from a third-party source that is in some way relevant to the book in question.

In the United Kingdom, Penguin responded to Amazon.co.uk's criticism of the agency model of pricing, with a note to literary agents, saying:

"Our first and foremost concern is that we protect the value of our authors' books, as well as the long-term health of this exciting new segment of the publishing industry. We believe that the agency model is more likely to provide authors with a just reward for their creative content, while establishing a fair price for the consumer. Under the agency model, publishers sell work directly to the consumer, enabling them to set the price. Under the traditional resale model, the retailer purchases books from the publisher at a pre-agreed discount to the recommended retail price (RRP), and then is free to resell them at whatever price they decide, even if it means making a loss.

"We understand that digital books are less expensive to produce than physical books, and that the benefit of this cost saving should be fairly allocated between readers, authors and publishers. With this in mind, we expect to price Penguin e-books below the list price of the comparable physical books, even though we will have to absorb the VAT that is levied on digital books but not on their physical counterparts."

Territorial issues. One literary agent is reported as having experienced pressure from American publishers to acquire worldwide rights on e-book editions when they have more limited territorial rights on the corresponding printed edition.

26–82

Payments to authors. There seems to be growing acceptance amongst publishers that the royalty payable to authors on e-books should be at least 25 per cent of the publisher's net receipts. One major publisher has agreed to pay an escalating royalty on backlist titles sold in e-books, starting at 25 per cent and rising to 40 per cent as sales increase. The Society of Authors considers that authors should be paid more than 25 per cent of the publisher's net receipts. One approach to this whole issue is to build in contractual provisions for reviewing royalty rates on a regular basis—perhaps even annually—to reflect changes in publishing practice as the market for e-books develops.

26–83

Licensing e-book rights. There is an old adage: "license in long and wide; license out short and narrow", meaning that a party acquiring rights should endeavour to obtain the widest rights for the longest period possible, and that a party licensing out rights should license the narrowest rights and for the shortest period possible. Given the pace of change in electronic publishing generally, and e-books in particular, this would appear to be sound advice. An author licensing e-book rights to a publisher might, for example, endeavour to limit the rights to a particular platform, e.g. the Kindle, and perhaps license corresponding rights on another

26–84

platform to another publisher. On the other hand, the publisher acquiring rights will seek to get the widest possible rights to publish the book on all electronic platforms, including those not yet developed.

(iv) Digitisation

26–85   **Google and Amazon digitisation programmes.** Google and Amazon (and others, such as Microsoft and Yahoo) have been busy trying to persuade publishers and libraries to allow them to scan large quantities of books and make the digitised texts available to be searched on the Google search engine, browsed on the Amazon website and otherwise accessed on the internet.

26–86   **Google.** There are two aspects to the Google Book Search project: the Partner Program and the Library Project.

The Partner Program enables publishers who control the relevant rights in the book to authorise Google to scan the full text of the book into Google's search database. Then when a user does a Google search, books that contain their search terms will show up in the search results. Users will be able to preview a limited number of pages to determine whether they have found what they were looking for, and they will be provided with links to online bookstores to buy the book and libraries to borrow the book. This program is put to publishers as free promotion for their books and a means to generate more sales.

In September 2008 Google announced a new feature as part of its Book Search program: Google Preview. By adding simple programming code to their websites, publishers, retailers and others can embed a Google-hosted preview of up to 20 per cent of any book that has been included in the Google Book Search database. The advantage for retailers of enabling the Google Preview function is that it allows consumers to browse books scanned by Google without leaving the retailer's website, simply by clicking the "Google Preview" button adjacent to the illustration of the book in question.

As part of the Google Partner Program, Google will be launching Google Editions in the United States late in 2010, and in most of Europe early in 2011. This program will allow consumers to easily purchase and read digital editions of books. Consumers will be able to preview a book, and will also have the option to purchase its Google Edition. After purchase, the book will, according to Google, "live in the consumer's online bookshelf", and will be available to be accessed and read on most devices with internet access and a web browser; as well as on supported devices. At launch, Google Editions will be available on the iPad but not on the Amazon Kindle. In the United States, there will be more than 400,000 paid-for titles available from publisher partners when the service launches, along with two million public domain titles, and more titles will become available when the service goes international. Once a Google Edition of a book has been purchased, it will be available for reading anywhere in the world— territorial rights will govern the sale, but not subsequent access. Google have announced that they will be working with US publishers on agency model pricing terms,[106] although not at Google's own request.

The Library Project involves Google scanning into its search database millions of published books from the libraries of Cornell University, Ghent University, Stanford University, the University of Michigan, the University of Wisconsin-Madison, the University of Virginia, Universidad Complutense of Madrid and the University of California, amongst others. The Bodleian Library, Oxford, the Columbia University Library, Harvard University Library, the New York Public

---

[106] See para.26–81 above.

Library and the Princeton University Library are also participating in the Library Project, but are only making available works that are out of copyright. In response to search queries, users will be able to browse the full text of materials that are out of copyright, but for materials that are still in copyright, users will only be able to see a few sentences of the text surrounding the search term.

Copies of Google's contracts with the University of California and the University of Michigan became available on the internet. Both contracts acknowledge that some of the works affected by the contract will be in copyright and others will be out of copyright, and that this may vary from jurisdiction to jurisdiction. Both contracts contain a statement that the parties intend to perform the contracts in compliance with copyright law. The sheer scale of what is involved is vast. For example, the contract with the University of California covers more than 100 libraries on the 10 campuses of the University, and the University is required to provide no fewer than two and a half million volumes for digitisation.

The Library Project gave rise to litigation in the United States alleging copyright infringement. Separate lawsuits were brought by The Authors Guild and by the Association of American Publishers (AAP) on behalf of five major publisher members of its organisation: The McGraw-Hill Companies, Pearson Education, Penguin Group (USA), Simon & Schuster and John Wiley & Sons. Google claimed to be entitled to scan and digitise copyright works under the "fair use" provisions of US copyright law, which are considered to be substantially wider than the "fair dealing" provisions of UK copyright law. Google carries out the scanning in the United States, claiming that it is entitled to do so under US law, notwithstanding that the publishers of some of the works in question may be based in other countries. It argues that the display of only very small portions of copyright works does not infringe the copyrights subsisting in other countries on the test of substantiality.

On October 28, 2008 it was announced that the litigation brought by The Authors Guild and the AAP had been settled, although the settlement still had to be approved by the Court in New York. On November 17, 2008 the New York judge in charge of the case preliminarily approved the Settlement and set a hearing date of June 11, 2009 for a final settlement/fairness hearing to decide if the Settlement is fair, reasonable and adequate.

Google established a settlement administration website,[107] with information about the Settlement and a procedure to register to receive notifications and further information. There is also a section on the Authors' Guild website dedicated to the Settlement and providing valuable resources about the Settlement.[108]

After opposition from many parties, including various authors' groups, consumer advocacy organisations, academics and competitors (including Amazon.com Inc, Yahoo and Microsoft) and the US Department of Justice (which opposed the proposed settlement particularly on anti-trust grounds), the parties to the settlement negotiated an Amended Settlement Agreement. The Amended Settlement Agreement received preliminary approval from the court on November 19, 2009, and the court set a date of February 18, 2010 for the fairness hearing, which duly took place. By that time, a great many objections had been filed. At the time of writing, it is not clear when a final decision will be made. It was pointed out in the US Department of Justice filing that the Anti-trust Division of the US Department of Justice is carrying out an anti-trust investigation into aspects of the Amended Settlement, and it may be that the Settlement

---

[107] *http://www.googlebooksettlement.com/* [Accessed October 18, 2010].
[108] *http://www.authorsguild.org/advocacy/articles/settlement-resources.html* [Accessed October 18, 2010].

cannot be finalised until anti-trust concerns have been satisfied by amendments to the proposed Settlement.

If and when finally approved, the Amended Settlement (as presently drafted and currently available to the public) will authorise Google on a non-exclusive basis to:

- Continue to digitise Books and Inserts (as defined);
- Sell subscriptions to an electronic Books database to institutions;
- Sell online access to individual Books;
- Sell advertising on pages from Books;
- Display portions of Books in a "preview" format to encourage sales of on-line access to Books;
- Display Snippets (three or four lines of text) from Books; and
- Display bibliographic information (the Book's title page, copyright page, table of contents and index) from Books.

In return:

- Google will pay Rightsholders (as defined) 63 per cent of all revenues Google receives from the commercial uses Google makes of the Books.
- Google will pay $34.5 million to establish and maintain a Book Rights Registry ("the Registry"), to locate Rightsholders and create a database of their contact information and copyright interests in Books and Inserts, and to collect revenues from Google and distribute those revenues to Rightsholders, and for notice and settlement administration costs. A significant development under the Amended Settlement Agreement is that the Board of the Registry will have at least one author and one publisher director from each of Canada, the United Kingdom and Australia. Furthermore, the Registry will include a fiduciary with responsibility to represent the interests of Rightsholders with respect to the exploitation of unclaimed Books and Inserts, and the Registry will, from its inception, use settlement funds to attempt to locate Rightsholders.
- Rightsholders will have the right to determine whether and to what extent Google may use their copyrighted writings.
- Google will pay a minimum of $45 million to compensate Rightsholders whose works Google has scanned without permission as of May 5, 2009. Rightsholders of works Google has scanned without permission as of May 5, 2009 are eligible for Cash Payments, which will be at least $60 per Principal Work, $15 per Entire Insert, and $5 per Partial Insert. A "Principal Work" is the main work in a Book (that is, the part of the Book that does not include forewords, afterwards, footnotes and other material).

Rightsholders who are included in the Amended Settlement Class are all persons and entities that, as of January 5, 2009, own a "US copyright interest" in one or more books or inserts that are "implicated by a use" authorised by the Amended Settlement.

A person or entity owns a "US copyright interest" if he or it owns, or has an exclusive license in, a copyright protected by US copyright law. For example, an author owns the US copyright in his or her Book, unless he or she has completely assigned all of his or her copyright interests to another person or entity, or unless he or she wrote the book as a "work for hire" for the purposes of US copyright law. A person or entity also owns a US copyright in a book if he or it has the exclusive right to publish that book in the United States or if he or it has the legal right to sue another for infringing his or its rights in the Book. Several persons may have US copyright interests in the same Book, such as co-authors, an author and a publisher, and the heirs of an author.

A person or entity owns a copyright interest that is "implicated by a use" authorised by the Amended Settlement, if the right that he or it owns is one that Google will be exploiting in using the book. Such uses would include the reproduction or display of any content from a Book.

For the purposes of the Amended Settlement Agreement, a US work (as defined in US copyright law) is only included in the Amended Settlement if it has been published and registered with the United States Copyright Office on or before January 5, 2009. Works other than US works are only included in the Amended Settlement if they were published on or before January 5, 2009 and either were registered in the United States Copyright Office by that date or their place of publication was in Canada, the United Kingdom or Australia.

A Rightsholder who did not previously opt out of the Original Settlement nor out of the Amended Settlement is "in" the Amended Settlement and has the following choices:

- Claim their Books and Inserts on the Settlement administration website;
- Claim a payment for any Books and Inserts that Google digitised on or before May 5, 2009;
- Request that one or more of their Books be removed or that one or more of their Books not be digitised;
- Exclude or include one or more of their Books in various Display Uses under the Amended Settlement;
- Exclude or include one or more of their Inserts in all Display Uses under the Amended Settlement.

A Rightsholder who remains in the Amended Settlement Class will be bound by the Amended Settlement. If they do not claim their Books, they will not receive any cash payment or be able to participate in future revenue from Google's use of their Books. By staying in the Amended Settlement, they will, however, release all copyright infringement claims they might have against Google for digitizing their Books without permission.

Whether a Book is "in-print" or "out-of-print" can affect what rights Google would have under the Amended Settlement to use the Book and whether (and which) Rightsholders would receive revenues from uses of the Book.

The Amended Settlement Agreement uses the term "Commercially Available", which generally means that a Book is in-print. If a Book is not Commercially Available, that means, in general, that it is out-of-print. Google would be authorised under the Amended Settlement to make Display Uses and Non-Display Uses of each Book that is not Commercially Available for the term of the US copyright for that Book, unless the Rightsholder directs Google not to do so or directs Google to remove the Book.

Google may not make any Display Uses of any Commercially Available Book unless the Rightsholder of the Book authorises Google to include the Book in such uses. If a Rightsholder authorises Display Uses, he or she will be entitled to the settlement benefits for that Book. However, a Rightsholder may be able to negotiate different terms with Google separately from this settlement. Google may make Non-Display Uses of an in-print Book for the term of the US Copyright for that Book unless the Rightsholder timely removes the Book.

For the purposes of the Amended Settlement Agreement, "Display Uses" include the following:

Access Uses: this includes viewing and annotating the entire Book, and printing and copying and pasting portions of the Book, subject to page number limitations. The uses include institutional subscriptions, consumer purchase of online access and public access at libraries and elsewhere.

Preview Uses: this allows a searcher to view up to 20 per cent of a book before making a purchase decision, but will not allow a searcher to copy and paste, annotate or print any pages from the Book. Preview uses are designed to serve as a marketing tool to sell the Book.

Snippet Displays: this allows a searcher to view three or four lines of text from a Book, with up to three snippet uses per user for the Book.

Display of Bibliographic Pages: this means that users can see the Book's title page, copyright page, table of contents and index.

"Non-Display Uses" are uses that do not involve displaying any content from a Book to the public. Examples include display of bibliographic information (but not displaying Book pages themselves), full-text indexing without displaying the text; geographic indexing of Books; algorithmic listings of key terms for chapters of Books; and internal research and development at Google.

Rightsholders will have the ability to direct Google not to make various Display Uses of their Books and Inserts. Rightsholders of in-print Books will have to notify the Registry if they want Google to make their Books available for any or all of the Display Uses. Out-of-print Books will automatically be included in all Display Uses unless the rightsholder(s) of the Book directs Google not to do so.

Documents filed with the court in the *Author's Guild et al v Google Inc.* case, including the hundreds of objections from the various interested parties, can be viewed on the Justia.com website.[109]

Concern has been expressed that if the Settlement goes ahead, then Google will have obtained through settlement of litigation what should really only, if at all, have been the result of carefully considered legislation. The US Department of Justice also said that the agreement was "an attempt to use the class-action mechanism to implement forward-looking business arrangements that go far beyond the dispute before the court" and "one of the most far-reaching class-action settlements of which the United States is aware".

The Settlement is important for UK publishers, authors, agents and others in the UK publishing industry, as it will potentially provide sources of revenue for them and they need to ensure that their own interests and/or the interests of those whom they represent are registered in accordance with the procedures on the Google settlement administration website. Currently, there is a deadline of March 31, 2011 for Rightsholders to claim Books and Inserts for cash payments, and there is a deadline of March 9, 2012 for removal of Books.

26–87   **Amazon.** Amazon operates its Search Inside program in a way similar to the Google Partner Program. Publishers are asked to allow Amazon to reproduce all of the authorised books in digital form so that they will be searchable by visitors to the various Amazon websites, enabling visitors to display portions of each such book on the Amazon websites.

In the United Kingdom, Penguin Books have joined the Search Inside program, after Penguin in the United States had deemed it a success. Apparently, in the United States Penguin found that sales of books included in the Search Inside program were between 7 and 10 per cent up. Oxford University Press have joined the program, as have Faber and Faber, Canongate and others.

26–88   **Yahoo!**, in conjunction with Adobe Systems, HP Labs, MSN, O'Reilly Media, Xerox Corporation and the libraries of the University of California and the University of Toronto, are involved in a project, known as the Open Content Alliance (*http://www.opencontentalliance.org* [Accessed October 29, 2010]), to make digitised texts available through the Yahoo! search engine and through

---

[109] *http://dockets.justia.com/docket/new-york/nysdce/1:2005cv08136/273913/* [Accessed October 18, 2010].

other search engines and websites, including the Internet Archive website—
http://www.archive.org [Accessed October 29, 2010]. The works to be included
in the project would only be those for which rights holders' permission has been
obtained or works that are in the public domain. A large number of other libraries
and organisations have now been brought on board in this project.

Microsoft also launched a similar project, limited to out-of-copyright works or,   **26–89**
in the case of books that are in copyright, only by agreement with rights-holders.
The Windows Live Books Publisher Program was launched in May 2006, but
was terminated by Microsoft in May 2008. Up until the end of the project, Microsoft had indexed the contents of 750,000 books and 80 million scholarly
journal articles. Microsoft said that it will provide publishers with digital copies
of books that were already scanned.

Project Gutenberg. Project Gutenberg (*http://www.gutenberg.org* [Accessed   **26–90**
October 29, 2010]) was the first and is the largest single collection of free
electronic books. All of the e-books available there are out of copyright. There
are over 25,000 free e-books available on the Project Gutenberg website and
many more available through associated websites.

"Orphan works". Orphan works are generally considered to be those works for   **26–91**
which no rightsholders can be traced. There are some estimates that up to 40 per
cent of the printed works held in libraries are orphan works, and given the various projects underway to digitise and make available the works held in libraries
(e.g. the Google Library Project and the EU Digital Libraries Initiative[110]), the issue of orphan works is of considerable importance. The ARROW project, funded
under the European Commission's eContentplus programme, aims to enable a
process of "diligent search" that will result in many orphan works being traced to
their rightsholders. The idea is to bring together data from multiple sources—
national libraries, books-in-print publishers, and reproduction rights organisations (RROs)—to provide the necessary "rights information infrastructure" to enable diligent searches to be carried out with a view to obtaining legal permission
to use a work. ARROW (which stands for "Accessible Registries of Rights Information and Orphan Works") is being delivered by an alliance of national libraries, authors' organisations, publishers' organisations, and collective management
organisations around Europe and in the United Kingdom. It will work by joining
together existing databases of rights information, currently held by a dispersed
range of sources, but not creating one gigantic database—that would be
completely impracticable. ARROW is, in effect, Europe's answer to the Book
Rights Registry, to be created in the United States under the Google Books
Settlement. The United Kingdom Publishers Association urges publishers and
others engage with the ARROW project, since if the project does not succeed,
one possible consequence could be that a new exception to copyright for orphan
works might be introduced.

(v) Access to scientific publications

Background. Technology has made possible a fundamental change to the way   **26–92**
scientific articles are published. By removing some of the non-editorial overheads associated with print publications, digitisation makes it relatively cheap to
set up and run new journals. The internet makes it feasible, in theory, for readers
to access the articles they need online, without charge. Several publishing models

---

[110] See para.26–105, below.

based around the central concept of free online access have emerged: collectively their proponents form the "Open Access" movement.

Traditionally, STM publishing works on the "subscriber-pays" publishing model. Authors submit articles to journals, usually free of charge. The publishers send the articles out for peer review. Those articles that are deemed to be of a sufficiently high standard are edited and published. The journal is then sold to readers, usually by means of a subscription. Commercial, learned and professional society and academic publishers all currently use this model, although some of them are also experimenting with the "author-pays" model. Under this model, authors, or more usually their research funders, pay to publish their article in a journal. The publishers send the articles out for peer review. Those articles that are deemed to be of a sufficiently high standard are edited and published. The journal is disseminated free of charge, primarily via the internet, although sometimes in paper form too. In some cases the author, or funder, pays a submission fee in advance of the publication fee in order to cover the administrative costs of processing their article, whether or not it is accepted for publication.

26–93   **Open Access.** The debate about Open Access (the provision of free online access for all to scholarly research articles) continues. There are primarily two ways of achieving the objective of Open Access: the first is Open Access publishing itself; and the second is self-archiving.

Open Access publishing requires that the funding comes otherwise than from the subscribers to the journal. Usually, there will be a subsidy (for example, from the publication's parent organisation or from a third-party grant) or from the author or his or her research funder. In a recent survey, the Association of Learned and Professional Society Publishers ("ALPSP") found that over 20 per cent of publishers were experimenting with Open Access journals. One variation on Open Access publishing is "Delayed Open Access", whereby the content of a journal is made freely available to all after a certain period—sometimes as short as six months. The idea of the delay is to protect subscription income. However, this might work for some journals but not for others. If material were made Open Access after, say, only six months, the publisher might be giving away a very significant part of the value of the material. For example, if librarians know that the articles in the journal would be free in six months' time, they might decide not to subscribe to the journal, and just wait for the material to be available free of charge. That could damage the publisher's financial viability and could also be damaging to the research process, since researchers would not have access to the most up-to-date material until it became Open Access.

The Open Access Scholarly Publishers Association ("OASPA") has recently been established, with a mission to "represent the interests of Open Access (OA) journal publishers globally in all scientific, technical and scholarly disciplines". OASPA says that its mission will be carried out in the following ways:

- Exchange Information—provide a forum for the exchange of information and experiences related to OA delivery of scientific content.
- Set Standards—promote a uniform definition of OA publishing, best practices for maintaining and disseminating OA scholarly communications, and ethical standards.
- Advance Models—support the development of business and publishing models that support OA journal publishing.
- Advocate for Gold OA[111]—promote Gold OA journals, and policies that support their viability.

---

[111] "Gold OA" refers to implementing the free and open dissemination of original scholarship by publishers, as opposed to Green OA, in which free and open dissemination is achieved by archiv-

- Educate—educate the research community and public on benefits of OA journals, on the value publishers bring to the publication process and on various policies that enhance and support the delivery of OA publications.
- Promote Innovation—contribute to the development and dissemination of innovative approaches to scientific communications pertaining to OA and of related activities that leverage the opportunities afforded by OA to scholarly content.

The Directory of Open Access Journals can be accessed at *http://www.doaj.org* [Accessed November 1, 2010].

Another variation on Open Access publishing is hybrid journals, where some of the content is Open Access and the rest is not. Among publishers to offer this option are Blackwell, Cambridge University Press, Oxford University Press, Springer and Wiley.

Self-archiving. Self-archiving involves authors being allowed to self-archive pre-publication versions of their own work or sometimes a PDF version of the published article. However, this can give rise to a number of problems. Some publishers have found that where all or most of a journal's content can be found in an archive, users appear to use that version rather than the one on the publisher's website, even though only the version on the publisher's website has undergone peer review and editing, and despite the fact that the version on the publisher's website also has additional functionality, such as reference linking. The other serious problem is that self-archiving will result in different versions of the material appearing in different places, and researchers may not know whether any particular version is or is not the official version or even whether it has actually been peer reviewed and published. This problem never arose with printed paper journals, since publication in the printed journal necessarily constituted the definitive version of the work. ALPSP wants publishers to retain the ability to control the manner and timing of self-archiving, in order to preserve the journals and the valuable functions they perform for the scientific community.

26–94

Scientific Publications: free for all? In July 2004 the House of Commons Select Committee on Science and Technology published its report "Scientific Publications: free for all?". The Committee's aim was to: examine the provision of scientific journals to the academic community and wider public; to establish whether the market for scientific publications was working well; how trends in journal pricing affected libraries and other users; the impact that new publishing trends would have on the scientific process; and what provisions were in place to support a secure national archive. This investigation took place in the context of intense scrutiny of the scientific, technical and medical ("STM") publishing industry. Whilst the volume of research output and the price of scientific journals has been steadily increasing, library budgets have seen funding decreases. As a consequence, the ability of libraries to purchase journals has come under severe pressure.

26–95

The Select Committee Report recommended:

(a) All UK higher education institutions establish institutional repositories on which their published output can be stored and from which it can be read, free of charge, online.

(b) Research Councils and other Government funders mandate their funded researchers to deposit a copy of all of their articles in this way.

(c) The Government to appoint a central body to oversee the implementation

ing and making freely available copies of scholarly publications that may or may not have been previously published.

of the repositories; to help with networking; and to ensure compliance with the technical standards needed to provide maximum functionality.

(d) Whilst institutional repositories will help to improve access to journals, a more radical solution may be required in the long term, and early indications suggest that the author-pays publishing model could be viable—but further experimentation is necessary.

(e) In order to encourage such experimentation, Research Councils each to establish a fund to which their funded researchers can apply should they wish to pay to publish.

(f) The British Library to receive sufficient funding to enable it to carry out the preservation of digital material.

(g) Work on new regulations for the legal deposit of non-print publications to begin immediately.

The government response was a distillation of responses from all the government departments and other government organisations that have an interest in the Report. Whilst the government said that it endorses much of the Report "in principle", in practice it undertook to implement none of the main recommendations. The Select Committee declared itself disappointed with the "unsatisfactory" government response. The Committee said that the government argued against the wholesale adoption of the "author-pays" publishing model as if that is what the Committee had recommended, whereas the Committee points out that it had not in fact made such a recommendation. The Committee instead recommended further investigation and has asked the government to reconsider its position.[112] A similar debate is taking place within the American STM publishing industry.

K. Deposit of Printed and Non-Printed Publications

(i) Deposit of books

26–96 **History of the privilege.** The 1911 Act, in obedience to art.4 of the Revised Convention of Berne, which provided that the enjoyment and exercise of the rights conferred by the Convention should not be subject to the performance of any formality, abolished all necessity for registration of copyright, but substantially re-enacted ss.6 to 9 of the Copyright Act 1842[113] relating to the deposit of published books at the British Museum and other libraries.[114] The old law was slightly extended by the 1911 Act in as much as the National Library of Wales was added to the list of libraries which can, under certain circumstances, demand delivery of a copy of a published book.

Representations were made to the 1952 Copyright Committee that the delivery of copies of books to the libraries free of charge was unfair to publishers, but the Committee recommended that the privilege of the libraries of deposit to receive copies of published works should be continued.[115] The 1956 Act in fact left unrepealed s.15 of the 1911 Act under which this privilege was conferred.[116]

Although the 1977 Copyright Committee received evidence on a number of topics relating to libraries of deposit, it considered that, since the link between

---

[112] The Select Committee Report and the government response can be accessed on the UK Parliament website at: *http://www.publications.parliament.uk/pa/cm/cmsctech.htm.*

[113] 5 & 6 Vict. c. 45.

[114] Copyright Act 1911 s.15.

[115] Cmnd.8662. para.58.

[116] Copyright Act 1956 s.50(2) and Sch.9, both repealed by the Statute Law (Repeals) Act 1974 (c. 22).

the legal recognition of property rights in published literary matter and its deposit in one or more designated libraries ceased to exist at a date now remote, there was no reason why the law of copyright should any longer concern itself with the subject of legal deposit. The Committee therefore made no formal recommendations on the subject although the Report set out the Committee's views on certain matters,[117] for instance that all deposit libraries should be on the same footing. The 1988 Act also left unrepealed s.15 of the 1911 Act.[118]

Background to the Legal Deposit Libraries Act 2003: the future of Legal   **26–97**
Deposit. Advances in publication technology and the rising popularity of non-print media prompted the Government to review the then current legal deposit requirements. A consultation paper was published in February 1997, inviting comments on whether legislation should be extended to cover electronic publications, sound recordings, film and video recordings, and microfilm. Following the extensive responses to the paper, a working party was set up in December 1997 which reported in July 1998 to the Secretary of State for Culture, Media and Sport. It concluded that in the longer term only statutory deposit could secure a comprehensive national published archive. It recommended that the archive should be a distributed one, including (but not necessarily restricted to) the six current legal deposit libraries. The Secretary of State, in a parliamentary answer in December 1998, accepted that the report "makes a convincing case for moving towards legislation for the legal deposit of non-print publications on the basis of minimum burden on publishers and minimum loss of sales". He asked the chairman of the Working Party to do further work on definitions and the impact on business through the medium of the technical group of library and publishing experts, with a view to then moving towards legislation. He asked that in the meantime a code of practice for the voluntary deposit of non-print publications should be drawn up and agreed between publishers and the deposit libraries and that a Regulatory Impact Assessment of the costs and benefits of the statutory deposit of non-print publications should be prepared before the proposed legislation was drafted. Following the Secretary of State's request, a code of practice was drawn up and agreed by representatives of the legal deposit libraries and publishing trade bodies.[119]

The code of practice applies to new publications published after January 4, 2000, but publishers are also encouraged to deposit publications which were published before this date. The scheme is voluntary and publishers are under no legal obligation to comply with it, but publishers are requested to do so in order to help plug the gap in the national published archive before new legislation eventually comes into force. In addition, the scheme operates as a pilot phase during which various issues can be agreed and monitored, so that when the new legislation is brought into force, it should be workable and effective.

The code of practice applies to UK non-print publications in microform and offline electronic media, which are primarily text-based or which are intended as information rather than entertainment products. Publications originally published abroad, but distributed in the United Kingdom, are liable for deposit as well as those first published in the United Kingdom. Online publications do not formally come within the code of practice, but it does contain recommendations for arrangements relating to online publications which are substantially fixed at the time of first publication, and the online elements of hybrid offline/online

---

[117] Cmnd.6732, paras 833 and 834.
[118] CDPA 1988 s.303 and Sch.8.
[119] A copy of the code of practice, and other resources relating to legal and voluntary deposit of works, can be found on the web site of the Association of Learned and Professional Society Publishers at *http://www.alpsp.org* [Accessed November 1, 2010].

publications. Continuously updated publications, such as "dynamic" databases, are not addressed in the code of practice.

26–98   The code of practice does not cover film, sound or Ordnance Survey digital mapping products, which are subject to separate voluntary schemes. Publishers are not requested to deposit any publication which substantially duplicates the content of a print publication from the same publisher which has already been deposited, nor a publication published only for private internal use within an organisation, nor certain categories of publications specified by the legal deposit libraries as not being required for deposit, such as computer software and computer games. Publishers are asked to deposit a minimum of one copy of all new microform or offline electronic publications, normally to the British Library, who will in turn issue a list of items received to the other deposit libraries. These other deposit libraries may then each request the deposit to them of an additional copy, and publishers are asked, at their discretion, to deposit such copies if so requested.

The code of practice makes proposals for access arrangements for the deposited publications and for printing out up to the limits for photocopying from printed publications. However, the code of practice does not allow for electronic downloading and saving from deposited publications by users. The code of practice assumes, in the absence of an express prohibition by the publisher, that the holding deposit libraries may copy a publication onto other media for preservation purposes only, subject to the preservation of the individual publication's identity and integrity, and so that the copied version may not be used to provide user access. This is to help ensure the long-term accessibility and usability of offline media, such as CD-ROMs, which cannot otherwise at present be assured because of the frequent advances in technology, which render older technologies obsolete and leads to the hardware necessary to access the software becoming unavailable.

26–99   **The Legal Deposit Libraries Act 2003.** The Legal Deposit Libraries Act 2003 ("the 2003 Act") repeals s.15 of the 1911 Act but effectively re-enacts it so far as printed publications are concerned and extends it to cover works published in non-print form. The 2003 Act has necessitated amendments to the 1988 Act to ensure that the various acts required or enabled by the 2003 Act do not infringe copyright. These are dealt with elsewhere.[120]

26–100   **The libraries entitled to the privilege.** Section 1(1) of the 2003 Act requires a person who publishes in the United Kingdom a work to which the 2003 Act applies to deliver, at his own expense, a copy of the work to an address (being an address in the United Kingdom or an electronic address) specified (generally or in a particular case) by any deposit library entitled to delivery under the section. If a deposit library has not specified an address, the copy is to be delivered to the library.[121] Generally the copy to be delivered should be in the same medium as that in which the work was published.[122] The deposit libraries are the British Library Board, the National Library of Scotland, the National Library of Wales, the Bodleian Library, Oxford, the University Library, Cambridge and the Library of Trinity College, Dublin.[123] In the case of works published in print, the 2003 Act applies (subject to any prescribed exception) to—

(a) a book (including a pamphlet, magazine or newspaper);

---

[120] See Ch.9, above.
[121] Legal Deposit Libraries Act 2003 s.1(2).
[122] Legal Deposit Libraries Act 2003 s.1 (6), the exception being works published online, where Regulations under s.6(h) may specify the medium in which the copy is to be delivered.
[123] Legal Deposit Libraries Act 2003 s.14.

(b) a sheet of letterpress or music;

(c) a map, plan, chart or table; and

(d) a part of any such work.[124]

In relation to a work published otherwise than in printed form, the 2003 Act applies to a work of a prescribed description,[125] but that must not include works that consist only of a sound recording or film or such material and other material which is merely incidental to it.[126]

The 2003 Act does not apply to a work which is substantially the same as one already published in the same medium in the United Kingdom.[127] Where substantially the same work is published in the United Kingdom in more than one medium, the obligation to deliver a copy to the deposit libraries applies only to publication in one of those media, and the question of which medium is to be determined in accordance with regulations to be made by the Secretary of State, and the regulations may also provide for how to determine whether or not particular works are or are not to be regarded as substantially the same.[128]

The British Library Board is entitled to delivery of a copy of every work published in print[129] and the copy must be delivered within one month of the date of publication.[130] The Board must give a written receipt (which may be sent by electronic or other means). The Bodleian Library, Oxford, the University Library, Cambridge, the National Library of Scotland, the Library of Trinity College, Dublin and the National Library of Wales, are entitled to delivery of a copy of any work published in print which it requests (by electronic or other means) in writing.[131] Such copy is to be delivered at any time within a month after such request, which must be made within 12 months after publication or within one month after publication if the request is made before publication.[132] In the case of an encyclopaedia, newspaper, magazine or other work, the written request may include all numbers or parts of the work which may be subsequently published.[133]   **26–101**

What copies are to be delivered. The copy to be delivered to the British Library Board must be one of the best copies produced for publication in the United Kingdom,[134] but the copy for each of the other libraries is to be one of the copies of which the largest number have been produced for publication in the United Kingdom.[135]   **26–102**

Effect of failure to deliver copies. The 2003 Act does not make delivery of the copies a condition of copyright. If the publisher, upon whom the duty is imposed of delivering the requisite copies of the work, fails to deliver a copy to a particu-   **26–103**

---

124 Legal Deposit Libraries Act 2003 s.1(3).

125 Legal Deposit Libraries Act 2003 s.1(4).

126 Legal Deposit Libraries Act 2003 s.1(5).

127 Legal Deposit Libraries Act 2003 s.2(1).

128 Legal Deposit Libraries Act 2003 s.2(2) and (3).

129 Legal Deposit Libraries Act 2003 s.(1).

130 Legal Deposit Libraries Act 2003 s.4(2).

131 The Agency for the Legal Deposit Libraries ("ALDL") requests and receives copies of publications for distribution to these five legal deposit libraries. It is maintained by these libraries and ensures that they receive legal deposit copies of British and Irish publications. The previous ALDL operation was supported by Cambridge University and operated from leased premises in central London. The agency outgrew this accommodation, and there was no room for flexibility or capacity for expansion. The National Library of Scotland ("NLS") has now taken over ownership and management of the agency on behalf of the five legal deposit libraries. Since March 2, 2009, the agency has been operating within the NLS Causewayside Building in Edinburgh.

132 Legal Deposit Libraries Act 2003 s.5(5).

133 Legal Deposit Libraries Act 2003 s.5(3)(b).

134 Legal Deposit Libraries Act 2003 s.4(3).

135 Legal Deposit Libraries Act 2003 s.5(6).

lar library, that library may apply to the county court (or to the sheriff in Scotland) for an order requiring the publisher to comply.[136] If on an application to the court (or sheriff) it appears that the publisher is unable to comply or for any other reason it is not appropriate to make an order requiring the publisher to comply, then the court or the sheriff can order the publisher instead to pay to the library an amount up to the cost of making good the failure to comply.[137] There is no criminal penalty, unlike under the previous legislation.

26–104   **Foreign works published in England.** The 2003 Act applies to works published in the United Kingdom, making no requirement that they must be entitled to copyright protection in the United Kingdom, nor that they be "first published" in the United Kingdom. It is understood that in the past, while the libraries of deposit did not claim that every book, copies of which are issued to the public in the United Kingdom, falls within the obligation to deliver copies, they have made this claim where the imprint of a London publisher appears on the work, whether alone or jointly with a foreign publisher, and whether or not the work has been first published in another country.[138]

In the wake of the enactment of the 2003 Act, the Joint Committee on Legal Deposit ("JCLD") has been established to (amongst other things)—

(a) further the mutual understanding between publishers and the legal deposit libraries of their respective positions and interests regarding the legal and voluntary deposit of printed, offline and online material, and to promote collaboration in the implementation of the 2003 Act;

(b) resolve issues that might arise between publishers and the libraries;

(c) maintain and monitor the voluntary code of practice[139];

(d) develop and administer pilot schemes for online material considered to be a priority for libraries; and

(e) advise government on the way forward regarding the establishment of a Legal Deposit Advisory Panel and to inform the Panel and government of the interests and requirements of publishers and libraries with respect to legal deposit.

The JCLD is made up of interested parties, including representatives from the British Library and the other deposit libraries, the Publishers Association, the ALPSP and the Digital Content Forum. One of the JCLD's priorities will be to provide input on proposed regulations under the 2003 Act.

26–105   **Further developments in preserving electronic works.** In September 1999 Book Industry Communication ("BIC") published a study entitled "Digital Preservation: an introduction to the standards issues surrounding the deposit of non-print publications". It is available on the BIC website,[140] which contains information about technical standards in relation to the publishing industry and also useful links. It is also available on the website of The Association of Learned and Professional Society Publishers.[141]

There are many digital initiatives currently in progress grappling with the complex issues involved in promoting the wide dissemination of works in digital formats and the preservation of electronically published works. One project is the

---

[136] Legal Deposit Libraries Act 2003 s.3(2).
[137] Legal Deposit Libraries Act 2003 s.3(3).
[138] See discussion in the Report of 1952 Copyright Committee, Cmnd. 8662, paras 60–65.
[139] See paras 26–97 et seq., above.
[140] *http://www.bic.org.uk* [Accessed November 1, 2010].
[141] *http://www.alpsp.org* [Accessed November 1, 2010].

UK Web Archive.[142] The UK Web Archive is provided by the British Library in partnership with the National Library of Wales, JISC and the Wellcome Library. In the past, the National Archives and the National Library of Scotland have also been involved. The British Library also works with the Live Art Development Agency, the Society of Friends Library, the Women's Library at London Metropolitan University and other key institutions to build Special Collections within the UK Web Archive. Websites are gathered for the UK Web Archive with the Web Curator Tool (WCT) which was developed collaboratively by the National Library of New Zealand and the British Library, under the auspices of the International Internet Preservation Consortium. WCT is an open source software, freely available under the terms of the Apache Public Licence. WCT manages the selective web harvesting process. Contributors to the UK Web Archive seek permission from the website owner for every website it archives. This is costly and difficult (many owners simply don't respond to the request) so the UK Web Archive have been advising the Government on the necessary regulations required to gather all in-scope UK websites automatically. The British Library and other "legal deposit libraries" have this right in principle under the Legal Deposit Libraries Act 2003 s.8, which amended the Copyright, Designs and Patents Act 1988 for this purpose,[143] but regulations are required in order to go ahead.

Because websites are revisited and snapshots (or "instances") are taken at regular intervals, users of the archive can see how a website evolves over time. The archive is free to view, is accessed directly from the Web itself and, since archiving began in 2004, has collected thousands of websites.

Another initiative is the Digital Preservation Coalition.[144] It was established in 2001 "to foster joint action to address the urgent challenges of securing the preservation of digital resources in the United Kingdom and to work with others internationally to secure our global digital memory and knowledge base" and members include the British Library, the National Archives, the National Archives of Scotland, National Library of Scotland, Publishers Licensing Society, Research Libraries UK, JISC and the Council for Museums, Archives and Libraries.

Information about and links to these and other initiatives are available from various industry websites, including those listed in this section. As part of the European Commission's digital libraries initiative, the High Level Expert Group (HLEG) on European Digital Libraries published in April 2007 a report on digital preservation, orphan works and out-of-print works,[145] together with a model licence agreement on digitisation of out-of-print works.[146] The report contains a number of practical recommendations for rights-holders and libraries to consider, and follows on from an Interim Report presented by the Copyright Subgroup of the HLEG in October 2006.

Another development is the EU Digital Libraries Initiative.[147] It was launched in 2005 as part of the Commission's i2010 strategy to boost the digital economy, building on work already done by the Commission over a number of years. This initiative sets out to make all Europe's cultural resources and scientific records—books, journals, films, maps, photographs, music, etc.—accessible to all, and

---

[142] *http://www.webarchive.org.uk* [Accessed November 1, 2010].

[143] See Copyright, Designs and Patents Act 1988 s.44A.

[144] *http://www.dpconline.org* [Accessed November 1, 2010].

[145] *http://ec.europa.eu/information_society/newsroom/cf/ document.cfm?action=display&doc_id=295* [Accessed October 18, 2010].

[146] *http://ec.europa.eu/information_society/newsroom/cf/ document.cfm?action=display&doc_id=296* [Not freely accessible online].

[147] *http://ec.europa.eu/information_society/activities/digital_libraries/index_en.htm* [Accessed October 18, 2010].

preserve it for future generations—a very ambitious plan, made all the more complicated by copyright implications. A number of copyright issues need to be resolved before material can be put online, e.g. how to deal with out-of-print works and what to do when the copyright holder cannot be found ("orphan works"). One solution would be to include only material already in the public domain—but that would rule out most of the twentieth century's output. This Initiative stresses accessibility of material and also preservation and storage, without which accessibility would become impossible to achieve. The Initiative points out that:

"Like books and paintings, digital materials have to be managed and maintained, otherwise:

- Files may be unreadable when the hardware and software used to store them becomes obsolete;
- Material will be lost when storage devices deteriorate over time (some CD-ROMs have a lifetime of just 10 years); and
- Storage systems could be overwhelmed by the sheer volume of new and changing content."

Most EU countries have no clear policy on digital preservation, though the issue is now being given more attention. National authorities agreed to step up their efforts following the Commission's 2006 recommendation on digitisation and digital preservation.[148]

(ii) Deposit of scripts

26–106   **Deposit of scripts of new plays.** Quite apart from the above provisions relating to deposit, the Theatres Act 1968[149] requires delivery of copies of scripts of plays to the Trustees of the British Museum. In practice, delivery was made to the British Museum's Department of Manuscripts. Since the British Library Act 1972[150] makes no reference to the 1968 Act, strictly speaking, delivery should still be made to the Trustees and not to the Board. Thus, the 1968 Act provides that,[151] with certain limited exceptions,[152] where there is given in Great Britain a public performance of a new play, being a performance based on a script, a copy of the actual script on which that performance was based must be delivered to the Trustees of the British Museum free of charge within the period of one month beginning with the date of the performance; the Trustees are required to give a written receipt for every script so delivered. However, delivery continues to be made to the Department of Manuscripts (the collections of which were transferred under the 1972 Act from the Trustees to the Board).

26–107   **Definitions.** The 1968 Act contains definitions of "script", "play", "public performance" and "public performance of a new play". Thus, "script" is defined as the text of the play (whether expressed in words or in musical or other notation) together with any stage or other directions for its performance, whether contained in a single document or not.[153] "Play" is defined as (a) any dramatic piece, whether involving improvisation or not, which is given wholly or in part by one or more persons actually present and performing and in which the whole or a major

---

[148] Commission Recommendation of August 24, 2006 on the digitisation and online accessibility of cultural material and digital preservation— *http://eur-lex.europa.eu/LexUriServ/ LexUriServ.do?uri=CELEX:32006H0585:EN:NOT* [Accessed October 18, 2010].
[149] c.54.
[150] c.54.
[151] Theatres Act 1968 s.11(1).
[152] Theatres Act 1968 s.11(4).
[153] Theatres Act 1968 s.9(2).

proportion of what is done by the person or persons performing, whether by way of speech, singing or action, involves the playing of a role, and (b) any ballet given wholly or in part by one or more persons actually present and performing, whether or not it falls within paragraph (a) of this definition.[154] "Public performance" is defined as including any performance in a public place within the meaning of the Public Order Act 1936,[155] and any performance which the public or any section thereof are permitted to attend, whether on payment or otherwise.[156] Section 18 of the London Local Authorities Act 1990[157] extends the definition of "public performance" in the 1968 Act. The extended definition is confined to performances in London boroughs and takes effect in a particular borough on a date appointed by resolution of the relevant borough council.[158] In a borough where the extension is in force, the expression "public performance" includes "any performance which is not open to the public but which is promoted for private gain".[159] The phrase "promoted for private gain" is defined in a new s.18A of the 1968 Act which is inserted by s.18(3) of the 1990 Act. Finally, "public performance of a new play" is defined as a public performance of a play of which no previous public performance has ever been given in Great Britain, but does not include a public performance of a play which either is based on a script substantially the same as that on which a previous public performance of a play given there was based, or is based substantially on a text of the play which has been published in the United Kingdom.[160]

Effect of failure to deliver copies. If the above-mentioned requirements as to delivery are not complied with, then any person who presented the relevant performance is liable, on summary conviction, to a fine not exceeding level 1 on the standard scale.[161] However, it is provided that a person is not to be treated as presenting a performance of a play by reason only of his taking part therein as a performer.[162] **26–108**

2. THE NEWSPAPER INDUSTRY

A. GENERAL NATURE OF THE INDUSTRY

The United Kingdom continues to have a lively and diverse printed press industry, incorporating not only a range of national broadsheets and tabloids, but also some 1,200 regional and local newspapers. However, the industry is currently facing profound changes which are re-shaping it fundamentally. The past three decades may already have witnessed enormous changes (the advent of free newspapers; consolidation of ownership; structural changes in employment patterns; shifts in trade union power). All these changes have, however, been completely overshadowed in recent years by the impact of the internet and related new technologies, and especially the rise of search. **26–109**

Impact of the internet. Search engines have developed from browser applica- **26–110**

[154] Theatres Act 1968 s.18(1).
[155] 1 Edw. 8 and 1 Geo. 6, s.9; see now Criminal Justice Act 1972 (c.71) s.33 and Roads (Scotland) Act 1984 (c.54) Sch.9.
[156] Theatres Act 1968 s.18(1).
[157] c.13.
[158] London Local Authorities Act 1990 ss.3 and 18(1).
[159] London Local Authorities Act 1990 s.18(2).
[160] Theatres Act 1968 s.11(3).
[161] Theatres Act 1968 s.11(2); as amended by Criminal Justice Act 1982 (c.48) ss.37 and 38. In relation to offences committed on or after October 1, 1992 the figure for level 1 on the standard scale is £200: see Criminal Justice Act 1991 (c.53) ss.17(1) and 101(1) and Sch.12 para.6.
[162] Theatres Act 1968 s.18(2).

tions designed simply to locate material on the internet, to extraordinarily power-ful systems capable of selecting, ranking and organising content to meet the searcher's needs. Few, if any, newspaper publishers believe that they can dispense with an online presence. However, the future of the printed product,[163] and the very role of a newspaper publisher in terms of editing, compiling and distributing content, has been called into question by search engines' ability to serve content direct to users, often by-passing the publisher's home page. Further, the internet in effect creates a single channel in which newspaper publishers compete with broadcasters for online consumers of news content.

These changes are associated not only with new methods of creating, consum-ing and distributing content, including social networking, and the rapid spread of new mobile platforms, but have also prompted a vigorous debate both within and outside the industry about its future. Declining print circulation and increased competition for advertising revenue have created unprecedented pressures in the industry, and are forcing publishers to experiment with different business models to support continued investment in content creation, and indeed ensure survival. Various solutions have been adopted, ranging from the erection of so-called "pay walls" (allowing online access to content only in return for payment),[164] to the abandonment of a cover price for printed copies.[165] At the time of writing, it remains unclear whether any of these models will emerge triumphant, or whether the industry will be able to continue offering diametrically opposed visions of how to survive in the electronic world.[166] Whatever the outcome, the newspaper industry is rapidly evolving into one where print is simply one among a wide range of options for delivering news content.

26–111   **National and regional press sectors.** The growing impact of the internet has coincided with a shrinkage in the overall UK newspaper market. This was estimated to be worth just under £7 billion in 2009,[167] but that reflected a decline since 2004 of almost 22 per cent.[168] While over half of newspaper revenue used to come from advertising, the exact proportion is significantly affected by the strength of advertising demand. The share of advertising going to print newspa-pers has been declining for the last decade, reflecting a migration of classified advertising to other media (specialised print classifieds or online sites), declining circulations, an increasing diversification of news outlets and the rise of the internet.

The national sector comprises 11 daily newspapers and nine Sunday newspapers. Total (average) daily circulation is 10,287,339 copies for daily newspapers and 10,423,311 for Sunday newspapers.[169] However all national newspapers are now seeing year-on-year declines in print circulation.[170] Reader-ship (as opposed to circulation) is relatively low compared to other OECD

---

[163] In a BBC Radio 4 debate held on May 18, 2010, Alan Rusbridger, Editor of *The Guardian* and John Witherow, Editor of *The Sunday Times* agreed that their currently installed presses would be their last.

[164] For example, the decision by *The Times* and *The Sunday Times* to start charging for online content from June 2010.

[165] For example the decision to drop a cover price for the print editions of the *London Evening Stan-dard* from October 12, 2009.

[166] A recent in-depth treatment of the global newspaper publishing market is the OECD report *The Evolution of News and the Internet*: DSTI/ICCP/IE(2009)14/FINAL (June 11, 2010).

[167] In 2008 the national press generated 58.6% of total revenue; the regional press generated 41.4%.

[168] Source: OECD (*The Evolution of News and the Internet*: DSTI/ICCP/IE(2009)14/FINAL June 11, 2010).

[169] Audit Bureau of Circulation January–June 2010.

[170] As reported in the *Press Gazette* on August 13, 2010, referring to the latest ABC figures.

countries.[171] The local and regional press sector comprises approximately 1,200 titles in the United Kingdom, generating £3 billion in turnover.[172] Of this, close to £2.3 billion is advertising revenue.[173] Each week, 28.5 million regional paid-for newspapers are sold and 33.3 million free newspapers are delivered. Just over 80 per cent of the population read a regional or local newspaper, compared with just over 61 per cent who read a national newspaper.[174] The regional press has not been immune to the declines affecting the market as a whole.

However, while print circulation is falling, the number of unique visitors to newspaper websites has grown very strongly in recent years. Online UK newspapers draw substantial domestic audiences, and many attract even larger international audiences.[175] It remains to be seen what impact charging for online content will have on this online audience growth.

General regulatory regime. There is no single definition of a newspaper, statutory or otherwise. Rather, newspapers are defined differently for different purposes, including libel,[176] for tax purposes,[177] for media ownership,[178] and other purposes.[179] Nor is there a specific regulatory regime governing the industry in the form of licensing or other permissions to publish a newspaper. In contrast with the broadcasting industries that are subject to a statutory licensing regime,[180] the newspaper sector regards its freedom from government control licensing systems as an essential historical prerequisite to maintain the tradition of a free press.[181] General legal and commercial constraints exist in the context of choosing a title (trade-mark law, passing-off law), acquiring a newspaper company or group of companies,[182] distribution networks (such as competition law considerations in respect of acceptance or refusal to supply particular outlets) and the need to ensure an imprint appears on the first or last page of each newspaper edition.[183] There is a requirement that any person who prints "any paper for hire, reward, gain or profit" preserves at least one copy for a period of six months and marks on it in "fair and legible" letters the name and address of the person who employed him to print it.[184] Failure to do so may incur a fine of up to £500 per copy (level 2).[185] One copy must be given to the British Library. The Libraries of Oxford, Cambridge, Scotland, Wales and Trinity College, Dublin are entitled to

26–112

---

[171] As a percentage of all adults claiming to have read a newspaper recently or the day before: OECD (*The Evolution of News and the Internet*: June 11, 2010), based on data from the World Association of Newspapers (WAN).

[172] Analysis of the Annual Local Media Survey findings for 2008, Newspaper Society.

[173] AA/WARC Advertising statistics Yearbook.

[174] BMRB/TGI 2010.

[175] Specifically, the Mail Online derived 73% of its worldwide audience from outside of the United Kingdom, followed by FT.com (67%), and Metro.co.uk (61%)—see: OECD (*The Evolution of News and the Internet*: June 11, 2010), page 48.

[176] Newspaper Libel and Registration Act 1881, to the extent not repealed by the Defamation Act 1996.

[177] See for example, Value Added Tax Act 1994 Sch.8 Pt II.

[178] Enterprise Act 2002; Communications Act 2003, repealing Fair Trading Act 1973 s.57.

[179] Statutory definitions may also be found in, for example, the Betting, Gaming and Lotteries Act 1963, Lotteries and Amusements Act 1976, and the Accommodation Agencies Act 1953.

[180] Communications Act 2003. See generally, as to broadcasting industry, paras 26–276 et seq., below.

[181] As to relevant self-regulatory controls, see para.26–137, below.

[182] Communications Act 2003, amending the Enterprise Act 2002 specifying new public interest considerations to be applied to mergers involving newspaper enterprises.

[183] Newspapers, Printers and Reading Rooms Repeal Act 1869 Sch.2 of which re-enacted s.2, Printers and Publishers Act 1839, as amended by Criminal Law Act 1977 s.31(6).

[184] Newspapers, Printers and Reading Rooms Repeal Act 1869, re-enacting the Unlawful Societies Act 1799 s.29.

[185] Criminal Law Act 1977 s.31; Criminal Justice Act 1982 s.46.

copies on demand. A myriad of statutory, case law and self-regulatory restrictions on content of published material exists.[186]

26–113   **Continuing relevance of copyright.** While print remains, for the time being, a key means of bringing editorial and advertising content to both domestic and business customers, it is now only one among a number of delivery platforms. Recent years have witnessed rapid expansion in both the formats in which information may be presented and the media by which it can be delivered.

A striking recent phenomenon has been the explosion in new digital delivery platforms, driven by the increased sophistication of mobile technologies, battery power and screen quality. Publishers must now ensure that content is capable of being accessed not only in the form of web pages and electronic facsimiles of the print edition, but also for delivery on devices such as the BlackBerry, Apple's iPad, Amazon's Kindle and Samsung's Galaxy Tab. Key characteristics of these devices are that publishers have to adapt electronic content files for each platform (i.e. there is no universal standard); and, since (unlike print and web pages) the publishers do not control the platforms, content has to be licensed for delivery on each platform.[187] This developing choice of delivery systems underlines the importance of copyright, as the transactions between publishers, intermediaries and readers are all constructed on the basis of copyright licences.

At the same time, content is now almost exclusively "born digital" and then adapted for different formats. Journalists create or capture most content in digital form. Often, material is captured in audiovisual form. Rights-clearance in relation to journalists and other traditional contributors (and in particular, ensuring that the publisher has secured the rights needed to publish in all formats and media) has, in general, declined as an issue, as commissioning terms were overhauled during the first wave of "new media" publishing.[188] However, the use of moving images, sound and music requires more sophisticated rights management, and engagement with collecting societies, for example to deal with performers' rights and recording rights.[189]

26–114   The industry is an active participant in debates on the domestic, European and international level in relation to adapting copyright to meet the demands of new technology.[190] The industry sees itself as one of the key players in the new media environment, both as provider of content and as investor in new media products and infrastructure.

Much, though not all, of the industry's representation takes place through its trade association links. The United Kingdom's national press is represented by the Newspaper Publishers' Association.[191] The Newspaper Society, representing regional and local publishers in the United Kingdom,[192] is a member of the

---

[186] The most important of which include contempt of court, defamation, and advertising regulation, both statutory and self-regulatory, in respect of advertisement content, and see paras 26–356, and 26–359, below.

[187] There are intermediaries that enable material to be read across multiple devices.

[188] Though see the case of *Alan Grisbrook v MGN Limited and others* [2009] EWHC 2520 (Ch), October 16, 2009 and para.26–125 below.

[189] As to these rights, see Ch.12, above. As to the role of collecting Societies, see Ch.27, below. See also *Experience Hendrix LLC and another v Times Newspapers Ltd* [2010] EWHC 1986 (Ch), July 30, 2010.

[190] Most recently in response to the Council Directive on Copyright and Related Rights in the Information Society (2001/29/EC) now implemented in the form of the Copyright and Related Rights Regulations 2003 (SI 2003/2498).

[191] Newspaper Publishers Association, 34 Southwark Bridge Road, London, SE1 9EU, Tel: 020 7207 2200. Fax: 020 7928 2067.

[192] Newspaper Society, Bloomsbury House, 74–77 Great Russell Street, London, WC1B 3DA, Tel:

European Newspaper Publishers' Association (ENPA), based in Brussels,[193] as well as the World Association of Newspapers (WAN) based in Paris.[194] ENPA and WAN operate a joint copyright committee which plays an active part in oral and written consultations by the European Commission, the European Parliament and WIPO (World Intellectual Property Organisation). The Newspaper Society was also instrumental in an all-industry challenge in 1993 before the Copyright Tribunal[195] to the royalty levels set by the BBC, ITV companies and Channel Four in respect of their television listings following the ending of the duopoly in seven-day television listings.

However, latterly there have been notable divergences of approach by newspaper groups in responding to the challenges posed by new technology. The decision by News Corporation to charge for online content, starting in June 2010, has provoked opposition and criticism from within the industry. Technical and commercial models have, for the time being, taken precedence over amendments to legislation as the industry seeks ways to engage with the power of search engines.

B. SOURCES OF COPYRIGHT

General. The fundamental tenet that there is no copyright in ideas, only in the form in which they are expressed, manifests itself in the newspaper context by the principle that there is no copyright in "news". There is nevertheless copyright in the form in which it is expressed in particular articles and reports.[196] Copyright may also subsist in the whole newspaper by way of the compilation of these items[197] and, in addition, will subsist in the typographical arrangement of the published newspaper.[198] This latter right protects a publisher's skill and effort in creating the layout of each edition, and may form the basis of an infringement action in circumstances in which a substantial part of a printed edition (perhaps comprising third-party copyright in editorial or advertising material), has been copied for use in another publication. The photocopying of individual articles, none of which sufficiently reproduces the layout of any page to amount to a substantial part of its typographical arrangement, has been held not to infringe the copyright in the layout.[199]

26–115

Multiplicity of sources. The content incorporated into the published edition of a newspaper always originated from a wide variety of sources: salaried employees (including journalists, photographers and illustrators); freelance journalists; news agencies and photo libraries; occasional contributors (the most common examples being readers' letters to the editor and classified advertising); advertising agencies; and third-party contributors of databases of information such as weather and sport information, arts and entertainment and the like. Digital technology has only increased the range of external sources. Newspaper websites can include, for example, reader-generated content, comments on blog posts, contributions to discussion boards and information (including sound and images) uploaded via

26–116

020 7636 7014. Fax: 020 7631 5119. *http://www.newspapersoc.org.uk* [Accessed November 1, 2010].
[193] ENPA, Rue des Pierres 29, bte 8, 1000 Brussels, Belgium, Tel: 003225 510190. Fax: 00 322 5510199. *http://www.enpa.be* [Accessed November 1, 2010].
[194] WAN, 25 Rue d'Astorg, 75008, Paris, France. Tel: 00 331 47428500. Fax: 00 331 47424948. *http://www.wan-press.org* [Accessed November 1, 2010].
[195] *News Group Newspapers Ltd v Independent Television Productions* [1993] E.M.L.R. 1.
[196] See Ch.7, above, as to the protection generally afforded to literary and artistic works.
[197] As to copyright in compilations, see paras 3–21 et seq., above.
[198] As to such copyright, see paras 3–104 et seq., above.
[199] *Newspaper Licensing Agency Ltd v Marks & Spencer Plc* [2003] 1 A.C. 551; [2002] R.P.C. 4; [2001] E.M.L.R. 43.

online data-sharing facilities. Where newspapers have introduced ancillary electronic services such as recorded audiotext material, there may be other third-party right-holders in recorded music or sports, weather messages, or other recorded information.

26–117   **Employee's works.** The rule whereby an employer is normally the first owner of works created by employees during the course of their employment[200] is now regarded by newspaper proprietors as axiomatic.[201] It gives a newspaper publisher wide scope to deal with employed journalists' works, both in-house and commercially, without the financial and administrative burden of entering into a substantial number of licence agreements or negotiating royalty fees over and above paid salaries. Its practical effect is to permit, in the absence of an agreement to the contrary,[202] use of employed journalists' material in electronic media, magazines and spin-off publications, and to enable newspaper proprietors to publish such material in book form, to sell articles or photographs to radio or television companies, to pass them to other media owned by the same group and to store and retrieve them in databases for internal or external use, all without the need to obtain licences from employees.

26–118   **Employee or independent contractor?** Given that the ownership of copyright in the works of journalists depends upon the employment status of the journalist, the question of whether a journalist is working under a contract for service or contract for services is of crucial importance in the industry. Although as a general rule the status is clear, the gradual extension over recent years of "employee-style" benefits to freelancers, new ways of working and varying methods of payment has in some cases blurred the original, relatively distinct freelance status, and may create a risk that freelancers might be deemed to be employees. There is much general case law on the subject of the criteria and consequences of the differing status of employees and independent contractors.[203]

26–119   **Commissioned and unsolicited works.** The exception to the general rule in the 1988 Act that the author of a work is the first owner of the copyright applies only to employees' works. Copyright ownership of material submitted by anyone other than an employee of the newspaper (whether journalist, graphic artist, illustrator and whether commissioned or unsolicited material) is therefore dependent upon such contractual arrangements as may exist between the parties.[204] It should be noted, however, that a newspaper publisher may be entitled to be taken to be the "author" of (and hence potentially first owner of copyright in) sound recordings and films made by non-employed journalists, to the extent that the publisher is the "producer".[205] Copy from advertising agencies and private advertisers (whether domestic or business) will generally be subject to a newspaper's standard terms and conditions of acceptance of advertising, subject to contractual principles relating to incorporation of such terms.

Copyright in unsolicited materials intended for publication, such as letters to

---

[200] CDPA 1988 s.11(2). See paras 5–08 et seq., above.
[201] Compare with the position under the 1911 and 1956 Acts where, in some circumstances, the copyright was split between the journalist and his publisher-employer: see paras 5–29 and 5–30. The point is still important in the case of works made under the 1956 and 1911 Acts.
[202] Agreements to the contrary are very rare in the newspaper industry.
[203] See paras 5–11 et seq., above.
[204] As may ownership of materials produced by an employee otherwise than during the course of his employment.
[205] CDPA 1988 s.9(2). "Producer" is defined as "the person by whom the arrangements necessary for the making of the sound recording or film are undertaken": CDPA 1988 s.178.

the editor will normally remain with the author[206] although some national newspapers have sought to obtain assignments of the copyright in such letters and to accept them only on the basis that they have not been submitted for publication elsewhere. On the other hand, the submission of material online, for example on bulletin boards, blogs or "tips" pages, is generally governed by terms of use which seek to make explicit the publisher's right to use, retain and delete such material.

Agreements with news agencies and external photolibraries will govern permitted use of material received by virtue of a subscription service. Such agreements generally reserve to the agency copyright and all other intellectual property rights in material supplied by them, granting subscribers to their services non-exclusive, non-transferable licences for a set time period, normally between three to five years. Newspapers are generally able under the terms of the licence to extract from the stream of material received via the service as much or as little as is relevant to them, to edit the material, and publish it for the duration of the licence. Downloading of agency material onto a newspaper's database is normally prohibited.

Journalists' interviews. Spoken words qualify for copyright protection once recorded in any manner, in writing or otherwise, provided they constitute a "literary" work and are "original".[207] Thus, copyright may well subsist in the words of an interviewee, once recorded by a reporter.[208] Because the "author" of and thus owner of the copyright in the interviewee's words is the interviewee himself and not the person recording the spoken words,[209] an infringement action might lie[210] by the speaker following publication of the words were it not for the exception in s.58 of the 1988 Act.[211] The effect of this section is that, provided no relevant prohibitions were imposed by the interviewee before the reporter made the recording, no express agreement need be obtained for subsequent use of the recording for the purpose of reporting current events or communicating the words to the public. It appears that any prohibition must be expressly made[212] and it is suggested that the stipulation by an interviewee that his comments were "off the record" would usually constitute a valid prohibition, given the well accepted understanding that such words are meant to prohibit use in the form of news reports or otherwise.

26–120

It is a further condition that the person who is lawfully in possession of the record must consent to the use of it.[213] This would appear to indicate that publication of the interview requires the consent of the reporter in order to ensure that the proprietor or other officer of the newspaper company does not infringe the interviewee's copyright. It is likely, however, that the reporter's consent would be inferred from the fact that the particular story had been submitted by him for publication. Presumably, also, where this tape is in "possession" of an employed reporter, his "possession" is that of his employer.

---

[206] The submission of a letter or article for publication will however usually imply a licence to publish. See paras 5–224 et seq., above.

[207] CDPA 1988 s.3(2). As to "originality", see paras 3–125 et seq., above.

[208] "Record" is not defined but would include a record in any form including writing, a sound recording or a film. "Writing" includes any form of notation or code: CDPA 1988 s.178.

[209] See para.4–16, above. As to the separate copyright belonging to the interviewer, see further in the text and para.4–17, above.

[210] Often, of course, publication of the interview will have been impliedly licensed by the interviewee.

[211] For a detailed discussion of this section, see paras 9–174 et seq. and see CDPA 1988 s.58(2)(b), (c).

[212] Where an interviewee is unaware that a recording is being made, the law of confidence may apply.

[213] CDPA 1988 s.58(2)(d).

There is a quite separate copyright which may subsist in the journalists' work, consisting of his record of the interview.[214] The standard of independent skill and labour required of a reporter in the taking down of notes to a speech or interview for the separate work to qualify for copyright protection is low. The mere taking of a *verbatim* shorthand note of an oral speech not previously written down has been held sufficient for the written record to qualify for copyright protection.[215] Given that most interviews are now recorded using digital sound recorders or video cameras, the newspaper publisher may (as noted above) be entitled to claim ownership of the copyright, or a joint share of the copyright, in any sound recordings and films made by non-employed journalists, to the extent that the publisher is the "producer".[216]

26–121 **News stories obtained from other sources.** It is a relatively commonplace practice for media to take note of other media sources for news stories to be then either followed up independently or rewritten by their own staff for publication. The rewriting of news stories may be permissible, provided that this does not involve the substantial reproduction of an article from another newspaper or radio, television or cable broadcast, which would infringe the copyright in that item. Even where the taking has been of a substantial part, however, this can sometimes be justified on the basis of fair dealing for the purposes of reporting current events, provided a sufficient acknowledgment is included.[217] Where the defence does not apply, and what has been taken are extracts consisting of an interviewee's own words, it is sometimes argued that a custom exists in the industry whereby it is accepted that this will happen.[218] The question of what is a substantial part of a newspaper article must now be considered in light of the ECJ's decision in *Infopaq International A/S v Danske Dagblades Forening*,[219] that the storing and printing out by a media monitoring business of eleven-word extracts from newspaper articles amounted to a reproduction in part within art.2 of the Information Society Directive[220] if the elements reproduced were the expression of the author's own intellectual creation.[221]

26–122 **Other material obtained from other sources.** Newspapers publish a huge range of other material obtained from a wide variety of sources. In doing so, reliance is often placed on the "fair dealing" defences. While the defence of "fair dealing" for the purposes of reporting current events is to be construed liberally, there are limits to its scope. Where extracts quoted from a private journal form a substantial part of the whole, the copy of the journal has been obtained via a breach of confidence, and the articles are not confined to current events, their purpose being to report on the revelation of the contents of the journal as itself as an event of interest, the defence is unlikely to apply.[222] Newspaper content is itself as much prone to "fair dealing" uses by third parties as it is likely to benefit from such

---

[214] See paras 3–125 et seq., above, as to the requirement of sufficient skill and labour, or originality.
[215] *Walter v Lane* [1900] A.C. 539; *Express Newspapers Plc v News (UK) Ltd* [1990] 1 W.L.R. 1320.
[216] See para.26–119, above.
[217] CDPA 1988 s.30(2).
[218] See, e.g. *Express Newspapers Plc v News (UK) Ltd* [1990] 1 W.L.R. 1320. This is because it would be contrary to pubic interest if further dissemination of news items was prohibited absolutely as a copyright infringement. But the argument has never succeeded, for good reason it is suggested. See *Walter v Steinkopff* [1892] 3 Ch. 489; *Banier v News Group Newspapers Ltd* [1997] F.S.R. 812.
[219] Case C–5/08, July 16, 2009; [2009] E.C.D.R. 16; [2009] F.S.R. 20.
[220] Directive 2001/29/EC.
[221] The ECJ left it to the national court to decide whether, on the facts, the extracts in issue did amount to the author's own intellectual creation.
[222] *HRH Prince of Wales v Associated Newspapers Ltd* [2006] EWHC 522; [2006] E.C.D.R. 20.

uses.[223] It is not however fair dealing for the purposes of criticism and review to reproduce the entire front page of a title published by a competitor in a comparative advertisement where a simple identification of the original title would have sufficed.[224]

Advertisements, compilations and databases. Insofar as newspaper employees expend sufficient skill and labour in the creation of text, design and illustration for an advertisement, whether classified or display, the newspaper proprietor will prima facie own the copyright subsisting in the work. Where advertisements are created in part by newspaper staff and in part by a private advertiser or agency, copyright in the advertisement will be split accordingly. The same is true for newspaper promotions or other marketing tools in the form of games or competitions, many of which may contain sufficient skill and labour to qualify for copyright protection as a compilation.[225] Newspaper-compiled business directories and other lists of, say, restaurants, entertainments, educational courses or facilities may also qualify for protection provided that sufficient work goes into the selecting and arranging of the data; and that sufficient skill and judgment is applied during the process to make the work the "intellectual creation" of the journalist.[226] Alternatively, they may qualify for protection under database right.[227]

26–123

However, where journalists consult databases to gather source material for their articles, including website content that falls within the definition of a database[228] then there is a risk of infringement of database right. Transferring[229] may occur even if no physical copying takes place. What is required is that a part of the database is found in a new medium. This may, for example, occur where the transferor consults the original database in order to assess each piece of data on whether to incorporate it into the new medium and in doing so displays it on a screen.[230]

C. RIGHTS REQUIRED FOR EXPLOITATION

Employees. Notwithstanding the employee provisions of s.11(2) of the 1988 Act, it is common practice to include an express assignment of copyright in any work created by an employee at any time while in the newspaper's employment. There are a number of reasons for this. First, an express assignment avoids arguments about whether a particular piece of work was produced "in the course of employment".[231] Express and clear provision in an employment contract can render less likely subsequent disputes about whether a verbal agreement was made as to copyright ownership, or whether a course of conduct was such that in respect of a particular article, photograph or illustration, there was a contrary agreement as to ownership. Lastly, an express assignment is useful in cases where other jurisdictions are involved, particularly in the event that the newspaper wishes to secure foreign rights in the material.

26–124

---

[223] *Fraser-Woodward Ltd v BBC* [2005] EWHC 472; [2005] F.S.R. 36.

[224] *IPC Media Ltd v News Group Newspapers Ltd* [2005] EWHC 317; [2005] F.S.R. 36.

[225] CDPA 1988 s.1(1)(c) and see, for example, *Express Newspapers v Liverpool Daily Post and Echo* [1985] 1 W.L.R. 1089 where copyright was held to subsist in a game consisting of reader cards comprising a five-letter sequence and daily varying grid-letter sequences.

[226] *Football DataCo Limited and Ors v Brittens Pools Limited and Ors* [2010] EWHC 841 (Ch).

[227] See Ch.18, above.

[228] As to which, see para.18–11, above.

[229] See para.18–28, above.

[230] *Directmedia Publishing GmbH v Albrecht-Ludwigs-Universität Freiburg*, October 9, 2008 (C–304/07) [2009] 1 C.M.L.R. 7; [2009] R.P.C. 10.

[231] For example, if an employee created a particular piece of work outside official working hours or if an employee argued that his work was outside his ordinary duties.

26–125   **Freelances: express terms.** The need to secure rights for re-use of material in a range of different digital formats and editions (including syndication in the United Kingdom and overseas), and litigation over whether such rights have been secured,[232] have driven the industry to adopt a more systematic approach to commissioning of freelances. Most, if not all, newspaper publishers have adopted written commissioning terms that include the right to use contributions in all formats and editions (including print, electronic and audiovisual) of the newspaper, and to store and display commissioned material on internal and external databases. Other rights include those required to be passed on to the Newspaper Licensing Agency,[233] and the right to syndicate. Although there are no industry wide standard commissioning terms, there has been a convergence in approach by publishers. There are, of course, other advantages in securing an express grant of rights on a formal basis. An assignment or exclusive licence of copyright will not be effective unless in writing and signed.[234] For a newspaper proprietor to have *locus standi* to institute infringement proceedings relating to the work, a written, signed agreement would be required from the freelancer either making the proprietor an exclusive licensee or amounting to an assignment of copyright.[235]

26–126   **Freelances: implied terms.** Nevertheless, given the news industry's abiding need for urgency, contributions are not infrequently commissioned without a written agreement between the newspaper and freelance. While repeated commissions may bring the publisher's standard terms to the freelance's attention, this may not happen in the case of "one-off" commissions. In the absence of a written agreement, a publisher will have an implied permission "to use the work in the manner and for the purpose in which and for which it was contemplated between the parties that it would be used at the time of the engagement".[236] This implied permission will generally be regarded by custom and practice as including a non-exclusive licence to publish the work in printed form. In addition, it is likely that the non-exclusive right to permit photocopying of the article, post it up as part of the online version of the newspaper and store it on archival databases may also be implied into the arrangement, since these are now likely to be understood as the normal consequences of publication in a newspaper. However, there is always a risk that the terms of the implied contract with the contributor may remain unclear, including the scope, permitted media of publication, territorial limitations, syndication rights and duration of the licence. An implied licence may also not extend to re-publication of archived articles, or syndication of the newspaper's commercial databases to third parties, including news agencies or other media companies. With time, assuming a custom develops, the courts may be willing to imply a wider licence to permit reproduction in other formats.

26–127   **Electronic commissioning of material.** Publishers are increasingly looking to streamline the commissioning process, both to ensure that the commissioning terms are binding on freelance journalists, and to make the process easier to administer for commissioning editors. Commissioning freelances by electronic

---

[232] Notably in the United States, for example, *New York Times Co Inc et al v Tasini et al* (Case no:00–21, Supreme Court, June 25, 2001); In re Freelance Works in Literary Databases Copyright Litigation MDL No.1379 (S.D.N.Y). See also *Alan Grisbrook v MGN Ltd and others* [2009] EWHC 2520 (Ch), October 16, 2009.

[233] See para.26–136, below.

[234] CDPA 1988 ss.90(3) and 92(1).

[235] CDPA 1988 ss.101(1) and 96(1), respectively. The new s.101A (see paras 21–30 et seq., above) is unlikely to be of much application to the newspaper industry because, while non-exclusive licences are not unusual in freelance commissioning terms, they are often not signed by the contributors.

[236] *Robin Ray v Classic FM Plc* [1998] FSR 622, at 643.

means is the inevitable result of combining these objectives with new technology. The question arises of whether electronic commissioning terms are capable of meeting the statutory requirements for a valid assignment of copyright or grant of an exclusive licence.[237] Section 8 of the Electronic Communications Act 2000 allows ministers to amend statutes to authorise or to facilitate the use of electronic communications or storage. As yet, no statutory instrument has been made to resolve the ambiguity in the law at present relating to whether signatures in an electronic form will suffice as a signature for the purposes of s.90 (3). However, it could be argued that an effect of EU legislation[238] and international model laws[239] is that the status of a "signature" must not be prejudiced solely by virtue of its electronic form. In the absence of definitive guidance a publisher commissioning material using electronic terms can argue that any agreement to assign or grant an exclusive licence is contractually enforceable by the publisher against the contributor.

Right to exploit advertising material. As with freelance commissioning terms, terms governing the booking of advertising space have evolved to reflect the opportunities for digital display, and now routinely include the right to publish the advertisement irrespective of the medium or platform in or on which it is published. Newspapers may insert in their standard terms and conditions for advertising a provision that the copyright for all purposes in all artwork, copy, and other material which the newspaper company or its employees have originated, contributed to or reworked belongs to the company. Such terms and conditions also authorise the company to record, reproduce, publish, distribute and broadcast (or permit such acts) in respect of all advertisements accepted for publication (including, but not limited to text, artwork and photographs) and to include and make them available in any information service, electronic or otherwise. A warranty to the effect that advertising copy submitted does not infringe any third-party intellectual property rights is another common provision, as is an indemnity from advertisers and advertising agencies in respect of all costs, damages and other charges falling upon the newspaper company in respect of legal actions or threatened legal actions arising from the publication of advertisements accepted for publication.

26–128

Photographs. In-house photographic libraries, the content of which comprise photographs taken solely by staff photographers after August 1, 1989, will generally be free from ownership restrictions on use. However, rights-clearance issues become more complicated where libraries comprise photographs taken by freelances (where use will be governed by contractual terms or implied licences), or in respect of older photographs where the law in force at the time the photograph was taken will apply. Newspaper publishers may not, of course, assume that contemporary industry custom takes precedence over prior agreements, so as to permit the online marketing of photographs, contrary to licence terms agreed in a consent order.[240] Nor should they seek to rely on it to imply terms into an (unwritten) agreement that pre-dated the use by many years, before a time when such online marketing could be said to have been in the contemplation of the parties.[241]

External photo libraries are becoming increasingly concerned that once their

26–129

---

[237] CDPA s.90(3) and s.92(1).

[238] Directive 2000/31/EC ('the Electronic Commerce Directive') and Directive 1999/93/EC ("the Electronic Signatures Directive").

[239] UNCITRAL Model Law on Electronic Signatures 2001 art.6.

[240] *Alan Grisbrook v MGN Ltd and others* [2009] EWHC 2520 (Ch), October 16, 2009.

[241] *Alan Grisbrook v MGN Ltd and others* [2009] EWHC 2520 (Ch), per Patten L.J. at 65, applying *Robin Ray v Classic FM PLC* [1998] F.S.R. 622.

photographs have been digitised, there is almost unlimited scope for them to be copied, digitised and altered. Photographers and agencies have therefore become more reluctant to grant licences for online newspaper publications without strict limitations on the right to adapt or alter the works. Where ancillary services are offered by newspaper companies, such as audiotext facilities linking newspaper text to telephone facilities, there may be a need for clearing rights via collecting societies such as the Performing Rights Society (PRS) or the Mechanical Copyright Protection Society (MCPS).[242] Such commercial projects are increasingly becoming integrated in newspaper operations.

The defence of "fair dealing" for the purposes of reporting current events does not apply to photographs.[243] Nor is it acceptable, in circumstances in which publication is time-critical, to reproduce photographs and pay licence fees for publication after the event.[244] In such circumstances the court may reach a finding of flagrancy and award additional damages.

26–130   **Right to privacy of certain photographs and films.** Section 85 of the 1988 Act provides for a moral right restricting publication of photographs and films commissioned for private and domestic purposes. In certain circumstances waiver of this right will be required if such a photograph is to be included in a newspaper or posted up on a newspaper website. However, the section amounts to a very limited exception to the general common law position that there is no right to prevent a photographer from taking a photograph of a person and subsequently using the photograph commercially for publication and distribution. The section is narrow in scope and was intended to cover, for example, commissioned wedding photographs and family portraits in a non-commercial context.[245] Nevertheless, developments in the law of privacy and data protection may in due course require that greater care will need to be taken in the use of photographs of a private nature, even if s.85 does not apply.[246]

26–131   **Exceptions to paternity and integrity right.** In specific circumstances the 1988 Act gives the author of a literary, dramatic, musical or artistic work the right to be identified as author of that work[247] (the "paternity right") and to object to the work being subjected to "derogatory treatment", (the "integrity right").[248] A number of exceptions to the paternity and integrity rights are relevant to publication of a copyright work in a newspaper apply, namely:

(i) Where a work is made for the purpose of reporting current events.[249]

(ii) In relation to the publication in a newspaper, magazine or similar periodical of any literary, dramatic musical or artistic work (including photographs, illustration, editorials or news stories) made for the purposes of

---

[242] As to such societies see paras 27–65 and 27–63, below.

[243] CDPA 1988 s.30(2).

[244] *Banier v News Group Newspapers Ltd* [1997] F.S.R. 812.

[245] In May 1993, the Photographs and Films (Unauthorised Use) Bill sought to extend the moral rights provision in s.85 to create what was in effect a right of privacy. The Bill, ultimately withdrawn, would have extended the moral right to cover non-commissioned photographs, effectively covering all photographs intended for commercial exploitation. The Bill would have created severe restrictions on use of journalistic material in the ordinary course of newspaper production.

[246] *Von Hannover v Germany* (59320/00) [2004] E.M.L.R. 21.

[247] CDPA 1988 ss.77, 78.

[248] CDPA 1988 s.80. The treatment would have to be held to amount to a "distortion or mutilation" of the work or be otherwise prejudicial to the honour or reputation of the journalist or photographer.

[249] CDPA 1988 ss.81(3) and 79(6).

such publication, or made available with the consent of the author for the purposes of such publication.[250]

(iii) Where the employer of the author is the first owner of the copyright pursuant to s.11(2) and where what is done has the authority of the copyright owner.[251]

Implications of exceptions of paternity right. One practical effect of the Act's exceptions to the paternity right is that no action will lie where a freelance or employed journalist is not identified in a published article by way of a by-line. In the case of freelancers, the exception applies whether the published work was specifically commissioned by the newspaper or whether it was an unsolicited work submitted to the newspaper. The rationale behind the exception lies partly in the practical difficulties which can ensue in ascertaining which of the persons who contributed to a final published version of an article (researchers, journalists, contributions, sub-editors) should be accorded a by-line. It has also been argued that the clarity of representation of newspapers and the flexibility of editors and publishers to determine an attractive format and appearance might be hindered if a paternity right imposed an obligation to provide by-lines to journalists. In some cases publishers and editors identify authors voluntarily or in satisfaction of a contractual obligation. However, since it is arguable that the exception to the paternity right does not extend to electronic publications, express waivers are frequently included in contractual agreements. Terms for online submission or posting of content (for example on bulletin boards) may contain waivers, or may remain silent, relying on the fact that (under UK law) the paternity right cannot be infringed unless asserted.[252]   **26–132**

Implications of exceptions to integrity right. The Act's exceptions to the integrity right[253] mean that staff journalists, freelancers and readers who have submitted letters for publication and agencies who have submitted illustrations or text in advertising copy cannot (subject to contractual agreements) object to the editing of their contributions. The exception also applies to subsequent exploitation of the work elsewhere, for example online, without modification to the published version.[254] Photographers cannot sue in respect of alterations to the size, colour or proportions of their published photographs. The electronic or manual alteration of a photograph, including cropping, has been justified in terms of the requirement to conform to space constraints or to align with the content of a particular news story. Some journalists' employment contracts may contain waivers of the integrity right (conditional or unconditional, and sometimes expressed to be subject to revocation). These are unlikely to be necessary, given that the moral right of integrity does not apply to a work prepared for publication in a newspaper, magazine or similar periodical. However, since it is unclear whether the exception applies to newspaper websites, terms for online submission or post-   **26–133**

---

[250] CDPA 1988 s.81(4)(a) and 79(6)(a).
[251] CDPA 1988 ss.79(3), 82(1)(a). In the case of derogatory treatment, a disclaimer may have to be published if the author has been named. See s.82(2). Note that where a newspaper publishes only with a licence of the copyright owner, the licence may not extend to publication in altered form. See para.5–228, above.
[252] CDPA 1988 s.78.
[253] CDPA 1988 ss.81(4), 82(1)(a). Note that the third exception identified above does not apply to the integrity right where the author, journalist or photographer is identified at the time of the relevant act (i.e. publication) or has previously been identified in or on published copies of the work, unless there is a sufficient disclaimer. A "sufficient disclaimer" is defined as a clear and reasonably prominent indication given at the time of publication (which, if the author is then identified, must appear along with the identification) that the work has been subjected to treatment to which the author has not consented: CDPA 1988 s.178. See generally as to these rights, Ch.11, above.
[254] CDPA 1988 s.81(4).

ing of content often entitle the publisher to make additions or deletions to the text or graphics prior to publication.

26–134   **False attribution.** Contracts with freelancers and employees (whether in respect of text, photographs, graphic illustrations or design) frequently contain a waiver of the moral right not to have work falsely attributed to the author.[255] In a newspaper context, such a right could be infringed by normal distribution to the public of a newspaper containing an article, photograph or advertising material where a false attribution had been made. The attribution may be express or implied. In contrast with the paternity and integrity rights, there is no exception applicable in a news-reporting context.[256]

D. REPRESENTATIVE COLLECTING SOCIETIES AND LICENSING AGENCIES RESPONSIBLE FOR ADMINISTERING THE RIGHTS

26–135   In marked contrast with the industrial relations position in a number of member states, there is little involvement in the print industry in the United Kingdom with systems of pooled copyright management, house agreements, collective agreements and the like. Rights are generally agreed and exploited on the basis of bilateral agreements between creators of commissioned works and publishers. That is, individual management is the norm.

26–136   **The Newspaper Licensing Agency.** In January 1996, a number of national newspapers launched the Newspaper Licensing Agency (NLA).[257] The NLA was designed to complement the service offered by the Copyright Licensing Agency (CLA) which licenses the copying of magazines, books and periodicals. The NLA is a limited company, owned by the United Kingdom's eight national newspaper groups. It licenses the copying of newspaper content on behalf of the copyright owners, and represents over 1,400 titles in total. Over 150,000 organisations rely on the NLA's annual licences. Since its inception the NLA has distributed more than £100 million in royalties to represented rightsholders. The NLA offers a selection of licences dependent upon the type of organisation and its requirements. These licences permit the copying of UK national and regional newspapers, in both print and online editions, as well as foreign and specialist titles. The licensed activities include photocopying, faxing and printing, digital reproduction (scanning, emailing and hosting on an intranet site) and the receipt and distribution of content supplied by a third party such as a public relations or media monitoring agency. Since January 2010 newspaper website content has been included, offering a complete feed of newspapers' online content direct to cuttings aggregators and press cuttings agencies.[258]

Following the litigation in the case of *The Newspaper Society Ltd v Marks & Spencer Plc*[259] the NLA amended the terms of its mandate and licences to cover the grant of licences of the copyright in individual articles, where that copyright had not been assigned to the applicable publisher. Its Distribution Scheme aims to identify contributors who have not assigned copying rights to the publisher ("Special Contributors"), who are entitled to a share of the sums paid by the NLA to newspaper publishers.

---

[255] CDPA 1988 s.84.

[256] See, for example *Clark v Associated Newspapers Ltd* [1998] 1 All E.R. 959.

[257] The Newspaper Licensing Agency Ltd, Wellington Gate, Church Road, Tunbridge Wells, TN1 1NL. Tel. 01892 525273. Fax 01892 525275. *http://www.nla.co.uk* [Accessed October 1, 2010].

[258] For further details, see the NLA website and para.26–143, below.

[259] [2001] UKHL 38, [2003] 1 A.C. 551.

E. OTHER INDUSTRY CONTROLS

Self-regulatory controls. In both the editorial and advertising spheres, there are   **26–137**
well-established self-regulatory controls in respect of content. Editorial content is
overseen by the Press Complaints Commission (PCC), funded by means of a levy
on all British newspapers, magazines and periodicals. The PCC enforces a Code
of Practice with provisions relating to accuracy, payment for articles, harassment,
opportunity to reply, interviewing or photographing children, intrusion into grief
or shock and other matters.[260] The PCC was created in 1991 to replace the old
Press Council in response to recommendations to the Home Office by The Committee on Privacy and Related Matters.[261] Self-regulation in the advertising and
marketing area is administered by the Advertising Standards Authority (ASA)[262]
on the basis the CAP Code.[263] This topic is dealt with in more detail elsewhere.[264]

F. CURRENT INDUSTRY ISSUES

The major current issues of concern to the newspaper sector relate to the impact   **26–138**
of new technology. This, more than anything else, dictates the industry stance to
proposed reforms to copyright law, wherever these emanate from.

Online re-use and infringement. The exponential growth of search engines and   **26–139**
online data aggregation has, from the perspective of newspaper publishers, been
a blessing and a curse. It has provided access to content for millions of users, and
opened up new markets. At the same time, it has facilitated re-use of content,
much of it unauthorised, on a grand scale. The activities of linking, spidering and
caching routinely undertaken by search engines and other intermediaries are
designed to make material available to wider audiences. However, whilst the
intermediaries argue that they are providing a beneficial service to the owner, by
presenting their content to huge numbers of web users, the publishers argue that
these activities do not always drive traffic to their sites, with the result that they
are missing out on substantial advertising revenue and losing their basic right to
control their own content.

Search engines. Search engine algorithms typically gather and rank thousands of   **26–140**
news stories every day. The search page ranks the results, displaying the headline
and a very short extract from the article. The headline is hyperlinked to the original newspaper publisher's website. Whether such reproduction and display of
headlines and stories infringes copyright has been considered in other countries,[265]
but not yet in the United Kingdom. In *Copiepresse v Google* it was held that
creating a memory "cache" of articles, and communicating the titles of articles
and the short extracts to the public, infringed copyright. The use of the hyperlink
itself was not the infringement; rather, it was the reproduction and communication to the public of the titles and extracts on Google's home page that infringed.
The Court held that the news reporting defence under Belgian copyright law did
not apply, and dismissed the argument that the publishers had granted an express

---

[260] The current Code of Practice was framed by the newspaper and periodical industry and was ratified by the PCC on June 13, 2005. It can be seen at *http://www.pcc.org.uk/cop/practice.html* [Ac-
cessed November 1, 2010].

[261] Chaired by Sir David Calcutt (Cmnd.1102) July 1990.

[262] Advertising Standards Authority, Mid City Place, 71 High Holborn, London WC1V 6QT. Tel.
020 7492 2222.

[263] The 12th edition of The UK Code of Non-Broadcast Advertising, Sales Promotion and Direct
Marketing (CAP Code) came into force on September 1, 2010.

[264] See the section on the Advertising Industry, paras 26–341 et seq., below.

[265] *Copiepresse SCRL v Google Inc* No 06/10.928/C (Court of First Instance, Brussels) February 13,
2007; [2007] E.C.D.R. 5.

or implied licence permitting copying, simply by virtue of making the articles available to the public on the internet.[266] The impact of *Infopaq*[267] on the *Copiepresse* decision remains to be seen.

26–141 **Linking and deep linking.** Many search engines and content aggregators include links in their presentation of search results, including "deep links".[268] An unauthorised communication to the public of a copyright work is an infringement. A communication to the public includes *"the making available to the public of the work by electronic transmission in such a way that members of the public may access it from a place and at a time individually chosen by them"*.[269] It has been suggested that linking involves the "making available" of a copyright work and therefore needs the copyright owner's consent. The very limited case law on this issue pre-dates the adoption of the "communication to the public" right, though it does suggest that the courts might seek to assist a claimant publisher.[270] It might be thought that, since linking does not involve the copying of the original site's pages (until someone clicks onto the link and views the page on his computer), this should not be an infringing act. However, the original act of "communication to the public" by the publisher does not involve the distribution of the copies of a site's pages either. Depending on the facts, consideration should also be given to possible secondary liability or liability for authorisation. Much may depend on whether the material in question is freely available for the public to access or hidden behind security systems.

26–142 **Spidering and screen-scraping.** There is very little case law in the United Kingdom or elsewhere on the extent to which "spidering" involves an infringement of copyright, or indeed of database right. This may well be because of the difficulties of proving infringement where small quantities of factual data are harvested. However, it is likely that aspects of "spidering" can infringe. The gathering of data and retrieval of web pages results in copies of the data or pages being made; if the data or pages are a copyright work, there would be an infringement. These activities would also be an "extraction" for database right purposes.[271] Case law is equally scarce relating to the closely related activity of screen-scraping, that is to say, the extraction of data from screen outputs of other websites. This issue was examined in *RyanAir v Vtours* by a German court.[272] In that case, RyanAir succeeded in obtaining relief against the operator of a website which posted large quantities of data scraped from Ryanair's site. It argued that Vtours' activities breached RyanAir's terms and conditions and infringed its copyright. Other causes of action should be considered too. In the United States, the courts have held that "spidering" constitutes a trespass to property.[273] If an unauthorised change is made to the rights holder's computer an offence may be committed under the Computer Misuse Act 1990. Finally, depending on the website's terms and conditions, there may be contractual issues.

---

[266] Google tried to argue that the publishers could have used technical restrictions (e.g. Robots.txt) to prevent copying, but the Court was not persuaded that publishers who failed to use such restrictions tolerated copying.

[267] See para.26–121, above.

[268] That is, a hyperlink that points to a specific page or image on another website, rather than the main or home page of that website.

[269] CDPA s.20(2)(b).

[270] *Shetland Times Ltd v Wills* (OH) Court of Session (Outer House) October 24, 1996 [1997] F.S.R. 604 (though this was based on the old law and treated websites as "cable programmes") and *Danske Dagblades Forening (DDF) v Newsbooster* Byret (Copenhagen) July 5, 2002 [2003] E.C.D.R. 5.

[271] See Ch.18.

[272] Unreported. Information on the case is available in *IT Law Today*, September 2008, pp.2–3 and in RyanAir's report to the US Securities and Exchange Commission of July 10, 2008.

[273] *Ticketmaster Corp. v Tickets.com, Inc.* (District Court of Central California, March 6, 2003) 2003 U.S. Dist. Lexis 6483.

Media monitoring. Media-monitoring services (which include the descendants   **26–143**
of press clipping agencies and public relations agencies) gather articles and
extracts from newspaper websites, aggregating such material with content drawn
from other sources for provision to their clients. There is no UK authority specifically on whether such copying and distribution of online newspaper content, and
its receipt and use by clients of media-monitoring services, infringes copyright,
or whether such activity is "fair dealing" for the purposes of reporting current
events. Following a referral to the Copyright Tribunal of the NLA's[274] new web
licensing scheme for media-monitoring services, the NLA has applied to the
High Court for a determination on whether the activities of media-monitoring
services infringe copyright.[275]

Non-legal solutions. Pending judicial clarification of whether the access to   **26–144**
newspaper content provided by search engines is a copyright infringement, several solutions of a technical or commercial nature have been proposed or piloted.
Among the technical solutions are the Automated Content Access Protocol,[276]
which offers a new universal permissions protocol on the internet, which can be
automatically recognised and interpreted by web crawlers. The purpose of this is
to allow any online publisher to express its access and use policies on its copyright material at source. Other technical solutions are emerging that are designed
to enable publishers to regain control of their content online by scanning the internet for unauthorised copies.[277] Commercial solutions are likely to involve
agreements between publishers and search companies, perhaps involving a limit
on the amount of content that can be accessed via search engines.

"Videograbbing". This is the practice of using video technology to capture im-   **26–145**
ages from broadcast material (either live or film footage) for subsequent use in
other publications. This should be understood in the context of the increasing use
of video technology by newspaper journalists as a routine means of gathering
information. The capture and publication of such images without authorisation is
prima facie an infringement of copyright.[278] In the absence of licence agreements,
therefore, publishers are limited to reliance on the defence of fair dealing for the
purpose of reporting current events, relying on the fact that a frame from a
broadcast film is not a photograph.[279] Clearly, such reliance brings with it numerous limitations on the commercial use of such images by newspapers. Given that
the defence applies only to the reporting of current events, care must be taken as
to the nature of newspaper articles accompanied by a videograbbed image. General features or documentary material on historical events, for example, unless
relevant to a current topical issue, fall outside the fair dealing provisions.[280] The
specific exclusion in s.30(2) of photographs means that publication of videograbbed images which reproduce broadcast photographs would not be subject to
the fair dealing defence, although it may be possible in certain circumstances to
rely on the defence of incidental inclusion of the image.[281] In an effort to remove
the uncertainty and limitation on use of such material occasioned by reliance
solely on the fair dealing defence, some newspaper publishers have given serious
consideration to entering into licences for publication of such images and other

---

[274] See para.26–136 above.
[275] See May 2010 press release on the NLA website.
[276] ACAP—see: *http://www.the-acap.org* [Accessed November 1, 2010].
[277] For example, "Attributor": see *http://www.attributor.com/* [Accessed November 1, 2010].
[278] CDPA 1988 s.17(4).
[279] CDPA 1988 s.4(2).
[280] In any event, a sufficient acknowledgement would be required on the reproduced image to fall
within the defence.
[281] CDPA 1988 s.31, and see paras 9–61 et seq., above.

material, such licences being increasingly offered by broadcasters as part of a general subscription service.

26–146   **Public interest defence.** The availability of a public interest defence to a claim for infringement of copyright has been the subject of consideration on at least two occasions[282] and is of particular interest to newspaper publishers and editors. It is now clear that the question must be considered in the context of an analysis of the defences available and whether these conflict with the right to freedom of expression, and that in these rare cases it is necessary to have close regard to the facts of the individual case. The court is required to apply the 1988 Act in a way that accommodates the right to freedom of expression. However, the right to freedom of expression does not normally include a right to make free use of another person's work. Where a newspaper considers it necessary to use exact extracts, it is appropriate for it to indemnify the author of such extracts or provide him with any profits that stems from the use of them. But it has been observed that since there is a clear public interest in giving effect to the right of freedom of expression, where such right overrides the rights conferred under the 1988 Act s.171(3) of that Act does permit the defence of public interest to be raised.[283]

3. THE MUSIC INDUSTRY

A. OVERVIEW

26–147   The music industry is a major cultural and economic force in the United Kingdom, and copyright and related rights provide much of the legal framework on which the industry is built. This section covers how the music market works in the United Kingdom; which copyright and related rights are relevant; how those rights are managed and licensed in various sectors of the industry; what changes are taking place in the music market that are affecting both the licensing and infringement of music-related copyrights; and what amendments to copyright and related laws are under discussion to deal with new developments in the music industry.

Music Industry Structure and Stakeholders

26–148   **(i) Market size and trends.** The music sector remains one of the many success stories amongst the United Kingdom's copyright-based industries. The United Kingdom is the third largest music market in the world, after the United States and Japan, and represents 9 per cent of the world-wide market for recorded music sales. The music industry in the United Kingdom accounts for approximately £4 billion in economic activity (measured by Gross Value Added), 31,200 businesses and 272,100 direct and related jobs.[284]

Consistent with world-wide trends,[285] sales of music on compact discs (CDs) and other physical formats have declined substantially in the United Kingdom over the past ten years, but online, mobile and broadcasting revenues as well as

---

[282] *Hyde Park Residence Ltd v Yelland* [2001] Ch. 143 and *Ashdown v Telegraph Group Ltd* [2001] EWCA Civ 1142; [2002] Ch. 149; [2002] R.P.C. 5. See paras 21–93 et seq., above.

[283] *Ashdown v Telegraph Group Ltd* [2002] Ch. 149.

[284] Department for Culture, Media and Sport, Creative Industries Economic Estimates (February 2010).

[285] Recorded music sales world-wide declined 7.2 per cent to $17bn in 2009. Global physical sales were down by 12.7 per cent to $11.9bn, but digital (internet and mobile) sales grew 9.2 per cent to $4.3bn. Digital sales thus represented 25.3 per cent of all world-wide recorded music sales at trade value in 2009 (source: IFPI).

public performance royalties have increased. Total UK revenues from sales of recorded music in 2009 amounted to £928.8 million at trade value (up 1.4 per cent
from 2008). However, there was a 6.1 per cent drop in sales of CD and other
physical formats to £739.9 million. By contrast, digital sales grew by 48.8 per
cent to £188.9m, and represented 20.3 per cent of all sales. Sales of digital singles
now account for 98 per cent of all singles sold in the United Kingdom. Internet
downloads and subscriptions outpaced mobile music sales by more than fourteen
to one. Albums as collections of related recorded music tracks remained popular,
even in the digital environment.[286]

The various UK collecting societies reported growth in overall broadcasting,
public performance and digital revenues in 2009, albeit with some declines in
mechanical, ringtones and commercial radio broadcasting revenues.[287]

(ii) Industry sectors: music publishing ("authors"), record companies ("pro-   **26–149**
ducers") and artists ("performers"). The music industry involves a broad and
complex matrix of different rights owners, roles and representatives, which must
be understood and dealt with in navigating copyright issues related to music.
There are three major groupings of music industry rights owners:

(1) Those involved in what is often called *music publishing* in the United
    Kingdom. These are the writers of song lyrics and the composers of musi-
    cal scores (often denominated "authors" internationally), and their various
    representatives including music publisher firms (large "major" companies
    and smaller independent music publishers) and licensing societies (PRS
    for Music and MCPS in the United Kingdom). Those involved in the
    music publishing business deal with various copyrights in the underlying
    musical composition and lyrics of a song, that is, the relevant musical and
    literary works.

(2) *Record companies.* Record companies own or manage rights in audio
    recordings of performances of the underlying musical and literary works.
    Like music publisher firms, record companies also comprise large "ma-
    jor" firms and smaller independent companies. Record companies can
    perform a wide range of different roles, and typically have principal
    responsibility for marketing and promoting recorded music. Sound record-
    ings are given protection under copyright in the United Kingdom,[288] but
    are subject to analogous "neighbouring" or "related" rights in continental
    European countries. Record companies' rights are typically called "pro-
    ducers' rights" in international copyright treaties and EU copyright
    legislation; this should not be confused with the role of individual "record
    producers" who might be involved in overseeing the development of a
    particular recording.[289]

(3) *Artists.* The artist who performs a musical and literary work—the well-
    known or obscure performer who sings or plays a song publicly or makes
    a recording—benefits from a separate set of rights. These are denominated
    as "performers' rights" rather than copyright as such in the United King-
    dom,[290] and are included among the "neighbouring" or "related" rights
    elsewhere. Artists can and often do have representatives that deal with
    various aspects of their careers, including relevant copyright licensing,
    such as managers and licensing societies (PPL in the United Kingdom).

---

[286] BPI, Statistical Handbook (2010). Recorded music sales in the UK amounted to £1,355.9 million
    at retail value in 2009 (the same as in 2008). Artist albums accounted for 88.9 per cent of digital
    recorded music sales in the UK.
[287] Source: BPI, PRS for Music, PPL, IFPI
[288] CDPA 1988 s.1(1)(b).
[289] See para.26–191 below.
[290] CDPA 1988 ss.182–184.

In a particular case, these roles may all be embodied in the same person: a performing artist may also be the songwriter and make his own recording, retaining all of the various rights that someone wanting to use the music might need to clear. More commonly, however, several different people or firms may own or manage the different rights that need to be cleared with respect to any particular use ("exploitation") of music. The use of a piece of music in a broadcast programme, for example, typically involves the songwriter's or music publisher's rights in the underlying music and lyrics, a record company's rights in the particular recording, and the artist's performer's rights. A variety of different representatives—publishers, sub-publishers, licensing societies, producers, managers and others described in this section—often handle various aspects of the licensing of these rights. Ownership or licensing responsibility for the different sets of rights may be held by different parties from country to country.

The industry has a long history of now-familiar agreements covering all aspects of the inter-relationships between the various music industry participants, and for the assignment or licensing of others to use these copyright and related rights. The explosion in cross-border activity that the internet and other new media services have heralded, the licensing, accounting and payment challenges resulting from large numbers of digital transactions and the financial pressures under which the music industry has laboured in recent years have all been catalysts for ongoing changes to the music industry's business and licensing practices, as outlined in this section.

26–150   **(iii) Majors and independents.** The industry has been characterised by a limited number of multinational companies that control the so-called "major" music publishing companies which own and/or exploit musical and literary works, and the "major" record companies which own and/or exploit sound recordings.[291] The major music publishers (EMI, Sony/ATV, Universal and Warner/Chappell) accounted for approximately 67.9 per cent of the UK music publishing market in 2009, and the major record companies (EMI, Sony Music (formerly Sony BMG), Universal and Warner Music) accounted for an approximate 81.4 per cent market share of recorded music sales in the United Kingdom in 2009, according to published album-related statistics.[292] These companies own large catalogues of copyright works and sound recordings and generally operate on such a scale as to afford them advantages in terms of marketing, promotion and distribution, both domestically and internationally, and the ability to lobby for changes to industry practice and applicable legislation.

A wide range of independent music publishers and independent record companies compete with the majors in the United Kingdom, and promote themselves on the basis that they offer a distinctive "indie" approach, can be more responsive to new forms of music and may be able to offer more flexible contract terms. More than thirty-five independent record companies, led by such companies as XL Beggars, Union Square, Domino Recordings, Cooking Vinyl, Ministry of Sound/Hed Kandi, Dirtee Stank, Demon and Sanctuary, appear on published reports listing significant sales of music singles and albums.

26–151   **(iv) Representative body.** UK Music is a cross-industry alliance that represents a broad spectrum of the music business nationally.[293] Its members include groups

---

[291] There has been a trend of consolidation in the industry over the past several years.
[292] Music & Copyright, April 18, 2009; BPI.
[293] UK Music, British Music House, 26 Berners Street, London, W1T 3LR. Tel.: 020 7306 4446, fax: 020 7306 4449, website: *http://www.ukmusic.org* [Accessed November 1, 2010]. UK Music is headed by Feargal Sharkey (CEO) and Andy Heath (Chairman).

from all of the industry sectors.[294] UK Music engages in public policy and lobbying, public communications and public awareness, research and analysis, and industry relevant education and skills training on behalf of the wider industry.

Industry Changes and Related Copyright Developments

The music industry historically has profited from the introduction of new forms of exploitation and advances in technology. For example, the introduction of digital sound recordings in the form of compact discs in the 1980s was responsible for a substantial growth in industry revenues. Perhaps perversely, the ubiquity of compact disc digital recordings combined with the widespread use of personal computers and the connectivity provided by the internet has resulted in a dramatic challenge to the music industry and the legal framework within which it operates.

26–152

Since the late 1990s, the music industry has witnessed a global decline in sales of physical copies of sound recordings, a growth in alternative forms of personal entertainment, and an increase in the means and scale of high-quality copying and distribution of music without authorisation or payment—activities engaged in not only by counterfeiting and on-line enterprises for financial gain, but also by consumers themselves.

Despite these difficulties, legitimate means for the exploitation of music in various new media are showing promise. Industry practice and the applicable laws are adapting to recognise new forms of exploitation and to develop the licensing regimes necessary to allow them to flourish. Many "digital issues" are now largely settled and routine, for example, the delineation and application of copyright rights to online and mobile uses of music, the inclusion of digital uses in the industry's various agreements, and the licensing of a variety of digital uses by rights owners and their collection societies.

It is likely that there will be further changes to established industry practices and relevant copyright and other legislation as new means for the delivery and exploitation of music continue to spread. The end of this section outlines developments in these areas.

B. Music Publishing

The copyrights in musical and literary works were the earliest of the rights related to the music industry to have been recognised, and are the underlying rights on which much of the industry is built. With the exception of works that are in the public domain, practically any commercial or public exploitation of sound recordings or performances requires a licence of the copyright in the underlying musical and literary works that are embodied in those recordings or performed by the performers. The fact that these rights endure for the life of the author plus 70 years—the longest period of protection afforded to any of the rights examined in this section—means that the vast majority of works that are the subject of commercial exploitation remain in copyright, with the notable exception of most classical compositions written before the twentieth century.

26–153

Most of the major sources of income in the music publishing sector are reliant on performances being made of the relevant copyright works, which performances are either live or, more typically, fixed and further exploited in the form of sound recordings. The principal forms of exploitation and relevant copyright rights in music publishing are as follows:

---

[294] UK Music members include the Association of Independent Music (AIM), the British Academy of Songwriters, Composers & Authors (BASCA), BPI (British Recorded Music Industry) Limited, PRS for Music, the Music Managers Forum (MMF), the Music Producers Guild (MPG), the Music Publishers Association Limited (MPA), the Musicians Union (MU) and Phonographic Performance Limited (PPL).

(i) the copying and issuing of copies to the public of the works in sheet-music form;

(ii) the public performance of the works[295];

(iii) the manufacture for distribution and sale to the public of physical copies of audio or audio-visual recordings of the works (which involves both copying and issuing of copies to the public)[296];

(iv) the communication and making available to the public of the works[297] (which may also involve copying and issuing copies of the works);

(v) the inclusion or combination of the works in or with other copyright works or goods or services[298] (which involves copying and may also involve the issuing of copies to the public, making an adaptation and/or exercising other rights in the work).

First Owner of Copyright

26–154   The copyright in a musical or literary work will ordinarily vest on creation in the composer or lyricist, usually referred to in the popular music business as the songwriter or simply the writer.[299] Typically, key rights in the relevant copyrights will be regulated by one or more agreements with collecting societies if the works have been the subject of any commercial exploitation or the writer has had previous success.[300] A writer may also enter into a publishing agreement with a music publisher which will regulate the writer's copyrights and may also regulate certain of the writer's services.[301] The writer and, to the extent applicable, the collecting societies and/or publisher will own, control and/or administer the rights in the copyright work.

Authors' Collecting Societies

26–155   Writers and the publishers that they appoint typically rely on collecting societies to license the exploitation of certain of their rights. The key rights in this context are the right to publicly perform a musical or literary work,[302] the right to communicate that work to the public[303] and the right to reproduce and issue to the public copies of that work, including in the form of copies in audio or audio-visual recordings such as compact discs.[304] The collective licensing of these rights enables many types of exploitation that would be practically and economically impossible if clearances from individual writers and publishers had to be negotiated on each occasion.

The majority of UK writers will seek to become members of the Performing

---

[295] This may take the form of live performances or the playing in public of sound recordings embodying the relevant works.

[296] This predominantly comprises traditional audio products (such as compact discs) released by record companies and consisting of commercial sound recordings, but also includes embodiments of the works in other formats including DVDs, CD-ROMs and promotional sound carriers distributed with other goods or services.

[297] This includes traditional radio and television broadcasting as well as the more recent forms of communication and making available to the public, ranging from on-line streaming of music to the making available of music for download by means of telecommunication devices and networks.

[298] This includes the synchronisation of the works with moving images such as films, advertisements and computer games.

[299] For exceptions to first ownership of copyright see paras 5–08 et seq., above.

[300] As to collecting societies, see para.26–155, below.

[301] As to music publishers, see para.26–157, below.

[302] CDPA 1988 s.16(1)(c).

[303] CDPA 1988 s.16(1)(d).

[304] CDPA 1988 s.16(1)(a) and (b).

Rights Society ("PRS"), whose operating company is Performing Right Society Limited and which trades under the name PRS for Music.[305] By joining they assign to PRS their so-called "performing rights", being the right to authorise the public performance and communication to the public of their copyright works. PRS operates a number of licensing schemes, the most important of which are licences offered to broadcasters (including radio and television), venues where live or other public performances take place (including live venues, clubs, bars and retailers), and licences to operators of music services in new media.[306] Tariffs are set after consultation with licensees but are subject to referral to the Copyright Tribunal.[307] PRS makes quarterly distributions of the monies it receives from licensees after deducting an administration charge. Distributions are apportioned between writers based on information included in accounts or returns PRS receives from its licensees.[308]

A writer or publishing company may also appoint a collecting society to issue so called "mechanical" licences on its behalf. In the United Kingdom the relevant collecting society to license the reproduction of music for physical products is the Mechanical-Copyright Protection Society Limited ("MCPS"), which together with PRS also trades under the name PRS for Music.[309] MCPS acts as an agent in respect of these "mechanical" rights, unlike the PRS which benefits from a full assignment of its members' "performing" rights.

MCPS operates a range of licensing schemes, the most important of which is the licensing of the rights to manufacture and distribute physical audio or audio-visual products in many formats including CD, video and DVD. Different schemes apply to different forms of distribution so that, for example, retail sales are licensed differently from products given away with other goods or services, such as compact discs distributed with newspapers or magazines. MCPS charges a commission for its services on a variety of different scales. The terms upon which MCPS grants licences vary between different licensing schemes; these are approved by MCPS board and subject to review by the UK Copyright Tribunal.[310] A writer or publisher does not have to appoint MCPS as its agent. It could issue or refuse to issue licences itself for some or all of the works in its catalogue. However, once a writer or publisher has appointed the collecting society as its agent, whilst it may reserve some rights to itself, the primary task of issuing mechanical licences will then fall to the collecting society.

Details of the current tariffs and terms of the various types of PRS and MCPS

---

[305] PRS for Music, Copyright House, 29–33 Berners Street, London, W1T 3AB. Tel.: 020 7580 5544, fax: 020 7306 4455, website: *http://www.prsformusic.com* [Accessed November 1, 2010].

[306] These include streaming and download services offered via the internet or mobile telephone.

[307] As to the Copyright Tribunal see paras 28–81 et seq., below.

[308] The level of detail in returns will depend on the licensee. Major licensees including broadcasters such as the BBC and large live venues are typically required to submit a complete list of all copyright works broadcast or publicly performed. Medium-sized licensees are only required to provide samples, and very small licensees may be exempt from submitting returns.

[309] The contact details for MCPS are the same as for PRS for Music, see para.26–155, above.

[310] MCPS's current scheme for licensing the manufacture of commercial, physical audio product has been approved by the Copyright Tribunal. The scheme provides for payment of a fixed percentage of the dealer price (presently 8.5%) or if unavailable the retail price (presently 6.5%) of the record in question. The MCPS/PRS first combined licence for various online and mobile download and streaming services (the "Joint Online Licence") was challenged in the Copyright Tribunal in July 2007. MCPS/PRS had initially sought a headline royalty rate of 12% of gross retail revenues for such services, temporarily discounted to 8%. The Tribunal approved tariffs of 8% of gross revenues for on-demand music services, 6.5% for interactive webcasting services, and 5.75% for non-interactive webcasting, subject to certain minimums. The BPI, mobile telecommunication companies and iTunes had settled most of their issues with the MCPS/PRS, including applicable rates (8% for on-demand services, and 6.5% for non-interactive services) in September 2006. The Tribunal decision resolved remaining issues with respect to the definition of gross revenues and the internet music service providers' objections to the rates. See *BPI v MCPS/PRS*, No. CT84–90/05 (Copyright Tribunal, July 19, 2007; [2008] E.M.L.R. 5).

licences, and how to apply for a licence, are listed on the PRS for Music website.[311]

26–156   Authors' collecting societies similar to the PRS and the MCPS operate in most territories of the world. In many cases there is one single society that licenses both the performing right and the reproduction right, for example GEMA in Germany.[312] These societies offer similar licensing schemes with respect to writers' and publishers' reproduction, public performance and other rights. The collecting societies have detailed reciprocal agreements that permit each society to license the repertoire of the other affiliated societies in its local territory, ensuring relevant licences include not only local repertoire but a vast body of copyrights from around the world.

Whilst public performance and national broadcast rights are generally licensed from the society in the territory in which the public performance or broadcast takes place, collecting societies (particularly within the European Union) compete with each other to offer favourable terms to the major international record companies for mechanical reproduction rights. These competitive terms have encouraged major record companies to deal directly with one European society for all of their European manufacturing licences.[313] Attempts to expand such "one-stop shopping" to cross-border activities have proved one of the most difficult challenges for the collective licensing of new digital services, however.[314]

Publishers

26–157   Commercially successful composers and lyricists will typically enter into an agreement with a music publisher to administer various aspects of their rights in original music and lyrics as well as their services as writers.

The music publisher may be a "major" international company with branches or affiliated group companies in all countries where the songs are likely to be exploited. Such a company is more likely to be in a position to administer copyrights on an international basis through its networks of overseas companies in an economic and efficient manner. Through intra-group arrangements these companies specify how much of the locally generated income a local affiliate may retain and enable relatively speedy accounting of income to UK composers and lyricists.[315] The network of international affiliates also means that to the extent that profits are made at a local level, such profits benefit the group as a whole. The size of these companies and their inter-company arrangements usually enable a major international music publisher to offer higher advances and calculate royalties due to the songwriter on an "at-source" basis.[316]

Smaller, independent music publishers may only have a presence in a limited number of countries or indeed only in the United Kingdom. In order to be able to

---

[311] *http://www.prsformusic.com/users/Pages/default.aspx* [Accessed November 1, 2010].

[312] Gesellschaft für Musikalische Aufführungs und Mechanische Vervielfältigungsrechte.

[313] For example, in July 2004 Universal Group's recording arm, which previously had a European mechanical central licence deal with MCPS, entered into a three-year agreement with the Belgian publishers' society SABAM instead.

[314] See para.26–210, below.

[315] Foreign accounting arrangements have a definite impact on the speed in which a writer is paid. For example, a sub-publisher in Germany may account to the UK music publisher every six months, accounting for example for income received in the period January 1 to June 30 within 90 days, i.e. by September 30. Assuming the UK music publisher also accounts to the writer at the same six-monthly intervals, the income received in the UK on September 30 is finally paid through to the writer on March 30 of the following year, i.e. 90 days after December 31. Thus it can take a year or more for the income to reach the songwriter. If the UK publisher received accounting quarterly within 60 days the writer would be accounted to 6 months earlier.

[316] As to "at source", see para.26–166, below.

exploit songs and collect revenue in other countries, such music publishers may enter into "sub-publishing" agreements with music publishers in various countries. These arrangements are generally on arms-length, commercial terms under which the UK publisher and its composers and lyricists may not benefit from profits retained by the sub-publisher, and thus may realise lower receipts from foreign territories than those that might be achieved by a local affiliate of a major UK publisher. Smaller music publishers may calculate royalties for their composers and lyricists on a "receipts"[317] rather than an "at-source" basis. Smaller publishers promote themselves as being more "writer friendly" and, since they generally control smaller catalogues, more determined to secure exploitation of and full accounting for the copyrights they administer.

Publishing Agreements

Agreements for a composer or lyricist to license or assign copyrights in musical and literary works to a music publisher vary significantly. This section will be limited to an examination of several types of agreements whereby substantially all of the rights of the owner of copyright are assigned or exclusively licensed to a publisher.[318] A licence may be for the world or a specified territory, and for the life of copyright[319] or for a shorter period. Outlined here are the typical types of matters covered in (i) an exclusive songwriter agreement, (ii) a single song assignment, (iii) an administration agreement, (iv) a commissioning agreement, and (v) a library music agreement.[320] The publisher or owner of the relevant rights may also enter into a variety of other agreements with third parties for specific forms of exploitation, for example, the printing of sheet music.   **26–158**

Types of agreement

(i) Exclusive Songwriter Agreement. An exclusive songwriter agreement regulates a common form of relationship between a writer and a publisher. In addition to effecting the assignment of existing and/or future copyrights to the publisher, this type of agreement grants the publisher exclusive rights over the writer's services and the products thereof during the term of the agreement.   **26–159**

The term of an exclusive songwriter agreement may be for a fixed contract period but it is commonly for a period that extends by reference to a specified event.[321] This event is typically the fulfilment of a minimum requirement known as the "minimum commitment". A writer's minimum commitment will vary depending on the circumstances and the relative bargaining power of the writer and publisher. It is common for the agreement to include options to extend the term by further contract periods each of equal or similar length to the initial period. The publisher will not usually have more than three such options (four contract periods in total). The options are generally only exercisable by the publishing company.

For a writer who is not also a performer able to record his songs for a record company which is able to procure a commercial release, a fixed contract period with no minimum commitment may be more appropriate. If there is a minimum commitment, it is likely to be that the writer writes a specified number of songs.

---

[317] As to "receipts", see para.26–166, below.

[318] As to the distinction between licences and assignments, see paras 5–204 to 5–206, above.

[319] As to duration of copyright, see Ch.6, above.

[320] For a detailed discussion of publishing agreements, see *Bagehot & Kanaar on Music Business Agreements* 3rd edn (London: Sweet & Maxwell, 2009).

[321] The period will often be for a minimum of 1 year, and the extension will normally be capped so as not to exceed 3 to 5 years.

There may be no requirement that the songs be commercially exploited, or there may be a requirement that a minimum number of them be exploited.[322]

For a so-called "singer songwriter",[323] the minimum commitment may entail a requirement not only that the writer write and deliver a number of new and original songs but also that these be commercially released as audio recordings. In order to fulfil the minimum commitment the publisher might require that these songs be included in an album,[324] and that they be sufficient in number to enable the publisher to collect a minimum percentage of the total mechanical royalties payable in respect of that album. This percentage varies, with a typical range being between 50 and 100 per cent, but it may be less, particularly if the writer is one of several in a band and can therefore only hope to control a low percentage of the works embodied in an album.

Where the writer is a member of a group of performing artists, the publisher may seek to enter into one exclusive agreement with all members of the group whereby the writers' obligations (including any minimum commitments) would be joint and several. A well-drafted agreement will also cover how the rights of parties will be dealt with if one or more members leave the group. There is a balance to be negotiated between the desire of the publishing company to protect its investment by retaining exclusive rights over all the writers, and the interests of the writers who may well wish to ensure that the agreement applies in a manner that reflects any changes to the group.[325]

26–160   **(ii) Single Song.** This type of agreement typically does not include any rights over a songwriter's services, or a minimum commitment. The single-song assignment or licence provides for an assignment or licence of the copyright to the music publisher of one or more specified songs (or a part thereof). This is typically done in return for an entitlement to receive a royalty and, in some cases, an advance against those royalties.

26–161   **(iii) Administration.** This type of agreement is intended to grant rights to administer the copyright in certain songs. These rights may be granted to an administrator by a songwriter, publisher (typically a small publisher) or other owner or licensee of the relevant copyrights, principally so that the administrator may effect the registration of the songs with all relevant collecting societies and collect any income generated by exploitation of the works. This may take the form of an assignment or licence of copyright, but sometimes consists solely of an appointment of the administrator as an agent on behalf of the copyright owner.

It is unusual for the administrator actively to seek additional exploitation for these songs or to be obliged to do so. The percentage of income retained by the administrator is typically less than that retained by a publisher under other publishing agreements,[326] which is reflected in the fact that there is rarely an advance paid under such agreements.

The administration agreement must be distinguished from a sub-publishing agreement. A sub-publishing agreement usually grants the sub-publisher materially all of the rights that the publisher has in certain songs albeit usually for a limited territory or duration. An advance may be payable against royalties in a

---

[322] This would typically include being recorded by a third party as a "cover".

[323] This could apply when a writer is also a vocalist or a musician or a member of a band.

[324] The album or "long play record" has traditionally been a more profitable format than the single, which as a format has in recent years seen a substantial drop in sales volume as well as price.

[325] Among other things to be negotiated here would be changes to the minimum commitment to reflect what may be reasonably expected from the new group and the departing members, as well as the treatment of songs that are written prior to and after any change in the group.

[326] For example, this may be 10–15% of "at source" income as opposed to the 20–30% that a publisher would expect to retain under an exclusive publishing agreement.

sub-publishing agreement, and there is usually an obligation on the sub-publisher to do more than merely administer the songs. A sub-publisher usually retains a larger percentage of income than an administrator.[327]

(iv) Commissioning Agreement. This type of agreement is similar in many ways to a songwriter agreement but is specific to a particular project such as a film or theatrical production. The commissioning agreement will not normally include a requirement of exclusivity but will include very specific requirements for the writing and delivery by the writer of the material required for the relevant project. The term will be linked to the delivery of the commissioned works. Delivery requirements will typically include the making and delivery or the overseeing of the making of recordings of the relevant copyright works.

26–162

(v) Library Music. This type of agreement generally assigns rights in specified works and compositions together with recordings thereof to a library music publisher primarily for the purpose of exploitation in conjunction with audio-visual productions, although increasingly library music agreements are non-exclusive licences. Library music (which includes both sound recordings and the underlying works) is typically available for exploitation in synchronisation with television and other audio-visual programmes without restrictions or rights of approval and is collectively licensed on standard terms making it easy to clear and therefore commercially attractive where its use is appropriate.

26–163

Rights

The publishing agreement will regulate the scope and duration of the rights granted or licensed to the publisher. The duration of the publisher's rights will vary, but the publisher will usually seek to maximise both the scope and the duration of the agreement so far as consistent with the doctrine of restraint of trade.[328] A rights period equal to the life of copyright is often sought by independent publishing companies[329] or under a commissioning agreement. The period for which a major publisher can administer the rights granted under an exclusive songwriter agreement is likely to be between 10 and 15 years following the expiry of the term of the agreement. Until the 1980s, rights periods under exclusive songwriting agreements for the life of copyright were relatively common. However, such lengthy periods are now very rare, even in the case of independent publishers.

26–164

Competition between major publishers for high-profile or desirable writers and catalogues has led to rights periods falling (in some cases significantly below 10 years after the expiry of the term of the agreement). Life of copyright remains the standard duration of rights under a commissioning or library music agreement. Under an administration agreement, it is common for the rights to be granted for periods as short as one to three years. The publisher's rights may be limited to specified territories, although this is usually resisted by publishers and rarely accepted by major international publishers.

The principal rights a publisher will seek to control are:

26–165

    (i) The exclusive right to license mechanical reproduction and the issuing of copies to the public. These rights are most commonly administered on

---

[327] This traditionally has been about 15–25% of income "at source"

[328] As to which, see paras 28–330 et seq., below.

[329] This is in the publisher's interest as it is building a catalogue of rights, which forms a valuable asset of its business.

behalf of the publisher by collecting societies such as the MCPS.[330] Licences are typically granted by such collecting societies at standard rates[331] and without a requirement for the specific consent of the publisher or the writer. It is common for a writer who is also a performer to seek to restrict the granting of a first mechanical licence by the publisher or a collecting society so that no third party may successfully apply for and obtain a mechanical licence to record a "cover" of the writer's song before the writer has had the opportunity to do so.

(ii) The exclusive right to collect income from public performance and communication to the public (but not the "grand rights"[332]). These rights are, however, almost always devolved to performing right societies such as PRS.[333] If the writer is a member of PRS, the publisher takes subject to PRS's rights, and the publisher's right is limited to an entitlement to receive a proportion of the revenues distributed by PRS.[334] PRS or similar societies in turn regulate the collecting of income and the granting of licences by centrally negotiated "blanket" licence schemes with licensees, including broadcasters, live venues and, more recently, new-media services. Under a blanket licence a collecting society's entire repertoire is licensed, and neither the publisher nor the writer exercises any rights of approval over particular licensees or licence terms.

(iii) The exclusive right to grant licences to synchronise the works with visual images, notably for films and other audio-visual works. Some synchronisation licences are granted under licence schemes administered by collecting societies,[335] but the most commercially significant of these licences[336] are granted directly by the publisher on terms negotiated by the publisher and often subject to a writer's approval.

(iv) The exclusive right to reproduce the song graphically and to license that reproduction. This includes the right to publish or license the publication of sheet music. This right is particularly important in the context of classical music where the publisher licenses and is paid for the various sheet music "parts" printed for orchestras. A writer will rarely be entitled to exercise a right of approval over the exercise by the publisher of this right.

(v) The exclusive right to authorise alterations, adaptations, translations and the use of extracts of a song.[337] A writer will commonly seek to be entitled to exercise rights of approval over material alterations to a work or the granting of clearances for "sampling".

(vi) The exclusive right to authorise public performance outside the scope of collecting society licensing. This consists of "grand rights" exploitation,

---

[330] As to collecting societies, see paras 26–165 to 26–166, above, and Ch.27, below.

[331] The rates applied in the UK have been reviewed and approved by the Copyright Tribunal and are currently 8.5% of the "dealer price". See para.26–176, below. In other territories there are similar standard rates established by agreement between industry bodies or by law.

[332] As to grand rights see para.26–165 at (vi), below.

[333] As to the PRS, see para.26–155, above.

[334] A writer's membership of PRS assigns to PRS exclusively the public performance and communication to the public rights of the writer. The PRS's membership rules prevent a writer from assigning these rights to a publisher and restrict the amount of income the publisher may claim directly from PRS to 50% of the relevant income. This 50% of PRS income is commonly referred to as the "publisher's share" and the other 50% is referred to as the "writer's share".

[335] Major UK broadcasters such as the BBC benefit under their blanket licences from a synchronisation licence for their own productions for limited uses such as recordings of live performances and background use.

[336] These include licences for the inclusion of songs in motion pictures, advertisements and computer games.

[337] This could include authorisation of the inclusion of a sample of the work in another work or of the use of the title of the song or an extract from it.

namely the right to publicly perform the work as part of a theatrical production where the work is being performed in a dramatico-musical
context. A writer will typically seek to approve grand rights exploitation.

Remuneration

It is common for a publisher to pay a writer advances under an exclusive song-   **26–166**
writer agreement.[338] The amount of such advance will depend on a combination
of three factors, namely the anticipated income from the relevant songs (which
may not yet be written), the songwriter's bargaining power (this will often depend
on the number of publishers competing to sign the writer) and the publisher's
budget. Different amounts may be payable by way of advance during the term of
a publishing agreement. These will often be linked to certain events, most commonly one or more of (i) the signature of the agreement; (ii) the exercise by the
publisher of options to extend the term; and (iii) the satisfaction of a minimum
commitment for a particular contract period. The amounts of such advances may
either be specified in the publishing agreement or, for option periods, may be
determined by means of a formula, such as a percentage of the revenue generated
from previous songs subject to minimum and maximum amounts.[339] Advances
paid under publishing agreements are typically recoupable from the writer's
share of any income under the publishing agreement but are generally not repayable by the writer. The publisher bears the risk that insufficient income may be
generated from exploitation of the songs to recoup the advances and any other
recoupable payments they may have made under the agreement.

Subject to recoupment of any advances (if applicable), a publishing agreement
will regulate the payment of royalties and other remuneration to the songwriter.
There are two fundamentally different bases on which royalties are usually
calculated: an "at source" basis and a "receipts" basis. In an "at source" agreement, the royalties are calculated on the basis of the gross amounts generated by
the exploitation of the songs net only of certain very limited deductions. These
deductions are typically limited to sales taxes, fees paid to collecting societies for
actually collecting in the income[340] and fees paid to arrangers and translators on
industry standard terms. In a "receipts" agreement, the publisher pays the royalty
on the basis of an amount which is equal to the "at source" amount but after
deduction of other costs or amounts retained by third parties including amounts
retained by sub-publishers or licensees. The royalty rate itself will vary from one
agreement to another and from one form of exploitation to another.[341]

The publishing agreement should also set out how the income is to be accounted for, in what form and how regularly. Typically, an accounting will be
made every six months.

Representative Bodies

The main organisation in the United Kingdom that represents the interests of   **26–167**

---

[338] Advances may equally be payable under any other publishing agreement.
[339] This is referred to as a "mini-max" formula.
[340] As to collecting societies, see Ch.27, below.
[341] A songwriter could expect to receive, from a UK music publisher, a royalty for most forms of
exploitation of between 60 and 80%. In a commissioning agreement this rate is likely to be in the
region of 50%, and in an administration agreement the rights owner will receive as much as between 85 and 95%. Different considerations apply to publishing agreements outside the UK,
where percentages as low as 50% are not uncommon. Lower percentages also tend to apply to
publishing agreements in the classical music field. The royalty rate in respect of library music is
typically 50% of receipts in respect of all income except income collected by PRS where the
publisher typically receives the 50% "publisher's share" and the writer collects directly the 50%
"writer's share" from PRS (as to the writer's share and publisher's share see para.26–165, fn.335).

songwriters is the British Academy of Songwriters, Composers and Authors (BASCA).[342] BASCA was founded in 1947 as the Songwriters Guild. It represents the interests of contemporary songwriters and is represented on the boards of industry bodies such as PRS, MCPS and UK Music. BASCA runs regular legal and creative workshops, sponsors annual awards and competitions, and makes available professional advice and standard agreements to members.

The Music Publishers Association (MPA) represents UK music publishers.[343] On behalf of publishers and the writers signed to them, the MPA lobbies the government and represents publishers to the music industry more generally, as well as to the media and the public. MPA provides a variety of services, information and training courses to members, and also administers International Standard Music Numbers for the identification of songs.

British Music Rights acted as the lobbying arm of the music publishing sector until October 2008, when it was dissolved into the pan-industry organisation UK Music.[344]

C. THE RECORDING BUSINESS

26–168   Under copyright law, a sound recording is a fixation of a performance of a musical and/or literary work. There is a copyright in a sound recording itself that is separate from and additional to the copyrights in the underlying musical and literary works (compositions and lyrics) and any rights in the performances that are embodied in the sound recording.[345] Creation and exploitation of rights in a sound recording do require, however, that any underlying publishing and performance rights are also cleared or are capable of being cleared.

This right to control the exploitation of a sound recording is at the heart of a record company's business. The principal forms of exploitation of sound recordings and the relevant copyright rights are:

(i) the public performance of the sound recordings[346];

(ii) the manufacture for distribution and sale to the public of physical copies of the recordings[347] (which involves both copying and issuing copies to the public);

(iii) the communication and making available to the public of the recordings[348] (which may also involve copying and issuing copies of the works to the public); and

(iv) the inclusion or combination of the recordings in or with other recordings or products[349] (which involves copying and may also involve the issuing of copies to the public, making an adaptation and/or exercising other rights in the work).

---

[342] British Academy of Songwriters, Composers and Authors, British Music House, 26 Berners Street, London W1T 3LR. Tel.: 020 7636 2929, fax: 020 7636 2212, website: http://www.basca.org.uk [Accessed November 1, 2010].

[343] Music Publishers Association, 6th Floor, British Music House, 26 Berners Street, London, W1T 3LR. Tel.: 020 7580 0126, fax: 020 7637 3929, website: http://www.mpaonline.org.uk [Accessed November 1, 2010].

[344] See para.26–151, above.

[345] See Ch.12, above.

[346] Unlike publishing, this does not include live performances which, by definition, do not rely on recordings. It does include the playing in public of recordings.

[347] This still predominantly takes the form of traditional audio products (such as compact discs) released by record companies and consisting of commercial sound recordings.

[348] This includes traditional radio and television broadcasting as well as the more recent forms of communication and making available to the public in various forms, from on-line streaming to the making available of downloadable files by means of telecommunication devices and networks.

[349] This includes the synchronisation of the recordings with moving images such as films, advertisements and computer games.

First Owner of Rights in a Sound Recording

The first owner of copyright in the sound recording is the "producer".[350] Under **26–169** the 1988 Act, the producer is the person by whom the arrangements necessary for the making of the sound recording are undertaken[351] and is in most circumstances the person or entity that has paid for or made available the facilities for the creation of the sound recording. Depending on the circumstances, this person may be the performer, publisher, manager, record producer or recording studio owner, but in many cases it is the record company.

Producer Collecting Societies

The owners of rights in sound recordings generally seek either to exploit or to **26–170** license reproductions of their works directly, and will generally do so only if the circumstances and commercial terms of such exploitation meet with their approval. However, they also rely on collecting societies—albeit far less extensively than writers and publishers do. The rights in sound recordings that are typically exercised collectively are the rights to publicly perform and broadcast a sound recording.[352]

In the United Kingdom those who control the copyright in commercial sound recordings typically give Phonographic Performance Limited (PPL)[353] a mandate to administer and license these particular rights collectively on their behalf. PPL operates a number of licensing schemes[354] the most important of which are licences offered to broadcasters (including radio and television), and venues where public performances take place (including clubs, bars and retailers). Tariffs are set by negotiation between licensees' representative bodies and PPL and, after deducting an administration charge, PPL distributes 50 per cent of its revenues to the owners of the copyright in the sound recordings that PPL administers and the other 50 per cent as equitable remuneration[355] to performers and/or collecting societies mandated by performers to collect such income. Distributions are based on information included in accounts or returns that PPL receives from its licensees, from which PPL determines the extent to which specific sound recordings have been exploited.

Producer collecting societies similar to PPL operate in many territories of the world, administering the rights of owners of sound recordings and/or performers with respect to public performance and broadcasts in their territories. Unlike the collecting societies representing writers and publishers, producer societies do not have a full complement of reciprocal agreements, but rights owners seeking accurate and regular payments can and generally do seek to give mandates to each local producer collecting society. It is of note that in the United States of Amer-

---

[350] CDPA 1988 s.9(2)(aa).

[351] CDPA 1988 s.178. The term "producer" as used in the context of the ownership of sound recordings should not be confused with the technical "producer", who is engaged to oversee the creation of the sound recording in the recording studio. As to record producers, see para.26–191, below.

[352] CDPA 1988 ss.19 and 20(2)(a).

[353] Phonographic Performance Ltd. (PPL), 1 Upper James Street, London, W1F 9DE. Tel.: 020 7534 1000, fax: 020 7534 1111, website: *http://www.ppluk.com* [Accessed November 1, 2010].

[354] These include radio and television (analogue and digital), cable, satellite and internet simulcasts, suppliers of jukeboxes, background music systems or music services to business sites or users and licensing premises, such as night-clubs, pubs or even an individual using music such as a dance teacher or aerobics instructor. PPL's tariffs for these various uses are listed on its website, at *http://www.ppluk.com/en/Music-Users/Playing-Music-and-Videos-In-Public/* [Accessed November 1, 2010].

[355] This is payable by the copyright owners to performers pursuant to CDPA 1988 s.182D. As to performers' rights to equitable remuneration, see para.26–185, below.

ica, owners of sound recordings and performers are not entitled to receive payment for the broadcast of recordings on radio or television at all.

PPL has substantially expanded its reciprocal arrangements with other producer collecting societies outside the United Kingdom to enable the collection of public performance, broadcast and certain online royalties in multiple territories on behalf of member record companies and performers. At the time of writing, PPL had bilateral agreements covering various licensing activities with 42 other collecting societies.[356] Some of these agreements involve arrangements authorising PPL and the other society to collect traditional broadcasting and public performance royalties on each other's behalf. So far, this has had principal relevance for independent record companies that are members of PPL but that are not members of producer collection societies in other countries.

More broadly, these agreements set up "one-stop shops" for certain internet licences valid throughout these territories. The agreements establish reciprocal representation for each participating society to license "simulcasting" (internet streaming of traditional broadcast stations' programming), as well as "webcasting" (internet-originated streaming) with some limited interactivity, in the participating territories. As approved by the European Commission, the simulcasting and webcasting tariffs are based upon the relevant tariff of the country into which each recording is streamed (the "country of destination" principle). Under these agreements there are no territorial restrictions within the European Union as to which collecting society a licensee can go to get a licence.[357] Pursuant to revised mandates from their members, PPL and other producer societies are expanding the online uses that they can license to include certain podcasts and television 'play it again' services, for example.

A separate producer collecting society, Video Performance Limited ("VPL") administers licences for audio-visual recordings for public performance and broadcast on behalf of record companies.[358] PPL and VPL tariffs are subject to review by the Copyright Tribunal.[359]

Some independent record companies license certain of their rights collectively or through "aggregators", particularly for new digital services. The independent sector established a global licensing agency Merlin in 2007 "outside the space occupied by collecting societies", through which independent record companies can jointly and non-exclusively license new media deals. Merlin explicitly excludes physical reproduction from the mandates with its members.[360]

Record Companies

26–171   A record company is typically engaged in creating and acquiring rights in sound recordings, marketing and promoting those recordings, and commercialising those recordings, primarily through the distribution of copies of those recordings

---

[356] Source: PPL.

[357] See para.28–237.

[358] Video Performance Ltd. (VPL), 1 Upper James Street, London, W1F 9DE. Tel.: 020 7534 1000, fax: 020 7534 1111, website: *http://www.ppluk.com* [Accessed November 1, 2010].

[359] Recent Copyright Tribunal reviews have overturned PPL tariffs for public houses, bars, restaurants, cafes and hotels, shops and stores, and factories and offices, and VPL tariffs for music television operator CSC Media Group Ltd. See Copyright Tribunal Cases CT 91/05, 92/05, 93/05, and 94/05. The High Court has upheld the Tribunal's decision in the PPL case but overturned its decision in the VPL case. See *Phonographic Performance Ltd v The British Hospitality Association* [2009] EWHC 209 (Ch); *CSC Media Group Ltd v Video Performance Ltd* [2010] EWHC 2094 (Ch).

[360] Merlin UK Ltd, 29-33 Berners Street, London, W1T 3AB. Tel.: 0207 436 7387, fax: 0207 183 2445, website: *http://www.merlinnetwork.org* [Accessed November 1, 2010]. Merlin also is engaged in anti-piracy activities on behalf of its members, and reported $3.5 million in annual licensing deals and settlement proceeds in August 2010 (source: AIM).

to the public in physical and digital form. Each of these aspects of a record company's business generally involves substantial costs and investment. The record industry has therefore tended to face substantially greater financial risks than the publishing industry, where a publisher's financial exposure tends to be limited to advance payments (if applicable) and overhead and administration costs.

With the advent of affordable computer-based recording facilities, it is now more feasible for performers to become producers themselves, making high-quality sound recordings at home or in rented studio facilities at relatively low cost. They may want to promote and distribute their recordings themselves on the internet, or may employ others to carry out various manufacturing, promotion or distribution activities. The lower potential barriers to entry and the potential of online marketing and distribution have helped some artists to launch their careers and many to promote digital or physical sales of their recordings.[361] These developments have meant, however, that an even larger number of recordings are competing for consumers' attention and purchase decisions, leaving record companies' substantial marketing and promotion capabilities as an attractive option for many performers as they seek commercial success.

In order to exploit sound recordings a record company must:

- acquire rights in sound recordings. This is achieved either by virtue of the record company being the first owner of rights in those sound recordings or by acquiring the relevant rights pursuant to an assignment or licence;
- clear the underlying rights in the songs that are embodied in the sound recordings it controls for the forms of exploitation it intends to undertake. The most important of these rights, the rights to copy and issue copies to the public (termed "mechanical" rights), are typically available at standard rates through MCPS or an equivalent collecting society; and
- secure the consents it requires from the performers whose performances are embodied in the sound recording. This is typically done pursuant to a recording agreement with the featured performers by reference to whom the recordings will be marketed and, in the case of non-featured performers, agreements securing the consent of those performers or those administering their rights.[362]

Acquiring Rights in Recordings—Exclusive Recording Agreements

Due to the level of investment that is often required in order to create, promote, market and distribute sound recordings, a record company will generally seek to enter into exclusive arrangements with the performer or group of performers whose performances it intends to record and/or commercially release and by reference to whom those recordings will be marketed and promoted.[363] These agreements tend to regulate exclusively such performer's entire recording output during the term of the agreement. The record company will usually seek to ensure that the recording agreement confirms that the rights in the resulting recordings will vest in the record company as first owner of copyright and to the extent that any such rights vest in the performer that such rights are assigned to the record company.

26–172

---

[361] For example, the artist Gnarls Barkley achieved a number one status with the single "Crazy" before the release of the recording in physical format. The artists The Arctic Monkeys achieved the highest ever number of first week album sales in the UK with their first album, in part as the result of building a reputation through online communities such as *myspace.com*.

[362] As to agreements with performers see paras 26–172 to 26–177, below.

[363] This is to be distinguished from circumstances where record labels acquire the rights in specified recordings by assignment or licence of those recordings. For a description of such agreements see paras 26–178 to 26–181, below.

Exclusivity, Term and Minimum Commitment

26–173   A recording contract will generally seek to govern exclusively for a period of time the performers' rights in recordings. Generally the record company will seek to control all such recordings but where a performer operates in different and distinct genres of music or under distinct and different professional names, the record company may occasionally limit the scope of the recording agreement to one genre or one title, leaving the performer free to enter into separate agreements in relation to the excluded category of performances. This is generally resisted by record companies, however, which prefer to control all of a performer's output in all genres exclusively.

The term of an agreement will typically be for an initial period which is linked in duration to the required minimum commitment. There will usually be options exercisable by the record company to extend the term by further contract periods of equal length.[364]

The performer will in most cases be required to deliver to the record company a minimum number of recordings of performances in each contract period. The minimum commitment for each contract period is typically the recording and delivery of a new studio-recorded album[365] although the commitment for the initial period may consist of one or more singles. Each contract period is usually extendible by the record company until a fixed period of time after the delivery[366] or release of the minimum commitment for that period. The record company will prefer the period to end by reference to release[367] in order to evaluate the performance of the relevant album before deciding whether to exercise its option for the next album. It is usual for a performer to seek (i) to limit the periods of extension so that each contract period is not capable of being extended indefinitely and (ii) a commitment from the record company to make the recordings commercially available for sale to the public within a fixed period of time from delivery.[368]

A number of high-profile cases culminating in the *George Michael* case[369] brought significant changes to the way that record contracts operate. After the decisions in the *Gilbert O'Sullivan*[370] and *Holly Johnson*[371] cases, recording agreements that tied a performer to one company exclusively for up to seven or eight albums became open to criticism as being unreasonably restrictive. Record companies have too much invested to risk having an unenforceable contract and, as a result, recording agreements in the United Kingdom now tend to be for a maximum of far fewer albums, typically four or less. In the classical music field, long-term deals are uncommon. A conductor or soloist will occasionally sign a "tie-in" deal for a two or three album series of a particular type of music. "Popular" classical performers, who are perceived as having the commercial potential to cross over from the classical music market into the mainstream marketplace, often have recording contracts similar to those of pop performers.

---

[364] For a detailed discussion of recording contract terms, see *Bagehot & Kanaar on Music Business Agreements* 3rd edn (London: Sweet & Maxwell, 2009).

[365] Other recordings, including live recordings, will typically be agreed to belong to the record company but may not satisfy the minimum commitment. If recordings in excess of the minimum commitment are made during the term, these will also typically be subject to the recording agreement and belong to the record company.

[366] Delivery is determined by reference to the standard of the recordings. This will usually require that the recordings are technically satisfactory for manufacture of recordings for commercial sale and of a reasonable artistic standard, sometimes fixed by reference to the standard of previous recordings by that performer.

[367] Between three and six months after release is common.

[368] A period of between three and six months is common. This is referred to as the "release commitment".

[369] *Panayiotou v Sony Music Entertainment (UK) Ltd* [1994] E.M.L.R 229.

[370] *O'Sullivan v Management Agency and Music Ltd* [1985] Q.B. 428.

[371] *Zang Tumb Tuum Records Ltd v Holly Johnson* [1993] E.M.L.R. 61.

In the case of a group of performers, the recording contract may make provision for the possibility that the group may decide to cease performing together either because one or more leave the group or the entire group disbands. As occurs in publishing agreements,[372] the record company will seek to protect its investment by securing options to continued exclusivity not only over those performers who remain in the group but also individuals who leave. The continued use of the professional name of the group also is a matter of fundamental importance not only to the group but also to the record company since it is often central to the promotion of the group and its recordings. Well-negotiated contracts therefore cover not only the record company's rights to the performers' services and how the group name is dealt with but also the manner of division of income from recordings made before and after any change to the group has occurred.

Whilst major label recording agreements have for some time governed all audio or audio-visual recordings of an artist's musical performances and included requirements for the delivery of audio-visual performances in the context of promotional videos of singles, the scope of such agreements may now also include obligations to create and grant rights over a broader range of audio and audio-visual recordings and other products of the artist's services embodying the artist's name and image. This is intended to provide the record label with material that can be used in a wider variety of new media, including for example internet video streaming and mobile video ringtones. Some artists seek to retain rights over such audio-visual material.

Rights

An exclusive recording agreement will typically result in the ownership by the record company of all the rights in recordings of musical performances made by the performer during the term of the agreement, and confirm the grant to the record company of the performer's rights and consents. Such an agreement also typically restricts the performer from re-recording the songs that the performer has recorded and delivered to the record company for a period following the end of the term of the agreement.[373] Whilst the record company will wish for unfettered rights of exploitation, it is common for the agreement to provide for restrictions on certain aspects of the exploitation of the sound recordings together with obligations that the record company must honour. Restrictions or consents can relate to matters including:

   (i) artistic matters—these may relate to the choice of artwork, choice of singles, choice of producer or remixer, choice of songs for an album and their order, and/or the concept and directors of promotional videos;
   (ii) financial matters—these will typically include matters that affect the amount of advances or royalties payable to the performer, for example, amounts that may be recoupable from or reduce payments to a performer, including recording costs, remix costs and video budgets; and
   (iii) exploitation outside the context of singles or albums—performers may seek to retain approval over exploitation which is not part of the mainstream exploitation of sound recordings by the record company. These may include the right to approve synchronisation of the recordings with

26–174

---

[372] See para.26–159, above.

[373] This is intended to protect the record company against the eventuality that, after the performer has made recordings of the songs for the record label, he makes a new recording of these songs in direct competition with the record company's recordings following the expiry of the recording agreement. This restriction is typically limited to recordings that have been commercially released by the record company during or within a certain period (often one year) after the end of the term, and generally applies for a fixed period from the end of the term only (often five years).

advertisements and feature films, and/or uses in which recordings are given away or otherwise used to promote another product or service.

The featured performer will also typically seek additional agreements and undertakings from the record company. The most important of these is an obligation for the record company to pay (as applicable) advances, recording costs and royalties, and an obligation to commercially release the recordings subject to the minimum commitment. This release commitment is often limited to particular territories and in some cases only to the "home" territory of the record company.[374]

In addition to rights over the performer's recording services and the sound recordings, the exclusive recording agreement may also seek to govern the performers' rights in relation to audio-visual recordings of musical performances, and will generally grant the record company rights to require that the performer is available to make so-called promotional videos to promote the sale of the sound recordings. The agreement will usually contain obligations for the performer to make himself available to promote the product of his services. The contract will also usually place an obligation on the performer to procure that the record company will be entitled to acquire a mechanical licence from the owner of the copyright in the works to be recorded and that this licence will be available on terms accepted as standard in the industry.[375] This will be required whether or not the performer is the writer of the works to be recorded, since the record company will need such licences to release the recordings. (Note that, as described above, the MCPS and similar authors societies outside the United Kingdom have established collective licensing schemes by which such licences can be granted and administered.[376])

In a growing number of cases—particularly with new artists—record companies have also agreed with the performer to participate in the performer's other revenue streams including, for example, income from live performances and merchandise. It is also not uncommon for a record company to seek to secure rights over an artist's website or domain name.[377] Such agreements for broader revenue sharing between artists and record companies do not readily fit every artist's situation, and are resisted by many artists and their managers. Nonetheless, the BPI reported that record company income from such "360-degree deals" with artists had grown 16.7 per cent to £58.6m in 2009, as part of an overall trend of revenue growth outside of album and singles sales.[378]

Remuneration

26–175   A performer or group of performers will in most cases receive advances under an exclusive recording agreement. As with the advances payable to a writer under a publishing agreement, such advances (i) are recoupable but typically non-returnable; (ii) will vary in amount considerably; and (iii) may be payable at vari-

---

[374] A performer's remedies for a record company's failure to release may vary, but generally will include a right to terminate the agreement (and therefore any further options) and/or a right to require an assignment of the rights in the sound recordings to the performer or a right to require the record company to license the sound recordings to a third party willing to release them.

[375] As to mechanical licences, see paras 26–155 to 26–156, above.

[376] As to the MCPS and other collecting societies, see Ch.27, below, and paras 26–155 to 26–156, above.

[377] EMI Records entered into perhaps the best-known of such agreements with the artist Robbie Williams in October 2002 pursuant to which EMI and the artist invested in a joint entity entitled to a broad range of the artist's services and income. EMI entered into other early deals of this sort with the band Korn and a few artists in Asia, and Interscope struck a deal in 2003 with the Pussycat Dolls by which the two sides split the profits from all the act's ventures (source: CFOEurope.com, *The Economist*).

[378] Source: BPI.

ous points during the term[379] either in amounts fixed under the agreement or determined by a formula specified in the agreement.[380] The advances paid to a performer are either inclusive or exclusive of recording costs for the minimum commitment recordings. Whether they are inclusive or exclusive will generally depend on the circumstances, and in particular whether the performer already has access to recording facilities or wishes to control the recording process. Unless the performer has access to recording facilities of sufficient quality to deliver the minimum commitment recordings to the record company's satisfaction, the performer in an inclusive deal takes a risk that advances will either be insufficient to meet the recording costs or that there may not be a significant sum available to the performer personally after the payment of recording costs. An advance that is exclusive of recording costs is generally referred to as the "personal advance".

The performer's personal advance is typically fully recoupable from the performer's royalties. Whether other amounts are also recoupable from the performer's royalties depends on the type of royalty arrangement negotiated in the agreement. There are two principle methods of paying royalties to a performer from the exploitation of the recordings:

(i) Royalties based on the price of records. This is the method traditionally used by major record companies and larger independent record companies. Royalties from the most significant form of exploitation, being the sale of "records",[381] are calculated according to a formula by reference to the number of records sold and the price of those records. The price used is typically the "dealer price" or the "retail price" of those records.[382] In respect of exploitation other than in the form of "records"—for example use in an advertisement or motion picture—the record company will typically account to the performer for a percentage of its actual or its net receipts. Under this method of calculation the record company typically seeks to recoup from the performer's royalties the performer's advances and recording costs.[383] Other costs incurred by the record company do not, however, affect the performer's royalties. These may be substantial and include the costs of marketing, promotion, manufacture (including mechanical royalties) and distribution of recordings. Some record companies have sought to apply the royalty rate applicable to the sale of physical records to digital distribution (audio and audio-visual downloading and/or streaming),

26–176

---

[379] Most commonly the advances will be paid by reference to some or all of the following events: (i) signature of the agreement; (ii) commencement and/or completion of recording of the minimum commitment; (iii) the exercise of an option; and (iv) success milestones, including achieving certain chart positions or numbers of sales.

[380] This is often done under what is commonly known as a "mini-max" formula, which typically sets advances for option periods by reference to the royalties accrued to the artist in respect of the recordings made in the preceding contract period, subject to a minimum and a maximum amount.

[381] This includes various formats of sound recordings, with the compact disc album format still the most popular.

[382] The dealer price is usually defined as the price that distributors of records charge to retailers, and the retail price is defined as the price at which the records are sold to the public. The royalty rate payable may typically be in the range of 15% to 21% for popular music if it is calculated on the dealer price, and at a substantially lower percentage if calculated on a retail-price basis (given that retail price traditionally has been about 30% higher than dealer price). The rate itself is slightly misleading in that it is usually subject to detailed calculation provisions that seek either to reduce the base price of the records—typically for example the dealer price may be reduced by a 25% packaging deduction in the case of a CD format—or to reduce the rate itself for certain types of sales.

[383] These will typically include recording costs of any nature, including studio costs, payments to producers, engineers and session musicians, mastering costs, remix costs and video costs, although video costs are typically only partly recoupable from audio-only forms of exploitation, the remainder being recoupable from audio-visual exploitation.

whilst featured performers have tried to increase their remuneration for such digital distribution.[384]

26–177   **(ii) Royalties based on net receipts.** This basis for calculating royalties, where applied, is more often used by independent record companies and under so-called "production agreements". A production agreement commonly refers to an exclusive recording agreement entered into by a performer with a party that intends to fund the making and/or promotion of recordings in the hope of securing a licence agreement with a record company to distribute those recordings.[385] In a so called "net receipts" agreement, the performer's royalty is based on a percentage[386] of the total income derived from the relevant recordings after deduction of the total costs incurred in making and exploiting the recordings. Under this model the amounts typically recoupable from the performer's share of income are the performer's personal advances, with all other costs—including recording costs (recoupable against the artist in the alternative, above), marketing, promotion, manufacture and distribution costs (not recoupable in the alternative, above)—being deductible from gross income. A record company that traditionally has used the "net receipts" method would typically continue to use such basis of accounting in the context of new forms of exploitation.

Acquiring Rights in Recordings—Other Examples

26–178   Whilst record companies will seek to enter into exclusive recording agreements with performers in whose careers they intend to make a substantial investment, record companies and third parties also may acquire rights in sound recordings under a variety of other types of agreements:

Exclusive licences and assignments

26–179   These may be used when the party seeking to exploit the rights wishes to control them exclusively but is not the first owner. Examples include:

- a performer who makes the relevant recordings and thereby is the first owner of the rights in such recordings. The performer may seek to license rather than assign his rights in the recordings in order to provide for a reversionary interest on the expiry of the licence or to restrict the rights licensed to certain territories or certain forms of exploitation.
- an agreement for the acquisition of a catalogue of recordings by one record company from another.
- a commissioning agreement whereby recordings are made for a specific purpose and are assigned or licensed to the commissioning party. This approach is used, for example, where recorded music is commissioned by a film producer for a motion picture.

Non-exclusive licences

26–180   These may be used where the party exploiting the recordings only requires certain non-exclusive rights. Examples include recordings licensed for inclusion in a compilation, an advertisement or a computer game.

---

[384] See para.26–177, below.

[385] The royalty paid by a record company for such recordings will often be higher than the royalty it would otherwise pay since the creative and financial risk involved in the making of the recordings has already been taken. Royalties in these circumstances can be more than 20% of the dealer price.

[386] The percentage is typically 50% or more in favour of the performer, sometimes with increases up to 70% or more, particularly in later contract periods.

Non-exclusive recording agreements

With the exception of "popular" classical performers whose recordings are a **26–181**
"crossover" success, recording agreements for the creation of classical recordings rarely include exclusive rights over a performer's on-going services. It is
also common that only certain performers such as the conductor or a soloist
receive royalties from the exploitation of the recordings, with other musicians being paid session fees according to rates fixed with the Musician's Union.[387] The
royalties that are payable to "featured" classical performers are also generally
lower than those payable to pop performers. This reflects the fact that the financial
return to the record industry from classical recordings is generally lower than that
of pop records, among other things due to the smaller size of the market.

Representative Bodies

The representative bodies for UK record companies are the BPI (British Re- **26–182**
corded Music Industry Limited)[388] and the Association of Independent Music
("AIM").[389] The BPI and AIM are members of the UK Music alliance.[390]

The BPI has 400 members consisting of the four major record companies and a
few hundred independent record companies. The BPI represents its membership
in lobbying, negotiates with other organisations including the Musicians' Union
and PRS for Music, conducts anti-piracy activities and puts on the annual BRIT
Awards show. It is also an important source of industry information and statistics.
The BPI is affiliated with similar organisations in other territories through the
global umbrella organisation IFPI, the International Federation of the Phonographic Industry.[391]

AIM represents independent record companies, with over 800 independent
labels and other members—an estimated 25 per cent of the market. AIM likewise
engages in lobbying and represents its members among other industry groups,
and focuses on support, advice, information and resources to help its members'
business. The services AIM offers include legal and business affairs guidance,
master class and networking events, and guidance and support on breaking into
digital and international markets. AIM is also affiliated with similar organisations
abroad.

D. Performers

Performers were the last of the music industry's major groupings to be granted **26–183**
rights related to copyright. In this context, a "performer" includes vocalists,
musicians and conductors. Performers may perform publicly or "live" (for
example on stage), or perform for the purpose of their performances being recorded for further exploitation. Performers broadly fall into two categories,
described here as contracted (or featured) performers, and session performers. A
typical example of a contracted performer is one who is a party to an exclusive
recording agreement. A session performer is a performer who is typically engaged

---

[387] As to the Musicians' Union, see para.26–188, below.

[388] BPI (British Recorded Music Industry Ltd.), Riverside Building, County Hall, Westminster
Bridge Road, London, SE1 7JA. Tel.: 020 7803 1300, fax: 020 7803 1310, website: *http://
www.bpi.co.uk* [Accessed November 1, 2010].

[389] AIM, Lamb House, Church Street, Chiswick, London, W4 2PD. Tel.: 020 8994 5599, fax: 020
8994 5222, website: *http://www.musicindie.com* [Accessed November 1, 2010].

[390] See para.26–151, above.

[391] IFPI Secretariat, International Federation of the Phonographic Industry, 10 Piccadilly, London,
W1J 0DD. Tel.: 020 7878 7900, fax: 020 7878 7950, website: *http://www.ifpi.org* [Accessed
November 1, 2010].

for a specific performance or series of performances, more often than not on the basis of his ability rather than public renown.

Consent

26–184   Quite apart from a performer's right and ability to impose by contract any condition with respect to his performance, all performers have the right to grant or withhold their consent to certain forms of exploitation of their performance under specific rights recognised under the copyright law, including:

(i) the making of a recording of a live performance[392];

(ii) the copying of a recording of a performance (the reproduction right)[393];

(iii) the issuing of a copy of a recording of a performance to the public[394];

(iv) the making available of a recording of a performance to the public on demand.[395]

Equitable Remuneration

26–185   In addition to the right to grant or withhold consent with respect to the activities described above, a performer has a right to receive equitable remuneration from the relevant copyright owner in respect of the public performance and communication to the public of a commercially published recording of his performance, except where that communication to the public constitutes the act of a "making available" on demand.[396] Communication to the public for these purposes therefore includes all traditional forms of broadcast and any form of transmission of a recording that is akin to a broadcast—in other words where the recipient is not able to determine when and where he receives the transmission. This right to receive equitable remuneration may not be assigned by the performer except to a collecting society.[397]

Moral Rights

26–186   Performers' moral rights of paternity (the right to be identified as the performer) and of integrity (the right to object to modifications that would be prejudicial to the reputation of the performer) were introduced in the United Kingdom in 2006.[398]

Recording Rights under Exclusive Recording Agreements

26–187   It should be noted that a record company with the benefit of an exclusive recording agreement with a performer will have certain rights akin to the performers' rights by virtue of that agreement.[399]

---

[392] CDPA 1988 s.182.
[393] CDPA 1988 s.182A.
[394] CDPA 1988 s.182B.
[395] CDPA 1988 s.182CA.
[396] CDPA 1988 s.182D.
[397] CDPA 1988 s.182D(2).
[398] The Performances (Moral Rights, etc.) Regulations 2006 (SI 2006/18) enacted new ss.205C to 205N into the 1988 Act.
[399] See CDPA 1988 ss.185–188 and Ch.12, above. As to more detailed provisions usually found in exclusive recording contracts, see paras 26–172 to 26–177, above.

Clearance of Performers' Rights

The performer's consent

Consents are typically secured through a recording contract or other agreement **26–188**
with the performer, although certain consents may be implied by conduct, for
example, where a performer willingly performs in a recording studio knowing
that his performance will be recorded with the intention that the recording be
commercially exploited. In the case of featured performers subject to an exclusive
recording agreement, such agreement will typically include the broadest possible
consents in favour of the record company. Where performances are contracted
other than under an exclusive recording agreement, for example in the case of
session performances, the contract for the specific performance or recording session normally includes as a minimum the performer's consent to the exploitation
of the product of his services that is anticipated but may include the grant of all
possible consents to any form of exploitation.

The agreement with the performer regulates the remuneration payable with respect to the performance and the various forms of exploitation as to which the
consents are granted. In the case of a session musician the remuneration is usually a one-off fee. Many session performers will be members of the Musicians'
Union ("MU").[400] The MU develops minimum rates for the remuneration of its
members in respect of certain forms of exploitation of their performances.
Industry bodies often formally adopt and agree these rates by negotiation with
the MU. If, for example, a recording is made by or for a record company which is
a member of BPI, or by or for a film or TV programme producer which is a
member of Producers Alliance for Cinema and Television (PACT), the minimum
rates will be set down in collective agreements negotiated between the MU and
the BPI or PACT respectively.[401]

The MU was set up to represent the interests of performers. It has more than
32,000 musician members that work in all sectors of the industry. Besides
negotiating with major employers of musicians, the MU provides contractual,
professional and practical advice and assistance to members. Another body that
represents the interests of musicians is the Incorporated Society of Musicians
("ISM").[402] ISM has as its overall aim the promotion of the art of music and of
higher standards in the musical profession, and the provision of advice and service to its members.

The right to receive equitable remuneration

The right to equitable remuneration does not entitle performers to grant or with- **26–189**
held consent to the broadcast or public performance of their performances, but
rather to claim equitable remuneration through a collecting society.[403] PPL
income is now split to give 50 per cent of broadcast and public performance
royalties to the record companies and 50 per cent to the performers. The Copyright Tribunal has jurisdiction over any disagreement between performers and

---

[400] Musicians' Union, 60-62 Clapham Road, London, SW9 0JJ. Tel.: 020 7582 5566, fax: 020 7582
9805, website: *http://www.musiciansunion.org.uk* [Accessed November 1, 2010].
[401] The rates that the MU has negotiated with the BPI, PACT, BBC, ITV and other parties are summarised for MU members on its website. *http://www.musiciansunion.org.uk/site/cms/
contentviewarticle.asp?article=439* [Accessed November 1, 2010].
[402] Incorporated Society of Musicians (ISM), 10 Stratford Place, London, W1C 1AA. Tel.: 020 7629
4413, fax: 020 7408 1538, website: *http://www.ism.org* [Accessed November 1, 2010].
[403] CDPA 1988 s.182D.

the record companies over such remuneration.[404] PPL collects and distributes all equitable remuneration payments for all broadcasting and public performance, and certain internet uses, on behalf of performers in the United Kingdom.[405]

E. OTHER MUSIC INDUSTRY PARTICIPANTS

26–190   Beside the major groupings of copyright and related rights owners—the authors, producers and performers—a wide range of other industry participants acts in many cases on behalf of one or more of these rights owners. In carrying out their activities, these other individuals and firms may or may not acquire or administer copyrights or other rights. An overview follows of the roles and activities of some of these other music industry participants: record producers, mixers, remixers, managers and distributors.

Record Producers, Mixers, Remixers

26–191   The "record producer", mixer and remixer, traditionally viewed as being responsible for the technical aspects of making recordings, are now often recognised as much for their creative role as for their technical expertise, and in some cases more so.

The traditional role of the record producer primarily has been to oversee the recording process to ensure that sound recordings are of a standard suitable for release to the public. The producer is often also responsible for ensuring that a sound recording is completed on time and within budget and that all consents have been obtained from session performers and other contributors to the recordings.[406] Although many record producers fulfil this role, certain producers[407] have become well known for the artistic quality of their recordings. These producers may determine key creative matters and even be involved in the writing of the underlying musical works embodied in the recordings. In some cases these producers may not be technically proficient or actively involved in the organisation of recording sessions, leaving such tasks to recording studio engineers or A&R[408] co-ordinators.

The role of the record producer is usually governed by a contract with the person commissioning the making of the recordings. This is usually the record company that seeks to exploit the sound recording. The contract will usually stipulate the services required and provide that the producer must complete an agreed number of recordings for delivery to the record label. The agreement will typically require the producer to acknowledge that the record company is the "producer" (as the term is used in the 1988 Act) of the sound recording and therefore the first owner of the sound recording copyright, and will also require the producer to assign all rights in the sound recordings to the record company. This will include a grant of consent and assignment of all rights in any performances of the producer.

The remuneration payable to the record producer will be one or more of (i) a

---

[404] CDPA 1988 s.182D(4).

[405] The performers' organisations PAMRA and AURA merged into PPL following approval by the Office of Fair Trading in May 2006. PPL established a new Performer Board, which included former PAMRA and AURA directors as well as Equity and Musicians' Union representatives.

[406] As to consents, see para.26–188, above.

[407] This is particularly true in the area of pop and rhythm and blues music (R&B), where producers have become as famous as and, in some cases more important than, the featured artist.

[408] A&R refers to "Artist and Repertoire".

(non-recoupable) fee, (ii) a recoupable advance, and (iii) a royalty[409]. These amounts may or may not include some or all of the recording costs. The producer's royalty will usually be calculated and paid on the same accounting basis and at the same time as the featured performer's royalties are paid.

The record producer may or may not also be the "mixer". The mixer will usually **26–192** become involved once the performances have been recorded. A mixer is typically engaged to ensure that the sound quality of the whole recording, each individual performance and the level of volume of each of the performances relative to the others are optimised. As with record producers, some mixers have developed a reputation for achieving a particular quality of sound and are highly sought after and well remunerated. The agreement with a mixer will typically provide for the assignment of rights to the person commissioning the mix (generally the record company), with remuneration most likely to consist of a fixed fee but occasionally to include an advance and/or a royalty.[410]

A remixer is usually a record producer or mixer engaged to rework or alter a sound recording to produce a different sound. Traditionally a remixer takes the elements of the original recording and changes the quality of the sound or the arrangement to produce a recording that changes the emphasis of the relevant performances, alters the order of the performances or extends or shortens certain sections. More recently, remixers have been engaged to produce recordings that in many cases share little in common with the original recording, often using nothing more than a vocal performance or only a part of it. Depending on the degree of change, a new musical or literary copyright work may be created.[411] As a matter of practice, however, it is extremely unusual, regardless of the contribution of the remixer, for the remixer to be acknowledged as a writer or to be recognised as the owner of any new musical or literary works embodied in the remix, ownership of which is usually attributed to the writers of the works embodied in the original recording.

The contract with the remixer usually specifies that any rights in a new sound recording are assigned to the person commissioning the remix (often the record company). The remixer typically receives a one-off fee and waives any applicable moral rights. The remixer will usually be entitled to receive a credit on the packaging of the sound recordings.

Managers

A manager in this context is a representative of a performer, songwriter, producer, mixer or remixer (referred to here as the "artist"). Managers of classical performers are often referred to as agents. The precise nature of the manager's role varies from artist to artist and may include advising and assisting an artist in raising his profile, seeking opportunities and resolving differences with record companies and publishers, making arrangements for live performances and promotional appearances[412] and negotiating agreements on behalf of the artist either directly or in conjunction with a lawyer specialising in the entertainment industry. Whilst it is not essential that an artist appoint a manager, most successful artists do retain an experienced manager. **26–193**

---

[409] UK producers' royalties vary but typically range between 2 and 5% of the dealer price, depending on the standing of the producer.

[410] The royalty payable to a mixer, if any, may be in the region of 1 per cent of the dealer price and will rarely exceed 2% of the dealer price.

[411] As to the requirement of originality, see paras 3–125 to 3–149, above. The new sound recording itself will inevitably be a new copyright work.

[412] A live agent and/or tour manager may also be engaged to assist with live work.

It is common for a manager to have a formal written contract with the artist.[413] A management contract will usually deal with two key elements:

26–194   *Scope of the management contract.* The appointment of a manager is usually exclusive and will apply to a defined set of the artist's activities. The scope of activities covered may be very broad and extend to anything relating to "the entertainment industry", or may be limited to "the music industry" or even to a specific activity such as songwriting. The term of the agreement may be measured in terms of a rolling period terminable by either side on notice, a fixed term,[414] or a period determined by milestones in the artist's career.[415] The manager may be appointed for the world or for a specified territory. Even if the appointment is world-wide, an artist appointing a UK-based manager may seek to secure an option to require the appointment of a manager in North America.

26–195   *The remuneration payable to the manager.* The manager will receive a fee, commonly described as a "commission", which typically is a percentage of the artist's earnings from the activities in respect of which the manager has been appointed.[416] The manager will seek to receive commission in respect of activities carried out during the term but will also seek to ensure that the commission is payable even if the income from those activities arises after the term. The artist will seek to limit any such post-term commissions.[417] The artist may account to the manager directly. Alternatively, the manager may seek to receive the artist's income himself or may require the appointment of an accountant to receive the artist's income and to account to the manager for the manager's commission. In addition to the commission, the manager will usually also be entitled to reimbursement of certain out-of-pocket expenses incurred in the course of his services.

The UK representative body for managers is the Music Managers Forum (MMF).[418]

Distributors

26–196   In the present context, "distributors" means distributors of physical copies of sound recordings—predominantly in compact disc format—to retail outlets. Given that the sale of sound recordings is still dominated by physical products, efficient distribution systems are vital to the music industry to ensure that retail customers receive supplies of recordings. A record company's agreement with a distributor may be limited to the distribution of product manufactured by the record company or it may appoint the distributor to carry out manufacturing as well. The latter is referred to as a "production and distribution" or a "P&D" deal.

The major international record companies traditionally owned their own

---

[413] Some managers, including very successful ones, dispense with formal contracts altogether and rely simply on a relationship of trust with the artist. Of course this does not necessarily make the course of any disagreements among the manager and the artist straightforward, predictable or easily manageable.

[414] This is often between three and five years.

[415] These are often "album cycles", referring to the time from commencement of recording of an album to the end of the main promotional activity in relation to that album after its commercial release.

[416] The percentage for a United Kingdom manager has traditionally been between 15 and 25%, calculated on the basis of the artist's gross income and net only of a limited number of costs. Increasingly, however, managers' commissions are subject to limitations to particular revenue streams, greater deductions of costs, or even net income as the basis for calculation.

[417] A typical compromise may see the manager receiving commission at the full rate for a period of three years following the end of the term and at half rate for a period of three years thereafter, for example.

[418] Music Managers Forum: British Music House, 26 Berners Street, London, W1T 3LR. Tel: 020 7306 4888, website: *http://www.themmf.net* [Accessed November 1, 2010].

manufacturing and distribution companies, but now largely benefit from advantageous terms negotiated for the manufacture and distribution of their products by large manufacturers and distributors.[419] Large distributors in turn have advantageous relationships with retailers and in particular retail chains that are responsible for the sale of large volumes of the most "commercial" recorded-music products. Smaller independent record companies may have less advantageous distribution terms or may not have access to a large distributor. In some cases smaller record companies enter into agreements with small distributors that aggregate products from several independent record companies in order to create sufficient volume.

A distribution agreement normally provides for the distributor to be appointed exclusively by a record company in respect of its entire catalogue of recordings for a specified territory and for a specified period of time. It is common for a distributor to seek international distribution rights even if the distributor is based in one territory. The distributor will in those circumstances seek to export and distribute the product outside its territory through affiliated distributors in other territories or to sell product to exporters based in its home territory.

Distribution agreements grant the distributor the right to issue copies of recordings to the public and, in a P&D deal, the right to make copies of the recordings. A UK-based distributor will typically receive a percentage of the dealer price[420] in respect of recordings sold and, in addition, will charge the record company for other costs or services. These may include charges for manufacturing (in a P&D deal), charges for promotional activities, charges for storage and/or charges in respect of records distributed and then returned.

F. NEW THREATS AND NEW OPPORTUNITIES

New technologies have always had an impact on the music industry. In some **26–197** cases the impact has been profound. The invention of the means for making recordings of performances of musical works resulted in the eventual creation of a new category of "producers' rights" on which the entire recording business is built. Whilst some technologies such as the compact disc format have been embraced by the industry with great success, other developments have proved less welcome and more difficult to turn into a commercial success. The hostile reaction and legal disputes relating to the introduction of the first "tape-to-tape" recording devices are echoed in the more recent disputes that have surrounded technologies and services that facilitate the making and rapid dissemination of large quantities of unauthorised, high-quality digital copies of sound recordings.[421]

Most previous technological developments were reliant on specialised hardware, much of which was initially expensive. The time required for any technology to reach a significant market penetration often allowed the music industry and, if applicable, the law, the opportunity to develop a model for maintaining legitimate offerings. By contrast, technological advances have become much more rapid in recent years, the cost of reproduction and distribution of sound recordings has dropped dramatically, and consumers all over the world themselves have access to much of the latest technology. Much of the technology for enjoying, copying and disseminating music now relies on software

---

[419] The trend in the industry, given for example the majors' sale of their major manufacturing facilities and the sale of Sony and Warner's distribution joint venture to CINRAM, is toward outsourcing of manufacturing and distribution.

[420] This has traditionally ranged between approximately 5% and 25%, although higher and lower percentages are possible. For "dealer price", see para.26–176, above.

[421] See paras 26–198 to 26–201, below.

that is freely available and can operate on hardware that already has substantial market penetration in the western world, such as personal computers and mobile telephones.

The rapid growth of these new technologies and the speed at which they have become readily available—not only to infringers engaged in counterfeiting and piracy for profit, but also to consumers—are among the fundamental challenges that the music industry faces today. Litigation and new legislative efforts are helping to define the rights and responsibilities of various parties under copyright and related laws in the "digital age". Licensing and other practices are evolving to deal more effectively with various new-media uses of music. Finally, new technologies continue to represent an opportunity for the music industry, particularly as legitimate digital services are appearing that build on technologies once only used for unauthorised copying and dissemination of music. Each of these developments is explored in the remainder of this section.

New Threats—The Changing Face of Counterfeiting and Piracy

26–198   Counterfeiting and piracy—the unauthorised reproduction, distribution and other infringing use of copyright music and sound recordings—have always represented a challenge to the music industry. The traditional threat for the music industry was from the organised wholesale manufacture and distribution of unauthorised physical copies of music, first sheet music and then sound recordings.

The digital compact disc format allowed for counterfeit physical copies of sound recordings to be all but indistinguishable in quality from authorised copies. Whilst physical piracy of sound recordings remains a popular undertaking of commercial counterfeiters, the possibilities (in many cases the reality) of unauthorised digital copying and distribution offered by new technology are of an entirely different order. Unauthorised copying by individuals has always been a concern, but it has recently been viewed as a significant threat to the music industry's health and sustainability.

The internet and in particular the introduction of high speed or broadband access for domestic consumers[422], together with the widespread availability of hardware for the making or storage of digital copies of sound recordings[423], have made it possible for individual consumers not only to make unauthorised copies with ease but to distribute them in previously unimaginable quantities at negligible cost. So-called "file-sharing" or "peer-to-peer" ("P2P") networks[424] have made it possible for millions of individuals to copy and transmit copies of sound recordings, videos, computer games and even complete feature films.[425]

The industry has adopted several approaches over the years—with varying degrees of success and failure—to deal with the perceived threats of unauthorised copying and dissemination carried out via various technological means.

The hardware

26–199   Initial efforts were targeted at outlawing devices that allowed the copying and

---

[422] This permits the fast and cheap downloading of large audio and audio-visual files.

[423] This includes "burning" CD copies or storing such copies on a personal computer's hard-disc storage or on portable playback devices.

[424] These networks allow their users or "peers" to make available files from their own personal computers and to search the hard-drive storage and take copies of files from the computers of other users on the P2P network.

[425] In a recent quantitative online survey conducted by Harris Interactive, 23% of UK respondents aged 16–54 confirmed that they engaged in file sharing, much of it infringing. Jupiter Research has reported that approximately 21% of internet users in Europe's major markets are engaged in frequent unauthorised file sharing. Source: BPI, IFPI.

storage of digital sound recordings. In the United Kingdom, the *Amstrad* litigation targeted tape-to-tape recorders, and failed on the basis that the equipment manufacturers were not "authorising" reproduction of the works and were not joint infringers with the purchasers of their machines.[426] The similar *Sony Betamax* case brought by the film industry in the United States had failed to outlaw Betamax video recorders, on the ground that they had a "substantial non-infringing use".[427]

A decade later, the Recording Industry Association of America (RIAA)[428] attempted and failed to ban one of the early portable music devices,[429] the RIO MP3 player, which involved changing the format of sound recordings and copying them onto the device.[430] It is clear from these and other cases both in the United Kingdom and the United States that attempts to ban hardware that has legitimate as well as illegitimate applications are almost certainly doomed to failure without further evidence of the provider's control, knowledge, intention, and/or involvement in its users' infringements.

The P2P networks

Perceived by many in the music industry and other entertainment industries to be a much greater threat than stand-alone devices capable of making or storing digital copies of sound recordings or other materials, the peer-to-peer file-sharing networks were targeted next. Although it is now the name of a licensed service, Napster was the first of the peer-to-peer services that came to prominence and provided simple and effective means for its users to exchange files of copyrighted sound recordings. Napster was estimated to have had 70 million users at its peak. The original Napster was effectively shut down following a series of legal challenges in the United States, in which the court found that Napster had engaged in "contributory copyright infringement".[431] Amongst the arguments unsuccessfully advanced by Napster was a defence based on "*Sony* Betamax". However, whilst the service was capable of legitimate applications, the evidence was that it was used overwhelmingly to trade unlicensed recordings. Crucially, the service itself operated through servers under Napster's control. Napster had access to information about its users and was in a position both to monitor the exchange of files and to terminate user accounts, and thereby prevent infringement.

26–200

The following generation of peer-to-peer (P2P) networks with names like Kazaa,[432] Aimster, Blubster, Morpheus and Grokster evolved to exhibit less technical control over users' activities. These new variants eschewed centrally based directories of users in favour of decentralised networks that largely resided and operated on users' own computers. The providers of these new services argued that they had no control over users or infringements, and that they should benefit from a *Sony* Betamax-type defence on the basis that they merely supplied software to users that could have legitimate application. Despite some initial successes by such "decentralised" P2P services, copyright litigation against them has taken a very different path from earlier hardware-related cases.

---

[426] See *CBS Songs Ltd v Amstrad Consumer Electronics* [1988] A.C. 1013; [1988] R.P.C. 567.

[427] *Sony Corp of America v Universal City Studios Inc* 104 S.Ct. 774 (US S.Ct. 1984).

[428] The RIAA is the record company representative body in the United States of America.

[429] *Recording Industry Association of America Inc v Diamond Multimedia Systems Inc* 180 F.3d 1072 (US 9th Cir. 1999).

[430] MP3 refers to a common format used to encode sound recordings into digital files.

[431] These culminated in two successful applications by the recording industry in *A&M Records Inc v Napster Inc* 114 F.Supp.2d 896 (US N.D. Cal 2000) and *A&M Records Inc v Napster Inc* 239 F.3d 1004 (US 9th Cir 2001).

[432] By the end of 2002 Kazaa estimated that it had 140 million users.

Grokster. The United States Supreme Court's unanimous ruling against the P2P services Grokster and Streamcast,[433] overturned the decision of the US Court of Appeals for the Ninth Circuit and found that the P2P services could not escape liability if they *promoted* the infringement of copyright. In the view of the US Supreme Court, such promotion need not be subjective or overt to result in liability—it could be proven by the presence of more than one objective activity evidencing such promotion, including communications (e.g. soliciting infringing users), failure to prevent or curtail infringement (i.e. to filter), or profiting from the infringement. In such circumstances, actual or potentially lawful uses, even if substantial, would be no defence. This legal theory, referred to as "inducing infringement", has been used to find similar defendants liable in subsequent litigation, notably in the 2010 District Court decision involving P2P service LimeWire.[434]

Universal v Sharman. Within the Commonwealth, companies and individuals involved in the Kazaa P2P service have paid a reported US$100 million in settlement damages to record company claimants and agreed to filter their P2P service after being found liable for "authorising infringement" by the Federal Court in Australia following a protracted and costly lawsuit. Rejecting familiar "blindness" defences, the court found in September 2005 that six of the Kazaa-related respondents had "long known" that the system was "widely used" for sharing copyright files; had encouraged infringement; had offered a system the "primary", "major" or "predominant" use of which was to share infringing material; had a financial interest in maximising infringement; and had failed to take steps to prevent or curtail infringement. The court had issued an injunction ordering the Kazaa service to filter out users' infringing copies of music files. The settlement was reached prior to the court's determination of damages.[435]

Both the *Grokster* and the *Sharman* decisions indicate that the greater the service provider's control, knowledge, intention and involvement in a third party's infringement, the less likely the service will be able to avoid liability and obligations to prevent such infringement through such measures as filtering. The application of this reasoning to other types of internet-related services has begun to be explored in recent cases in the United Kingdom and elsewhere in the Commonwealth.[436]

26–201 *Individual users*. The record industry has also pursued claims against individual users of P2P networks in addition to the networks themselves. At last report, the industry had brought more than 100,000 cases—civil claims or criminal complaints—against such individuals in at least 22 countries including the United

---

[433] *MGM Studios Inc. v Grokster, Ltd.*, 545 U.S. 913 (US S.Ct. 2005).

[434] *Arista Records LLC v Lime Group LLC*, No. 06 CV 5936 (KMW) (US S.D.N.Y. May 25, 2010). In granting summary judgement for the plaintiff record companies, the court found that several LimeWire related defendants were aware of the substantial infringement being committed by LimeWire users; purposefully marketed LimeWire to individuals who were known to use file-sharing programs to share copyrighted recordings or who expressed an interest in doing so; assisted users in committing infringement; experienced business growth that depended greatly on LimeWire users' ability to commit infringement; and did not implement in a meaningful way any technological barriers or design choices to diminish infringement.

[435] See *Universal Music Australia Pty Ltd v Sharman License Holdings Ltd* [2005] F.C.A. 1242 (Australia September 5, 2005); Kazaa to pay record groups $100m, *Financial Times* (July 27, 2006).

[436] See, for example, *Twentieth Century Fox Film Corp v Newzbin Ltd* [2010] E.W.H.C. 608 (Ch) (finding premium Usenet service operator liable for authorising, procuring and engaging in a common design with respect to users' infringement); *Roadshow Films Pty Ltd v iiNet Ltd* [2010] F.C.A. 24 (Australia February 4, 2010) (finding internet service provider not engaged in authorising infringement with respect to users that infringed copyright via the BitTorrent P2P system); *L'Oreal SA v Ebay International AG* [2009] EWHC 1094 (Ch); [2009] R.P.C. 21 (finding no "procurement" of users' infringements, whether by inducement, incitement or persuasion, by online auction site eBay with respect to counterfeits sold through its service).

Kingdom. Many of these cases were settled, for an average of approximately US$2,500 each. At least nine such cases went to court in the United Kingdom, all of which resulted in judgements for the record companies. The decision in *Polydor Ltd v Brown*[437] made clear that connecting a computer to the internet, where the computer is running P2P software and where music files containing copies of copyright works are placed in a shared directory, constitutes an infringement of the copyright owner's "making available" rights by the person in control of the computer. This litigation was subject to some public criticism, but the record industry claimed that the cases produced the desired deterrent effect.[438]

New Opportunities—Legitimate New Forms of Exploitation

The online boom

In the face of substantial challenges from widespread copyright infringement, there have been some notable success stories in legitimate digital distribution and use of music, perhaps none greater than iTunes. Apple's iTunes online music download service offers 12 million licensed recorded music tracks, and has sold over ten billion tracks since its launch in April 2003.[439]   **26–202**

There are an estimated 400 legitimate online music services operating in 60 countries—more than 66 of which are available in the United Kingdom—and new ones are announced on a regular basis. Various types of digital music sales—online and mobile—have grown substantially over the past several years.[440]

(i) Download services. These permit users to receive and retain copies of sound recordings for future playback, in some cases subject to certain "digital rights management" ("DRM") restrictions. Unlike the purchase of a physical copy, the download of a digital copy can be subject to usage terms that vary among different download services. Most download services offer a combination of usage rights which may include the right to make a copy on one (or more) personal computer, one (or more) storage device or portable player, and one (or more) copy onto a recordable compact disc.   **26–203**

Some downloads are provided on the basis that they will be available to the buyer for an unlimited period of time. Some are provided on a more restricted basis. Restrictions may be by reference to a specified period of time, which might be the duration of the user's subscription with the applicable service, or some other condition.[441] In addition to the now relatively established download services for audio recordings, there has been a growth in the delivery of audio-visual

---

[437] [2005] EWHC 3191.

[438] See IFPI, Digital Music Report 2010: "Surveys have showed both in the US and Europe that these waves of well publicised legal actions had a very significant impact in raising awareness of the law on unauthorised file-sharing. Research by GfK in Europe showed that after legal actions awareness of illegality levels reached 70 per cent." Litigation against individual users does not seem to be actively pursued in the UK at the time of writing. In its response to the Government's Digital Britain report, UK Music remarked, "[W]e do not believe that the form of intervention proposed by today's Report – suing consumers – is the best way forward." (*www.ukmusic.org/policy/117-uk-music-statement-on-digital-britain*) [Accessed November 1, 2010].

[439] Apple has reportedly sold more than 275 million iPods and enjoyed an estimated 70% market share of the legitimate online music market. Source: Apple Press Release, February 25, 2010; *Financial Times*, August 5, 2009.

[440] At the time of writing, the newest type of digital music service to launch in the UK involved advertising supported offerings including Spotify and We7. Source: BPI, Pro-Music (*http://www.pro-music.org* [Accessed November 1, 2010]). As regards the level and trends of UK and world-wide digital sales, see para.26–148, above.

[441] Napster, for example, is at the time of writing offering a subscription-based service with unlimited access to streamed music so long as the subscription is paid, plus a certain number of track downloads that can be downloaded and kept permanently. Napster also offers a full "à la carte"

recordings (assisted by Apple's launch of video-enabled versions of its iPod player) as well as the development of download products such as podcasts. Podcasts consist of a downloadable audio or audio-visual programme, which may be a radio or television programme made available at the time of broadcast or posted later for download, or which may be specially created for download purposes.

26–204   **(ii) Streaming services.** These permit users to listen to a sound recording that is transmitted to their personal computer or similar device but without a copy being made for later playback. As with download services there is a wide range of streaming services. They include services ("webcasts") that are akin to traditional radio broadcasts insofar as they consist of continuous non-interactive transmissions that are communicated to all users simultaneously at the time determined by the service. Indeed, many traditional terrestrial broadcasters themselves now offer simultaneous internet transmissions (sometimes called "simulcasts") of their terrestrial broadcast programming.

At the other end of the spectrum are fully "on-demand" services in which specific sound recordings selected by the consumers are transmitted to and accessed by them at the time and place of their choosing. In between these two models lies a range of possible services that include archives of broadcast programmes that are available online to members of the public on demand, and online "radio" services that offer multiple channels aimed at different types of listeners and that in some cases even adapt to the listener's feedback and requirements. There has been a growth in streaming services in recent years, particularly with the advent of advertising supported on-demand streaming services such as Spotify and We7, available without payment of a subscription fee by the consumer.

Mobile music

26–205   Services akin to the internet downloading and streaming services described above are also available for mobile telephones. The delivery of downloads or the streaming of music via mobile telecommunication networks is a natural extension of delivery via wired and wireless internet services and evidences a further convergence of information and communication technologies. Many mobile telephones now include music storage and playback functionality similar to that of personal computers and portable digital music devices. The mobile medium offers new means of disseminating music that have already generated significant revenues for both the music industry and service providers.

There are other types of exploitation of music that are mobile phone specific:

26–206   **(i) Ringtones.** A ringtone refers to the sound made by a telephone to alert the user to an incoming call. Early offerings were referred to as monophonic ringtones, which consisted of one or a short series of single tones reproducing a melody. More advanced telephones permitted the use of so-called polyphonic ringtones. These also consisted of a series of tones but were more complex and rich in texture than a monophonic tone. As handsets developed, it became possible for mobile telephones to reproduce not just a series of electronic tones but a faithful copy of a studio recording as a ringtone. These are sometimes known as "truetones" or "mastertones".

26–207   **(ii) Ring-back.** Another similar development was so-called "ring-back" services. These allow a consumer to substitute the ringing tone normally heard by his callers with music that the consumer has selected. Despite success in some territories

---

download service under which payments are made per copy of recording purchased, and downloaded tracks can be kept permanently.

including Japan, ringback tones have not achieved a significant market in the United Kingdom.

Changes to Industry Business and Licensing Practices

Technical challenges: DRM and interoperability

One element in the music industry's transition to the digital on-line and mobile telecommunications market has been the use of technical protection measures. These offer some possibility of ensuring that once disseminated, digitised music will be secure—in other words, that the uses made of the music are the uses that have been paid for. Such technical measures in principle also allow a wider variety of different usage models to be offered at different price points. Technical measures have been implemented in different ways using various encryption and digital rights management ("DRM") technologies, which among other things can control who can access a file and/or the ways that the file can be used.[442] There have been several challenges to the use of such technologies:

26–208

  (i) No technology is impervious to "hacking". Despite the fact that hacking technologies are largely illegal,[443] any technical protection measure remains susceptible to being "cracked" by determined hackers, sometimes through the use of software designed to circumvent technical protections that has been made freely available on the internet.

 (ii) Universal standards and full interoperability among DRM and other technical protection devices and methods have not yet been achieved. Several formats are used for the encoding of files for delivery, storage and playback, and new or updated formats are implemented as they are developed. Although multi-purpose devices such as personal computers may be able to handle a variety of such technologies in ways that stand-alone devices never could, consumers, industry participants and even governments sometimes have called for better interoperability and consumer information regarding technical measures.[444]

(iii) Consumers and others sometimes complain about the use of *any* technical restrictions on the digital use of music. In the view of some, technical measures impair the consumer experience and compare unfavourably with the unrestricted use offered by pirate copies. This is sometimes an argument for improving DRM and other such technologies or making them more transparent, and sometimes for removing technical measures altogether such that every paid use is an unlimited use.

Apple iTunes initially was a DRM-protected music download service, but following a salvo from Apple CEO Steve Jobs against DRM in February 2007, Apple gradually removed technical protections from all iTunes tracks by 2009 with the consent of the record labels. EMI was the first major record company to offer DRM-free tracks for download on iTunes, announcing in April 2007 that it would offer unprotected tracks in the MP3 format.[445]

---

[442] DRM commonly restricts the number and type of storage or playback devices to which files may be copied and/or the number of times a file may be copied onto a physical format such as recordable compact disc.

[443] See CDPA ss.296 to 296ZG.

[444] The UK's Gowers Review, for example, recommended that better information on DRM be made available to consumers through such vehicles as a complaint procedure or a labelling system. No such legislation has been adopted in the UK to date.

[445] See S. Jobs, "Thoughts on Music" (February 6, 2007), *http://www.apple.com/hotnews/thoughtsonmusic/* [Accessed November 1, 2010]; EMI and Apple agree iTunes music deal,

Business and licensing challenges

26–209   As described above, the music industry has traditionally been both highly organised and relatively regimented in terms of the agreements entered into by the various rights owners and the licensing models that each uses. New media technologies have challenged the established business models and relationships between publishers, record companies, performers, collecting societies, distributors and retailers. New forms of exploitation also have raised particular challenges as to the way in which rights are licensed between various industry participants, and licensed to new-media services and users.

26–210   **(i) Music publishing.** The music publishing sector has generally embraced new media exploitation enthusiastically, and has sought, principally through collecting societies, to make licences available for most mainstream forms of new media exploitation. For example, ringtones have been licensed with success by authors' collecting societies for several years.[446] Indeed, writers and publishers have sometimes benefited from new forms of exploitation in circumstances where others have not.

Cross-border licensing of internet-based and other new-media services has been an on-going challenge for the music publishing sector. Given that these services do not readily recognise geographical boundaries, national authors' collecting societies have tried various ways of delivering writers' and composers' rights to their counterpart societies in other countries, such that each might license the repertoire of the others to new-media services in their country, and potentially offer multi-territorial licences (i.e. become "one-stop shops") for new-media services operating in multiple territories. The European Commission has challenged these societies' arrangements twice to date, and changes that have been implemented in the wake of such challenges have resulted in cross-border licensing that remains piecemeal.

In the first instance, PRS and MCPS entered into multilateral agreements (the "Santiago" and "Barcelona" agreements in 2000 and 2001, respectively) with performing and mechanical rights societies in other countries with the principal aim of making it possible for collecting societies to license each other's repertoire to services based in their own territory, even if those services disseminated music to users based outside the territory. The publishers' collection societies let their multi-territorial reciprocal licensing system for internet-based activities lapse, however, following the European Commission's Statement of Objections in 2001 to the effect that these agreements contained anti-competitive territorial and membership restrictions.[447]

Some early attempts by record companies and music services to secure Europe-wide licences for digital distribution from one sole authors' collecting society met with strong resistance from the other societies. The Universal record company agreed with the Belgian society SABAM to clear publishing rights for online and mobile activities Europe-wide in 2003. In a complaint filed with the European Commission in 2004, however, Universal alleged that the other societies punished SABAM for "breaking rank", with some major publishers and societies reportedly threatening to withdraw rights from SABAM, and the French society SACEM suing Universal in 2004 for failing to secure those rights in

---

Financial Times, April 1, 2007). EMI's arrangement with iTunes was initially to offer higher-quality DRM-free files at a 20p premium.

[446] Publishing income from digital uses of music has continued to rise. In 2009 PRS for Music realised revenues of £30.4 million for online music uses, a 72.7% increase over the previous year, although ringtone income declined 56.1% to £2.5 million. Source: PRS for Music, "Expanding Music's Frontiers" (2010).

[447] See para.28–238, below.

France.[448] The Commission did not take any action or make any allegation of illegal activity on the part of the collection societies in response to the complaint,
and the Universal/SABAM deal lapsed.

Online music services eMusic and Beatport experienced similar difficulties
when they tried to clear Europe-wide publishing rights through the Netherlands
authors' society Buma/Stemra. After eMusic sought a pan-European licence
from Buma in 2006: "[MCPS/PRS] made it clear to eMusic and to Dutch collecting society Buma/Stemra that it (Buma/Stemra) is not able to grant such a pan-
European licence since it does not have the MCPS or PRS rights to do so." In
2008, PRS took legal action in court in the Netherlands and secured an injunction
against Buma's announced pan-European licence to Beatport.[449]

The European Commission challenged authors societies' licensing practices
again in the context of RTL's and Music Choice Europe's EU competition complaint against these societies' traditional reciprocal agreements covering "communication to the public". The complainants had sought pan-European public-
performance licences for traditional broadcasting, in particular, cable and satellite
transmissions, and objected to restrictions in the societies' reciprocal agreements
that they alleged precluded EU-wide licences. The allegations were later
expanded to include claims that the societies also were restricting membership
and licensing territories in ways that discouraged competitive pan-European
licensing of on-line services.

In July 2008, the Commission found that EU competition law was violated by
provisions in the societies' agreements that (1) limited membership to nationals
of a society's own country, (2) granted exclusive licences to other societies with
respect to those societies' own territory, and (3) granted licences to other societies limited only to those societies' own territory in a concerted practice that
reinforced national monopolies. The Commission ordered the societies to end
such practices immediately. The societies have appealed against this decision to
the European Court of First Instance.[450]

Some pan-EU licensing is underway. MCPS/PRS and GEMA announced an
agreement with EMI Music Publishing whereby these two national societies
would have mandates for and license EMI's Anglo-American catalogue for on-
line and mobile usage Europe-wide through a joint venture called CELAS.[451]
Universal Music Publishing has entered into a similar arrangement called DEAL
(Direct European Administration and Licensing) with SACEM in France, and
Warner/Chappell has organised a similar agreement with a group of at least seven
European societies including PRS for Music under an arrangement called PEDL
(Pan-European Licensing (PEDL).[452] Independent publishers recently have been
offered the possibility of pan-European licensing of their works through the
IMPEL initiative developed by PRS for Music.[453]

These arrangements potentially involve full or partial withdrawals of the
publisher's licensing mandates from some European publishers' societies and the
giving of those mandates to the selected society or societies, resulting in the
set-up of a "one-stop" shop at least with respect to the particular catalogue of that

---

[448] See Universal Files Antitrust Complaint Against Euro Collecting Agencies, Billboard (October 22, 2005).
[449] Music Week, August 22, 2008; "MCPS-PRS Rebukes eMusic's Pan-Europe System", Billboard.biz (September 15, 2006).
[450] Commission decision relating to a proceeding under art.81 of the EC Treaty and art. 53 of the EEA Agreement, Case COMP/C2/38.698 (July 16, 2008), appealed, *CISAC v Commission* (T–442/08) (Eur.Ct. October 3, 2008).
[451] Source: PRS for Music.
[452] Warner/Chappell adds new name to Euro initiative, *Music Week* (October 21, 2009); Midem: Universal and SACEM name DEAL, *Music Week* (January 19, 2009).
[453] PRS for Music, "Indy publishers and PRS for Music launch IMPEL" (January 25, 2010).

particular publisher. The practical but perhaps unintended consequence of the European Commission's legal challenges and the industry licensing developments to date, however, has been effectively to eliminate a true "one-stop shop" where a multinational online music service might secure publishing licences to cover all repertoire and all of its activities throughout Europe. Pan-EU online services must typically clear public performance (not to mention relevant mechanical) rights country-by-country with national authors' societies. Given that some publishers have entered into separate deals with different societies, and that individual writers not represented by those publishers still largely belong only to their national collecting societies, *additional* "stops" are being added to the publishers' "multi-stop shopping" for multi-territorial online licences at present.

The publisher societies' tariffs for digital services have also been the subject of debate, negotiation and, in some cases, litigation in several key markets including the United Kingdom, Denmark, Germany and the United States.[454]

26–211   **(ii) The record companies**

The changes brought about by the advent of new digital media do not seem to have diminished the industry's need for substantial investment and expertise in the development, marketing and promotion of recorded music—a role that remains fulfilled largely by record companies. Considering the investments that remain necessary to launch successful artists, and recent declines in income from physical sales that have not yet been recovered through digital sales, record companies have explored other ways of generating revenues including "360-degree deals" and other revenue sharing with artists, as described above.[455]

Licensing practices also have evolved among record companies such that the producer collecting societies have been given mandates to license "simulcasting" and "webcasting" streaming services. Record companies largely license the whole range of downloading and interactive digital services directly. In some cases independent record labels have banded together—through aggregators or their Merlin licensing agency—to license downloading and other interactive services.[456]

26–212   **(iii) Performers**

Performers have enthusiastically embraced new media in all of its forms. One of the issues that digital distribution of recordings of their performances has raised is the basis and the amount of remuneration that performers receive from new forms of exploitation.

In a traditional recording agreement, for example, it has been common for the royalty payable to an artist for the sale of recordings to be a percentage of the "dealer price".[457] One question has been whether the licence fee or price charged by record companies in the context of online or mobile distribution of downloads is treated as a *de facto* "dealer price" for that form of distribution. The traditional dealer price of a CD on which an artist's royalty is calculated is not subject to any deduction for elements of cost that are absorbed by the record company, such as mechanical licence fees, manufacturing costs and distribution fees. Given that some of these costs are now commonly absorbed by the on-line or mobile distributor, the net result may be that record companies will realise a greater percentage

---

[454] The record companies' and music service providers' challenge to an early MCPS/PRS combined licence for various online and mobile download and streaming services was resolved by a September 2006 settlement with the record companies and a July 2007 interim decision of the Copyright Tribunal with respect to other parties and issues. (See para.26–155, above.)

[455] See para.26–174, above.

[456] See para.26–170, above.

[457] As to dealer price, see para.26–176, above.

of the "dealer price" from non-physical sales than physical sales, whilst the performer might see the same or a smaller[458] percentage.

Featured performers have sought to increase the remuneration that they receive under recording agreements, particularly with respect to new digital uses. The Music Managers Forum has taken out advertisements in the industry and national press, and made a submission to the Government's Gowers Review consultation, to the effect that performers' remuneration should be raised for digital uses, given the lower attendant manufacturing and distribution costs. Record companies have argued, among other things, that digital distribution has its own costs, and that it benefits from all of the record companies' other activities in artist and repertoire development, marketing, promotion and physical distribution, and thus does not merit a different royalty treatment.[459]

Some performers are as a matter of practice relatively unaffected by new technology. Performers' exclusive rights to grant or withhold their consent to the "making available" of recordings of their performances[460]—which covers download services, interactive streaming and similar "on demand" digital uses—are typically assigned or licensed when recordings are made. As with performers' other exclusive rights, remuneration is paid for these activities under the terms of the relevant contract. The performers' equitable remuneration rights do not cover such activities or provide a separate basis for remuneration.

(iv) Distributors and retailers

26–213

As the industry has changed, traditional distributors and retailers have been among the most severely affected as physical sales have declined, digital piracy has grown and new forms of digital distribution have taken hold. Having well-respected brand names has helped some traditional retailers to launch online music services, but their traditional "bricks-and-mortar" strengths of geographic location and investment in infrastructure for the delivery of physical products have given them little advantage in the new media market. New distributors and retailers have stepped into digital delivery. Traditional "record shops" have seen poor profitability, diversification into other businesses (notably video and games), mergers and closures.

Iconic US music retailer Tower Records filed for Ch.11 bankruptcy protection in 2004 and sold or shut its UK stores, citing illegal music downloading as one of the main causes.[461] Zavvi, which took over Virgin Megastores in a management buy-out in 2007, went into administration shortly thereafter and survives principally as the brand of The Hut Group's online shop that sells physical music CDs and a wide variety of other entertainment and consumer products.[462] The HMV chain of records stores is promoting more sales of games and other entertainment products given lacklustre sales of CDs, but has launched HMV Digital offering downloads of music and audio books.[463]

---

[458] Some recording agreements provide for the reduction of royalty rates from new formats or for a high "packaging deduction" to be applied to reduce the dealer price for new formats.

[459] At the time of writing, this debate has not been resolved, given the difficulty of reaching solutions with respect to new media that are both equitable in the current market and "future-proof". See paras 27–176 to 27–177, above.

[460] CDPA 1988 s.182CA.

[461] Source: BBC, February 9, 2004.

[462] Zavvi saw music sales drop from 40% to 31% of its business almost immediately after it purchased Virgin Megastores, and went into administration in December 2008. The Zavvi brand was sold to the Hut Group in March 2009. (Source: *Financial Times*, March 3, 2009; December 24, 2008; January 2, 2008.)

[463] Website: *http://www.hmvdigital.com* [Accessed November 1, 2010]. HMV chief executive Simon Fox has pointed to downloading and other new ways of consuming music as putting pressure on traditional retail traffic. (Source: *Financial Times*, July 2, 2008; BBC, June 28, 2007.)

Legislative Proposals and Changes

26–214   The major changes to copyright and related laws that were needed to deal with new media uses of music—principally to provide new "making available" rights with respect to on-demand activities; to protect digital rights management and other technical measures for managing digital distribution and use; and to define the liabilities of third-party services that transmit, cache or host infringing material posted by their users—are by now reasonably well defined and understood.

Consideration of further possible changes to legislation and practice has been under way in five major areas over the past several years. Some of these issues have arisen principally, although not exclusively, with respect to digital uses of music. Many of these issues were outlined in the Gowers Review of Intellectual Property, commissioned by the Treasury and released in December 2006. The Government has conducted various consultations on these issues, which remain under review. The European Union has also engaged in stakeholder dialogues and has promised legislative proposals in some of these areas. The issues are as follows.

(i) Term extension

26–215   Under European and UK legislation at present, sound recording producers' and performers' rights are protected for 50 years from the date of fixation of the performance, whilst other rights owners typically enjoy protection in their works for the life of the author plus 70 years.[464] Although the Gowers Report rejected the notion of extending the term of producers' and performers' rights, the House of Commons Culture, Media and Sport Committee and subsequently the Secretary of State for Culture, Media and Sport accepted by late 2008 that "there is a case for extending the term to a period of something like 70 years".[465]

On April 23, 2009, the European Parliament adopted an amended EU proposal that would extend music producers' and performers' rights within the European Union to 70 years after fixation of a performance. A "use it or lose it" rule would return assigned copyrights to performers in the event the producer did not continue publishing the recording after the initial 50 years, and to the public domain if the performers did not publish it either. A new technical rule would harmonise the term of the underlying musical copyright (70 years after the last of all composers and lyricists dies).[466] This proposal remains under discussion among the United Kingdom and other EU Member States meeting as the European Council, in consultation with the European Commission.

(ii) Exceptions to protection

26–216   **Private copying.** The United Kingdom at present does not have an exception for "private copying" of musical works or sound recordings along the lines of exceptions in most other EU countries. The Gowers Review recommended a "format shifting" exception to allow for the copying of such works from, for example,

---

[464] CDPA 1988 ss.12–15A, 191.

[465] The Committee's May 2007 report "New Media and the Creative Industries" endorsed extending the term of copyright for sound recordings and performers. The Government initially announced on July 17, 2007, that it would follow the Gowers recommendations and not support such an extension (source: Department of Culture, Media and Sport), but Culture Minister Andy Burnham backtracked and announced "A moral case for extending copyright" at the end of 2008 (source: *Financial Times*, December 15, 2008).

[466] Proposal for a European Parliament and Council Directive amending Directive 2006/116/EC of the European Parliament and of the Council on the term of protection of copyright and related rights (July 16, 2008).

compact discs to digital music players, subject to compensation that would be deemed to have been included in the price of products purchased following the date such an exception is adopted. The music industry has reached broad consensus that it would support a narrow copyright exception for private "format shifting" of legitimate CDs to portable digital music devices. This would be subject to collective licensing and payment of negotiated licence fees by manufacturers and distributors of devices "substantially used or marketed for making copies of music".[467] No format shifting or other private copying exception has been proposed or endorsed by the Government to date.

Other exceptions and limitations. The European Commission has announced that it will propose a new Directive on "orphan works", which it defines as works that are still in copyright but whose owners cannot be identified or located. This is contemplated as a way of "facilitat[ing] the digitisation and dissemination of cultural works in Europe."[468] A proposal for an orphan works registry, conditional licensing (subject to a diligent search being made for the owner) and collection of royalties in respect of orphan works was included in the 2010 UK Digital Economy Bill but was not enacted. "Orphan works" issues are expected to have relatively little relevance in the music industry, given that most musical works and recordings already contain notices of copyright ownership, and the industry and its collection societies maintain large databases of information about the rights owners of music and sound recording works.

26–217

(iii) Collective licensing

Concerns over difficulties in cross-border licensing of music for digital uses has led the European Commission to convene various "stakeholder dialogues" among rights owners, collecting societies and digital services to try to address such issues. A recent EU "Licensing Roundtable" convened by the Commission's competition directorate concluded with a joint statement of the various participants to pursue new EU-wide licensing platforms, to adhere to transparent, non-discriminatory licensing criteria, and to develop a common framework for exchanging rights ownership information.[469]

26–218

The Commission also plans to propose a directive on collective rights management to expand online access to copyrighted material and to address the governance, transparency and pan-European licensing of collection societies.

(iv) Copyright enforcement

Damages. Rules about damages, including damages for infringement of music and other copyrights, have been the subject of a consultation by the UK Department of Constitutional Affairs, now the Ministry of Justice. The Ministry's report proposed not to provide any additional remedies of exemplary or pre-established damages (as sought by copyright owners), but rather to rename "additional damages" as "aggravated and restitutionary damages" and to clarify that corporate claimants are entitled to such damages. The Ministry promised further consider-

26–219

---

[467] Source: Music Business Group, Response to UKIPO Consultation on Copyright Exceptions, *http://www.mpaonline.org.uk/files/pdf/MBG_Formatshifting_Response_-_FINAL.pdf* [Accessed November 1, 2010].

[468] European Commission, A Digital Agenda for Europe, Communication from the Commission to the European Parliament, the Council, the European Economic and Social Committee and the Committee of the Regions, COM(2010) 245, pp.9, 37 (May 19, 2010); European Commission, Copyright in the Knowledge Economy COM(2009) 532 final (December 2009).

[469] General principles for the online distribution of music, October 20, 2009, *http://ec.europa.eu/competition/sectors/media/joint_statement_1.pdf* [Accessed November 1, 2010].

ation as to whether appropriate civil or criminal sanctions should be introduced for situations in which licences have not been acquired prior to use.[470] None of these changes has been introduced into legislation at the time of writing.

26–220   EU Observatory. The European Commission has set up the European Observatory on Counterfeiting and Piracy to bring government officials, consumers and the private sector together to develop more effective means of combating copyright piracy. The group's work is focussed on collecting better statistics on the problem, identifying best practice enforcement strategies and techniques, and promoting better public awareness. The Observatory's legal experts' group has conducted several studies to date on various legal issues relating to anti-piracy enforcement among all EU Member States.[471]

(v) ISP co-operation

**26–221   **One of the highest and most heavily debated priorities of the music industry has been to address online infringement, in particular widespread peer-to-peer infringements among internet users, through increased co-operation from internet service providers. European and UK rules under the E-Commerce Directive have produced reasonably settled mechanisms among rights owners and ISPs for "notice and take-down" of infringements on-line where the ISP is "hosting" infringing materials posted by its users. With respect to P2P infringements, however, there has been far less consensus between rights owners and ISPs about how to proceed, given that the ISP's role has been largely considered to be that of a "mere conduit".[472]

Under a Memorandum of Understanding entered into between the BPI and other rights owner representatives and five ISPs in 2008,[473] approximately 50,000 notices were sent to the ISPs for onward forwarding to subscribers whose accounts had been alleged by rights owners to have been used for P2P infringement of music copyrights.

When in force, new provisions introduced by the Digital Economy Act 2010[474] will enshrine this practice into law and impose other requirements on rights owners and ISPs. An ISP will be required to notify a subscriber when it has received a report from a rights owner to the effect that the subscriber's account has allegedly been used for copyright infringement. The Act also requires ISPs to maintain records and provide anonymised "copyright infringement lists" of subscribers who have been sent a number of such notices above a certain threshold. Details of the subscribers to which such anonymous information relates will only be available by court order in legal proceedings brought by the rights owners. Details of the specific procedures, cost sharing and other requirements of this system remain to

---

[470] Ministry of Justice, The Law on Damages: Response to Consultation (July 1, 2009), *http://www.justice.gov.uk/consultations/docs/law-damages-response.pdf* [Accessed November 1, 2010].

[471] *http://ec.europa.eu/internal_market/iprenforcement/observatory/index_en.htm* [Accessed November 1, 2010].

[472] Electronic Commerce (EC Directive) Regulations 2002 (SI 2002/2013) arts 17–29, See Vol.2 B10.i and paras 21–105 to 21–107, above.

[473] Joint Memorandum of Understanding on an Approach to Reduce Unlawful File-Sharing, Annex F, Department for Business, Innovation and Skills, Consultation on Legislation to Address Illicit Peer-To-Peer (P2P) File-Sharing (June 16, 2009), *http://www.bis.gov.uk/assets/biscore/corporate/docs/migrated-consultations/consultation-legislation-p2p-filesharing.pdf* [Accessed November 1, 2010].

[474] See the amendments made to the Communications Act 2003 by the Digital Economy Act 2010 s. 24, in Vol.2 B11.ii.

be worked out.[475] ISPs British Telecom and Talk Talk have brought court proceedings in the High Court seeking a judicial review of this legislation.[476] The music industry continues to promote these sorts of "graduated response" mechanisms to address P2P infringement.

4. THE FILM INDUSTRY

A. THE GENERAL NATURE OF THE INDUSTRY

Background. Although the world's economies slid into recession in 2009, in the United Kingdom the film industry appeared to buck the trend. There were 174 million cinema admissions (the second highest figure since 1971) and £944 million was taken at the UK box office. This is partly explained by Harry Potter, the advent of 3D productions and the increasing number of digital cinemas (365— more than any other European country).   **26–222**

Buoyed by the weakness of sterling, total film production activity in the United Kingdom rose in 2009 to £957 million (2008: £613 million), of which £753 million represented spend in the United Kingdom on 32 "inward investment" films (2008: £357 million). These are films originating overseas but filmed mainly in the United Kingdom. However, the number of UK indigenous or "domestic" films declined from 77 to 71 and the production spend to £169 million (2008: £207 million). The median budgets for such domestic films fell to £1.5 million (2008: £1.7 million) and these productions continue to find it difficult to secure finance in the marketplace and suffer from the ongoing low numbers of international co-productions. By way of a benchmark, the comparable number of domestic films intended for theatrical exhibition (feature-length, otherwise known as "feature" films) in 2003 was 170.

Nevertheless, the industry remains a major employer—42,500 people, of whom 25,500 work in film and video production—and clearly attracts significant inward investment. Moreover, these bald statistics do not include those films made overseas, particularly in Hollywood, where writers, directors or actors from the United Kingdom make a contribution to any film.

In these circumstances it was surprising that the Secretary of State for Culture, Media and Sport should announce in July 2010 that the Government would abolish the United Kingdom Film Council ("UKFC"), which incidentally supplies these statistics. The UKFC distributes national lottery funding for film (£26 million in 2010). The task of distributing this money and its other functions will be transferred elsewhere but the future for other government funding for film (£25 million in 2010) was unclear.

Film-making. There are three stages involved in turning an initial idea into a film which is exhibited in theatres, on television screens and exploited in various DVD[477] and other formats around the world: development, production and distribution. Each stage raises different copyright issues. Film creation is a collaborative process in which artistic and technical contributions are made by many people. As a general rule, the director is responsible for refining the screenplay,[478] taking charge of filming the scenes and editing the footage shot into the completed work. The producer is responsible for raising the funding, engaging the director,

---

[475] See paras 21–301 et seq., above.
[476] T. Bradshaw, "Broadband providers contest Digital Economy Act", *Financial Times* (July 8, 2010).
[477] "DVD" or digital versatile disc has replaced video cassette as the home-viewing format of choice. In 2009 the UK DVD market was estimated to be worth US$2 billion.
[478] "Screenplay" is the script for the film including dialogue and scene directions.

camera crew and actors and arranging distribution of the completed work. The following outline is intended to simplify what can be an extremely intricate process involving creation by collaboration.

(i) Development

26–223   The development of a film includes all the activity on the part of the producer which is necessary to prepare a film project for the production stage. It consists of:

(a) acquisition of the necessary rights in any literary or dramatic work on which the film is to be based; this may be a novel or play (usually referred to as an "underlying work"), a story outline or "treatment" upon which a screenplay might be based, or simply a screenplay itself;

(b) engaging personnel required at the development stage, for example the writer of the screenplay, then the casting director who will conduct auditions for the actors;

(c) creation of works necessary to make the film, e.g. screenplay, production or costume designs;

(d) scouting possible filming locations and negotiating for use of studio facilities;

(e) preparation of a production budget and shooting schedule, financing plan and cash-flow schedule.

Development finance for the above may be provided by a film distributor, a broadcaster or the UKFC. In return for this, the financier will usually expect to take an assignment by way of security or a charge over the producer's rights in any underlying work and the copyright in works and other materials created for the film project.[479] Unless the development financier is also financing the production of the film,[480] these rights will be reassigned to the producer once all sums lent by the development financier have been repaid.[481]

(ii) Production

26–224   Production itself can be divided into three phases. First, there is *pre-production*, which involves activities such as storyboarding,[482] casting, engaging the production crew, set building, hire or manufacture of costumes and props and securing locations or studios. Next is the *production* phase, commonly referred to as "principal photography". During this phase, in addition to the filming or "shooting", prints are taken from each section of negative that has been shot to create the "rushes".[483] Additional scenes may be filmed by a second unit, often away from the principal location. The soundtrack is recorded, usually towards the end. Lastly, during the *post-production* phase at a studio, the editing, dubbing and recording of any voice-overs are undertaken, music and sound effects are added, and a scene may be reshot if appropriate. The first version of the film assembled during post-production is commonly called the "rough cut". The second is called

---

[479] For mortgages and charges of copyright, see paras 5–194 et seq., above.

[480] See Production, paras 26–244 et seq., below.

[481] Some development financiers have been known to require credit and an ongoing financial participation.

[482] A "storyboard" is a plot outline.

[483] "Rushes" are the prints of all material which has been filmed, which are viewed on a daily basis by the director in order to ensure the quality of what has been filmed and that no retakes are required. Digital technology is facilitating greater use of shooting on high definition (HD) videotape, although celluloid remains the technology of choice at present. Computer-generated imagery (CGI) is of increasingly wider application.

the "director's cut", which is the version delivered by the director to the producer. Thereafter the producer will make such changes as he may wish, or be permitted, to make before delivering the final version (or "final cut") to one or more distributors.

The decision whether or not to proceed with production will usually depend upon whether someone can be found to finance the budget for that production. Frequently the development financier will also finance all or part of production, so retaining his investment and any rights previously acquired in the project. The producer will charge a producing fee to the budget and will receive a share (typically 50 per cent) of any eventual profits derived following the recoupment from receipts of the cost of marketing and production of the film.

The producer may, before commencement of principal photography, agree to sell rights in the film by way of pre-sale to a theatrical or DVD distributor or broadcaster. The distributor will acquire certain rights of exploitation in the film once it has taken delivery of materials from the producer. In return the distributor will pay an advance on account of receipts from the exploitation of the film which advance will be paid on or by reference to delivery.

In order to fund the costs of production of the film, the producer may seek bank finance which can be raised against the security of completed distribution agreements which provide for the payment of an advance on a date certain. In return for a fee and an interest margin, the bank will usually agree to advance funds on the strength of bankable distribution agreements coupled with additional security over the copyright and other rights in the film.

The circumstances surrounding the manufacture of props for the first of the "Star Wars" films were considered by the courts in *Lucasfilm Ltd v Ainsworth*.[484] The props in question were various uniforms worn by several of the characters. Even though the claimant film producer had supplied drawings and a clay model to the prop manufacturer, this part of the producer's claim for copyright infringement did not succeed. It was held that the props were not artistic works, being neither sculptures, nor works of artistic craftsmanship.

An investor or the financier of a film will usually require a security interest, often **26-225** by a mortgage of the copyright in the film and in the underlying rights, together with the benefit of the agreements entered into by the production company. This arrangement will result in ownership of the copyright in the film being assigned to the financier by way of security only and therefore subject to reassignment to the producer on repayment of the loan. The documentation may afford certain rights of approval but a bank will typically not wish to become involved in creative aspects of the project. It will not want to exercise any of those rights except in extreme circumstances.

In addition to the sources of repayment, the bank considering the financing of a film will need to consider the security which is available and is being offered to it by the producer. While the bank may require a fixed and floating charge over the assets of the production company, in many cases the independent production company may have no other assets than the film being produced. The bank will need to look for repayment of its loan to the distribution agreements concluded by the producer and the advances payable under those agreements, together with its security over the copyright in the film and other rights and the benefit of insurance (such as a completion bond).[485] If a number of financiers are involved in the financing of a film, each will require a security interest over the production company and/or the film. The priority and enforcement procedures for their respective security interests will be dealt with in an intercreditor agreement.

---

[484] [2008] EWHC 1878 (Ch); on appeal [2010] F.S.R. 10.
[485] As to completion bonds, see para.26–261, below.

The production agreement between the producer and the financier will not merely involve provision of production finance, the grant of rights and the taking of security. It will also be concerned with such issues as the financier's approval rights, liability for cost overruns, ownership or sale of any artwork or props, allocation of any budgetary underspend, insurances (with particular reference to the financier's interest in payment of any claim), administration of the production account, entitlements to credits and the producer's delivery obligations.

26–226   **Producer Tax Credits.** In his budget in March 2005 the Chancellor of the Exchequer announced that the Government would replace the previous film tax reliefs with a new regime targeted directly at filmmakers. Chapter 3 of the Finance Act 2006 reformed the taxation of the film industry and introduced a new tax relief for the production of "British" films. The new provisions were brought into force from January 1, 2007.[486] The new film tax credit is available for films that (i) commenced principal photography on or after January 1, 2007; or (ii) commenced principal photography before January 1, 2007 but were still uncompleted on that date (subject to meeting the conditions listed in (a), (b) and (c) below). This replaces the relief previously available under s.42 of the Finance (No.2) Act 1992 and s.48 of the Finance (No.2) Act 1997. The new tax relief is given to film production companies not individuals or partnerships, nor to investors, financial institutions or those whose involvement in filmmaking is confined to providing or arranging finance. The Finance Act 2006 makes provision for the film production company to claim the tax relief in instalments during production of the film rather than only upon completion.

Such companies only receive the relief in respect of their films if:

(a) the film is intended for theatrical release (i.e. exhibition to the paying public at the commercial cinema). The film is only regarded as intended for theatrical release if it is intended that a significant proportion of the earnings of the film should be obtained from such exhibition (the timing and measurement of this "intention" is set out in detail in the HM Revenue and Customs Guidance Notes on Film Tax Relief); and

(b) it is British Qualifying, i.e. if it is certified by the UKFC (see para.26–259, below) as a British film under the revised Sch.1 to the Films Act 1985 (see para.26–259, below) or as an official co-production (see para.26–262, below); and

(c) at least 25 per cent of the film's core expenditure is incurred in the United Kingdom. Core expenditure is production expenditure on activities involved in pre-production, principal photography and post production of a film. It excludes expenditure on development and distribution.

To qualify as a film production company, a company must, in general, be responsible for:

(a) the pre-production, principal photography and post production of the film; and

(b) the delivery of the film on completion.

The film tax relief consists of two elements being an enhanced deduction and a payable tax credit. The amount of the relief is based on the UK core expenditure, up to a maximum of 80 per cent of the total core expenditure incurred by the film production company. This means that a film production company can claim film tax relief on whichever is the lower of: (i) 80 per cent of the total core expenditure or (ii) the actual UK core expenditure incurred. United Kingdom core expen-

---

[486] Finance Act 2006 s.53(1) (Films and Sound Recordings) (Appointed Day) Order 2006 (SI 2006/3399). Certain transitional provisions were included in the Corporation Tax (Taxation of Films) (Transitional Provisions) Regulations 2007 (SI 2007/1050).

diture is the amount of the core expenditure incurred by the film production company, which is also UK expenditure. United Kingdom expenditure is defined as that which is incurred on goods and services which are used or consumed in the United Kingdom. The nationality of those providing such goods and services has no bearing on whether the expenditure qualifies as UK expenditure.

In March 2007 HM Revenue and Customs announced that it was severely restricting "sideways loss relief" which allows partners to use losses in one business to set off against income derived elsewhere for tax purposes. This relief formed a backbone of much of the investment made by film finance partnerships into British films. The question to be answered in the forthcoming years is whether the film tax relief will compensate for the restriction of the sideways loss relief.

(iii) Distribution

After completion, the producer will then want to exploit the finished film and, un-   **26–227**
less he or his financier is a distributor or has been granted distribution rights, he will be looking to secure a distribution agreement. Often he will do this through a sales agent (formerly called a producer's "rep" or representative), who will charge expenses and a commission of typically between 10 per cent and 25 per cent of the income realised from the distribution agreements which he procures on the producer's behalf. The distributor will generally receive an exclusive licence from the producer of those rights in the film that are necessary for its exploitation, including the right to cut (usually for reasons of length or because of censorship requirements), the rights to dub or sub-title the soundtrack of the film into other languages and the right to promote the film, e.g. by creating "trailers". The distributor will also want the right to license to sub-distributors, as he may not have the necessary infrastructure in all the territories in which the film is to be distributed, and to authorise such sub-distributors themselves to cut, dub or sub-title and promote the film.

The master negative of the film will normally be retained at the processing laboratory. The distributor can only expect to own the title to the original physical negative outright if he has distribution rights in all media worldwide. The producer will arrange for the laboratory to provide copies of the negative and other materials to distributors in particular territories, as appropriate. The distributor will often own the materials delivered to it on the agreed date by the producer and will supply copies of the film to exhibitors. If further materials have to be ordered from the laboratory, the distributor will be permitted to do so direct if he holds a "laboratory access letter" from the producer authorising this. Under the Finance Act 2006 (see para.26–226, above) there is no requirement for the film production company to own the master negative of the film. This contrasts with the previous tax regime where the film production company had to own the master negative at the time when the sale and leaseback of the film took place.

The distributor's income (known as "gross income") will principally consist of receipts from the cinema box office, fees paid by licensed broadcasters and revenue from the sale of copies of the film by DVD retailers. Once the cinema exhibitors and retailers have deducted their cut (for which there is currently no typical percentage or fixed fee), the distributor will deduct from the gross income ("distributor's gross") all distribution expenses as well as his commission (typically 25 to 30 per cent of distributor's gross) before passing on the balance ("distributor's net income") to the financier.

B. THE SOURCES AND RIGHTS

The producer must acquire from the rights owners sufficient rights to produce and   **26–228** exploit the film. These may be obtained from the creators of the works or their successors in title. The rights may be in pre-existing or "underlying" works, or in specially created works, such as an original screenplay. The main sources upon which the film will be based are as follows:

(i) Underlying works

26–229 If underlying works (such as a novel, play or biography) are to be reproduced in or adapted for the screenplay and the film, the film producer must acquire the necessary rights in them so as not to infringe the rights of the copyright owner.[487] The rights needed are those to:

(i) adapt the work in the form of a screenplay[488];

(ii) reproduce the work in the form of a film[489];

(iii) perform the work in public by exhibition of such film[490];

(iv) communicate the work to the public[491];

(v) issue copies of the work (in the form of the film) to the public, i.e. usually in DVD format[492];

(vi) rent or lend copies of the work (in the form of the film) to the public, i.e. usually in DVD format.[493]

There are other (often referred to as "ancillary" or "subsidiary") rights which may need to be acquired, namely the rights to:

(a) adapt the work in the form of scripts for a television series or serial or "movie-of-the-week" (often referred to as "TV spin offs");

(b) adapt the work in the form of a dramatic work for radio broadcast or performance on stage;

(c) adapt the work in the form of a synopsis (for promotional purposes);

(d) adapt the screenplay for publication in the form of a "novelisation";

(e) publish the screenplay in the form of a "book of the film"[494];

(f) copy the work in the form of a remake[495] of the film;

(g) copy the work in the form of a prequel[496] or sequel to the film.

26–230 To the extent that the rights owner has the capacity to grant them, the producer will also be concerned to acquire the right to produce and distribute a soundtrack music album, the right to use the writer's name and likeness, and the "merchan-

---

[487] In theory it would be possible for the producer to acquire the entire copyright in any underlying work. In practice, the entire copyright is rarely acquired and the copyright owner reserves to himself rights not required for film purposes (e.g. book and other publication rights).

[488] CDPA 1988 s.21.

[489] s.17.

[490] s.19.

[491] CDPA 1988 s.20 as amended by the Copyright and Related Rights Regulations 2003 (SI 2003/2498). See generally paras 7–112 et seq.

[492] s.18 as amended by reg.10(2) of the Copyright and Related Rights Regulations 1996 (SI 1996/2967).

[493] CDPA 1988 s.18A as amended by reg.10(2) of the Copyright and Related Rights Regulations 1996 (SI 1996/2967).

[494] "Book of the film" is generally understood to be a publication in which the screenplay is juxtaposed with other writing (such as director's notes) and with still photographs taken on the production set.

[495] A film is remade when the screenplay of the earlier film is filmed a second time, invariably by a different director; one of the best examples is "Ben Hur".

[496] A "prequel" to a film is another film using one or more of the characters, the characterisations, the designs and the genre (perhaps even some of the plot lines or settings) of the script of the original, but portraying the characters at an earlier moment in time. The more customary "sequel" to a film portrays the characters at a later moment in time than the original. The extent to which either a prequel or a sequel infringes the copyright in the original work is a moot point since it is invariably the custom to seek a grant of such rights where contemplated.

dising rights".[497] Merchandising rights are often pieced together from disparate sources, for example the name and features of characters described in the underlying work, the set or costume designer's drawings, specially designed artwork and logos, and registered trade marks.

It would be usual for the producer to require the author either to hold back from granting film (or television) rights in any sequel or prequel to the underlying work written by him, or at least to afford to the producer the right to match the terms of any third-party offer to acquire such rights. Provided that the grant of rights from the author to the producer is drafted sufficiently widely, this restriction will not arise in respect of sequels or prequels to the film based on the characters and settings of the original film because the copyright in them (to the extent that the same subsists) will vest in the producer.

At the start of the development stage it is common for a producer to acquire an option to purchase the film rights in the underlying work for a consideration which is typically 10 per cent of the agreed purchase price. This sum will be on account of and deductible from the purchase price due on exercise of the option. An initial option period of one year is customary; this period might be extended by further periods for an additional consideration which may or may not be deductible from the purchase price. The producer thus ensures that his initial financial exposure is not massive and he has a window of opportunity to develop the project, but the rights are available to enable him to make the film and he can grant security over such option to any funding source.

(ii) Original screenplay

Where a writer is commissioned to write an original screenplay, as opposed to a film based on a pre-existing work, it is usual for the producer to take a full assignment of any rights the writer may have in his screenplay. No such assignment would technically be required where the writer is employed by the producer under a contract of service.[498] However, even in such circumstances, the prudent producer will use a full assignment incorporating provisions dealing with entitlements to credits and moral rights. A producer with insufficient funds to pre-purchase all rights, or who only envisages certain types of exploitation, may choose simply to acquire those rights which are required for immediately foreseeable uses.

26–231

Unless he is deemed to be employed by the producer under a contract of service, the writer has the moral right to be identified as the author of the work (his paternity right).[499] This obligation will normally be satisfied by giving the writer a screen credit, e.g. in accordance with the provisions of the current WGGB/PACT Screenwriting Credits Agreement. The producer must also have regard to the writer's integrity right, protecting him from "derogatory treatment" of his work (which might result from editing, dubbing, etc. of the film).[500] Since moral rights are inalienable, or unassignable, producers should ensure that they are waived by their owners if there is any possibility of their being infringed.[501] The application of moral rights is examined in more detail at para.26–241, below.

---

[497] The producer will require the right to register the copyright in the film in those jurisdictions in which it is necessary to do so, e.g. the United States of America.

[498] CDPA 1988 s.11(2). This remains a rarity outside the United States of America where such works are frequently written by screenplay writers contracted under so-called "work-for-hire" agreements.

[499] CDPA 1988 s.77. See Ch.11, above.

[500] CDPA 1988 s.80. Again, see Ch.11, above.

[501] As permitted by CDPA 1988 s.87.

(iii) Musical works

26–232   Although music will frequently not be added to the sound track until the film has been edited in the post production stage, it may be featured or performed as part of the live action. Whether the producer uses a pre-existing musical work or a work specially commissioned for use within the soundtrack of the film, it will be necessary to obtain a "synchronisation" licence to record (or "dub") the music (and naturally any lyrics to be performed alongside the music) onto the soundtrack. In the case of pre-existing music, this will be under the control of the owner of the copyright in the work or, in the case of music specially composed for the film, the composer.[502] If the composer has an exclusive publishing contract, the publisher will also have to be party to the licence. The producer will also require a grant of the "mechanical" right, that is the right to copy or transpose the work onto other media, e.g. DVDs, and for all media of distribution (including those technologies not yet invented). Both such rights—synchronisation and mechanical—are often administered by the Mechanical-Copyright Protection Society ("MCPS").[503]

A recurrent problem is that music for the soundtrack is invariably left to a later stage in the production process (sometimes because the composer wishes to view the "rough cut" first); requests for synchronisation licences are given a low priority by publishers and record companies (resulting in delays) and the budget available to "clear" music is usually small. The fact that both time and money are tight can often combine to reduce the strength of the producer's negotiating position with the copyright owner. A similar timing problem can also occur where the score is commissioned from a composer. Whether or not the producer pays for the recording of the score (and especially if he does not), it is imperative to agree in advance issues such as the composer's duties; the grant (or waiver) of rights; and the engagement of, and the obtaining of grants and consents from, musicians.

(iv) Sound recordings

26–233   Where an existing sound recording is to be used as part of the soundtrack, a synchronisation (or "recording synchronisation" or "master use") licence will be required in respect of such sound recording from the owner of the copyright in that recording, usually a record company. A grant of the right to copy the recording onto other carriers will also be required from the record company.

(v) Artistic works

26–234   Copyright in the set and costume designs and any storyboard should be expressly assigned in the producer's agreements with the relevant "behind the camera" personnel. Copyright in such artistic works as appear in the background of a film (architectural works, paintings, etc.) will usually not be infringed in a film which displays those works since the 1988 Act allows for the *incidental* inclusion of artistic works[504] in a film and the filming of works of architecture and sculpture on public display.[505] The producer will, however, still need a grant of rights or "clearance" from the copyright owner in order to feature an artistic work prominently in his film.

---

[502] As to which see para.26–239, below.
[503] MCPS and PRS together trade as "PRS for Music". As to MCPS, see para.26–155, above.
[504] CDPA 1988 s.31. See paras 9–61 et seq., above, for a discussion of the "incidental inclusion" exception.
[505] CDPA 1988 s.62.

(a) *Assignments from actors/director*

Contracts for the services of all performers and the director should contain an   **26–235**
express assignment of the copyright in any material which may be created during
the course of filming. In this way copyright in "on-the-floor" dialogue changes
suggested by such individuals and incorporated into the film will vest in the production company.

(b) *Public domain works*

A producer may wish to use material in which the copyright has expired. Al-   **26–236**
though it will not be necessary for the producer to acquire rights in such public
domain material, it will be necessary to establish the position in all countries in
which the film is to be distributed.

(c) *Duration of grant of rights*

A producer would certainly be advised to take an outright assignment of copy-   **26–237**
right or film rights for the full period of copyright to enable the film to be exploited
without reference to the owners of the underlying rights. In addition the assignment should be expressed to include all renewals, reversions and extensions or
revivals of the period of copyright because, although the Berne and Universal
Copyright Conventions provide minimum periods of copyright, it may be that
national laws provide varying degrees of protection.

C. The Works which are Created and the Main Rights which are Required for Exploitation

The film

The producer, as part of the development process of his film project, will need to   **26–238**
acquire all of the rights in the film which are necessary to enable him to exploit it
in all media of exploitation. The optimal position is for the producer to acquire
the copyright or the exclusive film, television and DVD rights in the underlying
work throughout the world together with the sole right to exploit the film based
on the work in any and all media for the full period of copyright plus any renewals, extensions or revivals.[506] The principal media are theatrical exhibition, free
or pay television broadcasts (including the relay of such signals over cable television networks) and the sale ("sell-through") or rental of DVDs.[507] However,
video (or near video) on demand services have increased over recent years.
Digital downloading via the internet has also increased as a method of exploitation of films in recent years. Hollywood studios have previously been wary of
putting films on the internet for fear of piracy and undermining DVD sales. In
April 2006 six studios began selling online and in May 2006 the remake of "King
Kong" became the first significant DVD release to offer a downloading option in
the United Kingdom. In March 2007 the first authorised "download to burn" service for films was offered in the United Kingdom. Several companies now rent
digital films online. In June 2007 Warner Bros announced its plans to release

---

[506] There may be a "turnaround" provision requiring these rights to be returned to the previous
owner if the film has not been made within a fixed period. Such return must be by way of reassignment, although the prudent owner will include a power of attorney in his favour to enable
him to execute the reassignment as attorney for the producer, in the event that the producer fails
to reassign when the provision becomes operative.
[507] These rights are those contained in CDPA 1988 (as amended), ss.18, 19 and 20.

selected video on demand services at the same time as certain films were released on DVD. This deviated from the traditional windows of exploitation adopted by the US studios.

The soundtrack

26–239   Notwithstanding that the soundtrack of a film is to be treated as part of the film, film soundtracks are entitled to copyright separately as sound recordings under the Act.[508] The film producer should therefore ensure that he takes either an assignment of copyright from the soundtrack owner or a licence entitling him to reproduce the work in any material form. In many cases, he alone arranges for the soundtrack to be made.[509]

The right to perform in public any music or lyrics (the "performance right"), as opposed to the sound recording of that work, will invariably have been assigned by the composer (assuming he is British—there are similar affiliated societies in other countries) to the Performing Right Society (the "PRS"). This assignment will also include the right to synchronise specially commissioned music with the film soundtrack. In an ideal world, the composer will be required in his agreement with the producer to procure the grant of such synchronisation right by the PRS to the producer. Since no royalty is collected for public performance in the United States of America, the PRS in practice refuses to grant a film synchronisation licence unless the producer agrees to provide for payment of fees to the composer via the PRS in respect of the theatrical exhibition of the film in the United States.

As the assignee of the right to perform any composition in public, the PRS controls the performance right of works of its members. However, since the public performance of such works will be undertaken by others, e.g. theatrical exhibitors, it is not the producer who obtains performing right licences from the PRS.

If the producer intends to issue a recording of the soundtrack or "soundtrack album", this may prove lucrative if the requisite rights are obtained in a timely manner and on favourable terms. If the producer has to return to negotiate the acquisition of this right with the composer, if he does not own the copyright in the sound recording of the score, if the fullest consents have not been obtained from the performers, or if he intends to use various recordings owned by different recording companies, he may find that to release such a soundtrack album presents grave difficulties.

Ancillary rights

26–240   As explained at para.26–229, above, the producer would be well advised to acquire as far as possible all ancillary or subsidiary rights, including the right to exploit recordings of the soundtrack, the merchandising elements of the underlying works, the right to publish synopses of the works and the right to make adaptations from them. Although the "merchandising rights"[510] (i.e. the right to sell products bearing attributes of a film, such as a toy or T-shirt) are potentially lucrative, there is no generic merchandising right. Nevertheless, a book of a film may infringe copyright or another intellectual property right in the screenplay, or

---

[508] CDPA 1988 s.5B(2). In *Experience Hendrix LLC and anor v Times Newspapers Ltd* [2010] EWHC 1986 (Ch) it was postulated that 8 songs included in a CD distributed by *The Sunday Times* were actually taken from the filmed soundtrack of the 1969 Royal Albert Hall concert by the Jimi Hendrix Experience.

[509] For first owner of copyright in a soundtrack, see paras 5–52 et seq., above.

[510] As to merchandising rights in relation to the film industry, see para.26–230, above.

a toy based on an animated film character may infringe copyright in the drawings or designs used in the film. There is no copyright in film titles, although the film owner can benefit from the sale of goods bearing the film title by registration of trade marks of particular classes of goods. The tort of passing off may offer further protection to film owners. Sequel and prequel rights to the film made by the producer should be acquired in order to prevent the situation where such rights are granted to a third party who may go on to produce a film the commercial success of which is derived almost entirely from the success of the earlier film.

Moral rights

A waiver of the moral rights of authors, without which it may not be possible to make desired changes or "cuts" to the film and thus ensure its successful exploitation, should be included in any agreement to acquire film rights.[511] It should be noted that in certain circumstances the right to object to derogatory treatment may still apply even if the work is created under a contract of service.[512]   **26–241**

Performers' property rights

Following the creation of performers' property rights by the Duration of Copyright and Rights in Performances Regulations 1995,[513] it is imperative that the producer obtains the written consent of all performers in the film. This is usually obtained by a clause to this effect in the contract of engagement. These rights extend to all performers whether they are seen in the film or whether their performance is only included in the soundtrack. Where a performing artiste with an exclusive recording contract appears, the consent of the person having the benefit of such contract, i.e. the record company, must also be obtained.[514] The recent Court of Appeal case *Experience Hendrix LLC v Purple Haze Records Ltd*[515] confirmed that performers' rights exist in performances that predate CDPA 1988.   **26–242**

Rental and lending right

Following the creation of the rental and lending right by the Copyright and Related Rights Regulations 1996[516] it is anticipated that, in due course, one or more test cases, and possibly collective bargaining agreements, will ensue. The potential problem areas for the film industry are: **26–243**

(a) the lack of a presumption of transfer of rental right in a film production agreement with the film director;

(b) the uncertainty created by the jurisdiction of the Copyright Tribunal generally and, in particular, the outlawing of provisions purporting to prevent a person from questioning the amount of equitable remuneration[517];

(c) the fact that the rental right is partly retrospective in scope,[518] resulting in difficulty in tracing the successors in title of rights owners many years after the event, and difficulty in assessing the impact of the right on the operations and valuations of film libraries and catalogues.

---

[511] As to moral rights generally, see Ch.11, above.
[512] See CDPA 1988 s.82.
[513] As to performers' property rights generally, see Ch.12, above.
[514] As to such right of a record company, see para.26–187, above.
[515] [2007] EWCA Civ 501, [2007] F.S.R. 31.
[516] As to rental and lending right generally, see para.7–93, above.
[517] As to which see s.93C(5) of CDPA 1988 (as amended by reg.14 of the Copyright and Related Rights Regulations 1996 (SI 1996/2967).
[518] reg.26 of the Copyright and Related Rights Regulations 1996 (SI 1996/2967).

Copyright notice

26–244   To secure protection in those countries which are not party to the Berne Convention, but are members of the Universal Copyright Convention,[519] it is essential to
ensure that the © symbol, the name of the copyright owner and the year of first
publication appear on all film prints and negatives.

D. THE ORGANISATIONS BY MEANS OF WHICH FILMS ARE EXPLOITED

26–245   **Distributors (including so-called "majors", or Hollywood film studios).** These
are the companies which market the film and incur significant expenditures on the
cost of prints of the film and on advertising in the press, on posters and billboards,
on television and through other publicity. Unless they control their own means of
distribution they license the film through some or all of the other media, as follows:

(a) Theatre owners. Films are booked into cinemas through which the film
can achieve a "theatrical'" release. Some cinemas are part of a chain, others are independently owned/operated.

(b) Non-theatrical distribution. This is the term given to describe all means of
distribution, other than those specifically identified in (a) and (c)–(g). The
most obvious are exhibition on airlines, ships and oil rigs, or by relay to
bedrooms in a hotel. Other methods include exhibition in institutions such
as hostels, schools, colleges and prisons.

(c) Dial-up online distributors ("video on demand" or "pay per view"). This
is a growing market by which a customer can order the viewing of a film
by connection to an interactive network.

(d) DVD rental outlets. These outlets have grown up since the early 1980s,
some operating under the brand name of a chain, others independently
owned.

(e) "Sell through" retailers. Many DVDs are offered for sale by retailers also
offering copies to rent. Increasing numbers of units are sold by large high-
street retail stores.

(f) Pay TV broadcasters and pay cable TV. These are the broadcasting channels and cablecasting networks which will offer films to their subscribers.

(g) Free TV broadcasters and basic cable TV. Exhibitions of the film on "free-
to-air" television and by basic (i.e. free) cable can deliver the largest audiences, but yield no return to the producer/distributor other than the basic
licence fee.

E. THE TRADE UNIONS OR TRADE ASSOCIATIONS WHICH REPRESENT VARIOUS INTERESTS

26–246   Bodies representing producers or their representatives:

(a) Motion Picture Association of America ("MPAA") represents six major
producers and distributors of films based primarily in the United States of
America;

(b) The Independent Film and Television Alliance ("IFTA"), formerly known
as the American Film Marketing Association, represents independent film
producers and their representatives. IFTA's membership includes 150
companies from 22 countries;

(c) Producers Alliance for Cinema and Television ("PACT"). Membership

---

[519] As to which, see Ch.23, above. Note also that the United States of America is a member of Berne.

includes independent feature film companies operating in the United
Kingdom.

Bodies representing creators: **26–247**
  (a) British Academy of Composers, Songwriters and Authors represents
      composers of music and lyrics;
  (b) British Film Designers Guild represents film designers of every type;
  (c) Directors Guild of Great Britain represents film, television and theatre
      directors;
  (d) Guild of British Film and Television Editors represents film and sound
      editors;
  (e) Music Publishers Association represents music publishers;
  (f) Society of Authors represents principally novelists and dramatists;
  (g) Writers' Guild of Great Britain ("WGGB") represents all freelance writ-
      ers in the United Kingdom but principally writers for film and television.

Bodies representing performers: **26–248**
  (a) Equity represents actors and other performers including singers and
      dancers. As well as negotiating in traditional TV and film works, Equity
      negotiates individual agreements for the use of its members' services in
      developing media such as interactive CD-ROM games;
  (b) Film Artistes Association, now operating as a sub-division of BECTU,
      represents film "extras";
  (c) Musicians' Union represents performing musicians.

Bodies representing film technicians and others involved in the creative pro-   **26–249**
cess[520]:
  (a) Association of Motion Picture Sound represents sound technicians and
      editors;
  (b) British Society of Cinematographers represents (by invitation) cinematog-
      raphers and lighting cameramen;
  (c) Broadcasting, Entertainment, Cinematograph and Theatre Union
      ("BECTU"), formed by a merger between ACTT and NATKE, represents
      the technical staff used in film productions (e.g. set designers, cameramen,
      editors, etc.) throughout the United Kingdom;
  (d) Guild of British Camera Technicians represents camera operators and
      crew;
  (e) Guild of Location Managers represents those who scout for film locations;
  (f) Guild of Stunt and Action Co-ordinators represents stunt co-ordinators;
  (g) Production Guild of Great Britain, formed by a merger between the Guild
      of Film Production Accountants and Financial Administrators and the
      Guild of Film Production Executives, represents film production ac-
      countants;
  (h) Production Managers Association represents film production managers.

Bodies representing distributors or those involved in the distribution process: **26–250**
  (a) British Phonographic Industry represents the producers and distributors of
      sound recordings in the United Kingdom and internationally through the
      International Federation of the Phonographic Industry;
  (b) Cinema Exhibitors Association represents operators of cinemas in the
      United Kingdom;

---

[520] Several of these "craft" guilds come together under the umbrella organisation of the Cine Guilds
of Great Britain.

(c) Film Distributors' Association represents theatrical film distributors (currently 22) in the United Kingdom;

(d) British Video Association represents publishers and rights owners of video home entertainment.

Guild agreements

26–251　The various individuals involved in film production are represented by different professional bodies which agree minimum terms and conditions of service. PACT has collective bargaining agreements with Equity, Film Artistes Association,[521] Musicians' Union,[522] BECTU, WGGB and Directors' and Producers' Rights Society ("DPRS")[523] governing the employment of their respective members. These standard film industry agreements are worth a brief examination insofar as they differ regarding the treatment of copyright and other similar rights.

26–252　**PACT—Equity agreement for cinema.**[524] Actors have no copyright in their work but enjoy performers' property rights. These rights allow performers to control the reproduction, distribution, rental and lending of recordings of their performances. The text of the PACT—Equity agreement grants all consents necessary under the 1988 Act for exploitation of such recordings although it is advisable to ensure that the producer's agreement with the individual actor confirms this. The agreement also provides that artists are no longer engaged on a buy out basis but have the right to share in the profits of a film.

26–253　**PACT—WGGB agreement.**[525] According to this agreement, full copyright in the work for which the writer is engaged vests in the producer. However, the writer is given the right to buy back an original script for 50 per cent of sums previously paid if principal photography has not begun within two years of delivery of the last material for which the writer had been commissioned.

26–254　**PACT—BECTU agreement.**[526] Again, this agreement grants to the producer all the necessary grants and consents under the 1988 Act as he may reasonably require. This might be in respect of copyright in a set or costume design.

26–255　The American principal professional organisations involved in film production are:

(a) Writers Guild of America ("WGA")—the counterpart of WGGB;

(b) Directors Guild of America ("DGA")—the counterpart of Directors UK;

(c) Screen Actors Guild ("SAG")—the counterpart of Equity.

Generally, each of the above three bodies negotiates a standard agreement with the Alliance of Motion Picture and Television Producers ("AMPTP"), which is the multi-employer bargaining unit representing the "major" film studios and the leading independents. Production companies are obviously only bound by such agreements if they are signatories to them. This has resulted in the practice of requiring co-producers, distributors or other parties contracting with AMPTP members to execute so-called "affiliation" agreements. The intended effect of such an "affiliation" agreement is to extend the provisions of the agreement between the guild and AMPTP so as to bind the non-member for the purposes of the specific film.

---

[521] The current amended version is dated 2010.
[522] The current version is dated 2010.
[523] The current version is dated 2005.
[524] The current PACT—Equity agreement for cinema is dated 2010.
[525] The PACT—WGGB Agreement is dated February 2002 but is under negotiation.
[526] The versions of the PACT—BECTU Agreement relating to feature films are dated 2010.

F. COLLECTING SOCIETIES/LICENSING AGENCIES WHICH ARE RESPONSIBLE FOR ADMINISTERING THE RIGHTS

Authors Licensing and Collecting Society administers photocopying, lending and **26–256** certain recording and retransmission rights on behalf of authors in the United Kingdom[527];

Design and Artists Copyright Society administers the rights of painters, sculptors, photographers and other visual artists;

Directors UK, formerly DPRS, administers secondary rights payments received from United Kingdom broadcasters and via agreements with collecting societies overseas on behalf of film and television directors;

Educational Recording Agency administers the recording of works for educational use in educational establishments;

Phonographic Performance Limited administers the rights to broadcasting and the public use of sound recordings and issues licences to radio and television broadcasters and performance venues, such as dance halls and discotheques;

PRS for Music (combining both PRS and MCPS-PRS Alliance) administers the rights to perform a work in public, broadcast it or include it in a cable programme service and any film synchronisation rights if a work has been commissioned for a film soundtrack. It also administers the rights to broadcasting, online and public use of music recordings and issues licences to film companies allowing them to include their members' works in films and commercials.

G. RELEVANT INDUSTRY CONTROLS

Licensing of films

For a film to be shown in cinemas it must be licensed. The British Board of Film **26–257** Classification ("BBFC") was established in 1912 to bring a degree of uniformity to the censorship standards imposed by local authorities in the exercise of their licensing function. The BBFC has for approximately 100 years regulated the content of films distributed in the United Kingdom. The BBFC classifies films on behalf of the local authorities who license cinemas under the Licensing Act 2003. Local authorities retain the right to ban a film which may have been passed by the BBFC, to alter the category for a film to be exhibited under their jurisdiction or to impose or waive cuts to be made to a film. However, in general, local authorities accept the decisions of the BBFC. Since 1985 the BBFC has also classified and controlled the content of video recordings offered for sale or hire commercially in the United Kingdom, which definition was later expanded to include computer games.[528] It does this as the designated authority and in conjunction with the Video Standards Council, which was established in 1989 and administers a voluntary scheme making age-suitability recommendations for computer and video games that do not require legal classification.

The BBFC is responsible for the certification of films to be exhibited in cinemas. There are a number of tests laid down within its memorandum which must be applied before the granting of a certificate. There are six categories of certificate: U-Universal; PG-Parental Guidance; 12A, 15, 18 and R18 for restricted distribution only. If a film or video is obscene within the meaning of the Obscene Publications Acts or offends against other provisions of the law in

---

[527] As to Collecting Societies generally, see Ch.27, below.
[528] Video Recordings Act 1984. See also Sch.9 para.22(a) of the Criminal Justice and Public Order Act 1994 which extends the definition of video recordings to include computer-generated games and works.

such a manner that in the view of the BBFC no amount of cutting can make it acceptable, the work will be refused a certificate altogether.[529] Uc is an additional classification category that indicates that a film is particularly suitable for pre-school children. Film companies are free to submit their product to any local authority if it is felt that a different view might be taken.[530] For videos, there is the Video Appeals Committee.

Quotas

26–258   The "Television Without Frontiers" Directive[531] was intended to serve as a means to promote European productions and the distribution of audio-visual products. Article 4 of the Directive obliges all television channels licensed in Europe to devote to European works a majority of certain parts of the transmission schedule (this rule does not apply to those parts of the schedule devoted to news, sports events, games, advertising and teletext services). "European works" are, broadly speaking, works made, or at least supervised and controlled, by producers established in EU Member States.[532] However, the obligation to make transmissions involving 51 per cent European works is qualified insofar as it only applies "where practicable".[533]

The "Television Without Frontiers" Directive was substantially updated by the Audiovisual Media Services (AVMS) Directive,[534] which was adopted by the European Parliament and the European Council on December 11, 2007. Member States were required to transpose the new provisions into national law by the end of 2009. The AVMS Directive does not vary the wording of art.4 of the existing "Television Without Frontiers" Directive and the requirement for all broadcasters licensed in Europe to devote to European works a majority of certain parts of the transmission schedule remains unaltered.

Films Act 1985

26–259   Schedule 1 to the Films Act 1985 sets out the circumstances in which a film will be regarded as a British film under the Act and therefore can be certified by the UKFC as a qualifying film for the purpose of certain tax and other legislation.[535] For a film to qualify as a British film, each of the following three requirements must be satisfied:

     (a) The maker of the film must, throughout the time the film was made, be either: (i) a person ordinarily resident in an EU Member State; or (ii) a company registered in an EU Member State, being a company whose central management and control is exercised in an EU Member State. The maker is defined as the person (i.e. the legal entity) by whom the arrangements necessary for the making of the film are undertaken.

---

[529] The age definition in the Protection of Children Act 1978 of a "child" as portrayed in a film was raised to age 18 by the Sexual Offences Act 2003. This makes it an offence to portray onscreen the sexual exploitation of an under-18, irrespective of the actual age of the actor.

[530] An example of a local authority taking a different view was in the case of David Cronenberg's film "Crash".

[531] The Co-ordination of Certain Provisions Laid Down by Law, Regulation or Administrative Action in Member States Concerning the Pursuit of Television Broadcasting Activities: 89/552/EC and 97/36/EC.

[532] art.6 of Directive 89/552.

[533] art.4 of Directive 89/552.

[534] Directive 2007/65/EC amending Council Directive 89/552/EC on the co-ordination of certain provisions laid down by Law, Regulation or Administrative Action in Member States concerning the Pursuit of Television Broadcasting Activities.

[535] For tax treatment of British films, see paras 29–52 et seq., below.

(b) At least 70 per cent of the expenditure on production of the film must have
     been incurred on activity carried out in the United Kingdom.
(c) Not less than the requisite amount of labour costs must have been paid to:
     (i) Commonwealth citizens or citizens of any EU Member State; or (ii)
     persons ordinarily resident in a Commonwealth country or an EU Member
     State.[536]

Schedule 1 to the Films Act 1985 sets out the requirements to be satisfied in order for a film to be a British film for the purpose of that Schedule. Schedule 1 to
the Films Act 1985 was modified by the Films (Definition of "British Film") Order 2006,[537] which was further modified by the Films (Definition of "British
Film") (No.2) Order.[538] These orders introduce a requirement to pass the "cultural
test" before a film can be certified as "British". The reason a new test was required
was that the film tax relief is a form of state aid which needs to be cleared by the
European Commission. The promotion of culture is an exceptional reason for the
granting of state aid and therefore the new test ensures that the tax relief is more
clearly aimed at promoting culture.[539]

Each year an estimated €1.6 billion is spent on national film support across
Europe. On January 28, 2009 the European Commission adopted a Communication extending until December 31, 2012 the current rules on state aid to
cinematographic and other audiovisual works. These rules were laid down in the
previous Cinema Communications of 2001, 2004 and 2007. The extension of the
rules until December 31, 2012 followed a public consultation launched by the
European Commission in October 2008. The 2009 Communication requires the
"general legality principle" to be respected (e.g. that the aid must not affect the
internal market) and sets out four additional specific compatibility criteria according to which aid for the production of films for cinema and TV can be approved as cultural aid. These criteria are that:

(i)   aid must benefit a cultural product;
(ii) the producer must be free to spend at least 20 per cent of the production
      budget in other Member States without suffering any reduction in the aid
      provided under the scheme;
(iii) the aid intensity in principle must be limited to 50 per cent of the produc-
      tion budget (except for difficult and low budget films); and
(iv) aid supplements for specific filmmaking activities are not allowed.

The UK Government submitted a state aid notification to obtain approval from
the Commission for the new tax relief. An initial version of the cultural test was
submitted but the Commission subsequently agreed a revised cultural test.[540] This
new test changed the allocation of points within the categories set out in the
initial version and introduced into the test a new category to reflect the contribution which a film makes to British culture. A film will pass the cultural test if it is
awarded 16 out of a possible 31 points. The Order sets out how the points will be
allocated. There are four categories of points, namely:

(i)   cultural content (16 points) assessing the British subject matter of the
      film;
(ii) cultural contribution (4 points) assessing the contribution of the film to the
      promotion, development and enhancement of British culture;

---

[536] Sch.1 para.4(2)(c) to Films Act 1985. Sch.1 para.7 to Films Act 1985 sets out in detail how the
requisite amount of labour costs is to be calculated.
[537] SI 2006/643.
[538] SI 2006/3430.
[539] Between April 1, 2007 and October 31, 2008 118 films received certification as a British Film, of
which 111 were certified through applying the "cultural test" and only 7 were certified as co-
productions. This dramatic decline from the 69 co-productions which were certified in 2006 occurred following changes in the applicable tax regimes (see para.26–226, above).
[540] Which is set out in SI 2006/3430.

(iii) cultural hubs (3 points) assessing the use of the United Kingdom's film making facilities;

(iv) cultural practitioners (8 points) assessing the use of all personnel with creative input.

The UKFC is also responsible for awarding European certificates of British Nationality (formerly known as EC Certificates). Some Member States impose limits on the number of non-European films to be exhibited in their countries. A European certificate of British Nationality would enable a film to be included within such a quota of European films.

H. PROBLEMS WHICH CONFRONT THE INDUSTRY IN PRACTICE

(i) Colourisation

26–260   The case of *Turner Entertainment v Huston*[541] highlights a potential problem which can arise in relation to colourisation of monochrome films. Turner Entertainment had acquired the rights to the 1950 film "Asphalt Jungle" and had "colourised" the film, which had originally been created in black and white. Turner Entertainment applied to register copyright in the new version and consented to the broadcast of the colourised version on French television. The heirs to the estate of the film's director, John Huston, tried to prevent its broadcast on the basis that the colourisation was an infringement of the author's moral right not to have his work subjected to derogatory treatment. The issue turned on whether the disputed modification was compatible with the original artistic concept of the film. The Court of Appeal of Versailles felt there was evidence to suggest that John Huston would have opposed the broadcast of a colourised version of one of his works and so held that his moral right of integrity had been infringed. The case represents persuasive authority that colourisation may constitute derogatory treatment of a film under the Act. It added colourisation to a list of technical alterations held by the French courts to constitute an infringement of a film-maker's right of integrity. Previous illustrations had involved the addition of credits, the addition of a sound track, excessive editing and the superimposing of a logo on the broadcast of a film.

(ii) Completion bonds

26–261   A financier will frequently obtain a performance guarantee or "completion bond" from an independent guarantor that the film will be completed and delivered to the distributors, or in the alternative the financier's investment will be repaid. In return for providing such bond, the completion guarantor might expect a fee of approximately 3 per cent of the "negative cost" (i.e. all the cost up to the completion of the master negative and delivery of the film). This negative cost figure is commonly known as the "strike price". The guarantor will also seek an agreement with the producer to protect his position, which agreement will grant to the guarantor the ultimate right to take over production of the film if the producer should run into insoluble difficulties. Problems have occurred[542] in circumstances where the distributor refuses to accept delivery and to pay the distribution advance, the guarantee of repayment is called under the completion bond and the guarantor has to pursue the remedies under his agreement with the producer.

---

[541] *Turner Entertainment v Heirs to the Estate of John Huston*, Court of Appeal of Versailles, *Revue Internationale des droits d'auteur* No.164 April 1995 at p.389.
[542] An example was a film entitled "Mesmer".

(iii) Co-productions

Because film is such an international commodity, and funding difficult to come   **26–262**
by, it is hardly surprising that producers should want to shoot or edit their films in
different territories or to co produce with producers from other countries. This
process can create difficulties in various different ways, for example availability
of work permits for cast and crew, attribution of nationality for subsidy or awards
purposes, and so on. These difficulties have been reduced by the creation of a
series of bilateral agreements or co-production treaties. The United Kingdom has
seven active treaties with, respectively, Australia, Canada, France, India, Jamaica,
New Zealand and South Africa. A treaty was signed with Morocco in October
2009 and is awaiting ratification. A negotiation with China is in progress.

These treaties facilitate co-productions between co-producers resident in the
respective countries, which qualify according to the treaty regulations to be
treated as a production of each such country (at least to the extent of the expenditure in such country). Although each treaty is bilateral, it is possible to construct
three-way co-productions using the provisions of each of any two treaties. Since
1992, the European Convention on Cinematographic Co-productions has been
promoted by the Council of Europe and 31 countries have now adhered to it
including the United Kingdom. The Convention can operate as a framework either for a three-way co-production between producers located in signatory states,
or for a bilateral co-production between two such producers.

Co-production status brings with it significant benefits, for example such films
are not required to pass the "cultural test".[543] Nevertheless, although these treaties
(and the Convention) have facilitated the production of international films, actual
and potential problems remain, many resulting from the conflicts between the applicable legal regimes. For instance, could a completion guarantor enforce its
contractual right to replace the director of a co-production film in both jurisdictions, including one where the moral rights of authors carry great weight?

(iv) Copyright in characters and titles

Where characters from a film are copied borrowing the name and other identify-   **26–263**
ing features but without details of plot or dialogue, a claim for infringement of
copyright is unlikely to be successful. A claim for passing off a different film as a
sequel to, or spin-off from, the original film by reason of the unauthorised use of
the character will be the most likely cause of action available to the owner. It is
very difficult to protect titles of films by an action for infringement of copyright
due to the requirements of originality and that a substantial part of a work be
copied.[544] If a well-known title of a film is used without authority, the owner's
remedy is likely to lie in passing off. Protection by registration as a trade mark
may be available provided the title is sufficiently distinctive.

The MPAA has a voluntary subscription registration scheme for titles of theatrical motion pictures. Over 125,000 titles have been registered since 1925. The
primary purpose of the MPAA Title Registration Bureau is not to assist copyright
owners but to avoid confusion in the US theatrical marketplace. The register,
which can be used for a fee by non-MPAA members, helps prevent the release of
two or more films with similar or identical titles. Subscribers agree to resolve
disputes through arbitration, and any arbitration decision can be enforced by a
court.

---

[543] As to the "cultural test", see para.26–259, above.
[544] As to copyright in titles, see para.3–16, above.

(v) Downloading

26–264   As available bandwidth increases, the film industry is beginning to experience problems of unauthorised downloading akin to those which the music industry has suffered for many years. *Twentieth Century Fox Film Corp. and Ors v Newzbin Ltd*[545] is an example of the efforts made by FACT and its members to halt this unwelcome trend. In that case, the defendant operated a website on a worldwide internet discussion system called Usenet. This site was said to locate and categorise unlawful copies of films and display their titles in its indices and to provide both a facility for its users to search for particular copies (and to display the results) and a one-click facility for users to acquire unlawful copies of their choice. When granting injunctive relief Kitchin J. held that Newzbin had infringed the claimants' copyrights by authorising copying of their films, had procured and engaged with its members in a common design to copy their films and had communicated the same to the public.

This welcome news for copyright owners, whose works are vulnerable to online piracy via peer-to-peer networks, followed shortly after enactment of the Digital Economy Act 2010. This contains a provision[546] empowering the Secretary of State to order the blocking of internet locations which the court is satisfied have been, are being or are likely to be used for or in connection with an activity which infringes copyright.

Lawful downloading of films (so-called download-to-own) under licence from the copyright owners appears set to increase as efforts to halt the spread of unlawful downloads intensify and as digital technology advances.

(vi) DVD and other piracy

26–265   Piracy remains a major cause of concern for all those in the film industry, over 30 years since it first manifested itself. There are a number of laws dealing with counterfeiting in the United Kingdom and an agency, Federation Against Copyright Theft (FACT), which acts to combat piracy and other forms of copyright theft. The manufacture of pirate DVD copies is prevalent in the South East Asia region, where it is frequently controlled by organised crime. The reduction of DVD sales in the UK market in 2009 was estimated by the British Video Association as over 7 per cent.

This issue poses a significant problem because many films, if deemed to be unsuitable, are not released theatrically and go "direct to DVD". Their opportunity to earn revenues is thus limited principally to this market. Whilst one strategy to deal with the piracy problem would be to release the film simultaneously in the cinema and on DVD, this would require the calculation of the number of DVDs to be manufactured to be made in advance of the film's performance at the box office. Whatever strategy the industry adopts, it is clear that the traditional distribution pattern of successive "windows" of exploitation is not immune from amendment.

Piracy is not a problem originating solely in other countries. In September 2010, a cinema goer was convicted and sentenced to a term of six months imprisonment for copying from his seat films which were subsequently uploaded to a free website. The films were traced using an embedded security code. Although the accused made no profit from his actions, he was nevertheless convicted of possession of a mobile phone and copying a film for use in fraud contrary to

---

[545] [2010] EWHC 608 (Ch); [2010] E.C.C. 13; [2010] E.C.D.R. 8; [2010] E.M.L.R. 17; [2010] F.S.R. 21.
[546] Digital Economy Act 2010 s.17.

the Fraud Act 2006 ss.6 and 7, and of infringing copyright by distributing a film contrary to CDPA 1988 s.107(1)(e). In mitigation, he pleaded that his work was of an amateur quality. FACT asserted that this was the first conviction of this type in the United Kingdom.

(vii) Incidental inclusion

A substantial part of a copyright work, such as a painting or a film clip, but not music or lyrics, may be included in the film even though the owner may not have consented to its use. In such a case the defence of "incidental inclusion" may be available, but it will be a matter of degree.[547] In practice, permission for inclusion (or "clearance") is usually sought.   **26–266**

(viii) ISAN system

The ISAN system is a voluntary standard numbering system for the unique and international identification of audiovisual works. Any such work to which the system applies is allocated a 16-digit ISAN (International Standard Audio-visual Number). Each version of the work may have a different ISAN. The system could be used to assist allocation of royalties among rightholders and to track use of audio-visual works. However, the system cearly states that the issuance of an ISAN shall in no way be related to any process of copyright registration, nor shall the issuance of an ISAN provide evidence of the ownership of rights in a work. The ISAN Registration Agency for the United Kingdom, ISAN UK, was finally launched in December 2007. ISAN UK was established as a result of a collaboration between PACT, MCPS-PRS Alliance and Soundmouse (an online programme metadata platform). In October 2008, ITV announced that it was adopting ISAN for the content identification of all of its programmes. All Blu-ray and HD-DVD releases must have an ISAN.[548]   **26–267**

(ix) Plagiarism

The issue of plagiarism, particularly allegations of plagiarism, is ever-present in the film industry.[549] Screenplays are often submitted on an unsolicited basis. Nevertheless it is the desire of some production companies to read or review all such screenplays. In response to the former trend, some companies have adopted a policy either to return all such unsolicited screenplays marked "unread" or to invite the writer to sign a waiver of all appropriate rights as a condition precedent to the reading of any such unsolicited screenplay.   **26–268**

(x) Portrayal of living persons

Portraying a living person in a film is not a copyright infringement in itself. However, a film-maker undertaking such a project should beware of a possible claim for infringement of privacy or for defamation by such a person who may feel the film has lowered his reputation in the eyes of others. This is why the credits of a film (other than a biographical study) usually purport to state that any   **26–269**

---

[547] As to incidental inclusion and CDPA 1988 s.31, see paras 9–61 et seq., above.

[548] Further information regarding the ISAN system is available at *http://www.isan.org.uk* [Accessed November 1, 2010].

[549] The authors of a 1987 stage play entitled "Ladies Night" commenced proceedings in California against the makers of "The Full Monty", claiming that the award-winning film plagiarised the setting, premise and some character development of the earlier work. "Errors and omissions" insurance was devised with this type of claim in mind.

resemblance of any character to a living person is entirely coincidental. One sure way to avoid the possibility of a defamation action where the film portrays a living person is to collaborate with such person when making the film. Such collaboration should involve the agreement of those depicted in the film not to work with any other film-maker who is contemplating the making of a competing film. It is also advisable to acquire the exclusive rights to use any published biography on which the portrayal is to be based, not only to avoid any copyright infringement, but also to avoid such material being available for use in any competitive project.

(xi) Public domain films

26–270   A film producer will always be advised to take an assignment or an irrevocable licence for the full term of copyright in the underlying rights he seeks to acquire, especially where the underlying works were not originally created for the purposes of the film. This is because the periods of copyright of the underlying works may, in theory, extend beyond the expiry of copyright in the film and its exploitation could thereafter be subject to the licence of the owners of the copyright in the underlying works. Given the extension of the term of copyright in films,[550] this issue may in the future pose less of a problem in practice.[551]

(xii) Publishers' quitclaims

26–271   It is standard in many publishing agreements for a book publisher to take some interest (either a licence or an agency) in the film, television and radio rights to the published work. A "quitclaim" is often sought from the publisher(s) in all major territories in order to confirm that no such interest is asserted by such publisher(s).

(xiii) Screen credits

26–272   The author of a literary, dramatic, artistic or musical work has the right under certain circumstances to be identified as the author of that work.[552] This right extends to an author from whose work an adaptation has been made, which would include for example where a screenplay has been adapted from a novel. The director of a film has the right to be identified as the director in similar circumstances.[553]

Credits are the lifeblood of the film industry. Although they (and their order, size, whether sole or shared, etc.) are sometimes negotiated at great length, no standard industry credits have evolved. Only select directors will command a "possessory" credit.[554] However, the provisions of the WGGB/PACT Screenwriting Credits Agreement will sometimes be incorporated into an agreement with a writer, even where the parties are not contracting in accordance with another collective bargaining agreement and the DGA has very strict requirements to be adhered to for distribution in the United States of America. Thus, certain conventions have become established—for example that the director will have a credit on the final card, i.e. the final frame on which credits appear, whether at the beginning or end of the film. The issue remains a contractual art, not a science.

---

[550] Duration of Copyright and Rights in Performances Regulations 1995 (SI 1995/3297) reg.6(1).

[551] Any extension of the period of copyright in the United States of America also reduces the scale of the problem there.

[552] CDPA 1988 s.77(1).

[553] CDPA 1988 s.77(2)(a) and (b).

[554] For example "John Carpenter's 'The Thing'", "A film by John Carpenter" or "A John Carpenter film".

(xiv) Storylines

Since there is no monopoly of source material and no copyright in an idea, there **26–273**
is frequently a multiplicity of projects concerning a topical or popular subject in
development at any time. There are several independent registration services for
writers. These accept registrations of screenplays and scripts submitted for a
limited period of time so that the author can verify his authorship with effect from
an independently certifiable date. Registration with one of these services does not
however confer any proprietary rights.[555] It is rare, however, for more than two
similar big-budget projects to reach the screen at the same or similar time.[556] The
MPAA title register,[557] although technically available only to MPAA members,
can alert a film producer to the existence of a storyline which may resemble one
he is thinking of using in his next project.

(xv) United States Library of Congress

The United States of America is the most important source of making films and **26–274**
frequently the most lucrative market—at least for American films. It is also one
of the few jurisdictions to maintain a register of copyrights.[558] Although registration is no longer a prerequisite for subsistence of copyright, the register is
extensively used and offers several benefits to producers of UK films:

  (a) a search against the title of an underlying work may reveal interests other
       than those of the copyright owner, for example that of a mortgagee or
       owner of a prior contractual option;

  (b) registration of the producer's interest in an underlying work or a
       screenplay would operate as notice of it to third parties who conduct sim-
       ilar searches[559];

  (c) a search against the title will reveal the existence of any work with the
       same or a similar title.

(xvi) WIPO Register

The World Intellectual Property Organisation ("WIPO") has sponsored a Treaty **26–275**
on the International Registration of Audiovisual Works, which entered into force
on February 27, 1991.[560] The Treaty has established a self-supporting International Film Register ("IFR") to record statements concerning rights in audiovisual works. These statements show who owns the work or which other rights in
the work exist, the territory for which the rights are valid and other details
concerning the work. Problems have dogged the scheme to the extent that the
Treaty was suspended in 1993 and is, for all practical purposes, defunct.

---

[555] Examples of such registration services include the Raindance Script Registration Service and the
Script Factory Script Registration Service.
[556] The films "Robin Hood" and "Robin Hood: Prince of Thieves" both released in 1991 were a
notable exception to this generalisation.
[557] See para.26–263, above.
[558] The register is kept at the United States Library of Congress in Washington, DC.
[559] To facilitate such registration and to preserve confidentiality, the practice has grown up of executing a supplemental or "short-form" document which reflects the principal grant of rights but
not the commercial terms contained in the long-form documents.
[560] "International Property Laws and Treaties, Multilateral Treaties 1–01"; *Copyright*, June 1989
published by WIPO.

5. THE BROADCASTING INDUSTRY

A. O*VERVIEW*

26–276   The broadcasting industry is a user on a massive scale of copyright works and of performances of actors and musicians. Its expenditure on acquiring the rights to broadcast such works and performances and, increasingly, to make them available on demand in catch-up and archive services forms a significant proportion of the annual revenues that flow from copyright users to rights owners. For example, UK radio and television broadcasters paid PRS for Music[561] (the joint venture between the Performing Right Society ("PRS")[562] and the Mechanical Copyright Protection Society ("MCPS")[563]) some £147 million in 2009 for the right to record and broadcast musical works.[564]

Broadcasters are not merely users of existing copyright works and of live or recorded performances given by actors and musicians. They also commission and finance the creation of new works for use in their services: new television and radio programmes, and the music, sound recordings, screenplays, scripts, photographs, film clips, other works and performances they may include. Broadcasters own the copyright or hold extensive rights in such specially created works and they turn that ownership to account not only by broadcasting them but also by licensing their secondary use by others in a variety of media. The turnover of BBC Worldwide Limited, the commercial arm of the BBC, in 2009/2010 derived from programme distribution and channel licensing was some £906 million.[565]

Broadcasters create programme services designed to appeal to mass, minority or special-interest audiences, as well as services which are aimed at local, national or overseas audiences. The broadcasters own the copyright in their broadcasts and need adequate legislation to enable them to protect the integrity of their services when these are carried on third parties' transmission platforms and to enable them to preserve and obtain the benefit of the economic value of their rights. Encryption allows broadcasters to limit reception of their services to those prepared to pay to receive them and to those territories which the broadcasts are designed to serve. However, it has proved necessary to supplement broadcasters' basic protection under copyright law with additional "associated rights" to enable them to take effective action against those who manufacture or market devices designed to circumvent encryption controls. These were introduced, along with related criminal law sanctions, in the 1988 Act, and were then supplemented by the Broadcasting Acts of 1990 and 1996, and again by the Copyright and Related Rights Regulations 2003.[566] The efficacy of these instruments to ensure territorial exclusivity has been put into question in the reference made to the European Court of Justice in the case *Football Association Premier League Limited and Others v QC Leisure and Others.*[567]

As broadcasters enter the second decade of the twenty-first century, perhaps their greatest challenge in the copyright sphere is to obtain solutions to the rights clearance problems that hamper their ability to make their services available "any place, any time, anywhere". Broadcasters' proposals for solutions to these problems are described below.

---

[561] As to PRS for Music, see para.27–65, below.
[562] As to the PRS, see para.27–65, below.
[563] As to MCPS, see para.27–63, below.
[564] PRS for Music press release "Financial Results 2009", April 2010.
[565] BBC Worldwide Annual Review 2009/10, p.5.
[566] See Ch.15, above.
[567] [2008] EWHC 1411 (Ch); [2008] F.S.R. 32.

B. THE STRUCTURE OF THE BROADCASTING INDUSTRY IN THE UNITED KINGDOM

Regulation

Broadcasting is, in most countries, a highly regulated industry. In part this is **26–277** because, until the advent of satellite broadcasting and the development of digital cable and the internet, the limited range of frequencies available for over-the-air broadcasting restricted the number of broadcasters able to operate without unacceptable levels of signal interference. Further, it has always been considered that the right to use these limited public assets, the wireless frequencies, should be allocated with the public interest in mind. A third reason for the high degree of regulation is the pervasive and invasive nature of broadcasting. Radio and television signals enter every home; if individuals in the home turn on a radio or television set they hear or see whatever is being broadcast at that moment on the channel to which their set is tuned. Regulation of the content of broadcasting services is aimed, at the minimum, to ensure that what they hear or see is within acceptable social, cultural and political limits. At the maximum, regulation is intended to enhance the quality of life. For instance, the BBC's main object, as set out in its Charter of September 19, 2006 is the promotion of its "Public Purposes", defined as:

"(a) sustaining citizenship and civil society;
(b) promoting education and learning;
(c) stimulating creativity and cultural excellence;
(d) representing the UK, its nations, regions and communities;
(e) bringing the UK to the World and the World to the UK;
(f) in pursuing its other purposes, helping to deliver to the public the benefit of emerging communications technologies and services and, in addition, taking a leading role in the switchover to digital television."

Likewise, the chief European regulatory instrument, the EU Audiovisual Media Services Directive,[568] regulates the provision of such services across frontiers because, according to para.5 of the Directive's preamble, such services "are as much cultural services as they are economic services. Their growing importance for societies, democracy,…education and culture justifies the application of special rules to these services".

Regulation of commercial broadcasters

The regulation of commercial broadcasting in the United Kingdom is undertaken **26–278** by the Office of Communications—Ofcom—under powers vested in it by the Communications Act 2003. It is an offence for anyone other than the BBC to operate a broadcasting service in the United Kingdom without a licence from Ofcom. Licensed broadcasters are required by the terms of their licences to observe Ofcom's codes as to programme content, as to advertising standards and the duration and placement of advertising,[569] and as to impartiality and other matters.

Regulation of the BBC

Established by Royal Charter, with its Governors appointed by the Queen in **26–279**

---

568 Directive 2007/65/EC, codified version of March 10, 2010.
569 As to the advertising codes, see paras 26–355 and 26–359, below.

Council, the BBC is essentially self-regulating. The Communications Act 2003 has, however, subjected the BBC to regulation by Ofcom in respect of programme content standards and certain quantifiable elements of its public service obligations, such as the requirement that 25 per cent of its television programmes be commissioned from independent producers.[570]

The broadcasting landscape in the UK

26-280   A brief account of the range of television and radio services available in the United Kingdom and of the platforms on which they are carried will provide some context for the description in the next section of this chapter of the organisation of rights clearances for these media.

Television

The regulatory structure in the United Kingdom classifies as public service channels all the television channels broadcast by the BBC and funded by the public through payment of the television licence fee. In addition the commercially funded channels ITV1, Daybreak, Channel 4, S4C and Five all have public service broadcasting obligations, a reflection of the allocation to them of the scarce analogue frequencies available for terrestrial broadcasting. These channels will retain that status even after the analogue frequencies cease to be available for broadcasting purposes in 2012, although it is possible for the broadcasters of ITV1 and Five to relieve the channels of that status and of the concomitant obligations and advantages by handing back their licences to Ofcom.

All of the above-mentioned public service channels are also broadcast on digital terrestrial television, by digital cable and by direct to home satellite broadcasting ("DTH"). The latter platform has the largest capacity; over 240 channels are offered by BSkyB in its basic DTH package. Such channels include:

- services intended for reception in the United Kingdom, such as the public service channels identified above;
- services intended for reception in the United Kingdom and Europe: examples are CNN International, Discovery, Sky News and National Geographic;
- services broadcast from but not intended for reception in the United Kingdom: for example TV3 (aimed at Scandinavia) and BBC World News.

Some of these services are general entertainment and information channels, others are thematic channels, consisting entirely of feature films, news, sport, children's or music programming.

Radio

Although the thrust of broadcasting policy is towards digital audio broadcasting becoming the primary distribution network for radio, the take-up of digital technology by radio listeners has been slower than by television viewers, with no deadline having been set for cessation of analogue radio broadcasting.

In fulfilling its public purposes, the BBC provides:

- 10 national radio services, 5 of which are broadcast in analogue as well as digital form;
- 3 national regional services, for Scotland, Wales and Northern Ireland respectively, together with services in Welsh and Gaelic;

---

[570] ss.198 and 338 Communications Act 2003.

- over 40 local and community radio services;
- the World Service, broadcasting in 32 languages.

As for commercial radio:

- there are 3 national commercial radio services broadcasting on analogue frequencies:
  Absolute, Classic FM and Talksport;
- national digital commercial stations have commenced broadcasting;
- there are over 200 local commercial radio stations, mostly providing music-based services, and over 180 community radio stations have been licensed;
- some 90 satellite radio stations have been licensed.

Other broadcasting services

These include:

- teletext services of general interest;
- data broadcasting services, most conveying information services for commercial customers.[571]

Cable

By the end of 2009, 3.7 million homes in the United Kingdom were receiving television broadcasts by way of cable rather than through off-air reception from terrestrial or satellite transmitters.[572] All but a few of the channels transmitted are ones that are also broadcast over-the-air from terrestrial and satellite transmitters. Also offered on cable are video-on-demand services and a number of radio services.   **26–281**

Internet broadcasting

A very large number of sound broadcasting services are transmitted via the internet. Many are "simulcasts" of services also being broadcast over-the-air, while others are transmitted only in this medium. Internet relays from concerts and sports events—also now treated as acts of broadcasting under the 1988 Act— have also become common. The provision of television services over the internet is in its infancy, but the rapid pace of technical development means that this form of broadcasting is likely to be widespread before the next edition of this book appears. Internet technology is ideally suited to the provision of programming on demand and many individual television and radio programmes are now made available in this way. The principal broadcasters have introduced catch-up services and these are heavily used; for example, requests for streaming and downloading from the BBC's iPlayer were running at over two million a day by the end of 2009. Such has been the growth of on-demand listening and viewing that some foresee the demise of linear scheduled broadcasting, a prediction that has been somewhat confounded by audience research showing an increase in viewing of linear channels in 2010.   **26–282**

Programme production

Until the arrival of Channel Four in the early 1980s the UK television industry   **26–283**

---

[571] These broadcast the "other information" referred to in the definition of broadcasting in s.6 of the 1988 Act. See para.3–93, above.
[572] Ofcom Digital Television Update, Quarter 1, 2009.

was vertically integrated. That is, the broadcasters also had substantial programme-making capacity to meet their programming requirements. Channel Four adopted the publisher-broadcaster model, commissioning most of its programming from independent production companies. The Broadcasting Act 1990 further encouraged the growth of an independent production sector by imposing on the BBC and the ITV companies a requirement that a minimum of 25 per cent of the time they allocate to the broadcasting of certain defined categories of programmes should be reserved for the broadcasting of a range and diversity of independent productions, with a quota of 10 per cent on other commercial broadcasters. The Communications Act 2003 gave further support to production companies by putting Ofcom under a duty to require the commercial public sector broadcasters to draw up and comply with codes of practice in respect of programme commissioning.

Radio remains by and large a vertically integrated sector, although independent production has secured a foothold. Independent radio productions make up some 8.4 per cent of the hours of broadcasting on the BBC's national services.[573]

C. The Use of Copyright Works and Protected Performances in Broadcasting

Rights usage

26–284   A given hour of broadcasting may use almost no copyright works or protected performances at all, while another may involve the use of a multiplicity of works and performances, many simultaneously. For instance, a live broadcast of cricket from Lord's or tennis from Wimbledon will as a rule not involve the use of protected works of third parties, other than to a trivial extent. Coverage of a football match may include some singing by the crowd of well-known tunes[574] but little else in the way of copyright material. Advertisers' and sponsors' logos and other copyright works may appear in shot, but the broadcaster's contract with the event organiser will generally place the onus on the organiser to effect any necessary clearances of them. Synchronised swimming may cross the borderline between sport and performance of a dramatic work, provided, of course, that it is choreographed.[575] But at the other extreme, an hour of a television drama-documentary programme dramatising the life of a public figure could involve all of the following:

- the use of a published biography as the basis for the programme;
- commissioning a researcher to analyse other sources or to carry out fresh research into the subject, and to provide a written report for the screenplay writer to use;
- commissioning a writer to provide a dramatic screenplay;
- use of extracts from letters, speeches, diaries or other literary works to be quoted in the programme;
- engaging a director to direct the filming[576];
- use of existing photographs and commissioning of a photographer to take fresh ones for use in the production;

---

[573] Radio Independents Group press release, May 13, 2010.

[574] Accompanied sometimes by rather less-well-known words.

[575] Note, however, the rejection of the argument that there is a copyright in a sports game such as American football, in which individual movements are intended to follow a pre-set plan, in *FWS Joint Sports Claimants v Copyright Board* (1991) 22 I.P.R. 429 (Fed Ct App Canada).

[576] Following the implementation of the EC Term and Rental Directives (93/98 and 92/100), the principal director will be a co-author of the programme. See para.5–48, above.

- use of historic film or television footage of the events, period or characters being portrayed;
- commissioning a composer to write opening, closing and incidental music;
- use of existing music to be played by musicians in or out of vision or to be dubbed into the programme from commercial sound recordings;
- use of such commercial sound recordings;
- engaging actors and musicians to perform in the production, who will have rights in respect of the fixations made of their performances[577];
- use of excerpts from films or programmes that include performances by actors or musicians.

Rights clearances

Just as the extent to which various types of programmes use copyright works and performances may differ markedly, so too may the rights clearances which broadcasters and their programme suppliers obtain. A commercial radio broadcaster may need to acquire nothing more than the right to give one live broadcast of a work, because the broadcast will have little or no prospect of further exploitation. Conversely, a television production company will typically acquire very extensive rights in order to be able to realise the full commercial value of the programme over a period of many years. **26–285**

Using again the example of a television drama-documentary, the producer will, ideally, acquire all rights for all media in perpetuity, but where that cannot be achieved for economic or practical reasons, the following are the rights clearances that will usually be required:

Primary Rights
- the right to adapt the source material as required for the purposes of the programme. In this connection a waiver of the author's moral right of integrity will usually be sought;
- the right to copy all the works and performances to be used. This is needed to permit them to be recorded or filmed in the course of production of the programme. Apart from being reproduced in the final master recording, there will be a number of intermediate reproductions which the clearance must permit;
- the right to broadcast each work and performance included in the programme, and the programme itself, by all methods of broadcast transmission;
- the right to include the works and performances in the broadcaster's catch-up on-demand service;

Secondary exploitation rights, including:
- the right to make and distribute copies of the programme in the form of DVDs, both by way of sale and by way of rental and lending;
- the right to make and distribute copies of the soundtrack of the programme in the form of CDs;
- the right to permit the programme to be transmitted via cable, either by way of licensing of the programme for inclusion in a third party's cable channel or by way of cable retransmission (by reception and immediate retransmission) of broadcasts;
- the right to permit the programme to be included in internet services, including on-demand services;

---

[577] See Ch.12, above.

- the right to adapt and distribute the programme in nonlinear media (e.g. CD-ROM or CDi);
- the right to permit the programme to be shown in public, certainly to non-paying audiences and, in some instances, to paying audiences too;
- the right to publish the screenplay or an adaptation of it in a book related to the programme and likewise the right to publish in such a book other elements such as photographs and extracts from the source material;
- the right to publish the screenplay in the form of a novelisation of it;
- the right to use any of the works or performances in connection with the promotion and advertising of the programme;
- the right to make further recordings of any of the works or performances, as recorded for the purposes of the programme, for archival purposes[578];
- the right to produce and market merchandise related to the programme.

Acquisition of rights

26–286   The acquisition of such rights can be extremely straightforward, as some may be acquired by the simple method of acquiring the complete copyright in the work throughout the world, in perpetuity, in return for payment of a single fee at the outset. More often, the clearance process will involve the painstaking negotiation of the acquisition of specified rights, for limited territories and for limited periods, not infrequently from several rightsowners for a single work, and against payment of an initial fee payable in instalments at different stages of the production process, with further fees or royalties becoming due upon further exploitation of the programme. The parties' freedom to negotiate may, moreover, be constrained by the terms of agreements between, on the one hand, trade unions or collecting societies representing rightsowners, and on the other hand the broadcaster or a trade association representing producers. Some of these are minimum terms agreements, setting the minimum rates that must be paid and the working practices that must be observed when writers are commissioned or performers engaged for productions. Others set out standard terms for certain uses of certain types of works. Others again are "blanket agreements" allowing specified uses to be made of a body of works in a collecting society's repertoire, against payment of annual lump sums or fixed rates per unit of usage.

The following is a representation in schematic form of the collecting society and trade union agreements that govern the process of rights clearances for broadcasting in the United Kingdom.

---

[578] CDPA 1988 s.75, which enables designated broadcasts to be recorded for archival purposes can at present only be taken advantage of by The British Film Institute, The British Library, The British Medical Association, The British Music Information Centre, The Imperial War Museum, The Music Performance Research Centre, The National Library of Wales and The Scottish Film Council. See para.9–234, above and Vol.2 A4.xii.

TYPE OF WORK OR PERFOR-MANCE	ARE CLEAR-ANCES PRI-MARILY MADE INDIVIDU-ALLY RATHER THAN UNDER A COLLEC-TIVE AGREE-MENT?	ARE ANY CLEAR-ANCES (OR PAYMENTS) MADE UNDER COL-LECTIVE AGREE-MENTS?	WHICH TRADE UNION, COLLECTING SOCIETY OR OTHER OR-GANISATION IS INVOLVED?
Literary works used as source material	Yes	For certain cable re-transmissions of terrestrial broadcasts, and for some BBC satellite televi-sion programme services[579]	Authors Licens-ing and Collecting Society ("ALCS")[580]
Screenplays and radio drama scripts	Yes	For certain cable re-transmissions of terrestrial broadcasts, and for some BBC satellite televi-sion broadcasts	ALCS. In addi-tion, the Writers Guild of Great Britain[581] has minimum terms agreements for the writing of drama scripts with the Producers Alliance for Cin-ema and Televi-sion ("PACT"), ITV, and the BBC which deal with rights clearance. The Personal Managers As-sociation also participates in the agreement with the BBC.

TYPE OF WORK OR PERFOR-MANCE	ARE CLEAR-ANCES PRI-MARILY MADE INDIVIDU-ALLY RATHER THAN UNDER A COLLEC-TIVE AGREE-MENT?	ARE ANY CLEAR-ANCES (OR PAYMENTS) MADE UNDER COL-LECTIVE AGREE-MENTS?	WHICH TRADE UNION, COLLECTING SOCIETY OR OTHER OR-GANISATION IS INVOLVED?
Directors	Yes	Directors UK[582] collects remu-neration for British directors in respect of cable re-transmissions in Europe of Brit-ish television programmes and under the licensing scheme of the Educational Recording Agency.	The Broadcasting, Entertainment, Cinema and The-atre Union ("BECTU"),[583] the Directors Guild[584] and Directors UK have agreements with PACT, the BBC, ITV, Chan-nel Four, S4C, Five and BSkyB relating to the engagement of directors. Direc-tors UK makes distributions to directors in re-spect of sales of programmes out of an annual pay-ment made by the broadcasters and PACT under the agreements.

---

[582] As to Directors UK, see para.27–61, below.
[583] *http://www.bectu.org.uk.* [Accessed November 1, 2010].
[584] *http://www.dggb.co.uk.* [Accessed November 1, 2010].

TYPE OF WORK OR PERFOR- MANCE	ARE CLEAR- ANCES PRI- MARILY MADE INDIVIDU- ALLY RATHER THAN UNDER A COLLEC- TIVE AGREE- MENT?	ARE ANY CLEAR- ANCES (OR PAYMENTS) MADE UNDER COL- LECTIVE AGREE- MENTS?	WHICH TRADE UNION, COLLECTING SOCIETY OR OTHER OR- GANISATION IS INVOLVED?
Commissioned Composers	Yes, other than for communica- tion and public performance rights pre- assigned by the composer to the Performing Right Society ('PRS')	For com- munication to the public and public perfor- mance rights	PRS[585]
Existing music	Only if "grand rights"[586] usage is involved, or for secondary exploitation rights falling outside the scope of the mandate given by composers and publishers to the Mechani- cal Copyright Protection Soci- ety ('MCPS')[587] or outside the scope of the blanket agree- ments referred to in column 4	For (a) communica- tion to the pub- lic and public performance rights, and (b) synchronisa- tion and record- ing rights	(a) The Music Publishers As- sociation[588] has negotiated agree- ments on synchro- nisation and broadcasting fees for grand rights use; (b) PRS has negotiated blanket agreements with broadcasters for communication to the public and public perfor- mance rights;

[585] As to PRS, see para.27–65, below.
[586] As to the meaning of this expression, see para.26–325, below.
[587] As to MCPS, see para.27–63, below.
[588] *http://www.mpaonline.org.uk.*[Accessed November 1, 2010].

TYPE OF WORK OR PERFOR-MANCE	ARE CLEAR-ANCES PRI-MARILY MADE INDIVIDU-ALLY RATHER THAN UNDER A COLLEC-TIVE AGREE-MENT?	ARE ANY CLEAR-ANCES (OR PAYMENTS) MADE UNDER COL-LECTIVE AGREE-MENTS?	WHICH TRADE UNION, COLLECTING SOCIETY OR OTHER OR-GANISATION IS INVOLVED?
			(c) MCPS has negotiated blanket agreements for synchronisation and recording rights with broadcasters and some independent producers; (d) The PRS and MCPS blanket licences are now usually negotiated jointly by PRS for Music.

TYPE OF WORK OR PERFORMANCE	ARE CLEARANCES PRIMARILY MADE INDIVIDUALLY RATHER THAN UNDER A COLLECTIVE AGREEMENT?	ARE ANY CLEARANCES (OR PAYMENTS) MADE UNDER COLLECTIVE AGREEMENTS?	WHICH TRADE UNION, COLLECTING SOCIETY OR OTHER ORGANISATION IS INVOLVED?
Commercial sound recordings	Even if a blanket agreement has been entered into between the broadcaster and Phonographic Performance Limited ("PPL"),[589] the consent of individual record companies may be required for certain kinds of further exploitation of television programmes containing dubbed commercial records	For dubbing and communication to the public rights	PPL has blanket agreements with both radio and television broadcasters.
Music videos	Yes, except to the extent that usage may be covered by a blanket agreement between a broadcaster and Video Performance Limited ("VPL")[590]	For communication to the public rights	VPL has negotiated blanket agreements or standard rates with broadcasters and producers.

---

[589] As to PPL, see para.27–66, below.
[590] As to VPL, see para.27–68, below.

TYPE OF WORK OR PERFORMANCE	ARE CLEARANCES PRIMARILY MADE INDIVIDUALLY RATHER THAN UNDER A COLLECTIVE AGREEMENT?	ARE ANY CLEARANCES (OR PAYMENTS) MADE UNDER COLLECTIVE AGREEMENTS?	WHICH TRADE UNION, COLLECTING SOCIETY OR OTHER ORGANISATION IS INVOLVED?
Artistic works	Yes	Only for certain cable re-transmissions, through the Design and Artists Copyright Society ('DACS')[591]	DACS has negotiated a model form of clearance agreement with the BBC. Likewise, the British Association of Picture Libraries and Agencies ("BAPLA")[592] has negotiated a model form of agreement with the BBC for the use of its members' photographs.
Film and television programme footage	Yes	For cable re-transmission of foreign broadcasts	The Association de Gestion Internationale Collective des Oeuvres Audiovisuelles ("AGICOA")[593] is mandated to license cable retransmission.

---

[591] As to DACS, see para.27–60, below.
[592] *http://www.bapla.org.uk.*[Accessed November 1, 2010].
[593] As to AGICOA, see para.27–27, below.

TYPE OF WORK OR PERFORMANCE	ARE CLEARANCES PRIMARILY MADE INDIVIDUALLY RATHER THAN UNDER A COLLECTIVE AGREEMENT?	ARE ANY CLEARANCES (OR PAYMENTS) MADE UNDER COLLECTIVE AGREEMENTS?	WHICH TRADE UNION, COLLECTING SOCIETY OR OTHER ORGANISATION IS INVOLVED?
Actors	Yes	No	British Actors Equity Association ('Equity')[594] has negotiated minimum terms agreements with PACT, the BBC and the ITV companies for the engagement of actors.
Musicians	Yes	No	The Musicians' Union[595] has negotiated minimum terms agreements with PACT, the BBC and the ITV companies for the engagement of musicians.

Copies of the agreements entered into by the Writers' Guild, the Musicians' Union and Equity can be obtained from those unions. PACT[596] should be contacted for information on the agreements it has entered into. Information about the blanket and other agreements entered into by the various collecting societies with broadcasters is published on the broadcasters' websites in sections provided for the information of independent production companies. A considerable amount of information about collecting societies' licensing terms is also available on their respective websites.

---

[594] *http://www.equity.org.uk.* [Accessed November 1, 2010].
[595] *http://www.musiciansunion.org.uk* [Accessed November 1, 2010].
[596] *http://www.pact.co.uk* [Accessed November 1, 2010].

D. REGULATORY CONTROLS RELEVANT TO RIGHTS CLEARANCES

Copyright Tribunal

26–287 A critically important role is played by the Copyright Tribunal[597] in relation to the terms on which collecting societies license the use of works in their repertoires by broadcasters.

The table below identifies the most significant references to the Tribunal in the broadcasting field.

PARTIES	REFERENCE NUMBER	OUTCOME
1. The Independent Television Companies Association Limited 2. Independent Television News Limited 3. The Performing Right Society Limited	38/81	The Tribunal rejected PRS's claim for a percentage of ITV's net advertising revenue.
1. The Association of Independent Radio Companies & Others 2. Phonographic Performance Limited	9/91	The Tribunal altered the formula under which the commercial radio broadcasters pay percentages of their net advertising revenue so that they would pay as follows: Music stations: 5% of relevant revenue; Speech stations: 1% of relevant revenue.

---

[597] As to the Copyright Tribunal and its predecessor, the Performing Right Tribunal, generally, see paras 28–76 et seq., below.

PARTIES	REFERENCE NUMBER	OUTCOME
1. BSkyB and Sky TV 2. The Performing Right Society Limited	38/96	In this reference, BSkyB sought a continuation of the terms on which its predecessors were licensed to broadcast music. The PRS sought a percentage (1% initially, rising to 3% after two years) of BSkyB's net advertising revenues and (discounted) revenues from cable operators. The Tribunal rejected a revenue-based approach and awarded a flat fee, adjustable for the future as to one part by percentage changes in viewer hours and RPI and as to another part by an incremental payment for each new channel.
1. CSC Media Group Limited 2. Video Performance Limited	CT/94/05	The Tribunal reduced VPL's royalty from 20% to 12.5% of the same proportion of the broadcaster's revenues as the proportion of music video hours to total hours of broadcasting. VPL appealed successfully and there is to be a re-hearing before a differently constituted Tribunal.

As many broadcasters now simulcast their services and make programmes available on-demand online, the decision by the Copyright Tribunal in the reference made by record companies, online music service providers and mobile network operators in respect of the Joint Online Licence offered by PRS for Music has been of particular interest.[598]

Tribunal licensing of performers' rights

26–288 The Copyright Tribunal was given another important jurisdiction by the 1988 Act, in respect of "orphan" performances. Broadcasters had lobbied for this in order to overcome difficulties they had experienced in exploiting their programme archives. The difficulties arose from the need to obtain additional consents from performers for the making of copies of programmes for supply to new categories of users, such as (at that time) satellite broadcasters. The 1988 Act empowered the Tribunal to grant consent on behalf of a performer to the making of a copy of a recording which included the performer's performance, if the performer could

---

[598] CT84-90/05.

not be identified or traced after reasonable enquiry.[599] This provision was invoked to enable a 1954 BBC radio production of Dylan Thomas's "Under Milk Wood" to be used as the sound-track of an animated television production of that work.[600]

For the same reason, the Tribunal was also given power under the 1988 Act to give consent to the making of further recordings in the case of a performer who was unreasonably withholding consent.[601] It was considered unacceptable that a "tenth spear carrier" (i.e. a minor member of the cast) should be able to prevent exploitation of a production by withholding his consent unreasonably when all other cast members might have consented to the making of the necessary copies. This power was abolished on implementation of the EC Directive on Rental and Lending Rights.[602] The overall enhancement of performers' rights required by the Directive was considered to be incompatible with this compulsory licence mechanism.

E. RIGHTS-CLEARANCE ISSUES IN THE BROADCASTING FIELD

Overview of developments 1988–2010

26–289   The 1988 Act introduced, as broadcasters had requested, a number of provisions designed to facilitate their use of copyright works and protected performances. The process continued in the Broadcasting Act 1990, which made a number of amendments to the 1988 Act helpful to broadcasters. Although the thrust of subsequent EC legislation on copyright and neighbouring rights has been to enhance the rights of authors and performers, the Satellite Broadcasting and Cable Retransmission Directive[603] recognised that the rights-clearance burden on satellite broadcasters needed to be lightened in the interests of encouraging the development of transfrontier television services. Likewise the transitional provisions of the Regulations implementing that Directive, the Rental and Lending Rights Directive[604] and the Term Directive[605] bear the imprint of representations made by producers and broadcasters concerned to ensure that the making of productions for which they had already entered into commitments, and the exploitation of productions already completed, should not be impeded. Although producers and broadcasters regretted the loss of the "tenth spear carrier"[606] provision because of its incompatibility with the terms of the Rental and Lending Rights Directive, their representations in respect of the drafting of the transitional provisions succeeded to a limited degree in ensuring that their programme archives would not be locked up by rights-clearance difficulties, just at the point at which the new media were promising to offer fresh opportunities for their exploitation. No sooner had broadcasters achieved these concessions, however, than they found themselves having to make representations to the European Parliament and Commission over the treatment, in the proposed Directive on Copyright and Related Rights in the Information Society, of the key exceptions to copyright protection. Once that Directive[607] had been adopted, their attention focussed on ensuring that the United Kingdom's regulations implementing it dealt appropriately with the new forms of broadcasting then coming onstream. The salient details of these developments are outlined below.

---

[599] CDPA 1988 s.190 (1)(a).
[600] *Ex p. Sianel Pedwar Cymru* [1993] E.M.L.R. 251.
[601] CDPA 1988 s.190(1)(b).
[602] The Copyright and Related Rights Regulations 1996 reg.23 (SI 1996/2967).
[603] 93/83/EEC.
[604] 92/100/EEC.
[605] 93/98/EEC.
[606] See para.26–288, above.
[607] 2001/29/EC.

By the latter stage of this 22-year period, however, it had become apparent that a more radical approach was needed if broadcasters were to be able to make their programmes and services available to the public in the way the public increasingly wished to receive them. Broadcasters now need to have the ability to ensure that their programmes and services can be delivered on all transmission platforms, whether in linear schedules or as part of an on-demand service. Broadcasters with extensive programme archives want to make their older programmes available again, which the virtually unlimited capacity of the internet makes possible. All this is hampered by the legacy of past rights clearance practices when all too frequently the rights that could be obtained in respect of a copyright work or performance were to use it for a limited range of purposes for a limited period. In addition, many works and performances in those older programmes are orphan. After conducting a trial rights-clearance exercise in 2007 on 1,000 hours of archive television programmes, the BBC calculated that to meet the objective of making its entire radio and television archive available online would require the effort of 800 people working full time for three years. For this reason the BBC strongly endorsed the inclusion in the Digital Economy Bill of 2010 of provisions paving the way for collective licensing of orphan works and for the introduction of extended collective licensing of the kind established in the Nordic countries. Those provisions were refined in the Committee stage of the Bill in the House of Lords, but were a casualty of the accelerated legislative procedure (the wash-up) necessitated by the calling of the 2010 General Election. The European Broadcasting Union has lobbied in parallel at the European Union level for such provisions to be the subject of a new Directive, along with other provisions designed to facilitate rights clearances, so that broadcasters can make their programmes and services available any time, any place, anywhere.

The 1988 Act

For broadcasters, the most important of the rights clearances facilitating provisions introduced by the 1988 Act were as follows: **26–290**

Recording of the spoken word: section 58

The 1988 Act put it beyond doubt that a speaker's words, recorded while being spoken, could constitute a literary work.[608] The making of such recordings is an everyday activity for broadcasters, who were therefore concerned that the implied licences on which they would often have to rely when using such contributions would not protect them in all circumstances. For instance, would a speaker who regretted what he had said be entitled to revoke such a licence? What would be the position as regards recordings made surreptitiously, for which no implied licence could be invoked? The validity of such concerns was recognised and dealt with by s.58 of the 1988 Act, which provides that where a recording of spoken words is made for the purposes of broadcasting, it is not an infringement of copyright in the words as a literary work to use the recording (or to copy it and use the copy) for broadcasting, provided certain conditions are met. These conditions have not detracted from the protection which s.58 gives to broadcasting journalism.[609]   **26–291**

---

[608] See CDPA 1988 s.3(1) and para.3–115, above.
[609] As to these conditions and s.58 generally, see paras 9–174 et seq., above.

Fair dealing: extension to sound recordings, film, broadcasts and performers' rights

26–292   Under the Copyright Act 1956 the fair dealing exceptions did not apply to sound recordings or films. Further, the civil rights of performers which had been recognised by the court in *Rickless v United Artists Corp*[610] were not subject to a statutory fair dealing exception. These defects were remedied by the 1988 Act.[611] The BBC, having pressed for these changes to be introduced, mounted the first challenge to their scope, but failed to convince the court that the broadcasting by British Satellite Broadcasting of highlights from the BBC's coverage of the 1990 Football World Cup was not fair dealing for the purpose of reporting a current event.[612]

The availability of this fair dealing exception was subsequently underpinned by the inclusion in the Broadcasting Act 1996 of a provision making void any clause in an agreement which seeks to prohibit the taking of visual images from a broadcast in circumstances where the exception would apply.[613]

The application to films of the exception allowing criticism or review had its first test in court in 1994 when Channel Four succeeded in persuading the Court of Appeal that the use of excerpts from Stanley Kubrick's film "A Clockwork Orange", in a programme evaluating the film and arguing that Kubrick's ban on its showing in the United Kingdom should be lifted, fell within the scope of the exception.[614]

These fair dealing exceptions were the subject of further amendments introduced by the Copyright and Related Rights Regulations 2003, most notably a new requirement that fair dealing with a work for the purposes of reporting a current event by way of a broadcast must be accompanied by a sufficient acknowledgement, except where this would be impossible for reasons of practicality or otherwise. There are not likely to be many instances where it can safely be said that it would be impossible to give an acknowledgement.[615]

Exception for incidental inclusion

26–293   Broadcasters gave a warm welcome to the introduction of a defence of incidental inclusion in the Bill that became the 1988 Act. Had the Act included only the wording of cl.31(1) from the Bill (i.e. "Copyright in a work is not infringed by its incidental inclusion in an artistic work, sound recording, film, broadcast or cable programme"), it would have produced a very satisfactory degree of protection for broadcasters against claims from copyright owners for payments for the use of their works in such *de minimis* circumstances. However, lobbying by music copyright owners resulted in the inclusion in the Act of s.31(3), which provides that a musical work, words spoken or sung with music, or so much of a sound recording, broadcast or cable programme as includes a musical work or such words, shall not be regarded as incidentally included in another work if it is deliberately included. This has complicated the analysis that needs to be made when a pro-

---

[610] [1988] Q.B. 40.
[611] By CDPA 1988, s.30 for films, sound recordings and broadcasts and by s.189 and Sch.2 para.2 for performances.
[612] *BBC v British Satellite Broadcasting Ltd* [1992] Ch. 141. As to the fair dealing provisions, see paras 9–49 et seq., above.
[613] Broadcasting Act 1996 s. 137.
[614] *Time Warner Entertainment Co v Channel Four Television Corp* [1994] E.M.L.R. 1, CA. See paras 9–40 et seq., above.
[615] See para.9–33, above.

ducer or broadcaster is considering whether this exception is applicable.[616] Broadcasters were subsequently dismayed to find that the exception did not appear at all in the exhaustive list of exceptions permitted by the Information Society Directive in its draft form, but their concerted lobbying succeeded in having it included in the final version.

Filming and broadcasting of artistic works on public display

Broadcasters filming in public places or in premises open to the public are at risk   **26–294** of including artistic works that happen to be in shot. Section 62 of the 1988 Act is a useful safeguard for them in circumstances where they might not readily be able to argue that they are covered by the exception for "incidental inclusion". It provides that the copyright in (a) buildings and (b) sculptures, models for buildings and works of artistic craftsmanship, if permanently situated in a public place or in premises open to the public, will not be infringed by making a film of them or broadcasting or including in a cable programme service a visual image of them.[617] This exception also survived unscathed the narrowing effect of the Information Society Directive's exhaustive list of exceptions.

The Broadcasting Act 1990: use of sound recordings

The Broadcasting Act 1990 introduced into the 1988 Act an important change to   **26–295** the basis on which broadcasters may acquire the right to use sound recordings.[618] This followed an enquiry by the Monopolies and Mergers Commission[619] into practices in the collective licensing of public performance and broadcasting rights in sound recordings, which recommended that Phonographic Performance Limited[620] should be obliged to permit the use of its repertoire in return for equitable remuneration, and that users should be entitled to a statutory licence. The statutory licence is available when the licensing body refuses to grant a licence whose terms as to payment would be acceptable to the broadcaster, or a licence allowing unlimited needletime or such needletime as the broadcaster has demanded (needletime being the amount of time for which sound recordings may be broadcast in any given period). The reference to the Tribunal made in 1991 by the Association of Independent Radio Companies[621] was made under the terms of this new provision, not surprisingly since it had been the Association which had made the representations which led to the reference of PPL's practices to the Monopolies and Mergers Commission. The Copyright and Related Rights Regulations, 2003 have restricted the scope of this statutory licence so that it will not apply to on-demand services, nor to internet broadcasts other than simulcasts.

EC copyright harmonisation Directives

The key provisions of the EC copyright harmonisation Directives facilitating   **26–296** broadcasters' rights clearances are as follows:

---

[616] As to CDPA 1988 s.31 generally, see para.9–61, above.
[617] As to CDPA 1988 s.62 generally, see para.9–188, above.
[618] CDPA 1988 ss.135A–G. See, generally paras 28–25 et seq., below.
[619] CM 530. December 1988.
[620] As to PPL, see para.27–66, below.
[621] para.28–36, above.

Place of broadcast

26–297   The Satellite Broadcasting and Cable Retransmission Directive[622] adopts the "emission theory" of broadcasting, that is, that a broadcast receivable in more than one country should be deemed to take place only in the country where the broadcast originates, rather than in each country where the broadcast is receivable. This means that a broadcaster only has to clear rights in one territory, not wherever the signal may be received. This was already the position as far as the United Kingdom was concerned under the 1988 Act, although refining amendments were introduced by the Copyright and Related Rights Regulations 1996.[623] This principle now applies throughout the EC and EEA. In practice, of course, the commercial terms on which rights are licensed to the transfrontier satellite broadcaster will reflect the fact that audiences in other countries within the satellite footprint will be reached. It is noteworthy that in relation to the forms of Internet transmission defined as broadcasting by the Copyright and Related Rights Regulations 2003, there is no similar adoption of the emission theory, a defect that the European Broadcasting Union proposes should be remedied in a new Directive.[624]

Mandatory collective licensing of cable retransmissions

26–298   Article 9 of the Satellite Broadcasting and Cable Retransmission Directive requires Member States to ensure that the right of copyright owners and holders of related rights to grant or refuse authorisation to a cable operator for a cable retransmission of a broadcast may be exercised only through a collecting society. Further, where a rights holder has not transferred the management of his rights to a collecting society, the collecting society which manages rights of the same category shall be deemed to manage his rights. These provisions removed the risk that an individual rights holder might be able to prevent retransmission of a broadcast of the work he controlled, thereby disturbing the commercial relationship between cable operators as licensees on the one hand and broadcasters and collecting societies as licensors of cable retransmissions of television channels on the other.

Transitional provisions

26–299   The three copyright Directives adopted in the 1990s contained a number of transitional provisions intended to give protection to persons with "legitimate expectations", that is, persons who had entered into contractual arrangements on the basis of existing law and who would be adversely affected by a change in the law applicable to those arrangements which resulted from implementation of the Directives.[625] In giving effect to the transitional provisions, the UK Government responded in a number of respects to concerns expressed by producers and broadcasters wishing to ensure that rights clearances for production and exploitation of programmes should not be made yet more complicated. Key provisions which reflect these concerns include the following:

- the revival of copyright in a work included in or adapted by a film or television or radio programme at a time before July 1, 1995 when that work was out of copyright will not affect the continued exploitation of the film or programme;

---

[622] 93/83/EEC art.1.2(b).
[623] See para.7–126, above.
[624] But see para.7–135, above.
[625] For a discussion of the transitional arrangements, see paras 5–148 et seq., above.

- the revived copyright in a work will not be infringed by acts done after 1 January 1996 in pursuance of arrangements to exploit the work entered into before January 1, 1995 when it was in the public domain;
- the revived copyright in a work will not be infringed by a restricted act done at a time when, or done in pursuance of arrangements made at a time when, the name and address of a person entitled to authorise the act cannot be ascertained by reasonable enquiry;
- a copyright licence subsisting on December 31, 1995 which was valid for the entire period of the copyright under the 1988 Act is extended so as to have effect throughout the duration of any extended copyright (subject to any agreement to the contrary);
- the presumption of transfer of rental rights is applied to agreements concluded before December 1, 1996, with no exclusion in relation to screenplay, dialogue or music specifically created for the film.

F. PROTECTION OF BROADCASTERS' RIGHTS

The 1988 Act introduced a number of specific protections of broadcasters' rights additional to the protection of the broadcast themselves. Two in particular are worth special attention as they have come under recent scrutiny.   **26–300**

Protection of encrypted broadcasts

The 1988 Act included, at the request of broadcasters, specific protection in respect of fraudulent reception of broadcast programmes, which was made a criminal offence,[626] and in respect of dealings in equipment or publishing of information to enable or assist unauthorised reception, which was made the subject of civil rights and remedies.[627] Broadcasters of pay television services had foreseen that such a package of criminal and civil law deterrents would be needed to deal with circumvention of payment for reception of their encrypted services. These provisions were strengthened by amendments introduced by the Broadcasting Act 1990, which made it a criminal offence to make, import, sell or let for hire an unauthorised decoder, and by further amendments in the Broadcasting Act 1996 adding offences of offering, exposing or advertising such decoders for sale or hire, and increasing the penalties for the offences.[628] These provisions, and such counterparts as had been enacted in other EU Member States, were reinforced by the EU Directive on the legal protection of services based on, or consisting of, conditional access.[629] The Directive requires Member States to prohibit the manufacture, import, sale or possession for commercial purposes of illicit devices; their installation, maintenance or replacement for commercial purposes; and the use of commercial communications to promote them. An illicit device is defined as any equipment or software designed or adapted to enable unauthorised access to a radio, television or online service where these are provided on the basis of conditional access. Broadcasters were concerned that conditional access was defined in the Directive in such a way that it would only be protected when it is aimed at ensuring remuneration for provision of a service. Broadcasters want conditional access to be protected when it is used to restrict access for other reasons, such as territorial rights limitations. Now the efficacy of the legislation has been called into question by the reference made to the ECJ from the High   **26–301**

---

[626] See CDPA 1988 s.297 and para.16–07, above.
[627] See s.298 and para.16–27, above.
[628] See s.297A and para.16–12, above.
[629] 98/84/EC.

Court in *Football Association Premier League and others v QC Leisure and others.*[630]

Cable retransmission of certain UK broadcasts

26–302   The 1988 Act narrowed the scope, just in time for the new era of satellite broadcasting and the proliferation of television channels it ushered in, of the provision which had made its first appearance as s.40(3) of the Copyright Act 1956. This had provided that a cable operator would not infringe the copyright in a work included in a UK television or radio broadcast by retransmitting the broadcast to its subscribers. The justification for this exception was that cable operators were under obligation to retransmit BBC and ITV television broadcasts; the so-called "must-carry" rule. They were therefore seen as vulnerable to claims from copyright owners for excessive fees.

Section 73 of the 1988 Act continued the exception and further extended it to the copyright in the broadcasts themselves. However, the 1988 Act restricted the exception to the retransmission only of unencrypted broadcasts from terrestrial transmitters and to retransmissions of broadcasts intended for reception in the area where the cable operator's network is located or to broadcasts which a number of cable operators were obliged to carry as a condition of their operating licences granted under the Cable and Broadcasting Act 1984. The Broadcasting Act 1996 substituted a new s.73, applying the exception only to "must-carry" broadcasts (it was envisaged that some digital terrestrial broadcasts would be in this category) and to a defined list of public service channels, namely those of the BBC, ITV, Channel 4, Channel 5 and S4C, as well as the teletext services associated with them. Other commercial television broadcasters are therefore at liberty to negotiate terms for the carriage of their services with cable operators,[631] of which there is now only one, Virgin Media.[632] In the lead-up to the Digital Economy Act, proposals were made for s.73 to be abolished but these were rejected in the "Digital Britain: Final Report".[633]

G. International Protection of Broadcasters' Rights

26–303   Many broadcasters consider that, at the international level, insufficient recognition is given to their status as copyright owners of the broadcasts they create, and in particular to their need for enhanced protection in the face of the challenges posed by the new technologies. Whereas many of those challenges were addressed for other rights owners and for performers in the WIPO Treaties adopted in December 1996,[634] broadcasters' rights were not on the agenda.

In April 1997, WIPO held a World Symposium on Broadcasting, New Communication Technologies and Intellectual Property, at which a catalogue of rights was identified as a core for up-to-date neighbouring rights protection of broadcasters. Subsequent meetings of the WIPO Standing Committee on Copyright and Related Rights took matters forward to the point where it appeared that a Diplomatic Conference might be convened as the final step in developing a new international treaty. The broadcasters' hopes for a new treaty were dashed when in June 2007 the WIPO General Assembly decided that there was insufficient agreement to justify the convening of a Diplomatic Conference to adopt a treaty.

---

[630] See para.16–30, above.

[631] Broadcasting Act 1996 s.138 and Sch.9. See para.9–226, above.

[632] At least one internet-based operator has claimed to be entitled to rely on the section.

[633] Cm 7650 paras 54 to 61.

[634] As to the WIPO Treaties, see paras 23–66 et seq. and paras 23–119 et seq., above.

Brazil and India led the opposition to the treaty proposals, the harshest critics arguing that the creation of new rights for broadcasters would overlay other copyrights in broadcast content, restrict access to programmes in the public domain, prevent legitimate copying for private use and stifle technological innovation. The Standing Committee has continued to work, but as of mid-2010 it appeared unlikely that a Diplomatic Conference would be called in the near future.

Progress has, however, been made in the Council of Europe, which has decided to support the development of a possible Convention to update the neighbouring rights protection of broadcasting organisations. Work on this is at an early stage, but builds on the consensus achieved within the European Union in the course of the work on the proposed WIPO treaty. The content of any Convention is unlikely to require the United Kingdom to extend significantly the rights accorded to broadcasters by the 1988; Act the real value of a Convention will be as a model for adoption by other countries in which broadcasters are not presently given a high level of protection against unauthorised use of their services.

6. THE THEATRE INDUSTRY

A. THE AUTHORS OF COPYRIGHT MATERIAL

Introduction

The principal focus of the theatre industry is on live public performances of liter-   **26–304**
ary, dramatic and musical works, which are acts restricted by copyright under CDPA 1988 ss.16(1)(c) and 19, although it must be remembered that performance itself is not enough to constitute "publication", which necessitates the issue of copies to the public or public electronic availability.[635] This may explain why copies of a play or other theatrical work are sometimes offered on sale or handed out free to members of the public within the precincts of the theatre or elsewhere, in cases where the author is a foreign national.

Publication by the issue of copies to the public is an act restricted by copyright under s.18(1) of the Act. Lack of publication may have little or no practical consequence in cases where the status of the author as a qualifying person under s.154 of the Act is clear, since the author is the person who creates the work,[636] and also the first copyright owner[637] with the exclusive right to publish the work concerned. However, where the status of the author as a qualifying person is unclear, copyright protection under the Act will depend on the place of first publication under s.155 of the Act, and mere live public performance will not suffice. Thus, an unauthorised public performance in the United Kingdom of a play by a foreign author of non-qualifying status will not be an infringement of copyright under English law if the play has not yet been "published" at all or if the place of its first publication was not in the United Kingdom or another qualifying country within the meaning of the Act. Nevertheless it would be a bold UK producer who would take the risk of presenting unauthorised live public performances of such a hitherto unpublished work, since it would be relatively easy for the foreign author to arrange qualifying first publication in the United Kingdom or other qualifying

---

[635] CDPA 1988 ss.175(1)(a) and (4)(a)(i). To constitute publication, an alternative to issuing copies to the public is inclusion in an electronic retrieval system which is made available to the public, e.g publication on the internet— CDPA 1988 s. 175(1)(b).

[636] CDPA 1988 s.9(1).

[637] CDPA 1988 s.11(1).

country, and so stop any continuation of the unauthorised production in its tracks.[638]

An unlicensed performance of a theatrical work which is not given in public will not be an infringement of copyright.[639] There are numerous cases falling on one side of the line or the other as to what constitutes performance "in public".[640] It is considered that a rehearsal of a forthcoming theatrical production would not itself be a performance in public, even if one or two guests were to be invited in addition to production personnel, provided the rehearsal was not open to the public, and the same applies to auditions. In this connection it should be borne in mind that making an action-film will of necessity involve live performances, whether on a fixed set or "on location", of excerpts from a dramatic work (the screenplay) while these are in the process of being filmed, but in most cases this activity is unlikely to take place in public. Whether the presence in the background of a crowd scene of any members of the public who happened to be around would make the performance of the actors in the foreground a performance in public is debatable, but perhaps the question is academic.[641]

It is not uncommon for writers of new theatrical, copyright material to deposit a copy of their work as soon as it is completed with a trusted potential witness, such as a lawyer or other professional person, in order to establish beyond doubt the date when it came into existence, so as to pre-empt any future allegation of copying by another author of a later work, and to establish a foundation for copyright in the original work itself, i.e. to establish which came first.

In common parlance the word "author" is usually used to connote the writer of a literary work and "playwright" to connote the writer of a dramatic work, but in copyright terms the word "author" is defined by s.8 of the 1988 Act as meaning simply in relation to any "work" the person who creates it. The word "author" can thus be used to apply, among other things, to a musical composer or indeed to the creator of any literary, dramatic, musical and/or artistic work.

The issue of copyright obviously looms large in most contracts for the creation and/or live performance of all "works"[642] of a theatrical nature. However, the law of copyright in its application to the practical and contractual aspects of the theatre industry, can best be illustrated by reference to a live stage dramatico-musical work, which usually contains all the elements of drama, speech, music, song and dance, stage direction and production design, one or more of which may be missing from other forms of entertainment attraction, such as a non-musical play, concert, variety act or ballet. Indeed, the production on stage of a dramatico-musical work ("stage musical") will usually also contain all four copyright elements of literary, dramatic,[643] musical and artistic material combined.

The principal parties or *dramatis personae* involved in the creation or acquisition of copyright and other rights in relation to the production of a stage musical are as follows:

---

[638] For foreign authors and foreign works generally see paras 3–154 et seq, 3–192 et seq. and 17–36.

[639] CDPA 1988 s.19 and s.34.

[640] See paras 7–108 and 7–109. By CDPA 1988 s.34, certain performances in an educational establishment are deemed not to be public performances provided the public (including parents) are not invited. Other "permitted acts" are set out in Ch.III of the Act.

[641] For a detailed analysis of the criteria to be considered in deciding whether or not a performance took place in public see the Court of Appeal decision in *Jennings v Stephens* [1936] Ch.469

[642] As to what constitutes a "work" for copyright protection see CDPA 1988 s.1.

[643] For meaning of "dramatic work" see CDPA 1988 s.2 and *Norowzian v Arks Ltd (No.2)* [2000] F.S.R. 363, [2000] E.M.L.R. 67 and paras 3–37, 3–43 et seq. and 7–63. In the latter case, the CA held that the definition of dramatic work being at large, it must be given its natural and ordinary meaning: "a work of action, with or without words or music, which is capable of being performed before an audience", and could thus include a film. For the meaning of "musical work" see para.3–48 and for the relative unimportance of the copyright distinction between "dramatic" and "musical" works see para.3–50.

  (i) Writers and composers.
 (ii) Creative team:
       (a) Stage director.
       (b) Choreographer or musical stager.
       (c) Designers of:
             (i) Sets and properties.
            (ii) Costumes and wigs.
           (iii) Lighting.
            (iv) Sound.
       (d) Orchestrator and musical "arrangers".
(iii) Logo and artwork designer.
(iv) Performers.
 (v) Translators.
(vi) Producers.
(vii) Other adaptors of the written work (if any).

(i) Writers and composers

Clearly the fundamental elements of these works are the basic words and music   **26–305**
which are to be performed, but plot, characterisation and situations may also in
the right circumstances be separately protected as dramatic works, ballet being an
obvious example.[644] Rarely will there be just one playwright or dramatist who
has written the entire work and also composed the music. More often the music,
text and lyrics will be composed or written by different persons, and even one
such element alone may involve a number of collaborators.[645] In addition, there
may be separate individuals who have created the conceptual treatment, some or
all of the plot or the characterisation.[646] Sometimes adaptors or new writers will
be engaged to adapt or make changes to a pre-existing novel, film or play on
which a new work is to be based. Sometimes a so-called "dramaturge" is engaged
for the sole purpose of enhancing the dramatic effect of a new, pre-existing
dramatico-musical work. The different bases for the acquisition of writers' and
composers' rights by the producer are considered below.[647] Note also that where
the writer or composer is a member of the Performing Right Society Ltd
("PRS"),[648] the PRS will very likely have acquired certain rights in his work,
including in particular, in this context, the so-called "small" performing right.[649]
Authors also have important moral rights in respect of their work.[650]
   Often the contractual terms between authors and producers will be governed
by the minimum terms of a collective bargaining agreement between bodies

---

[644] See para.7–63.
[645] As to whether such collaborators will be "joint" authors, see paras 4–32 et seq. and 5–163 above,
  and *Brighton v Jones* [2004] E.M.L.R. 26; [2005] F.S.R. 16. See also *Beckingham v Hodgens*
  [2002] E.M.L.R. 45 and *Bamgboye v Reed* [2004] E.M.L.R. 5. As to copyright in a "composite
  work", see paras 4–20, 26–318 and 26–336. As to implied licences to re-use existing material,
  see *Brighton v Jones* at paras 72 to 77.
[646] As to the protection given by the law of copyright to such elements, see para.3–43, above.
[647] paras 26–320 to 26–323. Note that where a writer is commissioned to write new material, the
  Court will be slow, in the absence of express agreement, to imply that this will be of any particular (other than "reasonable") length— *Artlamb Productions Ltd v Goude* [2004] EWHC 3029
  (QB); [2005] BLD 2212045481.
[648] As to the role of the PRS generally, see Ch.27, and also in particular paras 26–323 and 26–325.
[649] See paras 26–325 and 26–330, below. As to the full extent of the rights administered by the PRS,
  see the Society's Handbook.
[650] As to these, see Ch.11, above and para.26–331, below.

representing the two sides respectively.[651] However, it will be noted that there is no such standard collective bargaining agreement between producers and writers/composers for commercial West End of London theatre productions, where the usual practice is for terms to be negotiated between the parties to suit individual circumstances.[652] Typically such agreements will provide for an advance and royalties, comprising a percentage of net weekly box office receipts,[653] payable to the author or other copyright owner,[654] and for all royalties to be calculated in the same way. Royalties may be expressed to escalate after recoupment of pre-production capital expenditure, or to be "capped" or "pooled" prior to such recoupment, or in some cases may be calculated on "weekly running surplus" rather than box office receipts. The advance will usually be expressed as non-returnable but recoupable in whole or in part from royalties. The producer will be granted an option to present the production within a specific period, possibly extendible by payment of further advances within specified time limits. If the production is presented within the option period and continued for a specified number of consecutive performances (usually 21), the producer may acquire specified "subsidiary" or "ancillary" rights to produce in other territories and/or to exploit the work in other media.[655] The producer's rights may be limited to a specified period of time, or they may be open-ended and subject to lapse only if, after the closure of the initial run or another specified period, either fewer than a specified number of performances per annum (usually 50 first class, professional performances) are presented by the producer, or no specified optional payment is made to the author in order to compensate for any shortfall in the number of such performances so as thereby to preserve the rights for the further specified period concerned.

The grantor of the rights will, usually, be expected to "hold back" on releasing other stage rights or subsidiary rights so long as the producer's rights subsist or for a specified period or territory, and even when such other rights are released from hold-back, it is frequently agreed that the producer will share in revenue from their exploitation on the ground that such revenue is generated in part by his contribution to the reputation of the work, at least in the case of new work as distinct from "revivals".[656]

Other typical provisions commonly found in such agreements relate to warranties as to title and as to non-obscene and non-defamatory content, billing credits, house-seats allocation (seats held back for management disposal or priority reservation), approval or consultation rights, attendance at auditions and rehearsals, travel, accommodation and subsistence expenses (the latter being known as "per diems"), payment and accounting procedures. An interpretation clause, containing numerous definitions of commonly used theatrical terms, is an essential feature in contracts of this nature.

---

[651] For details of relevant collective bargaining agreements see para.26–335, below.

[652] The expression "West End" of London in a theatrical context is normally taken to mean those theatres which are represented in the Society of London Theatre, as distinct from the geographical location of London's West End. Such theatres may not necessarily have a West End postal address. Sometimes they may be identified by being individually listed in the contract between the parties.

[653] Usually defined as subject to certain standard deductions, such as VAT, credit card, charge card and ticket agents' commissions and block-booking discounts.

[654] In theatrical contracts, as the copyright ownership often becomes fragmented and the subject of sub-licensing arrangements, the obligation to pay royalties to a variety of royalty participants is frequently passed on to licensees and sub-licensees, but the possibly unwelcome effect in this context of the Contracts (Rights of Third Parties) Act, 1999 should be noted, and the appropriate steps taken to negate its impact, if desired.

[655] See para.26–238.

[656] For contractual restrictions in restraint of trade on authors generally see paras 28–330, et seq.

(ii) The creative team

The creative team, together with and in consultation with the producer, is **26–306**
responsible for converting the basic written work (that is to say the music, text
and lyrics) into the audio-visual representation of that basic work which is presented on stage. Inevitably this often involves a considerable degree of creativity.
It may also involve the creation of new copyright works, such as the set and
costume designs, the choreography and, more controversially, stage directions,
lighting and sound designs[657], in so far as these contain a sufficient degree of
originality. The creative team will usually be engaged as self-employed independent contractors under contracts for services and will therefore start off as owners
of the copyright in their works,[658] although occasionally they may be employees
under a contract of service, for example if they are part of a resident stage
company, when the copyright will vest in the employer unless otherwise agreed.[659]
It is also not uncommon for individual members of the creative team to contract
their services through their own so-called "lend-out" companies which have the
exclusive right to dispose of such services,[660] in which case a personal guarantee
of his company's contractual obligations by the individual concerned, in what is
often called an "inducement letter", will usually be required.

The creative team will usually be remunerated for their work by a fixed fee,
possibly payable by instalments at fixed intervals. Usually such fees are expressed
as being non-returnable but recoverable, in whole or in part, from the whole or
part of future royalties. The use of their copyright material or the product of their
services on a repetitive basis will usually be remunerated by reference to royalties expressed as a fixed percentage of net weekly box office receipts (after standard deductions such as VAT, credit card, charge card, and ticket agency commissions and block-booking discounts), possibly in some cases escalating after a
specified number of performances or after so-called "recoupment" of the pre-
production capital costs incurred prior to opening.[661]

(a) Directors

There seems to be no reason in principle why a director's stage directions,   **26–307**
whether relating to vocal or facial expressions, gestures or movements, should
not attract copyright as part of the whole dramatic work,[662] provided that they are
not merely contributions to the interpretation or theatrical presentation of the
work,[663] are original and are recorded in some permanent form.

The view has been expressed that despite a stage director giving life and vital-
ity to the printed text of a dramatic work, his creative contribution has no protection in law.[664] This view needs to be treated with caution as a statement of

---

[657] See paras 26–307, 26–311 and 26–312.

[658] As to the rights acquired by the producer, see paras 26–318 and 26–321 to 26–323, below.

[659] CDPA 1988 s.11(2). As to works of employees generally, see paras 5–11 et seq., above, and
para.26–337, below, and note in particular *Intercase UK Ltd v Time Computers Ltd* [2004]
E.C.D.R. 8 and *Ultraframe (UK) Ltd v Fielding* [2004] R.P.C. 24.

[660] Such companies generally employ their "owners" under a contract of service and so will in the
first instance own the copyright in any work made by the employee. Their tax effectiveness is
now less than it was.

[661] See para.26–305, above, as to alternative bases of royalty calculation.

[662] As to what constitutes a dramatic work, see para.26–304, above and para 3–37, above.

[663] See *Brighton v Jones* [2004] EWHC 1157 (Ch), [2004] E.M.L.R. 26 and [2005] F.S.R. 16 at
para.56(iii).

[664] See L. E. Cotterell, *Performance* 3rd edn, p.371.

principle.[665] As a matter of practice, the collective bargaining agreements for directors between the Society of London Theatre (SOLT) and Equity, and between the Theatrical Management Association (TMA) and Equity proceed on the assumption that copyright subsists in the product of a stage director's services, which may or may not be justified, and which contrasts with the position of a film director as a joint copyright owner under ss.9(2)(ab) and 10(1A) of the 1988 Act. The absence of any provisions similar to those for a film director under s.9(2)(ab) of the Act in relation to the work of a live stage director appears to leave it an open question. The reason for this may well be that the work of a film director, unlike that of a stage director, involves camera angles, zooming in and out, and other moving photographic techniques, which add considerably to the creative process and originality of the basic work, which in turn cannot help but affect, for good or ill, the quality and dramatic impact of the finished product.

No doubt where a director adds stage directions which are commonplace or largely dictated by the script, no question of copyright will arise, there being no sufficient contribution to the dramatic work as a whole or no originality. In each case it will be a matter of degree. In many cases it will be fortuitous whether the further requirement, namely that the directions be recorded in some permanent form, is satisfied, depending on whether the stage directions were noted down at any stage or whether, for example, the production was filmed.[666] In practice, the point may not be so important in relation to directors' remuneration, since the stage director's contract will usually provide for him to be remunerated whenever and wherever "the product of his services"[667] is used by the other contracting party. It is only where his work is described for the purpose of remuneration as being confined to that which is protected by copyright, or where he has placed some limitation on the right to use his copyright material, that a problem may arise.

(b) Choreographers and musical stagers

26–308   The work of choreographers will be protected if the usual conditions for subsistence of copyright apply.[668] The function of a choreographer is, of course, similar to that of a stage director, but relates specifically to dance and movement. Consequently, similar considerations apply as in the case of a director, save that, in contrast to the stage director, the choreographer's position is expressly recognised by s.3(1) of the 1988 Act.

26–309   **Stage fights.** Stage fights, although not works of "dance", are clearly capable of constituting one of the elements of a dramatic work. Fight direction has developed into a separate specialist art form of its own to such an extent that a standard form

---

[665] See also D. Michael Rose, "Copyright in Stage Production Elements." [1998] Ent. L.R. 30. Also on the issue of substantiality see *Baigent and Anor v Random House Group Limited* [2007] EWCA Civ 247; [2007] F.S.R. 24 (the *Da Vinci Code* case) in which Mummery L.J. (with whose judgment Rix L.J. agreed) said that the resolution of this issue in that case required a careful assessment or evaluation of all the relevant evidence by the fact-finding tribunal in the context of the pleaded case (para.143 of the judgment). This observation seems particularly apposite in its application to a claim for infringement of that part of the copyright in a dramatic work which consists of stage directions.

[666] As to the requirement that a copyright work be recorded, in writing or otherwise, see CDPA 1988 s.3(2) and paras 3–107 et seq., above. As to the operation of this requirement in relation to dramatic works, see para.3–117, above.

[667] The expression "product of his services" is one which appears frequently in this field.

[668] As to subsistence of copyright in works of dance generally, see para.3–37, above, and CDPA 1988 s.3, and for choreography recorded in notation or code see para.3–17. Note also that it has been held that a sports game did not constitute choreography, and was therefore not a dramatic work, even though partly intended to follow a pre-determined plan, as to which see para.3–43 and the cases there cited.

of Agreement for Fight Directors was set up in 1991 and updated in January 1995 between SOLT/TMA/ITC (formerly and collectively known as the Theatres National Committee) (TNC)[669] and British Actors Equity Association ("Equity"), applicable to theatrical productions throughout the United Kingdom. It requires SOLT/TMA/ITC members presenting a production which involves a fight to engage a suitably qualified fight director, and any member of the Equity Fight Director's Register is regarded as suitably qualified for this purpose. A "fight" for this purpose is defined by such agreement as "a specialised performance involving two or more people using fists, implements or weapons, which requires choreography[670] and supervision for safety".

(c) Designers

Costumes and stage sets. Clearly the room for originality is limited in, for example, the exact re-creation of military uniforms and period costumes, the design and colours of which are largely dictated by historical fact and are to be found in most public libraries. Similarly, a playwright's description of a scene in a play may in some instances leave the set-designer little room for manoeuvre to demonstrate much originality of design, particularly where commonplace "props" or a spartan set are required. However, there are many other cases where considerable scope for originality[671] exists in relation to the design of costumes and stage sets.

26–310

Costume and set designs, being by their very nature three-dimensional objects, will normally qualify for design right rather than copyright,[672] but copyright protection may be available for such works as artistic works.[673] In principle artistic works which qualify for design right may also qualify for copyright and vice versa, subject to certain limitations such as those contained in ss.51 and 52 of the Act, which render important the distinction between designs intended for surface decoration and those for three-dimensional objects.[674] Thus, the fact that it may also qualify for design right is no defence to a claim for infringement of copyright in a design document intended primarily for surface decoration.[675] This may be of particular importance in relation to sets and costumes designs for a theatrical production, as well as logos and artwork on bill posters, show merchandise, souvenir programmes and the like.

The question was considered in some depth in *Shelley Films Ltd v Rex Features Ltd*[676] which related to an alleged infringement of copyright by the taking of photographs of a scene of actors in costume on a film set. The plaintiff claimed copyright in the set and costumes and prostheses as works of artistic craftsmanship. It was held that there was a serious question to be tried on this issue. For example, the evidence was that the script's perception of a particular character had led the designer of his costume to base it upon a Prussian military uniform which he then adapted, using his researches into contemporary artwork and the sort of fabrics, buttons and braiding appropriate for the period and partly

---

[669] The TNC has since ceased to exist, and the former "British Actors Equity Association" is now called simply "Equity".

[670] Strictly (according to the O.E.D), choreography refers to the act of dancing. However, fight movement may be regarded as "mime" and therefore a dramatic work within the meaning of CDPA 1988 s.3(1).

[671] As to the meaning of originality in this context, see Ch.3, above.

[672] See Ch.13, above.

[673] As to works of artistic craftsmanship, see *Guild v Eskander* [2001] F.S.R. 645, and para.3–67.

[674] See *Lucasfilm Limited v Ainsworth* [2008] EWHC 1878 (Ch); on appeal [2010] F.S.R. 10; [2010] E.M.L.R. 12.

[675] *Flashing Badge Co. Ltd v Groves* [2007] EWHC 1372; [2007] F.S.R. 36.

[676] [1994] E.M.L.R. 34

his own imaginative conceptions of what the character should look like. There then followed a process of fabric and colour selection, distressing and breaking down in order to produce a garment which would have been worn by the character concerned. In this way, he had created some 120 costumes so that, besides being technically correct, they blended in and constituted part of the overall artistic texture of the film.[677] It was also held that it was plainly arguable that copyright could subsist in a film set as a work of artistic craftsmanship.[678] Here, the evidence was that the set and every detail of it were the result of hundreds of little drawings, loosely based on the designer's researches, yet imaginatively conceived as original creations bearing in mind the artistic concepts of the film. Although that case related to a film, there can be no difference in principle for present purposes between the costumes and sets of a film and those of a live stage production.

As in the case of directors and choreographers, there are collective bargaining agreements,[679] which proceed on the assumption of the existence of copyright in designs of stage sets and costumes. Indeed, most commercial contracts between designer and producer will ignore any difficulties in establishing copyright by assuming its existence and providing for payment by the producer whenever the product of the designer's services is used. Problems are likely to arise in such cases, however, when, for example, a designer alleges that his designs have been used without his consent, and where in response it is said that only unoriginal or public domain elements of the designs, if any, have been used to which no copyright protection attaches. The outcome of each such case will turn on its own facts. Clearly designers should beware of warranting that *all* parts of their designs are wholly original, when this may be open to challenge. Warranties as to originality are commonly requested in creative team contracts, but ought to be confined to the totality of the work (as distinct from its component parts) and to the absence of breach of any third party's copyright, or alternatively should exclude commonplace elements and any which are in the public domain.

26–311   **Lighting design.** Lighting design has long been recognised as a means of contributing to the appearance of the stage, sets and costumes, which in turn contribute to the dramatic impact of the visual presentation to the audience. For example, stage scenery may be made to appear very different indeed from its daylight appearance by the use of clever lighting to enhance its dramatic appeal.

Lighting designs will usually be recorded in the form of a specification of the equipment required, a "plot" or plan of the positioning of that equipment and lighting cues. It is obviously desirable in particular that there be some record of the form and sequence of lighting effects. Whether they are capable in law of forming an element of the dramatic work as a whole, and thus in principle capable of copyright protection, is an open question which remains to be tested.[680] Clearly, the records themselves of lighting plots, plans and specifications are likely to be protected under ss.3 or 4 of the 1988 to the extent that they are "original".

---

[677] The scrupulous re-creation of an authentic, albeit well-used uniform cannot, however, be an original work. See para.3–133, above. Note, however, that a "uniform" which is merely functional or utilitarian or intended to give a particular impression, and has no aesthetic, visual appeal in itself (such as certain body armour) will not be considered a work of artistic craftsmanship, and consequently, even though the article may be made to another person's copyright design, CDPA 1988 s.51 (and possibly also s.52) will afford a good defence to an action by that designer for infringement of copyright: see *Lucasfilm Limited v Ainsworth* [2008] EWHC 1878 (Ch); on appeal [2010] F.S.R. 10; and paras 3–60 and 3–69, above.

[678] Depending on the circumstances it might also be capable of being a work of architecture, being a fixed structure or part of a fixed structure: see CDPA 1988 s.4(1)(b) and paras 3–62 and 3–67. Very often of course, there will be preliminary drawings for the set.

[679] See para.26–335, below.

[680] See *Vermaat v Boncrest Ltd* [2001] F.S.R. 43, and as to works of artistic craftsmanship generally

If a written record of the lighting designs is protected by copyright as a substantial part of a dramatic work, which itself is arguable and remains to be determined[681], then the unlicensed use of such designs in a dramatic performance on stage will infringe s.16(1)(c) of the 1988 Act. The same can be said of stage directions and sound designs. The process of lighting design, unlike sound design, also creates a visual image, which may amount to an artistic work. If this is reproduced in a real sense without a licence in the course of a performance, that too would amount to an infringement.[682]

Sound design. Sound design is of comparatively recent origin, and is a manifestation of the huge advances in sound technology during the last 50 years or so, which has made the role of the sound designer in the production of a stage musical one of primary and increasing importance. The West End of London has seen the advent of recorded music to replace or partially replace live orchestral accompaniment of a stage musical, despite initial strenuous opposition from the Musicians' Union. This and the continuing development of new sound technology, such as digital audio systems, is expected to enhance even further the important role of sound designers in musical theatre.   **26–312**

There are three basic elements of sound design, namely the specification of equipment, the positioning of that equipment in the theatre, and the movement of certain parts of the equipment (such as microphones) during the performance. The "sound desk" with its console of myriad moveable keys is a very important piece of sound equipment in a first class production of a stage musical, sometimes displacing a block of seats in the back of the auditorium, and being operated during the performance by a sound engineer in accordance with instructions given to him by the sound designer.

Some elements of sound design are peculiar to the structure and configuration of the theatre. Others are peculiar to the production itself, irrespective of venue, and other elements are peculiar to the voice characteristics of individual performers. There may also be special sound effects, such as those created by a motor car or aeroplane, to be reproduced at the appropriate time in the course of a performance. All these various elements will be plotted, specified and cued by the sound designer. The extent to which they are capable of copyright protection as part of a dramatic or musical work will depend on the facts, but the diagrams, written specifications and "plots" clearly will be protected under ss.3 or 4 of the 1988 Act; the latter section provides that diagrams, maps, charts and plans are regarded as artistic works for copyright purposes, irrespective of artistic quality.

Much the same considerations apply to sound design as to lighting design, for which, in order to avoid repetition, reference should be made to para.26–311 above.[683]

(d) *Orchestrators*

The function of an orchestrator is usually to create musical, instrumental and vocal arrangements from a piano-vocal score to full orchestral and vocal rendering. Invariably this process involves the creation of new musical sounds and therefore a new copyright work by the orchestrator.[684] An orchestrator will usually be engaged to carry out his work by someone, possibly the original composer, but   **26–313**

---

para.3–67, above. See also D. Michael Rose, "Copyright in Stage Production Elements." [1998] Ent. L.R. 30.

[681] As to this see para.3–67.

[682] See para.7–02, above.

[683] See also D. Michael Rose, "Copyright in Stage Production Elements." [1998] Ent. L.R. 30.

[684] See paras 3–139 et seq., above, and, e.g. *Redwood Music Ltd v Chappell & Co Ltd* [1982] R.P.C.

more probably a producer who has acquired the right to create or commission the creation of orchestrations,[685] since the contents of orchestrations for a stage production are to some extent dictated by the venue of the performance.

Orchestrations are an important element in the presentation of a stage musical, and orchestrators for that reason are customarily treated in much the same way as other members of the creative team. They are usually remunerated by substantial fees for their initial work and by performance fees or box-office royalties in relation to future use of their orchestrations in the production. In return for a substantial fee they may well be expected to assign the copyright in their orchestrations to whoever commissioned them, since they will be working as adaptors of pre-existing copyright material, namely the music of the composer. Sometimes vocal, instrumental and dance "arrangements" of the musical score will (possibly by inadvertence) be created separately and attract separate copyright protection from the orchestrations by individuals separately engaged for that purpose.[686]

Orchestrations and musical arrangements are, of course, adaptations of the original musical composition and as such will require the consent of the original "author" (composer) of the music or his assignees or licensees of the adaptation right.

(iii) Logo and artwork designers

26–314   The importance of a distinctive logo and artwork to the marketing and promotion of modern, first class, stage musical production has grown greatly, and has given rise to exploitation in other important areas such as merchandising and commercial usage. Thus, souvenir brochures, T-shirts, toys, pens, drinking-mugs and the like, emblazoned with the show's logo, are frequently to be found on sale within the precincts of theatres where the show is in production, and sometimes in an even wider retail market. A kind of livery or uniform is frequently created for the musical, which is intensively used as a means of enhancing the reputation of the work in all its possible means of exploitation. Thus, the producer of a stage musical will, at a comparatively early planning stage, devote a great deal of time and thought to the graphic designer's work, which he will usually commission on the basis that the copyright will vest in or be assigned to the producer. The use of such artwork will often lead to its being identified by the public exclusively with the particular production, so establishing a valuable goodwill, protectable in a passing-off action.[687] For this reason such logos are frequently made the subject of registration as trade marks by the copyright owner in jurisdictions where such registration exists and where the production concerned is likely to be performed or the logo to be used for any ancillary purpose, or where possible infringement is anticipated.

Where such logos or artwork are used in conjunction with unauthorised im-

---

109; *Godfrey v Lees* [1995] E.M.L.R. 307; and *Sawkins v Hyperion Records Ltd* [2004] E.M.L.R. 27; [2005] R.P.C. 4; on appeal [2005] EWCA Civ 565; [2005] 1 W.L.R. 3281; [2005] R.P.C. 32.

[685] See CDPA 1988 ss.21(3)(b) and 16(1)(e).

[686] See, for example, *Beckingham v Hodgens* [2002] E.M.L.R. 45, where a session musician, performing a violin part, was held on the facts to be a joint author of a musical arrangement and entitled to a royalty by virtue of having made a "significant and original" contribution to the arrangement. See also *Bamgboye v Reed* [2004] E.M.L.R. 5 to similar effect in relation to a copyright contribution by a tape operator and sound engineer, and *Sawkins v Hyperion Records Ltd* [2005] R.P.C. 4; on appeal [2005] EWCA Civ 565; [2005] 1 W.L.R. 3281; [2005] R.P.C. 32, as to copyright in a new edition of an out-of-copyright work. See, finally, *Fisher v Brooker* [2009] UKHL 41; [2009] 1 W.L.R. 1764 to like effect as *Beckingham* above.

[687] See *Griggs v Evans* [2004] F.S.R. 31; on appeal [2005] EWCA Civ 11; [2005] E.C.D.R. 30; [2005] F.S.R. 31 and para.5–178, above, as to ownership of copyright in commissioned logos.

ages from the production, the question whether or not there is a defence of incidental inclusion under s.31 of the 1988 Act must be determined by the circumstances existing at the time the images were made.[688]

(iv) Performers

Although performers have extensive property rights in relation to their performances, these are not of immediate concern to live stage producers since they relate to their fixation or broadcast only,[689] and do not therefore attract copyright protection as such. It is for this reason that impersonators and "tribute" artistes are able to perform on the live stage without authorisation and with impunity. Performers' rights will, however, assume great significance to a stage producer if it is desired to make a film or sound recording of the stage production, or to make a live broadcast, for which, with certain limited exceptions for specific permitted acts, the performers' consent will be required, even if the producer intends to make such a film or sound recording only for his own private, archival purposes or only for a "demo-recording" or publicity purposes.[690] It is obviously desirable that any such performers' consents should be obtained in writing, but this is not an essential requirement under the Act.

26–315

Performers are usually engaged on standard minimum terms and/or printed collective contracts in one or other of the forms agreed by their trade union, Equity, (or in the case of musicians, the Musicians Union) with various bodies representing producers and theatre managers, such as Society of London Theatre (SOLT), Theatrical Management Association (TMA), Independent Theatre Council (ITC), and Variety and Light Entertainment Council (VLEC)[691]. There are separate forms for play actors, variety artists and musicians, the latter being agreed by the Musicians Union rather than Equity. Performers now have statutory, non-assignable moral rights to be identified as the performer, and to object to derogatory treatment, subject to certain exceptions and supplementary provisions.[692]

(v) Translators

The lyrics and text of a finished work written in one particular language may be required to be translated into another language or languages for the purposes of foreign stage productions. The right to make or authorise such a translation is an adaptation right, which will in the first instance belong to the original author.[693] Where, for example, the right is assigned or licensed to a stage producer, it is usual for the author or copyright owner to reserve a right of approval over such translation as well as over the translator, although the producer will usually seek to provide that any right of approval by the author will not be unreasonably withheld. Although constituting an adaptation of a pre-existing copyright work,

26–316

[688] See *The Football Association Premier League Ltd v Panini UK Ltd* [2003] EWCA Civ. 995; [2004] 1 W.L.R. 1147; [2004] F.S.R. 1, and for a detailed discussion of the point see para.9–64 et seq., above.

[689] For a full discussion of performers' rights, see Ch.12, and para.26–344.

[690] CDPA 1988 s.182, as amended by the Copyright and Related Rights Regulations 1996, applicable to performances by "qualifying individuals" or given in a "qualifying country".

[691] In the case of VLEC, it issues guidance notes and minimum rates of pay, but no separate standard form of agreement.

[692] See CDPA 1988 ss.205C(1) and 205F(1), inserted with effect from February 1, 2006 by the Performances (Moral Rights etc) Regulations 2006 (SI 2006/18). See also para.26 331 and Ch.12.

[693] See CDPA 1988 s.21(3)(a)(i), para.26–319 and paras 7–136 et seq., above. It must also be borne in mind that the person who has the right to authorise performances of a work in a foreign jurisdiction will be determined by the law of that jurisdiction.

the translation will itself be a new copyright work,[694] and where it has been commissioned it is usual for the party engaging the translator to stipulate that the copyright in the translation will vest in or be assigned to that party or as he may direct.[695]

It is now common for English language productions of stage musicals to be recreated and re-presented overseas in local foreign languages, requiring approved translations and translators, and in such cases, if the producer of the original English language production licenses the foreign language reproduction to a local producer the latter will usually be required to engage an approved translator (possibly at his own or as a production expense) and to direct the translator to assign copyright in the translation to the original English language producer. If the copyright owner of the original work is not the producer, then the copyright owner's consent to the translation will also be required if he has not already granted the producer the right to commission and exploit it.

(vi) The producer

26–317   The role of the producer in relation to a live stage production is manifold and varied. It embraces all arrangements necessary or desirable for presenting a play, a musical, an opera, a ballet or other work to the paying public on the live stage. The principal aspects in which the producer will be involved may be summarised as follows, although the list is not intended by any means to be exhaustive:

(1) *Acquiring the rights,* i.e. acquiring the legal right to present the work from the authors and all other copyright owners such as the creative team, including the negotiation of remuneration, the extent and duration of the producer's copyright licence or assignment and all other contractual terms between the parties.

(2) *Preparing the budget.*

(3) *Raising the money.*

(4) *Selecting and engaging the creative team and cast.*

(5) *Organising auditions and rehearsals.*

(6) *Selecting and hiring the theatre.*

(7) *Arranging logo and artwork design and printing.*

(8) *Promotion, publicity and advertising.*

(9) *Ticket retailing arrangements.*

(10) *Arrangements for sets and properties.*

(11) *Managing the administration and accounts of the production.*

(12) *Arrangements for "get-in", "fit-up" and "get-out" at the theatre.*

26–318   As to raising the money for the production, non-profit-making production companies (usually having charitable status) are likely to be heavily subsidised by grants from public bodies such as the Arts Council of England, the National Lottery and local authorities or by public donation. Commercial production companies which are unable to self-finance their own productions will usually seek financial investment from backers who are colloquially known as "angels". In such cases the producer will estimate the cost of preparing the production up to the first paid public performance. This estimate is referred to as the "capitalisation" to which investors are invited to contribute by purchasing units, each of

---

[694] As to copyright in translations, see para.3–137, above.

[695] And see paras 5–32 and 26–323, as to "commissioned works", and *Griggs v Evans* [2004] F.S.R. 31; see also the judgment on appeal ([2005] EWCA Civ 11; [2005] F.S.R. 31). A comparison may be made with orchestrations and arrangements of pre-existing music, where the same position applies.

which units is entitled to a pro rata share of (usually) 60 per cent of production profits, the remainder being reserved to the producer.

A producer will usually be more involved with the acquisition or licensing of rights in the exploitation of copyright works than with their creation. It is more than likely, however, that in the course of preparing to mount a production, and particularly during the consultation process with his creative team and during rehearsals, the producer will contribute ideas and suggestions which may lead to changes in the creative material or its manner of presentation. The producer will, however, rarely claim copyright for himself in the product of his ideas and suggestions.[696] If they are adopted, they are in practice likely to be recorded as the original contributions of the authors and creative team. However, a producer who commissions for value various production elements of a composite dramatic work, as for example, in the case of a ballet, the stage direction, music and choreography, may, in the absence of agreement to the contrary and depending on the facts, be held to be the owner in equity of the copyrights in the composite work and can thereby claim copyright in "his production".[697] If scenic designs and costumes are not protected by the copyright in the dramatic work they may of course qualify for separate protection as artistic works, but see para.26–310, above.

A commercial producer of a stage musical is usually remunerated in a variety of ways. He will usually charge the production with a producer's royalty, up to about 2 per cent of net weekly box-office receipts[698] after prior deduction from such receipts of VAT, block-blocking discounts and credit card, charge card, and agency commissions, and he will usually share any "profits" (as contractually defined) with his investors on the basis of 40 per cent for himself and 60 per cent for his investors, unless of course he finances the production himself or with the aid of loan capital without any profit-sharing arrangements. He will also usually charge to the production a weekly office management fee, usually from two weeks prior to first rehearsal until two weeks after closure. If he has obtained the right to subsidiary exploitation, such as merchandising, cast album sound recording, and motion picture, he will control, and therefore expect to retain a substantial share of the net revenue generated by any such exploitation. On the other hand, any losses in excess of the amount contributed by his "investors" will have to be borne by him.

(vii) Other adaptors of written work

The work of orchestrators and translators has already been considered above, **26–319** each of them being both an adaptor and an "author" in his own right. Other forms of adaptation arise in the present context where, for example, the copyright owners of a novel and/or film and/or straight play or collection of songs grant to a third party the right to turn their original work(s) into a stage musical, in which case the grantee will in turn go out and commission writers of his choice to create

---

[696] In any event, mere suggestions or ideas or "inspiration" from another work will rarely be of sufficient substance to qualify for copyright protection. See paras 3–18, 4–22, 4–35 and 7–140. See also *Ultra (United Kingdom) Ltd v Universal Components Ltd* [2004] EWHC 468; *Stoddard International Plc v William Lomas Carpets Ltd* [2001] F.S.R. 14; and *Wiseman v Weidenfeld & Nicholson Ltd* [1985] F.S.R. 525. It was suggested in *Kelly v Cinema Houses Ltd* [1933] Mac G. Cop Cas (1928–1935) 362 that there is "probably" no copyright in a fictitious character such as Falstaff or Sherlock Holmes, but it is doubtful if that view would prevail today.

[697] Such a work will comprise two separate copyright works: the dramatic work and the musical work. See para.3–50, above. By the same token, there is no copyright in a song as a single hybrid work, but only in the words and music separately— *Chappell &Co Ltd v Redwood Music Ltd* [1981] R.P.C. 337. As to equitable ownership generally see paras 5–174 et seq., above.

[698] As to basis of calculation of royalties see para.26–305, above.

the new material required for such adaptation. Projects of this nature have become increasingly common, and, of course, the same considerations apply as for any original copyright work, which is to be adapted for exploitation in some other medium, whatever its nature,[699] since making an adaptation of any copyright work is a restricted act under s.16(1)(e) of the 1988 Act.

In such cases the contractual terms negotiated by the grantee of the adaptation rights in a theatrical work may in many respects be complex, but, so far as copyright is concerned, the contractual arrangements usually involve the copyright owners of the underlying works retaining their pre-existing rights in their own material, and the grantee (or his successors in title) acquiring copyright in the adapted work which he commissions, and separately in his own new material, subject perhaps to "qualification" by completion and exploitation within a specified time limit. If, for example, a novel is turned into a film, which is turned into a play, which is turned into a stage musical, the creator(s) of the latter, or more likely the party commissioning the musical, will require the consents of the original novelist and each subsequent adaptor for the creation of the new composite work.[700]

Copyright in a dramatic work will be infringed by an unauthorised adaptation into a non-dramatic work,[701] and the making of any adaptation of a literary, dramatic or musical work is an act restricted by copyright under s.21(1) of the 1988 Act, but the borderline between an "adaptation" and a mere "synopsis" may be a very fine one.[702] Furthermore, if the new work is merely "inspired" by or "derived" from the earlier work, there may be no infringement of copyright.[703] Of course, if the underlying work which is the subject of adaptation is out of copyright, there will be no infringement by an unauthorised adaptation, as in the case, for example, of a Shakespearean play adapted into a stage musical.

B. LICENCE OR ASSIGNMENT?

26–320   The right to present a single specific production of a live stage play, stage musical, opera or ballet at a specified venue, for a fixed term or even an open-ended run, with no intention to promote the work any further, would normally be expected to be granted by way of an exclusive licence for a specified period at the particular venue or venues concerned. An alternative would be an exclusive licence for an indefinite period, subject to lapse by reference to predetermined criteria, such as failure to present a minimum number of performances over a specified period or make payment in lieu. Usually such a licence would be expressed to be exclusive within a defined territory for the obvious reason that the producer would not wish to find himself in competition with other producers of the same work.[704]

26–321   **The authors and composers.** In the case, however, of a production of a major, big-budget stage musical which is expected, if successful, to have a relatively long life under the stewardship of the producer to whom the rights are originally being granted, the producer may (subject to "qualifying") ask for an assignment of the right to present performances of the work, either worldwide or within a

---

[699] For adaptation rights generally see paras 7–137 et seq. and in particular para.7–140 and CDPA 1988 s.21.

[700] For a similar analogy see judgment of Park J. in *Brighton v Jones* [2004] E.M.L.R.26; [2005] F.S.R. 16.

[701] CDPA 1988 s.21(3)(a)(ii) and para.7–141.

[702] See paras 2–06, 3–18 and 7–141 and CDPA 1988 s.21(3).

[703] See paras 2–06, 3–18, 7–63 and 26–313, above.

[704] As to the distinction between licensing or assignment generally, see paras 5–204 et seq.

specified territory or territories,[705] as distinct from a mere licence, exclusive or otherwise. The point may be the subject of much contention and negotiation, but the distinction between an assignment and an exclusive licence (particularly if the licence is described as "perpetual", i.e. for the full period of copyright) may be largely negated if, as is sometimes the case, an exclusive licence stipulates that the licensor's remedies for breach shall be confined to an action for damages and shall not give rise to any right of termination.[706] Alternatively, an outright assignment may contain provision for reverter or reassignment in specified circumstances such as, for example, failure either to present a minimum number of performances per annum or to pay compensation instead. Any exclusive licence or assignment must be in writing.[707] It is important to make clear what the intended legal effect is.

Whether an assignment or a mere licence is created is not always clear from the language used by the parties, particularly where one simply "grants to the other the right" (or the "exclusive" right") to exploit the copyright work concerned, either in all media or in a particular medium. Thus (perhaps surprisingly), it was held in one case that the grant of an exclusive right to perform a play is an assignment of the performing right, even though the parties had described themselves as "Licensor" and "Licensee" and even though there were territorial and other limitations, a reversion of rights clause being one of the principal determining factors.[708] Clearly an assignment of copyright can sometimes be implied from the particular circumstances.

The creative team. The same point frequently arises in relation to the copyright   **26–322**
material of the creative team. They will obviously be willing to grant licences for the use of their material in the particular production concerned, and may even be prepared to grant a general exclusive licence (limited to use in connection with the musical or play or other work concerned) for a long or indefinite period. On the other hand, they may be resistant to assigning their rights in creative material, even with reverter or reassignment provisions, and most of their collective bargaining agreements reserve copyright to them, although others provide for the parties to elect between outright assignment of copyright to the producer or manager (either in perpetuity or for a restricted period) on the one hand and a mere copyright licence on the other, which suggests that either course may be regarded as reasonable, depending on the circumstances and the relative bargaining strengths of the parties.[709]

Commissioned work. The question of whether to seek a licence or an assign-   **26–323**

---

[705] He may fear that with only a licence, which may be terminable on breach, the production may be forced to close after a minor or disputed violation.

[706] In *Harbinger United Kingdom Ltd v GE Information Services Ltd* [2000] 1 All E.R. (Comm) 166; [2000] 1 P.L.C. 56; the High Court held that the use of the words "in perpetuity" as the term of the licence negated any possibility of termination on reasonable notice and meant that the licence continued until the licensee no longer required it. This was despite termination procedures in the licence itself, thus, in effect, making even more ephemeral the distinction between an assignment and an exclusive licence in perpetuity. The negation of any right to terminate a licence for breach was given judicial sanction in *NIC v PW Allen* [2004] BL 0/026/04. For judicial consideration and rejection of a submission that a termination-for-breach clause constituted an unenforceable contract penalty see *Python (Monty) Pictures Ltd v Paragon Entertainment Corporation* [1998] E.M.L.R. 640 at 686.

[707] See ss.90(3) and 92(1) of CDPA 1998.

[708] *Messager v BBC* [1929] A.C. 151; *Loew's Inc v Littler* [1958] 2 All E.R. 200.

[709] See, for example, the SOLT/Equity Agreement for West End Theatre Designers (1989) and the TMA/Equity/BECTU Agreement for Theatre Designers outside West End (1999) and the SOLT/Equity Agreement for West End Theatre Choreographers (2003) and the TMA/Equity Agreement for Subsidised Repertory and Commercial Theatres (2004). Interestingly, and in contrast to most other creative team collective agreements, the last two mentioned agreements contain, in addition to the option for an outright assignment of copyright, alternative terms for a licence covering not just the United Kingdom but also the rest of the world, which in the case of the

ment also frequently arises where one party engages or commissions another to create copyright material for a particular purpose, for example the logo and artwork for a stage musical, or the music to go with the lyrics of a partly written work.[710] In these circumstances the party doing the commissioning will often insist, as a condition of the engagement, that the other agrees in advance to the copyright in the product of his services vesting in or being assigned to the commissioning party, a concession which is often made where there is a substantial fee being paid in advance and there are others who would be willing to do the work on the terms offered. A factor which may induce an agreement to assign, rather than license, is if the writer is being commissioned to adapt a pre-existing work (e.g. a film or novel into a stage play), so that the commissioned work will have no stand-alone life of its own without the consent of the owner of the adaptation rights (usually the intended producer who is doing the commissioning).

Where, as is common in the case of theatrical productions, a person is commissioned to create new copyright material on the terms that copyright in that new material is to be assigned to the commissioner, such assignment will take effect as an assignment of future copyright to the commissioner as prospective owner at the time when (if ever) the new material comes into existence.[711] However, it has been held that the remedy of specific performance is not available for breach of a commission to compose and write law reports[712] and this decision is likely to be applied by analogy to contracts for the creation of new material for theatrical productions. Also, the Court will be slow, in the absence of express agreement, to imply that the commissioned work will be of any particular, other than "reasonable" length.[713]

If the contract between a producer and an independent contractor for creation by the latter for value of material capable of forming part of a composite copyright work is silent as to ownership of the commissioned material, the facts of the case are likely to give rise to a "necessary implication" that the producer, as the paying party, is the equitable owner of that part of the copyright and accordingly has the right to require it to be assigned to him. This is analogous to the American doctrine of "work for hire" which carries a similar implication, but such an implication will not necessarily be made in every case of a commissioned work.[714]

C. CLASSIFICATION OF RIGHTS

26–324   **General.** The rights in the various works may be classified in a number of differ-

---

TMA/Equity Agreement is described as being for "the copyright period". Why provision for a similarly broad licence is not included in corresponding collective agreements for other members of the creative team between SOLT/TMA and Equity is not explained. Thus, the current SOLT and TMA/Equity collective agreements for West End of London and provincial stage directors provide for copyright to be reserved to the director and only licensed to the producer, which perhaps is surprising since, by its very nature, his work can have no stand-alone life of its own.

[710] As to the ownership of copyright in a commissioned work generally, see paras 5–32, 5–33 and 5–174, and as to copyright in a logo see para.26–314, above, and *Griggs v Evans* [2004] F.S.R. 31; see also the judgment on appeal [2005] EWCA Civ 11; [2005] F.S.R. 31.

[711] CDPA 1988 s.91(1).

[712] *Clarke v Price* [1819] 2 Wils.Ch.157.

[713] *Artlamb Productions Ltd v Goude* [2004] EWHC 3029 (QB); [2005] BLD 2212045481.

[714] See paras 5–32 and 5–174 above and also *Massine v de Basil* [1936–1945] Mac C.C. 223, in which such a term was held to be implied. The circumstances in *Lucasfilm Limited v Ainsworth* [2008] EWHC 1878 (Ch); [2008] E.C.D.R. 17 were described at first instance as a "classic case for saying that there is an implication that the commissioner would have the copyright in the [work], if any" (para.185) and it was held to be "implicit in the relationship" that the party commissioned to do the work would not retain copyright (para.187). This element of the decision was upheld on appeal: [2010] 3 W.L.R. 333; [2010] F.S.R. 10; [2010] E.M.L.R. 12 at paras 196–208. See also *Societa Esplosivi Industriali SPA v Ordnance Technologies Limited* [2008] EWHC 2875 (Ch); [2008] 2 All E.R. 622; [2008] R.P.C. 12, for the circumstances in which a sole director and shareholder of an infringing company may be held personally liable for infringement by his company in the case of a commissioned work.

ent ways, the importance of which is two-fold. First, copyright is divisible,[715] and one particular classification of rights may be licensed, assigned or otherwise disposed of differently from another. Secondly, the exploitation of one class of rights may be differently remunerated from another. Again, it is proposed to take the classification of rights in a stage musical as the example with the widest scope.

"Grand rights" and "small rights". This classification is solely concerned with performing rights in stage musicals. As a matter of convention the expression "grand rights" is usually understood to mean the right to present live performances of dramatico-musical works for which the music has been specially composed.[716] In contrast, the "small performing right", or "small right", usually means the right to perform non-dramatic performances of individual songs or other short musical excerpts from a dramatico-musical work.   **26–325**

The Performing Right Society, ("PRS")[717] limits its jurisdiction in respect of these "small rights" in live performances of excerpts from dramatico-musical works which have been vested in the Society by its members to circumstances where:

   (i) the performance is not dramatic[718]; and

   (ii) it does not exceed 25 minutes; and

   (iii) it is not a performance of a complete act of the work; and

   (iv) it is not a so-called "potted" or condensed version of the whole work;[719] and

   (v) it has not been released back to the copyright owner by the PRS at the former's request under PRS art.7(f) of the PRS's constitution.

Thus, for example, a non-vocal performance of the music alone, or the singing of one or two songs from a dramatico-musical work by a singer in street dress on a plain stage in cabaret or on television or in a variety bill will not be within the domain of the grand rights owner.

A PRS licence is required for the performance of overture, entre-act and exit music in the theatre, and also for incidental music used to add atmosphere to a play or between scene changes, or used for background or featured music in theatre foyers, bars or restaurants.[720] Interpolated music, meaning "music not specially written for a particular theatrical production but performed by a character(s) which is to be heard by another character(s) in that production", e.g an actor singing or playing a musical instrument to another actor as part of a production, either separately or as a series or as part of a compilation show, also needs PRS clearance, and in each such case there are PRS procedures to be fol-

---

[715] As to divisibility of copyright, see paras 5–97 et seq.

[716] The PRS Rules define a dramatico-musical work as "an opera, operetta, musical play, review or pantomime, in so far as it consists of words and music written expressly therefor", and the PRS Members' Handbook (1994 edn) defines a ballet as "a choreographic work having a story, plot or abstract idea, devised or used for the purpose of interpretation by dancing and/or miming, but does not include country or folk dancing, nor tap dancing, nor precision dancing sequences". As to changes in PRS nomenclature see footnote to para.26–334.

[717] As to the Performing Right Society Ltd and its affiliated societies overseas, see para.27–65, below.

[718] Whether or not it is dramatic depends on all the circumstances, including the use of costume, stage scenery, dramatic movement or mime and any other means to convey the dramatic impact of the piece to the audience, such as narration of the plot or storyline, either as part of the performance itself or in a theatre programme, as to which see the PRS publications entitled "Music in Theatres" and "Music in Live Venues" (Jan. 2009 edn in both cases) and for a more detailed analysis see the section on "Rights" in the PRS Members' Handbook (1994 edn)

[719] See the section on "Rights" in the PRS Members' Handbook (1994 edn)

[720] See PRS publication entitled "Music in Theatres" (Jan. 2009 edn) and the Society's handbook mentioned above.

lowed, including the giving of at least 30 days prior notice to the PRS whenever practicable.[721] However, PRS may release its right to license interpolated music back to the copyright owner or the latter's music publisher under art.7(f) of its constitution on request within 21 days of first public performance.

The distinction between the two rights is important, because the grand rights are usually not within the rights which are assigned to the PRS by its members, so that even in the case where the author, composer or music publisher is a member of the PRS, these rights will be controlled by the author (or his music publisher) and not the PRS, unless the author as a matter of convenience to himself, with PRS approval, unusually chooses to vest the grand rights also in the PRS. In contrast, the small rights are assigned to the PRS by its members and so are controlled by the PRS. The distinction between the two types of rights has been brought into sharp relief by a proliferation in recent years of so-called "compilation shows", featuring short excerpts from a number of well-known stage musicals. Often such shows are presented with dramatic staging and costume, and thus dramatically, without the consent of the grand rights owner and so potentially will be an infringement of the latter's copyright. Compilation shows are also a common feature of cruise line productions, the producers of which are usually alive to the importance of the distinction and the need to ensure that the requisite licences are in place.

In addition to the small rights, the PRS also administers the performing rights in dramatico-musical works and ballets of its members when such works are performed by means of films made primarily for the purpose of exhibition in cinemas, and the television broadcasting of such films.[722] It also controls performances of such works when given in public by means of radio or television sets (for example in a hotel lounge or public house).[723]

It should be noted, however, that not every author, composer and music publisher is necessarily a member of the PRS and that the separation of grand rights and small rights into different ownerships (if any) is essentially a contractual matter for the original copyright owner. Usually, though not always, composers and songwriters will place the administration and disposition of the rights in their music and lyrics into the control of a "music-publisher", who may license their exploitation directly, or stand between them and collection societies, such as the PRS, as to which see paras 26–154 to 26–165 inclusive. Thus, a stage producer may find himself dealing with the composer and songwriter, or with the latter's music-publisher or with the PRS or other collection society in relation to the acquisition of stage rights in music and songs, depending on the nature of the work and which of them controls the copyright in the music and lyrics at the time concerned, and the extent to which, if at all, the music was specially composed for the dramatico-musical work concerned. For this purpose song-lyrics will very likely, though not necessarily, be similarly controlled as the music, although royalties and fees may, in whole or in part, pass to and be divided among separate composers and lyricists.

The PRS has very complex tariffs and systems for calculating royalties and their fragmentation and distribution amongst copyright owners of the works which the Society administers. It also settles disputes and stipulates that no legal proceedings may be taken by any of its members in respect of any performing

---

[721] See PRS publication entitled "Music in Theatres " (Jan. 2009 edn) and its Members' Handbook (1994)

[722] See the PRS publication entitled "Music in Live Venues" (Jan. 2009 edn) and above Handbook.

[723] See the PRS publication entitled "Are you Listening?" and above Handbook As to what constitutes a performance "in public" in such circumstances, see para.7–108, above.

right in any works controlled by the Society without the sanction of the Society's General Council.[724]

Professional rights and amateur rights. These classifications mostly speak for themselves. Professional rights are performing rights which are exercised with the use of only paid professional performers. Amateur rights relate to performances using amateur performers. It is rare for amateur rights in a new dramatico-musical work to be released before at least the initial first-class professional production has run its course. Amateur rights, at least in relation to well-known, established works, will often be administered through a specialist agency, offering a "catalogue" of such works available to amateur production companies. Sometimes a performance may be classified as a "pro-am", meaning that both professional and amateur performers are used. In such a case a licence will be required from whoever controls each of the professional and amateur rights. Pro-am productions are not easy to mount because of potential trade union intervention.

26–326

First-class and second-class rights. There is no standard uniform definition of the expression "first-class" in relation to a theatrical production, but it is widely recognised that the size, location and importance of the theatre venue are essential elements, as also are the use of exclusively professional performers and an experienced, professional creative team. A theatre with fewer than 400 seats would not normally be regarded as a first-class venue. The size of the budgeted capitalisation of pre-production costs and the length of the production run, whether open-ended or for a fixed season or touring, will also be relevant factors. In cases where the distinction has contractual importance the usual and best approach is to define precisely what is meant by "first class" performances in the particular case and then to define "second class" performances as meaning all other than "first class". Another approach is to define first class and second class performances by reference to how such expressions are theatrically understood and leave it to expert evidence to resolve any dispute. In the final analysis it is up to the contracting parties to say what they mean by these expressions or how their meaning is to be determined.

26–327

Amateur, concert-version, cabaret-version, condensed, tabloid, and dinner-theatre performances will all usually be regarded as second-class, and the same frequently applies to repertory performances. The expression "repertory" is usually applied to performances either by a "resident" stage company under the same management, or as part of a repertoire of a number of works pre-programmed for a fixed season at a fixed venue or venues or both.

Second-class performances will also include so-called try-out, showcase, and festival productions and "readings", where the purpose is to test audience reaction and attract the interest of producers and investors, sometimes before an invited audience (as often is the case with showcases and readings) and sometimes before the general public (as in the case of try-outs and festival productions) in the hope of raising sufficient interest and finance to launch a full scale production at a more important venue elsewhere. Often such second class performances will be presented for obvious reasons in so-called "fringe" or "alternative" theatre venues of an unconventional nature (e.g. pubs, village halls, assembly rooms, end-of-pier venues, and the like) but sometimes in well-appointed, purpose-built theatres, depending on how "second class" is defined or understood. Both London and Edinburgh, for example, are particularly well known for their thriving, well-established "fringe" theatre venues, some of a temporary and others of a permanent nature.

---

[724] See r.10 of the PRS's Rules and Regulations.

26–328   **Subsidiary rights.** A production contract for a major stage production will often be expected to include the grant to the producer, conditional upon his "qualifying" by presenting a first-class live stage production for a specified minimum number of performances, within a specified period at a specified venue or in a specified place or territory, of one or more so called "subsidiary" or "ancillary" or "residual" or "secondary" rights, in addition to the specified live performance rights. These subsidiary rights may include any one or more of the following, namely the right to exploit the work by:

(i) merchandising, sponsorship and commercial usage;

(ii) motion picture (film, television, DVD, video-cassette) (whether "as staged" or as an adaptation of the live stage version);

(iii) second-class stage performances;

(iv) cast album sound recordings, featuring members of the cast of the specified production;

(v) electronic transmission (CD-ROM, internet and other multi-media); and

(vi) translation into another language or other languages.

Merchandising, sponsorship and commercial usage exploitation will in practice usually relate to the title, logo and artwork of a show, rather than the text or lyrics or music, although the latter may sometimes be used as, for example, in respect of a souvenir programme-brochure or a coffee-table book about the history and origins of a work. Copyright in the logo and artwork will probably be acquired by the producer from the graphic designer in any event,[725] and will rarely have originated from the author or composer and other copyright owner of the written work. As to the title of the show, there will rarely be any copyright in it,[726] and so the consent of the author or composer to merchandising exploitation will rarely be needed. Nevertheless, it is usual for the author, composer or copyright owner of the written work to require and be given a share of merchandising revenue on the ground that the reputation of the written work contributes materially to the generation of the revenue concerned. Multimedia rights are, of course, a modern phenomenon, akin to motion picture rights and in certain respects indistinguishable from them. As a matter of practicality it may be convenient simply to include them in the same contractual definition as motion picture rights, since attempts at separation can cause problems of both technological and remunerative differentiation.

Cast album records of a major stage musical may be the source of considerable revenue for all the parties involved, and much thought will be given to the decision by the producer whether to release the album before, during or after the production. The producer will or should be able to deliver the cast for the making of the album, usually in a recording studio. The division of royalties and profit shares and the contractual arrangements involved are all matters of some complexity. Copyright issues in relation to sound recordings are, of course, considered elsewhere in this work.[727]

26–329   **New productions, reproductions, revivals and transfers.** "New production" is an expression which may be used either to describe a production of a work which may be long established and may already have been presented on the live stage before, but is now to be presented in a different way with a different creative team and with different production designs and other elements than before, or it may

---

[725] As to this, see paras 26–314 and 26–317, above.

[726] As to copyright in titles, see para.3–16, above. Depending on the facts, a title may be protected by a passing-off action.

[727] See the specialist section 3 of Pt VIII of this work entitled "The Music Industry" at paras 26–147 et seq.

be used to describe the stage production of a new work which is now to be presented for the first time.

"Reproductions" used to be a comparatively rare phenomenon, but are becoming increasingly common. Since about 1985 the global reproduction market has opened up, such that it is now common for "reproductions", namely recreations of the original stage production, which perhaps is still being presented to the public at its original location, to be presented at the same time in a number of different countries and languages around the world, either directly by the original producer or under licence from him on a kind of franchise basis, using the same stage directions, choreography and production designs as the original production on which the copycat "repro" is based. For this purpose, of course, the producer has to acquire the necessary rights from the creative team of the core production which is being recreated, as well as from the authors and/or copyright-owners of the written work, bearing in mind the various territories in which such rights, and their spin-off subsidiary rights, may need to be exploited.

It follows that the copyright elements of the work of the creative team in relation to stage musicals have assumed far greater importance. As a result, copyright terms are usually much more complex and difficult to negotiate in respect of a contract geared to the worldwide reproduction market in stage musicals than a simple licence for a single production run at a single specified theatre. Licensed reproductions, where the original producer licenses another to recreate the same production elements of stage directions, choreography and designs at another venue, are akin to franchise operations, and usually involve conditions of close artistic quality control. The creative team will usually require to be given options for their engagement in reproducing their work at other venues, and also to be involved in the appointment of "deputies" engaged to re-create their work if they do not take up their option due to non-availability or otherwise.

A "revival", as the word implies, refers to a production of an established work which has been presented before, perhaps many times, but has been out of production for a long time and is now being "revived".

A "transfer" refers to an entire production with its physical assets, and possibly including the whole of the original stage company, being transferred from one venue to another, possibly even from one country to another, as from the West End of London to Broadway or vice versa, or from an out-of-town venue to a major West End or Broadway theatre.

Reserved rights and music publishing rights. Most contracts between author **26–330** and producer can be expected to stipulate that all other rights apart from the specific rights expressly granted are reserved to the grantors. Even where a full range of subsidiary rights is granted to the producer, however, the authors or copyright owners will expect to reserve to themselves the so-called "music publishing rights" which are usually expressed to include sound recording rights, motion-picture-with-music synchronisation rights, the publication of sheet music and the "small" non-dramatic performance rights in the individual musical compositions, such as are customarily administered by music publishers or local collection societies. It is, however, up to the contracting parties to establish what they mean by such expressions in each individual case.

D. Moral Rights

Authors have important moral rights in this field, including in particular, the right **26–331** (if asserted) not to have their work subjected to derogatory treatment and the right to be identified as the author of their work.[728] Although the moral rights of authors cannot be assigned,[729] they may be waived or be the subject of consent, but only by the original author during his lifetime.[730] Frequently a stage play or musical is adapted from a film, novel or other original work, a process that involves a risk of the author claiming that his work has been subjected to derogatory treatment within the meaning of the Act.[731] Consequently, an adaptor will be at risk unless either a waiver of the moral right or consent in some form to make the adaptation is obtained from the author. Where an author is persuaded to waive his moral rights in a particular work, it is not uncommon for him to stipulate that, in the event of his considering that his work is being subjected to derogatory treatment, he should be entitled to require cancellation of his accreditation as the author of a work, of the adaptation of which he no longer approves. Indeed, certain collective bargaining agreements provide specifically for a designer to have such a right of cancellation of his accreditation.[732]

The translation of a lyric set to music needs to be in harmony with the corresponding musical composition, requiring a certain amount of poetic licence and freedom of expression on the part of the translator, whose task is to maintain the right balance between being faithful to the sense and object of the original words, whilst finding the best way of expressing the meaning in harmony and synchronisation with the music, even if this means departing from a more literal translation. However, a translation of a literary or dramatic work is in any event excluded from the scope of derogatory treatment.[733]

E. THEATRE PREMISES AND DEPOSIT OF SCRIPTS

26–332   The Theatres Act, 1968, provides, among other things, for the prohibition of obscene performances in public, and requires delivery of scripts of new plays to the Trustees of the British Museum free of charge (for archiving purposes) within one month of the first public performance. For a more detailed treatment of this topic see paras 26–106 et seq. It is mentioned here in a specialist section on theatre for the sake of completeness, but does not raise any particular copyright issues. Section 18 of the 1968 Act contains definitions of, among others, "play", "script" and "public performance",[734] but they are for the purpose of that Act only.

F. UNIONS, TRADE ASSOCIATIONS AND OTHER ORGANISATIONS

26–333   The principal "trade union"[735] or trade association for performers is Equity (formerly called British Actors Equity Association), and for theatre staff and technicians is the Broadcasting, Entertainment, Cinematography and Theatre

---

[728] As to moral rights generally, see Ch.11, and for performers' moral rights generally see Ch.11 paras 11–33 and 11–52. CDPA 1988 ss. 205C(1) and 205F(1), inserted with effect from February 1, 2006 by the Performances (Moral Rights etc) Regulations 2006 (SI 2006/18), created two new statutory, non-assignable moral rights for performers, similar to those already existing for copyright owners, namely a right to be identified as the performer, and a right to object to derogatory treatment. These new rights are subject to certain exceptions and supplementary provisions, for which see details in CDPA 1988 s.250(c) et seq..

[729] See paras 11–67 et seq.

[730] CDPA 1988 s.94. As to waiver of moral rights, see s.87 and paras 11–75 et seq., above. As to the position following the author's death, see s.95 and paras 11–67 et seq.. The position varies in other jurisdictions.

[731] But see the next sub-paragraph.

[732] See, for example, the TMA/Equity/BECTU Agreement for Theatre Designers (1999).

[733] CDPA 1988 s.80(2)(a)(i).

[734] See para.26–107.

[735] The expression "trade union" may be regarded as a misnomer when applied to those performers, who are self-employed and enter into contracts for services rather than contracts of service.

Union (BECTU). The principal trade associations for theatre managers are the Society of London Theatre (SOLT)[736]; the Theatrical Management Association (TMA), which is to provincial theatre managers and subsidised repertory theatre managers what SOLT is to managers of theatres in the West End of London and pre-West End touring managers; and the Independent Theatre Council (ITC) which covers small-scale independent theatres in much the same way as SOLT and TMA operate in relation to the larger ones.

There are, however, a great many other representative bodies in the theatre industry such as, for example, the Writers Guild of Great Britain (WGGB) (now incorporating the former Theatre Writers Union), the British Academy of Composers and Songwriters (BACS), and the Musicians' Union. A full list of theatre-related societies and organisations is to be found in the British Theatre Directory,[737] which is updated annually. Among these organisations are listed separate associations for, by way of example, stage directors, lighting designers, choreographers, theatre designers and stage managers. The same directory also contains details of Arts Councils and Regional Arts Boards which are dedicated to providing financial support to the subsidised sector of the theatre industry. Other organisations include:

- The London Theatre Council, which is run by representatives of Equity and SOLT, its purpose being to regulate relations between producers and performers in the West End of London, to require and hold deposits against default in payment to performers in West End productions and to provide a structure for conciliation and arbitration.

- The Theatres Trust, which was established by Act of Parliament in 1976 to promote the better protection of the theatre industry for the benefit of the nation. It administers a charitable fund and maintains contact with other organisations with related concerns

- The Variety and Light Entertainment Council of Great Britain (VLEC), which includes a number of other bodies such as SOLT, TMA and Equity among its constituent members, and is concerned primarily with performances by variety artistes.

- The Agents Association (Great Britain) which has over 400 entertainment agencies in its membership, and its sister organisation the National Entertainment Agents Council (NEAC).

G. Collecting Societies and Licensing Agencies

The role of the Performing Right Society Ltd (PRS) in relation to live stage performances of dramatico-musical works has already been considered above.[738] A licence from both the PRS and Phonographic Performance Ltd (PPL) will also be required for the playing of a copyright recording of copyright music incidental to the action of a live stage non-musical play, assuming the copyright owners have assigned their copyrights to those organisations. In the absence of such assignments a licence will be needed from the author/composer or their respective assignees or music publishers (in the case of the music) and from the record

26–334

---

[736] The Society of London Theatre (SOLT) was formerly known as the Society of West End Theatre (SWET) and is an operating name of West End Theatre Managers Ltd.

[737] Published by Richmond House Publishing Company Ltd of Douglas House, 3 Richmond Buildings, London W1V 5AE.

[738] See para.26–325, and for more general coverage of the PRS see para.27–65, below. In 1996 the PRS formed an alliance with the MCPS (The Mechanical Copyright Protection Society), which administers and collects royalties on music recordings on behalf of its members. This alliance was called "The MCPS-PRS Alliance" or simply "The Music Alliance," but each remains a separate society in terms of income, constitution, membership and guardianship of rights. In 2009 the alliance again changed its name to "PRS for Music".

company (in the case of the sound recording). The same applies to incidental recorded music prior to curtain-up or in the interval or between scene changes. There are collective bargaining agreements between SOLT/TMA and the Musicians' Union, which have no copyright implications, but contain detailed provisions for reporting to, and in some cases obtaining prior approval of the Union for the use in a stage production of recorded music (including archive recordings) and as to use in such production of electronic instruments. However, there are important and substantial differences between the SOLT and TMA agreements with the Union in this respect, which require careful study and the reasons for which are not obvious, the current SOLT Agreement having been made in October 2007 and seeming less favourable to the producer than that of the TMA made in April of the same year.

There are a number of privately owned and operated agencies, which specialise in the licensing of plays (including stage musicals) to repertory companies, schools, colleges, amateur dramatic societies and the like, that is to say in the licensing of so-called "second-class rights."[739] This is regarded as a convenient method of marketing and exploiting such second-class rights with a view to maximising the revenue from such exploitation in a way which the rights owners would find difficult to do themselves. Agencies of this kind will frequently reach out to the market by issuing "catalogues" of the available works in their licensing "repertoire", and will set standard tariffs, sometimes by reference to a percentage of box office receipts and sometimes fixed performance fees or a mixture of both. They operate off commission which will be deducted when accounting to their principals, the rights owners. Often they are appointed on fixed, long-term contracts at specified commission rates.

H. COLLECTIVE BARGAINING AGREEMENTS

26–335 There are a great many collective bargaining agreements relating to live stage performances. All of them regulate the minimum remuneration and other minimum terms and conditions of engagement of the members of the contracting organisations concerned.[740] Some relate only to performers, stage managers and theatre staff, and are accordingly outside the scope of this work as having no particular copyright significance. The principal such agreements relating to creators of copyright material are as follows:

Date	
1989	SOLT/Equity Agreement for West End of London Theatre Designers.
1993	Agreement between the Writers' Guild of GB and the "English Stage Companies", namely Royal National Theatre, Royal Shakespeare Company and Royal Court Theatre, applicable to productions staged at those theatres.
1993	TMA/Writers' Guild of GB/Scottish Society of Playwrights Agreement, relating to works to be produced by members using the TMA/Equity Subsidised Repertory Agreement.
1995	SOLT/TMA/Equity Agreement for Fight Directors.
1999	TMA/Equity/BECTU Agreement for Designers outside West End of London.

---

[739] As to the use of the expression "second-class rights" see para.26–327, above.
[740] For collecting societies in general and the work of individual collecting societies in particular, as well as the constitution and work of the Copyright Tribunal, see Chs 27 and 28.

Date

2002	TMA/Equity Agreement for Directors in Subsidised Repertory and Commercial Theatres.
2003	SOLT/Equity Agreement for West End Theatre Choreographers.
2004	TMA/Equity Agreement for Choreographers for Subsidised Repertory and Commercial Theatres.
2006	SOLT/Equity Agreement for West End Theatre Directors.
2006	SOLT/TMA/Equity Agreement for Opera Directors and Staff Directors.

The 1989, 1995 and 1999 Agreements listed above are presently in renegotiation, and replacements are expected to be issued shortly.

There is at this time no collective agreement for contracts between commercial producers and authors/composers in relation to West End of London live stage productions, which are therefore the subject of free negotiation between the parties. However, the relevant "minimum" terms of collective agreements between producers and members of the creative team of directors, choreographers and designers for West End productions are frequently incorporated by reference where applicable into their West End contracts, but are often extensively supplemented, particularly in relation to further exploitation of their work in "reproductions" on tour and/or overseas.

The ITC (Independent Theatre Council) also has a number of collective agreements with various bodies, on similar lines to those of SOLT/TMA, which are regarded as compulsory for ITC members registered as "approved managers". The ITC has over 600 members (only a proportion of whom have "approved manager" status), who are concerned principally with small- to medium-sized stage performances outside the West End of London, including non-traditional performance spaces. Its collective agreements for owners of copyright material comprise:

1993 ITC/Equity Agreement for Resident and Freelance Theatre Directors.

1993 ITC/Equity Agreement for Freelance Designers.

2003 ITC/Writers Guild of GB Agreement for Writers of Plays first professionally presented in the provinces by ITC approved managers.

2004 ITC/Equity Agreement for Freelance Choreographers.

Unlike SOLT/TMA, doubtless because the latter focus on larger productions of completed dramatico-musical works, ITC in its 1993 Agreement with Equity for Theatre Directors grapples, where applicable and in considerable detail, with contractual issues relating to so-called "devised plays" which have no working script at commencement of the workshop/rehearsal period but are allowed to develop and devolve during such period from contributions by various participants in the creative process including, prominently, the Director. Reference should be made to this agreement for its somewhat complex treatment of the copyright issues concerned.

The VLEC (Variety and Light Entertainment Council) also maintains minimum rates of remuneration for contracts between its member organisations and variety artistes, but does not have any collective agreements dealing with copyright matters separately from Equity.

The WGGB (Writers Guild of Great Britain), in addition to the collective Agreements listed above, also publishes very detailed "Guidelines" and checklists and a model Collaborators Agreement for its members. The last issue of these Guidelines was published in 2006 and contains detailed guidance on a wide range of matters including copyright in dramatic and dramatico-musical works written for the live stage.

I. OPERA AND BALLET

26–336   In theory there is no reason why both opera and ballet should not follow the same course as stage musicals, and indeed precisely the same copyright considerations apply in all three cases. After all, an opera is merely one particular type of stage musical with a more limited appeal and profitability than its more popular counterpart. Many productions, however, tend to be of classical works which are out of copyright, and are most often presented by national or regional, heavily subsidised, opera or ballet companies, with "resident" or "semi-resident" performers, management and production personnel. Nevertheless contemporary dance and opera works by new writers do play a significant part in the continuing development of these performing arts. Sometimes classical ballet may be re-choreographed almost as a wholly new work. The choreography will usually be recorded by notation or other appropriate means, in which case, it will ordinarily be protected as a dramatic work.[741]

In *Massine v de Basil*,[742] a case decided before the passing of the 1956 Act, the Court of Appeal proceeded on the basis (which was common ground) that a ballet in its entirety was a composite work protected by copyright, comprising collectively the elements of music, story, choreography, scenery and costumes. However, given the way in which the 1988 Act defines the works which may be subject to copyright this can no longer be the case.[743] To the extent that *Massine v de Basil* suggests that the copyright in a dramatic work extends to and includes the scenic designs and costumes for that work, the decision is no longer good authority either.[744] Of course, such scenic designs may qualify for separate protection as artistic works, but see para.26–310, above, It is also possible that a stage producer who puts together other separate component parts of an opera, ballet or other dramatico-musical work, such as the text, music, stage direction and choreography created by third parties, may justifiably have a claim in equity to copyright protection in the composite whole separately from its component parts.[745]

It is important to bear in mind, when considering the way in which the work is staged, that it has been held that copyright may not subsist in contributions to the mere interpretation and theatrical presentation of a dramatic work.[746] The outcome in each case will depend on its own facts.

26–337   **The creative team.** In the case of opera and ballet productions the creative team of director, choreographer[747] and designers are more likely to be employed as part of a resident company than in the case of "popular" stage musicals or regular theatre. If so, the copyright in their work, created in the course of such employment, will usually vest in the employer, i.e. the production company.[748] If independent and self-employed, they may be expected to assign any copyright in their

---

[741] CDPA 1988 s.3(1) which defines a "dramatic work" as including a work of dance or mime. See paras 3–37, and 26–308.

[742] [1936–1945] Mac C.C. 223.

[743] See para.3–02. By the same token, there is no copyright in a song as a "hybrid work" but only in the words and music separately: *Chappell & Co. Ltd v Redwood Music Ltd* [1981] R.P.C. 337.

[744] See para.3–32, above.

[745] See paras 26–318 and 5–174 et seq..

[746] *Brighton v Jones* [2004] EWHC 1157.

[747] In ballet the roles of director and choreographer are often combined under the title of "artistic director".

[748] CDPA 1988 s.11(2). As to works of employees, see paras 5–11 et seq. and note in particular *In-*

work to the company engaging them.[749] However, if the contract with an independent contractor is silent as to ownership of copyright, it is likely that the circumstances will give rise to a "necessary implication" that copyright in the material concerned should in equity be the property of the paying party who should in that event be entitled to have the rights assigned to him.[750]

Just as the role of the choreographer in ballet assumes a heightened importance, so too in the case of opera does the role of the musical director. Making a written record of choreography for copyright and reproduction purposes in the form of special choreographer's "notation" is a highly skilled task,[751] the result of which is likely to unintelligible to the uninitiated. An opera, however, as with a stage musical, is usually recorded in permanent form by written music and words, and thus unlikely to present any problems of establishing an adequate permanent record for copyright purposes.

Opera producers are usually regarded by national and major opera companies in much the same way as members of the creative team of a stage musical. They are engaged to perform the function of producer either for a single production or series of productions for which they will usually be remunerated by fees or a salary, plus expenses but no royalties. They will not have to raise finance for the production but will be expected to put together all the artistic elements required. They will usually be engaged under the 2006 standard, collective form of agreement established by SOLT/TMA/EQUITY, which also includes opera directors. Apart from the above, there is no standard agreement for commercial productions of contemporary opera and ballet, the producers of which will either adopt or adapt one or other of the SOLT/ TMA/Equity forms of agreement for opera or regular theatre productions, or negotiate special terms for such copyright licences as they require.

J. Variety Acts and other Forms of Live Entertainment

In the context of copyright the word "theatre" may in its narrowest sense be thought to be confined to live stage performances of dramatic or dramatico-musical works in a purpose-built theatre. However, in a wider sense it may also include live performances of any "pre-set" form of entertainment attraction, whether in a purpose built theatre, or in an enclosed or open air auditorium or in a so-called "arena" venue, such as a skating-rink or circus tent. For example, both dramatic and non-dramatic works, usually accompanied by recorded music, are now not infrequently performed, even sometimes in a conventional, specially adapted theatre, by a stage company of ice-skaters or roller-skaters, where, as in the case of ballet, the choreographic content assumes a considerably enhanced degree of importance.

26–338

Rock concerts, are an example of works frequently performed live on a temporary stage in the open air. The Open Air Theatre in Regents Park, London, regularly presents dramatic productions in the summer months, and is itself one of the theatres represented in SOLT. Some circus acts are frequently performed,

---

tercase United Kingdom Ltd v Time Computers Ltd [2004] E.C.D.R. 8 and *Ultraframe (United Kingdom) Ltd v Fielding* [2004] R.P.C. 24.

[749] The former 1987 SOLT/TMA/Equity Agreement for Opera Directors required copyright in the product of a freelance producer's and director's services to be assigned to the opera company concerned on specified terms, but when this was replaced in 2006, the new version provided for the director to retain copyright in "the product of his services", subject to the producer having an exclusive licence for the initial production and tour (if any) with a conditional option for exploitation in other media. Both agreements assumed the existence of copyright in such services, but as to whether such assumption is justified see para.26–307 and its footnotes.

[750] See para.26–323 and para.26–325, above.

[751] See para.3–17 and CDPA 1988 s.4.

either with or without animals, to a "pre-set" formulation in a circus tent or "big top". Then there are live stage performances in a so-called "variety bill" by, for example, comedians, conjurers, illusionists, song and dance artistes, acrobats, jugglers, comedy sketch actors and the like. Cruise liners, particularly the bigger ones, often have large, very well-appointed theatre venues which alone would merit being regarded as "first class". The same may or may not be said of the staging and presentation of their theatrical productions, which are sometimes of a "compilation nature" and sometimes include members of the crew as enthusiastic amateurs in their cast of performers. In relation to copyright issues each such case will need to be considered on its own particular facts.

In most cases where the "dramatic" nature of a performance is in doubt, the attraction of the audience is likely to lie primarily, though not entirely, in the skill of the performers, but also, perhaps to a lesser extent, in the subject matter of their performance. In so far as any copyright issue may arise, which by virtue of the nature of the subject matter is likely to be comparatively rare, the content of the performance and the manner of its staging and presentation will need to be carefully analysed in order to determine to what extent, if at all, it is capable of copyright protection. The usual basic tests, all of which have been considered elsewhere in this work, will need to be applied. Thus, it will be necessary to ask:

   (i) Is it within the definition of a literary, dramatic, musical and/or artistic work?

   (ii) Is it original to the copyright claimant or his predecessor in title?

   (iii) Has it been recorded in writing or on film or in some other permanent form?

   (iv) To what extent, if at all, were any "original" elements created within the period of copyright protection, and are they of sufficient substance, either alone or in relation to the whole, to qualify for such protection as a "work" (as to which see paras 3–125 et seq., above)?

   (v) Was the work created by a "qualifying author" under s.154 of the 1988 Act or first published in the United Kingdom or in another qualifying country under s.155 of the 1988 Act?

In some such cases the answers to these questions will be clear, but in many cases they will not. For example, a joke told on stage by a comedian, possibly to persons, some of whom may claim to have heard it before, may well have some literary or dramatic content, but its origin and originality may be obscure, although this is less likely where it relates to a recently reported event or person in the news, who was previously relatively unknown.[752] Then again, the methodology of a conjuring trick or illusion may not be original but the manner of its staging and presentation may be of a nature which is both dramatic and artistic in terms of its characterisation, costume, "props" and storyline.

To qualify for copyright protection the dramatic elements must be identifiable with sufficient certainty and must be sufficiently linked or connected so as to be capable of performance. It is for this reason that copyright has been denied to a sports game or competition or so-called "reality" situation where the performers and/or participants react to unforeseeable events or circumstances. However, much depends on the facts and the format of such situations may in some instances attract copyright protection.[753]

It must be noted in this context that no copyright (as distinct from performers'

---

[752] Comedians are said to have an "unwritten", non-legal copyright code, at least in the US, as to which see Ollar, Dotan and Sprigman, Christopher Jon of University of Virginia Law School, " *Intellectual Property Norms in Stand-up Comedy*" (2010), available at SSRN: *http://ssrn.com/abstract=1635023* [Accessed November 1, 2010].

[753] See paras 2–06 and 3–18 and the cases cited in their footnotes.

rights) will attach to the mere manner of performance by a comedian, conjurer or other performing artiste of the kind concerned. Further, the mere performance of a dramatic work will not of itself constitute publication of it, in those cases where publication is required in order to qualify for copyright protection under s.155 of the 1988 Act.

Pantomime. Pantomime is an interesting theatrical genre so far as copyright is concerned. Hundreds of pantomime productions with well-known titles are presented annually around the United Kingdom, especially at Christmas time. The plot synopses are invariably based on fairy tales and folklore originating many hundreds of years ago, their precise origin being very often indeterminate, although some of the lesser-known ones may be based on tales by known authors such as Hans Christian Andersen and the brothers Grimm. Most pantomimes have well-known character-names, such as "Cinderella" and "Aladdin", and characteristics such as the cross-gender roles of the "principal boy" and "principal girl", the "panto dame", the wicked "baddy" and audience participation. Such characteristics and the basic plots and characters themselves are for the most part long since out of copyright.

26–339

Although it is possible in theory for a playwright to write an entirely new and original pantomime as a wholly copyright protected work, this is unlikely since part of the genre's public appeal lies in the long-established storylines and in the special characteristics described above. Some pantomime productions, even those of which the basic material is long since out of copyright, may nevertheless contain some original new writing and new production elements by writers commissioned for that purpose by the producer, unless they are in a fixed, unchangeable form licensed from one of the licensing agencies.[754] Thus, it will be possible to identify numerous variations, some large and some small, between one production and another of the same pantomime, and these "variations" (possibly also "additions") will in some instances comprise modifications constituting new copyright material. Thus, it is not now uncommon for pantomime producers to introduce new material specially tailored for "celebrity performers" as a perceived additional attraction. However, productions of well-known pantomimes have become so prolific and formulaic that the room for originality in the written work and staging is greatly diminished. In the result, any claim of copyright infringement is quite likely to be met with a defence of unoriginality and/or insubstantiality in relation to the work as a whole, but each case will turn on its own facts. For example, pantomimes on ice, performed by ice-skaters, are not uncommon, and will obviously allow for considerable more originality, particularly in their choreography, than would otherwise be the case. Many pantomime productions will be accompanied by music, either live or recorded, and usually of more recent origin, in which cases copyright in such music and any songs will fall to be separately assessed in accordance with general principles considered elsewhere in this work.[755]

K. BILLING CREDITS

The inclusion of so-called "production billing credits" in theatre programmes, bill posters, flyers and other publicity material is a sensitive area and fertile ground for contention in the theatre industry. Much time may be spent in contract negotiation as to, not only whether and where accreditation should be given, but also as to the size, prominence, positioning and general appearance of the individual billing relative to that accorded to other recipients.

26–340

---

[754] See para.26–326 and CDPA 1988 s.175.
[755] See paras 26–147 et seq.

Moral rights, including the right (if asserted) of an author or adaptor of a copyright work and the director of a copyright film to be identified as such whenever the work is published commercially or performed in public, was first introduced into English law by CDPA 1988 Ch.IV, so as to bring it broadly in conformity with the law in much of continental Europe, but in reality this only gave statutory effect to what had long before then been the custom and practice of the theatre industry to an even greater extent than the Act provided. Thus, by long-established custom and practice, credits are usually given, not only to those entitled by s.77 of the Act, but also to producers, associates and certain others involved in mounting a production without their necessarily having created copyright material. By virtue of s.78 of the Act the statutory right to be identified as author or director is conditional upon such right being asserted in writing, either generally or in relation to a particular act or description of acts, by the person claiming it. The same statutory right of identification has since to a limited extent been extended by statutory instrument to performers.[756]

Billing credits in theatre programmes and bill-posters and flyers are usually under the control of the producer, occasionally subject to approval of or in consultation with the theatre-manager. The principal billing page in the programme, which is invariably also the title-page, will usually contain the names of the producer, the authors and copyright-owners, any adaptors, and the creative team of director, choreographer and designers.

Posters and flyers often do not contain the same full billing complement as the corresponding theatre programmes, their purpose being to place emphasis on and draw particular attention to the title, authors and theatre venue (sometimes also "star" performers) without cluttering the page with a lot of subsidiary nomenclature.

The names of the producer and copyright-owners will usually appear above the title on the principal billing page where the producer may be described as presenting the production "by arrangement with" the copyright-owners "or in association with" a co-producer or very large investor or sponsor, although the latter persons should be alive to the legal implications of allowing themselves to be held out to the public in this way. The names of big star performers are also very occasionally introduced above the title after the word "present".

The author's billing is usually placed immediately below the title for obvious reasons in no less size than that of the producer. The director will usually expect his billing credit to appear whenever and wherever the name of the producer appears and will usually stipulate the size of his billing by comparison with that of the producer or author. The creative team will expect their billing to be equal in size to or at least of a size no less than a specified proportion of that of the director. To avoid arguments it has become increasingly common for all members of the creative team to be billed in the same size and with the same prominence, but the director's billing is usually on a separate line of its own. For the same reason it is also sometimes regarded as convenient to attach a mock-up of the complete billing page to the particular contract concerned.

It is common for contractual terms to provide (for obvious reasons of limited space) that billing credits shall not be required in classified or small or so-called "teaser" advertisements. Some contracts also give the individual concerned the right to have his billing withdrawn if he later wishes for any reason to dissociate himself from the production.

In the case of a local producer presenting a "copycat repro" under licence from

---

[756] See CDPA 1988 ss.205(C) and 205(F), inserted with effect from February 1, 2006 by the Performances (Moral Rights etc) Regulations 2006 (SI 2006/18). As to moral rights generally see Ch.11 and para.26–331. As to performers' moral rights generally, see Ch.11.

the original producer, he may be described as presenting the original producer's production. Where a revival or reproduction is being presented it is frequently the case that reference will be made at the bottom of the page to the date and venue of the "original" production, which is being revived or re-created.

The theatre programme, will, of course, invariably contain a cast list of performers, usually on a separate page, and often accompanied by "biogs" of all or most of the principal members of the cast, (as well as the authors, the producer and creative team). It is also common for there to appear towards the back of the programme lists of company personnel, and sometimes professional advisors, of the theatre management and the producer respectively, even including sometimes, office personnel, stage managers, carpenters and electricians. All this, of course, when added to a number of advertisements, tends to swell the length of the programme and its cost to the public which may be regarded by some as prohibitive. In the case of big budget stage musicals souvenir programmes containing numerous colour photographs and a cover bearing the show's distinctive logo are often to be found on sale in the precincts of the theatre at comparatively substantial cost, designed to enhance the merchandising revenue of the production concerned.

It must be emphasised that some of the above accreditation arises by virtue of statutory requirements, some by contractual arrangement, and some by mere custom and practice of the industry. In so far as statutory requirements are concerned these relate to the moral rights referred to in CDPA 1988 as amended and described elsewhere in this work.

7. THE ADVERTISING INDUSTRY

A. COMPONENTS OF ADVERTISING

(i) Television, radio and cinema commercials

A television or cinema commercial is typically the product of the creative and administrative work of many separate individuals. The intellectual property rights involved are often complex. Many of the rights will vest in the advertiser or its advertising agency, but advertisers are often surprised to learn what rights remain with other contributors.   **26–341**

Production companies. Most television and cinema commercials are produced for an advertising agency by one of a relatively small number of specialist production companies. Advertising agency creative staff are the initial source of a joint creative enterprise which is then managed by the agency in conjunction with the production company. The first work involved in this process and the most important work underlying the end product is the script, which may be either a literary or dramatic work. Its author will typically be a copywriter employed by the advertising agency and the copyright in the script will in such cases usually vest initially in the advertising agency.[757] In some cases, storyboards will be produced by agency staff or by artists commissioned for this purpose.[758] These graphic representations of scenes from the intended film may be significant in infringement actions as artistic works underlying the end product.   **26–342**

The division of labour between advertising agency and production company varies. The production company will assemble a team of film technicians and a director approved by the advertising agency. The advertising agency may be

---

[757] CDPA 1988 s.11(2), see paras 5–08 et seq., above.
[758] As to the ownership of copyright in commissioned works, see para.5–178, above.

responsible for selecting and hiring actors and for commissioning or licensing any music required. It may be difficult to determine whether the producer of the resulting film is the production company, the advertising agency or both.[759] The author of the film will be the producer and the principal director.[760] The first owner of the copyright in the film will be the producer and the principal director, or their employers.[761] The sound track of the commercial is treated as part of the film.[762]

A television commercial can be not only a film but also a dramatic work if, as is often the case, it is a work of action which is capable of being performed before an audience.[763] The author of the commercial, *qua* dramatic work, will be the person who creates it. This may include different persons, for example the writer of the script, from the authors of the commercial *qua* film (the producer and principal director).

In most cases the identity of the producer will be of little significance since production companies and advertising agencies normally contract on standard terms approved by their respective trade associations.[764] These provide for an assignment to the advertising agency of "all copyright and similar rights throughout the world for all purposes and for their full duration in the Commercial(s) and in all other footage shot by the production company in the production of the Commercial(s) whether or not included in the completed Commercial(s)".[765] As to the director, he is normally an employee or sub-contractor of the production company and it is the production company's duty to ensure that it procures from the director and passes on to the advertising agency an assignment of the director's interest, if any, in the copyright.[766]

Many of the individuals employed or hired by the production company, such as cameramen, lighting and sound technicians, will have no copyright interest. Others, such as set designers and model makers, may be the authors of copyright artistic works. Except in the case of animated cartoon characters and models created by third parties for the commercial, if they are created by third parties the production company undertakes to obtain from the third party either an assignment of copyright or, if an assignment cannot be negotiated on reasonable terms, a licence on terms to be approved by the advertising agency.[767]

It is also the production company's responsibility to procure the irrevocable and unconditional waiver of all moral rights, wherever in the world enforceable, vesting in the director and all other persons engaged in the creation or production of the commercial.[768] It is provided, however, that the use of the commercial in connection with the production of any other commercial for a different advertiser is subject to the production company's prior written consent.[769]

26–343   **Music.** Many commercials include music in their soundtrack. That music may be

---

[759] As to who is the "producer" of a film and a sound recording, see paras 4–49 and 4–42, above.
[760] CDPA 1988 s.9(2) and see para.4–48, above.
[761] CDPA 1988 ss.11(2) and 10(1A). See para.5–08, above.
[762] CDPA 1988 s.5B(2), but see s.5B(5). See also para.3–78, above.
[763] *Norowzian v Arks Ltd (No. 2)* [2000] F.S.R. 363.
[764] The Advertising Producers Association, the Institute of Practitioners in Advertising and the Incorporated Society of British Advertisers.
[765] But note that animation "exclusively designed and created by the production company" remains the property of the production company unless a copyright assignment is separately agreed; see Agreement for the Production of Commercials (2004) cl.12(b).
[766] Agreement for the Production of Commercials (2004) cl.12(c).
[767] Agreement for the Production of Commercials (2004) cl.12(c).
[768] Agreement for the Production of Commercials (2004) cl.12(e). International advertisers should note that, notwithstanding the terms of the production company's warranty, a waiver of moral rights may be unenforceable under the laws of certain other jurisdictions including France and Germany.
[769] cl.12(f).

original or it may be copied from an existing sound recording. Alternatively, an existing musical work may be adapted and re-recorded so as to fit the timing and other requirements of the commercial. Where a music production company is commissioned by the advertising agency to produce a sound recording incorporating either original music or a version of an existing work, the music production company will normally be the producer of the resulting sound recording and therefore its author and the first owner of the copyright in it.[770] If the sound recording embodies an original musical work the author of that work will be the composer hired or employed by the music production company.

Copyright in a sound recording created by a music production company and in any musical work created for the commercial is dealt with quite differently from the copyright in the film itself and its associated sound recording. Under the terms of the standard agreements approved by the trade associations of the music production companies (Producers and Composers of Applied Music) and advertising agencies, the copyrights in both the sound recording and any original composition are retained by the music production company (as between the production company and the composer, the production company will usually have taken the copyright either as the composer's employer or under the terms of his engagement). In the case of a re-recording of an existing musical work, the music production company retains the copyright in the sound recording but the copyright in any arrangement of the existing musical work becomes the property of the owner of the copyright in the work that has been arranged. The standard agreements are the Agreement for the Production and Licensing of Original Musical Composition and the Agreement for the Licensing and Re-Recording of an Existing Copyright Work (April 2009). An exclusive licence is granted to the advertising agency to exploit the works in specified media and territories and for a specified period of time. With limited qualifications relating to credits,[771] however, the music production company warrants that all moral rights of all persons engaged in the production of the work have been waived.

Where an existing copyright musical work, or a version reproducing any substantial part of an existing musical work, is to be included in an advertisement the advertising agency must obtain a licence from the copyright owner, normally a music publishing company. See the Synchronisation Licence for Music in Commercials, approved by the Music Publishers Association and the Institute of Practitioners in Advertising (December 2005). Phonographic Performance Limited ("PPL") takes an assignment of the performing right and dubbing right under its standard form agreement with member record companies who own copyright. Where the member is an exclusive licensee, PPL is appointed to act as the member's exclusive agent for the exercise of these rights. In practice, however, PPL does not grant dubbing licences for advertisements or where the sound recording is to be associated with brands or trade marks, but leaves this to the individual record companies.

Actors. An entirely separate set of rights is created when an actor's audio or visual performance is recorded for inclusion in a commercial.[772] An actor engaged by an advertising agency will necessarily give consent, either expressly or impliedly, for the recording of his live performance. Subsequent exploitation of the commercial is subject to contractual restrictions agreed by the advertising

26–344

---

[770] CDPA 1988 s.9(2)(aa). See para.5–41, above.
[771] The composer and his publisher/agent are entitled to a printed credit wherever the advertising agency, advertiser and film director receive such a credit. An arranger is entitled to a credit in such circumstances "wherever possible".
[772] As to rights in performances generally, see Ch.12, above.

agency, normally under the terms of a standard contract agreed with Equity.[773] The actor's ability to enforce those restrictions is in practice reinforced by his reproduction right to authorise or prohibit the making of direct or indirect copies of the original master recording made by the production company.[774] The reproduction right is a property right[775] but is retained by the actor under the terms of the standard Equity agreement.[776] Under this agreement the actor grants consent for the exploitation of the commercial "limited to television transmission in the United Kingdom for the purpose of advertising the product(s) or service(s) specified". Any extension to other media such as cinema, radio or press advertising, or inclusion in a film or television documentary or other programme, or use outside the United Kingdom, requires the actor's further consent. The Form of Engagement covers overseas use and gives "the right to use such commercial(s) for agency/production company promotion, awards entries and websites, and for use in all showreels".

The Equity agreement requires the advertising agency to obtain the actor's specific consent for use of still photographs in "paid-for advertising space, packaging, or point-of-sale material". Exploitation of stills from a commercial in this manner without such consent would not, however, infringe an actor's reproduction right.[777]

26–345   **Performers' moral rights.** Performers of qualifying performances now have the right to be identified as such[778] and the right to object to derogatory treatment of their performance.[779] The right to be identified does not apply where it is not reasonably practicable to identify the performer,[780] nor does it apply in relation to performances given for the purposes of advertising any goods or services.[781]

(ii) Printed advertisements

26–346   Copyright will often subsist in press and poster advertisements, either as artistic or literary works (including compilations) or both. They are frequently the work of a number of individuals, some of whom may have copyright interests. As with broadcast and cinema advertising, the creative process typically starts within an advertising agency. Copy for the advertisement will be written within the agency and employees of the agency may also produce a "concept" or "visual" to illustrate how the advertisement is intended to look. If the advertisement is to include photographic or other graphic material, external creative suppliers will be commissioned by the agency.

26–347   **Advertising copy.** In the past, copyright protection was denied to a short advertis-

---

[773] Agreement for the Employment of Featured Artists in Television Commercials (November 1, 1991). This agreement is not officially approved but is used in practice, as supplemented by a Form of Engagement approved by the Advertising Producers Association, the Institute of Practitioners in Advertising and the Incorporated Society of British Advertisers (October 2007).

[774] CDPA 1988 s.182A. See para.12–20, above.

[775] CDPA 1988 s.191A(1).

[776] Agreement for the Employment of Featured Artists in Television Commercials (November 1, 1991). This Agreement is not officially approved but is used in practice, as supplemented by further standard terms approved by the Advertising Producers Association, the Institute of Practitioners in Advertising and the Incorporated Society of British Advertisers.

[777] Stills would not amount to a recording of part of an actor's "performance". cf. the position in relation to infringement of copyright in a film, para.7–81, above.

[778] CDPA 1988, s.205C(1).

[779] s.205F(1).

[780] s.205E(2).

[781] s.205E(4).

ing slogan.[782] However, the Court of Justice has now held that extracts of 11 words from newspaper articles will be protected if they "contain elements which are the expression of the individual expression of the creator of the work".[783] It remains to be seen what impact this decision will have on the protection of advertising slogans, particularly in the light of the amount of time and effort which may now be invested in their creation. More substantial copy, if original, has always been capable of protection as a literary work. As in the case of scripts for television commercials, the copyright in advertising copy written by copywriters employed by an advertising agency will normally vest initially in the advertising agency,[784] unless assigned by the advertising agency to the advertiser.

Photographs and illustrations. The author of a photograph is the person who   **26–348**
creates it and this will normally be the photographer. The role of the photographer in the creation of some advertising photographs may, however, be largely technical, the main creative input coming from the advertising agency's art director who may specify the precise content of the photograph. In these circumstances authorship may be joint, particularly if each has collaborated in the creation of the work and each has contributed a significant part of the skill and labour protected by the copyright.[785]

Photographs and illustrations are usually commissioned by an advertising agency from outside photographers and artists. The copyright in such circumstances is frequently retained by the photographer or illustrator. The Association of Photographers has agreed a negotiating framework with representatives of advertising agencies under which the copyright in commissioned photographs is retained by photographers whose works are licensed for use for specified media, territories and time periods. Most advertisers will require exclusive use of commissioned photographs and other artistic works, at least in the field of advertising and for the duration of the campaign in question. It is likely that exclusivity is, at least to this extent, implied in most commissions.

B. Issues between Rights Owners

(i) Rights of action against third parties

Since advertisements are often made up of a number of distinct copyright works   **26–349**
and ownership of the copyright in some of these works will not always vest in the advertiser or its agency, complex questions may arise when an advertisement is copied without permission by some third party. Who, for example, has rights of action when a commissioned artistic work included in an advertisement is reproduced without permission in a television drama and copyright has been retained by the artist?

Unauthorised use for non-advertising purposes of an image associated with a particular advertising campaign may be damaging to the campaign itself. In extreme cases the image may need to be replaced and a new work commissioned for the campaign. This will involve substantial additional costs for the advertiser. If the artist has retained copyright in the work, the advertiser will be unlikely to have any right of action against the infringer, even if an exclusive licence has been granted by the artist. This is because the licence will have given the

---

[782] *Sinanide v La Maison Kosmeo* (1928) 139 L.T. 365; *Kirk v Fleming* (1928–1935) MacG. Cop. Cas. 44. It is, however, common for advertising slogans to be registered as trade marks.
[783] *Infopaq International A/S v Danske Dagblades Forening* (C–5/08) [2009] E.C.D.R 16.
[784] CDPA 1988 s.11(2).
[785] See para.4–28, above, where the question of authorship of photographs is discussed.

advertiser exclusive rights only in the field of advertising[786]: the advertiser has no cause of action where the infringement is outside the scope of the exclusive licence (unless the infringing act was directly connected to a prior licensed act and the artist has expressly granted a right of action in respect of non-exclusive rights).[787] The artist will be able to sustain an infringement action, but will only be able to recover damages referable to the damage to his own interest in the copyright. Such damage may be limited, for example, to the loss of opportunity to negotiate a reuse fee in the event that the advertiser decided to renew the licence at the end of its term. The artist will not be able to recover damages by reference to the far greater costs incurred by the advertiser in replacing the advertisement with one based on a different, uncompromised image.

(ii) Rights in physical works

26–350   Title to photographic transparencies, original illustrations and models incorporated in photographs is a matter for agreement, just as with the copyright in such works.[788] There is no fixed trade practice. Disputes as to ownership of transparencies are unusual owing to the widespread use in the production process of digital technology. If an advertising agency has a digital scan of a photograph it is unlikely to have any further requirement for the transparency. Original physical materials are generally regarded by photographers as belonging to themselves. The value of an original illustration, unlike a photographic transparency or negative, lies primarily in its status as an *objet d'art*. An illustration commissioned for an advertisement may be a desirable object for the advertiser to display in its boardroom. It is normal trade practice, however, for illustrators to grant advertisers and their agencies reproduction rights only. The original artwork is owned by the illustrator and an additional price must usually be paid for its purchase. Some models created for advertising photographs may have equivalent status to illustrations as physical objects. Trade practice in relation to models is less clear. A model of artistic value is more likely to be regarded as belonging to the model maker.

(iii) Rights of advertisers vis-à-vis agencies

26–351   The suggested contract provisions published in 2005 by the Incorporated Society of British Advertisers, the Chartered Institute of Purchasing and Supply and the Institute of Practitioners in Advertising have gone some way towards standardising the terms of contracts between advertisers and agencies. However, the suggested contract no longer includes provisions concerning ownership of copyright in advertising. A menu of options and guidance for clauses dealing with copyright is now contained in a separate document to the standard agreement: Handbook of Intellectual Property Clauses.

Where no written contract is entered into, the copyright in materials created by an advertising agency's employees (and by sub-contractors such as television commercial production companies who have assigned copyright to the agency) will normally belong to the advertising agency. In particular circumstances, for

---

[786] As to the rights of an exclusive licensee, see para.5–209, above.

[787] CDPA 1988 s.101A.

[788] As to the distinction between ownership of physical materials and the copyright in the works embodied in them, see para.5–02, above.

example, where the design of a logo is commissioned,[789] the advertising agency may be held to have assigned copyright to the advertiser in equity.[790] In many cases it may be possible to imply a licence for advertising created by the advertising agency to continue to be used by the advertiser after the termination of the contract, but this will depend upon a number of factors including the manner in which the advertising agency has been remunerated. Advertising agencies will not be in a position to assign to the advertiser copyright in materials created by third parties who have retained copyright, for example licensors of existing or commissioned musical works.

Where an advertising agency presents creative proposals to an advertiser as part of a "pitch", copyright will remain with the advertising agency if the pitch is unsuccessful. Where a pitch is successful and an advertising agency agrees to assign to the advertiser "copyright in work created by [it] for [the advertiser's] advertising", this will only extend to material created after the appointment of the advertising agency.[791] Copyright will not protect ideas imparted by advertising agencies to advertisers during a pitch, although an action for breach of confidence would in many circumstances lie against an advertiser who made use of ideas disclosed to it by an advertising agency in the course of an unsuccessful pitch.

Advertising agencies are under an implied obligation to their clients to carry out their work with reasonable skill and care. This would include a duty to use reasonable care not to include material knowingly copied from a third party. Alternatively, the copying of material from a third party without a licence may breach an implied obligation to deliver work to the advertiser which is fit for the purpose for which it was commissioned.[792]

C. COPYING OF OTHER ADVERTISEMENTS

(i) Copyright and passing off

Copyright. It is unusual for one advertiser simply to reproduce material included in another advertiser's advertisement. When this occurs, the other advertiser may be concerned to prevent any damage to the integrity of its campaign or the advertising agency whose work has been plagiarised may wish to warn off a competing agency from taking further liberties in future. In either case, issues as to title may arise and appropriate assignments may need to be executed in order to give appropriate rights of action to the party who wishes to take proceedings. There is no equivalent in copyright law to the provisions in trade mark law allowing the use of marks in comparative advertising.[793] Reproduction in an advertisement of a competitor's copyright work is unlikely to be fair dealing for the purposes of criticism or review: *IPC Media v News Group Newspapers Ltd*[794]; and see *IPC Magazines v MGN Ltd*.[795]

26–352

Imitations or parodies. More commonly, one advertiser will merely imitate or parody another's campaign, whether to score points against a competitor in a comparative campaign or simply to entertain its audience by a witty cultural

26–353

---

[789] *R Griggs Group Ltd v Evans* ([2004] F.S.R. 31) was upheld on appeal: [2005] EWCA Civ 11; [2005] F.S.R. 31.
[790] *Drabble (Harold) Ltd v Hycolite Manufacturing Co* (1928) 44 T.L.R. 264. But see also *Robin Ray v Classic FM Plc* [1998] F.S.R. 622; see para.5–178, above.
[791] *Hutchison Personal Communications Ltd v Hook Advertising Ltd* [1996] F.S.R. 549.
[792] *Antiquesportfolio.com v Rodney Fitch Y Co Ltd* [2001] F.S.R. 345.
[793] Trade Marks Act 1994 s.10(6).
[794] [2005] EWHC 317 (Ch); (2005) E.M.L.R. 532; (2005) F.S.R. 35.
[795] [1998] F.S.R. 431.

reference. The main issue raised by a parody of an advertisement is the same as in any other infringement claim. Neither the fact of parody nor the advertising context affects the issue of substantiality.[796]

26–354   **Passing off.** Similarities between the campaigns of competing advertisers may give rise to a passing-off claim. The tort of passing off is wide enough to encompass slogans or visual material associated with an advertiser's product by means of an advertising campaign. The product must have derived from the advertising a distinctive character recognised by the market.[797] An advertisement which makes use of a competitor's brand name in such a manner as to give rise to confusion as to the source or origin from which that product may be obtained may also amount to a passing off.[798]

(ii) Advertising codes

26–355   Broadcast and non-broadcast advertisements are governed by codes of practice for which the Advertising Standards Authority and Ofcom are responsible. These codes contain provisions concerning the imitation of others' advertisements.

D. REFERENCES TO INDIVIDUALS

(i) Defamation and passing off

26–356   In many other countries unauthorised references in advertising to living (and in some cases deceased) individuals are restricted by clearly defined privacy laws. The United Kingdom has a developing law of privacy but the extent to which this will govern advertising is uncertain. The use of photographs of individuals in advertisements may arguably be controlled under the Data Protection Act 1998 in certain circumstances. References to deceased individuals will rarely infringe any legal rights of their heirs. Unauthorised references to living individuals do, however, give rise to clear defamation or passing off claims in certain circumstances.

26–357   **Defamation.** An advertisement may defame an individual either directly or indirectly. Both types of defamation were held to have been present when a photograph of a policeman on duty bore the caption: "Phew! I am going to get my feet into a Jeyes' Fluid foot-bath." Not only did this suggest that the policeman's feet smelt, but also that he was engaged in publicity for which the public would assume that he had received payment, this being inconsistent with his position as a public servant.[799] The following have also been held to be defamatory: to portray an amateur golfer in such a manner as to suggest a paid endorsement, thereby imperilling his amateur status[800]; the superimposition of a professional model's head and shoulders upon some other woman's legs, thereby implying that the model had consented to being photographed in an indecent manner, in an advertisement for silk stockings[801]; the use of a person's features

---

[796] *AGL Sydney Ltd v Shortland County Council* (1990) A.I.P.C. 90–661. As to parodies generally, see para.7–33, above. See below as to Codes of Practice.

[797] *Cadbury Schweppes Pty Ltd v Pub Squash Co Pty Ltd* [1981] All E.R. 213.

[798] *McDonald's Hamburgers Ltd v Burgerking (UK) Ltd* [1986] F.S.R. 45.

[799] *Plumb v Jeyes Sanitary Compounds Co Ltd, The Times*, April 15, 1937.

[800] *Tolley v Fry* [1931] A.C. 333.

[801] *Griffiths v Bondor, The Times*, December 11, 1935.

on the body of a very tall man dressed in an exaggeratedly foppish manner[802]; a circular stating that a professional footballer would give advice on football pool entries, footballers being forbidden by the Football Association from gambling in this manner.[803]

The principle of strict liability for unintentional defamation, in relation to "lookalikes" of persons whose photographs are included in advertisements, has been held to be incompatible with a publisher's right to freedom of speech under art.10 of the European Convention on Human Rights.[804] Although this decision is open to criticism it would appear to apply also to the more usual problem of unintentional references in advertising to individuals and companies when real names are used in fictional contexts, giving rise to "namesake" claims.

Passing off. A passing-off claim may arise when a celebrity is portrayed or referred to in an advertisement without permission in such a manner as to suggest to the public that permission has been given for reference to be made to that person.[805] The claimant must show not only that the advertisement contains an express or implied misrepresentation to this effect but also that a business goodwill of his has been damaged. This is unlikely to be the case in the case of a private individual or of a person such as a senior politician who, although prominent, is not in the business of accepting fees for commercial endorsements.

26–358

A passing-off claim may also lie when a copyright work is used in an advertisement without permission if it will be wrongly assumed that permission has in fact been granted.

(ii) Advertising codes

Broadcast and non-broadcast advertisements are governed by codes of practice for which the Advertising Standards Authority and Ofcom are responsible. These codes contain important provisions concerning the circumstances in which permission should be obtained for portrayals of or references to individual living persons.

26–359

8. THE COMPUTER SOFTWARE INDUSTRY

A. The Industry

Once confined to bulky machines operated by technicians in air-conditioned rooms, software is now embedded in a wide range of consumer products, as well as providing the means of managing ever-more complex processes in the financial and business worlds and in scientific research. Software producers create products for an enormously diverse range of uses and budgets. Consciously or unconsciously, virtually everyone in the developed world today uses computer software on a regular basis.

26–360

These changes are the result of multiple innovations that have opened up everyday computing for large sectors of the population in the work and home environment. The 1980s were the decade of the widespread adoption of stand alone personal computers, while the 1990s saw the penetration of networked

---

[802] *Dunlop Rubber Co v Dunlop* [1921] 1 A.C. 367.
[803] *Rutherford v Turf Publishers Ltd*, *The Times*, October 30, 1925.
[804] *O'Shea v MGN Ltd* [2001] E.M.L.R. 943.
[805] *Irvine v TalkSport Ltd* [2002] 1 W.L.R. 2355; [2002] E.M.L.R. 32; [2002] F.S.R. 60 (liability at first instance); [2003] E.M.L.R. 6 (damages); and [2003] F.S.R. 25 and [2003] E.M.L.R. 26 (on appeal).

communications, and the popularisation of online computing and the internet. In the 2000s, wireless computing and the widespread adoption of mobile telephones and other mobile communications devices further extended the reach of software into people's daily lives, facilitating on-demand access to massive amounts of information and stimulating the growth of social media and accessible user-generated content.

The software industry shaped copyright law relating to exploitation of products in digital form. It was the application of copyright law to computer programs that first established the concept that reproduction which was incidental to use and/or transient implicated the reproduction right, meaning that use of copyright software required a licence. This concept became clear as regards programs in Europe from adoption of Directive 91/250 on the legal protection of computer programs ("the Software Directive"—now Directive 2009/24/EC in codified version). It has since been extended to databases and to all forms of work by Directive 96/9/EC on the legal protection of databases ("the Database Directive") and Directive 2001/29/EC on the 1996 harmonisation of certain aspects of copyright and related rights in the information society ("the Information Society Directive"—implementing similar principles from the WIPO Copyright and Performances and Phonograms Treaties of 1996). Software was also the testbed for copyright law reinforcement of the use of copy protection technologies by making it unlawful to take steps to circumvent copy protection applied to programs, or to deal in programs from which copy protection had been removed. This type of protection was first introduced in Europe by the Software Directive, and has since been elaborated and extended to works of all types, through the WIPO Copyright and Performances and Phonograms Treaties and the Information Society Directive.

26–361   In a world of rapidly changing terminology and technology, there has been understandable reluctance to engage in precise legal definition of terms—the term "computer program" is not defined at all in the 1988 Act, for example, and the Software Directive merely says that programs include "preparatory design material".

Some software is bespoke (or "custom")—i.e. purpose written. Other software is "off-the-shelf", i.e. a standard package intended for supply to multiple users on a non-exclusive basis. Other software may be a mix of "off-the-shelf" and bespoke elements. Many "off-the-shelf" packages are intended for widespread commercial distribution. Traditionally, this mainly occurred by means of the supply of copies in electronic form on physical media such as tape, floppy discs or CD-ROMs, often through intermediary wholesalers and retailers. The mixed physical and intangible nature of the product generated enormous debate about the legal nature of the transaction and how a software publisher could effectively establish direct contractual relations with the user in order to establish limitations on liability and scope of licence. In mass-market sectors, the practice grew up of "shrink-wrap licensing", i.e. the supply of contractual terms as between software publisher and user in conjunction with product "sold" though intermediaries in the distribution channel.

The internet has enabled direct electronic distribution, for example by internet download from the software vendor's own website bypassing the need to provide a physical copy, or to have intermediary suppliers. Software distribution is ideally suited to all-electronic commerce, subject to there being adequate legal and technological infrastructure to prevent unlicensed copying. "Click-wrap" agreements in electronic distribution (which require the acquirer positively to assent to terms and conditions before goods are supplied) are likely to provide a more secure contractual basis for software licensing than their shrink-wrap precedessors.

Another trend in licensing has been the growth of so-called "open-source" software. Open-source licensing began as a reaction to closed licensing models based on ownership of copyright and trade secrets in program code. In open-source licensing, software suppliers make their source code available and permit its modification and inclusion in derivative products, provided that the recipient agrees that if it decides to redistribute derivative code it will similarly make available its source code and will pass on the terms of licence and any notices applicable to the original code. By doing this, software developers potentially allow their software to evolve, grow and be disseminated much more rapidly and simply. Open-source software licensing has particularly taken off in the areas of operating systems, core internet applications, and programming tools. Methods of open-source licensing are subject to a commonly understood set of principles as to the rules of open-source licensing, which can be found in documents published on the internet (see, e.g. *http://www.opensource.org* [Accessed November 1, 2010]), but terms of licence vary between products. Open-source concepts can now be seen in evolving practices in other areas of collaborative endeavour, such as the Creative Commons movement, and the web encyclopaedia, Wikipedia.

Innovations in virtualisation and greater availability of high-speed connectivity may now be encouraging a shift in the way some software is used towards on-demand usage on a services basis—so-called "cloud computing"—rather than ownership or long-term licence business models.

B. WRITING SOFTWARE

(i) Authorship/ownership

One feature of the industry is that, while most software is the product of teamwork, the programming labour force is relatively mobile, with people often moving employment and working on a freelance, consultancy basis. It is common to find that there are problems in proving legal title to software, and it is no coincidence that in both *Richardson (John) Computers Ltd v Flanders*[806] and *Ibcos Computers Ltd v Barclays Mercantile Highland Finance Ltd*,[807] the first two reported English software copyright trials, the claimants had problems in establishing full legal title and had to rely on title in equity to parts of their software. For more recent cases dealing with disputes over ownership as between software developers and their customers see *Cyprotex Discovery Ltd v University of Sheffield*[808]; *Clearsprings Management Ltd v Businesslinx Ltd*[809]; *Wrenn Integrated Multi-Media Solutions Ltd v Landamore*[810]; *Meridian International Services Ltd v Richardson*[811]; *Cantor Gaming Ltd v Gameaccount Global Ltd*[812]; and *Infection Control Enterprises Ltd v Virage Industries Ltd.*[813]

The mobility of programmers means that questions frequently arise about possible copying of software in which a previous employer or customer owns rights. This may be a clear infringement resulting from programmers innocently or deliberately re-using copied software. On the other hand, there may be much more subtle arguments about whether similarities between two separate pieces of

26–362

---

[806] [1993] F.S.R. 497.
[807] [1994] F.S.R. 275.
[808] [2004] EWCA Civ 380 (CA); [2004] R.P.C. 44.
[809] [2005] EWHC 1487 (Ch); [2006] F.S.R. 3.
[810] [2007] EWHC 1833 (Ch); [2008] EWCA Civ 496 (appeal dismissed).
[811] [2008] EWCA Civ 609.
[812] [2007] EWHC 1914.
[813] [2009] EWHC 2602 (QB).

software represent infringing copying, or are merely the natural result of the same person doing something similar in a similar way. In *Cantor Fitzgerald v Tradition (UK) Ltd*[814] programmers who wrote the defendants' program modules had also previously written the claimants'. They were held to have infringed copyright and misused confidential information by loading the claimants' source code on to the defendants' computers and to have infringed by some, but not all, of the alleged acts of copying of the claimants' code, including uses involving consulting the claimants' code during development and using the claimants' code during testing and debugging.

Methods of writing software have evolved extensively over the years. Things which were once hand-coded can now be generated automatically through the use of programming tools. Increasingly "intelligence" is being built into computer programs and data. These trends tend to exacerbate the already inherent difficulties in determining the boundary between "idea" and "expression" in computer programs, and may also challenge concepts of originality. Inbuilt intelligence has also raised questions about the concept of authorship. In a simple case it is easy to draw an analogy between a computer program used to achieve a result and a pen or other tool, which does not challenge human authorship of the result.[815] But, as the 1988 Act has already recognised,[816] there may be a need for a rule to determine the deemed human author in cases where the machine appears to be the author, rather than any human being.

(ii) Bug fixing and maintenance

26–363   Computer programs tend to evolve, both during initial development, and subsequently, to enhance their functionality or to correct programming errors or "bugs". Testing and bug fixing are important in all but the most trivial software development programme. Even after extensive testing, few software publishers would ever warrant that their software is "bug-free". Among other things, most programs are designed to work with other programs in an overall computer environment, in response to input, such that their operation is affected by factors outside the control of the developer.

Because software is not generally warranted bug-free, maintenance and error correction are important issues for users of software. The Software Directive recognised these concerns by specifically requiring member states to provide that "in the absence of specific contactual provisions" it is not an infringement of copyright to carry out acts restricted by copyright in a computer program where this is necessary for the use of the computer program by the lawful acquirer in accordance with its intended purpose, including for error correction.[817]

Because programs can fail, and may require to be reloaded into computer memory, many users also require the right to make "back-up copies" of programs supplied to them. This practice was also recognised by the Software Directive, which required that national laws provide that the making of a back-up copy of a program by a person who has the right to use it may not be prevented by contract in so far as it is necessary for that use.[818]

In its April 2000 communication on the implementation and effect of the

---

[814] [2000] R.P.C. 95.

[815] This was the approach taken in *Express Newspapers Plc v Liverpool Daily Post and Echo Plc* [1985] F.S.R. 306.

[816] See CDPA 1988 s.9(3) and the definition of "computer-generated work" in s.178.

[817] Directive 2009/24/EC art.5.1. See CDPA 1988 s.50C, added by the Copyright (Computer Programs) Regulations 1992 (SI 1992/3233).

[818] Directive 2009/24/EC art.5.2. See CDPA 1988 ss.50A and 296A, added by The Copyright (Computer Programs) Regulations 1992 (SI 1992/3253) and para.9–150. In practice, where software is

Software Directive, the Commission clarified its position as regards the scope of the back-up copy exception. The Commission is of the opinion that the wording and objective of art.5(2) means that only "a" (i.e. one) copy is permitted and that the purpose may not be other than as a "back-up" to ensure that normal use of the program can continue in the event of loss or defect of the original. The making of unauthorised copies for private use is not permitted, and consitutes an act of software piracy.

C. RELEVANT WORKS

The 1988 Act[819] makes computer programs a subset of "literary works", as does the Software Directive. The international status of computer programs as literary works appears to have been confirmed by adoption in December 1996 of the WIPO Copyright Treaty.[820] However, as mentioned above, there is considerable scope for debate over what is, and is not, a computer program for these purposes. The 1988 Act does not define the term at all, while the Directive only does so partially, by including "preparatory design material" for computer programs[821] but excluding from protection "ideas and principles which underlie any element of a computer program, including those which underlie its interfaces".[822]   **26–364**

Methods of program development vary depending upon the programming environment, and have evolved over time as programs have become more powerful and more complex in response to repeated and drastic falls in cost of memory and processing power. Programs can be expressed at multiple levels, from levels which involve methods of expression which are more intelligible to the human mind, such as code written in popular programming languages of their day, to the lowest levels of machine-intelligible code. Subject to any questions of substantiality and originality which may arise, any level of code should be protectable as a computer program for copyright purposes. The 1988 Act confirms that making a version of a program in which it is converted into or out of a computer language or code into a different computer language or code may be an act of infringing adaptation.[823]

There are levels, however, at which it is not so clear what is within the scope of a computer program for these purposes. One of these is the reference to "preparatory design materials" in the Software Directive. Does this embrace, for example, manuscript notes or flow diagrams which a programmer might have generated in sketching out initial design thoughts, and, if so, how much is protection for high-level design precluded by virtue of this being "idea" and not "expression"?   **26–365**

Complex and difficult questions may arise about the limits of protection for computer programs and the interrelationship of that protection with the protection available for other forms of works—in the digital environment, it can be less easy to distinguish between "works" than was traditionally the case. These questions matter because the attributes of the right may vary depending on the characterisation of the work. By way of example, in an electronic database, where is the boundary between what is protected as "program" and what is protected by database copyright or under the sui generis right created as a result of the

---

acquired on a physical medium for loading into computer memory, it is common for the original copy to be kept as the back-up copy.
[819] See CDPA 1998 s.3.
[820] Directive 2009/24/EC art.4 provides that computer programs are protected as literary works within the meaning of art.2 of the Berne Convention.
[821] Directive 2009/24/EC art.1.1.
[822] Directive 2009/24/EC art.1.2. See also recital 11.
[823] See CDPA 1988 s.21.

Database Directive?[824] Under the 1988 Act, the "back-up right" contained in s.50A is limited to computer programs. If this means that it is not permissible to back up databases unless this is expressly licensed, uncertainty about what is and is not protected as a program may raise questions about the value of the back-up right in relation to database software. Following implementation of the Information Society Directive, the statutory provisions applicable to circumvention of copy-protection technology in relation to programs are also differently worded from those applicable to other types of work in digital form.[825] Similarly, ss.79 and 81 of the 1988 Act exclude computer programs from the moral rights to be identified as author and to object to derogatory treatment of the work, but these rights may still apply to non-program elements.

At the user interface level it is also very unclear what is protected as a computer program. Program protection may be argued, for example, to extend to input commands, screen layout, text or images on screen generated by the program, or other forms of data output to devices to which the computer is connected. In *Navitaire Inc v easyJet Airline Co Ltd* [2004] EWHC 1725 (Ch); [2006] R.P.C. 3, Pumfrey J. held that individual commands in issue in that case were not copyright works and that the compilation of commands should also not be protected. In his view, to protect these amounted to protecting ideas, which is excluded under recital 11 and art.1(2) of Directive 2009/24/EC. On his analysis, computer languages, as opposed to computer programs written in specific languages, are not themselves protected by copyright. However, he acknowledged that the exclusion of programming languages from protection was not entirely clear, and would require to be referred to the European Court of Justice. Protection of programming languages resurfaced in *SAS Institute Inc. v World Programming Limited* [2010] EWHC 1829 (Ch), and is the subject of one of a series of questions referred by Arnold J. in that case to the European Court of Justice for clarification about the scope of copyright protection for programs.

D. RELEVANT TRADE ASSOCIATIONS, COLLECTING SOCIETIES/LICENSING AGENCIES

26–366 The software industry has not established significant collective licensing. It is a very dynamic and varied market in terms both of products and of means of distribution and exploitation. These conditions have militated against the establishment of collective licensing. On the other hand, because there is interdependency between software products which are designed to work together, and between software products and hardware products, it is common in the industry for products of different vendors to be combined prior to sale to end users. For example, manufactures of hardware may act as resellers of third-party software (and vice versa). The practice of open-source licensing is also discussed above.

---

[824] Directive 2009/24/EC does not give any guidance on this issue. Directive 96/9 specifically excludes protection under that Directive for "computer programs used in the making or operation of databases accessible by electronic means" (art.1.3). In *Navitaire Inc v easyJet Airline Co Ltd* [2004] EWHC 1725 (Ch); [2006] R.P.C. 3 Pumfrey J. considered the dividing line between program copyright and database copyright. This arose in respect of data migration and the design of a substitute database. In *SAS Institute Inc v World Programming Limited* [2010] EWHC 1829 (Ch) Arnold J. considered whether it would be an infringement of copyright in a program for a third party to write a second program to read from and write to data files in the same format, or whether protection for file formats was excluded by art.1.2 of Directive 2009/24/EC. This became one of the questions referred to the European Court of Justice in that case.

[825] As was highlighted in *Kabushiki Kaisha Sony Computer Entertainment Inc v Ball* at [2005] F.S.R. 9. See also *R v Higgs* [2008] EWCA Crim 1324; [2008] All E.R. (D) 318 (Jun) for consideration of s.296ZF. S.296 of the 1988 Act has been retained in relation to computer programs only; new ss.296ZA–F apply to other types of work. The retention of different treatment for programs was thought to be required by the terms of the Information Society Directive 2001/29.

There has been collective activity in connection with enforcement in the United Kingdom and elsewhere. For example, FAST, the Federation Against Software Theft,[826] was established in the mid-1980s, when the United Kingdom first enacted legislation confirming subsistence of copyright in computer programs, to act as an anti-piracy body acting on behalf of the industry. ELSPA, the European Leisure Software Publishers Association, represents its members in the games software industry on software piracy issues.[827] The Business Software Alliance (BSA)[828] has also carried out anti-piracy work in the United Kingdom on behalf of its members. All of these bodies, and other computer industry bodies such as Intellect[829] (formerly the CSSA) and BCS (the Chartered Institute for IT)[830], take an active role in representing their members on issues which affect them, including copyright protection.

E. CONTROLS ON THE INDUSTRY

There are no specific controls on the exercise of copyright in computer software outside the normal principles of competition law. It is clear, however, that there are certain areas of particular sensitivity so far as the application of competition law is concerned, and in particular in the areas of interoperability, the making available of interface specifications and bundling of products. In March 2004, the European Commission adopted a decision finding that Microsoft had infringed (what is now) art.102 of the Treaty on European Union by (1) refusing to supply interoperability information and (2) tying Windows Media Player with the Windows PC operating system.[831] These findings were subsequently upheld by the General Court.[832] In January 2008, the European Commission opened two new investigations into Microsoft's practices with respect to interoperability and tying. In one of these investigations, which concerned the tying of Internet Explorer to Windows, the Commission issued a Statement of Objections in January 2009 and then adopted, in December 2009, a decision under art.9 of Regulation 1/2003 (on the implementation of EU antitrust rules) accepting undertakings by Microsoft with respect to Internet Explorer.[833] Additionally, in July 2009, Microsoft provided public undertakings concerning the disclosure of interoperability information.[834]

26–367

Software maintenance is also an area in which competition issues may potentially arise, in particular because third parties carrying out maintenance may need to perform restricted acts of copying by running some or all of the software on their customer's machine in the process of performing their service.[835]

---

[826] York House, 18 York Road, Maidenhead, Berkshire SL6 1SF. See also *http://www.fastiis.org* [Accessed November 1, 2010].

[827] See *http://www.elspa.com* [Accessed November 1, 2010]/

[828] BSA Europe, 2 Queen Anne's Gate Building, Dartmouth Street, London, SW1H 9BP. See also *http://www.bsa.org*.

[829] See *http://www.intellect.org* [Accessed November 1, 2010].

[830] See *http://www.bcs.org*[Accessed November 1, 2010].

[831] See the Commission Decision of March 24, 2004 (Case COMP/C–3/37.792 Microsoft) notified under document number C(2004) 900. See also [2007] OJ L32/23 for the main content of the decision.

[832] See General Court judgment dated September 17, 2007 (Case T–201/04 *Microsoft v Commission*). See also [2007] E.C.R. II–1491 and [2007] OJ C269/44.

[833] See European Commission Decision of December 16, 2009 (Case COMP/C–3/39.530 *Microsoft (tying)*). See also summary decision at [2010] OJ C36/7.

[834] See *http://europa.eu/rapid/pressReleasesAction.do?reference=IP/10/216&format =HTML&aged=0&language=EN&guiLanguage=en* [Accessed November 1, 2010].

[835] See *Digital Equipment Corp v LCE Computer Maintenance Ltd* (Mervyn Davies J., May 22, 1992 (transcript available on LEXIS)).

F. PROBLEMS AND ISSUES

(i) Problems of subsistence and infringement inherent in the nature of software

26–368   Most lawyers and judges have read books, listened to music, seen plays, watched films, and visited museums and art galleries. Traditional forms of work are relatively familiar to them. This assists in forming views on questions such as whether a work or an aspect of a work is sufficiently original to be protected by copyright, or about whether a substantial part has been copied. Most lawyers and judges are much less familiar with computer programs and computer programming. As a result, in those software copyright disputes which involve comparison of non-identical products, it is common for there to be detailed and extensive expert evidence going to matters of originality and substantiality. The functional nature of software, and trends in types of software for different uses, also tend to raise difficult questions about whether similarities result from copying protected expression or underlying idea.

There has been limited UK case law on these issues. Courts in the United States, on the other hand, quickly decided a number of cases exploring these issues under US law. Given that country's important role in the development of the software industry, these cases tended to have the effect of determining the development of the industry's understanding of what aspects of a program may be protected by copyright. As a very broad generalisation, early US cases tended to confirm protection of software under copyright law, whereas later cases have tended to qualify its scope. A consequence of the tendency for US cases to develop industry thinking on these issues was that in the first reported English software copyright infringement trial, *John Richardson Computers Ltd v Flanders*,[836] Ferris J. based his approach to analysing originality and infringement on the "abstraction and filtration" analysis from the US case of *Computer Associates Inc. v Altai Inc.*[837] This analysis seeks to exclude systematically from consideration elements dictated by efficiency, elements dictated by external factors, and elements taken from the public domain. In *Ibcos Computers Ltd v Barclays Mercantile Highland Finance Ltd*[838] Jacob J. rejected this route as unhelpful, pointing out that US copyright law is different in certain material respects from the copyright law of the United Kingdom. He went back to basic principles of UK copyright law to determine considerations of the distinction between idea and expression in the context of deciding whether a substantial part had been copied. He reconfirmed that only "mere general ideas" and "general principles" are excluded from protection, but that "detailed ideas" may be protected. He found that the test of substantiality was a question of degree, "where a good guide is the notion of overborrowing of the skill, labour and judgment which went into the copyright work". He analysed the various programs which were common between the parties' software and determined infringement or non-infringement of each on its specific facts. The law remains difficult to apply with certainty in this area, however. In *Navitaire Inc v easyJet Airline Co Ltd*[839] Pumfrey J. rejected the claimant's argument based on infringement by copying of the "business logic" underlying its programs, in circumstances where the disputed systems had been specifically designed to replace the claimant's software. The defendant's software acted upon identical or very similar inputs and produced

---

[836] [1993] F.S.R. 497.
[837] 982 F. 2d. 693, 23 U.S.P.Q. 2d. 1241 (1992).
[838] [1994] F.S.R. 275.
[839] [2004] EWHC 1725 (Ch); [2006] R.P.C. 3.

very similar results but without copying code. The questions referred to the Court of Justice in *SAS Institute Inc. v World Programming Limited*[840] continue to explore aspects of scope of protection against copying of functionality.

(ii) Protection of user interfaces

Screen outputs may not be part of the program, as such, but be characterised as other forms of work, such as (non-program) literary works,[841] or artistic works. The outcome of a dispute may depend on characterisation. In *Navitaire Inc v easyJet Airline Co Ltd*[842] Pumfrey J. held that character-based screens in dispute in that action were properly viewed as tables and therefore literary in character, while other screen layouts were artistic works. The claimants succeeded in respect of the screens held to be artistic works, but not in respect of the screens held to be literary works. In *Nova Productions Ltd v Mazooma Games Ltd*,[843] a case relating to computer games based on the game pool, Kitchin J. held that each of bitmap files stored in computer memory and composite frames generated from those files during game play were artistic works within CDPA 1988 s.4. On appeal,[844] it was common ground between the parties that the individual frames stored in memory were "graphic works". Jacob L.J. found the case based on graphic works "falls at the first hurdle" given the concession that there was no frame-for-frame reproduction, and that the similarity was in the sequence of events depicted through the series of frames. The appellant did not pursue its claims based on rights in film or dramatic works on appeal. The 1988 Act defines a "film" as "a recording on any medium from which a moving image may by any means be reproduced",[845] a definition which obviously embraces many digital products, which also are or include computer programs. The provisions of the 1988 Act dealing with films differ significantly from those dealing with literary works generally, and, particularly, computer programs.

There are additional questions about whether prescribed forms of user inputs for a program, such as the use of a particular keyboard function key or keystroke to achieve a particular result, form part of a program, or whether these should be excluded from consideration of whether a substantial part has been copied. Arguments for exclusion could be that these are not of their nature protectable under UK copyright law, or because they are not sufficiently original. It is also sometimes argued that such features of computer systems should be deprived of protection because they have become "industry standard".

26–369

(iii) Compatibility; protection of interfaces; reverse engineering

The fact that programs do not work in isolation has various implications. Programmers have to make their programs work with the hardware and software with which they are designed to run, and have to enable them to operate on the types of inputs they may receive. So, they have to understand the environments in which their programs will be used. Producers of hardware and software commonly recognise that it is in their own interests to make available information about at least some of the "interfaces" to their products to enable third parties to develop "compatible" or "interoperable" products. This reflects the industry

26–370

---

[840] [2010] EWHC 1829 (Ch).
[841] For example, in the form of text on screen generated by the program, or "compilations".
[842] [2004] EWHC 1725 (Ch); [2006] R.P.C. 3.
[843] [2006] EWHC 24 (Ch); [2006] R.P.C. 14; [2006] E.M.L.R. 14.
[844] [2007] R.P.C. 25.
[845] CDPA 1988 s.5B, introduced by The Duration of Copyright and Rights in Performances Regulations 1995 (SI 1995/3297).

symbiosis between hardware and software manufacturers, and developers of "operating" and "applications" software.

The Software Directive reflected these issues, both in describing the limits on the scope of copyright in a computer program,[846] and in establishing a limited exception to the restricted acts where reproduction of copyright code "is "indispensable to obtain the information necessary to achieve the interoperability of an independently created computer program with other programs", subject to numerous limiting conditions.[847]

In *Mars UK Ltd v Teknowledge Ltd*[848] the defendants had used reverse engineering techniques to establish the communications protocol used to communicate with program-controlled coin receiving and changing mechanisms. Parts of the communications process involved encryption to protect data contained in the mechanisms from unauthorised modification. The defendants' purpose in doing this was to enable them to offer after-sales services in relation to the mechanisms, including updating and changing coinset data contained in the mechanisms to enable the mechanisms to accept or change different coins from those originally programmed into them. The defendants' main argument in defence was based on an implied licence to repair (*British Leyland*[849]) argument. Jacob. J. held that the Software Directive and Database Directive did not provide for such a defence, and that—had it otherwise been applicable on the facts—the defence was not available in relation to programs and databases.[850] Accordingly, various acts carried out by the defendants both during the reverse engineering process and subsequently in developing their own reprogramming software and in reprogramming mechanisms infringed the claimant's copyrights and database rights. There was no detailed consideration of which acts specifically infringed and the judge did not consider the claimant's allegation of infringement by circumvention of copy-protection.

In *Navitaire Inc v easyJet Airline Co Ltd*[851], Pumfrey J. had to consider whether the defendants had infringed program copyright, and/or database copyright in designing and developing a replacement system to perform similar functions on the same data types, and/or in migrating data to the new system. He held most of the acts done by the defendants in this process were permitted uses under s.50B (acts necessary for the purpose of access to and use of the contents of the database by a lawful user, implementing art.6.1 of the Database Directive).

Article 6 of the Software Directive requires that acts of reproduction of computer programs during decompilation be limited to those parts of the program necessary to achieve interoperability, something which may be difficult to do until one has established what the different parts of the program do. This preliminary analysis may, however, be permitted under art.5(3)[852] (which permits lawful users to observe, study or test the functioning of a program in order to determine the ideas and principles which underlie any element of it, so long as this is done in the course of performing acts which the user is permitted to do). The questions referred by Arnold J. to the European Court of Justice in *SAS Institute Inc v*

---

[846] Directive 2009/24/EC art.1.2 provides "Protection in accordance with this Directive shall apply to the expression in any form of a computer program. Ideas and principles which underlie any element of a computer program, including those which underlie its interfaces, are not protected by copyright under this Directive". CDPA 1988 does not specifically include this language.

[847] Directive 2009/24/EC art.6. See CDPA 1988 s.50B, introduced by The Copyright (Computer Programs) Regulations 1992 (SI 1992/3233).

[848] [2000] F.S.R. 138.

[849] *British Leyland Motor Corp. Ltd v Armstrong Patents Co. Ltd* [1986] A.C. 577.

[850] See, also, para.5–236, above.

[851] [2004] EWHC 1725 (Ch); [2006] R.P.C. 3. See also [2005] EWHC 0282 (Ch).

[852] art.5 (3) is implemented by CDPA 1988 s.50BA.

World Programming Limited[853] include questions about the correct application of
art.5(3).

(iv) Protection for hardware implementations/circuit designs

At their most basic level, computer programs consist of very simple instructions   **26–371**
to hardware to carry out very simple functions. These instructions may be stored
as program instructions, or by hardware implementation, for example, in a
semiconductor chip. As noted above, there is no comprehensive definition of
"computer program". Arguably, a hardware implementation of a set of instructions which could also be implemented in program code should benefit from the
same form of protection. This appears to be confirmed by recital 7 of the Software
Directive, although not expressly imported into the 1988 Act.

In the mid-1980s, the United States enacted[854] sui generis protection for
semiconductor chip-masks works, being a series of related images, however fixed
or encoded, representing the patterns on the layers of a semiconductor chip.
Protection for foreign mask works was based on reciprocity. In response to this,
Council Directive 87/54/EEC on the legal protection of topographies of
semiconductor products was adopted in December 1986. Directive 87/54/EEC
required Member States to provide protection for the topographies of semiconductor chips. The Directive includes, inter alia, specific limitations relevant to reverse engineering of semiconductor topographies. It is currently implemented in
the United Kingdom via a modified form of the design right.[855]

At the same time, industry has continued to seek patent protection for inventions involving circuits for computers, including in the semiconductor area. In
addition, there may in some circumstances be potential for reliance on circuit
layout diagrams and lists of electronic components included in the circuitry as
artistic or literary (non-program) works.[856]

(v) Enforceability of shrink-wrap licences

In mass-market physical software distribution, many aspects of the transaction   **26–372**
are approached as a contractual licence directly between rightholder and end
user, but there is typically a "channel" of wholesalers and retailers through whose
hands passes the physical item on which the software is recorded, i.e. floppy
discs or CD-ROM, plus associated documentation. As between retailer and
purchaser, the transaction is one of sale and purchase. It is not normal for the
customer to be asked to read and sign the licence terms before buying the product.
In many cases, the terms are not even visible until the user has made the purchase
and opened the box. Although licensor terms and conditions typically cover similar issues, such as scope of licence and limitations and exclusions of the software
publisher's liability, the details of the terms and conditions vary and certainly
could not be said to be "industry standard".

Since copyright law makes it clear that incidental and transitory copying is
prima facie restricted unless licensed, copyright owners are in a strong position to
argue that the sale of a copy of a program does not imply an unlimited licence to
do any act restricted by the copyright and that it is clearly within the contempla-

---

[853] [2010] EWHC 1829 (Ch).
[854] Semiconductor Chip Protection Act 1984.
[855] See, The Design Right (Semiconductor Topographies) Regulations 1989 (SI 1989/1100), as
  amended. For a detailed discussion of the right, see Ch.14, above.
[856] See *Anacon Corp Ltd v Environmental Research Technology Ltd* [1994] F.S.R. 659.

tion of users that their use will be subject to the scope of licence restrictions.[857] However, traditional contract analysis requires offer and acceptance between vendor and purchaser, or licensor and licensee, for terms to be agreed. The fact these terms are not agreed to at time of purchase therefore raises questions about enforceability of shrink-wrap licence terms.

Nonetheless, the practice of shrink-wrap licensing has been widely used. In 1996, an important test case was fought in the United States, *Pro CD v Zeidenberg*.[858] The outcome appears to have brought some measure of certainty to enforceability of shrink-wrap licence terms in the United States. The Scots Court of Session decision of *Beta Computers v Adobe Systems*,[859] also recognised the industry practice.

Electronic distribution reduces or removes the need for a distribution channel, enabling software publishers to deal directly with their customers without establishing traditional distribution infrastructure. Electronic distribution has grown rapidly, and is expected to grow further, with consequential reduction of shrink-wrap distribution. Nonetheless, electronic commerce has not yet completely replaced physical distribution. Furthermore, in the online environment related questions will continue to arise, as to whether, for example, notices as to licence limitations necessarily have contractual effect. In this respect, the use of "click-wrap" agreements (requiring licensees positively to indicate acceptance of licence terms) is now widespread.

(vi) Scope of licensed use

26–373   There are many different types of software, and many different types of use of software. So, it is not surprising that there is no single type of licence. On the other hand, many licences cover similar issues. Typical software licences cover:

1. type of machine on which the software may be used (e.g. specific hardware model, whether stand-alone or networked);
2. restrictions on types of use (e.g. internal data processing or bureau use, permitted number of users on a network, personal use only);
3. maintenance, right to make back ups and, in some cases, escrow of source code (i.e. a copy to be deposited with a third party on terms that it will be made available to the customer on specified triggering events, such as insolvency of the licensor).

These, and other, scope of licence issues are frequently covered with a fairly high level of specificity in supplier standard-form licences.

As is discussed elsewhere, the ability of a software copyright owner to restrict scope of use is to some extent circumscribed by statute, in particular as a result of the implementation of the Software Directive. For example, the "decompilation right" cannot be excluded by contract, any more than the right to make back-ups where this is necessary for the licensed use. However, the circumstances in which the exceptions to the restricted acts arise have been carefully defined, such that it may be possible to limit their application by the manner in which the licence is drafted or by establishing business practices which obviate their application, such as the routine publication of interface specification information.[860] Disputes or at least licence re-negotiations are relatively common between software licensors and licensees. This is often due to changes in technology, rendering scope of

---

[857] See *Creative Technology v Aztech Systems Pte Ltd* 1997–1 S.L.R. 621; 1996 S.L.R. LEXIS 486.
[858] United States Court of Appeals (7th Cir.) 86 F. 3d. 1447.
[859] [1996] F.S.R. 367.
[860] art.6 of Directive 2009/24/EC only applies, inter alia, to the extent the information necessary to achieve interoperability has not previously been readily available.

licence language which may have seemed appropriate at time of signature less clear and certain over time. Other interpretation uncertainties may arise from loose grants of rights language not mirroring the actual acts restricted by copyright. See *Cantor Gaming Ltd v Gameaccount Global Ltd*.[861]

---

[861] [2007] EWHC 1914 (Ch).

CHAPTER TWENTY SEVEN

COLLECTING SOCIETIES

1. INTRODUCTION

A. RATIONALE FOR COLLECTING SOCIETIES

27–01 **Individual exercise of rights.** Copyright confers exclusive rights which are vested in the copyright owner and give him the right to forbid others to exploit the work without authorisation. Ideally these rights are exercised on an individual basis by agreement between the copyright owner and the individual user of the work and there are many cases in which rights continue to be exercised individually. Such individual exercise of rights is the norm, for example, so far as agreements between authors of literary works and publishers are concerned with respect to the conditions for publication of the author's work. Similarly, the author of a dramatic work will likely have no difficulty in making an individual contract with a theatre company. Producers of cinematographic works also generally control the use of their works directly. Likewise, owners of rights in computer programs manage their products themselves.

27–02 **Need for collective administration of certain rights.** There are, however, certain rights which are difficult if not impossible to exercise individually and in respect of which rights owners have for many years banded together to exercise rights on a collective basis. The need for such collective administration of rights was felt first in the second half of the nineteenth century[1] by composers and music publishers as regards the performance in places of public entertainment of non-dramatic musical works. Since then, new technologies have given rise to new, high-volume markets for works in respect of which individual exercise and control of rights is at worst impossible, or at best impractical. Public performance and broadcasting of works were the first uses to give rise to collective licensing, and in that area collective administration has been traditional. Over the past fifty years, the emergence of secondary mass usage by new means of exploitation of works such as reprographic reproduction of literary and graphic works, commercial rental, satellite broadcasting, cable distribution of television programmes and films, and the use of computer technology to digitise and store protected works of all kinds and to transmit them in digital form throughout the world, by means of a combination of computer, telephone and satellite and cable technologies on the global information infrastructure that has produced the internet,[2] has made the need for collective administration of rights even more acute. Increasingly, therefore, since 1990, when the first commercial provider of internet dial-up access came on line, and the invention of the worldwide web a year later,[3] collective administration has become the most realistic way for copyright owners to exercise many of their rights in the online environment.[4]

27–03 **Collecting societies.** The term "collecting societies" is generally used internation-

---

[1] See para.27–08.

[2] For a brief history of the internet, see Cunard, Hill and Barlas, "Current Developments in the Field of Digital Rights Management", August 1, 2003, WIPO doc. SCCR/10/2, pp.5, et seq..

[3] Cunard, Hill and Barlas, "Current Development in the Field of Digital Rights Management", August 1, 2003, WIPO doc. SCCR/10/2, p.6.

[4] D. Gervais (ed.) *Collective Management of Copyright and Related Rights* 3rd edn (London: Sweet & Maxwell, 2008).

ally to describe the organisations set up by the various categories of rights owners to administer their rights collectively. A collecting society has been defined
by the European Unionto mean "any organisation which manages or administers
copyright or rights related to copyright as its sole purpose or as one of its main
purposes".[5]

As regards the United Kingdom, the 1988 Act uses the term licensing body,
with the following similar, but more precise definition:

> "A 'licensing body' means a society or other organisation which has as its
> main object, or one of its main objects, the negotiation or granting, either as
> owner or prospective owner of copyright or as agent for him, of copyright
> licences, and whose objects include the granting of licences covering works
> of more than one author."[6]

Copyright licences are defined as meaning 'licences to do, or authorise the doing of, any of the acts restricted by copyright.'[7]

In the United Kingdom and other EU Member States, collecting societies or
licensing bodies are private sector organisations established and controlled by the
rights owners' themselves. However, in most countries, for the protection of the
public, there is some kind of government supervision or control over the practices of collecting societies. In the United Kingdom, the 1988 Act provides a
regulatory framework for the operation of licensing schemes and licensing bodies in certain areas and also provides for the Copyright Tribunal to oversee the
proper functioning of such licensing schemes and the activities of the licensing
bodies generally.[8]

Purposes of collective administration. Collective administration of copyrights   **27–04**
serves two principal purposes:

(a) to do for members of collecting societies what they cannot practically and
economically do for themselves by providing a service to enable rights
owners to enforce and administer certain of their copyrights effectively
and cheaply, and

(b) to provide a service to users by facilitating access to copyright works and
making it possible for users to comply with their obligations under the
law to obtain licences for the use of copyright works.

As the Monopolies and Mergers Commission stated in 1988:

> "The principal functions of collective licensing bodies are to license the use
> of the copyrights they manage; to monitor that use in order to enforce the
> conditions upon which the licence has been granted; and to collect and dis-
> tribute the royalties payable as the result of licensed use. The licensing func-
> tion includes the negotiation of appropriate rates of royalty with the pro-
> spective user, and is inevitably contentious because it is concerned with how
> much the user should pay for the copyright material. Collective licensing
> should provide a mechanism so that payment of the required royalty:
>
>> (a) guarantees users immediate access to the licensor's repertoire;
>>
>> (b) keeps to a minimum the administrative costs incurred by users and
>> owners;
>>
>> (c) provides for the use of copyright of recordings that have yet to be
>> made (and hence are of unknown value); and

---

[5] Satellite and Cable Directive 93/83 art.1(4).
[6] CDPA 1988 ch.VII, Copyright Licensing s.116(2); see paras 28–30 and 28–88, below.
[7] CDPA 1988 s.116(3).
[8] CDPA 1988 Ch.VII. See also paras 27–15 and 27–20 and Ch.28, paras 28–84 et seq.

    (d) meets the needs of owners and users whatever the scale of their business."[9]

The Commission concluded that collective licensing bodies are the best available mechanism for licensing copyright works provided they can be restrained from using their monopoly unfairly.[10]

In a system of collective administration, rights owners authorise one or more collecting societies to administer their rights on their behalf. The societies then generally organise and make available to prospective users, or associations of users, blanket licences, which authorise the users to make use of the entire repertoire, national and foreign, represented by the society in question, for certain purposes and for a prescribed period. Blanket licences are granted on a take-it-or-leave-it basis with respect to the society's entire repertoire; societies do not license the use of a part only of their repertoire. Such blanket licences generally cover "commercially marketable repertoires, in which the value of the whole is greater than the sum of the values of the parts: the difference reflects the benefit of the aggregation" to the user.[11] In some circumstances, collecting societies issue individual licences, although on standard terms.

Licences are granted in return for royalties or fees and the collecting societies collect and distribute the resulting remuneration among their members. Such organisations either acquire copyrights from their members by assignment or act as agents or licensees on behalf of their members to enforce copyright. Collecting societies are also empowered to monitor the uses made of the works to ensure that unauthorised uses of the works controlled by them do not take place. Where necessary, they enforce the rights of their members by legal action for infringement. For example, in the field of music, no individual composer, producer of a sound recording or other copyright owner has the resources, in practice, to secure adequate protection for his work or deal with the very large number of broadcasters and the many thousands of different public performance users in thousands of different places wishing to exploit such works.

Various collecting societies undertake additional activities on behalf of their members, other than collective administration of rights. Such activities include the provision of social and legal services to rights owners, educational and public relations activities aimed at ensuring a better understanding and respect on the part of the public and users for the rights they administer and representation of their members' interests in relation to government departments and intergovernmental organisations.

27–05   **Advantages of collecting societies.** Collecting societies are practically, economically and legally both viable and essential: practically, because copyright owners cannot be in an indefinite number of places at the same time exercising individual rights, and foreign rights owners would be unable to exercise their rights outside their country of origin without extreme expense and difficulty; economically, because it is cheaper to share the financial expenses of negotiation, supervision and collection among the greatest possible number of rights owners; and, legally, because it is impossible for users of works to obtain permission from every individual copyright owner, both national and foreign. From the point of view of the

---

[9] Monopolies and Mergers Commission, *Collective Licensing, A report on certain practices in the Collective Licensing of Public Performance and Broadcasting Rights in Sound Recordings*, Cm.530 HMSO December 1988, para.7.12. The report referred specifically to the activities of PPL in relation to the licensing of sound recordings but its conclusions on the merits of collective licensing are equally applicable in respect of other works protected by copyright. The reference in point (c) of the passage quoted refers to the fact that licences cover the use of both existing sound recordings and those yet to be produced.

[10] Cm.530 HMSO December 1988, para.7.14.

[11] Cm.530 HMSO December 1988, para.7.15.

World Programming Limited[853] include questions about the correct application of art.5(3).

(iv) Protection for hardware implementations/circuit designs

At their most basic level, computer programs consist of very simple instructions **26–371** to hardware to carry out very simple functions. These instructions may be stored as program instructions, or by hardware implementation, for example, in a semiconductor chip. As noted above, there is no comprehensive definition of "computer program". Arguably, a hardware implementation of a set of instructions which could also be implemented in program code should benefit from the same form of protection. This appears to be confirmed by recital 7 of the Software Directive, although not expressly imported into the 1988 Act.

In the mid-1980s, the United States enacted[854] sui generis protection for semiconductor chip-masks works, being a series of related images, however fixed or encoded, representing the patterns on the layers of a semiconductor chip. Protection for foreign mask works was based on reciprocity. In response to this, Council Directive 87/54/EEC on the legal protection of topographies of semiconductor products was adopted in December 1986. Directive 87/54/EEC required Member States to provide protection for the topographies of semiconductor chips. The Directive includes, inter alia, specific limitations relevant to reverse engineering of semiconductor topographies. It is currently implemented in the United Kingdom via a modified form of the design right.[855]

At the same time, industry has continued to seek patent protection for inventions involving circuits for computers, including in the semiconductor area. In addition, there may in some circumstances be potential for reliance on circuit layout diagrams and lists of electronic components included in the circuitry as artistic or literary (non-program) works.[856]

(v) Enforceability of shrink-wrap licences

In mass-market physical software distribution, many aspects of the transaction **26–372** are approached as a contractual licence directly between rightholder and end user, but there is typically a "channel" of wholesalers and retailers through whose hands passes the physical item on which the software is recorded, i.e. floppy discs or CD-ROM, plus associated documentation. As between retailer and purchaser, the transaction is one of sale and purchase. It is not normal for the customer to be asked to read and sign the licence terms before buying the product. In many cases, the terms are not even visible until the user has made the purchase and opened the box. Although licensor terms and conditions typically cover similar issues, such as scope of licence and limitations and exclusions of the software publisher's liability, the details of the terms and conditions vary and certainly could not be said to be "industry standard".

Since copyright law makes it clear that incidental and transitory copying is prima facie restricted unless licensed, copyright owners are in a strong position to argue that the sale of a copy of a program does not imply an unlimited licence to do any act restricted by the copyright and that it is clearly within the contempla-

---

[853] [2010] EWHC 1829 (Ch).

[854] Semiconductor Chip Protection Act 1984.

[855] See, The Design Right (Semiconductor Topographies) Regulations 1989 (SI 1989/1100), as amended. For a detailed discussion of the right, see Ch.14, above.

[856] See *Anacon Corp Ltd v Environmental Research Technology Ltd* [1994] F.S.R. 659.

tion of users that their use will be subject to the scope of licence restrictions.[857] However, traditional contract analysis requires offer and acceptance between vendor and purchaser, or licensor and licensee, for terms to be agreed. The fact these terms are not agreed to at time of purchase therefore raises questions about enforceability of shrink-wrap licence terms.

Nonetheless, the practice of shrink-wrap licensing has been widely used. In 1996, an important test case was fought in the United States, *Pro CD v Zeidenberg*.[858] The outcome appears to have brought some measure of certainty to enforceability of shrink-wrap licence terms in the United States. The Scots Court of Session decision of *Beta Computers v Adobe Systems*,[859] also recognised the industry practice.

Electronic distribution reduces or removes the need for a distribution channel, enabling software publishers to deal directly with their customers without establishing traditional distribution infrastructure. Electronic distribution has grown rapidly, and is expected to grow further, with consequential reduction of shrink-wrap distribution. Nonetheless, electronic commerce has not yet completely replaced physical distribution. Furthermore, in the online environment related questions will continue to arise, as to whether, for example, notices as to licence limitations necessarily have contractual effect. In this respect, the use of "click-wrap" agreements (requiring licensees positively to indicate acceptance of licence terms) is now widespread.

(vi) Scope of licensed use

26-373 There are many different types of software, and many different types of use of software. So, it is not surprising that there is no single type of licence. On the other hand, many licences cover similar issues. Typical software licences cover:

1. type of machine on which the software may be used (e.g. specific hardware model, whether stand-alone or networked);
2. restrictions on types of use (e.g. internal data processing or bureau use, permitted number of users on a network, personal use only);
3. maintenance, right to make back ups and, in some cases, escrow of source code (i.e. a copy to be deposited with a third party on terms that it will be made available to the customer on specified triggering events, such as insolvency of the licensor).

These, and other, scope of licence issues are frequently covered with a fairly high level of specificity in supplier standard-form licences.

As is discussed elsewhere, the ability of a software copyright owner to restrict scope of use is to some extent circumscribed by statute, in particular as a result of the implementation of the Software Directive. For example, the "decompilation right" cannot be excluded by contract, any more than the right to make back-ups where this is necessary for the licensed use. However, the circumstances in which the exceptions to the restricted acts arise have been carefully defined, such that it may be possible to limit their application by the manner in which the licence is drafted or by establishing business practices which obviate their application, such as the routine publication of interface specification information.[860] Disputes or at least licence re-negotiations are relatively common between software licensors and licensees. This is often due to changes in technology, rendering scope of

---

[857] See *Creative Technology v Aztech Systems Pte Ltd* 1997–1 S.L.R. 621; 1996 S.L.R. LEXIS 486.
[858] United States Court of Appeals (7th Cir.) 86 F. 3d. 1447.
[859] [1996] F.S.R. 367.
[860] art.6 of Directive 2009/24/EC only applies, inter alia, to the extent the information necessary to achieve interoperability has not previously been readily available.

user, there is a clear advantage in being able to obtain a licence from a national collecting society, giving him the right to use virtually any work from its worldwide repertoire. Given that national collecting societies control the rights administered by their sister societies in other countries by means of the reciprocal representation agreements already referred to, the user with a Performing Rights Society (PRS) or Phonographic Performance Ltd (PPL) licence (see para.27–09, below) is generally safe from actions for infringement, whatever music or sound recordings he uses.

There is an additional advantage to the individual right owner whose personal standing or size would put them in a weak bargaining position in relation to powerful users, if they were to try to exercise their rights on an individual basis. Collective licensing increases their marketing power, putting them on the same footing as their better known or more influential colleagues.

In certain cases, there is a need for rights owners to mandate more than one collecting society. This lies in the fact that some of these societies administer only one particular right for one category of right owner. For example, in the United Kingdom, the Mechanical Copyright Protection Society (MCPS) administers composers' and songwriters' rights to copy their works, issue copies to the public and to rent or lend their works to the public, whereas the PRS administers those composers' and songwriters' public performance and communication to the public rights. These latter PRS rights are collectively referred to as performing rights.[12]

The public interest. There is a general consensus that such collective administration bodies provide the best available mechanism for licensing and administering copyrights and is to be encouraged wherever individual licensing is not practicable. They represent the best means of protecting the rights owners' interests, enabling copyright owners to license and monitor the use of their works, to collect and distribute royalties, and to bring actions for infringement. At the same time, they facilitate access to copyright protected works for the consumer and minimise the number of persons with whom users must negotiate licensing contracts.

27–06

The convenience offered by such bodies both to the owner and user of copyright cannot be matched by any other means and, in their absence, in a totally free market, individual users and copyright owners would be at a serious disadvantage in negotiating and subsequently enforcing contractual arrangements for the exploitation of rights. Thus, collecting societies make the copyright system more effective and efficient, promote the dissemination of works and tend to enlarge the choice of works made available to the public. They benefit rights owners and users alike and in principle operate for the benefit of the public.

Collective administration of rights through such societies operates worldwide. While the precise nature, representation and practices of collecting societies vary from country to country, collective administration of copyright by licensing bodies is standard practice.

Technical progress is such that in the modern world there exist innumerable possibilities for the exploitation of protected works. Such technology, whilst facilitating access to works by the consumer, has increased the difficulties of enforcing exclusive rights. Collective administration provides the only practical

---

[12] For details of the activities of these societies, see para.27–10 and Section 4 of this Chapter, below. Since 1997, these two bodies have been brought under joint management as the MCPS-PRS Alliance, and although they retain their separate identities and conduct the majority of their licensing activities separately, in certain areas (primarily those in relation to online exploitation), the societies issue joint licences that cover both the "mechanical" and the "performing" rights. For further information about the PRS and MCPS, see paras 25–59 and 28–56.

means for rights owners to safeguard their rights and, in particular, those new rights introduced to enable rights owners to control new methods of exploitation of their works. Indeed, the law now provides that certain rights may only be exercised through collecting societies, both in the United Kingdom and elsewhere. For example, under the amendments introduced by the Copyright and Related Rights Regulations 1996,[13] which implement, inter alia, the EU Directive on rental right and that on satellite broadcasting and cable distribution,[14] the cable-redistribution rights of copyright owners may be exercised against a cable operator only through a licensing body.[15] Other examples of rights in respect of which legislation makes their exercise conditional on collective administration are the reprographic reproduction right, the right to remuneration in respect of private copying of works (a right which has been introduced in a majority of Member States of the European Union and elsewhere but which is not yet part of the law of the United Kingdom), and the artist's resale right (*droit de suite*), which has only recently been introduced in the law of the UK (see Ch.20, above).

27–07   **Benefits of collective administration for foreign nationals.** Collective administration of rights also greatly facilitates the exercise of the rights of foreign rights owners, entitled to national treatment under the international copyright and related rights conventions and pursuant to EU law (see Chs 23 and 24, above). Most established collecting societies belong to international networks, consisting of federations of societies representing the same categories of rights owners and which enter into reciprocal representation agreements for the exercise of rights in their respective members' repertoire.[16] Thus, one collecting society in any given country is able to represent both foreign and national rights owners within its territory and to license practically the entire world repertoire of the rights owners it represents; at the same time a rights owner will be able to exercise his rights and receive royalties when his work is used abroad. The system is thus of benefit both to United Kingdom and non-United Kingdom nationals.

B. ORIGINS OF COLLECTING SOCIETIES

27–08   **The first collecting societies.** The establishment of the first collective licensing body predates the adoption of the Berne Convention for the Protection of Literary and Artistic Works in 1886 (the Berne Convention).[17] SACEM (Society of Authors, Composers and Music Publishers), the French society representing authors and composers, was established in France in 1852 to administer public performance rights in musical works. Following the adoption of the Berne Convention, which recognised the public performance right as a principal feature of the protection to be afforded to all authors from the Berne Union countries, it became apparent to authors in many other countries that, in practice, it was impossible to safeguard such a right on an individual basis. The need for collective licensing bodies was soon felt, therefore, in every country in Europe and led to the establishment of more such bodies representing, in the first place, authors and composers. Subsequently, by the turn of the century, technical developments led to the advent of new categories of works protected by copyright, such as

---

[13] SI 1996/2967.

[14] Directive 92/100 on rental right and lending right and on certain rights related to copyright in the field of intellectual property [1992] OJ L346/61, repealed and replaced by Directive 2006/115/EC (codified version) [2006] OJ L376 of December 27, 2006. Directive 93/83 on the co-ordination of certain rules concerning copyright and rights related to copyright applicable to satellite broadcasting and cable retransmission of September 27, 1993 [1993] OJ L248/15).

[15] CDPA 1988 s.144A. See paras 28–74 et seq., below.

[16] See also paras 27–25 et seq. below.

[17] As to the Berne Convention, generally, see Ch.23 s.2.

photographs, films and sound recordings. Following the recognition of public performance rights in sound recordings, collective licensing bodies representing producers and performers were set up in the countries which recognised these rights. The emergence of radio and television broadcasting as a major user of copyright works in the first half of the twentieth century,[18] as well as the other new technologies which have developed in the meantime and given rise to new uses of works, such as reprography, satellite transmission and cable distribution, commercial rental, computer storage of protected works in databases and nowadays digital storage and distribution of works online over the internet and so on, has led to the extension of collective licensing schemes to new areas. Likewise, new categories of works have emerged and been afforded copyright protection, such as computer programs, broadcasts, cable programmes and databases. As a result of all these developments, new collecting societies have been set up to safeguard, enforce and obtain payment for the exploitation of new rights recognised by legislation in favour of authors and other copyright owners.

The establishment of collecting societies in the United Kingdom. In the United Kingdom, the first collecting societies to be set up were the Mechanical Copyright Licences Company Ltd (Mecolico), now the Mechanical Copyright Protection Society (MCPS), and the Performing Right Society Ltd (PRS). Mecolico was established by music publishers at the time of the 1911 Act to collect and distribute royalties from producers of sound recordings for the recording rights in music and lyrics (these rights are sometimes referred to as "mechanical rights"). The PRS was set up in 1914 to administer the public performance rights of authors, composers and music publishers in musical works, which at the time were published mainly in the form of sheet music. At that time, music publishers derived most of their income from theatrical performances of their works and from the sale of sheet music; the recording industry was still in its infancy. The PRS now administers all non-dramatic performing rights in musical works, including broadcasting, cable distribution and non-theatrical use of excerpts from dramatico-musical works (these rights are known as "small" rights as opposed to "grand" rights). Grand rights are the rights of authors and composers in dramatic and dramatico-musical works, opera, operetta and ballet, which it is feasible to exercise individually since the use of such works is limited to a comparatively small number of users and locations. The PRS also plays a limited role in the licensing of its members' film synchronisation rights. Phonographic Performance Ltd (PPL) came into being in 1934 to administer performing rights in sound recordings on behalf of record producers, following the decision in the *Cawardine* case,[19] which decided that the rights conferred on record producers by the 1911 Act included public performance and broadcasting rights. Organisations equivalent to those in the United Kingdom are established in most other European countries and, outside Europe, particularly in the English-speaking world, including, for example, in Australia, Canada and the United States of America. **27–09**

Collecting societies operating in the United Kingdom in 2010. Today, the following additional collective licensing bodies are operating in the United Kingdom; their activities, as well as those of the MCPS, PRS and PPL, are described in more detail in Section 4 of this Chapter, below: **27–10**

(a) Artists' Collecting Society (ACS) collects artists' resale right royalties (*droit de suite*) on behalf of UK artists;

---

[18] Marconi developed wireless communication (radio) in the closing years of the last century. The first radio programme broadcast in the USA took place in 1906. The BBC was established by charter in 1927 with a monopoly over sound broadcasting. Television was invented by Baird in 1926 and the first television programmes to be broadcast in the UK took place in July 1936.

[19] *Gramophone Co Ltd v Stephen Cawardine and Co* [1934] Ch. 450.

(b) Artists' Rights Administration Ltd (ARA) collects artists' resale rights royalties, primarily on behalf of Russian artists;

(c) Authors' Licensing and Collecting Society Ltd (ALCS) administers a wide variety of rights in literary and dramatic works on behalf of authors, including inter alia the reprographic right, the cable distribution right and the private recording right;

(d) British Equity Collecting Society Ltd (BECS) administers performers' remuneration;

(e) Compact Collections Ltd (CCL) collects secondary television royalties for film and television content owners;

(f) Copyright Licensing Agency Ltd (CLA) licenses the reprographic rights of authors and publishers in published literary and artistic works;

(g) Design and Artists Copyright Society Ltd (DACS) administers rights in artistic works, including the artists' resale right;

(h) Directors UK (DUKL) (formerly Directors and Producers Rights Society (1992) Ltd) administers certain rights on behalf of film and television directors and producers;

(i) Educational Recording Agency Ltd (ERA) licenses the recording by educational establishments of broadcasts and cable programmes;

(j) Newspaper Licensing Agency Ltd (NLA) licenses the reprographic rights of newspaper publishers in news articles;

(k) Publishers Licensing Society Limited (PLS) administers the reprographic rights on behalf of publishers of book, journal, and magazine publishers;

(l) Video Performance Ltd (VPL) administers the rights of producers of music videos.

A number of other trade associations, including the Music Publishers' Association (MPA), the British Phonographic Industry (BPI) and the International Federation of the Phonographic Industry (IFPI) also administer certain rights on behalf of their members. The Open University Educational Enterprises Ltd licenses the off-air recording of Open University programmes. The Association of United Recording Artists (AURA) and the Performing Artists Media Rights Association Ltd (PAMRA) both of which previously collected equitable remuneration arising from the exploitation of sound recordings on behalf of performers went into voluntary liquidation in late 2006, following a merger with PPL.

C. CHARACTERISTICS OF EFFECTIVE COLLECTING SOCIETIES

27-11   **Structure and functions of collecting societies.** There have been a number of studies carried out at the international level under the auspices of the World Intellectual Property Organisation (WIPO, Geneva) into the structure and functions of appropriate and effective collecting societies. These gave rise to the adoption in 1979 of guidelines for the establishment and operation of collecting societies for the rights of producers of phonograms and performers under the Rome Convention for the Protection of Performers, Producers of Phonograms and Broadcasting Organisations 1961 (the Rome Convention).[20] In 1983, WIPO published model statutes for organisations administering authors' rights.[21] Subsequently, both WIPO and Unesco published studies on the establishment and operation of col-

---

[20] Recommendations concerning the protection of performers, producers of phonograms and broadcasting organisations, adopted by the Intergovernmental Committee of the Rome Convention in 1979 [1979] *Copyright* 105. As to the Rome Convention, generally, see Section 5, Ch.23.

[21] Model Statutes for Public Institutions Administering Authors' Rights and for Private Societies Administering Authors' Rights, October 1983, [1983] *Copyright* 351 and 353.

lective administration organisations to serve as a basis for advice to governments.[22]

In the United Kingdom, the activities of the PRS and PPL in particular have been under scrutiny in recent years as a result of investigations by and subsequent recommendations of the Competition Commission.[23]

From the foregoing, some characteristics of effective collecting societies may be identified.

Benefits of a single organisation representing a single category of rights owner. As a rule, there should be only one organisation for any one category of rights owners open for membership to all rights owners of that category on reasonable terms. A long-established exception to this principle is the alliance between authors and publishers in performing right societies such as the PRS. By means of reciprocal representation agreements with foreign societies or federations of societies, a collecting society should represent in its territory both national and foreign rights owners.

27–12

The existence of two or more organisations in the same field may diminish the advantages of collective administration for both rights owners and users. For the rights owners, competing societies lead to duplication of functions and reduction in economies of scale in operation and thus are unlikely to bring benefits to their members.[24] For the user, a multiplicity of societies representing a single category of rights owner would also cause uncertainty, duplication of effort and extra expense. The user would have to check, for each work he wished to use, which society controlled it and whether he had the appropriate licence. For both parties, administration costs would be greater, reducing the revenue available for distri-

---

[22] WIPO, *Collective administration of copyright and neighbouring rights*, Geneva 1990 (WIPO publication No.688(E)); P. Schepens, *Guide to the collective administration of authors' rights (The Administration Society at the Service of Authors and Users)*, Unesco, 2002 (doc. CLT-2000/WS/4). M. Ficsor, *Collective Management of Copyright and Related Rights* (WIPO Publication no.855).

[23] See the following reports of the Monopolies and Merger Commission, *Performing rights—A report on the supply in the United Kingdom of the services of administering performing rights and film synchronisation rights*, (Cm. 3147 HMSO, London 1996). Monopolies and Mergers Commission, *Collective Licensing—A report on certain practices in the Collective Licensing of Public Performance and Broadcasting Rights in Sound Recordings*, (Cm. 530 HMSO, London 1988). The Monopolies and Mergers Commission has meantime been replaced by the Competition Commission, established by the Competition Act 1998 with effect from April 1, 1999, see para.28–287 below.

[24] As noted in para.9–1 of the MMC PRS report (see previous fn.), there are only two major jurisdictions, Brazil and the USA, where there are competing societies. In Brazil, there are 13: ABRAC (Associação Brasileira de Autores, Compositores, Intérpretes e MÚsicos), ABRAMUS (Associação Brasileira de MÚsicos); ACIMBRA (Associação de Compositóres e Intérpretes Musicais do Brasil), AMAR (Associação de MÚsicos, Arranjadores e Regentes); ANACIM (Associação Nacional de Autores, Compositores e Intérpretes de MÚsica); ASSIM (Associação de Intérpretes e MÚsicos); ATIDA (Associação de Titulares de Direitos Autorais); SADEMBRA (Sociedade Administradora de Direitos de Execução Musical do Brasil); SBACEM (Sociedade Brasileira de Autores, Compositores e Escritores de MÚsica); SBAT (Sociedade Brasileira de Autores Teatrais) which administers "grand rights"; SICAM (Sociedade Independente de Compositores e Autores Musicais); SOCINPRO (Sociedade Brasileira de Administração e Protecão de Direitos Intelectuais) and UBC (União Brasileira de Compositores). In the USA, there are three: ASCAP (American Society of Composers, Authors and Publishers); BMI (Broadcast Music Inc.); and SESAC (Society of European Stage Authors and Composers). In Brazil, so far as performing rights in musical works and phonograms are concerned, the situation is different from that in the USA. Collection on behalf of all the societies, with the exception of ATIDA and SBAT, is effected by one organisation, ECAD (Escritório Central de Arrecadação e Distribuição). ECAD is a private monopoly organisation imposed by law, which collects remuneration on behalf of the societies it represents and distributes it to rights owners through the specific society to which the rights owner is affiliated (Law no.9.610/98). The following societies are members of ECAD: ABRAMUS, AMAR, SPACEM, SICAM, SOCINPRO and UBC and four societies are simply administered by ECAD, without the right to vote: ASSIM, SADEMBRA, ABRAC AND ANACIM). As to the position in the USA, see para.27–17, below.

bution to rights owners and increasing the overall cost of obtaining licences for the user.

27–13   Adequate mandates. Collecting societies should have valid mandates to act as agent or licensee of their members, or take assignments of their individual rights, and have the legal personality required:

    (a) to enter into binding contracts, both at the national and international level;

    (b) to exercise the mandates or assignments received from their members;

    (c) to enforce their members' rights by means of legal action, where necessary.

Societies should provide an efficient, transparent and equitable service to their members. Monitoring of uses and the collection of royalties should be as comprehensive as possible, subject to reasonable costs. Members should receive regular and sufficiently detailed information about the manner in which their rights are being exercised. Such information should also be available to foreign collecting societies with which the society has entered into reciprocal representation contracts. Societies should provide for a suitable internal appeal procedure to deal with matters of dispute between them and their members.

27–14   Collection and distribution of revenue. Decisions about the methods and rules of collection and distribution of remuneration, on the basis of statistically valid sampling procedures, should be taken by the rights owners concerned. There should be no discrimination between rights owners, members or non-members, nationals or foreigners. Indeed, foreign rights owners should receive the same treatment in all respects as national rights owners. Remuneration collected should be distributed among individual rights owners as much in proportion to the actual use of their works as possible, subject only to deduction of the actual costs of administration and of any other deductions (e.g. for cultural or social purposes) which have been expressly agreed by the members. Such costs should be subject to the effective scrutiny of the membership.

Government supervision of, and interference in, the establishment and operation of tariffs and other licensing conditions applied by collective administration organisations, which are in a de facto monopoly position vis-à-vis users, is justified to the extent that such supervision is required to prevent abuse of such a monopoly position.[25]

D. PRINCIPLES GOVERNING THE REGULATION OF COLLECTING SOCIETIES

27–15   Public interest and need for public control. Any collecting society by its nature and as a matter of fact, will be in a dominant position because it will represent the rights of a majority of a particular category of rights owners, both national and foreign in any given territory. Thus, collective administration may not be in the public interest if there is no mechanism for ensuring that monopolistic collecting agencies do not abuse this position. As mentioned above, the existence of collecting societies is considered to be of advantage to the public as being the most effective means of, on the one hand, administering and protecting rights owners' interests whilst, on the other, facilitating the ease of access of copyright protected works to the consumer. The potential conflict between the public interest in collective administration and the de facto monopolistic nature of collecting societies has on occasion been illustrated by users challenging their role on the grounds

---

[25] Monopolies and Mergers Commission Cm. 3147 HMSO 1996. Cm. 3147; Conclusions, para.306 (m); see also paras 28–57 et seq., below.

that they are monopolies and abuse their monopoly position. In the United Kingdom, there have been complaints of abuse of monopoly rights against, in particular, the PRS and PPL, since virtually all popular music is now controlled by these organisations and their counterparts in other countries. It has therefore come to be felt, in a number of countries and at the international level, that to ensure against abuse of monopoly some measure of public control over the activities of such organisations is necessary in the public interest[26]; and that:

> "... it is better to accept the usefulness, in the public interest, of the fact of monopoly but to control it in other ways".[27]

Supervision of establishment and operation of collecting societies. In many countries, therefore, collecting societies are subject to some form of supervision which may be exercised in a variety of ways. Some countries make the establishment of a collecting society conditional upon the approval of a competent authority (e.g. the Ministry of Culture, the Ministry of Justice or the Patent Office); this is the case, for example, in France, Germany and Spain.[28] In France, the Ministry of Culture is responsible; but if for any reason it opposes the incorporation of a society, the courts have jurisdiction to decide the matter after assessing the professional qualifications of the founders of such society, the human and material means that they intend to use to collect royalties and to exploit their repertoire. By law, such societies are obliged to make available blanket licences covering the complete repertoire of the French and foreign rights owners they represent.[29] In Germany, the supervising authority for collecting societies is the Patent Office.[30] In Spain, as in France, authorisation to operate as a collecting society must be obtained from the Ministry of Culture. Due account is taken, in particular, of the degree to which the proposed society is representative of the category of right owner it purports to represent, the volume of potential users, the suitability of its statutes and the means whereby it proposes to achieve its aims, the potential efficiency of its administration abroad, and the views of existing collecting societies operating in Spain.[31] Where such systems for supervision by a competent authority of the establishment and operation of collecting societies exist, provision is made for continued monitoring of the societies' activities. In the United Kingdom, the means of control are the Copyright Tribunal the Office of Fair Trading and the Competition Commission, whose respective powers are considered in detail below.[32]

27–16

The monopoly position of collecting societies. Various jurisdictions have dealt differently with the reality that collecting societies, having a de facto monopoly position, may abuse that position. Some provide for settlement of disputes by the civil courts. Elsewhere, governments have opted to establish, as in the United

27–17

---

[26] See, as to the position of such organisations under the Treaty on the Functioning of the European Union (TFEU), arts 101 and 102 (ex arts 81 and 82, previously arts 85 and 86), para.27–20 and para.28–285, below.

[27] See W. Wallace, "Control over the Monopoly Exercise of Copyright" [1973] I.I.C. 382.

[28] See A. Dietz, "Legal Regulation of Collective Management of Copyright (Collecting Societies Law) in Western and Eastern Europe" [2002] No.4, 49 *Journal of the Cop. Soc. of the USA*, 897.

[29] Law on the Intellectual Property Code (No.92–597 of July 1, 1992, amended up to January 3, 1995), Title II concerning royalty collection and distribution societies, arts L.321–3 and L.321–7

[30] Law of September 9, 1965, on the Administration of Copyright and Related Rights, as amended to May 23, 1985 art.18(1).

[31] Revised Law on Intellectual Property, regularising, clarifying and harmonising the applicable statutory provisions (approved by Royal Legislative Decree 1/1996 of April 12, 1996 arts 142 et seq.).

[32] See paras 28–93 and 28–287 et seq.

Kingdom and Australia,[33] some form of compulsory arbitration or specialist tribunal having jurisdiction to review the activities of collecting societies and power to determine or vary the rates charged and to order the grant of licences. Others provide for review of licensing conditions by an administrative authority.

In Germany, collecting societies are specifically exempted from the antitrust law, in recognition of the fact that the very nature of a collective licensing body is by necessity a monopoly. In order to avoid any abuse of this monopoly, a special arbitration board (*Schiedstelle*) was established to control the activities of collective licensing bodies and to settle any conflicts which might arise between them and users.[34] As a rule, claims may not be asserted in court proceedings unless they have been preceded by proceedings before the arbitration board.[35] The Canadian Government has also recognised the need to exempt collecting societies from certain provisions of its Competition Act and has set up a system of voluntary submission to regulatory review; the Competition Act does not apply in respect of any royalties or related terms and conditions arising under an agreement submitted for review.[36]

In 1985, the Australian Trade Practices Commission had to decide whether to allow the Phonographic Performance Company of Australia Ltd (PPCA) to become the collective licensing body representing copyright owners in sound recordings throughout Australia. The Commission concluded that there was public benefit in terms of efficiencies and cost savings and that such benefit outweighed any detriment to competition. Since this collective arrangement was justified on "public benefit" grounds, it was found to be eligible for exemption from the Trade Practices Act of 1974. This finding is equally applicable to collecting societies representing other rights owners.[37]

In the United States of America, litigation concerning the operations of collecting societies has given rise to an exhaustive examination of the question whether the operations of these societies are contrary to the public interest by reason of incompatibility with US antitrust law. The benefits to rights owner and user alike of collective licensing is recognised and the societies' activities are not per se considered to be unlawful.[38] There is, however, competition for the collective administration of performing rights in music in the United States of America, where three competing organisations, ASCAP, BMI and SESAC, exist. ASCAP is a composers' society, representing and controlled by its members. BMI is a corporate body with full trading powers owned and managed by broadcasters, i.e. music users, with the writers and publishers it represents playing no part in its operations. SESAC is a privately owned corporation representing writers and publishers. These organisations carry out identical functions, competition between them lying in competing for members. Users have to obtain licences from all three.

27–18   **Collective administration and the copyright conventions.** The international conventions on copyright and related rights do not explicitly address the question

---

[33] Copyright Act 1968 Pt IV. For a comparative law study of the role of copyright tribunals, see M. Freegard, " *Quis Custodiet? The Role of Copyright Tribunals*" [1994] 7 E.I.P.R. 286.

[34] The Law of September 9, 1965, on the Administration of Copyright and Related Rights arts 14, 14a–14c, and 15.

[35] The Law of September 9, 1965 on the Administration of Copyright and Related Rights art.16.

[36] Copyright Act 1988 s.50.5(3).

[37] Determination of the Trade Practices Commission of Australia on applications for authorisation under s.88(1) of the Trade Practices Act 1974 by EMI Records (Australia) Ltd on their own behalf and that of Phonographic Performance Company of Australia Ltd dated August 28, 1985.

[38] For an authoritative finding on this issue, see *Broadcast Music Inc v Columbia Broadcasting Sys., Inc*, 441 U.S. 1, 201 U.S.P.Q. 497 (1979), 5.9.

of collective administration of rights.[39] Their basic philosophy is the protection of individual rights owners and individual exercise of rights. Article 2(6) of the Berne Convention provides that "protection shall operate for the benefit of the author and his successors in title". According to this principle, collective administration should not operate in such a way as to reduce the protection established by the Convention. However, the Berne Convention provides that members of the Union may determine by legislation the conditions under which certain rights may be exercised, in particular, the broadcasting and cable distribution rights as well as the right of recording musical works (both of which may be subject to compulsory licensing in certain circumstances).[40] These provisions provide a basis in convention law for non-voluntary licences or for obligatory collective administration. Collective administration is also considered appropriate in other cases where the right is established as a mere right to remuneration[41] or where it represents a compromise between an exclusive right and a fair use exception to it, permitted under the conventions, as in the case of remuneration schemes established to compensate for home taping and reprography.

The compatibility of tribunals, supervisory authorities, etc. with the Berne   **27–19**
Convention. It is relevant here to mention art.17 of the Berne Convention, which deals with the right of governments to take measures to control the circulation, performance and exhibition of works for the preservation of public order. According to the "WIPO Guide to the Berne Convention": "Authors may exercise their rights only if that exercise does not conflict with public order. The former must give way to the latter".[42] The article is mainly but not solely concerned with censorship; according to the report on the discussions relating to art.17 at the Stockholm Conference in 1967, "questions of public policy should always be a matter for domestic legislation" and "the countries of the Union would therefore be able to take all necessary measures to restrict possible abuse of monopolies".[43] It is, therefore, understood that under the Berne Convention, tribunals and other supervisory bodies may only interfere with the setting of tariffs and other licensing conditions in cases where there is an actual abuse of monopoly position and should only serve the purpose of taking measures against possible abuses of monopolies.[44] Thus, such tribunals may not be used arbitrarily as a means to impose a régime of statutory control over the exercise of the exclusive rights guaranteed to authors under the Berne Convention.

E. COLLECTIVE ADMINISTRATION AND EU LAW

EU action on collecting societies. The Commission of the European Union (the   **27–20**
Commission) first announced its intention to study the need for action within the European Union on the subject of the collective management of copyright and related rights and collecting societies in its document "Follow-up to the Green

---

[39] The WIPO Copyright Treaty (WCT) and the WIPO Performances and Phonograms Treaty (WPPT), both adopted on December 20, 1996, contain respectively arts 12 and 19, which impose certain obligations on Contracting Parties concerning the protection of rights management information; for further details, see paras 23–73 et seq. and paras 23–129 et seq., above.

[40] Berne Convention art.11*bis*(2) and art.13(1).

[41] For example, the Rome Convention art.12 which provides for equitable remuneration to be paid to producers of phonograms and performers for the broadcasting and public performance of sound recordings in certain circumstances.

[42] "WIPO Guide to the Berne Convention" [1978] *Geneva* 99.

[43] Records of the Stockholm Conference, 1967, Report of Main Committee I, para.263.

[44] See WIPO "Collective Administration of Copyright and Neighbouring Rights" [1990] *Geneva* para.281.

Paper" issued in January 1991.[45] To date, no firm proposals for legislation relating to collective administration generally have been published by the Commission, although the question of the governance of collective rights management in the European Union has been continually under discussion ever since and a public hearing on the subject was held as recently as April 2010.[46] A legislative proposal was foreshadowed in a communication published in April 2004 entitled "The Management of Copyright and Related Rights in the Internal Market".[47] However, in October 2005, after a short consultation, the Commission instead issued a Recommendation on collective cross-border management of copyright and related rights for legitimate online music services.[48] The Recommendation is limited in its scope (although that limitation is not entirely clear from the wording of the recommendation) to the online sale of recorded music. This ambiguity, the scope of the consultation and the Commission's attempt to achieve regulation by this soft law approach were heavily criticised by the European Parliament in its Resolution of March 13, 2007, on cross-border collective copyright management.[49] The Commission monitored the effect of the Recommendation from the time of its adoption but formally commenced an assessment of the development of the online music market under the Recommendation with a Call for Comments on January 17, 2007.[50] It released a Summary Report of the findings of that monitoring on February 7, 2008.[51] The view of the Commission was that the Recommendation had "produced an impact on the licensing marketplace and is endorsed by a number of collective rights managers, music publishers and users." The Commission further indicated that it would "follow further developments and repeat the monitoring should a clear need to do so arise." If such repeated monitoring becomes necessary, it seems that further and tougher action, presumably in the form of legislation, will be taken by the Commission if it considers sufficient progress is not being made.[52] For further discussion of the Recommendation, see para.27–22, below.

The 2004 communication remains relevant, therefore. It was the result of a wide-ranging process of consultation with interested parties begun in 1995/96 and continued through 2002 on the basis of the Commission's Green Paper on Copyright and Related Rights in the Information Society, published in July 1995.[53]

The Green Paper included a chapter concerning questions on the exploitation of rights, in which it raised issues for discussion with regard to the acquisition and management of rights and technical systems of identification and protection,

---

[45] Commission Communication to the Council: Follow-up to the Green Paper: Working Programme of the Commission in the Field of Copyright and Neighbouring Rights COM(90) 584 final, January 17, 1991.

[46] Public hearing on the governance of collective rights management in the European Union, April 23, 2010.

[47] Communication from the Commission to the Council, The European Parliament and the European Economic and Social Committee COM(2004) 261 final, April 16, 2004.

[48] Recommendation 2005/737/EC on collective cross-border management of copyright and related rights for legitimate online music services [2005] OJ L276/54. This edition of the Official Journal, of October 21, 2005, mistakenly records the date of the Recommendation as May 18, 2005. Shortly thereafter a corrigendum was issued, correcting the date to October 18, 2005: OJ L284/10.

[49] P6_TA(2007)0064 OJ C301E/64.

[50] *http://ec.europa.eu/internal_market/copyright/docs/management/monitoring_en.pdf* [Accessed November 13, 2010].

[51] *http://ec.europa.eu/internal_market/copyright/docs/management/monitoring-report_en.pdf* [Accessed November 13, 2010].

[52] Statement of Internal Market and Services Commissioner, Charlie McCreevy, October 12, 2005, IP/05/1261.

[53] Green Paper on Copyright and Related Rights in the Information Society, COM (95) 382 final, Brussels, July 19, 1995.

having regard particularly to new multimedia works and the exploitation of works on digital networks.[54] That paper did not comment on the structure of collecting societies. Following consultation with interested parties, in November 1996, the Commission issued a Communication entitled: Follow-up to the Green Paper on Copyright and Related Rights in the Information Society ("1996 Follow-up Communication"),[55] which set out the Commission's Single Market policy at the time in the area of copyright and related rights in the Information Society.[56] The document identified management of rights as an issue requiring further evaluation, rather than as a priority item for legislative action.[57] This further evaluation included a study on certain aspects of collective management carried out at the Commission's request and completed in early 2000.[58] Discussions continued at a series of conferences organised by the European Union in the year 2000, culminating in a hearing on collective management, held in Brussels in November 2000, with a view to assisting the Commission to determine appropriate action in the field.[59]

In its April 2004 communication, the Commission announced that it had concluded that EU legislation on the collective management of rights, and particularly on the governance of collecting societies, would be highly desirable, stating that the marketing of intellectual property rights needed to be facilitated in order to create a true single market in this area.[60] Following the publication of the document, the Commission launched a further consultation exercise on what such legislation might consist of.

Collective management in EU instruments. It should be recalled that the issue   **27–21**
of collective management has been addressed already in several Community instruments. There is a definition of collecting societies in the Satellite and Cable Directive art.1(4); it is stated to be for the purposes of that particular Directive but is clearly of general application. Directives in the field of copyright and related rights explicitly tolerate or recommend the mandatory assignment of certain rights, such as the rights of authors and performers to equitable remuneration for rental, to collecting societies.[61] European Union law also stipulates mandatory rights administration by collecting societies in the case of cable distribution:

---

[54] Green Paper on Copyright and Related Rights in the Information Society, COM (95) 382 final, Ch.2, Pt 3, ss.VIII and IX, at pp.69 et seq.

[55] Communication from the Commission: Follow-up to the Green Paper on Copyright and Related Rights in the Information Society, COM(96) 568 final, Brussels, November 20, 1996.

[56] See also the answer given by Mr M. Monti in the European Parliament on behalf of the Commission on November 12, 1996, to a written question (E 2255/96) by Mr K.-L. Lehne to the Commission on the subject of "Competition between copyright management societies (music collecting societies" [1997] OJ C105/5.

[57] 1996 Follow-up to the Green Paper Com(96) 568 final, at 3.

[58] *"Etude sur la gestion collective des droits d'auteur dans l'Union européenne"* (Deloitte & Touche, ITEC Group 2000).

[59] Conference organised by the Portuguese Presidency at Evora, March 2000; International Conference organised by the Commission entitled "The Management and Legitimate Use of Intellectual Property", Strasbourg, July 2000; Public Hearing on Collective Management, Brussels, November 2000; the conclusions of the hearing are available on the Commission website: *http://europa.eu.int.*

[60] Com (2004) 261 final of April 16, 2004. Note also that the European Parliament adopted a resolution on January 15, 2004, on a Community framework for collective management societies in the field of copyright and neighbouring rights. The resolution noted, inter alia, "that collecting societies require a degree of regulation, bringing greater harmonisation, democratisation and transparency in relation to the management of copyright and neighbouring rights, and ... a Community approach in the area of the exercise and management of copyright and neighbouring rights must be pursued while respecting and complying with the principles of copyright and competition law and in accordance with the principles of subsidiarity and proportionality". Bull. EU 1/2–2004 para.1.3.61. See also Report on a Community Framework for collecting societies for authors' rights adopted by the Committee on Legal Affairs and the Internal Market, December 11, 2003 (doc. A5–0578/2003 final).

[61] Rental Right Directive 92/100 art.4(3) and (4).

"Member States shall ensure that the right of copyright owners and holders of related rights to grant or refuse authorisation to a cable operator for a cable retransmission may be exercised only through a collecting society".[62] Likewise Community law provides for the extension of a collective agreement with a collecting
society to unrepresented right-holders.[63] In several cases, the Directives refer to
collecting societies as an accepted way of rights management. However, recital
17 of the Directive on the harmonisation of certain aspects of copyright and related rights in the information society[64] states:

> "It is necessary, especially in the light of the requirements arising out of the
> digital environment, to ensure that collecting societies achieve a higher level
> of rationalisation and transparency with regard to compliance with competi-
> tion rules."

This is followed by a qualifying statement to the effect that the Directive is
without prejudice to the arrangements in the Member States concerning the
management of rights such as extended collective licences.[65]

27–22   **Commission recommendation on management of online rights in musical
works.**[66] Presenting the recommendation to the public, the Commission stated
that it:

> "puts forward measures for improving the EU-wide licensing of copyright
> and related rights for on-line services. Improvements are necessary because
> new internet-based services such as webcasting or on-demand music
> downloads need a licence that covers their activities throughout the EU. The
> absence of EU-wide copyright licences has been one factor that has made it
> difficult for new internet-based music services to develop their full
> potential".[67]

In order to improve EU-wide online licensing of music, which it considered
unsatisfactory due to the cost and complexity of clearing online rights in musical
works on a territory-by-territory basis, the Commission considered three options:
(1) do nothing; (2) improve cooperation among collecting societies allowing
each society in the EU to grant a EU-wide licence covering the other societies'
repertoires; or (3) give right holders the choice to appoint a collective rights
manager for the online use of their musical works across the entire European
Union ("EU-wide direct licensing"). A consultation of "stakeholders" (rights
holders, rights management societies and commercial users) was undertaken in
July 2005. Having reached a broad consensus that doing nothing was not an option, views of these stakeholders were divided as regards the other two options.
The Commission concluded that right holders and commercial users of copyright-
protected material should be given a choice as to their preferred model of licensing and that different online services might require different forms of EU-wide
licensing policies. Multi-territorial licensing should be provided for in order to
enhance greater legal certainty to commercial users in relation to their activity
and to foster the development of legitimate online services, increasing, in turn,

---

[62] Cable and Satellite Directive 92/183 art.9.

[63] Cable and Satellite Directive art.3(2) to the benefit of collecting societies. cf. S. von Lewinski,
"Mandatory Collective Administration of Exclusive Rights—A Case Study on its Compatibility
with International and EC Copyright Law", [2004] January–March *E.Copyright Bulletin*
No.WW1.

[64] Directive 2001/29/EC of May 22, 2001 [2001] OJ L167/10; see para.24–106, above.

[65] Directive 2001/29/EC recital 18.

[66] Recommendation 2005/737/EC on collective cross-border management of copyright and related
rights for legitimate online music services [2005] OJ L276/54, see the Supplement to Vol.2 I2.

[67] IP/05/1261.

the revenue stream for right holders.[68] The Recommendation invites Member States to facilitate the growth of legitimate online services[69] and states that right holders should have the right to entrust the management of any of the online rights necessary to operate legitimate online music services, on a territorial scope of their choice, irrespective of the Member State of residence or the nationality of either the collective rights manager or the right holder.[70] The recommendation also includes provisions on the governance of collecting societies, the distribution of royalties, equal treatment of right holders, transparency, dispute settlement and accountability of collective rights managers, aimed at introducing "a culture of transparency and good governance enabling all relevant stakeholders to make an informed decision as to the licensing model best suited to their needs".[71] The recommendation is addressed to EU Member States as well as to all economic operators involved in the clearance of copyright across the European Union.[72] The Commission was required to assess the development of the online music sector and the need for further action at EU level.[73] The consultation that took place as part of this assessment drew contributions from 89 interested parties. The summary report of that assessment[74] reported that the first EU-wide licence for online music was granted on January 26, 2008, providing mobile phone users access to the EMI repertoire throughout Europe. Stakeholders reported various barriers to further EU-wide licences, which included litigation between various collecting societies, taxation in different member states and difficulties in the identification of the works to be licensed. Nevertheless, the Commission appeared to be satisfied with the effects of the Recommendation, and did not suggest at that time that any further action was necessary.

Recognition of advantages of collective administration by the European Union. The Commission and the Court of Justice have long acknowledged the factual dependence of right-holders on collective licensing in relation to certain rights, accepting that in practice an individual rights owner does not have the resources or power to exercise his rights himself and cannot avoid joining a collecting society. Moreover, rights owners depend on such societies to counterbalance the users' market strength.[75] However, as stated in the 1996 Follow-up document:

27–23

---

[68] Recommendation 2005/737/EC on collective cross-border management of copyright and related rights for legitimate online music services recital 8.

[69] art.2.

[70] art.3.

[71] IP/05/1261.

[72] art.19.

[73] arts 17 and 18. On February 2, 2008, the Commission issued a summary report on the results of the monitoring of the 2005 Recommendation. No new proposals for action are made. The Commission will follow further developments and repeat the monitoring, should a clear need to do so arise. See also Creative content online in the Single market COM(2007) 836 final, January 3, 2008.

[74] See previous fn., above, at p.5.

[75] See, e.g. *BRT v SABAM & FONIOR* (127/73) [1974] E.C.R. 51 and 313; [1974] 2 C.M.L.R. 238; *Re GEMA (No.1)* [1971] OJ L134/15; [1971] C.M.L.R. D 35; *Re GEMA (No.2)* [1972] OJ L182/24; [1971] C.M.L.R. D 115; *GEMA Statutes* [1982] OJ L94/12; [1982] 2 C.M.L.R. 482. In 1994, the Commission, however, issued a statement of objections (no decision has been issued) against the collective licensing activities of VPL and IFPI, with respect to their members' broadcasting rights in music videos. Following a complaint from MTV, which had previously negotiated a collective licence covering the whole repertoire of VPL and IFPI for its pan-European satellite broadcasting service but which, at the conclusion of a five-year contract, alleging that the collective licensing of their members' repertoire by VPL and IFPI represented an abuse of monopoly, it wished to replace by separate licences from major, individual record companies, the Commission stated that the refusal of the major companies to negotiate individually had the result "that competition between the members of VPL, and between the majors in particular, is restricted since by giving an exclusive mandate to VPL ... they refrained from conducting price negotiations on an individual basis". The position of the small independent rec-

"copyright licensing and collecting societies as such are subject to the EU competition rules. Collecting societies are 'undertakings' for the purposes of applying Article 85 (restrictive agreements) and 86 (abuse of dominant position) of the Treaty. They cannot be regarded as "undertakings entrusted with the operation of services of general economic interest" benefiting from the special regime laid down in Article 90(2) of the Treaty".[76]

Thus, collecting societies, drawing up their rules, must take account of all relevant interests in such a way that a balance is ensured between the requirement of maximum freedom for authors, composers and publishers to dispose of their works and that of the effective management of their rights. They should not, therefore, impose obligations on its members which are not absolutely necessary for the attainment of the object of collective licensing and which encroach unfairly on a member's freedom to exercise his copyright.[77]

A number of practices of collective licensing bodies have been found to be an abuse under art.101 (ex art.82) TFEU, including the following:

(a) imposing an obligation on members to assign all their rights, present and future, to the licensing body[78];

(b) unreasonable refusal to supply services to persons in need of the licensing body who do not come within a certain category of persons defined by that body on the basis of nationality or residence[79];

(c) conducting their activities so that their effect is to partition the common market and thereby restrict the freedom to supply services which constitute one of the objectives of the Treaty[80];

(d) discriminating between persons seeking services or customers on the ground of nationality alone.[81]

For a full discussion of these issues, see paras 28–180 et seq. and para.28–285, below.

27–24   **Future EU legislative action.** The adoption of the Commission recommendation referred to in paras 27–20 and 27–22, above, does not mean that binding legislation on the governance of collecting societies in Europe may not be introduced in the future. The legislative proposal foreshadowed in the Commission's communication on the management of copyright and related rights in the internal market already referred to therefore remains relevant. The proposal came to four main conclusions[82]:

> — "An internal market for collective rights management will be more firmly established if a legislative framework on the governance of collecting societies is implemented at Community level. Such a framework would address the issues surrounding the establishment and use of collecting societies, the relationship they have with right holders and commercial users, and lastly, their external supervision.

---

ord companies was completely overlooked in the Commission's statement. The Commission's attitude in this case is at variance with its past decisions on the subject of collective licensing and with the case law of the court. See H. Porter, "European Union Competition Policy: Should the Role of Collecting Societies Be Legitimised? *MTV v VPL*", [1996] 12 E.I.P.R. 672. C. Jackson, "European Union Competition Policy: Collecting Societies", [1997] 3 E.I.P.R. 161.

[76] Follow-up to the Green Paper COM(96) 568 final, at p.25. Note that thearticles referred to are now arts 101 and 102, respectively.

[77] *BRT v SABAM & FONIOR* [1974] E.C.R. 51 and 313; [1974] 2 C.M.L.R. 238.

[78] *Re GEMA (No.1)* [1971] OJ L134; [1971] C.M.L.R. D 35. See also *Bangalter v SACEM*, COMP/C2/37.219; cf. para.28–285, below.

[79] *GVL v Commission* (7/82) [1983] E.C.R. 483.

[80] *Greenwich Film Production v SACEM* (22/79) [1979] E.C.R. 3275.

[81] *Re GEMA (No.I)*, [1971] OJ L134; [1971] C.M.L.R D 35; *GVL* [1983] E.C.R 483; *Basset v SACEM* (402/85) [1983] E.C.R. 483.

[82] Commission Press release IP/04/492.

This would make it possible to ensure that collecting societies are transparent, and that established Community law in the field of intellectual property is properly applied. It would foster the emergence of Community-wide licensing for the exploitation of rights via one-stop shops.

— The development of Digital Rights Management (DRM) systems should, in principle, be based on their acceptance by all stakeholders, including consumers, as well as on copyright policy of the legislature. A prerequisite to ensure Community wide accessibility to DRM systems and services by right holders as well as users and, in particular, consumers, is that DRM systems and services are interoperable.

— For the time being, there is no need for action at Community level with regard to individual rights management as differences in national law have not given rise to concern with respect to the functioning of the Internal Market; national developments will, however, be kept under review.[83] An internal market in the collective management of rights can be best achieved if the monitoring of collecting societies under competition rules is complemented by the establishment of a legislative framework on good governance. Common ground on the following features of collective rights management would be required: the establishment and status of collecting societies (persons who may establish a society, the status thereof, the necessary evidence of efficiency, operability, accounting obligations, and a sufficient number of represented right holders); the relation of collecting societies to users (users must be in a position to contest tariffs, through the courts, specially created mediation tribunals or with the assistance of public authorities); however, use without payment should not be permitted. These principles would promote and safeguard access to protected works on appropriate terms."[84]

It appears, however, that this laissez-faire approach is not supported by the European Parliament. In its Resolution of March 13, 2007, on cross-border collective copyright management,[85] the Parliament stated that the Commission's failure to formally consult with the Parliament prior to issuing its Recommendation was unacceptable,[86] particularly in light of the Parliament's earlier Resolution of January 15, 2004.[87] It further stated[88] that the Commission's Recommendation was an unacceptable approach as it:

"was chosen without prior consultation and without the formal involvement of Parliament and the Council, thereby circumventing the democratic process, especially as the initiative taken has already influenced decisions in the market to the potential detriment of competition and cultural diversity."

As a consequence of these perceived defects in the Commission's approach, the Parliament invited the Commission to present, as soon as possible after a broad consultation, a framework directive to be adopted by the Parliament and the Council.

More recently, as mentioned in para.27–20, above, a public hearing on the

---

[83] COM(96) 568 final, para.2.
[84] COM(96) 568 final, para.3.5.
[85] See fn.49, above.
[86] Recital B.
[87] OJ C92E April 16, 2004, p.293.
[88] Recital C.

governance of collective rights management was held in April 2010. The following month the Commission announced that it will put forward a proposal for a framework Directive on the subject in the course of 2010.[89]

F. RELATIONS WITH FOREIGN COLLECTING SOCIETIES

27–25   **Application of principle of national treatment.** The principle of national treatment under the copyright conventions[90] requires that authors of literary and artistic works protected under the Berne Convention or the Universal Copyright Convention shall enjoy the same rights of protection of their works in all the other States of the Berne Union or UCC as do nationals of those States.[91] Article 5, para.(1) of the Berne Convention defines the principle of national treatment as follows:

> "Authors shall enjoy, in respect of works for which they are protected under this Convention, in countries of the Union other than the country of origin, the rights which their respective laws do now or may hereafter grant to their nationals, as well as the rights specially granted by this Convention."

Article II of the Universal Copyright Convention similarly lays down:

> "Published works of nationals of any Contracting State and works first published in that State shall enjoy in each other Contracting State the same protection as that other State accords to works of its nationals first published in its own territory, as well as the protection especially granted by this Convention."

The principle of national treatment in relation to copyright works and performers' rights is recognised also by the Agreement Establishing the World Trade Organisation (including the Agreement on Trade-Related Aspects of Intellectual Property Rights), 1994,[92] and by the Rome Convention.[93] The United Kingdom implements its obligations under these international agreements by extending protection to the works of nationals of other countries by means of statutory instruments issued pursuant to ss.159 and 208 of the 1988 Act.[94]

27–26   **Need for international co-operation to implement national treatment.** The principle of national treatment was incorporated in the original text of the Berne Convention adopted in 1886. In order for this principle to be fully applied, the need was felt from the early days of the Convention for international cooperation between organisations representing rights owners in different countries in order to enforce the rights of their members not only in their countries of origin but elsewhere. International cooperation with regard to the performing rights of authors and composers of musical works was the first to develop. In the last years

---

[89] Communication on a Digital Agenda for Europe COM(2010)245 of May 19, 2010 p.9. At the time of writing (October 2010), no such proposal has been published. For further information on the Commission's activities in the area, see Ch.24, paras 24–161 and 24–162.

[90] See Ch.23.

[91] WIPO Copyright Treaty art.3 (WCT) of December 20, 1996, and WIPO Performances and Phonograms Treaty art.4 (WPPT) of the same date, also provide for the application of the national treatment principle.

[92] TRIPS Agreement art.1(3): "Members shall accord the treatment provided for in this Agreement to the nationals of other Members."

[93] Rome Convention art.2. However, national treatment is subject to the protection specifically guaranteed, and the limitations specifically provided for, in the Convention (art.2(2)). So far as performing rights in phonograms are concerned, which are protected under art.12, reservations are permitted under art.16 excluding such protection in whole or in part and there is no obligation to give national treatment.

[94] The Copyright and Performances (Application to Other Countries) Order 2008 (SI 2008/677), which entered into force on April 6, 2008, as amended by the Copyright and Performances (Application to Other Countries) (Amendment) Order 2009(SI 2009/ 2745), which entered into force of November 12, 2009 (see Vol.2 C4).

of the nineteenth century and in the first quarter of the twentieth century, performing rights societies were established in nearly all European countries as well as
overseas. Cooperation developed rapidly between these organisations and in
1926 an international confederation of such societies was established, the
International Confederation of Societies of Authors and Composers (CISAC),
which groups 229 societies in 121 countries,[95] representing rights owners of
musical, dramatic, literary and audio-visual works and works of graphic and visual art.[96] It has five Regional Committees (Africa, Asia-Pacific, Canada/USA,
Europe and Ibero-America) to facilitate cooperation between societies in the
same region. Subsequently, as new collecting societies were formed at the
national level to administer rights in new categories of works and in respect also
of new uses of works in response to new technical developments, these new collecting societies also established international non-governmental organisations to
coordinate their activities.

International federations of collecting societies. Thus, most of the collecting   **27–27**
societies operating in the United Kingdom belong to such international federations of societies representing the same category of rights owners in other
countries. The UK societies have reciprocal representation agreements with the
other member societies of such federations for the exercise of rights in their respective members' repertoire. Agreements in the field of performing rights in
works, where the network of collecting societies is the most developed, are based
on the CISAC "Model Contract of Reciprocal Representation between Public
Performance Rights Societies" (the CISAC Model Contract). Under art.3(1) of
that contract:

> "each of the contracting parties undertakes to enforce, within the territory in
> which it operates, the rights of the members of the other party in the same
> way and to the same extent as it does for its own members, and to do this
> within the limits of the legal protection afforded to a foreign work in the
> country where protection is claimed, unless, in virtue of the present contract,
> such protection not being specifically provided in law, it is possible to ensure
> an equivalent protection ...
>
> In particular, each society shall apply to works in the repertoire of the other
> society the same tariffs, methods and means of collection and distribution of
> royalties as those which it applies to works in its own repertoire."[97]

A second powerful international organisation, which groups 53 national societies in 56 countries concerned with the collective administration of authors
rights to authorise the reproduction of works in the form of recordings (sound
recordings or audiovisual fixations), sometimes referred to as mechanical rights,
is the International Bureau of Societies Administering the Rights of Mechanical
Recording and Reproduction (BIEM—*Bureau international des Sociétés gérant
les droits d'enregistrement et de reproduction mécanique*), founded in 1929.[98]
BIEM's principal function is to act as a centralised negotiating body fixing the
conditions for the use of the repertoire of its member societies. Its main negotiating partner is the International Federation of the Phonographic Industry (IFPI),

---

[95] As at October 15, 2010.
[96] The address of CISAC is 20–26 Boulevard du Parc, 92200 Neuilly-sur-Seine, France; *http://
www.cisac.org*. It has regional offices in Budapest, Buenos Aires, Johannesburg and Singapore.
[97] CISAC document "CISAC/40.700, July 1974", updated to July 1, 1974. According to the CISAC
Secretariat, this remains the applicable text.
[98] Membership as at October 15, 2010. The address of BIEM is 20–26 Boulevard du Parc, 92200
Neuilly-sur-Seine, France; *http://www.BIEM.org*.

established in 1933.[99] As at October 15, 2010, IFPI has more than 1,400 members in 66 countries and affiliated industry associations in 45 countries.[100] The contract is renegotiated from time to time and is implemented by means of individual contracts between national BIEM societies and individual producers and is subject to some nationally negotiated variations.

Other international organisations representing collecting societies operating in non-musical fields include AGICOA[101] and IFFRO.[102] The Association for the International Collective Management of Audiovisual Works (AGICOA), established in 1981, groups national associations and societies of producers of audiovisual works. Its purpose is the representation and defence, within collective management, of its members' interests.[103] AGICOA has two principal functions, namely negotiations in cooperation with its national member organisations in respect of the simultaneous, cable retransmission of unchanged broadcasts including the audiovisual works in AGICOA's repertoire, and the collection and distribution of remuneration resulting from such negotiations. The International Federation of Reproduction Rights Organisations (IFRRO) was established in 1988. Its statutory purpose is to facilitate, on an international basis, the collective and/or centralised management of reproduction and other relevant rights in copyright-able works through the cooperation of national Reproduction Rights Organisations (RROs).[104] Its main objectives are: (1) to foster the creation of RROs worldwide; (2) to facilitate formal and informal agreements and relationships between and on behalf of its members; and (3) to increase public and institutional awareness of copyright and the role of RROs in conveying rights and royalties between right-holders and users.

International cooperation between national collecting societies in the music field is promoted and supervised by means of the joint activities of three international non-governmental organisations, the International Federation of Musicians (FIM)[105] (representing mainly session musicians and members of orchestras), the International Federation of Actors (FIA)[106] (representing soloists, conductors and singers) and the International Federation of the Phonographic Industry (IFPI), which represents producers of sound recordings and music videos.

2. THE CONTROL OF COLLECTING SOCIETIES IN THE UNITED KINGDOM

27–28   **Variety of controls over collecting societies.** Control over the operations of col-

---

[99] The IFPI Secretariat is located at 10 Piccadilly, London, W1J 0DD, UK. It has regional offices also in Brussels, Hong Kong, Miami (for Latin America) and Moscow.

[100] The RIAA (Recording Industry Association of America) is affiliated to IFPI. See *http://www.ifpi.org* and *http://www.riaa.org*.

[101] AGICOA has 47 member associations in 30 countries. Its address is 26, Rue de Saint-Jean, 1203 Geneva, Switzerland. *http://www.Agicoa.org*.

[102] IFFRO groups 58 member organisations and 60 associate members in 54 countries. Its address is Rue du Prince Royal 87, B-1050 Brussels, Belgium. *http://www.iffro.org*.

[103] Agicoa By-Laws art.3.

[104] Statutes of the International Federation of Reproduction Rights Organisations art.1.

[105] As at October 15, 2008, FIM, founded in 1948, represents 65 musicians' organisations in 57 countries. It has three regional groups, in Africa, Europe and Latin America. Its objects are to protect and further the economic, social and artistic interests of musicians organised in its member unions. Its address is 21*bis*, Rue Victor Massé, 75009 Paris, France; *http://www.Fim-musicians.com*.

[106] FIA, established in 1952, has 101 member organisations in 73 countries. Its objects are the protection and promotion of the artistic, economic, social and legal interests of the actors, singers, dancers, variety and circus artists, choreographers, directors, professional broadcasters, etc. organised in its affiliated or associated unions. It has offices in London at Guild House, Upper St. Martin's Lane, London, WC2H 9EG, UK and in Brussels at 31 Rue de l'Hôpital, B-1000, Brussels, Belgium; *http://www.fia-actors.com*.

lecting societies is exercised in a variety of ways. First, there is the democratic control exercised by the members of such societies through their governing bodies by means of guarantees for their protection written into the memoranda and articles of association of the various societies. Secondly, the collecting societies' activities are subject to compliance with the copyright licensing provisions of the 1988 Act[107] and to the international obligations of the United Kingdom under the Copyright Conventions.[108] Thirdly, the terms of licences and licensing schemes operated by collecting societies may be referred to the Copyright Tribunal for review, confirmation or variation by actual or potential licensees.[109] Fourthly, collecting societies are subject to powers exercisable under UK domestic legislation to control anti-competitive or monopolistic practices.[110] Finally, as seen above,[111] collecting societies are subject to the EU competition rules. Each of these means of control is discussed briefly below.

A. INTERNAL CONTROLS EXERCISED BY THE MEMBERS OF COLLECTING SOCIETIES

Effect of de facto monopoly position of collecting societies on their members.　**27–29**
The de facto monopoly position of collecting societies prevails generally in respect both of the rights owners, who are the members of the organisations, and of the users. Rights owners, as a rule, do not have any choice other than to entrust the administration of their rights to the particular collecting society representing their respective category of rights owner. For this reason, as seen above,[112] in some countries there is government supervision of the establishment and operation of collecting societies in order to guarantee their effective and proper operation for the benefit of their members. In the United Kingdom, there are no legislative provisions making the establishment or recognition of collecting societies conditional on the approval of a government department. Collecting societies are private companies, established and controlled by their members and subject to the requirements of UK company law, including the obligations imposed thereby on the directors of companies.

The rights owners who make up the membership of collecting societies have the ability to influence the way in which their rights are administered and to control the operating methods of such societies, provided that certain guarantees to that effect are written into the constitutions of the collecting societies in question. There should be guarantees therefore for the rights owners who are members of any given society to participate democratically in the policy making process of the society's operations. In conformity with EU law, members should retain the option of managing certain rights themselves, where appropriate, or of mandating the society to administer them on their behalf.[113] Decisions concerning terms of membership, and the methods and rules of monitoring uses of works, collecting and distributing remuneration and enforcing rights should be taken by all the individual rights owners represented by the society, or by bodies representing them. Members should also have access to regular, full and detailed information enabling them to judge whether the rules are being correctly applied, whether the costs of administration are reasonable and whether the distribution of remuneration is actually taking place as prescribed. There is also a need for appeal

---

[107] CDPA 1988 Ch.VII ss.116–144.
[108] See Ch.24 and paras 28–06 et seq. below.
[109] CDPA 1988 Ch.VII ss. 145–152.
[110] CDPA 1988 Ch.VII s.144; and see paras 27–31, 28–54 and 28–286, et seq., below.
[111] See paras 27–20 et seq., above and 28–180 et seq., and in particular, para.28–285, below.
[112] See para.27–16.
[113] *GEMA (No.1)* [1971] OJ L134; [1971] C.M.L.R. D35.

procedures enabling members to challenge distributions on the ground that the distribution policies of the society have been incorrectly implemented. Members should also expressly authorise any decisions to use fees collected by their society to undertake additional activities for the defence and promotion of their members' interests, such as, for example, anti-piracy campaigns or the promotion of cultural or social activities.

27–30 **Monopolies and Mergers Commission recommendations concerning rights of members.** Guidance to collecting societies with regard to maintaining correct relations with their members emerged following a 1995 report of the Monopolies and Mergers Commission ("MMC")[114] into the practices of the PRS. In 1994, complaints that the PRS was operating against the interests of certain of its members were referred to the MMC. Complaints had been received from writers of "less popular" forms of music to the effect that: they were receiving inadequate royalty payments; under the Society's rules, they lacked sufficient representation to be able to pursue their interests effectively; and the revenue policies adopted by PRS unduly favoured the writers and publishers of "more popular" forms of music. Criticisms were also made by some of the highest-earning members of the Society about the exclusive nature of their assignment of performing rights to the Society and the restrictions applied to members who wished to leave. Concerns were also raised about the amounts spent on administration and whether the PRS was managed efficiently.[115] In November 1995, the MMC issued a report into the PRS' activities, in which it came to a number of conclusions concerning its management practices and decided that the PRS had failed to provide adequate information to its members and to operate with sufficient transparency. It had failed to make clear to its members: its responsibilities to them, its policies and procedures and the limitations of its services; how it allocated costs; and their right to self-administer certain performance rights in accordance with the *GEMA* decision.[116] The PRS had further failed to consult the membership adequately in order to allow them to contribute to policy-making and to choose whether they wished cross-subsidies from one group of members to another to occur or not. It had also failed to ensure that its members had a right of appeal in matters of dispute to deal with their grievances and had refused to allow members to administer their own rights in respect of live performances. To remedy these deficiencies, the MMC made a series of recommendations[117] to strengthen the position and influence of members within the PRS, including: the establishment of an Appeals Board to resolve disputes which members may have from time to time with the PRS about their personal rights; the introduction of a formal consultative process to take members' views on proposed changes in policy or strategy; the amendment of voting rules to allow writer members to send representatives to speak and vote for them at meetings; amendment of the Articles of Association to allow self-administration of the live performance right

---

[114] Which was replaced, from April 1, 1999, by the Competition Commission.

[115] Performing Rights: A report on the supply in the United Kingdom of the services of administering performing rights and film synchronisation rights, (Cm.3147) London, HMSO, paras 2.2 and 2.3. Note that the IMMC has in the meantime been replaced by the Competition Commission, established by the Competition Act 1998, see para.28–287, below.

[116] These rights are listed in the MMC Report, (Cm.3147) HMSO, p.52, as follows: the general performing right; the broadcasting right; the public performing right of broadcast works; the televising right; the public performing right of televised works; the right of cinematographic exhibition; the right of mechanical reproduction and diffusion; the public performing right of mechanically reproduced works; the cinematographic production right; the right to produce, reproduce and diffuse on video tape; the public performing right of works reproduced on video tape; and the exploitation rights resulting from technical development or future change in the law. See *Re GEMA (No.1)* [1971] OJ L134/15; [1971] C.M.L.R. D35; *Re GEMA (No.2)* [1972] OJ L182/24; [1972] C.M.L.R. D115. See further para.28–285, below.

[117] MMC Report, (Cm. 3147) HMSO, summary of recommendations, pp.34–36.

and to make it clear that members have the right to self-administer the categories of performing rights specified in the *GEMA* decision.[118]

The PRS Memorandum and Articles of Association were revised in 1995 to permit self-administration of certain performance rights to take account of the MMC's recommendations. These recommendations may also be expected to serve as guidelines for the operational practices of other UK collecting societies in the future.

B. PUBLIC CONTROL OF COLLECTING SOCIETIES IN THE UNITED KINGDOM

Public control of collecting societies in the public interest. As seen above,[119]   **27–31**
some measure of public control over the activities of collecting societies is now considered to be necessary in the public interest. Some mechanism is required to guard against the possibility that monopoly rights are abused in the conditions demanded for licensing their use, and to prevent the customer suffering from unjustifiably high prices, since collecting societies may in some cases control worldwide repertoires over which they exercise a de facto monopoly in any given country.

The position prior to the 1956 Act. Prior to the 1956 Act, there were no controls   **27–32**
over the activities of collecting societies of which there were only four operating at the time (the PRS, MCPS, PPL and the Sound Film Music Bureau). The PRS and PPL were then, as now, concerned respectively with the control of performing rights in musical works and sound recordings. The other two were solely concerned with the exercise of the right to record the music under their control.

Brussels Act of the Berne Convention. The exclusive right of the author to au-   **27–33**
thorise the public performance and transmission of dramatic, dramatico-musical or musical works was formally established in the Berne Convention in a new text of art.11 at the Brussels Conference in 1948.[120] At the time, the UK delegation made the following Declaration:

> "The United Kingdom Delegation accepts the provisions of Article 11 of the Convention on the understanding that His Majesty's Government remains free to enact such legislation as it may consider necessary in the public interest to prevent or deal with any abuse of the monopoly rights conferred upon owners of copyright by the law of the United Kingdom."[121]

This declaration by the United Kingdom would appear to have been prompted by representations made to it by a number of organisations as regards the licensing practices of PRS and PPL.[122] Complaints were also made to the 1952 Copyright Committee,[123] to the effect that these two societies had exercised their rights to fix and to alter their tariffs of charges in an arbitrary way, and that one of them had unjustifiably withheld its licences or only issued them subject to unduly re-

---

[118] cf. fn.81.
[119] See para.27–15.
[120] These rights were made subject, however, to minor reservations allowing Member States to preserve their law on exceptions covering performances at religious ceremonies and performances by military bands at public fêtes.
[121] See Records of the Brussels Conference June 5–26, 1948, *Documents de la Conférence, Bureau de l'Union internationale pour la protection des oeuvres littéraires et artistiques*, Berne, 1951, pp.82 and 264. See also S. Ricketson, *The Berne Convention for the Protection of Literary and Artistic Works 1886–1986* (London: Sweet & Maxwell) para.3.43.
[122] Report of the Gregory Committee, HMSO 1952 (Cmd. 8662), Pt VIII, para.205.
[123] Report of the Gregory Committee, HMSO 1952 (Cmd. 8662), Pt VII, paras 137 et seq. and see Pt VIII, paras 204 et seq.

strictive conditions.[124] In view of the Government Declaration made at Brussels, it was open to the Gregory Committee, notwithstanding that it was recommending adherence to the Brussels Act of the Berne Convention, to make proposals for the compulsory adjustment of tariffs charged by the copyright organisations. One method suggested was that of compulsory arbitration, but this did not seem wholly satisfactory, in that it was necessary to envisage not only disputes between a collecting society and organisations representing performers, but also cases where individual persons were aggrieved, and moreover, what was really required was some method of arriving at tariffs which would be binding not only between the parties, but also in respect of any other persons wishing to exercise similar rights. The Committee therefore proposed that a standing tribunal should be established to decide disputes between collecting societies and would-be users of controlled works.[125] This proposal was accepted by the legislature and was embodied in ss.23 to 30 of the 1956 Act.

27–34 **Performing Right Tribunal.** Section 23 of the 1956 Act established the Performing Right Tribunal (PRT) with the jurisdiction conferred by the provisions of the 1956 Act.[126] The PRT had two principal functions.[127] The first was to confirm or vary licence schemes put into operation by organisations under which licences were to be granted to the public in certain classes of cases.[128] The second was to deal with applications by individuals who were aggrieved, either because an organisation operating a licence scheme refused or failed to grant the individual a licence in accordance with the scheme, or to procure the grant to him of such a licence, or because the individual claimed that he required a licence in a case where there was no applicable licence scheme and the organisation refused or failed to grant him a licence, or the terms and conditions proposed were unreasonable.[129] The PRT was concerned with licences dealing with only three types of right. First, the right to perform in public, broadcast or diffuse, a literary, dramatic or musical work or an adaptation thereof.[130] Secondly, the right to cause a sound recording to be heard in public or to be broadcast.[131] Thirdly, the right to cause a television broadcast to be seen or heard in public.[132] The rights, therefore, covered in effect the whole of the performing and broadcasting rights conferred by the 1956 Act, other than the right to include an artistic work in a television broadcast, the right to cause a film to be seen or heard in public or to be broadcast, and the right to re-broadcast a sound or television broadcast.

27–35 **Proposals for reform.** The functions of the PRT were considered by the Whitford Committee,[133] which recommended that it should be given jurisdiction over a wider range of matters, including reprographic licences, video recording, licences to use music on film soundtracks, and copyright clearances where the copyright owner cannot be traced.[134] The Committee also proposed that the tribunal's name should be changed to the Copyright Tribunal, in view of the recommended increase in its jurisdiction. The 1986 White Paper, in its belated

---

[124] Report of the Gregory Committee, HMSO 1952 (Cmd. 8662), paras 204 and 205.
[125] Report of the Gregory Committee, HMSO 1952 (Cmd. 8662), paras 210 et seq.
[126] 1956 Act ss.24–27A.
[127] 1956 Act s.24(1).
[128] 1956 Act ss.25 and 26.
[129] 1956 Act ss.27(1) and (2) and 27A.
[130] 1956 Act s.24(2)(a); a right (as to musical works and associated works) usually controlled by PRS.
[131] 1956 Act s.24(2)(b) a right usually controlled by PPL.
[132] 1956 Act s.24(2)(c) a right controlled by broadcasting organisations, such as the BBC.
[133] Report of the Committee to consider the Law on Copyright and Designs, HMSO, March 1977 (Cmnd.6732).
[134] Cmnd.6732, paras 788–790.

response to the Committee's report, generally followed these recommendations in relation to the change of name of the tribunal and the extension of its functions,[135] and also made recommendations as to the introduction of more specific criteria for the tribunal to base its decisions on, and for improvements in the procedure before the tribunal. These recommendations were enacted in the 1988 Act, Ch.VIII of which established the Copyright Tribunal as the successor to the PRT.

C. The Copyright Tribunal

The Copyright Tribunal. The constitution of the Copyright Tribunal established   **27–36** under the 1988 Act is described elsewhere,[136] as also is its procedure under the Copyright Tribunal Rules 1989.[137] The Copyright Tribunal has been given an extended jurisdiction, covering not only the functions previously carried out by the PRT, but also a number of new specific functions introduced by the 1988 Act, as amended by the Broadcasting Act 1990. Since the 1988 Act came into force, the functions of the Copyright Tribunal have more than doubled as a result of new legislation, including inter alia the Broadcasting Act 1996 and the Copyright and Related Rights Regulations 1996 and 2003.[138] Broadly, the Tribunal's jurisdiction is such that anyone who has unreasonably been refused a licence by a collecting society or considers the terms of an offered licence to be unreasonable may refer the matter to the Tribunal. It should be noted that the Tribunal's jurisdiction does not extend to all copyright licences. It would be contrary to the Berne Convention to subject the exercise of all the exclusive rights of authors of literary, dramatic, musical and artistic works and films to public control by the Tribunal. Licences offered by individual authors do not fall within the Tribunal's jurisdiction. Thus, as regards the works protected by the Berne Convention, jurisdiction relates to licences and schemes of a licensing body, such as a collecting society, having as its main object the negotiating or granting of licences, including licences covering works of more than one author in relation to copying the work, rental or lending of copies of the work to the public, performing, showing or playing the work in public, or communicating the work to the public. In summary, the proceedings heard by the Tribunal and which concern collecting societies are inter alia proceedings brought by, or on behalf of, actual or potential licensees, relating to the following: applications to determine remuneration payable with respect to cable re transmission and rental; proposed or existing licensing schemes[139]; entitlement to a licence under licensing scheme[140]; licensing by a licensing body[141]; coverage of a licensing scheme or licence in respect of reprographic copying by an educational establishment[142]; terms of a copyright licence available as of right consequent on the exercise of their powers by the Secretary of State, the Office of Fair Trading and the Competition Commission[143] and applications to settle the terms of payment as to the reasonableness of any condition

---

[135] Cmnd.9712 (1986) Ch.18, broadly following proposals set out in the 1981 Green Paper, Cmnd. 8302.

[136] See para.28–81, below.

[137] See paras 28–154, et seq., below.

[138] The Copyright Tribunal issued a decision dated February 26, 2008, concerning the scope of the Tribunal's new jurisdiction following the amendments to the CDPA 1988 made in 2003 (CT 91/05, CT 92/05 and CT 93/05 Appeal of Phonographic Performance Limited). The decision is under appeal.

[139] CDPA 1988 ss.73(4), 73A, 118, 119 and 120; and see further paras 28–89, et seq., below.

[140] CDPA 1988 ss.121 and 122; and see further paras 28 98, et seq., below.

[141] CDPA 1988 ss.125, 126 and 127; and see further paras 28–101, et seq., below.

[142] CDPA 1988 s.139; and see further para.28–124, below.

[143] CDPA 1988 s.144(4); and see further para.28–325, below.

in relation to the use as of right of sound recordings in broadcasts or cable programme services.[144] The Tribunal's jurisdiction also extends to applications
concerning the exercise and licensing of the rights of performers and the determination of royalties and equitable remuneration payable in relation thereto.[145]

Following a consultation by the Intellectual Property Office which considered
whether improvements could be made to the way in which the Copyright Tribunal
works, new rules governing its procedure came into force on April 6, 2010.[146]
Other matters recommended by this consultation were that: the fees of the CT
should be abolished; the emphasis should be on written rather than oral evidence;
expert evidence should be allowed only if strictly necessary; Alternative Dispute
Resolution (ADR) should be used when appropriate; the CT should have a permanent staff of two located at permanent premises to be made available at the offices of the Intellectual Property Office in London; the chairman should be called
the President and the position should be salaried and filled by an open recruit-
ment exercise; there should be no restriction on the number of deputy chairmen
but lay members should be abolished. On October 18, 2010, the Department for
Business, Innovation and Skills announced that the Copyright Tribunal was to
merge with the Tribunals service with the intention of achieving greater
efficiencies.

D. UNITED KINGDOM COMPETITION LAW

27–37   **The Office of Fair Trading and the Competition Commission**. The role of
these bodies under the UK legislation aimed at anti-competitive practices is
discussed in Ch.28.[147] Such legislation has particular application to collecting societies as regards both their dealings with their members and with their
licensees.[148]

E. EU LAW

27–38   **Application of EU Competition Law.** The application of EU competition law to
the exercise of intellectual property rights is discussed elsewhere.[149] Again, such
law has particular application to collecting societies, as regards their dealings
both with their members and with their licensees.[150]

3. THE FUTURE OF COLLECTING SOCIETIES

A. THE IMPACT OF TECHNICAL DEVELOPMENT AND THE INFORMATION SOCIETY ON COLLECTING SOCIETIES AND THE MARKET

27–39   **The Information Society.**
"The world is undergoing a technological revolution and entering the age of
the Information Society. The combination of information technology and
high-speed communications is breaking down the traditional barriers to the
movement of information (distance, location, time and volume) at an un-

---

[144] CDPA 1988 ss.135D, 135E and 135F, introduced into the CDPA 1988 and into CDPA 1988
s.149 by amendment of the Broadcasting Act 1990 s.175(1) and (2); see further paras 28–25 et
seq., below.
[145] See para.28–83, below.
[146] For which, see para.28–154, below.
[147] See paras 28–287 et seq., below.
[148] See paras 28–300, et seq.
[149] See paras 28–181, et seq., below.
[150] See paras 28–202 and 28–285, et seq., below.

precedented rate. Information technology is becoming widely accessible and as a result a vast new range of applications and opportunities is arising".[151]

As the 1996 Select Committee of the House of Lords predicted, these developments have exacerbated the well-established tensions between copyright owners and those who wish to use works subject to copyright. The internet has increased these problems exponentially. A networked, digital environment making use of digital recording and transmission techniques gives users access to large quantities of material for inspection, down-loading, storing, printing and dissemination.[152] Copyright law has changed over the years in response to technical development and the copyright owners and their collecting societies are in the process of responding to these latest changes, which present not so much new problems as problems of scale and technical control to the copyright owner.

Fifteen years later, the Monti Report to the President of the European Commission "A New Strategy for the Single Market" published in May 2010[153] describes the present situation as follows:

"Digital technologies are radically transforming the way we live, work and interact. The propagation of digital technology is a spontaneous process of innovation and transformation... Yet, regulatory and social conditions influence the speed and extent of the uptake of new technologies and the spread of the benefits of a digital economy. Europe is moving at a slower speed than the US. A number of obstacles reduce the capacity of industry in Europe to innovate and generate value added in the digital sphere: the fragmentation of online markets, **ill-adapted intellectual property legislation,** the lack of high-speed transmission infrastructure and the lack of digital skills. Many of these obstacles point to a simple cause: a lack of a digital single market [emphasis added].[154]

The report recommends further harmonisation of copyright, creation of an EU copyright title, and an EU framework for copyright clearance and management.[155]

The achievement of a single market in the European Union for digital online content is a laudable aim but in pursuing its goals the European Commission needs to maintain cooperation and trust of right owners and the collecting societies. Digitisation and the internet make possible the dissemination of copyright works and open up new markets. However, they also bring challenges. Digital technology makes copying much easier and research in the UK estimates that around 25 per cent of UK internet users engaged in online piracy in 2007.[156] The collecting societies of Europe have been transforming their practices in response to pressure from the European Union and from national governments to facilitate pan-European licensing and these efforts of which an overview is given at paras 27–43 and 27–45, below should be respected and supported.

---

[151] House of Lords, Select Committee on Science and Technology, report entitled *Information Society: Agenda for Action in the United Kingdom*, HL Paper 77, See ss.1995–96, 5th Report, July 1996, para.1.6.

[152] House of Lords, Select Committee on Science and Technology, report entitled *Information Society: Agenda for Action in the United Kingdom*, HL Paper 77, See ss.1995–96, 5th Report, July 1996, paras 2.18 and 2.19.

[153] "A New Strategy for the Single Market—At the Service of Europe's Economy and Society", report to the President of the European Commission, by Mario Monti, May 9, 2010.

[154] Monti Report, p.44.

[155] Monti Report, p.46.

[156] "© the Future—Developing a Copyright Agenda for the 21st Century", Intellectual Property Office, December 2008, p.2.

27–40   **Expansion of fields of collective administration.** As already discussed,[157] collective administration is justified when use of protected works takes place on such a scale and in such circumstances that it is impractical for the rights owners and the users to negotiate on an individual basis. In recent years, the fields in which individual exercise of rights have become impractical or impossible have been constantly expanding as a result of technical developments which have led to new uses and methods of exploitation of works. Collective administration by performing rights societies no longer applies only in the field of music but has expanded to embrace rental rights, broadcasting rights, satellite transmission and cable distribution of broadcasts and audiovisual works. Under the increasing pressure of technical developments, other categories of rights owners have established collective licensing systems to control repeated, high volume uses; one example is the blanket licensing of the reprographic copying of literary works; another is the administration of remuneration schemes for private copying where these are in place. Film producers have also established mechanisms for negotiating collectively as regards cable television use. Most recently, the artist's resale right has been introduced into the law of the United Kingdom; this right may only be exercised through a collecting society.[158] In the European Union there are other examples of rights which by law may only be exercised through collecting societies, in particular, rights to remuneration for reprography and private copying.

27–41   **The impact of digital technology on the market.** Since the beginning of the 1990s, the landscape of the market for copyright works has changed dramatically. New methods of exploitation of protected works have developed rapidly and the digital and communications revolution continues to transform the ways in which works are made available to the public. Digital storage media has been essential to the growth of e-Commerce in digital goods but it is also used to store large quantities of copyright infringing material. In the United Kingdom, the BBC and commercial broadcasters are entering the digital broadcasting market and the consumer already has access via his computer and telephone to the internet,[159] from which he is able to obtain access to copyright works of all kinds to use, store, transmit and copy at will. As the 2003 WIPO Report has put it:

> "The situation becomes even more problematic when the personal computer is linked to the internet, because the owner's compilations can then be made available to anyone else on a file-sharing network. ... All content is now vulnerable to illegal copying and distribution over the internet, irrespective of media type".[160]

Meanwhile, digital technology also makes possible widespread, interactive legitimate services making all kinds of works available on a commercial basis to consumers. Such digital services are beginning to get established on the internet,, which these days operates worldwide and reaches over 1.46 billion people.[161] Thus, the packaged product, the CD or video cassette, for example, is fast being

---

[157] See para.27–02, above.

[158] The Artist's Resale Right Regulations 2006 (SI 2006/346) reg.14.

[159] Over two million people accessed the internet in the year to August 1995, para.3.39. By 2002, it was estimated that about 10 per cent of the world's population was online, representing more than 605 million users. It was also predicted that by 2005 the world online population could reach one billion (cf. *Intellectual Property on the internet: A Survey of Issues*, WIPO, December 2002, para.7.

[160] Cunard, Hill and Barlas, "Current Developments in the Field of Digital Rights Management", WIPO doc. SCCR/10/2, August 1, 2003, paras 1.2.3 and 1.2.6. See also P. Gilliéron, "Collecting Societies and the Digital Environment" [2006] I.I.C. 939.

[161] On June 30, 2008, and based on figures from, amongst others Nielsen/Netratings and the International Telecommunications Union, the website *http://www.internetworldstats.com/ stats.htm* estimated that the internet was used by 1.46 billion people worldwide.

displaced by delivery to the consumer by electronic means in interactive services such as video-on-demand, pay-per-view and musical juke boxes online. In the new electronic networks, households have direct access to multimedia works and services and interactive technology enables the consumer to play an active role; they are no longer passive recipients of programmes but are able to communicate directly with the distribution network, to select their favourite films and music from a wide range of databases to copy and even edit them. In this fast moving environment the copyright system is hard pressed to keep up.

The challenge to collecting societies. The exact way in which the information society and the EU digital single market will develop over the next decades cannot be predicted with any certainty. Collecting societies are facing the challenge of monitoring and securing reward for the use of their members' works in all these new services. It is apparent, however, that an important element for the successful development of the information society will be the ability of right owners to control access to protected works by means of technological copy protection measures and to monitor and obtain payment for use of such works through digital rights management (DRM) techniques. The role, organisation and operation of collecting societies in the management of rights must evolve to adapt to this new environment and, as seen above,[162] the societies are under pressure to do so. "The challenge is both to secure reward for use and also to ensure that securing that reward is for the users as fast, simple and painless as possible."[163] Moreover, it is plain that international cooperation between collecting societies will play a vital role in meeting this challenge. "No one country can protect the intellectual property of its citizens satisfactorily: global agreement and enforcement will be ever more necessary in the digital age,"[164] and this applies not only to the legislative framework for copyright but also to collective administration. A further challenge to right owners and collecting societies is the problem of reconciling the use of technological protection measures and rights management information with the need to respect the limitations and exceptions provided for by copyright legislation. Technical protection measures and rights management systems are crucial to a secure and balanced distribution of content in the electronic environment and, following the adoption of the 1996 WIPO Internet Treaties,[165] have found wide acceptance in national legislation. However, the Internet Treaties and, indeed, the Information Society Directive,[166] also establish principles for the development of limitations and exceptions in national legislation, laying the ground work for adaptation of limitations and exceptions to the digital environment. Future avenues of work towards facilitating the coexistence of limitations and technological measures have been identified in a recent WIPO Study.[167]

27–42

Supranational central licensing schemes. Hitherto, collective licensing has

27–43

---

[162] See para.27–40, above.
[163] C. Clark, *The Copyright Environment for the Publisher in the Digital World* (International Publishers' Association: March 1996). See also T.C. Vinje, "A Brave New World of Technical Protection Systems: Will there Still Be Room for Copyright?" [1996] 8 E.I.P.R. 431. See also, B. Hugenholtz, (ed.) *The Future of Copyright in a Digital Environment* (The Hague: Kluwer, 1996) and I.A.Stamatoudi and P.L.C. Torremans (eds) *Copyright in the New Digitals, London, Environment*, (London: Sweet & Maxwell, 2000).
[164] House of Lords Select Committee Report, Information Society: Agenda for Action in the United Kingdom, HL Paper 77, para.5.45.
[165] See Ch.23, above.
[166] See Ch.24, above.
[167] N. Garnett, *Automated Rights Management Systems and Copyright Limitations and Exceptions* WIPO document SCCR/14/5, April 27, 2006. See also P. Akester, *A Practical Guide to Digital Copyright Law* (London: Sweet & Maxwell, 2008) and "The new challenges of striking the right balance between copyright protection and access to knowledge, information and culture" [2010] E.I.P.R. 372.

been effected mainly at national level by national societies separately representing the traditional sectors of music, text and picture, with foreign repertoire being
protected by means of reciprocal representation agreements with sister collecting
societies in other countries. However, the harmonisation of copyright and related
rights in the European Union achieved so far[168] has paved the way, for example,
for a real single market in satellite broadcasting and cable distribution and
national boundaries are irrelevant in the context of the internet and the information society. The traditional territorial basis for the operations of collecting societies is becoming outdated and inappropriate and the desirability of supranational
or pan-European central licensing schemes being established to clear rights is
increasingly recognised.

> "In the long term it is difficult to see the need for separate national societies
> in each Community Member State. A single community society could
> achieve the same results more efficiently than the present over-complex
> structure, and might not be significantly less competitive."[169]

The suggestion has even been made that a single, worldwide, international collecting society for rights in works in digital form should be founded to license all
repertoires on a central basis to avoid compatibility problems. "One central
institution will then install the international numbering system, provide necessary
information on the product and licensing terms, collect and distribute royalties
and deliver digital copies of the work".[170] The Recommendation of October 18,
2005, on cross-border management of copyright and related rights for legitimate
online music services (on which see paras 27–20 and 27–22, above) had as its
aim to promote collective licensing across borders.[171]

27–44   **Multimedia works.** Multimedia works pose a particular problem for collective
administration due to the large number of licences required to produce them.
They bring together in one product, text, music and images, all these components
having different rights owners from whom licences have to be obtained by the
maker of the multimedia work. The multimedia work, moreover, is itself a work
in its own right and has an author or producer of its own, the natural or legal
person who created it, and the user must obtain a licence from him.[172] The rights
in the various components have traditionally been represented by different collecting societies divided according to the traditional distinctions between music,
text and image. To cope with the changing situation, it has been suggested that
"one-stop-shops" be established by rights owners to represent them all and facilitate access to works. As the Commission has suggested:

> "With the development of the Information Society, currently adequate
> means of administering rights must be reassessed. In particular, the question
> must be addressed of whether and how copyright administration needs to be
> rationalised in view of the possibilities created by digital technology for
> creating complex works or other protected matter, such as multimedia

---

[168] See Ch.24, above.

[169] Temple Lang J., "Media, Multimedia and European Community Antitrust Law", paper delivered
at 24th Annual Conference of the Fordham Corporate Law Institute on International Antitrust
Law and Policy, October 16–17, 1997.

[170] Hoeren, T., "An assessment of long-term solutions in the context of copyright and electronic
delivery systems and multimedia products", European Commission DG XIII E-1, document EUR
16069 EN, pp.35 et seq., and 50.

[171] 2005/737/EC.

[172] art.5 of the new WIPO Copyright Treaty of December 20, 1996, contains the following provision
relating to compilations of data, which is applicable to multimedia works: "Compilations of data
or other material, in any form, which by reason of the selection or arrangement of their contents
constitute intellectual creations, are protected as such. This protection does not extend to the data
or the material itself and is without prejudice to any copyright subsisting in the data or material
contained in the compilation."

products or services. In fact, the creation and exploitation of multimedia products and services may imply that the individual exercise of rights will become even less practicable than it is today due to the great number of new or pre-existing works, productions and uses involved. This may call for new forms of centralised administration which facilitate rights management or, in some cases, for more collective management."[173]

The concept of a one-stop-shop. In this context it is worth noting that within the European Union a number of national one-stop-shops have been set up by coalitions of national collecting societies which have pooled their resources and repertoires in new joint representative organisations, the purpose of which is to manage the rights of their members in multimedia works or, in the case of the music industry, for example, to licence joint repertoires for cross-border use.[174] The Commission has suggested that such alliances: **27–45**

> "would give authors, performers and also editor/producers, a tool which would allow them to identify the origin of very diverse works, by bringing together the repertoires which might be valuable to the new technologies. Users could obtain information which interested them, such as the level of the fees and the rights given. Such provision of information could be possible if different societies operated together and combined their databases and systems if identification were progressively introduced".[175]

Such one-stop-shops are envisaged as being the means to centralise the identification of individual rights; they would not replace the collecting societies but would make the current system more efficient and easier to deal with for the user. In the past, the European Commission took the view that the creation and development of one-stop-shops for "Multimedia Rights Clearance Systems" should be left to the market and limited itself to supporting studies and pilot projects financially.[176] The collecting societies responded to the need for one-stop-shops by means of reciprocal representation agreements so that each authors' society offered in its territory a one-stop-shop for users to obtain licences for a worldwide repertoire from a single source. The European Commission, however, now argues that in the online environment it is appropriate to provide for multi-territorial licensing and that there should be freedom to provide collective management services across national borders. This entails that right holders are able to freely appoint the collective rights manager of their choice for the management of the rights necessary to operate legitimate online music services across the European Union. As the Commission Recommendation on collective cross-border management of copyright and related rights for legitimate online music services makes clear:

> "That right implies the possibility to entrust or transfer all or a part of the online rights to another collective rights manager irrespective of the member

---

[173] Communication from the Commission: Follow-up to the Green Paper on Copyright and Related Rights in the Information Society, COM(96) 568 final, Brussels, November 20, 1996, p.24.

[174] These new coalitions include: SESAM (France); *Clearingstelle Multimedia* (CMMV GmbH) (Germany); *Centrum voor Dienstveerlening Auteurs-en aanverwante rechten* (CEDAR) (Netherlands); *Oficina Multimedia* (OM) (Spain); *Copyswede* (Sweden) and *KOPIOSTO* (Finland). For further information on these developments, see Clark, C. and Koskinen-Olsson, T., "New Alternatives for Centralised Management One-Stop-Shops—A Review", paper delivered at the WIPO International Forum on the Exercise and Management of Copyright and Neighbouring Rights in the Face of the Challenges of Digital Technology, Seville, May 1997. For an account of the Commission's recent decision in relation to a new one-stop licensing scheme for simulcasts, see para.28–221.

[175] Commission Green Paper on Copyright and Related Rights in the Information Society COM(95) 382 final, Brussels, July 19, 1995, p.76.

[176] See M. Shippan, "Purchase and Licensing of Digital Rights: The VERDI Project and the Clearing of Multimedia Rights in Europe" [2000] E.I.P.R. 24; *Multimedia Rights Clearance Systems* (European Commission, DG XIII/E).

state of residence or the nationality of either the collective rights manager or the rights holder."[177]

B. EU Approach to the Role of Collecting Societies in the Information Society

27–46   **The approach of the European Union.** As seen above, the European Union has already addressed the issue of collective management in several EU instruments, endorsing their role in rights management and in some situations providing for mandatory rights administration by collecting societies, as in the Satellite and Cable Directive.[178] In its "Follow-up to the Green Paper on Copyright and Related Rights in the Information Society", the Commission stated:

> "It seems essential that the Single Market provides both right holders and users with similar and transparent conditions (level playing field) for the exploitation/management of rights, both with respect to individual and collective licensing conditions."[179]

This need for a "level playing field" approach has been reflected in the Commission's studies and reports on the subject ever since but the need for and role of collecting societies has not been called into question, as such. The Commission has been concerned rather with the governance of the societies and facilitating cross-border licensing as demonstrated by the adoption of the Recommendation on collective cross-border management of copyright and related rights for legitimate online music services[180] which, as described above in paras 27–20 and 27–22, made clear that the European Commission's policy is to encourage multi-territorial licensing by pan-European collecting societies. Since the adoption of the Recommendation in 2005, ever more attention has been given to the need for the European Union to establish a Single Digital Market in Europe and the spotlight has been put on the role of collecting societies in this context.[181]

In January 2007, the Commission announced its intention to assess the development of Europe's online music sector in the light of the Recommendation and issued an invitation to Member States and collective rights managers to report to the Commission by July 1, 2007, on measures they had taken in relation to the recommendation and on the management, at Community level, of copyright and related rights for the provision of legitimate online music services. Meanwhile, the Commission has issued a summary report of the results of the monitoring of the Recommendation and of current EU-wide licensing initiatives; it noted that a nascent market for EU-wide licensing of music for online services is being established.[182] The Commission stated that it would follow further developments

---

[177] Recommendation 2005/737/EC, recitals 9 and 10.

[178] See paras 27–21 et seq., above. See also Chs 24 and 28.

[179] Follow-up to the Green Paper, p.26.

[180] See paras 27–20, 27–22 and 27–43, above.

[181] On this subject, see V. Dehin, "The future of legal online music services in the European Union: a review of the EU Commission's recent initiatives in cross-border copyright management", [2010] E.I.P.R. 220.

[182] In April 2007, IFPI announced that in response to the 2005 Recommendation arrangements had been put in place between IFPI and more than 40 collecting societies representing the record industry to facilitate online music and broadcasting services. Two new licensing agreements will create the framework for collective licensing of producers' rights for certain streaming and podcast services across several markets. In practice, the participating collecting societies will be able to license rights in each others' territories and repertoire. Online music services and broadcasters established in the EEA will be able to approach any European society for a licence, which will enable them to approach and choose the society they consider provides the best service for their needs. Users will continue also to have the option to approach record companies directly for a licence.

and repeat the monitoring should a clear need to do so arise.[183] From the outset the Commission had made it clear that if it considered that sufficient progress was not being made, legislation might be necessary.

A digital agenda for Europe. The soft law approach of the Recommendation **27–47** has now been abandoned by the Commission.

The recent Monti Report published in May 2010, already referred to in para.27–39, above, views the present fragmentation along national borders of rights clearance mechanisms as a "bottleneck" still hampering the rapid development of the EU goal of a single market for online digital content. The Report puts the problem as follows:

> "The European markets for online digital content are still underdeveloped as the complexity and lack of transparency of the copyright regime creates an unfavourable business environment. It is urgent to simplify copyright clearance and management by facilitating pan-European content licensing, by developing EU-wide copyright rules, **including a framework for digital rights management**" [emphasis added].[184]

The Monti report was followed up by a Commission document "A Digital Agenda for Europe"[185] which states that it is time for a new single market to deliver the benefits of the digital era.

> "The internet is borderless, but online markets, both globally and in the EU, are still separated by multiple barriers affecting not only access to pan-European telecom services but also to what should be global internet services and content. This is untenable. First, the creation of attractive online content and services and its free circulation inside the EU and across its borders are fundamental to stimulate the virtuous cycle of demand. However, persistent fragmentation is stifling Europe's competitiveness in the digital economy. …The single market therefore needs a fundamental update to bring it into the internet era".

One aim of the Commission in this connection is to open up access to content online, on the basis that consumers expect to be able to access content online at least as effectively as in the offline world. The lack of a unified market in the content sector holds the European Union back, because (it is said) to set up a pan-European online music store it would be necessary to negotiate with numerous rights management societies based in 27 countries. Another example given is that consumers can buy CDs in every shop but are often unable to buy music from on-line platforms across the European Union because rights are licensed on a national basis. This, the Commission suggests, compares unfavourably with the business environment in the USA.[186]

Proposed framework Directive on collective rights management. The Com- **27–48** munication states that one of the key actions of the Commission in the coming year will, therefore, be to take action to simplify copyright clearance, management and cross-border licensing by enhancing the governance, transparency and pan-European licensing for (online) rights management by means of a framework Directive on collective rights management. In the Commission's opinion, more uniform and technologically neutral solutions for cross-border and pan-European licensing is the audiovisual sector will stimulate creativity and help the content

---

[183] Summary report, Brussels, February 7, 2008. See also paras 27–20 and 27–22, above. For an overview of the situation, see M. Frabboni, "From copyright collectives to exclusive "clubs": the changing faces of music rights administration in Europe" [2008] Ent. L.R 19(5), 100.
[184] Monti Report, p.45
[185] Commission Communication on A digital agenda for Europe COM(2010) 245, May 19, 2010.
[186] Commission Communication on A digital agenda for Europe COM(2010) 245, p.7.

producers and broadcasters. Such solutions should, it is proposed, preserve the contractual freedom of right holders. They would not be obliged to license for all European territories, but would remain free to restrict their licences to certain territories and to contractually set the level of licence fees.[187]

27-49   **Collective Management and Competition.** The approach of the EU competition authorities to collective management will also need to be taken into account. At present, there is a need to clarify the application of Community competition rules to collecting societies and collective management, if centralised, voluntary licensing schemes to facilitate rights clearance on a pan-European basis are to be encouraged in the form of one-stop-shops. The need for such clarification was brought into focus more than twenty years ago as a result of the intervention of the Commission competition authorities in the activities of Video Performance Ltd (VPL), which administers the rights in its members' videos, and the International Federation of the Phonographic Industry, representing international music video repertoire. In 1987, VPL and IFPI entered into pan-European licensing agreements with satellite broadcasters, including MTV for a period of five years, in which they licensed the use of their members' music videos for the entire satellite footprint. At that time, MTV had welcomed the opportunity given by VPL and IFPI to obtain such a licence, which enabled them to clear the entire worldwide music video repertoire by one licence in what represented a real "one-stop-shop". Without the licence, MTV would not have been able to enter the market so quickly and effectively. As has been pointed out, in this case, a collecting society not only facilitated competition within the European Community, but also acted as a springboard to promote the emergence of a new pan-European broadcaster.[188] In 1992, however, MTV approached the major record companies seeking to make individual direct deals with them and to avoid taking the VPL/IFPI licence. The majors demurred, preferring to continue to licence their repertoire collectively. MTV then lodged a complaint with the Commission competition authorities alleging that VPL and IFPI were acting in breach of art.101(1) (former art.81(1)) of the TFEU. In 1994, the Commission issued a statement of objections in response to the complaint in which they said that the refusal of the five major companies to negotiate individually and the fact that they had instead given a mandate to VPL and IFPI to conduct collective negotiations on their behalf and to conclude blanket, rather than individual, licences, restricted competition between members of VPL and between the majors in particular and was contrary to the Community's competition rules. No decision of the Commission was issued in this case but the statement of objections left the law on collective licensing in some doubt and it would appear that the policy of the competition directorate is to favour individual licensing and is inconsistent with the views that the Commission has expressed in other contexts about the usefulness of collective management for the promotion of cross-border licensing by means of one-stop-shops. For example, in its Green Paper on Copyright and Related Rights in the Information Society, the Commission said:

> "It is reasonable to suppose that certain alliances would be a major step forward for collecting societies, which are currently organised by category of work or class of right holder (*e.g.* authors, performers, etc.). To allow centralised management or administration of the rights over all works, performances and other protected matter incorporated into multimedia works, the collecting societies and other rights managers ought to be encouraged to

---

[187] Commission Communication on A digital agenda for Europe COM(2010) 245, pp.8 and 9.
[188] For a full account of these proceedings, see H. Porter, "European Union Competition Policy: Should the Role of Collecting Societies be Legitimised?" [1996] 12 E.I.P.R. 672 at 674.

set up joint bodies allowing a simplification of right management. ...[189] The competition rules are fundamental, but there is no reason why they should be in contradiction with the idea of centralised schemes, at least so far as the creation of 'one-stop-shops' are concerned. ...[190] Centralised schemes for the administration of rights, which would be voluntary in character, would be an appropriate response to the information society."[191]

In a more recent decision, the Commission held that:

"The absence of territorial boundaries in the on-line environment induced by the internet and digital format of the products enables users to choose any collecting society in the EEA which is a member of the one-stop-shop mechanism for the delivering of the licence. ... This way, commercial users will be able to recognise the most efficient societies in the EEA and seek their licences from the collecting societies that provide them at lower cost".[192]

The CISAC Decision. In 2006, the European Commission Competition Department intervened once more in collective licensing and sent a Statement of Objections to CISAC, the International Federation of Societies of Authors and Composers, and to 24 of its members in the EEA. The objections followed complaints filed by RTL against the German authors' society GEMA in 2000 and by Music Choice Europe against CISAC in 2003. The objections deal with the transmission of music via the internet, satellite and cable and targeted aspects of the reciprocal representation agreements signed between authors' societies, alleging that these were in breach of EU competition laws.   **27–50**

In response to the Statement of Objections, CISAC, along with 18 EEA authors' societies, announced that it had reached an agreement in principle with the European Commission in response to the issues raised in the statement of objections. *Exclusivity*: CISAC agreed formally to reconfirm the absence of exclusivity from its Model Contract, whilst the societies agreed to ensure such an absence from their representation contracts with other EEA-based societies. *Membership*: CISAC agreed that the Model Contract would re-emphasise the right of an EEA creator and publisher to move freely between EEA authors' societies, whilst the societies agreed to ensure that such a right was present in their representation contract with other EEA-based societies. *Territoriality*: The societies agreed to mandate each other to grant multi-territorial EEA internet, satellite and cable re-transmission service licenses (subject to certain qualifications aimed at protecting the creative community and ensuring that authors and their works do not suffer the effects of a potentially harmful downward spiral in royalty rates). In June 2007, the European Commission invited comments from interested parties on the commitments proposed by CISAC and indicated that, if the results of the market test were positive, it would adopt a decision under art.9 of Regulation 1/2003, rendering the commitments legally binding.[193] However, on July 16, 2008, the Commission's Directorate General for Competition issued its Decision in the case under art.7 of Regulation 1/2003,[194] announcing at the same time[195] that the interested parties' comments on the commitments were negative—in par-

---

[189] Commission Green Paper on Copyright and Related Rights in the Information Society, Com(95) 382 final, p.76.

[190] Commission Green Paper on Copyright and Related Rights in the Information Society, Com(95) 382 final, p.77.

[191] Commission Green Paper on Copyright and Related Rights in the Information Society, Com(95) 382 final, p.77.

[192] Decision IFPI Simulcasting—COMP/C2/38.014, October 8, 2002, [2003] OJ L107/58.

[193] Details of the proposed commitments have been published at [2007] OJ C128.

[194] CISAC—COMP/C–2/38.698, July 16, 2008. The full decision is available on the Competition DG website and a Summary was published in [2008] OJ C323 on December 18, 2008.

ticular, it was suggested that the proposed commitments would continue to make pan-European licences difficult to obtain.

The Decision concerned the conditions of management and licensing by collecting societies of authors' public performance rights in musical works. It identified specific clauses contained in the reciprocal representation agreements between collecting societies which relate to membership and exclusivity and held that the 24 European collecting societies subject to the investigation had each entered into reciprocal agreements restricting their ability to offer services outside their domestic territories. These clauses were restrictive business practices which offended against art.101 of the TFEU (the prohibition on agreements, decisions and concerted practices, which may affect trade or which are intended to prevent, restrict or distort competition). The societies were, by the Decision, required to modify their agreements so as to remove these restrictions. Thus, 23 of the EEA-based collecting societies were required to no longer apply the membership clauses that prevented authors from choosing to appoint another collecting society in the European Union to administer their repertoire. Secondly, the collecting societies were prohibited from conferring exclusive rights to each other in their reciprocal representation agreements. The decision objected to the coordinated approach (concerted practice) by all CISAC members as regards the delineation of the scope of their respective mandates. No fines were applied and the societies were required to agree on a territorial scope of their mandates not limited to their domestic territory.

The Decision did not challenge the existence of the reciprocal representation agreements or the collecting societies' right to set levels of royalty payments due in their domestic territory.[196]. Furthermore, it stated that it would make it easier for an author to select which collecting society/societies will manage his or her performance rights and that efficiency, quality of service and conditions of membership differ appreciably between collecting societies. It also allows collecting societies to licence their repertoire to more than one other collecting society per territory. It suggested that:

> "For internet, satellite and cable exploitation, the Decision improves the opportunities for commercial users (including broadcasters and content providers) to obtain a licence which covers more than one territory. By opening up the market to more competition between collecting societies, the Decision would provide incentives to collecting societies to improve their efficiency and the quality of their services, thereby benefitting both authors and users".

On October 3, 2008, CISAC and 22 authors' societies appealed the Decision.[197]

C. THE POTENTIAL CONTRIBUTION OF DIGITAL TECHNOLOGY TO COLLECTIVE ADMINISTRATION

27–51   **Technical systems of identification and protection.** In the new digital world of the information society, technical systems of identification and protection are being applied to facilitate the administration of rights in the digital environment and to allow more individual management of certain rights. Digital technology offers scope for identifying, controlling access to, tracing, monitoring and rewarding all uses of works. It provides rights owners for the first time with tools to control uses such as private copying, which could not be monitored or controlled before.

---

[195] IP/08/1165 of July 16, 2008
[196] Commission Rules of European Collecting Societies' Practices, EU Focus 2008, 239
[197] For further information on the appeal, see the CISAC website, *http://www.CISAC.org*. See also P. Gyertyanfy, "Collective management of music rights in Europe after the CISAC decision", [2010] 1 *International Review of Intellectual Property and Competition Law* 59.

As the Commission has stated "at least with respect to some new forms of copyright applications, new digital means of identification of protected material and of automatic licensing of their uses may allow more individualised management".[198] The need for compulsory statutory licensing of certain rights, often in the past introduced because of the perceived difficulty of clearing rights on an individual basis, and for private copying levies on the sale of blank tapes and equipment to provide remuneration of previously uncontrollable private use, can now in principle be replaced by payments for use paid directly by the user to the rights owner. In relation to multimedia products, where thousands of rights-holders may be involved, electronic clearing of rights is essential. "Technical devices have no disadvantages *per se*; they are instead mandatory for solving multimedia licensing problems".[199]

The organisations and collecting societies representing the various copyright owners are fully aware of these possibilities and the development of digital rights management systems (DRM systems) have been a key issue for many years now. DRM systems can be used to identify works and right owners, "to clear rights, to secure payment, to trace behaviour and to enforce rights .... [They] are, therefore, crucial for the development of new high volume, low transactional value business models".[200]

Since DRM systems became available, much work has been done by right owners to establish product identification codes which take advantage of digital technology to provide for digital identification of works. Such digital identification is the first step in building DRM systems, which will enable the use of copyright materials to be tracked, the users to be identified, recorded and charged in order for appropriate payment to be made for the use made.[201]

In 1995, the US NII Report pointed out that digital identification of works would be critical to the efficient operation and success of the information superhighway:

> "Copyright management information will serve as a kind of license plate for a work on the information superhighway, from which a user may obtain important information about the work. The accuracy of such information will be crucial to the ability of consumers to find and make authorised uses of works on the NII. Reliable information will also facilitate efficient licensing and reduce transaction costs for licensable usesof copyright works (both fee-based and royalty-free)."[202]

For copyright identification systems to be useful, all works and protected subject-matter need to carry identification of the work and its respective rights owner. Moreover, international standards for such codes are necessary if they are to be recognised and to be effective globally. The Commission of the European Union has provided funds for research projects and efforts towards establishing open standards for interoperability of data in E-commerce systems and the

---

[198] Green Paper on Copyright and Related Rights in the Information Society COM(95) 382 final, p.75.

[199] T. Hoeren "An assessment of long-term solutions in the context of copyright and electronic delivery systems and multimedia products", European Commission DG-XIII E-1, document EUR 16069EN, p.43. See also M. Frabboni, "From copyright collectives to exclusive 'clubs': the changing faces of music rights administration in Europe" [2008] Ent.L.R. 19(5), 100.

[200] EC Communication, p.10.

[201] See generally D.J. Gervais, "Electronic Rights Management Systems (ERMS): The Next Logical Step in the Evolution of Rights Management", paper delivered at the WIPO International Forum on the Exercise and Management of Copyright and Neighbouring Rights in the Face of the Challenges of Digital Technology, Seville, May 1997.

[202] Report of the Working group on Intellectual Property Rights (NII Report), B.A. Lehman, Assistant Secretary of Commerce and Commissioner of Patents and Trademarks, Chair, Washington, September 1995, p.235.

International Bureau of WIPO has also worked to promote such systems. To date, identification codes, most of which are recognised by the International Standards Organisation (ISO), are in use for books (ISBN-ISO 2108),[203] journals (ISSN-ISO 3297),[204] recorded music tracks (ISRC-ISO 3901),[205] CDs (UPC), sheet music (ISMN-ISO 10957), music (ISWC-ISO 15707)[206] musical works (ISWC-ISO 21047), releases of music for electronic distribution (GRid—Global Release Identifier),[207] audiovisual (ISAN-ISO 15706), and audiovisual works (V-ISAN- ISO 15706-2). Interested party identifier (IPI) is a new identifier for composers, authors and publishers ("compositeurs, auteurs, éditeurs", previously identified as CAE) and there is a such an identifier also for performers (IPDN—International Performers' Database Number). BIEM and CISAC have also developed a Common Information System (CIS), which is a standardised identification system for the works administered by their member societies and in use via the CIS network around the world.[208] Such universal product identification codes are a pre-requisite for electronic copyright clearance systems. Some of these codes are insufficient because they identify, for example like the ISBN, the packaging (the book) not the work or works contained therein. In such cases, the codes need to be adapted to the new requirements. Suitable codes, of global application, would in principle make it possible to establish signalling methods, incorporated in the subcodes of digital works, which would provide encoded business information capable of being automatically read electronically. The rights owners would be identified and paid by means of schemes of individual invoicing to consumers in respect of the actual use made by them of protected works. For such schemes to work, the systems sold to consumers would have to incorporate systems for the reading of the codes.

Electronic licensing and clearance systems are now ubiquitous in the collective management world and the situation is evolving rapidly in this area. There is a great deal of research and experimentation on the subject being undertaken by interested parties in Europe, Japan and the United States of America.[209] For example, in an initiative on a global scale, the international trade bodies BIEM, CISAC, IFPI and the RIAA, representing music publishers, authors, composers and the recording industry, have worked jointly to develop a global infrastructure to support the efficient management of the electronic delivery of music in an online environment. The project is known as the Music Integrated Identifiers Proj-

---

[203] The International Standard Book Number (ISBN) consists of 10 digits identifying the group, publisher and title.

[204] The International Standard Serial Number (ISSN) is used to identify periodicals.

[205] The International Standard Recording Code (ISRC) consists of twelve digits including information on the original producer, the year of recording and the country of origin.

[206] The International Standard Music Number and the International Standard Work Code.

[207] Administered by IFPI on behalf of the global recording industry.

[208] See "CIS, The Common Information System", proposed by the BIEM/CISAC Information Systems Steering Committee in December 1994 and approved by the Executive Bureau at Cannes, February 1995. Updated in July 1995, available from CISAC, (see para.27–27, above). See K. Hill, "CIS-A Collective Solution for Copyright Management in the Digital Age" [1997] 76 *Copyright World*, 18–25.

[209] See generally with regard to Europe, Japan and the USA: R. Oman, "Technological Means of Protection and Rights Management Information", paper delivered at the WIPO International Forum on the Exercise and Management of Copyright and Neighbouring Rights in the Face of the Challenges of Digital Technology, Seville, May 1997. As regards Europe, see "Handbook listing the various initiatives and existing techniques for the identification of rights holders and works in the context of management and clearance of rights in the digital area", Council of Europe, doc. MM-S-PR 4 Rev., February 13, 1998 and inter alia, D. S. Marks and B. H. Turnbull, "Technical Protection Measures: The Intersection of Technology, Law and Commercial Licences" [2000] E.I.P.R. 198; N. Hanbridge, "DRM: Can it Deliver? [2001] Ent. L.R. 138; J. Selby, "The Legal and economic implications of the digital distribution of music" [2000] E.I.P.R. 4, 25.

ect (MI3P).[210] This is an infrastructure for the music industry which will enable the development of automated transaction processing in a music e-commerce environment, through integrated standards for identification and description of releases, sound recordings' musical works and licences. A number of key standards have been developed. These include the Global Release Identifier Standard (GRid) and the Musical Work Licence Identifier Standard (MWLI). The system is fully integrated with existing industry identifiers already in common use, such as the CIS, ISRC and ISWC.

Anti-copying devices. Another positive result of digital technology is its application to anti-piracy measures. New types of anti-copying devices, such as encryption and scrambling systems, designed to prevent unauthorised copying of copyright works distributed over the internet have been developed and are constantly being perfected. Likewise, devices permitting the limitation of reproductions made for private purposes such as the serial copy management system (SCMS), first introduced twenty years ago and now an ISO standard for digital sound recording machines, have been developed. SMCS permits such machines to copy from a CD or digital tape but prevents copies being made from those first copies. In this area also, uniform standards which are inter-operable and recognised throughout the world are a prerequisite for success. **27–52**

Much work continues to be done to develop systems to deliver digital files of copyright subject-matter over the internet, to receive payment for that delivery and to protect the file from unauthorised distribution and reproduction. Such systems already benefit in the European Union from the legal protection afforded by the Information Society Directive, already referred to, and by the WIPO Copyright Treaty (WCT) and the WIPO Performances and Phonograms Treaty (WPPT), referred to in the next paragraph.[211]

D. LEGISLATIVE BACK-UP FOR TECHNICAL SYSTEMS OF IDENTIFICATION AND PROTECTION

Internationally, there is a consensus that legislative back-up is needed to provide effective legal remedies against the circumvention of copyright protection systems and the removal or alteration of electronic copyright management information without authority. The two so-called WIPO Internet Treaties adopted on December 20, 1996, the WIPO Copyright Treaty (WCT) and the WIPO Performances and Phonograms Treaty (WPPT) include provisions to this effect.[212] **27–53**

In the USA, legislative back-up for such systems was introduced in 1998 in the "Digital Millenium Copyright Act" (DMCA). The Act provides that the following should give rise to criminal offences and penalties: the circumvention of copyright protection systems, the providing of false copyright management information, and the removal or alteration of copyright management information.[213]

Within the European Union, the adoption of the Information Society Directive provides for legal protection of electronic information attached to works and re-

---

[210] See *http://www.mi3p-standard.org.*

[211] See also Marks and Turnbull, "Technical Protection Measures: The Intersection of Technology, Law and Commercial Licences" [2000] E.I.P.R 198; G. Davies, "Technical Devices as a Solution to Private Copying" in P. Torremans and I. Stamatoudi, *Copyright in the New Digital Environment, The Need to Redesign Copyright* (London: Sweet & Maxwell, 2000); G. Davies, "Copyright in the Information Society-Technical Devices to Control Private Copying", in *Festschrift für Adolf Dietz* (Munich: Verlag C.H. Beck, 2001); L. Jones, Artist's Entry into Cyberspace: Intellectual Property on the internet" [2000] E.I.P.R. 79.

[212] WIPO Copyright Treaty arts 11 and 12; WIPO Performances and Phonograms Treaty arts 18 and 19. Both Treaties were adopted at Geneva on December 20, 1996 (see Vol.2 F13 and F14, below).

[213] Pub.L. No.105–304, 112 Stat. 2760 (1998), adding new paras 512 and 1201–1203 to the Copyright Act 1976.

lated subject-matter for the purpose of copyright management and protection systems and to prevent any circumvention, removal or alteration of such electronic information without authority.[214]

Community law first legislated in this area in the context of the Computer Programs Directive. Article 7(1)(c) thereof stipulates that Member States are to provide appropriate remedies against persons putting into circulation, or possessing for commercial purposes, "any means the sole intended purpose of which is to facilitate the unauthorised removal or circumvention of any technical device which may have been applied to protect a computer program".

Finally, this is one area of the law where the United Kingdom was in advance of its Community partners. The 1988 Act already provided rights owners with protection equivalent to the rights obtaining in respect of infringement against devices designed to circumvent electronic copy-protection systems.[215]

4. INDIVIDUAL COLLECTING SOCIETIES OPERATING IN THE UNITED KINGDOM

A. ARTISTS' COLLECTING SOCIETY ("ACS")

27–54   ACS was formally established as a collecting society in June 2006 in response to Directive 2001/84/EC[216] and the new UK legislation on artists' resale right.[217] ACS is an independent collecting society, established to collect resale royalties for British artists in the United Kingdom. Its aim is to provide artists with an alternative agency which maximises revenue due to its members, while minimising interference in the art trade. It is run on a not-for-profit basis and charges 15 per cent for administration costs but has undertaken to reimburse artists with any excess money on a pro-rata basis. Its members are artists represented by the Society of London Art Dealers and the British Art Market Federation. As at August 31, 2010, ACS had 339 members. ACS is a community interest company. Its website is at *http://www.artistscollectingsociety.org.uk*.

B. ARTISTS' RIGHTS ADMINISTRATION LTD ("ARA")

27–55   The ARA is a company limited by shares and was established in July 2007. It was established to collect artists' resale royalties, principally for Russian artists. Its website at *http://www.aradmin.com*, indicates that the ARA "look[s] after rights, including copyright, resale right and moral right, on behalf of visual artists and their heirs".

C. AUTHORS' LICENSING & COLLECTING SOCIETY LTD ("ALCS")

27–56   The ALCS administers a wide variety of rights in literary and dramatic works on behalf of any writer and their heirs and personal representatives.[218] The rights assigned by members to the ALCS as at August 2010 are set out in art.7(c) of the ALCS's Articles of Association. The principal rights were as follows. The reproduction right, defined as the right exercisable anywhere in the world to reproduce or authorise the reproduction of the work by means of any appliance or

---

[214] The relevant provisions of the Directive are arts 6 and 7. See also paras 24–116 et seq., above.
[215] CDPA 1988 s.296 (see Ch.15).
[216] Council Directive 2004/48/EC on the enforcement of intellectual property rights [2004] OJ L195/16.
[217] Artists' Resale Right Regulations SI 2006/346.
[218] Articles of Association arts 3 and 4.

process capable of producing multiple copies of the work.[219] This reproduction right is administered by ALCS through the CLA (as to which see para.27–59, below), which acts as agent for ALCS. The communication to the public right, defined by the ALCS as the right to communicate a work to the public by electronic transmission and includes the broadcasting of the work and inclusion of the work in an interactive service for making a work available to the public by electronic transmission in such a way that members of the public may access the work from a place and at a time individually chosen by them.[220] The educational off-air recording right which is administered by the ALCS as a member of the ERA (as to which see para.27–62, below).[221] The private copying right, which gives ALCS the right to recover monies from blank tape levies where they exist.[222] The cable retransmission right. The performing right.[223] The ALCS also administers the lending right and the rental right and collects fees from the German, Dutch, French, Spanish, Italian and Irish public lending rights.[224] A number of other rights were also assigned to the ALCS, but not all of these are administered.[225]

As at March 2009, ALCS had 45,173 Ordinary Members, and 7,791 Associate Members[226] and had arrangements with 55 similar societies in 46 countries. The ALCS is seeking to remove the distinction between Ordinary and Associate Members and is currently undergoing a transition process whereby Associate Members become Ordinary Members by the payment of a one-off fee of £10. Members assign to the ALCS the rights specified in the Articles of Association. ALCS now charges a one-off £25 joining fee for new members and has abolished the £10 annual fee previously charged. Existing Associate Members transferring to Ordinary Member status are charged a one-off £10 administration fee.

In the financial year to March 31, 2010, the ALCS received an income of £27,663,467, an increase of 9.6 per cent over the previous year. Over £19 million of this income came from the CLA, just over £1 million came from the ERA and £6.7 million came from international bilateral agreements. The remainder (£833,868) came from the BBC PRIME and DTH licences, in relation to which a significant one-off payment was received in the course of the year. The net distribution to ALCS' members and overseas societies was £24,036,785, of which £23,057,403 was paid in the course of the year. ALCS charges a commission rate for members of 9.5 per cent.

The ALCS is a company limited by guarantee. Its website is at *http://www.alcs.co.uk.*

---

[219] Articles of Association art.1(xv).

[220] Articles of Association art.1(xxvii).

[221] Articles of Association art.7(c)(v).

[222] Articles of Association art.7(c)(iii) and 7(d)(i). ALCS now collects monies from blank tape levies in Austria, Belgium, Denmark, France, Germany, Italy, the Netherlands and Switzerland.

[223] Such as the right to read poems at poetry festivals (administered under an agreement with the British Federation of Music and Drama Festivals)

[224] i.e. the entitlement of authors to a fee in respect of loans of copies of their works by a public library.

[225] The ALCS also collected remuneration for its members from payments for what it terms "small literary rights, such as the readings of excerpts of literary works on television and radio in certain countries; the public reception of broadcasts; and certain rights related to visual impairment". ALCS also licensed BBC Worldwide Ltd for the use of BBC programmes containing literary and dramatic material. These covered the direct reception and cable retransmission of the BBC's entertainment satellite channel, BBC PRIME, in Europe and Africa, the information satellite channel, BBC WORLD worldwide, and the satellite transmission of BBC digital channels from the Republic of Ireland. While these licences are no longer current, fees for past uses are still being received and are distributed to writers for every transmission of programmes falling within the ALCS repertoire.

[226] Whose rights it administers as their agent, charging a commission of 14% at the point of distribution.

D. BRITISH EQUITY COLLECTING SOCIETY LTD ("BECS")

27-57   BECS was incorporated in April 1998 with the principal object of collecting, distributing and administering "performers' remuneration".[227] It has strong links to the performers' and artists' trade union, Equity, and a majority of its directors must be drawn from the Council of Management of Equity.[228] "Performers' remuneration" is defined by BECS as any income or remuneration arising or payable to performers in any of the following ways: first, in respect of the rental of a sound recording or film either by way of the exercise of the rental right under s.182C of the 1988 Act or of the right to equitable remuneration where the rental right has been transferred under s.191G of the 1988 Act or of any equivalent rights in other countries; secondly, from any blank tape levy or other levies on copying media or devices; and thirdly, in respect of the cable retransmission of programmes incorporating their performances.[229] There is power to add to the definition any income or remuneration which is of a similar collective character and which the Board of Management resolves should be collected by BECS.[230] For example BECS is now responsible for administering the revenue generated from contractual licences with BBC 7 (Digital Archive Radio) and from certain BBC programmes that are simulcast by cable and satellite in Belgium, Ireland and the Netherlands.

   BECS also acts as agent either for Equity or for the relevant UK broadcaster to distribute sums negotiated between Equity and those broadcasters for the use of performances by Equity members in programmes made available through the following catch-up television services: the BBC iPlayer service, the ITV-Player, and Channel 4's 4-o-D service. Members sign a mandate appointing BECS as their exclusive agent to collect this remuneration on their behalf.

   In 2009, BECS collected in excess of £7 million for its membership of approximately 23,000. There is no membership charge, but BECS charges commission. The commission levels vary according to approved distribution policies and take into account the level of data input and checking carried out by BECS (as opposed to third-party collecting societies). Commission is not levied on all sources of revenue. Where performances are identified individually by a foreign society, BECS does not generally charge commission, nor does it levy a charge for distribution of revenue from the BBC 7 and catch-up TV schemes (where it obtains a contribution from the broadcaster). However, where commission is charged, it is solely for the purpose of covering BECS's overheads. For Equity members, BECS rates of commission vary up to 10 per cent. Payments made to non-Equity members are subject to higher commission rates. At European level, BECS is affiliated to aepo-artis (see *http://www.aepo-artis.org* [Accessed November 8, 2010]). At UK level, it is affiliated to the British Copyright Council.

E. COMPACT COLLECTIONS LTD ("CCL")

27-58   Compact Collections Ltd was incorporated in 1995 for the purposes of collecting secondary television royalties for film and television content owners. It is a limited company incorporated by shares. As at April 2007 CCL represented over 250 media companies worldwide including production companies, distributors, sales agents and broadcasters. The rights administered were as follows: the cable

---

[227] Memorandum of Association art.(1).
[228] Articles of Association arts 33–35 and art.38(h).
[229] Articles of Association, art.1(1)–(4).
[230] Articles of Association art.1(5).

and satellite retransmission right[231]; the private copying right[232]; the educational off-air recording right[233]; the German rental right; and the right to show films by televised broadcast in public places. CCL provides a full administration service from registering the audio-visual works of its clients with each of the rights societies through to distributing the collected returns. In order to facilitate this process, the relevant right is assigned by the right holder. This enables CCL to furnish warranties to the rights societies and to collect receipts. The member retains all other rights. The website of CCL is at *http:// www.compactcollections.com* [Accessed November 8, 2010].

F. COPYRIGHT LICENSING AGENCY LTD ("CLA")

CLA represents the copyright interests of authors, artists and publishers in the United Kingdom. Its Articles of Association permit it to license the copying of published literary, dramatic, musical and artistic works[234] using photocopiers and other methods of multiple copying such as scanning.[235] In March 2008, CLA announced that it was launching a new series of collective licences which, in addition to the photocopying and scanning rights granted under existing licences, would also permit copying from opted-in digital publications together with electronic circulation (such as e-mailing) and in some instances, limited storage. As at October 2010 CLA represented some 2,770 mandating publishers via the PLS[236] and had reciprocal rights exchange agreements with similar societies in 30 countries. It also represented some 80,000 authors.[237] Artistic works are licensed under an agency agreement with DACS.[238]

27–59

CLA is a company limited by guarantee. Its members are the ALCS[239] and PLS. It is empowered by its Articles of Association to negotiate the terms of and to grant licences to collect royalties and to institute and prosecute such proceedings as may be necessary for the enforcement of the rights entrusted to it.[240] Its licences typically authorise the licensee and those authorised by the licensee to make reprographic copies for the licensee's internal use at specified premises over a particular period in return for a fixed annual fee. CLA issues licences to schools, colleges and universities.[241] Where a group of colleges or universities or

---

[231] This right is administered in respect of royalties arising in Austria, Belgium, Canada, Denmark, the Republic of Ireland, Finland, France, Germany, Liechtenstein, Luxembourg, the Netherlands, Norway, Spain, Sweden, Switzerland and the USA.

[232] This right is administered in respect of Austria, Belgium, Denmark, France, Germany, the Netherlands, Spain, Sweden and Switzerland.

[233] This right is administered in respect of Australia, New Zealand and Switzerland.

[234] Articles of Association art.9.1.

[235] See Articles of Association art.1.2 which defines "reprographic right" as "the right to reproduce or authorise the reproduction of the work by means of any appliance or process (including but not limited to any Electronic appliance or process) capable of producing multiple copies of the work in such a form that the work may be perceived visually", and cf. the definition of reprographic copying in CDPA 1988 s.178.

[236] For PLS, see para.27–67, below

[237] As agent for the ALCS, as to which see para.27–56, above.

[238] For DACS, see para.27–60, below.

[239] As to which see para.27–56, above.

[240] Articles of Association art.10.

[241] This scheme is the subject of a decision of the Copyright Tribunal: *Universities UK v Copyright Licensing Agency Ltd and Design and Artists Copyright Society Ltd*, CT71/00, 72/00, 73/00, 74/ 00, 75/01, [2002] R.P.C. 36; [2002] E.M.L.R. 35. The availability of licences from the CLA for educational establishments means that s.36 of the CDPA 1988 is of very limited practical effect: see s.36(3). The licence ordered by the Tribunal has now expired. CLA and Universities UK/ Guild of Higher Education have negotiated renewals to include scanning and digital rights in addition to the photocopying rights in the licence scheme adjudicated upon by the Copyright Tribunal.

other organisations is represented by a negotiating body[242] CLA will negotiate with that body and issue a licence to the individual organisations it represents. In October 2010 CLA launched its new schools' licence which, in addition to photocopying and scanning permits the reproduction of material from opted-in digital originators and "free-to-view" websites. CLA also issues increasing numbers of blanket licences to public bodies, government departments (including central government and local authorities), corporate and other commercial organisations and charities.[243] In addition it offers transactional licences such as its document supply licences and press cuttings licence. CLA operates a special licensing scheme ("the CLA Print Disability Licensing Scheme") in respect of the making by bodies not conducted for profit of multiple copies for persons who are visually impaired or otherwise disabled as a result of which they are unable to read or access part or the whole of a copyright work for circulation outside their organisations.[244]

In order to enable CLA to distribute royalties in proportion to actual use, licences require the licensee to take part in a data gathering exercise by recording the copyright works copied on its premises over a specified period. All licences contain conditions as to the proportion of a work which may be copied.[245] Some categories of works[246] and a number of specific works are excluded altogether.[247] Licensees are provided with an indemnity by CLA in respect of infringement claims which is expressed to be in addition to the indemnity implied by s.136 of the 1988 Act.[248] Royalties are attributed to the works copied and CLA pays ALCS, DACS and PLS, representing authors, artists and publishers respectively, in the proportions agreed between those parties. CLA pays royalties for international works to the overseas collecting societies with whom it has exchanged reciprocal representation agreements. In the year ending 31 March 2010, CLA received royalties totalling £51.8 million from UK licences and £10.9 million from international licences. It distributed £57 million. During the year CLA's administration costs were £6.7 million. CLA's website is at *http://www.cla.co.uk*. [Accessed November 8, 2010].

The editors are grateful to CLA's Martin Delaney, Legal Director and

---

[242] Such as Universities UK or the Law Society and City of London Law Society.

[243] As with the education sector, CLA negotiates sector-specific licences (examples include the licence for pharmaceutical companies) with representative bodies taking into consideration factors such as the type of industry or profession concerned and the amount of research involved in that industry or profession... As at October 2010 the current rates for business licences for businesses with more than 51 employees ranged from £13.55 to £40.40 per year per professional, managerial or technical employee depending upon the type of business which is determined according to the SIC (Standard Industry Classification) code. Smaller businesses were subject to a flat rate. For those with between 1 and 10 employees, the rate was £136.50, while for those with 11 to 50 employees, the rate was £414.75. All rates are subject to VAT.

[244] This scheme covers books, journals and periodicals published in the United Kingdom, together with some foreign works. It also includes databases where these are included in books, journals and periodicals. There is a list of excluded works. The scheme is intended to comply with CDPA 1988 s.31D, with the effect that s.31B (which provides for the making of multiple copies for visually impaired persons) is disapplied by s.31D(1). For s.31B, see paras 9–85 et seq., above. Where educational establishments make copies for print disabled persons for internal use only, this will be covered by an extension of the existing CLA licence.

[245] In general, with minor exceptions, no more than 5% or one complete chapter of a book or one article in a periodical publication (whichever is the greater) may be copied at a time; cf. CDPA 1988 s.36(2).

[246] They are as follows: printed music (including the words); newspapers (as to which see para.28–279, below); maps and charts; workbooks, workcards and assignment sheets; and any work on which the copyright owner has expressly and prominently stipulated that it may not be copied under a CLA Licence.

[247] The CLA's list of excluded categories and works, as amended periodically, is available on CLA's website at *http://www.cla.co.uk/licences/excluded__works/excluded__categories__works/* [Accessed October 15, 2010].

[248] Note the limited application of s.136.

Company Secretary, and Polly Swan, Legal Adviser, for their assistance in updating this paragraph.

G. Design and Artists Copyright Society Ltd ("DACS")

DACS exists to protect and promote the copyright and similar rights in artistic works of artists and other visual creators[249] and their successors in title.[250] It is a company limited by guarantee and operates as a not-for-profit organisation. DACS is currently governed by a board of non-executive directors comprising representatives from a range of artistic disciplines alongside others from business and the legal profession. **27–60**

Licensing is divided into "primary" and "collective" licensing. Primary licensing means the exercise on behalf of members of those rights which are exercisable individually such as the right to make copies of the work, the right to issue copies of the work to the public and moral rights. Representation is authorised by way of direct agreements with UK artists and through reciprocal agreements with the Associated Societies. Collective licensing concerns those rights which it is impracticable or impossible for a member to exercise individually. Rights administered by DACS by way of collective licensing as at August 2010 included certain reprographic rights,[251] the educational off-air recording right[252] and the satellite and cable retransmission right.[253] To avoid confusion with the services it has provided since 2006 in relation to the artists resale right, DACS now refers to what was "primary licensing" and then, briefly, "Individual Rights Management" as simply "Copyright Licensing". Collective Licensing is now referred to as the "Payback" scheme. Licence fees received in respect of this Payback scheme are distributed to individual visual creators who claim through the scheme each year.

Members are divided into ordinary members (the authors of the works and their nominees) and successor members (defined as surviving spouses and relatives, beneficiaries under a will or personal representatives of the authors).[254] As at April 2010 DACS had a membership of nearly 60,000 artists and their successors in title. Licence fees received in respect of collective rights management are distributed annually through the DACS Payback scheme. In 2009, 11,628 visual artists successfully claimed a share of £3.1 million of collective licensing revenue. All visual creators, whether or not they are members of DACS, are entitled to seek a share of annual collective licensing revenue, and are entitled to a royalty subject to certain criteria. An ordinary member grants to DACS an exclusive licence to exercise and to authorise others to exercise all the primary and secondary rights in all of that member's artistic works throughout the world for primary and collective advertising purposes.[255] The membership also includes associate members (individuals or organisations which own, manage, administer or otherwise control relevant rights), and governing members (any person ap-

---

[249] Including sculptors, photographers and other visual creators of artistic works as defined by CDPA 1988 s.4.

[250] Memorandum of Association para.3.

[251] Administered through the CLA, as to which see para.27–59, above.

[252] Which DACS administers as a member of the ERA, as to which see para.27–62, below.

[253] In respect of retransmissions in the Republic of Ireland, revenue is collected through the Irish Music Rights Organisation, a group of broadcasters and collecting societies. In respect of retransmissions in Belgium, France and Holland, revenue is collected through the relevant local collecting society. The full list of rights which DACS may administer collectively is as follows (see Articles of Association art.1.18): cable retransmission right, digital and electronic imaging rights, lending right, off-air recording right, private audio-visual recording right, public display right, rental right, reprographic right, resale right (droit de suite), terrestrial and satellite broadcast rights, and such other rights as may hereafter come into existence.

[254] Articles of Association arts 4.1 and 4.2.

[255] Membership Agreement (Ordinary Member) arts 1 and 2m.

pointed as a director of DACS): see arts 3.2 and 3.3 of the Articles of Association respectively. Members retain the right to exercise any of the primary or secondary rights on notice to DACS.[256] Since March 2006 new members have been able to join DACS without payment of a membership fee. In addition, a member may if he or she wishes retain control over the grant of licences in respect of any type of use which he or she specifies in the membership agreement. DACS automatically refers requests for licences for the use of works in advertising or merchandising to the member concerned.[257] DACS agrees to use its reasonable endeavours to preserve the member's rights[258] and to collect royalties,[259] but is not obliged to institute legal proceedings.[260] However, if proceedings are commenced in the name of the member, DACS is granted the right to have the conduct of those proceedings and to compromise them as it sees fit.[261] Licences are granted both on an individual basis by reference to a standard published tariff (which varies in accordance with the type of reproduction) and on a collective basis where appropriate.

The Artist's Resale Right Service (ARR) is a new service of collection and distribution of resale royalties launched by DACS in February 2006 as a result of the UK implementation of the Artist's Resale Right Directive. The ARR service is offered to all artists and visual creators, and with its online facility is designed to offer administrative ease in the collection and distribution of the royalties for both art market professionals and artists. In particular DACS is aiming to ensure that all artists are eligible to receive royalties through DACS whether or not DACS manages their copyright through the Individual Rights Management Service. Artists can mandate DACS to act on their behalf in respect of resale royalties by completing a simple registration form. Distribution is not yet "real time": an artist who has registered does not receive an immediate payment if a resale generates a royalty. Art market professionals have a certain period of time within which to provide information on completed sales to DACS via its online portal. On receipt of that information DACS will calculate any royalty liability and invoice them accordingly. A distribution of collected royalties is made at the end of each calendar month.

In 2009, £2.4 million of Artists' Resale Right royalties were paid to over 840 artists.

In July 2007 DACS retained a commission of 25 per cent of all copyright revenue collected through the Payback scheme, but by 2010 this had reduced to 22 per cent. In the financial year ending December 31, 2009, DACS charged a commission of 25 per cent of UK copyright revenues, 15 per cent of overseas revenues collected through Copyright Licensing and 15 per cent of all Artists' Resale Right royalties in the United Kingdom. In general, royalties are distributed every six months. DACS operates a special blanket licensing scheme[262] for the reproduction of artistic works on to slides, acetates and transparencies by educational establishments. Royalties in respect of works which have been licensed individually are distributed on the basis of actual use. DACS's total turnover for 2009 was £9.48 million with £7.61 million payable to artists. The DACS website is at *http://www.dacs.org.uk* [Accessed November 8, 2010].

DACS belongs to an international network of visual artists' organisations and

---

[256] Membership Agreement (Ordinary Member) arts 3 and 5.
[257] Membership Guide para.11.
[258] Membership Agreement (Ordinary Member) art.9.
[259] Membership Agreement (Ordinary Member) art.10.
[260] Membership Agreement (Ordinary Member), art.9.
[261] Membership Agreement (Ordinary Member) art.9.
[262] The Slide Collection Licensing Scheme.

currently holds reciprocal agreements with 30 other copyright societies ("Associated Societies") in 27 countries. All agreements cover individual and collective rights management (including the administration of artist's resale right). DACS also belongs to the following international federations: EVA (European Visual Artists: *http://www.europeanvisualartists.org* [Accessed November 8, 2010]), IFRRO (International Federation of Reproduction Rights Organisations: *http://www.ifrro.org*) and CISAC (International Confederation of Authors and Composers Societies). In the first year of administering the Artists' Resale Right, DACS distributed over £1 million to artists and visual creators.

H. DIRECTORS UK LTD ("DUKL")

On June 12, 2008, the Directors and Producers Rights Society (1992) Ltd, usually abbreviated to DPRS, changed its name to Directors UK Ltd. Since then, while continuing to act as a collecting society for the distribution of secondary rights payments to directors, DUKL has also acted as a campaigning body which aims to protect and enhance the creative, economic and contractual rights of directors in the United Kingdom.[263] DUKL represents individual film and television directors and producers and their estates. The producers represented by DUKL are individual documentary makers who produce, direct, and write their works and frequently take an on-screen credit as "producer". As at August 2010, it administered on their behalf the cable retransmission right, the private copying right and the video rental right through collecting societies in the European Community, Norway, Mexico and Switzerland. It also has exchange arrangements with collecting societies in the USA, Canada, Ireland and Australia.[264] DUKL also represents freelance television directors in respect of the exploitation of their works throughout the world. As a matter of industry practice, such directors are required to assign all their rights in programmes of which they are the authors to the producer. The fee paid on such assignment is deemed to cover the first transmission. However, in July 2001, DUKL reached an agreement with the United Kingdom broadcasters and producers[265] ("the Rights Agreement") in relation to remuneration for any further transmissions within the United Kingdom ("secondary use"). The agreement also covers sales and DVD releases. Under an initial five-year arrangement, DUKL receives a fixed annual sum in respect of such secondary use. Payments are distributed to individual directors in accordance with a scheme devised and administered by DUKL.[266] DUKL is a company limited by guarantee. As at August 2010, DUKL had around 4,000 members. The DUKL website is at *http://www.directors.uk.com* [Accessed August 31, 2010].

27–61

I. EDUCATIONAL RECORDING AGENCY LTD ("ERA")

Section 35(1) of the 1988 Act, as amended by the Copyright and Related Rights Regulations, permits educational establishments[267] and persons acting on their behalf to make recordings of broadcasts and to copy such recordings for

27–62

---

[263] From the DUKL website is at *http://www.directors.uk.com* [Accessed August 31, 2010].

[264] As at October 2008, it had agreements with collecting societies in Austria, Belgium, Bulgaria, the Czech Republic, Denmark, Finland, France, Germany, Hungary, Italy, Lithuania, Mexico, the Netherlands, Norway, Poland, Portugal, Slovakia, Spain and Switzerland.

[265] The BBC, ITV Network, Channel 4, Channel 5, BSkyB, PACT, S4C and TAC.

[266] The terms of the scheme are available on DUKL's website.

[267] Which expression includes schools and any other educational establishment specified by order of the Secretary of State: CDPA 1988 s.174(1). The Secretary of State has specified universities and institutions providing further or higher education under this section: see the Copyright (Educational Establishments) (No.2) Order 1989 No.1068. ERA has published a statement on the meaning of the term "educational establishment".

educational purposes without infringing copyright. Section 35(1A) provides that where a recording is made in this way without infringing copyright, copyright is not infringed if it is communicated to the public within the premises of an educational establishment provided that the communication cannot be received by any person situated outside the premises of that establishment. Similar provision is made in respect of rights in performances by para.6 of Sch.2 to the 1988 Act (as to which see para.12–84). However, these provisions do not apply if or to the extent that there is a certified licensing scheme in force.[268] On May 30, 1990, a certified licensing scheme operated by ERA came into force.[269] This scheme and then its successor have been replaced such that the current scheme, which came into force on April 1, 2007, is brought into force by the Copyright (Certification of Licensing Scheme for Educational Recording of Broadcasts) (Educational Recording Agency Ltd) Order 2007 (SI 2007/266), as amended, which was made under s.143 of and para.16 of Sch.2A to the 1988 Act. The scheme itself ("the 2007 Scheme") is contained within the schedule to that statutory instrument. Details of the evolution of the various schemes are contained in previous editions of this work.

The 2007 Scheme is limited to specified categories of material, the copyright in which is owned or controlled by specified Licensor Members of the ERA and, as the new licensing scheme extends to rights to performances, to the performances by persons represented by other specified Licensor Members such as Equity, the Musician's Union and The Incorporated Society of Musicians.

The list of Licensor Members is contained in para.8 of the 2007 Scheme. That paragraph was amended by SI 2008/211 so that, as from April 1, 2008, it included the following bodies: ALCS, AGICOA (the Association of International Collective Management of Audiovisual Works—Association de Gestion Internationale Collective des Oeuvres Audiovisuelles. A typographical error in the word "Gestion" was corrected (from "Geston") by art.2(2) of SI 2009/20), BPI, BBC Worldwide Ltd, Channel Four Television Corporation, Channel Five Broadcasting Limited, DACS, Directors UK Limited (the new name of the DPRS—see para.27–61, above), Equity, Incorporated Society of Musicians, ITV Network Limited, MCPS, Musicians Union, PRS, PPL and Sianel Pedwar, Cymru (Channel 4, Wales). It does not apply to Open University programmes[270] (the Open University has its own licensing scheme[271]).

The ERA Scheme permits licensees to cause or authorise the making of recordings of a broadcast and copies of such a recording and (only as a direct result of their inclusion in a broadcast) of copyright works and/or performances contained in the recorded broadcast by or on behalf of an Educational Establishment for the educational purposes of that Educational Establishment ("ERA Recordings") (para.7(a)); and to authorise ERA Recordings to be communicated to the public by a person situated within the premises of an Educational Establishment but only to the extent that the communication cannot be received by any person situated outside the premises of that Educational Establishment (para.7(b)). Rates are set in para.17 of the 2007 Scheme, as amended most recently by SI 2009/20. These are as follows: Primary/Preparatory schools: 32p per head; secondary schools: 56p per head; further education establishments: £1.06 per head; and

---

[268] CDPA 1988 s.35(2).

[269] Under the Copyright (Certification of Licensing Scheme for Educational Recording of Broadcasts and Cable Programmes) (Educational Recording Agency Ltd) Order 1990 (SI 1990/879). See Vol.2 B2.i. This has been amended by the following statutory instruments: SI 1992/211, SI 1993/193, SI 1994/247, SI 1996/191, SI 1998/203, SI 1999/3452 and SI 2003/188.

[270] ERA Scheme para.8.

[271] Certified under the Copyright (Certification of Licensing Scheme for Educational Recording of Broadcasts)(Open University) Order 2003 (SI 2003/187). See Vol.2 B2.ii.

higher education establishments or otherwise uncategorised establishments: £1.67 per head. ERA has negotiated discounted licence fees with umbrella organisations representing large numbers of educational establishments.[272] Under the terms of ERA's licence, all recordings or copies must be marked with a statement that the recording is to be used only for educational purposes.[273] ERA reserves the right to require licensees to carry out a survey of the material they copy and record[274] and to inspect all recordings and copies made by licensees under the terms of the licence.[275]

In December 2006 the Gowers Review published its recommendations. These included that steps should be taken to enable educational provisions to cover distance learning and interactive white boards by 2008 by amending s.35 of the Copyright Designs and Patents Act 1988. As a result, since August 1, 2007 ERA has offered a new "ERA Plus Licence". This will permit Licensor Members to authorise ERA Recordings to be accessed by students and teachers online whether they are on the premises of their school, college or university, at home, or working elsewhere in the United Kingdom.

Educational establishments and bodies acting on behalf of educational establishments which hold ERA licences will be eligible for ERA Plus licences. The right to record broadcasts for non-commercial educational purposes by making ERA Recordings will continue to be governed by the terms of the ERA licence.

The annual tariff for the ERA Plus Licence will be calculated according to the number of full-time or full-time equivalent students who have the benefit of the licence. For licences taking effect on or after April 1, 2009 the tariffs are as follows: Primary/Preparatory schools: 16p per head; secondary schools: 28p per head; further education establishments: 53p per head; and higher education establishments: 84p per head. The ERA Plus Licence will offer the same discounts as an ordinary licence where blanket licences have been taken out.

It was initially anticipated by ERA that the recommended changes to ss.35 and 36 of the 1988 Act would be made in 2008. However, by October 2010, no such changes have been made, and no timetable for those changes is apparent. ERA is therefore unable to guarantee that establishments seeking to make off-air recordings available online to students not present on their premises will be protected from copyright infringement either by the ERA Plus licence or by a defence to infringement like that in s.35(1).

ERA is a company limited by guarantee. For the year ending March 31, 2009, the ERA distributed £6.7 million in relation to the membership agreement and a further £520,480 as a result of the ERA Plus Licence. It charges a commission of about 4.5 per cent. If fees are not paid when due or a licensee is in substantial breach of the licence terms, for example by permitting an unauthorised use of an ERA recording, the ERA may give the licensee 28 days' notice of termination. The notice will take effect at the end of the 28-day period unless the licensee has paid the outstanding fees or remedied the breach: see para.20 of the Scheme. Interest may be charged at the rate prescribed by the Late Payment of Commercial Debts (Interest) Act 1998: see para.22 of the Scheme. Overheads are recouped against a budget approved by members which equates to a commission

---

[272] *Off-Air Recording for Educational Establishments*, ERA, 1999.
[273] See para.11 of the ERA Scheme. The ERA now produces labels suitable for this purpose for video cassettes and DVDs. These are available to licensees at cost. When ERA recordings are made and stored in digital form for access through a computer, labelling must take the form of a written opening credit or webpage which must be viewed or listened to before access to the recording is permitted.
[274] See para.13 of the ERA Scheme.
[275] See para.14 of the ERA Scheme.

of around 6.5 per cent. Its website is at *http://www.era.org.uk* [Accessed November 8, 2010].

J. MECHANICAL-COPYRIGHT PROTECTION SOCIETY LTD ("MCPS")

27–63   MCPS exists to protect the "mechanical" copyright in musical works. This is defined in its current membership agreement as the right to make sound-bearing copies of musical works, to issue such copies to the public, to import such copies and to authorise any of these things.[276] As at July 2007 MCPS had 40 reciprocal agreements with societies in foreign countries. MCPS is a company limited by shares. It is a wholly owned subsidiary of Music Publishers' Association Ltd, a company limited by guarantee. The normal membership agreement,[277] involves the appointment of MCPS as the member's agent to manage and administer its mechanical copyright in the United Kingdom and (in certain circumstances) throughout the world.[278] The agreement empowers MCPS to grant licences and collect royalties on the member's behalf[279] and obliges MCPS to use its best endeavours to prevent infringement.[280] It entitles (but does not oblige) MCPS to take proceedings for infringement in the member's name.[281] MCPS's licensing arrangements in relation to phonorecords[282] were the subject of a Copyright Tribunal decision in 1992,[283] which fixed royalty rates at 8.5 per cent of that part of the published price for dealers attributable to music the copyright in which is administered by MCPS. Pursuant to the Copyright Tribunal decision, MCPS offers three types of licence agreement to record companies.[284] The AP.1 agreement[285] permits the record company to record any work within MCPS's repertoire provided MCPS is notified at least seven working days before release. Royalties are paid quarterly in arrears. However, consent for a first recording must still be obtained in advance.[286] The AP.2A agreement is intended for companies which have a trading history with MCPS but do not fulfil the financial and accounting criteria for the AP.1 agreement. The record company must obtain a licence before manufacture, but is given a 60-day credit period up to an agreed sum for the payment of royalties. The AP.2 agreement is similar to the AP.2A agreement but there is no credit period. There are other standard agreements for other specialist areas, such as videos, music-DVD videos and newspaper/magazine covermounts.[287] There are blanket licensing arrangements with substantially all UK television and radio stations,[288] schools[289] and many other specialist music providers, such as in-flight radio programme providers, online music service providers, karaoke disc producers, mobile phone ringtone suppli-

---

[276] cl.16.21 of MA2. Note, however, that authorising the importation of infringing copies is not an infringement of copyright.

[277] Agreement MA2 dated August 1994.

[278] cl.1.1.

[279] cl.1.2.

[280] cl.9.1.

[281] cl.11.

[282] i.e. CDs, cassettes, and vinyl records made for the purpose of retail sale to the public.

[283] *BPI v MCPS* [1993] E.M.L.R. 86, 139.

[284] Terms and Conditions of Business, Product Licensing (MCPS).

[285] As at July 2006 about 180 record companies and associated labels were parties to an AP.1 Agreement.

[286] In addition, there are specific restrictions as to the making of adaptations of works. The licence does not cover reproduction where the licence of the owner of the sound recording copyright or the consent of the performer has not been obtained.

[287] Terms and Conditions of Business, Product Licensing (MCPS).

[288] Terms and Conditions of Business, Broadcast Blanket Licensing (MCPS).

[289] Through the ERA. See para.27–62, above.

ers and video jukebox software suppliers.[290] MCPS levies commission on royalties before they are distributed to members. As at October 2010 commission rates were fixed at between 3.6 per cent and 20 per cent depending on the product and the nature of the licensing agreement. The AP.1 agreement had a commission rate of 6.25 per cent, the AP.2 agreement, 12.5 per cent and the AP.2A agreement 7.5 per cent. In the year ending December 31, 2009, royalties of £187,660 was distributed with a commission of a little over £16.2m levied. MCPS administers the off-air educational recording right on behalf of its members through the ERA.[291] Some time ago, MCPS established an operational alliance with the PRS under which both societies are managed by a limited company which is jointly owned by them. This company employs the staff and owns assets such as buildings. However, the rights continue to be vested in or administered by the societies separately and there is no intention to merge the two organisations. On January 18, 2009, the name of this alliance was changed to "PRS for Music". Its website is at *http://www.prsformusic.com* [Accessed November 8, 2010]. As at August 2010, PRS for Music had a combined membership of 63,952 writers and composers and 7,587 publishers.

K. NEWSPAPER LICENSING AGENCY LTD ("NLA")

The NLA was launched in January 1996 in order to license certain types of copying of newspaper articles. Its repertoire comprises works appearing in all the national newspapers and over 1,400 regional newspapers in the United Kingdom, the Channel Islands, and a number of foreign newspapers.[292] The publishers assign to the NLA the reproduction right in the literary and artistic works and in the typographical arrangement of the published editions of any works appearing in those newspapers.[293] However, as a result of the decision of the House of Lords in *Newspaper Licensing Agency Ltd v Marks & Spencer Plc*[294] the NLA now concentrates on enforcing its literary and artistic copyrights rather than those in the typographical arrangements of the newspapers of its members.

27–64

There is a basic licence fee which covers ad hoc copying for internal management purposes of national newspapers and is based on the size of the licensee, measured either by number of staff or by turnover.[295] The basic licence also permits the occasional digital copying of national newspapers other than the *Financial Times* (for which digital licences have been available direct from its publishers since July 1, 2010) and those published by News International (for

---

[290] Terms and Conditions of Business, Other Licensing (MCPS).

[291] See para.27–62, above.

[292] Including the major newspapers in Australia, Austria, Belgium, Canada, Finland, France, the Republic of Ireland, the Netherlands, Norway, Russia, Switzerland, and the United States.

[293] Publisher Mandate, cl.1(a). For these purposes, "works" are defined as including advertisements, photographs, cartoon and strip illustrations, graphic designs, drawings, illustrations, charts, diagrams, paintings and other works of fine art: Publisher Mandate cl.1(c). The full list of reproduction rights assigned is: photocopying; faxing; digital scanning and transmission; and any copying, reproduction or other act which takes place as a necessary incident to one of these acts throughout the world: Publisher Mandate cl.1(a). The right to pursue claims of copyright infringement in respect of unlicensed copying extends to all these forms of reproduction together with any other unlicensed act of copying or reproduction. By cl.1(c) the assignment extends to all works previously published in the newspaper.

[294] [2001] UKHL 38; [2003] 1 A.C. 551; [2002] R.P.C. 4. This case is discussed at length at para.3–106, above. It is understood that Marks & Spencer Plc has now taken a standard NLA licence to copy newspaper cuttings for its internal management and information purposes.

[295] Thus, for example, in the year commencing July 1, 2010, a company with 51 to 100 employees or with a turnover of £2–5 million paid an annual fee of £362. Higher licence fees are charged as regional titles are added to the licensed publications, or if the organisation undertakes "frequent copying", defined to be regularly repeated copying, with a view to distributing articles to a predetermined set of recipients. Further charges also apply to PR agencies copying newspaper extracts for supply to third parties.

which a digital licence is available as part of the NLA's "eClips" service). This digital extension permits the receipt of electronic newspaper cuttings either in the form of email attachments or links to a media monitoring website, the distribution of such cuttings internally to staff and the continued access to such cuttings for 28 days from receipt[296].

From January 2010 this basic licence can also permit (subject to the payment of an increased licence fee) the copying of content from websites operated by NLA members, but notably excluding websites operated by News International and the website at *http://www.FT.com* [Accessed November 8, 2010]. Licensees have a choice of paying for this digital license extension under one of two schemes: a variable basis based on the total volume of estimated links in a year (at a rate of 5p per link per staff member); or by a fixed fee depending on the organisation's number of staff and the number of people set to receive website links. By way of example, a company of 51–100 employees distributing clippings to 9–15 members of staff would pay £444 for the year commencing July 1, 2010). If an organisation is taking a licence from the NLA for the first time and wishing to take advantage of this service, it pays 1.5 times these rates.

Additional fees are payable for the copying of other newspapers, for systematic copying, for digital copying, and for public relations consultancies and trade or professional organisations who make copies for their clients. The licences expressly permit the reproduction of photographs, illustrations or advertisements.[297] There is a limit of 250 copies of any particular article.[298] Special licences are available for professional partnerships[299] and educational establishments.[300] Non-educational charities are entitled to apply for a discount.[301] Except in the case of public relations consultancies, trade or professional organisations, professional partnerships and educational establishments, licensees are not generally permitted to use copies of press cuttings otherwise than for distribution to personnel for their internal use.[302] The NLA's website is at *http://www.nla.co.uk* [Accessed November 8, 2010]. It is a company limited by shares.

L. PERFORMING RIGHT SOCIETY LTD ("PRS")

27–65   The PRS exists to administer the performing rights in musical works (which expression includes any words associated with musical works,[303]) i.e. the rights to perform such works in public, to communicate them to the public and to authorise others to do the same.[304] It also administers the film synchronisation right in musical works, which is defined as the exclusive right in any part of the world to record them on the soundtrack of a film.[305] As noted in the discussion of the

---

[296] Clause 10 of the NLA Licence terms and conditions.

[297] Definition of "Cutting" in the NLA Licence terms and conditions.

[298] Clause 4.2 of the NLA Licence terms and conditions.

[299] The licence contains specific provisions as to the supply of copies to clients.

[300] Schools where the normal admission age is under 16 can obtain a licence free of charge: Clause 7.6 of the NLA Licence terms and conditions.

[301] Clause 9 of the NLA Licence terms and conditions.

[302] Clauses 4.1 and 11 of the NLA Licence terms and conditions.

[303] art.1(a)(xvii) of the PRS Articles of Association defines "musical work" as including "(a) any part of a musical work, (b) any vocal or instrumental music recorded on the soundtrack of any film, (c) any musical accompaniment to non-musical plays, (d) any words or music of monologues having a musical introduction or accompaniment, [and] (e) any other words (or part of words) which are associated with a musical work even if the musical work itself is not in copyright, or even if the performing rights in the musical work are not administered by [the PRS]".

[304] Articles of Association art.1(xix). See CDPA 1988 ss.19 and 16(2).

[305] Articles of Association art.1(a)(xii). In *Music Gallery Ltd v Direct Line Insurance Plc* [1998] E.M.L.R. 551, it was held that the film synchronisation right granted to the PRS by its members

MCPS,[306] some time ago, PRS and MCPS established an operational alliance under which both societies are managed by a limited company which is jointly owned by them. On January 18, 2009, the name of this alliance was changed to "PRS for Music". As at August 2010, PRS for Music had a combined membership of 63,952 writers and composers and 7,587 publishers.[307] As at November 2008, the PRS had 89 affiliations with societies in foreign countries. In the year ending December 31, 2009, £166.9 million was collected from those international income sources. The PRS has claimed that its licence is necessary for the public performance[308] of "just about all the copyright music in the world".[309] The PRS is a company limited by guarantee registered under the Companies Act 1985. The Articles of Association require members on election (or at any time thereafter if so requested) to assign or cause to be assigned to the PRS the following rights in "all or any works or parts of works,[310] present or future, of which the member is the writer, publisher or proprietor", namely: the performing right; (in the case of writer members only) the film synchronisation right in every work composed or written primarily for the soundtrack of a film; and such other rights as the Board of the PRS may direct.[311] Provision is made for members to reserve to themselves on admission one or more "categories of rights" or "forms of utilisation" of their rights in all of their works,[312] and for existing members to require the PRS on notice to reassign any such rights to them.[313] It is further provided that any assignment of the film synchronisation right must expressly require the PRS at the request of the composer or author of a work to assign or license the film synchronisation right in the work to the film producer or any other person who commissioned the composition or writing of the work on terms as to the payment to the PRS by the film producer of royalties in respect of cinema showings of the film in the United States of America.[314] It is also provided that any member may require the PRS to reassign the right to perform the work live in public.[315] Finally, it is provided that the PRS may "decline to exercise" the performing right in a speci-

---

in works written primarily for the purpose of being included in the soundtrack of a particular film or films in contemplation when the work was commissioned, applies only to that film or those films and not to any film.

[306] For which, see para.27–63, above.

[307] For eligibility, see Articles of Association art.4.

[308] As to what constitutes a performance "in public" see paras 7–103 et seq., above.

[309] *http://www.prsformusic.com/users/businessesandliveevents/musicforbusinesses/Pages/ WhatisPRSforMusic.aspx* [Accessed October 15, 2010].

[310] Presumably this is intended to be a reference to musical works as defined in art.1(a)(xvii).

[311] Articles of Association, arts 7(a) and 7(c). The terms of art.7(c)(iii) are intended to permit the Board of the PRS to specify particular parts of the performing and film synchronisation right which are not to be administered by it. If they are not to be administered by the PRS then they are not within the ambit of any assignment to it: art.7(a). The Board has directed that the PRS shall not in fact administer the so-called "grand rights", i.e. the performing right in "dramatico-musical works" (defined in the Rules of the PRS as "an opera, operetta, musical play, revue or pantomime, in so far as it consists of words and music written expressly therefor": see r.1(e)) or ballets. For a more detailed account of the rights which the PRS does not administer, see its *Member Information Pack "Dramatic presentations of music"*.

[312] arts 7(cc) and (cd). The terminology derives from *Re Gema* [1971] C.M.L.R. (R.P. Supplement) D35 at D49 and *Re Gema (No.2)* [1972] C.M.L.R. (R.P. Supplement) D115 at D116. The "categories of rights" are expressed as follows "(i) the general performing right; (ii) the broadcasting right, including the public performing right of broadcast works (transmission right); (iii) the right of cinematographic exhibition; (iv) the right of mechanical reproduction and diffusion, including the public performing right of mechanically reproduced works (transmission right); (v) the cinematographic production right; (vi) the exploitation rights resulting from technical developments or future change in the law." The "forms of utilisation of rights" are the same as the categories of rights but also include the "televising right", the "public performing right of televised works" and the "public performing right of works reproduced on video tape".

[313] Articles of Association arts 7(cc) and (cd). For the notice periods, which may be up to three years, see art.9(f).

[314] art.7(b). *BPI v MCPS* (the "Downloading" decision) [2008] E.M.L.R. 5.

[315] art.7(g).

fied work or works.[316] The PRS is obliged by the Rules to enforce the rights assigned to it.[317] As well as individual licences, there are a number of different licensing schemes, the tariff for each of which depends on the category of user.[318] Because blanket licences are granted, the system of royalty distribution is complex and sophisticated. Some licensees (including the BBC, ITV and many concert venues) are required to submit a full census of all performances. Otherwise, licence fees are distributed on the basis of sample returns from users together with analogous data such as radio usage. Royalties in respect of a particular work are divided between publishers and authors in a set proportion, subject to any prior agreement there may be between them.[319] In the financial year ending December 31, 2009, PRS received £438.8 million in licence revenue resulting in a net distributable income of £387.9 million. On February 1, 1996, the Monopolies and Mergers Commission ("MMC") published a report on the PRS.[320] It found that a monopoly situation existed in favour of PRS and made 44 recommendations, all of which have now been implemented.[321] The website of PRS for Music (the alliance of PRS with MCPS) is at *http://www.prsformusic* [Accessed November 8, 2010].

M. PHONOGRAPHIC PERFORMANCE LTD ("PPL")

27–66 PPL was established in 1934 to administer certain rights in sound recordings on behalf of its record company members. Since the implementation of the Rental and Related Rights Directive on December 1, 1996, PPL has paid equitable remuneration to performers. PPL is a company limited by guarantee. As at October 2010, it had around 5,750 record company members and 45,000 performer members. The record company members assign to PPL (or, where they are not the owner of the relevant rights, appoint PPL as their exclusive agent in respect of) all their current and future broadcast and public performance rights together with the related "dubbing" rights, that is the rights to make copies for the purposes of subsequent broadcasts or public performances.

PPL licenses over 200,000 premises for public performance, and is a frequent applicant for injunctions to restrain the unlicensed playing of sound recordings from its repertoire in public. The approach it takes to obtaining injunctive relief in most cases was approved by the Court of Appeal in *PPL v Saibal Maitra*.[322] PPL has about 60 different tariffs which depend on the category into which the user of the sound recordings falls. The revenue is distributed to members and performers according to the way in which the sound recordings were used, which is determined by a variety of means including detailed track-based usage reports received from licensees and specialist chart data. Once PPL has received all of this information, it compares it with the PPL Repertoire Database to identify exactly which tracks have been played. The PPL Repertoire Database now contains information relating to over 10 million sound recordings. For each track on the Repertoire Database a substantial amount of information is held, such as the record company that owns the track and the full performer line-up, which often includes many orchestral and other performers as well as the featured

---

[316] art.7(f). See also *Member Information Pack "Dramatic presentations of music"*. This right is in practice exercised at the member's request.

[317] Rules and Regulations r.2(a).

[318] See in respect of Tariff D (dance halls) *PRS v BEDA* [1993] E.M.L.R. 325.

[319] For details see *Member Information Pack "Registering works and agreements"*.

[320] Cm. No.3147. See further para.27–30, above

[321] Examples are the member's entitlement to require a reassignment of the right to perform the work in public.

[322] *Phonographic Performance Limited v Saibal Maitra and Others* [1998] 1 W.L.R. 870; [1998] F.S.R. 749.

artist(s). PPL allocates money to each track depending upon the amount of use each has received. PPL then distributes this to members and performers along with information showing how much each track has earned.

Members may also appoint PPL as their agent to administer and license their "new media" rights, which are the right to communicate any sound recording, via the internet or otherwise, to the public and the right to make copies for the purpose of such communication. Therefore, in addition to the public performance licences, PPL also grants licences to radio and television broadcasters who wish to incorporate sound recordings in their broadcasts and licences the simultaneous transmission over the internet of a radio station's broadcasts. The standard licences that permit communication to the public via internet services are limited to those activities that would fall within the right to broadcast, such as the provision of radio via the internet. These licences do not grant permission to carry out acts that fall within the making available right, and as such each internetservice permitted by the licence must be streamed only, and must not permit the user to download, fast forward, rewind or repeat the content. However, other licences that would provide the right to do these things, and which have been agreed with broadcasters to permit archived programmes to be made available on demand, may be available by individual negotiation. PPL also grants licences to commercial suppliers of background music, who wish to dub sound recordings for subsequent public performance in their customers' premises. By its Articles of Association and by virtue of these assignments, PPL is granted sole power and authority in the name of its members to collect licence fees, to recover damages for infringement of the broadcasting, public performance or dubbing right and to take, defend and compromise proceedings in relation to such rights.[323]

Members may also appoint PPL as their agent to exploit their repertoire overseas and collect payment from overseas collecting societies. PPL offers international services to collect overseas public performance, broadcast and associated income from a growing number of territories on behalf of record company members and registered performers. This service involves the member or performer giving PPL a legal mandate to collect overseas income, either in all territories or on a country-by-country basis. As at October 2010, PPL had 26 arrangements with foreign producer societies and 21 arrangements with foreign performer societies. In the financial year ending December 31, 2009, PPL collected £21.6 million from foreign societies.

Following the implementation of the Rental and Related Rights Directive on December 1, 1996, PPL has paid equitable remuneration to performers. The split between the record company as owner of the copyright in the sound recording and the performer has been agreed at 50:50. In late 2006, PPL took over the businesses of two other performers' collecting societies,[324] removing a duplication of work by the three societies and thereby reducing administration costs. As a consequence of this responsibility for performers' remuneration, PPL's Memorandum and Articles of Association provide for a "Performer Board" controlled by performer representatives to oversee the distribution of income and secure the repatriation of overseas earnings. In addition, a Director of Performer Affairs has been appointed and Annual Performer Meetings are be held.

In the year ending December 31, 2009, PPL's gross revenue was £129.6 million, but a reduced sum of £111.4 million was available as licence fee income

---

[323] Articles of Association art.9(i).
[324] The Association of United Recordings Artists ("AURA") and the Performing Artists' Media Rights Association Ltd ("PAMRA"). Both AURA and PAMRA went into members' voluntary liquidation following the merger. Some information about them is available in previous editions of this book.

because of substantial repayments that had to be made following an adverse decision of the Copyright Tribunal.[325] After deducting administration costs, £91.5 million was available for distribution from collections in the year ending December 31, 2009. PPL's website is at *http://www.ppluk.com* [Accessed November 8, 2010].

N. Publishers Licensing Society Ltd ("PLS")

27–67   PLS was established in 1981 and exists in part to oversee a collective licensing scheme in the United Kingdom for book, journal, and magazine copying. It is a company limited by guarantee, owned by three trade associations, the Association of Learned and Professional Society Publishers, the Periodical Publishers Association, and the Publishers Association. As at October 2010, its board of directors had nine members, consisting of three representatives from each of those associations. In turn, together with the ALCS,[326] it owns the CLA.[327]

PLS takes a licence from its mandating publishers consisting of the non-exclusive right to do or to authorise the doing of any of the acts restricted by copyright, database right and other intellectual property rights with respect to that publisher's publications but only to the extent that the publisher owns or controls the rights and only to the extent required for the purpose of various collective licences. The licence may also include the collection of public lending right revenues from overseas.[328] Having aggregated these licences from its mandating publishers, the PLS realises revenue by sublicensing those rights through the CLA or through similar bodies overseas. At the end of the financial year ending March 31, 2010, the PLS had 2,746 mandating publishers, to whom it distributed £28.4 million from an income of £29.6 million.

O. Video Performance Ltd ("VPL")

27–68   VPL exists to exercise and enforce certain rights in music videos. It is a company limited by guarantee. Its members are the owners or exclusive licensees of the rights to broadcast and perform music videos in public together with the "dubbing right" which permits the copying of videos for the purpose of subsequent broadcast or public performance. VPL and PPL have very close ties: while they remain separate companies, they have a centralised management. As at October 2010, over half of the members of the VPL Board were also members of the PPL Board. The administrative functions VPL and PPL are carried out in the same building and by the same people. VPL licences are frequently referred to as PPL Video licences to further emphasise this common management.

Various tariffs are available depending upon the nature of the licensee's exploitation of music videos. There is a background tariff suitable for playing such videos on no more than five TV monitors (defined to have a screen size up to and including 41"). The cost of this tariff for licences taken out between January 1, 2010 and December 31, 2010 is £235.37 plus VAT. There is a foreground tariff where larger screens or more than five TV monitors are used. There are also tariffs for exhibition uses, airlines, concert/stage events, a video jukebox operators' tariff, a mobile DJ tariff and finally a tariff for spectator sports venues.

As at October 2010, VPL had over 1,200 members (including major record companies in the United Kingdom) and controlled the copyright in over 80,000

---

[325] For Copyright Tribunal cases to which PPL has been a party, see the notes to para.28–77, fn.424, below.
[326] For which, see para.27–56, above
[327] For which, see para.27–59, above.
[328] PLS General terms and conditions, definition of "Licensed Rights".

music videos. VPL's gross revenue for the year ending December 31, 2009 was £11.4 million and its administrative costs were £2.2 million. VPL has no dedicated website, instead sharing the website of PPL at *http://www.ppluk.com* [Accessed November 8, 2010].

CHAPTER TWENTY EIGHT

CONTROL OF THE EXERCISE OF COPYRIGHTS AND RELATED RIGHTS

Contents   *Para.*

1. INTRODUCTION

Scheme of this chapter. The exercise of copyright and related rights by their **28–01** owner is subject to a variety of legal restraints. It is the purpose of this Chapter to examine the different legal restraints which may operate to fetter the free exercise of exclusive rights accorded under the 1988 Act and the Database Regulations. The second section deals with nine situations where the owner's right may be, or become, subject to a compulsory licence. The third section deals with certain anomalous circumstances where there is some interference with the free exercise of such rights, but which stop short of a compulsory or statutory licence. The fourth section sets out the jurisdiction of the Copyright Tribunal, and its control over the exercise of rights in a wide variety of different circumstances. The procedure before the Tribunal is also described in this section. The fifth section describes the effect of rules of European and domestic competition law. The sixth section covers the application of the doctrine of restraint of trade to the exercise of such rights.

2. COMPULSORY LICENCES

A. INTRODUCTION

Nature of compulsory licences. Although copyright is a property right, in certain **28–02** limited circumstances the law permits uses of works without the consent of the copyright owner if the user complies with specified conditions, including the payment of a fee.[1] In such circumstances, the copyright owner is compelled to license the particular use of the work and the licence is referred to as a "compulsory licence" or "licence of right".[2] Although the conceptual distinction is sometimes blurred,[3] such licences differ from permitted acts in that payment is required. The effect of a compulsory licence is not dissimilar to the refusal by a court of injunctive relief or to a statutory right of "equitable remuneration" in that the right owner is left with the possibility of financial compensation for uses of the work rather than control over such uses. A further useful distinction can be drawn between statutory licences and compulsory licences properly so called. In the case of a statutory licence the rate is fixed by law, whereas in the case of a compulsory licence the rate is left to be negotiated, but in neither case can use be refused or prevented.[4] Collectively these licences can be referred to as non-voluntary licences.

Nature of compulsory licences: a summary. Under existing domestic law **28–03**

---

[1] Thus, in jurisprudential terms, the grant of a compulsory licence converts a property rule into a liability rule. See further, Ayres and Talley, "Solomonic Bargaining: Dividing a Legal Entitlement to facilitate Coasean Trade" (1995) 104 Yale L.J. 1027; Kaplow and Sharell, "Property Rules Versus Liability Rules: An Economic Analysis" (1996) 109 Harv. L.Rev. 713. For consideration in the context of intellectual property, see Merges, "Contracting into Liability Rules: Intellectual Property Rights and Collective Rights Organizations" (1996) 84 Cal. L.Rev. 1293.

[2] Compare Patents Act 1977 (c.37) ss.46–54.

[3] In particular, note that a number of the permitted acts only take effect in the absence of a licensing arrangement, thereby encouraging the grant of licences: CDPA 1988 ss.31B, 35, 36, 60, 74.

[4] Historically, the United Kingdom has adopted a mixture of statutory and compulsory licences, although since 1989 the preference has clearly been for compulsory licences.

compulsory licences are available in eight distinct circumstances: where the copyright work comprises broadcast schedules and a person wishes to reproduce those schedules[5]; where the work is a sound recording, and it is proposed to broadcast it or include it in a cable programme[6]; where copyright had lapsed but has been revived by the Duration Regulations[7]; where the work is a document embodying a design which was in existence on January 1, 1989 and therefore subject to transitional provisions[8]; where the Secretary of State has made an order regarding the lending of works[9]; where a copyright work is included in a wireless broadcast which is retransmitted by cable under a statutory requirement but beyond the original broadcast area[10]; where the work is of "enemy origin"[11]; and where the Secretary of State, the Office of Fair Trading or the Competition Commission so provide under their statutory powers in relation to competition.[12] Compulsory licences may also be made available if a copyright owner is found to have violated art.102 of the Treaty on the Functioning of the European Union ("TFEU") or the Competition Act 1998 by abusing a dominant position.[13] Further compulsory licences exist in relation to unregistered design right, in particular, to allow for the reproduction of a design during the last five years of its protection, but these provisions are dealt with elsewhere.[14]

B. OVERVIEW

(i) History of compulsory and statutory licences in the United Kingdom

28–04   Apart from the existing provisions, the United Kingdom has historically recognised four other situations where non-voluntary licences were made available. The first compulsory licence was introduced into the United Kingdom by the Literary Copyright Act 1842.[15] This provision was aimed at preventing the newly increased term of protection from being used in such a way as to be detrimental to the public interest. It gave the Judicial Committee of the Privy Council a power to grant compulsory licences any time after the death of the author where the owner of the copyright was preventing a work that had previously been published from being republished. This provision was re-enacted in the 1911 Act and the powers of the Judicial Committee of the Privy Council were extended to cover cases where the owner was refusing to grant a licence to allow a work to be performed in public.[16] These provisions were not repeated in the 1956 Act.[17] A second non-voluntary licence was available after 1847 to permit the importation

---

[5] Broadcasting Act 1990 (c.42) s.176, Sch.17, paras 28–09 et seq., below.

[6] CDPA 1988 ss.135A–H, paras 28–25 et seq., below.

[7] Duration of Copyright and Rights in Performances Regulations (SI 1995/3297) reg.24(1), paras 28–41 et seq., below.

[8] CDPA 1988 Sch.1, para.28–44, below.

[9] CDPA 1988 s.66, paras 28–45 et seq., below.

[10] CDPA 1988 s.73(4), paras 28–48 et seq., below.

[11] The Patents, Designs, Copyright and Trade Marks (Emergency) Act 1939 (c.107) s.2, paras 28–52 et seq., below.

[12] CDPA 1988 s.144, paras 28–54 et seq., below.

[13] Previously art.82 and previously to that art.84 of the Treaty of Rome.

[14] See paras 13–127 et seq., above.

[15] Literary Copyright Act 1842 (5 & 6 Vict. c.45) s.5. It might be noted, however, that the Statute of Anne 1709 (8 Anne c.19) contained a provision which allowed for a maximum price to be set on the sale of particular books, a provision which has been described as "analogous" to a compulsory licence. See Latman, Gorman & Ginsburg, *Copyright for the Nineties* 3rd edn (New York: Matthew Bender, 1989) p.4.

[16] Copyright Act 1911 s.4.

[17] The powers under the 1911 Act were never in fact used and repeal occurred in the light of the recommendations of the Gregory Committee: Report of the Copyright Committee, 1952 (Cmnd. 8662). This enabled the United Kingdom to comply with the Brussels Act (1948) revising the

of reprints of works into the colonies, on payment of a customs duty which was to be redistributed to authors.[18] This scheme was abandoned in 1911.[19] A third such licence was introduced by the proviso to s.3 of the 1911 Act and gave a statutory licence to reproduce for sale any work after the expiration of 25 (or, in the case of pre-1911 works, 30) years from the date of death of the author, with the rate being calculated at 10 per cent on the price at which the work was published. Concern existed as to whether such a provision conflicted with the requirements of the Berne Convention, and the provision was not re-enacted in the 1956 Act.[20]

The fourth licence—the statutory recording licence—was introduced in 1911 and was maintained in the 1956 Act.[21] Under this licence manufacturers were entitled to make records of musical works which had previously been recorded with the consent of the copyright owner, provided the manufacturer gave the copyright owner notice of his intention to do so and paid a royalty. Further provision was made so that words previously associated with such a recording might also be reproduced.[22] The 1956 Act fixed the royalty payable at an amount equal to 6.25 per cent of the ordinary retail selling price of the record,[23] although this was subject to alteration following a public inquiry.[24] Regulations were prescribed setting out the particulars to be given by the manufacturer, including the estimated number of records intended to be sold or supplied.[25] This licence was originally introduced to encourage the growth of the then infant recording industry.[26] Despite the Whitford Committee's recommendation that the licence should remain (subject to alterations of detail),[27] the 1981 Green Paper suggested[28] and the 1986 White Paper recommended[29] its abolition. Consequently, the provisions of the 1956 Act were repealed by the 1988 Act and no equivalent scheme was substituted.[30] The decision to abolish the statutory recording licence was taken in recognition of the fact that the conditions of the market had long

---

Berne Convention. As to the international concern these provisions had caused, see Ricketson & Ginsburg, *International Copyright and Neighbouring Rights* (2006), paras 9.19, 9.20 and 9.24.

[18] Colonial Copyright Act 1847 (10 & 11 Vict. c.95). This was introduced primarily at the behest of the Canadians, who subsequently charged a duty of 12.5 per cent. However, very little was collected: Report of the Commission on Copyright, 1878 (C–2036) paras 182–197.

[19] Copyright Act 1911 s.37, Sch.2.

[20] Again, repeal occurred in the light of the recommendations of the Gregory Committee: Report of the Copyright Committee, 1952 (Cmnd.8662), para.23. However, it should be noted that although the 1956 Act repealed s.3 of the 1911 Act it maintained the effect of the proviso as a defence after 1956 in relation to reproductions of pre-1957 works in respect of which the requisite notice had been given.

[21] Copyright Act 1956 s.8; Copyright Act 1911 s.19. For a detailed discussion of the provisions, see *Copinger* 12th edn, paras 827 et seq. See also *Discount Inter-Shopping Co Ltd v Micrometre Ltd* [1984] Ch. 369; [1984] R.P.C. 198.

[22] Copyright Act 1956 s.8(5).

[23] Copyright Act 1956 s.8(2).

[24] Copyright Act 1956 s.8(3). An inquiry was held in 1977, but no change in the rate resulted.

[25] Copyright Royalty System (Records) Regulations, 1957 (SI 1957/866): *Copinger* 12th edn, paras 1737 et seq.

[26] Intellectual Property and Innovation, 1986 (Cmnd.9712) para.11.2. In the United States of America the introduction of a statutory mechanical recording licence was a response to the acts of the Aeolian Company, a piano-roll manufacturer, in purchasing the exclusive recording rights from over 80 music publishers. It was feared that this would give the Company an unbreakable hold on the market. The recording licence was thus introduced to ensure that, subject to the payment of a reasonable royalty, potential competitors would be free to release their own versions of popular recordings. See further, Rosenlund, "Compulsory Licensing of Musical Compositions for Phonorecords Under the Copyright Act of 1976," (1979) 30 Hastings L.J. 683 at 686–7.

[27] Whitford Committee: Report of the Committee to consider the Law on Copyright and Designs, 1977 (Cmnd.6732), paras 341–368.

[28] Reform of the Law relating to Copyright, Designs and Performers Protection 1981 (Cmnd.8302), pp.18–21.

[29] Intellectual Property and Innovation 1986 (Cmnd.9712), para.11.5.

[30] The 1988 Act contained transitional provisions such that the provisions of the 1956 Act continued

since changed and that there had been a breakdown of the consensus in its favour.[31] Nor was the Government convinced that the statutory recording licence was necessary in order to maintain diversity within the recording industry.[32]

28–05 Proposed licences. A number of proposals for the introduction of other non-voluntary licences have been made, but not adopted: these have included proposals to replace the copyright system with a system of royalties,[33] as well as more specific proposals for compulsory licences to publish foreign works,[34] to televise any event,[35] to use musical works in television programmes,[36] for the inclusion of sound recordings in cinematographic works,[37] for the making of ephemeral recordings,[38] for the public performance and broadcasting of musical and literary works[39] and to allow for the creation of multimedia works.[40] More recently interest has focused on the possibility of introducing compulsory licences or making similar provision for use of "orphan works", that is works whose owners are difficult or impossible to trace.[41]

(ii) International standards and policy considerations

28–06 International standards: Berne Convention.[42] One reason why so few non-voluntary licences exist in the United Kingdom is that international standards to which the United Kingdom has committed itself are generally antipathetic to such provisions. However, two provisions of the Berne Convention explicitly permit the national legislature to grant such licences.[43] Article 13 empowers each country to limit the rights of the authors of musical works and accompanying lyrics who have already authorised the making of a sound recording of their works to a right to equitable remuneration in respect of the making of future such

---

to apply where the prescribed notice was given by the manufacturer before August 1, 1989, but only in respect of the making of records within one year of that date and up to the number of records stated in the notice as intended to be sold. As regards licences thereafter, the matter is one of negotiation between the owners of copyright and the recording company. In general, this is effected in the UK by the Mechanical Copyright Protection Society (as to which, see para.27–63, above). In 1991, on a reference from British Phonographic Industry Ltd, the Copyright Tribunal set the rate at 8.5%: *The British Phonographic Industry Ltd v Mechanical-Copyright Protection Society Ltd (No. 2)* [1993] E.M.L.R. 86. This remains the rate.

[31] Intellectual Property and Innovation 1986 (Cmnd.9712), para.11.4.

[32] Intellectual Property and Innovation 1986 (Cmnd.9712), para.11.4.

[33] Such a proposal was considered, but rejected, in the Report of the Royal Commission on Copyright, 1878 (C–2036), paras 16–22. Recently, however, there has been renewed interest in this proposal, with some commentators arguing that this might be the best way of ensuring remuneration for authors over electronic networks. For example, see Rheingold, *The Virtual Community* (London: Minerva, 1995), p.103.

[34] Scrutton, *The Law of Copyright* (London: John Murray, 1883), pp.276–77. But compare the UK's obligations under the Berne Convention. These are considered below.

[35] Gregory Committee: Report of the Copyright Committee, 1952 (Cmnd.8662), para.159

[36] Whitford Committee: Report of the Committee to consider the Law on Copyright and Designs, 1977 (Cmnd.6732), para.357.

[37] Whitford Committee: para.357.

[38] Whitford Committee: paras 359–60.

[39] Monopolies and Merger Commission: A Report on the supply in the UK of the services of administering performing rights and film synchronisation rights, 1996 (Cm.3147) paras 2.96, 2.131, 10.5, 10.21, 10.31, 10.38, 10.41, 10.48, 14.134.

[40] For a detailed discussion, see *Copinger* 15th edn, paras 29–69 to 29–72.

[41] This was considered by the Whitford Committee: paras 774–5. For more recent developments, see the UK IPO/BIS report © *the way ahead A Strategy for Copyright in the Digital Age* (October 28, 2009), cl.42 of the Digital Economy Bill 2010 (this clause was never enacted) and the Commission's Communications *Europeana-next steps*, August 28, 2009, para.3.2 and *A Digital Agenda for Europe* COM (2010) 245 p.9.

[42] As to the Berne Convention generally, see paras 23–04 et seq, above.

[43] For a useful analysis of Berne in the context of the US jukebox licence, see Martin, "The Berne Convention and the US Compulsory License for Jukeboxes: Why the Song Could not remain the Same" (1990) J Copyright Socy USA 262 at 296–307.

recordings.[44] Similarly, art.11*bis*(2) allows the author's exclusive right to authorise the communication to the public of the work, by broadcasting or related means, to be restricted to a right of equitable remuneration.[45] Although the WIPO Treaty adopted at Geneva in December 1996[46] had proposed to remove these provisions, in the end the status quo was maintained.[47] It may be possible to justify certain other licences under art.9(2) as regards reproduction of works "provided that such reproduction does not conflict with a normal exploitation of the work and does not unreasonably prejudice the legitimate interests of the author"; and under art.10(2) as regards use by way of illustration in publications for teaching provided such utilisation is compatible with fair practice.[48] It has also been suggested[49] that there might be a power to grant compulsory licences under art.17 of the Convention, which provides that "the provisions of this Convention cannot in any way affect the right of the Government of each country of the Union to *permit*, to control, or to prohibit, by legislation or regulation, the circulation, presentation, or exhibition of any work or production".[50] The better view, however, seems to be that art.17 is not intended to permit any general system of compulsory licences but to cover such things as the maintenance of public order and morality.[51] Over and above these provisions the UK delegation made a declaration (as opposed to a reservation) in relation to art.11 of the Brussels Act to the effect that the Government remained free to enact such legislation as it might consider necessary in the public interest to prevent or deal with any abuse of the monopoly rights conferred upon owners of copyright.[52] At the Stockholm revision conference in 1967, the UK Government put forward a proposal to amend art.17 to make express provision for abuse of monopoly by owners of substantial numbers of copyrights. This proposal was withdrawn upon it being accepted in principle that nothing in the Convention prevented members from taking action

---

[44] "Each country of the Union may impose for itself reservations and conditions on the exclusive right granted to the author of a musical work and to the author of any words, the recording of which together with the musical work has already been authorised by the latter, to authorise the sound recording of that musical work, together with such words, if any." see Ricketson and Ginsburg, *International Copyright and Neighbouring Rights* (2006), paras 13.59 et seq. Art.14 makes it explicit that this does not apply to cinematographic reproductions. For the full text of the Berne Convention (Paris Act 1971), see Vol.2 F1.

[45] "It shall be a matter for legislation in the countries of the Union to determine the conditions under which the rights mentioned in the preceding paragraph may be exercised, but those conditions ... shall not in any circumstances be prejudicial to the moral rights of the author, nor to his right to obtain equitable remuneration." Note that arts 13 and 11*bis* state that the right to equitable remuneration shall " *in the absence of agreement* be fixed by competent authority" (emphasis added). A literal reading of these provisions would suggest that countries of the Union are only entitled to grant compulsory licences, they are not free to introduce a statutory licence (see para.28–04, above). This is not, however, how the effect of this provision has historically been understood. For the full text of the Berne Convention (Paris Act 1971), see Vol.2 at F1.

[46] See paras 23–66 et seq, above.

[47] art.11 of the draft Treaty proposed the abolition of Certain Non-Voluntary Licenses within three years. It stated, "(1) Within three years of ratifying or acceding to this Treaty, Contracting Parties shall no longer provide for non-voluntary licenses under art.11*bis*(2) of the Berne Convention in respect of the broadcasting of a work. (2) Within three years of ratifying or acceding to this Treaty, Contracting Parties shall no longer apply the provisions of art.13 of the Berne Convention". At the meeting in Geneva, several delegations proposed a longer phase-out period and others favoured eliminating para.(2), many expressing concerns over possible anti-competitive conduct by recording companies. Ultimately, it was agreed that the article be deleted in its entirety and the existing provisions of the Berne Convention were maintained.

[48] See further, Ricketson and Ginsburg, *International Copyright and Neighbouring Rights* (2006), paras 13.03 and 13.43 et seq., respectively.

[49] See Ricketson and Ginsburg, *International Copyright and Neighbouring Rights* (2006), paras 13.91–13.92.

[50] Berne Convention (Paris Act 1971) art.17 (emphasis added); Vol.2 F1.

[51] See further, Ricketson and Ginsburg, *International Copyright and Neighbouring Rights* (2006), para.13.91.

[52] Ricketson and Ginsburg, *International Copyright and Neighbouring Rights* (2006), para.13.91.

against abuse of monopoly.[53] It seems, therefore, that compulsory licences can be imposed to control an abuse of monopoly.[54]

28–07   **Rome and Phonograms Conventions.**[55] The Rome Convention states that any Contracting State is permitted to provide for the same kinds of limitations in respect of the works covered by the Convention "as it provides for, in its domestic laws and regulations, in connection with the protection of copyright in literary and artistic works", but that "compulsory licences may be provided for only to the extent to which they are compatible with this Convention".[56] Consequently, compulsory licences may not be imposed as regards reproduction of phonograms since that would be inconsistent with art.10, nor in relation to the rebroadcasting, fixation or reproduction of broadcasts (which would be inconsistent with art.13) but may be imposed as regards secondary uses of phonograms under art.12, since this article only requires that Contracting States ensure that a remuneration is paid for the broadcasting or communication to the public of phonograms.[57]

Article 6 of the Convention for the Protection of Producers of Phonograms Against Unauthorised Duplication of their Phonograms (1971)[58] states that compulsory licences to make or import duplicates of phonograms may not be permitted unless (a) duplication is for use solely for the purpose of teaching or scientific research; (b) the licence does not permit export of the duplicates; and (c) an equitable remuneration, linked to the number of duplicates to be made, is paid.

28–08   **Policy considerations.** A second reason why the law has rarely allowed for non-voluntary licences is that they are seen as a "suspect device in copyright law generally".[59] They are "administratively cumbersome, unlikely to arrive at a correct rate,[60] and contrary to copyright's overall free market philosophy".[61] Nevertheless, such licences provide a compromise of the unrestricted exercise of intellectual property rights that the legislature occasionally finds attractive. It is not possible to characterise by way of a single principle the circumstances in which the legislature has in the past made copyright subject to such licences. Rather they have been employed to deal with a number of difficult situations. Some of the factors which seem to influence the choice of non-voluntary licences are as follows:

> (i) where a change in the law (such as extension of the term of copyright, or the addition of new rights) alters the assumptions upon which owners may have acquired copyright and potential users planned their activities[62];
>
> (ii) where in the light of technological change (such as the emergence of sound recordings), the refusal to license the use of copyright works might

---

[53] Ricketson and Ginsburg, *International Copyright and Neighbouring Rights* (2006), para.13.92.

[54] Note however that some states adopted different views as to the extent of measures which might be taken to prevent such abuse: Ricketson and Ginsburg, *International Copyright and Neighbouring Rights* (2006), para.13.92.

[55] As to these, see paras 23–88 et seq. and 23–109 et seq., above, respectively.

[56] Rome Convention for the Protection of Performers, Producers of Phonograms and Broadcasting Organisations 1961 art.15(2). For the text of the Convention, see Vol.2 F5. It might also be possible to justify a limited number of compulsory licences under art.15(1), which allows for exceptions to the protection guaranteed as regards private use, reporting of current events, ephemeral recordings and teaching and scientific research.

[57] See para.28–25, below.

[58] The text of the Convention is set out in Vol.2 F8.

[59] Ginsburg, "Creation and Commercial Value: Copyright Protection of Works of Information" (1990) 90 Col. L.Rev. 1865 at 1872.

[60] See further, Scrutton, *The Law of Copyright* (London: John Murray, 1883), at 14.

[61] Ginsburg, "Creation and Commercial Value: Copyright Protection of Works of Information" (1990) 90 Col. L.Rev. 1865 at 1924.

[62] See, for example, the provisions relating to revived copyright (see paras 28–41 et seq., below).

impede the emergence of certain industries or activities, or a negotiated price might give the copyright owner an unjustified windfall[63];

(iii) where the copyright owner has failed to supply the needs of the public and other producers and distributors are available[64];

(iv) where copyright owners have refused to license use of their works or have imposed conditions which do not reflect the purposes for which copyright is granted;

(v) where there is evidence of abuse of monopoly[65];

(vi) where there exist otherwise insuperable transaction costs or delays[66];

(vii) where a negotiated price would be too high and it is deemed desirable to subsidise users, for example those which are public institutions.[67]

C. Existing Compulsory Licences

(i) Information about programmes

Introduction. The Broadcasting Act 1990 introduced provisions into the 1988 **28–09** Act entitling publishers, once certain conditions are satisfied, to reproduce information about programmes which are to be broadcast. The scheme of the Broadcasting Act is that these provisions are to take effect as if they were included in Ch.III of Pt I of the 1988 Act (acts permitted in relation to copyright works).[68] Some minor amendments to these provisions were made by the Broadcasting Act 1996 and the Communications Act 2003.[69] Since the implementation of the Database Directive[70] by the Copyright and Rights in Databases Regulations[71] the significance of these provisions may well be very limited, for two reasons. First, depending on the facts, copyright may well not subsist in the material which is the subject of the compulsory licence, that is works embodying information as to

---

[63] See, for example, the provisions relating to the statutory recording licence (see para.28–04, above).

[64] Scrutton, *The Law of Copyright* (London: John Murray, 1883), suggests that compulsory licences should be available in the following exceptional circumstances: (i) as regards works first published abroad where the author's interests do not immediately lead them to supply the work; (ii) where the social organisation of a country is in its infancy; and (iii) where a publisher fails to supply works within a reasonable time at a reasonable price. Also note the special regime for developing countries contained in the Berne Convention, as to which, see Ricketson and Ginsburg, *International Copyright and Neighbouring Rights* (2006), Ch.14. See also, Ch.23.

[65] See paras 28–277 et seq., below.

[66] See further, Cassler, "Copyright Compulsory Licences—are they Coming or Going?" (1990) 37 Jo. Copyright Socy USA 231 at 249–250. Professor Merges has criticised the use of compulsory licences in these circumstances, arguing that copyright owners will often form collecting societies in order to overcome transaction cost problems and that such societies tend to be more efficient than compulsory licence schemes, in particular, because of their ability to tailor schemes to the needs of different classes of user. It should be noted, however, that Professor Merges' criticisms are primarily aimed at statutory licensing schemes, that is where the rate is fixed by statute. Although Professor Merges argues that collective licensing will still tend to be more efficient than "judicially administered" schemes he only refers in passing to the possibility of setting up a "a special rate court" (such as the Copyright Tribunal). See Merges, "Contracting into Liability Rules: Intellectual Property Rights and Collective Rights Organizations" (1996) 84 Cal. L.Rev. 1293, in particular, at 1316–1317.

[67] See, e.g. the Australian Copyright Act 1968 (Cth).

[68] Broadcasting Act 1990 Sch.17 para.7(1): "This Schedule and the Copyright, Designs and Patents Act 1988 shall have effect as if the Schedule were included in Ch.III of Pt I of that Act, and that Act shall have effect as if proceedings under this Schedule were listed in s.149 of that Act (jurisdiction of the Copyright Tribunal)." The provisions of the 1990 Act are set out at in Vol.2 A2.

[69] 1996 (c.55) and 2003 (c.21) respectively.

[70] Directive 96/9/EC. See Vol.2 H3.

[71] SI 1997/3032.

the titles of programmes and the time of their broadcast.[72] Second, to the extent that such material is only covered by database right (which again may well not be the case), the compulsory licence is not available.[73]

28–10   **Background.** The proprietors of the *Radio Times* and *TV Times* had a long-standing policy of asserting copyright in the listings of their programmes. By refusing to grant licences to publish such listings more than two or three days prior to broadcast they were each able to use this copyright to create a monopoly over weekly listings of their respective programmes. As a result, no comprehensive weekly guide to programme schedules was available. This remained the position until the owners of *Time Out* magazine decided to produce a comprehensive weekly listing by publishing in advance details of dates, titles and times of transmission of selected television programmes for the following week, those details having been taken from the proprietors' listings. In the resulting litigation[74] *Time Out* argued that the listings were not protected by copyright on the basis that there is no copyright in information. This argument was rejected, however, and the injunctions sought by the proprietors were granted.[75] This case caused some disquiet,[76] and in 1984 the Office of Fair Trading produced a report in which it concluded that broadcasters were involved in a course of conduct which constituted an anti-competitive practice which affected the public interest and therefore referred the situation to the Monopolies and Mergers Commission (MMC) under s.5 of the Competition Act 1980.[77] In 1985, the MMC reported. While it found that refusal to grant licences amounted to an anti-competitive practice within s.2 of the Competition Act, it was divided equally as to whether that was contrary to the public interest.[78]

Despite the MMC's inconclusive report, the Government decided to take action to bring the two monopolies to an end following the findings of the Select Committee on Home Affairs in June 1988, and a ruling of the European Commission in relation to an analogous situation in the Republic of Ireland in December 1988.[79] The Home Secretary thus announced in September 1989 the Government's intention of introducing a compulsory licensing scheme. Accordingly, the

---

[72] For the material covered, see below, para.28–13. For copyright in such material, see above paras 3–21 et seq.

[73] For the inapplicabilty of the provisions to database right, see para.28–24, below. For database right, see Ch.18, above.

[74] *ITP v Time Out and Elliott* and *BBC v Time Out and Elliott* [1984] F.S.R. 64.

[75] The position in the United Kingdom is this respect was quite different from that which operated in most other countries, except the Republic of Ireland (as which see *Radio Telefís Eireann and others v Magill TV Guide Ltd* [1990] F.S.R. 561). See *Copinger* 14th edn, para.29–10, fn.72.

[76] Earlier criticism of the publishing arrangements appeared in the Third Report of the House of Commons Estimates Committee (Session 1968–9) P.P. Vol.13 xxvii, para.71 (suggesting a single combined weekly listings journal) and Report of the Committee on the Future of Broadcasting, 1977 (Cmnd.6753) paras 29.33–29.42 (the majority taking the view that the monopoly did not operate in the public interest and that the broadcasters should be obliged to waive their copyright in programme information, if necessary on payment of an agreed fee).

[77] *BBC and ITP Ltd: The Publication of Programme Information*, Office of Fair Trading, December 13, 1984.

[78] *The British Broadcasting Corporation and Independent Television Publications Limited: A report on the policies and practices on the BBC and ITP of limiting the publication by others of advance programme information*, 1985 (Cmnd. 9614). It should be noted that the European Court of First Instance and the European Court of Justice later declared that a refusal to license the use of such listings was an abuse of dominant position and contrary to art.86 of the Treaty of Rome. See para.28–279, below.

[79] Commission Decision 89/205/EEC of December 21, 1988, [1989] OJ L78/43; [1989] 4 C.M.L.R. 757. In July 1991, the Court of First Instance of the European Communities (Second Chamber) decided *Radio Telefis Eireann v EC Commission* [1991] 4 C.M.L.R. 586, rejecting the broadcasting organisations' appeal against the finding of the Commission that it had infringed art.86. In June 1994, Advocate-General Gulmann delivered his opinion in support of the broadcasters, but in April 1995 the ECJ upheld the decision of the Commission and the Court of First Instance. See para.28–279, below.

Broadcasting Act 1990 introduced provisions into the 1988 Act entitling publishers, provided certain conditions are satisfied, to reproduce information about programmes which are to be broadcast. These provisions are to be found in s.176 of and Sch.17 to the Broadcasting Act 1990.[80]

The duty. By s.176(1) a person providing a programme service to which the section applies has a duty to make available information relating to the programmes to be included in the service to any person wishing to publish in the United Kingdom any such information. The term "making available" is distinguishable from that of supplying, since making available suggests notions of accessibility rather than delivery.[81]   **28–11**

The providers. Persons providing a programme service to which the section applies are:[82] the BBC for television and national radio services provided by it for reception in the United Kingdom; licensees of television programme services subject to regulation by OFCOM[83]; the Welsh Authority for public television services provided by it[84]; and licensees of any national service subject to regulation by OFCOM,[85] any simulcast radio service,[86] and any national digital sound programme service subject to regulation by OFCOM.[87]   **28–12**

The information. The information which is to be provided consists of the titles of the programmes and the time of their proposed inclusion in a programme service,[88] but need not include information about any advertisement.[89] This matches the information with respect to which copyright was claimed in the *Time Out* case.[90] There is no requirement that the person make available "billing" material, that is the copyright material which adds flesh to this skeleton,[91] though this may be available from a variety of sources.[92] However, it may have been more signif-   **28–13**

---

[80] Set out in Vol.2 A2. The original Bill (Broadcasting Bill No.9 (1989–90) December 12, 1989) did not include such provisions, which were added in Standing Committee. See further, the Report of the Debates of House of Commons Standing Committee F in 1990, cols 1346–1384; cols 1465–1501.

[81] *News Group Newspapers v ITP Ltd* [1993] R.P.C. 173 at 190. Thus a broadcaster could meet the obligation by allowing staff or agents to copy the master copy, although in practice copies were made and sent to broadcasters: ibid. However, where the broadcaster has assigned future copyright it may be that the making and supplying of copies will infringe that copyright, as there is no obligation to make such copies and thus no defence of statutory authority will apply. (As to the defence of statutory authority see CDPA 1988 s.50, see para.9–148.)

[82] Broadcasting Act 1990 s.176(7).

[83] OFCOM (the Office of Communications) was established under s.1 of the Office of the Communications Act 2002 (c.11). The ITC's functions under Pt I of the Broadcasting Act 1990 (as to which see *Copinger* 14th edn, para.29–13 fn.80) were transferred to OFCOM by s.2 of the Communications Act 2003 (c.21) with effect from December 29, 2003: see the Office of Communications Act 2002 (Commencement No.3) and Communications Act 2003 (Commencement No.2) Order 2003, SI 2003/3142, reg.3(1) and Sch.1. The television services regulated by OFCOM are listed in s.211 of the Communications Act 2003.

[84] Within the meaning of Pt 2 of Sch.12 to the Communications Act 2003.

[85] See Broadcasting Act 1990 s.126(1) and Communications Act 2003 s.245(4)(a).

[86] Added by the Broadcasting Act 1996 s.148(1), Sch.10 para.10. "Simulcast radio service" means a service provided by a person for broadcasting in digital form and corresponding to a service which is a national radio service within the meaning of Pt 3 of [the Broadcasting Act 1990] and is provided by that person: Broadcasting Act 1996 s.41(2), as substituted by s.256(1) of the Communications Act 2003.

[87] Added by the Broadcasting Act 1996 s.148(1), Sch.10 para.10.

[88] Broadcasting Act 1990 s.176(2).

[89] Broadcasting Act 1990 s.176(8).

[90] *ITP v Time Out and Elliott* and *BBC v Time Out and Elliott* [1984] F.S.R. 64. Also see *Hansard*, HL Vol.521, col.1700. The *Magill* decision was also limited to consideration of this information.

[91] *News Group Newspapers v ITP Ltd* [1993] R.P.C. 173.

[92] Consequently, it is probably not information with respect to which the broadcasting companies have a dominant position.

icant that the Act failed to provide any duty to provide information as to bar codings which set automatic video recording machines.[93]

28–14   **Timing.** The duty is to make the information available as soon after it has been prepared as is reasonably practicable. Moreover, this general requirement is limited by a principle of equity between publishers to the effect that information must be made available to any publisher not later than when it is made available to any other publisher. Failure to provide listings to all publishers at the same time would thus be a breach of statutory duty.[94] As regards weekly listings, the statute also lays down a minimum period. It says that in the case of information in respect of all the programmes to be included in the service in any period of seven days, the duty is to make the information available not later than the beginning of the preceding period of 14 days, or such other number of days as may be prescribed by the Secretary of State by order.[95] Early versions of the Bill referred simply to a duty to make available at the publisher's request such information as he might reasonably require.[96] However, the issue of timing was sensitive, since the aim was to provide a realistic opportunity of allowing others to publish a rival weekly publication, without giving unwarranted information to rival broadcasters who could then alter their schedules.[97] The period of 14 days reflected previous practice according to which the final listings went to the *TV Times* 10–17 days before transmission.[98] A publisher may ask for skeleton schedules before that point and the general duty applies. There does not appear to be an entitlement to updating information.[99]

28–15   **Conditions.** The obligation to provide information is not satisfied if the information is provided on terms, other than terms as to copyright, prohibiting or restricting publication in the United Kingdom by the publisher.[100]

28–16   **The recipient/licensee.** The information is to be made available to a publisher, not in respect of each publication, so when calculating the terms of payment one flat fee must be paid per publisher, with rates thereafter calculated according to circulation and usage—not per title.[101]

28–17   **The compulsory licence.** The Broadcasting Act 1990 makes further provision to enable information provided under the duty outlined above to be reproduced and published, by providing for a compulsory licence scheme, the provisions of which are set out in Sch.17 to that Act.[102]

28–18   **The licensor.** For the purposes of the compulsory licence, the Broadcasting Act proceeds on the basis that the provider of the programme service has the right to grant licences. Thus the person to be approached for the licence is the programme service provider, even though any copyright in works containing information as

---

[93] Report of the Debates of the House of Commons Standing Committee F in 1990, col.1375 (Mr Gale).

[94] *Hansard*, HL Vol.521, col.1701.

[95] Broadcasting Act 1990 s.176(3)(b).

[96] House of Commons Bill No. 100, Parliamentary Papers Vol.3 (1989–1990), cl.164(1).

[97] Report of the Debates of the House Standing Committee F in 1990, cols 1351–2; 1376; *Hansard*, HL Vol.521, col.1701.

[98] Report of the Debates of the House of Commons Standing Committee F in 1990, col.1371. This was a House of Lords' Amendment: Lords Amendments to the Broadcasting Bill, House of Commons Bill No. 202, 26 October 1990 Parliamentary Papers (1989–1990) Vol.5.

[99] *News Group Newspapers v ITP Ltd* [1993] R.P.C. 173 at 190.

[100] Broadcasting Act 1990 s.176(5). Note that this provision does not appear broad enough to prevent a broadcaster from relying on database right. See further para.28–24, below.

[101] *News Group Newspapers v ITP Ltd* [1993] R.P.C. 173 at 184–5.

[102] For transitional provisions, see *Copinger* 14th edn, para.29–19.

to scheduling may have been assigned to another person. Schedule 17 to the Broadcasting Act 1990 therefore provides that the person providing the programme service, rather than the assignee, is to be treated as the owner of the copyright for the purposes of licensing any act restricted by the copyright,[103] but the broadcaster must then account to the assignee for payments received for the rights to publish.[104]

Obtaining the compulsory licence. The compulsory licence is available where   **28–19**
the programme service provider[105] refuses to grant the publisher a licence on terms as to duration and payment which are acceptable to the publisher.[106] The publisher must first give notice of his intention to exercise the right to the programme service provider, asking him to propose terms of payment.[107] After receipt of any such proposal (assuming that it is unacceptable) or after the expiry of a reasonable time, the publisher must then give the programme service provider reasonable notice of the date on which he proposes to begin exercising the right and the terms of payment which he proposes. It seems that one month's notice would in most situations be reasonable.[108] The publisher must also give reasonable notice to the Copyright Tribunal of his intention to exercise the right and of the date on which he proposes to do so, and also apply to the Tribunal to settle terms of payment.[109]

The licence. Once a publisher has done all these things, and whether or not the   **28–20**
Tribunal has yet settled terms of payment, the publisher, after the date specified in his notice to the programme service provider, and if he makes the required payments, shall be in the same position as if he held a licence.[110] Thus, where the publisher "does any act in circumstances in which the paragraph applies", he shall be in the same position as regards infringement of copyright as if he had at all material times been the holder of a licence granted by the programme service provider to do such acts. This licence also covers anything done on his behalf,[111] and applies to any act restricted by the copyright in works containing the information. Thus where, for example, the information is contained in a literary work, it apparently follows that the licence will extend to any act restricted by the copyright in such work. The publisher may therefore reproduce and publish the information in a newspaper or magazine (though this involves the restricted acts

---

[103] Broadcasting Act 1990 Sch.17 para.1(2). Prior to the Broadcasting Act such assignments had been made by BBC to BBC Enterprises, and by ITV and Channel 4 to ITP, which in turn had been acquired by Reed International.

[104] See the Report of the Debates of the House of Commons Standing Committee F in 1990, cols 1358, 1377.

[105] Or the assignee in the case of an assignment made before September 29, 1989: Broadcasting Act 1990 Sch.17 para.1(3)(b).

[106] Broadcasting Act 1990 Sch.17 para.2(1)(b). Note that the reference to refusing to grant a licence includes failing to do so within a reasonable time of being asked: Broadcasting Act 1990 Sch.17 para.2(2).

[107] Broadcasting Act 1990 Sch.17 para.3(1).

[108] An amendment proposed in the Committee stage of the House of Lords suggested requiring a prospective publisher to give both the broadcaster and the Copyright Tribunal three months' notice. This was rejected as unduly slanting the scheme against the publisher: *Hansard*, HL Vol.521, col.1702–3. The Government suggested that one month's notice would be reasonable as regards notice to the broadcaster and the Tribunal: *Hansard*, HL Vol.522, col.852. In *News Group Newspapers v ITP Ltd* [1993] R.P.C. 173, MGN applied on February 28, 1991 to publish commencing on March 1, 1991. No objection was made, but this hardly appears to be reasonable notice. In contrast, ITP had applied on January 30, 1991, to commence on March 1, 1991.

[109] Broadcasting Act 1990 Sch.17 para.3(2).

[110] Broadcasting Act 1990 Sch.17 para.4(1).

[111] Broadcasting Act 1990 Sch.17 para.7(2).

of reproduction, adaptation and issuing)[112] and presumably may broadcast the information, including, for example, on teletext.

28–21   **Payment.** The required payments, which are to be made at not less than quarterly intervals in arrears,[113] are those determined by the Copyright Tribunal. If no such determination has yet been made, the required payments are those proposed by the programme service provider in response to the request from the publisher or, if no such proposal has been made or is considered by the publisher to be unreasonably high, those proposed by the publisher in his notice to the programme service provider.[114] If the publisher were to offer a derisory sum, the Tribunal might well award costs against him.[115]

28–22   **The Copyright Tribunal.** Where an application is made to the Copyright Tribunal to settle terms of payment, the Tribunal may make such order as it may determine to be reasonable in the circumstances.[116] During the passage of the Broadcasting Act, calls were made for the Copyright Tribunal to be provided with guidance to help it with its "Solomonic task" of determining rates of payment.[117] More specifically, it was suggested that the statute should make clear whether the purpose of the payment was to reimburse costs incurred by the broadcaster or to compensate for loss of copyright.[118] The Government declined to include any such directions, arguing that it was for the parties to a dispute to bring any relevant considerations to the Tribunal's attention. In particular, it rejected an amendment requiring the Tribunal to distinguish between the copyright and information elements of the value of a work and to ignore the latter when assessing the licence fee. The jurisdiction is thus "wide and unfettered"[119] and previous decisions over licensing schemes do not provide a compelling analogy.[120]

In *News Group Newspapers v ITP Ltd*[121] a number of publishers sought to have the terms of payment set for use of information concerning BBC and ITV schedules.[122] The publishers argued that the terms should not exceed the cost of supply of the information, whereas the broadcasters asserted that the rates should reflect the value of the copyright in the statutory information. This represented "a great gulf both in terms of principle and of money".[123] The Copyright Tribunal, in exercising its discretion, was concerned about evidence that after the enactment of the 1990 Act a large number of local papers had stopped publishing listings. Indeed the Copyright Tribunal called this "a serious matter, contrary to the public interest and not in accordance with the policy and objects of the 1990 Act". The Tribunal saw its task as being to promote dissemination of the information, rather

---

[112] *News Group Newspapers v ITP Ltd* [1993] R.P.C. 173 at 180.

[113] Broadcasting Act 1990 Sch.17 para.4(2).

[114] Sch.17 para.4(3). The publisher's fee was preferred to the copyright owner's "because the principal reason for the legislation is to open up the market:" Report of the Debates of the House of Commons Standing Committee F in 1990, col.1381.

[115] See previous note.

[116] Broadcasting Act 1990 Sch.17 para.5(1). As to the Copyright Tribunal generally, see paras 28–81 et seq. below, and as to its procedure see paras 28–154 et seq., below. As to "reasonableness", see paras 28–110 et seq., below.

[117] See *Hansard*, HL Vol.521, col.1704. Also see the Report of the Debates of the House of Commons Standing Committee F in 1990, col.1353.

[118] Report of the Debates of the House of Commons Standing Committee F in 1990, col.1383; *Hansard*, HL Vol.521, col.1700.

[119] *News Group Newspapers v ITP Ltd* [1993] R.P.C. 173 at 180.

[120] *News Group Newspapers v ITP Ltd* [1993] R.P.C. 173 at 187.

[121] See previous note.

[122] The Tribunal held there was no reason to treat the BBC and ITV differently: *News Group Newspapers v ITP Ltd* [1993] R.P.C. 173 at 185.

[123] *News Group Newspapers v ITP Ltd* [1993] R.P.C. 173 at 186.

than to protect the financial interests of the broadcaster as copyright owner.[124] This was because "[t]he objects of the 1990 Act include making a wide range of programmes and types of broadcasting available and that is only worth doing if individuals can easily find out what is on so that they can choose for themselves what they want to see and hear". It rejected the relevance of any exercise to second guess what "free negotiations" would have produced as "entirely theoretical and unreliable".[125]

The Tribunal indicated that little assistance was provided by analogies with other licensing schemes or patent licences.[126] Moreover, it took the view that the inclusion of the statutory information could not be shown to be responsible for any "significant and calculable incremental profit" to publishers. However, while the Tribunal said that the problem of proving a causative link between the use of the information and the profits made by newspapers was insuperable, it held that the rate to be paid should relate to the extent of usage by the publisher. This was best calculated by reference to circulation and to the number of days for which the information was published, with a minimum set to ensure that the marginal costs of supply were met. The Tribunal assessed the basic costs of the broadcasters at £125,000 each and the administrative costs at £200 per publisher. Consequently, it imposed a rate of 0.003p for each day multiplied by the circulation with a £200 minimum per publisher. It calculated that this would give a return to the broadcasters of £500,000 above costs, but stated that even were this as high as £1,600,000 that would not be unreasonable. The BBC and ITP appealed, but a hearing was avoided by a compromise of 0.004p.[127]

The Order. The order has effect from the date the publisher begins to exercise the right, so that any necessary adjustments in the amounts which have fallen due must be made.[128] An application may subsequently be made to review the order.[129] However, an application for review shall not be made, except with the special leave of the Tribunal, within 12 months from the date of the order or of the decision on a previous application. Similarly, for orders intended to be in force for 15 months or less, no review is to take place until the last three months before expiry.[130] The provisions relating to such applications are analogous to those relating to the Tribunal's jurisdiction over licensing schemes, which are dealt with elsewhere.[131] On such an application, the Tribunal shall consider the matter and confirm or vary the original order as it may determine to be reasonable in the circumstances.[132] The order made on such an application is to have effect from the date on which it is made or such later date as may be specified by the Tribunal.[133]

28–23

The impact of the Database Directive. As has been noted, the Database Directive may affect the provisions considered above in two key respects. First, depending on the facts, a work embodying television listings may well fall squarely

28–24

---

[124] *News Group Newspapers v ITP Ltd* [1993] R.P.C. 173 at 186. Thus, although the interests of the broadcasters were taken into account, these were considered to be of only secondary importance: see at 188.

[125] *News Group Newspapers v ITP Ltd* [1993] R.P.C. 173 at 187.

[126] *News Group Newspapers v ITP Ltd* [1993] R.P.C. 173 at 187.

[127] [1993] E.M.L.R. 133.

[128] Broadcasting Act 1990 Sch.17 para.5(2).

[129] Sch.17 para.6(1).

[130] Sch.17 para.6(2).

[131] See paras 28–89 et seq., below.

[132] Sch.17 para.6(3).

[133] Sch.17 para.6(4).

within the definition of a "database" in s.3A of the 1988 Act[134] but yet not satisfy the requirement of originality imposed by s.3A(2).[135] If so, copyright will not subsist in the work in question. Second, again depending on the facts, database right may well not subsist in such listings either because the investment in their creation relates directly to the *production* of the information, rather than to obtaining, verifying or presenting it.[136]

If database right can be shown to subsist in programme lists, at first sight this might seem to present the possibility that broadcasters would seek to use the database right to re-establish their previous monopoly. This is because the compulsory licence does not appear to extend to database right (the Act refers to the "copyright owner" and does not mention database right, and there is no general provision in the Database Regulations which extends such a licence to incorporate database right).[137]

However, such an approach would be unlikely, since to do so would be a breach of competition law and the Competition Commission (and in some cases the Secretary of State) has a separate power to order that licences in respect of the database right shall be available as of right following an adverse market investigation report.[138] Moreover, the market for weekly television listings has changed beyond all recognition since the compulsory licence was introduced and it is by no means certain that broadcasters would wish to return to the previous position, even if they could legally do so. Nevertheless, it might well be possible for broadcasters to argue for a higher licence fee for use of their programme listings. In particular, it could be said that the rate set by the Tribunal under the compulsory licence applicable to the copyright in the database is not appropriate for a licence of database right, since, as has been seen, in arriving at a rate the Tribunal saw its task as being to promote dissemination of the information, rather than to protect the financial interests of the broadcaster, a conclusion which was based on the objects of the Broadcasting Act 1990, which (it could be argued) have no relevance to the database right.

(ii) Use as of right of sound recordings in broadcasts and cable programme services

28–25   **General.** The Broadcasting Act 1990 introduced a new compulsory licence allowing the inclusion of sound recordings in broadcasts or cable programme

---

[134] See Ch.18.

[135] See *Football Dataco Ltd v Brittens Pools Ltd* [2010] EWHC 841 (Ch); [2010] R.P.C. 17 and para.3–22 above.

[136] See in particular the *Fixtures Marketing* cases (*Fixtures Marketing Ltd v Oy Veikkaus AB* (C–46/02) [2004] E.C.R. I–10365; *Fixtures Marketing Ltd v Svenska Spel AB* (C–338/02) [2005] E.C.D.R. 4; and *Fixtures Marketing Ltd v Organismos prognostikon agonon podosfairou AE (OPAP)*) (C–444/02) [2004] E.C.R. I–10549; *The British Horseracing Board Ltd v William Hill Organization Ltd* (C–203/02) [2004] E.C.R. I–10415; and *Football Dataco Ltd v Brittens Pools Ltd* [2010] EWHC 841 (Ch).

[137] Note that the Database Regulations (SI 1997/3032) do provide a general defence of statutory authority (Sch.1 para.6). However, this would not assist a publisher since the compulsory licence only refers to infringement of copyright. As has been seen, the compulsory licence provisions apply as if they were included in Ch.III of Pt 1 of the 1988 Act and s.28(1) of that Act provides that "the provisions of this Chapter ... relate only to the question of infringement of copyright and do not affect any other right or obligation".

[138] Database Regulations (SI 1997/3032) Sch.2 para.15(1), as amended by the Enterprise Act 2002 (Consequential and Supplemental Provisions) Order 2003 (SI 2003/1398) art.2 and Sch. para.31, with effect from June 20, 2003. This provision closely follows the wording of s.144, as to which see para.28–54, below.

services.[139] The statutory right is available against a licensing body which either restricts the amount of needletime, that is imposes restrictions on the total or proportionate time in which such recordings can be played, or imposes unacceptable terms as to payment. After complying with certain procedural formalities, the broadcaster may broadcast the recording and "shall be in the same position as regards infringement of copyright as if he had at all material times been the holder of a licence granted by the owner of the copyright in question".[140] Some minor amendments to these provisions were made by the Broadcasting Act 1996 and the Copyright and Related Rights Regulations 2003.[141] These limitations on the copyright in sound recordings are permissible under the Rome Convention, which merely requires Contracting States to guarantee to the producers of phonograms an equitable remuneration from (as opposed to an exclusive right to control) the broadcasting or communication to the public of published phonograms.[142]

Background. Under the 1911 Act sound recordings were equated with musical works, but the scope of this copyright was initially unclear. In the *Cawardine* case decided in 1934[143] it was held that the right conferred on the manufacturers of sound recordings by the 1911 Act included a public performance right. Thereafter, these performance rights were administered on behalf of most record companies by Phonographic Performance Limited (PPL).[144] It remained unclear whether the broadcasting of a work amounted to a public performance, but to the extent that the right to control broadcasts existed, these rights fell to be administered on behalf of record companies by PPL, as part of its collective exercise of public performance rights more generally.[145] Hence, when the Copyright Act 1956 expressly granted the owner of copyright in a sound recording the exclusive right to broadcast the work, these rights also came to be administered by PPL. It remains the case that broadcasting rights in respect of sound recordings are usually exercised collectively in the United Kingdom by PPL. The licensing terms are therefore subject to review by the Copyright Tribunal (formerly the Performing Right Tribunal).

28–26

Prior to 1988 the licences granted by PPL to radio broadcasters were typically limited as regards the length of the periods in which the broadcaster could perform PPL's repertoire.[146] In 1988 the Monopolies and Mergers Commission (MMC) was requested to report on practices relating to the collective licensing of sound recordings for broadcasting and public performance. Pending the completion of the Report, moves to introduce provisions to force an end to needletime restrictions were stifled.[147] The MMC Report[148] concluded that the needletime restriction was an anti-competitive practice which adversely affected radio licensees

---

[139] These provisions are additional to the general jurisdiction of the Copyright Tribunal to control licensing bodies and licensing schemes, as to which see paras 28–84 et seq., below.

[140] CDPA 1988 s.135C(1).

[141] SI 2003/2498.

[142] Rome Convention for the Protection of Performers, Producers of Phonograms and Broadcasting Organisations art.12 (and see para.23–99, above).

[143] *Gramophone Co. Ltd v Stephen Cawardine & Co.* [1934] Ch.450.

[144] As to PPL, see para.27–66, above.

[145] See *Copinger* 13th edn, para.8–102, fn.8 and further discussion in earlier editions.

[146] These "needletime" restrictions were first imposed in 1946 in response to pressure from the Musicians' Union. Independent radio companies were generally limited to a total of nine hours per day: MMC Report, Collective Licensing: A Report on Certain Practices in the Collective Licensing of Public Performances and Broadcasting Rights in Sound Recordings, 1988 (Cm. 530) paras 7.44–7.48.

[147] See, *Hansard*, HL Vol.491, cols 509–511.

[148] Collective Licensing: A report on certain practices in the collective licensing of public performances and broadcasting rights in sound recordings, 1988 (Cm.530).

and that it should be abandoned.[149] The MMC therefore recommended the imposition of an obligation on PPL to permit the use of its repertoire in return for equitable remuneration, initially on the basis of what the licensee thought "appropriate", pending determination by the Copyright Tribunal as to equitable remuneration.[150]

28–27   **The 1988 Act amended.** The 1990 Broadcasting Act gave effect to the recommendations of the MMC.[151] With effect from February 1, 1991, a compulsory licence of the kind proposed, with unlimited needletime, was incorporated into the 1988 Act by introducing into it seven new sections, ss.135A to 135G, which provided for a statutory right to include sound recordings in broadcasts and cable programme services. The scheme of the new provisions followed that of the provisions dealing with the right to use information about programmes. This has already been considered.[152] Sections 135A to 135G were further amended by the Copyright and Related Rights Regulations 2003.[153] The sections now apply only to non-internet "broadcasts" within the meaning of s.6 of the 1988 Act and to "simulcasts", that is transmissions taking place simultaneously on the internet and by other means (s.6(1A)(a)).[154] The result is a significant narrowing of the ambit of the sections. Before the amendment, the sections applied to cable programmes as well as broadcasts. As a result, they almost certainly applied to the other two forms of internet transmission which are within the new definition of "broadcast" (that is, concurrent transmissions of live events (s.6(1A)(b)) and transmissions of recorded moving images or sounds forming part of a programme service offered by the person responsible for making the transmission, being a service in which programmes are transmitted at scheduled times determined by that person (s.6(1A)(c)). They also applied to "on-request" or "on-demand" services. This is no longer the case.[155]

Given that prior to 1991 the terms of licences granted by PPL for the broadcast of its sound recordings were reviewable by the Copyright Tribunal,[156] the critical change effected by the introduction of ss.135A to 135G concerned "needletime". Under the provisions in effect prior to 1991, conditions concerning needletime were subject only to a reasonableness requirement. Therefore, as long as PPL could demonstrate a legitimate reason to restrict needletime, the Tribunal could not object to it. Under the new law, the term "needletime" means the time in any period (whether determined as a number of hours in the period or a proportion of the period, or otherwise) in which recordings may be included in a broadcast.[157]

28–28   **Scope.** The provisions are confined to uses of "sound recordings". Consequently, they do not confer any right to include in the broadcast the musical works or associated lyrics embodied in the recording, which must therefore be the subject of

---

[149] Collective Licensing: Report, 1988 (Cm.530), paras 7.44, 7.48, 7.49.

[150] Collective Licensing: Report, 1988 (Cm.530), para.7.49.

[151] The original Bill did not include such provisions, which were added in Standing Committee. See the Report of the Debates of the House of Commons, Standing Committee F in 1990, cols 1454–1464.

[152] See paras 28–09 et seq. above.

[153] SI 2003/2498.

[154] CDPA 1988 s.135A(5).

[155] See Consultation on UK Implementation of Directive 2001/29/EC on Copyright and Related Rights in the Information Society: *Analysis of Responses and Government Conclusions*, para.3.15.

[156] See generally, paras 28–76 et seq., below.

[157] CDPA 1988 s.135A(5).

a separate agreement with the owner of these rights.[158] Nor do the provisions allow for the broadcasting of "music videos" since these are films.[159] Moreover, s.135A(5) states that the term "sound recording" does not include a film sound track when accompanying a film. However, the Secretary of State may now extend the scope of these provisions by Order so as to include works of any description.[160] For example, the Secretary of State might wish to extend the system to music videos[161] and it has been suggested that a parallel licence should apply as regards the performance or broadcast of musical and literary works.[162]

Licensed acts. The licence is only available where the licensee intends to "broadcast" the sound recording. This term bears the same meaning as in s.6 of the 1988 Act save that the only form of internet transmission to which the sections apply is a "simulcast".[163] The licence thus covers both radio and television broadcasts, whether national or local, as well as satellite broadcasts and digital broadcasts and simulcasts. From November 1, 1996, the Secretary of State may by order amend these provisions so as to limit the types of broadcast to which the licence applies.[164] This provision was enacted so that digital broadcasts and broadcasts designed to provide background music in shops (sometimes referred to as "narrowcasts") can be excluded from the scope of the licence should that prove necessary.[165]   **28–29**

The licensor. The licence is only available where the rights are administered by a licensing body, as defined in s.116(2) of the 1988 Act.[166] The section is drafted to cover both the situation where the licensing body has been given the right to grant licences, and the situation where it has the ability to procure the grant of such a licence.[167] The requirement that the rights be administered by a licensing body may prove significant if changes in commercial practice lead individual record companies to license the broadcasting of records themselves (for example on a Europe-wide basis). In such a situation the question will arise as to whether a   **28–30**

---

[158] These will be administered in the main by the Performing Right Society, as to which, see para.27–65, above.

[159] *The Association of Independent Radio Companies Ltd (AIRC) v Phonographic Performance Ltd* [1994] R.P.C. 143 at 173. See also CDPA 1988 s.5B.

[160] CDPA 1988 s.135H(1)(a), added by the Broadcasting Act 1996 s.139(1); no order has yet been made under this provision.

[161] In the early 1990s, MTV Europe objected to the collective licensing practices of Video Performance Limited (VPL) since it wished to obtain Europe-wide licences directly from the record companies. Consequently, MTV complained to the European Commission which in turn issued a statement of objections to VPL's practices in 1994. The dispute is referred to at p.173 of the *AIRC* case (*Association of Independent Radio Companies Ltd v Phonographic Performance Ltd* [1994] R.P.C. 143). It seems that following the Commission's statement, VPL allowed MTV to enter into direct agreement with the major record companies: see *CSC Media Group Ltd v Video Performance Ltd* (CT/94/05) at paras 147–8 and *Music and Copyright* Vol.68/1 21.6.1995.

[162] Such an extension was considered by the MMC: A Report on the supply in the UK of the services of administering performing rights and film synchronisation rights, 1996 (Cm.3147) paras 10.5, 10.21, 10.31, 10.38, 10.48, 14.134. The MMC concluded, however, that such an extension was not necessary: ibid. paras 2.96, 2.131. Such an extension to literary, dramatic, musical or artistic works or films would not contravene the Berne Convention, as art.11*bis*(2) allows for limitations to be placed on an author's right to authorise the broadcasting or communication to the public of the work (whether by wireless or by wire or by public communication of a broadcast): "It shall be a matter for legislation in the countries of the Union to determine the conditions under which the rights mentioned in the preceding paragraph [Broadcasting and Related Rights] may be exercised, but these conditions ... shall not in any circumstances be prejudicial to the moral rights of the author, nor to his right to obtain equitable remuneration".

[163] CDPA 1988 s.135A(5). For the background to this, see para.28–27, above.

[164] s.135H(1)(b), added by the Broadcasting Act 1996 s.139(1); no order has yet been made under this provision.

[165] See *Hansard*, HL Vol.568, cols 547–8; Vol.569, cols 761–3. See also *AEI Rediffusion Music Ltd v Phonographic Performance Ltd* [1998] R.P.C. 335.

[166] As to which, see para.28–88, below.

[167] CDPA 1988 s.135A(1)(a).

record company with a catalogue of recordings itself constitutes a licensing body. This may raise difficult questions about whether a record company has such licensing activities as one of its "main objects", and whether the record company grants licences only relating to works of which it is the "author".[168]

The licensing body may not refuse the licence, it seems, even if the prospective licensee is of dubious financial standing or if it has engaged in activities damaging to the record companies.[169]

28–31　　**Necessary conditions.** A person who wishes to include sound recordings in a broadcast must then show that one of two sets of conditions is satisfied. These two sets of conditions differentiate between the situations where a broadcaster has obtained a licence but is unhappy with the terms thereof and where a licence does not exist (for example, because it was never granted or has lapsed without being renewed). Where the broadcaster already has a licence, the statutory right only applies if the licence limits the needletime available to the broadcaster. In those circumstances, if the broadcaster is refused greater (including unlimited) needletime, or is only offered extended needletime on terms as to payment which are unacceptable or is not offered different terms within a reasonable time, then the statutory licence will potentially be available.[170] Where a broadcaster does not hold a licence the statutory licence will be available if the licensing body refuses within a reasonable time to grant a licence either on terms as to payment which would be acceptable to the broadcaster (or on terms laid down in an order of the Copyright Tribunal under s.135D) or if the licensing body restricts the needletime that the broadcaster has demanded.[171]

28–32　　**Proposal of terms.** Before a broadcaster can avail itself of the statutory licence, various steps must be taken.[172] These involve at least three stages, and they are mandatory not directory.[173] First, the broadcaster must give notice to the licensing body of its intention to use the right and ask the body to propose terms of payment.[174] This gives the licensing body the opportunity to set the rate which the broadcaster will have to pay pending the determination by the Copyright Tribunal. Secondly, once the proposed terms have been received from the licensing body (or a reasonable period has passed), the broadcaster must give reasonable notice of the date on which it proposes to commence broadcasting of sound recordings under the right, and the terms of payment that the broadcaster intends to employ.[175] At this time, the broadcaster must also give reasonable notice to the Copyright Tribunal of its intention to exercise the right, and of the date on which

---

[168] As to the definition of "author" in relation to a sound recording see CDPA 1988 s.9(2)(aa) and see para.4–42, above.

[169] cf. MMC Report, Collective Licensing: A Report on Certain Practices in the Collective Licensing of Public Performances and Broadcasting Rights in Sound Recordings 1988 (Cm.530) paras 7.16–7.17, suggesting an injunction should be available in such circumstances.

[170] CDPA 1988 ss.135A(3), (4).

[171] s.135A(2) and (4).

[172] CDPA 1988 s.135B.

[173] However, where a broadcaster fails to comply with these requirements it is questionable whether the broadcaster's liability for damages for infringement of copyright in the sound recording will exceed what is awarded by the Copyright Tribunal, together with any interest the Court may award. In certain circumstances, this could have substantial implications as to costs. See further, *Phonographic Performance Ltd v Retail Broadcast Services Ltd* [1995] F.S.R. 813 at 817, per Jacob J.

[174] CDPA 1988 ss.135B(1)(a). In *Phonographic Performance Ltd v Retail Broadcast Services Ltd* [1995] F.S.R. 813, the defendant and PPL had been in voluntary negotiations during which PPL proposed terms for payment. Jacob J. held that the requirement that the licensing body be asked to propose terms of payment had not been satisfied: "Section 135B(1) sets up a particular machinery. The person intending to avail themselves of the right must send the notice called for by subsection (1)(a). Some other notice or negotiation will not do". [1995] F.S.R. 813 at para.816.

[175] s.135B(1)(b).

it proposes to begin to do so, and apply to the Tribunal under s.135D to settle the terms of payment.[176]

The licence. Once all these conditions are satisfied, then, after the date that was **28–33** specified in the notice, if a person includes in a broadcast any sound recordings, he is to be in the same position as regards infringement of copyright as if he had at all material times been the holder of a licence granted by the owner of the copyright, provided three further conditions are satisfied[177]: (a) he complies with any reasonable condition, notice of which has been given to him by the licensing body, as to the inclusion of those recordings[178]; (b) he provides the licensing body with such information about their inclusion in the broadcast as it may reasonably require; and (c) he makes payments as required at not less than quarterly intervals in arrears. The terms of payment are to be either those specified by the Copyright Tribunal or, if there are none, those proposed by the licensing body or, if those are "unreasonably high", those specified in the broadcaster's notice to the licensing body. Once a person is treated as being the holder of a licence in accordance with these provisions, any existing licence is replaced.[179]

The Copyright Tribunal. As has been seen, before being entitled to the licence **28–34** the broadcaster must have applied to the Copyright Tribunal to settle the terms of payment. The provisions relating to the application to the Copyright Tribunal to settle the terms of payment, and the right to apply for review of any order, follow the same form as those which relate to the right to use information about programmes.[180] Section 135D requires the Copyright Tribunal to consider such applications and provides it with a discretion to make such order as it may determine to be reasonable in the circumstances.[181] In addition, a person exercising the right may also request that the Copyright Tribunal consider the reasonableness of any conditions or requirements as to information imposed by the licensing body and again the Tribunal is given the power to make such order as it may determine to be reasonable in the circumstances.[182] The Tribunal does not have jurisdiction to limit the forms of broadcast by which the sound recording may be transmitted, for example, by excluding digital audio broadcasting.[183]

References about conditions, etc. The test as to whether a condition may be at- **28–35** tached to the exercise of the statutory right is that of reasonableness. This presumably means reasonable from both parties' point of view, judged by reference to the objective which the statutory right was intended to achieve. A condition as to providing security for the licence fees would probably not be deemed reasonable, given that the provisions are intended to assist the establishment of niche radio stations which may well lack the resources to provide such security.[184] However, the Tribunal has held that a requirement that a licensee identify which programmes are supplied by third parties and the identity of the supplier is

---

[176] s.135B(3).
[177] CDPA 1988 s.135C(1).
[178] See further, paras 28–35, et seq., below.
[179] CDPA 1988 s.135C(4).
[180] See paras 28–22 et seq., above and as to the procedure of the Tribunal, see paras 28–154 et seq., below.
[181] See, generally, paras 28–110 et seq., below.
[182] CDPA 1988 s.135E.
[183] But see para.28–29, above.
[184] During the passage of the Broadcasting Bill there were attempts to introduce an amendment which would have required a broadcaster to provide security for the differences between the amount asked for by the licensing body and the amount the broadcaster declared it was willing to pay. This amendment was rejected by the Government because of the adverse affect this might have on small broadcasters. See *Hansard*, HL Vol.521, cols 1678–80.

reasonable.[185] During the passage of these provisions through Parliament, it was suggested that conditions could be imposed so as to prohibit certain disreputable practices which might be damaging to record companies. Thus, for example, it would, no doubt, be reasonable to impose conditions so as to prevent the playing of a particular recording whenever a particular product is advertised in such a way as to imply an endorsement of that product by the artist involved.[186] Moreover, the MMC took the view that conditions designed to restrict home taping were reasonable.

The power to review the conditions of the licence does not enable the Tribunal to require the licensing body to grant related ancillary rights, such as the right to dub[187] recordings and keep copies indefinitely,[188] or to provide to other stations copies of programmes compiled by the licensee. Pending a finding by the Tribunal that a condition is unreasonable, the licensee should comply with it. If it declines to do so, the licensing body may seek injunctive relief requiring compliance with the condition. However, were the condition unreasonable, it is unlikely that such relief would be forthcoming.[189]

28–36   **Payment: general approach.** It has been said that it is "notoriously difficult to arrive at a decision as to an appropriate royalty in the absence of equivalent consensual licences".[190] Ultimately, the decision will be "a 'judgment call' taking into account a large number of factors".[191]

In *AIRC v PPL*[192] the Copyright Tribunal considered the effect of the removal of needletime restrictions on the terms of licences between PPL and the AIRC. PPL sought a substantial increase in the rates that had been determined when airplay was restricted to nine hours per day. PPL argued that such an increase was justified by the huge increase in the applicant's use of its records since the rates were last set by the Tribunal. AIRC argued that PPL's proposals were unreasonable as they represented a 54 per cent increase on the expiring licence and that the promotional benefit to the respondent's members should be taken into account, as should lower royalty rates in other European countries. In reaching its decision the Tribunal held that the position in other European countries was not helpful as the structure and function of the radio industries there was so different.[193] It also thought existing agreements on video licensing by VPL to MTV Europe and patent licences were of no assistance. It held that the most useful comparator was the PRS agreement with the AIRC, particularly as regarded the overall yield which the Tribunal considered "should be in the same general

---

[185] *The Association of Independent Radio Companies Ltd (AIRC) v Phonographic Performance Ltd* [1994] R.P.C. 143 at 188–189.

[186] See *Hansard*, HL Vol.521, col.1671; Vol.522, col.840.

[187] That is to make a further copy of recorded music.

[188] In *Phonographic Performance Ltd v AEI Rediffusion Music Ltd* [1998] Ch. 187 it was held that there was no right to make copies under s.135C of the Act. Broadcasters must therefore rely on s.68 of the Act which requires copies to be destroyed within 28 days (see para.9–206) or they must negotiate a separate dubbing licence. During the passage of the Broadcasting Bill some concern was expressed that the dubbing right might be used to reimpose needletime restrictions: *Hansard*, HL Vol.521, col.1658. However, a review of dubbing licence arrangements might fall within the general powers of the Tribunal. See further, *AEI Rediffusion Music Ltd v Phonographic Performance Ltd* [1998] R.P.C. 335, in particular, at 358 and see para.28–36, below.

[189] See *Hansard*, HL Vol.542, col.841.

[190] *AEI Rediffusion Music Ltd v Phonographic Performance Ltd* [1998] R.P.C. 335 at 343.

[191] *AEI Rediffusion Music Ltd v Phonographic Performance Ltd* [1998] R.P.C. 335 at 343 and see the cases cited at para.28–110, below.

[192] *The Association of Independent Radio Companies Ltd (AIRC) v Phonographic Performance Ltd* [1994] R.P.C. 143. Also see Arnold, (1993) Ent. L.Rev. 145.

[193] But note that the MMC has emphasised the potential importance of international comparisons: MMC, *A Report on the supply in the UK of the services of administering performing rights and film synchronisation rights*, 1996 (Cm.3147) para.2.91.

range".[194] In rejecting the respondent's argument for a substantial increase the Tribunal held that, whilst the amount of needletime was a relevant consideration in assessing payment, on the facts, the abolition of needletime had worked not only to the benefit of the broadcasters but also to the benefit of PPL.[195] Nor could such an increase be justified by reference to the loss of revenue caused by home taping.[196]

AEI Rediffusion v PPL[197] involved a dispute between PPL and the operators of a subscription narrowcast service delivered by satellite. The Tribunal had to consider the appropriate royalty rate and the revenue on which it should be based. The Tribunal emphasised that it had a duty to arrive at a figure "which is both fair to the licensor in terms of the value to the licensee of having access to the copyright sound recordings, and also fair to the licensee in giving him a proper reward for the effort put into the exploitation of the licensor's intellectual property rights. This includes in particular making full allowance for the added value provided by the licensee".[198] The Tribunal also said that where the licensee makes part of its profit from equipment sales or rental then it will be appropriate to take this into account in cases where "without the provision of the music the opportunity to sell or lease equipment would not arise".[199] Moreover, it seems that in cases where a licensor's rights are to be exploited overseas under a licence granted in the United Kingdom, the right to broadcast in the United Kingdom will be made subject to conditions that a proper royalty rate should be paid in respect of all sites taking the service. In this case this meant that the rate payable for use of the copyrights overseas should be the same as that charged domestically.[200] When deciding on a useful comparator the driving consideration should be commercial reality. Thus the decision in the *AIRC* case that patent licences were of no assistance could not be taken to have decided as a matter of principle that licences of different legal rights could be of no assistance.[201] However, the best comparator in this case was the existing commercial dubbing licences, even though the markets for delivery on tape or CD or delivery by satellite were "not exactly co-terminous".[202]

Virgin v PPL[203] concerned Virgin Megastores Radio, a radio station located in Virgin's Oxford Street store, which played music introduced by disc jockeys for satellite broadcast to all Virgin's stores. The Tribunal rejected comparisons with the *AEI* decision because, in its view, the activities of Virgin's radio station (which involved "live"[204] music, DJs, news bulletins and advertisements) did not constitute narrowcasting.[205] By contrast, it accepted that there were enough similarities between Virgin's radio station and an independent local radio station

---

[194] *The Association of Independent Radio Companies Ltd (AIRC) v Phonographic Performance Ltd* [1994] R.P.C. 143 at 185.

[195] *Association of Independent Radio Companies Ltd v Phonographic Performances Ltd* [1994] R.P.C. 143 at 183–4.

[196] *Association of Independent Radio Companies Ltd v Phonographic Performances Ltd* [1994] R.P.C. 143 at 184.

[197] *AEI Rediffusion Music Ltd v Phonographic Performance Ltd* [1998] R.P.C. 335.

[198] *AEI Rediffusion Music Ltd v Phonographic Performance Ltd* [1998] R.P.C. 335 at 343.

[199] *AEI Rediffusion Music Ltd v Phonographic Performance Ltd* [1998] R.P.C. 335 at 343.

[200] *AEI Rediffusion Music Ltd v Phonographic Performance Ltd* [1998] R.P.C. 335 at 343.

[201] *AEI Rediffusion Music Ltd v Phonographic Performance Ltd* [1998] R.P.C. 335 at 348.

[202] *AEI Rediffusion Music Ltd v Phonographic Performance Ltd* [1998] R.P.C. 335 at 353.

[203] *Virgin Retail Ltd v Phonographic Performance Ltd* [2000] E.M.L.R. 323.

[204] In the sense that it was played "live" by a DJ.

[205] *Virgin Retail Ltd v Phonographic Performance Ltd* [2000] E.M.L.R. 323 at para.50. The Tribunal defined "narrowcasting" by reference to the *AEI* decision. It noted that AEI had originally been a "commercial dubber", that is it had delivered background music to its subscribers in the form of a hard copy, typically a tape, which was then played by the subscriber on commercially available equipment. It went on to point out that the service which was the subject of the *AEI* decision, *AEI Rediffusion Music Ltd v Phonographic Performance Ltd* [1998] R.P.C. 335, was exactly the same as this except that material was broadcast rather than supplied in hard copy. Accordingly,

for the royalty rates ordered in the *AIRC* case to provide useful guidance.[206] Nevertheless, because Virgin's radio station did not have to make a profit and its advertising revenue might be lower than a comparable local radio station, the royalty rate was set at a higher level than for a local radio station with comparable advertising revenue.[207] The Tribunal rejected an argument that there should be a discount because Virgin's radio station was itself involved in marketing the records of PPL's members.[208] It also held that it should ignore the possibility that if too high a royalty was charged, this might force Virgin to discontinue its radio station.[209] Finally, to guard against the possibility that Virgin might cease to pursue a policy of maximising advertising revenue, thus reducing the royalty, the Tribunal imposed a minimum royalty on Virgin, based on square footage of Virgin's sites.[210] On appeal, the Judge accepted that the Tribunal was entitled to reject the comparison with the *AEI* decision, but held that there was no evidence to support its finding that the *AIRC* decision provided useful guidance: the whole commercial raison d'être, commercial financing and business of an independent local radio station was completely different from that of Virgin's radio station.[211] Accordingly, he remitted the matter to the Tribunal. The dispute was then settled and the application withdrawn.

28–37   **Factors to be taken into account.** In considering what is reasonable on any application to review the conditions of the licence or to settle or review the terms of payment, the Tribunal is expressly required to consider certain factors[212]:

(i) **Non-discrimination.** The Tribunal is required to have regard to the terms of any orders which it has made in the case of persons in similar circumstances exercising the right conferred by s.135C, and to exercise its powers so as to ensure that there is no unreasonable discrimination between persons exercising that right against the same licensing body.[213] In the *AIRC* case, the Tribunal declined to discriminate on the basis of usage, except in determining whether a station was a music station or talk station. It held that talk stations should be able to make reasonable use of recorded music without incurring the full rigours of normal rates. It also held that low-revenue stations should benefit from a lower rate, so that the tariff encouraged "small and specialist incremental stations which add to the diversity in broadcasting".[214] Apart from those two concessions, it imposed a single standard revenue-based royalty applicable to the generality of stations.

(ii) **Other orders.** Secondly, the Tribunal is directed, when settling the terms

---

the Tribunal defined narrowcasting as "the business analogous to a commercial dubber of a company which uses the broadcasting medium to supply pre-recorded material to its clients rather than supplying them with hard copies of the pre-recorded material" (para.43).

[206] *Virgin Retail Ltd v Phonographic Performance Ltd* [2000] E.M.L.R. 323, para.64.

[207] *Virgin Retail Ltd v Phonographic Performance Ltd* [2000] E.M.L.R. 323, para.68.

[208] *Virgin Retail Ltd v Phonographic Performance Ltd* [2000] E.M.L.R. 323, para.71.

[209] *Virgin Retail Ltd v Phonographic Performance Ltd* [2000] E.M.L.R. 323, para.73; but the Tribunal stated that it was "singularly unimpressed" by Virgin's evidence as to this: para.72.

[210] *Virgin Retail Ltd v Phonographic Performance Ltd* [2000] E.M.L.R. 323, para.77.

[211] *Phonographic Performance Ltd v Virgin Retail Ltd* [2001] E.M.L.R. 139 at para.38.

[212] These factors do not expressly include those set out in s.129 of CDPA 1988. Nevertheless, the wide language of s.135D ("reasonable in the circumstances") requires those factors to be taken into account: *Phonographic Performance Ltd v Virgin Retail Ltd* [2001] E.M.L.R. 139, para.11.

[213] CDPA 1988 s.135G(1).

[214] *Association of Independent Radio Companies Ltd (AIRC) v Phonographic Performance Ltd* [1994] R.P.C. 143 at 179. This reflects Government policy as represented in the Green Paper, *Radio: Choices and Opportunities*, 1987 (Cm.92) and the White Paper, *Broadcasting in the '90s: Competition, Choice and Quality*, 1988 (Cm.517). The MMC Report, *Collective Licensing: A Report on Certain Practices in the Collective Licensing of Public Performances and Broadcasting Rights in Sound Recordings*, 1988 (Cm.530) also suggested that new stations should be given preferential rates: para.7.42.

of payment, not to be guided by any order it has made under any enactment other than s.135D.[215] This might appear to exclude from consideration comparisons with voluntary licensing schemes, the compulsory
licence for broadcast information, as well as decisions made by the
Performing Right Tribunal and the Copyright Tribunal prior to 1991.
However, the requirement that the Tribunal is not to be "guided by" previous orders[216] does not require it to ignore previous decisions; it merely
indicates that the Tribunal should not regard such orders as the basis or
starting-point for determination of a decision under the section.[217] The
Tribunal should not simply extrapolate, but should consider matters
afresh. In the *AIRC* case, the terms of the agreement between the parties
had been reviewed in 1980 by the PRT and again in 1986.[218] The Copyright Tribunal considered that it could refer to these previous orders as
"an essential part of the history of the matter", but that in this case the
previous orders were of little help because of changes in the independent
radio and record industries and because of difficulty in following the reasoning of the PRT.[219] In *Virgin v PPL*, the Tribunal held that the *AIRC* decision provided useful guidance, but this holding was overruled on
appeal.[220]

(iii) **Re-transmissions.** The Act makes further provision to deal with the situation where a broadcast is further broadcast by reception and immediate
retransmission.[221] Where the retransmission is confined to the original
broadcast area, the Act provides that the Copyright Tribunal, in considering what charges (if any) should be paid for licences for either transmission, should have regard to the extent to which the owner of copyright in
the sound recording has already received, or is entitled to receive, payment for the other transmission in that area.[222] Where a retransmission
extends beyond the original broadcast area, the Tribunal is further directed
to leave out of consideration of the terms of the licence for the first transmission any further transmission to an area outside that to which the first
transmission was made.[223] The aim of these provisions is thus to ensure
that the copyright owner is not remunerated twice over, and to protect the
original broadcaster from having to pay royalties for transmission beyond
its service area.[224]

Effect of the Order. The effect of the order is retrospective, relating back to the   **28–38**
date when the applicant began to use the statutory licence. If the Tribunal
increases the financial remuneration due to the licensing body from that which
the applicant has been paying pending determination, the broadcaster is liable for
the amounts that have fallen due. If the broadcaster has been paying the licensing

---

[215] CDPA 1988 s.135G(2).
[216] For criticism of the width of this phrase see *Hansard,* HL Vol.522, col.842 (Lord Jenkins).
[217] *The Association of Independent Radio Companies Ltd (AIRC) v Phonographic Performance Ltd* [1994] R.P.C. 143 at 175.
[218] *AIRC v PPL*, Decision of July 15, 1980; *AIRC v PPL*, Decision of October 23, 1986.
[219] *The Association of Independent Radio Companies Limited (AIRC) v Phonographic Performance Ltd* [1994] R.P.C. 143 at 175.
[220] For a fuller account, see the previous paragraph.
[221] CDPA 1988 ss.135G(3) and 134.
[222] s.134(2).
[223] s.134(3).
[224] These provisions should thus be compared to the provisions relating to the re-transmission of broadcasts in a cable programme service, as to which see paras 28–48 et seq., below.

body too much, the difference must be repaid.[225] In *AIRC v PPL* the Tribunal held that since there was no express provision in the 1990 scheme permitting the Tribunal to order that interest be paid, such power was not available.[226] Following criticism of this by the Monopolies and Mergers Commission,[227] the Government introduced a new s.151A into the 1988 Act which empowers the Tribunal to award simple interest at such rate and for such period after the first payment became due as the Tribunal thinks reasonable in the circumstances.[228] Having set out the basis on which the order is to be made, the Tribunal usually refers the matter back to the parties to produce an agreed form of licence which in due course is incorporated in the Tribunal's final order. If the parties fail to do so, the Tribunal will determine the form of wording of the order.

28–39   **Costs.** The Tribunal has considerable discretion over the award of costs.[229] The MMC suggested that, where the licensee adopted an unreasonably low figure the Copyright Tribunal should order it to bear the costs of both parties[230]; the same might apply if the licensing body made an unreasonably high demand.[231]

28–40   **Review.** The Order is open to review at the behest of either party. On such an application the Tribunal must consider the matter and make such order confirming or varying the original order as it may determine to be reasonable in the circumstances.[232] Such an application cannot be made without special leave within 12 months following an existing order or decision.[233] Similarly, if the order was made so as to be in force for 15 months or less, or as a result of a decision on a previous application is due to expire within 15 months of that decision, no application for review is permitted (without special leave) until the last three months before the expiry date.[234]

(iii) Duration: transitional provisions

28–41   **General.** As is noted elsewhere, the effect of the implementation of the Term Directive[235] was that certain copyrights which had lapsed were revived.[236] In the United Kingdom the revived right is, however, limited, if certain conditions are satisfied, to a right to remuneration. The regulations thus provide that where such conditions are satisfied, in the case of a work in which revived copyright subsists, any acts restricted by the copyright shall be treated as licensed by the copyright

---

[225] CDPA 1988 s.135D(2).

[226] *The Association of Independent Radio Companies Ltd (AIRC) v Phonographic Performance Ltd* [1994] R.P.C. 143 following *Swift v Board of Trade* [1925] A.C. 520 and distinguishing *Knibb v NCB* [1987] 1 Q.B. 906.

[227] MMC, A Report on the supply in the UK of the services of administering performing rights and film synchronisation rights 1996 (Cm.3147) paras 2.93, 2.130. But note the BBC evidence that the absence of such a power provides an incentive for matters to be dealt with expeditiously: para.10.5. See also, The Reports of the Debates of the House of Commons Standing Committee D in 1996, col.760.

[228] CDPA 1988 s.151A, added by the Broadcasting Act 1996 s.139(2). More generally see para.28–96, below.

[229] CDPA 1988 s.151; Copyright Tribunal Rules 2010 (SI 2010/791) r.31 and see para.28–175, below.

[230] MMC Report, Collective Licensing: A Report on Certain Practices in the Collective Licensing of Public Performances and Broadcasting Rights in Sound Recordings, 1988 (Cm.530) para.7.19(e).

[231] *Hansard,* HL Vol.521, col.1664; Vol.522, col.840.

[232] CDPA 1988 s.135F(3).

[233] s.135F(2)(a).

[234] s.135F(2)(b).

[235] Directive 93/98/EEC. This Directive has now been repealed and replaced (but only in order to codify amendments) by Directive 2006/116/EC on the term of protection of copyright and certain related rights [2006] OJ L372/12. See Vol.2 H13.

[236] See para.6–17, above.

owner, subject only to the payment of such reasonable royalty or other remuneration as may be agreed or determined in default of agreement by the Copyright Tribunal.[237] A person intending to avail himself of this right must give reasonable notice of his intention to the copyright owner, stating when he intends to begin to do the acts.[238] If he fails to give such notice his acts are not to be treated as licensed.[239] If he does give such notice, the acts are to be treated as if they were licensed and a reasonable royalty or other remuneration will be payable in respect of them despite the fact that the amount of such royalty or other remuneration is not yet agreed or determined.[240] Thus, for example, when the UK copyright lapsed in Joyce's *Ulysses* in 1991 and was revived on January 1, 1996, a person wishing to publish a copy of that work was obliged to give notice of his intention to the owner of the copyright and agree a royalty or apply to the Copyright Tribunal to settle a reasonable royalty.[241] This compulsory licence does not, however, apply if or to the extent that a licence to do the acts could be granted by a licensing body,[242] whether under a licensing scheme or otherwise.[243] Moral rights, which are also revived, continue to be subject to any waiver which subsisted immediately before the expiry of the old term and are otherwise exercisable as with any other copyright work.[244] Equivalent provisions for rights in performances are dealt with below.[245]

The notice. The Regulations require the notice to state the date on which the person giving it intends to do the acts in question.[246] However, a notice which fails to state that date may be sufficient where it can be shown that when the notice was served the copyright owner knew that date by other means, for example as a result of publicity material or having been informed of it orally.[247] Since the copyright owner cannot stop the publication, the purpose of the requirement to give notice appears to be to ensure that the acts in question are open and not clandestine and that a person who hoped to get away with an infringement in secret cannot justify his act retrospectively by reference to the Regulations. Accordingly, it is arguable that only a short period of notice need be given.[248] The notice does not need to include a copy of the intended publication.[249] There is no reason why a notice should not be expressed in contingent terms, for example, that it is without prejudice to an argument that the acts in question would not infringe, for example because reg.23 applies.[250]   **28–42**

The Copyright Tribunal. An application to settle the royalty or other remuneration payable in respect of the right outlined above may be made to the Tribunal by either the owner or the licensee.[251] The Tribunal is required to consider such applications and may make such an order as it may determine to be reasonable in   **28–43**

---

[237] Duration of Copyright and Rights in Performances Regulations 1995 (SI 1995/3297) reg.24(1).
[238] reg.24(2).
[239] reg.24(3).
[240] reg.24(4).
[241] *Sweeney v Macmillan Publishers Ltd* [2002] R.P.C. 35.
[242] For the definition of a licensing body see CDPA 1988 s.116(2) and para.28–88, below.
[243] Duration of Copyright and Rights in Performances Regulations 1995 (SI 1995/3297) reg.24(5).
[244] reg.22. See further, Ch.11, above.
[245] See notes to para.28–150.
[246] Duration of Copyright and Rights in Performances Regulations 1995 (SI 1995/3297) reg.24(2).
[247] *Sweeney v Macmillan Publishers Ltd* [2002] R.P.C. 35, para.62.
[248] *Sweeney v Macmillan Publishers Ltd* [2002] R.P.C. 35, para.63. On the facts, notice in March in respect of publication in June was held to be reasonable "on any basis".
[249] *Sweeney v Macmillan Publishers Ltd* [2002] R.P.C. 35, para.63.
[250] *Sweeney v Macmillan Publishers Ltd* [2002] R.P.C. 35, paras 64 to 65.
[251] Duration of Copyright and Rights on Performances Regulations 1995 (SI 1995/3297) reg.25(1).

the circumstances.[252] Either party may subsequently apply to the Tribunal to vary the order, and the Tribunal shall consider the matter and make such order confirming or varying the original order as it may determine to be reasonable in the circumstances.[253] Restrictions exist, similar to those already considered, so that an application for review may not normally be made within 12 months from the date of the original order.[254]

(iv) Copyright in design documents

28–44 As is explained in detail elsewhere, where copyright subsists in a document or model embodying a design for anything other than an artistic work or a typeface, s.51 of the 1988 Act provides a "defence" to an action for infringement to any person who makes an article to the design or copies such an article.[255] This is effective as regards design documents created after January 1, 1989. However, to avoid the drastic effects that the introduction of such a defence would have had on established rights in works already in existence, para.19 of Sch.1 to the 1988 Act provided that s.51 should not apply to designs recorded in design documents or models prior to August 1, 1989 for 10 years thereafter. The effect of this provision was that full copyright protection was maintained during this period. However, para.19(2) provided that licencesof right were available in relation to such design documents on the same conditions as such licences are available in relation to unregistered designs under ss.237 to 239 of the 1988 Act.[256] Paragraph 19(3) explained that s.237 was to be read as applying to the last five years of the 10-year period. The net effect of this was that from August 1, 1989 until July 31, 1994 full copyright applied (subject to the non-derogation from grant doctrine) but that from then until July 31, 1999, licences of right were available in relation to such design documents. The scope of the licence was confined to acts which would have been permitted under s.51 had it applied.[257] Since July 31, 1999, s.51 has applied fully to design documents created before August 1, 1989.

(v) Lending to the public of copies of certain works

28–45 **Overview.** Under s.66 of the 1988 Act, power is provided to the Secretary of State to subject the lending of certain works to compulsory licensing. The new s.66 was introduced by the Copyright and Related Rights Regulations 1996[258] and came into force on December 1, 1996. It replaced the power given to the Secretary of State under the 1988 Act to subject the rental of sound recordings, films or computer programs to such licences. The new power has not been exercised.[259]

28–46 **Background.** The implementation of the Rental and Related Rights Directive[260] required extension of the rental right to include lending, and the works to which

---

[252] See further, paras 28–110 et seq., below.

[253] reg.25(3).

[254] reg.25(4).

[255] See further, paras 13–315 et seq., above.

[256] See, e.g. *In the matter of an application by Stafford Engineering Services Ltd* [2000] R.P.C. 797. These provisions were challenged on the grounds that they contravened GATT-TRIPS, which requires Member States to protect industrial designs for at least 10 years. This argument was rejected on the grounds that the Registered Designs Act 1949 fulfilled the UK's obligations in this respect. The unregistered design right grants additional protection over and above that required by TRIPS. See *Re Azrak-Hamway International Inc. Licence of Right (Design Right and Copyright) Application* [1997] R.P.C. 134 at 150–1.

[257] CDPA 1988 Sch.1 para.19(7).

[258] SI 1996/2967 reg.11(3).

[259] Neither has the original power.

[260] Council Directive 92/100 on rental and lending right and on certain rights related to copyright in

the right applies include literary, dramatic, musical and some artistic works as well as sound recordings and films.[261] The amended s.66 extends the Secretary of State's power to order compulsory licences to all such works, but confines the power to deal only with cases of lending. Such a limitation is consistent with the provisions of the Directive[262] and existing international conventions.[263] Rental remains an exclusive right outside the scope of any potential order, as is required under the Directive.

The amended section also repeals, but does not replace, former s.66(5). This stated that copyright in a computer program would not be infringed by the rental of copies to the public after the end of a period of 50 years from the end of the calendar year in which copies of it were first issued to the public in electronic form. The effect of this repeal is that the rental right in such works is retained for the full copyright term.

The Order. The Secretary of State may by order specify that in certain situations the lending to the public of copies of literary, dramatic, musical or artistic works, sound recordings or films shall be treated as licensed by the copyright owner subject only to the payment of such reasonable royalty or other payment as may be agreed or determined in default of agreement by the Copyright Tribunal.[264] No such order shall apply if, or to the extent that, there is a licensing scheme certified for the purposes of this section under s.143 providing for the grant of licences.[265] The order shall be made by statutory instrument; and laid before and approved by a resolution of each House of Parliament.[266] The terms of the order may make different provision for different cases and may specify cases by reference to any factor relating to the work, the copies lent, the lender or the circumstances of the lending.[267] Such an order would not operate to exempt from liability a person lending or renting infringing copies.[268]

28–47

(vi) Cable retransmission

Overview. A further compulsory licence is available permitting the retransmission by cable of copyright works and performances included in certain wireless broadcasts, where the cable area falls outside the original broadcast area. The licence represents a compromise between copyright owners, cable service providers and broadcasters where the cable provider is obliged to carry certain broadcasting services. These provisions were introduced by the Broadcasting Act 1996. They supplement the exceptions available under s.73(2) and 73(3) of the 1988 Act.[269] Section 73(2) deals with copyright in the broadcasts themselves, and provides a defence where the retransmission is in pursuance of a "must-carry"

28–48

---

the field of intellectual property ([1992] OJ L346/61). The Directive was repealed and replaced (but only in order to codify amendments) by Directive 2006/115/EC on the rental and lending right and on certain rights related to copyright in the field of intellectual property [2006] OJ L376/28 ("the 2006 Directive"). See Vol.2 H12.

[261] arts 1 to 3 of the 2006 Directive.

[262] art.6 of the 2006 Directive. For background see Reinbothe and von Lewinski, *The EC Directive on Rental and Lending Rights and on Piracy* (London: Sweet & Maxwell, 1993) pp.34–35, 77–83.

[263] There is no lending right under either the Berne or Rome Conventions. cf. the exclusive rental right under the WIPO Copyright Treaty 1996 art.7; and under the WIPO Performances and Phonograms Treaty 1996 art.13.

[264] CDPA 1988 s.66(1).

[265] s.66(2). No such scheme has yet been certified.

[266] s.66(4).

[267] s.66(3). Member States are free to determine the amount of remuneration in accordance with their cultural objectives: Dir. 2006/115/EC art.6(1).

[268] s.66(5).

[269] See *Hansard*, HL Vol.570, cols 194–5; HC July 1, 1996, col.593. See paras 9–226 et seq., above.

requirement or is in the same service area. Section 73(3) and (4) concern copy-right in the works included in the broadcast. Thus, s.73(3) provides a defence to an action for infringement of copyright in works contained in the broadcast as regards retransmissions within the broadcast area.[270] Section 73(4) provides for a compulsory licence where inclusion is pursuant to a relevant requirement, but diffusion extends beyond the broadcast area. The compulsory licence under s.73(4) is therefore of no application where the retransmission is within the broadcast area and the s.73(3) defence applies, nor does it have any relevance to copyright in the broadcast itself. These provisions were amended by the Copy-right and Related Rights Regulations 2003[271] in order to give effect to the new definition of "broadcast" introduced by those Regulations. The provisions as amended continue to be confined to wireless broadcasts. Accordingly, the amend-ments appear to be purely ones of terminology.

These provisions must also be viewed alongside s.144A of the 1988 Act. This section applies to the right of the owner of copyright in a literary, dramatic, musi-cal or artistic work, sound recording or film to control the cable retransmission of a wireless broadcast from another EEA State.[272] This right can only be exercised against a cable operator through a licensing body.[273]

It should also be noted that equivalent provisions exist as regards the retrans-mission of performances.[274]

28–49   **The licence.** The licence applies to works included in a broadcast which has been retransmitted beyond the original broadcast area in fulfilment of a "must-carry" obligation. In these circumstances, the Act provides that the retransmission by cable shall be treated as licensed by the owner of the copyright in the work, subject only to the payment to him by the person making the broadcast of such reasonable royalty or other payment as may be agreed or determined in default of agreement by the Copyright Tribunal. The idea appears to be that the original broadcaster must pay a royalty to the copyright owner of a work included in the broadcast because the original licence negotiated between the broadcaster and the owner of copyright may not have accounted for the additional audience reached by the retransmission.[275] At first sight it may perhaps seem surprising that it is the broadcaster who has to pay the royalty to the copyright owner and not the person operating the retransmission service, in particular because the broadcaster's potential liability is dependent upon the actions of a third party over whom the broadcaster has no control. The justification for this arrangement is that the "must-carry" provisions are designed to protect traditional broadcast-ers by ensuring that their broadcasts remain widely available, whereas the person operating the retransmission service might well prefer not to have to include the broadcasts concerned. Moreover, in the case of broadcasters whose income depends upon advertising revenue, such retransmission may allow the broadcaster to charge more for advertising time, as the advertisements will reach a larger audience. Further justification for placing the obligation on the broadcaster can be obtained by reference to the relative transaction costs: identifying and locating all the relevant copyright holders might involve considerable extra expense for

---

[270] See further, para.9–230, above.
[271] SI 2003/2498.
[272] As to which countries are EEA States, see para.24–02, above.
[273] CDPA 1988 s.144A(3). This section was introduced in order to comply with art.9 of the Direc-tive on the co-ordination of certain rules concerning copyright and rights related to copyright ap-plicable to satellite broadcasting and cable retransmission 93/83/EEC [1993] OJ L248/15 (see paras 24–00 et seq., above); see generally as to s.144A, para.28–59, below.
[274] CDPA 1988 Sch.2 para.19 inserted by the Broadcasting Act 1996 Sch.9 para.5.
[275] The compulsory licence does not operate where the retransmission of the work by cable is licensed by the owner of copyright in the work: CDPA 1988 s.73(5), and see below.

the cable retransmitter, whereas the broadcaster will in any event have to negotiate with the copyright owners to get permission to include their works in the broadcast.

Qualification. In order to qualify for the licence a number of conditions must be satisfied: **28–50**

> First, the retransmission must be of a wireless broadcast made from a place in the United Kingdom and it must be received and immediately retransmitted by cable.[276] However, this restriction should be viewed alongside s.144A, considered above, which mandates the collective administration of cable retransmission rights in respect of wireless broadcasts made from another EEA State.[277]
>
> Secondly, the inclusion of the broadcast in the cable retransmission must be in pursuance of a relevant requirement. This is defined as a requirement imposed by a general condition within the meaning of Ch.I of Pt 2 of the Communications Act 2003, the setting of which is authorised under s.64 of that Act, that is "conditions making any provision that OFCOM consider appropriate for securing that particular services are broadcast or otherwise transmitted by means of the electronic communications networks described in the conditions".[278] Section 64(3) lists the services which may be made the subject of such "must-carry" conditions.
>
> Thirdly, the section only operates where the area in which the cable retransmission takes place ("the cable area") falls outside the area for reception in which the broadcast is made ("the broadcast area"). To the extent that the retransmission falls within the broadcast area, an absolute defence exists under s.73(3).[279]
>
> Finally, the licence does not apply if, or to the extent that, the retransmission of the work by cable is licensed by the owner of the copyright in the work.[280]

The Copyright Tribunal. An application to settle the royalty or other sum payable in respect of the compulsory licence may be made to the Copyright Tribunal by the copyright owner or the person making the broadcast.[281] The Tribunal is required to consider such applications and may make such order as it determines to be reasonable in the circumstances.[282] Either party may subsequently apply to the Tribunal to vary the order, and the Tribunal shall consider the matter and make such order confirming or varying the original order as it may determine to be reasonable in the circumstances.[283] Restrictions exist, similar to those already considered, so that an application for review may not normally be made within 12 months from the date of the original order.[284]   **28–51**

---

[276] CDPA 1988 s.73(1).

[277] See further, para.28–59, below.

[278] s.64(1).

[279] See further, para.9–230, above.

[280] CDPA 1988 s.73(5).

[281] CDPA 1988 s.73A(1).

[282] s.73A(2). Such an order has effect from the date on which it is made or such later date as may be specified by the Tribunal: s.73A(5). For "reasonableness", see generally paras 28–110 et seq., below. For the procedure before the Tribunal see paras 28–154 et seq., below. It should also be noted that s.134 of the 1988 Act (duty of the Copyright Tribunal to leave retransmission out of account in considering what charges should be paid for licences for the original transmission) does not apply in relation to such applications: s.134(3A) (added by the Broadcasting Act 1996 Sch.9 para.2(3)).

[283] CDPA 1988 s.73A(3).

[284] s.73A(4).

(vii) Works of enemy origin

28–52   **Background: The First World War.** Where works were made or published before or during the First World War the copyright in this country, if the property of an enemy, became vested in the Public Trustee as the Custodian of Enemy Property under the Trading with the Enemy Acts 1914 to 1918.[285] After the termination of the war such copyrights were revested, but this was subject to a complex system of disabilities and restrictions.[286] In the light of these complexities, the emergency legislation adopted on the outbreak of war in 1939,[287] created a simpler system so that the war did not affect the continuance or creation of British copyrights in works originating in enemy countries. The 1939 provisions remain in force[288] and have been amended by successive Acts of Parliament dealing with intellectual property matters.

28–53   **The Patents, Designs, Copyright and Trade Marks (Emergency) Act 1939.** Under the 1939 Act, enemy owned copyrights are preserved[289] but made subject to the possibility of compulsory licensing. Power is vested in the Comptroller to grant licences in respect of copyrights owned by an enemy or enemy subject on any terms that the comptroller may think expedient.[290] This power also applies where an enemy or enemy subject is a joint owner of copyright.[291] Owners of copyright to which the Act applies remain free to exercise their rights unless and until some order affecting them is made by the Comptroller. Where an order has been made by the Comptroller this will override any exercise of the owner's rights which is inconsistent with the terms of that licence. But, provided the Comptroller has granted a non-exclusive licence, there is nothing to stop the owner, if not disqualified by trading with the enemy legislation, from granting additional non-exclusive licences.[292]

Before making an order the Comptroller is under a duty to give any interested party an opportunity to be heard, except in cases where this would be impossible or inexpedient.[293] Where the Comptroller orders royalties to be paid he shall also give directions as to the person to whom or the manner in which the licensee is to pay or deal with such royalties.[294] For these purposes the "Comptroller" means the Comptroller-General of Patents, Designs and Trade Marks and "enemy" and "enemy subject" have the meanings assigned to them by the Trading with the Enemy Act 1939.[295]

(viii) Control of monopoly: powers exercisable under domestic law

28–54   **Licences as of right.** The 1988 Act and the Rights in Databases Regulations supplement, with reference to copyright, design right, performers' property rights

---

[285] 4 & 5 Geo. 5, c.87; 5 Geo. 5, c.12; 5 & 6 Geo. 5, c.79; 5 & 6 Geo. 5, c.98; 5 & 6 Geo. 5, c.105; 8 & 9 Geo. 5, c.31.

[286] See *Copinger* 10th edn, para.1186.

[287] The Patents, Designs, Copyright and Trade Marks (Emergency) Act 1939 (c.107).

[288] For a discussion of this see *Novello & Co Ltd v Hinrichsen Edition Ltd* [1951] Ch. 1026 at 1032; (1951) 68 R.P.C. 243.

[289] The Patents, Designs, Copyright and Trade Marks (Emergency) Act 1939 s.5.

[290] s.2. Note that the Comptroller also has the power to vary existing licences by virtue of this provision.

[291] s.2(1).

[292] See *Novello & Co Ltd v Hinrichsen Edition Ltd* [1951] Ch. 1026, in particular, at 1038; (1951) 68 R.P.C. 243.

[293] The Patents, Designs, Copyright and Trade Marks (Emergency) Act 1939 s.8.

[294] s.2(6). Note that under s.2(5) of the Act a licensee also has exceptional powers to "institute proceedings in his own name as though he were the owner of copyright". See, as to the effect of this provision, *Novello & Co. Ltd v Eulenberg* [1950] 1 All E.R. 44.

[295] s.10.

and database right, the general controls under UK legislation over anti-competitive or monopolistic practices.[296] Thus, s.144 of the 1988 Act provides that where whatever needs to be remedied, mitigated or prevented by the Secretary of State, the Office of Fair Trading or (as the case may be) the Competition Commission under various specified statutory provisions consists of or includes (a) conditions in copyright licences restricting the use of the work by the licensee or the right of the copyright owner to grant other licences, or (b) a refusal on the part of the copyright owner to grant licences on reasonable terms, then the Secretary of State, Office of Fair Trading or Competition Commission as the case may be is given the power to cancel or modify the licensing conditions, and (instead or in addition) the power to provide that licences shall be available as of right.[297] However, these powers may only be exercised if the person or body exercising them is satisfied that to do so does not contravene any Convention relating to copyright to which the United Kingdom is a party.[298] Equivalent provision is made in respect of design right,[299] performers' property rights[300] and database right.[301]

The Copyright Tribunal. If the terms of a licence available under any of these provisions except s.238 cannot be agreed, then the person requiring the licence may apply to the Copyright Tribunal to settle the terms.[302] The licence, as so settled, must authorise the licensee to do everything in respect of which a licence under the relevant provision is available.[303] When the terms of the licence have been settled by the Tribunal, the licence takes effect from the date of application to the Tribunal.[304] The terms of a licence under s.238 are to be settled by the comptroller in default of agreement.[305]

28–55

---

[296] See, generally, as to such legislation, para.28–288, below.

[297] CDPA 1988 s.144(1A), as amended by the Enterprise Act 2002 (c.40) Sch.25 para.18(2) with effect from June 20, 2003: see the Enterprise Act (Commencement No. 3, Transitional and Transitory and Savings) Order 2003 (SI 2003/1397) art.2 (except for the purposes of references under s.32 of the Water Industry Act 1991: see art.3(1)). This provision is discussed at paras 28–325 et seq., below.

[298] CDPA 1988 s.144(3); see further para.28–328, below.

[299] CDPA 1988 s.238, as amended by the Enterprise Act 2002 (c.40) Sch.25 para.18(3) with effect from June 20, 2003: see the Enterprise Act (Commencement No. 3, Transitional and Transitory and Savings) Order 2003 (SI 2003/1397) art.2 (except for the purposes of references under s.32 of the Water Industry Act 1991: see art.3(1)). Since design right is not covered by any relevant international convention, there is no requirement that the powers in respect of it should only be exercised if the person or body exercising them is satisfied that to do so does not contravene such a convention.

[300] CDPA 1988 Sch.2A para.17, as amended by the Enterprise Act 2002 (c.40) Sch.25 para.18(5) with effect from June 20, 2003: see the Enterprise Act (Commencement No. 3, Transitional and Transitory and Savings) Order 2003 (SI 2003/1397) art.2 (except for the purposes of references under s.32 of the Water Industry Act 1991: see art.3(1)).

[301] The Copyright and Rights in Databases Regulations 1997 (SI 1997/3032) Sch.2 para.15, as amended by the Enterprise Act 2002 (Consequential and Supplemental Provisions) Order 2003 (SI 2003/1398) art.2 and Sch. para.31 with effect from June 20, 2003 (except for the purposes of references under s.32 of the Water Industry Act 1991: ibid. art.3(1)). Since database right is not covered by any relevant international convention, there is no requirement that the powers in respect of it should only be exercised if the person or body exercising them is satisfied that to do so does not contravene such a convention.

[302] CDPA 1988 s.144(4), CDPA 1988 Sch.2A para.17(4) and Sch.2 para.15(3) of the Regulations, respectively; as to the Copyright Tribunal generally, see paras 28–81 et seq., below, and as to such applications and the procedure before the Tribunal see paras 28–154 et seq., below.

[303] CDPA 1988 s.144 (4), CDPA 1988 Sch.2A para.17(4) and Sch.2 para.15(3) of the Regulations, respectively.

[304] CDPA 1988 s.144(5), CDPA 1988 Sch.2A para.17(5) and Sch.2 para.15(4) of the Regulations, respectively.

[305] s.238(3).

(ix) Control of monopoly: European Law

28–56   **Article 102 TFEU.** In addition to the domestic provisions considered above, compulsory licences may also be made available under European law, where a copyright owner is found to have violated art.102 of the TFEU by abusing a dominant position.[306] This is considered elsewhere.[307]

3. MISCELLANEOUS CONTROLS ON THE EXERCISE OF RIGHTS

28–57   **Introduction.** There are two areas where the legislature has interfered with the exercise of exclusive rights accorded under the 1988 Act, but stopping short of imposing a compulsory or statutory licence. In these two cases, the Act has left the right to be exercised consensually, but has provided how it is to be exercised. In the first case, that of the exercise of the cable retransmission right, the Act provides that the right may only be exercised by a collecting society. In the second case, that of the exercise of the reproduction right by reprographic copying of published literary, dramatic, musical and artistic works and typographical arrangements of published editions, the Act provides that existing consensual arrangements for the exercise of such right in respect of certain such works may be compulsorily extended to include other such works. In a third area, the Act provides a procedure for the certification or (in one case) notification of licensing schemes for certain works for the purpose of displacing the permitted acts which would otherwise apply to those works. In a fourth area, until very recently the Act provided a procedure for compulsory notification of proposed licences or licensing schemes to the Secretary of State, who might decide to refer them to the Copyright Tribunal. The effect in all these cases is to subject the exercise of such rights to the control of the Copyright Tribunal.

A. Compulsory Collective Administration of Rights: the Cable Retransmission Right

28–58   **Cable retransmission right.** The Satellite and Cable Directive[308] was adopted as part of the programme of harmonisation of the national laws of Member States of the European Union undertaken at the instigation of the Commission,[309] aimed, in the case of this Directive, at the creation of a single audio visual area.[310] One of the aims of the Directive is to facilitate the cable retransmission across national boundaries of broadcast and cable transmissions. For these purposes the Directive defines cable retransmission as "the simultaneous, unaltered and unabridged retransmission by a cable or microwave system for reception by the public of an initial transmission from another Member State, by wire or over the air".[311] The Directive requires Member States to ensure that when programmes from other Member States are retransmitted by cable in their territory the applicable copyright and related rights are observed, and that such retransmission takes place on the basis of individual or collective contractual agreements between right owners

---

[306] Formerly art.82 (and before that art.86) of the Treaty of Rome.

[307] See paras 28–277 et seq., below.

[308] September 27, 1993, [1993] OJ L248/15; for the text of the Directive, see Vol.2 H2.

[309] See generally paras 24–75 et seq.

[310] See Council Directive 89/552, [1989] OJ L298/23, on the co-ordination of certain provisions laid down by law, regulation or administrative action in Member States concerning the pursuit of television broadcasting activities.

[311] Directive 89/552 art.1(3).

and cable operators.[312] However, the Directive also requires that the cable retransmission right should only be capable of being exercised as regards a cable operator through a collecting society.[313] Where a right owner has not transferred the management of the cable retransmission right in his work to a collecting society, he is to be treated as having mandated the collecting society which manages rights of the same category to manage his right. Where there is more than one such collecting society, the right owner is to have the right to choose which he wishes to be mandated to manage his right.[314] A right owner who has not mandated his right to a collecting society is to have the same rights and obligations arising from an agreement between a collecting society and a cable operator as one who has.[315] According to the Court of Justice, the object of these provisions is to enable cable operators to be sure that they have actually acquired all the underlying rights and to prevent owners of such rights from challenging the smooth operation of the contractual arrangements authorising the retransmission. Accordingly, the Directive restricts the number of parties with which the cable operators have to negotiate in order to obtain authorisation for retransmission whilst observing the copyright and related rights of all right-holders.[316]

Section 144A of the 1988 Act. These provisions of the Satellite and Cable Directive were implemented in the United Kingdom by the Copyright and Related Rights Regulations 1996,[317] which introduced into the 1988 Act, with effect from December 1, 1996, s.144A. Although the wording of the section often closely follows the provisions of the Directive, it remains questionable whether the section properly implements the Directive in all respects. Section 144A has in turn been amended to give effect to the Information Society Directive.[318]   **28–59**

The section first identifies as a specific right in a work, being part of the bundle of rights comprising the copyright in that work under the 1988 Act, the right to grant or refuse authorisation for cable retransmission of a wireless broadcast from another EEA State in which the work is included.[319] A "cable retransmission" is defined as the reception and immediate retransmission by cable, including the transmission by microwave energy between terrestrial fixed points, of a wireless broadcast.[320] This right is defined as the cable retransmission right and the works in respect of which it exists are all literary, dramatic, musical and artistic works, sound recordings and films.[321] The policy behind the Directive was that collective administration of the cable retransmission right was only required in relation to the numerous underlying works reproduced in the broadcast, but was not necessary in respect of the broadcast itself, as the broadcaster should remain free to decide for itself whether to grant or refuse authorisation for the cable retransmission of its broadcast in another EEA State. Thus this list does not include the broadcast itself, and it is expressly provided that the section does not

---

[312] art.8(1).
[313] art.9(1). This was considered necessary in order to ensure the smooth operation of contractual arrangements for retransmission in other Member States of the broadcast and cable transmissions; see recital 28.
[314] art.9(2).
[315] art.9(2).
[316] *Uradex SCRL v Union Professionelle de la Radio et de la Télédistribution (RTD)* (C–169/05) [2006] E.C.R. I–4973, para.20.
[317] SI 1996/2967; those provisions of the Regulations not incorporated into the 1988 Act are set out in Vol.2 A3.iii.
[318] The amendments are effected by the Copyright and Related Rights Regulations 2003 (SI 2003/2498), with effect from October 31, 2003.
[319] CDPA 1988 s.144A(1); as to which countries are EEA States, see para.24–02, above.
[320] CDPA 1988 s.144A(7); the term does not appear elsewhere in the 1988 Act and the definition is therefore expressed to be for the purposes of s.144A.
[321] s.144A(1).

affect any rights exercisable by the maker of the broadcast, either in respect of the broadcast, or any underlying works included in it.[322] The omission of cable programmes from this list is explained on the same basis. What is less easy to understand is why the cable retransmission right is expressed to be limited to the retransmission of a wireless broadcast, thus excluding cable retransmission where the initial transmission is by cable, since such a retransmission would also appear to be within the terms of the Directive.[323]

The section then provides that the cable re-transmission right may only be exercised against a cable operator through a licensing body.[324] For these purposes a cable operator means a person responsible for cable retransmission of a wireless broadcast[325]; this is the person who will be committing the act restricted by the copyright in the work when re-transmitting the initial broadcast by means of cable.[326] A copyright owner who has not transferred the management of the cable retransmission right in his work to a licensing body is deemed to have mandated the licensing body which manages rights of the same category to manage his right.[327] The effect is that the collecting society has the right not only to collect remuneration but also to grant or refuse authorisation for the cable retransmission.[328] Where there are two or more such licensing bodies, the copyright owner may specify which of them is to manage the right in his work.[329] Such a copyright owner who has not transferred the management of the cable retransmission right to a licensing body nevertheless has the same rights and obligations resulting from any relevant agreement between the cable operator and the licensing body as those who have transferred their right to that body,[330] but he must claim those rights within the period of three years from the date of the cable retransmission of his work.[331] The structure effected by the Directive as implemented by s.144A leaves the copyright intact and accordingly is unaffected by any assignment (deemed or otherwise) of any of the underlying rights.[332]

B. COMPULSORY EXTENSION AND CREATION OF LICENSING SCHEMES AND LICENCES FOR REPROGRAPHIC COPYRIGHT OF CERTAIN WORKS

28–60   **Reprographic copying by educational establishments.** The 1988 Act provides a special regime in ss.137 to 141 in respect of reprographic copying[333] of published literary, dramatic, musical or artistic works or of typographical ar-

---

[322] s.144A(6).

[323] See the definition in art.1(3) of Directive 93/83, cited in para.28–58, above, which governs the extent of art.9(1).

[324] CDPA 1988 s.144A(2); as to the definition of a licensing body, see para.28–88, below.

[325] s.144(7); again, the term cable operator is not one which appears elsewhere in the 1988 Act, and the definition is expressed to be for the purposes of this section.

[326] See ss.16(1)(d) and 20.

[327] s.144A(3).

[328] *Uradex SCRL v Union Professionelle de la Radio et de la Télédistribution (RTD)* (C–169/05) [2006] E.C.R. I–4973, para.25 (the decision concerns art.9(2) of the Directive, which is implemented by s.144A(3)).

[329] s.144A(3).

[330] s.144A(4).

[331] s.144A(5); the Directive gave Member States the freedom to stipulate the length of this period, subject to a minimum of three years. In implementing this provision the Government simply applied this minimum.

[332] Recital 28 to the Directive and *Uradex SCRL v Union Professionelle de la Radio et de la Télédistribution (RTD)* (C–169/05) [2006] E.C.R. I–4973, para.24.

[333] Reprographic copying means copying by a process for making facsimile copies or involving the use of an appliance for making multiple copies, or, in the case of a work held in electronic form, copying by electronic means: CDPA 1988 s.178. The definition does not include the making of a film (or a sound recording).

rangements of published editions by educational establishments.[334] Where a licensing scheme, to which ss.118 to 123 of the 1988 Act apply,[335] or a licence, to which ss.125 to 128 of that Act apply,[336] exists and provides for the licensing of reprographic copying of such works by educational establishments, then the Secretary of State has power to extend the coverage of such scheme or licence to works which he considers to be of a description similar to those covered but unreasonably excluded from it.[337] The Secretary of State may not exercise this power in relation to a work unless he considers that to do so would not conflict with the normal exploitation of the works or unreasonably prejudice the legitimate interests of the copyright owners.[338]

Where the Secretary of State proposes to make such an order, he must give notice to the copyright owners, the licensing body in question and appropriate persons or organisations representative of educational establishments.[339] Such notice must inform the persons of their right to make written or oral representations to the Secretary of State within six months of the notice, and if any person wishes to make oral representations, the Secretary of State will appoint a person to hear them.[340] The Secretary of State, in making his decision, must take into account representations made to him and all other matters as appear to him to be relevant.[341] There is provision for the variation or discharge by the Secretary of State of any order previously made by him under s.137 of the 1988 Act on the application of the copyright owner.[342] Such variation cannot be made within two years of the original order or of a previous application seeking to vary it, unless the Secretary of State is satisfied that the circumstances are exceptional.[343] The Secretary of State may proceed to confirm the previous order on considering the grounds for the application without further representations,[344] but if he does not, the procedure to be followed is the same as that described above for the making of a decision under s.137 of the 1988 Act.[345] The Secretary of State's decision under each of these sections is subject to a right of appeal to the Copyright Tribunal.[346]

Inquiry whether scheme or licence required. The Secretary of State may appoint a person to inquire into whether new provision is required, by way of a licensing scheme or general licence, to authorise the making by or on behalf of educational establishments of reprographic copies of published literary, dramatic, musical or artistic works or of the typographical arrangements of published editions.[347] The procedure to be followed on such an inquiry is to be laid down by

28–61

---

[334] Educational establishment means any school (as further defined) and other description of educational establishment specified for such purpose by an order of the Secretary of State: CDPA 1988 s.174.

[335] See para.28–85, below.

[336] See para.28–101, below.

[337] CDPA 1988 s.137(2)(a).

[338] s.137(2)(b); this provision is necessary for the derogation of the owner's rights in such works not to be in breach of the Berne Convention, and follows the wording of the permitted exception to the owner's exclusive rights in such works: see Berne Convention (Paris Act 1971) art.9(2), the text of which is set out in Vol.2 F1.

[339] s.137(3).

[340] s.137(4).

[341] s.137(5).

[342] s.138(1).

[343] s.138(2).

[344] s.138(3).

[345] s.138(4).

[346] s.139; see, as to the procedure, paras 28–124 and 28–154 et seq., below.

[347] CDPA 1988 s.140; as to the meaning of reprographic copying and educational establishments, see para.28–60, above.

regulation by statutory instrument.[348] The person holding the inquiry is not to recommend the making of new provision unless he is satisfied that it would be to the advantage of educational establishments and that to do so would neither conflict with the normal exploitation of the works nor unreasonably prejudice the legitimate interests of the copyright owners.[349] A recommendation for new provision shall also specify any terms, other than terms as to charges payable, on which authorisation under the new provision should be available.[350] Where provision has not been made in accordance with such a recommendation within one year,[351] the Secretary of State has power to order that the making of reprographic copies of the works to which the recommendation relates by educational establishments for the purposes of instruction shall be treated as if licensed by the owners of the copyrights in the works.[352] The order is to be made by statutory instrument, and shall not come into force until at least six months after it is made.[353] The order may provide that any existing more restrictive licence shall cease to have effect, and shall provide for the terms of the licence, which shall be royalty-free.[354] The order may also provide that copies made pursuant to the order (and, therefore, when made not infringing copies[355]) are to be treated as infringing copies if sold, let for hire, offered or exposed for sale or hire or exhibited in public.[356]

C. Certification or Notification of Licensing Schemes for Purposes of Excluding Permitted Acts

28–62　　**Certification of licensing schemes: s.143.** The Secretary of State is given power to certify a licensing scheme on the application of the person operating or proposing to operate it for the purposes of displacing other provisions of the 1988 Act which permit certain acts in relation to the works the subject of the scheme.[357] The sections affected are: s.35 (educational recording of broadcasts),[358] s.60 (copying or issuing to the public copies of abstracts of scientific or technical articles),[359] s.66 (lending to the public of copies of certain works),[360] s.74 (subtitled copies of broadcasts for people who are deaf or hard of hearing)[361] and s.141 (reprographic copying of published works by educational establishments).[362] The scheme may be certified if the Secretary of State is satisfied that it enables the works to which it relates to be identified with sufficient certainty by persons likely to require licences and sets out clearly the charges, if any, payable and other terms on which licences will be granted.[363] The order is to be made by statutory instrument and the scheme is to be scheduled to the order; the order is not to take effect before eight weeks after it is made.[364] A certified scheme may not be effectively varied unless a corresponding amendment is made

---

[348] s.140(2), (3) and (6).
[349] s.140(4).
[350] s.140(5).
[351] i.e. no licensing scheme or licence complying with the recommendation has been established or granted: s.141(2).
[352] CDPA 1988 s.141(1).
[353] s.141(7) and (8).
[354] s.141(3) and (4).
[355] s.27.
[356] s.141(5).
[357] CDPA 1988 s.143(1).
[358] s.35(2); and see para.9–105, above.
[359] s.60(2); and see para.9–182, above.
[360] s.66(2); and see para.9–119, above.
[361] s.74(4); and see para.9–232, above.
[362] See paras 9–107 and 28–60, above.
[363] CDPA 1988 s.143(2).
[364] s.143(3).

to the order; the Secretary of State must make such an amendment where the scheme has been varied by the Copyright Tribunal.[365] The Secretary of State may revoke an order if it appears to him that the scheme has ceased to be operated, or is no longer being operated according to its terms.[366]

Schemes certified under s.143. Two schemes have been certified under s.143.   **28–63**
They both relate to the educational recording of broadcasts. The first came into force in 1990 but has since been substantially amended and expanded.[367] It concerns the repertoire of the Educational Recording Agency Limited, which comprises a large number of works, sound recordings, films, broadcasts and performances the rights in which are owned or controlled by a variety of collecting societies, broadcasters and industry bodies.[368] The second scheme came into force in 2003[369] and concerns television programmes broadcast on behalf of the Open University.[370]

Notification of licensing schemes. Rather different provision is made in respect   **28–64**
of licensing schemes which may displace the permitted acts provided for in s.31B of the 1988 Act, which permits in certain circumstances the making or supplying of multiple accessible copies of works to visually impaired persons.[371] It is provided that s.31B does not apply if a licensing scheme is in force, is not unduly restrictive and the scheme and any modification to it have been notified to the Secretary of State.[372] Section 31D(2) provides that a scheme is "unreasonably restrictive" if it includes a term or condition which purports to prevent or limit the steps which may be taken under ss.31B or 31C or has that effect.[373] However, s.31D(2) does not apply if the work in question is no longer published by or with the authority of the copyright owner and there are reasonable grounds for preventing or restricting the making of accessible copies of the work.[374] It appears, therefore, that where, for example, a book is out of print, the scheme will not be unreasonably restrictive if it prevents or restricts the making of copies provided there are reasonable grounds for doing so. It is not clear what grounds might be considered to be reasonable. Where ss.31B and 31C are displaced by a licensing scheme, s.31D(4) applies the normal provisions of the 1988 Act concerning references of the scheme to the Copyright Tribunal and applications to the Copyright Tribunal for individual licences under the scheme.[375]

D. COMPULSORY NOTIFICATION OF SOUND RECORDING LICENSING SCHEMES TO THE SECRETARY OF STATE

Background. Before the coming into force of the Copyright and Related Rights   **28–65**

---

[365] s.143(4).

[366] s.143(5).

[367] See the Copyright (Certification of Licensing Scheme for Educational Recording of Broadcasts and Cable Programmes) (Educational Recording Agency Limited) Order 1990 (SI 1990/879). The present scheme is scheduled to the Copyright (Certification of Licensing Scheme for Educational Recording of Broadcasts and Cable Programmes) (Educational Recording Agency Limited) Order 2007 (SI 2007/266) as amended. See Vol.2 B2.i.

[368] See para.8 of the Schedule to SI 2007/266.

[369] See the Copyright (Certification of Licensing Scheme for Educational Recording of Broadcasts) (Open University) Order 2003 (SI 2003/187) as amended. See Vol.2 B2.ii.

[370] See the definition of "Designated Programmes" in the Schedule to SI 2003/187.

[371] See paras 9–85 et seq., above.

[372] CDPA 1988 s.31D(1). See para.9–93, above.

[373] s.31D(2). S.31C permits the holding of intermediate copies of the master copy used to make copies under s.31B.

[374] s.31D(3).

[375] This is effected by providing that ss.119 to 122 of CDPA 1988 apply to the scheme as if it were one to which they applied under s.117. As to ss.119 to 122, see paras 28–89 et seq., below.

Regulations 2003,[376] the showing or playing in public of a broadcast or cable programme to an audience who had not paid for admission to the place where this occurred (e.g. a shop or public house) did not infringe any copyright in any sound recording included in the broadcast.[377] This has now changed. Such showing or playing does infringe the sound recording copyright if the recording is an "excepted" recording, that is a recording of music whose author is not the author of the broadcast (there are exemptions where the playing is by a non-profit-making organisation or is necessary for demonstrating or repairing equipment).[378] As will be apparent, most recordings which are likely to be played in these circumstances are in fact "excepted" recordings and accordingly a licence will be necessary. In practice, such a licence will need to be obtained from PPL, which owns the UK rights to play substantially all commercially released sound recordings in public.[379]

28–66   **Section 128A of the 1988 Act: general.** Given the large number of persons who will require a licence to play excepted recordings in public, it was inevitable that PPL would introduce a licensing scheme. Any such scheme would ordinarily have been subject to review by the Copyright Tribunal under the general provisions as to licensing schemes.[380] However, the 2003 Regulations do not simply leave the position subject to the general law. Rather, they make provision (in s.128A of the 1988 Act) for any proposed licence or licensing scheme to be referred to the Secretary of State before it comes into operation. The Secretary of State then has a choice as to whether to notify the proposed licence or scheme to the Copyright Tribunal or to allow it to be implemented. It seems that the Government's intention in adopting this approach was to create a procedure which would minimise costs for users because (it was thought) they would not need to be parties to the proceedings and thus risk having to pay costs in the event of an unsuccessful challenge.[381]

28–67   **Repeal of s.128A.** However, following a consultation in 2008, the Government has now repealed s.128A and its counterpart s.128B, with effect from January 1, 2011.[382] The Government's grounds for proposing the repeal were as follows.[383] First, concerns had been expressed about the length of time cases referred to the Tribunal had taken to be resolved. Second, the supposed benefit to users of not having liability for their litigation costs if the licensing scheme was found to be reasonable had not been borne out in practice because users (contrary to expectations) had become parties to the proceedings and incurred substantial costs. Third, there would be other measures to assist users: the reform of the Tribunal,[384] the use of mediation and the PPL/PRS Code of Conduct and independent complaints reviewer.

---

[376] SI 2003/2498, which came into force on October 31, 2003.

[377] CDPA 1988 s.72(1)(b).

[378] s.72(1B). The exemption for non-profit making organisations is repealed with effect from January 1, 2011 by the Copyright, Designs and Patents Act 1988 (Amendment) Regulations 2010 (SI 2010/2694) reg.4.

[379] As to which, see para.27–66, above. For a more detailed discussion of these provisions, see paras 132 et seq., above.

[380] See paras 28–132, et seq.

[381] See the Government's *Consultation on changes to exemptions from public performance rights in sound recordings and performers' rights*, June 2008 para.151; *Phonographic Performance Ltd v The British Hospitality Association* [2008] EWHC 2715 (Ch); [2009] R.P.C. 7 para.10; and *Phonographic Performance Ltd v The British Hospitality Association* [2009] EWHC 209 (Ch) para.21.

[382] Copyright, Designs and Patents Act 1988 (Amendment) Regs 2010 (SI 2010/2694) reg.6.

[383] *Government Response to the Consultation on Changes to Exemptions from Public Performance rights in Sound Recordings and Performers' Rights*, p.12.

[384] As to which see para.28–154, below.

Notification of licence or scheme to the Secretary of State. The provisions of   **28–68**
s.128A apply to a proposed licence or licensing scheme that will authorise the
playing in public of excepted sound recordings included in broadcasts where that
would otherwise infringe the copyright in them.[385] For these purposes, the term
"licence" means a licence granted by a licensing body otherwise than in pursuance of a licensing scheme and which covers works of more than one author.[386]
The meaning of the terms "licensing scheme" and "licensing body" are discussed
below.[387] If a scheme which covers the playing of sound recordings included in
broadcasts also covers the playing of sound recordings by other means, for
example on CD, the sections still apply to the scheme as a whole.[388] A licensing
body that wishes to operate a licence or scheme which falls within s.128A must
notify its details to the Secretary of State before it comes into operation and may
not operate such a licence or licensing scheme until 28 days have elapsed since
the notification.[389] The Secretary of State may then refer the licence or scheme to
the Copyright Tribunal for a determination of whether it is reasonable in the
circumstances. Alternatively, he may notify the licensing body that he does not
intend to refer it to the Tribunal.[390] The only sanction for failure to notify the
licence or scheme to the Secretary of State before it comes into operation or for
operating the licence or scheme before the 28-day period has elapsed is that if the
Secretary of State becomes aware of this, he may refer the licence or scheme to
the Tribunal for a determination as above.[391] It is clear that once the 28-day period has elapsed, the licence or scheme may come into operation even though the
Secretary of State has referred it to the Copyright Tribunal.[392] These provisions
apply to a proposed modification of an existing licence or scheme as they apply
to proposed licences or schemes.[393]

Factors the Secretary of State must take into account. The Secretary of State   **28–69**
is obliged to take into account five factors, as follows. First, whether the terms
and conditions of the proposed licence or scheme have taken into account four
additional factors. These are considered in the next paragraph. Secondly, any
written representations received by the Secretary of State. No doubt this will
include any representations from the licensing body and potential licensees.
However, there is no obligation on the Secretary of State to engage in a public
consultation.[394] Thirdly, previous determinations of the Tribunal. This is not
limited in any way. However, presumably the Secretary of State is only obliged
to take account of determinations about licences or schemes which are genuinely
similar or comparable to the licence or scheme in question. Fourthly, the availability of other schemes, or the granting of other licences, to persons in similar
circumstances, and the terms of those schemes or licences. Clearly, this is directed
at comparables. It does not appear to be limited to comparables in the United
Kingdom, although in practice there may be few genuine comparables abroad.
Fifthly, the extent to which the licensing body has consulted any persons who

---

[385] CDPA 1988 s.128A(1). For the term "excepted recording", see para.28–65, above.
[386] s.128A(13).
[387] See paras 28–88 and 28–85.
[388] *Phonographic Performance Ltd v The British Hospitality Association* [2008] EWHC 2715 (Ch);
[2009] R.P.C. 7.
[389] CDPA 1988 s.128A(2), (3).
[390] s.128A(4).
[391] s.128A(5).
[392] See, e.g. s.128B(4) which gives the Tribunal a power to backdate its order and provides for the
repayment of excessive licence fees which have been paid prior to the date of the order.
[393] s.128A(12).
[394] Note, however, that the existence of the fifth factor (discussed below) will have the effect that the
licensing body will be obliged to consult.

would be affected by the proposed licence or scheme, or organisations represent-ing such persons, and the steps, if any, it has taken as a result. It is not entirely clear what "steps" are meant here. Presumably, however, this is a reference to changes made to the terms of the licence or scheme as a result of representations made by record companies and potential licensees.

28–70 **The four additional factors.** As has been stated in the previous paragraph, the Secretary of State is obliged to take account of whether the terms and conditions of the proposed licence or scheme themselves have taken into account four ad-ditional factors.[395] These are as follows. First, the extent to which the broadcasts to be shown or played by a potential licensee are likely to include excepted sound recordings. The presence of this factor is presumably aimed at avoiding a scheme under which charges are based solely on the number of hours of broadcasting. However, it is not easy to see how it will be applied in practice. Secondly, the size and nature of the audience that the licence or scheme would permit to hear the excepted sound recordings. This is already a factor in PPL's licensing scheme in respect of the playing of sound recordings in night clubs and public houses. Thirdly, what commercial benefit a potential licensee is likely to obtain from playing the excepted sound recordings. No doubt this factor is aimed at distinguishing between situations where the playing of the sound recording can be shown to encourage the public to enter the premises (for example, the playing of an appropriate radio station in a specialist music shop) and situations where the fact that the broadcast is being played is unlikely to have any bearing on the number of customers who attend (for example, a radio which is played in the kitchen of a café but is audible at the counter).[396] Fourthly, the extent to which the owners of the copyright in the sound recordings will receive equitable remunera-tion from sources other than the proposed licence or scheme for the inclusion of their recordings in the broadcasts.

28–71 **Interaction with the Copyright Tribunal's general jurisdiction.** As has al-ready been made clear, in the absence of this machinery, the Tribunal would have jurisdiction over the licence or scheme under its general jurisdiction, which is discussed below.[397] Accordingly, it was necessary for provision to be made as to the interaction of the two regimes. That provision is as follows. First, the terms of a licence or scheme which must be notified to the Secretary of State under s.128A may be referred to the Tribunal under its general jurisdiction over *proposed* licences or schemes (under ss.118 and 125 of the 1988 Act), but only if this is done before the notification to the Secretary of State takes place.[398] If this occurs, two special provisions apply. First, the reference is not to be considered prema-ture[399] merely because the licence or scheme has not been notified to the Secre-tary of State. Secondly, if the Tribunal decides to entertain the reference, the s.128A machinery ceases to have effect; thus, there is no obligation to refer the proposed licence or scheme to the Secretary of State and the Secretary of State has no power to refer it to the Tribunal.[400] The second express provision in rela-tion to the interaction of the two regimes is that if a proposed licensing scheme

---

[395] CDPA 1988 s.128A(7).
[396] In its Analysis of Responses and Government Conclusions on this point, the Government empha-sised that "the circumstances in which broadcasts are heard in commercial situations will vary considerably, and will not always be the same as with [sic] a conscious or deliberate decision to play sound recordings in public by way of CDs, tapes or the like": see at para.5.20.
[397] paras 28–132 et seq., below.
[398] CDPA 1988 s.128A(8).
[399] s.128(10)(a). This is a reference to the Tribunal's power under ss.118(2) and 125(2) to refuse to entertain a reference on the ground that it is premature.
[400] s.128(10)(b).

has been notified to the Secretary of State, but has then come into operation, the entitlement to refer it to the Copyright Tribunal under s.119 of the 1988 Act (that is, as an *existing* scheme) is postponed until the Secretary of State has notified the licensing body that he does not intend to refer it to the Tribunal.[401] Finally, it is provided that nothing in s.128A is to prejudice any right to make a reference or application to the Tribunal under certain specified sections of the 1988 Act. These sections, which are all considered below,[402] provide for the following (in brief): the right to refer a scheme back to the Tribunal after it has already ruled on it under ss.118, 119 or 128A (s.120); the right to apply for a licence under an existing scheme (s.121) and to apply for a review of a decision made on such an application (s.122); the right to refer an expiring licence to the Tribunal (s.126); and the right to apply for a review of an order of the Tribunal made under ss.125, 126 or 126B of the 1988 Act, in the latter case where the order did not relate to a licensing scheme (s.127).[403]

Role of the Tribunal. The Tribunal's role is inquisitorial rather than adversarial.[404] Section 128B(1) of the 1988 Act states that the Tribunal may make "appropriate enquiries" to establish whether the licence or scheme is reasonable in the circumstances.[405] This does not impose any obligation on the Tribunal to investigate but instead gives rise to a discretion (which must be exercised on a proper basis) as to whether to make enquiries and if so as to what enquiries to make.[406] Where a substantial volume of material had been put before the Tribunal over a period of four years in circumstances where both sides were represented by specialist legal teams and each side had been able to set out its case in detail, the Tribunal had been entitled to conclude that it did not need to make any additional enquiries.[407]   **28–72**

The Tribunal's Practice Direction.[408] This provides that the following procedure will take place. Within 21 days of receipt of notice that the Secretary of State has notified a proposed licence or licensing scheme to the Tribunal, the licensing body is obliged to serve on all other parties which to its knowledge have made representations to it or to the Secretary of State copies of all documents it has put before the Secretary of State. At the same time, it is obliged to serve on the Secretary to the Tribunal (with copies to all such other parties) such other representations as it may wish to make to the Tribunal, together with a list of the names and addresses of the other parties (para.1). The other parties then have 21 days to make any further representations (para.2) and the licensing body has a further 14 days to reply (para.3). The Tribunal will then address such ques-   **28–73**

---

[401] s.128A(9).

[402] See paras 28–97 et seq., below.

[403] s.125 provides for the reference to the Tribunal of the terms of a proposed licence.

[404] *Phonographic Performance Ltd v The British Hospitality Association* [2009] EWHC 209 (Ch) para.85.

[405] CDPA 1988 s.128B(1). The recently retired Chairman of the Tribunal reportedly said that it does not have the appropriate remit or resources to make these enquiries and that it is not intended to act as an investigatory body but as an adjudicator to settle disputes between parties: see the Government's *Consultation on changes to exemptions from public performance rights in sound recordings and performers' rights*, June 2008 para.150; and *Phonographic Performance Ltd v The British Hospitality Association* [2008] EWHC 2715 (Ch); [2009] R.P.C. 7 para.10. This was mentioned in the Consultation as a reason for repealing ss.128A and B (see para.153) but is not mentioned in the Government's Response to the Consultation (in which such repeal was however proposed).

[406] *Phonographic Performance Ltd v The British Hospitality Association* [2009] EWHC 209 (Ch) para.85.

[407] *Phonographic Performance Ltd v The British Hospitality Association* [2009] EWHC 209 (Ch) para.87.

[408] See para.41 of *Phonographic Performance Ltd v The British Hospitality Association* [2009] EWHC 209 (Ch).

tions (if any) as it considers appropriate to the licensing body and/or any of the other parties and will inform any third party that it considers should be notified of the existence of the reference. At the same time the Tribunal will set such time limits for the answering of such questions or for the making of representations by the third parties or further representations by the licensing body and/or the other parties as it sees fit (para.4). Following this process, the Tribunal will issue its formal decision (para.5). The Practice Direction states that the Tribunal will only hold an oral hearing in exceptional circumstances.

28–74   **Decision of the Copyright Tribunal.** The Tribunal is obliged to take account of whether the terms and conditions of the scheme have taken into account the four additional factors referred to above. It is also obliged to take into account any other factors it considers relevant.[409] In the case of a licensing scheme, it is then obliged to make an order either confirming or varying the scheme, either generally or so far as it relates to cases of any description. In the case of a licence, it is obliged either to confirm or vary the licence.[410] The Tribunal may direct that the order, so far as it reduces the amount of the charges payable, has effect from a date before the date on which it is made. If it so directs, any necessary payments shall be repaid and the Tribunal may award simple interest on the repayments.[411]

28–75   **Review of Copyright Tribunal's order.** The normal provisions apply as to the review of the order. Thus, while the order remains in force, the operator of the scheme, a person claiming that he requires a licence in a case to which the order applies or an organisation claiming to be representative of such persons may refer the scheme again to the Tribunal so far as it relates to cases of that description.[412] Special leave is required if the reference is sought to be made within 12 months of the order or, if the order was made for 15 months or less, before the start of the last three months before its expiry.[413] The scheme remains in operation until proceedings on the reference are concluded.[414] The Tribunal may make such order either confirming, varying or further varying the scheme so far as it relates to cases of the description to which the reference relates as the Tribunal may consider to be reasonable in the circumstances.[415] The order may be made so as to be in force indefinitely or for such period as the Tribunal may determine.[416] Analogous provision is made in respect of licences.[417]

4. CONTROL OF THE EXERCISE OF COPYRIGHT AND RELATED RIGHTS BY THE COPYRIGHT TRIBUNAL

A. INTRODUCTION

28–76   **Organisations controlling the exercise of copyright.** In most countries a development in the field of copyright has been the creation of organisations to control the exercise of specific rights restricted by the copyright in particular types of works, collectively, on behalf of the various authors and owners of the copyright in such works. In particular the rights so controlled have been the

---

[409] s.128B(2).
[410] s.128B(3).
[411] s.128B(4), (5).
[412] CDPA 1988 s.120(1).
[413] s.120(2).
[414] s.120(3).
[415] s.120(4).
[416] s.120(5).
[417] s.127.

performing,[418] broadcasting and recording rights in musical works and sound recordings. Such organisations either acquire the relevant rights from their members, or act as agents on behalf of their members to enforce such rights. They issue licences in respect of the works of all their members and, in the last resort, enforce the rights of their members by legal action. Because their principal activity is to exercise the rights under their control by granting licences and collecting royalties due under such licences, such organisations are often referred to as Collecting Societies.[419] From the point of view of composers of music and owners of musical copyright the system has great advantages, in that no individual composer or copyright owner can, in practice, secure adequate protection for his work, or deal with the very large number of persons and bodies wishing to exploit such works. The system also has considerable advantages, from the point of view of those wishing to exploit such works, in that licences relating to all of a great number of works ("blanket licences") can be obtained from a single organisation, whereas, without such a system, it would be necessary to obtain individual licences from a large number of owners of copyright, and the delay and inconvenience, and the risk of exploiting such works without having obtained a licence from the person entitled to give one, would greatly add to the difficulty and expense of exploiting such works.[420] A number of such organisations have been established in the United Kingdom. The longest established and largest of these are Performing Right Society Limited (PRS),[421] controlling the right to perform musical works in public, Mechanical-Copyright Protection Society Limited (MCPS),[422] controlling the right to make recordings of musical works, and Phonographic Performance Limited (PPL),[423] controlling the right to play sound recordings in public, and broadcast them and, in limited circumstances, to rerecord them. There are also equivalent organisations established in most other European countries and in the United States, Canada and Australia.[424]

Public interest and need for public control. The existence of such organisa-   **28–77**
tions is therefore to the advantage of the public in facilitating wider access by the public to such works. However, it has also given rise to complaints of the abuse of what have become monopoly rights, since (for example) virtually all popular music is now controlled by such organisations.[425] It therefore came to be felt, in a

---

[418] The performing right under the law of the United Kingdom is, with regard to literary dramatic or musical works: the right to perform them in public by any mode of visual or acoustic presentation, including presentation by means of a sound recording, film or broadcast of the work; with regard to sound recordings: the right to play them in public; and with regard to films or broadcasts: the right to show them in public; see CDPA 1988 ss.16(1)(c) and 19 which correspond to the provisions of the previous law contained in the Copyright Act 1956 ss.2(5)(c), 12 to 14A and 48(1).

[419] For a detailed consideration of the role and workings of the different Collecting Societies, see Ch.27.

[420] See the 1977 Copyright Committee, Cmnd. 6732, para.390 in relation to musical works. The respective advantages of collective licensing of specific rights in copyright works to authors and copyright owners on the one hand and users of copyright works on the other are however the same whenever works of various authors are likely to be regularly used by a number of different users. Accordingly Collecting Societies, for example, exist to control the exercise of the right to photocopy literary and artistic works, to photocopy material from newspapers and to make recordings of broadcast or cable programmes for educational purposes: see Ch.27.

[421] See para.27–65, above.

[422] See para.27–63, above.

[423] See para.27–66, above.

[424] See Gervais (ed.), *Collective Management of Copyright and Related Rights* (2006).

[425] See *The British Phonographic Industry Ltd v Mechanical-Copyright Protection Society Ltd* (CT 84–90/05), [2008] E.M.L.R. 5 at paras 44 to 46 and most recently the statements of the Copyright Tribunal in *Phonographic Performance Ltd v The British Hospitality Association* (CT 91–93/05) at paras 4 and 5. This decision was upheld on appeal: *Phonographic Performance Ltd v The British Hospitality Association* [2009] EWHC 209 (Ch).

number of countries, that some measure of public control over the activities of such organisations was necessary in the public interest.[426]

28–78   **Copyright Committee 1952.** At the Brussels Copyright Conference, the United Kingdom, in accepting the provisions of art.11 of the Brussels Act of the Berne Convention (1948), declared that it remained free to enact such legislation as it might consider necessary in the public interest to prevent or deal with any abuse of the monopoly rights conferred upon owners of copyright by the law of the United Kingdom.[427] It was therefore open to the 1952 Copyright Committee, notwithstanding that it was recommending adherence to the Brussels Act, to make proposals for the compulsory adjustment of tariffs charged by collecting societies. One method suggested was that of compulsory arbitration, but the Committee did not consider this wholly satisfactory, in that it was necessary to envisage not only disputes between a collecting organisation and an organisation of potential users of copyright works, but also cases where individual persons were aggrieved, and moreover, what was really required was some method of arriving at tariffs which would be binding not only between the parties to the reference, but also in respect of any other persons wishing to exercise similar rights. The Committee therefore proposed that a standing tribunal should be established to decide disputes between collecting organisations and would-be users of controlled works.[428] This proposal was accepted by the legislature and was embodied in ss.23 to 30 of the 1956 Act.

28–79   **Performing Right Tribunal.** Section 23 of the 1956 Act established the Performing Right Tribunal (PRT) with the jurisdiction conferred by the provisions of the 1956 Act. The PRT had three principal functions.[429] The first was to confirm or vary licence schemes put into operation by organisations under which licences to do certain acts restricted by the copyright in particular works were to be granted to the public in certain classes of cases.[430] The second was to deal with applications by persons who were aggrieved because an organisation operating a licence scheme refused to grant them a licence in accordance with the scheme.[431] The third was to deal with applications by persons who were aggrieved because they claimed that there was no licence scheme applicable to them and that the organisation concerned with granting licences of the type required unreasonably refused to grant them a licence or proposed terms that were unreasonable.[432] The PRT was concerned with licences dealing with only three types of right. First, the right to perform in public, broadcast or diffuse, a literary, dramatic or musical work or an adaptation thereof.[433] Secondly, the right to cause a sound recording to be heard in public or to be broadcast.[434] Thirdly, the right to cause a television broadcast to be seen or heard in public.[435] The rights, therefore, covered in effect, the whole of the performing and broadcasting rights conferred by the 1956 Act,

---

[426] See, as to the position of such organisations under art.102 of the Treaty on the Functioning of the European Union, para.28–285, below.

[427] This declaration was not repeated in relation to the Stockholm Act (1967), since it was accepted at the Stockholm Conference that Convention countries remain free to enact measures to restrict possible abuses of monopoly (albeit there were some reservations about the extent of the measures which might be permissible). See Ricketson and Ginsburg, *International Copyright and Neighbouring Rights* (2006), para.13.92.

[428] Cmnd.8662, para.210.

[429] Copyright Act 1956 ss.24 to 27A.

[430] s.24(1).

[431] ss.27(1) and (2) and 27A.

[432] s.27(3).

[433] s.24(2)(a); a right (as to musical works and associated words) usually controlled by PRS.

[434] s.24(2)(b); a right usually controlled by PPL.

[435] s.24(2)(c); a right then controlled by the BBC or the IBA.

other than the right to include an artistic work in a television broadcast, the right to cause a film to be seen or heard in public or to be broadcast, and the right to re-broadcast a sound or television broadcast.

Proposals for reform. The functions of the PRT were considered by the 1977 Copyright Committee, which recommended that it should be given jurisdiction over a wider range of matters, including reprographic licences, video recording, licences to use music on film sound-tracks, and copyright clearances where the copyright owner could not be traced.[436] The Committee also proposed that the tribunal's name should be changed to the Copyright Tribunal, in view of the recommended increase in its jurisdiction. The White Paper generally followed these recommendations in relation to the change in name of the tribunal and the extension of its functions,[437] and also made recommendations as to the introduction of more specific criteria for the tribunal to base its decision on, and for improvements in the procedure before the tribunal. These recommendations were enacted in the 1988 Act, Ch.VIII of which established the Copyright Tribunal as the successor to the PRT.

28–80

B. THE COPYRIGHT TRIBUNAL

(i) Background and constitution

The Copyright Tribunal. By s.145 of the 1988 Act the Tribunal established under s.23 of the 1956 Act was renamed the Copyright Tribunal.[438] The Tribunal's membership was enlarged in view of its increased jurisdiction, and now consists of a chairman and two deputy chairmen appointed by the Lord Chancellor. Each must satisfy the judicial-appointment eligibility condition on a five-year basis[439]; or be an advocate or solicitor in Scotland of at least five years' standing; or be a barrister or solicitor in Northern Ireland of at least five years' standing; or be a person who has held judicial office.[440] In addition, the Tribunal must consist of not less than two and not more than eight ordinary members appointed by the Secretary of State.[441]

28–81

Constitution of the Tribunal. For the purposes of any proceedings the Copyright Tribunal shall consist of a chairman (who shall be either the chairman or a deputy chairman of the Tribunal) and two or more ordinary members.[442] In the absence of unanimity, decisions are arrived at by majority, with the chairman exercising a casting vote.[443] There are provisions ensuring that the Tribunal remains duly constituted where a member is unable to continue after proceedings are part heard,[444] and for the appointment of one of the ordinary members to act as chairman together with a suitably qualified person to advise on law, where it is

28–82

---

[436] Cmnd.6732, paras 788–90; the Committee also recommended that the Tribunal should have jurisdiction in respect of royalties payable under s.8 of the 1956 Act (assuming the statutory licence was to be retained) and over the amount of levy on blank tape (assuming that such levy was to be introduced).

[437] Cmnd.9712 (1986) Ch.18, broadly following proposals set out in the 1981 Green Paper, Cmnd.8302.

[438] For transitional provisions, see *Copinger* 15th edn, para.29–93.

[439] That is, broadly, must be a solicitor or barrister who has been qualified for over 5 years: Tribunals Courts and Enforcement Act 2007 s.50.

[440] CDPA 1988 s.145(3).

[441] CDPA 1988 ss.145(2).

[442] CDPA 1988 s.148(1), derived from Copyright Act 1956 Sch.4 para.3.

[443] CDPA 1988 s.148(2), derived from Copyright Act 1956 Sch.4 para.3.

[444] s.148(3).

the chairman who is unable to continue.[445] It is not inappropriate for a deputy chairman to act as advocate before a Tribunal comprising lay members with whom he has never previously sat as chairman.[446]

(ii) Jurisdiction

28–83   **General.** Following the proposals for reform discussed above,[447] the Copyright Tribunal was given an extended jurisdiction, covering not only the three functions previously carried out by the PRT in relation to licence schemes and licences by licensing bodies (but in relation to a wider variety of copyright licences), but also five further specific functions introduced by the 1988 Act and two further specific functions later introduced into the 1988 Act by the Broadcasting Act 1990.[448] Subsequently, the jurisdiction of the Copyright Tribunal has been extended very considerably. As to the functions inherited from the PRT in relation to licensing schemes and licensing bodies dealing with copyright licences, the variety of copyright licences in relation to which the functions are exercisable has been further extended. Furthermore, principally as a result of (1) the introduction of performers' property rights[449] and the right to equitable remuneration for the playing in public or broadcasting of sound recordings of performances,[450] (2) the introduction of rights for authors to receive equitable remuneration for the rental of sound recordings and films,[451] (3) the increase in the duration of copyright and of rights in performances (and consequent provisions for use as of right, subject to a reasonable royalty, of works in which revived copyright subsists and performances in which revived performance rights subsist),[452] (4) the introduction of the database right[453], and (5) the introduction of the publication right for those who publish previously unpublished works in which copyright has expired,[454] the number of specific functions of the Copyright Tribunal has more than doubled since the 1988 Act came into force. Specifically it now has the following jurisdiction[455]:

(1) Jurisdiction under Pt I of the 1988 Act

    (a) applications to determine the royalty or other remuneration to be paid to a copyright owner with respect to the cable re-transmission in certain circumstances of a wireless broadcast including a work owned by him[456];

    (b) applications to determine the amount of equitable remuneration payable to authors of literary, dramatic, musical and artistic works and principal directors of films where their rental right concerning a

---

[445] s.148(4) and (5).

[446] *Meltwater Holding BV v. NLA Ltd* (CT 114/09), April 19, 2010.

[447] See para.28–80, above.

[448] For a list of the specific functions of the Tribunal as at the beginning of 1991, see *Copinger* 13th edn, para.15–57.

[449] See para.12–20.

[450] Under CDPA 1988 s.182D, see para.12–47, above.

[451] Under CDPA 1988 s.93B, see para.7–101, above.

[452] See paras 6–17 and 12–35, above.

[453] See Ch.18, above.

[454] See Ch.17, above.

[455] The version of the following list which appeared in the 15th edn of this work (which included reference to the now repealed s.128B of the 1988 Act: see para.28–67, above) was adopted in the UK IPO's Review of the Copyright Tribunal: see pp.10–12.

[456] CDPA 1988 ss.73(4) and 73A, introduced into the 1988 Act and into s.149 of the 1988 Act by the Broadcasting Act 1996 s.138 and Sch.9; see further paras 28–48 et seq., above.

sound recording or film has been transferred to the producer of the sound recording or film[457];

(c) references of proposed or existing licensing schemes dealing with copyright licences[458];

(d) applications with respect to entitlement to a copyright licence under a licensing scheme[459];

(e) references or applications with respect to licensing by a licensing body dealing with copyright licences[460];

(f) applications to settle the terms of payment or as to the reasonableness of any condition in relation to the use as of right of sound recordings in broadcasts[461];

(g) appeals against an order by the Secretary of State as to the coverage of a licensing scheme or licence in respect of reprographic copying by an educational establishment[462];

(h) applications to settle a royalty or other sum payable for lending of certain works to the public[463];

(i) applications to settle the terms of a copyright licence available as of right consequent on the exercise of their powers by the Secretary of State, the Office of Fair Trading and the Competition Commission[464];

(j) applications to settle the terms of payment under a compulsory licence in respect of information about a programme service[465];

(2) Jurisdiction under Pt II of the 1988 Act

(k) applications to determine the amount of equitable remuneration payable to performers where commercially published sound recordings of their performances are played in public or communicated to the public[466];

(l) applications to give consent to the making of a recording of a performance on behalf of a performer who cannot be traced[467];

(m) applications to determine the amount of equitable remuneration payable to performers where their rental right concerning a sound

---

[457] CDPA 1988 s.93C, introduced into Ch.V of Pt I and s.149 of the 1988 Act by the Copyright and Related Rights Regulations 1996 (SI 1996/2967), para.14; and see para.7–101, above and para.28–128, below.

[458] CDPA 1988 ss.118, 119 and 120; and see further paras 28–89 et seq., below.

[459] ss.121 and 122; and see further paras 28–98 et seq., below.

[460] ss.125, 126 and 127; and see further paras 28–101 et seq., below.

[461] CDPA 1988 ss.135D and 135E, introduced into Ch.III of Pt I, and s.149 of the 1988 Act by the Broadcasting Act 1990 Sch.17 para.7(1) and amended by the Copyright and Related Rights Regulations 2003 (SI 2003/2498) Sch.2 para.1; see further paras 28–25 et seq., above.

[462] CDPA 1988 s.139; and see further para.28–124, below.

[463] s.142, as inserted by the Copyright and Related Rights Regulations 1996 (SI 1996/2967) reg.13(2); and see further para.28–125, below.

[464] s.144(4) as amended by the Enterprise Act 2002 (c.40) Sch.25 para.18; and see further paras 28–304 et seq., below.

[465] Broadcasting Act 1990 Sch.17 paras 5 and 6 introduced into Ch.III of Pt I and s.149 of the 1988 Act by the Broadcasting Act 1990 Sch.17 para.7(1); see further paras 28–09, et seq., above.

[466] CDPA 1988 182D, introduced into the 1988 Act by the Copyright and Related Rights Regulations 1996 (SI 1996/2967) reg.20, as amended by the Copyright and Related Rights Regulations 2003 (SI 2003/2498), reg.7(2); and see further para.28–147, below.

[467] s.190, as amended by the Copyright and Related Rights Regulations 1996 (SI 1996/2967) reg.23; and see further para.28–149, below.

recording or film has been transferred to the producer of the sound recording or film[468];

(n) applications to determine the royalty or other remuneration to be paid to the owners of the rights conferred by Pt II of the 1988 Act in relation to a performance or recording of a performance with respect to the re-transmission by cable of a wireless broadcast including the performance or recording[469];

(o) references of proposed or existing licensing schemes relating to performers' property right licences, namely for copying a recording of a performance or renting or lending of copies of such a recording to the public[470];

(p) applications with respect to entitlement to a licence under a licensing scheme relating to performers' property right licences[471];

(q) references and applications with respect to licensing by a licensing body dealing with performers' property right licences[472];

(r) applications to settle the royalty or other sum payable for the lending of certain recordings treated as licensed by performers by virtue of an order of the Secretary of State[473];

(s) applications to settle the terms of licences in respect of performers' property rights available as of right consequent on the exercise of their powers by the Secretary of State, the Office of Fair Trading and the Competition Commission[474];

(3) Other jurisdiction

(t) applications to settle the royalty or other remuneration payable in respect of the use as of right of works in which revived copyright subsists[475];

(u) applications to settle the remuneration payable in respect of the doing as of right with regard to performances in which revived performance right subsists of any acts which require the consent of the owner of such rights[476];

(v) references and applications with respect to licensing schemes, licences and licensing bodies relating to licences in respect of the database right conferred in respect of the contents of databases ("database right licences")[477]; and in particular:

---

[468] ss.191G and 191H, introduced into the 1988 Act by the Copyright and Related Rights Regulations 1996 (SI 1996/2967) reg.21; and see further para.28–148, below.

[469] Sch.2 paras 19 and 19A, introduced into the 1988 Act by the Broadcasting Act 1996 s.138 and Sch.9, as amended by the Copyright and Related Rights Regulations 2003 (SI 2003/2498) reg.22; and see further para.28–150, below.

[470] Sch.2A paras 3, 4 and 5 introduced into the 1988 Act by the Copyright and Related Rights Regulations 1996 (SI 1996/2967) reg.22; and see further paras 28–130 et seq., below.

[471] Sch.2A paras 6 and 7; and see further para.28–139, below.

[472] Sch.2A paras 10, 11 and 12; and see further paras 28–141 et seq., below.

[473] Sch.2A para.15; and see para.28–150, below.

[474] Sch.2A para.17, as amended by the Enterprise Act 2002 (c.40) Sch.25 para.18; and see paras 28–150 and 28–325 et seq., below.

[475] Under the Duration of Copyright and Rights in Performances Regulations 1995 (SI 1995/3297) reg.25; and see further paras 28–41 et seq., above.

[476] Under the Duration of Copyright and Rights in Performances Regulations 1995 (SI 1995/3297) reg.35; and see further para.28–150, below.

[477] Under the Copyright and Rights in Databases Regulations 1997 (SI 1997/3032) reg.25 and Sch.2; and see further para.28–152, below.

(i) references of proposed or existing licensing schemes relating to database right licences[478];

(ii) applications with respect to entitlement to licences under a licensing scheme relating to database right licences[479];

(iii) references or applications with respect to licensing by a licensing body dealing with database right licences[480];

(iv) applications to settle the terms of a database right licence available as of right consequent on the exercise of their powers by the Secretary of State, the Office of Fair Trading and the Competition Commission[481];

(w) equivalent references and applications with respect to licensing schemes, licences and licensing bodies relating to licences in respect of the publication right conferred on publishers of previously unpublished works in which copyright has expired[482];

(x) applications to determine the royalty or other remuneration payable to the trustees for the Hospital for Sick Children in respect of the use of the play "Peter Pan" by Sir James Matthew Barrie.[483]

C. CONTROL BY THE COPYRIGHT TRIBUNAL OF LICENSING SCHEMES AND LICENSING BODIES DEALING WITH COPYRIGHT LICENCES

Introduction. The aim of the provisions establishing control by the Copyright Tribunal over licensing schemes and licences by licensing bodies is to prevent copyright owners abusing what has come to be recognised as a monopoly or near monopoly power in their dealings with those wishing to be licensed to exploit their copyright works. However, this control is only exercisable (apart from certain other situations discussed below[484]) in a situation involving either a licensing scheme or a licensing body, as these terms are defined.[485] A copyright owner is not obliged to operate or join a licensing scheme,[486] or to agree to a licensing body exercising or administering his copyright,[487] and, in general, if he does neither and refuses to grant a licence, then such refusal is not subject to the overriding jurisdiction of the Copyright Tribunal. It is only, therefore, when a copyright owner himself chooses to operate a tariff for licences of his works, or agrees to his works being owned or administered by a collecting society acting on his behalf, that the grant and the terms of a licence affecting his works may be referred to the Copyright Tribunal.

28–84

---

[478] Copyright and Rights in Databases Regulations 1997 (SI 1997/3032) Sch.2 paras 3, 4 and 5.

[479] Sch.2 paras 6 and 7.

[480] Sch.2 paras 10, 11 and 12.

[481] Sch.2 para.15(3), as amended by the Enterprise Act 2002 (Consequential and Supplemental Provisions) Order 2003 (SI 2003/1398) with effect from June 20, 2003.

[482] Under the Copyright and Related Rights Regulations 1996 (SI 1996/2967) reg.17; and see further para.28–153 below and Ch.17.

[483] CDPA 1988 Sch.6 para.5, as amended by the Copyright and Related Rights Regulations 1996 (SI 1996/2967); and see further para.28–127, below.

[484] See para.28–123, below.

[485] See paras 28–85 and 28–88, below.

[486] But, in relation to the making in some cases of copies for the visually impaired, the educational recording of broadcasts, the copying of abstracts of scientific or technical articles, the lending of certain works and adding sub-titles to broadcasts for the hard of hearing, certain acts are deemed not to be infringements if there is no licensing scheme in existence under which royalties are payable: CDPA 1988 ss.31B, 35, 60, 66 and 74; see paras 9–93, 9–105, 9–182, 9–119 and 9–232, above.

[487] But in relation to the cable re-transmission right, this may only be exercised against a cable operator by a collecting society: see paras 28–48 et seq., above.

(i) Definitions

28–85   **Licensing scheme.** "Licensing scheme" is defined[488] as a scheme setting out the classes of cases in which the operator of the scheme, or the person on whose behalf he acts, is willing to grant copyright licences and the terms on which licences would be granted in those classes of cases. The term "scheme" is to include anything in the nature of a scheme, whether described as such, or as a tariff, or by any other name.[489] The question of whether a licensing scheme exists depends on the circumstances of each case, and thus where a particular type of licence was not available on demand from a licensing body and each inquiry for such a licence was considered individually there was no scheme even though each inquiry was dealt with in the same methodical manner.[490] A "copyright licence" is defined as a licence to do, or to authorise the doing of,[491] any of the acts restricted by copyright.[492]

28–86   **Restrictions.** The *Universities UK* reference[493] concerned reprographic copying at educational establishments. The Copyright Licensing Agency (CLA)[494] operated a scheme which covered all such copying except when it involved the creation of "course packs" (defined compilations of photocopied material provided to support a course of study). Although it was possible to obtain a licence from the CLA to create a course pack (under the "CLARCS" scheme), the CLA did not hold itself out as willing to grant licences in respect of course packs because it did not have a mandate from all its members to license them; furthermore, the terms of the licences for course packs varied depending on the transaction. Accordingly, the Tribunal held that CLARCS was not a licensing scheme.[495] Nevertheless, the Tribunal held that it had jurisdiction to consider the reasonableness of the restriction contained in the scheme on copying course packs and if it considered it unreasonable, to require its removal.[496] The fact that the CLA had no mandate to grant blanket licences for course packs was irrelevant.[497] Section 119(1) of the 1988 Act allows a reference on behalf of a person who claims he requires a licence in a case of "a description to which the scheme applies". The scheme which had been referred related only to copying which did not involve the creation of course packs. However, the scheme related to copying of "licensed material", which was what the course packs contained. Thus, the copying involved in the creation of course packs involved copying of the same material,

---

[488] CDPA 1988 s.116(1): derived from Copyright Act 1956 s.24(4) where the term defined was "licence scheme".

[489] CDPA 1988 s.116(1).

[490] *Candy Rock Recording Ltd v Phonographic Performance Ltd* (CT 34/96), *The Performing Right Society Ltd v Working Men's Club and Institute Ltd* [1988] F.S.R. 586 and *Universities UK v Copyright Licensing Agency Ltd and Design and Artists Copyright Society Ltd* (CT 71/00, 72/00, 73/00, 74/00, 75/01), [2002] R.P.C. 36; at para.58. For the facts of the last of these, see the next paragraph.

[491] The express inclusion of these words reverses the decision of Whitford J. on the different wording of s.24(2) of the 1956 Act to the effect that the PRT's jurisdiction was limited to the right itself and not the right to authorise as well: *Reditune Limited v PRS* [1981] F.S.R. 165.

[492] CDPA 1988 s.116(3); compare the much narrower definition under the 1956 Act in s.24(2), and see para.28–79, above; but see the further definitions in ss.117 and 124 (as inserted by the Copyright and Related Rights Regulations 1996 (SI 1996/2967) which limit the schemes and licences which fall within the jurisdiction of the Copyright Tribunal, paras 28–90 and 28–101, below.

[493] *Universities UK v Copyright Licensing Agency Ltd and Design and Artists Copyright Society Ltd* (CT 71/00, 72/00, 73/00, 74/00, 75/01), [2002] R.P.C. 36, para.59

[494] See para.27–59 above.

[495] para.58.

[496] para.59.

[497] para.60.

by the same people as were involved when copying took place under the licensing scheme.[498]

Related arrangements. *Meltwater v NLA*[499] concerned a reference in respect of   **28–87**
a licensing scheme relating to the provision of online media monitoring services.
The scheme referred to the terms of a separate scheme for customers of such
services. On a reference in respect of the providers' scheme, the Tribunal held
that it had jurisdiction to consider the customers' scheme as well, either because
the two schemes were in reality a single scheme or (by analogy with *Universities
UK*) because the providers' scheme prohibited providers from supplying customers who had not entered into the customers' scheme or been otherwise licensed
by the licensor.[500]

Licensing body. "Licensing body" is defined[501] as meaning a society or other or-   **28–88**
ganisation which has as its main object, or one of its main objects, the negotiation
or granting of copyright licences,[502] either as owner or prospective owner of
copyright, or as agent for the owner or prospective owner of copyright, and whose
main objects include the granting of licences covering works of more than one
author. Collective works[503] are not "works of more than one author" for these
purposes, nor are works made by employees of one person, firm, company or
group of companies.[504] The definition is therefore intended to cover collective
licensing societies and agencies rather than individual publishers or authors,
whose activities fall within the jurisdiction of the Copyright Tribunal only if they
operate a licensing scheme.

(ii) References and applications with respect to licensing schemes

References and applications involving licensing schemes. The distinction,   **28–89**
introduced in the 1956 Act, between references and applications relating to general tariffs and those relating to individual complaints, is maintained in the 1988
Act. Under ss.118, 119 and 120 of the 1988 Act the subject of the reference is the
scheme itself whereas under ss.121 and 122 of that Act the subject of the application is the availability of an individual licence to a person claiming to be covered
by the scheme or claiming to have been unreasonably excluded from it.

Jurisdiction over licensing schemes. The jurisdiction of the Copyright Tribunal   **28–90**
over licensing schemes depends both on the licensing scheme being operated by
a licensing body and on the nature of the right the subject of the licensing scheme.
Thus the Tribunal has jurisdiction over licensing schemes operated by licensing
bodies, covering works of more than one author, in so far as they relate to licences

---

[498] paras 62 and 63.
[499] *Meltwater Holding BV v The Newspaper Licensing Agency Ltd* (CT 114/09); decision dated
March 18, 2010.
[500] para.68.
[501] CDPA 1988 s.116(2); derived from Copyright Act 1956 s.24(3), but without drawing the distinctions previously made as between the different forms of licences set out in s.24(2) of that Act. See
also para.28–79, above.
[502] That is a licence to do, or to authorise the doing of any of the acts restricted by copyright: CDPA
1988 s.116(3); compare the much narrower definition under the 1956 Act in s.24(2), and see
paras 28–79 and 28–80, above.
[503] That is a single work of more than one author, or a number of such works where the authors are
the same.
[504] CDPA 1988 s.116(4).

for copying the works, rental or lending of the works to the public or performing, showing or playing the works in public or communicating them to the public.[505]

28–91   **Reference of a proposed scheme.** Under the 1956 Act, a licence scheme could be referred to the PRT at any time whilst in operation.[506] The 1988 Act, whilst retaining this jurisdiction,[507] has, in s.118, introduced the possibility of referring a proposed licensing scheme to the Copyright Tribunal before it has begun to be operated.[508] A proposed scheme may be referred to the Copyright Tribunal by an organisation claiming to be representative of persons claiming that they require licences in cases of a description to which the scheme would apply.[509] The validity of such an organisation's claim to be representative of such class of persons is a matter which the Copyright Tribunal will decide.[510] The Copyright Tribunal must first consider whether the reference is premature, in which case it will refuse to entertain it.[511]

28–92   **Reference of an existing scheme.** In the case of an existing scheme, where a dispute arises with respect to the scheme between the licensing body operating it and any person claiming that he requires a licence in cases of a description to which the scheme applies,[512] or an organisation claiming to be representative of persons requiring such licences, the scheme may be referred to the Copyright Tribunal either by such person or by such organisation.[513] The expression "person claiming that he requires a licence" includes a person who wishes to have a licence even if that person also contends that no licence is necessary. Accordingly, an applicant cannot be forced, as a precondition for commencing proceedings, to make an admission that in the absence of a licence under the scheme its activities would infringe.[514] An existing scheme which has been referred to the Copyright Tribunal remains in operation until the reference has been determined.[515]

28–93   **Order confirming or varying the scheme.** Where an existing or proposed licensing scheme is referred under s.118 or 119 of the 1988 Act, the Copyright Tribunal is empowered to make such order, either confirming or varying the scheme, in so far as it relates to cases of the description to which the reference relates, or, in the case of a proposed scheme, generally, as the Tribunal may determine to be reasonable in the circumstances.[516] There is no presumption that a referred scheme

---

[505] CDPA 1988 s.117, as amended by the Copyright and Related Rights Regulations 1996 (SI 1996/2967) and the Copyright and Related Rights Regulations 2003 (SI 2003/2498).

[506] Copyright Act 1956 s.25(1); and see *The Performing Right Society Ltd v Working Men's Club and Institute Union Ltd* [1988] F.S.R. 586.

[507] CDPA 1988 s.119; see para.28–92, below.

[508] Proposed schemes were referred to the Tribunal in *British Amusement Catering Trades Association v Phonographic Performance Ltd* [1992] R.P.C. 149 and *The British Phonographic Industry Ltd v Mechanical-Copyright Protection Society Ltd* [1993] E.M.L.R. 139.

[509] s.118(1).

[510] Copyright Tribunal Rules 2010 (SI 2010/791) r.9(1)(b). The rules are in Vol.2 B1.i.

[511] CDPA 1988 s.118(2); Copyright Tribunal Rules 2010 (SI 2010/791) r.9(1)(b). For a decision as to whether a reference in respect of a proposed licence was premature, see *Candy Rock Recording Ltd v Phonographic Performance Ltd* (CT 35/96).

[512] For the meaning of this expression, see above, para.28–86.

[513] CDPA 1988 s.119(1).

[514] *Meltwater Holding BV v The Newspaper Licensing Agency Ltd* (CT 114/09); decision dated March 18, 2010, paras 59–66.

[515] CDPA 1988 s.119(2).

[516] CDPA 1988 s.118(3) and 119(3); as to reasonableness, see s.129 and para.28–110, below and as to other factors to be considered, see paras 28–112 to 28–122, below.

should either be confirmed or varied.[517] The Copyright Tribunal's order may be either for an indefinite period, or for such period as the Tribunal may determine.[518]

Effect of order. A licensing scheme confirmed or varied by the Copyright Tribunal remains in operation (or in the case of a proposed scheme comes into and remains in force) for so long as the Tribunal's order remains in force.[519] The effect of an order of the Tribunal with respect to a licensing scheme is that if, during the continuance of the order, a person has complied with the terms and conditions which, in accordance with the licensing scheme as confirmed or varied by the order, would be applicable to a licence granted in accordance with the scheme, and has paid any charges payable in respect of such licence (or, if the amount payable could not be ascertained, has given an undertaking to pay such charges) then he is to be in the same position as if he had at all material times been the holder of a licence granted by the owner of the copyright in question in accordance with the scheme.[520] The exact effect of these provisions will therefore depend on the precise form of any scheme as varied or confirmed by the Tribunal. It would seem, however, that once a licensing scheme has been confirmed or varied by the Tribunal, as covering a particular description of cases, it will not be necessary for an actual licence to be issued to a person wishing to carry out activities falling within the scheme with regard to a case covered by that description, since it will be sufficient if he complies with the terms and conditions of the licensing scheme and pays fees as required under it. If, however, a licence is actually issued, the parties are bound by the terms of the licence and the protection of the order is irrelevant.

28–94

Date from which order takes effect. Under the 1956 Act the PRT had no power to backdate its order, which took effect on the scheme from the date the order was made.[521] The 1988 Act introduced a limited ability for the Copyright Tribunal to backdate the effect of its order on the scheme referred to it. Thus, where the order of the Tribunal varies the amount of charges payable under a licensing scheme, the Tribunal may direct that the order has such effect from a date earlier than that on which the order is made, but not earlier than the date on which the reference was made or, if later, on which the scheme came into operation.[522] Any necessary repayments, or further payments, in respect of charges already paid must then be made.[523]

28–95

Power to award interest in certain cases. The Tribunal has no general power to

28–96

---

[517] *The British Phonographic Industry Ltd v Mechanical-Copyright Protection Society Limited* [1993] E.M.L.R. 86 at 99.

[518] CDPA 1988 ss.118(4), 119(4). Once the Tribunal has made a final order either confirming or varying the scheme under ss.118(4) or 119(4), then while such order remains in force it can only be reviewed on a further reference under s.120, see para.28–97, below. See *The Working Men's Club and Institute Union Ltd v The Performing Right Society Ltd* [1992] R.P.C. 227 in which a matter of months after the Tribunal's order varying the tariff in question until further notice, an attempt was made to substitute, by agreement, a revised version of the tariff. There was no attempt to invoke s.120 or to vary the substance of the order but merely to make presentational and stylistic changes to the licensing scheme set out in it. The Tribunal accordingly held that in such circumstances it had no jurisdiction to vary the order it had made.

[519] CDPA 1988 s.123(1).

[520] s.123(2); presumably protecting such person both from proceedings for infringement of copyright and from prosecution for offences under s.107.

[521] See *The Performing Right Society Ltd v Working Men's Club and Institute Union Ltd* [1988] F.S.R. 586; *The British Broadcasting Corporation v The Performing Right Society Ltd* (1967) PRT 22/67.

[522] CDPA 1988 s.123(3); as a matter of construction of s.123 it would appear that this provision does not apply to an application under s.121.

[523] CDPA 1988 s.123(3).

award interest.[524] However, where the Tribunal directs that the order varying the amount of charges payable under a licensing scheme relating to licences for communicating works to the public has effect from a date earlier than that on which it is made, the Tribunal has power to award simple interest.[525] Interest may be awarded for such period, beginning not earlier than the date on which the reference was made and ending not later than the date of the order, as the Tribunal thinks is reasonable in the circumstances.[526] There is also a power to award interest where the Tribunal settles the terms of payment for the use as of right of sound recordings in broadcasts or confirms or varies such an order.[527] On the passage of the Broadcasting Bill through Parliament the Government spokesman stated that because of the scope of the Bill the new s.151A (giving the Tribunal power to award interest) had been limited to cases involving broadcasting and cable programmes,[528] but that when a suitable legislative opportunity arose the Government intended to apply the change to all disputes that can be heard by the Tribunal. To date no such change has been introduced.

28–97   **Further reference.** Where the Copyright Tribunal has made an order with respect to a licensing scheme,[529] the scheme may be referred again to the Tribunal in relation to cases of the description to which the order applies.[530] On the second and any subsequent reference, application may be made not only by such an organisation or person as may initiate a first reference, but also by the licensing body operating the scheme.[531] In order, however, to avoid constant references with regard to the same description of cases, a licensing scheme may not, without the special leave of the Copyright Tribunal, be referred back to the Tribunal within 12 months from the date of the order on the previous reference, or, if the previous order was made so as to be in force for 15 months or less, until the last three months before expiry of the order.[532] A licensing scheme which is made the subject of a further reference remains in operation until the reference is determined.[533] On a further reference, the Copyright Tribunal has the same powers with regard to the order it can make as in the case of an initial reference.[534]

28–98   **Application for individual licence where scheme exists.** Under the 1956 Act, an application for an individual licence in relation to a scheme could only be made where the scheme applied, but the licensing body operating the scheme

---

[524] See, e.g. *The Association of Independent Radio Companies Ltd v Phonographic Performance Ltd* [1994] R.P.C. 143

[525] s.151A(1)(a) and (b) inserted into the 1988 Act by s.139(2) of the Broadcasting Act 1996, as amended by the Copyright and Related Rights Regulations 2003.

[526] CDPA 1988 s.151A(1).

[527] Under ss.135D or 135F. See s.151A(1)(c) and (d) inserted into the 1988 Act by s.139(2) of the Broadcasting Act 1996. It had been held in the *AIRC* case (*The Association of Independent Radio Companies Ltd v Phonographic Performance Ltd* [1994] R.P.C. 143), which was a reference under s.135D but was decided before the introduction of s.151A, that the provisions of s.135D (which are similar to those of s.123(3) in that they provide for backdating and the making of any necessary payments by way of adjustment but are themselves silent as to interest) impliedly excluded a power to award interest.

[528] Now communication to the public.

[529] i.e. under any of ss.118, 119 or 120 of the 1988 Act.

[530] CDPA 1988 s.120(1). This statutory provision deals with subsequent referral of a scheme in relation to the same description of classes previously the subject of the order; the same scheme may be referred any number of times to the Tribunal under s.119, quite apart from this provision, if the reference is in relation each time to a description of classes within the scheme but not the subject of a previous order (cf. s.26(7) of the 1956 Act, not specifically re-enacted).

[531] CDPA 1988 s.120(1); this allows the operator of the scheme to seek to have the terms as to payment, or other terms, varied.

[532] s.120(2).

[533] CDPA 1988 s.120(3).

[534] s.120(4) and (5); see para.28–93, above.

would not grant a licence to the applicant in accordance with the scheme.[535] Thus, no application could be made in relation to the scheme where it contained terms or conditions, other than those relating to the amount of a charge for a licence, which excluded from the scheme the class of case in respect of which the applicant sought a licence.[536] Under the 1988 Act, however, an applicant may make an application to the Copyright Tribunal for an individual licence where a licensing scheme exists in two situations, depending, again, whether the licence sought is or is not covered by the scheme. The first, which re-enacted the position under the 1956 Act, is where the applicant claims, in a case covered by the scheme, that the operator has refused or failed within a reasonable time to grant to him, or to procure the grant to him of, a licence in accordance with the scheme.[537] The second, which was new in the 1988 Act, is where the applicant seeks a licence in respect of a case which is excluded from the scheme and claims that the operator of the scheme has either unreasonably refused to grant a licence, or has proposed unreasonable terms for a licence.[538] A case is treated as excluded from a licensing scheme for this purpose if either the case falls within exceptions provided for in the scheme or is so similar to a case in which a licence is granted under the scheme that it is unreasonable that it should not be dealt with in the same way.[539] On an application under s.121 of the 1988 Act, the Copyright Tribunal, if satisfied that the claim is well founded, must make an order declaring that, in respect of the matters specified in the order, the applicant is entitled to a licence on such terms and conditions as the Tribunal may determine to be applicable in accordance with the scheme, or, as the case may be, reasonable in the circumstances.[540] The order may be made either for an indefinite period, or for such period as the Tribunal may determine.[541]

Effect of order. Where the Copyright Tribunal has made an order under s.121, **28–99** and, during the continuance of the order, the person in whose favour the order is made pays any charges payable in accordance with the order (or, if the amount payable cannot be ascertained, gives an undertaking to pay such charges) and complies with the other terms of the order, then such person is to be in the same position as if he had at all material times been the holder of a licence granted by the owner of the copyright in question.[542]

Further reference. Where the Copyright Tribunal has made an order under s.121 **28–100**

---

[535] Copyright Act 1956 s.27(2).

[536] This being the effect of ss.24(5) and 27(1) of the 1956 Copyright Act.

[537] CDPA 1988 s.121(1).

[538] s.121(2). No application may be made under this subsection by an organisation claiming to be representative of persons requiring a licence: *Universities UK v Copyright Licensing Agency Ltd and Design and Artists Copyright Society Ltd* (CT71/00, 72/00, 73/00, 74/00, 75/01) [2002] R.P.C. 36; [2002] E.M.L.R. 35, para.29.

[539] s.121(3). On the passage of the legislation through Parliament and in speaking to an amendment to substitute the word "excluded" for the word "excepted" in what is now subs.121(3) the Minister stated: "The point to bear in mind is that the word 'cases' does not refer to 'works' which may be outside a licensing scheme but types of licensing situations which may not be covered by it. For example, where a scheme covers the use of the licensing body's repertoire in village halls but not in church halls. Substituting the word "excluded" for the word "excepted" should help to bring out the fact that we are dealing with cases where a particular class of potential licensee has been prevented from having access to the works in question under the terms of the scheme. This exclusion is unreasonable. Thus it might be held that the circumstances in which church halls required a licence to use music or records were sufficiently similar to those in which village halls might do so for it to be unreasonable not to treat them in the same way." (*Hansard*, HL Vol.493, col.1375.)

[540] CDPA 1988 s.121(4); as to reasonableness, see s.129 and para.28–110, below and as to other factors to be considered, see paras 28–112 to 28–122, below.

[541] s.121(5).

[542] CDPA 1988 s.123(5), presumably protecting such person both from proceedings for infringement of copyright and from prosecution for offences under s.107; and see s.123(2), para.28–94, above. As a matter of construction of s.123 it would appear that subs.(3) does not apply to an ap-

of the 1988 Act that a person is entitled to a licence under a licensing scheme, the operator of the scheme or the original applicant may apply to the Tribunal for a review of its order.[543] As with other provisions in the 1988 Act dealing with subsequent references,[544] such an application may not be made, without the special leave of the Copyright Tribunal, within 12 months from the date of the order on the previous reference, or, if the previous order was made so as to be in force for 15 months or less, until the last three months before expiry of the order.[545] On an application for review the Copyright Tribunal is empowered to confirm or vary its previous order as the Tribunal may determine to be reasonable having regard to the terms applicable in accordance with the licensing scheme, or, as the case may be, reasonable in all the circumstances.[546]

(iii) References and applications with respect to licensing bodies

28–101   **Jurisdiction over licences by licensing bodies.** Where no licensing scheme exists or is proposed, the Copyright Tribunal has jurisdiction in relation to the granting and terms of licences only when the party from whom the licence is sought is a licensing body.[547] The jurisdiction of the Tribunal then depends, as in the case of licensing schemes,[548] on the nature of the right the subject of the licence. Thus, the Copyright Tribunal has jurisdiction over licences to copy works, rent or lend works to the public, to perform, play or show works in public or communicate works to the public.[549]

28–102   **Reference of a proposed licence.** A person seeking a licence[550] from a licensing body may refer the terms of the proposed licence to the Copyright Tribunal under s.125(1) of the 1988 Act. As with a reference of a proposed licensing scheme,[551] the Tribunal must first decide whether the reference is premature, in which case it will refuse to entertain it.[552] If the Tribunal does entertain the reference, it may make such order, either confirming or varying the terms of the proposed licence, as the Tribunal may determine to be reasonable in the circumstances.[553] The

---

plication under s.121, so that there is no ability to backdate the effect of the order as to the amount payable.

[543] CDPA 1988 s.122(1). This allows the operator of the scheme to seek to have the terms as to payment, or other terms, varied.

[544] See paras 28–97, above, and 28–107, below.

[545] CDPA 1988 s.122(2). The Tribunal's jurisdiction is not, however, limited to cases where there has been a material change of circumstances. An amendment to the Bill which would have had this effect was resisted, it being said on behalf of the Government that there might be other cases in which an early return to the Tribunal might be appropriate, such as where it turned out that it had been misled, inadvertently or deliberately, about the facts or an existing error of fact was subsequently discovered: *Hansard*, HL Vol.491, col.496.

[546] CDPA 1988 s.122(3).

[547] CDPA 1988 s.124, as amended by the Copyright and Related Rights Regulations 1996 (SI 1996/2967). As to the definition of a licensing body, see para.28–88, above.

[548] See para.28–90, above.

[549] CDPA 1988 s.124, as amended by the Copyright and Related Rights Regulations 1996 (SI 1996/2967) and the Copyright and Related Rights Regulations 2003 (SI 2003/2498).

[550] i.e. one falling within the jurisdiction of the Tribunal; see para.28–101, above.

[551] See para.28–91, above.

[552] CDPA 1988 s.125(2). In *Candy Rock Recording Ltd v Phonographic Performance Ltd* (CT 35/96), November 6, 1996, the Tribunal held on a preliminary issue that a letter which stated that a licensing body was prepared in principle to grant a licence provided that the intended licensee gave certain undertakings contained terms on which a licensing body proposed to grant a licence and thus that the Tribunal had jurisdiction to hear the reference. The Tribunal stated that its discretion whether to entertain the reference was an unusual discretion which was to be exercised sparingly and judicially on a practical view of the disputes between the parties.

[553] CDPA 1988 s.125(3); as to reasonableness, see s.129 and para.28–110, below, and as to other factors to be considered, see paras 28–112 to 28–122, below.

Copyright Tribunal's order may be either for an indefinite period or for such period as the Tribunal may determine.[554]

Reference of an expiring licence. A licensee under a licence[555] which is due to   **28–103**
expire, whether by effluxion of time or as a result of notice given by the licensing body, may apply under s.126(1) of the 1988 Act to the Copyright Tribunal within the last three months before the licence is due to expire,[556] on the ground that it is unreasonable in the circumstances that the licence should cease to be in force. The effect of such an application is to continue the licence in force until the application has been determined.[557] On such an application the Copyright Tribunal may make such order, either confirming or varying the terms of the proposed licence, as the Tribunal may determine to be reasonable in the circumstances.[558] The Copyright Tribunal's order may be either for an indefinite period or for such period as the Tribunal may determine.[559]

Effect of order. Where the Copyright Tribunal has made an order under s.125 or   **28–104**
s.126 of the 1988 Act, and, during the continuance of the order, the person entitled to the benefit of the order pays any charges payable in accordance with the order (or, if the amount payable cannot be ascertained, gives an undertaking to pay such charges) and complies with the other terms of the order, then such person is to be in the same position as if he had at all material times been the holder of a licence granted by the owner of the copyright in question.[560]

Date from which order takes effect. As in the case of orders relating to licens-   **28–105**
ing schemes,[561] the 1988 Act introduced a limited ability for the Copyright Tribunal to backdate the effect of its order under s.125 or s.126 of the 1988 Act with regard to the charges payable.[562] Thus, the Tribunal may direct that the order has effect with regard to the charges payable from a date earlier than that on which the order is made, but not earlier than the date on which the reference was made or, if later, on which the licence was granted or, as the case may be, was due to expire.[563] Any necessary repayments, or further payments, in respect of charges already paid must then be made.[564] Where the direction relates to a licence for communicating works to the public the Tribunal has power to award simple interest.[565]

Transfer of benefit of order. The benefit of an order made by the Copyright   **28–106**
Tribunal under s.125 or s.126 of the 1988 Act may be assigned, provided such as-

---

[554] s.125(4).
[555] i.e. one falling within the jurisdiction of the Tribunal; see para.28–101, above.
[556] CDPA 1988 s.126(2).
[557] CDPA 1988 s.126(3).
[558] s.126(4); as to reasonableness, see s.129 and para.28–110, below, and as to other factors to be considered, see paras 28–112 to 28–122, below. For a reference of an expiring licence, see *British Sky Broadcasting Ltd and Sky Television Ltd v The Performing Right Society Ltd* [1988] R.P.C. 467.
[559] CDPA 1988 s.126(5).
[560] CDPA 1988 s.128(1); presumably protecting such person both from proceedings for infringement of copyright and from prosecution for offences under s.107; and see s.123(2), and para.28–94, above.
[561] See para.28–95, above.
[562] CDPA 1988 s.128(3).
[563] s.128(3).
[564] s.128(3).
[565] s.151A.

signment was not prohibited under the terms of the order, or the original licence, as the case may be.[566]

28–107   **Further reference.** Where the Copyright Tribunal has made an order with respect to a licence,[567] the licence may be referred back to the Tribunal for review.[568] On the second and any subsequent reference, application may be made not only by the licensee who initiated the initial reference (or by a person subsequently becoming entitled to the benefit of the order),[569] but also by the licensing body.[570] In order, however, to avoid constant references, a licence may not, without the special leave of the Copyright Tribunal, be referred back to the Tribunal within 12 months from the date of the order on the previous reference, or, if the previous order was made so as to be in force for 15 months or less, until the last three months before expiry of the order.[571] On an application for review the Tribunal is directed to confirm or vary its previous order as it may determine to be reasonable in the circumstances.[572]

(iv) Implied indemnity in certain licensing schemes and licences

28–108   **Implied indemnity.** In the case both of licensing schemes and licences granted by licensing bodies which license the reprographic copying[573] of published literary, dramatic, musical or artistic works, or the typographical arrangement of published editions, there is implied into the scheme or the licence an undertaking by the operator of the scheme, or the licensing body granting the licence, as the case may be, to indemnify the licensee against any liability, including as to costs,[574] which he may incur by infringing copyright by making or authorising the making of reprographic copies of a work within the apparent scope of his licence.[575]

28–109   **Conditions for availability of indemnity.** A licensee is taken to act within the scope of his licence in respect of a work which is not in fact within the licence where it is not apparent, from an inspection both of the licence and of the work, that the work does not fall within the description of works to which the licence applies.[576] It is to be noted that, whilst it is not a condition of availability of the indemnity that the licensee should in fact have checked the terms both of the licence and the work, he would in all cases be wise to do so. The scheme or licence may also contain provisions, provided they are reasonable,[577] regulating the manner in which and the time within which the licensee may make a claim

---

[566] CDPA 1988 s.128(2).

[567] i.e. under CDPA 1988 ss.125, 126 or 127.

[568] s.127.

[569] See para.28–106, above.

[570] CDPA 1988 s.127(1); this allows the licensing body to seek to have the terms as to payment, or other terms, varied.

[571] s.127(2).

[572] CDPA 1988 s.127(3).

[573] As defined in CDPA 1988 s.178.

[574] Which include those reasonably incurred in relation to actual or contemplated proceedings: CDPA 1988 s.136(4).

[575] s.136(1) and (2). This provision, which was new in the 1988 Act, gives statutory force to the scheme previously operated voluntarily by the Copyright Licensing Agency (an association of publishers and authors; see para.27–59, above); see the White Paper, Cmnd.9712, para.8.7.

[576] CDPA 1988 s.136(3)(a). Given the terms of this sub-paragraph, it is not clear what sub-para.(b) adds.

[577] s.136(5); presumably a court would refuse to give effect to any conditions which it considered unreasonable.

under the indemnity,[578] and for the operator of the scheme or the licensing body to take over the conduct of the licensee's defence in any proceedings affecting the amount of the liability under the indemnity.[579]

(v) Determination of references and applications: reasonableness[580]

General approach of the Tribunal. In exercising its task to set terms which are "reasonable in the circumstances", the Tribunal has a discretion in the widest possible terms.[581] Its job is to favour neither copyright owners nor users, but to maintain a balance between them.[582] In the case of an existing or proposed scheme, the Tribunal's function is not limited to one of review. Rather it has to form its own judgment as to whether the referred scheme is reasonable in all the circumstances.[583] Accordingly, there is no presumption for or against an existing scheme.[584] On the other hand, where the parties have argued the case on a particular basis, it would be a rare case where the Tribunal (although not bound by their agreement[585]) should depart from that basis.[586] It has been said that ultimately what the Tribunal has to determine is how much of the licensee's total profit should be paid by way of licence fee. In so doing, the Tribunal has to arrive at a figure from the total receipts which is both fair to the licensor in terms of the value of the licensee having access to the copyright works and fair to the licensee in giving him a proper reward for the effort put into the exploitation of the licensor's intellectual property rights.[587]

28–110

Determination of substantive copyright issues. The extent to which the Tribunal may determine substantive copyright issues which arise in the course of an application or reference is not clear. In one case, the PRT appears to have decided the question whether the operator of a scheme owned copyright in the material which was its subject of the scheme.[588] However, the Tribunal has stated that it is not a general court existing to determine copyright disputes, pointing to

28–111

---

[578] s.136(5)(a).

[579] s.136(5)(b).

[580] A list of the Tribunal's decisions together with copies is on its website. Although "reasonableness" is not only applicable when the Tribunal is considering references relating to licensing schemes and bodies, it is dealt with at this point because most of the Tribunal's decisions on reasonableness have related to such schemes and bodies.

[581] *Association of Independent Radio Companies Ltd v Phonographic Performance Ltd* Unreported, January 16, 1986, Harman J.; cited with apparent approval in *CSC Media Group Ltd v Video Performance Ltd* [2010] EWHC 2094 (Ch) para.14.

[582] See *The British Phonographic Industry Ltd v Mechanical-Copyright Protection Society Ltd* (CT 84–90/05), [2008] E.M.L.R. 5 at paras 45 and 46 and, most recently, *Phonographic Performance Ltd v The British Hospitality Association* (CT 91–93/05) at para.6. This decision was upheld on appeal: *Phonographic Performance Ltd v The British Hospitality Association* [2009] EWHC 209 (Ch).

[583] *The British Phonographic Industry Ltd v Mechanical-Copyright Protection Society Ltd (No. 2)* [1993] E.M.L.R. 86 at p.99; *Phonographic Performance Ltd v The British Hospitality Association* (CT 91–93/05) at para.6. This decision was upheld on appeal: *Phonographic Performance Ltd v The British Hospitality Association* [2009] EWHC 209 (Ch).

[584] *The British Phonographic Industry Ltd v Mechanical-Copyright Protection Society Ltd* (CT 84–90/05), [2008] E.M.L.R. 5 para.46.

[585] *British Airways v The Performing Right Society Ltd* [1998] R.P.C. 581 at 564.

[586] *CSC Media Group Ltd v Video Performance Ltd* [2010] EWHC 2094 (Ch) para.61.

[587] See *AEI Rediffusion Music Ltd v Phonographic Performance Ltd* [1998] R.P.C. 335, in a passage which the Tribunal approved in *Candy Rock Recording Ltd v Phonographic Performance Ltd* [1999] E.M.L.R. 155 at 168.

[588] *Barrington Electronics Ltd v Phonographic Performance Ltd* PRT 6/60 October 10, 1960, as analysed in *Meltwater Holding BV v The Newspaper Licensing Agency Ltd* (CT 114/09); decision dated March 18, 2010, para.44.

s.149 of the Act.[589] In the most recent decision on this point, the Tribunal accepted the proposition (which was agreed by the parties) that it had jurisdiction to decide substantive issues which were "incidental" to the reference, but that there were limitations on the Tribunal's powers to decide "substantive" issues.[590] It suggested that if the law was uncertain that might be a factor in the determination as to the reasonableness of the terms of a licence.[591] It seems that the Tribunal no longer has the power to refer questions of law to the court.[592] Accordingly, if it were necessary to determine an issue which the Tribunal decided that it did not have jurisdiction to determine, it would presumably have to adjourn the matter pending an application to the court. Difficult questions might arise as to who should be joined in such proceedings.

28–112   **Factors taken into account by the Tribunal.** The Tribunal is obliged to take account of certain factors in all proceedings. These are considered first.[593] Next, consideration is given to the factors which the Tribunal is obliged to take into account in proceedings relating to particular matters.[594] Finally, consideration is given to a wide range of factors which the Tribunal has taken into account although not expressly obliged to.[595]

28–113   **Factors the Copyright Tribunal is required to take into account in all proceedings.** Under the 1956 Act the PRT was required to make such orders as were reasonable in all the circumstances,[596] but the 1956 Act set out no guidance as to what was reasonable. The general requirement under the 1988 Act remains that the Copyright Tribunal should make such orders as are reasonable in all the circumstances.[597] However, the 1988 Act, whilst providing that the Copyright Tribunal has a general obligation in any case to have regard to all relevant considerations,[598] gives further general guidance by providing that the Copyright Tribunal shall, in determining what is reasonable, have regard to the availability and the terms of other schemes or licences to other persons in similar circumstances, and shall exercise its powers so as to secure that there is no unreasonable

---

[589] *The British Phonographic Industry Ltd v Mechanical-Copyright Protection Society Ltd* July 11, 1990. The parties had asked the Tribunal to determine certain issues as to the term of any scheme and as to the effect of s.119(2) CDPA 1988 on the scheme. In view of the Tribunal's finding that there was no scheme, these issues did not arise, but the Tribunal stated that it would not in any event have had jurisdiction to determine them. The Tribunal characterised the issues as "a matter of construction of the existing arrangements" and "matters of copyright law outside this s.119 reference". However, the correctness of the Tribunal's observations seems open to question. There seems little doubt that the Tribunal may determine issues as to the construction of a scheme so far as is necessary to make its determination. The effect of s.119(2) is far less likely to be in point, except (conceivably) when claims to interest are made.

[590] *Meltwater Holding BV v The Newspaper Licensing Agency Ltd* (CT 114/09); decision dated March 18, 2010 paras 42 and 48.

[591] para.48.

[592] para.51.

[593] paras 28–113 et seq., below.

[594] paras 28–116 et seq., below.

[595] paras 28–120 et seq., below.

[596] Copyright Act 1956 ss.25(5), 26(4), 27(5) and 27A(4).

[597] CDPA 1988 ss.73A(2), 93C(3), 118(3), 119(3), 120(4), 121(4), 122(3), 125(3), 126(4), 127(3), 135D(1), 135E(2), 142(2), 182D(6), 191H(3), Sch.2, para.19A(2), Sch.2A paras 3(3), 4(3), 5(4), 6(4), 7(3), 10(3), 11(4), 12(3), 15(3) and Sch.6 para.5(1). The requirement that the Tribunal should make such orders as are reasonable in the circumstances is also contained in paras 25(2) and 35(3) of the Duration of Copyright and Rights in Performances Regulations 1995 (SI 1995/3297) (jurisdiction to settle the royalty or other remuneration payable in respect of the use as of right of works and performances in which revived copyright and performance rights subsist) and the Copyright and Rights in Databases Regulations 1997 (SI 1997/3032) (jurisdiction with respect to licensing schemes, licences and licensing bodies dealing with the database right).

[598] CDPA 1988 s.135 and see *Phonographic Performance Ltd v Candy Rock Recording Ltd* [2000] E.M.L.R. 618(CA) at para.29: "Nothing is excluded provided it is relevant to determining the terms of the licence".

discrimination between the actual or prospective licensees making the application and licensees under alternative schemes or licences being operated or granted by the same person.[599] Beyond this, the 1988 Act gives no further general guidance.

General obligatory factors (i): availability and terms of other schemes or licences. Because the Tribunal is seeking to fix a price for a commodity where there is no market in the conventional sense, it has paid particular regard to previously negotiated agreements between the parties.[600] Unlike the non-discrimination factor considered below, this factor is not limited to a comparison between licences granted by the same person.[601] Nor is it limited to other schemes or licences in relation to rights identical to those before it.[602] In principle the Tribunal may take account of other schemes and licences from outside the United Kingdom.[603] However, the relevance of such material may be limited. Thus for example in *British Phonographic Industry Ltd v Mechanical-Copyright Protection Society Ltd*,[604] the royalty payable in Europe for making recordings was held not to be a meaningful comparator because the British record industry was of a different order of magnitude and the commercial risks were commensurately greater. As regards other schemes and licences generally, the Tribunal has said that it is necessary for it to consider carefully the circumstances surrounding any particular negotiated tariff as there may be special considerations depriving a particular negotiated rate of its cogency in support of the tariff under review.[605] Matters to consider in relation to postulated comparables include whether they were at arm's length, whether either side was affected by stress, whether they were affected by legal factors which were irrelevant to the case at hand[606] and changes in the market since they were agreed.[607] Another factor which may be relevant is any practice which a licensing body may have of negotiating tariffs sequentially, relying upon gains achieved in each negotiation to support later increases in other

28–114

---

[599] s.129 (and see Sch.2A para.14 with regard to applications concerning licensing of performers' rights and see the Copyright and Rights in Databases Regulations 1997 (SI 1997/3032) Sch.2 para.14 with regard to applications relating to database right licensing).

[600] See *British Phonographic Industry Ltd v Mechanical-Copyright Protection Society Ltd* [1993] E.M.L.R. 86, *British Sky Broadcasting Ltd and Sky Television Ltd v The Performing Right Society Ltd* [1998] R.P.C. 467 and *The British Phonographic Industry Ltd v Mechanical-Copyright Protection Society Ltd* (CT 84–90/05); [2008] E.M.L.R. 5; where it was said (at para.49) that the willing buyer/seller test was "a classic test in this jurisdiction".

[601] *Candy Rock Recording Ltd v Phonographic Performance Ltd* [2000] E.M.L.R. 618.

[602] In *AEI Rediffusion Music Ltd v Phonographic Performance Ltd* [1998] R.P.C. 335, the Tribunal expressly stated that it was entitled to find that a licence of a different right to the one in dispute was a comparator if in all the circumstances that was appropriate (licences to "dub" sound recordings for playing in public held to be a relevant comparator to narrowcast licence to broadcast recordings for playing in public). See also for comparison of rates under PRS licences in respect of musical works and PPL licences in respect of sound recordings, *The Manx Radio Case* (PRT 18/64), where it was held that as regards the PRS rights in musical works and those of PPL in sound recordings neither was superior to the other.

[603] During the passage of the Bill through Parliament an amendment requiring the Tribunal to look specifically at data from other Member States of the EEC was resisted on the grounds that there was nothing in what became s.129 to preclude it from considering comparisons from anywhere in the world if they were relevant (*Hansard*, Reports of Standing Committee E, 1988, col.432).

[604] *British Phonographic Industry Ltd v Mechanical-Copyright Protection Society Ltd* [1993] E.M.L.R. 86.

[605] See *Working Men's Club and Institute Union Ltd v The Performing Right Society Ltd* [1992] R.P.C. 227 at 238.

[606] *Association of Independent Radio Companies v Phonographic Performance Ltd* [1993] E.M.L.R 181 at 218. This statement was cited with apparent approval in *CSC Media Group Ltd v Video Performance Ltd* [2010] EWHC 2094 (Ch) at para.15.

[607] In *CSC Media Group Ltd v Video Performance Ltd* [2010] EWHC 2094 (Ch) the Judge, while setting aside the overall decision, upheld the Tribunal's finding that changes in the market since some of the postulated comparable agreements had been made diminished their value: see paras 34 and 54(iii).

tariffs.[608] If the Tribunal is satisfied that there exist other licences which are sufficiently comparable to the licence it is being asked to settle, the Tribunal should adopt a similar rate absent any special circumstances.[609] However, it has been said that in practice comparable schemes appear to have been more of a legitimate quarry (or template) for particular terms and figures than full precedents for a particular licence.[610]

28–115 **General obligatory factors (ii): non-discrimination.** *Candy Rock Recording Ltd v Phonographic Performance Ltd*[611] concerned the terms of a proposed licence to "dub", that is rerecord, sound recordings onto cassettes and CDs for hire to public houses, restaurants and chain stores for use as background music. The Tribunal held that it was entitled to take account of the *AEI* "narrowcasting" decision[612] because narrowcasters and dubbers were in competition. However, it took into account the fact that the customer of a dubber has to pay PPL a further fee in order to play its recordings in public whereas a narrowcaster (in reliance on s.72 of the 1988 Act) does not. Accordingly, it set a fee at a level which it stated would permit the licensee to compete with narrowcasters. On appeal, the Court of Appeal held that the Tribunal was obliged to ensure that there was no unreasonable discrimination but not to secure fair competition. Nevertheless, although the use of the word "compete" was unfortunate, the Tribunal had not erred. The product to be licensed was the same but the way PPL obtained recompense for its use was different. The effect of s.72 was a relevant factor for the Tribunal in seeking to avoid unreasonable discrimination between licensees. Read in context, the Tribunal was attempting to avoid unreasonable discrimination between dubbers and narrowcasters and this was the correct approach.

28–116 **Specific obligatory factors: (i) licences for reprographic copying.** Proceedings relating to the licensing for reprographic copying of published literary, dramatic, musical or artistic works or of the typographical arrangement of published editions may come before the Copyright Tribunal either under the general provisions relating to licensing schemes or under the provisions relating to licences granted by licensing bodies,[613] or, where the party seeking the licence is an educational establishment, under the specific provisions relating to such copying by educational establishments.[614] In all such proceedings the Copyright Tribunal is obliged to have regard to the extent of the availability of other published editions of the work, the proportion of the work to be copied and the nature of the use to which the copies are likely to be put.[615] These factors are clearly of importance not only to whether it is reasonable that a licence is not available (e.g. because too large a part of the work is to be photocopied and published editions are available, or because the use to which the photocopies are to be put is damag-

---

[608] See *Working Men's Club and Institute Union Ltd v The Performing Right Society Ltd* [1992] R.P.C 227 at 238.

[609] *AEI Rediffusion Music Ltd v Phonographic Performance Ltd* [1998] R.P.C. 335 at 347, adopted in *Candy Rock Recording Ltd v Phonographic Performance Ltd* [1999] E.M.L.R. 155 at 168 and approved and applied in *CSC Media Group Ltd v Video Performance Ltd* [2010] EWHC 2094 (Ch) at para.52. In the latter case it was held on appeal that it was wrong in principle to arrive at a view of the worth of the product without considering the comparable licence(s) and available profits (see para.54(ii)).

[610] *The British Phonographic Industry Ltd v Mechanical-Copyright Protection Society Ltd* (CT 84–90/05), [2008] E.M.L.R. 5 at paras 50 to 51.

[611] *Candy Rock Recording Ltd v Phonographic Performance Ltd* [1999] E.M.L.R. 155 (on appeal [1999] E.M.L.R. 806 and on further appeal [2000] E.M.L.R. 618).

[612] *AEI Rediffusion Music Ltd v Phonographic Performance Ltd* [1998] R.P.C. 335. See para.28–36, above.

[613] CDPA 1988 ss.116–128; see paras 28–84 et seq., above.

[614] s.139; see para.28–124, below.

[615] s.130.

ing to the copyright owner's own commercial exploitation of his copyright), but also to what is a reasonable fee for the licence sought. This provision provides the means for the Copyright Tribunal to ensure that excessive photocopying does not become a substitute for the normal access to such works through the purchase of published editions.

Specific obligatory factors: (ii) licences in respect of recordings, films, broadcasts or cable programmes including an entertainment or event. In proceedings relating to licences for sound recordings, films or broadcasts which include any entertainment or other event,[616] the Copyright Tribunal is obliged to have regard to any conditions imposed by the promoter of the entertainment or other event (other than conditions which seek to regulate the charges to be imposed in respect of licences or which relate to payment for the grant of facilities to make the recording, etc.),[617] and may not regard the refusal or failure to grant a licence as unreasonable if it could not have been granted consistently with those conditions.[618] The situation envisaged here is analogous to those discussed under (iii) below, except that there may be no underlying work by means of the copyright in which the promoter can control the subsequent exploitation of his entertainment or event, and his only opportunity to do so is through the contract with the maker of the recording. The aim of the 1988 Act is, therefore, to ensure that the reasonable rights of the promoter of the entertainment or event to control the making of a recording of his entertainment or event and its further use, by means of contractual terms imposed on the maker of the recording, are not circumvented by the possibility of others being entitled to obtain licences from the maker to exploit the recording under the general provisions of the 1988 Act in relation to licensing schemes and licences granted by licensing bodies. Unless promoters of such entertainments and events can be assured that such conditions will be respected, they might well be unwilling to permit the recording to be made and exploited at all.

28–117

Specific obligatory factors: (iii) Payments in respect of underlying copyright works and other rights. In these cases the aim of the 1988 Act is to ensure that any consideration already received or stipulated for by the owner of the copyright in the underlying work or other right at the time he authorises the making and showing of the subsequent copyright work, or which he may otherwise be entitled to obtain in respect of any further use by others of that subsequent copyright work, is taken into account, so as to ensure, in effect, that his overall remuneration from the licensing of his work, both directly by himself and indirectly by the owner of the subsequent copyright work, is neither unreasonably high (because he is paid in respect of some uses twice), nor unreasonably low (because he is not paid at all in respect of some uses).

28–118

This principle applies to proceedings relating to licences for educational establishments for the recording by them or on their behalf of broadcasts which include copyright works, or for the making of copies of such recordings, for educational purposes[619]; proceedings relating to licences in respect of the rental

---

[616] i.e. proceedings brought under the general provisions applying to licensing schemes and licences granted by licensing bodies, see paras 28–84 et seq., above.

[617] CDPA 1988 s.132(3).

[618] s.132(2); this provision is based on s.29(4) of the 1956 Act which applied to television broadcasts, and is now extended to cover sound recordings, films, cable programmes and sound broadcasts.

[619] CDPA 1988 s.131(1) and (2); such proceedings would be brought under the general provisions applying to licensing schemes and licences granted by licensing bodies, see paras 28–84 et seq, above.

or lending of copies of a work[620]; proceedings relating to licences in respect of the copyright in sound recordings, films or broadcasts[621]; and proceedings relating to licences in respect of works to be included in immediate retransmissions of broadcasts.[622]

In the last mentioned case, there are further special provisions which apply, depending on whether the retransmission is to be in the same area as that of the original transmission, or partly or wholly in an area outside that of the original transmission. Where the retransmission is to be in the same area as the original transmission, the Copyright Tribunal, in considering what charges, if any, should be made in respect of either transmission, must take into account any charges the copyright owner is entitled to receive in respect of the other transmission, thus preventing the copyright owner obtaining remuneration twice over in respect of the same area.[623] Where the retransmission is to an area wholly or partly outside the area of the original transmission, then, to the extent that it is, the Copyright Tribunal must leave the further transmission out of account in considering what charges, if any, should be paid in respect of the first transmission, thus leaving the copyright owner to make his own terms with the party making the retransmission.[624] (These special provisions do not, however, apply in relation to any applications to the Tribunal to determine the reasonable royalty or other sum payable to a copyright owner by a broadcaster in respect of works included in a wireless broadcast which is retransmitted by cable where or to the extent that the retransmission falls outside the area of the original transmission and occurs as a result of the statutory obligations imposed under the Broadcasting Act 1990.[625] In the case of such retransmissions the inclusion in the retransmission (to the extent that it falls outside the area of the original transmission) of any work included in the broadcast is treated as licensed by the copyright owner subject to the payment to him by the person making the broadcast of a reasonable royalty and the Copy-

---

[620] CDPA 1988 s.133(1) as amended by the Copyright and Related Rights Regulations 1996 (SI 1996/2967); and see further para.28–125, below.

[621] CDPA 1988 s.133(2); such proceedings would be brought under the general provisions applying to licensing schemes and licences granted by licensing bodies, see paras 28–84, et seq., below. Foreign broadcasts and cable transmissions may therefore be relevant where charges under UK licences or foreign licences have been negotiated to take account of foreign retransmission (see as to the former position under s.28 of the 1956 Act: *Copinger* 12th edn, para.1271).

[622] CDPA 1988 s.134; such proceedings would be brought under the general provisions applying to licensing schemes and licences granted by licensing bodies, see paras 28–84 et seq., above. Reception and retransmission may be a permitted act, see CDPA 1988 s.73 and para.9–226, above; and see further below.

[623] CDPA 1988 s.134(2).

[624] CDPA 1988 s.134(3). S.134(2) and (3) were explained in Parliament as being "intended, first, to ensure that if copyright owners license inclusion of their material in a foreign broadcast or cable programme service on terms which cover retransmission of that broadcast or service in the United Kingdom, any tribunal award that they may obtain in the UK in respect of royalties due from UK cable operators or broadcasters for retransmitting the foreign broadcast are (sic) abated to the extent that this retransmission was allowed for in the terms of the initial licence. The intention is to avert double payments to rights owners in respect of what is essentially a single transmission (or chain of transmissions) reaching the same audience. This policy is unchanged from the 1956 Act, where it is implemented by Section 28. The second objective is to ensure that, when broadcasts or cable programme services are retransmitted within the intended reception area of the broadcast or service (and this applies particularly to 'in area' retransmissions abroad of UK satellite broadcasts), and rights owners obtain payment from the cable operator for the retransmission under local law, tribunal decisions on licences in respect of the original broadcast shall take this into account. The third objective is to ensure that when broadcasts or cable programme services are retransmitted beyond or outside the intended reception area of the broadcast or service, the broadcaster or provider of the cable programme service which is retransmitted cannot be made to pay royalties in respect of the retransmission. It is up to the rights owners concerned to use any rights available in the country or area of the retransmission to reach an agreement with those responsible for it. If such rights do not exist it should not fall to the broadcaster to reimburse copyright owners for that fact" (*Hansard*, HL Vol.491, cols 524, 525).

[625] s.78A and Sch.12, Pt III para.4; see CDPA 1988 s.134(3A) as inserted into the 1988 Act by s.138 and Sch.9 of the Broadcasting Act 1996.

right Tribunal has a separate specific jurisdiction to determine the amount of such royalty).[626]

Finally, with regard to payments in respect of underlying copyright works, such payments made by the owners of subsequent works (such as sound recordings, films and broadcasts) in which the underlying works are included are an expense incurred by the owners of such subsequent works in creating those works and, as such, relevant to the licence fees that they should receive for their exploitation.

Specific obligatory factors: (iv) factors relevant to determining equitable remuneration. On applications to determine the amount payable by way of equitable remuneration to the author of a literary, dramatic, musical or artistic work or the principal director of a film for the rental of a sound recording or film (where such author or director has transferred his rental right concerning the recording or film) the Copyright Tribunal, in being directed to make such order as to the method of calculating and paying such remuneration as it may determine to be reasonable in all the circumstances, is specifically directed to take into account the importance of the contribution of the author or director to the recording or film.[627] Similarly, on applications to determine the amount of equitable remuneration payable to performers for rental of sound recordings or films where they have transferred their rental rights concerning such recordings or films the Tribunal is directed to take into account the importance of the contribution of the performers to the recording or film,[628] and the Tribunal is given a similar direction when determining the equitable remuneration payable to performers where sound recordings containing their performances are played in public or included in a broadcast or cable programme.[629] European case law on equitable remuneration is considered below.[630]

28–119

Other factors: (i) causal link between use of copyright works and revenue. In cases where the licensing body seeks to base payment for a licence on the revenue or profits of the licensee there must be a sufficient causal link between the use by the licensee of the copyright work in question and the revenue or profits of that licensee.[631] Thus in *British Sky Broadcasting Ltd and Sky Television Ltd v The Performing Right Society Ltd*,[632] PRS's contention that the licence fee for the broadcasting of musical works in its repertoire on Sky should be a percentage of Sky's relevant revenues was rejected on the ground that there was no sufficient correlation between the use of the works and Sky's revenues (which were derived mainly from subscribers who paid to watch programmes the main feature of which was sport or which otherwise contained many different elements). It was

28–120

---

[626] Under CDPA 1988 ss.73(4) and 73A, inserted into the 1988 Act by s.138 and Sch.9 of the Broadcasting Act 1996. See para.28–48, above.

[627] CDPA 1988 s.93C(3), inserted into the 1988 Act by the Copyright and Related Rights Regulations 1996 (SI 1996/2967).

[628] s.191H(3) inserted into the 1988 Act by the Copyright and Related Rights Regulations 1996 (SI 1996/2967).

[629] s.182D(6) inserted into the 1988 Act by the Copyright and Related Rights Regulations 1996 (SI 1996/2967).

[630] para.28–147.

[631] *British Sky Broadcasting v The Performing Right Society Ltd* [1998] E.M.L.R., cited with apparent approval in *CSC Media Group Ltd v Video Performance Ltd* [2010] EWHC 2094 (Ch) at para.17. See also *The British Phonographic Industry Ltd v Mechanical-Copyright Protection Society Ltd* (CT 84–90/05); [2008] E.M.L.R. 5 at para.61. In some cases whether the royalty is to be a percentage of income is not of concern to the licensee, the real issue being not the basis of the calculation but the result, see *British Airways Plc v The Performing Right Society Ltd* [1998] R.P.C. 581. See also J. Rayner James and A. Norris, "A Common Thread in Collective Licensing?" [1998] Ent. L.R. 205.

[632] *British Sky Broadcasting Ltd and Sky Television Ltd v The Performing Right Society Ltd* [1998] R.P.C. 467.

further held relevant that Sky's revenues were a product of substantial capital investment made at high risk which risk PRS had not shared. This case may be contrasted with the *AEI* "narrowcasting" decision,[633] where the question was the amount to be paid by AEI for the compulsory licence to include sound recordings in "narrowcast" broadcasts to particular outlets. There the Tribunal set a minimum royalty to take into account not only revenue of the licensee generated directly by the narrowcasts (which consisted preponderantly of recordings) but also income generated by sales of equipment to receive the narrowcasts which the licensee was only able to make by reason of supplying the narrowcasts.

28–121   **Other factors: (ii) available profits of licensee.** Even where the basis of the payment is not in issue the available profits of the licensee may be taken into account in order to ensure that the impact on the licensee's business is not disproportionate.[634] This does mean that rich licensees should pay more or that licensees who make a loss should pay nothing but is a cross check to ensure that the royalty is not too high. In *AEI*,[635] the Tribunal stated that ultimately what it had to determine was how much of the licensee's total profit should be paid by way of licence fee. In so doing, the Tribunal had to arrive at a figure from the total receipts which was both fair to the licensor in terms of the value of the licensee having access to the copyright works and fair to the licensee in giving him a proper reward for the effort put into the exploitation of the licensor's intellectual property rights. In *Virgin Retail Ltd v Phonographic Performance Ltd*,[636] the Tribunal refused to take any account of the possibility (which it found was not made out on the facts) that a high royalty might force Virgin to discontinue its radio service. In that case, however, the radio station was a marketing tool rather than a profit-making exercise in its own right.[637]

28–122   **Other factors: (iii) miscellaneous.** Other factors which the Tribunal has taken into account include the audience for musical works and sound recordings,[638] any incidental benefit derived by the licensor from the public exploitation of its copyright works,[639] profits which the licensee has been able to make out of the sale of ancillary equipment and out of the jurisdiction,[640] the strength of the market in which the licensee operates,[641] whether the licensor has assumed any risk in issuing the material in question to the public,[642] guidelines laid down for similar

---

[633] *AEI Rediffusion Music Ltd v Phonographic Performance Ltd* [1998] R.P.C. 335.

[634] See *British Phonographic Industry Ltd v Mechanical-Copyright Protection Society Ltd* [1993] E.M.L.R. 86 at 124, referring to dicta in *Smith Kline & French Ltd's (Cimetidine) Patents* [1990] R.P.C. 203.

[635] *AEI Rediffusion Music Ltd v Phonographic Performance Ltd* [1998] R.P.C. 335, in a passage which it approved in *Candy Rock Recording Ltd v Phonographic Performance Ltd* [1999] E.M.L.R. 155 at 168.

[636] *Virgin Retail Ltd v Phonographic Performance Ltd* [2000] E.M.L.R. 323; on appeal [2001] E.M.L.R. 139.

[637] See at para.68.

[638] See *British Sky Broadcasting Ltd and Sky Television Ltd v The Performing Right Society Ltd* [1998] R.P.C. 467.

[639] See *Association of Independent Radio Contractors Ltd v Phonographic Performance Ltd* [1994] R.P.C. 143 and *CSC Media Group Ltd v Video Performance Ltd* [2010] EWHC 2094 (Ch) at paras 22 and 54(iii). However, in *Virgin Retail Ltd v Phonographic Performance Ltd* [2000] E.M.L.R. 323 (on appeal [2001] E.M.L.R. 139), an application under CDPA 1988 s.135D, the Tribunal refused to award a discount to reflect the fact that Virgin's business was to a significant extent involved in selling the records of PPL's record company members, which were marketed on Virgin's radio station.

[640] See *AEI Rediffusion Music Ltd v Phonographic Performance Ltd* [1998] R.P.C. 335.

[641] *Candy Rock Recording Ltd v Phonographic Performance Ltd* [1999] E.M.L.R. 155; upheld on appeal [1999] E.M.L.R. 806; point not pursued on further appeal [2000] E.M.L.R. 618.

[642] *The British Phonographic Industry Ltd v Mechanical-Copyright Protection Society Ltd* (CT 84–90/05), [2008] E.M.L.R. 5 at para.71.

tribunals in other jurisdictions and decisions from other jurisdictions[643] and the need for a simple and workable tariff.[644]

D. CONTROL BY THE COPYRIGHT TRIBUNAL OF OTHER COPYRIGHT LICENSING AND OF THE RIGHT TO EQUITABLE REMUNERATION FOR RENTAL

Other controls exercised by the Copyright Tribunal. In addition to its general   **28–123**
jurisdiction in respect of licensing schemes and licences granted by licensing bodies, discussed above,[645] the Copyright Tribunal exercises control over licensing of copyright works in a number of other areas. It is given such control by reason of various provisions in the 1988 Act, dealing with schemes for reprographic copying by educational establishments,[646] the lending right in respect of literary, dramatic, musical or artistic works, sound recordings or films,[647] licences of right available consequent on the exercise of their powers by the Secretary of State, the Office of Fair Trading or the Competition Commission,[648] and the determination of a royalty payable to the trustees of the Hospital for Sick Children in respect of the play *Peter Pan*,[649] compulsory licences in respect of works included in wireless broadcasts which are re-transmitted by cable,[650] compulsory licences in respect of information about a programme service[651] and compulsory licences in respect of use as of right of sound recordings in broadcasts.[652] Additionally, control over copyright licensing is conferred on the Copyright Tribunal by provisions dealing with compulsory licences in respect of works in which copyright had lapsed but has been revived.[653] Lastly, the Tribunal is given control over the rights of authors of certain works and directors of films to equitable remuneration for rental of films and sound recordings, where such persons have transferred their rental rights concerning such films or recordings by the specific provisions of the 1988 Act introducing the right to such remuneration in such circumstances.[654]

Power to extend coverage of scheme or licence for reprographic copying.   **28–124**
The 1988 Act establishes a system of control by the Secretary of State over licensing schemes and licences granted by a licensing body which license educational establishments to make reprographic copies of published literary, dramatic, musi-

---

[643] See *British Phonographic Industry Ltd v Mechanical-Copyright Protection Society Ltd* [1993] E.M.L.R. 86, and *British Sky Broadcasting Ltd and Sky Television Ltd v The Performing Right Society Ltd* [1998] R.P.C. 467.

[644] *The British Phonographic Industry Ltd v Mechanical-Copyright Protection Society Ltd* (CT 84–90/05); [2008] E.M.L.R. 5 at para.57.

[645] See paras 28–84 et seq., above.

[646] CDPA 1988 s.139; see para.28–124, below.

[647] s.142, as amended by the Copyright and Related Rights Regulations 1996 (SI 1996/2967); see para.28–125, below.

[648] s.144(4); see para.28–126, below.

[649] Sch.6 para.5; see para.28–127, below.

[650] s.73A inserted into the 1988 Act by the Broadcasting Act 1996, s.138 and Sch.9; see further paras 28–48 et seq., above.

[651] Broadcasting Act 1990 Sch.17 paras 5 and 6, introduced into Ch.III of Pt I, and s.149, of the 1988 Act by the Broadcasting Act 1990 Sch.17 para.7(1); see further paras 28–09 et seq., above.

[652] CDPA 1988 ss.135D, 135E and 135F, introduced into the 1988 Act and into s.149 of the 1988 act by amendment by the Broadcasting Act 1990 s.175(1) and (2); see further paras 28–25 et seq., above.

[653] The Duration of Copyright and Rights in Performances Regulations 1995 (SI 1995/3297) regs 24 and 25; see further paras 28–41 et seq., above.

[654] CDPA 1988 ss.93B and 93C, inserted into the 1988 Act by the Copyright and Related Rights Regulations 1996 (SI 1996/2967); see paras 7–101 above and 28–127, below.

cal or artistic works or of the typographical arrangements of published editions.[655] The Copyright Tribunal is given jurisdiction to hear appeals from orders made by the Secretary of State in the exercise of this control.[656] Thus, where the Secretary of State has made an order extending the coverage of a scheme or licence[657] or an order confirming, varying or discharging any previous such order,[658] the owner of the copyright in a work which is the subject of the order and, in the case of a subsequent order, any organisation representative of educational establishments which was given notice of the initial application for the order and made representations in respect of it, may appeal to the Tribunal.[659] The appeal must be brought within six weeks of the making of the order (which does not take effect for such period).[660] Although the Tribunal has power to entertain an appeal brought after such period, its decision will not then affect the validity of anything done in reliance on the order before the decision of the Tribunal takes effect.[661] In deciding the appeal the Tribunal is required to have regard, in addition to all other relevant circumstances,[662] to the extent to which published editions of the works in question are otherwise available, to the proportion of the work to be copied and to the nature of the use to which the copies are likely to be put.[663]

28–125   **Settling royalty in respect of lending right.** Section 66 of the 1988 Act empowers the Secretary of State to subject the lending of certain types of work to compulsory licensing by order.[664] In such cases, where no scheme exists, the acts may be carried out subject only to the payment of reasonable royalties.[665] In default of agreement between the copyright owner and the person claiming to be treated as being licensed by him under s.66(1) of the 1988 Act, either of them may apply to the Copyright Tribunal to determine the royalty or other sum to be paid to the copyright owner.[666] Upon such an application, the Tribunal shall make such order as it may determine to be reasonable in all the circumstances,[667] and such order takes effect from the date on which it was made, or such later date as the Tribunal shall specify.[668] Either party may subsequently apply to the Tribunal to vary its order,[669] but not, without the special leave of the Tribunal, within 12 months of the original order or previous application. On a further application the Copyright Tribunal has the same powers with regard to the order it can make as in the case of an initial application.[670]

28–126   **Settling terms of licence of right consequent on the exercise of their powers by the Secretary of State, the Office of Fair Trading or the Competition**

---

[655] CDPA 1988 ss.137–141; see para.28–60, above.

[656] CDPA 1988 s.139(1) and (2).

[657] Under CDPA 1988 s.137.

[658] Under CDPA 1988 s.138.

[659] s.139(1) and (2).

[660] s.139(3) and (4).

[661] s.139(5).

[662] s.135; see para.28–114, above.

[663] s.130; see para.28–116, above.

[664] See paras 28–45 et seq., above.

[665] CDPA 1988 s.66(1), as amended by the Copyright and Related Rights Regulations 1996 (SI 1996/2967); see para.28–47, above.

[666] s.142(1) as amended by the Copyright and Related Rights Regulations 1996 (SI 1996/2967).

[667] s.142(2), as amended by the Copyright and Related Rights Regulations 1996 (SI 1996/2967); as to reasonableness, see s.135 and para.28–113, above, and as to the other factors to be considered, see s.133(1) and paras 28–110 et seq., above.

[668] s.142(5) as inserted by the Copyright and Related Rights Regulations 1996 (SI 1996/2967).

[669] s.142(3) and (4); as amended by the Copyright and Related Rights Regulations 1996 (SI 1996/2967).

[670] CDPA 1988 s.142(3), as amended by the Copyright and Related Rights Regulations 1996 (SI 1996/2967).

Commission. Section 144 of the 1988 Act supplements, with reference to copyright, the general controls under UK legislation over anti-competitive or monopolistic practices.[671] Under this section,[672] where whatever needs to be remedied, mitigated or prevented by the Secretary of State, the Office of Fair Trading or (as the case may be) the Competition Commission under various specified statutory provisions consists of or includes conditions in licences granted by a copyright owner restricting the use by the licensee of the copyright work or preventing the copyright owner granting other licences, or a refusal of a copyright owner to grant licences on reasonable terms, then the powers conferred on the Secretary of State, the Office of Fair Trading or (as the case may be) the Competition Commission by Sch.8 to the Enterprise Act 2002 include the power to cancel or modify those conditions as well as the power to provide (in addition or instead) that licences in respect of the copyright shall be available as of right.[673] The Secretary of State, the Office of Fair Trading or (as the case may be) the Competition Commission may only exercise such powers if he or it is satisfied that to do so will not contravene any Convention relating to copyright to which the United Kingdom is a party.[674] If the terms of a licence available under this section cannot be agreed, then the person requiring the licence may apply to the Copyright Tribunal to settle the terms,[675] and the licence, as so settled, takes effect from the date of application to the Tribunal.[676] There are analogous provisions in respect of performers' property rights and database right.[677]

Settling the royalty or other remuneration payable to the trustees for the Hospital for Sick Children in respect of the use of the play "Peter Pan". The   **28–127** Copyright Tribunal has a similar jurisdiction to that discussed above in relation to the lending right, to settle the royalty or other remuneration payable to the trustees of The Hospital for Sick Children, Great Ormond Street, London in respect of the public performance, commercial publication, or communication to the public of the play *Peter Pan* written by Sir James Barrie, under the right conferred by the 1988 Act on the trustees.[678] In default of agreement as to the amount to be paid to the trustees, an application may be made to the Copyright Tribunal to determine the royalty or other remuneration to be paid,[679] and the Tribunal shall make such order as it considers reasonable in all the circumstances.[680] Application may be made to the Tribunal subsequently to vary its order, but not, without the special leave of the Tribunal, within 12 months from the original order or application. On a further application the Copyright Tribunal has the same powers with regard to the order it can make as in the case

---

[671] This legislation is discussed, together with the background to the enactment of s.144, at paras 28–304 et seq., below. As to the possible application of European law see paras 28–181 et seq., below.

[672] A provision which is closely modelled on Patents Act 1977 (c.37) s.53. The section has been significantly amended by para.18 of Sch.25 to the Enterprise Act 2002 (c.40).

[673] CDPA 1988 s.144(1A).

[674] s.144(3); the exercise of such powers in respect of the exercise of copyright may be inconsistent with the Berne Convention; see Greaves [1987] 1 E.I.P.R. 3, 5; and see further para.28–304, above.

[675] s.144(4). As to the factors to be considered by the tribunal, see paras 28–110 et seq., above.

[676] s.144(5).

[677] CDPA 1988 Sch.2A para.17 and the Copyright (Rights in Databases) Regs 1997 (SI 1997/3032), Vol.2 A3.iv, Sch.2 para.15.

[678] CDPA 1988 s.301 and Sch.6, para.2(1); see para.6–52, above.

[679] Sch.6 para.5(1).

[680] Sch.6 para.5(1); as to reasonableness, see s.135 and paras 28–110 et seq., above.

of an initial application,[681] and any variation made by the Tribunal has effect from the date when made or such later date specified by the Tribunal.[682]

28–128   **Control exercised by the Copyright Tribunal over rights of authors and principal directors of films to equitable remuneration for rental.** Section 93B of the 1988 Act[683] provides that authors of literary, dramatic, musical or artistic works copies of whose works have been included in a sound recording or film and who have transferred their rental right concerning the sound recording or film[684] to the producer of such recording or film (or are deemed to have done so[685]) retain a right to equitable remuneration for the rental.[686] Equally, if principal directors of films[687] have transferred their rental rights concerning the films, they too retain the right to equitable remuneration for the rental.[688] In default of agreement as to the amount payable by way of equitable remuneration, the person by or to whom it is payable[689] may apply to the Copyright Tribunal to determine the amount payable[690] and such persons may also apply to the Tribunal to vary a previous agreement or previous determination of the Tribunal as to the amount of such remuneration[691] but such application may not, except with the special leave of the Tribunal, be made within 12 months from the date of a previous determination.[692] On an application to it regarding equitable remuneration, the Tribunal is directed to make such order as to the method of calculating and paying such remuneration as it may determine to be reasonable in the circumstances, specifically taking into account the importance of the author, or, in the case of a film, the director, to the recording or film.[693] Moreover it is specifically also provided that remuneration is not to be considered inequitable merely because it is paid by way of a single payment or at the time of the transfer of the rental

---

[681] CDPA 1988 Sch.6 para.5(2).

[682] Sch.6 para.5(4).

[683] As inserted into the 1988 Act by the Copyright and Related Rights Regulations 1996 (SI 1996/2967).

[684] i.e. the exclusive right arising under CDPA 1988 s.18A (inserted into the 1988 Act by the Copyright and Related Rights Regulations 1996 (SI 1996/2967)) to rent copies of their works (which in this case would be constituted by the film or recording in which the works were included) to the public.

[685] Where an agreement concerning film production is concluded between the author or prospective author of a literary, dramatic, musical, or artistic work and a film producer, the author is to be presumed, unless the agreement provides to the contrary, to have transferred to the film producer any rental right in relation to the film arising by virtue of the inclusion of a copy of the author's work in the film: CDPA 1988 s.93A(1) and (2) (inserted into the 1988 Act by the Copyright and Related Rights Regulations 1996 (SI 1996/2967) and see para.5–107, above. This does not apply to any rental right arising by virtue of the inclusion in the film of the screenplay, dialogue or music specifically created for and used in the film: s.93A(3)).

[686] CDPA 1988 s.93B(1)(a), inserted into the 1988 Act by the Copyright and Related Rights Regulations, above; and see para.7–101, above.

[687] Who would be co-authors of the films under CDPA 1988 s.9(2)(ab), inserted into the 1988 Act by the Copyright and Related Rights Regulations 1996 (SI 1996/2967).

[688] CDPA 1988 s.93B(1)(b) and see para.7–101, above.

[689] Equitable remuneration is payable by the person for the time being entitled to the rental right, that is the person to whom the right was transferred or any successor in title of his: CDPA 1988 s.93B(3) (i.e. in the first instance the producer of the recording or film). As regards the person to whom it is payable, this is the person on whom the right is conferred and it is provided that the right may not be assigned by the author or film director except to a collecting society for the purpose of enabling it to enforce the right on his behalf: s.93A(2). It is understood that the Authors Licensing and Collecting Society ("ALCS", see para.27–56, above) has the power to administer the right to such remuneration on behalf of authors of literary works and that Directors UK Limited ("DUKL", see para.27–61, above) has been established to administer such rights on behalf of film directors. The right is, however transmissible by testamentary disposition or by operation of law as personal or moveable property and may be assigned or further transmitted by any person into whose hands it passes: s.93A(2).

[690] CDPA 1988 s.93C(1).

[691] s.93C(2).

[692] s.93C(2).

[693] s.93C(3).

right.[694] For European case law on the assessment of equitable remuneration, see below.[695]

E. CONTROL BY THE COPYRIGHT TRIBUNAL OF PERFORMERS' RIGHTS AND OVER EQUITABLE REMUNERATION PAYABLE TO PERFORMERS

Introduction. The creation of performers' property rights giving performers rights, analogous to copyright, to prevent the copying, issue to the public or rental or lending to the public of copies of recordings of their performances[696] gave performers, collectively, the same monopoly or near monopoly power with regard to those wishing to be licensed to exploit their performances as that collectively enjoyed by copyright owners with regard to those wishing to be licensed to exploit their copyright works.[697] Accordingly, at the same time as such rights were conferred upon performers, the Copyright Tribunal was given control over licensing schemes and licensing bodies dealing with performers' property right licences, equivalent to that which it has over such schemes and bodies dealing with copyright licences.[698] In addition to performers' property rights, amendments to the 1988 Act also conferred upon performers the right to equitable remuneration, where sound recordings of their performances are played in public or included in a broadcast or cable programme,[699] and the right to such remuneration for rental of sound recordings or films,[700] and control over the amount of such remuneration was given to the Copyright Tribunal. Finally, the Copyright Tribunal is given control over licensing of performers' rights in a number of other specific situations, most of which mirror situations in which the Tribunal exercises control over copyright licensing.[701]

28–129

(i) Control by the Copyright Tribunal of licensing schemes and licensing bodies dealing with performers' property right licences

Licensing scheme. A "licensing scheme" is defined as a scheme setting out: (a) the classes of case in which the operator of the scheme, or the person on whose behalf he acts, is willing to grant performers' property right licences, and (b) the terms on which licences would be granted in those classes of case.[702] The term "scheme" is to include anything in the nature of a scheme, whether described as a scheme or a tariff or by any other name.[703] A "performers' property right licence"

28–130

---

[694] s.93C(4).

[695] para.28–147.

[696] i.e. under CDPA 1988 ss.182A, 182B and 182C, inserted into the 1988 Act by the Copyright and Related Rights Regulations 1996 (SI 1996/2967) para.12–20, above.

[697] See para.28–08, above.

[698] The Tribunal was given control over licensing schemes and licensing bodies concerned with performers' property right licences by CDPA 1988 Sch.2A, inserted into the 1988 Act by the Copyright and Related Rights Regulations 1996 (SI 1996/2967); and see paras 28–130 et seq., below.

[699] CDPA 1988 s.182D, inserted into the 1988 Act by the Copyright and Related Rights Regulations 1996 (SI 1996/2697). See para.28–147, below.

[700] CDPA 1988 s.191H, inserted into the 1988 Act by the Copyright and Related Rights Regulations 1996 (SI 1996/2697); see further para.28–148, below. This right corresponds to the right conferred upon authors of copyright works under CDPA ss.93B and 93C, see paras 28–128, above.

[701] See para.28–150, below.

[702] CDPA 1988 Sch.2A para.1(1). Sch.2A was inserted into the 1988 Act by the Copyright and Related Rights Regulations 1996 (SI 1996/2957). See the parallel definition of "licensing scheme" in relation to copyright rights in CDPA 1988 s.116(1) and para.28–85, above.

[703] CDPA 1988 Sch.2A para.1(1). Whether a licensing scheme exists depends on the circumstances of each case, see para.28–85, above.

is a licence to do or authorise the doing of any of the acts for which consent is required under ss.182A, 182B, 182C or 192CA of the 1988 Act.[704]

28–131   **Licensing body.** A "licensing body" is defined as a society or other organisation which has as its main object, or one of its main objects, the negotiating or granting, whether as owner or prospective owner of a performer's property rights or as agent for him, of performers' property right licences, and whose objects include the granting of licences covering the performances of more than one performer.[705] Licences or licensing schemes covering the performances of more than one performer do not include licences or schemes covering only performances recorded in a single recording, or performances recorded in more than one recording where the performers giving the performances are the same or the recordings are made by, or by employees of or commissioned by, a single individual, firm, company or group of companies.[706]

(a) *References and applications with respect to licensing schemes*

28–132   **References and applications involving licensing schemes.** Licensing schemes operated by licensing bodies may be referred to the Copyright Tribunal. Applications for licences in connection with such schemes may be made to the Tribunal, so far as they relate to licences for copying a recording of the whole or any substantial part of a qualifying performance, making such a recording available to the public in the way mentioned in s.182CA(1) of the 1988 Act, or renting or lending copies of a recording to the public.[707]

28–133   **Reference of a proposed licensing scheme.** The terms of a proposed licensing scheme may be referred to the Copyright Tribunal by an organisation claiming to be representative of persons claiming that they require licences in cases of a description to which the scheme would apply.[708] The Tribunal may decline to entertain the reference on the ground that it is premature.[709] The Tribunal must decline to entertain the reference unless it is satisfied that the organisation is reasonably representative of the class of persons it claims to represent.[710]

28–134   **Reference of an existing scheme.** If a licensing scheme is already in operation, a reference to the Copyright Tribunal may be made by a person claiming that he requires a licence in a case of a description to which the scheme applies, or by an organisation claiming to be representative of such persons.[711] The scheme remains in operation until all proceedings on the reference are concluded.[712] Where the reference is made by an organisation, the Tribunal must decline to entertain the

---

[704] i.e. making, issuing to the public, renting, lending or making available to the public copies of recordings of performers' performances; see further Ch.12. The reference to the "making available" right was added by the Copyright and Related Rights Regulations 2003 (SI 2003/2498) reg.7(4)(a).

[705] CDPA 1988 Sch.2A para.1(2). See the parallel definition of "licensing body" in relation to copyright rights in CDPA 1988 s.116(2) and para.28–88 above.

[706] Sch.2A para.1(4).

[707] CDPA 1988 Sch.2A para.2, as amended by the Copyright and Related Rights Regulations 2003 (SI 2003/2498) reg.7(4)(b).

[708] CDPA 1988 Sch.2A para.3(1). See the parallel jurisdiction of the Tribunal with regard to proposed licensing schemes dealing with copyright licences, CDPA 1988 s.118 and para.28–91, above.

[709] CDPA 1988 Sch.2A para.3(2).

[710] CDPA 1988 s.205B(3) provides for the making of provision to this effect by rules. The relevant rule is r.9(1)(b)(ii) of the Copyright Tribunal Rules 2010 (SI 2010/791).

[711] CDPA 1988 Sch.2A para.4(1).

[712] CDPA 1988 Sch.2A para.4(2).

reference unless it is satisfied that the organisation is reasonably representative of the class of persons it claims to represent.[713]

Order confirming or varying the scheme. Where an existing or proposed scheme is referred to the Copyright Tribunal, the Tribunal is empowered to make such order either confirming or varying the scheme, in so far as it relates to cases of the description to which the reference relates, and additionally in the case of a proposed scheme, generally, as the Tribunal may determine to be reasonable in the circumstances.[714] The Tribunal's order may be either for an indefinite period, or for such period as the Tribunal may determine.[715]   **28–135**

Effect of order. A licensing scheme confirmed or varied by the Copyright Tribunal remains in operation (or in the case of a proposed scheme comes into and remains in force) for so long as the Tribunal's order remains in force.[716] Where the Tribunal has made an order confirming or varying a licensing scheme following a reference or application, a person who, in a case of a class to which the order applies, pays the scheme's operator any charges payable under the scheme in respect of a licence covering the case in question (or, if the charges cannot be ascertained, gives an undertaking to pay them when ascertained) and complies with any other applicable terms, is deemed to be licensed as regards performers' property rights.[717]   **28–136**

Date from which order takes effect. Where the order of the Tribunal varies the amount of the charges payable under a licensing scheme, the Tribunal may direct that the order has such effect from a date earlier than that on which the reference was made, or, if later, on which the scheme came into operation.[718] Any necessary repayments, or further payments, in respect of charges already made must then be made.[719] The Tribunal does not have power to award interest when backdating its order.[720]   **28–137**

Further reference. Where the Tribunal has made a previous order in respect of a licensing scheme under paras 3, 4 or 5 of Sch.2A, any of the following may make a further reference to the Tribunal: the operator of the scheme: a person claiming that he requires a licence in a case of the description to which the order applies, or an organisation claiming to be representative of such persons.[721] However, without the special leave of the Tribunal, such further reference may not be made within 12 months from the date of the previous order, or (if the order was made to be in force for 15 months or less) within three months of the expiry of the previous order.[722] Again, where the reference is made by an organisation, the Tribunal must decline to entertain the reference unless it is satisfied that the organisation is   **28–138**

---

[713] CDPA 1988 s.205B(3) and r.9(1)(b)(ii) of the Copyright Tribunal Rules 2010 (SI 2010/791).

[714] CDPA 1988 Sch.2A paras 4(3) and 3(3). As to reasonableness, see paras 28–110 et seq., above dealing with the requirement that the Tribunal should make such orders as are reasonable in all the circumstances in relation to licensing schemes dealing with copyright licences.

[715] Sch.2A paras 4(4) and 3(4).

[716] CDPA 1988 Sch.2A para.8(1).

[717] Sch.2A paras 8(2) and (5), mirroring CDPA 1988 s.123(2), see para.28–94, above.

[718] CDPA 1988 Sch.2A para.8(3).

[719] Sch.2A para.8(3)(a).

[720] The power to order further payments or repayments impliedly excludes the power to award interest: see notes to para.28–96, above, discussing directly equivalent provisions relating to licensing schemes relating to copyright licences. However in the case of copyright licensing schemes the 1988 Act gives the Tribunal express power to award interest in limited circumstances.

[721] CDPA 1988 Sch.2A para.5(1).

[722] Sch.2A para.5(2).

reasonably representative of the class of persons it claims to represent.[723] A licensing scheme which is made the subject of a further reference remains in operation until the reference is determined.[724] On a further reference the Tribunal has the same powers with respect to the order it can make as in the case of an initial reference.[725]

28–139   **Applications for individual licences in connection with licensing scheme.** A person may make an application to the Copyright Tribunal for an individual licence where a licensing scheme exists in two situations, depending on whether the licence sought is or is not covered by the scheme. A person who claims, in a case covered by a licensing scheme, that the operator of the scheme has refused to grant him, or procure the grant to him of, a licence in accordance with the scheme, or has failed to do so within a reasonable time after being asked, may apply to the Tribunal for a declaration that he is entitled to a licence.[726] Alternatively if the case is excluded from the scheme, either because it falls within an exception to the scheme or because it falls outside the scheme altogether, an application for a declaration may still be made. If the case falls outside the scheme altogether, the case must be so similar to those in which licences are granted that it is unreasonable that it should not be dealt with in the same way.[727] In such cases (i.e. where the case falls within an exception or outside the scheme), application for a declaration may be made not only where the operator has refused or failed to grant a licence, but also where the operator proposes terms for a licence which are claimed to be unreasonable.[728] The Tribunal may make an order declaring that the applicant is entitled to a licence, either on the terms applicable under the scheme, or on such terms as it considers reasonable.[729] Again the order may be indefinite or for a fixed period.[730]

28–140   **Further reference.** Where the Tribunal has made a previous order in respect of the entitlement of a person to a licence in connection with a licensing scheme, either the operator of the scheme or the original applicant may make a further reference to the Tribunal.[731] However, without the special leave of the Tribunal, such further reference may not be made within 12 months from the date of the previous order, or (if the order was made to be in force for 15 months or less) within three months of the expiry of the previous order.[732]

(b)   *References and applications with respect to licensing by licensing bodies*

28–141   **Jurisdiction over licensing by licensing bodies.** The Copyright Tribunal also has jurisdiction over references and applications in respect of licences relating to a performer's property rights which cover the performance of more than one performer granted by a licensing body otherwise than in connection with a licensing scheme, in so far as the licences authorise the copying of a recording, the

---

[723] CDPA 1988 s.205B(3).

[724] Sch.2A para.5(3).

[725] Sch.2A para.5(4).

[726] CDPA 1988 Sch.2A para.6(1), mirroring CDPA 1988 s.121(1), see para.28–98, above.

[727] Sch.2A paras 6(2) and (3), mirroring CDPA 1988 s.121(2), see para.28–98, above.

[728] Sch.2A para.6(2).

[729] Sch.2A para.6(4).

[730] Sch.2A para.6(5).

[731] CDPA 1988 Sch.2A para.7(1).

[732] Sch.2A para.7(2); and see para.28–100, above, as to the parallel provisions relating to copyright licensing.

electronic "on-demand" transmission of a recording or the rental and lending of copies of a recording to the public.[733]

Reference to Tribunal of proposed licence. The terms on which a licensing body proposes to grant a licence may be referred to the Copyright Tribunal by the prospective licensee.[734] The Tribunal may decline to entertain the reference on the ground that the reference is premature.[735] If the Tribunal decides to entertain the reference it may make such order as it thinks reasonable in the circumstances, either confirming or varying the terms of the licence.[736] The order may be indefinite or for a fixed period determined by the Tribunal.[737]   **28–142**

Reference to Tribunal of expiring licence. Where a licence is due to expire, either by effluxion of time or as a result of notice given by the licensing body, the licensee may apply to the Copyright Tribunal on the ground that it is unreasonable in the circumstances that the licence should cease to be in force.[738] The application may not be made until the last three months before the licence is due to expire.[739] The licence remains in operation until the proceedings on the reference are concluded.[740] The Tribunal may make an order declaring that the licensee continues to be entitled to the benefit of the licence on such terms as the Tribunal determines to be reasonable in the circumstances.[741] The order may be indefinite or for a fixed period.[742]   **28–143**

Effect of order of Tribunal as to licence. Where the Tribunal has made an order on a reference or application relating to a licence not under a licensing scheme, the person entitled to the benefit of the order is deemed to be licensed as regards performers' property rights if he pays the licensing body any charges payable in accordance with the order (or, if the charges cannot be ascertained, gives an undertaking to pay them when ascertained) and complies with any other applicable terms.[743] In so far as it varies the charges payable, the order may be backdated to the date when the reference or application was made, or, if later, the date on which the licence was granted or was due to expire.[744]   **28–144**

Further reference. Where the Tribunal has made a previous order in respect of a licence under paras 10 or 11 of Sch.2A, either the licensing body or the person entitled to the benefit of the order may apply to the Tribunal to review its order.[745] However, without the special leave of the Tribunal, such further application may not be made within 12 months from the date of the previous order, or (if the order was made to be in force for 15 months or less) within three months of the expiry of the previous order.[746]   **28–145**

General considerations: unreasonable discrimination. When considering a   **28–146**

---

[733] CDPA 1988 Sch.2A para.9, as amended by the Copyright and Related Rights Regulations 2003 (SI 2003/2498) reg.7(4)(b). S.182CA(1) refers to "on-demand" transmissions. For the definition of "licensing body" see para.28–88, above.

[734] CDPA 1988 Sch.2A para.10(1).

[735] Sch.2A para.10(2).

[736] Sch.2A para.10(3).

[737] Sch.2A para.10(4).

[738] CDPA 1988 Sch.2A para.11(1). This mirrors the provisions of CDPA 1988 s.126(1), see para.28–103, above.

[739] Sch.2A para.11(2).

[740] Sch.2A para.11(3).

[741] Sch.2A para.11(4). As to reasonableness, see paras 28–110 et seq., above.

[742] Sch.2A para.11(5).

[743] CDPA 1988 Sch.2A para.13(1).

[744] Sch.2A para.13(3).

[745] CDPA 1988 Sch.2A para.12(1).

[746] Sch.2A para.12(2).

reference or application, whether relating to a licensing scheme or a licence, in determining what is reasonable the Tribunal must have regard to the same factors. These are: the availability of other schemes, or the granting of other licences, to other persons in similar circumstances; and the terms of those schemes or licences. The Tribunal must exercise its powers so as to secure that there is no unreasonable discrimination between licensees, or prospective licensees, under the scheme or licence to which the reference or application relates and licensees under other schemes operated by, or other licences granted by, the same person.[747] The Tribunal also has a general obligation to have regard to all relevant circumstances.[748]

(ii) Control by the Copyright Tribunal of performers' rights to equitable remuneration and other performers' rights

28–147　**Section 182D of the 1988 Act: playing in public and communication to the public.** Under this section, the Tribunal is given control over the amount of equitable remuneration payable to performers by owners of the copyright in commercially published sound recordings including the performers' performances, where such sound recordings are played in public or communicated to the public otherwise than by way of electronic "on-demand" transmission.[749] In default of agreement as to the amount payable by way of equitable remuneration, the person by or to whom equitable remuneration is payable may apply to the Tribunal to determine the amount.[750] Such persons may also apply to the Tribunal either to vary any agreement as to the amount payable or any previous determination by the Tribunal, but no such application may be made within 12 months of a previous determination except with the special leave of the Tribunal.[751] There is no power to back-date an order varying any agreement or previous determination by the Tribunal as to the amount of remuneration. On an application, the Tribunal is directed to make such order as to the method of calculating and paying equitable remuneration as the Tribunal may determine to be reasonable in the circumstances, specifically taking into account the importance of the contribution of the performer to the sound recording.[752] In *Stichting ter Exploitatie van Naburige Rechten v Nederlandse Omroep Stichting*,[753] the European Court of Justice had to consider the method used in the Netherlands to calculate the amount of equitable remuneration. It held as follows. Although the concept of equitable remuneration must be interpreted in the same way in all Member States, there is no universally applicable method for determining the amount of such remuneration for all Member States. It is for each Member State to determine the relevant criteria

---

[747] CDPA 1988 Sch.2A para.14 (1).

[748] Sch.2A para.14(2). See also paras 28–110 et seq., above dealing with the requirement that the Tribunal should make such orders as are reasonable in all the circumstances in relation to copyright licensing schemes and licences.

[749] CDPA 1988 s.182D(4), as amended by the Copyright and Related Rights Regulations 2003 (SI 2003/2498) reg.7(2), with effect from October 31, 2003; and see further Ch.12. The right to such remuneration is collectively controlled on behalf of performers by Phonographic Performance Limited (which also controls the public performance rights in sound recordings on behalf of the owners of the copyright in such recordings (see para.27–66, above)).

[750] CDPA 1988 s.182D(4). The person to whom such remuneration is in the first instance payable is the performer, and he may not assign his right to such remuneration except to a collecting society: s.182D(1) and (2). The right is however transmissible by testamentary disposition or operation of law as personal or moveable property and may be assigned or further transmitted by any person into whose hands it passes: s.182D(2).

[751] CDPA 1988 s.182D(5).

[752] s.182D(6).

[753] Case C–245/00 [2003] E.C.R. I–1251. See also *Lagardère Active Broadcast v Société pour la perception de la rémunération équitable (SPRE)* (C–28/04) [2005] E.C.R. I–7199; [2005] 3 C.M.L.R. 48; [2006] E.C.D.R. 1.

consistent with the objectives of the Directive, which are to enable a proper balance to be achieved between, on the one hand, the interests of performing artists and producers in obtaining remuneration for the broadcast of a particular sound recording and, on the other, the interests of third parties in being able to broadcast the sound recording on terms that are reasonable. Whether the remuneration is equitable is to be assessed, in particular, in the light of the value of the use of the sound recording in trade. The European Court of Justice therefore has no role in laying down the criteria for determining equitable remuneration, only to provide the national courts with direction in order for them to assess whether the criteria actually used are such that they ensure that performers and record producers receive equitable remuneration in a manner that is consistent the Directive. The Dutch model for calculating equitable remuneration by reference to variable and fixed factors, such as the number of hours of broadcasts of recordings, the viewing and listening numbers, agreed tariffs in the relevant field, tariffs set in bordering states and the amounts paid by commercial broadcasters, having as its object the achievement of a proper balance of the respective interests, did not therefore contravene Community Law.

Section 191H of the 1988 Act: rental. Under this section,[754] the Tribunal is given control over the amount payable by way of equitable remuneration to performers for the rental of sound recordings or films including recordings of their performances, where they have transferred (or are presumed to have transferred) their rental right concerning such recordings or films.[755] Again, an application to determine the amount of such remuneration may be made by the person by or to whom it is payable,[756] and such persons may also apply to the Tribunal to vary a previous agreement or previous determination of the Tribunal as to the amount of such remuneration.[757] Again, without the special leave of the Tribunal, no application may be made within 12 months from the date of a previous determination.[758] As with remuneration for public exploitation of commercial sound recordings, the Tribunal on an application with respect to equitable remuneration for rental is directed to make such order as it determines to be reasonable in the circumstances, taking into particular account the importance of the contribution of the performer to the film or sound recording.[759] It is however specifically provided that remuneration is not to be considered inequitable merely because it is paid by way of a single payment or at the time of the transfer of the rental right.[760]

28–148

Granting consent on behalf of a performer to the making of a copy of a recording of a performance. The Copyright Tribunal has power to grant consent on behalf of a performer to the making of a copy of a recording of a performance, where the identity or whereabouts of the person entitled to the reproduction right

28–149

---

[754] Inserted into the 1988 Act by the Copyright and Related Rights Regulations 1996 (SI 1996/2967).

[755] CDPA 1988 s.191H(1); and see further para.12–66, above.

[756] s.191H(1). The remuneration is payable in the first instance to the performer, and he may not assign it except to a collecting society (though it is transmissible by testamentary disposition or by operation of law): s.191G(2). The British Equity Collecting Society Limited ("BECS") has been formed to collect such remuneration, see para.27–57, above. It is payable by the person for the time being entitled to the rental right, namely, the person to whom the rental right was transferred or any successor in title: s.191G(3).

[757] CDPA 1988 s.191H(2).

[758] s.191H(2).

[759] s.191H(3).

[760] s.191H(4).

in the performance cannot be ascertained by reasonable inquiry.[761] The consent has effect as consent of the person entitled to the reproduction right for the purposes of the provisions of Pt II of the 1988 Act relating to performers' rights and as consent of the performer for the purposes of the criminal provisions of the 1988 Act in relation to rights in performances.[762] The Tribunal shall not give consent except after the service or publication of such notices as are required by The Copyright Tribunal Rules or by direction of the Tribunal.[763] In deciding whether to grant consent on behalf of the performer, the Tribunal is bound to take into account two factors, namely whether the original recording was made with his consent and is lawfully in the possession or control of the person wishing to make the further recording, and whether the making of the further recording is consistent with the obligations of the parties to the arrangements under which the original recording was made.[764] Where the Tribunal gives consent on behalf of a performer, it may attach such conditions as it considers appropriate,[765] and, in default of agreement between the applicant and the person entitled to the reproduction right, the Tribunal shall also determine what payment is to be made to such person.[766] To date there is only one reported case in relation to the Tribunal's power to grant consent on behalf of performers.[767]

28–150 **Other controls exercised by the Copyright Tribunal over performers' rights.** In addition to the jurisdiction of the Tribunal, discussed above, with regard to licensing schemes and licensing bodies dealing with performers' property rights and its jurisdiction with regard to equitable remuneration and the granting of consent on behalf of performers who cannot be identified or traced, the Tribunal exercises control over the licensing of performers' rights in a number of other specific situations. These largely mirror the other controls exercised by the Tribunal over licensing of copyright works[768] and the Tribunal is given such control by various provisions inserted into the 1988 Act dealing with the lending right in respect of sound recordings or films treated as licensed by performers by virtue of an order of the Secretary of State,[769] licences of right of performers' property rights available as a result of the exercise of powers consequent on a

---

[761] CDPA 1988 s.190, as amended by the Copyright and Related Rights Regulations 1996 (SI 1996/2967).

[762] Thus enabling the applicant to copy the recording (s.182A), issue those copies to the public (s.182B), or rent or lend those copies to the public (s.182C).

[763] CDPA 1988 s.190(3). There is no specific rule but r.14 of the Copyright Tribunal Rules 2010 (SI 2010/791) provides for publication of details of any application on the Copyright Tribunal website.

[764] s.190(5).

[765] s.190(2).

[766] s.190(6). Under the Practice Direction previously in force, if the Tribunal was satisfied that the identity or whereabouts of a performer could not be ascertained by reasonable enquiry and that all particulars required (including particulars of the terms upon which the previous recording was made) had been supplied, the Tribunal might make an Order simply giving consent, with a provision for liberty to apply for an Order as to payment or other terms as the Tribunal might think fit: see Copyright Tribunal Practice Direction (April 7, 2004) para.18. An example was *Chris Sawyer*, CT 63/98.

[767] *Ex p. Sianel Cymru* [1993] E.M.L.R. 251, where the applicant (the Welsh Fourth Television Channel Authority) wished to make an animated version of Under Milk Wood and rerecord the original 1954 BBC radio production onto the soundtrack. (The copyright owner of that recording had no objection to the proposed rerecording.) The cast of the radio production had included members of a school. The applicant had managed to ascertain the identity of some of the school children but not all. It applied to the Tribunal under s.190(1) for consent on behalf of those performers whose identity or whereabouts could not be ascertained and also for consent on behalf of the personal representatives of one deceased performer whose identity could not be ascertained. The order of the Tribunal giving consent included an express liberty for the performers and the personal representatives to apply to the Tribunal for payment. See also the unreported case of *Chris Sawyer* (CT 63/98), where a similar order was made.

[768] See para.28–83, above.

[769] CDPA 1988 Sch.2A para.15. The provisions of para.15 mirror the provisions in s.142 of the 1988

competition report[770] and compulsory licences in respect of performances or recordings of performances included in wireless broadcasts which are retransmitted by cable pursuant to statutory requirement but beyond the original broadcast area.[771] In one further case control over the licensing of performers' rights is conferred upon the Copyright Tribunal by regulations providing for compulsory licences in respect of performances in which performance rights had lapsed but have been revived.[772]

F. CONTROL BY THE COPYRIGHT TRIBUNAL OF THE LICENSING OF DATABASE RIGHT AND PUBLICATION RIGHT

Introduction. The creation of new intellectual property rights, analogous to copyright (1) in respect of the contents of databases ("the database right")[773] and (2) conferred on those who, after the expiry of copyright protection, for the first time publish previously unpublished works ("the publication right"),[774] also gives the owners of such rights as a group the same kind of monopoly power with regard to those wishing to exploit their works as that enjoyed by copyright owners. Thus, as with the new performers' rights, the provisions introducing the database and publication rights at the same time also provided for control of their licensing by the Copyright Tribunal.[775]   **28–151**

Database right licensing. With regard to database right there exist provisions, equivalent to those under the 1988 Act regulating copyright licensing schemes and licensing bodies,[776] giving the Copyright Tribunal control over licensing schemes and licensing bodies dealing with database right licences,[777] and in respect of database right licences available as of right consequent on a report of the   **28–152**

Act relating to the settling of a royalty in respect of the lending of copies of certain copyright works treated as licensed by the copyright owner by order of the Secretary of State (see para.28–125, above) but the subject matter of para.15 is a royalty in respect of the lending of recordings or films containing performers' performances treated as licensed by the Secretary of State's order (under CDPA 1988 Sch.2 para.14A) in the absence of a licensing scheme.

[770] CDPA 1988 Sch.2A para.17, as amended by the Enterprise Act 2002 (c.40) Sch.25 para.18. The provisions of para.17 giving the Tribunal power to settle the terms of licences of right of performers' property rights directed consequent on a competition report mirror the provisions in s.144 of the 1988 Act giving the Tribunal power to settle the terms of a licence of right in respect of copyright; see para.28–126, above.

[771] CDPA 1988 Sch.2 paras 19 and 19A as amended by the Copyright and Related Rights Regulations 2003 (SI 2003/2498) reg.22. Again, these provisions mirror provisions of the 1988 Act dealing with copyright works (i.e. s.73A giving the Tribunal power to settle the royalty payable to copyright owners under the compulsory licence of their works where such works are included in a wireless broadcast which is by statutory requirement retransmitted by cable outside the broadcast area) discussed at para.28–51, above.

[772] The Duration of Copyright and Rights in Performances Regulations 1995 (SI 1995/3297) regs 34 and 35. In the case of a performance in which revived performance rights subsist any acts which require the consent of any person under Pt II of the 1988 Act are treated as having that consent subject only to the payment of such reasonable remuneration as may be agreed or in default of agreement determined by the Copyright Tribunal (reg.34(1)). In order for a person to take advantage of such compulsory licence he must give reasonable notice to the rights owner stating when he intends to begin to do the acts (reg.34(2)). If he does so his acts are treated as having consent and reasonable remuneration shall be payable in respect of them despite the fact that its amount is not agreed or determined until later (reg.34(4)). An application to settle the remuneration payable may be made to the Tribunal by the rights owner or the person claiming to be treated as having his consent and on an application the Tribunal may make such order as it may determine to be reasonable in the circumstances (reg.35(1) and (2)). For the equivalent copyright provisions see paras 28–41 et seq., above.

[773] See Ch.18.

[774] See Ch.17.

[775] Copyright and Rights in Databases Regulations 1997 (SI 1997/3032) regs 24 and 25 and Sch.2; and the Copyright and Related Rights Regulations 1996 (SI 1996/2967) reg.17.

[776] See paras 28–84 et seq., above.

[777] Copyright and Rights in Databases Regulations 1997 (SI 1997/3032) Sch.2 regs 1 to 14. As to the database right, see Ch.18. The form and wording of these provisions dealing with licensing

Monopolies and Mergers Commission.[778] Again, following the provisions of the 1988 Act with regard to copyright licensing, the Tribunal in exercising its jurisdiction in relation to references and applications relating to licensing schemes and licensing bodies concerned with database right licences is directed to make such order as it may determine to be reasonable in the circumstances.[779] Further, again imitating the provisions of the 1988 Act regulating copyright licensing, the Tribunal in determining what is reasonable on a reference or application relating to a licensing scheme or licence dealing with the database right is to have regard to the availability of other schemes or the granting of other licences in similar circumstances and the terms of those licences. The Tribunal must then exercise its powers so as to secure that there is no unreasonable discrimination between licensees or prospective licensees under the scheme or licence to which the reference or application relates and licensees under other schemes operated by, or other licences granted by, the same person.[780]

28–153   **Publication right licensing.** With regard to control over licensing of publication right, the substantive provisions of Ch.VII of the 1988 Act (i.e. those dealing with copyright licensing) are, with minor amendments, simply applied in relation to publication right as in relation to copyright.[781] Moreover the provisions of Ch.VIII, dealing with the constitution and procedure of and appeals from the Copyright Tribunal are also applied for the purpose of supplementing such substantive provisions as so applied.[782] The modifications of the substantive provisions are twofold. First, s.116(4)[783] (which excludes from licences and licensing schemes over which the Tribunal has jurisdiction, licences or schemes covering only a single collective work or collective works of which the authors are the same or the works of employees of a single individual firm or company or group of companies) does not apply.[784] Licensing schemes dealing with licences of the publication right relating to such works are accordingly within the jurisdiction of the Tribunal. Secondly, in ss.116(2), 117 and s124 (which define the schemes and licences subject to the Tribunal's jurisdiction) the words "works of more than one author" are replaced by the words "works of more than one publisher."[785] This is necessary since the right is given to the publisher, and in the same way that copyright licensing schemes have to cover the works of more than one author to come within the jurisdiction of the Tribunal, publication right licensing schemes have to cover freshly published works of more than one publisher.

---

schemes and licensing bodies concerned with database right licences follows the form and wording of the provisions of the 1988 Act dealing with such schemes and bodies concerned with copyright licences; see paras 28–84 to 28–107, above. Thus there is provision for reference of proposed or existing licensing schemes (Sch.2 paras 3 to 5), for applications for the grant of individual licences in connection with a licensing scheme (Sch.2 paras 6 to 8), for references and applications with respect to the grant of licences by licensing bodies not in connection with a licensing scheme (Sch.2 paras 9 to 13).

[778] Copyright and Rights in Databases Regulations 1997 (SI 1997/3032) Sch.2 para.15; and see equivalent provisions relating to copyright licences paras 28–54, above and 28–325 et seq., below.

[779] Sch.2 paras 3(3), 4(3), 5(3), 6(3), 7(3), 10(3) and 11(3).

[780] Sch.2 para.14. See also paras 28–114 and 28–115, above, dealing with the requirement that the Tribunal should take such factors into account in relation to copyright licensing schemes and licences.

[781] The Copyright and Related Rights Regulations 1996 (SI 1996/2967) reg.17.

[782] reg.17(4).

[783] See para.28–88, above.

[784] The Copyright and Related Rights Regulations 1996 (SI 1996/2967) reg.17(2)(c).

[785] reg.17(3)(b).

G. PROCEDURE BEFORE THE COPYRIGHT TRIBUNAL

General. Copyright Tribunal Rules were made in 1989[786] and in 1995 the Chairman issued a general Practice Direction, giving guidance on a number of procedural matters.[787] In 2006 a further Practice Direction was issued, dealing specifically with references under s.128A of the 1988 Act.[788] In May 2007, the UK Intellectual Property Office published a Review of the Copyright Tribunal whose authors recommended a large number of changes to its procedures, including the adoption of the Civil Procedure Rules and Practice Directions.[789] This was followed in April 2009 by a consultation document to which draft new rules were annexed ("the Consultation"). Following the Consultation, new rules were made by statutory instrument dated March 15, 2010.[790] The new rules came into force on April 6, 2010. They are based on an amalgam of the Civil Procedure Rules and the Competition Appeal Tribunal Rules 2003.[791] They include a suitably tailored version of the overriding objective and require the parties to help the Tribunal to further that objective.[792] The Tribunal retains the right, subject to the provisions of the Act and of the Rules, to regulate its own procedure,[793] e.g. by Practice Direction. At the time of writing the general Practice Direction is being revised in line with the new rules.[794] The principal aspects of the procedure before the Tribunal are dealt with below.

28–154

Secretary and service of documents. The business of the Tribunal is administered by the Secretary, who is a civil servant working in the Intellectual Property Office.[795] Notices and documents may be served by sending them by prepaid post to the recipient's address for service, or, where no such address has been given, at its registered office, principal place of business or last known address.[796] Service on a licensing body or organisation which is not a body corporate may be effected by sending the document to the secretary, manager or other similar officer.[797] Service on a party's solicitor or agent is deemed to be service on that party.[798] The Tribunal may direct that service of any notice or other document be dispensed with or effected otherwise than in the manner provided by the Rules.[799]

28–155

The overriding objective. As with the Civil Procedure Rules, the overriding

28–156

---

[786] The Copyright Tribunal Rules 1989 (SI 1989/1129), based, to a large extent, on the Performing Right Tribunal Rules (as amended), made under the Copyright Act 1956) as amended by the Copyright Tribunal (Amendment) Rules 1991 (SI 1991/201) and the Copyright Tribunal (Amendment) Rules 1992 (SI 1992/467).

[787] The latest version is reproduced in *Copinger* 15th edn, Vol.2 B1.ii.

[788] These sections have now been repealed: see para.28–67, above.

[789] *http://www.ipo.gov.uk/ctribunalreview.pdf* [Accessed October 1, 2010] para.7.12.

[790] SI 2010/791. See Vol.2 B1.i.

[791] Consultation: "General observations".

[792] r.3. See para.28–156, below.

[793] r.43.

[794] E-mail exchange with Catherine Worley, Secretary to the Tribunal, September 16, 2010.

[795] The Tribunal's postal address is 21 Bloomsbury Street, London, WC1B 3HF (for office hours, see r.41). That or such other address as may be notified in the London, Edinburgh and Belfast Gazettes and on the Tribunal Website is the Tribunal's address for service of documents: r.4. The Tribunal's website is at *http://www.ipo.gov.uk/ctribunal.htm* [Accessed October 1, 2010] or such other location as may be notified from time to time in such manner as the Chairman may direct: r.5.

[796] r.39(1).

[797] r.39(2).

[798] r.39(4). A party may be represented by a person authorised to exercise a right of audience or conduct litigation under the Legal Services Act 2007, an advocate or solicitor in Scotland, a barrister or solicitor in Northern Ireland or any other person allowed by the Tribunal to appear on his behalf: r.6.

[799] r.39(3).

objective is to enable the Tribunal to deal with cases justly.[800] This includes, so far as practicable:[801] ensuring that the parties are on an equal footing; saving expense; dealing with the case in ways which are proportionate to the amount of money involved, the importance of the case, the complexity of the issues involved and the financial position of each party; ensuring that the case is dealt with expeditiously and fairly; and allotting to the case an appropriate share of the resources available to the Tribunal, while taking into account the need to allot resources to other cases. The parties are required to help the Tribunal to further the overriding objective.[802]

28–157   **Commencement of proceedings.** The Rules appear to apply to all types of proceedings before the Tribunal. Rule 7 provides that proceedings must be commenced by filing an application form, a statement of grounds and the relevant fee. There is now a single application form for all applications.[803] The statement of grounds must contain a concise statement of the facts on which the applicant relies, state the statutory provision under which the application is made, where appropriate include the terms of payment or terms of licence which the applicant believes to be unreasonable and specify the relief sought; the grounds must be verified by a statement of truth.[804] Fees remain low by comparison with High Court fees.[805] An application may be amended or withdrawn but only with the permission of the Tribunal, which may impose such terms as it thinks fit.[806] If permission to amend is granted, the Tribunal must give such further or consequential directions as may be necessary.[807] If the application is withdrawn, the Tribunal may instruct the Secretary to publish notice of the withdrawal on the Tribunal website or in such manner as the Tribunal may direct;[808] any interim order (other than an order in respect of costs) shall immediately cease to have effect, unless the Tribunal directs otherwise.[809]

28–158   **Initial filtering process.** If the Tribunal considers that an application does not comply with r.7 (see the previous paragraph) or is materially incomplete, or is lacking in clarity, the Tribunal may give such directions as may be necessary to ensure that those defects are remedied.[810] The Tribunal may, if satisfied that the efficient conduct of the proceedings so requires, defer service on the respondent until such directions have been complied with.[811] The Tribunal also has a power to reject an application in whole or in part at any stage of the proceedings.[812] However, this power may only be exercised after giving the parties an opportunity

---

[800] r.3(1)

[801] r.3(2).

[802] r.3(2).

[803] See Sch.1 and rr.7(1)(a) and 2(1). The previous rules prescribed a multiplicity of application forms. The use of a single form for all proceedings was recommended in the Review (para.7.14).

[804] r.7(1)(b), 7(2). The object is the early identification of the issues: Consultation "Part II". A statement of truth is defined in the same way as in the Civil Procedure Rules. It must be signed by the party or his legal representative.

[805] The fees are set out in Sch.2. They vary between £15 and £50 depending on the application. The aim is not to discourage users: Consultation "Part I". The Review suggested that fees at the then existing levels (between £10 and £30) would not deter frivolous applications or contribute significantly to the costs of the Tribunal, would simply be viewed as an annoyance and ought to be abolished: para.7.15.

[806] rr.10 and 11.

[807] r.10(2).

[808] r.11(2)(b).

[809] r.11(3).

[810] r.8(1).

[811] r.8(2).

[812] r.9.

to be heard.[813] The application may be rejected if the Tribunal considers that[814]: it has no jurisdiction to hear the application; the applicant does not have a sufficient interest in the application or is not an organisation that is representation of a class or persons that have a sufficient interest in the application; in accordance with "relevant provision" of the 1988 Act[815] the application is premature; the application is an abuse of the Tribunal's process; or the application discloses no reasonable grounds for bringing the application. When the Tribunal rejects the application it may make any consequential orders it considers appropriate.[816]

Service of application and response. On receipt of an application, the Secretary must send an acknowledgement of its receipt to the applicant and (subject to the filtering process described in the previous paragraph) send a copy to the respondent which copy must be marked to show the date on which it is sent.[817] The respondent must send to the Secretary a response so as to arrive with 28 days (or such further time as the Tribunal may allow)[818] of the date on which the Secretary sent a copy of the application to the respondent.[819] The response must state the name and address of the respondent and its legal representatives if any and give an address for service in the EEA.[820] It must be signed and dated by the respondent or its duly authorised officer or legal representative.[821] It must contain a concise statement of the facts on which the respondent relies, any relief sought by the respondent and any directions the respondent seeks.[822] It must be supported by a statement of truth.[823] As with an application, if the response does not comply with the rules, is materially incomplete or lacking in clarity the Tribunal may give such directions as may be necessary to ensure those defects are remedied and defer service until such directions have been complied with.[824] A response may be amended, but only with the permission of the Tribunal, which may impose such terms as it thinks fit.[825] If permission to amend is granted, the Tribunal must give such further or consequential directions as may be necessary.[826]

28–159

Publication of application. Subject to any directions made by the Tribunal in the exercise of its powers to require defects in applications to be cured[827] and to the Tribunal's power to reject applications altogether, the Secretary must as soon as practicable upon receipt of the application publish a notice on the Tribunal website and in any other manner the Chairman may direct.[828] The notice must state that the application has been received, identify the section of the 1988 Act under which it is made, state the name of the applicant, state the particulars of the

28–160

---

[813] r.9(1).
[814] r.9(1)(a)–(e).
[815] i.e. ss.118(2), 125(2) or Sch.2A paras 3(2) or 10(2): see r.9(3).
[816] r.9(2).
[817] r.12.
[818] For provisions in the Rules about time, see r.40.
[819] r.13(2).
[820] r.13(2).
[821] See previous note.
[822] r.13(3).
[823] r.13(4). As to which see para.28–157, above.
[824] r.13(5) applying r.8.
[825] r.10(1), applied by r.13(5).
[826] r.10(2), applied by r.13(5).
[827] Presumably directions under r.8(1) might include a stay on publication pending cure of the defects.
[828] r.14(1).

relief sought, summarise the principal grounds relied on and set out the grounds on which and time within which a person may apply to intervene.[829]

28–161 **Intervention: general.** The Rule dealing with publication of the application states that the notice must include a statement that any person may apply to intervene if he has a substantial interest in the proceedings, objects to the application on the basis that the applicant does not have a sufficient interest in them or objects to the application on the basis that the applicant is not representative of a class of persons that have a sufficient interest in the application.[830] These grounds are stated as alternatives. However, the rule relating to intervention[831] states that a person with a substantial interest in the outcome of the proceedings may make a request to intervene, without referring to persons who object that the applicant does not have sufficient interest or is not representative.[832] It goes on to say that the Tribunal may permit the intervention if satisfied that the intervening party has a substantial interest.[833] It follows that it is necessary to have "a substantial interest" before any application to intervene may be made.

28–162 **Intervention: procedure.** The request to intervene must be sent to the Secretary within 28 days of the publication of the notice.[834] The request must state the title of the proceedings, the name and address of the person wishing to intervene and of any legal representative, an address for service in the EEA, the facts on which the person wishing to intervene relies and the relief sought.[835] The request must be verified by a statement of truth and accompanied by the relevant fee.[836] The Secretary must then notify the respondent and all other parties and invite representations within a specified period.[837] Having taken into account the parties' observations, the Tribunal may permit the intervention if satisfied that the intervening party has a substantial interest.[838] If permission is granted, the Tribunal will give all consequential directions it considers necessary with regard in particular to service of documents on the intervener, submission by the intervener of a statement of intervention and (if appropriate) the submission by the principal parties of a response to that statement.[839]

28–163 **Statement of intervention and response.** The statement and any response must contain a concise statement of the facts supporting the intervention or response and any relief sought by the intervener or the party responding.[840] It must be supported by a statement of truth.[841] If the statement or response does not comply with the rules, is materially incomplete or lacking in clarity the Tribunal may give such directions as may be necessary to ensure those defects are remedied.[842] A response may be amended but only with the permission of the Tribunal, which

---

[829] r.14(2).
[830] r.14(2)(f).
[831] r.15.
[832] r.15(1).
[833] r.15(6).
[834] r.16(2). This time period can presumably be extended under r.20(3)(m).
[835] r.15(4).
[836] r.15(5).
[837] r.15(2).
[838] r.15(6).
[839] r.15(7).
[840] r.15(8).
[841] r.15(9); see para.28–157 above.
[842] r.8(1), applied by r.15(10). Presumably r.8(2) does not apply because service is by the intervener/respondent.

may impose such terms as it thinks fit.[843] If permission to amend is granted, the Tribunal must give such further or consequential directions as may be necessary.[844]

Allocation. The authors of the Review did not explain how they envisaged that the allocation provisions in the Civil Procedure Rules and Practice Directions would be adapted to cover cases before the Tribunal.[845] The Rules provide for two "tracks": a "small applications track" and a "standard applications track".[846] They require the Tribunal, when making an allocation, to have regard to: the financial value of the application to each of the parties; whether the facts, legal issues, relief requested or procedures involved are simple or complex; and the importance of the outcome of the application to other licensees or putative licensees.[847] In addition, there is a presumption in favour of the small applications track when the financial value is less than £50,000 to each party and the facts and legal issues are "simple".[848] In all other cases there is a presumption in favour of the standard track.[849] The rules do not require the Tribunal to receive representations as to allocation although it could do so.[850] However, the allocation once made may be changed on the request of a party or on the Tribunal's own initiative, in each case applying the criteria referred to above.[851]

28–164

Consolidation. Where two or more applications relate to the same scheme or proposed scheme or involve the same or similar issues, the Tribunal may on its own initiative or on request order that the proceedings or particular issues or matters be consolidated or heard together.[852] The Tribunal must invite observations from the parties before making such an order.[853]

28–165

Case management: general. In determining applications, the Tribunal is required actively to exercise specified procedural powers with a view to ensuring that the application is dealt with justly.[854] The Tribunal may in particular encourage and facilitate the use of alternative dispute resolution and dispense with the need for the parties to attend any hearing.[855]

28–166

Case management: small applications. Rule 21 provides that as soon as possible after an allocation is made the Tribunal shall give directions and notify the parties of the date on which the decision shall be delivered. The rules do not require the Tribunal to receive representations as to directions although it could do so.[856] If a party requests a hearing or the Tribunal considers that one is required, the Tribunal must give directions (which may include directions for a case management conference or a pre-hearing review), fix a date for the hearing

28–167

---

[843] r.10(1), applied by r.15(10).
[844] r.10(2), applied by r.15(10).
[845] para.7.12.
[846] r.17(1).
[847] r.17(2). According to the Consultation (under "Part V") the last of these criteria follows from the requirement in s.129 of the 1988 Act that the Tribunal must exercise its powers so as to ensure that there is no unreasonable discrimination between licensees. If an application by an individual has implications for many other licensees the small track might well be inappropriate.
[848] r.17(3).
[849] r.17(4).
[850] Under r.43.
[851] r.18.
[852] r.16(1).
[853] r.16(2).
[854] r.19(1). The powers are those relating to consolidation, allocation, change of track, directions, procedure for small applications, case management of standard applications, evidence of fact, expert evidence, summoning of witnesses and failure to comply with directions.
[855] r.19(2).
[856] Under r.43.

and notify the parties in writing of the date, time and place of the hearing.[857] This appears to give a party a right to a hearing if it wants one. If the Tribunal gives directions leading to a hearing, the rules for case management conferences in standard applications apply.[858]

28–168   **Case management: standard applications.** Unless the Tribunal directs otherwise, a case management conference must be held as soon as possible after allocation.[859] In addition, where it appears to it that any proceedings would be facilitated by holding a case management conference or pre-hearing review, the Tribunal may on its own initiative or on request direct that there be one.[860] A case management conference or pre-hearing review will be held in private unless the Tribunal directs otherwise.[861] According to the Rules, the purpose of a case management conference is to ensure the efficient conduct of the proceedings; to determine the points on which the parties must present further argument or which call for further evidence; to clarify the forms of order sought by the parties, their arguments of fact and law and the points at issue between then; to ensure that all agreements that can be reached between the parties about the matters in issue and the conduct of the proceedings are made and recorded; to facilitate settlement; to set a timetable outlining the steps to be taken by the parties pursuant to directions in preparation for the oral hearing of the proceedings; and to set the dates within which the hearing shall take place.[862]

28–169   **Directions: general.** At a case management conference, pre-hearing review, application for appeal or otherwise, the Tribunal may, on request or on its own initiative, give directions of the type listed in r.20(3) or such other directions as it thinks fit to secure the just, expeditious and economical conduct of the proceedings. The matters which may be directed under r.20(3) are as follows: the manner of conduct of the proceedings, including the imposition of time limits on oral hearings; the provision of further statements or particulars; the determination of preliminary issues; striking out, dismissal or stay; skeleton arguments; witness summonses and summonses to produce documents[863]; evidence and whether it should be oral or written[864]; submission of witness statements or expert reports[865]; cross-examination; the fixing, extension or abridgement of time limits; disclosure of documents; expert evidence; restrictions on the use of documents disclosed in the proceedings; costs; and the hearing of non-parties in relation to whom orders or directions are proposed to be made. Requests for directions must be made in writing as soon as practicable and will be served by the Secretary on any other party who might be affected.[866] In determining them the Tribunal will take into account the observations of the parties.[867] Failure to comply with directions may lead to a party being debarred from taking further part in the proceedings without the permission of the Tribunal.[868]

---

[857] r.21(3).
[858] See below, para.28–168.
[859] r.22(3).
[860] r.22(2).
[861] r.22(4).
[862] r.22(5).
[863] More detail on this power is given in r.26.
[864] See para.28–171, below.
[865] See para.28–171, below.
[866] r.20(5).
[867] r.20(5).
[868] r.27.

Procedural powers of the Tribunal acting on its own initiative.[869] The authors   **28–170**
of the Review strongly favoured greater intervention by the Tribunal[870] and this
approach was endorsed in the Consultation.[871] Accordingly, the Rules expressly
provide that the Tribunal may, in particular, of its own initiative put questions to
the parties, invite written or oral submissions on certain aspects of the proceedings, ask the parties or other persons for information or particulars, ask for documents or any papers relating to the case to be produced and summon the parties'
representatives or the parties in person to meetings.[872]

Evidence. The high costs of Tribunal proceedings have been a source of concern   **28–171**
since before the passing of the 1988 Act[873] and the Rules seek to grapple with the
problem by empowering the Tribunal to control the amount of evidence adduced
by the parties. As to evidence of fact the Tribunal is empowered to direct the issues on which evidence is required, the nature of the evidence required to decide
those issues and the way in which the evidence is to be placed before the
Tribunal.[874] In addition, the Tribunal is empowered to exclude otherwise admissible evidence if it was not provided within the time allowed by a direction; if it
was provided in a manner which did not comply with a direction; if it would be
unfair to admit it; if it is not proportionate to the issues in the case; or if it is not
necessary for the fair disposal of the case.[875] The Tribunal may direct that evidence is given by statement rather than orally and by video link.[876] There are also
controls on expert evidence.[877] It may only be adduced with permission.[878] Any
permission will be limited to a named expert and to a named field and specified
issues.[879] Expert evidence is to be restricted to that which is proportionate to the
issues in the case and necessary for the fair disposal of the case.[880] The Tribunal
may limit the fees and expenses of an expert that can be recovered from the parties who did not instruct the expert.[881]

Interim orders and awards. The Rules permit the Tribunal to order on a provi-   **28–172**
sional basis any relief which it would have power to grant in a final decision.[882]

The hearing. There are few rules in relation to the conduct of the hearing, as to   **28–173**
which the Tribunal has a very broad discretion. The rules are as follows[883]: the
proceedings must be opened and directed by the Chairman, who is responsible
for the conduct of the hearing; the Tribunal must so far as appropriate seek to
avoid formality; the Tribunal must conduct the hearing in such manner as it
considers most appropriate "for the clarification of the issues before it and gener-

---

[869] r.20(4).
[870] See recommendations 7–11 (p.5).
[871] See under "General observations" and "Case management".
[872] r.20(4).
[873] See, e.g. the 1986 White Paper, Cmnd.9712 para.18.19; Report para.7.34; Consultation p.10;
Universities UK v Copyright Licensing Agency Ltd (CT 71/00 etc.), [2002] R.P.C. 36; [2002]
E.M.L.R. 35 paras 13–16; *The British Phonographic Industry Ltd v Mechanical-Copyright
Protection Society Ltd* (CT 84–90/05), [2008] E.M.L.R. 5 at paras 11 and 284.
[874] r.24(1).
[875] r.24(2).
[876] r.24(3) and (4).
[877] Under the previous rules the Tribunal held that the principles relating to experts' duties to the
court applied equally in the Tribunal: *The British Phonographic Industry Ltd v Mechanical-
Copyright Protection Society Ltd* (CT 84–90/05) [2008] E.M.L.R. 5 at paras 107–108. Presumably the same principles apply under the 2010 Rules.
[878] r.25(2).
[879] r.25(4); these must be specified in the application to adduce the evidence: r.25(3).
[880] r.25(1).
[881] r.25(5).
[882] r.35.
[883] r.29.

ally to the just, expeditious and economical handling of the proceedings"; unless the Tribunal otherwise directs, no evidence may be adduced unless a written statement or report has been submitted in advance of the hearing in accordance with directions; and the Tribunal may limit cross-examination to any extent or in any manner it deems appropriate.

28–174   **The decision and order.** Decisions must be in writing and reasoned. They must be served on every party and published in such manner as is considered appropriate.[884] There is a slip rule.[885] Orders take effect from and remain in force for such period as is specified in them.[886] The Tribunal may make more than one award at different times on different aspects of the matters to be determined.[887] In England and Wales and Northern Ireland decisions may be enforced by leave of court in the same manner as a judgment or order of the court to the same effect.[888]

28–175   **Incidence of costs.** In accordance with s.151(1) of the 1988 Act, the Rules provide that the Tribunal may, at its discretion, at any stage of the proceedings, make any order it thinks fit in relation to the payment of costs by one party to another in respect of the whole or part of the proceedings. This seems to continue the previous practice, under which the Tribunal's jurisdiction as to costs differed from that of the courts in two important respects. First, there was no general rule that the unsuccessful party should pay the successful party's costs. Second, the breadth of the Tribunal's discretion meant that the outcome was often one in which there was no clear winner or loser. Accordingly, there was far more room for flexibility in relation to costs in the Tribunal than in the ordinary courts.[889] In Practice Directions made before the introduction of the 2010 Rules, the Tribunal warned that it would consider exercising its power to award costs against any party which it considered responsible for undue prolixity in its evidence at the hearing. It also stated that, whilst it was not the Tribunal's practice that in all cases costs would follow the event, the fact that a party's case might have been unreasonably maintained would be an important factor in considering the exercise of its discretion as to costs.[890] The Tribunal further stated that offers "without prejudice as to costs"[891] would be considered in relation to any application for costs.[892] It is expected that these practices will continue.

28–176   **Amount of costs.** The Tribunal has the power to direct a party to pay any other party a lump sum by way of costs "or such proportion of the costs as may be just" and in the latter case may assess the sum to be paid or direct that it be assessed or, where appropriate, taxed by the Chairman, a costs officer of the High Court, the Master (Taxing Office) of the High Court of Northern Ireland or the Auditor of the Court of Session.[893]

28–177   **Appeal to the Court on point of law.** Under the 1956 Act[894] any question of law arising in the course of proceedings before the PRT could be referred by the PRT,

---

[884] r.30.
[885] r.42.
[886] r.32.
[887] r.36.
[888] r.37. In Scotland they are enforceable in the same way as a recorded decree arbitral: r.38.
[889] *AEI Rediffusion Music Ltd v Phonographic Performance Ltd* [1999] 1 W.L.R. 1507.
[890] See *Practice Direction 1995* as amended, para.16.
[891] So-called "*Calderbank*" letters, following the procedure commended by the Court of Appeal in *Calderbank v Calderbank* [1976] Fam. 93.
[892] *Practice Direction* para.17.
[893] r.31(2).
[894] Copyright Act 1956 s.30.

at the request of any party, to the High Court[895] for decision, whether before or after the PRT gave its decision in the proceedings. The procedure was by way of case stated.[896] The legislature did not adopt this approach in the 1988 Act,[897] which makes provision for an appeal to the High Court on any point of law arising from a decision of the Copyright Tribunal.[898] Such an appeal can therefore be made only after the Copyright Tribunal has made a decision, and the Court has no power to refuse to entertain the appeal.[899] The Rules provide that an appeal must be brought within 28 days of the date of decision or within such further period as the court may, on application to it, allow.[900] Notice must be served on the Secretary (accompanied by the relevant fee) and the other parties.[901] The appeal itself is a "statutory appeal" as defined in para.17 of Practice Direction 52. The procedure is therefore governed by CPR Pt 52 as modified by para.17.[902]

Stay pending appeal. The Rules provide that unless the Tribunal orders otherwise an appeal does not operate as a stay of any decision or order.[903] However, as is permitted by s.152(3)(a) of the 1988 Act, the Rules provide that the Tribunal may suspend the operation of any order on its own initiative[904] or by endorsing a consent order.[905] It seems to follow from the use of the phrase "unless the Tribunal orders otherwise" that the Tribunal also has the power to suspend the operation of an order on a contested application.[906] Notice of a suspension will be served on all parties and, if particulars of the order have been advertised on the Tribunal's website, the notice must be so advertised as well.[907] **28–178**

Approach of the court on appeal. An appeal lies only on a point of law.[908] Since the Tribunal is a specialist tribunal created by Parliament specifically for the **28–179**

---

[895] In Scotland, the Court of Session.

[896] Copyright Act 1956 s.30(5); and see rr.19 to 21 of the Performing Right Tribunal Rules 1965 (as amended) and *Copinger* 12th edn, paras 1776–1778.

[897] In the light of representations made by the Council on Tribunals. See *Meltwater Holding BV v NLA Ltd* (CT 114/09), March 18, 2010 at para.51.

[898] CDPA 1988 s.152. There is no restriction on further appeals from the decision of the Court. A decision for these purposes includes, it would seem, an interim decision. Appeals under s.152 on a point of law have been made to the High Court in *The Performing Right Society Limited v British Entertainment and Dancing Association* [1993] E.M.L.R. 325; *AEI Rediffusion Music Limited v Phonographic Performance Ltd* [1999] E.M.L.R. 129, (costs; appeal to the Court of Appeal dismissed: [1999] 1 W.L.R. 1507); *Phonographic Performance Ltd v Virgin Retail Ltd* [2001] E.M.L.R. 139; *Phonographic Performance Ltd v Candy Rock Recording Ltd* [1999] E.M.L.R. 806; *Phonographic Performance Ltd v The British Hospitality Association* [2008] EWHC 2715 (Ch); [2009] R.P.C. 7 (appeal on jurisdiction; as to the costs of this appeal see [2009] EWHC 175 (Ch)) and [2009] EWHC 209 (Ch) (appeal on substantive decision); and *CSC Media Group Ltd v Video Performance Ltd* [2010] EWHC 2094 (Ch).

[899] Under the 1956 Act, a case could be stated on a point of law at any time in the proceedings, and the Court could refuse to entertain the reference where the PRT refused to state a case (but see *AIRC Ltd v Phonographic Performance Ltd* [1983] F.S.R. 637).

[900] Copyright Tribunal Rules 2010 (SI 2010/791) rr.33(1) and 34, Vol.2 B1.i.

[901] r.33(2).

[902] para.17 provides that the time for filing the appellant's notice is 28 days after the date of the decision (para.17.3) or, where a statement of reasons is given later than the notice of the decision, 28 days after that statement is received by the appellant (para.17.4). However, such a time lag should not occur because the decision is to include reasons: Copyright Tribunal Rules 2010 r.30(1). Para.17.5 provides that as well as serving the appellant's notice on the respondent, the appellant must serve it on the Chairman of the Tribunal. This requirement seems unnecessary in view of r.33(2) of the Copyright Tribunal Rules which requires a copy of the notice of appeal to be served on the Secretary to the Tribunal.

[903] r.34(1).

[904] r.33(3).

[905] r.34(2). The relevant fee must be paid.

[906] See also Consultation under "Part IX": "a decision to suspend … requires either the consent of all parties or a hearing".

[907] r.34(4), (5).

[908] *Phonographic Performance Ltd v The British Hospitality Association* [2009] EWHC 209 (Ch) at para.77.

purposes of regulating collective copyright licensing, the court will approach appeals with an appropriate degree of caution: it is probable that in understanding and applying the law in its specialist field the Tribunal will have got it right.[909] Errors of law include misinterpretation of a statute or other legal document or a rule of common law; asking oneself or answering the wrong question; taking irrelevant considerations into account or failing to take relevant considerations into account when purporting to apply the law to the facts[910]; giving reasons which disclose faulty legal reasoning or which are inadequate to fulfil any express duty to give reasons; and making a finding unsupported by any evidence.[911] The issue is not whether the court agrees with the Tribunal's conclusions but whether as a matter of law the Tribunal was entitled to reach them. Accordingly, the appeal is not just another hearing of the self-same issue what was decided by the Tribunal.[912] Many of the questions faced by the Tribunal are of fact and degree. For example, there lies a "no man's land" where it is for the Tribunal to evaluate whether a prior agreement or decision is an appropriate comparator or not. The court can only interfere where the degree of fact is so inclined towards one frontier or the other as to lead it to believe that there is only one conclusion to which the Tribunal could reasonably have come.[913] Likewise, in so far as an appeal is in respect of the amount of royalty determined by the Copyright Tribunal, establishing an error of law is likely to be difficult. If the Tribunal has expressly directed itself in accordance with the requirement to make such order as is reasonable[914] then it will only have erred in law if it did something which no Tribunal, if it thought about the matter, could have regarded as reasonable. Such irrationality could be shown either if the royalty fixed by the Tribunal was so large or so small that no rational Tribunal could have arrived at such a figure, or if the reasons given by the Tribunal disclosed some non sequitur which invalidated its reasoning,[915] or if there was no evidential basis for an essential factual finding.[916]

5. COMPETITION LAW AND THE EXERCISE OF COPYRIGHT AND OTHER RIGHTS COVERED IN THIS WORK

28–180　　**Introduction.** This section considers the restraints which are imposed on the free exercise of copyright and other rights covered in this work by competition law and related legislative and common law rules, dealing first with European Community competition law and then with UK competition law. The common law doctrine of restraint of trade is dealt with in the next section.[917] The restraint

---

[909] *Phonographic Performance Ltd v The British Hospitality Association* [2009] EWHC 209 (Ch) at para.80, adopting dicta of Baroness Hale in *AH (Sudan) v Secretary of State for the Home Department* [2007] UKHL 49; [2008] 1 A.C. 678 at para.30.

[910] It is not however necessary for the Tribunal to mention expressly every relevant matter that has been placed before it: *Phonographic Performance Ltd v Candy Rock Recording Ltd* [1999] E.M.L.R. 806 at 822.

[911] 1 *Halsbury's Laws* 4th edn, para.70 applied by Scott V.-C. in *Phonographic Performance Ltd v Candy Rock Recording Ltd* [1999] E.M.L.R. 806 at 812.

[912] *Phonographic Performance Ltd v The British Hospitality Association* [2009] EWHC 209 (Ch) at para.81, adopting dicta of Mummery L.J. in *Commissioners for Her Majesty's Revenue and Customs v Procter & Gamble (UK) Ltd* [2009] EWCA Civ 407; [2009] S.T.C. 1990.

[913] *Phonographic Performance Ltd v Virgin Retail Ltd* [2001] E.M.L.R. 139 at para.16.

[914] See paras 28–110 et seq., above.

[915] *The Performing Right Society v British Entertainment and Dancing Association* [1993] E.M.L.R. 325 at 330, per Hoffmann J.

[916] As was found in *Phonographic Performance Ltd v Virgin Retail Ltd* [2001] E.M.L.R. 139 at para.38.

[917] paras 28–330 et seq.

imposed on the free exercise of copyright and related rights by the Community law principle of free movement of goods and services is dealt with elsewhere.[918]

A. EUROPEAN COMMUNITY COMPETITION LAW

Introduction. As is discussed elsewhere,[919] the principal aims of the European Union require the establishment within the Union of a common market, and this in turn requires the removal of all obstacles to the free movement of goods, persons, services and capital within the territory of the European Union, and therefore across the boundaries of the Member States. Such obstacles may be caused by the trading activities of undertakings which seek to restrict competition and isolate national markets. The institution of a system which ensures that competition within the common market is not distorted in this way is one of the primary activities which the Community is charged by the Treaty on the Functioning of the European Union ("TFEU") to undertake. Articles 101 to 109 of the Treaty, comprising Ch.1 (the Rules on Competition) of Title VII of the Treaty, are the specific provisions directed at achieving this. Of this Chapter of the Treaty, arts 101 and 102 in s.1 (the rules applying to undertakings), are the most important for present purposes. This section of the work discusses these articles and their application to the exercise of copyright and the other rights covered in this work.

28–181

Nomenclature. With effect from December 1, 2009, arts 101 and 102 of the TFEU replaced arts 81 and 82 of the Treaty of Rome which were in identical terms. Articles 81 and 82 of the Treaty of Rome were renumbered in 1997 having previously been numbered 85 and 86. For ease of exposition, references in this section to arts 101 and 102 include references to their predecessor articles where appropriate. Changes of name have also affected the European Court of Justice (now simply Court of Justice) and the Court of First Instance (now the General Court). Again, for ease of exposition, present day terminology is used throughout.

28–182

International obligations. At the 1967 Stockholm revision conference in relation to the Berne Convention, the UK Government put forward a proposal to amend art.17 of the Convention to make express provision for abuse of monopoly by owners of substantial numbers of copyrights. This proposal was withdrawn upon it being accepted in principle that nothing in the Convention prevented members from taking action against abuse of monopoly.[920] In *Magill*, the Court of Justice rejected a submission to the effect that the grant of a compulsory copyright licence as a remedy for an abusive failure to license was contrary to the Berne Convention. The Court observed that the Community was not a party to that convention, and noted that provisions of an international agreement entered into before the Treaty could not be relied on if the rights of non-Member States were not involved. More recently, the General Court has held that international agreements (such as TRIPS) do not prevail over primary Community law, such as art.102.[921] By contrast, where a Community measure expressly implements or refers to an international agreement the Community judicature is obliged to review the legality of the measure in the light of the agreement.[922]

28–183

---

[918] See Ch.24.
[919] See Ch.24.
[920] Ricketson & Ginsburg, *International Copyright and Neighbouring Rights* (2006), para.13.92.
[921] *Microsoft* (T–201/04) paras 798 and 1190.
[922] *Microsoft* (T–201/04) para.802. See also para.1192 where the Court stated that there is nothing in TRIPS which prevents members of the WTO from limiting or regulating the exercise of intellectual property rights when they are exercised in a anti-competitive manner.

(i) Article 101: general

28–184   **General.** Article 101 comprises three paragraphs: art.101(1) prohibits certain restrictive agreements; art.101(2) declares prohibited agreements to be void; and art.101(3) provides for exemption in certain cases of individual agreements or types of agreements from the prohibition in art.101(1). The Court of Justice has held that art.101 aims to protect not only the interests of competitors or of consumers, but also the structure of the market and, in so doing, competition as such. Consequently, it is not necessary to find that final consumers are deprived of the advantages of effective competition in terms of supply or price before a finding that an agreement has an anti-competitive object can be made.[923] Article 101 is effectively reproduced in art.53 of the EEA Agreement[924] with respect to restrictive agreements that may affect trade between the EEA States.[925]

28–185   **Agreements, decisions and concerted practices.** Article 101(1) applies to agreements, decisions and concerted practices. The definitions of "agreement", "decisions by associations of undertakings" and "concerted practice" are intended, from a subjective point of view, to catch forms of collusion having the same nature which are distinguishable from each other only by their intensity and the forms in which they manifest themselves.[926] Accordingly, there is little need to draw any hard-and-fast line between these concepts, which often overlap.[927] An "agreement" may be oral.[928] It need not be legally binding, but can consist of an informal understanding between the parties.[929] It may also exist, for the purposes of art.101(1), in the terms of a compromise of legal proceedings brought by the owner of an industrial property right for the enforcement of such right.[930] An example of a "decision" is a regulation imposed on its members by a professional body or an association of right holders.[931] A "concerted practice" will exist where there is no agreement between undertakings, but where undertakings by one means or another have reached the stage where they are knowingly co-ordinating their behaviour so as to substitute practical co-operation between them for the risks of competition.[932]

28–186   **Apparently unilateral behaviour.** What at first sight appears to be unilateral conduct may, particularly in the context of distribution arrangements, turn out on analysis to infringe art.101(1).[933] Thus, if an undertaking chooses to operate a selective distribution system (for example, where dealers are appointed only if (a) they satisfy certain criteria and (b) they agree not to supply to dealers outside the authorised network), the undertaking's decisions as to whom it is prepared to

---

[923] Joined cases C'–501/06P etc., *GlaxoSmithKline Services Unlimited v Commission* para.63.

[924] The Agreement on the European Economic Area, signed at Oporto on May 2, 1992, as adjusted by the Protocol signed at Brussels on March 17, 1993.

[925] That is to say, the 27 Member States of the EU and Iceland, Liechtenstein and Norway (that is to say all the EFTA States other than Switzerland, which decided not to take part in the EEA).

[926] *T-Mobile Netherlands BV v Raad van bestuur van de Nederlandse Mededingingsautoriteit* (Case C–8/08), para.23.

[927] See, e.g. the remarks of Advocate General Reischl in *Van Landewyck v Commission* (Case 209/78) [1980] E.C.R. 3125 at 3310; [1981] 3 C.M.L.R. 134.

[928] e.g. *Tepea v Commission* (Case 28/77) [1978] E.C.R. 1391; [1978] 3 C.M.L.R. 392.

[929] e.g. Case 41/69 *ACF Chemiefarma v Commission* [1970] E.C.R. 661, grounds 110–114.

[930] *Nungesser v Commission* (Case 258/78) [1982] E.C.R. 2015, grounds 82–89; [1983] 1 C.M.L.R. 278.

[931] *Wouters v Algemene Raad van de Nederlandse Orde van Advocaten* (Case C309/99) [2002] E.C.R. I–01577. See also Commission Decision 93/403 *EBU/Eurovision System*: non-binding rules and recommendations of an association of broadcasting organisations which were generally followed constituted a "decision".

[932] *ICI v Commission* (Case 48/69) [1972] E.C.R. 619, para.64; [1972] C.M.L.R. 557 ("Dyestuffs").

[933] For a summary by the English Court of Appeal of the European cases in this area, see *Argos Ltd v OFT* [2006] EWCA Civ 1318; [2006] U.K.C.L.R. at para.21.

admit to its dealer network may be considered as part of the agreement between the undertaking and its dealers, and, therefore, as potentially falling under art.101(1).[934] In another case, a supplier who stamped "Not for export" on invoices to his dealers was held to infringe art.101(1), as the dealers tended to comply with that indication.[935] However, where a supplier refused to supply dealers with as much product as they wanted on the ground that some of what they wanted would be exported but the dealers, while reducing their orders, continued to do their best to export what they could, there was no agreement within art.101(1) because there was no relevant "concurrence of wills", nor was there any tacit acquiescence by the dealers in anti-competitive practices on the part of the suppliers.[936]

Undertakings. There is no definition of the term "undertaking" in the treaty. **28–187** However, it has been held that every entity engaged in economic activity is an undertaking, regardless of its legal status or how it is funded.[937] Sole traders may be undertakings.[938] However, an employee of an undertaking, being incorporated into and forming an economic unit with it, cannot himself be an undertaking.[939] Non-profit-making organisations may be undertakings.[940] The question is whether the entity is an undertaking for the purposes of carrying on the activity in issue.[941] Accordingly, state corporations may be undertakings, but not in so far as they are exercising what are essentially the sovereign functions of the state.[942]

Single economic entity. Two or more legal persons may be treated as a single **28–188** undertaking if they form part of the same economic unit. If the only parties to an agreement that engage in economic activity are all part of a single undertaking, art.101(1) will not apply, as the conduct is essentially unilateral. The test for determining whether one company is part of the same economic unit as another is whether that company enjoys real autonomy in determining its course of action in the market, or whether it carries out the instructions of its parent company.[943] The Commission can generally assume that a wholly-owned subsidiary essentially follows the instructions given to it by its parent company without need-

---

[934] *AEG v Commission* (Case 107/82) [1983] E.C.R. 3151; [1984] 3 C.M.L.R. 325.

[935] *Sandoz v Commission* (Case C–277/87) [1990] E.C.R. I–45.

[936] *Bayer v Commission* [2000] E.C.R. II–3383; [2001] 4 C.M.L.R. 126 (CFI); upheld on appeal: Joined Cases C–2/01P and C–3/01P *Bundesverband der Arzneimittel-Importeure eV v Commission*, January 6, 2004. See Stothers, "Who Needs Intellectual Property? Competition Law and Restrictions on Parallel Trade within the European Economic Area" [2005] 12 E.I.P.R. 458.

[937] See, e.g. *Höfner v Macroton GmbH* (C–41/90) [1991] E.C.R. I–1979; [1994] C.M.L.R. 306 at para.21. See also, *Federación Española de Empresas de Tecnología Sanitaria (FENIN) v Commission* (C–205/03 P) [2006] 5 C.M.L.R. 7, para.25, emphasising that it is the activity consisting in offering goods and services on a given market which is the characteristic feature of an economic activity. The term undertaking includes individuals such as authors, artists, artistes, inventors and plant breeders: *Re Unitel* [1978] OJ L157/39; [1978] 3 C.M.L.R. 306; *A.O.I.P. v Beyrard* [1976] OJ L6/8; [1976] 1 C.M.L.R. D14; *H. Vaessen B.V. v Alex Morris* [1979] OJ L19/32; [1979] 1 C.M.L.R. 511; *Nungesser v Commission* (Case 258/78) [1982] E.C.R. 2015; [1983] 1 C.M.L.R. 278. A performer's service company is, of course, an undertaking for these purposes: *Panayiotou v Sony Music Entertainment (UK) Ltd* [1994] E.M.L.R. 229, para.B1.

[938] e.g. *COAPI* [1995] OJ L122/37 (Spanish intellectual property agents).

[939] e.g. *Becu* (Case C–22/98) [1999] E.C.R. I–5665, [2001] 4 C.M.L.R. 968.

[940] e.g. *Fédération Française des Sociétés d'Assurance* (C–244/94) [1995] E.C.R. I–4013 (organisation entrusted with managing a voluntary State supplementary old-age insurance scheme).

[941] When this involves the purchase of goods, the question whether the purchasing activity amounts to an economic one depends on the purpose for which the goods are to be used: *P FENIN* (C–205/01) [2003] E.C.R. I–6295.

[942] e.g. *Eurocontrol* (C–364/92) [1994] E.C.R. I–43 and *SELEX Sistemi Integrati SpA v Commission* (T–155/04) [2007] 4 C.M.L.R. 10; note that the activities of State entities are to some extent protected against the application of the competition rules by art.106(2) of the Treaty, which lies outside the scope of this work.

[943] *Centrafarm v Sterling Drug* (Case 15/74) [1974] E.C.R. 1147; [1974] 2 C.M.L.R. 480; *Viho Europe v Commission* (C–73/95P) [1997] 4 C.M.L.R. 419 at 450.

ing to check whether the parent company has in fact exercised that power.[944] An agent too may be considered to be part of the same economic unit as its principal for these purposes.[945]

28–189   **Object or effect of preventing, distorting, or restricting competition within the common market: general.** Examples of the types of restrictions that fall within art.101(1) are given in sub-paras (a) to (e) of art.101(1). These restrictions, which are often known as the "hardcore" restrictions, can be broadly summarised as terms fixing selling prices or conditions, limiting or controlling production, sharing markets, applying dissimilar conditions to equivalent transactions and tying the other party to extraneous obligations. However, this list is expressly not exhaustive. The issue of what restrictions will be regarded as having the object or effect of preventing, distorting, or restricting competition[946] under art.101(1) is the most complex question in Community competition law, and it is beyond the scope of this work to examine it in detail. However, in the context of intellectual property rights generally, and the rights covered in this work in particular, a number of points can be made.

28–190   **Distinction between horizontal and vertical agreements.** Although the distinction defies precise legal definition, horizontal agreements are agreements between undertakings at the same level of trade, whereas vertical agreements are between undertakings at different levels of trade. In the present context, the best example of a vertical agreement would be a copyright licensing agreement between an author and a publisher. On the other hand, an agreement between publishers in different countries to grant each other licences in certain works in their respective countries would be regarded as a horizontal agreement, or as a mixed horizontal/vertical agreement. It has been clear since 1966 that art.101(1) applies to vertical as well as horizontal agreements,[947] but the distinction is still of importance in analysing the applicability of art.101(1).[948]

28–191   **The "object"/"effect"distinction.** Article 101 applies where the agreement either has as its object the prevention, restriction or distortion of competition or where that is its effect. These criteria are alternative.[949] Accordingly, the Court of Justice has held on numerous occasions that where an agreement can be shown to have an anti-competitive object, it is not necessary to prove in addition that it might have an anti-competitive effect.[950] By contrast, where such an object cannot be proved, it is necessary to show, usually by market analysis, that the agreement would have such an effect.[951] The "object" of an agreement is to be ascertained on an objective assessment of the aims of the agreement in question

---

[944] Joined Cases T–71/03, T–74/03, T–87/03 and T–91/03 *Tokai Carbon Co. Ltd v Commission (CFI)* [2005] C.M.L.R. 13.

[945] See e.g. T–325/01, *Daimler Chrysler AG v Commission (CFI)* [2007] 4 C.M.L.R. 215, paras 86–88.

[946] As to the meaning of "competition", see *Bookmakers' Afternoon Greyhound Services Ltd v Amalgamated Racing Ltd* [2008] EWHC 1978 (Ch) at paras 310–319.

[947] *Consten and Grundig v Commission* (Cases 56 & 58/64) [1966] E.C.R. 299; [1966] C.M.L.R. 418.

[948] See, for example, the Commission's notice on agreements of minor importance [2001] OJ C368/07, paras 7 to 9, where differing guidance is given as to the application of art.101(1) depending on whether the agreement is horizontal or vertical.

[949] *Société Technique Minière v Machinenbau Ulm* (Case 56/65) [1966] E.C.R. 235 at 249; [1966] C.M.L.R. 357 at 375.

[950] e.g. *Société Technique Minière v Machinenbau Ulm* (Case 56/65) [1966] E.C.R. 235 at 249; [1966] C.M.L.R. 357 at 375.

[951] *European Night Services v Commission* (T–374/94 etc.) [1998] E.C.R. II–3141; [1998] 5 C.M.L.R. 718, para.136.

and does not depend on the parties' subjective intentions,[952] although these may be taken into account.[953] In determining the object of an agreement, regard must be had amongst other things to the content of its provisions, the objectives it seeks to attain and the economic and legal context of which it forms a part.[954] In order for a concerted practice to infringe under this head it is sufficient that it has the potential to have a negative impact on competition. In other words, the concerted practice must simply be capable, in an individual case, having regard to the specific legal and economic context, of resulting in the prevention, restriction or distortion of competition within the common market.[955] It is generally considered that in any case there is only an infringement of art.101 if, in addition to meeting one of the criteria referred to above, the agreement appreciably affects competition *and* has an appreciable effect on trade between Member States.[956] Some analysis of the market may therefore be necessary even in a case where the agreement has been shown to have an anti-competitive object.[957] Finally, it should be said that even if all these criteria are satisfied, art.101 will not be infringed if it is declared inapplicable under art.101(3).[958]

Provisions which are intrinsically likely to have the object or effect of preventing, distorting, or restricting competition. Horizontal agreements to fix prices or to share out markets have consistently been held to have the object of preventing, distorting, or restricting competition. Similarly, vertical agreements that contain absolute restrictions on dealers supplying outside their allocated territories,[959] or which fix resale prices, have consistently been found to have such an object. Even where an agreement is between undertakings with such a low aggregate market share that the Commission would not usually hold an agreement between them to be capable of falling within art.101(1), an agreement containing such "hardcore" provisions may be held to have the object of preventing, distorting, or restricting competition.[960] Such restrictions are sometimes referred to as *"per se"* restrictions on competition. This term (which is derived from American anti-trust law) is acceptable shorthand provided that it is remembered: (a) that there is no restriction on competition that cannot be exempted under art.101(3)[961];

28–192

---

[952] See e.g. Cases 29/83 and 30/83 *Compagnie Royale Asturienne des Mines SA v Commission* [1984] E.C.R. 1679, para.26.

[953] Joined cases C–501/06P etc., *GlaxoSmithKline Services Unlimited v Commission* para.58.

[954] Joined cases C–501/06P etc., *GlaxoSmithKline Services Unlimited v Commission* para.58.

[955] *T-Mobile Netherlands BV v Raad van bestuur van de Nederlandse Mededingingsautoriteit* (C–8/08), para.31.

[956] See Whish, *Competition Law* 6th edn, p.117; Bellamy & Child, *European Community Law of Competition* 6th edn, paras 1.124 and 2.121. See however *Bpb Plc v Commission* (T–53/03), in which the General Court stated (at para.90) that "Undertakings which conclude an agreement whose purpose is to restrict competition cannot, in principle, avoid the application of art.[101(1)] by claiming that their agreement was not intended to have an appreciable effect on competition". For the requirements of appreciability, see paras 28–197 and 28–198 respectively, below.

[957] See Whish, *Competition Law* 6th edn, p.117.

[958] See para.28–200, below.

[959] In *Javico AG v Yves Saint Laurent Parfums SA* (C–306/96) [1999] Q.B. 477, the Court of Justice discussed the applicability of art.101(1) to a restriction imposed on a dealer based in the EEA requiring him to supply only in a territory outside the EEA. In essence, the Court held that, in contrast to the case where the territory was a part of the EEA, such a restriction was not intrinsically likely to contravene art.101(1), although it might do so if competition in the relevant market was limited in the EEA, there was a marked difference in prices between the EEA and outside it, and the volume of products covered by such a clause was not very small in comparison to the market for the products in the EEA. In the *Murphy* and *FAPL* cases questions as to whether an export ban on decoder cards infringed art.101 were referred to the Court of Justice. See paras 16–10 and 16–33, above.

[960] Notice on Agreements of Minor Importance [2001] OJ C368/07, para.11. See paras 28–195 et seq., below.

[961] *Matra Hachette v Commission* (T–17/93) [1994] E.C.R. II–595, para.85.

and (b) that if the effect of the restriction on competition or on trade between Member States is insignificant, there will be no contravention of art.101(1).[962]

28–193   **A balancing exercise?** It has been suggested that for the purposes of art.101(1) the decision maker should ask whether any anti-competitive effects of the agreement are counter-balanced by its pro-competitive aspects (the so-called "rule of reason"). The General Court has held that it is inappropriate to weigh the anti-competitive effects of the agreement against the pro-competitive effects at this stage of the analysis.[963] Rather, this exercise should be carried out later, when considering the applicability of art.101(3).[964] However, it has been suggested[965] that it is difficult to resolve the General Court's approach with earlier and later cases of the Court of Justice, including *Wouters*.[966]

28–194   **Market analysis.** The Court of First Instance has said that a full analysis of the relevant market is necessary before any finding can be made of anti-competitive behaviour under art.101 or art.102.[967] This proposition, however, has to be approached with caution in the context of art.101(1). If the parties to an agreement are clearly of a substantial size, or if the restriction in question is a so-called per se restriction, then it may not be necessary to conduct any detailed market analysis.[968] However, as has been said above, even so-called per se restrictions may be regarded as having no appreciable effect on competition if an analysis of the parties' positions on the relevant markets shows that they have insignificant market power.[969] Where the restrictions are not per se restrictions, an analysis of the parties' positions on the relevant market may reveal that they have an aggregate share of the market which is low enough to benefit from the presumptions in the Commission's notice on agreements of minor importance[970] (as to which, see below[971]). Moreover, market analysis has been held to be essential where it is alleged that the agreement in question has to be considered in the light of other similar agreements. The leading case on this point is *Delimitis v Henniger Bräu*.[972] In that case, the owner of a bar agreed to purchase his supplies of beer exclusively from one supplier. In analysing that restriction, the Court of Justice stated that it was first necessary to define the relevant market (being, in that case, "on-licence" beer), and then it was necessary to examine how far access to that market was foreclosed to potential new suppliers of beer for "on-licence" sale, taking account

---

[962] e.g. *Volk v Vervaecke* (Case 5/69) [1969] E.C.R. 295; [1969] C.M.L.R. 273, in which, since the supplier's market share was between 0.2 and 0.5 per cent, a provision conferring absolute territorial protection on a distributor did not contravene art.101(1). Note, though, that an agreement with an anti-competitive object, but which failed to achieve that object because it was not implemented properly, will be regarded as falling under art.81(1): *ICI v Commission* (T–13/89) [1992] E.C.R. II–1021, para.293.

[963] *Métropole Télévision v Commission* (T–112/99) [2001] E.C.R. II–2459; [2001] 5 C.M.L.R. 1236, para.72.

[964] *Métropole Télévision v Commission* (T–112/99) [2001] E.C.R. II–2459; [2001] 5 C.M.L.R. 1236, para.74.

[965] See *The Racecourse Association v OFT* [2005] CAT 29. For a contrary view, see Whish, *Competition Law* 6th edn, p.133.

[966] *Wouters v Algemene Raad van de Nederlandse Orde van Advocaten* [2002] ECR I–1577. See also Bellamy & Child, *European Community Law of Competition* 6th edn, para.2.091.

[967] *Società Italiana Vetro v Commission* (T–68/89, T–77/89 and T–78/89) [1992] E.C.R. II–1403, para.159.

[968] *Musique Diffusion Française v Commission* (Cases 100–103/80) [1983] E.C.R. 1825, para.87; [1983] 3 C.M.L.R. 221.

[969] *Volk v Vervaecke* (Case 5/69) [1969] E.C.R. 295; [1969] C.M.L.R. 273.

[970] [2001] OJ C368/13.

[971] paras 28–195 et seq., below.

[972] [1991] E.C.R. I–935; [1992] 5 C.M.L.R. 210 (C–234/89). This case was followed in the English case of *Crehan v Inntrepreneur Pub Company CPC* [2004] E.C.C. 28. See also the judgment of the House of Lords, [2006] UKHL 38; [2007] 1 A.C. 333, also following *Delimitis* but reinstating the Judge's original decision.

of the agreement in question and the other similar agreements between breweries and outlets. Finally, the Court stated that the agreement in question would only contravene art.101(1) if it significantly contributed to that foreclosure.

The Commission's notice on agreements of minor importance: general.[973]   **28–195**
The Court of Justice has consistently held that art.101(1) is not applicable unless there is an appreciable effect on competition. The purpose of this notice is to quantify, with the help of market share thresholds, what is not an appreciable restriction on competition. The notice is not concerned with the requirement that the agreement be shown to have an appreciable effect on trade between Member States. However, in the notice the Commission acknowledges that agreements between small and medium-sized undertakings[974] are rarely capable of appreciably affecting trade between Member States.[975] In cases covered by the notice, the Commission will not institute proceedings either on application or on its own initiative.[976] Where undertakings assume in good faith that an agreement is covered by the notice, the Commission will not impose fines.[977] Although not binding on them, the notice is intended to give guidance to the national courts and authorities.[978]

The Commission's notice on agreements of minor importance: specific   **28–196**
provisions. The notice applies to agreements between undertakings which affect trade between Member States.[979] Where such an agreement is between actual or potential competitors[980] on the relevant markets affected by the agreement, the Commission's view is that it will not appreciably restrict competition if the aggregate market share held by the parties does not exceed 10 per cent on any relevant market.[981] Where such an agreement is between non-competitors, it will not appreciably restrict competition if the market share held by each of the parties does not exceed 15 per cent on any relevant market.[982] Where it is difficult to classify the parties as competitors or non-competitors, the 10 per cent threshold applies.[983] Where, in a relevant market, competition is restricted by the cumulative effect of agreements for the sale of goods or services entered into by different suppliers or distributors,[984] the thresholds are both reduced to 5 per cent.[985] Agreements are also not restrictive of competition if they do not exceed the relevant

---

[973] [2001] OJ C368/13.

[974] Defined in the Notice as undertakings with fewer than 250 employees and either an annual turnover not exceeding EUR 40 million or an annual balance-sheet total not exceeding EUR 27 million. The appropriate figures are now EUR 50 million and 43 million respectively: Commission Recommendation of May 6, 2003 [2003] OJ L124/36.

[975] Notice, para.3.

[976] para.4.

[977] para.4.

[978] para.4. The Notice is without prejudice to any interpretation of art.101 which may be given by the Court of Justice or the Court of First Instance: para.6.

[979] para.7.

[980] An undertaking is an actual competitor if it is either active on the same relevant market or in the absence of the agreement it is able to switch production to the relevant products and market them in the short term without incurring significant additional costs or risks in response to a small and permanent increase in relative prices ("immediate supply-side substitutability"). An undertaking is a potential competitor if there is evidence that, absent the agreement, the firm could and would be likely to undertake the necessary additional investments or other necessary switching costs so that it could enter the relevant market in response to a small and permanent increase in relative prices: para.7, n.4, citing the Commission's guidelines on the applicability of art.101 to horizontal cooperation agreements [2001] OJ C 3/2, nn.8 and 9.

[981] para.7(a).

[982] para.7(b).

[983] para.7.

[984] This is called a "cumulative foreclosure effect of parallel networks of agreements having similar effects on the market". Individual suppliers or distributors with a market share not exceeding 5 per cent are not generally considered to contribute significantly to a such an effect. Furthermore,

threshold by two per cent during 2 successive years.[986] However, these provisions do not apply to agreements containing any of a list of "hardcore" restrictions. If the agreement is between competing undertakings, the hardcore restrictions may be summarised as follows: price fixing, the limitation of output or sales and the allocation of customers.[987] Between non-competing undertakings, they are (in summary): the restriction of the buyer's ability to determine its sale price (but genuine maximum and recommended prices are permitted), territorial restrictions (with significant exceptions), certain restrictions in relation to selective distribution systems and restrictions on a supplier's ability to sell components as spare parts.[988]

28–197   **Agreement contains restrictions but has no anti-competitive effects.** The Court of Justice has in some cases been prepared to regard prima facie restrictions on competition as not having an appreciable anti-competitive effect under art.101(1) because they are necessary to facilitate a commercial activity such as the penetration of a new market or the successful operation of a purchasing cooperative. In the present context, the best example of this approach is *Nungesser v Commission*.[989] The Court of Justice there held that an agreement by which the holder of certain plant breeder's rights granted Nungesser the exclusive right to produce and sell the relevant seeds in West Germany did not contravene art.101(1). The Court accepted that without such an agreement it would be commercially impossible to introduce the new seeds onto the West German market, and hence that the agreement promoted competition between the new seeds and existing products. However, the Court drew a clear distinction between that case, and a case where the agreement, or the parties' behaviour, sought to prevent any competition between the exclusive licensee and parallel exporters into the licensee's territory. More recently, in *Gøttrup-Klim v Dansk Landbrugs Grovvareselskab AmbA*,[990] a rule of a Danish agricultural purchasing co-operative that prevented members from joining other purchasing co-operatives was held not to contravene art.101(1) if it went no further than was necessary to maintain the position of the co-operative in relation to producers. An analogous approach was adopted in *Wouters v Algemene Raad van de Dederlandsche Orde van Advocaten*[991] in which the Court of Justice held that art.101(1) might not be infringed by a professional rule which restricted lawyers' freedom of action if it could reasonably be considered necessary in order to ensure the proper practice of the profession.[992]

28–198   **Effect on trade between Member States.**[993] Articles 101(1) and 102 apply only where the agreement[994] or conduct has an actual or potential effect on trade between Member States. This test serves to define the boundary between agreements and conduct which are subject to the Community competition rules and

---

such an effect is unlikely to exist if less than 30 per cent of the relevant market is covered by parallel networks of agreements having similar effects: para.8.

[985] para.8.

[986] para.9.

[987] para.11(1).

[988] para.11(2).

[989] *Nungesser v Commission* (Case 258/78) [1982] E.C.R. 2015; [1983] 1 C.M.L.R. 278.

[990] (C–250/92) [1996] E.C.R. I–5641.

[991] (C–309/99) [2002] C.M.L.R. 913; [2002] E.C.R. I–1577.

[992] For a discussion of this controversial decision, see Whish, *Competition Law* 6th edn, pp.126–130.

[993] See generally the Commission's guidelines on the effect on trade concept contained in arts [101] and [102] of the Treaty, OJ [2004] C101/81 and Cases C–295/04 to C–298/04, *Manfredi v Lloyd Adriatico Assicurazioni SpA* (ECJ).

[994] Note that a provision of an agreement that does not affect trade between Member States when viewed in isolation may nonetheless be subject to art.101(1) if the agreement as a whole has such

agreements which are left to be dealt with exclusively by national competition law.[995] The Court of Justice has consistently held that the test is satisfied if "it is possible to foresee, with a sufficient degree of probability on the basis of a set of objective factors of law or of fact, that the agreement [or conduct] in question may have an influence, direct or indirect, actual or potential, on the pattern of trade between Member States".[996] It is enough that the pattern of trade between two Member States is affected, e.g. the pattern of trade between the United Kingdom and Ireland[997] (a point of some practical importance when the relevant products are English-language publications). The fact that an agreement, decision or practice relates only to the marketing of products in a single Member State does not exclude the possibility that trade between Member States may be affected;[998] and an agreement or practice extending over the whole of the territory of a Member State has by its very nature the effect of reinforcing the partitioning of markets on a national basis, thereby holding up the economic interpenetration which the Treaty is designed to bring about.[999] It is irrelevant that the effect of the agreement or conduct is to increase, rather than reduce, trade between Member States.[1000] An agreement or conduct which has the effect of partitioning national markets will be particularly likely to have an effect on trade between Member States.[1001] One way in which an agreement or conduct may be found to have an effect on trade between Member States is if it affects the structure of competition within the common market.[1002] However, the fact that an agreement or conduct prevents transactions which could in theory have been attempted, or which in fact have been attempted, is not of itself enough to show an effect on trade between Member States for these purposes, if the transactions affected would be or are entirely abnormal transactions (e.g. transactions attempted in order to demonstrate an effect on trade between Member States).[1003] In the United Kingdom, the practical importance of this aspect of arts 101(1) and 102 is much diminished following the enactment of the Competition Act, as the Chapter I and II prohibitions substantially replicate arts 101(1) and 102 respectively, but without the reference to an effect on trade between Member States.[1004]

Article 101(2): effects of prohibition. An agreement which contravenes art.101(1) is automatically void under art.101(2). The consequences of this, for example in relation to existing orders or deliveries and related agreements, are a   **28–199**

---

an effect: *Windsurfing International v Commission* (Case 193/83) [1986] E.C.R. 611; [1986] 3 C.M.L.R. 489.

[995] *Hugin v Commission* (Case 22/78) [1979] E.C.R. 1869, para.17; [1979] 3 C.M.L.R. 345.

[996] This phrase, which appears in *Société Technique Minière v Machinenbau Ulm* (Case 56/65) [1966] E.C.R. 235 at 249; [1966] C.M.L.R. 357 at 375, is to be found in a number of judgments of the Court; see, for example, *Lancôme v Etos* (Case 99/79) [1980] E.C.R. 2511, para.23; [1981] 2 C.M.L.R. 164. The phrase "such as might prejudice the aim of a single market in all the Member States" is sometimes appended to the test (see, e.g. *Bodson v Pompes Funèbres* (Case 30/87) [1988] E.C.R. 2479, para.25; [1989] 4 C.M.L.R. 984) but it is not clear what, if anything, this adds.

[997] See, for example, *Irish Sugar* [1997] OJ L258/1, para.159 ("border rebate" affected pattern of imports from Northern Ireland to Ireland), and *Publishers' Association v Commission* (T–66/89) [1992] E.C.R. II–1995, para.56; [1992] 5 C.M.L.R. 120 (annulled on appeal on other grounds, Case C–360/92P [1995] E.C.R. I–23).

[998] *Manfredi v Lloyd Adriatico Assicurazioni SpA* (C–295/04 to C–298/04) [2006] E.C.R. I–6619, (ECJ) para.44.

[999] *Manfredi v Lloyd Adriatico Assicurazioni SpA* (C–295/04 to C–298/04) [2006] E.C.R. I–6619, (ECJ) para.45.

[1000] e.g. *Napier Brown* [1988] OJ L284/41; [1990] 4 C.M.L.R. 196.

[1001] e.g. *Miller v Commission* (Case 19/77) [1978] E.C.R. 131; [1978] 2 C.M.L.R. 334.

[1002] e.g. *Commercial Solvents v Commission* (Cases 6 & 7/73) [1974] E.C.R. 223; [1974] 1 C.M.L.R. 309.

[1003] *Hugin v Commission* (Case 22/78) [1979] E.C.R. 1869; [1979] 3 C.M.L.R. 345.

[1004] See below, paras 28–288 et seq. For the English decisions on art.101 prior to the introduction of the Competition Act, see *Copinger* 14th edn, para.29–167.

matter of national law.[1005] Article 101(2) does not, however, affect provisions of an agreement that are severable from those provisions that fall under art.101(1)[1006]; whether provisions are severable is a matter of national law.[1007] The only agreements falling under art.101(1) that are not affected by art.101(2) are those which have been declared inapplicable under art.101(3), or which fall into a category of agreements which, pursuant to art.101(3), has been prescribed as exempt from the prohibition of art.101(1) pursuant to a block exemption.

28–200   **Article 101(3).**[1008] From what has been said above, it will be appreciated that a large number of agreements fall under art.101(1). It may, of course, be that the anti-competitive aspects of many such agreements are more than offset by their beneficial aspects. Article 101(3) provides the legal framework for conducting such a balancing exercise. Under art.101(3), art.101(1) can be "declared inapplicable" to an agreement or category of agreements if it satisfies each of four conditions, namely that:

(i) it may contribute to an improvement in the production or distribution of goods or services,[1009] or to technical or economic progress[1010];

(ii) a fair share of the resulting benefit is passed on to consumers;[1011]

(iii) the restrictions are indispensable to the achievement of the aims of agreement;[1012] and

(iv) the agreement does not eliminate competition in a particular sector.[1013]

These conditions are cumulative in that all must be satisfied before the benefit of art.101(3) may be claimed.[1014] They are also exhaustive, in that the objectives of other Treaty provisions may only be taken into account to the extent that they are subsumed under the four conditions.[1015]

28–201   **Article 101(3): procedure** Before May 1, 2004, art.101(3)[1016] operated by the grant of individual exemptions, which could only be granted by the

---

[1005] *Société de Vente de Ciments et Bétons v Kerpen & Kerpen* (Case 319/82) [1983] E.C.R. 4173; [1985] 1 C.M.L.R. 511. In *Bookmakers' Afternoon Greyhound Services Ltd v Amalgamated Racing Ltd* [2008] EWHC 1978 (Ch) at paras 409–410 the judge held that where the supplier of goods is a party to a horizontal price-fixing agreement which is void, a vertical contract of supply made by the supplier with a consumer will not be void unless the vertical contract is part of a more complex arrangement involving the supplier, the consumer and the other parties to the horizontal agreement.

[1006] *Société Technique Minière v Machinenbau Ulm*(Case 56/65) [1966] E.C.R. 235 at 249; [1966] C.M.L.R. 357.

[1007] *Société de Vente de Ciments et Bétons v Kerpen & Kerpen* (Case 319/82) [1983] E.C.R. 4173; [1985] 1 C.M.L.R. 511.

[1008] See generally the Commission's guidelines on the application of art.[101(3)] of the Treaty [2004] OJ C101/8.

[1009] Although art.101(3) refers to "goods", there is no doubt that improvements relating to services are also covered; see e.g. BT/MCI [1994] OJ L223/36 (improvements relating to telecommunications) and the Commission's Guidelines on the application of art.[101(3)], [2004] OJ C101/97, para.48 (which states that this provision applies by analogy to services).

[1010] The Commission has interpreted this phrase widely, to include such matters as: cost savings (LH/SAS [1996] OJ L54/36; see also the Commission's guidelines on the application of art.81(3), [2004] OJ C101/97, paras 64 to 68); the protection of a large investment (*Eurotunnel III* [1994] OJ L354/66); the restructuring of an industry under acceptable social conditions (*Stichting Baksteen* [1994] OJ L131/15); and qualitative efficiencies (see the Commmission's guidelines on the application of art.[101(3)], [2004] OJ C101/97, paras 69 to 72).

[1011] Commission's guidelines on the application of art.[101(3)], [2004] OJ C101/97, paras 83 to 104.

[1012] Commission's guidelines, paras 73 to 82.

[1013] paras 105 to 116.

[1014] para.42.

[1015] para.42.

[1016] Exemptions under art.53(3) of the EEA Agreement were (and at the time of writing still are) granted by the EFTA Surveillance Authority where (a) the only trade affected is between participating EFTA Member States or (b) where (i) there is no effect on trade between EU

Commission.[1017] Since May 1, 2004, a new procedure has been in operation. Article 101(3) is now "directly effective". Thus, agreements which are caught by art.101(1) but which satisfy the conditions of art.101(3) are not prohibited, and no prior decision to that effect is required.[1018] Furthermore, art.101(3) can be applied by national competition authorities and courts as well as the Commission. As before, however, an agreement that falls within a block exemption is automatically exempt from the operation of art.101(3).[1019] As before, the burden of proving that the conditions of art.101(3) apply lies on the undertaking claiming the benefit of art.101(3).[1020]

(ii) Article 102: general

Article 102. Whereas art.101 in essence deals with agreements between undertakings, art.102 regulates unilateral behaviour by single undertakings.[1021] Article 102 prohibits the abuse by an undertaking of a dominant position within the common market or a substantial part of it, where that abuse may affect trade between Member States. It should be noted at the outset that art.102 does *not* prohibit dominance; it addresses abuses of that dominance. In the words of the Court of Justice:

28–202

> "A finding that an undertaking has a dominant position is not in itself a recrimination but simply means that, irrespective of the reasons for which it has such a dominant position, the undertaking concerned has a special responsibility not to allow its conduct to impair genuine undiluted competition on the common market".[1022]

It has been said that the principal purpose of art.102 is to prevent distortion of competition and to safeguard the interests of consumers.[1023] Article 102 is effectively reproduced in art.54 of the EEA Agreement.[1024]

Dominant position. The classic definition of a dominant position is that it is:

28–203

> "A position of economic strength enjoyed by an undertaking which enables it to prevent effective competition being maintained on the relevant market by giving it the power to behave to an appreciable extent independently of its competitors, customers and, ultimately, of its consumers."[1025]

In practice, there are two key elements in assessing whether an undertaking enjoys such a position of economic strength.

Member States and (ii) the turnover of the undertakings concerned equals 33 per cent or more of their EEA turnover: art.56 of the EEA Agreement.

[1017] Reg.17, First Regulation implementing arts 85 and 86 of the Treaty [1962] OJ Sp. Ed. No. 204/87, art.9(1). See previous editions of this work.

[1018] Council Regulation (EC) No 1/2003 on the implementation of the rules of competition laid down in arts [101] and [102] of the Treaty ("the Modernisation Regulation"), [2003] OJ L1/1, art.1(2).

[1019] All existing block exemption regulations remain in force: Commission Guidelines on the application of art.[101(3)], [2004] OJ C101/97, para.2.

[1020] Modernisation Regulation 1/2003, art.2. The standard of proof is the civil standard of balance of probabilities: see *Bookmakers' Afternoon Greyhound Services Ltd v Amalgamated Racing Ltd* [2008] EWHC 1978 (Ch) at para.392 and the cases cited in that paragraph. Where a restriction is prima facie contrary to art.101(1) but a party seeks to persuade a court that it is justified, the legal burden remains on the party alleging an infringement of art.101(1) but the evidential burden of proving justification falls on the person advancing such assertion: The *Racecourse Association v OFT* [2005] CAT 29 para.131.

[1021] See, however, "collective dominance" below, para.28–206. For the meaning of the term "undertaking", see para.28–187, above.

[1022] *Michelin v Commission* (Case 322/81) [1983] E.C.R. 3461, para.57; [1985] 1 C.M.L.R. 282.

[1023] *Attheraces Ltd v British Horseracing Board* [2007] EWCA Civ 38; [2007] U.K.C.L.R. 309 at para.100.

[1024] The Agreement on the European Economic Area, signed at Oporto on May 2, 1992, as adjusted by the Protocol signed at Brussels on March 17, 1993.

[1025] *United Brands Company v Commission* (Case 27/76) [1978] E.C.R. 207; [1978] 1 C.M.L.R. 429, para.65.

28–204   **Relevant market.** The first element is the assessment of the correct relevant market; this element is so important a constituent of the analysis of conduct under art.102 that an error will vitiate any finding of breach.[1026] There are two aspects to the definition of the relevant market: the product market and the geographical market. The relevant market comprises those goods (or services) to which the conduct relates and those goods (or services), defined by their nature and their geographical location, which are interchangeable or substitutable for them. This can be looked at from the point of view of the customer[1027] (what other goods or services could he buy instead, and from where?) and of the supplier (what suppliers could easily switch from production of other goods or services to those goods or services, and where could they do this?).[1028] It is beyond the scope of this work to enter further into these questions, but a valuable guide to the Commission's thinking on can be found in its Notice on the definition of the relevant market.[1029]

28–205   **Dominance.** The obvious case where an undertaking is dominant in a relevant market is where it is unlawful to compete with that undertaking on that market.[1030] This point is important in the context of copyright, since the essence of that right is that others are unable to supply copies of a work in which such a right is held, without permission of the right holder. In most cases, of course, the work to which the right relates is not a relevant market, since a number of alternative works exist, each of which is an acceptable substitute from the point of view of the customer.[1031] But this may not be the case with some works, e.g. TV listings information.[1032] In cases where there is no legal restriction on competition, the starting point is to consider the undertaking's share of the relevant market. As the Court of Justice has observed,[1033] a high market share makes an undertaking an unavoidable trading partner for most customers (unless smaller competitors can rapidly expand production). However, there is no hard-and-fast market share above which an undertaking can be said to be dominant.[1034] Other things being equal, an undertaking is more likely to be dominant if: its market share has been stable over time[1035]; it faces no competitors of any size,[1036] or only one or two large competitors[1037]; its size, financial strength and reputation confer advantages

---

[1026] e.g. *Continental Can v Commission* (Case 6/72) [1973] E.C.R. 215, para.32.

[1027] It may be that some customers can use alternatives but others cannot; if relatively few can use an alternative to the product in question, the product in question is more likely to be a relevant market. In *Michelin v Commission* (Case 322/81) [1983] E.C.R. 3461; [1985] 1 C.M.L.R. 282, the fact that some customers could easily use retread tyres did not prevent new tyres from being the relevant market. Similarly, spare parts or software packages designed for particular equipment are not in the same relevant market as equivalent parts or packages designed for other equipment if customers are unable to change the equipment that they have; see e.g. *Hugin v Commission* (Case 22/78) [1979] E.C.R. 1869; [1979] 3 C.M.L.R. 345.

[1028] In *Continental Can v Commission* (Case 6/72) [1973] E.C.R. 215, above, the Court of Justice accepted that the market for light metal containers for meat and fish was not a relevant market unless manufacturers of other metal containers were unable easily to switch production into making such containers.

[1029] [1997] OJ C372/3; [1998] 4 C.M.L.R. 177.

[1030] e.g. *CBEM v CLT and IPB* (Case 311/84) [1985] E.C.R. 3261 ("Telemarketing").

[1031] *Parke, Davis v Probel* [1968] E.C.R. 81; [1968] C.M.L.R. 47.

[1032] *RTE and ITP v Commission* (C–241 & 242/91P) [1995] E.C.R. I–743; [1995] 4 C.M.L.R. 718 ("Magill TV Guide"); discussed more fully at para.28–279, below.

[1033] *Hoffmann-La Roche v Commission* (Case 85/76) [1979] E.C.R. 461, para.41; [1979] 3 C.M.L.R. 211.

[1034] Hence, in the Commission decision in *Tetra Pak II* [1992] OJ L72/1; [1992] 4 C.M.L.R. 551, the Commission found that a market share of 48–52 per cent did not confer dominance; but in Case 27/76 *United Brands v Commission* [1978] E.C.R. 207; [1978] 1 C.M.L.R. 429, a market share of 40–45 per cent was found to do so.

[1035] *Hoffmann-La Roche v Commission* (Case 85/76) [1979] E.C.R. 461, para.58.

[1036] *United Brands v Commission* (Case 27/76) [1978] E.C.R. 207; [1979] 1 C.M.L.R. 429, para.111.

[1037] *Hoffmann-La Roche v Commission* (Case 85/76) [1979] E.C.R. 461, para.51.

on the relevant market[1038]; or there are no large purchasers of the product in a position to exercise countervailing market power.[1039]

Collective dominance. Since art.102 refers to an abuse "by one or more undertakings", it is clear that two or more undertakings can hold a collective dominant position. Such a position may exist if the entities present themselves or act together on a particular market as a collective entity.[1040] The existence of such a position may flow from the existence of an agreement or from other links between the undertakings in question. However, the existence of an agreement or such links is not essential: a finding of collective dominance may be based on other connecting factors; it is necessary to make an economic assessment and, in particular, an assessment of the market in question.[1041] An example of a case where such a position of collective dominance has been established is the relationship between members of a liner shipping conference.[1042]   **28–206**

Relationship between the dominance and the abuse. Four situations can be distinguished; in each of them, an undertaking may be found to be abusing its dominant position.   **28–207**

    (i)   The abuse affects the market in which the undertaking is dominant ("the dominated market"). In this case there is no need to show any causal link between the dominance and the abuse.[1043]

   (ii)   The undertaking uses its position in the dominated market to produce effects in another market (e.g. by refusing in the dominated market to supply competitors in the other market), a practice often known as "leveraging".[1044]

  (iii)   The undertaking behaves in the other market in a way designed to protect its position in the dominated market.[1045]

  (iv)   The undertaking behaves on another market in a way that produces effects on that other market. This is at first sight a surprising case, as the conduct does not appear to relate to the dominant position at all. However, there is a breach of art.102 in such cases if the other market is "associated" with the dominated market, and if there are "special circumstances".[1046]

Abuse. Article 102 itself contains a non-exhaustive list of practices that may be considered to be abuses. The following are examples of practices that have been   **28–208**

[1038] Case 85/76 *Hoffmann-La Roche v Commission* [1979] E.C.R. 461, paras 45–47; *Michelin v Commission* (Case 322/81) [1983] E.C.R. 3461, para.55; [1985] 1 C.M.L.R. 282.

[1039] *Alcatel/Telettra* [1991] OJ L122/48; [1991] 4 C.M.L.R. 778.

[1040] *P Compagnie Maritime Belge Transports SA v Dafra-Lines A/S* (Joined Cases C–395/96P and C–396/96) [2000] E.C.R. I–1365; [2000] 4 C.M.L.R. 1076, para.36.

[1041] *P Compagnie Maritime Belge Transports SA v Dafra-Lines A/S* (Joined Cases C–395/96P and C–396/96) [2000] E.C.R. I–1365, [2000] 4 C.M.L.R. 1076, paras 41 to 45.

[1042] *P Compagnie Maritime Belge Transports SA v Dafra-Lines A/S* (Joined Cases C–395/96P and C–396/96) [2000] E.C.R. I–1365, [2000] 4 C.M.L.R. 1076.

[1043] *Continental Can v Commission* (Case 6/72) [1973] E.C.R. 215; the ability to acquire a competitor did not depend on the undertaking's dominance.

[1044] e.g. *CBEM v CLT and IPB* (Case 311/84) [1985] E.C.R. 3261 ("Telemarketing"). Another example in this category is *British Airways Plc v Commission* (T–219/99), ECJ December 17, 2003.

[1045] e.g. *BPB v Commission* (C–310/93P) [1995] E.C.R. I–865, para.11; see also, *RTE and ITP v Commission* (C–241 & 242/91P) [1995] E.C.R. 1-743; [1995] 4 C.M.L.R. 718.

[1046] *Tetra Pak v Commission* (C–333/94P) [1996] E.C.R. I–5951. In that case, the markets were associated because both T and its competitors were present on both markets; T was the leading supplier in both; the customers in one were at least potential customers in the other; and T's position in the dominated market allowed it to concentrate on protecting its position in the other market.

considered to be abuses; the list concentrates on those abuses which are likely to be of most relevance in the context of this work.[1047]

28–209   **Excessive prices.** Although this might be thought to be the most obvious way in which a monopolist might seek to abuse his market power, there are relatively few cases[1048] where excessive pricing has been found to be an abuse, even though the setting of unfairly high prices is listed as an abuse in art.102(a). The principal difficulty is that in the absence of appropriate comparators[1049] in order to determine whether a price is excessive,[1050] a comparison has to be made with the costs of production[1051]; but these costs can be very difficult to determine objectively.

28–210   **Price discrimination.** There are a number of cases where it will almost certainly be regarded as an abuse for a dominant undertaking to charge different prices[1052] to different purchasers for his product. One is where the favoured purchasers are those that have purchased, or are particularly liable to purchase, from the dominant undertaking's competitors.[1053] Another is where discounts are given to dealers who buy all or a high proportion of their supplies from the dominant undertaking,[1054] or who achieve a large turnover in the dominant undertaking's products.[1055] Price discrimination based on the nationality of the purchaser with a view to maintaining national boundaries between markets is very likely to be considered to be an abuse.[1056] Differing royalty fees charged by a dominant copyright owner may well constitute price discrimination in the absence of objective justification.

28–211   **Refusal to supply.** It will be an abuse for a dominant undertaking to refuse to supply raw material to a purchaser because that purchaser will use it to compete with the dominant undertaking on another, ancillary market.[1057] So, for example, it was an abuse for a company dominant in the supply of TV listings information to refuse to supply a company that wished to compete with it on the market for

---

[1047] See, generally, the Commission's Guidance on the Commission's enforcement priorities in applying art.[102] of the EC Treaty to abusive exclusionary conduct by dominant undertakings [2009] OJ C45/7.

[1048] One being *United Brands v Commission* (Case 27/76) [1978] E.C.R. 207; [1978] 1 C.M.L.R. 429. Note, however, that in this case the Commission's decision was quashed by the ECJ.

[1049] As to which, see, e.g. *Bodson v Pompes Funèbres* (Case 30/87) [1988] E.C.R. 2479; [1989] 4 C.M.L.R. 984.

[1050] That is "it has no reasonable relation to the economic value of the product supplied": see *Attheraces Ltd v British Horseracing Board Ltd* [2007] EWCA Civ 38; [2007] E.C.C. 7 at para.152, applying Case 27/76 United *Brands v Commission* [1978] E.C.R. 207; [1978] 1 C.M.L.R. 429.

[1051] *United Brands v Commision* (Case 27/76) [1978] E.C.R. 207; [1978] 1 C.M.L.R. 429, para.251.

[1052] Or to treat more favourably in other ways, such as shorter delivery times; e.g. *BPB Industries v Commission* (C–310/93P) [1995] E.C.R. I–865 (priority given to those who purchased plasterboard from the dominant undertaking).

[1053] e.g. *AKZO v Commission* (C–62/86) [1991] E.C.R. I–3359 (discounts to purchasers who have bought from a competitor); *Irish Sugar* [1997] OJ L258/1 (discounts to customers who were particularly accessible to competing cross-border suppliers).

[1054] e.g. *Suiker-Unie v Commission* (Case 40/73) [1975] E.C.R. 1663 at 2003; [1976] 1 C.M.L.R. 295; *Hoffmann-La Roche v Commission* (Case 85/76) [1979] E.C.R. 461; [1979] 3 C.M.L.R. 211.

[1055] e.g. *Michelin v Commission* (Case 322/81) [1983] E.C.R. 3461, para.57; [1985] 1 C.M.L.R. 282.

[1056] e.g. *United Brands v Commission* (Case 27/76) [1978] E.C.R. 207; [1978] 1 C.M.L.R. 429; *British Leyland v Commission* (Case 226/84) [1986] E.C.R. 3263; [1987] 1 C.M.L.R. 184.

[1057] e.g. *Commercial Solvents v Commission* (Case 6/73) [1974] E.C.R. 223; *Attheraces Ltd v British Horseracing Board Ltd* [2007] EWCA Civ 38; [2007] E.C.C. 7: refusal to supply data which was unprotected by intellectual property rights except on particular terms held not to be abusive on the facts.

weekly TV guides[1058]; and it was an abuse for a broadcasting company to refuse to accept advertisements showing telephone numbers of a telemarketer that competed with the broadcaster's own telemarketing arm.[1059] A "constructive" refusal to supply, for example a refusal to supply except on terms which make the purchase unviable, may also be an abuse.[1060] Refusal to license in the copyright field is dealt with at length below.[1061]

Essential facilities. In a line of cases which can be seen as a development of the cases discussed in the previous paragraph, an abuse has been found where the owner of an "essential facility"—and thereby dominant in the supply of that facility—refused to grant access to that facility to a potential competitor, or discriminated in price against that competitor. Thus, in *Port of Rødby*,[1062] the Commission found that it was an abuse of a ferry company's dominant position in the market for port facilities at Rødby (where it owned the port) for it to refuse to allow a potential competitor to use the port on reasonable terms. There have been similar decisions concerning other ports and airports.[1063] A similar line of reasoning was employed in the *Magill* case,[1064] where TV listings information was regarded as "essential" to the publication of weekly TV guides. It will be seen in the context of this work that this line of case-law could affect the conduct of copyright and related right owners if the right that they possess can be described as an "essential facility".[1065]   **28–212**

Miscellaneous abuses. Other abuses include: making the supply of products conditional on the purchase of some other product[1066] ("tying"); and pricing below the average variable cost[1067] of producing a product, or pricing at below average total cost with the intent of eliminating a competitor ("predatory pricing").[1068]   **28–213**

(iii) Enforcement and direct effect of arts 101(1) and 102

Enforcement. The Modernisation Regulation provides that arts 101 and 102 are to be enforced both by the Commission and by the competition authorities and courts of the Member States.[1069] The Commission's powers are as follows.[1070]   **28–214**

[1058] *RTE and ITP v Commission* (Cases C–241 & 242/91P) [1995] E.C.R. I–743; [1995] 4 C.M.L.R. 718.

[1059] *CBEM v CLT and IPB* (Case 311/84) [1985] E.C.R. 3261 ("Telemarketing").

[1060] See most recently *Intecare Direct Ltd v Pfizer Ltd* [2010] EWHC 600 (Ch).

[1061] paras 28-00 et seq.

[1062] [1994] OJ L55/52.

[1063] e.g. *Brussels Airport* [1995] OJ L216/8; *Sea Containers/Stena Sealink* [1994] OJ L15/8.

[1064] *RTE and ITP v Commission* (C–241 & 242/91P) [1995] E.C.R. I–743; [1995] 4 C.M.L.R. 718.

[1065] See paras 28–277 et seq., below, for a discussion of the *Magill* decision and subsequent ECJ cases.

[1066] e.g. *Hilti v Commission* (T–30/89) [1991] E.C.R. II–1439; [1992] 4 C.M.L.R. 16 (upheld on appeal (C–53/92P) [1994] E.C.R. I–667) (supply of nail guns made conditional on purchase of nails). See also the *Microsoft* cases, discussed at length below (para.28–274). See also the Commission's Guidance on the Commission's enforcement priorities in applying art.[102] of the EC Treaty to abusive exclusionary conduct by dominant undertakings [2009] OJ C45/7 at paras 48–50.

[1067] That is to say, costs such as energy and raw materials that are not fixed in the short term however much is produced; contrast management overheads and depreciation, which do not vary with the amount produced.

[1068] *AKZO v Commission* (C–62/86) [1991] E.C.R. I–3359. See, the Commission's Guidance on the Commission's enforcement priorities in applying art.82 of the EC Treaty to abusive exclusionary conduct by dominant undertakings [2009] OJ C45/7 paras 63–74

[1069] arts 4, 5 and 6 of the Modernisation Regulation 1/2003. See, generally, the Commission's report on the functioning of the Modernisation Regulation COM(2009)206 final.

[1070] See, generally, as to enforcement, the Commission's Annual Reports on Competition Policy

First, where, acting on a complaint[1071] or on its own initiative, it finds that there is an infringement, it may by decision impose any behavioural or structural remedies which are proportionate to the infringement and necessary to end it.[1072] In the case of intentional or negligent infringements of arts 101 and 102, it may also impose a fine of up to 10 per cent of the preceding year's turnover of the relevant undertaking.[1073] In cases of urgency, it may order interim measures.[1074] It may accept binding "commitments" in lieu of imposing remedies.[1075] Where the Community public interest so requires, it may, acting on its own initiative, by decision find that art.101 is not applicable to a particular agreement or that art.102 does not apply.[1076] In addition, the Commission is empowered to investigate a particular sector of the economy or a particular type of agreement across various sectors.[1077] For these purposes, the Commission may compel undertakings and associations to supply information,[1078] and may take statements[1079] and conduct all necessary inspections.[1080] The Modernisation Regulation grants similar enforcement powers to the competition authorities of Member States.[1081] In addition, it provides that national courts shall have the power to apply arts 101 and 102.[1082]

28–215   **Relationship between the work of the Commission and the national competition authorities: general.**[1083] The Modernisation Regulation requires Member States to designate the authority or authorities responsible for the application of arts 101 and 102 in such a way that its provisions are effectively complied with.[1084] It also provides that the Commission and the national authorities shall apply the Community competition rules in close cooperation.[1085] To that end, it contains detailed provision for the exchange of information, including confidential information,[1086] and requires the Commission to consult with an Advisory Committee on Restrictive Practices and Dominant Positions consisting of representatives of the national authorities before taking enforcement or investigatory action.[1087] It also contains provisions to avoid duplication in enforcement procedures.[1088] Finally, it expressly provides that when national authorities make rulings on agreements, decisions or practices which are already the subject of a Commission

---

[1071] Which may be made by any person with a legitimate interest or a Member State: Modernisation Regulation art.7(2).

[1072] art.7(1). In relation to settlement procedures, see the Commission's Regulation (EC) No 622/2008 [2008] OJ L171/3 and its Notice on the conduct of settlement procedures [2008] OJ C167/1.

[1073] art.23(2)(a).

[1074] art.8(1). The Commission may impose fines for intentional or negligent breaches of such measures: art.23(2)(b).

[1075] art.9(1).

[1076] art.10.

[1077] art.17.

[1078] art.18. There are financial penalties for supplying incorrect or misleading information: art.23.

[1079] art.19. Only those who consent may be interviewed.

[1080] arts 20 and 21. This provision includes sweeping powers of search and seizure.

[1081] art.5.

[1082] art.6 .

[1083] See, generally, the Commission Notice on co-operation within the Network of Competition Authorities [2004] OJ C101/43 and the Commission's Annual Reports on Competition Policy. See also *Inntrepreneur Pub Company (CPC) v Crehan* [2006] UKHL 38; [2007] 1 A.C. 333.

[1084] Modernisation Regulation 1/2003 art.35. For the United Kingdom authorities, see the next paragraph.

[1085] art.11(1).

[1086] arts 11(2) and 12. See also the Commission Notice on cooperation within the Network of Competition Authorities [2004] OJ C101/43, paras 26 to 30.

[1087] Modernisation Regulation 1/2003 art.14. See also the Commission Notice on co-operation within the Network of Competition Authorities [2004] OJ C101/43, paras 58 to 68.

[1088] arts 11 and 13. See also the Commission Notice on cooperation within the Network of Competition Authorities [2004] OJ C101/43, paras 6 to 25, 31 to 57.

decision, they cannot take decisions which would run counter to the Commission's decision.[1089]

Enforcement of arts 101 and 102 by national competition authorities in the United Kingdom. In accordance with the requirements of the Modernisation Regulation, the Office of Fair Trading ("OFT") and certain regulators have been designated as national competition authorities for the United Kingdom.[1090] Since May 1, 2004, the OFT has been empowered to conduct an investigation where there are reasonable grounds to suspect an infringement of either art.101 or art.102.[1091] For the purposes of such an investigation, the OFT is given extensive powers to require the production of documents and information[1092]; to enter premises[1093]; to accept commitments in lieu of enforcement[1094]; to make decisions that art.101 or art.102 have been infringed; and to give directions for the purposes of ending the infringements and enforcing those directions.[1095] Appeals from the OFT lie to the Competition Commission.[1096] The OFT is also given extensive powers in relation to the enforcement of inspections under arts 20(4), 21 and 22(2) of the Modernisation Regulation.[1097] On October 14, 2010, the Government announced its intention to consult on a merger of the OFT's competition functions with the Competition Commission.

28–216

Relationship between the work of the Commission and litigation in national courts.[1098] When national courts rule on agreements, decisions or practices which are already the subject of a Commission decision, they are expressly prohibited by the terms of the Modernisation Regulation from taking decisions running counter to the decision adopted by the Commission.[1099] They must also avoid giving decisions which would conflict with a decision contemplated by the Commission in proceedings it has initiated and in order to do so may consider whether to stay the proceedings.[1100] At the same time, the Modernisation Regulation provides for three forms of co-operation between the Commission and national courts. First, national courts may ask the Commission to transmit to them information

28–217

[1089] art.16(2).

[1090] The Competition Act 1998 and Other Enactments (Amendment) Regulations 2004 (SI 2004/1261) reg.3(1). The regulators are those referred to in s.54(1) of the Competition Act 1998 (c.41), i.e. (at the time of writing) the Office of Communications; the Gas and Electricity Markets Authority; the Director General of Electricity Supply for Northern Ireland; the Water Services Regulation Authority; the Office of Rail Regulation; the Director General of Gas for Northern Ireland; and the Civil Aviation Authority.

[1091] Competition Act 1998 s.25(3) and 25(5), inserted by the Competition Act 1998 and Other Enactments (Amendment) Regulations 2004 (SI 2004/1261) Sch.1 para.10.

[1092] Competition Act 1998 s.26. Failure to comply may be an offence under ibid., s.42.

[1093] ss.27 to 29. Again, failure to comply may be an offence under s.42.

[1094] ss.31A to 31E, inserted by the Competition Act 1998 and Other Enactments (Amendment) Regulations 2004 (SI 2004/1261) Sch.1 para.18.

[1095] ss.32 to 34. There is power to take interim measures in s.35 and power to impose penalties in ss.36 to 38.

[1096] s.46.

[1097] These powers are set out in Pts 2 and 2A of the Competition Act, as amended by the Competition Act 1998 and Other Enactments (Amendment) Regulations 2004 (SI 2004/1261), Sch.1. Arts 20(4) and 21 concern inspections by the Commission. Art.22 concerns investigations by competition authorities of other Member States.

[1098] See, generally, the Commission Notice on the co-operation between the Commission and the courts of the EU Member States in the application of arts [101 and 102] [2004] OJ C101/54.

[1099] Modernisation Regulation 1/2003 art.16(1).

[1100] Modernisation Regulation 1/2003 art.16(1). This is stated to be without prejudice to the rights and obligations under what is now art.267 of the Treaty (which gives the Court of Justice jurisdiction to make preliminary rulings as to the Treaty etc.).

which is in its possession,[1101] Secondly, they may ask the Commission for its opinion on questions concerning the applicability of the Community competition rules.[1102] Thirdly, the Commission may make written or (if they request) oral observations to the national courts.[1103]

28–218   **Direct effect: general.** The Modernisation Regulation makes clear that, as before, arts 101(1) and 102 have direct effect in the national courts of the Member States.[1104] Their application in the English Courts is governed by a Practice Direction.[1105] Prior to 2001, the English courts (including the House of Lords) had held that a right to damages would arise from breach of art.102 on the basis of breach of statutory duty.[1106] In 2001, the European Court of Justice held in *Courage v Crehan* that the same applies in respect of a breach of art.101.[1107] The main issue in *Courage v Crehan* was whether a claimant was precluded from claiming damages under art.101 if he was a party to the agreement and thus arguably *in pari delicto* with the defendant. The Court of Justice stated the general principle that in the absence of Community rules governing the matter, it is for the domestic legal system of each Member State to lay down the detailed procedural rules governing actions for safeguarding rights which individuals derive directly from Community law, provided that such rules are not less favourable than those governing similar domestic actions (the principle of equivalence) and that they do not render practically impossible or excessively difficult the exercise of rights conferred by Community law (the principle of effectiveness).[1108] Having regard to these principles, the Court confirmed that a remedy in damages for breach of art.101 was necessary in order to give the provision its full effectiveness.[1109] The Court went on to hold that art.101 precludes a rule of national law which disqualifies a claimant from claiming damages merely because he was a party to the agreement in question.[1110] However, it held, Community law does not preclude a rule of national law which disqualifies a claimant from relying on his own unlawful acts to obtain damages where it is established that he bore significant responsibility for the distortion of competition.[1111] In deciding whether the claimant bore such responsibility, it is relevant to consider such matters as the parties' respective bargaining positions, their conduct and whether the

---

[1101] art.15(1). See also Commission Notice on the co-operation between the Commission and the courts of the EU Member States in the application of arts [101 and 102] [2004] OJ C101/54, paras 21 to 26.

[1102] art.15(1). See also Commission Notice on the co-operation between the Commission and the courts of the EU Member States in the application of arts [101 and 102] [2004] OJ C101/54, paras 27 to 30.

[1103] Modernisation Regulation, art.15(3). See also Commission Notice on the co-operation between the Commission and the courts of the EU Member States in the application of arts [101 and 102] [2004] OJ C101/54, paras 31 to 35.

[1104] Modernisation Regulation 1/2003 art.6. There are certain exceptions to the applicability of arts 101 and 102, but these apply in the transport sector and are unlikely to be material to the rights covered in this work.

[1105] Practice Direction — Competition Law — Claims relating to the application of arts [101] and [102] of the EC Treaty. See the Ministry of Justice website.

[1106] *Garden Cottage Foods v Milk Marketing Board* [1984] A.C. 130; [1983] 3 C.M.L.R. 43; *Bourgoin v Ministry of Agriculture* [1986] Q.B. 716; [1986] 1 C.M.L.R. 267; see also *Cutsforth v Mansfield Inns* [1986] 1 W.L.R. 588.

[1107] *Courage Ltd v Crehan* (C–453/99) [2004] E.C.C. 28. See also *Manfredi v Lloyd Adriatico Assicurazioni SpA* (Joined Cases C–295/04 to C–298/04) [2006] E.C.R. I–6619, (ECJ), paras 56 to 63 (*"Manfredi"*) and the Commission's White Paper Damages actions for breach of the EC antitrust rules (COM (2008) 165 final).

[1108] *Courage Ltd v Crehan* (C–453/99) [2004] E.C.C. 28, para.29. In *Manfredi* (above) the Court of Justice held that "the detailed procedural rules" included the applicable limitation period (para.82) and the rules for the assessment of damages (para.98).

[1109] *Courage Ltd v Crehan* (C–453/99) [2004] E.C.C. 28, para.26.

[1110] *Courage Ltd v Crehan* (C–453/99) [2004] E.C.C. 28, para.36.

[1111] *Courage Ltd v Crehan* (C–453/99) [2004] E.C.C. 28, para.36.

agreement in question was part of a network of agreements which had a cumulative effect on competition and to which the claimant was not a party.[1112]

Direct effect: claims in England and Wales. Procedure is governed by a   **28–219**
Practice Direction.[1113] The Court has the power to grant an injunction to prevent a
breach or threatened breach of arts 101 or 102. Normal principles apply.[1114]
Claims for damages may be brought in the Court or in the Competition Appeal
Tribunal.[1115] Although the claim under art.101 is a claim for breach of statutory
duty, it is not necessary for the claimant to establish that the duty imposed by
art.101 exists in respect of the kind of loss he has suffered.[1116] Neither exemplary
damages nor an account of profits are available to a victim of a breach of
art.101.[1117] Otherwise, it appears that damages are assessed in accordance with
the normal tort principles.[1118] The Commission is reviewing various aspects of
the remedy of damages including their quantification.[1119]

Direct effect: defences in England and Wales. Breaches of arts 101 and 102   **28–220**

[1112] *Courage Ltd v Crehan* (C–453/99) [2004] E.C.C. 28, paras 32–34, 36. The case concerned two beer-tie agreements to which Crehan (as publican) was a party. The judge held that he was not significantly responsible for the distortion of competition and this was upheld by the Court of Appeal [2004] EWCA Civ 637 at para.153: "He was not of course compelled to enter into any agreement with Inntrepreneur. To that extent he had bargaining power. But he was dealing with the single largest tied-house landlord in the United Kingdom who made it clear that the offending tying terms in their agreement were not negotiable. There was no equality of bargaining power in any real sense. Mr. Crehan was in a markedly weaker position than Inntrepreneur: if he wanted to lease the pubs he had to agree to the tie. In practice Inntrepreneur imposed the tie on him".

[1113] Practice Direction — Competition Law — Claims relating to the application of arts [101] and [102] of the EC Treaty. See the Ministry of Justice website. As to the application of the Judgments Regulation to claims under art.102, see *Roche Products Ltd v Provimi* [2003] EWHC 961 (Comm); [2003] U.K.C.L.R. 493; [2003] E.C.C. 29; and *Sandisk Corporation v Koninklijke Philips Electronics NV* [2007] EWHC 332; [2007] F.S.R. 22.

[1114] Mandatory injunctions are frequently sought in this field. See *AAH Pharmaceuticals Ltd v Pfizer Ltd* [2007] EWHC 565 (Ch) [2007] U.K.C.L.R. 1561; *Software Cellular Network Ltd v T-Mobile (UK)) Ltd* [2007] EWHC (1790) Ch; and *Intecare Direct Ltd v Pfizer Ltd* [2010] EWHC 600 (Ch).

[1115] Under s.47A of the Competition Act 1998. As to the limitation period for claims in the Tribunal, see *BCL Old Co Ltd v BASF SE* [2009] EWCA Civ 434; [2009] Bus. L.R. 1516; [2009] U.K.C.L.R. 789. As to jurisdiction in damages claims arising from findings of pan-European infringement see *Cooper Tire & Rubber Company Europe Ltd v DOW Deutschland Inc* [2010] EWCA Civ 864.

[1116] *Crehan v Inntrepreneur Pub Company CPC* [2004] EWCA Civ 637; [2004] E.C.C. 28; at paras 162 and 167. Thus, on the facts of that case, the tie agreements offended against art.81 because they had adverse effects on the market for the distribution of beer. The claimant was not a beer distributor and had not suffered loss as a result of those adverse effects. His claim was that as a result of having entered into the tie agreements he was obliged to pay more for beer than independent competitors. Applying the normal principles in respect of damages for breach of statutory duty (as stated in *South Australia Asset Management Corporation v York Montague Ltd* [1997] A.C. 191 at 211), his loss would have been irrecoverable. The Court of Appeal held that as a matter of construction of the ECJ's decision and in accordance with the principle of effectiveness, this loss was nevertheless recoverable. The question of the quantification of damages did not arise on the appeal to the House of Lords: *Inntrepreneur Pub Company (CPC) v Crehan* [2006] UKHL 38; [2007] 1 A.C. 333; para.73.

[1117] *Devenish Nutrition Ltd v Sanofi-Adventis SA (France)* [2007] EWHC 2394 (Ch); [2008] 2 W.L.R. 637; [2008] 2 All E.R. 249; [2008] E.C.C. 4. On appeal, the ruling in relation to exemplary damages was not challenged and the ruling in relation to accounts of profits was upheld: [2008] EWCA Civ 1086; [2004] E.C.C. 28; [2009] Ch. 390.

[1118] In *Crehan v Inntrepreneur Pub Company CPC*, [2004] EWCA Civ 637; [2004] E.C.C. 28, the Court of Appeal, in ruling on questions of causation and quantum, did not suggest otherwise: see at paras 169–183. In *Manfredi* (above) the Court of Justice held (at para.61) that individuals could claim compensation for the harm suffered "where there is a causal relationship between that harm and an agreement or practice prohibited under art.81 EC" but that in the absence of Community rules governing the matter it was for domestic legal systems to prescribe the detailed rules on the application of the concept of "causal relationship" provided that the principles of equivalence and effectiveness are observed (para.64).

[1119] See *http://ec.europa.eu/competition/antitrust/actionsdamages/index.html* [Accessed September 25, 2010].

can also be relied on as a defence in proceedings to enforce an agreement[1120] or in proceedings for infringement of an intellectual property right. Before such a breach can give rise to a successful defence, it is necessary for the defendant to establish a nexus between the abuse and the claimant's cause of action. Thus, for example, the mere fact that an intellectual property right is being used by a dominant undertaking to secure a market environment in which price fixing may occur will not prevent the enforcement of that right, e.g. to prevent unlawful importation of infringing goods.[1121] However, it has been held well arguable that to be able to prove that a relevant agreement was in breach of art.101 would give a defendant a stronger basis for saying that a claimant did not have legitimate reasons to oppose further dealings in the goods for the purposes of s.12(2) of the Trade Marks Act 1994.[1122]

(iv) Application of Community competition law to copyright and related rights

(a) *General*

28–221   **Introduction.** There are three main areas where Community competition law can affect the exercise of the rights covered in this work. The first is that art.101(1) of the Treaty can affect the agreements by which a right holder assigns his rights or licenses others to make copies of the work in which he has those rights. The second is that art.102 of the Treaty can restrict the ability of rightholders to decline to license others to copy the work, and can restrict the terms on which they can license, and their ability to discriminate between licensees, if they do grant a licence. Finally, both arts 101 and 102 can affect the activities of copyright collecting societies.

28–222   **Relationship between the competition rules and copyright and similar rights.** Questions as to whether there is an inherent conflict between intellectual property rights and competition itself are beyond the scope of this work and the reader is referred to the specialist texts.[1123] As to the relationship between such rights and competition *law*, the early cases sought to distinguish between the *existence* of intellectual property rights, which was not considered to be amenable to regulation by competition law,[1124] and the *exercise* of such rights, which was.[1125] This distinction has been extensively criticised.[1126] Nevertheless, the early cases continue to be cited and followed.

(b) *Article 101 and licences and assignments*

28–223   **Article 101: general.** In general it may be said that although an intellectual prop-

---

[1120] See Bellamy & Child, *European Community Law of Competition* 6th edn, paras 14.136 et seq.

[1121] *Hewlett Packard Development Company LP v Expansys UK Ltd* [2005] EWHC 1495; [2005] E.T.M.R. 111.

[1122] *Sportswear SpA v Stonestyle Ltd* [2006] EWCA Civ 380; [2007] F.S.R. 2; [2006] E.T.M.R. 66. See also *Oracle America, Inc v M-Tech Data Ltd* [2010] EWCA Civ 997.

[1123] See e.g. Whish, *Competition Law* 6th edn, pp.758-9; Turner, *Intellectual Property and EU Competition Law* (2010), para.1.02.

[1124] *Parke, Davis v Probel* (Case 24/67) [1968] E.C.R. 55; [1968] C.M.L.R. 47; *EMI Records Ltd v CBS United Kingdom Ltd* (Case 51/75) [1968] E.C.R. 811.

[1125] *Keurkoop BV v Nancy Kean Gifts BV* (Case 144/81) [1982] E.C.R. 2853 at 2873; [1983] 2 C.M.L.R. 47.

[1126] A recent example is Korah, *Intellectual Property Rights and the EC Competition Rules* (2006) pp.3–4: "In ruling that an important difference rests on a distinction, which cannot be drawn by logical analysis, the ECJ created a very flexible instrument for it to develop the law and reduce the possibilities of dividing the Common Market".

erty right, as a "legal entity", will not fall within the class of agreements, decisions or concerted practices prohibited by art.101(1), the exercise of that right may be subject to the prohibitions in the Treaty when it is the purpose, the means or the result of an agreement, decision or concerted practice.[1127]

Article 101: application to assignments. In the English copyright case of *Panayiotou v Sony Music Entertainment (UK) Ltd* it was held (obiter) that art.101 did not apply to an assignment of copyright because the assignment concerned the existence rather than the exercise of intellectual property rights.[1128] However, the European courts have not recognised a distinction between assignments and licences. Thus, for example, in *Sirena SRL v Eda SRL*[1129] the Court of Justice held that the simultaneous assignment to several concessionaires of national trade mark rights for the same product may prejudice trade between Member States and distort competition in the Common Market, if this has the effect of re-establishing rigid frontiers between Member States. The Court went on to state that it was sufficient for art.101(1) to apply, in that case to an agreement concluded before the date the Treaty took effect, if the effects of the agreement continued after that date. The judgment left it unclear when an agreement such as an assignment could be considered as continuing to have its effects. What if the assignment were a bare assignment containing no other terms as to the future exercise of the right by the assignee, or if any such terms as it may have contained had become spent by the passing of time? In *EMI Records Ltd v CBS United Kingdom Ltd*[1130] the Court stated that an agreement could continue to produce its effects after it had formally ceased to be in force, but should only be regarded as doing so if, from the behaviour of the persons concerned, there might be inferred the existence of elements of concerted practice peculiar to the agreement and producing the same result as that envisaged by the agreement. The Court added that such an inference should not be drawn when the effects do not exceed those flowing from the mere exercise of national trade-mark rights. Neither *Sirena* nor *EMI v CBS* appears to have been cited in *Panayiotou*, which it is suggested does not represent the law.

28–224

No rights at all in absence of assignment or licence. It might be thought that restrictions on the assignee or licensee as to their use or reproduction of the work in question under a copyright assignment or licence should raise few competition issues, given that in the absence of the agreement the assignee or licensee would not have been able to reproduce or use the work at all.[1131] However, it is unlikely that such an approach can be relied upon. Thus, in *Windsurfing*,[1132] the Court of Justice upheld the Commission's view (in a patents case) that a restriction on the licensee to the effect that he could mount the patented rig only on a particular type of surfboard was contrary to art.101(1). It might also be thought that if a licensor or licensee would not have entered into an agreement at all in the absence of a particular clause (thus preventing the dissemination of the work at all), then that should be an argument against its being regarded as anti-competitive. That

28–225

[1127] *Keurkoop BV v Nancy Kean Gifts BV* (Case 144/81) [1982] E.C.R. 2853 at 2873; [1983] 2 C.M.L.R. 47.

[1128] [1994] E.M.L.R.229 at para.C4.16 (p.425 of the report).

[1129] (Case 40/70) [1971] E.C.R. 69; [1971] C.M.L.R. 260.

[1130] (Case 51/75) [1976] E.C.R. 811; [1976] 2 C.M.L.R. 235.

[1131] Compare, under the UK Restrictive Trade Practices Act 1976, *Ravenseft Properties v DGFT* [1978] Q.B. 352, where it was held that a restriction of this type upon the licensee or assignee was not a relevant restriction for the purposes of that Act. The Commission's 1964 Patent Notice reflected this approach until it was withdrawn in 1984.

[1132] (Case 193/83) [1986] E.C.R. 611; [1986] 3 C.M.L.R. 489.

argument does carry some weight under art.101(1), as the case of *Nungesser v Commission*[1133] shows; it may also affect the analysis under art.101(3).

28–226   **Exclusive licences.** An important distinction was drawn in the *Nungesser* case[1134] between so-called "open" exclusive licences (which prevent the licensor from competing with the licensee in the licensee's territory or from granting further licences in respect of that territory, but do not preclude other licensees selling into the territory) and "closed" exclusive licences (where the agreement is designed to protect the licensee from any competition with respect to the licensed goods).[1135] "Open" exclusive licences may well not fall under art.101(1) at all, provided that (as in *Nungesser*) they do not last for an undue period of time,[1136] are necessary to provide the licensee with the degree of protection that he needs in order to develop a market for the product,[1137] and relate to a new product with which purchasers may not be familiar.[1138] In *Nungesser*, the Court of Justice accepted the argument that this was a case where the licensee would not have been prepared to take the risk of developing and marketing the licensed product without protection of this kind; as a result, competition was not affected by the restriction and art.101(1) did not apply to it. In any event, an open exclusive licence which is not unlimited in time may benefit from an exemption under art.101(3) even if the conditions in *Nungesser* do not apply.[1139] The Commission may be more inclined to take an adverse view of such a clause if the effect of the exclusivity is that a product is not supplied at all in a part of the common market.[1140]

28–227   **Right to perform a copyright work.** In *Coditel II*,[1141] the Court of Justice stated that an exclusive licence to exhibit a film would not, as such, be subject to art.101. The Court of Justice took the view that the right of the owner of the copyright in a film to require fees for the showing of that film was part of the essential function of copyright; unless the grant of a sole and exclusive licence to show a film could be shown to be the purpose, the means or the result of an agreement prohibited by the Treaty, the restriction was unaffected by art.101. However, the

---

[1133] (Case 258/76) [1982] E.C.R. 2015; [1983] 1 C.M.L.R. 278.

[1134] Case 258/78 *Nungesser v Commission* [1982] E.C.R. 2015; [1983] 1 C.M.L.R. 278.

[1135] For an example of such a licence, see Commission Decision 87/123 *Boussois* [1987] OJ L50/30 (know-how; exemption granted).

[1136] See *RAI/Unitel* [1978] OJ L157/39; [1978] 3 C.M.L.R. 306, Commission XIIth Report on Competition Policy, point 90; the Commission held that Unitel's exclusive contract for opera singers for one operatic work and one means of exploitation was not caught by art.101(1); it is not clear what period may be imposed.

[1137] In *Velcro/Aplix* [1985] OJ L233/22; [1989] 4 C.M.L.R. 157, the Commission held that *Nungesser* did not apply to take an exclusive licence outside art.101(1) once the technology in question had ceased to be novel. See also Commission Decision 88/501, *Tetra Pak I (BTG Licence)* [1990] 4 C.M.L.R. 47, upheld on appeal: *Tetra Pak Rausing SA v Commission* (T–51/89) [1990] E.C.R. II–309; [1991] 4 C.M.L.R. 334, where it was held that an open exclusive patent licence would have infringed art.101 even though it fell within the block exemption provided for by reg.2349/84 because the licensee was dominant in the field of activity which was the object of the licence and barriers to entry were particularly high.

[1138] Compare art.4 of the TTBER, which does not include open exclusive licences in the list of hardcore restrictions. Note also *Knoll-Hille Form*, Commission XIIIth annual report on competition policy, point 142, where the Commission records its view that neither the newness of the product nor the necessary investment justified an "open" exclusive licence with a duration of eight years. Given the market position of the companies involved, the Commission would not have been prepared to grant an exemption under art.101(3).

[1139] For examples in the field of know-how licensing, see Commission Decisions 87/123 *Boussois* [1987] OJ L50/30; 87/100 [1987] OJ L31/41 *Mitchell Cotts (joint venture)*; 88/143 *Rich Products* [1988] OJ L69/21; and 88/563 *Delta Chemie* [1988] OJ L309/34. Compare art.4 of the TTBER, and para.28–200, above.

[1140] See *The Old Man and the Sea* [1977] 1 C.M.L.R. D121.

[1141] (Case 262/81) *Coditel v Cine Vog Films* [1982] E.C.R. 3381; [1983] 1 C.M.L.R. 49.

Court of Justice also held[1142] that if artificial and unjustifiable barriers were created, or if there was a possibility of charging excessive royalties, or if the period
of exclusivity was disproportionate, then the agreement would fall under art.101.
This dictum was applied in *Film Purchases for German Television Stations*,[1143]
where the Commission held that the purchase of the exclusive right to show a
large number of films in Germany and Luxembourg for a long period was contrary to art.101(1), and required modification of the agreement to allow third parties to show films at times that did not clash with those chosen by the licensees.[1144]
The case law of the Court of Justice relating to the public performance and rental
of commercially released sound recordings and videos is considered
elsewhere.[1145]

Other objectionable provisions in the case-law and Commission decisions.   **28–228**
The fields of sports broadcasting and collecting societies are dealt with separately
below.[1146] Outside those fields, such provisions have included (or might include)
the following:

> A restriction on the licensee selling copyright works outside the allocated
> territory.[1147]
>
> Agreements between sound recording copyright owners and a pan-
> European retailer pursuant to which consumers could only purchase cop-
> ies for download in their country of residence.[1148]
>
> Restrictions in settlement agreements arising out of litigation in respect of
> the infringement of copyright,[1149] such as: a "no-challenge" clause
> preventing the licensee from challenging the licensor's rights,[1150] a non-
> competition clause, a royalties clause extending to goods which are not
> the subject of the licensed rights[1151] and a clause requiring the licensee to
> transfer to the licensor title to any licensee's copyright in improvements

---

[1142] (Case 262/81) *Coditel v Cine Vog Films* [1982] E.C.R. 3381; [1983] 1 C.M.L.R. 49, para.19.

[1143] [1989] OJ L284/36; [1990] 4 C.M.L.R. 841.

[1144] For the application of these principles to territorial exclusive licences in relation to televised
horse races, see Commission decision 95/373, *PMI-DSV* [1995] OJ L221/34 and *Tiercé-Ladbroke
v Commission* (T–504/93) [1997] E.C.R. II–923. In Commission decision of December 29, 2003,
Telenor/Canal+/Canal Digital C(2003)5192 final, the Commission exempted exclusive distribution arrangements relating to pay TV content which were entered into when one joint venturer
bought out the other inter alia because they allowed continued competition. See also Commission
decision 199/242 *TPS*.

[1145] See para.24–30, above.

[1146] See paras 28–229 et seq. and 28–237 et seq. respectively.

[1147] See para.28–192, above; *Dutch Publishers' Association*, VIth Report on Competition Policy
points 153-5; *BBC*, VIth Report on Competition Policy point 166; *Ernest Benn*, IXth Report on
Competition Policy points 118 and 119; and *Knoll/Hille-Form* XIIIth Report on Competition
Policy points 142 to 146. However, such a restriction may not be a hardcore restriction for the
purposes of the Technology Transfer Block Exemption: see below para.28–249.

[1148] Case COMP/39.154— *iTunes*. See MEMO/07/126. On investigation it emerged that no such
agreements actually existed. See IP/08/22 in which the Commission nevertheless noted that
"some record companies, publishers and collecting societies still apply licensing practices which
can make it difficult for iTunes to operate stores accessible for a European consumer anywhere in
the EU".

[1149] *NeilsonHordell/Reichmark*, Commission, XIIth Report on Competition Policy, points 88–89.
The case concerned technical drawings and "by extension" the products they represented.

[1150] In *Bayer AG v Süllhöfer* [1988] E.C.R. 5249 the ECJ held that no challenge clauses in patent
agreements did not restrict competition when the agreement in which they were contained granted
a free licence and the licensee did not, therefore, suffer the competitive disadvantage involved in
the payment of royalties or when the licence was granted subject to payment of royalties but related to a technically outdated process which the undertaking accepting the no-challenge agreement did not use. See now the TTBER and Guidelines.

[1151] As to whether clauses requiring payment of royalties after the expiry of a patent infringe art.101,
see *Ottung v Klee und Weilbach A/S* [1989] E.C.R. 1177.

to the licensed products.[1152] According to the Commission all such clauses would normally be regarded as infringing art.101(1) and not capable of exemption under art.101(3).

Clauses in licensing agreements for the development of games compatible with Sega and Nintendo's consoles which required the licensee to obtain the licensor's approval of any game before it was marketed, restricted the range of sub-contractors the licensee could use and limited the number of games licensees could release per year.[1153]

Terms of agreements between Microsoft and Internet service providers for the licensing and distribution of Microsoft's Internet Explorer products which provided for termination if minimum distribution volumes or percentages of the Internet Explorer were not achieved and which restricted ISPs from promoting and advertising competing browser software.[1154]

So-called "most favoured nation" clauses in agreements between Hollywood film studios and pay-TV companies in Europe.[1155] According to the Commission the studios typically sold to broadcasters their entire film production for a given period of years. These clauses gave the studios the right to enjoy the most favourable terms agreed between a pay-TV company and any one of them and according to the Commission's preliminary assessment the cumulative effect was an alignment of the prices paid to the studios.[1156]

(c) Sports broadcasting and art.101

28–229 ***Eurovision/the European Broadcasting Union.*** The European Broadcasting Union ("EBU") is an association of radio and television organisations which coordinates and supports television programme exchanges among its members through the Eurovision system. The EBU has operated a system of rules governing the acquisition of television rights to sports events, the exchange of programmes within the Eurovision framework and contractual access to such programmes for third parties.

In 1989, following a complaint that the EBU was refusing to grant sub-licences for sporting events, which gave rise to a statement of objections, the EBU revised its rules to allow sub-licensing. It then sought negative clearance or exemption for its rules. The Commission held[1157] that the revised rules restricted competition between EBU's members (who would otherwise compete with themselves for

---

[1152] As to such clauses in the patent field, see also *Velcro/Aplix* [1985] OJ L233/22; [1989] 4 C.M.L.R. 157.

[1153] *Sega and Nintendo*, Commission XXVIIth Report on Competition Policy (1997), pp.125–6. These cases were resolved by comfort letter following deletion of the offending clauses. The following year, the Commission dealt with the following restrictions in Sony's game development licensing agreements: a requirement that the licensee obtain Sony's approval before starting development and before launching the game; a requirement that all developing and publishing sub-contractors be approved by Sony; and a requirement that the licensee have its games manufactured by Sony: *Sony*, Commission XXVIIIth Report on Competition Policy (1998), pp.159–160. Proceedings were terminated on the basis that these restrictions were removed and replaced with "non-restrictive" pre-release approval rights. All game software would be tested either by an independent testing service or by Sony's testing service, but only for compliance with clear, non-objectionable specifications and well-defined criteria.

[1154] *Microsoft*, Commission XXIXth Report on Competition Policy (1999), point 56 and p.162. This case was resolved by comfort letter on deletion of the offending clauses.

[1155] Case COMP/38.427.

[1156] Commission Press Release IP/04/1314. Without admitting a violation of competition law, all but two of the studios waived the MFN clauses in their existing agreements. See Commission Press Release IP/04/1314 and the Commission's Report on Competition Policy 2004, paras 88–91.

[1157] Commission decision 93/403.

the acquisition of rights) and disadvantaged purely commercial channels who were outside the EBU (because the EBU had acquired considerable market power). However, it held that the arrangements did provide certain benefits (including an improvement in purchasing conditions, programme coordination at national level, the facilitation of cross-border broadcasting and a cheaper and better service). For this and other reasons the Commission went on to declare art.101(1) inapplicable for a period of five years subject to conditions designed to ensure access to third parties. However, in 1996 this decision was annulled by the General Court[1158] on two grounds. First, EBU's membership rules were not clear enough to enable them to be applied uniformly and in a non-discriminatory manner, as a result of which it was not possible to assess whether the restrictions on competition were indispensable. Second, the Commission had wrongly taken account of the EBU's public mission.

Thereafter the EBU rules were referred again. The Commission held that the rules fell within art.101(1) but, having regard to their provision for the grant of sublicences to non EBU members, adopted a decision conditionally exempting them under art.101(3).[1159] However, this decision too was annulled by the Court of First Instance on the ground that the system of sublicensing did not guarantee access to non EBU members and therefore failed to avoid the elimination of competition in the market.[1160] In 2007 the Commission closed its investigation.[1161]

Telefónica/Sogecable/Audiovisual Sport.[1162] This case followed the notification to the Commission by a Spanish pay-TV company ("Sogecable") and a Spanish telecommunications operator ("Telefónica") of an agreement concerning a joint venture company ("AVS") which had been set up by them to exploit the broadcasting rights to the Spanish "Liga" and "Copa" football matches. In broad terms, under the agreement, Sogecable, which held exclusive pay-per-view broadcasting rights in respect of the Liga, granted Telefónica and its cable subsidiaries a licence to broadcast Liga matches. In return, Telefónica, which held pay-per-view rights to Champions League matches, granted a licence to Sogecable to broadcast such matches jointly with Telefónica. It was agreed that the parties would cooperate in the exploitation of these rights through AVS, which determined the prices and conditions for their exploitation. The Commission's preliminary view was that the agreement might have as its object and effect both price-fixing and the sharing of markets.[1163] Following notification of this, the parties agreed to grant access to the relevant rights to new cable and digital terrestrial television entrants, to modify their agreements and to introduce contractual guarantees that the competitors were free to set the prices of pay-per-view matches to viewers. The investigation was suspended when it was announced that Via Digital would merge with Sogecable. Following the merger, Sogecable agreed to buy Telefónica's stake in AVS, thus terminating the agreement notified to the Commission.[1164]

28–230

GTR/FIA.[1165] This case concerned amongst other things the broadcasting rights in respect of the FIA Formula One Championship. Following a notification by

28–231

[1158] *Métropole Télévision SA v Commission* (Joined Cases T–528/93, T–542/93, T–543/93 and T–546/93).
[1159] Decision 2004/400, [2000] OJ L151/18.
[1160] *Métropole Télévision SA v Commission* (Joined Cases T–185/00, T–216/00, T–299/00 and T–300/00). An appeal to the Court of Justice was dismissed: Case C470/02.
[1161] Report on Competition Policy 2007 point 64.
[1162] Case COMP/C2/37.652.
[1163] Press Release IP/00/372, April 12, 2000.
[1164] Press Release IP/03/655, May 8, 2003.
[1165] Case COMP/C2/36.776.

the Commission, the organisers and promoters of the championship made various alterations to their broadcasting arrangements. These included the removal of provisions which would have entitled the organisers to appropriate all media rights in a given championship together with a reduction in the length of periods of exclusivity granted to individual broadcasters. Accordingly, the Commission indicated that it intended to take a favourable view of the arrangements.[1166] It later closed its investigation.[1167]

28–232   *UEFA's broadcasting regulations.*[1168] This case concerned UEFA regulations which enable national football associations to "block" a limited number of hours during which football may not be broadcast on television. Their purpose is to provide national football associations with a limited opportunity to schedule domestic football fixtures at times when attendance and amateur participation are not liable to be disrupted by contemporaneous broadcasting. The Commission decided that UEFA's regulations did not have any anti-competitive object: the object was to promote the development of football and the variety of the competition rather than restricting broadcasters' possibilities of acquiring rights to football events or of competing for advertising revenues or subscribers. Nor was there an appreciable restriction of competition. Accordingly, the Commission decided that it had no grounds for action under art.101(1).[1169]

28–233   *UEFA: Champions League.*[1170] This case concerned the sale of media rights in respect of that league. UEFA applied for negative clearance or exemption in respect of its proposed arrangements for the sale of these rights. Under the proposed arrangements, UEFA was granted the exclusive right to sell these rights, thus excluding the football clubs from taking independent commercial actions relating to their exploitation. UEFA's commercial policy was to sell the television rights in a single package on an exclusive basis to a single broadcaster per Member State. The Commission issued a statement of objections finding that the notified arrangement restricted competition. Subsequently, UEFA notified a new commercial policy which would give the football clubs much greater control over the sale of these rights. In particular, the clubs would be allowed to sell certain media rights on a non-exclusive basis in parallel with UEFA and the media rights would be split into several different rights packages that would be offered for sale in separate packages to different third parties. The Commission later adopted a final decision exempting the new policy subject to conditions.[1171]

28–234   *Joint Selling of the media rights of the FA Premier League.*[1172] In this case the Commission concluded (following its own initiative investigation and thereafter an application for negative clearance or exemption) that certain aspects of the agreement between the Premier League clubs and Football Association Premier League Limited ("FAPL", a company owned by the clubs) restricted competition. The clubs granted FAPL the exclusive right to sell the media rights to the Premier League. Any sale of the rights required approval of two thirds of the clubs in general meeting. Thus, individual clubs were prevented from taking independent commercial actions regarding the exploitation of the rights. The Commission found that this restricted competition in the upstream market for the acquisition

---

[1166] [2001] OJ C169/5.
[1167] Press Release IP/01/1523, October 30, 2001.
[1168] Case COMP/C2/37.576.
[1169] [2001] OJ L171/12.
[1170] Case COMP/C.2/37.398.
[1171] *Joint selling of the commercial rights of the UEFA Champions League* (Case 2003/778) [2003] OJ L 291/25.
[1172] Cases COMP/C2/38.173 and 38.453.

of media rights and that this also affected the downstream markets on which those rights are used to provide services to consumers, in particular the television markets where free-TV broadcasters compete for advertisers and pay-TV broadcasters compete for subscribers. In response to the Commission's objections, FAPL offered and the Commission accepted commitments which would involve the television rights being offered in several packages and would give the individual clubs greater rights to exploit the broadcasting rights themselves.[1173]

3G mobile rights to sports events. In September 2005 the Commission concluded a sector inquiry into this market. Four main areas of concern were identified. First, bundling: situations where powerful media operators had bought all audio-visual rights to premium sports in a bundle in order to secure exclusivity over all platforms with no view to exploiting or sublicensing 3G rights. Second, embargoes: situations where overly restrictive conditions (serious time embargoes or unnecessary limitations of clip length) were imposed upon mobile rights that limited the practical availability of 3G content. Third, joint selling: situations where 3G rights remained unexploited because collective selling organisations did not manage to sell the 3G rights of individual sports clubs. Fourth, exclusivity: the exclusive attribution of 3G rights in situations leading to the monopolisation of premium content by powerful operators. The report invited market players to review their business practices and to redress possible anti-competitive effects resulting from them.[1174]   **28–235**

English cases. In *The Racecourse Association v OFT*[1175] it was held that the joint selling of media rights to horse races did not infringe the Chapter I prohibition of the Competition Act[1176] being necessary to secure a proper commercial objective, namely the creation of a new broadcasting channel and linked interactive betting website.   **28–236**

Bookmakers' Afternoon Greyhound Services Ltd v Amalgamated Racing Ltd[1177] concerned the provision of live broadcasts of horseracing to licensed betting offices ("LBOs"). After it became lawful to show such broadcasts in 1987 the operators of LBOs paid a single distributor for the rights to show them. Following dissatisfaction with the amount they were being paid for these rights, a majority of the racecourses established a joint venture to market them. As a result, prices charged to LBOs increased and the LBOs contended that the emergence of the joint venture and its entry into the market infringed art.101. The Court of Appeal upheld the Judge's decision that neither the object nor the effect of the arrangements was restrictive of competition.

[1173] Notice [2004] OJ C115/3. Commission Press Release IP/06/356. Similar issues have arisen is respect of the German Bundesliga: see Commission decision 2005/396 [2005] OJ L134/46.

[1174] See the report at *ec.europa.eu/comm/competition/sectors/media/inquiries/final_report/pdf* [Accessed November 16, 2008]. Its contents are summarised at points 78 to 83 of the Commission's Report on Competition Policy 2005 (SEC (2006) 761 final). See also Penny, "Sports Rights—How Mobile are they?" [2005] 8 Ent. L.R. 201 and Hatton, Wagner and Armengod, "Fair Play: How Competition Authorities have regulated the Sale of Football Media Rights in Europe" [2007] E.C.L.R. 346.

[1175] [2005] CAT 29.

[1176] See para.28–290, below.

[1177] [2008] EWHC 1978 (Ch); on appeal [2009] EWCA Civ 750.

(d) *Collecting societies*[1178]

28–237   **IFPI "Simulcasting".**[1179] This case arose from the notification by the IFPI[1180] of a model agreement between record companies' collecting societies in relation to the simultaneous broadcast via the internet in multiple territories of sound recordings incorporated in radio and television programmes. The purpose of the agreement was to enable broadcasters to obtain a single multi-territorial licence from a single collecting society rather than having to obtain a separate licence in respect of each territory in which the broadcasts would be received. In its original form, the agreement required broadcasters to obtain a licence from the collecting society for the territory in which the signal in question originated. Following discussions with the Commission, the agreement was amended so that broadcasters whose signals originated anywhere in the EEA would be able to approach any participating EEA collecting society for a licence, thus encouraging competition between the various collecting societies (there were participating societies in all EEA countries except France and Spain; other participants included societies in the Far East, Latin America and New Zealand). In 2001, the Commission indicated that it took a favourable view of the amended agreement[1181] and in 2002 it issued a decision exempting the agreement until its expiry.[1182] The Commission's reasoning can be summarised as follows. There were two relevant product markets: "multi-territorial simulcasting rights administration services between record producers' collecting societies" and "multi-territorial and multi-repertoire licensing of the record producers' simulcasting right".[1183] In respect of each product market, the geographical market was the whole of the EEA apart from France and Spain.[1184] The proposed agreement was an agreement between undertakings.[1185] Article 5(2) of the agreement, which provided that the tariff applicable to the clearance of rights was that of the country of destination, appreciably restricted competition.[1186] The proposed agreement was clearly capable of affecting trade between Member States.[1187] Although the agreement would create a new product, improve the distribution of music and benefit the consumer,[1188] the Commission identified two major concerns in respect of art.5(2). The first was that neither the national tariffs nor the global licence fee distinguished between the copyright royalty and the administration fee. The parties resolved this concern by undertaking to separate these two elements and to identify them separately when charging users. This could not be done immediately and the parties undertook to achieve it by December 31, 2004. The Commission accepted that

---

[1178] See generally Ch.27, above. For a detailed assessment by the Commission of some of the competition issues relevant to the European music industry, see decision C(2007)2160 in the merger case COMP/M.4402— *Universal/BMG Publishing*.

[1179] Case COMP/C2/38.014. See Capobianco: "Licensing of Music Rights: Media Convergence, Technological Developments and EC Competition Law" [2004] E.I.P.R. 113 and Aitman & Jones: "Competition Law and Copyright: Has the Copyright Owner Lost the Ability to Control his Copyright?" [2004] E.I.P.R. 137.

[1180] For the IFPI, see para.26–182, above.

[1181] [2001] OJ C231/18.

[1182] [2003] OJ L107/58.

[1183] Case COMP/C2/38.014 IFPI, para.32. The term "multi-repertoire licence" was defined by the Commission as "a multi-territory licence to a user including, beside its own, the repertoire of a represented sister-society": ibid., para.16.

[1184] paras 39 and 44.

[1185] para.60.

[1186] para.76.

[1187] para.83.

[1188] paras 87, 92 and 95 respectively.

this time period was indispensable within the meaning of art.101(3).[1189] The Commission's second concern was that the global licence fee to be charged in respect of multi-territory/multi-repertoire licences would include a royalty element which resulted from the aggregation of all the copyright royalties determined at national level. As a result, the royalty element would remain predetermined and unchangeable by the society granting the licence. Ultimately, however, the Commission accepted that such a provision was indispensable within the meaning of art.101(3).[1190] The Commission further concluded that the agreement did not eliminate competition in respect of a substantial part of the relevant products within the meaning of art.101(3).[1191]

The Santiago Agreement. In April 2001, BUMA, GEMA, PRS and SACEM   **28–238**
(which were later joined by all similar societies in the EEA apart from SPA in Portugal) notified to the Commission a proposed amendment to their existing bilateral reciprocal representation agreements[1192] to cover the licensing of the public performance of music on the internet ("the Santiago agreement").[1193] The amendment authorised each society to grant non-exclusive licences for the online public performance (including webcasting, streaming, music on demand and music included in online video transmission) of musical works in the repertoire of all the other societies on a worldwide basis. The licence was granted by the society operating in the country where the content provider had its economic residence. In its Notice of Objections, the Commission stated that it supported the "one-stop-shop" principle embodied in the agreement, but that the agreement failed to provide for competition between collecting societies and thus hampered the achievement of a genuine single market in the field of copyright management services. The Commission believed that this might result in unjustified inefficiencies as regards the offer of online music services to the ultimate detriment of consumers. It also considered that the territorial exclusivity embodied in the agreement was not justified by technical reasons and was irreconcilable with the worldwide reach of the internet.[1194] In April and May 2005, two of the parties to the Santiago agreement (BUMRA and SABEM) undertook to the Commission pursuant to art.9(1) of the Modernisation Regulation not to be party to any agreement in relation to the licensing of public performance of music on the internet which contained an "economic residency" clause of the type to which the Commission objected.[1195]

The Cannes Extension Agreement. This is an agreement between 13 European   **28–239**
mechanical copyright collecting societies and the five major music publishers which was notified to the Commission under Regulation 17. On January 24, 2006, the Commission notified the parties of its preliminary assessment within the

---

[1189] para.107.

[1190] para.115.

[1191] para.123.

[1192] As to which, see *Tournier v Ministere Public* (C–395/87) and Cases C–110, 241 and 242/88 *Lucazeau v SACEM; SACEM v Deiselle; SACEM v Sougmagnac* [1989] E.C.R. 2521; [1991] C.M.L.R. 248, para.28–285, below.

[1193] Case COMP/C2/38.126, [2001] OJ C145/2. For the rights administered by PRS, see para.27–65, above. See also Capobianco: "Licensing of Music Rights: Media Convergence, Technological Developments and EC Competition Law" [2004] E.I.P.R. 113.

[1194] Press release IP/04/586. The Commission contrasted the Santiago agreement unfavourably with the IFPI Simulcasting agreement (see para.28–237, above) and the standard agreement produced in 2003 by the record companies' collecting societies, pursuant to which commercial users would also have freedom of choice as regards the licensor society in Europe.

[1195] The Commission invited comments: Cases COMP/C2/39152— *BUMRA* and COMP/C2/39151— *SABEM* [2005] OJ C200/11. The Commission's website does not refer to any subsequent proceedings in this matter.

meaning of art.9(1) of the Modernisation Regulation.[1196] The Commission raised two serious concerns. The first concerned Clause 9(a), which made provision for the grant of rebates to record companies who negotiated Central Licensing Agreements (defined by the Commission as "multi-repertoire one stop shop licences for the whole EEA territory"). The effect of Clause 9(a) was that a collecting society would have to obtain the consent of all its members before granting such a rebate. Given that each collecting society might have thousands of members, the Commission took the view that Clause 9(a) would effectively prevent the grant of rebates. The second concerned Clause 7(a)(i), which provided that collecting societies should never engage in activities which might be the activities of a publisher or record company. The Commission took the view that this clause had the object and might have the effect of crystallising current market structures and preventing future competition. The parties to the agreement then offered commitments. Clause 9(a) would be modified to permit a collecting society to grant a rebate out of retained administrative expenses if so decided by the competent body of the society without the need for consent. Clause 7(a)(i) would be deleted. Those commitments were accepted.[1197]

28–240   **CISAC.** CISAC (International Confederation of Societies of Authors and Composers) is the international association of authors' collecting societies. It has 24 members in the EEA including PRS[1198] in the United Kingdom and GEMA in Germany. The relations between its members are governed by a standard model contract for reciprocal representation in relation to the management of public performance rights.

On November 30, 2000, the RTL Group filed a complaint to the Commission against GEMA concerning GEMA's refusal to grant a Community-wide licence for all RTL Group's music broadcasting activities. On April 4, 2003, Music Choice Europe plc filed a complaint to the Commission concerning CISAC's model contract. The two cases were later merged as the CISAC Case.[1199]

At the time of the complaints, each member of CISAC enjoyed an exclusive position on its domestic market and had its own portfolio of works (or "repertoire"). Each EEA member of CISAC had a reciprocal representation contract with each of the other EEA members, giving it a "global portfolio" of musical works ("a multirepertoire") which enabled each member to deliver a multirepertoire licence to be exploited in its domestic market only.

For the purposes of the case, there were two important categories of clause in the CISAC model contract. The "membership clause" provided that while a reciprocal representation contract was in force neither of the contracting collecting societies might without the consent of the other accept as a member any member of the other society or any natural or legal person having the nationality of one of the countries in which the other collecting society operated. The "territoriality clauses" provided first that a collecting society could only grant licences to users within its own territory ("the exclusivity clause"); and secondly that the licence was limited to the domestic territory of the society which granted it ("the territorial delineation"). This limitation applied even for the internet, cable retransmission and (with certain exceptions) satellite transmission rights.

On February 7, 2006 the Commission announced that it had sent a statement of objections to CISAC concerning three forms of copyright exploitation: internet,

---

[1196] Case COMP/C.2/38.681 *Universal International Music BV/MCPS (the Cannes Extension Agreement).*
[1197] Commission decision of October 4, 2006 [2007] OJ L296/27.
[1198] As to which, see para.27–65.
[1199] COMP 38.698.

satellite transmission and cable retransmission of music. The Commission was not concerned about the reciprocal representation agreements as such, but considered that the membership clause and the territoriality clauses might infringe art.101. The Commission also expressed concerns about the "network effect" of the agreements. It stated that it believed that the effect of the network of the agreements was that the membership and territorial restrictions multiplied and guaranteed to collecting societies an absolutely exclusive position on their domestic market, thus strengthening their historical de facto monopoly and preventing new entrants from entering the market for the management of copyright.

Following written replies and an oral hearing, CISAC and 18 of its members (including PRS) offered commitments. The commitments involved the removal of the "membership clause" and the "exclusivity clause". As to the "territorial delineation", each society offered either to license its own repertoire directly across the EEA or to mandate under certain conditions each signatory society which fulfilled certain criteria to grant multirepertoire multi territorial licences. On June 9, 2007, the Commission indicated its intention, subject to market testing, to adopt a decision under Article 9 of the Modernisation Regulation.[1200]

However, according to the Commission,[1201] market players generally expressed the view that the commitments would not be effective. Although the objectionable clauses had all been removed from the CISAC model contract, a number of collecting societies still had the membership clause in some of their contracts and the other clauses continued to exist in a number of reciprocal agreements. On July 16, 2008, the Commission therefore adopted a Decision[1202] that the members of CISAC had infringed art.101 and required them to cease to apply the membership clause, the exclusivity clause and the territorial delineation (in the case of the latter, in relation to internet, cable and satellite exploitation only), which it now described as a concerted practice.

This decision is under appeal.[1203] So far as can be gleaned from the Official Journal, two grounds have been raised. First that the territorial delineation is not the product of a concerted practice but "exists because all societies find it in the interest of their members to include such a clause in their reciprocal representation agreements". Alternatively, any concerted practice on territorial delineations "concerns a form of competition that is not worthy of protection"; and if it restricts competition it is "necessary and proportionate to the legitimate objective".

Proposed legislation. Proposed community legislation in this area is dealt with elsewhere.[1204]   **28–241**

(e) The technology transfer block exemption

The technology transfer block exemption ("TTBER"): background.[1205] As   **28–242**
has been seen, art.101(3) of the Treaty provides that art.101(1) may be declared inapplicable in the case of any category of agreements between undertakings.

[1200] [2007] OJ C128/12.

[1201] MEMO/08/511 of July 16, 2008 and IP/08/1165.

[1202] Commission decision of July 16, 2008, C(2008) 3435 final.

[1203] Case T–442/08. See [2009] OJ C82/25.

[1204] paras 24–160 et seq.

[1205] Commission Regulation 772/2004/EC [2004] OJ L123/11. For the position in the EEA, see EFTA Surveillance Authority Decision No. 228/05/COL issuing a Notice entitled "Guidelines on the application of art.53 of the EEA Agreement to technology transfer agreements" [2005] OJ L259/1.

Article 1(1)(b) of Regulation 19/65/EEC[1206] provides that the Commission may by regulation declare that art.101(1) shall not apply to categories of agreements to which only two undertakings are party and which include restrictions imposed in relation to the acquisition or use of industrial property rights, in particular of patents, utility models, designs or trade marks, or to the rights arising out of contracts for assignment of, or the right to use, a method of manufacture or knowledge relating to the use or application of industrial processes. In 1984, pursuant to this provision, the Commission made a Regulation in respect of patent licensing agreements.[1207] In 1988, it made a further Regulation in respect of know-how licensing agreements.[1208] In 1996, these provisions were repealed and replaced by a new Regulation covering technology transfer agreements.[1209] This Regulation in turn was repealed and replaced with effect from May 1, 2004 but subject to transitional provisions.[1210] The aim of the Regulation is to simplify the regulatory framework and its application. The Commission considered it appropriate to move away from the previous approach which involved listing exempted clauses and to place greater emphasis on defining the categories of agreements which are exempted up to a certain level of market power and on specifying the restrictions or clauses which are not to be contained in such agreements. The Commission considered that this was consistent with an "economics-based" approach which assesses the impact of agreements on the relevant market.[1211] The block exemption of categories of agreement is based on a presumption that to the extent that they are caught by art.101(1) they fulfil the four conditions laid down by art.101(3).[1212] Block exempted agreements are legally valid and enforceable. They can only be prohibited for the future and only on withdrawal of the block exemption by the Commission or a national competition authority. They cannot be prohibited under art.101 by national courts in the context of private litigation.[1213]

28–243   **The TTBER: direct application to the rights covered in this Work.** The 1996 block exemption did not apply to licences of intellectual property rights other than patents unless they were ancillary to patent or know-how licences.[1214] This caused a lack of certainty in the computer software field, which the Commission considered particularly regrettable in view of the economic importance of software products.[1215] Accordingly, for the first time, the technology transfer block exemption applies to copyright licences, albeit only to licences relating to

---

[1206] [1965] OJ 036/533 as amended by Council Regulation 1215/99/EC [1999] OJ L148/1.

[1207] reg.2349/84/EEC.

[1208] reg.556/89/EEC.

[1209] reg.240/96 EC [1996] OJ L31/2. See *Copinger* 14th edn, para.29–189.

[1210] Commission Regulation No. 772/2004/EC on the application of art.[101](3) to categories of technology transfer agreements [2004] OJ L123/1, "the TTBER". Art.9 repeals reg.240/96 EC. Art.10 provides that where an agreement was in force on April 30, 2004 and was exempt from art.101 under reg.240/96 EC on that date, but does not satisfy the conditions of the TTBER, art.101(1) shall nevertheless not apply to it until March 31, 2006.

[1211] TTBER, recital 4. See also the Commission's Evaluation Report on reg.240/96 EC, COM(2001) 786 final.

[1212] Guidelines on the application of art.81 of the EC Treaty to technology transfer agreements [2004] OJ C101/2 ("TTBER Guidelines"), para.35.

[1213] TTBER Guidelines, para.34. As to withdrawal, see para.28–258, below.

[1214] reg.240/96 art.1(1).

[1215] The Commission's Evaluation Report COM(2001) 786 final, refers to two forms of uncertainty (para.114). First, a single licence often includes a complex package of intellectual property rights and it may be difficult to determine what is the preponderant element of the licence. Secondly, while the Commission was generally inclined to treat copyright licences in the same way as patent licences (as in *Sicasov* [1999] OJ L4/27; [1999] C.M.L.R. 192), it had never clearly stated that all the principles applicable to patents were also applicable to copyright. The Report goes on to say that this is of particular importance to the software industry, because many software licensing agreements do not fall within the block exemption for vertical agreements (Reg.2790/99), for

computer software. Since the Regulation applies to patent licensing agreements and for these purposes, the term "patent" includes designs and semiconductor topographies,[1216] the Regulation also applies to licensing agreements in respect of these rights as well.

The TTBER: application by analogy to the rights covered in this work. More-   **28–244**
over, although the block exemption does not apply to copyright other than software copyright, the Commission has made clear that as a general rule it will apply the principles set out in the Regulation to copyright licences which are granted for the purpose of the reproduction and distribution of copies of a copyright work, that is, the production of copies for resale.[1217] On the other hand, the Commission does not intend to apply the TTBER by way of analogy to rights in performances or "other rights related to copyright" (this appears to be a reference to copyright in sound recordings and broadcasts).[1218] Such rights are considered to raise different considerations. The Commission's reasoning is not always easy to follow. According to the Commission, in the case of "the various rights related to performances", value is created not by the reproduction and sale of copies of a product but by each individual performance of the protected work. Such exploitation can take various forms including the performance, showing or renting of protected material such as films, music or sporting events.[1219] The Commission goes on to emphasise the importance of taking account of "the specificities of the work and the way in which it is exploited".[1220] In that context, the Commission believes that resale restrictions may give rise to fewer competition concerns,[1221] while particular concerns may arise where licensors impose on their licensees to extend to each of the licensors more favourable conditions obtained by one of them.[1222]

The TTBER: general. Recital 5 to the Regulation states that technology transfer   **28–245**
agreements usually improve economic efficiency and are usually pro-competitive because they can reduce duplication of research and development, strengthen the incentive for initial research and development, spur incremental innovation, facilitate diffusion and generate product market competition. Accordingly, art.2 of the Regulation declares that art.101(1) of the Treaty does not apply to technology transfer agreements entered into between two undertakings[1223] permitting the production of contract products (that is, products produced with the licensed technology).[1224] The term "technology transfer agreement" means a patent licens-

---

example if they involve distribution licences where the distributor duplicates the software and provides the physical medium on which the program is stored; or so-called "value-added" licences, whereby the software producer allows the licensee to modify the software for particular purposes, such as the creation of a local language version (ibid., para.115).

[1216] TTBER art.1(h).

[1217] TTBER Guidelines, para.51.

[1218] TTBER Guidelines, para.52. When used by the Commission, the term "related rights" usually refers to the rights granted by the 1961 Rome Convention for the Protection of Performers, Producers of Phonograms and Broadcasting Organisations: see below, paras 23–88 et seq., above.

[1219] Presumably a protected sporting event is an event in respect of which exclusive broadcasting rights have been granted.

[1220] Citing *Coditel SA v Ciné Vog Films SA* (Case 262/81) [1982] E.C.R. 3381; [1983] 1 C.M.L.R. 49, discussed at para.28–227, above.

[1221] The reason for this is not stated.

[1222] Again, the Commission does not elaborate.

[1223] In the TTBER Guidelines, the Commission notes that the block exemption does not apply to agreements between more than two undertakings but states that the principles in the Regulation will be applied to agreements between more than two undertakings which are of the same nature as those covered by the block exemption (paras 39 and 40).

[1224] TTBER art.1(f). The term "product" means a good or service, including both intermediary and final goods or services. In the TTBER Guidelines, the Commission notes that in order to be

ing agreement, a know-how[1225] licensing agreement, a software copyright licensing agreement or a mixed patent, know-how and software copyright licensing agreement. For these purposes, the term "patent" includes designs and semiconductor topographies.[1226] Such agreements are included even if they contain provisions which relate to the sale and purchase of products or the licensing of other intellectual property rights provided those provisions do not constitute the primary object of the agreement and are directly related to the production of the contract products.[1227] The definition also includes assignments of patents, know-how, software copyright or a combination thereof where part of the risk associated with the exploitation of the technology remains with the assignor.[1228] The exemption applies to the extent that the agreement contains restrictions on competition falling within art.101(1) and as long as to the intellectual right in question has not expired, lapsed or been declared invalid or (in the case of know-how) ceased to be secret.[1229]

28–246   **The TTBER: "competing undertakings".** This term, which appears regularly in the TTBER, is defined in art.1(j) to mean undertakings which compete on the relevant technology market and/or the relevant product market. There are lengthy sub-definitions as follows. Competing undertakings on the relevant technology market are undertakings which license out competing technologies without infringing each others' intellectual property rights. The relevant technology market includes technologies which are regarded by the licensees as interchangeable with or substitutable for the licensed technology, by reason of the technologies' characteristics, royalties and intended use.[1230] Potential competition on the technology market is not taken into account for these purposes.[1231] Competing undertakings on the relevant product market are undertakings which, in the absence of the technology transfer agreement, are both active on the relevant product and geographic market(s) on which the contract products are sold without infringing each others' intellectual property rights; or would on realistic grounds undertake the necessary additional investments or other necessary switching costs so that they could timely enter, without infringing each others' intellectual property rights, the relevant product and geographic markets in response to a small and permanent increase in relative prices (thus, to this extent, potential competition is relevant).[1232] The relevant product market comprises products which are regarded by the buyers as interchangeable with or substitutable for the

---

covered by the block exemption the licence must permit the licensee to exploit the licensed technology (para.41). It goes on to say that the exemption does not cover "technology pools" (agreements whereby the parties agree to pool their respective technologies and license them as a package or authorise a third party to license them on (ibid.)). Guidance as to technology pools is given in the TTBER Guidelines at paras 210 to 235.

[1225] "Know-how" is defined as a package of non-patented practical information resulting from experience and testing, which is secret, substantial and identified: TTBER, art.1(i).

[1226] See para.28–243, above.

[1227] TTBER art.1(b). Thus, according to the Commission, an agreement containing provision for the sale and purchase of products would be included in the exemption where, for example, the tied products take the form of equipment or process input which is specifically tailored to exploit the licensed technology efficiently: TTBER Guidelines, para.49. Similarly, where an agreement contains a provision for a licence in respect of copyright other than software copyright, it will only be block exempted to the extent that the copyright licence serves to enable the licensee better to exploit the licensed technology: para.50.

[1228] TTBER art.1(b). A particular example of this is stated to be where the consideration is dependent on the turnover obtained by the assignee in respect of products produced with the assigned technology, the quantity of such products produced or the number of operations carried out using the technology.

[1229] TTBER art.2. Where the know-how becomes publicly known as a result of action by the licensee, the exemption applies for the duration of the agreement.

[1230] TTBER art.1(j)(i).

[1231] TTBER Guidelines, para.66.

[1232] TTBER art.1(j)(ii). TTBER Guidelines, para.67.

contract products, by reason of the products' characteristics, prices and intended use.[1233]

The TTBER: "reciprocal agreements". This term also appears frequently in the TTBER. An agreement is reciprocal where the parties grant each other in the same or separate contracts a patent, know-how or software copyright licence or a mixed patent, know-how or software copyright licence and where these licences concern competing technologies or can be used for the production of competing products.[1234] An agreement is not reciprocal merely because it contains a grant back obligation or because the licensee licenses back its own improvements to the licensed technology.[1235] An agreement is non-reciprocal where one party grants the other a patent, know-how or software copyright licence or a mixed patent, know-how or software copyright licence or where the parties grant each other such a licence but those licences do not concern competing technologies and cannot be used for the production of competing products.[1236]

28–247

The TTBER: market share thresholds. The block exemption of restrictive agreements is subject to market share thresholds. Outside the "safe harbour" created by these thresholds, individual assessment is required. However, the fact that market shares exceed the thresholds does not give rise to any presumption that the agreement is caught by art.101(1) or does not fulfil the conditions of art.101(3).[1237] The threshold depends on whether the parties to the agreement are competing. Where they are competing, the exemption only applies if their combined market share is less than 20 per cent on the affected relevant technology and product market.[1238] Where the parties are not competing, the exemption applies if the market share of each of the parties does not exceed 30 per cent on the affected relevant technology and product market.[1239] The Regulation contains specific rules as to the calculation of market share.[1240]

28–248

The TTBER: hardcore restrictions: general. The TTBER contains a list of so-called "hardcore" restrictions, which the Commission considers to be restrictive of competition by their very object.[1241] Where a technology transfer agreement contains a hardcore restriction, the agreement as a whole falls outside the block exemption; for the purposes of the Regulation, such restrictions cannot be severed.[1242] The list of hardcore restrictions depends on whether the parties are or are not competing undertakings.[1243] Where the parties to the agreement are not competing at the time it is concluded but become competitors afterwards, they are to be treated as if they are competing undertakings for the full length of the agreement unless it is materially amended.[1244] Where the parties are competing undertakings, the exemption does not apply to agreements which directly or indirectly, in isolation or in combination with other factors under the parties'

28–249

[1233] TTBER art.1(j)(ii).
[1234] TTBER art.1(c). The TTBER Guidelines use the term "cross-licensing agreement": para.78.
[1235] TTBER Guidelines, para.78.
[1236] TTBER art.1(d).
[1237] TTBER Guidelines, para.65.
[1238] TTBER art.3(1). For these purposes, the market share of a party on the relevant technology market(s) is defined in terms of the presence of the licensed technology on the relevant product market(s). A licensor's market share is the combined market share on the relevant product market of the contract products produced by the licensor and its licensees: TTBER art.3(3).
[1239] TTBER art.3(2). For the definition of market share, see the previous footnote.
[1240] TTBER art.8.
[1241] TTBER Guidelines, para.14.
[1242] TTBER Guidelines para.75.
[1243] For when undertakings are competing, see above, para.28–246.
[1244] TTBER art.4(3).

control, have any of the following objects[1245]: restrictions on the prices at which the product is to be sold[1246]; the limitation of output[1247]; the allocation of markets or customers (but there are numerous exceptions to this)[1248]; and the restriction of the licensee's ability to exploit its own technology or of the ability of any party to carry out research and development unless the latter is indispensable to prevent the disclosure of the licensed know-how to third parties.[1249] Where the parties are not competing undertakings,[1250] the exemption does not apply to agreements which directly or indirectly, in isolation or in combination with other factors under the control of the parties have any of the following objects: first, the restriction of a party's ability to determine its prices when selling products to third parties (but this is without prejudice to the possibility of imposing a maximum sale price or recommending a sale price, provided it does not amount to a fixed or minimum sale price as a result of pressure from, or incentives offered by, any of the parties)[1251]; secondly, the restriction of the territory into which, or the customers to whom, the licensee may passively sell the contract products (but there are numerous exceptions to this)[1252]; and thirdly, the restriction of active or passive sales to end-users by a licensee which is a member of a selective distribution system and which operates at the retail level (but this is without prejudice to the possibility of prohibiting a member of the system from operating out of an unauthorised place of establishment).[1253]

28–250   **Competing undertakings: price fixing.** The exemption does not apply where the agreement has as its object the restriction of a party's ability to determine its prices when selling products to third parties,[1254] including products incorporating the licensed technology.[1255] According to the Commission,[1256] it is immaterial whether the agreement concerns fixed, minimum or maximum prices. Direct restrictions which will offend include direct agreement on the price to be charged and direct agreement on a price list with certain allowed maximum rebates. Price-fixing may also be implemented indirectly by applying disincentives to deviate from an agreed price level, for example by providing that the royalty rate will increase if product prices are reduced below a certain level. However, an obligation to pay a certain minimum royalty does not in itself amount to price-fixing.[1257] Where royalties are calculated on the basis of individual product sales, the amount of the royalty has a direct impact on product prices. Accordingly, competitors can use cross-licensing with reciprocal running royalties as a means of co-ordinating prices on downstream product markets. The Commission will only treat such cross licences as price-fixing where the agreement is devoid of competitive purpose.[1258] The restriction on price fixing also applies to agreements whereby royalties are calculated on the basis of all products sold irrespective of

---

[1245] TTBER art.4(1). These are analogous to the so-called "blacklisted" restrictions which appeared in art.3 of Regulation 240/96/EC (see *Copinger* 14th edn, para.29–189). See generally the TT-BER Guidelines, paras 77 to 95.
[1246] TTBER art.4(1)(a). See para.28–250, below.
[1247] TTBER art.4(1)(b). See para.28–251, below.
[1248] TTBER art.4(1)(c). See para.28–252, below.
[1249] TTBER art.4(1)(d).
[1250] For the meaning of the term "competing undertakings", see para.28–246, above.
[1251] TTBER art.4(2)(a). See para 28–250, below.
[1252] TTBER art.4(2)(b). See paras 28–255 to 28–256, below.
[1253] TTBER art.4(2)(c).
[1254] TTBER art.4(1)(a).
[1255] TTBER Guidelines, para.79.
[1256] TTBER Guidelines, para.79.
[1257] TTBER Guidelines, para.79.
[1258] TTBER Guidelines, para.80.

whether the licensed technology is being used.[1259] Such agreements restrict competition because they raise the cost of using the licensee's own technology and reduce competition which would otherwise have existed.[1260] Exceptionally, however, art.101(3) may apply to such an agreement, for example where, in the absence of the restriction, it would be impossible for the licensor to calculate and monitor royalties because the licensor's technology leaves no visible trace in the final product and there are no practicable alternative monitoring methods.[1261]

Competing undertakings: limitation of output. The exemption does not apply where the agreement has as its object the limitation of output,[1262] that is a restriction on how much a party may produce or sell.[1263] However, limitations on the output of contract products imposed on the licensee in a non-reciprocal agreement or imposed on only one of the licensees in a reciprocal agreement are permissible.[1264] The effect is that the TTBER identifies as hardcore restrictions reciprocal output restrictions on both parties and output restrictions on the licensor in respect of his own technology.[1265] According to the Commission, when competitors agree to impose reciprocal output limitations, the object and likely effect of the agreement is to reduce output in the market. The same is true of agreements which reduce the parties' incentive to expand output, for example by obliging each other to make payments if a certain level of output is exceeded.[1266] However, a "one-way" restriction on the licensee does not necessarily lead to a lower output. Rather, it is likely that the agreement leads to a real integration of complementary technologies or an efficiency enhancing integration of the licensor's superior technology with the licensee's productive assets.[1267] Where an output restriction is imposed on only one of the licensees in a non-reciprocal agreement, the Commission considers that this is likely to reflect the higher value of the technology licensed by one of the parties and may serve to promote pro-competitive licensing.[1268]

28–251

Competing undertakings: allocation of markets or customers. The exemption does not apply where the agreement has as its object the allocation of markets and customers.[1269] This applies whether or not the licensee remains free to use its own technology.[1270] However, there are numerous exceptions: first, an obligation on the licensee or licensees to produce with the licensed technology only within one or more technical fields of use or one or more product markets[1271]; secondly, an obligation on either party to a non-reciprocal agreement not to produce with

28–252

[1259] TTBER Guidelines, para.81. Such agreements are also caught by art.4(1)(d): see para.28–253, below.

[1260] See the *Windsurfing* case, *Windsurfing International v Commission* (Case 193/83) [1986] E.C.R. 611; [1986] 3 C.M.L.R. 278.

[1261] TTBER Guidelines, para.81.

[1262] TTBER art.4(1)(b).

[1263] TTBER Guidelines, para.82.

[1264] TTBER art.4(1)(b). For what is a reciprocal agreement, see above, para.28–247. In general, the hardcore list is stricter for reciprocal agreements than for non-reciprocal agreements: TTBER Guidelines, para.78.

[1265] TTBER Guidelines, para.82.

[1266] TTBER Guidelines, para.82.

[1267] TTBER Guidelines, para.83.

[1268] TTBER Guidelines, para.83.

[1269] TTBER art.4(1)(c).

[1270] TTBER Guidelines, para.85. This is because once the licensee has tooled up to use the licensor's technology it may be costly to maintain a separate production line using another technology in order to serve customers covered by the restrictions. Furthermore, given the anti-competitive potential of the restraint, the licensee may have little incentive to produce under its own technology.

[1271] It is, however, a condition of the exemption that the field of use restrictions do not go beyond the scope of the licensed technologies: TTBER Guidelines, para.90. It is also a condition that

the licensed technology within one or more technical fields of use or one or more product markets or one or more exclusive territories reserved for the other[1272]; thirdly, an obligation on the licensor not to license the technology to another licensee in a particular territory[1273]; fourthly, the restriction in a non-reciprocal agreement of active or passive sales by either party into the exclusive territory or to the exclusive customer group reserved for the other party[1274]; fifthly, the restriction in a non-reciprocal agreement of active sales by the licensee into the exclusive territory or to the exclusive customer group allocated by the licensor to another licensee provided the latter was not a competing undertaking of the licensor at the time of the grant of its own licence[1275]; sixthly, a "captive use restriction", that is an obligation on the licensee to produce the contract products only for its own use, provided the licensee is not restricted in selling the contract products actively and passively as spare parts for its own products[1276]; and seventhly, an obligation on the licensee in a non-reciprocal agreement to produce the contract products only for a particular customer where the licence was granted in order to create an alternative source of supply for that customer.[1277]

28–253   **Competing undertakings: restrictions on licensee's ability to exploit its own technology and on research and development.** The exemption does not apply where the agreement has as its object the restriction of the licensee's ability to exploit its own technology.[1278] When restrictions are imposed on the licensee's use of its own technology the competitiveness of that technology is reduced.[1279] Accordingly, when the licensee is using its own technology, it is not to be subject to limitations as to where it produces or sells, how much it produces or sells or at what price it sells; it must not be obliged to pay royalties on products produced with its technology; and must not be restricted in licensing its technology to third

---

licensees are not limited to use of their own technology: TTBER art.4(1)(d): see para.28–253, below.

[1272] For what is a reciprocal agreement, see para.28–247 above. The reason for this exception is that the purpose of the agreement may be to give the licensee an incentive to invest in and develop the licensed technology rather than to share markets: TTBER Guidelines, para.86.

[1273] This exception permits the licensor to appoint a sole licensee in a particular territory. The exemption applies whether or not the agreement is reciprocal because it does not affect the parties' abilities fully to exploit their own technology in the respective territories: TTBER Guidelines, para.88.

[1274] Again, the reason for this exception is that the purpose of the agreement may be to give the licensee an incentive to invest in and develop the licensed technology rather than to share markets: TTBER Guidelines, para.87. Active selling to an exclusive territory or group involves making active approaches to customers in that territory or group; passive selling to an exclusive territory or group involves making supplies to that territory or group in response to unsolicited requests together with general advertising which reaches that territory, provided it is a reasonable way to reach the seller's own public or the public in non-exclusive territories: see para.51 of the Commission's Guidelines on Vertical Restraints [2010] OJ C130/1.

[1275] The Commission believes that such restrictions are likely to induce the licensee to exploit the licensed technology more efficiently: TTBER Guidelines, para.89. However, if the licensees agree between themselves not to sell into certain territories or to certain customer groups, that agreement amounts to a cartel.

[1276] Captive use restrictions are permitted because they may be necessary to encourage the dissemination of technology, particularly between competitors: TTBER Guidelines, para.92. Thus, where the contract product is a component, the licensee can be obliged to produce that component only for incorporation in its own products. However, the licensee must not be prohibited from supplying third parties that perform after-sale services on the contract products.

[1277] The Commission considers that the potential of such agreements to share markets is limited and that it cannot be assumed that the agreement will cause the licensee to cease exploiting his own technology: TTBER Guidelines, para.93. The Commission points out that it is not a condition for the operation for this exception that only one such licence is granted and that this exception includes situations where more than one person is licensed to supply the same specified customer.

[1278] TTBER art.4(1)(d).

[1279] TTBER Guidelines, para.95.

parties.[1280] The exemption is also inapplicable where the agreement has as its object the restriction of either party's ability to carry out research and development, unless that restriction is indispensable to prevent the disclosure of the licensed know-how to third parties.[1281] This applies whether or not the restriction concerns the licensed technology.[1282] The Commission considers that each party must be free to carry out independent research and development.[1283] However, it considers that the mere fact that the parties agree to provide each other with future improvements of their respective technologies does not amount to a restriction on independent research and development.[1284] Restrictions imposed to protect know-how must be necessary and proportionate. For example, where the agreement designates particular employees to be trained in and responsible for the use of the licensed know-how, it may be sufficient to oblige the licensee to prohibit those employees from being involved in research and development with third parties.[1285]

Non-competing undertakings: price-fixing. The exemption does not cover agreements between non-competitors which have as their object the restriction of a party's ability to determine its prices when selling products to third parties.[1286] However, this is stated to be without prejudice to the possibility of imposing a maximum sale price or recommending a sale price, provided it does not amount to a fixed or minimum sale price as a result of pressure from, or incentives offered by any of the parties.[1287] This category of hardcore restriction includes agreements that directly establish the selling price. It also includes indirect price-fixing, for example by fixing the margin, fixing the maximum level of discounts, linking the sales price to that of a competitor, threats, intimidation, warnings, penalties or contract terminations in relation to observance of a given price level.[1288] The Commission notes that direct or indirect means of price-fixing can be made more effective when combined with measures to identify price-cutting, such as the implementation of a price-monitoring system or imposing an obligation on licensees to report price deviations.[1289] It also notes that price-fixing may be made more effective when combined with measures that reduce the licensee's incentive to reduce its selling price, for example where the licensor obliges the licensee to apply a most-favoured-customer clause.[1290] The Commission goes on to state that the same means can be used to make maximum or recommended prices work as fixed or minimum selling prices, but that the provision of a list of recommended prices or the imposition of a maximum price is not considered in itself as leading to fixed or minimum prices.[1291]

28–254

Non-competing undertakings: the general rule as to territorial restrictions. The exemption does not cover agreements between non-competitors which have as their object the restriction of the territory into which, or the customers to

28–255

[1280] TTBER Guidelines, para.95.
[1281] TTBER art.4(1)(d).
[1282] TTBER Guidelines, para.94.
[1283] TTBER Guidelines, para.94.
[1284] TTBER Guidelines, para.94.
[1285] TTBER Guidelines, para.94.
[1286] TTBER art.4(2)(a).
[1287] TTBER art.4(2)(a).
[1288] TTBER Guidelines, para.97.
[1289] TTBER Guidelines, para.97.
[1290] TTBER Guidelines, para.97.
[1291] TTBER Guidelines, para.97.

whom, the licensee may passively sell the contract products.[1292] Passive sales restrictions may be the result of direct obligations (including an obligation to refer orders from particular customers or customers in particular territories to other licensees) or of indirect obligations aimed at inducing the licensee to refrain from making such sales, such as financial incentives or the implementation of a monitoring system aimed at verifying the effective destination of the licensed products.[1293] The Commission notes that quantity sales may be an indirect means to restrict passive sales. However, it will not assume that this is the case unless the limitations are used to implement an underlying market partitioning agreement. Indications of such an agreement include: the adjustment of quantities over time to cover only local demand; the combination of quantity limitations and an obligation to sell minimum quantities in the territory; minimum royalty obligations linked to sales in the territory; differentiated royalty rates depending on the destination of the products; and the monitoring of the destination of products sold by individual licensees.[1294] It will be seen that sales restrictions on the licensor are not treated as hardcore restrictions. The same applies in general to restrictions on active sales by the licensee (other than by a licensee in a selective distribution system).[1295] The block exemption of restrictions on active selling is based on the assumption that such restrictions promote investments, non-price competition and improvements in the quality of services provided by licensees by solving "free-rider" problems and "hold-up" problems.[1296]

28–256   **Non-competing undertakings: exceptions to the general rule as to territorial restrictions.** There are the following exceptions to the general rule. First, the restriction of passive sales into an exclusive territory or to an exclusive customer group reserved for the licensor.[1297] Secondly, the restriction of such sales into an exclusive territory or customer group allocated by the licensor to another licensee during the first two years that that other licensee is selling the contract products in that territory or to that contract group.[1298] Thirdly, an obligation on the licensee to produce the contract products only for its own use (provided that the licensee is not restricted in selling the contract products actively and passively as spare parts of its own products).[1299] Fourthly, the obligation to produce the contract products only for a particular customer, where the licence was granted in order to create an alternative source of supply for that customer.[1300] Fifthly, the restriction of sales

---

[1292] TTBER art.4(2)(b). For the meaning of the term "passive sales", see notes to para.28–252, above.

[1293] TTBER Guidelines, para.98.

[1294] TTBER Guidelines, para.98.

[1295] TTBER Guidelines, para.99.

[1296] TTBER Guidelines, para.99. A "free-rider" problem arises if a licensee takes a free ride on the investment of another in building up the brand and creating a demand for it. A "hold-up" problem arises where a licensee will not commit the investment necessary to sell the contract products without the protection of an exclusive distribution agreement, usually because of fears that its business will be dominated or expropriated by the licensor.

[1297] TTBER art.4(2)(b)(i). It is presumed that such restraints promote pro-competitive dissemination of technology and the integration of such technology into the production assets of the licensee: TTBER Guidelines, para.100.

[1298] TTBER art.4(2)(b)(ii). Given the amount of investment often required in order for a licensee to start up in a particular territory, the Commission believes that it is often the case that a licensee would not enter into the licence agreement without protection for a certain period of time against sales into its territory from other licensees: TTBER Guidelines, para.101.

[1299] TTBER art.4(2)(b)(iii). The effect of this is that where the product is a component, the licensee can be obliged to use it only for incorporation into its own products and not to sell it to other producers. However, the licensee must be able to sell the products as spare parts for its own products and therefore to be able to supply third parties that perform after sales services on those products: TTBER Guidelines, para.102.

[1300] TTBER art.4(2)(b)(iv).

to end-users by a licensee operating at the wholesale level.[1301] Finally, the restriction of sales to unauthorised distributors by the members of a selective distribution system.[1302]

The TTBER: excluded restrictions.[1303] The Regulation also lists four types of restriction which are not block exempted and require individual assessment.[1304] Unlike the hardcore restrictions, these restrictions may be severed.[1305] The rationale behind the exclusion of the first three of the four restrictions is to avoid block exemption of agreements which may reduce licensees' incentives to innovate.[1306] They are as follows. First, any direct or indirect obligation on the licensee to grant an exclusive licence to the licensor or to a third party designated by the licensor in respect of its own severable improvements to or its own new applications of the licensed technology.[1307] Secondly, any direct or indirect obligation on the licensee to assign, in whole or in part, to the licensor or a third party designated by the licensor, rights to its own severable improvements to or its own new applications of the licensed technology.[1308] Thirdly, any direct or indirect obligation on the licensee not to challenge the validity of intellectual property rights which the licensor holds in the common market (without prejudice to the possibility of providing for termination of the technology transfer agreement in the event that the licensee challenges the validity of one or more of the licensed intellectual property rights).[1309] The fourth exclusion applies where the parties are not competing and concerns any direct or indirect obligation limiting the licensee's ability to exploit its own technology or limiting the ability of any of the parties to the agreement to carry out research and development, unless the latter restriction is indispensable to prevent the disclosure of the licensed know-how to third parties.[1310]

28–257

Withdrawal and disapplication of the TTBER. In certain circumstances, the benefit of the Regulation may be withdrawn by the Commission if it finds in any particular case that an agreement to which it applies nevertheless has effects which are incompatible with art.101(3).[1311] Particular examples given in the Regulation are as follows: first, where the access of third parties' technologies to

28–258

[1301] TTBER art.4(2)(b)(v).

[1302] TTBER art.4(2)(b)(vi). This permits the licensor to impose on licensees an obligation to form part of a selective distribution system. However, in that case licensees must be allowed to sell to end users (unless restricted to a wholesale function under art.4(2)(b)(v), art.4(2)(c); TTBER Guidelines, para.105. The Commission notes that the agreements between the licensee and its buyers must comply with the Vertical Agreements Block Exemption Regulation (Reg.2790/1999 EC). See now Regulation 330/2010 [2010] OJ L102/1 considered below, paras 28–263 et seq.

[1303] See generally TTBER Guidelines, paras 107 to 116.

[1304] TTBER art.5.

[1305] TTBER Guidelines, para.107.

[1306] TTBER Guidelines, para.108.

[1307] TTBER art.5(1)(a). Non-exclusive grant-backs are considered to promote innovation: TTBER Guidelines, para.109.

[1308] TTBER art.5(1)(b).

[1309] TTBER, art.5(1)(c). Intellectual property rights are defined as including "industrial property rights, know-how, copyright and neighbouring rights" art.1(g). Note that in *Neilson Hordell/ Reichmark*, Commission XIIth Report on Competition Policy, points 88–89, the Commission had objected to a no-challenge clause. The Commission's reasoning is that invalid intellectual property stifles innovation and the licensee is likely to be in the best position to say whether a particular right is or is not valid: TTBER Guidelines, para.112. However, the Commission takes a favourable view of no-challenge clauses relating to know-how where once disclosed it is likely to be impossible or very difficult to recover the licensed know-how. In such a case, a no-challenge clause promotes innovation, in particular by allowing weaker licensors to license stronger licensees without fear of a challenge once the know-how has been absorbed by the licensee.

[1310] TTBER art.5(2). See also TTBER Guidelines paras 114–116.

[1311] TTBER art.6, applying art.29(1) of the Modernisation Regulation 1/2003. TTBER Guidelines paras 117 to 122.

the market is restricted, for example by the cumulative effect of parallel networks of similar restrictive agreements restricting licensees from using third parties' technologies; secondly, where potential licensees' access to the market is restricted, for example by the cumulative effect of parallel networks of similar re- strictive agreements prohibiting licensors from licensing to other licensees; and third where without any objectively valid reason, the parties do not exploit the licensed technology.[1312] National competition authorities are given an analogous power of withdrawal where a particular agreement has effects which are incompatible with art.101(3) in the territory of a Member State or a part thereof, which has all the characteristics of a distinct geographic market.[1313] The Commis- sion is also given power by Regulation to declare that where parallel networks of similar technology transfer agreements cover more than 50 per cent of a relevant market, the block exemption Regulation does not apply to technology transfer agreements containing specific restraints relating to that market.[1314]

28–259   **Non-block exempted agreements: the TTBER Guidelines.** Where a technol- ogy transfer agreement is not block exempted, then unless it contains hardcore restrictions, there is no presumption that it infringes art.101, and individual as- sessment is necessary.[1315] The Commission has issued guidelines as to how it will approach such agreements. As is the case with the TTBER, the Commission will apply the guidelines by analogy to copyright licensing, but not to the licensing of rights in performances or other related rights.[1316] The guidelines are lengthy and detailed and accordingly no more than a brief sketch will be presented here.

28–260   **A further safe harbour.** The guidelines make clear that outside the area of hard- core restrictions, art.101 is unlikely to be infringed where there are four or more independently controlled technologies in addition to the technologies controlled by the parties to the agreement, provided that these independent technologies may be substitutable for the licensed technology at a comparable cost to the user.[1317] Where this condition is met, there is a further "safe harbour". Otherwise, individual assessment is required.

28–261   **Individual assessment: general.** The guidelines begin by emphasising the need to take due account of the way in which competition operates on the market in question. The Commission considers the following factors to be particularly rele- vant in this respect: the nature of the agreement; the market position of the par- ties; the market position of competitors; the market position of buyers of the licensed products; entry barriers; and the maturity of the market. This list is not, however, exhaustive.[1318] The guidelines go on to note the potential negative ef- fects on competition which may arise from restrictive technology transfer agreements. They are stated to be as follows (again the list is not exhaustive): the reduction of inter-technology competition on a technology market or on a market for the products in question; the foreclosure of competitors by raising their costs, restricting their access to essential inputs or otherwise raising barriers to entry; and the reduction of intra-technology competition between undertakings that pro- duce products on the basis of the same technology.[1319] The guidelines then note that even restrictive licence agreements mostly also produce pro-competitive ef-

---

[1312] TTBER art.6(1)(a) to (c).
[1313] TTBER art.6(2).
[1314] TTBER art.7(1). TTBER Guidelines paras 123 to 129.
[1315] TTBER Guidelines, para.37.
[1316] TTBER Guidelines, para.52.
[1317] TTBER Guidelines, para.131.
[1318] TTBER Guidelines, para.132.
[1319] para.141.

fects in the form of efficiencies which may outweigh their anti-competitive effects.[1320] There follows a detailed discussion of when such efficiencies will be sufficient to satisfy art.101(3).[1321]

Types of clause covered by the guidelines. The guidelines go on to discuss specific types of clause. First, there is a non-exhaustive list of obligations which the Commission believes are generally not restrictive of competition within the meaning of art.101. The list, which is similar to but shorter than the so-called "white list" contained in the previous block exemption regulation,[1322] is as follows: confidentiality obligations; obligations not to use the licensed technology after the expiry of the agreement, provided that the technology remains valid and in force; obligations to assist the licensor in enforcing the licensed intellectual property rights; obligations to pay minimum royalties or to produce a minimum quantity of products incorporating the licensed technology; and obligations to use the licensor's trade mark or indicate the name of the licensor on the product.[1323] There is then guidance on the application of art.101 to a variety of different types of clause.[1324] The types of clause are as follows: royalty obligations; exclusive and sole licences which restrict production within a given territory; restrictions on sales into a given territory or to a given customer group; output restrictions; "field of use restrictions", that is restrictions under which the licensee is limited to one or more technical fields of application or one or more product markets; "captive use restrictions", that is obligations on the licensee to limit its production of the licensed product to the quantities required for the production of its own products and the maintenance and repair of its own products; "tying", that is making the licensing of one technology conditional on the licensee taking a licence for another technology or purchasing a particular product; "bundling", which occurs where two technologies or a technology and a product are only sold together as a bundle; and "non-compete obligations", that is obligations on the licensee not to use third-party technologies which compete with the licensed technology. The guidance on these particular clauses is detailed and defies summary. The reader is accordingly referred to the Commission's text itself.[1325] Finally, the guidelines deal with licensing in settlement and non-assertion agreements (which are treated like other licence agreements)[1326] and technology pools.[1327]

28–262

(f) *The vertical agreements block exemption*

General. The Commission's view is that for most vertical restraints, competition concerns can only arise if there is insufficient competition at one or more levels of trade, that is if there is some degree of market power at the level of the supplier, the buyer or both.[1328] In that context, Commission Regulation 330/2010

28–263

[1320] para.146.

[1321] paras 146 to 152.

[1322] See *Copinger*, 14th edn, para.29–189.

[1323] TTBER Guidelines, para.162.

[1324] TTBER Guidelines, paras 156 to 203.

[1325] [2004] OJ C 101/2.

[1326] TTBER Guidelines, paras 204 to 209.

[1327] TTBER Guidelines, paras 210 to 235.

[1328] Commission Notice Guidelines on Vertical Restraints [2010] OJ C130/1, para.6. These guidelines, which were published on May 19, 2010, replace the previous guidelines published on October 13, 2000, as to which see *Copinger* 15th edn, paras 29–234 et seq.

("the VABER")[1329] provides block exemption to vertical agreements, subject to certain qualifications and exceptions. For these purposes, a vertical agreement is an agreement or concerted practice entered into between two or more undertakings each of which operates for the purposes of the agreement or practice at a different level of the production or distribution chain and relating to the conditions under which the parties may purchase, sell or resell certain goods or services.[1330] The block exemption applies to such agreements to the extent that they contain vertical restraints.[1331] A separate Regulation applies to restraints in vertical agreement for the purchase, sale or resale of new motor vehicles, spare parts for motor vehicles and repair and maintenance services for motor vehicles.[1332]

28–264   **Agreements to which the exemption does not apply.** First, some vertical agreements between an association of undertakings and its members are excluded.[1333] Second, there are limits to the application of the exemption to agreements which contain certain provisions about intellectual property rights.[1334] Third, in general the exemption does not apply to vertical agreements between competing undertakings.[1335] Fourth, it is a condition for the operation of the exemption that the market share of the supplier does not exceed 30 per cent of the market on which it sells the contract goods or services and that the market share of the buyer does not exceed 30 per cent of the market on which it purchases the contract goods or services.[1336] Fifth, the exemption does not apply to an agreement which has as its object one of a list of "hardcore" restrictions, including restrictions on the buyer's ability to determine its sale price, territorial restrictions on the buyer, restrictions on certain sales by members or distributors of selective distribution systems and certain restrictions relating to spare parts.[1337] Sixth, the exemption also does not apply to certain specified obligations contained in vertical agreements, such as certain non-compete obligations.[1338] Finally, the benefit of the exemption may be withdrawn by the Commission.[1339]

28–265   **Provisions of the VABER relating to intellectual property rights.** The exemption applies to vertical agreements containing provisions which relate to the assignment to the buyer or use by the buyer of intellectual property rights, provided those provisions do not constitute the primary object of such agreements and are directly related to the use, sale or resale of goods or services by the buyer or its

---

[1329] Commission Regulation (EU) No. 330/2010 on the application of art.101(3) of the TFEU to categories of vertical agreements and concerted practices [2010] OJ L102/1. This replaces Commission Regulation 2790/1999 of December 22, 1999 [1999] OJ L336/21, which expired on May 31, 2010. Agreements which were in force on May 31, 2010 and were exempted by the 1999 Regulation remain exempted until May 31, 2011 even if they do not meet the criteria for exemption in the 2010 Regulation: art.9.

[1330] VABER art.1(1)(a). An agreement between a supplier and a person assisting purchasers (and not acting as a distributor or reseller) was held not to be a vertical agreement: *Jones v Ricoh UK Ltd* [2010] EWHC 1743 (Ch) at para.46.

[1331] art.2(1). A vertical restraint is "a restriction on competition in a vertical agreement falling within the scope of art.101(1)": art.1(b).

[1332] Commission Regulation (EC) 1400/2002 [2001] OJ L203/30. See Report on Competition Policy 2007 points 66–67.

[1333] art.1(2). The limits concern the annual turnover of the members. For calculation of annual turnover, see art.8.

[1334] art.2(3). See the next paragraph.

[1335] art.2(4).

[1336] VABER art.3(1). For multi party agreements, see art.3(2). For the calculation of market share, see, art.7.

[1337] VABER art.4. If a "hardcore" restriction is present, the agreement will be subject to assessment: see Guidelines on Vertical Restraints para.47.

[1338] VABER art.5. Provided that an obligation in this category is severable, its presence does not mean that the whole agreement is void, merely that the obligation itself is not exempt: Guidelines on Vertical Restraints, para.65.

[1339] VABER art. 6.

customers.[1340] For these purposes, the term "intellectual property rights" includes industrial property rights, know how, copyright and neighbouring rights,[1341] and thus the vast majority of the rights covered in this work. It is clear, however, that the exemption does not apply to a copyright assignment between an author and a publisher because the assignment would be the primary object of the agreement.

Application of the vertical agreements block exemption to intellectual property rights: general guidance. In its Guidelines, the Commission notes that five conditions must be fulfilled before an agreement containing provisions in relation to intellectual property rights will fall within the exemption and then gives examples of the types of agreement which, in the Commission's opinion, are and are not exempt.[1342]   **28–266**

First, in order to be exempt, the intellectual property provisions must be part of a vertical agreement, that is an agreement with conditions under which the parties may purchase, sell or resell certain goods or services. Accordingly, neither an agreement concerning the assignment or licensing of intellectual property rights for the manufacture of goods nor a pure licensing agreement is exempt. Examples of agreements which are not exempt for this reason are as follows: where one party provides another with a recipe and licenses that other to produce a drink with it; where one party provides the other with a mould or master and licenses the other to produce or distribute copies; the "pure" licence of a trade mark or sign for the purposes of merchandising; sponsorship contracts concerning the right to advertise oneself as the official sponsor of an event; and copyright licensing such as broadcasting contracts concerning the right to record or broadcast an event.

Secondly, the intellectual property rights must be assigned to or licensed for use by the buyer. Accordingly, the exemption does not apply when the rights are supplied by the buyer to the supplier, even if the rights concern the manner of manufacture or distribution. Thus, for example, sub-contracting involving the transfer of know-how to the sub-contractor is not exempt. However, vertical agreements under which the buyer provides the supplier with no more than specifications which describe the goods or services to be supplied are exempt.

Thirdly, the assignment or licensing of the intellectual property rights must not constitute the primary object of the agreement. The primary object must be the purchase or distribution of goods or services and the intellectual property provision must serve the implementation of the vertical agreement.

Fourthly, the intellectual property provisions must be directly related to the use, sale or resale of goods or services by the buyer or his customers. They will normally concern the marketing of goods and services. Examples include: a franchise agreement where the franchisor sells the franchisee goods for resale and licenses to the franchisee the use of his trade mark and know-how to market the goods; and a contract under which the supplier of a concentrated extract licenses the buyer to dilute and bottle the extract before selling it as a drink.

Finally, the intellectual property provisions must not contain restrictions on competition having the same object or effect as vertical restraints which are not exempted under the Regulation.

Application of the vertical agreements block exemption to copyright: specific provisions which are exempt. The Notice goes on to give specific examples of provisions in agreements concerning copyright which the Commission considers   **28–267**

[1340] VABER art.2(3).
[1341] VABER art.1(f).
[1342] Guidelines on Vertical Restraints, paras 31 to 38.

will be exempt to the extent that they fall within art.101(1) at all.[1343] First, an obligation imposed by a copyright owner on a reseller of goods covered by copyright (for example, books or software) under which the reseller may only resell on condition that the buyer (whether another reseller or the end user) shall not infringe the copyright. Second, agreements under which hard copies of software are supplied for resale and under which the reseller does not acquire a licence to any rights over the software (such rights being granted to the end-user, for example under a "shrink-wrap" licence). These are agreements for the supply of goods for resale for the purposes of the Regulation and are exempt. Thirdly, obligations imposed by a software copyright owner on the buyers of hardware incorporating that software not to make copies of the software for resale or for use in combination with other hardware.

28–268   **Block-exempted horizontal agreements.**[1344] There are two relevant horizontal block exemptions. The first concerns categories of specialisation agreement.[1345] The term "specialisation agreement" includes a joint production agreement by virtue of which two or more parties agree to produce certain products jointly.[1346] The exemption may apply to provisions concerning the assignment or use of intellectual property rights, but only if they do not constitute the primary object of the agreement and are directly related to and necessary for their implementation.[1347] The second exemption concerns categories of research and development agreement.[1348] The kinds of agreement which may be exempt are agreements which relate to the conditions under which the parties pursue either joint research and development of products or processes and joint exploitation of the results of that research and development or joint exploitation of the results of research and development carried out by them pursuant to a prior agreement between them.[1349] It is clear that the exemption may include provisions as to the licensing of intellectual property rights between the parties to a research and development agreement as defined.[1350] Any licences granted by way of the exploitation of the research and development will be governed by the TTBER so far as they concern rights to which it applies.[1351]

[1343] Guidelines on Vertical Restraints, paras 40 to 42.

[1344] See, generally, Commission Notice: Guidelines on the applicability of art.81 of the EC Treaty to horizontal co-operation agreements [2001] OJ C3/2. Draft revised guidelines have recently been published: see *http://ec.europa.eu/competition/consultations/2010__horizontals/index.html* [Accessed September 26, 2010].

[1345] Commission Regulation (EC) No. 2658/2000 on the application of art.81(3) of the Treaty to categories of specialisation agreements. A draft revised Regulation has been published for consultation: see *http://ec.europa.eu/competition/consultations/2010__horizontals/index.html* [Accessed September 26, 2010].

[1346] Commission Regulation (EC) No. 2658/2000, art.1(1)(c). This provision is repeated in the draft revised Regulation.

[1347] Commission Regulation (EC) No. 2658/2000, art.1(2). The term "intellectual property" is not defined. Art.2(2) of the draft revised Regulation provides that the exemption may apply to agreements containing provisions concerning the assignment or licensing of intellectual property rights, but only if they do not constitute the primary object of the agreement and are directly related to and necessary for their implementation.

[1348] Commission Regulation (EC) No. 2659/2000 on the application of art.81(3) of the Treaty to categories of research and development agreements. A draft revised Regulation has been published for consultation: see *http://ec.europa.eu/competition/consultations/2010__horizontals/index.html* [Accessed September 26, 2010].

[1349] Commission Regulation (EC) No. 2659/2000, art.1(1). Art. 2(1) of the draft revised Regulation is to much the same effect.

[1350] art.2(2) of the draft revised Regulation provides that the exemption may apply to agreements containing provisions concerning the assignment or licensing of intellectual property rights, but only if they do not constitute the primary object of the agreement and are directly related to and necessary for their implementation.

[1351] See TTBER Guidelines, para.60. For the rights to which the TTBER applies, see paras 28–243 and 28–244, above.

(g) *Application of art.102 to the exercise of copyright and related rights*[1352]

Article 102 and intellectual property rights. The question of intellectual prop-   **28–269**
erty rights and art.102 first arose in the *Parke, Davis* case,[1353] where the Court of
Justice held that the ownership and exercise of a patent right does not in itself
give its holder a dominant position for the purpose of art.102. This was repeated
in the *Deutsche Grammophon* case[1354] in relation to the distribution right.
However, if the subject matter of the right is itself a relevant market (i.e. in essence, where there is no substitute for the work in question) then the owner of a
copyright is likely to have a dominant position and art.102 will potentially apply.
Moreover, if an undertaking enjoys a dominant position for reasons unconnected
with the right, it may find that its behaviour with respect to copyright is restrained
by art.102. In *Tetra Pak I*[1355] the Commission held that it was an abuse of Tetra-
Pak's dominant position in aseptic packaging for it to purchase the company that
held the exclusive licence to use a competing technology.

Types of abusive conduct: excessive pricing. In *Basset v SACEM*[1356] the Court   **28–270**
of Justice upheld the right of a copyright management society to charge a supplementary mechanical reproduction royalty in addition to the performance royalty
for the public performance of sound recordings, as this was a power granted to it
by national legislation, even though that right was not provided for by the
Member State where the recordings were lawfully placed on the market. But the
Court added that it was possible for the level of royalties to be such that art.102
might be invoked. Since the national court had found that SACEM had a
dominant position, it followed that its conduct would be contrary to art.102 if
anything it did amounted to an abuse, particularly by imposing unreasonable
conditions.[1357] In *Attheraces Ltd v British Horseracing Board Ltd*,[1358] the English
Court of Appeal overturned a finding that excessive prices had been charged for
the supply of pre-race information which was not protected by any intellectual
property rights. The case illustrates some of the difficulties a claimant may face in
establishing that prices are excessive.

Terms of licences. It may be an abuse of an undertaking's dominant position for   **28–271**
it to enter into licence agreements which have the effect of preventing or restricting the other party from dealing with a competitor. Thus, in a Microsoft case
from 1994,[1359] the Commission intervened to prevent the following conduct by
Microsoft: entering into "per-processor" licences under which equipment
manufacturers had to pay a licence fee to Microsoft based on the number of
computers sold, whether or not they were loaded with Microsoft software; entering into long licences going beyond the lifetime of most operating systems; and
entering into confidentiality agreements with software firms that had the effect of
preventing their dealing with competitors. Microsoft agreed to desist from such
conduct in future.

[1352] See, generally, the Commission's Guidance on the Commission's enforcement priorities in applying art.82 of the EC Treaty to abusive exclusionary conduct by dominant undertakings [2009]
OJ C45/7

[1353] *Parke, Davis v Probel* [1968] E.C.R. 55; [1968] C.M.L.R. 47 (Case 24/67) .

[1354] *Deutsche Grammophon GmbH v Metro-SB-Grossmärkte GmbH & Co.* (Case 78/70) [1971]
E.C.R. 487; [1971] C.M.L.R. 631.

[1355] [1988] OJ L272/27; [1990] 4 C.M.L.R. 47.

[1356] (Case 402/85) [1987] E.C.R. 1747; [1987] 3 C.M.L.R. 173.

[1357] See also *Volvo v Veng* (Case 238/87) [1988] E.C.R. 6211; [1989] 4 C.M.L.R. 122 and *Hilti v
Commission* (T–30/89) [1991] E.C.R. II–1439; [1992] 4 C.M.L.R. 16 (upheld on appeal Case
C–53/92P [1994] E.C.R. I–667).

[1358] [2007] EWCA Civ 38; [2007] E.C.C. 7.

[1359] Commission press release IP/94/653.

28–272   **Infringement actions.** Another example of an abusive exercise of industrial property is where a number of undertakings owning similar industrial property rights, and together enjoying a dominant position, commence several infringement actions against a competitor, which are then stayed on condition that the competitor enter into an agreement with such undertakings.[1360]

28–273   **Spare parts and related copyrights.** Further, it can amount to an abuse within art.102 for an undertaking which occupies a dominant position in spare parts for its products to refuse to supply such spare parts.[1361] Spare parts for industrial machines are often the subject of drawings in which intellectual property rights subsist, and such rights may be exercised in such a way as to seek to maintain a dominant position enjoyed in respect of the spare parts; such exercise may, in certain circumstances, amount to an abuse of the dominant position, and be prohibited by art.102.

28–274   **Tying: the *Microsoft Windows Media* case: the Commission's decision.** This case involved the tying by Microsoft of Microsoft Windows Media Player with Microsoft Windows. The Commission held[1362] that through tying these products, Microsoft used Windows as "a distribution channel to anti-competitively ensure for itself a significant competition advantage in the media player market", placing competitors at a disadvantage irrespective of the quality of their products.[1363] This interfered with the normal competitive process which would benefit users in terms of quicker cycles of innovation due to unfettered competition on the merits.[1364] Moreover, tying enabled Microsoft "to anti-competitively expand its position in adjacent media-related software markets and weaken effective competition to the eventual detriment of consumers".[1365] The tying also deterred innovation in any technologies which Microsoft could conceivably take an interest in and tie with Windows in future. There was therefore a reasonable likelihood that the tying would lead to a lessening of competition so that the maintenance of an effective competition structure would not be ensured for the foreseeable future.[1366] Accordingly, there was a violation of art.102(d).[1367] There was an appreciable effect on trade between Member States and between the Contracting Parties to the EEA.[1368] Accordingly, Microsoft was ordered to offer a version of Windows for client PCs which did not include Windows Media Player and to refrain from using any technological, commercial, contractual or other means which would have the equivalent effect of tying Windows Media Player to Windows.[1369]

28–275   **Tying: the *Microsoft Windows Media* case: the General Court's decision.**[1370] The General Court upheld the Commission's decision. The Commission had

---

[1360] *Zip Fasteners* [1977] 3 C.M.L.R. 44. See also *ITT Promedia NV v Commission* (T–111/96) [1998] ECR II–2937; [1998] 5 C.M.L.R. 491, discussed in *Sandisk Corporation v Koninklijke Philips Electronics NV* [2007] EWHC 332; [2007] F.S.R. 22.

[1361] *Hugin v Commission* (Case 22/78) [1979] E.C.R. 1869; [1979] 3 C.M.L.R. 345, upholding the Commission decision ([1978] OJ L122/23) on finding of abuse, but quashing the decision on the basis that there was no effect on trade between Member States.

[1362] Case COMP/C–3/37.792 *Microsoft*, C(2004) 900 final.

[1363] Recital 979.

[1364] Recitals 980 and 981.

[1365] Recitals 980 and 982.

[1366] Recital 983.

[1367] Recital 984.

[1368] Recital 993.

[1369] Recitals 1011 and 1012. For enforcement, see the Commission's 2009 Report on Competition Policy, para.112.

[1370] Case T–21/04.

adopted a four-stage analysis.[1371] First, the tying product (Windows client PC operating systems) and the tied product (Windows Media Player) were two separate products. Second, Microsoft was dominant in the market for the tying product. Third, Microsoft did not give customers a choice to obtain the tying product without the tied product. Fourth, the practice in question foreclosed competition. Microsoft criticised the Commission's third stage on the grounds that it amounted to a departure from art.102(d), which provides as an example of abusive conduct "making the conclusion of contracts subject to acceptance by the other parties of supplementary obligations which, by their nature or according to commercial usage, have no connection with the subject of such contracts". The Court observed that art.102(d) is not intended to be exhaustive but held in any event that the Commission's third step merely expressed in different words the concept that "bundling assumes that consumers are compelled, directly or indirectly, to accept 'supplementary obligations', such as those referred to in art.[102(d)]".[1372] Microsoft also criticised the Commission's fourth stage as introducing a new requirement, not justified in the case law. The Court dismissed this argument: "the fact remains that, in principle, conduct will be regarded as abusive only if it is capable of restricting competition".[1373]

Tying: the *Microsoft Internet Explorer* case.[1374] On January 14, 2009 the Commission adopted a statement of objections against Microsoft on the basis of a preliminary assessment that it had technically and contractually tied Internet Explorer to Windows by licensing the latter only with Internet Explorer included. While not agreeing with the assessment, Microsoft offered commitments aimed at allowing for an unbiased choice both for "original equipment manufacturers" ("OEMs") and end users, as follows. First, Microsoft would make available a mechanism in Windows to enable OEMs and end users to make Internet Explorer inaccessible. Second, OEMs would be free to pre-install any web browser of their choice and set it as the default without retaliation from Microsoft. Third, users of Windows who had set Internet Explorer as their default browser would be offered (via Windows Update and in an unbiased manner) the option to choose a competing browser.[1375] The Commission invited observations and having been informed of the observations Microsoft amended the detail of the third commitment and undertook to make regular reports on the implementation of the commitment. On December 16, 2009 the Commission adopted a decision that the commitments as amended should be binding for five years from the adoption of the decision.[1376]

28–276

Refusal to license: general. The law in relation to the refusal by a dominant undertaking to grant licences to use its intellectual property has developed rapidly over the last decade. The position was summarised by the General Court in 2007 as follows: "the Community judicature considers that the fact that the holder of an intellectual property right can exploit that right solely for his own benefit constitutes the very substance of his exclusive right. Accordingly, a simple refusal, even on the part of an undertaking in a dominant position, to grant a licence to a third party cannot in itself constitute an abuse of a dominant position within the meaning of art.[102]. It is only when it is accompanied by exceptional circumstances such as those hitherto envisaged in the case-law that such a refusal can be

28–277

[1371] Recital 794.
[1372] paras 861, 864.
[1373] Applying *Michelin III* [2003] E.C.R. II–4071.
[1374] Case COMP/C–3/39.530— *Microsoft (tying).*
[1375] Commission Notice October 9, 2009 [2009] OJ C242/20.
[1376] Commission Decision of December 16, 2009. For implementation, see Press Release IP/10/216.

characterised as abusive". If such an abuse is found, "it is permissible, in the public interest in maintaining effective competition on the market, to encroach upon the exclusive right of the holder of the intellectual property right by requiring him to grant licences to third parties seeking to enter or remain on that market."[1377] However, the Commission recognises that such an intervention "requires careful consideration" because it may damage the interest of consumers by undermining undertakings' incentives to invest and innovate or by permitting competitors to free-ride on the undertakings' investments.[1378] In what follows, the development of the law will be traced before an attempt is made to summarise the present position.

28–278   *Volvo v Veng.* In *Volvo AB v Erik Veng (UK) Ltd*[1379] the Court of Justice had to consider the question of a refusal to license the manufacture of spare body panels for cars in connection with registered design rights. Volvo, the registered proprietor in the United Kingdom for the design of the body panels, sought to prevent Veng importing into the United Kingdom Volvo body panels manufactured without authority from Volvo. The Court of Justice in a brief judgment, answering only one of the three questions referred to it, stated that in the absence of harmonised laws within the Community, the individual is entitled to the protection of the subject-matter of his rights to the extent determined by the national legislature. In this case the right of a proprietor of a registered design included, as part of the subject-matter of his exclusive right, the right to prevent third parties manufacturing and selling, or importing, products identical to the design. Thus, forcing a proprietor to grant a licence, even in return for a reasonable royalty, would deprive the proprietor of the substance of his rights. However, the Court added that the exercise of an exclusive right by the proprietor of a registered design in respect of car body panels may be prohibited by art.102 if it involves, on the part of an undertaking holding a dominant position, certain abusive conduct, such as the arbitrary refusal to supply spare parts to independent repairers, the fixing of prices for spare parts at an unfair level or a decision no longer to produce spare parts for a particular model, even though many cars of that model are still in circulation, provided such conduct is liable to affect trade between Member States.

28–279   *Magill.* In *Magill*,[1380] the Court of Justice, upholding the General Court,[1381] held that the refusal by Radio Telefis Eireann and ITP (as agent for the ITV companies) to grant licences to third parties to reproduce their schedules amounted to an abuse of their dominant positions in the supply of that information.[1382] The Court accepted that refusal to grant a licence could not "in itself" amount to an abuse.[1383] However, there were exceptional circumstances in the *Magill* case: the refusal prevented the emergence of a product for which there was potential consumer demand (a comprehensive TV guide); there was no justification for the refusal;

[1377] *Microsoft v Commission* (T–201/04) [2007] E.C.R. II–3601 para.691.
[1378] See, generally, the Commission's Guidance on the Commission's enforcement priorities in applying art.[102] to abusive exclusionary conduct by dominant undertakings [2009] OJ C45/7.
[1379] (Case 238/87) [1988] E.C.R. 6211; [1989] 4 C.M.L.R. 47. See also (Case 53/87) *Consorzio Italiano della Componentistica di Ricambio per Autoveicoli v Régie Nationale des Usines Renault* [1988] E.C.R. 6039.
[1380] *RTE and ITP v Commission* (C–241& 242/91P) [1995] E.C.R. I–743; [1995] 4 C.M.L.R. 718.
[1381] (T–69/89) [1991] E.C.R. II–485.
[1382] The Court found that these undertakings enjoyed a "de facto monopoly over [that] information"; (para.47) there were, in effect, no substitutes for that information, which could not be obtained in any other way but from the undertakings.
[1383] *RTE and ITP v Commission* (C–241& 242/91P) [1995] E.C.R. I–743; [1995] 4 C.M.L.R. 718, para.49.

and by refusing, the undertakings reserved the TV guide market to themselves.[1384] Although the Court did not itself allude to this point, it may well be that the Court had in mind the nature of the "work" in question; it was difficult to argue that the copyright at issue protected any substantial investment or provided a reward for creativity.[1385] The Court went on to hold that the Commission was entitled, under art.3 of Council Regulation 17/62, to require RTE and ITP to put an end to the infringement by ordering them to supply the scheduling information at issue.[1386]

Tiercé Ladbroke.[1387] This case concerned a refusal by the owners of the exclusive television rights in respect of French racing to provide a Belgian betting company (Ladbroke) with the sound and pictures of French races for its betting outlets in Belgium. The Court of First Instance held that *Magill* was not in point. In *Magill*, the refusal to licence prevented the applicant from entering the market. By contrast, Ladbroke had the largest share of the betting market in Belgium. Furthermore, the refusal to supply would not fall within the prohibition of art.102 unless it concerned a product or service which was either essential for the exercise of the activity in question (in that there was no real or potential substitute) or was a new product the introduction of which might be prevented despite specific, constant and regular demand. In this case, the availability of televised broadcasts was not indispensable for the taking of bets. Accordingly there was no abuse of dominant position.

28–280

Bronner.[1388] This case concerned the question whether a refusal by a newspaper proprietor in a dominant position to include another's product in its home-delivery scheme could amount to an abuse of that position. The Court of Justice emphasised that it would only be in exceptional circumstances that the refusal by a dominant owner to license another would amount to an abuse. It stated that in *Magill* those exceptional circumstances were that the refusal concerned a product (information on the schedules) the supply of which was indispensable for carrying on the business in question (publication of a television guide); prevented the appearance of a new product for which there was potential demand; was not justified by objective considerations; and was likely to exclude all competition in the secondary market of television guides. The Court went on to state that the effect of *Magill* was that three cumulative requirements needed to be satisfied before an abuse existed: elimination of competition, absence of objective justification and the fact that the service being refused is indispensable to the proposed business inasmuch as there is no actual or potential substitute. On the facts, at least the third of these requirements was not satisfied and accordingly there could be no abuse.

28–281

IMS Health: **(i) general.**[1389] In this case, both parties were engaged in the business of tracking sales of pharmaceutical and healthcare products and marketing

28–282

[1384] *RTE and ITP v Commission* (C–241& 242/91P) [1995] E.C.R. I–743; [1995] 4 C.M.L.R. 718, paras 53–56.

[1385] Indeed, depending on the facts, such listings may well not attract any protection at all. See above para.28–24.

[1386] *RTE and ITP v Commission* (C–241& 242/91P) [1995] E.C.R. I–743; [1995] 4 C.M.L.R. 718, paras 88–94.

[1387] *Tiercé Ladbroke SA v Commission* (T–504/93) [1997] E.C.R. II–923; [1997] 5 C.M.L.R. 309.

[1388] *Oscar Bronner GmbH & Co KG v Mediaprint Zeitungs- und Zeitschriftenverlag GmbH & Co KG* (C–7/97) [1998] E.C.R. I–7791, [1999] 4 C.M.L.R. 112.

[1389] *IMS Health GmbH & Co. OHG v NDC Health GmbH & Co KG* (C–418/01) [2004] 4 C.M.L.R. 28. See Stothers, " *IMS Health* and its implications for compulsory licensing in Europe" [2004] 10 E.I.P.R. 467; Ong, "Anti-competitive Refusals to Grant Copyright Licences: Reflections on the *IMS* Saga" [2004] 11 E.I.P.R. 505; Ridyard, "Compulsory Access Under EC Competition Law—A New Doctrine of "Convenient Facilities" and the Case for Price Regulation" [2004] E.C.L.R. 669; Ong, "Building Brick Barricades and other Barriers to Entry: Abusing a Dominant

the resulting regional sales data to pharmaceutical companies. At issue was the assumed copyright in a "brick structure" which had been developed by the claimant ("IMS") in conjunction with a working group which included many of its clients and which had become the *de facto* industry standard for the presentation of such data. The defendant ("NDC") had attempted to market data based on a different brick structure, but clients were reluctant to use it. It therefore contended that IMS's refusal to grant it a licence to use the brick structure infringed art.102. The German court referred a number of questions to the Court of Justice.

(ii) Indispensability. Two of the questions referred concerned the criteria for determining whether the refusal concerned a product or service which was indispensable for carrying on a particular business (the first exceptional circumstance identified in *Bronner* as having applied in *Magill*). The first of these was as to the relevance of the degree of participation by users in the development of IMS's brick structure.[1390] NDC and the Commission contended that the considerable role played by users had contributed to a relationship of dependency by them on the structure. The second question was as to the relevance of the outlay, particularly in terms of cost, which potential users would have to provide in order to be able to purchase sales data based on a different brick structure.[1391]

The Court held, applying *Bronner*, that it is necessary to determine whether there are products or services which provide alternative solutions even if they are less advantageous, and whether there are technical, legal or economic obstacles capable of making it impossible or at least unreasonably difficult for any undertaking to create such alternatives. Economic obstacles are only relevant to the extent that the creation of such alternatives is not economically viable for production on a scale comparable to that of the copyright owner. Accordingly, in considering the question of indispensability, any dependency on the part of clients (if proven) would be relevant. If there were such dependency, it would be likely that such clients would have to make exceptional organisational and financial efforts in order to acquire the sales data presented on the basis of a different brick structure. The supplier of such a structure might therefore be obliged to offer terms which were such as to rule out any economic viability of doing business on a scale comparable to the copyright owner.[1392]

(iii) Abuse: general. The other question referred by the German court was whether there was an abuse where potential clients rejected any competing product not based on IMS's brick structure because their set-up relied on products manufactured on the basis that structure.[1393] In answering this question, the Court began by stating that it was clear from the case law that in order for a refusal by a copyright owner to give access to a product or service which was indispensable for carrying on a particular business to be abusive, it was sufficient for three cumulative conditions to be satisfied: first, that the refusal was preventing the emergence of a new product for which there was a potential consumer demand; secondly, that the refusal was unjustified; and thirdly, that the refusal was such as

---

Position by Refusing to Licence Intellectual Property Rights" [2005] E.C.L.R. 215; Meinberg, "From *Magill* to *IMS Health*: The New Product Requirement and the Diversity of Intellectual Property Rights" [2006] 7 E.I.P.R. 398.

[1390] *IMS Health GmbH & Co OHG v NDC Health GmbH & Co KG* (C–418/01) [2004] 4 C.M.L.R. 28, para.17.

[1391] *IMS Health GmbH & Co OHG v NDC Health GmbH & Co KG* (C–418/01) [2004] 4 C.M.L.R. 28.

[1392] *IMS Health GmbH & Co OHG v NDC Health GmbH & Co KG* (C–418/01) [2004] 4 C.M.L.R. 28, paras 28 and 29.

[1393] *IMS Health GmbH & Co OHG v NDC Health GmbH & Co KG* (C–418/01) [2004] 4 C.M.L.R. 28, para.17.

to exclude any competition on a secondary market.[1394] The Court stated that the conditions were "sufficient", not "necessary".

(iv) New product or service. The parties disputed whether NDC was intending to produce a new product or service. The Court emphasised that free competition would only prevail (in the form of a compulsory licence) where the refusal to grant a licence prevented the development of a secondary market to the detriment of consumers. It was not sufficient that the competitor merely intended to duplicate the copyright owner's goods and services. The competitor must intend to produce new goods and services not offered by the copyright owner and for which there is a potential consumer demand.[1395] It was for the national court to resolve this issue.

(v) Unjustified. The Court reiterated that it was for the national court to decide on the facts whether the refusal was justified by objective considerations.[1396] However, it did not provide further guidance on this point, as to which no specific observations were made by the parties.

(vi) Exclusion of competition on a secondary market. The Court noted that in *Bronner*, the national court had been invited to determine whether home-delivery schemes constituted a separate market on which the owner of the scheme held a dominant position. Accordingly, it had been relevant to distinguish an upstream market for a product or service (in *Bronner*, the market for home delivery) and a (secondary) downstream market on which the upstream product or service was used for the production of another product or supply of another service (in *Bronner*, the market for daily newspapers). The Court noted that in *Bronner* the fact that the home-delivery service was not marketed separately did not preclude the possibility of identifying it as a separate market. It followed, according to the Court, that it was sufficient that a potential, even hypothetical, market could be identified. If two different stages of production could be identified, even if they were interconnected, the condition would be fulfilled provided the upstream product was indispensable for the supply of the downstream product. On the facts of the case, therefore, the question for the national court was whether IMS's brick structure constituted, upstream, an indispensable factor in the downstream supply of regional sales data. If so, the question was whether IMS's refusal to grant a licence was capable of excluding all competition on the market for sales data.[1397]

Microsoft: **interoperability information:**[1398] **(i) the Commission.**[1399] One of the   **28–283** abuses identified by the Commission in this case was the refusal to supply the specifications for the protocols used by Windows workgroup servers in order to provide file, print and group and user administration services to Windows work group networks and allow third parties to implement such specifications for the purpose of developing and distributing interoperable work group server operating system products.[1400] The Commission summarised its reasoning as follows. Microsoft had had a dominant (quasi-monopoly) position on the client PC operating system market for many years. This had enabled it to determine to a large extent the set of coherent communications rules that would govern the de facto

---

[1394] *IMS Health GmbH & Co OHG v NDC Health GmbH & Co KG* (C–418/01) [2004] 4 C.M.L.R. 28, para.38.
[1395] paras 48 and 49.
[1396] *IMS Health GmbH & Co OHG v NDC Health GmbH & Co KG* (C–418/01) [2004] 4 C.M.L.R. 28, para.51.
[1397] *IMS Health GmbH & Co OHG v NDC Health GmbH & Co KG* (C–418/01) [2004] 4 C.M.L.R. 28, paras 40 to 47.
[1398] For the part of the decision which concerns tying, see para.28–274, above.
[1399] Case COMP/C–3/37.792 *Microsoft*, C(2004) 900 final.
[1400] Recital 576.

standard of interoperability in work group networks. As such, interoperability with the Windows domain architecture was necessary for a work group server operating system vendor in order viably to stay in the market.[1401] Microsoft had refused to disclose to third parties the information necessary to achieve such interoperability.[1402] As a result of the interoperability advantage enjoyed by Microsoft, it had reached a dominant position in the market. There was no actual or potential substitute for disclosures by Microsoft.[1403] Microsoft's refusal to supply such information had the result of stifling innovation in the market and of diminishing consumers' choices by locking them into a homogeneous Microsoft solution.

This was inconsistent with art.102(b).[1404] On balance, the possible negative impact on Microsoft's incentives to innovate which would result from a disclosure order was outweighed by the positive effects of such an order on the level of innovation in the whole industry (including Microsoft). For this and other reasons there was no objective justification for Microsoft's conduct.[1405] There was an appreciable effect on trade between Member States and between the Contracting Parties to the EEA.[1406] Accordingly, applying the pre-*IMS Health* case law, Microsoft was ordered to disclose the information.[1407]

(ii) The General Court. The Commission's decision was upheld by the General Court.[1408] In reaching its decision, the Court, like the Commission, assumed that the interoperability information was subject to intellectual property rights.[1409]

(iii) Were the *Magill, IMS Health* and *Bronner* conditions necessary or just sufficient? It seems that Microsoft sought to contend that a refusal by a person in a dominant position to license an intellectual property right would only be abusive if the conditions identified in the previous case law were met.[1410] By contrast, the Commission contended that the enquiry needed to be more general, taking account of all the particular circumstances and not merely those identified in the existing case law.[1411] This was potentially a significant issue because the Commission was relying on factors other than those in the existing case law albeit it was contending in the alternative that the conditions identified in that case law were met.[1412]

The Court stated that in this particular case the correct approach was to decide whether the conditions identified in the earlier case law were present but that if one or more of them was absent it would proceed to assess the particular circumstances invoked by the Commission.[1413] In the event, the Court held that Microsoft had not satisfied it that any of these conditions was absent or that there was any objective justification for the refusal to license.[1414] Accordingly, it did not examine the other particular circumstances invoked by the Commission.[1415]

(iv) Indispensability. The Court upheld the Commission's approach, which

---

[1401] Recital 799.
[1402] Recital 780.
[1403] Recital 781.
[1404] Recital 782.
[1405] Recital 783.
[1406] Recital 993.
[1407] Recital 998 et seq.
[1408] T–21/04.
[1409] para.289.
[1410] para.315.
[1411] para.316.
[1412] paras 317–318.
[1413] para.336.
[1414] paras 436, 620, 665, 711 and 712.
[1415] paras 436, 620, 665, 711 and 712. See also para.691, in which the Court appeared to state that these conditions were examples of the type of circumstances in which a refusal might be abusive.

was first to consider what degree of interoperability with the Windows domain architecture non-Microsoft work group server operating systems must achieve in order for competitors to be able to remain viably on the market and secondly to appraise whether the information that Microsoft refused to disclose was indispensable to the attainment of that degree of interoperability.[1416]

(v) Exclusion of effective competition. Microsoft criticised the Commission on the ground that it had considered that this condition would be met if there was a "risk", rather than a "likelihood" or "high probability", that competition on the work group operating systems market would be eliminated.[1417] The Court rejected this argument. It stated that the expressions "risk of elimination of competition" and "likely to eliminate competition" are used without distinction by the Community judicature to reflect the same idea, namely that art.102 does not apply only from the time when there is no more, or practically no more, competition on the market. If the Commission were required to wait until competitors were eliminated from the market, or until their elimination was sufficiently imminent, before being able to take action under art.102, that would run counter to the objective of that provision, which is to maintain undistorted competition in the common market and, in particular, to safeguard the competition that still exists on the relevant market.[1418] In this case it had been particularly important for the Commission to act when it did because the market in question was characterised by significant network effects.[1419] The Court made the further point that it is not necessary to demonstrate that *all* competition on the market will be eliminated. What matters is that the refusal at issue is liable to, or is likely to, eliminate all *effective* competition on the market. The fact that the competitors of the dominant undertaking retain a marginal presence in certain niches on the market cannot suffice to substantiate the existence of such competition.[1420]

(vi) New product. There were already a number of server operating systems in the market. The Commission's case was that the supply of the interoperability information would enable the products of Microsoft's competitors to behave in the same way as Windows server operating systems and to develop the advanced features of their existing products.[1421] The Court held that the "new product" requirement must seen in the context of art.102(b), which gives, as an example of abusive conduct, "limiting production, markets or technical development to the prejudice of consumers".[1422] Accordingly, "the circumstance relating to the appearance of a new product, as envisaged in *Magill* and *IMS Health* … cannot be the only parameter which determines whether a refusal to license an intellectual property right is capable of causing prejudice to consumers within the meaning of art.[102](b)".[1423] Thus, the Commission had been entitled to find that the "new product" condition was satisfied because the refusal limited technical development to the prejudice of consumers.[1424]

(vii) Objective justification. Microsoft's only argument had been that the interoperability information was covered by intellectual property rights and the Court held that this was inconsistent with the raison d'être of the *Magill*

[1416] paras 370 et seq.
[1417] ara.560.
[1418] para.561.
[1419] para.562.
[1420] paras 563.
[1421] paras 623 and 624.
[1422] para.643.
[1423] para.647.
[1424] paras 648, 665. This has been described as a "somewhat benign approach" to the 'new product' rule, which may have to be examined further: Whish *Competition Law* 6th edn, p.791.

exception.[1425] It made no difference that the material was secret, valuable and innovative.[1426] Further, Microsoft had failed to establish that the order for disclosure would have a sufficient negative effect on its incentives to innovate.[1427]

(viii) Enforcement and a later case. The enforcement of the decision can be traced through the Commission's Annual Reports on Competition Policy.[1428] In a subsequent case[1429] Microsoft gave a public undertaking to make interoperability information available in relation to a number of applications and operating systems.

28–284   **Refusal to license: summary of the law.**[1430] The following propositions may be tentatively put forward:

(1) A refusal to license intellectual property is not in itself an abuse. It will only amount to an abuse in exceptional circumstances.

(2) The categories of exceptional circumstances are not closed. However, certain conditions have been identified in the case law which if satisfied will amount to exceptional circumstances.

(3) In particular, where use of the intellectual property is indispensable for carrying on a business which comprises the provision of a new product or service for which there is potential demand and a refusal to license the intellectual property will exclude competition on the market for that new product, the refusal will be an abuse unless it is objectively justified.

(4) Use of the intellectual property will be indispensable for carrying on a business if would be impossible or at least unreasonably difficult to provide the new product or service without it.

(5) The earlier cases suggest that the "new" product or service must be one which is not offered by the copyright owner and must be on a market which would be downstream from the market in which the intellectual property in question was used or developed. However, according to the General Court in *Microsoft*, it is sufficient that the product or service amounts to a technical development of an existing product.

(6) The earlier cases suggest that the refusal to license must be capable of excluding all competition on the market for the new product. However, according to the General Court in *Microsoft*, it is sufficient that there is a "risk" that all "effective" competition will be excluded.

(7) As to objective justification, according to the General Court in *Microsoft*, a refusal to license will not be objectively justified merely because the material to be licensed is secret, valuable and innovative.[1431]

28–285   **Collecting societies.** Collecting societies have come under particular scrutiny under art.102.[1432] In *Re GEMA*[1433] the Commission held that the German performing right society had a dominant position within the meaning of art.102, and had

---

[1425] para.690.

[1426] paras 693–695.

[1427] para.701. As to objective justification, see also the Commission's Guidance on the Commission's enforcement priorities in applying art.[102] of the EC Treaty to abusive exclusionary conduct by dominant undertakings [2009] OJ C45/7 paras 89–90.

[1428] See, e.g. the 2007 Report points 53-54 and the 2008 Report point 23.

[1429] Comp C–3/39.294.

[1430] See also the Commission's Guidance on the Commission's enforcement priorities in applying art.[102] of the EC Treaty to abusive exclusionary conduct by dominant undertakings [2009] OJ C45/7 paras 75–90.

[1431] For the Commission's view as to when conduct will be objectively justified, see Guidance on the Commission's enforcement priorities in applying art.[102] of the EC Treaty to abusive exclusionary conduct by dominant undertakings [2009] OJ C45/7 paras 28–31.

[1432] For the Commission's current thinking in this area, see para.24–160 above.

abused that position by the following practices: discriminating against authors from other Member States; binding its members to unjustified obligations, such as the assignment by the author of all his rights to GEMA; preventing foreign publishers from becoming ordinary members of GEMA; extending copyright through contractual means to non-copyright works; and discriminating against (i) independent importers of gramophone records as compared with manufacturers of records and (ii) importers of tape and optical sound recorders as compared with German manufacturers of such recorders.

In *BRT v SABAM*[1434] the Court of Justice had to consider questions referred to it raising the validity under art.102 of practices carried out by the Belgian association of authors, composers and publishers, SABAM. The Court held that in determining whether a national copyright society is imposing unfair conditions on its members or on third parties, account is to be taken of all relevant interests so as to ensure a balance between the needs of the members for freedom from restraint, and for effective management of their rights.[1435] The Court went on to hold that for the society to require a compulsory assignment by an author to it of all his copyrights, present and future, may amount to an unfair condition, especially if the assignment is to remain effective for a considerable time after the author has left the society.[1436]

In *GVL v Commission*[1437] the Court was asked to overturn the Commission's decision[1438] that the German collecting society GVL had abused a dominant position by refusing to conclude management contracts or otherwise manage the performer's rights for artistes of other Member States not resident in Germany. Upholding the Commission's decision and finding that GVL had a monopoly on the relevant market for the secondary exploitation of copyright, the Court held that a refusal by a *de facto* monopoly to provide its services to all who might be in need of them, but who are not in a category defined by that undertaking by nationality or residence, is an abuse of a dominant position. Thus GVL could not refuse its services to foreign artistes not resident in Germany; they might also wish to assert rights of secondary exploitation. GVL knew it was preventing those artistes from being paid the royalties they were entitled to.

In *Basset v SACEM*,[1439] the Court held that the French copyright management society SACEM would not be infringing art.102 by exercising the powers granted to it by national legislation. However, it was possible that the level of royalty or combined royalties charged by the society might be such as to bring art.102 into operation. The French court had already found that the royalties charged by SACEM were not unreasonable, so the Court of Justice made no further comment in this particular case.

The practices of SACEM received further attention from the Court of Justice in a series of cases[1440] challenging the restrictions it imposed on discotheques using the repertoire of authors registered with SACEM and collecting societies in other Member States having reciprocal agreements with SACEM. The challenge

---

[1433] [1971] OJ L134/15; [1971] C.M.L.R. D35; see also *Re Gema (No.2)* [1972] OJ L166/22; [1972] C.M.L.R. D115.

[1434] (Case 127/73) [1974] E.C.R. 313; [1974] 2 C.M.L.R. 238.

[1435] *BRT v SABAM* (Case 127/73) [1974] 2 C.M.L.R. 238 at 283, para.8.

[1436] *BRT v SABAM* (Case 127/73) [1974] 2 C.M.L.R. 238 at 283, para.12; see also *Greenwich Films SA v SACEM* [1979] 2 C.M.L.R. 535 and (Case 22/79) [1979] E.C.R. 3275; [1980] 1 C.M.L.R. 629.

[1437] Case 7/82 [1983] E.C.R. 483; [1983] 3 C.M.L.R. 645.

[1438] [1981] OJ L370/49; [1982] 1 C.M.L.R. 221.

[1439] [1981] OJ L370/49; [1982] 1 C.M.L.R. 221.

[1440] *Ministère Public v Tournier* (Case 395/87) [1989] E.C.R. 2521; *Lucazeau v SACEM* (Cases 110/88, 241/88 & 242/88); *SACEM v Debelle*; *SACEM v Sougmagnac* [1989] E.C.Rl. 2811; [1991] 4 C.M.L.R. 248.

under art.102 was to the level of royalties charged by SACEM to discotheques for the performance of the protected works in comparison with copyright societies in other Member States. In the judgment of the Court, if those rates were significantly higher than those charged by the other copyright societies, when compared on an equal basis, the difference would be an indication of abuse. It would then be for the society in question to justify the difference objectively.[1441] An attempt by SACEM to justify the difference on the basis of its greater administrative zeal was rejected by the Court as also being capable of explanation by the lack of competition on the market, allowing SACEM to develop an unnecessarily burdensome administration.

In *Ministère Public v Tournier*[1442] the Court went slightly further than in the other cases by adding that the imposition of any inequitable contractual term by a dominant undertaking is an abuse of art.102. As to the method of calculation of royalties, it stated that a flat rate royalty charged on a discotheque by reference to turnover could only be attacked under art.102 if other methods might be capable of attaining the same legitimate aim (the protection of copyright owners' interests) without thereby increasing the costs of management and monitoring. This statement was applied in *Kanal 5 Ltd v Föreningen Svenska Tonsättares Internationella Musikbyrå (STIM)*.[1443] In that case royalties for television broadcasting of music were calculated both on the basis of revenue and on the amount of music broadcast. The Court of Justice held that such a remuneration model might amount to an abuse if another method existed which enabled a more precise identification and quantification of the works and the audience without leading to a disproportionate increase in management and supervision costs. The Court also considered whether charging lower royalties to a public broadcaster than those charged to commercial broadcasters was capable of amounting to an abuse. As to this, the Court stated that the following considerations needed to be taken into account. First, whether on the facts dissimilar conditions were applied to equivalent services. Second, if so, whether the commercial companies were thereby placed at a commercial disadvantage. Third, whether the public and commercial broadcasters were competitors on the same market. Fourth, whether there was any objective justification for the practice, for example as a result of "the task and method of financing of public service undertakings".[1444]

In *Banghalter v SACEM*,[1445] the Commission held that a mandatory requirement in the statute of a collecting society that all rights of an author, including those of online exploitation, be assigned, amounted to an abuse since it corresponded to the imposition of an unfair trading condition.

B. UNITED KINGDOM COMPETITION LAW

(i) Introduction

28–286 Current United Kingdom legislation. United Kingdom competition law is

---

[1441] *Ministère Public v Tournier* (Case 395/87) [1989] E.C.R. 2521; *Lucazeau v SACEM* (Cases 110/88, 241/88 & 242/88) ; *SACEM v Debelle*; *SACEM v Sougmagnac* [1989] E.C.Rl. 2811; [1991] 4 C.M.L.R. 248, paras 38 and 25 of the respective judgments.

[1442] [1989] E.C.R. 251, para.34 of the judgment.

[1443] (C–52/07.)

[1444] The Court did not elaborate on this last point.

[1445] Case COMP/C2/37.219, as reported in the Commission's Communication The Management of Copyright and Related Rights in the Internal Market, COM (2004) 261 final, April 16, 2004, pp.16 to 17. The French Competition Council case *SACD* (reported at [2005] E.C.L.R. N–132) is to the same effect.

governed by the Competition Act 1998[1446] and the Enterprise Act 2002. In broad terms, the Competition Act covers anti-competitive agreements and conduct,[1447] while the Enterprise Act covers issues of market structure, in particular, mergers[1448] and market investigations.[1449] A residual part of the Competition Act 1980 remains in force and covers the regulation of the conduct of certain public bodies.[1450] Community competition law and national competition law apply in parallel, since they consider restrictive practices from different points of view. Whereas arts 101 and 102 regard them in the light of the obstacles which may result for trade between Member States, national law proceeds on the basis of considerations peculiar to it and considers restrictive practices only in that context.[1451]

The Office of Fair Trading and the Competition Commission. The two major institutions of relevance to the rights covered in this work are the Office of Fair Trading ("OFT") and the Competition Commission.

28–287

The OFT is a body corporate established under the Enterprise Act 2002.[1452] Its role so far as relevant to this work includes the enforcement of the Chapter I and II prohibitions in the Competition Act 1998 and the conduct of preliminary investigations into mergers and markets and decisions as to whether to make references to the Competition Commission. The OFT's extensive investigation and enforcement powers are outlined below.[1453]

The Competition Commission is body corporate established by the Competition Act 1998.[1454] It conducts inquiries into mergers, markets and the regulation of the major regulated industries in response to references by the OFT, the Secretary of State and specific regulators. The Commission has no power to conduct inquiries on its own initiative.[1455] Its rules of procedure are available on its website.[1456]

On October 14, 2010, the Government announced its intention to consult on a merger of the OFT's competition functions with the Competition Commission.

(ii) The Competition Act 1998

(a) *General principles*

General principles of interpretation. Section 2 of the Act provides for a prohibition ("the Chapter I prohibition") of anti-competitive agreements closely modelled on art.101(1) of the Treaty,[1457] although without the reference to an effect on trade between Member States. Likewise, s.18 provides for a prohibition ("the Chapter II prohibition") on abuse of a dominant position closely modelled

28–288

[1446] For the transitional provisions applicable on the commencement of the Act, see *Copinger* 15th edn, paras 29–256—29–258.

[1447] See paras 28–288 et seq., below.

[1448] See paras 28–307 et seq., below.

[1449] See paras 28–318 et seq., below.

[1450] See paras 28–324 et seq., below.

[1451] *Manfredi v Lloyd Adriatico Assicurazioni SpA* (Joined Cases C–295/04 to C–298/04) [2006] E.C.R. I–6619.

[1452] Enterprise Act 2002 s.1(1).

[1453] para.28–305.

[1454] Competition Act 1998 s.45.

[1455] See the article "About us" on its website *www.competition-commission.org.uk* [Accessed November 22, 2010].

[1456] Publication CC1 at *www.competition-commission.org.uk* [Accessed November 22, 2010.].

[1457] As to which, see paras 28–184 et seq., above.

on art.102 of the Treaty.[1458] In interpreting these provisions, the starting point is s.60 of the Act. That section is as follows:

"(1) The purpose of this section is to ensure that so far as is possible (having regard to any relevant differences between the provisions concerned), questions arising under this Part in relation to competition within the United Kingdom are dealt with in a manner which is consistent with the treatment of corresponding questions arising in Community law in relation to competition within the Community.

(2) At any time when the court determines a question arising under this Part, it must act (so far as is compatible with the provisions of this Part and whether or not it would otherwise be required to do so) with a view to securing that there is no inconsistency between:

(a) the principles applied, and decision reached, by the court in determining that question; and

(b) the principles laid down by the [EC] Treaty and the European Court,[1459] and any relevant decision of that Court, as applicable at that time in determining any corresponding question arising in Community law.

(3) The court must, in addition, have regard to any relevant decision or statement of the [European] Commission.

(4) Subsections (2) and (3) also apply to—

(a) the [OFT][1460]; and

(b) any person acting on behalf of the OFT, in connection with any matter arising under this Part.

(5) In subsections (2) and (3), 'court' means any court or tribunal.

(6) In subsections (2)(b) and (3), 'decision' includes a decision as to

(a) the interpretation of any provision of Community law;

(b) the civil liability of an undertaking for harm caused by its infringement of Community law".

The effect of this provision is that in applying the Act both the courts and the OFT are, in essence, required to interpret the Act in the same way as equivalent provisions of Community law are interpreted by the European Community Courts and the European Commission. Thus, concepts such as "agreement", "undertaking", "prevention, distortion or restriction of competition", "abuse", and "dominant position" are left undefined in the Act. In order to extract their meaning, reference must be made to the case law of the European Community Courts, and (on the basis that its views have, by virtue of s.60(3), persuasive authority) to decisions and statements of the European Commission.[1461] It is therefore suggested that the reader should refer, before reading the following discussion of the

---

[1458] As to which, see paras 28–202 et seq., above.

[1459] That is to say, the Court of Justice and the Court of First Instance: Competition Act 1998 s.59(1).

[1460] The Act originally gave powers to the Director General of Fair Trading. However, with effect from April 1, 2003, this post was abolished by s.2(2) of the Enterprise Act 2002 (c.40) and its functions were transferred to the Office of Fair Trading by s.2(1) of the same Act. For commencement, see the Enterprise Act 2002 (Commencement No. 2, Transitional and Transitory Provisions) Order 2003 (SI 2003/766) art.2 and Sch. S.60 was amended to give effect to this: Enterprise Act 2002 Sch.25 para.38, also with effect from April 1, 2003: ibid. The powers of the OFT under the Act are shared with a number of specialist utility regulators in their respective fields. This complication is unlikely to affect the rights that are the subject of this work, and is ignored in what follows.

[1461] In the OFT's view, this is limited to decisions or statements which have the authority of the European Commission as a whole, such as, for example, decisions on individual cases under arts 101 and/or 102; European Commission Notices; and clear statements about its policy approach which the European Commission has published in its Annual Reports on Competition Policy: *Modernisation*: OFT Guideline 442 (December 2004).

Act, to the discussion above of European Community competition law.[1462] The following discussion will concentrate mainly on matters where there is or may be a difference in approach between the Act and equivalent provisions of Community competition law, or where there is no equivalent provision of Community law. In addition, however, reference will be made to the OFT's guidelines where that assists in illuminating the understanding that body has of the Community law.

Market integration. One area where the approach of the OFT and of the courts under the Act may well differ from the approach of the Community authorities under arts 101 and 102 is that of agreements and conduct that have the effect of segmenting the market. The Community authorities have consistently condemned vertical agreements that confer absolute territorial protection on distributors or licensees, and have condemned as abusive conduct by a dominant undertaking that is intended to partition the market for its products on a geographical basis. However, it is doubtful that this strict approach to such agreements or conduct will be appropriate in the context of the Act; there is no evidence that United Kingdom legislators or policy-makers have shared in relation to the United Kingdom the concern to promote market integration that is evident in the Treaty. It remains to be seen how this distinction is developed.   **28–289**

(b) *The Chapter I prohibition*

The Chapter I prohibition. Subsections 2(1) and (2) of the Act set out the Chapter I prohibition in terms that substantially replicate art.101(1) of the Treaty.[1463] Agreements[1464] between undertakings[1465] that (a) may affect trade within the United Kingdom[1466] and (b) have as their object or effect the prevention, restriction or distortion of competition within the United Kingdom are prohibited unless exempt. There is no reference to an effect on trade between Member States; the Act therefore applies to agreements that have a purely do-   **28–290**

[1462] See paras 28–181 et seq., above.

[1463] See paras 28–184 et seq., above. In December 2004 the OFT published a Guideline as to its interpretation of the Ch.1 prohibition (OFT 401)

[1464] The section refers (as does art.101(1)) to agreements between undertakings, decisions by associations of undertakings and concerted practices; in what follows, references to agreements include references to decisions and concerted practices. According to the OFT: "Agreement has a wide meaning and covers agreements whether legally enforceable or not, written or oral; it includes so-called gentlemen's agreements. There does not have to be a physical meeting of the parties for an agreement to be reached: an exchange of letters or telephone calls may suffice." See OFT 401 para.2.7. The OFT has published a Guideline on the application of the Ch.I and Ch.II prohibitions to the activities of trade association, professional bodies and self-regulating bodies: OFT 408 (December 2004).

[1465] According to the OFT, the term "undertaking" "covers any natural or legal person engaged in economic activity, regardless of its legal status and the way in which it is financed. It includes companies, firms, businesses, partnerships, individuals operating as sole traders, agricultural co-operatives, associations of undertakings (e.g. trade associations), non profit-making organisations and (in some circumstances) public entities that offer goods or services on a given market." See OFT 401, para.2.5. As under Community law, the prohibition is not applied to agreements between entities which form a single economic unit: ibid., para.2.6.

[1466] The effect of this provision is rather obscure. Art.101(1) refers (as does art.102) to an effect on trade between Member States; it is clear that this imposes an additional requirement to the requirement that there be an effect on competition within the common market, because it is clearly possible to have both effect on competition in the common market and yet no effect on trade between Member States (where the effect is confined to one Member State forming part of the common market). But it is not clear how an agreement or conduct could affect competition within the UK but not affect trade within the UK. In para.2.25 of Guideline OFT 401, the OFT acknowledges that in practice it is very unlikely that an agreement which restricts competition in the United Kingdom does not also affect trade in the United Kingdom and states that in applying the Ch.I prohibition the focus will be on the effect on competition.

mestic effect.[1467] Subsection 2(4) renders void any agreement or decision prohibited by subs.2(1); it is analogous to art.101(2). In *P&S Amusements Ltd v Valley House Leisure Ltd*[1468] it was submitted that[1469] there was no requirement that the effect on trade in the United Kingdom should be appreciable. The Judge[1470] stated that he would need "much persuasion" before accepting such a submission.

28–291   **Territorial effect.** In addition to the requirements of subs.2(1) (to the effect that an agreement must affect trade and competition within the United Kingdom to be caught by the prohibition), subs.2(3) provides that an agreement will not be prohibited unless it is, or is intended to be, implemented in the United Kingdom. This provision is intended to replicate the test at Community level set out by the Court of Justice in *Wood Pulp*.[1471]

28–292   **Appreciability.** Although the Act makes no mention of it, the requirement that the effect on competition should be appreciable is implicit in the application of established Community case law to the Chapter I prohibition by s.60 of the Act. In determining whether an agreement has an appreciable effect on competition for the purposes of the Chapter I prohibition (or indeed art.101), the OFT will have regard to the Commission's approach as set out in its Notice on Agreements of Minor Importance.[1472] As a matter of practice the OFT is likely to consider that an agreement will not fall within the Chapter I prohibition when it is covered by the Commission's Notice.[1473] Furthermore, where the OFT considers that undertakings have relied in good faith on the terms of the Notice it will not impose financial penalties.[1474] The mere fact that the parties' market shares exceed the thresholds provided for in the Notice does not mean that the effect on competition is appreciable. Other factors, such as the content of the agreement and the structure of the market, will be considered.[1475] In *Burgess v The OFT*,[1476] the CAT was prepared to accept that a material effect on competition must be shown, but rejected the OFT's submission that it was necessary to show "substantial harm".

28–293   **Exemptions.** Since May 1, 2004 it has no longer been possible to notify an agreement for exemption under s.4 of the Competition Act 1998.[1477] Section 6 of the Act gives the Secretary of State power, on the recommendation of the OFT, to exempt a class of agreements which are likely in the view of the OFT to be ones to which s.9 applies. The effect of these provisions is to reproduce the substance of art.101(3) of the Treaty, although set out in a different way. To date, no block exemptions have been made which are of any relevance to the rights covered in this work.

[1467] Where an agreement does have an effect on trade between Member States, the effect of art.3 of the Modernisation Regulation (2003/1) is that Community law must be applied as well as national law and that an agreement may not be sanctioned unless it infringes art.101.

[1468] [2006] EWHC 1510 (Ch); [2006] U.K.C.L.R. 876.

[1469] As a result of the Competition Appeal Tribunal's decision in *Aberdeen Journals Ltd v OFT* [2003] CAT 11 (see para.28–300, below).

[1470] Morritt C. (obiter).

[1471] *Åhlström v Commission* (C–89/95) [1993] E.C.R. I–1307.

[1472] Guideline OFT 401, para.2.18, As to the Notice, see paras 28–195 and 28–196, above.

[1473] Guideline OFT 401, para.2.19.

[1474] See previous note.

[1475] Guideline OFT 401, para.2.20.

[1476] [2005] CAT 25.

[1477] The effect of reg.4 and para.2 of Sch.1 to the Competition Act and Other Enactments (Amendment) Regulations 2004 (SI 2004/1261) was that on May 1, 2004, s.4 ceased to have effect. Individual exemptions granted before May 1, 2004 and still in force on that day remain effective, but this does not permit the OFT to extend the period of the exemption under s.4(6) of the Competition Act 1998 after May 1, 2004: ibid., reg.6(2).

Relationship with Community provisions; parallel exemptions. Article 3(1) **28–294**
of the Modernisation Regulation[1478] provides that where an agreement affects
trade between Member States, national competition authorities must apply art.101
as well as national competition law. Article 3(2) provides that such an agreement
may not be prohibited[1479] if it would not be prohibited under art.101. This provision is complemented by s.10 of the 1988 Act, which provides that an agreement
that is exempt from art.101(1) by virtue of a Commission or Council Regulation
(such as a block exemption regulation)[1480] or because of a decision by the Commission under art.10 of the Modernisation Regulation[1481] is exempt from the
Chapter I prohibition. Such Regulations and decisions only apply where
art.101(1) is otherwise satisfied, and in particular where the agreement in question affects trade between Member States. In order to exempt agreements which
only fall outside such Regulations and decisions because they have no actual or
potential effect on trade between Member States, subs.10(2) provides that an
agreement is exempt from the Chapter I prohibition if it does not affect trade between Member States but otherwise falls within a category of agreement which is
exempt from the Community prohibition by virtue of a Commission or Council
Regulation. The 1998 Act gives the OFT power to cancel such a "parallel
exemption".[1482] The power is exercisable where the OFT finds that the agreement
nevertheless has effects in the United Kingdom, or a part of it, which are
incompatible with the conditions laid down in s.9 of the 1998 Act.[1483]

Exclusions. A number of agreements (and various types of conduct) are excluded **28–295**
from the Chapter I prohibition (and the Chapter II prohibition). These relate to
mergers and concentrations (Schedule 1); agreements and conduct scrutinised for
competition implications under other enactments (Schedule 2); planning obligations and other general exclusions (Schedule 3)[1484]; and professional rules (Schedule 4). As to vertical agreements, the Act proceeds by granting the Secretary of
State the power to prescribe exclusions and exemptions in relation to both the
Chapter I and Chapter II provisions by subordinate legislation; see s.50. Such
exclusions may, however, be made subject to withdrawal by the OFT.[1485] The
meaning of "vertical agreement" is itself left to be prescribed by the Secretary of
State.[1486]

Vertical agreements. The power to exclude vertical agreements was exercised **28–296**
by the making of an Order ("the Exclusion Order"),[1487] but the Order was revoked

---

[1478] Regulation 2003/1.

[1479] For example under national restraint of trade law: *Jones v Ricoh UK Ltd* [2010] EWHC 1743 (Ch) at para.49.

[1480] e.g. Commission Regulation 330/2010 which creates a block exemption for certain vertical agreements (see above, paras 28–263 et seq.).

[1481] Council Regulation (EC) No. 1/2003, [2003] OJ L1/1. Art.10 gives the Commission the power, acting on its own initiative and where the Community public interest requires, to make findings that art.101 or 102 is inapplicable.

[1482] Competition Act 1998 s.10(5).

[1483] See r.12 in the Schedule to the Competition Act (Office of Fair Trading's Rules) Order 2004 (SI 2004/2751).

[1484] Exclusions in this Schedule that may be worth noting are: the exclusion for agreements which have benefited from a direction by the Secretary of State under RTPA 1976, s.21(2)—see *Copinger* 14th edn, para.29–207; and the exclusion for an agreement entered into or conduct engaged in so as to comply with a legal requirement having legal effect in the UK.

[1485] Competition Act 1998 s.50(3). See also r.14 of the Office of Fair Trading's Rules (Sch. to SI 2004/2751).

[1486] Competition Act 1998 s.50(5).

[1487] The Competition Act 1998 (Land and Vertical Agreements Exclusion) Order 2000 (SI 2000/310).

with effect from May 1, 2005.[1488] As a result, vertical agreements are only exempt if they satisfy the requirements of the VABER, which will apply by way of parallel exemption.[1489] Accordingly, a vertical agreement which may affect trade between Member States but satisfies the requirements of the VABER will continue to be exempt. Furthermore, a vertical agreement which has no actual or potential effect on trade between Member States but otherwise satisfies the requirements of the VABER will also be exempt. The application of the VABER to the rights covered in this work is considered above.[1490]

28–297   **Guidance from the OFT.** The OFT has issued a considerable amount of guidance as to how it operates the provisions of the Competition Act. Furthermore, it has stated that it will continue to offer informal advice.[1491] Finally, where a case raises novel or unresolved questions about the application of the Chapter I or Chapter II prohibitions, and where the OFT considers there is an interest in issuing clarification for the benefit of a wider audience, it may publish written guidance in the form of an opinion.[1492] Such an opinion cannot prejudge the assessment of the same question by the Competition Appeal Tribunal and does not bind any court having the power to apply the prohibitions in the Competition Act[1493]; nor can it bind the subsequent assessment of the same or similar issues, although the OFT will have regard to its opinion when carrying out the assessment.[1494]

28–298   **The OFT's draft guideline on intellectual property rights: general.** In November 2001 the OFT issued a draft guideline in respect of the application of the Competition Act to intellectual property rights.[1495] This draft guideline was never finalised and has since been withdrawn from the OFT's website. It seems doubtful whether it is of any value other than as an indication of the OFT's thinking on the subject in November 2001. Nevertheless, an account follows. According to this guideline, the OFT recognised the importance of intellectual property rights, on the grounds that they tend to encourage innovation and thus benefit consumers.[1496] The OFT acknowledged that much of the European case law concerning intellectual property rights had been driven by the single market objective. It considered that it was not obliged by s.60 to follow that case law. In practice, however, it intended to follow the principles developed in the European case law in relation to intellectual property rights where they were relevant in a domestic context.[1497] The guideline contained a statement of the general approach which the OFT expected to take when assessing the most common forms of restrictions in intellectual property licensing agreements. It emphasised that in practice, each agreement would be assessed on a case by case basis by examining it in its market and economic context.[1498] The OFT's main concerns in respect of

---

[1488] By the Competition Act (Land Agreements Exclusion and Revocation) Order 2004 (SI 2004/1260) art.2.

[1489] For the VABER, see paras 28–263 et seq., above. For parallel exemptions, see para.28–294, above. For the Government's reasoning in revoking the Exclusion Order, see *Copinger* 15th edn para.29–268, fn.20.

[1490] See paras 28–265 et seq., above.

[1491] See *Modernisation*, OFT Guideline 442, para.3.5.

[1492] See *Modernisation*, OFT Guideline 442, para.7.4.

[1493] See *Modernisation*, OFT Guideline 442, para.7.18.

[1494] See *Modernisation*, OFT Guideline 442, para.7.19.

[1495] OFT 418. This guideline was issued in draft in November 2001 and consultation closed on February 28, 2002.

[1496] OFT 418, para.1.3.

[1497] para.1.8.

[1498] para 2.17.

such agreements were price-fixing, market sharing and provisions which foreclosed the market.[1499]

The OFT's draft guideline on intellectual property rights: specific provisions in licences. Specific guidance was given as to the application of the Chapter I prohibition to intellectual property licences as follows. First, any provisions in a licence which directly or indirectly imposed minimum resale prices for the products or services covered by the licensed intellectual property right were likely to infringe the prohibition. The OFT considered that the licensee must remain free to determine its own pricing policy. The setting of royalty rates in a way intended to fix the prices at which the goods or products are sold was likely to infringe.[1500] Secondly, any provisions which shared markets were likely to infringe. However, the grant of an exclusive right to manufacture and sell the goods in a particular territory and/or the grant of a particular field of exploitation were unlikely to infringe unless, having regard to the conditions of competition in the relevant market, they had the effect of foreclosing competition in that market and therefore had an appreciable effect on competition.[1501] Thirdly, a provision preventing sub-licensing or assignment would generally not infringe.[1502] Fourthly, a provision which required a licensee to grant back to the licensor the exclusive right to improvements might infringe.[1503] Fifthly, any provision preventing the exploitation of the right after the expiry of the licence would infringe if it exceeded the lifetime of the right. Other provisions in a licence which continued to apply even after the right had expired, such as a royalty obligation, might also infringe.[1504] Sixthly, an obligation to meet certain specifications as to minimum quality of the licensed product (including provisions as to marketing and labelling) was unlikely to infringe.[1505] Seventhly, provisions which required the licensee to purchase certain products from the licensor might infringe where they had the effect of foreclosing the market, but not if they were necessary for quality control.[1506] Finally, a requirement that the licensee produce a minimum quantity of products made using the right might infringe if it prevented the licensee from using other intellectual property rights to compete with products made using the right and if it foreclosed the market and therefore had an appreciable effect on competition.[1507]

28–299

(c) The Chapter II prohibition

The Chapter II prohibition. Section 18[1508] prohibits any "conduct" which amounts to the abuse of a dominant position "in a market ... if it may affect trade within the United Kingdom [or any part of it]".[1509] Although the word "conduct" does not appear in art.102, it is not thought that its inclusion leads to any difference between the interpretation of s.18 and that of art.102. The dominant position

28–300

[1499] para.2.18.
[1500] OFT 418, para.2.19.
[1501] para.2.21.
[1502] para.2.22.
[1503] para.2.23.
[1504] para.2.24.
[1505] para.2.25.
[1506] para.2.26.
[1507] para.2.27.
[1508] The OFT has published a guideline as to its interpretation of the Ch.II prohibition: *Abuse of a Dominant Position*, OFT 402 (December 2004).
[1509] See Competiton Act 1998 s.18(3). In *Aberdeen Journals Ltd v OFT* [2003] CAT 11, the Competition Appeal Tribunal held that there was no requirement that the effect on trade should be appreciable. In *P&S Amusements Ltd v Valley House Leisure Ltd* [2006] EWHC 1510 (Ch); [2006] U.K.C.L.R. 876, Morritt C. (*obiter*) expressed considerable misgivings about this.

must be within the United Kingdom or any part of it.[1510] As in relation to the Ch.I prohibition, there is no reference to an effect on trade between Member States; the Act therefore potentially applies to conduct that has a purely domestic effect. An illustrative list of abuses—identical to the equivalent list in art.102—is set out in s.18(2). Article 3 of the Modernisation Regulation requires national competition authorities to apply art.102 when they apply national laws to abuses of a dominant position.[1511] However, by contrast with the position under art.101, Member States are not precluded from adopting and applying stricter national laws in this area.[1512]

28–301   **Exclusions.** Schedules 1 and 3 to the Competition Act set out a number of exclusions from the Chapter II prohibition. These exclusions also apply in relation to the Chapter I prohibition and are set out above.[1513]

28–302   **Notifications.** As in the case of the Ch.I prohibition, the Competition Act originally provided for the possibility of notifying conduct for guidance or a decision as to whether it contravened the Ch.II prohibition. Again, however, this system was abolished with effect from May 1, 2004[1514] and replaced by the same system of published guidance, informal advice and Opinions as applies in respect of the Chapter I prohibition.[1515]

28–303   **The OFT's draft guideline on intellectual property rights: general points about the Chapter II prohibition.** The status of this draft guideline is considered elsewhere.[1516] According to the draft guideline, in applying the Chapter II prohibition, the OFT accepted the general Community law position that ownership of an intellectual property right does not necessarily create a dominant position. However, the OFT believed that whether dominance resulted from the ownership of an intellectual property right depended on the extent to which there were substitutes for the product, work or process to which it related.[1517] In assessing dominance, the OFT stated that it would follow the approach set out in its guidelines on market definition and the Chapter II prohibition and would take account of factors such as the market shares of the undertaking in question as well as barriers to entry in the relevant market. It would also consider whether there were other constraints on the behaviour of the undertaking in question, such as strong buyer power or government regulation.[1518] The draft guideline went on to state that although the existence of an intellectual property right might impede entry into a market in the short term, any other undertaking might in the long term be able to enter the market with its own innovation. A persistently high market share might indicate no more than persistently successful innovation. Accordingly, dominance would be assessed on a case-by-case basis.[1519]

28–304   **The OFT's draft guideline: specific types of conduct.** The draft guideline went on to identify certain types of conduct which might or might not infringe the

---

[1510] Competiton Act 1998, s.18(3).

[1511] art.3(1).

[1512] art.3(2).

[1513] See para.28–295, above.

[1514] By reg.4 of and para.9 of Sch.1 to the Competition Act and Other Enactments (Amendment) Regulations 2004 (SI 2004/1261).

[1515] See para.28–297, above. See the OFT's guidelines "The Ch.II prohibition" (OFT 402), "Market definition" (OFT 403) and "Assessment of market power" (OFT 415).

[1516] See para.28–298, above.

[1517] Draft Guideline OFT 418, Intellectual property rights, para.3.3.

[1518] Draft Guideline OFT 481. The guideline on market definition is OFT 403. The guideline on the Ch.II prohibition is OFT 402. Both OFT 403 and OFT 402 were reissued in December 2004. All these documents are available on the OFT's website.

[1519] Draft Guideline OFT 418, Intellectual property rights, para.3.4.

Ch.II prohibition. They were as follows. First, refusal to licence. The OFT stated that this would not generally infringe, but might do so in certain stated circumstances.[1520] That part of the draft guideline has clearly been superseded by recent European case law.[1521] Secondly, tying and bundling. Again, the OFT's views[1522] have been superseded by later European case law.[1523] Thirdly, other contractual provisions of the type listed in the guideline as potentially infringing the Ch.I prohibition might also infringe the Ch.II provision.[1524] Fourthly, pricing. The OFT's view was that intellectual property rights provide an incentive to innovate by preventing for a period of time the commercial appropriation of ideas that have resulted from that innovation. Successful innovation would naturally lead to an undertaking earning post-innovation profits which were significantly higher than those of its competitors. Accordingly, there would not necessarily be an infringement if the owner of the right held a dominant position and charged a higher selling price or royalty rate for a product, process or work protected by its right as compared with that of an unprotected product, process or work.[1525]

(d) *Enforcement and civil liability*

Enforcement. The Competition Act gives the OFT wide powers to require the production of documents and information where it suspects that there has been a breach of one of the prohibitions.[1526] It also has wide powers to enter premises (with or without a warrant) in order to seek documents.[1527] Once the OFT has established the existence of an infringement, it may impose a penalty of up to 10 per cent of an undertaking's annual turnover.[1528] It will also issue directions requiring the undertaking concerned to bring the infringement to an end[1529]; such directions may also be made on an interim basis pending a final determination of whether there has been an infringement.[1530] An appeal on the merits and on the law lies to the Competition Appeal Tribunal established by s.12 of and Schedule 2 to the Enterprise Act 2002; a further appeal on a point of law or on penalty lies to the Court of Appeal, with the permission of that court.[1531]   **28–305**

Civil liability. The effect of s.60(6)(b)[1532] appears to be that the existence of, and conditions attaching to, civil liability by undertakings in breach of the prohibitions to third parties depend on the existence of, and conditions attaching to, an   **28–306**

[1520] Draft Guideline OFT 418, Intellectual property rights, para.3.7.
[1521] See paras 28–277 et seq., above.
[1522] Draft Guideline OFT 418, Intellectual property rights, para.3.8.
[1523] See paras 28–274 et seq., above.
[1524] Draft Guideline OFT 418, Intellectual property rights, para.3.9. For these, see above, para.28–299.
[1525] Draft Guideline OFT 418, Intellectual property rights, para.3.11.
[1526] Competition Act 1998 s.27.
[1527] ss.28–29.
[1528] s.36. These terms are defined in the Competition Act 1998 (Small Agreements and Conduct of Minor Significance) Regulations 2000 (SI 2000/262). See also the OFT's Guidance as to the appropriate amount of a penalty, OFT 423 (December 2004).
[1529] ss.33 and 34. These provisions are analogous to art.3(1) of Council Reg.17/62 (now art.7(1) of the Modernisation Regulation 1/2003), which has been held to permit the Commission to require the compulsory licensing of copyright material; see paras 28–261 et seq., above.
[1530] Competition Act 1998 s.35.
[1531] s.49. In *Argos Ltd v OFT* [2006] EWCA Civ 1318; [2006] U.K.C.L.R. 1135 the Court of Appeal approved the approach of the CAT to the OFT's guidance on penalties (para.163). The Court went on to say that it recognised that the CAT is an expert and specialised body, and that, subject to any difference in the basis on which the infringements are to be considered as a result of any appeal on liability, the Court of Appeal should hesitate before interfering with its assessment of the appropriate penalty (para.165).
[1532] Set out at para.28–288, above.

equivalent liability in Community law under arts 101(1) and 82. This is considered above.[1533]

(iii) Mergers: Part 3 of the Enterprise Act 2002

28–307   **Introduction.** As is the case in the antitrust field, there are parallel regimes for the regulation of mergers in the United Kingdom and in Europe. Only the United Kingdom regime is dealt with here. That is not because the European merger regime cannot result in an interference with the rights dealt with in this work but because the operation of the UK regime may lead to the exercise of powers under s.144 of the 1988 Act,which is considered below.[1534] For European merger laws, the reader should consult the specialist texts.

28–308   **Power of the OFT to make a reference to the Competition Commission.**[1535] A reference may be made by the OFT if a "relevant merger situation" exists or is anticipated. Such a situation exists if two or more enterprises have ceased to be distinct enterprises and either (a) the value of the turnover in the United Kingdom of the enterprise being taken over exceeds £70 million ("the turnover test") or (b) at least one quarter or all the goods or services of a particular description which are supplied in the United Kingdom or a substantial part of the United Kingdom are supplied by or to one and the same person or are supplied by or to the persons by whom the enterprises concerned are carried on ("the share of supply test").[1536] If the OFT believes that a relevant merger situation has been or will be created and a substantial lessening of competition within any UK market or markets for goods or services has resulted or may result, it is obliged to make a reference to the Competition Commission.[1537] However, the OFT may decide not to make a reference if the market is or the markets concerned are not of sufficient importance to justify it, any relevant consumer benefits outweigh the substantial lessening of competition (or any effects thereof) or (in the case of an anticipated merger) the arrangements are not sufficiently far advanced or likely to proceed to justify the reference.[1538] For these purposes relevant customer benefits are: lower prices, higher quality or greater choice of goods or services and greater innovation in relation to goods or services.[1539] The OFT may also make a reference if the European Commission has by decision referred the whole or part of a case to it

---

[1533] See para.28–218.

[1534] See para.28–325, below.

[1535] See, generally, *Merger Assessment Guidelines*, September 2010 (published by the Competition Commission and the OFT); *Mergers — Substantive Assessment Guidance*, May 2003 (as amended by OFT Guidance Note 516a, October 2004), Ch.7 and 8; and *Mergers — Jurisdictional and procedural Guidance*, OFT, June 2009.

[1536] Enterprise Act 2002 s.23.

[1537] Enterprise Act 2002 s.22(1) and 33(1). The "substantial lessening of competition" test did not appear in the Fair Trading Act 1973. In *OFT v IBA Health Ltd* [2004] 4 All E.R. 1003; [2005] E.C.C. 1 the CAT had held that in reaching a decision as to whether to make a reference under 33(1) (anticipated mergers) the OFT was obliged to decide first, whether as far as it was concerned there was a significant prospect of a substantial lessening of competition ("SLC") and secondly (if not) whether there was a significant prospect of an alternative view being taken in the context of a fuller investigation by the Commission. The Court of Appeal rejected this: the relevant belief is that the merger may be expected to result in SLC, not that the Commission may in due course decide that it may be expected to result in SLC. Further, the body which is to hold that belief is the OFT, not the Commission (see para.38). The test is one of belief, not mere suspicion (para.44). The belief must be reasonable and objectively justified by relevant facts (para.45). The likelihood of SLC must be more than merely fanciful but need not be as high as "a significant prospect" (para.48). More than an arguable issue of SLC is required (para.84). By contrast, where the Competition Commission has to decide under ss.35(1) or 36(1) whether the merger may be expected to result in SLC, the test is the balance of probabilities (paras 46 and 81).

[1538] Enterprise Act 2002 ss.22(2) and 33(2).

[1539] s.30.

under art.4(4) or 9 of the EC Merger Regulation, or is deemed to have taken such a decision, unless an intervention notice is in force in relation to that case.[1540]

When the OFT may not make a reference. The OFT is prohibited from making a reference under the following circumstances. First, while it is considering whether to accept undertakings in lieu of a reference.[1541] Secondly, once it has accepted undertakings in lieu of making a reference, provided all material facts were notified to it or made public before the undertakings were accepted.[1542] Thirdly, the Act contains a "merger notice procedure" pursuant to which notice may be given to the OFT of proposed arrangements which might result in the creation of a relevant merger situation.[1543] In general, no reference may be made in respect of such arrangements if the period for considering the merger notice has expired without a reference being made.[1544] Fourthly, if the Secretary of State has accepted undertakings in lieu of making a reference under sections 45 or 63 of the Enterprise Act, provided all material facts were notified to the Secretary of State or the OFT or made public before the undertakings were accepted.[1545] Fifthly, if there is in force an intervention notice under s.42 of the Enterprise Act, or the matter to which such a notice relates has been finally determined under Chapter 2 otherwise than in circumstances where a notice is given to the OFT under s.56(1).[1546] Sixthly, where the matter is being considered or has been dealt with by the European Commission.[1547]

28–309

Undertakings in lieu of reference. The power to accept undertakings in lieu of a reference may be exercised if the OFT considers that it is under a duty to make a reference.[1548] The power must be exercised for the purpose of remedying, mitigating or preventing the substantial lessening of competition concerned or any adverse effect thereof.[1549] In exercising its power, the OFT is obliged to have particular regard to the need for as comprehensive a solution as is reasonable and practicable and may have particular regard to the effect of any action on any relevant customer benefits in relation to the creation of the relevant merger situation.[1550] Neither the OFT nor the Secretary of State may make a reference in relation to the creation of a relevant merger situation if it is the situation by reference to which the undertakings were accepted.[1551] Where the OFT considers that an undertaking has not been or will not be fulfilled or that false or misleading in-

28–310

[1540] s.34A(1). The Merger Regulation is Council Regulation (EC) No. 139/2004 of 20 January 2004 on the control of concentrations between undertakings [2004] OJ L24/1. For intervention notices, see para.28–316, below.
[1541] Enterprise Act 2002 ss.22(3)(b) and 33(3)(b). The power to accept undertakings is considered in the next paragraph.
[1542] ss.22(3)(a), 33(3)(a), 74(1) and 74(2).
[1543] ss.96 to 102. See also the Enterprise Act 2002 (Merger Prenotification) Regulations 2003 (SI 2003/1369).
[1544] Enterprise Act 2002 ss.22(3)(a), 33(3)(a) and 96(3). Note, however, that there are numerous exceptions to this: see s.100.
[1545] ss.22(3)(a), 33(3)(a) and Sch.7, para.4. For ss.45 and 63, see para.28–316, below. The Secretary of State's power to accept undertakings derives from Sch.7, para.3.
[1546] Enterprise Act 2002 s.22(3)(d).
[1547] Pursuant to a request by the United Kingdom under art.22(1) of the EC Merger Regulation 139/2004: Enterprise Act 2002 s.22(3)(e); or where a reasoned submission requesting referral to the European Commission has been submitted to the European Commission under art.4(5) of the EC Merger Regulation 139/2004 and no Member State competent to examine the concentration under its national competition law has, within the time permitted by art.4(5) of the EC Merger Regulation, expressed its disagreement as regards the request to refer the case to the European Commission, s.22(3)(f).
[1548] Enterprise Act 2002 s.73(1).
[1549] s.73(2).
[1550] s.73(3), (4).
[1551] Enterprise Act 2002 s.74(1). However, this prohibition does not apply if material facts were not notified to the OFT or made public before the undertaking was accepted: s.74(2).

formation has been given to it in relation to an undertaking, it may make an order instead.[1552] In *Tetra Laval*[1553] the OFT accepted in lieu of a reference undertakings to grant to a suitable purchaser an exclusive irrevocable EEA-wide licence of intellectual property rights relating to cheese equipment.

28–311   **Determination by the Competition Commission.**[1554] On a reference the Commission is obliged to decide whether a relevant merger situation has been created or will be created and if so whether that has resulted or may be expected to result in a substantial lessening of competition within any market or markets in the United Kingdom ("an anti-competitive outcome").[1555] If the Commission decides that there is an anti-competitive outcome, it must decide whether to take action itself, or recommend action to be taken by others, for the purpose of remedying, mitigating or preventing the substantial lessening of competition or any adverse effect thereof.[1556] If it decides that action should be taken, it must also decide what action should be taken and what is to be remedied, mitigated or prevented.[1557] Like the OFT when considering whether to accept undertakings in lieu, the Commission is obliged to have particular regard to the need for as comprehensive a solution as is reasonable and practicable and may have particular regard to the effect of any action on any relevant customer benefits in relation to the creation of the relevant merger situation.[1558] The Commission's decisions must be published in a report on the reference.[1559]

28–312   **Action on the report.** Following publication of the report, the Commission is under a duty to take such action as it considers to be reasonable or practicable in order to remedy, mitigate or prevent the substantial lessening of competition and any adverse effects thereof.[1560] Again it must have particular regard to the need for as comprehensive a solution as is reasonable and practicable and may have particular regard to the effect of any action on any relevant customer benefits in relation to the creation of the relevant merger situation.[1561] To that end, it may accept undertakings or make an order, which may contain anything permitted by Schedule 8 of the Act, together with such supplementary, consequential or incidental provision as it considers appropriate.[1562] Where the Commission considers that an undertaking has not been or will not be fulfilled or that false or misleading information has been given to it in relation to an undertaking, it may make an order instead.[1563]

28–313   **Schedule 8: general restrictions and obligations.** Schedule 8 also applies where authorities other than the Competition Commission are taking action. Accord-

---

[1552] s.75(2).

[1553] See Press Release 162/06.

[1554] See, generally, Merger Assessment Guidelines, September 2010 (published by the Competition Commission and the OFT); Mergers — Substantive Assessment Guidance, May 2003 (as amended by OFT Guidance Note 516a, October 2004), Chs 7 and 8; and Mergers — Jurisdictional and procedural Guidance, OFT, June 2009.

[1555] Competition Act 1998 ss.35(1) and 36(1). This is a significant departure from the "public interest" test in s.84 of the Fair Trading Act 1973. In *OFT v IBA Health Ltd* [2004] 4 All E.R. 1003; [2005] E.C.C. 1, the CA held that where the Competition Commission has to decide under ss.35(1) or 36(1) whether the merger may be expected to result in a significant lessening of competition, the test is the balance of probabilities (paras 46 and 81).

[1556] Competition Act 1998 ss.35(3) and 36(2).

[1557] ss.35(3)(c), 36(2)(c).

[1558] ss.35(4), (5) and 36(3), (4).

[1559] s.38.

[1560] Competition Act 1998 s.41.

[1561] Competition Act 1998 s.41(4), (5).

[1562] Enterprise Act 2002 ss.82 to 84.

[1563] Enterprise Act 2002 s.83(2).

ingly, some of its provisions are expressed in terms of what "the authority", rather than "the Competition Commission", may do. The range of permitted provisions is extensive. Under the heading "General restrictions on conduct", it includes provisions prohibiting: the making or performance of an agreement[1564]; the withholding from any person of any goods or services or any orders for goods or services[1565]; the requiring as a condition of the supply of goods or services the buying of any goods, the making of any payment in respect of services other than the goods or services supplied or the doing of or refraining from the doing of any other such matter[1566]; discrimination (or anything which the authority considers to be discrimination) between persons in the prices charged for goods or services[1567]; giving or agreeing to give any preference (or anything which the authority considers to be a preference) in respect of the supply of goods or services or of orders for goods or services[1568]; or charging prices for goods or services which differ from those in any published list or notification or doing anything which the authority considers to be charging such prices.[1569] An order may regulate the prices charged for goods or services, provided the relevant report identifies the prices as requiring remedial action.[1570] An order may prohibit the exercise of a right to vote exercisable by virtue of the holding of any shares, stocks or securities.[1571] Under the heading "General obligations to be performed", an order may require a person to supply goods or services or to do anything which the relevant authority considers appropriate to facilitate the supply of goods or services.[1572] An order may require a person to supply goods or services to a particular standard or in a particular manner or to do anything which the relevant authority considers appropriate to facilitate the provision of goods or services to that standard or in that manner.[1573]

Schedule 8: acquisitions and divisions. Under this head an order may: prohibit or restrict the acquisition by any person of the whole or part of an undertaking or assets of another person's business or the doing of anything which will or may result in two or more bodies corporate becoming interconnected bodies corporate[1574]; require that if such an acquisition occurs or the bodies corporate become interconnected, the persons concerned shall observe any prohibitions or restrictions[1575]; or provide for the division of any business or group of interconnnected bodies corporate.[1576]   **28–314**

Schedule 8: supply and publication of information. Under this head, an order may: require a supplier of goods or services to publish or otherwise notify prices   **28–315**

[1564] Or ordering a party to terminate an agreement Sch.8 para.2(1). However, such an order may not affect an agreement (or proposed agreement) so far as it relates to the terms and conditions of employment of any workers or to the physical conditions in which any workers are required to work: ibid., Sch.8 para.2(2).

[1565] Sch.8 para.3(1). References to withholding include references to agreeing or threatening to withhold and procuring others to withhold or to do such acts: Sch.8 para.3(2).

[1566] Sch.8 para.4.

[1567] Sch.8 para.5. The order may also prohibit the procuring of such acts.

[1568] Sch.8 para.6. Again, the order may also prohibit the procuring of such acts.

[1569] Sch.8 para.7.

[1570] Sch.8 para.8.

[1571] Sch.8 para.9.

[1572] Sch.8, para.10(1).

[1573] Sch.8 para.10(2).

[1574] Sch.8 para.12(1). Bodies corporate are "interconnected" if one is a subsidiary of the other or if both are subsidiaries of the same parent: Enterprise Act 2000 s.129(2).

[1575] Sch.8 para.12(2).

[1576] Sch.8 para.13(1). Such an order may contain such provision as the relevant authority considers appropriate to effect or take account of the division, e.g. provision as to transfer of property, rights, liabilities or obligations: ibid. Sch.8 para.13(3).

and other information[1577]; prohibit the notification of recommended or suggested prices[1578]; require a supplier of goods or services to publish accounting information about the goods or services as well as information as to the quantities supplied and the geographical areas in which they are supplied[1579]; and require information to be supplied to the relevant authority.[1580]

28–316 **Public interest, special public interest cases and European merger cases.** In exceptional circumstances, the Secretary of State may give the OFT an "intervention notice" where he considers that one or more public interest considerations is or may be relevant to a consideration of a merger situation.[1581] A "public interest consideration" is one which is specified in s.58 of the Act or is not so specified but in the opinion of the Secretary of State ought to be so specified.[1582] The only specified public interest consideration (except in the case of media mergers, which are considered below)[1583] specified in s.58 of the Act is the interests of national security. The effect of an intervention notice is that the OFT is obliged to report to the Secretary of State on both the competition and the public interest considerations.[1584] On receipt of the report, the Secretary of State may make a reference to the Commission,[1585] which is then obliged to report to the Secretary of State on competition and public interest considerations and remedies.[1586] The Secretary of State may then take such action under paragraph 9 or 11 of Schedule 7 to the Act as he considers to be reasonable or practicable to remedy, mitigate or prevent any of the effects adverse to the public interest which have resulted from or may be expected to result from the creation of the relevant merger situation.[1587] A similar procedure applies to "special public interest cases" concerning merger situations which involve government contractors holding confidential information relating to defence matters.[1588] The Secretary of State's powers to take action are set out in s.66(6). A similar procedure also applies where there is a relevant merger situation which is also a concentration with a Community dimension and the Secretary of State wishes to take appropriate measures to protect legitimate interests as permitted by art.21(4) of the EC Merger Regulation.[1589] Any person aggrieved by a decision of the OFT, the Secretary of State or the Commission

---

[1577] Sch.8 para.15. The order can also prohibit the publication or notification of information: ibid.

[1578] Sch.8 para.16.

[1579] Sch.8 para.17.

[1580] Sch.8 para.19.

[1581] Enterprise Act 2002 s.42.

[1582] s.42(3).

[1583] See para.28–317, below.

[1584] Enterprise Act 2002 s.44.

[1585] Enterprise Act 2002 s.45. The Secretary of State may accept an undertaking in lieu of making a reference: Sch.7 para.3. If he considers that the undertaking has not been or will not be fulfilled or that false or misleading information has been given in relation to it, he may make an order instead: para.5(2).

[1586] Enterprise Act 2002 s.50.

[1587] s.55. Para.9 gives the Secretary of State power to accept final undertakings. Para.10(2) gives the Secretary of State power to make an order in the event of the non-fulfilment of the final undertakings or if false or misleading information has been supplied in relation to them. Para.11 gives the Secretary of State power to make orders containing anything permitted under Sch.8 (see paras 28–313 and 28–314, above) together with such supplementary, consequential or incidental provision as the Secretary of State considers appropriate.

[1588] ss.59 to 66. The Secretary of State's powers to accept undertakings and make orders are the same as in relation to public interest mergers.

[1589] Council Regulation (EC) No.139/2004 of January 20, 2004 on the control of concentrations between undertakings, [2004] OJ L24/1, which came into effect on May 1, 2004. For the Secretary of State's powers in this regard, see Enterprise Act 2002 ss.67 to 68 and the Enterprise Act 2002 (Protection of Legitimate Interests) Order 2003 (SI 2003/1592).

under these provisions may apply to the Competition Appeal Tribunal for a review of that decision.[1590]

Media mergers.[1591] Media mergers are now assimilated to the general mergers regime, but special rules apply to them.[1592] First, additional public interest considerations are specified for the purposes of s.58 of the Act, such as the need for accurate presentation of news and free expression of opinion in newspapers.[1593] This brings many media mergers into the category of public interest mergers. When that occurs, OFCOM are obliged to report to the Secretary of State.[1594] Secondly, certain media mergers are now subject to the "special public interest cases" regime.[1595] Again, OFCOM are to report to the Secretary of State.[1596] Any person aggrieved by a decision of the OFT, OFCOM, the Secretary of State or the Commission under these provisions may apply to the Competition Appeal Tribunal for a review of that decision.[1597] Finally, in relation to newspaper mergers, the Schedule 8 powers are supplemented by the addition of new powers, including the power to alter the constitution of a body corporate, and attach conditions to the operation of a newspaper.[1598]

28–317

(iv) Market investigations: Part 4 of the Enterprise Act 2002

Introduction. The operation of the Part 4 of the Enterprise Act may lead to the exercise of powers under s.144 of the 1988 Act. Accordingly, Part 4 is dealt with briefly here.

28–318

Power of OFT and Minister to make references.[1599] The OFT may make a reference to the Competition Commission if it has reasonable grounds for suspecting that any feature, or combination of features, of a market in the United Kingdom for goods or services prevents, restricts or distorts competition in connection with the supply or acquisition of any goods or services in the United Kingdom or a part of the United Kingdom.[1600] For these purposes, the following are features of the market: the structure of the market or any aspect of that structure; any conduct (whether or not in the market concerned) of one or more than one person who supplies or acquires goods or services in the market; and any conduct in relation to the market concerned of customers of any person who supplies or acquires goods or services.[1601] A reference may not be made by the

28–319

[1590] s.120. See *British Sky Broadcasting Group Plc v The Competition Commission* [2010] EWCA Civ 2.

[1591] See, generally, the DTI's Guidance Document: Enterprise Act 2002: Public Interest Intervention in Media Mergers, May 2004, which is available on the BIS website, *http://www.bis.gov.uk* [Accessed November 22, 2010].

[1592] By the insertion in the Enterprise Act 2002 of a number of additional sections by the Communications Act 2003, with effect from December 29, 2003: see the Office of Communications Act 2002 (Commencement No.3) and Communications Act 2003 (Commencement No.2) Order 2003 (SI 2003/3142) art.3 and Sch.1.

[1593] Enterprise Act 2002 s.58(2A) to (2C).

[1594] s.44A.

[1595] s.59(3) to (3D).

[1596] s.61A.

[1597] s.120. See *British Sky Broadcasting Group Plc v The Competition Commission* [2010] EWCA Civ 2.

[1598] Sch.8 para.20A.

[1599] See, generally, OFT 511: Market Investigation References, March 2006. The OFT may decide to make such a reference as a result of a market study pursuant to s.5 of the Enterprise Act. For market studies, see generally, "Market Studies: Guidance" (OFT, June 2010).

[1600] Enterprise Act 2002 s.131(1).

[1601] Enterprise Act 2002 s.131(2). "Conduct" includes any failure to act, whether intentional or not, and any other unintentional conduct., s.131(3).

OFT where a reference by the appropriate Minister is pending.[1602] The appropriate Minister has the power to make a reference (a) in the same circumstances as the OFT,[1603] (b) where he is not satisfied with a decision of the OFT not to make a reference[1604] or (c) when he has brought to the OFT's attention information which he considers relevant to the question of whether it should made a reference, but is not satisfied that it will decide within such period as he considers reasonable whether to make such a reference.[1605] The effect of an earlier acceptance of undertakings in lieu of a reference on these powers to refer is dealt with in the next paragraph.

28–320   **Undertakings in lieu of reference.** The power to accept undertakings in lieu of a reference may be exercised if the OFT considers that it has the power to make a reference and otherwise intends to make one.[1606] The power must be exercised for the purpose of remedying, mitigating or preventing any adverse effect on competition concerned or any detrimental effect on customers so far as it has resulted from or may be expected to result from the adverse effect on competition.[1607] In exercising its power, the OFT is obliged to have particular regard to the need to achieve as comprehensive a solution as is reasonable and practicable and may have particular regard to the effect of any action on any relevant customer benefits of the feature or features of the market concerned.[1608] Neither the OFT nor the relevant Minister may make a reference in relation to any feature of a market for goods or services where the OFT has accepted undertakings in lieu of a reference within the previous 12 months in relation to the same description of goods or services to which the feature relates.[1609]

28–321   **Questions to be decided on reference.**[1610] On receipt of a reference, the Competition Commission is obliged to decide whether any feature or combination of features of each relevant market prevents, restricts or distorts competition in connection with the supply or acquisition of any goods or services in the United Kingdom or a part of the United Kingdom.[1611] If the Commission decides that there is such an adverse effect on competition, it must also decide whether action should be taken by itself for the purposes of remedying, mitigating or preventing the adverse effect on competition or any resultant detrimental effect on customers.[1612] For these purposes, the term "detrimental effect on customers" means higher prices, lower quality of goods or services or less innovation.[1613] If the Commission decides that action should be taken, it should decide what action is to be taken and what is to be remedied, mitigated or prevented.[1614] Like the OFT when considering whether to accept undertakings, the Commission is obliged to have particular regard to the need to achieve as comprehensive a solution as is reasonable and practicable and may have particular regard to the effect

---

[1602] s.131(4)(b).
[1603] s.132(3).
[1604] s.132(1).
[1605] s.132(2).
[1606] Enterprise Act 2002 s.154(1).
[1607] s.154(2).
[1608] ss.154(3) and (4).
[1609] Enterprise Act 2002 s.156(1), unless the OFT considers that any undertaking concerned has been breached or the person responsible for giving the undertaking concerned gave the OFT false or misleading information in connection with the matter: ibid., s.156(2).
[1610] See, generally, Market Investigation References: Competition Commission Guidelines, CC3, June 2003.
[1611] Enterprise Act 2002 s.134(1).
[1612] s.134(4)(a), (b).
[1613] s.134(5).
[1614] s.134(4)(c).

of any action on any relevant customer benefits of the feature or features of the market concerned.[1615] The Commission is obliged to prepare and publish a report on its decisions.[1616]

Action on report. Following publication of the report, the Commission is under a duty to take such action as it considers to be reasonable or practicable in order to remedy, mitigate or prevent the adverse effect on competition and any detrimental effects on customers.[1617] Again it must haveparticular regard to the need for as comprehensive a solution as is reasonable and practicable and may have particular regard to the effect of any action on any relevant customer benefits of the feature or features of the market concerned.[1618] To that end, it may accept undertakings or make an order, which may contain anything permitted by Schedule 8 of the Act, together with such supplementary, consequential or incidental provision as the Commission considers appropriate.[1619] The provisions permitted by Schedule 8 are considered above.[1620] Where the Commission considers that an undertaking has not been or will not be fulfilled or that false or misleading information has been given in relation to an undertaking, it may make an order instead.[1621]

28–322

Public interest cases. Where the OFT is considering whether to accept undertakings in lieu of a reference or the Commission is considering a reference, the Secretary of State may serve an "intervention notice" if he considers that it is or may be the case that a public interest consideration is relevant to the case.[1622] For these purposes, a public interest consideration is a consideration specified as such in the Act or which is not so specified but which the Secretary of State considers ought to be so specified.[1623] At the time of writing, the only consideration which is specified is the interests of national security.[1624] If an intervention notice is served at a time when the OFT is considering whether to accept undertakings in lieu, the Secretary of State obtains a power of veto over the undertakings which the OFT may accept.[1625] Where an intervention notice is served at a time when the Commission is considering a reference, the Commission is obliged to determine the same questions as in a normal case, but to decide whether the Secretary of State should take action.[1626] If the Commission's report contains a decision that there is an adverse effect on competition and that action should be taken, the Secretary of State must then decide whether a public interest consideration is relevant to any action recommended by the Commission.[1627] If so, he may take remedial action,[1628] by way of accepting undertakings or making an order in accordance with Sch.8.[1629] Where the Secretary of State considers that an undertaking has not been or will not be fulfilled or that false or misleading information has

28–323

[1615] s.134(6), (7).
[1616] s.136(2).
[1617] Enterprise Act 2002 s.138(2). For the meaning of the expression "detrimental effects on customers", see the previous paragraph.
[1618] s.138(4), (5).
[1619] ss.159 to 161.
[1620] See paras 28–313 and 28–314.
[1621] Enterprise Act 2002 s.160(2).
[1622] Enterprise Act 2002 s.139.
[1623] s.139(5).
[1624] s.153(1).
[1625] s.150.
[1626] s.141.
[1627] s.146.
[1628] s.147.
[1629] s.147.

been given to him in relation to an undertaking, he may make an order instead.[1630] If the Secretary of State does not act, the matter reverts to the Commission to be dealt with in the normal way.[1631]

(v) The Competition Act 1980

28–324   **Competition Act 1980 s.11.** The operation of this section too may result in an order under section 144 of the 1988 Act. It empowers the Secretary of State to refer to the Competition Commission any question relating to the efficiency and costs of or the service provided by certain public bodies.[1632] Following a reference, the Commission must report on the questions referred and any recommended action.[1633] On receipt of the report, the Secretary of State has the power to make an order for the purpose of remedying or preventing what he considers are the adverse effects of any course of conduct specified in the report as operating against the public interest.[1634] An order made under this power may contain anything permitted by Schedule 8 of the Enterprise Act 2002 with some specified omissions.[1635]

(vi) Section 144 of the 1988 Act

28–325   **Introduction and background.** As initially introduced, this section contained special powers exercisable in cases where the matters identified by the Monopolies and Mergers Commission as operating against the public interest included conditions in licences granted by the owner of copyright in a work restricting the use of the work by the licensee or the right of the copyright owner to grant other licences; or a refusal of a copyright owner to grant licences on reasonable terms.

This followed two reports from the MMC. The first of these reports concerned the licensing of copyright in respect of spare body panels for cars by the Ford Motor Company Limited.[1636] The MMC concluded that Ford's refusal to grant licences to would-be manufacturers of replacement parts was anti-competitive and contrary to the public interest.[1637] However, the MMC went on to say that there was no remedy against such practices under existing legislation because "the ability to make an order for the grant of a licence is not among the limited powers exercisable by the Secretary of State following a report of the

---

[1630] s.160(2).

[1631] s.148.

[1632] Competition Act 1980 s.11(1). The public bodies are as follows: any body corporate that supplies goods or services by way of business, whose affairs are managed by its members and whose members hold office by virtue of a statutory appointment by a Minister (s.11(3)(a)); certain public transport companies and service providers (s.11(3)(aa) to (bb)); the National Rivers Authority (s.11(3)(c)); Scottish Water (s. 11(3)(ca)); a board administering a scheme under the Agricultural Marketing Act or equivalent Northern Ireland legislation (s.11(3)(d)); any body corporate with a duty to promote and assist the supply of goods and services by any of these bodies (s.11(3)(e)); and any subsidiary of such a body (s.11(3)(f)).

[1633] Competition Act 1980 s.11(8), (10).

[1634] Competition Act 1980 s.12(5).

[1635] Competition Act 1980 s.12(5A). The omitted paras are 8 (regulation of prices charged for goods or services), 13 (division of business or group) and 14 (division by sale of part of an undertaking).

[1636] Ford Motor Company Ltd: *A report on the policy of the Ford Motor Company of not granting licences to manufacture or sell in the United Kingdom certain replacement body parts for Ford Vehicles*, 1985 (Cmnd 9437). This Report followed an investigation under Competition Act 1980 s.3 (as to which see *Copinger* 14th edn, para.29–242) by the DGFT, who concluded that Ford was engaged in an anti-competitive practice and who referred the matter to the MMC. See further, *Ford Motor Company Ltd, Licensing for the Manufacture or Sale of Replacement Body Parts*, published on March 21, 1984 by the Office of Fair Trading: paras 9.1–9.4.

[1637] Cmnd.9437, paras 6.51; 6.29–6.50.

Commission".[1638] The MMC also pointed out that whilst an order prohibiting Ford from engaging in this practice might appear to oblige Ford indirectly to grant licences, there would be nothing to stop Ford from only offering licences at a prohibitively high rate.[1639]

The second report concerned the refusal of the owners of the *Radio Times* and *TV Times* to license newspapers and magazines to publish comprehensive weekly listings of television programmes.[1640] Although the MMC concluded that the BBC and ITP were engaged in an anti-competitive practice, in this case the MMC was equally divided on the question of whether this practice operated against the public interest.[1641] Nevertheless, the MMC also made it clear that even if it had concluded that the practice did operate against the public interest it would not have been able to recommend an effective course of action.[1642] Section 144 was thus introduced to ensure that in future a remedy would be available in these circumstances.

Prior to its introduction there was some concern that such a power would contravene the United Kingdom's international obligations under the Berne Convention.[1643] It might be thought that such a power would fall within art.17 of the Convention, which provides that "The provisions of this Convention cannot in any way affect the right of the Government of each country of the Union to permit, to control, or to prohibit, by legislation or regulation, the circulation, presentation, or exhibition of any work or production". The better view, however, seems to be that art.17 should be confined to matters of public order and morality.[1644] Nevertheless, the regulation of monopolistic activity may still be justified under the general principle, agreed at the Rome, Brussels and Stockholm revision conferences, that Member States remain free to regulate certain matters in the public interest, and that this includes restricting potential abuses of monopoly. Moreover, the Act expressly provides that the powers under s.144 and para.17 of Sch.2A shall only be exercised if the person exercising them is satisfied that to do so does not contravene any Convention relating to copyright to which the United Kingdom is a party.[1645]

The present s.144. The section (as amended)[1646] applies where whatever needs to be remedied, mitigated or prevented by the Secretary of State, the OFT or (as the case may be) the Competition Commission under a list of specified provisions consists of or includes conditions in licences granted by the owner of copyright   **28–326**

[1638] MMC Report, Cmnd.9437, para.6.57.

[1639] MMC Report, Cmnd.9437, paras 6.58–6.59.

[1640] *The British Broadcasting Corporation and Independent Television Publications Limited: A report on the policies and practices on the BBC and ITP of limiting the publication by others of advance program information*, 1985 (Cmnd 9614). Again, this Report followed an investigation under Competition Act 1980, s.3 (as to which see *Copinger*, 14th edn, para.29–242) by the Director General of Fair Trading who referred the matter to the MMC. See further, *British Broadcasting Corporation and Independent Television Publications: The Publication of Programme Information*, published on December 13, 1984 by the Office of Fair Trading. See further, paras 28–09 et seq., above.

[1641] Cmnd.9614, paras 6.11; 6.26–6.36; 6.37–6.40.

[1642] MMC Report, Cmnd.9614, para.6.42.

[1643] See para.28–06, above and see further, Greaves, "Copyright: Public interest and statutory powers under the CA 1980", [1987] 1 E.I.P.R. 3 at 5.

[1644] See further, Ricketson and Ginsburg, *International Copyright and Neighbouring Rights* (2006), para.13.90. It should also be noted that attempts by the UK and Australian Governments to amend art.17 so as to include expressly a reference to the control of monopolies were rejected at the Stockholm revision conference (1967), at least partly on the grounds that any such amendment would be superfluous: ibid., para.13.92.

[1645] CDPA 1988 s.144(3), Sch.2A para.17(3).

[1646] By the Enterprise Act 2002 Sch.25 para.18(2) and (3) with effect from June 20, 2003 (with limited exceptions): see the Enterprise Act 2002 (Commencement No.3, Transitional and Transitory Provisions and Savings) Order 2003 (SI 2003/1397) art.2 and Sch.

in a work restricting the use of the work by the licensee or the right of the copyright owner to grant other licences; or a refusal of a copyright owner to grant
licences on reasonable terms.[1647] In such a case, the powers conferred by Schedule 8 to the Enterprise Act 2002 include power to cancel or modify those conditions and, instead or in addition, to provide that licences in respect of the copyright be available as of right.[1648]

28–327 **Circumstances where s.144 may apply.** As has been explained, s.144 applies
where something needs to be remedied by the Secretary of State, the OFT or the
Competition Commission under a list of specified provisions. They are as follows: s.12(5) of the Competition Act 1980, which empowers the Secretary of
State to make an order to remedy or prevent the adverse effects of a course of
conduct by certain public authorities[1649]; s.41(2) of the Enterprise Act 2002,
which obliges the Competition Commission in some circumstances to take action
in relation to mergers[1650]; ss.55(2) and 66(6) of the Enterprise Act, which
empower the Secretary of State to take action in relation to mergers in public
interest cases[1651] and special public interest cases[1652]; s.75(2) of the Enterprise
Act, which empowers the OFT to make orders in relation to mergers when
undertakings in lieu of a reference are not or will not be fulfilled or false or
misleading information has been given[1653]; s.83(2) of the Enterprise Act, which
gives the same powers to the Commission in relation to final undertakings[1654];
s.138(2) of the Enterprise Act, which obliges the Competition Commission in
some circumstances to take action following a market investigation[1655]; s.147(2)
of the Enterprise Act, which empowers the Secretary of State to take action following a market investigation to which a public interest consideration applies[1656];
s.160(2) of the Enterprise Act, which permits the Competition Commission or
the Secretary of State to make orders following a market investigation where
undertakings are nor or will not be fulfilled or false or misleading information has
been given[1657]; and paras 5(2) and 10(2) of Sch.7 to the Enterprise Act, which
empower the Secretary of State to make orders in relation to public interest and
special public interest mergers when undertakings in lieu of a reference or final
undertakings are not or will not be fulfilled or false or misleading information has
been given.[1658]

28–328 **Exercise of powers under s.144.** The powers available under s.144 may only be
exercised if the Secretary of State, the OFT or (as the case may be) the Competition Commission is satisfied that to do so does not contravene any Convention relating to copyright to which the United Kingdom is a party.[1659] The terms of any
licence available by virtue of these provisions fall to be settled, in default of
agreement, by the Copyright Tribunal on an application by the person requiring

---

[1647] CDPA 1988 s.144(1).
[1648] CDPA 1988 s.144(1A). For Sch.8, see paras 28–313 to 28–314, above.
[1649] See para.28–324, above.
[1650] See para.28–312, above.
[1651] See para.28–316, above.
[1652] See para.28–316, above.
[1653] See para.28–310, above. The reference to s.66(6) has effect as if it includes a reference to art.12(7)
  of the Enterprise Act 2002 (Protection of Legitimate Interests) Order 2003 (SI 2003/192): see
  Sch.4 para.7. For this Order, see note to para.28–316, above.
[1654] See para.28–312, above.
[1655] See para.28–322, above.
[1656] See para.28–323, above.
[1657] See paras 28–322 and 28–323, above.
[1658] See para.28–316, above. The references to paras 5(2) or 10(2) have effect as if they included a
  reference to paras 5(2) or 10(2) to the Enterprise Act 2002 (Protection of Legitimate Interests)
  Order 2003 (SI 2003/192): see ibid., Sch.4 para.7. For this Order, see above, para.28–316.
[1659] CDPA 1988 s.144(3). For the reason for this, see para.28–325, above

the licence.[1660] The terms so settled shall authorise the licensee to do everything in respect of which a licence is so available.[1661] Where the terms of a licence are so settled by the Tribunal, the licence has effect from the date on which the application to the Tribunal was made.[1662]

Application to design right, rights in performances and database right. Section 238 of the 1988 Act[1663] contains parallel powers in relation to design right. The section is in substantially the same terms as s.144 but there are the following differences. First, there is no reference to compliance with international Conventions, no doubt because the United Kingdom is not a party to any relevant Convention in respect of design right. Secondly, in default of agreement the terms of the licence are to be settled by the comptroller rather than the Copyright Tribunal.[1664] Paragraph 17 of Schedule 2A to the 1988 Act[1665] contains parallel powers in relation to performers' property rights. These are in substantially identical terms to those of s.144. Finally, para.15 of Sch.2 to the Database Regulations[1666] contains parallel powers in relation to database right. This paragraph is in substantially the same terms but again, since there is no relevant Convention in respect of database right, there is no reference to compliance with international Conventions.

28–329

6. RESTRAINT OF TRADE

General principles. The common law doctrine of restraint of trade is an example of the application of public policy to contracts. Under the doctrine, covenants which are in restraint of trade are prima facie unenforceable at common law and are enforceable only if they are reasonable as between the parties and so far as the public interest is concerned.[1667] Covenants in restraint of trade are void in the sense that the courts will not enforce them, but the parties are not acting illegally if they choose to do so.[1668] The doctrine is one to be "applied to factual situations with a broad and flexible rule of reason".[1669]

28–330

Macaulay v Schroeder Music Publishing Co Ltd.[1670] This case dispelled whatever doubts may previously have existed as to the applicability of the principles established in cases on agreements in restraint of trade to agreements for the exclusive provision of services for a definite period. It is therefore now clear that

28–331

[1660] CDPA 1988 s.144(4); as to the Copyright Tribunal generally, see paras 28–81 et seq., and as to an application under this provision see para.28–55, above.

[1661] CDPA 1988 s.144(4)

[1662] CDPA 1988 s.144(5).

[1663] As amended by the Enterprise Act 2002 (c.40) Sch.25 para.18(3) with effect from June 20, 2003 (with limited exceptions): see the Enterprise Act (Commencement No.3, Transitional and Transitory and Savings) Order 2003 (SI 2003/1397) art.2.

[1664] CDPA 1988 s.238(3).

[1665] As amended by the Enterprise Act 2002 (c.40) Sch.25 para.18(5) with effect from June 20, 2003 (with limited exceptions): see the Enterprise Act (Commencement No.3, Transitional and Transitory and Savings) Order 2003 (SI 2003/1397) art.2.

[1666] As amended by the Enterprise Act 2002 (Consequential and Supplemental Provisions) Order 2003 (SI 2003/1398), art.2 and Sch., para.31 with effect from June 20, 2003 (with limited exceptions).

[1667] See in particular *Esso Petroleum Ltd v Harper's Garage (Stourport) Ltd* [1968] A.C. 269. For a general discussion of the principles of the doctrine see *Chitty on Contracts* 30th edn (London: Sweet & Maxwell) at paras 16–075 et seq.

[1668] *Boddington v Lawton* [1994] I.C.R. 478.

[1669] Per Lord Reid in *Esso Petroleum Ltd v Harper's Garage (Stourport) Ltd* [1968] A.C. 269 at 331.

[1670] [1974] 1 W.L.R. 1308, HL. See also *Clifford Davis Management Ltd v WEA Records Ltd* [1975] 1 W.L.R. 61, CA.

the doctrine is capable of applying to agreements relating to publishing and recording.[1671]

In *Macaulay v Schroeder*, the House of Lords, affirming the Court of Appeal and Plowman J., held that an agreement between a songwriter and music publishers, whereby the publishers engaged the songwriter's exclusive services for the term of the agreement was, having regard to all its terms, unduly restrictive and in unreasonable restraint of trade and was therefore contrary to public policy and unenforceable, and that this was so, notwithstanding that the agreement was in the publishers' standard form, which was a form in common use between music publishers and songwriters.

Whilst the agreement was in the form of an agreement for exclusive services, which contained an express restriction on the songwriter's ability to work for any other music publishers, with an assignment of the product of the writer's talent created during the period of the agreement,[1672] it was the restriction inherent in this assignment of future works which was throughout seen as the restriction which brought the agreement within the principles applicable to agreements in restraint of trade. It follows, therefore, that these principles are equally applicable to an agreement which in its form is simply an assignment of present and future works, or even of future works only, to be composed during the period of the agreement, and which contains no express restrictions on the songwriter's ability to pursue his profession, but only terms directly connected with the assignment, such as for the payment by the publishers of royalties on works published under the agreement. All such agreements and assignments have therefore to be considered in the light of the decision in *Macaulay v Schroeder*. What is required is a consideration of the agreement as a whole, and an assessment of the cumulative effect of the restrictions in it, whether such restrictions are expressed, or merely follow, by necessary implication, from the very fact of an assignment of future works. An artist's contract is in restraint of trade if the artist can effectively be prevented by the contract from reaching the public over a prolonged period. It makes no difference that meanwhile the artist has a living wage.[1673]

In *Macaulay v Schroeder* certain terms were singled out as pointing to a conclusion that the agreement in that case was unduly restrictive; they are set out in the speech of Lord Reid, and are a helpful guide for those seeking to avoid entering into a publishing agreement which may subsequently be found to be unduly restrictive. Of particular importance is the duration of the term of the agreement,[1674] and this will include any possible extension, whether automatic in certain events, or at the option of the publishers. Then the exclusivity of the services and the extent of the works covered by the agreement must be considered. Are all outlets for the writer's creative talents covered, or only those in certain fields, leaving him free to exploit his talents in other fields? Are all the writer's

---

[1671] See also *Zang Tumb Tuum Records Ltd v Johnson* [1993] E.M.L.R. 61.

[1672] The material terms of the agreement are set out in the speech of Lord Reid: *Macaulay v Schroeder* [1974] 1 W.L.R. 1308 at 1310.

[1673] See *Silvertone Records Ltd v Mountfield* [1993] E.M.L.R. 152 and *Provident Financial Group plc v Hayward* [1989] 3 All E.R. 298.

[1674] *Macaulay v Schroeder Music Publishing Co. Ltd* [1974] 1 W.L.R. 1308, per Lord Reid at 1312G. The term under consideration was for five years, extendable for a further five years on royalties payable in the first five years exceeding a stated amount. Such agreements often contain a string of option clauses enabling the publisher or record company to prolong the agreement. If the total possible length of the agreement is such as to make it unfair, the publisher or record company will not be able to save the agreement by arguing that some of the option clauses can be severed: see *Silvertone Records Ltd v Mountfield* [1993] E.M.L.R. 152. A publisher is entitled to a reasonable period to obtain a proper reward for taking on a new writer, with all the incidental costs involved: *John v James* [1991] F.S.R. 397 at para.451. In that case, six years was considered too long, even in respect of unknown artists. In the case of the recording agreement, a five-year tie was held to be reasonable in respect of unknown artists, given the expense involved in breaking a new artist and the low success rate: 452.

past and future works created during the term of the agreement covered? Clearly the narrower the scope of the restriction in these two respects, the less likely that it would be found unreasonable. The right to assign the benefit of the agreement may be a relevant consideration; an unqualified right in this respect on the part of the publishers, coupled with a qualified right or an express prohibition against such assignment on the part of the writer may well be unreasonable. Are the publishers under any meaningful obligation to publish and exploit any of the writer's works?[1675] If it is not practicable to provide for such an obligation, it may be advisable to give the writer a right to terminate the agreement, and to call for reassignment of the copyright in unpublished works, if the publishers do not publish his works.[1676]

Looked at as a whole, can it be said that the agreement could, whether by deliberate manipulation or not, result in the sterilisation of the earning output of the writer for a considerable time?[1677] If so, it will be for the party imposing the restrictions to show that they are both reasonably necessary for the protection of that party's legitimate interests, and commensurate with the benefits secured to the party restricted. This brings the test applicable to such agreements closer to the approach of Lord Diplock in *Macaulay v Schroeder*, who agreed with Lord Reid's analysis of the restrictive effect of the terms of the agreement, and stated that the question to be asked was the same as in all cases where the court was faced with a bargain that on its face appeared unconscionable, by reason of the unequal bargaining power of the parties, that is, "was the bargain fair?".[1678]

Whichever formulation was adopted, the publishers in *Macaulay v Schroeder* were held not to have discharged the onus on them in the light of the restrictive nature of the agreement, to justify its restrictions, or to show that the agreement as a whole was fair. Lord Reid summarised the position as follows:

"Any contract by which a person engages to give his exclusive services to another for a period necessarily involves extensive restriction during that period of the common law right to exercise any lawful activity he chooses in such manner as he thinks best. Normally the doctrine of restraint of trade has no application to such restrictions: they require no justification. But if contractual restrictions appear to be unnecessary or to be reasonably capable of enforcement in an oppressive manner, then they must be justified before they can be enforced. In the present case the respondent assigned to the appellants 'the full copyright for the whole world' in every musical composition 'composed, created or conceived' by him alone or in collaboration with any other person during a period of five or it might be 10 years. He received no payment (apart from an initial £50) unless his work was published and the appellants need not publish unless they chose to do so. And if they did not publish he had no right to terminate the agreement or to have copyrights

---

[1675] As to which see Lord Reid, *Macaulay v Schroeder Music Publishing Co. Ltd* [1974] 1 W.L.R. 1308 at para.1313H; as to the meaning of an undertaking to use "best endeavours", see *IBM United Kingdom Ltd v Rockware Glass Ltd* [1980] F.S.R. 335 and *Imasa Ltd v Technic Incorporated* [1981] F.S.R. 554.

[1676] Such a provision would considerably mitigate the otherwise restrictive effect of the agreement: per Lord Reid, *Macaulay v Schroeder Music Publishing Co. Ltd* [1974] 1 W.L.R. 1308 at 1314A/B; see for a case where the reassignment provisions failed to save the agreement *Zang Tumb Tuum Records Ltd v Johnson* [1993] E.M.L.R. 61; see also *Silvertone Records Ltd v Mountfield* [1993] E.M.L.R. 152.

[1677] For examples of cases where that was held to be so see *Zang Tumb Tuum Records Ltd v Johnson* [1993] E.M.L.R. 61, above, and *Silvertone Records* [1993] E.M.L.R. 152.

[1678] *Macaulay v Schroeder Music Publishing Co. Ltd* [1974] 1 W.L.R. 1308 at paras 1315H–1316A. And see further as to the court's jurisdiction to refuse to enforce such bargains, *Lloyd's Bank v Bundy* [1975] Q.B. 326, CA and *Clifford Davis Management Ltd v WEA Records Ltd* [1975] 1 W.L.R. 61; but see *National Westminster Bank Plc v Morgan* [1985] A.C. 686 disapproving Lord Denning M.R. in *Bundy*, ibid. at 339, to the effect that English courts will grant relief where there has been "inequality of bargaining power".

reassigned to him. I need not consider whether in any circumstances it would be possible to justify such a one-sided agreement. It is sufficient to say that such evidence as there is falls far short of justification. It must therefore follow that the agreement, so far as unperformed, is unenforceable".[1679]

28–332   **Other cases.** In *Sunshine Records (Pty) Ltd v Frohling*,[1680] the court held that an exclusive recording contract for an initial term of three years renewable for a further three years was in undue restraint of trade, because of the nature, extent and duration of the obligations and restrictions imposed on the artists, together with the absence of any real reciprocal obligation on the recording company.

In *John v James*[1681] it was held that an experienced and successful publisher assumed a dominating influence over young inexperienced writers. Even after a short acquaintance they were apprehensive of the publisher and anxious to have him as their publisher, trusting and relying on him that the terms of the contract proposed were reasonable. The publisher took charge of the arrangement and failed to explain the terms of the agreement. The agreement was liable to be set aside even though the publisher had acted in good faith and had made no conscious attempt to obtain an unfair bargain.[1682]

In *Silvertone Records Ltd v Mountfield*[1683] the following terms of an exclusive recording agreement were held to be unfair: the term of the agreement which made it possible to sterilise the artist's output for seven years; a rerecording restraint of 10 years; the record company's unrestricted right to authorise the use of the artist's records to endorse products; the right to withhold advances in the event of a breach of any kind; the unequal power to terminate the agreement; the record company's right to decide on all aspects of the recording process and the denial of any artistic control to the artists; and the record company's unlimited right of assignment, given the degree of co-operation required.

In *Panayiotou v Sony Music Entertainment (UK) Ltd*[1684] the pop star, George Michael, alleged that his exclusive recording agreement dated January 4, 1988, with the defendant, Sony, (the 1988 Agreement) was void or unenforceable (in so far as it remained unperformed) as being in unreasonable restraint of trade. The allegation that the agreement was void was not pursued at first instance. The plaintiff further alleged that the agreement was prohibited by art.101(1) of the TFEU.[1685] Although the only agreement in issue was the 1988 Agreement, the background to that agreement was important. The plaintiff and one Ridgeley, who at the time were both young, unknown and inexperienced, had entered into an exclusive recording agreement dated March 25, 1982, with Melodyshire Ltd, trading as Inner Vision (the 1982 Agreement). The 1982 Agreement was for their exclusive performances for up to four singles and 10 albums. Inner Vision had a licence agreement with Sony, and the 1982 Agreement incorporated Sony's then standard artists' conditions. In late 1983 the plaintiff and Ridgeley were in dispute with Inner Vision, claiming that the 1982 Agreement was unenforceable as being in restraint of trade. Inner Vision commenced proceedings, which in due course were compromised by the plaintiff and Ridgeley entering into a recording agreement with Sony (the 1984 Agreement) on Sony's then standard form of recording contract, including an option to acquire the exclusive recording services of each artist if they ceased to perform together as a group. The plaintiff and Ridgeley

---

[1679] *Macaulay v Schroeder Music Publishing Co. Ltd* [1974] 1 W.L.R. 1308 at 1314H.
[1680] [1990] (4) S.A.782.
[1681] [1991] F.S.R. 397.
[1682] See p. 451; similar considerations applied to the recording agreement: ibid. at 453.
[1683] [1993] E.M.L.R. 152.
[1684] [1994] E.M.L.R. 229, Parker J.
[1685] See paras 28–184 et seq., above.

subsequently ceased to perform together as a group, and in 1986 Sony exercised its option against the plaintiff, thereby acquiring the exclusive right to his performances as a solo artist. Sony took delivery of the plaintiff's first solo album, *Faith*, which was very successful.

The plaintiff then renegotiated the terms of his recording agreement with Sony, and entered into the 1988 Agreement, whereupon the 1984 Agreement ceased to have effect. The plaintiff was obliged to deliver three albums in the initial period of the 1988 Agreement. *Faith* was treated as the first, and the plaintiff delivered *Listen Without Prejudice* as the second in July 1990. Further variations were negotiated and agreed to in the 1988 Agreement. Before delivery of the third album, the present dispute arose and the plaintiff commenced proceedings in October 1992.[1686]

The terms of the 1988 Agreement were held to contain restraints of trade, as understood for the purposes of the common law doctrine, which were not dispensed from the necessity of justification, so that, apart from arguments based on public policy, the restraint of trade doctrine was applicable to the 1988 Agreement and its provisions required to be justified by reference to the test in *Nordenfelt v Maxim Nordenfelt Guns and Ammunition Company Ltd*.[1687]

However, the judge then went on to hold that the 1988 Agreement had to be considered as a renegotiation of the 1984 Agreement, which was itself a compromise of proceedings which raised the issue of the enforceability of the 1982 Agreement. The plaintiff had expressly not sought to assert the unenforceability of the 1984 Agreement in the current proceedings. The court concluded that the 1984 Agreement had to be treated for the purposes of the current proceedings as an enforceable agreement. In these circumstances the court accepted Sony's argument that reasons of public policy relating to the compromise of disputes precluded the plaintiff from alleging that the 1988 Agreement was in restraint of trade. For that reason, the plaintiff's claim failed.[1688]

The judge then proceeded to consider whether, on the basis that the restraint of trade doctrine did apply to the 1988 Agreement, its terms were justified. His conclusion, after considering each of the relevant terms and the evidence before him, was that the restrictions contained were reasonably necessary for the protection of the legitimate interests of Sony and were commensurate with the benefits secured to the plaintiff under the agreement.[1689]

It is clear that, for the purposes of deciding whether an agreement is in unreasonable restraint of trade or unduly restrictive, the agreement must be considered as at the date it is entered into.[1690] The court is not therefore entitled to have regard to how the agreement has in practice been operated, nor to the motives of the party under the restraint who now wishes to be free of his bargain.

[1686] The material terms of the 1988 Agreement were: it covered the plaintiff's worldwide performing services for the production of records; it was for an initial contract period and five further contract periods at Sony's option; each contract period continued until after delivery of a minimum commitment for that period; the agreement was for an overall maximum term of 15 years; the total minimum commitment, assuming that all options were exercised, was sufficient for eight albums; Sony could reject product on the ground that it was not of the artistic or commercial quality of prior recorded performances; Sony was entitled to copyright in the master recordings throughout the world for the full period of copyright; the plaintiff was not entitled to perform for recording purposes any composition contained in a master recording before the later of three years after expiry of the agreement or five years from release of the master recording of the composition; Sony's obligation to exploit the product of the plaintiff's services was limited to the release of no less than three and no more than four single play records; Sony was free to assign its copyrights and, indirectly, its contractual rights under the agreement.

[1687] [1894] A.C. 535.

[1688] *Panayiotou v Sony Music Entertainment (UK) Ltd*. [1994] E.M.L.R. 229 at paras 345–347.

[1689] *Panayiotou v Sony Music Entertainment (UK) Ltd*. [1994] E.M.L.R. 229 at para.380.

[1690] *Macaulay v Schroeder Music Publishing Co Ltd* [1974] 1 W.L.R. 1308, per Lord Reid at 1309H.

28–333   **Parties to proceedings.** In *Peer International Corporation v Termidor Music Publishers Ltd*,[1691] the question arose as to whether the doctrine of restraint of trade could be relied on by a stranger to a contract in circumstances where the "innocent" party was not represented in the proceedings. Lindsay J. noted that standing in contractual matters is normally confined to the parties to the contract but that the public interest in every person being able to carry on his trade freely arguably justified a broader approach. However, he concluded that the public interest did not provide a "wholly compelling reason" for such an approach. Even if there was scope for such an approach, on the particular facts of the case there was no basis for holding that the third party should have standing to challenge the agreements in question.[1692]

28–334   **Contractual provisions as to legal advice and reasonableness.** In *Proactive Sports Management Ltd v Rooney*,[1693] a footballer's management agreement contained a clause by which the footballer acknowledged that he had "taken and understood" legal advice (which, it was held, he had not) and that the terms of the agreement were reasonable. It was held that this did not prevent the doctrine of restraint of trade applying to the agreement.

28–335   **Estoppel and affirmation.** Equitable defences in the nature of waiver, laches, estoppel and acquiescence are available in restraint of trade cases.[1694] In *Panayiotou v Sony Music Entertainment (UK) Ltd*[1695] Jonathan Parker J. held that the common law defence of affirmation also applied. However, in *Proactive Sports Management Ltd v Rooney*,[1696] HH Judge Hegarty QC stated (obiter) that it did not.

28–336   **Effect of a finding of restraint of trade.** The declaration granted in *Macaulay v Schroeder*, above, was that the agreement was contrary to public policy and void. However, agreements found to be in restraint of trade are usually voidable, not void and it may be that such an agreement is better described as unenforceable.[1697] Clearly the writer is not bound by the agreement from the moment it is held to be in restraint of trade, and it would follow that any assignment in the agreement of the copyright in future works would not be effective to vest in the publishers the copyright in works brought into existence after the agreement is held to be in restraint of trade. What the position is regarding copyrights in works already brought into existence at that date is far from clear.[1698] If such an agreement were truly void, it would follow that no assignment of such copyright would have

---

[1691] [2006] EWHC 2883 (Ch); [2007] E.C.D.R. 1.
[1692] Para. 31.
[1693] [2010] EWHC 1807 (QB).
[1694] *Panayiotou v Sony Music Entertainment (UK) Ltd* [1994] E.M.L.R. pp.384–385.
[1695] [1994] E.M.L.R. pp.384–385.
[1696] [2010] EWHC 1807 (QB) at para.708.
[1697] See Lord Reid, *Macaulay v Schroeder Music Publishing Co. Ltd* [1974] 1 W.L.R. 1308 at para.1315A/B; see also *Clifford Davis Management Ltd v WEA Records Ltd* [1975] 1 W.L.R. 61 and *Zang Tumb Tuum Records Ltd v Johnson* [1993] E.M.L.R. 61. Severance of objectionable clauses is not permissible where it is the whole agreement which is objectionable, and the court will not strike out clauses so as to change the nature of the contract: *Silvertone Records Ltd v Mountfield* [1993] E.M.L.R. 152.
[1698] The judgment of the Court of Appeal in *Macaulay v Schroeder Music Publishing Co. Ltd*, delivered by Russell L.J., [1974] 1 All E.R. 171 at 181f, confirmed that the assignment was ineffective as to the copyright in works not in existence at the time the agreement was avoided, but the statement that the assignment of copyright in works already brought into existence at that time remained effective, per Russell L.J. [1974] 1 All E.R. 171 at 181e/f, was based on a concession made to such effect by counsel for the plaintiffs. See also the brief discussion in *Proactive Sports Management Ltd v Rooney* [2010] EWHC 1807 (QB) at para.741. Compare the position where the agreement is set aside in equity for undue influence and breach of fiduciary duty: *O'Sullivan v Management Agency and Music Ltd* [1985] Q.B. 428 at 459 C/D.

taken place but if, as it is thought, such an agreement is merely voidable as to the future, then the position may be that the legal title to such works in existence before the agreement is avoided is effectively assigned to the assignee at law by such agreement, and notwithstanding the subsequent avoidance of the agreement remains vested in the assignee, subject to the Court ordering, in the exercise of its equitable jurisdiction, reassignment of the copyright in such works. This question will be particularly important in the case of any such works which the publishers have already at that date exploited, either themselves, or by granting rights to others. A further unanswered problem arises in connection with any separate assignment of copyright in particular works in which a songwriter engaged under such an agreement is asked by the publishers to execute. Such assignments are often taken, for no further consideration than the publishers' promise to pay royalties on the work being published, usually in the same terms as in the principal agreement. In themselves such individual assignments are clearly not within the principles applied in *Macaulay v Schroeder*, above, but, in that the only reason for their execution is the pre-existing obligation under the principal agreement, if this latter agreement is subsequently found to be unenforceable, should not the same apply to any such individual assignments?[1699]

Effect of the doctrine on construction of agreements. In *Taylor v Rive Droite*   **28–337**
Music Ltd[1700] Neuberger L.J. stated that there was no principle requiring a court to lean in favour of a construction of a recording agreement which would give the production company a monopoly over all the output of an artist during its term. He concluded on the facts of that case that if there was any presumption it was to the opposite effect, for two reasons. First, the agreement was in a standard form prepared by the production company and accordingly the *contra proferentem* rule applied against the company. Second, any bias in the court's approach should be one which is "against monopoly, restraint of trade and impairing an artist's freedom to exploit his work commercially".

[1699] This was the court's approach in *O'Sullivan v Management Agency and Music Ltd* [1985] Q.B. 428, at 459C/D.
[1700] [2005] EWCA Civ 1300; [2006] E.M.L.R. 4 at para.142.

CHAPTER TWENTY NINE

TAXATION OF COPYRIGHT

1. OVERVIEW OF UNITED KINGDOM TAX SYSTEM FOR INTELLECTUAL PROPERTY

Historically, the UK tax treatment of intellectual property expenditure and **29–01**
receipts has been developed through a combination of case law and legislation—
the result has been very different treatments of different types of intellectual property and many gaps which are filled by the general rules relating to expenditure
and receipts. This chapter is principally concerned with the tax treatment of
copyright and other related forms of intellectual property covered by this work,
whose exploitation may give rise to taxable receipts. Save where specific rights
are dealt with, these rights are referred to collectively as intellectual property.

Exactly how copyright is taxed depends upon the manner in which a number
of factors are combined. At the outset it may be helpful to summarise the most
important of these:

   (a) whether the recipient is a company;
   (b) if the recipient is not a company, whether the recipient is or has been car-
       rying on a trade, profession or vocation which involves the creation or
       exploitation of intellectual property, etc. for example, authors, composers,
       designers, etc.;
   (c) if the recipient is not a company, whether the receipt is a royalty or a lump
       sum;
   (d) whether the recipient is resident or domiciled in the United Kingdom;
   (e) whether the receipt has a UK source.

For individuals, partnerships and other unincorporated entities (and pre-April   **29–02**

2002 assets of companies), it is convenient to treat (b) above as the primary classification and to categorise taxpayers as either traders or non-traders. The other factors are considered as each of the categories are dealt with.

The overall approach to the taxation of intellectual property is being considered in some detail in the forthcoming autumn 2010 consultation on the United Kingdom's approach to taxing intellectual property. The issues around intellectual property holding companies continue to be discussed in the consultations on controlled foreign companies, with interim legislation expected in 2011 and final legislation in this area expected in 2012.

2. UNINCORPORATED PERSONS AND ENTITIES AND COMPANIES PRE-APRIL 2002

A. INCOME TAX

Trade, profession or vocation

29–03   For income tax purposes, the profits of a trade, profession or vocation are charged collectively under the Income Tax (Trading and Other Income) Act 2005 ("IT-TOIA 2005") ss.5–8. However, as these provisions largely apply to professions and vocations as they apply to trades, it is convenient to classify as "traders" not only persons who carry on a trade which involves the creation or exploitation of intellectual property, for example, persons involved in publishing or distribution, etc. but also individuals who carry on a profession or vocation which involves the creation or exploitation of intellectual property for example, authors, composers and designers.

The rules discussed below generally have no application to employees who produce intellectual property in the course of their employment. This is because the rights usually vest in the employer and so it is the employer who is usually taxable on any receipts generated by the exploitation of the rights. The employee is taxable under the employment income provisions of ITEPA 2003 (Pts 2 to 7) on his general earnings and specific employment income. The distinction between works made by employees in the course of their employment under a contract of service and other works is discussed elsewhere.[1]

Distinguishing between trade, profession and vocation

29–04   It is outside the scope of this work to discuss in any detail what constitutes a trade, profession or vocation and reference should be made to specialist works on income tax for a full treatment of the topic.[2] In most cases it will be relatively clear whether the creator or owner of intellectual property is carrying on a trade, profession or vocation. Examples include professional authors, composers, recording artists, designers and others who systematically exploit their creative activities on a commercial basis. The more difficult cases concern people whose creative activities are casual or sporadic, for example, individuals who create a copyright work by an isolated piece of writing.

29–05   In *Billam v Griffith*[3] an individual who had written three or four plays in his spare time, only one of which was successful, was held to be carrying on the profession

---

[1] See paras 5–12 et seq., above.
[2] e.g. see *Whiteman and Sherry on Income Tax* 4th edn (London: Sweet & Maxwell, 2009), Ch.4.
[3] (1941) 23 T.C. 757

of a dramatist. By contrast, in *Nethersole v Withers*,[4] an actress who dramatised a single novel was held not to have been carrying on the profession or vocation of a dramatist when she subsequently disposed of the film rights. In *Beare v Carter*[5] there was no suggestion that a taxpayer who merely edited five versions of one book over a 36-year period was carrying on the profession or vocation of authorship.

The fact that a person creates a copyright work by an isolated piece of writing, rather than in the course of a profession, does not mean, in itself, that any profit escapes tax.[6] Where, for example, an independent individual collaborates with a journalist to produce a series of articles, the individual is taxable upon sums received from the transaction unless the individual is being paid mainly for publication rights, any services that he renders being incidental.[7]   **29–06**

Trading receipts

A person who is resident in the United Kingdom and carrying on a trade, profession or vocation here which involves exploiting intellectual property is taxable upon any sums which he receives from such exploitation whether or not they are received in the United Kingdom.[8] This includes royalties and licence fees. It also includes lump sums for the grant of a licence to exploit the right[9] or for the total or partial assignment of the right or as compensation or damages for infringements.[10]   **29–07**

Trading profits are assessed by reference to the income of the accounting period which ends in the year of assessment concerned. The profits must be computed on a basis which gives a "true and fair view" of the profits, subject to adjustments required (or permitted) by tax law.[11] This requires the person carrying on the trade, profession or vocation to bring in expenses, income and stock (or work in progress[12]) at the beginning and end of the accounting period.   **29–08**

Taxpayers are required to file annual tax returns which include a self-assessment of the individual's income tax and capital gains tax liabilities. The tax self-assessed in the return is due for payment automatically. No further action is required on the part of HMRC.   **29–09**

---

[4] (1948) 28 T.C. 501.

[5] [1940] 2 K.B. 187; 23 T.C. 353.

[6] But note that the income would be taxed as miscellaneous income under ITTOIA 2005 s.579 rather than as income of a trade, profession or vocation under ITTOIA 2005 ss.5–8.

[7] See *Hobbs v Hussey* [1942] 1 K.B. 491, *Housden v Marshall* [1959] 1 W.L.R. 1; 38 T.C. 233, *Alloway v Phillips* [1980] 1 W.L.R. 888.

[8] See para.29–72 for the tax position of a non-resident.

[9] *Glasson v Rougier* [1944] 1 All E.R. 535; 26 T.C. 86; *Housden v Monsell* [1950] 2 All E.R. 1239; 31 T.C. 529. The principle is that a professional receipt is incapable of being capital for tax purposes. See also *Mackenzie v Arnold* 33 T.C. 363.

[10] Because any sum which a trader derives from carrying on of his trade is income. See *Raja's Commercial College v Gian Singh & Co Ltd* [1977] A.C. 312; [1976] S.T.C. 282; *Rolfe v Nagel* [1982] S.T.C. 53 and *Deeny v Gooda Walker Ltd* [1996] 1 W.L.R. 426; [1996] S.T.C. 299. For a case concerning a theatrical production company, see *Vaughan v Archie Parnell and Alfred Zeitlin Ltd* 23 T.C. 505.

[11] ITTOIA 2005 s.25: the profits of a trade, profession or vocation must be calculated in accordance with generally accepted accounting practice, which requires that accounts give a true and fair view of the profits.

[12] Although see para.29–16 below as to stock and work-in-progress of authors.

Public lending right payments

29–10   Public lending right payments are treated as copyright payments for tax purposes[13] and are regarded as part of an author's professional income.

Averaging provisions

29–11   An averaging relief for fluctuating profits can be claimed in respect of the profits of creators, relating to the profits of an entire year rather than to the profits relating to a particular piece of work.[14] This is to relieve the distortion that could otherwise affect the taxpayer's taxable profits for the year of receipt, giving rise to a disproportionate charge to tax, where lump sums are received. The relief is available to partnerships as well as individuals.

The relief is available for a trade, profession or vocation where the income comes wholly or mainly from creative works,[15] which are literary, dramatic, musical or artistic works or designs created by the taxpayer personally (or, in the case of a partnership, created by one of the partners personally).[16]

A claim for the relief can be made if the business is more than two years old[17] and either:

(a) relevant profits for one year are less than 75 per cent of the relevant profits for the other year (regardless of whether that year is immediately before or immediately after); or

(b) profits for one—not both—years are nil.[18]

"Profits" are the profits of the business for the year before deduction of any losses.[19] Where there is a loss in the business for the year, the profits are deemed to be nil for averaging purposes.[20]

Claims need to be made chronologically,[21] so a claim cannot be made if there has already been a claim made in respect of a later year.[22] For example, a claim can be made to average years 2 and 3 where a claim has already been made to average years 1 and 2; but where a claim has been made to average years 2 and 3, a claim cannot then be made to average years 1 and 2.

The claim must be made within 12 months of the January 31 following the end of the second year for which a claim is made.[23] If, after an averaging claim has been made, the profits of either of the years concerned are adjusted for any other reason, the averaging claim is nullified and a new claim must be made if necessary, no later than 12 months after the January 31 following the end of the tax year in which the adjustment was made.[24]

The relief is given:

(a) by simple averaging of the profits for the two years if the profits of one

---

[13] Income Tax Act (ITA) 2007 s.907(1)(c).
[14] ITTOIA 2005 ss.221–225.
[15] ITTOIA 2005 s.221(2)(c)
[16] ITTOIA 2005 s.221(3).
[17] No claims can be made for the opening and closing years of a trade; ITTOIA 2005 s.222(4).
[18] ITTOIA 2005 s.222(1).
[19] ITTOIA 2005 s.221(4).
[20] ITTOIA 2005 s.221(5).
[21] ITTOIA 2005 s.222(2).
[22] ITTOIA 2005 s.222(3)
[23] ITTOIA 2005 s.222(5).
[24] ITTOIA 2005 s.225

year are less than 70 per cent of the profits of the other (including where the profits for one year are nil)[25]; or

(b) where profits of one year are more than 70 per cent (and less than 75 per cent) of the other year then a formula[26] is applied:

$$(D \times 3) - (P \times 0.75)$$

where D is the difference between the relevant profits for the two years, and P is the profit of the higher year.

The result is deducted from the profits of the higher year and added to the profits of the lower year. The adjusted profits are treated as the relevant profits of the two tax years to which the claim relates for all income tax purposes.[27] However, if the relevant profits in one of the tax years are nil, these rules do not prevent the taxpayer from claiming loss relief in that or any other tax year.[28]

Prizes and grants

HMRC accept that literary, etc. prizes which are both unsolicited and awarded as "a mark of honour, distinction or public esteem in recognition of outstanding achievement in a particular field" are not taxable receipts.[29] The key point is that there is no application process for these awards (regardless of any informal promotion by publishers and authors), so they are not part of the exercise of the winner's profession.   **29–12**

Any other prizes, awards, grants or bursaries received by a professional author, musician, etc. will be taxable on the basis that entering competitions or seeking awards is a normal part of the profession of authors and other creative persons.[30] This is the case even if the author, etc. does not apply for the award personally but, instead, the publisher or some other person makes the application.[31]

Where an award is taxable, the tax treatment of that award will depend on the context in which it is received. Receipts of a professional author, etc. will be taxed as part of his trading income.[32] Where the recipient is not carrying on a profession, the receipt will be taxable as miscellaneous income.[33] Where the recipient is an employee and receives the award as part of their employment, the award will be taxed as employment income.

HMRC also accepts that the following awards made by the Arts Council are not taxable[34]:

(a) Training bursaries to trainee directors, associate directors, actors and actresses, technicians and stage managers, students attending the City University Arts Administration Courses, people attending full-time

---

[25] ITTOIA 2005 s.223(3)

[26] ITTOIA 2005 s.223(4)

[27] ITTOIA 2005 s.224(1)

[28] ITTOIA 2005 s.224(3).

[29] HMRC Manual BIM50710; for example, the Booker Prize and the Whitbread Award. One of the Whitbread winners, Andrew Boyle, apparently won at the Special Commissioners in 1979 against HMRC and obtained confirmation that the award was not subject to tax.

[30] HMRC manual BIM50710.

[31] HMRC's view is based on a number of cases relating to awards for the exercise of a trade, profession or vocation generally; the point has not been directly tested by a creator of a copyright work who has won an award.

[32] See para.29–7 above.

[33] See para.29–17, below. Note that ITTOIA 2005 s.776 provides an exemption for scholarship awards made to full-time students, even where the prize is awarded for an essay or thesis. There are financial limits to this exemption, set out in HMRC's Statement of Practice 4/86.

[34] Formerly in the HMRC Inspectors Manual at IM2691b, but not reproduced in the current HMRC manuals.

courses in arts administration (the practical training course) and in-service bursaries for the theatre designers scheme.

(b) "Buying Time Awards" to dramatists, authors, composers and artists to maintain the recipient to enable him to take time off to develop and explore his personal talents. These at present include the awards and bursaries known as the:

  (i) Theatre Writing Bursaries;

  (ii) Awards and Bursaries to Composers;

  (iii) Awards and Bursaries to Painters, Sculptors and Printmakers;

  (iv) Literature Awards and Bursaries.

It is understood that the Arts Council will normally indicate whether a particular award is taxable.

Post-cessation receipts

29-13 Under generally accepted accounting practice, since the tax year 1999/2000, traders must normally make up their accounts under the accruals basis for the purposes of establishing taxable profits. This means that income is taxed as soon as it is earned (accrued) even if not yet received. In that case, receipts after discontinuance do not normally give rise to any tax liability as they would have already been accounted for in a prior period of account.

As a matter of general Revenue law, a person carrying on a trade, profession or vocation is not subject to income tax as profits of the trade, profession or vocation[35] on:

(a) lump sums received pursuant to contracts entered into after the discontinuance of his or her trade, profession or vocation[36]; or

(b) lump sums, royalties, etc. received after the discontinuance of his or her trade, profession or vocation which are paid pursuant to contracts made before that discontinuance.[37]

Sums falling within (b), however, may be taxable under the "post-cessation receipts" rules[38] which apply to "... sums arising from the carrying on of the trade, profession or vocation during any period before the discontinuance (not being sums otherwise chargeable to tax)".[39] Although it is widely believed that sums falling within (a) above are also caught, it is far from clear that this is correct. It is suggested that such sums "arise" from the sale of intellectual property rights after discontinuance, not from the carrying on of the profession before the discontinuance, and thus fall outside the "post-cessation receipts" rules. However, so long as significant sales continue to take place, it may be difficult for a person carrying on a trade, profession or vocation which involves creating and exploiting such rights to establish that a discontinuance has occurred.[40]

29-14 The "post-cessation receipts" rules apply to lump sums and royalties received by

---

[35] But note that the receipt may still be subject to capital gains tax or taxed as miscellaneous income.

[36] Such sums will only be taxable as capital receipts: see para.29–21 onwards, below. Note, however, that where a trader who has permanently discontinued his trade transfers, the right to receive sums to which the post-cessation receipts provisions apply, he is taxable on the amount or value of the consideration received for the transfer or (if the transfer is not at arm's length) on the value of the right transferred: ITTOIA 2005 ss.98 and 251.

[37] *Purchase v Stainers Executors* [1952] A.C. 280; 32 T.C. 367; *Carson v Peter Cheyney's Executors* [1959] A.C. 412; 38 T.C. 240.

[38] ITTOIA 2005 ss.241 to 253.

[39] ITTOIA 2005 ss.243(1) and 246(1), which apply to any sums "... received after a person permanently ceases to carry on a trade ... which arise from the carrying on of the trade before cessation" only insofar as such sums are not otherwise chargeable to income tax.

[40] Because it is just as much part of such a person's trade, profession or vocation to turn such rights

third parties, as well as by the person who previously carried on the trade, profession or vocation concerned. Accordingly, a lump sum or royalties received by a third party or personal representatives[41] will be subject to income tax under these provisions if payable under a contract entered into by a person carrying on a trade, profession or vocation prior to discontinuance.

As the "post-cessation receipts" rules only apply to sums received after the discontinuance, only royalties and lump sums received after the original author, musician or composer has ceased carrying on his trade, profession or vocation will be caught. Accordingly, sums received by a third party under a contract assigned to him by an author, composer or musician are not subject to tax under the post-cessation receipts rules so long as the original author, etc. continues to practise, although such sums will be taxable under other provisions.

Further, where a trader who has permanently discontinued his trade, profession or vocation transfers the right to receive sums to which the post-cessation receipts provisions apply, for example the benefit of an existing royalty contract, the trader is taxable on the amount or value of the consideration received for the transfer or (if the transfer is not at arm's length) on the value of the right transferred.[42] No further liability falls on the transferee.

It is considered that lump sums received by persons who are not carrying on a trade, profession or vocation on the sale by them of intellectual property rights fall outside the "post-cessation receipts" rules altogether.[43] In the case of lump sums paid to the personal representatives of the author of a literary, dramatic, musical or artistic work or as consideration for the assignment by them, wholly or partially, of the copyright in the work, it is expressly provided that the "post-cessation receipts" rules do not apply.[44] It is thought that, this is a declaratory provision, intended for the avoidance of doubt,[45] and does not imply that such sums would be caught if received by a person who used to carry on a trade, profession or vocation or by a third party other than the personal representatives of a person who used to carry on a trade, profession or vocation.[46]

Deductible expenses

Traders are not taxed on their gross receipts, but on their profits. Such profits are computed in accordance with ordinary principles of commercial accounting and adjusted to reflect the statutory disallowances contained in ITTOIA 2005.[47]   **29–15**

Expenses of creating copyright material will be deductible if they fall within the general rules for deduction of revenue expenditure from trading profits (in general, where they are incurred wholly and exclusively for the purposes of the trade, profession or vocation).

Specific disallowances are contained primarily in Ch.4 of ITTOIA 2005 and

---

to account as it is to create such rights: see *Carson v Peter Cheyney's Executors* [1959] A.C. 412; 38 T.C. 240.

[41] This includes the personal representatives of a person who previously carried on a trade, profession or vocation, as the deceased's trade, profession or vocation will have been discontinued on his death.

[42] ITTOIA 2005 ss.98 and 251.

[43] Post-discontinuance sales by a person who used to carry on a trade, profession or vocation are discussed at above. The position of third parties is a fortiori.

[44] ITTOIA 2005 s.253: this exclusion also has effect in relation to assignments of public lending right (ITTOIA 2005 s.253(1)(b)) and there is a corresponding provision relating to design rights; ITTOIA 2005 s.253(2).

[45] cf. the dictum of Lord Herschell in *West Derby Union v Metropolitan Life Assurance Society* [1897] A.C. 647 at 656.

[46] For example, a legatee of a copyright, design right or public lending right.

[47] See *Odeon Associated Theatres Ltd v Jones* [1973] Ch. 288; 48 T.C. 257 CA and *Gallagher v Jones* [1993] S.T.C. 537 CA.

elsewhere throughout the Act; these amounts must be added back to the accounting profit to establish the taxable profits. The prohibitions most relevant to persons carrying on a trade, profession or vocation which involves exploiting intellectual property are the prohibitions on deducting:

(a) disbursements or expenditure not wholly and exclusively laid out or expended for the purposes of the trade, profession or vocation[48]; and

(b) capital expenditure.[49]

Capital expenditure incurred by a trader may qualify for capital allowances, for example, capital expenditure on plant or machinery or for the accelerated research and development capital allowances, which give a 100 per cent deduction in the year the expenditure is incurred.[50]

Where expenditure is classified as being capital in nature, this is deductible when the copyright is finally disposed of; generally the cost of acquisition and any associated costs of sale are deductible from the proceeds of sale. Entrepreneur's relief may be available to reduce the chargeable gain if the necessary conditions are fulfilled.[51]

Trading stock

29–16   Where a trader disposes of an item of trading stock otherwise than in the course of his trade (for example by giving an item away otherwise than to forward the interests of the trade), he is treated for tax purposes as if he had earned, as a trading receipt, an amount equal to the market value of the item at the time of the disposal.[52]

It has been held that this rule does not apply to persons carrying on a profession in respect of copyright, as such persons have no trading stock and their copyrights are considered a form of circulating capital.[53] This is confirmed in ITTOIA 2005 s.172B which refers only to disposals of trading stock of a trade; there is no clause applying the provisions of Ch.11A to professions or vocations.

A gift of intellectual property may still be subject to the capital gains tax rules.[54] It may also be part of arrangements which are subject to income tax under the sale of income from personal occupation rules.[55]

Casual receipts

29–17   A lump sum received by a person otherwise than in the course of trade, profession or vocation for the assignment or partial assignment of an intellectual property right is a capital receipt.[56] Accordingly, it will generally be subject to capital gains tax,[57] rather than income tax. By contrast, a lump sum received otherwise than in the course of a trade, profession or vocation for the grant of a licence may

---

[48] ITTOIA 2005 s.34(1)(a).

[49] ITTOIA 2005 s.33.

[50] See para.29–61 below.

[51] See para.29–29 below.

[52] *Sharkey v Wernher* [1956] A.C. 58; 36 T.C. 275, now given statutory effect in ITTOIA 2005, Pt 2 Ch.11A.

[53] *Mason v Innes* [1967] Ch. 1079; [1967] 3 W.L.R. 816; 44 T.C. 326, which confirmed that the rule in *Sharkey* does not apply to gifts of copyright by the author; the judgment suggests that the decision may have been at least partly because the judges were offended by the idea of an artist being taxed if he painted a picture of his mother and then gave it to her.

[54] See paras 29–21 onwards, below.

[55] ITA 2007 s.777; see para.29–19 below.

[56] *Nethersole v Withers* [1948] 1 All E.R. 400; 28 T.C. 501, which involved a partial assignment of a copyright.

[57] See paras 29–21, onwards, below.

be either capital or income, depending upon the true character of the transaction[58]. Thus, a lump sum has been held to be capital where the grant of the licence substantially diminished the value of a copyright work.[59] But a lump sum, which is quantified by reference to some anticipated quantum of user, which is received for or on account of royalties or represents a share of gross receipts will normally be income.

The nature of the transaction and therefore the categorisation of the payment is generally a question of fact.

In general, copyright royalties of a person who is a UK resident but is not carrying business as an author are taxable as miscellaneous income.[60] Lump sum payments for services rendered in relation to copyright will also usually be chargeable as miscellaneous income under Pt 5. For example, in *Housden v Marshall*[61] the income received by a jockey who worked with a professional author to produce newspaper articles about his racing days was taxable as miscellaneous income on the payment received, as it was for services to be rendered to the newspaper.

Lump sum payments received in respect of the sale of copyright, however, are generally subject to capital gains tax where the vendor is not carrying on a trade, profession or vocation in respect of that copyright.[62]

Payments of royalties

A copyright royalty (which includes any other payment similar to a royalty) paid by a trader will be deductible in computing the profits of his trade provided it is a trading expense, that is to say expenditure which is neither capital nor disallowed by Ch.4 of ITTOIA 2005, or elsewhere in that Act. The same principle applies to a lump sum paid by a trader for the grant of a licence to exercise intellectual property rights. Such a sum may be either a revenue expense or a capital expense, depending on the circumstances of the case, in particular the nature and duration of the rights granted by the licence and the purpose for which they have been acquired. Damages paid by a trader for infringement of an intellectual property right will normally be deductible in computing the profits of his trade if the infringement was incidental to the carrying on of the trade.

29–18

Copyright royalties paid by a person who is not carrying on a trade, and royalties paid by traders which are not trading expenses, are not allowable for income tax purposes. Such royalties must be paid gross unless the recipient is normally resident abroad,[63] in which case the payer is obliged to deduct tax at the basic rate from the payment and account to the Revenue for the taxes. It is then up to the non-resident, if entitled to do so, to claim from the Revenue the tax deducted. Any agreement for making such a payment without deduction of income tax is rendered void.

Where any royalty payment is made through the hands of an agent resident in the United Kingdom who is entitled to deduct commission from the payment, the agent need only deduct basic rate tax from the residue of the royalty payment remaining after deduction of his commission. If the amount of the commission is not ascertained at the time of the payment, tax is deductible from the gross amount of the payment.

---

[58] *Nethersole v Withers* [1948] 1 All E.R. 400; 28 T.C. 501.
[59] *Haig's Trustees v IRC* [1939] S.C. 676; 22 T.C. 725.
[60] Under ITTOIA 2005 s.579.
[61] 38 T.C. 233
[62] For example, *Nethersole v Withers* [1948] 1 All ER 400; 28 T.C. 501.
[63] See para.29–72, below.

Every person carrying on a trade or business may be required by notice to make a return of periodical or lump sum payments made in respect of any copyright, public lending right, design right or the right in a registered design. The same applies to any person carrying on an activity which does not constitute a trade or a business.

Anti-avoidance: sales of income from personal occupation

29–19   One way for a trader to minimise the income tax consequences of exploiting his intellectual property would be to arrange for the receipts of such exploitation to accrue to a person not carrying on a trade, profession or vocation (for example, the author's spouse). To counter this, a person such as an author, musician or composer who is carrying on a profession or vocation will be chargeable to income tax on any capital amounts received by another person which come into the recipient's hands as a result of arrangements which:

     (a)   are designed to exploit the earning capacity of the person carrying on the profession or vocation; and

     (b)   have as one of their main objectives the avoidance or reduction of liability to income tax.[64]

Thus, an author, musician or composer can be assessed to income tax on capital sums paid for the grant of a licence to exploit his copyright in a work, even though those capital sums may be payable to a service company or to members of his family.

Anti-avoidance: settlement provisions

29–20   Any income arising under a settlement during the lifetime of the settlor is treated for the purposes of the Taxes Acts as the settlor's income unless it derives from property in which he has no interest. The same applies to income arising under a settlement which is paid to or for the benefit of an unmarried minor child of the settlor during his lifetime.

Settlement is widely defined[65] to include "any disposition, trust, covenant, agreement, arrangement or transfer of assets", although the width of the definition is limited by the rule that there must be an element of bounty before there can be a "settlement". The term "settlor" is also widely defined to include any person who has contributed funds directly or indirectly for the purposes of the settlement.

Accordingly, if an author, musician or composer settles intellectual property rights, he will be subject to income tax on any income arising during his lifetime which could be applied for the benefit of himself or his spouse (e.g. by virtue of the exercise of a power). He will also be subject to income tax on any income which is actually used during his life to benefit an unmarried minor child of his.

B. CAPITAL GAINS TAX

Disposal of assets

29–21   Capital gains tax is payable on gains realised from the disposal of assets, unless the receipt is subject to income tax. All forms of property are assets for this purpose including incorporeal property such as copyrights and other forms of

---

[64] ITA 2007 Pt 13 Ch. 4.
[65] ITTOIA 2005 s.620(1).

intellectual property. Indeed the Taxation of Chargeable Gains Act 1992 makes express reference to copyright, design rights or licences to use any copyright work or design in which design right subsists.[66]

A person who is resident or ordinarily resident[67] in the United Kingdom is chargeable to capital gains tax on the disposal[68] of assets wherever situated, save that an individual who is not domiciled in the United Kingdom is taxable only on a remittance basis[69] in respect of gains arising on the disposal of intellectual property situated abroad.[70] Non-residents are outside the scope of capital gains tax, save that a non-resident carrying on a trade, profession or vocation in the United Kingdom through a branch or agency here is subject to capital gains tax on assets used for the purpose of the trade or held for the purposes of the branch or agency.[71]

Although a person who disposes of intellectual property is prima facie liable to capital gains tax, there are special rules designed to prevent double taxation which ensure that sums taken into account for income tax purposes are left out of account for capital gains tax.[72] So a professional author, musician, etc. who disposes of copyright will not be subject to capital gains tax if the consideration is taken into account for income tax as a professional receipt.[73] The same principle applies to a person who buys and sells copyright as a trade.

Calculation of gain

Unless the consideration is chargeable to income tax, an arm's length disposal of intellectual property to a person who is not connected[74] to the vendor will give rise to a capital gains tax charge on the difference between (a) the consideration for that disposal and (b) any allowable expenditure[75] attributable to the right. Entrepreneur's relief may be available to reduce the tax payable on the gain.[76]

29–22

The requirement that any sums chargeable to income tax must be excluded from the consideration received for the disposal does not require the Revenue to exclude the capitalised value of any right to receive royalties.[77] If the right is such that it cannot be valued, the vendor's liability to capital gains tax is computed on

---

[66] Taxation of Capital Gains Act 1992 ("TCGA 1992") s.275(j); see also the reference to registered designs in TCGA 1992 s.275(h).

[67] Resident" and "ordinarily resident" have the same meanings as for income tax; see TCGA 1992 s.9 and the discussion at para.29–71 below.

[68] Or part disposal; see TCGA 1992 s.21(2)(a). On a part disposal, only part of the acquisition cost of the asset is deductible; see para.29–25 below.

[69] TCGA 1992 s.12(1) and see s.12(2) for the definition of remittance for these purposes.

[70] Copyright, design right and franchises, and rights or licences to use any copyright work or design in which design right subsists, are situated in the United Kingdom if they or any right derived from them, are exercisable in the United Kingdom: TCGA 1992 s.275(j). And see *Redwood Music Ltd v B. Feldman & Co. Ltd* [1981] R.P.C. 337.

[71] TCGA 1992 s.10.

[72] TCGA 1992 s.37(1).

[73] See para.29–07 above.

[74] Broadly, a person is connected with his relatives, his spouse's relatives, the trustees of any settlement of which he (or anyone connected to him) is settlor, his partners (and their spouses) and any companies of which he has control; see TCGA 1992 s.286.

[75] See para.29–27, below.

[76] See para.29–29, below.

[77] TCGA 1992 s.37(3). Thus, where intellectual property is assigned in return for royalties, the assignor (whether author or third party) is exposed to the risk of double taxation, namely capital gains tax on the capitalised value of the royalties and income tax on the royalties as they come in. No case is known in practice where the Revenue have invoked this subsection in the context of copyright royalties, and it may be that the Revenue view the rather odd words "are not precluded" as being permissive. However, then the provision is declaratory and confers no such discretion on the Revenue.

the basis that he received the market value of the right.[78] Market value is also substituted for the actual consideration where there is a sale of copyright otherwise than by way of a bargain at arm's length or to a connected person.[79]

Gifts

29–23   A gift of intellectual property is a disposal otherwise than by way of bargain at arm's length and is therefore treated as a disposal at market value. The donor will be subject to capital gains tax on the difference between (a) the market value of the right at the date of the gift[80] and (b) the acquisition cost[81] of that asset. Entrepreneur's relief may be available to reduce the tax payable on the gain.[82]

The donor may be able to postpone part or all of the capital gains tax arising on a gift, or any other disposal at an undervalue, by claiming hold-over relief.[83] Hold-over relief is available in two situations. The first is where the gift amounts to a chargeable transfer for inheritance tax purposes (for example, where the right is given to a company or to discretionary trustees).[84] The second is where the right is used for the purposes of a trade, profession or vocation carried on by (a) the donor, (b) his personal company[85] or (c) a member of a trading group of which the holding company is the donor's personal company.[86]

Where a person makes a gift of a right to receive intellectual property as and when it comes into existence, it is considered that the gift of the right is not a disposal. The reason lies in the fact that in order for property to be disposed of, it must exist at the time of the purported gift, and the person making the gift must have a beneficial or proprietary right in that property.[87]

Note that anti-avoidance provisions may apply where a gift is part of arrangements which will be subject to income tax.[88]

Realisation of investments

29–24   Receipts on the disposal of copyright by a person who has acquired the copyright as an investment are subject to capital gains tax, rather than income tax.[89]

Part disposals

29–25   There is a part disposal of an asset where an interest or right in or over an asset is

---

[78] TCGA 1992 s.17(1)(b).

[79] TCGA 1992 s.18(2).

[80] TCGA 1992 s.17(1)(a).

[81] See para.29–27, below.

[82] See para.29–29, below.

[83] Hold-over relief operates by reducing both the chargeable gain accruing to the donor and the donee's acquisition cost; TCGA 1992 ss.165(4) and 260(3). Accordingly, the gain becomes chargeable when the donee disposes of the right (or emigrates; see TCGA 1992 s.168).

[84] TCGA 1992 s.260(2) and see para.29–32 for what constitutes a "chargeable transfer".

[85] i.e. a company in which the donor exercises at least 5% of the voting rights: TCGA 1992 s.165(8)(a).

[86] TCGA 1992 s.15(2)(a).

[87] See *Kirby v Thorn EMI* [1986] 1 W.L.R. 851; [1986] S.T.C. 200 and *Whiteman on Capital Gains Tax* 5th edn (London: Sweet & Maxwell, 2008) paras 7.24 et seq. Though note *Jerome v Kelly (Inspector of Taxes)* [2004] UKHL 25; [2004] 1 W.L.R. 1409, where the necessity for an asset to *exist* at the time of a disposal was distinguished from the case where the disposal of an asset for capital gains tax purposes may properly *precede* its acquisition, such as where an investor sells short.

[88] See paras 29–19, 29–20 and 29–77.

[89] *Shiner v Lindblom* [1961] 1 W.L.R. 248; (1960) 39 T.C. 367 confirmed that acquisition of copyright with no intention to trade in that copyright was an acquisition of an investment. The later disposal of the copyright on receipt of a favourable offer was not therefore subject to income tax; it would now be subject to capital gains tax.

created and where any property derived from the asset remains undisposed of.[90] The copyright in a work is regarded as a single asset so that any partial assignment is a part disposal as the owner still retains overall ownership of that intellectual property, even though he is constrained in his ability to exploit the intellectual property and has acquired proceeds of exploitation.

Capital gains tax on a part disposal is charged on the excess of:

- the sale proceeds, over
- the relevant proportion of the expenditure incurred on acquiring or creating the asset.

Capital gains tax will generally only be applicable where a copyright is held by an individual and does not relate to a trade, profession or vocation of that individual; receipts of a trade, profession or vocation will be taxed as income.[91]

Deemed disposals

29–26 A person is deemed to have disposed of intellectual property whenever he derives a capital sum from that asset.[92] Thus, unless it is taxable as income, any sum received on the grant of (or under the terms of) a licence to exploit such a right or as damages for infringement[93] will be subject to capital gains tax.

Allowable expenditure

29–27 For capital gains tax purposes, the gain on a disposal is arrived at by deducting from the actual or notional consideration the amount of any allowable expenditure. Allowable expenditure for capital gains tax purposes consists of acquisition cost plus enhancement expenditure and incidental costs of acquisition.

Where a person disposes of intellectual property which he has owned since March 31, 1982, the acquisition cost of that asset is its market value on March 31, 1982.[94] In any other case, the acquisition cost of the right acquired depends on the circumstances in which the acquisition took place. If the acquisition was from a connected person[95] or otherwise than by way of a bargain at arm's length, the acquisition cost will be the market value of the asset at the time of acquisition.[96] Otherwise it will be the amount of the consideration actually given for the right or in the case of the creator of the right, the expenditure incurred in its creation. Allowable enhancement expenditure is any expenditure wholly and exclusively incurred on the right for the purpose of enhancing the value of the asset, being expenditure reflected in the state or nature of the asset at the time of disposal, and any expenditure wholly and exclusively incurred in establishing, preserving or defending title to, or a right over the intellectual property.[97] Where the asset in question is intangible (as will be the case with intellectual property), "state or

---

[90] For example, on the sale of the film rights to a novel or on the grant of an exclusive licence in respect of software. See TCGA 1992 s.21(2)(b).

[91] See para.29–07, above.

[92] TCGA 1992 s.22. Particular examples of situations where capital sums are derived from assets are set out in TCGA 1992 s.22(1)(a)–(d). Where this occurs there is a part disposal of the asset.

[93] The concessionary treatment by which the Revenue does not tax certain damages awards does not apply to damages for infringement of an intellectual property right because there is an "underlying asset"; see Extra-Statutory Concession D33.

[94] TCGA 1992 s.35.

[95] Broadly, a person is connected with his relatives, his spouse's relatives, the trustees of any settlement of which he (or anyone connected to him) is settlor, his partners (and their spouses) and any companies of which he has control; see TCGA 1992 s.286.

[96] TCGA 1992 ss.17(1)(a) and 18(1)(2).

[97] TCGA 1992 s.38(1).

nature" has been held to mean something more than merely the value of the asset.[98]

Any expenditure which is allowable for income tax purposes, such as expenditure incurred in the creation of copyright by a professional author, is not allowable expenditure for capital gains tax.[99]

Personal representatives are treated as having acquired assets from the deceased at their market value at the date of death.[100] Accordingly, the acquisition cost of any intellectual property deemed to be so disposed and re-acquired by the personal representatives will be the market value of the intellectual property at the date of the deceased's death.

Where an intellectual property right is only disposed of in part (e.g. by the grant of a right to exploit the right for a limited period or in a limited location), only part of the acquisition cost is deductible in computing the chargeable gain. Each element of the acquisition cost is deductible in computing the chargeable gain. Each element of the acquisition cost is reduced according to an A/A-B formula, where A is the consideration for the disposal and B is the market value of the right remaining undisposed of.[101]

Wasting assets

29–28   Intellectual property rights with less than 50 years to run[102] are "wasting assets".[103] The acquisition cost of such assets is written off (on a straight line basis) from the date of acquisition to the date on which it expires,[104] so that the acquisition cost brought into account on a disposal is the written down cost.

Entrepreneur's relief

29–29   Schedule 3 of Finance Act 2008 introduced entrepreneurs' relief for disposals on or after April 6, 2008 to counteract (to an extent) the loss of the business assets taper relief previously available. Broadly speaking, entrepreneurs' relief operates by reducing the effective rate of capital gains tax to 10 per cent in respect of so-called "qualifying business disposals", up to a maximum lifetime limit of £5 million of chargeable gains.[105]

Moral and performer's rights

29–30   It is suggested that because moral rights are personal and not proprietary rights,[106] they are not a form of property and hence do not count as "assets" for capital gains tax.[107] Sums received in return for a waiver of, or by way of compensation for infringement of, moral rights would not on this view be derived from "assets"

---

[98] See *Trustees of the F D Fenston Will Trusts v Revenue and Customs Commissioners* [2007] STC (SCD) 316 where the words were held to require a change in the rights or restrictions attaching to the asset—here, shares.

[99] TCGA 1992 s.37(1).

[100] TCGA 1992 s.62(1)(a). Where the value of any assets has been ascertained for the purposes of inheritance tax (see para.29–31 onwards below) that value is taken to be their market value at the date of death for the purposes of capital gains tax: TCGA 1992 s.274.

[101] TCGA 1992 s.42.

[102] Such as copyright material more than twenty years after the author's death.

[103] TCGA 1992 s.44.

[104] TCGA 1992 s.46.

[105] Increased from £2m in the 2010 Emergency Budget.

[106] See para.11–05, above.

[107] Some support for this view is found in para.12 of Extra-Statutory Concession D33. cf. the view expressed in the 14th edition of this work that, although moral rights are not assignable, they are

and would therefore escape the charge to capital gains tax. The point may be of limited practical significance because in infringement cases the exemption for compensation or damages "for any wrong or injury suffered by an individual in his person" is likely to apply given the wide meaning attributed by the Revenue to the phrase "in his person".[108] Further, in the case of professional authors, etc. sums received by way of compensation for infringement of moral rights are liable to be taxed, if at all, as income.

It is thought that performers' rights and recording rights are commercial in nature and would be held to be an asset for capital gains tax purposes.

C. INHERITANCE TAX

Death

When a person dies, inheritance tax will be payable on the value of any intellectual property which immediately before his death was vested in him or comprised in a settlement in which he had an interest in possession.[109] Further, inheritance tax will be payable on the value of any intellectual property which the deceased gave away during his lifetime, if he reserved a benefit in the gifted property.[110] The value of property given away by a person to another individual or to a particular settlement within seven years of his death will also form part of that person's estate on his death.[111]   **29–31**

The value of the property for inheritance tax purposes is the price which it might reasonably be expected to fetch if sold in the open market immediately before the deceased's death.[112] A valuation by the publisher or literary agent is evidence[113] of open market value, although HMRC is not bound to accept it.

Lifetime gifts and settlements

It is not uncommon for people to make lifetime gifts or settlements of intellectual property. Such gifts and settlements will not divest the donor's estate of the property (for the purposes of inheritance tax) if he reserves a benefit in the gifted property[114] or settles such property on trusts in which he retains an interest in possession.[115]   **29–32**

As inheritance tax is payable on certain lifetime gifts, a gift or settlement of intellectual property may give rise to an inheritance tax charge. If the gift is to an individual, or to a settlement in which an individual has an interest in possession

---

nonetheless "assets" for the purposes of capital gains tax because they can be waived and thus turned to account.

[108] See Extra-Statutory Concession D33 para.12 where it is stated that the words "in his person" embrace more than physical injury so that distress, embarrassment, loss of reputation or dignity are covered; damages for libel or slander are given as an example.

[109] Inheritance Tax Act 1984 ("IHTA 1984") ss.4(1), 5 and 49(1). For new interest in possession settlements, i.e. those created after March 22, 2006, the value of the settled property in which the interest in possession subsists will no longer be deemed to fall within the person's estate on death (para.4 of Sch.20 to the Finance Act 2006). This ties in with the aim of ensuring that all new interest in possession settlements are taxed in the same way as discretionary settlements.

[110] Finance Act 1986 s.102(2).

[111] IHTA 1984 s.3A(4).

[112] IHTA 1984 s.160. If the death of the holder affects the value of the property, the change in value is taken into account as though it had occurred immediately before the death: IHTA 1984 s.171.

[113] It is admissible as expert evidence.

[114] Finance Act 1986 s.102.

[115] IHTA 1984 s.49(1). For new interest in possession settlements, i.e. those created after March 22, 2006, the value of the settled property in which the interest in possession subsists will no longer be deemed to fall within the person's estate on death (para.4 of Sch.20 to the Finance Act 2006).

or an accumulation or maintenance trust, the gift or settlement will be a "potentially exempt transfer".[116] A potentially exempt transfer only gives rise to an inheritance tax charge if the donor dies within seven years of making the gift or settlement.[117] Although the tax charge is calculated by reference to the value of the property at the time of the gift (less the value of any consideration received by the donor), it will be charged at the rate in force when the donor dies[118] and, if tax is chargeable, tapering relief will be available if the donor survives for at least three years after making the gift or settlement.[119]

29–33   Any other gift or settlement will be a "chargeable transfer"[120] at the time it is made, and inheritance tax will be payable at the lifetime rates[121] on the value of the rights comprised in the gift or settlement. If the donor dies within seven years, the tax payable on the chargeable transfer is recomputed at the full death rates in force at the time of death and, if this results in a higher amount of tax, the balance becomes payable.

   Where the gift is an effective assignment of future copyright or design right, it is apprehended that the Revenue may invoke the so-called "associated operations" provisions[122] if (as will usually be the case) it can be said that the assignment and the creation of the right were effected with reference to one another. If so, the assignment will be treated as having taken place at the time when the right comes into existence.

   In order for a transfer of a right to attract inheritance tax there must be an intention to confer gratuitous benefit. Consequently, a sale of intellectual property at arm's length will not attract inheritance tax even if the sale is at an undervalue.[123]

Business property relief

29–34   In the absence of any authority on the point, it is unclear whether intellectual property comprised in the estate of a person whose trade, profession or vocation involves exploiting such rights (e.g. an author, musician, composer, etc.) qualifies for business property relief.[124] However, it is understood that in practice the Revenue do afford business property relief on the death of such a person provided he was carrying on his trade, profession or vocation at (or shortly before) his death. Although the Revenue regard this treatment as concessionary, it is suggested that there are persuasive arguments in favour of the view that, on the death of a professional author, musician, composer, artist, etc., the rights comprised in his estate qualify for business property relief as a matter of law.[125] On the other hand, where an author, musician, etc. makes a lifetime gift or settlement of copy-

---

[116] IHTA 1984 s.3A. The Finance Act 2006 made significant erosions into the realm of potentially exempt transfers. No transfers made after March 22, 2006 are potentially exempt transfers unless, broadly, they are to an individual or to a disabled trust (defined by s.89 of IHTA 1984). The concept of accumulation and maintenance trusts has been abolished for assets settled after March 22, 2006.

[117] IHTA 1984 s.3A.

[118] IHTA 1984 Sch.2 para.1A.

[119] IHTA 1984 s.7(4).

[120] A chargeable transfer is a transfer of value made by an individual other than an exempt transfer (IHTA 1984 s.2). A transfer of value is any disposition which reduces the value of the transferor's estate. Apart from the exemptions mentioned in para.29–35, below, there is also an exemption for transfers not exceeding £3,000 in any one year: IHTA 1984 s.19.

[121] Lifetime transfers are charged at half of the death rates: IHTA 1984 s.7(2).

[122] IHTA 1984 s.268.

[123] IHTA 1984 s.10.

[124] IHTA 1984 ss.103 et seq.

[125] See *Foster's Inheritance Tax* at G1.71.

right, etc. it is difficult to see how business property relief can be available because there is no transfer of a business, merely a transfer of individual business assets.[126]

Exemptions

There is no charge to inheritance tax where intellectual property passes to the owner's spouse or a charity.[127] This is so whether the copyright passes by way of lifetime gift, settlement or on the holder's death. As a result of the Finance Act 2006, no new lifetime settlements in favour of the spouse will attract the spouse exemption. For lifetime gifts, it will now only be possible to attract the spouse exemption on outright gifts to the spouse.

29–35

Non-domiciled individuals

There are two special rules in relation to intellectual property rights held by non-UK domiciled persons. First, inheritance tax is only payable in respect of intellectual property rights held by persons who are domiciled[128] outside the United Kingdom where such rights are situated in the United Kingdom.[129] Second, where the intellectual property is comprised in a settlement and is situated outside the United Kingdom, no inheritance tax is payable on a transfer of such property if the settlor of that settlement was not UK domiciled at the time the settlement was created.

29–36

In respect of any particular work, separate copyrights or equivalent rights subsist in different territories throughout the world. Copyright is only situated here in so far as it is protected here by the Copyright, Designs and Patents Act 1988. The rights in works which are protected in other countries by other laws are situate in those countries and not in the United Kingdom.[130] Such rights, if held by a non-UK domiciled person or within a settlement created by a non-domiciled person, will be outside the scope of UK inheritance tax.

3. CORPORATE TAX

A. PRE-APRIL 2002 ASSETS

Scope

The corporate rules for taxation of intellectual property and other intangible fixed assets[131] generally apply to such assets where they are acquired or created by companies *only* on or after April 1, 2002. Assets acquired before April 1, 2002 or created by the taxpayer company before April 1, 2002 remain subject to the same

29–37

---

[126] cf. the capital gains tax cases of *McGregor v Adcock* [1977] 3 All E.R. 65, [1977] S.T.C. 206, 51 T.C. 692; *Mannion v Johnston* [1988] S.T.C. 758; *Pepper v Daffurn* [1993] S.T.C. 466 and *Wase v Bourke* [1996] S.T.C. 18.

[127] IHTA 1984 ss.18 and 23.

[128] A person is domiciled in the United Kingdom for inheritance tax purposes if (a) he is domiciled here as a matter of general law, (b) he was domiciled here within the previous three years (IHTA 1984 s.267(1)(a) or (c) he was resident in the United Kingdom in 17 of the previous 20 years of assessment (IHTA 1984 s.267(1)(b)).

[129] IHTA 1984 s.6(1).

[130] For inheritance tax purposes, there is no "situs" code comparable to TCGA 1992 s.275 (discussed at para.29–21, above).

[131] See para.29–41, below.

rules as individuals, except in respect of royalties.[132] It is therefore primarily the capital gains rules (see para.29–38 below) that will be applicable to such assets.

Royalties

29–38   The exception to this is in respect of royalties: royalty payments received on or after April 1, 2002 will be taxed under the post-April 1, 2002 rules, *regardless* of when the intellectual property to which they relate was acquired or created by the taxpayer company.[133]

Capital gains

29–39   Capital gains arising from pre-April 1, 2002 assets will be taxed under the same rules as those for individuals and other unincorporated entities[134] save that companies are subject to corporation tax on gains, rather than capital gains tax.[135] A capital gain of a company is reduced by the indexation allowance[136], rather than entrepreneur's relief.[137]

Indexation allowance

29–40   Indexation allowance is designed to prevent gains due to inflation from being subject to capital gains tax; it is now only available for capital gains of companies. The allowance is given by means of a deduction in computing the chargeable gain accruing on a disposal.[138] The amount deductible is a fraction of each component of the asset's allowable expenditure, that fraction being given by dividing:

     (a) the increase in the RPI between the date on which the expenditure was incurred and the date on which the asset is disposed of, by

     (b) the RPI on the date when the expenditure was incurred.[139]

In practice, HMRC publish a table listing such relevant fractions, updated each month.

The indexation allowance is only available to reduce or extinguish a gain, and not to create a loss.[140]

B. Post-April 1, 2002 assets

Accounts basis

29–41   These rules[141] relate to intellectual property and other intangible assets created by the taxpayer company or acquired by the taxpayer company (regardless of when it was created by others) only on or after April 1, 2002.

The key point of the corporate tax rules for intellectual property is that they treat expenditure on the creation or acquisition of intellectual property fixed as-

---

[132] See para.29–39, below.
[133] Corporation Tax Act 2009 ("CTA 2009") s.896.
[134] See paras 29–21, onwards above.
[135] CTA 2009 s.2.
[136] See para.29–40, below.
[137] See para.29–29, above.
[138] TCGA 1992 s.53(1).
[139] TCGA 1992 s.54(1).
[140] Finance Act 1994 s.93, amending TCGA 1992 s.53.
[141] CTA 2009 Pt 8 (ss.711–906).

sets—those created or acquired for enduring use in a business—as revenue expenditure, if it is treated as such in the company's profit and loss account. That is, it is brought into account for tax purposes if it is recognised in the company's profit and loss account. This overrides the general computational rules in respect of capital and revenue expenditure on the creation or acquisition of intangible assets. Receipts are similarly taxed when they are recognised in the profit and loss account, rather than according to the general corporate tax rules.

Where an intangible asset is created by a change in accounting policy (for example, on the adoption of International Accounting Standards, which may result in the re-classification of a tangible asset as an intangible asset) then such an asset does not qualify as a corporate IP asset for the purposes of these rules if capital allowances were deducted in respect of that asset when it was categorised as tangible.[142]

Where the intellectual property is held for the purposes of the trade, any debits and credits on disposal are treated as expenses and receipts of the trade, respectively, when calculating the profits of the business for tax purposes.

Where the intellectual property is acquired and held for non-trade purposes (for example, where it is held as an investment) the debits and credits are pooled to create a non-trading gain or loss. A non-trading gain for the period is charged to tax as miscellaneous income. A company which has a non-trading loss in an accounting period can elect for that non-trading loss to be set against the total profits of the company for that period, or carried forward.

If, for any reason, the company does not draw up accounts that follow generally accepted accounting practice ("correct accounts"), the expenditure which can be deducted for tax purposes is that which would have been deducted in the accounts if correct accounts had been produced.[143]

"Generally accepted accounting practice" is defined by the Corporation Tax Act 2010 ("CTA 2010") s.1127 as being that used to produce accounts that are intended to give a "true and fair view"—essentially, the practice codified in the Companies Act 1985 and the standards and statements of the United Kingdom's Accounting Standards Board.

This requirement will generally affect foreign companies with UK branches or dependent agents, whose accounts may not reflect UK generally accepted accounting practice—those accounts will need to be restated for UK tax purposes to reflect "correct accounts".

Expenses

Debits for tax purposes relating to intellectual property are brought into account **29–42** when they are recognised in a company's profit and loss account, particularly:

- (a) the writing-off for accounting purposes, as it is incurred, of expenditure on intellectual property; and
- (b) the writing-down of the capitalised costs of the intellectual property.

The amount of the expenditure that can be deducted for tax purposes is generally the same as the amount recognised for accounting purposes; however, the amounts may differ where, for example, roll-over relief has been granted.

Expenditure on research and development is specifically excluded from the corporate IP tax rules to enable companies to claim R&D relief.[144] To allow for incentives to boost British film-making, these rules also do not to apply to

---

[142] CTA 2009 s.804.
[143] CTA 2009 s.717.
[144] See para.29–53 onwards below for the special reliefs for research and development expenditure.

intangible fixed assets held by film production companies where the expenditure on such assets represents production expenditure on a qualifying film, so that the film tax incentive rules apply to that expenditure instead.[145]

Written-off expenditure

29–43   Under Financial Reporting Standard 10 (FRS10), expenditure on intangible assets, including intellectual property, is written off when incurred when it is either:

(a) abortive expenditure; or

(b) royalties paid for the use of third-party intellectual property; or

(c) expenditure on internally generated intellectual property.

This will cover most expenses of creating intellectual property; FRS10 effectively denies the capitalisation of internally generated intangible assets, including intellectual property. Intellectual property expenditure may be capitalised for accounting purposes if the research and development expenditure involved in creating an intellectual property asset meets specific criteria, including the requirement to have a reasonable likelihood of commercial success. However, as noted at para.29–42, above, research and development expenditure is specifically excluded from the corporate IP tax rules.

FRS10 does allow expenditure on internally-generated intellectual property to be capitalised when it belongs to a homogenous population of assets that are equivalent in every respect and for which an active market exists, as evidenced by frequent transactions. It is rare for intellectual property to fulfil the conditions for this exemption—in fact, the exemption is designed to ensure that expenditure on internally created brands cannot be capitalised.

Hence, the capitalised intellectual property assets carried in the balance sheet of companies will generally relate to the cost of acquiring rights to or ownership of intellectual property developed by a third party. The corporate IP tax rules do specifically include internally generated IP assets within the definition of intangible assets,[146] but the accounts basis means that it is unlikely that companies will often have to consider such IP assets under these rules.

Amortisation/impairment

29–44   There are two types of profit and loss account charge which may appear in the accounts in relation to capitalised costs of intellectual property; the amortisation charge for the period (the most usual charge—the asset is amortised over its useful economic life, to spread the acquisition cost against profits derived from the asset) or a charge as a result of an impairment review where the value of the asset has been assessed to have fallen below the amortised value.

On capitalisation, the amount of the debit for tax purposes is,[147] in the accounting period in which the intellectual property is capitalised:

$$L \times \frac{E}{CE}$$

Where:

L = the amount recognised in the profit and loss account;

---

[145] CTA 2009 s.808; similar provisions also apply to sound recordings under CTA 2009 s.811.
[146] CTA 2009 s.712.
[147] CTA 2009 s.729.

E = the expenditure on the intellectual property recognised for tax purposes; and

CE = the expenditure capitalised in the accounts.

In subsequent periods, the amount of the debit for tax purposes is[148]:

$$L \times \frac{WDV}{AV}$$

Where:

L = the amount recognised in the profit and loss account;

WDV = the tax written-down value of the asset immediately before the amortisation charge is made (or before an impairment review); and

AV = the value of the asset for accounting purposes immediately before the amortisation charge is made (or before an impairment review).

The *tax written-down value* of the intellectual property is[149]:

$$\text{Tax cost} - \text{Debits} + \text{Credits}$$

The *tax cost* is the cost of creating the intellectual property which is recognised for tax purposes. *Debits* includes all debits previously brought into account for tax purposes (i.e. previous periods' writing down), and *credits* includes any credits previously brought into account for tax purposes on a revaluation.

Fixed rate allowance

A company can elect for the cost of the asset to be written down at a fixed rate for tax purposes,[150] regardless of whether, or for how long, it is amortised in the accounts. This allows intellectual property to be written down for tax purposes where no amortisation is given in the accounts.   **29–45**

Once an election is made, the debit that can be brought into account for tax purposes is the lower of:

(a) 4 per cent of the expenditure recognised for tax purposes; and

(b) the balance of the tax written-down value.

This amount must be proportionately reduced if the accounting period is less than 12 months.

The tax written-down value for the purposes of a debit under this election is slightly different to that for a debit on written-down expenditure[151] as no revaluation is possible for tax purposes:

$$\text{Tax cost} - \text{Debits}$$

The tax cost is the cost of creating the intellectual property which is recognised for tax purposes. Debits includes all debits previously brought into account for tax purposes (i.e. previous periods' writing down).

The election must be made in writing within two years of the end of the accounting period in which the asset is created or acquired, and is made in respect of all the expenditure on the asset created that is capitalised for accounting purposes. The election is irrevocable. This election needs to be considered by any

---

[148] CTA 2009 s.729.
[149] CTA 2009 s.742.
[150] CTA 2009 s.730.
[151] See para.29–42, above.

company adopting International Accounting Standards, which do not permit amortisation of goodwill; if an election is not (or cannot) be made in respect of the goodwill, no writing down allowance will be available for goodwill within the corporate IP tax rules.

Royalties

29–46   As noted above, royalty payments are taxed when they are reflected in the profit and loss account of the company, regardless of when the intellectual property to which they relate was acquired or created[152] and regardless of whether the payment is a lump sum or a series of payments.

Disposals

29–47   An intellectual property asset will be realised when it ceases to be recognised in the company's balance sheet and a credit or debit will be brought into account for tax purposes on that realisation.

Where the intellectual property asset has been written down under the corporate IP tax rules, either on an accounting basis or under a fixed rate election, the amount that needs to be brought into account for tax purposes on a realisation is as follows[153]:

(a) where the proceeds of the realisation exceed the tax written-down value of the asset—a credit equal to the excess;

(b) where the proceeds of the realisation are less than the tax written-down value of the asset—a debit equal to the shortfall;

(c) where there are no proceeds from the realisation (e.g. on a gifted licence)—a debit equal to the tax written-down value of the asset.

The tax written-down value in the above cases is the value immediately before the realisation.

Where the intellectual property is shown in the company's balance sheet but has not been written down for tax purposes (usually where it is licensed soon after acquisition), then the amount brought into account for tax purposes is as follows[154]:

(a) where the proceeds of the realisation exceed the cost of the asset—a credit equal to the excess;

(b) where the proceeds of the realisation are less than the cost of the asset—a debit equal to the shortfall;

(c) where there are no proceeds from the part realisation (e.g. on a gifted licence)—a debit equal to the cost of the asset.

The cost of the asset is that recognised for tax purposes.

Where intellectual property assets are disposed of as part of a scheme of reconstruction, the disposal of those assets is treated as tax-neutral provided certain conditions are fulfilled.[155]

Where the accounting value of an intellectual property asset changes from one accounting period to another as the result of a change of accounting policy, a corresponding debit or credit is brought into account for tax purposes.[156] The amount brought into account is:

---

[152] CTA 2009 s.896.
[153] CTA 2009 s.735.
[154] CTA 2009 s.736.
[155] CTA 2009 s.818.
[156] CTA 2009 s.872.

$$D \times \frac{\text{WDVE}}{\text{AVE}}$$

Where:

> D = the difference between the accounting value at the end of the accounting period prior to the change in accounting policy and the accounting value at the beginning of the accounting period immediately after the change in accounting policy;
>
> WDVE = the tax value of the asset at the end of the accounting period prior to the change; and
>
> AVE = the accounting value of the asset at the end of the accounting period prior to the change.

This does not apply to assets in respect of which an election has been made for fixed-rate writing down.[157]

Up-front payments in respect of intellectual property licences must be charged as royalties and not as realisation proceeds, so that the taxable credit cannot be reduced by the accounting cost of the intangible.[158]

A part realisation is dealt with in the same way as a realisation, comparing the proceeds of the part realisation to the appropriate portion of the cost of the asset.[159]

The effect of a part realisation of an intellectual property asset under the corporate IP tax rules is to alter the tax written-down value of the asset so that immediately after the part realisation occurs, the tax value is effectively "reset", so that debits and credits which were brought into account in relation to periods before the part realisation are no longer taken into account for tax purposes.[160]

Roll-over relief

The corporate IP tax rules contain a wide roll-over relief for dealing with gains on intellectual property assets.[161]   **29–48**

A company can defer gains on realisations of intellectual property by acquiring other intellectual property assets and can also defer such gains by utilising the IP asset acquisitions of other group companies.

The amount available for relief is the amount by which the proceeds of realisation (or, if less, the qualifying expenditure on reinvestment assets) exceed the cost of the old asset.[162]

The roll-over is given by deducting the amount of the relief from both:

(a) the proceeds of realisation of the old asset[163]; and

(b) the cost recognised for tax purposes of the reinvestment assets.[164]

Note that the amortisation debits taken into account for tax purposes will mean that this rollover relief is a cashflow benefit rather than a potentially indefinite deferral—the relief on the gain will be clawed back over the amortisation period as the reduction in the cost recognised will mean that the amortisation debits in each accounting period will be lower.

---

[157] See para.29–45, above.
[158] This is consistent with the income tax treatment, following cases such as *Glasson v Rougier* [1944] 1 All E.R. 535; 26 T.C. 86.
[159] CTA 2009 s.737.
[160] CTA 2009 s.744.
[161] CTA 2009 Pt 8 Ch.7 (ss.754 to 763).
[162] CTA 2009 s.755.
[163] Which can be a pre-April 1, 2002 asset.
[164] CTA 2009 s.758.

In addition, the amortisation debits for tax purposes will not be the same as the amortisation debits in the accounts, as the cost recognised for tax purposes of the new asset will be lower than the accounts value. The amortisation debits on an asset that has provided roll-over relief for a disposal will need to be calculated for tax purposes on each return as a result: the gain on accounts amortisation costs will need to be added back in the return.

Intra-group transfers

29–49   Broadly, where there is a disposal of an intellectual property asset by one group member to another, the transfer will be treated as tax-neutral[165] so that there is no tax charge for the transferring company.

The original cost of the asset is treated as though it was the transferee's original cost, and all amortisation and other costs and receipts which have been brought into account for tax purposes as debits and credits are treated as though the transferee had incurred them.[166]

Degrouping

29–50   Where a company ceases to be a member of the group, there is a deemed disposal and re-acquisition at market value of any intangible assets owned by the company which were transferred to the company ceasing to be a member of the group by another group member within the six years prior to the date of the company ceasing to be a member of the group.[167]

The company and a continuing group member can elect for the continuing group member to be treated as incurring the gain[168]; the tax on the reallocated gain can be deferred by roll-over relief if the continuing group member makes, or has made, a qualifying acquisition.[169]

Investment assets

29–51   Where copyright is acquired and held for non-trade purposes (generally, where it is held as an investment—although not all investments qualify as relevant assets to which the corporate IP tax rules apply), the debits and credits are pooled.

A non-trading loss arises where there are only non-trading debits, or if the total non-trading debits exceed the total of non-trading credits received (in respect of any intellectual property held as an investment).[170]

A non-trading gain arises where there are only non-trading credits, or if the total non-trading credits exceed the total of non-trading debits.[171]

If the accounting period is not the same as the period of account for tax purposes, the gain or loss will need to be adjusted on a time basis.[172]

A company which has a non-trading loss in an accounting period can make a claim for that loss to be set against the total profits of the company for that period. The claim must be made within two years of the end of the accounting period. Where the loss is not absorbed by that period's profits, and is not surrendered by

---

[165] CTA 2009 s.775.
[166] CTA 2009 s.776.
[167] CTA 2009 s.780.
[168] CTA 2009 s.792.
[169] CTA 2009 s.794.
[170] CTA 2009 s.751(5).
[171] CTA 2009 s.751(2).
[172] CTA 2010 s.1172.

way of group relief, it can be carried forward to the next accounting period to be treated as a non-trading loss of that period and so on.[173]

Where a company has a non-trading gain for the period, it is subject to corporation tax as income.[174]

C. FILM PRODUCTION COMPANIES

Film tax relief is available for a "film production company" in respect of expenditure on a film that commences principal photography on or after January 1, 2007, or to acquisition expenditure that is incurred on or after October 1, 2007 on a film (whenever made) and which is expenditure that qualifies for relief.[175] As the relief applies only to film production companies it is clear that this relief does not apply to individuals or to partners in partnerships.

29–52

Expenditure qualifies for relief if it satisfies three conditions,[176] namely, that the film is "intended for theatrical release", that it is a "British film" and that the expenditure is "UK expenditure". These are defined terms. A film is "intended for theatrical release" where, broadly, it is intended to be exhibited to the paying public at a commercial cinema and it is intended that a significant proportion of the earnings from the film are to arise from such exhibition. A film is a "British film" if it is so certified under Sch.1 to the Films Act 1985. "UK expenditure" is expenditure on services performed in the United Kingdom or on goods supplied in the United Kingdom. In order for the third condition (as to UK expenditure) to be satisfied, it is necessary that not less than 25 per cent of the core expenditure on the film is UK expenditure.

Where these conditions are satisfied, the film production company is entitled to an additional deduction in respect of "qualifying expenditure" in calculating the profit and loss of that particular film; each film is treated as a separate trade for film tax relief purposes. "Qualifying expenditure" is, broadly, the core expenditure of the film taken into account in calculating the profit or loss of the particular film trade.[177] There is a formula for calculating the amount of the additional deduction[178]: $E \times R$, where E is the lesser of the amount of qualifying expenditure that is UK expenditure and 80 per cent of the total amount of qualifying expenditure and R is the rate of enhancement. The R figure (the rate of enhancement) is set at 100 per cent for films with budgets of less than £20m and at 80 per cent for films with budgets of over £20m.

A film production company qualifying for the additional deduction is also entitled to a payable tax credit.[179] A film production company is entitled to claim the payable tax credit where it has a "surrenderable loss" in an accounting period. The "surrenderable loss" is either the trading loss of the company or the available qualifying expenditure, whichever is less. The amount of the available qualifying expenditure is the figure for "E" in the calculation of the additional deduction—in other words, the lesser of the qualifying expenditure that is UK expenditure and 80 per cent of the total amount of the qualifying expenditure. A film production company may surrender all or part of its surrenderable loss for a period.[180] The

---

[173] CTA 2009 s.753.
[174] CTA 2009 s.752.
[175] CTA 2009 Pt 15.
[176] Set out in CTA 2009 ss.1196 to 1198 inclusive.
[177] CTA 2009 s.1199(3).
[178] CTA 2009 s.1200.
[179] CTA 2009 s.1201(1).
[180] CTA 2009 s.1202.

amount of the payable tax credit is determined by using the formula[181]: $L \times R$, where L is the amount of loss surrendered and R is the payable credit rate. The payable credit rate for films with budgets of less than £20m is 25 per cent and for films with budgets of over £20m it is 20 per cent.

The payable tax credit is not automatic but must be claimed.[182] The credit may be set against the corporation tax liability of the film production company.

There are, not surprisingly, anti-avoidance provisions built into the film tax relief. These provisions deny film tax relief (the additional deduction and the payable tax credit) if, and to the extent that, the relief arises from arrangements entered into wholly or partly for a disqualifying purpose, i.e. arrangements where the main object, or one of the main objects, is to enable the film production company to obtain an additional deduction or a payable tax credit to which it would not otherwise have been entitled or one greater than the one to which it would otherwise have been entitled.

Companies can opt out of the provisions for relief in Finance Act 2006 and into general tax treatment.[183] To do this, the clause allows a company to make an election in its tax return to be regarded as not meeting the conditions to be a Film Production Company in respect of any present or future film. Once an election has been made, it may be withdrawn only within the time limit for amending the return in which it is contained.[184]

D. CORPORATE TAX RELIEF AND CREDIT

29–53   In an effort to increase the attractiveness of the United Kingdom as a place to do research and development ("R&D"), tax incentives for companies undertaking R&D were introduced in 2000 (for small and medium-sized companies) and 2002 (for large companies). Since introduction, the reliefs have been gradually widened to cover more companies and costs.

The R&D tax reliefs are only available for companies, not partnerships or individuals. There are three reliefs:

    (a) small or medium-sized enterprise ("SME") relief, for small and medium-sized companies;

    (b) the large company relief; and

    (c) the repayable tax credit, for loss-making SME companies.

There is a cap of €7.5m on the total R&D relief that may be claimed by an SME on a particular project[185]; the cap was a concession to the European Union to gain approval for other improvements in the relief (such as the extension of SME R&D relief to larger SMEs).

The tax reliefs are available for R&D activities which relate to a project representing an advance in science or technology (in the context of copyright, this is most likely to arise in the area of software development)[186]. This was confirmed in *B E Studios Ltd v Smith & Williamson Ltd*[187] in which the court noted that it was not sufficient that the company believed the products being created (which were software products) to be innovative or cutting edge and held

---

[181] CTA 2009 s.1202(2).

[182] CTA 2009 s.1201(1).

[183] CTA 2009 s.1182(7).

[184] CTA 2009 s.1182(8).

[185] CTA 2009 s.1113.

[186] For more details on what qualifies as R&D for the tax relief, see the 2004 Guidelines published by the DTI (as it was then), now on the BIUS website.

[187] [2005] EWHC 1506 (Ch)—technically the case was a claim for professional negligence, but it remains the only substantive case on what constitutes research and development for the purposes of the tax relief.

that the company did not qualify for R&D relief, even though HMRC had granted the relief and paid the repayable tax credit to the company (this was a claim for professional negligence, not a tax case against HMRC). Following the decision, it seems HMRC may have been embarrassed by this as it became rather difficult to obtain R&D relief for software development for a while. Anecdotal evidence indicates that HMRC is no longer quite so suspicious of software-related R&D claims.

SME relief

The SME relief is taken as a deduction for tax purposes,[188] reducing a profit or increasing a loss (to reduce future profits). If the SME company is loss-making, the additional loss arising from the relief can then be surrendered in exchange for an immediate repayment from HMRC.[189]   **29–54**

The relief is given by allowing an SME company to deduct 75 per cent of its qualifying expenditure when calculating profits/losses for tax purposes,[190] in addition to the 100 per cent deduction already available under the general rules. For a tax-paying SME company, this will reduce the company's tax liability. For a loss-making SME company it will increase the trading loss available to carry forwards or backwards, use against other income of the period, or surrender as group relief.

Definition of SME

A company is regarded as small or medium-sized[191] if it, considered together with its linked and partner enterprises: **29–55**

  (a) has fewer than 500 employees and either or both of:

      (i) an annual turnover not exceeding €100 million; and

      (ii) a period-end balance sheet total not exceeding €86 million; and

  (b) has less than 25 per cent of its capital or voting rights owned by one or more companies that are not small or medium-sized (unless such companies are certain types of investment company).

The thresholds in (a) above are double the standard EU thresholds in the definition of an SME; this is a concession obtained by the United Kingdom for the SME R&D relief only, it does not extent the meaning of an SME for any other purpose.

In addition, the accounts of a company claiming the SME relief must not be qualified on a going concern basis.[192] The SME accounts must also not be prepared on a going concern basis only because of an expectation that R&D relief would be received—there must be other reasons for enabling the accounts to be prepared on a going concern basis.

Qualifying expenditure

Expenditure which qualifies for the relief is revenue expenditure attributable to   **29–56**

---

[188] CTA 2009 s.1044(7).
[189] CTA 2009 s.1054; see para.29–59, below.
[190] CTA 2009 s.1044(8).
[191] CTA 2009 ss.1119, 1120.
[192] CTA 2009 s.1046.

R&D which is related to the trade of the company and is carried out by the company or on its behalf[193] and relating to:

(a) the cost of qualifying staff involved; and
(b) consumable stores used; and
(c) certain sub-contractor costs; and
(d) payments to clinical trials volunteers.

Ownership requirement

29–57　Up until December 9, 2009, SMEs were required to own any intellectual property resulting from the R&D to qualify for relief. This requirement is removed by s.13 of the Finance (No.2) Bill 2010.

Grants

29–58　If all or part of the costs of a project are met by a notified State Aid (notified to and approved by the European Commission), then none of the costs of the project will qualify for the SME R&D tax relief (because the SME R&D tax relief is also classed as a State Aid), regardless of whether all of the costs of the project are covered by the State Aid.[194] All that is required for the SME R&D relief to be lost is the grant of a State Aid; even if the payment is subsequently returned or is refused after grant, the SME R&D relief will not be restored. However, SMEs who cannot claim the SME R&D tax relief because they benefit from a notified State Aid can claim the large company R&D tax relief (detailed below) because that relief is not classed as a State Aid.[195]

If the grant or subsidy is not a notified State Aid, then the R&D tax relief can only be claimed on relevant expenditure which is not met by the grant or subsidy.[196] In many cases, subsidies/grants are given for capital expenditure and so may not affect the R&D relief claim at all, as the expenditure met by the grant or subsidy would not qualify for relief in any case.

Repayment tax credit

29–59　If an SME company is loss-making once the relief has been deducted, the option of surrendering the loss and taking the credit as immediate cash is available—but the payment from HMRC is less than the tax ultimately saved if the relief is carried forward as a loss. The repayment option may be preferable for a company which has cash flow issues, where the longer-term financial disadvantage is less important than the short-term need for cash.

The SME can surrender a loss equal to the lower of[197]:

(a) 175 per cent of the qualifying R&D expenditure; and
(b) the total loss of the trade in the period, less
　(i) any claim made, or which could be made, to set the loss against other profits or gains of the same accounting period, and
　(ii) any other relief claimed in respect of the losses, including losses carried back to earlier accounting periods or surrendered by group or consortium relief.

---

[193] CTA 2009 ss.1052, 1053.
[194] CTA 2009 ss.1138(a), 1052(6), 1053(5).
[195] CTA 2009 ss.1071–1072.
[196] CTA 2009 s.1138(b), (c).
[197] CTA 2009 ss.1055–1056.

In exchange for such a surrender, the company can claim a repayment of the lower of[198]:

(a) 14 per cent of the surrenderable loss (which equates to 24.5 per cent of the qualifying expenditure where (a) above applies); and

(b) the total amount of relevant PAYE and Class 1 National Insurance Contributions paid by the company in the relevant accounting period (the PAYE and NICs relating to all staff employed by the company, not just those engaged in R&D activity).

Large company relief

A large company is a company that does not meet the definition of a small or medium-sized company.[199] Note that there is a year of grace where a company falls below or goes above the employee or financial thresholds for a single year; it is only where the thresholds are breached for two years running that the company will change status, and then only with effect from the second year. This year of grace is not available where the thresholds are exceeded or the independence test is failed as a result of an SME being acquired by another company.

29–60

Large companies' relief can be claimed by companies that do not meet the SME threshold tests noted above, and also by SMEs that do not qualify for the SME company relief—for example, where a grant has been received in respect of the R&D project.[200]

There are several differences between the SME relief and the large companies' relief, particularly:

(a) the overall cap on R&D relief for SMEs (see 29–53 above) does not apply to the large companies' relief as this relief is not regarded as a State Aid;

(b) there has never been a requirement for large companies to own any intellectual property resulting from the R&D; and

(c) relief for costs of contracted out work is only available in very limited circumstances for large companies.

The R&D tax relief for large companies is given by allowing the company to deduct 30 per cent of its qualifying expenditure on R&D (in addition to the 100 per cent deduction given under the normal rules) when calculating its profits for tax purposes; this will either reduce the tax payable by the company or, if it is loss-making, increase the loss available to the company.

Claiming R&D relief

The SME company relief, the large company relief, and the repayment relief must be claimed within one year of the filing date for the self-assessment return for the accounting period to which the claim relates (i.e. in the company's corporation tax return or amended return).[201]

29–61

4. RESEARCH & DEVELOPMENT CAPITAL ALLOWANCES

R&D capital allowances can be claimed by both companies and unincorporated businesses, unlike the R&D tax relief incentives, which are for companies only.

29–62

---

[198] CTA 2009 s.1058.
[199] See para.29–55, above.
[200] CTA 2009 Pt 13 Ch.4.
[201] Finance Act 1998 Sch 18 para.83B.

This capital allowance is given for purchases of capital expenditure (equipment and buildings, primarily) used in R&D,[202] defined as for the R&D tax reliefs.[203]

R&D capital allowances provide a deduction of 100 per cent for tax purposes of the value of the capital expenditure in the period in which the expenditure is incurred,[204] unless the taxpayer elects to deduct a smaller percentage. Where a smaller deduction is taken, the balance cannot be deducted later.

The tax saving of this immediate write off of the expenditure means that the effective cost of equipment and buildings for R&D purposes can be substantially reduced for the acquiring company. The R&D allowance is one of very few tax deductions now available for the cost of acquiring buildings.

5. VALUE ADDED TAX

Background

29–63   One of the treaty obligations assumed by the United Kingdom on joining the European Economic Community in 1972 was an obligation to introduce the common system of VAT.[205] VAT is an indirect tax levied on consumption which is administered in the United Kingdom by HM Revenue & Customs. It is collected at each stage in the commercial chain from the supplier, who must account for tax on the supply he makes ("output tax") but can recover tax on supplies made to him ("input tax"). The result is that the burden of VAT falls on the person who is unable to recover the tax charged on supplies made to him. This is generally the ultimate consumer, but in the case of an exempt supply[206] is the person making the exempt supply.

The principal current source of UK VAT legislation is the consolidating Value Added Tax Act ("VATA 1994"), together with Regulations made under Statutory Instrument. Domestic legislation is designed to give effect to the common system of VAT which predominantly originated as the Sixth Directive of May 17, 1977 and was required to be implemented in all Member States' VAT legislation. On December 11, 2006, the revised versions of the First and Sixth Directives were published.[207] The Council Directive 2006/112/EC entered into force on January 1, 2007.[208] In general, this latest Directive does not bring any major changes to the current VAT rules and principles and domestic legislation will continue to be construed accordingly. In case of conflict between domestic and directly applicable Community legislation, taxpayers (but not HMRC) may rely on the latter.

VAT charge

29–64   VAT is charged on any supply of goods or services made in the United Kingdom where it is a taxable supply made by a taxable person in the course or furtherance

---

[202] Capital Allowances Act (CAA) 2001 s.437(1).
[203] See para.29–53, above.
[204] CAA 2001 s.441.
[205] The European Communities Act 1972 provides for the implementation of Community legislation in UK law and for it to take precedence over domestic law.
[206] i.e. supplies of goods and services within Sch.9 to VATA 1994.
[207] [2006] OJ L347/1.
[208] art.413 of the Directive.

of any business carried on by him.[209] VAT is currently charged at 17.5 per cent[210] on the value of the supply and is a liability of the person making the supply.[211]

The grant or assignment of copyright or any other intellectual property right is a supply of services if done for a consideration.[212] An author, musician, composer, etc. who assigns or licenses copyright will thus be subject to VAT if the other conditions for chargeability are met.

First, the supply must be a taxable supply. To constitute a taxable supply, the supply must be made in the United Kingdom and can be any supply of goods or services other than an exempt supply.[213]

Secondly, the person granting or assigning the right must be a taxable person.[214] A taxable person is a person who is either registered for VAT or is required to be so registered.[215] A person is required to be registered if, at the end of any month, he has made taxable supplies exceeding the VAT threshold[216] in the preceding year or there are reasonable grounds for believing that the value of his taxable supplies in the next 30 days will exceed the VAT threshold.[217] So, for example, an author who is about to receive an advance of £70,000 would become a taxable person even if he was previously below the threshold for registration.

Thirdly, the supply must be made by the taxable person in the course or furtherance of a business carried on by him.[218] The term "business" extends beyond trades, professions or vocations,[219] to include any occupation or function actively pursued with a reasonable and recognisable continuity and which involves the making of taxable supplies,[220] even if it is not done with the object of making profit.[221] However there are limits. Merely exercising rights of ownership does not amount to the carrying on of a business, for example, the buying and selling of securities in the course of managing an investment portfolio.[222] Difficult questions may therefore arise where a copyright or the benefit of a royalty agreement is inherited or acquired by gift. It is thought that the mere receipt of royalties does not amount to the carrying on of a business.

Finally, the supply must be made for a consideration, which may be in monetary or non-monetary form and includes everything received in return for the supply. VAT is charged on the "value" of the supply, namely the amount which, with the addition of VAT thereon, equals the consideration.[223] Where the consideration for the grant of a right takes the form of royalties, there is a separate supply of services on each occasion when payment is received or, if earlier, when an invoice is issued.[224]

Credit for input tax

It is a fundamental principle of the VAT system that a taxable person is entitled   **29–65**

---

[209] VATA 1994 s.4.
[210] Rising to 20 per cent with effect from January 4, 2011.
[211] VATA 1994 s.2.
[212] VATA 1994 s.5(2). A gift of a right will not be a supply because "supply" does not include anything done otherwise than for consideration: CTA 2009 s.5(2).
[213] VATA 1994 s.4. The place of supply rules are discussed at para.29–65, below.
[214] VATA 1994 s.4(1).
[215] VATA 1994 s.3(1).
[216] £70,000 in 2010/11.
[217] VATA 1994 Sch.1 para.1(1).
[218] VATA 1994 s.4(1).
[219] VATA 1994 s.94(1).
[220] See *C&E Commissioners v Morrison's Academy* [1978] S.T.C. 1.
[221] *C&E Commissioners v Morrison's Academy* [1978] S.T.C. 1 at 5c–d.
[222] *Wellcome Trust v C&E Commissioners* [1996] S.T.C. 945.
[223] VATA 1994 s.19.
[224] VAT Regulations 1995 (SI 1995/2518) regs 90 and 91.

to recover VAT on supplies made to him to the extent that the supplies are attributable to taxable supplies he makes.[225]

Place of supply

29–66 Prior to January 1, 2010 the general rule was that a supply of services took place where the supplier belonged. However, intellectual property fell within an exemption in VATA 1994 Sch.5 and so the supply was treated as taking place where the customer belonged, provided that the customer received the supply for the purposes of a business. Following the changes to the rules on the place of supply of services with effect from January 1, 2010 which changed the general rule for the place of supply of services to be where the customer belongs, the supply of intellectual property falls within the general rules for the place of supply of services. As a result, the place of supply of intellectual property will still be where the recipient belongs for VAT purposes unless the supply is not to a relevant business person.[226]

The Value Added Tax Act 1994 contains detailed rules to determine where a person belongs. The supplier will belong in the United Kingdom if he has his only business establishment or fixed establishment in the United Kingdom.[227] If the supplier has business establishments or fixed establishments in more than one country, the supplier is treated as belonging in that country which is most directly concerned with the supply in question.[228] If the supplier has no business establishment or fixed place of business anywhere, he is treated as belonging in the country where he has his usual place of residence.[229] Similar rules apply to determine where the recipient of the supply belongs save that, where a supply of services is made to an individual and is received by him otherwise than for the purposes of any business carried on by him, he is treated as belonging where he has his usual place of residence.[230]

A supply of intellectual property to a business in another Member State is therefore not subject to UK VAT as it is supplied outside the United Kingdom; the recipient will be required to effectively self-assess for local VAT under the reverse charge provisions. Where a UK business receives such a supply from outside the United Kingdom, it will similarly be required to self-assess for UK VAT under the reverse charge provisions.

There are, however, important exceptions to the general rule. Of particular importance in the present context, some supplies of services are treated as made

---

[225] VATA 1994 ss.24–26. There are detailed rules for attributing input tax between taxable supplies and supplies which are either outside the scope of VAT or are exempt: See Pt XIV of the VAT Regulations 1995 (SI 1995/2518).

[226] Supplies of intellectual property to a consumer anywhere will be subject to UK VAT; it should be noted that it would be unusual to supply intellectual property to a consumer. The more usual transaction is a supply of goods a book, or a CD, for example, and the rules on VAT on goods will apply. The supply of electronic books, music and software (over the internet, for example), is regarded as a supply of digitised goods rather than a supply of intellectual property. A supply of digitised goods is treated as a supply of services, and so will be subject to UK VAT where supplied by a UK VAT registered person.

[227] VATA 1994 s.9(2)(a). A person carrying on business through a branch or agency in any country is treated as having a business establishment there: VATA 1994 s.9(5)(a). As to fixed establishment, see *C&E Commissioners v DFDS A S* [1997] 1 W.L.R. 1037; [1997] S.T.C. 384.

[228] VATA 1994 s.9(2).

[229] VATA 1994 s.9(2)(b). In the case of a body corporate, this means the place where it is legally constituted.

[230] VATA 1994 s.9.

where the supplies are physically carried out. These include cultural, artistic, sporting, scientific, educational or entertainment services.[231]

It should be noted that "use and enjoyment" provisions may apply to change the place of supply of services in certain circumstances. The United Kingdom has relatively limited use and enjoyment provisions (these are primarily in connection with telecoms and broadcasting, where the European Union has set out the provisions) but other Member States have made more extensive provisions which may result in a change in the place of supply; although this could affect any supply of services, it is in connection with intellectual property and similar intangible services that use and enjoyment are most often applied.

In summary, the changes on January 1, 2010 have had little practical impact on the VAT treatment of supplies of intellectual property beyond the (not to be underestimated) need to complete EC Sales Lists in respect of such supplies.

Reverse charge

As mentioned in the previous paragraph, all services, including transfers and as-   **29–67** signments of copyright, patents, licences, trademarks and similar supplies, are supplied where received.[232] Where the supply is made by a person outside the United Kingdom, the supply will be subject to the so-called "reverse charge" where the service is received by a person who belongs in the United Kingdom for the purpose of any business carried on by him.[233]

The "reverse charge" rules treat the recipient as if he had himself supplied the services in the United Kingdom in the course or furtherance of his business and the supply were a taxable supply. If the recipient is a taxable person, he is both liable to account for output tax and eligible for input tax credit (to the extent that the services which are the subject matter of the reverse supply are attributable to taxable supplies). So, for example, a publishing company which acquires copyright from an author who belongs abroad will have to pay VAT on the consideration for the copyright but (assuming the company is entitled to full credit for its input tax) will be able to recover the VAT as input tax in exactly the same way as if the VAT had been charged by a third-party supplier.

Zero-rating and digitised goods

Books, booklets, brochures, pamphlets, leaflets, newspapers, journals, periodicals,   **29–68** children's picture books and painting books, music (printed, duplicated or manuscript), maps, charts and topographical plans (excluding plans or drawings for industrial, architectural, engineering, commercial or similar purposes) are all zero-rated.[234] This means that the supplier does not need to account for VAT but is entitled to credit for input tax attributable to the supply.[235]

However, digitised versions of books and similar material are not zero-rated and so are subject to VAT at the standard rate when supplied to a consumer. This

---

[231] VAT (Place of Supply of Services) Order 1992 (SI 1992/3121) art.15.

[232] Supplies are not taxable supplies for reverse charge purposes, if the recipient belongs outside the EC or belongs in the EC and receives the supply otherwise than for the purpose of a business carried on by him.

[233] VATA 1994 s.8.

[234] VATA 1994 s.30 and Sch.8.

[235] Zero-rated supplies are those supplies described in VATA 1994 Sch.8. Unlike exempt supplies, these are "taxable supplies" so input tax attributable to zero-rated supplies is recoverable: input tax attributable to exempt supplies is irrecoverable. Zero-rating is also referred to as "exemption with credit".

is because the sale of digitised books is regarded for VAT purposes as the supply of services, rather than the supply of goods.[236]

6. STAMP DUTY

No application to intellectual property

29–69 The Finance Act 2000 s.129 and Sch.34 abolished stamp duty in respect of instruments for the sale, transfer or other disposition of intellectual property. This abolition applies to instruments executed on or after March 28, 2000. The Finance Act 2002 s.116 abolished stamp duty in respect of an instrument for the sale transfer or other disposition of goodwill. The abolition applies to instruments executed on or after April 23, 2002.

7. TAXATION OF DAMAGES

29–70 Damages for infringement of an intellectual property right may also be taxable as income if they represent compensation for the unauthorised use of the right rather than the diminution of its capital value.[237]

Where damages are not subject to tax, tax may in some circumstances be taken into account in determining the quantum of the damages payable. It was established in *British Transport Commission v Gourley*[238] that where a plaintiff receives compensation for loss of income which would have been taxable and the compensation is not itself subject to tax, the defendant is entitled to have the damages reduced by an amount equivalent to the tax which the plaintiff would have had to pay. The reason behind the *Gourley* principle is to prevent the plaintiff from being over-compensated. However, the principle only applies where the court is satisfied that the compensation is not subject to either income tax or capital gains tax[239] and will not in practice be applied where calculation of the appropriate deduction will be unduly complex.[240]

8. CROSS-BORDER ISSUES

Residence

29–71 Historically, it has been a feature of UK tax law that there is no statutory test of residence, and that "resident" must be given its ordinary meaning.[241] Accordingly, the question of whether an individual is resident or not is generally determined by reference to such factors as the regularity, purpose and duration of

---

[236] VATA 1994 para.7C, Sch.5.
[237] *Raja's Commercial College v Gian Singh & Co Ltd* [1977] A.C. 312; [1976] S.T.C. 282. What matters is the character of the payment and not the authority under which it is paid.
[238] [1956] A.C. 185 HL.
[239] *Pennine Raceway Ltd v Kirklees Metropolitan Council (No.2)* [1989] S.T.C. 122.
[240] See *John v James* [1986] S.T.C. 352, where damages received by Elton John against a music publisher who failed to account for sums due under various publishing and recording agreements were not reduced under the *Gourley* principle.
[241] In July 1988, the Revenue produced a consultative document entitled "Residence in the United Kingdom: The Scope of United Kingdom Taxation for Individuals" which proposed the introduction of a statutory test of residence based on days of presence in the United Kingdom. The proposals were subsequently shelved. However, there have been renewed calls for a statutory residence test following the decision of the Special Commissioners in *Gaines-Cooper v Revenue and Customs Commissioners* [2007] EWHC 2617 (Ch); [2007] STC (SCD) 23, where the Special Commissioners chose not to follow their guidance in IR20 (now superseded by the leaflet HMRC6), but instead counted the number of nights the taxpayer spent in the United Kingdom.

his visits to the United Kingdom. Whilst a comprehensive survey of the meaning of residence is beyond the scope of this work, attention is drawn to the following points:

(a) A person who is present in the United Kingdom for six months or more in any financial year is resident in that year[242];

(b) A person who lives and works abroad with a full-time contract of employment for a period including a full financial year will not be resident or ordinarily resident in the United Kingdom in that year[243];

(c) It is the Revenue's view that a person who visits the United Kingdom for periods averaging at least three months per year becomes resident after four years of such visits, unless his arrangements indicated from the start that regular visits of such duration were to be made, in which case he would be resident from the first year[244];

(d) If a British subject who has hitherto been resident leaves the United Kingdom for some temporary purpose only, he does not cease to be resident here.[245]

Different rules apply to companies. A company incorporated in the United Kingdom is automatically deemed to be resident here.[246] Foreign incorporated companies are resident where their central management and control is located.[247]

Non-residents

Income from a trade, profession or vocation carried on in the United Kingdom by a non-UK resident is prima facie liable to UK taxation, and will generally be liable to tax in the country of residence as well. Where there is a double tax treaty between the United Kingdom and the country of residence, there will normally be exemption from UK tax unless the trade or profession is carried on through a permanent establishment in this country.   **29–72**

The test for determining where a trade profession or vocation is carried on is: where do the operations take place from which the profits in substance arise?[248] The test was applied in *Commissioners of Inland Revenue v HK-TVB Interna-*

---

[242] ITA 2007 s.831(1)(b). In determining whether an individual has been present in the United Kingdom for six months or more, days of arrival in the United Kingdom are counted, but days of departure are ignored: ITA 2007 s.831(1A).

[243] See *Reed v Clark* [1986] Ch.1; [1985] S.T.C. 323.

[244] See the HMRC leaflet on "Residents and non-residents. Liability to tax in the United Kingdom" (HMRC 6, 2010).

[245] In *Reed v Clark* [1986] Ch.1; [1985] S.T.C. 323, a British subject who lived and worked abroad for a period of one year was held not to have left the United Kingdom for a temporary purpose only. In *Gaines-Cooper v Revenue and Customs Commissioners* [2007] EWHC 2617 (Ch), the taxpayer's presence in the United Kingdom for the years under appeal was held not to have been for a temporary purpose, notwithstanding that he had no subjective intention of establishing a residence in the United Kingdom. The taxpayer subsequently lost his appeal to the High Court, reported at [2008] S.T.C. 1665.

[246] CTA 2009 s.14; see also CTA 2009 s.18 which treats certain dual resident companies as non-resident.

[247] *Unit Construction Ltd v Bullock* [1960] A.C. 351 and see Revenue Statement of Practice SP1/90. See the recent cases of *Wood and another v Holden (Inspector of in Taxes)* [2006] EWCA Civ 26; [2006] 1 W.L.R. 1393 and *Laerstate BV v Revenue & Customs* [2009] UKFTT 209 (TC) as to what constitutes central management and control.

[248] *FL Smidth & Co v Greenwood* [1921] 3 K.B. 583. The place where contracts are concluded is not decisive: *Firestone Tyre and Rubber Co. v Llewellin* [1957] 1 W.L.R. 464; 37 T.C. 111. See also *IRC v Padmore* [1987] S T.C. 36. Nor does it matter that the party contracting with the taxpayer may itself be non-resident and the taxpayer receives no income in the United Kingdom pursuant to that contract: see *Agassi v Robinson (H.M. Inspector of Taxes)* [2006] UKHL 23; 77 TC 686. See also *IR Manuals International Manual*, para.INTM263000 for the current HM Revenue & Customs guidance on non-residents trading in the United Kingdom, the determining factors and a discussion of the case law.

tional Ltd,[249] where a company incorporated and carrying on business in Hong Kong was granted the sole and exclusive right to exploit the copyright in Chinese dialect video films outside Hong Kong which it exercised by granting sub-licences to customers abroad. The company argued that this did not amount to carrying on a trade or business in Hong Kong: the company was either providing services to its customers in the overseas territories concerned, or it was exploiting property assets outside Hong Kong by sub-licensing rights which were only capable of use in the overseas territories concerned. The Court rejected the company's argument, saying "the relevant business of the taxpayer company was the exploitation of film rights exercisable overseas and it was a business carried on in Hong Kong. The fact that the rights which they exploited were only exercisable outside Hong Kong was irrelevant in the absence of any financial interest in the subsequent exercise of the rights by the sub-licensee". It was held to be a factor of great importance that the company's principal place of business was in Hong Kong.

Foreign business

29–73   A trade or profession carried on wholly outside the United Kingdom by a non-resident person is outside the scope of UK taxation.[250] This is so even if the trade is one that had previously been carried on in the United Kingdom: the post-cessation receipts rules will not apply because there will have been no discontinuance.

However, the "post-cessation receipts" rules apply to non-residents whose trade or profession was being carried on in the United Kingdom at the time when it was discontinued, for example, authors who emigrate on retirement.[251]

The taxation of an individual who is resident in the United Kingdom, but carries on a trade, profession or vocation wholly abroad, depends upon whether or not he is domiciled in the United Kingdom. If he is domiciled here, he is subject to income tax on all his income arising worldwide under ITTOIA 2005 s.6; but under ITTOIA 2005 s.243(3), the post-cessation receipts rules[252] do not apply where the trade was carried on wholly outside the United Kingdom. Accordingly, sums arising after the discontinuance of the foreign trade, profession or vocation escape the charge to tax.

If an individual is resident but not domiciled in the United Kingdom and the remittance basis applies,[253] he is liable to tax only to the extent that income from the wholly foreign trade or profession is remitted to the United Kingdom[254]. Remittances in a year of assessment after the trade or profession has been discontinued escape the charge to tax, because there is no longer any taxable source.

Very broadly speaking, an individual's income or chargeable gains are remitted to the United Kingdom if they are received in the United Kingdom in cash (or if property deriving from the income or chargeable gains has been brought to the United Kingdom) for the benefit of the individual or some other relevant person,

---

[249] *Commissioners of Inland Revenue v HK-TVB International Ltd* [1992] S.T.C. 723 PC.
[250] See *Colquhoun v Brooks* 2 T.C. 490, where the so-called "principle of territoriality" was established. Though see *Clark (Inspector of Taxes) v Oceanic Contractors Inc.* [1983] 2 A.C. 130 as referred to in *Agassi v Robinson (HM. Inspector of Taxes)* [2006] UKHL 23; [2006] 1 W.L.R. 1380 for subsequent limitations to this principle.
[251] Save that the rules do not catch receipts which represent income arising outside the United Kingdom: ITTOIA 2005 s.243(3). See para.29–13, above.
[252] See para.29–13, above.
[253] ITA 2007 ss.809B–809E.
[254] ITA 2007 s.809F.

or if services are performed in the United Kingdom and the consideration paid for those services is or derives from the overseas income or gains.

There are also rules relating to the payment of debts arising overseas but which nevertheless have a connection to property, or services performed, in the United Kingdom. The remittance basis rules are extremely wide with limited exemptions, and there are various anti-avoidance provisions to prevent the alienation of income or chargeable gains abroad.

Because the remittance basis only applies to individuals, UK resident companies are fully taxable on the profits of a foreign trade (subject to any available double taxation relief).

Double tax relief

The United Kingdom is party to a comprehensive range of Double Tax Treaties, the majority of which deal expressly with royalties arising in one contracting state which are paid to a resident of the other contracting state. The majority of treaties, though by no means all, give exclusive taxing rights to the contracting state where the recipient is resident; the other contracting state may not then impose a withholding tax.

29–74

Most treaties contain two exceptions to the general rule. First, relief is not available if the recipient carries on business in the contracting state where the royalties arise through a permanent establishment or fixed base of business and the right or property in respect of which the royalties are paid is effectively connected with the permanent establishment or fixed base. Secondly, where there is a special relationship between the payer and the recipient, and the royalties exceed the amount that would have been agreed upon in the absence of any special relationship, there is no treaty relief for the excess.

Where treaty relief is not available, the country of residence usually gives unilateral relief for the foreign tax. The United Kingdom's provisions for unilateral relief are provided for in the Taxation (International and Other Provisions) Act 2010 s.18.

Withholding tax

Basic rate income tax must be deducted from copyright royalty payments made by a UK taxpayer if the copyright licensor is not resident in the United Kingdom.[255] The licensee must account to HMRC for any tax deducted.[256]

29–75

Payments in respect of copyright which are paid to a professional author (that is, where the work was created in the ordinary course of a profession as an author) are regarded as fees for professional services and are not subject to deduction of income tax at source.[257]

There is also no requirement to withhold tax on royalties paid by UK companies (or UK permanent establishments of EU companies) to associated EU companies.[258]

Deductions are also required in respect of certain payments to non-resident entertainers and sportsmen.[259]

---

[255] ITA 2007 s.906.
[256] ITA 2007 Pt 15, Ch.16.
[257] HMRC manual INTM342590.
[258] ITTOIA 2005 s.758.
[259] ITA 2007 Pt 15, Ch.18.

Leasing

29–76 A lease of copyright material (particularly in respect of software) gives the lessee the right to use the material for a specified period of time, rather than user. Accordingly, payments under the lease are not payments of royalties[260] and no withholding needs to be made from the payments.

Anti-avoidance: transfer of assets abroad

29–77 The Income Tax Act 2007 ("ITA 2007") Pt 13 Ch.2 prevents avoidance of UK tax by a transfer of assets to non-residents. Where an individual who is ordinarily resident in United Kingdom seeks to avoid tax[261] by transferring (or procuring the transfer of) assets to a non-resident, s.21 imposes a charge to income tax on "individuals with a power to enjoy income as a result of relevant transactions", and s.728 on "individuals receiving capital sums as a result of relevant transactions". The section also applies where the transferor is not ordinarily resident at the time of the transfer if he or his spouse subsequently becomes ordinarily resident.[262] Section 732 applies to "non-transferors receiving a benefit as a result of relevant transactions".

A "relevant transaction" is a transfer of assets (including the creation of new rights) where, as a result of the transfer or associated operations, income becomes payable to a person abroad.[263] An "associated operation" is widely defined, being any operation by any person relating to: the assets transferred, or any assets representing those assets, the income arising from those assets, or any assets representing accumulated income from the assets.[264]

Individuals will not be liable for income tax under these provisions if they fall into one of the categories for exemption or partial exemption at ITA 2007 ss.736–742. Broadly, the exemptions apply where there is no tax avoidance purpose or the transactions are genuine commercial transactions.[265] The conditions for exemption effectively make clear that the existence or otherwise of a tax avoidance purpose must be determined objectively in light of all the circumstances and not subjectively.

The anti-avoidance provisions are not confined to transfers of income producing assets. In *Brackett v IRC*[266] there was held to be a transfer of assets for the purpose of (what is now) s.721 where the taxpayer entered into a service contract with a Jersey company whose shares were owned by a settlement created by the taxpayer. As a result the trading income of the Jersey company derived from the taxpayer's activities was deemed to be the taxpayer's income. The case considerably restricts the scope for high-earning UK residents, for example, entertainers, sportsmen, etc. to avoid UK income tax by entering into a service contract with an offshore company.

---

[260] *Carson v Cheyney's Executor* [1959] A.C. 412; (1958) 38 T.C. 240.

[261] The intention need not be to avoid income tax; the avoidance of any form of UK taxation is sufficient; see ITA 2007 ss.721(5), 728(3), 737 and 739.

[262] ITA 2007 ss.721(5) and 728(3).

[263] ITA 2007 s.716.

[264] ITA 2007 s.719.

[265] ITA 2007 s.738.

[266] *Brackett v IRC* [1986] S.T.C. 521.

Index

LEGAL TAXONOMY
FROM SWEET & MAXWELL

This index has been prepared using Sweet and Maxwell's Legal Taxonomy. Main index entries conform to keywords provided by the Legal Taxonomy except where references to specific documents or non-standard terms (denoted by quotation marks) have been included. These keywords provide a means of identifying similar concepts in other Sweet & Maxwell publications and online services to which keywords from the Legal Taxonomy have been applied. Readers may find some minor differences between terms used in the text and those which appear in the index. Suggestions to *sweetandmaxwell.taxonomy@thomson.com*

All references are to paragraph numbers. General cross-references appear at the beginning of certain main headings, referring to entries for specific offences or subjects. Specific cross-references are either to sub-headings elsewhere under the same main heading or to other main headings.

Literary works—*cont.*
  generally, 3-11—3-20
  history of protection
    Berne Convention, 3-10
    CA 1911, 3-09
    CA 1956, 3-10
    introduction, 3-08
  ideas
    expression by words, 3-14
    generally, 3-18
  information, 3-20
  integrity right, 11-45
  joint authorship
    agreements, 4-38
    collaboration requirement, 4-36
    definition, 4-34
    distinct contributions, 4-37
    distinction from co-authorship, 4-33
    introduction, 4-32
    rights inter se and against third parties, 4-39
    skill and labour requirement, 4-35
  lending right, 7-95
  'literary', 3-15
  mere copy, 3-133
  musical works, and, 3-12
  names and titles, 3-16
  new version of existing work, 3-138
  news, 3-19
  notation, 3-17
  originality
    Berne Convention, 3-127
    compilations, 3-146—3-147
    computer-generated works, 3-149
    Database Directive, 3-128
    derivative works, 3-133—3-143
    EU Directives, 31-28
    expression not content, 3-129
    historical background, 3-126
    introduction, 3-125
    non-derivative works, 3-131—3-132
    principles, 3-129—3-130
    TRIPs, 3-127
  ownership
    author as first owner, 5-06—5-07
    commissioned works, 5-32—5-39
    employees, by, 5-08—5-27
    joint authors, 5-07
    pre-CA 1911 works, 5-40
    publication in newspapers, etc, for, 5-28—5-31
    reporters, by, 5-28—5-3
  paternity right, 11-11
  précis, 3-140
  protected subject matter, 3-13—3-20
  public performance right, 7-103
  publication right
    examples, 17-32
    expiry of copyright, 17-29
    generally, 17-05
  rental right, 7-95
  reproduction right
    abridgments, 7-42
    abstracts, 7-42

Literary works—*cont.*
  reproduction right—*cont.*
    adaptation right, and, 7-35
    anthologies, 7-48
    betting coupons, 7-48
    catalogues, 7-48
    compilations, 7-45
    computer programs, 7-48
    databases, 7-46—7-47
    defendant's work to represent claimant's, 7-37
    derivative works, 7-39
    dictionaries, 7-48
    directories, 7-48
    encyclopedias, 7-48
    generally, 7-34
    fixture lists, 7-48
    historical works, 7-48
    introduction, 7-36—7-37
    'little and often', 7-51
    maps, 7-48
    newspaper reports, 7-44
    non-literal copying, 7-40
    non-textual copying, 7-40
    parodies, 7-43
    précis, 7-42
    programme schedules, 7-48
    rearrangement of databases, 7-49
    software, 7-48
    statistical information, 7-48
    substantial part, 7-38—7-44
    tables, 7-47
    technical data, 7-48
    verbatim extracts, 7-41
    wholly new works, 7-39
  skill or labour, 3-130
  software
    functionality, 3-30
    history of protection, 3-28
    ideas vs expression dichotomy, 3-30
    interfaces, 3-30
    meaning, 3-29
    nature of protected subject matter, 3-30
    preparatory design materials, 3-31
    programming languages, 3-30
  style or merit, 3-15
  substantial part
    abridgments, 7-42
    abstracts, 7-42
    derivative works, 7-39
    general considerations, 7-38
    newspaper reports, 7-44
    non-literal copying, 7-40
    non-textual copying, 7-40
    parodies, 7-43
    précis, 7-42
    verbatim extracts, 7-41
    wholly new works, 7-39
  successive versions, 3-136
  tables and compilations
    collections of works, 3-26
    databases, 3-21—3-23
    definition, 3-24